Bill James presents . . .

STATS™ 1995
Minor League
Handbook

STATS, Inc.
and
Howe Sportsdata International

STATS
PUBLISHING

Published by STATS Publishing
A division of Sports Team Analysis & Tracking Systems, Inc.
Dr. Richard Cramer, Chairman • John Dewan, President

**This book is dedicated to
STATS' Rookie of the Year:**

Annabelle Christine (A.C.) Miller

Cover by John Grimwade, New York, NY

Photo provided by the Tucson Toros

First Edition: November, 1994

Printed in the United States of America

ISBN 1-88406408-6

Acknowledgments

Each October, we go through the "Fall book crunch," putting together three books—the *Major League Handbook*, *Minor League Handbook* and *Player Profiles*—in the space of about 11 days. It's a true group effort, and we'd like to thank the following people.

Dick Cramer, founder and Chairman of the Board of STATS, remains heavily involved with the company from his St. Louis-area home. John Dewan, President and CEO, has managed the company through a period of incredible growth, and continues to play a very active role in the production of these books. They remain a tribute to John's efforts.

Sue Dewan manages the Systems Department, which produces the programming needed to produce this book. Mike Canter is assistant director of Systems, and Bob Mecca is chief programmer for the book. They are assisted by Stefan Kretschmann, Rob McQuown, David Mundo, David Pinto, Jeff Schinski, and Madison Smith. Art Ashley is responsible for the hardware and software used by the programmers and all of the rest of us at STATS, a vital part of our operation.

Steve Moyer, who heads the Operations Department, has also managed the production of this book for the past few years, and continued to help manage this edition. Steve's staff, which consists of Ethan Cooperson, Allan Spear, Peter Woelflein and a host of others in the field, is the vital first link in producing all our sports data. Ross Schaufelberger, Director of Marketing, heads the team which sells our products and services to STATS clients. Thanks also to his staff: Jim Capuano, Jason Gumbs, Mike Hammer, Jim Husbands, Chuck Miller, Jim Musso, Kenn Ruby, Jeff Schwarze and Lisa Suarez.

Michael Coulter and Rob Neyer are my assistants in the Publications Department, and help produce the prose parts of this book. They also review every page of the manuscript to check for clarity, accuracy and completeness. Bob Meyerhoff heads the Department of Finances and Human Resources, the people who man the phones, get out the mailings and manage the finances. He is assisted by Jules Aquino, Drew Faust, Patti Foy, Virginia Hamill, Marge Morra, Betty Moy, Pat Quinn and Wendy Walshe. Stephanie Seburn, John Dewan's assistant, handles many of the important details of John's job.

Howe Sportsdata International is responsible for the collection and tracking of our minor league statistics, and we'd like to offer our thanks to President Jay Virshbo, Executive Vice President William Weiss, and the following people: Bob Townsend, Tom Graham, Jim Keller, Mike Walczak, John Foley, Vin Vitro, Paul La Rocca, Brian Joura, Bob Chaban and Dan Landesman. Special thanks go to Chris Pollari, who, as usual, was particularly helpful in the production of this book.

Last, a special thanks to Bill James, who developed the concept and format of the Handbooks and the Major League Equivalency formula. More than that, he has helped make STATS the company that it is.

— Don Zminda

Table of Contents

Introduction

Welcome to the fourth edition of the *STATS Minor League Handbook*. Doing the book each year has become a habit with us. We hope studying it each year will become a habit with you—if it isn't already.

Why would you want to take a good look at this book? Well, here's some names you probably know by now. A year ago, they were "just minor leaguers" whose career lines were included in the *Minor League Handbook*:

Mark Acre, Athletics	James Mouton, Astros
Garret Anderson, Angels	Jose Oliva, Braves
Rusty Greer, Rangers	Paul Shuey, Indians
Darren Hall, Blue Jays	Dave Stevens, Twins
John Hudek, Astros	Mark Thompson, Rockies
Brian Hunter, Astros	Ismael Valdes, Dodgers
Ray McDavid, Padres	Brad Woodall, Braves

Every year, some minor league players develop quickly and change from relative unknowns to prospects, or even major league stars. Probably the best example on the above list was John Hudek, who went from a guy buried in the Tiger system to the ace closer for the Astros in less than a year. Are there more Hudeks in this year's *Minor League Handbook*? You better believe it. There are also a few guys like Eddie Williams, the sort of "career prospect" who fails in a few chances, gets labeled a "minor league ballplayer" and waits, usually in vain, for a chance. Williams got his last year, and made the most of it.

For the second year in a row, we present our exclusive Park Data and AAA Lefty/Righty Stats. These are both sections of never-seen-before information that only STATS/Howe—and the *Minor League Handbook*—present to the general public.

— John Dewan and Don Zminda

Career Stats

Chances are, you're a longtime fan of this book, so you know who's in here and who's not. Like always, any player who spent time at the AAA and/or AA levels in 1994, and did *not* play in the majors, gets a full career spread. There are minor league totals and major league totals where applicable. Major league data accompanies any player who played in the majors as recently as 1991. Thanks to the "work stoppage" (can someone tell me the difference between a work stoppage and a strike?), there are more players in this year's *Minor League Handbook* than ever before. This is because a lot of guys who would have been September call-ups, and hence ineligible for this book, *weren't*. One player not technically eligible for this book is Brian Hunter, Houston's stellar outfield prospect, because he played briefly with the big-league club. We wanted him for our cover, so you'll find his stats in this book.

Just like in the *Major League Handbook*:

- **Age** is seasonal age based on July 1, 1995. This means our age is the player's age as of July 1. By choosing this particular date, almost exactly mid-season, we get the age at which each player will play during most of the 1995 season.

- **TBB** and **IBB** are Total Bases on Balls and Intentional Bases on Balls.

- **SB%** is Stolen Base Percentage (stolen bases divided by attempts). **OBP** and **SLG** are On-Base Percentage and Slugging Percentage.

- **BFP**, **Bk**, and **ShO** are Batters Faced Pitcher, Balks, and Shutouts.

Note: For some players, minor league statistics prior to 1984 are not available.

Chris Abbe

Bats: Right **Throws:** Right **Pos:** C **Ht:** 6'4" **Wt:** 215 **Born:** 02/06/71 **Age:** 24

Year	Team	Lg	G	AB	H	2B	3B	HR	TB	R	RBI	TBB	IBB	SO	HBP	SH	SF	SB	CS	SB%	GDP	Avg	OBP	SLG
1992	Yakima	A	52	192	58	9	0	9	94	25	37	17	2	43	7	0	0	0	0	.00	1	.302	.380	.490
1993	San Antonio	AA	82	254	52	7	1	13	100	32	36	35	5	61	6	0	4	0	3	.00	3	.205	.311	.394
1994	San Antonio	AA	73	236	62	14	1	7	99	24	25	25	2	55	4	1	1	1	1	.50	5	.263	.342	.419
	3 Min. YEARS		207	682	172	30	2	29	293	81	98	77	9	159	17	1	5	1	4	.20	9	.252	.341	.430

Paul Abbott

Pitches: Right **Bats:** Right **Pos:** P **Ht:** 6'3" **Wt:** 194 **Born:** 09/15/67 **Age:** 27

Year	Team	Lg	G	GS	CG	GF	IP	BFP	H	R	ER	HR	SH	SF	HB	TBB	IBB	SO	WP	Bk	W	L	Pct.	ShO	Sv	ERA
1985	Elizabethtn	R	10	10	1	0	35	172	33	32	27	3	1	0	0	32	0	34	7	1	1	5	.167	0	0	6.94
1986	Kenosha	A	25	15	1	7	98	462	102	62	49	13	3	2	2	73	3	73	7	0	6	10	.375	0	0	4.50
1987	Kenosha	A	26	25	1	0	145.1	620	102	76	59	11	5	6	3	103	0	138	11	2	13	6	.684	0	0	3.65
1988	Visalia	A	28	28	4	0	172.1	799	141	95	80	9	8	6	4	143	5	205	12	9	11	9	.550	2	0	4.18
1989	Orlando	AA	17	17	1	0	90.2	389	71	48	44	6	2	1	0	48	0	102	7	7	9	3	.750	0	0	4.37
1990	Portland	AAA	23	23	4	0	128.1	568	110	75	65	9	3	3	1	82	0	129	8	5	5	14	.263	1	0	4.56
1991	Portland	AAA	8	8	1	0	44	193	36	19	19	2	0	1	3	28	0	40	1	0	2	3	.400	1	0	3.89
1992	Portland	AAA	7	7	0	0	46.1	191	30	13	12	2	0	0	0	31	0	46	0	0	4	1	.800	0	0	2.33
1993	Charlotte	AAA	4	4	0	0	19	91	25	16	14	4	3	1	0	7	0	12	3	0	0	1	.000	0	0	6.63
	Canton-Akrn	AA	13	12	1	0	75.1	315	71	34	34	4	1	0	1	28	2	86	6	0	4	5	.444	0	0	4.06
1994	Omaha	AAA	15	10	0	4	57.1	262	57	32	31	8	1	0	2	45	0	48	3	0	4	1	.800	0	0	4.87
1990	Minnesota	AL	7	7	0	0	34.2	162	37	24	23	0	1	1	1	28	0	25	1	0	0	5	.000	0	0	5.97
1991	Minnesota	AL	15	3	0	1	47.1	210	38	27	25	5	7	3	0	36	1	43	5	0	3	1	.750	0	0	4.75
1992	Minnesota	AL	6	0	0	5	11	50	12	4	4	1	0	1	1	5	0	13	1	0	0	0	.000	0	0	3.27
1993	Cleveland	AL	5	5	0	0	18.1	84	19	15	13	5	0	0	0	11	1	7	1	0	0	1	.000	0	0	6.38
	10 Min. YEARS		176	159	14	11	911.2	4062	778	502	434	71	27	20	16	620	10	913	65	24	59	58	.504	4	0	4.28
	4 Maj. YEARS		33	15	0	6	111.1	506	106	70	65	11	8	5	2	80	2	88	8	0	3	7	.300	0	0	5.25

Bob Abreu

Bats: Left **Throws:** Right **Pos:** INF **Ht:** 6'0" **Wt:** 160 **Born:** 03/11/74 **Age:** 21

Year	Team	Lg	G	AB	H	2B	3B	HR	TB	R	RBI	TBB	IBB	SO	HBP	SH	SF	SB	CS	SB%	GDP	Avg	OBP	SLG
1991	Astros	R	56	183	55	7	3	0	68	21	20	17	0	27	1	2	3	10	6	.63	3	.301	.358	.372
1992	Asheville	A	135	480	140	21	4	8	193	81	48	63	1	79	3	0	3	15	11	.58	5	.292	.375	.402
1993	Osceola	A	129	474	134	21	17	5	204	62	55	51	1	90	1	1	3	10	14	.42	8	.283	.352	.430
1994	Jackson	AA	118	400	121	25	9	16	212	61	73	42	3	81	3	0	6	12	10	.55	2	.303	.368	.530
	4 Min. YEARS		438	1537	450	74	33	29	677	225	196	173	5	277	8	3	15	47	41	.53	18	.293	.364	.440

Juan Acevedo

Pitches: Right **Bats:** Right **Pos:** P **Ht:** 6'2" **Wt:** 195 **Born:** 05/05/70 **Age:** 25

Year	Team	Lg	G	GS	CG	GF	IP	BFP	H	R	ER	HR	SH	SF	HB	TBB	IBB	SO	WP	Bk	W	L	Pct.	ShO	Sv	ERA
1992	Bend	A	1	0	0	0	2	13	4	3	3	0	1	0	0	1	0	3	0	0	0	0	.000	0	0	13.50
	Visalia	A	12	12	1	0	64.2	289	75	46	39	2	2	2	3	33	0	37	1	2	3	4	.429	0	0	5.43
1993	Central Val	A	27	20	1	3	118.2	529	119	68	58	8	5	4	9	58	0	107	12	4	9	8	.529	0	0	4.40
1994	New Haven	AA	26	26	5	0	174.2	697	142	56	46	16	4	3	5	38	0	161	4	5	17	6	.739	2	0	2.37
	3 Min. YEARS		66	58	7	3	360	1528	340	173	146	26	12	9	18	130	0	308	17	11	29	18	.617	2	0	3.65

Dave Adam

Pitches: Right **Bats:** Right **Pos:** P **Ht:** 6'3" **Wt:** 202 **Born:** 02/14/69 **Age:** 26

Year	Team	Lg	G	GS	CG	GF	IP	BFP	H	R	ER	HR	SH	SF	HB	TBB	IBB	SO	WP	Bk	W	L	Pct.	ShO	Sv	ERA
1990	Bellingham	A	19	7	4	7	69.1	269	40	13	11	0	4	0	4	22	1	76	6	1	4	4	.500	1	1	1.43
1992	San Berndno	A	26	26	0	0	155	702	178	110	97	17	3	10	4	64	1	112	16	3	7	12	.368	0	0	5.63
1993	Riverside	A	27	27	1	0	169	730	180	91	76	11	7	7	10	51	0	98	8	1	12	8	.600	0	0	4.05
1994	Jacksonville	AA	24	20	2	1	117.1	513	135	75	66	12	6	4	8	33	3	74	7	0	6	10	.375	0	0	5.06
	4 Min. YEARS		96	80	7	8	510.2	2214	533	289	250	40	20	21	26	170	5	360	37	5	29	34	.460	1	1	4.41

Tommy Adams

Bats: Right **Throws:** Right **Pos:** OF **Ht:** 6'1" **Wt:** 205 **Born:** 11/26/69 **Age:** 25

Year	Team	Lg	G	AB	H	2B	3B	HR	TB	R	RBI	TBB	IBB	SO	HBP	SH	SF	SB	CS	SB%	GDP	Avg	OBP	SLG
1991	Bellingham	A	46	150	39	12	0	3	60	27	18	34	2	39	5	0	1	7	2	.78	0	.260	.411	.400
1992	San Berndno	A	94	339	95	21	0	13	155	56	75	38	4	68	5	2	10	20	9	.69	6	.280	.352	.457
	Jacksnville	AA	17	50	11	2	0	0	13	4	5	2	0	13	1	0	0	1	0	1.00	3	.220	.264	.260
1993	Jacksnville	AA	61	232	64	12	2	4	92	19	20	14	2	34	1	0	2	4	0	1.00	5	.276	.313	.397
1994	Riverside	A	8	30	7	0	0	0	7	5	3	6	0	3	1	0	0	2	2	.50	2	.233	.378	.233
	Jacksnville	AA	71	251	58	12	1	8	96	31	19	23	1	55	1	2	1	8	8	.50	4	.231	.297	.382
	4 Min. YEARS		297	1052	274	59	3	28	423	142	140	117	9	212	13	6	15	42	21	.67	20	.260	.338	.402

3

William Adams
Pitches: Right Bats: Right Pos: P   Ht: 6'7" Wt: 215 Born: 10/08/72 Age: 22

Year Team	Lg	G	GS	CG	GF	IP	BFP	H	R	ER	HR	SH	SF	HB	TBB	IBB	SO	WP	Bk	W	L	Pct.	ShO	Sv	ERA
1993 Madison	A	5	5	0	0	18.2	84	21	10	7	2	1	1	0	8	0	22	1	1	0	2	.000	0	0	3.38
1994 Modesto	A	11	5	0	6	45.1	181	41	17	17	7	2	0	0	10	0	42	2	3	7	1	.875	0	2	3.38
Huntsville	AA	10	10	0	0	60.2	256	58	32	29	3	2	3	5	23	2	33	1	1	4	3	.571	0	0	4.30
2 Min. YEARS		26	20	0	6	124.2	521	120	59	53	12	5	4	5	41	2	97	4	5	11	6	.647	0	2	3.83

Joel Adamson
Pitches: Left Bats: Left Pos: P   Ht: 6'4" Wt: 180 Born: 07/02/71 Age: 23

Year Team	Lg	G	GS	CG	GF	IP	BFP	H	R	ER	HR	SH	SF	HB	TBB	IBB	SO	WP	Bk	W	L	Pct.	ShO	Sv	ERA
1990 Princeton	R	12	8	1	3	48	204	55	27	21	2	1	0	3	12	1	39	6	7	2	5	.286	0	1	3.94
1991 Spartanburg	A	14	14	1	0	81	333	72	29	23	5	2	4	3	22	0	84	3	2	4	4	.500	1	0	2.56
Clearwater	A	5	5	0	0	29.2	125	28	12	10	1	2	1	1	7	0	20	2	1	2	1	.667	0	0	3.03
1992 Clearwater	A	15	15	1	0	89.2	378	90	35	34	4	2	3	7	19	0	52	0	1	5	6	.455	1	0	3.41
Reading	AA	10	10	2	0	59	255	68	36	28	10	3	1	0	13	1	35	3	0	3	6	.333	0	0	4.27
1993 Edmonton	AAA	5	5	0	0	26	125	39	21	20	5	1	1	0	13	0	7	0	1	1	2	.333	0	0	6.92
High Desert	A	22	20	6	1	129.2	571	160	83	66	13	3	4	4	30	0	72	5	7	5	5	.500	3	0	4.58
1994 Portland	AA	33	11	2	16	91.1	402	95	51	44	9	5	2	5	32	5	59	0	0	5	6	.455	2	7	4.34
5 Min. YEARS		116	88	13	20	554.1	2393	607	294	246	49	19	16	23	148	7	368	19	19	27	35	.435	7	8	3.99

Steve Adkins
Pitches: Left Bats: Right Pos: P   Ht: 6'6" Wt: 215 Born: 10/26/64 Age: 30

Year Team	Lg	G	GS	CG	GF	IP	BFP	H	R	ER	HR	SH	SF	HB	TBB	IBB	SO	WP	Bk	W	L	Pct.	ShO	Sv	ERA
1986 Oneonta	A	14	12	2	1	80.1	325	59	23	15	1	6	0	0	36	2	74	8	0	8	2	.800	1	1	1.68
1987 Ft.Laudrdle	A	5	3	0	1	21.1	91	26	11	11	2	1	1	0	8	0	7	3	1	1	1	.500	0	0	4.64
Pr William	A	21	20	0	0	115.2	527	120	72	62	11	3	3	3	70	1	84	12	1	9	8	.529	0	0	4.82
1988 Pr William	A	31	6	2	13	94.1	404	88	44	35	6	6	3	3	40	4	92	5	4	6	4	.600	1	0	3.34
1989 Ft.Laudrdle	A	11	4	0	4	45.2	185	40	15	12	2	1	2	1	14	0	48	2	1	3	3	.500	0	0	2.36
Albany	AA	16	16	7	0	117.2	467	67	31	27	5	3	0	1	58	1	132	2	0	12	1	.923	5	0	2.07
1990 Columbus	AAA	27	27	6	0	177	764	153	72	57	9	4	6	5	98	0	138	4	1	15	7	.682	2	0	2.90
1991 Columbus	AAA	14	13	3	1	80.1	360	75	59	50	7	4	5	0	57	1	52	5	2	4	5	.444	0	0	5.60
Iowa	AAA	13	12	0	0	63	273	57	41	36	6	5	3	2	32	0	48	8	0	4	4	.500	0	0	5.14
1992 Iowa	AAA	33	22	0	3	135	632	161	103	92	18	6	5	3	74	0	89	15	0	7	13	.350	0	0	6.13
1993 Syracuse	AAA	5	0	0	0	3.2	17	4	2	2	0	1	0	0	3	0	0	1	0	0	0	.000	0	0	4.91
Birmingham	AA	26	3	0	8	50	213	46	25	23	2	1	1	1	20	2	40	2	0	1	4	.200	0	2	4.14
1994 Bowie	AA	6	0	0	4	8	31	6	2	2	0	1	0	0	4	0	4	0	0	0	1	.000	0	1	2.25
Rochester	AAA	41	0	0	26	48	228	63	36	25	2	4	2	0	23	6	35	5	0	0	7	.000	0	7	4.69
1990 New York	AL	5	5	0	0	24	115	19	18	17	4	1	1	0	29	0	14	2	0	1	2	.333	0	0	6.38
9 Min. YEARS		263	138	20	61	1040	4517	965	536	449	71	46	31	19	537	17	843	72	10	70	60	.538	9	16	3.89

Sharnol Adriana
Bats: Right Throws: Right Pos: 2B   Ht: 6'1" Wt: 185 Born: 11/13/70 Age: 24

Year Team	Lg	G	AB	H	2B	3B	HR	TB	R	RBI	TBB	IBB	SO	HBP	SH	SF	SB	CS	SB%	GDP	Avg	OBP	SLG
1991 St.Cathmes	A	51	170	35	8	0	5	58	27	20	26	0	33	5	1	4	9	4	.69	6	.206	.322	.341
1992 Dunedin	A	69	210	58	6	3	0	70	25	18	31	1	43	0	4	0	9	4	.69	5	.276	.369	.333
1993 Knoxville	AA	64	177	38	3	1	0	43	19	18	24	2	59	2	2	2	8	8	.53	4	.215	.312	.243
1994 Syracuse	AAA	17	30	4	2	0	0	6	2	0	6	0	8	0	1	0	1	0	1.00	1	.133	.278	.200
Knoxville	AA	69	189	47	7	1	3	65	28	21	31	1	39	2	3	1	7	7	.50	5	.249	.359	.344
4 Min. YEARS		270	776	182	26	5	8	242	101	77	118	4	182	9	11	7	35	23	.60	21	.235	.340	.312

Pat Ahearne
Pitches: Right Bats: Right Pos: P   Ht: 6'3" Wt: 195 Born: 12/10/69 Age: 25

Year Team	Lg	G	GS	CG	GF	IP	BFP	H	R	ER	HR	SH	SF	HB	TBB	IBB	SO	WP	Bk	W	L	Pct.	ShO	Sv	ERA
1992 Lakeland	A	1	1	0	0	4.2	17	4	2	1	0	0	0	0	0	0	4	0	0	0	0	.000	0	0	1.93
1993 Lakeland	A	25	24	2	0	147.1	650	160	87	73	8	7	4	6	48	0	51	3	1	6	15	.286	0	0	4.46
1994 Trenton	AA	30	13	2	3	108.2	467	126	55	48	8	1	6	5	25	1	57	5	0	7	5	.583	0	0	3.98
3 Min. YEARS		56	38	4	3	260.2	1134	290	144	122	16	8	10	11	73	1	112	8	1	13	20	.394	0	0	4.21

Jose Alberro
Pitches: Right Bats: Right Pos: P   Ht: 6'2" Wt: 190 Born: 06/29/69 Age: 26

Year Team	Lg	G	GS	CG	GF	IP	BFP	H	R	ER	HR	SH	SF	HB	TBB	IBB	SO	WP	Bk	W	L	Pct.	ShO	Sv	ERA
1991 Rangers	R	19	0	0	16	30.1	121	17	6	5	1	1	0	4	9	0	40	1	2	2	0	1.000	0	6	1.48
Charlotte	A	5	0	0	0	5.2	33	8	9	6	0	1	0	1	7	2	3	3	0	0	1	.000	0	0	9.53
1992 Gastonia	A	17	0	0	6	20.2	84	18	8	8	2	0	1	1	4	0	26	1	0	1	0	1.000	0	1	3.48

4

Year	Team	Lg	G	GS	CG	GF	IP	BFP	H	R	ER	HR	SH	SF	HB	TBB	IBB	SO	WP	Bk	W	L	Pct.	ShO	Sv	ERA
	Charlotte	A	28	0	0	20	45	175	37	10	6	0	2	0	3	9	0	29	1	1	1	1	.500	0	15	1.20
1993	Tulsa	AA	17	0	0	16	19	78	11	2	2	2	1	0	0	8	1	24	2	1	0	0	.000	0	5	0.95
	Okla City	AAA	12	0	0	7	17	85	25	15	13	2	1	2	0	11	0	14	4	0	0	0	.000	0	0	6.88
1994	Okla. City	AAA	52	0	0	35	69.2	314	79	40	35	6	6	4	5	36	8	50	3	0	4	3	.571	0	11	4.52
	4 Min. YEARS		150	0	0	100	207.1	890	195	90	75	13	12	7	14	84	11	186	15	4	8	5	.615	0	38	3.26

Manny Alexander

Bats: Right **Throws:** Right **Pos:** SS · Ht: 5'10" **Wt:** 165 **Born:** 03/20/71 **Age:** 24

						BATTING												BASERUNNING				PERCENTAGES		
Year	Team	Lg	G	AB	H	2B	3B	HR	TB	R	RBI	TBB	IBB	SO	HBP	SH	SF	SB	CS	SB%	GDP	Avg	OBP	SLG
1989	Bluefield	R	65	274	85	13	2	2	108	49	34	20	1	49	3	0	2	19	8	.70	2	.310	.361	.394
1990	Wausau	A	44	152	27	3	1	0	32	16	11	12	1	41	1	1	3	8	3	.73	2	.178	.238	.211
1991	Frederick	A	134	548	143	17	3	3	175	81	42	44	0	68	2	3	1	47	14	.77	4	.261	.318	.319
	Hagerstown	AA	3	9	3	1	0	0	4	3	2	1	0	3	1	0	1	0	0	.00	0	.333	.417	.444
1992	Hagerstown	AA	127	499	129	23	8	2	174	69	41	25	0	62	6	4	4	43	12	.78	10	.259	.300	.349
	Rochester	AAA	6	24	7	1	0	0	8	3	3	1	0	3	0	1	0	2	2	.50	0	.292	.320	.333
1993	Rochester	AAA	120	471	115	23	8	6	172	55	51	22	0	60	4	2	1	19	7	.73	11	.244	.283	.365
1994	Rochester	AAA	111	426	106	23	6	6	159	63	39	16	0	67	3	4	5	30	8	.79	7	.249	.278	.373
1992	Baltimore	AL	4	5	1	0	0	0	1	1	0	0	0	3	0	0	0	0	0	.00	0	.200	.200	.200
1993	Baltimore	AL	3	0	0	0	0	0	0	1	0	0	0	0	0	0	0	0	0	.00	0	.000	.000	.000
	6 Min. YEARS		610	2403	615	104	28	19	832	339	223	141	2	353	20	15	17	168	54	.76	36	.256	.301	.346
	2 Maj. YEARS		7	5	1	0	0	0	1	2	0	0	0	3	0	0	0	0	0	.00	0	.200	.200	.200

Edgar Alfonzo

Bats: Right **Throws:** Right **Pos:** 3B · Ht: 6'0" **Wt:** 167 **Born:** 06/10/67 **Age:** 28

						BATTING												BASERUNNING				PERCENTAGES		
Year	Team	Lg	G	AB	H	2B	3B	HR	TB	R	RBI	TBB	IBB	SO	HBP	SH	SF	SB	CS	SB%	GDP	Avg	OBP	SLG
1985	Quad City	A	8	21	6	0	0	0	6	3	0	2	0	2	1	0	0	0	2	.00	0	.286	.375	.286
	Salem	A	56	209	57	10	2	4	83	29	25	17	0	28	2	2	2	0	3	.00	3	.273	.330	.397
1986	Quad City	A	67	219	47	8	1	1	60	21	12	22	0	42	2	6	0	1	1	.50	9	.215	.292	.274
1987	Palm Spngs	A	36	92	28	4	0	1	35	13	15	13	0	21	0	3	1	1	1	.50	1	.304	.387	.380
	Quad City	A	51	198	50	9	3	4	77	25	25	12	0	35	2	3	3	3	7	.30	3	.253	.298	.389
1988	Palm Spngs	A	5	9	1	0	0	0	1	0	2	1	0	3	0	0	0	0	0	.00	0	.111	.200	.111
	Quad City	A	102	406	83	12	2	2	105	36	36	23	1	58	6	8	6	5	5	.50	4	.204	.254	.259
1989	Palm Spngs	A	77	242	58	10	2	3	81	31	27	40	0	37	3	3	3	8	3	.73	4	.240	.351	.335
1990	Edmonton	AAA	4	11	2	0	0	0	2	1	1	0	0	0	0	1	0	0	0	.00	1	.182	.182	.182
	Midland	AA	37	121	36	4	1	1	45	20	9	8	0	18	2	1	1	1	0	1.00	4	.298	.348	.372
	Palm Spngs	A	57	203	56	4	2	2	70	44	12	30	0	37	0	5	2	5	4	.56	2	.276	.366	.345
1991	Palm Spngs	A	81	292	81	11	4	4	112	43	38	38	3	32	1	10	2	5	7	.42	8	.277	.360	.384
	Midland	AA	26	83	23	1	1	4	38	13	13	2	0	7	1	2	0	0	0	.00	2	.277	.302	.458
1992	Palm Spngs	A	65	257	92	18	2	3	123	52	42	31	3	25	2	0	3	1	4	.20	8	.358	.427	.479
	Midland	AA	61	220	65	9	1	4	88	39	30	26	0	30	5	1	0	2	2	.50	8	.295	.382	.400
1993	Bowie	AA	130	459	121	22	3	5	164	45	49	37	1	49	4	5	11	14	4	.78	15	.264	.317	.357
1994	Bowie	AA	124	463	143	35	1	11	213	75	73	40	2	63	4	3	6	13	8	.62	13	.309	.365	.460
	10 Min. YEARS		987	3505	949	157	25	49	1303	490	409	342	10	487	35	53	40	59	51	.54	85	.271	.338	.372

Edgardo Alfonzo

Bats: Right **Throws:** Right **Pos:** INF · Ht: 5'11" **Wt:** 178 **Born:** 08/11/73 **Age:** 21

						BATTING												BASERUNNING				PERCENTAGES		
Year	Team	Lg	G	AB	H	2B	3B	HR	TB	R	RBI	TBB	IBB	SO	HBP	SH	SF	SB	CS	SB%	GDP	Avg	OBP	SLG
1991	Mets	R	54	175	58	8	4	0	74	29	27	34	0	12	2	3	7	6	4	.60	1	.331	.431	.423
1992	St. Lucie	A	4	5	0	0	0	0	0	0	0	0	0	0	0	0	0	0	0	.00	0	.000	.000	.000
	Pittsfield	A	74	298	106	13	5	1	132	41	44	18	1	31	0	2	4	7	5	.58	6	.356	.388	.443
1993	St.Lucie	A	128	494	145	18	3	11	202	75	86	57	3	51	5	4	9	26	16	.62	13	.294	.366	.409
1994	Binghamton	AA	127	498	146	34	2	15	229	89	75	64	6	55	0	5	7	14	11	.56	9	.293	.369	.460
	4 Min. YEARS		387	1470	455	73	14	27	637	234	232	173	10	149	7	14	27	53	36	.60	29	.310	.379	.433

Jeffrey Alkire

Pitches: Left **Bats:** Right **Pos:** P · Ht: 6'1" **Wt:** 200 **Born:** 11/15/69 **Age:** 25

			HOW MUCH HE PITCHED						WHAT HE GAVE UP										THE RESULTS					
Year	Team	Lg	G	GS	CG	GF	IP	BFP	H	R	ER	HR	SH	SF	HB	TBB	IBB	SO	WP	Bk	W	L	Pct.	ShO	Sv	ERA
1993	Savannah	A	28	28	0	0	171.2	711	143	56	47	10	5	3	11	68	0	175	8	0	15	6	.714	0	0	2.46
1994	Arkansas	AA	8	8	0	0	37.1	171	50	27	25	0	2	0	0	17	0	31	3	0	4	3	.571	0	0	6.03
	St. Pete	A	12	12	2	0	70	289	61	32	22	2	3	5	3	22	0	56	4	1	4	5	.444	0	0	2.83
	2 Min. YEARS		48	48	2	0	279	1171	254	115	94	12	10	8	14	107	0	262	15	1	23	14	.622	0	0	3.03

Andy Allanson

Bats: Right **Throws:** Right **Pos:** C · Ht: 6'5" **Wt:** 225 **Born:** 12/22/61 **Age:** 33

						BATTING												BASERUNNING				PERCENTAGES		
Year	Team	Lg	G	AB	H	2B	3B	HR	TB	R	RBI	TBB	IBB	SO	HBP	SH	SF	SB	CS	SB%	GDP	Avg	OBP	SLG
1990	Okla City	AAA	13	40	4	0	0	0	4	3	4	6	0	7	0	1	0	0	0	.00	2	.100	.217	.100
	Salinas	A	36	127	37	6	1	3	54	21	18	19	0	22	2	0	2	6	5	.55	4	.291	.387	.425

Year	Team	Lg	G	AB	H	2B	3B	HR	TB	R	RBI	TBB	IBB	SO	HBP	SH	SF	SB	CS	SB%	GDP	Avg	OBP	SLG
1992	Denver	AAA	72	266	79	16	3	4	113	42	31	23	0	29	1	3	1	9	4	.69	4	.297	.354	.425
1993	Phoenix	AAA	50	161	57	15	2	6	94	31	23	10	1	18	1	1	2	7	4	.64	4	.354	.391	.584
1994	San Bernrdo	A	20	61	14	2	1	1	21	13	9	15	0	8	3	0	0	6	2	.75	2	.230	.405	.344
	Vancouver	AAA	40	138	36	11	0	3	56	18	22	10	1	15	2	1	2	4	1	.80	7	.261	.316	.406
1986	Cleveland	AL	101	293	66	7	3	1	82	30	29	14	0	36	1	11	4	10	1	.91	7	.225	.260	.280
1987	Cleveland	AL	50	154	41	6	0	3	56	17	16	9	0	30	0	4	5	1	1	.50	2	.266	.298	.364
1988	Cleveland	AL	133	434	114	11	0	5	140	44	50	25	2	63	3	8	4	5	9	.36	6	.263	.305	.323
1989	Cleveland	AL	111	323	75	9	1	3	95	30	17	23	2	47	4	6	3	4	4	.50	7	.232	.289	.294
1991	Detroit	AL	60	151	35	10	0	1	48	10	16	7	0	31	0	2	0	0	1	.00	1	.232	.266	.318
1992	Milwaukee	AL	9	25	8	1	0	0	9	6	0	1	0	2	0	2	0	3	1	.75	3	.320	.346	.360
1993	San Francisco	NL	13	24	4	1	0	0	5	3	2	1	0	2	0	1	0	0	0	.00	1	.167	.200	.208
	4 Min. YEARS		231	793	227	50	7	17	342	128	107	83	2	99	9	6	7	32	16	.67	23	.286	.358	.431
	7 Maj. YEARS		477	1404	343	45	4	13	435	140	130	80	4	211	8	34	16	23	17	.58	27	.244	.286	.310

Ronnie Allen

Pitches: Right Bats: Right Pos: P Ht: 5'11" Wt: 185 Born: 05/10/70 Age: 25

			HOW MUCH HE PITCHED						WHAT HE GAVE UP												THE RESULTS					
Year	Team	Lg	G	GS	CG	GF	IP	BFP	H	R	ER	HR	SH	SF	HB	TBB	IBB	SO	WP	Bk	W	L	Pct.	ShO	Sv	ERA
1991	Batavia	A	8	7	0	1	46	171	33	18	16	5	1	1	1	7	0	39	2	2	3	3	.500	0	0	3.13
	Spartanburg	A	2	2	2	0	14	57	14	5	5	1	0	0	0	4	0	7	0	1	2	0	1.000	0	0	3.21
1992	Clearwater	A	15	15	1	0	91.1	372	87	36	29	6	3	2	1	24	0	49	1	3	6	6	.500	1	0	2.86
	Reading	AA	5	5	1	0	31	133	35	18	17	2	0	3	1	9	1	17	0	1	1	3	.250	0	0	4.94
1993	Scranton/wb	AAA	5	5	0	0	24.1	110	30	15	14	3	1	2	1	8	1	12	1	0	0	2	.000	0	0	5.18
	Reading	AA	15	15	0	0	85	367	82	45	42	8	2	2	1	35	0	63	6	1	4	5	.444	0	0	4.45
1994	Clearwater	A	2	2	0	0	13.2	51	10	2	2	0	0	0	0	5	0	10	0	2	2	0	1.000	0	0	1.32
	Reading	AA	24	10	0	5	81.2	373	95	62	61	10	5	5	2	40	1	46	7	0	3	4	.429	0	0	6.72
	4 Min. YEARS		76	61	4	6	387	1634	386	201	186	35	12	15	7	132	3	243	17	9	21	23	.477	1	0	4.33

Steve Allen

Pitches: Right Bats: Right Pos: P Ht: 6'3" Wt: 210 Born: 07/27/66 Age: 28

			HOW MUCH HE PITCHED						WHAT HE GAVE UP												THE RESULTS					
Year	Team	Lg	G	GS	CG	GF	IP	BFP	H	R	ER	HR	SH	SF	HB	TBB	IBB	SO	WP	Bk	W	L	Pct.	ShO	Sv	ERA
1988	Butte	R	17	6	0	3	46.1	225	74	53	48	2	0	2	3	14	0	30	4	7	2	2	.500	0	1	9.32
1989	Gastonia	A	51	0	0	20	89	364	60	33	20	1	1	1	10	31	5	84	2	2	6	2	.750	0	3	2.02
1990	Tulsa	AA	54	0	0	23	89.1	408	97	43	38	4	7	3	7	42	6	84	7	0	8	4	.667	0	5	3.83
1991	San Antonio	AA	12	0	0	7	20.1	92	22	10	10	1	0	1	3	10	0	25	0	0	1	0	1.000	0	1	4.43
1992	San Antonio	AA	43	0	0	22	79	315	62	31	23	2	2	3	7	17	4	64	5	2	5	2	.714	0	5	2.62
1993	Albuquerque	AAA	2	0	0	0	1.2	9	3	2	2	0	0	0	0	2	0	1	0	0	1	0	1.000	0	0	10.80
	Colo Spmgs	AAA	35	0	0	16	62	272	70	32	27	5	5	3	0	26	4	31	1	0	5	4	.556	0	2	3.92
1994	Colo. Spmg	AAA	46	1	0	17	75.1	366	109	62	56	11	6	4	6	29	5	56	7	3	2	5	.286	0	2	6.69
	7 Min. YEARS		260	7	0	108	463	2051	497	266	224	29	21	17	36	171	24	375	26	15	30	19	.612	0	19	4.35

Jermaine Allensworth

Bats: Right Throws: Right Pos: OF Ht: 5'11" Wt: 180 Born: 01/11/72 Age: 23

			BATTING															BASERUNNING				PERCENTAGES		
Year	Team	Lg	G	AB	H	2B	3B	HR	TB	R	RBI	TBB	IBB	SO	HBP	SH	SF	SB	CS	SB%	GDP	Avg	OBP	SLG
1993	Welland	A	67	263	81	16	4	1	108	44	32	24	0	38	12	2	1	18	3	.86	2	.308	.390	.411
1994	Carolina	AA	118	452	109	26	8	1	154	63	34	39	0	79	11	5	3	16	14	.53	2	.241	.315	.341
	2 Min. YEARS		185	715	190	42	12	2	262	107	66	63	0	117	23	7	4	34	17	.67	4	.266	.343	.366

Dana Allison

Pitches: Left Bats: Right Pos: P Ht: 6'3" Wt: 215 Born: 08/14/66 Age: 28

			HOW MUCH HE PITCHED						WHAT HE GAVE UP												THE RESULTS					
Year	Team	Lg	G	GS	CG	GF	IP	BFP	H	R	ER	HR	SH	SF	HB	TBB	IBB	SO	WP	Bk	W	L	Pct.	ShO	Sv	ERA
1989	Madison	A	13	0	0	11	24	100	24	6	3	0	3	0	1	3	2	16	1	0	2	3	.400	0	1	1.13
	Sou Oregon	A	11	2	0	6	29.1	108	17	8	6	0	0	1	1	4	0	27	2	1	0	2	.000	0	4	1.84
1990	Modesto	A	10	0	0	8	19.1	76	13	9	5	0	0	1	0	3	0	19	0	1	0	0	.000	0	4	2.33
	Huntsville	AA	35	0	0	14	52.2	216	52	14	14	2	7	2	0	6	3	36	1	0	7	1	.875	0	2	2.39
	Tacoma	AAA	2	0	0	1	1.1	5	1	0	0	0	0	0	0	1	0	2	0	0	0	0	.000	0	0	0.00
1991	Tacoma	AAA	18	0	0	4	22.2	101	25	12	11	2	2	0	1	11	2	13	0	1	3	1	.750	0	0	4.37
1992	Huntsville	AA	22	6	0	6	61.1	237	51	24	20	8	3	2	1	5	0	40	1	1	4	1	.800	0	1	2.93
	Tacoma	AAA	19	4	0	6	44.2	215	63	32	24	6	2	5	1	17	2	17	0	0	2	3	.400	0	0	4.84
1993	Huntsville	AA	19	0	0	6	40	159	40	9	8	5	0	0	0	4	2	18	1	0	2	3	.400	0	0	1.80
	Tacoma	AAA	23	5	0	5	62.1	270	75	35	31	7	6	2	0	19	1	30	0	0	3	3	.500	0	0	4.48
1994	Tacoma	AAA	33	21	2	3	151	674	204	105	97	16	3	7	3	31	3	60	6	1	10	8	.556	2	0	5.78
1991	Oakland	AL	11	0	0	4	11	49	16	9	9	0	1	1	0	5	1	4	0	0	1	1	.500	0	0	7.36
	6 Min. YEARS		205	38	2	70	508.2	2162	565	254	219	46	26	20	7	104	15	278	12	5	33	25	.569	2	12	3.87

Tom Allison

Bats: Both Throws: Right Pos: 2B Ht: 5'10" Wt: 165 Born: 09/13/67 Age: 27

			BATTING															BASERUNNING				PERCENTAGES		
Year	Team	Lg	G	AB	H	2B	3B	HR	TB	R	RBI	TBB	IBB	SO	HBP	SH	SF	SB	CS	SB%	GDP	Avg	OBP	SLG
1990	Mets	R	1	4	0	0	0	0	0	0	0	0	0	0	1	0	0	0	0	.00	0	.000	.000	.000

Year	Team	Lg	G	AB	H	2B	3B	HR	TB	R	RBI	TBB	IBB	SO	HBP	SH	SF	SB	CS	SB%	GDP	Avg	OBP	SLG
	Pittsfield	A	59	160	40	4	2	1	51	35	15	25	0	32	4	6	2	10	4	.71	3	.250	.361	.319
1991	Columbia	A	43	121	39	11	1	1	55	26	10	17	0	24	4	3	0	9	2	.82	2	.322	.423	.455
	Williamsprt	AA	31	89	20	4	1	0	26	13	9	11	0	19	1	2	1	2	1	.67	1	.225	.314	.292
	St. Lucie	A	22	74	12	1	0	0	13	7	7	9	0	24	0	3	2	8	0	1.00	1	.162	.247	.176
1992	Tidewater	AAA	5	10	4	1	1	0	7	4	1	2	0	0	0	0	0	0	0	.00	1	.400	.500	.700
	Binghamton	AA	59	117	29	4	0	2	39	19	14	18	0	37	1	3	1	1	2	.33	0	.248	.350	.333
1993	Norfolk	AAA	13	34	8	0	0	0	8	9	3	8	0	7	0	0	1	0	0	.00	0	.235	.372	.235
	Binghamton	AA	63	130	26	7	2	0	37	16	5	20	0	34	1	3	0	5	0	1.00	4	.200	.311	.285
1994	Binghamton	AA	7	5	1	0	0	0	1	1	0	0	0	3	0	2	0	0	0	.00	0	.200	.200	.200
	5 Min. YEARS		303	744	179	32	7	4	237	130	64	110	0	181	11	22	7	35	9	.80	13	.241	.344	.319

Beau Allred

Bats: Left Throws: Left Pos: OF　　　　**Ht: 6' 0" Wt: 193 Born: 06/04/65 Age: 30**

			BATTING															BASERUNNING				PERCENTAGES		
Year	Team	Lg	G	AB	H	2B	3B	HR	TB	R	RBI	TBB	IBB	SO	HBP	SH	SF	SB	CS	SB%	GDP	Avg	OBP	SLG
1987	Burlington	R	54	167	57	14	1	10	103	39	38	35	3	33	1	2	4	4	0	1.00	1	.341	.449	.617
1988	Kinston	A	126	397	100	23	3	15	174	66	74	59	4	112	5	0	8	6	0	1.00	5	.252	.350	.438
1989	Canton-Akrn	AA	118	412	125	23	5	14	200	67	75	56	2	88	2	2	8	16	5	.76	8	.303	.383	.485
	Colo Sprngs	AAA	11	47	13	3	0	1	19	8	4	2	1	10	0	0	0	3	3	.00	2	.277	.306	.404
1990	Colo Sprngs	AAA	115	378	105	23	6	13	179	79	74	60	1	54	4	2	7	6	3	.67	5	.278	.376	.474
1991	Colo Sprngs	AAA	53	148	37	12	3	6	73	39	21	34	1	55	3	0	2	1	1	.50	0	.250	.396	.493
1992	Colo Sprngs	AAA	135	434	125	23	10	17	219	79	76	57	8	75	7	2	10	1	1	.50	11	.288	.372	.505
1993	Charlotte	AAA	120	347	85	13	3	20	164	59	61	45	3	57	7	2	8	4	3	.57	5	.245	.337	.473
1994	Richmond	AAA	60	169	38	9	1	6	67	27	23	27	2	29	2	0	3	4	1	.80	2	.225	.333	.396
1989	Cleveland	AL	13	24	6	3	0	0	9	0	1	2	0	10	0	0	0	0	0	.00	0	.250	.308	.375
1990	Cleveland	AL	4	16	3	1	0	1	7	2	2	2	0	3	0	0	0	0	0	.00	0	.188	.278	.438
1991	Cleveland	AL	48	125	29	3	0	3	41	17	12	25	2	35	1	3	2	2	2	.50	1	.232	.359	.328
	8 Min. YEARS		792	2499	685	143	32	102	1198	463	446	375	25	513	31	10	50	42	17	.71	39	.274	.369	.479
	3 Maj. YEARS		65	165	38	7	0	4	57	19	15	29	2	48	1	3	2	2	2	.50	1	.230	.345	.345

Garvin Alston

Pitches: Right Bats: Right Pos: P　　　　**Ht: 6'1" Wt: 175 Born: 12/08/71 Age: 23**

			HOW MUCH HE PITCHED					WHAT HE GAVE UP									THE RESULTS					
Year	Team	Lg	G	GS	CG	GF	IP	BFP	H	R	ER	HR	SH	SF	HB	TBB	IBB	SO	WP	Bk	W	L	Pct.	ShO	Sv	ERA
1992	Bend	A	14	12	0	0	73	320	71	40	32	1	5	5	9	29	0	73	7	8	5	4	.556	0	0	3.95
1993	Central Val	A	25	24	1	0	117	538	124	81	71	11	6	6	8	70	0	90	10	2	5	9	.357	0	0	5.46
1994	Central Val	A	37	13	0	20	87	382	91	51	35	9	5	0	6	42	1	83	5	2	5	9	.357	0	8	3.62
	New Haven	AA	4	0	0	1	4.1	22	5	6	6	1	0	0	0	3	0	8	0	0	0	0	.000	0	1	12.46
	3 Min. YEARS		80	49	1	21	281.1	1262	291	178	144	22	16	11	23	144	1	254	22	12	15	22	.405	0	9	4.61

Clemente Alvarez

Bats: Right Throws: Right Pos: C　　　　**Ht: 5'11" Wt: 180 Born: 05/18/68 Age: 27**

			BATTING															BASERUNNING				PERCENTAGES		
Year	Team	Lg	G	AB	H	2B	3B	HR	TB	R	RBI	TBB	IBB	SO	HBP	SH	SF	SB	CS	SB%	GDP	Avg	OBP	SLG
1987	White Sox	R	25	55	10	1	0	1	14	8	4	7	0	8	0	0	0	1	1	.50	1	.182	.274	.255
1988	South Bend	A	15	41	3	0	0	0	3	0	1	3	0	19	0	0	0	0	0	.00	2	.073	.136	.073
	Utica	A	53	132	31	5	1	0	38	15	14	11	0	36	2	4	1	5	2	.71	2	.235	.301	.288
1989	South Bend	A	86	230	51	15	0	0	66	22	22	16	0	59	0	9	1	4	1	.80	6	.222	.271	.287
1990	Sarasota	A	37	119	19	4	1	1	28	9	9	8	0	24	0	2	0	0	0	.00	5	.160	.213	.235
	South Bend	A	48	127	30	5	0	2	41	14	12	20	0	38	1	5	2	2	1	.67	1	.236	.340	.323
1991	Sarasota	A	71	194	40	10	2	1	57	14	22	20	0	41	4	7	1	3	2	.60	6	.206	.292	.294
1992	Birmingham	AA	57	169	24	8	0	1	35	7	10	10	0	52	2	3	0	1	1	.50	5	.142	.199	.207
1993	White Sox	R	2	5	0	0	0	0	0	0	0	1	0	2	0	0	0	0	1	.00	0	.000	.167	.000
	Nashville	AAA	11	29	6	0	0	0	6	1	2	1	0	4	0	2	0	0	0	.00	0	.207	.233	.207
	Birmingham	AA	35	111	25	4	0	1	32	8	8	11	0	28	1	1	1	0	4	.00	3	.225	.298	.288
1994	Nashville	AAA	87	223	48	8	1	3	67	18	14	17	0	48	2	12	2	0	2	.00	2	.215	.275	.300
	8 Min. YEARS		527	1435	287	60	5	10	387	116	118	125	0	359	12	45	8	16	15	.52	33	.200	.268	.270

Jorge Alvarez

Bats: Right Throws: Right Pos: 2B　　　　**Ht: 5'10" Wt: 155 Born: 10/30/68 Age: 26**

			BATTING															BASERUNNING				PERCENTAGES		
Year	Team	Lg	G	AB	H	2B	3B	HR	TB	R	RBI	TBB	IBB	SO	HBP	SH	SF	SB	CS	SB%	GDP	Avg	OBP	SLG
1988	Dodgers	R	55	167	49	13	2	0	66	23	24	17	1	25	2	2	2	5	3	.63	2	.293	.362	.395
1989	Salem	A	76	291	78	14	6	6	122	46	33	49	1	58	3	1	0	22	11	.67	1	.268	.379	.419
1990	Vero Beach	A	124	454	131	19	5	1	163	56	48	31	0	58	9	3	2	31	12	.72	10	.289	.345	.359
1991	San Antonio	AA	66	225	67	14	2	3	94	33	23	18	2	32	3	2	1	9	6	.60	4	.298	.356	.418
1992	San Antonio	AA	103	305	74	11	4	5	108	33	32	21	1	64	2	4	3	8	4	.67	6	.243	.293	.354
1993	San Antonio	AA	93	251	68	24	0	4	104	26	34	20	3	34	1	1	3	9	8	.53	7	.271	.324	.414
1994	Portland	AA	89	189	39	13	1	1	57	22	16	8	0	32	1	1	2	2	5	.29	2	.206	.242	.302
	7 Min. YEARS		606	1882	506	108	20	20	714	239	210	164	8	303	21	14	11	86	49	.64	32	.269	.333	.379

7

Cliff Anderson

Bats: Left **Throws:** Right **Pos:** SS **Ht:** 5'8" **Wt:** 165 **Born:** 07/04/70 **Age:** 24

Year Team	Lg	G	AB	H	2B	3B	HR	TB	R	RBI	TBB	IBB	SO	HBP	SH	SF	SB	CS	SB%	GDP	Avg	OBP	SLG
1992 Yakima	A	51	142	31	11	2	3	55	24	18	24	2	29	4	2	4	2	4	.33	2	.218	.339	.387
1993 Yakima	A	23	81	18	4	0	1	25	7	7	7	2	19	2	0	1	1	0	1.00	2	.222	.297	.309
Bakersfield	A	12	36	5	3	0	0	8	4	3	1	0	13	0	3	0	0	1	.00	2	.139	.162	.222
Great Falls	R	37	141	42	9	2	1	58	19	22	5	1	27	1	3	1	1	3	.25	3	.298	.324	.411
1994 Vero Beach	A	23	72	24	4	0	0	28	7	9	3	0	12	1	1	1	0	0	.00	2	.333	.364	.389
San Antonio	AA	41	99	24	9	0	1	36	8	15	4	1	25	2	1	1	0	0	.00	0	.242	.283	.364
3 Min. YEARS		187	571	144	40	4	6	210	69	74	44	6	125	10	10	8	4	8	.33	11	.252	.313	.368

Mike Anderson

Pitches: Right **Bats:** Right **Pos:** P **Ht:** 6'3" **Wt:** 205 **Born:** 07/30/66 **Age:** 28

Year Team	Lg	G	GS	CG	GF	IP	BFP	H	R	ER	HR	SH	SF	HB	TBB	IBB	SO	WP	Bk	W	L	Pct.	ShO	Sv	ERA
1988 Reds	R	2	2	0	0	7.1	34	6	7	4	0	0	0	0	5	0	11	3	4	0	1	.000	0	0	4.91
Billings	R	17	4	0	12	44.1	192	36	17	16	1	0	4	2	21	1	52	4	0	3	1	.750	0	2	3.25
1989 Greensboro	A	25	25	4	0	154.1	647	117	64	49	7	2	3	8	72	0	154	9	2	11	6	.647	2	0	2.86
1990 Cedar Rapds	A	23	23	2	0	138.1	613	134	67	52	6	8	7	5	62	0	101	10	0	10	5	.667	0	0	3.38
1991 Chattanooga	AA	28	26	3	1	155.1	698	142	94	76	8	4	4	8	93	2	115	17	1	10	9	.526	3	0	4.40
1992 Chattanooga	AA	28	26	4	1	171.2	716	155	59	48	4	0	3	7	61	1	149	15	3	13	7	.650	4	0	2.52
1993 Chattanooga	AA	2	2	1	0	15	54	10	3	2	0	1	1	0	1	0	14	0	0	1	1	.500	0	0	1.20
Indianapols	AAA	23	23	2	0	151	647	150	73	63	10	7	7	4	56	5	111	8	0	10	6	.625	1	0	3.75
1994 Iowa	AAA	40	14	0	9	110	510	132	90	75	6	6	7	5	57	6	78	12	0	4	8	.333	0	0	6.14
1993 Cincinnati	NL	3	0	0	0	5.1	30	12	11	11	3	0	0	0	3	0	4	0	0	0	0	.000	0	0	18.56
7 Min. YEARS		188	145	16	23	947.1	4111	882	474	385	42	28	36	39	428	15	785	78	10	62	44	.585	10	2	3.66

Paul Anderson

Pitches: Right **Bats:** Right **Pos:** P **Ht:** 6'4" **Wt:** 215 **Born:** 12/19/68 **Age:** 26

Year Team	Lg	G	GS	CG	GF	IP	BFP	H	R	ER	HR	SH	SF	HB	TBB	IBB	SO	WP	Bk	W	L	Pct.	ShO	Sv	ERA
1990 Cardinals	R	4	1	0	0	12	51	9	2	2	1	0	0	1	3	0	13	0	0	0	0	.000	0	0	1.50
1991 Springfield	A	27	27	5	0	174.2	730	171	98	72	13	8	6	3	38	2	109	13	2	9	14	.391	0	0	3.71
1992 St. Pete	A	5	2	0	0	16	65	13	9	5	1	0	2	1	5	0	4	2	0	0	2	.000	0	0	2.81
Arkansas	AA	22	20	2	0	123	500	117	49	46	13	2	3	3	27	4	73	7	0	4	11	.267	0	0	3.37
1993 Arkansas	AA	17	17	4	0	107.2	449	102	52	45	9	3	0	2	24	4	81	5	2	6	9	.400	2	0	3.76
Louisville	AAA	11	11	2	0	70	297	74	41	38	7	2	3	2	14	0	32	7	2	3	5	.375	0	0	4.89
1994 Louisville	AAA	11	3	0	1	28.2	124	29	22	22	4	4	1	3	8	1	20	2	0	4	2	.667	0	0	6.91
Arkansas	AA	14	4	0	3	37.2	178	60	33	27	3	3	3	1	9	1	30	4	1	0	4	.000	0	0	6.45
5 Min. YEARS		111	85	13	4	569.2	2394	576	306	257	51	22	18	16	128	12	362	40	7	26	47	.356	2	0	4.06

Scott Anderson

Pitches: Right **Bats:** Right **Pos:** P **Ht:** 6'6" **Wt:** 190 **Born:** 05/01/62 **Age:** 33

Year Team	Lg	G	GS	CG	GF	IP	BFP	H	R	ER	HR	SH	SF	HB	TBB	IBB	SO	WP	Bk	W	L	Pct.	ShO	Sv	ERA
1984 Burlington	A	14	13	2	0	86.1	366	79	33	24	8	3	4	4	28	0	81	2	1	3	6	.333	0	0	2.50
1985 Tulsa	AA	28	27	2	0	174.1	735	177	87	71	15	4	0	4	51	1	123	3	1	9	6	.600	1	0	3.67
1986 Tulsa	AA	10	0	0	7	18.2	76	11	4	3	0	2	2	0	8	0	13	0	0	0	0	.000	0	5	1.45
Okla City	AAA	48	0	0	39	82	355	82	36	27	6	5	7	1	28	3	51	1	0	5	7	.417	0	15	2.96
1987 Okla City	AAA	49	0	0	36	64	294	79	44	40	4	1	1	2	35	7	39	2	0	5	3	.625	0	0	5.63
1988 Okla City	AAA	38	10	0	10	97	421	101	51	49	6	5	4	3	49	3	44	2	3	4	6	.400	0	2	4.55
1989 Indianapols	AAA	29	19	1	3	127.2	560	139	62	45	7	12	6	4	44	1	88	5	2	7	8	.467	0	0	3.17
1990 Indianapols	AAA	27	25	6	2	182	750	166	74	67	16	8	5	0	61	2	116	6	1	12	10	.545	2	0	3.31
1993 Edmonton	AAA	44	1	0	14	66.1	285	74	30	26	6	2	0	2	15	2	52	1	0	5	4	.556	0	4	3.53
1994 New Orleans	AAA	8	3	0	1	24.1	111	34	20	19	4	0	1	0	6	0	17	0	0	0	2	.000	0	0	7.03
1987 Texas	AL	8	0	0	2	11.1	59	17	12	12	1	0	1	0	8	2	6	2	0	0	1	.000	0	0	9.53
1990 Montreal	NL	4	3	0	1	18	71	12	6	6	1	1	1	0	5	0	16	0	0	0	1	.000	0	0	3.00
9 Min. YEARS		295	98	11	112	922.2	3953	942	441	371	72	37	30	21	325	19	624	22	8	50	52	.490	3	34	3.62
2 Maj. YEARS		12	3	0	3	29.1	130	29	18	18	2	1	1	1	13	2	22	2	0	0	2	.000	0	0	5.52

Shane Andrews

Bats: Right **Throws:** Right **Pos:** 3B **Ht:** 6'1" **Wt:** 205 **Born:** 08/28/71 **Age:** 23

Year Team	Lg	G	AB	H	2B	3B	HR	TB	R	RBI	TBB	IBB	SO	HBP	SH	SF	SB	CS	SB%	GDP	Avg	OBP	SLG
1990 Expos	R	56	190	45	7	1	3	63	31	24	29	0	46	3	1	1	10	4	.71	7	.237	.345	.332
1991 Sumter	A	105	356	74	16	7	11	137	46	49	65	2	132	3	0	0	5	4	.56	8	.208	.335	.385
1992 Albany	A	136	453	104	18	1	25	199	76	87	107	4	174	7	0	3	8	3	.73	4	.230	.382	.439
1993 Harrisburg	AA	124	442	115	29	1	18	200	77	70	64	2	118	1	1	4	10	6	.63	8	.260	.352	.452
1994 Ottawa	AAA	137	460	117	25	2	16	194	79	85	80	5	126	5	0	5	6	5	.55	11	.254	.367	.422
5 Min. YEARS		558	1901	455	95	12	73	793	309	315	345	13	596	19	2	13	39	22	.64	38	.239	.360	.417

Juan Andujar

Bats: Both **Throws:** Right **Pos:** SS   **Ht:** 6'0" **Wt:** 150 **Born:** 08/14/71 **Age:** 23

Year	Team	Lg	G	AB	H	2B	3B	HR	TB	R	RBI	TBB	IBB	SO	HBP	SH	SF	SB	CS	SB%	GDP	Avg	OBP	SLG
1989	Johnson Cty	R	67	240	61	9	0	7	91	40	31	21	0	61	4	1	3	12	5	.71	2	.254	.321	.379
1990	Springfield	A	105	366	78	13	2	3	104	32	30	23	1	109	1	8	1	9	4	.69	6	.213	.261	.284
1991	Springfield	A	27	100	18	3	2	0	25	14	6	3	0	23	0	1	0	7	0	1.00	1	.180	.204	.250
	Savannah	A	100	320	67	9	5	3	95	39	29	28	0	80	1	5	1	27	4	.87	4	.209	.274	.297
1992	St. Pete	A	104	359	97	11	9	2	132	37	29	20	0	77	3	6	3	14	12	.54	3	.270	.312	.368
1993	Kinston	A	111	407	103	12	5	3	134	42	31	17	0	92	2	8	1	15	9	.63	4	.253	.286	.329
1994	Kinston	A	118	454	118	27	1	8	171	56	46	34	0	98	3	0	4	14	11	.56	5	.260	.313	.377
	Canton-Akrn	AA	12	40	8	1	0	0	9	4	0	1	0	10	0	1	0	1	1	.50	0	.200	.220	.225
6 Min. YEARS			644	2286	550	85	24	26	761	264	202	147	1	550	14	30	13	99	46	.68	25	.241	.289	.333

Luis Andujar

Pitches: Right **Bats:** Right **Pos:** P   **Ht:** 6'2" **Wt:** 175 **Born:** 11/22/72 **Age:** 22

Year	Team	Lg	G	GS	CG	GF	IP	BFP	H	R	ER	HR	SH	SF	HB	TBB	IBB	SO	WP	Bk	W	L	Pct.	ShO	Sv	ERA
1991	White Sox	R	10	10	1	0	62.1	255	60	27	17	0	1	2	4	10	0	52	3	1	4	4	.500	1	0	2.45
1992	South Bend	A	32	15	1	11	120.1	516	109	49	39	5	2	0	6	47	0	91	5	1	6	5	.545	1	3	2.92
1993	Sarasota	A	18	11	2	4	86	345	67	26	19	2	7	0	3	28	0	72	1	0	6	6	.500	0	1	1.99
	Birmingham	AA	6	6	0	0	39.2	169	31	9	8	3	3	1	5	18	0	48	1	0	5	0	1.000	0	0	1.82
1994	White Sox	R	2	0	0	0	6	22	3	1	0	0	0	0	1	1	0	6	0	0	1	0	1.000	0	0	0.00
	Birmingham	AA	15	15	0	0	76.2	344	90	50	43	5	1	2	8	25	0	64	5	0	3	7	.300	0	0	5.05
4 Min. YEARS			83	57	4	15	391	1651	360	162	126	15	14	5	27	129	0	333	15	2	25	22	.532	2	4	2.90

Kurt Archer

Pitches: Right **Bats:** Right **Pos:** P   **Ht:** 6'4" **Wt:** 215 **Born:** 04/27/69 **Age:** 26

Year	Team	Lg	G	GS	CG	GF	IP	BFP	H	R	ER	HR	SH	SF	HB	TBB	IBB	SO	WP	Bk	W	L	Pct.	ShO	Sv	ERA
1990	Helena	R	10	0	0	9	19.2	83	19	9	8	0	0	0	2	3	2	23	0	1	0	2	.000	0	3	3.66
	Beloit	A	11	0	0	3	29.1	122	24	11	5	1	1	3	1	9	1	27	2	1	5	0	1.000	0	1	1.53
1991	Stockton	A	27	6	0	9	46.1	219	45	36	22	1	3	4	7	29	3	26	5	0	2	4	.333	0	1	4.27
1992	Stockton	A	55	0	0	42	76.2	317	60	19	16	2	5	3	5	32	8	49	2	0	11	3	.786	0	15	1.88
1993	El Paso	AA	54	5	0	28	104.2	457	129	63	57	10	6	6	8	38	8	50	6	0	9	8	.529	0	11	4.90
1994	Stockton	A	5	0	0	4	5	22	6	2	2	0	0	0	0	1	1	5	0	0	0	1	.000	0	2	3.60
	El Paso	AA	44	1	0	16	77	327	87	40	35	6	4	4	2	17	2	58	2	0	5	3	.625	0	9	4.09
5 Min. YEARS			206	12	0	111	358.2	1547	370	180	145	20	19	20	25	129	25	238	17	2	32	21	.604	0	41	3.64

Marcos Armas

Bats: Right **Throws:** Right **Pos:** OF   **Ht:** 6'5" **Wt:** 195 **Born:** 08/05/69 **Age:** 25

Year	Team	Lg	G	AB	H	2B	3B	HR	TB	R	RBI	TBB	IBB	SO	HBP	SH	SF	SB	CS	SB%	GDP	Avg	OBP	SLG
1988	Athletics	R	17	58	17	2	1	0	21	14	10	5	0	17	0	0	0	0	0	.00	2	.293	.349	.362
1989	Sou Oregon	A	36	136	43	5	2	3	61	18	22	6	0	42	0	1	1	1	0	1.00	6	.316	.343	.449
1990	Madison	A	75	260	62	13	0	7	96	32	33	10	0	80	2	1	3	3	5	.38	11	.238	.269	.369
1991	Modesto	A	36	140	39	7	0	8	70	21	33	10	0	41	2	1	5	0	0	.00	5	.279	.325	.500
	Huntsville	AA	81	305	69	16	1	8	111	40	53	18	1	89	0	2	4	2	1	.67	11	.226	.266	.364
1992	Huntsville	AA	132	509	144	30	6	17	237	83	84	41	4	133	3	0	6	9	1	.90	11	.283	.336	.466
1993	Tacoma	AAA	117	434	126	27	8	15	214	69	89	35	1	113	3	1	6	4	0	1.00	7	.290	.343	.493
1994	Tacoma	AAA	113	443	127	26	5	18	217	57	73	19	1	117	5	0	1	1	2	.33	16	.287	.323	.490
1993	Oakland	AL	15	31	6	2	0	1	11	7	1	1	0	12	1	0	0	0	1	.00	0	.194	.242	.355
7 Min. YEARS			607	2285	627	126	23	76	1027	334	397	144	7	632	15	6	26	20	9	.69	69	.274	.318	.449

Ken Arnold

Bats: Right **Throws:** Right **Pos:** SS   **Ht:** 6'1" **Wt:** 180 **Born:** 05/10/69 **Age:** 26

Year	Team	Lg	G	AB	H	2B	3B	HR	TB	R	RBI	TBB	IBB	SO	HBP	SH	SF	SB	CS	SB%	GDP	Avg	OBP	SLG
1992	Peoria	A	91	271	57	4	3	1	70	41	22	42	0	65	3	4	1	11	4	.73	11	.210	.322	.258
1993	Thunder Bay	IND	55	183	54	7	0	0	61	22	19	11	1	36	1	2	1	12	6	.67	4	.295	.337	.333
1994	Bowie	AA	86	228	61	8	1	5	86	29	27	23	0	48	1	9	1	4	5	.44	3	.268	.336	.377
3 Min. YEARS			232	682	172	19	4	6	217	92	68	76	1	149	5	15	3	27	15	.64	18	.252	.330	.318

Ivan Arteaga

Bats: Left **Throws:** Right **Pos:** P   **Ht:** 6'2" **Wt:** 220 **Born:** 07/20/72 **Age:** 22

Year	Team	Lg	G	GS	CG	GF	IP	BFP	H	R	ER	HR	SH	SF	HB	TBB	IBB	SO	WP	Bk	W	L	Pct.	ShO	Sv	ERA
1993	Wst Plm Bch	A	4	4	0	0	15.2	80	23	15	14	1	1	0	1	9	0	10	0	0	0	3	.000	0	0	8.04
	Burlington	A	20	20	2	0	127.0	549	114	57	40	7	2	5	7	47	0	111	10	4	6	5	.545	0	0	2.83
1994	New Haven	AA	27	24	2	1	150.0	631	123	74	58	13	5	3	2	70	0	101	4	5	8	9	.471	0	0	3.48
2 Min. YEARS			51	48	4	1	292.2	1260	260	146	112	21	8	8	10	126	0	222	14	9	14	17	.452	0	0	3.44

9

Kym Ashworth

Pitches: Left **Bats: Left** **Pos: P** | Ht: 6'2" Wt: 185 Born: 07/31/76 Age: 18

		HOW MUCH HE PITCHED					WHAT HE GAVE UP											THE RESULTS					
Year	Team	Lg	G	GS	CG	GF	IP	BFP	H	R	ER	HR	SH	SF	HB	TBB	IBB	SO	WP	Bk	W	L	Pct.	ShO	Sv	ERA
1993	Great Falls	R	11	11	0	0	59	236	43	25	16	4	1	3	1	14	0	52	9	3	3	3	.500	0	0	2.44
1994	San Antonio	AA	1	1	0	0	4	18	5	3	2	0	0	0	0	0	0	6	0	0	0	1	.000	0	0	4.50
	Bakersfield	A	24	24	1	0	127.2	536	112	63	56	9	2	0	1	69	0	109	26	2	6	7	.462	1	0	3.95
	2 Min. YEARS		36	36	1	0	190.2	790	160	91	74	13	3	3	2	83	0	167	35	5	9	11	.450	1	0	3.49

Derek Aucoin

Pitches: Right **Bats: Right** **Pos: P** | Ht: 6'7" Wt: 226 Born: 03/27/70 Age: 25

		HOW MUCH HE PITCHED					WHAT HE GAVE UP											THE RESULTS					
Year	Team	Lg	G	GS	CG	GF	IP	BFP	H	R	ER	HR	SH	SF	HB	TBB	IBB	SO	WP	Bk	W	L	Pct.	ShO	Sv	ERA
1989	Expos	R	7	3	0	1	23.2	106	24	10	7	2	1	0	0	12	0	27	3	1	2	1	.667	0	1	2.66
1990	Jamestown	A	8	8	1	0	36.1	152	28	20	18	3	1	1	1	18	0	27	6	0	1	3	.250	0	0	4.46
1991	Sumter	A	41	4	0	8	90.1	408	85	55	43	7	4	2	10	44	3	70	6	1	3	6	.333	1	4	4.28
1992	Rockford	A	39	2	0	17	69	289	48	32	23	2	1	2	4	34	2	65	6	3	3	2	.600	0	3	3.00
1993	Wst Plm Bch	A	38	6	0	6	87.1	387	89	48	41	5	6	2	0	44	3	62	8	2	4	4	.500	0	1	4.23
1994	W. Palm Bch	A	7	0	0	5	7.1	26	3	0	0	0	0	0	0	2	0	10	0	0	0	0	.000	0	2	0.00
	Harrisburg	AA	31	0	0	12	47	208	36	19	17	4	1	0	2	29	0	48	3	0	3	4	.429	0	4	3.26
	6 Min. YEARS		171	23	1	49	361	1576	313	184	149	21	14	7	17	183	8	309	32	7	16	20	.444	0	12	3.71

Rich Aude

Bats: Right **Throws: Right** **Pos: 1B** | Ht: 6' 5" Wt: 180 Born: 07/13/71 Age: 23

		BATTING														BASERUNNING				PERCENTAGES		
Year	Team	Lg	G	AB	H	2B	3B	HR	TB	R	RBI	TBB	IBB	SO	HBP	SH	SF	SB	CS	SB%	GDP	Avg	OBP	SLG
1989	Pirates	R	24	88	19	3	0	0	22	13	7	5	0	17	3	0	1	2	0	1.00	1	.216	.278	.250
1990	Augusta	A	128	475	111	23	1	6	154	48	61	41	1	133	7	0	4	3	1	.75	11	.234	.302	.324
1991	Salem	A	103	366	97	12	2	3	122	45	43	27	5	72	9	0	0	3	0	1.00	7	.265	.331	.333
1992	Salem	A	122	447	128	26	4	9	189	63	60	50	2	79	8	0	1	11	2	.85	10	.286	.368	.423
	Carolina	AA	6	20	4	1	0	2	11	4	3	1	0	3	0	0	0	0	0	.00	0	.200	.238	.550
1993	Buffalo	AAA	21	64	24	9	0	4	45	17	16	10	0	15	1	0	1	0	0	.00	1	.375	.461	.703
	Carolina	AA	120	422	122	25	3	18	207	66	73	50	7	79	12	1	6	8	4	.67	6	.289	.376	.491
1994	Buffalo	AAA	138	520	146	38	4	15	237	66	79	41	3	83	11	0	2	9	5	.64	14	.281	.345	.456
1993	Pittsburgh	NL	13	26	3	1	0	0	4	1	4	1	0	7	0	0	0	0	0	.00	0	.115	.148	.154
	6 Min. YEARS		662	2402	651	137	14	57	987	322	342	225	18	481	51	1	15	36	12	.75	50	.271	.344	.411

Don August

Pitches: Right **Bats: Right** **Pos: P** | Ht: 6' 3" Wt: 190 Born: 07/03/63 Age: 31

		HOW MUCH HE PITCHED					WHAT HE GAVE UP											THE RESULTS					
Year	Team	Lg	G	GS	CG	GF	IP	BFP	H	R	ER	HR	SH	SF	HB	TBB	IBB	SO	WP	Bk	W	L	Pct.	ShO	Sv	ERA
1985	Columbus	AA	27	27	4	0	176.1	752	183	77	58	11	1	7	3	49	4	78	9	1	14	8	.636	2	0	2.96
1986	Tucson	AAA	24	24	3	0	154.2	659	166	78	58	7	3	10	1	44	4	60	7	1	8	9	.471	0	0	3.38
	Vancouver	AAA	3	3	1	0	24.1	102	26	10	9	0	0	3	0	7	1	10	0	0	2	1	.667	0	0	3.33
1987	Denver	AAA	28	27	8	1	179.1	787	220	124	111	16	2	6	5	55	3	91	4	0	10	9	.526	0	0	5.57
1988	Denver	AAA	10	10	3	0	71.2	302	79	37	28	6	0	1	1	14	0	58	2	3	4	1	.800	0	0	3.52
1989	Denver	AAA	4	4	0	0	23.2	108	35	18	13	3	1	0	1	5	0	12	1	0	1	1	.500	0	0	4.94
1990	Denver	AAA	22	22	3	0	124	553	164	98	93	17	0	2	5	27	1	67	1	1	7	7	.500	1	0	6.75
1991	Denver	AAA	1	1	0	0	5	18	3	0	0	0	0	0	0	0	0	1	0	0	1	0	1.000	0	0	0.00
1992	London	AA	11	6	1	0	53	210	47	16	16	5	1	1	0	10	2	39	2	0	3	2	.600	1	0	2.72
	Toledo	AAA	5	3	0	2	14.2	75	25	17	14	2	0	1	0	7	0	6	1	0	0	2	.000	0	0	8.59
1993	Charlotte	AAA	14	5	0	5	44.1	195	57	29	27	9	2	0	1	10	0	24	1	0	3	1	.750	0	0	5.48
1994	Wichita	AA	4	0	0	0	11.2	57	18	7	5	1	0	0	0	5	1	7	1	0	0	0	.000	0	0	3.86
1988	Milwaukee	AL	24	22	6	0	148.1	614	137	55	51	12	4	3	0	48	6	66	5	0	13	7	.650	1	0	3.09
1989	Milwaukee	AL	31	25	2	2	142.1	648	175	93	84	17	2	7	2	58	2	51	3	1	12	12	.500	1	0	5.31
1990	Milwaukee	AL	5	0	0	1	11	51	13	10	8	0	2	0	0	5	0	2	2	0	0	3	.000	0	0	6.55
1991	Milwaukee	AL	28	23	1	3	138.1	613	166	87	84	18	9	3	3	47	2	62	5	0	9	8	.529	1	0	5.47
	10 Min. YEARS		153	132	23	8	882.2	3818	1023	511	432	77	10	31	17	233	16	453	29	6	53	41	.564	4	0	4.40
	4 Maj. YEARS		88	70	9	6	440	1926	491	245	227	47	17	13	5	158	10	181	15	1	34	30	.531	3	0	4.64

Sam August

Pitches: Right **Bats: Right** **Pos: P** | Ht: 6'2" Wt: 170 Born: 11/24/67 Age: 27

		HOW MUCH HE PITCHED					WHAT HE GAVE UP											THE RESULTS					
Year	Team	Lg	G	GS	CG	GF	IP	BFP	H	R	ER	HR	SH	SF	HB	TBB	IBB	SO	WP	Bk	W	L	Pct.	ShO	Sv	ERA
1986	Astros	R	13	13	1	0	83	338	71	23	14	0	2	1	4	20	0	66	6	0	6	5	.545	0	0	1.52
1987	Asheville	A	18	18	5	0	115	468	82	35	22	4	3	2	4	39	0	110	4	1	12	1	.923	3	0	1.72
1988	Osceola	A	5	5	0	0	30	119	20	9	5	1	0	0	0	10	0	28	0	0	2	0	1.000	0	0	1.50
1989	Columbus	AA	2	2	0	0	8.2	36	4	3	3	1	1	1	0	6	0	8	1	0	0	0	.000	0	0	3.12
1990	Astros	R	7	7	0	0	29.1	113	25	10	5	1	1	0	0	2	0	22	1	0	4	2	.667	0	0	1.53
	Asheville	A	5	4	0	0	20	79	17	6	5	0	0	0	1	6	0	17	1	0	3	0	1.000	0	0	2.25
1991	Jackson	AA	7	7	0	0	34.1	149	27	22	20	2	1	1	2	19	0	25	1	0	1	2	.333	0	0	5.24
1992	Jackson	AA	4	4	0	0	19.2	82	15	6	4	1	0	0	2	8	0	16	0	1	1	1	.500	0	0	1.83
1994	Riverside	A	10	6	0	1	47.2	195	39	16	13	2	2	0	2	14	0	23	4	0	4	1	.800	0	0	2.45

		G	GS	CG	GF	IP	BFP	H	R	ER	HR	SH	SF	HB	TBB	IBB	SO	WP	Bk	W	L	Pct.	ShO	Sv	ERA
Jacksonville	AA	11	6	0	3	37.1	190	59	34	27	4	0	2	3	20	2	17	5	1	1	3	.250	0	0	6.51
8 Min. YEARS		82	72	6	4	425	1769	359	164	118	16	10	7	18	144	2	332	23	3	34	15	.694	3	0	2.50

Rich Aurilia

Bats: Right Throws: Right Pos: SS Ht: 6'0" Wt: 170 Born: 09/02/71 Age: 23

			BATTING												BASERUNNING				PERCENTAGES		
Year Team	Lg	G	AB	H	2B	3B	HR	TB	R	RBI	TBB	IBB	SO	HBP	SH	SF	SB	CS	SB%	GDP	Avg	OBP	SLG
1992 Butte	R	59	202	68	11	3	3	94	37	30	42	0	18	0	5	2	13	9	.59	2	.337	.447	.465
1993 Charlotte	A	122	440	136	16	5	5	177	80	56	75	4	57	3	9	7	15	18	.45	9	.309	.408	.402
1994 Tulsa	AA	129	458	107	18	6	12	173	67	57	53	0	74	4	8	5	10	13	.43	8	.234	.315	.378
3 Min. YEARS		310	1100	311	45	14	20	444	184	143	170	4	149	7	22	14	38	40	.49	19	.283	.378	.404

Joe Aversa

Bats: Both Throws: Right Pos: SS Ht: 5'10" Wt: 150 Born: 05/20/68 Age: 27

			BATTING												BASERUNNING				PERCENTAGES		
Year Team	Lg	G	AB	H	2B	3B	HR	TB	R	RBI	TBB	IBB	SO	HBP	SH	SF	SB	CS	SB%	GDP	Avg	OBP	SLG
1990 Cardinals	R	9	34	8	1	0	0	9	5	4	8	0	8	1	0	0	2	3	.40	1	.235	.395	.265
Johnson Cy	R	41	93	15	1	0	0	16	10	8	10	0	18	1	0	0	2	1	.67	2	.161	.250	.172
1991 Springfield	A	78	184	43	2	0	1	48	19	14	43	0	37	0	5	0	5	6	.45	2	.234	.379	.261
1992 St. Pete	A	25	44	7	1	0	0	8	4	3	8	0	8	0	0	1	0	1	.00	3	.159	.283	.182
Arkansas	AA	49	106	25	4	1	0	31	16	3	21	0	20	0	2	0	3	2	.60	1	.236	.362	.292
1993 Arkansas	AA	95	199	36	4	2	0	44	23	5	17	0	34	1	2	1	3	1	.75	3	.181	.248	.221
1994 St. Pete	A	15	31	5	2	0	0	7	6	3	8	0	2	0	0	0	0	0	.00	0	.161	.333	.226
Arkansas	AA	52	99	20	5	2	0	29	10	6	7	1	25	1	1	0	0	1	.00	2	.202	.262	.293
5 Min. YEARS		364	790	159	20	5	1	192	93	46	122	1	152	4	10	2	15	15	.50	14	.201	.310	.243

Bob Ayrault

Pitches: Right Bats: Right Pos: P Ht: 6'4" Wt: 235 Born: 04/27/66 Age: 29

		HOW MUCH HE PITCHED						WHAT HE GAVE UP												THE RESULTS					
Year Team	Lg	G	GS	CG	GF	IP	BFP	H	R	ER	HR	SH	SF	HB	TBB	IBB	SO	WP	Bk	W	L	Pct.	ShO	Sv	ERA
1989 Reno	A	24	14	3	5	109.2	478	104	56	46	7	3	4	11	57	3	91	3	3	7	4	.636	1	0	3.78
Batavia	A	4	3	2	1	26	93	13	5	4	2	1	0	2	7	0	20	0	0	2	1	.667	1	0	1.38
Reading	AA	2	1	0	0	8.2	33	3	1	1	0	0	0	0	4	0	8	0	0	0	0	.000	0	0	1.04
1990 Reading	AA	44	9	0	29	109.1	432	77	33	28	4	3	5	2	34	1	84	2	2	4	6	.400	0	10	2.30
1991 Scranton-Wb	AAA	68	0	0	21	98.2	433	91	58	53	11	6	5	5	47	4	103	4	1	8	5	.615	0	3	4.83
1992 Scranton/wb	AAA	20	0	0	14	25.1	110	19	15	14	4	3	2	1	15	3	30	0	0	5	1	.833	0	6	4.97
1993 Scranton/wb	AAA	5	1	0	3	7.1	33	8	2	1	0	0	0	0	3	1	9	0	0	0	1	.000	0	1	1.23
Calgary	AAA	3	0	0	2	4.1	22	8	5	5	0	0	0	0	2	0	3	0	0	0	0	.000	0	1	10.38
Albuquerque	AAA	11	0	0	1	14.2	74	21	10	10	2	1	0	2	7	3	13	0	0	2	2	.500	0	0	6.14
1994 Edmonton	AAA	5	0	0	1	9.1	41	11	6	6	0	0	0	0	4	0	8	0	0	0	0	.000	0	0	5.79
1992 Philadelphia	NL	30	0	0	7	43.1	178	32	16	15	0	4	3	1	17	1	27	0	0	2	2	.500	0	0	3.12
1993 Philadelphia	NL	10	0	0	3	10.1	59	18	11	11	1	0	0	1	10	1	8	1	0	2	0	1.000	0	0	9.58
Seattle	AL	14	0	0	6	19.2	80	18	8	7	1	1	2	0	6	1	7	0	0	1	1	.500	0	0	3.20
6 Min. YEARS		186	28	5	77	413.1	1749	355	191	168	30	17	16	23	180	15	369	9	6	28	20	.583	2	20	3.66
2 Maj. YEARS		54	0	0	16	73.1	317	68	35	33	2	5	5	2	33	3	42	1	0	5	3	.625	0	0	4.05

Joe Ayrault

Bats: Right Throws: Right Pos: C Ht: 6'3" Wt: 190 Born: 10/08/71 Age: 23

			BATTING												BASERUNNING				PERCENTAGES		
Year Team	Lg	G	AB	H	2B	3B	HR	TB	R	RBI	TBB	IBB	SO	HBP	SH	SF	SB	CS	SB%	GDP	Avg	OBP	SLG
1990 Braves	R	30	87	24	2	2	0	30	8	12	9	0	14	1	2	0	1	1	.50	1	.276	.351	.345
1991 Pulaski	R	55	202	52	12	0	3	73	22	27	13	0	49	0	2	0	0	0	.00	4	.257	.302	.361
1992 Macon	A	90	297	77	12	0	6	107	24	24	24	0	68	4	2	1	1	1	.50	7	.259	.322	.360
1993 Durham	A	119	390	99	21	0	6	138	45	52	23	0	103	7	8	3	1	4	.20	8	.254	.305	.354
1994 Greenville	AA	107	350	80	24	0	6	122	38	40	19	1	74	7	6	4	2	2	.50	6	.229	.279	.349
5 Min. YEARS		401	1326	332	71	2	21	470	137	155	88	1	308	19	20	8	5	8	.38	26	.250	.305	.354

Brett Backlund

Pitches: Right Bats: Right Pos: P Ht: 6'0" Wt: 195 Born: 12/16/69 Age: 25

		HOW MUCH HE PITCHED						WHAT HE GAVE UP												THE RESULTS					
Year Team	Lg	G	GS	CG	GF	IP	BFP	H	R	ER	HR	SH	SF	HB	TBB	IBB	SO	WP	Bk	W	L	Pct.	ShO	Sv	ERA
1992 Augusta	A	5	4	0	1	25	91	10	3	1	1	1	0	0	4	0	31	1	0	3	0	1.000	0	0	0.36
Carolina	AA	3	3	0	0	19	71	11	6	4	0	1	1	0	3	0	17	0	1	1	1	.500	0	0	1.89
Buffalo	AAA	4	4	2	0	25	101	15	8	6	2	0	0	0	11	0	9	0	0	3	0	1.000	0	0	2.16
1993 Buffalo	AAA	5	5	0	0	21.1	109	30	25	25	5	3	1	2	14	0	10	0	0	0	4	.000	0	0	10.55
Carolina	AA	20	20	0	0	106	457	115	66	54	22	1	4	2	28	3	94	7	2	7	5	.583	0	0	4.58
1994 Carolina	AA	25	25	4	0	147	627	147	81	59	14	5	7	7	47	0	86	7	1	5	13	.278	0	0	3.61
3 Min. YEARS		62	61	6	1	343.1	1456	328	189	149	44	11	13	11	107	3	247	15	4	19	23	.452	0	0	3.91

Mike Badorek

Pitches: Right Bats: Right Pos: P Ht: 6'5" Wt: 230 Born: 05/15/69 Age: 26

		HOW MUCH HE PITCHED						WHAT HE GAVE UP												THE RESULTS					
Year Team	Lg	G	GS	CG	GF	IP	BFP	H	R	ER	HR	SH	SF	HB	TBB	IBB	SO	WP	Bk	W	L	Pct.	ShO	Sv	ERA

Year	Team	Lg	G	GS	CG	GF	IP	BFP	H	R	ER	HR	SH	SF	HB	TBB	IBB	SO	WP	Bk	W	L	Pct.	ShO	Sv	ERA
1991	Hamilton	A	13	11	1	1	63.1	282	56	33	19	2	1	1	3	30	0	48	9	0	2	5	.286	0	0	2.70
1992	Springfield	A	29	28	1	0	187.1	780	175	74	61	6	3	4	9	39	1	119	10	0	17	8	.680	0	0	2.93
1993	St.Pete	A	29	28	2	1	170	712	170	76	65	6	4	5	4	53	1	60	3	0	15	7	.682	0	0	3.44
1994	Arkansas	AA	40	15	2	4	123.1	528	119	61	43	8	5	2	3	36	4	95	4	0	8	8	.500	0	0	3.14
	4 Min. YEARS		111	82	6	6	544	2302	520	244	188	22	13	12	19	158	6	322	26	0	42	28	.600	0	0	3.11

Kevin Baez

Bats: Right Throws: Right Pos: SS **Ht: 6' 0" Wt: 170 Born: 01/10/67 Age: 28**

			BATTING														BASERUNNING				PERCENTAGES		
Year	Team	Lg	G	AB	H	2B	3B	HR	TB	R	RBI	TBB	IBB	SO	HBP	SH	SF	SB	CS	SB%	GDP	Avg	OBP	SLG
1988	Little Fls	A	70	218	58	7	1	1	70	23	19	32	1	30	2	2	3	7	3	.70	3	.266	.361	.321
1989	Columbia	A	123	426	108	25	1	5	150	59	44	58	3	53	6	9	3	11	9	.55	5	.254	.349	.352
1990	Jackson	AA	106	327	76	11	0	2	93	29	29	37	4	44	2	11	2	3	4	.43	7	.232	.313	.284
1991	Tidewater	AAA	65	210	36	8	0	0	44	18	13	12	1	32	4	5	4	0	1	.00	5	.171	.226	.210
1992	Tidewater	AAA	109	352	83	16	1	2	107	30	33	13	1	57	4	5	5	1	1	.50	9	.236	.267	.304
1993	Norfolk	AAA	63	209	54	11	1	2	73	23	21	20	1	29	1	2	1	0	2	.00	3	.258	.325	.349
1994	Rochester	AAA	110	359	85	17	1	2	110	50	42	40	0	52	2	5	5	2	7	.22	13	.237	.313	.306
1990	New York	NL	5	12	2	1	0	0	3	0	0	0	0	0	0	0	0	0	0	.00	2	.167	.167	.250
1992	New York	NL	6	13	2	0	0	0	2	0	0	0	0	0	0	0	1	0	0	.00	1	.154	.154	.154
1993	New York	NL	52	126	23	9	0	0	32	10	7	13	1	17	0	4	0	0	0	.00	1	.183	.259	.254
	7 Min. YEARS		646	2101	500	95	5	14	647	232	201	212	11	297	21	39	23	24	27	.47	45	.238	.311	.308
	3 Maj. YEARS		63	151	27	10	0	0	37	10	7	13	1	17	0	4	0	0	0	.00	4	.179	.244	.245

Bob Bailey

Bats: Both Throws: Right Pos: 2B **Ht: 6'0" Wt: 170 Born: 08/04/68 Age: 26**

			BATTING														BASERUNNING				PERCENTAGES		
Year	Team	Lg	G	AB	H	2B	3B	HR	TB	R	RBI	TBB	IBB	SO	HBP	SH	SF	SB	CS	SB%	GDP	Avg	OBP	SLG
1989	Welland	A	18	57	16	1	0	1	20	11	6	6	0	11	0	2	0	5	1	.83	0	.281	.349	.351
	Augusta	A	51	185	37	3	2	0	44	20	14	37	0	44	0	0	0	9	3	.75	3	.200	.333	.238
1990	Salem	A	74	227	41	6	2	1	54	28	19	25	0	71	2	6	4	12	4	.75	5	.181	.264	.238
	Augusta	A	36	131	31	3	3	0	40	26	10	18	0	37	2	2	1	14	5	.74	1	.237	.336	.305
1991	Salem	A	75	213	50	7	0	2	63	30	19	23	0	69	0	4	1	15	5	.75	3	.235	.308	.296
1992	Salem	A	108	353	92	15	2	4	123	56	31	61	1	78	1	4	1	44	16	.73	8	.261	.370	.348
1993	Rochester	IND	70	284	69	8	1	2	85	37	23	24	1	52	1	2	4	30	8	.79	2	.243	.300	.299
1994	New Haven	AA	4	7	3	0	0	0	3	2	0	1	0	0	0	0	0	0	0	.00	0	.429	.500	.429
	Lake Elsino	A	66	202	50	10	3	0	66	30	27	30	0	44	1	0	2	16	11	.59	3	.248	.345	.327
	6 Min. YEARS		502	1659	389	53	13	10	498	240	149	225	2	406	7	20	13	145	53	.73	25	.234	.326	.300

Roger Bailey

Pitches: Right Bats: Right Pos: P **Ht: 6'1" Wt: 180 Born: 10/03/70 Age: 24**

			HOW MUCH HE PITCHED						WHAT HE GAVE UP												THE RESULTS					
Year	Team	Lg	G	GS	CG	GF	IP	BFP	H	R	ER	HR	SH	SF	HB	TBB	IBB	SO	WP	Bk	W	L	Pct.	ShO	Sv	ERA
1992	Bend	A	11	11	1	0	65.1	271	48	19	16	4	2	1	4	30	0	81	2	1	5	2	.714	0	0	2.20
1993	Central Val	A	22	22	1	0	111.2	515	139	78	60	9	1	3	6	56	1	84	7	1	4	7	.364	1	0	4.84
1994	New Haven	AA	25	24	1	1	159	675	157	70	57	8	5	7	5	56	1	112	6	0	9	9	.500	1	0	3.23
	3 Min. YEARS		58	57	3	1	336	1461	344	167	133	21	8	11	15	142	2	277	15	2	18	18	.500	2	0	3.56

Scott Baker

Pitches: Left Bats: Left Pos: P **Ht: 6'2" Wt: 175 Born: 05/18/70 Age: 25**

			HOW MUCH HE PITCHED						WHAT HE GAVE UP												THE RESULTS					
Year	Team	Lg	G	GS	CG	GF	IP	BFP	H	R	ER	HR	SH	SF	HB	TBB	IBB	SO	WP	Bk	W	L	Pct.	ShO	Sv	ERA
1990	Johnson Cy	R	32	0	0	7	51.1	223	44	21	12	2	1	3	0	29	2	62	6	3	4	2	.667	0	0	2.10
1991	Savannah	A	8	8	0	0	46.2	200	42	27	15	1	1	3	1	25	0	41	2	0	2	3	.400	0	0	2.89
	St. Pete	A	19	16	1	2	93.2	401	98	47	45	2	4	6	3	42	0	50	5	0	3	9	.250	0	0	4.32
1992	St. Pete	A	24	24	0	0	151.2	610	123	48	33	3	9	4	5	54	0	125	11	8	10	9	.526	0	0	1.96
1993	Huntsville	AA	25	25	1	0	130.1	589	141	73	60	7	3	1	4	84	0	97	8	4	10	4	.714	1	0	4.14
1994	Huntsville	AA	30	14	3	5	111	453	86	28	22	4	7	2	0	46	2	67	4	2	10	4	.714	2	1	1.78
	5 Min. YEARS		138	87	5	14	584.2	2476	534	244	187	19	25	19	13	280	4	442	36	17	39	31	.557	3	2	2.88

Scott Bakkum

Pitches: Right Bats: Right Pos: P **Ht: 6'4" Wt: 205 Born: 11/20/69 Age: 25**

			HOW MUCH HE PITCHED						WHAT HE GAVE UP												THE RESULTS					
Year	Team	Lg	G	GS	CG	GF	IP	BFP	H	R	ER	HR	SH	SF	HB	TBB	IBB	SO	WP	Bk	W	L	Pct.	ShO	Sv	ERA
1992	Red Sox	R	4	1	0	2	11	52	19	11	11	0	1	1	0	5	0	8	0	1	0	1	.000	0	0	9.00
	Winter Havn	A	5	4	2	0	27.2	109	19	9	9	1	3	1	1	10	0	10	0	0	1	3	.250	0	0	2.93
1993	Lynchburg	A	26	26	6	0	169.2	717	201	87	71	23	1	3	2	31	0	98	7	2	12	11	.522	4	0	3.77
1994	Sarasota	A	12	12	1	0	69	311	86	50	40	8	2	2	2	26	0	43	3	0	3	6	.333	0	0	5.22
	New Britain	AA	3	3	0	0	15	68	20	8	8	1	1	0	0	9	0	7	3	0	0	2	.000	0	0	4.80
	Lynchburg	A	11	8	0	1	44.2	206	58	39	35	3	1	1	0	18	0	37	1	0	1	6	.143	0	0	7.05
	3 Min. YEARS		61	54	9	3	337	1463	403	204	174	36	9	9	5	99	0	203	11	3	17	29	.370	4	0	4.65

James Baldwin

Pitches: Right **Bats:** Right **Pos:** P   **Ht:** 6'4" **Wt:** 210 **Born:** 07/15/71 **Age:** 23

			HOW MUCH HE PITCHED					WHAT HE GAVE UP									THE RESULTS					
Year	Team	Lg	G	GS	CG	GF	IP	BFP	H	R	ER	HR	SH	SF	HB	TBB	IBB	SO	WP	Bk	W	L	Pct.	ShO	Sv	ERA
1990	White Sox	R	9	7	0	1	37.1	164	32	29	17	1	1	2	0	18	0	32	6	3	1	6	.143	0	0	4.10
1991	White Sox	R	6	6	0	0	34	132	16	8	8	0	0	1	1	16	0	48	3	1	3	1	.750	0	0	2.12
	Utica	A	7	7	1	0	37.1	180	40	26	22	0	0	1	2	27	0	23	4	2	1	4	.200	0	0	5.30
1992	South Bend	A	21	21	1	0	137.2	570	118	53	37	6	2	2	3	45	0	137	8	2	9	5	.643	1	0	2.42
	Sarasota	A	6	6	1	0	37.2	149	31	13	12	2	3	0	1	7	0	39	1	0	1	2	.333	0	0	2.87
1993	Birmingham	AA	17	17	4	0	120	491	94	48	30	6	9	3	6	43	0	107	7	2	8	5	.615	0	0	2.25
	Nashville	AAA	10	10	1	0	69	279	43	21	20	5	2	2	0	36	0	61	3	1	5	4	.556	0	0	2.61
1994	Nashville	AAA	26	26	2	0	162	696	144	75	67	14	2	2	1	83	1	156	9	4	12	6	.667	0	0	3.72
	5 Min. YEARS		102	100	10	1	635	2661	518	273	213	34	19	13	14	275	1	603	41	15	40	33	.548	1	0	3.02

Jeff Ball

Bats: Right **Throws:** Right **Pos:** 3B   **Ht:** 5'10" **Wt:** 185 **Born:** 04/17/69 **Age:** 26

			BATTING												BASERUNNING				PERCENTAGES		
Year	Team	Lg	G	AB	H	2B	3B	HR	TB	R	RBI	TBB	IBB	SO	HBP	SH	SF	SB	CS	SB%	GDP	Avg	OBP	SLG
1990	Auburn	A	66	263	76	18	1	5	111	40	38	22	1	35	4	3	5	20	5	.80	4	.289	.347	.422
1991	Osceola	A	118	392	96	15	3	5	132	53	51	49	4	74	10	3	4	20	8	.71	9	.245	.341	.337
1992	Jackson	AA	93	278	53	14	1	5	84	27	24	20	1	58	10	2	1	5	3	.63	9	.191	.269	.302
1993	Quad City	A	112	389	114	28	2	14	188	68	76	58	3	63	7	1	5	40	19	.68	11	.293	.390	.483
1994	Jackson	AA	111	358	113	30	3	13	188	65	57	34	3	74	5	5	3	9	8	.53	9	.316	.380	.525
	5 Min. YEARS		504	1680	452	105	10	42	703	253	246	183	12	304	36	14	18	94	43	.69	42	.269	.350	.418

Travis Baptist

Pitches: Left **Bats:** Both **Pos:** P   **Ht:** 6'0" **Wt:** 190 **Born:** 12/30/71 **Age:** 23

			HOW MUCH HE PITCHED					WHAT HE GAVE UP									THE RESULTS					
Year	Team	Lg	G	GS	CG	GF	IP	BFP	H	R	ER	HR	SH	SF	HB	TBB	IBB	SO	WP	Bk	W	L	Pct.	ShO	Sv	ERA
1991	Medcine Hat	R	14	14	1	0	85.1	379	100	52	39	5	2	2	1	21	0	48	4	1	4	4	.500	1	0	4.11
1992	Myrtle Bch	A	19	19	2	0	118	455	81	24	19	2	6	2	4	22	0	97	5	4	11	2	.846	1	0	1.45
1993	Knoxville	AA	7	7	0	0	33	139	37	17	15	2	2	3	2	7	0	24	3	0	1	3	.250	0	0	4.09
1994	Syracuse	AAA	24	22	1	0	122.2	539	145	80	62	20	3	4	0	33	2	42	6	2	8	8	.500	0	0	4.55
	4 Min. YEARS		64	62	4	0	359	1512	363	173	135	29	13	11	7	83	2	211	18	7	24	17	.585	2	0	3.38

Donald Barbara

Bats: Left **Throws:** Left **Pos:** 1B   **Ht:** 6'2" **Wt:** 220 **Born:** 10/27/68 **Age:** 26

			BATTING												BASERUNNING				PERCENTAGES		
Year	Team	Lg	G	AB	H	2B	3B	HR	TB	R	RBI	TBB	IBB	SO	HBP	SH	SF	SB	CS	SB%	GDP	Avg	OBP	SLG
1990	Palm Sprngs	A	66	220	64	8	0	4	84	22	39	24	0	27	2	1	3	1	0	1.00	6	.291	.361	.382
1991	Quad City	A	66	226	65	15	2	5	99	29	48	59	10	49	0	0	6	2	1	.67	5	.288	.426	.438
	Midland	AA	63	224	81	13	0	10	124	43	40	37	6	45	0	0	1	0	0	.00	3	.362	.450	.554
1992	Edmonton	AAA	118	396	118	26	1	4	158	70	63	78	4	78	4	4	6	9	4	.69	11	.298	.413	.399
1993	New Orleans	AAA	84	255	75	10	1	4	99	34	38	42	2	38	1	1	6	1	3	.25	5	.294	.388	.388
1994	San Antonio	AA	8	30	11	3	0	1	17	4	10	5	0	8	0	0	0	0	0	.00	1	.367	.457	.567
	Albuquerque	AAA	81	168	59	14	1	12	111	37	37	32	1	22	0	0	2	1	0	1.00	5	.351	.450	.661
	5 Min. YEARS		486	1519	473	89	5	40	692	239	275	277	23	267	7	6	24	14	8	.64	36	.311	.414	.456

Brian Barber

Pitches: Right **Bats:** Right **Pos:** P   **Ht:** 6'1" **Wt:** 172 **Born:** 03/04/73 **Age:** 22

			HOW MUCH HE PITCHED					WHAT HE GAVE UP									THE RESULTS					
Year	Team	Lg	G	GS	CG	GF	IP	BFP	H	R	ER	HR	SH	SF	HB	TBB	IBB	SO	WP	Bk	W	L	Pct.	ShO	Sv	ERA
1991	Johnson Cty	R	14	13	0	0	73.1	325	62	48	44	5	1	1	5	38	0	84	4	6	4	6	.400	0	0	5.40
1992	Springfield	A	8	8	0	0	50.2	215	39	21	21	7	2	0	1	24	0	56	2	1	3	4	.429	0	0	3.73
	St. Pete	A	19	19	1	0	113.1	473	99	51	41	7	1	2	5	46	0	102	4	0	5	5	.500	0	0	3.26
1993	Arkansas	AA	24	24	1	0	143.1	625	154	70	64	19	7	4	4	56	2	126	10	2	9	8	.529	0	0	4.02
	Louisville	AAA	1	1	0	0	5.2	25	4	3	3	0	1	0	0	4	0	5	0	1	0	1	.000	0	0	4.76
1994	Arkansas	AA	6	6	0	0	36	152	31	15	13	4	1	0	0	16	2	54	2	0	1	3	.250	0	0	3.25
	Louisville	AAA	19	18	0	1	85.1	376	79	58	51	7	4	3	5	46	1	95	7	0	4	7	.364	0	0	5.38
	4 Min. YEARS		91	89	2	1	507.2	2191	468	266	237	49	17	10	20	230	5	522	29	10	26	34	.433	0	1	4.20

Marc Barcelo

Pitches: Right **Bats:** Right **Pos:** P   **Ht:** 6'3" **Wt:** 210 **Born:** 01/10/72 **Age:** 23

			HOW MUCH HE PITCHED					WHAT HE GAVE UP									THE RESULTS					
Year	Team	Lg	G	GS	CG	GF	IP	BFP	H	R	ER	HR	SH	SF	HB	TBB	IBB	SO	WP	Bk	W	L	Pct.	ShO	Sv	ERA
1993	Ft.Myers	A	7	3	0	3	23	89	18	10	7	1	0	1	1	4	0	24	1	0	1	1	.500	0	0	2.74
	Nashville	AA	2	2	0	0	9.1	42	9	5	4	2	1	1	1	5	0	5	1	1	1	0	1.000	0	0	3.86
1994	Nashville	AA	29	28	4	0	183.1	760	167	74	54	11	5	2	9	45	0	153	8	0	11	6	.647	0	0	2.65
	2 Min. YEARS		38	33	4	3	215.2	891	194	89	65	14	6	4	11	54	0	182	10	1	13	7	.650	0	0	2.71

John Barfield

Pitches: Left Bats: Left Pos: P Ht: 6'1" Wt: 195 Born: 10/15/64 Age: 30

			HOW MUCH HE PITCHED							WHAT HE GAVE UP												THE RESULTS					
Year	Team	Lg	G	GS	CG	GF	IP	BFP	H	R	ER	HR	SH	SF	HB	TBB	IBB	SO	WP	Bk	W	L	Pct.	ShO	Sv	ERA
1986	Daytona Bch	A	3	3	0	0	17.1	69	14	9	8	0	0	0	1	1	0	13	0	0	1	1	.500	0	0	4.15
	Salem	A	13	11	0	0	56	250	71	43	31	7	2	0	1	22	0	39	3	1	2	5	.286	0	0	4.98
1987	Charlotte	A	25	25	3	0	153.2	654	145	75	63	3	1	8	3	55	0	79	6	3	10	7	.588	2	0	3.69
1988	Tulsa	AA	24	24	5	0	169	702	159	69	54	8	6	2	3	66	2	125	13	2	9	9	.500	0	0	2.88
1989	Okla City	AAA	28	28	7	0	175.1	739	178	93	79	14	6	6	2	68	2	58	11	1	10	8	.556	3	0	4.06
1990	Okla City	AAA	19	3	0	2	43.1	182	44	21	17	3	6	0	1	21	3	25	0	2	1	6	.143	0	1	3.53
1992	Charlotte	A	3	0	0	2	7	30	10	7	6	0	0	0	0	1	0	4	0	0	0	1	.000	0	1	7.71
	Okla City	AAA	42	0	0	12	71.2	306	75	39	33	6	4	0	2	26	0	26	1	3	7	1	.875	0	2	4.14
1993	Birmingham	AA	13	5	1	5	42	185	57	24	18	1	2	1	1	5	0	18	0	1	5	2	.714	1	1	3.86
	Nashville	AAA	14	4	0	4	35	147	36	19	16	3	1	1	1	11	2	15	3	0	3	1	.750	0	1	4.11
1994	San Antonio	AA	51	0	0	24	73.1	298	63	27	22	3	8	2	3	24	6	45	4	2	6	5	.545	0	3	2.70
1989	Texas	AL	4	2	0	1	11.2	52	15	10	8	0	1	0	0	4	0	9	1	0	0	1	.000	0	0	6.17
1990	Texas	AL	33	0	0	10	44.1	178	42	25	23	2	3	4	1	13	3	17	1	1	4	3	.571	0	1	4.67
1991	Texas	AL	28	0	0	4	83.1	361	96	51	42	11	3	4	0	22	3	27	0	2	4	4	.500	0	1	4.54
	8 Min. YEARS		235	103	16	49	843.2	3562	852	426	347	48	36	20	18	300	15	447	41	15	54	46	.540	6	9	3.70
	3 Maj. YEARS		65	11	0	15	139.1	591	153	86	73	13	7	8	1	39	6	53	2	3	8	8	.500	0	2	4.72

Brian Bark

Pitches: Left Bats: Left Pos: P Ht: 5'9" Wt: 170 Born: 08/26/68 Age: 26

			HOW MUCH HE PITCHED							WHAT HE GAVE UP												THE RESULTS					
Year	Team	Lg	G	GS	CG	GF	IP	BFP	H	R	ER	HR	SH	SF	HB	TBB	IBB	SO	WP	Bk	W	L	Pct.	ShO	Sv	ERA
1990	Pulaski	R	5	5	0	0	23.2	100	17	19	7	3	1	0	1	13	0	33	2	0	2	2	.500	0	0	2.66
1991	Durham	A	13	13	0	0	82.1	330	66	23	23	0	3	2	6	24	0	76	4	3	4	3	.571	0	0	2.51
	Greenville	AA	9	3	1	2	17.2	79	19	10	7	0	0	0	2	8	1	15	3	1	2	1	.667	0	1	3.57
1992	Greenville	AA	11	11	2	0	55	215	36	11	7	1	0	1	3	13	0	49	3	0	5	0	1.000	1	0	1.15
	Richmond	AAA	22	4	0	4	42	197	63	32	28	3	1	2	1	15	1	50	1	1	1	2	.333	0	2	6.00
1993	Richmond	AAA	29	28	1	0	162	705	153	81	66	13	6	7	9	72	4	110	9	0	12	9	.571	1	0	3.67
1994	Richmond	AAA	37	16	0	8	126.2	543	128	76	67	15	8	4	3	51	5	87	8	0	4	9	.308	0	0	4.76
	5 Min. YEARS		126	80	4	14	509.1	2169	482	252	205	35	19	16	25	196	11	420	30	5	30	26	.536	2	3	3.62

Timothy Barker

Bats: Right Throws: Right Pos: 2B-SS Ht: 6'0" Wt: 175 Born: 06/30/68 Age: 27

			BATTING															BASERUNNING				PERCENTAGES		
Year	Team	Lg	G	AB	H	2B	3B	HR	TB	R	RBI	TBB	IBB	SO	HBP	SH	SF	SB	CS	SB%	GDP	Avg	OBP	SLG
1989	Great Falls	R	59	201	63	9	6	5	99	54	36	37	0	55	2	1	1	25	9	.74	2	.313	.423	.493
1990	Bakersfield	A	125	443	120	22	6	8	178	83	62	71	1	116	5	4	4	33	14	.70	7	.271	.375	.402
1991	San Antonio	AA	119	401	117	20	4	2	151	70	46	80	2	61	6	8	5	32	13	.71	6	.292	.413	.377
1992	San Antonio	AA	97	350	95	17	3	1	121	47	26	33	2	91	5	6	1	25	9	.74	2	.271	.342	.346
1993	Harrisburg	AA	49	185	57	10	1	4	81	40	16	30	1	32	2	6	2	7	4	.64	1	.308	.406	.438
	Ottawa	AAA	51	167	38	5	1	2	51	25	14	26	0	42	3	7	1	5	3	.63	3	.228	.340	.305
1994	New Orleans	AAA	128	436	115	25	7	5	169	71	44	76	2	97	6	10	4	41	17	.71	6	.264	.380	.388
	6 Min. YEARS		628	2183	605	108	28	27	850	390	244	353	7	494	29	42	15	168	69	.71	27	.277	.383	.389

Jeff Barns

Bats: Both Throws: Right Pos: 2B Ht: 6'0" Wt: 185 Born: 11/18/63 Age: 31

			BATTING															BASERUNNING				PERCENTAGES		
Year	Team	Lg	G	AB	H	2B	3B	HR	TB	R	RBI	TBB	IBB	SO	HBP	SH	SF	SB	CS	SB%	GDP	Avg	OBP	SLG
1987	Quad City	A	64	221	57	7	2	1	71	29	18	22	2	26	1	3	0	8	2	.80	4	.258	.328	.321
1988	Palm Spngs	A	103	376	91	11	5	2	118	42	42	51	1	66	0	3	3	5	5	.50	14	.242	.330	.314
1989	Midland	AA	70	226	67	7	3	1	83	32	27	13	2	30	2	6	1	3	4	.43	5	.296	.339	.367
1990	Midland	AA	58	177	51	7	0	2	64	17	24	7	1	18	1	1	2	3	2	.60	7	.288	.316	.362
1992	Modesto	A	76	221	62	7	1	0	71	27	21	21	4	17	0	5	2	3	0	1.00	11	.281	.340	.321
1993	Modesto	A	53	143	44	8	0	0	52	17	14	24	0	9	0	8	2	1	1	.50	3	.308	.402	.364
1994	Midland	AA	22	73	12	2	0	0	14	5	5	4	0	8	1	0	0	1	1	.50	2	.164	.218	.192
	7 Min. YEARS		446	1437	384	49	11	6	473	169	151	142	10	174	5	26	10	24	15	.62	46	.267	.333	.329

Richard Barnwell

Bats: Right Throws: Right Pos: OF Ht: 6'0" Wt: 190 Born: 02/29/68 Age: 27

			BATTING															BASERUNNING				PERCENTAGES		
Year	Team	Lg	G	AB	H	2B	3B	HR	TB	R	RBI	TBB	IBB	SO	HBP	SH	SF	SB	CS	SB%	GDP	Avg	OBP	SLG
1989	Oneonta	A	69	256	74	17	5	2	107	58	29	33	1	57	6	4	2	39	9	.81	2	.289	.380	.418
1990	Ft.Laudrdle	A	71	274	75	15	5	4	112	54	20	32	1	62	4	0	1	23	11	.68	2	.274	.357	.409
1991	Ft.Laudrdle	A	86	298	86	15	3	5	122	50	37	43	2	76	9	6	0	29	7	.81	3	.289	.394	.409
	Albany	AA	5	19	5	0	0	0	5	4	0	1	0	6	0	0	0	2	0	1.00	0	.263	.300	.263
1992	Albany	AA	123	434	113	26	5	1	152	80	31	48	1	102	11	4	3	42	18	.70	5	.260	.347	.350
1993	Albany	AA	131	463	138	24	7	11	209	98	50	77	3	101	13	3	2	33	13	.72	8	.298	.411	.451
1994	Columbus	AAA	50	112	22	2	1	1	29	17	5	13	1	30	1	1	1	8	3	.73	3	.196	.283	.259
	Albany-Colo	AA	55	218	54	11	3	4	83	30	18	16	1	54	2	4	0	8	3	.73	6	.248	.305	.381
	6 Min. YEARS		590	2074	567	110	29	28	819	391	190	263	10	488	46	22	9	184	64	.74	30	.273	.366	.395

Tony Barron

Bats: Right **Throws:** Right **Pos:** OF **Ht:** 6'0" **Wt:** 185 **Born:** 08/17/66 **Age:** 28

Year	Team	Lg	G	AB	H	2B	3B	HR	TB	R	RBI	TBB	IBB	SO	HBP	SH	SF	SB	CS	SB%	GDP	Avg	OBP	SLG
1987	Great Falls	R	53	171	51	13	2	3	77	33	30	13	2	49	5	1	3	5	3	.63	1	.298	.359	.450
1988	Bakersfield	A	12	20	5	2	0	0	7	1	4	1	1	5	0	0	0	0	0	.00	1	.250	.286	.350
	Salem	A	73	261	79	6	3	9	118	54	38	25	1	75	10	6	0	36	7	.84	2	.303	.385	.452
1989	Vero Beach	A	105	324	79	7	5	4	108	45	40	17	1	90	4	2	3	26	12	.68	9	.244	.287	.333
1990	Vero Beach	A	111	344	102	21	3	6	147	58	60	30	1	82	7	2	5	42	7	.86	9	.297	.360	.427
1991	San Antonio	AA	73	200	47	2	2	9	80	35	31	28	2	44	3	0	1	8	3	.73	11	.235	.336	.400
1992	San Antonio	AA	28	97	39	4	1	7	66	18	22	6	1	22	2	0	1	7	3	.70	3	.402	.443	.680
	Albuquerque	AAA	78	286	86	18	2	6	126	40	33	17	1	65	2	2	0	6	4	.60	15	.301	.344	.441
1993	Albuquerque	AAA	107	259	75	22	1	8	123	42	36	27	1	59	2	2	2	6	5	.55	7	.290	.359	.475
1994	Jacksonville	AA	108	402	119	19	3	18	198	60	55	26	1	85	4	1	3	18	5	.78	19	.296	.343	.493
	Calgary	AAA	2	8	2	0	0	2	8	2	2	0	0	0	0	0	0	0	0	.00	1	.250	.250	1.000
	8 Min. YEARS		750	2372	684	114	22	72	1058	388	351	190	12	576	39	16	18	154	49	.76	78	.288	.349	.446

Jeffrey Barry

Bats: Both **Throws:** Right **Pos:** OF **Ht:** 6'1" **Wt:** 192 **Born:** 09/22/68 **Age:** 26

Year	Team	Lg	G	AB	H	2B	3B	HR	TB	R	RBI	TBB	IBB	SO	HBP	SH	SF	SB	CS	SB%	GDP	Avg	OBP	SLG
1990	Jamestown	A	51	197	62	6	1	4	82	30	23	17	2	25	0	2	0	25	5	.83	1	.315	.369	.416
1991	Wst Plm Bch	A	116	437	92	16	3	4	126	47	31	34	4	67	4	2	2	20	14	.59	7	.211	.273	.288
1992	St. Lucie	A	3	9	3	2	0	0	5	0	1	0	0	0	0	0	0	0	0	.00	0	.333	.333	.556
	Mets	R	8	23	4	1	0	0	5	5	2	6	1	2	0	0	0	2	0	1.00	1	.174	.345	.217
1993	St.Lucie	A	114	420	108	17	5	4	147	68	50	49	4	37	5	2	6	17	14	.55	7	.257	.338	.350
1994	Binghamton	AA	110	388	118	24	3	9	175	48	69	35	1	62	6	1	8	10	11	.48	10	.304	.364	.451
	5 Min. YEARS		402	1474	387	66	12	21	540	198	176	141	12	193	15	7	16	74	44	.63	26	.263	.330	.366

Shawn Barton

Pitches: Left **Bats:** Right **Pos:** P **Ht:** 6'3" **Wt:** 190 **Born:** 05/14/63 **Age:** 32

Year	Team	Lg	G	GS	CG	GF	IP	BFP	H	R	ER	HR	SH	SF	HB	TBB	IBB	SO	WP	Bk	W	L	Pct.	ShO	Sv	ERA
1984	Bend	A	13	8	1	1	58.1		46	28	14	3	0	0	4	24	0	47	2	1	4	5	.444	0	0	2.16
1985	Peninsula	A	22	22	7	0	140.2	555	108	45	36	5	5	4	1	43	1	82	4	2	12	4	.750	5	0	2.30
1986	Reading	AA	17	17	3	0	92.2	404	92	53	39	10	5	2	2	41	2	62	2	1	8	7	.533	1	0	3.79
1987	Maine	AAA	7	4	0	3	26.2	119	25	14	13	2	2	1	0	15	1	19	3	2	1	1	.500	0	1	4.39
	Reading	AA	32	12	3	9	82.1	367	108	50	45	8	1	2	1	31	2	53	5	1	6	5	.545	0	3	4.92
1988	Jackson	AA	22	8	0	8	71.2	305	74	33	26	5	2	1	1	26	3	58	3	3	2	4	.333	0	1	3.27
	Tidewater	AAA	19	2	0	5	32.1	140	34	13	11	1	1	1	0	11	0	27	2	2	2	2	.500	0	0	3.06
1989	Tidewater	AAA	38	0	0	20	33.2	152	41	22	16	3	4	1	3	9	2	27	1	1	0	3	.000	0	5	4.28
1990	Tidewater	AAA	16	0	0	4	21.2	103	27	17	14	1	0	1	1	10	0	23	1	0	0	0	.000	0	1	5.82
	Greenville	AA	15	0	0	11	16.2	79	24	15	15	2	1	0	1	9	1	8	0	0	0	1	.000	0	1	8.10
1991	Jacksnville	AA	14	4	1	3	34.2	143	36	16	12	0	2	0	1	8	0	24	0	1	3	3	.500	1	0	3.12
	Calgary	AAA	17	0	0	6	31	127	25	11	9	3	1	0	0	8	0	22	1	0	2	0	1.000	0	1	2.61
1992	Calgary	AAA	30	0	0	17	53	231	57	31	25	4	3	1	2	24	4	31	1	1	3	5	.375	0	4	4.25
1993	Calgary	AAA	51	0	0	18	60.2	266	64	29	24	5	1	2	2	27	6	29	3	0	3	1	.750	0	4	3.56
1994	Phoenix	AAA	38	0	0	17	54.2	230	51	16	12	2	5	3	2	22	4	39	3	0	1	2	.333	0	4	1.98
1992	Seattle	AL	14	0	0	2	12.1	50	10	5	4	1	1	0	0	7	2	4	2	0	0	1	.000	0	0	2.92
	11 Min. YEARS		351	77	15	122	810.2	3221	812	393	311	54	33	19	21	308	26	551	31	15	47	43	.522	7	24	3.45

Michael Basse

Bats: Left **Throws:** Left **Pos:** OF **Ht:** 6'0" **Wt:** 185 **Born:** 03/07/70 **Age:** 25

Year	Team	Lg	G	AB	H	2B	3B	HR	TB	R	RBI	TBB	IBB	SO	HBP	SH	SF	SB	CS	SB%	GDP	Avg	OBP	SLG
1991	Helena	R	55	218	80	15	4	3	112	55	26	29	1	43	5	0	3	16	9	.64	1	.367	.447	.514
1992	Stockton	A	115	407	110	16	3	2	138	77	37	62	1	87	3	4	2	36	15	.71	2	.270	.369	.339
1993	El Paso	AA	108	386	103	14	5	1	130	65	36	51	2	72	4	4	2	26	13	.67	7	.267	.357	.337
1994	New Orleans	AAA	75	238	68	6	7	2	94	44	28	46	2	52	3	3	5	23	7	.77	5	.286	.401	.395
	El Paso	AA	42	137	46	6	2	0	56	36	19	30	1	31	2	4	2	11	4	.73	1	.336	.456	.409
	4 Min. YEARS		395	1386	407	57	21	8	530	277	146	218	7	285	17	15	14	112	48	.70	16	.294	.393	.382

Richard Batchelor

Pitches: Right **Bats:** Right **Pos:** P **Ht:** 6'1" **Wt:** 195 **Born:** 04/08/67 **Age:** 28

Year	Team	Lg	G	GS	CG	GF	IP	BFP	H	R	ER	HR	SH	SF	HB	TBB	IBB	SO	WP	Bk	W	L	Pct.	ShO	Sv	ERA
1990	Greensboro	A	27	0	0	18	51.1	200	39	15	9	1	0	2	0	14	1	38	0	0	2	2	.500	0	8	1.58
1991	Ft.Laudrdle	A	50	0	0	41	62	269	55	28	19	1	6	1	1	22	5	58	4	0	4	7	.364	0	25	2.76
	Albany	AA	1	0	0	1	1	9	5	5	5	0	1	0	0	1	0	0	0	0	0	0	.000	0	0	45.00
1992	Albany	AA	58	0	0	34	70.2	320	79	40	33	1	2	6	2	34	3	45	4	0	4	5	.444	0	7	4.20
1993	Albany	AA	36	0	0	32	40.1	162	27	9	4	1	1	0	1	12	1	40	3	0	1	3	.250	0	19	0.89
	Columbus	AAA	15	0	0	14	16.1	74	14	5	5	0	0	0	1	8	1	17	3	0	1	1	.500	0	6	2.76

15

Year Team	Lg	G	GS	CG	GF	IP	BFP	H	R	ER	HR	SH	SF	HB	TBB	IBB	SO	WP	Bk	W	L	Pct.	ShO	Sv	ERA
1994 Louisville	AAA	53	0	0	13	81.1	347	85	40	32	7	5	3	3	32	6	50	7	0	1	2	.333	0	0	3.54
1993 St. Louis	NL	9	0	0	2	10	45	14	12	9	1	1	2	0	3	1	4	0	0	0	0	.000	0	0	8.10
5 Min. YEARS		240	0	0	153	323	1381	304	142	107	15	14	8	12	123	16	248	23	0	13	20	.394	0	65	2.98

Jason Bates

Bats: Both **Throws:** Right **Pos:** SS **Ht:** 5'11" **Wt:** 170 **Born:** 01/05/71 **Age:** 24

								BATTING										BASERUNNING				PERCENTAGES		
Year Team	Lg	G	AB	H	2B	3B	HR	TB	R	RBI	TBB	IBB	SO	HBP	SH	SF	SB	CS	SB%	GDP	Avg	OBP	SLG
1992 Bend	A	70	255	73	10	3	6	107	31	16	9	1	55	5	2	4	18	4	.82	5	.286	.419	.420
1993 Colo Spngs	AAA	122	449	120	21	2	13	184	76	62	45	4	99	10	3	3	9	8	.53	8	.267	.345	.410
1994 Colo. Spng	AAA	125	458	131	19	5	10	190	68	76	60	4	57	4	2	5	4	6	.40	11	.286	.370	.415
3 Min. YEARS		317	1162	324	50	10	29	481	201	169	161	9	211	19	7	12	31	18	.63	24	.279	.372	.414

Miguel Batista

Pitches: Right **Bats:** Right **Pos:** P **Ht:** 6' 0" **Wt:** 160 **Born:** 02/19/71 **Age:** 24

			HOW MUCH HE PITCHED					WHAT HE GAVE UP										THE RESULTS					
Year Team	Lg	G	GS	CG	GF	IP	BFP	H	R	ER	HR	SH	SF	HB	TBB	IBB	SO	WP	Bk	W	L	Pct.	ShO	Sv	ERA
1990 Expos	R	9	6	0	1	40.1	167	31	16	9	0	1	2	1	19	0	22	1	1	4	3	.571	0	0	2.01
Rockford	A	3	2	0	0	12.1	63	16	13	12	2	0	1	4	5	0	7	3	0	0	1	.000	0	0	8.76
1991 Rockford	A	23	23	2	0	133.2	592	126	74	60	1	6	8	6	57	0	90	12	2	11	5	.688	1	0	4.04
1992 Wst Plm Bch	A	24	24	1	0	135.1	585	130	69	57	3	4	4	6	54	1	92	9	4	7	7	.500	0	0	3.79
1993 Harrisburg	AA	26	26	0	0	141	627	139	79	68	11	4	5	4	86	0	91	8	0	13	5	.722	0	0	4.34
1994 Harrisburg	AA	3	3	0	0	11.1	49	8	3	3	0	0	0	0	9	0	5	2	0	0	1	.000	0	0	2.38
1992 Pittsburgh	NL	1	0	0	1	2	13	4	2	2	1	0	0	0	3	0	1	0	0	0	0	.000	0	0	9.00
5 Min. YEARS		88	84	3	1	474	2083	450	254	209	17	15	20	21	230	1	307	35	7	35	22	.614	1	0	3.97

Allen Battle

Bats: Right **Throws:** Right **Pos:** OF **Ht:** 6'0" **Wt:** 170 **Born:** 11/29/68 **Age:** 26

								BATTING										BASERUNNING				PERCENTAGES		
Year Team	Lg	G	AB	H	2B	3B	HR	TB	R	RBI	TBB	IBB	SO	HBP	SH	SF	SB	CS	SB%	GDP	Avg	OBP	SLG
1991 Johnson Cty	R	17	62	24	6	1	0	32	26	7	14	0	6	1	1	0	7	1	.88	2	.387	.506	.516
Savannah	A	48	169	42	7	1	0	51	27	20	27	0	34	1	0	2	12	3	.80	0	.249	.352	.302
1992 Springfield	A	67	235	71	10	4	4	101	49	24	41	0	34	10	1	2	22	12	.65	1	.302	.424	.430
St. Pete	A	60	222	71	9	2	1	87	34	15	35	2	38	4	4	2	21	11	.66	2	.320	.418	.392
1993 Arkansas	AA	108	390	107	24	12	3	164	71	40	45	0	75	6	2	3	20	12	.63	4	.274	.356	.421
1994 Louisville	AAA	132	520	163	44	7	6	239	104	69	59	2	82	6	1	7	23	8	.74	14	.313	.385	.460
4 Min. YEARS		432	1598	478	100	27	14	674	311	175	221	4	269	28	9	16	105	47	.69	23	.299	.390	.422

Howard Battle

Bats: Right **Throws:** Right **Pos:** 3B **Ht:** 6'0" **Wt:** 197 **Born:** 03/25/72 **Age:** 23

								BATTING										BASERUNNING				PERCENTAGES		
Year Team	Lg	G	AB	H	2B	3B	HR	TB	R	RBI	TBB	IBB	SO	HBP	SH	SF	SB	CS	SB%	GDP	Avg	OBP	SLG
1990 Medicne Hat	R	61	233	62	17	1	5	96	25	32	15	2	38	2	0	0	5	2	.71	2	.266	.316	.412
1991 Myrtle Bch	A	138	520	147	33	4	20	248	82	86	49	2	88	3	0	4	15	7	.68	1	.283	.345	.477
1992 Dunedin	A	136	520	132	27	3	17	216	76	85	49	3	89	5	1	5	6	8	.43	5	.254	.321	.415
1993 Knoxville	AA	141	521	145	21	5	7	197	66	70	45	3	94	7	1	3	12	9	.57	8	.278	.342	.378
1994 Syracuse	AAA	139	517	143	26	8	14	227	72	75	40	4	82	3	1	7	26	2	.93	15	.277	.328	.439
5 Min. YEARS		615	2311	629	124	21	63	984	321	348	198	14	391	20	3	19	64	28	.70	31	.272	.332	.426

Matt Bauer

Pitches: Left **Bats:** Left **Pos:** P **Ht:** 6'1" **Wt:** 195 **Born:** 03/25/70 **Age:** 25

			HOW MUCH HE PITCHED					WHAT HE GAVE UP										THE RESULTS					
Year Team	Lg	G	GS	CG	GF	IP	BFP	H	R	ER	HR	SH	SF	HB	TBB	IBB	SO	WP	Bk	W	L	Pct.	ShO	Sv	ERA
1991 Bristol	R	15	2	0	10	36.2	157	33	16	13	1	0	1	5	8	1	39	1	1	5	3	.625	0	4	3.19
Fayettevlle	A	4	0	0	1	10	38	7	2	2	0	0	0	0	3	0	9	0	0	2	0	1.000	0	0	1.80
1992 Lakeland	A	7	0	0	2	9.1	48	15	13	11	0	0	1	1	3	0	12	0	0	1	2	.333	0	0	10.61
Niagara Fls	A	31	0	0	10	33	144	22	18	8	1	7	1	2	18	4	33	4	0	0	3	.000	0	2	2.18
1993 Fayettevlle	A	40	0	0	16	62	268	57	30	20	2	6	1	3	23	1	81	4	0	6	5	.545	0	5	2.90
1994 Trenton	AA	14	0	0	9	25.1	99	17	4	3	0	0	0	0	13	0	30	0	0	2	0	1.000	0	3	1.07
Toledo	AAA	37	0	0	13	36.1	172	29	25	22	3	3	1	2	34	5	24	2	0	2	1	.667	0	0	5.45
4 Min. YEARS		148	2	0	61	212.2	926	180	107	79	7	16	5	13	102	11	228	11	1	18	14	.563	0	14	3.34

Bob Baxter

Pitches: Left **Bats:** Right **Pos:** P **Ht:** 6'1" **Wt:** 180 **Born:** 02/17/69 **Age:** 26

			HOW MUCH HE PITCHED					WHAT HE GAVE UP										THE RESULTS					
Year Team	Lg	G	GS	CG	GF	IP	BFP	H	R	ER	HR	SH	SF	HB	TBB	IBB	SO	WP	Bk	W	L	Pct.	ShO	Sv	ERA
1990 Jamestown	A	13	13	2	0	74.1	321	85	44	32	4	2	1	0	25	1	67	4	0	5	4	.556	0	0	3.87
1991 Rockford	A	45	0	0	39	65	262	56	20	18	1	4	1	1	16	6	52	2	0	6	5	.545	0	19	2.49
Wst Plm Bch	A	1	0	0	0	1.1	8	4	3	3	0	0	0	0	0	0	5	0	0	0	0	.000	0	0	20.25
1992 Wst Plm Bch	A	42	0	0	27	46	212	46	12	10	1	2	1	0	9	1	54	2	0	6	2	.750	0	7	1.41
1993 Wst Plm Bch	A	33	0	0	18	59.1	232	55	20	15	1	4	4	0	5	1	29	2	1	2	2	.500	0	6	2.28
1994 Harrisburg	AA	40	11	0	6	105	451	107	61	49	10	3	3	0	32	0	56	4	0	11	3	.786	0	0	4.20
5 Min. YEARS		174	24	2	90	368.2	1505	353	160	127	17	15	10	1	87	9	259	14	1	30	16	.652	0	32	3.10

Trey Beamon

Bats: Left   Throws: Right   Pos: OF Ht: 6'3" Wt: 195 Born: 02/11/74 Age: 21

					BATTING													BASERUNNING				PERCENTAGES		
Year	Team	Lg	G	AB	H	2B	3B	HR	TB	R	RBI	TBB	IBB	SO	HBP	SH	SF	SB	CS	SB%	GDP	Avg	OBP	SLG
1992	Pirates	R	13	39	12	1	0	1	16	9	6	4	1	0	0	0	0	0	1	.00	0	.308	.372	.410
	Welland	A	19	69	20	5	0	3	34	15	9	8	0	9	0	0	0	4	3	.57	6	.290	.364	.493
1993	Augusta	A	104	373	101	18	6	3	131	64	45	48	2	60	6	0	4	19	6	.76	12	.271	.360	.351
1994	Carolina	AA	112	434	140	18	9	5	191	69	47	33	4	53	5	4	3	24	9	.73	8	.323	.375	.440
	3 Min. YEARS		248	915	273	42	15	9	372	157	107	93	7	122	11	4	7	47	19	.71	26	.298	.367	.407

Garrett Beard

Bats: Right   Throws: Right   Pos: 3B Ht: 6'1" Wt: 190 Born: 02/01/69 Age: 26

					BATTING													BASERUNNING				PERCENTAGES		
Year	Team	Lg	G	AB	H	2B	3B	HR	TB	R	RBI	TBB	IBB	SO	HBP	SH	SF	SB	CS	SB%	GDP	Avg	OBP	SLG
1989	Salem	A	75	274	66	11	2	6	99	38	54	31	1	58	4	0	3	6	4	.60	6	.241	.324	.361
1990	Vero Beach	A	6	16	4	1	0	0	5	1	3	2	0	2	0	0	0	0	0	.00	0	.250	.333	.313
	Yakima	A	60	232	63	13	1	5	93	29	39	17	2	30	4	1	10	5	6	.45	2	.272	.319	.401
	Bakersfield	A	5	15	3	2	1	0	7	2	3	1	0	2	0	0	0	0	0	.00	0	.200	.250	.467
1991	Bakersfield	A	48	152	42	14	0	6	74	22	30	27	0	30	2	5	1	0	1	.00	2	.276	.390	.487
1992	Modesto	A	98	348	94	12	2	10	140	55	59	51	1	84	9	4	5	4	6	.40	11	.270	.373	.402
1993	Huntsville	AA	18	61	16	3	1	0	21	8	6	6	0	13	1	0	1	1	1	.50	3	.262	.333	.344
	Modesto	A	83	284	76	17	2	6	115	46	33	63	0	55	3	3	3	2	2	.60	7	.268	.402	.405
	Tacoma	AAA	19	49	7	4	0	0	11	3	2	4	0	8	0	2	0	1	1	.50	3	.143	.208	.224
1994	Huntsville	AA	88	279	71	15	0	7	107	38	35	38	1	44	6	4	2	3	5	.38	5	.254	.354	.384
	6 Min. YEARS		500	1710	442	92	9	40	672	242	264	240	5	326	29	19	25	23	26	.47	39	.258	.355	.393

Blaine Beatty

Pitches: Left   Bats: Left   Pos: P Ht: 6'2" Wt: 185 Born: 04/25/64 Age: 31

				HOW MUCH HE PITCHED					WHAT HE GAVE UP										THE RESULTS					
Year	Team	Lg	G	GS	CG	GF	IP	BFP	H	R	ER	HR	SH	SF	HB	TBB	IBB	SO	WP	Bk	W	L	Pct.	ShO	Sv	ERA
1986	Newark	A	15	15	8	0	119.1	475	98	37	28	6	5	2	1	30	3	93	6	0	11	3	.786	3	0	2.11
1987	Hagerstown	A	13	13	4	0	100	389	81	32	28	7	3	1	1	11	0	65	5	0	11	1	.917	1	0	2.52
	Charlotte	AA	15	15	3	0	105.2	438	110	38	36	2	1	4	1	20	2	57	4	0	6	5	.545	1	0	3.07
1988	Jackson	AA	30	28	12	1	208.2	824	191	64	57	13	12	6	0	34	3	103	3	7	16	8	.667	5	0	2.46
1989	Tidewater	AAA	27	27	6	0	185	764	173	86	68	14	4	8	1	43	0	90	3	2	12	10	.545	3	0	3.31
1991	Tidewater	AAA	28	28	3	0	175.1	750	192	86	80	18	7	4	5	43	6	74	0	1	12	9	.571	1	0	4.11
1992	Indianapolis	AAA	26	12	2	3	94	412	109	52	45	8	4	1	1	24	3	54	4	1	7	5	.583	0	0	4.31
1993	Carolina	AA	17	13	2	1	94.1	378	67	42	30	8	3	0	2	35	0	67	4	0	7	3	.700	0	0	2.86
	Buffalo	AAA	20	4	0	5	36	168	51	25	22	2	2	2	2	8	0	14	3	0	2	3	.400	0	1	5.50
1994	Chattanooga	AA	27	26	6	1	196.1	770	146	66	52	15	6	3	8	43	0	162	4	0	14	7	.667	4	0	2.38
1989	New York	NL	2	1	0	0	6	25	5	1	1	1	0	0	0	2	0	3	0	0	0	0	.000	0	0	1.50
1991	New York	NL	5	0	0	1	9.2	42	9	3	3	0	1	1	0	4	1	7	1	0	0	0	.000	0	0	2.79
	8 Min. YEARS		218	181	46	11	1314.2	5368	1218	528	446	93	47	34	22	291	17	779	36	11	98	54	.645	18	1	3.05
	2 Maj. YEARS		7	1	0	1	15.2	67	14	4	4	1	1	1	0	6	1	10	1	0	0	0	.000	0	0	2.30

Kash Beauchamp

Bats: Right   Throws: Right   Pos: OF Ht: 6'3" Wt: 165 Born: 01/08/63 Age: 32

					BATTING													BASERUNNING				PERCENTAGES		
Year	Team	Lg	G	AB	H	2B	3B	HR	TB	R	RBI	TBB	IBB	SO	HBP	SH	SF	SB	CS	SB%	GDP	Avg	OBP	SLG
1984	Kinston	A	130	463	123	23	9	8	188	63	58	51	0	92	1	1	3	10	9	.53	11	.266	.338	.406
	Knoxville	AA	3	10	4	0	0	1	7	3	3	1	0	2	0	0	0	1	0	1.00	0	.400	.455	.700
1985	Knoxville	AA	137	496	137	14	5	4	173	68	35	60	3	62	6	6	8	25	16	.61	10	.276	.356	.349
1986	Knoxville	AA	51	193	65	10	1	8	101	32	25	17	0	40	2	0	1	5	4	.56	0	.337	.394	.523
	Syracuse	AAA	55	198	52	11	1	7	86	23	21	13	0	44	1	1	0	6	4	.60	5	.263	.311	.434
1987	Knoxville	AA	59	188	56	10	2	5	85	28	24	24	0	39	3	1	2	3	5	.38	4	.298	.382	.452
1988	Knoxville	AA	8	28	4	1	0	0	5	2	3	5	0	9	0	0	0	0	0	.00	0	.143	.273	.179
	Greenville	AA	62	198	62	15	2	5	96	35	30	23	1	31	0	1	4	6	2	.75	2	.313	.378	.485
	Richmond	AAA	3	9	2	0	0	0	2	1	0	0	0	1	0	0	0	0	0	.00	0	.222	.222	.222
1989	Richmond	AAA	91	278	66	15	3	5	102	26	29	13	0	45	3	1	1	4	3	.57	2	.237	.278	.367
1990	Phoenix	AAA	55	121	34	4	2	1	45	12	15	7	1	21	1	0	1	2	3	.40	2	.281	.323	.372
	Shreveport	AA	38	141	45	11	0	5	71	15	18	8	0	16	2	1	1	7	2	.78	2	.319	.362	.504
1993	Rochester	IND	47	166	61	8	1	9	98	32	33	24	2	24	3	0	3	2	1	.67	1	.367	.449	.590
	Chattanooga	AA	18	60	24	6	1	5	47	16	15	10	0	9	2	1	0	1	1	.50	1	.400	.500	.783
1994	Albuquerque	AAA	6	18	4	2	1	0	8	3	0	0	0	5	0	0	0	0	1	.00	0	.222	.222	.444
	San Antonio	AA	82	224	57	13	1	6	90	30	28	26	2	44	2	1	5	2	2	.50	4	.254	.331	.402
	9 Min. YEARS		845	2791	796	143	29	69	1204	389	337	282	9	484	26	14	29	74	53	.58	44	.285	.353	.431

Todd Beckerman

Pitches: Right   Bats: Left   Pos: P Ht: 6'1" Wt: 185 Born: 12/21/69 Age: 25

				HOW MUCH HE PITCHED					WHAT HE GAVE UP										THE RESULTS					
Year	Team	Lg	G	GS	CG	GF	IP	BFP	H	R	ER	HR	SH	SF	HB	TBB	IBB	SO	WP	Bk	W	L	Pct.	ShO	Sv	ERA
1992	Pittsfield	A	21	0	0	17	32.2	128	21	8	5	2	1	0	0	12	1	31	3	0	0	3	.000	0	5	1.38

1993	Capital Cty	A	25	0	0	22	30	117	19	5	3	0	4	0	1	10	0	41	2	1	5	1	.833	0	10	0.90
	St.Lucie	A	20	0	0	19	23.2	89	16	3	1	0	0	1	1	2	0	28	1	0	2	0	1.000	0	14	0.38
1994	Binghamton	AA	55	0	0	44	65.1	290	71	33	28	6	6	1	6	23	6	46	2	0	3	5	.375	0	19	3.86
	3 Min. YEARS		121	0	0	102	151.2	624	127	49	37	8	11	2	8	47	7	146	8	1	10	9	.526	0	48	2.20

Robbie Beckett

Pitches: Left Bats: Right Pos: P Ht: 6'5" Wt: 235 Born: 07/16/72 Age: 22

			HOW MUCH HE PITCHED						WHAT HE GAVE UP											THE RESULTS					
Year	Team	Lg	G	GS	CG	GF	IP	BFP	H	R	ER	HR	SH	SF	HB	TBB	IBB	SO	WP	Bk	W	L	Pct.	ShO	Sv	ERA
1990	Padres	R	10	10	0	0	49.1	236	40	28	24	1	3	1	2	45	0	54	8	3	2	5	.286	0	0	4.38
	Riverside	A	3	3	0	0	16.2	76	18	13	13	0	1	0	0	11	0	11	1	1	2	1	.667	0	0	7.02
1991	Chston-Sc	A	28	26	1	0	109.1	545	115	111	100	5	1	8	3	117	0	96	20	2	2	14	.125	0	0	8.23
1992	Waterloo	A	24	24	1	0	120.2	578	77	88	64	4	1	1	6	140	0	147	20	4	4	10	.286	1	0	4.77
1993	Rancho Cuca	A	37	10	0	14	83.2	413	75	62	56	7	1	7	2	93	1	88	25	3	2	4	.333	0	4	6.02
1994	Wichita	AA	33	0	0	14	40	188	30	28	26	2	4	2	1	40	0	59	10	0	1	3	.250	0	2	5.85
	Las Vegas	AAA	23	0	0	11	23.2	134	27	36	31	4	0	3	0	39	0	30	7	0	0	1	.000	0	0	11.79
	5 Min. YEARS		158	73	2	39	443.1	2170	382	366	314	23	11	22	14	485	1	485	91	13	13	38	.255	1	6	6.37

Tim Belk

Bats: Right Throws: Right Pos: OF Ht: 6'3" Wt: 200 Born: 04/06/70 Age: 25

			BATTING														BASERUNNING				PERCENTAGES		
Year	Team	Lg	G	AB	H	2B	3B	HR	TB	R	RBI	TBB	IBB	SO	HBP	SH	SF	SB	CS	SB%	GDP	Avg	OBP	SLG
1992	Billings	R	73	273	78	13	0	12	127	60	56	35	0	33	4	0	6	15	2	.88	6	.286	.368	.465
1993	Winston-Sal	A	134	509	156	23	3	14	227	89	65	48	3	76	6	2	2	9	7	.56	8	.306	.372	.446
1994	Indianapols	AAA	6	18	2	1	0	0	3	1	0	1	0	5	0	1	0	0	1	.00	1	.111	.158	.167
	Chattanooga	AA	118	411	127	35	3	10	198	64	86	60	5	41	3	0	11	13	8	.62	7	.309	.392	.482
	3 Min. YEARS		331	1211	363	72	6	36	555	214	207	144	8	155	13	3	19	37	18	.67	22	.300	.375	.458

David Bell

Bats: Right Throws: Right Pos: 3B Ht: 5'10" Wt: 170 Born: 09/14/72 Age: 22

			BATTING														BASERUNNING				PERCENTAGES		
Year	Team	Lg	G	AB	H	2B	3B	HR	TB	R	RBI	TBB	IBB	SO	HBP	SH	SF	SB	CS	SB%	GDP	Avg	OBP	SLG
1990	Indians	R	30	111	29	5	1	0	36	18	13	10	1	8	4	0	1	1	1	.50	5	.261	.341	.324
	Burlington	R	12	42	7	1	1	0	10	4	2	2	0	5	1	0	1	2	1	.67	1	.167	.217	.238
1991	Columbus	A	136	491	113	23	1	5	153	47	63	37	2	49	5	3	7	3	2	.60	22	.230	.287	.312
1992	Kinston	A	123	464	117	17	2	6	156	52	47	54	1	66	1	2	7	2	4	.33	13	.252	.327	.336
1993	Canton-Akm	AA	129	483	141	20	2	9	192	69	60	43	1	54	3	2	6	3	4	.43	12	.292	.350	.398
1994	Charlotte	AAA	134	481	141	17	4	18	220	66	88	41	5	54	9	1	7	2	5	.29	9	.293	.355	.457
	5 Min. YEARS		564	2072	548	83	11	38	767	256	273	187	9	236	23	8	29	13	17	.43	62	.264	.328	.370

Eric Bell

Pitches: Left Bats: Left Pos: P Ht: 6'0" Wt: 165 Born: 10/27/63 Age: 31

			HOW MUCH HE PITCHED						WHAT HE GAVE UP											THE RESULTS					
Year	Team	Lg	G	GS	CG	GF	IP	BFP	H	R	ER	HR	SH	SF	HB	TBB	IBB	SO	WP	Bk	W	L	Pct.	ShO	Sv	ERA
1984	Hagerstown	A	3	1	0	0	3.2	23	6	4	4	0	0	1	1	5	0	6	0	0	0	0	.000	0	0	9.82
	Newark	A	15	15	4	0	102.1	424	82	40	28	6	2	2	2	26	0	114	8	1	8	3	.727	1	0	2.46
1985	Hagerstown	A	26	26	5	0	158.1	664	141	73	55	7	3	3	1	63	0	162	4	0	11	6	.647	2	0	3.13
1986	Charlotte	AA	18	18	6	0	129.2	539	109	49	44	7	3	1	1	66	0	104	5	0	9	6	.600	1	0	3.05
	Rochester	AAA	11	11	4	0	76.2	323	68	26	26	3	0	1	0	35	1	59	7	0	7	3	.700	0	0	3.05
1988	Rochester	AAA	7	7	0	0	36.1	148	28	10	8	0	3	1	0	13	0	33	1	2	3	1	.750	0	0	1.98
1989	Hagerstown	AA	9	7	0	1	43	170	32	11	9	3	1	0	1	11	1	35	0	1	4	2	.667	0	1	1.88
	Rochester	AAA	7	7	0	0	39.2	172	40	24	22	5	1	2	0	15	0	27	4	2	1	2	.333	0	0	4.99
1990	Rochester	AAA	27	27	3	0	148	667	168	90	80	16	4	8	9	65	0	90	11	1	9	6	.600	0	0	4.86
1991	Canton-Akm	AA	18	16	1	0	93.1	402	82	47	30	1	3	5	2	37	1	84	6	0	9	5	.643	0	0	2.89
	Colo Sprngs	AAA	4	4	1	0	25.1	108	23	6	6	1	1	0	0	11	1	16	1	0	2	1	.667	1	0	2.13
1992	Colo Sprngs	AAA	26	18	5	8	137.2	575	161	64	57	10	5	4	0	30	1	56	6	2	10	7	.588	0	1	3.73
1993	Tucson	AAA	22	16	3	1	106.2	474	131	59	48	8	7	4	1	39	0	53	5	0	4	6	.400	1	0	4.05
1994	Tucson	AAA	30	29	0	0	171.1	769	209	112	85	12	7	11	6	60	1	82	4	2	8	8	.500	0	0	4.46
1985	Baltimore	AL	4	0	0	3	5.2	24	4	3	3	1	0	0	0	4	0	4	0	0	0	0	.000	0	0	4.76
1986	Baltimore	AL	4	4	0	0	23.1	105	23	14	13	4	1	1	0	14	0	18	0	0	1	2	.333	0	0	5.01
1987	Baltimore	AL	33	29	2	1	165	729	174	113	100	32	4	2	2	78	0	111	11	1	10	13	.435	0	0	5.45
1991	Cleveland	AL	10	0	0	3	18	61	5	2	1	0	0	0	1	5	0	7	0	0	4	0	1.000	0	0	0.50
1992	Cleveland	AL	7	1	0	2	15.1	75	22	13	13	1	1	1	1	9	0	10	1	0	0	2	.000	0	0	7.63
1993	Houston	NL	5	0	0	0	7.1	34	10	5	5	0	0	0	0	2	0	2	0	0	0	1	.000	0	0	6.14
	10 Min. YEARS		223	202	32	11	1272	5458	1280	615	502	79	40	43	24	476	6	921	62	11	85	56	.603	6	2	3.55
	6 Maj. YEARS		68	34	2	11	234.2	1028	238	150	135	38	6	4	4	112	0	152	12	1	15	18	.455	0	0	5.18

Carlos Bellidard

Pitches: Left Bats: Left Pos: P Ht: 6'1" Wt: 150 Born: 11/04/72 Age: 22

			HOW MUCH HE PITCHED						WHAT HE GAVE UP											THE RESULTS					
Year	Team	Lg	G	GS	CG	GF	IP	BFP	H	R	ER	HR	SH	SF	HB	TBB	IBB	SO	WP	Bk	W	L	Pct.	ShO	Sv	ERA
1992	Athletics	R	13	5	1	5	46	201	36	19	15	0	2	2	2	27	0	55	4	3	1	2	.333	0	0	2.93
1993	Madison	A	26	11	0	1	86.2	391	81	44	35	3	4	4	2	54	2	64	8	3	5	3	.625	0	0	3.63

1994 Modesto	A	6	2	0	3	23	88	10	5	5	0	0	1	2	10	0	22	1	1	1	2	.333	0	2	1.96
Huntsville	AA	3	2	0	1	4.2	21	6	4	4	0	0	1	0	3	0	4	1	0	1	0	1.000	0	0	7.71
3 Min. YEARS		48	20	1	10	160.1	701	133	72	59	3	6	8	6	94	2	145	14	7	8	7	.533	0	2	3.31

Clay Bellinger

Bats: Right **Throws:** Right **Pos:** SS   **Ht:** 6'3" **Wt:** 195 **Born:** 11/18/68 **Age:** 26

					BATTING											BASERUNNING				PERCENTAGES		
Year Team	Lg	G	AB	H	2B	3B	HR	TB	R	RBI	TBB	IBB	SO	HBP	SH	SF	SB	CS	SB%	GDP	Avg	OBP	SLG
1989 Everett	A	51	185	37	8	1	4	59	29	16	19	0	47	1	1	0	3	2	.60	4	.200	.278	.319
1990 Clinton	A	109	382	83	17	4	10	138	52	48	28	0	102	7	5	3	13	6	.68	5	.217	.281	.361
1991 San Jose	A	105	368	95	29	2	8	152	65	62	53	3	88	11	7	6	13	4	.76	3	.258	.363	.413
1992 Shreveport	AA	126	433	90	18	3	13	153	45	50	36	1	82	3	4	4	7	8	.47	15	.208	.271	.353
1993 Phoenix	AAA	122	407	104	20	3	6	148	50	49	38	4	81	4	7	5	7	7	.50	8	.256	.322	.364
1994 Phoenix	AAA	106	337	90	15	1	7	128	48	50	18	0	56	7	2	3	6	1	.86	8	.267	.315	.380
6 Min. YEARS		619	2112	499	107	14	48	778	289	275	192	8	456	33	26	21	49	28	.64	43	.236	.307	.368

Rigoberto Beltran

Pitches: Left **Bats:** Left **Pos:** P   **Ht:** 5'11" **Wt:** 185 **Born:** 11/13/69 **Age:** 25

		HOW MUCH HE PITCHED						WHAT HE GAVE UP											THE RESULTS					
Year Team	Lg	G	GS	CG	GF	IP	BFP	H	R	ER	HR	SH	SF	HB	TBB	IBB	SO	WP	Bk	W	L	Pct.	ShO	Sv	ERA
1991 Hamilton	A	21	4	0	4	48	206	41	17	14	4	4	2	2	19	0	69	3	12	5	2	.714	0	0	2.63
1992 Savannah	A	13	13	2	0	83	316	38	20	20	4	1	0	4	40	0	106	8	6	6	1	.857	1	0	2.17
St. Pete	A	2	2	0	0	8	30	6	0	0	0	1	0	0	2	0	3	0	0	0	0	.000	0	0	0.00
1993 Arkansas	AA	18	16	0	1	88.2	376	74	39	32	8	5	0	6	38	1	82	11	4	5	5	.500	0	0	3.25
1994 Arkansas	AA	4	4	1	0	28	95	12	3	2	2	1	0	0	3	0	21	0	0	4	0	1.000	1	0	0.64
Louisville	AAA	23	23	1	0	138.1	624	147	82	78	15	7	7	5	68	2	87	18	5	11	11	.500	0	0	5.07
4 Min. YEARS		81	62	4	5	394	1647	318	161	146	33	19	9	17	170	3	368	40	27	31	19	.620	2	0	3.34

Marvin Benard

Bats: Left **Throws:** Left **Pos:** OF   **Ht:** 5'10" **Wt:** 180 **Born:** 01/20/71 **Age:** 24

					BATTING											BASERUNNING				PERCENTAGES		
Year Team	Lg	G	AB	H	2B	3B	HR	TB	R	RBI	TBB	IBB	SO	HBP	SH	SF	SB	CS	SB%	GDP	Avg	OBP	SLG
1992 Everett	A	64	161	38	4	2	1	55	31	17	24	0	39	6	1	0	17	3	.85	1	.236	.356	.342
1993 Clinton	A	112	349	105	14	2	5	138	84	50	56	1	66	4	2	0	42	10	.81	1	.301	.403	.395
1994 Shreveport	AA	125	454	143	32	3	4	193	66	48	31	5	58	4	7	4	24	13	.65	14	.315	.361	.425
3 Min. YEARS		301	964	286	56	7	10	386	181	115	111	6	163	14	10	4	83	26	.76	16	.297	.376	.400

Omar Bencomo

Pitches: Right **Bats:** Right **Pos:** P   **Ht:** 6'2" **Wt:** 195 **Born:** 06/26/64 **Age:** 31

		HOW MUCH HE PITCHED						WHAT HE GAVE UP											THE RESULTS					
Year Team	Lg	G	GS	CG	GF	IP	BFP	H	R	ER	HR	SH	SF	HB	TBB	IBB	SO	WP	Bk	W	L	Pct.	ShO	Sv	ERA
1994 Midland	AA	6	4	0	0	25.1	118	34	22	17	3	5	3	1	12	1	18	1	0	1	3	.250	0	0	6.04

Bill Bene

Pitches: Right **Bats:** Right **Pos:** P   **Ht:** 6'4" **Wt:** 205 **Born:** 11/21/67 **Age:** 27

		HOW MUCH HE PITCHED						WHAT HE GAVE UP											THE RESULTS					
Year Team	Lg	G	GS	CG	GF	IP	BFP	H	R	ER	HR	SH	SF	HB	TBB	IBB	SO	WP	Bk	W	L	Pct.	ShO	Sv	ERA
1988 Great Falls	R	13	12	0	0	65.1	302	53	43	33	3	1	5	5	45	0	56	14	4	5	0	1.000	0	0	4.55
1989 Bakersfield	A	7	5	0	2	13.1	82	14	20	17	1	0	0	2	29	0	11	8	0	0	2	.000	0	0	11.48
Salem	A	7	4	0	0	13.2	85	13	18	14	1	0	1	3	27	0	13	10	0	0	2	.000	0	0	9.22
1990 Vero Beach	A	17	14	0	2	56.2	307	49	55	44	3	1	2	6	96	0	34	23	1	1	10	.091	0	0	6.99
1991 Vero Beach	A	31	1	0	12	52	267	39	37	24	0	3	3	2	65	1	57	21	0	1	1	.500	0	0	4.15
1992 San Antonio	AA	18	1	0	5	32	144	19	15	11	1	2	1	0	34	1	25	10	1	0	2	.000	0	0	3.09
Vero Beach	A	18	0	0	12	18	82	11	4	4	0	1	1	1	16	0	30	5	0	2	2	.500	0	0	2.00
1993 San Antonio	AA	46	0	0	12	70.2	313	50	43	38	3	3	5	4	53	1	82	15	2	5	6	.455	0	1	4.84
1994 Albuquerque	AAA	9	0	0	3	13.1	74	18	17	15	4	0	1	1	16	0	6	5	0	0	1	.000	0	0	10.13
San Antonio	AA	20	0	0	5	37.1	176	34	23	19	4	3	0	2	33	3	34	7	1	1	0	1.000	0	0	4.58
7 Min. YEARS		186	37	0	53	372.1	1832	300	275	219	20	14	19	26	414	6	348	118	9	15	26	.366	0	1	5.29

Alan Benes

Pitches: Right **Bats:** Right **Pos:** P   **Ht:** 6'5" **Wt:** 215 **Born:** 01/21/72 **Age:** 23

		HOW MUCH HE PITCHED						WHAT HE GAVE UP											THE RESULTS					
Year Team	Lg	G	GS	CG	GF	IP	BFP	H	R	ER	HR	SH	SF	HB	TBB	IBB	SO	WP	Bk	W	L	Pct.	ShO	Sv	ERA
1993 Glens Falls	A	7	7	0	0	37	162	39	20	15	2	0	1	2	14	0	29	2	1	0	4	.000	0	0	3.65
1994 Savannah	A	4	4	0	0	24.1	95	21	5	4	1	0	0	2	7	0	24	1	0	2	0	1.000	0	0	1.48
St. Pete	A	11	11	0	0	78.1	299	55	18	14	0	3	0	2	15	0	69	4	1	7	1	.875	0	0	1.61
Arkansas	AA	13	13	1	0	87.2	341	58	38	29	8	1	2	4	26	0	75	3	1	7	2	.778	0	0	2.98
Louisville	AAA	2	2	1	0	15.1	61	10	5	5	1	0	0	0	4	0	16	3	0	1	0	1.000	0	0	2.93
2 Min. YEARS		37	37	2	0	242.2	958	183	86	67	12	4	3	9	66	0	213	13	3	17	7	.708	0	0	2.48

Brandy Bengoechea

Bats: Right **Throws:** Right **Pos:** SS   Ht: 5'10" Wt: 162 Born: 08/02/71 Age: 23

Year	Team	Lg	G	AB	H	2B	3B	HR	TB	R	RBI	TBB	IBB	SO	HBP	SH	SF	SB	CS	SB%	GDP	Avg	OBP	SLG
1993	Sou Oregon	A	31	72	21	1	1	0	24	11	11	8	0	16	3	2	1	2	1	.67	0	.292	.381	.333
1994	Sou. Oregon	A	48	162	43	5	1	3	59	30	21	23	0	29	7	5	1	7	5	.58	3	.265	.378	.364
	Tacoma	AAA	4	14	3	1	0	0	4	0	0	1	0	4	1	0	0	0	0	.00	0	.214	.313	.286
	2 Min. YEARS		83	248	67	7	2	3	87	41	32	32	0	49	11	7	2	9	6	.60	3	.270	.375	.351

Yamil Benitez

Bats: Right **Throws:** Right **Pos:** OF   Ht: 6'2" Wt: 180 Born: 10/05/72 Age: 22

Year	Team	Lg	G	AB	H	2B	3B	HR	TB	R	RBI	TBB	IBB	SO	HBP	SH	SF	SB	CS	SB%	GDP	Avg	OBP	SLG
1990	Expos	R	22	83	19	1	0	1	23	6	5	8	0	18	0	0	0	0	0	.00	1	.229	.297	.277
1991	Expos	R	54	197	47	9	5	5	81	20	38	12	1	55	1	1	5	10	5	.67	3	.239	.279	.411
1992	Albany	A	23	79	13	3	2	1	23	6	6	5	1	49	0	0	0	2	2	.00	1	.165	.214	.291
	Jamestown	A	44	162	44	6	6	3	71	24	23	14	0	52	2	1	0	19	1	.95	5	.272	.337	.438
1993	Burlington	A	111	411	112	21	5	15	188	70	61	29	1	99	3	6	3	18	7	.72	8	.273	.323	.457
1994	Harrisburg	AA	126	475	123	18	4	17	200	58	91	36	2	134	2	1	4	18	15	.55	12	.259	.311	.421
	5 Min. YEARS		380	1407	358	58	22	42	586	184	224	104	5	407	8	9	12	65	30	.68	30	.254	.307	.416

Erik Bennett

Pitches: Right **Bats:** Right **Pos:** P   Ht: 6'2" Wt: 205 Born: 09/13/68 Age: 26

Year	Team	Lg	G	GS	CG	GF	IP	BFP	H	R	ER	HR	SH	SF	HB	TBB	IBB	SO	WP	Bk	W	L	Pct.	ShO	Sv	ERA
1989	Bend	A	15	15	2	0	96	422	96	58	37	4	3	2	3	36	0	96	8	6	6	8	.429	0	0	3.47
1990	Quad City	A	18	18	3	0	108.1	453	91	48	36	9	5	6	4	37	0	100	2	4	7	7	.500	1	0	2.99
1991	Palm Sprngs	A	8	8	1	0	43	192	41	15	12	2	3	0	3	27	0	31	0	0	2	3	.400	0	0	2.51
1992	Quad City	A	8	8	1	0	57.1	238	46	20	17	0	3	5	4	22	0	59	3	1	3	3	.500	1	0	2.67
	Palm Sprngs	A	6	6	1	0	42	171	27	19	17	0	2	1	4	15	0	33	2	1	4	2	.667	0	0	3.64
	Midland	AA	7	7	0	0	46	195	47	22	20	3	3	2	7	16	0	36	1	0	1	3	.250	0	0	3.91
1993	Midland	AA	11	11	0	0	69.1	308	87	57	50	12	2	6	6	17	1	33	1	0	5	4	.556	0	0	6.49
	Vancouver	AAA	18	12	0	1	80.1	353	101	57	54	10	1	0	4	21	0	51	3	0	6	6	.500	0	0	6.05
1994	Vancouver	AAA	45	1	0	14	89.2	375	71	32	28	9	2	4	10	28	2	83	8	2	1	4	.200	0	3	2.81
	6 Min. YEARS		136	86	8	15	632	2707	607	328	271	49	24	26	45	219	3	522	28	14	35	40	.467	2	4	3.86

Gary Bennett

Bats: Right **Throws:** Right **Pos:** C   Ht: 6'0" Wt: 190 Born: 04/17/72 Age: 23

Year	Team	Lg	G	AB	H	2B	3B	HR	TB	R	RBI	TBB	IBB	SO	HBP	SH	SF	SB	CS	SB%	GDP	Avg	OBP	SLG
1990	Martinsvle	R	16	52	14	2	1	0	18	3	10	4	0	15	0	0	1	0	1	.00	0	.269	.316	.346
1991	Martinsvle	R	41	136	32	7	0	1	42	15	16	17	0	26	5	1	1	0	1	.00	5	.235	.340	.309
1992	Batavia	A	47	146	30	2	0	0	32	22	12	15	0	27	2	3	0	2	1	.67	2	.205	.288	.219
1993	Spartanburg	A	42	126	32	4	1	0	38	18	15	12	0	22	1	2	1	2	0	.00	0	.254	.321	.302
	Clearwater	A	17	55	18	0	0	1	21	5	6	3	0	10	1	2	0	0	1	.00	0	.327	.373	.382
1994	Clearwater	A	19	55	13	3	0	0	16	6	10	8	0	6	0	0	1	0	0	.00	1	.236	.328	.291
	Reading	AA	63	208	48	9	0	3	66	13	22	14	0	26	0	3	3	0	1	.00	6	.231	.276	.317
	5 Min. YEARS		245	778	187	27	2	5	233	82	91	73	0	132	9	11	7	2	7	.22	16	.240	.310	.299

Joel Bennett

Pitches: Right **Bats:** Right **Pos:** P   Ht: 6'1" Wt: 170 Born: 01/31/70 Age: 25

Year	Team	Lg	G	GS	CG	GF	IP	BFP	H	R	ER	HR	SH	SF	HB	TBB	IBB	SO	WP	Bk	W	L	Pct.	ShO	Sv	ERA
1991	Red Sox	R	2	2	0	0	10	38	6	2	2	0	0	1	1	4	0	8	2	1	0	0	.000	0	0	1.80
	Elmira	A	13	12	1	0	81	325	60	29	22	3	3	1	6	30	0	75	7	0	5	3	.625	1	0	2.44
1992	Winter Havn	A	26	26	4	0	161.2	690	161	86	76	7	7	5	7	55	2	154	7	3	7	11	.389	0	0	4.23
1993	Lynchburg	A	29	29	3	0	181	754	151	93	77	17	7	9	4	67	6	221	18	0	7	12	.368	1	0	3.83
1994	New Britain	AA	23	23	1	0	130.2	560	119	65	59	9	2	2	4	56	0	130	10	0	11	7	.611	1	0	4.06
	Pawtucket	AAA	4	4	0	0	21	91	19	16	16	8	0	0	1	12	0	24	1	0	1	3	.250	0	0	6.86
	4 Min. YEARS		97	96	9	0	585.1	2458	516	291	252	44	19	18	23	224	8	612	45	4	31	36	.463	3	0	3.87

Cesar Bernhardt

Bats: Right **Throws:** Right **Pos:** 2B   Ht: 5'9" Wt: 148 Born: 01/18/69 Age: 26

Year	Team	Lg	G	AB	H	2B	3B	HR	TB	R	RBI	TBB	IBB	SO	HBP	SH	SF	SB	CS	SB%	GDP	Avg	OBP	SLG
1986	Appleton	A	19	76	21	2	2	1	30	9	12	4	0	11	1	1	1	1	2	.33	3	.276	.317	.395
	White Sox	R	42	103	19	3	0	0	22	6	10	10	3	15	1	1	2	1	1	.50	2	.184	.259	.214
1987	Chston-Wv	A	122	444	112	28	5	5	165	56	53	25	1	59	7	0	2	15	9	.63	9	.252	.301	.372
1988	South Bend	A	124	482	136	17	2	1	160	47	51	16	4	32	2	3	6	26	16	.62	13	.282	.304	.332
1989	South Bend	A	127	493	148	26	7	6	206	73	81	32	2	40	5	2	8	18	12	.60	11	.300	.344	.418
1990	Birmingham	AA	142	574	160	26	9	6	222	96	82	46	0	53	3	3	7	30	15	.67	7	.279	.332	.387
1991	Vancouver	AAA	87	323	84	10	5	1	107	40	30	18	1	26	1	2	2	12	6	.67	5	.260	.299	.331
	Birmingham	AA	26	103	28	2	0	3	39	15	16	12	0	8	2	0	0	3	4	.43	4	.272	.359	.379

1992	Birmingham	AA	24	94	17	0	0	0	17	12	5	7	0	14	0	2	1	3	1	.75	1	.181	.235	.181
	Memphis	AA	42	146	26	4	0	1	33	12	6	7	0	20	1	1	0	2	3	.40	4	.178	.221	.226
	Stockton	A	47	173	53	13	3	1	75	34	16	26	2	22	2	0	2	6	3	.67	6	.306	.399	.434
1994	Orlando	AA	48	156	41	8	0	0	49	16	9	14	0	5	3	2	0	1	0	1.00	5	.263	.335	.314
	8 Min. YEARS		850	3167	845	139	33	25	1125	416	371	217	13	305	28	17	31	118	72	.62	80	.267	.317	.355

Harold Berrios

Bats: Right **Throws:** Right **Pos:** OF · **Ht:** 5'11" **Wt:** 205 **Born:** 12/02/71 **Age:** 23

			BATTING															BASERUNNING				PERCENTAGES		
Year	Team	Lg	G	AB	H	2B	3B	HR	TB	R	RBI	TBB	IBB	SO	HBP	SH	SF	SB	CS	SB%	GDP	Avg	OBP	SLG
1993	Albany	A	46	145	30	5	1	3	46	16	16	18	1	20	5	0	2	2	0	1.00	3	.207	.312	.317
1994	Albany	A	42	162	54	12	2	6	88	42	35	18	1	23	9	0	1	14	0	1.00	4	.333	.426	.543
	Frederick	A	86	325	113	13	0	13	165	70	71	32	2	47	18	2	2	42	14	.75	6	.348	.432	.508
	Bowie	AA	1	4	1	1	0	0	2	1	0	0	0	1	0	0	0	0	0	.00	0	.250	.250	.500
	2 Min. YEARS		175	636	198	31	3	22	301	129	122	68	4	91	32	2	5	58	14	.81	13	.311	.402	.473

Mike Bertotti

Pitches: Left **Bats:** Left **Pos:** P · **Ht:** 6'1" **Wt:** 185 **Born:** 01/18/70 **Age:** 25

			HOW MUCH HE PITCHED						WHAT HE GAVE UP										THE RESULTS				
Year	Team	Lg	G	GS	CG	GF	IP	BFP	H	R	ER	HR	SH	SF	HB	TBB	IBB	SO	WP	Bk	W	L	Pct.	ShO	Sv	ERA
1991	Utica	A	14	5	0	3	37.1	186	38	33	24	2	1	3	2	36	0	33	9	0	3	4	.429	0	0	5.79
1992	South Bend	A	11	0	0	5	19.1	86	12	8	8	1	1	1	1	22	0	17	1	1	0	3	.000	0	1	3.72
	Utica	A	17	1	0	5	33.1	164	36	28	23	2	0	1	2	31	0	23	7	1	2	2	.500	0	1	6.21
1993	Hickory	A	9	9	2	0	59.2	248	42	19	14	2	4	0	1	29	1	77	2	3	3	3	.500	0	0	2.11
	South Bend	A	17	16	2	0	111	466	93	51	43	5	6	6	6	44	2	108	7	1	5	7	.417	2	0	3.49
1994	Pr. William	A	16	15	2	0	104.2	435	90	48	41	13	2	1	3	43	0	103	8	1	7	6	.538	1	0	3.53
	Birmingham	AA	10	10	1	0	68.1	273	55	25	22	1	2	3	0	21	1	44	5	0	4	3	.571	1	0	2.90
	4 Min. YEARS		94	56	7	13	433.2	1858	366	212	175	26	16	15	15	226	4	405	39	7	24	28	.462	4	2	3.63

Andres Berumen

Pitches: Right **Bats:** Right **Pos:** P · **Ht:** 6'1" **Wt:** 205 **Born:** 04/05/71 **Age:** 24

			HOW MUCH HE PITCHED						WHAT HE GAVE UP										THE RESULTS				
Year	Team	Lg	G	GS	CG	GF	IP	BFP	H	R	ER	HR	SH	SF	HB	TBB	IBB	SO	WP	Bk	W	L	Pct.	ShO	Sv	ERA
1989	Royals	R	12	10	0	0	49	223	57	29	26	2	2	2	4	17	1	24	6	0	2	4	.333	0	0	4.78
1990	Royals	R	5	4	0	1	22.2	95	24	9	6	0	0	1	0	8	1	18	0	0	0	2	.000	0	1	2.38
	Baseball Cy	A	9	9	1	0	44	197	30	27	21	0	2	5	4	28	0	35	2	1	3	5	.375	1	0	4.30
1991	Baseball Cy	A	7	7	0	0	37	161	34	18	17	0	1	0	4	18	0	24	5	0	0	5	.000	0	0	4.14
	Appleton	A	13	13	0	0	56.1	254	55	33	22	0	3	4	3	26	0	49	2	1	2	6	.250	0	0	3.51
1992	Appleton	A	46	0	0	38	57.2	245	50	25	17	3	1	3	1	23	2	52	3	0	5	2	.714	0	13	2.65
1993	High Desert	A	14	13	1	0	92	396	85	45	37	8	0	4	7	36	1	74	6	1	9	2	.818	0	0	3.62
	Wichita	AA	7	7	0	0	26.2	120	35	17	17	2	1	1	1	11	2	17	3	0	3	1	.750	0	0	5.74
1994	Las Vegas	AAA	43	6	0	14	75.2	375	93	70	55	5	2	22	5	57	1	49	6	1	4	7	.364	0	1	6.54
	6 Min. YEARS		156	69	2	53	461	2066	463	273	218	20	12	22	29	224	8	342	33	4	28	34	.452	1	15	4.26

Johnny Bess

Bats: Both **Throws:** Right **Pos:** C · **Ht:** 6'1" **Wt:** 190 **Born:** 04/06/70 **Age:** 25

			BATTING															BASERUNNING				PERCENTAGES		
Year	Team	Lg	G	AB	H	2B	3B	HR	TB	R	RBI	TBB	IBB	SO	HBP	SH	SF	SB	CS	SB%	GDP	Avg	OBP	SLG
1992	Princeton	R	48	173	36	9	1	2	53	22	21	15	2	55	4	1	0	3	2	.60	0	.208	.286	.306
1993	Winston-Sal	A	11	33	8	0	0	2	14	4	7	6	1	7	0	0	0	2	1	.67	0	.242	.359	.424
	Chston-Wv	A	106	358	82	16	7	5	127	35	67	47	2	107	6	2	2	10	5	.67	4	.229	.327	.355
1994	Winston-Sal	A	58	186	56	7	0	8	87	41	29	34	1	51	2	3	2	8	6	.57	1	.301	.411	.468
	Chattanooga	AA	37	103	21	5	1	0	28	9	9	13	0	34	2	2	2	1	1	.50	1	.204	.300	.272
	3 Min. YEARS		260	853	203	37	9	17	309	111	133	115	6	254	14	8	6	24	15	.62	6	.238	.336	.362

Steve Bethea

Bats: Both **Throws:** Right **Pos:** 3B · **Ht:** 5'10" **Wt:** 172 **Born:** 06/20/67 **Age:** 28

			BATTING															BASERUNNING				PERCENTAGES		
Year	Team	Lg	G	AB	H	2B	3B	HR	TB	R	RBI	TBB	IBB	SO	HBP	SH	SF	SB	CS	SB%	GDP	Avg	OBP	SLG
1989	Spokane	A	62	215	47	7	1	1	59	36	22	41	0	45	1	2	0	4	2	.67	2	.219	.346	.274
1990	Riverside	A	104	315	54	9	3	0	69	38	21	57	0	108	1	0	1	13	9	.59	4	.171	.299	.219
1991	High Desert	A	79	206	57	8	2	1	72	43	33	37	0	44	1	3	2	9	5	.64	4	.277	.386	.350
1992	Wichita	AA	93	253	63	12	3	1	84	32	32	35	2	66	6	2	2	11	4	.73	3	.249	.351	.332
1993	Wichita	AA	15	49	13	0	0	0	13	2	1	4	0	16	0	0	0	0	1	.00	2	.265	.321	.265
	Las Vegas	AAA	39	61	11	2	0	0	13	7	2	14	1	22	0	1	0	0	1	.00	0	.180	.333	.213
1994	Rancho Cuca	A	9	29	6	2	0	0	8	4	4	7	0	7	0	0	0	0	0	.00	0	.207	.361	.276
	Las Vegas	AAA	2	4	0	0	0	0	0	0	0	0	0	1	0	0	0	0	0	.00	0	.000	.000	.000
	Wichita	AA	18	59	10	1	0	0	11	3	3	9	0	12	0	1	1	2	1	.67	0	.169	.275	.186
	6 Min. YEARS		421	1191	261	41	9	3	329	165	118	204	3	321	9	9	6	39	23	.63	15	.219	.336	.276

Brian Bevil

Pitches: Right Bats: Right Pos: P Ht: 6'3" Wt: 190 Born: 09/05/71 Age: 23

			HOW MUCH HE PITCHED						WHAT HE GAVE UP												THE RESULTS					
Year Team	Lg	G	GS	CG	GF	IP	BFP	H	R	ER	HR	SH	SF	HB	TBB	IBB	SO	WP	Bk	W	L	Pct.	ShO	Sv	ERA
1991 Royals	R	13	12	2	1	65.1	262	56	20	14	0	1	0	2	19	0	70	3	3	5	3	.625	0	0	1.93
1992 Appleton	A	26	26	4	0	156	646	129	67	59	17	5	4	5	63	0	168	9	0	9	7	.563	2	0	3.40
1993 Wilmington	A	12	12	2	0	74.1	286	46	21	19	2	2	2	4	23	0	61	4	0	7	1	.875	0	0	2.30
Memphis	AA	6	6	0	0	33	146	36	17	16	4	2	2	0	14	0	26	3	0	3	3	.500	0	0	4.36
1994 Memphis	AA	17	17	0	0	100	408	75	42	39	6	3	5	3	40	0	78	12	0	5	4	.556	0	0	3.51
4 Min. YEARS		74	73	8	1	428.2	1748	342	167	147	29	13	13	14	159	0	403	31	3	29	18	.617	2	0	3.09

Joe Biasucci

Bats: Right Throws: Right Pos: 2B Ht: 5'11" Wt: 180 Born: 04/28/70 Age: 25

				BATTING												BASERUNNING				PERCENTAGES		
Year Team	Lg	G	AB	H	2B	3B	HR	TB	R	RBI	TBB	IBB	SO	HBP	SH	SF	SB	CS	SB%	GDP	Avg	OBP	SLG
1990 Huntington	R	6	16	3	1	0	0	4	2	1	2	0	3	0	0	0	0	0	.00	0	.188	.278	.250
Geneva	A	51	168	50	8	2	4	74	29	29	16	0	43	2	3	1	4	1	.80	4	.298	.364	.440
1991 Winston-Sal	A	67	211	58	10	3	1	77	35	34	30	0	58	4	4	3	2	3	.40	2	.275	.371	.365
Charlotte	AA	24	50	11	2	0	0	13	4	2	6	0	18	0	0	1	2	0	1.00	0	.220	.298	.260
1992 Peoria	A	74	268	70	25	1	5	112	51	32	32	1	61	5	5	2	9	1	.90	1	.261	.349	.418
Winston-Sal	A	30	93	22	6	2	1	35	13	9	9	0	22	1	2	0	1	1	.50	1	.237	.311	.376
1993 Springfield	A	119	398	115	30	3	26	229	76	86	62	3	111	7	4	5	15	5	.75	3	.289	.390	.575
1994 Arkansas	AA	112	355	90	18	1	15	155	45	48	50	4	98	3	3	1	1	7	.13	6	.254	.350	.437
5 Min. YEARS		483	1559	419	100	12	52	699	255	241	207	8	414	22	21	13	34	18	.65	17	.269	.360	.448

Greg Bicknell

Pitches: Right Bats: Right Pos: P Ht: 6'1" Wt: 185 Born: 06/01/69 Age: 26

			HOW MUCH HE PITCHED						WHAT HE GAVE UP												THE RESULTS					
Year Team	Lg	G	GS	CG	GF	IP	BFP	H	R	ER	HR	SH	SF	HB	TBB	IBB	SO	WP	Bk	W	L	Pct.	ShO	Sv	ERA
1989 St.Cathrnes	A	17	11	1	2	86	370	80	56	40	6	0	1	4	35	0	60	9	2	6	5	.545	0	0	4.19
1990 Myrtle Bch	A	34	15	0	5	120.2	529	118	63	49	8	2	6	2	45	3	89	12	4	5	4	.556	0	0	3.65
1991 Myrtle Bch	A	27	4	0	10	61	276	68	45	30	7	3	2	0	20	0	60	8	0	3	5	.375	0	0	4.43
1992 Peninsula	A	28	28	3	0	179	760	170	80	62	11	6	4	3	53	1	140	5	0	10	7	.588	2	0	3.12
1993 Jacksnville	AA	24	12	2	4	94	403	96	59	45	14	3	3	5	28	0	45	5	0	6	6	.500	1	1	4.31
1994 San Bernrdo	A	1	0	0	0	3	10	1	0	0	0	0	0	0	0	0	4	0	0	1	0	1.000	0	0	0.00
Stockton	A	1	0	0	0	2	7	1	0	0	0	0	0	0	0	0	2	0	0	0	0	.000	0	0	0.00
El Paso	AA	18	3	0	10	35	168	50	29	24	3	2	2	2	21	1	21	7	0	2	4	.333	0	2	6.17
High Desert	A	9	9	0	0	46	232	79	50	44	13	0	1	2	17	0	29	0	0	1	6	.143	0	0	8.61
6 Min. YEARS		159	82	6	31	626.2	2755	663	382	294	62	16	19	18	219	5	450	46	6	34	37	.479	3	4	4.22

Steve Bieser

Bats: Both Throws: Right Pos: OF Ht: 5'10" Wt: 170 Born: 08/04/67 Age: 27

				BATTING												BASERUNNING				PERCENTAGES		
Year Team	Lg	G	AB	H	2B	3B	HR	TB	R	RBI	TBB	IBB	SO	HBP	SH	SF	SB	CS	SB%	GDP	Avg	OBP	SLG
1989 Batavia	A	25	75	18	3	1	1	26	13	13	12	0	20	2	2	2	2	1	.67	1	.240	.352	.347
1990 Batavia	A	54	160	37	11	1	0	50	36	12	26	1	27	1	2	2	13	2	.87	3	.231	.339	.313
1991 Spartanburg	A	60	168	41	6	0	0	47	25	13	31	0	35	3	4	3	17	4	.81	4	.244	.366	.280
1992 Clearwater	A	73	203	58	6	5	0	74	33	10	39	3	28	9	8	0	8	8	.50	2	.286	.422	.365
Reading	AA	33	139	38	5	4	0	51	20	8	6	0	25	4	4	0	8	3	.73	3	.273	.322	.367
1993 Reading	AA	53	170	53	6	3	1	68	21	19	15	1	24	2	1	0	9	5	.64	2	.312	.374	.400
Scranton/wb	AAA	26	83	21	4	0	0	25	3	4	2	0	14	1	1	0	3	0	1.00	0	.253	.279	.301
1994 Scranton-Wb	AAA	93	228	61	13	1	0	76	42	15	17	1	40	5	4	2	12	8	.60	2	.268	.329	.333
6 Min. YEARS		417	1226	327	54	15	2	417	193	94	148	6	213	27	26	9	72	31	.70	17	.267	.356	.340

Mike Birkbeck

Pitches: Right Bats: Right Pos: P Ht: 6'2" Wt: 185 Born: 03/10/61 Age: 34

			HOW MUCH HE PITCHED						WHAT HE GAVE UP												THE RESULTS					
Year Team	Lg	G	GS	CG	GF	IP	BFP	H	R	ER	HR	SH	SF	HB	TBB	IBB	SO	WP	Bk	W	L	Pct.	ShO	Sv	ERA
1984 Beloit	A	26	25	6	1	177.2	721	134	57	43	5	3	5	1	64	3	164	13	1	14	3	.824	2	0	2.18
1985 El Paso	AA	24	24	4	0	155	654	154	67	59	9	7	2	1	64	4	103	11	1	9	9	.500	0	0	3.43
1986 Vancouver	AAA	23	23	2	0	134.1	597	160	82	69	9	2	2	2	39	4	81	6	0	12	6	.667	0	0	4.62
1987 Beloit	A	1	1	0	0	4.1	19	4	4	1	0	0	0	0	1	0	7	0	0	0	0	.000	0	0	2.08
Denver	AAA	1	1	0	0	4.2	29	9	11	5	0	1	0	0	3	0	1	0	1	0	1	.000	0	0	9.64
1988 Denver	AAA	5	5	4	0	44.2	169	30	10	10	1	0	0	0	10	0	30	1	2	4	1	.800	0	0	2.01
1989 Denver	AAA	5	5	0	0	23.2	103	26	9	8	2	1	1	0	10	1	9	2	1	2	2	.500	0	0	3.04
1990 Denver	AAA	21	20	0	0	96.1	425	102	73	57	6	4	2	2	36	0	69	7	2	3	8	.273	0	0	5.33
1991 Canton-Akrn	AA	21	2	0	14	39.1	170	39	17	17	1	2	0	0	18	3	40	2	2	2	3	.400	0	5	3.89
Colo Sprngs	AAA	3	1	0	2	7	26	4	1	0	0	0	0	0	3	0	3	0	0	0	0	.000	0	0	0.00
1992 Tidewater	AAA	21	19	3	0	117	481	108	61	53	9	4	2	2	31	0	101	9	3	4	10	.286	0	0	4.08
1993 Richmond	AAA	27	26	1	0	159.1	654	143	67	55	10	4	9	1	41	0	136	11	1	13	8	.619	0	0	3.11
1994 Richmond	AAA	28	28	1	0	164.2	658	145	58	50	8	5	3	2	46	0	143	5	2	13	6	.684	0	0	2.73

Year	Team	Lg	G	GS	CG	GF	IP	BFP	H	R	ER	HR	SH	SF	HB	TBB	IBB	SO	WP	Bk	W	L	Pct.	ShO	Sv	ERA
1986	Milwaukee	AL	7	4	0	2	22	97	24	12	11	0	0	0	0	12	0	13	1	0	1	1	.500	0	0	4.50
1987	Milwaukee	AL	10	10	1	0	45	210	63	33	31	8	1	2	0	19	0	25	2	0	1	4	.200	0	0	6.20
1988	Milwaukee	AL	23	23	0	0	124	538	141	69	65	10	4	2	1	37	1	64	0	11	10	8	.556	0	0	4.72
1989	Milwaukee	AL	9	9	1	0	44.2	214	57	32	27	4	2	3	3	22	2	31	1	0	0	4	.000	0	0	5.44
1992	New York	NL	1	1	0	0	7	33	12	7	7	3	1	0	0	1	1	2	1	0	0	1	.000	0	0	9.00
	11 Min. YEARS		206	180	21	17	1128	4706	1058	517	427	60	29	21	19	366	15	887	67	16	76	57	.571	2	5	3.41
	5 Maj. YEARS		50	47	2	2	242.2	1092	297	153	141	25	8	7	4	91	4	135	5	11	12	18	.400	0	0	5.23

Dirk Blair

Pitches: Right Bats: Right Pos: P **Ht: 6'3" Wt: 215 Born: 05/19/69 Age: 26**

			HOW MUCH HE PITCHED						WHAT HE GAVE UP										THE RESULTS					
Year	Team	Lg	G	GS	CG	GF	IP	BFP	H	R	ER	HR	SH	SF	HB	TBB	IBB	SO	WP	Bk	W	L	Pct.	ShO	Sv	ERA
1991	Pulaski	R	18	1	0	10	45.2	197	47	21	17	2	1	2	0	15	0	41	5	4	8	1	.889	0	4	3.35
1992	Macon	A	41	0	0	22	67.1	279	66	25	17	1	3	2	2	12	1	60	2	1	2	1	.667	0	9	2.27
1993	Durham	A	44	0	0	33	81.1	340	78	32	29	7	2	2	3	17	1	69	3	1	4	5	.444	0	12	3.21
1994	Greenville	AA	49	0	0	21	86.2	370	93	38	34	6	6	3	3	18	6	59	5	1	8	3	.727	0	3	3.53
	4 Min. YEARS		152	1	0	76	281	1186	284	116	97	16	12	9	8	62	8	229	15	7	22	10	.688	0	28	3.11

Henry Blanco

Bats: Right Throws: Right Pos: 3B **Ht: 5'11" Wt: 168 Born: 08/29/71 Age: 23**

			BATTING														BASERUNNING				PERCENTAGES		
Year	Team	Lg	G	AB	H	2B	3B	HR	TB	R	RBI	TBB	IBB	SO	HBP	SH	SF	SB	CS	SB%	GDP	Avg	OBP	SLG
1990	Dodgers	R	60	178	39	8	0	1	50	23	19	26	0	43	1	0	4	7	2	.78	6	.219	.316	.281
1991	Vero Beach	A	5	7	1	0	0	0	1	0	0	2	0	0	0	0	0	0	0	.00	0	.143	.333	.143
	Great Falls	R	62	216	55	7	1	5	79	35	28	27	0	39	1	2	3	3	6	.33	5	.255	.336	.366
1992	Bakersfield	A	124	401	94	21	2	5	134	42	52	51	3	91	9	10	9	10	6	.63	10	.234	.328	.334
1993	San Antonio	AA	117	374	73	19	1	10	124	33	42	29	0	80	4	2	1	3	3	.50	7	.195	.260	.332
1994	San Antonio	AA	132	405	93	23	2	6	138	36	38	53	2	67	2	5	3	6	6	.50	12	.230	.320	.341
	5 Min. YEARS		500	1581	355	78	6	27	526	169	179	188	5	320	17	19	20	29	23	.56	40	.225	.310	.333

Ben Blomdahl

Pitches: Right Bats: Right Pos: P **Ht: 6'2" Wt: 185 Born: 12/30/70 Age: 24**

			HOW MUCH HE PITCHED						WHAT HE GAVE UP										THE RESULTS					
Year	Team	Lg	G	GS	CG	GF	IP	BFP	H	R	ER	HR	SH	SF	HB	TBB	IBB	SO	WP	Bk	W	L	Pct.	ShO	Sv	ERA
1991	Niagara Fls	A	16	13	0	2	78.2	344	72	43	39	2	1	3	2	50	0	30	7	6	6	6	.500	0	0	4.46
1992	Fayetteville	A	17	17	2	0	103.1	423	94	46	31	5	2	0	4	26	0	65	6	3	10	4	.714	2	0	2.70
	Lakeland	A	10	10	2	0	62	264	77	35	32	3	2	1	3	5	0	41	2	0	5	3	.625	0	0	4.65
1993	London	AA	17	17	3	0	119	498	108	58	49	7	4	6	7	42	1	72	4	3	6	6	.500	0	0	3.71
	Toledo	AAA	11	10	0	0	62.2	264	67	34	34	8	1	4	2	19	0	27	4	0	3	4	.429	0	0	4.88
1994	Toledo	AAA	28	28	0	0	165.1	729	192	92	82	18	6	10	7	47	3	83	5	0	11	11	.500	0	0	4.46
	4 Min. YEARS		99	95	7	2	591	2522	610	308	267	43	16	24	25	189	4	318	28	12	41	34	.547	2	0	4.07

Doug Bochtler

Pitches: Right Bats: Right Pos: P **Ht: 6'3" Wt: 200 Born: 07/05/70 Age: 24**

			HOW MUCH HE PITCHED						WHAT HE GAVE UP										THE RESULTS					
Year	Team	Lg	G	GS	CG	GF	IP	BFP	H	R	ER	HR	SH	SF	HB	TBB	IBB	SO	WP	Bk	W	L	Pct.	ShO	Sv	ERA
1989	Expos	R	9	9	1	0	47.2	209	46	22	17	0	2	2	0	20	1	45	3	1	2	2	.500	0	0	3.21
1990	Rockford	A	25	25	1	0	139	602	142	82	54	3	6	4	8	54	2	109	6	5	9	12	.429	1	0	3.50
1991	Wst Plm Bch	A	26	24	7	1	160.1	647	148	63	52	6	6	2	6	54	2	109	7	0	12	9	.571	2	0	2.92
1992	Harrisburg	AA	13	13	2	0	77.2	310	50	25	20	1	2	2	0	36	1	89	4	0	6	5	.545	1	0	2.32
1993	Central Val	A	8	8	0	0	47.2	205	40	23	18	2	1	0	1	28	0	43	2	0	3	1	.750	0	0	3.40
	Colo Sprngs	AAA	12	11	0	0	50.2	239	71	41	39	3	2	2	1	26	1	38	2	0	1	4	.200	0	0	6.93
	Las Vegas	AAA	7	7	1	0	39.2	177	52	26	23	2	1	1	0	11	1	30	1	0	0	5	.000	0	0	5.22
1994	Las Vegas	AAA	22	20	2	1	100.1	458	116	67	58	11	5	3	3	48	2	86	10	0	3	7	.300	1	0	5.20
	6 Min. YEARS		122	117	14	2	663	2847	665	349	281	28	25	16	19	277	10	549	35	6	36	45	.444	5	0	3.81

Brian Boehringer

Pitches: Right Bats: Both Pos: P **Ht: 6'2" Wt: 180 Born: 01/08/69 Age: 26**

			HOW MUCH HE PITCHED						WHAT HE GAVE UP										THE RESULTS					
Year	Team	Lg	G	GS	CG	GF	IP	BFP	H	R	ER	HR	SH	SF	HB	TBB	IBB	SO	WP	Bk	W	L	Pct.	ShO	Sv	ERA
1991	Utica	A	4	4	0	0	19	78	14	8	5	0	0	0	2	8	0	19	0	2	1	1	.500	0	0	2.37
1992	White Sox	R	2	2	0	0	12	47	9	3	2	0	1	0	1	2	0	8	0	0	1	1	.500	0	0	1.50
	South Bend	A	15	15	2	0	86.1	381	87	52	42	5	3	3	6	40	0	59	6	4	6	7	.462	0	0	4.38
1993	Sarasota	A	18	17	3	0	119	495	103	47	37	2	3	6	1	51	2	92	2	2	10	4	.714	0	0	2.80
	Birmingham	AA	7	7	1	0	40.2	173	41	20	16	3	1	1	2	14	0	29	1	1	2	1	.667	0	0	3.54
1994	Albany-Colo	AA	27	27	5	0	171.2	722	165	85	69	10	7	10	4	57	1	145	7	5	10	11	.476	1	0	3.62
	4 Min. YEARS		73	72	11	0	448.2	1896	419	215	171	20	15	20	16	172	3	352	16	14	30	25	.545	1	0	3.43

Frank Bolick

Bats: Both Throws: Right Pos: 3B **Ht: 5'10" Wt: 180 Born: 06/28/66 Age: 29**

			BATTING														BASERUNNING				PERCENTAGES		
Year	Team	Lg	G	AB	H	2B	3B	HR	TB	R	RBI	TBB	IBB	SO	HBP	SH	SF	SB	CS	SB%	GDP	Avg	OBP	SLG
1987	Helena	R	52	156	39	8	1	10	79	41	28	41	1	44	3	1	0	4	0	1.00	3	.250	.415	.506

Year	Team	Lg	G	AB	H	2B	3B	HR	TB	R	RBI	TBB	IBB	SO	HBP	SH	SF	SB	CS	SB%	GDP	Avg	OBP	SLG
1988	Beloit	A	55	180	41	14	1	2	63	28	16	43	0	49	1	1	0	3	3	.50	3	.228	.379	.350
	Brewers	R	23	80	30	9	3	1	48	20	20	22	0	8	0	0	3	1	0	1.00	0	.375	.495	.600
	Helena	R	40	131	39	10	1	10	81	35	28	32	2	31	1	1	2	5	1	.83	2	.298	.434	.618
1989	Beloit	A	88	299	90	23	0	9	140	44	41	47	5	52	6	0	2	9	6	.60	3	.301	.404	.468
1990	Stockton	A	50	164	51	9	1	8	86	39	36	38	1	33	2	0	5	5	3	.63	0	.311	.435	.524
	San Berndno	A	78	277	92	24	4	10	154	61	66	53	6	53	2	0	8	3	6	.33	2	.332	.432	.556
1991	Jacksnville	AA	136	468	119	19	0	16	186	69	73	84	3	115	5	2	7	5	4	.56	7	.254	.369	.397
1992	Jacksnville	AA	63	224	60	9	0	13	108	32	42	42	1	38	1	0	4	1	4	.20	3	.268	.380	.482
	Calgary	AAA	78	274	79	18	6	14	151	35	54	39	2	52	1	1	4	4	4	.50	4	.288	.374	.551
1993	Ottawa	AAA	2	8	1	0	0	0	1	0	0	0	0	0	0	0	0	0	0	.00	0	.125	.125	.125
1994	Buffalo	AAA	35	95	25	6	0	2	37	18	8	27	3	29	2	1	2	0	1	.00	1	.263	.429	.389
	New Haven	AA	85	301	76	13	0	21	152	53	63	41	3	57	3	1	2	2	2	.50	10	.252	.346	.505
1993	Montreal	NL	95	213	45	13	0	4	70	25	24	23	2	37	4	0	2	1	0	1.00	4	.211	.298	.329
	8 Min. YEARS		785	2657	742	162	17	116	1286	475	475	509	27	561	27	8	39	42	34	.55	38	.279	.395	.484

Rodney Bolton

Pitches: Right Bats: Right Pos: P Ht: 6' 2" Wt: 190 Born: 09/23/68 Age: 26

			HOW MUCH HE PITCHED						WHAT HE GAVE UP												THE RESULTS					
Year	Team	Lg	G	GS	CG	GF	IP	BFP	H	R	ER	HR	SH	SF	HB	TBB	IBB	SO	WP	Bk	W	L	Pct.	ShO	Sv	ERA
1990	Utica	A	6	6	1	0	44	168	27	4	2	0	1	0	3	11	0	45	0	0	5	1	.833	1	0	0.41
	South Bend	A	7	7	3	0	51	196	34	14	11	0	1	1	1	12	1	50	1	1	5	1	.833	1	0	1.94
1991	Sarasota	A	15	15	5	0	103.2	412	81	29	22	2	5	1	2	23	0	77	3	1	7	6	.538	2	0	1.91
	Birmingham	AA	12	12	3	0	89	360	73	26	16	3	0	2	8	21	1	57	3	0	8	4	.667	2	0	1.62
1992	Vancouver	AAA	27	27	3	0	187.1	781	174	72	61	9	9	4	1	59	2	111	9	2	11	9	.550	2	0	2.93
1993	Nashville	AAA	18	16	1	1	115.2	486	108	40	37	10	2	3	3	37	2	75	11	0	10	1	.909	0	1	2.88
1994	Nashville	AAA	17	17	1	0	116	480	108	43	33	4	6	1	4	35	2	63	2	0	7	5	.583	0	0	2.56
1993	Chicago	Al	9	8	0	0	42.1	197	55	40	35	4	1	4	1	16	0	17	4	0	2	6	.250	0	0	7.44
	5 Min. YEARS		102	100	17	1	706.2	2883	605	228	182	28	24	12	22	198	8	478	29	4	53	27	.663	8	1	2.32

Bobby Bonds

Bats: Right Throws: Right Pos: OF Ht: 6'4" Wt: 180 Born: 03/07/70 Age: 25

			BATTING															BASERUNNING				PERCENTAGES		
Year	Team	Lg	G	AB	H	2B	3B	HR	TB	R	RBI	TBB	IBB	SO	HBP	SH	SF	SB	CS	SB%	GDP	Avg	OBP	SLG
1992	Padres	R	12	41	13	2	2	0	19	10	2	7	0	11	0	0	0	5	0	1.00	0	.317	.417	.463
	Spokane	A	25	84	15	2	2	0	21	5	5	13	0	37	0	2	0	13	2	.87	1	.179	.289	.250
1993	Waterloo	A	102	359	89	12	3	4	119	44	35	30	0	124	4	4	3	30	11	.73	6	.248	.311	.331
1994	Las Vegas	AAA	4	4	0	0	0	0	0	0	0	0	0	1	0	0	0	0	0	.00	0	.000	.000	.000
	Rancho Cuca	A	37	103	18	5	3	1	32	14	6	7	0	36	1	2	0	5	0	1.00	0	.175	.234	.311
	Springfield	A	46	163	45	8	4	2	67	35	23	26	0	46	2	0	0	10	3	.77	1	.276	.382	.411
	3 Min. YEARS		226	754	180	29	14	7	258	118	71	83	0	255	7	8	3	63	16	.80	10	.239	.319	.342

Ken Bonifay

Bats: Left Throws: Right Pos: 1B Ht: 6'1" Wt: 185 Born: 09/01/70 Age: 24

			BATTING															BASERUNNING				PERCENTAGES		
Year	Team	Lg	G	AB	H	2B	3B	HR	TB	R	RBI	TBB	IBB	SO	HBP	SH	SF	SB	CS	SB%	GDP	Avg	OBP	SLG
1991	Pirates	R	20	64	22	1	0	1	26	13	9	14	0	8	1	0	1	4	1	.80	3	.344	.463	.406
	Welland	A	37	140	33	5	3	2	50	17	13	11	1	38	0	0	0	2	1	.67	2	.236	.291	.357
1992	Augusta	A	15	47	12	2	0	2	20	8	9	11	2	10	2	0	2	2	0	1.00	1	.255	.403	.426
	Salem	A	71	209	42	6	0	1	51	20	20	28	0	36	3	1	2	1	2	.33	4	.201	.302	.244
1993	Salem	A	100	361	100	19	1	18	175	59	60	42	1	63	4	0	6	12	2	.86	3	.277	.354	.485
1994	Carolina	AA	95	290	64	21	2	6	107	36	28	32	3	58	4	2	2	3	1	.75	4	.221	.305	.369
	4 Min. YEARS		338	1111	273	54	6	30	429	153	139	138	7	213	14	3	13	24	7	.77	17	.246	.333	.386

Pedro Borbon

Pitches: Left Bats: Left Pos: P Ht: 6'1" Wt: 205 Born: 11/15/67 Age: 27

			HOW MUCH HE PITCHED						WHAT HE GAVE UP												THE RESULTS					
Year	Team	Lg	G	GS	CG	GF	IP	BFP	H	R	ER	HR	SH	SF	HB	TBB	IBB	SO	WP	Bk	W	L	Pct.	ShO	Sv	ERA
1988	White Sox	R	16	11	1	2	74.2	299	52	28	20	1	3	3	2	17	0	67	5	14	5	3	.625	1	1	2.41
1990	Burlington	A	14	14	6	0	97.2	381	73	25	16	3	0	0	3	23	0	76	4	1	11	3	.786	2	0	1.47
	Durham	A	11	11	0	0	61.1	266	73	40	37	8	2	2	2	16	0	37	2	1	4	5	.444	0	0	5.43
1991	Durham	A	37	6	1	21	90.2	388	85	40	23	2	5	4	2	35	2	79	4	2	4	3	.571	0	5	2.28
	Greenville	AA	4	4	0	0	29	120	23	12	9	1	1	0	3	10	0	22	2	0	0	1	.000	0	0	2.79
1992	Greenville	AA	39	10	0	14	94	384	73	36	32	6	1	3	3	42	1	79	2	0	8	2	.800	0	3	3.06
1993	Richmond	AAA	52	0	0	15	76.2	344	71	40	36	7	10	3	2	42	9	95	3	1	5	5	.500	0	1	4.23
1994	Richmond	AAA	59	0	0	20	80.2	337	66	29	25	3	2	3	1	41	5	82	1	0	3	4	.429	0	4	2.79
1992	Atlanta	NL	2	0	0	2	1.1	7	2	1	1	0	0	0	0	1	1	1	0	0	0	1	.000	0	0	6.75
1993	Atlanta	NL	3	0	0	0	1.2	11	3	4	4	0	1	0	0	3	0	2	0	0	0	0	.000	0	0	21.60
	6 Min. YEARS		232	56	8	72	604.2	2519	516	250	198	31	24	18	18	226	17	537	23	19	40	26	.606	3	14	2.95
	2 Maj. YEARS		5	0	0	2	3	18	5	5	5	0	1	0	0	4	1	3	0	0	0	1	.000	0	0	15.00

Joe Borowski

Ht: 6'2" Wt: 225 Born: 05/04/71 Age: 24

Year Team	Lg	G	GS	CG	GF	IP	BFP	H	R	ER	HR	SH	SF	HB	TBB	IBB	SO	WP	Bk	W	L	Pct.	ShO	Sv	ERA
1990 White Sox	R	12	11	0	0	61.1	286	74	47	38	3	1	2	2	25	0	67	2	2	2	8	.200	0	0	5.58
1991 Kane County	A	49	0	0	28	81	344	60	26	23	2	4	4	3	43	2	76	4	0	7	2	.778	0	13	2.56
1992 Frederick	A	48	0	0	36	80.1	362	71	40	33	3	5	6	3	50	3	85	2	0	5	6	.455	0	10	3.70
1993 Frederick	A	42	2	0	27	62.1	280	61	30	25	5	2	2	3	37	0	70	8	0	1	1	.500	0	11	3.61
Bowie	AA	9	0	0	5	17.2	75	11	0	0	0	3	0	0	11	3	17	0	1	3	0	1.000	0	0	0.00
1994 Bowie	AA	49	0	0	37	66	277	52	14	14	3	4	1	0	28	3	73	4	0	3	4	.429	0	14	1.91
5 Min. YEARS		209	13	0	133	368.2	1624	329	157	133	16	19	15	11	194	11	388	20	3	21	21	.500	0	48	3.25

Dean Borrelli

Ht: 6'2" Wt: 210 Born: 10/20/66 Age: 28

Year Team	Lg	G	AB	H	2B	3B	HR	TB	R	RBI	TBB	IBB	SO	HBP	SH	SF	SB	CS	SB%	GDP	Avg	OBP	SLG
1988 Sou Oregon	A	43	140	28	7	1	0	37	10	6	10	1	18	1	1	2	0	1	.00	5	.200	.255	.264
1989 Madison	A	20	59	9	1	0	1	13	2	6	4	0	18	0	0	0	0	0	.00	1	.153	.206	.220
Huntsville	AA	5	13	2	1	0	0	3	0	2	2	0	6	1	1	0	0	0	.00	0	.154	.313	.231
1990 Huntsville	AA	27	78	14	4	1	1	23	7	4	5	0	20	1	0	2	0	0	.00	4	.179	.233	.295
Modesto	A	52	148	34	9	1	1	48	22	11	24	0	25	7	1	0	0	2	.00	5	.230	.363	.324
1991 Huntsville	AA	64	184	35	4	1	0	41	9	7	15	0	45	3	4	1	1	1	.50	6	.190	.261	.223
1992 Huntsville	AA	85	238	48	5	0	1	56	20	23	26	0	45	2	3	2	3	3	.50	5	.202	.284	.235
1993 Tacoma	AAA	76	210	51	7	2	1	65	29	19	18	0	37	2	3	2	1	0	1.00	3	.243	.306	.310
1994 Tacoma	AAA	101	369	103	21	0	3	133	32	42	31	3	64	3	3	1	0	1	.00	8	.279	.339	.360
7 Min. YEARS		473	1439	324	59	6	8	419	131	120	135	4	278	20	16	10	5	8	.38	42	.225	.299	.291

Brent Bowers

Ht: 6'3" Wt: 200 Born: 05/02/71 Age: 24

Year Team	Lg	G	AB	H	2B	3B	HR	TB	R	RBI	TBB	IBB	SO	HBP	SH	SF	SB	CS	SB%	GDP	Avg	OBP	SLG
1989 Medicne Hat	R	54	207	46	2	2	0	52	16	13	19	0	55	0	0	1	6	2	.75	5	.222	.286	.251
1990 Medicne Hat	R	60	212	58	7	3	3	80	30	29	31	0	35	1	1	0	19	8	.70	2	.274	.369	.377
1991 Myrtle Bch	A	120	402	101	8	4	2	123	53	44	31	1	76	2	9	4	35	12	.74	11	.251	.305	.306
1992 Dunedin	A	128	524	133	10	3	3	158	74	46	34	0	99	3	8	1	31	15	.67	4	.254	.302	.302
1993 Knoxville	AA	141	577	143	23	4	5	189	63	43	21	1	121	3	13	0	36	19	.65	5	.248	.278	.328
1994 Knoxville	AA	127	472	129	18	11	4	181	52	49	20	4	75	1	7	2	15	8	.65	8	.273	.303	.383
6 Min. YEARS		630	2394	610	68	27	17	783	288	222	156	6	461	10	38	8	142	64	.69	35	.255	.302	.327

Tyrone Boykin

Ht: 6'0" Wt: 195 Born: 04/25/68 Age: 27

Year Team	Lg	G	AB	H	2B	3B	HR	TB	R	RBI	TBB	IBB	SO	HBP	SH	SF	SB	CS	SB%	GDP	Avg	OBP	SLG
1991 Boise	A	52	162	34	8	3	4	58	26	22	33	0	54	0	1	2	4	1	.80	4	.210	.340	.358
1992 Quad City	A	119	383	87	18	1	7	128	77	43	93	1	108	4	2	6	20	12	.63	5	.227	.379	.334
1993 Palm Sprngs	A	77	286	93	13	1	3	117	48	40	51	0	52	0	2	3	22	8	.73	13	.325	.424	.409
Midland	AA	35	132	37	3	3	2	52	29	17	17	0	17	2	0	2	0	1	1.00	8	.280	.366	.394
1994 Midland	AA	119	426	100	21	3	5	142	67	63	73	1	78	1	5	8	9	10	.47	9	.235	.343	.333
4 Min. YEARS		402	1389	351	63	10	21	497	247	185	267	2	309	7	10	21	56	31	.64	39	.253	.371	.358

Marshall Boze

Ht: 6'1" Wt: 212 Born: 05/23/71 Age: 24

Year Team	Lg	G	GS	CG	GF	IP	BFP	H	R	ER	HR	SH	SF	HB	TBB	IBB	SO	WP	Bk	W	L	Pct.	ShO	Sv	ERA
1990 Brewers	R	15	0	0	5	20.2	104	28	22	17	0	0	0	3	13	1	17	3	0	1	0	1.000	0	3	7.40
1991 Beloit	A	3	1	0	2	6.1	34	8	4	4	0	0	0	0	7	0	4	0	1	0	1	.000	0	0	5.68
Helena	R	16	8	0	1	56	271	59	49	43	3	2	3	3	47	0	64	6	2	3	3	.500	0	0	6.91
1992 Beloit	A	26	22	4	4	146.1	635	117	59	46	6	6	2	12	82	4	126	18	1	13	7	.650	1	0	2.83
1993 Stockton	A	14	14	0	0	88.1	379	82	36	26	4	2	4	7	41	2	54	6	0	7	2	.778	0	0	2.65
El Paso	AA	13	13	1	0	86.1	357	78	36	26	5	0	3	4	32	2	48	6	0	10	3	.769	0	0	2.71
1994 New Orleans	AAA	29	29	2	0	171.1	746	182	101	90	18	9	4	10	74	2	81	16	1	6	10	.375	0	0	4.73
5 Min. YEARS		116	87	7	12	575.1	2526	554	307	252	36	19	16	39	296	11	394	55	5	40	26	.606	1	3	3.94

Troy Bradford

Ht: 6'2" Wt: 200 Born: 02/25/69 Age: 26

Year Team	Lg	G	GS	CG	GF	IP	BFP	H	R	ER	HR	SH	SF	HB	TBB	IBB	SO	WP	Bk	W	L	Pct.	ShO	Sv	ERA
1990 Geneva	A	7	7	1	0	45.1	167	27	9	9	2	0	1	0	14	0	54	1	1	5	0	1.000	0	0	1.79
Peoria	A	8	8	1	0	52.1	225	51	30	26	2	0	5	1	19	0	35	6	1	2	6	.250	0	0	4.47
1991 Winston-Sal	A	19	19	4	0	118	496	103	44	34	10	2	2	2	48	2	72	10	0	9	5	.643	2	0	2.59
1992 Peoria	A	6	6	0	0	39.1	167	33	19	13	1	2	1	0	20	0	31	4	0	2	2	.500	0	0	2.97
Charlotte	AA	2	2	0	0	11.1	50	16	5	4	0	0	0	0	3	0	8	1	0	1	1	.500	0	0	3.18
Winston-Sal	A	6	4	1	0	26.2	115	25	21	20	3	1	1	1	14	0	7	2	0	2	4	.333	0	0	6.75

Year	Team	Lg																						
1993	Daytona	A	11	10	0	0	53.2	243	58	35	33	7	1	3	3	27	1	39	3	0	3	5	.375	0	0	5.53
1994	Orlando	AA	18	13	1	2	72.1	323	74	45	40	8	5	2	1	42	4	48	4	0	3	9	.250	1	0	4.98
	Daytona	A	9	9	0	0	40.1	191	45	31	28	3	1	2	1	26	0	23	6	0	1	3	.250	0	0	6.25
	5 Min. YEARS		86	78	8	2	459.1	1977	432	239	207	36	12	17	9	213	7	317	37	2	28	35	.444	3	0	4.06

Scott Bradley

Bats: Left **Throws:** Right **Pos:** C **Ht:** 5'11" **Wt:** 185 **Born:** 03/22/60 **Age:** 35

						BATTING													BASERUNNING				PERCENTAGES		
Year	Team	Lg	G	AB	H	2B	3B	HR	TB	R	RBI	TBB	IBB	SO	HBP	SH	SF	SB	CS	SB%	GDP	Avg	OBP	SLG
1984	Columbus	AAA	138	538	180	31	2	6	233	84	84	33	7	31	2	5	6	1	2	.33	15	.335	.371	.433
1985	Albany	AA	6	24	3	1	0	0	4	2	2	2	0	1	0	0	0	0	0	.00	5	.125	.192	.167
	Columbus	AAA	43	163	49	10	0	4	71	17	27	8	2	12	1	0	4	2	0	1.00	5	.301	.330	.436
1986	Buffalo	AAA	33	126	42	3	3	5	66	14	20	6	0	6	0	0	2	2	0	1.00	2	.333	.358	.524
1992	Nashville	AAA	24	59	15	3	0	0	18	7	6	3	0	4	2	0	0	1	0	1.00	2	.254	.313	.305
	Tidewater	AAA	35	111	23	1	0	1	27	8	7	7	1	9	1	0	0	0	1	.00	2	.207	.261	.243
1993	Greenville	AA	26	57	19	2	0	1	24	6	11	5	1	8	1	0	0	0	0	.00	1	.333	.397	.421
1994	Colo. Sprng	AAA	5	10	3	1	0	0	4	1	0	0	0	1	0	0	0	0	0	.00	0	.300	.300	.400
1984	New York	AL	9	21	6	1	0	0	7	3	2	1	0	1	0	0	0	0	0	.00	0	.286	.318	.333
1985	New York	AL	19	49	8	2	1	0	12	4	1	1	0	5	1	0	0	0	0	.00	2	.163	.196	.245
1986	Chicago	AL	9	21	6	0	0	0	6	3	0	1	0	0	2	0	0	0	2	.00	1	.286	.375	.286
	Seattle	AL	68	199	60	8	3	5	89	17	28	12	4	7	2	2	2	1	0	1.00	12	.302	.344	.447
1987	Seattle	AL	102	342	95	15	1	5	127	34	43	15	1	18	3	2	4	0	1	.00	13	.278	.310	.371
1988	Seattle	AL	103	335	86	17	1	4	117	45	33	17	1	16	2	3	2	1	1	.50	11	.257	.295	.349
1989	Seattle	AL	103	270	74	16	0	3	99	21	37	21	4	23	1	1	6	1	1	.50	5	.274	.322	.367
1990	Seattle	AL	101	233	52	9	0	1	64	11	28	15	2	20	0	3	6	0	1	.00	6	.223	.264	.275
1991	Seattle	AL	83	172	35	7	0	0	42	10	11	19	2	19	0	5	2	0	0	.00	2	.203	.280	.244
1992	Seattle	AL	2	1	0	0	0	0	0	0	0	1	0	1	0	0	0	0	0	.00	0	.000	.500	.000
	Cincinnati	NL	5	5	2	0	0	0	2	1	1	1	0	0	0	0	0	0	0	.00	0	.400	.500	.400
	6 Min. YEARS		310	1088	334	52	5	17	447	139	157	64	11	72	7	5	12	6	3	.67	32	.307	.346	.411
	9 Maj. YEARS		604	1648	424	75	6	18	565	149	184	104	14	110	11	16	22	3	6	.33	52	.257	.302	.343

Terry Bradshaw

Bats: Left **Throws:** Right **Pos:** OF **Ht:** 6'0" **Wt:** 180 **Born:** 02/03/69 **Age:** 26

						BATTING													BASERUNNING				PERCENTAGES		
Year	Team	Lg	G	AB	H	2B	3B	HR	TB	R	RBI	TBB	IBB	SO	HBP	SH	SF	SB	CS	SB%	GDP	Avg	OBP	SLG
1990	Hamilton	A	68	236	55	5	1	3	71	37	13	24	1	60	1	2	1	15	3	.83	5	.233	.305	.301
1991	Savannah	A	132	443	105	17	1	7	145	90	42	99	1	117	10	4	5	64	15	.81	6	.237	.384	.327
1993	St.Pete	A	125	461	134	25	6	5	186	84	51	82	1	60	7	7	5	43	17	.72	8	.291	.402	.403
1994	Arkansas	AA	114	425	119	25	8	10	190	65	52	50	4	69	7	2	4	13	10	.57	5	.280	.362	.447
	Louisville	AAA	22	80	20	4	0	4	36	16	8	6	0	10	2	1	0	5	1	.83	2	.250	.318	.450
	4 Min. YEARS		461	1645	433	76	16	29	628	292	166	261	7	316	27	16	15	140	46	.75	25	.263	.370	.382

Doug Brady

Bats: Both **Throws:** Right **Pos:** SS **Ht:** 5'11" **Wt:** 165 **Born:** 11/23/69 **Age:** 25

						BATTING													BASERUNNING				PERCENTAGES		
Year	Team	Lg	G	AB	H	2B	3B	HR	TB	R	RBI	TBB	IBB	SO	HBP	SH	SF	SB	CS	SB%	GDP	Avg	OBP	SLG
1991	Utica	A	65	226	53	6	3	2	71	37	31	31	0	31	1	3	4	21	6	.78	5	.235	.324	.314
1992	South Bend	A	24	92	27	5	1	0	34	12	7	17	1	13	0	2	1	16	3	.84	4	.293	.400	.370
	White Sox	R	3	8	1	0	0	0	1	1	2	1	0	1	0	0	2	0	0	.00	0	.125	.182	.125
	Sarasota	A	56	184	50	6	0	2	62	21	27	25	1	33	3	6	2	5	7	.42	4	.272	.364	.337
1993	Sarasota	A	115	449	113	16	6	5	156	75	44	55	2	54	6	4	5	26	9	.74	4	.252	.338	.347
	Nashville	AAA	2	3	0	0	0	0	0	0	0	0	0	0	0	0	0	0	0	.00	0	.000	.000	.000
1994	Birmingham	AA	127	516	128	18	8	4	174	59	47	38	1	59	1	6	5	34	12	.74	4	.248	.298	.337
	4 Min. YEARS		392	1478	372	51	18	13	498	205	158	167	5	191	11	21	19	102	37	.73	17	.252	.328	.337

Pat Brady

Bats: Left **Throws:** Right **Pos:** 3B **Ht:** 6'0" **Wt:** 180 **Born:** 03/25/66 **Age:** 29

						BATTING													BASERUNNING				PERCENTAGES		
Year	Team	Lg	G	AB	H	2B	3B	HR	TB	R	RBI	TBB	IBB	SO	HBP	SH	SF	SB	CS	SB%	GDP	Avg	OBP	SLG
1988	Everett	A	63	221	52	10	0	7	83	38	38	57	6	52	0	1	3	9	3	.75	7	.235	.388	.376
1989	Salinas	A	126	435	101	21	3	2	134	52	28	81	1	84	0	1	2	5	10	.33	4	.232	.351	.308
	San Jose	A	8	26	6	3	0	0	9	1	1	6	0	11	0	0	0	0	0	.00	1	.231	.375	.346
1990	Clinton	A	49	156	35	6	1	2	49	23	20	23	1	25	0	0	2	2	4	.33	7	.224	.320	.314
	San Jose	A	54	151	32	5	1	1	42	22	17	24	0	32	0	2	2	2	2	.50	6	.212	.316	.278
1991	Clearwater	A	117	369	91	18	9	4	139	52	52	41	2	63	2	1	4	3	3	.50	7	.247	.322	.377
1992	Clearwater	A	65	209	56	7	1	10	95	34	39	38	2	28	3	1	4	7	4	.64	6	.268	.382	.455
	Reading	AA	67	233	61	10	1	7	94	40	44	37	2	39	2	0	1	3	1	.75	5	.262	.366	.403
	Scranton/wb	AAA	3	9	0	0	0	0	0	0	0	1	2	1	0	0	0	0	0	.00	0	.000	.182	.000
1993	Reading	AA	46	140	33	8	0	5	56	23	14	30	1	28	2	2	1	1	3	.25	2	.236	.376	.400
	Scranton/wb	AAA	63	189	43	10	4	6	85	26	28	49	0	40	1	0	3	1	4	.20	6	.228	.384	.450
1994	Scranton-Wb	AAA	29	66	10	1	0	0	11	2	2	7	0	21	0	0	0	0	0	.00	1	.152	.233	.167
	Toledo	AAA	64	207	50	5	0	4	67	20	29	26	0	47	1	2	0	5	5	.50	5	.242	.329	.324
	7 Min. YEARS		754	2411	570	104	20	50	864	335	311	421	15	471	11	10	22	38	39	.49	57	.236	.350	.358

Mark Brandenburg

Pitches: Right **Bats:** Right **Pos:** P
Ht: 6'0" **Wt:** 170 **Born:** 07/14/70 **Age:** 24

Year Team	Lg	G	GS	CG	GF	IP	BFP	H	R	ER	HR	SH	SF	HB	TBB	IBB	SO	WP	Bk	W	L	Pct.	ShO	Sv	ERA
1992 Butte	R	24	1	0	16	62	268	70	32	28	3	1	1	5	14	1	78	1	0	7	1	.875	0	2	4.06
1993 Chston-Sc	A	44	0	0	18	80	320	62	23	13	2	4	2	3	22	6	67	0	0	6	3	.667	0	4	1.46
1994 Charlotte	A	25	0	0	15	41.1	159	23	5	4	1	2	1	2	15	4	44	0	0	0	2	.000	0	5	0.87
Tulsa	AA	37	0	0	26	62	248	50	17	12	2	2	2	1	12	6	63	0	0	5	4	.556	0	8	1.74
3 Min. YEARS		130	1	0	75	245.1	995	205	77	57	8	9	6	11	63	17	252	1	0	18	10	.643	0	19	2.09

Scott Bream

Bats: Both **Throws:** Right **Pos:** SS
Ht: 6'1" **Wt:** 170 **Born:** 11/04/70 **Age:** 24

Year Team	Lg	G	AB	H	2B	3B	HR	TB	R	RBI	TBB	IBB	SO	HBP	SH	SF	SB	CS	SB%	GDP	Avg	OBP	SLG
1989 Padres	R	28	97	17	3	1	0	22	15	8	18	0	22	1	0	0	9	5	.64	2	.175	.310	.227
1990 Chston-Sc	A	4	14	1	0	0	0	1	2	0	4	0	7	0	1	0	1	0	1.00	0	.071	.278	.071
1991 Chston-Sc	A	52	174	24	2	1	0	28	17	7	20	0	61	1	1	1	10	6	.63	1	.138	.230	.161
Spokane	A	68	262	56	4	5	0	70	37	26	25	1	57	5	3	3	16	7	.70	5	.214	.292	.267
1992 Waterloo	A	124	392	90	9	6	1	114	50	29	33	0	126	2	4	0	17	9	.65	4	.230	.293	.291
1993 Rancho Cuca	A	113	405	114	15	6	4	153	70	52	74	3	85	2	4	3	30	14	.68	10	.281	.393	.378
1994 Wichita	AA	109	333	100	8	3	5	129	40	35	42	4	81	3	3	2	18	8	.69	4	.300	.382	.387
6 Min. YEARS		498	1677	402	41	22	10	517	231	157	216	8	439	14	16	9	101	49	.67	26	.240	.330	.308

Bill Brennan

Pitches: Right **Bats:** Right **Pos:** P
Ht: 6'3" **Wt:** 200 **Born:** 01/15/63 **Age:** 32

Year Team	Lg	G	GS	CG	GF	IP	BFP	H	R	ER	HR	SH	SF	HB	TBB	IBB	SO	WP	Bk	W	L	Pct.	ShO	Sv	ERA
1985 Vero Beach	A	22	21	5	0	142	616	121	64	45	1	8	6	5	59	1	74	11	2	10	9	.526	1	0	2.85
1986 San Antonio	AA	26	21	3	2	146.2	642	149	75	63	11	2	5	2	61	7	83	7	0	7	9	.438	0	0	3.87
1987 Albuquerque	AAA	28	28	4	0	171.1	747	188	95	82	9	9	3	7	67	0	95	20	0	10	9	.526	1	0	4.31
1988 Albuquerque	AAA	29	28	5	0	167.1	719	177	85	71	15	4	2	5	51	0	83	3	4	14	8	.636	2	0	3.82
1989 Albuquerque	AAA	34	17	2	2	129	573	149	87	75	7	3	3	1	57	0	104	15	1	6	9	.400	0	0	5.23
1990 Tucson	AAA	41	8	2	5	110.1	521	104	68	58	6	5	3	10	89	3	88	10	1	8	7	.533	0	0	4.73
1991 Harrisburg	AA	21	0	0	6	34.2	162	35	21	12	1	2	1	4	30	1	33	9	0	3	2	.600	0	1	3.12
1992 Toledo	AAA	12	3	0	4	26.2	130	29	29	24	1	0	0	2	23	0	28	8	0	0	4	.000	0	1	8.10
Iowa	AAA	19	1	0	9	29.2	147	43	27	21	4	0	0	2	12	1	34	3	0	1	4	.200	0	0	6.37
1993 Iowa	AAA	28	28	2	0	179	773	180	96	88	13	7	4	15	64	0	143	23	0	10	7	.588	1	0	4.42
1994 Iowa	AAA	41	5	1	19	85.2	399	99	57	52	10	8	4	7	42	5	79	15	0	2	6	.182	0	6	5.46
1988 Los Angeles	NL	4	2	0	2	9.1	44	13	7	7	0	0	0	0	6	1	7	2	1	0	1	.000	0	0	6.75
1993 Chicago	NL	8	1	0	0	15	65	16	8	7	2	0	1	1	8	1	11	0	0	2	1	.667	0	0	4.20
10 Min. YEARS		301	160	24	47	1222.1	5429	1274	704	591	77	48	31	60	555	18	844	124	8	71	77	.480	5	8	4.35
2 Maj. YEARS		12	3	0	2	24.1	109	29	15	14	2	0	1	1	14	2	18	2	1	2	2	.500	0	0	5.18

Greg Briley

Bats: Left **Throws:** Right **Pos:** OF
Ht: 5'9" **Wt:** 170 **Born:** 05/24/65 **Age:** 30

Year Team	Lg	G	AB	H	2B	3B	HR	TB	R	RBI	TBB	IBB	SO	HBP	SH	SF	SB	CS	SB%	GDP	Avg	OBP	SLG
1986 Bellingham	A	63	218	65	12	4	7	106	52	46	50	1	29	3	0	7	26	5	.84	1	.298	.424	.486
1987 Chattanooga	AA	137	539	148	21	5	7	200	81	61	41	0	58	2	2	8	34	14	.71	10	.275	.324	.371
1988 Calgary	AAA	112	445	139	29	9	11	219	74	66	40	5	51	3	2	8	27	10	.73	2	.312	.368	.492
1989 Calgary	AAA	25	94	32	8	1	4	54	27	20	13	1	10	2	0	0	14	2	.88	8	.340	.431	.574
1994 Charlotte	AAA	31	69	13	1	1	1	19	12	7	7	1	15	0	0	1	3	1	.75	1	.188	.256	.275
1988 Seattle	AL	13	36	9	2	0	1	14	6	4	5	1	6	0	0	1	0	1	.00	0	.250	.333	.389
1989 Seattle	AL	115	394	105	22	4	13	174	52	52	39	1	82	5	1	5	11	5	.69	9	.266	.336	.442
1990 Seattle	AL	125	337	83	18	2	5	120	40	29	37	0	48	1	1	4	16	4	.80	6	.246	.319	.356
1991 Seattle	AL	139	381	99	17	3	2	128	39	26	27	0	51	0	1	3	23	11	.68	7	.260	.307	.336
1992 Seattle	AL	86	200	55	10	0	5	80	18	12	4	0	31	1	0	2	9	2	.82	4	.275	.290	.400
1993 Florida	NL	120	170	33	6	0	3	48	17	12	12	0	42	1	1	1	6	2	.75	4	.194	.250	.282
5 Min. YEARS		368	1365	397	71	20	30	598	246	200	151	8	163	10	4	24	104	32	.76	22	.291	.360	.438
6 Maj. YEARS		598	1518	384	75	9	29	564	172	135	124	2	260	8	4	16	65	25	.72	31	.253	.310	.372

Bernardo Brito

Bats: Right **Throws:** Right **Pos:** OF
Ht: 6'1" **Wt:** 190 **Born:** 12/04/63 **Age:** 31

Year Team	Lg	G	AB	H	2B	3B	HR	TB	R	RBI	TBB	IBB	SO	HBP	SH	SF	SB	CS	SB%	GDP	Avg	OBP	SLG
1984 Batavia	A	76	297	89	19	3	19	171	41	57	14	1	67	1	2	2	3	4	.43	7	.300	.333	.576
1985 Waterloo	A	135	498	128	27	1	29	244	66	78	24	1	133	4	0	3	1	4	.20	15	.257	.295	.490
1986 Waterbury	AA	129	479	118	17	1	18	191	61	75	22	0	127	3	3	3	0	1	.00	10	.246	.282	.399
1987 Williamsprt	AA	124	452	125	20	4	24	225	64	79	24	2	121	5	0	6	2	6	.25	15	.277	.316	.498
1988 Orlando	AA	135	508	122	20	4	24	222	55	76	20	2	138	1	0	9	2	2	.50	12	.240	.266	.437
1989 Portland	AAA	111	355	90	12	7	22	182	51	74	31	4	111	4	2	2	1	3	.25	7	.254	.319	.513
1990 Portland	AAA	113	376	106	26	3	25	213	48	79	27	3	102	2	2	4	1	4	.20	13	.282	.330	.566
1991 Portland	AAA	115	428	111	17	2	27	213	65	83	28	2	110	7	0	7	1	0	1.00	9	.259	.311	.498

Year	Team	Lg	G	AB	H	2B	3B	HR	TB	R	RBI	TBB	IBB	SO	HBP	SH	SF	SB	CS	SB%	GDP	Avg	OBP	SLG
1992	Portland	AAA	140	564	152	27	7	26	271	80	96	32	6	124	6	0	5	0	1	.00	19	.270	.313	.480
1993	Portland	AAA	85	319	108	18	3	20	192	64	72	26	5	65	4	0	6	0	2	.00	8	.339	.389	.602
1994	Salt Lake	AAA	108	437	135	24	2	29	250	85	122	30	5	120	4	0	8	3	0	1.00	7	.309	.353	.572
1992	Minnesota	AL	8	14	2	1	0	0	3	1	2	0	0	4	0	0	1	0	1	.00	0	.143	.133	.214
1993	Minnesota	AL	27	54	13	2	0	4	27	8	9	1	0	20	0	0	0	0	0	.00	0	.241	.255	.500
11 Min. YEARS			1271	4713	1284	227	37	263	2374	680	891	278	31	1218	41	9	53	14	27	.34	122	.272	.315	.504
2 Maj. YEARS			35	68	15	3	0	4	30	9	11	1	0	24	0	0	1	0	1	.00	1	.221	.229	.441

Jorge Brito

Bats: Right Throws: Right Pos: C Ht: 6'1" Wt: 188 Born: 06/22/66 Age: 29

			BATTING															BASERUNNING				PERCENTAGES		
Year	Team	Lg	G	AB	H	2B	3B	HR	TB	R	RBI	TBB	IBB	SO	HBP	SH	SF	SB	CS	SB%	GDP	Avg	OBP	SLG
1986	Medford	A	21	59	9	2	0	0	11	4	5	4	0	17	2	0	1	0	2	.00	3	.153	.227	.186
1987	Medford	A	40	110	20	1	0	1	24	7	15	12	0	54	1	1	2	0	0	.00	3	.182	.264	.218
1988	Modesto	A	96	300	65	15	0	5	95	38	27	47	0	104	8	3	3	0	0	.00	6	.217	.335	.317
1989	Modesto	A	16	54	13	2	0	1	18	8	6	5	0	14	1	1	0	0	0	.00	2	.241	.317	.333
	Tacoma	AAA	5	15	3	1	0	0	4	2	0	2	0	6	0	0	0	0	1	.00	2	.200	.294	.267
	Huntsville	AA	24	73	16	2	2	0	22	13	8	20	0	23	0	2	0	1	1	.50	2	.219	.387	.301
	Madison	A	43	143	30	4	1	3	45	20	14	22	1	46	2	1	0	1	0	1.00	9	.210	.323	.315
1990	Huntsville	AA	57	164	44	6	1	2	58	17	20	30	1	49	3	3	1	0	1	.00	6	.268	.389	.354
1991	Tacoma	AAA	22	73	17	2	0	1	22	6	3	4	0	20	0	0	0	0	0	.00	1	.233	.273	.301
	Huntsville	AA	65	203	41	11	0	1	55	26	23	28	0	50	4	2	1	0	1	.00	6	.202	.309	.271
1992	Tacoma	AAA	18	35	5	2	0	0	7	4	1	2	0	17	0	0	0	0	0	.00	0	.143	.189	.200
	Huntsville	AA	33	72	15	2	0	2	23	10	6	13	0	21	1	3	0	2	0	1.00	1	.208	.337	.319
1993	Huntsville	AA	18	36	10	3	0	4	25	6	11	10	1	10	2	0	1	0	0	.00	0	.278	.449	.694
1994	New Haven	AA	63	200	46	11	1	5	74	18	25	18	3	59	2	1	2	2	0	1.00	6	.230	.297	.370
	Colo. Sprng	AAA	21	64	24	5	0	3	38	13	19	7	1	14	0	1	0	0	0	.00	3	.375	.437	.594
9 Min. YEARS			542	1601	358	69	5	28	521	192	183	224	7	504	26	18	11	6	6	.50	50	.224	.327	.325

Luis Brito

Bats: Both Throws: Right Pos: SS Ht: 6'0" Wt: 155 Born: 04/12/71 Age: 24

			BATTING															BASERUNNING				PERCENTAGES		
Year	Team	Lg	G	AB	H	2B	3B	HR	TB	R	RBI	TBB	IBB	SO	HBP	SH	SF	SB	CS	SB%	GDP	Avg	OBP	SLG
1989	Martinsville	R	9	16	5	0	0	0	5	1	1	0	0	3	0	0	0	0	0	.00	0	.313	.313	.313
1990	Princeton	R	27	95	23	2	0	0	25	15	4	2	0	11	2	1	0	4	2	.67	1	.242	.273	.263
1991	Martinsvlle	R	31	123	33	5	0	0	38	17	9	5	0	21	2	1	0	5	2	.71	3	.268	.303	.309
	Batavia	A	22	76	24	2	1	0	28	13	10	6	0	8	0	2	0	9	3	.75	1	.316	.366	.368
1992	Spartanburg	A	34	105	23	1	1	0	26	11	9	4	0	17	0	1	0	7	8	.47	1	.219	.248	.248
	Clearwater	A	65	188	41	4	0	0	45	18	11	5	0	21	1	6	1	4	7	.36	0	.218	.241	.239
1993	Spartanburg	A	127	467	146	16	4	0	170	56	33	11	0	47	1	8	3	9	12	.43	12	.313	.328	.364
1994	Clearwater	A	31	108	35	4	3	1	48	18	13	2	0	3	0	1	1	2	1	.67	4	.324	.333	.444
	Reading	AA	86	284	63	6	2	3	82	33	21	13	0	38	2	4	2	4	4	.50	4	.222	.259	.289
6 Min. YEARS			432	1462	393	40	11	4	467	182	111	48	0	169	8	24	9	44	39	.53	26	.269	.294	.319

Mario Brito

Pitches: Right Bats: Right Pos: P Ht: 6'3" Wt: 179 Born: 04/09/66 Age: 29

			HOW MUCH HE PITCHED						WHAT HE GAVE UP												THE RESULTS					
Year	Team	Lg	G	GS	CG	GF	IP	BFP	H	R	ER	HR	SH	SF	HB	TBB	IBB	SO	WP	Bk	W	L	Pct.	ShO	Sv	ERA
1986	Expos	R	11	11	1	0	59.1	254	58	29	27	4	3	4	4	24	0	40	4	1	5	3	.625	0	0	4.10
1987	Jamestown	A	15	15	3	0	95.1	414	83	50	32	6	5	3	2	40	0	89	3	0	6	5	.545	0	0	3.02
1988	Rockford	A	27	27	7	0	186	775	161	83	62	11	2	2	5	52	1	144	4	7	13	8	.619	2	0	3.00
1989	Wst Plm Bch	A	23	23	4	0	149.1	624	134	64	48	2	3	3	4	49	2	90	5	2	11	8	.579	1	0	2.89
1990	Jacksnville	AA	18	18	1	0	115.2	488	100	57	41	6	4	3	3	34	1	49	4	0	9	7	.563	0	0	3.19
1991	Vancouver	AAA	19	13	1	2	78.1	366	106	69	62	8	2	6	3	25	2	41	0	0	0	10	.000	0	0	7.12
	Birmingham	AA	10	10	4	0	71	284	53	31	26	4	2	0	2	16	0	37	5	0	2	4	.333	1	0	3.30
1992	Indianapols	AAA	2	0	0	0	5.1	23	5	2	2	1	0	0	0	3	0	1	0	0	2	0	1.000	0	0	3.38
	Harrisburg	AA	46	0	0	15	77.1	317	65	25	19	3	3	0	3	24	4	66	4	0	6	4	.600	0	3	2.21
1993	Harrisburg	AA	36	0	0	22	50.1	207	41	17	15	5	3	0	1	11	3	51	0	0	4	3	.571	0	10	2.68
	Ottawa	AAA	23	0	0	7	34	139	25	6	5	0	2	0	1	17	0	29	3	0	2	0	1.000	0	2	1.32
1994	New Orleans	AAA	40	0	0	32	57.2	225	39	18	16	3	3	0	1	20	0	74	5	0	6	2	.750	0	11	2.50
9 Min. YEARS			270	117	21	80	979.2	4116	870	451	355	53	32	21	31	315	13	711	37	10	66	54	.550	4	26	3.26

Tilson Brito

Bats: Right Throws: Right Pos: INF Ht: 6'0" Wt: 170 Born: 05/28/72 Age: 23

			BATTING															BASERUNNING				PERCENTAGES		
Year	Team	Lg	G	AB	H	2B	3B	HR	TB	R	RBI	TBB	IBB	SO	HBP	SH	SF	SB	CS	SB%	GDP	Avg	OBP	SLG
1992	Blue Jays	R	54	189	58	10	4	3	85	36	36	22	1	22	6	0	5	16	8	.67	5	.307	.387	.450
	Knoxville	AA	7	24	5	1	0	0	10	2	2	0	0	9	0	0	0	0	0	.00	0	.208	.208	.417
1993	Dunedin	A	126	465	125	21	3	6	170	80	44	59	0	60	10	10	3	27	16	.63	8	.269	.361	.366
1994	Knoxville	AA	139	476	127	17	7	5	173	61	57	35	2	68	8	9	7	33	12	.73	7	.267	.323	.363
3 Min. YEARS			326	1154	315	49	16	14	438	179	139	116	3	159	24	19	15	76	36	.68	20	.273	.348	.380

Chris Brock

Pitches: Right **Bats:** Right **Pos:** P **Ht:** 6'0" **Wt:** 175 **Born:** 02/05/70 **Age:** 25

Year	Team	Lg	G	GS	CG	GF	IP	BFP	H	R	ER	HR	SH	SF	HB	TBB	IBB	SO	WP	Bk	W	L	Pct.	ShO	Sv	ERA
1992	Idaho Falls	R	15	15	1	0	78	333	61	27	20	3	3	2	3	48	0	72	12	8	6	4	.600	0	0	2.31
1993	Macon	A	14	14	1	0	80	333	61	37	24	3	1	0	2	33	0	92	8	1	7	5	.583	0	0	2.70
	Durham	A	12	12	1	0	79	335	63	28	22	7	1	2	5	35	0	67	6	0	5	2	.714	0	0	2.51
1994	Greenville	AA	25	23	2	0	137.1	576	128	68	57	9	4	4	5	47	0	94	8	3	7	6	.538	2	0	3.74
	3 Min. YEARS		66	64	5	0	374.1	1577	313	160	123	22	9	8	15	163	0	325	34	12	25	17	.595	2	0	2.96

Russell Brock

Pitches: Right **Bats:** Right **Pos:** P **Ht:** 6'5" **Wt:** 210 **Born:** 10/13/69 **Age:** 25

Year	Team	Lg	G	GS	CG	GF	IP	BFP	H	R	ER	HR	SH	SF	HB	TBB	IBB	SO	WP	Bk	W	L	Pct.	ShO	Sv	ERA
1991	Sou Oregon	A	8	8	1	0	43.1	180	37	19	15	2	1	0	1	12	1	48	4	1	4	0	1.000	1	0	3.12
	Modesto	A	4	4	0	0	27	111	25	15	12	3	1	0	1	6	0	12	1	0	1	2	.333	0	0	4.00
1992	Reno	A	25	23	0	0	90	414	109	61	44	10	1	3	5	34	3	72	3	0	3	10	.231	0	0	4.40
1993	Modesto	A	27	26	1	0	139.1	586	137	69	59	12	2	3	6	44	0	121	4	1	12	4	.750	0	0	3.81
1994	Huntsville	AA	10	9	1	0	64.2	269	58	27	21	4	3	2	2	23	3	49	1	1	2	3	.400	1	0	2.92
	Tacoma	AAA	19	18	1	0	119.2	514	115	61	50	13	2	1	3	54	0	85	0	0	6	8	.429	0	0	3.76
	4 Min. YEARS		93	88	4	0	484	2074	481	252	201	44	10	9	17	173	7	387	13	3	28	27	.509	2	0	3.74

Tarrik Brock

Bats: Left **Throws:** Left **Pos:** OF **Ht:** 6'3" **Wt:** 170 **Born:** 12/25/73 **Age:** 21

Year	Team	Lg	G	AB	H	2B	3B	HR	TB	R	RBI	TBB	IBB	SO	HBP	SH	SF	SB	CS	SB%	GDP	Avg	OBP	SLG
1991	Bristol	R	55	177	47	7	3	1	63	26	13	22	0	42	3	1	1	14	6	.70	3	.266	.355	.356
1992	Fayettevlle	A	100	271	59	5	4	0	72	35	17	31	1	69	4	5	1	15	10	.60	2	.218	.306	.266
1993	Fayettevlle	A	116	427	92	8	4	3	117	60	47	54	2	108	5	5	4	25	16	.61	5	.215	.308	.274
1994	Lakeland	A	86	331	77	17	14	2	128	43	32	38	2	89	2	2	2	15	6	.71	5	.233	.314	.387
	Trenton	AA	34	115	16	1	4	2	31	12	11	13	0	43	2	1	0	3	3	.50	2	.139	.238	.270
	4 Min. YEARS		391	1321	291	38	29	8	411	176	120	158	5	351	16	14	8	72	41	.64	17	.220	.309	.311

Eric Brooks

Bats: Right **Throws:** Right **Pos:** C **Ht:** 6'2" **Wt:** 195 **Born:** 05/18/69 **Age:** 26

Year	Team	Lg	G	AB	H	2B	3B	HR	TB	R	RBI	TBB	IBB	SO	HBP	SH	SF	SB	CS	SB%	GDP	Avg	OBP	SLG
1988	St.Cathrnes	A	47	152	34	3	1	1	42	10	9	29	0	49	2	0	0	2	5	.29	3	.224	.355	.276
1989	Myrtle Bch	A	75	270	70	7	0	1	80	33	35	32	0	48	2	2	2	2	1	.67	4	.259	.340	.296
1990	Myrtle Bch	A	68	213	56	8	0	3	73	26	22	44	1	34	2	1	1	1	1	.50	7	.263	.392	.343
1991	Dunedin	A	47	133	24	3	0	0	27	7	11	18	0	37	0	2	0	1	1	.50	6	.180	.278	.203
1992	Knoxville	AA	6	8	0	0	0	0	0	0	0	0	0	3	0	0	0	0	0	.00	0	.000	.000	.000
	Dunedin	A	30	82	19	3	0	1	25	7	6	6	1	16	1	0	0	0	0	.00	2	.232	.292	.305
1993	Dunedin	A	43	142	28	4	0	1	35	18	10	17	2	21	3	2	1	1	2	.33	4	.197	.294	.246
1994	Knoxville	AA	57	157	30	7	0	1	40	14	24	20	1	34	3	2	3	0	3	.00	7	.191	.290	.255
	7 Min. YEARS		373	1157	261	35	1	8	322	115	117	166	5	242	13	9	7	7	13	.35	33	.226	.328	.278

Jerry Brooks

Bats: Right **Throws:** Right **Pos:** OF **Ht:** 6'0" **Wt:** 195 **Born:** 03/23/67 **Age:** 28

Year	Team	Lg	G	AB	H	2B	3B	HR	TB	R	RBI	TBB	IBB	SO	HBP	SH	SF	SB	CS	SB%	GDP	Avg	OBP	SLG
1988	Great Falls	R	68	285	99	21	3	8	150	63	60	24	0	25	4	0	9	7	4	.64	9	.347	.394	.526
1989	Bakersfield	A	141	565	164	39	1	16	253	70	87	25	0	79	6	0	8	9	6	.60	10	.290	.323	.448
1990	San Antonio	AA	106	391	118	19	0	9	164	52	58	26	4	39	4	1	5	5	8	.38	7	.302	.347	.419
1991	Albuquerque	AAA	125	429	126	20	7	13	199	64	82	29	5	49	6	1	4	4	3	.57	14	.294	.344	.464
1992	Albuquerque	AAA	129	467	124	36	1	14	204	77	78	39	1	68	4	0	7	3	2	.60	9	.266	.323	.437
1993	Albuquerque	AAA	116	421	145	28	4	11	214	67	71	21	2	44	2	3	7	3	4	.43	11	.344	.373	.508
1994	Albuquerque	AAA	115	390	125	23	1	16	198	76	79	31	3	34	5	0	3	4	1	.80	13	.321	.375	.508
1993	Los Angeles	NL	9	9	2	1	0	1	6	2	1	0	0	2	0	0	0	0	0	.00	0	.222	.222	.667
	7 Min. YEARS		800	2948	901	186	17	87	1382	469	515	195	15	338	31	5	43	35	28	.56	73	.306	.350	.469

Jason Brosnan

Pitches: Left **Bats:** Left **Pos:** P **Ht:** 6'1" **Wt:** 190 **Born:** 01/26/68 **Age:** 27

Year	Team	Lg	G	GS	CG	GF	IP	BFP	H	R	ER	HR	SH	SF	HB	TBB	IBB	SO	WP	Bk	W	L	Pct.	ShO	Sv	ERA
1989	Great Falls	R	13	13	0	0	67	294	41	24	19	1	1	1	3	55	0	89	10	4	6	2	.750	0	0	2.55
1990	Bakersfield	A	26	25	0	0	136	607	113	63	47	4	3	4	7	91	1	157	7	2	12	4	.750	0	0	3.11
1991	San Antonio	AA	2	2	0	0	7.2	49	15	15	15	2	0	0	0	11	0	8	0	0	0	1	.000	0	0	17.61
	Vero Beach	A	11	9	0	0	36.1	164	34	27	23	2	1	2	2	21	0	25	5	0	1	2	.333	0	0	5.70
1992	Albuquerque	AAA	8	0	0	3	8.2	44	13	9	8	2	1	0	1	4	0	12	2	0	0	0	.000	0	1	8.31
	San Antonio	AA	8	8	0	0	32.1	163	44	33	28	9	2	2	1	21	1	27	4	0	1	7	.125	0	0	7.79
	Vero Beach	A	18	8	2	3	58	255	69	32	30	2	2	1	2	26	2	51	11	1	3	4	.429	0	0	4.66
1993	Vero Beach	A	23	0	0	9	25.2	127	30	22	13	1	4	1	1	19	2	32	4	0	0	2	.000	0	1	4.56

	Lg	G	GS	CG	GF	IP	BFP	H	R	ER	HR	SH	SF	HB	TBB	IBB	SO	WP	Bk	W	L	Pct.	ShO	Sv	ERA
Bakersfield	A	9	6	0	1	36.1	161	36	20	14	2	1	1	2	15	0	34	4	0	4	1	.800	0	0	3.47
San Antonio	AA	3	3	0	0	20.1	83	21	11	10	1	0	0	0	7	0	10	1	0	0	2	.000	0	0	4.43
1994 San Antonio	AA	17	1	0	8	30.2	141	34	16	12	3	0	1	2	12	1	29	3	0	2	3	.400	0	1	3.52
Albuquerque	AAA	24	7	0	5	61.2	275	75	36	36	4	2	1	0	30	0	43	3	2	2	4	.333	0	1	5.25
6 Min. YEARS		162	82	2	29	520.2	2363	525	308	255	33	14	14	21	312	7	517	54	9	31	32	.492	0	4	4.41

Terry Bross

Pitches: Right Bats: Right Pos: P   Ht: 6' 9" Wt: 240 Born: 03/30/66 Age: 29

		HOW MUCH HE PITCHED						WHAT HE GAVE UP												THE RESULTS					
Year Team	Lg	G	GS	CG	GF	IP	BFP	H	R	ER	HR	SH	SF	HB	TBB	IBB	SO	WP	Bk	W	L	Pct.	ShO	Sv	ERA
1987 Little Fls	A	10	3	0	1	28	129	22	23	12	3	2	1	0	20	0	21	1	1	2	0	1.000	0	0	3.86
1988 Little Fls	A	20	6	0	8	55.1	248	51	25	19	2	1	2	1	38	0	59	2	2	2	1	.667	0	1	3.09
1989 St.Lucie	A	35	0	0	26	58	234	39	21	18	1	0	4	1	26	3	47	3	1	8	2	.800	0	11	2.79
1990 Jackson	AA	58	0	0	48	71.2	289	46	21	21	4	5	3	2	40	5	51	4	4	3	4	.429	0	28	2.64
1991 Tidewater	AAA	27	0	0	10	33	159	31	21	16	0	1	1	1	32	2	23	3	2	2	0	1.000	0	2	4.36
Williamsprt	A	20	0	0	16	25.1	98	13	12	7	1	2	1	0	11	0	28	1	1	2	0	1.000	0	5	2.49
1992 Las Vegas	AAA	49	0	0	12	85.2	356	83	36	31	4	5	6	0	30	3	42	5	1	7	3	.700	0	5	3.26
1993 Phoenix	AAA	54	0	0	28	79.1	343	76	37	35	5	1	5	1	37	1	69	3	2	4	4	.500	0	5	3.97
1994 Indianapols	AAA	38	14	0	1	110.1	449	86	42	37	8	4	2	1	43	3	82	4	0	6	2	.750	0	3	3.02
1991 New York	NL	8	0	0	4	10	39	7	2	2	1	1	0	0	3	0	5	0	0	0	0	.000	0	0	1.80
1993 San Francisco	NL	2	0	0	1	2	10	3	2	2	1	0	0	0	1	0	1	0	0	0	0	.000	0	0	9.00
8 Min. YEARS		311	23	0	150	546.2	2305	439	238	196	28	21	25	7	277	17	422	26	14	36	16	.692	0	52	3.23
2 Maj. YEARS		10	0	0	5	12	49	10	4	4	2	1	0	0	4	0	6	0	0	0	0	.000	0	0	3.00

Adam Brown

Bats: Left Throws: Right Pos: C   Ht: 6'0" Wt: 203 Born: 08/10/66 Age: 28

		BATTING														BASERUNNING				PERCENTAGES		
Year Team	Lg	G	AB	H	2B	3B	HR	TB	R	RBI	TBB	IBB	SO	HBP	SH	SF	SB	CS	SB%	GDP	Avg	OBP	SLG
1986 Great Falls	R	64	209	63	13	1	8	102	30	41	37	1	62	4	0	3	6	5	.55	7	.301	.411	.488
1988 Bakersfield	A	92	318	112	18	3	9	163	66	80	54	4	50	8	3	8	5	2	.71	5	.352	.448	.513
San Antonio	AA	30	98	29	5	0	2	40	14	13	7	0	20	3	1	1	0	1	.00	5	.296	.355	.408
1989 San Antonio	AA	42	124	35	6	0	6	59	19	20	13	1	20	3	1	0	1	0	1.00	3	.282	.364	.476
1990 Albuquerque	AAA	5	11	4	0	0	0	4	2	1	0	0	1	0	0	0	0	0	.00	0	.364	.364	.364
San Antonio	AA	43	120	36	10	1	2	54	13	21	11	4	27	1	2	1	1	0	1.00	4	.300	.361	.450
1991 Vero Beach	A	58	183	52	10	1	6	82	26	35	25	4	29	3	0	3	1	1	.50	2	.284	.374	.448
San Antonio	AA	15	37	10	1	0	1	14	3	4	2	1	11	0	0	0	0	0	.00	0	.270	.308	.378
1992 San Antonio	AA	31	76	16	4	0	2	26	4	9	3	0	16	0	0	0	0	0	.00	2	.211	.241	.342
Albuquerque	AAA	6	9	4	1	0	1	8	3	3	0	0	1	0	0	0	0	0	.00	0	.444	.444	.889
1993 Daytona	A	36	109	31	8	0	4	51	17	23	15	1	21	0	1	0	0	1	.00	3	.284	.362	.468
Orlando	AA	2	6	3	1	0	0	4	0	1	0	0	1	0	0	0	0	0	.00	0	.500	.500	.667
1994 Orlando	AA	11	29	10	2	0	0	12	3	2	2	0	6	0	0	0	0	0	.00	1	.345	.387	.414
Iowa	AAA	60	133	32	8	1	5	57	14	18	5	1	23	1	1	2	0	0	.00	6	.241	.270	.429
8 Min. YEARS		495	1462	437	87	7	46	676	214	271	174	17	288	23	8	22	14	10	.58	38	.299	.377	.462

Brant Brown

Bats: Left Throws: Left Pos: 1B   Ht: 6'3" Wt: 220 Born: 06/22/71 Age: 24

		BATTING														BASERUNNING				PERCENTAGES		
Year Team	Lg	G	AB	H	2B	3B	HR	TB	R	RBI	TBB	IBB	SO	HBP	SH	SF	SB	CS	SB%	GDP	Avg	OBP	SLG
1992 Peoria	A	70	248	68	14	0	3	91	28	27	24	2	49	1	3	5	3	4	.43	4	.274	.335	.367
1993 Daytona	A	75	266	91	8	7	3	122	26	33	11	0	38	1	4	0	8	7	.53	5	.342	.371	.459
Orlando	AA	28	110	35	11	3	4	64	17	23	6	1	18	4	0	1	2	1	.67	2	.318	.372	.582
1994 Orlando	AA	127	470	127	30	6	5	184	54	37	37	3	86	5	2	0	11	15	.42	10	.270	.330	.391
3 Min. YEARS		300	1094	321	63	16	15	461	125	120	78	6	191	11	9	6	24	27	.47	21	.293	.345	.421

Greg Brown

Pitches: Right Bats: Right Pos: P   Ht: 6'2" Wt: 200 Born: 03/28/70 Age: 25

		HOW MUCH HE PITCHED						WHAT HE GAVE UP												THE RESULTS					
Year Team	Lg	G	GS	CG	GF	IP	BFP	H	R	ER	HR	SH	SF	HB	TBB	IBB	SO	WP	Bk	W	L	Pct.	ShO	Sv	ERA
1991 Batavia	A	16	7	0	3	50.2	230	47	35	30	6	0	0	3	30	1	33	14	2	1	4	.200	0	1	5.33
1992 Spartanburg	A	17	17	1	0	98.2	432	107	60	46	8	0	2	3	35	0	66	8	2	6	5	.545	0	0	4.20
1993 Clearwater	A	11	11	1	0	67.1	289	76	29	22	1	0	1	3	11	0	21	4	1	8	3	.727	1	0	2.94
Reading	AA	18	17	1	0	94.1	426	119	72	60	10	5	6	5	29	1	42	4	1	5	6	.455	0	0	5.72
1994 Reading	AA	15	0	0	4	27.1	135	41	32	28	2	1	5	2	17	0	11	3	0	2	0	1.000	0	0	9.22
4 Min. YEARS		77	52	3	7	338.1	1512	390	228	186	27	6	14	16	122	2	173	33	6	22	18	.550	1	1	4.95

Mike Brown

Bats: Left Throws: Left Pos: 1B   Ht: 6'7" Wt: 245 Born: 11/04/71 Age: 23

		BATTING														BASERUNNING				PERCENTAGES		
Year Team	Lg	G	AB	H	2B	3B	HR	TB	R	RBI	TBB	IBB	SO	HBP	SH	SF	SB	CS	SB%	GDP	Avg	OBP	SLG
1989 Pirates	R	39	140	31	5	2	0	40	18	11	19	0	28	2	0	1	2	3	.40	2	.221	.321	.286
1990 Welland	A	66	194	57	7	0	2	70	23	32	22	4	35	1	0	1	4	3	.57	5	.294	.367	.361
1991 Augusta	A	94	314	73	13	4	3	103	24	34	47	1	77	3	0	6	12	6	.67	7	.232	.332	.328

Year	Team	Lg	G	AB	H	2B	3B	HR	TB	R	RBI	TBB	IBB	SO	HBP	SH	SF	SB	CS	SB%	GDP	Avg	OBP	SLG
1992	Augusta	A	102	322	82	11	9	2	117	34	33	37	5	69	1	4	5	11	5	.69	10	.255	.329	.363
1993	Salem	A	126	436	118	25	3	21	212	71	70	61	4	109	2	0	7	6	4	.60	15	.271	.358	.486
1994	Carolina	AA	117	377	94	24	2	7	143	49	45	44	8	94	3	1	0	3	1	.75	10	.249	.333	.379
	6 Min. YEARS		544	1783	455	85	20	35	685	219	225	230	22	412	12	5	20	38	22	.63	49	.255	.341	.384

Randy Brown

Bats: Right Throws: Right Pos: SS   Ht: 5'11" Wt: 160 Born: 05/01/70 Age: 25

			BATTING															BASERUNNING				PERCENTAGES		
Year	Team	Lg	G	AB	H	2B	3B	HR	TB	R	RBI	TBB	IBB	SO	HBP	SH	SF	SB	CS	SB%	GDP	Avg	OBP	SLG
1990	Team	A	74	212	50	4	0	1	57	27	8	17	0	47	4	9	0	17	4	.81	1	.236	.305	.269
1991	Red Sox	R	44	143	27	7	0	0	34	25	10	23	0	31	2	3	1	19	1	1.00		.189	.308	.238
	Winter Havn	A	63	135	21	3	0	0	24	14	5	16	0	42	1	4	0	10	3	.77	2	.156	.250	.178
1992	Winter Havn	A	121	430	101	18	2	2	129	39	24	28	0	115	6	8	4	8	9	.47	1	.235	.288	.300
1993	Lynchburg	A	128	483	114	25	7	2	159	57	45	25	0	127	13	2	4	10	8	.56	6	.236	.290	.329
1994	New Britain	AA	114	389	87	14	2	8	129	51	30	30	0	102	5	7	4	9	5	.64	1	.224	.285	.332
	5 Min. YEARS		544	1792	400	71	11	13	532	213	122	139	0	464	31	33	13	73	29	.72	15	.223	.289	.297

Byron Browne

Pitches: Right Bats: Right Pos: P   Ht: 6'7" Wt: 190 Born: 08/08/70 Age: 24

			HOW MUCH HE PITCHED					WHAT HE GAVE UP											THE RESULTS					
Year	Team	Lg	G	GS	CG	GF	IP	BFP	H	R	ER	HR	SH	SF	HB	TBB	IBB	SO	WP	Bk	W	L	Pct.	ShO	Sv	ERA
1991	Brewers	R	13	11	0	0	58	312	68	65	52	2	0	4	5	67	1	68	14	2	1	6	.143	0	0	8.07
1992	Beloit	A	25	25	2	0	134.2	621	109	84	76	8	8	4	11	114	0	111	24	6	9	8	.529	0	0	5.08
1993	Stockton	A	27	27	0	0	143.2	661	117	73	65	9	7	6	11	117	1	110	13	0	10	5	.667	0	0	4.07
1994	Stockton	A	11	11	1	0	62	260	46	30	19	4	4	1	3	30	0	67	3	0	2	6	.250	0	0	2.76
	El Paso	AA	5	5	0	0	29	124	26	11	8	3	0	1	0	13	0	33	1	0	2	1	.667	0	0	2.48
	4 Min. YEARS		81	79	3	0	427.1	1978	366	263	220	26	19	16	30	341	2	389	55	8	24	26	.480	0	0	4.63

Andy Bruce

Bats: Right Throws: Right Pos: 3B   Ht: 6'0" Wt: 220 Born: 04/15/69 Age: 26

			BATTING															BASERUNNING				PERCENTAGES		
Year	Team	Lg	G	AB	H	2B	3B	HR	TB	R	RBI	TBB	IBB	SO	HBP	SH	SF	SB	CS	SB%	GDP	Avg	OBP	SLG
1991	Johnson Cty	R	50	198	57	21	0	9	105	34	42	13	1	50	2	0	5	1	2	.33	4	.288	.330	.530
	Savannah	A	20	76	14	5	0	1	22	6	6	4	1	27	0	0	0	0	0	.00	2	.184	.225	.289
1992	St. Pete	A	89	295	51	6	0	13	96	28	35	19	0	102	3	2	7	0	0	.00	2	.173	.225	.325
1993	Springfield	A	105	364	93	13	1	21	171	61	70	44	3	136	6	0	3	1	2	.33	5	.255	.343	.470
1994	Arkansas	AA	62	133	23	6	0	2	38	10	11	14	1	61	0	0	2	0	0	.00	2	.173	.248	.286
	4 Min. YEARS		326	1066	238	51	1	47	432	139	164	94	6	376	11	2	17	2	4	.33	17	.223	.289	.405

J.T. Bruett

Bats: Left Throws: Left Pos: OF   Ht: 5'11" Wt: 175 Born: 10/08/67 Age: 27

			BATTING															BASERUNNING				PERCENTAGES		
Year	Team	Lg	G	AB	H	2B	3B	HR	TB	R	RBI	TBB	IBB	SO	HBP	SH	SF	SB	CS	SB%	GDP	Avg	OBP	SLG
1988	Elizabethtn	R	28	91	27	3	0	0	30	23	3	19	0	15	0	0	0	17	4	.81	3	.297	.418	.330
	Kenosha	A	3	10	2	0	0	0	2	2	0	3	0	0	0	0	0	1	1	.50	0	.200	.385	.200
1989	Kenosha	A	120	445	119	9	1	3	139	82	29	89	2	64	0	2	1	61	27	.69	6	.267	.389	.312
1990	Portland	AAA	10	34	8	2	0	0	10	8	3	11	0	4	0	0	1	2	1	.67	0	.235	.413	.294
	Visalia	A	123	437	134	15	3	1	158	86	33	101	4	60	4	8	3	50	21	.70	8	.307	.439	.362
1991	Portland	AAA	99	345	98	6	3	0	110	51	35	40	1	41	3	9	0	21	9	.70	10	.284	.363	.319
1992	Portland	AAA	77	280	70	10	3	0	86	41	17	60	3	27	1	3	3	29	12	.71	5	.250	.381	.307
1993	Portland	AAA	90	320	103	17	6	2	138	70	40	55	3	38	3	10	3	12	11	.52	7	.322	.423	.431
1994	Salt Lake	AAA	46	151	42	8	0	3	59	25	29	29	1	18	2	2	1	7	5	.58	5	.278	.399	.391
	Charlotte	AAA	64	163	41	7	2	1	55	23	8	15	2	20	4	2	0	2	0	1.00	3	.252	.330	.337
1992	Minnesota	AL	56	76	19	4	0	0	23	7	2	6	1	12	1	1	0	6	3	.67	0	.250	.313	.303
1993	Minnesota	AL	17	20	5	2	0	0	7	2	1	1	0	4	1	0	0	0	0	.00	1	.250	.318	.350
	7 Min. YEARS		660	2276	644	77	18	10	787	411	197	422	16	287	17	36	12	202	91	.69	47	.283	.397	.346
	2 Maj. YEARS		73	96	24	6	0	0	30	9	3	7	1	16	2	1	0	6	3	.67	1	.250	.314	.313

Greg Brummett

Pitches: Right Bats: Right Pos: P   Ht: 6'0" Wt: 180 Born: 04/20/67 Age: 28

			HOW MUCH HE PITCHED					WHAT HE GAVE UP											THE RESULTS					
Year	Team	Lg	G	GS	CG	GF	IP	BFP	H	R	ER	HR	SH	SF	HB	TBB	IBB	SO	WP	Bk	W	L	Pct.	ShO	Sv	ERA
1989	San Jose	A	2	2	0	0	9.2	49	15	7	6	2	0	1	1	8	0	3	0	0	0	1	.000	0	0	5.59
	Everett	A	14	10	1	2	72	311	63	34	23	1	0	3	6	24	0	76	6	4	4	2	.667	0	0	2.88
1990	Clinton	A	6	4	0	0	25.2	107	18	14	10	0	1	0	3	9	0	22	1	0	2	2	.500	0	0	3.51
1991	Clinton	A	16	16	5	0	112.1	445	91	39	34	2	2	2	3	32	2	74	5	1	10	5	.667	0	0	2.72
1992	San Jose	A	19	13	2	1	100	379	74	32	29	2	6	1	4	21	0	68	1	0	10	4	.714	2	0	2.61
	Phoenix	AAA	3	1	0	2	4.2	21	8	4	4	0	0	0	0	1	0	2	1	1	0	1	.000	0	0	7.71
1993	Phoenix	AAA	18	18	1	0	107	454	114	56	44	3	1	2	2	27	3	84	3	3	7	7	.500	0	0	3.70
1994	Salt Lake	AAA	13	13	0	0	71.2	330	90	49	44	10	2	4	2	28	1	44	6	0	4	3	.571	0	0	5.53
	Pawtucket	AAA	8	4	0	0	27.1	128	34	19	16	1	1	1	0	16	0	9	0	0	1	1	.500	0	0	5.27
1993	San Francisco	NL	8	8	0	0	46	196	53	25	24	9	1	2	0	13	1	20	2	2	2	3	.400	0	0	4.70
	Minnesota	AL	5	5	0	0	26.2	115	29	17	17	3	0	3	0	15	1	10	0	0	1	0	.667	0	0	5.74
	6 Min. YEARS		99	81	9	5	530.1	2224	507	254	210	21	13	14	21	166	6	382	23	12	38	26	.594	4	0	3.56

Dave Brundage

Pitches: Left Bats: Left Pos: P Ht: 6'3" Wt: 190 Born: 10/06/64 Age: 30

Year	Team	Lg	G	GS	CG	GF	IP	BFP	H	R	ER	HR	SH	SF	HB	TBB	IBB	SO	WP	Bk	W	L	Pct.	ShO	Sv	ERA
1988	Vermont	AA	1	0	0	1	1	3	0	0	0	0	0	0	0	0	0	0	0	0	0	0	.000	0	0	0.00
1989	Williamsprt	AA	1	0	0	1	0.1	2	0	0	0	0	0	0	0	1	0	0	0	0	0	0	.000	0	0	0.00
1990	Calgary	AAA	2	0	0	2	2.2	15	4	4	4	1	0	0	0	3	0	5	1	0	0	0	.000	0	0	13.50
1991	Calgary	AAA	4	0	0	4	4	16	5	1	1	0	0	0	0	0	0	4	2	0	0	0	.000	0	0	2.25
1992	Calgary	AAA	5	0	0	4	6.2	32	7	5	5	0	0	0	1	4	0	5	0	0	0	0	.000	0	0	6.75
1993	Calgary	AAA	4	1	0	2	8	36	8	4	2	0	0	0	1	4	0	4	1	0	0	1	.000	0	0	2.25
1994	Calgary	AAA	24	0	0	8	24.1	109	21	10	8	1	1	1	0	17	4	15	6	0	1	4	.200	0	3	2.96
	7 Min. YEARS		41	1	0	22	47	213	45	24	20	3	1	1	2	29	4	33	10	0	1	5	.167	0	3	3.83

Julio Bruno

Bats: Right Throws: Right Pos: 3B Ht: 5'11" Wt: 190 Born: 10/15/72 Age: 22

Year	Team	Lg	G	AB	H	2B	3B	HR	TB	R	RBI	TBB	IBB	SO	HBP	SH	SF	SB	CS	SB%	GDP	Avg	OBP	SLG
1990	Chston-Sc	A	19	75	17	1	1	0	20	11	5	1	0	21	0	1	1	0	0	.00	0	.227	.234	.267
	Spokane	A	68	251	63	7	2	2	80	36	22	25	1	78	2	0	0	7	5	.58	10	.251	.324	.319
1991	Waterloo	A	86	277	64	10	3	1	83	34	25	29	0	78	4	4	1	11	6	.65	8	.231	.312	.300
1992	High Desert	A	118	418	116	22	5	3	157	57	62	33	4	92	1	5	3	2	3	.40	8	.278	.330	.376
1993	Rancho Cuca	A	54	201	62	11	2	3	86	37	16	19	2	56	1	1	2	15	6	.71	7	.308	.368	.428
	Wichita	AA	70	246	70	17	1	3	98	34	24	11	3	46	2	1	1	3	5	.38	9	.285	.319	.398
1994	Rancho Cuca	A	6	25	14	2	1	2	24	11	7	4	0	4	1	0	0	2	0	1.00	0	.560	.633	.960
	Las Vegas	AAA	123	450	117	25	4	6	168	48	52	24	3	83	4	5	5	4	5	.44	15	.260	.300	.373
	5 Min. YEARS		544	1943	523	95	19	20	716	268	213	146	13	458	15	17	13	44	30	.59	57	.269	.323	.369

Jim Bruske

Pitches: Right Bats: Right Pos: P Ht: 6'1" Wt: 185 Born: 10/07/64 Age: 30

Year	Team	Lg	G	GS	CG	GF	IP	BFP	H	R	ER	HR	SH	SF	HB	TBB	IBB	SO	WP	Bk	W	L	Pct.	ShO	Sv	ERA
1986	Batavia	A	1	0	0	1	1	7	1	2	2	0	0	0	0	3	0	3	2	0	0	0	.000	0	0	18.00
1989	Canton-Akrn	AA	2	0	0	2	2	11	3	3	3	0	0	0	0	2	0	1	1	0	0	0	.000	0	0	13.50
1990	Canton-Akrn	AA	32	13	3	6	118	511	118	53	43	6	2	3	4	42	2	62	5	0	9	3	.750	2	0	3.28
1991	Canton-Akrn	AA	17	11	0	3	80.1	337	73	36	31	3	0	1	2	27	3	35	2	0	5	2	.714	0	1	3.47
	Colo Spgs	AAA	7	1	0	3	25.2	100	19	9	7	3	0	1	0	8	0	13	1	1	4	0	1.000	0	2	2.45
1992	Colo Spgs	AAA	7	0	0	1	17.2	83	24	11	9	2	0	0	2	6	1	8	2	0	2	0	1.000	0	0	4.58
	Jackson	AA	13	9	1	1	61.2	258	54	23	18	2	2	2	4	14	1	48	1	0	4	3	.571	0	0	2.63
1993	Jackson	AA	15	15	1	0	97.1	391	86	34	25	6	1	1	2	22	1	83	2	0	9	5	.643	0	0	2.31
	Tucson	AAA	12	9	0	1	66.2	290	77	36	28	4	2	1	0	18	2	42	3	0	2	1	.667	0	1	3.78
1994	Tucson	AAA	7	7	0	0	39	170	47	22	18	2	1	0	1	8	0	25	2	0	3	1	.750	0	0	4.15
	7 Min. YEARS		113	65	5	18	509.1	2158	502	229	184	28	8	9	15	150	10	320	21	2	40	16	.714	2	4	3.25

Renay Bryand

Pitches: Left Bats: Left Pos: P Ht: 5'10" Wt: 170 Born: 09/22/66 Age: 28

Year	Team	Lg	G	GS	CG	GF	IP	BFP	H	R	ER	HR	SH	SF	HB	TBB	IBB	SO	WP	Bk	W	L	Pct.	ShO	Sv	ERA
1988	Spokane	A	18	6	2	10	80	329	71	29	22	5	4	5	1	23	1	75	3	0	6	3	.667	0	2	2.47
1989	Chston-Sc	A	48	0	0	21	91.2	395	90	46	36	9	3	3	3	40	5	70	1	1	8	5	.615	0	3	3.53
1990	Riverside	A	47	6	0	14	88.1	418	128	66	52	9	5	6	1	31	4	68	4	0	7	2	.778	0	0	5.30
1991	High Desert	A	10	0	0	4	11.2	50	12	6	5	0	2	1	0	4	1	13	0	0	3	1	.750	0	0	3.86
	Wichita	AA	37	1	0	14	55.1	230	53	23	19	3	3	5	2	14	5	34	3	1	3	2	.600	0	1	3.09
1992	Las Vegas	AAA	6	0	0	1	8	37	12	8	8	2	0	1	0	3	0	5	0	0	0	0	.000	0	0	9.00
	Wichita	AA	49	0	0	17	52.2	233	59	27	25	3	4	4	4	19	2	39	4	2	2	3	.400	0	1	4.27
1993	Wichita	AA	52	0	0	15	71	313	67	29	19	4	3	0	0	32	2	63	5	0	3	5	.375	0	2	2.41
1994	Las Vegas	AAA	11	0	0	3	11	56	16	11	11	1	1	0	0	6	2	4	1	0	1	0	1.000	0	0	9.00
	Wichita	AA	13	0	0	1	14.1	66	19	8	8	0	0	1	1	4	1	10	0	0	1	1	.500	0	0	5.02
	7 Min. YEARS		291	14	2	100	484	2127	527	253	205	36	25	25	12	176	23	381	21	4	34	22	.607	0	9	3.81

Pat Bryant

Bats: Right Throws: Right Pos: OF Ht: 5'11" Wt: 182 Born: 10/27/72 Age: 22

Year	Team	Lg	G	AB	H	2B	3B	HR	TB	R	RBI	TBB	IBB	SO	HBP	SH	SF	SB	CS	SB%	GDP	Avg	OBP	SLG
1990	Indians	R	17	51	10	2	0	0	12	3	3	8	0	18	4	0	1	2	0	1.00	0	.196	.344	.235
	Burlington	R	17	50	5	0	0	1	8	3	2	7	0	23	0	0	0	7	1	.88	0	.100	.211	.160
1991	Columbus	A	100	326	68	11	0	7	100	51	27	49	0	108	7	2	2	30	6	.83	2	.209	.323	.307
1992	Columbus	A	49	151	33	14	2	2	57	36	19	30	2	52	7	2	0	10	2	.83	1	.219	.372	.377
	Watertown	A	63	220	58	13	1	7	94	41	30	33	1	61	5	1	1	35	8	.81	0	.264	.371	.427
1993	Columbus	A	121	483	127	26	2	16	205	82	61	43	1	117	13	0	2	43	11	.80	6	.263	.338	.424
1994	Canton-Akrn	AA	124	377	89	14	2	12	143	61	53	48	0	87	5	5	3	23	14	.62	4	.236	.328	.379
	5 Min. YEARS		491	1658	390	80	7	45	619	277	195	218	4	466	41	10	9	150	42	.78	13	.235	.337	.373

Scott Bryant

Bats: Right　Throws: Right　Pos: OF　　　　　　　Ht: 6'2"　Wt: 215　Born: 10/31/67　Age: 27

							BATTING										BASERUNNING				PERCENTAGES		
Year	Team	Lg	G	AB	H	2B	3B	HR	TB	R	RBI	TBB	IBB	SO	HBP	SH	SF	SB	CS	SB%	GDP	Avg	OBP	SLG
1989	Cedar Rapds	A	49	186	47	7	0	9	81	26	39	30	0	46	0	1	1	2	4	.33	7	.253	.355	.435
1990	Cedar Rapds	A	67	212	56	10	3	14	114	40	48	50	5	47	1	0	3	6	4	.60	7	.264	.402	.538
	Chattanooga	AA	44	131	41	10	3	6	75	23	30	22	0	28	2	0	0	1	1	.50	5	.313	.419	.573
1991	Chattanooga	AA	91	306	93	14	6	8	143	42	43	34	1	77	3	0	2	2	3	.40	8	.304	.377	.467
1992	Charlotte	AA	6	20	3	1	1	1	9	3	2	1	0	9	0	0	0	0	0	.00	0	.150	.190	.450
	Iowa	AAA	98	315	79	22	3	18	161	35	49	25	2	73	3	2	2	0	2	.00	8	.251	.310	.511
1993	Ottawa	AAA	112	364	103	19	1	12	160	48	65	53	3	90	2	0	6	1	2	.33	11	.283	.372	.440
1994	Calgary	AAA	105	416	133	32	3	20	231	69	87	39	2	66	1	0	5	1	2	.33	12	.320	.375	.555
	6 Min. YEARS		572	1950	555	115	20	88	974	286	363	254	13	436	12	3	19	13	18	.42	58	.285	.367	.499

Shawn Bryant

Pitches: Left　Bats: Right　Pos: P　　　　　　　Ht: 6'3"　Wt: 205　Born: 06/10/69　Age: 26

			HOW MUCH HE PITCHED						WHAT HE GAVE UP										THE RESULTS					
Year	Team	Lg	G	GS	CG	GF	IP	BFP	H	R	ER	HR	SH	SF	HB	TBB	IBB	SO	WP	Bk	W	L	Pct.	ShO	Sv	ERA
1990	Burlington	R	2	2	0	0	10.2	42	5	2	1	0	0	0	0	6	0	17	2	0	1	0	1.000	0	0	0.84
	Watertown	A	10	10	2	0	61.2	253	49	24	19	3	1	1	3	23	1	56	8	4	6	3	.667	0	0	2.77
	Kinston	A	2	2	0	0	8.2	43	10	6	5	0	0	0	0	7	0	13	1	2	1	1	.500	0	0	5.19
1991	Kinston	A	29	28	2	0	154.2	701	154	91	69	12	6	4	4	106	0	112	13	6	11	9	.550	1	0	4.02
1992	Kinston	A	27	27	3	0	167.2	713	152	85	71	8	7	6	5	69	0	121	15	8	10	8	.556	1	0	3.81
1993	Canton-Akm	AA	27	27	0	0	172	740	179	80	71	11	7	4	7	61	3	111	11	7	10	5	.667	0	0	3.72
1994	Salt Lake	AAA	33	21	1	5	139.1	643	168	112	97	16	3	5	5	65	1	59	13	1	5	9	.357	0	2	6.27
	5 Min. YEARS		130	117	8	5	714.2	3135	717	400	333	50	24	24	24	337	5	489	63	28	44	35	.557	2	2	4.19

James Buccheri

Bats: Right　Throws: Right　Pos: OF　　　　　　　Ht: 5'11"　Wt: 165　Born: 11/12/68　Age: 26

							BATTING										BASERUNNING				PERCENTAGES		
Year	Team	Lg	G	AB	H	2B	3B	HR	TB	R	RBI	TBB	IBB	SO	HBP	SH	SF	SB	CS	SB%	GDP	Avg	OBP	SLG
1988	Sou Oregon	A	58	232	67	8	1	0	77	42	17	20	0	35	4	0	3	25	7	.78	7	.289	.351	.332
1989	Madison	A	115	433	101	9	0	2	116	56	28	26	1	61	5	3	3	43	12	.78	5	.233	.283	.268
1990	Modesto	A	36	125	35	4	1	0	41	27	7	25	0	16	2	2	0	15	9	.63	2	.280	.408	.328
	Huntsville	AA	84	278	58	2	1	0	62	39	22	40	0	38	3	7	1	14	6	.70	5	.209	.314	.223
1991	Huntsville	AA	100	340	72	15	0	0	87	48	22	71	0	60	7	5	4	35	7	.83	5	.212	.355	.256
1992	Huntsville	AA	20	60	9	2	1	1	16	8	5	9	0	18	0	1	1	5	3	.63	2	.150	.257	.267
	Reno	A	63	259	95	14	2	4	125	65	38	56	3	40	2	2	2	33	13	.72	5	.367	.480	.483
	Tacoma	AAA	46	127	38	6	3	0	50	24	5	27	1	25	2	0	0	10	5	.67	2	.299	.429	.394
1993	Modesto	A	2	7	2	0	0	0	2	3	1	2	0	2	1	0	0	0	0	.00	1	.286	.500	.286
	Tacoma	AAA	90	293	81	9	3	2	102	45	40	39	1	46	2	10	1	12	9	.57	6	.276	.364	.348
1994	Tacoma	AAA	121	448	136	8	3	3	159	59	39	42	1	45	4	7	2	32	14	.70	8	.304	.367	.355
	7 Min. YEARS		735	2602	694	77	15	12	837	416	232	357	7	386	32	37	17	224	85	.72	48	.267	.360	.322

Travis Buckley

Pitches: Right　Bats: Right　Pos: P　　　　　　　Ht: 6' 4"　Wt: 208　Born: 06/15/70　Age: 25

			HOW MUCH HE PITCHED						WHAT HE GAVE UP										THE RESULTS					
Year	Team	Lg	G	GS	CG	GF	IP	BFP	H	R	ER	HR	SH	SF	HB	TBB	IBB	SO	WP	Bk	W	L	Pct.	ShO	Sv	ERA
1989	Rangers	R	16	4	0	2	50.1	211	41	28	19	1	1	2	0	24	1	34	3	5	3	3	.500	0	0	3.40
1990	Gastonia	A	27	26	3	0	161.2	684	149	66	51	10	3	5	4	61	0	149	7	0	12	6	.667	0	0	2.84
1991	Charlotte	A	28	21	3	3	128	553	115	58	46	7	8	5	6	67	4	131	8	1	8	9	.471	3	1	3.23
1992	Harrisburg	AA	26	26	1	0	160	676	146	58	51	8	2	4	12	64	2	123	4	1	7	7	.500	0	0	2.87
1993	Colo Sprngs	AAA	6	1	0	1	9	48	12	13	6	0	1	1	3	7	0	5	2	0	1	2	.333	0	0	6.00
	Chattanooga	AA	2	2	0	0	8	37	7	6	3	1	0	1	1	4	0	6	2	0	0	1	.000	0	0	3.38
	Jacksnville	AA	10	9	0	0	48.1	216	57	35	33	7	0	5	3	18	0	38	1	1	2	3	.400	0	0	6.14
1994	Jacksonvlle	AA	14	11	0	2	71.1	308	70	41	38	3	2	6	3	30	2	31	8	0	2	6	.250	0	0	4.79
	Chattanooga	AA	13	13	2	0	85	351	75	32	26	6	2	3	4	26	1	65	6	0	7	2	.778	0	0	2.75
	6 Min. YEARS		142	113	8	8	721.2	3084	672	337	273	43	19	32	36	301	10	582	41	8	42	39	.519	3	1	3.40

Troy Buckley

Bats: Right　Throws: Right　Pos: C　　　　　　　Ht: 6'4"　Wt: 215　Born: 03/03/68　Age: 27

							BATTING										BASERUNNING				PERCENTAGES		
Year	Team	Lg	G	AB	H	2B	3B	HR	TB	R	RBI	TBB	IBB	SO	HBP	SH	SF	SB	CS	SB%	GDP	Avg	OBP	SLG
1990	Visalia	A	117	404	124	24	4	5	171	69	64	43	2	58	11	2	5	5	2	.71	8	.307	.384	.423
1991	Portland	AAA	3	5	2	0	0	0	2	2	0	0	0	1	0	0	0	0	0	.00	0	.400	.400	.400
	Visalia	A	98	323	82	10	2	5	111	42	56	47	1	60	2	1	5	4	4	.50	8	.254	.347	.344
1992	Miracle	A	121	434	111	20	0	1	134	26	44	29	1	59	3	1	6	1	2	.33	10	.256	.303	.309
1993	Chattanooga	AA	14	43	11	1	0	1	15	4	4	1	0	5	0	1	0	0	0	.00	2	.256	.273	.349
	Winston-Sal	A	64	215	57	10	1	4	81	19	29	15	0	31	0	1	3	0	3	.00	13	.265	.309	.377
1994	Chattanooga	AA	75	219	51	11	0	3	71	15	19	8	1	32	2	4	2	0	1	.00	5	.233	.264	.324
	5 Min. YEARS		492	1643	438	76	7	19	585	177	216	143	5	246	18	10	21	10	12	.45	46	.267	.328	.356

Scott Bullett

Bats: Left Throws: Left Pos: OF   Ht: 6' 2" Wt: 190 Born: 12/25/68 Age: 26

Year Team	Lg	G	AB	H	2B	3B	HR	TB	R	RBI	TBB	IBB	SO	HBP	SH	SF	SB	CS	SB%	GDP	Avg	OBP	SLG
1988 Pirates	R	21	61	11	1	0	0	12	6	8	7	1	9	0	1	1	2	5	.29	0	.180	.261	.197
1989 Pirates	R	46	165	42	7	3	1	58	24	16	12	2	31	5	1	0	15	5	.75	2	.255	.324	.352
1990 Welland	A	74	256	77	11	4	3	105	46	33	13	2	50	2	1	0	30	6	.83	7	.301	.339	.410
1991 Augusta	A	95	384	109	21	6	1	145	61	36	27	2	79	2	1	1	48	17	.74	1	.284	.333	.378
Salem	A	39	156	52	7	5	2	75	22	15	8	1	29	0	0	0	15	7	.68	0	.333	.366	.481
1992 Carolina	AA	132	518	140	20	5	8	194	59	45	28	5	98	10	2	7	29	21	.58	7	.270	.316	.375
Buffalo	AAA	3	10	4	0	2	0	8	1	0	0	0	2	0	0	0	0	0	.00	0	.400	.400	.800
1993 Buffalo	AAA	110	408	117	13	6	1	145	62	30	39	0	67	1	8	0	28	17	.62	5	.287	.350	.355
1994 Iowa	AAA	135	530	163	28	4	13	238	75	69	19	4	110	5	11	6	27	16	.63	5	.308	.334	.449
1991 Pittsburgh	NL	11	4	0	0	0	0	0	0	0	0	0	3	1	0	0	1	1	.50	0	.000	.200	.000
1993 Pittsburgh	NL	23	55	11	0	2	0	15	2	4	3	0	15	0	0	0	3	2	.60	1	.200	.237	.273
7 Min. YEARS		655	2488	715	108	35	29	980	356	252	153	17	475	25	25	15	194	94	.67	27	.287	.333	.394
2 Maj. YEARS		34	59	11	0	2	0	15	4	4	3	0	18	1	0	0	4	3	.57	1	.186	.234	.254

Kirk Burgess

Pitches: Left Bats: Left Pos: P   Ht: 6'0" Wt: 175 Born: 06/10/69 Age: 26

Year Team	Lg	G	GS	CG	GF	IP	BFP	H	R	ER	HR	SH	SF	HB	TBB	IBB	SO	WP	Bk	W	L	Pct.	ShO	Sv	ERA
1991 Braves	R	20	0	0	17	29.2	119	21	8	5	1	5	1	1	7	0	25	2	4	1	0	1.000	0	8	1.52
1992 Macon	A	51	0	0	20	70.2	302	66	34	23	3	8	1	4	19	4	65	8	3	3	6	.333	0	6	2.93
1993 Durham	A	48	0	0	25	75.2	330	84	40	37	4	5	3	2	20	3	61	5	1	6	5	.545	0	5	4.40
1994 High Desert	A	24	1	0	11	51.2	225	63	29	26	11	2	1	3	6	2	35	2	1	1	4	.200	0	3	4.53
Durham	A	4	0	0	1	6	25	4	5	4	0	1	0	1	1	1	7	0	0	0	0	.000	0	0	6.00
Greenville	AA	9	0	0	3	12.2	56	9	7	2	0	1	1	1	5	1	6	1	0	0	0	.000	0	1	1.42
4 Min. YEARS		156	1	0	77	246.1	1057	247	123	97	19	22	7	12	58	11	199	18	9	11	15	.423	0	23	3.54

Enrique Burgos

Pitches: Left Bats: Left Pos: P   Ht: 6' 4" Wt: 195 Born: 10/07/65 Age: 29

Year Team	Lg	G	GS	CG	GF	IP	BFP	H	R	ER	HR	SH	SF	HB	TBB	IBB	SO	WP	Bk	W	L	Pct.	ShO	Sv	ERA
1993 Omaha	AAA	48	0	0	26	62.2	263	36	26	22	4	2	3	1	37	0	91	9	0	2	4	.333	0	9	3.16
1994 Omaha	AAA	57	0	0	45	56.1	248	44	24	18	5	2	1	1	33	3	68	8	1	1	4	.200	0	19	2.88
1993 Kansas City	AL	5	0	0	3	5	28	5	5	5	0	0	0	0	6	1	6	3	0	0	1	.000	0	0	9.00
2 Min. YEARS		105	0	0	71	119	511	80	50	40	9	4	4	2	70	3	159	17	1	3	8	.273	0	28	3.03

John Burgos

Pitches: Left Bats: Left Pos: P   Ht: 5'11" Wt: 170 Born: 08/02/67 Age: 27

Year Team	Lg	G	GS	CG	GF	IP	BFP	H	R	ER	HR	SH	SF	HB	TBB	IBB	SO	WP	Bk	W	L	Pct.	ShO	Sv	ERA
1986 Rangers	R	12	12	0	0	63.2	256	55	18	11	4	0	1	0	22	1	53	2	2	3	3	.500	0	0	1.55
1987 Gastonia	A	21	3	0	6	55	241	61	34	32	4	1	3	2	14	2	42	4	0	0	2	.000	0	0	5.24
Butte	R	10	10	2	0	62.2	278	77	48	39	4	1	3	1	20	0	38	5	0	4	6	.400	0	0	5.60
1988 Gastonia	A	28	2	0	11	58	252	54	28	19	4	3	8	1	28	2	52	3	2	4	1	.800	0	2	2.95
1989 Savannah	A	4	4	1	0	27.1	100	16	4	2	2	0	1	0	7	0	16	2	0	3	0	1.000	1	0	0.66
St.Pete	A	1	1	0	0	6	21	4	0	0	0	0	0	0	0	0	4	0	0	1	0	1.000	0	0	0.00
1990 St. Pete	A	19	14	0	1	92.2	382	77	37	32	5	3	2	1	36	1	67	3	3	7	4	.636	0	0	3.11
Arkansas	AA	6	6	1	0	39	160	37	13	12	1	1	2	3	10	1	15	0	1	2	3	.400	1	0	2.77
1991 Reading	AA	15	0	0	8	23	105	27	13	12	2	1	2	0	13	3	10	0	0	2	0	1.000	0	0	4.70
Scranton-Wb	AAA	24	6	1	1	64	265	54	25	21	4	7	1	1	29	1	32	3	0	1	3	.250	1	0	2.95
1992 Quad City	A	4	0	0	3	7.1	33	9	2	2	0	0	0	0	3	0	7	1	0	0	0	.000	0	0	2.45
1993 Chattanooga	A	31	1	0	14	48	189	33	21	19	2	2	4	2	14	4	35	4	0	2	2	.500	0	1	3.56
1994 Charlstn-Sc	A	8	4	0	4	35.1	135	31	5	5	2	1	1	1	2	0	26	1	0	3	0	1.000	0	0	1.27
Winston-Sal	A	5	4	0	0	21.2	112	35	26	23	5	0	1	3	11	1	16	3	0	0	3	.000	0	0	9.55
Chattanooga	AA	34	2	0	21	53.2	218	43	20	18	3	4	3	1	16	5	33	1	0	1	3	.250	0	3	3.02
9 Min. YEARS		222	69	5	70	657.1	2747	613	294	247	39	24	32	16	225	21	446	32	8	33	30	.524	3	7	3.38

John Burke

Pitches: Right Bats: Both Pos: P   Ht: 6'4" Wt: 220 Born: 02/09/70 Age: 25

Year Team	Lg	G	GS	CG	GF	IP	BFP	H	R	ER	HR	SH	SF	HB	TBB	IBB	SO	WP	Bk	W	L	Pct.	ShO	Sv	ERA
1992 Bend	A	10	10	0	0	41	173	38	13	11	3	1	0	0	18	0	32	0	0	2	0	1.000	0	0	2.41
1993 Central Val	A	20	20	2	0	119	521	104	62	42	5	7	2	3	64	0	114	8	1	7	8	.467	0	0	3.18
Colo Sprngs	AAA	8	8	0	0	48.2	206	44	22	17	0	3	2	2	23	0	38	1	0	3	2	.600	0	0	3.14
1994 Colo. Sprng	AAA	8	0	0	3	11	72	16	25	24	0	1	2	2	22	0	6	5	0	0	0	.000	0	0	19.64
Asheville	A	4	4	0	0	17	61	5	3	2	1	0	0	0	5	0	16	1	0	0	1	.000	0	0	1.06
3 Min. YEARS		50	42	2	3	236.2	1033	207	125	96	9	11	5	7	132	0	206	15	4	12	11	.522	0	0	3.65

Ben Burlingame

Pitches: Right **Bats:** Right **Pos:** P   **Ht:** 6'5" **Wt:** 210 **Born:** 01/31/70 **Age:** 25

		HOW MUCH HE PITCHED						WHAT HE GAVE UP											THE RESULTS					
Year Team	Lg	G	GS	CG	GF	IP	BFP	H	R	ER	HR	SH	SF	HB	TBB	IBB	SO	WP	Bk	W	L	Pct.	ShO	Sv	ERA
1991 Geneva	A	14	5	0	4	50.2	207	49	22	16	2	1	0	1	12	0	38	1	1	5	2	.714	0	1	2.84
1992 Winston-Sal	A	31	25	3	2	160.2	666	164	79	65	13	5	8	3	44	1	82	3	0	8	12	.400	0	0	3.64
1993 Daytona	A	8	1	0	2	17.1	85	27	16	15	4	0	2	2	9	0	10	0	0	0	1	.000	0	0	7.79
Peoria	A	20	20	4	0	126.1	537	122	59	50	9	0	4	15	32	0	102	3	3	9	7	.563	1	0	3.56
1994 Orlando	AA	25	22	0	0	139	586	132	75	60	14	7	4	10	41	1	84	7	0	4	11	.267	0	0	3.88
4 Min. YEARS		98	73	7	8	494	2081	494	251	206	42	13	18	31	138	2	316	14	4	26	33	.441	1	1	3.75

Roger Burnett

Bats: Right **Throws:** Right **Pos:** SS   **Ht:** 6'1" **Wt:** 185 **Born:** 11/14/69 **Age:** 25

		BATTING														BASERUNNING				PERCENTAGES		
Year Team	Lg	G	AB	H	2B	3B	HR	TB	R	RBI	TBB	IBB	SO	HBP	SH	SF	SB	CS	SB%	GDP	Avg	OBP	SLG
1991 Oneonta	A	62	232	64	6	2	4	86	36	28	17	0	40	8	0	2	3	4	.43	2	.276	.344	.371
1992 Pr William	A	101	341	64	11	3	1	84	38	32	23	0	81	6	5	8	1	3	.25	9	.188	.246	.246
1993 Pr William	A	18	53	10	1	0	2	17	3	7	6	0	7	1	1	0	1	0	1.00	0	.189	.283	.321
San Berndno	A	72	245	70	15	0	6	103	34	33	25	1	39	2	4	1	3	2	.60	6	.286	.355	.420
1994 Tampa	A	6	20	2	0	0	1	5	2	4	2	0	8	0	0	1	0	1	.00	1	.100	.174	.250
Albany-Colo	AA	74	196	42	8	2	0	54	19	9	16	0	43	3	7	1	0	4	.00	10	.214	.282	.276
4 Min. YEARS		333	1087	252	41	7	14	349	132	113	89	1	218	20	17	13	8	14	.36	31	.232	.299	.321

Todd Burns

Pitches: Right **Bats:** Right **Pos:** P   **Ht:** 6'2" **Wt:** 195 **Born:** 07/06/63 **Age:** 31

		HOW MUCH HE PITCHED						WHAT HE GAVE UP											THE RESULTS					
Year Team	Lg	G	GS	CG	GF	IP	BFP	H	R	ER	HR	SH	SF	HB	TBB	IBB	SO	WP	Bk	W	L	Pct.	ShO	Sv	ERA
1984 Medford	A	22	0	0	18	36.1	0	21	4	2	0	0	0	0	12	1	63	0	0	3	0	1.000	0	8	0.50
Madison	A	10	0	0	9	14	55	11	4	4	1	3	0	0	3	0	20	0	1	3	2	.600	0	1	2.57
1985 Madison	A	20	19	5	0	123	506	109	55	50	8	1	3	3	40	0	94	12	0	8	8	.500	3	0	3.66
Huntsville	AA	4	4	1	0	22.2	94	16	6	3	0	0	2	0	13	0	8	0	0	3	1	.750	1	0	1.19
1986 Huntsville	AA	20	18	5	1	124.2	525	122	59	52	16	1	6	3	39	1	77	6	3	7	7	.500	3	0	3.75
Tacoma	AAA	11	0	0	9	16.2	66	11	4	4	1	0	1	0	12	1	14	0	0	0	1	.000	0	2	2.16
1987 Huntsville	AA	34	0	0	27	63.2	257	49	24	21	4	3	1	1	17	4	54	3	0	3	4	.429	0	7	2.97
Tacoma	AAA	21	0	0	10	27.2	122	27	16	15	3	1	2	0	16	1	30	0	2	2	2	.500	0	4	4.88
1988 Tacoma	AAA	21	5	1	3	73.1	310	74	39	30	4	3	2	1	26	2	59	2	4	4	3	.571	0	1	3.68
1991 Modesto	A	2	1	0	0	6	31	9	7	7	1	0	1	1	3	0	8	3	0	1	0	1.000	0	0	10.50
Tacoma	AAA	13	0	0	4	25.1	112	30	16	15	5	1	3	0	7	2	24	2	0	0	2	.000	0	5	5.33
1992 Okla City	AAA	8	7	0	1	42.1	169	32	15	12	3	0	1	0	13	0	16	1	1	3	2	.600	0	0	2.55
1994 Calgary	AAA	37	13	1	10	104	461	133	90	78	24	1	8	2	18	1	62	5	0	9	6	.600	0	2	6.75
1988 Oakland	AL	17	14	2	3	102.2	425	93	38	36	8	2	2	1	34	1	57	3	6	8	2	.800	0	1	3.16
1989 Oakland	AL	50	2	0	22	96.1	374	66	27	24	3	7	1	1	28	5	49	4	0	6	5	.545	0	8	2.24
1990 Oakland	AL	43	2	0	9	78.2	337	78	28	26	8	5	3	0	32	1	43	5	0	3	3	.500	0	3	2.97
1991 Oakland	AL	9	0	0	5	13.1	57	10	5	5	2	1	2	0	8	1	3	1	0	1	0	1.000	0	0	3.38
1992 Texas	AL	35	10	0	9	103	433	97	54	44	8	2	4	4	32	1	55	5	0	3	5	.375	0	1	3.84
1993 Texas	AL	25	5	0	8	65	288	63	36	33	6	2	3	2	32	3	35	3	2	0	4	.000	0	0	4.57
St. Louis	NL	24	0	0	5	30.2	131	32	21	21	8	3	2	0	9	6	10	0	1	0	4	.000	0	0	6.16
8 Min. YEARS		223	67	13	93	679.2	2708	644	339	293	70	14	30	11	219	13	529	34	11	46	38	.548	7	23	3.88
6 Maj. YEARS		203	33	2	61	489.2	2045	439	209	189	43	22	17	8	175	21	252	21	9	21	23	.477	0	13	3.47

Darren Burton

Bats: Both **Throws:** Right **Pos:** OF   **Ht:** 6'1" **Wt:** 185 **Born:** 09/16/72 **Age:** 22

		BATTING														BASERUNNING				PERCENTAGES		
Year Team	Lg	G	AB	H	2B	3B	HR	TB	R	RBI	TBB	IBB	SO	HBP	SH	SF	SB	CS	SB%	GDP	Avg	OBP	SLG
1990 Royals	R	15	58	12	0	1	0	14	10	2	4	0	17	0	1	2	6	0	1.00	6	.207	.250	.241
1991 Appleton	A	134	532	143	32	6	2	193	78	51	45	4	122	1	3	6	37	12	.76	18	.269	.324	.363
1992 Baseball Cy	A	123	431	106	15	6	4	145	54	36	49	7	93	6	4	3	16	14	.53	7	.246	.329	.336
1993 Wilmington	A	134	549	152	23	5	10	215	82	45	48	1	111	1	13	4	30	10	.75	7	.277	.334	.392
1994 Memphis	AA	97	373	95	12	3	3	122	55	37	35	4	53	1	4	5	10	6	.63	5	.255	.316	.327
5 Min. YEARS		503	1943	508	82	21	19	689	279	171	181	16	396	9	25	20	99	42	.70	37	.261	.324	.355

Mike Busch

Bats: Right **Throws:** Right **Pos:** 1B   **Ht:** 6'5" **Wt:** 222 **Born:** 07/07/68 **Age:** 26

		BATTING														BASERUNNING				PERCENTAGES		
Year Team	Lg	G	AB	H	2B	3B	HR	TB	R	RBI	TBB	IBB	SO	HBP	SH	SF	SB	CS	SB%	GDP	Avg	OBP	SLG
1990 Great Falls	R	61	220	72	18	2	13	133	48	47	39	2	50	3	0	3	3	2	.60	8	.327	.430	.605
1991 Bakersfield	A	21	72	20	3	1	4	37	13	16	12	0	21	0	0	1	0	1	.00	1	.278	.376	.514
1992 San Antonio	AA	115	416	99	14	2	18	171	58	51	36	2	111	4	0	3	3	2	.60	7	.238	.303	.411
1993 Albuquerque	AAA	122	431	122	32	4	22	228	87	70	53	4	89	8	0	5	1	2	.33	12	.283	.368	.529
1994 Albuquerque	AAA	126	460	121	23	3	27	231	73	83	50	0	101	4	0	1	2	3	.40	8	.263	.340	.502
5 Min. YEARS		445	1599	434	90	12	84	800	279	267	190	8	372	19	0	13	9	10	.47	36	.271	.353	.500

Homer Bush

Bats: Right **Throws:** Right **Pos:** SS   **Ht:** 5'11" **Wt:** 180 **Born:** 11/11/72 **Age:** 22

					BATTING											BASERUNNING				PERCENTAGES		
Year	Team	Lg	G	AB	H	2B	3B	HR	TB	R	RBI	TBB	IBB	SO	HBP	SH	SF	SB	CS	SB%	GDP	Avg	OBP	SLG
1991	Padres	R	32	127	41	3	2	0	48	16	16	4	1	33	1	0	0	11	7	.61	2	.323	.348	.378
1992	Chston-Sc	A	108	367	86	10	5	0	106	37	18	13	0	85	3	0	2	14	11	.56	3	.234	.265	.289
1993	Waterloo	A	130	472	152	19	3	5	192	63	51	19	0	87	1	1	1	39	14	.74	10	.322	.349	.407
1994	Rancho Cuca	A	39	161	54	10	3	0	70	37	16	9	0	29	4	1	1	9	2	.82	2	.335	.383	.435
	Wichita	AA	59	245	73	11	4	3	101	35	14	10	0	39	3	1	0	20	7	.74	6	.298	.333	.412
	4 Min. YEARS		368	1372	406	53	17	8	517	188	115	55	1	273	12	3	4	93	41	.69	23	.296	.328	.377

Chris Bushing

Pitches: Right **Bats:** Right **Pos:** P   **Ht:** 6' 0" **Wt:** 183 **Born:** 11/04/67 **Age:** 27

			HOW MUCH HE PITCHED					WHAT HE GAVE UP										THE RESULTS					
Year	Team	Lg	G	GS	CG	GF	IP	BFP	H	R	ER	HR	SH	SF	HB	TBB	IBB	SO	WP	Bk	W	L	Pct.	ShO	Sv	ERA
1986	Bluefield	R	13	1	0	7	26.1	104	14	5	4	1	0	2	0	12	0	30	4	0	2	0	1.000	0	2	1.37
1987	Bluefield	R	20	0	0	11	37	157	27	20	15	2	1	0	1	18	0	51	1	1	2	0	1.000	0	6	3.65
1989	Peninsula	A	35	14	1	13	99.2	472	96	64	48	4	3	5	6	79	0	99	10	5	2	7	.222	1	3	4.33
1990	Rockford	A	46	0	0	32	79.2	344	62	38	29	5	8	2	2	38	6	99	3	0	3	6	.333	0	12	3.28
1991	Wst Plm Bch	A	46	0	0	26	65	274	41	15	14	1	6	1	1	41	3	68	4	7	2	1	.667	0	9	1.94
	Harrisburg	AA	3	1	0	0	8.2	37	3	2	1	0	0	0	1	8	0	8	2	0	1	0	1.000	0	0	1.04
1992	Reading	AA	22	8	0	2	70.1	305	68	38	34	9	2	3	2	30	0	72	4	0	3	6	.333	0	1	4.35
	Nashville	AAA	5	0	0	1	10.1	42	8	4	4	1	1	1	0	6	0	6	0	0	1	0	1.000	0	0	3.48
1993	Chattanooga	AA	61	0	0	50	70	279	50	20	18	7	2	2	2	23	3	84	2	1	6	1	.857	0	29	2.31
1994	Nashville	AAA	9	0	0	0	12	55	12	7	6	1	0	1	0	9	3	16	0	0	0	0	.000	0	0	4.50
1993	Cincinnati	NL	6	0	0	2	4.1	25	9	7	6	1	0	1	0	4	0	3	2	0	0	0	.000	0	0	12.46
	8 Min. YEARS		260	24	1	142	479	2069	381	213	173	31	24	17	15	264	15	533	30	14	22	22	.500	1	62	3.25

Albert Bustillos

Pitches: Right **Bats:** Right **Pos:** P   **Ht:** 6'1" **Wt:** 230 **Born:** 04/08/68 **Age:** 27

			HOW MUCH HE PITCHED					WHAT HE GAVE UP										THE RESULTS					
Year	Team	Lg	G	GS	CG	GF	IP	BFP	H	R	ER	HR	SH	SF	HB	TBB	IBB	SO	WP	Bk	W	L	Pct.	ShO	Sv	ERA
1988	Dodgers	R	17	6	1	7	68	261	46	13	11	2	3	1	1	12	1	65	2	1	6	3	.667	0	2	1.46
1989	Vero Beach	A	7	7	1	0	43	183	42	19	14	4	2	0	1	11	0	30	4	1	2	4	.333	0	0	2.93
	Bakersfield	A	19	19	2	0	125	521	115	53	44	7	2	5	1	42	0	80	3	1	8	4	.667	1	0	3.17
1990	San Antonio	AA	5	0	0	1	8.1	38	8	6	6	0	1	1	0	5	0	6	1	1	0	1	.000	0	1	6.48
	Vero Beach	A	22	20	2	0	136	563	131	50	46	3	3	2	0	45	5	89	6	0	11	5	.688	1	0	3.04
1991	Bakersfield	A	11	5	1	4	42.2	176	31	15	7	2	2	1	1	16	0	37	5	0	2	3	.400	0	1	1.48
	San Antonio	AA	16	14	1	1	93	402	113	51	48	6	1	3	1	23	0	47	1	1	5	5	.500	0	0	4.65
1992	San Antonio	AA	6	0	0	2	13	52	8	3	1	0	1	0	0	3	0	10	0	0	1	0	1.000	0	2	0.69
	Albuquerque	AAA	26	0	0	13	37.2	164	41	20	20	4	4	1	0	16	5	23	2	0	1	2	.333	0	3	4.78
1993	Albuquerque	AAA	20	0	0	4	30.1	139	37	15	15	4	5	2	0	13	4	17	2	0	2	1	.667	0	2	4.45
1994	San Antonio	AA	16	8	0	3	65.2	272	75	28	23	3	2	2	0	16	2	34	0	2	5	2	.714	0	1	3.15
	Albuquerque	AAA	15	4	0	2	42.2	194	57	37	29	5	1	1	0	14	1	25	2	0	2	2	.500	0	1	6.12
	7 Min. YEARS		180	83	8	37	705.1	2965	704	310	264	40	27	19	5	216	18	463	28	7	45	32	.584	2	13	3.37

Rich Butler

Bats: Left **Throws:** Right **Pos:** OF   **Ht:** 6'1" **Wt:** 180 **Born:** 05/01/73 **Age:** 22

					BATTING											BASERUNNING				PERCENTAGES		
Year	Team	Lg	G	AB	H	2B	3B	HR	TB	R	RBI	TBB	IBB	SO	HBP	SH	SF	SB	CS	SB%	GDP	Avg	OBP	SLG
1991	Blue Jays	R	59	213	56	6	7	0	76	30	13	17	1	45	0	4	0	10	6	.63	6	.263	.317	.357
1992	Myrtle Bch	A	130	441	100	14	1	2	122	43	43	37	1	90	7	6	0	11	15	.42	6	.227	.297	.277
1993	Dunedin	A	110	444	136	19	8	11	204	68	65	48	10	64	3	1	4	11	13	.46	4	.306	.375	.459
	Knoxville	AA	6	21	2	0	1	0	4	3	0	3	0	5	0	0	0	0	0	.00	0	.095	.208	.190
1994	Knoxville	AA	53	192	56	7	4	3	80	29	22	19	1	31	2	1	1	7	4	.64	1	.292	.360	.417
	Syracuse	AAA	94	302	73	6	2	3	92	34	27	22	0	66	0	0	2	8	8	.50	6	.242	.292	.305
	4 Min. YEARS		452	1613	423	52	23	19	578	207	170	146	13	301	12	14	6	47	46	.51	17	.262	.327	.358

Chris Butterfield

Bats: Both **Throws:** Right **Pos:** 3B   **Ht:** 6'1" **Wt:** 193 **Born:** 08/27/67 **Age:** 27

					BATTING											BASERUNNING				PERCENTAGES		
Year	Team	Lg	G	AB	H	2B	3B	HR	TB	R	RBI	TBB	IBB	SO	HBP	SH	SF	SB	CS	SB%	GDP	Avg	OBP	SLG
1989	Pittsfield	A	71	260	79	13	8	8	132	51	47	30	2	63	5	2	3	14	4	.78	3	.304	.383	.508
1990	St. Lucie	A	118	386	76	10	5	4	108	50	36	64	5	128	4	7	2	21	9	.70	6	.197	.316	.280
1991	St. Lucie	A	121	426	96	24	7	3	143	41	40	53	4	87	2	6	2	8	8	.50	5	.225	.313	.336
1992	Binghamton	AA	138	483	108	20	3	14	176	59	51	57	8	126	3	4	3	9	4	.69	4	.224	.308	.364
1993	Binghamton	AA	77	237	50	10	5	9	97	32	37	24	1	72	1	2	4	0	4	.00	2	.211	.282	.409
1994	Norfolk	AAA	24	66	12	3	0	2	21	4	9	4	0	29	0	0	0	0	1	.00	0	.182	.229	.318
	Charlotte	AAA	22	39	9	2	0	2	17	5	7	5	1	11	0	0	0	1	0	1.00	1	.231	.318	.436
	Canton-Akm	AA	22	65	13	2	0	2	21	5	10	3	0	16	0	1	0	1	1	.50	0	.200	.235	.323
	6 Min. YEARS		593	1962	443	84	28	44	715	247	237	240	21	532	15	22	14	54	31	.64	21	.226	.313	.364

John Byington

Bats: Right **Throws:** Right **Pos:** 3B **Ht:** 5'8" **Wt:** 165 **Born:** 11/04/67 **Age:** 27

						BATTING												BASERUNNING				PERCENTAGES		
Year	Team	Lg	G	AB	H	2B	3B	HR	TB	R	RBI	TBB	IBB	SO	HBP	SH	SF	SB	CS	SB%	GDP	Avg	OBP	SLG
1989	Beloit	A	44	149	31	7	2	1	45	14	14	14	2	26	3	0	2	0	3	.00	6	.208	.286	.302
1990	Beloit	A	127	438	115	23	1	17	191	75	89	49	2	68	8	2	7	2	4	.33	4	.263	.343	.436
1991	El Paso	AA	129	501	137	27	1	9	193	60	89	25	1	63	4	5	15	3	3	.50	17	.273	.305	.385
1992	El Paso	AA	130	468	143	39	4	4	202	60	64	32	2	54	7	1	11	5	9	.36	15	.306	.351	.432
1993	New Orleans	AAA	123	436	122	33	2	11	192	58	63	35	4	32	6	2	5	3	2	.60	17	.280	.338	.440
1994	New Orleans	AAA	134	506	157	32	4	9	224	71	86	36	3	29	8	0	5	8	2	.80	16	.310	.362	.443
	6 Min. YEARS		687	2498	705	161	14	51	1047	338	405	191	14	272	36	10	45	21	23	.48	75	.282	.336	.419

Jim Byrd

Bats: Right **Throws:** Right **Pos:** SS **Ht:** 6'1" **Wt:** 186 **Born:** 10/03/68 **Age:** 26

						BATTING												BASERUNNING				PERCENTAGES		
Year	Team	Lg	G	AB	H	2B	3B	HR	TB	R	RBI	TBB	IBB	SO	HBP	SH	SF	SB	CS	SB%	GDP	Avg	OBP	SLG
1988	R.S./mamrs	R	33	121	36	7	2	2	53	18	13	6	0	19	2	0	1	7	1	.88	3	.298	.338	.438
1989	Winter Havn	A	126	447	88	17	2	3	118	42	25	25	0	104	4	11	0	22	10	.69	13	.197	.246	.264
1990	Lynchburg	A	131	511	115	20	1	8	161	59	45	38	0	139	15	1	4	24	11	.69	14	.225	.296	.315
	New Britain	AA	2	5	1	1	0	0	2	1	0	0	0	1	0	0	0	0	0	.00	1	.200	.200	.400
1991	Lynchburg	A	52	206	49	10	0	1	62	29	18	13	0	50	3	0	1	9	3	.75	6	.238	.291	.301
	New Britain	AA	79	292	70	9	1	0	81	28	15	28	1	53	1	5	2	14	10	.58	12	.240	.307	.277
1992	Winter Havn	A	18	71	19	2	1	0	23	12	1	5	0	7	0	1	0	4	0	1.00	3	.268	.316	.324
	New Britain	AA	20	63	14	1	2	0	19	5	6	3	0	13	1	0	0	2	3	.40	1	.222	.269	.302
	Pawtucket	AAA	72	246	55	5	1	2	68	27	18	7	0	48	4	4	0	2	3	.40	5	.224	.257	.276
1993	Pawtucket	AAA	117	378	67	12	4	3	96	33	26	18	1	111	9	5	0	10	9	.53	5	.177	.232	.254
1994	New Britain	AA	12	26	2	0	0	0	2	3	0	2	0	5	0	0	0	0	0	.00	2	.077	.143	.077
	El Paso	AA	71	219	50	8	1	2	66	25	23	16	1	54	4	3	1	4	7	.36	4	.228	.292	.301
1993	Boston	AL	2	0	0	0	0	0	0	0	0	0	0	0	0	0	0	0	0	.00	0	.000	.000	.000
	7 Min. YEARS		733	2585	566	92	15	21	751	282	190	161	3	604	43	30	9	98	57	.63	69	.219	.275	.291

Paul Byrd

Pitches: Right **Bats:** Right **Pos:** P **Ht:** 6'1" **Wt:** 185 **Born:** 12/03/70 **Age:** 24

			HOW MUCH HE PITCHED						WHAT HE GAVE UP												THE RESULTS					
Year	Team	Lg	G	GS	CG	GF	IP	BFP	H	R	ER	HR	SH	SF	HB	TBB	IBB	SO	WP	Bk	W	L	Pct.	ShO	Sv	ERA
1991	Kinston	A	14	11	0	0	62.2	263	40	27	22	7	3	3	0	36	0	62	6	7	4	3	.571	0	0	3.16
1992	Canton-Akrn	AA	24	24	4	0	152.1	654	122	68	51	4	5	4	4	75	2	118	10	0	14	6	.700	0	0	3.01
1993	Canton-Akrn	AA	2	1	0	1	10	41	7	4	4	1	0	1	0	3	0	8	1	0	0	0	.000	0	0	3.60
	Charlotte	AAA	14	14	1	0	81	351	80	43	35	9	1	3	6	30	0	54	4	1	7	4	.636	1	0	3.89
1994	Canton-Akrn	AA	21	20	4	0	139.1	594	135	70	59	10	5	5	2	52	3	106	1	2	5	9	.357	1	0	3.81
	Charlotte	AAA	9	4	0	2	36.2	149	33	19	16	5	3	3	0	11	1	15	3	0	2	2	.500	0	1	3.93
	4 Min. YEARS		84	74	9	3	482	2052	417	231	187	36	17	19	12	207	6	363	25	10	32	24	.571	2	1	3.49

Tony Byrd

Bats: Right **Throws:** Right **Pos:** OF **Ht:** 5'11" **Wt:** 180 **Born:** 11/13/70 **Age:** 24

						BATTING												BASERUNNING				PERCENTAGES		
Year	Team	Lg	G	AB	H	2B	3B	HR	TB	R	RBI	TBB	IBB	SO	HBP	SH	SF	SB	CS	SB%	GDP	Avg	OBP	SLG
1992	Kenosha	A	46	150	35	5	3	0	46	15	10	12	0	35	0	3	0	7	1	.88	2	.233	.290	.307
1993	Ft.Wayne	A	123	479	140	19	10	16	227	84	79	58	4	78	3	0	3	24	11	.69	6	.292	.370	.474
1994	Nashville	AA	132	512	121	25	6	7	179	62	38	37	0	114	3	4	3	28	10	.74	10	.236	.290	.350
	3 Min. YEARS		301	1141	296	49	19	23	452	161	127	107	4	227	6	7	6	59	22	.73	18	.259	.325	.396

Clayton Byrne

Bats: Right **Throws:** Right **Pos:** OF **Ht:** 6'1" **Wt:** 180 **Born:** 02/12/72 **Age:** 23

						BATTING												BASERUNNING				PERCENTAGES		
Year	Team	Lg	G	AB	H	2B	3B	HR	TB	R	RBI	TBB	IBB	SO	HBP	SH	SF	SB	CS	SB%	GDP	Avg	OBP	SLG
1991	Kane County	A	26	104	22	6	0	0	28	14	3	2	0	26	2	1	2	2	0	1.00	2	.212	.236	.269
	Bluefield	R	54	221	71	9	4	3	97	39	25	18	0	38	2	2	1	8	17	.32	2	.321	.376	.439
1992	Kane County	A	109	347	78	14	1	2	100	42	35	13	0	74	3	6	1	12	5	.71	7	.225	.258	.288
1993	Albany	A	122	457	126	26	3	6	176	64	55	42	0	69	3	0	4	23	11	.68	13	.276	.338	.385
1994	Rochester	AAA	3	2	0	0	0	0	0	0	0	0	0	2	0	0	0	0	0	.00	0	.000	.000	.000
	Frederick	A	77	290	83	20	2	8	131	48	39	19	0	45	3	2	3	14	6	.70	7	.286	.333	.452
	Bowie	AA	26	95	21	4	0	0	25	12	9	2	0	16	0	2	1	5	2	.71	1	.221	.235	.263
	4 Min. YEARS		417	1516	401	79	10	19	557	219	166	96	0	270	13	13	12	64	41	.61	32	.265	.312	.367

Jolbert Cabrera

Bats: Right **Throws:** Right **Pos:** SS **Ht:** 6'0" **Wt:** 177 **Born:** 12/08/72 **Age:** 22

						BATTING												BASERUNNING				PERCENTAGES		
Year	Team	Lg	G	AB	H	2B	3B	HR	TB	R	RBI	TBB	IBB	SO	HBP	SH	SF	SB	CS	SB%	GDP	Avg	OBP	SLG
1991	Sumter	A	101	324	66	4	0	1	73	33	20	19	0	62	4	4	2	10	11	.48	5	.204	.255	.225
1992	Albany	A	118	377	86	9	2	0	99	44	23	34	0	77	1	6	0	22	11	.67	8	.228	.294	.263
1993	Burlington	A	128	507	129	24	2	0	157	62	38	39	0	93	7	11	4	31	11	.74	13	.254	.314	.310
1994	W. Palm Bch	A	83	266	54	4	0	0	58	32	13	14	0	48	8	4	0	7	10	.41	4	.203	.264	.218

	Lg	G	AB	H	2B	3B	HR	TB	R	RBI	TBB	IBB	SO	HBP	SH	SF	SB	CS	SB%	GDP	Avg	OBP	SLG
San Bernrdo	A	30	109	27	5	1	0	34	14	11	14	0	24	0	4	2	2	2	.50	1	.248	.328	.312
Harrisburg	AA	3	2	0	0	0	0	0	0	0	0	0	1	0	0	0	0	0	.00	0	.000	.000	.000
4 Min. YEARS		463	1585	362	46	5	1	421	185	105	120	0	305	20	29	8	72	45	.62	31	.228	.290	.266

Edgar Caceres

Bats: Both Throws: Right Pos: 3B   Ht: 6'1" Wt: 170 Born: 06/06/64 Age: 31

		BATTING															BASERUNNING				PERCENTAGES		
Year Team	Lg	G	AB	H	2B	3B	HR	TB	R	RBI	TBB	IBB	SO	HBP	SH	SF	SB	CS	SB%	GDP	Avg	OBP	SLG
1984 Dodgers	R	20	77	23	3	1	0	28	11	11	10	0	6	0	1	0	5	2	.71	0	.299	.379	.364
1985 Dodgers	R	53	176	53	6	0	0	59	37	22	18	1	11	2	2	0	5	2	.71	4	.301	.372	.335
1986 Wst Plm Bch	A	111	382	106	9	5	0	125	52	37	24	2	28	2	4	4	25	6	.81	4	.277	.320	.327
1987 Jacksnville	AA	18	62	8	0	1	0	10	7	3	3	0	7	0	0	0	2	0	1.00	2	.129	.169	.161
Wst Plm Bch	A	105	390	105	14	1	2	127	55	37	27	0	30	5	7	1	30	5	.86	4	.269	.324	.326
1988 Rockford	A	36	117	31	2	0	0	33	25	8	12	0	12	0	5	1	13	3	.81	2	.265	.331	.282
Tampa	A	32	74	15	2	0	1	20	5	8	10	2	8	1	2	3	3	0	1.00	2	.203	.295	.270
1989 Sarasota	A	106	373	110	16	4	0	134	45	50	24	4	38	2	9	2	8	3	.73	12	.295	.339	.359
1990 Birmingham	AA	62	213	56	5	1	0	63	31	17	16	0	26	1	3	1	7	4	.64	7	.263	.316	.296
1992 El Paso	AA	114	378	118	14	6	2	150	50	52	23	4	41	2	5	1	9	2	.82	8	.312	.354	.397
1993 New Orleans	AAA	114	420	133	20	2	5	172	73	45	35	5	39	1	3	3	7	4	.64	14	.317	.368	.410
1994 Omaha	AAA	67	236	64	7	3	2	83	39	18	16	1	23	0	6	3	5	3	.63	7	.271	.314	.352
10 Min. YEARS		838	2898	822	98	24	12	1004	430	308	218	19	269	16	47	19	119	34	.78	66	.284	.335	.346

Tim Cain

Pitches: Right Bats: Both Pos: P   Ht: 6'1" Wt: 180 Born: 10/09/69 Age: 25

		HOW MUCH HE PITCHED						WHAT HE GAVE UP											THE RESULTS				
Year Team	Lg	G	GS	CG	GF	IP	BFP	H	R	ER	HR	SH	SF	HB	TBB	IBB	SO	WP	Bk	W	L	Pct.	ShO	Sv	ERA
1990 Rangers	R	16	1	0	4	36	146	27	22	15	1	0	0	5	6	0	38	2	2	0	3	.000	0	1	3.75
1991 Bend	A	17	6	0	4	58	267	65	49	37	2	0	1	4	25	0	59	8	0	1	3	.250	0	2	5.71
1993 Rochester	IND	20	12	2	1	102.1	428	76	37	27	4	7	1	13	28	0	73	1	1	4	4	.500	1	1	2.37
1994 Winnipeg	IND	6	6	1	0	43	167	30	11	11	2	1	0	1	6	0	50	1	0	5	1	.833	0	0	2.30
New Britain	AA	10	10	0	0	50.2	226	65	39	32	8	2	0	3	18	0	37	1	1	2	4	.333	0	0	5.68
4 Min. YEARS		69	35	3	9	290.1	1234	263	158	122	17	10	2	26	83	0	257	15	4	12	15	.444	1	4	3.78

Cameron Cairncross

Pitches: Left Bats: Right Pos: P   Ht: 6'2" Wt: 212 Born: 05/11/72 Age: 23

		HOW MUCH HE PITCHED						WHAT HE GAVE UP											THE RESULTS				
Year Team	Lg	G	GS	CG	GF	IP	BFP	H	R	ER	HR	SH	SF	HB	TBB	IBB	SO	WP	Bk	W	L	Pct.	ShO	Sv	ERA
1991 Chston-Sc	A	24	24	2	0	131.1	545	111	72	52	10	4	3	7	74	0	102	6	9	8	5	.615	1	0	3.56
1992 Waterloo	A	24	24	1	0	137	578	127	68	55	14	3	3	14	61	2	138	8	9	8	8	.500	1	0	3.61
1993 Rancho Cuca	A	29	26	0	0	154.2	706	182	112	88	10	5	6	13	81	1	122	8	9	10	11	.476	0	0	5.12
1994 Las Vegas	AAA	4	0	0	0	6.1	32	8	3	3	0	0	0	0	6	2	4	0	0	0	1	.000	0	0	4.26
Rancho Cuca	A	29	0	0	6	34.2	139	26	19	17	3	0	1	2	14	0	40	1	2	3	1	.750	0	3	4.41
Wichita	AA	31	0	0	13	37	162	37	19	15	5	0	2	1	15	1	33	6	1	2	3	.400	0	3	3.65
4 Min. YEARS		141	74	3	19	501	2162	491	293	230	42	12	15	37	251	6	439	29	30	31	29	.517	2	6	4.13

Sergio Cairo

Bats: Right Throws: Right Pos: OF   Ht: 6'1" Wt: 165 Born: 10/22/70 Age: 24

		BATTING															BASERUNNING				PERCENTAGES		
Year Team	Lg	G	AB	H	2B	3B	HR	TB	R	RBI	TBB	IBB	SO	HBP	SH	SF	SB	CS	SB%	GDP	Avg	OBP	SLG
1989 Bluefield	R	57	207	55	13	2	2	78	30	40	13	0	19	2	1	2	1	7	.13	5	.266	.313	.377
1990 Wausau	A	111	333	80	8	4	3	105	31	29	25	0	49	3	2	3	12	7	.63	8	.240	.297	.315
1991 Frederick	A	90	299	94	20	2	3	127	38	40	47	2	39	0	1	2	4	7	.36	8	.314	.405	.425
1992 Hagerstown	AA	121	409	115	13	4	2	142	43	46	33	1	53	1	3	5	5	8	.38	11	.281	.333	.347
1993 Birmingham	AA	68	189	43	2	0	2	51	20	13	28	0	28	1	0	1	6	3	.67	6	.228	.329	.270
Charlotte	AA	34	122	45	4	1	5	66	15	25	15	0	11	2	2	0	3	4	.43	3	.369	.446	.541
1994 Tulsa	AA	123	454	124	24	1	14	192	48	76	40	1	88	2	2	3	1	3	.25	12	.273	.333	.423
6 Min. YEARS		604	2013	556	84	14	31	761	225	269	201	4	287	11	11	16	32	39	.45	53	.276	.343	.378

Danny Calcagno

Bats: Right Throws: Right Pos: C   Ht: 5'9" Wt: 165 Born: 03/12/68 Age: 27

		BATTING															BASERUNNING				PERCENTAGES		
Year Team	Lg	G	AB	H	2B	3B	HR	TB	R	RBI	TBB	IBB	SO	HBP	SH	SF	SB	CS	SB%	GDP	Avg	OBP	SLG
1991 Everett	A	4	6	1	0	0	0	1	0	0	0	0	1	0	1	0	0	0	.00	1	.167	.167	.167
San Jose	A	4	10	0	0	0	0	0	1	0	1	0	2	1	0	0	0	0	.00	0	.000	.167	.000
Clinton	A	24	47	13	3	0	0	16	7	5	12	0	9	0	6	0	0	0	.00	1	.277	.424	.340
1992 San Jose	A	39	96	16	1	0	0	17	8	7	13	0	14	1	7	0	2	0	1.00	2	.167	.273	.177
Clinton	A	32	87	20	0	0	0	20	14	5	13	0	15	2	5	0	4	1	.80	2	.230	.343	.230
1993 Shreveport	AA	3	4	2	0	0	0	2	1	0	1	0	1	0	0	0	0	0	.00	0	.500	.600	.500
Phoenix	AAA	16	34	7	1	0	0	8	4	2	8	1	8	0	0	0	1	0	1.00	0	.206	.372	.235
San Jose	A	25	64	16	1	0	0	17	10	6	11	0	8	0	0	3	1	1	.50	0	.250	.346	.266
1994 El Paso	AA	16	41	2	0	0	0	2	3	1	6	0	11	0	4	0	0	1	.00	1	.049	.170	.049
Stockton	A	2	4	2	0	0	0	2	0	0	0	0	0	0	0	0	0	0	.00	1	.500	.500	.500
4 Min. YEARS		165	393	79	6	0	0	85	48	30	65	1	69	5	23	3	8	4	.67	8	.201	.320	.216

Stanton Cameron

Bats: Right **Throws:** Right **Pos:** OF **Ht:** 6'5" **Wt:** 195 **Born:** 07/05/69 **Age:** 25

							BATTING										BASERUNNING				PERCENTAGES		
Year	Team	Lg	G	AB	H	2B	3B	HR	TB	R	RBI	TBB	IBB	SO	HBP	SH	SF	SB	CS	SB%	GDP	Avg	OBP	SLG
1987	Kingsport	R	26	53	7	1	0	1	11	6	5	10	0	24	0	1	1	1	1	.50	1	.132	.266	.208
1988	Mets	R	51	171	40	10	1	1	55	24	15	25	0	33	3	1	0	10	5	.67	7	.234	.342	.322
1989	Pittsfield	A	71	253	65	13	1	10	110	35	50	41	2	71	4	1	1	7	2	.78	3	.257	.368	.435
1990	Columbia	A	87	302	90	19	1	15	156	57	57	52	1	68	4	0	7	3	2	.60	7	.298	.400	.517
1991	St. Lucie	A	83	232	43	7	0	2	56	25	26	46	0	82	4	3	1	1	1	.50	2	.185	.329	.241
1992	Frederick	A	127	409	101	16	1	29	206	76	92	90	3	121	11	2	5	2	3	.40	7	.247	.392	.504
1993	Bowie	AA	118	384	106	27	1	21	198	65	64	84	2	103	6	0	6	6	7	.46	11	.276	.408	.516
1994	Buffalo	AAA	38	139	24	4	0	4	40	10	14	8	1	29	2	0	0	3	0	1.00	5	.173	.228	.288
	Carolina	AA	88	327	102	28	3	11	169	58	56	34	2	74	2	0	4	10	2	.83	7	.312	.376	.517
	8 Min. YEARS		689	2270	578	125	8	94	1001	356	379	390	11	605	36	8	25	43	23	.65	50	.255	.369	.441

Robert Campillo

Bats: Right **Throws:** Right **Pos:** C **Ht:** 6'0" **Wt:** 195 **Born:** 11/02/71 **Age:** 23

							BATTING										BASERUNNING				PERCENTAGES		
Year	Team	Lg	G	AB	H	2B	3B	HR	TB	R	RBI	TBB	IBB	SO	HBP	SH	SF	SB	CS	SB%	GDP	Avg	OBP	SLG
1992	Jamestown	A	18	46	12	3	0	1	18	9	7	3	0	12	2	1	0	0	0	.00	2	.261	.333	.391
	Rockford	A	16	37	5	2	0	0	7	4	3	4	0	7	1	1	0	0	0	.00	2	.135	.238	.189
1993	El Paso	AA	4	11	0	0	0	0	0	0	0	0	0	3	0	0	0	0	0	.00	0	.000	.000	.000
	Helena	R	33	92	23	3	0	2	32	13	19	17	0	22	3	0	0	3	2	.60	2	.250	.384	.348
1994	New Orleans	AAA	1	3	0	0	0	0	0	0	0	0	0	1	0	0	0	0	0	.00	0	.000	.000	.000
	Beloit	A	11	25	3	0	0	0	3	2	2	1	0	7	0	1	0	0	0	.00	0	.120	.154	.120
	Helena	R	43	143	39	6	0	6	63	23	27	11	0	25	3	1	2	5	3	.63	2	.273	.333	.441
	3 Min. YEARS		126	357	82	14	0	9	123	51	58	36	0	77	9	4	2	8	5	.62	8	.230	.314	.345

Frank Campos

Pitches: Right **Bats:** Right **Pos:** P **Ht:** 6'1" **Wt:** 168 **Born:** 05/11/68 **Age:** 27

			HOW MUCH HE PITCHED					WHAT HE GAVE UP											THE RESULTS					
Year	Team	Lg	G	GS	CG	GF	IP	BFP	H	R	ER	HR	SH	SF	HB	TBB	IBB	SO	WP	Bk	W	L	Pct.	ShO	Sv	ERA
1987	Wytheville	R	18	2	0	11	39.2	172	29	23	21	4	0	2	4	24	0	34	4	0	0	3	.000	0	4	4.76
1988	Chston-Wv	A	39	14	1	18	113	530	119	71	61	4	4	6	6	87	1	87	11	0	9	13	.409	0	2	4.86
1989	Chston-Wv	A	38	18	2	7	131	582	113	67	50	3	6	3	4	87	1	82	11	0	2	11	.154	0	2	3.44
	Winston-Sal	A	2	0	0	1	6	21	2	1	1	0	0	1	0	2	0	2	1	0	0	0	.000	0	0	1.50
1990	Peoria	A	1	0	0	0	0.2	4	0	2	2	0	0	0	0	2	0	1	2	1	0	0	.000	0	0	27.00
	South Bend	A	12	1	0	8	14.2	75	19	15	14	2	1	3	0	14	0	12	2	0	1	0	1.000	0	1	8.59
	Utica	A	19	6	1	9	60	258	41	27	20	0	3	3	2	47	1	37	3	0	3	1	.750	0	1	3.00
1991	South Bend	A	37	14	2	9	113.2	517	116	73	54	3	3	1	5	62	1	98	18	0	7	9	.438	0	1	4.28
1992	Sarasota	A	22	0	0	16	30	121	20	11	6	0	3	2	1	10	0	23	5	0	1	2	.333	0	10	1.80
	Birmingham	AA	31	2	0	15	53.2	250	56	37	32	4	4	3	0	41	3	31	9	0	5	3	.625	0	3	5.37
1993	Birmingham	AA	9	9	0	0	55.1	241	49	29	20	4	3	2	3	26	0	41	7	1	2	4	.333	0	0	3.25
	Nashville	AAA	19	19	2	0	116.2	509	104	60	46	13	5	1	7	58	0	86	14	0	7	5	.583	0	0	3.55
1994	White Sox	R	11	0	0	5	13	59	5	6	1	0	0	0	5	6	2	14	2	0	0	0	.000	0	1	0.69
	Birmingham	AA	2	0	0	1	2	12	5	2	2	1	0	0	1	0	0	2	0	0	1	0	1.000	0	0	9.00
	Pr. William	A	11	0	0	10	19.2	92	17	9	3	1	3	0	1	15	1	14	2	0	1	3	.250	0	5	1.37
	8 Min. YEARS		271	85	8	110	769	3443	695	433	333	39	35	27	39	481	10	564	91	2	38	55	.409	0	26	3.90

Miguel Campos

Bats: Right **Throws:** Right **Pos:** SS **Ht:** 6'1" **Wt:** 185 **Born:** 03/28/76 **Age:** 19

							BATTING										BASERUNNING				PERCENTAGES		
Year	Team	Lg	G	AB	H	2B	3B	HR	TB	R	RBI	TBB	IBB	SO	HBP	SH	SF	SB	CS	SB%	GDP	Avg	OBP	SLG
1994	Cubs	R	19	42	11	4	0	1	18	3	8	2	0	15	1	1	1	0	0	.00	0	.262	.304	.429
	Orlando	AA	4	8	1	0	0	0	1	0	0	1	0	4	0	0	0	0	0	.00	1	.125	.222	.125
	1 Min. YEARS		23	50	12	4	0	1	19	3	8	3	0	19	1	1	1	0	0	.00	1	.240	.291	.380

George Canale

Bats: Left **Throws:** Right **Pos:** 1B **Ht:** 6'1" **Wt:** 190 **Born:** 08/11/65 **Age:** 29

							BATTING										BASERUNNING				PERCENTAGES		
Year	Team	Lg	G	AB	H	2B	3B	HR	TB	R	RBI	TBB	IBB	SO	HBP	SH	SF	SB	CS	SB%	GDP	Avg	OBP	SLG
1986	Helena	R	65	221	72	19	0	9	118	48	49	54	0	65	0	2	5	6	4	.60	2	.326	.450	.534
1987	Stockton	A	66	246	69	18	1	7	110	42	48	38	3	59	1	2	2	5	4	.56	8	.280	.376	.447
	El Paso	AA	65	253	65	10	2	7	100	38	36	20	1	69	2	0	0	3	2	.60	4	.257	.316	.395
1988	El Paso	AA	132	496	120	23	2	23	216	77	93	59	5	152	2	0	2	9	3	.75	12	.242	.324	.435
1989	Denver	AAA	144	503	140	33	9	18	245	80	71	71	1	134	2	2	6	5	8	.38	3	.278	.366	.487
1990	Denver	AAA	134	468	119	18	6	12	185	76	60	69	4	103	1	3	3	12	5	.71	10	.254	.349	.395
1991	Denver	AAA	88	274	64	10	2	10	108	36	47	51	0	49	2	0	3	6	2	.75	6	.234	.355	.394
1992	Canton-Akm	AA	54	194	59	10	1	15	116	47	49	30	1	37	1	0	1	2	1	.67	1	.304	.398	.598
	Colo Sprngs	AAA	46	163	48	12	2	5	79	33	31	16	1	27	0	0	2	0	0	.00	2	.294	.354	.485
1993	Charlotte	AAA	73	208	45	8	0	6	71	32	27	26	3	47	0	0	1	1	1	.50	4	.216	.302	.341

39

Year	Team	Lg	G	AB	H	2B	3B	HR	TB	R	RBI	TBB	IBB	SO	HBP	SH	SF	SB	CS	SB%	GDP	Avg	OBP	SLG
	Colo Spmgs	AAA	39	115	33	9	1	5	59	15	15	10	2	20	1	0	1	2	1	.67	1	.287	.346	.513
1994	Memphis	AA	114	426	98	25	2	12	163	54	51	51	8	79	0	0	2	7	1	.88	12	.230	.311	.383
1989	Milwaukee	AL	13	26	5	1	0	1	9	5	3	2	0	3	0	1	0	0	1	.00	0	.192	.250	.346
1990	Milwaukee	AL	10	13	1	1	0	0	2	4	0	2	0	6	0	0	0	0	1	.00	0	.077	.200	.154
1991	Milwaukee	AL	21	34	6	2	0	3	17	6	10	8	0	6	0	0	0	0	0	.00	5	.176	.318	.500
	9 Min. YEARS		1020	3567	932	195	28	129	1570	578	577	495	29	841	12	9	28	58	32	.64	65	.261	.351	.440
	3 Maj. YEARS		44	73	12	4	0	4	28	15	13	12	0	15	0	1	2	0	2	.00	5	.164	.276	.384

Willie Canate

Bats: Right **Throws:** Right **Pos:** OF **Ht:** 6' 0" **Wt:** 170 **Born:** 12/11/71 **Age:** 23

Year	Team	Lg	G	AB	H	2B	3B	HR	TB	R	RBI	TBB	IBB	SO	HBP	SH	SF	SB	CS	SB%	GDP	Avg	OBP	SLG
1989	Indians	R	11	24	5	2	0	0	7	4	0	0	0	8	0	0	0	0	0	.00	0	.208	.208	.292
1990	Watertown	A	57	199	52	6	2	2	68	28	15	10	0	43	3	1	0	9	4	.69	6	.261	.307	.342
1991	Kinston	A	51	189	41	3	1	1	49	28	12	14	0	29	3	5	0	4	2	.67	5	.217	.282	.259
	Columbus	A	62	204	49	13	2	4	78	32	20	25	0	32	4	7	3	14	5	.74	10	.240	.331	.382
1992	Columbus	A	133	528	167	37	8	5	235	110	63	56	3	66	10	3	6	25	9	.74	3	.316	.388	.445
1993	Indianapols	AAA	3	5	0	0	0	0	0	0	0	0	0	1	0	0	0	0	0	.00	0	.000	.000	.000
	Knoxville	AA	9	37	10	2	0	1	15	8	4	5	0	2	0	0	0	2	1	.67	1	.270	.357	.405
	Syracuse	AAA	7	24	6	0	0	2	12	3	5	5	0	3	0	0	0	0	2	.00	1	.250	.379	.500
1994	Syracuse	AAA	45	153	28	6	0	0	34	14	10	7	0	27	1	2	0	1	1	.50	1	.183	.224	.222
	Knoxville	AA	85	326	80	12	1	0	94	39	28	22	0	52	4	2	5	16	7	.70	8	.245	.297	.288
1993	Toronto	AL	38	47	10	0	0	1	13	12	3	6	0	15	1	2	1	1	1	.50	2	.213	.309	.277
	6 Min. YEARS		463	1689	438	81	14	15	592	266	157	144	3	263	25	20	14	71	31	.70	35	.259	.324	.351

Casey Candaele

Bats: Both **Throws:** Right **Pos:** OF-2B **Ht:** 5' 9" **Wt:** 165 **Born:** 01/12/61 **Age:** 34

Year	Team	Lg	G	AB	H	2B	3B	HR	TB	R	RBI	TBB	IBB	SO	HBP	SH	SF	SB	CS	SB%	GDP	Avg	OBP	SLG
1984	Jacksnville	AA	132	532	145	23	2	2	178	68	53	30	1	35	1	5	6	26	18	.59	13	.273	.309	.335
1985	Indianapols	AAA	127	390	101	13	5	0	124	55	35	44	2	33	0	11	1	13	10	.57	15	.259	.333	.318
1986	Indianapols	AAA	119	480	145	32	6	2	195	77	42	46	6	29	1	11	2	16	10	.62	8	.302	.363	.406
1988	Indianapols	AAA	60	239	63	11	6	2	92	23	36	12	0	20	0	1	7	5	1	.83	5	.264	.291	.385
	Tucson	AAA	17	66	17	3	0	0	20	8	5	4	0	6	0	0	0	4	2	.67	5	.258	.300	.303
1989	Tucson	AAA	68	206	45	6	1	0	53	22	17	20	4	37	0	4	1	6	3	.67	7	.218	.286	.257
1990	Tucson	AAA	7	28	6	1	0	0	7	2	2	3	1	2	1	1	0	1	2	.33	1	.214	.313	.250
1993	Tucson	AAA	6	27	8	1	0	0	9	4	4	3	1	2	0	0	0	1	2	.33	2	.296	.367	.333
1994	Indianapols	AAA	131	511	144	31	7	4	201	66	52	32	4	65	0	3	4	8	6	.57	21	.282	.322	.393
1986	Montreal	NL	30	104	24	4	1	0	30	9	6	5	0	15	0	0	1	3	5	.38	3	.231	.264	.288
1987	Montreal	NL	138	449	122	23	4	1	156	62	23	38	3	28	2	4	2	7	10	.41	5	.272	.330	.347
1988	Montreal	NL	36	116	20	5	1	0	27	9	4	10	0	11	0	2	0	1	0	1.00	7	.172	.238	.233
	Houston	NL	21	31	5	3	0	0	8	2	1	1	0	6	0	1	0	0	1	.00	0	.161	.188	.258
1990	Houston	NL	130	262	75	8	6	3	104	30	22	31	5	42	1	4	0	7	5	.58	5	.286	.364	.397
1991	Houston	NL	151	461	121	20	7	4	167	44	50	40	7	49	0	1	3	9	3	.75	5	.262	.319	.362
1992	Houston	NL	135	320	68	12	1	1	85	19	18	24	3	36	3	7	6	7	1	.88	5	.213	.269	.266
1993	Houston	NL	75	121	29	8	0	1	40	18	7	10	0	14	0	0	0	2	3	.40	0	.240	.298	.331
	8 Min. YEARS		667	2479	674	121	27	10	879	325	246	194	19	229	3	36	21	80	54	.60	77	.272	.323	.355
	7 Maj. YEARS		716	1864	464	83	20	10	617	193	131	159	19	201	6	19	12	36	28	.56	29	.249	.308	.331

Ozzie Canseco

Bats: Right **Throws:** Right **Pos:** OF **Ht:** 6' 3" **Wt:** 220 **Born:** 07/02/64 **Age:** 30

Year	Team	Lg	G	AB	H	2B	3B	HR	TB	R	RBI	TBB	IBB	SO	HBP	SH	SF	SB	CS	SB%	GDP	Avg	OBP	SLG
1984	Greensboro	A	8	1	0	0	0	0	0	1	0	0	0	0	0	0	0	0	0	.00	0	.000	.000	.000
1985	Yankees	R	20	39	7	0	1	1	12	2	5	2	0	18	0	0	0	0	0	.00	0	.179	.220	.308
1986	Yankees	R	7	15	2	1	0	1	6	3	3	5	0	9	0	0	0	0	0	.00	0	.133	.350	.400
	Madison	A	42	128	20	1	1	3	32	17	17	22	0	47	0	0	3	1	1	.50	2	.156	.275	.250
1987	Madison	A	92	309	82	12	4	11	135	64	54	67	3	104	1	0	1	6	7	.46	6	.265	.397	.437
1988	Madison	A	99	359	98	17	7	12	165	63	68	49	3	84	3	1	7	15	8	.65	8	.273	.359	.460
	Huntsville	AA	27	99	22	7	0	3	38	6	12	6	1	31	0	0	0	3	0	1.00	1	.222	.267	.384
1989	Huntsville	AA	91	317	74	17	2	12	131	52	52	51	0	88	5	2	4	1	2	.33	4	.233	.345	.413
1990	Huntsville	AA	97	325	73	21	0	20	154	50	67	47	2	103	7	2	2	2	2	.50	5	.225	.333	.474
1992	Louisville	AAA	98	308	82	19	1	22	169	53	57	43	0	96	2	1	2	1	1	.50	3	.266	.358	.549
1993	Louisville	AAA	44	154	37	6	1	13	84	20	33	15	4	59	0	0	1	1	2	.33	2	.240	.306	.545
1994	New Orleans	AAA	117	403	95	29	1	14	168	54	67	55	6	139	4	0	7	3	5	.38	11	.236	.328	.417
1990	Oakland	AL	9	19	2	1	0	0	3	1	1	1	0	10	0	0	0	0	0	.00	0	.105	.150	.158
1992	St. Louis	NL	9	29	8	5	0	0	13	7	3	7	0	4	0	0	0	0	0	.00	1	.276	.417	.448
1993	St. Louis	NL	6	17	3	0	0	0	3	0	0	3	0	3	0	0	0	0	0	.00	0	.176	.222	.176
	10 Min. YEARS		742	2457	592	130	18	112	1094	385	435	362	19	778	22	6	27	33	28	.54	43	.241	.340	.445
	3 Maj. YEARS		24	65	13	6	0	0	19	8	4	9	0	17	0	0	0	0	0	.00	1	.200	.297	.292

Nick Capra

Bats: Right **Throws:** Right **Pos:** OF **Ht:** 5' 8" **Wt:** 165 **Born:** 03/08/58 **Age:** 37

Year	Team	Lg	G	AB	H	2B	3B	HR	TB	R	RBI	TBB	IBB	SO	HBP	SH	SF	SB	CS	SB%	GDP	Avg	OBP	SLG
1984	Okla City	AAA	123	442	113	18	1	2	139	68	21	76	1	67	0	12	1	47	18	.72	4	.256	.364	.314
1985	Okla City	AAA	97	353	96	17	1	0	115	53	27	68	1	45	4	2	1	25	16	.61	5	.272	.394	.326
1986	Buffalo	AAA	36	123	25	2	0	2	33	14	9	20	1	13	0	2	2	6	9	.40	2	.203	.310	.268
	Okla City	AAA	72	283	80	16	2	5	115	54	22	46	0	36	2	6	2	26	6	.81	5	.283	.384	.406
1987	Okla City	AAA	97	353	107	18	3	1	134	69	39	62	3	53	0	6	3	21	13	.62	6	.303	.404	.380
1988	Omaha	AAA	93	346	100	11	6	1	126	53	43	50	0	49	1	4	2	28	9	.76	9	.289	.378	.364
1989	Omaha	AAA	128	500	145	27	3	7	199	84	44	70	1	67	4	5	1	31	18	.63	8	.290	.381	.398
1990	Okla City	AAA	122	451	125	26	3	5	172	80	45	68	0	61	3	7	1	34	14	.71	4	.277	.375	.381
1991	Okla City	AAA	127	485	132	33	4	5	188	74	38	87	1	58	4	8	1	27	13	.68	7	.272	.386	.388
1992	Nashville	AAA	90	287	67	14	1	5	98	48	27	51	1	36	3	12	2	31	10	.76	3	.233	.353	.341
	Scranton/wb	AAA	18	56	16	3	0	1	22	12	3	10	1	7	0	1	0	3	2	.60	0	.286	.394	.393
1993	Edmonton	AAA	106	389	108	19	4	7	156	71	44	58	0	42	2	4	4	20	13	.61	9	.278	.371	.401
1994	Edmonton	AAA	109	382	116	26	6	7	175	71	41	43	0	25	4	2	3	25	10	.71	7	.304	.377	.458
1982	Texas	AL	13	15	4	0	0	1	7	2	1	3	0	4	1	0	0	2	1	.67	1	.267	.421	.467
1983	Texas	AL	8	2	0	0	0	0	0	2	0	0	0	0	0	0	0	0	0	.00	0	.000	.000	.000
1985	Texas	AL	8	8	1	0	0	0	1	1	0	0	0	0	0	0	0	0	0	.00	0	.125	.125	.125
1988	Kansas City	AL	14	29	4	1	0	0	5	3	0	2	0	3	0	0	0	1	0	1.00	0	.138	.194	.172
1991	Texas	AL	2	0	0	0	0	0	0	1	0	1	0	0	0	0	0	0	0	.00	0	.000	1.000	.000
	11 Min. YEARS		1218	4450	1230	230	34	48	1672	751	403	709	10	559	27	71	23	324	151	.68	69	.276	.377	.376
	5 Maj. YEARS		45	54	9	1	0	1	13	9	1	6	0	7	1	0	0	3	1	.75	4	.167	.262	.241

Gary Caraballo

Bats: Right **Throws:** Right **Pos:** 3B **Ht:** 5'11" **Wt:** 205 **Born:** 07/11/71 **Age:** 23

Year	Team	Lg	G	AB	H	2B	3B	HR	TB	R	RBI	TBB	IBB	SO	HBP	SH	SF	SB	CS	SB%	GDP	Avg	OBP	SLG
1989	Royals	R	46	160	38	6	0	1	47	18	25	16	0	18	6	0	4	4	4	.50	2	.238	.323	.294
	Baseball Cy	A	3	9	3	0	0	0	3	0	0	0	0	2	0	0	0	0	0	.00	0	.333	.333	.333
1990	Appleton	A	123	406	87	14	3	6	125	37	50	39	1	62	12	0	7	6	5	.55	8	.214	.297	.308
1991	Appleton	A	79	275	69	16	1	2	93	39	44	34	0	33	7	0	7	13	1	.93	7	.251	.341	.338
	Baseball Cy	A	50	179	40	9	3	3	64	28	24	22	0	32	3	0	2	3	2	.60	5	.223	.316	.358
1992	Baseball Cy	A	67	239	69	9	4	4	98	30	40	24	1	43	6	3	4	6	3	.67	3	.289	.363	.410
	Memphis	AA	58	195	41	6	2	3	60	17	17	7	0	37	5	3	1	1	3	.25	2	.210	.255	.308
1993	Wilmington	A	39	145	44	8	3	2	64	20	26	20	1	25	5	0	0	3	0	1.00	5	.303	.406	.441
1994	Memphis	AA	127	429	106	21	1	10	159	45	59	32	0	69	7	3	3	6	3	.67	16	.247	.308	.371
	6 Min. YEARS		592	2037	497	89	17	31	713	234	285	194	3	321	51	9	28	42	21	.67	48	.244	.321	.350

Ramon Caraballo

Bats: Both **Throws:** Right **Pos:** 2B **Ht:** 5' 7" **Wt:** 150 **Born:** 05/23/69 **Age:** 26

Year	Team	Lg	G	AB	H	2B	3B	HR	TB	R	RBI	TBB	IBB	SO	HBP	SH	SF	SB	CS	SB%	GDP	Avg	OBP	SLG
1989	Braves	R	20	77	19	3	1	1	27	9	10	10	0	14	0	1	1	5	4	.56	0	.247	.330	.351
	Sumter	A	45	171	45	10	5	1	68	22	32	16	0	38	2	1	3	9	4	.69	5	.263	.328	.398
1990	Burlington	A	102	390	113	18	14	7	180	84	54	49	2	69	7	2	2	41	20	.67	9	.290	.377	.462
1991	Durham	A	120	444	111	13	8	6	158	73	52	38	1	91	3	3	2	53	23	.70	5	.250	.312	.356
1992	Greenville	AA	24	93	29	4	4	1	44	15	8	14	0	13	0	0	1	10	6	.63	1	.312	.398	.473
	Richmond	AAA	101	405	114	20	3	2	146	42	40	22	1	60	3	7	1	19	16	.54	6	.281	.323	.360
1993	Richmond	AAA	126	470	128	25	9	3	180	73	41	30	3	81	7	7	5	20	14	.59	3	.272	.322	.383
1994	Richmond	AAA	22	75	10	1	0	0	11	5	0	7	0	12	1	0	0	4	4	.50	1	.133	.217	.147
	Greenville	AA	72	243	58	4	6	9	101	32	30	12	1	46	7	2	5	4	7	.36	3	.239	.288	.416
1993	Atlanta	NL	6	0	0	0	0	0	0	0	0	0	0	0	0	0	0	0	0	.00	0	.000	.000	.000
	6 Min. YEARS		632	2368	627	98	50	30	915	355	267	198	8	424	30	23	20	165	98	.63	33	.265	.327	.386

Paul Carey

Bats: Left **Throws:** Right **Pos:** OF **Ht:** 6' 4" **Wt:** 215 **Born:** 01/08/68 **Age:** 27

Year	Team	Lg	G	AB	H	2B	3B	HR	TB	R	RBI	TBB	IBB	SO	HBP	SH	SF	SB	CS	SB%	GDP	Avg	OBP	SLG
1990	Miami	A	49	153	50	5	3	4	73	23	20	43	1	39	2	0	1	4	3	.57	2	.327	.477	.477
1991	Hagerstown	AA	114	373	94	29	1	12	161	63	65	68	8	109	4	2	5	5	4	.56	11	.252	.369	.432
1992	Frederick	A	41	136	41	6	0	9	74	24	26	28	5	22	2	0	1	0	1	.00	2	.301	.425	.544
	Rochester	AAA	30	87	20	4	1	1	29	9	7	6	0	16	2	0	0	0	0	.00	2	.230	.292	.333
	Hagerstown	AA	48	163	44	8	0	4	64	17	18	15	5	37	2	0	1	3	2	.60	4	.270	.337	.393
1993	Rochester	AAA	96	325	101	20	4	12	165	63	50	65	11	92	5	1	2	0	0	.00	10	.311	.431	.508
1994	Frederick	A	16	54	20	1	1	6	41	16	12	11	0	7	2	0	0	1	0	.00	2	.370	.493	.759
	Rochester	AAA	47	172	43	5	0	8	72	29	28	28	2	47	2	0	3	1	0	1.00	2	.250	.356	.419
1993	Baltimore	AL	18	47	10	1	0	0	11	1	3	5	0	14	0	0	0	0	0	.00	4	.213	.288	.234
	5 Min. YEARS		441	1463	413	78	10	56	679	244	226	264	32	369	21	3	14	13	11	.54	38	.282	.396	.464

Dan Carlson

Pitches: Right Bats: Right Pos: P Ht: 6'1" Wt: 185 Born: 01/26/70 Age: 25

		HOW MUCH HE PITCHED						WHAT HE GAVE UP								THE RESULTS					
Year Team	Lg	G	GS	CG	GF	IP	BFP	H	R	ER	HR	SH	SF	HB	TBB	IBB	SO	WP	Bk	W	L	Pct.	ShO	Sv	ERA
1990 Everett	A	17	11	0	3	62.1	279	60	42	37	5	1	4	1	33	1	77	9	5	2	6	.250	0	0	5.34
1991 Clinton	A	27	27	5	0	181.1	740	149	69	62	11	3	3	2	76	0	164	18	5	16	7	.696	3	0	3.08
1992 Shreveport	AA	27	27	4	0	186	765	166	85	66	15	5	3	1	60	3	157	4	0	15	9	.625	1	0	3.19
1993 Phoenix	AAA	13	12	0	0	70	320	79	54	51	12	2	1	5	32	1	48	4	0	5	6	.455	0	0	6.56
Shreveport	AA	15	15	2	0	100.1	397	86	30	25	9	4	4	0	26	3	81	5	0	7	4	.636	1	0	2.24
1994 Phoenix	AAA	31	22	0	2	151.1	665	173	80	78	21	3	9	1	55	1	117	10	0	13	6	.684	0	1	4.64
5 Min. YEARS		130	114	11	5	751.1	3166	713	360	319	73	18	24	10	282	9	644	50	10	58	38	.604	5	1	3.82

Ken Carlyle

Pitches: Right Bats: Right Pos: P Ht: 6'1" Wt: 185 Born: 09/16/69 Age: 25

		HOW MUCH HE PITCHED						WHAT HE GAVE UP								THE RESULTS					
Year Team	Lg	G	GS	CG	GF	IP	BFP	H	R	ER	HR	SH	SF	HB	TBB	IBB	SO	WP	Bk	W	L	Pct.	ShO	Sv	ERA
1992 Niagara Fls	A	1	1	0	0	6	26	6	1	1	0	0	0	0	1	0	9	1	1	1	0	1.000	0	0	1.50
Fayetteville	A	14	14	1	0	79.2	319	64	21	17	3	0	1	4	24	0	59	6	1	8	4	.667	1	0	1.92
1993 Toledo	AAA	15	14	1	0	75.2	339	88	59	54	13	2	2	1	36	1	43	4	2	2	10	.167	0	0	6.42
London	AA	12	12	1	0	78	341	72	40	32	8	1	3	5	35	1	50	0	2	4	6	.400	0	0	3.69
1994 Trenton	AA	19	19	5	0	116.1	519	125	75	53	6	4	3	3	47	3	69	5	2	3	9	.250	1	0	4.10
Toledo	AAA	12	1	0	3	24.1	104	23	13	11	2	1	2	2	8	0	12	1	0	1	0	1.000	0	1	4.07
3 Min. YEARS		73	61	8	3	380	1648	378	209	168	32	8	11	15	151	5	242	17	8	19	29	.396	2	1	3.98

Don Carman

Pitches: Left Bats: Left Pos: P Ht: 6' 3" Wt: 201 Born: 08/14/59 Age: 35

		HOW MUCH HE PITCHED						WHAT HE GAVE UP								THE RESULTS					
Year Team	Lg	G	GS	CG	GF	IP	BFP	H	R	ER	HR	SH	SF	HB	TBB	IBB	SO	WP	Bk	W	L	Pct.	ShO	Sv	ERA
1984 Portland	AAA	39	2	0	24	55.2	0	66	36	33	8	0	0	3	22	6	53	3	0	3	3	.500	0	3	5.34
1991 Omaha	AAA	14	2	0	1	25	112	29	12	11	0	2	0	0	13	1	14	2	0	3	3	.500	0	0	3.96
1992 Tulsa	AA	12	7	0	1	57	230	45	23	17	2	3	4	3	12	1	36	2	0	3	3	.500	0	0	2.68
Okla City	AAA	20	12	1	1	80.2	350	80	39	36	5	4	5	3	31	0	43	5	0	4	6	.400	1	1	4.02
1993 Calgary	AAA	6	0	0	1	12.2	54	12	6	5	1	2	0	1	2	1	6	0	1	1	0	1.000	0	0	3.55
1994 Scranton-Wb	AAA	3	0	0	2	4.1	22	6	4	4	1	0	1	0	3	0	3	2	0	0	0	.000	0	0	8.31
1983 Philadelphia	NL	1	0	0	1	1	3	0	0	0	0	0	0	0	0	0	0	0	0	0	0	.000	0	1	0.00
1984 Philadelphia	NL	11	0	0	9	13.1	61	14	9	8	2	0	0	0	6	4	16	3	0	0	1	.000	0	0	5.40
1985 Philadelphia	NL	71	0	0	33	86.1	342	52	25	20	6	5	5	2	38	3	87	1	0	9	4	.692	0	7	2.08
1986 Philadelphia	NL	50	14	2	13	134.1	545	113	50	48	11	5	3	3	52	11	98	6	2	10	5	.667	1	1	3.22
1987 Philadelphia	NL	35	35	3	0	211	886	194	110	99	34	11	5	5	69	7	125	3	1	13	11	.542	2	0	4.22
1988 Philadelphia	NL	36	32	2	0	201.1	873	211	101	96	20	9	8	4	70	6	116	8	3	10	14	.417	0	0	4.29
1989 Philadelphia	NL	49	20	0	5	149.1	683	152	98	87	21	5	5	3	86	6	81	7	3	5	15	.250	0	0	5.24
1990 Philadelphia	NL	59	1	0	11	86.2	368	69	43	40	13	6	4	4	38	7	58	6	1	6	2	.750	0	1	4.15
1991 Cincinnati	NL	28	0	0	10	36	164	40	23	21	8	3	1	1	19	1	15	2	0	0	2	.000	0	0	5.25
1992 Texas	AL	2	0	0	0	2.1	11	4	3	2	0	0	0	0	0	0	2	0	0	0	0	.000	0	0	7.71
5 Min. YEARS		94	23	1	30	235.1	768	238	120	106	17	11	10	10	83	9	155	14	1	14	15	.483	1	4	4.05
10 Maj. YEARS		342	102	7	83	921.2	3936	849	462	421	115	44	31	22	378	45	598	36	10	53	54	.495	3	11	4.11

Bubba Carpenter

Bats: Left Throws: Left Pos: 1B Ht: 6'1" Wt: 185 Born: 07/23/68 Age: 26

		BATTING													BASERUNNING				PERCENTAGES		
Year Team	Lg	G	AB	H	2B	3B	HR	TB	R	RBI	TBB	IBB	SO	HBP	SH	SF	SB	CS	SB%	GDP	Avg	OBP	SLG
1991 Pr William	A	69	236	66	10	3	6	100	33	34	40	3	50	2	1	3	4	1	.80	7	.280	.384	.424
1992 Albany	AA	60	221	51	11	5	4	84	24	31	25	0	41	2	0	1	2	3	.40	8	.231	.313	.380
Pr William	A	68	240	76	15	2	5	110	41	41	35	2	44	1	1	6	4	4	.50	4	.317	.397	.458
1993 Albany	AA	14	53	17	4	0	2	27	8	14	7	0	4	0	0	1	2	2	.50	2	.321	.393	.509
Columbus	AAA	70	199	52	9	0	5	77	29	17	29	3	35	3	0	1	2	2	.50	4	.266	.366	.387
1994 Albany-Colo	AA	116	378	109	14	1	13	164	47	51	58	5	65	3	3	3	9	5	.64	3	.288	.385	.434
Columbus	AAA	7	15	4	0	0	0	4	0	1	2	0	7	0	0	0	0	0	.00	1	.267	.267	.267
4 Min. YEARS		404	1342	376	63	11	35	566	182	190	194	13	246	11	5	15	23	17	.58	29	.280	.372	.422

Mark Carper

Pitches: Right Bats: Right Pos: P Ht: 6'2" Wt: 200 Born: 09/29/68 Age: 26

		HOW MUCH HE PITCHED						WHAT HE GAVE UP								THE RESULTS					
Year Team	Lg	G	GS	CG	GF	IP	BFP	H	R	ER	HR	SH	SF	HB	TBB	IBB	SO	WP	Bk	W	L	Pct.	ShO	Sv	ERA
1991 Frederick	A	26	9	1	5	87.2	401	92	59	42	5	3	3	2	51	1	49	3	2	3	8	.273	0	0	4.31
1992 Hagerstown	AA	11	9	0	1	59	258	59	23	22	2	2	2	1	37	0	38	4	1	4	3	.571	0	0	3.36
Albany	AA	20	10	1	3	74.1	309	62	22	20	4	0	1	2	30	1	36	8	0	5	4	.556	0	0	2.42
1993 Albany	AA	25	25	0	0	155.1	667	148	96	78	9	5	6	4	70	3	98	17	4	7	10	.412	0	0	4.52
1994 Columbus	AAA	26	18	2	4	117.2	520	128	68	57	9	3	3	10	48	1	58	6	0	8	6	.571	1	1	4.36
4 Min. YEARS		108	71	4	13	494	2155	489	268	219	29	13	15	19	236	6	279	38	7	27	31	.466	1	1	3.99

42

Giovanni Carrara

Pitches: Right Bats: Right Pos: P Ht: 6'2" Wt: 210 Born: 03/04/68 Age: 27

			HOW MUCH HE PITCHED					WHAT HE GAVE UP									THE RESULTS				
Year	Team	Lg	G	GS	CG	GF	IP	BFP	H	R	ER	HR	SH	SF	HB	TBB	IBB	SO	WP	Bk	W	L	Pct.	ShO	Sv	ERA
1991	St.Cathrnes	A	15	13	2	0	89.2	363	66	26	16	5	0	4	8	21	0	83	4	2	5	2	.714	2	0	1.61
1992	Dunedin	A	5	4	0	1	23.1	101	22	13	12	1	0	0	2	11	0	16	4	0	0	1	.000	0	0	4.63
	Myrtle Bch	A	22	16	1	2	100.1	416	86	40	35	12	0	2	4	36	0	100	9	3	11	7	.611	1	0	3.14
1993	Dunedin	A	27	24	1	1	140.2	601	136	69	54	14	4	4	4	59	0	108	10	0	6	11	.353	0	0	3.45
1994	Knoxville	AA	26	26	1	0	164.1	705	158	85	71	16	2	7	7	59	0	96	9	0	13	7	.650	0	0	3.89
	4 Min. YEARS		95	83	5	4	518.1	2186	468	233	188	48	6	17	25	186	0	403	36	5	35	28	.556	3	0	3.26

Glenn Carter

Pitches: Right Bats: Right Pos: P Ht: 6'0" Wt: 175 Born: 11/29/67 Age: 27

			HOW MUCH HE PITCHED					WHAT HE GAVE UP									THE RESULTS				
Year	Team	Lg	G	GS	CG	GF	IP	BFP	H	R	ER	HR	SH	SF	HB	TBB	IBB	SO	WP	Bk	W	L	Pct.	ShO	Sv	ERA
1988	Bend	A	9	9	1	0	45	197	46	25	23	6	0	3	2	15	0	47	5	4	3	4	.429	0	0	4.60
1989	Quad City	A	25	25	5	0	166.2	646	109	48	38	10	2	2	2	57	1	190	4	8	15	6	.714	1	0	2.05
1990	Midland	AA	20	20	1	0	102.2	483	132	84	67	9	0	5	1	46	0	66	4	2	3	8	.273	0	0	5.87
1991	Midland	AA	8	8	0	0	40.1	214	69	46	37	5	2	1	0	26	1	13	3	1	1	6	.143	0	0	8.26
1992	El Paso	AA	15	14	2	1	78	340	91	47	41	7	2	5	4	23	2	40	5	1	6	5	.545	2	0	4.73
1993	El Paso	AA	18	9	0	4	63.1	270	65	44	36	10	3	3	2	22	1	47	2	1	3	5	.375	0	0	5.12
	New Britain	AA	12	12	2	0	80.1	331	67	31	28	5	2	2	1	35	0	55	6	2	5	4	.556	1	0	3.14
1994	New Britain	AA	5	5	1	0	31.2	130	30	11	8	3	0	2	1	9	0	20	2	0	2	2	.500	1	0	2.27
	Pawtucket	AAA	22	20	1	0	124	542	140	81	66	21	2	6	3	44	0	73	6	2	8	7	.533	0	0	4.79
	7 Min. YEARS		134	122	13	5	732	3153	749	417	344	76	13	29	16	277	5	551	37	21	46	47	.495	5	0	4.23

Jeff Carter

Bats: Both Throws: Right Pos: OF Ht: 5'10" Wt: 160 Born: 10/20/63 Age: 31

			BATTING													BASERUNNING				PERCENTAGES		
Year	Team	Lg	G	AB	H	2B	3B	HR	TB	R	RBI	TBB	IBB	SO	HBP	SH	SF	SB	CS	SB%	GDP	Avg	OBP	SLG
1985	Everett	A	54	207	63	9	4	4	92	45	22	36	0	33	2	1	1	28	8	.78	2	.304	.411	.444
1986	Clinton	A	128	472	107	13	3	3	135	62	47	58	0	76	3	3	2	60	20	.75	2	.227	.314	.286
1987	Fresno	A	135	510	140	14	11	6	194	109	50	94	4	75	5	4	7	49	25	.66	6	.275	.388	.380
1988	Shreveport	AA	124	409	101	9	8	3	135	50	41	51	0	52	6	6	4	15	10	.60	6	.247	.338	.330
1989	Shreveport	AA	127	445	129	16	4	3	162	77	52	63	2	47	4	8	5	33	16	.67	4	.290	.379	.364
1990	Phoenix	AAA	121	435	127	21	9	2	172	80	63	63	1	81	5	2	2	28	11	.72	4	.292	.386	.395
1991	Phoenix	AAA	92	246	67	5	2	2	82	47	24	34	1	51	0	2	1	11	7	.61	2	.272	.359	.333
1992	Tacoma	AAA	123	379	102	14	5	1	129	60	36	70	0	63	5	9	5	22	9	.71	6	.269	.386	.340
1993	Portland	AAA	101	381	124	21	7	0	159	73	48	63	1	53	3	1	3	17	12	.59	7	.325	.422	.417
1994	Salt Lake	AAA	122	460	149	18	6	5	194	105	70	89	2	78	7	0	3	26	12	.68	14	.324	.438	.422
	10 Min. YEARS		1127	3944	1109	140	59	29	1454	708	453	621	11	609	40	36	31	289	130	.69	53	.281	.382	.369

John Carter

Pitches: Right Bats: Right Pos: P Ht: 6'1" Wt: 195 Born: 02/16/72 Age: 23

			HOW MUCH HE PITCHED					WHAT HE GAVE UP									THE RESULTS				
Year	Team	Lg	G	GS	CG	GF	IP	BFP	H	R	ER	HR	SH	SF	HB	TBB	IBB	SO	WP	Bk	W	L	Pct.	ShO	Sv	ERA
1991	Pirates	R	10	9	0	0	41	179	42	20	15	0	0	0	5	13	0	28	5	2	5	4	.556	0	0	3.29
1992	Augusta	A	1	1	0	0	5	19	3	0	0	0	1	0	2	1	0	4	0	1	0	0	.000	0	0	0.00
	Welland	A	3	3	0	0	15.2	68	12	11	6	2	0	1	1	7	0	15	1	1	0	3	.000	0	0	3.45
	Watertown	A	13	11	3	0	63	269	55	36	29	2	0	3	2	32	0	39	4	4	4	4	.500	0	0	4.14
1993	Columbus	A	29	29	1	0	180.1	731	147	72	56	7	4	2	7	48	0	134	8	2	17	7	.708	0	0	2.79
1994	Canton-Akrn	AA	22	22	3	0	131	564	134	68	63	15	4	2	6	53	1	73	7	1	9	6	.600	1	0	4.33
	4 Min. YEARS		78	75	7	0	436	1830	393	207	169	26	9	8	23	154	1	293	25	11	35	24	.593	1	0	3.49

Mike Carter

Bats: Right Throws: Right Pos: OF Ht: 5'9" Wt: 170 Born: 05/05/69 Age: 26

			BATTING													BASERUNNING				PERCENTAGES		
Year	Team	Lg	G	AB	H	2B	3B	HR	TB	R	RBI	TBB	IBB	SO	HBP	SH	SF	SB	CS	SB%	GDP	Avg	OBP	SLG
1990	Helena	R	61	241	74	11	3	0	91	45	30	16	0	20	6	2	5	22	7	.76	0	.307	.358	.378
1991	Beloit	A	123	452	126	24	4	2	164	62	40	26	5	42	4	4	3	46	13	.78	5	.279	.322	.363
1992	Stockton	A	67	252	66	9	1	3	86	38	26	17	1	26	2	3	5	31	8	.79	4	.262	.308	.341
	El Paso	AA	50	165	42	4	4	1	57	20	15	16	2	31	0	3	1	10	8	.56	3	.255	.319	.345
1993	El Paso	AA	17	73	27	4	1	2	39	16	16	3	0	7	0	0	0	6	4	.60	1	.370	.395	.534
	New Orleans	AAA	104	369	102	18	5	3	139	49	31	17	0	52	4	11	4	20	11	.65	6	.276	.312	.377
1994	Iowa	AAA	122	421	122	24	3	6	170	56	30	14	1	43	4	12	4	16	14	.53	7	.290	.316	.404
	5 Min. YEARS		544	1973	559	94	21	17	746	286	188	109	9	221	20	33	22	151	65	.70	26	.283	.324	.378

Tommy Carter

Pitches: Left Bats: Left Pos: P Ht: 6'8" Wt: 215 Born: 04/30/70 Age: 25

			HOW MUCH HE PITCHED					WHAT HE GAVE UP									THE RESULTS				
Year	Team	Lg	G	GS	CG	GF	IP	BFP	H	R	ER	HR	SH	SF	HB	TBB	IBB	SO	WP	Bk	W	L	Pct.	ShO	Sv	ERA
1991	Yankees	R	7	3	0	1	11	47	7	5	5	0	0	1	0	4	0	11	3	3	0	0	.000	0	0	4.09

1992	Ft. Laud	A	10	8	0	1	36.1	171	35	32	22	1	0	2	1	30	0	23	9	0	3	5	.375	0	0	5.45
	Greensboro	A	13	13	0	0	74.2	319	77	41	35	2	1	1	3	29	0	59	13	0	3	3	.500	0	0	4.22
1993	Pr William	A	26	26	1	0	145.2	641	160	87	71	11	9	5	0	53	0	105	11	1	8	10	.444	0	0	4.39
1994	Albany-Colo	AA	24	15	0	4	92.2	431	128	66	61	8	3	4	4	28	0	73	11	2	2	8	.200	0	0	5.92
	4 Min. YEARS		80	65	1	6	360.1	1609	407	231	194	22	13	13	8	144	1	271	47	6	16	26	.381	0	0	4.85

Joe Caruso

Pitches: Right Bats: Right Pos: P   Ht: 6'3" Wt: 195 Born: 09/16/70 Age: 24

| | | | HOW MUCH HE PITCHED | | | | | | WHAT HE GAVE UP | | | | | | | | | | THE RESULTS | | | | | |
Year	Team	Lg	G	GS	CG	GF	IP	BFP	H	R	ER	HR	SH	SF	HB	TBB	IBB	SO	WP	Bk	W	L	Pct.	ShO	Sv	ERA
1991	Red Sox	R	2	0	0	0	6	24	6	3	3	0	0	0	0	4	0	4	0	0	2	0	1.000	0	0	4.50
	Elmira	A	21	4	0	7	66.2	289	56	23	21	2	4	2	5	29	2	68	8	0	2	1	.667	0	2	2.84
1992	Lynchburg	A	49	0	0	27	118	470	68	36	26	5	6	2	3	40	3	133	6	0	6	4	.600	0	15	1.98
1993	Pawtucket	AAA	36	17	2	6	122.1	562	138	82	72	15	0	3	7	68	0	65	5	1	5	10	.333	0	0	5.30
1994	New Britain	AA	56	2	0	28	91.2	413	93	47	37	6	3	2	4	45	3	76	6	1	7	4	.636	0	0	3.63
	4 Min. YEARS		164	23	2	68	404.2	1758	361	191	159	28	13	9	19	186	8	346	27	2	22	19	.537	0	17	3.54

Mike Case

Bats: Right Throws: Right Pos: OF   Ht: 6'2" Wt: 185 Born: 12/26/68 Age: 26

| | | | BATTING | | | | | | | | | | | | | | BASERUNNING | | | | PERCENTAGES | | |
Year	Team	Lg	G	AB	H	2B	3B	HR	TB	R	RBI	TBB	IBB	SO	HBP	SH	SF	SB	CS	SB%	GDP	Avg	OBP	SLG
1992	Bend	A	49	170	43	10	1	5	70	30	20	22	0	48	2	0	1	10	2	.83	7	.253	.344	.412
1993	Colo Spmgs	AAA	3	3	1	0	0	0	1	0	0	0	0	0	0	0	0	0	0	.00	0	.333	.333	.333
	Central Val	A	124	449	124	20	2	11	181	54	80	53	2	120	7	6	7	21	6	.78	8	.276	.357	.403
1994	New Haven	AA	118	369	96	20	2	7	141	47	39	39	1	100	1	3	2	10	4	.71	10	.260	.331	.382
	3 Min. YEARS		294	991	264	50	5	23	393	131	139	114	3	268	10	9	10	41	12	.77	25	.266	.345	.397

Pedro Castellano

Bats: Right Throws: Right Pos: 3B   Ht: 6'1" Wt: 195 Born: 03/11/70 Age: 25

| | | | BATTING | | | | | | | | | | | | | | BASERUNNING | | | | PERCENTAGES | | |
Year	Team	Lg	G	AB	H	2B	3B	HR	TB	R	RBI	TBB	IBB	SO	HBP	SH	SF	SB	CS	SB%	GDP	Avg	OBP	SLG
1989	Wytheville	R	66	244	76	17	4	9	128	55	42	46	2	44	3	1	3	5	2	.71	9	.311	.422	.525
1990	Peoria	A	117	417	115	27	4	2	156	61	44	63	2	72	3	3	4	7	1	.88	9	.276	.372	.374
	Winston-Sal	A	19	66	13	0	0	1	16	6	8	10	0	11	2	2	0	1	0	1.00	1	.197	.321	.242
1991	Winston-Sal	A	129	459	139	25	3	10	200	59	88	72	4	97	3	2	5	11	10	.52	13	.303	.397	.436
	Charlotte	AA	7	19	8	0	0	0	8	2	2	1	0	6	1	0	1	0	0	.00	1	.421	.455	.421
1992	Iowa	AAA	74	238	59	14	4	2	87	25	20	32	0	42	1	8	1	2	2	.50	6	.248	.338	.366
	Charlotte	AA	45	147	33	3	0	1	39	16	15	19	0	21	4	3	2	0	1	.00	2	.224	.326	.265
1993	Colo Spmgs	AAA	90	304	95	21	2	12	156	61	60	36	0	63	6	1	8	3	5	.38	8	.313	.387	.513
1994	Colo. Sprng	AAA	33	120	42	11	2	4	69	23	24	13	1	17	2	0	2	1	1	.50	3	.350	.416	.575
1993	Colorado	NL	34	71	13	2	0	3	24	12	7	8	0	16	0	0	1	1	1	.50	1	.183	.266	.338
	6 Min. YEARS		580	2014	580	118	19	41	859	308	303	292	9	373	25	20	26	30	22	.58	54	.288	.381	.427

Berto Castillo

Bats: Right Throws: Right Pos: C   Ht: 6'0" Wt: 170 Born: 02/10/70 Age: 25

| | | | BATTING | | | | | | | | | | | | | | BASERUNNING | | | | PERCENTAGES | | |
Year	Team	Lg	G	AB	H	2B	3B	HR	TB	R	RBI	TBB	IBB	SO	HBP	SH	SF	SB	CS	SB%	GDP	Avg	OBP	SLG
1987	Kingsport	R	7	9	1	0	0	0	1	1	0	5	0	3	0	1	0	1	0	1.00	1	.111	.429	.111
1988	Mets	R	22	68	18	4	0	0	22	7	10	4	0	4	2	2	3	2	0	1.00	3	.265	.312	.324
	Kingsport	R	24	75	22	3	0	1	28	7	14	15	1	14	0	1	1	0	1	.00	1	.293	.407	.373
1989	Kingsport	R	27	74	19	4	0	3	32	15	12	11	1	14	1	0	0	2	1	.67	2	.257	.360	.432
	Pittsfield	A	34	123	29	8	0	1	40	13	13	7	0	26	1	2	2	2	0	1.00	3	.236	.278	.325
1990	Columbia	A	30	103	24	4	3	1	37	8	14	10	0	21	0	2	2	1	1	.50	2	.233	.296	.359
	Pittsfield	A	58	185	41	8	1	4	63	19	24	28	2	35	5	1	2	3	3	.50	7	.222	.336	.341
	St. Lucie	A	3	11	4	0	0	1	7	4	3	1	0	1	0	0	0	0	0	.00	0	.364	.417	.636
1991	Columbia	A	90	267	74	20	3	3	109	35	47	43	0	44	5	6	4	6	6	.50	6	.277	.382	.408
1992	St. Lucie	A	60	162	33	6	0	3	48	11	17	16	0	37	2	3	2	0	0	.00	4	.204	.280	.296
1993	St.Lucie	A	105	333	86	21	0	5	122	37	42	28	1	46	3	2	7	0	2	.00	5	.258	.315	.366
1994	Binghamton	AA	90	315	78	14	0	7	113	33	42	41	0	46	0	3	1	1	3	.25	11	.248	.333	.359
	8 Min. YEARS		550	1725	429	92	7	29	622	190	238	209	5	291	19	23	24	18	17	.51	46	.249	.332	.361

Kevin Castleberry

Bats: Left Throws: Right Pos: 2B   Ht: 5'10" Wt: 170 Born: 04/22/68 Age: 27

| | | | BATTING | | | | | | | | | | | | | | BASERUNNING | | | | PERCENTAGES | | |
Year	Team	Lg	G	AB	H	2B	3B	HR	TB	R	RBI	TBB	IBB	SO	HBP	SH	SF	SB	CS	SB%	GDP	Avg	OBP	SLG
1989	Burlington	A	64	224	55	8	0	1	66	27	20	20	1	32	0	2	2	14	8	.64	5	.246	.305	.295
1990	Durham	A	119	372	90	18	4	7	137	59	27	23	1	64	2	3	2	15	4	.79	5	.242	.288	.368
1991	Miami	A	20	64	14	4	2	0	22	12	4	9	0	9	0	2	0	8	1	.89	1	.219	.315	.344
	Birmingham	AA	1	0	0	0	0	0	0	0	0	0	0	0	0	0	0	0	0	.00	0	.000	.000	.000
	Sarasota	A	94	346	94	14	3	4	126	70	39	54	3	54	4	6	7	23	9	.72	2	.272	.370	.364
1992	Sarasota	A	24	98	28	4	0	0	32	16	10	14	0	12	2	1	1	8	3	.73	2	.286	.383	.327
	Birmingham	AA	104	382	98	9	5	2	123	57	26	48	1	59	3	1	3	13	10	.57	3	.257	.343	.322
1993	El Paso	AA	98	327	98	9	5	2	123	46	49	26	3	38	2	0	3	13	3	.81	9	.300	.352	.376

Year	Team	Lg	G	AB	H	2B	3B	HR	TB	R	RBI	TBB	IBB	SO	HBP	SH	SF	SB	CS	SB%	GDP	Avg	OBP	SLG
1994	El Paso	AA	74	251	69	6	8	1	94	44	35	26	1	50	3	2	0	12	7	.63	4	.275	.350	.375
	6 Min. YEARS		598	2065	546	72	27	17	723	331	210	220	10	318	16	16	16	106	45	.70	29	.264	.338	.350

Bats: Right Throws: Right Pos: SS

Juan Castro

Ht: 5'10" Wt: 163 Born: 06/20/72 Age: 23

			BATTING															BASERUNNING				PERCENTAGES		
Year	Team	Lg	G	AB	H	2B	3B	HR	TB	R	RBI	TBB	IBB	SO	HBP	SH	SF	SB	CS	SB%	GDP	Avg	OBP	SLG
1991	Great Falls	R	60	217	60	4	2	1	71	36	27	33	1	31	0	3	2	7	6	.54	2	.276	.369	.327
1992	Bakersfield	A	113	446	116	15	4	4	151	56	42	37	2	64	1	20	7	14	11	.56	7	.260	.314	.339
1993	San Antonio	AA	118	424	117	23	8	7	177	55	41	30	3	40	2	17	3	12	11	.52	14	.276	.325	.417
1994	San Antonio	AA	123	445	128	25	4	4	173	55	44	31	2	66	1	10	2	4	7	.36	9	.288	.334	.389
	4 Min. YEARS		414	1532	421	67	18	16	572	202	154	131	8	201	4	50	14	37	35	.51	32	.275	.331	.373

Pitches: Right Bats: Right Pos: P

Nelson Castro

Ht: 6'1" Wt: 185 Born: 12/10/71 Age: 23

			HOW MUCH HE PITCHED						WHAT HE GAVE UP												THE RESULTS					
Year	Team	Lg	G	GS	CG	GF	IP	BFP	H	R	ER	HR	SH	SF	HB	TBB	IBB	SO	WP	Bk	W	L	Pct.	ShO	Sv	ERA
1990	Dodgers	R	10	10	0	0	55	202	65	30	26	2	1	0	0	7	0	35	1	5	3	1	.750	0	0	4.25
1991	Great Falls	R	14	14	1	0	75.1	325	81	51	44	7	0	4	5	13	0	63	2	4	7	4	.636	1	0	5.26
1993	Bakersfield	A	20	20	0	0	86.1	390	100	47	41	5	1	5	4	37	0	54	2	6	4	7	.364	0	0	4.27
	San Antonio	AA	5	5	0	0	27.1	117	35	16	15	2	1	2	1	4	0	15	0	3	2	1	.667	0	0	4.94
1994	San Antonio	AA	6	6	0	0	36	157	36	21	21	3	3	2	2	21	1	14	1	0	3	2	.600	0	0	5.25
	Bakersfield	A	22	12	0	4	91.1	409	96	57	36	8	3	7	5	45	1	74	5	0	7	5	.583	0	1	3.55
	4 Min. YEARS		77	67	1	4	371.1	1631	413	222	183	27	9	20	17	127	2	255	11	18	26	20	.565	1	1	4.44

Pitches: Right Bats: Right Pos: P

Blas Cedeno

Ht: 6'0" Wt: 165 Born: 11/15/72 Age: 22

			HOW MUCH HE PITCHED						WHAT HE GAVE UP												THE RESULTS					
Year	Team	Lg	G	GS	CG	GF	IP	BFP	H	R	ER	HR	SH	SF	HB	TBB	IBB	SO	WP	Bk	W	L	Pct.	ShO	Sv	ERA
1991	Bristol	R	14	2	0	6	45	202	47	36	19	7	0	3	2	18	1	37	3	4	1	4	.200	0	0	3.80
1992	Bristol	R	13	13	3	0	80.2	335	64	21	18	2	3	1	5	41	0	77	6	0	8	2	.800	2	0	2.01
	Fayettevlle	A	2	1	1	1	9	32	3	3	3	0	0	0	0	4	0	12	6	0	0	1	.000	0	1	3.00
1993	Fayettevlle	A	28	22	1	3	148.2	621	145	64	52	11	5	3	11	55	0	103	6	0	6	6	.500	1	0	3.15
1994	Lakeland	A	5	0	0	3	14	52	9	3	2	1	1	1	0	4	0	16	1	0	1	0	1.000	0	0	1.29
	Trenton	AA	34	0	0	18	52.1	228	50	18	15	5	4	0	2	27	2	40	4	0	1	3	.250	0	3	2.58
	4 Min. YEARS		96	38	5	31	349.2	1470	318	145	109	26	13	8	20	149	3	285	20	4	17	16	.515	3	4	2.81

Bats: Both Throws: Right Pos: OF

Roger Cedeno

Ht: 6'1" Wt: 165 Born: 08/16/74 Age: 20

			BATTING															BASERUNNING				PERCENTAGES		
Year	Team	Lg	G	AB	H	2B	3B	HR	TB	R	RBI	TBB	IBB	SO	HBP	SH	SF	SB	CS	SB%	GDP	Avg	OBP	SLG
1992	Great Falls	R	69	256	81	6	5	2	103	60	27	51	3	53	2	4	2	40	9	.82	4	.316	.431	.402
1993	San Antonio	AA	122	465	134	13	8	4	175	70	30	45	2	90	1	4	1	28	20	.58	5	.288	.352	.376
	Albuquerque	AAA	6	18	4	1	1	0	7	1	4	3	0	9	0	0	0	1	0	1.00	0	.222	.333	.389
1994	Albuquerque	AAA	104	383	123	18	5	4	163	84	49	51	0	57	0	3	7	30	13	.70	6	.321	.395	.426
	3 Min. YEARS		301	1122	342	38	19	10	448	215	110	150	5	203	3	11	10	98	43	.70	13	.305	.385	.399

Bats: Both Throws: Right Pos: INF

Henri Centeno

Ht: 5'11" Wt: 159 Born: 01/01/70 Age: 25

			BATTING															BASERUNNING				PERCENTAGES		
Year	Team	Lg	G	AB	H	2B	3B	HR	TB	R	RBI	TBB	IBB	SO	HBP	SH	SF	SB	CS	SB%	GDP	Avg	OBP	SLG
1991	Astros	R	31	85	27	4	0	0	31	12	7	5	0	10	3	4	0	4	4	.50	1	.318	.376	.365
1992	Asheville	A	126	461	115	15	1	1	135	62	24	37	0	65	16	6	2	14	7	.67	7	.249	.326	.293
1993	Quad City	A	102	296	74	5	3	1	88	42	24	30	0	50	8	4	3	23	9	.72	11	.250	.332	.297
1994	Tucson	AAA	4	9	1	1	0	0	2	0	0	1	0	2	0	0	0	0	0	.00	1	.111	.200	.222
	Osceola	A	49	175	49	8	1	0	59	21	29	20	1	24	1	2	1	11	1	.92	3	.280	.355	.337
	Jackson	AA	18	42	12	3	0	2	21	6	7	4	1	7	2	1	0	0	0	.00	2	.286	.375	.500
	4 Min. YEARS		330	1068	278	36	5	4	336	143	91	97	1	158	30	17	6	52	21	.71	23	.260	.337	.315

Bats: Left Throws: Right Pos: 1B

Scott Cepicky

Ht: 6'4" Wt: 220 Born: 07/29/66 Age: 28

			BATTING															BASERUNNING				PERCENTAGES		
Year	Team	Lg	G	AB	H	2B	3B	HR	TB	R	RBI	TBB	IBB	SO	HBP	SH	SF	SB	CS	SB%	GDP	Avg	OBP	SLG
1989	White Sox	R	40	133	42	8	2	0	54	14	23	12	0	13	2	0	1	5	6	.45	3	.316	.378	.406
1990	South Bend	A	128	462	144	30	5	7	205	65	77	55	7	72	3	6	6	12	12	.50	12	.312	.384	.444
1991	Sarasota	A	124	442	128	33	4	8	193	62	76	62	11	99	4	2	6	13	6	.68	8	.290	.377	.437
1992	Birmingham	AA	138	502	124	30	1	14	198	56	87	44	5	140	5	3	5	1	2	.33	6	.247	.311	.394
1993	Nashville	AAA	45	137	29	3	1	12	70	22	27	19	0	51	1	0	0	0	1	.00	3	.212	.312	.511
	Birmingham	AA	66	236	57	12	1	7	92	30	35	34	3	67	1	2	2	4	0	1.00	6	.242	.337	.390
1994	Nashville	AA	96	307	69	10	3	8	109	44	32	39	5	66	4	2	1	8	4	.67	8	.225	.319	.355
	6 Min. YEARS		637	2219	593	126	17	56	921	293	357	265	31	508	20	15	21	43	31	.58	46	.267	.348	.415

Tony Chance

Bats: Right **Throws:** Right **Pos:** OF **Ht:** 6'1" **Wt:** 191 **Born:** 10/26/64 **Age:** 30

								BATTING									BASERUNNING				PERCENTAGES		
Year	Team	Lg	G	AB	H	2B	3B	HR	TB	R	RBI	TBB	IBB	SO	HBP	SH	SF	SB	CS	SB%	GDP	Avg	OBP	SLG
1984	Watertown	A	41	115	17	2	0	3	28	13	14	17	1	47	3	2	2	5	2	.71	1	.148	.270	.243
	Pirates	R	16	55	12	1	0	0	13	9	10	5	0	11	0	0	1	2	2	.50	3	.218	.279	.236
1985	Pirates	R	10	33	11	1	1	0	14	7	2	4	0	4	0	0	0	2	0	1.00	0	.333	.405	.424
	Macon	A	6	17	2	0	0	0	2	3	1	2	0	10	0	0	0	1	0	1.00	0	.118	.211	.118
	Gastonia	A	56	214	54	8	0	5	77	31	18	16	0	47	0	2	0	16	7	.70	3	.252	.304	.360
1986	Pr William	A	19	60	14	1	2	2	25	5	11	3	0	15	0	0	0	4	2	.67	0	.233	.270	.417
	Macon	A	108	366	85	12	3	17	154	52	55	38	3	99	3	5	5	18	2	.90	7	.232	.306	.421
1987	Salem	A	133	525	167	23	6	23	271	99	96	50	1	104	10	1	5	26	13	.67	15	.318	.385	.516
1988	Harrisburg	AA	56	196	43	8	2	3	64	26	10	20	0	48	2	1	0	9	4	.69	4	.219	.298	.327
	Salem	A	54	207	44	7	0	5	66	25	26	9	0	51	3	2	1	3	3	.50	5	.213	.255	.319
1989	Augusta	A	5	22	3	1	1	1	9	3	5	0	0	5	0	0	0	0	0	.00	0	.136	.136	.409
	Harrisburg	AA	4	14	2	1	0	0	3	1	2	0	0	4	0	0	0	0	0	.00	0	.143	.143	.214
	Hagerstown	AA	67	246	66	15	4	8	113	34	44	14	0	65	5	0	2	11	3	.79	2	.268	.318	.459
1990	Rochester	AAA	130	454	122	17	4	14	189	55	75	41	2	115	1	1	3	14	9	.61	10	.269	.329	.416
1991	Rochester	AAA	111	355	89	14	3	14	151	61	55	41	0	98	2	2	4	4	3	.57	6	.251	.332	.425
1992	Iowa	AAA	131	434	117	23	1	11	175	60	52	34	1	100	4	4	3	5	3	.63	16	.270	.326	.403
1993	Iowa	AAA	101	294	83	23	4	16	154	50	46	38	2	73	1	2	4	5	5	.50	2	.282	.362	.524
1994	Charlotte	AAA	11	16	4	0	0	1	7	3	1	1	0	7	0	0	0	1	0	1.00	2	.250	.294	.438
	11 Min. YEARS		1059	3623	935	157	27	123	1515	537	523	333	10	903	34	22	26	126	58	.68	78	.258	.324	.418

Darrin Chapin

Pitches: Right **Bats:** Right **Pos:** P **Ht:** 6' 0" **Wt:** 170 **Born:** 02/01/66 **Age:** 29

			HOW MUCH HE PITCHED						WHAT HE GAVE UP										THE RESULTS					
Year	Team	Lg	G	GS	CG	GF	IP	BFP	H	R	ER	HR	SH	SF	HB	TBB	IBB	SO	WP	Bk	W	L	Pct.	ShO	Sv	ERA
1986	Yankees	R	13	13	2	0	83.1	341	71	42	30	2	3	3	2	27	1	67	10	1	4	3	.571	2	0	3.24
1987	Oneonta	A	25	0	0	21	40	170	31	8	3	1	2	1	0	17	5	26	6	0	1	1	.500	0	12	0.68
1988	Albany	AA	3	0	0	3	4	26	11	7	5	0	0	0	1	2	0	4	0	0	0	0	.000	0	0	11.25
	Ft.Laudrdle	A	38	0	0	33	63	234	39	8	6	1	4	1	0	19	5	57	3	1	6	4	.600	0	15	0.86
1989	Albany	AA	7	0	0	7	8.2	32	5	0	0	0	0	0	0	1	1	16	2	0	1	0	1.000	0	3	0.00
	Columbus	AAA	27	0	0	21	40	167	33	15	13	3	3	1	1	15	4	38	3	1	2	4	.333	0	5	2.93
1990	Columbus	AAA	6	0	0	5	8.2	41	10	8	7	0	0	0	0	6	0	8	1	0	0	1	.000	0	2	7.27
	Albany	AA	43	0	0	40	52.2	223	43	20	16	2	1	4	1	21	1	61	4	0	3	2	.600	0	21	2.73
1991	Columbus	AAA	55	0	0	28	78.1	328	54	23	17	5	5	3	1	40	3	69	5	1	10	3	.769	0	12	1.95
1992	Scranton/wb	AAA	40	0	0	16	61.2	291	72	39	35	5	2	3	0	33	5	67	7	0	5	4	.556	0	4	5.11
1993	Portland	AAA	47	0	0	35	56.1	244	58	28	27	5	3	1	1	24	2	43	6	0	5	2	.714	0	14	4.31
1994	Edmonton	AAA	53	2	0	17	91.1	421	110	72	63	13	1	6	5	41	1	64	5	0	3	2	.600	0	2	6.21
1991	New York	AL	3	0	0	2	5.1	25	3	3	3	0	0	0	0	6	0	5	2	0	0	1	.000	0	0	5.06
1992	Philadelphia	NL	1	0	0	0	2	8	2	2	2	1	0	0	0	0	0	1	1	0	0	0	.000	0	0	9.00
	9 Min. YEARS		357	15	2	226	588	2518	537	270	222	37	24	23	12	246	28	520	52	4	40	26	.606	2	90	3.40
	2 Maj. YEARS		4	0	0	2	7.1	33	5	5	5	1	0	0	0	6	0	6	3	0	0	1	.000	0	0	6.14

Rafael Chaves

Pitches: Right **Bats:** Right **Pos:** P **Ht:** 6'0" **Wt:** 195 **Born:** 11/01/68 **Age:** 26

			HOW MUCH HE PITCHED						WHAT HE GAVE UP										THE RESULTS					
Year	Team	Lg	G	GS	CG	GF	IP	BFP	H	R	ER	HR	SH	SF	HB	TBB	IBB	SO	WP	Bk	W	L	Pct.	ShO	Sv	ERA
1986	Charleston	A	39	2	0	8	81	354	77	46	30	6	2	2	2	37	2	43	1	3	5	3	.625	0	1	3.33
1987	Chston-Sc	A	53	0	0	32	87	371	86	36	29	2	2	1	3	21	6	59	3	0	8	5	.615	0	11	2.99
1988	Riverside	A	46	0	0	34	64.2	273	58	20	17	1	1	3	2	28	1	49	2	4	2	3	.400	0	19	2.37
1989	Wichita	AA	37	2	0	12	76	338	84	51	45	4	4	2	2	32	9	43	9	3	1	5	.167	0	3	5.33
1990	Wichita	AA	46	1	0	36	84	354	85	46	39	4	3	4	3	16	1	46	8	1	6	5	.545	0	9	4.18
1991	Wichita	AA	38	0	0	11	71	338	80	54	41	6	3	2	6	41	3	49	7	0	3	0	1.000	0	3	5.20
1992	High Desert	A	68	0	0	53	88.1	356	64	28	18	5	5	4	3	36	3	67	2	0	4	5	.444	0	34	1.83
1993	Bowie	AA	45	0	0	40	48	210	56	23	21	4	1	1	1	16	2	39	4	0	2	5	.286	0	20	3.94
1994	Portland	AA	12	0	0	6	16	82	17	14	12	0	0	3	1	13	1	10	3	1	0	0	.000	0	1	6.75
	9 Min. YEARS		384	5	0	232	616.1	2676	607	318	252	32	21	22	23	240	28	405	39	12	31	31	.500	0	101	3.68

Raul Chavez

Bats: Right **Throws:** Right **Pos:** SS **Ht:** 5'11" **Wt:** 175 **Born:** 03/18/73 **Age:** 22

								BATTING									BASERUNNING				PERCENTAGES		
Year	Team	Lg	G	AB	H	2B	3B	HR	TB	R	RBI	TBB	IBB	SO	HBP	SH	SF	SB	CS	SB%	GDP	Avg	OBP	SLG
1990	Astros	R	48	155	50	8	1	0	60	23	23	7	0	12	2	2	1	5	3	.63	7	.323	.358	.387
1991	Burlington	A	114	420	108	17	0	3	134	54	41	25	1	64	10	3	4	1	4	.20	13	.257	.312	.319
1992	Asheville	A	95	348	99	22	1	2	129	37	40	16	1	39	4	1	4	1	0	1.00	11	.284	.320	.371
1993	Osceola	A	58	197	45	5	1	0	52	13	16	8	0	19	1	1	1	1	1	.50	12	.228	.261	.264
1994	Jackson	AA	89	251	55	7	0	1	65	17	22	17	3	41	2	2	1	1	0	1.00	5	.219	.273	.259
	5 Min. YEARS		404	1371	357	59	3	6	440	144	142	73	5	175	19	9	11	9	8	.53	48	.260	.305	.321

46

Pitches: Right **Bats:** Right **Pos:** P

Dan Chergey

Ht: 6'2" **Wt:** 195 **Born:** 01/29/71 **Age:** 24

Year Team	Lg	HOW MUCH HE PITCHED						WHAT HE GAVE UP												THE RESULTS					
		G	GS	CG	GF	IP	BFP	H	R	ER	HR	SH	SF	HB	TBB	IBB	SO	WP	Bk	W	L	Pct.	ShO	Sv	ERA
1993 Elmira	A	15	10	1	1	79.2	329	85	34	31	5	3	3	8	14	0	53	3	1	3	5	.375	0	0	3.50
1994 Edmonton	AAA	13	0	0	6	19.2	88	22	13	13	2	0	1	2	5	0	17	0	0	2	1	.667	0	0	5.95
Brevard Cty	A	32	0	0	21	42	160	29	12	8	1	1	0	1	11	1	41	0	0	1	3	.250	0	9	1.71
2 Min. YEARS		60	10	1	28	141.1	577	136	59	52	8	4	4	11	30	1	111	3	1	6	9	.400	0	9	3.31

Pitches: Right **Bats:** Left **Pos:** P

Scott Chiamparino

Ht: 6'2" **Wt:** 205 **Born:** 08/22/66 **Age:** 28

Year Team	Lg	HOW MUCH HE PITCHED						WHAT HE GAVE UP												THE RESULTS					
		G	GS	CG	GF	IP	BFP	H	R	ER	HR	SH	SF	HB	TBB	IBB	SO	WP	Bk	W	L	Pct.	ShO	Sv	ERA
1987 Medford	A	13	11	3	1	67.2	288	64	29	19	2	1	3	3	20	0	65	6	0	5	4	.556	1	0	2.53
1988 Modesto	A	16	16	5	0	106.2	456	89	40	32	1	2	2	0	56	0	117	17	4	5	7	.417	3	0	2.70
Huntsville	AA	13	13	4	0	84	365	88	36	30	3	1	7	1	26	2	49	5	1	4	5	.444	0	0	3.21
1989 Huntsville	AA	17	17	2	0	101.2	440	109	60	52	8	4	3	4	29	0	87	8	0	8	6	.571	1	0	4.60
1990 Tacoma	AAA	26	26	4	0	173	744	174	79	63	10	5	4	5	72	1	110	9	1	13	9	.591	2	0	3.28
1992 Rangers	R	1	1	0	0	7	26	8	2	0	0	0	0	0	0	0	5	1	0	0	1	.000	0	0	0.00
Charlotte	A	2	2	0	0	11.2	46	6	3	3	0	0	1	4	3	0	8	0	0	1	1	.500	0	0	2.31
Tulsa	AA	3	3	0	0	18.2	72	17	5	4	0	1	0	0	5	0	18	1	0	0	0	.000	0	0	1.93
Okla City	AAA	5	5	0	0	31.1	133	29	11	10	1	1	1	0	13	0	9	1	0	2	1	.667	0	0	2.87
1994 Las Vegas	AAA	7	7	0	0	39	167	45	19	17	1	3	2	1	11	0	17	2	0	2	2	.500	0	0	3.92
1990 Texas	AL	6	6	0	0	37.2	160	36	14	11	1	1	1	2	12	0	19	5	0	1	2	.333	0	0	2.63
1991 Texas	AL	5	5	0	0	22.1	101	26	11	10	1	1	0	0	12	0	8	0	0	1	0	1.000	0	0	4.03
1992 Texas	AL	4	4	0	0	25.1	102	25	11	10	2	0	1	0	5	0	13	1	0	0	4	.000	0	0	3.55
6 Min. YEARS		103	101	18	1	640.2	2737	629	284	230	26	18	23	18	235	3	485	50	6	40	36	.526	7	0	3.23
3 Maj. YEARS		15	15	0	0	85.1	363	87	36	31	4	2	2	2	29	0	40	6	0	2	6	.250	0	0	3.27

Bats: Right **Throws:** Right **Pos:** OF

Bruce Chick

Ht: 6'4" **Wt:** 210 **Born:** 03/07/69 **Age:** 26

Year Team	Lg	BATTING															BASERUNNING				PERCENTAGES		
		G	AB	H	2B	3B	HR	TB	R	RBI	TBB	IBB	SO	HBP	SH	SF	SB	CS	SB%	GDP	Avg	OBP	SLG
1990 Red Sox	R	24	93	30	5	2	1	42	12	23	12	0	11	0	0	2	4	2	.67	1	.323	.393	.452
Winter Havn	A	37	128	29	2	0	0	31	10	4	11	0	23	0	0	0	4	2	.67	4	.227	.288	.242
1991 Lynchburg	A	134	513	139	23	4	10	200	58	73	44	2	119	2	2	5	10	8	.56	11	.271	.328	.390
1992 New Britain	AA	128	436	96	19	0	9	142	52	51	28	3	122	2	3	5	8	5	.62	6	.220	.268	.326
1993 Ft.Laud	A	39	159	46	9	0	1	58	13	14	4	2	34	0	2	0	1	2	.33	3	.289	.307	.365
Pawtucket	AAA	29	82	25	6	0	2	37	8	12	6	0	24	0	2	1	0	3	.00	1	.305	.348	.451
New Britain	AA	55	193	50	8	1	3	69	20	14	8	0	39	1	2	2	2	3	.40	6	.259	.289	.358
1994 New Britain	AA	12	45	10	2	0	1	15	6	7	2	0	10	0	0	1	1	0	1.00	2	.222	.250	.333
Central Val	A	50	196	73	12	2	3	98	29	31	12	1	24	2	2	3	3	5	.38	5	.372	.408	.500
New Haven	AA	13	39	7	1	1	0	10	3	1	0	0	12	0	0	1	1	0	1.00	1	.179	.179	.256
5 Min. YEARS		521	1884	505	87	10	30	702	211	230	127	8	418	7	13	19	34	30	.53	40	.268	.314	.373

Bats: Right **Throws:** Right **Pos:** 3B

Joel Chimelis

Ht: 6'0" **Wt:** 165 **Born:** 07/27/67 **Age:** 27

Year Team	Lg	BATTING															BASERUNNING				PERCENTAGES		
		G	AB	H	2B	3B	HR	TB	R	RBI	TBB	IBB	SO	HBP	SH	SF	SB	CS	SB%	GDP	Avg	OBP	SLG
1988 Sou Oregon	A	61	225	62	8	0	1	73	40	28	31	1	35	1	1	2	14	7	.67	4	.276	.363	.324
1989 Modesto	A	69	211	40	1	0	1	44	18	14	33	0	41	3	3	1	2	3	.40	8	.190	.306	.209
1990 Reno	A	85	343	96	12	9	2	132	58	47	31	4	36	3	3	2	20	10	.67	17	.280	.343	.385
Modesto	A	46	188	65	14	1	2	87	29	23	18	0	20	0	3	1	10	5	.67	4	.346	.401	.463
1991 Huntsville	AA	68	238	51	10	2	1	68	26	16	18	0	30	0	7	3	4	3	.57	4	.214	.266	.286
San Jose	A	42	126	31	5	1	0	38	19	14	16	0	22	1	1	4	9	4	.69	3	.246	.327	.302
1992 Shreveport	AA	75	279	89	13	1	9	131	47	32	18	3	34	1	4	1	6	6	.50	4	.319	.361	.470
Phoenix	AAA	49	185	56	9	3	1	74	26	23	5	1	24	1	5	2	1	4	.20	3	.303	.321	.400
1993 Shreveport	AA	36	114	23	5	0	6	46	10	18	8	0	14	2	0	2	3	0	1.00	2	.202	.262	.404
Phoenix	AAA	80	262	81	14	3	13	140	40	46	22	1	41	3	1	2	4	3	.57	9	.309	.367	.534
1994 Shreveport	AA	127	478	141	43	1	10	216	74	72	41	2	58	13	1	5	8	6	.57	10	.295	.363	.452
7 Min. YEARS		738	2649	735	134	21	46	1049	387	333	241	12	355	28	29	25	81	51	.61	62	.277	.341	.396

Pitches: Right **Bats:** Right **Pos:** P

Steve Chitren

Ht: 6'0" **Wt:** 180 **Born:** 06/08/67 **Age:** 28

Year Team	Lg	HOW MUCH HE PITCHED						WHAT HE GAVE UP												THE RESULTS					
		G	GS	CG	GF	IP	BFP	H	R	ER	HR	SH	SF	HB	TBB	IBB	SO	WP	Bk	W	L	Pct.	ShO	Sv	ERA
1989 Sou Oregon	A	2	0	0	1	5	20	3	2	1	0	0	1	0	2	0	3	0	0	0	0	.000	0	0	1.80
Madison	A	20	0	0	18	22.2	85	13	3	3	1	0	2	2	4	0	17	0	0	2	1	.667	0	7	1.19
1990 Huntsville	AA	48	0	0	39	53.2	218	32	18	10	4	0	0	3	22	1	61	2	0	2	4	.333	0	27	1.68
Tacoma	AAA	1	0	0	1	0.2	3	1	0	0	0	0	0	0	0	0	2	0	0	0	0	.000	0	0	0.00
1992 Tacoma	AAA	29	7	0	3	62	296	64	53	47	5	5	3	10	46	5	37	4	2	4	7	.364	0	0	6.82
1993 Huntsville	AA	32	0	0	13	55.2	266	53	38	32	7	2	5	10	35	3	39	7	0	2	1	.667	0	1	5.17

Year	Team	Lg	G	GS	CG	GF	IP	BFP	H	R	ER	HR	SH	SF	HB	TBB	IBB	SO	WP	Bk	W	L	Pct.	ShO	Sv	ERA
	Tacoma	AAA	14	0	0	6	24	107	21	9	8	0	0	0	1	14	2	27	2	0	1	0	1.000	0	1	3.00
1994	Bowie	AA	41	1	0	21	70	299	64	34	23	5	2	4	5	26	3	53	10	1	4	5	.444	0	2	2.96
1990	Oakland	AL	8	0	0	4	17.2	64	7	2	2	0	0	0	0	4	0	19	2	0	1	0	1.000	0	1	1.02
1991	Oakland	AL	56	0	0	20	60.1	271	59	31	29	8	4	2	4	32	4	47	2	1	1	4	.200	0	4	4.33
	5 Min. YEARS		187	8	0	102	293.2	1294	251	157	124	22	9	15	31	149	14	239	25	3	15	18	.455	0	38	3.80
	2 Maj. YEARS		64	0	0	24	78	335	66	33	31	8	4	2	4	36	4	66	4	1	2	4	.333	0	4	3.58

Dan Cholowsky

Bats: Right Throws: Right Pos: 2B Ht: 6'0" Wt: 195 Born: 10/30/70 Age: 24

			BATTING																BASERUNNING				PERCENTAGES		
Year	Team	Lg	G	AB	H	2B	3B	HR	TB	R	RBI	TBB	IBB	SO	HBP	SH	SF	SB	CS	SB%	GDP	Avg	OBP	SLG
1991	Hamilton	A	20	69	16	1	1	1	22	9	6	9	0	17	1	0	0	6	3	.67	0	.232	.329	.319
1992	Savannah	A	69	232	76	6	4	8	114	44	34	51	2	48	3	0	2	34	16	.68	1	.328	.451	.491
	St.Pete	A	59	201	57	8	0	1	68	19	17	33	0	31	2	1	4	14	10	.58	8	.284	.383	.338
1993	St.Pete	A	54	208	60	12	0	2	78	30	22	20	2	54	2	0	6	6	8	.43	5	.288	.357	.375
	Arkansas	AA	68	212	46	10	2	3	69	31	16	38	3	54	2	1	1	10	2	.83	7	.217	.340	.325
1994	Arkansas	AA	131	454	101	18	4	14	169	57	51	65	2	114	4	1	1	20	9	.69	9	.222	.324	.372
	4 Min. YEARS		401	1376	356	55	11	29	520	190	146	216	9	318	14	3	8	90	48	.65	30	.259	.363	.378

Eddie Christian

Bats: Both Throws: Left Pos: OF Ht: 5'11" Wt: 180 Born: 08/26/71 Age: 23

			BATTING																BASERUNNING				PERCENTAGES		
Year	Team	Lg	G	AB	H	2B	3B	HR	TB	R	RBI	TBB	IBB	SO	HBP	SH	SF	SB	CS	SB%	GDP	Avg	OBP	SLG
1992	Marlins	R	59	219	61	10	3	0	77	33	29	31	2	35	1	0	3	14	5	.74	6	.279	.366	.352
1993	Kane County	A	112	366	98	21	5	3	138	49	46	58	6	77	0	3	10	9	11	.45	7	.268	.359	.377
1994	Portland	AA	65	228	53	11	0	1	67	27	21	19	0	52	1	3	2	1	4	.20	7	.232	.292	.294
	Brevard Cty	A	54	192	50	11	0	2	67	20	22	18	0	35	1	4	3	3	2	.60	5	.260	.322	.349
	3 Min. YEARS		290	1005	262	53	8	6	349	129	118	126	8	199	3	10	18	27	22	.55	25	.261	.339	.347

Jason Christiansen

Pitches: Left Bats: Right Pos: P Ht: 6'5" Wt: 235 Born: 09/21/69 Age: 25

			HOW MUCH HE PITCHED						WHAT HE GAVE UP												THE RESULTS					
Year	Team	Lg	G	GS	CG	GF	IP	BFP	H	R	ER	HR	SH	SF	HB	TBB	IBB	SO	WP	Bk	W	L	Pct.	ShO	Sv	ERA
1991	Pirates	R	6	0	0	4	8	29	4	0	0	0	0	0	0	1	0	8	0	0	1	0	1.000	0	1	0.00
	Welland	A	8	1	0	1	21.1	85	15	9	6	1	0	0	1	12	1	17	5	0	0	1	.000	0	0	2.53
1992	Augusta	A	10	0	0	4	20	73	12	4	4	0	3	0	0	8	0	21	1	0	1	0	1.000	0	0	1.80
	Salem	A	38	0	0	15	50	212	47	20	18	7	3	1	1	22	2	59	0	1	3	1	.750	0	2	3.24
1993	Salem	A	57	0	0	22	71.1	287	48	30	25	5	5	1	4	24	2	70	2	0	1	1	.500	0	4	3.15
	Carolina	AA	2	0	0	1	2.2	12	3	0	0	0	0	0	0	1	0	2	0	0	0	0	.000	0	0	0.00
1994	Carolina	AA	28	0	0	9	38.2	158	30	10	9	2	3	1	1	14	1	43	2	0	2	1	.667	0	2	2.09
	Buffalo	AAA	33	0	0	12	33.2	132	19	9	9	3	1	2	0	16	0	39	1	0	3	1	.750	0	0	2.41
	4 Min. YEARS		182	1	0	68	245.2	988	178	82	71	18	15	5	7	98	6	259	11	1	11	5	.688	0	11	2.60

Mike Christopher

Pitches: Right Bats: Right Pos: P Ht: 6'5" Wt: 205 Born: 11/03/63 Age: 31

			HOW MUCH HE PITCHED						WHAT HE GAVE UP												THE RESULTS					
Year	Team	Lg	G	GS	CG	GF	IP	BFP	H	R	ER	HR	SH	SF	HB	TBB	IBB	SO	WP	Bk	W	L	Pct.	ShO	Sv	ERA
1985	Oneonta	A	15	9	2	3	80.1	317	58	21	13	2	1	2	3	22	0	84	3	0	8	1	.889	2	0	1.46
1986	Albany	AA	11	11	2	0	60.2	273	75	48	34	6	2	4	3	12	1	34	3	0	3	5	.375	0	0	5.04
	Ft.Laudrdle	A	15	14	3	0	102.2	421	92	37	30	2	4	2	1	36	0	56	1	1	7	3	.700	1	0	2.63
1987	Ft.Laudrdle	A	24	24	9	0	169.1	694	183	63	46	5	6	4	0	28	1	81	4	0	13	8	.619	4	0	2.44
1988	Albany	AA	24	24	5	0	152.2	648	166	75	65	7	4	5	6	44	3	67	2	4	13	7	.650	1	0	3.83
1989	Columbus	AAA	13	11	1	0	73	331	95	45	39	6	6	5	3	21	3	42	1	0	5	6	.455	0	0	4.81
	Albany	AA	8	8	3	0	53.2	213	48	17	15	1	0	1	1	7	0	33	0	0	6	1	.857	0	0	2.52
1990	Albuquerque	AAA	54	0	0	25	68.2	287	62	20	15	3	5	4	2	23	3	47	0	0	6	1	.857	0	8	1.97
1991	Albuquerque	AAA	63	0	0	34	77.1	334	73	25	21	2	4	1	3	30	5	67	7	1	7	2	.778	0	16	2.44
1992	Colo Spngs	AAA	49	0	0	45	58.2	240	59	21	19	2	5	4	0	13	6	39	3	0	4	4	.500	0	26	2.91
1993	Charlotte	AAA	50	0	0	46	50.1	204	51	21	18	2	3	2	0	14	4	36	2	0	3	6	.333	0	22	3.22
1994	Toledo	AAA	63	0	0	48	71.2	309	76	33	28	10	4	3	0	18	7	60	4	0	3	6	.333	0	10	3.52
1991	Los Angeles	NL	3	0	0	2	4	15	2	0	0	0	0	0	0	3	0	2	0	0	0	0	.000	0	0	0.00
1992	Cleveland	AL	10	0	0	4	18	79	17	8	6	2	1	1	0	10	1	13	2	0	0	0	.000	0	0	3.00
1993	Cleveland	AL	9	0	0	3	11.2	51	14	6	5	3	0	0	0	2	1	8	0	0	0	0	.000	0	0	3.86
	10 Min. YEARS		389	101	25	201	1019	4271	1038	426	343	48	44	37	22	260	33	646	30	6	78	50	.609	8	83	3.03
	3 Maj. YEARS		22	0	0	9	33.2	145	33	14	11	5	1	1	0	15	2	23	2	0	0	0	.000	0	0	2.94

Eric Christopherson

Bats: Right Throws: Right Pos: C Ht: 6'1" Wt: 190 Born: 04/25/69 Age: 26

			BATTING																BASERUNNING				PERCENTAGES		
Year	Team	Lg	G	AB	H	2B	3B	HR	TB	R	RBI	TBB	IBB	SO	HBP	SH	SF	SB	CS	SB%	GDP	Avg	OBP	SLG
1990	San Jose	A	7	23	4	0	0	0	4	1	3	0	6	0	0	0	0	0	0	.00	0	.174	.269	.174
	Everett	A	48	162	43	8	1	1	56	20	22	31	1	28	0	1	2	7	2	.78	2	.265	.379	.346
1991	Clinton	A	110	345	93	18	0	5	126	45	58	68	1	54	1	1	6	10	7	.59	10	.270	.386	.365
1992	Shreveport	AA	80	270	68	10	1	6	98	36	34	37	0	44	1	0	2	1	6	.14	5	.252	.342	.363

Year	Team	Lg	G	AB	H	2B	3B	HR	TB	R	RBI	TBB	IBB	SO	HBP	SH	SF	SB	CS	SB%	GDP	Avg	OBP	SLG
1993	Giants	R	8	22	9	1	1	0	12	7	4	9	0	1	0	0	0	0	0	.00	0	.409	.581	.545
	Shreveport	AA	15	46	7	2	0	0	9	5	2	9	0	10	0	0	0	1	1	.50	1	.152	.291	.196
1994	Shreveport	AA	88	267	67	22	0	6	107	30	39	42	4	55	0	1	2	5	5	.83	2	.251	.350	.401
	5 Min. YEARS		356	1135	291	61	3	18	412	147	160	199	6	198	2	3	12	24	17	.59	20	.256	.365	.363

Joe Ciccarella

Pitches: Left Bats: Left Pos: P **Ht: 6' 3" Wt: 200 Born: 12/29/69 Age: 25**

			HOW MUCH HE PITCHED						WHAT HE GAVE UP											THE RESULTS					
Year	Team	Lg	G	GS	CG	GF	IP	BFP	H	R	ER	HR	SH	SF	HB	TBB	IBB	SO	WP	Bk	W	L	Pct.	ShO	Sv	ERA
1992	Winter Havn	A	38	0	0	30	40.2	177	35	13	12	2	4	3	0	26	1	45	0	0	2	1	.667	0	12	2.66
1993	Pawtucket	AAA	12	0	0	2	17.2	89	27	13	11	2	0	0	2	12	0	8	0	0	0	1	.000	0	0	5.60
	New Britain	AA	30	0	0	30	32	151	31	19	15	1	1	1	1	23	4	34	5	0	0	4	.000	0	15	4.22
1994	New Britain	AA	31	18	0	1	113.2	524	134	68	53	11	5	3	7	54	0	95	5	2	6	6	.500	0	0	4.20
	3 Min. YEARS		111	18	0	63	204	941	227	113	91	16	10	7	10	115	5	182	10	2	8	12	.400	0	27	4.01

Dera Clark

Pitches: Right Bats: Right Pos: P **Ht: 6'1" Wt: 204 Born: 04/14/65 Age: 30**

			HOW MUCH HE PITCHED						WHAT HE GAVE UP											THE RESULTS					
Year	Team	Lg	G	GS	CG	GF	IP	BFP	H	R	ER	HR	SH	SF	HB	TBB	IBB	SO	WP	Bk	W	L	Pct.	ShO	Sv	ERA
1987	Royals	R	21	0	0	8	56.1	230	42	20	14	1	3	1	1	17	5	51	3	0	3	4	.429	0	4	2.24
1988	Baseball Cy	A	34	0	0	13	79.2	335	73	28	24	2	3	4	1	31	6	46	9	2	5	2	.714	0	4	2.71
1989	Memphis	AA	30	13	1	5	106.1	459	103	63	52	11	2	5	8	29	0	93	15	2	5	5	.500	1	1	4.40
1990	Omaha	AAA	17	17	0	0	91.2	396	82	40	38	14	1	5	3	44	0	66	6	1	8	3	.727	0	0	3.73
1991	Omaha	AAA	25	23	0	1	129.2	577	126	76	65	10	5	6	4	74	0	108	17	0	6	9	.400	0	0	4.51
1992	Royals	R	2	1	0	0	8.2	40	7	4	2	0	0	1	0	2	0	13	2	0	0	0	.000	0	0	2.08
	Baseball Cy	A	3	3	0	0	16	63	15	3	3	0	0	0	0	3	0	7	0	0	2	0	1.000	0	0	1.69
	Omaha	AAA	9	9	0	0	43	197	57	39	38	9	1	3	1	16	0	32	3	0	1	6	.143	0	0	7.95
1993	Omaha	AAA	51	0	0	19	82.1	355	86	43	40	16	1	6	0	30	2	53	4	1	4	4	.500	0	5	4.37
1994	Richmond	AAA	8	0	0	1	10.1	48	9	8	7	1	0	2	0	7	0	11	0	1	0	0	.000	0	0	6.10
	8 Min. YEARS		200	66	1	47	624	2700	600	324	283	64	16	33	18	253	13	480	59	7	34	33	.507	1	14	4.08

Terry Clark

Pitches: Right Bats: Right Pos: P **Ht: 6' 2" Wt: 195 Born: 10/10/60 Age: 34**

			HOW MUCH HE PITCHED						WHAT HE GAVE UP											THE RESULTS					
Year	Team	Lg	G	GS	CG	GF	IP	BFP	H	R	ER	HR	SH	SF	HB	TBB	IBB	SO	WP	Bk	W	L	Pct.	ShO	Sv	ERA
1979	Johnson Cty	R	23	0	0	20	32	134	31	10	7	1	3	2	0	11	0	22	0	1	4	2	.667	0	0	1.97
1980	Gastonia	A	49	0	0	38	88	365	82	34	31	8	4	5		22	0	50	3	0	4	7	.364	0	0	3.17
1981	Gastonia	A	53	0	0	51	75	304	56	23	18	4	2	1	1	25	0	66	2	1	4	5	.444	0	0	2.16
1982	St. Pete	A	58	0	0	51	88.1	385	81	32	25	1	11	4	3	34	0	61	6	0	10	7	.588	0	0	2.55
1983	Arkansas	AA	52	0	0	39	81.1	323	68	31	29	9	3	1	2	19	0	63	4	0	6	6	.500	0	15	3.21
1984	Louisville	AAA	18	1	0	9	34.1	156	41	19	18	5	0	1	1	12	2	24	2	0	1	3	.250	0	1	4.72
1985	Arkansas	AA	42	7	0	8	96.2	420	102	64	53	9	7	5	4	38	2	67	0	1	6	5	.545	0	2	4.93
1986	Midland	AA	57	2	0	32	90.1	386	98	49	33	6	2	4	4	28	3	66	1	0	9	4	.692	0	4	3.29
1987	Edmonton	AAA	33	20	5	6	154.2	654	140	79	66	13	6	2	7	56	8	88	4	4	8	9	.471	1	4	3.84
1988	Edmonton	AAA	16	16	3	0	113.2	488	128	62	57	7	4	4	4	33	0	59	0	3	7	6	.538	0	0	4.51
1989	Edmonton	AAA	21	20	4	1	138.1	569	130	62	55	7	5	3	6	33	5	90	8	1	11	5	.688	2	0	3.58
1990	Tucson	AAA	29	22	3	2	155	657	172	73	61	9	9	8	8	41	2	80	3	5	11	4	.733	1	1	3.54
1991	Tucson	AAA	26	26	2	0	164	705	199	104	85	5	4	5	6	37	0	97	9	2	14	7	.667	0	0	4.66
1992	Colo Spngs	AAA	9	9	2	0	59.2	248	62	30	25	3	1	3	1	13	0	33	3	0	4	4	.500	0	0	3.77
1993	Rancho Cuca	A	8	0	0	2	9.2	39	7	5	5	1	1	0	0	4	2	7	0	0	0	2	.000	0	0	4.66
	Wichita	AA	19	0	0	3	29.2	125	27	10	8	2	1	2	1	7	0	30	2	0	3	0	1.000	0	0	2.43
1994	Richmond	AAA	61	0	0	45	83.1	342	72	33	28	6	7	3	0	27	5	74	1	0	5	4	.556	0	26	3.02
1988	California	AL	15	15	2	0	94	410	120	54	53	8	2	5	0	31	6	39	5	2	6	6	.500	1	0	5.07
1989	California	AL	4	4	2	0	11	48	13	8	6	0	2	1	0	3	0	7	2	1	0	2	.000	0	0	4.91
1990	Houston	NL	1	1	0	0	4	25	9	7	6	0	1	0	0	3	0	2	1	0	0	0	.000	0	0	13.50
	16 Min. YEARS		574	123	19	307	1494	6300	1496	720	604	96	74	52	53	440	29	977	48	18	107	80	.572	4	53	3.64
	3 Maj. YEARS		20	18	2	2	109	483	142	69	65	8	5	6	0	37	6	48	7	3	6	8	.429	1	0	5.37

Tim Clark

Bats: Left Throws: Left Pos: OF **Ht: 6'3" Wt: 210 Born: 02/10/69 Age: 26**

			BATTING															BASERUNNING				PERCENTAGES		
Year	Team	Lg	G	AB	H	2B	3B	HR	TB	R	RBI	TBB	IBB	SO	HBP	SH	SF	SB	CS	SB%	GDP	Avg	OBP	SLG
1990	Beloit	A	67	219	57	13	1	4	84	27	44	31	1	45	3	2	3	3	4	.43	10	.260	.355	.384
1991	Stockton	A	125	424	116	19	4	9	170	51	56	57	4	60	8	1	5	9	7	.56	5	.274	.366	.401
1992	Salt Lake	R	69	272	97	25	2	11	159	57	53	28	1	36	3	1	4	1	2	.33	8	.357	.417	.585
1993	High Desert	A	128	510	185	42	10	17	298	109	126	56	3	65	4	0	13	2	5	.29	13	.363	.420	.584
1994	Portland	AA	135	486	129	30	0	14	201	63	65	50	0	112	3	0	4	3	7	.30	15	.265	.335	.414
	5 Min. YEARS		524	1911	584	129	17	55	912	307	344	222	9	318	21	4	29	18	25	.42	51	.306	.379	.477

Tony Clark

Bats: Both   Throws: Right   Pos: OF   Ht: 6'8" Wt: 240 Born: 06/15/72 Age: 23

Year	Team	Lg	G	AB	H	2B	3B	HR	TB	R	RBI	TBB	IBB	SO	HBP	SH	SF	SB	CS	SB%	GDP	Avg	OBP	SLG
1990	Bristol	R	25	73	12	2	0	1	17	2	8	6	0	28	1	0	0	0	0	.00	0	.164	.238	.233
1992	Niagara Fls	A	27	85	26	9	0	5	50	12	17	9	0	34	0	0	0	1	0	1.00	0	.306	.372	.588
1993	Lakeland	A	36	117	31	4	1	1	40	14	22	18	2	32	0	2	2	0	1	.00	1	.265	.358	.342
1994	Trenton	AA	107	394	110	25	0	21	198	50	86	40	5	113	1	0	2	0	4	.00	9	.279	.346	.503
	Toledo	AAA	25	92	24	4	0	2	34	10	13	12	1	25	0	0	2	2	0	1.00	1	.261	.340	.370
	4 Min. YEARS		220	761	203	44	1	30	339	88	146	85	8	232	2	2	6	3	5	.38	11	.267	.340	.445

Marty Clary

Pitches: Right   Bats: Right   Pos: P   Ht: 6'4" Wt: 190 Born: 04/03/62 Age: 33

Year	Team	Lg	G	GS	CG	GF	IP	BFP	H	R	ER	HR	SH	SF	HB	TBB	IBB	SO	WP	Bk	W	L	Pct.	ShO	Sv	ERA
1984	Greenville	AA	30	30	5	0	186.1	790	172	77	66	10	6	6	3	82	1	125	10	4	14	9	.609	2	0	3.19
1985	Richmond	AAA	26	25	0	1	156.2	688	155	81	73	7	8	6	5	77	1	76	9	1	8	12	.400	0	0	4.19
1986	Richmond	AAA	24	22	3	1	132.1	581	118	72	64	12	5	6	1	82	1	56	9	4	7	6	.538	1	0	4.35
1987	Richmond	AAA	26	26	5	0	178	768	180	86	74	13	5	5	4	75	2	91	10	0	11	10	.524	0	0	3.74
1988	Richmond	AAA	27	25	2	1	143.2	604	142	65	54	10	5	6	2	37	3	73	10	2	6	11	.353	1	0	3.38
1989	Richmond	AAA	15	15	4	0	101.2	408	87	33	23	3	5	4	2	28	0	70	2	0	7	5	.583	0	0	2.04
1991	Louisville	AAA	33	7	0	7	70.1	309	77	40	35	6	3	0	2	26	1	28	6	0	2	8	.200	0	1	4.48
	Buffalo	AAA	7	5	1	0	30	130	31	13	13	2	0	0	0	10	0	14	1	2	3	0	1.000	1	0	3.90
1994	Orlando	AA	13	6	0	4	52.2	202	46	23	20	4	4	0	0	9	1	27	3	0	4	3	.571	0	0	3.42
1987	Atlanta	NL	7	1	0	2	14.2	68	20	13	10	2	1	1	1	4	0	7	0	0	0	1	.000	0	0	6.14
1989	Atlanta	NL	18	17	2	0	108.2	452	103	47	38	4	3	1	1	31	3	30	5	0	4	3	.571	1	0	3.15
1990	Atlanta	NL	33	14	0	5	101.2	466	128	72	64	9	5	5	1	39	4	44	5	1	1	10	.091	0	0	5.67
	8 Min. YEARS		201	161	20	14	1051.2	4480	1008	490	422	67	41	33	19	426	10	560	60	13	62	64	.492	5	1	3.61
	3 Maj. YEARS		58	32	2	7	225	986	251	132	112	17	10	9	3	74	7	81	10	1	5	14	.263	1	0	4.48

Craig Clayton

Pitches: Right   Bats: Right   Pos: P   Ht: 6'0" Wt: 185 Born: 11/29/70 Age: 24

Year	Team	Lg	G	GS	CG	GF	IP	BFP	H	R	ER	HR	SH	SF	HB	TBB	IBB	SO	WP	Bk	W	L	Pct.	ShO	Sv	ERA
1991	Bellingham	A	1	0	0	1	0.2	3	1	0	0	0	0	0	0	0	0	0	0	0	0	0	.000	0	0	0.00
1993	Jacksnville	AA	3	0	0	3	4	17	3	0	0	0	0	0	1	1	0	1	0	0	0	0	.000	0	0	0.00
1994	Jacksnville	AA	10	0	0	6	12.1	52	8	6	5	1	0	0	1	6	0	13	3	4	0	0	.000	0	1	3.65
	Riverside	A	20	1	0	4	26.1	135	29	24	23	2	2	1	1	26	0	35	1	0	1	1	.500	0	0	7.86
	3 Min. YEARS		34	1	0	14	43.1	207	41	30	28	3	2	1	3	33	0	49	4	4	1	1	.500	0	1	5.82

Royal Clayton

Pitches: Right   Bats: Right   Pos: P   Ht: 6'2" Wt: 210 Born: 11/25/65 Age: 29

Year	Team	Lg	G	GS	CG	GF	IP	BFP	H	R	ER	HR	SH	SF	HB	TBB	IBB	SO	WP	Bk	W	L	Pct.	ShO	Sv	ERA
1987	Oneonta	A	2	0	0	1	4	16	4	1	1	0	0	0	0	2	0	3	0	0	0	1	.000	0	0	2.25
	Yankees	R	3	1	0	2	10.1	44	12	5	4	0	0	1	0	2	1	5	0	0	0	2	.000	0	1	3.48
	Pr William	A	9	4	0	4	37.1	181	49	25	19	4	0	0	0	17	0	20	1	2	2	1	.667	0	0	4.58
1988	Pr William	A	22	11	3	8	91.1	372	81	31	24	2	3	1	2	25	1	44	1	2	5	5	.500	1	0	2.36
	Ft.Laudrdle	A	6	6	5	0	43.2	166	38	10	7	2	0	0	0	3	0	16	1	0	4	2	.667	2	0	1.44
1989	Albany	AA	25	25	6	0	175	715	166	72	58	8	1	3	4	48	2	74	5	3	16	4	.800	0	0	2.98
1990	Columbus	AAA	4	4	0	0	26	111	33	12	11	1	0	0	0	7	0	15	1	0	1	2	.333	0	0	3.81
	Albany	AA	21	21	6	0	141.2	590	148	58	50	13	8	3	1	43	4	68	2	3	10	9	.526	2	0	3.18
1991	Columbus	AAA	32	19	1	2	150	650	152	76	64	15	2	4	2	53	1	100	2	1	11	7	.611	0	0	3.84
1992	Columbus	AAA	36	15	1	10	130.2	557	132	62	52	5	2	6	3	45	2	72	6	3	10	5	.667	1	1	3.58
1993	Columbus	AAA	47	11	0	21	117	489	119	56	46	12	5	3	2	31	3	66	3	0	7	6	.538	0	8	3.54
1994	Columbus	AAA	58	3	0	21	90	394	103	47	42	2	3	2	0	30	4	54	7	0	12	7	.632	0	5	4.20
	8 Min. YEARS		265	120	22	69	1017	4285	1037	455	378	64	24	23	14	306	18	537	29	14	78	51	.605	6	15	3.35

Troy Clemens

Bats: Left   Throws: Right   Pos: C   Ht: 6'1" Wt: 195 Born: 01/12/68 Age: 27

Year	Team	Lg	G	AB	H	2B	3B	HR	TB	R	RBI	TBB	IBB	SO	HBP	SH	SF	SB	CS	SB%	GDP	Avg	OBP	SLG
1988	Pirates	R	15	37	5	0	0	0	5	1	5	4	0	5	0	0	1	1	1	.50	2	.135	.214	.135
1989	Cardinals	R	47	146	39	6	2	1	52	18	26	12	0	19	1	0	2	4	2	.67	3	.267	.323	.356
1990	Springfield	A	105	316	86	16	2	2	112	37	40	30	1	44	5	5	3	0	5	.00	11	.272	.342	.354
1991	Reno	A	69	152	34	5	0	2	45	22	19	30	1	21	1	1	0	0	1	.00	9	.224	.353	.296
1992	Shreveport	AA	3	6	1	0	0	0	1	0	1	0	0	2	0	0	0	0	0	.00	0	.167	.167	.167
	San Jose	A	65	159	42	8	1	0	52	12	20	12	2	27	1	0	3	0	0	.00	6	.264	.314	.327
1993	San Jose	A	96	306	89	15	1	0	106	36	31	35	4	34	3	2	4	1	1	.50	4	.291	.365	.346
1994	San Jose	A	39	115	29	8	1	0	39	15	10	13	0	18	2	1	0	2	0	1.00	2	.252	.338	.339
	Shreveport	AA	4	5	0	0	0	0	0	0	0	1	0	1	0	0	0	0	0	.00	0	.000	.167	.000
	7 Min. YEARS		443	1242	325	58	7	5	412	141	152	137	8	171	13	8	14	8	10	.44	37	.262	.338	.332

Jim Clinton

Bats: Right **Throws:** Right **Pos:** SS **Ht:** 6'2" **Wt:** 185 **Born:** 06/17/67 **Age:** 28

						BATTING											BASERUNNING				PERCENTAGES		
Year	Team	Lg	G	AB	H	2B	3B	HR	TB	R	RBI	TBB	IBB	SO	HBP	SH	SF	SB	CS	SB%	GDP	Avg	OBP	SLG
1989	Butte	R	60	137	30	7	0	0	37	14	15	12	2	37	2	0	0	3	3	.50	3	.219	.291	.270
1990	Gastonia	A	61	128	26	6	1	0	34	12	7	13	0	35	1	4	0	3	7	.30	1	.203	.282	.266
1991	Charlotte	A	86	244	47	12	1	1	64	19	17	16	0	63	3	4	0	16	8	.67	8	.193	.251	.262
1992	Charlotte	A	92	239	42	5	2	1	54	27	15	19	0	64	2	9	0	9	2	.82	7	.176	.242	.226
1993	Tulsa	AA	6	12	1	0	0	0	1	0	2	1	0	3	0	0	0	0	0	.00	0	.083	.154	.083
	Charlotte	A	86	285	50	9	0	1	62	26	23	18	1	72	4	7	2	4	3	.57	9	.175	.233	.218
1994	Okla. City	AAA	6	22	4	1	0	0	5	1	2	0	0	4	0	0	0	1	0	1.00	0	.182	.182	.227
	Tulsa	AA	69	203	48	4	0	0	52	21	14	6	0	54	1	3	2	10	4	.71	3	.236	.259	.256
	6 Min. YEARS		466	1270	248	44	4	3	309	120	95	85	3	332	13	27	4	46	27	.63	31	.195	.252	.243

Brad Clontz

Pitches: Right **Bats:** Right **Pos:** P **Ht:** 6'1" **Wt:** 180 **Born:** 04/25/71 **Age:** 24

			HOW MUCH HE PITCHED						WHAT HE GAVE UP										THE RESULTS				
Year	Team	Lg	G	GS	CG	GF	IP	BFP	H	R	ER	HR	SH	SF	HB	TBB	IBB	SO	WP	Bk	W	L	Pct.	ShO	Sv	ERA
1992	Pulaski	R	4	0	0	3	5.2	23	3	1	1	0	0	0	2	2	0	7	1	0	0	0	.000	0	1	1.59
	Macon	A	17	0	0	14	23	103	19	14	10	2	2	1	3	10	0	18	1	0	2	1	.667	0	2	3.91
1993	Durham	A	51	0	0	38	75.1	325	69	32	23	5	8	0	4	26	1	79	6	0	1	7	.125	0	10	2.75
1994	Greenville	AA	39	0	0	38	45	178	32	13	6	5	3	1	1	10	2	49	2	0	1	2	.333	0	27	1.20
	Richmond	AAA	24	0	0	22	25.2	101	19	6	6	1	0	1	0	9	2	21	0	0	0	0	.000	0	11	2.10
	3 Min. YEARS		135	0	0	115	174.2	730	142	66	46	13	13	3	10	57	5	174	10	0	4	10	.286	0	51	2.37

Alan Cockrell

Bats: Right **Throws:** Right **Pos:** OF **Ht:** 6'2" **Wt:** 210 **Born:** 12/05/62 **Age:** 32

						BATTING											BASERUNNING				PERCENTAGES		
Year	Team	Lg	G	AB	H	2B	3B	HR	TB	R	RBI	TBB	IBB	SO	HBP	SH	SF	SB	CS	SB%	GDP	Avg	OBP	SLG
1984	Everett	A	2	8	3	0	0	0	3	1	3	1	0	2	0	0	0	0	0	.00	0	.375	.444	.375
	Fresno	A	61	214	46	6	0	1	55	20	32	28	0	66	5	0	2	0	1	.00	10	.215	.317	.257
1985	Shreveport	AA	126	455	115	25	3	11	179	53	68	54	2	137	3	3	2	12	3	.80	16	.253	.335	.393
1986	Shreveport	AA	124	438	113	31	3	14	192	66	78	61	3	126	3	3	3	4	2	.67	11	.258	.350	.438
1987	Phoenix	AAA	129	432	111	23	5	11	177	82	72	69	4	131	3	5	4	7	3	.70	9	.257	.360	.410
1988	Phoenix	AAA	102	347	105	16	2	8	149	65	39	48	1	93	1	1	1	3	3	.50	6	.303	.388	.429
	Portland	AAA	18	63	15	1	1	2	24	9	8	5	0	25	0	0	0	1	0	1.00	0	.238	.294	.381
1989	Portland	AAA	127	433	116	15	3	11	170	60	61	57	0	127	2	5	6	5	3	.62	11	.268	.351	.393
1990	Portland	AAA	6	23	5	1	1	0	8	2	1	0	0	5	1	0	0	1	0	1.00	0	.217	.250	.348
	Colo Sprngs	AAA	113	352	116	23	4	17	198	75	70	50	2	68	2	0	3	5	3	.63	12	.330	.413	.563
1991	Calgary	AAA	117	435	126	27	2	11	190	77	81	45	1	74	4	1	3	7	4	.64	17	.290	.359	.437
1992	Colo Sprngs	AAA	82	259	61	6	2	7	92	31	38	22	1	51	4	2	2	0	2	.00	6	.236	.303	.355
1993	Charlotte	AAA	96	275	76	12	2	8	116	31	39	23	0	59	2	2	3	0	0	.00	9	.276	.333	.422
1994	New Haven	AA	12	43	13	4	0	1	20	6	8	3	1	6	1	0	1	2	0	1.00	1	.302	.354	.465
	Colo. Sprng	AAA	84	271	83	15	2	13	141	50	60	29	0	58	4	1	1	1	1	.50	6	.306	.380	.520
	11 Min. YEARS		1199	4048	1104	205	30	115	1714	628	658	495	15	1028	35	23	31	51	27	.65	114	.273	.355	.423

Emmitt Cohick

Bats: Left **Throws:** Left **Pos:** OF **Ht:** 6'2" **Wt:** 175 **Born:** 08/08/68 **Age:** 26

						BATTING											BASERUNNING				PERCENTAGES		
Year	Team	Lg	G	AB	H	2B	3B	HR	TB	R	RBI	TBB	IBB	SO	HBP	SH	SF	SB	CS	SB%	GDP	Avg	OBP	SLG
1991	Quad City	A	112	350	96	22	9	11	169	52	53	56	3	97	5	2	3	8	4	.67	2	.274	.379	.483
1992	Palm Sprngs	A	117	402	121	17	6	8	174	69	78	49	2	91	3	2	7	15	12	.56	8	.301	.375	.433
1993	Midland	AA	105	356	96	18	5	11	157	59	53	35	2	91	5	9	2	6	2	.75	4	.270	.342	.441
1994	Midland	AA	96	330	86	25	5	8	145	41	62	32	1	99	4	2	3	3	4	.43	4	.261	.331	.439
	4 Min. YEARS		430	1438	399	82	25	38	645	221	246	172	8	378	17	15	15	32	22	.59	18	.277	.358	.449

Craig Colbert

Bats: Right **Throws:** Right **Pos:** C **Ht:** 6' 0" **Wt:** 214 **Born:** 02/13/65 **Age:** 30

						BATTING											BASERUNNING				PERCENTAGES		
Year	Team	Lg	G	AB	H	2B	3B	HR	TB	R	RBI	TBB	IBB	SO	HBP	SH	SF	SB	CS	SB%	GDP	Avg	OBP	SLG
1986	Clinton	A	72	263	60	12	0	1	75	26	17	23	1	53	3	0	1	4	1	.80	7	.228	.297	.285
1987	Fresno	A	115	388	95	12	4	6	133	41	51	22	2	89	4	3	5	5	5	.50	11	.245	.289	.343
1988	Clinton	A	124	455	106	19	2	11	162	56	64	41	0	100	1	2	2	8	9	.47	4	.233	.297	.356
1989	Shreveport	AA	106	363	94	19	3	7	140	47	34	23	5	67	0	2	2	3	7	.30	11	.259	.302	.386
1990	Phoenix	AAA	111	400	112	22	2	8	162	41	47	31	3	80	3	1	2	4	5	.44	8	.280	.335	.405
1991	Phoenix	AAA	42	142	35	6	2	2	51	9	13	11	2	38	0	0	1	0	1	.00	4	.246	.299	.359
1992	Phoenix	AAA	36	140	45	8	1	1	58	16	12	3	0	16	1	2	2	0	1	.00	4	.321	.336	.414
1993	Phoenix	AAA	13	45	10	2	1	1	17	5	7	0	0	11	1	0	1	0	0	.00	1	.222	.234	.378
1994	Charlotte	AAA	69	182	47	7	1	4	68	19	25	19	1	40	0	1	1	1	1	.50	9	.258	.327	.374
1992	San Francisco	NL	49	126	29	5	2	1	41	10	16	9	0	22	0	2	2	1	0	1.00	8	.230	.277	.325
1993	San Francisco	NL	23	37	6	2	0	1	11	2	5	3	1	13	0	0	0	0	0	.00	0	.162	.225	.297
	9 Min. YEARS		688	2378	604	107	16	41	866	260	270	173	14	494	13	11	17	25	30	.45	62	.254	.306	.364
	2 Maj. YEARS		72	163	35	7	2	2	52	12	21	12	1	35	0	2	2	1	0	1.00	8	.215	.266	.319

Stu Cole

Bats: Right **Throws:** Right **Pos:** 2B **Ht:** 6' 1" **Wt:** 175 **Born:** 02/07/66 **Age:** 29

Year	Team	Lg	G	AB	H	2B	3B	HR	TB	R	RBI	TBB	IBB	SO	HBP	SH	SF	SB	CS	SB%	GDP	Avg	OBP	SLG
1987	Eugene	A	63	243	74	17	1	3	102	42	51	34	1	45	1	3	4	3	1	.75	3	.305	.387	.420
1988	Virginia	A	70	257	70	10	0	1	83	41	22	32	0	52	4	0	2	10	5	.67	6	.272	.359	.323
	Baseball Cy	A	15	41	6	0	0	0	6	7	4	9	0	10	0	1	1	2	1	.67	4	.146	.294	.146
1989	Memphis	AA	90	299	64	8	3	6	96	30	32	25	0	67	0	4	2	11	3	.79	7	.214	.273	.321
1990	Memphis	AA	113	357	110	18	2	1	135	61	49	55	2	55	3	4	3	20	5	.80	8	.308	.402	.378
1991	Omaha	AAA	120	441	115	13	7	3	151	64	39	42	0	60	1	5	2	11	10	.52	12	.261	.325	.342
1992	Omaha	AAA	63	205	40	8	0	4	60	30	17	25	0	27	3	6	0	3	5	.38	5	.195	.292	.293
	Memphis	AA	49	174	41	8	1	0	51	19	12	18	2	23	1	2	1	7	7	.50	7	.236	.308	.293
1993	Colo Spmgs	AAA	104	324	91	22	3	5	134	54	35	36	1	36	1	2	2	10	6	.63	14	.281	.353	.414
1994	Colo. Spmg	AAA	97	285	86	22	2	6	130	39	38	22	1	45	4	2	4	7	3	.70	9	.302	.356	.456
1991	Kansas City	AL	9	7	1	0	0	0	1	1	0	2	0	2	0	0	0	0	0	.00	0	.143	.333	.143
	8 Min. YEARS		784	2626	697	126	19	29	948	387	299	298	7	420	18	29	22	84	46	.65	75	.265	.342	.361

Victor Cole

Pitches: Right **Bats:** Both **Pos:** P **Ht:** 5'10" **Wt:** 160 **Born:** 01/23/68 **Age:** 27

Year	Team	Lg	G	GS	CG	GF	IP	BFP	H	R	ER	HR	SH	SF	HB	TBB	IBB	SO	WP	Bk	W	L	Pct.	ShO	Sv	ERA
1988	Eugene	A	15	0	0	13	23.2	94	16	6	4	0	0	0	2	8	0	39	3	0	1	0	1.000	0	9	1.52
	Baseball Cy	A	10	5	0	2	35	149	27	9	8	0	1	1	1	21	0	29	2	0	5	0	1.000	0	1	2.06
1989	Memphis	AA	13	13	0	0	63.2	303	67	53	45	4	4	1	5	51	1	52	4	1	1	9	.100	0	0	6.36
	Baseball Cy	A	9	9	0	0	42	186	43	23	18	2	1	1	1	22	0	30	2	1	3	1	.750	0	0	3.86
1990	Memphis	AA	46	0	0	15	107.2	479	91	61	52	6	4	1	3	70	2	102	2	2	3	8	.273	0	4	4.35
1991	Omaha	AAA	6	0	0	1	13	54	9	6	6	1	0	0	0	9	1	12	0	0	1	1	.500	0	0	4.15
	Carolina	AA	20	0	0	17	28.1	116	13	8	6	1	0	1	2	19	1	32	3	2	0	2	.000	0	12	1.91
	Buffalo	AAA	19	1	0	9	24	115	23	11	10	2	0	1	1	20	0	23	3	0	1	2	.333	0	0	3.75
1992	Buffalo	AAA	19	19	3	0	115.2	498	102	46	40	8	3	3	4	61	0	69	8	0	11	6	.647	1	0	3.11
1993	Buffalo	AAA	6	6	0	0	26.1	134	35	25	25	5	2	1	0	24	0	14	1	0	1	3	.250	0	0	8.54
	Carolina	AA	27	0	0	13	41	189	39	30	27	5	1	0	2	31	2	35	6	0	0	4	.000	0	8	5.93
	New Orleans	AAA	6	1	0	0	6	34	9	7	7	0	0	1	1	7	0	5	0	0	0	2	.000	0	0	10.50
1994	El Paso	AA	8	0	0	2	8	50	18	17	16	4	0	0	1	9	1	3	0	1	0	1	.000	0	0	18.00
	Memphis	AA	6	6	0	0	35.2	162	32	22	19	3	0	4	0	23	0	22	2	0	2	1	.667	0	0	4.79
1992	Pittsburgh	NL	8	4	0	2	23	104	23	14	14	1	1	1	0	14	0	12	1	0	0	2	.000	0	0	5.48
	7 Min. YEARS		210	66	3	72	570	2563	524	324	283	41	16	15	23	375	8	467	36	7	29	40	.420	1	34	4.47

John Coleman

Pitches: Right **Bats:** Right **Pos:** P **Ht:** 6'1" **Wt:** 185 **Born:** 01/18/69 **Age:** 26

Year	Team	Lg	G	GS	CG	GF	IP	BFP	H	R	ER	HR	SH	SF	HB	TBB	IBB	SO	WP	Bk	W	L	Pct.	ShO	Sv	ERA
1991	Oneonta	A	18	5	0	4	52.2	230	44	22	17	1	2	2	1	30	0	36	4	1	2	3	.400	0	1	2.91
1992	Greensboro	A	56	0	0	25	73	336	59	39	27	4	4	2	6	52	3	67	14	1	3	5	.375	0	7	3.33
1993	Greensboro	A	59	0	0	41	70	290	54	24	20	5	3	5	3	23	4	82	5	0	5	3	.625	0	14	2.57
1994	Albany-Colo	AA	12	1	0	4	16.2	73	17	12	10	1	1	1	0	6	0	14	3	1	1	2	.333	0	2	5.40
	Tampa	A	14	0	0	8	16.2	72	13	10	3	1	1	2	0	6	1	21	2	0	2	2	.500	0	1	1.62
	4 Min. YEARS		159	6	0	82	229	1001	187	107	77	12	11	12	10	117	8	220	28	3	13	15	.464	0	25	3.03

Kenneth Coleman

Bats: Both **Throws:** Right **Pos:** 2B **Ht:** 5'10" **Wt:** 175 **Born:** 02/06/67 **Age:** 28

Year	Team	Lg	G	AB	H	2B	3B	HR	TB	R	RBI	TBB	IBB	SO	HBP	SH	SF	SB	CS	SB%	GDP	Avg	OBP	SLG
1989	Utica	A	27	90	16	0	0	0	16	16	4	14	0	17	1	0	1	9	2	.82	2	.178	.292	.178
	White Sox	R	22	76	33	6	2	0	43	23	13	13	0	7	3	1	1	18	6	.75	3	.434	.527	.566
1990	Sarasota	A	65	225	56	6	1	1	67	23	22	14	0	30	2	7	3	14	8	.64	3	.249	.295	.298
1991	South Bend	A	8	26	9	1	0	0	10	5	4	0	0	4	0	1	1	0	0	.00	0	.346	.333	.385
	Sarasota	A	44	118	33	6	1	1	44	15	15	20	0	21	1	0	2	5	3	.63	2	.280	.383	.373
1992	Sarasota	A	100	299	78	16	4	2	108	52	31	35	1	41	10	10	3	14	7	.67	7	.261	.354	.361
1993	Sarasota	A	11	32	6	0	0	0	6	4	2	6	0	4	0	0	1	1	1	.50	0	.188	.308	.188
	Birmingham	AA	50	129	30	3	0	0	33	11	14	13	0	25	1	3	2	2	1	.67	3	.233	.303	.256
1994	Nashville	AAA	5	16	5	2	1	1	12	5	3	3	0	1	1	0	0	0	0	.00	1	.313	.450	.750
	Birmingham	AA	75	188	36	6	2	3	55	30	25	37	0	38	5	4	3	4	4	.50	7	.191	.335	.293
	6 Min. YEARS		407	1199	302	46	11	8	394	184	133	155	1	188	24	26	17	67	32	.68	28	.252	.345	.329

Cris Colon

Bats: Both **Throws:** Right **Pos:** 3B-SS **Ht:** 6' 2" **Wt:** 180 **Born:** 01/03/69 **Age:** 26

Year	Team	Lg	G	AB	H	2B	3B	HR	TB	R	RBI	TBB	IBB	SO	HBP	SH	SF	SB	CS	SB%	GDP	Avg	OBP	SLG
1987	Rangers	R	46	136	35	3	0	0	38	12	9	3	0	17	0	2	1	2	0	1.00	1	.257	.271	.279
1988	Gastonia	A	75	232	46	12	0	1	61	23	11	12	0	46	0	4	0	6	2	.75	5	.198	.238	.263

Year	Team	Lg	G	AB	H	2B	3B	HR	TB	R	RBI	TBB	IBB	SO	HBP	SH	SF	SB	CS	SB%	GDP	Avg	OBP	SLG
	Butte	R	49	190	37	3	4	1	51	21	19			34	0	1	1	3	0	1.00	4	.195	.206	.268
1989	Gastonia	A	125	473	107	9	8	3	141	58	49	10	0	95	2	11	4	8	5	.62	6	.226	.243	.298
1990	Gastonia	A	38	140	45	2	4	4	67	23	16	4	1	24	1	4	0	7	1	.88	2	.321	.345	.479
	Tulsa	AA	65	234	57	9	1	3	77	24	29	5	1	37	1	3	2	5	4	.56	6	.244	.260	.329
1991	Charlotte	A	66	249	78	9	5	3	106	33	27	9	2	44	3	5	0	4	5	.44	7	.313	.345	.426
	Tulsa	AA	26	102	40	6	2	3	59	20	28	4	0	11	0	1	3	0	1	.00	4	.392	.404	.578
1992	Tulsa	AA	120	415	109	16	3	1	134	35	44	16	3	72	0	3	5	7	4	.64	4	.263	.287	.323
1993	Tulsa	AA	124	490	147	27	3	11	213	63	47	13	0	76	5	4	5	6	3	.67	13	.300	.322	.435
1994	Iowa	AAA	123	434	118	31	2	12	189	57	55	14	3	68	7	3	3	2	2	.50	6	.272	.303	.435
1992	Texas	AL	14	36	6	0	0	0	6	5	1	1	0	8	0	1	0	0	0	.00	2	.167	.189	.167
	8 Min. YEARS		857	3095	819	127	32	42	1136	365	334	93	10	524	19	41	24	50	27	.65	62	.265	.288	.367

Dennis Colon

Bats: Left Throws: Right Pos: 3B Ht: 5'10" Wt: 165 Born: 08/04/73 Age: 21

						BATTING												BASERUNNING				PERCENTAGES		
Year	Team	Lg	G	AB	H	2B	3B	HR	TB	R	RBI	TBB	IBB	SO	HBP	SH	SF	SB	CS	SB%	GDP	Avg	OBP	SLG
1992	Burlington	A	123	458	116	27	6	6	175	54	63	32	1	50	2	2	6	4	7	.36	9	.253	.301	.382
1993	Osceola	A	118	469	148	20	6	2	186	51	59	17	1	41	0	0	3	10	4	.71	12	.316	.337	.397
1994	Jackson	AA	118	380	105	17	6	5	149	37	52	18	5	43	0	4	5	8	5	.62	12	.276	.305	.392
	3 Min. YEARS		359	1307	369	64	19	13	510	142	174	67	7	134	2	6	14	22	16	.58	33	.282	.315	.390

Felix Colon

Bats: Right Throws: Right Pos: 2B Ht: 6'0" Wt: 176 Born: 09/15/70 Age: 24

						BATTING												BASERUNNING				PERCENTAGES		
Year	Team	Lg	G	AB	H	2B	3B	HR	TB	R	RBI	TBB	IBB	SO	HBP	SH	SF	SB	CS	SB%	GDP	Avg	OBP	SLG
1989	Red Sox	R	58	214	48	9	1	6	77	29	21	22	2	43	4	1	1	2	1	.67	4	.224	.307	.360
1990	Winter Havn	A	89	275	54	14	2	6	90	21	25	38	0	80	3	1	0	1	3	.25	7	.196	.301	.327
	Red Sox	R	29	108	30	11	0	1	44	22	22	16	1	21	2	0	2	0	0	.00	2	.278	.375	.407
1991	Elmira	A	63	205	51	8	0	12	95	32	41	32	1	56	3	0	1	0	2	.00	4	.249	.357	.463
1992	Winter Havn	A	97	339	83	14	3	5	118	33	40	36	2	75	5	0	1	1	1	.50	6	.245	.325	.348
1993	Lynchburg	A	97	319	102	22	0	16	172	52	58	45	0	65	1	2	7	0	1	.00	8	.320	.398	.539
1994	New Britain	AA	129	439	99	24	3	7	150	51	53	69	2	103	3	1	6	3	3	.50	5	.226	.331	.342
	6 Min. YEARS		562	1899	467	102	9	53	746	240	260	258	8	443	21	5	18	7	11	.39	35	.246	.340	.393

Pat Combs

Pitches: Left Bats: Left Pos: P Ht: 6'4" Wt: 200 Born: 10/29/66 Age: 28

				HOW MUCH HE PITCHED					WHAT HE GAVE UP									THE RESULTS				
Year	Team	Lg	G	GS	CG	GF	IP	BFP	H	R	ER	HR	SH	SF	HB	TBB	IBB	SO	WP	Bk	W	L	Pct.	ShO	Sv	ERA
1989	Clearwater	A	6	6	0	0	41.2	165	35	8	6	0	3	0	1	11	0	24	0	1	2	1	.667	0	0	1.30
	Reading	AA	19	19	4	0	125	512	104	57	47	16	6	2	4	40	2	77	5	2	8	7	.533	0	0	3.38
	Scr Wil-Bar	AAA	3	3	2	0	24.1	94	15	4	1	0	0	1	0	7	0	20	1	0	3	0	1.000	1	0	0.37
1991	Scranton/wb	AAA	6	6	1	0	27	132	39	23	20	0	2	3	0	16	0	14	1	0	2	2	.500	0	0	6.67
1992	Scranton/wb	AAA	21	21	1	0	124.2	526	123	62	50	9	10	5	0	41	0	77	3	1	5	7	.417	0	0	3.61
1993	Scranton/wb	AAA	15	15	1	0	83.2	372	97	57	45	8	4	2	4	27	1	60	7	0	0	9	.000	0	0	4.84
1994	Scranton-Wb	AAA	28	22	3	0	137.1	626	167	106	96	13	4	3	0	75	1	70	4	0	6	11	.353	0	0	6.29
1989	Philadelphia	NL	6	6	1	0	38.2	153	36	10	9	2	2	0	0	6	1	30	5	0	4	0	1.000	1	0	2.09
1990	Philadelphia	NL	32	31	3	0	183.1	800	179	90	83	12	7	7	4	86	7	108	9	1	10	10	.500	2	0	4.07
1991	Philadelphia	NL	14	13	1	0	64.1	300	64	41	35	7	1	2	2	43	1	41	7	0	2	6	.250	0	0	4.90
1992	Philadelphia	NL	4	4	0	0	18.2	88	20	16	16	0	3	1	0	12	0	11	1	0	1	1	.500	0	0	7.71
	5 Min. YEARS		98	92	12	0	563.2	2427	580	317	265	46	29	16	9	217	4	342	21	4	26	37	.413	1	0	4.23
	4 Maj. YEARS		56	54	5	0	305	1341	299	157	143	21	13	10	6	147	9	190	22	1	17	17	.500	3	0	4.22

Fidel Compres

Pitches: Right Bats: Right Pos: P Ht: 6'0" Wt: 165 Born: 05/10/65 Age: 30

				HOW MUCH HE PITCHED					WHAT HE GAVE UP									THE RESULTS				
Year	Team	Lg	G	GS	CG	GF	IP	BFP	H	R	ER	HR	SH	SF	HB	TBB	IBB	SO	WP	Bk	W	L	Pct.	ShO	Sv	ERA
1984	Batavia	A	2	0	0	0	2	16	5	5	5	2	0	1	0	5	0	0	0	0	0	0	.000	0	0	22.50
	Utica	A	6	6	1	0	29	134	30	24	19	6	1	3	0	20	0	18	3	1	2	2	.500	0	0	5.90
1985	Batavia	A	4	1	0	3	4	22	5	6	6	0	0	0	0	6	0	4	0	0	0	1	.000	0	0	13.50
1986	Batavia	A	18	2	0	7	39.2	187	50	29	18	5	2	1	4	17	0	34	4	0	2	5	.286	0	0	4.08
1987	Waterloo	A	21	6	0	3	63	269	60	29	26	5	0	2	1	23	0	56	8	2	3	2	.600	0	0	3.71
1988	Waterloo	A	29	3	0	13	67.1	297	69	41	33	4	1	2	1	31	3	65	4	1	5	5	.500	0	2	4.41
1989	Gastonia	A	8	0	0	4	19.2	77	12	4	2	1	0	0	2	5	0	13	0	0	0	1	.000	0	1	0.92
1990	Tulsa	AA	6	0	0	3	10.1	54	12	10	7	0	0	1	0	11	1	9	2	0	0	1	.000	0	0	6.10
	Charlotte	A	22	16	2	2	116.2	476	89	38	29	0	4	3	3	43	0	69	8	1	9	2	.818	0	1	2.24
1991	Arkansas	AA	27	0	0	26	32	143	37	17	14	2	1	5	0	12	3	18	2	0	4	2	.667	0	9	3.94
	Louisville	AAA	10	0	0	4	14.2	70	22	5	5	0	1	0	0	8	2	7	1	0	0	2	.000	0	0	3.07
1992	Arkansas	AA	54	0	0	49	57.2	251	55	26	21	3	2	2	2	23	3	39	1	0	4	3	.571	0	28	3.28
1993	Louisville	AAA	21	0	0	11	27.1	144	41	26	21	5	0	0	2	19	5	18	2	1	3	5	.375	0	0	6.91
	Las Vegas	AAA	24	0	0	9	26	118	33	16	16	1	3	3	2	10	1	7	2	0	1	1	.500	0	4	5.54
1994	Las Vegas	AAA	2	0	0	0	3	14	2	2	2	0	1	0	0	2	0	1	0	0	0	0	.000	0	0	6.00
	11 Min. YEARS		254	34	3	134	512.1	2272	522	278	224	34	16	23	17	235	18	358	39	6	33	32	.508	0	45	3.93

Brian Conroy

Pitches: Right Bats: Both Pos: P Ht: 6'2" Wt: 185 Born: 08/29/68 Age: 26

Year	Team	Lg	G	GS	CG	GF	IP	BFP	H	R	ER	HR	SH	SF	HB	TBB	IBB	SO	WP	Bk	W	L	Pct.	ShO	Sv	ERA
1989	Red Sox	R	7	7	2	0	44	174	33	15	11	0	0	1	2	9	0	31	2	3	4	2	.667	0	0	2.25
	Winter Havn	A	8	6	2	1	39.2	172	38	19	13	3	1	1	4	11	0	30	3	2	3	3	.500	2	0	2.95
1990	Lynchburg	A	26	26	8	0	186.1	769	160	84	73	13	3	4	7	51	0	147	11	6	10	12	.455	4	0	3.53
	New Britain	AA	1	1	0	0	6	24	7	4	4	1	1	0	0	1	1	3	0	0	0	1	.000	0	0	6.00
1991	New Britain	AA	10	10	1	0	65.2	274	51	27	22	6	2	4	4	26	2	34	3	0	1	5	.167	1	0	3.02
	Pawtucket	AAA	17	16	1	1	98.1	431	95	60	50	13	3	8	2	51	1	66	3	1	6	4	.600	0	0	4.58
1992	New Britain	AA	11	11	3	0	75.1	303	70	33	32	9	1	3	0	17	0	40	1	0	4	6	.400	1	0	3.82
	Pawtucket	AAA	15	13	1	1	85.2	375	91	49	44	17	0	1	2	31	2	57	2	1	7	5	.583	1	0	4.62
1993	Pawtucket	AAA	19	19	0	0	106	478	126	74	69	24	1	3	2	40	0	64	6	0	5	7	.417	0	0	5.86
1994	Pawtucket	AAA	11	11	0	0	57.1	247	65	40	37	13	3	2	2	15	0	22	0	0	5	3	.625	0	0	5.81
	Colo. Spmg	AAA	16	15	1	0	87.2	411	121	80	70	22	2	2	3	29	3	42	0	1	8	3	.727	0	0	7.19
	6 Min. YEARS		141	135	19	3	852	3658	857	485	425	121	17	29	28	281	9	536	31	14	53	51	.510	9	0	4.49

Andy Cook

Pitches: Right Bats: Right Pos: P Ht: 6'5" Wt: 205 Born: 08/30/67 Age: 27

Year	Team	Lg	G	GS	CG	GF	IP	BFP	H	R	ER	HR	SH	SF	HB	TBB	IBB	SO	WP	Bk	W	L	Pct.	ShO	Sv	ERA
1988	Oneonta	A	16	16	2	0	102	444	116	50	41	2	2	1	4	21	0	65	2	3	8	4	.667	0	0	3.62
1989	Pr William	A	25	24	5	0	153	621	123	68	56	7	4	2	6	49	0	83	6	7	8	12	.400	1	0	3.29
1990	Albany	AA	24	24	5	0	156.2	648	146	69	60	12	4	5	4	52	2	53	5	4	12	8	.600	0	0	3.45
1991	Albany	AA	14	14	1	0	82	360	94	46	36	2	0	3	0	27	0	46	1	0	6	3	.667	0	0	3.95
	Columbus	AAA	13	13	2	0	79.1	338	63	34	31	0	5	3	4	38	1	40	1	1	5	5	.500	0	0	3.52
1992	Columbus	AAA	32	9	0	7	99.2	411	85	41	35	8	5	1	3	36	0	58	3	0	7	5	.583	0	2	3.16
1993	Columbus	AAA	21	20	0	0	118.1	543	149	91	86	14	6	5	7	49	3	47	4	3	6	7	.462	0	0	6.54
1994	Salt Lake	AAA	3	3	0	0	14.2	69	17	14	11	2	1	0	1	4	0	7	1	0	0	2	.000	0	0	6.75
	Columbus	AAA	34	8	0	5	80	341	86	36	33	6	3	1	4	26	2	49	2	0	3	5	.375	0	0	3.71
1993	New York	AL	4	0	0	3	5.1	28	4	3	3	1	1	0	0	7	0	4	2	0	0	1	.000	0	0	5.06
	7 Min. YEARS		182	131	15	12	885.2	3775	879	449	389	53	30	21	33	302	8	448	25	18	55	51	.519	1	2	3.95

Mike Cook

Pitches: Right Bats: Right Pos: P Ht: 6'3" Wt: 215 Born: 08/14/63 Age: 31

Year	Team	Lg	G	GS	CG	GF	IP	BFP	H	R	ER	HR	SH	SF	HB	TBB	IBB	SO	WP	Bk	W	L	Pct.	ShO	Sv	ERA
1985	Quad City	A	2	2	0	0	10	44	6	3	2	0	0	0	1	7	0	10	1	0	0	0	.000	0	0	1.80
1986	Midland	AA	15	15	2	0	105.1	453	101	54	41	2	1	4	2	52	0	82	10	2	4	6	.400	0	0	3.50
	Edmonton	AAA	9	9	0	0	55.1	245	49	42	33	10	1	2	3	24	0	35	3	1	4	1	.800	0	0	5.37
1987	Edmonton	AAA	15	15	4	0	83.1	376	81	64	60	8	2	5	1	54	1	54	12	2	4	7	.364	2	0	6.48
1988	Edmonton	AAA	51	5	0	34	91	402	93	56	49	11	4	3	2	41	6	84	6	0	5	9	.357	0	10	4.85
1989	Portland	AAA	42	0	0	36	64	273	53	29	26	1	4	0	1	35	0	55	5	0	5	3	.625	0	12	3.66
1990	Portland	AAA	19	19	2	0	115.1	496	105	54	41	8	4	3	5	59	0	63	4	0	6	8	.429	1	0	3.20
1992	Louisville	AAA	43	0	0	8	58.2	259	58	31	30	5	1	2	1	31	4	56	3	1	3	2	.600	0	4	4.60
1993	Rochester	AAA	57	0	0	38	81.1	373	77	39	28	3	7	1	5	48	9	74	11	0	6	7	.462	0	13	3.10
1994	Rochester	AAA	4	0	0	1	8.2	40	9	3	3	0	0	1	1	5	1	5	1	0	0	1	.000	0	0	3.12
	Norfolk	AAA	49	0	0	43	57	242	57	17	13	0	2	3	0	20	3	59	5	0	2	6	.250	0	19	2.05
1986	California	AL	5	1	0	1	9	46	13	12	9	3	0	0	0	7	1	6	0	0	0	2	.000	0	0	9.00
1987	California	AL	16	1	0	6	34.1	148	34	21	21	7	1	0	0	18	0	27	3	1	1	2	.333	0	0	5.50
1988	California	AL	3	0	0	1	3.2	15	4	2	2	0	0	0	1	1	0	2	1	0	0	1	.000	0	0	4.91
1989	Minnesota	AL	15	0	0	5	21.1	102	22	12	12	1	0	2	1	17	1	15	0	0	0	1	.000	0	0	5.06
1993	Baltimore	AL	2	0	0	0	3	13	1	0	0	0	0	0	0	2	1	3	1	0	0	0	.000	0	0	0.00
	9 Min. YEARS		306	65	8	160	730	3203	689	392	326	48	26	24	22	376	24	577	61	6	39	50	.438	3	54	4.02
	5 Maj. YEARS		41	2	0	13	71.1	324	74	47	44	11	1	2	2	45	3	53	5	1	1	6	.143	0	0	5.55

Brent Cookson

Bats: Right Throws: Right Pos: OF Ht: 5'11" Wt: 200 Born: 09/07/69 Age: 25

Year	Team	Lg	G	AB	H	2B	3B	HR	TB	R	RBI	TBB	IBB	SO	HBP	SH	SF	SB	CS	SB%	GDP	Avg	OBP	SLG
1991	Sou Oregon	A	6	9	0	0	0	0	0	0	0	0	0	7	0	0	0	0	0	.00	0	.000	.000	.000
	Athletics	R	1	1	0	0	0	0	0	0	0	0	0	1	0	0	0	0	0	.00	0	.000	.000	.000
1992	Clinton	A	46	145	31	5	1	8	62	30	20	22	0	48	3	1	1	9	3	.75	4	.214	.327	.428
	San Jose	A	68	255	74	8	4	12	126	44	49	25	0	69	3	0	2	9	5	.64	8	.290	.358	.494
1993	San Jose	A	67	234	60	10	1	17	123	43	50	43	1	73	3	2	5	14	6	.70	5	.256	.372	.526
1994	Shreveport	AA	62	207	67	21	3	11	127	32	41	18	2	57	1	2	2	4	1	.80	4	.324	.377	.614
	Phoenix	AAA	14	43	12	0	1	1	17	7	6	5	0	14	1	0	0	0	1	.00	1	.279	.367	.395
	4 Min. YEARS		264	894	244	44	10	49	455	156	166	113	3	269	11	5	10	36	16	.69	23	.273	.358	.509

Ron Coomer

Bats: Right **Throws:** Right **Pos:** 3B **Ht:** 5'11" **Wt:** 195 **Born:** 11/18/66 **Age:** 28

					BATTING											BASERUNNING				PERCENTAGES		
Year	Team	Lg	G	AB	H	2B	3B	HR	TB	R	RBI	TBB	IBB	SO	HBP	SH	SF	SB	CS	SB%	GDP	Avg	OBP	SLG
1990	Huntsville	AA	66	194	43	7	0	3	59	22	27	21	1	40	1	4	3	3	1	.75	5	.222	.297	.304
1991	Birmingham	AA	137	505	129	27	5	13	205	81	76	59	1	78	1	6	8	0	3	.00	21	.255	.330	.406
1992	Vancouver	AAA	86	262	62	10	0	9	99	29	40	16	3	36	0	3	4	3	0	1.00	14	.237	.277	.378
1993	Birmingham	AA	69	262	85	18	0	13	142	44	50	15	3	43	0	0	2	1	1	.50	8	.324	.358	.542
	Nashville	AAA	59	211	66	19	0	13	124	34	51	10	1	29	1	0	3	1	2	.33	5	.313	.342	.588
1994	Albuquerque	AAA	127	535	181	34	6	22	293	89	123	26	4	62	2	0	7	4	3	.57	12	.338	.367	.548
	5 Min. YEARS		544	1969	566	115	11	73	922	299	367	147	13	288	5	13	27	12	10	.55	65	.287	.334	.468

Gary Cooper

Bats: Right **Throws:** Right **Pos:** 3B **Ht:** 6'1" **Wt:** 200 **Born:** 08/13/64 **Age:** 30

					BATTING											BASERUNNING				PERCENTAGES		
Year	Team	Lg	G	AB	H	2B	3B	HR	TB	R	RBI	TBB	IBB	SO	HBP	SH	SF	SB	CS	SB%	GDP	Avg	OBP	SLG
1986	Auburn	A	76	275	86	16	3	11	141	52	54	47	0	47	2	0	2	16	4	.80	5	.313	.414	.513
1987	Osceola	A	123	427	119	17	4	4	156	66	74	66	2	69	5	4	5	14	5	.74	12	.279	.378	.365
1988	Columbus	AA	140	474	128	25	7	7	188	65	69	87	0	87	4	4	7	13	7	.65	20	.270	.383	.397
1989	Tucson	AAA	118	376	102	23	3	1	134	51	50	48	2	69	4	1	5	5	7	.42	2	.271	.356	.356
1990	Osceola	A	8	26	4	4	0	0	8	4	2	3	0	3	1	0	1	0	0	.00	1	.154	.258	.308
	Columbus	AA	54	160	42	7	0	8	73	29	30	30	0	32	1	0	1	1	2	.33	5	.263	.380	.456
1991	Tucson	AAA	120	406	124	25	6	14	203	86	75	66	5	108	3	2	5	7	8	.47	11	.305	.402	.500
1992	Tucson	AAA	127	464	139	31	3	9	203	66	73	47	0	86	3	3	7	8	6	.57	12	.300	.363	.438
1993	Buffalo	AAA	102	349	94	27	2	16	173	66	63	52	2	88	4	4	3	2	3	.40	12	.269	.368	.496
1994	Indianapols	AAA	76	226	73	19	3	10	128	43	36	37	0	57	4	2	0	7	3	.70	6	.323	.427	.566
1991	Houston	NL	9	16	4	1	0	0	5	1	2	3	0	6	0	0	0	0	0	.00	0	.250	.368	.313
	9 Min. YEARS		944	3183	911	194	31	80	1407	528	526	483	11	646	31	20	36	73	45	.62	86	.286	.382	.442

Archie Corbin

Pitches: Right **Bats:** Right **Pos:** P **Ht:** 6'4" **Wt:** 190 **Born:** 12/30/67 **Age:** 27

			HOW MUCH HE PITCHED						WHAT HE GAVE UP										THE RESULTS					
Year	Team	Lg	G	GS	CG	GF	IP	BFP	H	R	ER	HR	SH	SF	HB	TBB	IBB	SO	WP	Bk	W	L	Pct.	ShO	Sv	ERA
1986	Kingsport	R	18	1	0	9	30.1	149	31	23	16	3	0	1	0	28	0	30	8	1	1	1	.500	0	0	4.75
1987	Kingsport	R	6	6	0	0	25.2	128	24	21	18	3	0	0	2	26	0	17	6	0	2	3	.400	0	0	6.31
1988	Kingsport	R	11	10	4	0	69.1	277	47	23	12	5	2	0	3	17	0	47	1	1	7	2	.778	1	0	1.56
1989	Columbia	A	27	23	4	3	153.2	664	149	86	77	16	4	4	5	72	0	130	2	0	9	9	.500	2	1	4.51
1990	St. Lucie	A	20	18	3	2	118	494	97	47	39	2	4	3	7	59	0	105	10	0	7	8	.467	0	0	2.97
1991	Memphis	AA	28	25	1	0	156.1	692	139	90	81	7	4	6	8	90	1	166	13	0	8	8	.500	0	0	4.66
1992	Memphis	AA	27	20	2	1	112.1	503	115	64	59	7	3	1	1	73	0	100	11	0	7	8	.467	0	0	4.73
	Harrisburg	AA	1	1	0	0	3	11	2	0	0	0	0	0	0	1	0	3	0	0	0	0	.000	0	0	0.00
1993	Harrisburg	AA	42	2	0	21	73.1	314	43	31	30	0	1	5	2	59	1	91	5	1	5	3	.625	0	4	3.68
1994	Buffalo	AAA	14	1	0	3	22.2	99	14	13	12	0	1	1	1	18	0	23	2	0	0	0	.000	0	0	4.76
1991	Kansas City	AL	2	0	0	2	2.1	12	3	1	1	0	0	0	0	2	0	1	0	1	0	0	.000	0	0	3.86
	9 Min. YEARS		194	107	14	39	764.2	3331	661	398	344	43	19	21	29	443	2	712	58	3	46	42	.523	3	5	4.05

Ted Corbin

Bats: Both **Throws:** Right **Pos:** SS **Ht:** 5'9" **Wt:** 150 **Born:** 04/27/71 **Age:** 24

					BATTING											BASERUNNING				PERCENTAGES		
Year	Team	Lg	G	AB	H	2B	3B	HR	TB	R	RBI	TBB	IBB	SO	HBP	SH	SF	SB	CS	SB%	GDP	Avg	OBP	SLG
1992	Miracle	A	62	179	36	5	0	0	41	18	11	16	0	30	5	5	1	1	3	.25	3	.201	.284	.229
1993	Ft.Myers	A	91	339	80	11	2	0	95	46	22	36	0	47	8	5	3	22	8	.73	9	.236	.321	.280
	Nashville	AA	5	15	5	1	0	0	6	2	1	2	0	2	0	0	0	0	0	.00	0	.333	.412	.400
1994	Salt Lake	AAA	4	10	1	0	0	0	1	0	0	0	0	1	0	0	0	0	0	.00	0	.100	.100	.100
	Nashville	AA	51	152	32	2	0	0	34	13	13	10	1	26	0	1	1	0	2	.00	3	.211	.258	.224
	3 Min. YEARS		213	695	154	19	2	0	177	79	47	64	1	106	13	11	5	23	13	.64	16	.222	.297	.255

Marty Cordova

Bats: Right **Throws:** Right **Pos:** OF **Ht:** 6'0" **Wt:** 190 **Born:** 07/10/69 **Age:** 25

					BATTING											BASERUNNING				PERCENTAGES		
Year	Team	Lg	G	AB	H	2B	3B	HR	TB	R	RBI	TBB	IBB	SO	HBP	SH	SF	SB	CS	SB%	GDP	Avg	OBP	SLG
1989	Elizabethtn	R	38	148	42	2	3	8	74	32	29	14	1	29	3	0	0	2	1	.67	7	.284	.358	.500
1990	Kenosha	A	81	269	58	7	5	7	96	35	25	28	0	73	5	0	1	6	3	.67	5	.216	.300	.357
1991	Visalia	A	71	189	40	6	1	7	69	31	19	17	0	46	2	2	0	2	3	.40	3	.212	.284	.365
1992	Visalia	A	134	513	175	31	6	28	302	103	131	76	5	99	9	3	5	13	5	.72	20	.341	.431	.589
1993	Nashville	AA	138	508	127	30	5	19	224	83	77	64	3	153	13	0	3	10	5	.67	10	.250	.347	.441
1994	Salt Lake	AAA	103	385	138	25	4	19	228	69	66	39	0	63	8	0	2	17	6	.74	9	.358	.426	.592
	6 Min. YEARS		565	2012	580	101	24	88	993	353	347	238	9	463	40	5	11	50	23	.68	54	.288	.373	.494

55

Reid Cornelius

Pitches: Right Bats: Right Pos: P Ht: 6'0" Wt: 190 Born: 06/02/70 Age: 25

Year	Team	Lg	G	GS	CG	GF	IP	BFP	H	R	ER	HR	SH	SF	HB	TBB	IBB	SO	WP	Bk	W	L	Pct.	ShO	Sv	ERA
1989	Rockford	A	17	17	0	0	84.1	391	71	58	40	1	3	3	11	63	0	66	13	3	5	6	.455	0	0	4.27
1990	Wst Plm Bch	A	11	11	0	0	56	245	54	25	21	1	0	4	5	25	0	47	3	3	2	3	.400	0	0	3.38
1991	Wst Plm Bch	A	17	17	0	0	109.1	449	79	31	29	3	9	4	7	43	1	81	3	6	8	3	.727	0	0	2.39
	Harrisburg	AA	3	3	1	0	18.2	76	15	6	6	3	0	0	2	7	0	12	0	0	2	1	.667	1	0	2.89
1992	Harrisburg	AA	4	4	0	0	23	92	11	8	8	0	2	0	6	8	0	17	1	0	1	0	1.000	0	0	3.13
1993	Harrisburg	AA	27	27	1	0	157.2	698	146	95	73	10	3	5	13	82	1	119	8	0	10	7	.588	0	0	4.17
1994	Ottawa	AAA	25	24	1	1	148	661	149	89	72	18	1	4	8	75	2	87	10	0	9	8	.529	0	0	4.38
	6 Min. YEARS		104	103	3	1	597	2612	525	312	249	41	18	20	52	303	4	429	38	12	37	28	.569	1	0	3.75

John Corona

Pitches: Left Bats: Left Pos: P Ht: 6'0" Wt: 185 Born: 05/28/69 Age: 26

Year	Team	Lg	G	GS	CG	GF	IP	BFP	H	R	ER	HR	SH	SF	HB	TBB	IBB	SO	WP	Bk	W	L	Pct.	ShO	Sv	ERA
1989	Cardinals	R	28	0	0	18	38.1	181	48	25	22	1	3	1	1	14	4	31	0	0	0	1	.000	0	5	5.17
1990	Springfield	A	54	0	0	16	68	294	68	36	28	6	4	2	2	29	4	58	7	0	5	1	.833	0	3	3.71
1991	St. Pete	A	15	0	0	6	18.2	79	17	8	6	0	2	1	1	8	1	12	1	2	2	1	.667	0	0	2.89
	Louisville	AAA	12	0	0	3	16.2	77	18	12	10	2	0	1	0	11	1	19	2	0	0	1	.000	0	0	5.40
	Arkansas	AA	27	0	0	17	30.1	130	27	15	15	0	1	1	0	21	3	23	3	1	0	2	.000	0	1	4.45
1993	St.Pete	A	59	0	0	35	60.2	251	52	26	19	3	1	1	1	22	4	51	1	0	3	4	.429	0	16	2.82
1994	Arkansas	AA	33	0	0	11	40.1	181	41	19	13	4	3	0	2	23	3	37	4	1	3	1	.750	0	0	2.90
	5 Min. YEARS		228	0	0	106	273	1193	271	141	113	16	14	7	7	128	20	231	18	4	13	11	.542	0	22	3.73

Erick Corps

Bats: Both Throws: Right Pos: SS Ht: 6'0" Wt: 155 Born: 09/06/74 Age: 20

Year	Team	Lg	G	AB	H	2B	3B	HR	TB	R	RBI	TBB	IBB	SO	HBP	SH	SF	SB	CS	SB%	GDP	Avg	OBP	SLG
1992	Padres	R	36	126	27	3	0	0	30	19	4	20	0	20	4	1	1	10	2	.83	0	.214	.338	.238
1993	Spokane	A	4	7	0	0	0	0	0	1	1	0	0	3	0	0	0	0	0	.00	0	.000	.000	.000
	Padres	R	43	153	43	8	4	0	59	28	18	33	0	23	1	1	0	4	6	.40	3	.281	.412	.386
1994	Wichita	AA	4	16	4	1	0	0	5	0	1	2	0	2	0	0	0	1	2	.33	1	.250	.333	.313
	Springfield	A	94	243	62	7	1	1	74	36	32	37	0	51	5	1	2	2	6	.25	7	.255	.362	.305
	3 Min. YEARS		181	545	136	19	5	1	168	84	56	92	0	99	10	3	3	17	16	.52	11	.250	.366	.308

Miguel Correa

Bats: Both Throws: Right Pos: OF Ht: 6'2" Wt: 165 Born: 09/10/71 Age: 23

Year	Team	Lg	G	AB	H	2B	3B	HR	TB	R	RBI	TBB	IBB	SO	HBP	SH	SF	SB	CS	SB%	GDP	Avg	OBP	SLG
1990	Braves	R	33	109	26	6	0	0	32	19	10	6	1	20	0	3	2	10	4	.71	1	.239	.274	.294
1991	Braves	R	47	171	43	8	2	0	55	21	6	7	0	29	1	2	0	10	6	.63	2	.251	.285	.322
1992	Idaho Falls	R	66	266	79	7	5	3	105	43	28	14	0	49	4	0	0	14	10	.58	2	.297	.342	.395
1993	Macon	A	131	495	131	26	8	10	203	58	61	30	5	84	4	2	5	18	17	.51	6	.265	.309	.410
1994	Greenville	AA	38	124	25	2	0	0	27	11	6	6	2	22	1	6	0	4	4	.50	0	.202	.244	.218
	Durham	A	83	290	64	12	4	8	108	43	19	18	0	53	2	2	0	12	7	.63	3	.221	.271	.372
	5 Min. YEARS		398	1455	368	61	19	21	530	195	130	81	8	257	12	15	7	68	48	.59	14	.253	.296	.364

Ramser Correa

Pitches: Right Bats: Right Pos: P Ht: 6'5" Wt: 225 Born: 11/13/70 Age: 24

Year	Team	Lg	G	GS	CG	GF	IP	BFP	H	R	ER	HR	SH	SF	HB	TBB	IBB	SO	WP	Bk	W	L	Pct.	ShO	Sv	ERA
1987	Helena	R	3	2	0	0	6	38	10	12	11	1	1	1	0	8	0	0	1	0	0	1	.000	0	0	16.50
1988	Helena	R	13	7	0	2	43.1	187	38	22	19	2	0	2	0	24	0	34	4	4	2	2	.500	0	0	3.95
1989	Helena	R	2	1	0	1	9	14	3	0	0	0	0	0	0	2	0	2	1	0	0	0	.000	0	0	0.00
1990	Beloit	A	4	4	0	0	24.2	105	24	8	6	1	0	0	0	9	0	30	1	0	3	0	1.000	0	0	2.19
1991	Stockton	A	10	8	0	0	33.2	147	31	14	11	1	1	1	2	20	0	21	2	0	2	1	.667	0	0	2.94
1992	Stockton	A	35	4	0	9	70.1	309	71	31	28	2	3	3	2	38	2	55	5	1	3	2	.600	0	1	3.58
1993	Stockton	A	21	10	0	6	67.2	304	78	38	34	2	1	5	1	30	1	32	2	1	4	3	.571	0	3	4.52
	El Paso	AA	5	1	0	2	10.2	57	15	15	6	2	1	5	0	7	1	5	2	0	1	0	1.000	0	0	5.06
1994	Kinston	A	4	4	0	0	18.1	87	14	11	9	3	0	0	0	19	0	17	1	1	2	1	.667	0	0	4.42
	Canton-Akrn	AA	19	8	0	5	67.1	310	72	41	32	6	0	2	0	51	3	41	6	0	2	4	.333	0	0	4.28
	8 Min. YEARS		116	49	0	25	345	1558	356	192	156	20	7	19	5	208	7	237	25	7	19	14	.576	0	4	4.07

Jim Corsi

Pitches: Right Bats: Right Pos: P Ht: 6'1" Wt: 220 Born: 09/09/61 Age: 33

Year	Team	Lg	G	GS	CG	GF	IP	BFP	H	R	ER	HR	SH	SF	HB	TBB	IBB	SO	WP	Bk	W	L	Pct.	ShO	Sv	ERA
1985	Greensboro	A	41	2	1	36	78.2	363	94	49	37	1	4	3	4	23	3	84	4	0	5	8	.385	0	9	4.23
1986	New Britain	AA	29	0	0	19	51.1	220	52	13	13	2	6	0	1	20	5	38	2	0	2	3	.400	0	3	2.28
1987	Modesto	A	19	0	0	10	30	121	23	16	12	1	1	1	0	10	1	45	4	0	3	1	.750	0	6	3.60
	Huntsville	AA	28	0	0	18	48	182	30	17	15	1	2	0	0	15	1	33	5	0	8	1	.889	0	4	2.81

Year	Team	Lg	G	GS	CG	GF	IP	BFP	H	R	ER	HR	SH	SF	HB	TBB	IBB	SO	WP	Bk	W	L	Pct.	ShO	Sv	ERA
1988	Tacoma	AAA	50	0	0	45	59	247	60	25	18	2	4	1	1	23	10	48	5	2	2	5	.286	0	16	2.75
1989	Tacoma	AAA	23	0	0	18	28.1	131	40	17	13	1	2	0	1	9	4	23	2	1	2	3	.400	0	8	4.13
1990	Tacoma	AAA	5	0	0	2	6	26	9	2	1	0	0	0	0	1	0	3	2	0	0	0	.000	0	0	1.50
1991	Tucson	AAA	2	0	0	2	3	11	2	0	0	0	0	0	0	0	0	4	0	0	0	0	.000	0	0	0.00
1992	Tacoma	AAA	26	0	0	22	29.1	121	22	8	4	0	2	2	1	10	3	21	2	1	0	0	.000	0	12	1.23
1993	High Desert	A	3	3	0	0	9	38	11	3	3	1	0	0	0	2	0	6	0	0	0	1	.000	0	0	3.00
1994	Brevard Cty	A	6	0	0	2	11	43	8	3	2	0	0	0	0	0	0	11	0	0	0	1	.000	0	0	1.64
	Edmonton	AAA	15	0	0	0	22	103	29	15	11	1	2	0	0	10	0	15	0	0	0	1	.000	0	0	4.50
1988	Oakland	AL	11	1	0	7	21.1	89	20	10	9	1	3	3	0	6	1	10	1	1	0	1	.000	0	0	3.80
1989	Oakland	AL	22	0	0	14	38.1	149	26	8	8	2	2	2	1	10	0	21	0	0	1	2	.333	0	0	1.88
1991	Houston	NL	47	0	0	15	77.2	322	76	37	32	6	3	3	2	23	5	53	1	1	0	5	.000	0	0	3.71
1992	Oakland	AL	32	0	0	16	44	185	44	12	7	2	4	2	0	18	2	19	0	0	4	2	.667	0	0	1.43
1993	Florida	NL	15	0	0	6	20.1	97	28	15	15	1	3	1	0	10	3	7	0	0	0	2	.000	0	0	6.64
	10 Min. YEARS		247	5	1	175	375.2	1606	380	168	129	10	23	6	9	123	27	331	26	4	22	24	.478	0	58	3.09
	5 Maj. YEARS		127	1	0	58	201.2	842	194	82	71	12	15	10	1	67	11	110	2	2	5	12	.294	0	0	3.17

Pitches: Right Bats: Right Pos: P

Fred Costello

Ht: 6'4" Wt: 190 Born: 10/01/66 Age: 28

			HOW MUCH HE PITCHED						WHAT HE GAVE UP												THE RESULTS					
Year	Team	Lg	G	GS	CG	GF	IP	BFP	H	R	ER	HR	SH	SF	HB	TBB	IBB	SO	WP	Bk	W	L	Pct.	ShO	Sv	ERA
1986	Astros	R	14	12	1	0	66.1	301	74	42	35	1	2	1	6	26	0	51	1	0	4	5	.444	1	0	4.75
1987	Astros	R	13	12	0	1	72.2	320	74	40	26	1	2	2	1	28	1	45	9	0	5	7	.417	0	0	3.22
1988	Asheville	A	51	0	0	37	76	329	76	34	30	5	9	1	3	31	2	65	2	1	6	7	.462	0	11	3.55
1989	Columbus	AA	30	0	0	17	54	220	39	22	20	5	1	1	0	21	1	39	5	0	4	5	.444	0	3	3.33
1990	Columbus	AA	35	5	0	20	45.1	214	54	31	21	4	3	1	1	23	3	39	6	2	0	5	.000	0	7	4.17
1991	Osceola	A	5	0	0	2	6	29	8	5	5	2	0	1	0	3	0	5	0	0	1	0	1.000	0	0	7.50
1992	Osceola	A	10	0	0	2	13.1	57	14	7	4	0	2	0	0	2	0	10	0	0	1	2	.333	0	1	2.70
	Jackson	AA	36	0	0	10	53.1	215	51	22	16	3	1	2	0	13	3	35	2	0	2	2	.500	0	0	2.70
1993	Jackson	AA	12	12	0	0	60.2	248	57	24	19	2	4	1	3	13	0	45	1	1	8	3	.727	0	0	2.82
	Tucson	AAA	14	14	0	0	83	370	92	42	34	6	2	2	6	33	1	36	1	0	6	2	.750	0	0	3.69
1994	Phoenix	AAA	34	14	0	10	113.2	512	141	80	67	10	5	5	4	39	2	52	7	1	7	10	.412	0	2	5.30
	9 Min. YEARS		254	69	1	99	644.1	2815	680	349	277	39	31	17	24	232	13	422	34	5	44	48	.478	1	24	3.87

Bats: Right Throws: Right Pos: 1B

Tim Costo

Ht: 6'5" Wt: 230 Born: 02/16/69 Age: 26

			BATTING														BASERUNNING				PERCENTAGES		
Year	Team	Lg	G	AB	H	2B	3B	HR	TB	R	RBI	TBB	IBB	SO	HBP	SH	SF	SB	CS	SB%	GDP	Avg	OBP	SLG
1990	Kinston	A	56	206	65	13	1	4	92	34	42	23	0	47	6	0	8	4	0	1.00	3	.316	.387	.447
1991	Canton-Akrn	AA	52	192	52	10	3	1	71	28	24	15	0	44	0	0	6	2	1	.67	10	.271	.315	.370
	Chattanooga	AA	85	293	82	19	3	5	122	31	29	20	0	65	4	0	2	11	4	.73	5	.280	.332	.416
1992	Chattanooga	AA	121	424	102	18	2	28	208	63	71	48	1	128	11	1	2	4	5	.44	10	.241	.332	.491
1993	Indianapols	AAA	106	362	118	30	2	11	185	49	57	22	1	60	5	1	1	3	2	.60	5	.326	.372	.511
1994	Indianapols	AAA	19	36	7	3	0	0	10	6	5	6	0	4	1	1	0	0	0	.00	0	.194	.326	.278
1992	Cincinnati	NL	12	36	8	2	0	0	10	3	2	5	0	6	0	0	1	0	0	.00	4	.222	.310	.278
1993	Cincinnati	NL	31	98	22	5	0	3	36	13	12	4	0	17	0	0	2	0	0	.00	1	.224	.250	.367
	5 Min. YEARS		439	1513	426	93	11	49	688	211	228	134	2	348	27	3	19	24	12	.67	33	.282	.347	.455
	2 Maj. YEARS		43	134	30	7	0	3	46	16	14	9	0	23	0	0	3	0	0	.00	5	.224	.267	.343

Bats: Left Throws: Right Pos: 2B

John Cotton

Ht: 5'11" Wt: 170 Born: 10/30/70 Age: 24

			BATTING														BASERUNNING				PERCENTAGES		
Year	Team	Lg	G	AB	H	2B	3B	HR	TB	R	RBI	TBB	IBB	SO	HBP	SH	SF	SB	CS	SB%	GDP	Avg	OBP	SLG
1989	Burlington	R	64	227	47	5	1	2	60	36	22	22	0	56	3	4	1	20	3	.87	5	.207	.285	.264
1990	Watertown	A	73	286	60	9	4	2	83	53	27	40	3	71	2	2	1	24	7	.77	4	.210	.310	.290
1991	Columbus	A	122	405	92	11	9	13	160	88	42	93	1	135	3	3	3	56	15	.79	5	.227	.373	.395
1992	Kinston	A	103	360	90	7	3	11	118	67	39	48	1	106	2	1	2	23	7	.77	5	.200	.296	.328
1993	Kinston	A	127	454	120	16	3	13	181	81	51	59	1	130	11	5	2	28	24	.54	3	.264	.361	.399
1994	Springfield	A	24	82	19	5	3	1	33	14	8	12	0	19	0	0	0	7	1	.88	0	.232	.330	.402
	Wichita	AA	34	85	16	4	0	3	29	9	14	13	3	20	1	0	2	2	0	1.00	3	.188	.297	.341
	Rancho Cuca	A	48	171	35	3	2	4	54	35	19	22	0	48	2	0	0	9	3	.75	3	.205	.303	.316
	6 Min. YEARS		595	2070	461	60	25	49	718	383	222	309	9	585	24	15	11	169	60	.74	27	.223	.329	.347

Bats: Left Throws: Left Pos: OF

Kevin Coughlin

Ht: 6'0" Wt: 175 Born: 09/07/70 Age: 24

			BATTING														BASERUNNING				PERCENTAGES		
Year	Team	Lg	G	AB	H	2B	3B	HR	TB	R	RBI	TBB	IBB	SO	HBP	SH	SF	SB	CS	SB%	GDP	Avg	OBP	SLG
1989	White Sox	R	24	74	19	2	0	0	21	11	13	12	0	8	0	0	0	9	2	.82	1	.257	.360	.284
1990	Utica	A	68	215	59	6	3	0	71	37	16	27	2	41	0	3	2	17	8	.68	4	.274	.352	.330
1991	South Bend	A	131	431	131	12	2	0	147	60	38	62	3	67	2	19	3	19	17	.53	6	.304	.392	.341
1992	White Sox	R	4	15	5	0	0	0	5	1	2	2	0	1	0	0	0	0	0	.00	0	.333	.412	.333
	Sarasota	A	81	291	79	7	1	1	91	39	28	22	1	51	2	8	1	14	4	.78	5	.271	.326	.313
1993	Sarasota	A	112	415	128	19	2	2	157	53	32	42	5	51	0	4	2	4	4	.50	9	.308	.370	.378
	Nashville	AAA	2	7	4	1	0	0	5	0	3	0	0	1	0	0	0	0	0	.00	0	.571	.571	.714

Year Team	Lg	G	AB	H	2B	3B	HR	TB	R	RBI	TBB	IBB	SO	HBP	SH	SF	SB	CS	SB%	GDP	Avg	OBP	SLG
1994 Birmingham	AA	112	369	95	10	0	0	105	51	26	40	3	42	3	4	4	5	8	.38	9	.257	.332	.285
6 Min. YEARS		534	1817	520	57	8	3	602	252	158	207	14	262	7	38	12	68	43	.61	32	.286	.359	.331

Craig Counsell

Bats: Left Throws: Right Pos: SS Ht: 6'0" Wt: 177 Born: 08/21/70 Age: 24

| | | | | | | BATTING | | | | | | | | | | | | BASERUNNING | | | | PERCENTAGES | | |
Year Team	Lg	G	AB	H	2B	3B	HR	TB	R	RBI	TBB	IBB	SO	HBP	SH	SF	SB	CS	SB%	GDP	Avg	OBP	SLG
1992 Bend	A	18	61	15	6	1	0	23	11	8	9	1	10	1	1	0	1	2	.33	2	.246	.352	.377
1993 Central Val	A	131	471	132	26	3	5	179	79	59	95	1	68	3	5	4	14	8	.64	8	.280	.401	.380
1994 New Haven	AA	83	300	84	20	1	5	121	47	37	37	4	32	5	1	2	4	1	.80	6	.280	.366	.403
3 Min. YEARS		232	832	231	52	5	10	323	137	104	141	6	110	9	7	6	19	11	.63	16	.278	.386	.388

John Courtright

Pitches: Left Bats: Left Pos: P Ht: 6'2" Wt: 185 Born: 05/30/70 Age: 25

| | | | HOW MUCH HE PITCHED | | | | | WHAT HE GAVE UP | | | | | | | | | | THE RESULTS | | | | | |
Year Team	Lg	G	GS	CG	GF	IP	BFP	H	R	ER	HR	SH	SF	HB	TBB	IBB	SO	WP	Bk	W	L	Pct.	ShO	Sv	ERA
1991 Billings	R	1	1	0	0	6	21	2	0	0	0	0	0	0	1	0	4	0	1	1	0	1.000	0	0	0.00
1992 Chston-Vw	A	27	26	1	0	173	688	147	64	48	5	5	4	7	55	2	147	9	5	10	5	.667	1	0	2.50
1993 Chattanooga	AA	27	27	1	0	175	752	179	81	68	5	8	11	8	70	6	96	5	2	5	11	.313	0	0	3.50
1994 Chattanooga	AA	4	4	0	0	21.2	95	19	16	13	2	2	1	1	14	0	12	1	0	1	2	.333	0	0	5.40
Indianapols	AAA	24	23	2	0	142	595	144	61	56	9	8	1	4	46	3	73	2	1	9	10	.474	2	0	3.55
4 Min. YEARS		83	81	4	0	517.2	2151	491	222	185	21	23	17	20	186	11	332	17	9	26	28	.481	3	0	3.22

Darron Cox

Bats: Right Throws: Right Pos: C Ht: 6'1" Wt: 210 Born: 11/21/67 Age: 27

| | | | | | | BATTING | | | | | | | | | | | | BASERUNNING | | | | PERCENTAGES | | |
Year Team	Lg	G	AB	H	2B	3B	HR	TB	R	RBI	TBB	IBB	SO	HBP	SH	SF	SB	CS	SB%	GDP	Avg	OBP	SLG
1989 Billings	R	49	157	43	6	0	0	49	20	18	21	0	34	5	2	0	11	3	.79	1	.274	.377	.312
1990 Chston-Wv	A	103	367	93	11	3	1	113	53	44	40	2	75	7	4	3	14	3	.82	12	.253	.336	.308
1991 Cedar Rapds	A	21	60	16	4	0	0	20	12	4	8	0	11	4	1	0	7	1	.88	2	.267	.389	.333
Chattanooga	AA	13	38	7	1	0	0	8	2	3	2	0	9	0	1	1	0	0	.00	1	.184	.220	.211
Chston-Wv	A	79	294	71	14	1	2	93	37	28	24	0	40	2	1	7	8	4	.67	7	.241	.297	.316
1992 Chattanooga	AA	98	331	84	19	1	1	108	29	38	15	0	63	5	1	6	8	3	.73	7	.254	.291	.326
1993 Chattanooga	AA	89	300	65	9	5	3	93	35	26	38	2	63	3	7	1	7	4	.64	7	.217	.310	.310
1994 Iowa	AAA	99	301	80	15	1	3	106	35	26	28	4	47	4	3	0	5	2	.71	12	.266	.336	.352
6 Min. YEARS		551	1848	459	79	11	10	590	223	187	176	8	342	30	20	18	60	20	.75	49	.248	.321	.319

Tim Crabtree

Pitches: Right Bats: Right Pos: P Ht: 6'4" Wt: 205 Born: 10/13/69 Age: 25

| | | | HOW MUCH HE PITCHED | | | | | WHAT HE GAVE UP | | | | | | | | | | THE RESULTS | | | | | |
Year Team	Lg	G	GS	CG	GF	IP	BFP	H	R	ER	HR	SH	SF	HB	TBB	IBB	SO	WP	Bk	W	L	Pct.	ShO	Sv	ERA
1992 St.Cathmes	A	12	12	2	0	69	279	45	19	12	1	1	0	7	22	0	47	6	0	6	3	.667	0	0	1.57
Knoxville	AA	3	3	1	0	19	78	14	8	2	0	1	0	2	4	0	13	0	0	0	2	.000	0	0	0.95
1993 Knoxville	AA	27	27	2	0	158.2	707	178	93	72	11	10	7	10	59	0	67	7	3	9	14	.391	2	0	4.08
1994 Syracuse	AAA	51	9	0	15	108	474	125	58	50	5	4	2	2	49	6	58	4	0	2	6	.250	0	2	4.17
3 Min. YEARS		93	51	5	15	354.2	1538	362	178	136	17	16	9	21	134	6	185	17	3	17	25	.405	2	2	3.45

Jay Cranford

Bats: Right Throws: Right Pos: 3B Ht: 6'3" Wt: 175 Born: 04/07/71 Age: 24

| | | | | | | BATTING | | | | | | | | | | | | BASERUNNING | | | | PERCENTAGES | | |
Year Team	Lg	G	AB	H	2B	3B	HR	TB	R	RBI	TBB	IBB	SO	HBP	SH	SF	SB	CS	SB%	GDP	Avg	OBP	SLG
1992 Welland	A	60	223	57	9	6	0	78	22	27	14	1	58	0	0	2	7	7	.50	0	.256	.297	.350
1993 Augusta	A	128	469	125	31	0	6	174	55	72	32	0	101	6	3	9	17	2	.89	6	.267	.316	.371
1994 Salem	A	110	417	110	27	4	13	184	66	53	23	0	97	6	0	3	6	6	.50	8	.264	.310	.441
Carolina	AA	17	59	11	3	0	0	14	9	5	6	1	15	1	1	2	0	0	.00	1	.186	.265	.237
3 Min. YEARS		315	1168	303	70	10	19	450	152	157	75	2	271	13	4	16	30	15	.67	15	.259	.307	.385

Carlos Crawford

Pitches: Right Bats: Right Pos: P Ht: 6'1" Wt: 185 Born: 10/04/71 Age: 23

| | | | HOW MUCH HE PITCHED | | | | | WHAT HE GAVE UP | | | | | | | | | | THE RESULTS | | | | | |
Year Team	Lg	G	GS	CG	GF	IP	BFP	H	R	ER	HR	SH	SF	HB	TBB	IBB	SO	WP	Bk	W	L	Pct.	ShO	Sv	ERA
1990 Indians	R	10	9	0	0	53.2	257	68	43	26	0	0	2	8	25	0	39	6	4	2	3	.400	0	0	4.36
1991 Burlington	R	13	13	2	0	80.1	325	62	28	22	3	2	2	9	14	0	80	6	3	6	3	.667	1	0	2.46
1992 Columbus	A	28	28	6	0	188.1	805	167	78	61	7	5	4	12	85	4	127	3	2	10	11	.476	3	0	2.92
1993 Kinston	A	28	28	4	0	165	703	158	87	67	11	10	4	10	46	0	124	8	4	7	9	.438	1	0	3.65
1994 Canton-Akm	AA	26	25	3	0	175	734	164	83	67	15	3	7	6	59	2	99	8	2	12	6	.667	0	0	3.45
5 Min. YEARS		105	103	15	0	662.1	2824	619	319	243	36	20	19	45	229	6	469	31	15	37	32	.536	5	0	3.30

Joe Crawford

Pitches: Left Bats: Left Pos: P Ht: 6'4" Wt: 215 Born: 05/02/70 Age: 25

| | | | HOW MUCH HE PITCHED | | | | | WHAT HE GAVE UP | | | | | | | | | | THE RESULTS | | | | | |
Year Team	Lg	G	GS	CG	GF	IP	BFP	H	R	ER	HR	SH	SF	HB	TBB	IBB	SO	WP	Bk	W	L	Pct.	ShO	Sv	ERA
1991 Kingsport	R	19	0		16	32.1	118	16	5	4	0	0	0	1	8	0	43	3	1	0	0	.000	0	11	1.11

Year	Team	Lg	G	GS	CG	GF	IP	BFP	H	R	ER	HR	SH	SF	HB	TBB	IBB	SO	WP	Bk	W	L	Pct.	ShO	Sv	ERA
	Columbia	A	3	0	0	2	3	9	29	0	0	0	0	0	0	0	0	6	0	0	0	0	.000	0	0	0.00
1992	St.Lucie	A	25	1	0	16	43.2	174	29	18	10	1	1	3	0	15	3	32	1	3	3	3	.500	0	3	2.06
1993	St.Lucie	A	34	0	0	19	37	156	38	15	15	0	2	0	2	14	5	24	0	0	3	3	.500	0	0	3.65
1994	St.Lucie	A	33	0	0	15	42.2	155	22	8	7	1	1	2	2	9	2	31	1	0	1	1	.500	0	5	1.48
	Binghamton	AA	13	0	0	6	14.2	70	20	10	9	2	0	2	0	8	0	9	0	0	1	0	1.000	0	5	5.52
	4 Min. YEARS		127	1	0	74	173.1	682	125	56	45	4	4	7	5	54	10	145	5	4	8	7	.533	0	24	2.34

Doug Creek

Pitches: Left Bats: Left Pos: P Ht: 5'10" Wt: 205 Born: 03/01/69 Age: 26

			HOW MUCH HE PITCHED						WHAT HE GAVE UP										WP	Bk	THE RESULTS					
Year	Team	Lg	G	GS	CG	GF	IP	BFP	H	R	ER	HR	SH	SF	HB	TBB	IBB	SO	WP	Bk	W	L	Pct.	ShO	Sv	ERA
1991	Hamilton	A	9	5	0	1	38.2	169	39	22	22	2	0	3	3	18	0	45	3	0	3	2	.600	0	1	5.12
	Savannah	A	5	5	0	1	28.1	117	24	14	14	2	0	1	1	17	0	32	1	0	2	1	.667	0	0	4.45
1992	Springfield	A	6	6	0	0	38.1	155	32	11	11	4	1	0	0	13	1	43	0	1	4	1	.800	0	0	2.58
	St. Pete	A	13	13	0	0	73.1	300	57	31	23	5	0	4	1	37	1	63	4	1	5	4	.556	0	0	2.82
1993	Arkansas	AA	25	25	1	0	147.2	620	142	75	66	15	5	5	3	48	1	128	10	1	11	10	.524	1	0	4.02
	Louisville	AAA	2	2	0	0	14	60	10	5	5	0	2	0	1	9	0	9	2	0	0	0	.000	0	0	3.21
1994	Louisville	AAA	7	7	0	0	26.1	132	37	26	25	2	0	2	1	23	0	16	2	1	1	4	.200	0	0	8.54
	Arkansas	AA	17	17	1	0	92	405	96	54	45	8	11	4	3	36	0	65	7	1	3	10	.231	1	0	4.40
	4 Min. YEARS		84	80	2	1	458.2	1958	437	238	211	38	19	19	13	201	3	401	29	5	29	32	.475	1	1	4.14

Felipe Crespo

Bats: Both Throws: Right Pos: 3B Ht: 5'11" Wt: 190 Born: 03/05/73 Age: 22

			BATTING															BASERUNNING				PERCENTAGES		
Year	Team	Lg	G	AB	H	2B	3B	HR	TB	R	RBI	TBB	IBB	SO	HBP	SH	SF	SB	CS	SB%	GDP	Avg	OBP	SLG
1991	Medicne Hat	R	49	164	57	11	4	4	88	40	31	25	0	31	3	2	2	6	4	.60	2	.310	.397	.478
1992	Myrtle Bch	A	81	263	74	14	3	1	97	43	29	58	2	38	4	2	5	7	7	.50	1	.281	.412	.369
1993	Dunedin	A	96	345	103	16	8	6	153	51	39	47	3	40	4	5	2	18	5	.78	9	.299	.387	.443
1994	Knoxville	AA	129	502	135	30	4	8	197	74	49	57	3	95	2	4	1	20	8	.71	5	.269	.345	.392
	4 Min. YEARS		355	1294	369	71	19	19	535	208	148	187	8	204	13	13	10	51	24	.68	17	.285	.378	.413

Andy Croghan

Pitches: Right Bats: Right Pos: P Ht: 6'5" Wt: 205 Born: 10/26/69 Age: 25

			HOW MUCH HE PITCHED						WHAT HE GAVE UP												THE RESULTS					
Year	Team	Lg	G	GS	CG	GF	IP	BFP	H	R	ER	HR	SH	SF	HB	TBB	IBB	SO	WP	Bk	W	L	Pct.	ShO	Sv	ERA
1991	Oneonta	A	14	14	0	0	78.1	352	92	59	49	6	1	1	2	28	0	54	5	0	5	4	.556	0	0	5.63
1992	Greensboro	A	33	19	1	3	122.1	544	128	78	61	11	2	9	3	57	0	98	9	0	10	8	.556	0	0	4.49
1993	Pr William	A	39	14	1	19	105	455	117	66	56	9	4	4	3	27	0	80	6	0	5	11	.313	0	11	4.80
1994	Albany-Colo	AA	36	0	0	33	36.2	153	33	7	7	1	2	1	0	14	0	38	1	0	0	1	.000	0	16	1.72
	Columbus	AAA	21	0	0	17	24	110	25	11	11	6	5	0	0	13	1	28	3	0	2	2	.500	0	8	4.13
	4 Min. YEARS		143	47	2	72	366.1	1614	395	221	184	33	14	15	8	139	1	298	24	0	22	26	.458	0	35	4.52

Nate Cromwell

Pitches: Left Bats: Left Pos: P Ht: 6'1" Wt: 185 Born: 08/23/68 Age: 26

			HOW MUCH HE PITCHED						WHAT HE GAVE UP												THE RESULTS					
Year	Team	Lg	G	GS	CG	GF	IP	BFP	H	R	ER	HR	SH	SF	HB	TBB	IBB	SO	WP	Bk	W	L	Pct.	ShO	Sv	ERA
1987	Medicne Hat	R	15	11	1	2	54.1	246	54	36	26	1	3	3	1	37	0	47	10	0	4	6	.400	0	0	4.31
1988	Myrtle Bch	A	21	20	1	1	124.1	513	88	47	40	6	6	2	8	67	2	86	8	0	8	8	.500	1	0	2.90
1989	Dunedin	A	31	30	0	0	151.2	665	136	70	61	5	2	1	4	84	0	161	25	4	12	6	.667	0	0	3.62
1990	Knoxville	AA	27	23	2	2	121.1	563	119	85	75	11	9	10	4	91	1	79	8	4	5	14	.263	0	0	5.56
1991	Knoxville	AA	16	16	0	0	80	363	73	53	44	6	1	3	5	53	0	61	8	4	2	9	.182	0	0	4.95
1992	Knoxville	AA	37	10	0	11	101	465	102	68	58	4	5	3	3	69	1	101	17	1	5	5	.500	0	0	5.17
1993	Knoxville	AA	6	1	0	3	9	52	15	13	11	2	0	0	1	10	0	11	1	0	0	1	.000	0	0	11.00
	Wichita	AA	21	11	1	2	89.1	389	90	49	41	9	4	2	4	38	4	86	8	3	3	5	.375	1	0	4.13
1994	Wichita	AA	31	20	0	2	132.2	588	130	78	60	9	10	4	5	61	3	126	12	0	9	5	.643	0	0	4.07
	Las Vegas	AAA	2	2	1	0	14.2	66	19	8	8	2	0	0	0	5	0	16	2	0	0	2	.000	0	0	4.91
	8 Min. YEARS		207	144	6	23	878.1	3910	826	507	424	55	40	28	37	515	11	774	99	22	48	61	.440	2	0	4.34

Chris Cron

Bats: Right Throws: Right Pos: 1B Ht: 6'2" Wt: 200 Born: 03/31/64 Age: 31

			BATTING															BASERUNNING				PERCENTAGES		
Year	Team	Lg	G	AB	H	2B	3B	HR	TB	R	RBI	TBB	IBB	SO	HBP	SH	SF	SB	CS	SB%	GDP	Avg	OBP	SLG
1984	Pulaski	R	32	114	42	8	0	7	71	22	37	17	1	20	6	0	2	2	0	1.00	2	.368	.468	.623
1985	Sumter	A	119	425	102	20	0	7	143	53	59	51	2	98	18	0	1	5	2	.71	8	.240	.345	.336
1986	Durham	A	90	265	55	10	0	7	86	26	34	29	0	60	6	2	2	0	2	.00	2	.208	.298	.325
1987	Quad City	A	111	398	110	20	1	11	165	53	62	44	2	88	17	0	1	1	3	.25	5	.276	.372	.415
	Palm Sprngs	A	26	92	25	3	0	2	34	6	9	9	0	27	2	1	2	2	2	.50	3	.272	.343	.370
1988	Palm Sprngs	A	127	467	117	28	3	14	193	71	84	68	1	147	27	2	6	4	3	.57	10	.251	.373	.413
1989	Midland	AA	128	491	148	33	3	22	253	80	103	39	5	126	14	1	6	0	1	.00	10	.301	.365	.515
1990	Edmonton	AAA	104	401	115	31	0	17	197	54	75	28	1	92	5	1	5	7	5	.58	9	.287	.337	.491
1991	Edmonton	AAA	123	461	134	21	1	22	223	74	91	47	3	103	10	2	11	6	5	.55	12	.291	.361	.484
1992	Vancouver	AAA	140	500	139	29	0	16	216	76	81	94	12	111	17	2	3	12	4	.75	9	.278	.407	.432
1993	Nashville	AAA	126	460	118	27	0	22	211	69	68	61	5	114	8	3	4	2	1	.67	12	.257	.351	.459

Year	Team	Lg	G	AB	H	2B	3B	HR	TB	R	RBI	TBB	IBB	SO	HBP	SH	SF	SB	CS	SB%	GDP	Avg	OBP	SLG
1994	Charlotte	AAA	103	350	81	19	1	23	171	50	72	33	2	105	11	0	1	1	1	.50	10	.231	.316	.489
1991	California	AL	6	15	2	0	0	0	2	0	0	2	0	5	0	0	0	0	0	.00	0	.133	.235	.133
1992	Chicago	AL	6	10	0	0	0	0	0	0	0	0	0	4	0	0	0	0	0	.00	0	.000	.000	.000
	11 Min. YEARS		1229	4424	1186	249	9	170	1963	634	775	520	34	1091	141	14	44	42	29	.59	92	.268	.360	.444
	2 Maj. YEARS		12	25	2	0	0	0	2	0	0	2	0	9	0	0	0	0	0	.00	0	.080	.148	.080

Mike Crosby

Bats: Left   Throws: Right   Pos: C   Ht: 6'1"   Wt: 200   Born: 02/24/69   Age: 26

						BATTING												BASERUNNING				PERCENTAGES		
Year	Team	Lg	G	AB	H	2B	3B	HR	TB	R	RBI	TBB	IBB	SO	HBP	SH	SF	SB	CS	SB%	GDP	Avg	OBP	SLG
1992	Columbus	A	53	149	25	3	0	0	28	14	13	6	0	32	4	2	2	0	1	.00	3	.168	.217	.188
1993	Kinston	A	72	203	44	9	0	3	62	20	17	7	0	45	3	4	2	1	2	.33	6	.217	.251	.305
1994	Canton-Akrn	AA	55	162	36	7	1	2	51	12	10	4	0	44	2	4	0	1	1	.50	3	.222	.250	.315
	3 Min. YEARS		180	514	105	19	1	5	141	46	40	17	0	121	9	10	4	2	4	.33	12	.204	.241	.274

Jesse Cross

Pitches: Right   Bats: Right   Pos: P   Ht: 5'10"   Wt: 195   Born: 01/15/68   Age: 27

			HOW MUCH HE PITCHED						WHAT HE GAVE UP								THE RESULTS					
Year	Team	Lg	G	GS	CG	GF	IP	BFP	H	R	ER	HR	SH	SF	HB	TBB	IBB	SO	WP	Bk	W	L	Pct.	ShO	Sv	ERA
1989	Myrtle Bch	A	36	13	0	17	100	431	61	46	39	7	1	4	6	81	0	139	13	3	7	8	.467	0	4	3.51
1990	Dunedin	A	28	18	0	2	139.1	571	100	54	51	3	8	5	6	70	2	126	16	6	13	7	.650	0	0	3.29
1991	Knoxville	AA	31	26	4	2	172	722	141	72	54	10	4	8	10	71	3	128	3	2	10	9	.526	0	1	2.83
1992	Syracuse	AAA	4	0	0	1	6.2	35	11	8	7	3	1	0	0	3	1	3	0	0	0	0	.000	0	0	9.45
	Knoxville	AA	26	24	2	1	147.1	615	136	69	58	12	2	7	3	44	1	126	4	0	8	13	.381	1	0	3.54
1993	Syracuse	AAA	29	25	0	0	151	633	137	68	53	13	4	4	5	53	1	127	9	1	8	6	.571	0	0	3.16
1994	Syracuse	AAA	31	29	2	0	177.1	761	173	97	90	23	4	6	6	68	1	132	2	0	14	11	.560	1	0	4.57
	6 Min. YEARS		185	135	8	23	893.2	3768	759	414	352	71	24	34	36	390	9	781	47	12	60	54	.526	2	5	3.54

Jim Crowley

Bats: Right   Throws: Right   Pos: 3B   Ht: 6'0"   Wt: 190   Born: 10/16/69   Age: 25

						BATTING												BASERUNNING				PERCENTAGES		
Year	Team	Lg	G	AB	H	2B	3B	HR	TB	R	RBI	TBB	IBB	SO	HBP	SH	SF	SB	CS	SB%	GDP	Avg	OBP	SLG
1991	Elmira	A	71	249	52	13	1	10	97	36	34	38	0	51	1	0	3	5	3	.63	4	.209	.313	.390
1992	Lynchburg	A	119	392	100	20	1	12	158	62	59	34	1	75	2	1	3	2	1	.67	6	.255	.316	.403
1993	Pawtucket	AAA	12	35	6	0	0	0	6	2	2	2	0	10	0	0	0	0	0	.00	2	.171	.216	.171
	New Britain	AA	109	369	89	19	1	11	143	49	51	59	0	95	4	4	2	3	7	.30	6	.241	.350	.388
1994	Lynchburg	A	30	107	22	4	0	2	32	8	11	17	1	18	1	1	1	1	0	1.00	1	.206	.317	.299
	New Britain	AA	76	220	42	2	1	7	67	25	24	27	1	57	1	3	2	2	3	.40	4	.191	.280	.305
	4 Min. YEARS		417	1372	311	58	4	42	503	182	181	177	3	306	9	9	11	13	14	.48	23	.227	.317	.367

Ivan Cruz

Bats: Left   Throws: Left   Pos: 1B   Ht: 6'3"   Wt: 210   Born: 05/03/68   Age: 27

						BATTING												BASERUNNING				PERCENTAGES		
Year	Team	Lg	G	AB	H	2B	3B	HR	TB	R	RBI	TBB	IBB	SO	HBP	SH	SF	SB	CS	SB%	GDP	Avg	OBP	SLG
1989	Niagara Fls	A	64	226	62	11	2	7	98	43	40	27	3	29	3	0	1	2	0	1.00	2	.274	.358	.434
1990	Lakeland	A	118	414	118	23	2	11	178	61	73	49	3	71	5	2	4	8	1	.89	8	.285	.364	.430
1991	Toledo	AAA	8	29	4	0	0	1	7	2	4	2	0	12	1	0	0	0	0	.00	0	.138	.219	.241
	London	AA	121	443	110	21	0	9	158	45	47	36	5	74	4	1	2	3	3	.50	12	.248	.309	.357
1992	London	AA	134	524	143	25	1	14	212	71	104	37	1	102	4	0	6	1	1	.50	16	.273	.322	.405
1993	Toledo	AAA	115	402	91	18	4	13	156	44	50	30	2	85	3	0	2	1	1	.50	5	.226	.284	.388
1994	Toledo	AAA	97	303	75	11	2	15	135	36	43	28	1	83	2	0	3	1	0	1.00	7	.248	.313	.446
	6 Min. YEARS		657	2341	603	109	11	70	944	302	361	209	15	456	22	3	18	16	6	.73	50	.258	.322	.403

Calvain Culberson

Pitches: Right   Bats: Right   Pos: P   Ht: 5'10"   Wt: 195   Born: 11/14/66   Age: 28

			HOW MUCH HE PITCHED						WHAT HE GAVE UP								THE RESULTS					
Year	Team	Lg	G	GS	CG	GF	IP	BFP	H	R	ER	HR	SH	SF	HB	TBB	IBB	SO	WP	Bk	W	L	Pct.	ShO	Sv	ERA
1989	Sumter	A	1	0	0	1	1	7	3	2	2	1	0	0	0	0	0	1	0	0	0	0	.000	0	0	18.00
1990	Chston-Wv	A	14	14	0	0	79	325	62	32	27	4	3	2	2	32	1	57	8	3	5	5	.500	0	0	3.08
1991	Cedar Rapds	A	18	14	1	1	88.1	396	82	54	41	4	2	5	3	54	3	68	4	1	6	8	.429	0	0	4.18
1992	Cedar Rapds	A	28	20	2	5	125.1	521	102	50	39	7	6	5	1	52	0	93	4	3	5	4	.556	0	2	2.80
1993	Indianapls	AAA	2	2	0	0	13	52	9	2	1	1	0	0	0	9	0	9	0	0	1	0	1.000	0	0	0.69
	Chattanooga	AA	37	7	0	15	105.1	430	82	38	35	11	5	0	6	36	0	86	3	0	6	6	.500	0	1	2.99
1994	Chattanooga	AA	38	5	0	20	81	339	60	31	23	6	2	1	1	39	3	66	8	0	2	9	.182	0	9	2.56
	6 Min. YEARS		138	62	3	42	493	2070	400	209	168	34	18	13	13	220	7	380	27	7	25	32	.439	0	12	3.07

Glen Cullop

Pitches: Right   Bats: Right   Pos: P   Ht: 6'7"   Wt: 180   Born: 10/04/71   Age: 23

			HOW MUCH HE PITCHED						WHAT HE GAVE UP								THE RESULTS					
Year	Team	Lg	G	GS	CG	GF	IP	BFP	H	R	ER	HR	SH	SF	HB	TBB	IBB	SO	WP	Bk	W	L	Pct.	ShO	Sv	ERA
1992	Princeton	R	11	1	0	3	28.1	123	33	15	7	1	0	2	0	7	0	23	1	0	0	1	.000	0	2	2.22
1993	Winston-Sal	A	39	0	0	11	65	249	37	12	11	2	2	7	3	21	3	48	5	1	6	0	1.000	0	2	1.52
1994	Chattanooga	AA	40	0	0	8	59.1	267	54	28	25	2	5	2	4	36	2	41	8	1	3	3	.500	0	0	3.79
	3 Min. YEARS		90	1	0	22	152.2	639	124	55	43	5	7	11	7	64	5	112	14	2	9	4	.692	0	4	2.53

Brian Culp

Bats: Right Throws: Right Pos: OF Ht: 6'0" Wt: 195 Born: 07/05/70 Age: 24

Year	Team	Lg	G	AB	H	2B	3B	HR	TB	R	RBI	TBB	IBB	SO	HBP	SH	SF	SB	CS	SB%	GDP	Avg	OBP	SLG
1994	New Haven	AA	5	12	5	1	0	1	9	2	2	1	0	2	0	1	0	0	0	.00	0	.417	.462	.750
	Asheville	A	65	223	67	19	2	4	102	33	25	23	0	47	4	0	2	9	3	.75	6	.300	.373	.457
	Central Val	A	23	82	28	9	1	0	39	18	16	14	0	13	3	0	1	2	4	.33		.341	.450	.476
	1 Min. YEARS		93	317	100	29	3	5	150	53	43	38	0	62	7	1	3	11	7	.61	7	.315	.397	.473

Steve Curry

Pitches: Right Bats: Right Pos: P Ht: 6'6" Wt: 217 Born: 09/13/65 Age: 29

Year	Team	Lg	G	GS	CG	GF	IP	BFP	H	R	ER	HR	SH	SF	HB	TBB	IBB	SO	WP	Bk	W	L	Pct.	ShO	Sv	ERA
1984	Elmira	A	14	14	3	0	83.1	368	83	51	37	6	1	2	1	35	4	82	6	1	6	4	.600	0	0	4.00
1985	Winter Havn	A	27	25	4	0	161	688	157	75	66	9	6	8	5	63	1	81	14	11	9	10	.474	0	0	3.69
1986	New Britain	AA	24	24	12	0	177.1	752	163	66	55	5	6	3	6	76	4	94	7	5	11	9	.550	2	0	2.79
1987	Pawtucket	AAA	28	26	8	1	184.1	792	175	85	78	13	6	7	4	74	4	112	5	5	11	12	.478	1	0	3.81
1988	Pawtucket	AAA	23	23	3	0	146.1	612	125	56	50	9	7	3	7	69	2	110	7	11	11	9	.550	1	0	3.08
1989	Pawtucket	AAA	7	6	1	0	38.2	177	49	27	24	6	1	0	1	12	0	19	2	2	0	5	.000	0	0	5.59
1990	Red Sox	R	3	3	0	0	14	53	11	5	4	2	1	0	0	2	0	12	0	0	1	2	.333	0	0	2.57
	Pawtucket	AAA	5	3	0	1	9	48	21	11	11	2	0	0	0	2	0	5	0	1	0	1	.000	0	0	11.00
1992	Memphis	AA	27	27	2	0	161.2	691	156	79	71	9	1	6	5	72	0	110	12	0	8	12	.400	1	0	3.95
1993	Omaha	AAA	33	21	1	2	145.2	613	141	86	79	14	7	5	5	56	0	91	5	4	6	7	.462	0	0	4.88
1994	Okla. City	AAA	28	3	0	7	59	292	76	62	47	6	0	2	4	39	3	28	7	3	2	2	.500	0	0	7.17
1988	Boston	AL	3	3	0	0	11	59	15	10	10	0	1	2	0	14	2	4	2	1	0	0	.000	0	0	8.18
	10 Min. YEARS		219	175	34	11	1180.1	5086	1157	603	522	81	36	36	38	500	18	744	65	43	65	73	.471	5	0	3.98

Chris Curtis

Pitches: Right Bats: Right Pos: P Ht: 6'2" Wt: 185 Born: 05/08/71 Age: 24

Year	Team	Lg	G	GS	CG	GF	IP	BFP	H	R	ER	HR	SH	SF	HB	TBB	IBB	SO	WP	Bk	W	L	Pct.	ShO	Sv	ERA
1991	Butte	R	6	3	0	2	12.2	69	27	23	14	1	0	0	1	4	0	7	0	3	0	2	.000	0	0	9.95
	Rangers	R	7	7	0	0	35	134	27	9	8	1	0	4	2	9	0	23	0	2	1	0	1.000	0	0	2.06
1992	Gastonia	A	24	24	1	0	147	590	117	60	43	3	1	5	6	54	0	107	6	7	8	11	.421	1	0	2.63
1993	Charlotte	A	27	26	1	0	151	637	159	76	67	6	4	2	8	51	0	55	4	5	8	8	.500	0	0	3.99
1994	Tulsa	AA	25	23	3	1	142.2	639	173	102	85	17	4	7	7	57	5	62	9	7	3	13	.188	1	0	5.36
	4 Min. YEARS		89	83	5	3	488.1	2069	503	270	217	28	9	18	24	175	5	254	19	24	23	34	.404	2	0	4.00

Randy Curtis

Bats: Left Throws: Left Pos: OF Ht: 5'10" Wt: 180 Born: 01/16/71 Age: 24

Year	Team	Lg	G	AB	H	2B	3B	HR	TB	R	RBI	TBB	IBB	SO	HBP	SH	SF	SB	CS	SB%	GDP	Avg	OBP	SLG
1991	Pittsfield	A	75	299	86	12	1	2	106	72	33	60	1	63	2	2	2	25	9	.74	3	.288	.408	.355
1992	Columbia	A	102	353	104	11	5	1	128	53	56	62	2	80	5	3	3	33	16	.67	1	.295	.404	.363
1993	St.Lucie	A	126	467	149	30	12	2	209	91	38	93	2	72	5	4	4	52	17	.75	4	.319	.434	.448
1994	Las Vegas	AAA	30	77	16	1	0	2	23	8	6	11	0	27	0	1	0	3	1	.75	1	.208	.307	.299
	Wichita	AA	59	200	54	9	3	4	81	30	21	24	0	56	4	1	2	12	9	.57	1	.270	.357	.405
	4 Min. YEARS		392	1396	409	63	21	11	547	254	154	250	5	298	16	11	11	125	52	.71	10	.293	.403	.392

Fred Dabney

Pitches: Left Bats: Right Pos: P Ht: 6'3" Wt: 190 Born: 11/20/67 Age: 27

Year	Team	Lg	G	GS	CG	GF	IP	BFP	H	R	ER	HR	SH	SF	HB	TBB	IBB	SO	WP	Bk	W	L	Pct.	ShO	Sv	ERA
1988	Utica	A	19	13	1	3	87.2	382	83	40	26	1	2	0	1	41	1	69	2	5	9	4	.692	0	0	2.67
1989	South Bend	A	26	26	3	0	163.1	676	128	50	38	2	4	2	11	65	1	150	7	6	11	7	.611	0	0	2.09
1990	Sarasota	A	24	21	1	1	126.1	569	146	82	73	3	4	4	6	57	1	77	6	6	6	7	.462	0	0	5.20
1991	Sarasota	A	26	8	1	5	96.1	414	88	45	32	6	3	4	4	44	1	72	2	4	11	3	.786	1	1	2.99
1992	Birmingham	AA	25	14	0	5	105.1	460	116	57	45	9	5	7	1	41	1	86	6	1	2	8	.200	0	0	3.84
1993	Nashville	AAA	51	0	0	15	63	280	65	43	34	7	1	3	9	21	0	44	3	1	2	5	.286	0	3	4.86
1994	Canton-Akm	AA	39	0	0	17	58	243	50	20	18	4	4	2	5	19	2	44	2	0	4	3	.571	0	2	2.79
	7 Min. YEARS		210	82	6	46	700	3024	676	337	266	32	23	22	37	288	7	542	28	23	45	37	.549	1	6	3.42

Mike Daniel

Bats: Right Throws: Right Pos: C Ht: 6'1" Wt: 195 Born: 09/21/69 Age: 25

Year	Team	Lg	G	AB	H	2B	3B	HR	TB	R	RBI	TBB	IBB	SO	HBP	SH	SF	SB	CS	SB%	GDP	Avg	OBP	SLG
1991	Jamestown	A	66	221	56	7	1	4	94	37	62	51	1	53	0	0	6	2	0	1.00	0	.253	.385	.425
1992	Wst Plm Bch	A	72	237	51	13	1	4	78	28	27	24	0	53	4	1	6	3	3	.50	5	.215	.292	.329
1993	Harrisburg	AA	3	6	2	0	1	0	4	1	1	0	0	3	0	0	0	0	0	.00	0	.333	.333	.667
	Wst Plm Bch	A	106	359	88	27	1	5	132	39	48	43	3	71	0	0	5	2	1	.67	0	.245	.327	.368
1994	Fort Myers	A	5	20	3	0	1	0	5	1	2	3	1	5	0	0	1	0	0	.00	1	.150	.261	.250
	Nashville	AA	33	110	26	7	0	6	51	18	16	11	0	21	1	0	0	0	0	.00	2	.236	.311	.464
	Portland	AA	13	43	9	2	1	1	16	6	11	5	0	8	1	0	2	0	0	.00	1	.209	.294	.372

Year Team	Lg	G	AB	H	2B	3B	HR	TB	R	RBI	TBB	IBB	SO	HBP	SH	SF	SB	CS	SB%	GDP	Avg	OBP	SLG
Brevard Cty	A	10	35	7	1	0	2	14	5	4	5	0	4	0	0	0	0	0	.00	0	.200	.300	.400
4 Min. YEARS		308	1031	242	59	9	25	394	135	171	142	5	218	9	2	19	7	4	.64	10	.235	.327	.382

Vic Darensbourg

Pitches: Left   Bats: Left   Pos: P   Ht: 5'10"   Wt: 165   Born: 11/13/70   Age: 24

		HOW MUCH HE PITCHED						WHAT HE GAVE UP										THE RESULTS						
Year Team	Lg	G	GS	CG	GF	IP	BFP	H	R	ER	HR	SH	SF	HB	TBB	IBB	SO	WP	Bk	W	L	Pct.	ShO	Sv	ERA
1992 Marlins	R	8	4	0	2	42	161	28	5	3	1	0	0	3	11	2	37	0	0	2	1	.667	0	2	0.64
1993 Kane County	A	46	0	0	31	71.1	300	58	17	17	3	3	3	4	28	3	89	2	0	9	1	.900	0	16	2.14
High Desert	A	1	0	0	0	1	4	1	0	0	0	0	0	0	0	0	0	0	0	0	0	.000	0	0	0.00
1994 Portland	AA	34	21	1	9	149	631	146	76	63	18	7	4	6	60	3	103	4	2	10	7	.588	1	4	3.81
3 Min. YEARS		89	25	1	42	263.1	1096	233	98	83	22	10	7	13	99	8	230	6	2	21	9	.700	1	22	2.84

Doug Dascenzo

Bats: Both   Throws: Left   Pos: OF   Ht: 5' 8"   Wt: 160   Born: 06/30/64   Age: 31

		BATTING															BASERUNNING				PERCENTAGES		
Year Team	Lg	G	AB	H	2B	3B	HR	TB	R	RBI	TBB	IBB	SO	HBP	SH	SF	SB	CS	SB%	GDP	Avg	OBP	SLG
1985 Geneva	A	70	252	84	15	1	3	110	59	23	61	4	20	2	1	4	33	9	.79	1	.333	.461	.437
1986 Winston-Sal	A	138	545	178	29	11	6	247	107	83	63	5	44	2	12	5	57	13	.81	9	.327	.395	.453
1987 Pittsfield	AA	134	496	152	32	6	3	205	84	56	73	5	38	1	7	5	36	7	.84	5	.306	.393	.413
1988 Iowa	AAA	132	505	149	22	5	6	199	73	49	37	4	41	2	7	5	30	14	.68	7	.295	.342	.394
1989 Iowa	AAA	111	431	121	18	4	4	159	59	33	51	3	41	0	9	2	34	21	.62	7	.281	.355	.369
1993 Okla City	AAA	38	157	39	8	2	1	54	21	13	16	0	16	0	2	1	6	5	.55	7	.248	.316	.344
1994 Norfolk	AAA	68	246	68	13	1	4	95	30	27	22	3	23	0	4	1	5	7	.42	5	.276	.335	.386
1988 Chicago	NL	26	75	16	3	0	0	19	9	4	9	1	4	0	1	0	6	1	.86	2	.213	.298	.253
1989 Chicago	NL	47	139	23	1	0	1	27	20	12	13	0	13	0	3	2	6	3	.67	2	.165	.234	.194
1990 Chicago	NL	113	241	61	9	5	1	83	27	26	21	2	18	1	5	3	15	6	.71	3	.253	.312	.344
1991 Chicago	NL	118	239	61	11	0	1	75	40	18	24	2	26	2	6	1	14	7	.67	3	.255	.327	.314
1992 Chicago	NL	139	376	96	13	4	0	117	37	20	27	2	32	0	4	2	6	8	.43	3	.255	.304	.311
1993 Texas	AL	76	146	29	5	1	2	42	20	10	8	0	22	0	3	1	2	0	1.00	1	.199	.239	.288
7 Min. YEARS		691	2632	791	137	30	27	1069	433	284	323	24	223	7	42	23	201	76	.73	41	.301	.376	.406
6 Maj. YEARS		519	1216	286	42	10	5	363	153	90	102	7	115	3	22	9	49	25	.66	14	.235	.294	.299

Jimmy Daspit

Pitches: Right   Bats: Right   Pos: P   Ht: 6'7"   Wt: 210   Born: 08/10/69   Age: 25

		HOW MUCH HE PITCHED						WHAT HE GAVE UP										THE RESULTS						
Year Team	Lg	G	GS	CG	GF	IP	BFP	H	R	ER	HR	SH	SF	HB	TBB	IBB	SO	WP	Bk	W	L	Pct.	ShO	Sv	ERA
1990 Great Falls	R	14	9	0	1	51	222	45	26	23	0	3	2	5	30	0	40	1	0	5	2	.714	0	0	4.06
1991 Bakersfield	A	22	9	0	6	64.2	276	58	29	23	1	4	2	1	36	2	47	6	1	3	2	.600	0	2	3.20
1992 Vero Beach	A	26	25	0	0	149.1	625	135	67	57	10	6	3	7	57	1	109	7	1	6	12	.333	0	0	3.44
1993 Vero Beach	A	1	1	0	0	3	15	4	0	0	0	0	0	0	2	0	2	0	0	0	0	.000	0	0	0.00
San Antonio	AA	15	15	0	0	81.1	363	92	48	40	5	4	4	8	33	0	58	5	0	3	8	.273	0	0	4.43
1994 Jackson	AA	28	10	1	7	71	274	48	22	18	1	2	0	2	23	0	74	3	0	5	1	.833	1	1	2.28
5 Min. YEARS		106	69	1	14	420.1	1775	382	192	161	17	19	11	23	181	3	330	22	2	22	25	.468	1	3	3.45

Jack Daugherty

Bats: Both   Throws: Left   Pos: 1B   Ht: 6' 0"   Wt: 190   Born: 07/03/60   Age: 34

		BATTING															BASERUNNING				PERCENTAGES		
Year Team	Lg	G	AB	H	2B	3B	HR	TB	R	RBI	TBB	IBB	SO	HBP	SH	SF	SB	CS	SB%	GDP	Avg	OBP	SLG
1984 Helena	R	66	259	104	26	2	15	179	77	82	52	10	48	2	0	2	16	3	.84	2	.402	.502	.691
1985 Wst Plm Bch	A	133	481	152	25	3	10	213	76	87	75	11	58	0	0	5	33	6	.85	14	.316	.405	.443
1986 Jacksnville	AA	138	502	159	37	4	4	216	87	63	79	1	58	4	7	3	15	6	.71	14	.317	.412	.430
1987 Indianapols	AAA	117	420	131	35	3	7	193	65	50	42	5	54	1	2	4	11	0	1.00	12	.312	.373	.460
1988 Indianapols	AAA	137	481	137	33	2	6	192	82	67	56	4	50	1	7	7	18	6	.75	14	.285	.356	.399
1989 Okla City	AAA	82	311	78	15	3	3	108	28	32	39	5	35	0	2	3	2	2	.50	9	.251	.331	.347
1991 Okla City	AAA	22	77	11	2	0	0	13	4	4	8	2	14	0	0	0	1	0	1.00	1	.143	.224	.169
1992 Okla City	AAA	9	18	5	2	0	0	7	3	2	3	0	3	0	0	0	0	0	.00	1	.278	.381	.389
1993 Tucson	AAA	42	141	55	9	2	2	74	23	29	26	2	12	3	0	2	1	0	1.00	5	.390	.488	.525
1994 Syracuse	AAA	47	149	50	12	0	3	71	19	21	27	1	16	0	1	0	0	0	.00	5	.336	.438	.477
1987 Montreal	NL	11	10	1	1	0	0	2	1	1	0	0	3	0	2	0	0	0	.00	0	.100	.100	.200
1989 Texas	AL	52	106	32	4	2	1	43	15	10	11	0	21	1	0	3	2	1	.67	3	.302	.364	.406
1990 Texas	AL	125	310	93	20	2	6	135	36	47	22	2	49	2	2	3	0	0	.00	4	.300	.347	.435
1991 Texas	AL	58	144	28	3	2	1	38	8	11	16	1	23	0	4	3	1	0	1.00	2	.194	.270	.264
1992 Texas	AL	59	127	26	9	0	0	35	13	9	16	1	21	1	0	2	2	1	.67	3	.205	.295	.276
1993 Houston	NL	4	3	1	0	0	0	1	0	0	0	0	0	0	0	0	0	0	.00	0	.333	.333	.333
Cincinnati	NL	46	59	13	2	0	2	21	7	9	11	0	15	0	0	1	0	0	.00	2	.220	.338	.356
10 Min. YEARS		793	2839	882	196	19	50	1266	464	437	407	41	348	11	19	26	97	23	.81	73	.311	.396	.446
6 Maj. YEARS		355	759	194	39	6	10	275	80	87	76	2	132	4	8	12	5	2	.71	10	.256	.322	.362

Phil Dauphin

Bats: Left   Throws: Left   Pos: OF   Ht: 6'1"   Wt: 180   Born: 05/11/69   Age: 26

		BATTING															BASERUNNING				PERCENTAGES		
Year Team	Lg	G	AB	H	2B	3B	HR	TB	R	RBI	TBB	IBB	SO	HBP	SH	SF	SB	CS	SB%	GDP	Avg	OBP	SLG
1990 Geneva	A	73	233	55	8	1	12	101	47	47	51	1	45	7	8	3	8	6	.57	2	.236	.384	.433

Year	Team	Lg	G	AB	H	2B	3B	HR	TB	R	RBI	TBB	IBB	SO	HBP	SH	SF	SB	CS	SB%	GDP	Avg	OBP	SLG
1991	Peoria	A	120	426	126	27	5	11	196	74	49	72	9	66	4	4	7	15	7	.68	4	.296	.397	.460
1992	Charlotte	AA	136	515	131	24	3	10	191	83	43	55	2	71	6	6	4	17	10	.63	1	.254	.331	.371
1993	Orlando	AA	81	299	79	16	2	11	132	53	35	30	0	40	3	5	3	7	10	.41	3	.264	.334	.441
	Iowa	AAA	20	54	12	4	1	1	21	5	2	10	2	9	0	0	0	2	0	1.00	2	.222	.344	.389
	Indianapolis	AAA	8	21	6	0	0	0	6	0	2	2	0	4	0	0	0	0	0	.00	0	.286	.348	.286
1994	Chattanooga	AA	1	4	2	0	0	0	2	1	1	1	0	1	0	0	0	0	0	.00	0	.500	.600	.500
	Harrisburg	AA	113	331	88	16	5	10	144	40	40	42	3	56	1	4	4	10	9	.53	3	.266	.347	.435
	5 Min. YEARS		552	1883	499	95	17	55	793	303	219	263	17	292	21	27	21	59	42	.58	15	.265	.358	.421

Adell Davenport

Bats: Right Throws: Right Pos: 3B Ht: 5'11" Wt: 195 Born: 07/16/67 Age: 27

			BATTING															BASERUNNING				PERCENTAGES		
Year	Team	Lg	G	AB	H	2B	3B	HR	TB	R	RBI	TBB	IBB	SO	HBP	SH	SF	SB	CS	SB%	GDP	Avg	OBP	SLG
1988	Everett	A	61	229	54	14	1	5	85	40	29	31	1	65	5	0	0	0	0	.00	3	.236	.340	.371
1989	Clinton	A	128	436	103	16	2	14	165	50	65	35	2	98	13	5	4	1	4	.20	10	.236	.309	.378
1990	San Jose	A	132	495	124	20	5	17	205	76	66	46	3	108	16	2	3	3	6	.33	8	.251	.332	.414
1991	San Jose	A	67	242	70	16	0	6	104	34	42	40	1	61	10	0	1	1	3	.25	6	.289	.410	.430
	Shreveport	AA	59	165	38	3	0	7	62	19	24	14	0	44	6	3	1	0	1	.00	4	.230	.312	.376
1992	Shreveport	AA	124	441	127	31	5	19	225	54	88	28	6	78	8	1	2	2	4	.33	6	.288	.340	.510
1993	Phoenix	AAA	14	40	12	1	0	2	19	5	8	3	0	10	0	0	0	0	1	.00	0	.300	.349	.475
	Shreveport	AA	103	370	97	21	0	15	163	43	62	29	6	73	5	0	4	4	2	.67	6	.262	.321	.441
1994	Nashville	AA	123	457	108	20	0	20	188	55	71	27	3	111	8	2	5	1	1	.50	3	.236	.288	.411
	7 Min. YEARS		811	2875	733	142	13	105	1216	376	455	253	22	648	71	13	20	12	22	.35	46	.255	.328	.423

Doug Davis

Bats: Right Throws: Right Pos: C Ht: 6' 0" Wt: 180 Born: 09/24/62 Age: 32

			BATTING															BASERUNNING				PERCENTAGES		
Year	Team	Lg	G	AB	H	2B	3B	HR	TB	R	RBI	TBB	IBB	SO	HBP	SH	SF	SB	CS	SB%	GDP	Avg	OBP	SLG
1984	Peoria	A	43	127	28	2	0	2	36	15	14	18	0	41	4	5	2	1	3	.25	3	.220	.331	.283
1985	Midland	AA	79	252	65	11	0	6	94	26	29	20	2	48	2	7	1	2	1	.67	6	.258	.316	.373
1986	Midland	AA	48	138	31	5	0	4	48	24	16	18	0	32	0	0	0	1	0	1.00	3	.225	.314	.348
	Palm Sprngs	A	31	100	29	3	0	3	41	20	20	22	0	26	0	5	2	0	0	.00	3	.290	.411	.410
1987	Midland	AA	63	187	43	5	1	7	71	28	26	24	0	44	2	5	5	2	4	.33	5	.230	.317	.380
1988	Edmonton	AAA	79	245	63	10	0	1	76	28	29	28	0	48	1	5	1	2	2	.50	7	.257	.335	.310
1989	Edmonton	AAA	54	147	39	6	1	3	56	17	22	18	0	40	2	3	0	0	0	.00	6	.265	.353	.381
1990	Midland	AA	42	148	45	8	5	3	72	22	18	9	0	32	2	0	1	1	1	.50	2	.304	.350	.486
	Edmonton	AAA	53	162	40	12	0	2	58	18	23	25	1	31	1	2	0	0	4	.00	1	.247	.351	.358
1991	Edmonton	AAA	33	113	31	4	0	3	44	12	18	11	1	23	1	3	1	1	3	.25	3	.274	.341	.389
	Memphis	AA	31	89	15	3	0	0	18	9	11	11	0	20	3	0	0	0	5	.00	2	.169	.282	.202
1992	Tulsa	AA	14	39	8	2	0	0	10	3	1	3	0	6	0	0	0	0	0	.00	3	.205	.262	.256
	Okla City	AAA	61	194	36	10	0	4	58	20	25	22	0	35	3	4	2	0	5	.00	7	.186	.276	.299
1993	Okla City	AAA	83	241	50	10	2	4	76	34	21	43	0	48	6	2	2	2	1	.67	6	.207	.339	.315
1994	Okla City	AAA	75	216	49	10	0	3	68	25	27	34	0	58	3	4	2	2	2	.50	3	.227	.337	.315
1988	California	AL	6	12	0	0	0	0	0	1	0	0	0	3	1	0	0	0	0	.00	0	.000	.077	.000
1992	Texas	AL	1	1	1	0	0	0	1	0	0	0	0	0	0	0	0	0	0	.00	0	1.000	1.000	1.000
	11 Min. YEARS		789	2398	572	101	9	45	826	301	293	306	4	532	30	45	19	14	31	.31	59	.239	.330	.344
	2 Maj. YEARS		7	13	1	0	0	0	1	1	0	0	0	3	1	0	0	0	0	.00	0	.077	.143	.077

Glenn Davis

Bats: Right Throws: Right Pos: 1B Ht: 6' 3" Wt: 212 Born: 03/28/61 Age: 34

			BATTING															BASERUNNING				PERCENTAGES		
Year	Team	Lg	G	AB	H	2B	3B	HR	TB	R	RBI	TBB	IBB	SO	HBP	SH	SF	SB	CS	SB%	GDP	Avg	OBP	SLG
1984	Tucson	AAA	131	471	140	28	7	16	230	66	94	49	3	88	5	1	9	3	2	.60	14	.297	.363	.488
1985	Tucson	AAA	60	220	67	24	2	5	110	22	35	13	2	23	3	0	3	1	0	1.00	7	.305	.347	.500
1990	Columbus	AA	12	37	11	0	0	1	14	3	8	2	0	9	1	0	0	1	0	1.00	7	.297	.350	.378
1991	Hagerstown	AA	7	24	6	1	0	1	10	4	3	1	0	2	0	0	1	0	0	.00	1	.250	.269	.417
1993	Frederick	A	3	11	3	1	0	0	4	1	2	1	0	3	0	0	0	0	0	.00	0	.273	.333	.364
	Rochester	AAA	7	24	6	1	1	0	9	2	3	2	0	8	0	0	0	0	0	.00	0	.250	.308	.375
	Bowie	AA	2	6	2	1	0	1	6	2	1	1	0	1	0	0	0	0	0	.00	0	.333	.429	1.000
1994	Omaha	AAA	129	471	133	30	0	27	244	76	97	57	0	75	14	0	6	4	3	.57	10	.282	.372	.518
1984	Houston	NL	18	61	13	5	0	2	24	6	8	4	0	12	0	2	1	0	0	.00	0	.213	.258	.393
1985	Houston	NL	100	350	95	11	0	20	166	51	64	27	6	68	7	2	4	0	0	.00	12	.271	.332	.474
1986	Houston	NL	158	574	152	32	3	31	283	91	101	64	6	72	9	0	7	3	1	.75	11	.265	.344	.493
1987	Houston	NL	151	578	145	35	2	27	265	70	93	47	10	84	5	0	5	4	1	.80	16	.251	.310	.458
1988	Houston	NL	152	561	152	26	0	30	268	78	99	53	20	77	11	0	3	4	3	.57	11	.271	.341	.478
1989	Houston	NL	158	581	156	26	1	34	286	87	89	69	17	123	7	0	6	4	2	.67	9	.269	.350	.492
1990	Houston	NL	93	327	82	15	4	22	171	44	64	46	17	54	8	0	0	8	3	.73	5	.251	.357	.523
1991	Baltimore	AL	49	176	40	9	1	10	81	29	28	16	0	29	5	0	2	4	0	1.00	5	.227	.307	.460
1992	Baltimore	AL	106	398	110	15	2	13	168	46	48	37	2	65	2	1	4	1	0	1.00	12	.276	.338	.422
1993	Baltimore	AL	30	113	20	3	0	1	26	8	9	7	0	29	1	0	0	0	1	.00	2	.177	.230	.230
	6 Min. YEARS		351	1264	368	86	10	51	627	176	243	126	6	209	23	1	19	9	5	.64	32	.291	.361	.496
	10 Maj. YEARS		1015	3719	965	177	13	190	1738	510	603	370	78	613	55	6	39	28	11	.72	80	.259	.332	.467

63

Jay Davis

Bats: Left **Throws:** Left **Pos:** OF | **Ht:** 6'0" **Wt:** 160 **Born:** 10/03/70 **Age:** 24

Year	Team	Lg	G	AB	H	2B	3B	HR	TB	R	RBI	TBB	IBB	SO	HBP	SH	SF	SB	CS	SB%	GDP	Avg	OBP	SLG
1989	Mets	R	52	195	48	6	5	0	64	26	18	12	0	33	2	0	2	7	11	.39	3	.246	.294	.328
1990	Kingsport	R	68	261	60	6	0	5	81	39	28	8	1	37	1	1	4	19	9	.68	8	.230	.252	.310
1991	Columbia	A	132	511	152	29	8	0	197	79	63	30	2	72	7	2	5	25	18	.58	14	.297	.342	.386
1992	St. Lucie	A	134	524	147	15	7	1	179	56	36	7	0	70	6	2	3	21	17	.55	15	.281	.296	.342
1993	Binghamton	AA	119	409	114	15	4	1	140	52	35	21	2	71	1	2	3	5	8	.38	8	.279	.313	.342
1994	Norfolk	AAA	6	14	3	1	0	0	4	3	0	1	0	1	0	0	0	0	0	.00	0	.214	.267	.286
	Binghamton	AA	105	325	107	15	3	5	143	51	42	14	4	39	3	3	2	9	3	.75	4	.329	.360	.440
	6 Min. YEARS		616	2239	631	87	27	12	808	306	222	93	9	323	20	10	19	86	66	.57	52	.282	.314	.361

Kevin Davis

Bats: Both **Throws:** Right **Pos:** 3B | **Ht:** 5'9" **Wt:** 180 **Born:** 07/06/64 **Age:** 30

Year	Team	Lg	G	AB	H	2B	3B	HR	TB	R	RBI	TBB	IBB	SO	HBP	SH	SF	SB	CS	SB%	GDP	Avg	OBP	SLG
1984	Redwood	A	131	420	100	10	5	1	123	37	47	30	1	112	2	18	3	16	14	.53	5	.238	.290	.293
1985	Midland	AA	100	354	93	19	1	8	138	47	42	28	0	64	2	4	3	7	10	.41	6	.263	.318	.390
1986	Nashua	AA	135	509	126	22	2	2	158	57	46	17	2	84	4	11	3	11	10	.52	5	.248	.276	.310
1987	Salem	A	137	486	126	36	3	13	207	64	65	30	1	95	4	4	9	12	5	.71	5	.259	.302	.426
1988	Harrisburg	AA	41	133	39	8	0	0	47	15	9	7	1	18	1	0	1	5	3	.63	2	.293	.331	.353
1989	Vancouver	AAA	7	22	7	0	0	1	10	2	1	0	0	4	0	0	0	0	1	.00	1	.318	.318	.455
	Birmingham	AA	85	279	66	13	5	1	92	38	37	16	1	67	1	0	2	5	3	.63	8	.237	.279	.330
1990	Palm Sprngs	A	30	126	32	6	0	0	38	11	16	6	0	32	0	0	2	5	3	.63	2	.254	.284	.302
	Midland	AA	59	201	53	7	2	6	82	28	26	14	0	45	0	4	1	8	5	.62	1	.264	.310	.408
1991	Midland	AA	51	153	53	12	2	0	69	30	25	10	0	26	0	5	1	8	3	.73	3	.346	.384	.451
	Edmonton	AAA	35	121	29	7	2	2	46	14	22	4	0	22	0	6	2	2	3	.40	0	.240	.260	.380
1992	Salinas	A	72	234	68	6	5	4	96	38	31	26	1	37	1	2	4	4	2	.67	5	.291	.358	.410
	Edmonton	AAA	23	80	31	9	3	1	49	21	16	5	0	11	0	2	0	0	2	.00	2	.388	.424	.613
1993	Midland	AA	47	156	43	5	1	7	71	29	28	18	1	31	1	1	2	6	3	.67	1	.276	.350	.455
	Vancouver	AAA	62	210	57	8	3	2	77	24	25	7	0	41	1	3	3	3	4	.43	4	.271	.294	.367
1994	Memphis	AA	59	135	37	4	0	3	50	23	15	21	2	30	0	2	4	7	2	.78	1	.274	.363	.370
	11 Min. YEARS		1074	3619	960	172	34	51	1353	478	451	239	10	719	17	62	40	99	73	.58	54	.265	.311	.374

Matt Davis

Bats: Both **Throws:** Right **Pos:** SS | **Ht:** 6'3" **Wt:** 185 **Born:** 05/28/68 **Age:** 27

Year	Team	Lg	G	AB	H	2B	3B	HR	TB	R	RBI	TBB	IBB	SO	HBP	SH	SF	SB	CS	SB%	GDP	Avg	OBP	SLG
1990	Everett	A	39	141	38	9	0	4	59	23	18	14	0	21	4	0	0	8	3	.73	2	.270	.352	.418
1991	Clinton	A	121	398	107	26	4	6	159	62	64	71	8	49	5	4	6	3	4	.43	4	.269	.381	.399
1992	San Jose	A	123	415	114	17	6	1	146	67	67	84	4	75	1	2	6	9	10	.47	7	.275	.393	.352
	Phoenix	AAA	6	24	7	1	0	0	8	3	4	0	0	3	0	0	0	0	0	.00	0	.292	.292	.333
1993	Shreveport	AA	131	423	114	25	0	4	151	44	42	52	7	64	1	3	5	3	5	.38	6	.270	.349	.357
1994	New Orleans	AAA	2	5	1	0	0	0	1	1	1	0	0	0	0	0	0	1	0	1.00	1	.200	.200	.200
	El Paso	AA	24	66	11	4	0	0	15	11	5	9	1	18	0	0	1	0	2	.00	0	.167	.263	.227
	Sioux Falls	IND	69	254	79	16	1	10	127	45	43	30	0	19	0	4	3	0	0	.00	5	.311	.380	.500
	5 Min. YEARS		515	1726	471	98	11	25	666	256	244	260	20	249	11	12	18	24	24	.50	25	.273	.368	.386

Scott Davison

Pitches: Right **Bats:** Right **Pos:** P | **Ht:** 6'0" **Wt:** 175 **Born:** 10/16/70 **Age:** 24

			HOW MUCH HE PITCHED						WHAT HE GAVE UP										THE RESULTS					
Year	Team	Lg	G	GS	CG	GF	IP	BFP	H	R	ER	HR	SH	SF	HB	TBB	IBB	SO	WP	Bk	W	L	Pct.	ShO	Sv	ERA
1994	Bellingham	A	13	0	0	11	15	66	11	5	3	0	1	0	1	6	1	21	3	2	0	1	.000	0	7	1.80
	Appleton	A	4	0	0	2	7.1	30	7	4	3	0	0	2	0	2	0	7	0	2	0	1	.000	0	0	3.68
	Calgary	AAA	11	0	0	3	14.2	67	20	10	10	1	0	0	1	6	0	17	2	1	0	1	.000	0	0	6.14
	1 Min. YEARS		28	0	0	16	37	163	38	19	16	1	1	2	2	14	1	45	5	5	0	3	.000	0	7	3.89

Juan de la Rosa

Bats: Right **Throws:** Right **Pos:** OF | **Ht:** 6'1" **Wt:** 190 **Born:** 12/01/68 **Age:** 26

Year	Team	Lg	G	AB	H	2B	3B	HR	TB	R	RBI	TBB	IBB	SO	HBP	SH	SF	SB	CS	SB%	GDP	Avg	OBP	SLG
1986	St.Cathrnes	A	6	21	5	0	0	0	5	0	0	0	0	5	0	0	0	0	0	.00	0	.238	.238	.238
	Medicne Hat	R	51	182	41	8	2	0	53	19	15	4	0	46	0	1	0	5	3	.63	4	.225	.242	.291
1987	Medicne Hat	R	57	200	58	9	2	1	74	29	24	2	0	38	0	1	3	14	5	.74	3	.290	.293	.370
1988	Myrtle Bch	A	134	477	109	12	5	7	152	54	66	31	0	108	2	4	2	11	4	.73	14	.229	.277	.319
1989	Myrtle Bch	A	132	535	137	28	6	11	210	66	74	19	1	124	2	1	4	19	10	.66	11	.256	.282	.393
1990	Dunedin	A	131	529	136	19	8	10	201	57	76	19	2	98	3	0	7	19	3	.75	14	.257	.283	.380
1991	Knoxville	AA	122	382	82	11	1	4	107	37	33	17	0	95	3	3	2	17	11	.61	9	.215	.252	.280
1992	Knoxville	AA	136	508	167	32	12	12	259	68	53	15	0	94	8	2	5	16	12	.57	13	.329	.354	.510
1993	Syracuse	AAA	60	198	45	10	2	4	71	17	15	7	0	41	1	4	1	4	4	.50	6	.227	.256	.359

64

1994 Salt Lake	AAA	89	287	78	15	3	4	111	40	46	17	0	49	2	1	3	0	2	.00	9	.272	.314	.387
9 Min. YEARS		918	3319	858	144	41	53	1243	387	402	131	3	698	21	17	27	95	54	.64	83	.259	.289	.375

Mariano De los Santos

Pitches: Right   Bats: Right   Pos: P   Ht: 5'10"   Wt: 200   Born: 07/13/70   Age: 24

		HOW MUCH HE PITCHED						WHAT HE GAVE UP											THE RESULTS					
Year	Team	Lg	G	GS	CG	GF	IP	BFP	H	R	ER	HR	SH	SF	HB	TBB	IBB	SO	WP	Bk	W	L	Pct.	ShO	Sv	ERA
1989	Pirates	R	13	4	0	6	37.1	172	41	27	24	2	1	5	2	19	0	24	5	0	2	2	.500	0	2	5.79
1991	Pirates	R	9	5	0	3	33.1	127	23	5	5	1	1	1	0	5	0	50	0	2	3	2	.600	0	1	1.35
	Welland	A	8	6	0	0	32.2	156	41	24	20	6	1	1	3	21	0	22	7	0	1	3	.250	0	0	5.51
1992	Augusta	A	52	1	0	28	96	390	75	33	24	2	4	4	6	38	2	103	4	3	7	8	.467	0	12	2.25
1993	Salem	A	18	18	2	0	99	429	90	46	37	8	5	0	5	41	0	80	8	5	9	5	.643	1	0	3.36
	Carolina	AA	8	8	0	0	40	181	49	24	21	1	1	3	4	15	1	34	2	0	1	2	.333	0	0	4.72
1994	Carolina	AA	14	14	1	0	76.1	322	77	34	31	7	3	3	8	24	0	57	2	0	7	2	.778	1	0	3.66
	Buffalo	AAA	9	9	0	0	48.2	208	46	27	26	5	2	2	4	17	0	26	0	0	2	6	.250	0	0	4.81
	5 Min. YEARS		131	65	3	37	463.1	1985	442	220	188	32	18	19	32	180	3	396	28	10	32	30	.516	2	15	3.65

Brian Deak

Bats: Right   Throws: Right   Pos: C   Ht: 6'0"   Wt: 185   Born: 10/25/67   Age: 27

			BATTING														BASERUNNING				PERCENTAGES		
Year	Team	Lg	G	AB	H	2B	3B	HR	TB	R	RBI	TBB	IBB	SO	HBP	SH	SF	SB	CS	SB%	GDP	Avg	OBP	SLG
1986	Pulaski	R	62	197	64	15	2	12	119	45	43	49	0	57	3	0	3	12	2	.86	2	.325	.460	.604
1987	Sumter	A	92	252	51	6	0	15	102	50	49	68	2	89	2	0	5	7	1	.88	4	.202	.370	.405
1988	Burlington	A	119	345	85	19	1	20	166	58	59	79	1	130	10	0	4	3	4	.43	4	.246	.397	.481
1989	Durham	A	113	327	77	10	0	21	150	44	64	66	2	111	9	3	2	3	3	.50	6	.235	.376	.459
1990	Durham	A	43	133	25	3	1	3	39	14	16	23	2	41	3	1	0	2	0	1.00	2	.188	.321	.293
	Greenville	AA	66	188	41	13	0	3	63	24	26	43	1	47	4	2	3	2	2	.50	4	.218	.370	.335
1991	Greenville	AA	73	204	41	9	0	10	80	31	41	53	4	51	3	1	5	0	1	.00	4	.201	.366	.392
1992	Richmond	AAA	79	238	62	13	0	9	102	46	36	57	3	59	5	0	2	0	1	.00	4	.261	.411	.429
1993	Calgary	AAA	80	235	58	12	0	11	103	43	41	41	0	65	5	4	2	5	1	.83	5	.247	.367	.438
1994	Las Vegas	AAA	99	298	86	19	1	13	146	42	51	58	0	73	8	1	3	1	1	.50	11	.289	.414	.490
	9 Min. YEARS		826	2417	590	119	5	117	1070	397	426	537	15	723	52	12	29	35	16	.69	46	.244	.388	.443

Darrel Deak

Bats: Both   Throws: Right   Pos: 2B   Ht: 6'0"   Wt: 180   Born: 07/05/69   Age: 25

			BATTING														BASERUNNING				PERCENTAGES		
Year	Team	Lg	G	AB	H	2B	3B	HR	TB	R	RBI	TBB	IBB	SO	HBP	SH	SF	SB	CS	SB%	GDP	Avg	OBP	SLG
1991	Johnson Cty	R	66	215	65	23	2	9	119	43	34	43	1	44	5	0	4	1	6	.14	2	.302	.423	.553
1992	Springfield	A	126	428	122	28	4	16	212	84	79	65	2	71	7	1	5	12	2	.86	9	.285	.384	.495
1993	Arkansas	AA	121	414	100	22	1	19	181	63	73	58	6	103	10	1	5	4	8	.33	8	.242	.345	.437
1994	Louisville	AAA	133	486	132	23	2	18	213	65	73	50	5	107	4	1	3	1	2	.33	15	.272	.343	.438
	4 Min. YEARS		446	1543	419	96	12	62	725	255	259	216	14	325	26	3	17	18	18	.50	34	.272	.367	.470

Joe DeBerry

Bats: Left   Throws: Left   Pos: 1B   Ht: 6'2"   Wt: 195   Born: 06/30/70   Age: 25

			BATTING														BASERUNNING				PERCENTAGES		
Year	Team	Lg	G	AB	H	2B	3B	HR	TB	R	RBI	TBB	IBB	SO	HBP	SH	SF	SB	CS	SB%	GDP	Avg	OBP	SLG
1991	Billings	R	65	236	62	13	0	10	105	41	47	36	1	46	3	0	1	5	4	.56	4	.263	.366	.445
1992	Cedar Rapds	A	127	455	109	22	4	15	184	58	68	43	1	102	2	0	3	3	3	.50	5	.240	.306	.404
1993	Albany	A	125	446	114	19	7	12	183	58	63	24	1	111	3	2	5	3	7	.30	6	.256	.295	.410
1994	Albany-Colo	AA	15	53	15	4	1	0	21	3	3	5	0	11	0	0	0	0	1	.00	2	.283	.345	.396
	4 Min. YEARS		332	1190	300	58	12	37	493	160	181	108	3	270	8	2	9	11	15	.42	17	.252	.316	.414

Dean Decillis

Bats: Right   Throws: Right   Pos: SS   Ht: 5'11"   Wt: 180   Born: 07/09/67   Age: 27

			BATTING														BASERUNNING				PERCENTAGES		
Year	Team	Lg	G	AB	H	2B	3B	HR	TB	R	RBI	TBB	IBB	SO	HBP	SH	SF	SB	CS	SB%	GDP	Avg	OBP	SLG
1987	Fayetteville	A	49	160	38	6	1	0	46	24	10	17	1	31	1	2	1	5	5	.50	3	.238	.311	.288
1988	Lakeland	A	122	436	113	14	4	5	150	43	61	24	3	64	1	5	4	9	10	.47	11	.259	.297	.344
1989	London	AA	98	375	92	14	1	5	123	47	46	31	0	47	2	1	0	4	4	.50	7	.245	.306	.328
1990	Toledo	AAA	31	77	22	4	0	0	26	8	9	9	0	7	1	0	1	0	0	.00	2	.286	.364	.338
	London	AA	72	264	74	19	1	3	104	27	29	17	0	23	0	1	4	5	0	1.00	4	.280	.319	.394
1991	London	AA	59	225	60	8	1	1	73	25	32	18	0	27	0	0	7	2	3	.40	13	.267	.312	.324
	Toledo	AAA	39	143	44	7	0	2	57	20	18	17	3	11	1	3	1	3	2	.60	2	.308	.383	.399
1992	Toledo	AAA	86	268	66	7	0	2	79	23	16	15	2	37	2	3	0	0	3	.00	8	.246	.291	.295
1993	Shreveport	AA	2	5	1	0	0	0	1	0	1	0	0	0	0	0	0	0	0	.00	1	.200	.200	.200
	London	AA	54	208	61	13	0	5	89	28	26	25	1	22	0	0	1	1	0	1.00	1	.293	.368	.428
1994	Trenton	AA	88	295	76	18	2	6	116	33	32	27	2	40	1	0	1	2	2	.50	14	.258	.321	.393
	8 Min. YEARS		700	2456	647	110	10	29	864	278	280	200	12	309	9	15	21	31	30	.51	72	.263	.319	.352

Steve Decker

Bats: Right Throws: Right Pos: C Ht: 6' 3" Wt: 205 Born: 10/25/65 Age: 29

									BATTING										BASERUNNING				PERCENTAGES		
Year	Team	Lg	G	AB	H	2B	3B	HR	TB	R	RBI	TBB	IBB	SO	HBP	SH	SF	SB	CS	SB%	GDP	Avg	OBP	SLG
1988	Everett	A	13	42	22	2	0	2	30	11	13	7	0	5	1	0	3	0	0	.00	1	.524	.566	.714
	San Jose	A	47	175	56	9	0	4	77	31	34	21	1	21	1	1	0	0	2	.00	4	.320	.396	.440
1989	San Jose	A	64	225	65	12	0	3	86	27	46	44	3	36	0	0	5	8	5	.62	9	.289	.398	.382
	Shreveport	AA	44	142	46	8	0	1	57	19	18	11	0	24	0	1	1	0	3	.00	1	.324	.370	.401
1990	Shreveport	AA	116	403	118	22	1	15	187	52	80	40	2	64	2	0	7	3	7	.30	11	.293	.354	.464
1991	Phoenix	AAA	31	111	28	5	1	6	53	20	14	13	0	29	1	0	1	0	0	.00	1	.252	.336	.477
1992	Phoenix	AAA	125	450	127	22	2	8	177	50	74	47	2	64	3	0	9	2	4	.33	19	.282	.348	.393
1994	Edmonton	AAA	73	259	101	23	0	11	157	38	48	27	1	24	2	1	3	0	1	.00	7	.390	.447	.606
1990	San Francisco	NL	15	54	16	2	0	3	27	5	8	1	0	10	0	1	0	0	0	.00	1	.296	.309	.500
1991	San Francisco	NL	79	233	48	7	1	5	72	11	24	16	1	44	3	2	4	0	1	.00	7	.206	.262	.309
1992	San Francisco	NL	15	43	7	1	0	0	8	3	1	6	0	7	1	0	0	0	0	.00	0	.163	.280	.186
1993	Florida	NL	8	15	0	0	0	0	0	0	1	3	0	3	0	0	1	0	0	.00	2	.000	.158	.000
	6 Min. YEARS		513	1807	563	103	4	50	824	248	327	210	9	267	10	3	28	13	22	.37	57	.312	.381	.456
	4 Maj. YEARS		117	345	71	10	1	8	107	19	34	26	1	64	4	3	5	0	1	.00	10	.206	.266	.310

Jim Dedrick

Pitches: Right Bats: Both Pos: P Ht: 6'0" Wt: 185 Born: 04/04/68 Age: 27

			HOW MUCH HE PITCHED						WHAT HE GAVE UP												THE RESULTS					
Year	Team	Lg	G	GS	CG	GF	IP	BFP	H	R	ER	HR	SH	SF	HB	TBB	IBB	SO	WP	Bk	W	L	Pct.	ShO	Sv	ERA
1990	Wausau	A	3	1	0	1	10	41	6	4	3	0	0	0	0	4	0	8	0	3	1	0	1.000	0	0	2.70
1991	Kane County	A	16	15	0	0	88.1	380	84	38	29	2	1	2	5	38	1	71	5	2	4	5	.444	0	0	2.95
1992	Frederick	A	38	5	1	19	108.2	454	94	41	37	5	5	0	5	42	4	86	4	3	8	4	.667	0	3	3.06
1993	Bowie	AA	38	6	1	14	106.1	426	84	36	30	4	5	0	3	32	1	78	1	0	8	3	.727	1	3	2.54
	Rochester	AAA	1	1	1	0	7	27	6	2	2	2	0	0	0	0	0	3	0	0	1	0	1.000	0	0	2.57
1994	Rochester	AAA	44	1	0	18	99	421	98	56	42	7	3	1	3	35	7	70	4	1	3	6	.333	0	1	3.82
	5 Min. YEARS		140	29	3	52	419.1	1749	372	177	143	20	14	3	16	151	13	316	14	9	24	19	.558	1	7	3.07

Bobby DeJardin

Bats: Both Throws: Right Pos: 2B Ht: 5'11" Wt: 180 Born: 01/08/67 Age: 28

									BATTING										BASERUNNING				PERCENTAGES		
Year	Team	Lg	G	AB	H	2B	3B	HR	TB	R	RBI	TBB	IBB	SO	HBP	SH	SF	SB	CS	SB%	GDP	Avg	OBP	SLG
1988	Oneonta	A	69	289	85	8	4	1	104	45	24	33	1	47	0	4	3	15	6	.71	1	.294	.363	.360
1989	Pr William	A	131	475	132	19	1	1	156	66	36	52	2	69	10	15	3	38	11	.78	11	.278	.359	.328
1990	Albany	AA	103	388	102	21	0	1	126	52	27	43	0	75	10	8	5	13	8	.62	5	.263	.348	.325
1991	Albany	AA	129	482	142	21	0	2	169	74	53	62	1	55	2	8	1	18	13	.58	9	.295	.377	.351
1992	Columbus	AAA	124	416	99	14	3	3	128	51	42	40	1	80	1	8	6	13	6	.68	13	.238	.302	.308
1993	Columbus	AAA	103	360	99	17	7	5	145	45	37	34	0	45	1	4	3	10	8	.56	8	.275	.337	.403
1994	Columbus	AAA	44	119	21	6	1	0	29	16	10	18	0	17	0	0	2	4	3	.57	1	.176	.281	.244
	Albany-Colo	AA	14	49	10	1	0	0	11	6	4	7	1	8	0	2	0	1	1	.50	1	.204	.304	.224
	7 Min. YEARS		717	2578	690	107	16	13	868	355	236	289	6	396	24	49	23	112	56	.67	49	.268	.344	.337

Mike DeJean

Pitches: Right Bats: Right Pos: P Ht: 6'2" Wt: 205 Born: 09/28/70 Age: 24

			HOW MUCH HE PITCHED						WHAT HE GAVE UP												THE RESULTS					
Year	Team	Lg	G	GS	CG	GF	IP	BFP	H	R	ER	HR	SH	SF	HB	TBB	IBB	SO	WP	Bk	W	L	Pct.	ShO	Sv	ERA
1992	Oneonta	A	20	0	0	19	20.2	78	12	3	1	1	0	0	0	3	0	20	0	0	0	0	.000	0	16	0.44
1993	Greensboro	A	20	0	0	18	18	87	22	12	10	1	1	1	0	8	2	16	1	0	2	3	.400	0	9	5.00
1994	Tampa	A	34	0	0	33	34	156	39	15	9	1	1	2	2	13	0	22	2	0	0	2	.000	0	16	2.38
	Albany-Colo	AA	16	0	0	10	24.2	110	22	14	12	1	4	1	2	15	3	13	6	0	0	0	.000	0	4	4.38
	3 Min. YEARS		90	0	0	80	97.1	431	95	44	32	4	6	4	4	39	5	71	9	0	2	7	.222	0	45	2.96

Guido DeJesus

Pitches: Left Bats: Left Pos: P Ht: 5'11" Wt: 198 Born: 08/03/71 Age: 23

			HOW MUCH HE PITCHED						WHAT HE GAVE UP												THE RESULTS					
Year	Team	Lg	G	GS	CG	GF	IP	BFP	H	R	ER	HR	SH	SF	HB	TBB	IBB	SO	WP	Bk	W	L	Pct.	ShO	Sv	ERA
1992	Elizabethtn	R	2	0	0	0	2.1	12	3	3	2	0	0	0	0	3	0	3	1	0	0	0	.000	0	0	7.71
1993	Elizabethtn	R	12	12	0	0	78.1	323	55	27	26	9	3	1	3	36	0	79	5	0	9	0	1.000	0	0	2.99
1994	Fort Wayne	A	21	0	0	10	38.2	143	21	4	4	2	1	0	1	13	1	55	3	0	5	2	.714	0	2	0.93
	Nashville	AA	2	0	0	0	2	6	0	0	0	0	0	0	0	0	0	2	0	0	0	0	.000	0	0	0.00
	3 Min. YEARS		37	12	0	11	121.1	484	79	34	32	11	4	1	3	52	1	139	9	0	14	2	.875	0	2	2.37

Javier Delahoya

Pitches: Right Bats: Right Pos: P Ht: 6'2" Wt: 160 Born: 02/21/70 Age: 25

			HOW MUCH HE PITCHED						WHAT HE GAVE UP												THE RESULTS					
Year	Team	Lg	G	GS	CG	GF	IP	BFP	H	R	ER	HR	SH	SF	HB	TBB	IBB	SO	WP	Bk	W	L	Pct.	ShO	Sv	ERA
1989	Dodgers	R	9	8	2	1	55.1	212	28	13	9	0	1	1	4	19	0	70	3	1	4	3	.571	1	0	1.46
1990	Vero Beach	A	4	4	0	0	21	100	14	14	13	0	1	1	1	20	2	22	0	0	1	2	.333	0	0	5.57
	Bakersfield	A	9	7	0	0	39.1	190	50	30	26	5	0	1	1	24	0	37	6	0	4	1	.800	0	0	5.95

	Lg	G	GS	CG	SHO	IP	BF	H	R	ER	HR				BB		SO			W	L	Pct			ERA
Yakima	A	14	14	0	0	70.2	326	65	52	35	2	2	5	7	39	2	71	9	0	3	5	.375	0	0	4.46
1991 Bakersfield	A	27	11	1	7	98	425	92	47	40	6	2	3	1	44	1	102	3	3	6	4	.600	0	2	3.67
1992 Vero Beach	A	14	14	2	0	80	325	68	25	25	4	1	1	4	26	0	92	2	0	4	5	.444	2	0	2.81
San Antonio	AA	5	5	0	0	25.1	116	20	11	8	1	1	2	1	17	0	24	1	0	2	1	.667	0	0	2.84
1993 San Antonio	AA	21	21	1	0	125.1	537	122	61	51	14	4	3	8	42	0	107	2	1	8	10	.444	0	0	3.66
1994 Portland	AA	22	11	1	5	73.2	328	81	56	53	11	2	1	2	29	4	60	3	0	0	7	.000	0	2	6.48
Brevard Cty	A	9	7	0	1	50	201	39	17	14	2	1	2	3	12	1	45	1	0	4	3	.571	0	0	2.52
6 Min. YEARS		134	102	7	14	638.2	2760	579	326	274	45	15	20	32	272	10	630	30	5	36	41	.468	3	4	3.86

Alex Delgado

Bats: Right Throws: Right Pos: 2B   Ht: 6'0" Wt: 160 Born: 01/11/71 Age: 24

							BATTING											BASERUNNING				PERCENTAGES		
Year Team	Lg	G	AB	H	2B	3B	HR	TB	R	RBI	TBB	IBB	SO	HBP	SH	SF	SB	CS	SB%	GDP	Avg	OBP	SLG
1988 R.S./mamrs	R	34	111	39	10	0	0	49	11	22	6	0	5	1	3	2	2	4	.33	1	.351	.383	.441
1989 Winter Havn	A	78	285	64	7	0	0	71	27	16	17	0	30	1	5	0	7	3	.70	9	.225	.271	.249
1990 New Britain	AA	7	18	1	1	0	0	2	3	0	2	0	5	0	0	0	0	0	.00	1	.056	.150	.111
Winter Havn	A	89	303	68	9	2	1	84	37	25	37	0	37	3	5	3	10	4	.71	7	.224	.312	.277
1991 Lynchburg	A	61	179	38	8	0	0	46	21	17	16	0	19	2	1	1	2	1	.67	6	.212	.283	.257
1992 Winter Havn	A	56	167	35	2	0	2	43	11	12	16	0	11	1	4	1	1	1	.50	6	.210	.281	.257
1993 Ft.Laud	A	63	225	57	9	0	2	72	26	25	9	1	21	5	7	1	2	2	.50	4	.253	.296	.320
New Britain	AA	33	87	16	2	0	1	21	10	9	4	0	11	4	4	2	1	1	.50	5	.184	.247	.241
1994 Red Sox	R	7	24	4	1	0	0	5	3	7	2	1	2	2	0	1	0	0	.00	0	.167	.276	.208
New Britain	AA	40	140	36	3	0	2	45	16	12	4	0	21	2	1	1	1	1	.50	7	.257	.286	.321
7 Min. YEARS		468	1539	358	52	2	8	438	165	145	113	2	162	21	30	12	26	17	.60	46	.233	.292	.285

Joe Dellicarri

Bats: Right Throws: Right Pos: 3B   Ht: 6'1" Wt: 178 Born: 01/16/67 Age: 28

							BATTING											BASERUNNING				PERCENTAGES		
Year Team	Lg	G	AB	H	2B	3B	HR	TB	R	RBI	TBB	IBB	SO	HBP	SH	SF	SB	CS	SB%	GDP	Avg	OBP	SLG
1989 Pittsfield	A	7	24	9	1	0	0	10	3	5	4	0	4	0	0	0	1	0	1.00	0	.375	.464	.417
St.Lucie	A	44	107	28	3	0	4	43	17	18	14	0	18	2	4	1	1	3	.25	2	.262	.355	.402
1990 St. Lucie	A	40	126	26	1	2	0	31	16	13	17	0	34	3	0	3	5	2	.71	3	.206	.309	.246
Jackson	AA	49	120	33	7	3	1	49	18	9	15	0	34	1	1	0	1	3	.25	2	.275	.360	.408
1991 Williamsprt	AA	80	215	52	10	2	5	81	30	23	22	0	36	4	5	2	7	2	.78	4	.242	.321	.377
1992 Tidewater	AAA	5	16	4	0	0	1	7	1	1	1	0	3	0	0	0	0	0	.00	0	.250	.294	.438
Binghamton	AA	109	328	82	11	2	2	103	32	29	33	1	52	6	2	1	1	5	.17	6	.250	.329	.314
1993 Norfolk	AAA	7	13	1	0	0	0	1	0	1	2	0	5	0	0	0	1	0	1.00	0	.077	.200	.077
Binghamton	AA	85	252	63	16	1	1	84	37	19	30	2	49	3	6	2	2	1	.67	4	.250	.334	.333
1994 Trenton	AA	116	316	71	16	3	1	96	36	26	34	1	61	2	4	0	8	5	.62	8	.225	.304	.304
6 Min. YEARS		542	1517	369	65	13	15	505	190	144	172	4	296	21	22	9	27	21	.56	30	.243	.327	.333

Chris Demetral

Bats: Left Throws: Right Pos: 2B   Ht: 5'11" Wt: 175 Born: 12/08/69 Age: 25

							BATTING											BASERUNNING				PERCENTAGES		
Year Team	Lg	G	AB	H	2B	3B	HR	TB	R	RBI	TBB	IBB	SO	HBP	SH	SF	SB	CS	SB%	GDP	Avg	OBP	SLG
1991 Yakima	A	65	226	64	11	0	2	81	43	41	34	2	32	1	6	0	4	3	.57	2	.283	.379	.358
1992 Bakersfield	A	90	306	84	14	1	4	112	38	36	33	7	45	1	4	3	7	8	.47	3	.275	.344	.366
1993 Vero Beach	A	122	437	142	22	3	5	185	63	48	69	2	47	2	6	3	6	6	.50	9	.325	.417	.423
1994 San Antonio	AA	108	368	96	26	3	6	146	44	39	34	5	44	1	11	2	5	2	.71	8	.261	.323	.397
4 Min. YEARS		385	1337	386	73	7	17	524	188	164	170	16	168	5	27	8	22	19	.54	22	.289	.369	.392

Drew Denson

Bats: Right Throws: Right Pos: 1B   Ht: 6'5" Wt: 220 Born: 11/16/65 Age: 29

							BATTING											BASERUNNING				PERCENTAGES		
Year Team	Lg	G	AB	H	2B	3B	HR	TB	R	RBI	TBB	IBB	SO	HBP	SH	SF	SB	CS	SB%	GDP	Avg	OBP	SLG
1984 Braves	R	62	239	77	20	3	10	133	43	45	17	0	41	3	0	1	5	2	.71	8	.322	.373	.556
1985 Sumter	A	111	383	115	18	4	14	183	59	74	53	3	76	4	0	4	5	3	.63	16	.300	.387	.478
1986 Durham	A	72	231	54	6	3	4	78	31	23	25	0	46	2	1	0	6	1	.86	10	.234	.314	.338
1987 Greenville	AA	128	447	98	23	1	14	165	54	55	33	1	95	11	1	2	1	2	.33	15	.219	.288	.369
1988 Greenville	AA	140	507	136	26	4	13	209	85	78	44	1	116	14	3	4	11	9	.55	11	.268	.341	.412
1989 Richmond	AAA	138	463	118	32	0	9	177	50	59	42	2	116	12	1	5	0	1	.00	4	.255	.330	.382
1990 Richmond	AAA	90	295	68	4	1	7	95	25	29	26	2	57	9	0	3	0	0	.00	9	.231	.309	.322
1992 Vancouver	AAA	105	340	94	7	3	13	146	43	70	36	3	58	7	0	0	1	0	1.00	12	.276	.358	.429
1993 Nashville	AAA	136	513	144	36	0	24	252	82	103	46	7	98	23	0	8	0	0	.00	22	.281	.361	.491
1994 Nashville	AAA	138	505	133	31	2	30	258	94	103	56	7	74	35	0	7	3	2	.60	13	.263	.371	.511
1989 Atlanta	NL	12	36	9	1	0	0	10	1	5	3	0	9	0	0	0	1	0	1.00	0	.250	.308	.278
1993 Chicago	AL	4	5	1	0	0	0	1	0	0	0	0	2	0	0	0	0	0	.00	0	.200	.200	.200
10 Min. YEARS		1120	3923	1037	203	21	138	1696	566	639	378	26	777	120	6	34	32	20	.62	120	.264	.345	.432
2 Maj. YEARS		16	41	10	1	0	0	11	1	5	3	0	11	0	0	0	1	0	1.00	0	.244	.295	.268

John DeSilva

Pitches: Right Bats: Right Pos: P Ht: 6' 0" Wt: 195 Born: 09/30/67 Age: 27

			HOW MUCH HE PITCHED						WHAT HE GAVE UP											THE RESULTS					
Year	Team	Lg	G	GS	CG	GF	IP	BFP	H	R	ER	HR	SH	SF	HB	TBB	IBB	SO	WP	Bk	W	L	Pct.	ShO	Sv	ERA
1989	Niagara Fls	A	4	4	0	0	24	95	15	5	5	0	1	0	2	8	0	24	3	1	3	0	1.000	0	0	1.88
	Fayettevlle	A	9	9	1	0	52.2	215	40	23	16	4	1	2	0	21	0	54	2	3	2	2	.500	0	0	2.73
1990	Lakeland	A	14	14	0	0	91	349	54	18	15	4	1	2	4	25	0	113	3	1	8	1	.889	0	0	1.48
	London	AA	14	14	1	0	89	372	87	47	37	4	1	4	2	27	0	76	3	0	5	6	.455	1	0	3.74
1991	London	AA	11	11	2	0	73.2	294	51	24	23	4	2	2	0	24	0	80	1	0	5	4	.556	0	0	2.81
	Toledo	AAA	11	11	1	0	58.2	254	62	33	30	10	0	1	1	21	0	56	1	0	5	4	.556	0	0	4.60
1992	Toledo	AAA	7	2	0	3	19	89	26	18	18	5	1	0	0	8	0	21	0	0	0	3	.000	0	0	8.53
	London	AA	9	9	1	0	52.1	216	51	24	24	4	1	2	1	13	0	53	2	1	2	4	.333	1	0	4.13
1993	Toledo	AAA	25	24	1	0	161	675	145	73	66	13	2	5	0	60	2	136	3	1	7	10	.412	0	0	3.69
1994	Albuquerque	AAA	25	6	0	4	66.2	317	90	62	58	7	1	3	4	27	0	39	3	0	3	5	.375	0	1	7.83
	San Antonio	AA	25	2	0	7	46	202	46	29	26	3	2	1	1	18	2	46	2	1	1	3	.250	0	2	5.09
1993	Detroit	AL	1	0	0	1	1	4	2	1	1	0	0	1	0	0	0	0	0	0	0	0	.000	0	0	9.00
	Los Angeles	NL	3	0	0	2	5.1	23	6	4	4	0	0	0	0	1	0	6	0	0	0	0	.000	0	0	6.75
	6 Min. YEARS		154	106	7	14	734	3078	667	356	318	58	13	22	15	252	4	698	23	8	41	42	.494	3	3	3.90

Cesar Devarez

Bats: Right Throws: Right Pos: C Ht: 5'10" Wt: 175 Born: 09/22/69 Age: 25

						BATTING										BASERUNNING				PERCENTAGES		
Year	Team	Lg	G	AB	H	2B	3B	HR	TB	R	RBI	TBB	IBB	SO	HBP	SH	SF	SB	CS	SB%	GDP	Avg	OBP	SLG
1989	Bluefield	R	12	42	9	4	0	0	13	3	7	1	0	5	0	0	0	0	0	.00	3	.214	.233	.310
1990	Wausau	A	56	171	34	4	1	3	49	7	19	7	0	28	0	2	0	2	3	.40	3	.199	.230	.287
1991	Frederick	A	74	235	59	13	2	3	85	25	29	14	0	28	4	2	1	2	2	.50	9	.251	.303	.362
1992	Hagerstown	AA	110	319	72	8	1	2	88	20	32	17	0	49	6	1	2	2	5	.29	3	.226	.276	.276
1993	Frederick	A	38	124	36	8	0	2	50	15	16	12	1	18	1	1	1	1	4	.20	2	.290	.358	.403
	Bowie	AA	57	174	39	7	1	0	48	14	15	5	0	21	2	2	2	5	1	.83	6	.224	.251	.276
1994	Bowie	AA	73	249	78	13	4	6	117	43	48	8	1	25	1	3	4	7	2	.78	10	.313	.332	.470
	6 Min. YEARS		420	1314	327	57	9	16	450	127	166	64	2	174	14	12	9	19	17	.53	36	.249	.289	.342

Carlos Diaz

Bats: Right Throws: Right Pos: C Ht: 6' 3" Wt: 190 Born: 12/24/64 Age: 30

						BATTING										BASERUNNING				PERCENTAGES		
Year	Team	Lg	G	AB	H	2B	3B	HR	TB	R	RBI	TBB	IBB	SO	HBP	SH	SF	SB	CS	SB%	GDP	Avg	OBP	SLG
1986	Ventura	A	2	5	2	1	0	0	3	1	0	1	0	2	0	0	0	0	0	.00	0	.400	.500	.600
	Medicne Hat	R	20	83	26	5	2	0	35	11	16	6	0	17	0	0	1	1	0	1.00	1	.313	.356	.422
	St.Cathrnes	A	24	74	13	3	1	1	21	9	5	7	2	18	2	0	1	1	0	1.00	1	.176	.262	.284
1987	Dunedin	A	73	230	53	6	0	0	59	24	27	22	0	41	1	1	1	3	2	.60	3	.230	.299	.257
1988	Knoxville	AA	7	23	5	1	0	0	6	2	0	2	0	4	0	0	0	0	1	.00	1	.217	.280	.261
	Dunedin	A	68	235	46	11	0	6	75	20	23	20	0	56	2	2	1	2	2	.50	8	.196	.264	.319
	Syracuse	AAA	27	83	14	5	0	1	22	4	8	1	0	23	0	2	1	0	0	.00	0	.169	.176	.265
1989	Knoxville	AA	100	320	80	12	1	6	112	28	36	17	0	55	3	4	3	3	1	.75	6	.250	.292	.350
1990	Syracuse	AAA	77	251	51	10	0	1	64	18	19	17	1	51	0	5	2	2	2	.50	9	.203	.252	.255
1991	Denver	AAA	1	1	0	0	0	0	0	0	0	0	0	1	0	0	0	0	0	.00	0	.000	.000	.000
	Colo Sprngs	AAA	36	93	22	4	0	0	26	7	7	2	0	17	0	1	0	0	0	.00	0	.237	.253	.280
1992	Memphis	AA	37	101	19	5	0	1	27	4	12	3	0	15	3	1	3	1	1	.50	3	.188	.227	.267
	Omaha	AAA	22	68	12	2	1	0	16	3	5	0	0	9	0	1	1	0	1	.00	1	.176	.174	.235
1993	Memphis	AA	54	163	35	3	0	3	47	13	25	3	0	33	1	0	1	1	0	1.00	7	.215	.229	.288
1994	Memphis	AA	42	103	24	6	0	2	36	10	13	6	1	18	0	1	0	1	0	1.00	0	.233	.275	.350
1990	Toronto	AL	9	3	1	0	0	0	1	1	0	0	0	2	0	1	0	0	0	.00	0	.333	.333	.333
	9 Min. YEARS		590	1833	402	74	5	21	549	154	196	107	3	360	12	17	17	15	10	.60	44	.219	.265	.300

Eddy Diaz

Bats: Right Throws: Right Pos: INF Ht: 5'10" Wt: 160 Born: 09/29/71 Age: 23

						BATTING										BASERUNNING				PERCENTAGES		
Year	Team	Lg	G	AB	H	2B	3B	HR	TB	R	RBI	TBB	IBB	SO	HBP	SH	SF	SB	CS	SB%	GDP	Avg	OBP	SLG
1991	Bellingham	A	61	246	68	14	1	3	93	48	23	24	1	33	1	3	2	9	2	.82	4	.276	.341	.378
1992	San Berndno	A	114	436	119	15	2	9	165	80	39	38	0	46	6	12	2	33	16	.67	11	.273	.338	.378
1993	Appleton	A	46	189	63	14	2	3	90	28	33	15	2	13	0	0	0	13	9	.59	7	.333	.382	.476
	Jacksonville	AA	77	259	65	16	0	6	99	36	26	17	1	31	2	7	4	6	3	.67	5	.251	.298	.382
1994	Jacksonvlle	AA	104	340	84	20	0	8	128	43	42	21	1	23	2	9	3	13	5	.72	8	.247	.292	.376
	4 Min. YEARS		402	1470	399	79	5	29	575	235	163	115	5	146	11	31	11	74	35	.68	35	.271	.327	.391

Giomar Diaz

Bats: Right Throws: Right Pos: OF Ht: 5'8" Wt: 150 Born: 10/23/72 Age: 22

						BATTING										BASERUNNING				PERCENTAGES		
Year	Team	Lg	G	AB	H	2B	3B	HR	TB	R	RBI	TBB	IBB	SO	HBP	SH	SF	SB	CS	SB%	GDP	Avg	OBP	SLG
1993	Bellingham	A	62	211	48	8	3	1	65	31	23	34	2	46	2	4	0	4	7	.36	3	.227	.340	.308
1994	Appleton	A	110	385	116	23	3	8	169	57	46	42	1	77	2	5	1	9	16	.36	6	.301	.372	.439
	Jacksonvlle	AA	7	20	4	2	0	1	9	2	3	2	0	9	0	1	0	0	0	.00	0	.200	.273	.450
	2 Min. YEARS		179	616	168	33	6	10	243	90	72	78	3	132	4	10	1	13	23	.36	9	.273	.358	.394

68

Ralph Diaz

Pitches: Right Bats: Right Pos: P Ht: 6'1" Wt: 175 Born: 12/12/69 Age: 25

			HOW MUCH HE PITCHED						WHAT HE GAVE UP										THE RESULTS					
Year	Team	Lg	G	GS	CG	GF	IP	BFP	H	R	ER	HR	SH	SF	HB	TBB	IBB	SO	WP	Bk	W	L	Pct.	ShO	Sv	ERA
1989	Expos	R	11	8	1	1	54	225	62	27	22	1	1	0	1	9	0	50	3	2	2	8	.200	0	0	3.67
1990	Jamestown	A	24	4	0	14	41.2	174	33	18	14	2	2	0	2	15	2	39	2	0	4	3	.571	0	5	3.02
1991	Rockford	A	38	15	1	18	119.2	507	109	51	43	10	4	5	6	43	0	76	8	6	4	6	.400	1	3	3.23
1992	Indianapolis	AAA	1	1	0	0	4	17	3	2	2	0	0	1	1	3	0	2	0	0	0	0	.000	0	0	4.50
	Wst Plm Bch	A	24	12	3	5	119.2	460	88	34	29	5	3	4	3	24	0	77	2	1	8	4	.667	2	2	2.18
1993	Harrisburg	AA	31	8	0	7	91	394	86	46	36	4	1	3	5	31	1	62	8	1	5	4	.556	0	0	3.56
1994	Ottawa	AAA	7	5	0	0	28.2	135	41	25	20	5	0	1	0	15	1	14	3	0	0	4	.000	0	0	6.28
	Harrisburg	AA	24	22	0	0	136.2	583	126	77	67	16	6	7	4	69	0	98	4	2	9	8	.529	0	0	4.41
	6 Min. YEARS		160	75	5	45	595.1	2495	548	280	233	43	17	21	22	209	4	418	30	12	32	37	.464	3	10	3.52

Rob Dibble

Pitches: Right Bats: Left Pos: P Ht: 6'4" Wt: 220 Born: 01/24/64 Age: 31

			HOW MUCH HE PITCHED						WHAT HE GAVE UP										THE RESULTS					
Year	Team	Lg	G	GS	CG	GF	IP	BFP	H	R	ER	HR	SH	SF	HB	TBB	IBB	SO	WP	Bk	W	L	Pct.	ShO	Sv	ERA
1984	Tampa	A	15	11	2	1	64.2	279	59	31	21	2	1	3	1	29	4	39	3	1	5	2	.714	0	0	2.92
1985	Cedar Rapds	A	45	1	0	30	65.2	290	67	37	28	3	4	2	1	28	2	73	6	0	5	5	.500	0	12	3.84
1986	Vermont	AA	31	1	1	20	55.1	246	53	29	19	0	1	1	0	28	3	37	5	1	3	2	.600	0	10	3.09
	Denver	AAA	5	0	0	3	6.2	27	9	4	4	0	0	0	0	2	0	3	0	1	1	0	1.000	0	0	5.40
1987	Nashville	AAA	44	0	0	19	61	276	72	34	32	5	4	2	1	27	4	51	5	1	2	4	.333	0	4	4.72
1988	Nashville	AAA	31	0	0	25	35	140	21	9	9	2	1	2	1	14	0	41	3	0	2	1	.667	0	13	2.31
1994	Indianapols	AAA	6	5	0	0	4.1	27	5	11	11	1	0	1	0	10	0	5	2	0	0	0	.000	0	0	22.85
1988	Cincinnati	NL	37	0	0	6	59.1	235	43	12	12	2	2	3	1	21	5	59	3	2	1	1	.500	0	0	1.82
1989	Cincinnati	NL	74	0	0	18	99	401	62	23	23	4	3	4	3	39	11	141	7	0	10	5	.667	0	2	2.09
1990	Cincinnati	NL	68	0	0	29	98	384	62	22	19	3	4	6	1	34	3	136	3	1	8	3	.727	0	11	1.74
1991	Cincinnati	NL	67	0	0	57	82.1	334	67	32	29	5	5	3	0	25	2	124	5	0	3	5	.375	0	31	3.17
1992	Cincinnati	NL	63	0	0	49	70.1	286	48	26	24	3	2	2	2	31	2	110	6	0	3	5	.375	0	25	3.07
1993	Cincinnati	NL	45	0	0	37	41.2	196	34	33	30	8	1	0	2	42	0	49	4	0	1	4	.200	0	19	6.48
	6 Min. YEARS		177	18	3	98	292.2	1285	286	155	124	13	11	11	4	138	13	249	24	4	18	16	.529	0	39	3.81
	6 Maj. YEARS		354	0	0	196	450.2	1836	316	148	137	25	17	18	9	192	23	619	28	3	26	23	.531	0	88	2.74

Lance Dickson

Pitches: Left Bats: Right Pos: P Ht: 6'0" Wt: 185 Born: 10/19/69 Age: 25

			HOW MUCH HE PITCHED						WHAT HE GAVE UP										THE RESULTS					
Year	Team	Lg	G	GS	CG	GF	IP	BFP	H	R	ER	HR	SH	SF	HB	TBB	IBB	SO	WP	Bk	W	L	Pct.	ShO	Sv	ERA
1990	Geneva	A	3	3	0	0	17	56	5	1	1	1	0	0	0	4	0	29	0	0	2	1	.667	0	0	0.53
	Peoria	A	5	5	1	0	35.2	138	22	9	6	1	1	0	0	11	0	54	2	4	3	1	.750	0	0	1.51
	Charlotte	AA	3	3	1	0	23.2	87	13	1	1	0	1	0	0	3	0	28	2	0	2	1	.667	1	0	0.38
1991	Iowa	AAA	18	18	1	1	101.1	427	85	39	35	5	8	3	0	57	1	101	5	1	4	4	.500	1	0	3.11
1992	Iowa	AAA	1	1	0	0	2.1	15	6	5	5	1	0	0	0	2	0	2	1	0	0	1	.000	0	0	19.29
1993	Daytona	A	3	3	0	0	17	69	17	7	6	0	0	0	0	3	0	18	3	0	1	2	.333	0	0	3.18
	Orlando	AA	9	9	0	0	49.1	192	37	22	21	7	1	0	0	17	1	46	5	0	2	3	.400	0	0	3.83
	Iowa	AAA	2	2	0	0	4.1	20	6	5	5	0	0	1	0	1	0	3	1	0	0	1	.000	0	0	10.38
1994	Iowa	AAA	4	4	0	0	14.2	66	10	8	8	1	0	0	0	12	1	17	0	0	0	1	.000	0	0	4.91
1990	Chicago	NL	3	3	0	0	13.2	61	20	12	11	2	2	1	0	4	1	4	0	1	0	3	.000	0	0	7.24
	5 Min. YEARS		48	48	3	1	265.1	1070	201	97	88	16	11	4	0	110	3	298	19	5	14	15	.483	2	0	2.98

Mike Difelice

Bats: Right Throws: Right Pos: C Ht: 6'2" Wt: 205 Born: 05/28/69 Age: 26

			BATTING														BASERUNNING				PERCENTAGES		
Year	Team	Lg	G	AB	H	2B	3B	HR	TB	R	RBI	TBB	IBB	SO	HBP	SH	SF	SB	CS	SB%	GDP	Avg	OBP	SLG
1991	Hamilton	A	43	157	33	5	0	4	50	10	15	9	0	40	1	0	0	1	5	.17	3	.210	.257	.318
1992	Hamilton	A	18	58	20	3	0	2	29	11	9	4	1	7	1	1	0	2	0	1.00	0	.345	.397	.500
	St. Pete	A	17	53	12	3	0	0	15	0	4	3	0	11	0	0	2	0	0	.00	3	.226	.259	.283
1993	Springfield	A	8	20	7	1	0	0	8	5	3	2	0	3	1	0	0	0	1	.00	0	.350	.435	.400
	St. Pete	A	30	97	22	2	0	0	24	5	8	11	1	13	1	2	2	1	0	1.00	4	.227	.306	.247
1994	Arkansas	AA	71	200	50	11	2	2	71	19	15	12	0	48	2	1	2	0	1	.00	9	.250	.296	.355
	4 Min. YEARS		187	585	144	25	2	8	197	50	54	41	2	122	6	4	6	4	7	.36	19	.246	.299	.337

Tony Diggs

Bats: Both Throws: Right Pos: OF Ht: 6'0" Wt: 175 Born: 04/20/67 Age: 28

			BATTING														BASERUNNING				PERCENTAGES		
Year	Team	Lg	G	AB	H	2B	3B	HR	TB	R	RBI	TBB	IBB	SO	HBP	SH	SF	SB	CS	SB%	GDP	Avg	OBP	SLG
1989	Helena	R	51	148	36	1	1	0	39	24	20	14	0	29	1	5	1	5	3	.63	0	.243	.311	.264
1990	Beloit	A	2	4	0	0	0	0	0	0	0	0	0	0	0	0	0	0	0	.00	0	.000	.000	.000
	Helena	R	42	129	33	5	0	0	38	18	13	11	0	19	2	1	2	10	5	.67	1	.256	.319	.295
1991	Beloit	A	124	448	121	9	8	3	155	70	34	65	2	76	3	5	1	52	19	.73	6	.270	.366	.346
1992	El Paso	AA	107	281	61	6	3	0	73	47	20	29	2	48	3	7	3	31	8	.79	6	.217	.294	.260
1993	New Orleans	AAA	11	27	7	3	0	0	10	4	1	3	0	6	0	1	0	4	2	.67	0	.259	.333	.370

Year Team	Lg	G	AB	H	2B	3B	HR	TB	R	RBI	TBB	IBB	SO	HBP	SH	SF	SB	CS	SB%	GDP	Avg	OBP	SLG
El Paso	AA	18	63	9	1	0	1	13	5	3	1	0	14	1	3	0	3	0	1.00	0	.143	.169	.206
Stockton	A	81	285	84	14	3	1	107	48	31	43	2	34	1	1	3	31	11	.74	2	.295	.389	.375
1994 Arkansas	AA	105	288	62	13	4	0	83	33	13	20	4	36	3	4	0	7	6	54	2	.215	.273	.288
6 Min. YEARS		541	1673	413	52	19	5	518	249	135	186	10	262	16	27	10	143	54	.73	19	.247	.326	.310

Glenn Disarcina

Bats: Left   Throws: Right   Pos: SS   Ht: 6'1"   Wt: 180   Born: 04/29/70   Age: 25

					BATTING												BASERUNNING				PERCENTAGES		
Year Team	Lg	G	AB	H	2B	3B	HR	TB	R	RBI	TBB	IBB	SO	HBP	SH	SF	SB	CS	SB%	GDP	Avg	OBP	SLG
1991 Utica	A	56	202	51	9	1	0	62	27	27	22	0	30	0	2	0	11	2	.85	5	.252	.326	.307
1992 South Bend	A	126	467	123	29	6	1	167	60	50	44	4	105	0	3	6	12	5	.71	11	.263	.323	.358
Sarasota	A	1	4	0	0	0	0	0	0	0	0	0	1	0	0	0	0	0	.00	0	.000	.000	.000
1993 Sarasota	A	120	477	135	29	5	4	186	73	47	33	4	77	2	0	6	11	5	.69	7	.283	.328	.390
Birmingham	AA	3	5	2	0	0	0	2	1	1	2	0	2	0	0	1	1	0	1.00	0	.400	.500	.400
1994 Birmingham	AA	118	452	116	26	2	7	167	50	57	25	3	74	3	4	4	10	5	.67	12	.257	.298	.369
4 Min. YEARS		424	1607	427	93	14	12	584	211	182	126	11	289	5	9	17	45	17	.73	35	.266	.318	.363

Glenn Dishman

Pitches: Left   Bats: Right   Pos: P   Ht: 6'1"   Wt: 195   Born: 11/05/70   Age: 24

		HOW MUCH HE PITCHED						WHAT HE GAVE UP									THE RESULTS					
Year Team	Lg	G	GS	CG	GF	IP	BFP	H	R	ER	HR	SH	SF	HB	TBB	IBB	SO	WP	Bk	W	L	Pct.	ShO	Sv	ERA
1993 Spokane	A	12	12	2	0	77.2	307	59	25	19	3	2	1	1	13	0	79	3	1	6	3	.667	2	0	2.20
Rancho Cuca	A	2	2	0	0	11.1	52	14	9	9	0	0	0	1	5	0	6	1	1	0	1	.000	0	0	7.15
1994 Wichita	AA	27	27	1	0	169.1	693	156	73	53	6	8	3	3	42	2	165	4	1	11	8	.579	0	0	2.82
Las Vegas	AAA	2	2	0	0	13	55	15	7	5	1	0	2	0	1	0	12	0	0	1	1	.500	0	0	3.46
2 Min. YEARS		43	43	3	0	271.1	1107	244	114	86	10	10	6	5	61	2	262	8	3	18	13	.581	2	0	2.85

Jamie Dismuke

Bats: Left   Throws: Right   Pos: 1B   Ht: 6'1"   Wt: 210   Born: 10/17/69   Age: 25

					BATTING												BASERUNNING				PERCENTAGES		
Year Team	Lg	G	AB	H	2B	3B	HR	TB	R	RBI	TBB	IBB	SO	HBP	SH	SF	SB	CS	SB%	GDP	Avg	OBP	SLG
1989 Reds	R	34	98	18	1	0	1	22	6	5	8	2	19	3	0	0	0	1	.00	0	.184	.266	.224
1990 Reds	R	39	124	44	8	4	7	81	22	28	28	5	8	5	0	2	3	3	.50	4	.355	.484	.653
1991 Cedar Rapds	A	133	492	125	35	1	8	186	56	72	50	3	80	4	2	9	4	2	.67	10	.254	.323	.378
1992 Chston-Vw	A	134	475	135	22	0	17	208	77	71	67	5	71	15	3	5	3	4	.43	15	.284	.386	.438
1993 Chattanooga	AA	136	497	152	22	1	20	236	69	91	48	6	60	14	0	4	4	2	.67	10	.306	.380	.475
1994 Indianapols	AAA	121	391	104	22	0	13	165	51	49	47	6	52	7	2	2	1	0	1.00	13	.266	.353	.422
6 Min. YEARS		597	2077	578	110	6	66	898	281	316	248	27	290	48	7	22	15	12	.56	52	.278	.365	.432

Eddie Dixon

Pitches: Right   Bats: Right   Pos: P   Ht: 6'3"   Wt: 195   Born: 04/16/64   Age: 31

		HOW MUCH HE PITCHED						WHAT HE GAVE UP									THE RESULTS					
Year Team	Lg	G	GS	CG	GF	IP	BFP	H	R	ER	HR	SH	SF	HB	TBB	IBB	SO	WP	Bk	W	L	Pct.	ShO	Sv	ERA
1985 Wst Plm Bch	A	9	9	1	0	54.1	231	49	25	19	0	2	3	2	19	0	38	1	1	3	2	.600	1	0	3.15
Jamestown	A	23	1	0	10	43.2	184	41	19	16	3	2	0	4	13	1	34	5	0	1	3	.250	0	4	3.30
1986 Wst Plm Bch	A	43	0	0	21	75	303	66	36	28	1	5	1	4	22	0	45	1	0	5	7	.417	0	4	3.36
1987 Wst Plm Bch	A	43	0	0	18	87.1	366	82	35	22	5	4	0	0	28	7	72	2	0	10	5	.667	0	4	2.27
1988 Jacksonville	AA	61	0	0	38	92	397	80	40	28	6	6	3	0	42	5	52	4	3	7	6	.538	0	4	2.74
1989 Jacksonville	AA	14	3	0	5	33.1	126	23	6	3	0	1	0	0	3	0	29	1	0	3	1	.750	0	1	0.81
Indianapols	AAA	27	4	0	7	54.1	227	45	20	15	2	5	0	0	18	0	31	0	0	3	2	.600	0	1	2.48
1990 Indianapols	AAA	57	6	0	25	110.2	451	87	47	40	5	3	6	5	35	1	40	2	0	6	7	.462	0	5	3.25
1991 Indianapols	AAA	53	8	0	16	117.2	489	120	50	38	5	4	2	2	30	8	63	1	2	6	7	.462	0	5	2.91
1992 Carolina	AA	25	0	0	20	28	115	25	14	10	0	0	1	2	3	1	17	0	1	2	2	.500	0	4	3.21
Buffalo	AAA	26	2	0	3	42	190	60	31	26	8	5	0	0	8	3	10	0	0	2	3	.400	0	0	5.57
1993 Tucson	AAA	50	0	0	18	80.1	353	92	54	37	6	10	0	1	22	7	41	7	0	4	3	.571	0	4	4.15
1994 Chattanooga	AA	25	0	0	14	29.2	134	35	21	13	4	2	2	2	9	2	16	1	0	2	4	.333	0	4	3.94
Harrisburg	AA	13	0	0	6	15	57	9	2	2	1	0	0	0	4	1	10	0	0	3	0	1.000	0	0	1.20
10 Min. YEARS		469	33	1	201	863.1	3623	814	400	297	46	49	18	22	256	36	498	25	6	57	52	.523	1	36	3.10

Thomas Dodge

Bats: Both   Throws: Right   Pos: C   Ht: 6'0"   Wt: 195   Born: 09/19/68   Age: 26

					BATTING												BASERUNNING				PERCENTAGES		
Year Team	Lg	G	AB	H	2B	3B	HR	TB	R	RBI	TBB	IBB	SO	HBP	SH	SF	SB	CS	SB%	GDP	Avg	OBP	SLG
1991 Quad City	A	21	63	12	2	0	0	14	13	5	9	0	12	1	0	0	3	1	.75	2	.190	.301	.222
Palm Sprngs	A	49	149	39	5	1	2	52	19	16	14	3	21	1	0	1	4	1	.80	8	.262	.327	.349
1992 Palm Sprngs	A	79	244	66	9	2	0	79	27	26	38	4	34	4	1	1	10	8	.56	5	.270	.376	.324
1993 Vancouver	AAA	7	17	4	1	0	0	5	3	4	1	0	2	0	0	3	3	0	1.00	0	.235	.238	.294
Palm Sprngs	A	97	366	99	9	2	1	115	47	44	35	1	38	7	2	4	13	10	.57	11	.270	.342	.314
1994 El Paso	AA	8	16	5	1	1	0	8	1	6	2	0	3	0	0	1	0	0	.00	0	.313	.368	.500
Lake Elsino	A	19	57	9	1	0	1	13	6	5	3	0	12	2	0	0	0	0	.00	1	.158	.226	.228
4 Min. YEARS		280	912	234	28	6	4	286	116	106	102	8	122	15	3	10	33	20	.62	27	.257	.338	.314

Bo Dodson

Bats: Left **Throws:** Left **Pos:** 1B **Ht:** 6'2" **Wt:** 195 **Born:** 12/07/70 **Age:** 24

														BATTING				BASERUNNING				PERCENTAGES		
Year	Team	Lg	G	AB	H	2B	3B	HR	TB	R	RBI	TBB	IBB	SO	HBP	SH	SF	SB	CS	SB%	GDP	Avg	OBP	SLG
1989	Helena	R	65	216	67	13	1	6	100	38	42	52	2	52	4	1	3	5	1	.83	4	.310	.447	.463
1990	Stockton	A	120	363	99	16	4	6	141	70	46	73	2	103	3	1	1	1	1	.50	3	.273	.398	.388
1991	Stockton	A	88	298	78	13	3	9	124	51	42	66	7	63	4	0	2	4	2	.67	2	.262	.400	.416
1992	El Paso	AA	109	335	83	19	6	4	126	47	46	72	6	81	0	0	1	3	7	.30	7	.248	.380	.376
1993	El Paso	AA	101	330	103	27	4	9	165	58	59	42	4	69	6	0	2	1	6	.14	3	.312	.397	.500
1994	El Paso	AA	26	68	10	3	0	0	13	6	7	12	0	18	1	0	0	0	1	.00	2	.147	.284	.191
	New Orleans	AAA	79	257	67	13	0	2	86	41	29	42	2	44	2	3	1	2	3	.40	8	.261	.368	.335
	6 Min. YEARS		588	1867	507	104	18	36	755	311	271	359	23	430	20	5	10	16	21	.43	28	.272	.393	.404

Blake Doolan

Pitches: Right **Bats:** Right **Pos:** P **Ht:** 6'0" **Wt:** 178 **Born:** 02/11/69 **Age:** 26

				HOW MUCH HE PITCHED					WHAT HE GAVE UP											THE RESULTS					
Year	Team	Lg	G	GS	CG	GF	IP	BFP	H	R	ER	HR	SH	SF	HB	TBB	IBB	SO	WP	Bk	W	L	Pct.	ShO	Sv	ERA
1992	Batavia	A	19	9	3	3	85.1	354	78	33	27	8	5	1	3	25	0	62	6	3	6	2	.750	2	1	2.85
1993	Spartanburg	A	8	8	1	0	58.1	228	50	16	11	2	1	1	0	9	1	34	2	0	2	2	.500	0	0	1.70
	Reading	AA	27	15	1	3	109.2	491	135	70	62	13	0	3	5	36	0	61	3	2	7	8	.467	0	0	5.09
1994	Clearwater	A	9	0	0	9	10.1	35	3	0	0	0	0	0	0	0	0	12	0	0	0	0	.000	0	5	0.00
	Reading	AA	50	0	0	22	67.1	297	70	45	40	5	5	3	3	28	3	42	8	1	3	2	.600	0	6	5.35
	3 Min. YEARS		113	32	5	37	331	1405	336	164	140	28	11	8	11	98	4	211	19	6	18	14	.563	2	12	3.81

Aaron Dorlarque

Pitches: Right **Bats:** Right **Pos:** P **Ht:** 6'3" **Wt:** 180 **Born:** 02/16/70 **Age:** 25

				HOW MUCH HE PITCHED					WHAT HE GAVE UP											THE RESULTS					
Year	Team	Lg	G	GS	CG	GF	IP	BFP	H	R	ER	HR	SH	SF	HB	TBB	IBB	SO	WP	Bk	W	L	Pct.	ShO	Sv	ERA
1992	Eugene	A	32	0	0	31	40.1	162	30	12	8	0	1	0	1	10	2	46	2	1	1	2	.333	0	13	1.79
1993	Rockford	A	28	0	0	28	49.1	198	37	12	8	3	3	3	1	12	0	51	4	0	2	3	.400	0	16	1.46
1994	Memphis	AA	50	0	0	33	75	336	88	41	33	5	5	6	2	26	6	51	4	0	7	4	.636	0	14	3.96
	3 Min. YEARS		110	0	0	90	164.2	696	155	65	49	8	9	9	6	48	8	148	10	1	10	9	.526	0	43	2.68

Bruce Dostal

Bats: Left **Throws:** Left **Pos:** OF **Ht:** 6'0" **Wt:** 195 **Born:** 03/10/65 **Age:** 30

														BATTING				BASERUNNING				PERCENTAGES		
Year	Team	Lg	G	AB	H	2B	3B	HR	TB	R	RBI	TBB	IBB	SO	HBP	SH	SF	SB	CS	SB%	GDP	Avg	OBP	SLG
1987	Great Falls	R	62	201	56	6	1	1	67	27	27	23	1	38	1	6	2	14	9	.61	0	.279	.352	.333
1988	Bakersfield	A	122	367	92	14	2	1	113	59	34	58	2	78	5	5	4	32	9	.78	2	.251	.357	.308
1989	Vero Beach	A	118	348	86	10	5	2	112	58	24	43	2	49	3	1	1	41	6	.87	8	.247	.334	.322
1990	Vero Beach	A	58	192	58	9	2	6	89	43	29	24	1	20	2	1	1	31	5	.86	2	.302	.384	.464
	San Antonio	AA	53	127	33	3	4	0	44	16	16	18	2	29	3	4	1	10	8	.56	1	.260	.362	.346
1991	Reading	AA	96	364	114	11	5	5	150	68	34	58	5	55	5	1	4	38	16	.70	5	.313	.411	.412
1992	Reading	AA	33	122	29	3	1	2	40	19	6	17	2	20	0	0	1	9	4	.69	1	.238	.329	.328
	Scranton/wb	AAA	65	168	37	7	0	1	47	32	7	45	4	35	1	2	0	10	4	.71	1	.220	.388	.280
1993	Scranton/wb	AAA	6	13	3	0	0	0	3	0	1	2	1	5	0	1	1	1	1	.50	1	.231	.313	.231
	Rochester	AAA	88	297	88	12	5	3	119	46	29	39	3	73	2	3	2	13	7	.65	3	.296	.379	.401
1994	Rochester	AAA	87	230	66	10	2	1	83	47	36	46	0	48	3	4	5	8	3	.73	3	.287	.405	.361
	8 Min. YEARS		788	2429	662	85	27	22	867	415	243	373	23	450	25	28	22	207	72	.74	27	.273	.372	.357

Mariano Dotel

Bats: Both **Throws:** Right **Pos:** SS **Ht:** 6'1" **Wt:** 130 **Born:** 04/03/71 **Age:** 24

														BATTING				BASERUNNING				PERCENTAGES		
Year	Team	Lg	G	AB	H	2B	3B	HR	TB	R	RBI	TBB	IBB	SO	HBP	SH	SF	SB	CS	SB%	GDP	Avg	OBP	SLG
1991	Myrtle Bch	A	125	327	67	7	0	0	74	42	20	43	0	90	2	17	0	7	15	.32	3	.205	.301	.226
1992	Dunedin	A	116	372	71	8	1	1	84	48	19	26	0	99	1	19	1	7	4	.64	4	.191	.245	.226
1993	Hagerstown	A	99	270	56	10	4	0	74	31	16	20	0	91	1	10	3	6	9	.40	3	.207	.262	.274
1994	Rancho Cuca	A	46	86	14	1	0	2	21	11	9	7	0	36	0	4	0	6	0	1.00	1	.163	.226	.244
	Wichita	AA	12	27	4	1	0	0	5	3	2	3	0	4	0	1	0	1	0	1.00	1	.148	.233	.185
	4 Min. YEARS		398	1082	212	27	5	3	258	135	66	99	0	320	4	51	4	27	28	.49	12	.196	.265	.238

Chris Dotolo

Bats: Right **Throws:** Right **Pos:** 2B **Ht:** 5'11" **Wt:** 175 **Born:** 10/01/68 **Age:** 26

														BATTING				BASERUNNING				PERCENTAGES		
Year	Team	Lg	G	AB	H	2B	3B	HR	TB	R	RBI	TBB	IBB	SO	HBP	SH	SF	SB	CS	SB%	GDP	Avg	OBP	SLG
1991	Giants	R	13	39	7	1	0	0	8	4	5	4	0	12	1	0	0	3	0	1.00	1	.179	.273	.205
	Clinton	A	3	8	1	1	0	0	2	2	1	0	0	2	0	0	1	0	0	.00	0	.125	.111	.250
1992	Clinton	A	66	199	49	7	0	0	56	15	13	18	0	55	2	1	0	2	3	.40	1	.246	.315	.281
1993	San Jose	A	58	157	31	9	0	0	40	17	22	23	0	36	3	4	3	1	3	.25	5	.197	.306	.255
1994	San Jose	A	6	17	1	0	0	0	1	0	2	1	0	6	0	0	0	0	0	.00	1	.059	.105	.059
	Shreveport	AA	12	22	7	0	0	0	7	1	1	3	0	5	0	0	0	1	1	.50	0	.318	.400	.318
	Phoenix	AAA	4	7	2	1	0	0	3	0	1	0	0	0	0	0	0	0	0	.00	0	.286	.286	.429
	4 Min. YEARS		162	449	98	19	0	0	117	39	45	49	0	116	6	5	5	7	7	.50	8	.218	.301	.261

Jim Dougherty

Pitches: Right Bats: Right Pos: P

Ht: 6'0" Wt: 210 Born: 03/08/68 Age: 27

Year	Team	Lg	G	GS	CG	GF	IP	BFP	H	R	ER	HR	SH	SF	HB	TBB	IBB	SO	WP	Bk	W	L	Pct.	ShO	Sv	ERA
1991	Asheville	A	61	0	0	48	82	324	63	17	14	0	7	0	3	24	6	76	0	2	3	1	.750	0	27	1.54
1992	Osceola	A	57	0	0	52	81	325	66	21	14	1	4	2	2	22	4	77	0	1	5	2	.714	0	31	1.56
1993	Jackson	AA	52	0	0	50	53	207	39	15	11	3	0	0	1	21	0	55	0	0	2	2	.500	0	36	1.87
1994	Tucson	AAA	55	0	0	48	59	276	70	32	27	9	1	1	2	30	6	49	4	0	5	4	.556	0	21	4.12
	4 Min. YEARS		225	0	0	198	275	1132	238	85	66	13	12	3	8	97	16	257	4	3	15	9	.625	0	115	2.16

Kelly Downs

Pitches: Right Bats: Right Pos: P

Ht: 6' 4" Wt: 200 Born: 10/25/60 Age: 34

Year	Team	Lg	G	GS	CG	GF	IP	BFP	H	R	ER	HR	SH	SF	HB	TBB	IBB	SO	WP	Bk	W	L	Pct.	ShO	Sv	ERA
1984	Portland	AAA	30	25	5	2	163	0	166	106	96	12	0	0	4	65	3	104	7	2	7	12	.368	0	0	5.30
1985	Phoenix	AAA	37	19	2	6	137	0	138	69	61	9	0	0	4	56	4	109	7	4	9	10	.474	1	1	4.01
1986	Phoenix	AAA	18	18	4	0	108	466	116	54	41	11	2	3	3	28	1	68	6	2	8	5	.615	0	0	3.42
1989	Phoenix	AAA	3	3	0	0	9.1	42	11	9	9	1	0	0	0	5	0	9	0	2	1	1	.500	0	0	8.68
	San Jose	A	1	1	0	0	5	21	1	0	0	0	0	0	0	4	0	7	0	0	0	0	.000	0	0	0.00
1990	San Jose	A	1	1	0	0	5	19	5	2	1	0	0	0	0	0	0	3	0	0	0	1	.000	0	0	1.80
	Phoenix	AAA	1	1	0	0	5	20	5	3	1	1	1	1	0	0	0	4	0	0	0	0	.000	0	0	1.80
1994	Salt Lake	AAA	2	1	0	0	7	29	7	4	4	1	0	1	0	1	0	5	0	0	1	0	1.000	0	0	5.14
1986	San Francisco	NL	14	14	1	0	88.1	372	78	29	27	5	4	4	3	30	7	64	3	2	4	4	.500	0	0	2.75
1987	San Francisco	NL	41	28	4	4	186	797	185	83	75	14	7	1	4	67	11	137	12	4	12	9	.571	3	1	3.63
1988	San Francisco	NL	27	26	6	0	168	685	140	67	62	11	4	9	3	47	8	118	7	4	13	9	.591	3	0	3.32
1989	San Francisco	NL	18	15	0	1	82.2	349	82	47	44	7	4	4	1	26	4	49	3	3	4	8	.333	0	0	4.79
1990	San Francisco	NL	13	9	0	1	63	265	56	26	24	2	2	1	2	20	4	31	2	1	3	2	.600	0	0	3.43
1991	San Francisco	NL	45	11	0	4	111.2	479	99	59	52	12	4	4	3	53	9	62	4	1	10	4	.714	0	0	4.19
1992	San Francisco	NL	19	7	0	5	62.1	272	65	27	24	4	7	2	3	24	0	33	4	0	1	2	.333	0	0	3.47
	Oakland	AL	18	13	0	2	82	364	72	36	30	4	6	4	4	46	3	38	3	1	5	5	.500	0	0	3.29
1993	Oakland	AL	42	12	0	12	119.2	539	135	80	75	14	3	4	2	60	8	66	4	1	5	10	.333	0	0	5.64
	6 Min. YEARS		93	69	11	8	439.1	597	449	247	213	35	3	5	15	159	8	309	20	10	26	29	.473	1	1	4.36
	8 Maj. YEARS		237	135	11	29	963.2	4122	912	454	413	73	41	33	25	373	54	598	42	17	57	53	.518	6	1	3.86

Ian Doyle

Pitches: Right Bats: Right Pos: P

Ht: 6'2" Wt: 200 Born: 09/11/71 Age: 23

Year	Team	Lg	G	GS	CG	GF	IP	BFP	H	R	ER	HR	SH	SF	HB	TBB	IBB	SO	WP	Bk	W	L	Pct.	ShO	Sv	ERA
1991	Burlington	R	25	0	0	23	43.1	187	44	20	16	2	4	3	1	11	1	44	5	1	2	4	.333	0	11	3.32
1992	Columbus	A	53	0	0	44	68	276	55	31	25	6	2	1	2	25	3	55	4	1	4	5	.444	0	26	3.31
1993	Kinston	A	47	0	0	38	52.2	228	44	20	18	9	2	0	1	29	0	51	6	0	5	1	.833	0	23	3.08
1994	Canton-Akm	AA	8	0	0	2	12.2	64	15	9	8	2	1	0	1	7	1	9	1	0	0	0	.000	0	0	5.68
	4 Min. YEARS		133	0	0	107	176.2	755	158	80	67	19	9	4	5	72	5	159	16	2	11	10	.524	0	60	3.41

Mike Draper

Pitches: Right Bats: Right Pos: P

Ht: 6' 2" Wt: 175 Born: 09/14/66 Age: 28

Year	Team	Lg	G	GS	CG	GF	IP	BFP	H	R	ER	HR	SH	SF	HB	TBB	IBB	SO	WP	Bk	W	L	Pct.	ShO	Sv	ERA
1988	Oneonta	A	8	0	0	8	10.2	46	10	4	1	0	0	1	0	3	0	16	1	0	2	1	.667	0	3	0.84
	Pr William	A	9	5	1	1	35.1	155	37	22	13	1	1	3	4	4	1	20	4	2	2	3	.400	0	0	3.31
1989	Pr William	A	25	24	6	0	153.1	646	147	66	53	7	3	4	6	42	4	84	12	1	14	8	.636	1	0	3.11
1990	Albany	AA	8	8	0	0	43.1	196	51	34	31	4	0	1	2	19	0	15	0	1	2	2	.500	0	0	6.44
	Ft.Lauderdle	A	14	14	1	0	96	389	80	30	24	1	5	3	3	22	0	52	5	4	9	1	.900	1	0	2.25
	Pr William	A	5	4	1	0	22.2	107	31	20	16	2	1	1	2	9	0	8	4	0	0	2	.000	0	0	6.35
1991	Albany	AA	36	14	1	6	131.1	555	125	58	48	6	5	3	6	47	3	71	10	1	10	6	.625	1	2	3.29
	Columbus	AAA	4	4	2	0	28.2	132	36	21	12	1	0	1	0	5	0	13	0	0	1	3	.250	0	0	3.77
1992	Columbus	AAA	57	3	0	50	80	332	70	36	32	3	2	5	6	28	2	42	3	0	5	6	.455	0	37	3.60
1994	Las Vegas	AAA	54	2	0	37	69.2	324	92	58	53	9	3	4	4	29	4	38	2	0	7	8	.467	0	12	6.85
1993	New York	NL	29	1	0	11	42.1	184	53	22	20	2	3	5	0	14	3	16	0	1	1	1	.500	0	0	4.25
	6 Min. YEARS		220	78	12	102	671	2882	679	349	283	34	20	26	33	208	14	359	41	9	52	40	.565	3	54	3.80

Darren Dreyer

Pitches: Right Bats: Right Pos: P

Ht: 6'0" Wt: 208 Born: 05/21/71 Age: 24

Year	Team	Lg	G	GS	CG	GF	IP	BFP	H	R	ER	HR	SH	SF	HB	TBB	IBB	SO	WP	Bk	W	L	Pct.	ShO	Sv	ERA
1992	Geneva	A	13	13	3	0	81.2	326	67	35	28	4	0	2	4	12	0	87	1	0	7	4	.636	1	0	3.09
1993	Geneva	A	3	3	0	0	19.2	80	22	9	8	1	0	2	1	4	1	10	0	1	2	1	.667	0	0	3.66
	Daytona	A	4	4	1	0	30	113	22	8	6	1	3	2	1	3	0	17	1	0	2	2	.500	1	0	1.80
1994	Orlando	AA	17	7	0	3	43.2	193	52	30	30	6	3	2	2	15	0	30	2	1	1	4	.200	0	0	6.18
	Daytona	A	15	14	3	0	89.1	379	99	51	49	7	0	2	4	18	1	57	5	0	2	9	.182	1	0	4.94
	3 Min. YEARS		52	41	7	3	264.1	1091	262	133	121	19	6	10	12	52	2	201	9	2	14	20	.412	3	0	4.12

Sean Drinkwater

Bats: Right **Throws:** Right **Pos:** SS   **Ht:** 6'3" **Wt:** 195 **Born:** 06/22/71 **Age:** 24

Year	Team	Lg	G	AB	H	2B	3B	HR	TB	R	RBI	TBB	IBB	SO	HBP	SH	SF	SB	CS	SB%	GDP	Avg	OBP	SLG
1992	Spokane	A	66	256	77	12	2	4	105	35	41	25	0	27	0	1	6	7	4	.64	8	.301	.355	.410
1993	Rancho Cuca	A	121	486	131	29	1	10	192	69	84	35	1	78	2	1	12	2	0	1.00	6	.270	.314	.395
1994	Wichita	AA	91	299	71	17	3	5	109	34	39	21	1	40	1	1	6	4	0	1.00	11	.237	.284	.365
	Rancho Cuca	A	28	96	22	6	0	1	31	15	12	10	0	29	1	1	2	1	0	1.00	2	.229	.303	.323
	3 Min. YEARS		306	1137	301	64	6	20	437	153	176	91	2	174	4	4	26	14	4	.78	27	.265	.315	.384

Brian DuBois

Pitches: Left **Bats:** Left **Pos:** P   **Ht:** 5'10" **Wt:** 194 **Born:** 04/18/67 **Age:** 28

Year	Team	Lg	G	GS	CG	GF	IP	BFP	H	R	ER	HR	SH	SF	HB	TBB	IBB	SO	WP	Bk	W	L	Pct.	ShO	Sv	ERA
1985	Bluefield	R	10	9	2	1	57.2	231	42	23	16	1	3	1	2	20	0	67	5	0	5	4	.556	1	0	2.50
1986	Hagerstown	A	5	5	0	0	20.1	95	29	19	16	1	1	1	1	11	0	17	2	1	1	2	.333	0	0	7.08
	Bluefield	R	3	1	0	0	9.1	37	8	2	1	0	0	0	0	2	0	8	1	1	1	1	.500	0	0	0.96
1987	Hagerstown	A	27	25	3	0	155	662	162	81	67	13	7	5	5	73	2	96	5	0	8	9	.471	1	0	3.89
1988	Virginia	A	9	9	0	0	48.2	228	66	42	30	2	1	1	0	20	0	35	2	1	2	5	.286	0	0	5.55
	Hagerstown	A	19	19	7	0	135	556	129	71	55	5	4	2	0	30	0	112	6	3	12	4	.750	1	0	3.67
1989	Hagerstown	AA	15	15	6	0	112	440	93	36	31	5	6	1	1	18	0	82	4	0	6	4	.600	2	0	2.49
	Rochester	AAA	4	4	0	0	30	121	24	8	6	3	0	0	0	12	0	16	2	0	3	1	.750	0	0	1.80
	Toledo	AAA	3	3	0	0	24	93	17	6	6	3	0	1	0	6	0	13	0	0	1	1	.500	0	0	2.25
1990	Toledo	AAA	13	10	2	2	69.2	297	67	27	21	6	2	2	2	26	1	47	2	0	5	4	.556	1	0	2.71
1991	Orioles	R	1	1	0	0	0	0	0	0	0	0	0	0	0	0	0	0	0	0	0	0	.000	0	0	0.00
1993	Frederick	A	10	8	1	0	58	237	50	19	10	2	2	0	0	13	1	55	4	0	6	2	.750	1	0	1.55
	Bowie	AA	13	13	0	0	75	316	71	36	21	2	4	5	1	29	0	37	5	0	6	1	.857	0	0	2.52
	Rochester	AAA	3	3	0	0	13	62	20	13	13	3	2	0	1	4	0	10	0	0	2	0	.000	0	0	9.00
1994	Rochester	AAA	8	7	0	0	27.1	132	50	24	22	3	0	0	0	6	0	20	1	0	0	4	.000	0	0	7.24
	Reading	AA	4	4	1	0	25.1	99	22	8	6	1	3	1	1	2	0	16	0	0	2	1	.667	1	0	2.13
	Scranton-Wb	AAA	27	0	0	10	37.1	150	28	10	9	3	0	4	3	11	3	25	1	0	4	0	1.000	0	2	2.17
1989	Detroit	AL	6	5	0	1	36	153	29	14	7	2	0	1	2	17	3	13	0	1	0	4	.000	0	1	1.75
1990	Detroit	AL	12	11	0	0	58.1	255	70	37	33	9	2	4	1	22	1	34	5	1	3	5	.375	0	0	5.09
	9 Min. YEARS		174	136	22	13	897.2	3756	878	425	330	53	35	24	17	283	7	656	40	6	62	45	.579	7	2	3.31
	2 Maj. YEARS		18	16	0	1	94.1	408	99	51	40	11	2	5	3	39	4	47	5	2	3	9	.250	0	1	3.82

Brian DuBose

Bats: Left **Throws:** Right **Pos:** 1B   **Ht:** 6'3" **Wt:** 208 **Born:** 05/17/71 **Age:** 24

Year	Team	Lg	G	AB	H	2B	3B	HR	TB	R	RBI	TBB	IBB	SO	HBP	SH	SF	SB	CS	SB%	GDP	Avg	OBP	SLG
1990	Bristol	R	67	223	56	8	0	6	82	31	21	24	2	53	3	0	1	5	3	.63	1	.251	.331	.368
1991	Lakeland	A	15	35	7	2	0	1	12	7	6	10	0	12	1	0	0	0	1	.00	0	.200	.391	.343
	Niagara Fls	A	44	164	42	7	1	7	72	26	32	17	0	32	1	0	0	3	1	.75	6	.256	.330	.439
1992	Fayetteville	A	122	404	92	20	5	12	158	49	73	64	1	100	4	2	4	19	12	.61	8	.228	.336	.391
1993	Lakeland	A	122	448	140	27	11	8	213	74	68	49	5	97	4	0	4	18	18	.50	11	.313	.382	.475
1994	Trenton	AA	108	378	85	10	3	9	128	48	41	32	0	96	6	1	1	12	10	.55	8	.225	.295	.339
	5 Min. YEARS		478	1652	422	74	20	43	665	235	241	196	8	390	19	3	10	57	45	.56	34	.255	.339	.403

Kyle Duey

Pitches: Right **Bats:** Right **Pos:** P   **Ht:** 6'2" **Wt:** 215 **Born:** 11/08/67 **Age:** 27

Year	Team	Lg	G	GS	CG	GF	IP	BFP	H	R	ER	HR	SH	SF	HB	TBB	IBB	SO	WP	Bk	W	L	Pct.	ShO	Sv	ERA
1990	Medicne Hat	R	15	11	0	1	72.1	325	72	38	31	4	2	2	4	34	0	54	8	0	4	6	.400	0	0	3.86
1991	Myrtle Bch	A	38	1	0	18	82.1	356	77	42	30	4	4	2	2	31	0	84	7	0	6	5	.545	0	5	3.28
	Dunedin	A	9	0	0	4	15.2	77	19	10	5	0	3	0	0	12	2	8	2	0	1	3	.250	0	0	2.87
1992	Dunedin	A	48	0	0	21	77	341	84	31	22	4	5	2	1	33	7	51	17	0	7	3	.700	0	7	2.57
1993	Knoxville	AA	37	1	0	16	68	317	92	57	52	7	3	2	0	27	0	40	6	0	2	3	.400	0	0	6.88
	Syracuse	AAA	11	0	0	4	20	83	19	10	9	1	0	1	0	7	1	13	3	0	2	1	.667	0	1	4.05
1994	Syracuse	AAA	12	0	0	3	17.2	87	26	17	13	2	1	1	1	6	1	9	0	0	0	0	.000	0	0	6.62
	Knoxville	AA	12	2	0	3	33.2	147	37	17	16	4	1	2	0	9	1	15	1	0	1	1	.500	0	0	4.28
	Jackson	AA	16	0	0	7	24.2	112	26	9	6	2	4	0	1	12	4	20	2	0	1	3	.250	0	0	2.19
	5 Min. YEARS		198	15	0	76	411.1	1845	452	231	184	28	23	12	9	171	16	294	46	0	24	25	.490	0	13	4.03

Kyle Duke

Pitches: Left **Bats:** Both **Pos:** P   **Ht:** 6'2" **Wt:** 197 **Born:** 09/26/70 **Age:** 24

Year	Team	Lg	G	GS	CG	GF	IP	BFP	H	R	ER	HR	SH	SF	HB	TBB	IBB	SO	WP	Bk	W	L	Pct.	ShO	Sv	ERA
1990	Peninsula	A	14	12	0	2	54.1	273	78	54	47	3	1	1	1	36	0	36	4	0	0	8	.000	0	0	7.79
	Bellingham	A	12	11	0	0	60.2	272	57	30	25	1	2	6	1	46	0	40	3	0	4	5	.444	0	0	3.71
1991	Bend	A	15	14	0	0	81	368	79	50	31	2	1	3	3	51	0	70	11	1	6	6	.500	0	0	3.44
1992	San Berndno	A	34	4	0	16	62	296	67	48	42	6	0	0	3	46	1	56	6	1	3	1	.750	0	1	6.10
1993	Central Val	A	28	0	0	24	41	171	42	14	14	1	2	1	2	12	0	40	4	0	3	3	.500	0	9	3.07
1994	New Haven	AA	33	0	0	10	63	312	82	49	31	5	5	1	1	34	1	37	4	0	1	2	.333	0	1	4.43
	5 Min. YEARS		136	41	0	52	362	1692	405	245	190	18	11	12	9	225	2	279	32	2	17	25	.405	0	11	4.72

73

Matt Dunbar

Pitches: Left **Bats: Left** **Pos: P** **Ht: 6'0"** **Wt: 160** **Born: 10/15/68** **Age: 26**

Year	Team	Lg	G	GS	CG	GF	IP	BFP	H	R	ER	HR	SH	SF	HB	TBB	IBB	SO	WP	Bk	W	L	Pct.	ShO	Sv	ERA
1990	Yankees	R	3	0	0	2	6	24	4	2	2	0	1	0	2	3	0	7	0	1	0	0	.000	0	1	3.00
	Oneonta	A	19	2	0	8	30.1	145	32	23	14	1	2	2	1	24	2	24	5	1	1	4	.200	0	0	4.15
1991	Greensboro	A	24	2	1	14	44.2	184	36	14	11	1	0	1	3	15	0	40	2	0	2	2	.500	0	1	2.22
1992	Pr William	A	44	0	0	21	81.2	350	68	37	26	5	7	4	6	33	2	68	7	1	5	4	.556	0	2	2.87
1993	Pr William	A	49	0	0	20	73	292	50	21	14	0	6	0	3	30	1	66	6	0	6	2	.750	0	4	1.73
	Albany	AA	15	0	0	6	23.2	91	23	8	7	0	0	0	0	6	0	18	0	0	1	0	1.000	0	0	2.66
1994	Albany-Colo	AA	34	0	0	12	39.2	163	30	10	9	1	2	2	4	14	0	41	1	0	2	1	.667	0	4	2.04
	Columbus	AAA	19	0	0	6	26	104	20	5	5	1	0	1	1	10	1	21	2	1	0	1	.000	0	2	1.73
	5 Min. YEARS		207	4	1	89	325	1353	263	120	88	9	18	10	20	135	6	285	23	4	17	14	.548	0	14	2.44

Andres Duncan

Bats: Both **Throws: Right** **Pos: SS** **Ht: 5'11"** **Wt: 155** **Born: 11/30/71** **Age: 23**

Year	Team	Lg	G	AB	H	2B	3B	HR	TB	R	RBI	TBB	IBB	SO	HBP	SH	SF	SB	CS	SB%	GDP	Avg	OBP	SLG
1991	Clinton	A	109	347	77	6	5	1	96	49	24	31	1	106	3	8	2	36	8	.82	2	.222	.290	.277
1992	San Jose	A	109	308	71	7	3	1	87	46	32	35	2	76	9	13	4	19	9	.68	8	.231	.323	.282
1993	Shreveport	AA	35	75	11	2	1	1	18	4	9	5	1	25	1	1	1	2	0	1.00	1	.147	.207	.240
	Phoenix	AAA	5	4	2	0	0	0	2	1	0	1	0	0	0	0	0	0	0	.00	1	.500	.600	.500
	San Jose	A	36	111	25	1	2	1	33	17	12	12	0	28	2	2	2	14	3	.82	3	.225	.307	.297
	Ft.Myers	A	5	22	8	0	0	1	11	3	1	3	0	6	0	0	0	4	2	.67	0	.364	.440	.500
1994	Nashville	AA	122	397	101	15	0	9	143	50	46	28	1	98	5	7	3	20	8	.71	5	.254	.309	.360
	4 Min. YEARS		421	1264	295	31	11	14	390	170	124	115	5	339	20	31	12	95	30	.76	21	.233	.305	.309

Chip Duncan

Pitches: Right **Bats: Right** **Pos: P** **Ht: 5'11"** **Wt: 185** **Born: 06/27/65** **Age: 30**

Year	Team	Lg	G	GS	CG	GF	IP	BFP	H	R	ER	HR	SH	SF	HB	TBB	IBB	SO	WP	Bk	W	L	Pct.	ShO	Sv	ERA
1987	Watertown	A	24	0	0	16	49.2	222	45	20	13	1	5	2	3	22	3	57	4	0	4	2	.667	0	4	2.36
1988	Salem	A	28	28	0	0	156.2	713	168	103	79	18	5	4	5	70	2	102	17	8	8	10	.444	0	0	4.54
1989	Salem	A	26	4	0	10	68.2	305	64	49	39	4	3	8	6	33	1	55	5	4	2	4	.333	0	2	5.11
1990	Salem	A	37	3	2	17	84.2	406	105	61	49	5	4	3	4	48	3	95	9	1	6	4	.600	0	1	5.21
1991	Carolina	AA	6	0	0	6	8	45	17	8	7	1	0	0	1	4	0	9	1	0	0	0	.000	0	1	7.88
	Memphis	AA	22	9	2	5	80.1	342	82	42	40	11	2	1	3	28	0	58	5	1	6	3	.667	1	0	4.48
1992	Memphis	AA	33	2	1	12	73.1	316	72	49	38	7	6	4	2	24	1	51	3	1	0	3	.000	0	3	4.66
1994	Reading	AA	17	11	0	2	77.2	339	79	40	36	9	1	3	4	34	2	62	3	4	4	2	.667	0	0	4.17
	7 Min. YEARS		193	57	5	68	599	2688	632	372	301	56	26	25	28	263	12	489	47	19	30	28	.517	1	11	4.52

Mike Dunne

Pitches: Right **Bats: Left** **Pos: P** **Ht: 6'4"** **Wt: 212** **Born: 10/27/62** **Age: 32**

Year	Team	Lg	G	GS	CG	GF	IP	BFP	H	R	ER	HR	SH	SF	HB	TBB	IBB	SO	WP	Bk	W	L	Pct.	ShO	Sv	ERA
1985	Arkansas	AA	23	23	3	0	146	606	133	72	50	9	4	2	5	57	5	91	7	2	4	9	.308	1	0	3.08
1986	Louisville	AAA	28	28	7	0	185.2	804	182	102	94	11	6	5	5	82	7	94	11	9	9	12	.429	1	0	4.56
1987	Vancouver	AAA	9	9	3	0	61.1	259	61	21	12	2	0	0	2	23	1	41	1	1	3	5	.375	1	0	1.76
1989	Calgary	AAA	9	9	0	0	51.2	230	54	26	19	3	0	2	3	25	0	19	2	2	4	0	1.000	0	0	3.31
1990	Las Vegas	AAA	4	4	1	0	28	114	20	12	10	2	4	1	1	10	1	12	0	0	1	2	.333	1	0	3.21
1991	White Sox	R	1	0	0	1	3	10	0	0	0	0	0	0	0	1	0	5	0	0	0	0	.000	0	0	0.00
	Vancouver	AAA	17	5	1	7	55	248	66	37	33	2	5	2	6	19	0	21	1	3	2	2	.500	0	2	5.40
1992	Vancouver	AAA	21	21	2	0	132.2	568	128	61	41	4	2	8	2	46	2	78	6	3	10	6	.625	0	2	2.78
1993	White Sox	R	3	2	0	0	5.2	21	3	1	0	0	0	0	0	1	0	9	0	0	0	0	.000	0	0	0.00
	Sarasota	A	7	1	0	1	24.2	109	30	17	15	4	0	0	0	8	0	11	1	0	1	1	.500	0	0	5.47
1994	Scranton-Wb	AAA	6	6	0	0	29.1	132	36	21	17	1	0	1	2	8	0	12	1	0	2	2	.500	0	0	5.22
1987	Pittsburgh	NL	23	23	5	0	163.1	680	143	66	55	10	11	4	1	68	8	72	6	4	13	6	.684	1	0	3.03
1988	Pittsburgh	NL	30	28	1	1	170	752	163	88	74	15	11	8	5	88	3	70	12	7	7	11	.389	0	0	3.92
1989	Pittsburgh	NL	3	3	0	0	14.1	75	21	12	12	1	1	0	1	9	1	4	1	0	1	1	.500	0	0	7.53
	Seattle	AL	15	15	1	0	85.1	386	104	61	50	7	3	5	2	37	1	38	7	1	2	9	.182	0	0	5.27
1990	San Diego	NL	10	6	0	0	28.2	134	28	21	18	4	1	0	0	17	0	15	4	1	0	3	.000	0	0	5.65
1992	Chicago	AL	4	1	0	0	12.2	54	12	7	6	0	0	0	1	6	1	6	0	0	2	0	1.000	0	0	4.26
	9 Min. YEARS		128	108	17	9	723	3101	713	370	291	41	18	25	22	280	16	393	30	20	36	39	.480	4	2	3.62
	5 Maj. YEARS		85	76	7	1	474.1	2081	471	255	215	37	27	17	10	225	14	205	30	13	25	30	.455	1	0	4.08

Mike Durant

Bats: Right **Throws: Right** **Pos: C** **Ht: 6'2"** **Wt: 198** **Born: 09/14/69** **Age: 25**

Year	Team	Lg	G	AB	H	2B	3B	HR	TB	R	RBI	TBB	IBB	SO	HBP	SH	SF	SB	CS	SB%	GDP	Avg	OBP	SLG
1991	Kenosha	A	66	217	44	10	0	2	60	27	20	25	0	35	3	2	1	20	5	.80	4	.203	.293	.276
1992	Visalia	A	119	418	119	18	2	6	159	61	57	55	0	35	5	3	8	19	15	.56	10	.285	.368	.380
1993	Nashville	AA	123	437	106	23	1	8	155	58	57	44	1	68	6	4	3	16	4	.80	2	.243	.318	.355
1994	Salt Lake	AAA	103	343	102	24	4	4	146	67	51	35	0	47	4	5	0	9	3	.75	7	.297	.369	.426
	4 Min. YEARS		411	1415	371	75	7	20	520	213	185	159	1	185	18	14	12	64	27	.70	23	.262	.342	.367

Ray Durham

Bats: Both **Throws:** Right **Pos:** 2B **Ht:** 5'8" **Wt:** 165 **Born:** 11/30/71 **Age:** 23

Year	Team	Lg	G	AB	H	2B	3B	HR	TB	R	RBI	TBB	IBB	SO	HBP	SH	SF	SB	CS	SB%	GDP	Avg	OBP	SLG
1990	White Sox	R	35	116	31	3	3	0	40	18	13	15	0	35	4	0	1	22	9	.71	0	.267	.368	.345
1991	Utica	A	39	142	36	2	7	0	52	29	17	25	0	43	2	2	1	12	1	.92	0	.254	.371	.366
	White Sox	R	6	23	7	1	0	0	8	3	4	3	0	5	0	0	0	5	1	.83	0	.304	.385	.348
1992	White Sox	R	5	13	7	2	0	0	9	3	2	3	0	1	0	0	0	1	0	1.00	0	.538	.625	.692
	Sarasota	A	57	202	55	6	3	0	67	37	7	32	0	36	10	5	0	28	8	.78	2	.272	.398	.332
1993	Birmingham	AA	137	528	143	22	10	3	194	83	37	42	2	100	14	5	5	39	25	.61	5	.271	.338	.367
1994	Nashville	AAA	133	527	156	33	12	16	261	89	66	46	7	91	12	3	4	34	11	.76	5	.296	.363	.495
	5 Min. YEARS		412	1551	435	69	35	19	631	262	146	166	9	311	42	15	11	141	55	.72	12	.280	.363	.407

Tommy Eason

Bats: Right **Throws:** Right **Pos:** C **Ht:** 6'0" **Wt:** 200 **Born:** 07/08/70 **Age:** 24

Year	Team	Lg	G	AB	H	2B	3B	HR	TB	R	RBI	TBB	IBB	SO	HBP	SH	SF	SB	CS	SB%	GDP	Avg	OBP	SLG
1991	Batavia	A	15	51	16	3	0	1	22	8	4	8	0	2	0	0	0	1	1	.50	0	.314	.407	.431
	Spartanburg	A	27	86	24	9	0	1	36	10	10	6	0	7	0	0	0	1	0	1.00	1	.279	.326	.419
1992	Spartanburg	A	73	262	78	20	1	7	121	41	37	24	1	21	2	1	2	2	1	.67	9	.298	.359	.462
1994	Clearwater	A	50	193	59	14	1	1	78	26	23	13	0	16	0	0	3	1	3	.25	3	.306	.344	.404
	Reading	AA	41	143	42	9	0	6	69	25	21	11	0	21	1	0	0	1	1	.50	8	.294	.348	.483
	3 Min. YEARS		206	735	219	55	2	16	326	110	95	62	1	67	3	1	5	6	6	.50	21	.298	.353	.444

Angel Echevarria

Bats: Right **Throws:** Right **Pos:** OF **Ht:** 6'4" **Wt:** 215 **Born:** 05/25/71 **Age:** 24

Year	Team	Lg	G	AB	H	2B	3B	HR	TB	R	RBI	TBB	IBB	SO	HBP	SH	SF	SB	CS	SB%	GDP	Avg	OBP	SLG
1992	Bend	A	57	205	46	4	1	5	67	24	30	19	1	54	2	0	0	8	1	.89	5	.224	.296	.327
1993	Central Val	A	104	358	97	16	2	6	135	45	52	44	0	74	5	5	3	6	5	.55	7	.271	.356	.377
1994	Central Val	A	50	192	58	8	1	6	86	28	35	9	0	25	4	0	3	2	2	.50	6	.302	.341	.448
	New Haven	AA	58	205	52	6	0	8	82	25	32	15	1	46	2	0	2	2	4	.33	8	.254	.308	.400
	3 Min. YEARS		269	960	253	34	4	25	370	122	149	87	2	199	13	5	8	18	12	.60	26	.264	.331	.385

Chris Eddy

Pitches: Left **Bats:** Left **Pos:** P **Ht:** 6'3" **Wt:** 200 **Born:** 11/27/69 **Age:** 25

Year	Team	Lg	G	GS	CG	GF	IP	BFP	H	R	ER	HR	SH	SF	HB	TBB	IBB	SO	WP	Bk	W	L	Pct.	ShO	Sv	ERA
1992	Eugene	A	23	0	0	11	45.1	191	25	13	8	1	2	2	6	23	1	63	3	3	4	2	.667	0	5	1.59
1993	Wilmington	A	55	0	0	38	54	237	39	23	18	4	4	6	3	37	1	67	8	1	2	2	.500	0	14	3.00
1994	Memphis	AA	43	0	0	19	78.1	336	74	37	34	3	4	2	1	32	3	86	5	0	9	2	.818	0	1	3.91
	3 Min. YEARS		121	0	0	68	177.2	764	138	73	60	8	10	10	10	92	5	216	16	4	15	6	.714	0	20	3.04

Ken Edenfield

Pitches: Right **Bats:** Right **Pos:** P **Ht:** 6'1" **Wt:** 165 **Born:** 03/18/67 **Age:** 28

Year	Team	Lg	G	GS	CG	GF	IP	BFP	H	R	ER	HR	SH	SF	HB	TBB	IBB	SO	WP	Bk	W	L	Pct.	ShO	Sv	ERA
1990	Boise	A	31	0	0	24	54.1	225	38	15	10	1	5	1	4	20	3	57	2	0	8	4	.667	0	9	1.66
1991	Quad City	A	47	0	0	40	87	356	69	30	25	3	5	3	4	30	2	106	5	1	8	5	.615	0	15	2.59
1992	Palm Sprngs	A	13	0	0	13	18.1	70	12	1	1	0	0	0	0	7	0	20	0	0	0	0	.000	0	7	0.49
	Midland	AA	31	0	0	17	49.2	225	60	35	33	5	3	2	4	24	3	43	4	0	1	5	.167	0	2	5.98
1993	Midland	AA	48	3	1	19	93.2	404	93	56	48	10	2	5	8	35	5	84	14	2	5	8	.385	0	4	4.61
	Vancouver	AAA	2	0	0	2	3.2	13	1	0	0	0	0	0	1	1	0	5	0	0	0	0	.000	0	0	0.00
1994	Vancouver	AAA	51	0	0	28	87.2	368	69	38	33	7	3	4	9	36	3	84	12	0	9	4	.692	0	4	3.39
	5 Min. YEARS		223	3	1	143	394.1	1661	342	175	150	26	18	15	30	153	16	399	37	3	31	26	.544	0	41	3.42

Tim Edge

Bats: Right **Throws:** Right **Pos:** C **Ht:** 6'0" **Wt:** 210 **Born:** 10/26/68 **Age:** 26

Year	Team	Lg	G	AB	H	2B	3B	HR	TB	R	RBI	TBB	IBB	SO	HBP	SH	SF	SB	CS	SB%	GDP	Avg	OBP	SLG
1990	Welland	A	63	149	32	5	0	1	40	6	12	19	1	27	2	0	1	4	3	.57	1	.215	.310	.268
1991	Salem	A	96	298	67	16	2	6	105	36	30	44	1	67	5	5	0	4	2	.67	7	.225	.334	.352
1992	Carolina	AA	4	9	1	0	0	0	1	1	0	2	1	5	0	0	0	0	0	.00	0	.111	.273	.111
	Salem	A	68	216	39	5	1	6	64	18	26	21	0	55	5	0	1	3	2	.60	3	.181	.267	.296
1993	Buffalo	AAA	1	2	0	0	0	0	0	0	0	0	0	0	0	0	0	0	0	.00	0	.000	.000	.000
	Carolina	AA	46	160	35	8	0	3	52	12	16	11	0	41	1	2	0	1	2	.33	5	.219	.273	.325
1994	Augusta	A	11	29	9	3	0	0	12	2	4	3	0	5	0	0	0	0	0	.00	0	.310	.375	.414
	Carolina	AA	6	20	3	1	0	0	4	1	2	1	0	9	0	0	0	0	0	.00	0	.150	.190	.200
	Buffalo	AAA	8	18	4	2	0	0	6	1	0	1	0	4	0	0	0	0	0	.00	0	.222	.263	.333
	5 Min. YEARS		303	901	190	40	3	16	284	76	90	102	3	213	13	7	2	12	9	.57	16	.211	.300	.315

Brian Edmondson

Pitches: Right **Bats:** Right **Pos:** P | **Ht:** 6'2" **Wt:** 165 **Born:** 01/29/73 **Age:** 22

			HOW	MUCH	HE	PITCHED		WHAT	HE	GAVE	UP								THE	RESULTS			
Year	Team	Lg	G	GS	CG	GF	IP	BFP	H	R	ER	HR	SH	SF	HB	TBB	IBB	SO	WP	Bk	W	L	Pct.	ShO	Sv	ERA
1991	Bristol	R	12	12	1	0	69	289	72	38	35	7	1	2	3	23	1	42	5	2	4	4	.500	0	0	4.57
1992	Fayetteville	A	28	27	3	0	155.1	665	145	69	58	10	5	3	6	67	0	125	6	2	10	6	.625	1	0	3.36
1993	Lakeland	A	19	19	1	0	114.1	483	115	44	38	6	1	0	3	43	0	64	7	0	8	5	.615	0	0	2.99
	London	AA	5	5	1	0	23	109	30	23	16	2	1	0	0	13	0	17	1	0	0	4	.000	0	0	6.26
1994	Trenton	AA	26	26	2	0	162	703	171	89	82	12	2	6	6	61	1	90	11	2	11	9	.550	0	0	4.56
	4 Min. YEARS		90	89	8	0	523.2	2249	533	263	229	37	10	11	18	207	2	338	30	6	33	28	.541	1	0	3.94

Jay Edwards

Bats: Right **Throws:** Right **Pos:** OF | **Ht:** 6'2" **Wt:** 180 **Born:** 01/16/69 **Age:** 26

					BATTING											BASERUNNING				PERCENTAGES		
Year	Team	Lg	G	AB	H	2B	3B	HR	TB	R	RBI	TBB	IBB	SO	HBP	SH	SF	SB	CS	SB%	GDP	Avg	OBP	SLG
1990	Princeton	R	64	229	44	4	6	1	63	39	20	30	0	66	1	1	2	26	8	.76	0	.192	.286	.275
1991	Batavia	A	67	242	66	9	1	2	83	37	25	29	0	42	4	3	2	23	10	.70	3	.273	.357	.343
1992	Spartanburg	A	101	367	82	11	2	1	100	46	35	37	0	59	3	4	1	29	18	.62	6	.223	.299	.272
1993	Clearwater	A	124	430	109	23	4	0	140	57	53	48	1	63	1	6	5	21	11	.66	9	.253	.326	.326
1994	Reading	AA	75	247	57	3	3	3	75	32	29	13	0	49	1	4	1	10	3	.77	4	.231	.271	.304
	Clearwater	A	36	129	29	4	0	0	33	17	9	12	1	31	0	2	0	13	1	1.00	2	.225	.291	.256
	5 Min. YEARS		467	1644	387	54	16	7	494	228	171	169	2	310	10	20	11	122	50	.71	24	.235	.309	.300

Mike Edwards

Bats: Right **Throws:** Right **Pos:** 3B | **Ht:** 6'1" **Wt:** 205 **Born:** 03/09/70 **Age:** 25

					BATTING											BASERUNNING				PERCENTAGES		
Year	Team	Lg	G	AB	H	2B	3B	HR	TB	R	RBI	TBB	IBB	SO	HBP	SH	SF	SB	CS	SB%	GDP	Avg	OBP	SLG
1991	Butte	R	66	217	68	11	1	10	111	56	42	38	1	45	2	1	3	9	4	.69	3	.313	.415	.512
1992	Gastonia	A	109	375	90	10	0	11	133	39	48	43	0	72	1	1	3	7	11	.39	9	.240	.318	.355
1993	Charlotte	A	130	458	128	26	2	12	194	73	79	82	2	70	4	1	3	11	6	.65	14	.279	.391	.424
1994	Tulsa	AA	104	342	89	16	5	6	133	39	37	43	2	56	10	3	3	2	5	.29	15	.260	.357	.389
	4 Min. YEARS		409	1392	375	63	8	39	571	207	206	206	5	243	17	6	12	29	26	.53	41	.269	.368	.410

Wayne Edwards

Pitches: Left **Bats:** Left **Pos:** P | **Ht:** 6'5" **Wt:** 185 **Born:** 03/07/64 **Age:** 31

					HOW	MUCH	HE	PITCHED		WHAT	HE	GAVE	UP								THE	RESULTS			
Year	Team	Lg	G	GS	CG	GF	IP	BFP	H	R	ER	HR	SH	SF	HB	TBB	IBB	SO	WP	Bk	W	L	Pct.	ShO	Sv	ERA
1985	White Sox	R	11	11	3	0	68.2	274	52	26	19	0	1	1	3	18	0	61	2	0	7	3	.700	0	0	2.49
1986	Peninsula	A	24	21	0	2	128.1	574	149	80	60	10	6	2	2	68	1	86	8	2	8	8	.500	0	0	4.21
1987	Daytona Bch	A	29	28	15	0	199.2	862	211	91	80	4	5	6	9	68	3	121	17	0	16	8	.667	2	0	3.61
1988	Birmingham	AA	27	27	6	0	167	762	176	108	91	9	5	10	5	92	3	136	16	7	9	12	.429	1	0	4.90
	Vancouver	AAA	2	0	0	1	3	9	0	0	0	0	0	0	0	0	0	2	0	0	0	0	.000	0	0	0.00
1989	Birmingham	AA	24	19	5	1	158	660	131	69	56	6	4	1	5	65	1	122	6	4	10	4	.714	0	1	3.19
1991	Vancouver	AAA	14	12	0	1	64.2	304	73	50	45	4	3	2	5	37	0	35	4	0	3	9	.250	0	0	6.26
1992	Syracuse	AAA	41	12	0	10	130.2	583	127	71	65	13	6	3	4	76	3	108	22	0	4	6	.400	0	3	4.48
1994	Toledo	AAA	12	0	0	4	19.2	95	17	17	12	2	1	0	1	19	0	16	1	1	0	1	.000	0	0	5.49
1989	Chicago	AL	7	0	0	2	7.1	30	7	3	3	1	0	1	0	3	0	9	0	0	0	0	.000	0	0	3.68
1990	Chicago	AL	42	5	0	8	95	396	81	39	34	6	4	2	3	41	2	63	1	0	5	3	.625	0	2	3.22
1991	Chicago	AL	13	0	0	3	23.1	106	22	14	10	2	2	2	0	17	3	12	2	0	0	2	.000	0	0	3.86
	8 Min. YEARS		184	130	29	19	939.2	4123	936	512	428	48	31	25	34	443	11	687	76	14	57	51	.528	3	4	4.10
	3 Maj. YEARS		62	5	0	13	125.2	532	110	56	47	9	6	5	3	61	5	84	3	0	5	5	.500	0	2	3.37

Kurt Ehmann

Bats: Right **Throws:** Right **Pos:** SS | **Ht:** 6'1" **Wt:** 185 **Born:** 08/18/70 **Age:** 24

					BATTING											BASERUNNING				PERCENTAGES		
Year	Team	Lg	G	AB	H	2B	3B	HR	TB	R	RBI	TBB	IBB	SO	HBP	SH	SF	SB	CS	SB%	GDP	Avg	OBP	SLG
1992	Everett	A	64	215	57	9	0	2	72	25	20	31	0	51	4	4	0	6	3	.67	1	.265	.368	.335
1993	San Jose	A	123	439	115	20	1	5	152	81	57	75	2	69	11	3	4	12	9	.57	4	.262	.380	.346
1994	Shreveport	AA	124	426	104	20	0	1	127	46	40	27	1	85	11	13	6	9	3	.75	5	.244	.302	.298
	3 Min. YEARS		311	1080	276	49	1	8	351	152	117	133	3	205	26	20	10	27	15	.64	10	.256	.348	.325

Dave Eiland

Pitches: Right **Bats:** Right **Pos:** P | **Ht:** 6'3" **Wt:** 210 **Born:** 07/05/66 **Age:** 28

				HOW	MUCH	HE	PITCHED		WHAT	HE	GAVE	UP									THE	RESULTS			
Year	Team	Lg	G	GS	CG	GF	IP	BFP	H	R	ER	HR	SH	SF	HB	TBB	IBB	SO	WP	Bk	W	L	Pct.	ShO	Sv	ERA
1987	Oneonta	A	5	5	0	0	29.1	109	20	6	6	1	0	0	0	3	0	16	2	0	4	0	1.000	0	0	1.84
	Ft.Lauderdle	A	8	8	4	0	62.1	248	57	17	13	0	2	0	0	8	0	28	1	1	5	3	.625	1	0	1.88
1988	Albany	AA	18	18	7	0	119.1	472	95	39	34	8	4	5	1	22	3	66	2	0	9	5	.643	2	0	2.56
	Columbus	AAA	4	4	0	0	24.1	106	25	8	7	4	0	1	1	6	0	13	1	0	1	1	.500	0	0	2.59
1989	Columbus	AAA	18	18	2	0	103	427	107	47	43	10	1	3	1	21	0	45	1	1	9	4	.692	0	0	3.76
1990	Columbus	AAA	27	26	11	0	175.1	707	155	63	56	8	3	1	1	32	0	96	2	2	16	5	.762	3	0	2.87
1991	Columbus	AAA	9	9	2	0	60	244	54	22	16	5	1	1	2	7	0	18	1	0	6	1	.857	0	0	2.40
1992	Las Vegas	AAA	14	14	0	0	63.2	276	78	43	37	4	7	6	0	11	2	31	0	0	4	5	.444	0	0	5.23

76

Year	Team	Lg	G	GS	CG	GF	IP	BFP	H	R	ER	HR	SH	SF	HB	TBB	IBB	SO	WP	Bk	W	L	Pct.	ShO	Sv	ERA
1993	Charlotte	AAA	8	8	0	0	35.2	154	42	22	21	8	1	0	1	12	0	13	0	0	1	3	.250	0	0	5.30
	Okla City	AAA	7	7	1	0	35.2	155	39	18	17	1	1	1	1	9	0	15	0	0	3	1	.750	0	0	4.29
1994	Columbus	AAA	26	26	0	0	140.2	597	141	72	56	12	6	7	1	33	0	84	2	0	9	6	.600	0	0	3.58
1988	New York	AL	3	3	0	0	12.2	57	15	9	9	6	0	0	2	4	0	7	0	0	0	0	.000	0	0	6.39
1989	New York	AL	6	6	0	0	34.1	127	44	25	22	5	1	2	2	13	3	11	0	0	1	3	.250	0	0	5.77
1990	New York	AL	5	5	0	0	30.1	127	31	14	12	2	0	0	0	5	0	16	0	0	2	1	.667	0	0	3.56
1991	New York	AL	18	13	0	4	72.2	317	87	51	43	10	0	3	3	23	1	18	0	0	2	5	.286	0	0	5.33
1992	San Diego	NL	7	7	0	0	27	120	33	21	17	1	0	0	0	5	0	10	0	1	0	2	.000	0	0	5.67
1993	San Diego	NL	10	9	0	0	48.1	217	58	33	28	5	2	2	1	17	1	14	1	0	0	3	.000	0	0	5.21
	8 Min. YEARS		144	143	27	0	849.1	3495	813	357	306	61	26	25	9	164	5	425	12	4	67	34	.663	6	0	3.24
	6 Maj. YEARS		49	43	0	4	225.1	990	268	153	131	29	3	7	8	67	5	76	1	1	5	14	.263	0	0	5.23

Rocky Elli

Pitches: Left **Bats:** Left **Pos:** P — **Ht:** 6'5" **Wt:** 215 **Born:** 09/27/67 **Age:** 27

			HOW MUCH HE PITCHED						WHAT HE GAVE UP												THE RESULTS					
Year	Team	Lg	G	GS	CG	GF	IP	BFP	H	R	ER	HR	SH	SF	HB	TBB	IBB	SO	WP	Bk	W	L	Pct.	ShO	Sv	ERA
1986	Kingsport	R	16	3	0	3	33.2	167	43	34	25	4	1	0	1	24	0	28	3	0	0	2	.000	0	0	6.68
1987	Kingsport	R	14	14	3	0	94.2	426	77	43	28	3	1	1	8	50	0	54	9	1	9	3	.750	1	0	2.66
1988	Columbia	A	27	27	4	0	168.2	718	147	87	65	12	6	2	11	65	1	104	10	8	13	8	.619	2	0	3.47
1989	St.Lucie	A	26	24	3	1	152.2	664	151	72	58	5	0	2	11	66	0	82	10	2	9	6	.600	0	1	3.42
1990	Jackson	AA	17	15	1	1	75.1	327	74	43	38	8	2	4	4	34	1	52	5	3	3	6	.333	0	0	4.54
1991	Scranton-Wb	AAA	18	0	0	4	19	98	23	13	9	0	3	1	0	20	2	13	3	0	1	0	1.000	0	0	4.26
	Reading	AA	16	14	1	0	74.1	308	65	33	26	6	7	1	1	33	0	48	0	0	5	7	.417	0	0	3.15
1992	Clearwater	A	5	5	0	0	27	111	24	13	11	3	0	1	3	8	0	23	2	2	1	1	.500	0	0	3.67
	Reading	AA	12	12	0	0	65.1	284	77	41	34	5	5	3	3	23	0	20	2	1	2	6	.250	0	0	4.68
1994	Sarasota	A	26	0	0	8	33	147	36	25	18	1	2	1	4	17	1	24	3	0	2	4	.333	0	3	4.91
	New Britain	AA	15	4	0	6	36.1	169	36	16	16	2	0	1	4	25	0	31	1	0	0	3	.000	0	0	3.96
	8 Min. YEARS		192	118	12	23	780	3419	753	420	328	49	27	17	50	365	5	479	48	17	45	46	.495	3	4	3.78

Paul Ellis

Bats: Left **Throws:** Right **Pos:** C — **Ht:** 6'1" **Wt:** 205 **Born:** 11/28/68 **Age:** 26

			BATTING														BASERUNNING				PERCENTAGES		
Year	Team	Lg	G	AB	H	2B	3B	HR	TB	R	RBI	TBB	IBB	SO	HBP	SH	SF	SB	CS	SB%	GDP	Avg	OBP	SLG
1990	Hamilton	A	15	58	18	4	0	3	31	8	18	6	3	13	0	0	2	0	0	.00	1	.310	.364	.534
	Springfield	A	50	183	43	5	0	5	63	18	25	26	1	34	2	0	0	0	1	.00	2	.235	.336	.344
1991	St. Pete	A	119	402	82	11	0	6	111	26	42	52	1	35	6	0	4	0	0	.00	8	.204	.302	.276
1992	St. Pete	A	84	308	67	17	0	2	90	22	29	26	1	22	3	0	4	0	1	.00	4	.218	.282	.292
	Arkansas	AA	25	79	18	2	0	2	26	9	8	13	2	14	1	0	1	0	1	.00	0	.228	.340	.329
1993	Arkansas	AA	24	78	26	3	0	1	32	5	11	16	0	2	3	0	0	0	2	.00	0	.333	.464	.410
	Louisville	AAA	50	125	25	6	0	0	31	12	8	13	2	16	1	0	1	0	0	.00	3	.200	.279	.248
1994	Arkansas	AA	102	281	65	9	0	6	92	28	39	35	4	34	0	6	2	0	0	.00	11	.231	.314	.327
	5 Min. YEARS		469	1514	344	57	0	25	476	128	180	187	14	170	16	6	14	0	5	.00	30	.227	.316	.314

Robert Ellis

Pitches: Right **Bats:** Right **Pos:** P — **Ht:** 6'5" **Wt:** 220 **Born:** 12/15/70 **Age:** 24

			HOW MUCH HE PITCHED						WHAT HE GAVE UP												THE RESULTS					
Year	Team	Lg	G	GS	CG	GF	IP	BFP	H	R	ER	HR	SH	SF	HB	TBB	IBB	SO	WP	Bk	W	L	Pct.	ShO	Sv	ERA
1991	Utica	A	15	15	1	0	87.2	407	87	66	45	4	6	5	6	61	0	66	13	0	3	9	.250	1	0	4.62
1992	White Sox	R	1	1	0	0	5	24	10	6	6	0	0	0	0	1	0	4	0	0	1	0	1.000	0	0	10.80
	South Bend	A	18	18	1	0	123	481	90	46	32	3	4	2	4	35	0	97	7	2	6	5	.545	1	0	2.34
1993	Sarasota	A	15	15	8	0	104	414	81	37	29	3	4	3	3	31	1	79	6	1	7	8	.467	2	0	2.51
	Birmingham	AA	12	12	2	0	81.1	336	68	33	28	2	1	1	4	21	0	77	6	0	6	3	.667	1	0	3.10
1994	Nashville	AAA	19	19	1	0	105	483	126	77	71	19	5	6	2	55	1	76	1	4	4	10	.286	0	0	6.09
	4 Min. YEARS		80	80	13	0	506	2145	462	265	211	31	20	17	19	204	2	399	33	7	27	35	.435	5	0	3.75

Alan Embree

Pitches: Left **Bats:** Left **Pos:** P — **Ht:** 6'2" **Wt:** 185 **Born:** 01/23/70 **Age:** 25

			HOW MUCH HE PITCHED						WHAT HE GAVE UP												THE RESULTS					
Year	Team	Lg	G	GS	CG	GF	IP	BFP	H	R	ER	HR	SH	SF	HB	TBB	IBB	SO	WP	Bk	W	L	Pct.	ShO	Sv	ERA
1990	Burlington	R	15	15	0	0	81.2	351	87	36	24	3	1	3	0	30	0	58	5	4	4	4	.500	0	0	2.64
1991	Columbus	A	27	26	3	0	155.1	651	125	80	62	4	5	3	4	77	1	137	7	0	10	8	.556	1	0	3.59
1992	Kinston	A	15	15	1	0	101	418	89	48	37	10	3	1	2	32	0	115	6	3	10	5	.667	0	0	3.30
	Canton-Akrn	AA	12	12	0	0	79	316	61	24	20	2	3	1	2	28	1	56	2	1	7	2	.778	0	0	2.28
1993	Canton-Akrn	AA	1	1	0	0	5.1	20	7	2	2	0	0	0	0	3	0	4	0	0	0	0	.000	0	0	3.38
1994	Canton-Akrn	AA	30	27	2	1	157	698	183	106	96	15	2	6	4	64	3	81	8	1	9	16	.360	1	0	5.50
1992	Cleveland	AL	4	4	0	0	18	81	19	14	14	3	0	2	1	8	0	12	1	1	0	2	.000	0	0	7.00
	5 Min. YEARS		100	96	6	1	579.1	2454	548	296	241	34	14	14	12	234	5	451	28	9	40	35	.533	2	0	3.74

Angelo Encarnacion

Bats: Right **Throws:** Right **Pos:** C — **Ht:** 5'8" **Wt:** 180 **Born:** 04/18/73 **Age:** 22

			BATTING														BASERUNNING				PERCENTAGES		
Year	Team	Lg	G	AB	H	2B	3B	HR	TB	R	RBI	TBB	IBB	SO	HBP	SH	SF	SB	CS	SB%	GDP	Avg	OBP	SLG
1991	Welland	A	50	181	46	3	2	0	53	21	15	5	0	27	1	0	0	4	3	.57	5	.254	.278	.293

Year	Team	Lg	G	AB	H	2B	3B	HR	TB	R	RBI	TBB	IBB	SO	HBP	SH	SF	SB	CS	SB%	GDP	Avg	OBP	SLG
1992	Augusta	A	94	314	80	14	3	1	103	39	29	25	1	37	1	4	2	2	4	.33	5	.255	.310	.328
1993	Salem	A	70	238	61	12	1	3	84	20	24	13	1	27	1	0	1	1	4	.20	5	.256	.294	.353
	Buffalo	AAA	3	9	3	0	0	0	3	1	2	0	0	0	0	0	0	0	0	.00	0	.333	.333	.333
1994	Carolina	AA	67	227	66	17	0	3	92	26	32	11	1	28	2	0	4	2	2	.50	4	.291	.324	.405
	4 Min. YEARS		284	969	256	46	6	7	335	107	102	54	3	119	4	4	7	9	13	.41	19	.264	.304	.346

Scott Epps

Bats: Right Throws: Right Pos: 3B   **Ht: 5'11" Wt: 180 Born: 12/08/69 Age: 25**

			BATTING														BASERUNNING				PERCENTAGES		
Year	Team	Lg	G	AB	H	2B	3B	HR	TB	R	RBI	TBB	IBB	SO	HBP	SH	SF	SB	CS	SB%	GDP	Avg	OBP	SLG
1992	Oneonta	A	16	36	6	1	0	0	7	3	1	6	0	6	1	0	0	0	0	.00	1	.167	.302	.194
1993	Pr William	A	34	92	18	4	0	1	25	12	17	9	0	24	1	0	1	0	0	.00	4	.196	.272	.272
1994	Columbus	AAA	3	2	0	0	0	0	0	0	0	0	0	2	0	0	0	0	0	.00	0	.000	.000	.000
	Tampa	A	27	72	11	2	2	0	17	10	12	7	0	20	0	1	0	0	0	.00	2	.153	.228	.236
	3 Min. YEARS		80	202	35	7	2	1	49	25	30	22	0	52	2	1	1	0	0	.00	7	.173	.260	.243

Brad Erdman

Bats: Right Throws: Right Pos: C   **Ht: 6'3" Wt: 190 Born: 02/23/70 Age: 25**

			BATTING														BASERUNNING				PERCENTAGES		
Year	Team	Lg	G	AB	H	2B	3B	HR	TB	R	RBI	TBB	IBB	SO	HBP	SH	SF	SB	CS	SB%	GDP	Avg	OBP	SLG
1989	Geneva	A	26	85	15	2	0	0	17	6	3	6	1	26	0	0	1	1	1	.50	2	.176	.228	.200
1990	Peoria	A	37	119	23	3	0	0	26	9	4	12	0	42	1	1	0	0	0	.00	2	.193	.273	.218
	Geneva	A	34	111	25	4	0	0	29	12	15	11	0	31	1	3	0	2	0	1.00	0	.225	.301	.261
1991	Peoria	A	83	280	71	19	1	4	104	33	26	32	1	59	3	8	1	5	0	1.00	6	.254	.335	.371
1992	Winston-Sal	A	65	219	42	4	0	3	55	29	14	12	0	53	4	4	1	1	5	.17	5	.192	.246	.251
1993	Peoria	A	20	57	14	1	0	1	18	7	10	6	0	12	2	3	1	2	0	1.00	0	.246	.333	.316
	Orlando	AA	69	171	31	5	0	1	39	12	17	18	5	42	6	9	3	2	2	.50	2	.181	.278	.228
1994	Daytona	A	76	236	60	12	1	2	80	26	24	21	0	47	9	3	0	2	2	.50	8	.254	.338	.339
	Orlando	AA	1	0	0	0	0	0	0	0	0	0	0	0	0	0	0	0	0	.00	0	.000	.000	.000
	6 Min. YEARS		411	1278	281	50	2	11	368	134	113	118	7	312	26	31	7	15	10	.60	25	.220	.297	.288

John Ericks

Pitches: Right Bats: Right Pos: P   **Ht: 6'7" Wt: 220 Born: 06/16/67 Age: 28**

			HOW MUCH HE PITCHED					WHAT HE GAVE UP									THE RESULTS					
Year	Team	Lg	G	GS	CG	GF	IP	BFP	H	R	ER	HR	SH	SF	HB	TBB	IBB	SO	WP	Bk	W	L	Pct.	ShO	Sv	ERA
1988	Johnson Cty	R	9	9	1	0	41	174	27	20	17	1	1	2	0	27	0	41	5	4	3	2	.600	0	0	3.73
1989	Savannah	A	28	28	1	0	167.1	690	90	59	38	4	4	5	9	101	0	211	11	2	11	10	.524	1	0	2.04
1990	St. Pete	A	4	4	0	0	23	88	16	5	4	0	0	1	0	6	0	25	1	1	2	1	.667	0	0	1.57
	Arkansas	AA	4	4	1	0	15.1	83	17	19	16	2	0	2	1	19	0	19	3	1	1	2	.333	1	0	9.39
1991	Arkansas	AA	25	25	1	0	139.2	630	138	94	74	6	5	4	7	84	3	103	15	3	5	14	.263	0	0	4.77
1992	Arkansas	AA	13	13	1	0	75	316	69	36	34	4	4	3	3	29	1	71	6	0	2	6	.250	0	0	4.08
1994	Salem	A	17	5	0	3	52.1	219	42	22	18	4	1	2	3	20	0	71	3	0	4	2	.667	0	1	3.10
	Carolina	AA	11	11	0	0	57	234	42	22	17	2	2	1	3	19	0	64	5	0	2	4	.333	0	0	2.68
	6 Min. YEARS		111	99	5	3	570.2	2439	441	277	218	23	17	20	26	305	4	605	49	11	30	41	.423	1	1	3.44

Greg Erickson

Bats: Both Throws: Right Pos: SS   **Ht: 5'11" Wt: 175 Born: 10/26/69 Age: 25**

			BATTING														BASERUNNING				PERCENTAGES		
Year	Team	Lg	G	AB	H	2B	3B	HR	TB	R	RBI	TBB	IBB	SO	HBP	SH	SF	SB	CS	SB%	GDP	Avg	OBP	SLG
1991	Pr William	A	47	152	31	5	2	0	40	14	9	22	0	32	1	2	0	2	3	.40	6	.204	.309	.263
1992	Ft. Laud	A	74	258	67	7	1	0	76	27	26	24	0	48	4	0	4	9	6	.60	1	.260	.328	.295
1993	Albany	AA	3	10	1	0	0	0	1	2	0	2	0	1	0	0	0	0	0	.00	1	.100	.250	.100
	Pr William	A	80	288	79	11	3	0	96	44	21	25	0	54	0	3	0	10	5	.67	8	.274	.332	.333
1994	Tampa	A	14	53	14	0	0	1	17	5	3	4	0	9	0	0	0	0	1	.00	3	.264	.316	.321
	Albany-Colo	AA	19	62	13	0	1	0	15	7	5	6	0	14	0	1	0	0	1	.00	3	.210	.279	.242
	4 Min. YEARS		237	823	205	23	7	1	245	99	64	83	0	158	5	6	4	21	16	.57	22	.249	.320	.298

Mike Ericson

Pitches: Right Bats: Left Pos: P   **Ht: 6'2" Wt: 200 Born: 01/15/68 Age: 27**

			HOW MUCH HE PITCHED					WHAT HE GAVE UP									THE RESULTS					
Year	Team	Lg	G	GS	CG	GF	IP	BFP	H	R	ER	HR	SH	SF	HB	TBB	IBB	SO	WP	Bk	W	L	Pct.	ShO	Sv	ERA
1990	Miami	A	25	1	0	9	36	160	33	16	16	2	5	1	4	19	6	27	2	5	2	2	.500	0	1	4.00
1991	Miami	A	8	8	0	0	36.2	144	30	12	11	1	1	1	0	8	0	21	2	3	1	3	.250	0	0	2.70
1992	Visalia	A	35	0	0	21	62	283	77	26	20	2	5	2	1	19	8	70	3	1	2	5	.286	0	9	2.90
1993	Central Val	A	38	1	0	11	67	313	90	46	43	6	2	4	0	27	2	51	6	0	0	5	.000	0	0	5.78
1994	New Haven	AA	13	1	0	5	20.1	98	23	19	12	2	1	3	1	8	1	21	0	1	1	2	.333	0	1	5.31
	5 Min. YEARS		119	11	0	46	222	998	253	120	102	13	14	11	6	81	17	190	13	12	6	17	.261	0	11	4.14

Vaughn Eshelman

Pitches: Left Bats: Left Pos: P   **Ht: 6'3" Wt: 205 Born: 05/22/69 Age: 26**

			HOW MUCH HE PITCHED					WHAT HE GAVE UP									THE RESULTS					
Year	Team	Lg	G	GS	CG	GF	IP	BFP	H	R	ER	HR	SH	SF	HB	TBB	IBB	SO	WP	Bk	W	L	Pct.	ShO	Sv	ERA
1991	Bluefield	R	3	3	0	0	14	59	10	4	1	1	0	1	0	9	0	15	1	0	1	0	1.000	0	0	0.64

Year	Team	Lg	G	GS	CG	GF	IP	BFP	H	R	ER	HR	SH	SF	HB	TBB	IBB	SO	WP	Bk	W	L	Pct.	ShO	Sv	ERA
	Kane County	A	11	11	2	0	77.2	319	57	23	20	3	3	1	3	35	0	90	2	2	5	3	.625	1	0	2.32
1993	Frederick	A	24	24	2	0	143.1	608	128	70	62	10	4	3	7	59	0	122	7	1	7	10	.412	1	0	3.89
1994	Bowie	AA	27	25	2	0	166.1	713	175	81	74	13	7	3	3	60	1	133	8	0	11	9	.550	2	0	4.00
	3 Min. YEARS		65	63	6	0	401.1	1699	370	178	157	27	14	8	13	163	1	360	18	3	24	22	.522	4	0	3.52

Ramon Espinosa

Bats: Right Throws: Right Pos: OF Ht: 6'0" Wt: 175 Born: 02/07/72 Age: 23

				BATTING													BASERUNNING				PERCENTAGES		
Year	Team	Lg	G	AB	H	2B	3B	HR	TB	R	RBI	TBB	IBB	SO	HBP	SH	SF	SB	CS	SB%	GDP	Avg	OBP	SLG
1991	Pirates	R	19	63	15	2	0	0	17	7	5	2	0	7	0	0	0	3	0	1.00	2	.238	.262	.270
1992	Welland	A	60	208	56	12	5	4	90	27	22	9	0	23	0	0	2	10	5	.67	9	.269	.297	.433
1993	Augusta	A	70	266	79	9	3	2	100	32	27	12	2	51	2	1	3	17	5	.77	12	.297	.329	.376
	Salem	A	54	208	56	8	2	8	92	30	25	6	0	36	1	2	0	11	6	.65	6	.269	.293	.442
1994	Carolina	AA	82	291	78	16	3	2	106	44	40	11	1	38	1	2	4	12	10	.55	4	.268	.293	.364
	4 Min. YEARS		285	1036	284	47	13	16	405	140	119	40	3	155	4	5	9	53	26	.67	33	.274	.301	.391

Mark Ettles

Pitches: Right Bats: Right Pos: P Ht: 6'0" Wt: 185 Born: 10/30/66 Age: 28

			HOW MUCH HE PITCHED						WHAT HE GAVE UP										THE RESULTS					
Year	Team	Lg	G	GS	CG	GF	IP	BFP	H	R	ER	HR	SH	SF	HB	TBB	IBB	SO	WP	Bk	W	L	Pct.	ShO	Sv	ERA
1989	Niagara Fls	A	5	0	0	3	17.2	66	12	3	2	0	0	0	0	2	0	21	1	1	3	0	1.000	0	1	1.02
	Fayetteville	A	19	0	0	11	27.2	120	28	9	7	1	2	0	1	9	2	34	1	2	2	2	.500	0	4	2.28
1990	Lakeland	A	45	0	0	21	68	295	63	34	25	1	4	2	6	16	1	62	4	2	5	5	.500	0	3	3.31
1991	Lakeland	A	8	1	0	0	17	74	19	11	9	2	0	0	1	6	0	14	1	1	2	1	.667	0	0	4.76
	Chston-Sc	A	29	0	0	23	45.2	193	36	15	12	2	5	2	2	12	2	57	2	0	2	1	.667	0	12	2.36
	Waterloo	A	14	0	0	14	16	60	6	5	4	2	4	0	0	6	2	24	2	0	1	2	.333	0	8	2.25
1992	Wichita	AA	54	0	0	43	68.1	283	54	23	21	6	4	1	4	23	6	86	8	1	3	8	.273	0	22	2.77
1993	Las Vegas	AAA	47	0	0	41	49.2	224	58	28	26	2	3	1	2	22	6	29	13	0	3	6	.333	0	15	4.71
1994	Padres	R	7	0	0	6	6.2	29	7	3	2	0	1	1	0	1	0	9	0	0	0	0	.000	0	2	2.70
	Wichita	AA	3	0	0	3	3	13	3	2	1	0	1	0	0	1	0	1	1	0	0	0	.000	0	0	6.00
1993	San Diego	NL	14	0	0	5	18	81	23	16	13	4	0	2	0	4	1	9	3	0	1	0	1.000	0	0	6.50
	6 Min. YEARS		231	1	0	165	319.2	1357	286	133	110	16	24	7	16	98	19	337	33	7	21	26	.447	0	67	3.10

Dave Evans

Pitches: Right Bats: Right Pos: P Ht: 6'3" Wt: 185 Born: 01/01/68 Age: 27

			HOW MUCH HE PITCHED						WHAT HE GAVE UP										THE RESULTS					
Year	Team	Lg	G	GS	CG	GF	IP	BFP	H	R	ER	HR	SH	SF	HB	TBB	IBB	SO	WP	Bk	W	L	Pct.	ShO	Sv	ERA
1990	San Berndno	A	26	26	4	0	155	673	135	83	72	9	4	7	7	74	0	143	10	0	14	9	.609	0	0	4.18
1991	Jacksnville	AA	21	20	1	0	115.2	507	118	74	67	15	2	7	9	49	0	76	12	0	5	9	.357	0	0	5.21
1993	Appleton	A	5	5	0	0	27.2	117	21	9	7	0	0	0	2	15	0	23	5	2	2	1	.667	0	0	2.28
	Riverside	A	8	8	1	0	41.2	187	41	22	21	5	1	1	5	23	0	42	2	0	3	2	.600	1	0	4.54
1994	Jacksonvlle	AA	31	6	0	8	81.1	354	86	59	50	11	3	4	5	31	2	62	4	0	3	5	.375	0	2	5.53
	4 Min. YEARS		91	65	6	8	421.1	1838	401	247	217	40	10	19	28	192	2	346	33	2	27	26	.509	1	2	4.64

Tim Evans

Bats: Left Throws: Left Pos: OF Ht: 6'0" Wt: 195 Born: 06/18/69 Age: 26

				BATTING													BASERUNNING				PERCENTAGES		
Year	Team	Lg	G	AB	H	2B	3B	HR	TB	R	RBI	TBB	IBB	SO	HBP	SH	SF	SB	CS	SB%	GDP	Avg	OBP	SLG
1992	Osceola	A	75	253	62	8	6	0	82	44	20	26	0	47	0	7	2	8	6	.57	2	.245	.313	.324
1993	Quad City	A	123	436	121	24	5	6	173	62	52	35	2	76	6	3	3	11	7	.61	6	.278	.338	.397
1994	Tucson	AAA	3	3	0	0	0	0	0	0	0	0	0	1	0	0	0	0	0	.00	0	.000	.000	.000
	Jackson	AA	95	242	64	8	3	1	81	23	24	15	2	44	1	4	3	1	3	.25	4	.264	.307	.335
	3 Min. YEARS		296	934	247	40	14	7	336	129	96	76	4	168	7	14	8	20	16	.56	12	.264	.322	.360

Steve Fanning

Bats: Right Throws: Right Pos: 2B Ht: 6'3" Wt: 180 Born: 05/16/67 Age: 28

				BATTING													BASERUNNING				PERCENTAGES		
Year	Team	Lg	G	AB	H	2B	3B	HR	TB	R	RBI	TBB	IBB	SO	HBP	SH	SF	SB	CS	SB%	GDP	Avg	OBP	SLG
1988	Hamilton	A	60	175	39	8	0	0	47	22	2	28	0	58	4	1	0	5	1	.83	2	.223	.343	.269
1989	Savannah	A	112	407	108	13	2	5	140	59	40	44	1	94	5	5	0	7	1	.88	11	.265	.344	.344
1990	Arkansas	AA	126	404	91	23	4	4	134	50	34	59	3	91	5	0	2	0	2	.00	10	.225	.332	.332
1991	Arkansas	AA	60	162	39	7	0	1	49	19	15	29	1	45	4	2	0	3	5	.38	5	.241	.369	.302
	St. Pete	A	53	189	42	7	1	2	57	19	14	29	1	27	1	3	0	1	3	.25	3	.222	.329	.302
1992	St. Pete	A	1	0	0	0	0	0	0	0	0	0	0	0	0	0	0	0	0	.00	0	.000	.000	.000
	Louisville	AAA	19	49	9	1	2	0	14	8	4	8	1	14	0	0	0	0	0	.00	2	.184	.298	.286
	Arkansas	AA	58	117	26	5	0	2	37	17	14	10	0	37	0	1	3	2	1	.67	4	.222	.277	.316
1993	Arkansas	AA	97	249	53	14	0	3	76	28	20	26	1	71	2	1	1	5	3	.63	5	.213	.291	.305
1994	Louisville	AAA	65	61	15	3	0	0	18	7	5	10	0	22	1	1	0	0	1	.00	1	.246	.361	.295
	7 Min. YEARS		651	1813	422	81	9	17	572	229	148	243	8	459	22	14	6	23	17	.58	43	.233	.330	.315

Paul Faries

Bats: Right Throws: Right Pos: 2B Ht: 5'10" Wt: 165 Born: 02/20/65 Age: 30

Year	Team	Lg	G	AB	H	2B	3B	HR	TB	R	RBI	TBB	IBB	SO	HBP	SH	SF	SB	CS	SB%	GDP	Avg	OBP	SLG
1987	Spokane	A	74	280	86	9	3	0	101	67	27	36	0	25	5	4	5	30	9	.77	7	.307	.390	.361
1988	Riverside	A	141	579	183	39	4	2	236	108	77	72	1	79	8	7	7	65	30	.68	14	.316	.395	.408
1989	Wichita	AA	130	513	136	25	8	6	195	79	52	47	0	52	2	2	1	41	13	.76	13	.265	.329	.380
1990	Las Vegas	AAA	137	552	172	29	3	5	222	109	64	75	1	60	6	7	1	48	15	.76	16	.312	.399	.402
1991	High Desert	A	10	42	13	2	2	0	19	6	5	2	1	3	0	1	1	1	0	1.00	2	.310	.333	.452
	Las Vegas	AAA	20	75	23	2	1	1	30	16	12	12	0	5	0	2	1	7	3	.70	2	.307	.398	.400
1992	Las Vegas	AAA	125	457	134	15	6	1	164	77	40	40	1	53	3	4	2	28	9	.76	13	.293	.353	.359
1993	Phoenix	AAA	78	327	99	14	5	2	129	56	32	22	1	30	1	3	1	18	11	.62	8	.303	.348	.394
1994	Phoenix	AAA	124	503	141	21	4	2	176	77	50	28	0	53	6	7	3	31	16	.76	19	.280	.324	.350
1990	San Diego	NL	14	37	7	1	0	0	8	4	2	4	0	7	1	2	1	0	1	.00	0	.189	.279	.216
1991	San Diego	NL	57	130	23	3	1	0	28	13	7	14	0	21	1	4	0	3	1	.75	5	.177	.262	.215
1992	San Diego	NL	10	11	5	1	0	0	6	3	1	1	0	2	0	0	0	0	0	.00	0	.455	.500	.545
1993	San Francisco	NL	15	36	8	2	1	0	12	6	4	1	0	4	0	1	1	2	0	1.00	1	.222	.237	.333
	8 Min. YEARS		839	3328	987	156	36	19	1272	595	359	334	5	360	31	37	22	269	100	.73	94	.297	.364	.382
	4 Maj. YEARS		96	214	43	7	2	0	54	26	14	20	0	34	2	7	2	5	2	.71	6	.201	.273	.252

Monty Fariss

Bats: Right Throws: Right Pos: 2B Ht: 6'4" Wt: 205 Born: 10/13/67 Age: 27

Year	Team	Lg	G	AB	H	2B	3B	HR	TB	R	RBI	TBB	IBB	SO	HBP	SH	SF	SB	CS	SB%	GDP	Avg	OBP	SLG
1988	Butte	R	17	53	21	1	0	4	34	16	22	20	2	7	2	0	2	2	0	1.00	1	.396	.558	.642
	Tulsa	AA	49	165	37	6	6	3	64	21	31	22	0	39	0	1	1	2	0	1.00	2	.224	.314	.388
1989	Tulsa	AA	132	497	135	27	2	5	181	72	52	64	0	112	0	1	8	12	6	.67	13	.272	.351	.364
1990	Tulsa	AA	71	244	73	15	6	7	121	45	34	36	0	60	1	1	0	8	5	.62	9	.299	.391	.496
	Okla City	AAA	62	225	68	12	3	4	98	30	31	34	0	48	0	0	2	1	1	.50	7	.302	.391	.436
1991	Okla City	AAA	137	494	134	31	9	13	222	84	73	91	1	143	0	3	2	4	7	.36	11	.271	.383	.449
1992	Okla City	AAA	49	187	56	13	3	9	102	28	38	31	0	42	0	0	1	5	4	.56	5	.299	.397	.545
1993	Edmonton	AAA	74	254	65	11	4	6	102	32	37	43	0	74	2	1	2	1	5	.17	3	.256	.365	.402
1994	Edmonton	AAA	129	414	118	32	4	20	218	83	60	55	1	99	6	0	4	2	4	.33	10	.285	.374	.527
1991	Texas	AL	19	31	8	1	0	1	12	6	6	7	0	11	0	0	0	0	0	.00	0	.258	.395	.387
1992	Texas	AL	67	166	36	7	1	3	54	13	21	17	0	51	2	2	0	0	2	.00	3	.217	.297	.325
1993	Florida	NL	18	29	5	2	1	0	9	3	2	5	0	13	0	0	0	0	0	.00	5	.172	.294	.310
	7 Min. YEARS		720	2533	707	148	37	71	1142	411	378	396	5	624	11	14	20	37	32	.54	61	.279	.376	.451
	3 Maj. YEARS		104	226	49	10	2	4	75	22	29	29	0	75	2	2	0	0	2	.00	5	.217	.311	.332

Mike Farmer

Pitches: Left Bats: Both Pos: P Ht: 6'1" Wt: 175 Born: 07/03/68 Age: 26

Year	Team	Lg	G	GS	CG	GF	IP	BFP	H	R	ER	HR	SH	SF	HB	TBB	IBB	SO	WP	Bk	W	L	Pct.	ShO	Sv	ERA
1992	Clearwater	A	11	9	1	2	53	209	33	16	11	1	1	1	1	13	1	41	2	5	3	3	.500	1	0	1.87
1993	Reading	AA	22	18	0	3	102	455	125	62	57	18	5	5	1	34	2	64	8	4	5	10	.333	0	0	5.03
1994	Central Val	A	14	3	0	4	28.2	125	28	17	15	4	1	1	3	11	1	28	4	1	1	4	.200	0	1	4.71
	New Haven	AA	10	0	0	4	14	54	7	2	2	1	1	1	0	5	0	13	0	0	0	0	.000	0	2	1.29
	3 Min. YEARS		57	30	1	13	197.2	843	193	97	85	24	8	8	5	63	4	146	14	10	9	17	.346	1	3	3.87

Terry Farrar

Pitches: Left Bats: Left Pos: P Ht: 6'1" Wt: 180 Born: 09/10/69 Age: 25

Year	Team	Lg	G	GS	CG	GF	IP	BFP	H	R	ER	HR	SH	SF	HB	TBB	IBB	SO	WP	Bk	W	L	Pct.	ShO	Sv	ERA
1991	Bluefield	R	11	3	0	1	13	57	11	9	6	1	0	0	2	6	0	17	1	3	1	1	.500	0	0	4.15
	Kane County	A	12	11	0	1	65.2	292	73	33	27	4	3	1	6	28	1	35	6	6	6	3	.667	0	0	3.70
1992	Frederick	A	28	28	5	0	182.1	762	160	88	71	14	6	5	5	65	0	122	11	3	11	10	.524	1	0	3.50
1993	Bowie	AA	24	21	2	0	116	497	114	51	45	10	5	2	4	40	0	85	5	2	7	7	.500	0	0	3.49
1994	Carolina	AA	3	1	0	1	6	34	7	7	4	0	1	0	0	9	0	5	1	0	1	0	1.000	0	0	6.00
	Salem	A	30	3	0	7	50	236	68	39	36	9	2	2	3	22	3	41	4	0	0	2	.000	0	0	6.48
	4 Min. YEARS		100	67	7	9	433	1878	433	227	189	38	17	10	20	170	4	305	28	14	26	23	.531	1	0	3.93

Mike Farrell

Pitches: Left Bats: Left Pos: P Ht: 6'2" Wt: 184 Born: 01/28/69 Age: 26

Year	Team	Lg	G	GS	CG	GF	IP	BFP	H	R	ER	HR	SH	SF	HB	TBB	IBB	SO	WP	Bk	W	L	Pct.	ShO	Sv	ERA
1991	Brewers	R	6	2	0	1	21.1	100	25	15	11	1	0	1	0	3	0	17	0	1	2	1	.667	0	0	4.64
	Helena	R	5	3	2	1	32	119	17	5	3	2	1	0	0	8	1	22	0	3	4	0	1.000	0	0	0.84
	Beloit	A	6	5	0	1	36.1	148	33	13	8	2	0	1	2	8	0	38	1	1	2	3	.400	0	0	1.98
1992	Stockton	A	13	13	3	0	92.2	371	82	28	24	6	3	5	5	21	0	67	1	3	8	4	.667	1	0	2.33
	El Paso	AA	14	14	5	0	106.1	435	95	42	31	5	7	0	7	25	4	66	0	1	7	6	.538	0	0	2.62
1993	New Orleans	AAA	26	26	3	0	152	637	164	92	82	22	2	2	6	32	1	63	2	2	9	9	.500	1	0	4.86
1994	El Paso	AA	5	5	0	0	29	127	39	18	18	5	1	1	1	5	0	16	1	2	3	0	1.000	0	0	5.59
	New Orleans	AAA	30	11	0	7	89	401	110	67	57	8	8	4	8	27	3	51	6	3	6	4	.600	0	0	5.76
	4 Min. YEARS		105	79	13	10	558.2	2338	565	280	234	51	24	12	29	129	9	340	11	16	41	27	.603	2	0	3.77

Mike Farrell

Bats: Right **Throws:** Right **Pos:** SS   **Ht:** 6'0" **Wt:** 170 **Born:** 04/01/72 **Age:** 23

Year	Team	Lg	G	AB	H	2B	3B	HR	TB	R	RBI	TBB	IBB	SO	HBP	SH	SF	SB	CS	SB%	GDP	Avg	OBP	SLG
1992	Pittsfield	A	2	6	0	0	0	0	0	0	1	0	0	0	0	0	0	0	0	.00	0	.000	.000	.000
	Mets	R	34	126	29	4	0	0	33	17	3	6	0	29	1	0	0	2	0	1.00	0	.230	.271	.262
1993	Kingsport	R	44	112	23	5	1	0	30	18	10	21	0	31	2	1	2	2	1	.67	5	.205	.336	.268
1994	Binghamton	AA	3	3	0	0	0	0	0	0	0	0	0	2	0	0	0	0	0	.00	0	.000	.000	.000
	St. Lucie	A	15	24	4	1	0	0	5	0	0	2	0	5	0	1	0	0	0	.00	0	.167	.231	.208
	3 Min. YEARS		98	271	56	10	1	0	68	35	14	29	0	67	3	2	2	4	1	.80	5	.207	.289	.251

Craig Faulkner

Bats: Right **Throws:** Right **Pos:** C   **Ht:** 6'5" **Wt:** 235 **Born:** 10/18/65 **Age:** 29

Year	Team	Lg	G	AB	H	2B	3B	HR	TB	R	RBI	TBB	IBB	SO	HBP	SH	SF	SB	CS	SB%	GDP	Avg	OBP	SLG
1987	Batavia	A	75	275	75	13	0	16	136	38	51	26	3	58	3	0	0	2	0	1.00	6	.273	.342	.495
1988	Hagerstown	A	125	440	125	25	1	12	188	55	76	50	0	99	6	0	5	1	0	1.00	10	.284	.361	.427
1989	Rochester	AAA	3	7	0	0	0	0	0	1	0	1	0	2	0	0	0	0	0	.00	0	.000	.125	.000
	Hagerstown	AA	81	272	57	8	2	8	93	27	30	22	1	97	2	0	2	0	2	.00	8	.210	.272	.342
1990	Hagerstown	AA	104	370	92	18	0	5	125	36	44	22	1	75	5	0	5	0	3	.00	13	.249	.296	.338
1991	El Paso	AA	77	267	82	18	0	10	130	39	46	19	0	57	2	1	1	1	1	.50	10	.307	.356	.487
1992	El Paso	AA	103	324	88	19	2	5	126	38	51	20	1	67	8	2	5	1	7	.13	14	.272	.325	.389
1993	Arkansas	AA	104	299	71	18	0	15	134	34	55	26	0	78	3	1	1	1	0	1.00	5	.237	.304	.448
1994	Rochester	AAA	36	106	23	5	1	2	36	9	10	6	0	21	2	0	0	0	0	.00	3	.217	.272	.340
	8 Min. YEARS		708	2360	613	124	6	73	968	277	363	192	6	554	31	4	19	6	13	.32	69	.260	.321	.410

Brian Faw

Pitches: Right **Bats:** Right **Pos:** P   **Ht:** 6'0" **Wt:** 185 **Born:** 03/19/68 **Age:** 27

Year	Team	Lg	G	GS	CG	GF	IP	BFP	H	R	ER	HR	SH	SF	HB	TBB	IBB	SO	WP	Bk	W	L	Pct.	ShO	Sv	ERA
1990	Yankees	R	12	12	1	0	80.1	313	56	27	19	1	2	2	3	16	0	66	2	0	7	5	.583	1	0	2.13
	Oneonta	A	1	0	0	0	3	14	6	3	3	0	1	0	0	2	0	0	0	0	0	0	.000	0	0	9.00
1991	Greensboro	A	26	26	6	0	166.1	686	148	75	62	12	3	5	3	56	1	123	4	3	11	7	.611	3	0	3.35
1992	Ft. Laud	A	24	17	0	4	119.2	516	129	72	56	6	0	9	1	38	0	74	3	2	5	9	.357	0	2	4.21
1993	Albany	AA	45	5	1	17	86	395	95	61	50	5	5	6	6	36	2	52	4	0	9	5	.643	0	0	5.23
1994	Albany-Colo	AA	43	3	0	18	73.2	346	72	57	46	12	6	5	6	51	2	31	6	1	4	6	.400	0	0	5.62
	5 Min. YEARS		151	63	8	39	529	2270	506	295	236	36	17	27	19	199	5	346	19	6	36	32	.529	4	6	4.02

Lauro Felix

Bats: Right **Throws:** Right **Pos:** SS   **Ht:** 5'9" **Wt:** 150 **Born:** 06/24/70 **Age:** 25

Year	Team	Lg	G	AB	H	2B	3B	HR	TB	R	RBI	TBB	IBB	SO	HBP	SH	SF	SB	CS	SB%	GDP	Avg	OBP	SLG
1992	Sou Oregon	A	11	24	10	1	0	1	14	5	3	8	0	5	0	0	1	2	1	.67	0	.417	.545	.583
	Madison	A	53	199	42	4	0	1	46	29	13	29	0	41	3	8	0	7	6	.54	2	.211	.320	.231
1993	Modesto	A	102	302	62	6	2	2	78	55	35	69	0	70	1	8	2	7	4	.64	10	.205	.353	.258
1994	Modesto	A	49	141	34	12	1	3	57	17	16	15	0	40	3	3	0	4	1	.80	0	.241	.327	.404
	Tacoma	AAA	43	131	23	5	0	0	28	13	5	17	0	34	2	4	1	0	4	.00	5	.176	.278	.214
	3 Min. YEARS		258	797	171	28	3	6	223	119	72	138	0	190	9	23	4	20	16	.56	17	.215	.335	.280

Danny Fernandez

Bats: Right **Throws:** Right **Pos:** C   **Ht:** 5'11" **Wt:** 180 **Born:** 06/06/66 **Age:** 29

Year	Team	Lg	G	AB	H	2B	3B	HR	TB	R	RBI	TBB	IBB	SO	HBP	SH	SF	SB	CS	SB%	GDP	Avg	OBP	SLG
1988	Clinton	A	23	53	12	1	0	0	13	2	3	6	0	15	1	2	0	2	0	1.00	1	.226	.317	.245
1989	San Jose	A	50	136	24	0	0	1	27	17	11	25	0	35	2	1	0	3	3	.50	4	.176	.313	.199
1990	San Jose	A	36	76	20	2	0	1	25	19	14	13	0	21	0	3	2	0	1	.00	4	.263	.363	.329
1991	Phoenix	AAA	4	3	0	0	0	0	0	0	0	0	0	0	0	0	0	0	0	.00	0	.000	.000	.000
	Shreveport	AA	7	12	3	0	0	0	3	3	1	6	1	3	1	1	0	0	0	.00	0	.250	.526	.250
	San Jose	A	37	90	22	5	1	0	29	14	11	29	1	26	0	0	2	0	2	.00	5	.244	.421	.322
1992	Shreveport	AA	60	185	40	2	0	2	48	18	22	16	2	34	1	5	1	2	0	1.00	5	.216	.281	.259
1993	Shreveport	AA	48	128	24	5	1	1	34	12	13	14	2	32	0	4	1	1	2	.33	2	.188	.266	.266
	Phoenix	AAA	42	118	31	3	1	0	36	17	7	17	0	24	1	2	2	1	2	.33	6	.263	.355	.305
1994	Phoenix	AAA	44	143	39	5	0	1	49	15	18	12	0	28	0	1	0	1	0	1.00	4	.273	.329	.343
	7 Min. YEARS		351	944	215	23	4	6	264	117	100	138	6	218	6	19	8	10	10	.50	28	.228	.328	.280

Jose Fernandez

Bats: Left **Throws:** Right **Pos:** C   **Ht:** 6'3" **Wt:** 210 **Born:** 08/24/67 **Age:** 27

Year	Team	Lg	G	AB	H	2B	3B	HR	TB	R	RBI	TBB	IBB	SO	HBP	SH	SF	SB	CS	SB%	GDP	Avg	OBP	SLG
1989	Hamilton	A	52	165	33	7	1	5	57	24	23	25	1	47	1	0	3	3	2	.60	3	.200	.304	.345
1990	St. Pete	A	42	138	35	10	0	1	48	12	19	34	2	39	0	0	0	0	1	.00	2	.254	.401	.348
	Arkansas	AA	55	177	30	5	1	4	49	13	25	14	0	65	1	2	4	0	0	.00	4	.169	.230	.277

Year	Team	Lg	G	AB	H	2B	3B	HR	TB	R	RBI	TBB	IBB	SO	HBP	SH	SF	SB	CS	SB%	GDP	Avg	OBP	SLG
1991	Arkansas	AA	93	281	64	14	1	12	116	46	27	62	1	86	2	0	1	0	1	.00	4	.228	.370	.413
1992	Louisville	AAA	12	38	3	1	0	1	7	1	3	6	1	9	1	0	0	0	0	.00	1	.079	.222	.184
	Arkansas	AA	49	115	18	5	0	1	26	7	8	18	0	39	0	0	1	0	1	.00	0	.157	.269	.226
1993	Reading	AA	38	129	32	5	0	3	46	8	18	12	0	37	0	2	1	0	0	.00	3	.248	.310	.357
	Scranton/wb	AAA	16	32	6	1	0	0	7	2	1	4	0	11	0	1	0	0	0	.00	0	.188	.278	.219
1994	Louisville	AAA	14	35	10	1	0	0	11	7	6	4	0	10	0	0	0	0	0	.00	0	.286	.359	.314
	6 Min. YEARS		371	1110	231	49	3	27	367	114	130	179	5	343	5	5	10	3	5	.38	17	.208	.318	.331

Mike Fernandez

Bats: Right Throws: Right Pos: OF   Ht: 6'0" Wt: 195 Born: 08/21/69 Age: 25

						BATTING													BASERUNNING				PERCENTAGES		
Year	Team	Lg	G	AB	H	2B	3B	HR	TB	R	RBI	TBB	IBB	SO	HBP	SH	SF	SB	CS	SB%	GDP	Avg	OBP	SLG
1991	Elizabethtn	R	42	148	34	8	3	6	66	20	18	12	0	40	1	1	2	0	0	.00	5	.230	.288	.446
1992	Kenosha	A	80	271	72	13	3	7	112	36	31	22	0	69	4	1	1	2	2	.50	8	.266	.329	.413
1993	Ft.Myers	A	107	375	100	29	3	1	138	47	37	45	5	73	3	6	7	14	2	.88	14	.267	.344	.368
1994	Nashville	AA	1	4	0	0	0	0	0	0	0	0	0	1	0	0	0	0	0	.00	0	.000	.000	.000
	4 Min. YEARS		231	798	206	50	9	14	316	103	86	79	5	183	8	8	10	16	4	.80	27	.258	.327	.396

Mike Ferry

Pitches: Right Bats: Right Pos: P   Ht: 6'3" Wt: 195 Born: 07/26/69 Age: 25

				HOW MUCH HE PITCHED					WHAT HE GAVE UP								THE RESULTS					
Year	Team	Lg	G	GS	CG	GF	IP	BFP	H	R	ER	HR	SH	SF	HB	TBB	IBB	SO	WP	Bk	W	L	Pct.	ShO	Sv	ERA
1990	Billings	R	27	0	0	24	31.2	140	29	13	10	3	2	1	1	12	1	29	6	2	2	5	.286	0	11	2.84
1991	Cedar Rapds	A	16	0	0	12	25.2	122	25	19	19	1	2	1	1	21	2	27	2	0	2	2	.500	0	3	6.66
	Chston-Wv	A	22	1	0	11	44.1	191	41	23	22	2	4	2	1	21	2	51	4	0	1	3	.250	0	2	4.47
1992	Cedar Rapds	A	25	25	6	0	162.2	665	134	57	49	6	4	5	9	40	1	143	10	1	13	4	.765	0	0	2.71
1993	Chattanooga	AA	28	28	4	0	186.2	749	176	85	71	17	5	9	5	30	1	111	8	1	13	8	.619	1	0	3.42
1994	Indianapols	AAA	7	7	0	0	31	152	47	32	23	5	1	0	1	14	0	15	2	0	1	4	.200	0	0	6.68
	Chattanooga	AA	21	21	3	0	147	616	162	72	58	11	6	6	3	20	1	94	7	1	9	7	.563	0	0	3.55
	5 Min. YEARS		146	82	13	47	629	2635	614	301	252	45	24	24	21	158	8	470	39	5	41	33	.554	1	16	3.61

Sean Fesh

Pitches: Left Bats: Left Pos: P   Ht: 6'2" Wt: 165 Born: 11/03/72 Age: 22

				HOW MUCH HE PITCHED					WHAT HE GAVE UP								THE RESULTS					
Year	Team	Lg	G	GS	CG	GF	IP	BFP	H	R	ER	HR	SH	SF	HB	TBB	IBB	SO	WP	Bk	W	L	Pct.	ShO	Sv	ERA
1991	Astros	R	6	0	0	2	12.1	53	5	4	3	0	0	0	0	11	0	7	4	0	0	0	.000	0	0	2.19
1992	Osceola	A	3	0	0	2	5.1	24	5	3	1	0	0	0	0	1	0	5	3	0	0	1	.000	0	0	1.69
	Astros	R	18	0	0	12	36.1	142	25	7	7	0	3	0	4	8	0	35	4	0	1	0	1.000	0	6	1.73
1993	Asheville	A	65	0	0	58	82.1	353	75	39	33	4	11	6	5	37	8	49	4	1	10	6	.625	0	20	3.61
1994	Osceola	A	43	0	0	29	49.2	222	50	27	14	2	5	0	6	24	6	32	2	0	2	4	.333	0	11	2.54
	Jackson	AA	20	1	0	5	25.2	122	34	17	12	2	2	1	0	11	0	19	2	0	1	2	.333	0	0	4.21
	4 Min. YEARS		155	1	0	108	211.2	916	194	97	70	8	21	7	15	92	14	147	19	1	14	13	.519	0	37	2.98

Todd Fiegel

Pitches: Left Bats: Left Pos: P   Ht: 6'3" Wt: 190 Born: 10/16/69 Age: 25

				HOW MUCH HE PITCHED					WHAT HE GAVE UP								THE RESULTS					
Year	Team	Lg	G	GS	CG	GF	IP	BFP	H	R	ER	HR	SH	SF	HB	TBB	IBB	SO	WP	Bk	W	L	Pct.	ShO	Sv	ERA
1991	Kingsport	R	11	11	2	0	66.1	268	45	20	15	2	0	1	12	25	1	90	6	3	5	4	.556	0	0	2.04
	Columbia	A	2	1	0	1	9	40	7	6	6	0	0	0	1	6	0	11	3	0	0	1	.000	0	1	6.00
1992	Columbia	A	26	18	1	6	128.2	557	118	80	55	9	2	5	6	55	0	83	14	2	5	6	.455	0	2	3.85
1993	St.Lucie	A	25	16	0	5	116.2	505	122	60	44	7	3	5	3	42	0	71	4	2	10	7	.588	0	0	3.39
1994	Norfolk	AAA	4	0	0	1	8	34	9	8	8	0	0	1	0	3	0	4	1	0	0	0	.000	0	0	9.00
	St. Lucie	A	5	0	0	1	4	15	1	0	0	0	0	0	0	1	0	6	0	0	1	0	1.000	0	1	0.00
	Binghamton	AA	29	8	1	8	79.2	355	93	44	36	6	3	3	4	28	3	66	6	2	3	3	.500	0	1	4.07
	4 Min. YEARS		102	54	4	22	412.1	1774	395	218	164	24	8	15	26	160	4	331	34	9	24	21	.533	0	5	3.58

Michael Figga

Bats: Right Throws: Right Pos: C   Ht: 6'0" Wt: 200 Born: 07/31/70 Age: 24

						BATTING													BASERUNNING				PERCENTAGES		
Year	Team	Lg	G	AB	H	2B	3B	HR	TB	R	RBI	TBB	IBB	SO	HBP	SH	SF	SB	CS	SB%	GDP	Avg	OBP	SLG
1990	Yankees	R	40	123	35	1	1	2	44	19	18	17	2	33	1	0	1	4	2	.67	2	.285	.373	.358
1991	Pr William	A	55	174	34	6	0	3	49	15	17	19	0	51	0	2	1	2	1	.67	9	.195	.273	.282
1992	Pr William	A	3	10	2	1	0	0	3	0	0	2	0	3	0	0	0	1	0	1.00	0	.200	.333	.300
	Ft. Laud	A	80	249	44	13	0	1	60	12	15	13	1	78	2	3	0	3	1	.75	7	.177	.223	.241
1993	San Berndno	A	83	308	82	17	1	25	176	48	71	17	0	84	2	2	3	2	3	.40	7	.266	.306	.571
	Albany	AA	6	22	5	0	0	0	5	3	2	2	0	9	0	0	0	1	0	1.00	0	.227	.292	.227
1994	Albany-Colo	AA	1	2	1	1	0	0	2	1	0	0	0	1	0	0	0	0	0	.00	0	.500	.500	1.000
	Tampa	A	111	420	116	17	5	15	188	48	75	22	1	94	2	1	5	3	0	1.00	12	.276	.312	.448
	5 Min. YEARS		379	1308	319	56	7	46	527	146	198	92	4	353	7	8	10	16	7	.70	37	.244	.295	.403

Bien Figueroa

Bats: Right Throws: Right Pos: SS
Ht: 5'10" Wt: 167 Born: 02/07/64 Age: 31

								BATTING									BASERUNNING				PERCENTAGES		
Year	Team	Lg	G	AB	H	2B	3B	HR	TB	R	RBI	TBB	IBB	SO	HBP	SH	SF	SB	CS	SB%	GDP	Avg	OBP	SLG
1986	Erie	A	73	249	59	4	0	0	63	31	30	32	1	26	1	1	3	13	4	.76	9	.237	.323	.253
1987	Springfield	A	134	489	136	13	3	2	161	52	83	34	2	46	4	12	7	7	7	.50	16	.278	.326	.329
1988	Arkansas	AA	126	407	113	17	2	0	134	48	32	22	1	49	3	7	1	2	6	.25	16	.278	.319	.329
1989	Louisville	AAA	74	221	48	3	0	0	51	18	14	12	0	22	0	5	1	0	1	.00	7	.217	.256	.231
1990	Louisville	AAA	128	396	95	19	2	0	118	41	39	24	2	37	3	7	2	5	1	.83	15	.240	.287	.298
1991	Louisville	AAA	97	269	55	8	2	0	67	18	14	20	2	27	2	5	0	1	4	.20	10	.204	.265	.249
1992	Louisville	AAA	94	319	91	11	1	1	107	44	23	33	0	32	2	6	3	2	0	1.00	8	.285	.353	.335
1993	Louisville	AAA	93	272	65	17	1	0	84	44	15	16	1	27	3	1	1	1	1	.50	6	.239	.288	.309
1994	Harrisburg	AA	13	40	10	1	0	0	11	6	4	6	0	3	2	1	0	0	0	.00	2	.250	.375	.275
	Ottawa	AAA	72	223	54	13	1	1	72	22	26	14	0	28	0	0	3	2	0	1.00	9	.242	.283	.323
1992	St. Louis	NL	12	11	2	1	0	0	3	1	4	1	0	2	0	0	0	0	0	.00	0	.182	.250	.273
	9 Min. YEARS		904	2885	726	106	12	4	868	324	280	213	9	297	20	45	21	33	24	.58	98	.252	.306	.301

John Finn

Bats: Right Throws: Right Pos: 2B
Ht: 5'8" Wt: 168 Born: 10/18/67 Age: 27

								BATTING									BASERUNNING				PERCENTAGES		
Year	Team	Lg	G	AB	H	2B	3B	HR	TB	R	RBI	TBB	IBB	SO	HBP	SH	SF	SB	CS	SB%	GDP	Avg	OBP	SLG
1989	Beloit	A	73	274	82	8	7	1	107	49	20	38	0	27	4	5	2	29	11	.73	3	.299	.390	.391
1990	Stockton	A	95	290	60	4	0	1	67	48	23	52	0	50	1	6	6	29	15	.66	1	.207	.324	.231
1991	Stockton	A	65	223	57	12	1	0	71	45	25	44	1	28	9	6	3	19	9	.68	5	.256	.394	.318
	El Paso	AA	63	230	69	12	2	2	91	48	24	16	0	27	2	5	2	8	4	.67	0	.300	.348	.396
1992	El Paso	AA	124	439	121	12	6	1	148	83	47	71	3	44	11	9	7	30	12	.71	7	.276	.384	.337
1993	New Orleans	AAA	117	335	94	13	2	1	114	47	37	33	1	36	6	9	0	27	9	.75	8	.281	.356	.340
1994	New Orleans	AAA	76	229	66	12	0	2	84	36	24	35	1	21	7	6	4	15	10	.60	3	.288	.393	.367
	6 Min. YEARS		613	2020	549	73	18	8	682	356	200	289	6	233	40	46	24	157	70	.69	27	.272	.370	.338

David Fisher

Bats: Right Throws: Right Pos: 2B
Ht: 6'0" Wt: 160 Born: 02/26/70 Age: 25

								BATTING									BASERUNNING				PERCENTAGES		
Year	Team	Lg	G	AB	H	2B	3B	HR	TB	R	RBI	TBB	IBB	SO	HBP	SH	SF	SB	CS	SB%	GDP	Avg	OBP	SLG
1992	Martinsvlle	R	50	188	57	14	1	3	82	31	42	27	2	27	0	1	1	6	1	.86	2	.303	.397	.436
	Batavia	A	21	80	27	4	1	1	36	10	14	6	0	5	4	2	0	3	2	.60	2	.338	.411	.450
1993	Clearwater	A	126	430	103	25	2	6	150	54	54	52	1	42	8	8	10	11	16	.41	7	.240	.326	.349
1994	Reading	AA	118	412	103	24	3	7	154	57	42	57	0	65	7	8	4	5	6	.45	6	.250	.348	.374
	3 Min. YEARS		315	1110	290	67	7	17	422	152	152	145	3	139	19	19	15	25	25	.50	17	.261	.352	.380

Robert Fitzpatrick

Bats: Right Throws: Right Pos: C
Ht: 6'0" Wt: 190 Born: 09/14/68 Age: 26

								BATTING									BASERUNNING				PERCENTAGES		
Year	Team	Lg	G	AB	H	2B	3B	HR	TB	R	RBI	TBB	IBB	SO	HBP	SH	SF	SB	CS	SB%	GDP	Avg	OBP	SLG
1990	Jamestown	A	62	209	56	14	0	6	88	23	34	28	2	53	0	0	1	1	0	1.00	3	.268	.353	.421
1991	Rockford	A	93	296	70	15	0	6	103	39	35	34	0	82	3	2	2	1	5	.17	4	.236	.319	.348
1992	Wst Plm Bch	A	96	336	86	19	0	8	129	42	37	37	1	81	2	1	0	4	3	.57	8	.256	.333	.384
1993	Harrisburg	AA	99	341	77	10	1	11	122	44	46	36	0	82	5	2	2	6	7	.46	10	.226	.307	.358
1994	Harrisburg	AA	95	315	79	12	1	9	120	39	34	29	2	78	4	2	1	3	4	.43	7	.251	.321	.381
	5 Min. YEARS		445	1497	368	70	2	40	562	187	186	164	5	376	14	7	6	15	19	.44	32	.246	.325	.375

Benjamin Fleetham

Pitches: Right Bats: Right Pos: P
Ht: 6'1" Wt: 205 Born: 08/03/72 Age: 22

				HOW MUCH HE PITCHED				WHAT HE GAVE UP									THE RESULTS					
Year	Team	Lg	G	GS	CG	GF	IP	BFP	H	R	ER	HR	SH	SF	HB	TBB	IBB	SO	WP	Bk	W	L	Pct.	ShO	Sv	ERA
1994	Vermont	A	17	0	0	2	28.2	125	23	13	8	0	2	2	1	16	1	29	2	2	0	0	.000	0	2	2.51
	Burlington	A	6	0	0	2	13.1	51	5	4	3	1	0	0	0	4	0	27	2	3	1	0	1.000	0	0	2.03
	Harrisburg	AA	2	0	0	2	3	14	2	0	0	0	0	0	1	2	0	0	1	1	0	0	.000	0	0	0.00
	1 Min. YEARS		25	0	0	6	45	190	30	17	11	1	2	2	2	22	1	56	5	6	1	0	1.000	0	2	2.20

Carlton Fleming

Bats: Both Throws: Right Pos: 2B
Ht: 5'11" Wt: 175 Born: 08/25/71 Age: 23

								BATTING									BASERUNNING				PERCENTAGES		
Year	Team	Lg	G	AB	H	2B	3B	HR	TB	R	RBI	TBB	IBB	SO	HBP	SH	SF	SB	CS	SB%	GDP	Avg	OBP	SLG
1992	Oneonta	A	3	11	2	0	0	0	2	2	2	1	0	2	1	0	0	1	0	1.00	0	.182	.308	.182
	Greensboro	A	68	236	78	1	1	0	81	35	24	31	0	20	0	1	0	9	7	.56	2	.331	.408	.343
1993	Pr William	A	120	442	132	14	2	0	150	72	25	80	2	23	0	6	1	21	10	.68	14	.299	.405	.339
1994	Albany-Colo	AA	117	378	92	12	1	0	106	39	37	52	0	37	3	10	4	20	10	.67	8	.243	.336	.280
	3 Min. YEARS		308	1067	304	27	4	0	339	148	88	164	2	82	4	17	5	51	27	.65	24	.285	.381	.318

Huck Flener

Pitches: Left Bats: Both Pos: P Ht: 5'11" Wt: 175 Born: 02/25/69 Age: 26

			HOW MUCH HE PITCHED						WHAT HE GAVE UP									THE RESULTS					
Year	Team	Lg	G	GS	CG	GF	IP	BFP	H	R	ER	HR	SH	SF	HB	TBB	IBB	SO	WP	Bk	W	L	Pct.	ShO	Sv	ERA
1990	St. Cath	A	14	7	0	3	61.2	258	45	29	23	4	3	0	1	33	0	46	4	3	4	3	.571	0	1	3.36
1991	Myrtle Bch	A	55	0	0	44	79.1	334	58	28	16	1	5	3	0	41	0	107	7	2	6	4	.600	0	13	1.82
1992	Dunedin	A	41	8	0	19	112.1	451	70	35	28	4	5	2	7	50	2	93	2	1	7	3	.700	0	8	2.24
1993	Knoxville	AA	38	16	2	10	136.1	556	130	56	50	9	6	4	3	39	1	114	9	8	13	6	.684	2	4	3.30
1994	Syracuse	AAA	6	6	0	0	37	155	38	22	19	6	0	0	0	8	0	20	2	1	0	3	.000	0	0	4.62
1993	Toronto	AL	6	0	0	1	6.2	30	7	3	3	0	0	0	0	4	1	2	1	0	0	0	.000	0	0	4.05
	5 Min. YEARS		154	37	2	76	426.2	1754	341	170	136	24	19	12	11	171	3	380	24	15	30	19	.612	2	26	2.87

Paul Fletcher

Pitches: Right Bats: Right Pos: P Ht: 6' 1" Wt: 185 Born: 01/14/67 Age: 28

			HOW MUCH HE PITCHED						WHAT HE GAVE UP									THE RESULTS					
Year	Team	Lg	G	GS	CG	GF	IP	BFP	H	R	ER	HR	SH	SF	HB	TBB	IBB	SO	WP	Bk	W	L	Pct.	ShO	Sv	ERA
1988	Martinsville	R	15	14	1	1	69.1	320	81	44	36	4	1	3	4	33	0	61	3	1	1	3	.250	0	1	4.67
1989	Batavia	A	14	14	3	0	82.1	339	77	41	30	13	2	2	3	28	0	58	3	1	7	5	.583	0	0	3.28
1990	Spartanburg	A	9	9	1	0	49.1	207	46	24	18	3	1	1	2	18	0	53	7	1	2	4	.333	0	0	3.28
	Clearwater	A	20	18	2	1	117.1	498	104	56	44	3	6	6	13	49	0	106	7	2	5	8	.385	0	0	3.38
1991	Clearwater	A	14	4	0	5	29.1	119	22	6	4	1	1	2	0	8	1	27	2	0	0	1	.000	0	1	1.23
	Reading	AA	21	19	3	1	120.2	517	111	56	47	12	3	1	2	56	3	90	6	1	7	9	.438	1	0	3.51
1992	Reading	AA	22	20	2	0	127	521	103	45	40	10	1	1	5	47	2	103	7	0	9	4	.692	0	0	2.83
	Scranton/wb	AAA	4	4	0	0	22.2	85	17	8	7	1	0	0	1	2	0	26	2	0	3	0	1.000	0	0	2.78
1993	Scranton/wb	AAA	34	19	3	5	140	625	146	99	88	21	4	4	9	60	3	116	21	0	4	12	.250	1	0	5.66
1994	Scranton-Wb	AAA	42	13	3	8	138.1	604	144	78	72	12	4	1	6	54	0	92	6	0	4	9	.308	1	1	4.68
1993	Philadelphia	NL	1	0	0	0	0.1	1	0	0	0	0	0	0	0	0	0	0	1	0	0	0	.000	0	0	0.00
	7 Min. YEARS		195	134	17	21	896.1	3835	851	457	386	80	23	22	44	355	9	732	64	6	42	55	.433	4	6	3.88

Kevin Flora

Bats: Right Throws: Right Pos: 2B Ht: 6' 0" Wt: 180 Born: 06/10/69 Age: 26

			BATTING													BASERUNNING				PERCENTAGES		
Year	Team	Lg	G	AB	H	2B	3B	HR	TB	R	RBI	TBB	IBB	SO	HBP	SH	SF	SB	CS	SB%	GDP	Avg	OBP	SLG
1987	Salem	A	35	88	24	5	1	0	31	17	12	21	0	14	0	3	0	8	4	.67	2	.273	.413	.352
1988	Quad City	A	48	152	33	3	4	0	44	19	15	18	4	33	0	1	0	5	3	.63	4	.217	.300	.289
1989	Quad City	A	120	372	81	8	4	1	100	46	21	57	2	107	6	5	3	30	10	.75	3	.218	.329	.269
1990	Midland	AA	71	232	53	16	5	5	94	35	32	23	0	53	0	3	1	11	5	.69	6	.228	.297	.405
1991	Midland	AA	124	484	138	14	15	12	218	97	67	37	0	92	3	3	3	40	8	.83	2	.285	.338	.450
1992	Edmonton	AAA	52	170	55	8	4	3	80	35	19	29	0	25	1	4	2	9	8	.53	6	.324	.421	.471
1993	Vancouver	AAA	30	94	31	2	0	1	36	17	12	10	0	20	1	2	1	6	2	.75	2	.330	.396	.383
1994	Vancouver	AAA	6	12	2	1	0	0	3	5	1	4	0	4	0	1	0	1	0	1.00	1	.167	.375	.250
	Lake Elsino	A	19	72	13	3	2	0	20	13	6	12	0	17	0	1	1	7	1	.88	2	.181	.294	.278
1991	California	AL	3	8	1	0	0	0	1	1	0	1	0	5	0	0	0	1	0	1.00	1	.125	.222	.125
	8 Min. YEARS		505	1676	430	60	35	22	626	284	185	211	6	365	11	23	11	117	41	.74	28	.257	.342	.374

Don Florence

Pitches: Left Bats: Right Pos: P Ht: 6'0" Wt: 195 Born: 03/16/67 Age: 28

			HOW MUCH HE PITCHED						WHAT HE GAVE UP									THE RESULTS					
Year	Team	Lg	G	GS	CG	GF	IP	BFP	H	R	ER	HR	SH	SF	HB	TBB	IBB	SO	WP	Bk	W	L	Pct.	ShO	Sv	ERA
1988	Winter Havn	A	27	16	4	7	120.2	542	136	68	53	4	3	4	4	50	1	56	10	2	6	8	.429	0	0	3.95
1989	Winter Havn	A	51	2	0	31	93.2	395	81	46	30	1	7	2	2	34	3	71	7	1	2	7	.222	0	15	2.88
1990	New Britain	AA	34	4	0	12	79.2	341	85	37	31	3	2	3	1	26	3	39	4	0	6	4	.600	0	1	3.50
1991	New Britain	AA	55	2	0	28	84.1	382	85	59	52	7	6	5	7	43	4	73	4	1	3	8	.273	0	2	5.55
1992	New Britain	AA	58	0	0	30	74.2	311	65	23	20	0	8	0	3	27	3	51	4	0	3	1	.750	0	6	2.41
1993	Pawtucket	AAA	57	0	0	18	59	246	56	24	22	6	6	1	0	18	5	46	8	0	7	8	.467	0	2	3.36
1994	Pawtucket	AAA	61	0	0	24	59	259	66	24	24	2	3	1	1	24	4	43	1	0	1	4	.200	0	7	3.66
	7 Min. YEARS		343	24	4	150	571	2476	574	281	232	23	35	16	18	222	23	379	41	4	28	40	.412	0	33	3.66

Jose Flores

Bats: Both Throws: Right Pos: 2B Ht: 6'1" Wt: 155 Born: 01/01/71 Age: 24

			BATTING													BASERUNNING				PERCENTAGES		
Year	Team	Lg	G	AB	H	2B	3B	HR	TB	R	RBI	TBB	IBB	SO	HBP	SH	SF	SB	CS	SB%	GDP	Avg	OBP	SLG
1990	Auburn	A	42	109	20	2	0	0	22	13	6	18	0	16	0	7	0	3	3	.50	6	.183	.299	.202
1991	Asheville	A	87	223	49	7	1	2	64	22	16	25	0	28	2	4	3	3	2	.60	5	.220	.300	.287
1992	Asheville	A	121	457	122	15	2	3	150	54	47	53	0	48	0	1	5	15	6	.71	13	.267	.340	.328
1993	Osceola	A	124	452	110	11	1	0	123	47	39	39	0	64	1	6	4	12	11	.52	9	.243	.302	.272
1994	Jackson	AA	47	99	19	3	2	0	26	12	7	5	1	11	0	4	0	3	1	.75	2	.192	.231	.263
	5 Min. YEARS		421	1340	320	38	6	5	385	148	115	140	1	167	3	22	12	36	23	.61	35	.239	.310	.287

Miguel Flores

Bats: Right Throws: Right Pos: 2B   Ht: 5'11" Wt: 185 Born: 08/16/70 Age: 24

Year	Team	Lg	G	AB	H	2B	3B	HR	TB	R	RBI	TBB	IBB	SO	HBP	SH	SF	SB	CS	SB%	GDP	Avg	OBP	SLG
1990	Burlington	R	57	208	52	8	1	3	71	33	25	20	0	18	2	0	0	22	7	.76	3	.250	.322	.341
1991	Kinston	A	124	425	114	19	3	5	154	61	40	34	1	45	9	7	6	29	7	.81	13	.268	.331	.362
1992	Canton-Akrn	AA	126	456	124	20	4	1	155	45	43	35	3	39	5	3	5	25	11	.69	19	.272	.327	.340
1993	Canton-Akrn	AA	116	435	127	20	5	3	166	73	54	59	0	39	3	4	3	36	9	.80	11	.292	.378	.382
1994	Charlotte	AAA	87	248	68	10	1	2	86	35	31	23	0	30	2	5	1	9	6	.60	8	.274	.339	.347
	5 Min. YEARS		510	1772	485	77	14	14	632	247	193	171	4	171	21	19	15	121	40	.75	54	.274	.342	.357

Tim Florez

Bats: Right Throws: Right Pos: 2B   Ht: 5'10" Wt: 170 Born: 07/23/69 Age: 25

Year	Team	Lg	G	AB	H	2B	3B	HR	TB	R	RBI	TBB	IBB	SO	HBP	SH	SF	SB	CS	SB%	GDP	Avg	OBP	SLG
1991	Everett	A	59	193	48	8	4	0	64	33	25	12	1	33	1	2	1	7	1	.88	4	.249	.295	.332
1992	Clinton	A	81	292	68	12	2	2	90	39	25	30	2	53	3	0	2	20	5	.80	6	.233	.309	.308
	San Jose	A	38	131	32	6	1	1	43	15	17	4	0	21	0	4	4	3	3	.50	2	.244	.259	.328
1993	Shreveport	AA	106	318	81	17	2	1	105	33	26	16	4	43	2	3	2	3	5	.38	9	.255	.293	.330
1994	Phoenix	AAA	13	24	6	1	0	1	10	5	2	1	0	4	0	0	0	0	0	.00	1	.250	.280	.417
	Shreveport	AA	61	158	34	10	0	1	47	21	13	21	3	34	1	2	1	0	3	.00	4	.215	.309	.297
	4 Min. YEARS		358	1116	269	54	9	6	359	146	108	84	10	188	7	11	10	33	17	.66	26	.241	.296	.322

P.J. Forbes

Bats: Right Throws: Right Pos: 2B   Ht: 5'10" Wt: 160 Born: 09/22/67 Age: 27

Year	Team	Lg	G	AB	H	2B	3B	HR	TB	R	RBI	TBB	IBB	SO	HBP	SH	SF	SB	CS	SB%	GDP	Avg	OBP	SLG
1990	Boise	A	43	170	42	9	1	0	53	29	19	23	1	21	0	7	1	11	4	.73	5	.247	.335	.312
1991	Palm Sprngs	A	94	349	93	14	2	2	117	45	26	36	1	44	4	12	0	18	8	.69	7	.266	.342	.335
1992	Quad City	A	105	376	106	16	5	2	138	53	46	44	1	51	2	24	5	15	6	.71	4	.282	.356	.367
1993	Midland	AA	126	498	159	23	2	15	231	90	64	26	1	50	4	14	2	6	8	.43	13	.319	.357	.464
	Vancouver	AAA	5	16	4	2	0	0	6	1	3	0	0	3	0	1	0	0	0	.00	1	.250	.250	.375
1994	Angels	R	2	6	0	0	0	0	0	1	0	0	0	1	0	0	0	0	0	.00	0	.000	.000	.000
	Vancouver	AAA	90	318	91	21	2	1	119	39	40	22	0	42	2	7	5	4	2	.67	6	.286	.331	.374
	5 Min. YEARS		465	1733	495	85	12	20	664	258	198	151	4	212	12	65	13	54	28	.66	36	.286	.345	.383

Brook Fordyce

Bats: Right Throws: Right Pos: C   Ht: 6'1" Wt: 185 Born: 05/07/70 Age: 25

Year	Team	Lg	G	AB	H	2B	3B	HR	TB	R	RBI	TBB	IBB	SO	HBP	SH	SF	SB	CS	SB%	GDP	Avg	OBP	SLG
1989	Kingsport	R	69	226	74	15	0	9	116	45	38	30	1	26	1	3	2	10	6	.63	3	.327	.405	.513
1990	Columbia	A	104	372	117	29	1	10	178	45	54	39	0	42	0	1	2	4	1	.80	18	.315	.378	.478
1991	St. Lucie	A	115	406	97	19	3	7	143	42	55	37	2	51	4	0	6	5	4	.44	7	.239	.305	.352
1992	Binghamton	AA	118	425	118	30	0	11	181	59	61	37	1	78	4	3	6	1	2	.33	13	.278	.337	.426
1993	Norfolk	AAA	116	409	106	21	2	2	137	33	40	26	3	62	5	3	6	2	2	.50	10	.259	.307	.335
1994	Norfolk	AAA	66	229	60	13	3	3	88	26	32	19	1	26	1	2	1	0	1	1.00	9	.262	.320	.384
	6 Min. YEARS		588	2067	572	127	9	42	843	250	280	188	8	285	15	12	23	22	16	.58	60	.277	.338	.408

Rick Forney

Pitches: Right Bats: Right Pos: P   Ht: 6'4" Wt: 210 Born: 10/24/71 Age: 23

Year	Team	Lg	G	GS	CG	GF	IP	BFP	H	R	ER	HR	SH	SF	HB	TBB	IBB	SO	WP	Bk	W	L	Pct.	ShO	Sv	ERA
1991	Orioles	R	12	10	2	0	65.2	260	48	21	16	1	1	1	4	10	0	51	1	2	7	0	1.000	1	0	2.19
1992	Kane County	A	20	18	2	0	123.1	513	114	40	34	4	4	2	9	26	1	104	9	2	3	6	.333	1	0	2.48
1993	Frederick	A	27	27	2	0	165	704	156	64	51	11	4	4	7	64	0	175	12	2	14	8	.636	0	0	2.78
	Bowie	AA	1	1	0	0	7	24	1	1	1	1	0	0	1	1	0	4	0	0	0	0	.000	0	0	1.29
1994	Bowie	AA	28	28	4	0	165.2	715	168	105	85	17	4	7	3	58	1	125	9	2	13	8	.619	0	0	4.62
	4 Min. YEARS		88	84	10	0	526.2	2216	487	231	187	34	13	14	24	159	2	459	31	8	37	22	.627	4	0	3.20

Steve Foster

Pitches: Right Bats: Right Pos: P   Ht: 6'0" Wt: 180 Born: 08/16/66 Age: 28

Year	Team	Lg	G	GS	CG	GF	IP	BFP	H	R	ER	HR	SH	SF	HB	TBB	IBB	SO	WP	Bk	W	L	Pct.	ShO	Sv	ERA
1988	Billings	R	18	0	0	14	30.1	114	15	5	4	0	3	2	3	7	1	27	1	7	2	3	.400	0	7	1.19
1989	Cedar Rapds	A	51	0	0	47	59	245	46	16	14	2	2	1	5	19	6	55	5	5	0	3	.000	0	23	2.14
1990	Chattanooga	AA	50	0	0	42	59.1	277	69	38	35	6	3	8	4	33	4	51	2	2	5	10	.333	0	20	5.31
1991	Chattanooga	AA	17	0	0	16	15.2	64	10	4	2	0	1	0	3	4	0	18	2	1	0	2	.000	0	10	1.15
	Nashville	AAA	41	0	0	25	54.2	237	46	17	13	4	2	3	1	29	5	52	0	0	2	3	.400	0	12	2.14
1992	Nashville	AAA	17	7	0	6	50.1	212	53	20	15	3	4	0	1	22	0	28	1	1	5	3	.625	0	1	2.68
1994	Chattanooga	AA	3	3	0	0	3.1	13	1	0	0	0	0	0	0	2	0	1	0	0	0	0	.000	0	0	0.00
1991	Cincinnati	NL	11	0	0	5	14	53	7	5	3	1	0	0	0	4	0	11	0	0	0	0	.000	0	0	1.93
1992	Cincinnati	NL	31	1	0	7	50	209	52	16	16	4	5	2	0	13	1	34	1	0	1	1	.500	0	2	2.88
1993	Cincinnati	NL	17	0	0	7	25.2	105	23	5	5	1	2	0	1	5	2	16	0	0	2	2	.500	0	0	1.75

	G	GS	CG	GF	IP	BFP	H	R	ER	HR	SH	SF	HB	TBB	IBB	SO	WP	Bk	W	L	Pct.	ShO	Sv	ERA
6 Min. YEARS	197	10	0	150	272.2	1162	240	100	83	15	15	14	17	116	16	232	11	16	14	24	.368	0	73	2.74
3 Maj. YEARS	59	1	0	19	89.2	367	82	29	24	6	6	2	1	22	3	61	1	0	3	3	.500	0	2	2.41

Andy Fox

Bats: Left Throws: Right Pos: 3B Ht: 6'4" Wt: 185 Born: 01/12/71 Age: 24

Year Team	Lg	G	AB	H	2B	3B	HR	TB	R	RBI	TBB	IBB	SO	HBP	SH	SF	SB	CS	SB%	GDP	Avg	OBP	SLG
1989 Yankees	R	40	141	35	9	2	3	57	26	25	31	1	29	2	0	2	6	1	.86	1	.248	.386	.404
1990 Greensboro	A	134	455	99	19	4	9	153	68	55	92	5	132	4	1	2	26	5	.84	14	.218	.353	.336
1991 Pr William	A	126	417	96	22	2	10	152	60	46	81	3	104	6	1	9	15	13	.54	7	.230	.357	.365
1992 Pr William	A	125	473	113	18	3	7	158	75	42	54	1	81	6	4	0	28	14	.67	7	.239	.325	.334
1993 Albany	AA	65	236	65	16	1	3	92	44	24	32	1	54	0	2	0	12	6	.67	1	.275	.362	.390
1994 Albany-Colo	AA	121	472	105	20	3	11	164	75	43	62	3	102	2	4	1	22	13	.63	4	.222	.315	.347
6 Min. YEARS		611	2194	513	104	15	43	776	348	235	352	14	502	20	12	14	109	52	.68	34	.234	.343	.354

Matt Franco

Bats: Left Throws: Right Pos: 1B Ht: 6'3" Wt: 195 Born: 08/19/69 Age: 25

Year Team	Lg	G	AB	H	2B	3B	HR	TB	R	RBI	TBB	IBB	SO	HBP	SH	SF	SB	CS	SB%	GDP	Avg	OBP	SLG
1987 Wytheville	R	62	202	50	10	1	1	65	25	21	26	1	41	0	0	0	4	1	.80	3	.248	.333	.322
1988 Wytheville	R	20	79	31	9	1	0	42	14	16	7	0	5	0	0	1	0	1	.00	2	.392	.442	.532
Geneva	A	44	164	42	2	0	3	53	19	21	19	3	13	0	0	1	2	0	1.00	1	.256	.332	.323
1989 Chston-Wv	A	109	377	102	16	1	5	135	42	48	57	0	40	0	5	4	2	2	.50	10	.271	.363	.358
Peoria	A	16	58	13	4	0	0	17	4	9	5	0	5	1	0	1	0	1	.00	1	.224	.292	.293
1990 Peoria	A	123	443	125	33	2	6	180	52	65	43	2	39	1	1	2	4	4	.50	19	.282	.346	.406
1991 Winston-Sal	A	104	307	66	12	1	4	92	47	40	46	2	41	2	2	6	4	1	.80	6	.215	.316	.300
1992 Charlotte	AA	108	343	97	18	3	2	127	35	31	26	1	46	1	0	3	3	3	.50	6	.283	.332	.370
1993 Orlando	AA	68	237	75	20	1	7	118	31	37	29	2	30	2	1	2	3	6	.33	2	.316	.393	.498
Iowa	AAA	62	199	58	17	4	5	98	24	29	16	3	30	1	0	3	4	1	.80	6	.291	.342	.492
1994 Iowa	AAA	128	437	121	32	4	11	194	63	71	52	5	66	2	2	5	3	3	.50	7	.277	.353	.444
8 Min. YEARS		844	2846	780	173	18	44	1121	356	388	326	19	356	10	11	27	29	23	.56	67	.274	.348	.394

Micah Franklin

Bats: Both Throws: Right Pos: OF Ht: 6'0" Wt: 195 Born: 04/25/72 Age: 23

Year Team	Lg	G	AB	H	2B	3B	HR	TB	R	RBI	TBB	IBB	SO	HBP	SH	SF	SB	CS	SB%	GDP	Avg	OBP	SLG
1990 Kingsport	R	39	158	41	9	2	7	75	29	25	8	0	44	1	0	2	4	1	.80	2	.259	.296	.475
1991 Pittsfield	A	26	94	27	4	2	0	35	17	14	21	0	20	1	2	1	12	3	.80	3	.287	.419	.372
Erie	A	39	153	37	4	0	2	47	28	8	25	0	35	2	0	1	4	5	.44	3	.242	.354	.307
1992 Billings	R	75	251	84	13	2	11	134	58	60	53	3	65	15	0	3	18	17	.51	3	.335	.472	.534
1993 Winston-Sal	A	20	69	16	1	1	3	28	10	6	10	1	19	2	1	0	0	1	.00	0	.232	.346	.406
Chston-Wv	A	102	343	90	14	4	17	163	56	58	47	4	109	18	3	6	6	1	.86	4	.262	.374	.475
1994 Winston-Sal	A	42	150	45	7	0	21	115	44	44	27	5	48	6	0	1	7	0	1.00	1	.300	.424	.767
Chattanooga	AA	79	279	77	17	0	10	124	46	40	33	3	79	13	0	3	2	2	.50	3	.276	.375	.444
5 Min. YEARS		422	1497	417	69	11	71	721	288	265	224	16	419	58	6	17	53	30	.64	19	.279	.389	.482

Ryan Franklin

Pitches: Right Bats: Right Pos: P Ht: 6'3" Wt: 160 Born: 03/05/73 Age: 22

Year Team	Lg	G	GS	CG	GF	IP	BFP	H	R	ER	HR	SH	SF	HB	TBB	IBB	SO	WP	Bk	W	L	Pct.	ShO	Sv	ERA
1993 Bellingham	A	15	14	1	0	74	321	72	38	24	2	2	1	3	27	0	55	7	3	5	3	.625	1	0	2.92
1994 Appleton	A	18	18	5	0	118	493	105	60	41	6	3	1	17	23	0	102	6	3	9	6	.600	1	0	3.13
Calgary	AAA	1	1	0	0	5.2	28	9	6	5	2	0	0	0	1	0	2	0	0	0	0	.000	0	0	7.94
Riverside	A	8	8	1	0	61.2	261	61	26	21	5	1	3	4	8	0	35	0	1	4	2	.667	1	0	3.06
2 Min. YEARS		42	41	7	0	259.1	1103	247	130	91	15	6	5	24	59	0	194	13	7	18	11	.621	3	0	3.16

Ron Frazier

Pitches: Right Bats: Right Pos: P Ht: 6'2" Wt: 185 Born: 06/13/69 Age: 26

Year Team	Lg	G	GS	CG	GF	IP	BFP	H	R	ER	HR	SH	SF	HB	TBB	IBB	SO	WP	Bk	W	L	Pct.	ShO	Sv	ERA
1990 Oneonta	A	13	13	0	0	80.1	328	67	32	22	5	2	7	2	33	0	67	4	5	6	2	.750	0	0	2.46
1991 Greensboro	A	25	25	3	0	169	692	140	65	45	10	3	6	9	42	0	127	8	4	12	6	.667	1	0	2.40
1992 Pr William	A	16	7	0	4	56.1	236	51	27	20	10	2	0	5	11	0	52	2	1	4	3	.571	0	0	3.20
1993 Pr William	A	15	15	1	0	101	403	79	34	24	5	2	1	1	23	0	108	4	1	8	3	.727	0	0	2.14
Albany	AA	12	12	0	0	79.2	341	93	43	34	5	1	6	1	16	0	65	3	1	4	3	.571	0	0	3.84
1994 Columbus	AAA	20	17	1	1	104	454	108	59	54	9	5	2	5	43	0	62	3	2	6	6	.500	1	0	4.67
Albany-Colo	AA	10	10	1	0	60.1	257	53	30	21	5	3	1	3	21	3	29	2	0	3	4	.429	0	0	3.13
5 Min. YEARS		111	99	6	5	650.2	2711	591	290	220	49	18	23	26	189	3	510	26	14	43	27	.614	2	0	3.04

John Fritz

Pitches: Right **Bats:** Right **Pos:** P **Ht:** 6'1" **Wt:** 170 **Born:** 03/06/69 **Age:** 26

			HOW MUCH HE PITCHED					WHAT HE GAVE UP											THE RESULTS					
Year	Team	Lg	G	GS	CG	GF	IP	BFP	H	R	ER	HR	SH	SF	HB	TBB	IBB	SO	WP	Bk	W	L	Pct.	ShO	Sv	ERA
1988	Bend	A	14	7	0	3	44.1	202	46	25	18	0	2	3	5	23	1	30	3	0	0	0	.000	0	0	3.65
1989	Angels	R	14	14	0	0	85	377	86	50	39	0	2	4	3	38	1	70	10	12	4	5	.444	0	0	4.13
1990	Palm Sprngs	A	31	21	1	2	131	588	131	80	61	13	3	6	5	75	3	64	13	1	8	7	.533	1	0	4.19
1991	Miami	A	14	0	0	7	22.2	99	21	7	6	1	1	2	0	10	1	24	1	1	0	2	.000	0	1	2.38
	Quad City	A	25	5	0	9	61.1	260	52	27	25	3	2	5	4	24	1	72	2	3	2	3	.400	0	0	3.67
1992	Quad City	A	27	25	6	0	172.1	705	129	65	58	10	3	0	3	69	1	143	16	4	20	4	.833	1	0	3.03
1993	Midland	AA	20	20	2	0	129.2	547	125	61	52	12	2	3	8	42	0	85	12	0	9	5	.643	1	0	3.61
	Vancouver	AAA	8	7	0	0	42	187	52	22	19	3	2	2	0	18	1	29	2	0	3	1	.750	0	0	4.07
1994	Vancouver	AAA	10	9	1	0	54.1	240	61	33	30	12	2	3	1	23	0	29	3	0	3	2	.600	0	0	4.97
	Midland	AA	13	11	1	0	61.1	275	70	46	38	8	1	4	3	27	0	48	11	1	2	5	.286	0	0	5.58
	7 Min. YEARS		176	119	11	21	804	3480	773	416	346	62	20	32	32	349	9	594	73	22	51	34	.600	3	1	3.87

Jason Fronio

Pitches: Right **Bats:** Right **Pos:** P **Ht:** 6'2" **Wt:** 205 **Born:** 12/26/69 **Age:** 25

			HOW MUCH HE PITCHED					WHAT HE GAVE UP											THE RESULTS					
Year	Team	Lg	G	GS	CG	GF	IP	BFP	H	R	ER	HR	SH	SF	HB	TBB	IBB	SO	WP	Bk	W	L	Pct.	ShO	Sv	ERA
1991	Watertown	A	3	0	0	2	3.2	21	6	8	8	1	0	0	0	4	0	1	0	0	0	1	.000	0	0	19.64
	Bend	A	5	0	0	2	13.2	62	12	7	6	0	0	1	0	6	0	11	2	1	0	0	.000	0	1	3.95
1992	Watertown	A	5	0	0	1	10	43	8	5	5	1	0	0	0	4	1	13	0	0	1	2	.333	0	0	4.50
	Columbus	A	20	0	0	15	32.1	117	11	7	3	2	1	2	1	11	1	40	1	1	3	1	.750	0	4	0.84
1993	Kinston	A	32	20	2	3	138.1	574	95	46	37	6	5	3	15	66	0	147	11	2	7	9	.438	0	0	2.41
1994	Kinston	A	10	5	0	0	41	176	36	13	9	1	3	1	4	14	0	40	9	2	5	1	.833	0	0	1.98
	Canton-Akrn	AA	16	15	1	0	94	409	95	51	39	7	3	3	2	35	0	65	7	3	7	6	.538	1	0	3.73
	4 Min. YEARS		91	40	3	23	333	1402	263	137	107	18	12	10	22	140	2	317	30	9	23	20	.535	1	5	2.89

Troy Fryman

Bats: Left **Throws:** Right **Pos:** 1B **Ht:** 6'4" **Wt:** 195 **Born:** 10/02/71 **Age:** 23

			BATTING													BASERUNNING				PERCENTAGES		
Year	Team	Lg	G	AB	H	2B	3B	HR	TB	R	RBI	TBB	IBB	SO	HBP	SH	SF	SB	CS	SB%	GDP	Avg	OBP	SLG
1991	White Sox	R	7	26	6	3	0	0	9	2	3	4	0	7	0	0	1	1	0	1.00	1	.231	.323	.346
	Utica	A	52	178	43	15	1	2	66	23	16	14	1	45	1	1	2	1	0	1.00	2	.242	.297	.371
1992	South Bend	A	129	432	75	26	2	8	129	45	34	60	5	130	5	3	2	7	2	.78	3	.174	.281	.299
1993	South Bend	A	51	173	55	7	6	7	95	34	41	33	5	45	3	0	4	2	0	1.00	1	.318	.427	.549
	Sarasota	A	78	285	68	16	3	5	105	42	46	31	3	55	3	0	1	0	0	.00	0	.239	.319	.368
1994	Birmingham	AA	123	445	100	22	4	6	148	55	43	31	3	88	3	2	0	2	5	.29	11	.225	.280	.333
	4 Min. YEARS		440	1539	347	89	16	28	552	201	183	173	17	370	15	6	10	13	7	.65	18	.225	.308	.359

Jon Fuller

Bats: Right **Throws:** Right **Pos:** C **Ht:** 6'1" **Wt:** 210 **Born:** 05/07/69 **Age:** 26

			BATTING													BASERUNNING				PERCENTAGES		
Year	Team	Lg	G	AB	H	2B	3B	HR	TB	R	RBI	TBB	IBB	SO	HBP	SH	SF	SB	CS	SB%	GDP	Avg	OBP	SLG
1988	Billings	R	31	96	27	2	0	0	29	11	11	10	0	22	0	0	1	2	2	.50	2	.281	.346	.302
1989	Greensboro	A	30	84	16	4	0	0	20	8	10	4	0	18	0	0	4	0	0	.00	3	.190	.250	.238
1990	Chston-Wv	A	67	224	54	12	1	5	83	34	33	34	1	38	6	8	2	1	0	1.00	4	.241	.353	.371
1991	Cedar Rapids	A	92	281	57	8	2	9	96	33	40	55	3	78	7	1	2	1	0	1.00	4	.203	.345	.342
1992	Cedar Rapids	A	83	267	57	19	2	6	98	33	28	38	0	68	5	1	0	2	2	.50	4	.213	.323	.367
1993	Chattanooga	AA	46	148	40	8	1	3	59	22	17	12	0	41	2	1	4	3	1	.75	4	.270	.325	.399
1994	Chattanooga	AA	47	133	30	5	0	3	44	16	16	25	0	27	2	1	3	1	0	1.00	5	.226	.350	.331
	7 Min. YEARS		396	1233	281	58	6	26	429	157	155	182	4	292	22	12	16	10	5	.67	24	.228	.334	.348

Mark Fuller

Pitches: Right **Bats:** Left **Pos:** P **Ht:** 6'6" **Wt:** 212 **Born:** 08/05/70 **Age:** 24

			HOW MUCH HE PITCHED					WHAT HE GAVE UP											THE RESULTS					
Year	Team	Lg	G	GS	CG	GF	IP	BFP	H	R	ER	HR	SH	SF	HB	TBB	IBB	SO	WP	Bk	W	L	Pct.	ShO	Sv	ERA
1992	Pittsfield	A	26	0	0	18	50	207	39	15	9	0	2	0	3	10	0	44	4	2	2	1	.667	0	6	1.62
1993	St.Lucie	A	40	0	0	18	47.1	201	53	13	10	0	4	1	3	12	2	31	0	1	4	3	.571	0	2	1.90
1994	Binghamton	AA	19	0	0	2	30.1	140	35	23	20	2	1	3	7	9	0	24	0	0	0	2	.000	0	0	5.93
	St. Lucie	A	27	0	0	16	41.2	165	31	9	8	2	1	0	1	15	3	31	1	0	5	4	.556	0	3	1.73
	3 Min. YEARS		112	0	0	54	169.1	713	158	60	47	4	8	4	14	46	5	130	5	3	11	10	.524	0	11	2.50

Edwards Fully

Bats: Right **Throws:** Right **Pos:** OF **Ht:** 5'11" **Wt:** 175 **Born:** 07/14/71 **Age:** 23

			BATTING													BASERUNNING				PERCENTAGES		
Year	Team	Lg	G	AB	H	2B	3B	HR	TB	R	RBI	TBB	IBB	SO	HBP	SH	SF	SB	CS	SB%	GDP	Avg	OBP	SLG
1989	Mets	R	26	74	20	4	1	0	26	8	7	9	0	14	1	0	1	5	2	.71	2	.270	.353	.351
1990	Kingsport	R	66	235	66	17	1	0	85	29	35	16	0	57	3	0	2	14	5	.74	4	.281	.332	.362
1991	Columbia	A	122	448	124	27	5	5	176	69	56	40	3	71	3	4	0	17	15	.53	9	.277	.340	.393
1992	St. Lucie	A	127	397	100	20	2	6	142	58	36	29	1	76	4	5	3	14	15	.48	10	.252	.307	.358
1993	St.Lucie	A	117	393	94	12	5	2	122	49	29	17	1	66	2	6	3	15	9	.63	16	.239	.272	.310

Year	Team	Lg	G	AB	H	2B	3B	HR	TB	R	RBI	TBB	IBB	SO	HBP	SH	SF	SB	CS	SB%	GDP	Avg	OBP	SLG
1994	Binghamton	AA	83	217	54	10	2	5	83	27	22	8	0	35	1	0	1	4	5	.44	3	.249	.278	.382
	6 Min. YEARS		541	1764	458	90	16	18	634	240	185	119	2	319	14	15	10	69	51	.58	44	.260	.310	.359

Ed Fulton

Bats: Left Throws: Right Pos: C Ht: 6'0" Wt: 195 Born: 01/07/66 Age: 29

					BATTING													BASERUNNING				PERCENTAGES		
Year	Team	Lg	G	AB	H	2B	3B	HR	TB	R	RBI	TBB	IBB	SO	HBP	SH	SF	SB	CS	SB%	GDP	Avg	OBP	SLG
1987	Johnson Cty	R	67	245	71	16	1	13	128	36	59	36	3	42	2	0	5	4	2	.67	6	.290	.378	.522
1988	Springfield	A	110	374	100	20	6	7	153	46	55	44	3	69	1	2	5	0	0	.00	8	.267	.342	.409
1989	St.Pete	A	125	432	105	23	2	6	150	38	75	51	5	64	0	0	15	0	2	.00	11	.243	.313	.347
1990	Arkansas	AA	48	148	39	9	1	3	59	24	25	19	2	26	3	0	0	0	0	.00	6	.264	.351	.399
	Louisville	AAA	36	100	24	4	2	2	38	9	14	8	1	16	0	1	3	2	0	1.00	2	.240	.288	.380
1991	Louisville	AAA	45	132	26	8	0	0	34	10	15	15	1	35	0	0	0	0	0	.00	4	.197	.279	.258
1992	Arkansas	AA	9	23	6	2	0	0	8	3	5	3	1	8	0	0	0	0	0	.00	0	.261	.346	.348
	Louisville	AAA	77	234	47	5	0	12	88	19	29	22	1	56	0	2	2	0	0	.00	7	.201	.267	.376
1993	Louisville	AAA	61	147	31	5	0	3	45	13	18	11	0	27	1	1	3	0	0	.00	5	.211	.265	.306
1994	Toledo	AAA	59	159	36	6	0	5	57	19	18	15	1	38	0	0	1	1	1	.50	3	.226	.290	.358
	8 Min. YEARS		637	1994	485	98	12	51	760	217	313	224	18	381	7	7	39	7	5	.58	52	.243	.316	.381

Mike Fyhrie

Pitches: Right Bats: Right Pos: P Ht: 6'2" Wt: 190 Born: 12/09/69 Age: 25

			HOW MUCH HE PITCHED						WHAT HE GAVE UP										THE RESULTS					
Year	Team	Lg	G	GS	CG	GF	IP	BFP	H	R	ER	HR	SH	SF	HB	TBB	IBB	SO	WP	Bk	W	L	Pct.	ShO	Sv	ERA
1991	Eugene	A	21	0	0	13	39.1	176	41	17	11	0	3	0	1	19	1	45	1	2	2	1	.667	0	5	2.52
1992	Baseball Cy	A	26	26	2	0	162	670	148	65	45	6	10	6	7	37	1	92	4	6	7	13	.350	0	0	2.50
1993	Wilmington	A	5	5	0	0	29.1	124	32	15	12	3	0	2	0	8	0	19	1	0	3	2	.600	0	0	3.68
	Memphis	AA	22	22	3	0	131.1	579	143	59	52	11	0	4	9	59	0	59	7	1	11	4	.733	0	0	3.56
1994	Omaha	AAA	18	16	0	0	85	379	100	57	54	13	2	4	6	33	1	37	0	0	6	5	.545	0	0	5.72
	Memphis	AA	11	11	0	0	67	279	67	29	24	4	1	2	5	17	1	38	1	0	2	5	.286	0	0	3.22
	4 Min. YEARS		103	80	5	13	514	2207	531	242	198	37	16	18	28	173	4	290	14	9	31	30	.508	0	5	3.47

Bob Gaddy

Pitches: Left Bats: Right Pos: P Ht: 6'1" Wt: 202 Born: 01/11/67 Age: 28

			HOW MUCH HE PITCHED						WHAT HE GAVE UP										THE RESULTS					
Year	Team	Lg	G	GS	CG	GF	IP	BFP	H	R	ER	HR	SH	SF	HB	TBB	IBB	SO	WP	Bk	W	L	Pct.	ShO	Sv	ERA
1989	Batavia	A	16	11	1	3	75.2	302	61	29	25	9	1	3	0	22	0	72	1	1	4	6	.400	1	0	2.97
1990	Spartanburg	A	30	19	0	2	140.1	587	107	65	52	12	8	5	4	67	0	143	8	2	9	7	.563	0	2	3.33
1991	Reading	AA	10	2	0	3	21	98	20	12	11	2	0	3	2	15	0	16	1	1	1	1	.500	0	1	4.71
	Clearwater	A	34	0	0	17	52.1	222	48	19	13	0	1	1	4	22	0	34	2	1	4	1	.800	0	1	2.24
1992	Clearwater	A	44	0	0	17	64	273	58	30	25	3	0	3	5	21	2	54	4	0	5	5	.500	0	4	3.52
	Reading	AA	12	1	0	5	24.2	101	15	8	8	2	1	0	3	13	1	19	0	0	0	2	.000	0	1	2.92
1993	Scranton/wb	AAA	23	3	0	10	48.1	232	54	35	30	4	5	4	3	29	5	40	2	0	1	4	.200	0	0	5.59
	Reading	AA	22	8	1	2	75.1	308	64	22	21	3	3	2	3	29	0	55	3	1	6	4	.600	1	0	2.51
1994	Scranton-Wb	AAA	27	25	5	1	165.1	723	161	86	66	7	7	6	4	74	1	117	12	0	9	12	.429	2	0	3.59
	6 Min. YEARS		218	69	7	60	667	2846	588	306	251	42	26	27	28	292	9	550	33	6	39	42	.481	4	8	3.39

Jay Gainer

Bats: Left Throws: Left Pos: 1B Ht: 6'0" Wt: 188 Born: 10/08/66 Age: 28

					BATTING													BASERUNNING				PERCENTAGES		
Year	Team	Lg	G	AB	H	2B	3B	HR	TB	R	RBI	TBB	IBB	SO	HBP	SH	SF	SB	CS	SB%	GDP	Avg	OBP	SLG
1990	Spokane	A	74	284	100	21	0	10	151	41	54	31	3	49	5	1	4	4	3	.57	4	.356	.424	.537
1991	High Desert	A	127	499	131	17	0	32	244	83	120	52	3	105	3	0	16	4	3	.57	8	.263	.326	.489
1992	Wichita	AA	105	376	98	12	1	23	181	57	67	46	6	101	0	1	6	4	2	.67	5	.261	.336	.481
1993	Colo Sprngs	AAA	86	293	86	11	3	10	133	51	74	22	2	70	1	1	4	4	2	.67	6	.294	.341	.454
1994	Colo. Sprng	AAA	94	283	70	13	2	9	114	38	34	25	2	62	0	1	1	2	3	.40	6	.247	.307	.403
1993	Colorado	NL	23	41	7	0	0	3	16	4	6	4	0	12	0	0	0	1	1	.50	0	.171	.244	.390
	5 Min. YEARS		486	1732	485	74	6	84	823	270	349	176	16	387	9	4	31	18	13	.58	29	.280	.344	.475

Steve Gajkowski

Pitches: Right Bats: Right Pos: P Ht: 6'2" Wt: 200 Born: 12/30/69 Age: 25

			HOW MUCH HE PITCHED						WHAT HE GAVE UP										THE RESULTS					
Year	Team	Lg	G	GS	CG	GF	IP	BFP	H	R	ER	HR	SH	SF	HB	TBB	IBB	SO	WP	Bk	W	L	Pct.	ShO	Sv	ERA
1990	Burlington	R	14	10	1	1	63.2	287	74	34	29	0	0	3	3	23	0	44	0	1	2	6	.250	0	0	4.10
1991	Columbus	A	3	0	0	2	6	24	3	2	2	0	0	0	0	5	0	5	0	0	0	0	.000	0	0	3.00
	Watertown	A	20	4	0	7	48	221	41	36	28	0	1	2	6	32	1	34	7	2	3	3	.500	0	0	5.25
1992	Utica	A	29	0	0	26	47	184	33	14	7	1	0	2	1	10	1	38	6	0	3	2	.600	0	14	1.34
1993	Sarasota	A	43	0	0	38	69.2	273	52	21	16	1	3	3	4	17	5	45	5	1	3	3	.500	0	15	2.07
	Birmingham	AA	1	0	0	0	2.1	8	0	0	0	0	0	0	0	0	0	2	0	0	0	0	.000	0	0	0.00
1994	Birmingham	AA	58	0	0	32	82.1	355	78	35	28	6	6	3	5	26	1	44	2	0	11	5	.688	0	8	3.06
	5 Min. YEARS		168	14	1	106	319	1352	281	142	110	8	10	13	19	113	8	212	20	4	22	19	.537	0	37	3.10

Dan Gakeler

Pitches: Right Bats: Right Pos: P Ht: 6' 6" Wt: 215 Born: 05/01/64 Age: 31

Year	Team	Lg	G	GS	CG	GF	IP	BFP	H	R	ER	HR	SH	SF	HB	TBB	IBB	SO	WP	Bk	W	L	Pct.	ShO	Sv	ERA
1984	Elmira	A	14	13	0	1	76.2	341	67	47	35	9	5	2	7	41	3	54	2	2	4	6	.400	0	0	4.11
1985	Greensboro	A	23	16	3	2	108	509	135	86	66	8	2	3	3	54	0	51	4	0	7	5	.583	1	0	5.50
1986	Greensboro	A	24	23	5	1	154.1	679	158	73	57	6	4	4	4	69	1	154	11	2	7	6	.538	1	1	3.32
1987	New Britain	AA	30	25	5	3	173	769	188	112	89	14	2	7	7	63	5	90	7	3	8	13	.381	1	0	4.63
1988	New Britain	AA	26	25	5	0	153.2	660	157	74	63	4	3	1	5	54	1	110	9	3	6	13	.316	2	0	3.69
1989	Jacksnville	AA	14	14	2	0	86.2	365	70	31	23	1	4	1	3	39	1	76	6	1	5	4	.556	1	0	2.39
	Indianapols	AAA	11	11	1	0	66.1	280	53	29	23	1	4	1	3	28	1	41	4	0	3	6	.333	0	0	3.12
1990	Indianapols	AAA	22	21	1	0	120	509	101	55	43	2	7	2	7	55	1	89	6	0	5	5	.500	1	0	3.22
1991	Toledo	AAA	23	2	0	12	43.2	187	44	22	17	0	2	1	1	13	1	32	3	0	2	3	.400	0	4	3.50
1992	London	AA	1	1	0	0	2	9	3	0	0	0	0	0	0	1	0	1	0	0	0	0	.000	0	0	0.00
	Toledo	AAA	3	3	0	0	12.2	57	14	10	10	3	0	0	1	4	0	11	2	0	0	1	.000	0	0	7.11
1993	Lynchburg	A	30	0	0	19	42.1	162	31	13	7	3	3	0	2	11	0	28	2	1	3	3	.500	0	9	1.49
	Pawtucket	AAA	6	0	0	3	12	66	21	11	10	1	2	0	0	9	0	8	2	0	0	1	.000	0	0	7.50
1994	Pawtucket	AAA	3	2	0	0	17	73	18	13	9	3	1	0	0	4	0	10	0	0	0	1	.000	0	0	4.76
	New Britain	AA	25	25	2	0	151.2	660	164	90	76	7	6	7	5	52	0	107	7	0	9	12	.429	0	0	4.51
1991	Detroit	AL	31	7	0	11	73.2	331	73	52	47	5	3	3	1	39	6	43	7	0	1	4	.200	0	2	5.74
	11 Min. YEARS		255	181	24	41	1220	5326	1224	666	528	62	45	29	48	497	14	862	65	12	59	79	.428	7	14	3.90

Kevin Gallaher

Pitches: Right Bats: Right Pos: P Ht: 6'3" Wt: 190 Born: 08/01/68 Age: 26

Year	Team	Lg	G	GS	CG	GF	IP	BFP	H	R	ER	HR	SH	SF	HB	TBB	IBB	SO	WP	Bk	W	L	Pct.	ShO	Sv	ERA
1991	Auburn	A	16	8	0	3	48	243	59	48	37	2	3	9	9	37	0	25	6	1	2	5	.286	0	0	6.94
1992	Osceola	A	1	1	0	0	6.1	26	2	2	2	1	0	0	0	3	0	5	1	0	0	1	.000	0	0	2.84
	Burlington	A	20	20	1	0	117	529	108	70	50	5	7	4	9	80	0	89	9	1	6	10	.375	0	0	3.85
1993	Osceola	A	21	21	1	0	135	586	132	68	57	7	3	3	4	57	1	93	8	3	7	7	.500	1	0	3.80
	Jackson	AA	4	4	0	0	24	95	14	7	7	3	1	2	2	10	0	30	6	0	0	2	.000	0	0	2.63
1994	Jackson	AA	18	18	0	0	106	468	88	57	46	5	1	2	8	67	1	112	13	0	6	6	.500	0	0	3.91
	Tucson	AAA	9	9	2	0	53.2	240	55	35	32	5	3	2	3	25	0	58	3	0	3	4	.429	0	0	5.37
	4 Min. YEARS		89	81	4	3	490	2187	458	287	231	28	18	22	35	279	2	412	46	5	24	35	.407	1	0	4.24

Bob Gamez

Pitches: Left Bats: Left Pos: P Ht: 6'5" Wt: 185 Born: 11/18/68 Age: 26

Year	Team	Lg	G	GS	CG	GF	IP	BFP	H	R	ER	HR	SH	SF	HB	TBB	IBB	SO	WP	Bk	W	L	Pct.	ShO	Sv	ERA
1988	Rangers	R	2	0	0	0	2.2	10	0	0	0	0	0	0	0	4	0	1	0	0	0	0	.000	0	0	0.00
1989	Rangers	R	23	1	0	5	40.2	172	35	17	17	0	0	0	0	18	0	44	3	0	2	1	.667	0	2	3.76
1990	Boise	A	14	7	0	0	46.1	196	42	19	15	3	0	0	2	15	2	38	5	0	3	0	1.000	0	0	2.91
1991	Quad City	A	41	5	0	11	76.2	341	75	38	31	6	5	6	3	38	4	83	10	0	4	3	.571	0	1	3.64
1992	Palm Sprngs	A	38	13	0	8	98.1	431	106	63	54	4	7	6	2	44	5	70	10	1	8	8	.500	0	3	4.94
1993	Midland	AA	44	0	0	13	60.2	260	68	27	22	7	1	0	2	18	0	50	5	0	5	2	.714	0	0	3.26
	Vancouver	AAA	9	0	0	3	13.1	60	11	9	7	0	1	1	0	9	0	15	2	0	1	0	1.000	0	0	4.72
1994	Phoenix	AAA	39	14	0	13	98	459	130	73	66	11	4	4	2	51	2	60	9	0	5	10	.333	0	3	6.06
	7 Min. YEARS		210	40	0	53	436.2	1929	467	246	212	31	18	17	11	197	13	361	44	1	28	24	.538	0	9	4.37

Francisco Gamez

Pitches: Right Bats: Right Pos: P Ht: 6'2" Wt: 185 Born: 04/02/70 Age: 25

Year	Team	Lg	G	GS	CG	GF	IP	BFP	H	R	ER	HR	SH	SF	HB	TBB	IBB	SO	WP	Bk	W	L	Pct.	ShO	Sv	ERA
1990	Brewers	R	11	7	1	1	50.2	211	44	21	15	5	0	2	3	20	0	32	0	6	2	3	.400	0	0	2.66
1991	Beloit	A	25	24	1	0	146.1	639	140	76	59	2	11	6	11	57	1	92	7	4	9	12	.429	0	0	3.63
1992	Stockton	A	23	23	2	0	134	578	134	64	54	5	3	4	1	69	1	95	4	1	9	5	.643	0	0	3.63
1993	El Paso	AA	15	14	1	0	68.1	315	92	45	41	3	2	2	8	25	1	26	0	0	2	8	.200	0	0	5.40
1994	El Paso	AA	27	27	2	0	168.1	740	193	104	90	13	3	6	12	62	6	87	10	2	10	7	.588	1	0	4.81
	5 Min. YEARS		101	95	7	1	567.2	2483	603	310	259	28	19	20	35	233	9	332	21	13	32	35	.478	1	0	4.11

Gustavo Gandarillas

Pitches: Right Bats: Right Pos: P Ht: 6'0" Wt: 180 Born: 07/19/71 Age: 23

Year	Team	Lg	G	GS	CG	GF	IP	BFP	H	R	ER	HR	SH	SF	HB	TBB	IBB	SO	WP	Bk	W	L	Pct.	ShO	Sv	ERA
1992	Elizabethtn	R	29	0	0	29	36	148	24	14	12	1	0	0	3	10	2	34	4	1	1	2	.333	0	13	3.00
1993	Ft.Wayne	A	52	0	0	48	66.1	295	66	37	24	8	5	5	1	22	2	59	4	0	5	5	.500	0	25	3.26
1994	Fort Myers	A	37	0	0	34	46.2	190	37	7	4	0	3	2	2	13	4	39	5	0	4	1	.800	0	20	0.77
	Nashville	AA	28	0	0	20	37	156	34	13	13	1	2	1	4	10	0	29	6	0	2	2	.500	0	8	3.16
	3 Min. YEARS		146	0	0	131	186	789	161	71	53	10	10	8	10	55	8	161	19	1	12	10	.545	0	66	2.56

Dave Gandolph

Pitches: Left Bats: Left Pos: P   Ht: 6' 4" Wt: 220 Born: 03/20/70 Age: 25

			HOW MUCH HE PITCHED					WHAT HE GAVE UP									THE RESULTS				
Year	Team	Lg	G	GS	CG	GF	IP	BFP	H	R	ER	HR	SH	SF	HB	TBB	IBB	SO	WP	Bk	W	L	Pct.	ShO	Sv	ERA
1991	Rangers	R	7	1	0	0	10.1	52	11	12	11	0	1	2	0	10	0	9	5	5	0	3	.000	0	0	9.58
1992	Gastonia	A	30	2	0	7	52.1	221	32	18	13	0	0	3	0	34	1	52	12	1	4	2	.667	0	2	2.24
1993	Charlotte	A	34	0	0	9	43.2	203	49	23	19	0	0	1	2	29	0	24	1	0	4	2	.667	0	2	3.92
1994	Jackson	AA	37	0	0	14	45.1	191	29	15	8	1	2	1	3	22	6	41	10	0	5	3	.625	0	4	1.59
	4 Min. YEARS		108	3	0	30	151.2	667	121	68	51	1	3	7	5	95	7	126	28	6	13	10	.565	0	8	3.03

Joe Ganote

Pitches: Right Bats: Right Pos: P   Ht: 6'1" Wt: 185 Born: 01/22/68 Age: 27

			HOW MUCH HE PITCHED					WHAT HE GAVE UP									THE RESULTS				
Year	Team	Lg	G	GS	CG	GF	IP	BFP	H	R	ER	HR	SH	SF	HB	TBB	IBB	SO	WP	Bk	W	L	Pct.	ShO	Sv	ERA
1990	St. Cath	A	18	0	0	12	29.2	120	26	9	9	0	1	1	1	7	0	33	2	2	3	0	1.000	0	4	2.73
1991	Myrtle Bch	A	20	20	3	0	118.1	491	104	61	45	9	1	3	2	46	0	127	10	2	8	6	.571	1	0	3.42
	Dunedin	A	4	4	1	0	26.1	110	26	10	9	1	3	2	1	9	0	13	0	0	2	1	.667	1	0	3.08
1992	Dunedin	A	23	21	4	0	140.2	604	148	72	62	10	6	9	10	40	1	101	9	1	6	10	.375	1	0	3.97
1993	Knoxville	AA	33	19	1	6	138.2	589	150	70	64	11	3	10	5	52	0	88	13	0	8	6	.571	0	1	4.15
1994	Knoxville	AA	11	11	3	0	66	273	53	29	20	4	4	2	6	24	0	43	7	0	4	6	.400	1	0	2.73
	Syracuse	AAA	18	14	1	1	79	351	79	41	36	6	2	1	2	41	0	55	9	0	3	7	.300	0	0	4.10
	5 Min. YEARS		127	89	13	19	598.2	2538	586	292	245	41	20	28	29	219	1	460	50	5	34	36	.486	4	5	3.68

Jeff Garber

Bats: Right Throws: Right Pos: 2B   Ht: 5'11" Wt: 180 Born: 09/27/66 Age: 28

			BATTING														BASERUNNING				PERCENTAGES		
Year	Team	Lg	G	AB	H	2B	3B	HR	TB	R	RBI	TBB	IBB	SO	HBP	SH	SF	SB	CS	SB%	GDP	Avg	OBP	SLG
1988	Eugene	A	65	243	61	14	2	1	82	31	25	30	1	45	5	4	3	12	9	.57	6	.251	.342	.337
1989	Appleton	A	117	407	107	18	3	7	152	63	50	54	1	77	13	9	8	4	1	.80	6	.263	.361	.373
1990	Baseball Cy	A	129	446	96	12	2	6	130	53	46	53	0	96	8	4	6	17	4	.81	6	.215	.306	.291
	Omaha	AAA	1	1	0	0	0	0	0	0	0	0	0	1	0	0	0	0	0	.00	0	.000	.000	.000
1991	Memphis	AA	61	200	50	4	1	0	56	24	19	26	0	44	4	7	0	7	2	.78	1	.250	.348	.280
	Omaha	AAA	34	94	26	3	3	1	38	12	13	6	0	21	0	2	1	0	2	.00	2	.277	.317	.404
1992	Memphis	AA	108	326	72	17	2	7	114	37	38	29	1	66	7	4	3	9	3	.75	7	.221	.296	.350
1993	Memphis	AA	81	253	71	13	0	12	120	40	32	26	2	61	5	2	0	1	3	.25	4	.281	.359	.474
1994	Omaha	AAA	23	58	15	4	0	0	19	7	10	6	0	18	0	0	0	1	0	1.00	0	.259	.328	.328
	Memphis	AA	54	181	55	10	2	7	90	29	29	31	2	37	1	1	2	6	5	.55	2	.304	.405	.497
	7 Min. YEARS		673	2209	553	95	15	41	801	296	262	261	7	466	43	33	23	57	29	.66	34	.250	.338	.363

Rich Garces

Pitches: Right Bats: Right Pos: P   Ht: 6' 0" Wt: 215 Born: 05/18/71 Age: 24

			HOW MUCH HE PITCHED					WHAT HE GAVE UP									THE RESULTS				
Year	Team	Lg	G	GS	CG	GF	IP	BFP	H	R	ER	HR	SH	SF	HB	TBB	IBB	SO	WP	Bk	W	L	Pct.	ShO	Sv	ERA
1988	Elizabethtn	R	17	3	1	10	59	254	51	22	15	1	2	1	1	27	2	69	7	0	5	4	.556	0	5	2.29
1989	Kenosha	A	24	24	4	0	142.2	596	117	70	54	5	5	5	5	62	1	84	5	6	9	10	.474	1	0	3.41
1990	Visalia	A	47	0	0	42	54.2	212	33	14	11	2	1	1	1	16	0	75	6	0	2	2	.500	0	28	1.81
	Orlando	AA	15	0	0	14	17.1	81	17	4	4	0	1	0	0	14	2	22	2	0	2	1	.667	0	8	2.08
1991	Portland	AAA	10	0	0	8	13	58	10	7	7	1	0	0	1	8	1	13	0	1	0	1	.000	0	3	4.85
	Orlando	AA	10	0	0	5	16.1	75	12	6	6	0	2	1	2	14	2	17	0	0	2	1	.667	0	0	3.31
1992	Orlando	AA	58	0	0	42	73.1	334	76	46	37	6	8	7	2	39	1	72	6	0	3	3	.500	0	13	4.54
1993	Portland	AAA	35	7	0	5	54	293	70	55	50	4	3	2	0	64	0	48	3	3	1	3	.250	0	0	8.33
1994	Nashville	AA	40	1	0	22	77.1	335	70	40	32	5	4	4	2	31	0	76	6	0	4	5	.444	0	3	3.72
1990	Minnesota	AL	5	0	0	3	5.2	24	4	2	1	0	0	0	0	4	0	1	0	0	0	0	.000	0	2	1.59
1993	Minnesota	AL	3	0	0	1	4	18	4	2	0	0	0	0	0	2	0	3	0	0	0	0	.000	0	0	0.00
	7 Min. YEARS		256	35	5	148	507.2	2238	456	264	216	24	26	21	14	275	9	476	35	10	28	30	.483	1	60	3.83
	2 Maj. YEARS		8	0	0	4	9.2	42	8	4	1	0	0	0	0	6	0	4	0	0	0	0	.000	0	2	0.93

Apolinar Garcia

Pitches: Right Bats: Right Pos: P   Ht: 5'11" Wt: 165 Born: 01/30/68 Age: 27

			HOW MUCH HE PITCHED					WHAT HE GAVE UP									THE RESULTS				
Year	Team	Lg	G	GS	CG	GF	IP	BFP	H	R	ER	HR	SH	SF	HB	TBB	IBB	SO	WP	Bk	W	L	Pct.	ShO	Sv	ERA
1988	Tacoma	AAA	1	1	0	0	5	26	6	5	5	0	1	3	1	4	0	1	0	0	0	0	.000	0	0	9.00
	Athletics	R	2	2	0	0	13	63	19	14	12	2	0	1	0	4	0	8	5	0	1	1	.500	0	0	8.31
	Madison	A	10	7	0	1	36.2	177	49	39	33	6	1	2	6	16	1	17	2	0	2	4	.333	0	0	8.10
1989	Madison	A	27	25	3	0	139	633	146	87	71	6	5	3	15	65	0	110	9	4	5	14	.263	2	0	4.60
1990	Modesto	A	20	20	1	0	123	519	113	63	49	13	3	4	4	41	0	96	8	5	3	11	.214	0	0	3.59
	Huntsville	AA	7	7	2	0	54	223	45	24	21	5	0	1	2	18	0	29	3	1	5	1	.833	0	0	3.50
1991	Tacoma	AAA	7	5	0	0	29.2	158	49	45	36	5	0	2	1	20	1	12	4	1	0	4	.000	0	0	10.92
	Huntsville	AA	13	13	3	0	79.1	328	76	36	28	3	2	7	4	22	0	40	3	0	6	3	.667	0	0	3.18
	Canton-Akrn	AA	4	4	0	0	18.1	88	22	13	4	0	0	2	1	7	0	10	4	0	2	1	.667	0	0	1.96
1992	Miracle	A	14	14	1	0	82.2	339	85	36	32	9	1	4	4	16	0	78	4	0	2	6	.250	0	0	3.48
	Kinston	A	10	10	1	0	57	241	51	30	25	8	3	4	2	17	0	61	4	0	1	5	.167	1	0	3.95

90

Year	Team	Lg	G	GS	CG	GF	IP	BFP	H	R	ER	HR	SH	SF	HB	TBB	IBB	SO	WP	Bk	W	L	Pct.	ShO	Sv	ERA
1993	Canton-Akm	AA	42	7	0	9	111	464	103	53	48	12	5	2	7	37	2	110	5	4	8	4	.667	0	3	3.89
1994	Charlotte	AAA	2	0	0	1	1	9	3	3	3	0	0	0	0	3	0	0	2	0	0	0	.000	0	0	27.00
	Canton-Akm	AA	36	4	0	18	84.2	350	66	37	30	3	6	0	7	30	5	78	7	1	8	4	.667	0	5	3.19
	7 Min. YEARS		195	119	11	29	834.1	3618	833	485	397	72	27	32	55	300	9	650	60	16	43	58	.426	3	8	4.28

Jose Garcia

Pitches: Right **Bats:** Right **Pos:** P

Ht: 6'3" **Wt:** 146 **Born:** 06/12/72 **Age:** 23

Year	Team	Lg	G	GS	CG	GF	IP	BFP	H	R	ER	HR	SH	SF	HB	TBB	IBB	SO	WP	Bk	W	L	Pct.	ShO	Sv	ERA
1993	Bakersfield	A	27	0	0	22	29	142	47	23	22	6	1	4	0	12	1	25	3	2	0	3	.000	0	4	6.83
	Yakima	A	36	0	0	30	44.2	188	40	14	12	1	0	2	3	19	2	19	2	0	2	2	.500	0	5	2.42
1994	Vero Beach	A	20	0	0	13	32.2	129	32	7	5	0	1	1	0	2	0	24	2	1	3	1	.750	0	4	1.38
	San Antonio	AA	7	0	0	7	11	40	7	2	2	0	1	1	0	6	2	8	0	1	2	0	1.000	0	3	1.64
	Albuquerque	AAA	37	0	0	7	57.2	258	66	39	33	6	2	3	3	26	5	38	2	0	4	1	.800	0	0	5.15
	2 Min. YEARS		127	0	0	79	175	757	192	85	74	13	5	10	6	65	10	114	9	4	11	7	.611	0	16	3.81

Omar Garcia

Bats: Right **Throws:** Right **Pos:** 1B

Ht: 6'0" **Wt:** 188 **Born:** 11/16/71 **Age:** 23

Year	Team	Lg	G	AB	H	2B	3B	HR	TB	R	RBI	TBB	IBB	SO	HBP	SH	SF	SB	CS	SB%	GDP	Avg	OBP	SLG
1989	Mets	R	32	98	25	3	1	0	30	15	8	10	0	22	1	0	1	6	2	.75	1	.255	.327	.306
1990	Kingsport	R	67	246	82	15	2	6	119	42	36	24	1	24	0	0	2	10	5	.67	3	.333	.390	.484
1991	Columbia	A	108	394	99	11	4	4	130	63	50	31	0	55	0	1	3	12	5	.71	9	.251	.304	.330
1992	Columbia	A	126	469	136	18	5	3	173	66	70	55	1	37	1	0	11	35	11	.76	11	.290	.358	.369
1993	St.Lucie	A	129	485	156	17	7	3	196	73	76	57	2	47	2	2	5	25	8	.76	14	.322	.392	.404
1994	Binghamton	AA	64	246	88	14	4	5	125	38	42	22	1	31	1	0	4	3	5	.38	3	.358	.407	.508
	Norfolk	AAA	67	227	55	9	2	0	68	28	28	19	1	35	0	1	5	7	4	.64	6	.242	.295	.300
	6 Min. YEARS		593	2165	641	87	25	21	841	325	310	218	6	251	5	4	31	98	40	.71	47	.296	.357	.388

Mike Gardella

Pitches: Left **Bats:** Left **Pos:** P

Ht: 5'10" **Wt:** 195 **Born:** 01/18/67 **Age:** 28

Year	Team	Lg	G	GS	CG	GF	IP	BFP	H	R	ER	HR	SH	SF	HB	TBB	IBB	SO	WP	Bk	W	L	Pct.	ShO	Sv	ERA
1989	Oneonta	A	28	0	0	26	37.2	153	23	8	7	2	2	2	0	15	0	66	1	0	2	0	1.000	0	19	1.67
1990	Pr William	A	62	0	0	57	71.2	301	61	18	16	0	5	0	1	31	3	86	7	0	4	3	.571	0	30	2.01
1991	Albany	AA	53	0	0	27	77.2	344	70	37	33	1	10	3	1	55	6	76	3	0	4	5	.444	0	11	3.82
1992	Albany	AA	15	0	0	13	18	77	18	4	4	1	0	0	0	10	1	18	1	1	3	1	.750	0	5	2.00
	Canton-Akm	AA	33	3	0	14	55	241	43	30	22	5	1	2	4	32	1	45	3	1	2	2	.500	0	7	3.60
1993	Canton-Akm	AA	21	0	0	7	22.2	114	26	14	11	2	3	0	1	22	2	14	0	0	2	1	.667	0	4	4.37
	Shreveport	AA	5	0	0	3	8.2	32	4	1	1	0	1	0	0	3	0	11	0	0	0	0	.000	0	1	1.04
1994	Shreveport	AA	38	5	0	11	84	353	73	41	36	4	4	3	1	34	4	70	6	2	2	4	.333	0	3	3.86
	6 Min. YEARS		255	8	0	158	375.1	1615	318	153	130	15	26	10	8	202	16	386	21	4	19	16	.543	0	80	3.12

Chris Gardner

Pitches: Right **Bats:** Right **Pos:** P

Ht: 6'0" **Wt:** 175 **Born:** 03/30/69 **Age:** 26

Year	Team	Lg	G	GS	CG	GF	IP	BFP	H	R	ER	HR	SH	SF	HB	TBB	IBB	SO	WP	Bk	W	L	Pct.	ShO	Sv	ERA
1988	Astros	R	12	9	0	0	55.1	226	37	18	9	0	3	1	4	23	0	41	4	4	4	3	.571	0	0	1.46
1989	Asheville	A	15	15	2	0	77.1	360	76	53	33	5	1	3	1	58	0	49	8	10	3	8	.273	0	0	3.84
1990	Asheville	A	23	23	3	0	134	560	102	57	39	6	1	2	7	69	2	81	8	3	5	10	.333	1	0	2.62
1991	Jackson	AA	22	22	1	0	131.1	559	116	57	46	6	5	4	8	75	1	72	9	1	13	5	.722	1	0	3.15
1992	Tucson	AAA	20	20	0	0	110.2	515	141	80	70	1	9	5	5	63	1	49	6	3	6	9	.400	0	0	5.69
1994	Jackson	AA	10	10	0	0	51	214	44	25	20	1	2	4	1	21	0	34	7	0	3	2	.600	0	0	3.53
	Tucson	AAA	18	12	0	2	72.1	339	95	53	49	6	3	1	5	32	1	33	3	0	3	4	.429	0	0	6.10
1991	Houston	NL	5	4	0	0	24.2	103	19	12	11	5	2	0	0	14	1	12	0	0	2	2	.333	0	0	4.01
	6 Min. YEARS		120	111	6	2	632	2773	611	343	266	25	24	20	31	341	5	359	45	21	37	41	.474	2	0	3.79

Daniel Garibay

Pitches: Left **Bats:** Left **Pos:** P

Ht: 5'8" **Wt:** 154 **Born:** 02/14/73 **Age:** 22

Year	Team	Lg	G	GS	CG	GF	IP	BFP	H	R	ER	HR	SH	SF	HB	TBB	IBB	SO	WP	Bk	W	L	Pct.	ShO	Sv	ERA
1994	San Antonio	AA	3	1	0	0	0.2	17	10	10	9	2	0	0	0	4	0	0	0	1	0	1	.000	0	0	99.99

Kevin Garner

Bats: Left **Throws:** Right **Pos:** 1B

Ht: 6'2" **Wt:** 200 **Born:** 10/21/65 **Age:** 29

Year	Team	Lg	G	AB	H	2B	3B	HR	TB	R	RBI	TBB	IBB	SO	HBP	SH	SF	SB	CS	SB%	GDP	Avg	OBP	SLG
1987	Spokane	A	36	106	29	7	1	5	53	19	25	16	1	28	1	0	3	0	0	.00	1	.274	.365	.500
1988	Riverside	A	124	445	106	18	3	15	175	66	72	61	9	122	2	1	8	3	6	.33	4	.238	.328	.393
1989	Wichita	AA	103	350	87	17	2	19	165	51	63	30	1	102	2	3	2	0	0	.00	9	.249	.310	.471
1991	Birmingham	AA	119	430	107	19	3	14	174	54	74	59	6	106	4	0	6	0	0	.00	7	.249	.341	.405
1992	Birmingham	AA	13	43	11	2	0	4	25	8	11	4	0	13	1	0	0	0	0	.00	7	.256	.333	.581
	Nashville	AAA	8	24	8	3	0	2	17	4	7	4	0	8	0	1	0	0	1	.00	0	.333	.429	.708

Year Team	Lg	G	AB	H	2B	3B	HR	TB	R	RBI	TBB	IBB	SO	HBP	SH	SF	SB	CS	SB%	GDP	Avg	OBP	SLG
Chattanooga	AA	51	170	53	8	0	10	91	28	42	19	5	35	0	1	1	0	2	.00	5	.312	.379	.535
1993 Chattanooga	AA	19	53	8	1	0	2	15	6	5	9	1	26	0	0	0	2	1	.67	2	.151	.274	.283
Ottawa	AAA	36	99	27	9	0	7	57	15	28	15	6	31	0	0	1	0	0	.00	1	.273	.365	.576
1994 Scranton-Wb	AAA	54	187	50	12	1	14	106	30	39	20	3	61	3	0	1	0	0	.00	3	.267	.346	.567
7 Min. YEARS		563	1907	486	96	10	92	878	281	366	237	32	532	13	6	22	5	10	.33	31	.255	.338	.460

Webster Garrison

Bats: Right Throws: Right Pos: SS Ht: 5'11" Wt: 170 Born: 08/24/65 Age: 29

					BATTING												BASERUNNING				PERCENTAGES		
Year Team	Lg	G	AB	H	2B	3B	HR	TB	R	RBI	TBB	IBB	SO	HBP	SH	SF	SB	CS	SB%	GDP	Avg	OBP	SLG
1984 Florence	A	129	502	120	14	0	0	134	80	33	57	0	44	1	2	2	16	7	.70	9	.239	.317	.267
1985 Kinston	A	129	449	91	14	1	1	110	40	30	42	0	76	3	2	5	22	5	.81	6	.203	.273	.245
1986 Florence	A	105	354	85	10	0	3	104	47	40	56	3	53	2	0	3	4	7	.36	7	.240	.345	.294
Knoxville	AA	5	6	0	0	0	0	0	0	0	0	0	2	0	0	0	1	0	1.00	0	.000	.000	.000
1987 Dunedin	A	128	477	135	14	4	0	157	70	44	57	0	53	0	0	5	27	9	.75	12	.283	.356	.329
1988 Knoxville	AA	138	534	136	24	5	0	170	61	40	53	0	74	1	2	4	42	15	.74	7	.255	.321	.318
1989 Knoxville	AA	54	203	55	6	2	4	77	38	14	33	0	38	0	4	1	18	6	.75	5	.271	.371	.379
Syracuse	AAA	50	151	43	7	1	0	52	18	9	18	1	25	2	4	0	3	2	.60	5	.285	.368	.344
1990 Syracuse	AAA	37	101	20	5	1	0	27	12	10	14	0	20	0	3	1	0	3	.00	3	.198	.293	.267
1991 Tacoma	AAA	75	237	51	11	2	2	72	28	28	26	0	34	2	7	2	4	0	1.00	6	.215	.296	.304
Huntsville	AA	31	110	29	9	0	2	44	18	10	16	0	21	1	0	1	5	2	.71	1	.264	.359	.400
1992 Tacoma	AAA	33	116	28	5	1	2	41	15	17	2	0	12	0	1	2	1	1	.50	5	.241	.250	.353
Huntsville	AA	91	348	96	25	4	8	153	50	61	30	0	59	0	3	5	8	6	.57	12	.276	.329	.440
1993 Tacoma	AAA	138	544	165	29	5	7	225	91	73	58	2	64	2	2	5	17	9	.65	17	.303	.369	.414
1994 Colo. Spmg	AAA	128	514	155	32	5	13	236	94	68	46	2	65	0	1	4	18	5	.78	11	.302	.356	.459
11 Min. YEARS		1271	4646	1209	205	31	42	1602	662	477	508	8	640	14	31	40	186	77	.71	106	.260	.332	.345

Sean Gavaghan

Pitches: Right Bats: Right Pos: P Ht: 6'1" Wt: 185 Born: 12/19/69 Age: 25

		HOW MUCH HE PITCHED					WHAT HE GAVE UP										THE RESULTS				
Year Team	Lg	G	GS	CG	GF	IP	BFP	H	R	ER	HR	SH	SF	HB	TBB	IBB	SO	WP	Bk	W	L	Pct.	ShO	Sv	ERA
1992 Kenosha	A	20	6	0	8	57	243	63	22	13	2	5	4	2	18	1	39	3	3	2	3	.400	0	1	2.05
1993 Ft.Wayne	A	11	0	0	5	22	89	14	5	3	0	2	0	0	7	0	25	2	1	3	1	.750	0	1	1.23
Ft.Myers	A	19	0	0	13	31	134	37	10	9	1	1	0	0	8	1	24	2	0	1	3	.250	0	4	2.61
Nashville	AA	20	1	0	5	36.2	143	21	3	2	0	0	1	4	12	1	30	3	2	4	0	1.000	0	1	0.49
1994 Nashville	AA	56	0	0	35	85	366	59	35	22	5	6	4	1	56	1	63	3	0	5	5	.500	0	13	2.33
3 Min. YEARS		126	7	0	66	231.2	975	194	75	49	8	14	9	7	101	4	181	13	6	15	12	.556	0	20	1.90

Daryle Gavlick

Pitches: Left Bats: Left Pos: P Ht: 6'1" Wt: 185 Born: 08/28/69 Age: 25

		HOW MUCH HE PITCHED					WHAT HE GAVE UP										THE RESULTS				
Year Team	Lg	G	GS	CG	GF	IP	BFP	H	R	ER	HR	SH	SF	HB	TBB	IBB	SO	WP	Bk	W	L	Pct.	ShO	Sv	ERA
1992 Huntington	R	13	12	4	0	82.2	345	73	38	28	7	1	1	0	23	0	75	5	0	6	4	.600	2	0	3.05
1993 Peoria	A	51	0	0	36	55.1	226	43	17	8	1	7	2	0	18	3	49	2	1	6	7	.462	0	9	1.30
1994 Daytona	A	30	0	0	8	50.2	225	62	33	24	2	1	2	1	15	3	21	4	1	2	5	.286	0	4	4.26
Orlando	AA	18	0	0	7	21.1	104	32	18	16	0	1	1	2	9	1	12	2	0	2	1	.667	0	2	6.75
3 Min. YEARS		112	12	4	51	210	900	210	106	76	10	10	6	3	65	7	157	13	2	16	17	.485	2	15	3.26

Dave Geeve

Pitches: Right Bats: Right Pos: P Ht: 6'3" Wt: 190 Born: 10/19/69 Age: 25

		HOW MUCH HE PITCHED					WHAT HE GAVE UP										THE RESULTS				
Year Team	Lg	G	GS	CG	GF	IP	BFP	H	R	ER	HR	SH	SF	HB	TBB	IBB	SO	WP	Bk	W	L	Pct.	ShO	Sv	ERA
1991 Gastonia	A	14	14	1	0	79.1	323	74	40	38	7	2	2	1	20	1	69	0	1	6	4	.600	1	0	4.31
1992 Charlotte	A	25	24	0	1	139.1	572	138	61	52	8	4	3	6	22	1	97	6	0	8	8	.500	0	0	3.36
1993 Charlotte	A	24	23	1	1	132.2	539	141	52	42	7	3	2	3	19	0	80	8	1	11	8	.579	1	0	2.85
1994 Tulsa	AA	9	8	0	0	53	203	43	14	14	7	0	0	3	10	0	53	0	0	4	2	.667	0	0	2.38
4 Min. YEARS		72	69	2	2	404.1	1637	396	167	146	29	9	7	13	71	2	299	14	2	29	22	.569	2	0	3.25

Phil Geisler

Bats: Left Throws: Left Pos: 1B Ht: 6'3" Wt: 200 Born: 10/23/69 Age: 25

					BATTING												BASERUNNING				PERCENTAGES		
Year Team	Lg	G	AB	H	2B	3B	HR	TB	R	RBI	TBB	IBB	SO	HBP	SH	SF	SB	CS	SB%	GDP	Avg	OBP	SLG
1991 Martinsville	R	32	114	37	5	0	1	45	22	18	23	1	25	1	0	0	1	0	1.00	1	.325	.442	.395
Spartanburg	A	36	129	21	3	0	1	27	19	8	14	0	36	0	1	0	0	0	.00	2	.163	.245	.209
1992 Clearwater	A	120	400	87	10	3	6	121	39	33	41	1	88	4	1	2	4	9	.31	8	.218	.295	.303
1993 Clearwater	A	87	344	105	23	4	15	181	72	62	29	3	70	6	2	1	4	5	.44	5	.305	.368	.526
Reading	AA	48	178	48	14	1	3	73	25	14	17	2	50	3	1	0	4	2	.67	3	.270	.343	.410
1994 Scranton-Wb	AAA	54	183	36	5	1	0	43	14	11	18	3	48	1	1	2	2	2	.50	3	.197	.270	.235
Reading	AA	74	254	70	12	1	7	105	32	40	24	5	55	2	0	2	4	7	.36	5	.276	.340	.413
4 Min. YEARS		451	1602	404	72	10	33	595	223	186	166	15	372	17	6	7	19	25	.43	27	.252	.328	.371

Brad Gennero

Bats: Left Throws: Left Pos: OF Ht: 6'1" Wt: 175 Born: 08/02/71 Age: 23

Year	Team	Lg	G	AB	H	2B	3B	HR	TB	R	RBI	TBB	IBB	SO	HBP	SH	SF	SB	CS	SB%	GDP	Avg	OBP	SLG
1992	Chston-Sc	A	78	274	67	11	3	9	111	30	42	18	2	58	2	2	5	6	5	.55	6	.245	.291	.405
1993	Rancho Cuca	A	127	481	137	23	7	13	213	77	70	30	0	88	5	4	3	3	9	.25	11	.285	.331	.443
1994	Wichita	AA	128	500	139	19	7	16	220	71	60	38	6	88	6	1	1	8	4	.67	14	.278	.336	.440
	3 Min. YEARS		333	1255	343	53	17	38	544	178	172	86	8	234	13	7	9	17	18	.49	31	.273	.324	.433

Scott Gentile

Pitches: Right Bats: Right Pos: P Ht: 5'11" Wt: 210 Born: 12/21/70 Age: 24

Year	Team	Lg	G	GS	CG	GF	IP	BFP	H	R	ER	HR	SH	SF	HB	TBB	IBB	SO	WP	Bk	W	L	Pct.	ShO	Sv	ERA
1992	Jamestown	A	13	13	0	0	62.2	282	59	32	27	3	0	0	6	34	0	44	5	0	4	4	.500	0	0	3.88
1993	Wst Plm Bch	A	25	25	0	0	138.1	592	132	72	62	8	4	5	7	54	0	108	6	0	8	9	.471	0	0	4.03
1994	Harrisburg	AA	6	2	0	1	10.1	72	16	21	20	1	1	0	0	25	0	14	6	0	0	1	.000	0	0	17.42
	W. Palm Bch	A	53	1	0	40	65.1	255	44	16	14	0	3	0	1	19	0	90	4	2	5	2	.714	0	26	1.93
	3 Min. YEARS		97	41	0	41	276.2	1201	251	141	123	12	8	5	14	132	0	256	21	2	17	16	.515	0	26	4.00

Chris George

Pitches: Right Bats: Right Pos: P Ht: 6'2" Wt: 200 Born: 09/24/66 Age: 28

Year	Team	Lg	G	GS	CG	GF	IP	BFP	H	R	ER	HR	SH	SF	HB	TBB	IBB	SO	WP	Bk	W	L	Pct.	ShO	Sv	ERA
1988	Beloit	A	22	4	0	10	58	243	52	27	19	1	1	1	5	14	4	58	4	1	7	4	.636	0	6	2.95
1989	Stockton	A	55	0	0	52	79.2	345	61	30	19	1	6	5	1	37	8	85	8	2	7	7	.500	0	22	2.15
1990	Denver	AAA	7	0	0	1	5.1	36	17	11	11	1	0	0	0	4	0	4	1	0	1	1	.500	0	0	18.56
	El Paso	AA	39	0	0	30	55.2	226	41	16	11	1	7	1	3	20	7	38	7	1	8	3	.727	0	13	1.78
1991	Denver	AAA	43	1	0	16	85	350	74	31	22	6	6	7	0	26	5	65	4	0	4	5	.444	0	4	2.33
1992	Denver	AAA	12	8	0	2	42.2	190	54	30	22	2	4	0	4	10	0	20	2	1	2	3	.400	0	0	4.64
1994	El Paso	AA	7	7	0	0	24	108	31	13	11	1	0	1	2	5	0	15	1	2	2	1	.667	0	0	4.13
	New Orleans	AAA	36	0	0	12	46.2	216	60	31	27	6	2	2	1	26	2	23	8	0	3	1	.750	0	0	5.21
1991	Milwaukee	AL	2	1	0	1	6	25	8	2	2	0	0	1	0	0	0	2	0	0	0	0	.000	0	0	3.00
	6 Min. YEARS		221	20	0	123	397	1714	390	189	142	19	26	17	16	142	26	308	35	7	34	25	.576	0	45	3.22

Ed Gerald

Bats: Both Throws: Right Pos: OF Ht: 6'3" Wt: 205 Born: 07/18/70 Age: 24

Year	Team	Lg	G	AB	H	2B	3B	HR	TB	R	RBI	TBB	IBB	SO	HBP	SH	SF	SB	CS	SB%	GDP	Avg	OBP	SLG
1989	Royals	R	61	217	40	1	6	1	56	30	24	30	0	80	1	1	0	15	5	.75	3	.184	.286	.258
1990	Royals	R	15	51	11	1	2	1	19	8	5	6	0	15	1	0	0	5	0	1.00	1	.216	.310	.373
	Appleton	A	45	125	27	4	1	0	33	22	6	17	0	45	0	2	0	4	1	.80	2	.216	.310	.264
1991	Appleton	A	101	348	85	15	10	7	141	49	46	49	1	107	2	3	4	18	2	.90	6	.244	.337	.405
1992	Appleton	A	123	420	104	13	8	12	169	55	62	45	2	127	1	2	4	17	3	.85	3	.248	.319	.402
1993	St.Pete	A	52	176	35	12	4	0	55	17	17	17	0	58	0	1	2	2	1	.67	8	.199	.267	.313
1994	Nashville	AA	112	393	107	15	6	13	173	64	52	42	1	107	0	3	2	14	5	.74	3	.272	.341	.440
	6 Min. YEARS		509	1730	409	61	37	34	646	245	209	206	4	539	5	12	12	75	17	.82	26	.236	.317	.373

Ronald Gerstein

Pitches: Left Bats: Left Pos: P Ht: 6'1" Wt: 200 Born: 01/01/69 Age: 26

Year	Team	Lg	G	GS	CG	GF	IP	BFP	H	R	ER	HR	SH	SF	HB	TBB	IBB	SO	WP	Bk	W	L	Pct.	ShO	Sv	ERA
1990	Salt Lake	R	2	0	0	0	4.1	25	7	7	7	1	0	1	0	5	0	3	0	0	0	1	.000	0	0	14.54
1991	Sumter	A	7	0	0	5	9.1	37	5	1	0	0	0	1	0	5	0	6	0	0	0	1	.000	0	1	0.00
1992	Rockford	A	33	5	0	17	51	236	62	37	32	2	2	2	1	28	1	40	5	3	4	8	.333	0	5	5.65
1993	Stockton	A	36	7	1	9	86.1	421	103	59	51	2	5	6	2	63	3	49	7	0	8	4	.667	0	5	5.32
1994	El Paso	AA	27	26	1	0	163.2	716	184	94	80	8	8	5	3	70	2	92	10	1	12	3	.800	1	0	4.40
	5 Min. YEARS		105	39	2	31	314.2	1435	361	198	170	13	15	15	6	171	6	190	22	4	24	17	.585	1	5	4.86

Jason Giambi

Bats: Left Throws: Right Pos: 3B Ht: 6'2" Wt: 200 Born: 01/08/71 Age: 24

Year	Team	Lg	G	AB	H	2B	3B	HR	TB	R	RBI	TBB	IBB	SO	HBP	SH	SF	SB	CS	SB%	GDP	Avg	OBP	SLG
1992	Sou Oregon	A	13	41	13	3	0	3	25	9	13	9	1	6	0	0	0	1	1	.50	2	.317	.440	.610
1993	Modesto	A	89	313	91	16	2	12	147	72	60	73	7	47	10	1	3	2	3	.40	12	.291	.436	.470
1994	Huntsville	AA	56	193	43	9	0	6	70	31	30	27	2	31	2	3	4	0	0	.00	8	.223	.319	.363
	Tacoma	AAA	52	176	56	20	0	4	88	28	38	25	2	32	0	0	8	1	0	1.00	7	.318	.388	.500
	3 Min. YEARS		210	723	203	48	2	25	330	140	141	134	12	116	12	4	15	4	4	.50	21	.281	.395	.456

Ray Giannelli

Bats: Left Throws: Right Pos: OF Ht: 6'0" Wt: 195 Born: 02/05/66 Age: 29

Year	Team	Lg	G	AB	H	2B	3B	HR	TB	R	RBI	TBB	IBB	SO	HBP	SH	SF	SB	CS	SB%	GDP	Avg	OBP	SLG
1988	Medicne Hat	R	47	123	30	8	3	4	56	17	28	19	2	22	0	1	3	0	0	.00	6	.244	.338	.455

Year	Team	Lg	G	AB	H	2B	3B	HR	TB	R	RBI	TBB	IBB	SO	HBP	SH	SF	SB	CS	SB%	GDP	Avg	OBP	SLG
1989	Myrtle Bch	A	127	458	138	17	1	18	211	76	84	78	4	53	5	1	8	2	6	.25	10	.301	.403	.461
1990	Dunedin	A	118	416	120	18	1	18	194	64	57	66	7	56	1	1	3	4	8	.33	12	.288	.385	.466
1991	Knoxville	AA	112	362	100	14	3	7	141	53	37	64	6	66	2	5	2	8	5	.62	6	.276	.386	.390
1992	Syracuse	AAA	84	249	57	9	2	5	85	23	22	48	2	44	0	0	2	2	2	.50	4	.229	.351	.341
1993	Syracuse	AAA	127	411	104	18	4	11	163	51	42	38	1	79	2	2	5	1	6	.14	8	.253	.316	.397
1994	Syracuse	AAA	114	327	94	19	1	10	145	43	51	48	2	77	2	0	3	0	1	.00	5	.287	.379	.443
1991	Toronto	AL	9	24	4	1	0	0	5	2	0	5	0	9	0	0	0	1	0	1.00	0	.167	.310	.208
	7 Min. YEARS		729	2346	643	103	15	73	995	327	321	361	24	397	12	10	26	17	28	.38	51	.274	.370	.424

David Giberti

Pitches: Left Bats: Right Pos: P **Ht: 6'2" Wt: 175 Born: 11/20/70 Age: 24**

			HOW MUCH HE PITCHED						WHAT HE GAVE UP									THE RESULTS					
Year	Team	Lg	G	GS	CG	GF	IP	BFP	H	R	ER	HR	SH	SF	HB	TBB	IBB	SO	WP	Bk	W	L	Pct.	ShO	Sv	ERA
1989	Rangers	R	4	0	0	0	7	34	9	7	7	0	0	1	0	5	0	6	2	2	0	1	.000	0	0	9.00
1990	Rangers	R	13	12	0	0	64.1	260	59	29	19	5	0	0	2	16	0	60	3	6	4	5	.444	0	0	2.66
1991	Butte	R	17	6	0	9	48.2	217	59	37	24	3	1	4	1	22	0	39	7	0	5	1	.833	0	2	4.44
	Gastonia	A	9	2	0	1	17	75	17	9	8	0	1	0	0	8	0	17	1	0	1	2	.333	0	0	4.24
1992	Miracle	A	24	24	2	0	135.1	558	120	53	49	6	9	2	5	42	0	90	6	3	7	9	.438	1	0	3.26
1993	Charlotte	A	31	20	2	2	141	580	132	63	58	7	5	4	3	52	0	85	8	0	11	4	.733	1	1	3.70
1994	Tulsa	AA	11	4	0	5	23.2	118	35	20	18	2	2	0	0	17	1	16	3	1	0	2	.000	0	0	6.85
	Central Val	A	4	4	0	0	15.2	83	23	16	13	4	1	0	0	11	0	8	2	1	0	3	.000	0	0	7.47
	High Desert	A	4	0	0	2	4.1	32	14	11	10	2	0	0	1	4	2	1	1	0	0	1	.000	0	0	20.77
	6 Min. YEARS		117	72	4	19	457	1957	468	245	206	29	19	11	12	177	3	322	33	13	28	28	.500	2	3	4.06

Steve Gibralter

Bats: Right Throws: Right Pos: OF **Ht: 6'0" Wt: 170 Born: 10/09/72 Age: 22**

			BATTING													BASERUNNING				PERCENTAGES		
Year	Team	Lg	G	AB	H	2B	3B	HR	TB	R	RBI	TBB	IBB	SO	HBP	SH	SF	SB	CS	SB%	GDP	Avg	OBP	SLG
1990	Reds	R	52	174	45	11	3	4	74	26	27	23	1	30	3	3	1	8	2	.80	5	.259	.353	.425
1991	Chston-Wv	A	140	544	145	36	7	6	213	72	71	31	2	117	5	2	6	11	13	.46	14	.267	.309	.392
1992	Cedar Rapds	A	137	529	162	32	3	19	257	92	99	51	4	99	12	1	3	12	9	.57	8	.306	.378	.486
1993	Chattanooga	AA	132	477	113	25	3	11	177	65	47	20	2	108	7	3	4	7	12	.37	6	.237	.276	.371
1994	Chattanooga	AA	133	460	124	28	3	14	200	71	63	47	0	114	9	4	5	10	8	.56	5	.270	.345	.435
	5 Min. YEARS		594	2184	589	132	19	54	921	326	307	172	9	468	36	13	19	48	44	.52	38	.270	.331	.422

Benji Gil

Bats: Right Throws: Right Pos: SS **Ht: 6' 2" Wt: 180 Born: 10/06/72 Age: 22**

			BATTING													BASERUNNING				PERCENTAGES		
Year	Team	Lg	G	AB	H	2B	3B	HR	TB	R	RBI	TBB	IBB	SO	HBP	SH	SF	SB	CS	SB%	GDP	Avg	OBP	SLG
1991	Butte	R	32	129	37	4	3	2	53	25	15	14	1	36	0	0	1	9	3	.75	0	.287	.354	.411
1992	Gastonia	A	132	482	132	21	1	9	182	75	55	50	0	106	3	3	4	26	13	.67	16	.274	.343	.378
1993	Tulsa	AA	101	342	94	9	1	17	156	45	59	35	2	89	7	0	3	20	12	.63	9	.275	.351	.456
1994	Okla. City	AAA	139	487	121	20	6	10	183	62	55	33	2	120	4	7	6	14	8	.64	9	.248	.298	.376
1993	Texas	AL	22	57	7	0	0	0	7	3	2	5	0	22	0	4	0	1	2	.33	0	.123	.194	.123
	4 Min. YEARS		404	1440	384	54	11	38	574	207	184	132	5	351	14	10	14	69	36	.66	34	.267	.331	.399

Gustavo Gil

Pitches: Right Bats: Right Pos: P **Ht: 6'2" Wt: 188 Born: 09/22/70 Age: 24**

			HOW MUCH HE PITCHED						WHAT HE GAVE UP									THE RESULTS					
Year	Team	Lg	G	GS	CG	GF	IP	BFP	H	R	ER	HR	SH	SF	HB	TBB	IBB	SO	WP	Bk	W	L	Pct.	ShO	Sv	ERA
1993	Athletics	R	14	13	0	0	75.2	324	63	43	38	6	1	4	3	31	0	63	8	2	7	1	.875	0	0	4.52
1994	Huntsville	AA	1	1	0	0	4	18	6	3	3	0	0	0	0	1	0	1	0	0	0	0	.000	0	0	6.75
	W. Michigan	A	23	13	0	5	80.2	361	97	50	45	11	6	1	5	28	0	50	6	1	2	8	.200	0	0	5.02
	2 Min. YEARS		38	27	0	5	160.1	703	166	96	86	17	7	5	8	60	0	114	14	3	9	9	.500	0	0	4.83

Shawn Gilbert

Bats: Right Throws: Right Pos: OF **Ht: 5'9" Wt: 170 Born: 03/12/65 Age: 30**

			BATTING													BASERUNNING				PERCENTAGES		
Year	Team	Lg	G	AB	H	2B	3B	HR	TB	R	RBI	TBB	IBB	SO	HBP	SH	SF	SB	CS	SB%	GDP	Avg	OBP	SLG
1987	Visalia	A	82	272	61	5	0	5	81	39	27	34	0	59	7	4	4	6	4	.60	8	.224	.322	.298
1988	Visalia	A	14	43	16	3	2	0	23	10	8	10	0	7	1	0	0	1	1	.50	0	.372	.500	.535
	Kenosha	A	108	402	112	21	2	3	146	80	44	63	2	61	2	0	5	49	10	.83	6	.279	.375	.363
1989	Visalia	A	125	453	113	17	1	2	138	52	43	54	1	70	3	6	3	42	16	.72	11	.249	.331	.305
1990	Orlando	AA	123	433	110	18	2	4	144	68	44	61	0	69	5	4	3	31	9	.78	10	.254	.351	.333
1991	Orlando	AA	138	529	135	12	5	3	166	69	38	53	1	70	11	6	6	43	19	.69	18	.255	.332	.314
1992	Portland	AAA	138	444	109	17	2	3	139	60	52	36	2	55	4	5	2	31	8	.79	10	.245	.307	.313
1993	Nashville	AAA	104	278	63	17	2	0	84	28	17	12	0	41	2	2	1	6	2	.75	4	.227	.263	.302
1994	Scranton-Wb	AAA	141	547	139	33	4	7	201	81	52	66	3	86	7	3	3	20	15	.57	9	.254	.340	.367
	8 Min. YEARS		973	3401	858	143	20	27	1122	487	325	389	9	518	42	30	27	229	84	.73	76	.252	.334	.330

94

Brian Giles

Bats: Left   Throws: Left   Pos: OF   Ht: 5'11" Wt: 195 Born: 01/20/71 Age: 24

Year	Team	Lg	G	AB	H	2B	3B	HR	TB	R	RBI	TBB	IBB	SO	HBP	SH	SF	SB	CS	SB%	GDP	Avg	OBP	SLG
1989	Burlington	R	36	129	40	7	0	0	47	18	20	11	2	19	1	0	1	6	3	.67	0	.310	.366	.364
1990	Watertown	A	70	246	71	15	2	1	93	44	23	48	1	23	0	0	1	10	8	.56	3	.289	.403	.378
1991	Kinston	A	125	394	122	14	0	4	148	70	47	68	2	70	0	3	3	19	7	.73	5	.310	.411	.376
1992	Canton-Akrn	AA	23	74	16	4	0	0	20	6	3	10	1	10	0	0	0	3	1	.75	4	.216	.310	.270
	Kinston	A	42	140	37	5	1	3	53	28	18	30	1	21	1	0	0	3	5	.38	5	.264	.398	.379
1993	Canton-Akrn	AA	123	425	139	16	6	8	191	64	64	57	4	43	4	7	3	18	12	.60	9	.327	.409	.449
1994	Charlotte	AAA	128	434	136	18	3	16	208	74	58	55	10	61	2	1	4	8	5	.62	9	.313	.390	.479
	6 Min. YEARS		547	1842	561	79	12	32	760	304	233	279	21	247	10	11	12	67	41	.62	31	.305	.397	.413

Tim Gillis

Bats: Right   Throws: Right   Pos: 3B   Ht: 6'2" Wt: 195 Born: 02/09/68 Age: 27

Year	Team	Lg	G	AB	H	2B	3B	HR	TB	R	RBI	TBB	IBB	SO	HBP	SH	SF	SB	CS	SB%	GDP	Avg	OBP	SLG
1990	Burlington	A	131	463	119	28	2	12	187	66	62	41	0	95	8	3	2	4	2	.67	10	.257	.327	.404
1991	Durham	A	120	395	97	26	3	5	144	48	59	58	3	86	3	1	9	6	7	.46	13	.246	.340	.365
1992	Durham	A	137	482	115	22	3	21	206	63	84	64	2	128	3	2	5	3	10	.23	7	.239	.329	.427
	Greenville	AA	2	7	3	0	1	0	5	1	3	1	0	2	0	0	0	0	0	.00	1	.429	.444	.714
1993	Greenville	AA	135	451	113	22	3	14	183	58	62	51	3	103	7	2	3	1	6	.14	9	.251	.334	.406
1994	Greenville	AA	128	444	107	21	2	9	159	50	48	47	2	90	2	1	3	2	6	.25	14	.241	.315	.358
	5 Min. YEARS		653	2242	554	119	14	61	884	286	318	262	10	504	23	9	23	16	31	.34	54	.247	.329	.394

Tony Gilmore

Bats: Right   Throws: Right   Pos: C   Ht: 6'2" Wt: 195 Born: 10/15/68 Age: 26

Year	Team	Lg	G	AB	H	2B	3B	HR	TB	R	RBI	TBB	IBB	SO	HBP	SH	SF	SB	CS	SB%	GDP	Avg	OBP	SLG
1990	Auburn	A	33	106	23	8	0	0	31	9	7	6	0	23	0	1	1	2	1	.67	2	.217	.257	.292
1991	Burlington	A	82	276	75	12	0	1	90	25	27	25	2	45	3	5	1	2	2	.50	13	.272	.338	.326
1992	Osceola	A	80	266	55	7	0	1	65	26	21	17	2	46	4	1	1	1	5	.17	7	.207	.264	.244
1993	Jackson	AA	47	145	25	4	0	2	35	14	7	7	1	29	4	0	0	1	0	1.00	6	.172	.231	.241
1994	Tucson	AAA	2	5	0	0	0	0	0	1	0	0	0	0	0	1	0	0	0	.00	0	.000	.000	.000
	Jackson	AA	68	178	46	11	0	0	57	14	19	11	2	41	3	2	2	0	1	.00	5	.258	.309	.320
	5 Min. YEARS		312	976	224	42	0	4	278	89	81	66	7	184	14	10	5	6	9	.40	33	.230	.287	.285

Ed Giovanola

Bats: Left   Throws: Right   Pos: SS   Ht: 5'10" Wt: 170 Born: 03/04/69 Age: 26

Year	Team	Lg	G	AB	H	2B	3B	HR	TB	R	RBI	TBB	IBB	SO	HBP	SH	SF	SB	CS	SB%	GDP	Avg	OBP	SLG
1990	Idaho Falls	R	25	98	38	6	0	0	44	25	13	17	0	9	0	2	1	6	2	.75	0	.388	.474	.449
	Sumter	A	35	119	29	4	0	0	33	20	8	34	1	17	0	3	0	8	6	.57	0	.244	.412	.277
1991	Durham	A	101	299	76	9	0	6	103	50	27	57	1	39	2	0	3	18	11	.62	6	.254	.374	.344
1992	Greenville	AA	75	270	72	5	0	5	92	39	30	29	2	40	0	1	2	4	1	.80	1	.267	.336	.341
1993	Greenville	AA	120	384	108	21	5	5	154	70	43	84	3	49	2	4	6	6	7	.46	11	.281	.408	.401
1994	Greenville	AA	25	84	20	6	1	4	40	13	16	10	1	12	0	1	0	2	0	1.00	5	.238	.319	.476
	Richmond	AAA	98	344	97	16	2	6	135	48	30	31	5	49	3	5	2	7	4	.64	5	.282	.345	.392
	5 Min. YEARS		479	1598	440	67	8	26	601	265	167	262	13	215	7	16	14	51	31	.62	23	.275	.377	.376

Brian Givens

Pitches: Left   Bats: Right   Pos: P   Ht: 6'6" Wt: 220 Born: 11/06/65 Age: 29

Year	Team	Lg	G	GS	CG	GF	IP	BFP	H	R	ER	HR	SH	SF	HB	TBB	IBB	SO	WP	Bk	W	L	Pct.	ShO	Sv	ERA
1984	Kingsport	R	14	10	0	2	44.1	227	41	36	32	2	0	1	3	52	0	51	20	1	4	1	.800	0	0	6.50
1985	Little Fls	A	11	11	3	0	73.2	315	54	28	24	1	4	2	2	43	0	81	2	0	3	4	.429	1	0	2.93
	Columbia	A	3	3	1	0	21.1	88	15	7	7	2	0	0	0	13	0	25	6	0	1	2	.333	0	0	2.95
1986	Columbia	A	27	27	2	0	172	753	147	89	72	8	2	3	4	100	1	189	21	0	8	7	.533	1	0	3.77
1987	Tidewater	AAA	1	1	0	0	3.2	25	9	10	10	0	0	0	0	6	0	3	2	0	0	1	.000	0	0	24.55
	Lynchburg	A	21	20	3	0	112.1	523	112	79	58	8	5	2	4	69	0	96	19	2	6	8	.429	0	0	4.65
1988	Jackson	AA	26	26	4	0	164.1	689	140	78	69	6	13	5	1	68	2	156	14	11	6	14	.300	3	0	3.78
1989	St.Lucie	A	1	1	0	0	5	25	7	6	0	1	0	0	0	1	0	8	0	0	0	1	.000	0	0	0.00
	Jackson	AA	13	13	2	0	85	382	76	39	32	4	1	4	3	55	5	68	11	1	3	5	.375	0	0	3.39
1990	Tidewater	AAA	15	15	0	0	83	376	99	45	38	9	4	1	2	39	0	53	9	0	4	6	.400	0	0	4.12
	Calgary	AAA	2	2	0	0	5.2	29	7	8	8	1	0	0	0	8	0	1	1	0	0	1	.000	0	0	12.71
1991	San Berndno	A	1	1	0	0	5	20	4	2	1	0	1	0	0	1	0	4	0	0	1	0	1.000	0	0	1.80
	Calgary	AAA	3	3	0	0	14.2	65	16	8	8	1	1	0	1	6	0	8	4	1	1	0	1.000	0	0	4.91
1992	Memphis	AA	7	0	0	1	8.1	38	5	5	3	0	1	0	0	7	0	9	1	0	0	0	.000	0	0	3.24
1993	Royals	R	4	4	0	0	8	31	7	3	3	0	0	1	0	0	0	11	0	0	0	1	.000	0	0	3.38
	Memphis	AA	14	4	0	7	35.1	154	37	22	18	4	2	3	1	11	0	29	3	0	1	3	.250	0	2	4.58
1994	Birmingham	AA	36	13	1	8	110	480	103	57	45	8	4	1	8	52	6	111	11	0	4	7	.364	1	1	3.68
	11 Min. YEARS		199	154	16	18	951.2	4220	879	522	428	55	38	22	29	532	14	906	124	16	42	61	.408	6	3	4.05

Jim Givens

Bats: Both **Throws: Right** **Pos: 2B** **Ht: 6'1"** **Wt: 173** **Born: 11/11/67** **Age: 27**

						BATTING											BASERUNNING				PERCENTAGES		
Year	Team	Lg	G	AB	H	2B	3B	HR	TB	R	RBI	TBB	IBB	SO	HBP	SH	SF	SB	CS	SB%	GDP	Avg	OBP	SLG
1991	Bristol	R	4	12	3	0	0	0	3	3	1	1	0	1	1	0	0	1	1	.50	0	.250	.357	.250
	Fayettevlle	A	60	226	56	5	0	0	61	27	15	17	0	32	0	0	0	13	11	.54	7	.248	.300	.270
1992	Lakeland	A	124	456	110	15	3	0	131	51	29	27	2	50	1	12	3	18	13	.58	8	.241	.283	.287
1993	London	AA	82	262	69	8	3	3	92	24	28	16	2	45	2	5	4	17	8	.68	8	.263	.306	.351
	Toledo	AAA	44	148	38	4	2	0	46	18	13	10	0	18	1	2	1	6	3	.67	3	.257	.306	.311
1994	Toledo	AAA	105	283	66	7	4	0	81	25	11	30	0	64	1	4	0	16	10	.62	4	.233	.309	.286
	4 Min. YEARS		419	1387	342	39	12	3	414	148	97	101	4	210	6	23	8	71	46	.61	30	.247	.299	.298

Doug Glanville

Bats: Right **Throws: Right** **Pos: OF** **Ht: 6'2"** **Wt: 170** **Born: 08/25/70** **Age: 24**

						BATTING											BASERUNNING				PERCENTAGES		
Year	Team	Lg	G	AB	H	2B	3B	HR	TB	R	RBI	TBB	IBB	SO	HBP	SH	SF	SB	CS	SB%	GDP	Avg	OBP	SLG
1991	Geneva	A	36	152	46	8	0	2	60	29	12	11	0	25	1	3	1	17	3	.85	1	.303	.352	.395
1992	Winston-Sal	A	120	485	125	18	4	4	163	72	36	40	4	78	4	9	2	32	9	.78	6	.258	.318	.336
1993	Daytona	A	61	239	70	10	1	2	88	47	21	28	0	24	3	4	0	18	15	.55	2	.293	.374	.368
	Orlando	AA	73	295	78	14	4	9	127	42	40	12	0	40	2	6	5	15	7	.68	1	.264	.293	.431
1994	Orlando	AA	130	483	127	22	2	5	168	53	52	24	4	49	5	10	7	26	20	.57	7	.263	.301	.348
	4 Min. YEARS		420	1654	446	72	11	22	606	243	161	115	4	216	15	32	15	108	54	.67	17	.270	.320	.366

Gettys Glaze

Pitches: Right **Bats: Right** **Pos: P** **Ht: 6'1"** **Wt: 185** **Born: 09/23/70** **Age: 24**

			HOW MUCH HE PITCHED					WHAT HE GAVE UP									THE RESULTS					
Year	Team	Lg	G	GS	CG	GF	IP	BFP	H	R	ER	HR	SH	SF	HB	TBB	IBB	SO	WP	Bk	W	L	Pct.	ShO	Sv	ERA
1992	Elmira	A	18	11	1	5	83.1	343	77	40	31	2	3	3	4	19	1	88	3	2	6	4	.600	1	0	3.35
	New Britain	AA	2	1	1	1	10	36	5	2	2	1	0	0	0	5	0	6	0	0	0	1	.000	0	0	1.80
1993	Lynchburg	A	27	25	2	2	163.1	716	191	90	72	8	4	1	8	49	3	137	12	1	5	12	.294	0	1	3.97
1994	New Britain	AA	3	0	0	1	5.2	24	5	1	1	1	0	0	0	3	0	5	0	0	0	1	.000	0	0	1.59
	Lynchburg	A	49	0	0	39	91.1	382	90	47	40	8	5	6	3	28	4	76	9	0	5	5	.500	0	10	3.94
	3 Min. YEARS		99	37	4	48	353.2	1501	368	180	146	20	12	10	15	104	8	312	24	3	16	23	.410	1	11	3.72

Leon Glenn

Bats: Left **Throws: Right** **Pos: 1B** **Ht: 6'2"** **Wt: 200** **Born: 09/16/69** **Age: 25**

						BATTING											BASERUNNING				PERCENTAGES		
Year	Team	Lg	G	AB	H	2B	3B	HR	TB	R	RBI	TBB	IBB	SO	HBP	SH	SF	SB	CS	SB%	GDP	Avg	OBP	SLG
1988	Brewers	R	55	212	72	13	10	8	129	54	53	24	2	29	2	2	3	5	4	.56	2	.340	.407	.608
1989	Helena	R	6	15	0	0	0	0	0	0	0	0	0	6	0	0	0	0	0	.00	0	.000	.000	.000
	Brewers	R	51	212	81	10	7	7	126	42	50	14	5	46	2	0	2	21	9	.70	2	.382	.422	.594
1990	Beloit	A	65	202	39	4	3	5	64	19	29	20	1	93	0	2	0	10	6	.63	1	.193	.266	.317
	Helena	R	42	153	36	6	2	4	58	19	26	29	1	41	1	1	1	12	3	.80	1	.235	.359	.379
1991	Beloit	A	51	161	28	2	2	6	52	23	27	13	0	60	0	3	2	18	3	.86	2	.174	.233	.323
	Bend	A	73	262	59	9	3	15	119	46	55	36	2	96	0	0	4	16	3	.84	3	.225	.315	.454
1992	Stockton	A	88	275	57	12	2	10	103	36	36	40	0	86	0	1	1	17	8	.68	0	.207	.306	.375
1993	Stockton	A	114	431	119	27	3	15	197	77	76	49	4	110	4	1	6	35	15	.70	9	.276	.351	.457
1994	El Paso	AA	67	219	56	12	3	8	98	40	32	20	2	67	1	1	0	8	7	.53	4	.256	.321	.447
	New Orleans	AAA	48	155	37	9	2	4	62	22	22	15	0	56	0	1	4	7	0	1.00	4	.239	.299	.400
	7 Min. YEARS		660	2297	584	104	37	82	1008	378	406	260	17	690	10	12	24	149	58	.72	28	.254	.330	.439

Barry Goetz

Pitches: Right **Bats: Right** **Pos: P** **Ht: 6'2"** **Wt: 195** **Born: 08/28/68** **Age: 26**

			HOW MUCH HE PITCHED					WHAT HE GAVE UP									THE RESULTS					
Year	Team	Lg	G	GS	CG	GF	IP	BFP	H	R	ER	HR	SH	SF	HB	TBB	IBB	SO	WP	Bk	W	L	Pct.	ShO	Sv	ERA
1990	Butte	R	4	0	0	2	5.2	22	2	1	1	0	1	0	1	3	0	2	0	0	0	1	.000	0	1	1.59
1991	Charlotte	A	46	0	0	33	56	248	56	24	15	1	6	3	0	24	2	42	6	0	3	1	.750	0	12	2.41
1992	Charlotte	A	33	0	0	28	33.1	138	21	10	10	1	2	0	1	19	0	38	1	1	4	5	.444	0	11	2.70
	Tulsa	AA	10	0	0	5	14.1	59	10	2	1	0	2	0	0	6	0	7	1	0	2	1	.667	0	1	0.63
1993	Tulsa	AA	38	0	0	13	56.1	276	70	51	41	12	0	4	2	44	2	57	7	2	2	3	.400	0	1	6.55
1994	Okla. City	AAA	55	0	0	32	98.1	432	102	51	50	4	8	4	1	45	5	63	9	1	3	7	.300	0	9	4.58
	5 Min. YEARS		186	0	0	113	264	1175	261	139	118	18	19	11	5	141	9	209	24	4	14	18	.438	0	35	4.02

Doug Gogolewski

Pitches: Right **Bats: Right** **Pos: P** **Ht: 6'2"** **Wt: 190** **Born: 06/08/65** **Age: 30**

			HOW MUCH HE PITCHED					WHAT HE GAVE UP									THE RESULTS					
Year	Team	Lg	G	GS	CG	GF	IP	BFP	H	R	ER	HR	SH	SF	HB	TBB	IBB	SO	WP	Bk	W	L	Pct.	ShO	Sv	ERA
1987	Oneonta	A	15	14	0	0	73.1	359	81	73	54	6	1	7	3	51	0	62	15	0	3	7	.300	0	0	6.63
1988	Ft.Laudrdle	A	8	8	1	0	49.1	219	44	23	18	2	1	0	3	28	0	33	5	3	4	2	.667	0	0	3.28
	Pr William	A	13	12	2	1	58.1	293	60	60	50	6	2	4	6	53	1	38	5	2	1	9	.100	0	0	7.71
1989	Ft.Laudrdle	A	23	21	0	2	131.1	567	140	71	53	7	2	6	6	49	1	73	6	0	6	12	.333	1	0	3.63
1990	Albany	AA	5	5	0	0	14.1	81	17	24	22	1	1	1	1	19	0	21	3	1	1	3	.250	0	0	13.81

96

Year	Team	Lg	G	GS	CG	GF	IP	BFP	H	R	ER	HR	SH	SF	HB	TBB	IBB	SO	WP	Bk	W	L	Pct	ShO	Sv	ERA
	Ft.Laudrdle	A	16	16	2	0	88.2	399	87	58	46	7	3	6	4	50	0	88	9	4	5	9	.357	0	0	4.67
1991	Yankees	R	6	3	0	0	19	71	11	7	5	0	0	1	0	5	0	21	0	0	2	1	.667	0	0	2.37
	Ft.Laudrdle	A	1	1	0	0	3	13	3	1	1	0	0	0	0	0	0	5	0	1	0	1	.000	0	0	3.00
1992	Ft. Laud	A	37	0	0	33	46	196	36	21	18	1	1	2	4	18	2	38	2	0	0	5	.000	0	17	3.52
	Albany	AA	6	0	0	3	6.2	31	9	7	7	0	0	0	0	2	0	6	1	0	0	0	.000	0	1	9.45
1993	Albany	AA	13	0	0	8	20.1	83	20	7	5	2	1	1	0	4	0	10	0	1	4	1	.800	0	1	2.21
	Columbus	AAA	28	0	0	8	51.1	229	63	32	25	4	1	3	1	14	0	32	3	0	5	3	.625	0	3	4.38
1994	Shreveport	AA	3	0	0	1	5.2	24	5	1	1	0	0	0	0	2	0	5	0	0	0	0	.000	0	0	1.59
	8 Min. YEARS		174	80	7	56	567.1	2565	576	385	305	31	17	31	31	295	4	432	49	12	31	53	.369	1	22	4.84

Gary Goldsmith

Pitches: Right Bats: Right Pos: P   Ht: 6'2" Wt: 205 Born: 07/04/71 Age: 23

			HOW MUCH HE PITCHED						WHAT HE GAVE UP											THE RESULTS					
Year	Team	Lg	G	GS	CG	GF	IP	BFP	H	R	ER	HR	SH	SF	HB	TBB	IBB	SO	WP	Bk	W	L	Pct	ShO	Sv	ERA
1993	Niagara Fls	A	21	5	0	12	54.2	231	43	21	14	3	2	0	4	20	3	64	4	0	4	2	.667	0	0	2.30
1994	Lakeland	A	23	19	1	3	120.2	499	105	50	44	4	4	4	7	51	2	81	7	2	7	7	.500	0	0	3.28
	Trenton	AA	4	4	2	0	25.2	103	23	12	11	3	1	0	0	9	1	27	3	0	0	4	.000	0	0	3.86
	2 Min. YEARS		48	28	3	15	201	833	171	83	69	10	7	4	11	80	6	172	14	2	11	13	.458	0	0	3.09

Fabio Gomez

Bats: Right Throws: Right Pos: 3B   Ht: 6'0" Wt: 185 Born: 05/12/68 Age: 27

							BATTING										BASERUNNING				PERCENTAGES		
Year	Team	Lg	G	AB	H	2B	3B	HR	TB	R	RBI	TBB	IBB	SO	HBP	SH	SF	SB	CS	SB%	GDP	Avg	OBP	SLG
1987	Burlington	R	22	76	14	2	0	2	22	6	9	2	0	23	1	0	1	2	2	.50	3	.184	.213	.289
1988	Burlington	R	57	188	38	3	1	4	55	18	22	11	0	46	2	1	2	7	6	.54	3	.202	.251	.293
1989	Kinston	A	17	45	12	0	0	1	15	5	5	1	0	12	1	0	0	1	0	1.00	3	.267	.298	.333
	Watertown	A	73	296	98	15	4	9	148	64	57	15	2	56	1	2	2	6	3	.67	6	.331	.363	.500
1990	Kinston	A	121	430	106	18	8	8	164	72	52	53	0	91	4	4	2	13	8	.62	9	.247	.333	.381
1992	Reno	A	130	503	154	16	12	19	251	101	115	62	6	92	2	2	5	7	9	.44	19	.306	.381	.499
1993	Huntsville	AA	60	220	57	10	1	7	90	26	33	17	0	43	2	3	1	5	3	.63	3	.259	.317	.409
	Tacoma	AAA	67	252	71	10	1	2	89	28	29	20	1	47	3	0	5	5	9	.36	4	.282	.336	.353
1994	New Haven	AA	61	206	62	17	0	3	88	38	29	26	1	49	2	0	2	3	3	.50	6	.301	.381	.427
	Colo. Spmg	AAA	29	44	7	3	0	1	13	6	5	4	0	16	0	1	0	0	0	.00	0	.159	.229	.295
	7 Min. YEARS		637	2260	619	94	27	56	935	364	356	211	10	475	18	13	20	49	43	.53	56	.274	.338	.414

Mike Gomez

Bats: Right Throws: Right Pos: 2B   Ht: 5'11" Wt: 170 Born: 11/25/70 Age: 24

							BATTING										BASERUNNING				PERCENTAGES		
Year	Team	Lg	G	AB	H	2B	3B	HR	TB	R	RBI	TBB	IBB	SO	HBP	SH	SF	SB	CS	SB%	GDP	Avg	OBP	SLG
1992	Batavia	A	59	221	60	6	2	0	70	38	16	16	0	23	6	8	3	12	3	.80	5	.271	.333	.317
	Spartanburg	A	1	4	1	1	0	0	2	1	0	0	0	0	0	0	0	0	0	.00	1	.250	.250	.500
1993	Clearwater	A	124	496	142	21	2	1	170	63	44	26	2	23	4	6	2	7	11	.39	22	.286	.326	.343
1994	Reading	AA	82	252	62	11	2	1	80	30	16	5	2	17	1	1	5	5	1	.83	9	.246	.259	.317
	3 Min. YEARS		266	973	265	39	6	2	322	132	76	47	4	63	11	15	10	24	15	.62	37	.272	.310	.331

Rudy Gomez

Bats: Right Throws: Right Pos: SS   Ht: 5'10" Wt: 165 Born: 06/08/69 Age: 26

							BATTING										BASERUNNING				PERCENTAGES		
Year	Team	Lg	G	AB	H	2B	3B	HR	TB	R	RBI	TBB	IBB	SO	HBP	SH	SF	SB	CS	SB%	GDP	Avg	OBP	SLG
1991	Geneva	A	61	229	52	6	2	0	62	22	14	24	1	38	5	4	2	5	5	.50	8	.227	.312	.271
1992	Winston-Sal	A	112	363	84	13	1	1	102	43	25	28	0	60	4	7	2	8	6	.57	4	.231	.292	.281
1993	Daytona	A	40	147	39	4	1	0	45	20	12	19	0	24	0	3	3	3	5	.38	3	.265	.343	.306
	Iowa	AAA	9	20	3	0	0	0	3	0	0	1	0	8	0	0	0	0	0	.00	1	.150	.190	.150
1994	Orlando	AA	56	140	46	8	0	1	57	26	17	25	0	31	3	8	2	5	3	.63	4	.329	.435	.407
	Orlando	AA	91	229	58	10	0	2	74	26	16	18	0	45	2	1	0	4	7	.36	3	.253	.313	.323
	4 Min. YEARS		369	1128	282	41	4	4	343	137	84	115	1	206	14	23	9	25	26	.49	23	.250	.325	.304

Frank Gonzales

Pitches: Left Bats: Right Pos: P   Ht: 6'0" Wt: 185 Born: 03/12/68 Age: 27

			HOW MUCH HE PITCHED						WHAT HE GAVE UP											THE RESULTS					
Year	Team	Lg	G	GS	CG	GF	IP	BFP	H	R	ER	HR	SH	SF	HB	TBB	IBB	SO	WP	Bk	W	L	Pct	ShO	Sv	ERA
1989	Niagara Fls	A	10	5	1	3	38	160	36	20	16	2	1	2	0	16	1	35	0	0	3	3	.500	1	0	3.79
1990	Fayetteville	A	25	25	0	0	143	606	123	54	48	2	1	7	4	66	0	101	9	1	10	6	.625	0	0	3.02
1991	Lakeland	A	25	25	1	0	146	603	130	62	55	3	5	9	3	55	0	99	3	1	11	5	.688	0	0	3.39
1992	London	AA	10	10	0	0	65.2	269	64	25	22	5	0	0	1	10	0	37	2	0	5	4	.556	0	0	3.02
	Toledo	AAA	18	17	2	0	98.1	421	100	48	47	7	3	2	3	36	0	65	5	0	4	6	.400	1	0	4.30
1993	Toledo	AAA	29	15	2	3	109.1	464	116	56	48	12	2	2	3	37	1	71	4	0	6	3	.667	0	0	3.95
1994	Toledo	AAA	34	17	0	1	117	535	142	79	62	11	1	8	3	58	3	86	7	1	6	11	.353	0	0	4.77
	6 Min. YEARS		151	114	6	7	717.1	3058	711	344	298	42	13	30	17	278	5	494	30	6	45	38	.542	2	0	3.74

Larry Gonzales

Bats: Right **Throws:** Right **Pos:** C **Ht:** 6' 3" **Wt:** 200 **Born:** 03/28/67 **Age:** 28

Year	Team	Lg	G	AB	H	2B	3B	HR	TB	R	RBI	TBB	IBB	SO	HBP	SH	SF	SB	CS	SB%	GDP	Avg	OBP	SLG
1988	Palm Sprngs	A	35	100	20	0	0	0	20	11	11	22	0	25	1	1	0	0	0	.00	0	.200	.350	.200
1989	Quad City	A	69	195	38	3	1	6	61	24	20	39	1	34	4	2	1	2	5	.29	3	.195	.339	.313
1990	Quad City	A	99	309	95	16	1	8	137	44	75	36	1	56	8	2	2	2	1	.67	9	.307	.392	.443
1991	Edmonton	AAA	2	3	0	0	0	0	0	0	0	1	0	1	0	0	0	0	0	.00	0	.000	.250	.000
	Midland	AA	78	257	82	13	0	4	107	27	56	22	0	33	6	3	6	2	2	.50	9	.319	.378	.416
1992	Edmonton	AAA	80	241	79	10	0	3	98	37	47	38	0	24	4	3	4	2	1	.67	10	.328	.422	.407
1993	Vancouver	AAA	81	264	69	9	0	2	84	30	27	26	2	28	2	5	3	5	1	.83	9	.261	.329	.318
1994	Angels	R	3	8	2	1	0	0	3	2	1	0	0	1	0	0	0	0	0	.00	0	.250	.222	.375
	Midland	AA	22	70	21	6	0	2	33	11	18	13	1	13	1	0	1	0	0	.00	1	.300	.412	.471
1993	California	AL	2	2	1	0	0	0	1	0	1	1	0	0	0	0	0	0	0	.00	0	.500	.667	.500
	7 Min. YEARS		469	1447	406	58	2	25	543	186	255	197	5	215	26	16	18	13	10	.57	43	.281	.373	.375

Javier Gonzalez

Bats: Right **Throws:** Right **Pos:** C **Ht:** 6'0" **Wt:** 193 **Born:** 10/03/68 **Age:** 26

Year	Team	Lg	G	AB	H	2B	3B	HR	TB	R	RBI	TBB	IBB	SO	HBP	SH	SF	SB	CS	SB%	GDP	Avg	OBP	SLG
1986	Kingsport	R	25	55	16	4	0	5	35	12	14	14	0	13	0	0	0	0	0	.00	1	.291	.435	.636
1987	Little Fls	A	40	145	38	6	1	5	61	18	25	14	1	36	0	1	2	2	1	.67	3	.262	.323	.421
1988	Columbia	A	79	250	50	4	2	3	67	21	21	15	0	58	2	6	1	0	1	.00	7	.200	.250	.268
1989	St.Lucie	A	56	175	43	7	0	3	59	26	16	10	0	39	5	4	3	1	0	1.00	4	.246	.301	.337
1990	Jackson	AA	45	137	23	4	0	4	39	16	15	13	1	42	0	3	2	0	1	.00	2	.168	.237	.285
1991	Tidewater	AAA	1	3	1	0	0	0	1	0	0	0	0	1	0	0	0	0	0	.00	0	.333	.333	.333
	Williamsprt	AA	48	150	23	7	0	4	42	7	14	12	0	45	2	1	1	1	0	1.00	4	.153	.224	.280
1992	Tidewater	AAA	39	120	25	4	0	4	41	9	12	4	0	33	2	2	0	0	0	.00	4	.208	.246	.342
1993	Binghamton	AA	94	257	59	7	0	10	96	30	36	24	0	65	5	0	3	0	0	.00	8	.230	.304	.374
1994	New Britain	AA	30	88	17	4	0	1	24	6	8	10	0	24	1	1	1	0	1	.00	1	.193	.280	.273
	Norfolk	AAA	17	43	10	1	0	1	14	5	1	1	0	10	0	1	0	0	0	.00	2	.233	.250	.326
	9 Min. YEARS		474	1423	305	48	3	40	479	150	162	117	2	366	17	19	13	4	4	.50	34	.214	.280	.337

Jimmy Gonzalez

Bats: Right **Throws:** Right **Pos:** C **Ht:** 6'3" **Wt:** 210 **Born:** 03/08/73 **Age:** 22

Year	Team	Lg	G	AB	H	2B	3B	HR	TB	R	RBI	TBB	IBB	SO	HBP	SH	SF	SB	CS	SB%	GDP	Avg	OBP	SLG
1991	Astros	R	34	103	21	3	0	0	24	7	3	7	0	33	0	1	0	3	5	.38	1	.204	.255	.233
1992	Burlington	A	91	301	53	13	0	4	78	32	21	34	0	119	1	0	0	0	3	.00	6	.176	.262	.259
1993	Quad City	A	47	154	35	9	1	0	46	20	15	14	1	36	4	1	1	2	2	.50	4	.227	.306	.299
	Asheville	A	43	149	33	5	0	4	50	16	15	7	0	37	0	2	1	3	1	.75	3	.221	.255	.336
1994	Jackson	AA	4	6	0	0	0	0	0	0	0	0	0	0	0	0	0	0	0	.00	0	.000	.000	.000
	Osceola	A	99	321	74	18	0	5	107	33	38	20	0	80	4	2	2	2	0	1.00	10	.231	.282	.333
	4 Min. YEARS		318	1034	216	48	1	13	305	108	92	82	1	305	9	6	4	10	11	.48	24	.209	.272	.295

Paul Gonzalez

Bats: Left **Throws:** Right **Pos:** 3B **Ht:** 6'0" **Wt:** 185 **Born:** 04/22/69 **Age:** 26

Year	Team	Lg	G	AB	H	2B	3B	HR	TB	R	RBI	TBB	IBB	SO	HBP	SH	SF	SB	CS	SB%	GDP	Avg	OBP	SLG
1990	Spokane	A	1	4	1	1	0	0	2	0	2	1	0	1	0	0	0	0	0	.00	0	.250	.400	.500
	Chston-Sc	A	69	231	56	7	3	11	102	30	32	37	0	62	3	2	2	0	0	.00	4	.242	.352	.442
1991	High Desert	A	103	371	99	31	3	14	178	61	64	47	1	85	4	1	1	2	3	.40	5	.267	.355	.480
1992	Wichita	AA	120	432	110	18	2	15	177	59	54	48	3	124	4	0	3	7	3	.70	9	.255	.333	.410
1993	Wichita	AA	59	215	58	7	3	7	92	36	33	25	2	55	3	0	2	5	5	.50	2	.270	.351	.428
	Las Vegas	AAA	75	267	64	11	4	7	104	36	34	21	1	64	1	1	2	3	2	.60	7	.240	.296	.390
1994	Wichita	AA	73	215	52	9	4	6	87	23	24	27	6	63	3	0	3	3	2	.60	2	.242	.331	.405
	Las Vegas	AAA	4	13	2	0	0	0	2	0	2	2	0	2	0	0	0	0	0	.00	0	.154	.267	.154
	Pr. William	A	24	90	23	1	0	2	30	12	18	9	0	24	0	0	0	2	1	.67	3	.256	.323	.333
	5 Min. YEARS		528	1838	465	85	19	62	774	257	263	217	13	480	18	4	13	22	16	.58	32	.253	.336	.421

Pete Gonzalez

Bats: Right **Throws:** Right **Pos:** C **Ht:** 6'0" **Wt:** 190 **Born:** 11/24/69 **Age:** 25

Year	Team	Lg	G	AB	H	2B	3B	HR	TB	R	RBI	TBB	IBB	SO	HBP	SH	SF	SB	CS	SB%	GDP	Avg	OBP	SLG
1989	Dodgers	R	34	94	23	5	0	0	28	16	13	14	0	16	0	0	0	3	1	.75	2	.245	.343	.298
1990	Vero Beach	A	90	198	43	12	0	2	61	31	21	42	2	40	11	5	3	2	2	.50	5	.217	.378	.308
1991	Vero Beach	A	74	207	45	12	0	1	60	26	14	31	0	32	6	5	1	1	0	1.00	4	.217	.335	.290
1992	Fayetteville	A	42	110	25	5	0	0	30	17	19	38	0	23	6	1	3	5	2	.71	2	.227	.439	.273
	Toledo	AAA	9	17	2	2	0	0	4	1	0	1	0	3	0	0	0	0	0	.00	0	.118	.167	.235
	Lakeland	A	32	81	24	7	0	1	34	15	13	19	0	9	2	1	0	1	0	1.00	0	.296	.441	.420
1993	Lakeland	A	63	200	50	4	1	2	62	20	25	31	4	28	2	2	3	7	2	.78	8	.250	.352	.310
	London	AA	25	64	10	3	0	0	13	5	6	14	0	12	2	0	1	0	0	.00	0	.156	.321	.203

Year	Team	Lg	G	AB	H	2B	3B	HR	TB	R	RBI	TBB	IBB	SO	HBP	SH	SF	SB	CS	SB%	GDP	Avg	OBP	SLG
1994	Trenton	AA	16	55	15	3	0	0	18	3	8	4	0	7	1	0	0	2	1	.67	0	.273	.333	.327
	Toledo	AAA	60	151	41	9	0	3	59	24	18	26	1	35	1	1	1	2	6	.25	1	.272	.380	.391
	6 Min. YEARS		445	1177	278	62	1	9	369	158	137	220	7	205	31	16	12	23	14	.62	22	.236	.367	.314

Curt Goodwin

Bats: Left   Throws: Left   Pos: OF   **Ht: 5'11"   Wt: 180   Born: 09/30/72   Age: 22**

						BATTING												BASERUNNING				PERCENTAGES		
Year	Team	Lg	G	AB	H	2B	3B	HR	TB	R	RBI	TBB	IBB	SO	HBP	SH	SF	SB	CS	SB%	GDP	Avg	OBP	SLG
1991	Orioles	R	48	151	39	5	0	0	44	32	9	38	0	25	1	5	0	26	5	.84	3	.258	.411	.291
1992	Kane County	A	134	542	153	7	5	1	173	85	42	38	0	106	2	14	0	52	18	.74	1	.282	.332	.319
1993	Frederick	A	138	555	156	15	10	2	197	98	42	52	0	90	1	7	1	61	15	.80	8	.281	.343	.355
1994	Bowie	AA	142	597	171	18	8	2	211	105	37	40	0	78	3	13	2	59	10	.86	7	.286	.333	.353
	4 Min. YEARS		462	1845	519	45	23	5	625	320	130	168	0	299	7	39	3	198	48	.80	19	.281	.343	.339

Keith Gordon

Bats: Right   Throws: Right   Pos: OF   **Ht: 6' 2"   Wt: 200   Born: 01/22/69   Age: 26**

						BATTING												BASERUNNING				PERCENTAGES		
Year	Team	Lg	G	AB	H	2B	3B	HR	TB	R	RBI	TBB	IBB	SO	HBP	SH	SF	SB	CS	SB%	GDP	Avg	OBP	SLG
1990	Billings	R	49	154	36	5	1	1	46	21	14	24	1	49	3	2	1	6	4	.60	2	.234	.346	.299
1991	Chston-Wv	A	123	388	104	14	10	8	162	63	46	50	2	134	5	7	1	25	9	.74	5	.268	.358	.418
1992	Cedar Rapds	A	114	375	94	19	3	12	155	59	63	43	2	135	3	1	4	21	10	.68	5	.251	.329	.413
1993	Chattanooga	AA	116	419	122	26	3	14	196	69	59	19	0	132	4	0	2	13	17	.43	15	.291	.327	.468
1994	Indianapols	AAA	18	58	12	1	0	1	16	3	4	4	0	25	0	1	0	0	0	.00	1	.207	.258	.276
	Chattanooga	AA	82	254	71	16	2	8	115	46	38	21	0	74	1	0	2	11	7	.61	6	.280	.335	.453
1993	Cincinnati	NL	3	6	1	0	0	0	1	0	0	0	0	2	0	0	0	0	0	.00	0	.167	.167	.167
	5 Min. YEARS		502	1648	439	81	19	44	690	261	224	161	5	549	16	11	10	76	47	.62	34	.266	.336	.419

Tony Gordon

Pitches: Left   Bats: Right   Pos: P   **Ht: 6'0"   Wt: 185   Born: 12/08/68   Age: 26**

			HOW MUCH HE PITCHED					WHAT HE GAVE UP											THE RESULTS					
Year	Team	Lg	G	GS	CG	GF	IP	BFP	H	R	ER	HR	SH	SF	HB	TBB	IBB	SO	WP	Bk	W	L	Pct.	ShO	Sv	ERA
1988	R.S./mamrs	R	15	5	0	4	39.2	201	52	52	41	4	2	4	0	36	1	33	4	3	1	6	.143	0	0	9.30
1989	Bellingham	A	15	5	0	4	39	188	37	33	21	1	1	1	0	34	1	34	4	1	2	3	.400	0	0	4.85
1990	Peninsula	A	25	3	0	12	43	216	40	37	24	0	2	2	2	48	0	45	10	0	0	3	.000	0	0	5.02
1991	Baseball Cy	A	19	0	0	4	23.2	113	20	11	5	1	0	1	0	24	1	27	0	0	1	0	1.000	0	0	1.90
1992	Baseball Cy	A	9	0	0	1	14.2	67	13	9	9	0	1	0	0	12	2	21	3	0	1	1	.500	0	1	5.52
	Sarasota	A	30	3	0	9	46	212	48	34	22	3	3	2	1	29	1	39	5	0	1	1	.500	0	1	4.30
1993	Sarasota	A	2	0	0	2	6	26	4	1	1	0	0	0	1	4	0	6	1	0	0	0	.000	0	1	1.50
	Birmingham	AA	37	0	0	9	45.1	201	32	17	13	0	3	1	1	35	2	49	5	0	3	2	.600	0	1	2.58
1994	El Paso	AA	15	0	0	4	17	85	14	12	10	1	1	0	0	26	0	11	1	0	1	0	1.000	0	0	5.29
	7 Min. YEARS		167	16	0	49	274.1	1309	260	206	146	10	13	11	5	248	8	265	33	4	10	16	.385	0	3	4.79

Rick Gorecki

Pitches: Right   Bats: Right   Pos: P   **Ht: 6'3"   Wt: 180   Born: 08/27/73   Age: 21**

			HOW MUCH HE PITCHED					WHAT HE GAVE UP											THE RESULTS					
Year	Team	Lg	G	GS	CG	GF	IP	BFP	H	R	ER	HR	SH	SF	HB	TBB	IBB	SO	WP	Bk	W	L	Pct.	ShO	Sv	ERA
1991	Great Falls	R	13	10	0	0	51	219	44	34	25	3	2	0	1	27	0	56	4	5	0	3	.000	0	0	4.41
1992	Bakersfield	A	25	24	0	1	129	580	122	68	58	11	0	2	7	90	2	115	17	0	11	7	.611	0	0	4.05
1993	San Antonio	AA	26	26	1	0	156	653	136	76	58	6	3	5	5	62	2	118	5	1	6	9	.400	0	0	3.35
1994	Albuquerque	AAA	22	21	0	0	103	481	119	65	58	11	2	3	7	60	1	73	11	0	8	6	.571	0	0	5.07
	4 Min. YEARS		86	81	1	1	439	1933	421	243	199	31	7	10	20	239	5	362	37	6	25	25	.500	0	0	4.08

Sean Gousha

Bats: Right   Throws: Right   Pos: C   **Ht: 6'4"   Wt: 200   Born: 09/19/70   Age: 24**

						BATTING												BASERUNNING				PERCENTAGES		
Year	Team	Lg	G	AB	H	2B	3B	HR	TB	R	RBI	TBB	IBB	SO	HBP	SH	SF	SB	CS	SB%	GDP	Avg	OBP	SLG
1992	Erie	A	20	62	15	2	0	0	17	4	6	5	0	19	0	0	1	3	0	1.00	2	.242	.294	.274
1993	High Desert	A	45	126	23	2	0	0	25	22	11	26	0	47	5	3	3	0	1	.00	3	.183	.338	.198
1994	Portland	AA	44	73	14	1	0	0	15	5	7	19	1	31	0	1	1	0	0	.00	2	.192	.355	.205
	3 Min. YEARS		109	261	52	5	0	0	57	31	24	50	1	97	5	4	5	3	1	.75	7	.199	.333	.218

Rob Grable

Bats: Right   Throws: Right   Pos: 3B   **Ht: 6'2"   Wt: 200   Born: 01/20/70   Age: 25**

						BATTING												BASERUNNING				PERCENTAGES		
Year	Team	Lg	G	AB	H	2B	3B	HR	TB	R	RBI	TBB	IBB	SO	HBP	SH	SF	SB	CS	SB%	GDP	Avg	OBP	SLG
1991	Niagara Fls	A	73	251	76	18	2	7	119	48	46	46	0	55	2	3	0	2	4	.33	8	.303	.415	.474
1992	Fayettevlle	A	24	77	21	5	1	0	28	9	10	12	0	16	2	3	1	3	3	.50	3	.273	.380	.364
	Spartanburg	A	77	279	69	14	2	4	99	36	33	47	0	54	2	0	5	6	7	.46	8	.247	.356	.355
1993	Clearwater	A	98	351	110	27	5	5	162	60	55	49	3	72	7	0	5	16	9	.64	13	.313	.403	.462
	Reading	AA	37	120	28	4	1	1	37	10	10	18	1	27	1	0	1	2	1	.67	3	.233	.336	.308
1994	Reading	AA	42	161	43	6	3	2	61	19	18	13	0	34	4	1	4	7	4	.64	3	.267	.330	.379
	4 Min. YEARS		351	1239	347	74	14	19	506	182	172	185	4	258	18	7	14	36	28	.56	38	.280	.378	.408

Anthony Graffagnino

Bats: Right **Throws:** Right **Pos:** SS **Ht:** 6'1" **Wt:** 200 **Born:** 06/06/72 **Age:** 23

Year	Team	Lg	G	AB	H	2B	3B	HR	TB	R	RBI	TBB	IBB	SO	HBP	SH	SF	SB	CS	SB%	GDP	Avg	OBP	SLG
1990	Pulaski	R	42	131	27	5	1	0	34	23	11	26	0	17	2	1	1	6	3	.67	3	.206	.344	.260
1991	Idaho Falls	R	66	274	95	16	4	4	131	53	57	27	0	37	3	2	2	19	4	.83	2	.347	.408	.478
1992	Macon	A	112	400	96	15	5	10	151	50	31	50	1	84	8	4	4	9	6	.60	6	.240	.333	.378
1993	Durham	A	123	459	126	30	5	15	211	78	69	45	1	78	4	2	4	24	11	.69	10	.275	.342	.460
1994	Greenville	AA	124	440	132	28	3	7	187	66	52	50	7	53	2	7	3	29	7	.81	8	.300	.372	.425
	5 Min. YEARS		467	1704	476	94	18	36	714	270	220	198	9	269	19	16	14	87	31	.74	29	.279	.358	.419

Greg Graham

Bats: Both **Throws:** Right **Pos:** SS **Ht:** 6'0" **Wt:** 185 **Born:** 01/30/69 **Age:** 26

Year	Team	Lg	G	AB	H	2B	3B	HR	TB	R	RBI	TBB	IBB	SO	HBP	SH	SF	SB	CS	SB%	GDP	Avg	OBP	SLG
1990	Winter Havn	A	15	39	2	0	0	0	2	0	1	2	0	16	0	1	0	0	0	.00	1	.051	.098	.051
	Red Sox	R	26	94	21	2	0	0	23	16	11	20	0	13	1	1	2	1	1	.50	1	.223	.359	.245
1991	Winter Havn	A	9	20	7	0	0	0	7	2	0	1	0	5	0	1	0	1	1	.50	1	.350	.381	.350
	Lynchburg	A	82	275	54	6	1	1	65	31	24	36	1	65	1	4	1	6	5	.55	9	.196	.291	.236
1992	New Britain	AA	104	347	78	6	1	0	86	32	19	30	1	62	3	5	1	9	10	.47	8	.225	.291	.248
1993	St.Lucie	A	26	56	11	1	0	0	12	10	4	13	0	10	1	0	0	1	2	.33	2	.196	.357	.214
1994	Binghamton	AA	48	137	34	6	0	0	40	19	19	11	0	25	0	2	1	2	1	.67	4	.248	.302	.292
	Norfolk	AAA	35	90	16	4	0	0	20	7	7	16	0	24	0	8	2	0	0	.00	3	.178	.296	.222
	5 Min. YEARS		345	1058	223	25	2	1	255	117	85	129	2	220	6	22	7	20	20	.50	29	.211	.298	.241

Dennis Gray

Pitches: Left **Bats:** Left **Pos:** P **Ht:** 6'6" **Wt:** 225 **Born:** 12/24/69 **Age:** 25

Year	Team	Lg	G	GS	CG	GF	IP	BFP	H	R	ER	HR	SH	SF	HB	TBB	IBB	SO	WP	Bk	W	L	Pct.	ShO	Sv	ERA
1991	St.Cathmes	A	15	14	0	0	77	341	63	42	32	4	3	1	4	54	0	78	4	4	4	4	.500	0	0	3.74
1992	Myrtle Bch	A	28	28	0	0	155.1	659	122	82	66	8	2	5	6	93	0	141	13	4	11	12	.478	0	0	3.82
1993	Dunedin	A	26	26	0	0	141.1	607	115	71	56	7	7	6	7	97	1	108	6	0	8	10	.444	0	0	3.57
1994	Knoxville	AA	30	16	0	6	100.2	488	118	83	59	5	12	8	11	65	0	77	13	1	5	11	.313	0	0	5.27
	4 Min. YEARS		99	84	0	6	474.1	2095	418	278	213	21	24	20	25	309	1	404	36	9	28	37	.431	0	0	4.04

Richie Grayum

Bats: Left **Throws:** Right **Pos:** OF **Ht:** 5'10" **Wt:** 185 **Born:** 09/17/68 **Age:** 26

Year	Team	Lg	G	AB	H	2B	3B	HR	TB	R	RBI	TBB	IBB	SO	HBP	SH	SF	SB	CS	SB%	GDP	Avg	OBP	SLG
1989	Geneva	A	69	259	75	16	2	8	119	43	33	38	2	57	0	6	4	0	5	.00	4	.290	.375	.459
1990	Charlotte	AA	113	316	75	8	0	10	113	38	35	31	1	64	4	0	4	6	0	1.00	4	.237	.310	.358
1991	Winston-Sal	A	110	309	77	18	1	9	124	43	31	66	2	88	3	2	0	1	2	.33	4	.249	.386	.401
1992	Charlotte	AA	116	334	81	25	0	13	145	46	52	45	2	84	1	5	5	0	2	.00	3	.243	.330	.434
1993	Iowa	AAA	4	7	1	0	0	0	1	0	0	0	0	2	0	0	0	0	0	.00	0	.143	.143	.143
	Orlando	AA	92	234	69	13	1	10	114	45	33	45	1	66	3	3	1	1	10	.09	2	.295	.413	.487
1994	Orlando	AA	25	51	10	0	0	1	13	1	3	5	0	10	0	0	1	0	2	.00	2	.196	.263	.255
	6 Min. YEARS		529	1510	388	80	4	51	629	216	187	230	8	371	11	16	15	8	21	.28	21	.257	.356	.417

Brian Grebeck

Bats: Right **Throws:** Right **Pos:** SS **Ht:** 5'7" **Wt:** 160 **Born:** 08/31/67 **Age:** 27

Year	Team	Lg	G	AB	H	2B	3B	HR	TB	R	RBI	TBB	IBB	SO	HBP	SH	SF	SB	CS	SB%	GDP	Avg	OBP	SLG
1990	Boise	A	58	202	57	10	2	1	74	45	34	64	1	57	1	5	2	1	3	.25	3	.282	.454	.366
1991	Quad City	A	121	408	100	20	3	0	126	80	34	103	1	76	10	15	4	19	10	.66	8	.245	.406	.309
1992	Palm Sprngs	A	91	289	97	14	2	0	115	71	39	83	2	55	0	8	3	6	5	.55	10	.336	.480	.398
1993	Midland	AA	118	405	119	20	4	5	162	65	54	64	1	81	8	6	7	6	1	.86	8	.294	.395	.400
1994	Midland	AA	55	184	58	18	2	1	83	27	17	27	1	33	5	1	1	1	1	.50	7	.315	.415	.451
	Vancouver	AAA	38	127	38	7	0	2	51	23	18	16	0	14	3	2	3	1	2	.33	5	.299	.383	.402
	5 Min. YEARS		481	1615	469	89	13	9	611	311	195	357	5	316	27	37	20	34	22	.61	41	.290	.422	.378

Tyler Green

Pitches: Right **Bats:** Right **Pos:** P **Ht:** 6'5" **Wt:** 185 **Born:** 02/18/70 **Age:** 25

Year	Team	Lg	G	GS	CG	GF	IP	BFP	H	R	ER	HR	SH	SF	HB	TBB	IBB	SO	WP	Bk	W	L	Pct.	ShO	Sv	ERA
1991	Batavia	A	3	3	0	0	15	58	7	2	2	0	0	0	2	6	0	19	2	0	1	0	1.000	0	0	1.20
	Clearwater	A	2	2	0	0	13	50	3	2	2	0	0	0	0	8	0	20	2	0	2	0	1.000	0	0	1.38
1992	Reading	AA	12	12	0	0	62.1	249	46	16	13	2	4	1	1	20	0	67	5	0	6	3	.667	0	0	1.88
	Scranton/wb	AAA	2	2	0	0	10.1	50	7	7	7	1	0	0	1	12	0	15	0	1	0	1	.000	0	0	6.10
1993	Scranton/wb	AAA	28	14	4	6	118.1	496	102	62	52	8	3	4	5	43	2	87	8	2	6	10	.375	0	0	3.95
1994	Scranton-Wb	AAA	27	26	4	0	162	725	179	110	100	25	4	4	12	77	3	95	14	1	7	16	.304	0	0	5.56
1993	Philadelphia	NL	3	2	0	1	7.1	41	16	9	6	1	0	0	0	5	0	7	2	0	0	0	.000	0	0	7.36
	4 Min. YEARS		74	59	8	6	381	1628	344	199	176	36	11	9	21	166	5	303	31	4	22	30	.423	0	0	4.16

Charlie Greene

Bats: Right **Throws:** Right **Pos:** C **Ht:** 6'3" **Wt:** 170 **Born:** 01/23/71 **Age:** 24

Year Team	Lg	G	AB	H	2B	3B	HR	TB	R	RBI	TBB	IBB	SO	HBP	SH	SF	SB	CS	SB%	GDP	Avg	OBP	SLG
1991 Padres	R	49	183	52	15	1	5	84	27	39	16	0	23	3	2	6	6	1	.86	7	.284	.341	.459
1992 Chston-Sc	A	98	298	55	9	1	1	69	22	24	11	0	60	5	3	2	1	2	.33	7	.185	.225	.232
1993 Waterloo	A	84	213	38	8	0	2	52	19	20	13	0	33	3	6	3	0	0	.00	5	.178	.233	.244
1994 Binghamton	AA	30	106	18	4	0	0	22	13	2	6	1	18	1	0	1	0	0	.00	3	.170	.219	.208
St. Lucie	A	69	224	57	4	0	0	61	23	21	9	0	31	4	4	1	0	0	.00	3	.254	.294	.272
4 Min. YEARS		330	1024	220	40	2	8	288	104	106	55	1	165	16	15	13	7	4	.64	25	.215	.263	.281

Rick Greene

Pitches: Right **Bats:** Right **Pos:** P **Ht:** 6'5" **Wt:** 200 **Born:** 01/02/71 **Age:** 24

Year Team	Lg	G	GS	CG	GF	IP	BFP	H	R	ER	HR	SH	SF	HB	TBB	IBB	SO	WP	Bk	W	L	Pct.	ShO	Sv	ERA
1993 Lakeland	A	26	0	0	11	40.2	184	57	28	28	1	6	0	1	16	1	32	5	2	2	3	.400	0	2	6.20
London	AA	23	0	0	11	29	135	31	22	21	1	3	3	1	20	3	19	3	2	2	2	.500	0	0	6.52
1994 Trenton	AA	20	0	0	14	19.1	92	17	17	17	0	3	2	0	21	2	5	2	0	1	1	.500	0	3	7.91
Lakeland	A	19	2	0	11	33.1	158	50	23	16	0	1	1	0	10	1	28	6	0	0	4	.000	0	4	4.32
2 Min. YEARS		88	2	0	47	122.1	569	155	90	82	2	13	6	2	67	7	84	16	4	5	10	.333	0	9	6.03

Ken Greer

Pitches: Right **Bats:** Right **Pos:** P **Ht:** 6'3" **Wt:** 210 **Born:** 05/12/67 **Age:** 28

Year Team	Lg	G	GS	CG	GF	IP	BFP	H	R	ER	HR	SH	SF	HB	TBB	IBB	SO	WP	Bk	W	L	Pct.	ShO	Sv	ERA
1988 Oneonta	A	15	15	4	0	112.1	470	109	46	30	0	5	4	7	18	2	60	6	6	5	5	.500	0	0	2.40
1989 Pr William	A	29	13	3	7	111.2	461	101	56	52	3	2	2	7	22	0	44	4	1	7	3	.700	1	2	4.19
1990 Ft.Laudrdle	A	38	5	0	11	89.1	417	115	64	54	5	9	5	7	33	2	55	3	3	4	9	.308	0	1	5.44
Pr William	A	1	1	0	0	7.2	32	7	2	2	0	0	1	0	2	0	7	0	0	1	0	1.000	0	0	2.35
1991 Ft.Laudrdle	A	31	1	0	12	57.1	245	49	31	27	3	1	1	7	22	2	46	5	0	4	3	.571	0	0	4.24
1992 Pr William	A	13	0	0	6	27	112	25	11	11	1	0	0	1	9	0	30	1	0	1	2	.333	0	1	3.67
Albany	AA	40	1	0	18	68.2	280	48	19	14	1	2	1	0	30	4	53	6	0	4	1	.800	0	4	1.83
Columbus	AAA	1	0	0	1	1	7	3	2	1	0	0	0	0	1	0	1	0	0	0	0	.000	0	0	9.00
1993 Columbus	AAA	46	0	0	21	79.1	347	78	41	39	5	4	4	2	36	6	50	2	0	9	4	.692	0	6	4.42
1994 Mets	R	4	2	0	0	6	24	7	2	2	0	0	0	0	0	0	3	1	0	0	0	.000	0	0	3.00
Norfolk	AAA	25	0	0	12	31	138	35	14	13	2	0	1	3	11	2	8	3	0	1	1	.500	0	1	3.77
1993 New York	NL	1	0	0	1	1	3	0	0	0	0	0	0	0	0	0	2	0	0	1	0	1.000	0	0	0.00
7 Min. YEARS		243	38	7	88	591.1	2533	577	288	245	20	23	19	34	184	18	357	31	10	36	28	.563	1	15	3.73

Kris Gresham

Bats: Right **Throws:** Right **Pos:** C **Ht:** 6'1" **Wt:** 193 **Born:** 08/30/70 **Age:** 24

Year Team	Lg	G	AB	H	2B	3B	HR	TB	R	RBI	TBB	IBB	SO	HBP	SH	SF	SB	CS	SB%	GDP	Avg	OBP	SLG
1991 Bluefield	R	34	116	28	5	2	0	37	16	16	6	0	19	4	1	3	6	3	.67	6	.241	.295	.319
1992 Kane County	A	38	113	22	4	0	2	32	10	17	4	0	21	0	2	0	0	0	.00	1	.195	.222	.283
1993 Frederick	A	66	188	41	13	1	4	68	22	17	13	0	41	7	3	0	1	0	1.00	1	.218	.293	.362
1994 Bowie	AA	69	204	40	8	2	3	61	27	20	10	0	57	6	1	3	1	0	1.00	6	.196	.251	.299
4 Min. YEARS		207	621	131	30	5	9	198	75	70	33	0	138	17	7	6	8	3	.73	15	.211	.267	.319

Craig Griffey

Bats: Right **Throws:** Right **Pos:** OF **Ht:** 5'11" **Wt:** 175 **Born:** 06/03/71 **Age:** 24

Year Team	Lg	G	AB	H	2B	3B	HR	TB	R	RBI	TBB	IBB	SO	HBP	SH	SF	SB	CS	SB%	GDP	Avg	OBP	SLG
1991 Mariners	R	45	150	38	1	1	0	41	36	20	28	0	35	1	2	2	11	6	.65	0	.253	.370	.273
1992 Bellingham	A	63	220	55	6	1	1	66	30	21	22	0	35	3	2	2	15	8	.65	1	.250	.324	.300
1993 Appleton	A	37	102	26	7	0	2	39	14	20	12	0	18	1	1	3	9	3	.75	1	.255	.331	.382
Riverside	A	58	191	46	4	4	3	67	30	25	17	3	25	2	3	7	10	2	.83	3	.241	.300	.351
1994 Jacksonville	AA	106	327	72	13	1	3	96	37	29	33	0	68	3	10	5	20	10	.67	3	.220	.293	.294
4 Min. YEARS		309	990	237	31	7	9	309	147	115	112	3	181	10	18	19	65	29	.69	8	.239	.317	.312

Marc Griffin

Bats: Left **Throws:** Right **Pos:** OF **Ht:** 6'0" **Wt:** 170 **Born:** 09/15/68 **Age:** 26

Year Team	Lg	G	AB	H	2B	3B	HR	TB	R	RBI	TBB	IBB	SO	HBP	SH	SF	SB	CS	SB%	GDP	Avg	OBP	SLG
1989 Vero Beach	A	129	440	124	8	8	2	154	59	52	29	6	58	7	3	8	35	15	.70	9	.282	.331	.350
1990 Vero Beach	A	31	106	20	2	1	0	24	12	6	11	0	14	0	0	0	16	3	.84	0	.189	.265	.226
Bakersfield	A	106	429	118	14	4	3	149	77	32	39	1	70	0	2	4	33	18	.65	0	.275	.333	.347
1991 Vero Beach	A	114	400	96	15	5	0	121	68	33	55	3	62	4	5	1	42	12	.78	4	.240	.337	.303
1993 Wst Plm Bch	A	69	226	72	6	2	2	88	34	18	29	1	34	2	4	0	23	8	.74	3	.319	.401	.389
Harrisburg	AA	24	53	8	2	0	0	10	5	6	7	0	9	1	1	1	5	1	.83	2	.151	.258	.189
1994 Harrisburg	AA	10	26	6	1	1	0	9	6	2	2	0	2	1	1	0	3	0	1.00	0	.231	.310	.346
5 Min. YEARS		483	1680	444	48	21	7	555	261	149	172	11	253	15	16	14	157	57	.73	22	.264	.335	.330

Pedro Grifol

Bats: Right Throws: Right Pos: C   Ht: 6'1" Wt: 205 Born: 11/28/69 Age: 25

					BATTING												BASERUNNING				PERCENTAGES		
Year	Team	Lg	G	AB	H	2B	3B	HR	TB	R	RBI	TBB	IBB	SO	HBP	SH	SF	SB	CS	SB%	GDP	Avg	OBP	SLG
1991	Elizabethtn	R	55	202	53	12	0	7	86	24	36	16	0	33	2	0	4	0	1	.00	6	.262	.317	.426
	Orlando	AA	6	20	3	0	0	0	3	0	2	0	0	6	0	0	0	0	0	.00	0	.150	.150	.150
1992	Miracle	A	94	333	76	13	1	4	103	24	32	17	1	38	2	3	1	1	0	1.00	19	.228	.269	.309
	Orlando	AA	14	40	11	2	0	0	13	2	5	2	0	9	0	1	0	0	0	.00	2	.275	.302	.325
1993	Nashville	AA	58	197	40	13	0	5	68	22	29	11	0	38	2	5	3	0	1	.00	6	.203	.249	.345
	Portland	AAA	28	94	31	4	2	2	45	14	17	4	0	14	0	2	2	0	0	.00	5	.330	.350	.479
1994	Nashville	AA	20	55	7	0	0	1	10	4	4	10	0	7	1	0	1	0	0	.00	1	.127	.269	.182
	4 Min. YEARS		275	941	221	44	3	19	328	90	125	60	1	145	7	10	12	1	2	.33	39	.235	.282	.349

Benji Grigsby

Pitches: Right Bats: Right Pos: P   Ht: 6'1" Wt: 190 Born: 12/02/70 Age: 24

			HOW MUCH HE PITCHED						WHAT HE GAVE UP									THE RESULTS					
Year	Team	Lg	G	GS	CG	GF	IP	BFP	H	R	ER	HR	SH	SF	HB	TBB	IBB	SO	WP	Bk	W	L	Pct.	ShO	Sv	ERA
1992	Athletics	R	3	3	0	0	11	35	4	2	2	0	0	0	1	0	7	0	0	1	1	.500	0	1	1.64
1993	Modesto	A	39	10	0	10	90.1	396	90	49	48	12	2	1	3	42	2	72	9	1	5	6	.455	0	6	4.78
1994	Modesto	A	16	8	0	5	65.1	272	59	28	24	4	1	3	1	18	0	49	6	2	4	1	.800	0	4	3.31
	Huntsville	AA	17	7	0	5	47	205	43	17	15	2	1	1	2	23	2	30	1	0	3	2	.600	0	0	2.87
	3 Min. YEARS		75	28	0	20	213.2	908	196	96	89	20	4	5	6	84	4	158	16	3	13	10	.565	0	11	3.75

Kevin Grijak

Bats: Left Throws: Right Pos: OF   Ht: 6'2" Wt: 195 Born: 08/06/70 Age: 24

					BATTING												BASERUNNING				PERCENTAGES		
Year	Team	Lg	G	AB	H	2B	3B	HR	TB	R	RBI	TBB	IBB	SO	HBP	SH	SF	SB	CS	SB%	GDP	Avg	OBP	SLG
1991	Idaho Falls	R	52	202	68	9	1	10	109	33	58	16	1	15	1	2	4	4	1	.80	5	.337	.381	.540
1992	Pulaski	R	10	31	11	3	0	0	14	1	6	6	0	0	0	0	0	2	2	.50	1	.355	.459	.452
	Macon	A	47	157	41	13	0	5	69	20	21	15	2	16	3	0	2	3	0	1.00	3	.261	.333	.439
1993	Macon	A	120	389	115	26	5	7	172	50	58	37	4	37	6	2	12	9	5	.64	9	.296	.356	.442
1994	Durham	A	22	68	25	3	0	11	61	18	22	12	4	6	3	0	1	1	1	.50	1	.368	.476	.897
	Greenville	AA	100	348	94	19	1	11	148	40	58	20	1	40	6	0	7	2	3	.40	11	.270	.315	.425
	4 Min. YEARS		351	1195	354	73	7	44	573	162	223	106	12	114	19	4	26	21	12	.64	30	.296	.356	.479

Mike Groppuso

Bats: Right Throws: Right Pos: 3B   Ht: 6'3" Wt: 195 Born: 03/09/70 Age: 25

					BATTING												BASERUNNING				PERCENTAGES		
Year	Team	Lg	G	AB	H	2B	3B	HR	TB	R	RBI	TBB	IBB	SO	HBP	SH	SF	SB	CS	SB%	GDP	Avg	OBP	SLG
1991	Asheville	A	63	197	36	12	1	4	62	31	25	34	2	60	3	0	0	3	1	.75	3	.183	.312	.315
1992	Osceola	A	115	369	80	19	1	4	113	53	37	43	2	98	9	3	3	6	3	.67	4	.217	.311	.306
1993	Jackson	AA	114	370	89	18	0	10	137	41	49	35	4	121	5	0	1	3	3	.50	8	.241	.314	.370
1994	Jackson	AA	118	352	93	16	2	12	149	49	47	35	2	97	5	1	4	6	7	.46	10	.264	.336	.423
	4 Min. YEARS		410	1288	298	65	4	30	461	174	158	147	10	376	22	4	8	18	14	.56	25	.231	.319	.358

Kip Gross

Pitches: Right Bats: Right Pos: P   Ht: 6' 2" Wt: 194 Born: 08/24/64 Age: 30

			HOW MUCH HE PITCHED						WHAT HE GAVE UP									THE RESULTS					
Year	Team	Lg	G	GS	CG	GF	IP	BFP	H	R	ER	HR	SH	SF	HB	TBB	IBB	SO	WP	Bk	W	L	Pct.	ShO	Sv	ERA
1987	Lynchburg	A	16	15	2	0	89.1	379	92	37	27	1	2	3	6	22	1	39	1	1	7	4	.636	0	0	2.72
1988	St. Lucie	A	28	27	7	1	178.1	736	153	72	52	1	1	3	7	53	6	124	10	11	13	9	.591	3	0	2.62
1989	Jackson	AA	16	16	4	0	112	444	96	47	31	9	4	2	2	13	0	60	4	4	6	5	.545	0	0	2.49
	Tidewater	AAA	12	12	0	0	70.1	289	72	33	31	3	5	2	1	17	0	39	1	1	4	4	.500	0	0	3.97
1990	Nashville	AAA	40	11	2	11	127	521	113	54	47	6	6	2	7	47	3	62	6	3	12	7	.632	1	3	3.33
1991	Nashville	AAA	14	6	1	3	47.2	195	39	13	11	3	2	1	4	16	0	28	3	1	5	3	.625	1	0	2.08
1992	Albuquerque	AAA	31	14	2	16	107.2	437	96	48	42	1	4	4	2	36	5	58	3	1	6	5	.545	0	8	3.51
1993	Albuquerque	AAA	59	7	0	25	124.1	521	115	58	56	7	7	1	2	41	6	96	9	3	13	7	.650	0	13	4.05
1994	Albuquerque	AAA	10	0	0	3	16	65	14	9	9	0	0	0	1	6	1	11	1	0	1	1	.500	0	1	5.06
1990	Cincinnati	NL	5	0	0	2	6.1	25	6	3	3	0	0	1	0	2	0	3	0	0	0	0	.000	0	0	4.26
1991	Cincinnati	NL	29	9	1	6	85.2	381	93	43	33	8	6	2	0	40	2	40	5	1	6	4	.600	0	0	3.47
1992	Los Angeles	NL	16	1	0	7	23.2	109	32	14	11	1	0	0	0	10	1	14	1	1	1	1	.500	0	0	4.18
1993	Los Angeles	NL	10	0	0	0	15	59	13	1	1	0	0	0	0	4	0	12	0	0	0	0	.000	0	0	0.60
	8 Min. YEARS		226	108	18	59	872.2	3587	790	371	306	31	31	19	32	251	22	517	38	25	67	45	.598	5	25	3.16
	4 Maj. YEARS		60	10	1	15	130.2	574	144	61	48	9	6	3	0	56	3	69	6	2	7	5	.583	0	0	3.31

Matt Grott

Pitches: Left Bats: Left Pos: P   Ht: 6'1" Wt: 205 Born: 12/05/67 Age: 27

			HOW MUCH HE PITCHED						WHAT HE GAVE UP									THE RESULTS					
Year	Team	Lg	G	GS	CG	GF	IP	BFP	H	R	ER	HR	SH	SF	HB	TBB	IBB	SO	WP	Bk	W	L	Pct.	ShO	Sv	ERA
1989	Athletics	R	9	5	0	0	35	139	29	16	9	0	0	0	2	9	0	44	1	2	3	1	.750	0	0	2.31
1990	Madison	A	22	0	0	19	25	102	15	5	1	0	0	0	0	14	1	36	1	1	2	0	1.000	0	12	0.36
	Modesto	A	12	0	0	8	17.2	78	10	7	4	0	1	0	0	14	1	28	4	0	2	0	1.000	0	4	2.04
	Huntsville	AA	10	0	0	6	15.2	62	8	5	5	1	1	0	0	10	0	12	0	0	0	0	.000	0	1	2.87

Year Team	Lg	G	GS	CG	GF	IP	BFP	H	R	ER	HR	SH	SF	HB	TBB	IBB	SO	WP	Bk	W	L	Pct.	ShO	Sv	ERA
1991 Huntsville	AA	42	0	0	23	57.2	276	65	40	33	6	8	3	0	37	7	65	6	0	2	9	.182	0	3	5.15
Harrisburg	AA	10	1	0	2	15.1	69	14	8	8	4	0	0	0	8	0	16	0	0	2	1	.667	0	1	4.70
1992 Chattanooga	AA	32	0	0	20	40.1	180	39	16	12	4	4	1	0	25	4	44	5	2	1	2	.333	0	6	2.68
1993 Indianapols	AAA	33	9	0	10	100.1	423	88	45	40	8	3	4	1	40	2	73	7	1	7	5	.583	0	1	3.59
1994 Indianapols	AAA	26	16	2	2	116.1	468	106	44	33	10	5	1	0	32	0	64	7	1	10	3	.769	1	1	2.55
6 Min. YEARS		196	31	2	90	423.1	1797	374	180	145	33	22	12	3	189	15	382	31	7	29	21	.580	1	29	3.08

Mark Grudzielanek

Bats: Right Throws: Right Pos: SS Ht: 6'1" Wt: 170 Born: 06/30/70 Age: 25

							BATTING									BASERUNNING				PERCENTAGES		
Year Team	Lg	G	AB	H	2B	3B	HR	TB	R	RBI	TBB	IBB	SO	HBP	SH	SF	SB	CS	SB%	GDP	Avg	OBP	SLG
1991 Jamestown	A	72	275	72	9	3	2	93	44	32	18	0	42	3	3	3	14	4	.78	6	.262	.311	.338
1992 Rockford	A	128	496	122	12	5	5	159	64	54	22	1	59	5	0	0	25	4	.86	10	.246	.285	.321
1993 Wst Plm Bch	A	86	300	80	11	6	1	106	41	34	14	0	42	7	0	0	17	10	.63	6	.267	.315	.353
1994 Harrisburg	AA	122	488	157	37	3	11	233	92	66	43	2	66	8	5	5	32	10	.76	15	.322	.382	.477
4 Min. YEARS		408	1559	431	69	17	19	591	241	186	97	3	209	23	8	8	88	28	.76	37	.276	.327	.379

Keith Grunewald

Bats: Both Throws: Right Pos: SS Ht: 6'1" Wt: 185 Born: 10/15/71 Age: 23

							BATTING									BASERUNNING				PERCENTAGES		
Year Team	Lg	G	AB	H	2B	3B	HR	TB	R	RBI	TBB	IBB	SO	HBP	SH	SF	SB	CS	SB%	GDP	Avg	OBP	SLG
1993 Bend	A	56	183	50	4	2	3	67	29	21	30	1	44	0	1	0	7	2	.78	2	.273	.376	.366
1994 New Haven	AA	8	18	8	0	0	0	8	2	0	0	0	5	0	0	0	0	0	.00	1	.444	.444	.444
Asheville	A	111	406	109	11	0	10	150	47	37	36	2	98	0	4	1	4	5	.44	5	.268	.327	.369
2 Min. YEARS		175	607	167	15	2	13	225	78	58	66	3	147	0	5	1	11	7	.61	8	.275	.346	.371

Juan Guerrero

Bats: Right Throws: Right Pos: 3B Ht: 5'11" Wt: 160 Born: 02/01/67 Age: 28

							BATTING									BASERUNNING				PERCENTAGES		
Year Team	Lg	G	AB	H	2B	3B	HR	TB	R	RBI	TBB	IBB	SO	HBP	SH	SF	SB	CS	SB%	GDP	Avg	OBP	SLG
1987 Pocatello	R	34	81	17	5	1	1	27	13	7	17	0	28	1	0	0	1	1	.50	1	.210	.354	.333
1988 Clinton	A	111	385	106	17	3	13	168	57	54	13	0	95	5	1	5	7	4	.64	5	.275	.304	.436
1989 San Jose	A	108	409	115	24	2	13	182	61	78	36	1	68	7	0	5	7	5	.58	13	.281	.346	.445
1990 Shreveport	AA	118	390	94	21	1	16	165	55	47	26	0	74	5	2	2	4	8	.33	9	.241	.296	.423
1991 Shreveport	AA	128	479	160	40	2	19	261	78	94	46	2	88	5	0	4	14	9	.61	12	.334	.395	.545
1994 Tucson	AAA	89	290	84	17	6	7	134	44	49	26	0	45	4	2	3	1	2	.33	11	.290	.353	.462
1992 Houston	NL	79	125	25	4	2	1	36	8	14	10	2	32	1	1	2	1	0	1.00	4	.200	.261	.288
6 Min. YEARS		588	2034	576	124	15	69	937	308	329	164	3	398	27	5	19	34	29	.54	51	.283	.342	.461

Mike Guerrero

Bats: Right Throws: Right Pos: 2B Ht: 5'11" Wt: 155 Born: 01/08/68 Age: 27

							BATTING									BASERUNNING				PERCENTAGES		
Year Team	Lg	G	AB	H	2B	3B	HR	TB	R	RBI	TBB	IBB	SO	HBP	SH	SF	SB	CS	SB%	GDP	Avg	OBP	SLG
1987 Helena	R	52	181	40	3	1	0	45	22	14	16	0	43	0	4	0	8	6	.57	1	.221	.284	.249
1988 Brewers	R	8	29	8	1	0	0	9	9	7	5	0	5	0	1	0	0	0	.00	0	.276	.382	.310
Helena	R	10	31	9	0	0	0	9	4	5	3	0	1	0	0	0	2	1	.67	1	.290	.353	.290
Beloit	A	65	221	39	8	1	0	49	20	7	14	0	55	1	8	0	5	5	.50	5	.176	.229	.222
1989 Beloit	A	51	171	38	10	0	0	48	28	13	13	0	33	0	2	2	7	4	.64	1	.222	.274	.281
Brewers	R	11	47	13	3	1	1	21	10	11	6	0	5	1	1	2	3	2	.60	0	.277	.357	.447
Stockton	A	44	136	32	5	0	0	37	12	13	12	0	15	0	5	1	3	1	.75	2	.235	.295	.272
1990 Stockton	A	105	320	80	5	5	1	98	36	36	24	0	54	3	6	1	14	10	.58	13	.250	.307	.306
1991 El Paso	AA	37	117	24	2	0	0	26	23	13	18	1	16	0	2	0	2	1	.67	4	.205	.311	.222
Stockton	A	59	204	48	4	1	1	57	22	18	28	1	28	1	4	5	6	2	.75	5	.235	.324	.279
1992 El Paso	AA	96	257	63	11	4	1	85	36	28	31	2	38	1	12	3	6	6	.50	1	.245	.325	.331
1993 Memphis	AA	24	68	18	6	0	0	24	7	4	4	0	7	0	4	0	0	2	.00	0	.265	.306	.353
Wilmington	A	44	150	41	4	1	0	47	24	7	32	0	20	0	7	0	4	12	.25	0	.273	.401	.313
1994 El Paso	AA	8	11	3	1	0	0	4	2	3	0	0	2	0	0	0	0	0	.00	0	.273	.273	.364
Stockton	A	27	86	30	3	0	2	39	13	15	5	0	12	1	0	2	1	2	.33	3	.349	.383	.453
8 Min. YEARS		641	2029	486	66	14	6	598	268	194	211	5	334	8	56	16	61	54	.53	36	.240	.311	.295

Lee Guetterman

Pitches: Left Bats: Left Pos: P Ht: 6'8" Wt: 230 Born: 11/22/58 Age: 36

		HOW MUCH HE PITCHED						WHAT HE GAVE UP										THE RESULTS					
Year Team	Lg	G	GS	CG	GF	IP	BFP	H	R	ER	HR	SH	SF	HB	TBB	IBB	SO	WP	Bk	W	L	Pct.	ShO	Sv	ERA
1984 Chattanooga	AA	24	24	5	0	157	652	174	68	59	7	6	2	4	38	2	47	5	1	11	7	.611	2	0	3.38
1985 Calgary	AAA	20	18	2	1	110.1	0	138	86	71	7	0	0	1	44	0	48	6	0	5	8	.385	0	0	5.79
1986 Calgary	AAA	4	4	0	0	19.1	82	24	12	12	0	0	0	0	7	0	8	0	0	1	0	1.000	0	0	5.59
1987 Calgary	AAA	16	2	1	5	44	186	41	14	14	1	1	2	1	17	1	29	3	0	5	1	.833	0	1	2.86
1988 Columbus	AAA	18	18	6	0	120.2	493	109	46	37	2	5	5	3	26	2	49	4	0	9	6	.600	0	0	2.76
1993 Louisville	AAA	25	0	0	7	33.2	145	35	11	11	0	1	1	2	12	3	20	3	1	2	1	.667	0	2	2.94
1994 Las Vegas	AAA	15	1	0	5	21.1	88	21	6	5	1	1	1	0	4	0	18	1	0	1	1	.500	0	0	2.11
Calgary	AAA	12	0	0	8	19.2	80	19	9	6	0	0	0	0	3	0	17	1	1	4	0	1.000	0	2	2.75

Year	Team	Lg	G	GS	CG	GF	IP	BFP	H	R	ER	HR	SH	SF	HB	TBB	IBB	SO	WP	Bk	W	L	Pct.	ShO	Sv	ERA
1984	Seattle	AL	3	0	0	1	4.1	22	9	2	2	0	0	0	0	2	0	2	1	0	0	0	.000	0	0	4.15
1986	Seattle	AL	41	4	1	8	76	353	108	67	62	7	3	5	4	30	3	38	2	0	0	4	.000	0	0	7.34
1987	Seattle	AL	25	17	2	3	113.1	483	117	60	48	13	2	5	2	35	2	42	3	0	11	4	.733	1	0	3.81
1988	New York	AL	20	2	0	7	40.2	177	49	21	21	2	1	1	1	14	0	15	2	0	1	2	.333	0	0	4.65
1989	New York	AL	70	0	0	38	103	412	98	31	28	6	4	2	0	26	9	51	4	0	5	5	.500	0	13	2.45
1990	New York	AL	64	0	0	21	93	376	80	37	35	6	8	3	0	26	7	48	1	1	11	7	.611	0	2	3.39
1991	New York	AL	64	0	0	37	88	376	91	42	36	6	4	4	3	25	5	35	4	0	3	4	.429	0	6	3.68
1992	New York	AL	15	0	0	7	22.2	114	35	24	24	5	0	2	0	13	3	5	1	0	1	1	.500	0	9	9.53
	New York	NL	43	0	0	15	43.1	196	57	28	28	5	2	3	1	14	5	15	3	0	3	4	.429	0	2	5.82
1993	St. Louis	NL	40	0	0	14	46	192	41	18	15	1	1	2	2	16	5	19	1	0	3	3	.500	0	1	2.93
	7 Min. YEARS		134	67	14	26	526	1726	561	252	215	18	14	11	11	151	8	236	23	3	38	24	.613	2	5	3.68
	9 Maj. YEARS		385	23	3	151	630.1	2701	685	330	299	51	25	27	13	201	39	270	22	1	38	34	.528	1	24	4.27

Todd Guggiana

Bats: Left Throws: Right Pos: 1B Ht: 6'0" Wt: 180 Born: 08/06/68 Age: 26

Year	Team	Lg	G	AB	H	2B	3B	HR	TB	R	RBI	TBB	IBB	SO	HBP	SH	SF	SB	CS	SB%	GDP	Avg	OBP	SLG
1990	Butte	R	66	248	87	23	5	4	132	50	52	26	1	22	3	0	4	6	3	.67	5	.351	.413	.532
1991	Charlotte	A	36	132	39	7	2	2	56	14	18	19	2	21	1	0	1	9	2	.82	4	.295	.386	.424
1993	Charlotte	A	134	514	147	34	4	4	193	53	79	41	7	62	4	2	5	7	4	.64	19	.286	.340	.375
1994	Tulsa	AA	39	106	21	6	0	0	27	12	8	14	4	26	2	2	1	0	2	.00	2	.198	.301	.255
	4 Min. YEARS		275	1000	294	70	7	10	408	129	157	100	14	131	10	4	11	22	11	.67	30	.294	.360	.408

Michael Guilfoyle

Pitches: Left Bats: Left Pos: P Ht: 5'11" Wt: 187 Born: 04/29/68 Age: 27

Year	Team	Lg	G	GS	CG	GF	IP	BFP	H	R	ER	HR	SH	SF	HB	TBB	IBB	SO	WP	Bk	W	L	Pct.	ShO	Sv	ERA
1990	Bristol	R	16	7	0	3	64.2	278	54	35	22	6	3	1	1	25	0	80	4	3	4	6	.400	0	1	3.06
1991	Fayetteville	A	40	0	0	34	47.1	213	41	22	13	3	4	4	5	26	1	44	2	1	1	4	.200	0	8	2.47
1992	Lakeland	A	45	0	0	31	51	214	48	23	18	1	1	1	1	16	1	32	2	1	4	1	.800	0	11	3.18
1993	Lakeland	A	9	0	0	9	9.1	37	5	1	1	0	1	0	0	3	0	10	0	0	0	0	.000	0	5	0.96
	London	AA	49	0	0	18	41	181	43	19	17	2	5	2	2	16	0	35	0	1	1	2	.333	0	3	3.73
1994	Trenton	AA	42	0	0	32	50.1	227	60	27	25	4	4	2	1	25	0	36	1	1	7	8	.467	0	5	4.47
	5 Min. YEARS		201	7	0	127	263.2	1150	251	127	96	16	18	10	10	111	2	237	9	7	17	21	.447	0	33	3.28

Jim Gutierrez

Pitches: Right Bats: Right Pos: P Ht: 6'2" Wt: 190 Born: 11/28/70 Age: 24

Year	Team	Lg	G	GS	CG	GF	IP	BFP	H	R	ER	HR	SH	SF	HB	TBB	IBB	SO	WP	Bk	W	L	Pct.	ShO	Sv	ERA
1989	Bellingham	A	13	11	0	1	57.2	268	68	44	25	4	0	1	1	24	0	33	1	0	1	5	.167	0	0	3.90
1990	Peninsula	A	28	28	4	0	186	758	171	82	71	9	6	11	6	41	0	95	6	1	11	13	.458	2	0	3.44
1991	San Berndno	A	17	14	1	0	82.2	377	100	65	60	11	0	3	2	37	0	66	4	0	4	4	.500	0	0	6.53
1992	Jacksonville	AA	15	11	0	1	54	234	58	34	30	7	1	2	3	17	0	44	0	0	1	5	.167	0	0	5.00
1993	Riverside	A	27	27	2	0	171.1	742	182	95	72	15	11	6	4	53	2	84	5	1	12	9	.571	0	0	3.78
1994	Jacksonville	AA	28	21	6	4	151.2	655	175	76	72	16	4	3	4	42	4	89	1	0	8	11	.421	1	0	4.27
	6 Min. YEARS		128	112	13	6	703.1	3034	754	396	330	62	22	26	20	214	6	411	17	2	37	47	.440	3	0	4.22

Dave Hajek

Bats: Right Throws: Right Pos: OF Ht: 5'10" Wt: 165 Born: 10/14/67 Age: 27

Year	Team	Lg	G	AB	H	2B	3B	HR	TB	R	RBI	TBB	IBB	SO	HBP	SH	SF	SB	CS	SB%	GDP	Avg	OBP	SLG
1990	Asheville	A	135	498	155	28	0	6	201	86	60	61	1	50	2	6	10	43	24	.64	16	.311	.382	.404
1991	Osceola	A	63	232	61	9	4	0	78	35	20	23	0	30	1	4	1	8	5	.62	5	.263	.331	.336
	Jackson	AA	37	94	18	6	0	0	24	10	9	7	2	12	0	0	1	2	0	1.00	1	.191	.245	.255
1992	Osceola	A	5	18	2	1	0	0	3	3	1	1	0	1	0	0	0	1	0	1.00	0	.111	.158	.167
	Jackson	AA	103	326	88	12	3	1	109	36	18	31	2	25	0	10	3	8	3	.73	5	.270	.331	.334
1993	Jackson	AA	110	332	97	20	2	5	136	50	27	17	2	14	2	1	3	6	5	.55	10	.292	.328	.410
1994	Tucson	AAA	129	484	157	29	5	7	217	71	70	29	5	23	2	5	5	12	7	.63	10	.324	.362	.448
	5 Min. YEARS		582	1984	578	105	14	19	768	291	205	169	12	155	7	26	23	80	44	.65	47	.291	.345	.387

Billy Hall

Bats: Both Throws: Right Pos: 2B Ht: 5'9" Wt: 180 Born: 06/17/69 Age: 26

Year	Team	Lg	G	AB	H	2B	3B	HR	TB	R	RBI	TBB	IBB	SO	HBP	SH	SF	SB	CS	SB%	GDP	Avg	OBP	SLG
1991	Chston-Sc	A	72	279	84	6	5	2	106	41	28	34	1	54	0	0	2	25	9	.74	2	.301	.375	.380
1992	High Desert	A	119	495	176	22	5	2	214	92	39	54	2	77	1	1	3	49	27	.64	2	.356	.418	.432
1993	Wichita	AA	124	486	131	27	7	4	184	80	46	37	1	88	3	4	4	29	19	.60	6	.270	.323	.379
1994	Wichita	AA	29	111	40	5	1	1	50	14	12	11	1	19	1	0	0	10	5	.67	5	.360	.423	.450
	Las Vegas	AAA	70	280	74	11	3	3	100	43	21	32	0	61	1	5	1	24	6	.80	2	.264	.341	.357
	4 Min. YEARS		414	1651	505	71	21	12	654	270	146	168	5	299	6	10	10	137	66	.67	17	.306	.370	.396

Drew Hall

Pitches: Left   Bats: Left   Pos: P   **Ht: 6' 5"   Wt: 220   Born: 03/27/63   Age: 32**

Year	Team	Lg	G	GS	CG	GF	IP	BFP	H	R	ER	HR	SH	SF	HB	TBB	IBB	SO	WP	Bk	W	L	Pct.	ShO	Sv	ERA
1984	Lodi	A	8	8	2	0	48	0	43	31	26	1	0	0	0	44	0	43	7	0	3	3	.500	1	0	4.88
1985	Winston-Sal	A	24	23	6	0	140.2	638	131	92	73	12	4	4	8	83	1	135	19	0	10	7	.588	3	0	4.67
1986	Pittsfield	AA	24	24	6	0	158.1	678	130	77	63	7	6	3	6	84	3	115	10	0	8	11	.421	3	0	3.58
1987	Iowa	AAA	35	6	0	11	66.1	318	74	42	33	9	2	1	1	45	3	66	3	0	6	3	.667	0	1	4.48
1988	Iowa	AAA	49	0	0	37	65.1	256	41	20	17	1	3	5	2	26	0	75	5	1	4	3	.571	0	19	2.34
1989	Okla City	AAA	11	0	0	7	17.2	65	7	3	3	0	0	0	1	6	0	18	1	1	1	0	1.000	0	5	1.53
1991	Nashville	AAA	8	0	0	1	7.2	41	6	6	5	0	1	0	0	10	1	2	2	0	0	1	.000	0	0	5.87
	Okla City	AAA	15	1	0	8	24.1	116	28	22	19	3	1	0	0	17	0	15	3	0	1	2	.333	0	0	7.03
	Colo Spngs	AAA	5	0	0	3	9.2	41	6	5	2	0	2	2	0	6	2	8	0	0	1	0	1.000	0	0	1.86
1992	Buffalo	AAA	16	4	0	1	38	158	36	15	10	3	0	1	1	12	2	30	3	0	4	0	1.000	0	0	2.37
1993	Scranton/wb	AAA	61	0	0	29	65.1	274	55	25	20	3	6	4	5	23	5	62	3	0	2	2	.500	0	7	2.76
1994	Toledo	AAA	53	2	0	15	62.1	292	76	41	32	6	4	1	2	24	3	66	2	0	1	4	.200	0	3	4.62
1986	Chicago	NL	5	4	1	1	23.2	101	24	12	12	3	1	0	0	10	0	21	0	0	1	2	.333	0	1	4.56
1987	Chicago	NL	21	0	0	7	32.2	147	40	31	25	4	1	2	0	14	0	20	1	0	1	1	.500	0	0	6.89
1988	Chicago	NL	19	0	0	8	22.1	103	26	20	19	4	3	2	1	9	2	22	0	0	1	1	.500	0	1	7.66
1989	Texas	AL	38	0	0	6	58.1	242	42	24	24	3	2	1	3	33	1	45	1	0	2	1	.667	0	0	3.70
1990	Montreal	NL	42	0	0	13	58.1	254	52	35	33	6	6	4	0	29	5	40	3	0	4	7	.364	0	3	5.09
	10 Min. YEARS		309	68	14	112	703.2	2877	633	379	303	45	29	21	26	380	20	635	58	2	41	36	.532	6	35	3.88
	5 Maj. YEARS		125	4	1	35	195.1	847	184	122	113	20	13	9	4	95	8	148	5	0	9	12	.429	0	5	5.21

Shane Halter

Bats: Right   Throws: Right   Pos: SS   **Ht: 5'10"   Wt: 160   Born: 11/08/69   Age: 25**

Year	Team	Lg	G	AB	H	2B	3B	HR	TB	R	RBI	TBB	IBB	SO	HBP	SH	SF	SB	CS	SB%	GDP	Avg	OBP	SLG
1991	Eugene	A	64	236	55	9	1	1	69	41	18	49	0	59	3	2	1	12	6	.67	3	.233	.370	.292
1992	Appleton	A	80	313	83	22	3	3	120	50	33	41	1	54	1	5	3	21	6	.78	4	.265	.349	.383
	Baseball Cy	A	44	117	28	1	0	1	32	11	14	24	0	31	0	5	4	5	5	.50	4	.239	.359	.274
1993	Wilmington	A	54	211	63	8	5	5	96	44	32	27	2	55	2	12	4	5	4	.56	3	.299	.377	.455
	Memphis	AA	81	306	79	7	0	4	98	50	20	30	1	74	2	10	3	4	7	.36	3	.258	.326	.320
1994	Memphis	AA	129	494	111	23	1	6	154	61	35	39	0	102	3	15	6	10	14	.42	10	.225	.282	.312
	4 Min. YEARS		452	1677	419	70	10	20	569	257	152	210	4	375	11	49	21	57	42	.58	27	.250	.334	.339

Al Hammell

Bats: Right   Throws: Right   Pos: C   **Ht: 5'11"   Wt: 190   Born: 07/23/71   Age: 23**

Year	Team	Lg	G	AB	H	2B	3B	HR	TB	R	RBI	TBB	IBB	SO	HBP	SH	SF	SB	CS	SB%	GDP	Avg	OBP	SLG
1992	Mets	R	33	81	18	3	0	0	21	3	8	14	1	20	0	2	0	2	1	.67	1	.222	.337	.259
1993	Capital Cty	A	11	23	4	1	0	0	5	0	3	3	0	6	0	0	0	0	0	.00	0	.174	.269	.217
1994	Binghamton	AA	2	6	2	1	0	0	3	1	2	0	0	2	0	0	0	0	0	.00	0	.333	.333	.500
	St. Lucie	A	18	52	7	2	0	1	12	4	5	7	0	13	1	1	1	0	0	.00	1	.135	.246	.231
	Norfolk	AAA	1	1	0	0	0	0	0	0	0	0	0	1	0	0	0	0	0	.00	0	.000	.000	.000
	Columbia	A	22	65	18	5	0	1	26	11	7	6	0	14	0	1	0	0	1	.00	1	.277	.338	.400
	3 Min. YEARS		87	228	49	12	0	2	67	19	25	30	1	56	1	4	1	2	2	.50	3	.215	.308	.294

Chris Hancock

Pitches: Left   Bats: Left   Pos: P   **Ht: 6'3"   Wt: 205   Born: 09/12/69   Age: 25**

Year	Team	Lg	G	GS	CG	GF	IP	BFP	H	R	ER	HR	SH	SF	HB	TBB	IBB	SO	WP	Bk	W	L	Pct.	ShO	Sv	ERA
1988	Pocatello	R	12	11	0	0	42.2	241	60	54	42	2	2	3	0	43	0	31	12	1	2	5	.286	0	0	8.86
1989	Clinton	A	18	17	0	0	72	355	63	53	47	5	1	1	5	77	0	62	17	2	4	7	.364	0	0	5.88
	Everett	A	11	11	0	0	52.2	262	47	52	33	3	1	7	2	53	0	50	13	0	2	5	.286	0	0	5.64
1990	Clinton	A	18	17	2	0	110.2	445	78	33	28	4	2	2	3	43	0	123	5	1	11	3	.786	1	0	2.28
	San Jose	A	1	1	0	0	7.2	31	7	1	1	0	0	0	0	4	0	7	0	0	0	0	.000	0	0	1.17
1991	San Jose	A	9	9	0	0	53.1	227	42	16	12	4	0	0	1	33	1	59	5	0	4	3	.571	0	0	2.03
1992	San Jose	A	18	17	0	1	111.1	484	104	60	50	2	4	1	6	55	1	80	8	1	7	4	.636	0	0	4.04
	Shreveport	AA	8	8	2	0	49.1	204	37	22	17	0	2	2	4	18	0	30	3	1	2	4	.333	0	0	3.10
1993	Shreveport	AA	23	23	0	0	124	544	126	71	56	13	7	3	7	52	2	93	8	0	8	8	.500	0	0	4.06
1994	Shreveport	AA	19	19	1	0	98	435	104	60	55	9	5	4	8	48	0	83	10	1	6	6	.500	1	0	5.05
	Phoenix	AAA	9	1	0	2	16.1	86	27	17	14	2	1	1	0	14	2	12	1	0	1	0	1.000	0	0	7.71
	7 Min. YEARS		146	134	5	3	738	3314	695	439	355	44	25	24	36	440	6	630	82	7	47	45	.511	2	0	4.33

Lee Hancock

Pitches: Left   Bats: Left   Pos: P   **Ht: 6'4"   Wt: 215   Born: 06/27/67   Age: 28**

Year	Team	Lg	G	GS	CG	GF	IP	BFP	H	R	ER	HR	SH	SF	HB	TBB	IBB	SO	WP	Bk	W	L	Pct.	ShO	Sv	ERA
1988	Bellingham	A	16	16	2	0	100.1	411	83	37	29	3	2	3	2	31	0	102	5	2	6	5	.545	0	0	2.60
1989	San Berndno	A	26	26	5	0	173	720	131	69	50	5	5	3	5	82	2	119	11	2	12	7	.632	0	0	2.60
1990	Williamsprt	AA	7	7	0	0	47	193	39	20	14	2	0	1	0	20	1	27	1	0	3	2	.600	0	0	2.68
	Harrisburg	AA	20	19	3	0	117.2	513	106	51	45	4	5	0	1	57	1	65	8	4	6	7	.462	1	0	3.44

105

Year	Team	Lg	G	GS	CG	GF	IP	BFP	H	R	ER	HR	SH	SF	HB	TBB	IBB	SO	WP	Bk	W	L	Pct.	ShO	Sv	ERA
	Buffalo	AAA	1	0	0	0	0	1	0	0	0	0	0	0	0	1	0	0	0	0	0	0	.000	0	0	0.00
1991	Carolina	AA	37	11	0	10	98	420	93	48	41	3	5	3	2	42	4	66	8	0	4	7	.364	0	4	3.77
1992	Buffalo	AAA	10	0	0	7	9	38	9	2	2	0	1	0	0	3	1	5	2	1	0	2	.000	0	0	2.00
	Carolina	AA	23	1	0	6	40.1	166	32	13	10	2	0	0	0	12	4	40	6	0	1	1	.500	0	0	2.23
1993	Carolina	AA	25	11	0	3	99.2	409	87	42	28	3	2	1	4	32	2	85	5	0	7	3	.700	0	0	2.53
	Buffalo	AAA	11	11	0	0	66	278	73	38	36	4	4	3	0	14	0	30	2	0	2	6	.250	0	0	4.91
1994	Buffalo	AAA	37	7	0	8	86.2	371	103	35	33	8	0	3	1	22	3	39	1	0	4	5	.444	0	0	3.43
	7 Min. YEARS		213	109	10	34	837.2	3520	756	355	288	34	24	17	15	316	18	578	49	9	45	45	.500	1	5	3.09

Ryan Hancock

Pitches: Right Bats: Right Pos: P Ht: 6'2" Wt: 210 Born: 11/11/71 Age: 23

			HOW MUCH HE PITCHED						WHAT HE GAVE UP										THE RESULTS						
Year	Team	Lg	G	GS	CG	GF	IP	BFP	H	R	ER	HR	SH	SF	HB	TBB	IBB	SO	WP	Bk	W	L	Pct.	ShO	Sv	ERA
1993	Boise	A	3	3	0	0	16.1	69	14	9	6	1	1	0	0	8	1	18	0	0	1	0	1.000	0	0	3.31
1994	Lake Elsino	A	18	18	3	0	116.1	494	113	62	49	10	1	5	5	36	1	95	2	5	9	6	.600	1	0	3.79
	Midland	AA	8	8	0	0	48	219	63	34	31	1	1	1	6	11	0	35	0	2	3	4	.429	0	0	5.81
	2 Min. YEARS		29	29	3	0	180.2	782	190	105	86	12	3	6	11	55	2	148	2	7	13	10	.565	1	0	4.28

Greg Hansell

Pitches: Right Bats: Right Pos: P Ht: 6'5" Wt: 215 Born: 03/12/71 Age: 24

			HOW MUCH HE PITCHED						WHAT HE GAVE UP										THE RESULTS						
Year	Team	Lg	G	GS	CG	GF	IP	BFP	H	R	ER	HR	SH	SF	HB	TBB	IBB	SO	WP	Bk	W	L	Pct.	ShO	Sv	ERA
1989	Red Sox	R	10	8	0	2	57	246	51	23	16	1	3	1	4	23	0	44	3	3	3	2	.600	0	2	2.53
1990	Winter Havn	A	21	21	2	0	115.1	502	95	63	46	8	4	4	9	64	0	79	4	4	7	10	.412	1	0	3.59
	St. Lucie	A	6	6	0	0	38	168	34	22	11	0	1	1	3	15	0	16	3	0	2	4	.333	0	0	2.61
1991	Bakersfield	A	25	25	0	0	150.2	625	142	56	48	5	10	2	5	42	1	132	3	0	14	5	.737	0	0	2.87
1992	Albuquerque	AAA	13	13	0	0	68.2	321	84	46	40	9	1	1	1	35	3	38	4	0	1	5	.167	0	0	5.24
	San Antonio	AA	14	14	0	0	92.1	380	80	40	29	6	2	1	3	33	2	64	1	2	6	4	.600	0	0	2.83
1993	Albuquerque	AAA	26	20	0	3	101.1	478	131	86	78	9	1	4	3	60	1	60	10	0	5	10	.333	0	0	6.93
1994	Albuquerque	AAA	47	6	0	19	123.1	498	109	44	41	7	3	4	6	31	3	101	8	0	10	2	.833	0	8	2.99
	6 Min. YEARS		162	113	2	24	746.2	3218	726	380	309	45	25	18	34	303	10	534	36	9	48	42	.533	1	10	3.72

Terrel Hansen

Bats: Right Throws: Right Pos: OF Ht: 6'3" Wt: 210 Born: 09/25/66 Age: 28

			BATTING															BASERUNNING				PERCENTAGES		
Year	Team	Lg	G	AB	H	2B	3B	HR	TB	R	RBI	TBB	IBB	SO	HBP	SH	SF	SB	CS	SB%	GDP	Avg	OBP	SLG
1987	Jamestown	A	29	67	16	3	0	1	22	8	14	10	1	20	0	0	2	1	2	.33	3	.239	.329	.328
1988	Wst Plm Bch	A	58	190	49	9	0	4	70	17	28	10	1	38	6	0	2	2	2	.50	5	.258	.313	.368
1989	Rockford	A	125	468	126	24	3	16	204	60	81	25	4	120	23	1	7	5	2	.71	8	.269	.333	.436
1990	Jacksnville	A	123	420	109	26	2	24	211	72	83	43	2	88	24	1	3	3	4	.43	14	.260	.359	.502
1991	Tidewater	AAA	107	368	100	19	2	12	159	54	62	40	2	82	20	1	3	0	0	.00	20	.272	.371	.432
1992	Tidewater	AAA	115	395	98	18	0	12	152	43	47	24	1	96	7	1	3	4	2	.67	13	.248	.300	.385
1993	Ottawa	AAA	108	352	81	19	0	10	130	45	39	18	0	103	27	2	4	1	1	.50	7	.230	.314	.369
1994	Jacksonville	AA	110	404	128	21	1	22	217	57	76	18	0	88	16	0	2	2	4	.33	9	.317	.368	.537
	Calgary	AAA	2	8	4	1	0	0	5	0	3	0	0	0	0	0	0	0	0	.00	0	.500	.500	.625
	8 Min. YEARS		777	2672	711	140	8	101	1170	356	435	188	11	635	123	5	27	18	17	.51	79	.266	.340	.438

Mike Hardge

Bats: Right Throws: Right Pos: SS Ht: 5'11" Wt: 183 Born: 01/27/72 Age: 23

			BATTING															BASERUNNING				PERCENTAGES		
Year	Team	Lg	G	AB	H	2B	3B	HR	TB	R	RBI	TBB	IBB	SO	HBP	SH	SF	SB	CS	SB%	GDP	Avg	OBP	SLG
1990	Expos	R	53	176	39	5	0	1	47	33	13	15	0	43	2	0	2	5	2	.71	1	.222	.287	.267
1991	Expos	R	60	237	60	17	3	3	92	44	30	23	0	41	2	0	4	20	7	.74	3	.253	.320	.388
1992	Rockford	A	127	448	97	21	2	12	158	63	49	47	0	141	3	4	2	44	13	.77	7	.217	.294	.353
	Wst Plm Bch	A	4	15	5	1	0	0	6	3	0	2	0	5	0	0	0	2	0	1.00	0	.333	.412	.400
1993	Wst Plm Bch	A	27	92	21	2	1	1	28	14	12	14	0	16	0	4	3	5	6	.45	1	.228	.321	.304
	Harrisburg	AA	99	386	94	14	10	6	146	70	35	37	0	97	3	3	1	27	8	.77	3	.244	.314	.378
1994	Harrisburg	AA	121	453	101	10	2	6	133	60	42	56	0	109	0	8	1	30	18	.63	8	.223	.308	.294
	5 Min. YEARS		491	1807	417	70	18	29	610	287	181	194	0	452	10	19	13	133	54	.71	23	.231	.307	.338

Jason Hardtke

Bats: Both Throws: Right Pos: SS Ht: 5'10" Wt: 175 Born: 09/15/71 Age: 23

			BATTING															BASERUNNING				PERCENTAGES		
Year	Team	Lg	G	AB	H	2B	3B	HR	TB	R	RBI	TBB	IBB	SO	HBP	SH	SF	SB	CS	SB%	GDP	Avg	OBP	SLG
1990	Burlington	R	39	142	38	7	0	4	57	18	16	23	0	19	2	0	0	11	1	.92	3	.268	.377	.401
1991	Columbus	A	139	534	155	26	8	12	233	104	81	75	5	48	7	6	6	22	4	.85	6	.290	.381	.436
1992	Kinston	A	6	19	4	0	0	0	4	3	1	4	0	4	0	0	0	0	0	.00	0	.211	.348	.211
	Waterloo	A	110	411	125	27	4	8	184	75	47	38	3	33	5	1	5	9	7	.56	9	.304	.366	.448
	High Desert	A	10	41	11	1	0	2	18	9	4	4	0	4	1	0	1	1	1	.50	1	.268	.340	.439
1993	Rancho Cuca	A	130	523	167	38	7	11	252	98	85	61	2	54	2	2	6	7	8	.47	12	.319	.389	.482
1994	Wichita	AA	75	255	60	15	1	5	92	26	29	21	1	44	0	2	4	1	2	.33	4	.235	.289	.361
	Rancho Cuca	A	4	13	4	0	0	0	4	2	0	3	0	2	0	0	0	0	1	.00	0	.308	.438	.308
	5 Min. YEARS		513	1938	564	114	20	42	844	335	267	229	11	208	17	11	22	51	24	.68	35	.291	.367	.436

Bubba Hardwick

Pitches: Left Bats: Left Pos: P Ht: 5'10" Wt: 170 Born: 01/18/72 Age: 23

Year	Team	Lg	G	GS	CG	GF	IP	BFP	H	R	ER	HR	SH	SF	HB	TBB	IBB	SO	WP	Bk	W	L	Pct.	ShO	Sv	ERA
1992	Brewers	R	4	0	0	3	7.1	37	11	6	2	0	0	0	1	1	0	9	0	1	0	0	.000	0	0	2.45
	Helena	R	5	0	0	5	8	29	1	0	0	0	0	0	2	3	0	6	0	1	0	0	.000	0	4	0.00
	Beloit	A	17	4	2	3	47	180	26	10	7	0	4	1	2	13	1	42	2	2	3	2	.600	1	0	1.34
1993	Stockton	A	61	0	0	41	83.2	365	95	32	27	4	2	1	5	30	0	59	5	0	6	2	.750	0	14	2.90
1994	El Paso	AA	8	0	0	5	11.2	49	9	6	6	2	0	0	1	7	0	7	0	0	0	0	.000	0	2	4.63
	Stockton	A	35	1	0	19	45.2	222	65	40	30	1	5	2	4	20	3	32	2	0	1	5	.167	0	8	5.91
	3 Min. YEARS		130	5	2	76	203.1	882	207	94	72	7	11	4	15	74	4	155	9	4	10	9	.526	1	28	3.19

Tim Harikkala

Pitches: Right Bats: Right Pos: P Ht: 6'2" Wt: 185 Born: 07/15/71 Age: 23

Year	Team	Lg	G	GS	CG	GF	IP	BFP	H	R	ER	HR	SH	SF	HB	TBB	IBB	SO	WP	Bk	W	L	Pct.	ShO	Sv	ERA
1992	Bellingham	A	15	2	0	2	33.1	145	37	15	10	2	3	2	0	16	0	18	1	2	2	0	1.000	0	1	2.70
1993	Bellingham	A	4	0	0	0	8	30	3	1	1	0	0	0	1	2	0	12	0	0	1	0	1.000	0	0	1.13
	Appleton	A	15	4	0	5	38.2	175	50	30	28	3	2	1	2	12	2	33	4	3	3	3	.500	0	0	6.52
1994	Appleton	A	13	13	3	0	93.2	373	69	31	20	6	2	3	5	24	0	63	5	0	8	3	.727	0	0	1.92
	Riverside	A	4	4	0	0	29	108	16	6	2	1	0	1	0	10	0	30	1	0	4	0	1.000	0	0	0.62
	Jacksonville	AA	9	9	0	0	54.1	245	70	30	24	4	1	3	1	19	0	22	4	0	4	1	.800	0	0	3.98
	3 Min. YEARS		60	32	3	7	257	1076	245	113	85	16	8	10	9	83	2	178	15	5	22	7	.759	0	1	2.98

Timothy Harkrider

Bats: Both Throws: Right Pos: SS Ht: 6'0" Wt: 180 Born: 09/05/71 Age: 23

Year	Team	Lg	G	AB	H	2B	3B	HR	TB	R	RBI	TBB	IBB	SO	HBP	SH	SF	SB	CS	SB%	GDP	Avg	OBP	SLG
1993	Boise	A	3	10	4	2	0	0	6	4	1	5	0	0	0	0	0	0	0	.00	0	.400	.600	.600
	Cedar Rapds	A	54	190	48	11	0	0	59	29	14	22	0	28	1	8	0	7	4	.64	5	.253	.333	.311
1994	Midland	AA	112	409	111	20	1	1	136	69	49	64	2	51	5	17	5	13	12	.52	10	.271	.373	.333
	2 Min. YEARS		169	609	163	33	1	1	201	102	64	91	2	79	6	25	5	20	16	.56	15	.268	.366	.330

Doug Harrah

Pitches: Right Bats: Right Pos: P Ht: 6'0" Wt: 175 Born: 04/23/69 Age: 26

Year	Team	Lg	G	GS	CG	GF	IP	BFP	H	R	ER	HR	SH	SF	HB	TBB	IBB	SO	WP	Bk	W	L	Pct.	ShO	Sv	ERA
1991	Pirates	R	5	1	0	0	12	49	8	4	3	0	0	0	0	6	0	10	0	2	1	2	.333	0	0	2.25
	Welland	A	11	7	0	0	47	206	51	22	16	4	1	1	4	10	0	47	1	0	3	3	.500	0	0	3.06
1992	Salem	A	32	16	1	9	137.1	578	133	73	58	10	3	2	8	43	0	90	11	1	8	8	.500	0	3	3.80
1993	Carolina	AA	6	6	1	0	25.2	130	40	28	27	3	0	1	3	9	0	17	0	0	1	4	.200	0	0	9.47
	Salem	A	24	19	0	1	115	500	125	61	54	14	4	6	6	26	0	85	4	3	8	5	.615	0	0	4.23
1994	Orlando	AA	55	0	0	35	80.2	332	70	38	27	4	8	4	4	18	4	43	6	1	7	4	.636	0	7	3.01
	4 Min. YEARS		133	49	2	45	417.2	1795	427	226	185	35	16	14	25	112	4	292	22	7	28	26	.519	0	10	3.99

Denny Harriger

Pitches: Right Bats: Right Pos: P Ht: 5'11" Wt: 185 Born: 07/21/69 Age: 25

Year	Team	Lg	G	GS	CG	GF	IP	BFP	H	R	ER	HR	SH	SF	HB	TBB	IBB	SO	WP	Bk	W	L	Pct.	ShO	Sv	ERA
1987	Kingsport	R	12	7	0	2	43.2	198	43	31	21	3	4	1	4	22	0	24	1	0	2	5	.286	0	0	4.33
1988	Kingsport	R	13	13	2	0	92.1	375	83	35	22	3	1	1	0	24	1	59	2	1	7	2	.778	1	0	2.14
1989	Pittsfield	A	3	3	1	0	21	84	20	4	4	0	2	0	1	0	0	17	0	0	2	0	1.000	1	0	1.71
	St.Lucie	A	11	11	0	0	67.2	284	72	33	24	6	0	0	2	17	0	17	1	0	5	3	.625	0	0	3.19
1990	St. Lucie	A	27	7	1	9	71.2	293	73	36	28	0	0	0	1	20	0	47	2	1	5	3	.625	0	2	3.52
1991	Columbia	A	2	2	1	0	11	37	5	0	0	0	1	0	0	2	0	13	0	0	2	0	1.000	1	0	0.00
	St. Lucie	A	14	11	2	1	71.1	286	67	20	18	2	4	2	1	12	0	37	1	0	6	1	.857	2	0	2.27
1992	Binghamton	AA	11	0	0	5	21.1	88	22	9	9	2	2	0	1	7	0	8	0	0	2	2	.500	0	0	3.80
	St. Lucie	A	27	10	0	9	88.1	372	89	30	22	1	6	0	3	14	1	65	5	1	7	3	.700	0	3	2.24
1993	Binghamton	AA	35	24	4	4	170.2	716	174	69	56	8	6	2	7	40	0	89	9	1	13	10	.565	3	1	2.95
1994	Las Vegas	AAA	30	25	3	0	157.1	720	216	122	104	16	6	5	4	44	0	87	3	1	6	11	.353	0	0	5.95
	8 Min. YEARS		185	113	14	30	816.1	3453	864	391	308	41	32	11	24	202	2	463	24	5	57	40	.588	8	6	3.40

Donald Harris

Bats: Right Throws: Right Pos: OF Ht: 6' 1" Wt: 185 Born: 11/12/67 Age: 27

Year	Team	Lg	G	AB	H	2B	3B	HR	TB	R	RBI	TBB	IBB	SO	HBP	SH	SF	SB	CS	SB%	GDP	Avg	OBP	SLG
1989	Butte	R	65	264	75	7	8	6	116	50	37	12	0	54	6	0	3	14	4	.78	6	.284	.326	.439
1990	Tulsa	AA	64	213	34	5	1	1	44	16	15	7	0	69	3	3	0	7	3	.70	0	.160	.197	.207
	Gastonia	A	58	221	46	10	0	3	65	27	13	14	0	63	2	4	0	15	8	.65	2	.208	.262	.294
1991	Tulsa	AA	130	450	102	17	8	11	168	47	53	26	1	118	7	7	0	9	6	.60	11	.227	.278	.373
1992	Tulsa	AA	83	303	77	15	2	11	129	39	39	9	1	85	7	3	1	4	3	.57	11	.254	.286	.426
1993	Okla City	AAA	96	367	93	13	9	6	142	48	40	23	0	89	4	4	5	4	4	.50	5	.253	.301	.387
1994	Okla. City	AAA	127	478	116	14	5	16	188	59	59	26	1	107	8	3	2	6	12	.33	5	.243	.292	.393

Year	Team	Lg	G	AB	H	2B	3B	HR	TB	R	RBI	TBB	IBB	SO	HBP	SH	SF	SB	CS	SB%	GDP	Avg	OBP	SLG
1991	Texas	AL	18	8	3	0	0	1	6	4	2	1	0	3	0	0	0	1	0	1.00	0	.375	.444	.750
1992	Texas	AL	24	33	6	1	0	0	7	3	1	0	0	15	0	0	0	1	0	1.00	0	.182	.182	.212
1993	Texas	AL	40	76	15	2	0	1	20	10	8	5	0	18	1	3	1	0	1	.00	0	.197	.253	.263
	6 Min. YEARS		623	2296	543	81	33	54	852	286	256	117	3	585	37	24	13	59	40	.60	40	.236	.283	.371
	3 Maj. YEARS		82	117	24	3	0	2	33	17	11	6	0	36	1	3	1	2	1	.67	0	.205	.248	.282

Pitches: Right Bats: Right Pos: P

Doug Harris

Ht: 6'4" Wt: 205 Born: 09/27/69 Age: 25

			HOW MUCH HE PITCHED						WHAT HE GAVE UP									THE RESULTS					
Year	Team	Lg	G	GS	CG	GF	IP	BFP	H	R	ER	HR	SH	SF	HB	TBB	IBB	SO	WP	Bk	W	L	Pct.	ShO	Sv	ERA
1990	Eugene	A	15	15	0	0	69.1	309	74	46	34	5	3	2	4	28	0	46	6	2	4	5	.444	0	0	4.41
1991	Appleton	A	7	7	1	0	45	181	41	14	11	1	2	1	1	10	1	39	2	0	2	2	.500	1	0	2.20
	Baseball Cy	A	19	18	3	0	116.2	466	92	38	32	3	4	3	3	27	4	84	4	1	10	6	.625	1	0	2.47
1992	Baseball Cy	A	7	7	0	0	29.1	122	25	11	7	3	0	0	2	6	0	22	2	0	0	2	.000	0	0	2.15
1993	Memphis	AA	22	12	1	4	86.2	367	99	52	45	6	3	2	3	13	0	38	3	0	3	6	.333	0	1	4.67
1994	Memphis	AA	30	13	0	9	100	449	122	70	53	8	4	10	9	28	2	43	6	0	3	9	.250	0	2	4.77
	5 Min. YEARS		100	72	5	13	447	1894	453	231	182	26	16	18	22	112	7	272	23	3	22	30	.423	2	2	3.66

Bats: Left Throws: Left Pos: 1B

Mike Harris

Ht: 5'11" Wt: 195 Born: 04/30/70 Age: 25

			BATTING														BASERUNNING				PERCENTAGES		
Year	Team	Lg	G	AB	H	2B	3B	HR	TB	R	RBI	TBB	IBB	SO	HBP	SH	SF	SB	CS	SB%	GDP	Avg	OBP	SLG
1991	Beloit	A	50	145	31	4	2	1	42	27	12	27	1	30	1	5	0	16	3	.84	4	.214	.341	.290
1992	Stockton	A	40	101	27	6	4	1	44	15	16	11	0	21	0	0	0	6	0	1.00	1	.267	.339	.436
1993	Stockton	A	104	363	112	17	3	9	162	64	65	63	4	56	6	8	4	19	7	.73	5	.309	.415	.446
1994	El Paso	AA	105	372	102	22	12	5	163	76	61	55	4	68	5	1	4	12	6	.67	8	.274	.372	.438
	4 Min. YEARS		299	981	272	49	21	16	411	182	154	156	9	175	12	14	8	53	16	.77	18	.277	.380	.419

Pitches: Right Bats: Right Pos: P

Pep Harris

Ht: 6'2" Wt: 185 Born: 09/23/72 Age: 22

			HOW MUCH HE PITCHED						WHAT HE GAVE UP									THE RESULTS					
Year	Team	Lg	G	GS	CG	GF	IP	BFP	H	R	ER	HR	SH	SF	HB	TBB	IBB	SO	WP	Bk	W	L	Pct.	ShO	Sv	ERA
1991	Burlington	R	13	13	0	0	65.2	292	67	30	24	7	4	2	3	31	0	47	5	0	4	3	.571	0	0	3.29
1992	Columbus	A	18	17	0	0	90.2	400	88	51	37	10	3	6	2	51	1	57	11	0	7	4	.636	0	0	3.67
1993	Columbus	A	26	17	0	4	119	510	113	67	56	7	4	1	4	44	0	82	6	0	7	8	.467	0	0	4.24
1994	Kinston	A	27	0	0	20	32.2	140	21	14	7	1	0	0	2	16	0	37	2	0	4	1	.800	0	8	1.93
	Canton-Akrn	AA	24	0	0	22	20.1	86	9	5	5	0	1	0	2	13	2	15	1	0	2	0	1.000	0	12	2.21
	4 Min. YEARS		108	47	0	46	328.1	1428	298	167	129	25	12	9	13	155	3	238	25	0	24	16	.600	0	20	3.54

Pitches: Right Bats: Right Pos: P

Reggie Harris

Ht: 6'1" Wt: 190 Born: 08/12/68 Age: 26

			HOW MUCH HE PITCHED						WHAT HE GAVE UP									THE RESULTS					
Year	Team	Lg	G	GS	CG	GF	IP	BFP	H	R	ER	HR	SH	SF	HB	TBB	IBB	SO	WP	Bk	W	L	Pct.	ShO	Sv	ERA
1987	Elmira	A	9	8	1	0	46.2	212	50	29	26	3	1	1	6	22	0	25	3	0	2	3	.400	1	0	5.01
1988	Lynchburg	A	17	11	0	2	64	310	86	60	53	8	0	3	4	34	5	48	5	7	1	8	.111	0	0	7.45
	Elmira	A	10	10	0	0	54.1	237	56	37	32	5	1	3	2	28	0	46	1	2	3	6	.333	0	0	5.30
1989	Winter Havn	A	29	26	1	2	153.1	670	144	81	68	6	5	11	7	77	2	85	7	4	10	13	.435	0	0	3.99
1990	Huntsville	AA	5	5	0	0	29.2	131	26	12	10	3	1	1	4	16	0	34	4	0	0	2	.000	0	0	3.03
1991	Tacoma	AAA	16	15	0	0	83	380	83	55	46	11	0	4	3	58	0	72	5	0	5	4	.556	0	0	4.99
1992	Tacoma	AAA	29	28	1	0	149.2	676	141	108	95	12	3	5	6	117	0	111	20	6	6	16	.273	0	0	5.71
1993	Jacksnville	AA	9	8	0	1	37.2	167	33	24	20	4	1	1	3	22	0	30	3	2	1	4	.200	0	0	4.78
	Calgary	AAA	17	15	1	0	88.1	393	74	55	51	7	1	3	8	61	1	75	10	0	8	6	.571	0	0	5.20
1994	Calgary	AAA	20	18	0	0	98.2	481	137	99	89	21	0	4	8	51	1	73	5	2	6	9	.400	0	0	8.12
1990	Oakland	AL	16	1	0	9	41.1	168	25	16	16	5	1	2	2	21	1	31	2	0	1	0	1.000	0	0	3.48
1991	Oakland	AL	2	0	0	1	3	15	5	4	4	0	0	1	0	3	1	2	2	0	0	0	.000	0	0	12.00
	8 Min. YEARS		161	144	4	5	805.1	3657	830	560	490	80	13	35	51	486	9	599	63	23	42	71	.372	1	0	5.48
	2 Maj. YEARS		18	1	0	10	44.1	183	30	20	20	5	1	3	2	24	2	33	4	0	1	0	1.000	0	0	4.06

Pitches: Right Bats: Right Pos: P

Brian Harrison

Ht: 6'1" Wt: 175 Born: 12/18/68 Age: 26

			HOW MUCH HE PITCHED						WHAT HE GAVE UP									THE RESULTS					
Year	Team	Lg	G	GS	CG	GF	IP	BFP	H	R	ER	HR	SH	SF	HB	TBB	IBB	SO	WP	Bk	W	L	Pct.	ShO	Sv	ERA
1992	Appleton	A	16	15	1	0	98.2	419	114	47	40	5	1	5	1	16	0	54	2	1	5	6	.455	0	0	3.65
1993	Wilmington	A	26	26	1	0	173	707	168	76	63	16	7	6	2	38	0	98	6	1	13	6	.684	1	0	3.28
1994	Memphis	AA	28	28	1	0	172	717	180	87	69	11	5	9	5	31	0	94	2	0	9	10	.474	0	0	3.61
	3 Min. YEARS		70	69	3	0	443.2	1843	462	210	172	32	13	20	8	85	0	246	10	2	27	22	.551	1	0	3.49

Bats: Right Throws: Right Pos: C

Mike Harrison

Ht: 6'2" Wt: 210 Born: 11/30/69 Age: 25

			BATTING														BASERUNNING				PERCENTAGES		
Year	Team	Lg	G	AB	H	2B	3B	HR	TB	R	RBI	TBB	IBB	SO	HBP	SH	SF	SB	CS	SB%	GDP	Avg	OBP	SLG
1991	Billings	R	57	200	55	9	0	4	76	27	17	24	2	52	2	0	2	2	2	.50	1	.275	.355	.380
1992	Chston-Vw	A	117	395	95	20	1	10	147	38	51	33	0	122	8	4	6	5	2	.71	9	.241	.308	.372

Year	Team	Lg	G	AB	H	2B	3B	HR	TB	R	RBI	TBB	IBB	SO	HBP	SH	SF	SB	CS	SB%	GDP	Avg	OBP	SLG
1993	Winston-Sal	A	72	238	60	10	0	4	82	20	23	15	0	46	1	0	1	2	1	.67	6	.252	.298	.345
1994	Chattanooga	AA	5	17	2	1	0	0	3	1	1	1	0	5	0	0	0	0	0	.00	0	.118	.167	.176
	Winston-Sal	A	66	210	45	11	1	14	100	25	44	19	0	72	3	1	4	2	0	1.00	3	.214	.284	.476
	4 Min. YEARS		317	1060	257	51	2	32	408	111	136	92	2	297	14	5	13	11	5	.69	19	.242	.308	.385

Chris Hart

Bats: Right Throws: Right Pos: OF   Ht: 6'0" Wt: 190 Born: 05/02/69 Age: 26

			BATTING															BASERUNNING				PERCENTAGES		
Year	Team	Lg	G	AB	H	2B	3B	HR	TB	R	RBI	TBB	IBB	SO	HBP	SH	SF	SB	CS	SB%	GDP	Avg	OBP	SLG
1990	Sou Oregon	A	67	239	63	14	2	6	99	50	32	37	0	85	11	1	3	15	3	.83	7	.264	.383	.414
1991	Sou Oregon	A	9	21	3	1	0	0	4	3	1	1	0	5	1	0	0	0	0	.00	0	.143	.217	.190
	Modesto	A	37	88	22	4	0	0	26	9	13	8	0	22	3	0	2	2	2	.50	2	.250	.327	.295
1992	Modesto	A	120	450	128	20	3	13	193	76	86	35	4	135	18	0	2	15	9	.63	14	.284	.358	.429
1993	Huntsville	AA	103	301	77	7	3	6	108	39	42	10	0	82	11	5	1	12	9	.57	5	.256	.303	.359
1994	Huntsville	AA	117	365	85	13	5	9	135	45	52	23	0	101	11	7	4	7	7	.50	7	.233	.295	.370
	5 Min. YEARS		453	1464	378	59	13	34	565	222	226	114	4	430	55	13	12	51	30	.63	35	.258	.333	.386

Dean Hartgraves

Pitches: Left Bats: Right Pos: P   Ht: 6'0" Wt: 185 Born: 08/12/66 Age: 28

			HOW MUCH HE PITCHED						WHAT HE GAVE UP										THE RESULTS					
Year	Team	Lg	G	GS	CG	GF	IP	BFP	H	R	ER	HR	SH	SF	HB	TBB	IBB	SO	WP	Bk	W	L	Pct.	ShO	Sv	ERA
1987	Auburn	A	23	0	0	12	31.2	157	31	24	14	1	3	0	1	27	4	42	1	0	0	5	.000	0	2	3.98
1988	Asheville	A	34	13	2	7	118.1	523	131	70	59	9	2	8	5	47	2	83	8	5	5	9	.357	1	0	4.49
1989	Asheville	A	19	19	4	0	120.1	542	140	66	55	6	5	3	4	49	2	87	5	3	8	5	.385	0	0	4.11
	Osceola	A	7	6	1	0	39.2	165	36	20	13	0	2	2	2	12	0	21	4	0	3	3	.500	1	0	2.95
1990	Columbus	AA	33	14	0	6	99.2	454	108	66	52	8	7	4	3	48	1	64	6	0	8	8	.500	0	0	4.70
1991	Jackson	AA	19	9	3	5	74	302	60	25	22	3	6	4	2	25	3	44	4	0	6	5	.545	0	0	2.68
	Tucson	AAA	16	3	1	4	43.2	189	47	17	15	2	2	3	0	20	1	18	2	0	3	0	1.000	1	0	3.09
1992	Tucson	AAA	5	1	0	0	8	61	26	24	22	1	0	0	0	9	0	6	4	0	0	1	.000	0	0	24.75
	Jackson	AA	22	22	3	0	146.2	585	127	54	45	7	4	1	3	40	1	92	9	1	9	6	.600	2	0	2.76
1993	Tucson	AAA	23	10	0	2	77.2	369	90	65	55	7	2	6	4	40	0	42	5	0	1	6	.143	0	0	6.37
1994	Tucson	AAA	47	4	0	16	97.2	429	106	64	55	11	3	4	1	36	2	54	4	0	7	2	.778	0	3	5.07
	8 Min. YEARS		248	101	14	52	857.1	3776	902	495	407	55	36	35	25	353	16	553	52	9	47	53	.470	5	5	4.27

Jeff Hartsock

Pitches: Right Bats: Right Pos: P   Ht: 6'0" Wt: 190 Born: 11/19/66 Age: 28

			HOW MUCH HE PITCHED						WHAT HE GAVE UP										THE RESULTS					
Year	Team	Lg	G	GS	CG	GF	IP	BFP	H	R	ER	HR	SH	SF	HB	TBB	IBB	SO	WP	Bk	W	L	Pct.	ShO	Sv	ERA
1988	Great Falls	R	14	14	1	0	81	334	62	30	24	3	1	0	2	26	1	108	8	4	7	2	.778	0	0	2.67
1989	Bakersfield	A	26	26	5	0	164	670	123	64	48	5	4	2	4	62	0	146	11	2	12	5	.706	2	0	2.63
1990	San Antonio	AA	16	16	0	0	94	401	88	42	41	2	3	2	2	42	2	68	4	2	6	4	.600	0	0	3.93
	Albuquerque	AAA	11	10	0	0	46.1	226	62	38	32	5	1	0	0	30	1	33	4	2	3	3	.500	0	0	6.22
1991	Albuquerque	AAA	29	26	0	0	154	678	153	80	65	12	2	5	3	78	0	123	9	1	12	6	.667	0	0	3.80
1992	Iowa	AAA	27	27	2	0	173.1	744	177	91	84	13	9	8	10	61	2	87	3	1	5	12	.294	0	0	4.36
1993	Orlando	AA	8	8	1	0	49.1	204	43	24	19	3	2	0	2	17	0	24	2	1	3	4	.429	1	0	3.47
	Iowa	AAA	9	9	0	0	47	219	68	35	33	6	2	1	1	20	1	17	1	0	0	4	.000	0	0	6.32
	Phoenix	AAA	12	7	0	2	55.1	253	83	36	34	3	2	1	1	20	1	35	4	3	2	5	.286	0	0	5.53
1994	Louisville	AAA	9	4	0	0	33.1	152	41	24	23	4	2	4	0	14	3	16	0	0	1	2	.333	0	0	6.21
1992	Chicago	NL	4	0	0	0	9.1	46	15	7	7	2	1	1	0	4	0	6	2	0	0	0	.000	0	0	6.75
	7 Min. YEARS		161	146	9	3	897.2	3881	900	464	403	56	28	23	25	370	11	657	46	16	51	47	.520	3	0	4.04

Raymond Harvey

Bats: Left Throws: Left Pos: OF   Ht: 6'1" Wt: 185 Born: 01/01/69 Age: 26

			BATTING															BASERUNNING				PERCENTAGES		
Year	Team	Lg	G	AB	H	2B	3B	HR	TB	R	RBI	TBB	IBB	SO	HBP	SH	SF	SB	CS	SB%	GDP	Avg	OBP	SLG
1991	Columbus	A	129	443	124	22	7	10	190	75	80	71	6	66	10	2	9	7	4	.64	12	.280	.385	.429
1992	Kinston	A	97	331	94	18	0	2	118	35	45	36	4	43	4	1	2	2	1	.67	6	.284	.359	.356
1993	Canton-Akrn	AA	14	41	10	1	0	0	11	5	4	7	0	5	1	3	1	0	1	.00	1	.244	.360	.268
	Kinston	A	88	335	95	19	2	3	127	36	39	28	1	43	3	3	1	3	6	.33	8	.284	.343	.379
1994	Canton-Akrn	AA	137	508	149	24	5	6	201	66	72	61	6	88	5	2	3	1	5	.17	14	.293	.373	.396
	4 Min. YEARS		465	1658	472	84	14	21	647	217	240	203	17	245	23	11	16	13	17	.43	41	.285	.367	.390

Brad Hassinger

Pitches: Right Bats: Right Pos: P   Ht: 6'0" Wt: 195 Born: 11/29/67 Age: 27

			HOW MUCH HE PITCHED						WHAT HE GAVE UP										THE RESULTS					
Year	Team	Lg	G	GS	CG	GF	IP	BFP	H	R	ER	HR	SH	SF	HB	TBB	IBB	SO	WP	Bk	W	L	Pct.	ShO	Sv	ERA
1990	Princeton	R	13	13	5	0	91	353	66	30	22	6	2	3	6	20	1	47	4	2	7	4	.636	1	0	2.18
1991	Spartanburg	A	21	21	4	0	123.2	513	120	54	44	5	3	3	4	31	0	87	6	3	8	8	.500	2	0	3.20
1992	Spartanburg	A	20	2	0	14	46.2	187	38	9	7	1	2	1	1	11	2	34	5	0	4	1	.800	0	5	1.35
	Clearwater	A	12	10	0	0	63.2	260	63	22	18	0	1	0	3	10	0	29	1	0	6	1	.857	0	0	2.54
1993	Reading	AA	1	1	0	0	2	9	4	2	2	0	0	0	0	0	0	0	1	0	0	0	.000	0	0	9.00
	Durham	A	14	0	0	4	30.1	116	20	12	7	2	1	0	4	4	0	25	0	0	4	1	.800	0	0	2.08
	Greenville	AA	12	0	0	3	23	94	19	4	4	1	4	0	0	8	3	11	2	0	3	1	.750	0	1	1.57

		G	GS	CG	GF	IP	BFP	H	R	ER	HR	SH	SF	HB	TBB	IBB	SO	WP	Bk	W	L	Pct.	ShO	Sv	ERA
1994 Greenville	AA	42	2	0	12	85.1	361	88	36	33	6	2	3	0	22	3	57	2	0	3	8	.273	0	2	3.48
5 Min. YEARS		135	48	9	34	465.2	1893	418	169	137	21	15	10	18	106	9	290	21	5	35	24	.593	3	7	2.65

Chris Hatcher

Bats: Right **Throws:** Right **Pos:** OF   **Ht:** 6'3" **Wt:** 220 **Born:** 01/07/69 **Age:** 26

			BATTING														BASERUNNING				PERCENTAGES		
Year Team	Lg	G	AB	H	2B	3B	HR	TB	R	RBI	TBB	IBB	SO	HBP	SH	SF	SB	CS	SB%	GDP	Avg	OBP	SLG
1990 Auburn	A	72	259	64	10	0	9	101	37	45	27	3	86	5	0	5	8	2	.80	4	.247	.324	.390
1991 Burlington	A	129	497	117	23	6	13	191	69	65	46	4	180	9	0	4	10	5	.67	6	.235	.309	.384
1992 Osceola	A	97	367	103	19	6	17	185	49	68	20	1	97	5	0	5	11	0	1.00	5	.281	.322	.504
1993 Jackson	AA	101	367	95	15	3	15	161	45	64	11	0	104	11	0	3	5	8	.38	8	.259	.298	.439
1994 Tucson	AAA	108	349	104	28	4	12	176	55	73	19	0	90	4	0	6	5	1	.83	6	.298	.336	.504
5 Min. YEARS		507	1839	483	95	19	66	814	255	315	123	8	557	34	0	23	39	16	.71	29	.263	.317	.443

Hilly Hathaway

Pitches: Left **Bats:** Left **Pos:** P   **Ht:** 6'4" **Wt:** 195 **Born:** 09/12/69 **Age:** 25

		HOW MUCH HE PITCHED						WHAT HE GAVE UP												THE RESULTS					
Year Team	Lg	G	GS	CG	GF	IP	BFP	H	R	ER	HR	SH	SF	HB	TBB	IBB	SO	WP	Bk	W	L	Pct.	ShO	Sv	ERA
1990 Boise	A	15	15	0	0	86.1	337	57	18	14	1	1	3	2	25	0	113	7	5	8	2	.800	1	0	1.46
1991 Quad City	A	20	20	1	0	129	545	126	58	48	5	4	1	7	41	1	110	11	3	9	6	.600	1	0	3.35
1992 Palm Sprngs	A	3	3	2	0	24	98	25	5	4	1	0	0	0	3	0	17	0	0	2	1	.667	1	0	1.50
Midland	AA	14	14	1	0	95.1	378	90	39	34	2	1	1	8	10	0	69	2	2	7	2	.778	0	0	3.21
1993 Vancouver	AAA	12	12	0	0	70.1	291	60	38	32	5	1	2	2	27	0	44	4	1	7	0	1.000	0	0	4.09
1994 Las Vegas	AAA	26	15	0	1	95	453	121	82	66	15	2	5	5	48	0	68	6	2	2	9	.182	0	0	6.25
1992 California	AL	2	1	0	0	5.2	29	8	5	5	1	1	1	0	3	0	1	0	0	0	0	.000	0	0	7.94
1993 California	AL	11	11	0	0	57.1	253	71	35	32	6	1	3	5	26	1	11	5	1	4	3	.571	0	0	5.02
5 Min. YEARS		90	79	4	1	500	2102	479	240	198	29	9	12	24	154	1	421	30	13	35	20	.636	1	0	3.56
2 Maj. YEARS		13	12	0	0	63	282	79	40	37	7	2	4	5	29	1	12	5	1	4	3	.571	0	0	5.29

Scott Hatteberg

Bats: Left **Throws:** Right **Pos:** C   **Ht:** 6'1" **Wt:** 185 **Born:** 12/14/69 **Age:** 25

			BATTING														BASERUNNING				PERCENTAGES		
Year Team	Lg	G	AB	H	2B	3B	HR	TB	R	RBI	TBB	IBB	SO	HBP	SH	SF	SB	CS	SB%	GDP	Avg	OBP	SLG
1991 Winter Havn	A	56	191	53	7	3	1	69	21	24	22	4	22	0	2	2	1	2	.33	6	.277	.349	.361
Lynchburg	A	8	25	5	1	0	0	6	4	3	7	0	6	0	0	0	0	0	.00	0	.200	.375	.240
1992 New Britain	AA	103	297	69	13	2	1	89	28	30	41	2	49	2	1	3	1	3	.25	6	.232	.327	.300
1993 New Britain	AA	68	227	63	10	2	7	98	35	28	42	3	38	1	1	0	1	3	.25	6	.278	.393	.432
Pawtucket	AAA	18	53	10	0	0	1	13	6	2	6	0	12	1	2	0	0	0	.00	5	.189	.283	.245
1994 New Britain	AA	20	68	18	4	1	1	27	6	9	7	1	9	0	0	1	0	2	.00	2	.265	.329	.397
Pawtucket	AAA	78	238	56	14	0	7	91	26	19	32	1	49	3	2	1	2	1	.67	14	.235	.332	.382
4 Min. YEARS		351	1099	274	49	8	18	393	126	115	157	11	185	7	8	7	5	11	.31	39	.249	.345	.358

Ryan Hawblitzel

Pitches: Right **Bats:** Right **Pos:** P   **Ht:** 6'2" **Wt:** 170 **Born:** 04/30/71 **Age:** 24

		HOW MUCH HE PITCHED						WHAT HE GAVE UP												THE RESULTS					
Year Team	Lg	G	GS	CG	GF	IP	BFP	H	R	ER	HR	SH	SF	HB	TBB	IBB	SO	WP	Bk	W	L	Pct.	ShO	Sv	ERA
1990 Huntington	R	14	14	2	0	75.2	322	72	38	33	8	0	0	6	25	0	71	2	0	6	5	.545	1	0	3.93
1991 Winston-Sal	A	20	20	5	0	134	552	110	40	34	7	5	7	7	47	0	103	8	1	15	2	.882	2	0	2.28
Charlotte	AA	5	5	1	0	33.2	141	31	14	12	2	5	2	3	12	3	25	0	0	1	2	.333	1	0	3.21
1992 Charlotte	AA	28	28	3	0	174.2	727	180	84	73	18	5	5	4	38	3	119	8	0	12	8	.600	1	0	3.76
1993 Colo Sprngs	AAA	29	28	2	0	165.1	764	221	129	113	16	10	9	4	49	0	90	3	0	8	13	.381	0	0	6.15
1994 Colo. Spmg	AAA	28	28	3	0	163	732	200	119	111	21	6	2	10	53	2	103	5	0	10	10	.500	1	0	6.13
5 Min. YEARS		124	123	16	0	746.1	3238	814	424	376	72	31	25	34	224	8	511	26	1	52	40	.565	6	0	4.53

LaTroy Hawkins

Pitches: Right **Bats:** Right **Pos:** P   **Ht:** 6'5" **Wt:** 195 **Born:** 12/21/72 **Age:** 22

		HOW MUCH HE PITCHED						WHAT HE GAVE UP												THE RESULTS					
Year Team	Lg	G	GS	CG	GF	IP	BFP	H	R	ER	HR	SH	SF	HB	TBB	IBB	SO	WP	Bk	W	L	Pct.	ShO	Sv	ERA
1991 Twins	R	11	11	0	0	55	251	62	34	29	2	0	1	3	26	0	47	6	3	4	3	.571	0	0	4.75
1992 Twins	R	6	6	1	0	36.1	161	36	19	13	1	0	0	3	10	0	35	3	2	3	2	.600	0	0	3.22
Elizabethtn	R	5	5	1	0	26.2	115	21	12	10	2	0	0	0	11	0	36	0	1	0	1	.000	0	0	3.38
1993 Ft.Wayne	A	26	23	4	1	157.1	619	110	53	36	5	4	4	4	41	0	179	8	2	15	5	.750	3	0	2.06
1994 Fort Myers	A	6	6	1	0	38.2	153	32	10	10	1	2	0	2	6	0	36	0	0	4	0	1.000	1	0	2.33
Nashville	AA	11	11	0	0	73.1	297	50	23	19	2	3	1	3	28	0	53	2	1	9	2	.818	0	0	2.33
Salt Lake	AAA	12	12	1	0	81.2	353	92	42	37	8	2	2	5	33	0	37	4	2	5	4	.556	0	0	4.08
4 Min. YEARS		77	74	9	1	469	1949	403	193	154	21	11	8	20	155	0	423	23	11	40	17	.702	4	0	2.96

Scott Haws

Bats: Left **Throws:** Right **Pos:** C   **Ht:** 6'0" **Wt:** 190 **Born:** 01/11/72 **Age:** 23

			BATTING														BASERUNNING				PERCENTAGES		
Year Team	Lg	G	AB	H	2B	3B	HR	TB	R	RBI	TBB	IBB	SO	HBP	SH	SF	SB	CS	SB%	GDP	Avg	OBP	SLG
1992 Martinsvlle	R	36	128	27	3	0	0	30	20	9	18	2	12	0	0	0	0	0	.00	3	.211	.308	.234
1993 Spartanburg	A	73	234	57	7	0	1	67	23	21	37	0	44	0	1	1	2	3	.40	5	.244	.346	.286

Year	Team	Lg	G	AB	H	2B	3B	HR	TB	R	RBI	TBB	IBB	SO	HBP	SH	SF	SB	CS	SB%	GDP	Avg	OBP	SLG
1994	Clearwater	A	64	181	42	8	1	1	55	18	14	27	3	19	0	2	0	0	1	.00	4	.232	.332	.304
	Reading	AA	10	26	6	0	0	0	6	3	1	4	0	4	0	0	0	0	1	.00	3	.231	.333	.231
	3 Min. YEARS		183	569	132	18	1	2	158	64	45	86	5	79	0	3	1	2	5	.29	15	.232	.332	.278

Bats: Right   Throws: Right   Pos: SS

Dave Hayden

Ht: 5'11"   Wt: 170   Born: 12/01/69   Age: 25

			BATTING														BASERUNNING				PERCENTAGES		
Year	Team	Lg	G	AB	H	2B	3B	HR	TB	R	RBI	TBB	IBB	SO	HBP	SH	SF	SB	CS	SB%	GDP	Avg	OBP	SLG
1991	Batavia	A	50	158	35	2	0	0	37	16	9	13	0	24	3	2	0	3	1	.75	5	.222	.293	.234
1992	Spartanburg	A	125	394	88	11	2	0	103	46	29	35	1	66	3	9	3	7	1	.88	8	.223	.290	.261
1993	Clearwater	A	97	290	90	13	0	0	103	42	27	39	1	38	6	1	2	8	9	.47	5	.310	.401	.355
1994	Reading	AA	87	234	59	9	1	4	82	27	24	27	1	56	1	3	1	3	1	.75	4	.252	.331	.350
	4 Min. YEARS		359	1076	272	35	3	4	325	131	89	114	3	184	13	15	6	21	12	.64	22	.253	.330	.302

Pitches: Right   Bats: Right   Pos: P

Jimmy Haynes

Ht: 6'4"   Wt: 175   Born: 09/05/72   Age: 22

			HOW MUCH HE PITCHED					WHAT HE GAVE UP										THE RESULTS					
Year	Team	Lg	G	GS	CG	GF	IP	BFP	H	R	ER	HR	SH	SF	HB	TBB	IBB	SO	WP	Bk	W	L	Pct.	ShO	Sv	ERA
1991	Orioles	R	14	8	1	4	62	256	44	27	11	0	1	3	0	21	0	67	6	1	3	2	.600	0	2	1.60
1992	Kane County	A	24	24	4	0	144	616	131	66	41	2	4	9	4	45	0	141	12	7	7	11	.389	0	0	2.56
1993	Frederick	A	27	27	2	0	172.1	707	139	73	58	13	2	3	1	61	1	174	20	4	12	8	.600	1	0	3.03
1994	Rochester	AAA	3	3	0	0	13.1	68	20	12	10	3	0	1	0	6	0	14	0	0	1	0	1.000	0	0	6.75
	Bowie	AA	25	25	5	0	173.2	705	154	67	56	16	6	4	3	46	1	177	8	3	13	8	.619	1	0	2.90
	4 Min. YEARS		93	87	12	4	565.1	2352	488	245	176	34	13	20	9	179	2	573	46	15	36	29	.554	2	2	2.80

Bats: Right   Throws: Right   Pos: OF

Steve Hazlett

Ht: 5'11"   Wt: 170   Born: 03/30/70   Age: 25

			BATTING														BASERUNNING				PERCENTAGES		
Year	Team	Lg	G	AB	H	2B	3B	HR	TB	R	RBI	TBB	IBB	SO	HBP	SH	SF	SB	CS	SB%	GDP	Avg	OBP	SLG
1991	Elizabethtn	R	64	210	42	11	0	4	65	50	24	63	0	53	6	1	1	13	7	.65	0	.200	.396	.310
1992	Kenosha	A	107	362	96	23	4	6	145	68	32	52	0	77	7	2	4	20	9	.69	5	.265	.365	.401
1993	Ft.Myers	A	29	115	39	5	2	0	48	19	6	15	1	21	1	2	0	12	5	.71	0	.339	.420	.417
1994	Nashville	AA	123	457	134	31	1	14	209	63	54	37	1	99	8	6	3	9	3	.75	3	.293	.354	.457
	4 Min. YEARS		323	1144	311	70	7	24	467	200	116	167	2	250	22	11	8	54	24	.69	8	.272	.373	.408

Bats: Right   Throws: Right   Pos: OF

Lee Heath

Ht: 5'10"   Wt: 180   Born: 12/26/69   Age: 25

			BATTING														BASERUNNING				PERCENTAGES		
Year	Team	Lg	G	AB	H	2B	3B	HR	TB	R	RBI	TBB	IBB	SO	HBP	SH	SF	SB	CS	SB%	GDP	Avg	OBP	SLG
1988	Braves	R	48	139	28	3	0	0	31	10	5	5	0	38	1	3	2	7	6	.54	1	.201	.231	.223
1989	Pulaski	R	65	236	62	11	1	0	75	50	21	44	0	60	3	4	1	40	17	.70	1	.263	.384	.318
1990	Sumter	A	126	455	94	9	5	2	119	59	25	39	1	111	6	11	1	35	22	.61	7	.207	.277	.262
1991	Macon	A	126	399	94	9	3	3	118	55	44	29	0	83	5	9	3	60	21	.74	3	.236	.294	.296
1992	Durham	A	129	473	131	22	6	7	186	71	47	26	1	99	1	20	2	50	18	.74	2	.277	.315	.393
	Greenville	AA	2	4	1	0	0	1	4	2	3	1	0	1	1	0	0	1	1	.50	1	.250	.500	1.000
1993	Greenville	AA	112	432	105	15	6	6	150	47	36	23	0	108	7	1	2	16	18	.47	13	.243	.291	.347
1994	High Desert	A	102	402	109	16	5	20	195	72	71	33	0	98	2	3	2	22	9	.71	5	.271	.328	.485
	Richmond	AAA	13	27	6	0	1	0	8	4	1	0	0	6	1	1	0	1	0	1.00	0	.222	.250	.296
	7 Min. YEARS		723	2567	630	85	27	39	886	370	253	200	2	604	27	52	13	232	112	.67	33	.245	.305	.345

Pitches: Right   Bats: Right   Pos: P

Mike Heathcott

Ht: 6'3"   Wt: 180   Born: 05/16/69   Age: 26

			HOW MUCH HE PITCHED					WHAT HE GAVE UP										THE RESULTS					
Year	Team	Lg	G	GS	CG	GF	IP	BFP	H	R	ER	HR	SH	SF	HB	TBB	IBB	SO	WP	Bk	W	L	Pct.	ShO	Sv	ERA
1991	Utica	A	6	6	0	0	33	138	26	19	13	4	1	1	1	14	0	14	1	0	3	1	.750	0	0	3.55
1992	South Bend	A	15	14	0	1	82	340	67	28	14	3	5	2	0	32	0	49	8	0	9	5	.643	0	0	1.54
1993	Sarasota	A	26	26	6	0	179.1	739	174	90	72	5	12	10	4	62	7	83	16	1	11	10	.524	1	0	3.61
1994	Birmingham	AA	17	17	0	0	98	449	126	71	63	11	1	6	2	44	4	44	9	0	3	7	.300	0	0	5.79
	Pr. William	A	9	8	1	1	43	193	51	28	19	7	1	0	1	23	0	27	6	0	1	2	.333	0	0	3.98
	4 Min. YEARS		73	71	7	2	435.1	1859	444	236	181	30	20	19	8	175	11	217	40	1	27	25	.519	1	0	3.74

Pitches: Left   Bats: Left   Pos: P

Keith Heberling

Ht: 6'3"   Wt: 200   Born: 09/21/72   Age: 22

			HOW MUCH HE PITCHED					WHAT HE GAVE UP										THE RESULTS					
Year	Team	Lg	G	GS	CG	GF	IP	BFP	H	R	ER	HR	SH	SF	HB	TBB	IBB	SO	WP	Bk	W	L	Pct.	ShO	Sv	ERA
1993	Oneonta	A	4	3	0	0	27.1	105	20	4	3	0	0	1	0	8	0	27	0	0	2	1	.667	0	0	0.99
	Greensboro	A	11	11	0	0	69.2	271	47	18	16	3	0	3	3	18	0	74	3	0	8	1	.889	0	0	2.07
1994	Tampa	A	22	22	1	0	138.2	596	149	60	45	7	0	3	5	37	0	121	2	1	11	7	.611	0	0	2.92
	Albany-Colo	AA	6	6	1	0	35	152	44	23	22	3	0	2	2	6	0	21	1	0	1	3	.250	0	0	5.66
	2 Min. YEARS		43	42	2	0	270.2	1124	260	105	86	13	0	9	10	69	0	243	6	1	22	12	.647	0	0	2.86

Kurt Heble

Pitches: Right Bats: Right Pos: P   Ht: 6'3" Wt: 205 Born: 02/09/69 Age: 26

Year	Team	Lg	G	GS	CG	GF	IP	BFP	H	R	ER	HR	SH	SF	HB	TBB	IBB	SO	WP	Bk	W	L	Pct.	ShO	Sv	ERA
1991	St.Cathrnes	A	18	0	0	17	27	115	23	10	3	0	3	0	1	9	1	25	1	0	4	4	.500	0	3	1.00
1992	Myrtle Bch	A	8	0	0	5	9.2	42	7	5	4	0	0	1	0	7	0	13	3	0	0	0	.000	0	1	3.72
1993	Dunedin	A	41	0	0	21	50.2	217	35	16	14	1	2	1	3	34	1	66	4	1	6	1	.857	0	4	2.49
	Knoxville	AA	6	0	0	2	9.2	44	12	5	4	1	0	1	1	4	1	13	1	0	0	1	.000	0	0	3.72
1994	Knoxville	AA	46	1	0	20	71	339	77	46	38	8	2	5	2	48	2	63	5	0	5	3	.625	0	2	4.82
	4 Min. YEARS		119	1	0	65	168	757	154	82	63	10	7	8	7	102	4	180	14	1	15	9	.625	0	10	3.38

Steve Hecht

Bats: Left Throws: Right Pos: OF   Ht: 5'9" Wt: 165 Born: 11/12/65 Age: 29

Year	Team	Lg	G	AB	H	2B	3B	HR	TB	R	RBI	TBB	IBB	SO	HBP	SH	SF	SB	CS	SB%	GDP	Avg	OBP	SLG
1988	Everett	A	13	44	7	1	0	0	8	8	4	6	0	7	0	0	0	7	3	.70	1	.159	.260	.182
	Fresno	A	52	204	52	7	1	1	64	40	12	25	0	32	0	0	0	42	14	.75	3	.255	.336	.314
1989	Phoenix	AAA	3	9	4	1	0	0	5	3	0	1	0	0	0	0	0	2	1	.67	0	.444	.500	.556
	San Jose	A	127	501	133	17	8	3	175	83	43	52	3	57	4	1	3	56	25	.69	5	.265	.338	.349
1990	Shreveport	AA	64	200	60	12	7	2	92	37	27	12	2	15	2	0	1	12	5	.71	3	.300	.344	.460
	Indianapols	AAA	58	197	50	12	2	2	72	21	13	7	1	32	0	2	0	11	5	.69	0	.254	.279	.365
1991	Indianapols	AAA	89	210	51	8	2	4	75	34	26	12	0	51	0	6	1	9	2	.82	2	.243	.283	.357
1992	Harrisburg	AA	100	269	69	13	5	1	95	46	17	31	0	35	5	8	0	17	7	.71	1	.257	.344	.353
1993	Shreveport	AA	49	168	50	8	6	3	79	25	11	11	1	25	1	1	0	5	3	.63	2	.298	.344	.470
	Phoenix	AAA	48	169	53	8	1	2	69	27	20	20	0	23	0	1	2	9	1	.90	2	.314	.382	.408
1994	Shreveport	AA	14	31	7	1	1	0	10	9	3	6	0	2	0	0	0	3	0	1.00	1	.226	.351	.323
	Phoenix	AAA	98	332	106	17	9	10	171	66	44	26	2	52	5	3	1	18	5	.78	4	.319	.376	.515
	7 Min. YEARS		715	2334	642	105	42	28	915	399	220	209	9	331	17	22	8	191	71	.73	20	.275	.338	.392

Andy Heckman

Pitches: Left Bats: Right Pos: P   Ht: 6'3" Wt: 185 Born: 10/17/71 Age: 23

Year	Team	Lg	G	GS	CG	GF	IP	BFP	H	R	ER	HR	SH	SF	HB	TBB	IBB	SO	WP	Bk	W	L	Pct.	ShO	Sv	ERA
1992	Everett	A	22	2	0	12	40.1	158	26	12	12	6	1	1	2	14	2	41	1	0	2	3	.400	0	2	2.68
1993	Clinton	A	11	1	0	5	20.2	88	18	6	4	2	1	0	2	4	0	24	0	0	2	1	.667	0	1	1.74
	San Jose	A	30	0	0	19	59	242	45	20	16	3	2	4	2	23	0	40	2	0	5	1	.833	0	7	2.44
1994	San Jose	A	7	0	0	3	10	38	3	3	3	0	0	0	0	6	0	11	4	0	0	0	.000	0	0	2.70
	Shreveport	AA	20	14	0	4	97.2	398	84	30	27	9	2	1	5	25	1	59	1	0	7	1	.875	0	0	2.49
	3 Min. YEARS		90	17	0	43	227.2	924	176	71	62	20	6	6	11	72	3	175	8	0	16	6	.727	0	9	2.45

Derek Henderson

Bats: Right Throws: Right Pos: SS   Ht: 6'1" Wt: 180 Born: 06/02/68 Age: 27

Year	Team	Lg	G	AB	H	2B	3B	HR	TB	R	RBI	TBB	IBB	SO	HBP	SH	SF	SB	CS	SB%	GDP	Avg	OBP	SLG
1989	Pittsfield	A	47	152	40	11	2	1	58	24	19	14	0	36	1	2	2	6	1	.86	2	.263	.325	.382
1990	St. Lucie	A	59	184	38	2	2	0	44	16	26	15	0	34	5	3	3	7	5	.58	3	.207	.280	.239
1991	St. Lucie	A	83	282	68	10	4	0	86	31	15	20	0	51	3	2	0	2	7	.22	2	.241	.298	.305
1992	Knoxville	AA	127	425	107	12	4	2	133	37	39	25	0	72	6	11	2	6	9	.40	11	.252	.301	.313
	Syracuse	AAA	7	14	2	1	0	0	3	0	0	2	0	1	0	0	0	0	0	.00	0	.143	.250	.214
1993	Syracuse	AAA	14	27	10	1	0	0	11	2	3	3	0	7	0	2	0	0	2	.00	1	.370	.433	.407
	Knoxville	AA	13	29	7	0	0	0	7	4	1	3	0	7	2	1	0	1	1	.50	1	.241	.353	.241
1994	Knoxville	AA	8	12	0	0	0	0	0	2	0	1	0	5	1	0	0	0	0	.00	1	.000	.143	.000
	High Desert	A	29	102	27	2	1	3	40	15	15	13	0	17	1	0	0	0	1	.00	6	.265	.353	.392
	6 Min. YEARS		387	1227	299	39	13	6	382	131	118	96	0	230	19	21	7	22	26	.46	27	.244	.307	.311

Ryan Henderson

Pitches: Right Bats: Right Pos: P   Ht: 6'1" Wt: 190 Born: 09/30/69 Age: 25

Year	Team	Lg	G	GS	CG	GF	IP	BFP	H	R	ER	HR	SH	SF	HB	TBB	IBB	SO	WP	Bk	W	L	Pct.	ShO	Sv	ERA
1992	Great Falls	R	11	11	1	0	55	228	37	22	13	0	3	0	2	25	0	54	5	6	5	1	.833	1	0	2.13
	Bakersfield	A	3	3	0	0	16	72	17	10	9	1	0	0	0	9	1	15	0	0	0	2	.000	0	0	5.06
1993	Vero Beach	A	30	0	0	25	34	158	29	24	15	2	4	1	0	28	4	34	4	1	0	3	.000	0	10	3.97
	San Antonio	AA	23	0	0	20	25	110	19	10	7	0	3	1	0	16	2	22	1	1	0	0	.000	0	5	2.52
1994	Bakersfield	A	29	0	0	27	31.1	145	26	14	10	1	2	0	1	26	0	38	8	1	0	1	.000	0	14	2.87
	San Antonio	AA	11	1	0	0	21.2	105	25	18	17	2	0	1	1	18	1	15	3	1	1	2	.333	0	0	7.06
	3 Min. YEARS		107	15	1	72	183	818	153	98	71	6	12	3	4	122	8	178	21	13	6	9	.400	1	29	3.49

Jon Henry

Pitches: Right Bats: Right Pos: P   Ht: 6'5" Wt: 215 Born: 08/01/68 Age: 26

Year	Team	Lg	G	GS	CG	GF	IP	BFP	H	R	ER	HR	SH	SF	HB	TBB	IBB	SO	WP	Bk	W	L	Pct.	ShO	Sv	ERA
1990	Elizabethtn	R	14	13	1	1	87.1	365	82	40	35	11	0	2	7	28	0	89	1	3	7	2	.778	0	0	3.61

Year	Team	Lg	G	GS	CG	GF	IP	BFP	H	R	ER	HR	SH	SF	HB	TBB	IBB	SO	WP	Bk	W	L	Pct.	ShO	Sv	ERA
1991	Visalia	A	28	28	4	0	172.2	755	174	103	86	13	6	11	12	60	2	110	11	2	8	13	.381	0	0	4.48
1992	Orlando	AA	28	22	1	5	135.1	576	147	77	62	10	1	6	8	28	0	87	8	3	10	9	.526	0	0	4.12
1993	Nashville	AA	6	6	1	0	42.2	172	41	14	13	5	1	0	3	7	0	20	1	0	4	2	.667	1	0	2.74
	Portland	AAA	26	13	0	4	94.2	432	122	68	60	13	2	4	5	30	0	62	2	2	6	5	.545	0	1	5.70
1994	Nashville	AA	12	9	0	1	58.1	242	57	22	19	3	0	1	4	12	0	46	0	2	8	1	.889	0	1	2.93
	Salt Lake	AAA	10	10	0	0	57.1	254	72	42	36	7	0	1	6	17	0	27	2	0	4	4	.500	0	0	5.65
	5 Min. YEARS		124	101	7	11	648.1	2796	695	366	311	62	10	25	45	182	2	441	25	12	47	36	.566	1	1	4.32

Julian Heredia

Pitches: Right Bats: Right Pos: P Ht: 6'1" Wt: 160 Born: 09/22/69 Age: 25

Year	Team	Lg	G	GS	CG	GF	IP	BFP	H	R	ER	HR	SH	SF	HB	TBB	IBB	SO	WP	Bk	W	L	Pct.	ShO	Sv	ERA
1989	Angels	R	14	13	3	1	92.1	402	109	55	44	5	2	2	1	21	0	74	2	11	3	4	.429	0	0	4.29
1990	Angels	R	5	5	0	0	26	114	26	14	11	1	0	1	0	10	0	18	0	1	2	2	.500	0	0	3.81
	Quad City	A	5	0	0	3	7	34	6	6	3	0	0	1	0	6	0	10	0	2	0	0	.000	0	0	3.86
1991	Boise	A	25	0	0	10	77	290	42	17	9	1	3	1	1	16	1	99	4	3	8	1	.889	0	5	1.05
1992	Quad City	A	29	0	0	25	43.1	162	27	8	8	0	2	1	0	11	1	45	3	1	6	1	.857	0	10	1.66
	Palm Sprngs	A	30	0	0	27	28.1	121	28	16	15	2	2	3	1	9	3	36	3	1	3	1	.750	0	10	4.76
1993	Midland	AA	46	1	0	19	89.1	361	77	42	31	10	0	1	8	19	0	89	3	2	5	3	.625	0	0	3.12
1994	Midland	AA	45	2	0	10	97.2	414	87	47	35	10	5	4	6	37	5	109	11	3	5	3	.625	0	1	3.23
	6 Min. YEARS		199	21	3	95	461	1898	402	205	156	29	14	14	17	129	10	480	26	24	32	15	.681	0	26	3.05

Wilson Heredia

Pitches: Right Bats: Right Pos: P Ht: 6'0" Wt: 165 Born: 03/30/72 Age: 23

Year	Team	Lg	G	GS	CG	GF	IP	BFP	H	R	ER	HR	SH	SF	HB	TBB	IBB	SO	WP	Bk	W	L	Pct.	ShO	Sv	ERA
1991	Rangers	R	17	0	0	8	33.2	153	25	18	8	1	0	2	4	20	0	22	1	1	2	4	.333	0	4	2.14
1992	Gastonia	A	39	1	0	22	63.1	301	71	45	36	4	8	2	5	30	2	64	11	7	1	2	.333	0	5	5.12
1993	Charlotte	A	34	0	0	29	38.2	165	30	17	16	0	2	4	1	20	1	26	4	0	1	5	.167	0	15	3.72
1994	Tulsa	AA	18	1	0	5	43	171	35	23	18	6	4	1	0	8	0	53	5	2	3	2	.600	0	0	3.77
	4 Min. YEARS		108	2	0	64	178.2	790	161	103	78	11	14	9	10	78	3	165	21	10	7	13	.350	0	24	3.93

Dustin Hermanson

Pitches: Right Bats: Right Pos: P Ht: 6'3" Wt: 195 Born: 12/21/72 Age: 22

Year	Team	Lg	G	GS	CG	GF	IP	BFP	H	R	ER	HR	SH	SF	HB	TBB	IBB	SO	WP	Bk	W	L	Pct.	ShO	Sv	ERA
1994	Wichita	AA	16	0	0	14	21	82	13	1	1	0	1	0	1	6	2	30	2	1	1	0	1.000	0	8	0.43
	Las Vegas	AAA	7	0	0	7	7.1	33	6	5	5	1	0	1	0	5	0	6	0	0	0	0	.000	0	3	6.14
	1 Min. YEARS		23	0	0	21	28.1	115	19	6	6	1	1	1	1	11	2	36	2	1	1	0	1.000	0	11	1.91

Cesar Hernandez

Bats: Right Throws: Right Pos: OF Ht: 6'0" Wt: 170 Born: 09/28/66 Age: 28

Year	Team	Lg	G	AB	H	2B	3B	HR	TB	R	RBI	TBB	IBB	SO	HBP	SH	SF	SB	CS	SB%	GDP	Avg	OBP	SLG
1986	Burlington	A	38	104	26	11	0	1	40	12	12	7	0	24	4	1	2	7	0	1.00	2	.250	.316	.385
1987	Wst Plm Bch	A	32	106	25	3	1	2	36	14	6	4	0	29	1	0	1	6	1	.86	1	.236	.268	.340
1988	Rockford	A	117	411	101	20	4	19	186	71	60	25	1	109	4	1	1	28	8	.78	11	.246	.295	.453
1989	Wst Plm Bch	A	42	158	45	8	3	1	62	16	15	8	1	32	5	1	2	16	4	.80	2	.285	.335	.392
	Jacksnville	AA	81	222	47	9	1	3	67	25	13	22	2	60	0	1	0	11	4	.73	3	.212	.283	.302
1990	Jacksnville	AA	118	393	94	21	7	10	159	58	50	18	3	75	7	1	6	16	11	.59	4	.239	.281	.405
1991	Harrisburg	AA	128	418	106	16	2	13	165	58	52	25	2	106	8	1	6	34	8	.81	7	.254	.304	.395
1992	Nashville	AAA	1	2	2	0	0	0	2	0	0	0	0	0	0	0	0	0	0	1.00	0	1.000	1.000	1.000
	Chattanooga	AA	93	328	91	24	4	3	132	50	27	19	1	65	4	2	0	12	9	.57	5	.277	.325	.402
1993	Indianapols	AAA	84	272	70	12	4	5	105	30	22	9	0	63	3	1	2	5	7	.42	2	.257	.287	.386
1994	Buffalo	AAA	20	88	22	4	1	0	28	10	3	4	0	15	0	0	0	2	2	.50	2	.250	.283	.318
1992	Cincinnati	NL	34	51	14	4	0	0	18	6	4	0	0	10	0	0	0	3	1	.75	1	.275	.275	.353
1993	Cincinnati	NL	27	24	2	0	0	0	2	3	1	1	0	8	0	0	1	1	2	.33	0	.083	.120	.083
	9 Min. YEARS		754	2502	629	128	27	57	982	344	260	141	10	578	36	9	20	137	55	.71	39	.251	.299	.392
	2 Maj. YEARS		61	75	16	4	0	0	20	9	5	1	0	18	0	0	1	4	3	.57	1	.213	.224	.267

Fernando Hernandez

Pitches: Right Bats: Right Pos: P Ht: 6'2" Wt: 185 Born: 06/16/71 Age: 24

Year	Team	Lg	G	GS	CG	GF	IP	BFP	H	R	ER	HR	SH	SF	HB	TBB	IBB	SO	WP	Bk	W	L	Pct.	ShO	Sv	ERA
1990	Indians	R	11	11	2	0	69.2	289	61	36	31	3	2	2	1	30	0	43	2	7	4	4	.500	0	0	4.00
1991	Burlington	R	14	13	0	1	77	326	74	33	25	4	2	0	7	19	0	86	12	1	4	4	.500	0	0	2.92
1992	Columbus	A	11	11	1	0	68.2	268	42	16	12	4	1	0	6	33	1	70	4	1	5	5	.444	1	0	1.57
	Kinston	A	8	8	1	0	41.2	177	36	23	21	2	3	3	1	22	0	32	3	0	1	3	.250	0	0	4.54
1993	Kinston	A	8	8	0	0	51	200	34	15	10	1	2	1	2	18	0	53	1	0	2	3	.400	0	0	1.76
	Canton-Akrn	AA	2	2	0	0	7.2	40	14	11	10	1	0	1	1	5	0	8	0	0	0	1	.000	0	0	11.74
	Rancho Cuca	A	17	17	1	0	99.2	441	90	54	46	8	3	4	2	67	0	121	4	1	7	5	.583	0	0	4.15
1994	Wichita	AA	23	23	1	0	131.1	595	124	82	70	12	8	9	10	77	6	95	8	0	7	9	.438	1	0	4.80
	5 Min. YEARS		94	93	6	1	546.2	2336	475	270	225	35	21	20	30	271	7	508	34	10	29	34	.460	2	0	3.70

Kiki Hernandez

Bats: Right **Throws:** Right **Pos:** C   **Ht:** 5'11" **Wt:** 195 **Born:** 04/16/69 **Age:** 26

								BATTING										BASERUNNING				PERCENTAGES		
Year	Team	Lg	G	AB	H	2B	3B	HR	TB	R	RBI	TBB	IBB	SO	HBP	SH	SF	SB	CS	SB%	GDP	Avg	OBP	SLG
1988	Yankees	R	9	25	4	1	0	0	5	2	2	1	0	7	1	1	0	0	0	.00	1	.160	.222	.200
1989	Oneonta	A	29	94	21	4	0	2	31	12	7	15	0	21	1	0	0	1	1	.50	0	.223	.336	.330
1990	Pr William	A	107	360	90	20	2	6	132	39	47	40	0	88	2	1	1	0	0	.00	11	.250	.328	.367
1991	Greensboro	A	108	385	128	27	2	15	204	54	78	64	5	50	9	1	8	2	6	.25	9	.332	.431	.530
	Pr William	A	7	30	8	2	0	1	13	4	5	3	0	4	0	0	0	0	0	.00	1	.267	.333	.433
1992	Ft. Laud	A	3	9	1	0	0	0	1	1	1	2	0	2	0	0	0	0	0	.00	0	.111	.273	.111
	Albany	AA	99	328	92	18	0	4	122	46	40	38	1	45	3	2	3	0	0	.00	13	.280	.358	.372
1993	Columbus	AAA	22	54	13	4	0	1	20	8	8	6	1	12	1	1	2	0	0	.00	1	.241	.317	.370
1994	Albany-Colo	AA	4	11	1	0	0	0	1	0	0	3	0	2	0	0	0	0	0	.00	0	.091	.286	.091
	Columbus	AAA	48	134	36	7	1	4	57	17	22	12	0	29	1	1	1	1	3	.25	6	.269	.331	.425
	7 Min. YEARS		436	1430	394	83	5	33	586	183	210	184	7	260	18	7	15	4	10	.29	42	.276	.362	.410

Phil Hiatt

Bats: Right **Throws:** Right **Pos:** 3B   **Ht:** 6' 3" **Wt:** 200 **Born:** 05/01/69 **Age:** 26

								BATTING										BASERUNNING				PERCENTAGES		
Year	Team	Lg	G	AB	H	2B	3B	HR	TB	R	RBI	TBB	IBB	SO	HBP	SH	SF	SB	CS	SB%	GDP	Avg	OBP	SLG
1990	Eugene	A	73	289	85	18	5	2	119	33	44	17	1	69	1	1	4	15	4	.79	1	.294	.331	.412
1991	Baseball Cy	A	81	315	94	21	6	5	142	41	33	22	4	70	3	1	2	28	14	.67	8	.298	.348	.451
	Memphis	AA	56	206	47	7	1	6	74	29	33	9	1	63	3	0	6	6	1	.86	3	.228	.263	.359
1992	Memphis	AA	129	487	119	20	5	27	230	71	83	25	1	157	5	1	3	5	10	.33	11	.244	.287	.472
	Omaha	AAA	5	14	3	0	0	2	9	3	4	2	0	3	0	0	0	1	0	1.00	0	.214	.313	.643
1993	Omaha	AAA	12	51	12	2	0	3	23	8	10	4	0	20	1	0	0	0	0	.00	0	.235	.304	.451
1994	Omaha	AAA	6	22	4	1	0	1	8	2	2	0	0	4	1	1	0	1	0	1.00	2	.182	.217	.364
	Memphis	AA	108	400	120	26	4	17	205	57	66	40	4	116	13	2	2	12	8	.60	4	.300	.380	.513
1993	Kansas City	AL	81	238	52	12	1	7	87	30	36	16	0	82	7	0	2	6	3	.67	8	.218	.285	.366
	5 Min. YEARS		470	1784	484	95	21	63	810	244	275	119	11	502	27	6	17	68	37	.65	29	.271	.324	.454

Charlie Hicks

Pitches: Right **Bats:** Right **Pos:** P   **Ht:** 6'7" **Wt:** 230 **Born:** 06/20/69 **Age:** 26

			HOW MUCH HE PITCHED						WHAT HE GAVE UP											THE RESULTS					
Year	Team	Lg	G	GS	CG	GF	IP	BFP	H	R	ER	HR	SH	SF	HB	TBB	IBB	SO	WP	Bk	W	L	Pct.	ShO	Sv	ERA
1992	Everett	A	21	5	0	4	48.1	230	64	37	35	6	0	2	5	25	2	29	2	1	3	3	.500	0	1	6.52
1993	San Jose	A	36	0	0	20	68.1	304	63	48	40	5	3	4	5	42	0	48	5	0	5	4	.556	0	7	5.27
1994	Shreveport	AA	3	0	0	0	5.2	27	7	4	4	0	0	0	0	4	0	3	2	0	0	0	.000	0	0	6.35
	San Jose	A	4	2	0	1	13.1	60	16	8	4	0	0	1	0	6	0	5	0	0	1	1	.500	0	0	2.70
	Clinton	A	11	10	0	0	58	240	52	22	14	2	1	2	2	19	0	30	5	2	4	5	.444	0	0	2.17
	3 Min. YEARS		75	17	0	25	193.2	861	202	119	97	13	4	9	12	96	2	115	14	3	13	13	.500	0	8	4.51

Kevin Higgins

Bats: Left **Throws:** Right **Pos:** 1B   **Ht:** 5'11" **Wt:** 170 **Born:** 01/22/67 **Age:** 28

								BATTING										BASERUNNING				PERCENTAGES		
Year	Team	Lg	G	AB	H	2B	3B	HR	TB	R	RBI	TBB	IBB	SO	HBP	SH	SF	SB	CS	SB%	GDP	Avg	OBP	SLG
1989	Spokane	A	71	295	98	9	3	2	119	54	52	30	1	13	5	1	9	2	4	.33	8	.332	.392	.403
1990	Las Vegas	AAA	9	26	7	1	1	0	10	4	3	4	0	3	1	0	1	0	0	.00	1	.269	.375	.385
	Riverside	A	49	176	53	5	1	2	66	27	18	27	3	15	2	2	1	0	1	.00	6	.301	.398	.375
	Wichita	AA	52	187	67	7	1	1	79	24	23	16	3	8	1	1	4	5	0	1.00	6	.358	.404	.422
1991	Las Vegas	AAA	130	403	116	12	4	3	145	53	45	47	5	38	2	10	3	3	2	.60	13	.288	.363	.360
1992	Las Vegas	AAA	124	355	90	12	3	0	108	49	40	41	2	31	3	5	7	6	4	.60	10	.254	.330	.304
1993	Las Vegas	AAA	40	142	51	8	0	1	62	22	22	18	1	8	0	1	1	1	1	.50	3	.359	.429	.437
1994	Las Vegas	AAA	119	433	134	26	1	2	168	73	44	46	3	22	4	4	9	1	2	.33	8	.309	.374	.388
1993	San Diego	NL	71	181	40	4	1	0	46	17	13	16	0	17	3	1	1	0	1	.00	7	.221	.294	.254
	6 Min. YEARS		594	2017	616	80	14	11	757	306	247	229	18	138	18	24	35	18	14	.56	55	.305	.375	.375

Michael Higgins

Bats: Right **Throws:** Right **Pos:** C   **Ht:** 6'0" **Wt:** 205 **Born:** 06/03/71 **Age:** 24

								BATTING										BASERUNNING				PERCENTAGES		
Year	Team	Lg	G	AB	H	2B	3B	HR	TB	R	RBI	TBB	IBB	SO	HBP	SH	SF	SB	CS	SB%	GDP	Avg	OBP	SLG
1993	Bend	A	51	167	45	10	1	7	78	23	19	20	1	47	1	0	1	3	4	.43	1	.269	.349	.467
1994	New Haven	AA	1	1	0	0	0	0	0	0	0	0	0	0	0	0	0	0	0	.00	0	.000	.000	.000
	Asheville	A	56	205	55	14	0	3	78	29	15	18	0	35	2	0	1	1	2	.33	5	.268	.332	.380
	Central Val	A	45	157	34	4	0	0	38	15	16	15	0	37	1	1	1	2	1	.67	8	.217	.287	.242
	2 Min. YEARS		153	530	134	28	1	10	194	67	50	53	1	119	4	1	3	6	7	.46	14	.253	.324	.366

Bob Higginson

Bats: Left   Throws: Right   Pos: OF Ht: 5'11" Wt: 180 Born: 08/18/70 Age: 24

Year	Team	Lg	G	AB	H	2B	3B	HR	TB	R	RBI	TBB	IBB	SO	HBP	SH	SF	SB	CS	SB%	GDP	Avg	OBP	SLG
1992	Niagara Fls	A	70	232	68	17	4	2	99	35	37	33	0	47	1	2	0	12	8	.60	4	.293	.383	.427
1993	Lakeland	A	61	223	67	11	7	3	101	42	25	40	1	31	1	2	2	8	3	.73	6	.300	.406	.453
	London	AA	63	224	69	15	4	4	104	25	35	19	0	37	0	0	3	3	4	.43	6	.308	.358	.464
1994	Toledo	AAA	137	476	131	28	3	23	234	81	67	46	3	99	5	0	3	16	8	.67	9	.275	.343	.492
	3 Min. YEARS		331	1155	335	71	18	32	538	183	164	138	4	214	7	4	8	39	23	.63	25	.290	.367	.466

Chris Hill

Pitches: Left   Bats: Left   Pos: P Ht: 6'1" Wt: 175 Born: 04/13/69 Age: 26

Year	Team	Lg	G	GS	CG	GF	IP	BFP	H	R	ER	HR	SH	SF	HB	TBB	IBB	SO	WP	Bk	W	L	Pct.	ShO	Sv	ERA
1988	Little Fls	A	13	13	2	0	79.1	332	56	32	27	7	3	5	3	35	0	66	2	0	5	5	.500	1	0	3.06
1989	Columbia	A	29	25	2	1	165.2	705	140	74	56	5	7	2	4	78	1	157	9	1	11	7	.611	1	0	3.04
1990	St. Lucie	A	27	25	2	2	149.2	662	149	77	53	4	10	10	3	69	0	82	8	1	9	8	.529	0	1	3.19
1991	Williamsprt	AA	27	12	1	3	88.1	402	115	59	46	8	9	5	1	40	2	42	5	0	3	3	.500	0	1	4.69
	St. Lucie	A	6	4	0	1	32	110	18	6	4	1	1	1	0	4	0	24	0	0	4	0	1.000	0	0	1.13
1992	Osceola	A	30	26	1	0	159.2	677	154	73	52	4	4	3	5	58	1	126	11	1	16	7	.696	1	0	2.93
1993	Jackson	AA	58	3	0	27	105	453	90	52	45	9	4	2	7	53	6	93	8	0	6	4	.600	0	2	3.86
1994	Jackson	AA	45	8	0	15	100	446	95	55	42	11	2	3	7	57	3	83	3	0	5	3	.625	0	1	3.78
	7 Min. YEARS		235	116	8	49	879.2	3787	817	428	325	49	40	31	30	394	13	673	46	3	59	37	.615	3	5	3.33

Eric Hill

Pitches: Right   Bats: Right   Pos: P Ht: 6'2" Wt: 190 Born: 11/19/67 Age: 27

Year	Team	Lg	G	GS	CG	GF	IP	BFP	H	R	ER	HR	SH	SF	HB	TBB	IBB	SO	WP	Bk	W	L	Pct.	ShO	Sv	ERA
1990	Batavia	A	10	8	2	1	53.2	219	49	27	24	9	2	1	0	10	0	34	5	0	2	4	.333	0	1	4.02
1991	Spartanburg	A	27	21	2	1	143	599	126	64	50	13	2	7	1	48	0	143	11	3	7	10	.412	1	0	3.15
1992	Clearwater	A	5	5	0	0	27.2	116	26	13	10	3	1	1	0	7	0	18	0	1	4	1	.800	0	0	3.25
	Reading	AA	25	15	1	1	98	429	111	61	52	11	7	2	4	24	1	61	5	1	5	4	.556	0	0	4.78
1993	Reading	AA	21	7	0	3	68.2	303	72	44	35	10	2	4	1	30	2	37	5	3	2	3	.400	0	0	4.59
1994	Reading	AA	46	6	0	22	89.2	392	94	52	46	12	2	5	3	33	4	77	8	0	8	4	.667	0	2	4.62
	5 Min. YEARS		134	62	5	28	480.2	2058	478	261	217	58	16	20	9	152	7	370	34	8	28	26	.519	1	3	4.06

Lew Hill

Bats: Both   Throws: Right   Pos: OF Ht: 5'10" Wt: 190 Born: 04/16/69 Age: 26

Year	Team	Lg	G	AB	H	2B	3B	HR	TB	R	RBI	TBB	IBB	SO	HBP	SH	SF	SB	CS	SB%	GDP	Avg	OBP	SLG
1987	Oneonta	A	14	39	11	0	2	0	15	9	0	3	0	16	0	0	0	0	0	.00	0	.282	.333	.385
	Yankees	R	31	89	15	0	1	1	20	11	8	4	0	31	3	3	0	6	1	.86	1	.169	.229	.225
1988	Yankees	R	54	201	50	4	4	2	68	31	19	13	0	69	3	3	1	7	3	.70	1	.249	.303	.338
1989	Oneonta	A	48	164	35	5	3	4	58	36	24	14	0	60	13	0	1	7	2	.78	1	.213	.323	.354
1990	Greensboro	A	83	270	53	11	0	6	82	28	25	41	1	83	9	2	3	19	3	.86	4	.196	.319	.304
1991	Greensboro	A	125	426	97	17	3	6	138	69	45	67	0	112	14	1	1	36	16	.69	14	.228	.334	.324
1992	Greensboro	A	98	374	117	12	9	15	192	75	52	30	0	89	11	0	3	24	17	.59	3	.313	.378	.513
1993	Pr William	A	116	460	115	22	3	13	182	66	57	29	0	124	18	3	4	12	7	.63	9	.250	.317	.396
1994	Albany-Colo	AA	82	257	59	13	2	9	103	36	33	24	1	75	8	2	4	3	5	.38	4	.230	.311	.401
	8 Min. YEARS		651	2280	552	84	27	56	858	361	263	225	4	659	79	14	17	114	54	.68	37	.242	.329	.376

Rich Hines

Pitches: Left   Bats: Left   Pos: P Ht: 6'1" Wt: 185 Born: 05/20/69 Age: 26

Year	Team	Lg	G	GS	CG	GF	IP	BFP	H	R	ER	HR	SH	SF	HB	TBB	IBB	SO	WP	Bk	W	L	Pct.	ShO	Sv	ERA
1990	Yankees	R	11	9	0	0	61	242	44	18	12	0	0	3	2	19	0	73	9	1	5	2	.714	0	0	1.77
1991	Greensboro	A	26	26	0	0	155.1	667	147	76	55	8	5	2	2	68	1	126	7	3	8	9	.471	2	0	3.19
1992	Pr William	A	25	24	0	1	140	610	131	75	56	12	3	3	7	61	3	84	10	0	11	7	.611	0	0	3.60
1993	Albany	AA	14	0	0	3	26	102	17	9	6	1	1	1	0	11	2	27	0	0	0	1	.000	0	0	2.08
	Columbus	AAA	43	0	0	17	56	248	50	28	25	3	1	1	1	34	6	40	2	1	2	5	.286	0	4	4.02
1994	Columbus	AAA	49	2	0	12	84.1	367	87	48	43	11	1	2	0	41	4	54	6	0	3	2	.600	0	2	4.59
	5 Min. YEARS		168	61	6	33	522.2	2236	476	254	197	35	11	12	12	234	16	404	34	5	29	26	.527	2	6	3.39

Tommy Hinzo

Bats: Both   Throws: Right   Pos: 2B Ht: 5'10" Wt: 175 Born: 06/18/64 Age: 31

Year	Team	Lg	G	AB	H	2B	3B	HR	TB	R	RBI	TBB	IBB	SO	HBP	SH	SF	SB	CS	SB%	GDP	Avg	OBP	SLG
1986	Batavia	A	55	219	73	7	3	1	89	35	15	12	1	44	4	3	0	24	8	.75	4	.333	.379	.406
1987	Kinston	A	65	266	74	11	1	0	87	64	25	32	0	44	3	0	0	49	10	.83	1	.278	.362	.327
	Williamsprt	AA	26	99	24	2	1	0	28	16	9	13	0	18	0	1	0	11	3	.79	1	.242	.330	.283
1988	Colo Spngs	AAA	119	449	104	16	4	1	131	67	29	46	1	76	4	2	4	33	17	.66	7	.232	.306	.292
1989	Colo Spngs	AAA	102	410	104	13	7	1	134	65	35	31	2	68	1	1	2	22	16	.58	2	.254	.317	.327

115

Year	Team	Lg	G	AB	H	2B	3B	HR	TB	R	RBI	TBB	IBB	SO	HBP	SH	SF	SB	CS	SB%	GDP	Avg	OBP	SLG
1990	Richmond	AAA	17	49	11	0	0	2	17	9	5	5	0	12	2	0	0	1	1	.50	2	.224	.321	.347
	Greenville	AA	25	73	19	2	2	1	28	12	12	10	0	12	2	2	1	3	1	.75	4	.260	.360	.384
	Memphis	AA	20	48	8	1	1	0	11	3	2	4	0	9	1	2	0	3	3	.50	1	.167	.245	.229
	Omaha	AAA	35	111	27	5	1	0	34	16	9	2	0	22	1	0	1	6	2	.75	0	.243	.261	.306
1991	Omaha	AAA	9	20	5	1	0	0	6	4	4	1	0	3	2	1	0	0	1	.00	0	.250	.348	.300
1993	Rochester	AAA	136	560	152	25	5	6	205	83	69	37	0	78	11	8	6	29	12	.71	8	.271	.326	.366
1994	Mariners	R	5	15	6	1	0	0	7	1	1	0	0	3	2	0	0	0	0	.00	0	.400	.471	.467
	Calgary	AAA	47	142	35	10	0	0	45	20	13	8	0	21	2	1	1	1	2	.33	2	.246	.294	.317
1987	Cleveland	AL	67	257	68	9	3	3	92	31	21	10	0	47	2	10	1	9	4	.69	6	.265	.296	.358
1989	Cleveland	AL	18	17	0	0	0	0	0	4	0	2	0	6	0	2	0	1	2	.33	0	.000	.105	.000
	8 Min. YEARS		661	2461	642	94	25	12	822	395	228	201	4	410	41	22	13	182	76	.71	35	.261	.325	.334
	2 Maj. YEARS		85	274	68	9	3	3	92	35	21	12	0	53	2	12	1	10	6	.63	6	.248	.284	.336

Rick Hirtensteiner

Bats: Left Throws: Left Pos: OF **Ht: 5'11" Wt: 185 Born: 10/09/67 Age: 27**

			BATTING															BASERUNNING				PERCENTAGES		
Year	Team	Lg	G	AB	H	2B	3B	HR	TB	R	RBI	TBB	IBB	SO	HBP	SH	SF	SB	CS	SB%	GDP	Avg	OBP	SLG
1989	Bend	A	26	89	25	5	0	1	33	22	13	18	0	22	3	0	3	1	2	.33	0	.281	.407	.371
	Palm Sprngs	A	36	125	28	5	0	0	33	11	11	15	0	34	1	0	2	1	1	.50	3	.224	.308	.264
1990	Quad City	A	87	259	57	12	0	4	81	36	24	26	2	78	7	7	5	10	3	.77	5	.220	.303	.313
1992	Harrisburg	AA	127	449	118	18	5	5	161	68	50	33	3	95	13	2	6	18	4	.82	9	.263	.327	.359
1993	Ottawa	AAA	10	14	3	0	0	0	3	1	0	2	1	3	0	0	0	1	0	1.00	0	.214	.313	.214
	St. Paul	IND	69	271	84	10	3	4	112	52	35	27	0	46	11	3	2	8	6	.57	3	.310	.392	.413
1994	Portland	AA	59	183	44	12	1	4	70	21	20	13	0	47	6	3	0	3	1	.75	2	.240	.312	.383
	Brevard Cty	A	52	183	48	7	1	2	63	22	16	16	1	42	6	0	2	5	3	.63	0	.262	.338	.344
	5 Min. YEARS		466	1573	407	69	10	20	556	233	169	150	7	367	47	15	20	47	20	.70	22	.259	.337	.353

Darren Hodges

Pitches: Right Bats: Right Pos: P **Ht: 6'1" Wt: 190 Born: 11/03/69 Age: 25**

			HOW MUCH HE PITCHED					WHAT HE GAVE UP												THE RESULTS					
Year	Team	Lg	G	GS	CG	GF	IP	BFP	H	R	ER	HR	SH	SF	HB	TBB	IBB	SO	WP	Bk	W	L	Pct.	ShO	Sv	ERA
1990	Oneonta	A	14	14	1	0	86	347	81	30	16	1	4	0	2	24	0	85	4	0	6	3	.667	0	0	1.67
1991	Pr William	A	26	25	2	0	166	687	133	60	49	3	8	1	4	66	1	153	15	4	6	8	.429	0	0	2.66
1992	Albany	AA	15	13	0	0	64	300	78	54	43	4	1	4	2	38	0	43	10	4	4	7	.364	0	0	6.05
	Pr William	A	9	9	1	0	52	219	42	26	15	2	1	1	3	20	0	28	3	0	4	4	.500	0	0	2.60
1993	Albany	AA	30	24	2	1	152.2	651	161	89	80	18	1	5	2	61	2	96	6	2	10	10	.500	0	0	4.72
1994	Albany-Colo	AA	8	8	0	0	49.2	203	42	21	20	2	1	0	0	23	0	37	2	0	5	1	.833	0	0	3.62
	5 Min. YEARS		102	93	6	1	570.1	2407	537	280	223	30	16	11	13	232	3	442	46	10	35	33	.515	0	0	3.52

Steve Hoeme

Pitches: Right Bats: Right Pos: P **Ht: 6'6" Wt: 230 Born: 11/02/67 Age: 27**

			HOW MUCH HE PITCHED					WHAT HE GAVE UP												THE RESULTS					
Year	Team	Lg	G	GS	CG	GF	IP	BFP	H	R	ER	HR	SH	SF	HB	TBB	IBB	SO	WP	Bk	W	L	Pct.	ShO	Sv	ERA
1987	Royals	R	15	0	0	2	23.2	122	33	30	15	1	0	1	3	11	1	16	3	0	2	0	1.000	0	0	5.70
1988	Eugene	A	23	1	0	13	37.1	164	25	17	17	0	1	1	4	24	0	32	4	0	0	1	.000	0	0	4.10
1989	Appleton	A	29	12	0	1	89.1	402	83	47	33	9	4	1	7	57	0	73	10	2	4	5	.444	0	0	3.32
1990	Baseball Cy	A	33	1	0	7	60	268	49	28	22	2	1	2	5	40	0	51	13	2	2	2	.500	0	0	3.30
	Appleton	A	7	0	0	2	11.2	53	10	5	5	0	1	1	2	8	0	15	2	1	1	1	.500	0	0	3.86
1991	Chston-Sc	A	31	1	0	9	62.2	281	54	30	24	1	3	4	6	39	1	51	5	0	7	1	.875	0	2	3.45
1992	Waterloo	A	22	0	0	4	34.1	138	27	11	9	1	2	2	1	9	0	43	4	1	1	1	.500	0	1	2.36
	High Desert	A	7	0	0	5	9	40	10	2	2	0	1	1	0	5	2	6	1	0	2	0	1.000	0	0	2.00
	Wichita	AA	20	1	0	6	35.2	171	48	27	25	1	1	2	1	19	1	24	3	0	1	1	.500	0	0	6.31
1993	Rancho Cuca	A	8	0	0	4	8.1	39	8	9	6	1	1	0	1	5	0	4	0	0	1	0	1.000	0	0	6.48
	Wichita	AA	44	0	0	37	48.1	198	41	17	13	2	3	0	1	16	3	47	3	0	2	3	.400	0	19	2.42
1994	Harrisburg	AA	33	1	0	5	58.1	235	43	20	15	1	2	1	3	23	0	51	2	1	6	2	.750	0	0	2.31
	8 Min. YEARS		272	17	0	95	478.2	2111	431	236	186	19	20	16	34	256	8	413	50	7	29	17	.630	0	23	3.50

Aaron Holbert

Bats: Right Throws: Right Pos: SS **Ht: 6'0" Wt: 160 Born: 01/09/73 Age: 22**

			BATTING															BASERUNNING				PERCENTAGES		
Year	Team	Lg	G	AB	H	2B	3B	HR	TB	R	RBI	TBB	IBB	SO	HBP	SH	SF	SB	CS	SB%	GDP	Avg	OBP	SLG
1990	Johnson Cy	R	54	176	30	4	1	1	39	27	18	24	1	33	3	1	1	3	5	.38	2	.170	.279	.222
1991	Springfield	A	59	215	48	5	1	1	58	22	24	15	0	26	6	1	2	5	8	.38	3	.223	.290	.270
1992	Savannah	A	119	438	117	17	4	1	145	53	34	40	0	57	8	6	3	62	25	.71	4	.267	.337	.331
1993	St.Pete	A	121	457	121	18	3	2	151	60	31	28	2	61	4	15	1	45	22	.67	6	.265	.312	.330
1994	Cardinals	R	5	12	2	0	0	0	2	3	0	2	0	2	0	0	0	2	0	1.00	0	.167	.286	.167
	Arkansas	AA	59	233	69	10	6	2	97	41	19	14	0	25	2	4	1	9	7	.56	5	.296	.340	.416
	5 Min. YEARS		417	1531	387	54	15	7	492	206	126	123	3	204	23	27	8	126	67	.65	20	.253	.316	.321

David Holdridge

Pitches: Right **Bats:** Right **Pos:** P **Ht:** 6'3" **Wt:** 195 **Born:** 02/05/69 **Age:** 26

Year	Team	Lg	G	GS	CG	GF	IP	BFP	H	R	ER	HR	SH	SF	HB	TBB	IBB	SO	WP	Bk	W	L	Pct.	ShO	Sv	ERA
1988	Quad City	A	28	28	0	0	153.2	686	151	92	66	4	5	4	13	79	1	110	8	4	6	12	.333	0	0	3.87
1989	Clearwater	A	24	24	3	0	132.1	610	147	100	84	11	2	6	8	77	0	77	16	1	7	10	.412	0	0	5.71
1990	Reading	AA	24	24	1	0	127.2	571	114	74	64	13	3	5	6	79	0	78	8	0	8	12	.400	0	0	4.51
1991	Reading	AA	7	7	0	0	26.1	135	26	24	16	3	2	3	1	34	0	19	3	0	0	2	.000	0	0	5.47
	Clearwater	A	15	0	0	4	25	126	34	23	21	2	0	2	1	21	0	23	4	0	0	0	.000	0	1	7.56
1992	Palm Sprngs	A	28	27	3	0	159	726	169	99	75	5	5	3	5	87	4	135	21	0	12	12	.500	2	0	4.25
1993	Midland	AA	27	27	1	0	151	700	202	117	102	13	4	2	11	55	0	123	13	1	8	10	.444	1	0	6.08
1994	Vancouver	AAA	4	0	0	1	7	36	12	7	4	1	0	1	1	4	0	4	0	0	0	0	.000	0	0	5.14
	Midland	AA	38	2	0	17	66.1	286	66	33	29	4	1	3	5	23	0	59	2	0	7	4	.636	0	2	3.93
7 Min. YEARS			195	139	8	22	848.1	3876	921	569	461	56	22	29	51	459	5	628	75	6	48	62	.436	3	3	4.89

Rick Holifield

Bats: Left **Throws:** Left **Pos:** OF **Ht:** 6'2" **Wt:** 165 **Born:** 03/25/70 **Age:** 25

Year	Team	Lg	G	AB	H	2B	3B	HR	TB	R	RBI	TBB	IBB	SO	HBP	SH	SF	SB	CS	SB%	GDP	Avg	OBP	SLG
1988	Medicne Hat	R	31	96	26	4	1	1	35	16	6	9	0	27	4	0	0	6	0	1.00	2	.271	.358	.365
1989	St.Cathmes	A	60	209	46	7	1	4	67	22	21	15	1	74	1	0	2	4	7	.36	2	.220	.273	.321
1990	Myrtle Bch	A	99	279	56	9	2	3	78	37	18	28	0	88	6	1	0	13	8	.62	7	.201	.288	.280
1991	Myrtle Bch	A	114	324	71	15	5	1	99	37	25	34	1	94	7	1	1	14	15	.48	0	.219	.306	.306
1992	Myrtle Bch	A	93	281	56	15	2	8	99	32	27	23	1	81	5	3	3	6	5	.55	2	.199	.269	.352
1993	Dunedin	A	127	407	112	18	12	20	214	84	68	56	6	129	16	6	4	30	13	.70	4	.275	.381	.526
1994	Knoxville	AA	71	238	59	10	9	4	99	31	31	24	2	64	3	1	1	23	5	.82	2	.248	.323	.416
	Scranton-Wb	AAA	18	55	7	1	0	0	8	5	0	3	0	19	2	0	0	0	1	.00	0	.127	.200	.145
	Reading	AA	42	155	44	8	3	7	79	29	19	18	0	34	3	1	0	21	7	.75	1	.284	.369	.510
7 Min. YEARS			655	2044	477	87	35	48	778	293	215	210	11	610	47	13	11	117	61	.66	18	.233	.317	.381

Tim Holland

Bats: Right **Throws:** Right **Pos:** 3B **Ht:** 6'3" **Wt:** 180 **Born:** 06/15/69 **Age:** 26

Year	Team	Lg	G	AB	H	2B	3B	HR	TB	R	RBI	TBB	IBB	SO	HBP	SH	SF	SB	CS	SB%	GDP	Avg	OBP	SLG
1987	Bluefield	R	53	157	43	8	1	4	65	20	19	15	0	47	1	1	0	4	0	1.00	1	.274	.341	.414
1988	Erie	A	69	242	48	6	1	0	56	23	12	11	1	54	0	6	0	5	2	.71	1	.198	.233	.231
1989	Waterloo	A	113	391	79	19	0	5	113	42	32	31	4	82	0	3	2	4	4	.50	13	.202	.259	.289
1990	Frederick	A	115	424	128	26	4	8	186	63	68	38	0	75	4	4	2	6	4	.60	12	.302	.363	.439
1991	Hagerstown	AA	133	501	124	21	2	8	173	58	73	35	2	142	2	3	8	6	5	.55	15	.248	.295	.345
1992	Hagerstown	AA	86	263	62	9	3	1	80	29	22	15	0	63	0	1	2	8	3	.73	10	.236	.275	.304
1993	Rochester	AAA	9	28	3	2	0	0	5	4	0	1	0	9	0	0	0	0	0	.00	0	.107	.138	.179
	Bowie	AA	130	449	112	16	5	9	165	49	53	25	1	123	3	2	2	9	8	.53	11	.249	.292	.367
1994	Sarasota	A	4	12	3	0	0	0	3	3	0	1	1	3	0	0	0	0	0	.00	0	.250	.308	.250
	New Britain	AA	34	95	16	3	0	0	19	6	4	10	0	27	0	0	1	0	0	.00	3	.168	.245	.200
8 Min. YEARS			746	2562	618	110	16	35	865	294	284	182	8	625	10	20	17	42	26	.62	66	.241	.292	.338

Todd Hollandsworth

Bats: Left **Throws:** Left **Pos:** OF **Ht:** 6'2" **Wt:** 193 **Born:** 04/20/73 **Age:** 22

Year	Team	Lg	G	AB	H	2B	3B	HR	TB	R	RBI	TBB	IBB	SO	HBP	SH	SF	SB	CS	SB%	GDP	Avg	OBP	SLG
1991	Dodgers	R	6	16	5	0	0	0	5	1	0	0	0	6	0	0	0	0	0	.00	1	.313	.313	.313
	Yakima	A	56	203	48	5	1	8	79	34	33	27	3	57	4	0	0	11	1	.92	2	.236	.338	.389
1992	Bakersfield	A	119	430	111	23	5	13	183	70	58	50	5	113	3	0	2	27	13	.68	6	.258	.338	.426
1993	San Antonio	AA	126	474	119	24	9	17	212	57	63	29	2	101	5	2	5	23	12	.66	7	.251	.298	.447
1994	Albuquerque	AAA	132	505	144	31	5	19	242	80	91	46	5	96	0	1	3	15	9	.63	15	.285	.343	.479
4 Min. YEARS			439	1628	427	83	20	57	721	242	245	152	15	373	12	3	10	76	35	.68	31	.262	.328	.443

Adrian Hollinger

Pitches: Right **Bats:** Left **Pos:** P **Ht:** 6'0" **Wt:** 172 **Born:** 09/23/70 **Age:** 24

Year	Team	Lg	G	GS	CG	GF	IP	BFP	H	R	ER	HR	SH	SF	HB	TBB	IBB	SO	WP	Bk	W	L	Pct.	ShO	Sv	ERA
1991	Padres	R	8	0	0	3	12	76	21	20	17	1	1	1	0	16	2	14	1	2	1	1	.500	0	0	12.75
1992	Spokane	A	21	2	0	4	53.2	254	61	43	37	4	3	1	4	29	1	39	8	1	0	6	.000	0	1	6.20
1993	Waterloo	A	44	0	0	18	60.1	254	44	23	17	3	3	2	3	40	4	67	7	1	8	3	.727	0	5	2.54
1994	Rancho Cuca	A	19	0	0	9	23.2	111	20	17	15	3	1	0	3	19	0	32	3	2	0	1	.000	0	0	5.70
	Wichita	AA	25	0	0	10	46.2	218	47	32	25	4	0	2	3	33	2	42	7	0	1	3	.250	0	0	4.82
4 Min. YEARS			117	2	0	44	196.1	913	193	135	111	15	8	6	13	137	9	194	26	6	10	14	.417	0	7	5.09

117

Brad Holman

Pitches: Right Bats: Right Pos: P Ht: 6' 5" Wt: 200 Born: 02/09/68 Age: 27

Year	Team	Lg	G	GS	CG	GF	IP	BFP	H	R	ER	HR	SH	SF	HB	TBB	IBB	SO	WP	Bk	W	L	Pct.	ShO	Sv	ERA
1990	Eugene	A	17	4	0	3	43.1	184	43	28	23	3	2	0	4	17	0	31	4	2	0	3	.000	0	0	4.78
1991	Peninsula	A	47	0	0	35	78.1	334	70	34	28	4	5	3	2	33	7	71	5	3	6	6	.500	0	10	3.22
1992	Peninsula	A	13	0	0	12	17.2	74	15	8	6	0	0	0	0	4	1	19	2	0	1	1	.500	0	5	3.06
	Jacksnville	AA	35	0	0	15	73.2	305	67	24	21	6	0	2	4	21	3	76	3	0	3	3	.500	0	4	2.57
1993	Calgary	AAA	21	13	1	2	98.2	427	109	59	52	5	3	6	3	42	0	54	7	1	8	4	.667	0	0	4.74
1994	Calgary	AAA	24	2	0	8	38.2	209	65	54	48	3	1	4	4	27	0	19	4	0	0	1	.000	0	1	11.17
1993	Seattle	AL	19	0	0	9	36.1	152	27	17	15	1	1	0	5	16	2	17	2	0	1	3	.250	0	3	3.72
	5 Min. YEARS		157	19	1	75	350.1	1533	369	207	178	21	11	15	17	144	11	270	25	6	18	18	.500	0	20	4.57

Craig Holman

Pitches: Right Bats: Both Pos: P Ht: 6'2" Wt: 200 Born: 03/13/69 Age: 26

Year	Team	Lg	G	GS	CG	GF	IP	BFP	H	R	ER	HR	SH	SF	HB	TBB	IBB	SO	WP	Bk	W	L	Pct.	ShO	Sv	ERA
1991	Batavia	A	15	12	0	1	79.1	327	67	27	17	2	2	1	2	22	1	53	7	1	6	2	.750	0	0	1.93
1992	Spartanburg	A	25	24	3	1	143.1	611	153	72	59	9	4	4	4	39	0	129	10	2	9	6	.600	1	0	3.70
1993	Clearwater	A	7	1	0	2	18	71	17	7	5	1	0	0	0	1	0	7	1	0	0	0	.000	0	0	2.50
	Reading	AA	24	24	4	0	139	586	134	73	64	5	3	2	12	43	1	86	6	1	8	13	.381	1	0	4.14
1994	Reading	AA	7	4	0	1	27.2	126	33	22	19	3	0	0	1	13	1	18	1	0	2	5	.286	0	0	6.18
	4 Min. YEARS		78	65	7	5	407.1	1721	404	201	164	20	9	7	19	118	3	293	25	4	25	26	.490	2	0	3.62

Shawn Holman

Pitches: Right Bats: Right Pos: P Ht: 6' 2" Wt: 185 Born: 11/10/64 Age: 30

Year	Team	Lg	G	GS	CG	GF	IP	BFP	H	R	ER	HR	SH	SF	HB	TBB	IBB	SO	WP	Bk	W	L	Pct.	ShO	Sv	ERA
1984	Macon	A	9	6	1	2	46.2	210	48	19	10	1	3	1	1	25	0	32	3	0	3	2	.600	1	0	1.93
	Pr William	A	15	14	1	0	77.2	345	74	46	35	4	1	2	2	49	0	47	9	0	7	4	.636	0	0	4.06
1985	Pr William	A	24	23	4	0	142.1	596	123	69	56	11	3	8	6	53	2	65	11	2	10	11	.476	2	0	3.54
	Nashua	AA	2	2	0	0	8	38	10	6	4	0	1	1	0	7	0	2	0	0	0	1	.000	0	0	4.50
1986	Nashua	AA	25	17	1	3	109.1	484	108	61	58	9	5	2	4	67	3	39	8	0	4	13	.235	1	0	4.77
1987	Harrisburg	AA	27	0	0	11	62	277	67	32	25	6	4	2	4	35	2	27	0	0	4	3	.571	0	2	3.63
	Glens Falls	AA	18	5	0	5	42.1	201	49	33	29	4	0	1	4	25	2	22	6	0	1	3	.250	0	1	6.17
1988	Glens Falls	AA	52	0	0	26	91.2	377	82	36	19	3	7	2	7	26	1	44	7	2	8	3	.727	0	10	1.87
1989	Toledo	AAA	51	0	0	31	89.2	372	74	21	19	2	5	1	10	36	2	38	3	0	3	1	.750	0	11	1.91
1990	Toledo	AAA	17	0	0	3	20.1	110	27	22	17	3	0	1	3	14	0	10	0	0	2	1	.667	0	0	7.52
	London	AA	28	0	0	14	31	147	35	26	21	2	1	0	5	15	0	26	1	0	0	3	.000	0	8	6.10
1993	Richmond	AAA	37	22	0	3	155	661	174	88	72	12	5	4	5	46	3	101	8	0	12	7	.632	0	4	4.18
1994	Ottawa	AAA	59	0	0	52	69.1	301	65	28	23	1	2	2	3	35	4	44	4	1	2	4	.333	0	31	2.99
1989	Detroit	AL	5	0	0	3	10	50	10	7	2	0	0	0	0	11	1	9	0	0	0	0	.000	0	0	1.80
	9 Min. YEARS		364	89	7	150	945.1	4119	936	487	388	58	37	27	54	433	19	497	60	5	56	56	.500	4	63	3.69

Chris Holt

Pitches: Right Bats: Right Pos: P Ht: 6'4" Wt: 205 Born: 09/18/71 Age: 23

Year	Team	Lg	G	GS	CG	GF	IP	BFP	H	R	ER	HR	SH	SF	HB	TBB	IBB	SO	WP	Bk	W	L	Pct.	ShO	Sv	ERA
1992	Auburn	A	14	14	0	0	83	353	75	48	41	9	4	2	7	24	0	81	11	4	2	5	.286	0	0	4.45
1993	Quad City	A	26	26	10	0	186.1	775	162	70	47	10	8	2	3	54	1	176	9	3	11	10	.524	3	0	2.27
1994	Jackson	AA	26	25	5	0	167	679	169	78	64	11	6	4	9	22	2	111	5	1	10	9	.526	2	0	3.45
	3 Min. YEARS		66	65	15	0	436.1	1807	406	196	152	30	18	8	19	100	3	368	25	8	23	24	.489	5	0	3.14

Mark Holzemer

Pitches: Right Bats: Left Pos: P Ht: 6' 0" Wt: 165 Born: 08/20/69 Age: 25

Year	Team	Lg	G	GS	CG	GF	IP	BFP	H	R	ER	HR	SH	SF	HB	TBB	IBB	SO	WP	Bk	W	L	Pct.	ShO	Sv	ERA
1988	Bend	A	13	13	1	0	68.2	311	59	51	40	3	0	1	6	47	1	72	8	6	4	6	.400	1	0	5.24
1989	Quad City	A	25	25	3	0	139.1	603	122	68	52	4	3	5	5	64	1	131	12	4	12	7	.632	1	0	3.36
1990	Midland	AA	15	15	1	0	77	363	92	55	45	10	2	1	6	41	0	54	6	0	1	7	.125	0	0	5.26
1991	Midland	AA	2	2	0	0	6.1	28	3	2	1	0	1	0	1	5	0	7	2	0	0	0	.000	0	0	1.42
1992	Palm Sprngs	A	5	5	2	0	30	124	23	10	10	2	1	0	3	13	0	32	0	0	3	2	.600	0	0	3.00
	Midland	AA	7	7	2	0	44.2	188	45	22	19	4	0	1	1	13	0	36	3	1	2	5	.286	0	0	3.83
	Edmonton	AAA	17	16	4	1	89	416	114	69	66	12	2	6	7	55	1	49	6	1	5	7	.417	0	0	6.67
1993	Vancouver	AAA	24	23	2	0	145.2	642	158	94	78	9	6	4	4	70	2	80	5	5	9	6	.600	0	0	4.82
1994	Vancouver	AAA	29	17	0	5	117.1	540	144	93	86	19	4	5	6	58	1	77	15	0	5	10	.333	0	0	6.60
1993	California	AL	5	4	0	1	23.1	117	34	24	23	2	1	0	3	13	0	10	1	0	0	3	.000	0	0	8.87
	7 Min. YEARS		137	123	15	6	718	3215	760	464	397	63	19	23	39	366	6	538	57	17	41	50	.451	2	0	4.98

Dennis Hood

Bats: Right **Throws:** Right **Pos:** OF **Ht:** 6'2" **Wt:** 180 **Born:** 07/03/66 **Age:** 28

Year	Team	Lg	G	AB	H	2B	3B	HR	TB	R	RBI	TBB	IBB	SO	HBP	SH	SF	SB	CS	SB%	GDP	Avg	OBP	SLG
1984	Braves	R	49	155	31	7	0	1	41	16	18	15	0	40	0	1	2	4	2	.67	1	.200	.267	.265
1985	Braves	R	59	204	49	14	0	1	66	19	17	21	1	59	6	3	3	7	3	.70	2	.240	.325	.324
1986	Sumter	A	135	562	142	25	3	7	194	104	42	62	1	146	8	10	4	43	17	.72	9	.253	.333	.345
1987	Durham	A	120	438	118	19	4	13	184	73	62	51	0	115	4	3	2	32	12	.73	8	.269	.349	.420
1988	Greenville	AA	141	525	135	15	8	14	208	85	47	52	5	139	8	1	2	31	8	.79	6	.257	.332	.396
1989	Greenville	AA	136	464	117	20	5	11	180	68	44	48	4	124	8	3	3	32	14	.70	5	.252	.331	.388
1990	Richmond	AAA	121	389	96	15	5	8	145	50	36	33	2	120	4	5	3	13	9	.59	3	.247	.310	.373
1991	Calgary	AAA	102	314	56	9	2	11	102	52	42	34	0	97	2	7	0	18	6	.75	2	.178	.263	.325
1993	Thunder Bay	IND	69	261	84	13	7	7	132	36	34	19	2	75	4	5	3	30	7	.81	2	.322	.373	.506
1994	Rochester	AAA	2	9	1	1	0	0	2	1	0	0	0	3	0	0	0	0	0	.00	0	.111	.111	.222
	Regina	IND	71	284	93	14	3	9	140	69	54	31	2	50	4	0	3	39	3	.93	2	.327	.398	.493
	10 Min. YEARS		1005	3605	922	152	37	82	1394	573	396	366	17	968	48	38	25	249	81	.75	40	.256	.330	.387

Randy Hood

Bats: Right **Throws:** Right **Pos:** OF **Ht:** 5'11" **Wt:** 185 **Born:** 08/09/68 **Age:** 26

Year	Team	Lg	G	AB	H	2B	3B	HR	TB	R	RBI	TBB	IBB	SO	HBP	SH	SF	SB	CS	SB%	GDP	Avg	OBP	SLG
1990	Brewers	R	4	13	3	0	0	0	3	2	1	2	0	4	1	0	1	0	0	.00	0	.231	.353	.231
	Helena	R	48	178	56	11	4	3	84	44	20	37	0	30	5	3	0	7	3	.70	4	.315	.445	.472
1991	Stockton	A	42	128	23	3	0	2	32	16	10	21	0	37	6	2	0	2	3	.40	2	.180	.323	.250
	Helena	R	9	32	8	0	0	0	8	9	4	11	0	6	0	0	0	2	0	1.00	1	.250	.442	.250
	Erie	A	16	66	19	3	1	3	33	14	15	10	0	17	0	2	1	9	4	.69	0	.288	.377	.500
	South Bend	A	36	100	16	3	2	1	26	13	12	20	2	27	1	2	1	9	3	.75	4	.160	.303	.260
1992	Sarasota	A	67	138	31	5	1	0	38	19	12	13	0	28	5	6	1	7	3	.70	3	.225	.312	.275
1993	South Bend	A	6	17	4	2	0	0	6	5	1	6	0	3	3	0	0	1	1	.50	0	.235	.500	.353
	Sarasota	A	47	143	26	6	1	0	34	14	9	12	1	36	6	1	1	3	2	.60	2	.182	.272	.238
	Birmingham	AA	11	20	5	3	1	0	10	6	2	3	0	6	2	0	0	0	1	.00	1	.250	.400	.500
1994	Birmingham	AA	90	216	48	11	1	1	64	30	20	22	0	37	14	2	2	7	3	.70	6	.222	.331	.296
	5 Min. YEARS		376	1051	239	47	11	10	338	172	106	157	3	231	43	18	7	47	22	.68	23	.227	.349	.322

Chris Hook

Pitches: Right **Bats:** Both **Pos:** P **Ht:** 6'5" **Wt:** 195 **Born:** 08/04/68 **Age:** 26

			HOW MUCH HE PITCHED					WHAT HE GAVE UP										THE RESULTS					
Year	Team	Lg	G	GS	CG	GF	IP	BFP	H	R	ER	HR	SH	SF	HB	TBB	IBB	SO	WP	Bk	W	L	Pct.	ShO	Sv	ERA
1989	Reds	R	14	9	0	1	51	209	43	19	18	1	1	1	4	17	0	39	4	2	4	1	.800	0	0	3.18
1990	Chston-Wv	A	30	16	0	3	119.1	537	117	65	54	3	4	3	8	62	1	87	19	1	6	5	.545	0	0	4.07
1991	Chston-Wv	A	45	0	0	19	71	306	52	26	19	1	4	1	11	40	1	79	8	0	8	2	.800	0	2	2.41
1992	Cedar Rapds	A	26	25	1	1	159	664	138	59	48	2	7	5	10	53	0	144	5	6	14	8	.636	0	0	2.72
1993	Chattanooga	AA	28	28	1	0	166.2	723	163	85	67	7	11	7	12	66	2	122	9	1	12	8	.600	0	0	3.62
1994	Phoenix	AAA	27	11	0	8	90	401	109	48	46	6	3	4	5	29	0	57	4	1	7	2	.778	0	2	4.60
	6 Min. YEARS		170	89	2	32	657	2840	622	302	252	20	30	21	50	267	7	528	49	11	51	26	.662	0	4	3.45

Sam Horn

Bats: Left **Throws:** Left **Pos:** DH **Ht:** 6'5" **Wt:** 247 **Born:** 11/02/63 **Age:** 31

Year	Team	Lg	G	AB	H	2B	3B	HR	TB	R	RBI	TBB	IBB	SO	HBP	SH	SF	SB	CS	SB%	GDP	Avg	OBP	SLG
1984	Winston-Sal	A	127	403	126	22	3	21	217	67	89	76	5	107	4	1	3	5	4	.56	3	.313	.424	.538
1985	New Britain	AA	134	457	129	32	0	11	194	64	82	64	14	107	4	1	9	4	6	.40	5	.282	.369	.425
1986	Pawtucket	AAA	20	77	15	2	0	3	26	8	14	5	1	23	0	0	0	0	1	.00	1	.195	.244	.338
	New Britain	AA	100	345	85	13	0	8	122	41	46	49	4	80	1	0	5	1	0	1.00	6	.246	.338	.354
1987	Pawtucket	AAA	94	333	107	19	0	30	216	57	84	33	3	88	5	0	2	0	0	.00	9	.321	.389	.649
1988	Pawtucket	AAA	83	279	65	10	0	10	105	33	31	44	10	82	0	0	1	0	3	.00	9	.233	.336	.376
1989	Pawtucket	AAA	51	164	38	9	1	8	73	15	27	20	2	46	0	0	3	0	0	.00	4	.232	.310	.445
1990	Hagerstown	AA	7	23	6	2	0	1	11	2	3	6	1	5	0	0	0	0	1	.00	0	.261	.414	.478
	Rochester	AAA	17	58	24	4	0	9	55	16	26	9	1	13	0	0	0	0	1	.00	2	.414	.493	.948
1993	Charlotte	AAA	122	402	108	17	1	38	241	62	96	60	8	131	2	0	7	1	0	1.00	10	.269	.361	.600
1994	Columbus	AAA	59	197	48	9	1	8	83	22	26	22	1	58	0	0	1	0	0	1.00	6	.244	.320	.421
1987	Boston	AL	46	158	44	7	0	14	93	31	34	17	0	55	2	0	0	0	1	.00	5	.278	.356	.589
1988	Boston	AL	24	61	9	0	0	2	15	4	8	11	3	20	0	0	1	0	0	.00	1	.148	.274	.246
1989	Boston	AL	33	54	8	2	0	0	10	1	4	8	1	16	0	0	0	0	0	.00	4	.148	.258	.185
1990	Baltimore	AL	79	246	61	13	0	14	116	30	45	32	1	62	0	0	2	0	0	.00	4	.248	.332	.472
1991	Baltimore	AL	121	317	74	16	0	23	159	45	61	41	4	99	3	0	1	0	0	.00	10	.233	.326	.502
1992	Baltimore	AL	63	162	38	10	1	5	65	13	19	21	2	60	1	0	1	0	0	.00	8	.235	.324	.401
1993	Cleveland	AL	12	33	15	2	0	3	26	8	8	1	0	5	0	0	0	0	0	.00	0	.455	.472	.848
	9 Min. YEARS		814	2738	751	139	6	147	1343	387	524	388	50	740	16	2	30	12	16	.43	55	.274	.364	.491
	7 Maj. YEARS		378	1031	249	49	1	62	486	132	179	131	11	317	7	0	6	0	1	.00	37	.242	.329	.471

Tyrone Horne

Bats: Left Throws: Right Pos: OF Ht: 5'10" Wt: 185 Born: 11/02/70 Age: 24

Year	Team	Lg	G	AB	H	2B	3B	HR	TB	R	RBI	TBB	IBB	SO	HBP	SH	SF	SB	CS	SB%	GDP	Avg	OBP	SLG
1989	Expos	R	24	68	14	3	2	0	21	7	13	11	0	29	0	0	0	4	4	.50	0	.206	.316	.309
1990	Gate City	R	56	202	57	11	2	1	75	26	13	24	1	62	2	2	2	23	8	.74	1	.282	.361	.371
	Jamestown	A	7	23	7	2	1	0	11	1	5	4	0	5	0	0	0	3	0	1.00	1	.304	.407	.478
1991	Sumter	A	118	428	114	20	3	10	170	69	49	42	1	133	2	1	4	23	12	.66	4	.266	.332	.397
1992	Rockford	A	129	480	134	27	4	12	205	71	48	62	5	141	1	2	2	23	13	.64	3	.279	.361	.427
	Harrisburg	AA	1	1	1	0	0	0	1	0	0	0	0	0	0	0	0	0	0	.00	0	1.000	1.000	1.000
1993	Wst Plm Bch	A	82	288	85	19	2	10	138	43	44	40	1	72	0	1	3	11	10	.52	1	.295	.378	.479
	Harrisburg	AA	35	128	46	8	1	4	68	22	22	22	0	37	1	1	0	3	2	.60	3	.359	.457	.531
1994	Expos	R	7	29	7	1	0	1	11	3	7	4	0	9	0	0	0	1	0	1.00	1	.241	.333	.379
	Harrisburg	AA	90	311	89	15	0	9	131	56	48	50	1	92	1	1	2	11	13	.46	7	.286	.385	.421
	6 Min. YEARS		549	1958	554	106	15	47	831	298	249	259	9	580	7	8	13	102	62	.62	18	.283	.367	.424

Dwayne Hosey

Bats: Right Throws: Right Pos: OF Ht: 5'10" Wt: 175 Born: 03/11/67 Age: 28

Year	Team	Lg	G	AB	H	2B	3B	HR	TB	R	RBI	TBB	IBB	SO	HBP	SH	SF	SB	CS	SB%	GDP	Avg	OBP	SLG
1987	White Sox	R	41	129	36	2	1	1	43	26	10	18	1	22	3	0	2	19	4	.83	1	.279	.375	.333
1988	South Bend	A	95	311	71	11	0	2	88	53	24	28	2	55	5	4	2	36	15	.71	5	.228	.301	.283
	Utica	A	3	7	1	0	0	0	1	0	0	2	0	1	0	0	0	1	0	1.00	0	.143	.333	.143
1989	Madison	A	123	470	115	16	6	11	176	72	51	44	3	82	8	2	2	33	18	.65	9	.245	.319	.374
1990	Modesto	A	113	453	133	21	5	16	212	77	61	50	5	70	8	8	2	30	23	.57	2	.294	.372	.468
1991	Huntsville	AA	28	102	25	6	0	1	34	16	7	9	1	15	1	1	1	5	4	.56	1	.245	.310	.333
	Stockton	A	85	356	97	12	7	15	168	55	62	31	1	58	3	1	9	22	8	.73	4	.272	.328	.472
1992	Wichita	AA	125	427	108	23	9	16	168	56	68	40	3	70	10	1	7	16	11	.59	3	.253	.326	.393
1993	Wichita	AA	86	326	95	19	2	18	172	52	61	25	4	44	2	0	4	13	4	.76	4	.291	.342	.528
	Las Vegas	AAA	32	110	29	4	4	3	50	21	12	11	1	17	4	0	0	7	4	.64	0	.264	.352	.455
1994	Omaha	AAA	112	406	135	23	8	17	255	95	80	61	10	85	8	0	6	27	12	.69	3	.333	.424	.628
	8 Min. YEARS		843	3097	845	137	38	103	1367	523	436	319	31	519	52	17	35	209	103	.67	32	.273	.347	.441

Steve Hosey

Bats: Right Throws: Right Pos: OF Ht: 6'3" Wt: 225 Born: 04/02/69 Age: 26

Year	Team	Lg	G	AB	H	2B	3B	HR	TB	R	RBI	TBB	IBB	SO	HBP	SH	SF	SB	CS	SB%	GDP	Avg	OBP	SLG
1989	Everett	A	73	288	83	14	3	13	142	44	59	27	2	84	10	0	4	15	3	.83	3	.288	.367	.493
1990	San Jose	A	139	479	111	13	6	16	184	85	78	71	2	139	5	1	4	16	17	.48	7	.232	.335	.384
1991	Shreveport	A	126	409	120	21	5	17	202	79	74	56	5	87	6	5	4	24	11	.69	7	.293	.383	.494
1992	Phoenix	AAA	125	462	132	28	7	10	204	64	65	39	4	98	6	0	5	15	15	.50	11	.286	.346	.442
1993	Phoenix	AAA	125	453	133	40	4	16	229	70	85	66	5	129	3	0	5	16	10	.62	7	.292	.382	.503
1994	Vancouver	AAA	112	374	97	22	2	17	174	67	60	47	1	113	6	3	8	9	7	.56	8	.259	.345	.465
1992	San Francisco	NL	21	56	14	1	0	1	18	6	6	0	0	15	0	0	2	1	1	.50	1	.250	.241	.321
1993	San Francisco	NL	3	2	1	0	0	0	1	0	0	1	0	1	0	0	0	0	0	.00	0	.500	.667	1.000
	6 Min. YEARS		704	2467	676	138	27	89	1135	409	421	306	19	650	36	9	28	95	63	.60	43	.274	.359	.460
	2 Maj. YEARS		24	58	15	2	0	1	20	6	7	1	0	16	0	0	2	1	1	.50	1	.259	.262	.345

Mike Hostetler

Pitches: Right Bats: Right Pos: P Ht: 6'2" Wt: 195 Born: 06/05/70 Age: 25

Year	Team	Lg	G	GS	CG	GF	IP	BFP	H	R	ER	HR	SH	SF	HB	TBB	IBB	SO	WP	Bk	W	L	Pct.	ShO	Sv	ERA
1991	Pulaski	R	9	9	0	0	47	184	35	12	10	4	1	1	2	9	2	61	4	1	3	2	.600	0	0	1.91
1992	Durham	A	13	13	3	0	88	354	75	25	21	2	0	1	2	19	3	88	2	3	9	3	.750	2	0	2.15
	Greenville	AA	16	13	1	0	80.2	337	78	37	35	11	3	2	4	23	1	57	3	0	6	2	.750	0	0	3.90
1993	Richmond	AAA	9	9	0	0	48	212	50	29	27	5	1	0	4	18	2	36	0	1	1	3	.250	0	0	5.06
	Greenville	AA	19	19	2	0	135.2	559	122	48	41	9	6	2	7	36	3	105	6	0	8	5	.615	0	0	2.72
1994	Richmond	AAA	6	6	0	0	23.1	105	27	16	16	3	0	1	1	10	1	13	0	2	0	2	.000	0	0	6.17
	4 Min. YEARS		72	69	6	0	422.2	1753	387	167	150	34	11	7	20	115	12	360	15	6	27	17	.614	2	0	3.19

Tom Houk

Bats: Right Throws: Right Pos: 2B Ht: 6'0" Wt: 165 Born: 06/14/69 Age: 26

Year	Team	Lg	G	AB	H	2B	3B	HR	TB	R	RBI	TBB	IBB	SO	HBP	SH	SF	SB	CS	SB%	GDP	Avg	OBP	SLG
1989	Twins	R	47	158	45	15	2	0	64	26	23	28	0	26	1	0	3	1	3	.25	3	.285	.389	.405
1990	Twins	R	46	157	54	10	5	3	83	25	37	22	0	18	2	1	5	3	5	.38	2	.344	.419	.529
1991	Kenosha	A	101	253	53	10	2	2	73	16	25	39	0	57	2	3	0	3	6	.33	6	.209	.320	.289
1992	Visalia	A	93	278	64	7	1	5	88	42	35	47	0	55	1	3	3	7	4	.64	6	.230	.340	.317
1993	Nashville	AA	48	131	30	3	1	1	38	17	16	26	0	28	1	0	0	2	2	.50	4	.229	.361	.290
	Chattanooga	AA	43	147	36	3	3	1	48	19	13	22	0	29	1	0	1	4	4	.50	3	.245	.345	.327
1994	Chattanooga	AA	30	66	19	3	0	0	22	9	11	12	0	9	0	1	0	0	0	.00	1	.288	.397	.333
	6 Min. YEARS		408	1190	301	51	14	12	416	154	160	196	0	222	8	8	12	20	24	.45	25	.253	.359	.350

Wayne Housie

Bats: Both Throws: Right Pos: OF Ht: 5' 9" Wt: 165 Born: 05/20/65 Age: 30

Year Team	Lg	G	AB	H	2B	3B	HR	TB	R	RBI	TBB	IBB	SO	HBP	SH	SF	SB	CS	SB%	GDP	Avg	OBP	SLG
1986 Gastonia	A	90	336	87	10	6	2	115	55	29	43	0	85	4	4	1	38	13	.75	4	.259	.349	.342
1987 Lakeland	A	125	458	118	12	7	1	147	58	45	39	2	74	3	6	6	26	11	.70	7	.258	.316	.321
1988 Glens Falls	AA	63	202	38	4	2	1	49	26	16	28	1	34	3	5	2	9	5	.64	2	.188	.294	.243
Lakeland	A	55	212	57	11	3	0	74	31	23	13	0	40	3	2	1	24	6	.80	1	.269	.319	.349
1989 London	AA	127	434	103	17	2	5	139	56	28	52	3	90	4	3	3	23	14	.62	5	.237	.323	.320
1990 Salinas	A	92	367	99	20	6	5	146	51	49	22	1	72	4	5	3	27	11	.71	5	.270	.316	.398
New Britain	AA	30	113	31	8	3	1	48	13	12	6	0	33	1	5	0	7	2	.78	0	.274	.317	.425
1991 New Britain	AA	113	444	123	24	2	6	169	58	26	55	2	86	3	6	0	43	14	.75	5	.277	.361	.381
Pawtucket	AAA	21	79	26	9	0	2	41	14	8	6	0	20	1	0	0	2	2	.50	0	.329	.384	.519
1992 Pawtucket	AAA	134	456	100	22	5	2	138	53	28	32	1	102	3	10	1	20	8	.71	7	.219	.274	.303
1993 Norfolk	AAA	16	67	14	0	0	1	17	5	5	3	0	13	0	1	1	7	0	1.00	2	.209	.239	.254
New Orleans	AAA	64	113	31	6	1	0	39	22	7	18	0	21	1	4	0	6	2	.75	2	.274	.379	.345
1994 New Britain	AA	112	347	78	15	1	5	110	38	40	37	2	62	1	8	1	3	6	.27	7	.225	.306	.317
1991 Boston	AL	11	8	2	1	0	0	3	2	0	1	0	3	0	1	0	1	0	1.00	1	.250	.333	.375
1993 New York	NL	18	16	3	1	0	0	4	2	1	1	0	1	0	0	0	0	0	.00	0	.188	.235	.250
9 Min. YEARS		1042	3628	905	158	38	31	1232	480	316	354	12	732	34	59	19	235	96	.71	47	.249	.320	.340
2 Maj. YEARS		29	24	5	2	0	0	7	4	1	2	0	4	0	1	0	1	0	1.00	1	.208	.269	.292

Tyler Houston

Bats: Left Throws: Right Pos: C Ht: 6'2" Wt: 210 Born: 01/17/71 Age: 24

Year Team	Lg	G	AB	H	2B	3B	HR	TB	R	RBI	TBB	IBB	SO	HBP	SH	SF	SB	CS	SB%	GDP	Avg	OBP	SLG
1989 Idaho Falls	R	50	176	43	11	0	4	66	30	24	25	1	41	1	0	0	4	0	1.00	4	.244	.342	.375
1990 Sumter	A	117	442	93	14	3	13	152	58	56	49	1	101	2	2	7	6	2	.75	15	.210	.288	.344
1991 Macon	A	107	351	81	16	3	8	127	41	47	39	0	70	1	1	3	10	2	.83	8	.231	.307	.362
1992 Durham	A	117	402	91	17	1	7	131	39	38	20	0	89	1	3	5	5	6	.45	5	.226	.262	.326
1993 Greenville	AA	84	262	73	14	1	5	104	27	33	13	4	50	2	3	4	5	3	.63	12	.279	.313	.397
Richmond	AAA	13	36	5	1	1	1	11	4	3	1	0	8	0	0	0	0	0	.00	1	.139	.162	.306
1994 Richmond	AAA	97	312	76	15	2	4	107	33	33	16	1	44	0	0	5	3	3	.50	12	.244	.276	.343
6 Min. YEARS		585	1981	462	88	11	42	698	232	234	163	7	403	7	9	24	33	16	.67	57	.233	.291	.352

Matt Howard

Bats: Right Throws: Right Pos: 2B Ht: 5'10" Wt: 170 Born: 09/22/67 Age: 27

Year Team	Lg	G	AB	H	2B	3B	HR	TB	R	RBI	TBB	IBB	SO	HBP	SH	SF	SB	CS	SB%	GDP	Avg	OBP	SLG
1989 Great Falls	R	59	186	62	8	2	3	83	39	34	21	0	14	9	5	2	23	8	.74	3	.333	.422	.446
1990 Bakersfield	A	137	551	144	22	3	1	175	75	54	37	1	39	13	4	6	47	10	.82	8	.261	.320	.318
1991 Vero Beach	A	128	441	115	21	3	3	151	79	39	56	2	49	10	14	6	50	18	.74	6	.261	.353	.342
1992 San Antonio	AA	95	345	93	12	5	2	121	40	34	28	1	38	4	16	1	18	15	.55	12	.270	.331	.351
Albuquerque	AAA	36	116	34	3	0	0	37	14	8	9	0	7	0	2	0	1	2	.33	2	.293	.344	.319
1993 Albuquerque	AAA	18	26	4	0	1	0	6	3	4	3	0	2	0	1	1	1	1	.50	1	.154	.233	.231
San Antonio	AA	41	122	35	5	1	0	42	12	5	16	1	14	3	2	0	4	5	.44	4	.287	.383	.344
1994 Albuquerque	AAA	88	267	79	12	6	1	106	44	33	14	0	13	6	4	1	15	8	.65	12	.296	.344	.397
6 Min. YEARS		602	2054	566	83	21	10	721	306	211	184	5	176	45	48	17	159	67	.70	48	.276	.346	.351

Pat Howell

Bats: Both Throws: Right Pos: OF Ht: 5'11" Wt: 155 Born: 08/31/68 Age: 26

Year Team	Lg	G	AB	H	2B	3B	HR	TB	R	RBI	TBB	IBB	SO	HBP	SH	SF	SB	CS	SB%	GDP	Avg	OBP	SLG
1987 Kingsport	R	34	92	20	2	0	1	25	14	5	10	0	28	2	0	0	8	2	.80	0	.217	.308	.272
1988 Kingsport	R	66	251	67	6	3	0	79	43	16	12	0	52	1	2	3	27	6	.82	2	.267	.300	.315
1989 Pittsfield	A	56	231	67	4	3	1	80	41	26	7	0	46	3	6	1	45	10	.82	0	.290	.318	.346
1990 Columbia	A	135	573	151	15	5	1	179	97	37	22	2	111	7	10	3	79	11	.88	0	.264	.298	.312
1991 St. Lucie	A	62	246	54	8	2	0	66	36	10	14	0	47	3	6	0	37	9	.80	0	.220	.270	.268
Williamsprt	AA	70	274	77	5	1	1	87	43	26	21	0	50	6	8	0	27	11	.71	2	.281	.346	.318
1992 Tidewater	AAA	104	405	99	8	3	1	116	46	22	22	1	98	5	4	2	21	10	.68	2	.244	.290	.286
1993 Portland	AAA	114	369	77	11	3	2	100	57	29	12	0	77	1	6	3	36	10	.78	2	.209	.234	.271
1994 Binghamton	AA	8	35	9	3	0	0	12	7	3	3	0	10	0	0	0	3	0	1.00	0	.257	.316	.343
Norfolk	AAA	89	183	42	11	2	0	57	28	4	17	1	43	0	7	1	9	6	.60	1	.230	.294	.311
1992 New York	NL	31	75	14	1	0	0	15	9	1	2	0	15	1	1	0	4	2	.67	1	.187	.218	.200
8 Min. YEARS		738	2659	663	73	22	7	801	412	178	140	4	562	28	49	13	292	75	.80	11	.249	.293	.301

John Hrusovsky

Pitches: Right Bats: Right Pos: P Ht: 6'1" Wt: 195 Born: 09/12/70 Age: 24

		HOW MUCH HE PITCHED						WHAT HE GAVE UP											THE RESULTS					
Year Team	Lg	G	GS	CG	GF	IP	BFP	H	R	ER	HR	SH	SF	HB	TBB	IBB	SO	WP	Bk	W	L	Pct.	ShO	Sv	ERA
1991 Princeton	R	26	0	0	25	44.1	189	26	12	9	2	2	1	3	21	3	52	1	0	4	4	.500	0	7	1.83

Year	Team	Lg	G	GS	CG	GF	IP	BFP	H	R	ER	HR	SH	SF	HB	TBB	IBB	SO	WP	Bk	W	L	Pct.	ShO	Sv	ERA
1992	Chston-Vw	A	19	0	0	16	21.2	85	13	3	2	0	0	1	0	9	1	27	0	0	1	0	1.000	0	9	0.83
	Cedar Rapds	A	25	0	0	25	30.2	132	18	14	10	3	2	1	1	16	0	52	5	1	2	3	.400	0	7	2.93
1993	Winston-Sal	A	52	0	0	40	58.1	260	53	27	25	4	0	1	4	27	2	61	6	0	2	4	.333	0	25	3.86
1994	Chattanooga	AA	9	0	0	4	13.1	62	8	8	8	2	1	0	0	7	1	13	0	0	0	0	.000	0	0	5.40
	Canton-Akrn	AA	12	0	0	6	22	107	29	18	14	4	1	3	0	12	1	22	2	0	0	0	.000	0		5.73
	Kinston	A	19	1	0	15	23	113	28	19	16	2	0	1	1	16	0	16	4	0	0	3	.000	0	3	6.26
	4 Min. YEARS		162	1	0	131	213.1	948	181	101	84	17	6	8	9	108	8	243	18	1	9	14	.391	0	52	3.54

Mike Hubbard

Bats: Right Throws: Right Pos: C Ht: 6'1" Wt: 180 Born: 02/16/71 Age: 24

			BATTING														BASERUNNING				PERCENTAGES		
Year	Team	Lg	G	AB	H	2B	3B	HR	TB	R	RBI	TBB	IBB	SO	HBP	SH	SF	SB	CS	SB%	GDP	Avg	OBP	SLG
1992	Geneva	A	50	183	44	4	4	3	65	25	25	7	0	29	3	4	4	6	4	.60	2	.240	.274	.355
1993	Daytona	A	68	245	72	10	3	1	91	25	25	18	0	41	5	2	5	10	6	.63	4	.294	.348	.371
1994	Orlando	AA	104	357	102	13	3	11	154	52	39	29	4	58	8	2	2	7	7	.50	5	.286	.351	.431
	3 Min. YEARS		222	785	218	27	10	15	310	102	84	54	4	128	16	8	11	23	17	.58	11	.278	.333	.395

Daniel Hubbs

Pitches: Right Bats: Right Pos: P Ht: 6'2" Wt: 200 Born: 01/23/71 Age: 24

			HOW MUCH HE PITCHED						WHAT HE GAVE UP										THE RESULTS				
Year	Team	Lg	G	GS	CG	GF	IP	BFP	H	R	ER	HR	SH	SF	HB	TBB	IBB	SO	WP	Bk	W	L	Pct.	ShO	Sv	ERA
1993	Great Falls	R	3	0	0	1	7.2	29	3	1	1	0	0	0	2	2	0	12	0	1	1	1	.500	0	0	1.17
	Bakersfield	A	19	1	0	8	44.2	181	36	12	9	4	1	2	0	15	1	44	3	1	2	1	.667	0	1	1.81
1994	Bakersfield	A	13	0	0	6	35.1	145	29	17	15	3	3	0	1	10	0	51	0	0	3	1	.750	0	2	3.82
	San Antonio	AA	38	1	0	13	80	340	82	34	28	3	1	6	4	27	7	75	5	0	5	5	.500	0	1	3.15
	2 Min. YEARS		73	2	0	28	167.2	695	150	64	53	10	5	8	7	54	8	182	8	2	11	8	.579	0	4	2.84

Jeff Huber

Pitches: Left Bats: Right Pos: P Ht: 6'4" Wt: 220 Born: 12/17/70 Age: 24

			HOW MUCH HE PITCHED						WHAT HE GAVE UP										THE RESULTS				
Year	Team	Lg	G	GS	CG	GF	IP	BFP	H	R	ER	HR	SH	SF	HB	TBB	IBB	SO	WP	Bk	W	L	Pct.	ShO	Sv	ERA
1990	Padres	R	9	7	0	1	35.2	153	32	20	12	0	0	2	0	15	0	20	2	2	1	4	.200	0	1	3.03
1992	Chston-Sc	A	46	0	0	30	77.1	309	66	31	25	3	2	0	4	21	2	59	6	5	8	3	.727	0	9	2.91
	Waterloo	A	9	0	0	6	15	58	15	4	4	0	1	1	0	1	0	13	0	0	1	2	.333	0	1	2.40
1993	Rancho Cuca	A	42	0	0	41	48.2	199	43	22	17	4	2	0	0	18	0	43	4	0	4	1	.800	0	18	3.14
	Wichita	AA	15	0	0	8	19.1	82	16	9	7	2	1	0	3	9	0	18	1	1	3	1	.750	0	3	3.26
1994	Wichita	AA	38	0	0	29	39.2	193	56	37	31	7	4	3	0	17	2	32	3	0	3	2	.600	0	12	7.03
	4 Min. YEARS		159	7	0	115	235.2	994	228	123	96	16	10	6	7	81	4	185	16	8	20	13	.606	0	44	3.67

Ken Huckaby

Bats: Right Throws: Right Pos: C Ht: 6'1" Wt: 205 Born: 01/27/71 Age: 24

			BATTING														BASERUNNING				PERCENTAGES		
Year	Team	Lg	G	AB	H	2B	3B	HR	TB	R	RBI	TBB	IBB	SO	HBP	SH	SF	SB	CS	SB%	GDP	Avg	OBP	SLG
1991	Great Falls	R	57	213	55	16	0	3	80	39	37	17	0	38	4	1	3	3	2	.60	4	.258	.321	.376
1992	Vero Beach	A	73	261	63	9	0	0	72	14	21	7	0	42	1	2	2	1	1	.50	5	.241	.262	.276
1993	Vero Beach	A	79	281	75	14	1	4	103	22	41	11	1	35	2	3	2	2	1	.67	3	.267	.297	.367
	San Antonio	AA	28	82	18	1	0	0	19	4	5	2	1	7	2	0	1	0	0	.00	0	.220	.253	.232
1994	San Antonio	AA	11	41	11	1	0	1	15	3	9	1	1	1	0	0	0	1	0	1.00	1	.268	.286	.366
	Bakersfield	A	77	270	81	18	1	2	107	29	30	10	0	37	2	0	1	2	3	.40	7	.300	.329	.396
	4 Min. YEARS		325	1148	303	59	2	10	396	111	143	48	3	160	11	6	9	9	7	.56	20	.264	.298	.345

Joe Hudson

Pitches: Right Bats: Right Pos: P Ht: 6'1" Wt: 180 Born: 09/29/70 Age: 24

			HOW MUCH HE PITCHED						WHAT HE GAVE UP										THE RESULTS				
Year	Team	Lg	G	GS	CG	GF	IP	BFP	H	R	ER	HR	SH	SF	HB	TBB	IBB	SO	WP	Bk	W	L	Pct.	ShO	Sv	ERA
1992	Elmira	A	19	7	0	6	72	320	76	46	35	2	3	0	2	33	0	38	4	2	3	3	.500	0	0	4.38
1993	Lynchburg	A	49	1	0	30	84.1	372	97	49	38	1	2	2	2	38	2	62	10	2	8	6	.571	0	6	4.06
1994	Sarasota	A	30	0	0	21	48.1	215	42	20	12	0	1	1	2	27	0	33	6	0	3	1	.750	0	7	2.23
	New Britain	AA	23	0	0	11	39	183	49	18	17	0	3	1	2	18	1	24	1	1	5	3	.625	0	0	3.92
	3 Min. YEARS		121	8	0	68	243.2	1090	264	133	102	3	9	4	8	116	3	157	21	5	19	13	.594	0	13	3.77

Robert Hughes

Bats: Right Throws: Right Pos: C Ht: 6'4" Wt: 220 Born: 03/10/71 Age: 24

			BATTING														BASERUNNING				PERCENTAGES		
Year	Team	Lg	G	AB	H	2B	3B	HR	TB	R	RBI	TBB	IBB	SO	HBP	SH	SF	SB	CS	SB%	GDP	Avg	OBP	SLG
1992	Helena	R	11	40	7	1	1	0	10	5	6	4	0	14	2	0	0	0	0	.00	0	.175	.283	.250
1993	Beloit	A	98	321	89	11	3	17	157	42	56	23	0	77	6	5	0	1	3	.25	9	.277	.337	.489
1994	El Paso	AA	12	36	10	4	1	0	16	3	12	5	0	7	1	0	2	0	1	.00	1	.278	.364	.444
	Stockton	A	95	322	81	24	3	11	144	54	53	33	0	83	9	1	2	2	1	.67	1	.252	.336	.447
	3 Min. YEARS		216	719	187	40	8	28	327	104	127	65	0	181	18	6	4	3	5	.38	11	.260	.335	.455

Troy Hughes

Bats: Right Throws: Right Pos: OF Ht: 6'4" Wt: 212 Born: 01/03/71 Age: 24

Year	Team	Lg	G	AB	H	2B	3B	HR	TB	R	RBI	TBB	IBB	SO	HBP	SH	SF	SB	CS	SB%	GDP	Avg	OBP	SLG
1989	Braves	R	36	110	24	5	0	0	29	17	10	11	0	29	1	1	1	8	4	.67	0	.218	.293	.264
1990	Pulaski	R	46	145	39	7	1	1	51	22	17	16	0	39	0	2	1	5	1	.83	3	.269	.340	.352
1991	Macon	A	112	404	121	33	2	9	185	69	80	36	1	76	3	1	5	22	13	.63	6	.300	.357	.458
1992	Durham	A	128	449	110	21	4	16	187	64	53	49	3	97	1	2	6	12	7	.63	7	.245	.317	.416
1993	Greenville	AA	109	383	102	20	4	14	172	49	58	44	1	67	5	0	3	7	3	.70	10	.266	.347	.449
1994	Richmond	AAA	81	228	49	9	1	1	63	24	18	29	3	48	5	0	6	6	2	.75	7	.215	.310	.276
	Greenville	AA	27	89	27	7	0	3	43	14	12	11	0	11	0	0	1	4	0	1.00	2	.303	.376	.483
	6 Min. YEARS		539	1808	472	102	12	44	730	259	248	196	8	367	15	6	23	64	30	.68	35	.261	.334	.404

Rick Huisman

Pitches: Right Bats: Right Pos: P Ht: 6'3" Wt: 200 Born: 05/17/69 Age: 26

Year	Team	Lg	G	GS	CG	GF	IP	BFP	H	R	ER	HR	SH	SF	HB	TBB	IBB	SO	WP	Bk	W	L	Pct.	ShO	Sv	ERA
1990	Everett	A	1	0	0	0	2	10	3	1	1	0	0	0	0	2	1	0	0	0	0	0	.000	0	0	4.50
	Clinton	A	14	13	0	0	79	315	57	19	18	2	1	2	0	33	0	103	5	4	6	5	.545	0	0	2.05
1991	San Jose	A	26	26	7	0	182.1	720	126	45	37	5	11	3	3	73	1	216	13	3	16	4	.800	4	0	1.83
1992	Shreveport	AA	17	16	1	0	103.1	403	79	33	27	3	2	0	5	31	1	100	3	1	7	4	.636	1	0	2.35
	Phoenix	AAA	9	8	0	0	56	230	45	16	15	3	1	1	1	24	0	44	1	0	3	2	.600	0	0	2.41
1993	San Jose	A	4	4	1	0	23.1	97	19	6	6	0	2	1	2	12	0	15	1	0	2	1	.667	0	0	2.31
	Phoenix	AAA	14	14	0	0	72.1	333	78	54	48	5	1	1	1	45	0	59	8	4	3	4	.429	0	0	5.97
	Tucson	AAA	2	0	0	0	3.2	18	6	5	3	0	0	0	0	1	0	4	5	0	1	0	1.000	0	0	7.36
1994	Jackson	AA	49	0	0	46	50.1	204	32	10	9	1	1	1	2	24	2	63	1	0	3	0	1.000	0	31	1.61
	5 Min. YEARS		136	81	9	46	572.1	2330	445	189	164	19	19	9	14	245	4	606	38	12	41	20	.672	5	31	2.58

Mike Humphreys

Bats: Right Throws: Right Pos: OF Ht: 6'0" Wt: 185 Born: 04/10/67 Age: 28

Year	Team	Lg	G	AB	H	2B	3B	HR	TB	R	RBI	TBB	IBB	SO	HBP	SH	SF	SB	CS	SB%	GDP	Avg	OBP	SLG
1988	Spokane	A	76	303	93	16	5	6	137	67	59	46	1	57	0	0	4	21	4	.84	9	.307	.394	.452
1989	Riverside	A	117	420	121	26	1	13	188	77	66	79	4	79	7	3	5	23	10	.70	9	.288	.397	.448
1990	Wichita	AA	116	421	116	21	4	17	196	92	79	67	4	79	5	2	4	37	9	.80	6	.276	.378	.466
	Las Vegas	AAA	12	42	10	1	0	2	17	7	6	4	0	11	1	2	0	1	0	1.00	4	.238	.319	.405
1991	Columbus	AAA	117	413	117	23	5	9	177	71	53	63	3	61	3	1	6	34	9	.79	10	.283	.377	.429
1992	Columbus	AAA	114	408	115	18	6	6	163	83	46	59	0	70	1	3	5	37	13	.74	9	.282	.370	.400
1993	Columbus	AAA	92	330	95	16	2	6	133	59	42	52	2	57	3	2	2	18	15	.55	6	.288	.388	.403
1994	Columbus	AAA	135	487	121	25	1	8	172	83	51	64	0	92	5	6	8	28	12	.70	8	.248	.337	.353
1991	New York	AL	25	40	8	0	0	0	8	9	3	9	0	7	0	1	0	2	0	1.00	0	.200	.347	.200
1992	New York	AL	4	10	1	0	0	0	1	0	0	0	0	1	0	0	0	0	0	.00	2	.100	.100	.100
1993	New York	AL	25	35	6	2	1	1	13	6	6	4	0	11	0	0	1	2	1	.67	0	.171	.250	.371
	7 Min. YEARS		779	2824	788	146	24	67	1183	539	402	427	14	506	25	19	34	199	72	.73	61	.279	.375	.419
	3 Maj. YEARS		54	85	15	2	1	1	22	15	9	13	0	19	0	1	1	4	1	.80	2	.176	.283	.259

Brian L. Hunter

Bats: Right Throws: Right Pos: OF Ht: 6'4" Wt: 180 Born: 03/05/71 Age: 24

Year	Team	Lg	G	AB	H	2B	3B	HR	TB	R	RBI	TBB	IBB	SO	HBP	SH	SF	SB	CS	SB%	GDP	Avg	OBP	SLG
1989	Astros	R	51	206	35	2	3	0	37	15	13	7	0	42	1	0	0	12	6	.67	1	.170	.201	.180
1990	Asheville	A	127	445	111	14	6	0	137	84	16	60	1	72	8	1	1	45	13	.78	3	.249	.348	.308
1991	Osceola	A	118	392	94	15	3	1	118	51	30	45	2	75	1	5	5	32	9	.78	6	.240	.316	.301
1992	Osceola	A	131	489	146	18	9	1	185	62	62	31	0	76	5	6	4	39	19	.67	7	.299	.344	.378
1993	Jackson	AA	133	523	154	22	5	10	216	84	52	34	4	85	1	5	2	35	18	.66	11	.294	.338	.413
1994	Tucson	AAA	128	513	191	28	9	10	267	113	51	52	5	52	5	3	4	49	14	.78	11	.372	.432	.520
1994	Houston	NL	6	24	6	1	0	0	7	2	0	1	0	6	0	1	0	2	1	.67	0	.250	.280	.292
	6 Min. YEARS		688	2568	731	99	32	22	960	409	224	229	12	402	21	20	16	212	79	.73	39	.285	.346	.374

Jim Hunter

Pitches: Right Bats: Right Pos: P Ht: 6'3" Wt: 205 Born: 06/22/64 Age: 31

Year	Team	Lg	G	GS	CG	GF	IP	BFP	H	R	ER	HR	SH	SF	HB	TBB	IBB	SO	WP	Bk	W	L	Pct.	ShO	Sv	ERA
1985	Jamestown	A	14	13	1	1	70.2	310	65	30	22	1	2	1	1	34	1	41	3	0	3	3	.500	0	0	2.80
1986	Burlington	A	9	9	1	0	45	210	52	28	23	1	0	1	2	25	0	28	2	1	2	3	.400	0	0	4.60
	Beloit	A	15	15	2	0	89.1	382	91	47	37	4	2	1	5	22	3	52	5	1	4	5	.444	0	0	3.73
1987	Stockton	A	8	8	0	0	51.1	214	39	16	14	1	1	2	5	20	0	44	2	0	6	1	.857	0	0	2.45
	El Paso	AA	16	15	1	1	95.2	421	117	60	49	14	1	2	2	33	1	62	4	0	5	5	.500	0	0	4.61
1988	El Paso	AA	26	26	2	0	147.2	666	163	107	93	15	3	4	8	77	2	103	4	3	8	11	.421	0	0	5.67
1989	El Paso	AA	19	19	4	0	124.2	547	149	70	58	9	3	4	4	45	1	68	5	0	7	10	.412	0	0	4.19
1990	El Paso	AA	9	9	2	0	62	258	64	31	27	9	0	0	4	15	0	37	1	0	6	3	.667	0	0	3.92
	Denver	AAA	20	20	2	0	117	512	138	76	61	5	4	8	5	45	1	57	1	0	6	8	.429	0	0	4.69

Year	Team						IP	BFP	H	R	ER	HR				TBB	IBB	SO			W	L	Pct.			ERA
1991	Denver	AAA	14	14	0	0	87.1	374	94	38	32	6	4	1	5	27	0	43	2	0	7	4	.636	0	0	3.30
1992	El Paso	AA	3	3	0	0	18	69	18	6	6	0	0	1	1	3	0	9	0	1	1	1	.500	0	0	3.00
	Denver	AAA	34	18	3	9	134.2	590	144	68	55	13	4	4	4	46	2	56	2	2	6	7	.462	0	0	3.68
1993	New Orleans	AAA	39	3	0	8	68.2	301	82	40	32	8	2	1	6	25	2	35	1	0	5	2	.714	0	1	4.19
	El Paso	AA	14	0	0	2	22	89	20	8	6	1	1	1	0	6	1	10	0	0	3	1	.750	0	1	2.45
1994	Buffalo	AAA	5	5	0	0	22.2	96	22	11	11	1	3	1	2	6	0	9	1	0	1	0	.000	0	0	4.37
1991	Milwaukee	AL	8	6	0	0	31	152	45	26	25	3	1	1	4	17	0	14	3	0	0	5	.000	0	0	7.26
	10 Min. YEARS		245	177	18	21	1156.2	5039	1258	636	526	88	30	32	51	429	14	654	33	8	69	65	.515	0	4	4.09

Butch Huskey

Bats: Right Throws: Right Pos: 3B   Ht: 6' 3" Wt: 244 Born: 11/10/71 Age: 23

						BATTING												BASERUNNING				PERCENTAGES		
Year	Team	Lg	G	AB	H	2B	3B	HR	TB	R	RBI	TBB	IBB	SO	HBP	SH	SF	SB	CS	SB%	GDP	Avg	OBP	SLG
1989	Mets	R	54	190	50	14	2	6	86	27	34	14	0	36	1	0	0	4	1	.80	2	.263	.317	.453
1990	Kingsport	R	72	279	75	12	0	14	129	39	53	24	1	74	2	0	5	4	3	.57	2	.269	.326	.462
1991	Columbia	A	134	492	141	27	5	26	256	88	99	54	6	90	4	1	7	22	10	.69	11	.287	.357	.520
1992	St. Lucie	A	134	493	125	17	1	18	198	65	75	33	6	74	1	0	5	7	3	.70	5	.254	.299	.402
1993	Binghamton	AA	139	526	132	23	1	25	232	72	98	48	3	102	2	0	8	11	2	.85	14	.251	.312	.441
1994	Norfolk	AAA	127	474	108	23	3	10	167	59	57	37	2	88	3	4	5	16	7	.70	9	.228	.285	.352
1993	New York	NL	13	41	6	1	0	0	7	2	3	1	0	13	0	0	2	0	0	.00	0	.146	.159	.171
	6 Min. YEARS		660	2454	631	116	12	99	1068	350	416	210	18	464	13	5	30	64	26	.71	43	.257	.315	.435

Jeff Huson

Bats: Left Throws: Right Pos: SS   Ht: 6' 3" Wt: 180 Born: 08/15/64 Age: 30

						BATTING												BASERUNNING				PERCENTAGES		
Year	Team	Lg	G	AB	H	2B	3B	HR	TB	R	RBI	TBB	IBB	SO	HBP	SH	SF	SB	CS	SB%	GDP	Avg	OBP	SLG
1986	Burlington	A	133	457	132	19	1	16	201	85	72	76	4	68	2	2	3	32	6	.84	13	.289	.390	.440
	Jacksnville	AA	1	4	0	0	0	0	0	0	0	0	0	0	0	0	0	0	0	.00	0	.000	.000	.000
1987	Wst Plm Bch	A	131	455	130	15	4	1	156	54	53	50	4	30	1	6	8	33	9	.79	9	.286	.352	.343
1988	Jacksnville	AA	128	471	117	18	1	0	137	72	34	59	3	45	3	10	3	56	13	.81	15	.248	.334	.291
1989	Indianapols	AAA	102	378	115	17	4	3	149	70	35	50	1	26	1	2	2	30	17	.64	10	.304	.385	.394
1991	Okla City	AAA	2	6	3	1	0	0	4	0	2	0	0	1	0	0	0	0	0	.00	0	.500	.500	.667
1993	Okla City	AAA	24	76	22	5	0	1	30	11	10	13	0	10	0	0	0	1	3	.25	1	.289	.393	.395
1994	Okla City	AAA	83	302	91	20	2	1	118	47	27	30	2	32	1	6	2	18	5	.78	11	.301	.366	.391
1988	Montreal	NL	20	42	13	2	0	0	15	7	3	4	2	3	0	0	0	2	1	.67	2	.310	.370	.357
1989	Montreal	NL	32	74	12	5	0	0	17	1	2	6	3	6	0	3	0	3	0	1.00	6	.162	.225	.230
1990	Texas	AL	145	396	95	12	2	0	111	57	28	46	0	54	2	7	3	12	4	.75	8	.240	.320	.280
1991	Texas	AL	119	268	57	8	3	2	77	36	26	39	0	32	0	9	1	8	3	.73	6	.213	.312	.287
1992	Texas	AL	123	318	83	14	3	4	115	49	24	41	2	43	1	8	6	18	6	.75	7	.261	.342	.362
1993	Texas	AL	23	45	6	1	0	0	9	3	2	0	0	10	0	0	0	0	0	.00	0	.133	.133	.200
	7 Min. YEARS		604	2149	610	95	12	22	795	339	233	278	14	212	9	26	18	170	53	.76	59	.284	.366	.370
	6 Maj. YEARS		462	1143	266	42	9	6	344	153	85	136	7	148	3	28	10	43	14	.75	29	.233	.313	.301

David Hutcheson

Pitches: Right Bats: Right Pos: P   Ht: 6'2" Wt: 185 Born: 08/29/71 Age: 23

			HOW MUCH HE PITCHED					WHAT HE GAVE UP												THE RESULTS					
Year	Team	Lg	G	GS	CG	GF	IP	BFP	H	R	ER	HR	SH	SF	HB	TBB	IBB	SO	WP	Bk	W	L	Pct.	ShO	Sv	ERA
1993	Peoria	A	15	12	1	1	89	357	71	26	23	2	5	2	5	29	0	82	9	1	4	3	.571	1	0	2.33
1994	Daytona	A	25	24	4	0	162	663	139	57	46	6	4	6	8	35	0	102	3	3	13	5	.722	3	0	2.56
	Orlando	AA	3	3	1	0	19	80	12	10	7	2	0	0	1	7	0	12	0	0	1	2	.333	0	0	3.32
	2 Min. YEARS		43	39	6	1	270	1100	222	93	76	10	9	8	14	71	0	196	12	4	18	10	.643	4	0	2.53

Jason Hutchins

Pitches: Right Bats: Right Pos: P   Ht: 6'1" Wt: 185 Born: 03/20/70 Age: 25

			HOW MUCH HE PITCHED					WHAT HE GAVE UP												THE RESULTS					
Year	Team	Lg	G	GS	CG	GF	IP	BFP	H	R	ER	HR	SH	SF	HB	TBB	IBB	SO	WP	Bk	W	L	Pct.	ShO	Sv	ERA
1992	Bend	A	34	0	0	26	41.2	176	24	15	15	4	4	2	6	24	2	65	3	3	0	3	.000	0	18	2.59
1993	Central Val	A	20	0	0	9	20.2	116	14	21	21	4	0	1	5	37	0	27	7	0	1	3	.250	0	0	9.15
	Rockies	R	1	0	0	0	0	6	0	6	6	0	0	0	2	4	0	0	0	0	0	0	.000	0	0	0.00
1994	Central Val	A	19	0	0	18	24	99	15	6	5	1	0	1	1	14	0	29	5	0	0	1	.000	0	10	1.88
	New Haven	AA	25	1	0	15	39.1	189	36	33	32	6	2	2	4	34	1	33	3	0	0	1	.000	0	0	7.32
	3 Min. YEARS		99	1	0	68	125.2	586	89	81	76	15	6	6	18	113	3	154	18	3	1	9	.100	0	29	5.44

Gary Hymel

Bats: Right Throws: Right Pos: C   Ht: 6'2" Wt: 195 Born: 05/21/68 Age: 27

						BATTING												BASERUNNING				PERCENTAGES		
Year	Team	Lg	G	AB	H	2B	3B	HR	TB	R	RBI	TBB	IBB	SO	HBP	SH	SF	SB	CS	SB%	GDP	Avg	OBP	SLG
1991	Sumter	A	34	116	23	5	1	2	36	7	15	5	0	46	1	0	0	1	1	.50	0	.198	.238	.310
1992	Albany	A	87	286	54	11	1	4	79	29	23	31	0	97	6	1	1	2	4	.33	3	.189	.281	.276
1993	Ottawa	AAA	3	3	0	0	0	0	0	0	0	0	0	2	0	0	0	0	0	.00	0	.000	.000	.000
	Burlington	A	50	182	50	14	1	11	99	28	41	3	0	60	5	0	4	1	0	1.00	3	.275	.299	.544
	Wst Plm Bch	A	37	112	29	9	1	3	49	15	10	7	0	31	2	1	1	2	2	.50	0	.259	.311	.438
1994	Harrisburg	AA	77	233	58	16	0	12	110	36	36	9	0	67	3	2	7	1	0	1.00	1	.249	.278	.472
	4 Min. YEARS		288	932	214	55	4	32	373	115	125	55	0	303	17	4	13	7	7	.50	13	.230	.281	.400

Cole Hyson

Pitches: Right Bats: Right Pos: P   Ht: 6'4" Wt: 225 Born: 08/14/68 Age: 26

			HOW MUCH HE PITCHED						WHAT HE GAVE UP									THE RESULTS					
Year Team	Lg	G	GS	CG	GF	IP	BFP	H	R	ER	HR	SH	SF	HB	TBB	IBB	SO	WP	Bk	W	L	Pct.	ShO	Sv	ERA
1989 Auburn	A	15	12	2	2	78	349	77	42	32	7	5	2	5	36	1	78	4	2	4	5	.444	0	1	3.69
1990 Osceola	A	26	26	0	0	141.1	628	130	77	64	5	3		14	70	0	92	10	1	6	12	.333	0	0	4.08
1991 Osceola	A	25	23	3	1	131.1	578	134	68	61	6	5	6		63	1	91	16	0	8	10	.444	0	0	4.18
1992 Waterloo	A	17	0	0	16	22.2	101	18	10	8	0	2	1	3	12	2	25	3	0	0	1	.000	0	13	3.18
High Desert	A	7	0	0	3	5	37	10	12	11	2	0	0	0	12	0	6	3	0	0	0	.000	0	1	19.80
1994 Wichita	AA	1	0	0	0	0.2	6	2	4	4	0	0	1	0	2	0	0	0	0	0	0	.000	0	0	54.00
5 Min. YEARS		91	61	5	22	379	1699	371	213	180	20	15	13	27	195	4	292	36	3	18	28	.391	0	15	4.27

Adam Hyzdu

Bats: Right Throws: Right Pos: OF   Ht: 6'2" Wt: 210 Born: 12/06/71 Age: 23

			BATTING														BASERUNNING				PERCENTAGES		
Year Team	Lg	G	AB	H	2B	3B	HR	TB	R	RBI	TBB	IBB	SO	HBP	SH	SF	SB	CS	SB%	GDP	Avg	OBP	SLG
1990 Everett	A	69	253	62	16	1	6	98	31	34	28	1	78	2	0	5	2	4	.33	4	.245	.319	.387
1991 Clinton	A	124	410	96	14	5	5	135	47	50	64	1	131	3	7	2	4	5	.44	10	.234	.340	.329
1992 San Jose	A	128	457	127	25	5	9	189	60	60	55	4	134	1	1	8	10	5	.67	6	.278	.351	.414
1993 San Jose	A	44	165	48	11	3	13	104	35	38	29	0	53	0	1	2	1	1	.50	3	.291	.393	.630
Shreveport	AA	86	302	61	17	0	6	96	30	25	20	2	82	1	1	1	0	5	.00	5	.202	.253	.318
1994 Winston-Sal	A	55	210	58	11	1	15	116	30	39	18	0	33	2	0	2	1	5	.17	3	.276	.336	.552
Chattanooga	AA	38	133	35	10	0	3	54	17	9	8	0	21	1	1	0	0	2	.00	1	.263	.310	.406
Indianapls	AAA	12	25	3	2	0	0	5	3	3	3	1	5	0	0	2	0	0	.00	0	.120	.143	.200
5 Min. YEARS		556	1955	490	106	15	57	797	253	258	223	8	537	10	11	22	18	27	.40	32	.251	.327	.408

Todd Ingram

Pitches: Right Bats: Right Pos: P   Ht: 6'4" Wt: 200 Born: 04/01/68 Age: 27

			HOW MUCH HE PITCHED						WHAT HE GAVE UP									THE RESULTS					
Year Team	Lg	G	GS	CG	GF	IP	BFP	H	R	ER	HR	SH	SF	HB	TBB	IBB	SO	WP	Bk	W	L	Pct.	ShO	Sv	ERA
1991 Sou Oregon	A	19	12	1	1	81.1	355	72	39	31	4	2	2	6	39	0	64	5	3	6	5	.545	0	1	3.43
1992 Reno	A	41	9	0	23	67.1	332	91	69	54	8	0	3	3	40	4	44	12	2	1	7	.125	0	9	7.22
1993 Modesto	A	32	0	0	24	42.2	196	49	30	26	4	1	2	2	18	3	39	11	1	5	7	.417	0	9	5.48
1994 Huntsville	AA	48	0	0	28	59.1	278	63	40	36	4	5	0	1	37	4	55	7	0	3	8	.273	0	11	5.46
4 Min. YEARS		138	21	1	76	250.2	1161	275	178	147	20	8	7	12	134	11	202	35	6	15	27	.357	0	30	5.28

Jeff Innis

Pitches: Right Bats: Right Pos: P   Ht: 6'1" Wt: 170 Born: 07/05/62 Age: 32

			HOW MUCH HE PITCHED						WHAT HE GAVE UP									THE RESULTS					
Year Team	Lg	G	GS	CG	GF	IP	BFP	H	R	ER	HR	SH	SF	HB	TBB	IBB	SO	WP	Bk	W	L	Pct.	ShO	Sv	ERA
1984 Jackson	AA	42	0	0	27	59.1	283	65	34	28	3	4	0	0	40	8	63	6	1	6	5	.545	0	8	4.25
1985 Lynchburg	A	53	0	0	39	77	311	46	26	20	2	6	2	1	40	1	91	3	0	6	3	.667	0	14	2.34
1986 Jackson	AA	56	0	0	48	92	359	69	30	25	2	3	6	1	24	3	75	2	0	4	5	.444	0	25	2.45
1987 Tidewater	AAA	29	0	0	18	44.1	171	26	10	10	3	2	0	0	16	4	28	1	0	6	1	.857	0	5	2.03
1988 Tidewater	AAA	34	0	0	19	48.1	213	43	22	19	3	3	1	0	25	8	43	1	0	0	5	.000	0	4	3.54
1989 Tidewater	AAA	25	0	0	18	29.2	127	28	9	7	0	3	1	1	8	2	14	1	0	3	1	.750	0	10	2.12
1990 Tidewater	AAA	40	0	0	33	52.2	209	34	11	10	1	4	1	3	17	5	42	0	1	5	2	.714	0	19	1.71
1994 Salt Lake	AAA	7	0	0	2	10	44	10	4	3	0	0	1	0	4	0	4	0	0	0	0	.000	0	0	2.70
Las Vegas	AAA	33	0	0	8	36.1	176	41	32	16	1	1	1	0	23	3	34	0	0	1	2	.333	0	1	3.96
1987 New York	NL	17	1	0	8	25.2	109	29	9	9	5	0	0	1	4	1	28	1	1	0	1	.000	0	0	3.16
1988 New York	NL	12	0	0	7	19	80	19	6	4	0	1	1	0	2	1	14	0	0	1	1	.500	0	1	1.89
1989 New York	NL	29	0	0	12	39.2	160	34	18	14	2	1	1	1	8	0	16	0	0	0	1	.000	0	0	3.18
1990 New York	NL	18	0	0	12	26.1	104	19	9	7	4	0	2	1	10	3	12	1	1	1	3	.250	0	1	2.39
1991 New York	NL	69	0	0	29	84.2	336	66	30	25	2	6	5	0	23	6	47	4	0	0	2	.000	0	0	2.66
1992 New York	NL	76	0	0	28	88	373	85	32	28	4	7	4	6	36	4	39	1	0	6	9	.400	0	1	2.86
1993 New York	NL	67	0	0	30	76.2	345	81	39	35	5	9	1	6	38	12	36	3		2	3	.400	0	3	4.11
8 Min. YEARS		319	0	0	212	449.2	1893	362	178	138	15	26	13	6	197	34	394	14	2	31	24	.564	0	86	2.76
7 Maj. YEARS		288	1	0	126	360	1507	337	141	122	22	24	14	15	121	27	192	10	3	10	20	.333	0	5	3.05

Jason Isringhausen

Pitches: Right Bats: Right Pos: P   Ht: 6'3" Wt: 188 Born: 09/07/72 Age: 22

			HOW MUCH HE PITCHED						WHAT HE GAVE UP									THE RESULTS					
Year Team	Lg	G	GS	CG	GF	IP	BFP	H	R	ER	HR	SH	SF	HB	TBB	IBB	SO	WP	Bk	W	L	Pct.	ShO	Sv	ERA
1992 Mets	R	6	6	0	0	29	133	26	19	14	0	0	0	3	17	1	25	2	0	2	4	.333	0	0	4.34
Kingsport	R	7	6	1	0	36	160	32	22	13	2	0	3	1	12	1	24	2	1	4	1	.800	1	0	3.25
1993 Pittsfield	A	15	15	2	0	90.1	375	68	45	33	7	4	6	3	28	0	104	8	0	7	4	.636	0	0	3.29
1994 St. Lucie	A	14	14	6	0	101	391	76	31	25	2	1	1	2	27	2	59	4	0	6	4	.600	2	0	2.23
Binghamton	AA	14	14	2	0	92.1	368	78	35	31	6	4	5	2	23	0	69	5	1	5	4	.556	0	0	3.02
3 Min. YEARS		56	55	11	0	348.2	1427	280	152	116	17	9	15	11	107	4	281	21	2	24	17	.585	4	0	2.99

Damian Jackson

Bats: Right **Throws:** Right **Pos:** SS **Ht:** 5'10" **Wt:** 160 **Born:** 08/16/73 **Age:** 21

					BATTING													BASERUNNING				PERCENTAGES		
Year	Team	Lg	G	AB	H	2B	3B	HR	TB	R	RBI	TBB	IBB	SO	HBP	SH	SF	SB	CS	SB%	GDP	Avg	OBP	SLG
1992	Burlington	R	62	226	56	12	1	0	70	32	23	32	0	31	6	6	3	29	5	.85	1	.248	.352	.310
1993	Columbus	A	108	350	94	19	3	6	137	70	45	41	0	61	5	5	1	26	7	.79	1	.269	.353	.391
1994	Canton-Akrn	AA	138	531	143	29	5	5	197	85	46	60	2	121	5	10	5	37	16	.70	8	.269	.346	.371
	3 Min. YEARS		308	1107	293	60	9	11	404	187	114	133	2	213	16	21	9	92	28	.77	10	.265	.349	.365

Jeff Jackson

Bats: Right **Throws:** Right **Pos:** OF **Ht:** 6'2" **Wt:** 180 **Born:** 01/02/72 **Age:** 23

					BATTING													BASERUNNING				PERCENTAGES		
Year	Team	Lg	G	AB	H	2B	3B	HR	TB	R	RBI	TBB	IBB	SO	HBP	SH	SF	SB	CS	SB%	GDP	Avg	OBP	SLG
1989	Martinsvlle	R	48	163	37	5	1	2	50	16	21	14	1	66	2	0	1	11	2	.85	0	.227	.294	.307
1990	Batavia	A	63	227	45	11	3	3	71	30	22	30	1	81	4	3	0	12	11	.52	1	.198	.303	.313
1991	Spartanburg	A	121	440	99	18	1	5	134	73	33	52	0	123	6	3	1	29	13	.69	2	.225	.315	.305
1992	Clearwater	A	79	297	72	11	2	6	105	35	36	23	2	78	4	0	2	6	6	.50	4	.242	.304	.354
	Reading	AA	36	108	20	1	2	0	25	12	6	12	0	34	4	0	0	9	4	.69	2	.185	.290	.231
1993	Reading	AA	113	374	89	14	3	9	136	45	51	30	1	117	2	1	1	20	8	.71	7	.238	.297	.364
1994	Reading	AA	47	124	22	0	1	5	39	12	11	10	0	54	5	0	0	2	3	.40	3	.177	.266	.315
	6 Min. YEARS		507	1733	384	60	13	30	560	223	180	171	5	553	27	7	5	89	47	.65	19	.222	.301	.323

John Jackson

Bats: Left **Throws:** Left **Pos:** OF **Ht:** 6'0" **Wt:** 185 **Born:** 01/02/67 **Age:** 28

					BATTING													BASERUNNING				PERCENTAGES		
Year	Team	Lg	G	AB	H	2B	3B	HR	TB	R	RBI	TBB	IBB	SO	HBP	SH	SF	SB	CS	SB%	GDP	Avg	OBP	SLG
1990	Everett	A	26	92	28	2	2	1	37	26	7	27	0	11	4	1	1	14	4	.78	2	.304	.476	.402
1991	San Jose	A	14	44	13	0	2	0	17	8	3	8	0	5	1	0	0	1	2	.33	1	.295	.415	.386
1992	Midland	AA	40	151	44	4	3	0	54	19	16	17	0	20	3	3	0	12	5	.71	8	.291	.374	.358
1993	Midland	AA	70	243	79	18	2	3	110	43	34	40	1	43	10	6	4	12	8	.60	8	.325	.434	.453
	Vancouver	AAA	55	201	58	9	4	2	81	28	20	17	0	29	2	6	3	12	4	.75	3	.289	.345	.403
1994	Vancouver	AAA	102	358	105	16	5	2	137	62	38	46	1	37	7	3	4	18	11	.62	9	.293	.381	.383
	5 Min. YEARS		307	1089	327	49	18	8	436	186	118	155	2	145	27	19	12	69	34	.67	31	.300	.397	.400

Frank Jacobs

Bats: Left **Throws:** Left **Pos:** 1B **Ht:** 6'4" **Wt:** 245 **Born:** 05/22/68 **Age:** 27

					BATTING													BASERUNNING				PERCENTAGES		
Year	Team	Lg	G	AB	H	2B	3B	HR	TB	R	RBI	TBB	IBB	SO	HBP	SH	SF	SB	CS	SB%	GDP	Avg	OBP	SLG
1991	Pittsfield	A	74	287	67	12	5	9	116	52	50	46	3	56	0	0	2	5	2	.71	2	.233	.337	.404
1992	St. Lucie	A	123	434	108	23	3	12	173	55	55	35	2	78	4	0	5	3	3	.50	15	.249	.308	.399
1993	Binghamton	AA	109	346	93	17	3	9	143	50	46	42	3	72	4	0	0	2	3	.40	11	.269	.355	.413
1994	Binghamton	AA	121	431	123	26	0	13	188	64	67	51	3	65	1	0	7	2	1	.67	10	.285	.357	.436
	4 Min. YEARS		427	1498	391	78	11	43	620	221	218	174	11	271	9	0	14	12	9	.57	38	.261	.339	.414

Joe Jacobson

Pitches: Right **Bats:** Right **Pos:** P **Ht:** 6'3" **Wt:** 215 **Born:** 12/26/71 **Age:** 23

			HOW MUCH HE PITCHED						WHAT HE GAVE UP										THE RESULTS				
Year	Team	Lg	G	GS	CG	GF	IP	BFP	H	R	ER	HR	SH	SF	HB	TBB	IBB	SO	WP	Bk	W	L	Pct.	ShO	Sv	ERA
1992	Dodgers	R	6	3	0	2	26	100	17	7	5	0	0	0	0	6	0	25	2	1	1	1	.500	0	0	1.73
	Great Falls	R	6	6	1	0	32.1	143	37	22	19	2	0	1	1	9	0	24	3	0	2	2	.500	0	0	5.29
1993	Yakima	A	25	0	0	7	37.2	174	27	16	10	0	2	3	1	28	2	55	1	0	1	0	1.000	0	3	2.39
	Bakersfield	A	6	0	0	3	19.2	88	22	16	10	1	1	0	0	8	0	23	3	0	1	0	1.000	0	2	4.58
1994	Bakersfield	A	3	0	0	1	7.1	26	2	1	1	1	1	0	0	1	0	5	0	0	1	0	1.000	0	0	1.23
	San Antonio	AA	18	0	0	12	25	108	21	9	7	0	2	2	2	12	2	15	2	1	2	1	.667	0	1	2.52
	Vero Beach	A	37	0	0	34	43	193	40	15	13	1	3	0	2	23	2	44	3	0	0	5	.000	0	15	2.72
	3 Min. YEARS		101	9	1	59	191	832	166	86	65	5	9	6	6	87	6	191	14	3	8	9	.471	0	21	3.06

Mike James

Pitches: Right **Bats:** Right **Pos:** P **Ht:** 6'4" **Wt:** 216 **Born:** 08/15/67 **Age:** 27

			HOW MUCH HE PITCHED						WHAT HE GAVE UP										THE RESULTS				
Year	Team	Lg	G	GS	CG	GF	IP	BFP	H	R	ER	HR	SH	SF	HB	TBB	IBB	SO	WP	Bk	W	L	Pct.	ShO	Sv	ERA
1988	Great Falls	R	14	12	0	0	67	299	61	36	28	7	2	3	4	41	0	59	2	5	7	1	.875	0	0	3.76
1989	Bakersfield	A	27	27	1	0	159.2	706	144	82	67	11	3	3	12	78	1	127	13	0	11	8	.579	1	0	3.78
1990	San Antonio	AA	26	26	3	0	157	681	144	73	58	14	4	7	9	78	1	97	10	0	11	4	.733	0	0	3.32
1991	San Antonio	AA	15	15	2	0	89.1	402	88	54	45	10	2	1	4	51	1	74	5	0	9	5	.643	1	0	4.53
	Albuquerque	AAA	13	8	0	3	45	208	51	36	33	7	0	3	2	30	0	39	5	1	1	3	.250	0	0	6.60
1992	San Antonio	AA	8	8	0	0	54	214	39	16	16	3	2	0	1	20	0	52	1	1	2	1	.667	0	0	2.67
	Albuquerque	AAA	18	6	0	3	46.2	211	55	35	29	4	3	2	2	22	0	33	4	0	2	1	.667	0	1	5.59
1993	Albuquerque	AAA	16	0	0	5	31.1	154	38	28	26	5	1	2	4	19	3	32	2	0	1	0	1.000	0	2	7.47
	Vero Beach	A	30	1	0	15	60.1	271	54	37	33	2	2	2	5	33	5	60	5	1	2	3	.400	0	5	4.92
1994	Vancouver	AAA	37	1	0	18	91.1	402	101	56	53	15	1	3	6	34	1	66	3	0	5	3	.625	0	8	5.22
	7 Min. YEARS		204	113	6	44	801.2	3548	775	453	388	78	20	26	47	406	12	639	50	8	51	29	.638	2	16	4.36

126

Pete Janicki

Pitches: Right Bats: Right Pos: P Ht: 6'4" Wt: 190 Born: 01/26/71 Age: 24

Year	Team	Lg	G	GS	CG	GF	IP	BFP	H	R	ER	HR	SH	SF	HB	TBB	IBB	SO	WP	Bk	W	L	Pct.	ShO	Sv	ERA
1993	Palm Sprngs	A	1	1	0	0	1.2	10	3	2	2	0	0	0	0	2	0	2	0	1	0	0	.000	0	0	10.80
1994	Midland	AA	14	14	1	0	70	327	86	68	54	4	3	1	6	33	1	54	15	3	2	6	.250	0	0	6.94
	Lake Elsino	A	3	3	0	0	12	61	17	12	9	2	1	1	4	4	0	12	0	0	1	2	.333	0	0	6.75
	2 Min. YEARS		18	18	1	0	83.2	398	106	82	65	6	4	2	10	39	1	68	15	4	3	8	.273	0	0	6.99

Domingo Jean

Pitches: Right Bats: Right Pos: P Ht: 6'2" Wt: 175 Born: 01/09/69 Age: 26

Year	Team	Lg	G	GS	CG	GF	IP	BFP	H	R	ER	HR	SH	SF	HB	TBB	IBB	SO	WP	Bk	W	L	Pct.	ShO	Sv	ERA
1990	White Sox	R	13	13	1	0	78.2	312	55	32	20	1	0	1	6	16	0	65	10	2	4	5	.286	0	0	2.29
1991	South Bend	A	25	25	2	0	158	680	121	75	58	7	3	7	10	65	0	141	17	5	12	8	.600	0	0	3.30
1992	Ft. Laud	A	23	23	5	0	158.2	637	118	57	46	3	7	6	6	49	1	172	4	1	6	11	.353	1	0	2.61
	Albany	AA	1	1	0	0	4	17	3	2	1	0	0	0	0	3	0	6	1	0	0	0	.000	0	0	2.25
1993	Albany	AA	11	11	1	0	61	257	42	24	17	1	1	1	5	33	0	41	4	1	5	3	.625	0	0	2.51
	Columbus	AAA	7	7	1	0	44.2	180	40	15	14	2	0	2	2	13	1	39	3	0	2	2	.500	0	0	2.82
	Pr William	A	1	0	0	0	1.2	6	1	0	0	0	0	0	0	0	0	1	0	0	0	0	.000	0	0	0.00
1994	Tucson	AAA	6	3	0	1	19	88	20	13	12	3	0	1	0	11	1	16	0	0	0	0	.000	0	0	5.68
1993	New York	AL	10	6	0	0	40.1	176	37	20	20	7	0	1	0	19	1	20	1	0	1	1	.500	0	0	4.46
	5 Min. YEARS		87	83	10	1	525.2	2177	400	218	168	17	11	18	31	190	3	481	39	8	27	29	.482	1	0	2.88

Doug Jennings

Bats: Left Throws: Left Pos: OF Ht: 5'10" Wt: 175 Born: 09/30/64 Age: 30

Year	Team	Lg	G	AB	H	2B	3B	HR	TB	R	RBI	TBB	IBB	SO	HBP	SH	SF	SB	CS	SB%	GDP	Avg	OBP	SLG
1984	Salem	A	52	173	45	7	1	1	57	29	17	40	1	45	3	1	4	12	12	.50	2	.260	.400	.329
1985	Quad City	A	95	319	81	17	7	5	127	50	54	62	1	76	5	2	6	10	8	.56	7	.254	.378	.398
1986	Palm Sprngs	A	129	429	136	31	9	17	236	95	89	117	7	103	10	2	8	7	11	.39	6	.317	.466	.550
1987	Midland	AA	126	464	157	33	1	30	282	106	104	94	11	136	13	2	8	7	3	.70	8	.338	.459	.608
1988	Tacoma	AAA	16	49	16	1	0	0	17	12	9	18	1	13	2	2	0	5	1	.83	1	.327	.522	.347
1989	Tacoma	AAA	137	497	136	35	5	11	214	99	64	93	7	95	16	2	8	10	12	.45	8	.274	.399	.431
1990	Tacoma	AAA	60	208	72	19	1	6	111	32	30	31	4	36	2	1	3	4	2	.67	1	.346	.430	.534
1991	Tacoma	AAA	95	332	89	17	2	3	119	43	44	47	1	65	11	1	9	5	1	.83	6	.268	.368	.358
1992	Rochester	AAA	119	396	109	23	5	14	184	70	76	68	5	80	9	0	4	11	4	.73	10	.275	.390	.465
1993	Iowa	AAA	65	228	67	20	1	7	110	38	37	29	2	64	4	0	2	3	4	.43	5	.294	.380	.482
1994	Indianapls	AAA	130	436	129	34	4	23	240	77	92	72	5	105	12	1	5	6	4	.60	4	.296	.406	.550
1988	Oakland	AL	71	101	21	6	0	1	30	9	15	21	1	28	2	1	3	0	1	.00	1	.208	.346	.297
1989	Oakland	AL	4	4	0	0	0	0	0	0	0	0	0	2	0	0	0	0	0	.00	0	.000	.000	.000
1990	Oakland	AL	64	156	30	7	2	2	47	19	14	17	0	48	2	2	3	0	3	.00	1	.192	.275	.301
1991	Oakland	AL	8	9	1	0	0	0	1	0	0	2	0	2	0	0	0	0	1	.00	1	.111	.273	.111
1993	Chicago	NL	42	52	13	3	1	2	24	8	8	3	0	10	2	1	0	0	0	.00	0	.250	.316	.462
	11 Min. YEARS		1024	3531	1037	237	36	117	1697	651	616	671	45	818	87	14	53	80	62	.56	58	.294	.413	.481
	5 Maj. YEARS		189	322	65	16	3	5	102	36	37	43	1	90	6	3	6	0	5	.00	3	.202	.302	.317

John Jensen

Bats: Left Throws: Right Pos: OF Ht: 6'2" Wt: 215 Born: 11/30/66 Age: 28

Year	Team	Lg	G	AB	H	2B	3B	HR	TB	R	RBI	TBB	IBB	SO	HBP	SH	SF	SB	CS	SB%	GDP	Avg	OBP	SLG
1988	Chston-Wv	A	61	214	57	16	2	6	95	23	29	25	1	52	3	0	0	2	2	.50	6	.266	.351	.444
1989	Winston-Sal	A	69	217	52	8	1	2	68	20	23	22	1	63	2	0	1	5	5	.50	3	.240	.314	.313
	Peoria	A	47	168	38	13	0	4	63	11	21	14	1	47	3	0	3	1	0	1.00	5	.226	.293	.375
1990	Winston-Sal	A	126	403	99	17	4	12	160	59	67	77	8	95	5	2	4	4	4	.50	8	.246	.370	.397
1991	Winston-Sal	A	128	446	114	26	2	14	186	68	78	73	5	119	8	0	1	9	5	.64	7	.256	.369	.417
1992	Charlotte	AA	116	399	104	16	0	14	162	64	54	55	1	86	5	0	8	5	7	.42	1	.261	.351	.406
1993	Orlando	AA	62	192	51	10	2	6	83	27	34	18	2	45	2	0	2	4	3	.57	7	.266	.332	.432
	Iowa	AAA	25	62	11	3	0	2	20	5	8	7	0	18	0	0	0	2	1	.67	3	.177	.261	.323
1994	Orlando	AA	10	24	5	4	0	1	12	1	2	2	0	10	0	0	0	0	0	.00	0	.208	.269	.500
	7 Min. YEARS		644	2125	531	113	11	61	849	278	316	293	19	535	28	2	19	32	27	.54	40	.250	.346	.400

Derek Jeter

Bats: Right Throws: Right Pos: SS Ht: 6'3" Wt: 175 Born: 06/26/74 Age: 21

Year	Team	Lg	G	AB	H	2B	3B	HR	TB	R	RBI	TBB	IBB	SO	HBP	SH	SF	SB	CS	SB%	GDP	Avg	OBP	SLG
1992	Yankees	R	47	173	35	10	0	3	54	19	25	19	0	36	5	0	4	2	2	.50	4	.202	.296	.312
	Greensboro	A	11	37	9	0	0	1	12	4	4	7	0	16	1	0	0	0	1	.00	0	.243	.378	.324
1993	Greensboro	A	128	515	152	14	11	5	203	85	71	58	1	95	11	2	4	18	9	.67	9	.295	.376	.394
1994	Tampa	A	69	292	96	13	8	0	125	61	39	23	2	30	3	3	3	28	2	.93	4	.329	.380	.428
	Albany-Colo	AA	34	122	46	7	2	2	63	17	13	15	0	16	1	3	1	12	2	.86	3	.377	.446	.516
	Columbus	AAA	35	126	44	7	1	3	62	25	16	20	1	15	1	3	0	10	4	.71	6	.349	.439	.492
	3 Min. YEARS		324	1265	382	51	22	14	519	211	168	142	4	208	22	11	11	70	20	.78	26	.302	.379	.410

127

Manuel Jimenez

Bats: Right Throws: Right Pos: SS Ht: 5'11" Wt: 160 Born: 07/04/71 Age: 23

					BATTING													BASERUNNING				PERCENTAGES		
Year	Team	Lg	G	AB	H	2B	3B	HR	TB	R	RBI	TBB	IBB	SO	HBP	SH	SF	SB	CS	SB%	GDP	Avg	OBP	SLG
1991	Pulaski	R	57	234	66	10	7	1	93	37	29	12	2	48	1	2	0	19	8	.70	4	.282	.320	.397
1992	Macon	A	117	401	88	9	3	1	106	25	32	16	1	106	8	4	2	13	15	.46	7	.219	.262	.264
1993	Durham	A	127	427	96	16	4	6	138	55	29	21	0	93	7	10	1	9	12	.44	12	.225	.272	.323
1994	Greenville	AA	64	195	39	6	1	1	50	13	14	5	0	38	1	1	1	3	4	.43	6	.200	.223	.256
	Durham	A	31	104	20	6	0	0	26	6	9	2	0	18	2	0	0	1	1	.50	2	.192	.222	.250
	4 Min. YEARS		396	1361	309	47	15	9	413	136	113	56	3	303	19	17	4	43	37	.54	31	.227	.267	.303

Doug Johns

Pitches: Left Bats: Right Pos: P Ht: 6'2" Wt: 185 Born: 12/19/67 Age: 27

			HOW MUCH HE PITCHED						WHAT HE GAVE UP									THE RESULTS					
Year	Team	Lg	G	GS	CG	GF	IP	BFP	H	R	ER	HR	SH	SF	HB	TBB	IBB	SO	WP	Bk	W	L	Pct.	ShO	Sv	ERA
1990	Sou Oregon	A	6	2	0	4	11	57	13	9	7	0	0	0	0	11	1	9	2	2	0	2	.000	0	1	5.73
	Athletics	R	8	7	1	1	44	172	36	17	9	1	0	0	0	9	1	37	2	0	3	1	.750	0	1	1.84
1991	Madison	A	38	14	1	9	128.1	549	108	59	46	5	6	2	8	54	1	104	13	0	12	6	.667	1	2	3.23
1992	Reno	A	27	26	4	1	179.1	776	194	98	65	11	7	4	1	64	3	101	5	2	13	10	.565	1	0	3.26
	Huntsville	AA	3	1	0	1	16	74	21	11	7	0	1	0	0	5	0	4	1	0	0	0	.000	0	0	3.94
1993	Huntsville	AA	40	6	0	11	91	379	82	41	30	3	7	2	2	31	4	56	2	1	7	5	.583	0	1	2.97
1994	Huntsville	AA	9	0	0	2	15	70	16	2	2	1	2	0	1	12	5	9	1	3	3	0	1.000	0	1	1.20
	Tacoma	AAA	22	19	2	2	134	549	114	55	43	10	4	3	7	48	0	65	2	2	9	8	.529	1	0	2.89
	5 Min. YEARS		153	75	8	31	618.2	2626	584	292	209	31	27	11	19	234	15	385	28	10	47	32	.595	3	4	3.04

Barry Johnson

Pitches: Right Bats: Right Pos: P Ht: 6'4" Wt: 200 Born: 08/21/69 Age: 25

			HOW MUCH HE PITCHED						WHAT HE GAVE UP									THE RESULTS					
Year	Team	Lg	G	GS	CG	GF	IP	BFP	H	R	ER	HR	SH	SF	HB	TBB	IBB	SO	WP	Bk	W	L	Pct.	ShO	Sv	ERA
1991	Expos	R	7	1	0	3	12.2	55	10	9	5	0	0	0	4	6	0	10	2	0	0	2	.000	0	0	3.55
1992	South Bend	A	16	15	5	0	109.1	463	111	56	46	5	1	5	6	23	0	74	8	1	7	5	.583	1	0	3.79
1993	Sarasota	A	18	1	0	7	54.1	205	33	5	4	1	5	2	2	8	0	40	1	1	5	0	1.000	0	1	0.66
	Birmingham	AA	13	1	0	8	21.2	97	27	11	8	2	1	1	0	6	0	16	2	1	2	0	1.000	0	1	3.32
1994	Birmingham	AA	51	4	0	12	97.2	427	100	51	35	7	8	3	2	30	3	67	2	0	6	2	.750	0	1	3.23
	4 Min. YEARS		105	23	5	30	295.2	1247	281	132	98	15	15	11	14	73	3	207	15	3	20	9	.690	1	3	2.98

Chris Johnson

Pitches: Right Bats: Right Pos: P Ht: 6'8" Wt: 215 Born: 12/07/68 Age: 26

			HOW MUCH HE PITCHED						WHAT HE GAVE UP									THE RESULTS					
Year	Team	Lg	G	GS	CG	GF	IP	BFP	H	R	ER	HR	SH	SF	HB	TBB	IBB	SO	WP	Bk	W	L	Pct.	ShO	Sv	ERA
1987	Helena	R	12	11	0	0	60.1	257	55	32	27	8	3	3	3	21	0	54	5	2	5	0	1.000	0	0	4.03
1988	Beloit	A	26	26	0	0	130	566	137	66	57	9	4	4	4	42	3	99	5	9	8	10	.444	0	0	3.95
1989	Beloit	A	25	22	2	2	138.2	585	118	63	49	8	6	3	13	50	0	118	5	2	9	9	.500	1	0	3.18
1990	Stockton	A	23	23	1	0	142	592	121	56	47	7	5	5	9	54	1	112	4	1	13	6	.684	0	0	2.98
1991	El Paso	AA	13	12	0	1	66.2	322	85	56	48	4	6	3	4	40	4	43	5	0	4	4	.500	0	0	6.48
	Harrisburg	AA	10	10	1	0	56.2	243	59	25	21	2	0	1	1	28	0	42	2	1	3	2	.600	1	0	3.34
1992	Harrisburg	AA	28	23	0	1	142.1	616	149	71	63	9	6	5	4	43	1	95	7	1	9	10	.474	0	0	3.98
1993	Harrisburg	AA	1	0	0	0	1.1	6	1	2	2	0	0	0	0	3	1	0	0	0	0	0	.000	0	0	13.50
	Orlando	AA	15	1	0	3	27.1	133	31	12	9	1	3	1	4	15	2	14	3	0	0	1	.000	0	1	2.96
1994	Orlando	AA	20	1	0	9	38.1	146	33	15	13	2	4	1	0	8	1	28	0	0	1	1	.500	0	2	3.05
	8 Min. YEARS		173	129	4	16	803.2	3466	789	398	336	50	37	26	42	304	13	605	36	16	52	43	.547	2	3	3.76

Dom Johnson

Pitches: Right Bats: Right Pos: P Ht: 6'5" Wt: 230 Born: 08/09/68 Age: 26

			HOW MUCH HE PITCHED						WHAT HE GAVE UP									THE RESULTS					
Year	Team	Lg	G	GS	CG	GF	IP	BFP	H	R	ER	HR	SH	SF	HB	TBB	IBB	SO	WP	Bk	W	L	Pct.	ShO	Sv	ERA
1987	Pocatello	R	18	2	0	5	35	174	42	35	28	2	1	3	4	26	1	30	5	0	1	2	.333	0	2	7.20
1988	Clinton	A	24	18	1	1	101	463	87	63	52	4	0	3	4	85	1	67	13	7	4	8	.333	0	0	4.63
1989	Clinton	A	8	7	0	0	37.1	179	42	29	24	2	0	3	2	28	0	30	3	2	0	4	.000	0	0	5.79
	Salinas	A	17	14	1	1	87.1	393	75	42	37	4	1	0	5	63	0	60	15	5	6	4	.600	0	0	3.81
1990	San Jose	A	25	19	2	2	100	456	89	72	60	8	4	4	6	72	0	61	10	0	5	8	.385	0	0	5.40
1991	Reno	A	25	9	1	5	72	315	65	31	26	3	2	5	4	38	0	63	7	0	3	5	.375	0	0	3.25
1992	Palm Sprngs	A	22	4	0	6	40	196	44	32	30	4	1	0	3	35	1	23	10	1	0	4	.000	0	1	6.75
1993	Palm Sprngs	A	45	0	0	12	50.1	240	51	34	32	6	5	4	3	39	7	47	19	0	2	4	.333	0	5	5.72
1994	Midland	AA	31	16	0	3	128.2	580	136	84	67	11	2	3	7	64	0	116	12	2	7	9	.438	0	0	4.69
	8 Min. YEARS		215	89	5	35	651.2	2996	631	422	356	44	16	25	38	450	10	497	94	17	28	48	.368	0	5	4.92

Jeff Johnson

Pitches: Left Bats: Right Pos: P Ht: 6'3" Wt: 200 Born: 08/04/66 Age: 28

			HOW MUCH HE PITCHED						WHAT HE GAVE UP									THE RESULTS					
Year	Team	Lg	G	GS	CG	GF	IP	BFP	H	R	ER	HR	SH	SF	HB	TBB	IBB	SO	WP	Bk	W	L	Pct.	ShO	Sv	ERA
1988	Oneonta	A	14	14	0	0	87.2	371	67	35	29	2	3	3	2	39	0	91	3	2	6	1	.857	0	0	2.98

128

Year	Team	Lg	G	GS	CG	GF	IP	BFP	H	R	ER	HR	SH	SF	HB	TBB	IBB	SO	WP	Bk	W	L	Pct.	ShO	Sv	ERA
1989	Pr William	A	25	24	0	0	138.2	578	125	59	45	7	8	2	0	55	1	99	14	2	4	10	.286	0	0	2.92
1990	Ft.Laudrdle	A	17	17	1	0	103.2	439	101	55	42	2	5	2	3	25	0	84	5	2	6	8	.429	0	0	3.65
	Albany	AA	9	9	3	0	60.2	239	44	14	11	0	2	0	2	15	0	41	1	0	4	3	.571	1	0	1.63
1991	Columbus	AAA	10	10	0	0	62	261	58	27	18	1	4	1	1	25	0	40	1	3	4	0	1.000	0	0	2.61
1992	Columbus	AAA	11	11	0	0	58	229	41	15	14	0	2	2	2	18	0	38	3	1	2	1	.667	0	0	2.17
1993	Columbus	AAA	19	17	3	0	114.2	500	125	55	44	7	6	2	5	47	2	59	4	0	7	6	.538	1	0	3.45
1994	Charlotte	AAA	8	5	0	1	25.1	125	38	27	21	5	0	1	0	14	0	12	1	0	1	3	.250	0	0	7.46
1991	New York	AL	23	23	0	0	127	562	156	89	83	15	7	4	6	33	1	62	5	1	6	11	.353	0	0	5.88
1992	New York	AL	13	8	0	3	52.2	245	71	44	39	4	2	2	2	23	0	14	1	0	2	3	.400	0	0	6.66
1993	New York	AL	2	2	0	0	2.2	22	12	10	9	1	0	0	0	2	0	0	0	0	0	2	.000	0	0	30.38
	7 Min. YEARS		113	107	7	1	650.2	2742	599	287	224	24	30	13	15	238	3	464	32	10	34	32	.515	2	0	3.10
	3 Maj. YEARS		38	33	0	3	182.1	829	239	143	131	20	9	6	8	58	1	76	6	1	8	16	.333	0	0	6.47

Judd Johnson

Pitches: Left Bats: Right Pos: P
Ht: 6'0" Wt: 185 Born: 05/04/66 Age: 29

			HOW MUCH HE PITCHED						WHAT HE GAVE UP												THE RESULTS					
Year	Team	Lg	G	GS	CG	GF	IP	BFP	H	R	ER	HR	SH	SF	HB	TBB	IBB	SO	WP	Bk	W	L	Pct.	ShO	Sv	ERA
1989	Sumter	A	11	0	0	6	25.2	103	20	7	6	0	4	0	0	7	1	25	4	0	3	2	.600	0	3	2.10
	Durham	A	32	3	0	10	77.2	329	79	22	15	2	4	4	0	16	3	41	3	0	6	2	.750	0	4	1.74
1990	Greenville	AA	28	24	3	1	149	638	159	75	68	17	9	1	1	43	1	59	3	2	5	10	.333	2	1	4.11
1991	Greenville	AA	47	9	0	19	98.1	411	108	42	39	4	2	1	2	15	0	66	7	0	10	7	.588	0	6	3.57
1992	Greenville	AA	43	0	0	16	68.1	276	56	21	13	6	3	0	2	14	3	40	1	0	6	0	1.000	0	2	1.71
	Richmond	AAA	1	0	0	1	1	3	0	0	0	0	0	0	0	1	0	0	0	0	0	0	.000	0	0	0.00
1993	Richmond	AAA	49	2	0	8	85	358	85	28	25	3	4	0	3	22	2	55	3	0	4	2	.667	0	0	2.65
1994	Richmond	AAA	40	0	0	5	76.1	319	77	38	31	3	3	4	2	22	5	46	2	1	6	5	.545	0	1	3.66
	6 Min. YEARS		251	38	3	66	581.1	2437	584	233	197	35	29	10	10	140	15	332	23	3	40	28	.588	2	17	3.05

Mark Johnson

Bats: Left Throws: Left Pos: 1B
Ht: 6'4" Wt: 220 Born: 10/17/67 Age: 27

			BATTING												BASERUNNING				PERCENTAGES		
Year	Team	Lg	G	AB	H	2B	3B	HR	TB	R	RBI	TBB	IBB	SO	HBP	SH	SF	SB	CS	SB%	GDP	Avg	OBP	SLG
1990	Welland	A	5	8	3	1	0	0	4	2	2	2	0	0	0	0	0	0	0	.00	0	.375	.500	.500
	Augusta	A	43	144	36	7	0	0	43	12	19	24	2	18	0	0	2	4	2	.67	3	.250	.353	.299
1991	Augusta	A	49	139	36	7	4	2	57	23	25	29	1	14	0	1	2	4	2	.67	2	.259	.382	.410
	Salem	A	37	103	26	2	0	2	34	12	13	18	0	25	1	0	0	0	2	.00	2	.252	.369	.330
1992	Carolina	AA	122	383	89	16	1	7	128	40	45	55	4	94	3	1	0	16	11	.59	8	.232	.333	.334
1993	Carolina	AA	125	399	93	18	4	14	161	48	52	66	7	93	3	2	3	6	2	.75	4	.233	.344	.404
1994	Carolina	AA	111	388	107	20	2	23	200	69	85	67	11	89	4	0	4	6	6	.50	7	.276	.384	.515
	5 Min. YEARS		492	1564	390	71	11	48	627	206	241	261	25	333	11	4	11	36	25	.59	30	.249	.358	.401

Matt Johnson

Bats: Right Throws: Right Pos: SS
Ht: 5'10" Wt: 175 Born: 05/15/70 Age: 25

			BATTING												BASERUNNING				PERCENTAGES		
Year	Team	Lg	G	AB	H	2B	3B	HR	TB	R	RBI	TBB	IBB	SO	HBP	SH	SF	SB	CS	SB%	GDP	Avg	OBP	SLG
1992	Medcine Hat	R	67	234	60	10	2	2	80	33	28	38	0	36	6	3	2	6	6	.50	5	.256	.371	.342
1993	Dunedin	A	54	148	31	5	0	3	45	19	18	18	0	31	3	5	0	3	2	.60	3	.209	.308	.304
1994	Dunedin	A	82	243	62	15	0	4	89	33	35	28	0	47	5	3	1	4	2	.67	9	.255	.343	.366
	Knoxville	AA	5	10	0	0	0	0	0	0	1	2	0	2	0	0	0	0	1	.00	0	.000	.167	.000
	3 Min. YEARS		208	635	153	30	2	9	214	85	82	86	0	116	14	11	3	13	11	.54	17	.241	.343	.337

Barry Jones

Pitches: Right Bats: Right Pos: P
Ht: 6'4" Wt: 225 Born: 02/15/63 Age: 32

			HOW MUCH HE PITCHED						WHAT HE GAVE UP												THE RESULTS					
Year	Team	Lg	G	GS	CG	GF	IP	BFP	H	R	ER	HR	SH	SF	HB	TBB	IBB	SO	WP	Bk	W	L	Pct.	ShO	Sv	ERA
1984	Watertown	A	14	14	2	0	86.2	376	75	41	33	4	1	2	4	49	0	61	8	1	6	3	.667	1	0	3.43
1985	Pr William	A	28	0	0	23	37.1	154	26	7	5	0	6	0	0	19	3	42	9	0	3	2	.600	0	10	1.21
	Nashua	AA	23	0	0	20	29	111	19	6	5	1	2	1	0	10	0	24	4	0	3	2	.600	0	12	1.55
	Hawaii	AAA	1	0	0	1	3	10	5	5	3	0	0	0	0	1	0	2	0	0	0	0	.000	0	0	9.00
1986	Hawaii	AAA	35	0	0	32	48	203	41	20	19	3	5	1	2	20	4	28	0	0	3	6	.333	0	7	3.56
1987	Vancouver	AAA	20	0	0	20	25.1	112	21	9	9	2	0	2	0	14	1	27	0	0	1	2	.333	0	11	3.20
1989	White Sox	R	7	4	0	2	18.1	70	12	7	3	0	0	0	1	5	0	14	0	0	0	1	.000	0	1	1.47
	South Bend	A	3	0	0	1	3.2	17	6	3	2	0	1	0	0	0	0	2	0	0	0	0	.000	0	0	4.91
1993	Nashville	AAA	7	0	0	2	17.1	70	16	5	5	3	0	0	0	2	0	19	2	0	0	0	.000	0	2	2.60
1994	New Orleans	AAA	17	0	0	12	22.1	97	29	12	12	2	0	0	0	11	0	15	1	1	1	3	.250	0	6	4.84
1986	Pittsburgh	NL	26	0	0	10	37.1	159	29	16	12	3	2	1	0	21	2	29	2	0	3	4	.429	0	3	2.89
1987	Pittsburgh	NL	32	0	0	10	43.1	203	55	34	27	6	3	2	0	23	6	28	3	0	2	4	.333	0	1	5.61
1988	Pittsburgh	NL	42	0	0	15	56.1	241	57	21	19	3	5	4	1	21	6	31	7	1	1	1	.500	0	2	3.04
	Chicago	AL	17	0	0	10	26	106	15	7	7	3	0	1	0	17	1	17	6	1	2	2	.500	0	1	2.42
1989	Chicago	AL	22	0	0	8	30.1	121	22	12	8	2	4	2	1	8	0	17	1	0	3	2	.600	0	1	2.37
1990	Chicago	AL	65	0	0	9	74	310	62	20	19	2	7	5	1	33	7	45	0	1	11	4	.733	0	1	2.31
1991	Montreal	NL	77	0	0	46	88.2	353	76	35	33	8	7	3	1	33	8	46	1	1	4	9	.308	0	13	3.35
1992	Philadelphia	NL	44	0	0	10	54.1	243	65	30	28	3	2	2	2	24	4	19	1	2	5	6	.455	0	0	4.64

Team	Lg	G	GS	CG	GF	IP	BFP	H	R	ER	HR	SH	SF	HB	TBB	IBB	SO	WP	Bk	W	L	Pct.	ShO	Sv	ERA
New York NL		17	0	0	7	15.1	76	20	16	16	0	1	1	0	11	3	11	1	0	2	0	1.000	0	1	9.39
1993 Chicago AL		6	0	0	1	7.1	38	14	8	7	2	1	0	0	3	0	7	0	0	1	0	.000	0	0	8.59
7 Min. YEARS		155	18	2	113	291	1210	250	115	96	15	15	6	7	131	8	234	24	2	17	19	.472	1	49	2.97
8 Maj. YEARS		348	0	0	126	433	1850	415	199	176	32	32	21	6	194	37	250	22	6	33	33	.500	0	23	3.66

Calvin Jones

Pitches: Right Bats: Right Pos: P Ht: 6' 3" Wt: 185 Born: 09/26/63 Age: 31

		HOW MUCH HE PITCHED						WHAT HE GAVE UP												THE RESULTS					
Year Team	Lg	G	GS	CG	GF	IP	BFP	H	R	ER	HR	SH	SF	HB	TBB	IBB	SO	WP	Bk	W	L	Pct.	ShO	Sv	ERA
1984 Bellingham	A	10	9	0	0	59.2	0	29	23	16	0	0	0	7	36	0	59	8	1	5	0	1.000	0	0	2.41
1985 Wausau	A	20	19	1	0	106	473	96	59	46	10	0	2	5	65	1	71	9	2	4	11	.267	0	0	3.91
1986 Salinas	A	26	25	2	0	157.1	680	141	76	63	9	4	4	4	90	2	137	15	2	11	8	.579	0	0	3.60
1987 Chattanooga	AA	26	10	0	12	81.1	372	90	58	45	5	5	1	2	38	0	77	4	0	2	9	.182	0	2	4.98
1988 Vermont	AA	24	4	0	6	74.2	312	52	26	22	1	0	2	0	47	2	58	4	3	7	5	.583	0	0	2.65
1989 San Berndno	A	5	0	0	4	12.1	49	8	1	1	0	0	1	0	7	0	15	0	2	2	0	1.000	0	1	0.73
Williamsprt	AA	5	0	0	3	6.2	34	13	9	9	1	0	0	0	4	0	5	1	0	0	0	.000	0	0	12.15
1990 San Berndno	A	53	0	0	27	67	298	43	32	22	4	1	3	4	54	2	94	6	0	5	3	.625	0	8	2.96
1991 Calgary	AAA	20	0	0	15	23	109	19	12	10	1	0	0	2	19	1	25	6	2	1	1	.500	0	7	3.91
1992 Calgary	AAA	21	1	0	13	32.2	145	23	15	14	3	1	3	0	22	0	32	4	0	2	0	1.000	0	3	3.86
1993 Canton-Akrn	AA	43	0	0	36	62.2	253	40	25	23	1	3	1	1	26	2	73	9	1	5	5	.500	0	22	3.30
1994 Charlotte	AAA	55	0	0	35	62.2	275	64	30	27	7	1	3	1	27	2	47	10	0	3	3	.500	0	14	3.88
1991 Seattle	AL	27	0	0	6	46.1	194	33	14	13	0	6	0	1	29	5	42	6	0	2	2	.500	0	2	2.53
1992 Seattle	AL	38	1	0	14	61.2	275	50	39	39	8	1	4	2	47	1	49	10	0	3	5	.375	0	0	5.69
11 Min. YEARS		308	68	3	151	746	3000	618	366	298	42	15	20	26	435	12	693	76	13	47	45	.511	0	57	3.60
2 Maj. YEARS		65	1	0	20	108	469	83	53	52	8	7	4	3	76	6	91	16	0	5	7	.417	0	2	4.33

Dax Jones

Bats: Right Throws: Right Pos: OF Ht: 6'0" Wt: 170 Born: 08/04/70 Age: 24

		BATTING													BASERUNNING				PERCENTAGES		
Year Team	Lg	G	AB	H	2B	3B	HR	TB	R	RBI	TBB	IBB	SO	HBP	SH	SF	SB	CS	SB%	GDP	Avg	OBP	SLG
1991 Everett	A	53	180	55	5	6	5	87	42	29	27	0	26	1	1	3	15	8	.65	4	.306	.393	.483
1992 Clinton	A	79	295	88	12	4	1	111	45	42	21	0	32	1	1	1	18	5	.78	6	.298	.346	.376
Shreveport	AA	19	66	20	0	2	1	27	10	7	4	0	6	1	1	2	2	0	1.00	1	.303	.342	.409
1993 Shreveport	AA	118	436	124	19	5	4	165	59	36	26	6	53	4	3	2	13	8	.62	5	.284	.329	.378
1994 Phoenix	AAA	111	399	111	25	5	4	158	55	52	21	1	42	3	3	4	16	8	.67	14	.278	.316	.396
4 Min. YEARS		380	1376	398	61	22	15	548	211	166	99	7	159	10	9	12	64	29	.69	30	.289	.339	.398

Stacy Jones

Pitches: Right Bats: Right Pos: P Ht: 6' 6" Wt: 225 Born: 05/26/67 Age: 28

		HOW MUCH HE PITCHED						WHAT HE GAVE UP												THE RESULTS					
Year Team	Lg	G	GS	CG	GF	IP	BFP	H	R	ER	HR	SH	SF	HB	TBB	IBB	SO	WP	Bk	W	L	Pct.	ShO	Sv	ERA
1988 Erie	A	7	7	3	0	54.1	218	51	12	8	1	1	0	0	15	2	40	2	0	3	3	.500	2	0	1.33
Hagerstown	A	6	6	3	0	37.2	156	35	14	12	2	1	4	1	12	0	23	2	0	3	1	.750	2	0	2.87
1989 Frederick	A	15	15	3	0	82.2	374	93	57	45	11	1	3	2	35	0	58	3	4	5	6	.455	1	0	4.90
1990 Frederick	A	15	0	0	11	26.2	119	31	13	10	0	0	1	1	7	1	24	1	1	1	2	.333	0	2	3.38
Hagerstown	AA	19	0	0	11	40.1	176	46	27	23	1	4	1	1	11	1	41	2	0	1	6	.143	0	2	5.13
1991 Hagerstown	AA	12	0	0	4	30.1	130	24	6	6	1	2	0	1	15	1	26	1	0	0	1	.000	0	1	1.78
Rochester	AAA	33	1	0	21	50.2	221	53	22	19	4	7	2	0	20	2	47	2	1	4	4	.500	0	8	3.38
1992 Frederick	A	7	6	0	0	33.2	134	32	15	12	3	0	0	1	4	0	30	0	0	2	1	.667	0	0	3.21
Hagerstown	AA	11	9	0	0	69.2	290	62	30	27	1	1	3	1	25	0	45	0	2	2	5	.286	0	0	3.49
Rochester	AAA	2	0	0	1	2.2	11	2	2	2	0	0	0	0	1	0	1	0	0	0	0	.000	0	1	6.75
1993 Frederick	A	4	2	0	0	12.2	60	24	17	14	4	1	0	0	1	0	7	0	1	0	2	.000	0	0	9.95
Shreveport	AA	24	2	0	9	50.1	210	53	21	20	2	1	2	1	19	1	28	0	0	4	1	.800	0	1	3.58
1994 Shreveport	AA	56	0	0	53	64	270	73	21	17	2	5	0	2	12	2	64	1	1	3	6	.333	0	34	2.39
1991 Baltimore	AL	4	1	0	0	11	49	11	6	5	1	0	1	0	5	0	10	0	0	0	0	.000	0	0	4.09
7 Min. YEARS		211	48	9	110	555.2	2369	579	257	215	33	24	16	11	177	10	434	14	10	28	38	.424	5	49	3.48

Tim Jones

Bats: Left Throws: Right Pos: SS Ht: 5'10" Wt: 175 Born: 12/01/62 Age: 32

		BATTING													BASERUNNING				PERCENTAGES		
Year Team	Lg	G	AB	H	2B	3B	HR	TB	R	RBI	TBB	IBB	SO	HBP	SH	SF	SB	CS	SB%	GDP	Avg	OBP	SLG
1985 Johnson Cty	R	68	235	75	10	1	3	96	33	48	27	1	19	0	0	5	28	6	.82	1	.319	.382	.409
1986 St. Pete	A	39	142	36	3	2	0	43	19	27	30	0	8	1	0	3	8	6	.57	3	.254	.381	.303
Arkansas	AA	96	284	76	15	1	2	99	36	27	42	2	32	2	3	4	7	5	.58	7	.268	.364	.349
1987 Arkansas	AA	61	176	58	12	0	3	79	23	26	29	4	16	2	3	3	16	10	.62	3	.330	.424	.449
Louisville	AAA	73	276	78	14	3	4	110	48	43	29	1	27	0	2	0	11	3	.79	4	.283	.351	.399
1988 Louisville	AAA	103	370	95	21	2	6	138	63	38	36	3	56	3	5	1	39	12	.76	5	.257	.327	.373
1991 Louisville	AAA	86	305	78	9	1	5	104	34	29	37	1	59	0	4	3	19	5	.79	4	.256	.333	.341
1993 Louisville	AAA	101	408	118	22	10	5	175	72	46	44	1	67	2	2	4	13	8	.62	4	.289	.358	.429
1994 Charlotte	AAA	115	391	103	17	2	7	145	60	42	43	1	65	2	8	5	10	2	.83	8	.263	.336	.371
1988 St. Louis	NL	31	52	14	0	0	0	14	2	3	4	0	10	0	0	0	4	1	.80	1	.269	.321	.269

Year	Team	Lg	G	AB	H	2B	3B	HR	TB	R	RBI	TBB	IBB	SO	HBP	SH	SF	SB	CS	SB%	GDP	Avg	OBP	SLG
1989	St. Louis	NL	42	75	22	6	0	0	28	11	7	7	1	8	1	1	2	1	0	1.00	2	.293	.353	.373
1990	St. Louis	NL	67	128	28	7	1	1	40	9	12	12	1	20	1	4	0	3	4	.43	1	.219	.291	.313
1991	St. Louis	NL	16	24	4	2	0	0	6	1	2	2	1	6	0	0	1	0	1	.00	0	.167	.222	.250
1992	St. Louis	NL	67	145	29	4	0	0	33	9	3	11	1	29	0	2	0	5	2	.71	1	.200	.256	.228
1993	St. Louis	NL	29	61	16	6	0	0	22	13	1	9	0	8	1	2	0	2	2	.50	0	.262	.366	.361
	7 Min. YEARS		742	2587	717	123	22	35	989	388	326	317	14	349	12	27	26	151	57	.73	37	.277	.356	.382
	6 Maj. YEARS		252	485	113	25	1	1	143	45	28	45	4	81	3	9	3	15	10	.60	5	.233	.300	.295

Kevin Jordan

Bats: Right Throws: Right Pos: 2B Ht: 6'1" Wt: 185 Born: 10/09/69 Age: 25

			BATTING															BASERUNNING				PERCENTAGES		
Year	Team	Lg	G	AB	H	2B	3B	HR	TB	R	RBI	TBB	IBB	SO	HBP	SH	SF	SB	CS	SB%	GDP	Avg	OBP	SLG
1990	Oneonta	A	73	276	92	13	7	4	131	47	54	23	0	31	5	0	1	19	6	.76	3	.333	.393	.475
1991	Ft.Laudrdle	A	121	448	122	25	5	4	169	61	53	37	4	66	11	0	6	15	3	.83	13	.272	.339	.377
1992	Pr William	A	112	438	136	29	8	8	205	67	63	27	3	54	3	1	5	6	4	.60	9	.311	.351	.468
1993	Albany	AA	135	513	145	33	4	16	234	87	87	41	2	53	9	0	4	8	4	.67	8	.283	.344	.456
1994	Scranton-Wb	AAA	81	314	91	22	1	12	151	44	57	29	2	28	3	0	7	0	2	.00	9	.290	.348	.481
	5 Min. YEARS		522	1989	586	122	25	44	890	306	314	157	11	232	31	1	23	48	19	.72	42	.295	.352	.447

Michael Jordan

Bats: Right Throws: Right Pos: OF Ht: 6'6" Wt: 205 Born: 02/17/63 Age: 32

			BATTING															BASERUNNING				PERCENTAGES		
Year	Team	Lg	G	AB	H	2B	3B	HR	TB	R	RBI	TBB	IBB	SO	HBP	SH	SF	SB	CS	SB%	GDP	Avg	OBP	SLG
1994	Birmingham	AA	127	436	88	17	1	3	116	46	51	51	0	114	4	3	3	30	18	.63	4	.202	.289	.266

Rick Jordan

Pitches: Left Bats: Left Pos: P Ht: 5'11" Wt: 165 Born: 06/27/70 Age: 25

			HOW MUCH HE PITCHED					WHAT HE GAVE UP										THE RESULTS					
Year	Team	Lg	G	GS	CG	GF	IP	BFP	H	R	ER	HR	SH	SF	HB	TBB	IBB	SO	WP	Bk	W	L	Pct.	ShO	Sv	ERA
1990	Dunedin	A	13	2	0	4	22.2	103	15	9	6	0	1	1	1	9	3	16	1	5	0	2	.000	0	0	2.38
1991	Myrtle Bch	A	29	23	3	3	144.2	606	100	58	44	3	3	4	6	79	0	152	3	5	9	8	.529	1	1	2.74
1992	Dunedin	A	45	0	0	32	47	208	44	26	20	3	3	0	2	28	3	49	7	2	0	5	.000	0	15	3.83
1993	Dunedin	A	15	0	0	10	24.2	104	20	13	12	0	1	0	1	15	1	24	3	0	2	0	1.000	0	4	4.38
	Knoxville	AA	25	0	0	8	36.2	158	33	17	10	2	5	1	0	18	1	35	0	0	1	4	.200	0	2	2.45
1994	Knoxville	AA	53	0	0	40	64.1	273	54	25	19	2	4	2	4	23	2	70	4	0	4	3	.571	0	17	2.66
	5 Min. YEARS		180	25	3	90	340	1452	266	148	111	10	17	8	14	182	10	346	18	12	16	22	.421	1	36	2.94

Terry Jorgensen

Bats: Right Throws: Right Pos: 3B Ht: 6'4" Wt: 213 Born: 09/02/66 Age: 28

			BATTING															BASERUNNING				PERCENTAGES		
Year	Team	Lg	G	AB	H	2B	3B	HR	TB	R	RBI	TBB	IBB	SO	HBP	SH	SF	SB	CS	SB%	GDP	Avg	OBP	SLG
1987	Kenosha	A	67	254	80	17	0	7	118	37	33	18	0	43	2	0	1	1	0	1.00	7	.315	.364	.465
1988	Orlando	AA	135	472	116	27	4	3	160	53	43	40	3	62	6	2	6	4	1	.80	11	.246	.309	.339
1989	Orlando	AA	135	514	135	27	5	13	211	84	101	76	4	78	5	0	9	1	1	.50	6	.263	.358	.411
1990	Portland	AAA	123	440	114	28	3	10	178	43	50	44	2	83	0	1	4	0	4	.00	11	.259	.324	.405
1991	Portland	AAA	126	456	136	29	0	11	198	74	59	54	1	41	4	2	2	1	0	1.00	22	.298	.376	.434
1992	Portland	AAA	135	505	149	32	2	14	227	78	71	54	3	58	4	3	5	2	0	1.00	22	.295	.364	.450
1993	Portland	AAA	61	238	73	18	2	4	107	37	44	19	2	28	1	1	0	1	0	1.00	11	.307	.360	.450
1994	Portland	AA	124	471	136	23	0	14	201	65	72	40	0	50	3	0	1	0	0	.00	14	.289	.348	.427
1989	Minnesota	AL	10	23	4	1	0	0	5	1	2	4	0	5	0	0	0	0	0	.00	1	.174	.296	.217
1992	Minnesota	AL	22	58	18	1	0	0	19	5	5	3	0	11	1	0	1	1	2	.33	4	.310	.349	.328
1993	Minnesota	AL	59	152	34	7	0	1	44	15	12	10	0	21	0	0	1	1	0	1.00	7	.224	.270	.289
	8 Min. YEARS		906	3350	939	201	16	76	1400	471	473	345	15	443	25	9	28	10	10	.50	104	.280	.349	.418
	3 Maj. YEARS		91	233	56	9	0	1	68	21	19	17	0	37	1	0	2	2	2	.50	12	.240	.292	.292

Robert Juday

Bats: Both Throws: Right Pos: SS Ht: 6'0" Wt: 180 Born: 12/29/70 Age: 24

			BATTING															BASERUNNING				PERCENTAGES		
Year	Team	Lg	G	AB	H	2B	3B	HR	TB	R	RBI	TBB	IBB	SO	HBP	SH	SF	SB	CS	SB%	GDP	Avg	OBP	SLG
1992	Elmira	A	69	241	67	12	0	1	82	46	24	47	4	33	4	4	1	4	5	.44	6	.278	.403	.340
1993	Lynchburg	A	114	354	105	15	1	4	134	67	32	83	2	58	2	8	3	5	5	.50	9	.297	.430	.379
1994	Lynchburg	A	40	145	47	9	1	1	61	24	13	23	0	25	3	2	1	1	2	.33	3	.324	.424	.421
	New Britain	AA	93	315	61	16	1	1	82	42	17	56	0	63	5	6	4	2	7	.22	6	.194	.321	.260
	3 Min. YEARS		316	1055	280	52	3	7	359	179	86	209	6	179	14	20	9	12	19	.39	24	.265	.391	.340

Jarod Juelsgaard

Pitches: Right Bats: Right Pos: P Ht: 6'3" Wt: 190 Born: 06/27/68 Age: 27

			HOW MUCH HE PITCHED					WHAT HE GAVE UP										THE RESULTS					
Year	Team	Lg	G	GS	CG	GF	IP	BFP	H	R	ER	HR	SH	SF	HB	TBB	IBB	SO	WP	Bk	W	L	Pct.	ShO	Sv	ERA
1991	Everett	A	20	6	0	8	62	270	62	36	30	3	1	1	2	27	2	46	16	4	3	5	.375	0	3	4.35
1992	Clinton	A	35	9	1	11	76.2	368	86	58	45	2	4	4	3	52	6	60	12	1	6	9	.400	0	2	5.28
1993	Kane County	A	11	2	1	3	26	101	21	11	11	0	0	0	1	7	0	18	2	2	3	0	1.000	0	0	3.81
	High Desert	A	17	16	0	1	79.1	359	81	57	49	8	1	1	1	58	0	58	4	1	6	5	.545	0	0	5.56

		Lg	G	GS	CG	GF	IP	BFP	H	R	ER	HR	SH	SF	HB	TBB	IBB	SO	WP	Bk	W	L	Pct.	ShO	Sv	ERA
1994	Portland	AA	36	12	0	13	92.2	443	115	74	68	9	4	5	4	55	4	55	7	2	4	9	.308	0	0	6.60
	4 Min. YEARS		119	45	2	36	336.2	1541	365	236	203	22	10	11	11	199	12	237	41	10	22	28	.440	0	5	5.43

Bob Kappesser

Bats: Right Throws: Right Pos: C   **Ht: 5'9" Wt: 180 Born: 02/14/67 Age: 28**

			BATTING														BASERUNNING				PERCENTAGES		
Year	Team	Lg	G	AB	H	2B	3B	HR	TB	R	RBI	TBB	IBB	SO	HBP	SH	SF	SB	CS	SB%	GDP	Avg	OBP	SLG
1989	Helena	R	32	72	10	1	1	0	13	13	1	14	0	24	0	2	0	3	0	1.00	1	.139	.279	.181
1990	Stockton	A	63	147	27	2	1	0	31	17	12	15	0	39	2	2	1	2	6	.25	2	.184	.267	.211
	El Paso	AA	14	36	8	0	0	0	8	3	2	1	0	7	0	1	1	0	0	.00	0	.222	.237	.222
1991	Visalia	A	18	57	13	2	0	0	15	6	2	9	0	19	0	0	1	0	1	.00	3	.228	.328	.263
	Stockton	A	79	202	43	4	3	0	53	30	15	35	1	38	2	11	1	10	8	.56	3	.213	.333	.262
1992	El Paso	AA	88	233	55	7	1	1	67	32	33	22	0	49	3	2	2	6	7	.46	6	.236	.308	.288
1993	New Orleans	AAA	4	11	1	1	0	0	2	0	2	1	0	4	0	0	0	0	0	.00	1	.091	.167	.182
	El Paso	AA	67	173	43	9	1	2	60	25	28	20	0	29	2	3	2	7	3	.70	2	.249	.330	.347
1994	New Orleans	AAA	17	47	11	4	0	0	15	9	5	7	0	9	0	3	0	2	1	.67	1	.234	.333	.319
	El Paso	AA	53	140	33	0	1	0	35	15	10	16	0	32	0	1	0	4	2	.67	3	.236	.314	.250
	6 Min. YEARS		435	1118	244	30	8	3	299	150	105	140	1	250	9	25	8	34	28	.55	22	.218	.308	.267

Matt Karchner

Pitches: Right Bats: Right Pos: P   **Ht: 6'4" Wt: 245 Born: 06/28/67 Age: 28**

			HOW MUCH HE PITCHED						WHAT HE GAVE UP											THE RESULTS					
Year	Team	Lg	G	GS	CG	GF	IP	BFP	H	R	ER	HR	SH	SF	HB	TBB	IBB	SO	WP	Bk	W	L	Pct.	ShO	Sv	ERA
1989	Eugene	A	8	5	0	0	30	131	30	19	13	1	0	1	5	8	0	25	0	0	1	1	.500	0	0	3.90
1990	Appleton	A	27	11	1	5	71	308	70	42	38	3	2	1	6	31	2	58	4	1	2	7	.222	0	0	4.82
1991	Baseball Cy	A	38	0	0	16	73	295	49	28	16	1	5	0	5	25	3	65	7	1	6	3	.667	0	5	1.97
1992	Memphis	AA	33	18	2	2	141	606	151	83	70	5	6	2	11	35	0	88	8	1	8	8	.500	0	1	4.47
1993	Memphis	AA	6	5	0	1	30	126	34	16	14	2	2	0	4	4	0	14	1	0	3	2	.600	0	0	4.20
1994	Birmingham	AA	39	0	0	33	43	177	36	10	6	0	3	2	2	14	1	29	5	0	5	2	.714	0	6	1.26
	Nashville	AAA	17	0	0	11	26.1	101	18	5	4	0	4	1	1	7	2	19	1	0	4	2	.667	0	2	1.37
	6 Min. YEARS		168	39	3	68	414.1	1744	398	203	161	12	22	7	34	124	8	298	33	3	29	25	.537	0	14	3.50

Scott Karl

Pitches: Left Bats: Left Pos: P   **Ht: 6'2" Wt: 195 Born: 08/09/71 Age: 23**

			HOW MUCH HE PITCHED						WHAT HE GAVE UP											THE RESULTS					
Year	Team	Lg	G	GS	CG	GF	IP	BFP	H	R	ER	HR	SH	SF	HB	TBB	IBB	SO	WP	Bk	W	L	Pct.	ShO	Sv	ERA
1992	Helena	R	9	9	1	0	61.2	245	54	13	10	2	1	1	2	16	0	57	5	1	7	0	1.000	1	0	1.46
1993	El Paso	AA	27	27	4	0	180	732	172	67	49	9	6	3	6	35	0	95	6	7	13	8	.619	2	0	2.45
1994	El Paso	AA	8	8	3	0	54.2	219	44	21	18	2	2	1	1	15	1	51	3	0	5	1	.833	0	0	2.96
	New Orleans	AAA	15	13	2	0	89	375	92	38	38	10	3	2	4	33	1	54	2	0	5	5	.500	0	0	3.84
	3 Min. YEARS		59	57	10	0	385.1	1571	362	139	115	23	12	7	13	99	2	257	16	8	30	14	.682	3	0	2.69

Ryan Karp

Pitches: Left Bats: Left Pos: P   **Ht: 6'4" Wt: 205 Born: 04/05/70 Age: 25**

			HOW MUCH HE PITCHED						WHAT HE GAVE UP											THE RESULTS					
Year	Team	Lg	G	GS	CG	GF	IP	BFP	H	R	ER	HR	SH	SF	HB	TBB	IBB	SO	WP	Bk	W	L	Pct.	ShO	Sv	ERA
1992	Oneonta	A	14	13	1	0	70.1	300	66	38	32	2	1	1	3	30	0	58	2	0	6	4	.600	1	0	4.09
1993	Greensboro	A	17	17	0	0	109.1	436	73	26	22	2	0	2	2	40	0	132	6	1	13	1	.929	0	0	1.81
	Pr William	A	8	8	1	0	49	189	35	17	12	4	2	2	2	12	0	34	5	1	3	2	.600	1	0	2.20
	Albany	AA	3	3	0	0	13	60	13	7	6	1	0	1	0	9	0	10	1	0	0	0	.000	0	0	4.15
1994	Reading	AA	21	21	0	0	121.1	528	123	67	60	12	0	4	3	54	3	96	4	0	4	11	.267	0	0	4.45
	3 Min. YEARS		63	62	2	0	363	1513	310	155	132	21	3	10	10	145	3	330	18	2	26	18	.591	2	0	3.27

Robbie Katzaroff

Bats: Right Throws: Right Pos: OF   **Ht: 5'8" Wt: 190 Born: 07/29/68 Age: 26**

			BATTING														BASERUNNING				PERCENTAGES		
Year	Team	Lg	G	AB	H	2B	3B	HR	TB	R	RBI	TBB	IBB	SO	HBP	SH	SF	SB	CS	SB%	GDP	Avg	OBP	SLG
1990	Jamestown	A	74	294	107	15	7	1	139	57	20	29	4	18	5	1	0	34	13	.72	3	.364	.430	.473
1991	Harrisburg	AA	137	558	162	21	2	3	196	94	50	54	3	61	5	9	1	33	18	.65	5	.290	.358	.351
1992	Binghamton	AA	119	450	127	18	7	0	159	65	29	40	1	45	5	6	4	24	18	.57	4	.282	.345	.353
1993	Phoenix	AAA	9	26	4	0	0	0	4	2	3	1	0	4	0	0	1	0	0	.00	0	.154	.179	.154
	Shreveport	AA	104	406	122	22	4	0	152	52	30	35	3	33	8	5	4	15	13	.54	3	.300	.364	.374
1994	Midland	AA	32	105	29	3	2	0	36	22	11	15	0	10	1	5	1	10	4	.71	2	.276	.369	.343
	Lake Elsino	A	70	281	79	12	4	1	102	54	33	38	1	16	6	2	4	25	7	.78	8	.281	.374	.363
	5 Min. YEARS		545	2120	630	91	26	5	788	346	176	212	12	187	30	28	15	141	73	.66	25	.297	.367	.372

Gregory Keagle

Pitches: Right Bats: Right Pos: P   **Ht: 6'2" Wt: 185 Born: 06/28/71 Age: 24**

			HOW MUCH HE PITCHED						WHAT HE GAVE UP											THE RESULTS					
Year	Team	Lg	G	GS	CG	GF	IP	BFP	H	R	ER	HR	SH	SF	HB	TBB	IBB	SO	WP	Bk	W	L	Pct.	ShO	Sv	ERA
1993	Spokane	A	15	15	1	0	83	368	80	37	30	2	4	4	7	40	2	77	4	4	3	3	.500	0	0	3.25

Year	Team	Lg	G	GS	CG	GF	IP	BFP	H	R	ER	HR	SH	SF	HB	TBB	IBB	SO	WP	Bk	W	L	Pct.	ShO	Sv	ERA
1994	Rancho Cuca	A	14	14	1	0	92	377	62	23	21	2	1	3	5	41	1	91	1	0	11	1	.917	1	0	2.05
	Wichita	AA	13	13	0	0	70.1	321	84	53	49	5	5	2	2	32	1	57	3	1	3	9	.250	0	0	6.27
	2 Min. YEARS		42	42	2	0	245.1	1066	226	113	100	9	10	9	14	113	4	225	8	5	17	13	.567	1	0	3.67

Dave Keating

Pitches: Left Bats: Right Pos: P Ht: 6'1" Wt: 195 Born: 11/06/67 Age: 27

			HOW MUCH HE PITCHED						WHAT HE GAVE UP												THE RESULTS					
Year	Team	Lg	G	GS	CG	GF	IP	BFP	H	R	ER	HR	SH	SF	HB	TBB	IBB	SO	WP	Bk	W	L	Pct.	ShO	Sv	ERA
1992	Sarasota	A	19	0	0	8	27	119	25	17	15	2	2	0	0	17	0	18	2	0	0	1	.000	0	0	5.00
1993	Sarasota	A	22	0	0	14	33	151	37	16	13	0	3	2	0	16	2	28	2	0	2	0	1.000	0	3	3.55
	South Bend	A	6	0	0	2	8.2	33	6	3	3	0	0	0	0	2	0	6	0	0	1	0	1.000	0	1	3.12
1994	Pr. William	A	12	0	0	8	18.1	86	19	16	12	2	1	1	3	12	1	12	3	0	0	1	.000	0	1	5.89
	Birmingham	AA	22	0	0	7	29.1	130	30	14	14	3	0	1	1	17	0	9	6	0	1	1	.500	0	0	4.30
	3 Min. YEARS		81	0	0	39	116.1	519	117	66	57	7	6	4	4	64	3	73	13	0	4	3	.571	0	5	4.41

Jason Keeline

Bats: Right Throws: Right Pos: SS Ht: 6'2" Wt: 170 Born: 04/13/69 Age: 26

			BATTING														BASERUNNING				PERCENTAGES		
Year	Team	Lg	G	AB	H	2B	3B	HR	TB	R	RBI	TBB	IBB	SO	HBP	SH	SF	SB	CS	SB%	GDP	Avg	OBP	SLG
1991	Pulaski	R	36	91	17	1	0	0	18	9	7	8	0	30	1	0	2	3	1	.75	2	.187	.250	.198
1992	Macon	A	31	90	24	4	0	0	28	10	6	9	0	20	1	2	0	2	3	.40	3	.267	.340	.311
	Durham	A	69	213	50	3	0	0	53	17	5	14	0	35	1	8	0	2	2	.50	3	.235	.285	.249
1993	Macon	A	121	353	76	4	0	0	80	35	28	35	0	70	5	5	1	6	5	.55	12	.215	.294	.227
1994	Durham	A	14	39	6	1	0	0	7	3	1	2	0	8	1	0	0	1	1	.50	0	.154	.214	.179
	Greenville	AA	10	31	9	2	0	0	11	6	4	6	0	5	1	0	0	0	1	.00	1	.290	.421	.355
	4 Min. YEARS		281	817	182	15	0	0	197	80	51	74	0	168	9	17	2	14	13	.52	21	.223	.294	.241

Korey Keling

Pitches: Right Bats: Right Pos: P Ht: 6'5" Wt: 210 Born: 11/24/68 Age: 26

			HOW MUCH HE PITCHED						WHAT HE GAVE UP												THE RESULTS					
Year	Team	Lg	G	GS	CG	GF	IP	BFP	H	R	ER	HR	SH	SF	HB	TBB	IBB	SO	WP	Bk	W	L	Pct.	ShO	Sv	ERA
1991	Boise	A	15	14	0	1	83	340	71	31	28	3	5	1	3	30	0	96	5	4	6	2	.750	0	1	3.04
1992	Palm Sprngs	A	30	18	0	2	124	536	138	72	66	4	4	8	4	53	0	107	15	3	7	6	.538	0	0	4.79
1993	Palm Sprngs	A	31	21	2	1	158.2	667	152	69	58	9	3	7	3	62	1	131	7	2	8	8	.500	0	0	3.29
1994	Midland	AA	27	27	1	0	155	720	207	108	89	16	5	8	7	60	1	133	8	0	10	11	.476	0	0	5.17
	4 Min. YEARS		103	80	3	4	520.2	2263	568	280	241	32	17	24	17	205	2	467	35	9	31	27	.534	0	1	4.17

Rich Kelley

Pitches: Left Bats: Left Pos: P Ht: 6'3" Wt: 200 Born: 05/27/70 Age: 25

			HOW MUCH HE PITCHED						WHAT HE GAVE UP												THE RESULTS					
Year	Team	Lg	G	GS	CG	GF	IP	BFP	H	R	ER	HR	SH	SF	HB	TBB	IBB	SO	WP	Bk	W	L	Pct.	ShO	Sv	ERA
1991	Niagara Fls	A	15	13	0	1	81.1	341	76	38	30	7	0	2	1	33	1	78	4	0	4	8	.333	0	0	3.32
1992	Fayetteville	A	28	26	2	0	162.2	664	140	62	51	15	2	4	6	63	0	117	12	9	13	5	.722	0	0	2.82
1993	Lakeland	A	26	9	0	10	85.2	350	78	31	29	2	2	2	4	31	1	45	5	4	4	5	.444	0	2	3.05
	London	AA	7	0	0	5	5	25	7	5	5	1	0	0	0	5	0	3	3	1	0	0	.000	0	0	9.00
1994	Lakeland	A	13	0	0	10	38	156	32	15	10	2	2	5	0	15	1	23	0	0	4	2	.667	0	1	2.37
	Trenton	AA	16	4	0	2	42.1	178	46	28	27	8	1	1	0	20	0	29	3	1	1	2	.333	0	0	5.74
	4 Min. YEARS		105	52	2	23	415	1714	379	179	152	35	7	14	11	167	3	295	27	15	26	22	.542	0	3	3.30

Frank Kellner

Bats: Both Throws: Right Pos: SS Ht: 5'11" Wt: 175 Born: 01/05/67 Age: 28

			BATTING														BASERUNNING				PERCENTAGES		
Year	Team	Lg	G	AB	H	2B	3B	HR	TB	R	RBI	TBB	IBB	SO	HBP	SH	SF	SB	CS	SB%	GDP	Avg	OBP	SLG
1990	Osceola	A	109	369	91	9	7	0	114	43	34	65	2	65	1	9	3	14	7	.67	11	.247	.358	.309
	Tucson	AAA	19	60	18	1	0	0	19	13	7	15	0	6	0	2	0	1	0	1.00	0	.300	.440	.317
1991	Osceola	A	53	204	44	8	1	1	57	27	15	20	2	24	0	4	0	8	1	.89	6	.216	.286	.279
	Jackson	AA	83	311	84	7	4	2	105	47	25	29	2	37	0	2	2	6	5	.55	8	.270	.330	.338
1992	Jackson	AA	125	474	113	18	5	3	150	45	48	42	5	89	3	4	2	8	7	.53	9	.238	.303	.316
1993	Jackson	AA	121	355	107	27	2	4	150	51	36	38	5	51	2	2	6	11	12	.48	10	.301	.367	.423
1994	Tucson	AAA	106	296	88	13	5	1	114	32	35	46	3	40	0	3	2	5	4	.56	4	.297	.390	.385
	5 Min. YEARS		616	2069	545	83	24	11	709	258	200	255	19	312	6	26	15	53	36	.60	48	.263	.344	.343

John Kelly

Pitches: Right Bats: Right Pos: P Ht: 6'4" Wt: 185 Born: 07/03/67 Age: 27

			HOW MUCH HE PITCHED						WHAT HE GAVE UP												THE RESULTS					
Year	Team	Lg	G	GS	CG	GF	IP	BFP	H	R	ER	HR	SH	SF	HB	TBB	IBB	SO	WP	Bk	W	L	Pct.	ShO	Sv	ERA
1990	Johnson Cy	R	25	0	0	22	34.1	144	22	7	3	1	1	1	2	12	3	41	1	3	1	2	.333	0	13	0.79
1991	Savannah	A	56	0	0	50	58.2	230	43	14	9	5	3	0	0	16	6	62	2	0	6	5	.545	0	30	1.38
1992	St. Pete	A	56	0	0	52	62	243	47	15	14	1	3	3	1	13	2	59	3	1	4	4	.500	0	38	2.03
1993	Arkansas	AA	51	0	0	45	58.1	245	53	28	23	4	8	0	1	12	5	40	1	0	2	4	.333	0	27	3.55
1994	Arkansas	AA	27	0	0	24	30.2	134	37	23	18	2	3	3	1	5	1	29	0	0	3	3	.333	0	16	5.28
	Louisville	AAA	9	0	0	4	20.2	91	23	12	12	2	0	1	3	5	1	14	0	0	0	0	.000	0	0	5.23
	5 Min. YEARS		224	0	0	197	264.2	1087	225	99	79	15	18	8	8	63	18	245	7	4	14	17	.452	0	124	2.69

Pat Kelly

Bats: Right **Throws:** Right **Pos:** OF **Ht:** 5'11" **Wt:** 175 **Born:** 01/22/67 **Age:** 28

Year	Team	Lg	G	AB	H	2B	3B	HR	TB	R	RBI	TBB	IBB	SO	HBP	SH	SF	SB	CS	SB%	GDP	Avg	OBP	SLG
1989	Pulaski	R	50	163	54	4	1	0	60	25	21	18	2	17	5	8	0	5	7	.42	4	.331	.414	.368
1990	Sumter	A	121	437	97	12	2	1	116	57	44	61	0	65	8	9	6	22	8	.73	10	.222	.324	.265
1991	Durham	A	54	120	30	5	0	0	35	14	12	14	0	18	1	1	1	4	4	.50	2	.250	.331	.292
	Greenville	AA	30	90	27	6	2	0	37	14	5	13	1	10	0	2	1	5	1	.83	2	.300	.385	.411
1992	Greenville	AA	98	325	81	12	2	0	97	44	36	26	1	55	2	1	1	11	3	.79	6	.249	.308	.298
	Richmond	AAA	6	15	7	0	0	0	7	1	4	3	0	2	0	0	0	0	0	.00	0	.467	.556	.467
1993	Durham	A	35	128	36	6	0	1	45	27	12	13	1	19	2	2	0	5	4	.56	3	.281	.357	.352
	Greenville	AA	72	212	54	10	1	0	66	23	17	14	1	30	1	5	1	2	3	.40	4	.255	.303	.311
1994	Richmond	AAA	75	189	51	13	0	1	67	21	23	17	0	22	1	1	0	6	6	.50	3	.270	.333	.354
	6 Min. YEARS		541	1679	437	68	8	3	530	226	174	179	6	238	20	29	10	60	36	.63	34	.260	.337	.316

Jason Kendall

Bats: Right **Throws:** Right **Pos:** C **Ht:** 6'0" **Wt:** 170 **Born:** 06/26/74 **Age:** 21

Year	Team	Lg	G	AB	H	2B	3B	HR	TB	R	RBI	TBB	IBB	SO	HBP	SH	SF	SB	CS	SB%	GDP	Avg	OBP	SLG
1992	Pirates	R	33	111	29	2	0	0	31	7	10	8	1	9	2	0	2	2	2	.50	3	.261	.317	.279
1993	Augusta	A	102	366	101	17	4	1	129	43	40	22	1	30	7	0	5	8	5	.62	17	.276	.325	.352
1994	Salem	A	101	371	118	19	2	7	162	68	66	47	1	21	13	0	7	14	3	.82	15	.318	.406	.437
	Carolina	AA	13	47	11	2	0	0	13	6	6	2	0	3	2	0	0	0	0	.00	0	.234	.294	.277
	3 Min. YEARS		249	895	259	40	6	8	335	124	122	79	3	63	24	0	14	24	10	.71	35	.289	.358	.374

Kenny Kendrena

Pitches: Right **Bats:** Right **Pos:** P **Ht:** 5'11" **Wt:** 170 **Born:** 10/29/70 **Age:** 24

Year	Team	Lg	G	GS	CG	GF	IP	BFP	H	R	ER	HR	SH	SF	HB	TBB	IBB	SO	WP	Bk	W	L	Pct.	ShO	Sv	ERA
1992	Erie	A	22	0	0	10	54.2	229	47	33	23	5	5	3	5	12	2	61	2	1	5	4	.556	0	3	3.79
1993	High Desert	A	40	0	0	25	66.2	307	78	50	49	16	2	4	4	26	1	63	7	0	6	0	1.000	0	2	6.62
1994	Brevard Cty	A	21	1	0	7	38	141	19	5	5	0	3	1	0	10	0	32	1	0	5	1	.833	0	0	1.18
	Portland	AA	13	0	0	3	24.2	118	28	22	15	0	1	1	2	15	2	21	2	0	0	1	.000	0	0	5.47
	3 Min. YEARS		96	1	0	45	184	795	172	110	92	21	11	9	11	63	5	177	12	1	16	6	.727	0	5	4.50

Darryl Kennedy

Bats: Right **Throws:** Right **Pos:** C **Ht:** 5'10" **Wt:** 170 **Born:** 01/23/69 **Age:** 26

Year	Team	Lg	G	AB	H	2B	3B	HR	TB	R	RBI	TBB	IBB	SO	HBP	SH	SF	SB	CS	SB%	GDP	Avg	OBP	SLG
1991	Rangers	R	5	18	2	1	0	0	3	4	1	1	0	1	0	0	0	0	0	.00	0	.111	.158	.167
	Charlotte	A	23	68	7	3	0	0	10	5	4	5	0	11	2	1	2	0	0	.00	2	.103	.182	.147
1992	Gastonia	A	13	33	3	1	0	0	4	2	2	6	1	6	1	0	1	0	0	.00	1	.091	.244	.121
	Charlotte	A	13	28	13	4	0	0	17	3	6	3	0	3	0	0	0	0	1	.00	0	.464	.516	.607
	Tulsa	AA	30	98	22	2	0	0	24	6	9	8	0	18	2	2	1	0	0	.00	4	.224	.294	.245
1993	Okla City	AAA	6	16	1	0	0	0	1	2	0	3	0	4	0	1	0	0	0	.00	0	.063	.211	.063
	Charlotte	A	106	347	97	23	0	1	123	47	30	47	0	38	1	5	2	5	7	.42	7	.280	.365	.354
1994	Charlotte	A	53	177	47	5	2	1	59	24	22	25	1	20	1	2	0	1	2	.33	7	.266	.360	.333
	Tulsa	AA	23	70	16	3	0	1	22	5	5	8	0	10	0	2	0	1	1	.50	1	.229	.308	.314
	4 Min. YEARS		272	855	208	42	2	3	263	98	79	106	2	111	7	13	6	7	13	.35	22	.243	.330	.308

Keith Kessinger

Bats: Both **Throws:** Right **Pos:** 2B-SS **Ht:** 6' 2" **Wt:** 185 **Born:** 02/19/67 **Age:** 28

Year	Team	Lg	G	AB	H	2B	3B	HR	TB	R	RBI	TBB	IBB	SO	HBP	SH	SF	SB	CS	SB%	GDP	Avg	OBP	SLG
1989	Bluefield	R	28	99	27	4	0	2	37	17	9	8	0	12	1	2	0	1	0	1.00	1	.273	.333	.374
1990	Wausau	A	37	134	29	8	0	0	37	17	9	6	0	23	3	0	0	1	1	.50	2	.216	.266	.276
	Frederick	A	64	145	22	4	0	0	26	18	8	20	0	36	3	5	0	0	0	.00	2	.152	.268	.179
1991	Frederick	A	26	56	10	3	0	0	13	5	4	8	0	12	0	1	0	2	1	.67	3	.179	.281	.232
	Cedar Rapds	A	59	206	42	5	0	1	50	15	15	23	1	46	3	5	1	0	1	.00	4	.204	.292	.243
1992	Cedar Rapds	A	95	308	73	15	1	4	102	41	38	36	2	57	1	1	5	2	0	1.00	7	.237	.318	.331
1993	Chattanooga	AA	56	161	50	9	0	3	68	24	28	24	2	18	0	5	0	0	3	.00	4	.311	.400	.422
	Indianapls	AAA	35	120	34	9	0	2	49	17	15	14	4	14	1	1	0	0	0	.00	0	.283	.363	.408
1994	Indianapls	AAA	115	393	98	19	3	3	132	37	48	36	4	60	0	4	1	3	1	.75	11	.249	.312	.336
1993	Cincinnati	NL	11	27	7	1	0	1	11	4	3	4	0	4	0	0	0	0	0	.00	1	.259	.344	.407
	6 Min. YEARS		515	1622	385	76	4	15	514	191	174	175	13	278	12	28	3	9	8	.53	34	.237	.316	.317

Douglas Ketchen

Pitches: Right **Bats:** Right **Pos:** P **Ht:** 6'1" **Wt:** 190 **Born:** 07/09/68 **Age:** 26

Year	Team	Lg	G	GS	CG	GF	IP	BFP	H	R	ER	HR	SH	SF	HB	TBB	IBB	SO	WP	Bk	W	L	Pct.	ShO	Sv	ERA
1990	Auburn	A	19	12	1	2	92.2	393	81	43	35	4	7	2	4	40	2	76	8	2	6	5	.545	0	0	3.40

Year	Team	Lg	G	GS	CG	GF	IP	BFP	H	R	ER	HR	SH	SF	HB	TBB	IBB	SO	WP	Bk	W	L	Pct.	ShO	Sv	ERA
1991	Asheville	A	27	27	2	0	151.2	690	166	99	72	9	4	4	11	62	1	95	21	3	10	12	.455	1	0	4.27
1992	Osceola	A	34	12	0	9	116	500	121	43	36	6	3	1	1	28	4	72	9	0	8	3	.727	0	5	2.79
1993	Jackson	AA	27	27	3	0	159.2	689	160	91	73	12	7	6	6	50	2	104	10	0	7	12	.368	1	0	4.11
1994	Jackson	AA	38	15	0	11	124.1	551	127	69	56	8	12	6	4	53	3	73	10	1	6	9	.400	0	6	4.05
	Tucson	AAA	2	0	0	2	1.1	9	4	2	2	0	1	0	0	2	0	0	0	0	0	1	.000	0	0	13.50
	5 Min. YEARS		147	93	6	24	645.2	2832	659	347	274	39	34	19	26	235	14	420	58	6	37	42	.468	2	11	3.82

Brian Keyser

Pitches: Right Bats: Right Pos: P　　　　　　　　Ht: 6'1" Wt: 180 Born: 10/31/66 Age: 28

			HOW MUCH HE PITCHED						WHAT HE GAVE UP												THE RESULTS					
Year	Team	Lg	G	GS	CG	GF	IP	BFP	H	R	ER	HR	SH	SF	HB	TBB	IBB	SO	WP	Bk	W	L	Pct.	ShO	Sv	ERA
1989	Utica	A	14	13	2	0	93.2	374	79	37	31	6	2	2	4	22	0	70	5	3	4	4	.500	0	0	2.98
1990	Sarasota	A	38	10	2	13	115.2	475	107	54	47	5	3	6	1	40	1	83	6	3	6	7	.462	1	2	3.66
1991	Sarasota	A	27	14	2	9	129	527	110	43	33	5	8	3	6	45	8	94	3	3	6	7	.462	1	2	2.30
	Birmingham	AA	3	3	0	0	18	78	19	10	10	2	0	1	0	9	0	9	0	1	0	1	.000	0	0	5.00
1992	Birmingham	AA	28	27	7	1	183.1	754	173	86	76	12	1	7	4	60	1	99	9	0	9	10	.474	3	0	3.73
1993	Birmingham	AA	2	2	1	0	11	50	15	9	7	0	1	1	0	5	0	8	0	0	0	2	.000	0	0	5.73
	Nashville	AAA	30	18	2	4	121.2	511	142	70	63	8	2	4	1	27	4	44	4	1	9	5	.643	0	1	4.66
1994	Birmingham	AA	1	1	0	0	6	23	4	1	1	1	0	0	1	1	0	5	0	0	0	0	.000	0	0	1.50
	Nashville	AAA	37	10	2	15	135.2	556	123	49	42	9	7	5	3	36	4	76	9	0	9	5	.643	1	2	2.79
	6 Min. YEARS		180	98	18	42	814	3348	772	356	310	48	24	29	20	245	18	488	36	11	43	41	.512	6	7	3.43

John Kiely

Pitches: Right Bats: Right Pos: P　　　　　　　　Ht: 6'3" Wt: 215 Born: 10/04/64 Age: 30

			HOW MUCH HE PITCHED						WHAT HE GAVE UP												THE RESULTS					
Year	Team	Lg	G	GS	CG	GF	IP	BFP	H	R	ER	HR	SH	SF	HB	TBB	IBB	SO	WP	Bk	W	L	Pct.	ShO	Sv	ERA
1988	Bristol	R	8	0	0	6	11.2	53	9	9	8	0	2	0	0	7	0	14	2	0	2	2	.500	0	1	6.17
1989	Lakeland	A	36	0	0	22	63.2	267	52	26	17	2	4	3	0	27	4	56	1	2	4	3	.571	0	8	2.40
1990	London	AA	46	0	0	25	76.2	301	63	17	15	2	2	4	2	42	6	52	2	0	3	0	1.000	0	12	1.76
1991	Toledo	AAA	42	0	0	27	72	301	57	25	17	3	4	2	3	35	3	60	2	0	4	2	.667	0	6	2.13
1992	Toledo	AAA	21	0	0	17	31.2	125	25	11	10	1	0	0	0	7	0	31	1	0	1	1	.500	0	9	2.84
1993	Toledo	AAA	37	0	0	16	58	261	65	34	25	8	1	2	1	25	1	48	2	0	3	4	.429	0	4	3.88
1994	Toledo	AAA	7	0	0	1	12.2	58	14	8	8	1	0	2	0	7	0	6	0	0	1	0	1.000	0	0	5.68
1991	Detroit	AL	7	0	0	3	6.2	42	13	11	11	0	2	1	1	9	2	1	1	0	0	1	.000	0	0	14.85
1992	Detroit	AL	39	0	0	20	55	231	44	14	13	2	4	3	0	28	3	18	0	0	4	2	.667	0	0	2.13
1993	Detroit	AL	8	0	0	5	11.2	59	13	11	10	2	1	0	1	13	5	5	2	0	0	2	.000	0	0	7.71
	7 Min. YEARS		197	0	0	114	326.1	1386	285	130	100	17	13	13	6	150	14	267	10	2	18	12	.600	0	40	2.76
	3 Maj. YEARS		54	0	0	28	73.1	332	70	36	34	4	7	4	2	50	10	24	3	0	4	5	.444	0	0	4.17

Brooks Kieschnick

Bats: Left Throws: Right Pos: OF　　　　　　　　Ht: 6'4" Wt: 228 Born: 06/06/72 Age: 23

			BATTING													BASERUNNING				PERCENTAGES		
Year	Team	Lg	G	AB	H	2B	3B	HR	TB	R	RBI	TBB	IBB	SO	HBP	SH	SF	SB	CS	SB%	GDP	Avg	OBP	SLG
1993	Cubs	R	3	9	2	1	0	0	3	0	0	0	0	1	0	0	0	0	0	.00	0	.222	.222	.333
	Daytona	A	6	22	4	2	0	0	6	1	2	1	0	4	0	0	0	0	1	.00	1	.182	.217	.273
	Orlando	AA	25	91	31	8	0	2	45	12	10	7	1	19	0	0	0	1	2	.33	0	.341	.388	.495
1994	Orlando	AA	126	468	132	25	3	14	205	57	55	33	3	78	4	0	4	3	5	.38	10	.282	.332	.438
	2 Min. YEARS		160	590	169	36	3	16	259	70	67	41	4	102	4	0	4	4	8	.33	11	.286	.335	.439

Rusty Kilgo

Pitches: Left Bats: Left Pos: P　　　　　　　　Ht: 6'0" Wt: 175 Born: 08/09/66 Age: 28

			HOW MUCH HE PITCHED						WHAT HE GAVE UP												THE RESULTS					
Year	Team	Lg	G	GS	CG	GF	IP	BFP	H	R	ER	HR	SH	SF	HB	TBB	IBB	SO	WP	Bk	W	L	Pct.	ShO	Sv	ERA
1989	Jamestown	A	30	3	0	21	64.2	259	46	16	10	3	4	0	0	20	1	74	4	1	6	3	.667	0	8	1.39
1990	Rockford	A	45	0	0	31	88.2	347	62	26	22	1	2	1	3	20	1	85	6	2	4	4	.500	0	9	2.23
1991	Wst Plm Bch	A	33	1	0	10	74	286	56	14	13	1	3	0	2	24	1	48	1	0	6	3	.667	0	1	1.58
	Harrisburg	AA	14	0	0	10	25.2	105	24	11	10	1	3	1	1	4	1	20	3	0	1	0	1.000	0	1	3.51
1992	Rockford	A	4	0	0	2	8.2	28	3	0	0	0	0	0	0	0	0	8	0	0	0	0	.000	0	1	0.00
	Cedar Rapds	A	25	0	0	21	33.2	125	18	4	3	0	3	1	1	6	0	34	2	0	3	0	1.000	0	10	0.80
	Chattanooga	AA	24	0	0	10	31.2	123	22	16	11	3	1	3	0	11	1	11	2	0	1	3	.250	0	1	3.13
1993	Chattanooga	AA	53	1	0	20	80.1	360	92	30	25	2	5	0	5	31	6	61	4	1	11	7	.611	0	6	2.80
1994	Indianapols	AAA	50	0	0	11	62.1	274	75	32	28	6	4	2	0	17	5	30	2	0	5	6	.455	0	4	4.04
	6 Min. YEARS		278	5	0	136	469.2	1907	398	149	122	17	25	8	12	133	16	371	24	4	37	26	.587	0	41	2.34

Keith Kimberlin

Bats: Both Throws: Right Pos: SS　　　　　　　　Ht: 6'1" Wt: 170 Born: 07/25/66 Age: 28

			BATTING													BASERUNNING				PERCENTAGES		
Year	Team	Lg	G	AB	H	2B	3B	HR	TB	R	RBI	TBB	IBB	SO	HBP	SH	SF	SB	CS	SB%	GDP	Avg	OBP	SLG
1989	Niagara Fls	A	75	285	70	13	0	1	86	50	24	32	1	47	6	11	4	15	5	.75	6	.246	.330	.302
1990	Lakeland	A	122	419	109	16	5	0	135	56	35	54	1	68	1	21	1	16	3	.84	7	.260	.345	.322
1991	London	AA	107	331	77	16	5	2	109	27	34	24	1	55	3	7	5	4	2	.67	8	.233	.287	.329
1993	Reading	AA	137	504	133	12	3	2	157	56	29	57	1	70	5	11	3	19	7	.73	14	.264	.343	.312

Year	Team	Lg	G	AB	H	2B	3B	HR	TB	R	RBI	TBB	IBB	SO	HBP	SH	SF	SB	CS	SB%	GDP	Avg	OBP	SLG
1994	Reading	AA	21	82	14	2	0	1	19	4	5	6	0	21	0	2	0	1	1	.50	3	.171	.227	.232
	Scranton-Wb	AAA	20	37	4	1	0	0	5	2	1	4	0	9	0	0	1	0	0	.00	2	.108	.190	.135
	5 Min. YEARS		482	1658	407	60	13	6	511	195	128	177	7	270	15	52	14	55	18	.75	40	.245	.321	.308

Jack Kimel

Pitches: Left Bats: Left Pos: P Ht: 6'1" Wt: 175 Born: 12/24/69 Age: 25

			HOW MUCH HE PITCHED					WHAT HE GAVE UP												THE RESULTS					
Year	Team	Lg	G	GS	CG	GF	IP	BFP	H	R	ER	HR	SH	SF	HB	TBB	IBB	SO	WP	Bk	W	L	Pct.	ShO	Sv	ERA
1992	Butte	R	15	10	2	4	71	290	69	42	32	7	1	1	2	14	0	83	4	2	5	4	.556	0	1	4.06
1993	Chston-Sc	A	36	11	1	6	118	494	121	70	52	8	1	4	3	34	2	98	4	1	9	7	.563	0	0	3.97
1994	Tulsa	AA	10	0	0	3	11.1	69	27	21	19	1	0	0	1	8	0	8	2	0	0	1	.000	0	0	15.09
	Charlotte	A	38	0	0	20	45.2	191	41	17	13	2	3	1	1	19	3	31	2	0	3	1	.750	0	8	2.56
	3 Min. YEARS		99	21	3	33	246	1044	258	150	116	18	5	6	6	75	5	220	12	3	17	13	.567	0	9	4.24

Jeff Kipila

Bats: Right Throws: Right Pos: OF Ht: 6'4" Wt: 230 Born: 09/13/65 Age: 29

			BATTING															BASERUNNING				PERCENTAGES		
Year	Team	Lg	G	AB	H	2B	3B	HR	TB	R	RBI	TBB	IBB	SO	HBP	SH	SF	SB	CS	SB%	GDP	Avg	OBP	SLG
1988	Bend	A	69	253	52	12	2	9	95	34	42	40	0	71	3	0	3	2	0	1.00	3	.206	.318	.375
1989	Quad City	A	10	24	4	1	0	1	8	3	1	5	0	5	0	1	0	0	1	.00	1	.167	.310	.333
	Bend	A	66	238	64	10	1	15	121	48	49	45	1	63	4	0	4	3	0	1.00	3	.269	.388	.508
1990	Palm Sprngs	A	72	253	61	12	5	3	92	29	30	34	2	75	2	0	0	6	4	.60	2	.241	.333	.364
1991	Quad City	A	112	401	110	35	0	18	199	64	77	58	1	99	4	0	9	4	2	.67	5	.274	.364	.496
1992	Midland	AA	115	417	108	22	3	21	199	63	76	48	1	104	9	0	1	3	4	.43	3	.259	.347	.477
1993	Vancouver	AAA	32	99	31	7	0	5	53	18	21	15	0	20	0	1	0	2	1	.67	2	.313	.400	.535
	Midland	AA	59	203	47	7	1	12	92	32	47	32	1	67	3	0	4	0	0	.00	4	.232	.339	.453
1994	Harrisburg	AA	95	272	70	18	0	11	121	42	33	38	3	49	3	0	1	0	1	.00	1	.257	.354	.445
	7 Min. YEARS		630	2160	547	124	12	95	980	333	376	315	8	553	28	2	25	20	13	.61	23	.253	.352	.454

Bob Kipper

Pitches: Left Bats: Right Pos: P Ht: 6'2" Wt: 185 Born: 07/08/64 Age: 30

			HOW MUCH HE PITCHED					WHAT HE GAVE UP												THE RESULTS					
Year	Team	Lg	G	GS	CG	GF	IP	BFP	H	R	ER	HR	SH	SF	HB	TBB	IBB	SO	WP	Bk	W	L	Pct.	ShO	Sv	ERA
1984	Redwood	A	26	26	8	0	185	0	147	61	42	4	0	0	3	65	3	98	5	0	18	8	.692	3	0	2.04
1985	Midland	AA	9	9	1	0	49.2	204	52	22	17	5	2	3	0	10	0	31	1	1	3	3	.500	1	0	3.08
	Edmonton	AAA	1	1	0	0	8.1	0	7	3	2	1	0	0	0	2	0	8	0	1	0	0	.000	0	0	2.16
	Hawaii	AAA	6	5	1	1	41.1	0	29	12	9	3	0	0	1	10	0	34	1	0	3	0	1.000	1	0	1.96
1986	Nashua	AA	4	4	0	0	18.1	72	14	7	7	1	0	1	3	3	0	19	1	0	0	1	.000	0	0	3.44
1987	Vancouver	AAA	6	2	0	2	25.1	102	23	7	5	2	2	1	0	4	1	22	1	0	0	2	.000	0	1	1.78
1990	Buffalo	AAA	5	1	0	0	4.2	21	6	4	4	1	0	0	0	1	0	6	0	0	0	0	.000	0	0	7.71
1994	Norfolk	AAA	9	0	0	4	12.2	63	17	12	11	2	2	2	1	7	2	13	1	0	1	2	.333	0	0	7.82
1985	California	AL	2	1	0	0	3.1	20	7	8	8	1	0	2	0	3	0	0	0	0	0	1	.000	0	0	21.60
	Pittsburgh	NL	5	4	0	1	24.2	104	21	16	14	4	1	1	0	7	0	13	0	0	1	2	.333	0	0	5.11
1986	Pittsburgh	NL	20	19	0	1	114	496	123	60	51	17	3	3	2	34	3	81	3	3	6	8	.429	0	0	4.03
1987	Pittsburgh	NL	24	20	1	0	110.2	493	117	74	73	25	4	3	2	52	4	83	5	0	5	9	.357	1	0	5.94
1988	Pittsburgh	NL	50	0	0	15	65	267	54	33	27	7	5	3	2	26	4	39	1	1	2	6	.250	0	0	3.74
1989	Pittsburgh	NL	52	0	0	15	83	334	55	29	27	5	5	3	0	33	6	58	5	2	3	4	.429	0	4	2.93
1990	Pittsburgh	NL	41	1	0	7	62.2	260	44	24	21	7	2	3	3	26	1	35	1	5	5	2	.714	0	3	3.02
1991	Pittsburgh	NL	52	0	0	18	60	264	66	34	31	7	1	2	0	22	3	38	0	1	2	2	.500	0	4	4.65
1992	Minnesota	AL	25	0	0	12	38.2	168	40	23	19	8	2	0	3	14	2	22	1	0	3	3	.500	0	0	4.42
	6 Min. YEARS		66	48	10	7	345.1	462	295	128	97	19	6	7	8	102	6	231	10	2	25	16	.610	5	1	2.53
	8 Maj. YEARS		271	45	0	69	562	2406	527	301	271	81	23	21	12	217	24	369	16	12	27	37	.422	1	11	4.34

Jay Kirkpatrick

Bats: Left Throws: Right Pos: INF Ht: 6'4" Wt: 210 Born: 07/10/69 Age: 25

			BATTING															BASERUNNING				PERCENTAGES		
Year	Team	Lg	G	AB	H	2B	3B	HR	TB	R	RBI	TBB	IBB	SO	HBP	SH	SF	SB	CS	SB%	GDP	Avg	OBP	SLG
1991	Great Falls	R	50	168	54	11	1	2	73	25	26	13	0	23	3	0	0	1	2	.33	3	.321	.380	.435
1992	Vero Beach	A	114	385	108	22	2	6	152	32	50	31	4	82	4	1	6	2	2	.50	9	.281	.336	.395
1993	Bakersfield	A	103	375	108	21	0	8	153	42	63	35	2	78	4	1	3	1	4	.20	7	.288	.353	.408
	San Antonio	AA	27	97	31	6	1	6	57	17	17	14	4	15	0	0	0	0	1	.00	4	.320	.405	.588
1994	San Antonio	AA	123	449	133	40	1	18	229	61	75	45	7	91	3	0	6	2	2	.50	12	.296	.360	.510
	Albuquerque	AAA	3	5	1	1	0	0	2	0	1	1	0	0	0	0	0	0	0	.00	0	.200	.333	.400
	4 Min. YEARS		420	1479	435	101	5	40	666	177	232	139	17	290	14	2	15	6	11	.35	35	.294	.357	.450

Daron Kirkreit

Pitches: Right Bats: Right Pos: P Ht: 6'6" Wt: 225 Born: 08/07/72 Age: 22

			HOW MUCH HE PITCHED					WHAT HE GAVE UP												THE RESULTS					
Year	Team	Lg	G	GS	CG	GF	IP	BFP	H	R	ER	HR	SH	SF	HB	TBB	IBB	SO	WP	Bk	W	L	Pct.	ShO	Sv	ERA
1993	Watertown	A	7	7	1	0	36.1	156	33	14	9	1	1	0	0	11	0	44	1	1	4	1	.800	0	0	2.23
1994	Kinston	A	20	19	4	1	127.2	510	92	48	38	1	3	1	2	40	0	116	6	1	8	7	.533	0	0	2.68
	Canton-Akrn	AA	9	9	0	0	46.1	217	53	35	32	5	2	1	0	25	2	54	4	0	3	5	.375	0	0	6.22
	2 Min. YEARS		36	35	5	1	210.1	883	178	97	79	15	6	2	7	76	2	214	11	1	15	13	.536	0	0	3.38

Garland Kiser

Pitches: Left **Bats:** Left **Pos:** P Ht: 6' 3" Wt: 190 Born: 07/08/68 Age: 26

			HOW MUCH HE PITCHED						WHAT HE GAVE UP											THE RESULTS					
Year	Team	Lg	G	GS	CG	GF	IP	BFP	H	R	ER	HR	SH	SF	HB	TBB	IBB	SO	WP	Bk	W	L	Pct.	ShO	Sv	ERA
1986	Bend	A	14	12	0	2	70.2	0	79	58	43	4	0	0	2	48	2	46	6	1	4	5	.444	0	0	5.48
1987	Spartanburg	A	21	5	0	6	43	204	49	37	31	2	4	1	4	24	2	27	6	0	0	5	.000	0	1	6.49
1988	Indians	R	7	7	2	1	56	221	31	12	8	0	0	0	2	17	0	45	0	2	5	1	.833	0	0	1.29
	Burlington	R	7	5	1	1	31	123	22	11	7	0	0	0	0	9	0	29	1	2	2	2	.500	0	0	2.03
1989	Kinston	A	6	0	0	1	12.2	60	14	10	10	1	1	1	2	7	0	7	0	0	0	1	.000	0	0	7.11
	Watertown	A	12	9	2	2	74	304	66	36	28	4	4	0	2	18	0	74	5	2	7	1	.875	0	0	3.41
1990	Kinston	A	55	0	0	24	94.2	388	81	25	18	3	5	3	3	27	1	82	5	0	5	3	.625	0	9	1.71
1991	Kinston	A	31	0	0	19	48.1	197	35	11	8	2	3	0	1	14	2	52	3	0	6	1	.857	0	5	1.49
	Canton-Akrn	AA	17	4	0	6	44.1	170	35	13	10	1	1	0	1	11	2	34	3	0	2	3	.400	0	0	2.03
1992	Canton-Akrn	AA	39	1	0	19	53.1	231	52	25	21	6	3	2	0	18	1	36	1	0	3	2	.600	0	2	3.54
1993	New Orleans	AAA	50	4	0	12	66.2	287	69	43	40	10	2	2	3	24	3	42	2	2	5	4	.556	0	1	5.40
1994	Carolina	AA	2	0	0	0	2.1	12	5	3	3	0	0	0	0	0	0	1	0	0	0	0	.000	0	0	11.57
1991	Cleveland	AL	7	0	0	1	4.2	25	7	5	5	0	1	1	0	4	0	3	0	0	0	0	.000	0	0	9.64
	9 Min. YEARS		261	47	5	86	597	2197	538	284	227	33	23	9	20	217	13	475	32	9	39	28	.582	0	18	3.42

Stephen Kliafas

Bats: Right **Throws:** Right **Pos:** SS Ht: 5'10" Wt: 185 Born: 11/04/68 Age: 26

			BATTING														BASERUNNING				PERCENTAGES		
Year	Team	Lg	G	AB	H	2B	3B	HR	TB	R	RBI	TBB	IBB	SO	HBP	SH	SF	SB	CS	SB%	GDP	Avg	OBP	SLG
1990	Dodgers	R	20	79	27	7	0	0	34	9	17	3	0	5	1	1	1	2	1	.67	0	.342	.369	.430
	Yakima	A	39	118	22	2	0	1	27	8	12	8	0	19	0	1	0	5	3	.63	3	.186	.238	.229
1991	Vero Beach	A	31	73	19	1	0	0	20	11	2	5	0	10	1	0	0	1	3	.25	3	.260	.316	.274
	Yakima	A	49	165	46	7	2	0	57	28	18	10	0	30	4	2	2	7	4	.64	3	.279	.331	.345
1992	Vero Beach	A	15	52	13	1	0	0	14	7	3	2	0	9	1	1	0	4	0	1.00	2	.250	.291	.269
	Bakersfield	A	50	133	33	9	0	1	45	19	11	9	1	24	3	2	1	1	4	.20	2	.248	.308	.338
	San Antonio	AA	13	35	9	2	0	0	11	1	4	1	0	8	0	1	0	0	0	.00	0	.257	.278	.314
1993	San Antonio	AA	6	14	2	0	0	0	2	2	0	2	0	6	1	1	0	0	0	.00	0	.143	.294	.143
	Bakersfield	A	88	328	77	13	0	1	93	40	24	13	1	37	2	5	3	4	1	.80	3	.235	.267	.284
1994	San Antonio	AA	27	60	8	0	0	0	8	5	4	3	0	17	0	0	1	0	0	.00	0	.133	.172	.133
	5 Min. YEARS		338	1057	256	42	2	3	311	130	95	56	2	165	13	14	7	24	16	.60	16	.242	.287	.294

Joe Klink

Pitches: Left **Bats:** Left **Pos:** P Ht: 5'11" Wt: 175 Born: 02/03/62 Age: 33

			HOW MUCH HE PITCHED						WHAT HE GAVE UP											THE RESULTS					
Year	Team	Lg	G	GS	CG	GF	IP	BFP	H	R	ER	HR	SH	SF	HB	TBB	IBB	SO	WP	Bk	W	L	Pct.	ShO	Sv	ERA
1984	Columbia	A	31	0	0	27	38.2	172	30	19	15	1	4	3	1	28	0	49	5	1	5	4	.556	0	11	3.49
1985	Lynchburg	A	44	0	0	17	51.2	221	41	16	13	1	4	2	0	26	2	59	5	2	3	3	.500	0	5	2.26
1986	Orlando	AA	45	0	0	41	68	297	59	24	19	5	5	1	2	37	1	63	1	0	4	5	.444	0	11	2.51
1987	Portland	AAA	12	0	0	7	23	107	25	14	11	1	1	3	0	13	1	14	1	0	0	0	.000	0	0	4.30
1988	Huntsville	AA	21	0	0	12	34.2	143	25	6	3	0	0	0	0	14	1	30	3	4	1	2	.333	0	3	0.78
	Tacoma	AAA	27	0	0	15	38.2	185	48	29	22	0	5	3	1	17	1	32	3	6	2	1	.667	0	1	5.12
1989	Tacoma	AAA	6	0	0	5	6.2	23	2	0	0	0	0	0	1	2	0	5	0	0	0	0	.000	0	0	0.00
	Huntsville	AA	57	0	0	53	60.2	249	46	19	19	2	3	4	2	23	0	59	6	5	4	4	.500	0	26	2.82
1991	Modesto	A	3	3	0	0	5	19	4	2	2	2	0	0	0	1	0	1	0	0	0	0	.000	0	0	3.60
1994	Albuquerque	AAA	2	0	0	1	3	12	3	1	1	0	0	0	1	1	1	2	0	1	0	0	.000	0	0	3.00
1987	Minnesota	AL	12	0	0	5	23	116	37	18	17	4	1	1	0	11	0	17	1	0	0	1	.000	0	0	6.65
1990	Oakland	AL	40	0	0	19	39.2	165	34	9	9	1	1	0	0	18	0	19	3	1	0	0	.000	0	1	2.04
1991	Oakland	AL	62	0	0	10	62	266	60	30	30	4	8	0	5	21	5	34	4	0	10	3	.769	0	2	4.35
1993	Florida	NL	59	0	0	10	37.2	168	37	22	21	0	2	3	0	24	4	22	1	2	0	0	.000	0	0	5.02
	8 Min. YEARS		248	3	0	178	330	1428	283	130	105	12	22	16	8	162	7	314	24	19	19	19	.500	0	57	2.86
	4 Maj. YEARS		173	0	0	44	162.1	715	168	79	77	9	12	4	5	74	9	92	9	3	10	6	.625	0	3	4.27

Kevin Kloek

Pitches: Right **Bats:** Right **Pos:** P Ht: 6'3" Wt: 175 Born: 08/15/70 Age: 24

			HOW MUCH HE PITCHED						WHAT HE GAVE UP											THE RESULTS					
Year	Team	Lg	G	GS	CG	GF	IP	BFP	H	R	ER	HR	SH	SF	HB	TBB	IBB	SO	WP	Bk	W	L	Pct.	ShO	Sv	ERA
1992	Beloit	A	15	14	2	0	94	386	79	32	22	7	4	2	4	27	1	76	5	7	10	1	.909	1	0	2.11
1993	El Paso	AA	23	23	1	0	135.2	587	148	75	62	11	7	5	7	53	4	97	5	0	9	6	.600	0	0	4.11
1994	Brewers	R	3	3	0	0	19	71	9	3	3	0	0	0	0	3	0	19	1	0	2	0	1.000	0	0	1.42
	El Paso	AA	9	9	0	0	55.1	223	46	26	24	3	0	4	1	18	0	37	0	0	5	1	.833	0	0	3.90
	3 Min. YEARS		50	49	3	0	304	1267	282	136	111	21	11	11	12	101	5	229	11	7	26	8	.765	2	0	3.29

Joe Kmak

Bats: Right **Throws:** Right **Pos:** C Ht: 6' 0" Wt: 185 Born: 05/03/63 Age: 32

			BATTING														BASERUNNING				PERCENTAGES		
Year	Team	Lg	G	AB	H	2B	3B	HR	TB	R	RBI	TBB	IBB	SO	HBP	SH	SF	SB	CS	SB%	GDP	Avg	OBP	SLG
1985	Everett	A	40	129	40	10	1	1	55	21	14	20	0	23	3	0	2	0	1	.00	3	.310	.409	.426
1986	Fresno	A	60	163	44	5	0	1	52	23	9	15	0	38	3	0	1	3	2	.60	6	.270	.341	.319

137

Year Team	Lg	G	AB	H	2B	3B	HR	TB	R	RBI	TBB	IBB	SO	HBP	SH	SF	SB	CS	SB%	GDP	Avg	OBP	SLG
1987 Fresno	A	48	154	34	8	0	0	42	18	12	15	0	32	3	3	0	1	2	.33	3	.221	.302	.273
Shreveport	AA	15	41	8	0	1	0	10	5	3	3	0	4	1	0	0	0	0	.00	1	.195	.267	.244
1988 Shreveport	AA	71	178	40	5	2	1	52	16	14	11	2	19	4	1	1	0	0	.00	3	.225	.284	.292
1989 Reno	A	78	248	68	10	5	4	100	39	34	40	1	41	5	0	1	8	4	.67	9	.274	.384	.403
1990 El Paso	AA	35	109	31	3	2	2	44	8	11	7	0	22	2	3	2	0	0	.00	2	.284	.333	.404
Denver	AAA	28	95	22	3	0	1	28	12	10	4	0	16	3	5	0	1	1	.50	3	.232	.284	.295
1991 Denver	AAA	100	294	70	17	2	1	94	34	33	28	0	44	5	8	1	7	3	.70	5	.238	.314	.320
1992 Denver	AAA	67	225	70	11	4	3	98	27	31	19	0	39	3	5	2	6	3	.67	5	.311	.369	.436
1993 New Orleans	AAA	24	76	23	3	2	1	33	9	13	8	0	14	0	0	0	1	0	1.00	1	.303	.369	.434
1994 Norfolk	AAA	86	264	66	5	0	5	86	28	31	31	1	51	5	1	2	2	3	.40	0	.250	.339	.326
1993 Milwaukee	AL	51	110	24	5	0	0	29	9	7	14	0	13	2	1	0	6	2	.75	2	.218	.317	.264
10 Min. YEARS		652	1976	516	80	19	20	694	240	215	201	4	343	37	26	11	29	19	.60	47	.261	.339	.351

Chris Knabenshue

Bats: Left Throws: Right Pos: OF   Ht: 6'1" Wt: 185 Born: 10/30/63 Age: 31

Year Team	Lg	G	AB	H	2B	3B	HR	TB	R	RBI	TBB	IBB	SO	HBP	SH	SF	SB	CS	SB%	GDP	Avg	OBP	SLG
1985 Spokane	A	71	258	72	13	2	1	92	50	34	57	1	42	0	2	2	10	4	.71	3	.279	.407	.357
1986 Charleston	A	102	335	95	20	4	10	153	77	62	82	1	82	2	2	4	36	10	.78	7	.284	.423	.457
1987 Wichita	AA	128	473	146	31	3	15	228	91	65	66	11	99	1	0	0	20	14	.59	10	.309	.394	.482
1988 Wichita	AA	116	412	101	26	2	16	179	68	56	84	3	138	2	0	1	16	16	.50	6	.245	.375	.434
1989 Las Vegas	AAA	115	306	79	17	4	18	158	68	50	83	3	112	1	4	0	0	3	.00	5	.258	.418	.516
1990 Scr Wil-Bar	AAA	129	379	90	16	1	18	162	61	62	76	2	108	2	4	4	11	7	.61	7	.237	.364	.427
1991 Scranton-Wb	AAA	17	35	7	2	0	0	9	3	8	10	1	12	0	1	0	1	0	1.00	1	.200	.378	.257
Denver	AAA	12	29	6	1	0	1	10	5	3	9	1	9	0	0	0	0	0	.00	0	.207	.395	.345
Palm Sprngs	A	11	30	6	1	0	1	10	5	5	8	1	11	0	1	0	0	0	.00	0	.200	.368	.333
1992 Huntsville	AA	21	71	14	4	0	1	21	9	11	10	0	24	0	0	0	1	2	.33	0	.197	.293	.296
1994 Buffalo	AAA	45	131	38	8	1	2	54	17	18	24	2	27	0	0	0	0	0	.00	4	.290	.397	.412
9 Min. YEARS		767	2459	654	139	17	83	1076	454	374	509	26	664	8	14	13	95	56	.63	42	.266	.392	.438

Mike Knapp

Bats: Right Throws: Right Pos: C   Ht: 6'0" Wt: 195 Born: 10/06/64 Age: 30

Year Team	Lg	G	AB	H	2B	3B	HR	TB	R	RBI	TBB	IBB	SO	HBP	SH	SF	SB	CS	SB%	GDP	Avg	OBP	SLG
1986 Salem	A	64	224	66	12	1	3	89	31	39	31	1	37	3	1	3	4	4	.50	2	.295	.383	.397
1987 Quad City	A	91	327	84	14	3	1	107	34	31	27	0	48	4	0	7	1	6	.14	7	.257	.315	.327
1988 Midland	AA	100	327	86	12	1	3	109	34	33	35	0	64	2	6	5	1	3	.25	5	.263	.333	.333
1989 Midland	AA	20	64	21	2	0	2	29	7	6	3	0	8	2	1	0	0	0	.00	2	.328	.377	.453
Edmonton	AAA	51	144	38	8	0	1	49	15	22	15	0	27	4	3	1	0	4	.00	2	.264	.348	.340
1990 Midland	AA	57	193	50	8	0	2	64	16	21	16	0	29	0	0	1	1	1	.50	3	.259	.314	.332
Edmonton	AAA	12	39	8	0	1	0	10	3	4	4	0	6	0	0	0	0	0	.00	0	.205	.279	.256
1991 Charlotte	AA	92	266	68	12	0	1	83	19	33	19	3	53	1	7	1	4	0	1.00	8	.256	.307	.312
1992 Iowa	AAA	54	138	34	5	0	3	48	16	15	10	0	28	3	0	0	2	2	.50	1	.246	.311	.348
1993 Omaha	AAA	70	200	58	7	0	2	71	22	19	34	0	32	3	3	1	2	4	.33	6	.290	.399	.355
1994 Omaha	AAA	52	151	34	5	1	5	56	19	19	14	0	27	2	2	2	2	2	.50	1	.225	.296	.371
9 Min. YEARS		663	2073	547	85	7	23	715	216	242	208	4	359	24	23	21	17	26	.40	37	.264	.335	.345

Kerry Knox

Pitches: Left Bats: Left Pos: P   Ht: 6'0" Wt: 188 Born: 04/10/67 Age: 28

Year Team	Lg	G	GS	CG	GF	IP	BFP	H	R	ER	HR	SH	SF	HB	TBB	IBB	SO	WP	Bk	W	L	Pct.	ShO	Sv	ERA
1989 Spokane	A	12	12	1	0	75.1	306	74	30	22	7	1	3	1	10	0	76	1	3	8	2	.800	0	0	2.63
Chston-Sc	A	2	2	0	0	11	43	9	3	3	0	0	0	3	1	0	11	1	1	0	0	.000	0	0	2.45
1990 Riverside	A	27	27	3	0	179.2	768	188	97	73	14	9	6	3	49	2	111	8	4	11	12	.478	1	0	3.66
1991 Wichita	AA	28	15	1	1	113.2	504	133	72	62	13	2	2	4	36	1	51	5	2	4	4	.500	1	0	4.91
1992 Beloit	A	14	1	0	5	31	134	30	20	13	3	2	0	1	8	0	27	1	0	0	0	.000	0	4	3.77
El Paso	AA	13	1	0	2	15.2	76	16	14	12	1	1	1	2	12	1	12	1	1	0	1	.000	0	0	6.89
Stockton	A	5	4	0	0	24.2	99	26	6	6	1	1	1	0	5	0	15	1	0	1	1	.500	0	0	2.19
1993 Arkansas	AA	22	11	0	2	81	328	78	30	25	9	5	3	3	14	3	61	1	2	4	4	.500	0	0	2.78
Louisville	AAA	7	1	0	0	44	187	48	25	22	6	2	1	3	10	0	24	2	2	1	4	.200	1	0	4.50
1994 Louisville	AAA	32	24	1	1	149	673	185	104	95	21	8	9	10	43	4	83	4	5	8	9	.471	0	0	5.74
6 Min. YEARS		162	104	7	11	725	3118	787	401	333	75	31	26	30	188	11	471	25	20	37	37	.500	3	4	4.13

Brian Koelling

Bats: Right Throws: Right Pos: 2B   Ht: 6'1" Wt: 185 Born: 06/11/69 Age: 26

Year Team	Lg	G	AB	H	2B	3B	HR	TB	R	RBI	TBB	IBB	SO	HBP	SH	SF	SB	CS	SB%	GDP	Avg	OBP	SLG
1991 Billings	R	22	85	30	7	1	2	45	17	12	14	0	23	1	0	0	6	2	.75	0	.353	.450	.529
Cedar Rapids	A	35	147	38	6	0	1	47	27	12	14	0	39	3	0	1	22	6	.79	0	.259	.333	.320
1992 Cedar Rapids	A	129	460	121	18	7	5	168	81	43	49	0	137	1	9	2	47	16	.75	3	.263	.334	.365
1993 Chattanooga	AA	110	430	119	17	6	4	160	64	47	32	1	105	2	4	3	34	13	.72	2	.277	.328	.372

Year	Team	Lg	G	AB	H	2B	3B	HR	TB	R	RBI	TBB	IBB	SO	HBP	SH	SF	SB	CS	SB%	GDP	Avg	OBP	SLG
	Indianapols	AAA	2	9	2	0	0	0	2	1	0	0	0	1	1	0	0	0	1	.00	0	.222	.300	.222
1994	Indianapols	AAA	19	53	8	0	0	0	8	6	0	2	0	14	1	1	0	4	2	.67	0	.151	.196	.151
	Chattanooga	AA	92	343	96	11	5	3	126	54	31	24	1	64	4	7	1	27	18	.60	6	.280	.333	.367
1993	Cincinnati	NL	7	15	1	0	0	0	1	2	0	0	0	2	1	0	0	0	0	.00	0	.067	.125	.067
	4 Min. YEARS		409	1527	414	59	19	15	556	250	145	135	2	383	13	21	7	140	58	.71	11	.271	.334	.364

Jerry Koller

Pitches: Right Bats: Right Pos: P Ht: 6'3" Wt: 190 Born: 06/30/72 Age: 23

			HOW MUCH HE PITCHED						WHAT HE GAVE UP									THE RESULTS					
Year	Team	Lg	G	GS	CG	GF	IP	BFP	H	R	ER	HR	SH	SF	HB	TBB	IBB	SO	WP	Bk	W	L	Pct.	ShO	Sv	ERA
1990	Braves	R	13	8	1	1	51	210	45	24	12	0	0	1	4	13	2	45	4	8	4	3	.571	1	0	2.12
1991	Braves	R	2	2	0	0	8	40	9	6	3	0	0	0	0	3	0	10	1	0	0	0	.000	0	0	3.38
	Idaho Falls	R	9	9	0	0	36	171	49	29	25	1	0	2	1	14	0	29	7	2	2	2	.500	0	0	6.25
1992	Macon	A	21	21	2	0	133	526	104	41	35	8	2	4	5	31	0	114	8	2	10	5	.667	0	0	2.37
1993	Durham	A	27	26	1	0	157.2	666	168	91	80	20	7	6	8	47	1	102	7	2	8	10	.444	0	0	4.57
1994	Greenville	AA	22	22	0	0	119.2	498	110	60	56	8	4	5	3	42	0	56	7	4	7	5	.583	0	0	4.21
	5 Min. YEARS		94	88	4	1	505.1	2111	485	251	211	37	13	18	21	150	3	356	34	18	31	25	.554	1	0	3.76

Rod Koller

Pitches: Right Bats: Right Pos: P Ht: 6'4" Wt: 195 Born: 07/13/70 Age: 24

			HOW MUCH HE PITCHED						WHAT HE GAVE UP									THE RESULTS					
Year	Team	Lg	G	GS	CG	GF	IP	BFP	H	R	ER	HR	SH	SF	HB	TBB	IBB	SO	WP	Bk	W	L	Pct.	ShO	Sv	ERA
1991	Burlington	R	2	0	0	0	3	13	3	1	1	0	0	1	0	0	0	0	0	0	0	0	.000	0	0	3.00
1992	Burlington	R	1	1	0	0	3	15	3	4	4	0	0	0	0	3	0	2	2	0	0	1	.000	0	0	12.00
	Watertown	A	15	7	0	3	52.2	238	71	35	30	1	1	1	2	14	0	24	2	3	3	7	.300	0	1	5.13
1993	Columbus	A	47	0	0	23	68.1	273	51	21	17	4	2	2	1	19	1	37	1	0	9	5	.643	0	9	2.24
1994	Canton-Akrn	AA	7	0	0	2	13	63	14	12	11	4	2	0	0	9	0	7	1	0	0	1	.000	0	0	7.62
	Kinston	A	37	0	0	15	57.2	243	55	32	19	4	2	3	1	16	0	33	5	0	4	4	.500	0	8	2.97
	4 Min. YEARS		109	9	0	43	197.2	845	197	105	82	13	7	7	4	61	1	103	11	3	16	18	.471	0	18	3.73

Andy Kontorinis

Bats: Left Throws: Right Pos: 1B Ht: 6'0" Wt: 198 Born: 11/18/69 Age: 25

			BATTING														BASERUNNING				PERCENTAGES		
Year	Team	Lg	G	AB	H	2B	3B	HR	TB	R	RBI	TBB	IBB	SO	HBP	SH	SF	SB	CS	SB%	GDP	Avg	OBP	SLG
1992	Kenosha	A	75	273	77	12	0	5	104	26	44	28	2	39	4	0	5	2	4	.33	5	.282	.352	.381
1993	Ft.Myers	A	114	408	104	24	3	3	143	44	59	40	5	42	6	3	4	4	5	.44	11	.255	.328	.350
1994	Fort Myers	A	100	344	99	19	5	6	146	49	51	57	3	39	1	1	4	7	4	.64	9	.288	.387	.424
	Nashville	AA	9	31	5	0	0	1	8	5	2	2	1	6	0	0	0	0	0	.00	0	.161	.212	.258
	3 Min. YEARS		298	1056	285	55	8	15	401	124	156	127	11	126	11	5	13	13	13	.50	25	.270	.350	.380

Dennis Konuszewski

Pitches: Right Bats: Right Pos: P Ht: 6'3" Wt: 210 Born: 02/04/71 Age: 24

			HOW MUCH HE PITCHED						WHAT HE GAVE UP									THE RESULTS					
Year	Team	Lg	G	GS	CG	GF	IP	BFP	H	R	ER	HR	SH	SF	HB	TBB	IBB	SO	WP	Bk	W	L	Pct.	ShO	Sv	ERA
1992	Welland	A	2	2	0	0	7	30	6	1	1	0	1	0	0	4	0	4	1	1	0	0	.000	0	0	1.29
	Augusta	A	17	8	0	4	62.1	258	50	19	16	1	4	0	5	19	0	45	2	7	3	3	.500	0	1	2.31
1993	Salem	A	39	13	0	7	103	463	121	66	53	14	3	7	5	43	3	81	6	4	4	10	.286	0	1	4.63
1994	Carolina	AA	51	0	0	19	77.2	346	81	39	31	5	2	2	2	31	5	53	6	1	6	5	.545	0	1	3.59
	3 Min. YEARS		109	23	0	30	250	1097	258	125	101	20	10	9	12	97	8	183	15	13	13	18	.419	0	3	3.64

Bryn Kosco

Bats: Left Throws: Right Pos: 1B Ht: 6'1" Wt: 185 Born: 03/09/67 Age: 28

			BATTING														BASERUNNING				PERCENTAGES		
Year	Team	Lg	G	AB	H	2B	3B	HR	TB	R	RBI	TBB	IBB	SO	HBP	SH	SF	SB	CS	SB%	GDP	Avg	OBP	SLG
1988	Jamestown	A	63	229	65	19	2	8	112	26	42	18	4	48	1	0	3	1	0	1.00	7	.284	.335	.489
1989	Rockford	A	77	292	78	16	0	11	127	47	44	39	6	61	2	0	2	2	0	1.00	5	.267	.355	.435
	Wst Plm Bch	A	60	203	46	10	1	1	61	16	22	21	5	42	0	0	4	2	2	.50	4	.227	.294	.300
1990	Jacksnville	AA	33	113	28	8	0	0	36	7	15	11	2	23	0	2	1	0	0	.00	4	.248	.312	.319
1991	Harrisburg	AA	113	381	92	23	5	10	155	50	58	48	4	79	2	0	3	4	1	.80	9	.241	.327	.407
1992	Harrisburg	AA	106	341	78	17	0	5	110	35	41	31	2	75	1	1	5	2	0	1.00	6	.229	.291	.323
1993	High Desert	A	121	450	138	25	3	27	250	96	121	62	3	97	5	0	8	1	6	.14	13	.307	.390	.556
1994	New Haven	AA	132	479	116	24	3	22	212	64	90	59	6	124	4	1	6	2	2	.50	17	.242	.327	.443
	7 Min. YEARS		705	2488	641	142	14	84	1063	341	433	289	32	549	15	4	32	14	11	.56	65	.258	.335	.427

Mike Kotarski

Pitches: Left Bats: Left Pos: P Ht: 6'1" Wt: 195 Born: 09/18/70 Age: 24

			HOW MUCH HE PITCHED						WHAT HE GAVE UP									THE RESULTS					
Year	Team	Lg	G	GS	CG	GF	IP	BFP	H	R	ER	HR	SH	SF	HB	TBB	IBB	SO	WP	Bk	W	L	Pct.	ShO	Sv	ERA
1992	Bend	A	25	3	0	9	55.2	247	48	30	23	1	1	1	6	36	2	65	1	0	3	1	.750	0	0	3.72
1993	Central Val	A	52	0	0	32	88.1	396	87	44	38	9	11	2	3	37	3	81	3	1	6	2	.750	0	11	3.87
1994	New Haven	AA	18	0	0	12	21	109	29	29	23	7	0	3	0	13	0	14	3	0	0	1	.000	0	0	9.86
	Central Val	A	41	1	0	11	62.1	278	69	39	27	8	1	3	3	29	3	58	7	4	1	3	.250	0	2	3.90
	3 Min. YEARS		136	4	0	64	227.1	1030	233	142	111	25	13	9	12	115	8	218	14	5	10	7	.588	0	16	4.39

Tony Kounas

Bats: Right Throws: Right Pos: C Ht: 6'2" Wt: 210 Born: 11/06/67 Age: 27

					BATTING												BASERUNNING				PERCENTAGES		
Year	Team	Lg	G	AB	H	2B	3B	HR	TB	R	RBI	TBB	IBB	SO	HBP	SH	SF	SB	CS	SB%	GDP	Avg	OBP	SLG
1990	Bellingham	A	19	65	15	4	0	1	22	9	11	8	0	13	1	0	0	1	0	1.00	2	.231	.324	.338
1991	Peninsula	A	109	387	104	18	1	7	145	46	47	40	3	43	2	0	3	3	1	.75	11	.269	.338	.375
1992	San Berndno	A	111	378	99	23	2	10	156	51	55	40	1	43	1	1	1	2	5	.29	14	.262	.333	.413
1993	Jacksnville	AA	49	157	43	14	0	4	69	22	23	14	0	24	2	1	1	2	1	.67	3	.274	.339	.439
1994	Jacksnville	AA	68	212	54	14	0	7	89	26	23	15	0	32	1	1	1	0	1	.00	5	.255	.309	.420
	5 Min. YEARS		356	1199	315	73	3	29	481	154	159	117	4	155	8	3	6	8	8	.50	35	.263	.331	.401

Brian Kowitz

Bats: Left Throws: Left Pos: OF Ht: 5'10" Wt: 175 Born: 08/07/69 Age: 25

					BATTING												BASERUNNING				PERCENTAGES		
Year	Team	Lg	G	AB	H	2B	3B	HR	TB	R	RBI	TBB	IBB	SO	HBP	SH	SF	SB	CS	SB%	GDP	Avg	OBP	SLG
1990	Pulaski	R	43	182	59	13	1	8	98	40	19	16	2	16	1	2	2	12	6	.67	4	.324	.378	.538
	Greenville	AA	20	68	9	0	0	0	9	4	4	8	1	10	0	1	0	1	0	1.00	2	.132	.224	.132
1991	Durham	A	86	323	82	13	5	3	114	41	21	23	0	56	3	4	1	18	8	.69	3	.254	.309	.353
	Greenville	AA	35	112	26	5	0	3	40	15	17	10	0	7	2	2	2	1	4	.20	3	.232	.302	.357
1992	Durham	A	105	382	115	14	7	7	164	53	64	44	4	53	2	6	7	22	11	.67	3	.301	.370	.429
	Greenville	AA	21	56	16	4	0	0	20	9	6	6	0	10	0	0	0	1	4	.20	0	.286	.355	.357
1993	Greenville	AA	122	450	125	20	5	5	170	63	48	60	0	56	2	1	1	13	10	.57	7	.278	.365	.378
	Richmond	AAA	12	45	12	1	3	0	19	10	8	5	0	8	1	2	1	1	0	1.00	0	.267	.346	.422
1994	Richmond	AAA	124	466	140	29	7	8	207	68	57	43	2	53	2	1	7	22	8	.73	8	.300	.357	.444
	5 Min. YEARS		568	2084	584	99	28	34	841	303	244	215	9	269	13	19	21	91	51	.64	30	.280	.348	.404

Blaise Kozeniewski

Pitches: Right Bats: Right Pos: P Ht: 6'3" Wt: 185 Born: 11/02/69 Age: 25

			HOW MUCH HE PITCHED					WHAT HE GAVE UP										THE RESULTS					
Year	Team	Lg	G	GS	CG	GF	IP	BFP	H	R	ER	HR	SH	SF	HB	TBB	IBB	SO	WP	Bk	W	L	Pct.	ShO	Sv	ERA
1993	Oneonta	A	24	0	0	11	37	175	45	29	20	3	0	1	1	17	0	21	4	0	2	1	.667	0	1	4.86
1994	Greensboro	A	39	0	0	15	62	264	55	31	17	3	2	3	3	22	0	45	4	0	2	4	.333	0	3	2.47
	Albany-Colo	AA	2	0	0	0	4	14	1	0	0	0	0	0	0	1	1	4	1	0	0	0	.000	0	0	0.00
	2 Min. YEARS		65	0	0	26	103	453	101	60	37	6	2	4	4	40	1	70	9	0	4	5	.444	0	4	3.23

Randy Kramer

Pitches: Right Bats: Right Pos: P Ht: 6'2" Wt: 180 Born: 09/20/60 Age: 34

			HOW MUCH HE PITCHED					WHAT HE GAVE UP										THE RESULTS					
Year	Team	Lg	G	GS	CG	GF	IP	BFP	H	R	ER	HR	SH	SF	HB	TBB	IBB	SO	WP	Bk	W	L	Pct.	ShO	Sv	ERA
1984	Salem	A	12	11	0	0	53	261	63	66	58	14	0	0	4	34	0	35	7	0	2	8	.200	0	0	9.85
	Tri-Cities	A	15	15	0	0	84	0	83	62	47	6	0	0	5	58	1	74	13	0	5	6	.455	0	0	5.04
1985	Salem	A	25	24	1	0	115.1	565	143	99	86	11	5	3	3	77	0	86	20	0	7	11	.389	0	0	6.71
1986	Kinston	A	17	1	0	9	32.1	151	32	21	19	3	1	1	2	26	3	30	4	0	3	3	.500	0	4	5.29
	Salem	A	8	0	0	5	11	45	11	5	4	1	2	0	0	2	0	8	0	0	0	0	.000	0	0	3.27
	Tulsa	AA	26	0	0	17	39	172	40	22	19	0	1	1	2	19	1	32	3	1	0	3	.000	0	3	4.38
1987	Vancouver	AAA	11	1	0	1	17.2	86	16	14	12	2	0	3	0	19	1	16	3	0	0	0	.000	0	0	6.11
	Harrisburg	AA	26	4	1	14	49.2	235	62	43	35	2	4	3	0	29	4	43	8	0	4	5	.444	1	1	6.34
1988	Buffalo	AAA	28	28	6	0	198.1	797	161	85	69	15	5	4	4	50	4	120	9	4	10	8	.556	1	0	3.13
1989	Buffalo	AAA	5	2	0	2	14.1	65	15	5	2	0	2	1	0	7	1	8	2	0	1	0	1.000	0	0	1.26
1990	Buffalo	AAA	18	12	0	4	73.2	307	55	29	21	3	3	1	3	33	1	58	4	0	6	1	.857	0	3	2.57
1991	Richmond	AAA	11	10	1	0	64.1	268	60	22	20	2	5	2	2	24	0	26	7	0	3	3	.500	0	0	2.80
	Calgary	AAA	16	11	0	0	66	313	87	57	43	3	2	5	5	25	0	24	7	1	4	4	.500	0	0	5.86
1992	Calgary	AAA	27	6	0	6	64	309	87	57	43	5	4	2	4	30	1	30	10	1	1	4	.200	0	1	6.05
1993	Edmonton	AAA	46	0	0	20	62	287	76	45	38	3	3	2	1	24	2	44	8	2	5	4	.556	0	5	5.52
1994	Ottawa	AAA	7	1	0	0	14.1	74	22	21	19	7	0	2	0	10	0	6	2	0	0	0	.000	0	0	11.93
1988	Pittsburgh	NL	5	1	0	1	10	42	12	6	6	1	1	1	1	1	0	7	1	0	1	2	.333	0	0	5.40
1989	Pittsburgh	NL	35	15	1	7	111.1	482	90	53	49	10	9	4	7	61	4	52	1	0	5	9	.357	1	2	3.96
1990	Pittsburgh	NL	12	2	0	2	25.2	112	27	15	14	3	2	0	2	9	4	15	0	0	0	1	.000	0	0	4.91
	Chicago	NL	10	2	0	4	20.1	95	20	10	9	3	3	0	1	12	2	12	0	0	0	2	.000	0	0	3.98
1992	Seattle	AL	4	4	0	0	16.1	84	30	14	14	2	1	0	1	7	0	6	0	0	0	1	.000	0	0	7.71
	11 Min. YEARS		298	126	9	79	959	3935	1013	653	535	77	37	30	35	467	19	640	107	9	51	60	.459	2	17	5.02
	4 Maj. YEARS		66	24	1	14	183.2	815	179	98	92	19	16	5	12	90	10	92	2	0	6	15	.286	1	2	4.51

Tom Kramer

Pitches: Right Bats: Both Pos: P Ht: 6'0" Wt: 205 Born: 01/09/68 Age: 27

			HOW MUCH HE PITCHED					WHAT HE GAVE UP										THE RESULTS					
Year	Team	Lg	G	GS	CG	GF	IP	BFP	H	R	ER	HR	SH	SF	HB	TBB	IBB	SO	WP	Bk	W	L	Pct.	ShO	Sv	ERA
1987	Burlington	R	12	11	2	1	71.2	292	57	31	24	2	0	1	1	26	0	71	0	0	7	3	.700	1	1	3.01
1988	Waterloo	A	27	27	10	0	198.2	814	173	70	56	9	10	3	3	60	3	152	6	3	14	7	.667	2	0	2.54
1989	Kinston	A	18	17	5	1	131.2	527	97	44	38	7	5	3	4	42	3	89	4	1	9	5	.643	1	0	2.60
	Canton-Akm	AA	10	8	1	0	43.1	202	58	34	30	6	3	4	0	20	0	26	3	0	1	6	.143	0	0	6.23
1990	Kinston	A	16	16	2	0	98	402	82	34	31	5	1	2	1	29	0	96	2	1	7	4	.636	1	0	2.85

140

Year	Team	Lg	G	GS	CG	GF	IP	BFP	H	R	ER	HR	SH	SF	HB	TBB	IBB	SO	WP	Bk	W	L	Pct.	ShO	Sv	ERA
	Canton-Akrn	AA	12	10	2	0	72	287	67	25	24	3	2	1	0	14	1	46	1	0	6	3	.667	0	0	3.00
1991	Canton-Akrn	AA	35	5	0	13	79.1	320	61	23	21	5	6	1	1	34	3	61	3	0	7	3	.700	0	6	2.38
	Colo Spngs	AAA	10	1	0	6	11.1	43	5	1	1	1	0	0	0	5	0	18	1	0	1	0	1.000	0	4	0.79
1992	Colo Spngs	AAA	38	3	0	11	75.2	344	88	43	41	2	4	3	1	43	2	72	0	0	8	3	.727	0	3	4.88
1994	Charlotte	AAA	13	0	0	6	19	85	15	11	10	2	2	1	0	11	1	20	2	0	1	3	.250	0	0	4.74
	Indianapolis	AAA	23	13	0	3	102.2	431	109	55	51	12	5	3	2	32	2	54	6	0	5	4	.556	0	0	4.47
1991	Cleveland	AL	4	0	0	1	4.2	30	10	9	9	1	0	3	0	6	0	4	0	0	0	0	.000	0	0	17.36
1993	Cleveland	AL	39	16	1	6	121	535	126	60	54	19	3	2	2	59	7	71	1	0	7	3	.700	0	0	4.02
	7 Min. YEARS		214	111	22	41	903.1	3747	812	371	327	54	38	22	14	316	15	705	27	5	66	41	.617	5	14	3.26
	2 Maj. YEARS		43	16	1	7	125.2	565	136	69	63	20	3	5	2	65	7	75	1	0	7	3	.700	0	0	4.51

Frank Kremblas

Bats: Right **Throws:** Right **Pos:** 2B **Ht:** 5'11" **Wt:** 180 **Born:** 10/25/66 **Age:** 28

					BATTING												BASERUNNING				PERCENTAGES		
Year	Team	Lg	G	AB	H	2B	3B	HR	TB	R	RBI	TBB	IBB	SO	HBP	SH	SF	SB	CS	SB%	GDP	Avg	OBP	SLG
1989	Reds	R	60	213	49	10	1	1	64	32	18	28	1	44	1	1	2	8	4	.67	5	.230	.300	.300
1990	Cedar Rapds	A	92	266	67	13	0	5	95	18	26	23	0	54	1	4	3	2	7	.22	7	.252	.311	.357
1991	Chattanooga	AA	102	320	77	17	0	3	103	35	41	29	1	61	2	4	2	3	4	.43	9	.241	.306	.322
1992	Chattanooga	AA	100	282	65	16	1	0	83	29	28	18	1	58	1	5	2	4	5	.44	2	.230	.277	.294
1993	Indianapols	AAA	108	341	83	15	4	8	130	38	46	42	2	78	0	3	0	7	4	.64	4	.243	.326	.381
1994	Chattanooga	AA	47	144	37	3	2	1	47	11	14	8	0	31	1	1	0	8	4	.67	3	.257	.301	.326
	Indianapols	AAA	43	150	36	9	2	1	52	21	11	10	0	42	0	2	1	2	3	.40	1	.240	.286	.347
	6 Min. YEARS		552	1716	414	83	10	19	574	184	184	158	5	368	6	20	10	34	31	.52	31	.241	.306	.334

Jimmy Kremers

Bats: Left **Throws:** Right **Pos:** C **Ht:** 6' 3" **Wt:** 205 **Born:** 10/08/65 **Age:** 29

					BATTING												BASERUNNING				PERCENTAGES		
Year	Team	Lg	G	AB	H	2B	3B	HR	TB	R	RBI	TBB	IBB	SO	HBP	SH	SF	SB	CS	SB%	GDP	Avg	OBP	SLG
1988	Sumter	A	72	256	68	12	3	5	101	30	42	39	0	53	2	0	4	1	1	.50	3	.266	.362	.395
1989	Greenville	AA	121	388	91	19	1	16	160	41	58	34	5	95	0	2	2	5	5	.50	3	.235	.295	.412
1990	Richmond	AAA	63	190	44	8	0	6	70	25	24	35	1	47	1	0	1	1	0	1.00	4	.232	.352	.368
1991	Indianapols	AAA	98	290	70	14	0	11	117	34	42	40	6	97	0	5	4	2	1	.67	6	.241	.329	.403
1992	Indianapols	AAA	60	144	31	10	1	2	49	14	15	19	0	46	0	1	1	1	1	.50	4	.215	.300	.340
1993	Ottawa	AAA	4	15	3	0	0	1	6	1	2	1	1	2	0	0	0	0	0	.00	1	.200	.250	.400
	New Orleans	AAA	51	155	41	10	0	9	78	29	26	21	1	44	0	2	3	0	0	.00	1	.265	.346	.503
1994	El Paso	AA	1	1	1	1	0	0	2	0	0	0	0	0	0	0	0	0	0	.00	0	1.000	1.000	2.000
	New Orleans	AAA	58	158	34	4	1	6	58	19	23	16	2	41	0	2	0	0	0	.00	3	.215	.287	.367
1990	Atlanta	NL	29	73	8	1	1	1	14	7	2	6	1	27	0	0	0	0	0	.00	0	.110	.177	.192
	7 Min. YEARS		528	1597	383	78	6	56	641	193	232	205	16	425	3	11	15	10	8	.56	25	.240	.325	.401

Jim Krevokuch

Bats: Right **Throws:** Right **Pos:** 3B **Ht:** 5'11" **Wt:** 175 **Born:** 05/13/69 **Age:** 26

					BATTING												BASERUNNING				PERCENTAGES		
Year	Team	Lg	G	AB	H	2B	3B	HR	TB	R	RBI	TBB	IBB	SO	HBP	SH	SF	SB	CS	SB%	GDP	Avg	OBP	SLG
1991	Welland	A	58	196	44	9	0	2	59	22	17	26	0	30	7	0	4	8	6	.57	4	.224	.330	.301
1992	Augusta	A	65	239	68	13	1	3	92	32	39	20	0	19	4	2	2	10	2	.83	5	.285	.347	.385
	Salem	A	51	158	48	13	0	4	73	30	20	20	1	13	4	1	1	1	1	.50	2	.304	.393	.462
1993	Carolina	AA	125	395	100	15	3	4	133	58	30	53	1	38	15	3	2	4	3	.57	10	.253	.361	.337
1994	Carolina	AA	107	335	80	17	1	4	111	35	41	22	0	42	4	2	6	2	3	.40	7	.239	.289	.331
	4 Min. YEARS		406	1323	340	67	5	17	468	177	147	141	2	142	34	8	15	25	15	.63	28	.257	.340	.354

Rick Krivda

Pitches: Left **Bats:** Right **Pos:** P **Ht:** 6'1" **Wt:** 180 **Born:** 01/19/70 **Age:** 25

				HOW MUCH HE PITCHED					WHAT HE GAVE UP										THE RESULTS					
Year	Team	Lg	G	GS	CG	GF	IP	BFP	H	R	ER	HR	SH	SF	HB	TBB	IBB	SO	WP	Bk	W	L	Pct.	ShO	Sv	ERA
1991	Bluefield	R	15	8	0	2	67	265	48	20	14	0	2	1	0	24	0	79	1	4	7	1	.875	0	1	1.88
1992	Kane County	A	18	18	2	0	121.2	502	108	53	41	6	0	3	1	41	0	124	5	1	12	5	.706	0	0	3.03
	Frederick	A	9	9	1	0	57.1	236	51	23	19	7	0	0	1	15	0	64	1	1	5	1	.833	1	0	2.98
1993	Bowie	AA	22	22	0	0	125.2	522	114	46	43	10	2	1	2	50	0	108	1	2	7	5	.583	0	0	3.08
	Rochester	AAA	5	5	0	0	33.1	133	20	7	7	2	1	0	1	16	0	23	1	0	3	0	1.000	0	0	1.89
1994	Rochester	AAA	28	26	3	2	163	688	149	75	64	12	1	6	4	73	4	122	9	1	9	10	.474	2	0	3.53
	4 Min. YEARS		97	88	6	4	568	2346	490	224	188	37	6	11	9	219	4	520	18	9	43	22	.662	3	1	2.98

Jeff Kunkel

Bats: Right **Throws:** Right **Pos:** SS **Ht:** 6' 2" **Wt:** 180 **Born:** 03/25/62 **Age:** 33

					BATTING												BASERUNNING				PERCENTAGES		
Year	Team	Lg	G	AB	H	2B	3B	HR	TB	R	RBI	TBB	IBB	SO	HBP	SH	SF	SB	CS	SB%	GDP	Avg	OBP	SLG
1984	Tulsa	AA	47	177	56	16	1	4	86	30	22	6	0	32	4	0	1	7	2	.78	4	.316	.351	.486
1985	Okla City	AAA	99	370	72	8	6	5	107	40	43	20	0	81	3	2	5	8	9	.47	15	.195	.239	.289
1986	Okla City	AAA	111	409	100	16	4	11	157	50	51	18	0	101	5	6	4	10	6	.63	15	.244	.282	.384
1987	Okla City	AAA	58	193	49	9	3	9	91	31	34	20	0	58	0	1	0	2	4	.33	7	.254	.338	.472
1988	Okla City	AAA	56	203	44	11	4	5	78	28	21	12	1	50	0	0	5	7	2	.78	4	.217	.255	.384
1990	Okla City	AAA	4	19	8	1	0	0	9	0	3	0	0	2	0	0	1	0	0	.00	1	.421	.421	.474

141

Year	Team	Lg	G	AB	H	2B	3B	HR	TB	R	RBI	TBB	IBB	SO	HBP	SH	SF	SB	CS	SB%	GDP	Avg	OBP	SLG
1992	Denver	AAA	69	274	76	11	4	9	122	41	47	10	1	56	1	3	3	5	4	.56	13	.277	.302	.445
	Iowa	AAA	6	17	4	2	0	0	6	3	4	2	0	0	0	1	1	0	1	.00	0	.235	.300	.353
1993	Charlotte	AAA	115	430	121	34	3	11	194	65	46	13	0	104	9	5	0	12	8	.60	10	.281	.316	.451
1994	Toledo	AAA	103	346	86	17	1	11	138	46	45	7	0	82	3	5	1	21	5	.81	13	.249	.269	.399
1984	Texas	AL	50	142	29	2	3	3	46	13	7	2	0	35	1	3	2	4	3	.57	2	.204	.218	.324
1985	Texas	AL	2	4	1	0	0	0	1	1	0	0	0	3	0	0	0	0	0	.00	0	.250	.250	.250
1986	Texas	AL	8	13	3	0	0	1	6	3	2	0	0	2	0	0	0	0	0	.00	0	.231	.231	.462
1987	Texas	AL	15	32	7	0	0	1	10	1	2	0	0	10	1	1	0	0	1	.00	0	.219	.242	.313
1988	Texas	AL	55	154	35	8	3	2	55	14	15	4	1	35	1	1	1	0	1	.00	5	.227	.250	.357
1989	Texas	AL	108	293	79	21	2	8	128	39	29	20	0	75	3	10	0	3	2	.60	6	.270	.323	.437
1990	Texas	AL	99	200	34	11	1	3	56	17	17	11	0	66	2	5	0	2	1	.67	7	.170	.221	.280
1992	Chicago	NL	20	29	4	2	0	0	6	0	1	1	0	8	0	0	0	0	0	.00	0	.138	.138	.207
	9 Min. YEARS		668	2438	616	125	26	65	988	334	316	108	2	566	30	22	21	72	41	.64	82	.253	.290	.405
	8 Maj. YEARS		357	867	192	44	9	18	308	88	73	37	1	234	8	20	3	9	8	.53	21	.221	.259	.355

John Kupsey

Bats: Right Throws: Right Pos: 3B   **Ht: 6'1" Wt: 185 Born: 09/21/69 Age: 25**

Year	Team	Lg	G	AB	H	2B	3B	HR	TB	R	RBI	TBB	IBB	SO	HBP	SH	SF	SB	CS	SB%	GDP	Avg	OBP	SLG
1988	Braves	R	44	138	30	5	0	0	35	18	16	12	0	25	2	1	2	5	0	1.00	3	.217	.286	.254
1989	Pulaski	R	53	160	40	9	0	5	64	19	22	16	1	45	5	6	0	5	1	.83	3	.250	.337	.400
1990	Sumter	A	68	213	46	9	0	4	67	22	20	25	1	60	7	1	1	2	4	.33	4	.216	.317	.315
1992	Spartanburg	A	94	313	77	16	2	4	109	41	30	36	2	80	4	4	5	8	3	.73	4	.246	.327	.348
1993	Spartanburg	A	35	118	32	10	1	3	53	18	20	8	0	23	3	0	0	4	0	1.00	1	.271	.333	.449
1994	Reading	AA	32	65	13	5	0	1	21	5	5	2	0	17	0	0	0	0	0	.00	1	.200	.221	.323
	6 Min. YEARS		326	1007	238	54	3	17	349	143	113	99	4	250	21	12	9	24	8	.75	16	.236	.315	.347

Jerry Kutzler

Pitches: Right Bats: Left Pos: P   **Ht: 6'1" Wt: 175 Born: 03/25/65 Age: 30**

Year	Team	Lg	G	GS	CG	GF	IP	BFP	H	R	ER	HR	SH	SF	HB	TBB	IBB	SO	WP	Bk	W	L	Pct.	ShO	Sv	ERA
1987	White Sox	R	4	3	0	0	20	83	14	13	11	1	1	1	2	7	0	16	1	0	1	1	.500	0	0	4.95
	Peninsula	A	10	9	2	1	63.2	268	53	34	29	1	2	4	3	24	1	30	2	0	5	2	.714	1	0	4.10
1988	Tampa	A	26	26	12	0	184	733	154	73	57	10	3	2	6	39	1	100	9	2	16	7	.696	4	0	2.79
1989	Birmingham	AA	14	14	4	0	99.1	423	95	50	40	5	6	2	4	27	0	85	2	1	9	4	.692	0	0	3.62
	Vancouver	AAA	12	12	2	0	80	333	76	37	34	6	6	2	7	20	1	36	0	0	5	5	.500	0	0	3.83
1990	Vancouver	AAA	19	19	2	0	113.2	491	124	64	53	8	4	6	6	34	0	73	2	1	5	7	.417	0	0	4.20
1991	Vancouver	AAA	29	24	5	2	158.1	730	199	98	89	9	7	6	9	62	4	64	5	0	5	10	.333	1	0	5.06
1992	Iowa	AAA	2	0	0	1	3	14	5	2	1	0	0	0	0	0	0	0	0	0	0	0	.000	0	0	3.00
	Winston-Sal	A	6	6	1	0	37.1	152	41	14	14	3	1	0	0	6	0	21	0	0	4	0	1.000	1	0	3.38
	Charlotte	AA	12	2	0	3	38.1	153	33	12	9	2	1	0	0	4	0	28	2	0	1	2	.333	0	0	2.11
1993	San Antonio	AA	2	0	0	0	5.2	20	3	1	1	0	0	1	0	0	0	3	1	1	1	0	1.000	0	0	1.59
	Albuquerque	AAA	35	11	0	5	100	442	124	70	62	10	6	9	2	31	1	50	4	0	5	6	.455	0	1	5.58
1994	Omaha	AAA	37	7	0	15	102.2	434	114	47	43	10	4	3	4	24	1	38	2	0	5	7	.417	0	2	3.77
1990	Chicago	AL	7	7	0	0	31.1	141	38	23	21	2	1	1	0	14	1	21	1	0	2	1	.667	0	0	6.03
	8 Min. YEARS		208	133	28	27	1006	4276	1035	515	443	65	41	36	43	278	9	544	30	5	62	51	.549	7	3	3.96

Kerry Lacy

Pitches: Right Bats: Right Pos: P   **Ht: 6'2" Wt: 195 Born: 08/07/72 Age: 22**

Year	Team	Lg	G	GS	CG	GF	IP	BFP	H	R	ER	HR	SH	SF	HB	TBB	IBB	SO	WP	Bk	W	L	Pct.	ShO	Sv	ERA
1991	Butte	R	24	2	0	6	48	221	47	34	30	5	0	2	6	36	0	45	15	4	2	1	.667	0	1	5.63
1992	Gastonia	A	49	1	0	32	55.2	262	55	35	24	2	2	0	1	42	2	57	9	2	3	7	.300	0	17	3.88
1993	Chston-Sc	A	58	0	0	57	60	267	49	25	21	1	3	5	5	32	5	54	6	1	0	6	.000	0	36	3.15
	Charlotte	A	4	0	0	3	4.2	21	2	2	1	0	0	0	1	3	0	3	1	0	0	0	.000	0	2	1.93
1994	Tulsa	AA	41	0	0	35	63.2	270	49	30	26	4	3	2	3	37	4	46	3	1	2	6	.250	0	12	3.68
	4 Min. YEARS		176	3	0	133	232	1041	202	126	102	12	8	9	16	150	11	205	34	8	7	20	.259	0	68	3.96

Cleveland Ladell

Bats: Right Throws: Right Pos: OF   **Ht: 5'11" Wt: 170 Born: 09/19/70 Age: 24**

Year	Team	Lg	G	AB	H	2B	3B	HR	TB	R	RBI	TBB	IBB	SO	HBP	SH	SF	SB	CS	SB%	GDP	Avg	OBP	SLG
1992	Princeton	R	64	241	64	8	6	4	90	37	32	13	0	45	1	2	2	24	3	.89	1	.266	.304	.373
	Chston-Vw	A	8	30	6	0	0	0	6	3	0	3	0	14	0	0	0	3	1	.75	0	.200	.273	.200
1993	Winston-Sal	A	132	531	151	15	7	20	240	90	66	16	0	95	3	4	5	24	7	.77	13	.284	.306	.452
1994	Chattanooga	AA	33	99	16	4	1	1	25	9	9	4	0	26	0	0	1	4	1	.80	2	.162	.192	.253
	Winston-Sal	A	75	283	71	11	3	12	124	46	40	26	0	63	2	2	3	17	7	.71	3	.251	.315	.438
	3 Min. YEARS		312	1184	308	36	15	37	485	185	147	62	0	243	6	8	11	72	19	.79	19	.260	.298	.410

Tim Laker

Bats: Right Throws: Right Pos: C **Ht: 6' 2" Wt: 190 Born: 11/27/69 Age: 25**

Year	Team	Lg	G	AB	H	2B	3B	HR	TB	R	RBI	TBB	IBB	SO	HBP	SH	SF	SB	CS	SB%	GDP	Avg	OBP	SLG
1988	Jamestown	A	47	152	34	9	0	0	43	14	17	8	0	30	0	2	1	2	1	.67	4	.224	.261	.283
1989	Rockford	A	14	48	11	1	1	0	14	4	4	3	0	6	0	0	0	1	0	1.00	1	.229	.275	.292
	Jamestown	A	58	216	48	9	1	2	65	25	24	16	1	40	2	0	3	8	4	.67	4	.222	.278	.301
1990	Rockford	A	120	425	94	18	3	7	139	46	57	32	1	83	1	1	8	7	2	.78	9	.221	.273	.327
	Wst Plm Bch	A	2	3	0	0	0	0	0	0	0	0	0	1	0	0	0	0	0	.00	0	.000	.000	.000
1991	Harrisburg	AA	11	35	10	1	0	1	14	4	5	2	0	5	1	0	0	0	1	.00	1	.286	.342	.400
	Wst Plm Bch	AA	100	333	77	15	2	5	111	36	33	22	0	52	2	0	4	10	1	.91	9	.231	.280	.333
1992	Harrisburg	AA	117	409	99	19	3	15	169	55	68	39	2	89	5	0	5	3	1	.75	10	.242	.312	.413
1993	Ottawa	AAA	56	204	47	10	0	4	69	26	23	21	0	41	1	0	1	3	2	.60	10	.230	.304	.338
1994	Ottawa	AAA	118	424	131	32	2	12	203	68	71	47	2	96	3	2	1	11	6	.65	10	.309	.381	.479
1992	Montreal	NL	28	46	10	3	0	0	13	8	4	2	0	14	0	0	0	1	1	.50	1	.217	.250	.283
1993	Montreal	NL	43	86	17	2	1	0	21	3	7	2	0	16	1	3	1	2	0	1.00	2	.198	.222	.244
	7 Min. YEARS		643	2249	551	114	12	46	827	278	302	190	6	443	15	5	23	45	18	.71	58	.245	.305	.368
	2 Maj. YEARS		71	132	27	5	1	0	34	11	11	4	0	30	1	3	1	3	1	.75	3	.205	.232	.258

Tom Lampkin

Bats: Left Throws: Right Pos: C **Ht: 5'11" Wt: 183 Born: 03/04/64 Age: 31**

Year	Team	Lg	G	AB	H	2B	3B	HR	TB	R	RBI	TBB	IBB	SO	HBP	SH	SF	SB	CS	SB%	GDP	Avg	OBP	SLG
1986	Batavia	A	63	190	49	5	1	1	59	24	20	31	3	14	0	1	1	4	3	.57	4	.258	.360	.311
1987	Waterloo	A	118	398	106	19	2	7	150	49	55	34	2	41	2	1	6	5	0	1.00	7	.266	.323	.377
1988	Williamsprt	AA	80	263	71	10	0	3	90	38	23	25	3	20	3	0	0	1	2	.33	6	.270	.340	.342
	Colo Spmgs	AAA	34	107	30	5	0	0	35	14	7	9	1	12	2	1	0	0	0	.00	3	.280	.347	.327
1989	Colo Spmgs	AAA	63	209	67	10	3	4	95	26	32	10	1	18	2	2	1	4	2	.67	5	.321	.356	.455
1990	Colo Spmgs	AAA	69	199	44	7	5	1	64	32	18	19	0	19	2	0	1	7	2	.78	2	.221	.294	.322
	Las Vegas	AAA	4	2	1	0	0	0	1	0	0	0	0	1	0	0	0	0	0	.00	0	.500	.500	.500
1991	Las Vegas	AAA	45	164	52	11	1	2	71	25	29	10	1	20	2	0	1	2	1	.67	4	.317	.362	.433
1992	Las Vegas	AAA	108	340	104	17	4	3	138	45	48	53	7	27	6	1	3	15	8	.65	12	.306	.405	.406
1993	New Orleans	AAA	25	80	26	5	0	2	37	18	10	18	2	4	3	1	0	5	4	.56	2	.325	.463	.463
1994	Phoenix	AAA	118	453	136	32	8	8	208	76	70	42	1	49	12	0	6	8	7	.53	12	.300	.370	.459
1988	Cleveland	AL	4	4	0	0	0	0	0	0	0	1	0	0	0	0	0	0	0	.00	1	.000	.200	.000
1990	San Diego	NL	26	63	14	0	1	1	19	4	4	4	1	9	0	0	0	0	1	.00	2	.222	.269	.302
1991	San Diego	NL	38	58	11	3	1	0	16	4	3	3	0	9	0	0	0	0	0	.00	0	.190	.230	.276
1992	San Diego	NL	9	17	4	0	0	0	4	2	1	6	0	1	1	0	0	2	0	1.00	0	.235	.458	.235
1993	Milwaukee	AL	73	162	32	8	0	4	52	22	25	20	3	26	0	2	4	7	3	.70	2	.198	.284	.321
	9 Min. YEARS		724	2405	686	121	24	31	948	347	312	251	21	225	34	7	19	51	29	.64	57	.285	.358	.394
	5 Maj. YEARS		150	304	61	11	2	5	91	33	32	34	4	45	1	2	4	9	4	.69	5	.201	.280	.299

Les Lancaster

Pitches: Right Bats: Right Pos: P **Ht: 6' 2" Wt: 200 Born: 04/21/62 Age: 33**

Year	Team	Lg	G	GS	CG	GF	IP	BFP	H	R	ER	HR	SH	SF	HB	TBB	IBB	SO	WP	Bk	W	L	Pct.	ShO	Sv	ERA
1985	Wytheville	R	20	10	7	8	102	433	98	49	41	6	4	3	1	24	5	81	4	0	7	4	.636	1	3	3.62
1986	Winston-Sal	A	13	13	3	0	97	396	88	37	30	4	3	4	2	30	2	52	1	1	8	3	.727	0	0	2.78
	Pittsfield	AA	14	14	2	0	88	389	105	46	41	4	2	4	5	34	2	49	2	1	5	6	.455	0	0	4.19
1987	Iowa	AAA	15	6	0	6	67	268	59	24	24	9	3	1	1	17	3	62	0	1	5	3	.625	0	4	3.22
1989	Iowa	AAA	17	14	3	0	91.1	389	76	38	27	6	4	4	3	43	0	56	2	4	5	7	.417	2	0	2.66
1990	Iowa	AAA	6	0	0	2	17.2	74	20	10	8	0	0	1	0	5	0	15	1	0	0	1	.000	0	1	4.08
1994	Syracuse	AAA	64	1	0	19	89.2	391	95	44	36	6	5	5	4	25	4	69	3	0	14	3	.824	0	0	3.61
1987	Chicago	NL	27	18	0	4	132.1	578	138	76	72	14	5	6	1	51	5	78	7	8	8	3	.727	0	0	4.90
1988	Chicago	NL	44	3	1	15	85.2	371	89	42	36	4	3	7	1	34	7	36	3	3	4	6	.400	0	5	3.78
1989	Chicago	NL	42	0	0	15	72.2	288	60	12	11	2	3	4	0	15	1	56	2	1	4	2	.667	0	8	1.36
1990	Chicago	NL	55	6	1	26	109	479	121	57	56	11	6	5	1	40	8	65	7	0	9	5	.643	1	6	4.62
1991	Chicago	NL	64	11	1	21	156	653	150	84	61	13	9	4	4	49	7	102	9	7	9	7	.563	0	3	3.52
1992	Detroit	AL	41	1	0	17	82	404	101	66	61	11	2	4	2	51	12	35	2	0	3	4	.429	0	0	6.33
1993	St. Louis	NL	50	0	0	12	61.1	259	56	24	20	5	5	1	1	21	5	36	5	0	4	1	.800	0	0	2.93
	6 Min. YEARS		149	58	15	35	552.2	2340	541	248	207	35	21	22	16	178	16	384	13	7	44	27	.620	3	11	3.37
	7 Maj. YEARS		323	39	3	110	703.2	3032	715	345	317	60	33	31	11	261	45	408	28	14	41	28	.594	1	22	4.05

Dan Lane

Bats: Right Throws: Right Pos: SS **Ht: 6'2" Wt: 180 Born: 12/05/69 Age: 25**

Year	Team	Lg	G	AB	H	2B	3B	HR	TB	R	RBI	TBB	IBB	SO	HBP	SH	SF	SB	CS	SB%	GDP	Avg	OBP	SLG
1992	Jamestown	A	56	182	49	16	2	6	87	36	27	16	0	32	2	1	0	3	1	.75	6	.269	.335	.478
1993	Wst Plm Bch	A	66	193	44	9	0	2	59	25	24	26	3	31	2	4	1	2	2	.50	5	.228	.324	.306
1994	Harrisburg	AA	28	63	15	2	0	2	23	9	5	4	0	15	0	1	0	2	0	.00	2	.238	.284	.365
	W. Palm Bch	A	65	226	64	13	1	5	94	26	23	19	0	41	0	3	1	3	3	.50	6	.283	.337	.416
	3 Min. YEARS		215	664	172	40	3	15	263	96	79	65	3	119	4	9	2	8	8	.50	19	.259	.328	.396

Gregory Langbehn

Pitches: Left Bats: Right Pos: P Ht: 5'11" Wt: 182 Born: 11/14/69 Age: 25

Year Team	Lg	G	GS	CG	GF	IP	BFP	H	R	ER	HR	SH	SF	HB	TBB	IBB	SO	WP	Bk	W	L	Pct.	ShO	Sv	ERA
1988 Kingsport	R	7	4	0	1	28.1	124	26	15	11	2	0	2	0	11	0	29	3	1	3	3	.500	0	0	3.49
1989 Pittsfield	A	14	14	3	0	100	406	76	33	20	1	8	3	2	35	3	70	2	0	10	3	.769	2	0	1.80
1990 Columbia	A	26	25	7	1	174	732	165	84	64	6	6	3	5	59	1	132	9	0	13	11	.542	2	0	3.31
1991 St. Lucie	A	27	27	1	0	175.1	702	149	53	49	7	5	4	4	44	3	106	7	1	10	12	.455	0	0	2.52
1992 Binghamton	AA	52	1	0	30	71	307	63	31	25	2	3	2	4	41	3	45	3	0	5	5	.500	0	9	3.17
1993 Norfolk	AAA	49	0	0	16	69.2	319	76	46	42	5	3	2	3	34	3	58	4	1	2	2	.500	0	2	5.43
1994 Norfolk	AAA	19	0	0	6	19	81	13	8	6	1	1	0	1	14	2	11	2	0	0	2	.000	0	0	2.84
Binghamton	AA	32	0	0	10	46.1	213	45	31	28	2	1	2	5	28	2	42	0	0	3	3	.500	0	1	5.44
7 Min. YEARS		226	71	11	64	683.2	2884	613	301	245	26	27	18	24	266	17	493	30	3	46	41	.529	4	13	3.23

Michel LaPlante

Pitches: Right Bats: Right Pos: P Ht: 6'2" Wt: 180 Born: 12/09/69 Age: 25

Year Team	Lg	G	GS	CG	GF	IP	BFP	H	R	ER	HR	SH	SF	HB	TBB	IBB	SO	WP	Bk	W	L	Pct.	ShO	Sv	ERA
1992 Welland	A	11	11	1	0	69	282	54	34	24	1	3	1	5	13	1	75	8	2	1	5	.167	0	0	3.13
Augusta	A	3	3	0	0	18.1	77	20	7	7	1	1	1	0	6	0	7	1	0	1	1	.500	0	0	3.44
1993 Augusta	A	14	14	0	0	83.1	351	89	37	32	5	3	0	3	10	1	80	4	0	5	5	.500	0	0	3.46
Salem	A	11	11	0	0	65.1	278	71	35	25	6	1	3	0	19	0	44	10	1	3	2	.600	0	0	3.44
1994 Carolina	AA	28	26	3	0	163	705	180	110	89	20	6	8	6	41	1	110	5	0	7	12	.368	0	0	4.91
3 Min. YEARS		67	65	4	0	399	1693	414	223	177	33	14	13	14	89	3	316	28	3	17	25	.405	1	0	3.99

Edgardo Larregui

Bats: Right Throws: Right Pos: OF Ht: 6'0" Wt: 185 Born: 12/01/72 Age: 22

Year Team	Lg	G	AB	H	2B	3B	HR	TB	R	RBI	TBB	IBB	SO	HBP	SH	SF	SB	CS	SB%	GDP	Avg	OBP	SLG
1990 Huntington	R	34	102	19	3	0	2	28	13	16	7	0	12	0	2	3	3	0	1.00	1	.186	.232	.275
1991 Geneva	A	71	269	67	12	2	1	86	34	28	16	0	29	5	2	2	13	3	.81	10	.249	.301	.320
1992 Peoria	A	129	478	137	24	2	5	180	62	71	30	1	68	4	9	4	15	6	.71	12	.287	.331	.377
1993 Daytona	A	95	329	78	10	5	2	104	26	34	15	0	24	2	5	2	1	11	.08	13	.237	.273	.316
1994 Daytona	A	74	283	82	12	2	6	116	40	51	21	0	32	1	0	2	6	9	.40	10	.290	.339	.410
Orlando	AA	35	111	32	2	1	0	36	14	7	5	0	13	1	2	1	3	6	.33	0	.288	.322	.324
5 Min. YEARS		438	1572	415	63	12	16	550	189	207	94	1	178	13	20	14	41	35	.54	46	.264	.308	.350

Tim Layana

Pitches: Right Bats: Right Pos: P Ht: 6'2" Wt: 190 Born: 03/02/64 Age: 31

Year Team	Lg	G	GS	CG	GF	IP	BFP	H	R	ER	HR	SH	SF	HB	TBB	IBB	SO	WP	Bk	W	L	Pct.	ShO	Sv	ERA
1986 Oneonta	A	3	3	0	0	19	71	10	5	5	1	1	0	1	5	0	24	1	0	2	0	1.000	0	0	2.37
Ft.Laudrdle	A	11	10	3	1	68.1	276	59	19	17	1	2	0	4	19	1	52	5	1	5	4	.556	1	1	2.24
1987 Albany	AA	8	7	1	1	46.1	195	51	28	26	4	2	1	2	18	0	19	1	1	2	4	.333	0	0	5.05
Pr William	A	7	3	0	2	22.2	111	29	22	16	3	1	2	1	11	0	17	5	2	2	1	.667	0	0	6.35
Columbus	AAA	13	13	0	0	70	310	77	37	37	6	3	1	1	37	2	36	3	0	4	5	.444	0	0	4.76
1988 Albany	AA	14	14	1	0	87	378	90	52	42	3	3		6	30	2	42	2	8	5	7	.417	0	0	4.34
Columbus	AAA	11	9	0	0	47.2	216	54	34	32	2	0	1	6	25	0	25	2	4	1	7	.125	0	0	6.04
1989 Albany	AA	40	1	0	37	67.2	261	53	17	13	2	5	1	3	15	3	48	2	4	7	4	.636	0	17	1.73
1991 Nashville	AAA	26	2	0	4	47.1	210	41	17	17	3	3	0	2	28	0	43	5	1	3	1	.750	0	1	3.23
1992 Rochester	AAA	41	3	0	28	72.1	323	79	45	43	4	4	4	4	38	6	48	14	0	3	3	.500	0	4	5.35
1993 Phoenix	AAA	55	0	0	38	67.1	306	80	42	36	5	4	6	5	24	4	55	8	2	3	2	.600	0	9	4.81
1994 San Bernrdo	A	11	0	0	11	15.1	71	10	11	4	0	1	0	2	9	1	17	2	0	1	3	.250	0	3	2.35
Ottawa	AAA	42	0	0	19	59	280	72	47	33	6	6	3	2	28	6	35	4	1	1	5	.167	0	1	5.03
1990 Cincinnati	NL	55	0	0	17	80	344	71	33	31	7	4	3	2	44	5	53	5	4	5	3	.625	0	2	3.49
1991 Cincinnati	NL	22	0	0	9	20.2	95	23	18	16	1	1	0	0	11	0	14	3	0	0	2	.000	0	0	6.97
1993 San Francisco	NL	1	0	0	0	2	15	7	5	5	1	1	0	0	1	1	1	0	0	0	0	.000	0	0	22.50
8 Min. YEARS		282	65	5	141	690	3008	705	376	321	40	35	22	39	287	25	461	54	24	39	46	.459	1	36	4.19
3 Maj. YEARS		78	0	0	26	102.2	454	101	56	52	9	6	3	2	56	6	68	8	4	5	5	.500	0	2	4.56

Jalal Leach

Bats: Left Throws: Left Pos: OF Ht: 6'2" Wt: 200 Born: 03/14/69 Age: 26

Year Team	Lg	G	AB	H	2B	3B	HR	TB	R	RBI	TBB	IBB	SO	HBP	SH	SF	SB	CS	SB%	GDP	Avg	OBP	SLG
1990 Oneonta	A	69	257	74	7	1	2	89	41	18	37	3	52	0	4	0	33	13	.72	1	.288	.378	.346
1991 Ft.Laudrdle	A	122	468	119	13	9	2	156	48	42	44	3	122	0	0	3	28	12	.70	5	.254	.317	.333
1992 Pr William	A	128	462	122	22	7	5	173	61	65	47	2	114	0	3	5	18	9	.67	8	.264	.329	.374
1993 Albany	AA	125	457	129	18	9	14	208	64	79	47	3	113	1	0	4	16	12	.57	9	.282	.348	.455
1994 Columbus	AAA	132	444	116	18	9	6	170	56	56	39	3	106	1	3	4	14	12	.54	8	.261	.320	.383
5 Min. YEARS		576	2088	560	79	35	29	796	270	260	214	14	507	2	13	16	109	58	.65	27	.268	.334	.381

Pat Leahy

Pitches: Right **Bats:** Right **Pos:** P **Ht:** 6'6" **Wt:** 245 **Born:** 10/31/70 **Age:** 24

			HOW MUCH HE PITCHED						WHAT HE GAVE UP									THE RESULTS				
Year	Team	Lg	G	GS	CG	GF	IP	BFP	H	R	ER	HR	SH	SF	HB	TBB	IBB	SO	WP	Bk	W	L	Pct.	ShO	Sv	ERA
1992	Erie	A	26	0	0	18	37	153	37	11	7	3	2	2	2	12	0	27	3	1	2	0	1.000	0	5	1.70
1993	Kane County	A	25	25	2	0	139.2	594	124	68	50	6	9	3	23	43	2	106	12	7	8	11	.421	0	0	3.22
1994	Brevard Cty	A	13	12	0	0	84	340	72	32	29	4	1	4	7	18	0	59	7	1	7	3	.700	0	0	3.11
	Portland	AA	17	8	0	6	49.2	233	59	39	27	5	3	2	6	19	3	32	9	1	1	6	.143	0	0	4.89
	3 Min. YEARS		81	45	2	24	310.1	1320	292	150	113	18	15	11	38	92	5	224	31	10	18	20	.474	0	5	3.28

Aaron Ledesma

Bats: Right **Throws:** Right **Pos:** SS **Ht:** 6'2" **Wt:** 195 **Born:** 06/03/71 **Age:** 24

			BATTING												BASERUNNING				PERCENTAGES		
Year	Team	Lg	G	AB	H	2B	3B	HR	TB	R	RBI	TBB	IBB	SO	HBP	SH	SF	SB	CS	SB%	GDP	Avg	OBP	SLG
1990	Kingsport	R	66	243	81	11	1	5	109	50	38	30	2	28	8	0	4	23	6	.79	4	.333	.418	.449
1991	Columbia	A	33	115	39	8	0	1	50	19	14	8	0	16	4	3	3	3	2	.60	1	.339	.392	.435
1992	St. Lucie	A	134	456	120	17	2	2	147	51	50	46	1	66	11	2	7	20	12	.63	13	.263	.340	.322
1993	Binghamton	AA	66	206	55	12	0	5	82	23	22	14	0	43	2	4	1	2	1	.67	6	.267	.318	.398
1994	Norfolk	AAA	119	431	118	20	1	3	149	49	56	28	0	41	6	9	6	18	8	.69	16	.274	.323	.346
	5 Min. YEARS		418	1451	413	68	4	16	537	192	180	126	3	194	31	18	21	66	29	.69	40	.285	.350	.370

Derek Lee

Bats: Left **Throws:** Right **Pos:** OF **Ht:** 6'1" **Wt:** 200 **Born:** 07/28/66 **Age:** 28

			BATTING												BASERUNNING				PERCENTAGES		
Year	Team	Lg	G	AB	H	2B	3B	HR	TB	R	RBI	TBB	IBB	SO	HBP	SH	SF	SB	CS	SB%	GDP	Avg	OBP	SLG
1988	Utica	A	76	252	86	7	5	2	109	51	47	50	5	48	3	3	4	54	15	.78	2	.341	.450	.433
1989	South Bend	A	125	448	128	24	7	11	199	89	48	87	4	83	9	4	2	45	26	.63	5	.286	.410	.444
1990	Birmingham	AA	126	411	105	21	3	7	153	68	75	71	5	93	6	3	5	14	10	.58	8	.255	.369	.372
1991	Birmingham	AA	45	154	50	10	2	5	79	36	16	46	5	23	6	0	1	9	7	.56	1	.325	.493	.513
	Vancouver	AAA	87	319	94	28	5	6	150	54	44	35	2	62	2	3	1	4	2	.67	1	.295	.367	.470
1992	Vancouver	AAA	115	381	104	20	6	7	157	58	50	56	7	65	6	4	2	17	7	.71	11	.273	.373	.412
1993	Portland	AAA	106	381	120	30	7	10	194	79	80	60	2	51	4	4	4	16	5	.76	10	.315	.410	.509
1994	Ottawa	AAA	131	463	139	35	9	13	231	62	75	66	9	81	2	0	6	12	6	.67	7	.300	.385	.499
1993	Minnesota	AL	15	33	5	1	0	0	6	3	4	1	0	4	0	0	0	0	0	.00	0	.152	.176	.182
	7 Min. YEARS		811	2809	826	175	44	61	1272	497	435	471	39	506	38	21	25	171	78	.69	45	.294	.399	.453

Mark Lee

Pitches: Left **Bats:** Left **Pos:** P **Ht:** 6'3" **Wt:** 200 **Born:** 07/20/64 **Age:** 30

			HOW MUCH HE PITCHED						WHAT HE GAVE UP									THE RESULTS				
Year	Team	Lg	G	GS	CG	GF	IP	BFP	H	R	ER	HR	SH	SF	HB	TBB	IBB	SO	WP	Bk	W	L	Pct.	ShO	Sv	ERA
1985	Bristol	R	15	1	0	11	33	127	18	5	4	1	1	0	0	12	0	40	2	0	3	0	1.000	0	5	1.09
1986	Lakeland	A	41	0	0	31	62.2	281	73	44	36	4	4	1	2	21	8	39	5	0	2	5	.286	0	10	5.17
1987	Glens Falls	AA	7	0	0	4	8.1	38	13	9	8	1	1	1	0	1	0	3	0	0	0	0	.000	0	0	8.64
	Lakeland	A	30	0	0	15	53	223	48	17	15	1	0	1	1	18	3	42	1	0	3	2	.600	0	4	2.55
1988	Lakeland	A	10	0	0	2	19	73	16	7	3	0	2	3	0	4	1	15	0	1	1	0	1.000	0	1	1.42
1988	Glens Falls	AA	14	0	0	6	26	106	27	10	7	0	2	1	0	4	2	25	0	0	3	0	1.000	0	1	2.42
	Toledo	AAA	22	0	0	6	19.1	79	18	7	6	0	0	2	0	7	2	13	0	0	0	1	.000	0	2	2.79
1989	Memphis	AA	25	24	0	1	122.2	558	149	84	71	13	4	4	3	44	2	79	6	8	5	11	.313	0	0	5.21
1990	Stockton	A	5	0	0	2	7.2	32	5	2	2	0	1	0	0	3	0	7	0	0	1	0	1.000	0	1	2.35
	Denver	AAA	20	0	0	6	28	110	25	7	7	2	1	0	0	6	1	35	1	1	3	1	.750	0	4	2.25
1992	Denver	AAA	48	0	0	14	68.2	309	78	45	32	5	3	0	0	26	4	57	1	1	2	4	.333	0	1	4.19
1993	Okla City	AAA	52	1	0	21	101.2	454	112	61	49	4	3	7	0	43	5	65	4	1	5	3	.625	0	4	4.34
1994	Iowa	AAA	54	0	0	29	61.1	265	69	27	23	3	0	2	1	21	8	42	4	0	1	3	.250	0	10	3.38
1988	Kansas City	AL	4	0	0	4	5	21	6	2	2	0	0	0	0	1	0	6	0	0	0	0	.000	0	0	3.60
1990	Milwaukee	AL	11	0	0	1	21.1	85	20	5	5	1	1	2	0	4	1	14	0	0	1	0	1.000	0	0	2.11
1991	Milwaukee	AL	62	0	0	9	67.2	291	72	33	29	10	4	1	1	31	7	43	0	0	2	5	.286	0	1	3.86
	9 Min. YEARS		343	26	0	148	611.1	2655	651	325	263	34	22	22	7	210	36	462	24	12	29	30	.492	0	41	3.87
	3 Maj. YEARS		77	0	0	14	94	397	98	40	36	11	5	3	1	36	7	57	0	0	3	5	.375	0	1	3.45

Greg Legg

Bats: Right **Throws:** Right **Pos:** 2B **Ht:** 6'1" **Wt:** 185 **Born:** 04/21/60 **Age:** 35

			BATTING												BASERUNNING				PERCENTAGES		
Year	Team	Lg	G	AB	H	2B	3B	HR	TB	R	RBI	TBB	IBB	SO	HBP	SH	SF	SB	CS	SB%	GDP	Avg	OBP	SLG
1982	Peninsula	A	44	134	46	9	0	0	55	20	20	14	0	8	0	0	0	2	3	.40	0	.343	.405	.410
1983	Reading	AA	90	284	87	14	1	4	115	44	49	26	0	30	0	0	0	5	1	.83	0	.306	.365	.405
1984	Reading	AA	64	224	54	11	1	2	73	16	27	19	0	19	3	4	2	2	2	.50	4	.241	.306	.326
	Portland	AAA	50	141	34	8	0	1	45	17	15	14	1	13	3	0	2	0	1	.00	2	.241	.319	.319
1985	Portland	AAA	115	420	119	11	7	7	165	48	50	39	2	46	2	5	4	9	5	.64	6	.283	.344	.393
1986	Portland	AAA	120	461	149	27	5	6	204	72	66	41	4	43	3	1	8	8	6	.57	9	.323	.376	.443
1987	Maine	AAA	95	348	84	16	4	4	120	48	30	27	1	47	1	1	3	8	2	.80	10	.241	.296	.345
1988	Reading	AA	84	312	83	8	1	1	96	39	33	37	0	25	1	5	4	6	4	.60	6	.266	.342	.308

145

Year	Team	Lg	G	AB	H	2B	3B	HR	TB	R	RBI	TBB	IBB	SO	HBP	SH	SF	SB	CS	SB%	GDP	Avg	OBP	SLG
	Maine	AAA	49	149	36	7	0	1	46	20	9	25	1	21	1	2	1	3	3	.50	3	.242	.352	.309
1989	Scr Wil-Bar	AAA	109	379	94	10	0	2	110	41	33	36	1	44	3	5	2	5	5	.50	12	.248	.317	.290
1990	Scr Wil-Bar	AAA	61	169	52	5	0	1	60	25	21	31	1	27	1	2	1	1	0	1.00	7	.308	.416	.355
1991	Scranton-Wb	AAA	111	352	102	15	4	3	134	58	41	44	2	33	3	6	5	3	0	1.00	9	.290	.369	.381
1992	Scranton/wb	AAA	90	289	66	12	2	1	85	35	29	43	1	41	0	2	2	2	2	.50	6	.228	.326	.294
1993	Scranton/wb	AAA	73	225	63	13	3	0	82	27	25	19	1	23	1	3	0	2	2	.50	4	.280	.339	.364
1994	Scranton-Wb	AAA	29	84	25	4	0	2	35	10	10	8	1	5	0	4	0	0	0	.00	0	.298	.359	.417
1986	Philadelphia	NL	11	20	9	1	0	0	10	2	1	0	0	3	0	0	0	0	0	.00	0	.450	.450	.500
1987	Philadelphia	NL	3	2	0	0	0	0	0	1	0	0	0	0	0	0	0	0	0	.00	0	.000	.000	.000
	13 Min. YEARS		1184	3971	1094	170	28	35	1425	520	458	423	16	425	22	40	34	56	36	.61	78	.275	.346	.359
	2 Maj. YEARS		14	22	9	1	0	0	10	3	1	0	0	3	0	0	0	0	0	.00	0	.409	.409	.455

Tim Leiper

Bats: Left Throws: Right Pos: OF **Ht: 5'11" Wt: 175 Born: 07/19/66 Age: 28**

							BATTING											BASERUNNING				PERCENTAGES		
Year	Team	Lg	G	AB	H	2B	3B	HR	TB	R	RBI	TBB	IBB	SO	HBP	SH	SF	SB	CS	SB%	GDP	Avg	OBP	SLG
1985	Gastonia	A	31	106	30	4	2	1	41	16	14	9	0	17	1	2	1	4	3	.57	1	.283	.336	.387
	Lakeland	A	25	77	17	2	1	0	21	13	5	10	0	11	0	0	1	1	0	1.00	2	.221	.307	.273
	Bristol	R	61	211	65	16	0	3	90	37	47	15	1	18	1	0	2	7	4	.64	3	.308	.354	.427
1986	Lakeland	A	107	407	108	17	4	3	142	46	49	33	5	21	1	1	5	4	8	.33	23	.265	.318	.349
1987	Glens Falls	AA	46	176	56	12	0	4	80	31	26	12	2	12	0	1	4	4	1	.80	5	.318	.354	.455
1988	Toledo	AAA	22	48	8	1	0	0	9	6	4	6	0	7	0	1	0	0	1	.00	2	.167	.259	.188
	Glens Falls	AA	91	329	95	23	0	2	124	36	36	37	1	33	3	7	5	10	3	.77	10	.289	.361	.377
1989	London	AA	27	101	37	6	0	1	46	13	9	13	1	10	1	0	0	0	2	.00	0	.366	.443	.455
	Toledo	AAA	101	376	90	13	2	3	116	43	30	28	0	33	3	7	1	3	6	.33	1	.239	.297	.309
1990	London	AA	48	166	50	7	0	2	63	30	20	26	1	14	1	3	2	8	2	.80	3	.301	.395	.380
	Toledo	AAA	74	249	73	14	1	2	95	26	34	27	1	21	0	1	2	2	1	.67	2	.293	.360	.382
1991	Tidewater	AAA	93	282	71	11	1	2	90	33	30	35	5	32	1	4	4	0	3	.00	12	.252	.332	.319
1992	Memphis	AA	73	246	63	10	2	2	83	37	21	31	0	29	1	4	4	4	1	.80	6	.256	.337	.337
1993	Carolina	AA	44	132	34	4	0	1	41	11	11	10	0	6	2	1	0	0	1	.00	2	.258	.319	.311
	Buffalo	AAA	75	208	68	15	5	2	99	21	33	11	2	18	2	0	6	1	3	.25	3	.327	.357	.476
1994	Buffalo	AAA	114	349	92	20	2	4	128	36	39	21	5	39	1	7	1	3	3	.50	5	.264	.306	.367
	10 Min. YEARS		1032	3463	957	175	20	32	1268	462	408	324	24	321	17	39	38	51	42	.55	80	.276	.338	.366

Steve Lemke

Pitches: Right Bats: Right Pos: P **Ht: 6'0" Wt: 185 Born: 01/04/70 Age: 25**

			HOW MUCH HE PITCHED						WHAT HE GAVE UP												THE RESULTS					
Year	Team	Lg	G	GS	CG	GF	IP	BFP	H	R	ER	HR	SH	SF	HB	TBB	IBB	SO	WP	Bk	W	L	Pct.	ShO	Sv	ERA
1992	Sou Oregon	A	21	0	0	6	49.2	219	63	35	22	1	1	5	1	9	1	41	1	0	5	5	.500	0	1	3.99
1993	Sou Oregon	A	8	0	0	4	14.1	65	13	11	7	2	1	0	0	6	0	11	1	0	1	0	1.000	0	1	4.40
	Madison	A	16	0	0	9	36	156	41	17	14	1	1	0	4	6	1	22	1	0	7	0	1.000	0	0	3.50
1994	W. Michigan	A	10	4	0	0	43.2	209	38	13	11	1	2	1	3	6	1	29	2	0	4	2	.667	0	1	2.27
	Huntsville	AA	1	1	0	0	4.2	21	9	3	3	0	0	0	0	1	0	1	0	0	0	0	.000	0	0	5.79
	Modesto	A	20	18	0	1	116.1	462	93	36	30	7	1	4	4	23	1	63	5	0	12	2	.857	0	1	2.32
	3 Min. YEARS		76	23	0	26	264.2	1103	257	115	87	12	6	7	12	51	4	167	10	0	29	9	.763	0	4	2.96

Don Lemon

Pitches: Right Bats: Right Pos: P **Ht: 6'4" Wt: 195 Born: 06/02/67 Age: 28**

			HOW MUCH HE PITCHED						WHAT HE GAVE UP												THE RESULTS					
Year	Team	Lg	G	GS	CG	GF	IP	BFP	H	R	ER	HR	SH	SF	HB	TBB	IBB	SO	WP	Bk	W	L	Pct.	ShO	Sv	ERA
1989	Idaho Falls	R	9	6	0	1	40.1	183	50	31	29	6	0	1	1	17	0	20	2	3	2	1	.667	0	0	6.47
1990	Sumter	A	4	4	0	0	21.1	95	29	20	15	2	0	0	1	5	0	3	2	0	1	2	.333	0	0	6.33
	Braves	R	2	2	1	0	12	49	14	5	3	1	0	0	0	1	0	13	0	1	1	0	1.000	0	0	2.25
	Idaho Falls	R	11	11	2	0	70.2	300	78	38	35	3	1	3	1	17	1	36	2	1	6	2	.750	1	0	4.46
1992	Erie	A	17	11	1	4	72.2	297	60	27	23	4	2	0	2	28	1	55	5	1	6	3	.667	1	2	2.85
1993	High Desert	A	5	5	0	0	24.1	108	35	17	10	2	1	3	0	2	0	17	4	0	0	1	.000	0	0	3.70
	Edmonton	AAA	21	11	0	1	74.1	331	89	48	43	10	2	3	1	20	1	52	2	0	3	3	.500	0	0	5.21
1994	Portland	AA	14	4	0	5	37.2	163	34	26	24	6	1	1	3	16	0	25	2	1	2	3	.333	0	1	5.73
	Edmonton	AAA	19	15	0	0	87.1	377	120	55	50	10	5	4	0	17	0	42	6	1	4	7	.364	0	0	5.15
	5 Min. YEARS		102	69	4	11	440.2	1903	509	267	232	44	12	15	8	123	3	263	25	8	24	21	.533	2	3	4.74

Patrick Lennon

Bats: Right Throws: Right Pos: OF **Ht: 6' 2" Wt: 200 Born: 04/27/68 Age: 27**

							BATTING											BASERUNNING				PERCENTAGES		
Year	Team	Lg	G	AB	H	2B	3B	HR	TB	R	RBI	TBB	IBB	SO	HBP	SH	SF	SB	CS	SB%	GDP	Avg	OBP	SLG
1986	Bellingham	A	51	169	41	5	2	3	59	35	27	36	0	50	0	1	1	8	6	.57	3	.243	.374	.349
1987	Wausau	A	98	319	80	21	3	7	128	54	34	46	1	82	1	1	2	25	8	.76	10	.251	.345	.401
1988	Vermont	AA	95	321	83	9	3	9	125	44	40	21	1	87	3	3	4	15	4	.79	9	.259	.307	.389
1989	Williamsprt	AA	66	248	65	14	2	3	92	32	31	23	2	53	0	0	5	7	4	.64	9	.262	.319	.371
1990	San Berndno	A	44	163	47	6	2	8	81	29	30	15	0	51	0	0	1	6	0	1.00	4	.288	.346	.497
	Williamsprt	AA	49	167	49	6	4	5	78	24	7	10	0	37	3	2	3	10	4	.71	2	.293	.335	.467

Year	Team		G	AB	H	2B	3B	HR	TB	R	RBI				HBP	SH	SF	SB	CS	SB%	GDP	Avg	OBP	SLG
1991	Calgary	AAA	112	416	137	29	5	15	221	75	74	46	4	68	4	1	1	12	5	.71	9	.329	.400	.531
1992	Calgary	AAA	13	48	17	3	0	1	23	8	9	6	0	10	0	0	0	4	1	.80	1	.354	.426	.479
1993	Canton-Akm	AA	45	152	39	7	1	4	60	24	22	30	1	45	1	0	2	4	2	.67	4	.257	.378	.395
1994	New Britain	AA	114	429	140	30	5	17	231	80	67	48	1	96	5	0	1	13	9	.59	10	.326	.400	.538
1991	Seattle	AL	9	8	1	1	0	0	2	2	1	3	0	1	0	0	0	0	0	.00	0	.125	.364	.250
1992	Seattle	AL	1	2	0	0	0	0	0	0	0	0	0	0	0	0	0	0	0	.00	0	.000	.000	.000
	9 Min. YEARS		687	2432	698	130	27	72	1098	405	356	281	11	579	16	6	20	104	45	.70	61	.287	.362	.451
	2 Maj. YEARS		10	10	1	1	0	0	2	2	1	3	0	1	0	0	0	0	0	.00	0	.100	.308	.200

Dana Levangie

Bats: Right **Throws:** Right **Pos:** C
Ht: 5'10" **Wt:** 185 **Born:** 08/11/69 **Age:** 25

			BATTING															BASERUNNING				PERCENTAGES		
Year	Team	Lg	G	AB	H	2B	3B	HR	TB	R	RBI	TBB	IBB	SO	HBP	SH	SF	SB	CS	SB%	GDP	Avg	OBP	SLG
1991	Elmira	A	35	94	14	3	0	0	17	6	4	19	1	18	0	0	0	0	1	.00	1	.149	.231	.181
1992	Winter Havn	A	76	245	47	5	1	0	55	21	22	20	0	49	2	1	3	1	2	.33	6	.192	.256	.224
1993	Ft.Laud	A	80	250	47	5	0	0	52	17	11	26	0	46	0	2	0	0	2	.00	5	.188	.264	.208
1994	Lynchburg	A	79	239	56	8	2	3	77	19	21	25	2	36	3	6	0	1	2	.33	5	.234	.315	.322
	New Britain	AA	8	21	3	1	0	1	7	2	5	1	0	6	1	0	0	0	0	.00	0	.143	.217	.333
	4 Min. YEARS		278	849	167	22	2	5	208	65	63	82	3	155	6	9	3	2	7	.22	17	.197	.271	.245

Tom LeVasseur

Bats: Right **Throws:** Right **Pos:** SS
Ht: 5'11" **Wt:** 175 **Born:** 02/11/64 **Age:** 31

			BATTING															BASERUNNING				PERCENTAGES		
Year	Team	Lg	G	AB	H	2B	3B	HR	TB	R	RBI	TBB	IBB	SO	HBP	SH	SF	SB	CS	SB%	GDP	Avg	OBP	SLG
1986	Spokane	A	53	191	71	3	1	1	79	50	21	47	0	14	2	2	1	28	8	.78	4	.372	.498	.414
1987	Reno	A	106	389	107	7	3	0	120	68	48	55	1	53	1	3	4	19	16	.54	6	.275	.363	.308
1988	Riverside	A	133	489	139	21	2	1	167	81	57	71	0	64	1	7	3	26	16	.62	4	.284	.374	.342
1989	Wichita	A	87	296	80	16	4	1	107	41	36	38	0	33	0	2	3	8	7	.53	9	.270	.350	.361
1990	Las Vegas	AAA	90	257	56	10	3	5	87	35	37	36	2	37	1	3	7	7	4	.64	9	.218	.309	.339
1994	Calgary	AAA	43	114	28	5	1	1	38	19	16	9	0	19	1	1	2	5	1	.83	4	.246	.302	.333
	6 Min. YEARS		512	1736	481	62	14	9	598	294	215	256	3	220	6	18	20	93	52	.64	36	.277	.368	.344

Alan Levine

Pitches: Right **Bats:** Left **Pos:** P
Ht: 6'3" **Wt:** 180 **Born:** 05/22/68 **Age:** 27

			HOW MUCH HE PITCHED					WHAT HE GAVE UP									THE RESULTS					
Year	Team	Lg	G	GS	CG	GF	IP	BFP	H	R	ER	HR	SH	SF	HB	TBB	IBB	SO	WP	Bk	W	L	Pct.	ShO	Sv	ERA
1991	Utica	A	16	12	2	3	85	361	75	43	30	2	4	2	4	26	0	83	8	1	6	4	.600	1	1	3.18
1992	South Bend	A	23	23	2	0	156.2	650	151	67	49	6	6	2	8	36	1	131	9	1	9	5	.643	0	0	2.81
	Sarasota	A	3	2	0	0	15.2	68	17	11	7	1	3	2	0	5	1	11	0	1	0	2	.000	0	0	4.02
1993	Sarasota	A	27	26	5	0	161.1	696	169	87	66	6	11	3	7	50	3	129	11	3	11	8	.579	1	0	3.68
1994	Birmingham	AA	18	18	1	0	114.1	501	117	50	42	7	2	3	14	44	1	94	3	0	5	9	.357	0	0	3.31
	Nashville	AAA	8	4	0	1	24	116	34	23	21	2	1	3	2	11	0	24	0	0	0	2	.000	0	0	7.88
	4 Min. YEARS		95	85	10	4	557	2392	563	281	215	24	27	15	35	172	6	472	31	6	31	30	.508	2	1	3.47

Anthony Lewis

Bats: Left **Throws:** Left **Pos:** OF
Ht: 6'0" **Wt:** 185 **Born:** 02/02/71 **Age:** 24

			BATTING															BASERUNNING				PERCENTAGES		
Year	Team	Lg	G	AB	H	2B	3B	HR	TB	R	RBI	TBB	IBB	SO	HBP	SH	SF	SB	CS	SB%	GDP	Avg	OBP	SLG
1989	Cardinals	R	51	187	46	10	0	2	62	32	27	11	1	45	0	0	4	11	3	.79	1	.246	.282	.332
1990	Savannah	A	128	465	118	22	4	8	172	55	49	24	6	79	1	2	1	10	13	.43	13	.254	.291	.370
1991	St. Pete	A	124	435	100	17	7	6	149	40	43	50	7	100	2	0	2	5	5	.50	7	.230	.311	.343
1992	St. Pete	A	128	454	101	18	2	15	168	50	55	46	6	105	5	1	4	2	4	.33	7	.222	.299	.370
1993	Arkansas	AA	112	326	86	28	2	13	157	48	50	25	3	98	0	1	3	3	4	.43	5	.264	.314	.482
1994	Arkansas	AA	88	335	85	18	4	17	156	58	50	27	0	69	0	0	2	2	1	.67	9	.254	.308	.466
	Louisville	AAA	21	74	9	0	1	0	11	3	6	0	0	27	0	0	0	0	0	.00	1	.122	.122	.149
	6 Min. YEARS		652	2276	545	113	17	61	875	286	280	183	23	523	8	4	16	33	30	.52	43	.239	.296	.384

Dan Lewis

Bats: Left **Throws:** Left **Pos:** 1B
Ht: 6'0" **Wt:** 202 **Born:** 12/14/67 **Age:** 27

			BATTING															BASERUNNING				PERCENTAGES		
Year	Team	Lg	G	AB	H	2B	3B	HR	TB	R	RBI	TBB	IBB	SO	HBP	SH	SF	SB	CS	SB%	GDP	Avg	OBP	SLG
1986	Astros	R	38	116	34	4	2	1	45	22	18	17	1	24	2	0	2	8	3	.73	1	.293	.387	.388
1987	Auburn	A	70	230	64	11	2	3	88	39	32	40	2	48	6	1	4	9	5	.64	1	.278	.393	.383
1988	Asheville	A	107	326	78	11	0	12	125	52	45	47	2	84	5	3	2	2	4	.33	4	.239	.342	.383
1989	Osceola	A	86	264	66	11	1	3	88	33	28	33	3	59	5	2	1	7	3	.70	2	.250	.343	.333
1990	San Jose	A	116	415	121	23	3	14	192	58	93	61	1	78	10	2	10	7	5	.58	14	.292	.387	.463
1991	Shreveport	AA	118	422	123	30	1	13	194	66	90	50	8	76	9	2	6	6	10	.38	11	.291	.374	.460
1992	Phoenix	AAA	70	244	66	15	2	10	115	32	41	24	5	42	2	1	4	0	8	.00	12	.270	.336	.471
	Shreveport	AA	50	170	53	3	0	3	65	28	25	18	2	24	3	0	2	2	3	.40	7	.312	.383	.382
1993	Iowa	AAA	42	122	24	7	0	3	40	10	13	7	1	23	1	1	1	0	0	.00	2	.197	.244	.328
1994	Jacksonvle	AA	24	72	15	3	0	3	27	8	9	12	0	12	0	1	0	1	2	.33	2	.208	.321	.375
	9 Min. YEARS		721	2381	644	118	11	65	979	348	394	309	25	470	43	13	32	42	43	.49	56	.270	.360	.411

Jim Lewis

Pitches: Right Bats: Right Pos: P   Ht: 6'4" Wt: 190 Born: 01/31/70 Age: 25

		HOW MUCH HE PITCHED						WHAT HE GAVE UP												THE RESULTS					
Year	Team	Lg	G	GS	CG	GF	IP	BFP	H	R	ER	HR	SH	SF	HB	TBB	IBB	SO	WP	Bk	W	L	Pct.	ShO	Sv	ERA
1991	Auburn	A	7	7	0	0	38.1	157	30	20	16	3	1	1	3	14	0	26	2	1	3	2	.600	0	0	3.76
1992	Tucson	AAA	1	1	0	0	1	4	0	0	0	0	0	0	0	2	0	0	0	0	0	0	.000	0	0	0.00
	Osceola	A	13	13	1	0	80.1	324	54	18	10	0	6	1	2	32	0	65	5	0	5	1	.833	0	0	1.12
	Jackson	AA	12	12	2	0	70	291	64	33	32	4	5	6	2	30	0	43	4	0	3	5	.375	1	0	4.11
1993	Osceola	A	4	4	0	0	7.2	34	8	4	2	1	0	0	0	2	0	3	0	0	0	0	.000	0	0	2.35
1994	Osceola	A	16	16	0	0	63	265	64	37	22	3	1	0	1	16	0	33	3	0	1	8	.111	0	0	3.14
	Jackson	AA	8	8	0	0	48	191	41	13	13	2	2	1	1	10	2	39	4	0	2	1	.667	0	0	2.44
	4 Min. YEARS		61	61	3	0	308.1	1266	261	125	95	13	15	9	9	106	2	209	18	1	14	17	.452	1	0	2.77

T.R. Lewis

Bats: Right Throws: Right Pos: 3B   Ht: 6'0" Wt: 180 Born: 04/15/71 Age: 24

		BATTING															BASERUNNING				PERCENTAGES		
Year	Team	Lg	G	AB	H	2B	3B	HR	TB	R	RBI	TBB	IBB	SO	HBP	SH	SF	SB	CS	SB%	GDP	Avg	OBP	SLG
1989	Bluefield	R	40	151	50	11	1	10	93	31	32	9	0	21	0	0	2	0	0	.00	2	.331	.364	.616
1990	Wausau	A	115	404	115	24	2	8	167	60	45	46	0	64	5	1	1	10	5	.67	14	.285	.364	.413
	Frederick	A	22	80	26	4	3	1	39	12	11	11	1	11	2	0	0	5	0	1.00	1	.325	.419	.488
1991	Frederick	A	49	159	33	7	2	0	44	18	7	19	2	25	1	2	1	1	1	.50	4	.208	.294	.277
1992	Kane County	A	45	134	40	10	0	2	56	26	22	13	0	22	3	1	4	5	4	.56	3	.299	.364	.418
	Frederick	A	84	313	96	27	6	7	156	58	54	36	0	46	2	0	5	5	2	.71	5	.307	.376	.498
1993	Bowie	AA	127	480	146	26	2	5	191	73	64	36	4	80	3	0	7	22	8	.73	12	.304	.352	.398
1994	Orioles	R	5	20	6	1	0	1	10	2	5	2	0	3	0	0	0	1	1	.50	0	.300	.364	.500
	Bowie	AA	17	72	18	5	0	3	32	13	8	6	0	15	0	0	1	1	0	1.00	1	.250	.304	.444
	Rochester	AAA	55	174	53	10	0	6	81	25	31	16	2	33	3	0	2	6	1	.86	1	.305	.369	.466
	6 Min. YEARS		559	1987	583	125	16	43	869	318	279	194	9	320	19	4	23	56	24	.70	43	.293	.358	.437

Rich Linares

Pitches: Right Bats: Right Pos: P   Ht: 6'0" Wt: 170 Born: 08/31/72 Age: 22

		HOW MUCH HE PITCHED									WHAT HE GAVE UP								THE RESULTS					
Year	Team	Lg	G	GS	CG	GF	IP	BFP	H	R	ER	HR	SH	SF	HB	TBB	IBB	SO	WP	Bk	W	L	Pct.	ShO	Sv	ERA
1992	Dodgers	R	7	0	0	6	11.2	46	8	2	1	0	0	0	3	1	0	14	0	1	1	2	.333	0	1	0.77
	Great Falls	R	19	0	0	6	47.2	198	32	22	13	4	3	2	6	11	0	53	2	1	3	1	.750	0	3	2.45
1993	Vero Beach	A	45	7	0	29	109.1	440	97	36	22	4	4	2	2	28	5	80	1	3	4	4	.500	0	13	1.81
1994	San Antonio	AA	5	0	0	2	6	28	4	7	6	0	1	0	0	7	1	2	1	0	0	2	.000	0	0	9.00
	Bakersfield	A	41	3	1	14	107.1	434	95	45	41	13	5	5	8	20	2	65	4	0	5	3	.625	1	6	3.44
	3 Min. YEARS		117	10	1	57	282	1146	236	112	83	21	13	9	17	69	9	214	8	5	13	12	.520	1	23	2.65

Doug Lindsey

Bats: Right Throws: Right Pos: C   Ht: 6'2" Wt: 200 Born: 09/22/67 Age: 27

		BATTING															BASERUNNING				PERCENTAGES		
Year	Team	Lg	G	AB	H	2B	3B	HR	TB	R	RBI	TBB	IBB	SO	HBP	SH	SF	SB	CS	SB%	GDP	Avg	OBP	SLG
1987	Utica	A	52	169	41	7	0	1	51	23	25	22	2	34	1	0	3	1	3	.25	2	.243	.328	.302
1988	Spartanburg	A	90	324	76	19	0	4	107	29	46	29	1	68	4	2	3	4	2	.67	5	.235	.303	.330
1989	Spartanburg	A	39	136	31	7	0	3	47	14	17	23	2	31	0	1	1	2	2	.50	7	.228	.338	.346
	Clearwater	A	36	118	23	3	0	0	26	8	9	5	0	18	0	0	2	0	0	.00	4	.195	.224	.220
1990	Reading	AA	107	323	56	11	0	1	70	16	32	26	1	78	1	6	3	2	1	.67	10	.173	.235	.217
1991	Reading	AA	94	313	81	13	0	1	97	26	34	21	0	49	2	4	4	1	0	1.00	12	.259	.306	.310
1992	Scranton/wb	AAA	87	274	57	9	0	4	78	28	27	37	4	66	1	1	2	0	2	.00	11	.208	.303	.285
1993	Scranton/wb	AAA	38	121	21	4	1	2	33	9	7	5	0	24	0	0	0	0	0	.00	6	.174	.206	.273
1994	Nashville	AAA	57	164	34	8	0	5	57	21	14	10	0	36	0	2	1	0	0	.00	4	.207	.251	.348
	Bowie	AA	16	53	19	4	0	0	23	5	9	3	0	8	0	1	1	0	0	.00	0	.358	.386	.434
1991	Philadelphia	NL	1	3	0	0	0	0	0	0	0	0	0	3	0	0	0	0	0	.00	0	.000	.000	.000
1993	Philadelphia	NL	2	2	1	0	0	0	1	0	0	0	0	1	0	0	0	0	0	.00	0	.500	.500	.500
	Chicago	AL	2	1	0	0	0	0	0	0	0	0	0	0	0	0	0	0	0	.00	0	.000	.000	.000
	8 Min. YEARS		616	1995	439	85	1	21	589	179	220	181	10	412	9	17	20	10	10	.50	61	.220	.285	.295
	2 Maj. YEARS		5	6	1	0	0	0	1	0	0	0	0	4	0	0	0	0	0	.00	0	.167	.167	.167

Felipe Lira

Pitches: Right Bats: Right Pos: P   Ht: 6'0" Wt: 170 Born: 04/26/72 Age: 23

		HOW MUCH HE PITCHED									WHAT HE GAVE UP								THE RESULTS					
Year	Team	Lg	G	GS	CG	GF	IP	BFP	H	R	ER	HR	SH	SF	HB	TBB	IBB	SO	WP	Bk	W	L	Pct.	ShO	Sv	ERA
1990	Bristol	R	13	10	2	2	78.1	318	70	26	21	4	0	1	3	16	1	71	4	2	5	5	.500	1	1	2.41
	Lakeland	A	1	0	0	0	1.2	11	3	1	1	0	0	1	0	3	0	4	0	0	0	0	.000	0	0	5.40
1991	Fayetteville	A	15	13	0	2	73.1	315	79	43	38	8	4	2	1	19	0	56	6	4	5	5	.500	0	1	4.66
1992	Lakeland	A	32	8	2	2	109	441	95	36	29	6	3	1	7	16	1	84	4	0	11	5	.688	1	2	2.39
1993	London	AA	22	22	2	0	152	641	157	63	57	16	5	3	6	39	2	122	8	1	10	4	.714	0	0	3.38
	Toledo	AAA	5	5	0	0	31.1	135	32	18	16	5	0	3	1	11	1	23	0	0	1	2	.333	0	0	4.60
1994	Toledo	AAA	26	26	1	0	151.1	669	171	91	79	19	4	9	6	45	4	110	16	0	7	12	.368	1	0	4.70
	5 Min. YEARS		114	84	7	6	597	2530	607	278	241	58	16	20	24	149	9	470	38	8	39	33	.542	3	3	3.63

Joe Lis

Bats: Right Throws: Right Pos: 2B **Ht: 5'10" Wt: 170 Born: 11/03/68 Age: 26**

Year	Team	Lg	G	AB	H	2B	3B	HR	TB	R	RBI	TBB	IBB	SO	HBP	SH	SF	SB	CS	SB%	GDP	Avg	OBP	SLG
1991	St.Cathrnes	A	66	206	60	12	1	5	89	36	27	41	0	19	4	9	4	3	3	.50	5	.291	.412	.432
1992	Myrtle Bch	A	125	434	130	25	0	13	194	70	79	68	5	54	7	2	7	5	11	.31	11	.300	.397	.447
1993	Knoxville	AA	129	448	130	29	3	8	189	66	64	42	1	58	16	2	5	6	9	.40	12	.290	.368	.422
1994	Syracuse	AAA	89	319	93	20	0	11	146	53	49	25	2	39	2	4	3	3	1	.75	14	.292	.344	.458
	4 Min. YEARS		409	1407	413	86	4	37	618	225	219	176	8	170	29	17	19	17	24	.41	42	.294	.379	.439

Paul List

Bats: Right Throws: Right Pos: OF **Ht: 6'3" Wt: 200 Born: 11/17/65 Age: 29**

Year	Team	Lg	G	AB	H	2B	3B	HR	TB	R	RBI	TBB	IBB	SO	HBP	SH	SF	SB	CS	SB%	GDP	Avg	OBP	SLG
1987	Salem	A	13	18	0	0	0	0	0	2	0	4	0	7	0	0	0	0	0	.00	0	.000	.182	.000
1990	Mariners	R	14	44	11	1	3	1	21	7	8	12	1	5	1	0	0	1	2	.33	0	.250	.421	.477
1991	Augusta	A	12	33	9	3	0	1	15	7	10	7	1	10	0	0	2	1	0	1.00	0	.273	.381	.455
	Carolina	AA	7	20	3	0	1	0	5	1	2	0	0	6	0	0	0	0	0	.00	0	.150	.150	.250
	Salem	A	94	336	107	22	5	10	169	60	46	39	1	74	1	0	2	12	3	.80	6	.318	.389	.503
1992	Carolina	AA	9	24	5	1	0	0	6	3	1	3	1	3	0	0	0	0	0	.00	0	.208	.296	.250
	Gastonia	A	51	182	64	11	3	8	105	32	40	23	0	26	4	0	1	5	9	.36	2	.352	.433	.577
	Tulsa	AA	34	130	38	7	1	1	50	17	14	13	0	30	0	0	0	1	1	.50	1	.292	.357	.385
1993	Tulsa	AA	40	125	25	3	1	0	30	8	6	10	0	30	3	0	2	2	6	.25	6	.200	.271	.240
	Colo Sprngs	AAA	18	50	15	7	1	0	24	9	5	3	0	8	0	0	0	0	0	.00	2	.300	.340	.480
	Central Val	A	33	120	35	6	2	8	69	21	27	17	0	19	2	0	1	0	3	.00	5	.292	.386	.575
1994	New Haven	AA	81	271	68	13	1	8	107	45	40	32	5	69	5	1	0	1	2	.33	9	.251	.341	.395
	6 Min. YEARS		406	1353	380	74	18	37	601	212	199	163	9	287	16	1	8	23	26	.47	33	.281	.363	.444

Jeff Livesey

Bats: Right Throws: Right Pos: C **Ht: 6'0" Wt: 185 Born: 05/24/66 Age: 29**

Year	Team	Lg	G	AB	H	2B	3B	HR	TB	R	RBI	TBB	IBB	SO	HBP	SH	SF	SB	CS	SB%	GDP	Avg	OBP	SLG
1988	Oneonta	A	37	126	28	3	1	2	39	15	9	17	0	30	0	1	0	0	0	.00	4	.222	.315	.310
	Ft.Laudrdle	A	9	25	5	2	0	0	7	2	2	1	0	11	0	1	0	0	0	.00	0	.200	.231	.280
1989	Pr William	A	70	197	40	12	0	2	58	17	17	9	0	48	1	2	1	1	0	1.00	4	.203	.240	.294
1990	Ft.Laudrdle	A	45	148	26	6	0	4	44	11	15	15	0	55	2	2	1	0	3	.00	4	.176	.259	.297
	Albany	AA	9	19	3	0	0	0	3	0	1	1	0	6	0	0	0	0	0	.00	0	.158	.200	.158
1991	Albany	AA	23	61	14	1	0	2	21	5	6	0	0	14	2	1	0	0	0	.00	1	.230	.254	.344
	Pr William	AA	20	73	18	5	0	2	29	8	9	3	0	13	0	1	1	0	0	.00	2	.247	.273	.397
1992	Columbus	AAA	3	9	1	0	0	0	1	0	1	0	0	2	0	0	0	0	0	.00	0	.111	.111	.111
	Albany	AA	18	42	8	3	0	0	11	1	5	6	0	13	0	2	0	0	0	.00	0	.190	.292	.262
1993	Albany	AA	32	104	16	4	0	0	20	6	6	7	0	22	0	4	0	0	0	.00	0	.154	.207	.192
	Columbus	AAA	34	89	22	5	0	2	33	9	8	2	0	19	0	2	0	0	0	.00	4	.247	.264	.371
1994	Albany-Colo	AA	31	106	32	6	1	2	46	13	16	0	0	20	0	1	2	1	0	1.00	2	.302	.296	.434
	7 Min. YEARS		331	999	213	47	2	16	312	87	95	61	0	253	5	17	5	2	3	.40	21	.213	.261	.312

Esteban Loaiza

Pitches: Right Bats: Right Pos: P **Ht: 6'2" Wt: 172 Born: 12/31/71 Age: 23**

Year	Team	Lg	G	GS	CG	GF	IP	BFP	H	R	ER	HR	SH	SF	HB	TBB	IBB	SO	WP	Bk	W	L	Pct.	ShO	Sv	ERA
1991	Pirates	R	11	11	1	0	51.2	220	48	17	13	0	0	2	5	14	0	41	1	0	5	1	.833	1	0	2.26
1992	Augusta	A	26	25	3	1	143.1	613	134	72	62	7	2	3	10	60	0	123	7	4	10	8	.556	0	0	3.89
1993	Salem	A	17	17	3	0	109	462	113	53	41	7	2	4	4	30	0	61	8	0	6	7	.462	0	0	3.39
	Carolina	AA	7	7	1	0	43	176	39	18	18	5	0	2	0	12	1	40	3	0	2	1	.667	0	0	3.77
1994	Carolina	AA	24	24	3	0	154.1	647	169	69	65	15	5	3	5	30	0	115	1	1	10	5	.667	0	0	3.79
	4 Min. YEARS		85	84	11	1	501.1	2118	503	229	199	34	9	14	24	146	1	380	20	5	33	22	.600	1	0	3.57

Ron Lockett

Bats: Left Throws: Left Pos: 1B **Ht: 6'1" Wt: 190 Born: 09/05/69 Age: 25**

Year	Team	Lg	G	AB	H	2B	3B	HR	TB	R	RBI	TBB	IBB	SO	HBP	SH	SF	SB	CS	SB%	GDP	Avg	OBP	SLG
1990	Princeton	R	63	229	71	12	5	6	111	32	34	15	2	51	2	1	0	10	6	.63	3	.310	.358	.485
1991	Clearwater	A	128	459	123	13	7	10	180	81	71	70	8	109	3	0	7	10	3	.77	9	.268	.364	.392
1992	Reading	AA	116	400	91	17	2	5	127	42	36	17	1	91	2	1	1	12	4	.75	11	.228	.262	.318
1993	Reading	AA	105	368	89	18	5	11	150	53	53	27	3	79	2	2	3	12	2	.86	11	.242	.295	.408
1994	Scranton-Wb	AAA	90	267	61	10	1	5	88	34	18	11	0	56	0	2	1	6	4	.60	8	.228	.258	.330
	5 Min. YEARS		502	1723	435	70	20	37	656	242	212	140	14	386	9	6	12	50	19	.72	42	.252	.310	.381

149

Dean Locklear

Pitches: Left Bats: Right Pos: P　　　Ht: 6'1" Wt: 190 Born: 10/12/69 Age: 25

Year	Team	Lg	G	GS	CG	GF	IP	BFP	H	R	ER	HR	SH	SF	HB	TBB	IBB	SO	WP	Bk	W	L	Pct.	ShO	Sv	ERA
			HOW MUCH HE PITCHED						WHAT HE GAVE UP												THE RESULTS					
1990	White Sox	R	14	0	0	10	24.1	106	25	17	11	1	2	0	1	7	0	29	2	3	0	2	.000	0	1	4.07
1991	South Bend	A	44	0	0	21	60.2	256	40	27	20	3	4	2	3	31	2	47	2	1	5	1	.833	0	0	2.97
1992	Sarasota	A	41	0	0	15	60	247	52	28	21	3	5	0	4	21	5	43	2	1	7	3	.700	0	4	3.15
1993	Birmingham	AA	9	2	0	4	22	105	29	17	15	1	2	1	1	11	0	20	1	1	2	0	1.000	0	0	6.14
	Sarasota	A	18	2	1	6	53.2	230	55	25	22	2	3	1	2	16	0	37	1	0	7	0	1.000	1	0	3.69
1994	Pr.William	A	12	2	0	3	32.2	142	33	17	16	0	2	1	5	14	0	34	4	2	1	1	.500	0	0	4.41
	Birmingham	AA	4	4	0	0	18.1	89	22	15	9	0	0	1	0	15	1	11	2	3	1	2	.333	0	0	4.42
	Midland	AA	21	0	0	9	25	130	47	25	24	0	0	4	1	11	2	14	3	1	0	0	.000	0	0	8.64
5 Min. YEARS			163	10	1	68	296.2	1305	303	171	138	10	18	10	17	126	10	235	17	12	23	9	.719	1	6	4.19

Rod Lofton

Bats: Right Throws: Right Pos: 2B　　　Ht: 5'11" Wt: 185 Born: 10/07/67 Age: 27

Year	Team	Lg	G	AB	H	2B	3B	HR	TB	R	RBI	TBB	IBB	SO	HBP	SH	SF	SB	CS	SB%	GDP	Avg	OBP	SLG
			BATTING															BASERUNNING				PERCENTAGES		
1988	Erie	A	72	251	75	13	1	0	90	40	37	35	0	29	3	8	4	37	7	.84	8	.299	.386	.359
1989	Frederick	A	127	473	115	9	2	0	128	65	29	56	1	72	2	7	3	62	21	.75	3	.243	.324	.271
1990	Frederick	A	2	9	5	1	0	0	6	1	2	0	0	1	0	0	0	2	0	1.00	0	.556	.556	.667
	Rochester	AAA	14	28	4	0	0	0	4	3	0	2	0	7	0	1	0	1	1	.50	1	.143	.200	.143
	Hagerstown	AA	89	294	80	7	2	0	91	35	34	23	0	50	2	10	2	24	4	.86	8	.272	.327	.310
1991	Rochester	AAA	3	3	0	0	0	0	0	0	1	0	0	0	0	0	0	0	0	.00	0	.000	.000	.000
	Hagerstown	AA	118	437	124	8	4	1	143	78	33	48	1	74	3	9	2	56	10	.85	3	.284	.357	.327
1992	Hagerstown	AA	50	172	43	7	0	0	50	17	8	7	0	22	2	3	0	11	6	.65	4	.250	.287	.291
	Rochester	AAA	52	132	31	3	1	0	36	24	8	8	0	26	0	4	0	10	3	.77	6	.235	.279	.273
1993	Indianapols	AAA	2	3	2	0	0	0	2	0	2	0	0	1	0	0	1	0	0	.00	0	.667	.500	.667
	Chattanooga	AA	10	27	3	0	0	0	3	1	2	7	0	11	0	1	1	2	0	1.00	0	.111	.286	.111
	El Paso	AA	67	200	53	8	5	2	77	39	21	13	0	40	5	5	1	16	1	.94	5	.265	.324	.385
1994	El Paso	AA	92	354	117	25	5	2	158	70	54	26	0	68	3	1	3	21	5	.81	5	.331	.378	.446
7 Min. YEARS			698	2383	652	81	20	5	788	373	231	225	2	401	20	49	17	242	58	.81	43	.274	.339	.331

Kevin Logsdon

Pitches: Left Bats: Both Pos: P　　　Ht: 5'11" Wt: 215 Born: 12/23/70 Age: 24

Year	Team	Lg	G	GS	CG	GF	IP	BFP	H	R	ER	HR	SH	SF	HB	TBB	IBB	SO	WP	Bk	W	L	Pct.	ShO	Sv	ERA
			HOW MUCH HE PITCHED						WHAT HE GAVE UP												THE RESULTS					
1991	Watertown	A	13	11	0	0	59.1	272	58	42	28	2	5	3	1	41	3	38	6	0	2	5	.286	0	0	4.25
1992	Columbus	A	19	18	0	0	113.1	470	104	43	37	1	3	3	5	48	0	86	9	3	6	5	.545	0	2	2.94
1993	Kinston	A	31	20	1	10	124.2	566	146	94	85	11	10	6	5	57	0	105	6	2	6	7	.462	0	3	6.14
1994	Canton-Akm	AA	39	0	0	20	64.1	268	45	24	18	3	3	3	3	34	1	34	5	0	4	2	.667	0	1	2.52
4 Min. YEARS			102	49	1	30	361.2	1576	353	203	168	17	21	15	14	180	4	263	26	5	18	19	.486	0	4	4.18

Adin Lohry

Bats: Left Throws: Right Pos: C　　　Ht: 6'1" Wt: 180 Born: 01/12/71 Age: 24

Year	Team	Lg	G	AB	H	2B	3B	HR	TB	R	RBI	TBB	IBB	SO	HBP	SH	SF	SB	CS	SB%	GDP	Avg	OBP	SLG
			BATTING															BASERUNNING				PERCENTAGES		
1989	Yankees	R	38	124	33	4	3	0	43	24	12	28	0	34	0	0	0	5	2	.71	0	.266	.401	.347
1990	Oneonta	A	44	137	27	1	2	0	32	14	14	20	1	27	1	3	2	5	5	.50	1	.197	.300	.234
1991	Yankees	R	8	25	6	2	0	0	8	4	8	6	0	5	0	0	0	4	1	.80	1	.240	.387	.320
	Ft.Laudrdle	A	30	90	15	5	0	0	20	6	8	11	1	33	2	1	0	0	1	.00	0	.167	.272	.222
1992	Pr William	A	57	135	35	1	0	0	36	19	14	35	1	27	0	7	2	3	2	.60	5	.259	.407	.267
1993	San Berndno	A	28	84	21	3	0	0	24	13	7	13	0	17	3	2	1	2	1	.67	0	.250	.366	.286
	Pr William	A	1	2	0	0	0	0	0	0	0	1	0	2	0	0	0	0	0	.00	0	.000	.333	.000
1994	San Bernrdo	A	32	92	22	3	0	1	28	18	11	20	0	22	0	0	1	0	1	.00	4	.239	.372	.304
	Albany-Colo	AA	21	41	6	2	0	0	8	4	2	7	0	10	1	0	0	0	0	.00	0	.146	.286	.195
6 Min. YEARS			259	730	165	21	5	1	199	102	76	141	3	177	7	13	6	19	13	.59	12	.226	.354	.273

Kevin Lomon

Pitches: Right Bats: Right Pos: P　　　Ht: 6'1" Wt: 195 Born: 11/20/71 Age: 23

Year	Team	Lg	G	GS	CG	GF	IP	BFP	H	R	ER	HR	SH	SF	HB	TBB	IBB	SO	WP	Bk	W	L	Pct.	ShO	Sv	ERA
			HOW MUCH HE PITCHED						WHAT HE GAVE UP												THE RESULTS					
1991	Pulaski	R	10	5	1	1	44	168	17	9	3	0	0	1	4	13	0	70	4	6	6	0	1.000	1	1	0.61
	Macon	A	1	0	0	1	5	17	2	1	1	0	0	0	0	1	0	2	0	0	1	0	1.000	0	1	1.80
1992	Durham	A	27	27	0	0	135	609	147	83	74	13	5	3	11	63	1	113	16	3	8	9	.471	0	0	4.93
1993	Durham	A	14	14	1	0	85	358	80	36	35	6	0	1	2	30	1	68	5	3	4	2	.667	0	0	3.71
	Greenville	AA	13	13	1	0	79.1	338	76	41	34	4	3	3	4	31	2	68	4	0	3	4	.429	1	0	3.86
1994	Richmond	AAA	28	26	0	0	147	628	159	69	63	12	1	2	3	53	2	97	9	0	10	8	.556	0	0	3.86
4 Min. YEARS			93	85	3	2	495.1	2118	481	239	210	35	9	10	24	191	6	418	38	12	32	23	.582	2	1	3.82

Kevin Long

Bats: Left **Throws:** Left **Pos:** OF **Ht:** 5'9" **Wt:** 165 **Born:** 12/30/66 **Age:** 28

Year	Team	Lg	G	AB	H	2B	3B	HR	TB	R	RBI	TBB	IBB	SO	HBP	SH	SF	SB	CS	SB%	GDP	Avg	OBP	SLG
1989	Eugene	A	69	260	81	19	1	3	111	54	45	36	6	40	1	1	6	15	3	.83	7	.312	.389	.427
1990	Baseball Cy	A	85	308	87	17	5	2	120	53	33	32	0	28	0	7	2	22	6	.79	4	.282	.348	.390
1991	Memphis	AA	106	407	112	18	2	3	143	60	35	45	1	63	2	6	3	27	10	.73	8	.275	.348	.351
1992	Omaha	AAA	88	312	71	16	3	1	96	28	29	29	2	41	0	2	3	9	5	.64	4	.228	.291	.308
1993	Omaha	AAA	17	51	13	2	0	0	15	7	4	2	0	13	0	1	1	3	0	1.00	0	.255	.278	.294
	Memphis	AA	79	301	82	14	6	1	111	47	20	37	2	56	5	2	2	7	12	.37	4	.272	.359	.369
1994	Memphis	AA	10	24	5	3	0	0	8	5	1	5	0	2	0	0	0	2	0	1.00	2	.208	.345	.333
	6 Min. YEARS		454	1663	451	89	17	10	604	254	167	186	11	243	8	19	17	85	36	.70	29	.271	.344	.363

Steve Long

Pitches: Right **Bats:** Right **Pos:** P **Ht:** 6'4" **Wt:** 220 **Born:** 07/17/69 **Age:** 25

Year	Team	Lg	G	GS	CG	GF	IP	BFP	H	R	ER	HR	SH	SF	HB	TBB	IBB	SO	WP	Bk	W	L	Pct.	ShO	Sv	ERA
1990	Jamestown	A	22	0	0	11	39.1	173	26	15	6	1	5	1	3	24	0	35	2	3	4	2	.667	0	2	1.37
1991	Sumter	A	63	0	0	53	76.1	335	72	34	27	2	5	1	5	31	1	79	15	2	3	3	.500	0	17	3.18
1992	Wst Plm Bch	A	26	23	4	0	151.1	607	121	53	41	2	9	4	7	42	3	67	7	3	9	7	.563	0	0	2.44
1993	Binghamton	AA	38	19	4	4	156.2	682	165	87	70	9	5	7	7	58	0	70	6	1	12	8	.600	0	1	4.02
1994	Edmonton	AAA	29	29	2	0	172	781	224	119	101	15	5	7	17	59	1	85	14	0	10	11	.476	0	0	5.28
	5 Min. YEARS		178	71	10	68	595.2	2578	608	308	245	29	29	20	39	214	5	336	44	9	38	31	.551	0	20	3.70

Luis Lopez

Bats: Right **Throws:** Right **Pos:** OF **Ht:** 6'1" **Wt:** 190 **Born:** 09/01/64 **Age:** 30

Year	Team	Lg	G	AB	H	2B	3B	HR	TB	R	RBI	TBB	IBB	SO	HBP	SH	SF	SB	CS	SB%	GDP	Avg	OBP	SLG
1984	Great Falls	R	68	275	90	15	5	6	133	60	61	27	1	15	5	1	2	4	4	.50	10	.327	.395	.484
1985	Vero Beach	A	120	382	106	18	2	1	131	47	43	25	3	41	6	3	3	2	2	.50	19	.277	.329	.343
1986	Vero Beach	A	122	434	124	21	3	1	154	52	60	33	3	25	2	2	4	5	7	.42	21	.286	.336	.355
1987	Bakersfield	A	142	550	181	43	2	16	276	89	96	38	3	49	9	5	6	6	6	.50	9	.329	.378	.502
1988	San Antonio	AA	124	470	116	16	3	7	159	56	65	32	5	33	13	5	7	3	4	.43	12	.247	.308	.338
1989	San Antonio	AA	99	327	87	17	0	10	134	46	51	38	4	39	5	0	2	1	0	1.00	14	.266	.349	.410
	Albuquerque	AAA	19	75	37	7	0	2	50	17	16	6	0	7	1	0	2	1	0	1.00	1	.493	.524	.667
1990	Albuquerque	AAA	128	448	158	23	2	11	218	65	81	47	4	49	4	0	2	3	3	.50	12	.353	.417	.487
1991	Colo Sprngs	AAA	41	176	61	11	4	1	83	29	31	9	0	10	3	0	0	0	0	.00	4	.347	.388	.472
1992	Canton-Akrn	AA	20	82	21	1	0	0	22	4	7	3	0	8	0	0	0	1	0	1.00	4	.256	.282	.268
1993	Canton-Akrn	AA	60	231	64	16	0	2	86	30	41	13	0	16	5	2	3	0	3	.00	5	.277	.325	.372
	Charlotte	AAA	67	242	76	15	0	12	127	36	37	6	2	17	1	0	2	0	0	.00	8	.314	.331	.525
1994	Richmond	AAA	133	521	159	33	3	18	252	67	79	34	5	43	5	0	4	4	2	.67	20	.305	.351	.484
1990	Los Angeles	NL	6	6	0	0	0	0	0	0	0	0	0	2	0	0	0	0	0	.00	0	.000	.000	.000
1991	Cleveland	AL	35	82	18	4	1	0	24	7	7	4	1	7	0	0	1	0	0	.00	0	.220	.261	.293
	11 Min. YEARS		1143	4213	1280	236	24	87	1825	598	668	311	30	352	59	18	37	30	31	.49	139	.304	.357	.433
	2 Maj. YEARS		41	88	18	4	1	0	24	7	7	4	1	9	1	1	1	0	0	.00	0	.205	.245	.273

Pedro Lopez

Bats: Right **Throws:** Right **Pos:** C **Ht:** 6'0" **Wt:** 160 **Born:** 03/29/69 **Age:** 26

Year	Team	Lg	G	AB	H	2B	3B	HR	TB	R	RBI	TBB	IBB	SO	HBP	SH	SF	SB	CS	SB%	GDP	Avg	OBP	SLG
1988	Padres	R	42	156	44	4	6	1	63	18	22	10	0	24	0	0	0	9	4	.69	2	.282	.325	.404
1989	Waterloo	A	97	319	61	13	1	2	82	32	26	25	1	61	4	6	1	4	4	.50	12	.191	.258	.257
1990	Chston-Sc	A	32	101	20	2	0	0	22	9	5	7	0	18	4	0	2	0	1	.00	2	.198	.272	.218
1991	Waterloo	A	102	342	97	13	1	8	136	49	57	47	5	66	2	2	4	3	3	.50	4	.284	.370	.398
1992	Wichita	AA	96	319	78	8	4	6	112	35	48	13	0	68	7	2	6	4	3	.57	7	.245	.284	.351
1993	Rancho Cuca	A	37	103	26	10	0	1	39	25	9	24	1	19	2	0	0	0	1	.00	3	.252	.403	.379
	Wichita	AA	50	142	29	7	0	4	48	12	14	22	2	24	1	1	0	3	0	1.00	2	.204	.315	.338
1994	Wichita	AA	42	131	33	7	0	1	43	15	12	15	0	16	3	1	2	0	2	.00	2	.252	.338	.328
	Rancho Cuca	A	7	20	5	2	0	0	7	1	1	1	0	2	0	0	0	0	0	.00	1	.250	.286	.350
	Las Vegas	AAA	17	47	10	2	0	1	15	3	4	1	0	7	0	1	1	0	0	.00	2	.213	.224	.319
	7 Min. YEARS		522	1680	403	68	12	24	567	199	198	165	9	305	23	13	16	23	18	.56	36	.240	.314	.338

Mark Loretta

Bats: Right **Throws:** Right **Pos:** 1B **Ht:** 6'0" **Wt:** 175 **Born:** 08/14/71 **Age:** 23

Year	Team	Lg	G	AB	H	2B	3B	HR	TB	R	RBI	TBB	IBB	SO	HBP	SH	SF	SB	CS	SB%	GDP	Avg	OBP	SLG
1993	Helena	R	6	28	9	1	0	1	13	5	8	1	0	4	1	0	0	0	0	.00	1	.321	.367	.464
	Stockton	A	53	201	73	4	1	4	91	36	31	22	0	17	2	2	2	8	2	.80	6	.363	.427	.453
1994	El Paso	AA	77	302	95	13	6	0	120	50	38	27	0	33	2	9	5	8	5	.62	12	.315	.369	.397
	New Orleans	AAA	43	138	29	7	0	1	39	16	14	12	0	13	3	3	3	2	1	.67	2	.210	.282	.283
	2 Min. YEARS		179	669	206	25	7	6	263	107	91	62	0	67	8	14	10	18	8	.69	21	.308	.368	.393

151

Billy Lott

Bats: Right Throws: Right Pos: OF Ht: 6'4" Wt: 210 Born: 08/16/70 Age: 24

Year	Team	Lg	G	AB	H	2B	3B	HR	TB	R	RBI	TBB	IBB	SO	HBP	SH	SF	SB	CS	SB%	GDP	Avg	OBP	SLG
1989	Dodgers	R	46	150	29	2	4	0	39	18	9	10	0	48	1	1	0	5	1	.83	0	.193	.248	.260
1990	Bakersfield	A	38	133	27	1	1	2	36	11	14	6	0	46	1	1	1	3	2	.60	3	.203	.241	.271
	Yakima	A	65	240	66	13	2	4	95	37	38	10	0	62	3	0	4	4	0	1.00	1	.275	.307	.396
1991	Bakersfield	A	92	314	70	10	1	5	97	40	35	25	0	90	3	3	6	11	4	.73	8	.223	.282	.309
1992	Vero Beach	A	126	435	107	17	4	3	141	42	35	22	3	107	3	2	5	11	5	.69	18	.246	.284	.324
1993	San Antonio	AA	114	418	106	17	2	15	172	49	49	23	3	111	1	1	2	5	11	.31	8	.254	.293	.411
1994	San Antonio	AA	122	448	131	25	4	12	200	61	62	31	2	100	4	2	3	20	10	.67	7	.292	.342	.446
	6 Min. YEARS		603	2138	536	85	18	41	780	258	242	127	8	564	16	10	21	59	33	.64	45	.251	.295	.365

Vance Lovelace

Pitches: Left Bats: Left Pos: P Ht: 6'5" Wt: 235 Born: 08/09/63 Age: 31

Year	Team	Lg	G	GS	CG	GF	IP	BFP	H	R	ER	HR	SH	SF	HB	TBB	IBB	SO	WP	Bk	W	L	Pct.	ShO	Sv	ERA
1984	San Antonio	AA	16	16	0	0	65	309	48	39	28	5	2	1	1	73	1	52	10	1	3	7	.300	0	0	3.88
1985	San Antonio	AA	7	5	0	1	23.2	125	22	27	20	0	2	2	1	30	0	12	5	1	0	4	.000	0	0	7.61
	Vero Beach	A	11	3	0	4	29.1	140	31	22	20	0	0	1	1	23	1	26	4	2	1	2	.333	0	0	6.14
1986	Midland	AA	23	6	0	2	42.1	223	45	46	42	4	1	1	4	58	0	27	13	2	2	4	.333	0	0	8.93
	Palm Sprngs	A	6	5	0	1	17.2	103	21	23	18	0	1	1	1	30	0	16	5	0	0	1	.000	0	0	9.17
1987	Midland	AA	53	1	0	14	83.2	377	73	40	30	8	3	1	3	60	1	91	13	2	3	3	.500	0	4	3.23
1988	Edmonton	AAA	46	5	1	14	69.1	336	79	48	47	5	2	4	4	57	4	56	11	3	1	3	.250	0	1	6.10
1989	Edmonton	AAA	37	1	0	14	48.2	242	42	42	32	5	6	3	3	55	0	40	12	3	0	7	.000	0	2	5.92
1990	Calgary	AAA	56	0	0	29	70	307	64	33	27	0	1	3	2	44	0	40	2	0	5	5	.500	0	6	3.47
1992	Toledo	AAA	15	0	0	5	25.1	127	28	17	9	1	0	3	2	21	0	22	9	0	2	0	1.000	0	0	3.20
1993	Greenville	AA	11	0	0	3	16.1	67	10	4	3	1	0	1	1	12	1	21	1	0	2	0	1.000	0	0	1.65
	Richmond	AAA	5	0	0	1	9	42	10	5	5	0	0	0	0	6	0	7	1	0	0	0	.000	0	0	5.00
1994	Okla. City	AAA	15	1	0	9	20.1	94	18	12	12	1	1	1	1	16	0	19	4	1	0	0	.000	0	0	5.31
1988	California	AL	3	0	0	2	1.1	8	2	2	2	1	0	0	0	3	0	0	0	0	0	0	.000	0	0	13.50
1989	California	AL	1	0	0	1	1	4	0	0	0	0	0	0	0	1	1	1	0	0	0	0	.000	0	0	0.00
1990	Seattle	AL	5	0	0	1	2.1	17	3	1	1	0	0	0	1	6	0	1	2	0	0	0	.000	0	0	3.86
	10 Min. YEARS		301	43	1	97	520.2	2492	491	358	293	30	18	22	24	485	8	429	90	15	19	36	.345	0	14	5.06
	3 Maj. YEARS		9	0	0	4	4.2	29	5	3	3	1	0	0	1	10	1	2	2	0	0	0	.000	0	0	5.79

Derek Lowe

Pitches: Right Bats: Right Pos: P Ht: 6'6" Wt: 185 Born: 06/01/73 Age: 22

Year	Team	Lg	G	GS	CG	GF	IP	BFP	H	R	ER	HR	SH	SF	HB	TBB	IBB	SO	WP	Bk	W	L	Pct.	ShO	Sv	ERA
1991	Mariners	R	12	12	0	0	71	295	58	26	19	2	1	4	2	21	0	60	4	6	5	3	.625	0	0	2.41
1992	Bellingham	A	14	13	2	1	85.2	349	69	34	23	2	3	1	4	22	0	66	5	4	7	3	.700	1	0	2.42
1993	Riverside	A	27	26	3	1	154	687	189	104	90	9	2	2	2	60	0	80	12	9	12	9	.571	2	0	5.26
1994	Jacksonvlle	AA	26	26	2	0	151.1	676	177	92	83	7	6	3	9	50	1	75	11	7	7	10	.412	0	0	4.94
	4 Min. YEARS		79	77	7	2	462	2007	493	256	215	20	12	10	17	153	1	281	32	26	31	25	.554	3	0	4.19

Jon Lowe

Pitches: Right Bats: Right Pos: P Ht: 6'2" Wt: 200 Born: 03/29/71 Age: 24

Year	Team	Lg	G	GS	CG	GF	IP	BFP	H	R	ER	HR	SH	SF	HB	TBB	IBB	SO	WP	Bk	W	L	Pct.	ShO	Sv	ERA
1992	Hamilton	A	5	5	0	0	28	109	14	8	5	0	0	0	1	14	0	22	1	1	2	0	1.000	0	0	1.61
1993	St.Pete	A	25	25	0	0	132.2	594	152	80	63	6	2	5	6	62	1	87	4	5	6	11	.353	0	0	4.27
1994	St. Pete	A	21	21	0	0	114	488	119	51	44	6	3	2	5	37	0	92	3	0	5	6	.455	0	0	3.47
	Arkansas	AA	3	3	0	0	19.1	76	13	3	3	0	2	0	0	8	0	11	0	0	2	1	.667	0	0	1.40
	3 Min. YEARS		54	54	0	0	294	1267	298	142	115	12	7	7	12	121	1	212	8	6	15	18	.455	0	0	3.52

Terrell Lowery

Bats: Right Throws: Right Pos: OF Ht: 6'3" Wt: 175 Born: 10/25/70 Age: 24

Year	Team	Lg	G	AB	H	2B	3B	HR	TB	R	RBI	TBB	IBB	SO	HBP	SH	SF	SB	CS	SB%	GDP	Avg	OBP	SLG
1991	Butte	R	54	214	64	10	7	3	97	38	33	29	0	44	1	0	2	23	12	.66	2	.299	.382	.453
1993	Charlotte	A	65	257	77	7	9	3	111	46	36	46	2	47	2	1	1	14	15	.48	2	.300	.408	.432
	Tulsa	AA	66	258	62	5	1	3	78	29	14	28	1	50	1	1	1	10	12	.45	5	.240	.316	.302
1994	Tulsa	AA	129	496	142	34	8	8	216	89	54	59	0	113	5	5	5	33	15	.69	7	.286	.365	.435
	3 Min. YEARS		314	1225	345	56	25	17	502	202	137	162	3	254	9	7	9	80	54	.60	16	.282	.367	.410

Roger Luce

Bats: Right Throws: Right Pos: C Ht: 6'4" Wt: 215 Born: 05/07/69 Age: 26

Year	Team	Lg	G	AB	H	2B	3B	HR	TB	R	RBI	TBB	IBB	SO	HBP	SH	SF	SB	CS	SB%	GDP	Avg	OBP	SLG
1991	Gastonia	A	33	107	28	9	2	2	47	17	16	7	0	31	3	1	3	2	2	.50	1	.262	.317	.439
1992	Charlotte	A	91	303	70	9	0	1	82	18	20	19	1	77	3	1	2	3	4	.43	3	.231	.281	.271
1993	Tulsa	AA	101	321	62	14	2	8	104	35	29	17	0	107	4	0	1	2	1	.67	5	.193	.242	.324
1994	Tulsa	AA	59	191	54	11	4	6	87	27	22	16	0	56	0	1	0	2	2	.50	2	.283	.338	.455
	Okla. City	AAA	49	169	40	9	1	1	54	20	14	4	0	40	0	1	0	0	1	.00	1	.237	.254	.320
	4 Min. YEARS		333	1091	254	52	7	18	374	117	101	63	1	311	10	4	6	9	9	.50	12	.233	.279	.343

Larry Luebbers

Pitches: Right Bats: Right Pos: P Ht: 6'6" Wt: 205 Born: 10/11/69 Age: 25

Year	Team	Lg	G	GS	CG	GF	IP	BFP	H	R	ER	HR	SH	SF	HB	TBB	IBB	SO	WP	Bk	W	L	Pct.	ShO	Sv	ERA
1990	Billings	R	13	13	1	0	72.1	319	74	46	36	3	2	3	6	31	0	48	7	1	5	4	.556	1	0	4.48
1991	Cedar Rapds	A	28	28	3	0	184.2	781	177	85	64	8	12	6	10	64	5	98	11	4	8	10	.444	0	0	3.12
1992	Cedar Rapds	A	14	14	1	0	82.1	355	71	33	24	2	4	3	8	33	0	56	1	1	7	0	1.000	0	0	2.62
	Chattanooga	AA	14	14	1	0	87.1	368	86	34	22	5	2	1	4	34	1	56	5	2	6	5	.545	0	0	2.27
1993	Indianapols	AAA	15	15	0	0	84.1	380	81	45	39	7	6	2	6	47	5	51	1	0	4	7	.364	0	0	4.16
1994	Iowa	AAA	27	26	0	0	138.2	630	149	100	93	22	4	7	5	87	3	90	7	4	10	12	.455	0	0	6.04
1993	Cincinnati	NL	14	14	0	0	77.1	332	74	49	39	7	4	5	1	38	3	38	4	0	2	5	.286	0	0	4.54
	5 Min. YEARS		111	110	6	0	649.2	2833	638	343	278	47	30	22	39	296	14	399	32	12	40	38	.513	1	0	3.85

Rob Lukachyk

Bats: Left Throws: Right Pos: OF Ht: 6'0" Wt: 185 Born: 07/24/68 Age: 26

Year	Team	Lg	G	AB	H	2B	3B	HR	TB	R	RBI	TBB	IBB	SO	HBP	SH	SF	SB	CS	SB%	GDP	Avg	OBP	SLG
1987	White Sox	R	17	54	12	1	1	0	15	6	7	9	2	13	0	0	0	5	1	.83	1	.222	.333	.278
1988	Utica	A	71	227	64	10	8	7	111	42	48	31	1	48	3	2	1	9	6	.60	2	.282	.374	.489
1989	South Bend	A	122	430	125	16	4	3	158	60	63	35	7	78	2	5	6	18	15	.55	5	.291	.342	.367
1990	Sarasota	A	118	428	104	23	9	4	157	56	36	31	4	88	2	4	4	17	8	.68	6	.243	.295	.367
1991	Sarasota	A	125	399	108	27	2	9	166	63	49	63	4	100	15	9	2	22	8	.73	2	.271	.383	.416
1992	Stockton	A	105	359	99	21	14	15	193	77	81	53	3	86	9	0	5	44	15	.75	0	.276	.378	.538
1993	New Orleans	AAA	8	24	4	1	0	2	11	5	6	3	0	6	0	2	0	0	0	.00	0	.167	.259	.458
	El Paso	AA	113	362	96	24	7	9	161	58	63	52	3	75	7	2	5	8	10	.44	5	.265	.364	.445
1994	Bowie	AA	108	371	107	19	6	10	168	68	54	47	9	60	5	1	5	33	6	.85	5	.288	.371	.453
	8 Min. YEARS		787	2654	719	142	51	59	1140	435	407	324	33	554	43	25	28	156	69	.69	31	.271	.356	.430

Matt Luke

Bats: Left Throws: Left Pos: 1B Ht: 6'5" Wt: 225 Born: 02/26/71 Age: 24

Year	Team	Lg	G	AB	H	2B	3B	HR	TB	R	RBI	TBB	IBB	SO	HBP	SH	SF	SB	CS	SB%	GDP	Avg	OBP	SLG
1992	Oneonta	A	69	271	67	11	7	2	98	30	34	19	3	32	2	0	3	4	1	.80	9	.247	.298	.362
1993	Greensboro	A	135	549	157	37	5	21	267	83	91	47	4	79	7	0	6	11	3	.79	9	.286	.346	.486
1994	Albany-Colo	AA	63	236	67	11	2	8	106	34	40	28	0	50	2	3	1	6	4	.60	6	.284	.363	.449
	Tampa	A	57	222	68	11	2	16	131	52	42	28	2	27	1	0	1	4	1	.80	7	.306	.385	.590
	3 Min. YEARS		324	1278	359	70	16	47	602	199	207	122	9	188	12	3	11	25	9	.74	31	.281	.346	.471

Brent Lutz

Bats: Right Throws: Right Pos: C Ht: 6'1" Wt: 185 Born: 05/07/70 Age: 25

Year	Team	Lg	G	AB	H	2B	3B	HR	TB	R	RBI	TBB	IBB	SO	HBP	SH	SF	SB	CS	SB%	GDP	Avg	OBP	SLG
1991	Medicne Hat	R	41	115	31	4	2	3	48	23	23	21	0	34	7	1	0	6	1	.86	0	.270	.413	.417
1992	Myrtle Bch	A	49	90	15	2	0	2	23	10	10	13	0	31	4	2	1	2	1	.67	0	.167	.296	.256
1993	Hagerstown	A	1	0	0	0	0	0	0	0	0	0	0	0	0	0	0	0	0	.00	0	.000	.000	.000
	Dunedin	A	84	246	65	12	3	4	95	38	33	31	1	60	5	3	2	16	8	.67	5	.264	.356	.386
1994	Knoxville	AA	111	372	101	16	5	8	151	56	41	34	0	100	17	2	2	19	10	.66	8	.272	.358	.406
	4 Min. YEARS		286	823	212	34	10	17	317	127	107	99	1	225	33	8	5	43	20	.68	13	.258	.358	.385

Mitch Lyden

Bats: Right Throws: Right Pos: C Ht: 6'3" Wt: 225 Born: 12/14/64 Age: 30

Year	Team	Lg	G	AB	H	2B	3B	HR	TB	R	RBI	TBB	IBB	SO	HBP	SH	SF	SB	CS	SB%	GDP	Avg	OBP	SLG
1984	Greensboro	A	14	32	7	1	0	1	11	3	2	1	1	9	0	0	0	0	0	.00	3	.219	.242	.344
	Yankees	R	54	200	47	4	0	1	54	21	21	13	1	36	4	1	2	3	1	.75	3	.235	.292	.270
1985	Ft.Laudrdle	A	116	400	102	21	1	10	155	43	58	27	0	93	5	1	5	1	2	.33	15	.255	.307	.388
1986	Yankees	R	17	50	17	7	0	3	33	8	16	7	0	7	0	0	1	0	0	.00	1	.340	.414	.660
	Albany	AA	46	159	48	14	1	8	88	19	29	4	1	39	2	0	2	0	1	.00	5	.302	.323	.553
	Columbus	AAA	2	7	0	0	0	0	0	0	0	1	0	1	0	0	0	0	0	.00	0	.000	.125	.000
1987	Columbus	AAA	29	100	22	3	0	0	25	7	8	4	0	22	1	1	3	1	0	1.00	0	.220	.250	.250
	Albany	AA	71	233	59	12	2	8	99	25	36	11	0	47	2	1	1	0	0	.00	4	.253	.291	.425

153

Year	Team	Lg	G	AB	H	2B	3B	HR	TB	R	RBI	TBB	IBB	SO	HBP	SH	SF	SB	CS	SB%	GDP	Avg	OBP	SLG
1988	Pr William	A	67	234	66	12	2	17	133	42	47	19	3	59	4	0	2	1	0	1.00	5	.282	.344	.568
	Albany	AA	20	78	32	7	1	8	65	16	21	5	1	15	0	0	1	0	2	.00	1	.410	.440	.833
1989	Albany	AA	53	181	43	2	0	6	63	24	21	12	3	51	2	1	0	1	0	1.00	5	.238	.292	.348
	Pr William	A	30	105	29	2	1	7	54	17	28	8	0	26	8	0	1	1	0	1.00	2	.276	.369	.514
1990	Albany	AA	85	311	92	22	1	17	167	55	63	24	1	67	9	0	4	1	0	1.00	13	.296	.359	.537
	Columbus	AAA	41	147	33	8	0	7	62	18	20	7	0	34	4	0	1	0	0	.00	9	.224	.277	.422
1991	Toledo	AAA	101	340	76	11	2	18	145	34	55	15	3	108	0	0	7	0	0	.00	11	.224	.251	.426
1992	Tidewater	AAA	91	299	77	13	0	14	132	34	52	12	0	95	3	0	4	1	2	.33	11	.258	.289	.441
1993	Edmonton	AAA	50	160	49	15	1	8	90	34	31	5	0	34	0	0	2	1	1	.50	2	.306	.323	.563
1994	Edmonton	AAA	84	289	85	21	0	18	160	52	65	11	0	74	11	1	2	2	0	1.00	13	.294	.342	.554
1993	Florida	NL	6	10	3	0	0	1	6	2	1	0	0	3	0	0	0	0	0	.00	0	.300	.300	.600
	11 Min. YEARS		971	3325	884	175	12	151	1536	452	573	186	14	817	55	6	38	13	9	.59	112	.266	.312	.462

Scott Lydy

Bats: Right Throws: Right Pos: OF Ht: 6' 5" Wt: 195 Born: 10/26/68 Age: 26

			BATTING															BASERUNNING				PERCENTAGES		
Year	Team	Lg	G	AB	H	2B	3B	HR	TB	R	RBI	TBB	IBB	SO	HBP	SH	SF	SB	CS	SB%	GDP	Avg	OBP	SLG
1990	Madison	A	54	174	33	6	2	4	55	33	19	25	1	62	1	0	2	7	5	.58	1	.190	.292	.316
	Athletics	R	18	50	17	6	0	2	29	8	11	10	0	14	0	0	0	0	0	.00	1	.340	.450	.580
1991	Madison	A	127	464	120	26	2	12	186	64	66	66	5	109	5	0	5	24	9	.73	10	.259	.354	.401
1992	Reno	A	33	124	49	13	2	2	72	29	27	26	2	30	0	0	0	9	4	.69	1	.395	.500	.581
	Huntsville	AA	109	387	118	20	3	9	171	64	65	67	5	95	4	0	4	16	5	.76	4	.305	.409	.442
1993	Tacoma	AAA	95	341	100	22	6	9	161	70	41	50	3	87	1	2	3	12	4	.75	8	.293	.382	.472
1994	Tacoma	AAA	135	508	160	37	3	17	254	98	73	58	1	108	6	1	5	22	6	.79	14	.315	.388	.500
1993	Oakland	AL	41	102	23	5	0	2	34	11	7	8	0	39	1	0	0	2	0	1.00	2	.225	.288	.333
	5 Min. YEARS		571	2048	597	130	18	55	928	366	305	302	17	505	17	3	19	90	33	.73	39	.292	.384	.453

Dave Lynch

Pitches: Left Bats: Right Pos: P Ht: 6'3" Wt: 205 Born: 10/07/65 Age: 29

			HOW MUCH HE PITCHED						WHAT HE GAVE UP												THE RESULTS					
Year	Team	Lg	G	GS	CG	GF	IP	BFP	H	R	ER	HR	SH	SF	HB	TBB	IBB	SO	WP	Bk	W	L	Pct.	ShO	Sv	ERA
1987	Rangers	R	13	9	1	0	55	221	38	18	14	1	2	2	3	29	0	55	5	4	4	3	.571	1	0	2.29
1988	Rangers	R	1	0	0	0	1.2	5	0	0	0	0	0	0	0	0	0	3	0	0	0	0	.000	0	0	0.00
	Charlotte	A	36	0	0	24	58	242	43	21	13	1	4	1	5	22	1	58	1	2	6	2	.750	0	6	2.02
1989	Okla City	AAA	11	0	0	5	11.2	56	12	8	8	1	0	0	0	8	1	10	3	0	0	2	.000	0	0	6.17
	Tulsa	AA	39	0	0	24	51.2	209	39	7	5	2	0	0	2	24	0	53	3	2	8	0	1.000	0	7	0.87
1990	Okla City	AAA	14	2	0	10	26.2	135	34	24	17	4	4	0	5	14	1	20	1	3	0	4	.000	0	1	5.74
	Tulsa	AA	21	6	0	10	59	242	60	25	25	5	3	1	3	21	1	37	2	1	4	4	.500	0	5	3.81
1991	Albuquerque	AAA	33	0	0	8	36.2	182	51	28	27	2	0	2	0	26	1	29	2	0	1	3	.250	0	6	6.63
	San Antonio	AA	11	0	0	7	13.1	62	17	11	10	2	0	1	0	6	0	10	0	0	0	1	.000	0	1	6.75
1992	Nashville	AAA	1	0	0	0	1.1	4	1	0	0	0	0	0	0	0	0	0	0	0	0	0	.000	0	0	0.00
	Chattanooga	AA	37	0	0	12	51	200	39	19	17	4	1	0	1	15	2	44	5	2	3	1	.750	0	2	3.00
1993	Chattanooga	AA	3	0	0	2	2.1	7	0	0	0	0	0	0	0	0	0	3	0	0	0	0	.000	0	1	0.00
	Indianapols	AAA	59	0	0	27	84	370	73	41	30	3	8	2	2	48	8	76	3	1	9	4	.692	0	1	3.21
1994	Charlotte	AAA	57	0	0	21	57.2	256	62	32	30	5	7	1	3	22	6	50	3	0	2	7	.222	0	4	4.68
	8 Min. YEARS		336	17	1	150	510	2191	469	234	196	30	29	10	24	235	21	448	28	15	37	31	.544	1	28	3.46

Barry Lyons

Bats: Right Throws: Right Pos: C Ht: 6' 1" Wt: 200 Born: 06/03/60 Age: 35

			BATTING															BASERUNNING				PERCENTAGES		
Year	Team	Lg	G	AB	H	2B	3B	HR	TB	R	RBI	TBB	IBB	SO	HBP	SH	SF	SB	CS	SB%	GDP	Avg	OBP	SLG
1984	Lynchburg	A	115	412	130	17	3	12	189	59	87	45	1	40	2	1	7	1	3	.25	11	.316	.380	.459
1985	Jackson	AA	126	486	149	34	6	11	228	69	108	25	2	67	5	0	3	3	0	1.00	19	.307	.345	.469
1986	Tidewater	AAA	61	234	69	16	0	4	97	28	46	18	2	32	1	2	7	0	0	.00	6	.295	.338	.415
1989	Tidewater	AAA	5	20	2	0	1	0	4	1	2	0	0	4	0	0	0	0	0	.00	0	.100	.100	.200
1990	Tidewater	AAA	57	164	28	5	0	0	33	8	17	16	1	25	2	0	1	0	0	.00	3	.171	.251	.201
1992	Tucson	AAA	71	277	83	24	0	4	119	32	45	9	2	35	0	1	3	1	0	1.00	12	.300	.318	.430
1993	Louisville	AAA	107	401	108	19	0	18	181	36	65	15	1	64	2	1	4	0	1	.00	16	.269	.296	.451
1994	Indianapols	AAA	114	431	133	25	1	14	202	63	58	28	3	59	4	0	4	0	2	.00	10	.309	.353	.469
1986	New York	NL	6	9	0	0	0	0	0	1	2	1	1	2	0	0	0	0	0	.00	0	.000	.100	.000
1987	New York	NL	53	130	33	4	1	4	51	15	24	8	1	24	2	0	3	0	0	.00	1	.254	.301	.392
1988	New York	NL	50	91	21	7	1	0	30	5	11	3	0	12	0	3	1	0	0	.00	0	.231	.253	.330
1989	New York	NL	79	235	58	13	0	3	80	15	27	11	1	28	2	1	3	0	1	.00	7	.247	.283	.340
1990	New York	NL	24	80	19	0	0	2	25	8	7	2	0	9	1	0	0	0	0	.00	2	.238	.265	.313
	Los Angeles	NL	3	5	1	0	0	1	4	1	2	0	0	1	0	0	0	0	0	.00	0	.200	.200	.800
1991	Los Angeles	NL	9	9	0	0	0	0	0	0	0	0	0	2	0	0	0	0	0	.00	0	.000	.000	.000
	California	AL	2	5	1	0	0	0	1	0	0	0	0	0	0	0	0	0	0	.00	0	.200	.200	.200
	8 Min. YEARS		656	2425	702	140	11	63	1053	296	436	156	12	326	16	5	29	5	6	.45	78	.289	.333	.434
	6 Maj. YEARS		226	564	133	24	2	10	191	45	73	25	3	78	5	4	7	0	1	.00	13	.236	.271	.339

Kevin Maas

Bats: Left   Throws: Left   Pos: OF   Ht: 6' 3"   Wt: 204   Born: 01/20/65   Age: 30

Year	Team	Lg	G	AB	H	2B	3B	HR	TB	R	RBI	TBB	IBB	SO	HBP	SH	SF	SB	CS	SB%	GDP	Avg	OBP	SLG
1986	Oneonta	A	28	101	36	10	0	0	46	14	18	7	1	9	0	0	1	5	1	.83	1	.356	.394	.455
1987	Ft.Laudrdle	A	116	439	122	28	4	11	191	77	73	53	4	108	2	0	8	14	4	.78	5	.278	.353	.435
1988	Pr William	A	29	108	32	7	0	12	75	24	35	17	1	28	4	0	4	3	1	.75	0	.296	.398	.694
	Albany	AA	109	372	98	14	3	16	166	66	55	64	4	103	4	3	2	5	1	.83	5	.263	.376	.446
1989	Columbus	AAA	83	291	93	23	2	6	138	42	45	40	0	73	1	0	4	2	3	.40	3	.320	.399	.474
1990	Columbus	AAA	57	194	55	15	2	13	113	37	38	34	1	45	0	0	0	2	2	.50	5	.284	.390	.582
1993	Columbus	AAA	28	104	29	6	0	4	47	14	18	19	2	22	1	0	1	0	1	.00	1	.279	.392	.452
1994	Wichita	AA	4	15	8	3	0	3	20	4	8	3	0	0	0	0	0	0	0	.00	0	.533	.611	1.333
	Las Vegas	AAA	29	90	22	6	2	4	44	15	12	9	0	25	1	0	1	1	0	1.00	0	.244	.317	.489
	Indianapols	AAA	78	283	82	18	2	19	161	55	45	29	0	49	2	1	3	2	3	.40	4	.290	.356	.569
1990	New York	AL	79	254	64	9	0	21	136	42	41	43	10	76	3	0	1	1	2	.33	2	.252	.367	.535
1991	New York	AL	148	500	110	14	1	23	195	69	63	83	3	128	4	0	5	5	1	.83	2	.220	.333	.390
1992	New York	AL	98	286	71	12	0	11	116	35	35	25	4	63	0	0	4	3	1	.75	1	.248	.305	.406
1993	New York	AL	59	151	31	4	0	9	62	20	25	24	2	32	1	0	1	1	1	.50	2	.205	.316	.411
	7 Min. YEARS		561	1997	577	130	15	88	1001	348	347	275	13	462	15	4	24	34	16	.68	25	.289	.375	.501
	4 Maj. YEARS		384	1191	276	39	1	64	509	166	164	175	19	299	8	0	10	10	5	.67	9	.232	.332	.427

Bob MacDonald

Pitches: Left   Bats: Left   Pos: P   Ht: 6' 3"   Wt: 208   Born: 04/27/65   Age: 30

Year	Team	Lg	G	GS	CG	GF	IP	BFP	H	R	ER	HR	SH	SF	HB	TBB	IBB	SO	WP	Bk	W	L	Pct.	ShO	Sv	ERA
1987	St.Cathrnes	A	1	1	0	0	4	20	8	4	2	0	0	0	0	0	0	4	0	0	0	0	.000	0	0	4.50
	Medicne Hat	R	13	0	0	9	24.2	109	22	13	8	0	1	0	1	12	1	26	5	0	3	1	.750	0	2	2.92
	Myrtle Bch	A	10	0	0	4	20.2	94	24	18	13	1	2	1	0	7	1	12	2	0	2	1	.667	0	0	5.66
1988	Myrtle Bch	A	52	0	0	48	53.1	222	42	13	10	2	3	1	0	18	3	43	2	0	3	4	.429	0	15	1.69
1989	Knoxville	AA	43	0	0	27	63	264	52	27	23	0	5	0	2	23	2	58	0	1	3	5	.375	0	9	3.29
	Syracuse	AAA	12	0	0	4	16	75	16	10	10	0	3	1	1	6	0	12	0	0	1	0	1.000	0	0	5.63
1990	Knoxville	AA	36	0	0	29	57	237	37	17	12	2	9	1	0	29	4	54	3	0	1	2	.333	0	15	1.89
	Syracuse	AAA	9	0	0	5	8.1	35	4	5	5	1	0	0	0	9	0	6	0	0	0	2	.000	0	2	5.40
1991	Syracuse	AAA	7	0	0	5	6	29	5	3	3	1	0	0	0	5	0	8	3	0	1	0	1.000	0	1	4.50
1992	Syracuse	AAA	17	0	0	11	23.1	104	25	13	12	2	2	0	0	12	1	14	2	0	2	3	.400	0	2	4.63
1994	Calgary	AAA	25	0	0	9	31	144	39	28	26	3	1	3	0	14	1	26	3	0	2	2	.500	0	1	7.55
	Birmingham	AA	23	3	0	8	55.2	208	40	16	11	4	1	1	0	6	0	38	0	1	4	4	.500	0	2	1.78
	Nashville	AAA	2	0	0	0	1.2	5	1	0	0	0	0	0	0	0	0	0	0	0	0	0	.000	0	0	0.00
1990	Toronto	AL	4	0	0	1	2.1	8	0	0	0	0	0	0	0	2	0	1	0	0	0	0	.000	0	0	0.00
1991	Toronto	AL	45	0	0	10	53.2	231	51	19	17	5	2	2	0	25	4	24	1	1	3	3	.500	0	0	2.85
1992	Toronto	AL	27	0	0	9	47.1	204	50	24	23	4	1	1	1	16	3	26	0	0	1	0	1.000	0	0	4.37
1993	Detroit	AL	68	0	0	24	65.2	293	67	42	39	8	4	5	1	33	5	39	1	1	3	3	.500	0	3	5.35
	7 Min. YEARS		250	4	0	159	364.2	1546	315	167	135	16	27	8	4	141	13	301	20	2	22	24	.478	0	49	3.33
	4 Maj. YEARS		144	0	0	44	169	736	168	85	79	17	7	8	2	76	12	89	4	2	7	6	.538	0	3	4.21

Lance Madsen

Bats: Right   Throws: Right   Pos: 3B   Ht: 6'0"   Wt: 185   Born: 10/14/68   Age: 26

Year	Team	Lg	G	AB	H	2B	3B	HR	TB	R	RBI	TBB	IBB	SO	HBP	SH	SF	SB	CS	SB%	GDP	Avg	OBP	SLG
1989	Auburn	A	59	196	52	9	2	9	92	25	33	12	2	60	2	3	1	9	3	.75	4	.265	.313	.469
1990	Osceola	A	135	487	119	23	11	6	182	62	63	59	1	131	6	3	3	7	5	.58	9	.244	.332	.374
1991	Jackson	AA	123	407	90	20	5	7	141	54	50	41	8	122	5	2	3	8	3	.73	6	.221	.298	.346
1992	Jackson	AA	109	332	76	16	2	13	135	40	40	36	1	105	6	5	1	2	6	.25	4	.229	.315	.407
1993	Jackson	AA	116	350	78	19	1	23	168	58	65	43	3	136	4	2	4	2	6	.25	6	.221	.309	.476
1994	Tucson	AAA	41	93	14	3	0	0	17	10	7	14	1	36	2	2	0	2	1	.67	4	.151	.275	.183
	6 Min. YEARS		583	1868	429	90	21	58	735	249	258	205	16	590	25	17	12	30	24	.56	33	.230	.312	.393

Ever Magallanes

Bats: Left   Throws: Right   Pos: SS   Ht: 5'10"   Wt: 165   Born: 11/06/65   Age: 29

Year	Team	Lg	G	AB	H	2B	3B	HR	TB	R	RBI	TBB	IBB	SO	HBP	SH	SF	SB	CS	SB%	GDP	Avg	OBP	SLG
1987	Kinston	A	58	205	50	4	3	2	66	20	23	16	0	18	1	2	0	2	0	1.00	1	.244	.302	.322
1988	Kinston	A	119	396	104	13	3	1	126	67	45	76	3	48	2	3	3	12	6	.67	16	.263	.382	.318
1989	Canton-Akrn	AA	74	241	67	5	0	0	72	26	18	37	0	24	1	4	3	1	6	.14	5	.278	.372	.299
	Colo Spmgs	AAA	12	44	11	1	0	0	15	2	3	4	0	3	0	1	0	1	0	1.00	0	.250	.313	.341
1990	Colo Spmgs	AAA	125	377	116	17	3	1	142	60	63	43	0	49	1	5	6	3	2	.60	13	.308	.375	.377
1991	Colo Spmgs	AAA	94	305	87	13	1	1	105	37	33	23	1	36	2	1	1	1	2	.33	9	.285	.338	.344
1992	Vancouver	AAA	93	243	56	9	3	3	80	32	23	29	1	24	1	4	3	2	1	.67	3	.230	.312	.329
1993	Okla City	AAA	33	116	36	6	1	0	44	16	18	10	2	17	1	2	0	0	3	.00	4	.310	.370	.379
	Tulsa	AA	55	184	60	12	2	1	79	20	14	16	1	22	1	1	1	0	4	.00	2	.326	.381	.429
1994	Tulsa	AA	115	396	97	24	1	4	135	49	41	38	1	45	1	10	1	5	8	.38	7	.245	.312	.341
	Okla City	AAA	3	8	4	0	0	0	5	0	2	0	0	0	0	0	0	0	0	.00	0	.500	.500	.625

155

	Lg	G	AB	H	2B	3B	HR	TB	R	RBI	TBB	IBB	SO	HBP	SH	SF	SB	CS	SB%	GDP	Avg	OBP	SLG
1991 Cleveland	AL	3	2	0	0	0	0	0	0	0	1	0	1	0	0	0	0	0	.00	0	.000	.333	.000
8 Min. YEARS		781	2515	688	105	17	14	869	329	283	292	9	288	11	33	18	27	32	.46	68	.274	.349	.346

Dan Magee

Pitches: Left **Bats:** Right **Pos:** P   Ht: 6'4" Wt: 180 Born: 04/09/68 Age: 27

		HOW MUCH HE PITCHED						WHAT HE GAVE UP											THE RESULTS					
Year Team	Lg	G	GS	CG	GF	IP	BFP	H	R	ER	HR	SH	SF	HB	TBB	IBB	SO	WP	Bk	W	L	Pct.	ShO	Sv	ERA
1991 Butte	R	14	14	0	0	69.1	330	76	45	37	3	0	2	3	57	2	51	6	6	2	7	.222	0	0	4.80
1992 Gastonia	A	27	24	1	0	151	637	113	49	38	6	7	3	2	82	2	109	13	3	7	9	.438	1	0	2.26
1993 Charlotte	A	30	14	0	4	89	386	76	44	41	3	5	6	0	51	0	64	6	4	6	3	.667	0	0	4.15
1994 Kinston	A	28	0	0	13	44.1	200	35	31	25	5	0	3	0	29	0	51	4	0	0	1	.000	0	0	5.08
Canton-Akm	AA	14	1	0	10	26.2	114	21	13	10	3	1	1	1	11	0	20	3	0	1	1	.500	0	2	3.38
4 Min. YEARS		113	53	1	27	380.1	1667	321	182	151	20	13	15	6	230	4	295	32	13	16	21	.432	1	4	3.57

Brett Magnusson

Bats: Right **Throws:** Right **Pos:** OF   Ht: 5'10" Wt: 210 Born: 08/20/67 Age: 27

		BATTING															BASERUNNING				PERCENTAGES		
Year Team	Lg	G	AB	H	2B	3B	HR	TB	R	RBI	TBB	IBB	SO	HBP	SH	SF	SB	CS	SB%	GDP	Avg	OBP	SLG
1988 Great Falls	R	51	175	56	18	4	7	103	51	46	44	0	43	3	0	4	4	4	.50	4	.320	.456	.589
1989 Vero Beach	A	120	354	86	16	1	8	128	47	48	68	3	68	4	2	3	5	2	.71	10	.243	.337	.362
1990 Bakersfield	A	121	434	135	34	2	23	242	92	85	73	5	104	10	1	1	5	4	.56	8	.311	.421	.558
1991 San Antonio	AA	110	358	95	22	2	11	154	69	66	67	1	69	4	2	4	5	5	.50	8	.265	.383	.430
1992 Albuquerque	AAA	1	0	0	0	0	0	0	1	0	0	0	0	0	0	0	0	0	.00	0	.000	.000	.000
1993 San Antonio	AA	13	9	1	1	0	0	2	1	0	4	0	3	0	1	0	0	0	.00	1	.111	.385	.222
1994 San Antonio	AA	2	1	0	0	0	0	0	0	0	0	0	0	0	0	0	0	0	.00	0	.000	.000	.000
7 Min. YEARS		418	1331	373	91	9	49	629	261	245	236	9	287	21	6	12	19	15	.56	31	.280	.394	.473

Scott Makarewicz

Bats: Right **Throws:** Right **Pos:** C   Ht: 6'0" Wt: 200 Born: 03/01/67 Age: 28

		BATTING															BASERUNNING				PERCENTAGES		
Year Team	Lg	G	AB	H	2B	3B	HR	TB	R	RBI	TBB	IBB	SO	HBP	SH	SF	SB	CS	SB%	GDP	Avg	OBP	SLG
1989 Auburn	A	61	216	52	17	0	4	81	22	24	14	0	43	4	5	1	2	0	1.00	1	.241	.298	.375
1990 Osceola	A	94	343	95	12	2	4	123	35	49	21	0	63	4	8	3	0	1	.00	11	.277	.323	.359
Columbus	AA	28	85	20	1	0	2	27	5	11	10	2	14	1	0	2	0	1	.00	3	.235	.316	.318
1991 Jackson	AA	76	229	53	9	0	2	68	23	30	18	5	36	8	0	3	1	4	.20	7	.231	.306	.297
1992 Jackson	AA	105	345	99	15	0	7	135	39	39	23	3	62	6	3	5	2	2	.50	6	.287	.338	.391
1993 Jackson	AA	92	285	70	14	1	7	107	31	35	17	2	51	8	1	3	1	1	.50	7	.246	.304	.375
1994 Tucson	AAA	63	171	49	10	1	3	70	24	32	13	0	28	4	6	1	0	0	.00	5	.287	.349	.409
6 Min. YEARS		519	1674	438	78	4	29	611	179	220	116	12	297	35	23	18	6	9	.40	40	.262	.320	.365

Jose Malave

Bats: Right **Throws:** Right **Pos:** OF   Ht: 6'2" Wt: 195 Born: 05/31/71 Age: 24

		BATTING															BASERUNNING				PERCENTAGES		
Year Team	Lg	G	AB	H	2B	3B	HR	TB	R	RBI	TBB	IBB	SO	HBP	SH	SF	SB	CS	SB%	GDP	Avg	OBP	SLG
1990 Elmira	A	13	29	4	1	0	0	5	4	3	2	0	12	0	0	1	1	0	1.00	0	.138	.188	.172
1991 Red Sox	R	37	146	47	4	2	2	61	24	28	10	0	23	1	0	3	6	0	1.00	3	.322	.363	.418
1992 Winter Havn	A	8	25	4	0	0	0	4	1	0	0	0	11	0	1	0	0	0	.00	0	.160	.160	.160
Elmira	A	65	268	87	9	1	12	134	44	46	14	3	48	3	0	1	8	3	.73	0	.325	.364	.500
1993 Lynchburg	A	82	312	94	27	1	8	147	42	54	36	3	54	3	0	5	2	3	.40	8	.301	.374	.471
1994 New Britain	AA	122	465	139	37	7	24	262	87	92	52	1	81	4	0	7	4	7	.36	12	.299	.369	.563
5 Min. YEARS		327	1245	375	78	11	46	613	202	223	114	7	229	11	1	17	21	13	.62	25	.301	.360	.492

Carlos Maldonado

Pitches: Right **Bats:** Right **Pos:** P   Ht: 6'2" Wt: 215 Born: 10/18/66 Age: 28

		HOW MUCH HE PITCHED						WHAT HE GAVE UP											THE RESULTS					
Year Team	Lg	G	GS	CG	GF	IP	BFP	H	R	ER	HR	SH	SF	HB	TBB	IBB	SO	WP	Bk	W	L	Pct.	ShO	Sv	ERA
1986 Royals	R	10	4	0	2	34.1	136	29	10	7	1	1	1	1	10	1	16	3	0	0	2	.000	0	1	1.83
1987 Appleton	A	2	0	0	0	2.1	13	4	3	3	0	0	1	0	3	0	4	1	0	0	0	.000	0	0	11.57
Royals	R	20	0	0	8	58	223	32	18	16	2	2	0	2	19	2	56	2	1	5	1	.833	0	4	2.48
1988 Baseball Cy	A	16	7	0	2	52.2	242	46	35	31	5	2	1	7	39	0	44	3	0	1	5	.167	0	0	5.30
1989 Baseball Cy	A	28	0	0	19	76.2	300	47	14	10	3	3	1	1	24	4	66	2	0	11	3	.786	0	9	1.17
1990 Memphis	AA	55	0	0	48	77.1	325	61	29	25	5	3	4	1	39	0	77	5	0	4	5	.444	0	20	2.91
1991 Omaha	AAA	41	1	0	31	61	282	67	31	29	6	3	2	2	42	1	46	6	0	1	1	.500	0	9	4.28
1992 Omaha	AAA	47	0	0	36	75	315	61	34	30	6	9	6	2	35	0	60	1	1	7	4	.636	0	16	3.60
1993 New Orleans	AAA	12	0	0	9	19.1	77	13	1	1	0	1	1	0	7	1	14	0	0	1	0	1.000	0	7	0.47
1994 Tacoma	AAA	25	0	0	10	39	186	57	31	29	9	0	0	2	16	1	24	4	0	3	2	.600	0	0	6.69
1990 Kansas City	AL	4	0	0	2	6	31	9	6	6	0	0	0	0	4	0	9	1	0	0	0	.000	0	0	9.00
1991 Kansas City	AL	5	0	0	2	7.2	43	11	9	7	0	1	0	0	9	1	1	4	0	0	0	.000	0	0	8.22
1993 Milwaukee	AL	29	0	0	2	37.1	167	40	20	19	2	4	4	0	17	5	18	1	0	2	2	.500	0	1	4.58
9 Min. YEARS		256	12	0	166	495.2	2099	417	206	181	37	24	17	18	234	10	407	27	2	33	23	.589	0	67	3.29
3 Maj. YEARS		38	0	0	12	51	241	60	35	32	2	5	5	0	30	6	28	6	0	2	2	.500	0	1	5.65

Chris Malinoski

Bats: Right Throws: Right Pos: SS Ht: 5'9" Wt: 185 Born: 04/07/68 Age: 27

Year	Team	Lg	G	AB	H	2B	3B	HR	TB	R	RBI	TBB	IBB	SO	HBP	SH	SF	SB	CS	SB%	GDP	Avg	OBP	SLG
1990	Expos	R	26	78	23	2	1	0	27	16	14	8	0	12	5	1	2	3	3	.50	1	.295	.387	.346
	Rockford	A	21	66	17	2	2	0	23	4	7	5	0	8	0	0	1	2	2	.50	1	.258	.306	.348
1991	Rockford	A	130	455	120	20	0	0	140	71	55	87	1	80	12	7	6	4	6	.40	16	.264	.391	.308
1992	Wst Plm Bch	A	66	228	63	9	0	0	72	31	30	22	0	39	3	2	7	3	2	.60	7	.276	.338	.316
	Harrisburg	AA	32	88	19	1	0	0	20	9	10	15	0	21	4	1	2	2	0	1.00	2	.216	.349	.227
1993	High Desert	A	111	368	112	24	3	3	151	62	72	81	2	54	12	1	6	7	7	.50	14	.304	.439	.410
1994	Portland	AA	87	225	52	8	0	3	69	23	16	31	0	37	4	3	0	1	3	.25	7	.231	.335	.307
	5 Min. YEARS		473	1508	406	66	6	6	502	216	204	249	3	251	40	15	24	22	23	.49	48	.269	.382	.333

John Malzone

Bats: Left Throws: Right Pos: 3B Ht: 5'10" Wt: 170 Born: 10/29/67 Age: 27

Year	Team	Lg	G	AB	H	2B	3B	HR	TB	R	RBI	TBB	IBB	SO	HBP	SH	SF	SB	CS	SB%	GDP	Avg	OBP	SLG
1990	Lynchburg	A	65	187	48	4	1	2	60	18	15	27	0	63	1	1	0	3	1	.75	2	.257	.353	.321
1991	Winter Havn	A	103	266	66	11	2	1	84	40	28	60	4	58	4	3	4	2	5	.29	11	.248	.389	.316
1992	Lynchburg	A	117	386	118	24	6	4	166	49	52	29	0	53	2	2	2	1	2	.33	16	.306	.356	.430
1993	Pawtucket	AAA	75	207	49	7	0	2	62	14	15	12	0	24	1	0	0	2	1	.67	12	.237	.282	.300
1994	New Britain	AA	60	181	39	5	2	1	51	22	11	21	1	26	1	1	0	2	1	.67	7	.215	.300	.282
	5 Min. YEARS		420	1227	320	51	11	10	423	143	121	149	5	224	9	7	6	10	10	.50	48	.261	.344	.345

Austin Manahan

Bats: Both Throws: Right Pos: 2B Ht: 6'1" Wt: 185 Born: 04/12/70 Age: 25

Year	Team	Lg	G	AB	H	2B	3B	HR	TB	R	RBI	TBB	IBB	SO	HBP	SH	SF	SB	CS	SB%	GDP	Avg	OBP	SLG
1988	Princeton	R	64	227	41	4	4	6	71	31	33	24	0	102	1	0	2	12	4	.75	1	.181	.260	.313
1989	Princeton	R	19	73	17	5	0	1	25	8	8	6	1	24	0	0	1	1	1	.50	0	.233	.288	.342
	Welland	A	50	178	38	3	4	3	58	18	16	17	0	51	1	0	1	12	1	.92	3	.213	.284	.326
1990	Augusta	A	94	378	114	12	10	7	167	59	52	46	2	105	4	2	4	26	14	.65	4	.302	.380	.442
	Salem	A	41	154	43	6	2	4	65	22	24	11	0	51	1	1	1	8	1	.89	1	.279	.329	.422
1991	Salem	A	113	369	78	14	1	9	121	53	35	47	0	127	3	1	2	16	10	.62	1	.211	.304	.328
1992	Carolina	AA	107	340	75	18	6	5	120	44	33	29	1	101	4	1	0	7	6	.54	5	.221	.290	.353
1993	Wst Plm Bch	A	77	274	65	14	2	4	95	34	29	26	0	78	0	1	2	7	3	.70	4	.237	.301	.347
	Rancho Cuca	A	43	145	42	8	4	2	64	17	22	11	0	38	1	1	2	7	2	.78	3	.290	.340	.441
1994	Rancho Cuca	A	11	27	8	1	0	0	9	9	3	3	0	10	0	0	0	2	1	.67	0	.296	.367	.333
	Orlando	AA	55	128	37	7	2	2	54	11	10	6	0	37	0	1	1	2	2	.50	3	.289	.319	.422
	7 Min. YEARS		674	2293	558	92	35	43	849	306	265	226	4	724	15	8	16	100	45	.69	25	.243	.313	.370

Tony Manahan

Bats: Right Throws: Right Pos: SS Ht: 6'0" Wt: 190 Born: 12/15/68 Age: 26

Year	Team	Lg	G	AB	H	2B	3B	HR	TB	R	RBI	TBB	IBB	SO	HBP	SH	SF	SB	CS	SB%	GDP	Avg	OBP	SLG
1990	San Berndno	A	51	198	63	10	2	7	98	46	30	24	0	34	2	1	3	8	1	.89	4	.318	.392	.495
1991	Jacksnville	AA	113	410	104	23	2	7	152	67	45	54	0	81	6	2	3	11	5	.69	8	.254	.347	.371
1992	Jacksnville	AA	134	505	130	24	6	8	190	70	49	39	1	76	2	3	3	24	11	.69	12	.257	.311	.376
1993	Calgary	AAA	117	451	136	31	4	3	184	70	62	38	0	48	2	3	3	19	4	.83	12	.302	.356	.408
1994	Calgary	AAA	78	295	84	21	1	4	119	48	36	24	0	22	3	1	2	7	2	.78	5	.285	.343	.403
	5 Min. YEARS		493	1859	517	109	15	29	743	301	222	179	1	261	15	10	14	69	23	.75	41	.278	.344	.400

Dwight Maness

Bats: Right Throws: Right Pos: OF Ht: 6'3" Wt: 180 Born: 04/03/74 Age: 21

Year	Team	Lg	G	AB	H	2B	3B	HR	TB	R	RBI	TBB	IBB	SO	HBP	SH	SF	SB	CS	SB%	GDP	Avg	OBP	SLG
1992	Dodgers	R	44	139	35	6	3	0	47	24	12	14	0	36	8	3	3	18	9	.67	1	.252	.348	.338
1993	Vero Beach	A	118	409	106	21	4	6	153	57	42	32	0	105	15	8	7	22	13	.63	3	.259	.330	.374
1994	San Antonio	AA	57	215	47	9	5	5	77	32	20	25	0	54	6	2	0	15	16	.48	1	.219	.317	.358
	Bakersfield	A	74	248	62	13	1	3	86	38	26	29	3	67	11	5	5	21	9	.70	1	.250	.348	.347
	3 Min. YEARS		293	1011	250	45	13	14	363	151	100	100	3	262	40	18	15	76	47	.62	6	.247	.334	.359

Henry Manning

Bats: Right Throws: Right Pos: C Ht: 5'11" Wt: 185 Born: 07/03/68 Age: 26

Year	Team	Lg	G	AB	H	2B	3B	HR	TB	R	RBI	TBB	IBB	SO	HBP	SH	SF	SB	CS	SB%	GDP	Avg	OBP	SLG
1991	South Bend	A	23	67	19	3	0	0	22	5	10	1	0	4	2	2	0	0	2	.00	2	.284	.314	.328
	Sarasota	A	13	24	2	0	0	0	2	2	2	0	0	6	2	0	0	0	0	.00	0	.083	.154	.083
	Erie	A	12	44	7	1	0	0	8	3	8	2	0	7	0	0	2	0	0	.00	1	.159	.188	.182
1992	South Bend	A	66	213	60	9	0	1	72	26	30	14	1	22	5	0	1	4	2	.67	3	.282	.339	.338
1993	Birmingham	AA	30	106	19	3	1	2	30	7	9	3	0	25	3	0	0	0	1	.00	3	.179	.223	.283
	Sarasota	A	27	79	18	3	0	0	21	8	4	7	0	12	2	0	0	0	0	.00	1	.228	.307	.266
1994	Pr. William	A	31	105	27	5	0	2	38	10	10	1	0	22	2	0	0	0	0	.00	2	.257	.278	.362

Nashville	AAA	21	46	13	0	0	1	16	5	9	1	0	4	2	3	1	0	0	.00	1	.283	.320	.348
4 Min. YEARS		223	684	165	24	1	6	209	66	80	29	1	102	18	9	4	4	5	.44	13	.241	.288	.306

Jeff Mansur

Pitches: Left Bats: Left Pos: P Ht: 5'11" Wt: 185 Born: 08/02/70 Age: 24

		HOW MUCH HE PITCHED						WHAT HE GAVE UP										THE RESULTS					
Year Team	Lg	G	GS	CG	GF	IP	BFP	H	R	ER	HR	SH	SF	HB	TBB	IBB	SO	WP	Bk	W	L	Pct.	ShO	Sv	ERA
1992 Kenosha	A	11	10	1	0	65.1	266	69	27	21	6	3	2	1	8	1	46	1	2	6	3	.667	0	0	2.89
Visalia	A	17	16	0	0	100.2	448	130	67	46	11	7	4	1	25	3	61	6	1	5	7	.417	0	0	4.11
1993 Nashville	AA	33	19	4	4	158.2	677	180	82	75	22	6	5	0	38	3	89	5	1	10	8	.556	0	0	4.25
1994 Nashville	AA	34	11	0	6	93.2	426	115	58	50	10	0	4	5	36	1	52	7	0	1	9	.100	0	1	4.80
3 Min. YEARS		95	56	5	10	418.1	1817	494	234	192	49	16	15	7	107	8	248	19	4	22	27	.449	0	1	4.13

Jeff Manto

Bats: Right Throws: Right Pos: 3B Ht: 6' 3" Wt: 210 Born: 08/23/64 Age: 30

		BATTING														BASERUNNING				PERCENTAGES		
Year Team	Lg	G	AB	H	2B	3B	HR	TB	R	RBI	TBB	IBB	SO	HBP	SH	SF	SB	CS	SB%	GDP	Avg	OBP	SLG
1985 Quad City	A	74	233	46	5	2	11	88	34	34	40	0	74	5	1	3	3	1	.75	7	.197	.324	.378
1986 Quad City	A	73	239	59	13	0	8	96	31	49	37	0	70	4	1	2	2	1	.67	2	.247	.355	.402
1987 Palm Sprngs	A	112	375	96	21	4	7	146	61	63	102	1	85	8	5	5	8	2	.80	7	.256	.419	.389
1988 Midland	AA	120	408	123	23	3	24	224	88	101	62	5	76	8	3	4	7	5	.58	17	.301	.400	.549
1989 Edmonton	AAA	127	408	113	25	3	23	213	89	67	91	5	81	9	3	4	4	4	.50	12	.277	.416	.522
1990 Colo Sprngs	AAA	96	316	94	27	1	18	177	73	82	78	2	65	9	1	3	10	3	.77	9	.297	.446	.560
1991 Colo Sprngs	AAA	43	153	49	16	0	6	83	36	36	33	2	24	3	0	3	1	0	1.00	3	.320	.443	.542
1992 Richmond	AAA	127	450	131	24	1	13	196	65	68	57	4	63	7	0	7	1	2	.33	8	.291	.374	.436
1993 Scranton/wb	AAA	106	388	112	30	1	17	195	62	88	55	3	58	5	0	6	4	1	.80	9	.289	.379	.503
1994 Norfolk	AAA	37	115	30	6	0	4	48	20	17	27	0	28	3	0	1	1	0	1.00	1	.261	.414	.417
Rochester	AAA	94	329	102	25	2	27	212	61	83	43	1	47	8	0	2	2	2	.50	19	.310	.401	.644
1990 Cleveland	AL	30	76	17	5	1	2	30	12	14	21	1	18	0	0	0	0	1	.00	0	.224	.392	.395
1991 Cleveland	AL	47	128	27	7	0	2	40	15	13	14	0	22	4	1	1	2	0	1.00	3	.211	.306	.313
1993 Philadelphia	NL	8	18	1	0	0	0	1	0	0	0	0	3	1	0	0	0	0	.00	0	.056	.105	.056
10 Min. YEARS		1009	3414	955	215	17	158	1678	620	688	625	23	671	69	14	41	43	21	.67	94	.280	.397	.492
3 Maj. YEARS		85	222	45	12	1	4	71	27	27	35	1	43	5	1	1	2	1	.67	3	.203	.323	.320

Barry Manuel

Pitches: Right Bats: Right Pos: P Ht: 5'11" Wt: 185 Born: 08/12/65 Age: 29

		HOW MUCH HE PITCHED						WHAT HE GAVE UP										THE RESULTS					
Year Team	Lg	G	GS	CG	GF	IP	BFP	H	R	ER	HR	SH	SF	HB	TBB	IBB	SO	WP	Bk	W	L	Pct.	ShO	Sv	ERA
1987 Rangers	R	1	0	0	0	1	7	3	2	2	0	0	0	0	1	0	1	2	0	0	0	.000	0	0	18.00
Charlotte	A	13	5	0	3	30	138	32	24	22	2	1	2	3	18	0	19	4	0	1	2	.333	0	0	6.60
1988 Charlotte	A	37	0	0	22	60.1	259	47	24	17	4	6	1	4	32	0	55	8	3	4	3	.571	0	4	2.54
1989 Tulsa	AA	11	11	0	0	49.1	237	49	44	41	5	3	6	9	39	0	40	3	3	3	4	.429	0	0	7.48
Charlotte	A	15	14	0	0	76.1	330	77	43	40	6	4	3	8	30	0	51	6	1	4	7	.364	0	0	4.72
1990 Charlotte	A	57	0	0	56	56.1	238	39	23	18	2	4	2	2	30	2	60	1	0	1	5	.167	0	36	2.88
1991 Tulsa	AA	56	0	0	48	68.1	300	63	29	25	5	4	2	5	34	1	45	0	1	2	7	.222	0	25	3.29
1992 Okla City	AAA	27	0	0	22	27.1	143	32	24	16	1	1	2	2	26	0	11	1	0	1	8	.111	0	5	5.27
Tulsa	AA	16	1	0	8	27	122	28	12	12	4	0	0	1	16	0	28	0	0	2	0	1.000	0	2	4.00
1993 Charlotte	A	3	0	0	1	4.2	20	6	0	0	0	0	0	0	2	0	4	0	0	0	0	.000	0	0	0.00
Okla City	AAA	21	0	0	10	23.2	109	29	21	21	1	0	1	0	16	1	19	3	0	2	2	.500	0	2	7.99
Rochester	AAA	9	0	0	2	19.2	77	14	8	8	2	1	1	1	7	0	11	0	0	1	1	.500	0	0	3.66
1994 Rochester	AAA	35	20	1	10	139.2	629	161	87	85	21	2	7	3	58	2	107	7	1	11	8	.579	0	4	5.48
1991 Texas	AL	8	0	0	5	16	58	7	2	2	0	0	3	0	6	0	5	2	0	1	0	1.000	0	0	1.13
1992 Texas	AL	3	0	0	0	5.2	25	6	3	3	2	0	0	1	1	0	9	0	0	1	0	1.000	0	0	4.76
8 Min. YEARS		301	51	1	182	583.2	2609	581	341	307	53	26	27	39	309	6	451	35	9	32	47	.405	0	78	4.73
2 Maj. YEARS		11	0	0	5	21.2	83	13	5	5	2	0	3	1	7	0	14	2	0	2	0	1.000	0	0	2.08

Marc Marini

Bats: Left Throws: Left Pos: OF Ht: 6'1" Wt: 185 Born: 03/17/70 Age: 25

		BATTING														BASERUNNING				PERCENTAGES		
Year Team	Lg	G	AB	H	2B	3B	HR	TB	R	RBI	TBB	IBB	SO	HBP	SH	SF	SB	CS	SB%	GDP	Avg	OBP	SLG
1992 Columbus	A	132	488	150	30	5	8	214	78	70	86	5	63	4	1	9	7	3	.70	10	.307	.409	.439
1993 Kinston	A	124	440	132	34	4	5	189	65	53	63	4	70	3	6	9	7	6	.54	9	.300	.384	.430
1994 Canton-Akrn	AA	91	331	91	21	2	17	167	58	65	50	3	62	0	2	3	2	4	.33	9	.275	.367	.505
3 Min. YEARS		347	1259	373	85	11	30	570	201	188	199	12	195	7	9	21	16	13	.55	28	.296	.390	.453

Isidro Marquez

Pitches: Right Bats: Right Pos: P Ht: 6'3" Wt: 190 Born: 05/15/65 Age: 30

		HOW MUCH HE PITCHED						WHAT HE GAVE UP										THE RESULTS					
Year Team	Lg	G	GS	CG	GF	IP	BFP	H	R	ER	HR	SH	SF	HB	TBB	IBB	SO	WP	Bk	W	L	Pct.	ShO	Sv	ERA
1988 Bakersfield	A	20	20	1	0	125.1	546	114	54	43	7	7	2	9	77	1	106	5	1	8	3	.727	1	0	3.09
1989 San Antonio	AA	39	0	0	21	62.1	273	61	33	30	2	4	3	2	34	6	52	6	1	1	4	.200	0	4	4.33
Bakersfield	A	17	0	0	16	36	140	21	5	3	0	2	0	2	11	0	44	2	0	6	0	1.000	0	8	0.75

1990 San Antonio	AA	13	0	0	7	16.2	75	20	10	9	0	1	0	0	8	0	15	1	0	3	1	.750	0	0	4.86
1991 San Antonio	AA	34	0	0	22	47.1	199	42	16	11	1	1	0	1	19	8	36	1	0	4	1	.800	0	3	2.09
Albuquerque	AAA	1	0	0	1	1	5	1	0	0	0	0	0	0	1	0	1	0	0	0	0	.000	0	0	0.00
1993 San Antonio	AA	30	0	0	29	31.2	136	34	13	.10	1	2	0	1	8	3	25	1	0	1	4	.200	0	12	2.84
Albuquerque	AAA	9	0	0	3	12	42	7	2	2	0	2	1	0	3	0	10	2	0	1	0	1.000	0	2	1.50
1994 Nashville	AAA	39	0	0	24	63.2	268	48	32	20	4	4	0	3	27	6	63	1	0	3	3	.500	0	11	2.83
6 Min. YEARS		202	20	1	123	396	1684	348	165	128	15	21	8	18	188	24	352	19	2	27	16	.628	1	40	2.91

Oreste Marrero

Bats: Left Throws: Left Pos: 1B Ht: 6' 0" Wt: 195 Born: 10/31/69 Age: 25

								BATTING										BASERUNNING				PERCENTAGES		
Year Team	Lg	G	AB	H	2B	3B	HR	TB	R	RBI	TBB	IBB	SO	HBP	SH	SF	SB	CS	SB%	GDP	Avg	OBP	SLG
1987 Helena	R	51	154	50	8	2	7	83	30	34	18	3	31	1	1	0	2	1	.67	1	.325	.399	.539
1988 Beloit	A	19	52	9	2	0	1	14	5	7	3	0	16	0	0	0	0	1	.00	1	.173	.218	.269
Helena	R	67	240	85	15	0	16	148	52	44	42	2	48	0	1	1	3	4	.43	4	.354	.449	.617
1989 Beloit	A	14	40	5	1	0	0	6	1	3	3	0	20	0	0	1	1	0	1.00	0	.125	.182	.150
Brewers	R	10	44	18	0	1	3	29	13	16	2	0	5	0	0	0	2	2	.50	0	.409	.426	.659
Boise	A	54	203	56	8	1	11	99	38	43	30	3	60	0	0	4	1	2	.33	3	.276	.363	.488
1990 Beloit	A	119	400	110	25	1	16	185	59	55	45	3	107	0	0	1	8	4	.67	12	.275	.348	.463
1991 Stockton	A	123	438	110	15	2	13	168	63	61	57	8	98	0	1	7	4	5	.44	5	.251	.333	.384
1992 El Paso	AA	18	54	10	2	1	1	17	8	8	4	0	13	0	0	1	1	0	1.00	0	.185	.237	.315
Stockton	A	76	243	67	17	0	7	105	35	51	44	6	49	1	1	1	3	2	.60	0	.276	.388	.432
1993 Harrisburg	AA	85	255	85	18	1	10	135	39	49	22	2	46	0	3	4	3	3	.50	2	.333	.381	.529
1994 Ottawa	AAA	88	254	62	14	7	7	111	41	31	29	1	56	0	1	2	1	1	.50	5	.244	.319	.437
1993 Montreal	NL	32	81	17	5	1	1	27	10	4	14	0	16	0	0	0	1	3	.25	0	.210	.326	.333
8 Min. YEARS		724	2377	667	125	16	92	1100	384	402	299	28	549	2	8	23	29	25	.54	32	.281	.358	.463

Randy Marshall

Pitches: Left Bats: Left Pos: P Ht: 6'3" Wt: 170 Born: 10/12/66 Age: 28

		HOW MUCH HE PITCHED						WHAT HE GAVE UP												THE RESULTS					
Year Team	Lg	G	GS	CG	GF	IP	BFP	H	R	ER	HR	SH	SF	HB	TBB	IBB	SO	WP	Bk	W	L	Pct.	ShO	Sv	ERA
1989 Niagara Fls	A	6	0	0	2	12.2	57	18	11	11	3	1	0	0	3	0	14	0	2	0	2	.000	0	0	7.82
Fayetteville	A	34	3	0	7	64.1	276	62	32	23	3	2	1	0	21	3	61	3	0	5	3	.625	0	0	3.22
1990 Fayetteville	A	14	14	5	0	101.2	377	64	17	15	3	2	1	0	9	1	81	0	0	13	0	1.000	3	0	1.33
Lakeland	A	13	13	2	0	72	293	71	29	24	3	2	3	1	14	1	40	3	0	7	2	.778	2	0	3.00
1991 London	AA	27	27	4	0	159	672	186	92	79	13	4	5	2	27	0	105	4	2	8	10	.444	1	0	4.47
Toledo	AAA	1	1	0	0	5	22	5	6	5	1	0	1	0	2	0	2	0	0	1	0	1.000	0	0	9.00
1992 Tidewater	AAA	26	25	3	0	151.2	641	170	75	68	15	8	6	3	31	0	87	0	0	7	13	.350	1	0	4.04
1993 Norfolk	AAA	4	1	0	1	7.1	47	19	18	16	2	0	0	0	4	1	3	1	0	0	2	.000	0	0	19.64
Binghamton	AA	7	7	0	0	35	173	61	39	33	3	1	2	0	8	0	21	1	0	0	3	.000	0	0	8.49
Colo Sprngs	AAA	11	1	0	5	21	101	35	20	9	2	0	1	0	6	0	12	2	1	1	0	1.000	0	1	3.86
1994 Colo. Spmg	AAA	50	0	0	12	40.2	177	48	25	24	7	2	0	0	14	2	27	5	0	4	0	1.000	0	2	5.31
6 Min. YEARS		193	92	14	27	670.1	2836	739	364	307	55	22	20	6	139	8	453	19	5	46	35	.568	7	3	4.12

Chris Martin

Bats: Right Throws: Right Pos: SS Ht: 6'1" Wt: 170 Born: 01/25/68 Age: 27

								BATTING										BASERUNNING				PERCENTAGES		
Year Team	Lg	G	AB	H	2B	3B	HR	TB	R	RBI	TBB	IBB	SO	HBP	SH	SF	SB	CS	SB%	GDP	Avg	OBP	SLG
1990 Wst Plm Bch	A	59	222	62	17	1	3	90	31	31	27	6	37	1	1	2	7	5	.58	4	.279	.357	.405
1991 Harrisburg	AA	87	294	66	10	0	6	94	30	36	22	0	61	4	2	5	1	4	.20	8	.224	.283	.320
1992 Harrisburg	AA	125	383	87	22	1	5	126	39	31	49	1	67	2	1	3	8	6	.57	15	.227	.316	.329
1993 Harrisburg	AA	116	395	116	23	1	7	162	68	54	40	2	48	6	7	3	16	6	.73	13	.294	.365	.410
1994 Ottawa	AAA	113	374	89	24	0	3	122	44	40	35	0	46	2	7	5	5	4	.56	17	.238	.303	.326
5 Min. YEARS		500	1668	420	96	3	24	594	212	192	173	9	259	15	18	18	37	25	.60	57	.252	.324	.356

Jim Martin

Bats: Left Throws: Right Pos: OF Ht: 6'1" Wt: 195 Born: 12/10/70 Age: 24

								BATTING										BASERUNNING				PERCENTAGES		
Year Team	Lg	G	AB	H	2B	3B	HR	TB	R	RBI	TBB	IBB	SO	HBP	SH	SF	SB	CS	SB%	GDP	Avg	OBP	SLG
1992 Great Falls	R	56	204	63	5	7	5	97	37	30	28	2	52	7	0	3	8	2	.80	0	.309	.405	.475
1993 Bakersfield	A	118	441	114	17	3	12	173	60	50	45	2	131	13	0	4	27	12	.69	3	.259	.342	.392
1994 Bakersfield	A	93	360	96	15	8	12	163	50	58	36	3	90	7	0	2	37	16	.70	3	.267	.343	.453
San Antonio	AA	29	101	22	8	0	1	33	7	10	8	0	23	0	0	0	3	5	.38	1	.218	.275	.327
3 Min. YEARS		296	1106	295	45	18	30	466	154	148	117	7	296	27	0	9	75	35	.68	7	.267	.349	.421

Thomas Martin

Pitches: Left Bats: Left Pos: P Ht: 6'1" Wt: 185 Born: 05/21/70 Age: 25

		HOW MUCH HE PITCHED						WHAT HE GAVE UP												THE RESULTS					
Year Team	Lg	G	GS	CG	GF	IP	BFP	H	R	ER	HR	SH	SF	HB	TBB	IBB	SO	WP	Bk	W	L	Pct.	ShO	Sv	ERA
1989 Bluefield	R	8	8	0	0	39	176	36	28	20	3	1	1	0	25	0	31	2	1	3	3	.500	0	0	4.62
Erie	A	7	7	0	0	40.2	190	42	39	30	2	0	2	1	25	0	44	11	2	0	5	.000	0	0	6.64
1990 Wausau	A	9	9	0	0	40	183	31	25	11	1	3	0	5	27	0	45	4	0	2	3	.400	0	0	2.47
1991 Kane County	A	38	10	0	19	99	442	92	50	40	4	6	4	3	56	3	106	13	0	4	10	.286	0	6	3.64

159

Year	Team	Lg	G	GS	CG	GF	IP	BFP	H	R	ER	HR	SH	SF	HB	TBB	IBB	SO	WP	Bk	W	L	Pct.	ShO	Sv	ERA
1992	High Desert	A	11	0	0	8	16.1	85	23	19	17	4	0	0	0	16	0	10	2	0	0	2	.000	0	0	9.37
	Waterloo	A	39	2	0	11	55	248	62	38	26	3	5	1	4	22	4	57	5	0	2	6	.250	0	3	4.25
1993	Rancho Cuca	A	47	1	0	16	59.1	290	72	41	37	4	1	7	7	39	2	53	9	0	1	4	.200	0	0	5.61
1994	Greenville	AA	36	6	0	9	74	324	82	40	38	6	7	1	4	27	3	51	3	0	5	6	.455	0	0	4.62
	6 Min. YEARS		195	43	0	63	423.1	1938	440	280	219	27	23	16	24	237	12	397	49	3	17	39	.304	0	9	4.66

Ryan Martindale

Bats: Right **Throws:** Right **Pos:** C **Ht:** 6'3" **Wt:** 215 **Born:** 12/02/68 **Age:** 26

			BATTING														BASERUNNING				PERCENTAGES		
Year	Team	Lg	G	AB	H	2B	3B	HR	TB	R	RBI	TBB	IBB	SO	HBP	SH	SF	SB	CS	SB%	GDP	Avg	OBP	SLG
1991	Watertown	A	67	243	56	7	0	4	75	34	25	20	3	51	7	1	1	7	4	.64	7	.230	.306	.309
1992	Kinston	A	99	331	75	8	1	5	100	38	40	25	1	74	12	1	2	8	2	.80	7	.227	.303	.302
1993	Canton-Akrn	AA	105	310	68	18	1	10	118	44	39	23	0	71	9	4	3	1	3	.25	4	.219	.290	.381
1994	Canton-Akrn	AA	86	276	81	14	3	6	119	41	41	26	1	54	7	2	2	3	2	.60	6	.293	.367	.431
	4 Min. YEARS		357	1160	280	47	5	25	412	157	145	94	5	250	35	8	8	19	11	.63	24	.241	.315	.355

Chito Martinez

Bats: Left **Throws:** Left **Pos:** OF **Ht:** 5'10" **Wt:** 185 **Born:** 12/19/65 **Age:** 29

			BATTING														BASERUNNING				PERCENTAGES		
Year	Team	Lg	G	AB	H	2B	3B	HR	TB	R	RBI	TBB	IBB	SO	HBP	SH	SF	SB	CS	SB%	GDP	Avg	OBP	SLG
1984	Eugene	A	59	176	53	12	3	0	71	18	26	24	2	38	0	1	0	4	4	.50	3	.301	.385	.403
1985	Ft. Myers	A	76	248	65	9	5	0	84	35	29	31	3	42	1	1	3	11	5	.69	6	.262	.343	.339
1986	Memphis	AA	93	283	86	16	5	11	145	48	44	42	4	58	2	2	1	4	4	.50	2	.304	.396	.512
1987	Omaha	AAA	35	121	26	10	1	2	44	14	14	11	0	43	0	0	0	0	0	.00	0	.215	.280	.364
	Memphis	AA	78	283	74	10	3	9	117	34	43	33	0	94	1	0	2	5	3	.63	4	.261	.339	.413
1988	Memphis	AA	141	485	110	16	4	13	173	67	65	66	4	130	1	2	6	20	3	.87	6	.227	.317	.357
1989	Memphis	AA	127	399	97	20	2	23	190	55	62	63	7	137	1	4	4	3	3	.50	8	.243	.345	.476
1990	Omaha	AAA	122	364	96	12	8	21	187	59	67	54	5	129	3	0	3	6	6	.50	3	.264	.361	.514
1991	Rochester	AAA	60	211	68	8	1	20	138	42	50	26	3	69	0	0	2	2	2	.50	3	.322	.393	.654
1993	Bowie	AA	5	13	1	0	0	0	1	5	0	2	0	2	0	0	1	0	0	.00	1	.077	.200	.077
	Rochester	AAA	43	145	38	11	0	5	64	14	23	11	0	34	0	2	0	0	2	.00	2	.262	.314	.441
1994	Columbus	AAA	94	300	83	16	5	16	157	47	47	48	5	80	0	2	4	0	1	.00	3	.277	.372	.523
1991	Baltimore	AL	67	216	58	12	1	13	111	32	33	11	0	51	0	0	1	1	1	.50	2	.269	.303	.514
1992	Baltimore	AL	83	198	53	10	1	5	80	26	25	31	4	47	2	0	4	0	1	.00	9	.268	.366	.404
1993	Baltimore	AL	8	15	0	0	0	0	0	0	0	4	2	4	0	0	0	0	0	.00	0	.000	.211	.000
	10 Min. YEARS		933	3028	797	140	37	120	1371	438	470	411	33	856	9	14	25	55	31	.64	43	.263	.350	.453
	3 Maj. YEARS		158	429	111	22	2	18	191	58	58	46	6	102	2	0	5	1	2	.33	11	.259	.330	.445

Domingo Martinez

Bats: Right **Throws:** Right **Pos:** 1B **Ht:** 6'2" **Wt:** 215 **Born:** 08/04/67 **Age:** 27

			BATTING														BASERUNNING				PERCENTAGES		
Year	Team	Lg	G	AB	H	2B	3B	HR	TB	R	RBI	TBB	IBB	SO	HBP	SH	SF	SB	CS	SB%	GDP	Avg	OBP	SLG
1985	Blue Jays	R	58	219	65	10	2	4	91	36	19	12	0	42	2	0	0	3	4	.43	3	.297	.339	.416
1986	Ventura	A	129	455	113	19	6	9	171	51	57	36	2	127	4	3	3	9	9	.50	15	.248	.307	.376
1987	Dunedin	A	118	435	112	32	2	8	172	53	65	41	2	88	3	0	2	8	3	.73	9	.257	.324	.395
1988	Knoxville	AA	143	516	136	25	2	13	204	54	70	40	3	88	5	0	7	2	7	.22	13	.264	.319	.395
1989	Knoxville	AA	120	415	102	19	2	10	155	56	53	42	3	82	9	1	5	2	2	.50	7	.246	.325	.373
1990	Knoxville	AA	128	463	119	20	3	17	196	52	67	51	1	81	5	1	2	2	3	.40	24	.257	.336	.423
1991	Syracuse	AAA	126	467	146	16	2	17	217	61	83	41	0	107	6	5	6	6	4	.60	10	.313	.371	.465
1992	Syracuse	AAA	116	438	120	22	0	21	205	55	62	33	5	95	8	0	4	0	1	1.00	11	.274	.333	.468
1993	Syracuse	AAA	127	465	127	24	2	24	227	50	79	31	6	115	10	0	4	4	5	.44	11	.273	.329	.488
1994	Nashville	AAA	131	471	127	22	2	22	219	57	81	38	2	102	5	1	8	2	1	.67	12	.270	.326	.465
1992	Toronto	AL	7	8	5	0	0	1	8	2	3	0	0	1	0	0	0	0	0	.00	0	.625	.625	1.000
1993	Toronto	AL	8	14	4	0	0	1	7	2	3	1	0	7	0	0	0	0	0	.00	0	.286	.333	.500
	10 Min. YEARS		1196	4344	1167	209	23	145	1857	525	636	365	24	927	57	11	41	44	38	.54	115	.269	.331	.427
	2 Maj. YEARS		15	22	9	0	0	2	15	4	6	1	0	8	0	0	0	0	0	.00	0	.409	.435	.682

Francisco Martinez

Pitches: Right **Bats:** Right **Pos:** P **Ht:** 6'2" **Wt:** 180 **Born:** 04/24/68 **Age:** 27

			HOW MUCH HE PITCHED						WHAT HE GAVE UP										THE RESULTS					
Year	Team	Lg	G	GS	CG	GF	IP	BFP	H	R	ER	HR	SH	SF	HB	TBB	IBB	SO	WP	Bk	W	L	Pct.	ShO	Sv	ERA
1992	Springfield	A	18	3	0	7	31	133	28	18	11	0	0	1	0	12	0	22	6	1	1	3	.250	0	0	3.19
1993	Savannah	A	14	14	2	0	95.1	371	70	28	20	4	1	2	1	23	1	79	2	0	7	3	.700	0	0	1.89
	St.Pete	A	13	7	1	2	65.2	265	55	13	10	2	2	1	0	22	0	38	0	0	3	2	.600	1	0	1.37
	Arkansas	AA	2	2	0	0	7	31	8	5	5	0	1	0	0	1	0	3	0	0	0	1	.000	0	0	6.43
1994	Arkansas	AA	45	0	0	31	58	249	48	25	19	5	4	0	2	25	1	34	4	1	5	4	.556	0	16	2.95
	3 Min. YEARS		92	26	3	40	257	1049	209	89	65	11	8	4	4	83	2	176	12	2	16	13	.552	1	16	2.28

Jesus Martinez

Pitches: Left **Bats:** Left **Pos:** P **Ht:** 6'2" **Wt:** 145 **Born:** 03/13/74 **Age:** 21

			HOW MUCH HE PITCHED						WHAT HE GAVE UP										THE RESULTS					
Year	Team	Lg	G	GS	CG	GF	IP	BFP	H	R	ER	HR	SH	SF	HB	TBB	IBB	SO	WP	Bk	W	L	Pct.	ShO	Sv	ERA
1992	Great Falls	R	6	6	0	0	18.1	112	36	30	27	4	0	0	2	21	0	23	9	0	0	3	.000	0	0	13.25

Year	Team	Lg	G	GS	CG	GF	IP	BFP	H	R	ER	HR	SH	SF	HB	TBB	IBB	SO	WP	Bk	W	L	Pct.	ShO	Sv	ERA
	Dodgers	R	7	7	1	0	41	174	38	19	15	1	2	0	1	11	0	39	5	0	1	4	.200	0	0	3.29
1993	Bakersfield	A	30	21	0	2	145.2	653	144	95	67	12	5	11	5	75	0	108	6	5	4	13	.235	0	0	4.14
1994	San Antonio	AA	1	1	0	0	4	14	3	2	2	0	0	0	0	2	0	3	0	0	0	1	.000	0	0	4.50
	Vero Beach	A	18	18	1	0	87.2	386	91	65	61	7	2	3	6	43	0	69	3	0	7	9	.438	1	0	6.26
	3 Min. YEARS		62	53	2	2	296.2	1339	312	211	172	24	9	14	14	152	0	242	23	5	12	30	.286	1	0	5.22

Manuel Martinez

Bats: Right **Throws:** Right **Pos:** OF   **Ht:** 6'2" **Wt:** 169 **Born:** 10/03/70 **Age:** 24

						BATTING										BASERUNNING				PERCENTAGES		
Year	Team	Lg	G	AB	H	2B	3B	HR	TB	R	RBI	TBB	IBB	SO	HBP	SH	SF	SB	CS	SB%	GDP	Avg	OBP	SLG
1990	Sou Oregon	A	66	244	60	5	0	2	71	35	17	16	0	59	5	1	0	6	4	.60	5	.246	.306	.291
1991	Modesto	A	125	502	136	32	3	3	183	73	69	34	0	80	7	7	3	26	19	.58	7	.271	.324	.365
1992	Modesto	A	121	495	125	23	1	9	177	70	45	39	3	75	4	12	5	17	13	.57	7	.253	.309	.358
1993	San Berndno	A	109	459	148	26	3	11	213	88	52	41	2	60	5	6	4	28	21	.57	10	.322	.381	.464
	Tacoma	AAA	20	59	18	2	0	1	23	9	6	4	0	12	0	1	0	2	3	.40	2	.305	.349	.390
1994	Tacoma	AAA	137	536	137	25	5	9	199	76	60	28	3	72	10	9	5	18	10	.64	14	.256	.302	.371
	5 Min. YEARS		578	2295	624	113	12	35	866	351	235	162	10	358	31	36	17	97	70	.58	45	.272	.326	.377

Pablo Martinez

Bats: Both **Throws:** Right **Pos:** INF   **Ht:** 5'10" **Wt:** 155 **Born:** 06/29/69 **Age:** 26

						BATTING										BASERUNNING				PERCENTAGES		
Year	Team	Lg	G	AB	H	2B	3B	HR	TB	R	RBI	TBB	IBB	SO	HBP	SH	SF	SB	CS	SB%	GDP	Avg	OBP	SLG
1989	Spokane	A	2	8	2	0	0	0	2	3	0	0	0	0	0	0	0	1	0	1.00	1	.250	.250	.250
	Padres	R	45	178	42	3	1	0	47	31	12	22	1	25	2	0	0	29	4	.88	1	.236	.327	.264
	Chston-Sc	A	31	80	14	2	0	0	16	13	4	11	0	21	0	3	1	0	1	.00	2	.175	.272	.200
1990	Chston-Sc	A	136	453	100	12	6	0	124	51	33	41	0	104	4	7	2	16	10	.62	6	.221	.290	.274
1991	Chston-Sc	A	121	442	118	17	6	3	156	62	36	42	1	64	0	6	2	39	19	.67	8	.267	.329	.353
1992	High Desert	A	126	427	102	8	4	0	118	60	39	50	0	74	1	2	4	19	14	.58	16	.239	.317	.276
1993	Wichita	AA	45	130	36	5	1	2	49	19	14	11	1	24	1	1	1	8	5	.62	2	.277	.336	.377
	Las Vegas	AAA	76	251	58	4	1	2	70	24	20	18	3	46	3	10	2	8	2	.80	5	.231	.288	.279
1994	Norfolk	AAA	34	80	12	1	0	0	13	8	5	4	0	22	0	3	0	1	1	.50	0	.150	.190	.163
	Binghamton	AA	13	48	9	2	2	0	15	3	4	5	0	12	0	2	0	0	1	.00	3	.188	.264	.313
	St. Lucie	A	49	177	42	5	0	1	50	19	10	13	0	29	0	3	1	7	7	.50	4	.237	.288	.282
	6 Min. YEARS		678	2274	535	59	21	8	660	293	177	217	6	421	11	37	13	128	64	.67	48	.235	.303	.290

Ramiro Martinez

Pitches: Left **Bats:** Left **Pos:** P   **Ht:** 6'2" **Wt:** 185 **Born:** 01/28/72 **Age:** 23

			HOW MUCH HE PITCHED						WHAT HE GAVE UP											THE RESULTS					
Year	Team	Lg	G	GS	CG	GF	IP	BFP	H	R	ER	HR	SH	SF	HB	TBB	IBB	SO	WP	Bk	W	L	Pct.	ShO	Sv	ERA
1992	Rangers	R	10	10	1	0	45.2	184	28	15	6	0	0	1	4	22	0	52	3	1	4	1	.800	1	0	1.18
1993	Chston-Sc	A	27	27	2	0	124.2	588	129	91	81	10	2	3	10	90	4	129	11	0	6	10	.375	2	0	5.85
1994	Tulsa	AA	23	23	2	0	139.1	589	126	79	70	21	1	3	4	69	0	107	2	1	6	10	.375	0	0	4.52
	3 Min. YEARS		60	60	5	0	309.2	1361	283	185	157	31	3	7	18	181	4	288	16	2	16	21	.432	3	0	4.56

Ramon Martinez

Bats: Both **Throws:** Right **Pos:** SS   **Ht:** 6'0" **Wt:** 170 **Born:** 09/08/69 **Age:** 25

						BATTING										BASERUNNING				PERCENTAGES		
Year	Team	Lg	G	AB	H	2B	3B	HR	TB	R	RBI	TBB	IBB	SO	HBP	SH	SF	SB	CS	SB%	GDP	Avg	OBP	SLG
1990	Pirates	R	15	58	21	2	1	0	25	8	5	2	0	6	0	0	2	2	5	.29	0	.362	.371	.431
	Welland	A	48	151	35	3	1	0	40	26	15	7	0	37	0	1	2	19	6	.76	3	.232	.263	.265
1991	Augusta	A	106	345	88	7	2	0	99	51	13	10	0	82	2	6	0	35	7	.83	6	.255	.280	.287
1992	Salem	A	131	533	154	17	12	3	204	73	30	29	0	139	2	5	2	35	17	.67	2	.289	.327	.383
1993	High Desert	A	118	412	109	10	6	2	137	73	46	49	2	79	2	6	3	46	11	.81	5	.265	.343	.333
1994	Portland	AA	132	502	121	17	2	1	145	59	44	28	4	104	2	6	8	31	14	.69	8	.241	.280	.289
	5 Min. YEARS		550	2001	528	56	24	6	650	290	153	125	6	447	8	24	17	168	60	.74	22	.264	.307	.325

Tim Marx

Bats: Right **Throws:** Right **Pos:** C   **Ht:** 6'2" **Wt:** 190 **Born:** 11/27/68 **Age:** 26

						BATTING										BASERUNNING				PERCENTAGES		
Year	Team	Lg	G	AB	H	2B	3B	HR	TB	R	RBI	TBB	IBB	SO	HBP	SH	SF	SB	CS	SB%	GDP	Avg	OBP	SLG
1992	Augusta	A	44	138	30	7	0	0	37	20	9	23	0	16	1	3	0	0	1	.00	4	.217	.333	.268
1993	Salem	A	13	43	10	0	0	0	10	2	5	7	0	9	0	1	1	1	1	.50	2	.233	.333	.233
	Augusta	A	53	162	45	8	0	3	62	28	21	34	0	18	2	2	2	3	4	.43	3	.278	.405	.383
	Buffalo	AAA	4	14	2	1	0	0	3	0	0	2	0	4	0	0	0	0	0	.00	1	.143	.250	.214
1994	Carolina	AA	77	239	71	11	2	7	107	32	42	20	1	29	1	2	5	1	3	.25	4	.297	.347	.448
	3 Min. YEARS		191	596	158	27	2	10	219	82	77	86	1	76	4	8	8	5	9	.36	14	.265	.357	.367

John Marzano

Bats: Right **Throws:** Right **Pos:** C   **Ht:** 5'11" **Wt:** 195 **Born:** 02/14/63 **Age:** 32

						BATTING										BASERUNNING				PERCENTAGES		
Year	Team	Lg	G	AB	H	2B	3B	HR	TB	R	RBI	TBB	IBB	SO	HBP	SH	SF	SB	CS	SB%	GDP	Avg	OBP	SLG
1985	New Britain	AA	103	350	86	14	6	4	124	36	51	19	0	43	3	7	9	4	3	.57	14	.246	.283	.354
1986	New Britain	AA	118	445	126	28	2	10	188	55	62	24	2	66	12	0	6	2	0	1.00	10	.283	.333	.422

161

Year	Team	Lg	G	AB	H	2B	3B	HR	TB	R	RBI	TBB	IBB	SO	HBP	SH	SF	SB	CS	SB%	GDP	Avg	OBP	SLG
1987	Pawtucket	AAA	70	255	72	22	0	10	124	46	35	21	0	50	5	2	1	2	3	.40	10	.282	.348	.486
1988	Pawtucket	AAA	33	111	22	2	1	0	26	7	5	8	0	17	0	2	1	1	1	.50	4	.198	.250	.234
	New Britain	AA	35	112	23	6	1	0	31	11	5	10	2	13	3	1	1	1	0	1.00	6	.205	.286	.277
1989	Pawtucket	AAA	106	322	68	11	0	8	103	27	36	15	1	53	4	4	2	1	4	.20	7	.211	.254	.320
1990	Pawtucket	AAA	26	75	24	4	1	2	36	16	8	11	0	9	0	0	0	6	3	.67	2	.320	.407	.480
1992	Pawtucket	AAA	18	62	18	1	0	2	25	5	12	3	0	11	2	0	0	0	0	.00	1	.290	.343	.403
1993	Charlotte	AAA	3	9	1	0	0	0	1	0	0	1	0	1	0	0	0	0	0	.00	0	.111	.200	.111
1994	Scranton-Wb	AAA	88	280	59	19	2	1	85	25	19	24	2	32	5	1	2	2	3	.40	4	.211	.283	.304
1987	Boston	AL	52	168	41	11	0	5	67	20	24	7	0	41	3	2	2	0	1	.00	3	.244	.283	.399
1988	Boston	AL	10	29	4	1	0	0	5	3	1	1	0	3	0	0	0	0	0	.00	1	.138	.167	.172
1989	Boston	AL	7	18	8	3	0	1	14	5	3	0	0	2	0	1	1	0	0	.00	1	.444	.421	.778
1990	Boston	AL	32	83	20	4	0	0	24	8	6	5	0	10	0	2	1	0	1	.00	0	.241	.281	.289
1991	Boston	AL	49	114	30	8	0	0	38	10	9	1	0	16	1	1	2	0	0	.00	5	.263	.271	.333
1992	Boston	AL	19	50	4	2	1	0	8	4	1	2	0	12	1	1	0	0	0	.00	0	.080	.132	.160
	9 Min. YEARS		600	2021	499	107	13	37	743	228	233	136	7	295	34	17	22	19	17	.53	58	.247	.302	.368
	6 Maj. YEARS		169	462	107	29	1	6	156	50	44	16	0	84	5	7	6	0	2	.00	10	.232	.262	.338

Damon Mashore

Bats: Both   Throws: Right   Pos: OF   **Ht: 5'11" Wt: 195 Born: 10/31/69 Age: 25**

			BATTING															BASERUNNING				PERCENTAGES		
Year	Team	Lg	G	AB	H	2B	3B	HR	TB	R	RBI	TBB	IBB	SO	HBP	SH	SF	SB	CS	SB%	GDP	Avg	OBP	SLG
1991	Sou Oregon	A	73	264	72	17	6	6	119	48	31	34	1	94	2	2	3	15	5	.75	6	.273	.356	.451
1992	Modesto	A	124	471	133	22	3	18	215	91	64	73	3	136	6	5	1	29	17	.63	6	.282	.385	.456
1993	Huntsville	AA	70	253	59	7	2	3	79	35	20	25	0	64	4	1	2	18	4	.82	5	.233	.310	.312
1994	Athletics	R	11	34	14	2	0	0	16	6	6	4	0	3	1	0	1	1	1	.50	3	.412	.475	.471
	Huntsville	AA	59	210	47	11	2	3	71	24	21	13	1	53	0	1	3	6	1	.86	3	.224	.265	.338
	4 Min. YEARS		337	1232	325	59	13	30	500	204	142	149	5	350	13	9	10	69	28	.71	23	.264	.347	.406

Justin Mashore

Bats: Right   Throws: Right   Pos: OF   **Ht: 5'9" Wt: 190 Born: 02/14/72 Age: 23**

			BATTING															BASERUNNING				PERCENTAGES		
Year	Team	Lg	G	AB	H	2B	3B	HR	TB	R	RBI	TBB	IBB	SO	HBP	SH	SF	SB	CS	SB%	GDP	Avg	OBP	SLG
1991	Bristol	R	58	177	36	3	0	3	48	29	11	28	1	65	0	2	0	17	6	.74	1	.203	.312	.271
1992	Fayetteville	A	120	401	96	18	3	4	132	54	43	36	2	117	3	9	1	31	8	.79	3	.239	.306	.329
1993	Lakeland	A	118	442	113	11	4	3	141	64	30	37	4	92	6	16	5	26	13	.67	9	.256	.318	.319
1994	Trenton	AA	131	450	100	13	5	7	144	63	45	36	0	120	3	8	3	31	7	.82	9	.222	.283	.320
	4 Min. YEARS		427	1470	345	45	12	17	465	210	129	137	7	394	12	35	9	105	34	.76	22	.235	.303	.316

John Massarelli

Bats: Right   Throws: Right   Pos: OF   **Ht: 6'2" Wt: 200 Born: 01/23/66 Age: 29**

			BATTING															BASERUNNING				PERCENTAGES		
Year	Team	Lg	G	AB	H	2B	3B	HR	TB	R	RBI	TBB	IBB	SO	HBP	SH	SF	SB	CS	SB%	GDP	Avg	OBP	SLG
1987	Auburn	A	23	56	9	1	2	0	14	7	3	7	0	10	0	0	1	3	0	1.00	2	.161	.250	.250
	Asheville	A	6	17	6	0	0	0	6	6	1	2	0	1	0	0	0	3	0	1.00	0	.353	.421	.353
1988	Auburn	A	59	179	54	8	1	0	64	29	26	32	0	31	3	1	4	25	5	.83	1	.302	.408	.358
1989	Asheville	A	90	246	61	13	2	3	87	43	21	35	0	42	3	2	2	25	6	.81	2	.248	.346	.354
1990	Osceola	A	120	396	117	8	3	2	137	55	50	41	4	73	2	5	7	54	6	.90	9	.295	.359	.346
1991	Osceola	A	51	194	60	9	0	1	72	27	22	16	2	34	4	2	2	18	8	.69	4	.309	.370	.371
	Jackson	AA	12	38	8	2	0	0	10	3	0	1	0	2	0	0	0	4	0	1.00	0	.211	.231	.263
	Tucson	AAA	46	127	34	7	1	0	43	19	16	15	1	18	0	1	1	10	2	.83	3	.268	.343	.339
1992	Jackson	AA	27	98	27	4	1	1	36	15	10	5	0	20	0	1	1	10	2	.83	2	.276	.311	.367
	Tucson	AAA	50	143	34	4	0	0	38	21	6	14	1	27	1	1	0	14	3	.82	2	.238	.310	.266
1993	Tucson	AAA	114	423	119	28	4	2	161	66	42	46	4	61	2	5	2	37	13	.74	14	.281	.353	.381
1994	Edmonton	AAA	120	414	108	18	10	4	158	67	36	34	1	72	0	0	3	39	7	.85	4	.261	.315	.382
	8 Min. YEARS		718	2331	637	102	24	13	826	358	233	248	13	391	15	18	22	242	52	.82	43	.273	.344	.354

Billy Masse

Bats: Right   Throws: Right   Pos: OF   **Ht: 6'1" Wt: 190 Born: 07/06/66 Age: 28**

			BATTING															BASERUNNING				PERCENTAGES		
Year	Team	Lg	G	AB	H	2B	3B	HR	TB	R	RBI	TBB	IBB	SO	HBP	SH	SF	SB	CS	SB%	GDP	Avg	OBP	SLG
1989	Pr William	A	124	377	90	17	4	11	148	70	50	89	4	57	13	3	4	16	4	.80	6	.239	.398	.393
1990	Ft.Lauderdle	A	68	230	63	15	0	6	96	42	33	33	2	28	6	0	5	9	0	1.00	2	.274	.372	.417
	Albany	AA	31	96	18	1	0	3	28	12	8	22	0	19	1	0	1	0	1	.00	2	.188	.342	.292
1991	Albany	AA	108	356	105	17	2	11	159	67	61	74	3	60	6	0	7	10	4	.71	11	.295	.418	.447
1992	Columbus	AAA	110	357	95	13	2	12	148	52	60	51	0	51	5	2	3	7	6	.54	13	.266	.363	.415
1993	Columbus	AAA	117	402	127	35	3	19	225	81	91	82	0	68	8	1	4	17	7	.71	9	.316	.438	.560
1994	Columbus	AAA	71	221	57	17	0	5	89	37	14	31	1	43	6	1	0	1	6	.14	7	.258	.364	.403
	6 Min. YEARS		629	2039	555	115	11	67	893	361	317	382	10	326	45	7	24	60	28	.68	50	.272	.394	.438

Dan Masteller

Bats: Left   Throws: Left   Pos: OF   **Ht: 6'0" Wt: 185 Born: 03/17/68 Age: 27**

			BATTING															BASERUNNING				PERCENTAGES		
Year	Team	Lg	G	AB	H	2B	3B	HR	TB	R	RBI	TBB	IBB	SO	HBP	SH	SF	SB	CS	SB%	GDP	Avg	OBP	SLG
1989	Elizabethtn	R	9	38	13	0	0	2	19	8	9	6	0	2	0	0	0	2	2	.50	0	.342	.432	.500

Year Team	Lg	G	AB	H	2B	3B	HR	TB	R	RBI	TBB	IBB	SO	HBP	SH	SF	SB	CS	SB%	GDP	Avg	OBP	SLG
Visalia	A	53	181	46	5	1	3	62	24	16	18	2	36	1	0	1	0	0	.00	2	.254	.323	.343
1990 Visalia	A	135	473	133	20	5	4	175	71	73	81	0	76	9	4	3	2	5	.29	15	.281	.394	.370
1991 Orlando	AA	124	370	91	14	5	5	130	44	35	43	6	43	3	3	2	6	4	.60	5	.246	.328	.351
1992 Orlando	AA	116	365	96	24	4	8	152	42	42	23	1	36	4	3	1	2	4	.33	7	.263	.313	.416
1993 Nashville	AA	36	121	33	3	0	3	45	19	16	11	0	19	1	2	0	2	1	.67	0	.273	.338	.372
Portland	AAA	61	211	68	13	4	7	110	35	47	24	3	25	1	1	7	3	4	.43	2	.322	.383	.521
1994 Salt Lake	AAA	98	338	102	26	3	8	158	53	58	21	1	27	1	2	4	4	1	.80	9	.302	.341	.467
6 Min. YEARS		632	2097	582	105	22	40	851	296	296	227	13	264	20	15	18	21	21	.50	40	.278	.351	.406

Tim Mathews

Pitches: Right Bats: Right Pos: P Ht: 6'1" Wt: 200 Born: 01/19/70 Age: 25

		HOW MUCH HE PITCHED						WHAT HE GAVE UP												THE RESULTS				
Year Team	Lg	G	GS	CG	GF	IP	BFP	H	R	ER	HR	SH	SF	HB	TBB	IBB	SO	WP	Bk	W	L	Pct.	ShO	Sv	ERA
1992 Hamilton	A	14	14	1	0	86.2	351	70	25	21	4	3	0	2	30	0	89	4	2	10	1	.909	0	0	2.18
1993 Springfield	A	25	25	5	0	159.1	634	121	59	48	7	7	4	6	29	0	144	1	3	12	9	.571	2	0	2.71
1994 St. Pete	A	11	11	0	0	66.1	270	52	22	18	1	1	0	2	23	0	62	1	1	5	5	.500	0	0	2.44
Arkansas	AA	16	16	1	0	97	395	83	37	34	8	6	2	6	24	1	93	1	0	5	5	.500	0	0	3.15
3 Min. YEARS		66	66	8	0	409.1	1650	326	143	121	20	17	6	16	106	1	388	7	6	32	20	.615	2	0	2.66

Mike Mathile

Pitches: Right Bats: Right Pos: P Ht: 6'4" Wt: 220 Born: 11/24/68 Age: 26

		HOW MUCH HE PITCHED						WHAT HE GAVE UP												THE RESULTS				
Year Team	Lg	G	GS	CG	GF	IP	BFP	H	R	ER	HR	SH	SF	HB	TBB	IBB	SO	WP	Bk	W	L	Pct.	ShO	Sv	ERA
1990 Jamestown	A	14	14	1	0	90	377	95	40	25	4	6	0	1	28	1	54	2	0	2	5	.286	0	0	2.50
1991 Rockford	A	17	17	5	0	116.2	465	100	45	32	3	2	0	4	19	0	66	4	6	9	3	.750	2	0	2.47
1992 Harrisburg	AA	26	26	7	0	185.2	741	175	61	59	6	3	3	5	28	0	89	6	1	12	5	.706	3	0	2.86
1993 Ottawa	AAA	31	21	2	6	140.1	594	147	74	65	9	3	4	6	41	1	56	7	0	9	9	.500	2	1	4.17
1994 Ottawa	AAA	2	0	0	1	5.2	26	9	1	1	0	0	0	0	2	1	1	0	0	0	1	.000	0	0	1.59
Indianapolis	AAA	2	2	0	0	3.2	20	10	8	8	3	0	0	0	0	0	2	0	1	0	0	.000	0	0	19.64
5 Min. YEARS		92	80	15	7	542	2223	536	229	190	25	14	7	16	118	3	268	19	7	32	24	.571	7	1	3.15

Rob Maurer

Bats: Left Throws: Left Pos: 1B Ht: 6'3" Wt: 210 Born: 01/07/67 Age: 28

		BATTING															BASERUNNING				PERCENTAGES		
Year Team	Lg	G	AB	H	2B	3B	HR	TB	R	RBI	TBB	IBB	SO	HBP	SH	SF	SB	CS	SB%	GDP	Avg	OBP	SLG
1988 Butte	R	63	233	91	18	3	8	139	65	60	35	3	33	3	0	2	0	0	.00	2	.391	.473	.597
1989 Charlotte	A	132	456	126	18	9	6	180	69	51	86	6	109	8	0	4	3	4	.43	9	.276	.397	.395
1990 Tulsa	AA	104	367	110	31	4	21	212	55	78	54	6	112	6	0	2	4	2	.67	5	.300	.396	.578
1991 Okla City	AAA	132	459	138	41	3	20	245	76	77	96	8	134	3	0	6	2	3	.40	5	.301	.420	.534
1992 Okla City	AAA	135	493	142	34	2	10	210	76	82	75	3	117	4	1	7	1	1	.50	9	.288	.382	.426
1994 Okla City	AAA	61	194	50	8	4	11	99	34	30	48	4	83	4	0	1	0	0	.00	1	.258	.413	.510
1991 Texas	AL	13	16	1	1	0	0	2	0	2	2	0	6	1	0	0	0	0	.00	0	.063	.211	.125
1992 Texas	AL	8	9	2	0	0	0	2	1	1	1	0	2	0	0	0	0	0	.00	0	.222	.300	.222
6 Min. YEARS		627	2202	657	150	25	76	1085	375	378	394	30	588	28	1	22	10	10	.50	31	.298	.408	.493
2 Maj. YEARS		21	25	3	1	0	0	4	1	3	3	0	8	1	0	0	0	0	.00	0	.120	.241	.160

Ron Maurer

Bats: Right Throws: Right Pos: SS Ht: 6'1" Wt: 185 Born: 06/10/68 Age: 27

		BATTING															BASERUNNING				PERCENTAGES		
Year Team	Lg	G	AB	H	2B	3B	HR	TB	R	RBI	TBB	IBB	SO	HBP	SH	SF	SB	CS	SB%	GDP	Avg	OBP	SLG
1990 Great Falls	R	62	238	64	8	0	6	90	43	43	27	0	38	6	5	4	5	2	.71	4	.269	.353	.378
1991 Bakersfield	A	129	442	128	21	5	7	180	59	53	63	3	68	7	13	3	8	8	.50	15	.290	.384	.407
1992 San Antonio	AA	82	224	61	13	0	0	74	29	14	15	3	32	5	4	0	4	3	.57	6	.272	.332	.330
1993 San Antonio	AA	11	37	7	1	0	1	11	6	4	7	0	12	0	1	0	0	1	.00	0	.189	.318	.297
Albuquerque	AAA	58	116	34	7	0	3	50	19	14	11	1	17	0	4	0	1	1	.50	6	.293	.354	.431
1994 Albuquerque	AAA	55	125	35	8	1	2	51	20	16	4	0	15	3	1	1	0	1	1.00	4	.280	.316	.408
5 Min. YEARS		397	1182	329	58	6	19	456	176	144	127	7	182	21	28	8	19	15	.56	35	.278	.357	.386

David Maxcy

Pitches: Right Bats: Right Pos: P Ht: 6'1" Wt: 170 Born: 05/04/71 Age: 24

		HOW MUCH HE PITCHED						WHAT HE GAVE UP												THE RESULTS				
Year Team	Lg	G	GS	CG	GF	IP	BFP	H	R	ER	HR	SH	SF	HB	TBB	IBB	SO	WP	Bk	W	L	Pct.	ShO	Sv	ERA
1992 Bristol	R	14	7	2	7	49.1	204	41	24	19	4	0	2	8	17	1	43	3	1	4	2	.667	2	3	3.47
1993 Fayetteville	A	39	12	1	20	113.2	501	111	51	37	2	5	3	13	42	3	101	5	0	12	4	.750	1	9	2.93
1994 Trenton	AA	5	0	0	2	10.2	45	6	1	0	0	0	0	1	4	0	5	0	0	0	0	.000	0	1	0.00
Toledo	AAA	24	1	0	6	44.1	182	31	12	8	1	2	1	2	18	1	43	1	0	2	3	.400	0	3	1.62
3 Min. YEARS		82	20	3	35	218	932	189	88	64	7	7	6	16	81	5	192	9	1	18	9	.667	3	16	2.64

Pat Maxwell

Bats: Left Throws: Right Pos: 2B Ht: 6'0" Wt: 170 Born: 03/28/70 Age: 25

		BATTING															BASERUNNING				PERCENTAGES		
Year Team	Lg	G	AB	H	2B	3B	HR	TB	R	RBI	TBB	IBB	SO	HBP	SH	SF	SB	CS	SB%	GDP	Avg	OBP	SLG
1991 Watertown	A	16	55	10	0	0	0	10	5	5	3	0	9	0	2	1	1	1	.50	0	.182	.220	.182
Burlington	R	45	166	48	8	4	1	67	41	12	26	2	15	0	3	1	7	4	.64	1	.289	.383	.404

Year	Team	Lg	G	AB	H	2B	3B	HR	TB	R	RBI	TBB	IBB	SO	HBP	SH	SF	SB	CS	SB%	GDP	Avg	OBP	SLG
1992	Columbus	A	81	270	71	7	0	1	81	31	25	19	1	19	2	4	1	7	2	.78	4	.263	.315	.300
1993	Kinston	A	103	400	117	17	3	4	152	46	35	22	3	32	3	3	2	6	4	.60	5	.293	.333	.380
1994	Canton-Akm	AA	75	256	67	8	0	0	75	30	19	16	1	32	2	9	2	8	4	.67	2	.262	.308	.293
	4 Min. YEARS		320	1147	313	40	7	6	385	153	96	86	7	107	7	21	7	29	15	.66	14	.273	.326	.336

Darrell May

Pitches: Left   Bats: Left   Pos: P **Ht: 6'2"   Wt: 170   Born: 06/13/72   Age: 23**

			HOW MUCH HE PITCHED						WHAT HE GAVE UP								THE RESULTS					
Year	Team	Lg	G	GS	CG	GF	IP	BFP	H	R	ER	HR	SH	SF	HB	TBB	IBB	SO	WP	Bk	W	L	Pct.	ShO	Sv	ERA
1992	Braves	R	12	7	0	2	53	204	34	13	8	3	0	2	0	13	0	61	2	1	4	3	.571	0	1	1.36
1993	Macon	A	17	17	0	0	104.1	404	81	29	26	6	0	0	1	22	1	111	3	0	10	4	.714	0	0	2.24
	Durham	A	9	9	0	0	51.2	213	44	18	12	4	4	2	1	16	0	47	2	1	5	2	.714	0	0	2.09
1994	Durham	A	12	12	1	0	74.2	307	74	29	25	6	0	1	3	17	1	73	3	0	8	2	.800	0	0	3.01
	Greenville	AA	11	11	1	0	63.2	265	61	25	22	4	1	2	2	17	0	42	6	0	5	3	.625	0	0	3.11
	3 Min. YEARS		61	56	2	4	347.1	1393	294	114	93	20	7	5	9	85	2	334	16	2	32	14	.696	0	1	2.41

Matt Maysey

Pitches: Right   Bats: Right   Pos: P **Ht: 6'4"   Wt: 225   Born: 01/08/67   Age: 28**

			HOW MUCH HE PITCHED						WHAT HE GAVE UP								THE RESULTS					
Year	Team	Lg	G	GS	CG	GF	IP	BFP	H	R	ER	HR	SH	SF	HB	TBB	IBB	SO	WP	Bk	W	L	Pct.	ShO	Sv	ERA
1985	Spokane	A	7	4	0	2	29		27	18	15	3	0	0	1	16	0	18	5	0	0	3	.000	0	0	4.66
1986	Charleston	A	18	5	0	11	43	196	43	28	24	5	3	0	3	24	2	39	5	2	3	2	.600	0	1	5.02
1987	Chston-Sc	A	41	18	5	21	150.1	623	112	71	53	13	8	7	5	59	4	143	13	3	14	11	.560	0	7	3.17
1988	Wichita	A	28	28	4	0	187	789	180	88	77	15	7	6	5	68	1	120	18	5	9	9	.500	0	0	3.71
1989	Las Vegas	AAA	28	28	4	0	176.1	773	173	94	80	19	3	1	2	84	3	96	12	3	8	12	.400	1	0	4.08
1990	Las Vegas	AAA	26	25	1	1	137.2	634	155	97	86	10	6	5	5	88	5	72	12	1	6	10	.375	0	0	5.62
1991	Harrisburg	AA	15	15	2	0	104.2	419	90	26	22	3	2	3	2	28	0	86	8	0	6	5	.545	2	0	1.89
	Indianapols	AAA	12	12	0	0	63	272	60	45	36	7	0	1	2	33	2	45	6	0	3	6	.333	0	0	5.14
1992	Indianapols	AAA	35	1	0	14	67	286	63	32	32	9	4	2	0	28	5	38	2	1	5	3	.625	0	5	4.30
1993	New Orleans	AAA	29	5	0	6	52.1	215	48	25	24	8	1	2	0	14	1	40	2	1	0	3	.000	0	2	4.13
1994	Buffalo	AAA	10	0	0	1	15	57	11	7	7	0	2	1	1	2	0	9	2	0	2	0	1.000	0	1	4.20
1992	Montreal	NL	2	0	0	1	2.1	12	4	1	1	1	0	0	1	0	0	1	0	0	0	0	.000	0	0	3.86
1993	Milwaukee	AL	23	0	0	12	22	105	28	14	14	4	2	2	1	13	1	10	4	0	1	2	.333	0	1	5.73
	10 Min. YEARS		249	141	16	56	1025.1	4264	962	531	456	92	36	28	26	444	23	706	85	16	56	64	.467	3	15	4.00
	2 Maj. YEARS		25	0	0	13	24.1	117	32	15	15	5	2	2	2	13	1	11	4	0	1	2	.333	0	1	5.55

Roderick McCall

Bats: Left   Throws: Right   Pos: 1B **Ht: 6'7"   Wt: 220   Born: 11/04/71   Age: 23**

			BATTING														BASERUNNING				PERCENTAGES		
Year	Team	Lg	G	AB	H	2B	3B	HR	TB	R	RBI	TBB	IBB	SO	HBP	SH	SF	SB	CS	SB%	GDP	Avg	OBP	SLG
1990	Indians	R	10	36	10	2	0	0	12	5	6	5	1	10	0	0	0	0	0	.00	0	.278	.366	.333
	Burlington	R	31	92	15	5	0	1	23	8	11	10	0	43	2	0	2	0	1	.00	1	.163	.255	.250
1991	Columbus	A	103	323	70	14	1	5	101	34	35	61	3	128	3	0	1	2	2	.50	5	.217	.345	.313
1992	Columbus	A	116	404	97	15	0	20	172	55	80	68	4	121	4	0	6	1	1	.50	9	.240	.351	.426
1993	Kinston	A	71	245	51	13	0	9	91	32	33	32	2	85	3	0	4	3	1	.75	3	.208	.303	.371
1994	Kinston	A	58	205	44	14	0	11	91	32	27	26	1	75	7	1	0	1	1	.50	2	.215	.324	.444
	High Desert	A	48	183	51	14	0	17	116	40	43	20	0	63	5	0	1	2	1	.67	4	.279	.364	.634
	Canton-Akm	AA	20	66	13	4	0	3	26	8	9	2	0	27	2	0	1	0	0	.00	1	.197	.239	.394
	5 Min. YEARS		457	1554	351	81	1	66	632	214	244	224	11	552	26	2	15	9	7	.56	25	.226	.330	.407

Greg McCarthy

Pitches: Left   Bats: Left   Pos: P **Ht: 6'2"   Wt: 193   Born: 10/30/68   Age: 26**

			HOW MUCH HE PITCHED						WHAT HE GAVE UP								THE RESULTS					
Year	Team	Lg	G	GS	CG	GF	IP	BFP	H	R	ER	HR	SH	SF	HB	TBB	IBB	SO	WP	Bk	W	L	Pct.	ShO	Sv	ERA
1987	Utica	A	20	0	0	13	29.2	130	14	9	3	0	2	1	2	23	2	40	1	2	4	1	.800	0	3	0.91
1988	Spartanburg	A	34	1	0	20	64.2	297	52	36	29	3	3	3	10	52	0	65	8	3	4	2	.667	0	2	4.04
1989	Spartanburg	A	24	15	2	4	112	499	90	58	52	3	3	5	9	80	0	115	8	2	5	8	.385	1	0	4.18
1990	Clearwater	A	42	1	0	19	59.2	265	47	32	22	4	2	2	1	38	1	67	5	2	1	3	.250	0	5	3.32
1992	Kinston	A	23	0	0	21	27.1	105	14	0	0	0	1	0	5	9	0	37	8	0	3	0	1.000	0	12	0.00
1993	Kinston	A	9	0	0	6	10.2	51	8	4	2	0	0	0	0	13	0	14	2	0	0	0	.000	0	2	1.69
	Canton-Akm	AA	33	0	0	19	34.1	156	28	18	18	1	0	3	2	37	2	39	5	0	2	3	.400	0	6	4.72
1994	Canton-Akm	AA	22	0	0	19	32	133	19	12	8	0	0	0	1	23	2	39	2	0	2	3	.400	0	9	2.25
	Charlotte	AAA	18	0	0	11	23.1	118	17	22	18	1	1	2	6	28	1	21	5	0	1	0	1.000	0	0	6.94
	7 Min. YEARS		225	17	2	132	393.2	1754	289	191	152	12	12	16	36	303	8	437	44	9	22	20	.524	1	39	3.48

Scott McClain

Bats: Right   Throws: Right   Pos: 3B **Ht: 6'3"   Wt: 209   Born: 05/19/72   Age: 23**

			BATTING														BASERUNNING				PERCENTAGES		
Year	Team	Lg	G	AB	H	2B	3B	HR	TB	R	RBI	TBB	IBB	SO	HBP	SH	SF	SB	CS	SB%	GDP	Avg	OBP	SLG
1990	Bluefield	R	40	107	21	2	0	4	35	20	15	22	0	35	2	0	4	2	3	.40	4	.196	.333	.327
1991	Kane County	A	25	81	18	0	0	0	18	9	4	17	0	25	0	1	0	1	1	.50	4	.222	.357	.222
	Bluefield	R	41	149	39	5	0	0	44	16	24	14	0	39	3	0	1	5	3	.63	5	.262	.335	.295
1992	Kane County	A	96	316	84	12	2	3	109	43	30	48	1	62	6	6	1	7	4	.64	5	.266	.372	.345
1993	Frederick	A	133	427	111	22	2	9	164	65	54	70	0	88	6	3	2	10	6	.63	8	.260	.370	.384

Year Team	Lg	G	AB	H	2B	3B	HR	TB	R	RBI	TBB	IBB	SO	HBP	SH	SF	SB	CS	SB%	GDP	Avg	OBP	SLG
1994 Bowie	AA	133	427	103	29	1	11	167	71	58	72	2	89	1	2	7	6	3	.67	14	.241	.347	.391
5 Min. YEARS		468	1507	376	70	5	27	537	224	185	243	3	338	18	12	15	31	20	.61	35	.250	.357	.356

Chad McConnell

Bats: Right **Throws:** Right **Pos:** RF **Ht:** 6'1" **Wt:** 180 **Born:** 10/13/70 **Age:** 24

					BATTING												BASERUNNING				PERCENTAGES		
Year Team	Lg	G	AB	H	2B	3B	HR	TB	R	RBI	TBB	IBB	SO	HBP	SH	SF	SB	CS	SB%	GDP	Avg	OBP	SLG
1993 Clearwater	A	90	300	72	17	3	6	113	43	37	51	2	98	4	0	2	9	5	.64	6	.240	.356	.377
1994 Clearwater	A	29	101	32	3	3	4	53	19	19	16	0	28	0	0	0	2	1	.67	4	.317	.410	.525
Reading	AA	88	267	62	9	3	6	95	30	41	24	1	86	6	2	2	7	5	.58	6	.232	.308	.356
2 Min. YEARS		207	668	166	29	9	16	261	92	97	91	3	212	10	2	4	18	11	.62	16	.249	.345	.391

Tim McConnell

Bats: Right **Throws:** Right **Pos:** C **Ht:** 5'11" **Wt:** 195 **Born:** 10/03/68 **Age:** 26

					BATTING												BASERUNNING				PERCENTAGES		
Year Team	Lg	G	AB	H	2B	3B	HR	TB	R	RBI	TBB	IBB	SO	HBP	SH	SF	SB	CS	SB%	GDP	Avg	OBP	SLG
1992 Fayettevlle	A	53	176	43	6	3	4	67	21	22	19	1	28	3	6	3	0	2	.00	6	.244	.323	.381
1993 Lakeland	A	81	253	69	16	3	3	100	34	43	41	2	48	0	5	6	9	3	.75	1	.273	.367	.395
1994 Trenton	AA	42	118	29	6	0	2	41	16	13	12	0	17	2	2	2	1	1	.50	2	.246	.321	.347
3 Min. YEARS		176	547	141	28	6	9	208	71	78	72	3	93	5	13	11	10	6	.63	9	.258	.343	.380

Trey McCoy

Bats: Right **Throws:** Right **Pos:** 1B **Ht:** 6'3" **Wt:** 215 **Born:** 10/12/66 **Age:** 28

					BATTING												BASERUNNING				PERCENTAGES		
Year Team	Lg	G	AB	H	2B	3B	HR	TB	R	RBI	TBB	IBB	SO	HBP	SH	SF	SB	CS	SB%	GDP	Avg	OBP	SLG
1990 Charlotte	A	45	160	37	11	0	3	57	19	18	23	0	35	1	0	0	0	0	.00	0	.231	.332	.356
Gastonia	A	24	80	27	6	0	4	45	13	11	12	1	12	0	0	2	1	1	.50	0	.338	.415	.563
1991 Tulsa	AA	44	137	33	7	0	10	70	21	32	33	4	26	2	0	2	0	0	.00	6	.241	.391	.511
1992 Tulsa	AA	15	52	10	0	0	2	16	5	6	8	0	15	0	0	0	0	1	.00	0	.192	.300	.308
Gastonia	A	32	99	35	6	0	8	65	17	30	23	0	19	7	0	2	3	0	1.00	0	.354	.496	.657
1993 Tulsa	AA	125	420	123	27	3	29	243	72	95	65	4	79	19	0	2	3	2	.60	9	.293	.409	.579
Okla City	AAA	8	28	7	1	1	3	19	6	11	5	0	5	1	0	0	0	0	.00	0	.250	.382	.679
1994 Okla. City	AAA	101	353	108	29	1	15	184	54	67	41	1	65	10	0	5	1	0	1.00	9	.306	.389	.521
5 Min. YEARS		394	1329	380	87	5	74	699	207	270	210	10	256	40	0	13	8	4	.67	24	.286	.396	.526

Quinton McCracken

Bats: Both **Throws:** Right **Pos:** 2B **Ht:** 5'8" **Wt:** 170 **Born:** 03/16/70 **Age:** 25

					BATTING												BASERUNNING				PERCENTAGES		
Year Team	Lg	G	AB	H	2B	3B	HR	TB	R	RBI	TBB	IBB	SO	HBP	SH	SF	SB	CS	SB%	GDP	Avg	OBP	SLG
1992 Bend	A	67	232	65	13	2	0	82	37	27	25	0	39	0	7	2	18	6	.75	6	.280	.347	.353
1993 Central Val	A	127	483	141	17	7	2	178	94	58	78	4	90	2	12	4	60	19	.76	15	.292	.390	.369
1994 New Haven	AA	136	544	151	27	4	5	201	94	39	48	4	72	4	10	4	36	19	.65	6	.278	.338	.369
3 Min. YEARS		330	1259	357	57	13	7	461	225	124	151	8	201	6	29	10	114	44	.72	27	.284	.360	.366

Jim McCready

Pitches: Right **Bats:** Right **Pos:** P **Ht:** 6'1" **Wt:** 177 **Born:** 11/25/69 **Age:** 25

		HOW MUCH HE PITCHED					WHAT HE GAVE UP										THE RESULTS				
Year Team	Lg	G	GS	CG	GF	IP	BFP	H	R	ER	HR	SH	SF	HB	TBB	IBB	SO	WP	Bk	W	L	Pct.	ShO	Sv	ERA
1991 Mets	R	16	6	2	8	77.2	328	69	36	28	1	0	2	4	18	1	59	5	4	6	4	.600	0	1	3.24
1992 Columbia	A	35	9	1	17	87.1	362	85	35	24	3	3	0	5	23	0	54	4	0	5	3	.625	1	5	2.47
1993 St.Lucie	A	40	0	0	30	61.1	250	51	18	12	0	8	2	2	22	6	40	2	0	6	4	.600	0	16	1.76
Binghamton	AA	14	0	0	4	18.1	73	18	7	7	0	2	0	0	4	1	12	0	0	1	1	.500	0	0	3.44
1994 Binghamton	AA	63	0	0	26	83.2	359	78	35	30	4	6	5	9	28	3	52	7	0	6	6	.500	0	7	3.23
4 Min. YEARS		168	15	3	85	328.1	1372	301	131	101	8	19	9	20	95	11	217	18	4	24	18	.571	1	29	2.77

Jeff McCurry

Pitches: Right **Bats:** Right **Pos:** P **Ht:** 6'7" **Wt:** 210 **Born:** 01/21/70 **Age:** 25

		HOW MUCH HE PITCHED					WHAT HE GAVE UP										THE RESULTS				
Year Team	Lg	G	GS	CG	GF	IP	BFP	H	R	ER	HR	SH	SF	HB	TBB	IBB	SO	WP	Bk	W	L	Pct.	ShO	Sv	ERA
1991 Pirates	R	6	1	0	0	14	68	19	10	4	0	0	1	2	4	0	8	2	1	1	0	1.000	0	0	2.57
Welland	A	9	0	0	5	15.2	70	11	4	1	0	3	0	0	10	3	18	5	1	2	1	.667	0	0	0.57
1992 Augusta	A	19	0	0	13	30	142	36	14	11	1	6	1	3	15	1	34	4	1	2	1	.667	0	7	3.30
Salem	A	30	0	0	15	62.2	255	49	22	20	3	4	2	3	24	3	52	7	0	6	2	.750	0	3	2.87
1993 Salem	A	41	0	0	36	44	184	41	21	19	3	3	3	0	15	3	32	5	0	1	4	.200	0	22	3.89
Carolina	AA	23	0	0	5	29	121	24	11	9	1	2	1	0	14	2	14	2	0	2	1	.667	0	0	2.79
1994 Carolina	AA	48	2	0	32	81.1	350	74	35	29	7	5	1	6	30	3	60	9	1	6	5	.545	0	11	3.21
4 Min. YEARS		176	3	0	106	276.2	1190	254	117	93	15	23	9	14	112	15	218	34	4	20	14	.588	0	43	3.03

Shawn McDonnell

Bats: Both **Throws:** Right **Pos:** C **Ht:** 6'2" **Wt:** 205 **Born:** 04/04/70 **Age:** 25

					BATTING												BASERUNNING				PERCENTAGES		
Year Team	Lg	G	AB	H	2B	3B	HR	TB	R	RBI	TBB	IBB	SO	HBP	SH	SF	SB	CS	SB%	GDP	Avg	OBP	SLG
1993 Daytona	A	42	141	39	2	0	2	47	18	14	20	1	18	1	1	0	2	2	.50	3	.277	.370	.333

		G	AB	H	2B	3B	HR	TB	R	RBI	TBB	IBB	SO	HBP	SH	SF	SB	CS	SB%	GDP	Avg	OBP	SLG
	Orlando AA	18	47	10	2	0	0	12	2	8	4	1	14	1	2	0	0	0	.00	0	.213	.288	.255
1994	Peoria A	54	140	40	4	0	2	50	20	20	44	1	37	4	2	1	4	1	.80	3	.286	.466	.357
	Orlando AA	18	49	9	0	0	0	9	4	3	5	0	11	0	0	0	0	0	.00	1	.184	.259	.184
	2 Min. YEARS	132	377	98	8	0	4	118	44	45	73	3	80	6	5	1	6	3	.67	7	.260	.387	.313

Jason McFarlin

Bats: Left Throws: Left Pos: OF Ht: 6'0" Wt: 175 Born: 06/28/70 Age: 25

			BATTING															BASERUNNING				PERCENTAGES		
Year	Team	Lg	G	AB	H	2B	3B	HR	TB	R	RBI	TBB	IBB	SO	HBP	SH	SF	SB	CS	SB%	GDP	Avg	OBP	SLG
1989	Everett	A	37	131	34	4	3	0	44	17	12	5	1	25	1	2	2	7	3	.70	3	.260	.288	.336
1990	Clinton	A	129	476	108	9	5	0	127	68	34	47	2	79	9	7	1	72	19	.79	7	.227	.308	.267
1991	San Jose	A	103	407	95	10	5	2	121	65	33	47	2	72	14	10	2	46	20	.70	6	.233	.332	.297
1992	San Jose	A	70	276	84	7	3	1	100	61	24	27	1	43	9	5	1	32	11	.74	4	.304	.383	.362
	Shreveport	AA	28	106	22	3	3	1	34	13	3	5	0	20	4	2	0	10	1	.91	0	.208	.270	.321
1993	Shreveport	AA	21	59	11	2	1	0	15	12	1	4	0	12	2	1	0	4	1	.80	0	.186	.262	.254
	San Jose	A	97	395	123	20	4	7	172	71	53	29	0	67	3	7	4	49	10	.83	5	.311	.360	.435
1994	Shreveport	AA	106	306	87	11	4	5	121	37	29	17	5	31	6	2	4	21	8	.72	6	.284	.330	.395
	6 Min. YEARS		591	2156	564	66	28	16	734	344	186	181	11	349	48	36	14	241	73	.77	31	.262	.331	.340

Terric McFarlin

Pitches: Right Bats: Both Pos: P Ht: 6'0" Wt: 160 Born: 04/06/69 Age: 26

			HOW MUCH HE PITCHED						WHAT HE GAVE UP												THE RESULTS					
Year	Team	Lg	G	GS	CG	GF	IP	BFP	H	R	ER	HR	SH	SF	HB	TBB	IBB	SO	WP	Bk	W	L	Pct.	ShO	Sv	ERA
1991	Bakersfield	A	26	21	0	3	152	634	139	63	45	6	5	5	1	56	2	128	17	0	14	6	.700	0	0	2.66
1992	Bakersfield	A	6	5	0	1	27.1	115	16	10	8	2	0	0	1	19	0	30	1	0	2	0	1.000	0	0	2.63
1993	San Antonio	AA	52	0	0	24	95.1	407	87	37	30	2	6	2	3	37	4	77	7	0	4	7	.364	0	0	2.83
1994	Wichita	AA	30	0	0	10	41	169	30	16	10	3	0	0	0	17	3	38	5	1	1	2	.333	0	3	2.20
	Las Vegas	AAA	33	0	0	12	62.2	284	72	51	42	9	4	4	2	22	4	58	1	0	1	5	.167	0	2	6.03
	4 Min. YEARS		147	26	0	50	378.1	1609	344	177	135	22	18	11	7	151	13	331	31	1	22	20	.524	0	9	3.21

Kevin McGehee

Pitches: Right Bats: Right Pos: P Ht: 6' 0" Wt: 190 Born: 01/18/69 Age: 26

			HOW MUCH HE PITCHED						WHAT HE GAVE UP												THE RESULTS					
Year	Team	Lg	G	GS	CG	GF	IP	BFP	H	R	ER	HR	SH	SF	HB	TBB	IBB	SO	WP	Bk	W	L	Pct.	ShO	Sv	ERA
1990	Everett	A	15	14	1	0	73.2	333	74	48	39	6	3	2	4	38	0	86	16	5	4	8	.333	0	0	4.76
1991	San Jose	A	26	26	2	0	174	735	129	58	45	1	5	6	8	87	2	171	11	2	13	6	.684	0	0	2.33
1992	Shreveport	AA	25	24	1	0	158.1	654	146	61	52	10	3	7	5	42	0	140	8	1	9	7	.563	0	0	2.96
1993	Phoenix	AAA	4	4	0	0	22	104	28	16	12	1	1	3	5	8	1	16	1	0	0	3	.000	0	0	4.91
	Rochester	AAA	20	20	2	0	133.2	551	124	53	44	14	1	3	7	37	1	92	3	0	7	6	.538	0	0	2.96
1994	Rochester	AAA	25	24	1	0	149.1	638	165	85	79	24	2	7	9	35	2	89	7	1	10	8	.556	1	0	4.76
1993	Baltimore	AL	5	0	0	1	16.2	75	18	11	11	5	1	1	2	7	2	7	1	0	0	0	.000	0	0	5.94
	5 Min. YEARS		115	112	8	0	711	3015	666	321	271	56	15	28	38	247	6	594	46	9	43	38	.531	1	0	3.43

Russ McGinnis

Bats: Right Throws: Right Pos: 1B Ht: 6' 3" Wt: 225 Born: 06/18/63 Age: 32

				BATTING														BASERUNNING				PERCENTAGES		
Year	Team	Lg	G	AB	H	2B	3B	HR	TB	R	RBI	TBB	IBB	SO	HBP	SH	SF	SB	CS	SB%	GDP	Avg	OBP	SLG
1985	Helena	R	48	150	46	7	0	5	68	33	38	31	1	19	4	0	2	2	2	.50	5	.307	.433	.453
1986	Beloit	A	124	413	102	24	2	16	178	62	59	52	2	79	12	3	4	5	2	.71	13	.247	.345	.431
1987	Beloit	A	51	189	58	10	0	13	107	34	35	19	2	36	2	1	0	1	2	.33	4	.307	.376	.566
	Modesto	A	47	165	42	9	0	8	75	24	31	23	1	33	2	3	3	1	1	.50	4	.255	.347	.455
1988	Huntsville	AA	23	77	20	9	0	2	35	9	15	7	0	13	0	0	0	1	0	1.00	1	.260	.321	.455
	Tacoma	AAA	63	186	47	13	1	2	68	25	22	21	0	38	1	3	1	1	0	1.00	7	.253	.330	.366
1989	Tacoma	AAA	110	380	105	25	0	7	151	42	60	45	0	78	6	2	5	0	1	.00	6	.276	.358	.397
1990	Tacoma	AAA	110	359	89	19	1	13	149	57	77	75	2	70	6	1	7	2	1	.67	15	.248	.380	.415
1991	Iowa	AAA	111	374	105	18	2	15	172	70	70	63	6	68	6	1	4	3	1	.75	12	.281	.389	.460
1992	Okla City	AAA	99	330	87	19	1	18	162	63	51	79	1	52	7	2	2	0	6	.00	15	.264	.414	.491
1993	Omaha	AAA	78	275	80	20	2	16	152	53	54	42	1	44	7	0	5	1	0	1.00	11	.291	.392	.553
1994	Omaha	AAA	98	344	97	21	1	24	192	73	70	64	1	64	14	0	5	1	3	.25	11	.282	.410	.558
1992	Texas	AL	14	33	8	4	0	0	12	2	4	3	0	7	0	0	0	0	0	.00	0	.242	.306	.364
	10 Min. YEARS		962	3242	878	194	10	139	1509	545	582	521	17	594	67	16	38	18	19	.49	104	.271	.379	.465

Thomas McGraw

Pitches: Left Bats: Left Pos: P Ht: 6'2" Wt: 195 Born: 12/08/67 Age: 27

			HOW MUCH HE PITCHED						WHAT HE GAVE UP												THE RESULTS					
Year	Team	Lg	G	GS	CG	GF	IP	BFP	H	R	ER	HR	SH	SF	HB	TBB	IBB	SO	WP	Bk	W	L	Pct.	ShO	Sv	ERA
1990	Beloit	A	12	12	1	0	70	299	49	33	15	1	1	2	2	34	0	61	4	4	7	3	.700	1	0	1.93
1991	El Paso	AA	9	7	0	2	35.2	163	43	28	23	1	2	1	1	21	0	28	0	0	1	1	.500	0	0	5.80
	Stockton	A	11	7	0	1	47	183	35	15	12	2	2	1	2	13	0	39	3	1	3	0	1.000	0	0	2.30
1992	Stockton	A	15	15	1	0	97.1	414	97	44	29	1	4	3	2	31	5	70	5	0	6	4	.600	0	0	2.68
	El Paso	AA	11	10	1	1	69.1	299	75	24	21	2	2	0	2	26	1	53	2	0	6	0	1.000	0	0	2.73
1993	High Desert	A	6	6	1	0	38	153	38	17	15	3	1	2	1	7	0	31	1	0	2	3	.400	0	0	3.55

Year	Team	Lg	G	GS	CG	GF	IP	BFP	H	R	ER	HR	SH	SF	HB	TBB	IBB	SO	WP	Bk	W	L	Pct.	ShO	Sv	ERA
	Edmonton	AAA	5	2	0	1	9.2	45	12	7	6	1	0	1	0	4	0	8	1	0	2	0	1.000	0	0	5.59
1994	Portland	AA	37	7	0	11	74	327	81	44	38	9	3	1	5	35	3	56	6	0	3	5	.375	0	2	4.62
	5 Min. YEARS		106	66	4	16	441	1883	430	212	159	20	15	11	13	171	9	346	22	5	30	16	.652	1	3	3.24

Tim McIntosh

Bats: Right Throws: Right Pos: C   **Ht: 5'11" Wt: 195 Born: 03/21/65 Age: 30**

			BATTING														BASERUNNING				PERCENTAGES		
Year	Team	Lg	G	AB	H	2B	3B	HR	TB	R	RBI	TBB	IBB	SO	HBP	SH	SF	SB	CS	SB%	GDP	Avg	OBP	SLG
1986	Beloit	A	49	173	45	3	2	4	64	26	21	18	0	33	2	0	3	0	0	.00	3	.260	.332	.370
1987	Beloit	A	130	461	139	30	3	20	235	83	85	49	2	96	7	1	3	7	4	.64	4	.302	.375	.510
1988	Stockton	A	138	519	147	32	6	15	236	81	92	57	1	96	11	6	5	10	5	.67	6	.283	.363	.455
1989	El Paso	AA	120	463	139	30	3	17	226	72	93	29	3	72	8	2	9	5	4	.56	8	.300	.346	.488
1990	Denver	AAA	116	416	120	20	3	18	200	72	74	26	0	58	14	3	7	6	2	.75	9	.288	.346	.481
1991	Denver	AAA	122	462	135	19	9	18	226	69	91	37	4	59	11	0	7	2	5	.29	13	.292	.354	.489
1993	Ottawa	AAA	27	106	31	7	1	6	58	15	21	10	2	22	0	0	2	1	0	1.00	3	.292	.347	.547
1994	Salt Lake	AAA	118	464	157	34	0	18	245	87	96	26	0	48	14	2	6	1	0	1.00	10	.338	.386	.528
1990	Milwaukee	AL	5	5	1	0	0	1	4	1	1	0	0	2	0	0	0	0	0	.00	0	.200	.200	.800
1991	Milwaukee	AL	7	11	4	1	0	1	8	2	1	0	0	4	0	0	0	0	0	.00	0	.364	.364	.727
1992	Milwaukee	AL	35	77	14	3	0	0	17	7	6	3	0	9	2	1	1	1	3	.25	1	.182	.229	.221
1993	Milwaukee	AL	1	0	0	0	0	0	0	0	0	0	0	0	0	0	0	0	0	.00	0	.000	.000	.000
	Montreal	NL	20	21	2	1	0	0	3	2	2	0	0	7	0	0	0	0	0	.00	0	.095	.095	.143
	8 Min. YEARS		820	3064	913	175	27	116	1490	505	573	252	12	484	67	14	42	32	20	.62	56	.298	.360	.486
	4 Maj. YEARS		68	114	21	5	0	2	32	12	10	3	0	22	2	1	1	1	3	.25	1	.184	.217	.281

Walt McKeel

Bats: Right Throws: Right Pos: C   **Ht: 6'2" Wt: 200 Born: 01/17/72 Age: 23**

			BATTING														BASERUNNING				PERCENTAGES		
Year	Team	Lg	G	AB	H	2B	3B	HR	TB	R	RBI	TBB	IBB	SO	HBP	SH	SF	SB	CS	SB%	GDP	Avg	OBP	SLG
1990	Red Sox	R	13	44	11	3	0	0	14	2	6	3	0	8	0	0	1	0	2	.00	2	.250	.292	.318
1991	Red Sox	R	35	113	15	0	1	2	23	10	12	17	0	20	1	0	4	0	0	.00	5	.133	.244	.204
1992	Lynchburg	A	96	288	64	11	0	12	111	33	33	22	0	77	3	5	1	2	1	.67	3	.222	.283	.385
1993	Lynchburg	A	80	247	59	17	2	5	95	28	32	26	0	40	3	6	3	0	1	.00	6	.239	.315	.385
1994	Sarasota	A	37	137	38	8	1	2	54	15	15	8	1	19	1	0	0	1	0	1.00	1	.277	.322	.394
	New Britain	AA	50	164	30	6	1	1	41	10	17	7	1	35	3	1	2	0	0	.00	5	.183	.227	.250
	5 Min. YEARS		311	993	217	45	5	22	338	98	115	83	2	199	11	12	11	3	4	.43	22	.219	.283	.340

Craig McMurtry

Pitches: Right Bats: Right Pos: P   **Ht: 6'5" Wt: 192 Born: 11/05/59 Age: 35**

			HOW MUCH HE PITCHED						WHAT HE GAVE UP												THE RESULTS				
Year	Team	Lg	G	GS	CG	GF	IP	BFP	H	R	ER	HR	SH	SF	HB	TBB	IBB	SO	WP	Bk	W	L	Pct.	ShO	Sv	ERA
1985	Richmond	AAA	16	16	4	0	107.1	437	88	43	39	7	4	2	1	51	1	74	4	1	7	5	.583	2	0	3.27
1986	Greenville	AA	3	3	0	0	15	67	13	10	10	2	0	1	0	9	0	12	1	0	1	1	.500	0	0	6.00
1987	Knoxville	AA	12	11	1	0	78	313	64	28	24	3	2	3	0	20	0	56	2	0	4	2	.667	0	0	2.77
	Syracuse	AAA	9	8	1	0	53.2	212	46	23	21	6	0	1	0	15	0	31	2	0	5	3	.625	1	0	3.52
1988	Okla City	AAA	9	9	2	0	49.2	219	55	27	24	1	0	0	4	21	0	35	7	0	2	5	.286	0	0	4.35
1989	Rangers	R	4	2	0	0	8	27	3	2	1	0	0	0	0	2	0	10	0	0	0	1	.000	0	0	1.13
	Okla City	AAA	1	0	0	1	3	11	2	1	1	0	0	0	0	1	0	1	0	0	0	0	.000	0	0	3.00
1990	Okla City	AAA	6	5	0	0	26.2	129	31	15	8	0	0	0	1	21	0	19	3	0	1	1	.500	0	0	2.70
1991	Phoenix	AAA	27	15	1	4	113	489	117	70	55	8	3	3	2	44	1	67	4	1	10	6	.625	1	0	4.38
1992	Phoenix	AAA	40	14	1	10	129.2	566	140	71	61	5	9	5	4	59	4	83	6	0	5	8	.385	1	1	4.23
1993	Buffalo	AAA	30	13	1	6	96.2	422	102	44	37	6	6	3	3	38	4	63	2	0	6	4	.600	1	1	3.44
1994	Tucson	AAA	29	19	0	3	126.1	519	118	55	50	10	4	4	3	35	0	109	2	0	8	4	.667	0	2	3.56
1983	Atlanta	NL	36	35	6	0	224.2	943	204	86	77	13	9	5	1	88	1	105	1	2	15	9	.625	3	0	3.08
1984	Atlanta	NL	37	30	0	1	183.1	811	184	100	88	16	12	9	1	102	4	99	4	3	9	17	.346	0	0	4.32
1985	Atlanta	NL	17	6	0	3	45	220	56	36	33	6	7	2	1	27	1	28	3	0	0	3	.000	0	1	6.60
1986	Atlanta	NL	37	5	0	5	79.2	356	82	46	42	7	0	2	2	43	5	50	2	0	1	6	.143	0	0	4.74
1988	Texas	AL	32	0	0	14	60	236	37	16	15	5	3	3	1	24	4	35	2	2	3	3	.500	0	3	2.25
1989	Texas	AL	19	0	0	4	23	111	29	21	19	3	1	2	2	13	1	14	1	1	0	0	.000	0	0	7.43
1990	Texas	AL	23	3	0	6	41.2	188	43	25	20	4	2	2	1	30	0	14	3	0	0	0	.000	0	0	4.32
	10 Min. YEARS		186	115	11	24	807	3411	779	389	331	48	28	22	18	316	10	560	33	2	49	40	.551	6	4	3.69
	7 Maj. YEARS		201	79	6	33	657.1	2865	635	330	294	54	34	25	9	327	16	345	16	8	28	41	.406	3	4	4.03

Buck McNabb

Bats: Left Throws: Right Pos: OF   **Ht: 6'0" Wt: 180 Born: 01/17/73 Age: 22**

			BATTING														BASERUNNING				PERCENTAGES		
Year	Team	Lg	G	AB	H	2B	3B	HR	TB	R	RBI	TBB	IBB	SO	HBP	SH	SF	SB	CS	SB%	GDP	Avg	OBP	SLG
1991	Astros	R	48	174	51	3	3	0	60	34	9	12	0	33	4	3	2	23	8	.74	0	.293	.349	.345
1992	Burlington	A	123	456	118	12	3	1	139	82	34	60	0	80	10	3	2	56	19	.75	4	.259	.356	.305
1993	Osceola	A	125	487	139	15	7	1	171	69	35	52	2	66	6	4	1	28	15	.65	8	.285	.361	.351
1994	Jackson	AA	125	454	124	25	7	0	163	67	27	26	0	63	1	4	2	15	17	.47	10	.273	.313	.359
	4 Min. YEARS		421	1571	432	55	20	2	533	252	105	150	2	242	21	14	7	122	59	.67	22	.275	.345	.339

Fred McNair

Bats: Right **Throws:** Right **Pos:** SS **Ht:** 6'4" **Wt:** 215 **Born:** 01/31/70 **Age:** 25

							BATTING												BASERUNNING				PERCENTAGES		
Year	Team	Lg	G	AB	H	2B	3B	HR	TB	R	RBI	TBB	IBB	SO	HBP	SH	SF	SB	CS	SB%	GDP	Avg	OBP	SLG
1989	Mariners	R	36	142	40	6	2	4	62	24	18	7	0	38	2	0	2	4	2	.67	2	.282	.320	.437
1990	Bellingham	A	50	176	36	8	0	3	53	16	17	15	1	55	3	1	0	7	3	.70	3	.205	.278	.301
1992	Bellingham	A	69	255	84	9	2	8	121	41	54	21	4	69	4	0	0	13	10	.57	9	.329	.389	.475
1993	Riverside	A	112	400	108	21	1	14	173	70	65	41	2	91	5	1	4	6	7	.46	11	.270	.342	.433
1994	Jacksonvile	AA	57	200	44	11	0	4	67	17	21	12	1	47	1	0	1	3	1	.75	5	.220	.266	.335
	Appleton	A	60	222	67	15	3	9	115	34	49	11	0	48	2	0	3	7	0	1.00	6	.302	.336	.518
	5 Min. YEARS		384	1395	379	70	8	42	591	202	224	107	8	348	17	2	10	40	23	.63	36	.272	.329	.424

Jim McNamara

Bats: Left **Throws:** Right **Pos:** C **Ht:** 6'4" **Wt:** 210 **Born:** 06/10/65 **Age:** 30

							BATTING												BASERUNNING				PERCENTAGES		
Year	Team	Lg	G	AB	H	2B	3B	HR	TB	R	RBI	TBB	IBB	SO	HBP	SH	SF	SB	CS	SB%	GDP	Avg	OBP	SLG
1986	Everett	A	46	158	39	1	2	8	68	23	30	18	2	39	3	0	2	0	0	.00	3	.247	.331	.430
1987	Clinton	A	110	385	95	22	1	5	134	43	53	19	1	52	0	2	7	4	2	.67	15	.247	.277	.348
1988	San Jose	A	93	315	59	9	0	1	71	27	41	43	1	76	2	0	2	3	4	.43	18	.187	.287	.225
1989	Salinas	A	49	155	37	8	0	0	45	9	10	22	2	24	0	1	0	3	1	.75	3	.239	.333	.290
	Phoenix	AAA	27	69	12	3	0	0	15	3	4	4	0	13	0	2	0	1	2	.33	2	.174	.219	.217
	San Jose	A	19	65	18	2	0	1	23	2	8	1	0	13	0	0	1	0	1	.00	3	.277	.284	.354
1990	San Jose	A	53	158	32	2	2	1	41	20	22	18	0	30	1	1	1	0	4	.00	3	.203	.287	.259
	Phoenix	AAA	6	20	9	0	0	0	9	2	1	3	0	4	0	0	0	0	0	.00	0	.450	.522	.450
	Shreveport	AA	28	79	19	7	0	0	26	2	13	7	0	9	0	0	0	0	1	.00	7	.241	.302	.329
1991	Phoenix	AAA	17	53	9	1	0	0	10	3	2	6	0	12	0	1	0	0	0	.00	1	.170	.254	.189
	Shreveport	AA	39	109	30	8	2	2	48	13	20	21	3	11	0	1	1	2	1	.67	2	.275	.389	.440
1992	Phoenix	AAA	23	67	14	3	0	0	17	5	3	14	3	13	0	0	0	0	0	.00	5	.209	.346	.254
1993	Phoenix	AAA	50	158	31	5	0	1	39	10	23	12	1	29	0	1	2	1	0	1.00	8	.196	.250	.247
1994	Okla. City	AAA	42	138	33	3	0	1	39	10	13	5	0	30	1	0	0	0	1	.00	3	.239	.271	.283
	Columbus	AAA	27	69	9	2	0	0	11	1	2	2	0	12	1	1	0	0	0	.00	2	.130	.167	.159
1992	San Francisco	NL	30	74	16	1	0	1	20	6	9	6	2	25	0	2	0	0	0	.00	1	.216	.275	.270
1993	San Francisco	NL	4	7	1	0	0	0	1	0	0	0	0	1	0	0	0	0	0	.00	0	.143	.143	.143
	9 Min. YEARS		629	1998	446	76	7	20	596	173	245	195	13	367	8	10	16	14	17	.45	75	.223	.293	.298
	2 Maj. YEARS		34	81	17	1	0	1	21	6	10	6	2	26	0	2	0	0	0	.00	1	.210	.264	.259

Jeff McNeely

Bats: Right **Throws:** Right **Pos:** OF **Ht:** 6'2" **Wt:** 200 **Born:** 10/18/69 **Age:** 25

							BATTING												BASERUNNING				PERCENTAGES		
Year	Team	Lg	G	AB	H	2B	3B	HR	TB	R	RBI	TBB	IBB	SO	HBP	SH	SF	SB	CS	SB%	GDP	Avg	OBP	SLG
1989	Red Sox	R	9	32	13	1	1	0	16	10	4	7	0	3	0	0	1	5	1	.83	1	.406	.500	.500
	Elmira	A	61	208	52	7	0	2	65	20	21	26	0	54	4	1	0	16	8	.67	4	.250	.345	.313
1990	Winter Havn	A	16	62	10	0	0	0	10	4	3	3	0	19	0	0	0	7	1	.88	1	.161	.200	.161
	Elmira	A	73	246	77	4	5	6	109	41	37	40	5	60	3	8	2	39	10	.80	7	.313	.412	.443
1991	Lynchburg	A	106	382	123	16	5	4	161	58	38	74	3	74	4	4	1	38	21	.64	5	.322	.436	.421
1992	New Britain	AA	85	261	57	8	4	2	79	30	11	26	0	78	2	4	0	10	5	.67	10	.218	.294	.303
1993	Pawtucket	AAA	129	498	130	14	3	2	156	65	35	43	1	102	3	10	2	40	7	.85	4	.261	.322	.313
1994	Pawtucket	AAA	117	458	106	15	5	4	143	60	34	49	0	100	9	5	3	13	17	.43	6	.231	.316	.312
1993	Boston	AL	21	37	11	1	1	0	14	10	1	7	0	9	0	0	0	6	0	1.00	0	.297	.409	.378
	6 Min. YEARS		596	2147	568	65	23	20	739	288	183	268	9	490	25	32	9	168	70	.71	38	.265	.352	.344

Paul Meade

Bats: Both **Throws:** Right **Pos:** SS **Ht:** 6'0" **Wt:** 175 **Born:** 02/14/69 **Age:** 26

							BATTING												BASERUNNING				PERCENTAGES		
Year	Team	Lg	G	AB	H	2B	3B	HR	TB	R	RBI	TBB	IBB	SO	HBP	SH	SF	SB	CS	SB%	GDP	Avg	OBP	SLG
1991	Kinston	A	17	45	4	0	0	0	4	4	1	4	0	20	1	2	0	2	0	1.00	0	.089	.180	.089
	Columbus	A	29	89	18	4	1	4	36	11	8	9	0	24	1	0	0	0	1	.00	0	.202	.283	.404
1992	Columbus	A	94	352	94	15	3	4	127	47	31	25	1	77	3	2	2	4	3	.57	9	.267	.319	.361
1993	Kinston	A	117	404	97	17	1	9	143	47	45	23	2	80	3	5	3	5	5	.50	10	.240	.284	.354
1994	Canton-Akrn	AA	107	397	99	21	5	3	139	49	42	24	3	79	2	3	2	4	6	.40	8	.249	.294	.350
	4 Min. YEARS		364	1287	312	57	10	20	449	158	127	85	6	280	10	12	7	15	15	.50	27	.242	.293	.349

Jim Mecir

Pitches: Right **Bats:** Both **Pos:** P **Ht:** 6'1" **Wt:** 195 **Born:** 05/16/70 **Age:** 25

			HOW MUCH HE PITCHED						WHAT HE GAVE UP												THE RESULTS					
Year	Team	Lg	G	GS	CG	GF	IP	BFP	H	R	ER	HR	SH	SF	HB	TBB	IBB	SO	WP	Bk	W	L	Pct.	ShO	Sv	ERA
1991	San Berndno	A	14	12	0	2	70.1	314	72	40	33	2	3	3	3	37	0	48	8	4	3	5	.375	0	1	4.22
1992	San Berndno	A	14	11	0	1	61.2	283	72	40	32	8	1	2	5	26	0	53	5	1	4	5	.444	0	0	4.67
1993	Riverside	A	26	26	1	0	145.1	654	160	89	70	3	3	8	15	58	2	85	4	0	9	11	.450	0	0	4.33
1994	Jacksonvile	AA	46	0	0	34	80.1	343	73	28	24	5	4	2	4	35	3	53	6	0	6	5	.545	0	13	2.69
	4 Min. YEARS		100	49	1	37	357.2	1594	377	197	159	19	10	15	27	156	5	239	23	5	22	26	.458	0	14	4.00

Kevin Meier

Pitches: Right **Bats:** Right **Pos:** P **Ht:** 6'4" **Wt:** 200 **Born:** 02/20/66 **Age:** 29

Year	Team	Lg	G	GS	CG	GF	IP	BFP	H	R	ER	HR	SH	SF	HB	TBB	IBB	SO	WP	Bk	W	L	Pct.	ShO	Sv	ERA
1987	Pocatello	R	6	5	1	1	36.1	162	39	16	13	2	2	1	0	11	0	24	3	3	3	0	1.000	0	0	3.22
	Fresno	A	13	3	0	2	49.1	201	45	22	20	4	1	2	0	18	0	26	4	0	3	2	.600	0	1	3.65
1988	San Jose	A	17	17	0	0	99	450	112	64	53	4	3	4	2	44	0	59	1	2	7	6	.538	0	0	4.82
1989	San Jose	A	19	19	5	0	140.1	549	110	43	35	5	6	4	2	32	0	95	3	0	11	6	.647	4	0	2.24
	Shreveport	AA	6	6	1	0	38	158	34	24	20	7	1	1	0	7	0	23	1	0	3	2	.600	0	0	4.74
1990	Shreveport	AA	14	14	1	0	87.2	365	91	32	30	2	1	2	1	21	1	61	3	0	6	5	.545	1	0	3.08
	Phoenix	AAA	13	13	0	0	68.1	302	82	41	33	9	1	3	2	21	0	25	0	0	5	3	.625	0	0	4.35
1991	Shreveport	AA	33	18	2	3	135.2	595	157	86	76	15	6	8	1	38	2	79	10	0	9	6	.600	0	0	5.04
1992	Arkansas	AA	27	27	2	0	171	694	156	63	49	15	4	2	2	37	3	107	8	1	11	6	.647	1	0	2.58
1993	Louisville	AAA	27	24	1	0	135	597	156	95	87	21	0	5	7	44	0	98	5	1	8	6	.571	0	0	5.80
1994	Colo. Spmg	AAA	30	11	0	5	93.1	437	136	79	68	17	4	3	3	27	3	71	6	0	5	5	.500	0	2	6.56
	8 Min. YEARS		205	157	13	11	1054	4510	1118	565	484	101	29	35	20	300	9	668	44	7	71	47	.602	6	3	4.13

Juan Melo

Bats: Both **Throws:** Right **Pos:** SS **Ht:** 6'1" **Wt:** 160 **Born:** 05/11/76 **Age:** 19

Year	Team	Lg	G	AB	H	2B	3B	HR	TB	R	RBI	TBB	IBB	SO	HBP	SH	SF	SB	CS	SB%	GDP	Avg	OBP	SLG
1994	Spokane	A	3	11	4	1	0	1	8	4	2	1	0	3	0	0	0	0	0	.00	1	.364	.417	.727
	Las Vegas	AAA	1	0	0	0	0	0	0	0	0	0	0	0	0	0	0	0	0	.00	0	.000	.000	.000
	Padres	R	37	145	41	3	3	0	50	20	15	10	0	36	6	0	1	3	2	.60	5	.283	.352	.345
	1 Min. YEARS		41	156	45	4	3	1	58	24	17	11	0	39	6	0	1	3	2	.60	6	.288	.356	.372

Kirk Mendenhall

Bats: Right **Throws:** Right **Pos:** SS **Ht:** 5'9" **Wt:** 160 **Born:** 09/17/67 **Age:** 27

Year	Team	Lg	G	AB	H	2B	3B	HR	TB	R	RBI	TBB	IBB	SO	HBP	SH	SF	SB	CS	SB%	GDP	Avg	OBP	SLG
1990	Niagara Fls	A	63	216	54	9	0	0	63	28	15	36	0	29	4	2	1	16	7	.70	3	.250	.366	.292
1991	Lakeland	A	111	354	89	10	4	1	110	38	38	36	0	57	2	12	3	9	8	.53	9	.251	.322	.311
1992	London	AA	105	362	87	17	2	4	120	54	36	52	0	61	4	4	2	9	7	.56	9	.240	.340	.331
1993	London	AA	97	275	56	5	1	1	66	41	18	30	0	45	5	4	3	21	4	.84	6	.204	.291	.240
1994	Trenton	AA	115	384	83	17	3	8	130	56	35	47	1	89	6	5	5	24	3	.89	4	.216	.308	.339
	Toledo	AAA	10	35	10	0	0	0	10	5	3	2	0	8	1	2	0	4	1	.80	2	.286	.342	.286
	5 Min. YEARS		501	1626	379	58	10	14	499	222	145	203	1	289	22	29	14	83	30	.73	33	.233	.324	.307

Orlando Mercado

Bats: Right **Throws:** Right **Pos:** C **Ht:** 6'0" **Wt:** 195 **Born:** 11/07/61 **Age:** 33

Year	Team	Lg	G	AB	H	2B	3B	HR	TB	R	RBI	TBB	IBB	SO	HBP	SH	SF	SB	CS	SB%	GDP	Avg	OBP	SLG
1984	Salt Lk Cty	AAA	29	109	39	9	2	6	70	18	22	6	1	20	0	0	0	0	0	.00	1	.358	.391	.642
1985	Okla City	AAA	59	206	52	7	1	8	85	20	29	19	0	37	2	2	2	1	0	1.00	7	.252	.319	.413
1986	Okla City	AAA	48	172	47	11	1	3	69	20	25	26	1	21	0	0	1	0	1	.00	6	.273	.367	.401
1987	Albuquerque	AAA	69	205	57	18	0	2	81	22	27	15	1	29	1	0	2	1	0	1.00	3	.278	.327	.395
1988	Tacoma	AAA	53	148	33	6	0	2	45	16	19	19	1	25	0	1	4	0	0	.00	1	.223	.304	.304
1989	Portland	AAA	57	196	58	20	1	4	92	17	29	16	1	30	1	0	4	0	1	.00	5	.296	.346	.469
1990	Tidewater	AAA	24	72	19	4	0	1	26	5	10	7	2	11	1	0	1	0	0	.00	4	.264	.333	.361
1991	Tidewater	AAA	55	159	43	12	0	4	67	13	26	11	3	28	0	3	6	0	1	.00	6	.270	.307	.421
1992	Tidewater	AAA	54	178	44	7	0	8	75	16	19	15	2	37	0	0	1	1	0	1.00	6	.247	.304	.421
1993	Iowa	AAA	8	28	10	2	0	1	15	4	5	1	0	6	0	0	0	0	0	.00	0	.357	.379	.536
	Charlotte	AAA	10	21	3	0	0	0	3	0	0	2	1	5	1	0	0	0	0	.00	0	.143	.250	.143
1994	Vancouver	AAA	12	40	9	5	0	0	14	2	3	0	0	9	0	0	0	0	0	.00	1	.225	.225	.350
1982	Seattle	AL	9	17	2	0	0	1	5	1	6	0	0	5	0	0	0	0	0	.00	0	.118	.194	.294
1983	Seattle	AL	66	178	35	11	2	1	53	10	16	14	0	27	1	2	2	2	2	.50	3	.197	.256	.298
1984	Seattle	AL	30	78	17	3	1	0	22	5	5	4	0	12	1	1	0	1	0	1.00	1	.218	.265	.282
1986	Texas	AL	46	102	24	1	1	1	30	7	7	6	0	13	1	1	2	0	1	.00	5	.235	.279	.294
1987	Detroit	AL	10	22	3	0	0	0	3	2	1	2	0	0	0	0	0	0	0	.00	0	.136	.208	.136
	Los Angeles	NL	7	5	3	1	0	0	4	1	1	1	0	1	0	0	0	0	0	.00	0	.600	.667	.800
1988	Oakland	AL	16	24	3	0	0	1	6	3	1	3	0	8	0	0	0	0	0	.00	0	.125	.222	.250
1989	Minnesota	AL	19	38	4	0	0	0	4	1	1	4	0	4	0	0	0	1	0	1.00	0	.105	.190	.105
1990	New York	NL	42	90	19	1	0	3	29	10	7	8	3	11	2	0	0	0	0	.00	4	.211	.290	.322
	Montreal	NL	8	8	2	0	0	0	2	0	0	1	0	0	0	0	0	0	0	.00	0	.250	.250	.250
	11 Min. YEARS		478	1534	414	101	5	39	642	153	214	137	13	258	6	6	21	3	3	.50	39	.270	.328	.419
	8 Mai. YEARS		253	562	112	17	4	7	158	40	45	42	3	82	5	4	4	4	3	.57	13	.199	.259	.281

Henry Mercedes

Bats: Right **Throws:** Right **Pos:** C **Ht:** 5'11" **Wt:** 185 **Born:** 07/23/69 **Age:** 25

Year	Team	Lg	G	AB	H	2B	3B	HR	TB	R	RBI	TBB	IBB	SO	HBP	SH	SF	SB	CS	SB%	GDP	Avg	OBP	SLG
1988	Athletics	R	2	5	2	0	0	0	2	1	0	0	0	0	0	0	0	0	0	.00	0	.400	.400	.400

Year	Team	Lg	G	AB	H	2B	3B	HR	TB	R	RBI	TBB	IBB	SO	HBP	SH	SF	SB	CS	SB%	GDP	Avg	OBP	SLG
1989	Madison	A	51	152	32	3	0	2	41	11	13	22	1	46	1	3	0	0	0	.00	1	.211	.314	.270
	Modesto	A	16	37	3	0	0	1	6	6	3	7	0	22	0	0	0	0	0	.00	2	.081	.227	.162
	Sou Oregon	A	22	61	10	0	1	0	12	6	1	10	0	24	1	0	0	0	2	.00	0	.164	.292	.197
1990	Tacoma	AAA	12	31	6	1	0	0	7	3	2	3	0	7	0	2	0	0	1	.00	2	.194	.265	.226
	Madison	A	90	282	64	13	2	3	90	29	38	30	0	100	1	6	2	6	0	1.00	5	.227	.302	.319
1991	Modesto	A	116	388	100	17	3	4	135	55	61	68	1	110	2	3	3	5	8	.38	6	.258	.369	.348
1992	Tacoma	AAA	85	246	57	9	2	0	70	36	20	26	0	60	0	4	0	1	3	.25	8	.232	.305	.285
1993	Tacoma	AAA	85	256	61	13	1	4	88	37	32	31	2	53	1	3	7	1	2	.33	8	.238	.315	.344
1994	Tacoma	AAA	66	205	39	5	1	1	49	16	17	13	0	60	0	5	3	1	2	.33	6	.190	.235	.239
1992	Oakland	AL	9	5	4	0	1	0	6	1	1	0	0	1	0	0	0	0	0	.00	0	.800	.800	1.200
1993	Oakland	AL	20	47	10	2	0	0	12	5	3	2	0	15	1	0	0	1	1	.50	0	.213	.260	.255
	7 Min. YEARS		545	1663	374	61	10	15	500	200	187	210	4	482	6	26	15	14	18	.44	38	.225	.312	.301
	2 Maj. YEARS		29	52	14	2	1	0	18	6	4	2	0	16	1	0	0	1	1	.50	0	.269	.309	.346

Mark Merchant

Bats: Both Throws: Right Pos: OF Ht: 6'2" Wt: 185 Born: 01/23/69 Age: 26

						BATTING												BASERUNNING				PERCENTAGES		
Year	Team	Lg	G	AB	H	2B	3B	HR	TB	R	RBI	TBB	IBB	SO	HBP	SH	SF	SB	CS	SB%	GDP	Avg	OBP	SLG
1987	Pirates	R	50	185	49	5	1	3	65	32	17	30	4	29	1	0	0	33	13	.72	0	.265	.370	.351
1988	Augusta	A	60	211	51	6	0	2	63	36	19	41	2	38	2	0	2	14	3	.82	5	.242	.367	.299
1989	Augusta	A	15	59	19	6	1	0	27	11	8	7	1	13	0	0	1	3	1	.75	1	.322	.388	.458
	San Berndno	A	119	429	90	15	2	11	142	65	46	61	1	101	2	0	4	17	6	.74	12	.210	.308	.331
1990	Williamsprt	AA	44	156	28	5	0	0	33	16	10	14	2	36	1	0	2	7	2	.78	8	.179	.249	.212
	San Berndno	A	29	102	32	3	0	4	47	22	19	20	0	34	0	0	0	8	2	.80	1	.314	.426	.461
1991	Peninsula	A	78	270	68	8	1	6	96	31	34	51	6	70	0	0	0	11	4	.73	7	.252	.371	.356
	Jacksnville	AA	51	156	44	10	0	5	69	22	17	21	4	37	1	0	1	3	4	.43	2	.282	.369	.442
1992	Jacksnville	AA	109	381	93	9	1	13	143	42	47	37	2	91	2	1	6	3	2	.60	11	.244	.310	.375
1993	Indianapols	AAA	3	6	1	1	0	0	2	2	0	2	0	3	0	1	0	0	0	.00	0	.167	.375	.333
	Chattanooga	AA	109	336	101	16	0	17	168	56	61	50	2	79	3	0	3	3	5	.38	9	.301	.393	.500
1994	Chattanooga	AA	106	329	102	14	2	5	135	31	56	39	8	46	0	1	5	1	2	.33	10	.310	.378	.410
	8 Min. YEARS		773	2620	678	98	8	66	990	366	334	373	32	577	12	3	24	103	44	.70	66	.259	.351	.378

Marc Mesewicz

Pitches: Left Bats: Left Pos: P Ht: 6'3" Wt: 195 Born: 10/13/69 Age: 25

			HOW MUCH HE PITCHED						WHAT HE GAVE UP											THE RESULTS					
Year	Team	Lg	G	GS	CG	GF	IP	BFP	H	R	ER	HR	SH	SF	HB	TBB	IBB	SO	WP	Bk	W	L	Pct.	ShO	Sv	ERA
1992	Welland	A	29	0	0	17	47.1	197	43	19	13	1	2	0	1	16	2	55	5	0	5	3	.625	0	5	2.47
1993	Augusta	A	12	0	0	8	15.1	66	14	9	7	2	2	0	0	3	0	17	3	0	2	2	.000	0	0	4.11
	Salem	A	48	0	0	12	65.1	265	57	24	20	7	3	0	3	15	0	75	6	0	4	4	.500	0	1	2.76
1994	Carolina	AA	55	0	0	12	72	311	74	41	34	5	2	2	7	17	0	52	5	0	6	2	.750	0	6	4.25
	3 Min. YEARS		144	0	0	49	200	839	188	93	74	15	9	2	11	51	2	199	19	0	15	11	.577	0	6	3.33

Joe Mikulik

Bats: Right Throws: Right Pos: OF Ht: 5'11" Wt: 180 Born: 10/30/63 Age: 31

						BATTING												BASERUNNING				PERCENTAGES		
Year	Team	Lg	G	AB	H	2B	3B	HR	TB	R	RBI	TBB	IBB	SO	HBP	SH	SF	SB	CS	SB%	GDP	Avg	OBP	SLG
1984	Auburn	A	76	283	70	8	1	2	86	57	27	28	0	55	3	1	2	23	8	.74	4	.247	.320	.304
1985	Asheville	A	135	529	141	27	3	23	243	87	87	37	0	94	10	3	5	18	3	.86	10	.267	.324	.459
1986	Columbus	AA	130	502	151	21	11	9	221	80	69	33	0	92	7	1	3	18	13	.58	8	.301	.350	.440
1987	Columbus	AA	133	488	118	17	9	12	189	88	57	36	0	93	5	4	2	11	5	.69	11	.242	.299	.387
1988	Tucson	AAA	68	176	39	6	4	1	56	15	17	10	0	38	0	2	1	6	4	.60	6	.222	.262	.318
	Columbus	AA	48	189	52	8	4	3	77	33	34	16	0	34	1	0	3	13	6	.68	5	.275	.330	.407
1989	Tucson	AAA	8	17	5	0	0	0	5	2	3	0	0	5	1	0	1	0	0	.00	0	.294	.316	.294
1990	Columbus	AA	46	120	31	3	2	4	50	17	20	16	1	22	0	1	1	8	1	.89	3	.258	.343	.417
	Tucson	AAA	62	175	58	11	2	1	76	31	29	13	2	17	1	1	2	3	4	.43	7	.331	.377	.434
1991	Jackson	AA	133	492	144	17	4	15	214	76	94	41	8	62	4	0	5	20	8	.71	10	.293	.349	.435
	Tucson	AAA	2	4	2	0	0	0	2	2	0	0	0	0	0	0	0	1	0	1.00	0	.500	.500	.500
1992	Tucson	AAA	59	161	40	10	3	1	59	22	18	7	2	22	0	3	3	1	1	.50	4	.248	.275	.366
	Jackson	AA	46	168	44	7	2	3	64	20	20	7	0	30	0	1	1	4	4	.50	4	.262	.290	.381
1993	Tucson	AAA	94	296	89	24	2	4	129	48	45	14	2	39	1	1	1	9	6	.60	7	.301	.333	.436
1994	Tucson	AAA	13	34	12	2	1	0	16	8	7	1	0	8	0	0	0	0	0	.00	0	.353	.371	.471
	11 Min. YEARS		1053	3634	996	161	48	78	1487	586	527	259	15	611	33	18	30	135	63	.68	79	.274	.326	.409

Sam Militello

Pitches: Right Bats: Right Pos: P Ht: 6' 3" Wt: 195 Born: 11/26/69 Age: 25

			HOW MUCH HE PITCHED						WHAT HE GAVE UP											THE RESULTS					
Year	Team	Lg	G	GS	CG	GF	IP	BFP	H	R	ER	HR	SH	SF	HB	TBB	IBB	SO	WP	Bk	W	L	Pct.	ShO	Sv	ERA
1990	Oneonta	A	13	13	3	0	88.2	332	53	14	12	2	0	2	1	24	0	119	0	2	8	2	.800	2	0	1.22
1991	Pr William	A	16	16	1	0	103.1	397	65	19	14	1	1	4	4	27	1	113	1	1	12	2	.857	2	0	1.22
	Albany	AA	7	7	0	0	46	191	40	14	12	3	1	1	3	19	1	55	0	0	2	2	.500	0	0	2.35
1992	Columbus	AAA	22	21	3	0	141.1	576	104	45	36	5	2	5	11	46	1	152	4	1	12	2	.857	2	0	2.29

Year	Team	Lg	G	GS	CG	GF	IP	BFP	H	R	ER	HR	SH	SF	HB	TBB	IBB	SO	WP	Bk	W	L	Pct.	ShO	Sv	ERA
1993	Columbus	AAA	7	7	0	0	33	151	36	22	21	7	1	0	1	20	0	39	4	0	1	3	.250	0	0	5.73
1994	Columbus	AAA	4	4	0	0	3.2	36	4	16	13	0	0	0	3	19	0	2	5	0	0	3	.000	0	0	31.91
1992	New York	AL	9	9	0	0	60	255	43	24	23	6	0	0	2	32	1	42	1	0	3	3	.500	0	0	3.45
1993	New York	AL	3	2	0	0	9.1	46	10	8	7	1	0	0	2	7	1	5	0	0	1	1	.500	0	0	6.75
5 Min. YEARS			69	68	7	0	416	1683	302	130	108	18	5	12	23	155	3	480	14	4	35	14	.714	4	0	2.34
2 Maj. YEARS			12	11	0	0	69.1	301	53	32	30	7	0	0	4	39	2	47	1	0	4	4	.500	0	0	3.89

Jose Millares

Bats: Right **Throws:** Right **Pos:** 3B **Ht:** 5'11" **Wt:** 190 **Born:** 03/24/68 **Age:** 27

						BATTING											BASERUNNING				PERCENTAGES		
Year	Team	Lg	G	AB	H	2B	3B	HR	TB	R	RBI	TBB	IBB	SO	HBP	SH	SF	SB	CS	SB%	GDP	Avg	OBP	SLG
1990	Bluefield	R	48	176	49	12	0	3	70	25	25	10	1	27	0	0	1	6	5	.55	1	.278	.316	.398
1991	Kane County	A	114	425	115	28	2	5	162	57	71	20	4	71	11	2	6	3	4	.43	6	.271	.316	.381
1992	Frederick	A	129	452	98	21	1	10	151	48	68	25	2	79	9	3	10	8	5	.62	6	.217	.266	.334
1993	Bowie	AA	30	50	14	1	2	0	19	6	5	1	0	9	7	2	0	1	1	.50	2	.280	.379	.380
	Frederick	A	85	299	75	11	0	9	113	38	36	23	0	44	12	2	2	4	4	.50	10	.251	.327	.378
1994	Bowie	AA	89	231	52	13	1	3	76	24	39	13	1	39	3	0	6	4	2	.67	10	.225	.269	.329
5 Min. YEARS			495	1633	403	86	6	30	591	198	244	92	8	269	42	9	25	26	21	.55	35	.247	.300	.362

Barry Miller

Bats: Left **Throws:** Left **Pos:** 1B **Ht:** 6'5" **Wt:** 210 **Born:** 07/10/68 **Age:** 26

						BATTING											BASERUNNING				PERCENTAGES		
Year	Team	Lg	G	AB	H	2B	3B	HR	TB	R	RBI	TBB	IBB	SO	HBP	SH	SF	SB	CS	SB%	GDP	Avg	OBP	SLG
1990	Everett	A	38	136	36	12	0	2	54	19	15	13	1	25	0	0	0	1	1	.50	1	.265	.329	.397
1991	Clinton	A	117	397	97	19	2	5	135	43	51	53	5	66	3	5	5	1	1	.50	10	.244	.334	.340
1992	San Jose	A	124	420	118	32	4	10	188	69	70	72	14	76	4	4	6	4	1	.80	9	.281	.386	.448
1993	Shreveport	AA	129	452	130	30	2	13	203	59	82	49	7	91	5	1	8	5	4	.56	5	.288	.358	.449
1994	Shreveport	AA	124	415	115	27	2	12	182	55	73	66	7	84	2	0	7	2	2	.50	12	.277	.373	.439
5 Min. YEARS			532	1820	496	120	10	42	762	245	291	253	34	342	14	10	26	13	9	.59	37	.273	.361	.419

Brent Miller

Bats: Left **Throws:** Right **Pos:** 1B **Ht:** 6'0" **Wt:** 190 **Born:** 11/12/70 **Age:** 24

						BATTING											BASERUNNING				PERCENTAGES		
Year	Team	Lg	G	AB	H	2B	3B	HR	TB	R	RBI	TBB	IBB	SO	HBP	SH	SF	SB	CS	SB%	GDP	Avg	OBP	SLG
1990	Bluefield	R	32	118	38	10	1	10	80	21	28	7	0	23	0	0	2	0	0	.00	3	.322	.354	.678
	Wausau	A	19	83	25	7	0	1	35	9	8	2	0	18	1	1	1	2	0	1.00	2	.301	.322	.422
1991	Kane County	A	87	308	88	21	3	9	142	36	50	12	2	33	1	0	3	3	3	.50	8	.286	.312	.461
	Frederick	A	37	148	38	8	0	10	76	21	31	6	2	16	0	0	2	0	1	.00	2	.257	.282	.514
1992	Hagerstown	AA	125	440	114	28	1	4	156	47	51	23	8	74	0	0	5	5	3	.63	13	.259	.293	.355
1993	Bowie	AA	113	404	104	13	0	11	150	35	66	19	5	41	2	0	4	6	1	.86	17	.257	.291	.371
1994	Rochester	AAA	3	3	0	0	0	0	0	0	0	0	0	1	0	0	0	0	0	.00	0	.000	.000	.000
	Bowie	AA	53	172	51	12	1	5	80	30	28	20	2	33	0	0	2	7	2	.78	8	.297	.366	.465
5 Min. YEARS			469	1676	458	99	6	50	719	199	262	89	19	239	4	1	19	23	10	.70	53	.273	.308	.429

Damian Miller

Bats: Right **Throws:** Right **Pos:** C **Ht:** 6'2" **Wt:** 190 **Born:** 10/13/69 **Age:** 25

						BATTING											BASERUNNING				PERCENTAGES		
Year	Team	Lg	G	AB	H	2B	3B	HR	TB	R	RBI	TBB	IBB	SO	HBP	SH	SF	SB	CS	SB%	GDP	Avg	OBP	SLG
1990	Elizabethtn	R	14	45	10	1	0	1	14	7	6	9	0	3	0	0	0	1	0	1.00	2	.222	.352	.311
1991	Kenosha	A	80	267	62	11	1	3	84	28	34	24	1	53	2	2	3	3	2	.60	4	.232	.297	.315
1992	Kenosha	A	115	377	110	27	2	5	156	53	56	53	1	66	7	2	4	6	1	.86	13	.292	.385	.414
1993	Ft. Myers	A	87	325	69	12	1	1	86	31	26	31	0	44	0	1	0	6	3	.67	5	.212	.281	.265
	Nashville	AA	4	13	3	0	0	0	3	0	0	2	0	4	0	0	0	0	0	.00	0	.231	.333	.231
1994	Nashville	AA	103	328	88	10	0	8	122	36	35	35	2	51	1	2	5	4	6	.40	11	.268	.336	.372
5 Min. YEARS			403	1355	342	61	4	18	465	155	157	154	4	221	10	7	12	20	12	.63	35	.252	.331	.343

Paul Miller

Pitches: Right **Bats:** Right **Pos:** P **Ht:** 6'5" **Wt:** 220 **Born:** 04/27/65 **Age:** 30

						HOW MUCH HE PITCHED			WHAT HE GAVE UP												THE RESULTS				
Year	Team	Lg	G	GS	CG	GF	IP	BFP	H	R	ER	HR	SH	SF	HB	TBB	IBB	SO	WP	Bk	W	L	Pct.	ShO	Sv	ERA
1987	Pirates	R	12	12	1	0	70.1	292	55	34	25	3	1	2	2	26	0	62	3	0	3	6	.333	1	0	3.20
1988	Augusta	A	15	15	2	0	90.1	374	80	34	29	3	3	5	4	28	1	51	8	5	6	5	.545	2	0	2.89
1989	Salem	A	26	20	2	0	133.2	599	138	86	62	17	2	4	8	64	0	82	8	1	6	12	.333	1	0	4.17
1990	Salem	A	22	22	5	0	150.2	628	145	58	41	6	3	6	7	33	1	83	5	1	8	6	.571	1	0	2.45
	Harrisburg	AA	5	5	2	0	37	148	27	9	9	1	1	2	2	10	0	11	0	0	2	1	.667	1	0	2.19
1991	Carolina	AA	15	15	1	0	89.1	369	69	29	24	4	7	1	3	35	4	69	5	1	7	2	.778	0	0	2.42
	Buffalo	AAA	10	10	2	0	67	272	41	17	11	2	4	0	5	29	0	30	1	1	5	2	.714	0	0	1.48
1992	Buffalo	AAA	8	7	0	0	32.1	150	38	23	14	3	3	1	1	16	0	18	0	0	2	3	.400	0	0	3.90
1993	Carolina	AA	6	6	0	0	38.1	152	31	15	12	3	1	1	0	12	1	33	4	1	2	2	.500	0	0	2.82
	Buffalo	AAA	10	10	0	0	52.1	220	57	28	26	2	2	0	1	14	1	25	0	0	3	1	.750	0	0	4.47
1994	Buffalo	AAA	13	9	0	1	51.1	232	65	35	28	2	5	4	3	17	0	30	1	0	3	6	.333	0	0	4.91
1991	Pittsburgh	NL	1	1	0	0	5	21	4	3	3	0	0	0	0	3	0	2	0	0	0	0	.000	0	0	5.40
1992	Pittsburgh	NL	6	0	0	0	11.1	46	11	3	3	0	1	1	0	1	0	5	1	0	1	0	1.000	0	0	2.38

171

Year	Team	Lg	G	GS	CG	GF	IP	BFP	H	R	ER	HR	SH	SF	HB	TBB	IBB	SO	WP	Bk	W	L	Pct.	ShO	Sv	ERA
1993	Pittsburgh	NL	3	2	0	1	10	47	15	6	6	2	2	0	0	2	0	2	1	0	0	0	.000	0	0	5.40
	8 Min. YEARS		142	131	15	1	812.2	3436	746	368	281	46	35	25	36	284	8	494	35	10	47	46	.505	6	0	3.11
	3 Maj. YEARS		10	3	0	2	26.1	114	30	12	12	2	3	1	0	6	0	9	2	0	1	0	1.000	0	0	4.10

Travis Miller

Pitches: Left Bats: Right Pos: P Ht: 6'3" Wt: 205 Born: 11/02/72 Age: 22

			HOW MUCH HE PITCHED						WHAT HE GAVE UP											THE RESULTS					
Year	Team	Lg	G	GS	CG	GF	IP	BFP	H	R	ER	HR	SH	SF	HB	TBB	IBB	SO	WP	Bk	W	L	Pct.	ShO	Sv	ERA
1994	Fort Wayne	A	11	9	1	0	55.1	223	52	17	16	2	1	3	2	12	0	50	5	2	4	1	.800	0	0	2.60
	Nashville	AA	1	1	0	0	6.1	23	3	3	2	0	0	0	0	2	0	4	1	0	0	0	.000	0	0	2.84
	1 Min. YEARS		12	10	1	0	61.2	246	55	20	18	2	1	3	2	14	0	54	6	2	4	1	.800	0	0	2.63

Trever Miller

Pitches: Left Bats: Right Pos: P Ht: 6'3" Wt: 175 Born: 05/29/73 Age: 22

			HOW MUCH HE PITCHED						WHAT HE GAVE UP											THE RESULTS					
Year	Team	Lg	G	GS	CG	GF	IP	BFP	H	R	ER	HR	SH	SF	HB	TBB	IBB	SO	WP	Bk	W	L	Pct.	ShO	Sv	ERA
1991	Bristol	R	13	13	0	0	54	253	60	44	34	7	3	3	2	29	0	46	9	1	2	7	.222	0	0	5.67
1992	Bristol	R	12	12	1	0	69.1	316	75	45	38	4	3	3	1	27	0	64	4	1	3	8	.273	0	0	4.93
1993	Fayetteville	A	28	28	2	0	161	699	151	99	75	7	2	8	5	67	0	116	10	0	8	13	.381	0	0	4.19
1994	Trenton	AA	26	26	6	0	174.1	754	198	95	85	9	10	8	3	51	0	73	3	1	7	16	.304	0	0	4.39
	4 Min. YEARS		79	79	9	0	458.2	2017	484	283	232	27	18	22	11	174	0	299	26	3	20	44	.313	0	0	4.55

Joe Millette

Bats: Right Throws: Right Pos: SS Ht: 6'1" Wt: 175 Born: 08/12/66 Age: 28

			BATTING														BASERUNNING				PERCENTAGES		
Year	Team	Lg	G	AB	H	2B	3B	HR	TB	R	RBI	TBB	IBB	SO	HBP	SH	SF	SB	CS	SB%	GDP	Avg	OBP	SLG
1989	Batavia	A	11	42	10	3	0	0	13	4	4	4	0	6	0	0	0	3	0	1.00	0	.238	.304	.310
	Spartanburg	A	60	209	50	4	3	0	60	27	18	28	0	36	7	3	3	4	2	.67	5	.239	.344	.287
1990	Clearwater	A	108	295	54	5	0	0	59	31	18	29	0	53	7	7	6	4	4	.50	5	.183	.267	.200
1991	Clearwater	A	18	55	14	2	0	0	16	6	6	7	0	6	1	3	2	1	2	.33	1	.255	.338	.291
	Reading	AA	115	353	87	9	4	3	113	52	28	36	2	54	7	10	3	6	6	.50	5	.246	.326	.320
1992	Scranton/wb	AAA	78	256	68	11	1	1	84	24	23	15	0	30	6	7	0	3	2	.60	4	.266	.321	.328
1993	Scranton/wb	AAA	107	343	77	15	2	1	99	27	24	19	2	56	5	7	1	5	4	.56	9	.224	.274	.289
1994	Edmonton	AAA	118	406	107	22	3	4	147	41	38	13	3	73	6	6	2	5	5	.50	15	.264	.295	.362
1992	Philadelphia	NL	33	78	16	0	0	0	16	5	2	5	2	10	2	2	0	1	0	1.00	8	.205	.271	.205
1993	Philadelphia	NL	10	10	2	0	0	0	2	3	2	1	0	2	0	3	0	0	0	.00	1	.200	.273	.200
	6 Min. YEARS		615	1959	467	71	13	9	591	212	159	151	7	314	39	43	17	31	25	.55	48	.238	.303	.302
	2 Maj. YEARS		43	88	18	0	0	0	18	8	4	6	2	12	2	5	0	1	0	1.00	9	.205	.271	.205

Darren Milne

Bats: Right Throws: Right Pos: OF Ht: 6'1" Wt: 190 Born: 03/24/71 Age: 24

			BATTING														BASERUNNING				PERCENTAGES		
Year	Team	Lg	G	AB	H	2B	3B	HR	TB	R	RBI	TBB	IBB	SO	HBP	SH	SF	SB	CS	SB%	GDP	Avg	OBP	SLG
1992	Bristol	R	15	55	15	3	0	0	18	7	5	7	0	11	1	0	0	0	1	.00	3	.273	.365	.327
	Fayetteville	A	46	137	31	5	0	2	42	16	18	20	1	34	6	4	1	9	5	.64	2	.226	.348	.307
1993	London	AA	5	20	1	0	0	0	1	2	1	2	0	7	0	0	0	0	0	.00	0	.050	.136	.050
	Lakeland	A	71	204	40	6	1	5	63	19	18	23	0	33	0	2	2	6	5	.55	4	.196	.275	.309
1994	Trenton	AA	113	364	89	11	2	6	122	38	36	27	2	71	6	6	1	11	5	.69	10	.245	.307	.335
	3 Min. YEARS		250	780	176	25	3	13	246	82	78	79	3	156	13	12	4	26	16	.62	19	.226	.306	.315

Dave Milstien

Bats: Right Throws: Right Pos: SS-3B Ht: 6'0" Wt: 170 Born: 09/11/68 Age: 26

			BATTING														BASERUNNING				PERCENTAGES		
Year	Team	Lg	G	AB	H	2B	3B	HR	TB	R	RBI	TBB	IBB	SO	HBP	SH	SF	SB	CS	SB%	GDP	Avg	OBP	SLG
1986	Elmira	A	34	107	29	4	0	1	36	15	6	5	0	12	0	1	0	0	2	.00	4	.271	.304	.336
1987	Winter Havn	A	100	303	67	5	0	0	72	35	33	12	1	31	1	7	4	0	1	.00	9	.221	.250	.238
1988	Winter Havn	A	120	429	92	15	5	1	120	36	26	5	0	38	0	2	1	2	4	.33	10	.214	.223	.280
1989	New Britain	AA	106	345	87	10	0	0	97	34	27	23	0	50	2	10	2	5	5	.50	16	.252	.301	.281
1990	New Britain	AA	115	376	81	12	0	0	93	31	24	23	1	44	1	12	4	6	3	.67	13	.215	.260	.247
1991	New Britain	AA	86	309	86	6	1	4	106	36	31	46	1	38	1	2	5	3	5	.38	13	.278	.368	.343
	Pawtucket	AAA	19	59	12	0	0	0	12	2	4	3	0	8	3	0	0	0	0	.00	1	.203	.277	.203
1992	Pawtucket	AAA	85	266	66	11	1	1	82	29	34	13	0	23	1	0	2	0	2	.00	9	.248	.284	.308
1993	Pawtucket	AAA	88	258	65	8	3	1	82	28	18	10	0	31	2	2	1	1	3	.25	8	.252	.284	.318
1994	Nashville	AAA	57	174	41	6	0	2	53	26	8	14	0	20	1	4	1	0	3	.00	8	.236	.295	.305
	9 Min. YEARS		810	2626	626	77	10	10	753	272	211	154	3	295	12	40	20	17	28	.38	91	.238	.282	.287

Mark Mimbs

Pitches: Left Bats: Left Pos: P Ht: 6'2" Wt: 180 Born: 02/13/69 Age: 26

			HOW MUCH HE PITCHED						WHAT HE GAVE UP											THE RESULTS					
Year	Team	Lg	G	GS	CG	GF	IP	BFP	H	R	ER	HR	SH	SF	HB	TBB	IBB	SO	WP	Bk	W	L	Pct.	ShO	Sv	ERA
1990	Great Falls	R	14	14	0	0	78	325	69	32	28	3	0	0	1	29	0	94	4	3	7	4	.636	0	0	3.23
1991	Bakersfield	A	27	25	0	1	170	687	134	49	42	2	3	2	3	59	2	164	4	2	12	6	.667	0	0	2.22

Year	Team	Lg	G	GS	CG	GF	IP	BFP	H	R	ER	HR	SH	SF	HB	TBB	IBB	SO	WP	Bk	W	L	Pct.	ShO	Sv	ERA
1992	Albuquerque	AAA	12	7	0	0	48.2	217	58	34	33	4	1	1	0	19	1	32	4	0	0	4	.000	0	0	6.10
	San Antonio	AA	13	13	0	0	82.1	340	78	43	33	3	5	2	2	22	4	55	3	0	1	5	.167	0	0	3.61
1993	Albuquerque	AAA	19	1	0	3	18.2	90	20	21	21	0	2	2	0	16	1	12	2	1	0	1	.000	0	1	10.13
	San Antonio	AA	49	0	0	23	67.2	272	49	21	12	0	6	4	2	18	7	77	2	0	3	3	.500	0	10	1.60
1994	Bakersfield	A	1	0	0	0	1.2	7	3	0	0	0	0	0	0	0	0	0	0	0	0	0	.000	0	0	0.00
	Albuquerque	AAA	6	0	0	3	6.2	28	8	3	3	1	0	0	0	0	0	9	1	0	1	0	1.000	0	0	4.05
	5 Min. YEARS		141	60	0	30	473.2	1966	419	203	172	13	17	11	8	163	15	443	20	6	24	23	.511	0	11	3.27

Michael Mimbs

Pitches: Left Bats: Left Pos: P **Ht: 6'2" Wt: 182 Born: 02/13/69 Age: 26**

			HOW MUCH HE PITCHED						WHAT HE GAVE UP												THE RESULTS					
Year	Team	Lg	G	GS	CG	GF	IP	BFP	H	R	ER	HR	SH	SF	HB	TBB	IBB	SO	WP	Bk	W	L	Pct.	ShO	Sv	ERA
1990	Great Falls	R	3	0	0	0	6.2	32	4	5	3	0	0	0	2	5	0	7	0	1	0	0	.000	0	0	4.05
	Yakima	A	12	12	0	0	67.1	295	58	36	29	5	2	2	3	39	0	72	1	2	4	3	.571	0	0	3.88
1991	Vero Beach	A	24	22	1	0	141.2	601	124	52	42	6	9	1	6	70	2	132	15	3	12	4	.750	1	0	2.67
1992	San Antonio	AA	24	22	2	2	129.2	581	132	65	61	11	10	5	3	73	1	87	7	1	10	8	.556	0	1	4.23
1993	St. Paul	IND	20	16	1	1	98.1	430	94	48	35	4	3	4	5	45	0	97	12	0	8	2	.800	0	0	3.20
1994	Harrisburg	AA	32	21	2	0	153.2	644	130	69	59	11	7	2	3	61	0	145	9	0	11	4	.733	1	0	3.46
	5 Min. YEARS		115	93	6	3	597.1	2583	542	275	229	37	31	14	22	293	3	540	44	7	45	21	.682	2	1	3.45

Steve Mintz

Pitches: Right Bats: Left Pos: P **Ht: 5'11" Wt: 190 Born: 11/24/68 Age: 26**

			HOW MUCH HE PITCHED						WHAT HE GAVE UP												THE RESULTS					
Year	Team	Lg	G	GS	CG	GF	IP	BFP	H	R	ER	HR	SH	SF	HB	TBB	IBB	SO	WP	Bk	W	L	Pct.	ShO	Sv	ERA
1990	Yakima	A	20	0	0	12	26	113	21	9	7	1	3	1	1	16	1	38	2	1	2	3	.400	0	3	2.42
1991	Bakersfield	A	28	11	0	6	92	419	85	56	44	2	5	4	4	58	1	101	9	1	6	6	.500	0	3	4.30
1992	Vero Beach	A	43	2	0	21	77.2	323	66	29	27	7	5	3	3	30	2	66	7	3	3	6	.333	0	6	3.13
1993	New Britain	AA	43	1	0	20	69.1	287	52	22	16	3	5	1	2	30	5	51	7	0	2	4	.333	0	7	2.08
1994	Phoenix	AAA	24	0	0	13	36	161	40	24	22	8	1	3	1	13	3	27	3	0	0	1	.000	0	3	5.50
	Shreveport	AA	30	0	0	12	65.1	261	45	29	16	5	2	1	2	22	1	42	8	0	10	2	.833	0	0	2.20
	5 Min. YEARS		188	14	0	84	366.1	1564	309	169	132	26	21	13	13	169	13	325	36	5	23	22	.511	0	22	3.24

Gino Minutelli

Pitches: Left Bats: Left Pos: P **Ht: 6'0" Wt: 185 Born: 05/23/64 Age: 31**

			HOW MUCH HE PITCHED						WHAT HE GAVE UP												THE RESULTS					
Year	Team	Lg	G	GS	CG	GF	IP	BFP	H	R	ER	HR	SH	SF	HB	TBB	IBB	SO	WP	Bk	W	L	Pct.	ShO	Sv	ERA
1985	Tri-Cities	A	20	10	0	7	57	0	61	57	51	3	0	0	6	57	0	79	6	0	4	8	.333	0	0	8.05
1986	Cedar Rapds	A	27	27	3	0	152.2	671	133	73	62	14	4	6	5	76	1	149	16	2	15	5	.750	2	0	3.66
1987	Tampa	A	17	15	5	1	104.1	461	98	51	44	4	10	3	5	48	4	70	13	1	7	6	.538	1	0	3.80
	Vermont	AA	6	6	0	0	39.2	168	34	15	14	3	0	0	2	16	0	39	2	1	4	1	.800	0	0	3.18
1988	Chattanooga	AA	2	2	0	0	5.2	27	6	2	1	0	0	0	1	4	0	3	0	2	0	1	.000	0	0	1.59
1989	Reds	R	1	1	0	0	1	4	0	0	0	0	0	0	0	1	0	0	0	1	0	0	.000	0	0	0.00
	Chattanooga	AA	6	6	1	0	29	140	28	19	17	1	0	1	6	23	0	20	8	4	1	1	.500	0	0	5.28
1990	Chattanooga	AA	17	17	5	0	108.1	467	106	52	48	9	5	2	2	46	1	75	5	13	9	5	.643	0	0	3.99
	Nashville	AAA	11	11	3	0	78.1	315	65	34	28	5	1	1	1	31	0	61	1	0	5	2	.714	0	0	3.22
1991	Chston-Wv	A	2	2	0	0	8	28	2	0	0	0	0	0	0	4	0	8	0	0	1	0	1.000	0	0	0.00
	Nashville	AAA	13	13	1	0	80.1	325	57	25	17	3	6	2	1	35	2	64	6	1	4	7	.364	1	0	1.90
1992	Nashville	AAA	29	29	1	0	158	722	177	96	75	18	13	5	5	76	1	110	11	1	4	12	.250	0	0	4.27
1993	Phoenix	AAA	49	0	0	34	53.2	235	55	28	24	1	1	3	0	26	0	57	6	1	2	2	.500	0	11	4.02
1994	Tucson	AAA	35	0	0	14	60.1	275	87	50	45	13	4	3	1	11	2	50	5	0	4	4	.500	0	0	6.71
	Canton-Akm	AA	4	3	0	1	20	83	16	8	7	1	1	1	0	8	0	11	2	0	1	1	.500	0	0	3.15
1990	Cincinnati	NL	2	0	0	0	1	6	0	1	1	0	0	0	1	2	0	1	1	0	0	0	.000	0	0	9.00
1991	Cincinnati	NL	16	3	0	2	25.1	124	30	17	17	5	0	2	0	18	1	21	3	0	0	2	.000	0	0	6.04
1993	San Francisco	NL	9	0	0	4	14.1	64	7	9	6	2	1	2	0	15	0	10	1	0	0	1	.000	0	0	3.77
	10 Min. YEARS		239	142	19	57	956.1	3921	925	510	433	75	45	27	35	462	11	796	81	27	60	55	.522	4	11	4.07
	3 Maj. YEARS		27	3	0	6	40.2	194	37	27	24	7	1	4	1	35	1	31	5	0	0	3	.000	0	0	5.31

Doug Mirabelli

Bats: Right Throws: Right Pos: C **Ht: 6'1" Wt: 205 Born: 10/18/70 Age: 24**

			BATTING													BASERUNNING				PERCENTAGES		
Year	Team	Lg	G	AB	H	2B	3B	HR	TB	R	RBI	TBB	IBB	SO	HBP	SH	SF	SB	CS	SB%	GDP	Avg	OBP	SLG
1992	San Jose	A	53	177	41	11	1	0	54	30	21	24	0	18	4	2	2	1	3	.25	7	.232	.333	.305
1993	San Jose	A	113	371	100	19	2	1	126	58	48	72	1	55	4	2	4	4	0	.00	7	.270	.390	.340
1994	Shreveport	AA	85	255	56	8	0	4	76	23	24	36	5	48	0	2	0	3	1	.75	6	.220	.316	.298
	3 Min. YEARS		251	803	197	38	3	5	256	111	93	132	6	121	8	6	6	4	8	.33	20	.245	.355	.319

Giovanni Miranda

Bats: Right Throws: Right Pos: 3B **Ht: 5'11" Wt: 170 Born: 02/16/70 Age: 25**

			BATTING													BASERUNNING				PERCENTAGES		
Year	Team	Lg	G	AB	H	2B	3B	HR	TB	R	RBI	TBB	IBB	SO	HBP	SH	SF	SB	CS	SB%	GDP	Avg	OBP	SLG
1988	Royals	R	44	117	27	1	0	0	28	20	4	9	0	14	0	0	0	9	2	.82	2	.231	.286	.239
1989	Royals	R	55	193	60	4	3	0	70	38	24	19	0	15	1	2	4	23	9	.72	1	.311	.369	.363

Year	Team	Lg	G	AB	H	2B	3B	HR	TB	R	RBI	TBB	IBB	SO	HBP	SH	SF	SB	CS	SB%	GDP	Avg	OBP	SLG
1990	Eugene	A	42	145	49	3	0	0	52	30	15	15	0	30	1	3	2	16	6	.73	2	.338	.399	.359
	Appleton	A	55	141	32	1	2	0	37	15	7	16	0	26	3	1	0	8	4	.67	3	.227	.319	.262
1991	Appleton	A	122	416	98	11	2	0	113	57	27	33	0	67	4	11	2	28	12	.70	6	.236	.297	.272
1992	South Bend	A	2	3	0	0	0	0	0	0	0	0	0	1	0	0	0	0	0	.00	0	.000	.000	.000
	Baseball Cy	A	7	24	4	0	0	0	4	4	1	2	0	6	0	1	0	1	0	1.00	0	.167	.231	.167
	Sarasota	A	18	41	15	1	2	0	20	6	4	2	0	3	0	2	1	2	0	1.00	1	.366	.386	.488
	Miracle	A	43	120	32	2	0	0	34	10	8	5	0	23	2	0	0	4	5	.44	3	.267	.307	.283
1993	Birmingham	AA	12	32	3	0	0	0	3	2	0	1	0	6	0	1	0	0	0	.00	2	.094	.121	.094
	Sarasota	A	19	63	11	0	1	0	13	7	2	1	0	8	1	1	0	3	0	1.00	0	.175	.200	.206
	Hickory	A	33	107	25	3	0	0	28	13	6	5	1	8	0	4	2	4	2	.67	1	.234	.263	.262
1994	Nashville	AAA	16	42	14	3	0	0	17	7	8	1	0	3	0	1	1	0	0	.00	0	.333	.341	.405
	Pr. William	A	55	193	53	7	2	0	64	33	18	7	0	25	2	2	1	10	1	.91	1	.275	.305	.332
7 Min. YEARS			523	1637	423	36	12	0	483	242	124	116	1	235	14	29	13	108	41	.72	22	.258	.311	.295

Mike Misuraca

Pitches: Right   Bats: Right   Pos: P   Ht: 6'0"   Wt: 188   Born: 08/21/68   Age: 26

			HOW MUCH HE PITCHED						WHAT HE GAVE UP												THE RESULTS					
Year	Team	Lg	G	GS	CG	GF	IP	BFP	H	R	ER	HR	SH	SF	HB	TBB	IBB	SO	WP	Bk	W	L	Pct.	ShO	Sv	ERA
1989	Kenosha	A	9	9	0	0	46	204	47	32	27	9	3	0	5	15	0	30	1	4	1	5	.167	0	0	5.28
	Elizabethtn	R	13	13	9	0	103	424	92	34	29	3	4	4	5	33	0	89	8	6	10	3	.769	2	0	2.53
1990	Kenosha	A	26	26	1	0	167.1	718	164	81	62	6	5	4	12	57	1	116	6	8	9	9	.500	0	0	3.33
1991	Visalia	A	21	19	2	0	116	512	131	65	55	12	3	5	8	39	1	82	13	0	7	9	.438	1	0	4.27
1992	Miracle	A	28	28	3	0	157	687	163	84	63	7	4	4	9	63	1	107	4	0	7	14	.333	1	0	3.61
1993	Nashville	AA	25	17	2	2	113	483	103	57	48	9	6	1	5	40	0	80	7	1	6	6	.500	1	0	3.82
1994	Nashville	AA	17	17	0	0	106.2	450	115	56	43	10	1	2	5	22	0	80	4	0	8	4	.667	0	0	3.63
	Salt Lake	AAA	10	10	1	0	65.2	295	88	43	38	5	2	2	4	13	0	51	6	0	3	5	.375	0	0	5.21
6 Min. YEARS			149	139	18	2	874.2	3773	903	452	365	61	31	22	53	282	3	635	49	19	51	55	.481	5	0	3.76

John Mitchell

Pitches: Right   Bats: Right   Pos: P   Ht: 6' 2"   Wt: 189   Born: 08/11/65   Age: 29

			HOW MUCH HE PITCHED						WHAT HE GAVE UP												THE RESULTS					
Year	Team	Lg	G	GS	CG	GF	IP	BFP	H	R	ER	HR	SH	SF	HB	TBB	IBB	SO	WP	Bk	W	L	Pct.	ShO	Sv	ERA
1984	Winter Havn	A	27	27	4	0	183.2	775	160	84	64	9	3	6	5	66	2	109	21	2	16	9	.640	0	0	3.14
1985	New Britain	AA	26	26	10	0	190.1	766	143	71	57	4	7	2	2	61	4	108	11	1	12	8	.600	1	0	2.70
1986	Tidewater	AAA	27	27	5	0	172.1	729	162	78	65	10	3	4	6	59	2	83	7	1	12	9	.571	2	0	3.39
1987	Tidewater	AAA	8	8	1	0	48.2	212	44	24	18	2	1	2	3	20	0	16	4	1	3	2	.600	1	0	3.33
1988	Tidewater	AAA	27	27	7	0	190	767	164	76	60	8	6	5	6	45	1	65	7	5	10	9	.526	2	0	2.84
1989	Tidewater	AAA	26	26	7	0	178.1	744	169	78	60	5	11	2	4	57	2	86	8	2	11	11	.500	0	0	3.03
1990	Rochester	AAA	8	7	3	0	46	178	39	9	8	3	0	0	1	9	0	15	0	0	5	0	1.000	2	0	1.57
1993	New Britain	AA	8	1	0	4	17.1	67	15	2	2	0	0	0	0	2	0	8	2	3	1	1	.500	0	1	1.04
1994	New Britain	AA	5	5	0	0	23.1	113	37	23	21	1	0	1	0	7	0	17	2	0	0	4	.000	0	0	8.10
	Okla. City	AAA	14	11	3	2	78.1	328	80	38	33	5	2	1	2	18	0	30	1	0	3	5	.375	0	0	3.79
1986	New York	NL	4	1	0	0	10	40	10	4	4	1	0	0	0	4	0	2	2	0	0	1	.000	0	0	3.60
1987	New York	NL	20	19	1	0	111.2	493	124	64	51	6	6	5	2	36	3	57	7	1	3	6	.333	0	0	4.11
1988	New York	NL	1	0	0	0	1	5	2	0	0	0	0	0	0	0	0	1	0	0	0	0	.000	0	0	0.00
1989	New York	NL	2	0	0	0	3	17	3	7	2	0	0	0	0	4	1	4	1	0	0	1	.000	0	0	6.00
1990	Baltimore	AL	24	17	0	2	114.1	509	133	63	59	7	6	8	3	48	3	43	3	0	6	6	.500	0	0	4.64
9 Min. YEARS			176	165	40	6	1128.1	4679	1013	483	388	47	33	23	29	344	11	537	63	15	73	58	.557	12	1	3.09
5 Maj. YEARS			51	37	1	3	240	1064	272	138	116	14	12	13	5	93	7	107	13	1	9	14	.391	0	0	4.35

Larry Mitchell

Pitches: Right   Bats: Right   Pos: P   Ht: 6'1"   Wt: 200   Born: 10/16/71   Age: 23

			HOW MUCH HE PITCHED						WHAT HE GAVE UP												THE RESULTS					
Year	Team	Lg	G	GS	CG	GF	IP	BFP	H	R	ER	HR	SH	SF	HB	TBB	IBB	SO	WP	Bk	W	L	Pct.	ShO	Sv	ERA
1992	Martinsvle	R	3	3	0	0	19	78	17	8	3	0	0	0	1	6	0	18	0	0	1	0	1.000	0	0	1.42
	Batavia	A	10	10	3	0	65	267	63	25	19	6	2	2	1	11	0	58	4	1	7	2	.778	1	0	2.63
1993	Spartanwater	A	19	19	4	0	116.1	505	113	55	53	3	2	7	3	54	0	114	14	0	6	6	.500	2	0	4.10
	Clearwater	A	9	9	1	0	57	234	50	23	19	0	5	2	0	21	1	45	4	1	4	4	.500	0	0	3.00
1994	Reading	AA	30	30	2	0	165.1	737	143	91	73	5	13	8	2	103	1	128	15	0	10	13	.435	3	0	3.97
3 Min. YEARS			71	71	10	0	422.2	1820	386	202	167	14	22	19	7	195	2	363	37	2	28	25	.528	3	0	3.56

Mike Mitchell

Bats: Left   Throws: Right   Pos: 1B   Ht: 6'3"   Wt: 205   Born: 04/05/73   Age: 22

			BATTING															BASERUNNING				PERCENTAGES		
Year	Team	Lg	G	AB	H	2B	3B	HR	TB	R	RBI	TBB	IBB	SO	HBP	SH	SF	SB	CS	SB%	GDP	Avg	OBP	SLG
1994	Oneonta	A	28	104	31	6	0	2	43	13	12	10	0	9	1	0	1	0	0	.00	2	.298	.362	.413
	Greensboro	A	39	133	35	5	1	3	51	15	19	14	1	19	1	0	1	0	1	.00	4	.263	.336	.383
	Albany-Colo	AA	8	24	8	2	0	0	10	3	2	4	1	5	0	0	0	0	0	.00	0	.333	.429	.417
1 Min. YEARS			75	261	74	13	1	5	104	31	33	28	2	33	2	0	2	0	1	.00	7	.284	.355	.398

Tony Mitchell

Bats: Both Throws: Right Pos: OF **Ht: 6'4" Wt: 225 Born: 10/14/70 Age: 24**

									BATTING									BASERUNNING				PERCENTAGES		
Year	Team	Lg	G	AB	H	2B	3B	HR	TB	R	RBI	TBB	IBB	SO	HBP	SH	SF	SB	CS	SB%	GDP	Avg	OBP	SLG
1989	Pirates	R	13	40	11	0	0	0	11	4	1	4	0	10	0	0	1	1	0	1.00	3	.275	.333	.275
1990	Pirates	R	44	102	30	4	2	3	47	18	13	8	0	21	1	0	0	3	4	.43	3	.294	.351	.461
1991	Welland	A	59	211	57	9	4	10	96	30	38	17	0	62	1	1	1	7	2	.78	4	.270	.326	.455
1992	Augusta	A	66	219	65	8	3	13	118	34	47	29	1	60	0	0	1	6	3	.67	3	.297	.378	.539
	Columbus	A	55	202	59	8	2	10	101	36	36	22	3	54	0	0	0	1	6	.14	5	.292	.362	.500
1993	Kinston	A	96	318	78	16	2	8	122	43	44	33	2	88	3	2	5	5	4	.56	8	.245	.318	.384
1994	Canton-Akm	AA	130	494	130	24	0	25	229	70	89	41	0	114	5	0	5	6	1	.86	13	.263	.323	.464
	6 Min. YEARS		463	1586	430	69	9	69	724	235	268	154	6	409	10	3	13	29	20	.59	39	.271	.337	.456

Dave Mlicki

Pitches: Right Bats: Right Pos: P **Ht: 6'4" Wt: 190 Born: 06/08/68 Age: 27**

			HOW MUCH HE PITCHED						WHAT HE GAVE UP										THE RESULTS					
Year	Team	Lg	G	GS	CG	GF	IP	BFP	H	R	ER	HR	SH	SF	HB	TBB	IBB	SO	WP	Bk	W	L	Pct.	ShO	Sv	ERA
1990	Burlington	R	8	1	0	2	18	81	16	11	7	1	0	1	1	6	0	17	0	0	3	1	.750	0	0	3.50
	Watertown	A	7	4	0	3	32	139	33	15	12	3	0	1	0	11	0	28	2	0	3	0	1.000	0	0	3.38
1991	Columbus	A	22	19	2	1	115.2	516	101	70	54	3	0	1	6	70	1	136	10	2	8	6	.571	0	0	4.20
1992	Canton-Akm	AA	27	27	2	0	172.2	720	143	77	69	8	5	7	3	80	3	146	9	1	11	9	.550	0	0	3.60
1993	Canton-Akm	AA	6	6	0	0	23	92	15	2	1	0	0	1	2	8	0	21	2	0	2	1	.667	0	0	0.39
1994	Charlotte	AAA	28	28	0	0	165.1	732	179	85	78	26	4	7	9	64	1	152	5	0	6	10	.375	0	0	4.25
1992	Cleveland	AL	4	4	0	0	21.2	101	23	14	12	3	2	0	1	16	0	16	1	0	0	2	.000	0	0	4.98
1993	Cleveland	AL	3	3	0	0	13.1	58	11	6	5	2	0	0	2	6	0	7	2	0	0	0	.000	0	0	3.38
	5 Min. YEARS		98	85	4	6	526.2	2280	487	260	221	41	9	18	21	239	5	500	28	3	33	27	.550	0	0	3.78
	2 Maj. YEARS		7	7	0	0	35	159	34	20	17	5	2	0	3	22	0	23	3	0	0	2	.000	0	0	4.37

Doug Mlicki

Pitches: Right Bats: Right Pos: P **Ht: 6'3" Wt: 175 Born: 04/23/71 Age: 24**

			HOW MUCH HE PITCHED						WHAT HE GAVE UP										THE RESULTS					
Year	Team	Lg	G	GS	CG	GF	IP	BFP	H	R	ER	HR	SH	SF	HB	TBB	IBB	SO	WP	Bk	W	L	Pct.	ShO	Sv	ERA
1992	Auburn	A	14	13	0	0	81.1	330	50	35	27	4	1	3	6	30	0	83	9	2	1	6	.143	0	0	2.99
1993	Osceola	A	26	23	0	0	158.2	668	158	81	69	16	6	5	2	65	1	111	9	0	11	10	.524	0	0	3.91
1994	Jackson	AA	23	23	1	0	138.2	575	107	62	52	20	5	2	8	54	5	130	13	3	13	7	.650	0	0	3.37
	3 Min. YEARS		63	59	1	0	378.2	1573	315	178	148	40	12	10	16	149	6	324	31	5	25	23	.521	0	0	3.52

Dennis Moeller

Pitches: Left Bats: Right Pos: P **Ht: 6'2" Wt: 195 Born: 09/15/67 Age: 27**

			HOW MUCH HE PITCHED						WHAT HE GAVE UP										THE RESULTS					
Year	Team	Lg	G	GS	CG	GF	IP	BFP	H	R	ER	HR	SH	SF	HB	TBB	IBB	SO	WP	Bk	W	L	Pct.	ShO	Sv	ERA
1986	Eugene	A	14	11	0	0	61.2		54	22	21	1	0	0	2	34	0	65	7	2	4	0	1.000	0	0	3.06
1987	Appleton	A	18	13	0	0	55	292	72	63	44	5	2	3	1	45	3	49	6	0	2	5	.286	0	0	7.20
1988	Appleton	A	20	18	0	1	99	421	94	46	35	4	4	3	4	34	1	88	5	2	3	5	.375	0	0	3.18
1989	Baseball Cy	A	12	11	2	1	71	280	59	17	14	2	0	3	1	20	1	64	1	1	9	0	1.000	0	0	1.77
	Memphis	AA	5	5	0	0	25.1	100	16	9	8	2	2	0	1	10	0	21	0	0	1	1	.500	0	0	2.84
1990	Memphis	AA	14	14	0	0	67.2	307	79	55	47	11	3	3	2	30	1	42	3	2	7	6	.538	0	0	6.25
	Omaha	AAA	11	11	1	0	65	274	63	29	29	8	1	0	1	30	0	53	0	5	5	2	.714	1	0	4.02
1991	Memphis	AA	10	10	0	0	53	224	52	24	15	6	1	1	1	21	0	54	1	1	4	5	.444	0	0	2.55
	Omaha	AAA	14	14	0	0	78.1	342	70	36	28	4	3	1	3	40	0	51	3	3	7	3	.700	0	0	3.22
1992	Omaha	AAA	23	16	3	2	120.2	496	121	36	33	9	3	1	4	34	1	56	5	3	8	5	.615	1	2	2.46
1993	Buffalo	AAA	24	11	0	4	76.2	326	85	43	37	13	5	5	1	21	3	38	4	5	3	4	.429	0	0	4.34
1994	Omaha	AAA	50	1	0	24	70.1	300	80	35	30	4	5	7	2	25	2	46	4	2	7	6	.538	0	5	3.84
1992	Kansas City	AL	5	4	0	1	18	89	24	17	14	5	3	3	0	11	2	6	1	1	0	3	.000	0	0	7.00
1993	Pittsburgh	NL	10	0	0	3	16.1	82	26	20	18	2	1	0	1	7	1	13	1	2	1	0	1.000	0	0	9.92
	9 Min. YEARS		215	135	6	32	843.2	3362	845	415	341	69	29	27	23	344	12	627	39	26	60	42	.588	2	7	3.64
	2 Maj. YEARS		15	4	0	4	34.1	171	50	37	32	7	4	3	1	18	3	19	2	3	1	3	.250	0	0	8.39

Jason Moler

Bats: Right Throws: Right Pos: C **Ht: 6'1" Wt: 195 Born: 10/29/69 Age: 25**

									BATTING									BASERUNNING				PERCENTAGES		
Year	Team	Lg	G	AB	H	2B	3B	HR	TB	R	RBI	TBB	IBB	SO	HBP	SH	SF	SB	CS	SB%	GDP	Avg	OBP	SLG
1993	Clearwater	A	97	350	101	17	2	15	167	59	64	46	3	40	3	0	4	5	7	.42	10	.289	.372	.477
	Reading	AA	38	138	39	11	0	2	56	15	19	12	0	31	2	0	1	1	1	.50	4	.283	.346	.406
1994	Scranton-Wb	AAA	44	144	35	9	1	2	52	16	16	18	1	26	1	2	2	2	2	.50	5	.243	.327	.361
	Reading	AA	78	285	81	13	3	4	112	37	37	29	1	21	2	0	1	7	6	.54	8	.284	.353	.393
	2 Min. YEARS		257	917	256	50	6	23	387	127	136	105	5	118	8	2	8	15	16	.48	27	.279	.355	.422

Izzy Molina

Bats: Right Throws: Right Pos: C **Ht: 6'0" Wt: 200 Born: 06/03/71 Age: 24**

									BATTING									BASERUNNING				PERCENTAGES		
Year	Team	Lg	G	AB	H	2B	3B	HR	TB	R	RBI	TBB	IBB	SO	HBP	SH	SF	SB	CS	SB%	GDP	Avg	OBP	SLG
1990	Athletics	R	38	122	43	12	2	0	59	19	18	9	1	21	2	1	3	5	0	1.00	0	.352	.397	.484

175

Year	Team	Lg	G	AB	H	2B	3B	HR	TB	R	RBI	TBB	IBB	SO	HBP	SH	SF	SB	CS	SB%	GDP	Avg	OBP	SLG
1991	Madison	A	95	316	89	16	1	3	116	35	45	15	1	40	6	1	4	6	4	.60	9	.282	.323	.367
1992	Reno	A	116	436	113	17	2	10	164	71	75	39	0	57	7	7	6	8	7	.53	20	.259	.326	.376
	Tacoma	AAA	10	36	7	0	1	0	9	3	5	2	0	6	0	0	0	1	0	1.00	1	.194	.237	.250
1993	Modesto	A	125	444	116	26	5	6	170	61	69	44	0	85	3	4	11	2	8	.20	11	.261	.325	.383
1994	Huntsville	AA	116	388	84	17	2	8	129	31	50	16	0	47	5	7	7	5	1	.83	10	.216	.252	.332
	5 Min. YEARS		500	1742	452	88	13	27	647	220	262	125	2	256	23	20	31	27	20	.57	51	.259	.312	.371

Michael Mongiello

Pitches: Right Bats: Right Pos: P   Ht: 6'2" Wt: 215 Born: 01/19/68 Age: 27

Year	Team	Lg	G	GS	CG	GF	IP	BFP	H	R	ER	HR	SH	SF	HB	TBB	IBB	SO	WP	Bk	W	L	Pct.	ShO	Sv	ERA
1989	White Sox	R	8	4	0	3	32.2	135	28	16	13	2	0	0	2	13	0	28	3	1	1	3	.250	0	2	3.58
1990	South Bend	A	38	15	3	21	106.1	470	98	55	39	3	6	3	2	54	4	89	5	8	6	6	.500	1	13	3.30
1991	Sarasota	A	55	0	0	44	68	292	51	26	17	1	3	1	1	34	5	62	5	4	4	4	.500	0	23	2.25
1992	Birmingham	AA	44	3	0	25	82.1	351	76	38	35	3	2	2	5	38	3	73	12	0	5	2	.714	0	8	3.83
1993	Birmingham	AA	7	1	0	4	11.2	46	5	6	2	0	0	0	2	4	0	9	3	0	0	1	.000	0	1	1.54
	Nashville	AAA	39	9	1	19	91	391	88	44	43	10	4	2	4	41	3	73	7	0	6	4	.600	0	7	4.25
1994	Nashville	AAA	45	5	0	13	86.1	393	94	39	35	6	10	1	3	49	7	77	7	0	4	6	.400	0	0	3.65
	6 Min. YEARS		236	37	4	129	478.1	2078	440	224	184	25	25	9	19	233	22	411	42	13	26	26	.500	1	54	3.46

Rob Montalvo

Bats: Right Throws: Right Pos: 2B   Ht: 6'1" Wt: 165 Born: 03/25/70 Age: 25

Year	Team	Lg	G	AB	H	2B	3B	HR	TB	R	RBI	TBB	IBB	SO	HBP	SH	SF	SB	CS	SB%	GDP	Avg	OBP	SLG
1988	St.Cathmes	A	62	190	32	4	0	0	36	19	18	25	0	48	0	4	1	4	5	.44	3	.168	.264	.189
1989	Dunedin	A	14	41	6	1	0	0	7	3	4	12	0	13	0	0	1	0	0	.00	0	.146	.340	.171
	Myrtle Bch	A	52	148	28	2	0	0	30	15	10	32	0	37	0	1	0	1	2	.33	2	.189	.333	.203
1990	St. Cath	A	38	115	21	2	0	0	23	11	5	21	1	19	1	1	1	1	2	.33	4	.183	.312	.200
	Myrtle Bch	A	45	125	25	1	0	0	26	15	11	9	0	14	1	3	1	2	2	.50	2	.200	.257	.208
1991	Knoxville	AA	15	31	5	1	0	0	6	3	0	7	0	7	1	1	0	0	0	.00	0	.161	.333	.194
	Dunedin	A	86	291	67	3	1	0	72	21	21	21	0	54	1	21	4	4	1	.80	6	.230	.281	.247
	Syracuse	AAA	1	3	0	0	0	0	0	0	0	0	0	0	0	0	0	0	0	.00	0	.000	.000	.000
1992	Knoxville	AA	32	72	12	1	0	0	13	7	4	12	0	19	0	5	0	1	1	.50	3	.167	.286	.181
	Syracuse	AAA	66	168	39	8	0	2	53	20	14	15	0	22	3	6	2	2	0	1.00	4	.232	.303	.315
1993	Syracuse	AAA	85	234	50	6	1	0	58	25	16	21	0	47	0	10	3	1	1	.50	7	.214	.275	.248
1994	Dunedin	A	7	17	7	1	0	0	8	5	1	3	0	2	0	0	0	0	0	.00	0	.412	.500	.471
	Syracuse	AAA	74	179	41	8	0	1	52	24	16	12	1	43	0	6	1	3	3	.50	2	.229	.276	.291
	7 Min. YEARS		577	1614	333	38	2	3	384	168	120	190	2	325	7	58	13	19	17	.53	33	.206	.291	.238

Ray Montgomery

Bats: Right Throws: Right Pos: OF   Ht: 6'3" Wt: 195 Born: 08/08/69 Age: 25

Year	Team	Lg	G	AB	H	2B	3B	HR	TB	R	RBI	TBB	IBB	SO	HBP	SH	SF	SB	CS	SB%	GDP	Avg	OBP	SLG
1990	Auburn	A	61	193	45	8	1	0	55	19	13	23	1	32	1	4	1	11	5	.69	5	.233	.317	.285
1991	Burlington	A	120	433	109	24	3	3	148	60	57	37	1	66	8	11	2	17	14	.55	10	.252	.321	.342
1992	Jackson	AA	51	148	31	4	1	1	40	13	10	7	2	27	0	1	1	4	1	.80	5	.209	.244	.270
1993	Tucson	AAA	15	50	17	3	1	2	28	9	6	5	0	7	1	1	0	1	2	.33	1	.340	.411	.560
	Jackson	AA	100	338	95	16	3	10	147	50	59	36	1	54	6	1	6	12	6	.67	7	.281	.355	.435
1994	Tucson	AAA	103	332	85	19	6	7	137	51	51	35	6	54	2	2	3	5	3	.63	9	.256	.328	.413
	5 Min. YEARS		450	1494	382	74	15	23	555	202	196	143	11	240	18	20	13	50	31	.62	37	.256	.326	.371

Steve Montgomery

Pitches: Right Bats: Right Pos: P   Ht: 6'4" Wt: 200 Born: 12/25/70 Age: 24

Year	Team	Lg	G	GS	CG	GF	IP	BFP	H	R	ER	HR	SH	SF	HB	TBB	IBB	SO	WP	Bk	W	L	Pct.	ShO	Sv	ERA
1993	St.Pete	A	14	5	0	7	40.2	161	33	14	12	2	1	2	0	9	0	34	1	0	2	1	.667	0	3	2.66
	Arkansas	AA	6	6	0	0	32	140	34	17	14	2	2	0	0	12	2	19	2	0	3	3	.500	0	0	3.94
1994	Arkansas	AA	50	9	0	19	107	447	97	43	39	10	4	4	3	33	3	73	5	0	4	5	.444	0	2	3.28
	2 Min. YEARS		70	20	0	26	179.2	748	164	74	65	14	7	6	3	54	5	126	8	0	9	9	.500	0	5	3.26

Albert Montoya

Pitches: Left Bats: Left Pos: P   Ht: 6'2" Wt: 168 Born: 06/10/69 Age: 26

Year	Team	Lg	G	GS	CG	GF	IP	BFP	H	R	ER	HR	SH	SF	HB	TBB	IBB	SO	WP	Bk	W	L	Pct.	ShO	Sv	ERA
1991	Medicne Hat	R	15	14	5	1	82.1	359	94	46	37	4	2	2	2	21	0	56	10	9	5	7	.417	1	1	4.04
1992	Myrtle Bch	A	42	2	0	21	99	412	96	36	31	7	3	1	4	33	4	99	9	3	4	4	.500	0	10	2.82
1993	Dunedin	A	50	1	0	22	80.1	349	78	37	32	2	2	2	2	26	5	35	5	2	7	4	.636	0	5	3.59
	Knoxville	AA	5	0	0	0	7	32	8	4	4	1	0	1	1	3	0	9	3	0	1	0	1.000	0	0	5.14
1994	Knoxville	AA	36	2	1	19	80.2	362	103	48	36	5	0	3	8	26	2	42	5	3	3	5	.375	0	2	4.02
	4 Min. YEARS		148	19	6	63	349.1	1514	379	171	140	19	7	9	18	109	11	241	32	17	20	20	.500	1	18	3.61

Norm Montoya

Pitches: Left **Bats:** Left **Pos:** P **Ht:** 6'1" **Wt:** 190 **Born:** 09/24/70 **Age:** 24

Year	Team	Lg	G	GS	CG	GF	IP	BFP	H	R	ER	HR	SH	SF	HB	TBB	IBB	SO	WP	Bk	W	L	Pct.	ShO	Sv	ERA
1990	Angels	R	10	6	1	2	47	199	49	20	11	1	1	0	1	7	0	28	0	0	3	3	.500	0	1	2.11
	Quad City	A	4	4	1	0	28.2	117	30	12	10	0	1	1	0	6	0	13	0	1	3	1	.750	0	0	3.14
1991	Quad City	A	8	8	0	0	40.1	186	55	27	23	2	1	1	0	12	0	22	4	1	4	1	.800	0	0	5.13
	Palm Sprngs	A	17	17	1	0	105	455	117	64	48	10	3	2	2	26	4	45	3	1	4	7	.364	0	0	4.11
1992	Palm Sprngs	A	14	6	2	6	43.2	194	42	21	18	3	4	2	1	19	1	46	2	1	2	3	.400	0	0	3.71
1993	Palm Sprngs	A	28	4	0	8	63.2	286	83	38	34	0	3	4	3	21	5	35	6	0	1	3	.250	0	0	4.81
1994	Stockton	A	11	0	0	3	16.1	65	12	6	4	1	2	0	1	3	0	15	0	0	0	1	.000	0	1	2.20
	El Paso	AA	9	0	0	4	12.1	48	10	5	4	0	1	0	0	4	2	8	0	0	1	1	.500	0	1	2.92
	5 Min. YEARS		101	45	5	23	357	1550	398	193	152	17	16	10	8	98	12	212	15	4	18	20	.474	0	3	3.83

Charlie Montoyo

Bats: Right **Throws:** Right **Pos:** 2B **Ht:** 5'11" **Wt:** 170 **Born:** 10/17/65 **Age:** 29

						BATTING												BASERUNNING				PERCENTAGES		
Year	Team	Lg	G	AB	H	2B	3B	HR	TB	R	RBI	TBB	IBB	SO	HBP	SH	SF	SB	CS	SB%	GDP	Avg	OBP	SLG
1987	Helena	R	13	45	13	1	2	0	18	12	2	12	0	3	0	0	1	2	1	.67	0	.289	.431	.400
	Beloit	A	55	188	50	9	2	5	78	46	19	52	0	22	4	1	1	8	0	1.00	4	.266	.433	.415
1988	Stockton	A	132	450	115	14	1	3	140	103	61	156	0	93	5	6	2	16	6	.73	7	.256	.450	.311
1989	Stockton	A	129	448	111	22	2	0	137	69	48	102	3	40	11	6	4	13	9	.59	7	.248	.396	.306
1990	El Paso	AA	94	322	93	13	3	3	121	71	44	72	1	43	8	1	2	9	0	1.00	9	.289	.428	.376
1991	Denver	AAA	120	394	94	13	1	12	145	68	45	69	0	51	5	6	4	15	4	.79	6	.239	.356	.368
1992	Denver	AAA	84	259	84	7	4	2	105	40	34	47	0	36	1	2	1	3	5	.38	10	.324	.429	.405
1993	Ottawa	AAA	99	319	89	18	2	1	114	43	43	71	0	37	4	6	5	0	9	.00	11	.279	.411	.357
1994	Scranton-Wb	AAA	114	387	109	28	0	9	164	64	47	74	4	61	5	10	1	3	3	.50	10	.282	.403	.424
1993	Montreal	NL	4	5	2	1	0	0	3	1	3	0	0	0	0	0	0	0	0	.00	0	.400	.400	.600
	8 Min. YEARS		840	2812	758	125	17	35	1022	516	343	655	8	386	43	38	21	69	37	.65	64	.270	.412	.363

Jose Monzon

Bats: Right **Throws:** Right **Pos:** C **Ht:** 6'1" **Wt:** 178 **Born:** 11/08/68 **Age:** 26

						BATTING												BASERUNNING				PERCENTAGES		
Year	Team	Lg	G	AB	H	2B	3B	HR	TB	R	RBI	TBB	IBB	SO	HBP	SH	SF	SB	CS	SB%	GDP	Avg	OBP	SLG
1987	Bristol	R	7	12	3	1	0	0	4	3	1	0	0	1	0	0	0	0	0	.00	1	.250	.250	.333
	Lakeland	A	4	5	0	0	0	0	0	0	0	0	0	4	0	0	2	0	0	.00	0	.000	.000	.000
	Fayettevlle	A	11	19	1	0	0	0	1	1	0	2	0	5	0	0	0	0	0	.00	0	.053	.143	.053
1989	Dunedin	A	16	48	12	2	1	0	16	4	7	5	0	11	0	0	0	0	0	.00	1	.250	.321	.333
	Myrtle Bch	A	50	165	39	7	0	1	49	18	10	19	0	31	0	0	0	3	2	.60	7	.236	.315	.297
1990	Dunedin	A	30	76	23	5	1	0	30	11	7	10	0	18	1	1	0	1	0	1.00	0	.303	.391	.395
	Knoxville	AA	1	3	1	0	0	0	1	1	0	0	0	0	0	0	0	0	0	.00	0	.333	.333	.333
1991	Dunedin	A	46	144	31	6	0	3	46	14	17	17	0	31	0	6	2	2	0	1.00	4	.215	.294	.319
	Knoxville	AA	44	116	31	5	0	0	36	12	11	13	1	23	0	1	1	1	1	.50	5	.267	.338	.310
1992	Knoxville	AA	65	178	41	9	1	0	52	17	10	12	0	42	2	3	1	3	2	.60	3	.230	.285	.292
	Syracuse	AAA	9	18	1	0	0	0	1	3	1	2	0	1	0	0	0	0	0	.00	1	.056	.150	.056
1993	Syracuse	AAA	71	197	47	7	0	3	63	14	21	11	0	37	0	4	0	0	1	.00	9	.239	.279	.320
1994	Midland	AA	83	283	71	18	3	4	107	41	35	24	0	52	2	3	0	1	1	.50	7	.251	.314	.378
	7 Min. YEARS		437	1264	301	60	6	11	406	139	120	115	1	256	5	20	4	11	7	.61	38	.238	.303	.321

Richie Moody

Pitches: Left **Bats:** Right **Pos:** P **Ht:** 6'1" **Wt:** 185 **Born:** 02/22/71 **Age:** 24

Year	Team	Lg	G	GS	CG	GF	IP	BFP	H	R	ER	HR	SH	SF	HB	TBB	IBB	SO	WP	Bk	W	L	Pct.	ShO	Sv	ERA
1992	Gastonia	A	21	0	0	15	26.1	107	9	7	1	0	1	1	0	16	0	29	4	1	0	2	.000	0	11	0.34
	Tulsa	AA	7	0	0	7	6.1	26	3	2	1	0	0	0	1	2	0	6	1	0	0	0	.000	0	2	1.42
1993	Tulsa	AA	46	0	0	38	66	287	58	27	16	1	2	3	2	34	2	60	10	2	3	2	.600	0	16	2.18
1994	Okla. City	AAA	8	8	0	0	42	191	40	29	28	3	2	2	3	31	0	32	7	0	0	5	.000	0	0	6.00
	3 Min. YEARS		82	8	0	60	140.2	611	110	65	46	4	5	6	6	83	2	127	22	3	3	9	.250	0	29	2.94

Bobby Moore

Bats: Right **Throws:** Right **Pos:** OF **Ht:** 5'9" **Wt:** 165 **Born:** 10/27/65 **Age:** 29

						BATTING												BASERUNNING				PERCENTAGES		
Year	Team	Lg	G	AB	H	2B	3B	HR	TB	R	RBI	TBB	IBB	SO	HBP	SH	SF	SB	CS	SB%	GDP	Avg	OBP	SLG
1987	Eugene	A	57	235	88	13	4	1	112	40	25	14	2	22	1	2	1	23	1	.96	5	.374	.410	.477
1988	Baseball Cy	A	60	224	52	4	2	0	60	25	10	17	0	20	2	4	0	12	7	.63	4	.232	.292	.268
1989	Baseball Cy	A	131	483	131	21	5	0	162	85	42	51	1	35	6	6	3	34	19	.64	6	.271	.346	.335
1990	Memphis	AA	112	422	128	20	6	2	166	93	36	56	0	32	2	8	4	27	7	.79	5	.303	.384	.393
1991	Omaha	AAA	130	494	120	13	3	0	139	65	34	37	0	41	3	13	2	35	15	.70	10	.243	.299	.281
1992	Richmond	AAA	92	316	79	13	3	0	98	41	25	21	0	26	0	6	3	14	6	.70	6	.250	.294	.310
1993	Richmond	AAA	1	3	2	0	0	0	2	2	0	1	0	0	0	0	0	1	0	1.00	0	.667	.750	.667

1994	Memphis	AA	27	97	23	2	1	2	33	10	7	8	0	15	1	2	1	1	2	.33	3	.237	.299	.340
	Richmond	AAA	60	216	79	6	3	5	106	37	18	18	1	16	0	1	2	10	6	.63	4	.366	.411	.491
1991	Kansas City	AL	18	14	5	1	0	0	6	3	0	1	0	2	0	0	0	3	2	.60	0	.357	.400	.429
	8 Min. YEARS		670	2490	702	92	27	10	878	398	197	223	4	207	15	42	16	157	63	.71	43	.282	.343	.353

Brad Moore

Pitches: Right Bats: Right Pos: P Ht: 6' 1" Wt: 185 Born: 06/21/64 Age: 31

			HOW MUCH HE PITCHED					WHAT HE GAVE UP										THE RESULTS					
Year	Team	Lg	G	GS	CG	GF	IP	BFP	H	R	ER	HR	SH	SF	HB	TBB	IBB	SO	WP	Bk	W	L	Pct.	ShO	Sv	ERA
1986	Bend	A	16	0	0	14	33.2	0	32	29	22	4	0	0	1	22	5	35	7	0	2	5	.286	0	4	5.88
1987	Clearwater	A	53	0	0	42	67.1	287	63	23	15	0	2	2	0	21	5	42	2	0	4	7	.364	0	16	2.00
	Reading	AA	9	0	0	8	18.1	69	12	2	2	0	0	0	2	4	2	13	0	0	1	0	.000	0	4	0.98
1988	Reading	AA	57	0	0	43	70.2	301	57	30	24	5	8	2	2	33	6	39	6	0	4	6	.400	0	18	3.06
1989	Scr Wil-Bar	AAA	61	1	0	25	97	421	86	41	36	4	6	3	6	49	10	67	4	2	6	10	.375	0	5	3.34
1990	Reading	AA	1	1	0	0	6	21	2	0	0	0	0	0	0	1	0	4	0	0	1	0	1.000	0	0	0.00
	Scr Wil-Bar	AAA	35	12	1	5	101.2	426	97	48	42	8	5	3	4	28	4	45	2	1	3	7	.300	0	0	3.72
1991	Tidewater	AAA	50	1	0	35	78.1	344	73	36	29	3	8	2	5	45	8	53	4	1	8	5	.615	0	13	3.33
1992	Tidewater	AAA	50	1	0	24	79.1	370	80	55	48	5	4	4	5	52	4	55	14	0	6	6	.500	0	1	5.45
1993	Indianapolis	AAA	21	1	0	6	43	196	46	28	28	4	3	2	2	22	1	22	9	0	0	1	.000	0	0	5.86
1994	Buffalo	AAA	12	1	0	4	16.1	80	23	15	10	2	1	2	2	5	0	3	0	0	1	1	.500	0	0	5.51
1988	Philadelphia	NL	5	0	0	2	5.2	21	4	0	0	0	2	0	0	4	1	2	0	0	0	0	.000	0	0	0.00
1990	Philadelphia	NL	3	0	0	3	2.2	13	4	1	1	0	0	1	0	2	1	1	1	0	0	0	.000	0	0	3.38
	9 Min. YEARS		365	18	1	206	611.2	2515	571	307	256	35	37	20	29	282	45	378	48	4	35	49	.417	0	66	3.77
	2 Maj. YEARS		8	0	0	5	8.1	34	8	1	1	0	2	1	0	6	2	3	1	0	0	0	.000	0	0	1.08

Kerwin Moore

Bats: Both Throws: Right Pos: OF Ht: 6'1" Wt: 190 Born: 10/29/70 Age: 24

			BATTING													BASERUNNING				PERCENTAGES		
Year	Team	Lg	G	AB	H	2B	3B	HR	TB	R	RBI	TBB	IBB	SO	HBP	SH	SF	SB	CS	SB%	GDP	Avg	OBP	SLG
1988	Royals	R	53	165	29	5	0	0	34	19	14	19	1	49	2	1	0	20	3	.87	2	.176	.269	.206
1989	Baseball Cy	A	4	11	4	0	0	1	7	3	2	1	0	2	0	0	0	0	0	.00	0	.364	.417	.636
	Eugene	A	65	226	50	9	2	2	69	44	25	36	0	75	2	1	0	20	6	.77	0	.221	.333	.305
1990	Appleton	A	128	451	100	17	7	2	137	93	36	111	2	139	3	6	1	57	19	.75	1	.222	.378	.304
1991	Baseball Cy	A	130	485	102	14	2	1	123	67	23	77	0	141	3	5	1	61	15	.80	5	.210	.322	.254
1992	Baseball Cy	A	66	248	59	2	1	1	66	39	10	40	1	67	2	4	1	26	9	.74	3	.238	.347	.266
	Memphis	AA	58	179	42	4	3	4	64	27	17	24	0	39	2	1	1	16	4	.80	2	.235	.330	.358
1993	High Desert	A	132	510	137	20	9	6	193	120	52	114	3	95	6	3	5	71	16	.82	3	.269	.405	.378
1994	Huntsville	AA	132	494	120	16	5	5	161	97	33	96	0	99	1	5	5	54	19	.74	11	.243	.364	.326
	7 Min. YEARS		768	2769	643	87	29	22	854	509	212	518	7	706	21	26	14	325	91	.78	27	.232	.356	.308

Mike Moore

Bats: Right Throws: Right Pos: OF Ht: 6'4" Wt: 200 Born: 03/07/71 Age: 24

			BATTING													BASERUNNING				PERCENTAGES		
Year	Team	Lg	G	AB	H	2B	3B	HR	TB	R	RBI	TBB	IBB	SO	HBP	SH	SF	SB	CS	SB%	GDP	Avg	OBP	SLG
1992	Yakima	A	18	58	12	1	0	2	19	12	6	9	1	25	0	0	0	3	2	.60	1	.207	.313	.328
1993	Bakersfield	A	100	403	116	25	1	13	182	61	58	29	0	103	3	0	4	23	10	.70	6	.288	.337	.452
1994	San Antonio	AA	72	254	57	12	1	5	86	32	32	22	0	75	6	0	1	11	7	.61	2	.224	.300	.339
	Bakersfield	A	21	81	24	5	0	2	35	17	8	13	1	21	0	0	0	2	0	1.00	3	.296	.394	.432
	3 Min. YEARS		211	796	209	43	2	22	322	122	104	73	2	224	9	0	5	39	19	.67	12	.263	.330	.405

Tim Moore

Bats: Both Throws: Left Pos: OF Ht: 5'9" Wt: 215 Born: 08/27/71 Age: 23

			BATTING													BASERUNNING				PERCENTAGES		
Year	Team	Lg	G	AB	H	2B	3B	HR	TB	R	RBI	TBB	IBB	SO	HBP	SH	SF	SB	CS	SB%	GDP	Avg	OBP	SLG
1989	Twins	R	37	95	16	3	0	0	19	10	10	24	0	26	0	0	0	19	1	.95	2	.168	.336	.200
1990	Twins	R	27	77	20	2	3	3	37	19	15	13	0	24	1	0	1	6	3	.67	0	.260	.370	.481
1991	Elizabethtn	R	57	197	52	17	1	12	107	33	37	28	3	57	2	0	1	7	2	.78	0	.264	.360	.543
1992	Kenosha	A	112	382	104	26	2	12	170	76	52	68	3	99	4	2	5	40	20	.67	11	.272	.383	.445
	Visalia	A	4	9	4	1	2	0	9	2	4	0	0	2	0	0	0	1	0	1.00	0	.444	.444	1.000
1993	Ft.Myers	A	69	222	56	15	3	6	95	32	32	28	0	52	0	1	4	17	3	.85	3	.252	.331	.428
1994	Nashville	AA	123	436	108	25	0	18	187	50	67	38	3	130	8	2	4	9	10	.47	8	.248	.317	.429
	6 Min. YEARS		429	1418	360	89	11	51	624	222	217	199	9	390	15	5	15	99	39	.72	24	.254	.349	.440

Tim Moore

Pitches: Right Bats: Right Pos: P Ht: 6'4" Wt: 190 Born: 09/04/70 Age: 24

			HOW MUCH HE PITCHED					WHAT HE GAVE UP										THE RESULTS					
Year	Team	Lg	G	GS	CG	GF	IP	BFP	H	R	ER	HR	SH	SF	HB	TBB	IBB	SO	WP	Bk	W	L	Pct.	ShO	Sv	ERA
1992	Utica	A	14	13	0	0	84.2	360	82	46	30	7	3	2	3	21	0	66	8	1	6	5	.545	0	0	3.19
1993	South Bend	A	26	26	4	0	165.1	692	156	89	83	21	6	7	12	52	0	108	8	1	11	9	.550	0	0	4.52
1994	Pr. William	A	27	0	0	13	66	279	59	24	19	4	6	1	2	24	0	77	3	1	2	2	.500	0	5	2.59
	Birmingham	AA	8	0	0	5	12.2	55	16	12	8	2	0	1	1	3	1	10	1	0	0	0	.000	0	0	5.68
	3 Min. YEARS		75	39	4	18	328.2	1386	313	171	140	34	15	11	18	100	1	261	20	3	19	16	.543	0	5	3.83

Vincent Moore

Bats: Left   Throws: Left   Pos: OF   Ht: 6'1"   Wt: 177   Born: 09/22/71   Age: 23

Year	Team	Lg	G	AB	H	2B	3B	HR	TB	R	RBI	TBB	IBB	SO	HBP	SH	SF	SB	CS	SB%	GDP	Avg	OBP	SLG
1991	Braves	R	30	110	44	4	6	2	66	28	22	13	0	20	0	0	1	7	2	.78	1	.400	.460	.600
	Macon	A	35	120	24	5	1	0	31	17	12	7	0	24	0	0	0	6	0	1.00	2	.200	.244	.258
1992	Macon	A	123	436	99	15	5	6	142	52	48	48	2	118	1	4	3	25	11	.69	10	.227	.303	.326
1993	Durham	A	87	319	93	14	1	14	151	53	64	29	2	93	6	1	2	21	8	.72	5	.292	.360	.473
1994	Wichita	AA	48	132	20	5	0	2	31	15	9	16	1	46	1	0	1	4	2	.67	4	.152	.247	.235
	Rancho Cuca	A	6	23	5	1	0	1	9	5	2	3	0	9	0	0	0	0	0	.00	0	.217	.308	.391
	4 Min. YEARS		329	1140	285	44	13	25	430	170	157	116	5	310	8	5	7	63	23	.73	22	.250	.322	.377

Francisco Morales

Bats: Right   Throws: Right   Pos: C   Ht: 6'3"   Wt: 180   Born: 01/31/73   Age: 22

Year	Team	Lg	G	AB	H	2B	3B	HR	TB	R	RBI	TBB	IBB	SO	HBP	SH	SF	SB	CS	SB%	GDP	Avg	OBP	SLG
1992	Huntington	R	13	39	7	1	0	1	11	4	9	10	0	13	1	1	0	1	2	.33	1	.179	.360	.282
	Geneva	A	19	49	11	2	0	0	13	3	0	7	1	21	0	0	0	0	0	.00	3	.224	.321	.265
1993	Peoria	A	19	49	10	1	1	3	22	9	11	9	0	16	0	4	0	0	0	.00	2	.204	.328	.449
	Geneva	A	45	123	24	4	0	2	34	12	20	15	0	41	1	0	2	1	0	1.00	2	.195	.284	.276
1994	Orlando	AA	22	58	12	0	0	2	18	3	10	7	0	21	0	0	0	0	1	.00	2	.207	.292	.310
	Daytona	A	38	120	29	7	1	1	41	9	10	9	0	37	1	0	1	1	0	1.00	2	.242	.298	.342
	3 Min. YEARS		156	438	93	15	2	9	139	40	60	57	1	149	3	5	3	3	3	.50	10	.212	.305	.317

Mike Morland

Bats: Right   Throws: Right   Pos: C   Ht: 6'0"   Wt: 190   Born: 08/17/69   Age: 25

Year	Team	Lg	G	AB	H	2B	3B	HR	TB	R	RBI	TBB	IBB	SO	HBP	SH	SF	SB	CS	SB%	GDP	Avg	OBP	SLG
1991	St.Cathmes	A	46	146	38	8	1	2	54	10	21	22	0	33	0	2	4	0	1	.00	1	.260	.349	.370
1992	Myrtle Bch	A	104	265	45	9	0	4	66	21	26	29	0	60	2	1	4	2	1	.67	2	.170	.253	.249
1993	Knoxville	AA	45	112	26	4	1	0	32	7	15	10	0	31	0	3	0	1	1	.50	3	.232	.295	.286
1994	Syracuse	AAA	11	26	6	2	0	0	8	4	3	1	0	5	1	2	0	0	0	.00	3	.231	.286	.308
	Knoxville	AA	39	95	28	4	1	2	40	19	15	11	0	25	3	1	0	1	1	.50	3	.295	.385	.421
	4 Min. YEARS		245	644	143	27	3	8	200	61	80	73	0	154	6	9	8	4	4	.50	9	.222	.304	.311

Alvin Morman

Pitches: Left   Bats: Left   Pos: P   Ht: 6'3"   Wt: 210   Born: 01/06/69   Age: 26

Year	Team	Lg	G	GS	CG	GF	IP	BFP	H	R	ER	HR	SH	SF	HB	TBB	IBB	SO	WP	Bk	W	L	Pct.	ShO	Sv	ERA
1991	Astros	R	11	0	0	3	16.2	71	15	7	4	0	1	0	0	5	0	24	0	4	1	0	1.000	0	1	2.16
	Osceola	A	3	0	0	1	6	25	5	3	1	0	0	0	0	2	0	3	1	0	0	0	.000	0	0	1.50
1992	Asheville	A	57	0	0	37	75.1	313	60	17	13	3	3	1	3	26	2	70	2	0	8	0	1.000	0	15	1.55
1993	Jackson	AA	19	19	0	0	97.1	392	77	35	32	7	3	2	5	28	0	101	5	1	8	2	.800	0	0	2.96
1994	Tucson	AAA	58	0	0	23	74	327	84	51	42	7	5	9	2	26	4	49	3	0	3	7	.300	0	5	5.11
	4 Min. YEARS		148	19	0	63	269.1	1128	241	113	92	17	12	12	10	87	6	247	11	5	20	9	.690	0	21	3.07

Keith Morrison

Pitches: Right   Bats: Right   Pos: P   Ht: 6'4"   Wt: 190   Born: 11/22/69   Age: 25

Year	Team	Lg	G	GS	CG	GF	IP	BFP	H	R	ER	HR	SH	SF	HB	TBB	IBB	SO	WP	Bk	W	L	Pct.	ShO	Sv	ERA
1990	Pulaski	R	13	13	2	0	79	348	77	46	36	4	1	2	1	37	0	79	5	8	6	6	.500	0	0	4.10
1991	Macon	A	8	8	1	0	42.2	174	41	23	14	2	2	1	2	6	0	25	0	2	4	3	.571	0	0	2.95
	Sumter	A	7	7	1	0	36	151	36	20	18	3	0	1	0	12	0	26	2	2	2	4	.333	0	0	4.50
1992	Albany	A	15	15	2	0	111	464	113	46	30	2	5	2	3	28	1	85	3	1	8	4	.667	1	0	2.43
	Rockford	A	15	3	0	7	35	158	46	24	20	2	4	1	1	7	0	29	2	1	1	2	.333	0	0	5.14
1993	Palm Sprngs	A	27	27	2	0	176	772	200	108	81	16	3	12	10	55	0	107	7	0	14	6	.700	1	0	4.14
1994	Midland	AA	12	12	3	0	83.2	355	78	39	33	4	3	1	7	28	1	61	1	1	6	3	.667	0	0	3.55
	Vancouver	AAA	16	14	2	2	85.1	394	111	68	62	17	3	3	0	27	2	50	1	0	4	6	.400	1	0	6.54
	5 Min. YEARS		113	99	13	9	648.2	2816	702	374	294	50	21	23	24	200	4	462	21	15	45	34	.570	3	0	4.08

Timmie Morrow

Bats: Right   Throws: Right   Pos: OF   Ht: 6'3"   Wt: 180   Born: 02/07/70   Age: 25

Year	Team	Lg	G	AB	H	2B	3B	HR	TB	R	RBI	TBB	IBB	SO	HBP	SH	SF	SB	CS	SB%	GDP	Avg	OBP	SLG
1988	Rangers	R	32	113	28	2	4	2	44	15	9	9	0	30	1	1	1	3	2	.60	0	.248	.306	.389
1989	Butte	R	60	225	61	7	2	4	84	40	27	12	1	44	1	1	2	13	5	.72	2	.271	.308	.373
1990	Gastonia	A	105	378	78	10	2	7	113	55	34	33	0	99	4	6	3	19	15	.56	5	.206	.275	.299
1991	Charlotte	A	119	463	116	24	8	5	171	65	59	33	0	124	1	8	5	33	13	.72	8	.251	.299	.369
1992	Tulsa	AA	7	30	4	1	0	0	5	2	3	2	0	11	0	0	0	1	1	.50	1	.133	.188	.167
	Charlotte	A	108	383	89	11	5	11	143	48	40	23	2	64	8	3	1	17	10	.63	10	.232	.289	.373
1993	Tulsa	AA	108	390	96	25	2	9	152	46	45	19	1	98	8	3	2	11	14	.44	1	.246	.294	.390
	Okla City	AAA	7	27	7	2	0	0	9	2	5	1	0	6	1	0	0	0	0	.00	0	.259	.300	.333

179

1994 Tulsa	AA	81	285	58	14	3	6	96	34	31	18	1	59	4	5	5	5	6	.45	3	.204	.256	.337
Okla. City	AAA	5	10	0	0	0	0	0	2	0	0	0	5	0	0	0	0	0	.00	0	.000	.000	.000
7 Min. YEARS		632	2304	537	96	26	44	817	309	253	150	5	540	28	27	20	102	66	.61	30	.233	.286	.355

Kevin Morton

Pitches: Left Bats: Right Pos: P Ht: 6' 2" Wt: 185 Born: 08/03/68 Age: 26

		HOW MUCH HE PITCHED						WHAT HE GAVE UP										THE RESULTS					
Year Team	Lg	G	GS	CG	GF	IP	BFP	H	R	ER	HR	SH	SF	HB	TBB	IBB	SO	WP	Bk	W	L	Pct.	ShO	Sv	ERA
1989 Red Sox	R	2	1	0	1	6	22	2	0	0	0	0	0	1	1	0	11	0	0	1	0	1.000	0	1	0.00
Elmira	A	3	3	2	0	24	90	11	6	5	0	2	2	1	6	0	32	1	0	1	1	.500	0	0	1.88
Lynchburg	A	9	9	4	0	65	253	42	20	17	2	0	2	2	17	0	68	3	0	4	5	.444	2	0	2.35
1990 New Britain	AA	26	26	7	0	163	685	151	86	69	10	4	3	14	48	0	131	6	5	8	14	.364	2	0	3.81
1991 Pawtucket	AAA	16	15	1	0	98	412	91	41	38	8	2	2	2	30	1	80	3	2	7	3	.700	1	0	3.49
1992 Pawtucket	AAA	26	25	1	0	138.2	627	166	93	84	19	3	4	3	59	2	71	5	2	2	12	.143	0	0	5.45
1993 Memphis	AA	20	9	1	4	73	328	88	48	39	12	4	2	1	29	1	59	0	0	3	6	.333	0	1	4.81
1994 Norfolk	AAA	29	20	1	3	137	590	124	74	57	11	6	7	7	67	4	75	4	0	5	8	.385	1	1	3.74
1991 Boston	AL	16	15	1	0	86.1	379	93	49	44	9	3	7	1	40	2	45	1	1	6	5	.545	0	0	4.59
6 Min. YEARS		131	108	17	8	704.2	3007	675	368	309	62	21	22	31	257	8	527	25	9	31	49	.388	6	3	3.95

Andy Mota

Bats: Right Throws: Right Pos: 2B Ht: 5'10" Wt: 180 Born: 03/04/66 Age: 29

		BATTING													BASERUNNING				PERCENTAGES		
Year Team	Lg	G	AB	H	2B	3B	HR	TB	R	RBI	TBB	IBB	SO	HBP	SH	SF	SB	CS	SB%	GDP	Avg	OBP	SLG
1987 Auburn	A	70	255	67	9	1	4	90	26	14	16	0	42	5	5	1	6	5	.55	7	.263	.318	.353
1988 Auburn	A	72	271	95	15	3	3	125	56	47	38	2	34	5	1	0	31	6	.84	5	.351	.434	.461
1989 Osceola	A	131	505	161	21	4	4	202	68	69	42	3	61	11	3	10	28	9	.76	9	.319	.377	.400
1990 Columbus	AA	111	413	118	21	1	11	174	59	62	28	2	81	10	9	6	17	7	.71	5	.286	.341	.421
1991 Tucson	AAA	123	462	138	19	4	2	171	65	46	22	3	76	7	4	2	14	9	.61	6	.299	.339	.370
1992 Tucson	AAA	96	317	76	14	6	3	111	33	32	16	0	53	6	1	3	7	8	.47	9	.240	.287	.350
1993 Tucson	AAA	3	6	1	0	0	0	1	1	1	0	0	2	0	0	0	1	0	1.00	0	.167	.167	.167
Phoenix	AAA	29	71	13	6	0	0	19	9	10	8	1	17	1	2	2	1	2	.33	1	.169	.250	.247
Colo Sprngs	AAA	70	262	90	23	4	7	142	36	50	13	3	38	5	2	2	6	3	.67	6	.344	.383	.542
1994 Colo. Sprng	AAA	37	124	30	10	0	6	58	20	20	4	0	15	2	0	0	3	0	1.00	5	.242	.277	.468
Tulsa	AA	24	82	24	7	0	3	40	12	7	5	0	20	2	0	1	1	1	.50	3	.293	.348	.488
1991 Houston	NL	27	90	17	2	0	1	22	4	6	1	0	17	0	0	0	2	0	1.00	1	.189	.198	.244
8 Min. YEARS		766	2774	813	145	23	43	1133	385	358	192	14	439	54	27	30	115	50	.70	55	.293	.347	.408

Domingo Mota

Bats: Right Throws: Right Pos: 2B Ht: 5'8" Wt: 180 Born: 08/04/69 Age: 25

		BATTING													BASERUNNING				PERCENTAGES		
Year Team	Lg	G	AB	H	2B	3B	HR	TB	R	RBI	TBB	IBB	SO	HBP	SH	SF	SB	CS	SB%	GDP	Avg	OBP	SLG
1990 Dodgers	R	61	213	73	12	2	1	92	46	34	36	3	19	8	2	1	23	15	.61	4	.343	.453	.432
1991 Bakersfield	A	104	408	112	20	2	8	160	75	44	44	1	83	6	10	4	37	19	.66	1	.275	.351	.392
1992 Memphis	AA	119	430	114	16	0	4	142	46	23	19	1	67	4	9	1	14	17	.45	7	.265	.302	.330
1993 Memphis	AA	56	196	42	7	3	1	58	22	16	11	0	48	1	3	3	10	9	.53	4	.214	.256	.296
Wilmington	A	14	36	7	1	1	0	10	1	6	2	0	6	1	2	1	0	1	.00	1	.194	.250	.278
1994 Memphis	AA	48	156	37	3	2	3	53	23	11	8	1	26	3	4	0	6	3	.67	4	.237	.287	.340
5 Min. YEARS		402	1439	385	59	10	17	515	213	134	120	6	249	23	30	10	90	64	.58	21	.268	.332	.358

Gary Mota

Bats: Right Throws: Right Pos: OF Ht: 6'0" Wt: 195 Born: 10/06/70 Age: 24

		BATTING													BASERUNNING				PERCENTAGES		
Year Team	Lg	G	AB	H	2B	3B	HR	TB	R	RBI	TBB	IBB	SO	HBP	SH	SF	SB	CS	SB%	GDP	Avg	OBP	SLG
1990 Auburn	A	69	248	64	12	4	3	93	39	19	26	2	74	2	3	2	12	1	.92	5	.258	.331	.375
1991 Osceola	A	22	71	14	2	2	0	20	10	3	8	0	19	0	0	0	4	1	.80	0	.197	.278	.282
1992 Asheville	A	137	484	141	21	5	23	241	92	89	58	5	131	3	0	6	22	10	.69	13	.291	.367	.498
1993 Jackson	AA	27	90	13	2	0	3	24	7	8	2	0	25	0	2	1	1	1	.50	2	.144	.161	.267
1994 Jackson	AA	108	314	75	13	4	10	126	46	54	57	2	80	3	0	4	12	7	.63	5	.239	.357	.401
5 Min. YEARS		363	1207	307	50	15	39	504	194	173	151	9	329	8	5	13	51	20	.72	25	.254	.338	.418

Jose Mota

Bats: Both Throws: Right Pos: 2B Ht: 5' 9" Wt: 155 Born: 03/16/65 Age: 30

		BATTING													BASERUNNING				PERCENTAGES		
Year Team	Lg	G	AB	H	2B	3B	HR	TB	R	RBI	TBB	IBB	SO	HBP	SH	SF	SB	CS	SB%	GDP	Avg	OBP	SLG
1985 Buffalo	AAA	6	18	5	0	0	0	5	3	1	2	0	0	0	0	0	0	0	.00	1	.278	.350	.278
Niagara Fls	A	65	254	77	9	2	0	90	35	27	28	3	29	2	5	2	8	5	.62	1	.303	.374	.354
1986 Tulsa	AA	41	158	51	7	3	1	67	26	11	22	0	13	0	3	1	14	8	.64	0	.323	.403	.424
Okla City	AAA	71	255	71	9	1	0	82	38	20	24	1	43	3	5	0	7	5	.58	7	.278	.348	.322
1987 Tulsa	AA	21	71	15	2	0	0	17	11	4	13	0	12	0	0	1	2	2	.50	0	.211	.329	.239
San Antonio	AA	54	190	50	4	3	0	60	23	11	21	1	34	2	5	0	3	4	.43	3	.263	.343	.316
1988 Albuquerque	AAA	6	15	5	0	0	0	5	4	1	3	0	3	0	1	0	1	0	1.00	1	.333	.444	.333
San Antonio	AA	82	214	56	11	1	1	72	32	18	27	1	35	0	4	1	10	4	.71	7	.262	.343	.336
1989 Huntsville	AA	27	81	11	1	0	0	12	15	6	30	1	15	1	5	1	3	2	.60	0	.136	.372	.148

180

Year	Team	Lg	G	AB	H	2B	3B	HR	TB	R	RBI	TBB	IBB	SO	HBP	SH	SF	SB	CS	SB%	GDP	Avg	OBP	SLG
	Wichita	AA	41	109	35	5	1	1	45	17	9	17	0	21	0	4	0	3	2	.60	1	.321	.413	.413
1990	Las Vegas	AAA	92	247	74	4	4	4	98	44	21	42	2	35	3	3	1	2	1	.67	0	.300	.406	.397
1991	Las Vegas	AAA	107	377	109	10	2	1	126	56	37	54	2	48	2	6	3	15	10	.60	10	.289	.378	.334
1992	Omaha	AAA	131	469	108	11	0	3	128	45	28	41	1	56	2	7	1	21	8	.72	3	.230	.294	.273
1993	Omaha	AAA	105	330	93	11	2	3	117	46	35	34	0	34	2	3	5	27	10	.73	4	.282	.348	.355
1994	Omaha	AAA	100	358	92	13	6	0	117	60	32	47	1	41	1	6	3	25	11	.69	3	.257	.342	.327
1991	San Diego	NL	17	36	8	0	0	0	8	4	2	2	0	7	1	2	0	0	0	.00	0	.222	.282	.222
	10 Min. YEARS		949	3146	852	97	25	14	1041	455	261	405	12	419	18	56	19	141	72	.66	41	.271	.355	.331

Scott Moten

Pitches: Right Bats: Right Pos: P Ht: 6'1" Wt: 198 Born: 04/12/72 Age: 23

			HOW MUCH HE PITCHED					WHAT HE GAVE UP											THE RESULTS					
Year	Team	Lg	G	GS	CG	GF	IP	BFP	H	R	ER	HR	SH	SF	HB	TBB	IBB	SO	WP	Bk	W	L	Pct.	ShO	Sv	ERA
1992	Elizabethtn	R	13	12	1	0	78.2	334	60	31	21	1	1	1	6	32	0	71	2	2	8	1	.889	1	0	2.40
1993	Ft.Wayne	A	30	22	0	4	140.2	627	152	99	79	8	6	3	11	63	2	141	7	2	7	11	.389	0	1	5.05
1994	Fort Myers	A	44	1	0	17	96	404	87	32	23	1	4	0	2	38	3	68	2	0	8	4	.667	0	7	2.16
	Nashville	AA	3	0	0	0	4.2	23	5	4	2	0	0	0	1	2	0	4	1	0	0	1	.000	0	0	3.86
	3 Min. YEARS		90	35	1	21	320	1388	304	166	125	10	11	4	20	135	5	284	12	4	23	17	.575	1	8	3.52

Chad Mottola

Bats: Right Throws: Right Pos: OF Ht: 6'3" Wt: 215 Born: 10/15/71 Age: 23

			BATTING															BASERUNNING				PERCENTAGES		
Year	Team	Lg	G	AB	H	2B	3B	HR	TB	R	RBI	TBB	IBB	SO	HBP	SH	SF	SB	CS	SB%	GDP	Avg	OBP	SLG
1992	Billings	R	57	213	61	8	3	12	111	53	37	25	0	43	0	0	0	12	3	.80	4	.286	.361	.521
1993	Winston-Sal	A	137	493	138	25	3	21	232	76	91	62	2	109	2	0	3	13	7	.65	9	.280	.361	.471
1994	Chattanooga	AA	118	402	97	19	1	7	139	44	41	30	1	68	1	2	2	9	12	.43	12	.241	.294	.346
	3 Min. YEARS		312	1108	296	52	7	40	482	173	169	117	3	220	3	2	5	34	22	.61	25	.267	.337	.435

Jeff Motuzas

Bats: Right Throws: Right Pos: C Ht: 6'2" Wt: 205 Born: 10/01/71 Age: 23

			BATTING															BASERUNNING				PERCENTAGES		
Year	Team	Lg	G	AB	H	2B	3B	HR	TB	R	RBI	TBB	IBB	SO	HBP	SH	SF	SB	CS	SB%	GDP	Avg	OBP	SLG
1990	Yankees	R	29	82	12	0	0	1	15	9	9	15	0	34	3	0	1	0	3	.00	1	.146	.297	.183
1991	Yankees	R	39	145	28	8	1	1	41	17	17	13	0	44	4	2	1	5	1	.83	2	.193	.276	.283
	Oneonta	A	3	7	2	0	0	0	2	1	0	0	0	2	1	0	0	0	0	.00	0	.286	.375	.286
1992	Pr William	A	63	203	36	13	0	5	64	21	20	14	0	74	3	5	2	1	1	.50	6	.177	.239	.315
1993	Pr William	A	16	53	11	4	1	0	17	5	3	1	0	20	0	0	1	0	1	.00	2	.208	.218	.321
	San Berndno	A	52	154	24	7	0	2	37	16	13	13	1	45	2	1	3	2	3	.40	4	.156	.227	.240
1994	San Berrdo	A	69	244	50	9	1	8	85	25	26	14	0	91	4	1	1	3	2	.60	10	.205	.259	.348
	Albany-Colo	AA	13	44	5	0	0	0	5	3	1	3	0	14	0	1	0	0	0	.00	0	.114	.170	.114
	5 Min. YEARS		284	932	168	41	3	17	266	97	89	73	1	324	17	10	9	11	12	.48	25	.180	.250	.285

Lyle Mouton

Bats: Right Throws: Right Pos: OF Ht: 6'4" Wt: 240 Born: 05/13/69 Age: 26

			BATTING															BASERUNNING				PERCENTAGES		
Year	Team	Lg	G	AB	H	2B	3B	HR	TB	R	RBI	TBB	IBB	SO	HBP	SH	SF	SB	CS	SB%	GDP	Avg	OBP	SLG
1991	Oneonta	A	70	272	84	11	2	7	120	53	41	31	2	39	6	0	3	14	8	.64	1	.309	.388	.441
1992	Pr William	A	50	189	50	14	1	6	84	28	34	17	1	42	0	0	0	4	2	.67	3	.265	.319	.444
	Albany	AA	64	214	46	12	2	2	68	25	27	24	2	55	1	0	1	1	1	.50	9	.215	.296	.318
1993	Albany	AA	135	491	125	22	3	16	201	74	76	50	2	125	7	2	1	19	13	.59	13	.255	.332	.409
1994	Albany-Colo	AA	74	274	84	23	1	12	145	42	42	27	1	62	2	0	4	7	6	.54	8	.307	.368	.529
	Columbus	AAA	59	204	64	14	5	4	100	26	32	12	0	45	1	2	3	5	1	.83	1	.314	.356	.490
	4 Min. YEARS		452	1644	453	96	14	47	718	248	252	163	8	368	17	4	16	50	31	.62	35	.276	.344	.437

Sean Mulligan

Bats: Right Throws: Right Pos: C Ht: 6'2" Wt: 205 Born: 04/25/70 Age: 25

			BATTING															BASERUNNING				PERCENTAGES		
Year	Team	Lg	G	AB	H	2B	3B	HR	TB	R	RBI	TBB	IBB	SO	HBP	SH	SF	SB	CS	SB%	GDP	Avg	OBP	SLG
1991	Chston-Sc	A	60	215	56	9	3	4	83	24	30	17	0	56	6	1	1	4	1	.80	5	.260	.331	.386
1992	High Desert	A	35	118	19	4	0	4	35	14	14	11	1	38	3	0	1	0	0	.00	3	.161	.248	.297
	Waterloo	A	79	278	70	13	1	5	100	24	43	20	0	62	5	2	4	1	0	1.00	10	.252	.309	.360
1993	Rancho Cuca	A	79	268	75	10	3	6	109	29	36	34	0	33	3	0	4	1	3	.25	16	.280	.362	.407
1994	Rancho Cuca	A	66	243	74	18	1	9	121	45	49	24	1	39	5	1	8	1	0	1.00	4	.305	.368	.498
	Wichita	AA	56	208	73	14	0	1	90	29	30	11	2	25	5	0	3	2	3	.40	9	.351	.392	.433
	4 Min. YEARS		375	1330	367	68	8	29	538	165	202	117	4	253	27	4	21	9	7	.56	47	.276	.342	.405

Jarrod Munoz

Pitches: Left Bats: Left Pos: P Ht: 5'9" Wt: 170 Born: 11/01/67 Age: 27

			HOW MUCH HE PITCHED					WHAT HE GAVE UP											THE RESULTS					
Year	Team	Lg	G	GS	CG	GF	IP	BFP	H	R	ER	HR	SH	SF	HB	TBB	IBB	SO	WP	Bk	W	L	Pct.	ShO	Sv	ERA
1990	Martinsvlle	R	14	14	3	0	95	383	70	35	29	12	1	1	1	48	0	126	12	0	6	7	.462	2	0	2.75
1991	Spartanburg	A	20	20	2	0	115.2	486	112	55	46	5	4	3	3	51	0	103	11	0	8	6	.571	0	0	3.58
	Clearwater	A	2	0	0	0	1.1	8	0	0	0	0	0	1	0	4	0	0	0	0	0	0	.000	0	0	0.00

Year	Team	Lg	G	GS	CG	GF	IP	BFP	H	R	ER	HR	SH	SF	HB	TBB	IBB	SO	WP	Bk	W	L	Pct.	ShO	Sv	ERA
1992	Clearwater	A	32	0	0	19	44.2	172	34	13	11	2	0	3	1	12	3	34	3	0	2	3	.400	0	6	2.22
1993	Clearwater	A	56	0	0	33	76	313	59	22	21	2	3	3	2	26	4	81	11	0	5	2	.714	0	9	2.49
1994	Reading	AA	9	0	0	0	13	67	19	11	11	5	1	0	0	11	1	11	0	1	0	0	.000	0	0	7.62
	5 Min. YEARS		133	34	5	52	345.2	1429	294	136	118	26	9	11	7	152	8	355	37	1	21	18	.538	2	15	3.07

Jose Munoz

Bats: Both Throws: Right Pos: 2B Ht: 5'11" Wt: 165 Born: 11/11/67 Age: 27

			BATTING															BASERUNNING				PERCENTAGES		
Year	Team	Lg	G	AB	H	2B	3B	HR	TB	R	RBI	TBB	IBB	SO	HBP	SH	SF	SB	CS	SB%	GDP	Avg	OBP	SLG
1987	Dodgers	R	54	187	60	7	0	0	67	31	22	26	3	22	3	2	1	6	5	.55	2	.321	.410	.358
1988	Bakersfield	A	105	347	86	6	0	0	92	35	24	42	0	54	3	5	1	7	2	.78	9	.248	.333	.265
1989	Vero Beach	A	105	300	77	15	1	0	94	39	24	14	0	31	1	5	3	6	2	.75	11	.257	.289	.313
1990	Bakersfield	A	14	39	7	1	0	0	8	3	6	6	0	7	0	0	0	2	1	.67	0	.179	.289	.205
	Vero Beach	A	113	397	117	18	3	2	147	57	47	34	3	43	2	8	4	28	8	.78	3	.295	.350	.370
1991	San Antonio	AA	31	123	39	6	2	0	49	25	13	12	1	14	1	3	0	4	2	.67	5	.317	.382	.398
	Albuquerque	AAA	101	389	127	18	4	0	153	49	65	20	0	36	2	6	5	15	10	.60	14	.326	.358	.393
1992	Albuquerque	AAA	131	450	137	20	3	2	169	48	45	25	6	46	1	7	0	7	4	.64	22	.304	.342	.376
1993	Albuquerque	AAA	127	438	126	21	5	1	160	66	54	29	3	46	1	8	3	6	3	.67	19	.288	.331	.365
1994	Pawtucket	AAA	129	519	136	16	1	7	175	59	41	52	2	59	2	8	2	12	13	.48	16	.262	.330	.337
	8 Min. YEARS		910	3189	912	128	19	12	1114	412	341	260	18	358	16	52	19	93	50	.65	101	.286	.341	.349

Noe Munoz

Bats: Right Throws: Right Pos: C Ht: 6'2" Wt: 180 Born: 11/11/67 Age: 27

			BATTING															BASERUNNING				PERCENTAGES		
Year	Team	Lg	G	AB	H	2B	3B	HR	TB	R	RBI	TBB	IBB	SO	HBP	SH	SF	SB	CS	SB%	GDP	Avg	OBP	SLG
1994	Bakersfield	A	8	26	7	2	0	0	9	4	3	3	0	5	0	1	0	0	2	.00	0	.269	.345	.346
	San Antonio	AA	51	137	31	4	2	2	45	12	14	3	1	21	2	3	2	1	1	.50	5	.226	.250	.328
	1 Min. YEARS		59	163	38	6	2	2	54	16	17	6	1	26	2	4	2	1	3	.25	5	.233	.266	.331

Omer Munoz

Bats: Right Throws: Right Pos: SS Ht: 5'9" Wt: 156 Born: 03/03/66 Age: 29

			BATTING															BASERUNNING				PERCENTAGES		
Year	Team	Lg	G	AB	H	2B	3B	HR	TB	R	RBI	TBB	IBB	SO	HBP	SH	SF	SB	CS	SB%	GDP	Avg	OBP	SLG
1985	Clinton	A	47	121	25	4	0	0	29	9	11	7	0	7	0	4	0	3	2	.60	4	.207	.250	.240
1987	Wst Plm Bch	A	5	7	0	0	0	0	0	0	0	1	0	1	0	0	0	0	1	.00	0	.000	.125	.000
	Burlington	A	52	195	47	8	2	0	59	22	16	7	0	13	3	6	0	5	3	.63	4	.241	.278	.303
1988	Wst Plm Bch	A	103	369	95	15	1	0	112	36	27	14	0	28	1	8	2	8	6	.57	3	.257	.285	.304
1989	Wst Plm Bch	A	68	246	67	2	0	0	69	22	27	5	0	17	1	8	0	8	5	.62	12	.272	.290	.280
1990	Jacksnville	AA	70	197	50	5	0	1	58	19	18	5	0	18	2	1	1	3	0	1.00	4	.254	.273	.294
1991	Harrisburg	AA	63	214	66	7	1	1	78	27	21	3	0	17	0	11	1	1	0	1.00	4	.308	.317	.364
	Indianapols	AAA	26	92	26	2	0	0	28	7	12	3	1	14	3	6	0	0	0	.00	2	.283	.327	.304
1992	Indianapols	AAA	116	375	94	12	1	1	111	33	30	10	0	32	4	9	4	7	2	.78	15	.251	.275	.296
1993	Buffalo	AAA	40	129	28	4	1	2	40	7	16	3	2	11	1	2	1	0	0	.00	2	.217	.239	.310
1994	Carolina	AA	79	287	90	15	1	5	122	30	38	12	2	29	2	3	3	2	4	.33	7	.314	.342	.425
	9 Min. YEARS		669	2232	588	74	7	10	706	212	216	70	5	187	17	58	12	37	23	.62	54	.263	.290	.316

Orlando Munoz

Bats: Both Throws: Right Pos: SS Ht: 5'11" Wt: 175 Born: 05/04/71 Age: 24

			BATTING															BASERUNNING				PERCENTAGES		
Year	Team	Lg	G	AB	H	2B	3B	HR	TB	R	RBI	TBB	IBB	SO	HBP	SH	SF	SB	CS	SB%	GDP	Avg	OBP	SLG
1989	Angels	R	39	135	30	4	2	0	38	18	18	10	0	21	1	2	1	5	5	.50	3	.222	.279	.281
1991	Palm Sprngs	A	36	122	33	4	0	0	37	16	10	15	0	23	3	7	0	3	3	.50	2	.270	.364	.303
1992	Palm Sprngs	A	103	329	77	9	1	0	88	50	43	50	1	53	4	4	2	21	4	.84	14	.234	.340	.267
1993	Palm Sprngs	A	64	237	64	8	3	0	78	38	24	47	0	25	2	3	5	23	14	.62	7	.270	.388	.329
	Midland	AA	36	118	31	8	1	0	41	24	10	20	0	23	1	2	0	0	4	.00	4	.263	.374	.347
1994	Vancouver	AAA	63	187	62	8	0	0	70	26	20	23	0	27	1	7	3	2	5	.29	3	.332	.402	.374
	5 Min. YEARS		341	1128	297	41	7	0	352	172	125	165	1	172	12	25	11	54	35	.61	33	.263	.360	.312

Oscar Munoz

Pitches: Right Bats: Right Pos: P Ht: 6'2" Wt: 205 Born: 09/25/69 Age: 25

			HOW MUCH HE PITCHED						WHAT HE GAVE UP												THE RESULTS					
Year	Team	Lg	G	GS	CG	GF	IP	BFP	H	R	ER	HR	SH	SF	HB	TBB	IBB	SO	WP	Bk	W	L	Pct.	ShO	Sv	ERA
1990	Watertown	A	2	2	0	0	10.2	43	8	2	2	1	0	0	0	3	0	9	1	1	1	1	.500	0	0	1.69
	Kinston	A	9	9	2	0	64	248	43	18	17	6	1	1	1	18	0	55	3	0	7	0	1.000	1	0	2.39
1991	Kinston	A	14	14	2	0	93.2	375	60	23	15	2	4	0	5	36	0	111	6	0	6	3	.667	1	0	1.44
	Canton-Akm	AA	15	15	2	0	85	378	88	54	54	5	1	2	0	51	1	71	1	1	3	8	.273	1	0	5.72
1992	Orlando	AA	14	12	1	1	67.2	306	73	44	38	10	1	1	4	32	1	74	6	0	3	5	.375	0	0	5.05
1993	Nashville	AA	20	20	1	0	131.2	567	123	56	45	10	1	4	4	51	0	139	12	0	11	4	.733	0	0	3.08
	Portland	AAA	5	5	0	0	31.1	138	29	18	15	2	2	1	0	17	1	29	6	0	2	2	.500	0	0	4.31
1994	Nashville	AA	3	3	2	0	22	86	16	1	1	0	0	0	3	5	0	21	1	0	3	0	1.000	1	0	0.41
	Salt Lake	AAA	26	26	1	0	139.1	662	180	113	91	20	6	5	3	68	1	100	8	0	9	8	.529	0	0	5.88
	5 Min. YEARS		108	106	11	1	645.1	2803	620	329	278	56	16	14	18	281	4	609	44	2	45	31	.592	4	0	3.88

Calvin Murray

Bats: Right Throws: Right Pos: OF Ht: 5'11" Wt: 185 Born: 07/30/71 Age: 23

Year	Team	Lg	G	AB	H	2B	3B	HR	TB	R	RBI	TBB	IBB	SO	HBP	SH	SF	SB	CS	SB%	GDP	Avg	OBP	SLG
1993	Shreveport	AA	37	138	26	6	0	0	32	15	6	14	0	29	2	3	1	12	6	.67	0	.188	.271	.232
	San Jose	A	85	345	97	24	1	9	150	61	42	40	0	63	4	2	0	42	10	.81	4	.281	.362	.435
	Phoenix	AAA	5	19	6	1	1	0	9	4	0	2	0	5	0	0	0	1	1	.50	0	.316	.381	.474
1994	Shreveport	AA	129	480	111	19	5	2	146	67	35	47	0	81	5	8	4	33	13	.72	4	.231	.304	.304
	2 Min. YEARS		256	982	240	50	7	11	337	147	83	103	0	178	11	13	5	88	30	.75	8	.244	.322	.343

Glenn Murray

Bats: Right Throws: Right Pos: OF Ht: 6'2" Wt: 200 Born: 11/23/70 Age: 24

Year	Team	Lg	G	AB	H	2B	3B	HR	TB	R	RBI	TBB	IBB	SO	HBP	SH	SF	SB	CS	SB%	GDP	Avg	OBP	SLG
1989	Expos	R	27	87	15	6	2	0	25	10	7	6	0	30	2	0	1	8	1	.89	1	.172	.240	.287
	Jamestown	A	3	10	3	1	0	0	4	1	1	1	0	1	0	0	0	0	0	.00	0	.300	.364	.400
1990	Jamestown	A	53	165	37	8	4	1	56	20	14	21	0	43	3	0	0	11	3	.79	3	.224	.323	.339
1991	Rockford	A	124	479	113	16	14	5	172	73	60	77	3	137	2	0	8	22	19	.54	8	.236	.339	.359
1992	Wst Plm Bch	A	119	414	96	14	5	13	159	79	41	75	3	150	4	2	1	26	11	.70	4	.232	.354	.384
1993	Harrisburg	AA	127	475	120	21	4	26	227	82	96	56	1	111	8	0	2	16	7	.70	3	.253	.340	.478
1994	Pawtucket	AAA	130	465	104	17	1	25	198	74	64	55	4	134	4	0	2	9	3	.75	10	.224	.310	.426
	6 Min. YEARS		583	2095	488	83	30	70	841	339	283	291	11	606	23	2	14	92	44	.68	29	.233	.331	.401

Matt Murray

Pitches: Right Bats: Left Pos: P Ht: 6'6" Wt: 235 Born: 09/26/70 Age: 24

Year	Team	Lg	G	GS	CG	GF	IP	BFP	H	R	ER	HR	SH	SF	HB	TBB	IBB	SO	WP	Bk	W	L	Pct.	ShO	Sv	ERA
1988	Pulaski	R	13	8	0	3	54	234	48	32	25	4	4	1	1	26	0	76	5	2	4	4	.333	0	1	4.17
1989	Braves	R	2	2	0	0	7	27	3	0	0	0	0	0	1	0	0	10	0	0	1	0	1.000	0	0	0.00
	Sumter	A	12	12	0	0	72.2	295	62	37	35	10	2	2	1	22	0	69	4	1	3	5	.375	0	0	4.33
1990	Burlington	A	26	26	6	0	163	671	139	72	59	9	4	2	3	60	0	134	10	1	11	7	.611	3	0	3.26
1991	Durham	A	2	2	0	0	7	26	5	1	1	0	0	0	0	0	0	7	0	0	1	0	1.000	0	0	1.29
1993	Macon	A	15	15	3	0	83.2	338	70	24	17	3	2	0	3	27	0	77	0	1	7	3	.700	0	0	1.83
1994	Macon	A	15	15	1	0	97.1	398	93	43	41	20	0	1	7	22	3	76	6	0	6	7	.462	0	0	3.79
	Greenville	AA	12	12	0	0	67.1	312	89	43	38	7	1	2	2	31	0	48	3	0	3	4	.429	0	0	5.08
	6 Min. YEARS		97	92	10	3	552	2301	509	252	216	53	13	8	18	188	3	497	28	5	34	30	.531	3	1	3.52

James Musselwhite

Pitches: Right Bats: Right Pos: P Ht: 6'1" Wt: 190 Born: 10/25/71 Age: 23

Year	Team	Lg	G	GS	CG	GF	IP	BFP	H	R	ER	HR	SH	SF	HB	TBB	IBB	SO	WP	Bk	W	L	Pct.	ShO	Sv	ERA
1993	Oneonta	A	5	4	0	0	20	84	15	7	5	0	1	1	0	8	0	18	1	0	1	1	.500	0	0	2.25
	Greensboro	A	11	10	0	1	67.2	285	60	29	21	4	3	2	2	24	0	60	4	2	5	3	.625	0	0	2.79
1994	Tampa	A	17	17	3	0	107.2	429	87	50	41	8	0	3	3	23	0	106	4	0	9	6	.600	2	0	3.43
	Albany-Colo	AA	5	5	1	0	29.2	116	28	4	4	0	0	0	2	5	0	31	2	0	2	1	.667	1	0	1.21
	2 Min. YEARS		38	36	4	1	225	914	190	90	71	12	4	6	7	60	0	215	11	2	17	11	.607	3	0	2.84

Jose Musset

Pitches: Right Bats: Right Pos: P Ht: 6'3" Wt: 186 Born: 09/18/68 Age: 26

Year	Team	Lg	G	GS	CG	GF	IP	BFP	H	R	ER	HR	SH	SF	HB	TBB	IBB	SO	WP	Bk	W	L	Pct.	ShO	Sv	ERA
1990	Angels	R	13	13	0	0	62.2	298	63	54	42	2	1	1	6	41	2	49	7	1	2	7	.222	0	0	6.03
	Boise	A	1	0	0	1	0.2	3	0	0	0	0	0	0	0	1	0	0	0	0	0	0	.000	0	0	0.00
1991	Angels	R	10	0	0	10	14	63	14	7	5	0	0	1	1	5	0	10	1	0	1	1	.500	0	2	3.21
1992	Quad City	A	41	0	0	22	71.2	279	41	19	19	3	3	1	3	25	0	104	5	0	8	2	.800	0	6	2.39
1993	Midland	AA	59	0	0	49	62.1	278	59	38	38	9	0	4	5	32	2	59	4	0	2	6	.250	0	21	5.49
1994	Columbus	AAA	1	0	0	0	0.1	6	3	3	3	0	0	0	0	2	0	0	0	0	0	0	.000	0	0	81.00
	5 Min. YEARS		125	13	0	82	211.2	927	180	121	107	14	4	7	15	106	4	222	17	1	13	16	.448	0	29	4.55

Jimmy Myers

Pitches: Right Bats: Right Pos: P Ht: 6'1" Wt: 185 Born: 04/28/69 Age: 26

Year	Team	Lg	G	GS	CG	GF	IP	BFP	H	R	ER	HR	SH	SF	HB	TBB	IBB	SO	WP	Bk	W	L	Pct.	ShO	Sv	ERA
1987	Pocatello	R	10	2	0	4	19.2	92	29	21	19	1	1	1	1	16	1	12	5	2	0	2	.000	0	0	8.69
1988	Pocatello	R	12	12	0	0	58.1	283	72	50	35	3	2	1	1	32	1	39	7	1	4	5	.444	0	0	5.40
1989	Clinton	A	32	21	0	5	137.2	592	139	71	57	6	8	5	9	58	5	63	11	0	4	12	.250	0	0	3.73
1990	San Jose	A	60	0	0	50	84	361	80	44	30	2	3	3	4	34	6	61	3	1	5	8	.385	0	25	3.21
1991	Shreveport	AA	62	0	0	55	76.1	325	71	22	21	2	6	0	2	30	5	51	4	0	6	4	.600	0	24	2.48
1992	Phoenix	AAA	25	0	0	19	23.2	114	32	20	15	1	2	1	0	13	5	11	0	0	0	4	.000	0	10	5.70
	Shreveport	AA	33	0	0	32	32	141	39	17	17	0	2	2	2	10	1	15	1	0	2	4	.333	0	18	4.78
1993	Shreveport	AA	29	0	0	14	49.1	210	50	14	11	4	2	0	2	19	3	23	4	0	2	2	.500	0	1	2.01

	Lg	G	GS	CG	GF	IP	BFP	H	R	ER	HR	SH	SF	HB	TBB	IBB	SO	WP	Bk	W	L	Pct.	ShO	Sv	ERA
Phoenix	AAA	31	3	0	5	58.2	259	69	35	24	2	3	0	3	22	2	20	5	0	2	5	.286	0	0	3.68
1994 Memphis	AA	33	2	0	12	64.1	286	68	38	35	3	7	2	4	32	4	35	7	1	4	4	.500	0	3	4.90
Carolina	AA	11	0	0	5	11.2	49	7	3	3	0	0	1	3	7	1	7	1	0	1	1	.500	0	4	2.31
8 Min. YEARS		338	40	0	201	615.2	2712	656	335	267	21	36	16	29	273	34	337	48	5	30	51	.370	0	85	3.90

Mike Myers

Pitches: Left **Bats:** Left **Pos:** P   **Ht:** 6'3" **Wt:** 197 **Born:** 06/26/69 **Age:** 26

		HOW MUCH HE PITCHED						WHAT HE GAVE UP												THE RESULTS					
Year Team	Lg	G	GS	CG	GF	IP	BFP	H	R	ER	HR	SH	SF	HB	TBB	IBB	SO	WP	Bk	W	L	Pct.	ShO	Sv	ERA
1990 Everett	A	15	14	1	0	85.1	374	91	43	37	9	1	0	5	30	0	73	7	0	4	5	.444	0	0	3.90
1991 Clinton	A	11	11	1	0	65.1	263	61	23	19	3	2	2	0	18	0	59	4	3	5	3	.625	0	0	2.62
Giants	R	1	0	0	0	3	16	5	5	4	0	0	0	0	2	0	2	0	0	0	1	.000	0	0	12.00
1992 Clinton	A	7	7	0	0	37.2	147	28	11	5	0	1	1	2	8	0	32	4	0	1	2	.333	0	0	1.19
San Jose	A	8	8	0	0	54.2	215	43	20	14	1	1	0	2	17	0	40	3	1	5	1	.833	0	0	2.30
1993 Edmonton	AAA	27	27	3	0	161.2	733	195	109	94	20	5	7	10	52	1	112	7	1	7	14	.333	0	0	5.23
1994 Brevard Cty	A	3	2	0	0	11.1	43	7	1	1	1	1	0	0	4	0	15	0	0	0	0	.000	0	0	0.79
Edmonton	AAA	12	11	0	0	60	282	78	42	37	9	1	3	3	21	0	55	3	0	1	5	.167	0	0	5.55
5 Min. YEARS		84	80	5	0	479	2073	508	254	211	43	12	13	22	152	1	388	28	5	23	31	.426	0	0	3.96

Rodney Myers

Pitches: Right **Bats:** Right **Pos:** P   **Ht:** 6'1" **Wt:** 190 **Born:** 06/26/69 **Age:** 26

		HOW MUCH HE PITCHED						WHAT HE GAVE UP												THE RESULTS					
Year Team	Lg	G	GS	CG	GF	IP	BFP	H	R	ER	HR	SH	SF	HB	TBB	IBB	SO	WP	Bk	W	L	Pct.	ShO	Sv	ERA
1990 Eugene	A	6	4	0	0	22.2	98	19	9	3	2	0	1	0	13	0	17	1	1	0	2	.000	0	0	1.19
1991 Appleton	A	9	4	0	1	27.2	127	22	9	8	0	1	1	1	26	0	29	1	1	1	1	.500	0	0	2.60
1992 Lethbridge	R	15	15	5	0	103.1	452	93	57	46	3	4	2	5	61	1	76	14	2	5	8	.385	0	0	4.01
1993 Rockford	A	12	12	5	0	85.1	322	65	22	17	3	2	2	1	18	0	65	3	1	7	3	.700	2	0	1.79
Memphis	AA	12	12	1	0	65.2	294	73	46	41	8	2	2	10	32	0	42	3	3	3	6	.333	1	0	5.62
1994 Wilmington	A	4	0	0	2	9.1	37	9	6	5	1	0	0	0	1	0	9	1	0	1	1	.500	0	1	4.82
Memphis	AA	42	0	0	30	69.2	284	45	20	8	3	2	4	5	29	2	53	3	0	5	1	.833	0	9	1.03
5 Min. YEARS		100	47	11	33	383.2	1614	326	169	128	20	11	12	22	180	3	291	26	8	22	22	.500	3	10	3.00

David Mysel

Pitches: Right **Bats:** Right **Pos:** P   **Ht:** 6'5" **Wt:** 215 **Born:** 04/13/71 **Age:** 24

		HOW MUCH HE PITCHED						WHAT HE GAVE UP												THE RESULTS					
Year Team	Lg	G	GS	CG	GF	IP	BFP	H	R	ER	HR	SH	SF	HB	TBB	IBB	SO	WP	Bk	W	L	Pct.	ShO	Sv	ERA
1992 Niagara Fls	A	12	6	1	0	47.1	182	33	14	9	1	1	1	3	13	1	40	4	3	2	2	.500	1	0	1.71
1993 Fayetteville	A	12	12	1	0	72.1	299	69	25	21	2	1	2	6	16	0	46	0	1	5	2	.714	1	0	2.61
Lakeland	A	12	12	1	0	70	296	59	36	28	2	3	5	6	28	0	46	2	1	4	5	.444	0	0	3.60
1994 Trenton	AA	20	20	2	0	108	493	122	72	55	14	4	4	4	52	1	64	5	4	5	10	.333	0	0	4.58
3 Min. YEARS		56	50	5	0	297.2	1270	283	147	113	19	9	12	19	109	2	196	11	9	16	19	.457	2	0	3.42

Dan Naulty

Pitches: Right **Bats:** Right **Pos:** P   **Ht:** 6'6" **Wt:** 202 **Born:** 01/06/70 **Age:** 25

		HOW MUCH HE PITCHED						WHAT HE GAVE UP												THE RESULTS					
Year Team	Lg	G	GS	CG	GF	IP	BFP	H	R	ER	HR	SH	SF	HB	TBB	IBB	SO	WP	Bk	W	L	Pct.	ShO	Sv	ERA
1992 Kenosha	A	6	2	0	1	18	83	22	12	11	3	1	0	1	7	0	14	1	1	0	1	.000	0	0	5.50
1993 Ft.Myers	A	7	6	0	0	30	148	41	22	19	4	1	1	6	14	1	20	3	0	0	3	.000	0	0	5.70
Ft.Wayne	A	18	18	3	0	116	478	101	45	42	5	3	1	2	48	0	96	7	5	6	8	.429	2	0	3.26
1994 Fort Myers	A	16	15	1	1	88.1	380	78	35	29	6	1	5	3	32	2	83	5	0	8	4	.667	0	0	2.95
Nashville	AA	9	9	0	0	47.1	208	48	32	31	4	2	5	1	22	1	29	3	0	0	7	.000	0	0	5.89
3 Min. YEARS		56	50	4	2	299.2	1297	290	146	132	22	8	12	13	123	4	242	19	6	14	23	.378	2	0	3.96

Lipso Nava

Bats: Right **Throws:** Right **Pos:** SS   **Ht:** 6'2" **Wt:** 175 **Born:** 11/28/68 **Age:** 26

		BATTING													BASERUNNING				PERCENTAGES		
Year Team	Lg	G	AB	H	2B	3B	HR	TB	R	RBI	TBB	IBB	SO	HBP	SH	SF	SB	CS	SB%	GDP	Avg	OBP	SLG
1990 Bellingham	A	46	171	43	12	0	0	55	11	15	15	2	31	2	3	0	2	2	.50	5	.251	.319	.322
San Berndno	A	7	23	4	1	0	0	5	1	1	0	0	9	2	1	0	0	0	.00	1	.174	.240	.217
1991 San Berndno	A	86	258	70	5	0	2	81	19	33	20	0	44	6	3	2	5	4	.56	4	.271	.336	.314
1992 Peninsula	A	102	346	78	16	2	3	107	32	35	18	1	56	8	4	1	7	3	.70	8	.225	.279	.309
1993 Jacksonville	AA	114	396	101	20	0	7	142	52	41	31	1	43	13	12	3	5	6	.45	11	.255	.327	.359
1994 Riverside	A	28	102	26	9	1	0	37	15	13	12	1	19	2	0	2	0	0	.00	5	.255	.339	.363
Jacksonville	AA	41	131	25	6	1	3	42	13	10	7	0	20	2	6	0	2	2	.50	1	.191	.243	.321
5 Min. YEARS		424	1427	347	69	4	15	469	143	148	103	5	222	35	29	8	21	17	.55	35	.243	.308	.329

Tito Navarro

Bats: Right **Throws:** Right **Pos:** SS   **Ht:** 5'10" **Wt:** 155 **Born:** 09/12/70 **Age:** 24

		BATTING													BASERUNNING				PERCENTAGES		
Year Team	Lg	G	AB	H	2B	3B	HR	TB	R	RBI	TBB	IBB	SO	HBP	SH	SF	SB	CS	SB%	GDP	Avg	OBP	SLG
1988 Kingsport	R	54	172	42	3	2	0	49	26	23	30	0	27	3	2	3	3	4	.43	4	.244	.361	.285

Year Team	Lg	G	AB	H	2B	3B	HR	TB	R	RBI	TBB	IBB	SO	HBP	SH	SF	SB	CS	SB%	GDP	Avg	OBP	SLG
1989 Pittsfield	A	46	157	44	6	2	0	54	26	14	18	0	30	0	3	1	13	3	.81	8	.280	.352	.344
1990 Columbia	A	136	497	156	25	4	0	189	87	54	69	1	56	2	7	7	50	14	.78	4	.314	.395	.380
Jackson	AA	3	11	2	1	0	0	3	0	1	2	0	2	0	0	0	0	1	.00	0	.182	.308	.273
1991 Williamsprt	AA	128	482	139	9	4	2	162	69	42	73	2	63	1	12	4	42	19	.69	10	.288	.380	.336
1993 Mets	R	4	14	4	1	1	0	7	2	5	3	0	1	0	0	2	1	0	1.00	0	.286	.368	.500
Norfolk	AAA	96	273	77	11	1	0	90	35	16	33	1	39	0	7	2	19	3	.86	10	.282	.357	.330
1994 St. Lucie	A	34	125	33	5	0	0	38	19	7	15	0	20	2	1	0	5	4	.56	5	.264	.352	.304
Norfolk	AAA	51	167	46	7	3	0	59	25	18	17	1	24	1	2	3	8	2	.80	3	.275	.340	.353
1993 New York	NL	12	17	1	0	0	0	1	1	1	1	0	4	0	1	0	0	0	.00	1	.059	.059	.059
6 Min. YEARS		552	1898	543	68	17	2	651	289	180	260	5	262	9	34	22	141	50	.74	44	.286	.371	.343

Pitches: Right   Bats: Both   Pos: P

Jim Neidlinger

Ht: 6' 4"   Wt: 180   Born: 09/24/64   Age: 30

		HOW MUCH HE PITCHED						WHAT HE GAVE UP												THE RESULTS					
Year Team	Lg	G	GS	CG	GF	IP	BFP	H	R	ER	HR	SH	SF	HB	TBB	IBB	SO	WP	Bk	W	L	Pct.	ShO	Sv	ERA
1984 Macon	A	25	25	2	0	166	707	138	65	51	6	4	5	0	85	2	113	4	1	8	8	.500	0	0	2.77
1985 Pr William	A	26	26	4	0	165.1	713	141	86	79	14	7	11	7	83	0	143	8	0	8	13	.381	0	0	4.30
1986 Nashua	AA	22	22	8	0	163.2	663	135	57	44	6	6	3	3	44	0	98	5	1	12	7	.632	2	0	2.42
Hawaii	AAA	4	4	1	0	27.2	124	33	14	12	3	2	0	1	9	0	14	0	0	1	1	.667	0	0	3.90
1987 Harrisburg	AA	26	26	7	0	170.2	737	183	92	75	9	3	5	5	61	4	96	6	1	11	8	.579	0	0	3.96
1988 Harrisburg	AA	40	11	0	15	124.2	531	135	54	39	3	9	4	5	25	3	88	2	2	5	8	.385	0	2	2.82
Buffalo	AAA	3	0	0	1	4.1	22	7	3	3	0	0	0	0	1	0	4	1	0	0	0	.000	0	0	6.23
1989 Albuquerque	AAA	34	18	1	5	139.2	604	164	77	63	8	5	3	1	37	1	97	2	1	8	6	.571	0	1	4.06
1990 Albuquerque	AAA	20	18	4	2	119.2	516	129	70	57	13	2	2	1	34	3	81	2	0	8	5	.615	1	0	4.29
1991 Albuquerque	AAA	23	23	3	0	130.2	577	165	81	69	19	3	5	0	39	0	80	12	0	7	7	.500	1	0	4.75
1992 Albuquerque	AAA	34	20	1	1	145.2	617	153	75	71	12	7	5	1	45	4	81	3	0	8	9	.471	0	0	4.39
1993 Portland	AAA	29	24	3	1	157.2	695	175	106	91	22	5	6	5	54	3	112	4	0	9	8	.529	0	0	5.19
1994 Louisville	AAA	7	7	0	0	37.2	176	51	31	26	2	3	3	2	11	2	34	1	0	1	3	.250	0	0	6.21
1990 Los Angeles	NL	12	12	0	0	74	301	67	30	27	4	4	3	1	15	1	46	0	1	5	3	.625	0	0	3.28
11 Min. YEARS		293	224	34	25	1553.1	6682	1609	811	680	117	56	52	31	528	22	1041	50	6	88	83	.515	4	3	3.94

Bats: Left   Throws: Left   Pos: OF

Mike Neill

Ht: 6'2"   Wt: 189   Born: 04/27/70   Age: 25

		BATTING												BASERUNNING				PERCENTAGES		
Year Team	Lg	G	AB	H	2B	3B	HR	TB	R	RBI	TBB	IBB	SO	HBP	SH	SF	SB	CS	SB%	GDP	Avg	OBP	SLG
1991 Sou Oregon	A	63	240	84	14	0	5	113	42	42	35	3	54	0	4	1	9	8	.529	1	.350	.431	.471
1992 Reno	A	130	473	159	26	7	5	214	101	76	81	2	96	5	6	2	23	11	.68	15	.336	.437	.452
Huntsville	AA	5	16	5	0	0	0	5	4	2	2	0	7	0	1	1	1	0	1.00	0	.313	.368	.313
1993 Huntsville	AA	54	179	44	8	0	1	55	30	15	34	0	45	1	0	1	3	4	.43	4	.246	.367	.307
Modesto	A	17	62	12	3	0	0	15	4	4	12	0	12	0	1	0	0	1	.00	0	.194	.324	.242
1994 Tacoma	AAA	7	22	5	1	0	0	6	1	2	3	0	7	0	0	0	0	0	.00	2	.227	.320	.273
Modesto	A	47	165	48	4	1	2	60	22	18	26	1	50	1	2	1	1	1	.50	4	.291	.389	.364
4 Min. YEARS		323	1157	357	56	8	13	468	204	159	193	6	271	7	14	6	37	20	.65	26	.309	.409	.404

Bats: Left   Throws: Left   Pos: 1B

Rob Nelson

Ht: 6' 4"   Wt: 215   Born: 05/17/64   Age: 31

		BATTING												BASERUNNING				PERCENTAGES		
Year Team	Lg	G	AB	H	2B	3B	HR	TB	R	RBI	TBB	IBB	SO	HBP	SH	SF	SB	CS	SB%	GDP	Avg	OBP	SLG
1984 Madison	A	136	487	120	25	2	19	206	71	85	80	6	140	5	1	8	4	6	.40	11	.246	.353	.423
1985 Huntsville	AA	140	499	116	25	0	32	237	68	98	86	8	137	2	1	5	2	0	1.00	7	.232	.345	.475
1986 Tacoma	AAA	139	508	140	26	4	20	234	77	108	62	5	115	2	0	13	3	1	.75	9	.276	.349	.461
1987 Tacoma	AAA	120	413	89	19	3	20	174	68	74	97	4	133	3	0	6	5	2	.71	6	.215	.364	.421
1988 Las Vegas	AAA	116	388	101	23	1	23	195	68	77	62	7	130	0	1	4	0	1	.00	5	.260	.359	.503
1989 Las Vegas	AAA	56	185	49	11	1	7	83	35	26	38	4	59	1	0	3	0	0	.00	3	.265	.388	.449
1990 Las Vegas	AAA	112	390	103	18	1	20	183	56	90	68	3	129	1	0	6	1	0	1.00	13	.264	.370	.469
1991 Vancouver	AAA	86	271	65	11	1	13	117	26	37	37	2	73	1	1	1	0	1	.00	8	.240	.332	.432
Tucson	AAA	25	90	25	6	1	3	42	14	25	12	0	39	0	0	0	1	1	.50	0	.278	.363	.467
1992 Portland	AAA	31	92	18	2	0	5	35	12	9	22	2	26	1	0	0	1	0	1.00	0	.196	.357	.380
Phoenix	AAA	53	142	32	9	0	5	56	23	19	33	3	44	0	1	0	0	0	.00	3	.225	.369	.394
1994 Tulsa	AA	79	275	72	14	1	11	121	26	49	42	1	86	0	0	1	0	0	.00	2	.262	.358	.440
1986 Oakland	AL	5	9	2	1	0	0	3	1	0	1	0	4	0	0	0	0	0	.00	0	.222	.300	.333
1987 Oakland	AL	7	24	4	1	0	0	5	1	0	0	0	12	0	1	0	0	0	.00	0	.167	.167	.208
San Diego	NL	10	11	1	0	0	0	1	0	1	1	0	8	0	0	0	0	0	.00	0	.091	.167	.091
1988 San Diego	NL	7	21	4	0	0	1	7	4	3	2	0	9	0	0	0	0	0	.00	0	.190	.261	.333
1989 San Diego	NL	42	82	16	0	1	3	27	6	7	20	1	29	0	0	0	1	3	.25	2	.195	.353	.329
1990 San Diego	NL	5	5	0	0	0	0	0	0	0	0	0	4	0	0	0	0	0	.00	0	.000	.000	.000
10 Min. YEARS		1093	3740	930	189	15	178	1683	544	697	639	45	1111	16	5	48	17	12	.59	71	.249	.357	.450
5 Maj. YEARS		76	152	27	2	1	4	43	12	11	24	1	66	0	1	0	1	3	.25	2	.178	.290	.283

Tom Nevers

Bats: Right Throws: Right Pos: INF Ht: 6'1" Wt: 175 Born: 09/13/71 Age: 23

					BATTING										BASERUNNING				PERCENTAGES		
Year	Team	Lg	G	AB	H	2B	3B	HR	TB	R	RBI	TBB	IBB	SO	HBP	SH	SF	SB	CS	SB%	GDP	Avg	OBP	SLG
1990	Astros	R	50	185	44	10	5	2	70	23	32	27	0	38	3	0	3	13	3	.81	3	.238	.339	.378
1991	Asheville	A	129	441	111	26	2	16	189	59	71	53	0	124	3	2	5	10	12	.45	11	.252	.333	.429
1992	Osceola	A	125	455	114	24	6	8	174	49	55	22	1	124	3	2	1	6	2	.75	10	.251	.289	.382
1993	Jackson	AA	55	184	50	8	2	1	65	21	10	16	2	36	2	1	1	7	2	.78	5	.272	.335	.353
1994	Jackson	AA	125	449	120	25	2	8	173	54	62	31	2	101	4	1	7	10	5	.67	8	.267	.316	.385
	5 Min. YEARS		484	1714	439	93	17	35	671	206	230	149	5	423	15	6	17	46	24	.66	37	.256	.318	.391

Phil Nevin

Bats: Right Throws: Right Pos: 3B Ht: 6'2" Wt: 185 Born: 01/19/71 Age: 24

					BATTING										BASERUNNING				PERCENTAGES		
Year	Team	Lg	G	AB	H	2B	3B	HR	TB	R	RBI	TBB	IBB	SO	HBP	SH	SF	SB	CS	SB%	GDP	Avg	OBP	SLG
1993	Tucson	AAA	123	448	128	21	3	10	185	67	93	52	1	99	3	0	7	8	1	.89	12	.286	.359	.413
1994	Tucson	AAA	118	445	117	20	1	12	175	67	79	55	2	101	1	0	4	3	2	.60	21	.263	.343	.393
	2 Min. YEARS		241	893	245	41	4	22	360	134	172	107	3	200	4	0	11	11	3	.79	33	.274	.351	.403

Jim Newlin

Pitches: Right Bats: Right Pos: P Ht: 6'2" Wt: 205 Born: 09/11/66 Age: 28

			HOW MUCH HE PITCHED					WHAT HE GAVE UP									THE RESULTS				
Year	Team	Lg	G	GS	CG	GF	IP	BFP	H	R	ER	HR	SH	SF	HB	TBB	IBB	SO	WP	Bk	W	L	Pct.	ShO	Sv	ERA
1989	San Berndno	A	19	0	0	9	28.2	110	13	6	5	1	1	0	3	15	1	25	1	1	1	2	.333	0	4	1.57
1990	San Berndno	A	36	0	0	28	45	192	35	24	18	2	2	3	4	21	5	56	3	2	1	5	.167	0	12	3.60
	Williamsprt	AA	20	0	0	12	38.2	174	45	22	15	2	3	2	2	15	0	23	0	3	1	1	.500	0	0	3.49
1991	Jacksnville	AA	47	0	0	37	64	275	58	24	16	4	9	2	5	29	5	48	3	1	6	5	.545	0	12	2.25
1992	Calgary	AAA	30	0	0	13	43.2	217	60	33	28	1	0	3	2	29	2	24	1	0	1	1	.500	0	3	5.77
	Jacksnville	AA	12	0	0	11	22	90	22	5	5	1	2	0	2	10	0	13	3	0	1	1	.500	0	1	2.05
1993	Jacksnville	AA	8	0	0	3	17.1	77	22	12	9	3	2	1	1	3	0	11	0	1	1	1	.500	0	0	4.67
	Knoxville	AA	13	2	0	4	26.1	133	41	28	26	2	3	3	0	13	1	19	3	4	0	2	.000	0	0	8.89
	Edmonton	AAA	4	0	0	1	6	35	11	9	9	1	0	2	2	4	0	3	1	1	0	0	.000	0	0	13.50
	High Desert	A	17	0	0	9	28.1	124	30	15	9	3	1	1	2	9	1	23	0	0	3	0	1.000	0	3	2.86
1994	Edmonton	AAA	21	0	0	6	38.2	186	60	36	34	3	3	1	3	17	2	23	3	0	2	4	.333	0	0	7.91
	Portland	AA	30	0	0	15	44.2	182	32	12	10	2	4	1	3	18	2	49	2	0	1	3	.250	0	4	2.01
	6 Min. YEARS		257	2	0	148	403.1	1795	429	226	184	25	30	24	29	183	19	317	20	13	18	25	.419	0	39	4.11

Rod Nichols

Pitches: Right Bats: Right Pos: P Ht: 6'2" Wt: 190 Born: 12/29/64 Age: 30

			HOW MUCH HE PITCHED					WHAT HE GAVE UP									THE RESULTS				
Year	Team	Lg	G	GS	CG	GF	IP	BFP	H	R	ER	HR	SH	SF	HB	TBB	IBB	SO	WP	Bk	W	L	Pct.	ShO	Sv	ERA
1985	Batavia	A	13	13	3	0	84	361	74	40	28	10	0	2	3	33	0	93	6	0	5	5	.500	0	0	3.00
1986	Waterloo	A	20	20	3	0	115.1	493	128	56	52	8	3	4	13	21	1	83	3	1	8	5	.615	1	0	4.06
1987	Kinston	A	9	8	1	1	56	231	53	27	25	3	0	2	1	14	0	61	4	0	4	2	.667	1	0	4.02
	Williamsprt	AA	16	16	1	0	100	441	107	53	41	9	2	3	9	33	0	60	5	1	4	3	.571	0	0	3.69
1988	Kinston	A	4	4	0	0	24	109	26	13	12	1	0	2	0	15	0	19	2	0	3	1	.750	0	0	4.50
	Colo Spgs	AAA	10	9	2	1	58.2	256	69	41	37	8	1	2	3	17	2	43	3	2	2	6	.250	0	0	5.68
1989	Colo Spgs	AAA	10	10	2	0	65.1	274	57	28	26	2	1	3	1	30	0	41	1	2	8	1	.889	1	0	3.58
1990	Colo Spgs	AAA	22	22	4	0	133.1	602	160	84	76	12	0	4	11	48	3	74	3	2	12	9	.571	2	0	5.13
1992	Colo Spgs	AAA	9	9	1	0	54	233	65	39	34	6	0	4	1	16	1	35	4	1	3	3	.500	0	0	5.67
1993	Albuquerque	AAA	21	21	3	0	127.2	552	132	68	61	16	6	3	3	50	3	79	9	3	8	5	.615	1	0	4.30
1994	Omaha	AAA	33	22	3	3	142	634	163	102	89	21	9	4	9	52	2	92	7	0	5	10	.333	1	1	5.64
1988	Cleveland	AL	11	10	3	1	69.1	297	73	41	39	5	2	2	2	23	1	31	2	3	1	7	.125	0	0	5.06
1989	Cleveland	AL	15	11	0	2	71.2	315	81	42	35	9	3	2	2	24	0	42	0	0	4	6	.400	0	0	4.40
1990	Cleveland	AL	4	2	0	0	16	79	24	14	14	5	1	0	2	6	0	3	0	0	0	3	.000	0	0	7.88
1991	Cleveland	AL	31	16	3	4	137.1	578	145	63	54	6	6	4	6	30	3	76	3	0	2	11	.154	1	1	3.54
1992	Cleveland	AL	30	9	0	5	105.1	456	114	58	53	13	1	5	2	31	1	56	0	0	4	3	.571	0	0	4.53
1993	Los Angeles	NL	4	0	0	2	6.1	28	9	5	4	1	1	0	0	2	1	3	0	0	0	1	.000	0	0	5.68
	9 Min. YEARS		167	154	23	5	960.1	4186	1034	551	481	96	22	33	54	329	12	680	47	12	62	50	.554	7	1	4.51
	6 Maj. YEARS		95	48	6	14	406	1753	446	223	199	39	14	13	14	116	7	211	8	3	11	31	.262	1	1	4.41

Chris Nichting

Pitches: Right Bats: Right Pos: P Ht: 6'1" Wt: 205 Born: 05/13/66 Age: 29

			HOW MUCH HE PITCHED					WHAT HE GAVE UP									THE RESULTS				
Year	Team	Lg	G	GS	CG	GF	IP	BFP	H	R	ER	HR	SH	SF	HB	TBB	IBB	SO	WP	Bk	W	L	Pct.	ShO	Sv	ERA
1988	Vero Beach	A	21	19	5	2	138	545	90	40	32	7	0	2	2	51	0	151	7	0	11	4	.733	1	1	2.09
1989	San Antonio	AA	26	26	2	0	154	698	160	96	86	13	9	6	6	101	6	136	14	4	4	14	.222	0	0	5.03
1992	Albuquerque	AAA	10	9	0	0	42	205	64	42	37	2	2	4	0	23	1	25	5	1	1	3	.250	0	0	7.93
	San Antonio	AA	13	13	0	0	78.2	309	58	25	22	3	4	0	1	37	0	81	4	0	4	5	.444	0	0	2.52
1993	Vero Beach	A	4	4	0	0	17.1	75	18	9	8	2	0	0	0	6	0	18	1	0	0	1	.000	0	0	4.15
1994	Albuquerque	AAA	10	7	0	1	41.1	209	61	39	34	5	0	0	3	28	1	25	6	0	2	2	.500	0	0	7.40
	San Antonio	AA	21	8	0	8	65.2	277	47	21	12	1	4	1	2	34	1	74	7	1	3	4	.429	0	1	1.64
	5 Min. YEARS		105	86	7	11	537	2318	498	272	231	33	19	9	14	280	9	510	44	6	25	33	.431	1	2	3.87

186

Jackie Nickell

Pitches: Right Bats: Right Pos: P
Ht: 5'10" Wt: 175 Born: 04/20/70 Age: 25

Year	Team	Lg	G	GS	CG	GF	IP	BFP	H	R	ER	HR	SH	SF	HB	TBB	IBB	SO	WP	Bk	W	L	Pct.	ShO	Sv	ERA
1992	Bellingham	A	1	1	0	0	5	23	5	4	4	1	0	0	1	1	0	3	0	1	0	1	.000	0	0	7.20
	San Berndno	A	13	4	0	4	40	185	45	33	31	8	1	3	4	23	0	30	3	6	0	4	.000	0	0	6.97
1993	Appleton	A	24	23	2	1	150	602	135	54	51	8	10	2	7	41	0	151	7	12	7	7	.500	0	0	3.06
1994	Riverside	A	15	14	1	0	90.1	370	77	42	38	9	3	0	4	21	0	71	3	7	9	4	.692	1	0	3.79
	Jacksonville	AA	3	2	1	0	14	62	16	10	7	2	1	0	1	3	0	11	2	0	1	0	1.000	0	0	4.50
	3 Min. YEARS		56	44	4	5	299.1	1242	278	143	131	28	15	5	17	89	0	266	15	26	17	16	.515	1	0	3.94

Jerry Nielsen

Pitches: Left Bats: Left Pos: P
Ht: 6'1" Wt: 180 Born: 08/05/66 Age: 28

Year	Team	Lg	G	GS	CG	GF	IP	BFP	H	R	ER	HR	SH	SF	HB	TBB	IBB	SO	WP	Bk	W	L	Pct.	ShO	Sv	ERA
1988	Oneonta	A	19	1	0	8	38	158	27	6	3	0	3	0	3	18	0	35	0	4	6	2	.750	0	0	0.71
1989	Pr William	A	39	0	0	16	49.1	198	26	14	12	0	2	4	6	25	0	45	6	0	3	2	.600	0	4	2.19
1990	Pr William	A	26	26	1	0	151.2	665	149	76	66	9	4	2	11	79	1	119	9	2	7	12	.368	1	0	3.92
1991	Ft.Laudrdle	A	42	0	0	14	64.2	275	50	29	20	2	5	5	3	31	4	66	7	0	3	3	.500	0	4	2.78
	Albany	AA	6	0	0	2	8	38	9	6	5	1	1	0	0	8	0	5	0	0	0	1	.000	0	0	5.63
1992	Albany	AA	36	0	0	21	53	207	38	8	7	1	1	0	1	15	2	59	5	0	3	5	.375	0	11	1.19
	Columbus	AAA	4	0	0	2	5	18	2	1	1	0	0	2	1	2	0	5	1	0	0	0	.000	0	1	1.80
1993	Vancouver	AAA	33	5	0	10	55.2	252	70	32	26	4	7	2	0	20	3	45	2	1	2	5	.286	0	0	4.20
1994	Midland	AA	32	3	0	8	42.1	192	50	36	36	1	1	2	3	19	0	48	6	1	1	2	.333	0	0	7.65
	Birmingham	AA	9	8	0	1	37.2	174	28	24	22	3	0	1	0	36	2	20	9	2	1	4	.200	0	0	5.26
1992	New York	AL	20	0	0	12	19.2	90	17	10	10	1	1	1	0	18	2	12	1	0	1	0	1.000	0	0	4.58
1993	California	AL	10	0	0	3	12.1	62	18	13	11	1	1	3	1	4	0	8	0	1	0	0	.000	0	0	8.03
	7 Min. YEARS		246	43	1	82	505.1	2177	449	232	198	21	24	18	37	253	12	447	45	10	26	36	.419	1	20	3.53
	2 Maj. YEARS		30	0	0	15	32	152	35	23	21	2	2	4	1	22	2	20	1	1	1	0	1.000	0	0	5.91

Christopher Nitkowski

Pitches: Left Bats: Left Pos: P
Ht: 6'2" Wt: 185 Born: 03/09/73 Age: 22

Year	Team	Lg	G	GS	CG	GF	IP	BFP	H	R	ER	HR	SH	SF	HB	TBB	IBB	SO	WP	Bk	W	L	Pct.	ShO	Sv	ERA
1994	Chattanooga	AA	14	14	0	0	74.2	318	61	30	29	4	5	0	4	40	0	60	2	5	6	3	.667	0	0	3.50

J.D. Noland

Bats: Left Throws: Right Pos: OF
Ht: 5'9" Wt: 173 Born: 12/05/68 Age: 26

Year	Team	Lg	G	AB	H	2B	3B	HR	TB	R	RBI	TBB	IBB	SO	HBP	SH	SF	SB	CS	SB%	GDP	Avg	OBP	SLG
1989	Waterloo	A	99	331	79	4	0	0	83	40	18	39	1	86	2	9	1	31	15	.67	4	.239	.322	.251
1990	Waterloo	A	125	456	112	20	6	4	156	75	51	71	3	84	1	4	6	48	24	.67	4	.246	.345	.342
1991	High Desert	A	128	495	137	23	12	4	196	114	68	78	5	96	2	5	4	81	23	.78	8	.277	.375	.396
1992	Wichita	AA	118	452	122	21	6	5	170	59	52	36	0	80	3	4	0	40	23	.63	5	.270	.328	.376
1994	New Haven	AA	55	212	62	6	3	3	83	28	44	18	1	27	2	3	4	24	8	.75	4	.292	.347	.392
	Colo. Spmg	AAA	53	214	74	13	2	3	100	37	34	9	0	32	2	1	1	11	8	.58	5	.346	.376	.467
	5 Min. YEARS		578	2160	586	87	29	19	788	353	267	251	10	405	12	26	16	235	101	.70	31	.271	.348	.365

Les Norman

Bats: Right Throws: Right Pos: OF
Ht: 6'1" Wt: 185 Born: 02/25/69 Age: 26

Year	Team	Lg	G	AB	H	2B	3B	HR	TB	R	RBI	TBB	IBB	SO	HBP	SH	SF	SB	CS	SB%	GDP	Avg	OBP	SLG
1991	Eugene	A	30	102	25	4	1	2	37	14	18	9	0	18	1	2	1	2	1	.67	4	.245	.310	.363
1992	Appleton	A	59	218	82	17	1	4	113	38	47	22	0	18	1	2	3	8	6	.57	5	.376	.430	.518
	Memphis	AA	72	271	74	14	5	3	107	32	20	22	0	37	2	1	1	4	4	.50	2	.273	.331	.395
1993	Memphis	AA	133	484	141	32	5	17	234	78	81	50	3	88	14	7	2	11	9	.55	8	.291	.373	.483
1994	Omaha	AAA	13	38	7	3	0	1	13	4	4	6	0	11	1	1	0	0	1	.00	2	.184	.311	.342
	Memphis	AA	106	383	101	19	4	13	167	53	55	36	1	44	7	3	2	7	7	.50	19	.264	.336	.436
	4 Min. YEARS		413	1496	430	89	16	40	671	219	225	145	4	216	26	16	9	32	28	.53	21	.287	.359	.449

Bill Norris

Bats: Left Throws: Right Pos: 3B
Ht: 5'10" Wt: 180 Born: 01/29/69 Age: 26

Year	Team	Lg	G	AB	H	2B	3B	HR	TB	R	RBI	TBB	IBB	SO	HBP	SH	SF	SB	CS	SB%	GDP	Avg	OBP	SLG
1990	Red Sox	R	28	97	30	7	0	0	37	20	13	20	0	13	1	0	1	2	0	1.00	6	.309	.429	.381
	Winter Havn	A	27	91	18	2	0	0	20	8	11	9	1	19	0	0	1	0	0	.00	0	.198	.267	.220
1991	Lynchburg	A	134	484	122	20	2	10	176	61	59	47	2	100	3	2	3	5	1	.83	13	.252	.320	.364
1992	New Britain	AA	122	384	80	15	0	1	98	36	24	29	2	83	4	5	1	5	5	.50	8	.208	.270	.255
1993	New Britain	AA	119	398	103	17	4	3	137	43	36	21	1	69	2	8	2	4	6	.40	11	.259	.298	.344
1994	New Britain	AA	14	46	10	2	0	2	18	6	4	2	0	10	0	0	0	0	1	.00	1	.217	.250	.391
	Lynchburg	A	11	37	13	3	1	2	24	9	9	7	0	7	0	0	0	0	0	.00	1	.351	.455	.649
	5 Min. YEARS		455	1537	376	66	7	18	510	183	156	135	6	301	10	15	8	16	13	.55	40	.245	.308	.332

Joe Norris

Pitches: Right   Bats: Right   Pos: P   Ht: 6'4"   Wt: 215   Born: 11/29/70   Age: 24

		HOW MUCH HE PITCHED					WHAT HE GAVE UP										THE RESULTS			
Year Team	Lg	G	GS	CG	GF	IP	BFP	H	R	ER	HR	SH	SF	HB	TBB	IBB	SO	WP	Bk	W	L	Pct.	ShO	Sv	ERA
1990 Jamestown	A	13	13	1	0	62.1	290	63	48	36	2	1	2	4	43	0	72	9	5	3	7	.300	0	0	5.20
1991 Sumter	A	8	8	0	0	35	161	41	25	20	2	0	1	3	17	0	42	6	2	1	3	.250	0	0	5.14
1992 Rockford	A	27	27	1	0	163	723	160	88	68	5	11	5	10	79	2	143	21	3	5	15	.250	0	0	3.75
1993 Wst Plm Bch	A	26	13	0	4	81	336	62	27	24	3	2	4	9	29	0	63	6	0	7	4	.636	0	0	2.67
1994 Nashville	AA	36	13	0	8	111	474	106	58	52	6	4	7	7	45	2	83	10	3	6	8	.429	0	1	4.22
5 Min. YEARS		110	74	2	12	452.1	1984	432	246	200	18	18	19	33	213	4	403	52	13	22	37	.373	0	1	3.98

Kevin Northrup

Bats: Right   Throws: Right   Pos: OF   Ht: 6'1"   Wt: 190   Born: 01/27/70   Age: 25

		BATTING														BASERUNNING				PERCENTAGES		
Year Team	Lg	G	AB	H	2B	3B	HR	TB	R	RBI	TBB	IBB	SO	HBP	SH	SF	SB	CS	SB%	GDP	Avg	OBP	SLG
1992 Jamestown	A	18	72	21	4	1	4	39	14	15	8	0	17	3	0	0	8	1	.89	1	.292	.386	.542
1993 Wst Plm Bch	A	131	459	136	29	0	6	183	65	63	70	7	76	3	4	5	10	7	.59	9	.296	.389	.399
1994 Harrisburg	AA	92	341	113	21	0	11	167	53	55	34	2	38	4	2	3	6	3	.67	14	.331	.395	.490
Ottawa	AAA	33	102	29	7	1	3	47	19	16	16	0	16	1	0	0	2	0	1.00	4	.284	.387	.461
3 Min. YEARS		274	974	299	61	2	24	436	151	149	128	9	147	11	6	8	26	11	.70	28	.307	.391	.448

Rafael Novoa

Pitches: Left   Bats: Left   Pos: P   Ht: 6' 1"   Wt: 190   Born: 10/26/67   Age: 27

		HOW MUCH HE PITCHED					WHAT HE GAVE UP										THE RESULTS			
Year Team	Lg	G	GS	CG	GF	IP	BFP	H	R	ER	HR	SH	SF	HB	TBB	IBB	SO	WP	Bk	W	L	Pct.	ShO	Sv	ERA
1989 Everett	A	3	3	0	0	15	73	20	11	8	2	0	0	1	8	0	20	3	1	0	1	.000	0	0	4.80
Clinton	A	13	10	0	0	63.2	267	58	20	18	1	9	1	4	18	1	61	1	6	5	4	.556	0	0	2.54
1990 Clinton	A	15	14	3	0	97.2	397	73	32	26	6	2	3	4	30	0	113	2	2	9	2	.818	1	0	2.40
Shreveport	AA	11	10	2	1	71.2	297	60	21	21	3	1	2	3	25	0	66	1	0	5	4	.556	1	0	2.64
1991 Phoenix	AAA	17	17	0	0	93.2	450	135	83	62	16	5	6	5	37	3	46	3	1	6	6	.500	0	0	5.96
1992 El Paso	AA	22	21	6	1	146.1	617	143	63	53	6	4	3	9	48	3	124	8	1	10	7	.588	0	0	3.26
1993 New Orleans	AAA	20	18	2	0	113	471	105	55	43	20	1	3	5	38	3	74	4	1	10	5	.667	1	0	3.42
1994 Iowa	AAA	27	23	1	0	137.1	621	151	90	80	12	7	4	8	67	3	54	7	1	6	10	.375	0	0	5.24
1990 San Francisco	NL	7	2	0	2	18.2	88	21	14	14	3	0	1	0	13	1	14	0	0	0	1	.000	0	1	6.75
1993 Milwaukee	AL	15	7	2	0	56	249	58	32	28	7	4	2	4	22	2	17	1	0	0	3	.000	0	0	4.50
6 Min. YEARS		128	116	14	2	738.1	3193	745	375	311	66	29	22	39	271	13	558	29	13	51	39	.567	3	0	3.79
2 Maj. YEARS		22	9	2	2	74.2	337	79	46	42	10	4	3	4	35	3	31	1	0	0	4	.000	0	1	5.06

Thomas Nuneviller

Bats: Right   Throws: Right   Pos: OF   Ht: 6'3"   Wt: 210   Born: 05/15/69   Age: 26

		BATTING														BASERUNNING				PERCENTAGES		
Year Team	Lg	G	AB	H	2B	3B	HR	TB	R	RBI	TBB	IBB	SO	HBP	SH	SF	SB	CS	SB%	GDP	Avg	OBP	SLG
1990 Batavia	A	71	259	60	10	0	9	97	36	31	30	1	45	3	0	0	15	4	.79	10	.232	.318	.375
1991 Clearwater	A	124	446	126	31	5	2	173	77	54	48	2	52	9	8	5	16	9	.64	11	.283	.360	.388
1992 Reading	AA	47	165	50	6	2	4	72	31	21	14	0	25	2	2	2	3	4	.43	2	.303	.361	.436
1993 Reading	AA	71	226	52	11	0	2	69	24	32	16	0	23	3	0	1	3	0	1.00	5	.230	.289	.305
1994 Reading	AA	49	191	51	10	2	5	80	30	29	11	0	21	2	0	2	4	2	.67	6	.267	.311	.419
Scranton-Wb	AAA	80	266	69	16	1	2	93	25	28	19	1	35	2	1	5	4	0	1.00	8	.259	.308	.350
5 Min. YEARS		442	1553	408	84	10	24	584	223	195	138	4	201	21	11	15	45	19	.70	42	.263	.328	.376

Rogelio Nunez

Bats: Both   Throws: Right   Pos: C   Ht: 6'0"   Wt: 180   Born: 05/06/70   Age: 25

		BATTING														BASERUNNING				PERCENTAGES		
Year Team	Lg	G	AB	H	2B	3B	HR	TB	R	RBI	TBB	IBB	SO	HBP	SH	SF	SB	CS	SB%	GDP	Avg	OBP	SLG
1989 White Sox	R	38	106	24	1	0	0	25	8	10	1	0	21	0	3	1	8	4	.67	2	.226	.231	.236
1990 Utica	A	35	90	24	1	2	1	32	11	11	5	2	24	0	1	2	5	1	.83	1	.267	.299	.356
1991 South Bend	A	56	189	40	4	1	0	46	26	15	14	0	30	0	6	0	21	6	.78	4	.212	.266	.243
Sarasota	A	15	36	8	1	0	0	9	6	3	3	0	8	0	2	1	0	1	.00	1	.222	.275	.250
1992 Sarasota	A	101	282	61	3	3	0	70	24	32	23	0	68	1	5	1	19	13	.59	7	.216	.277	.248
1993 Birmingham	AA	83	257	55	10	3	0	71	22	21	5	0	53	1	6	2	2	4	.33	6	.214	.230	.276
1994 Birmingham	AA	66	210	62	7	2	0	73	23	21	8	0	38	0	4	0	7	3	.70	2	.295	.321	.348
6 Min. YEARS		394	1170	274	27	11	2	326	120	113	59	2	242	2	27	7	62	32	.66	23	.234	.271	.279

Kevin O'Connor

Bats: Left   Throws: Right   Pos: OF   Ht: 6'0"   Wt: 180   Born: 06/08/69   Age: 26

		BATTING														BASERUNNING				PERCENTAGES		
Year Team	Lg	G	AB	H	2B	3B	HR	TB	R	RBI	TBB	IBB	SO	HBP	SH	SF	SB	CS	SB%	GDP	Avg	OBP	SLG
1990 Idaho Falls	R	12	47	11	2	0	1	16	6	4	0	0	5	0	0	0	4	0	1.00	2	.234	.234	.340
1991 Macon	A	90	312	78	11	2	1	96	58	31	48	1	36	3	2	6	32	10	.76	3	.250	.350	.308
Durham	A	28	79	16	1	0	3	26	14	10	8	0	13	0	0	2	1	4	.20	1	.203	.270	.329
1992 Durham	A	122	438	123	17	2	6	162	79	35	48	4	49	3	5	2	31	17	.65	7	.281	.354	.370
1993 Greenville	AA	122	355	67	15	5	7	107	63	30	62	1	63	7	4	0	18	10	.64	7	.189	.321	.301
1994 Greenville	AA	126	471	128	19	1	3	158	49	33	33	3	69	5	4	1	24	13	.65	1	.272	.325	.335
5 Min. YEARS		500	1702	423	65	7	21	565	269	143	199	9	235	18	15	11	110	54	.67	16	.249	.332	.332

188

John O'Donoghue

Pitches: Left Bats: Left Pos: P Ht: 6' 6" Wt: 210 Born: 05/26/69 Age: 26

Year	Team	Lg	G	GS	CG	GF	IP	BFP	H	R	ER	HR	SH	SF	HB	TBB	IBB	SO	WP	Bk	W	L	Pct.	ShO	Sv	ERA
1990	Bluefield	R	10	6	2	3	49.1	200	49	13	11	2	2	0	1	10	0	67	2	1	4	2	.667	2	0	2.01
	Frederick	A	1	1	0	0	4	18	5	2	2	0	0	0	0	0	0	3	0	0	0	1	.000	0	0	4.50
1991	Frederick	A	22	21	2	1	133.2	567	131	55	43	6	0	2	2	50	2	128	8	1	7	8	.467	1	0	2.90
1992	Hagerstown	AA	17	16	2	1	112.1	459	78	37	28	6	4	2	4	40	0	87	7	4	7	4	.636	0	0	2.24
	Rochester	AAA	13	10	3	1	69.2	282	60	31	25	5	4	0	0	19	1	47	5	0	5	4	.556	1	0	3.23
1993	Rochester	AAA	22	20	2	1	127.2	543	122	60	55	11	8	3	3	41	0	111	3	0	7	4	.636	1	0	3.88
1994	Rochester	AAA	38	12	0	9	105.1	508	142	76	67	13	5	5	5	55	6	78	6	2	4	7	.364	0	1	5.72
1993	Baltimore	AL	11	1	0	3	19.2	90	22	12	10	4	0	0	1	10	1	16	0	0	0	1	.000	0	0	4.58
	5 Min. YEARS		123	86	11	16	602	2577	587	274	231	43	23	12	15	215	9	521	31	8	34	30	.531	5	1	3.45

Kelley O'Neal

Bats: Left Throws: Right Pos: 2B Ht: 5'10" Wt: 160 Born: 12/19/70 Age: 24

Year	Team	Lg	G	AB	H	2B	3B	HR	TB	R	RBI	TBB	IBB	SO	HBP	SH	SF	SB	CS	SB%	GDP	Avg	OBP	SLG
1989	Bristol	R	60	208	48	6	7	3	77	31	24	15	1	47	1	0	1	9	2	.82	1	.231	.284	.370
1990	Niagara Fls	A	53	192	46	6	1	3	63	28	11	17	0	33	1	1	0	10	6	.63	6	.240	.305	.328
1991	Fayetteville	A	114	395	99	10	3	1	118	66	26	48	1	76	10	3	1	22	11	.67	8	.251	.346	.299
1992	Lakeland	A	103	340	87	11	3	3	113	48	20	21	0	61	6	6	2	21	7	.75	8	.256	.309	.332
1993	Lakeland	A	117	436	120	14	3	3	149	66	36	48	1	73	7	4	3	28	10	.74	9	.275	.354	.342
1994	Trenton	AA	43	129	25	5	1	0	32	12	13	13	1	32	0	3	2	4	4	.50	1	.194	.264	.248
	Lakeland	A	34	109	18	4	1	1	27	10	9	6	1	25	1	1	0	1	1	.50	2	.165	.216	.248
	6 Min. YEARS		524	1809	443	56	19	14	579	261	139	168	5	347	26	18	9	95	41	.70	35	.245	.317	.320

Sherman Obando

Bats: Right Throws: Right Pos: OF Ht: 6' 4" Wt: 215 Born: 01/23/70 Age: 25

Year	Team	Lg	G	AB	H	2B	3B	HR	TB	R	RBI	TBB	IBB	SO	HBP	SH	SF	SB	CS	SB%	GDP	Avg	OBP	SLG
1988	Yankees	R	49	172	44	10	2	4	70	26	27	16	2	32	3	0	1	8	5	.62	3	.256	.328	.407
1989	Oneonta	A	70	276	86	23	3	6	133	50	45	16	1	45	6	1	2	8	5	.62	3	.312	.360	.482
1990	Pr William	A	121	439	117	24	6	10	183	67	67	42	1	85	11	0	6	5	3	.63	7	.267	.341	.417
1991	Yankees	R	4	17	5	2	0	0	7	3	1	1	0	2	1	0	0	0	0	.00	0	.294	.368	.412
	Pr William	A	42	140	37	11	1	7	71	25	31	19	2	28	2	0	2	0	1	.00	1	.264	.356	.507
1992	Albany	AA	109	381	107	19	3	17	183	71	56	32	1	67	8	2	4	3	1	.75	12	.281	.346	.480
1993	Bowie	AA	19	58	14	2	0	3	25	8	12	9	0	11	1	0	3	1	0	1.00	1	.241	.338	.431
1994	Rochester	AAA	109	403	133	36	7	20	243	67	69	30	4	53	6	0	7	1	1	.50	3	.330	.379	.603
1993	Baltimore	AL	31	92	25	2	0	3	36	8	15	4	0	26	1	0	0	0	0	.00	1	.272	.309	.391
	7 Min. YEARS		523	1886	543	127	22	67	915	317	308	165	11	323	38	3	25	26	16	.62	30	.288	.353	.485

Alex Ochoa

Bats: Right Throws: Right Pos: OF Ht: 6'0" Wt: 173 Born: 03/29/72 Age: 23

Year	Team	Lg	G	AB	H	2B	3B	HR	TB	R	RBI	TBB	IBB	SO	HBP	SH	SF	SB	CS	SB%	GDP	Avg	OBP	SLG
1991	Orioles	R	53	179	55	8	3	1	72	26	30	16	0	14	1	3	1	11	6	.65	2	.307	.365	.402
1992	Kane County	A	133	499	147	22	7	1	186	65	59	58	5	55	7	5	7	31	17	.65	14	.295	.371	.373
1993	Frederick	A	137	532	147	29	5	13	225	84	90	46	0	67	9	1	6	34	13	.72	15	.276	.341	.423
1994	Bowie	AA	134	519	156	25	2	14	227	77	82	49	0	67	1	5	12	28	15	.65	11	.301	.355	.437
	4 Min. YEARS		457	1729	505	84	17	29	710	252	261	169	5	203	18	14	26	104	51	.67	42	.292	.356	.411

Rouglas Odor

Bats: Right Throws: Right Pos: SS Ht: 5'11" Wt: 165 Born: 01/26/68 Age: 27

Year	Team	Lg	G	AB	H	2B	3B	HR	TB	R	RBI	TBB	IBB	SO	HBP	SH	SF	SB	CS	SB%	GDP	Avg	OBP	SLG
1988	Burlington	R	63	222	55	3	2	1	65	39	39	32	1	32	2	5	1	13	6	.68	2	.248	.346	.293
1989	Kinston	A	28	60	7	0	0	0	7	4	2	3	0	12	3	2	0	3	0	1.00		.117	.197	.117
	Watertown	A	52	195	53	9	2	4	78	30	24	17	1	34	2	2	2	10	1	.91	3	.272	.333	.400
1990	Kinston	A	114	445	116	21	1	2	145	64	42	42	2	99	2	11	2	30	10	.75	7	.261	.326	.326
1991	Canton-Akrn	AA	76	236	47	5	2	1	59	24	29	25	2	50	1	7	5	8	2	.80	1	.199	.273	.250
1992	Kinston	A	71	219	59	6	2	1	72	24	17	22	0	36	6	8	1	11	6	.65	5	.269	.351	.329
1993	Canton-Akrn	AA	86	263	55	8	2	3	76	39	18	22	0	65	1	3	3	10	4	.71	2	.209	.270	.289
1994	Canton-Akrn	AA	35	146	36	6	3	0	48	23	17	12	0	20	2	3	2	8	2	.80	2	.247	.305	.329
	7 Min. YEARS		525	1786	428	58	14	12	550	247	188	175	6	348	19	41	18	93	31	.75	22	.240	.311	.308

Mark Ohlms

Pitches: Right Bats: Right Pos: P Ht: 6'1" Wt: 175 Born: 01/15/67 Age: 28

Year	Team	Lg	G	GS	CG	GF	IP	BFP	H	R	ER	HR	SH	SF	HB	TBB	IBB	SO	WP	Bk	W	L	Pct.	ShO	Sv	ERA
1988	Yankees	R	24	0	0	19	36.2	149	19	4	3	0	0	1	0	16	3	64	2	5	4	3	.571	0	10	0.74
1989	Pr William	A	37	0	0	29	52.1	231	48	25	15	1	4	3	3	25	4	37	6	0	2	5	.286	0	6	2.58

Year	Team	Lg	G	GS	CG	GF	IP	BFP	H	R	ER	HR	SH	SF	HB	TBB	IBB	SO	WP	Bk	W	L	Pct.	ShO	Sv	ERA
1990	Ft.Laudrdle	A	21	19	1	1	115.1	461	103	57	44	9	7	2	1	15	0	104	8	2	8	8	.500	0	0	3.43
1991	Pr William	A	47	0	0	42	51	227	44	22	15	2	3	1	0	28	1	55	2	0	2	4	.333	0	26	2.65
1992	Knoxville	AA	52	0	0	43	69.2	284	49	15	12	2	3	5	6	26	4	50	5	1	3	2	.600	0	18	1.55
1993	Knoxville	AA	7	0	0	6	6.2	26	6	2	2	0	1	0	0	3	0	4	0	0	1	0	1.000	0	1	2.70
	Syracuse	AAA	47	0	0	24	60	296	85	50	47	7	4	5	3	42	4	37	8	0	3	6	.333	0	5	7.05
1994	Knoxville	AA	53	0	0	21	81.2	359	81	45	41	9	12	5	3	36	5	57	9	0	4	6	.400	0	3	4.52
	7 Min. YEARS		288	19	1	185	473.1	2033	435	220	179	30	34	22	17	191	21	408	40	8	27	34	.443	0	69	3.40

Kirt Ojala

Pitches: Left   Bats: Left   Pos: P

Ht: 6'2"   Wt: 200   Born: 12/24/68   Age: 26

			HOW MUCH HE PITCHED						WHAT HE GAVE UP												THE RESULTS					
Year	Team	Lg	G	GS	CG	GF	IP	BFP	H	R	ER	HR	SH	SF	HB	TBB	IBB	SO	WP	Bk	W	L	Pct.	ShO	Sv	ERA
1990	Oneonta	A	14	14	1	0	79	353	75	28	19	2	5	2	3	43	0	87	1	2	7	2	.778	0	0	2.16
1991	Pr William	A	25	23	1	0	156.2	636	120	52	44	5	3	4	4	61	1	112	3	1	8	7	.533	0	0	2.53
1992	Albany	AA	24	23	2	0	151.2	642	130	71	61	10	3	7	0	80	0	116	10	0	12	8	.600	1	0	3.62
1993	Albany	AA	1	1	0	0	6.1	26	5	0	0	0	0	0	0	2	0	6	2	0	1	0	1.000	0	0	0.00
	Columbus	AAA	31	20	0	3	126	575	145	85	77	13	4	5	3	71	2	83	13	0	8	9	.471	0	0	5.50
1994	Columbus	AAA	25	23	1	0	148	638	157	78	63	12	2	2	4	46	1	81	10	1	11	7	.611	1	0	3.83
	5 Min. YEARS		120	104	5	3	667.2	2870	632	314	264	42	17	20	14	303	4	485	39	5	47	33	.588	2	0	3.56

Jim Olander

Bats: Right   Throws: Right   Pos: OF

Ht: 6'2"   Wt: 175   Born: 02/21/63   Age: 32

			BATTING															BASERUNNING				PERCENTAGES		
Year	Team	Lg	G	AB	H	2B	3B	HR	TB	R	RBI	TBB	IBB	SO	HBP	SH	SF	SB	CS	SB%	GDP	Avg	OBP	SLG
1981	Helena	R	61	222	72	10	3	6	106	37	37	17	0	59	0	0	0	5	0	1.00	0	.324	.372	.477
1982	Spartanburg	A	121	423	129	25	6	12	202	77	63	61	0	86	0	0	0	12	0	1.00	0	.305	.393	.478
1983	Peninsula	A	126	503	125	21	3	15	197	62	79	43	0	146	0	0	0	12	0	1.00	0	.249	.308	.392
1984	Reading	AA	117	362	95	12	2	8	135	44	47	29	0	62	2	1	5	10	10	.50	10	.262	.317	.373
1985	Portland	AAA	44	72	16	2	0	0	18	6	6	2	0	17	0	0	2	3	0	1.00	1	.222	.237	.250
	Reading	AA	64	208	67	15	2	4	98	30	39	29	1	45	3	2	4	2	2	.50	4	.322	.411	.471
1986	Reading	AA	129	464	151	33	4	8	216	77	68	56	3	84	2	3	5	10	15	.40	5	.325	.397	.466
1987	Maine	AAA	43	145	31	7	0	1	41	17	8	13	1	30	0	1	0	2	2	.50	5	.214	.278	.283
1988	Maine	AAA	25	71	15	3	0	0	18	5	4	4	1	18	1	1	0	0	2	.00	1	.211	.263	.254
1989	Scr Wil-Bar	AAA	111	274	69	17	4	3	103	35	29	27	1	69	3	8	2	5	7	.42	3	.252	.324	.376
1990	Tucson	AAA	33	98	23	8	2	1	38	12	12	14	1	24	1	1	0	0	3	.00	3	.235	.336	.388
	Denver	AAA	74	233	67	12	4	3	96	33	36	20	1	47	4	9	6	2	5	.29	3	.288	.346	.412
1991	Denver	AAA	134	498	162	32	10	9	241	89	78	64	5	83	4	3	2	14	2	.88	10	.325	.405	.484
1992	Denver	AAA	21	78	29	4	1	5	50	23	15	13	0	9	2	0	2	2	3	.40	1	.372	.463	.641
1993	Colo Spngs	AAA	57	200	60	16	3	6	100	43	25	31	1	40	2	1	1	4	1	.80	7	.300	.397	.500
1994	Indianapols	AAA	29	113	26	6	1	3	43	18	11	7	0	35	1	0	4	1	0	1.00	4	.230	.272	.381
	Charlotte	AAA	11	24	5	2	0	0	7	1	3	7	0	6	0	0	0	1	0	1.00	0	.208	.375	.292
1991	Milwaukee	AL	12	9	0	0	0	0	0	2	0	2	0	5	0	0	0	0	0	.00	0	.000	.182	.000
	14 Min. YEARS		1200	3988	1142	225	45	84	1709	609	560	437	15	860	25	30	31	85	52	.62	59	.286	.358	.429

Jose Olmeda

Bats: Both   Throws: Right   Pos: 2B

Ht: 5'9"   Wt: 155   Born: 06/20/68   Age: 27

			BATTING															BASERUNNING				PERCENTAGES		
Year	Team	Lg	G	AB	H	2B	3B	HR	TB	R	RBI	TBB	IBB	SO	HBP	SH	SF	SB	CS	SB%	GDP	Avg	OBP	SLG
1989	Idaho Falls	R	61	230	57	5	5	1	77	36	27	31	0	40	0	0	1	9	4	.69	7	.248	.336	.335
1990	Sumter	A	103	367	93	14	6	7	140	60	40	55	2	49	2	4	4	17	9	.65	3	.253	.350	.381
	Burlington	A	27	112	29	3	0	0	32	6	7	8	0	17	0	0	1	1	1	.50	1	.259	.306	.286
	Greenville	AA	2	8	1	0	0	0	1	1	0	1	0	3	0	0	0	0	0	.00	0	.125	.222	.125
1991	Macon	A	81	305	84	16	8	3	125	66	30	38	0	38	1	2	1	34	7	.83	3	.275	.357	.410
	Greenville	AA	50	173	35	10	1	3	56	18	16	15	0	36	2	5	2	9	2	.82	2	.202	.271	.324
1992	Durham	A	24	89	23	6	1	2	37	17	9	14	0	14	0	1	0	7	4	.64	0	.258	.359	.416
	Greenville	AA	106	341	84	22	4	2	120	54	33	38	3	50	0	1	6	12	6	.67	8	.246	.317	.352
1993	Greenville	AA	122	451	126	33	2	9	190	61	51	29	2	63	0	5	9	15	7	.68	8	.279	.317	.421
1994	Richmond	AAA	109	387	89	19	6	4	132	49	39	30	6	74	1	8	1	17	4	.81	12	.230	.286	.341
	6 Min. YEARS		685	2463	621	128	34	31	910	368	252	259	13	384	6	26	25	121	44	.73	40	.252	.322	.369

Steve Olsen

Pitches: Right   Bats: Right   Pos: P

Ht: 6'4"   Wt: 225   Born: 11/02/69   Age: 25

			HOW MUCH HE PITCHED						WHAT HE GAVE UP												THE RESULTS					
Year	Team	Lg	G	GS	CG	GF	IP	BFP	H	R	ER	HR	SH	SF	HB	TBB	IBB	SO	WP	Bk	W	L	Pct.	ShO	Sv	ERA
1991	Utica	A	2	2	0	0	14	51	3	3	1	0	0	0	0	4	0	20	1	0	1	0	1.000	0	0	0.64
	South Bend	A	13	13	0	0	81.2	352	80	44	33	4	2	4	3	28	1	76	3	3	5	2	.714	0	0	3.64
1992	Sarasota	A	13	13	3	0	88	363	68	22	19	4	2	1	3	32	0	85	3	2	11	1	.917	1	0	1.94
	Birmingham	AA	12	12	1	0	77.1	320	68	28	26	5	0	2	0	29	1	46	2	0	6	4	.600	0	0	3.03
1993	Birmingham	AA	25	25	1	0	142	618	156	87	75	22	1	5	7	52	2	92	4	0	10	9	.526	1	0	4.75
1994	Birmingham	AA	16	16	1	0	102.2	432	100	47	42	8	2	2	3	28	1	69	9	0	5	7	.417	0	0	3.68
	Nashville	AAA	11	11	2	0	71.1	289	69	30	26	4	2	1	0	18	0	58	0	1	7	2	.778	0	0	3.28
	4 Min. YEARS		92	92	8	0	577	2425	544	261	222	47	9	15	16	191	5	446	22	6	45	25	.643	2	0	3.46

Rey Ordonez

Bats: Both Throws: Right Pos: SS Ht: 5'10" Wt: 170 Born: 01/11/72 Age: 23

Year	Team	Lg	G	AB	H	2B	3B	HR	TB	R	RBI	TBB	IBB	SO	HBP	SH	SF	SB	CS	SB%	GDP	Avg	OBP	SLG
1994	St. Lucie	A	79	314	97	21	2	2	128	47	40	14	0	28	0	6	2	11	6	.65	8	.309	.336	.408
	Binghamton	AA	48	191	50	10	2	1	67	22	20	4	0	18	1	1	1	4	3	.57	2	.262	.279	.351
	1 Min. YEARS		127	505	147	31	4	3	195	69	60	18	0	46	1	7	3	15	9	.63	10	.291	.315	.386

Bo Ortiz

Bats: Right Throws: Right Pos: OF Ht: 5'11" Wt: 170 Born: 04/04/70 Age: 25

Year	Team	Lg	G	AB	H	2B	3B	HR	TB	R	RBI	TBB	IBB	SO	HBP	SH	SF	SB	CS	SB%	GDP	Avg	OBP	SLG
1991	Bluefield	R	12	53	16	2	1	1	23	4	7	2	0	6	0	0	1	1	0	1.00	2	.302	.321	.434
	Kane County	A	57	215	58	8	1	0	68	34	27	17	1	38	2	4	2	2	2	.50	4	.270	.326	.316
1992	Frederick	A	54	182	50	11	3	0	67	26	19	18	0	40	3	2	1	7	3	.70	4	.275	.348	.368
1993	Frederick	A	104	351	99	18	7	10	161	72	60	44	0	65	7	6	1	12	11	.52	7	.282	.372	.459
	Bowie	AA	8	30	6	0	1	0	8	1	3	1	0	5	1	2	0	0	0	.00	0	.200	.250	.267
1994	Bowie	AA	85	320	99	21	3	10	156	58	54	28	2	47	4	1	0	13	4	.76	10	.309	.372	.488
	Midland	AA	22	80	14	4	0	0	18	9	6	6	0	11	1	0	0	3	1	.75	2	.175	.241	.225
	4 Min. YEARS		342	1231	342	64	16	21	501	204	176	116	3	212	18	15	5	38	21	.64	29	.278	.347	.407

Hector Ortiz

Bats: Right Throws: Right Pos: C Ht: 6'0" Wt: 178 Born: 10/14/69 Age: 25

Year	Team	Lg	G	AB	H	2B	3B	HR	TB	R	RBI	TBB	IBB	SO	HBP	SH	SF	SB	CS	SB%	GDP	Avg	OBP	SLG
1988	Salem	A	32	77	11	1	0	0	12	5	4	5	0	16	1	1	0	0	2	.00	5	.143	.205	.156
1989	Vero Beach	A	42	85	12	0	1	0	14	5	4	6	0	15	2	4	0	0	0	.00	1	.141	.215	.165
	Salem	A	44	140	32	3	1	0	37	13	12	4	0	24	1	2	0	2	1	.67	6	.229	.255	.264
1990	Yakima	A	52	173	47	3	1	0	52	16	12	5	0	15	1	1	0	1	1	.50	6	.272	.296	.301
1991	Vero Beach	A	42	123	28	2	0	0	30	3	8	5	0	8	3	0	0	0	0	.00	2	.228	.275	.244
1992	Bakersfield	A	63	206	58	8	1	1	71	19	31	21	0	16	5	3	2	2	3	.40	8	.282	.359	.345
	San Antonio	AA	26	59	12	1	0	0	13	1	5	11	0	13	1	1	0	0	0	.00	2	.203	.338	.220
1993	San Antonio	AA	49	131	28	5	0	1	36	6	6	9	2	17	0	3	0	0	2	.00	3	.214	.264	.275
	Albuquerque	AAA	18	44	8	1	1	0	11	0	3	0	0	6	1	2	0	0	0	.00	1	.182	.200	.250
1994	Albuquerque	AAA	34	93	28	1	1	0	31	7	10	3	0	12	0	0	1	0	0	.00	4	.301	.320	.333
	San Antonio	AA	24	75	9	0	0	0	9	4	4	2	0	7	1	0	2	0	0	.00	4	.120	.150	.120
	7 Min. YEARS		426	1206	273	25	6	2	316	79	99	71	2	149	16	17	5	5	9	.36	45	.226	.277	.262

Javier Ortiz

Bats: Right Throws: Right Pos: OF Ht: 6' 4" Wt: 220 Born: 01/22/63 Age: 32

Year	Team	Lg	G	AB	H	2B	3B	HR	TB	R	RBI	TBB	IBB	SO	HBP	SH	SF	SB	CS	SB%	GDP	Avg	OBP	SLG
1983	Burlington	A	101	378	133	23	4	16	212	72	79	42	3	94	2	2	3	10	6	.63	14	.352	.416	.561
1984	Tulsa	AA	94	325	97	21	3	8	148	42	53	47	2	67	5	4	4	4	5	.44	8	.298	.391	.455
1985	Tulsa	AA	86	304	75	12	3	5	108	47	31	52	2	75	4	0	1	11	3	.79	10	.247	.363	.355
1986	Tulsa	AA	110	378	114	29	3	14	191	52	65	54	2	94	7	3	1	15	10	.60	7	.302	.398	.505
1987	Okla City	AAA	119	381	105	23	7	15	187	58	69	58	2	99	4	1	10	5	2	.71	6	.276	.369	.491
1988	San Antonio	AA	51	182	53	13	2	8	94	35	33	22	0	38	5	0	5	6	3	.67	4	.291	.374	.516
1989	Albuquerque	AAA	70	220	59	10	0	11	102	42	36	34	1	54	4	1	0	2	2	.50	4	.268	.376	.464
	Tucson	AAA	11	40	7	0	0	0	7	5	0	2	0	9	0	0	0	0	0	.00	1	.175	.214	.175
1990	Tucson	AAA	49	179	63	16	2	5	98	36	39	22	1	36	1	0	3	2	3	.40	6	.352	.420	.547
1991	Tucson	AAA	34	127	41	13	0	3	63	20	22	10	0	22	0	0	2	0	3	.00	4	.323	.367	.496
1993	Omaha	AAA	3	7	2	0	0	0	2	0	2	1	0	0	0	0	1	0	1	.00	0	.286	.333	.286
	Pirates	R	8	23	7	3	0	0	10	5	6	8	0	7	0	0	1	0	0	.00	0	.304	.469	.435
	Carolina	AA	33	109	37	10	1	5	64	17	24	15	3	18	2	0	3	1	1	.50	1	.339	.419	.587
1994	Nashville	AAA	111	346	95	20	2	16	167	49	55	36	2	56	2	1	3	8	1	.89	10	.275	.344	.483
1990	Houston	NL	30	77	21	5	1	1	31	7	10	12	0	11	0	0	1	1	1	.50	1	.273	.367	.403
1991	Houston	NL	47	83	23	4	1	1	32	7	5	14	0	14	0	0	0	0	0	.00	3	.277	.381	.386
	11 Min. YEARS		880	2999	888	193	27	106	1453	480	514	403	18	669	36	12	37	64	40	.62	76	.296	.382	.484
	2 Maj. YEARS		77	160	44	9	2	2	63	14	15	26	0	25	0	0	1	1	1	.50	4	.275	.374	.394

Ray Ortiz

Bats: Left Throws: Left Pos: OF Ht: 6'2" Wt: 215 Born: 04/27/68 Age: 27

Year	Team	Lg	G	AB	H	2B	3B	HR	TB	R	RBI	TBB	IBB	SO	HBP	SH	SF	SB	CS	SB%	GDP	Avg	OBP	SLG
1989	Kenosha	A	51	175	43	8	1	3	62	19	21	24	2	32	3	1	2	4	0	1.00	4	.246	.343	.354
1990	Visalia	A	62	235	74	15	1	13	130	43	53	26	3	47	1	0	1	1	0	1.00	8	.315	.384	.553
	Orlando	AA	71	265	68	16	0	9	111	41	49	27	1	57	6	0	4	1	0	1.00	6	.257	.334	.419
1991	Orlando	AA	135	470	116	19	3	9	168	58	71	48	3	100	7	1	6	3	2	.60	10	.247	.322	.357
1992	Orlando	AA	78	266	70	16	1	10	118	40	47	21	1	46	1	0	2	0	1	.00	4	.263	.317	.444
	Portland	AAA	42	134	44	12	1	3	67	17	22	7	2	17	1	0	3	0	1	.00	5	.328	.359	.500

Year	Team	Lg	G	AB	H	2B	3B	HR	TB	R	RBI	TBB	IBB	SO	HBP	SH	SF	SB	CS	SB%	GDP	Avg	OBP	SLG
1993	Portland	AAA	111	357	101	18	2	5	138	42	53	14	2	58	1	0	6	2	1	.67	11	.283	.307	.387
1994	Phoenix	AAA	122	364	100	19	8	9	162	51	56	19	2	78	1	0	2	1	5	.17	7	.275	.311	.445
6 Min. YEARS			672	2266	616	123	17	61	956	311	372	186	16	435	21	1	26	12	10	.55	55	.272	.329	.422

John Orton

Bats: Right Throws: Right Pos: C **Ht: 6' 1" Wt: 192 Born: 12/08/65 Age: 29**

						BATTING												BASERUNNING				PERCENTAGES		
Year	Team	Lg	G	AB	H	2B	3B	HR	TB	R	RBI	TBB	IBB	SO	HBP	SH	SF	SB	CS	SB%	GDP	Avg	OBP	SLG
1987	Salem	A	51	176	46	8	1	8	80	31	36	32	1	61	7	1	2	6	2	.75	5	.261	.392	.455
	Midland	AA	5	13	2	1	0	0	3	1	0	2	0	3	1	0	0	0	0	.00	0	.154	.313	.231
1988	Palm Sprngs	A	68	230	46	6	1	1	57	42	28	45	0	79	10	2	0	5	2	.71	4	.200	.354	.248
1989	Midland	AA	99	344	80	20	6	10	142	51	53	37	1	102	7	6	7	2	1	.67	5	.233	.314	.413
1990	Edmonton	AAA	50	174	42	8	0	6	68	29	26	19	1	63	0	1	1	4	2	.67	7	.241	.314	.391
1991	Edmonton	AAA	76	245	55	14	1	5	86	39	32	31	1	66	5	4	2	5	0	1.00	4	.224	.322	.351
1992	Edmonton	AAA	49	149	38	9	3	3	62	28	25	28	0	32	3	4	2	3	5	.38	3	.255	.379	.416
1993	Palm Sprngs	A	2	7	0	0	0	0	0	0	0	1	0	1	0	0	0	0	0	.00	0	.000	.125	.000
1994	Richmond	AAA	36	81	10	3	0	1	16	3	2	5	0	30	0	0	1	0	0	.00	3	.123	.172	.198
1989	California	AL	16	39	7	1	0	0	8	4	4	2	0	17	0	1	0	0	0	.00	0	.179	.220	.205
1990	California	AL	31	84	16	5	0	1	24	8	6	5	0	31	1	2	0	0	1	.00	2	.190	.244	.286
1991	California	AL	29	69	14	4	0	0	18	7	3	10	0	17	1	4	0	0	1	.00	2	.203	.313	.261
1992	California	AL	43	114	25	3	0	2	34	11	12	7	0	32	2	2	0	1	1	.50	1	.219	.276	.298
1993	California	AL	37	95	18	5	0	1	26	5	4	7	0	24	1	2	0	1	2	.33	1	.189	.252	.274
8 Min. YEARS			436	1419	319	69	12	34	514	224	202	200	4	437	33	18	15	25	12	.68	31	.225	.331	.362
5 Maj. YEARS			156	401	80	18	0	4	110	35	29	31	0	121	5	11	0	2	5	.29	6	.200	.265	.274

Keith Osik

Bats: Right Throws: Right Pos: C **Ht: 6'0" Wt: 195 Born: 10/22/68 Age: 26**

						BATTING												BASERUNNING				PERCENTAGES		
Year	Team	Lg	G	AB	H	2B	3B	HR	TB	R	RBI	TBB	IBB	SO	HBP	SH	SF	SB	CS	SB%	GDP	Avg	OBP	SLG
1990	Welland	A	29	97	27	4	0	1	34	13	20	11	1	12	2	1	3	2	6	.25	1	.278	.354	.351
1991	Carolina	AA	17	43	13	3	1	0	18	9	5	5	0	5	0	0	0	0	0	.00	1	.302	.375	.419
	Salem	A	87	300	81	13	1	6	114	31	35	38	0	48	3	3	2	2	3	.40	13	.270	.356	.380
1992	Carolina	AA	129	425	110	17	1	5	144	41	45	52	1	69	15	0	4	2	9	.18	12	.259	.357	.339
1993	Carolina	AA	103	371	105	21	2	10	160	47	47	30	1	47	9	4	1	2	0	.00	13	.283	.350	.431
1994	Buffalo	AAA	83	260	55	16	0	5	86	27	33	28	0	41	3	0	2	0	1	.00	5	.212	.294	.331
5 Min. YEARS			448	1496	391	74	5	27	556	168	185	164	3	222	32	8	12	6	21	.22	45	.261	.344	.372

Gavin Osteen

Pitches: Left Bats: Right Pos: P **Ht: 6'0" Wt: 195 Born: 11/27/69 Age: 25**

			HOW MUCH HE PITCHED					WHAT HE GAVE UP										THE RESULTS					
Year	Team	Lg	G	GS	CG	GF	IP	BFP	H	R	ER	HR	SH	SF	HB	TBB	IBB	SO	WP	Bk	W	L	Pct.	ShO	Sv	ERA
1989	Sou Oregon	A	16	6	0	3	46.1	211	44	24	18	3	4	1	3	29	0	42	9	0	2	2	.500	0	0	3.50
1990	Madison	A	27	27	1	0	154	659	126	69	53	6	5	6	3	80	0	120	10	4	10	10	.500	1	0	3.10
1991	Huntsville	AA	28	28	2	0	173	742	176	82	68	4	6	9	4	65	2	105	4	2	13	9	.591	1	0	3.54
1992	Tacoma	AAA	4	4	0	0	14.1	77	21	18	16	4	2	3	2	13	0	7	1	1	0	2	.000	0	0	10.05
	Huntsville	AA	16	16	1	0	102.1	425	106	45	41	9	5	5	1	27	0	56	2	2	5	5	.500	0	0	3.61
1993	Huntsville	AA	11	11	2	0	70.1	288	56	21	18	1	1	1	2	25	1	46	2	0	7	3	.700	0	0	2.30
	Tacoma	AAA	16	15	0	0	83.1	356	89	51	47	4	4	5	1	31	1	46	0	1	7	7	.500	0	0	5.08
1994	Tacoma	AAA	24	24	2	0	138.1	618	169	95	81	17	3	12	4	39	0	71	0	0	8	9	.471	1	0	5.27
6 Min. YEARS			142	131	8	3	782	3376	787	405	342	48	30	42	20	309	4	493	28	10	52	47	.525	3	0	3.94

Pedro Osuna

Pitches: Right Bats: Right Pos: P **Ht: 5'11" Wt: 160 Born: 04/12/73 Age: 22**

			HOW MUCH HE PITCHED					WHAT HE GAVE UP										THE RESULTS					
Year	Team	Lg	G	GS	CG	GF	IP	BFP	H	R	ER	HR	SH	SF	HB	TBB	IBB	SO	WP	Bk	W	L	Pct.	ShO	Sv	ERA
1991	Dodgers	R	8	0	0	6	11	44	8	5	1	0	0	0	1	0	0	13	2	1	0	0	.000	0	4	0.82
	Yakima	A	13	0	0	11	25.1	101	18	10	9	1	1	0	4	8	0	38	1	0	0	0	.000	0	5	3.20
1993	Bakersfield	A	14	2	0	11	18.1	76	19	10	10	2	0	0	0	5	0	20	0	1	0	2	.000	0	2	4.91
1994	San Antonio	AA	35	0	0	32	46	172	19	6	5	0	2	0	2	18	1	53	0	3	1	2	.333	0	19	0.98
	Albuquerque	AAA	6	0	0	6	6	24	5	1	0	0	0	0	1	1	0	8	1	0	0	0	.000	0	4	0.00
3 Min. YEARS			76	2	0	66	106.2	417	69	32	25	3	3	0	8	32	1	132	4	5	1	4	.200	0	34	2.11

Ricky Otero

Bats: Both Throws: Right Pos: OF **Ht: 5'7" Wt: 150 Born: 04/15/72 Age: 23**

						BATTING												BASERUNNING				PERCENTAGES		
Year	Team	Lg	G	AB	H	2B	3B	HR	TB	R	RBI	TBB	IBB	SO	HBP	SH	SF	SB	CS	SB%	GDP	Avg	OBP	SLG
1991	Kingsport	R	66	235	81	16	3	7	124	47	52	35	5	32	2	1	6	12	4	.75	4	.345	.424	.528
	Pittsfield	A	6	24	7	0	0	0	7	4	2	2	0	1	0	0	0	4	0	1.00	0	.292	.346	.292
1992	Columbia	A	96	353	106	24	4	8	162	57	60	38	0	53	3	4	6	39	13	.75	4	.300	.368	.459
	St. Lucie	A	40	151	48	8	4	0	64	20	19	9	1	11	2	3	2	10	5	.67	1	.318	.360	.424
1993	Binghamton	AA	124	503	133	21	10	2	180	63	54	38	2	57	7	7	4	28	15	.65	5	.264	.322	.358
1994	Binghamton	AA	128	531	156	31	9	7	226	96	57	50	1	49	3	4	4	33	16	.67	7	.294	.355	.426
4 Min. YEARS			460	1797	531	100	30	24	763	287	244	172	9	203	17	19	22	126	53	.70	21	.295	.359	.425

Eric Owens

Bats: Right Throws: Right Pos: SS Ht: 6'1" Wt: 184 Born: 02/03/71 Age: 24

					BATTING										BASERUNNING				PERCENTAGES		
Year	Team	Lg	G	AB	H	2B	3B	HR	TB	R	RBI	TBB	IBB	SO	HBP	SH	SF	SB	CS	SB%	GDP	Avg	OBP	SLG
1992	Billings	R	67	239	72	10	3	3	97	41	26	23	0	22	0	3	0	15	4	.79	1	.301	.363	.406
1993	Winston-Sal	A	122	487	132	25	4	10	195	74	63	53	0	69	4	4	7	20	12	.63	8	.271	.343	.400
1994	Chattanooga	AA	134	523	133	17	3	3	165	73	36	54	0	86	2	8	2	38	14	.73	10	.254	.325	.315
	3 Min. YEARS		323	1249	337	52	10	16	457	188	125	130	0	177	6	15	9	73	30	.71	19	.270	.339	.366

William Owens

Bats: Both Throws: Right Pos: 1B Ht: 6'1" Wt: 210 Born: 04/12/71 Age: 24

					BATTING										BASERUNNING				PERCENTAGES		
Year	Team	Lg	G	AB	H	2B	3B	HR	TB	R	RBI	TBB	IBB	SO	HBP	SH	SF	SB	CS	SB%	GDP	Avg	OBP	SLG
1992	Kane County	A	73	283	72	16	0	2	94	23	33	26	1	63	0	2	4	4	3	.57	2	.254	.313	.332
1993	Albany	A	120	458	136	23	2	11	196	64	66	49	6	70	2	1	5	3	5	.38	8	.297	.364	.428
	Frederick	A	17	60	21	4	0	0	25	8	8	3	0	8	0	0	1	0	0	.00	2	.350	.375	.417
1994	Bowie	AA	43	145	33	7	1	4	54	13	19	10	1	37	0	0	1	1	0	1.00	3	.228	.276	.372
	Frederick	A	86	324	74	16	0	13	129	50	52	44	5	73	1	0	1	1	1	.50	3	.228	.322	.398
	3 Min. YEARS		339	1270	336	66	3	30	498	158	178	132	13	251	3	3	12	9	9	.50	18	.265	.332	.392

Gabriel Ozuna

Pitches: Right Bats: Right Pos: P Ht: 6'1" Wt: 160 Born: 04/10/69 Age: 26

			HOW MUCH HE PITCHED						WHAT HE GAVE UP									THE RESULTS				
Year	Team	Lg	G	GS	CG	GF	IP	BFP	H	R	ER	HR	SH	SF	HB	TBB	IBB	SO	WP	Bk	W	L	Pct.	ShO	Sv	ERA
1988	St. Pete	A	5	0	0	2	10	42	10	5	5	1	0	0	0	2	0	9	2	0	1	0	1.000	0	0	4.50
	Johnson Cty	R	21	0	0	19	25.1	99	19	8	3	1	1	1	1	9	3	29	3	2	0	4	.000	0	9	1.07
1989	Savannah	A	59	0	0	52	74	291	48	21	13	2	2	1	3	19	2	94	3	1	3	5	.375	0	28	1.58
1990	Arkansas	AA	54	0	0	15	71	319	82	36	26	2	3	3	2	26	5	61	4	1	3	2	.600	0	0	3.30
1991	St. Pete	A	31	0	0	23	43.2	170	27	9	4	0	2	1	1	12	2	44	1	0	2	3	.400	0	13	0.82
	Arkansas	AA	17	0	0	6	23.2	111	26	20	16	5	1	0	2	15	6	25	4	0	0	2	.000	0	2	6.08
1992	Arkansas	AA	57	0	0	22	78	326	64	22	18	5	5	1	4	27	11	63	1	1	3	6	.333	0	4	2.08
1993	Louisville	AAA	35	0	0	20	40	176	32	16	13	7	1	0	3	18	2	41	1	0	0	4	.000	0	4	2.93
1994	Arkansas	AA	42	0	0	19	60	248	58	31	27	8	0	1	1	13	1	69	2	0	3	2	.600	0	1	4.05
	7 Min. YEARS		321	0	0	178	425.2	1782	365	166	125	31	15	8	17	141	32	435	21	5	15	28	.349	0	61	2.64

Gary Painter

Pitches: Right Bats: Right Pos: P Ht: 6'2" Wt: 196 Born: 04/30/68 Age: 27

			HOW MUCH HE PITCHED						WHAT HE GAVE UP									THE RESULTS				
Year	Team	Lg	G	GS	CG	GF	IP	BFP	H	R	ER	HR	SH	SF	HB	TBB	IBB	SO	WP	Bk	W	L	Pct.	ShO	Sv	ERA
1990	Red Sox	R	5	5	1	0	32.2	128	23	8	5	0	0	1	1	9	0	27	1	0	2	0	1.000	0	0	1.38
	Winter Havn	A	4	4	0	0	21.1	94	17	9	9	1	0	0	0	12	0	15	5	1	1	3	.250	0	0	3.80
1991	Winter Havn	A	9	9	1	0	57.2	230	38	21	18	1	6	1	1	22	0	54	7	0	2	5	.286	0	0	2.81
	New Britain	AA	15	15	1	0	87.1	371	89	54	47	10	3	1	0	35	0	51	4	1	3	7	.300	0	0	4.84
1992	New Britain	AA	20	14	0	3	93	399	102	39	33	1	2	2	2	24	1	55	3	1	7	2	.778	0	0	3.19
1993	New Britain	AA	14	14	0	0	77.2	333	76	44	35	4	1	1	3	29	1	57	4	3	3	6	.333	0	0	4.06
	Lynchburg	A	15	1	0	10	29.1	118	24	8	7	1	0	0	1	8	1	26	1	0	2	2	.500	0	5	2.15
1994	Sarasota	A	16	0	0	1	27	115	26	9	4	0	1	0	1	8	0	22	0	0	1	0	1.000	0	1	1.33
	New Britain	AA	14	1	0	7	23.1	112	35	18	14	3	3	1	0	11	2	20	1	1	1	2	.333	0	0	5.40
	San Bernrdo	A	11	9	0	0	56	266	76	41	37	4	2	4	3	27	1	45	3	0	2	6	.250	0	0	5.95
	5 Min. YEARS		123	72	3	21	505.1	2166	506	251	209	25	18	11	12	185	6	372	29	7	24	33	.421	0	6	3.72

Orlando Palmeiro

Bats: Left Throws: Right Pos: OF Ht: 5'11" Wt: 155 Born: 01/19/69 Age: 26

					BATTING										BASERUNNING				PERCENTAGES		
Year	Team	Lg	G	AB	H	2B	3B	HR	TB	R	RBI	TBB	IBB	SO	HBP	SH	SF	SB	CS	SB%	GDP	Avg	OBP	SLG
1991	Boise	A	70	277	77	11	2	1	95	56	24	33	0	22	3	6	3	8	8	.50	8	.278	.358	.343
1992	Quad City	A	127	451	143	22	4	0	173	83	41	56	3	41	5	19	7	31	13	.70	5	.317	.393	.384
1993	Midland	AA	131	535	163	19	5	0	192	85	64	42	1	35	2	18	3	18	14	.56	13	.305	.356	.359
1994	Vancouver	AAA	117	458	150	28	4	1	189	79	47	58	4	46	1	4	3	21	16	.57	7	.328	.402	.413
	4 Min. YEARS		445	1721	533	80	15	2	649	303	176	189	8	144	11	47	16	78	51	.60	33	.310	.378	.377

Jhonny Pantoja

Pitches: Right Bats: Right Pos: P Ht: 6'3" Wt: 190 Born: 02/24/78 Age: 17

			HOW MUCH HE PITCHED						WHAT HE GAVE UP									THE RESULTS				
Year	Team	Lg	G	GS	CG	GF	IP	BFP	H	R	ER	HR	SH	SF	HB	TBB	IBB	SO	WP	Bk	W	L	Pct.	ShO	Sv	ERA
1994	Albany-Colo	AA	12	12	0	0	65	285	73	44	33	5	0	3	1	24	0	52	3	3	3	7	.300	0	0	4.57

George Parker

Bats: Right Throws: Right Pos: SS Ht: 5'11" Wt: 165 Born: 05/27/72 Age: 23

					BATTING										BASERUNNING				PERCENTAGES		
Year	Team	Lg	G	AB	H	2B	3B	HR	TB	R	RBI	TBB	IBB	SO	HBP	SH	SF	SB	CS	SB%	GDP	Avg	OBP	SLG
1994	Lake Elsino	A	16	30	6	0	0	1	9	6	4	2	0	6	2	1	0	1	0	1.00	0	.200	.294	.300

Midland	AA	13	44	9	0	0	0	9	3	3	3	0	8	0	0	1	0	0	.00	0	.205	.250	.205
1 Min. YEARS		29	74	15	0	0	1	18	9	7	5	0	14	2	1	1	1	0	1.00	0	.203	.268	.243

Jose Parra

Pitches: Right Bats: Right Pos: P   Ht: 5'11" Wt: 160 Born: 11/28/72 Age: 22

			HOW MUCH HE PITCHED					WHAT HE GAVE UP										THE RESULTS					
Year	Team	Lg	G	GS	CG	GF	IP	BFP	H	R	ER	HR	SH	SF	HB	TBB	IBB	SO	WP	Bk	W	L	Pct.	ShO	Sv	ERA
1990	Dodgers	R	10	10	1	0	57.1	228	50	22	17	1	0	3	1	18	0	50	1	1	5	3	.625	0	0	2.67
1991	Great Falls	R	14	14	1	0	64.1	298	86	58	44	5	2	7	2	18	0	55	0	4	4	6	.400	1	0	6.16
1992	Bakersfield	A	24	23	3	0	143	618	151	73	57	5	4	4	4	47	4	107	5	1	7	8	.467	0	0	3.59
	San Antonio	AA	3	3	0	0	14.2	74	22	12	10	0	2	1	1	7	0	7	0	1	2	0	1.000	0	0	6.14
1993	San Antonio	AA	17	17	0	0	111.1	452	103	46	39	10	9	3	6	12	2	87	1	0	1	8	.111	0	0	3.15
1994	Albuquerque	AAA	27	27	1	0	145	636	190	92	77	10	4	4	5	38	2	90	10	0	10	10	.500	0	0	4.78
	5 Min. YEARS		95	94	6	0	535.2	2306	602	303	244	31	21	22	19	140	8	396	17	7	29	35	.453	1	0	4.10

Jeff Parrett

Pitches: Right Bats: Right Pos: P   Ht: 6' 3" Wt: 195 Born: 08/26/61 Age: 33

			HOW MUCH HE PITCHED					WHAT HE GAVE UP										THE RESULTS					
Year	Team	Lg	G	GS	CG	GF	IP	BFP	H	R	ER	HR	SH	SF	HB	TBB	IBB	SO	WP	Bk	W	L	Pct.	ShO	Sv	ERA
1984	Beloit	A	29	5	1	6	91.2	413	76	50	46	8	5	6	1	71	1	95	13	0	4	3	.571	1	2	4.52
1985	Stockton	A	45	2	0	21	127.2	0	97	50	39	5	0	0	1	75	2	120	7	2	7	4	.636	0	11	2.75
1986	Indianapolis	AAA	25	8	0	7	69	297	54	44	38	6	3	3	0	35	2	76	7	0	2	5	.286	0	2	4.96
1987	Indianapolis	AAA	20	0	0	19	22.1	91	15	5	5	0	1	0	0	13	0	17	3	0	2	1	.667	0	9	2.01
1991	Richmond	AAA	19	14	0	2	79.2	352	72	45	40	2	2	2	1	46	1	88	5	0	2	7	.222	0	0	4.52
1994	Royals	R	2	2	0	0	8	28	3	1	1	1	0	0	0	0	0	17	0	0	0	0	.000	0	0	1.13
	Wilmington	A	4	4	0	0	14	57	12	5	5	0	1	0	0	6	0	17	1	0	0	1	.000	0	0	3.21
	Omaha	AAA	12	4	0	3	38.2	164	34	21	17	2	0	1	4	14	0	35	4	0	0	3	.000	0	0	3.96
1986	Montreal	NL	12	0	0	6	20.1	91	19	11	11	3	0	1	0	13	0	21	2	0	0	1	.000	0	0	4.87
1987	Montreal	NL	45	0	0	26	62	267	53	33	29	8	5	1	0	30	4	56	6	1	7	6	.538	0	6	4.21
1988	Montreal	NL	61	0	0	34	91.2	369	66	29	27	8	9	6	1	45	9	62	4	1	12	4	.750	0	6	2.65
1989	Philadelphia	NL	72	0	0	34	105.2	444	90	43	35	6	7	5	0	44	13	98	7	3	12	6	.667	0	6	2.98
1990	Philadelphia	NL	47	5	0	14	81.2	355	92	51	47	10	3	1	1	36	8	69	3	1	4	9	.308	0	1	5.18
	Atlanta	NL	20	0	0	5	27	124	27	11	9	1	4	4	1	19	2	17	2	0	1	1	.500	0	1	3.00
1991	Atlanta	NL	18	0	0	9	21.1	109	31	18	15	2	2	0	0	12	2	14	4	0	1	2	.333	0	1	6.33
1992	Oakland	AL	66	0	0	14	98.1	410	81	35	33	7	4	4	2	42	3	78	13	0	9	1	.900	0	0	3.02
1993	Colorado	NL	40	6	0	13	73.2	341	78	47	44	6	4	5	2	45	9	66	11	1	3	3	.500	0	1	5.38
	6 Min. YEARS		156	39	1	58	451	1402	363	221	191	24	12	12	8	260	6	465	40	2	17	24	.415	1	24	3.81
	8 Maj. YEARS		381	11	0	155	581.2	2510	537	278	250	51	38	27	7	286	50	481	52	7	49	33	.598	0	22	3.87

Bronswell Patrick

Pitches: Right Bats: Right Pos: P   Ht: 6'1" Wt: 205 Born: 09/16/70 Age: 24

			HOW MUCH HE PITCHED					WHAT HE GAVE UP										THE RESULTS					
Year	Team	Lg	G	GS	CG	GF	IP	BFP	H	R	ER	HR	SH	SF	HB	TBB	IBB	SO	WP	Bk	W	L	Pct.	ShO	Sv	ERA
1988	Athletics	R	14	14	2	0	96.1	390	99	37	32	7	1	2	2	16	1	64	1	2	8	3	.727	0	0	2.99
1989	Madison	A	12	10	0	1	54.1	238	62	29	22	3	2	0	0	14	0	32	3	2	2	5	.286	0	0	3.64
1990	Modesto	A	14	14	0	0	74.2	340	92	58	43	10	3	1	4	32	0	37	5	1	3	7	.300	0	0	5.18
	Madison	A	13	12	3	0	80	337	88	44	32	6	5	4	1	19	0	40	3	0	3	7	.300	0	0	3.60
1991	Modesto	A	28	26	3	1	169.2	716	158	77	61	9	4	4	1	60	4	95	7	0	12	12	.500	1	0	3.24
1992	Huntsville	AA	29	29	3	0	179.1	758	187	84	75	20	1	3	4	46	0	98	3	0	13	7	.650	0	0	3.76
1993	Tacoma	AAA	35	13	1	12	104.2	496	156	87	82	12	3	12	4	42	3	56	3	0	3	8	.273	0	1	7.05
1994	Huntsville	AA	7	3	0	1	27.2	120	31	11	9	2	1	0	2	10	0	16	1	1	2	0	1.000	0	1	2.93
	Tacoma	AAA	30	0	0	9	47.1	208	50	31	25	5	3	1	0	20	2	38	2	0	1	1	.500	0	2	4.75
	7 Min. YEARS		182	120	12	24	834	3603	923	458	381	74	23	27	18	259	10	476	28	6	47	50	.485	1	4	4.11

Danny Patterson

Pitches: Right Bats: Right Pos: P   Ht: 6'0" Wt: 168 Born: 02/17/71 Age: 24

			HOW MUCH HE PITCHED					WHAT HE GAVE UP										THE RESULTS					
Year	Team	Lg	G	GS	CG	GF	IP	BFP	H	R	ER	HR	SH	SF	HB	TBB	IBB	SO	WP	Bk	W	L	Pct.	ShO	Sv	ERA
1990	Butte	R	13	3	0	2	28.1	135	36	23	20	3	0	3	1	14	1	18	3	1	0	3	.000	0	1	6.35
1991	Rangers	R	11	9	0	0	50	201	43	21	18	1	1	0	3	12	0	46	2	3	5	3	.625	0	0	3.24
1992	Gastonia	A	23	21	3	0	105.1	447	106	47	42	9	2	2	4	33	3	84	5	13	4	6	.400	1	0	3.59
1993	Charlotte	A	47	0	0	24	68	286	55	22	19	2	5	1	1	28	4	41	5	0	5	6	.455	0	7	2.51
1994	Charlotte	A	7	0	0	4	13.2	57	13	7	7	1	0	1	0	5	0	9	1	0	1	0	1.000	0	0	4.61
	Tulsa	AA	30	1	0	19	44	181	35	13	8	2	3	3	1	17	1	33	5	2	1	4	.200	0	6	1.64
	5 Min. YEARS		131	34	3	49	309.1	1307	288	133	114	18	11	10	10	109	9	231	21	19	16	22	.421	1	14	3.32

Jeff Patterson

Pitches: Right Bats: Right Pos: P   Ht: 6'2" Wt: 200 Born: 10/01/68 Age: 26

			HOW MUCH HE PITCHED					WHAT HE GAVE UP										THE RESULTS					
Year	Team	Lg	G	GS	CG	GF	IP	BFP	H	R	ER	HR	SH	SF	HB	TBB	IBB	SO	WP	Bk	W	L	Pct.	ShO	Sv	ERA
1989	Martinsville	R	7	7	0	0	42.1	171	35	23	17	3	0	0	2	12	0	44	3	4	2	4	.333	0	0	3.61
	Batavia	A	9	7	1	2	53.1	208	44	19	17	4	2	1	1	11	0	41	2	2	2	4	.333	1	1	2.87
1990	Clearwater	A	11	11	0	0	67	283	63	34	22	2	0	2	2	22	0	28	1	2	3	6	.333	0	0	2.96

194

Year	Team	Lg	G	GS	CG	GF	IP	BFP	H	R	ER	HR	SH	SF	HB	TBB	IBB	SO	WP	Bk	W	L	Pct.	ShO	Sv	ERA
1991	Spartanburg	A	35	10	2	22	114	480	103	60	56	7	4	7	4	41	0	114	2	0	9	8	.529	1	9	4.42
1992	Clearwater	A	30	0	0	22	36.1	148	29	11	8	0	1	0	2	11	2	33	3	1	2	1	.667	0	14	1.98
	Reading	AA	26	0	0	21	31.1	133	30	16	16	2	1	2	2	14	2	22	2	0	3	1	.750	0	13	4.60
	Scranton/wb	AAA	11	0	0	10	13.2	58	10	4	4	0	1	1	0	8	3	11	2	1	2	1	.667	0	1	2.63
1993	Scranton/wb	AAA	62	0	0	31	93.2	390	79	32	28	3	8	3	2	42	11	68	8	1	7	5	.583	0	8	2.69
1994	Scranton-Wb	AAA	52	2	0	32	94	420	102	50	48	8	4	0	5	48	8	64	7	0	6	4	.600	0	5	4.60
	6 Min. YEARS		243	37	3	140	545.2	2291	495	249	216	29	21	16	18	209	26	425	30	11	36	34	.514	2	51	3.56

Dave Paveloff

Pitches: Right Bats: Right Pos: P Ht: 6'2" Wt: 190 Born: 12/06/67 Age: 27

			HOW MUCH HE PITCHED						WHAT HE GAVE UP												THE RESULTS					
Year	Team	Lg	G	GS	CG	GF	IP	BFP	H	R	ER	HR	SH	SF	HB	TBB	IBB	SO	WP	Bk	W	L	Pct.	ShO	Sv	ERA
1990	Wausau	A	28	1	0	11	57.1	245	51	29	19	4	4	1	1	20	2	44	2	1	2	3	.400	0	1	2.98
1991	Kane County	A	35	0	0	21	52.2	220	50	22	21	3	1	3	1	16	1	54	3	0	6	1	.857	0	8	3.59
	Frederick	A	5	0	0	1	6.1	28	7	2	2	2	0	0	0	2	0	8	1	0	0	0	.000	0	0	2.84
1992	Frederick	A	51	0	0	37	82.1	335	62	28	22	3	6	2	1	31	2	54	5	0	2	1	.667	0	16	2.40
1993	Frederick	A	24	0	0	22	24.2	102	16	4	2	2	1	0	2	8	1	28	1	0	2	1	.667	0	15	0.73
	Bowie	AA	32	0	0	21	57.1	241	50	21	11	1	3	1	1	19	3	31	1	2	5	4	.556	0	1	1.73
1994	Bowie	AA	35	1	0	11	60.1	256	66	26	25	5	3	1	1	17	0	38	2	1	3	3	.500	0	3	3.73
	5 Min. YEARS		210	2	0	124	341	1429	302	132	102	20	18	8	7	113	9	257	15	4	20	13	.606	0	41	2.69

Darrin Paxton

Pitches: Left Bats: Right Pos: P Ht: 6'4" Wt: 220 Born: 04/17/70 Age: 25

			HOW MUCH HE PITCHED						WHAT HE GAVE UP												THE RESULTS					
Year	Team	Lg	G	GS	CG	GF	IP	BFP	H	R	ER	HR	SH	SF	HB	TBB	IBB	SO	WP	Bk	W	L	Pct.	ShO	Sv	ERA
1991	Jamestown	A	13	6	0	1	58.1	230	37	13	13	2	1	1	3	27	1	62	2	0	5	1	.833	0	0	2.01
1992	Albany	A	33	15	2	5	129.1	545	102	56	43	8	2	2	1	62	4	120	9	3	6	9	.400	1	0	2.99
1993	Burlington	A	41	3	0	8	75	317	57	28	24	5	3	3	8	34	1	110	4	0	6	1	.857	0	1	2.88
1994	High Desert	A	12	12	0	0	76.2	311	64	38	37	9	2	3	1	18	0	70	3	1	5	3	.625	1	0	4.34
	Harrisburg	AA	17	15	1	0	83.2	360	83	39	35	7	2	1	2	37	0	80	2	0	4	6	.400	0	0	3.76
	4 Min. YEARS		116	51	5	14	423	1763	343	174	152	31	10	10	15	178	6	442	20	4	26	20	.565	2	1	3.23

Jason Payton

Bats: Right Throws: Right Pos: OF Ht: 5'11" Wt: 190 Born: 11/22/72 Age: 22

			BATTING															BASERUNNING				PERCENTAGES		
Year	Team	Lg	G	AB	H	2B	3B	HR	TB	R	RBI	TBB	IBB	SO	HBP	SH	SF	SB	CS	SB%	GDP	Avg	OBP	SLG
1994	Pittsfield	A	58	219	80	16	2	3	109	47	37	23	2	18	9	0	4	10	2	.83	1	.365	.439	.498
	Binghamton	AA	8	25	7	1	0	0	8	3	1	2	0	3	1	0	0	1	1	.50	1	.280	.357	.320
	1 Min. YEARS		66	244	87	17	2	3	117	50	38	25	2	21	10	0	4	11	3	.79	2	.357	.431	.480

Steve Peck

Pitches: Right Bats: Right Pos: P Ht: 6'3" Wt: 190 Born: 11/20/67 Age: 27

			HOW MUCH HE PITCHED						WHAT HE GAVE UP												THE RESULTS					
Year	Team	Lg	G	GS	CG	GF	IP	BFP	H	R	ER	HR	SH	SF	HB	TBB	IBB	SO	WP	Bk	W	L	Pct.	ShO	Sv	ERA
1989	Athletics	R	12	1	0	6	23.2	99	21	10	8	1	0	1	1	7	0	22	0	0	1	3	.250	0	1	3.04
1990	Madison	A	5	4	0	1	22.1	97	24	15	13	3	2	1	1	9	1	14	0	0	2	2	.500	0	0	5.24
	Modesto	A	30	2	0	10	58.2	255	58	29	27	6	4	1	2	27	3	46	5	0	4	2	.667	0	3	4.14
1991	Palm Sprngs	A	17	8	0	3	69	278	57	28	16	2	2	3	1	16	0	67	3	0	6	4	.600	0	1	2.09
1992	Midland	A	43	7	0	16	111.1	448	105	54	49	9	4	5	4	22	1	87	6	0	8	6	.571	0	0	3.96
1993	Vancouver	AAA	31	7	0	5	72.1	333	91	47	39	4	2	3	4	29	2	47	3	2	5	3	.625	0	0	4.85
1994	El Paso	AA	29	19	0	4	121.1	531	132	75	67	11	7	5	7	50	2	72	4	0	12	4	.750	0	1	4.97
	6 Min. YEARS		167	48	0	45	478.2	2041	488	257	219	36	21	19	20	160	9	355	21	2	38	24	.613	0	6	4.12

Rod Pedraza

Pitches: Right Bats: Right Pos: P Ht: 6'2" Wt: 210 Born: 12/28/69 Age: 25

			HOW MUCH HE PITCHED						WHAT HE GAVE UP												THE RESULTS					
Year	Team	Lg	G	GS	CG	GF	IP	BFP	H	R	ER	HR	SH	SF	HB	TBB	IBB	SO	WP	Bk	W	L	Pct.	ShO	Sv	ERA
1991	Jamestown	A	7	7	1	0	44	182	41	16	10	3	0	1	1	6	0	30	2	1	3	1	.750	1	0	2.05
	Sumter	A	8	8	1	0	49	212	61	29	24	3	0	3	1	10	0	22	5	1	2	2	.500	0	0	4.41
1992	Albany	A	27	26	2	0	176.2	742	187	90	64	7	4	8	9	30	0	106	10	5	13	8	.619	0	0	3.26
1993	San Berndno	A	24	23	2	0	141.2	601	145	74	50	7	4	7	3	33	1	95	9	0	9	7	.563	1	0	3.18
1994	Colo. Sprng	AAA	7	7	0	0	33	175	60	37	34	2	0	3	2	13	0	20	3	0	1	3	.250	0	0	9.27
	New Haven	AA	22	20	4	0	127.2	528	129	59	46	2	5	3	3	23	2	58	0	1	13	3	.813	2	0	3.24
	4 Min. YEARS		95	91	10	0	572	2440	623	305	228	24	13	25	19	115	3	331	29	8	41	24	.631	4	0	3.59

Jorge Pedre

Bats: Right Throws: Right Pos: C Ht: 5'11" Wt: 205 Born: 10/12/66 Age: 28

			BATTING															BASERUNNING				PERCENTAGES		
Year	Team	Lg	G	AB	H	2B	3B	HR	TB	R	RBI	TBB	IBB	SO	HBP	SH	SF	SB	CS	SB%	GDP	Avg	OBP	SLG
1987	Eugene	A	64	233	63	15	0	13	117	28	66	16	2	48	12	0	1	2	1	.67	10	.270	.347	.502
1988	Appleton	A	111	412	112	20	2	6	154	44	54	23	1	76	4	0	6	4	2	.67	7	.272	.312	.374
1989	Baseball Cy	A	55	208	68	17	2	5	104	39	40	13	1	31	4	0	3	1	2	.33	2	.327	.373	.500
	Memphis	AA	38	141	33	5	0	2	44	17	16	9	0	18	0	1	2	0	0	.00	4	.234	.276	.312
1990	Memphis	AA	99	360	93	14	1	9	136	55	54	27	1	47	6	0	7	6	1	.86	17	.258	.315	.378

195

Year	Team	Lg	G	AB	H	2B	3B	HR	TB	R	RBI	TBB	IBB	SO	HBP	SH	SF	SB	CS	SB%	GDP	Avg	OBP	SLG
1991	Memphis	AA	100	363	92	28	1	9	149	43	59	24	4	72	7	1	3	1	2	.33	7	.253	.310	.410
	Omaha	AAA	31	116	25	4	0	1	32	12	4	4	0	18	0	0	0	2	1	.67	1	.216	.242	.276
1992	Iowa	AAA	98	296	75	17	1	6	112	31	34	26	1	62	1	5	1	2	0	1.00	10	.253	.315	.378
1993	Iowa	AAA	68	232	49	12	1	7	84	27	21	13	0	47	2	5	1	2	1	.67	5	.211	.258	.362
1994	New Britain	AA	11	38	7	0	0	0	7	2	3	2	0	2	0	0	1	0	3	.00	1	.184	.220	.184
	Pawtucket	AAA	64	197	43	9	0	5	67	22	25	8	0	34	1	3	1	0	0	.00	7	.218	.251	.340
1991	Kansas City	AL	10	19	5	1	1	0	8	2	3	3	0	5	0	0	0	0	0	.00	0	.263	.364	.421
1992	Chicago	NL	4	4	0	0	0	0	0	0	0	0	0	1	0	0	0	0	0	.00	0	.000	.000	.000
	8 Min. YEARS		739	2596	660	141	8	63	1006	320	376	165	10	455	37	15	26	20	13	.61	72	.254	.305	.388
	2 Maj. YEARS		14	23	5	1	1	0	8	2	3	3	0	6	0	0	0	0	0	.00	0	.217	.308	.348

Al Pedrique

Bats: Right **Throws:** Right **Pos:** 3B **Ht:** 6' 0" **Wt:** 155 **Born:** 08/11/60 **Age:** 34

			BATTING															BASERUNNING				PERCENTAGES		
Year	Team	Lg	G	AB	H	2B	3B	HR	TB	R	RBI	TBB	IBB	SO	HBP	SH	SF	SB	CS	SB%	GDP	Avg	OBP	SLG
1984	Jackson	AA	109	362	103	15	5	1	131	47	35	37	2	32	6	9	1	3	2	.60	13	.285	.360	.362
1985	Tidewater	AAA	110	325	82	17	2	2	109	39	24	24	1	28	3	7	1	2	6	.25	7	.252	.309	.335
1986	Tidewater	AAA	112	379	111	13	2	0	128	49	41	28	1	31	2	9	8	7	0	1.00	15	.293	.338	.338
1987	Tidewater	AAA	10	27	7	0	0	0	7	2	3	0	0	6	0	0	1	0	1	.00	0	.259	.250	.259
1988	Buffalo	AAA	61	218	67	14	2	1	88	23	22	13	0	20	4	1	2	0	5	.00	3	.307	.354	.404
1989	Toledo	AAA	56	193	40	8	0	1	51	15	21	16	0	32	3	3	1	2	1	.67	3	.207	.277	.264
1990	Tacoma	AAA	123	380	99	16	2	0	119	54	46	49	0	37	3	8	6	3	4	.43	8	.261	.345	.313
1991	Tidewater	AAA	79	182	49	6	0	0	55	24	12	23	2	19	3	7	1	2	0	1.00	5	.269	.359	.302
1992	Omaha	AAA	66	198	42	3	0	0	45	11	9	10	0	25	2	3	1	5	3	.63	5	.212	.256	.227
1993	Edmonton	AAA	121	403	123	14	1	2	145	54	42	44	4	43	7	8	4	5	6	.45	13	.305	.380	.360
1994	Edmonton	AAA	74	228	53	9	0	0	62	21	17	33	4	32	3	2	4	0	2	.00	11	.232	.332	.272
1987	New York	NL	5	6	0	0	0	0	0	1	0	1	0	2	0	0	0	0	0	.00	0	.000	.143	.000
	Pittsburgh	NL	88	246	74	10	1	1	89	23	27	18	4	27	3	6	1	5	4	.56	7	.301	.354	.362
1988	Pittsburgh	NL	50	128	23	5	0	0	28	7	4	8	2	17	1	0	0	0	0	.00	4	.180	.234	.219
1989	Detroit	AL	31	69	14	3	0	0	17	1	5	2	0	15	0	0	0	0	0	.00	5	.203	.225	.246
	11 Min. YEARS		921	2895	776	115	14	7	940	339	272	277	14	305	36	57	30	29	30	.49	86	.268	.336	.325
	3 Maj. YEARS		174	449	111	18	1	1	134	32	36	29	6	61	4	6	1	5	4	.56	16	.247	.298	.298

Tim Peek

Pitches: Right **Bats:** Right **Pos:** P **Ht:** 6'2" **Wt:** 210 **Born:** 01/23/68 **Age:** 27

			HOW MUCH HE PITCHED					WHAT HE GAVE UP										THE RESULTS					
Year	Team	Lg	G	GS	CG	GF	IP	BFP	H	R	ER	HR	SH	SF	HB	TBB	IBB	SO	WP	Bk	W	L	Pct.	ShO	Sv	ERA
1987	Utica	A	4	4	0	0	25.2	100	20	4	4	0	1	1	0	7	0	13	2	0	1	1	.500	0	0	1.40
	Spartanburg	A	10	9	1	0	56	228	50	24	20	6	3	1	1	16	0	39	2	1	2	3	.400	0	0	3.21
1988	Spartanburg	A	37	4	0	23	105.2	417	77	26	22	6	5	3	5	30	0	80	8	3	6	3	.667	0	9	1.87
1989	Clearwater	A	8	0	0	4	18.1	87	23	13	12	1	1	0	1	6	0	13	0	0	1	0	1.000	0	0	5.89
	Spartanburg	A	19	1	0	13	45.1	192	32	15	10	4	1	1	3	20	1	42	1	1	3	1	.750	0	3	1.99
1990	Madison	A	39	0	0	30	56.2	223	41	19	17	4	3	1	1	10	2	70	0	1	5	3	.625	0	7	2.70
1991	Huntsville	AA	56	0	0	49	66.1	279	65	31	24	5	7	2	1	15	3	52	2	0	2	4	.333	0	26	3.26
1992	Tacoma	AAA	57	0	0	23	87.2	379	87	38	29	7	7	1	4	37	9	52	1	0	4	3	.571	0	3	2.98
1993	Tacoma	AAA	60	0	0	25	86.2	389	103	46	38	8	7	6	5	28	5	63	0	1	9	6	.600	0	5	3.95
1994	Memphis	AA	26	1	0	10	50	191	38	16	14	2	2	2	1	12	2	27	1	0	6	4	.600	0	2	2.52
	Omaha	AAA	9	2	0	1	21.2	97	25	18	15	5	1	0	2	8	0	9	1	0	0	2	.000	0	0	6.23
	8 Min. YEARS		325	21	1	178	620	2582	561	250	205	48	38	18	24	189	22	460	18	7	39	30	.565	0	53	2.98

Lloyd Peever

Pitches: Right **Bats:** Right **Pos:** P **Ht:** 5'11" **Wt:** 185 **Born:** 09/15/71 **Age:** 23

			HOW MUCH HE PITCHED					WHAT HE GAVE UP										THE RESULTS					
Year	Team	Lg	G	GS	CG	GF	IP	BFP	H	R	ER	HR	SH	SF	HB	TBB	IBB	SO	WP	Bk	W	L	Pct.	ShO	Sv	ERA
1992	Bend	A	11	8	0	0	43.1	180	44	18	14	2	1	2	0	10	0	48	3	0	3	2	.600	0	1	2.91
1993	Central Val	A	16	7	1	6	66.2	278	65	31	31	6	0	2	1	17	0	69	5	0	2	4	.333	1	4	4.18
1994	New Haven	AA	23	21	3	1	131.1	536	109	59	50	8	6	5	3	37	1	126	3	2	9	8	.529	2	1	3.43
	3 Min. YEARS		50	36	4	9	241.1	994	218	108	95	16	7	9	6	64	1	243	11	2	14	14	.500	3	6	3.54

Dan Peltier

Bats: Left **Throws:** Left **Pos:** OF **Ht:** 6' 1" **Wt:** 205 **Born:** 06/30/68 **Age:** 27

			BATTING															BASERUNNING				PERCENTAGES		
Year	Team	Lg	G	AB	H	2B	3B	HR	TB	R	RBI	TBB	IBB	SO	HBP	SH	SF	SB	CS	SB%	GDP	Avg	OBP	SLG
1989	Butte	R	33	122	49	7	1	7	79	35	28	25	2	16	1	0	0	10	1	.91	4	.402	.507	.648
1990	Tulsa	AA	117	448	125	19	4	11	185	66	57	40	2	67	6	1	2	8	6	.57	8	.279	.345	.413
1991	Okla City	AAA	94	345	79	16	4	3	112	38	31	43	2	71	0	2	2	6	5	.55	8	.229	.313	.325
1992	Okla City	AAA	125	450	133	30	7	7	198	65	53	60	3	72	3	3	1	1	7	.13	14	.296	.381	.440
1993	Okla City	AAA	48	187	60	15	4	5	98	28	33	19	4	27	0	0	2	2	2	.50	4	.321	.380	.524
1994	Okla City	AAA	125	418	112	21	4	9	168	62	60	51	3	86	4	2	4	5	3	.63	16	.268	.350	.402
1992	Texas	AL	12	24	4	0	0	0	4	1	2	0	0	3	0	0	0	0	0	.00	0	.167	.167	.167
1993	Texas	AL	65	160	43	7	1	0	55	23	17	20	0	27	1	1	1	0	4	.00	3	.269	.352	.344
	6 Min. YEARS		542	1970	558	108	24	42	840	294	262	238	16	339	14	8	11	32	24	.57	54	.283	.363	.426
	2 Maj. YEARS		77	184	47	7	1	0	59	24	19	20	0	30	1	1	1	0	4	.00	3	.255	.330	.321

Kurt Peltzer

Pitches: Left Bats: Right Pos: P Ht: 6'3" Wt: 190 Born: 01/13/69 Age: 26

		HOW MUCH HE PITCHED						WHAT HE GAVE UP											THE RESULTS				
Year	Team	Lg	G	GS	CG	GF	IP	BFP	H	R	ER	HR	SH	SF	HB	TBB	IBB	SO	WP	Bk	W	L	Pct.	ShO	Sv	ERA
1990	Everett	A	18	5	0	4	48	231	58	30	23	2	2	3	1	23	1	39	5	0	3	1	.750	0	0	4.31
1991	Shreveport	AA	5	0	0	3	6.1	39	13	9	6	0	2	0	0	7	1	1	0	0	0	1	.000	0	0	8.53
	Clinton	A	27	0	0	14	42	176	38	21	20	3	2	1	0	17	3	33	6	1	3	3	.500	0	2	4.29
1992	Clinton	A	7	0	0	1	12.1	47	5	2	2	1	0	0	1	4	0	13	0	0	1	0	1.000	0	0	1.46
	San Jose	A	46	0	0	22	83.2	359	74	35	24	4	5	3	7	35	4	66	3	1	2	2	.500	0	5	2.58
1993	San Jose	A	17	0	0	9	27.2	120	28	16	9	3	0	3	0	8	0	20	3	0	2	3	.400	0	3	2.93
	Shreveport	AA	30	0	0	15	42.1	166	33	16	15	2	2	0	3	9	0	28	0	0	4	3	.571	0	1	3.19
	Phoenix	AAA	12	0	0	8	16	72	16	13	12	0	0	1	1	7	3	16	0	0	2	0	1.000	0	2	6.75
1994	Shreveport	AA	39	0	0	25	76	311	70	29	24	4	2	3	3	13	0	46	5	0	4	5	.444	0	1	2.84
	5 Min. YEARS		201	5	0	101	354.1	1521	335	171	135	19	15	14	16	123	12	262	22	2	21	18	.538	0	14	3.43

Rudy Pemberton

Bats: Right Throws: Right Pos: OF Ht: 6'1" Wt: 185 Born: 12/17/69 Age: 25

		BATTING												BASERUNNING					PERCENTAGES					
Year	Team	Lg	G	AB	H	2B	3B	HR	TB	R	RBI	TBB	IBB	SO	HBP	SH	SF	SB	CS	SB%	GDP	Avg	OBP	SLG	
1988	Bristol	R	6	5	0	0	0	0	0	2	0	1	0	3	2	0	0	0	0	.00	1	.000	.375	.000	
1989	Bristol	R	56	214	58	9	2	6	89	40	39	14	0	43	4	0	1	19	3	.86	3	.271	.326	.416	
1990	Fayetteville	A	127	454	126	14	5	6	168	60	61	42	1	91	12	1	9	12	9	.57	12	.278	.348	.370	
1991	Lakeland	A	111	375	86	15	2	3	114	40	36	25	2	51	9	6	2	25	15	.63	5	.229	.292	.304	
1992	Lakeland	A	104	343	91	16	5	3	126	41	43	21	2	37	13	2	3	25	10	.71	4	.265	.329	.367	
1993	London	AA	124	471	130	22	4	15	205	70	67	24	1	80	12	0	3	14	12	.54	11	.276	.325	.435	
1994	Toledo	AAA	99	360	109	13	3	12	164	49	58	18	3	62	6	0	6	30	9	.77	8	.303	.341	.456	
	7 Min. YEARS		627	2222	600	89	21	45	866	302	304	145	9	367	58	9	24	125	58	.68	44	.270	.328	.390	

Shannon Penn

Bats: Both Throws: Right Pos: 2B Ht: 5'10" Wt: 163 Born: 09/11/69 Age: 25

		BATTING												BASERUNNING					PERCENTAGES					
Year	Team	Lg	G	AB	H	2B	3B	HR	TB	R	RBI	TBB	IBB	SO	HBP	SH	SF	SB	CS	SB%	GDP	Avg	OBP	SLG	
1989	Rangers	R	47	147	32	2	1	0	36	19	8	20	0	27	1	0	1	17	7	.71	1	.218	.314	.245	
1990	Butte	R	60	197	64	4	2	0	72	38	18	15	0	35	1	0	2	9	4	.69	0	.325	.372	.365	
1992	Niagara Fls	A	70	253	69	9	2	3	91	47	25	28	2	53	6	3	1	31	10	.76	2	.273	.358	.360	
1993	London	AA	128	493	128	12	6	0	152	78	36	54	1	95	8	7	4	53	16	.77	4	.260	.340	.308	
1994	Toledo	AAA	114	444	126	14	6	2	158	63	33	30	0	96	5	4	4	45	16	.74	4	.284	.333	.356	
	5 Min. YEARS		419	1534	419	41	17	5	509	245	120	147	3	306	21	14	12	155	53	.75	11	.273	.342	.332	

Troy Percival

Pitches: Right Bats: Right Pos: P Ht: 6'3" Wt: 200 Born: 08/09/69 Age: 25

		HOW MUCH HE PITCHED						WHAT HE GAVE UP											THE RESULTS				
Year	Team	Lg	G	GS	CG	GF	IP	BFP	H	R	ER	HR	SH	SF	HB	TBB	IBB	SO	WP	Bk	W	L	Pct.	ShO	Sv	ERA
1991	Boise	A	28	0	0	20	38.1	157	23	7	6	0	1	2	2	18	1	63	9	0	2	0	1.000	0	12	1.41
1992	Palm Sprngs	A	11	0	0	9	10.2	45	6	7	6	0	0	3	2	8	1	16	1	1	1	1	.500	0	2	5.06
	Midland	AA	20	0	0	17	19	84	18	5	5	1	0	1	1	11	1	21	1	0	3	0	1.000	0	5	2.37
1993	Vancouver	AAA	18	0	0	11	18.2	94	24	14	13	0	1	3	2	13	1	19	2	0	0	1	.000	0	4	6.27
1994	Vancouver	AAA	49	0	0	32	61	266	63	31	28	4	6	3	7	29	5	73	6	2	2	6	.250	0	15	4.13
	4 Min. YEARS		126	0	0	89	147.2	646	134	64	58	5	8	12	14	79	9	192	19	3	8	8	.500	0	38	3.53

Carlos Perez

Pitches: Left Bats: Left Pos: P Ht: 6'3" Wt: 200 Born: 04/14/71 Age: 24

		HOW MUCH HE PITCHED						WHAT HE GAVE UP											THE RESULTS				
Year	Team	Lg	G	GS	CG	GF	IP	BFP	H	R	ER	HR	SH	SF	HB	TBB	IBB	SO	WP	Bk	W	L	Pct.	ShO	Sv	ERA
1990	Expos	R	13	2	0	6	35.2	145	24	14	10	0	1	1	1	15	0	38	1	0	3	1	.750	0	2	2.52
1991	Sumter	A	16	12	0	2	73.2	306	57	29	20	3	0	7	0	32	0	69	3	1	2	2	.500	0	0	2.44
1992	Rockford	A	7	1	0	2	9.1	43	12	7	6	3	1	0	1	5	0	8	1	0	0	1	.000	0	1	5.79
1993	Burlington	A	12	1	0	5	16.2	69	13	6	6	0	3	0	0	9	0	21	0	1	1	0	1.000	0	0	3.24
	San Berndno	A	20	18	3	0	131	550	120	57	50	12	3	2	0	44	0	98	9	6	8	7	.533	0	0	3.44
1994	Harrisburg	AA	12	11	2	1	79	307	55	27	17	5	3	0	2	18	0	69	5	0	7	2	.778	2	1	1.94
	Ottawa	AAA	17	17	3	0	119	511	130	50	44	8	5	3	3	41	2	82	4	1	7	5	.583	0	0	3.33
	5 Min. YEARS		97	62	8	16	464.1	1931	411	190	153	31	16	13	7	164	2	385	23	9	28	18	.609	2	4	2.97

Cesar Perez

Pitches: Right Bats: Right Pos: P Ht: 5'11" Wt: 175 Born: 08/13/70 Age: 24

		HOW MUCH HE PITCHED						WHAT HE GAVE UP											THE RESULTS				
Year	Team	Lg	G	GS	CG	GF	IP	BFP	H	R	ER	HR	SH	SF	HB	TBB	IBB	SO	WP	Bk	W	L	Pct.	ShO	Sv	ERA
1988	Yankees	R	6	0	0	1	7	30	5	3	2	0	1	0	0	2	1	6	0	0	0	1	.000	0	0	2.57
1989	Yankees	R	11	3	0	6	25	99	13	8	8	1	2	0	3	9	0	23	1	0	1	0	1.000	0	3	2.88
1990	Greensboro	A	13	0	0	7	20	77	18	13	7	0	0	1	0	12	0	27	6	0	0	0	.000	0	0	3.15
	Oneonta	A	28	0	0	15	28.2	122	21	12	10	3	0	1	0	17	0	32	4	0	2	2	.500	0	2	3.14
1991	Greensboro	A	30	0	0	24	37.1	161	26	17	11	4	0	1	3	20	0	48	7	5	1	1	.500	0	1	2.65
1992	Ft. Laud	A	33	1	0	15	70	277	44	25	21	1	2	2	3	30	4	79	1	3	4	2	.667	0	2	2.70

Year	Team	Lg	G	GS	CG	GF	IP	BFP	H	R	ER	HR	SH	SF	HB	TBB	IBB	SO	WP	Bk	W	L	Pct.	ShO	Sv	ERA
1993	Kinston	A	10	0	0	3	13.1	53	7	4	4	0	0	1	0	7	0	20	0	1	0	0	.000	0	0	2.70
	Columbus	A	45	0	0	45	46	177	21	4	3	1	0	0	0	19	0	50	3	0	0	0	.000	0	35	0.59
1994	Canton-Akrn	AA	7	0	0	3	7.1	36	9	10	8	3	0	0	0	8	0	5	0	0	0	1	.000	0	0	9.82
	7 Min. YEARS		183	4	0	119	254.2	1046	164	96	74	13	5	5	10	124	5	290	22	9	8	7	.533	0	43	2.62

Danny Perez

Bats: Right Throws: Right Pos: OF Ht: 5'10" Wt: 188 Born: 02/26/71 Age: 24

						BATTING												BASERUNNING				PERCENTAGES		
Year	Team	Lg	G	AB	H	2B	3B	HR	TB	R	RBI	TBB	IBB	SO	HBP	SH	SF	SB	CS	SB%	GDP	Avg	OBP	SLG
1992	Helena	R	33	104	22	3	0	1	28	12	13	10	0	17	1	1	0	3	0	1.00	5	.212	.287	.269
1993	Beloit	A	106	377	113	17	6	10	172	70	59	56	0	64	5	1	2	23	8	.74	6	.300	.395	.456
	Stockton	A	10	24	7	3	1	0	12	4	0	2	0	5	0	0	0	2	1	.67	2	.292	.346	.500
1994	Stockton	A	9	33	9	0	0	0	9	7	3	7	0	7	0	0	0	2	2	.50	0	.273	.400	.273
	El Paso	AA	115	440	143	19	17	6	214	88	73	45	1	79	5	1	3	9	5	.64	11	.325	.391	.486
	3 Min. YEARS		273	978	294	42	24	17	435	181	148	120	1	172	11	3	5	39	16	.71	22	.301	.382	.445

David Perez

Pitches: Right Bats: Right Pos: P Ht: 5'11" Wt: 170 Born: 05/23/68 Age: 27

			HOW MUCH HE PITCHED						WHAT HE GAVE UP										THE RESULTS					
Year	Team	Lg	G	GS	CG	GF	IP	BFP	H	R	ER	HR	SH	SF	HB	TBB	IBB	SO	WP	Bk	W	L	Pct.	ShO	Sv	ERA
1989	Butte	R	17	4	1	3	54	242	57	30	15	2	1	2	2	19	0	45	0	0	3	2	.600	0	1	2.50
1990	Charlotte	A	14	14	0	0	83.1	339	63	35	31	3	2	4	3	28	0	83	2	1	6	4	.600	0	0	3.35
1991	Tulsa	AA	25	24	4	0	147	619	130	76	69	11	5	2	4	69	3	97	5	3	5	14	.263	2	0	4.22
1992	Charlotte	A	13	7	1	5	59.1	227	44	14	14	3	1	0	1	15	2	31	2	1	5	2	.714	1	3	2.12
	Tulsa	AA	15	11	1	1	59.2	258	61	36	31	5	2	2	2	26	1	30	6	0	4	3	.571	0	0	4.68
1993	Tulsa	AA	33	14	1	6	125.1	520	119	64	56	11	3	3	7	34	7	111	3	1	9	10	.474	0	2	4.02
	Okla City	AAA	2	1	0	0	7.1	34	8	10	10	1	0	1	0	4	0	3	2	0	1	0	1.000	0	0	12.27
1994	Okla City	AAA	30	25	4	3	177	747	190	85	80	16	3	3	7	56	2	93	11	7	11	14	.440	1	0	4.07
	6 Min. YEARS		149	100	12	18	713	2986	672	350	306	52	17	17	26	251	15	493	31	13	44	49	.473	4	6	3.86

Eddie Perez

Bats: Right Throws: Right Pos: 1B Ht: 6'1" Wt: 175 Born: 05/04/68 Age: 27

						BATTING												BASERUNNING				PERCENTAGES		
Year	Team	Lg	G	AB	H	2B	3B	HR	TB	R	RBI	TBB	IBB	SO	HBP	SH	SF	SB	CS	SB%	GDP	Avg	OBP	SLG
1987	Braves	R	31	89	18	1	0	1	22	8	5	8	0	14	1	1	1	0	0	.00	4	.202	.273	.247
1988	Burlington	A	64	186	43	8	0	4	63	14	19	10	0	33	0	2	1	1	0	1.00	6	.231	.269	.339
1989	Sumter	A	114	401	93	21	0	5	129	39	44	44	1	68	5	4	5	2	6	.25	10	.232	.312	.322
1990	Sumter	A	41	123	22	7	1	3	40	11	17	14	0	18	2	3	1	0	0	.00	7	.179	.271	.325
	Durham	A	31	93	22	1	0	3	32	9	10	1	0	12	1	0	1	0	0	.00	3	.237	.250	.344
1991	Durham	A	91	277	75	10	1	9	114	38	41	17	2	33	3	2	3	0	3	.00	1	.271	.317	.412
	Greenville	AA	1	4	1	0	0	0	1	0	0	0	0	1	0	0	0	0	0	.00	1	.250	.250	.250
1992	Greenville	AA	91	275	63	16	0	6	97	28	41	24	0	41	2	1	4	3	3	.50	11	.229	.292	.353
1993	Greenville	AA	28	84	28	6	0	6	52	15	17	2	0	8	0	0	2	1	1	1.00	4	.333	.341	.619
1994	Richmond	AAA	113	388	101	16	2	9	148	37	49	18	1	47	3	3	6	1	1	.50	4	.260	.294	.381
	8 Min. YEARS		605	1920	466	86	4	46	698	199	243	138	4	275	17	16	24	8	13	.38	57	.243	.296	.364

Vladimir Perez

Pitches: Right Bats: Right Pos: P Ht: 6'1" Wt: 180 Born: 03/08/69 Age: 26

			HOW MUCH HE PITCHED						WHAT HE GAVE UP										THE RESULTS					
Year	Team	Lg	G	GS	CG	GF	IP	BFP	H	R	ER	HR	SH	SF	HB	TBB	IBB	SO	WP	Bk	W	L	Pct.	ShO	Sv	ERA
1986	Utica	A	13	8	0	1	45	220	59	39	35	3	0	2	2	29	0	25	2	1	2	5	.286	0	0	7.00
1987	Spartanburg	A	46	1	0	17	74.1	337	81	46	36	9	2	2	1	42	4	50	2	0	3	2	.600	0	5	4.36
1988	Little Fls	A	17	12	4	4	76	340	78	46	39	3	1	4	3	25	0	53	7	2	6	5	.545	0	0	4.62
1989	Columbia	A	25	8	0	13	81.1	336	66	32	27	3	4	3	1	34	1	63	4	1	3	5	.375	0	5	2.99
1990	St. Lucie	A	19	0	0	14	36.2	160	34	15	14	2	2	1	1	20	2	41	1	1	2	2	.500	0	5	3.44
	Jackson	AA	26	0	0	5	49	204	42	16	12	2	7	3	1	19	1	33	1	0	2	1	.667	0	0	2.20
1991	Shreveport	AA	27	0	0	11	43	181	40	16	16	0	2	2	0	19	1	22	0	1	1	1	.500	0	1	3.35
1992	Baseball Cy	A	20	0	0	17	36.1	155	23	14	8	1	4	3	0	17	4	23	5	0	3	3	.500	0	4	1.98
	Memphis	AA	32	1	0	6	70	302	71	26	20	3	2	1	2	24	0	48	3	2	3	3	.500	0	1	2.57
1993	Memphis	AA	18	1	1	9	42	172	37	15	14	2	0	3	1	11	0	35	2	0	1	0	1.000	1	3	3.00
1994	Memphis	AA	3	0	0	3	5.1	22	4	3	3	0	0	0	0	2	0	4	1	0	0	0	.000	0	0	5.06
	9 Min. YEARS		246	31	5	100	559	2429	535	268	224	28	24	24	12	242	13	397	28	8	26	27	.491	1	24	3.61

Tony Perezchica

Bats: Right Throws: Right Pos: 2B Ht: 5'11" Wt: 165 Born: 04/20/66 Age: 29

						BATTING												BASERUNNING				PERCENTAGES		
Year	Team	Lg	G	AB	H	2B	3B	HR	TB	R	RBI	TBB	IBB	SO	HBP	SH	SF	SB	CS	SB%	GDP	Avg	OBP	SLG
1984	Everett	A	33	119	23	6	1	0	31	10	10	6	0	24	1	1	2	0	0	.00	4	.193	.234	.261
1985	Clinton	A	127	452	109	21	8	4	158	54	40	28	0	77	9	6	5	23	7	.77	9	.241	.296	.350
1986	Fresno	A	126	452	126	30	8	9	199	65	54	35	0	91	14	10	2	18	6	.75	11	.279	.348	.440
1987	Shreveport	AA	89	332	106	24	1	11	165	44	47	19	4	74	4	3	3	3	3	.50	10	.319	.360	.497
1988	Phoenix	AAA	134	517	158	18	10	9	223	79	64	44	2	125	3	7	3	10	13	.43	16	.306	.362	.431

Year	Team	Lg	G	AB	H	2B	3B	HR	TB	R	RBI	TBB	IBB	SO	HBP	SH	SF	SB	CS	SB%	GDP	Avg	OBP	SLG
1989	Phoenix	AAA	94	307	71	11	3	8	112	40	33	15	0	65	5	2	7	5	4	.56	8	.231	.272	.365
1990	Phoenix	AAA	105	392	105	22	6	9	166	55	49	34	3	76	7	0	4	8	5	.62	8	.268	.334	.423
1991	Phoenix	AAA	51	191	56	10	4	8	98	41	34	18	0	43	6	1	3	1	0	1.00	4	.293	.367	.513
1992	Colo Sprngs	AAA	20	70	12	1	0	2	19	8	9	4	0	20	1	3	0	1	1	.50	1	.171	.227	.271
1994	Albany-Colo	AA	44	166	56	11	5	8	101	32	33	14	1	35	5	1	5	1	2	.33	1	.337	.395	.608
	Columbus	AAA	28	102	30	6	2	3	49	19	9	7	2	19	1	1	0	2	1	.67	1	.294	.345	.480
1988	San Francisco	NL	7	8	1	0	0	0	1	1	1	2	0	1	0	0	1	0	0	.00	0	.125	.273	.125
1990	San Francisco	NL	4	3	1	0	0	0	1	1	0	1	0	2	0	0	0	0	0	.00	0	.333	.500	.333
1991	San Francisco	NL	23	48	11	4	1	0	17	2	3	2	0	12	0	0	0	0	1	.00	0	.229	.260	.354
	Cleveland	AL	17	22	8	2	0	0	10	4	0	3	0	5	0	0	0	0	0	.00	0	.364	.440	.455
1992	Cleveland	AL	18	20	2	0	0	3	2	1	2	0	6	0	0	2	0	0	.00	0	.100	.182	.150
	10 Min. YEARS		851	3100	852	160	48	71	1321	447	382	224	11	649	56	35	34	72	42	.63	73	.275	.332	.426
	4 Maj. YEARS		69	101	23	7	1	0	32	10	5	10	0	26	0	2	1	0	1	.00	0	.228	.295	.317

Donny Perigny

Pitches: Right Bats: Right Pos: P Ht: 5'11" Wt: 175 Born: 01/08/69 Age: 26

			HOW MUCH HE PITCHED						WHAT HE GAVE UP											THE RESULTS					
Year	Team	Lg	G	GS	CG	GF	IP	BFP	H	R	ER	HR	SH	SF	HB	TBB	IBB	SO	WP	Bk	W	L	Pct.	ShO	Sv	ERA
1990	White Sox	R	7	1	0	5	16.2	64	9	1	1	0	1	0	0	6	0	19	0	0	1	1	.500	0	3	0.54
1991	South Bend	A	56	0	0	18	91.2	380	91	31	19	1	5	3	2	22	3	54	6	2	6	4	.600	0	6	1.87
1992	Sarasota	A	52	0	0	35	70.2	292	55	10	6	0	7	4	4	23	6	59	3	1	6	1	.857	0	20	0.76
1993	Birmingham	AA	48	0	0	25	70.1	297	69	38	33	9	2	4	5	15	1	57	7	1	3	4	.429	0	3	4.22
1994	Portland	AA	49	2	0	22	88.2	376	82	42	38	9	3	2	4	27	5	84	1	0	6	9	.400	0	11	3.86
	5 Min. YEARS		212	3	0	105	338	1409	306	122	97	19	18	13	15	93	15	273	17	4	22	19	.537	0	43	2.58

Bobby Perna

Bats: Both Throws: Right Pos: 3B Ht: 6'0" Wt: 195 Born: 09/17/68 Age: 26

			BATTING														BASERUNNING				PERCENTAGES		
Year	Team	Lg	G	AB	H	2B	3B	HR	TB	R	RBI	TBB	IBB	SO	HBP	SH	SF	SB	CS	SB%	GDP	Avg	OBP	SLG
1990	Billings	R	14	48	16	2	0	1	21	11	8	9	0	3	0	0	0	3	1	.75	1	.333	.439	.438
	Reds	R	46	169	49	6	1	2	63	29	31	25	0	22	0	0	2	16	3	.84	5	.290	.378	.373
1991	Chston-Wv	A	136	460	114	24	5	9	175	71	57	83	3	71	0	2	5	7	10	.41	8	.248	.359	.380
1992	Chston-Vw	A	129	499	150	27	2	11	214	73	71	44	3	77	0	4	5	14	9	.61	18	.301	.354	.429
	Chattanooga	AA	3	10	4	1	1	0	7	3	1	3	1	1	0	0	0	0	0	.00	0	.400	.538	.700
1993	Winston-Sal	A	138	525	139	27	0	18	220	88	70	64	1	116	3	3	4	6	5	.55	12	.265	.346	.419
1994	Chattanooga	AA	20	57	10	2	0	0	12	2	3	7	0	11	0	0	0	0	0	.00	4	.175	.266	.211
	Trenton	AA	18	58	6	2	0	0	8	4	3	5	0	18	0	1	1	0	1	.00	0	.103	.172	.138
	Duluth-Sup.	IND	54	206	57	11	0	7	89	31	30	24	1	46	1	2	2	4	5	.44	3	.277	.352	.432
	5 Min. YEARS		558	2032	545	102	9	48	809	312	274	264	9	365	4	12	19	50	34	.60	51	.268	.351	.398

Joe Perona

Bats: Right Throws: Right Pos: C Ht: 6'0" Wt: 195 Born: 02/08/70 Age: 25

			BATTING														BASERUNNING				PERCENTAGES		
Year	Team	Lg	G	AB	H	2B	3B	HR	TB	R	RBI	TBB	IBB	SO	HBP	SH	SF	SB	CS	SB%	GDP	Avg	OBP	SLG
1991	Bristol	R	5	16	8	3	0	1	14	1	3	3	0	1	0	0	0	2	1	.67	1	.500	.579	.875
	Fayetteville	A	46	147	40	7	2	6	69	25	25	23	1	19	4	2	2	4	2	.67	3	.272	.381	.469
1992	Lakeland	A	94	286	63	6	0	4	81	28	37	24	0	27	5	6	4	2	2	.50	9	.220	.288	.283
1993	London	AA	102	349	94	17	2	5	130	34	29	28	1	56	4	3	2	2	5	.29	5	.269	.329	.372
1994	Trenton	AA	107	359	79	24	3	5	124	39	26	31	0	50	6	0	0	0	5	.00	9	.220	.293	.345
	4 Min. YEARS		354	1157	284	57	7	21	418	127	120	109	2	153	19	11	8	10	15	.40	27	.245	.319	.361

Greg Perschke

Pitches: Right Bats: Right Pos: P Ht: 6'3" Wt: 180 Born: 08/03/67 Age: 27

			HOW MUCH HE PITCHED						WHAT HE GAVE UP											THE RESULTS					
Year	Team	Lg	G	GS	CG	GF	IP	BFP	H	R	ER	HR	SH	SF	HB	TBB	IBB	SO	WP	Bk	W	L	Pct.	ShO	Sv	ERA
1989	Utica	A	14	0	0	14	17	61	5	3	3	0	0	0	1	4	0	20	0	3	0	0	.000	0	1	1.59
	South Bend	A	13	0	0	8	20.1	80	19	10	7	0	0	1	1	2	0	16	2	1	0	2	.000	0	1	3.10
1990	Sarasota	A	42	0	2	23	111.1	450	83	32	15	3	3	4	4	29	3	107	5	8	7	3	.700	0	9	1.21
	Birmingham	AA	4	4	1	0	27.2	110	20	9	8	3	0	1	3	6	0	18	1	0	3	1	.750	0	0	2.60
1991	Vancouver	AAA	27	27	3	0	176	759	170	104	91	18	7	10	7	62	0	98	8	3	7	12	.368	0	0	4.65
1992	Vancouver	AAA	29	28	1	0	165	692	159	83	69	13	1	7	7	44	0	82	4	2	12	7	.632	1	0	3.76
1993	Albuquerque	AAA	33	13	0	5	104.2	475	146	76	74	12	3	6	2	24	3	63	6	2	7	4	.636	0	0	6.36
1994	Orlando	AA	25	0	0	14	41	158	28	9	7	2	3	0	1	10	4	26	0	1	4	3	.571	0	3	1.54
	Iowa	AAA	21	2	0	9	53	228	51	37	32	7	3	2	8	14	2	33	3	0	1	1	.500	0	1	5.43
	6 Min. YEARS		208	84	7	73	716	3013	681	363	306	58	20	31	34	195	12	463	29	20	41	33	.554	1	23	3.85

Robert Person

Pitches: Right Bats: Right Pos: P Ht: 5'11" Wt: 180 Born: 10/06/69 Age: 25

			HOW MUCH HE PITCHED						WHAT HE GAVE UP											THE RESULTS					
Year	Team	Lg	G	GS	CG	GF	IP	BFP	H	R	ER	HR	SH	SF	HB	TBB	IBB	SO	WP	Bk	W	L	Pct.	ShO	Sv	ERA
1989	Burlington	R	10	5	0	3	34	145	23	13	12	1	0	1	5	17	0	19	5	0	0	1	.000	0	1	3.18
1990	Kinston	A	4	3	0	1	16.2	74	17	6	5	0	0	1	0	9	0	7	0	0	1	0	1.000	0	0	2.70
	Indians	R	8	0	0	7	7.1	34	10	7	6	0	1	0	0	4	1	8	1	0	0	0	.000	0	2	7.36

Year	Team	Lg	G	GS	CG	GF	IP	BFP	H	R	ER	HR	SH	SF	HB	TBB	IBB	SO	WP	Bk	W	L	Pct.	ShO	Sv	ERA
	Watertown	A	5	2	0	2	16.1	62	8	2	2	0	0	0	0	7	0	19	0	0	1	0	1.000	0	0	1.10
1991	Kinston	A	11	11	0	0	52	252	56	37	27	2	3	6	2	42	0	45	2	1	3	5	.375	0	0	4.67
	Bend	A	2	2	0	0	10	41	6	6	4	0	0	0	1	5	0	6	1	0	1	1	.500	0	0	3.60
	South Bend	A	13	13	0	0	76.1	321	50	35	28	3	3	1	0	56	1	66	4	0	4	3	.571	0	0	3.30
1992	Sarasota	A	19	18	1	0	105.1	458	90	48	42	7	4	0	1	62	1	85	7	0	5	7	.417	0	0	3.59
1993	High Desert	A	28	26	4	1	169	740	184	115	88	13	4	6	4	48	0	107	9	1	12	10	.545	0	0	4.69
1994	Binghamton	AA	31	23	3	4	159	649	124	68	61	18	6	4	3	68	3	130	6	0	9	6	.600	2	0	3.45
	6 Min. YEARS		131	103	8	18	646	2776	568	337	275	44	21	19	16	318	6	492	35	2	36	35	.507	2	3	3.83

Tom Peskievitch

Pitches: Right Bats: Right Pos: P **Ht: 6'3" Wt: 210 Born: 07/19/68 Age: 26**

			HOW MUCH HE PITCHED						WHAT HE GAVE UP												THE RESULTS					
Year	Team	Lg	G	GS	CG	GF	IP	BFP	H	R	ER	HR	SH	SF	HB	TBB	IBB	SO	WP	Bk	W	L	Pct.	ShO	Sv	ERA
1991	Erie	A	27	3	0	15	60	258	48	28	19	2	0	1	0	30	0	52	4	4	5	3	.625	0	3	2.85
1992	Waterloo	A	49	9	1	14	102.2	477	105	65	56	5	3	4	7	67	7	122	10	3	11	8	.579	0	4	4.91
1993	Rancho Cuca	A	31	0	0	10	45.1	182	26	9	6	1	2	0	4	18	4	45	5	0	3	0	1.000	0	1	1.19
	Wichita	AA	7	0	0	5	9	46	11	8	7	1	2	0	1	8	2	5	0	1	1	2	.333	0	0	7.00
1994	Kane County	A	7	0	0	7	6.1	30	8	3	3	0	0	0	1	2	0	13	3	0	0	0	.000	0	3	4.26
	Portland	AA	5	0	0	3	6.1	28	10	5	5	0	0	0	0	3	0	2	0	0	0	0	.000	0	0	7.11
	Duluth-Sup.	IND	21	14	3	3	115.1	476	109	50	41	3	6	1	8	26	0	82	3	0	3	7	.300	0	0	3.20
	4 Min. YEARS		147	26	4	57	345	1497	317	168	137	12	13	6	21	154	13	321	25	8	23	20	.535	0	7	3.57

Matt Petersen

Pitches: Right Bats: Right Pos: P **Ht: 6'4" Wt: 190 Born: 05/21/70 Age: 25**

			HOW MUCH HE PITCHED						WHAT HE GAVE UP												THE RESULTS					
Year	Team	Lg	G	GS	CG	GF	IP	BFP	H	R	ER	HR	SH	SF	HB	TBB	IBB	SO	WP	Bk	W	L	Pct.	ShO	Sv	ERA
1992	Erie	A	14	14	1	0	80.2	322	56	28	24	7	1	0	2	29	0	44	2	6	5	1	.833	0	0	2.68
1993	Kane County	A	30	22	1	3	141.2	608	139	85	77	15	4	2	10	46	2	118	9	3	9	11	.450	1	3	4.89
1994	Brevard Cty	A	13	11	1	1	78	311	57	28	25	3	1	2	4	28	0	61	2	3	9	3	.750	0	0	2.88
	Portland	AA	16	14	0	0	81.2	351	74	49	44	10	2	7	6	39	1	64	3	1	4	5	.444	0	0	4.85
	3 Min. YEARS		73	61	3	4	382	1592	326	190	170	35	8	11	22	142	3	287	16	13	27	20	.574	1	3	4.01

Chris Peterson

Bats: Right Throws: Right Pos: SS **Ht: 5'10" Wt: 160 Born: 11/06/70 Age: 24**

			BATTING														BASERUNNING				PERCENTAGES		
Year	Team	Lg	G	AB	H	2B	3B	HR	TB	R	RBI	TBB	IBB	SO	HBP	SH	SF	SB	CS	SB%	GDP	Avg	OBP	SLG
1992	Geneva	A	71	244	55	8	0	1	66	36	23	32	0	36	4	9	2	11	7	.61	4	.225	.323	.270
1993	Daytona	A	130	473	101	10	0	0	111	66	28	58	0	105	9	17	1	19	11	.63	10	.214	.311	.235
1994	Orlando	AA	117	376	85	12	3	1	106	34	26	37	0	89	2	16	1	8	11	.42	7	.226	.298	.282
	3 Min. YEARS		318	1093	241	30	3	2	283	136	77	127	0	263	15	42	4	38	29	.57	21	.220	.309	.259

Mark Peterson

Pitches: Left Bats: Left Pos: P **Ht: 5'11" Wt: 195 Born: 11/27/70 Age: 24**

			HOW MUCH HE PITCHED						WHAT HE GAVE UP												THE RESULTS					
Year	Team	Lg	G	GS	CG	GF	IP	BFP	H	R	ER	HR	SH	SF	HB	TBB	IBB	SO	WP	Bk	W	L	Pct.	ShO	Sv	ERA
1992	Everett	A	20	5	0	7	53	226	58	23	19	5	2	0	1	17	1	47	0	4	3	2	.600	0	2	3.23
1993	San Jose	A	37	7	1	19	81.1	349	95	36	31	5	3	3	2	15	0	45	3	0	4	1	.800	1	0	3.43
1994	San Jose	A	9	4	0	2	36	139	36	16	16	4	2	2	0	6	1	27	1	0	3	3	.500	0	0	4.00
	Shreveport	AA	28	3	1	11	55.2	223	56	24	21	1	2	2	1	6	1	31	0	0	3	2	.600	0	1	3.40
	3 Min. YEARS		94	19	2	39	226	937	245	99	87	15	9	7	4	44	3	150	4	4	13	8	.619	1	3	3.46

Mark Petkovsek

Pitches: Right Bats: Right Pos: P **Ht: 6'0" Wt: 195 Born: 11/18/65 Age: 29**

			HOW MUCH HE PITCHED						WHAT HE GAVE UP												THE RESULTS					
Year	Team	Lg	G	GS	CG	GF	IP	BFP	H	R	ER	HR	SH	SF	HB	TBB	IBB	SO	WP	Bk	W	L	Pct.	ShO	Sv	ERA
1987	Rangers	R	3	1	0	0	5.2	26	4	2	2	0	0	2	0	2	0	7	0	0	0	0	.000	0	0	3.18
	Charlotte	A	11	10	0	1	56	249	67	36	25	2	3	3	0	17	0	23	5	1	3	4	.429	0	0	4.02
1988	Charlotte	A	28	28	7	0	175.2	708	156	71	58	5	6	7	3	42	2	95	11	4	10	11	.476	5	0	2.97
1989	Okla City	AAA	6	6	0	0	30.2	147	39	27	25	3	1	1	3	18	1	8	2	0	0	4	.000	0	0	7.34
	Tulsa	AA	21	21	1	0	140	585	144	63	54	7	6	7	3	35	0	66	5	0	8	5	.615	0	0	3.47
1990	Okla City	AAA	28	28	2	0	151	669	187	103	88	9	3	2	4	42	1	81	8	0	7	14	.333	1	0	5.25
1991	Okla City	AAA	25	24	3	0	149.2	646	162	89	82	9	5	9	7	38	2	67	10	1	9	8	.529	1	0	4.93
1992	Buffalo	AAA	32	22	1	1	150.1	632	150	76	59	9	12	3	1	44	1	49	5	0	8	8	.500	0	1	3.53
1993	Buffalo	AAA	14	11	1	0	70.2	291	74	38	34	8	2	1	2	16	0	27	4	0	3	4	.429	0	0	4.33
1994	Tucson	AAA	25	23	1	0	138.1	620	176	87	71	11	2	4	4	40	2	69	10	0	10	7	.588	1	0	4.62
1991	Texas	AL	4	1	0	1	9.1	53	21	16	15	4	0	1	0	4	0	6	2	0	0	1	.000	0	0	14.46
1993	Pittsburgh	NL	26	0	0	8	32.1	145	43	25	25	7	4	1	0	9	2	14	4	0	3	0	1.000	0	0	6.96
	8 Min. YEARS		193	174	16	2	1068	4573	1159	592	498	63	40	37	35	294	9	492	60	6	58	65	.472	8	1	4.20
	2 Maj. YEARS		30	1	0	9	41.2	198	64	41	40	11	4	2	0	13	2	20	6	0	3	1	.750	0	0	8.64

Geno Petralli

Bats: Left **Throws:** Right **Pos:** C **Ht:** 6' 1" **Wt:** 190 **Born:** 09/25/59 **Age:** 35

Year	Team	Lg	G	AB	H	2B	3B	HR	TB	R	RBI	TBB	IBB	SO	HBP	SH	SF	SB	CS	SB%	GDP	Avg	OBP	SLG
1984	Maine	AAA	23	83	18	3	0	0	21	9	5	13	2	10	0	0	0	0	2	.00	5	.217	.323	.253
1985	Maine	AAA	2	7	1	0	0	0	1	0	1	0	0	0	0	1	0	0	0	.00	0	.143	.143	.143
	Okla City	AAA	27	80	21	8	0	1	32	11	5	10	1	9	0	1	0	0	0	.00	3	.263	.344	.400
1989	Tulsa	AA	5	13	3	0	0	1	6	2	1	2	0	2	0	0	0	0	0	.00	0	.231	.333	.462
1991	Okla City	AAA	4	15	4	1	0	0	5	1	2	2	0	1	0	0	0	0	0	.00	1	.267	.353	.333
1993	Okla City	AAA	6	20	4	1	0	1	8	2	1	3	0	3	0	0	0	0	0	.00	1	.200	.304	.400
1994	Orlando	AA	4	8	2	1	0	0	3	0	0	1	0	2	0	0	0	0	0	.00	1	.250	.333	.375
	Iowa	AAA	4	6	1	0	0	0	1	1	0	1	0	0	0	0	0	0	0	.00	0	.167	.286	.167
1982	Toronto	AL	16	44	16	2	0	0	18	3	1	4	0	6	0	1	0	0	0	.00	1	.364	.417	.409
1983	Toronto	AL	6	4	0	0	0	0	0	0	0	1	0	1	0	0	0	0	0	.00	0	.000	.200	.000
1984	Toronto	AL	3	3	0	0	0	0	0	0	0	0	0	0	0	0	0	0	0	.00	0	.000	.000	.000
1985	Texas	AL	42	100	27	2	0	0	29	7	11	8	0	12	1	3	4	1	0	1.00	4	.270	.319	.290
1986	Texas	AL	69	137	35	9	3	2	56	17	18	5	0	14	0	0	0	3	0	1.00	7	.255	.282	.409
1987	Texas	AL	101	202	61	11	2	7	97	28	31	27	2	29	2	0	1	0	2	.00	4	.302	.388	.480
1988	Texas	AL	129	351	99	14	2	7	138	35	36	41	5	52	2	1	5	0	1	.00	12	.282	.356	.393
1989	Texas	AL	70	184	56	7	0	4	75	18	23	17	1	24	2	1	1	0	0	.00	5	.304	.368	.408
1990	Texas	AL	133	325	83	13	1	0	98	28	21	50	3	49	3	1	3	0	2	.00	12	.255	.357	.302
1991	Texas	AL	87	199	54	8	1	2	70	21	20	21	1	25	0	7	1	2	1	.67	4	.271	.339	.352
1992	Texas	AL	94	192	38	12	0	1	53	11	18	20	2	34	0	1	0	0	0	.00	8	.198	.274	.276
1993	Texas	AL	59	133	32	5	0	1	40	16	13	22	3	17	0	1	0	2	0	1.00	5	.241	.348	.301
	6 Min. YEARS		75	232	54	14	0	3	77	26	15	32	3	27	0	2	0	0	2	.00	11	.233	.326	.332
	12 Maj. YEARS		809	1874	501	83	9	24	674	184	192	216	17	263	10	16	15	8	6	.57	62	.267	.344	.360

Cecil Pettiford

Pitches: Right **Bats:** Right **Pos:** P **Ht:** 6'3" **Wt:** 178 **Born:** 06/26/68 **Age:** 27

Year	Team	Lg	G	GS	CG	GF	IP	BFP	H	R	ER	HR	SH	SF	HB	TBB	IBB	SO	WP	Bk	W	L	Pct.	ShO	Sv	ERA
1988	Burlington	R	4	1	0	1	12.1	55	9	4	3	0	0	1	1	11	0	15	2	1	0	1	.000	0	1	2.19
1989	Burlington	R	11	10	1	0	67.2	290	61	35	27	6	1	1	6	26	0	71	5	2	4	2	.667	0	0	3.59
1990	Reno	A	24	24	2	0	142	615	151	91	75	8	3	4	3	62	1	87	5	1	12	9	.571	0	0	4.75
1991	Kinston	A	26	6	1	7	85.1	360	69	39	30	5	2	1	3	35	0	70	6	0	8	2	.800	1	0	3.16
1992	Salt Lake	R	14	12	1	1	79	329	73	32	26	3	1	0	9	19	0	61	6	0	5	2	.714	0	0	2.96
1993	Lakeland	A	32	2	0	12	73.2	301	58	25	19	3	3	1	2	32	1	71	2	0	2	1	.667	0	1	2.32
1994	Trenton	AA	29	0	0	14	41	192	39	23	23	2	0	1	1	32	1	33	3	1	1	2	.333	0	0	5.05
	7 Min. YEARS		140	55	5	35	501	2142	460	249	203	27	10	9	25	217	3	408	29	5	32	19	.627	1	2	3.65

Andy Pettitte

Pitches: Left **Bats:** Left **Pos:** P **Ht:** 6'5" **Wt:** 220 **Born:** 06/15/72 **Age:** 23

Year	Team	Lg	G	GS	CG	GF	IP	BFP	H	R	ER	HR	SH	SF	HB	TBB	IBB	SO	WP	Bk	W	L	Pct.	ShO	Sv	ERA
1991	Yankees	R	6	6	0	0	36.2	135	16	6	4	0	0	0	1	8	0	51	4	6	4	1	.800	0	0	0.98
	Oneonta	A	6	6	1	0	33	150	33	18	8	1	1	2	0	16	0	32	4	0	2	2	.500	0	0	2.18
1992	Greensboro	A	27	27	2	0	168	671	141	53	41	4	3	1	5	55	0	130	11	2	10	4	.714	1	0	2.20
1993	Pr William	A	26	26	2	0	159.2	651	146	68	54	7	6	4	5	47	0	129	8	1	11	9	.550	1	0	3.04
	Albany	AA	1	1	0	0	5	22	5	4	2	0	0	0	0	2	0	6	0	0	1	0	1.000	0	0	3.60
1994	Albany-Colo	AA	11	11	0	0	73	294	60	32	22	5	1	1	1	18	1	50	5	1	7	2	.778	0	0	2.71
	Columbus	AAA	16	16	3	0	96.2	401	101	40	32	3	3	4	2	21	0	61	5	0	7	2	.778	0	0	2.98
	4 Min. YEARS		93	93	8	0	572	2324	502	221	163	20	14	12	14	167	1	459	37	10	42	20	.677	2	0	2.56

Marty Pevey

Bats: Left **Throws:** Right **Pos:** C **Ht:** 6' 1" **Wt:** 185 **Born:** 09/18/61 **Age:** 33

Year	Team	Lg	G	AB	H	2B	3B	HR	TB	R	RBI	TBB	IBB	SO	HBP	SH	SF	SB	CS	SB%	GDP	Avg	OBP	SLG
1984	St. Pete	A	128	441	136	16	4	2	166	53	60	48	7	47	1	6	2	7	7	.50	13	.308	.376	.376
1985	St. Pete	A	104	393	114	12	4	3	143	48	41	28	6	56	1	2	2	5	2	.71	9	.290	.337	.364
1986	Louisville	AAA	12	37	6	3	0	0	9	6	0	4	0	4	0	0	0	0	1	.00	0	.162	.244	.243
	Arkansas	AA	55	172	56	11	2	2	77	28	20	16	0	18	1	1	2	6	0	1.00	4	.326	.382	.448
1987	Louisville	AAA	16	38	9	2	0	1	14	5	5	0	0	10	0	0	1	0	0	.00	1	.237	.231	.368
	Arkansas	AA	80	197	55	11	3	1	77	28	16	10	2	33	1	1	1	6	1	.86	5	.279	.316	.391
1988	Jacksnville	AA	31	111	29	11	2	4	52	21	17	8	0	13	0	3	0	3	0	1.00	5	.261	.311	.468
	Indianapols	AAA	48	119	27	4	1	3	42	16	16	8	4	20	0	3	2	1	2	.33	4	.227	.271	.353
1989	Indianapols	AAA	34	108	28	4	2	1	39	12	14	8	1	20	0	2	0	3	3	.50	2	.259	.310	.361
1991	Syracuse	AAA	55	193	54	8	2	3	75	24	23	20	5	41	0	1	4	1	2	.33	4	.280	.347	.389
1992	Toledo	AAA	48	136	41	6	0	3	56	16	16	7	0	18	0	2	1	1	1	.50	1	.301	.333	.412
1993	Toledo	AAA	62	175	48	8	1	2	64	11	18	16	2	36	0	1	1	3	3	.50	3	.274	.333	.366
1994	Syracuse	AAA	96	259	70	13	2	6	105	29	31	20	3	55	1	4	3	2	3	.40	3	.270	.322	.405
1989	Montreal	NL	13	41	9	1	1	0	12	2	3	0	0	8	0	1	0	0	0	.00	1	.220	.220	.293
	10 Min. YEARS		769	2379	673	109	19	33	919	297	277	193	30	371	5	26	15	38	25	.60	54	.283	.336	.386

Ronald Pezzoni

Bats: Right **Throws:** Right **Pos:** OF　　　　　　　**Ht:** 6'0" **Wt:** 180 **Born:** 08/22/67 **Age:** 27

Year	Team	Lg	G	AB	H	2B	3B	HR	TB	R	RBI	TBB	IBB	SO	HBP	SH	SF	SB	CS	SB%	GDP	Avg	OBP	SLG
1990	Peninsula	A	109	408	109	15	4	2	138	47	42	23	0	59	1	2	2	26	6	.81	11	.267	.306	.338
1991	Peninsula	A	106	405	117	9	3	5	147	57	43	44	2	52	4	2	4	20	3	.87	5	.289	.361	.363
	Jacksnville	AA	7	22	7	0	0	0	7	3	2	1	0	3	0	0	0	0	0	.00	0	.318	.348	.318
1992	San Berndno	A	60	239	68	17	0	6	103	45	31	18	0	36	2	2	0	20	7	.74	5	.285	.340	.431
	Jacksnville	AA	27	93	21	3	0	0	24	10	15	7	0	19	1	0	3	3	0	1.00	1	.226	.279	.258
	Peninsula		25	100	30	3	1	0	35	6	11	2	0	8	0	1	0	5	1	.83	2	.300	.314	.350
1993	San Jose	A	100	340	87	18	0	5	120	51	53	50	3	42	0	1	2	11	5	.69	10	.256	.349	.353
1994	Shreveport	AA	72	153	41	6	0	3	56	18	21	12	1	30	0	1	3	2	0	1.00	7	.268	.315	.366
	5 Min. YEARS		506	1760	480	71	8	21	630	237	218	157	6	249	8	9	14	87	22	.80	41	.273	.333	.358

Randy Phillips

Pitches: Right **Bats:** Right **Pos:** P　　　　　　　**Ht:** 6'3" **Wt:** 210 **Born:** 03/18/71 **Age:** 24

Year	Team	Lg	G	GS	CG	GF	IP	BFP	H	R	ER	HR	SH	SF	HB	TBB	IBB	SO	WP	Bk	W	L	Pct.	ShO	Sv	ERA
1992	Medcine Hat	R	15	13	1	0	91	390	44	28	34	9	1	2	9	25	0	69	4	3	2	4	.333	0	0	3.36
1993	Dunedin	A	17	17	0	0	110.1	453	99	51	47	12	4	2	5	30	3	87	5	6	7	6	.538	0	0	3.83
	Knoxville	AA	5	5	0	0	25	120	32	20	17	3	2	0	2	12	0	12	3	2	2	2	.500	0	0	6.12
1994	Knoxville	AA	8	8	0	0	48	192	37	16	13	4	1	2	1	12	0	31	2	2	3	2	.600	0	0	2.44
	Syracuse	AAA	22	19	0	1	108.2	493	126	81	73	16	1	4	7	45	1	81	4	2	6	9	.400	0	0	6.05
	3 Min. YEARS		67	62	1	1	383	1648	382	216	184	44	9	10	24	124	4	280	18	15	20	23	.465	0	0	4.32

Tony Phillips

Pitches: Right **Bats:** Right **Pos:** P　　　　　　　**Ht:** 6'4" **Wt:** 195 **Born:** 06/09/69 **Age:** 26

Year	Team	Lg	G	GS	CG	GF	IP	BFP	H	R	ER	HR	SH	SF	HB	TBB	IBB	SO	WP	Bk	W	L	Pct.	ShO	Sv	ERA
1992	San Berndno	A	37	0	0	29	51	227	44	23	18	1	4	4	2	28	2	40	3	3	4	3	.571	0	12	3.18
1993	Riverside	A	25	0	0	23	30	118	22	8	6	1	2	2	2	4	1	19	0	1	3	1	.750	0	15	1.80
	Jacksnville	AA	26	0	0	21	30.1	125	34	6	6	1	1	0	0	5	1	23	1	1	1	3	.250	0	5	1.78
1994	Jacksnville	AA	5	0	0	4	5.2	22	3	2	1	1	0	0	0	3	0	3	0	0	0	0	.000	0	1	1.59
	Calgary	AAA	55	1	0	29	98	438	132	66	61	11	2	5	2	23	5	51	2	4	6	3	.667	0	6	5.60
	3 Min. YEARS		148	1	0	106	215	930	235	105	92	15	9	11	6	63	9	136	6	9	14	10	.583	0	39	3.85

Eddie Pierce

Pitches: Left **Bats:** Left **Pos:** P　　　　　　　**Ht:** 6' 1" **Wt:** 190 **Born:** 10/06/68 **Age:** 26

Year	Team	Lg	G	GS	CG	GF	IP	BFP	H	R	ER	HR	SH	SF	HB	TBB	IBB	SO	WP	Bk	W	L	Pct.	ShO	Sv	ERA
1989	Eugene	A	27	0	0	24	39	175	24	19	12	0	0	0	3	26	0	71	9	2	2	2	.500	0	4	2.77
1990	Baseball Cy	A	37	0	0	22	50	228	49	21	18	3	3	0	0	32	0	52	7	2	3	1	.750	0	5	3.24
	Memphis	AA	1	0	0	0	1	3	0	0	0	0	0	0	0	1	0	1	0	0	0	0	.000	0	0	0.00
1991	Memphis	AA	31	20	2	4	136	595	136	73	58	6	6	1	2	61	1	90	3	1	5	11	.313	0	0	3.84
1992	Memphis	AA	25	25	1	0	153.2	662	159	74	65	11	8	3	3	51	1	131	8	1	10	10	.500	1	0	3.81
1993	Memphis	AA	37	2	0	18	67.1	300	65	35	28	5	3	1	3	34	3	53	3	0	6	5	.545	0	1	3.74
	Omaha	AAA	12	2	0	3	34.2	153	40	24	21	6	3	1	1	13	1	20	0	2	0	0	.000	0	5	5.45
1994	Memphis	AA	13	13	1	0	74	318	80	38	32	5	2	1	2	22	0	52	5	0	5	3	.625	1	0	3.89
	Omaha	AAA	12	12	0	0	76	337	87	47	37	8	3	2	1	31	0	46	7	0	4	3	.571	0	0	4.38
1992	Kansas City	AL	2	1	0	0	5.1	26	9	2	2	1	0	1	0	4	0	3	0	0	0	0	.000	0	0	3.38
	6 Min. YEARS		195	74	4	71	631.2	2771	640	331	271	44	28	9	15	271	6	516	42	6	35	37	.486	2	10	3.86

Jeff Pierce

Pitches: Right **Bats:** Right **Pos:** P　　　　　　　**Ht:** 6'1" **Wt:** 200 **Born:** 06/07/69 **Age:** 26

Year	Team	Lg	G	GS	CG	GF	IP	BFP	H	R	ER	HR	SH	SF	HB	TBB	IBB	SO	WP	Bk	W	L	Pct.	ShO	Sv	ERA
1992	South Bend	A	52	0	0	46	69.2	281	46	22	16	1	5	4	6	18	0	88	8	0	3	5	.375	0	30	2.07
	Sarasota	A	1	0	0	1	0.2	3	0	0	0	0	0	0	0	1	0	1	0	0	0	0	.000	0	0	0.00
1993	Birmingham	AA	33	0	0	26	48.2	188	34	16	14	3	4	2	3	7	0	45	1	1	3	4	.429	0	18	2.59
	Chattanooga	AA	13	0	0	8	20.2	87	17	6	6	1	0	1	0	9	1	22	2	0	0	0	.000	0	4	2.61
1994	New Britain	AA	29	0	0	25	39.1	163	31	13	10	3	1	0	2	12	3	54	4	0	1	2	.333	0	10	2.29
	Pawtucket	AAA	32	0	0	14	60.1	249	53	27	23	4	1	0	0	21	1	57	2	2	6	1	.857	0	2	3.43
	3 Min. YEARS		160	0	0	120	239.1	971	181	84	69	12	11	7	12	67	5	267	17	2	13	12	.520	0	64	2.59

Rob Pierce

Pitches: Right **Bats:** Right **Pos:** P　　　　　　　**Ht:** 6'2" **Wt:** 200 **Born:** 12/17/70 **Age:** 24

Year	Team	Lg	G	GS	CG	GF	IP	BFP	H	R	ER	HR	SH	SF	HB	TBB	IBB	SO	WP	Bk	W	L	Pct.	ShO	Sv	ERA
1991	Athletics	R	20	2	0	5	53	254	59	48	33	4	0	4	5	29	2	34	9	1	2	2	.500	0	1	5.60
1992	Madison	A	34	0	0	19	59	272	62	33	29	3	5	5	3	30	2	56	6	1	2	3	.400	0	4	4.42
	Reno	A	15	1	0	4	30.2	158	45	33	25	2	2	1	1	22	0	22	4	0	0	1	.000	0	0	7.34
1993	Modesto	A	36	0	0	27	53	229	41	11	11	2	4	3	2	28	1	44	1	0	1	1	.500	0	14	1.87
1994	Huntsville	AA	37	1	0	16	56.1	254	58	43	38	5	2	2	3	30	2	39	6	0	3	6	.333	0	5	6.07
	4 Min. YEARS		142	4	0	71	252	1167	265	168	136	16	13	16	14	139	7	195	26	2	8	13	.381	0	25	4.86

Kevin Pincavitch

Pitches: Right **Bats:** Right **Pos:** P **Ht:** 5'11" **Wt:** 170 **Born:** 07/05/70 **Age:** 24

Year	Team	Lg	G	GS	CG	GF	IP	BFP	H	R	ER	HR	SH	SF	HB	TBB	IBB	SO	WP	Bk	W	L	Pct.	ShO	Sv	ERA
1992	Great Falls	R	26	0	0	9	50.2	219	36	16	11	1	1	0	4	26	1	65	4	0	2	2	.500	0	1	1.95
1993	Vero Beach	A	6	0	0	0	9.2	52	11	10	5	0	0	0	0	10	1	3	1	1	0	0	.000	0	0	4.66
	Yakima	A	9	9	0	0	57	234	40	22	12	2	1	1	5	29	1	43	7	3	3	4	.429	0	0	1.89
	Bakersfield	A	6	5	0	0	31.2	141	27	11	7	2	2	0	1	25	2	32	6	0	1	2	.333	0	0	1.99
1994	San Antonio	AA	4	2	0	0	10.1	54	12	15	11	1	1	0	0	12	0	7	2	0	0	2	.000	0	0	9.58
	Bakersfield	A	27	16	1	4	111.2	469	94	53	43	9	3	3	3	48	0	113	13	1	7	4	.636	0	0	3.47
	3 Min. YEARS		78	32	1	13	271	1169	220	127	89	15	8	4	13	150	5	263	33	5	13	14	.481	0	2	2.96

Marc Pisciotta

Pitches: Right **Bats:** Right **Pos:** P **Ht:** 6'5" **Wt:** 240 **Born:** 08/07/70 **Age:** 24

Year	Team	Lg	G	GS	CG	GF	IP	BFP	H	R	ER	HR	SH	SF	HB	TBB	IBB	SO	WP	Bk	W	L	Pct.	ShO	Sv	ERA
1991	Welland	A	24	0	0	21	34	143	16	4	1	0	2	1	3	20	1	47	7	1	1	1	.500	0	8	0.26
1992	Augusta	A	20	12	1	5	79.1	372	91	51	40	4	5	1	10	43	2	54	12	2	4	5	.444	0	1	4.54
1993	Augusta	A	34	0	0	28	43.2	188	31	18	13	0	5	0	5	17	1	49	5	0	5	2	.714	0	12	2.68
	Salem	A	20	0	0	18	18.1	88	23	13	6	0	1	1	0	13	0	13	2	0	0	0	.000	0	12	2.95
1994	Carolina	AA	26	0	0	17	25.2	127	32	21	16	2	6	2	3	15	2	21	1	1	3	4	.429	0	5	5.61
	Salem	A	31	0	0	30	29.1	134	24	14	5	1	2	1	3	13	1	23	4	0	1	4	.200	0	19	1.53
	4 Min. YEARS		155	12	1	119	230.1	1052	217	121	81	7	21	6	24	121	7	207	31	4	14	16	.467	0	57	3.16

Kinnis Pledger

Bats: Left **Throws:** Right **Pos:** OF **Ht:** 6'4" **Wt:** 215 **Born:** 07/17/68 **Age:** 26

Year	Team	Lg	G	AB	H	2B	3B	HR	TB	R	RBI	TBB	IBB	SO	HBP	SH	SF	SB	CS	SB%	GDP	Avg	OBP	SLG
1987	White Sox	R	37	127	32	6	3	1	47	18	13	13	3	46	0	0	1	20	0	1.00	1	.252	.319	.370
1988	South Bend	A	107	371	75	13	4	3	105	42	34	39	2	106	0	4	3	18	10	.64	2	.202	.276	.283
1989	South Bend	A	89	293	78	13	5	3	110	49	39	56	3	79	0	4	4	26	14	.65	2	.266	.380	.375
1990	Sarasota	A	131	460	114	18	4	3	149	72	46	94	3	134	8	6	3	26	14	.65	10	.248	.382	.324
	Vancouver	AAA	1	1	0	0	0	0	0	0	0	0	0	0	0	0	0	0	0	.00	0	.000	.000	.000
1991	Birmingham	AA	117	363	79	16	8	9	138	53	51	60	3	104	4	4	1	15	10	.60	2	.218	.334	.380
1992	Sarasota	A	59	217	70	11	2	7	106	42	38	28	4	47	3	0	1	13	9	.59	6	.323	.406	.488
	Birmingham	AA	60	191	34	5	2	1	46	18	14	19	2	65	0	5	3	2	4	.33	5	.178	.249	.241
1993	Birmingham	AA	125	393	95	10	6	14	159	70	56	74	0	120	3	5	4	19	6	.76	9	.242	.363	.405
1994	Daytona	A	11	37	8	1	1	1	14	5	3	10	0	12	0	0	0	0	0	.00	0	.216	.383	.378
	Orlando	AA	23	70	19	3	1	2	30	4	8	7	1	17	1	0	0	3	1	.75	4	.271	.346	.429
	Iowa	AAA	69	230	65	17	3	8	112	47	34	24	1	54	1	6	3	2	5	.29	2	.283	.349	.487
	8 Min. YEARS		829	2753	669	113	39	52	1016	420	330	424	23	784	20	34	23	144	73	.66	43	.243	.346	.369

Kevin Polcovich

Bats: Right **Throws:** Right **Pos:** SS **Ht:** 5'9" **Wt:** 165 **Born:** 06/28/70 **Age:** 25

Year	Team	Lg	G	AB	H	2B	3B	HR	TB	R	RBI	TBB	IBB	SO	HBP	SH	SF	SB	CS	SB%	GDP	Avg	OBP	SLG
1992	Carolina	AA	13	35	6	0	0	0	6	1	1	4	0	4	2	0	0	0	2	.00	1	.171	.293	.171
	Augusta	A	46	153	40	6	2	0	50	24	10	18	0	30	8	3	0	7	7	.50	1	.261	.369	.327
1993	Augusta	A	14	48	13	2	0	0	15	9	4	7	0	8	0	2	1	2	1	.67	1	.271	.357	.313
	Carolina	AA	4	11	3	0	0	0	3	1	1	1	0	1	0	2	0	0	1	.00	1	.273	.333	.273
	Salem	A	94	282	72	10	3	1	91	44	25	49	0	42	12	6	3	13	6	.68	7	.255	.384	.323
1994	Carolina	AA	125	406	95	14	2	2	119	46	33	38	4	70	11	10	8	9	4	.69	6	.234	.311	.293
	3 Min. YEARS		296	935	229	32	7	3	284	125	74	117	4	155	33	23	12	31	20	.61	17	.245	.345	.304

Damon Pollard

Pitches: Right **Bats:** Right **Pos:** P **Ht:** 5'9" **Wt:** 167 **Born:** 09/29/67 **Age:** 27

Year	Team	Lg	G	GS	CG	GF	IP	BFP	H	R	ER	HR	SH	SF	HB	TBB	IBB	SO	WP	Bk	W	L	Pct.	ShO	Sv	ERA
1990	Eugene	A	14	14	1	0	70	292	46	35	26	4	0	3	6	42	0	77	7	1	3	3	.500	0	0	3.34
1991	Appleton	A	16	4	0	7	55.2	247	41	21	14	2	2	2	3	44	3	56	9	4	3	3	.500	0	1	2.26
	Baseball Cy	A	13	2	0	3	25.1	117	22	14	12	0	0	5	1	22	0	23	8	0	1	1	.500	0	0	4.26
1992	Baseball Cy	A	49	0	0	35	71	297	46	30	21	2	2	6	1	43	3	51	6	1	4	3	.571	0	13	2.66
1993	St. Paul	IND	29	0	0	25	31.2	145	25	11	8	1	2	1	2	24	0	35	2	0	2	2	.500	0	14	2.27
1994	El Paso	AA	4	0	0	2	8.1	43	9	3	2	0	0	0	0	12	1	6	2	1	0	0	.000	0	0	2.16
	Harrisburg	AA	21	0	0	7	32.1	172	47	44	38	10	1	3	1	32	1	31	5	0	3	0	1.000	0	0	10.58
	W. Palm Bch	A	13	1	0	6	18	89	20	13	12	0	0	0	2	16	0	13	4	1	0	1	.000	0	0	6.00
	5 Min. YEARS		159	21	1	85	312.1	1402	256	171	133	19	7	19	15	235	8	292	43	8	16	13	.552	0	28	3.83

Tom Popplewell

Pitches: Right **Bats:** Right **Pos:** P **Ht:** 6'3" **Wt:** 225 **Born:** 08/03/67 **Age:** 27

Year	Team	Lg	G	GS	CG	GF	IP	BFP	H	R	ER	HR	SH	SF	HB	TBB	IBB	SO	WP	Bk	W	L	Pct.	ShO	Sv	ERA
1987	Oneonta	A	16	9	0	5	65.1	309	79	53	37	3	5	4	2	38	2	54	4	0	4	6	.400	0	1	5.10

1988	Pr William	A	22	20	1	1	113.1	541	127	89	70	5	7	3	9	63	2	58	8	1	4	12	.250	0	0	5.56
1989	Ft.Laudrdle	A	32	14	0	5	119	522	119	67	53	6	2	8	3	60	1	70	9	0	3	5	.375	0	0	4.01
1990	Ft.Laudrdle	A	15	15	3	0	101	408	82	38	29	2	2	1	1	23	0	59	4	1	6	5	.545	1	0	2.23
	Albany	AA	14	12	0	0	64	275	56	31	29	4	0	0	3	36	0	34	2	0	8	2	.800	0	0	4.08
1991	Albany	AA	52	4	0	16	86	417	81	56	42	8	4	4	8	83	5	63	7	3	4	10	.286	0	3	4.40
1992	Albany	AA	28	2	0	11	50.2	242	52	46	41	4	1	4	3	34	2	33	4	1	2	1	.667	0	0	7.28
	Columbus	AAA	4	0	0	0	6.1	38	6	5	5	0	0	0	0	11	0	7	0	0	1	0	1.000	0	0	7.11
1993	Albany	AA	34	4	1	12	64.1	301	60	45	42	3	1	3	5	48	2	59	11	0	1	3	.250	0	1	5.88
	Columbus	AAA	1	0	0	0	2	8	2	1	1	0	0	0	0	1	0	2	0	0	0	0	.000	0	0	4.50
1994	El Paso	AA	36	0	0	20	36.1	181	36	34	33	4	2	3	5	41	1	30	7	0	2	4	.333	0	10	8.17
	New Orleans	AAA	15	0	0	4	16	65	13	9	7	3	0	1	0	5	0	9	2	0	0	0	.000	0	1	3.94
	8 Min. YEARS		269	80	5	74	724.1	3307	713	474	385	42	24	31	39	443	15	478	58	6	35	48	.422	1	15	4.78

Jorge Posada

Bats: Both Throws: Right Pos: C Ht: 6'0" Wt: 167 Born: 08/17/71 Age: 23

						BATTING											BASERUNNING				PERCENTAGES		
Year	Team	Lg	G	AB	H	2B	3B	HR	TB	R	RBI	TBB	IBB	SO	HBP	SH	SF	SB	CS	SB%	GDP	Avg	OBP	SLG
1992	Greensboro	A	101	339	94	22	4	12	160	60	58	58	2	87	6	0	3	11	6	.65	9	.277	.389	.472
1993	Pr William	A	118	410	106	27	2	17	188	71	61	67	4	90	6	1	6	17	5	.77	7	.259	.366	.459
	Albany	AA	7	25	7	0	0	0	7	3	0	2	0	7	0	0	0	0	0	.00	1	.280	.333	.280
1994	Columbus	AAA	92	313	75	13	3	11	127	46	48	32	1	81	1	4	5	5	5	.50	3	.240	.308	.406
	3 Min. YEARS		318	1087	282	62	9	40	482	180	167	159	7	265	13	5	14	33	16	.67	19	.259	.357	.443

Scott Pose

Bats: Left Throws: Right Pos: OF Ht: 5'11" Wt: 165 Born: 02/11/67 Age: 28

						BATTING											BASERUNNING				PERCENTAGES		
Year	Team	Lg	G	AB	H	2B	3B	HR	TB	R	RBI	TBB	IBB	SO	HBP	SH	SF	SB	CS	SB%	GDP	Avg	OBP	SLG
1989	Billings	R	60	210	74	7	2	0	85	52	25	54	3	31	1	1	1	26	3	.90	2	.352	.485	.405
1990	Chston-Wv	A	135	480	143	13	5	0	166	106	46	114	8	56	7	5	6	49	21	.70	5	.298	.435	.346
1991	Nashville	AAA	15	52	10	0	0	0	10	7	3	2	0	9	2	2	0	3	1	.75	0	.192	.250	.192
	Chattanooga	AA	117	402	110	8	5	1	131	61	31	69	3	50	2	7	3	17	13	.57	7	.274	.380	.326
1992	Chattanooga	AA	136	526	180	22	8	2	224	87	45	63	5	66	4	4	3	21	27	.44	8	.342	.414	.426
1993	Edmonton	AAA	109	398	113	8	6	0	133	61	27	42	3	36	1	5	1	19	9	.68	6	.284	.353	.334
1994	New Orleans	AAA	124	429	121	13	7	0	148	60	52	47	2	52	2	9	4	20	8	.71	7	.282	.353	.345
1993	Florida	NL	15	41	8	2	0	0	10	0	3	2	0	4	0	0	0	0	2	.00	0	.195	.233	.244
	6 Min. YEARS		696	2497	751	71	33	3	897	434	229	391	24	300	19	33	18	155	82	.65	37	.301	.397	.359

Lou Pote

Pitches: Right Bats: Right Pos: P Ht: 6'3" Wt: 190 Born: 08/27/71 Age: 23

			HOW MUCH HE PITCHED						WHAT HE GAVE UP									THE RESULTS					
Year	Team	Lg	G	GS	CG	GF	IP	BFP	H	R	ER	HR	SH	SF	HB	TBB	IBB	SO	WP	Bk	W	L	Pct.	ShO	Sv	ERA
1991	Giants	R	8	8	0	0	42.1	184	38	23	12	0	0	1	0	18	0	41	5	0	2	3	.400	0	0	2.55
	Everett	A	5	4	0	0	28.2	117	24	8	8	0	1	2	1	7	0	26	2	0	2	0	1.000	0	0	2.51
1992	Shreveport	AA	20	3	0	9	37.2	146	20	7	4	1	3	1	1	15	2	26	3	0	4	2	.667	0	0	0.96
	San Jose	A	4	3	0	1	9.2	46	11	5	5	0	1	1	0	7	0	8	3	0	0	1	.000	0	0	4.66
1993	Shreveport	AA	19	19	0	0	108.1	458	111	53	49	10	1	3	0	45	1	81	3	1	8	7	.533	0	0	4.07
1994	Giants	R	4	4	0	0	19.2	73	9	0	0	0	1	0	0	6	0	30	0	0	1	0	1.000	0	0	0.00
	Shreveport	AA	5	5	0	0	28.2	122	31	11	9	2	2	2	0	7	0	15	1	1	2	2	.500	0	0	2.83
	4 Min. YEARS		65	46	0	10	275	1146	244	107	87	15	8	9	3	105	3	227	17	2	19	15	.559	0	0	2.85

Mike Potts

Pitches: Left Bats: Left Pos: P Ht: 5'9" Wt: 170 Born: 09/05/70 Age: 24

			HOW MUCH HE PITCHED						WHAT HE GAVE UP									THE RESULTS					
Year	Team	Lg	G	GS	CG	GF	IP	BFP	H	R	ER	HR	SH	SF	HB	TBB	IBB	SO	WP	Bk	W	L	Pct.	ShO	Sv	ERA
1990	Braves	R	23	1	0	17	39	174	29	23	15	2	0	3	1	25	1	39	5	0	5	2	.714	0	4	3.46
1991	Macon	A	34	11	2	5	95.1	399	64	45	37	3	2	2	4	50	1	76	13	0	8	5	.615	2	1	3.49
1992	Durham	A	30	21	0	2	127.2	547	104	75	57	4	6	6	1	71	5	123	14	0	6	8	.429	0	1	4.02
1993	Greenville	AA	25	25	1	0	141.2	621	131	79	61	7	7	3	1	86	2	116	6	1	7	6	.538	0	0	3.88
1994	Richmond	AAA	52	0	0	18	85.2	369	75	41	35	3	7	3	2	43	6	66	6	0	6	3	.667	0	2	3.68
	5 Min. YEARS		164	58	3	42	489.1	2110	403	263	205	19	22	17	9	275	15	420	44	1	32	24	.571	2	8	3.77

Clyde Pough

Bats: Right Throws: Right Pos: OF Ht: 6'0" Wt: 173 Born: 12/25/69 Age: 25

						BATTING											BASERUNNING				PERCENTAGES		
Year	Team	Lg	G	AB	H	2B	3B	HR	TB	R	RBI	TBB	IBB	SO	HBP	SH	SF	SB	CS	SB%	GDP	Avg	OBP	SLG
1988	Indians	R	52	173	45	11	0	3	65	28	21	24	1	52	1	2	0	1	3	.25	3	.260	.354	.376
1989	Burlington	R	67	225	58	15	1	8	99	39	37	36	1	64	3	0	2	9	5	.64	1	.258	.365	.440
1990	Reno	A	16	53	8	0	1	0	10	1	2	6	1	18	0	0	0	0	1	.00	1	.151	.237	.189
	Watertown	A	76	285	72	15	1	9	116	47	49	40	0	71	2	0	4	21	4	.84	7	.253	.344	.407
1991	Kinston	A	11	30	5	1	0	0	6	2	2	1	0	9	0	0	0	1	0	1.00	1	.167	.219	.200
	Columbus	A	115	414	127	35	3	11	201	76	73	62	2	63	8	2	9	11	6	.65	6	.307	.400	.486
	Colo Sprngs	AAA	2	2	0	0	0	0	0	0	0	0	0	0	0	0	0	0	0	.00	0	.000	.000	.000

Year	Team	Lg	G	AB	H	2B	3B	HR	TB	R	RBI	TBB	IBB	SO	HBP	SH	SF	SB	CS	SB%	GDP	Avg	OBP	SLG
1992	Kinston	A	114	411	93	23	1	11	151	59	58	50	1	98	6	4	5	12	3	.80	13	.226	.316	.367
1993	Kinston	A	120	418	113	18	1	13	172	66	57	59	2	95	5	1	4	8	3	.73	8	.270	.364	.411
1994	Canton-Akrn	AA	105	379	113	24	3	20	203	69	66	43	3	86	5	0	6	3	2	.60	9	.298	.372	.536
	Charlotte	AAA	16	42	9	4	0	0	13	1	4	6	0	13	0	0	1	0	0	.00	0	.214	.306	.310
	7 Min. YEARS		694	2432	643	146	11	75	1036	388	369	327	10	569	31	9	31	66	27	.71	49	.264	.355	.426

Dennis Powell

Pitches: Left   Bats: Right   Pos: P   Ht: 6' 3"   Wt: 200   Born: 08/13/63   Age: 31

Year	Team	Lg	G	GS	CG	GF	IP	BFP	H	R	ER	HR	SH	SF	HB	TBB	IBB	SO	WP	Bk	W	L	Pct.	ShO	Sv	ERA
1984	Vero Beach	A	4	4	0	0	26	106	19	7	4	0	2	1	1	12	1	14	3	0	1	1	.500	0	1	1.38
	San Antonio	AA	24	24	5	0	168	721	153	81	63	8	3	4	2	87	0	82	3	2	9	8	.529	2	0	3.38
1985	Albuquerque	AAA	18	17	3	1	111.2	0	106	40	34	5	0	0	1	48	0	55	6	2	9	0	1.000	0	0	2.74
1986	Albuquerque	AAA	7	7	0	0	41.2	176	45	23	19	3	0	1	0	15	0	27	1	0	3	3	.500	0	0	4.10
1987	Calgary	AAA	20	20	2	0	117.1	538	145	80	64	12	4	3	2	48	1	65	3	1	4	8	.333	1	0	4.91
1988	Calgary	AAA	21	18	2	1	108	481	116	57	50	9	6	2	1	49	1	81	6	3	6	4	.600	1	1	4.17
1989	Calgary	AAA	18	0	0	14	25.1	109	21	10	6	0	0	2	1	12	0	15	0	0	3	2	.600	0	6	2.13
1990	Denver	AAA	11	11	2	0	62.1	263	63	34	25	6	2	2	0	21	0	46	3	1	4	4	.500	0	1	3.61
1991	Calgary	AAA	27	26	5	1	173.2	761	200	90	80	20	7	6	6	59	0	96	12	1	9	8	.529	1	0	4.15
1993	Calgary	AAA	12	4	0	2	40	164	37	16	16	3	1	0	1	19	1	30	0	0	3	2	.600	0	1	3.60
1994	Nashville	AAA	25	0	0	6	22	107	26	13	11	2	3	2	2	16	5	27	3	1	1	3	.250	0	1	4.50
1985	Los Angeles	NL	16	2	0	6	29.1	133	30	19	17	7	4	1	1	13	3	19	3	0	1	1	.500	0	1	5.22
1986	Los Angeles	NL	27	6	0	5	65.1	272	65	32	31	5	5	2	1	25	7	31	7	2	2	7	.222	0	0	4.27
1987	Seattle	AL	16	3	0	1	34.1	147	32	13	12	3	2	2	0	15	0	17	0	0	1	3	.250	0	0	3.15
1988	Seattle	AL	12	2	0	1	18.2	95	29	20	18	2	0	2	2	11	2	15	0	0	1	3	.250	0	0	8.68
1989	Seattle	AL	43	1	0	9	45	201	49	25	25	6	3	3	2	21	0	27	1	0	2	2	.500	0	2	5.00
1990	Seattle	AL	2	0	0	1	3	17	5	3	3	0	0	0	1	2	0	0	0	0	0	0	.000	0	0	9.00
	Milwaukee	AL	9	7	0	1	39.1	197	59	37	30	0	2	2	1	19	0	23	2	0	0	4	.000	0	0	6.86
1992	Seattle	AL	49	0	0	11	57	243	49	30	29	5	5	0	3	29	2	35	2	0	4	2	.667	0	0	4.58
1993	Seattle	AL	33	2	0	7	47.2	197	42	22	22	7	5	2	2	24	2	32	2	0	0	0	.000	0	0	4.15
	10 Min. YEARS		187	131	19	25	896	3426	931	451	372	68	28	23	17	386	9	538	40	11	52	43	.547	5	9	3.74
	8 Maj. YEARS		207	23	0	42	339.2	1502	360	201	187	35	26	14	12	159	16	199	17	2	11	22	.333	0	3	4.95

Terry Powers

Pitches: Right   Bats: Right   Pos: P   Ht: 6'1"   Wt: 175   Born: 02/14/71   Age: 24

Year	Team	Lg	G	GS	CG	GF	IP	BFP	H	R	ER	HR	SH	SF	HB	TBB	IBB	SO	WP	Bk	W	L	Pct.	ShO	Sv	ERA
1990	Red Sox	R	3	3	0	0	13	52	10	5	4	0	0	0	0	3	0	10	0	0	0	1	.000	0	0	2.77
	Lynchburg	A	11	10	0	0	54.2	249	60	40	27	4	4	2	2	28	0	27	3	1	0	7	.000	0	0	4.45
1991	Winter Havn	A	25	15	3	5	105.2	470	108	66	54	2	7	6	3	54	1	56	7	2	8	7	.533	0	0	4.60
1992	Winter Havn	A	21	21	4	0	133.2	560	129	72	67	4	4	4	1	62	1	105	4	0	5	10	.333	1	0	4.51
1993	Wst Plm Bch	A	24	13	0	1	91	401	89	52	43	1	4	2	3	45	0	57	1	2	6	3	.667	0	0	4.25
1994	W. Palm Bch	A	9	0	0	1	16.2	78	21	9	9	0	3	0	2	7	0	9	3	0	0	1	.000	0	0	4.86
	Harrisburg	AA	2	0	0	1	3.2	26	10	11	10	2	0	0	0	4	0	0	0	0	0	0	.000	0	0	24.55
	5 Min. YEARS		95	62	7	8	418.1	1836	427	255	214	13	22	14	11	203	2	284	18	5	19	29	.396	1	0	4.60

Arquimedez Pozo

Bats: Right   Throws: Right   Pos: 2B   Ht: 5'10"   Wt: 180   Born: 08/24/73   Age: 21

Year	Team	Lg	G	AB	H	2B	3B	HR	TB	R	RBI	TBB	IBB	SO	HBP	SH	SF	SB	CS	SB%	GDP	Avg	OBP	SLG
1992	San Berndno	A	54	199	52	8	4	3	77	33	19	20	0	41	2	1	0	13	8	.62	2	.261	.335	.387
	Bellingham	A	39	149	48	12	0	7	81	37	21	20	0	24	2	1	1	9	5	.64	1	.322	.407	.544
1993	Riverside	A	127	515	176	44	6	13	271	98	83	56	4	56	2	1	5	10	10	.50	22	.342	.405	.526
1994	Jacksonville	AA	119	447	129	31	5	14	204	70	54	32	0	43	7	3	6	11	8	.58	8	.289	.341	.456
	3 Min. YEARS		339	1310	405	95	11	37	633	238	177	128	4	164	13	6	12	43	31	.58	33	.309	.373	.483

Howard Prager

Bats: Left   Throws: Left   Pos: 1B   Ht: 6'2"   Wt: 190   Born: 04/06/67   Age: 28

Year	Team	Lg	G	AB	H	2B	3B	HR	TB	R	RBI	TBB	IBB	SO	HBP	SH	SF	SB	CS	SB%	GDP	Avg	OBP	SLG
1989	Auburn	A	73	251	84	15	3	8	129	54	58	36	3	45	2	1	4	21	4	.84	2	.335	.416	.514
1990	Osceola	A	99	331	82	11	4	1	104	44	45	61	5	48	2	3	2	2	4	.33	9	.248	.366	.314
1991	Osceola	A	14	43	12	2	2	0	18	6	7	10	1	10	1	2	1	2	0	1.00	3	.279	.418	.419
	Jackson	AA	109	357	109	26	2	11	172	57	65	52	6	75	2	4	3	9	6	.60	15	.305	.394	.482
1992	Jackson	AA	113	326	84	13	0	5	112	36	48	45	2	75	6	2	3	1	4	.20	2	.258	.355	.344
1993	Arkansas	AA	59	158	50	8	1	7	81	31	21	28	5	34	0	2	2	4	2	.67	4	.316	.415	.513
	Louisville	AAA	63	209	55	17	0	4	84	27	28	24	1	37	2	0	1	0	0	.00	6	.263	.343	.402
1994	Louisville	AAA	86	176	42	8	0	7	71	24	23	32	4	36	1	0	2	3	1	.75	2	.239	.355	.403
	6 Min. YEARS		616	1851	518	100	12	43	771	279	295	288	29	360	16	14	18	42	21	.67	44	.280	.378	.417

Evan Pratte

Bats: Both **Throws: Right** **Pos: 2B**   Ht: 5'10"   Wt: 175   Born: 12/18/68   Age: 26

			BATTING													BASERUNNING				PERCENTAGES		
Year Team	Lg	G	AB	H	2B	3B	HR	TB	R	RBI	TBB	IBB	SO	HBP	SH	SF	SB	CS	SB%	GDP	Avg	OBP	SLG
1991 Niagara Fls	A	77	291	85	10	2	0	99	53	29	53	2	45	1	5	3	14	11	.56	8	.292	.399	.340
1992 Fayetteville	A	131	465	132	17	6	3	170	73	43	82	4	80	5	4	4	13	6	.68	13	.284	.394	.366
1993 London	AA	121	408	97	24	2	3	134	44	46	45	2	77	3	1	3	5	2	.71	12	.238	.316	.328
1994 Lakeland	A	9	30	12	3	0	0	15	8	5	6	0	3	0	2	0	0	1	.00	1	.400	.500	.500
Trenton	AA	87	319	83	19	1	4	116	38	34	27	1	55	7	1	2	2	3	.40	6	.260	.330	.364
4 Min. YEARS		425	1513	409	73	11	10	534	216	157	213	9	260	16	13	12	34	23	.60	40	.270	.364	.353

John Pricher

Pitches: Right **Bats: Right** **Pos: P**   Ht: 5'10"   Wt: 200   Born: 11/13/70   Age: 24

		HOW MUCH HE PITCHED						WHAT HE GAVE UP										THE RESULTS				
Year Team	Lg	G	GS	CG	GF	IP	BFP	H	R	ER	HR	SH	SF	HB	TBB	IBB	SO	WP	Bk	W	L	Pct.	ShO	Sv	ERA
1992 Boise	A	32	0	0	30	43	169	34	8	5	1	1	0	8	3	65	1	4	2	1	.667	0	23	1.05
1993 Palm Sprngs	A	49	0	0	45	54	225	41	20	19	3	5	2	3	25	4	61	0	2	3	5	.375	0	26	3.17
1994 Midland	AA	40	0	0	19	49.1	225	60	33	30	6	2	1	1	22	1	30	3	0	2	3	.400	0	2	5.47
Lake Elsino	A	14	0	0	7	12.2	65	18	10	8	0	2	0	0	14	4	9	1	0	1	2	.333	0	0	5.68
3 Min. YEARS		135	0	0	101	159	684	153	71	62	10	10	4	4	69	12	165	5	6	8	11	.421	0	51	3.51

Curtis Pride

Bats: Left **Throws: Right** **Pos: OF**   Ht: 5'11"   Wt: 195   Born: 12/17/68   Age: 26

			BATTING													BASERUNNING				PERCENTAGES		
Year Team	Lg	G	AB	H	2B	3B	HR	TB	R	RBI	TBB	IBB	SO	HBP	SH	SF	SB	CS	SB%	GDP	Avg	OBP	SLG
1986 Kingsport	R	27	46	5	0	0	1	8	5	4	6	0	24	1	0	0	5	0	1.00	0	.109	.226	.174
1987 Kingsport	R	31	104	25	4	0	1	32	22	9	16	0	34	1	2	0	14	5	.74	0	.240	.347	.308
1988 Kingsport	R	70	268	76	13	1	8	115	59	27	50	1	48	1	2	1	23	7	.77	2	.284	.397	.429
1989 Pittsfield	A	55	212	55	7	3	6	86	35	23	25	1	47	2	2	1	9	2	.82	1	.259	.342	.406
1990 Columbia	A	53	191	52	4	4	6	82	38	25	21	3	45	0	0	1	11	8	.58	3	.272	.343	.429
1991 St. Lucie	A	116	392	102	21	7	9	164	57	37	43	4	94	2	3	0	24	5	.83	8	.260	.336	.418
1992 Binghamton	AA	118	388	88	15	3	10	139	54	42	47	1	110	4	0	1	14	11	.56	5	.227	.316	.358
1993 Harrisburg	AA	50	180	64	6	3	15	121	51	39	12	0	36	4	2	2	21	6	.78	2	.356	.404	.672
Ottawa	AAA	69	262	79	11	4	6	116	55	22	34	7	61	3	2	0	29	12	.71	3	.302	.388	.443
1994 W. Palm Bch	A	3	8	6	1	0	1	10	5	3	4	0	2	0	0	0	2	2	.50	0	.750	.833	1.250
Ottawa	AAA	82	300	77	16	4	9	128	56	32	39	1	81	2	1	1	22	6	.79	3	.257	.345	.427
1993 Montreal	NL	10	9	4	1	1	1	10	3	5	0	0	3	0	0	0	1	0	1.00	0	.444	.444	1.111
9 Min. YEARS		674	2351	629	98	29	72	1001	437	263	297	18	582	20	14	7	174	64	.73	27	.268	.354	.426

Chris Pritchett

Bats: Left **Throws: Right** **Pos: 1B**   Ht: 6'4"   Wt: 185   Born: 01/31/70   Age: 25

			BATTING													BASERUNNING				PERCENTAGES		
Year Team	Lg	G	AB	H	2B	3B	HR	TB	R	RBI	TBB	IBB	SO	HBP	SH	SF	SB	CS	SB%	GDP	Avg	OBP	SLG
1991 Boise	A	70	255	68	10	3	9	111	41	50	47	3	41	2	0	1.00	7					.267	.381	.435
1992 Quad City	A	128	448	130	19	1	13	190	79	72	71	6	88	5	2	5	9	4	.69	7	.290	.389	.424
1993 Midland	AA	127	464	143	30	6	2	191	61	66	61	2	72	2	6	7	3	7	.30	17	.308	.386	.412
1994 Midland	AA	127	460	142	25	4	6	193	86	91	92	9	87	2	3	7	5	3	.63	8	.309	.421	.420
4 Min. YEARS		452	1627	483	84	14	30	685	267	279	271	20	288	11	11	22	18	14	.56	39	.297	.396	.421

Brian Proctor

Bats: Both **Throws: Left** **Pos: OF**   Ht: 6'1"   Wt: 190   Born: 06/12/69   Age: 26

			BATTING													BASERUNNING				PERCENTAGES		
Year Team	Lg	G	AB	H	2B	3B	HR	TB	R	RBI	TBB	IBB	SO	HBP	SH	SF	SB	CS	SB%	GDP	Avg	OBP	SLG
1991 Yakima	A	74	282	87	25	2	7	137	48	61	42	7	31	2	3	1	5	4	.56	6	.309	.401	.486
1992 Bakersfield	A	71	261	83	15	2	4	114	38	42	23	1	33	0	1	9	0	2	.00	13	.318	.362	.437
San Antonio	AA	64	235	71	17	1	3	99	32	37	22	1	30	2	4	4	2	5	.29	1	.302	.361	.421
1993 San Antonio	AA	91	294	74	10	0	5	99	38	42	45	4	45	1	1	3	1	4	.20	5	.252	.350	.337
1994 Canton-Akm	AA	104	316	91	24	1	6	135	40	36	48	0	54	0	0	2	1	5	.17	5	.288	.380	.427
4 Min. YEARS		404	1388	406	91	6	25	584	196	218	180	13	193	5	9	19	9	20	.31	30	.293	.371	.421

Javier Puchales

Bats: Left **Throws: Left** **Pos: OF**   Ht: 6'0"   Wt: 170   Born: 03/29/72   Age: 23

			BATTING													BASERUNNING				PERCENTAGES		
Year Team	Lg	G	AB	H	2B	3B	HR	TB	R	RBI	TBB	IBB	SO	HBP	SH	SF	SB	CS	SB%	GDP	Avg	OBP	SLG
1989 Dodgers	R	41	120	40	2	0	0	42	15	9	4	0	14	2	2	0	8	6	.57	0	.333	.365	.350
1990 Dodgers	R	29	55	11	0	0	0	11	7	3	7	0	20	0	0	0	4	2	.67	1	.200	.290	.200
1991 Great Falls	R	40	111	40	5	1	0	47	21	15	5	1	10	1	1	1	13	6	.68	4	.360	.390	.423
1993 Vero Beach	A	77	279	94	6	0	0	100	46	27	17	0	44	3	6	1	4	5	.44	9	.337	.380	.358
1994 San Antonio	AA	20	35	4	0	0	0	4	3	1	4	0	6	0	1	0	2	0	1.00	1	.114	.205	.114
5 Min. YEARS		207	600	189	13	1	0	204	92	55	37	1	94	6	10	2	31	19	.62	15	.315	.360	.340

Scott Pugh

Bats: Left **Throws:** Left **Pos:** 1B **Ht:** 5'11" **Wt:** 180 **Born:** 06/18/70 **Age:** 25

								BATTING										BASERUNNING				PERCENTAGES		
Year Team	Lg	G	AB	H	2B	3B	HR	TB	R	RBI	TBB	IBB	SO	HBP	SH	SF	SB	CS	SB%	GDP	Avg	OBP	SLG
1991 Spokane	A	36	139	44	8	0	3	61	20	20	14	2	11	1	1	1	1	2	.33	8	.317	.381	.439
Waterloo	A	38	145	37	5	0	0	42	16	14	10	2	21	1	1	2	1	1	.50	2	.255	.304	.290
1992 Waterloo	A	137	522	126	26	0	6	170	62	44	33	3	84	3	4	2	1	1	.50	7	.241	.289	.326
1993 Rancho Cuca	A	96	327	96	19	2	5	134	39	43	26	2	52	5	4	2	3	2	.60	10	.294	.353	.410
Wichita	AA	26	79	25	1	0	4	38	15	11	4	0	17	2	0	0	0	1	.00	2	.316	.365	.481
1994 Wichita	AA	35	87	15	4	0	2	25	8	7	8	1	26	0	0	0	0	2	.00	3	.172	.242	.287
Daytona	A	77	248	63	7	0	2	76	22	21	26	1	51	1	0	2	3	4	.43	6	.254	.325	.306
4 Min. YEARS		445	1547	406	70	2	22	546	182	160	121	11	262	13	10	9	9	13	.41	36	.262	.320	.353

Benny Puig

Pitches: Left **Bats:** Left **Pos:** P **Ht:** 5'10" **Wt:** 183 **Born:** 10/16/65 **Age:** 29

			HOW MUCH HE PITCHED					WHAT HE GAVE UP											THE RESULTS					
Year Team	Lg	G	GS	CG	GF	IP	BFP	H	R	ER	HR	SH	SF	HB	TBB	IBB	SO	WP	Bk	W	L	Pct.	ShO	Sv	ERA
1985 Reno	A	28	25	4	0	153.2	0	164	101	83	14	0	0	6	78	1	121	8	2	9	7	.563	2	0	4.86
1986 Reno	A	25	25	7	0	178.2	762	184	100	81	16	10	6	3	58	3	130	8	1	14	9	.609	2	0	4.08
1987 El Paso	AA	1	1	0	0	6.1	32	12	5	5	0	0	0	0	3	0	5	0	0	0	1	.000	0	0	7.11
Stockton	A	27	23	7	0	167	702	161	78	61	10	6	4	9	64	3	123	11	1	11	8	.579	3	0	3.29
1988 El Paso	AA	54	0	0	23	92.1	394	92	55	45	12	3	3	3	31	1	62	7	9	8	4	.667	0	12	4.39
1989 El Paso	AA	47	0	0	43	64	269	62	30	26	5	1	3	1	22	0	47	3	0	1	3	.250	0	29	3.66
Denver	AAA	12	0	0	4	13.1	79	30	13	10	1	2	1	1	8	2	12	1	0	1	1	.500	0	2	6.75
1990 Denver	AAA	19	0	0	9	26.2	124	35	12	10	3	1	3	3	9	0	24	0	0	2	0	1.000	0	3	3.38
El Paso	AA	19	0	0	16	23.2	97	18	3	3	1	0	0	1	11	2	24	1	0	1	0	1.000	0	8	1.14
1992 Memphis	AA	68	0	0	59	75.2	289	45	17	17	4	6	5	1	21	1	64	1	0	4	2	.667	0	25	2.02
1993 Harrisburg	AA	14	0	0	3	18.1	75	16	5	5	1	0	1	2	7	0	10	0	1	0	1	.000	0	1	2.45
1994 Ottawa	AAA	9	0	0	2	14.2	72	20	9	9	0	0	2	1	9	1	10	2	0	0	1	.000	0	0	5.52
Sioux City	IND	4	4	0	0	24	105	24	11	10	1	0	0	1	14	0	16	1	0	2	1	.667	0	0	3.75
9 Min. YEARS		327	78	18	159	858.1	3000	863	439	365	68	29	28	32	335	14	648	43	14	53	38	.582	7	77	3.83

Harvey Pulliam

Bats: Right **Throws:** Right **Pos:** OF **Ht:** 6' 0" **Wt:** 205 **Born:** 10/20/67 **Age:** 27

								BATTING										BASERUNNING				PERCENTAGES		
Year Team	Lg	G	AB	H	2B	3B	HR	TB	R	RBI	TBB	IBB	SO	HBP	SH	SF	SB	CS	SB%	GDP	Avg	OBP	SLG
1986 Royals	R	48	168	35	3	0	4	50	14	23	8	1	33	3	2	3	3	2	.60	9	.208	.253	.298
1987 Appleton	A	110	395	109	20	1	9	158	54	55	26	0	79	3	1	3	21	7	.75	10	.276	.323	.400
1988 Baseball Cy	A	132	457	111	19	4	4	150	56	42	34	3	87	5	2	3	21	11	.66	13	.243	.301	.328
1989 Omaha	AAA	7	22	4	2	0	0	6	3	2	3	0	6	0	0	0	0	0	.00	0	.182	.280	.273
Memphis	AA	116	417	121	28	8	10	195	67	67	44	4	65	5	0	3	5	5	.50	12	.290	.362	.468
1990 Omaha	AAA	123	436	117	18	5	16	193	72	72	49	0	82	3	2	4	9	3	.75	14	.268	.343	.443
1991 Omaha	AAA	104	346	89	18	2	6	129	35	39	31	0	62	1	1	3	2	4	.33	4	.257	.318	.373
1992 Omaha	AAA	100	359	97	12	2	16	161	55	60	32	1	53	6	1	3	4	2	.67	15	.270	.338	.448
1993 Omaha	AAA	54	208	55	10	0	5	80	28	26	17	1	36	1	0	0	1	0	1.00	6	.264	.323	.385
1994 Las Vegas	AAA	95	314	72	10	0	20	142	48	53	21	0	65	4	0	2	0	1	.00	5	.229	.284	.452
1991 Kansas City	AL	18	33	9	1	0	3	19	4	4	3	1	9	0	1	0	0	0	.00	1	.273	.343	.576
1992 Kansas City	AL	4	5	1	1	0	0	2	2	0	1	0	3	0	0	0	0	0	.00	0	.200	.333	.400
1993 Kansas City	AL	27	62	16	5	0	1	24	7	6	2	0	14	1	0	0	0	0	.00	3	.258	.292	.387
9 Min. YEARS		889	3122	810	140	22	90	1264	432	439	265	10	568	31	9	24	66	35	.65	88	.259	.321	.405
3 Maj. YEARS		49	100	26	7	0	4	45	13	10	6	1	26	1	1	0	0	0	.00	4	.260	.308	.450

Bill Pulsipher

Pitches: Left **Bats:** Left **Pos:** P **Ht:** 6'4" **Wt:** 195 **Born:** 10/09/73 **Age:** 21

			HOW MUCH HE PITCHED					WHAT HE GAVE UP											THE RESULTS					
Year Team	Lg	G	GS	CG	GF	IP	BFP	H	R	ER	HR	SH	SF	HB	TBB	IBB	SO	WP	Bk	W	L	Pct.	ShO	Sv	ERA
1992 Pittsfield	A	14	14	0	0	95	413	88	40	30	3	0	1	3	56	0	83	16	1	6	3	.667	0	0	2.84
1993 Capital Cty	A	6	6	1	0	43.1	175	34	17	10	1	2	0	1	12	0	29	1	1	2	3	.400	0	0	2.08
St.Lucie	A	13	13	3	0	96.1	374	63	27	24	2	3	1	0	39	0	102	3	1	7	3	.700	0	0	2.24
1994 Binghamton	AA	28	28	5	0	201	849	179	90	72	18	7	1	3	89	2	171	9	5	14	9	.609	1	0	3.22
3 Min. YEARS		61	61	9	0	435.2	1811	364	174	136	24	12	3	7	196	2	385	29	8	29	18	.617	2	0	2.81

Shawn Purdy

Pitches: Right **Bats:** Right **Pos:** P **Ht:** 6'0" **Wt:** 205 **Born:** 07/30/68 **Age:** 26

			HOW MUCH HE PITCHED					WHAT HE GAVE UP											THE RESULTS					
Year Team	Lg	G	GS	CG	GF	IP	BFP	H	R	ER	HR	SH	SF	HB	TBB	IBB	SO	WP	Bk	W	L	Pct.	ShO	Sv	ERA
1991 Boise	A	15	15	1	0	95.2	394	87	37	32	3	3	2	4	27	2	78	6	0	8	4	.667	0	0	3.01
1992 Palm Sprngs	A	26	26	7	0	168	740	203	90	77	7	2	7	5	51	3	113	5	3	13	8	.619	0	0	4.13
1993 Angels	R	2	2	0	0	13	49	7	3	3	0	0	0	1	1	0	11	0	0	1	0	1.000	0	0	2.08
Boise	A	1	1	0	0	6	25	2	2	0	0	0	1	0	5	2	11	0	0	1	0	1.000	0	0	0.00
Palm Sprngs	A	5	3	0	2	27	120	30	12	11	2	1	0	3	5	2	17	1	0	1	1	.500	0	1	3.67

	Lg	G	GS	CG	GF	IP	BFP	H	R	ER	HR	SH	SF	HB	TBB	IBB	SO	WP	Bk	W	L	Pct.	ShO	Sv	ERA
Midland	AA	5	5	1	0	32	136	38	19	18	2	1	2	1	9	0	18	2	0	2	2	.500	0	0	5.06
1994 Midland	AA	10	5	0	1	36	170	48	39	35	2	2	2	2	15	1	19	6	1	1	6	.143	0	0	8.75
Lake Elsino	A	25	11	1	6	117.2	493	113	63	49	8	7	3	10	30	0	76	5	2	7	5	.583	0	0	3.75
4 Min. YEARS		89	68	10	9	495.1	2127	528	265	225	24	16	17	26	143	10	333	25	6	34	26	.567	0	1	4.09

Dave Pyc

Pitches: Left Bats: Left Pos: P Ht: 6'3" Wt: 235 Born: 02/11/71 Age: 24

		HOW MUCH HE PITCHED						WHAT HE GAVE UP												THE RESULTS					
Year Team	Lg	G	GS	CG	GF	IP	BFP	H	R	ER	HR	SH	SF	HB	TBB	IBB	SO	WP	Bk	W	L	Pct.	ShO	Sv	ERA
1992 Great Falls	R	25	0	0	19	34.2	155	32	15	11	0	3	1	1	16	5	34	1	0	2	3	.400	0	9	2.86
1993 Vero Beach	A	23	15	1	2	113.1	469	97	41	30	1	6	3	1	47	2	78	5	4	7	8	.467	0	0	2.38
1994 San Antonio	AA	25	25	0	0	154.2	656	165	77	64	2	9	4	3	47	5	120	3	0	4	11	.267	0	0	3.72
3 Min. YEARS		73	40	1	21	302.2	1280	294	133	105	3	18	8	5	110	12	232	9	4	13	22	.371	0	9	3.12

Luis Quinones

Bats: Both Throws: Right Pos: 3B Ht: 5'11" Wt: 185 Born: 04/28/62 Age: 33

		BATTING														BASERUNNING				PERCENTAGES		
Year Team	Lg	G	AB	H	2B	3B	HR	TB	R	RBI	TBB	IBB	SO	HBP	SH	SF	SB	CS	SB%	GDP	Avg	OBP	SLG
1984 Maine	AAA	131	473	127	27	3	8	184	71	64	39	3	73	1	1	5	5	6	.45	5	.268	.322	.389
1985 Maine	AAA	14	45	8	2	1	1	15	4	2	6	0	5	0	0	0	0	0	.00	0	.178	.275	.333
Phoenix	AAA	85	304	78	13	7	8	129	46	47	28	5	41	1	4	5	4	1	.80	8	.257	.317	.424
1986 Phoenix	AAA	14	55	14	4	1	0	20	7	7	4	0	8	1	0	2	0	1	.00	1	.255	.306	.364
1987 Iowa	AAA	77	287	91	14	12	11	162	44	62	16	1	30	1	0	4	2	3	.40	5	.317	.351	.564
1988 Nashville	AAA	114	417	115	28	6	9	182	42	53	29	3	51	0	3	5	3	7	.30	8	.276	.319	.436
1989 Nashville	AAA	45	176	40	9	2	4	65	19	24	8	1	22	1	3	5	1	0	1.00	2	.227	.258	.369
1992 Portland	AAA	88	276	67	7	4	12	118	45	49	41	5	42	2	1	6	1	0	1.00	11	.243	.338	.428
1993 Tucson	AAA	64	136	30	10	1	0	42	14	18	25	4	23	0	5	2	0	1	.00	0	.221	.337	.309
Calgary	AAA	12	39	15	3	2	3	31	7	7	9	1	10	0	0	1	0	2	.00	0	.385	.490	.795
1994 Calgary	AAA	65	236	72	19	1	6	111	42	29	21	1	41	1	0	3	1	2	.33	5	.305	.360	.470
Jacksonville	AA	52	168	44	7	0	8	75	29	29	23	2	27	0	0	2	4	2	.67	1	.262	.347	.446
1983 Oakland	AL	19	42	8	2	1	0	12	5	4	1	0	4	0	1	1	1	1	.50	0	.190	.205	.286
1986 San Francisco	NL	71	106	19	1	3	0	26	13	11	3	1	17	1	4	1	3	1	.75	1	.179	.207	.245
1987 Chicago	NL	49	101	22	6	0	0	28	12	8	10	0	16	0	0	0	0	0	.00	0	.218	.288	.277
1988 Cincinnati	NL	23	52	12	3	0	1	18	4	11	2	1	11	0	2	1	1	1	.50	0	.231	.255	.346
1989 Cincinnati	NL	97	340	83	13	4	12	140	43	34	25	0	46	3	8	2	2	4	.33	3	.244	.300	.412
1990 Cincinnati	NL	83	145	35	7	0	2	48	10	17	13	3	29	1	1	4	1	0	1.00	3	.241	.301	.331
1991 Cincinnati	NL	97	212	47	4	3	4	69	15	20	21	3	31	2	1	1	2	2	.33	2	.222	.297	.325
1992 Minnesota	AL	3	5	1	0	0	0	1	0	1	0	0	0	0	0	0	0	0	.00	0	.200	.167	.200
9 Min. YEARS		761	2612	701	143	40	70	1134	370	387	249	26	373	8	17	40	21	25	.46	46	.268	.329	.434
8 Maj. YEARS		442	1003	227	36	11	19	342	102	106	75	8	154	7	17	11	9	9	.50	9	.226	.282	.341

Carlos Quintana

Bats: Right Throws: Right Pos: 1B Ht: 6' 2" Wt: 220 Born: 08/26/65 Age: 29

		BATTING														BASERUNNING				PERCENTAGES		
Year Team	Lg	G	AB	H	2B	3B	HR	TB	R	RBI	TBB	IBB	SO	HBP	SH	SF	SB	CS	SB%	GDP	Avg	OBP	SLG
1985 Elmira	A	65	220	61	8	0	4	81	27	35	29	0	31	3	0	2	3	0	1.00	6	.277	.366	.368
1986 Greensboro	A	126	443	144	19	4	11	204	97	81	90	1	54	4	3	6	26	9	.74	16	.325	.438	.460
1987 New Britain	AA	56	206	64	11	3	2	87	31	31	24	3	33	1	0	4	3	3	.50	9	.311	.379	.422
1988 Pawtucket	AAA	131	471	134	25	3	16	213	67	66	38	3	72	3	2	3	3	5	.38	15	.285	.340	.452
1989 Pawtucket	AAA	82	272	78	11	2	11	126	45	52	53	1	39	0	0	5	6	0	1.00	7	.287	.397	.463
1994 Buffalo	AAA	39	110	26	6	0	0	32	10	11	11	0	22	1	0	1	1	2	.33	6	.236	.309	.291
1988 Boston	AL	5	6	2	0	0	0	2	1	2	2	0	3	0	0	0	0	0	.00	0	.333	.500	.333
1989 Boston	AL	34	77	16	5	0	0	21	6	6	7	0	12	0	0	0	0	0	.00	5	.208	.274	.273
1990 Boston	AL	149	512	147	28	0	7	196	56	67	52	0	74	2	4	2	1	2	.33	19	.287	.354	.383
1991 Boston	AL	149	478	141	21	1	11	197	69	71	61	2	66	2	6	3	1	0	1.00	17	.295	.375	.412
1993 Boston	AL	101	303	74	5	0	1	82	31	19	31	2	52	2	5	2	1	0	1.00	13	.244	.317	.271
6 Min. YEARS		499	1722	507	80	12	44	743	277	276	245	6	251	12	5	21	42	19	.69	59	.294	.382	.431
5 Maj. YEARS		438	1376	380	59	1	19	498	163	165	153	4	207	6	15	7	3	2	.60	54	.276	.350	.362

Rafael Quirico

Pitches: Left Bats: Left Pos: P Ht: 6'3" Wt: 170 Born: 09/07/69 Age: 25

		HOW MUCH HE PITCHED						WHAT HE GAVE UP												THE RESULTS					
Year Team	Lg	G	GS	CG	GF	IP	BFP	H	R	ER	HR	SH	SF	HB	TBB	IBB	SO	WP	Bk	W	L	Pct.	ShO	Sv	ERA
1989 Yankees	R	17	7	0	1	63.2	268	61	32	27	2	1	3	3	20	0	55	0	8	2	2	.500	0	1	3.82
1990 Greensboro	A	13	13	1	0	72	325	74	60	40	4	1	2	3	30	0	52	5	10	2	6	.250	0	0	5.00
Oneonta	A	14	14	1	0	87	359	69	38	31	2	2	4	4	39	0	69	9	9	6	3	.667	0	0	3.21
1991 Greensboro	A	26	26	1	0	155.1	641	103	59	39	5	1	2	7	80	0	162	12	9	12	8	.600	1	0	2.26
1992 Pr William	A	23	23	2	0	130.2	570	128	84	46	11	8	1	1	50	1	123	7	7	6	11	.353	0	0	3.17
Columbus	AAA	1	1	0	0	6	27	6	3	2	0	0	0	0	4	0	1	1	0	1	0	1.000	0	0	3.00
1993 Albany	AA	36	11	0	15	94.2	403	92	46	37	15	5	1	1	33	2	79	6	1	4	10	.286	0	7	3.52
Columbus	AAA	5	2	0	0	11	53	12	10	9	3	0	0	0	7	0	16	1	0	2	0	1.000	0	0	7.36
1994 Columbus	AAA	37	0	0	12	63.2	289	63	41	33	6	1	2	3	36	1	49	9	1	0	4	.000	0	0	4.66
6 Min. YEARS		172	97	5	28	684	2935	608	373	264	48	19	15	22	299	4	606	50	45	35	44	.443	1	9	3.47

Brian Raabe

Bats: Right **Throws:** Right **Pos:** 2B   Ht: 5'9" Wt: 170 Born: 11/05/67 Age: 27

Year	Team	Lg	G	AB	H	2B	3B	HR	TB	R	RBI	TBB	IBB	SO	HBP	SH	SF	SB	CS	SB%	GDP	Avg	OBP	SLG
1990	Visalia	A	42	138	34	3	2	0	41	11	17	10	0	9	1	1	0	5	1	.83	6	.246	.302	.297
1991	Visalia	A	85	311	80	3	1	1	88	36	22	40	0	14	4	3	2	15	5	.75	8	.257	.347	.283
1992	Miracle	A	102	361	104	16	2	2	130	52	32	48	1	17	8	1	3	7	6	.54	3	.288	.381	.360
	Orlando	AA	32	108	30	6	0	2	42	12	6	2	0	2	0	3	0	0	4	.00	2	.278	.291	.389
1993	Nashville	AA	134	524	150	23	2	6	195	80	52	56	1	28	10	10	4	18	8	.69	9	.286	.364	.372
1994	Salt Lake	AAA	123	474	152	26	3	3	193	78	49	50	1	11	1	0	8	9	8	.53	19	.321	.381	.407
	5 Min. YEARS		518	1916	550	77	10	14	689	269	178	206	3	81	24	18	17	54	32	.63	47	.287	.361	.360

Mike Raczka

Pitches: Left **Bats:** Left **Pos:** P   Ht: 6' 0" Wt: 200 Born: 11/16/62 Age: 32

Year	Team	Lg	G	GS	CG	GF	IP	BFP	H	R	ER	HR	SH	SF	HB	TBB	IBB	SO	WP	Bk	W	L	Pct.	ShO	Sv	ERA
1990	Las Vegas	AAA	4	2	0	0	11.2	52	11	10	10	2	1	0	0	9	0	7	1	0	1	0	1.000	0	0	7.71
	Tacoma	AAA	42	0	0	18	55.2	238	48	27	22	3	5	1	3	35	3	54	2	0	6	5	.545	0	2	3.56
1992	Modesto	A	6	0	0	3	9.1	43	13	9	7	1	1	0	1	3	0	5	1	0	1	1	.500	0	0	6.75
	Tacoma	AAA	31	1	0	11	48.2	196	38	22	19	3	3	4	0	24	6	26	2	1	0	1	.000	0	1	3.51
1993	Tacoma	AAA	55	0	0	11	60.1	269	65	39	36	6	3	2	3	30	2	40	3	0	2	1	.667	0	0	5.37
1994	New Britain	AA	34	0	0	6	41.2	162	34	20	16	2	1	1	0	16	0	25	4	0	3	1	.750	0	0	3.46
	Pawtucket	AAA	24	1	0	4	26.2	114	19	7	6	1	2	2	0	14	1	14	5	0	1	1	.500	0	0	2.03
1992	Oakland	AL	8	0	0	1	6.1	33	8	7	6	0	0	0	2	5	0	2	0	0	0	0	.000	0	0	8.53
	4 Min. YEARS		196	4	0	53	254	1074	228	134	116	18	16	10	7	131	12	171	18	1	14	10	.583	0	3	4.11

Brad Radke

Pitches: Right **Bats:** Right **Pos:** P   Ht: 6'2" Wt: 180 Born: 10/27/72 Age: 22

Year	Team	Lg	G	GS	CG	GF	IP	BFP	H	R	ER	HR	SH	SF	HB	TBB	IBB	SO	WP	Bk	W	L	Pct.	ShO	Sv	ERA
1991	Twins	R	10	9	0	1	49.2	205	41	21	17	0	1	2	2	14	0	44	0	2	3	4	.429	0	1	3.08
1992	Kenosha	A	26	25	4	1	165.2	680	149	70	54	8	7	6	6	47	1	127	4	0	10	10	.500	1	0	2.93
1993	Ft.Myers	A	14	14	0	0	92	376	85	42	39	3	0	1	4	21	0	69	3	0	3	5	.375	0	0	3.82
	Nashville	AA	13	13	1	0	76	327	81	42	39	6	1	1	6	16	0	76	5	0	2	6	.250	0	0	4.62
1994	Nashville	AA	29	28	5	0	186.1	741	167	66	55	9	4	2	5	34	0	123	8	1	12	9	.571	1	0	2.66
	4 Min. YEARS		92	89	10	2	569.2	2329	523	241	204	26	13	12	23	132	2	439	20	3	30	34	.469	2	1	3.22

Doug Radziewicz

Bats: Left **Throws:** Left **Pos:** 1B   Ht: 6'1" Wt: 195 Born: 04/24/69 Age: 26

Year	Team	Lg	G	AB	H	2B	3B	HR	TB	R	RBI	TBB	IBB	SO	HBP	SH	SF	SB	CS	SB%	GDP	Avg	OBP	SLG
1991	Johnson Cty	R	62	201	58	15	2	4	89	31	28	25	2	18	2	0	2	1	0	1.00	4	.289	.370	.443
1992	Springfield	A	55	165	50	12	2	2	72	25	33	26	1	17	4	0	3	2	1	.67	3	.303	.404	.436
	St. Pete	A	21	73	17	4	2	1	28	10	5	10	0	15	1	0	0	0	0	.00	2	.233	.333	.384
1993	St.Pete	A	123	439	150	36	2	4	202	66	72	73	11	58	5	1	5	6	8	.43	5	.342	.437	.460
1994	Arkansas	AA	121	342	76	16	2	8	120	33	40	43	2	65	3	1	6	1	0	1.00	8	.222	.310	.351
	4 Min. YEARS		382	1220	351	83	10	19	511	165	178	177	16	173	15	2	16	10	9	.53	22	.288	.380	.419

Curtis Ralph

Pitches: Right **Bats:** Right **Pos:** P   Ht: 6'0" Wt: 205 Born: 08/06/68 Age: 26

Year	Team	Lg	G	GS	CG	GF	IP	BFP	H	R	ER	HR	SH	SF	HB	TBB	IBB	SO	WP	Bk	W	L	Pct.	ShO	Sv	ERA
1988	Yankees	R	12	12	0	0	64.2	270	62	26	19	3	3	2	1	22	0	37	5	0	6	0	1.000	0	0	2.64
1989	Ft.Laudrdle	A	15	10	0	3	59.1	274	66	42	26	4	1	3	6	37	0	31	11	0	6	2	.750	0	0	3.94
1990	Pr William	A	43	0	0	16	80	345	69	30	28	3	5	2	5	40	3	75	5	1	4	3	.571	0	0	3.15
1991	Pr William	A	47	0	0	24	65.1	264	51	28	24	5	3	3	4	22	4	60	1	0	5	7	.417	0	6	3.31
1992	Ft. Laud	A	12	0	0	6	22	102	23	10	6	2	2	0	3	7	1	22	1	2	1	2	.333	0	1	2.45
	Pr William	A	32	0	0	22	59	240	54	22	21	3	5	3	4	16	2	37	3	3	3	2	.600	0	4	3.20
1993	Pr William	A	32	0	0	30	37	162	39	23	21	2	3	1	1	11	0	41	2	0	3	3	.500	0	15	5.11
1994	Albany-Colo	A	43	0	0	14	65	273	56	17	17	3	1	1	4	31	2	54	5	1	7	2	.778	0	1	2.35
	Columbus	AAA	1	0	0	0	1.2	0	0	0	0	0	0	0	0	2	0	1	0	0	0	0	.000	0	0	0.00
	7 Min. YEARS		237	22	0	115	454	1937	420	198	162	25	23	15	28	188	12	358	33	7	35	21	.625	0	27	3.21

Dan Rambo

Pitches: Right **Bats:** Right **Pos:** P   Ht: 6'0" Wt: 190 Born: 10/07/66 Age: 28

Year	Team	Lg	G	GS	CG	GF	IP	BFP	H	R	ER	HR	SH	SF	HB	TBB	IBB	SO	WP	Bk	W	L	Pct.	ShO	Sv	ERA
1989	Pocatello	R	2	2	0	0	14	55	11	2	2	0	0	0	0	3	0	11	0	1	0	1	.000	0	0	1.29
	Clinton	A	12	11	1	0	66.1	273	59	27	24	7	1	2	3	19	3	63	2	1	4	4	.500	0	0	3.26
1990	San Jose	A	26	17	2	3	143.2	575	104	47	35	8	6	2	4	42	1	142	3	2	12	2	.857	1	1	2.19
1991	Phoenix	AAA	3	2	0	0	13.2	63	18	8	7	1	2	0	0	6	0	10	0	0	0	1	.000	0	0	4.61
	Shreveport	AA	26	21	1	1	147	618	146	71	60	12	7	4	4	43	2	103	7	2	12	6	.667	1	0	3.67

Year	Team	Lg	G	GS	CG	GF	IP	BFP	H	R	ER	HR	SH	SF	HB	TBB	IBB	SO	WP	Bk	W	L	Pct.	ShO	Sv	ERA
1992	Phoenix	AAA	20	1	0	4	41	181	47	28	27	1	3	2	3	15	2	32	0	1	1	2	.333	0	1	5.93
	Shreveport	AA	28	2	0	11	60	255	56	23	19	2	3	0	2	19	5	45	6	2	6	3	.667	0	1	2.85
1993	Phoenix	AAA	18	5	0	2	51.2	266	77	44	41	6	2	4	0	33	7	31	10	0	1	3	.250	0	0	7.14
	Shreveport	AA	15	15	1	0	102	413	98	46	36	1	0	5	4	27	1	61	2	1	7	5	.583	0	0	3.18
1994	Brainerd	IND	6	6	1	0	40	167	41	21	20	3	0	2	6	6	0	33	2	0	2	3	.400	0	0	4.50
	El Paso	AA	13	1	0	3	25.1	100	24	7	6	2	1	1	0	4	1	20	2	0	1	3	.250	0	1	2.13
	6 Min. YEARS		169	83	6	24	704.2	2966	681	324	277	43	25	22	26	217	22	551	34	10	46	33	.582	2	4	3.54

J.D. Ramirez

Bats: Right Throws: Right Pos: 2B　　　Ht: 5'9" Wt: 160 Born: 11/19/66 Age: 28

						BATTING											BASERUNNING				PERCENTAGES		
Year	Team	Lg	G	AB	H	2B	3B	HR	TB	R	RBI	TBB	IBB	SO	HBP	SH	SF	SB	CS	SB%	GDP	Avg	OBP	SLG
1989	Salt Lake	R	38	150	55	11	1	2	74	23	26	11	0	13	2	1	2	2	3	.40	6	.367	.412	.493
	Jamestown	A	13	44	13	2	0	2	21	9	11	4	0	12	0	0	0	2	2	.50	0	.295	.354	.477
1990	Rockford	A	119	432	112	21	5	2	149	56	51	53	3	58	8	5	1	6	6	.50	8	.259	.350	.345
1991	Wst Plm Bch	A	94	328	77	14	0	4	103	38	30	20	0	39	6	5	5	13	6	.68	10	.235	.287	.314
1992	Salt Lake	R	44	173	60	9	2	2	79	46	24	32	0	18	4	2	2	2	6	.25	2	.347	.455	.457
1993	Sioux City	IND	55	216	73	10	1	3	94	30	30	16	0	26	5	4	0	5	5	.50	2	.338	.397	.435
1994	Midland	AA	123	449	129	27	3	14	204	81	58	52	0	96	7	4	2	3	4	.43	8	.287	.369	.454
	6 Min. YEARS		486	1792	519	94	12	29	724	283	230	188	3	262	32	21	12	33	32	.51	36	.290	.365	.404

Omar Ramirez

Bats: Right Throws: Right Pos: OF　　　Ht: 5'9" Wt: 170 Born: 11/02/70 Age: 24

						BATTING											BASERUNNING				PERCENTAGES		
Year	Team	Lg	G	AB	H	2B	3B	HR	TB	R	RBI	TBB	IBB	SO	HBP	SH	SF	SB	CS	SB%	GDP	Avg	OBP	SLG
1990	Indians	R	18	58	10	0	0	0	10	6	2	11	0	11	0	0	0	2	4	.33	2	.172	.304	.172
1991	Watertown	A	56	210	56	17	0	2	79	30	17	30	0	30	1	3	1	12	2	.86	2	.267	.360	.376
1992	Kinston	A	110	411	123	20	5	13	192	73	49	38	1	53	3	8	2	19	12	.61	5	.299	.361	.467
1993	Canton-Akrn	AA	125	516	162	24	6	7	219	116	53	53	2	49	5	4	1	24	6	.80	9	.314	.383	.424
1994	Charlotte	AAA	134	419	97	20	2	8	145	66	45	54	0	43	1	2	3	15	7	.68	11	.232	.319	.346
	5 Min. YEARS		443	1614	448	81	13	30	645	291	166	186	3	186	10	17	7	72	31	.70	29	.278	.354	.400

Robert Ramirez

Pitches: Left Bats: Right Pos: P　　　Ht: 5'11" Wt: 165 Born: 08/17/72 Age: 22

			HOW MUCH HE PITCHED						WHAT HE GAVE UP										THE RESULTS					
Year	Team	Lg	G	GS	CG	GF	IP	BFP	H	R	ER	HR	SH	SF	HB	TBB	IBB	SO	WP	Bk	W	L	Pct.	ShO	Sv	ERA
1990	Pirates	R	11	3	0	0	33.2	133	20	4	2	1	0	0	1	18	0	27	1	1	2	1	.667	0	0	0.53
1991	Welland	A	16	12	0	2	74.1	316	66	43	34	7	2	2	2	35	0	71	3	3	2	6	.250	0	1	4.12
1994	Carolina	AA	6	6	0	0	27.1	129	38	19	16	2	3	0	1	8	0	21	1	0	0	1	.000	0	0	5.27
	3 Min. YEARS		33	21	0	2	135.1	578	124	66	52	10	5	2	4	61	0	119	5	4	4	8	.333	0	1	3.46

John Ramos

Bats: Right Throws: Right Pos: C　　　Ht: 6' 0" Wt: 190 Born: 08/06/65 Age: 29

						BATTING											BASERUNNING				PERCENTAGES		
Year	Team	Lg	G	AB	H	2B	3B	HR	TB	R	RBI	TBB	IBB	SO	HBP	SH	SF	SB	CS	SB%	GDP	Avg	OBP	SLG
1986	Ft.Laudrdle	A	54	184	49	10	1	2	67	25	28	26	0	23	1	4	2	8	3	.73	5	.266	.357	.364
	Oneonta	A	3	8	4	2	1	0	8	3	1	2	0	1	0	0	0	0	0	.00	0	.500	.600	1.000
1987	Pr William	A	76	235	51	6	1	2	65	26	27	28	3	30	2	3	3	8	5	.62	10	.217	.302	.277
1988	Pr William	A	109	391	119	18	2	8	165	47	57	49	1	34	7	2	5	8	2	.80	7	.304	.387	.422
	Albany	AA	21	72	16	1	3	1	26	11	13	12	0	9	1	0	2	2	1	.67	1	.222	.333	.361
1989	Albany	AA	105	359	98	21	0	9	146	55	60	40	2	65	7	2	2	7	5	.58	14	.273	.355	.407
1990	Columbus	AAA	2	6	0	0	0	0	0	0	1	0	0	0	0	0	0	0	0	.00	0	.000	.000	.000
	Albany	AA	84	287	90	20	1	4	124	38	45	36	0	39	3	0	5	1	0	1.00	10	.314	.390	.432
1991	Columbus	AAA	104	377	116	18	3	10	170	52	63	56	3	54	3	1	9	1	5	.17	15	.308	.393	.451
1992	Columbus	AAA	18	64	11	4	1	1	20	5	12	8	0	14	0	0	1	1	0	1.00	1	.172	.260	.313
1993	Columbus	AAA	49	158	41	7	0	1	51	17	18	19	1	32	0	0	2	1	2	.33	6	.259	.335	.323
1994	Las Vegas	AAA	114	312	102	25	1	10	159	51	46	40	1	41	1	2	3	0	0	.00	9	.327	.402	.510
1991	New York	AL	10	26	8	1	0	0	9	4	3	1	0	3	0	0	2	0	0	.00	1	.308	.310	.346
	9 Min. YEARS		739	2453	697	132	14	48	1001	330	371	316	11	342	25	14	34	37	23	.62	78	.284	.367	.408

Ken Ramos

Bats: Left Throws: Left Pos: OF　　　Ht: 6'1" Wt: 185 Born: 06/08/67 Age: 28

						BATTING											BASERUNNING				PERCENTAGES		
Year	Team	Lg	G	AB	H	2B	3B	HR	TB	R	RBI	TBB	IBB	SO	HBP	SH	SF	SB	CS	SB%	GDP	Avg	OBP	SLG
1989	Indians	R	54	193	60	7	2	1	74	41	14	39	1	18	3	3	2	17	7	.71	4	.311	.430	.383
	Kinston	A	8	21	3	0	0	0	3	6	0	5	0	2	0	1	0	2	0	1.00	0	.143	.308	.143
1990	Kinston	A	96	339	117	16	6	0	145	71	31	48	4	34	1	5	2	18	14	.56	4	.345	.426	.428
	Canton-Akrn	AA	19	73	24	2	2	0	30	12	11	8	0	10	0	0	1	2	1	.67	1	.329	.390	.411
1991	Canton-Akrn	AA	74	257	62	6	3	2	80	41	13	28	0	22	1	4	1	8	4	.67	3	.241	.317	.311
1992	Canton-Akrn	AA	125	442	150	23	5	5	198	93	42	82	6	37	0	5	1	14	11	.56	8	.339	.442	.448
1993	Charlotte	AAA	132	480	140	16	11	3	187	77	41	47	4	41	0	7	3	12	8	.60	10	.292	.353	.390
1994	Tucson	AAA	121	393	118	19	7	1	154	81	32	74	5	27	0	3	5	22	12	.65	8	.300	.407	.392
	6 Min. YEARS		629	2198	674	89	36	12	871	422	184	331	20	191	5	28	15	95	57	.63	38	.307	.396	.396

Fernando Ramsey

Bats: Right **Throws:** Right **Pos:** OF **Ht:** 6' 1" **Wt:** 175 **Born:** 12/20/65 **Age:** 29

Year Team	Lg	G	AB	H	2B	3B	HR	TB	R	RBI	TBB	IBB	SO	HBP	SH	SF	SB	CS	SB%	GDP	Avg	OBP	SLG
1987 Geneva	A	39	56	9	1	0	0	10	9	3	5	1	10	0	2	0	2	0	1.00	0	.161	.230	.179
1988 Chston-Wv	A	121	381	92	5	1	0	99	36	15	14	1	68	4	6	0	15	7	.68	4	.241	.276	.260
1989 Peoria	A	131	410	100	7	5	0	117	56	34	25	0	70	10	11	3	16	10	.62	6	.244	.301	.285
1990 Winston-Sal	A	124	428	109	12	4	5	144	52	48	19	0	50	3	9	2	43	7	.86	4	.255	.290	.336
1991 Charlotte	AA	139	547	151	18	6	6	199	78	49	36	0	90	3	7	2	37	17	.69	8	.276	.323	.364
1992 Iowa	AAA	133	480	129	9	5	1	151	62	38	23	0	78	2	11	0	39	12	.76	14	.269	.305	.315
1993 Iowa	AAA	134	545	147	30	7	5	206	76	42	25	2	72	2	9	0	13	13	.50	7	.270	.304	.378
1994 Norfolk	AAA	19	49	5	0	1	0	7	5	1	3	0	8	0	0	0	1	2	.33	0	.102	.154	.143
Indianapolis	AAA	14	51	18	4	0	0	22	9	4	0	0	7	0	0	0	3	1	.75	1	.353	.353	.431
1992 Chicago	NL	18	25	3	0	0	0	3	0	2	0	0	6	0	0	0	0	0	.00	0	.120	.120	.120
8 Min. YEARS		854	2947	760	86	29	17	955	383	234	150	4	453	24	55	7	169	69	.71	44	.258	.299	.324

Joe Randa

Bats: Right **Throws:** Right **Pos:** 3B **Ht:** 5'11" **Wt:** 190 **Born:** 12/18/69 **Age:** 25

Year Team	Lg	G	AB	H	2B	3B	HR	TB	R	RBI	TBB	IBB	SO	HBP	SH	SF	SB	CS	SB%	GDP	Avg	OBP	SLG
1991 Eugene	A	72	275	93	20	2	11	150	53	59	46	4	30	6	0	4	8	1	.86	8	.338	.438	.545
1992 Appleton	A	72	266	80	13	0	5	108	55	43	34	0	37	6	0	6	6	2	.75	6	.301	.385	.406
Baseball Cy	A	51	189	52	7	0	1	62	22	12	12	0	21	2	1	1	4	3	.57	4	.275	.324	.328
1993 Memphis	AA	131	505	149	31	5	11	223	74	72	39	2	64	3	0	10	8	7	.53	10	.295	.343	.442
1994 Omaha	AAA	127	455	125	27	2	10	186	65	51	30	1	49	8	5	5	5	2	.71	18	.275	.327	.409
4 Min. YEARS		453	1690	499	98	9	38	729	269	237	161	7	201	25	6	26	29	15	.66	46	.295	.360	.431

Paul Rappoli

Bats: Left **Throws:** Right **Pos:** OF **Ht:** 6'1" **Wt:** 195 **Born:** 10/04/71 **Age:** 23

Year Team	Lg	G	AB	H	2B	3B	HR	TB	R	RBI	TBB	IBB	SO	HBP	SH	SF	SB	CS	SB%	GDP	Avg	OBP	SLG
1990 Red Sox	R	53	161	46	4	0	1	53	31	22	35	0	16	8	1	3	4	4	.50	4	.286	.430	.329
1991 Winter Havn	A	4	5	0	0	0	0	0	2	0	0	0	1	0	0	0	0	0	.00	0	.000	.000	.000
Elmira	A	69	209	55	15	1	3	81	37	19	34	0	38	6	2	2	11	3	.79	0	.263	.378	.388
1992 Lynchburg	A	111	344	92	17	2	6	131	47	42	48	1	66	6	4	3	11	13	.46	8	.267	.364	.381
1993 New Britain	AA	115	356	76	16	5	3	111	49	26	64	4	77	6	6	2	6	8	.43	5	.213	.341	.312
1994 Sarasota	A	20	72	25	7	1	1	37	14	12	6	0	15	2	0	0	1	2	.33	2	.347	.413	.514
New Britain	AA	109	355	99	14	6	4	137	52	40	50	1	56	7	3	0	18	10	.64	3	.279	.379	.386
5 Min. YEARS		481	1502	393	73	15	18	550	232	161	237	6	269	35	16	10	51	40	.56	22	.262	.373	.366

Dennis Rasmussen

Pitches: Left **Bats:** Left **Pos:** P **Ht:** 6' 7" **Wt:** 240 **Born:** 04/18/59 **Age:** 36

Year Team	Lg	G	GS	CG	GF	IP	BFP	H	R	ER	HR	SH	SF	HB	TBB	IBB	SO	WP	Bk	W	L	Pct.	ShO	Sv	ERA
1984 Columbus	AAA	6	6	3	0	43.2	177	24	15	15	1	1	1	0	27	0	30	8	0	4	1	.800	1	0	3.09
1985 Columbus	AAA	7	7	1	0	45	196	41	24	19	1	3	3	1	25	0	43	3	1	0	3	.000	0	0	3.80
1987 Columbus	AAA	1	1	0	0	7	26	5	1	1	0	0	1	0	0	0	4	0	0	1	0	1.000	0	0	1.29
1991 Las Vegas	AAA	5	5	1	0	26.1	114	23	18	16	2	1	1	2	15	0	12	1	1	1	3	.250	0	0	5.47
1992 Rochester	AAA	9	9	1	0	46	208	49	33	29	3	1	1	0	22	0	33	1	0	0	7	.000	0	0	5.67
Iowa	AAA	2	2	0	0	11.1	52	15	7	6	0	1	1	1	3	0	6	0	0	1	1	.500	0	0	4.76
Omaha	AAA	11	6	3	1	50.2	205	37	14	8	3	4	1	0	17	2	44	0	1	3	3	.500	2	0	1.42
1993 Omaha	AAA	17	17	3	0	105.2	451	124	68	59	16	4	5	1	27	0	59	4	2	7	8	.467	1	0	5.03
1994 Phoenix	AAA	5	5	1	0	30	128	39	17	14	2	1	0	0	7	0	12	3	0	1	2	.333	0	0	4.20
Omaha	AAA	20	18	9	0	139	567	135	59	50	12	3	4	5	36	0	84	2	0	10	7	.588	2	0	3.24
1983 San Diego	NL	4	1	0	0	13.2	58	10	5	3	1	0	0	0	8	0	13	1	0	0	0	.000	0	0	1.98
1984 New York	AL	24	24	1	0	147.2	616	127	79	75	16	3	7	4	60	0	110	8	2	9	6	.600	0	0	4.57
1985 New York	AL	22	16	2	0	101.2	429	97	56	45	10	1	5	1	42	1	63	3	1	3	5	.375	0	0	3.98
1986 New York	AL	31	31	3	0	202	819	160	91	87	28	1	5	2	74	0	131	5	0	18	6	.750	1	0	3.88
1987 New York	AL	26	25	2	0	146	627	145	78	77	31	5	5	4	55	1	89	6	0	9	7	.563	0	0	4.75
Cincinnati	NL	7	7	0	0	45.1	187	39	22	20	5	3	1	1	12	0	39	1	2	4	1	.800	0	0	3.97
1988 Cincinnati	NL	11	11	1	0	56.1	255	68	36	36	8	2	2	2	22	4	27	1	5	2	6	.250	1	0	5.75
San Diego	NL	20	20	6	0	148.1	599	131	48	42	9	8	2	2	36	0	85	6	0	14	4	.778	0	0	2.55
1989 San Diego	NL	33	33	1	0	183.2	799	190	100	87	18	9	11	3	72	6	87	4	2	10	10	.500	0	0	4.26
1990 San Diego	NL	32	32	3	0	187.2	825	217	110	94	28	14	4	3	62	4	86	9	1	11	15	.423	1	0	4.51
1991 San Diego	NL	24	24	1	0	146.2	633	155	74	61	12	4	6	2	49	3	75	1	1	6	13	.316	1	0	3.74
1992 Chicago	NL	3	1	0	0	5	24	7	6	6	2	0	1	1	2	1	0	0	0	0	0	.000	0	0	10.80
Kansas City	AL	5	5	1	0	37.2	134	25	7	6	0	1	0	0	6	0	12	3	0	4	1	.800	1	0	1.43
1993 Kansas City	AL	9	4	0	3	29	138	40	25	24	4	0	1	0	14	1	12	2	0	1	2	.333	0	0	7.45
7 Min. YEARS		83	76	22	1	504.2	2124	492	256	217	40	19	18	10	179	2	327	22	5	28	35	.444	6	0	3.87
11 Maj. YEARS		251	234	21	6	1450.2	6143	1411	737	663	172	51	50	26	514	21	829	50	14	91	76	.545	5	0	4.11

Mark Ratekin

Pitches: Right Bats: Right Pos: P Ht: 6'4" Wt: 215 Born: 11/14/70 Age: 24

Year Team	Lg	G	GS	CG	GF	IP	BFP	H	R	ER	HR	SH	SF	HB	TBB	IBB	SO	WP	Bk	W	L	Pct.	ShO	Sv	ERA
1991 Boise	A	14	13	1	1	70	287	59	31	26	1	1	2	3	22	0	49	3	2	2	5	.286	0	0	3.34
1992 Quad City	A	23	19	1	4	110	467	104	57	47	6	6	4	5	35	0	62	9	1	5	6	.455	0	0	3.85
1993 Palm Spmgs	A	21	21	6	0	143.1	618	151	78	62	5	5	6	6	46	0	66	5	1	7	7	.500	1	0	3.89
Midland	AA	7	6	2	0	44.1	191	50	25	23	5	0	0	4	11	0	24	2	0	3	1	.750	0	0	4.67
1994 Midland	AA	8	8	2	0	56.2	233	54	36	31	5	0	1	2	14	4	37	1	0	3	4	.429	0	0	4.92
Vancouver	AAA	21	20	1	0	123.2	549	159	78	69	10	1	4	4	40	2	55	8	0	12	5	.706	0	0	5.02
4 Min. YEARS		94	87	13	5	548	2345	577	305	258	32	13	17	24	168	6	293	28	4	32	28	.533	1	0	4.24

Daryl Ratliff

Bats: Right Throws: Right Pos: OF Ht: 6'1" Wt: 180 Born: 10/15/69 Age: 25

Year Team	Lg	G	AB	H	2B	3B	HR	TB	R	RBI	TBB	IBB	SO	HBP	SH	SF	SB	CS	SB%	GDP	Avg	OBP	SLG
1989 Princeton	R	66	208	51	2	0	0	53	28	21	24	1	31	0	0	1	10	3	.77	2	.245	.322	.255
1990 Augusta	A	122	417	123	11	6	1	149	70	55	67	2	62	0	1	0	24	7	.77	12	.295	.393	.357
1991 Salem	A	88	352	103	8	4	2	125	60	23	27	0	43	0	2	1	35	9	.80	6	.293	.342	.355
Carolina	AA	24	93	20	3	0	0	23	10	9	6	0	16	0	1	0	7	3	.70	1	.215	.263	.247
1992 Carolina	AA	124	413	99	13	3	0	118	45	26	41	0	50	0	5	4	25	11	.69	7	.240	.306	.286
1993 Carolina	AA	121	454	129	15	4	0	152	59	47	35	0	58	2	14	5	29	13	.69	9	.284	.335	.335
1994 Salem	A	36	138	44	9	2	1	60	25	19	12	0	18	0	1	0	5	5	.50	1	.319	.373	.435
Carolina	AA	78	253	70	7	2	0	81	38	29	23	1	34	1	1	5	11	4	.73	8	.277	.333	.320
6 Min. YEARS		659	2328	639	68	21	4	761	335	229	235	4	312	3	25	16	146	55	.73	46	.274	.340	.327

Jon Ratliff

Pitches: Right Bats: Right Pos: P Ht: 6'5" Wt: 200 Born: 12/22/71 Age: 23

Year Team	Lg	G	GS	CG	GF	IP	BFP	H	R	ER	HR	SH	SF	HB	TBB	IBB	SO	WP	Bk	W	L	Pct.	ShO	Sv	ERA
1993 Geneva	A	3	3	0	0	14	65	12	8	5	0	0	0	2	8	0	7	0	0	1	1	.500	0	0	3.21
Daytona	A	8	8	0	0	41	194	50	29	18	0	2	3	5	23	0	15	3	1	2	4	.333	0	0	3.95
1994 Daytona	A	8	8	1	0	54	227	64	23	21	5	2	1	4	5	0	17	4	0	3	2	.600	0	0	3.50
Iowa	AAA	5	4	0	0	28.1	131	39	19	17	7	1	1	2	7	0	10	3	0	1	3	.250	0	0	5.40
Orlando	AA	12	12	1	0	62.1	292	78	44	39	4	4	5	8	26	1	19	5	0	1	9	.100	0	0	5.63
2 Min. YEARS		36	35	2	0	199.2	909	243	123	100	16	9	10	21	69	1	68	15	1	8	19	.296	0	0	4.51

Luis Raven

Bats: Right Throws: Right Pos: 3B Ht: 6'4" Wt: 230 Born: 11/19/68 Age: 26

Year Team	Lg	G	AB	H	2B	3B	HR	TB	R	RBI	TBB	IBB	SO	HBP	SH	SF	SB	CS	SB%	GDP	Avg	OBP	SLG
1989 Angels	R	43	145	30	6	2	1	43	15	20	8	0	43	1	0	3	3	0	1.00	3	.207	.248	.297
1991 Boise	A	38	84	23	2	0	2	31	13	13	9	0	19	1	0	0	1	1	.50	6	.274	.351	.369
1992 Palm Spmgs	A	107	378	109	16	2	9	156	59	55	24	2	81	2	0	4	18	7	.72	5	.288	.331	.413
1993 Midland	AA	43	167	43	12	1	2	63	21	30	5	1	45	1	1	0	4	2	.67	4	.257	.283	.377
Palm Spmgs	A	85	343	95	20	2	7	140	38	52	22	0	84	3	1	2	15	11	.58	6	.277	.324	.408
1994 Midland	AA	47	191	58	8	5	18	130	41	57	5	2	51	3	0	3	4	1	.80	9	.304	.327	.681
Vancouver	AAA	85	328	100	13	4	13	160	66	59	22	1	88	2	0	8	7	0	1.00	6	.305	.344	.488
5 Min. YEARS		448	1636	458	77	16	52	723	253	286	95	6	411	13	2	20	52	22	.70	39	.280	.321	.442

Darren Reed

Bats: Right Throws: Right Pos: OF Ht: 6'1" Wt: 205 Born: 10/16/65 Age: 29

Year Team	Lg	G	AB	H	2B	3B	HR	TB	R	RBI	TBB	IBB	SO	HBP	SH	SF	SB	CS	SB%	GDP	Avg	OBP	SLG
1984 Oneonta	A	40	113	26	7	0	2	39	17	9	10	0	19	0	1	1	2	1	.67	2	.230	.290	.345
1985 Ft.Lauderdle	A	100	369	117	21	4	10	176	63	61	36	3	56	7	0	7	13	3	.81	9	.317	.382	.477
1986 Albany	AA	51	196	45	11	1	4	70	22	27	15	0	24	1	1	5	1	0	1.00	2	.230	.281	.357
1987 Columbus	AAA	21	79	26	3	3	8	59	15	16	4	0	9	0	0	0	0	2	.00	2	.329	.361	.747
Albany	AA	107	404	129	23	4	20	220	68	79	51	9	50	8	0	3	9	6	.60	10	.319	.403	.545
1988 Tidewater	AAA	101	345	83	26	0	9	136	31	47	32	2	66	3	3	4	0	3	.00	9	.241	.307	.394
1989 Tidewater	AAA	133	444	119	30	6	4	173	57	50	60	1	70	11	1	4	11	2	.85	15	.268	.366	.390
1990 Tidewater	AAA	104	359	95	21	6	17	179	58	74	51	4	62	6	0	4	15	4	.79	11	.265	.362	.499
1992 Indianapols	AAA	1	3	1	1	0	0	2	0	0	0	0	1	0	0	0	0	0	.00	0	.333	.333	.667
Wst Plm Bch	A	10	40	10	4	0	2	20	6	12	1	0	14	4	0	1	0	0	.00	0	.250	.326	.500
1994 Buffalo	AAA	12	39	10	2	0	2	18	5	5	1	0	8	0	1	0	0	0	.00	1	.256	.275	.462
1990 New York	NL	26	39	8	4	1	1	17	5	2	3	0	11	0	0	0	1	0	1.00	0	.205	.262	.436
1992 Montreal	NL	42	81	14	2	0	5	31	10	10	6	2	23	1	0	0	0	0	.00	3	.173	.239	.383
Minnesota	AL	14	33	6	2	0	0	8	2	4	2	0	11	0	0	0	0	0	.00	0	.182	.216	.242
9 Min. YEARS		680	2391	661	149	24	78	1092	342	380	261	19	379	40	7	29	51	21	.71	61	.276	.354	.457
2 Maj. YEARS		82	153	28	8	1	6	56	17	16	11	2	45	1	0	2	1	0	1.00	3	.183	.240	.366

Calvin Reese

Bats: Right Throws: Right Pos: SS Ht: 6'0" Wt: 160 Born: 06/10/73 Age: 22

								BATTING										BASERUNNING				PERCENTAGES		
Year	Team	Lg	G	AB	H	2B	3B	HR	TB	R	RBI	TBB	IBB	SO	HBP	SH	SF	SB	CS	SB%	GDP	Avg	OBP	SLG
1991	Princeton	R	62	231	55	8	3	3	78	30	27	23	0	44	0	0	2	10	8	.56	4	.238	.305	.338
1992	Chston-Vw	A	106	380	102	19	3	6	145	50	53	24	0	75	5	4	7	19	8	.70	2	.268	.315	.382
1993	Chattanooga	AA	102	345	73	17	4	3	107	35	37	23	1	77	1	3	7	8	5	.62	2	.212	.258	.310
1994	Chattanooga	AA	134	484	130	23	4	12	197	77	49	43	1	75	7	6	1	21	4	.84	6	.269	.336	.407
	4 Min. YEARS		404	1440	360	67	14	24	527	192	166	113	2	271	13	13	17	58	25	.70	14	.250	.307	.366

Derek Reid

Bats: Right Throws: Right Pos: OF Ht: 6'3" Wt: 195 Born: 02/04/70 Age: 25

								BATTING										BASERUNNING				PERCENTAGES		
Year	Team	Lg	G	AB	H	2B	3B	HR	TB	R	RBI	TBB	IBB	SO	HBP	SH	SF	SB	CS	SB%	GDP	Avg	OBP	SLG
1990	Everett	A	62	215	62	15	1	5	94	35	40	20	2	49	3	4	3	21	3	.88	3	.288	.353	.437
1991	San Jose	A	121	454	122	23	6	4	169	72	65	37	2	91	1	6	10	27	9	.75	7	.269	.319	.372
1992	Shreveport	AA	2	6	1	1	0	0	2	1	0	0	0	1	0	1	0	0	0	.00	0	.167	.167	.333
1993	Clinton	A	15	57	17	2	0	0	19	5	7	1	0	6	0	1	0	3	2	.60	1	.298	.310	.333
	San Jose	A	29	80	15	1	1	0	18	9	8	6	0	16	1	0	0	5	2	.71	1	.188	.253	.225
1994	San Bernrdo	A	59	238	70	18	1	6	108	34	38	21	2	60	1	2	2	15	1	.94	7	.294	.351	.454
	Shreveport	AA	51	137	30	4	0	4	46	11	9	4	2	36	1	3	0	5	2	.71	6	.219	.246	.336
	5 Min. YEARS		339	1187	317	64	9	19	456	167	167	89	8	259	7	17	15	76	19	.80	25	.267	.318	.384

Desmond Relaford

Bats: Both Throws: Right Pos: SS Ht: 5'8" Wt: 155 Born: 09/16/73 Age: 21

								BATTING										BASERUNNING				PERCENTAGES		
Year	Team	Lg	G	AB	H	2B	3B	HR	TB	R	RBI	TBB	IBB	SO	HBP	SH	SF	SB	CS	SB%	GDP	Avg	OBP	SLG
1991	Mariners	R	46	163	43	7	3	0	56	36	18	22	1	24	1	1	5	15	3	.83	0	.264	.346	.344
1992	Peninsula	A	130	445	96	18	1	3	125	53	34	39	1	88	1	4	6	27	7	.79	7	.216	.277	.281
1993	Jacksnville	AA	133	472	115	16	4	8	163	49	47	50	1	103	7	6	4	16	12	.57	4	.244	.323	.345
1994	Jacksonvlle	AA	37	143	29	7	3	3	51	24	11	22	0	28	0	2	2	10	1	.91	2	.203	.305	.357
	Riverside	A	99	374	116	27	5	5	168	95	59	78	6	78	4	3	6	27	6	.82	7	.310	.429	.449
	4 Min. YEARS		445	1597	399	75	16	19	563	257	169	211	9	321	13	16	23	95	29	.77	20	.250	.338	.353

Mike Rendina

Bats: Left Throws: Left Pos: 1B Ht: 6'4" Wt: 215 Born: 09/28/70 Age: 24

								BATTING										BASERUNNING				PERCENTAGES		
Year	Team	Lg	G	AB	H	2B	3B	HR	TB	R	RBI	TBB	IBB	SO	HBP	SH	SF	SB	CS	SB%	GDP	Avg	OBP	SLG
1988	Bristol	R	39	75	15	3	0	3	27	12	16	9	0	18	0	0	2	0	1	.00	3	.200	.279	.360
1989	Fayetteville	A	28	86	10	4	0	0	14	9	5	11	1	19	0	3	0	0	0	.00	4	.116	.216	.163
	Bristol	R	62	224	61	13	0	11	107	34	34	28	3	36	1	0	0	5	3	.63	4	.272	.356	.478
1990	Fayetteville	A	137	475	121	23	3	11	183	59	77	76	7	90	3	0	4	4	4	.50	13	.255	.358	.385
1991	Lakeland	A	115	359	77	7	2	4	100	36	41	54	5	61	4	2	3	2	2	.50	11	.214	.321	.279
1992	Lakeland	A	121	397	106	23	1	9	158	48	69	46	5	59	2	1	7	2	0	1.00	9	.267	.341	.398
1993	London	AA	135	475	134	30	1	10	196	59	77	55	1	96	0	0	3	8	4	.67	6	.282	.355	.413
1994	Trenton	AA	116	387	88	15	0	11	136	46	46	29	2	77	2	0	2	2	1	.67	5	.227	.283	.351
	7 Min. YEARS		753	2478	612	118	7	59	921	303	365	308	24	456	12	6	21	23	15	.61	55	.247	.331	.372

Steve Renko

Pitches: Right Bats: Right Pos: P Ht: 6'3" Wt: 205 Born: 08/01/67 Age: 27

			HOW MUCH HE PITCHED						WHAT HE GAVE UP												THE RESULTS					
Year	Team	Lg	G	GS	CG	GF	IP	BFP	H	R	ER	HR	SH	SF	HB	TBB	IBB	SO	WP	Bk	W	L	Pct.	ShO	Sv	ERA
1990	Expos	R	2	0	0	1	5	23	7	1	1	0	0	0	0	1	0	5	0	2	1	0	1.000	0	0	1.80
	Gate City	R	11	10	2	0	59.2	263	56	32	26	4	2	0	2	23	1	68	6	1	3	4	.429	0	0	3.92
1991	Wst Plm Bch	A	4	3	0	0	9	44	14	8	8	2	0	0	1	5	0	4	0	0	0	1	.000	0	0	8.00
	Rockford	A	16	16	1	0	99	431	95	43	35	3	3	3	4	34	0	102	16	1	4	5	.444	0	0	3.18
1992	Winter Havn	A	10	10	1	0	61.1	264	65	33	27	7	1	1	2	16	0	56	2	0	3	5	.375	0	0	3.96
	Lynchburg	A	6	6	0	0	34.1	153	39	18	15	6	2	4	0	14	0	23	6	0	1	1	.500	0	0	3.93
1993	Hagerstown	A	23	1	0	12	42.1	170	35	20	16	2	5	1	1	11	1	45	5	0	4	2	.667	0	5	3.40
	Knoxville	AA	12	5	0	1	34.2	149	38	21	14	1	6	2	1	8	0	30	7	0	1	3	.250	0	0	3.63
1994	Wichita	AA	42	0	0	16	78.2	375	90	56	44	4	7	5	1	49	8	59	10	1	3	8	.273	0	2	5.03
	5 Min. YEARS		126	51	4	30	424	1872	439	232	186	29	26	16	12	161	10	392	52	5	20	29	.408	0	7	3.95

Dave Renteria

Bats: Right Throws: Right Pos: 2B Ht: 6'0" Wt: 175 Born: 12/01/72 Age: 22

								BATTING										BASERUNNING				PERCENTAGES		
Year	Team	Lg	G	AB	H	2B	3B	HR	TB	R	RBI	TBB	IBB	SO	HBP	SH	SF	SB	CS	SB%	GDP	Avg	OBP	SLG
1992	Yankees	R	20	61	14	1	0	0	15	6	7	6	0	14	0	0	0	0	0	.00	1	.230	.299	.246
1993	Oneonta	A	43	129	30	7	0	0	37	19	16	14	0	25	0	3	1	1	3	.25	3	.233	.306	.287
1994	San Bernrdo	A	23	72	10	0	0	0	10	11	6	18	1	24	1	1	1	0	1	.00	1	.139	.315	.139
	Greensboro	A	38	101	23	3	0	0	29	12	11	12	0	16	0	1	1	1	2	.33	6	.228	.307	.287

Team	Lg	G	AB	H	2B	3B	HR	TB	R	RBI	TBB	IBB	SO	HBP	SH	SF	SB	CS	SB%	GDP	Avg	OBP	SLG
Tampa	A	3	8	0	0	0	0	0	3	0	1	0	0	0	0	0	0	0	.00	0	.000	.111	.000
Columbus	AAA	2	1	0	0	0	0	0	0	0	0	0	0	0	0	0	0	0	.00	0	.000	.000	.000
Albany-Colo	AA	3	11	1	0	1	0	3	1	0	0	0	6	1	0	0	0	0	.00	1	.091	.167	.273
3 Min. YEARS		132	383	78	11	1	1	94	52	40	51	1	85	2	5	3	2	6	.25	12	.204	.298	.245

Ed Renteria

Bats: Right Throws: Right Pos: 2B Ht: 5'11" Wt: 160 Born: 04/07/68 Age: 27

					BATTING												BASERUNNING				PERCENTAGES		
Year Team	Lg	G	AB	H	2B	3B	HR	TB	R	RBI	TBB	IBB	SO	HBP	SH	SF	SB	CS	SB%	GDP	Avg	OBP	SLG
1985 Astros	R	40	110	18	0	0	0	18	12	7	8	0	14	3	1	1	1	1	.50	3	.164	.238	.164
1986 Astros	R	52	182	54	11	1	1	70	23	26	13	1	9	1	0	2	6	2	.75	4	.297	.343	.385
1987 Auburn	A	71	275	83	16	0	1	102	37	29	33	0	30	5	5	4	10	7	.59	5	.302	.382	.371
1988 Asheville	A	132	439	102	16	2	0	122	62	35	51	0	40	5	9	5	19	4	.83	8	.232	.316	.278
1989 Osceola	A	99	340	81	11	3	0	98	42	23	41	0	46	9	7	4	13	9	.59	9	.238	.332	.288
1990 Columbus	AA	62	179	46	10	1	0	58	22	19	21	0	26	2	3	1	6	2	.75	4	.257	.340	.324
Tucson	AAA	35	110	32	2	0	1	37	15	12	7	0	14	2	3	2	2	2	.50	3	.291	.339	.336
1991 Jackson	AA	18	59	17	3	0	1	23	11	6	4	1	7	1	0	0	1	0	1.00	1	.288	.344	.390
Osceola	A	71	231	65	10	0	0	75	24	27	27	1	24	3	1	1	9	3	.75	5	.281	.363	.325
1993 Edmonton	AAA	24	68	18	0	0	1	21	6	8	7	1	12	1	1	1	0	1	.00	2	.265	.338	.309
High Desert	A	56	207	65	12	0	2	83	43	27	22	1	33	2	0	3	1	4	.20	4	.314	.380	.401
1994 Portland	AA	9	16	2	1	0	0	6	1	3	2	0	3	1	1	0	0	0	.00	0	.125	.263	.375
9 Min. YEARS		669	2216	583	92	7	8	713	298	222	236	5	258	35	31	24	68	35	.66	48	.263	.340	.322

Rafael Reyes

Pitches: Right Bats: Right Pos: P Ht: 6'0" Wt: 165 Born: 04/10/71 Age: 24

			HOW MUCH HE PITCHED						WHAT HE GAVE UP								THE RESULTS					
Year Team	Lg	G	GS	CG	GF	IP	BFP	H	R	ER	HR	SH	SF	HB	TBB	IBB	SO	WP	Bk	W	L	Pct.	ShO	Sv	ERA
1990 Wst Plm Bch	A	16	10	0	4	57	253	52	32	30	4	3	3	2	32	2	46	5	0	5	4	.556	0	1	4.74
1991 Rockford	A	3	3	0	0	11.1	50	14	8	7	1	0	0	2	2	0	10	0	0	0	1	.000	0	0	5.56
1992 Albany	A	27	0	0	18	27.1	122	24	14	12	0	0	0	3	13	0	29	4	1	0	2	.000	0	4	3.95
1993 Burlington	A	53	0	0	41	74	308	52	33	22	7	6	2	5	26	3	80	5	0	7	6	.538	0	11	2.68
1994 Harrisburg	AA	60	0	0	53	69.1	284	68	26	25	4	2	2	2	13	0	60	2	0	2	2	.500	0	35	3.25
5 Min. YEARS		159	13	0	116	239	1017	216	113	96	16	11	7	14	86	5	225	16	1	14	15	.483	0	51	3.62

Chuck Ricci

Pitches: Right Bats: Right Pos: P Ht: 6'2" Wt: 180 Born: 11/20/68 Age: 26

			HOW MUCH HE PITCHED						WHAT HE GAVE UP								THE RESULTS					
Year Team	Lg	G	GS	CG	GF	IP	BFP	H	R	ER	HR	SH	SF	HB	TBB	IBB	SO	WP	Bk	W	L	Pct.	ShO	Sv	ERA
1987 Bluefield	R	13	12	1	0	62.1	288	74	52	45	11	1	0	2	38	1	40	3	0	5	5	.500	0	0	6.50
1988 Bluefield	R	14	14	1	0	73	355	92	61	54	7	1	3	2	48	0	73	6	0	4	6	.400	0	0	6.66
1989 Waterloo	A	29	25	9	1	181.1	760	160	89	60	11	11	5	12	59	5	89	14	1	10	12	.455	0	0	2.98
1990 Frederick	A	26	18	2	5	122.1	539	126	79	60	8	6	3	6	47	3	94	8	0	7	12	.368	1	0	4.41
1991 Frederick	A	30	29	2	0	173.2	752	147	91	60	12	3	10	3	84	2	144	15	1	12	14	.462	0	0	3.11
1992 Frederick	A	1	0	0	0	2.1	11	2	1	0	0	0	0	0	1	0	2	0	0	0	0	.000	0	0	0.00
Hagerstown	AA	20	6	0	4	57.2	275	58	40	37	4	3	4	3	47	1	58	8	2	1	4	.200	0	0	5.77
1993 Rochester	AAA	4	0	0	3	8	36	11	5	5	1	0	0	0	3	0	6	0	0	0	0	.000	0	0	5.63
Bowie	AA	34	1	0	16	81.2	334	72	35	29	7	5	2	3	20	0	83	8	0	7	4	.636	0	5	3.20
1994 Reading	AA	14	0	0	2	19	71	10	1	0	0	0	0	2	4	2	23	0	0	1	0	1.000	0	0	0.00
Scranton-Wb	AAA	44	1	0	17	64.2	274	60	30	29	7	2	3	5	22	5	72	4	0	4	3	.571	0	6	4.04
8 Min. YEARS		229	106	15	48	846	3695	812	484	379	68	32	30	38	373	19	684	66	4	51	60	.459	1	11	4.03

Lance Rice

Bats: Both Throws: Right Pos: C Ht: 6'1" Wt: 195 Born: 10/19/66 Age: 28

					BATTING												BASERUNNING				PERCENTAGES		
Year Team	Lg	G	AB	H	2B	3B	HR	TB	R	RBI	TBB	IBB	SO	HBP	SH	SF	SB	CS	SB%	GDP	Avg	OBP	SLG
1988 Great Falls	R	47	159	45	8	2	0	57	31	27	31	0	29	1	2	2	4	2	.67	2	.283	.399	.358
1989 Bakersfield	A	126	406	90	15	1	5	122	41	53	53	2	83	3	1	5	1	4	.20	9	.222	.313	.300
1990 San Antonio	AA	79	245	59	11	2	0	74	25	35	24	3	46	1	3	4	3	1	.75	6	.241	.307	.302
1991 San Antonio	AA	78	215	43	8	0	3	60	23	28	31	2	30	1	2	3	2	1	.67	7	.200	.300	.279
Albuquerque	AAA	1	3	1	0	0	0	2	0	1	0	0	0	0	0	0	0	0	.00	0	.333	.333	.667
1992 San Antonio	AA	75	194	45	9	0	2	60	17	18	17	3	34	1	6	2	0	1	.00	2	.232	.294	.309
1993 Harrisburg	AA	46	136	32	10	0	1	45	12	20	16	0	22	0	0	0	0	0	.00	3	.235	.312	.331
1994 Harrisburg	AA	13	30	9	1	0	0	10	8	2	7	0	4	0	0	0	0	0	.00	2	.300	.432	.333
7 Min. YEARS		465	1388	324	63	5	11	430	157	184	179	10	248	7	16	18	10	10	.50	31	.233	.320	.310

Jeff Richardson

Bats: Right Throws: Right Pos: 3B-2B Ht: 6'2" Wt: 180 Born: 08/26/65 Age: 29

					BATTING												BASERUNNING				PERCENTAGES		
Year Team	Lg	G	AB	H	2B	3B	HR	TB	R	RBI	TBB	IBB	SO	HBP	SH	SF	SB	CS	SB%	GDP	Avg	OBP	SLG
1986 Billings	R	47	162	51	14	4	0	73	42	20	17	0	23	1	0	0	12	1	.92	0	.315	.383	.451
1987 Tampa	A	100	374	112	9	2	0	125	44	39	30	5	35	3	1	7	10	4	.71	16	.299	.350	.334
Vermont	AA	35	134	28	4	0	0	32	24	8	5	0	25	1	2	0	5	0	1.00	1	.209	.243	.239
1988 Chattanooga	AA	122	399	100	17	1	1	122	50	37	23	0	56	9	12	4	8	1	.89	7	.251	.303	.306

Year	Team	Lg	G	AB	H	2B	3B	HR	TB	R	RBI	TBB	IBB	SO	HBP	SH	SF	SB	CS	SB%	GDP	Avg	OBP	SLG
1989	Nashville	AAA	88	286	78	19	2	1	104	36	25	17	4	42	1	6	3	3	1	.75	13	.273	.313	.364
1990	Buffalo	AAA	66	164	34	4	0	1	41	15	15	14	0	21	2	3	0	1	2	.33	6	.207	.278	.250
1991	Buffalo	AAA	62	186	48	16	2	1	71	21	24	18	7	29	2	9	3	5	3	.63	3	.258	.325	.382
1992	Buffalo	AAA	97	328	95	23	2	3	131	34	29	19	3	46	1	11	2	5	2	.71	12	.290	.329	.399
1993	Pawtucket	AAA	9	28	9	1	0	0	10	2	1	1	0	6	0	1	1	0	0	.00	1	.321	.333	.357
1994	Louisville	AAA	89	247	64	13	1	4	91	29	21	16	0	38	1	6	0	1	1	.50	10	.259	.307	.368
1989	Cincinnati	NL	53	125	21	4	0	2	31	10	11	10	0	23	1	3	1	1	0	1.00	3	.168	.234	.248
1991	Pittsburgh	NL	6	4	1	0	0	0	1	0	0	0	0	3	0	0	0	0	0	.00	0	.250	.250	.250
1993	Boston	AL	15	24	5	2	0	0	7	3	2	1	0	3	0	2	0	0	0	.00	0	.208	.240	.292
	9 Min. YEARS		715	2308	619	120	14	11	800	297	217	160	19	321	21	51	20	50	15	.77	72	.268	.319	.347
	3 Maj. YEARS		74	153	27	6	0	2	39	13	13	11	0	29	1	5	1	1	0	1.00	3	.176	.235	.255

Pitches: Right Bats: Right Pos: P

Dana Ridenour

Ht: 6'2" Wt: 205 Born: 11/15/65 Age: 29

			HOW MUCH HE PITCHED						WHAT HE GAVE UP										THE RESULTS					
Year	Team	Lg	G	GS	CG	GF	IP	BFP	H	R	ER	HR	SH	SF	HB	TBB	IBB	SO	WP	Bk	W	L	Pct.	ShO	Sv	ERA
1986	Oneonta	A	23	0	0	20	34.2	135	21	6	6	0	1	0	1	11	3	47	3	0	4	2	.667	0	8	1.56
1987	Ft.Laudrdle	A	43	0	0	39	66	268	38	14	13	3	3	2	3	34	1	90	10	0	5	4	.556	0	21	1.77
1988	Albany	AA	30	0	0	29	43.2	193	29	19	19	2	2	2	2	29	4	56	4	2	5	4	.556	0	14	3.92
	Columbus	AAA	14	0	0	11	21.1	99	16	9	5	1	2	1	0	19	2	24	3	0	1	2	.333	0	2	2.11
1989	Williamsprt	AA	6	0	0	4	11	41	5	3	2	0	0	0	1	3	0	13	2	0	1	0	1.000	0	0	1.64
	Calgary	AAA	18	0	0	8	37.2	166	43	27	23	3	2	1	3	14	1	25	5	1	2	1	.667	0	1	5.50
1990	Williamsprt	AA	45	2	1	29	78.2	352	75	31	25	2	7	0	1	41	7	70	15	2	4	7	.364	1	6	2.86
1991	Indianapols	AAA	57	0	0	21	80.2	365	69	31	28	2	4	2	6	50	7	93	15	0	5	3	.625	0	6	3.12
1992	Indianapols	AAA	30	0	0	19	46.2	188	44	16	16	4	1	1	2	9	3	37	3	0	1	1	.500	0	6	3.09
	Edmonton	AAA	5	0	0	1	10.1	48	12	7	7	0	1	0	0	8	1	8	2	0	1	0	1.000	0	0	6.10
1993	Colo Spmgs	AAA	39	16	1	6	121	563	156	83	70	9	8	5	6	58	5	105	16	1	8	8	.500	0	0	5.21
1994	Edmonton	AAA	25	14	2	3	99	446	111	73	59	18	2	1	5	40	0	83	10	1	4	9	.308	1	2	5.36
	9 Min. YEARS		335	32	4	190	650.2	2864	619	319	273	44	33	15	30	316	34	651	88	7	41	41	.500	2	64	3.78

Bats: Left Throws: Right Pos: 3B

Kevin Riggs

Ht: 5'11" Wt: 190 Born: 02/03/69 Age: 26

			BATTING															BASERUNNING				PERCENTAGES		
Year	Team	Lg	G	AB	H	2B	3B	HR	TB	R	RBI	TBB	IBB	SO	HBP	SH	SF	SB	CS	SB%	GDP	Avg	OBP	SLG
1990	Billings	R	57	192	61	9	2	1	77	49	21	50	2	27	2	0	0	16	3	.84	5	.318	.463	.401
	Chston-Wv	A	2	4	1	0	0	0	1	0	1	0	0	1	0	0	0	0	1	.00	0	.250	.250	.250
1991	Cedar Rapds	A	118	406	109	21	2	2	140	72	43	91	2	50	3	2	6	23	8	.74	11	.268	.401	.345
	Chston-Wv	A	1	2	1	0	0	0	1	0	0	1	0	0	0	0	0	0	0	.00	0	.500	.667	.500
1992	Cedar Rapds	A	126	457	132	24	4	2	170	87	44	97	3	63	5	4	5	23	15	.61	10	.289	.415	.372
1993	Stockton	A	108	377	131	18	3	3	164	84	45	101	3	46	1	1	4	12	15	.44	8	.347	.482	.435
1994	El Paso	AA	66	230	68	10	2	1	85	38	22	46	1	39	1	0	0	3	7	.30	2	.296	.415	.370
	5 Min. YEARS		478	1668	503	82	13	9	638	330	176	386	11	226	12	7	15	77	49	.61	36	.302	.433	.382

Pitches: Right Bats: Right Pos: P

Ron Rightnowar

Ht: 6'3" Wt: 190 Born: 09/05/64 Age: 30

			HOW MUCH HE PITCHED						WHAT HE GAVE UP										THE RESULTS					
Year	Team	Lg	G	GS	CG	GF	IP	BFP	H	R	ER	HR	SH	SF	HB	TBB	IBB	SO	WP	Bk	W	L	Pct.	ShO	Sv	ERA
1987	Fayetteville	A	39	10	2	19	101.2	450	115	70	56	7	5	6	4	37	1	65	4	1	7	7	.500	0	6	4.96
1988	Lakeland	A	17	2	0	4	49.1	197	41	19	8	1	2	0	4	11	2	32	5	2	2	0	1.000	0	0	1.46
1989	London	AA	36	7	2	14	108	478	132	63	60	10	4	5	4	34	4	46	2	2	2	8	.200	0	5	5.00
1990	Toledo	AAA	28	0	0	16	38	165	46	24	20	5	2	2	0	10	3	28	0	0	4	5	.444	0	5	4.74
	Niagara Fls	A	1	1	1	0	7	26	4	1	0	0	0	0	0	1	0	9	0	0	1	0	1.000	0	0	0.00
	London	AA	23	0	0	18	44.1	182	40	20	16	4	1	2	2	9	0	33	1	0	2	2	.500	0	5	3.25
1991	Toledo	AAA	23	0	0	14	29.2	130	30	15	13	2	1	2	1	15	2	5	0	0	1	1	.500	0	3	3.94
	London	AA	15	0	0	9	25.1	110	28	13	11	0	2	1	0	8	1	18	1	0	2	1	.667	0	3	3.91
1992	Toledo	AAA	34	0	0	20	57	258	68	43	39	10	2	5	5	18	4	33	5	0	3	2	.600	0	3	6.16
1993	Toledo	AAA	22	6	0	4	58.1	255	57	32	23	3	1	2	7	19	0	32	2	0	2	2	.500	0	1	3.55
	New Orleans	AAA	4	0	0	1	8.2	45	19	10	10	1	1	0	1	2	0	8	0	0	0	0	.000	0	0	10.38
1994	New Orleans	AAA	51	2	0	24	88	343	62	25	22	8	3	2	3	21	2	79	3	0	8	2	.800	0	11	2.25
	8 Min. YEARS		293	28	5	143	615.1	2639	642	335	278	51	24	27	31	185	19	388	23	5	34	30	.531	0	43	4.07

Bats: Left Throws: Right Pos: SS

Ernest Riles

Ht: 6' 1" Wt: 180 Born: 10/02/60 Age: 34

			BATTING															BASERUNNING				PERCENTAGES		
Year	Team	Lg	G	AB	H	2B	3B	HR	TB	R	RBI	TBB	IBB	SO	HBP	SH	SF	SB	CS	SB%	GDP	Avg	OBP	SLG
1984	Vancouver	AAA	123	424	113	19	7	3	155	59	54	67	8	67	1	1	8	1	2	.33	15	.267	.362	.366
1985	Vancouver	AAA	30	118	41	7	1	2	56	19	20	17	4	13	1	0	2	2	2	.50	1	.347	.428	.475
1987	El Paso	AA	41	153	52	10	0	6	80	45	24	28	1	24	0	0	2	1	1	.50	4	.340	.437	.523
1992	Tucson	AAA	60	202	62	17	3	1	88	37	35	30	4	33	0	1	4	2	1	.67	2	.307	.390	.436
1993	Pawtucket	AAA	6	18	5	0	0	2	11	4	6	3	0	0	0	0	2	0	0	.00	1	.278	.348	.611
1994	Vancouver	AAA	99	326	101	20	0	14	181	54	58	47	2	68	0	1	2	2	3	.40	2	.310	.395	.555
1985	Milwaukee	AL	116	448	128	12	7	5	169	54	45	36	2	54	2	6	3	2	2	.50	16	.286	.339	.377

Year	Team	Lg	G	AB	H	2B	3B	HR	TB	R	RBI	TBB	IBB	SO	HBP	SH	SF	SB	CS	SB%	GDP	Avg	OBP	SLG
1986	Milwaukee	AL	145	524	132	24	2	9	187	69	47	54	0	80	1	6	3	7	7	.50	14	.252	.321	.357
1987	Milwaukee	AL	83	276	72	11	1	4	97	38	38	30	1	47	1	3	6	3	4	.43	6	.261	.329	.351
1988	Milwaukee	AL	41	127	32	6	1	1	43	7	9	7	0	26	0	1	0	2	2	.50	3	.252	.291	.339
	San Francisco	NL	79	187	55	7	2	3	75	26	28	10	2	33	0	0	4	1	2	.33	5	.294	.323	.401
1989	San Francisco	NL	122	302	84	13	2	7	122	43	40	28	3	50	2	1	4	0	6	.00	7	.278	.339	.404
1990	San Francisco	NL	92	155	31	2	1	8	59	22	21	26	3	26	0	2	1	0	0	.00	2	.200	.313	.381
1991	Oakland	AL	108	281	60	8	4	5	91	30	32	31	3	42	1	4	4	3	2	.60	8	.214	.290	.324
1992	Houston	NL	39	61	16	1	0	1	20	5	4	2	0	11	0	0	1	1	0	1.00	0	.262	.281	.328
1993	Boston	AL	94	143	27	8	0	5	50	15	20	20	3	40	2	2	3	1	3	.25	3	.189	.292	.350
	6 Min. YEARS		359	1241	374	73	20	28	571	218	197	192	19	205	2	3	20	8	9	.47	20	.301	.390	.460
	9 Maj. YEARS		919	2504	637	92	20	48	913	309	284	244	15	409	9	25	29	20	28	.42	64	.254	.319	.365

Ed Riley

Pitches: Left Bats: Left Pos: P Ht: 6'2" Wt: 195 Born: 02/10/70 Age: 25

			HOW MUCH HE PITCHED						WHAT HE GAVE UP												THE RESULTS					
Year	Team	Lg	G	GS	CG	GF	IP	BFP	H	R	ER	HR	SH	SF	HB	TBB	IBB	SO	WP	Bk	W	L	Pct.	ShO	Sv	ERA
1988	R.S./mamrs	R	9	6	2	2	44.1	199	39	29	20	3	2	1	2	34	0	41	2	3	1	4	.200	0	1	4.06
1989	New Britain	AA	1	1	0	0	4.1	19	4	4	4	1	0	0	0	2	0	1	0	0	0	1	.000	0	0	8.31
	Elmira	A	17	15	2	0	92	404	81	42	32	2	5	3	2	50	0	102	3	1	4	6	.400	1	0	3.13
1990	Winter Havn	A	31	24	0	4	159	682	152	79	55	5	6	3	1	64	0	107	5	9	4	9	.308	0	0	3.11
1991	Lynchburg	A	27	27	2	0	163	685	169	80	64	11	3	9	6	56	0	122	7	0	8	10	.444	0	0	3.53
1992	Pawtucket	AAA	1	1	0	0	6	25	7	3	3	1	0	0	0	1	0	4	0	0	0	0	.000	0	0	4.50
	New Britain	AA	19	19	1	0	121	489	108	38	33	7	0	2	2	38	1	63	1	4	10	8	.556	1	0	2.45
1993	New Britain	AA	14	14	1	0	83.2	356	85	39	33	5	6	4	0	29	0	50	1	3	4	6	.400	0	0	3.55
	Pawtucket	AAA	14	13	2	0	70	321	90	45	39	8	3	2	1	23	0	45	6	1	4	4	.500	0	0	5.01
1994	New Britain	AA	57	5	0	16	76	328	74	48	39	7	0	4	1	34	3	70	3	0	2	4	.333	0	2	4.62
	7 Min. YEARS		190	125	10	22	819.1	3508	809	407	322	50	25	28	15	331	4	605	28	21	37	52	.416	2	3	3.54

Marquis Riley

Bats: Right Throws: Right Pos: OF Ht: 5'10" Wt: 170 Born: 12/27/70 Age: 24

			BATTING															BASERUNNING				PERCENTAGES		
Year	Team	Lg	G	AB	H	2B	3B	HR	TB	R	RBI	TBB	IBB	SO	HBP	SH	SF	SB	CS	SB%	GDP	Avg	OBP	SLG
1992	Boise	A	52	201	48	12	1	0	62	47	12	37	0	29	2	2	0	7	4	.64	3	.239	.363	.308
1993	Palm Sprngs	A	130	508	134	10	2	1	151	93	42	90	1	117	0	5	2	69	25	.73	3	.264	.373	.297
1994	Midland	AA	93	374	107	12	4	1	130	68	29	35	3	57	6	7	4	32	5	.86	10	.286	.353	.348
	Vancouver	AAA	4	14	3	0	0	0	3	3	1	3	0	3	0	0	0	1	0	1.00	1	.214	.353	.214
	3 Min. YEARS		279	1097	292	34	7	2	346	211	84	165	4	206	8	14	6	109	34	.76	17	.266	.364	.315

Todd Ritchie

Pitches: Right Bats: Right Pos: P Ht: 6'3" Wt: 185 Born: 11/07/71 Age: 23

			HOW MUCH HE PITCHED						WHAT HE GAVE UP												THE RESULTS					
Year	Team	Lg	G	GS	CG	GF	IP	BFP	H	R	ER	HR	SH	SF	HB	TBB	IBB	SO	WP	Bk	W	L	Pct.	ShO	Sv	ERA
1990	Elizabethtn	R	11	11	1	0	65	261	45	22	14	5	2	2	6	24	0	49	2	3	5	2	.714	0	0	1.94
1991	Kenosha	A	21	21	0	0	116.2	498	113	52	46	3	4	1	7	50	0	101	10	1	7	6	.538	0	0	3.55
1992	Visalia	A	28	28	3	0	172.2	763	193	113	97	13	6	6	7	65	2	129	16	1	11	9	.550	1	0	5.06
1993	Nashville	AA	12	10	0	0	46.2	194	46	21	19	2	1	1	0	15	0	41	5	1	3	2	.600	0	0	3.66
1994	Nashville	AA	4	4	0	0	17	74	24	10	8	1	1	0	0	7	0	9	2	0	0	2	.000	0	0	4.24
	5 Min. YEARS		76	74	4	0	418	1790	421	219	184	24	14	10	20	161	2	329	35	6	26	21	.553	1	0	3.96

Wally Ritchie

Pitches: Left Bats: Left Pos: P Ht: 6'2" Wt: 180 Born: 07/12/65 Age: 29

			HOW MUCH HE PITCHED						WHAT HE GAVE UP												THE RESULTS					
Year	Team	Lg	G	GS	CG	GF	IP	BFP	H	R	ER	HR	SH	SF	HB	TBB	IBB	SO	WP	Bk	W	L	Pct.	ShO	Sv	ERA
1985	Bend	A	2	1	0	0	10	11	10	11	5	0	0	0	1	5	0	3	0	0	1	0	1.000	0	0	4.50
	Clearwater	A	14	6	0	3	46.2	196	49	30	18	5	1	2	0	12	0	24	0	0	3	1	.750	0	0	3.47
1986	Clearwater	A	32	0	0	22	52.2	206	40	15	13	0	4	3	0	16	2	39	2	0	4	1	.800	0	10	2.22
	Reading	AA	28	0	0	15	30	129	29	13	9	4	3	5	1	9	0	13	0	0	4	1	.800	0	4	2.70
1987	Maine	AAA	13	0	0	9	22	91	17	6	5	1	1	0	0	8	1	16	1	0	3	1	.750	0	2	2.05
1988	Maine	AAA	16	14	0	0	78.2	340	88	49	41	4	3	4	0	29	2	49	6	1	4	5	.444	0	0	4.69
1989	Scr Wil-Bar	AAA	34	20	4	6	135.2	582	143	70	63	16	2	7	2	38	2	73	3	0	7	4	.636	1	0	4.18
1990	Scr Wil-Bar	AAA	20	13	1	1	82.1	350	75	46	38	7	5	1	2	28	1	47	2	0	4	3	.571	1	0	4.15
1991	Scranton-Wb	AAA	7	2	0	3	26	99	17	8	7	2	0	0	0	7	0	25	0	0	1	0	1.000	0	2	2.42
1992	Scranton/wb	AAA	15	0	0	8	16.2	64	11	5	5	2	0	0	0	3	2	12	1	0	1	0	1.000	0	5	2.70
1993	Toledo	AAA	62	0	0	14	45.1	200	44	26	24	5	5	3	0	15	2	29	2	0	1	0	1.000	0	4	4.76
1994	Chattanooga	AA	31	0	0	13	33.2	151	41	21	20	5	0	0	1	13	4	27	0	0	0	2	.000	0	1	5.35
1987	Philadelphia	NL	49	0	0	13	62.1	273	60	27	26	8	5	2	1	29	11	45	2	3	3	2	.600	0	3	3.75
1988	Philadelphia	NL	19	0	0	8	26	115	19	14	9	1	2	3	1	17	2	8	2	0	0	0	.000	0	0	3.12
1991	Philadelphia	NL	39	0	0	13	50.1	213	44	17	14	4	2	4	2	17	5	26	1	0	1	2	.333	0	2	2.50
1992	Philadelphia	NL	40	0	0	13	39	174	44	17	13	3	4	0	0	17	3	19	0	0	2	1	.667	0	1	3.00
	10 Min. YEARS		274	56	5	94	579.2	2408	564	300	248	51	24	25	7	183	16	357	17	1	33	18	.647	2	29	3.85
	4 Maj. YEARS		147	0	0	47	177.2	775	167	75	62	16	13	9	4	80	21	98	5	3	6	5	.545	0	4	3.14

Mariano Rivera

Pitches: Right **Bats:** Right **Pos:** P **Ht:** 6'4" **Wt:** 168 **Born:** 11/29/69 **Age:** 25

			HOW MUCH HE PITCHED						WHAT HE GAVE UP													THE RESULTS					
Year	Team	Lg	G	GS	CG	GF	IP	BFP	H	R	ER	HR	SH	SF	HB	TBB	IBB	SO	WP	Bk	W	L	Pct.	ShO	Sv	ERA
1990	Yankees	R	22	1	1	12	52	180	17	3	1	0	2	2	2	7	0	58	2	0	5	1	.833	1	1	0.17
1991	Greensboro	A	29	15	1	6	114.2	480	102	48	35	2	1	5	3	36	0	123	3	0	4	9	.308	0	0	2.75
1992	Ft. Laud	A	10	10	3	0	59.1	217	40	17	15	5	2	1	0	5	0	42	0	0	5	3	.625	1	0	2.28
1993	Yankees	R	2	2	0	0	4	15	2	1	1	0	0	0	0	1	0	6	1	0	0	1	.000	0	0	2.25
	Greensboro	A	10	10	0	0	39.1	161	31	12	9	0	0	1	0	15	0	32	0	0	1	0	1.000	0	0	2.06
1994	Tampa	A	7	7	0	0	36.2	148	34	12	9	2	1	1	2	12	0	27	0	0	3	0	1.000	0	0	2.21
	Albany-Colo	AA	9	9	0	0	63.1	252	58	20	16	5	3	1	0	8	0	39	1	1	3	0	1.000	0	0	2.27
	Columbus	AAA	6	6	1	0	31	137	34	22	20	5	0	0	0	10	0	23	0	0	4	2	.667	0	0	5.81
	5 Min. YEARS		95	60	6	18	400.1	1590	318	135	106	19	9	11	7	94	0	350	9	2	25	16	.610	2	1	2.38

Roberto Rivera

Pitches: Left **Bats:** Left **Pos:** P **Ht:** 6'0" **Wt:** 175 **Born:** 01/01/69 **Age:** 26

			HOW MUCH HE PITCHED						WHAT HE GAVE UP													THE RESULTS					
Year	Team	Lg	G	GS	CG	GF	IP	BFP	H	R	ER	HR	SH	SF	HB	TBB	IBB	SO	WP	Bk	W	L	Pct.	ShO	Sv	ERA
1988	Indians	R	14	12	1	1	69.1	295	64	32	25	2	2	4	3	21	1	38	2	4	6	5	.545	1	0	3.25
1989	Burlington	R	18	2	1	8	51.1	214	44	24	20	4	4	2	1	16	3	42	0	2	3	4	.429	0	2	3.51
1990	Watertown	A	14	13	2	0	85	345	85	43	34	9	2	1	1	10	0	63	0	0	4	4	.500	1	0	3.60
1991	Columbus	A	30	1	0	17	49	207	48	15	9	1	2	0	2	12	3	36	2	2	7	1	.875	0	3	1.65
	Kinston	A	10	0	0	5	10.1	46	10	6	5	1	1	1	0	2	0	9	0	0	1	0	1.000	0	0	4.35
1992	Kinston	A	24	8	4	5	88.2	353	83	35	32	7	3	3	3	11	3	56	4	0	3	5	.375	1	1	3.25
1993	Canton-Akrn	AA	8	0	0	4	14.1	68	22	8	8	0	0	0	2	3	0	6	0	2	0	1	.000	0	0	5.02
	Kinston	A	19	1	0	9	35	150	44	26	24	1	4	2	1	4	0	32	0	0	2	3	.400	0	0	6.17
1994	Peoria	A	14	0	0	6	19.1	90	27	6	5	1	2	0	3	3	1	13	2	0	3	1	.750	0	0	2.33
	Orlando	AA	34	0	0	19	45.2	192	45	14	14	1	2	0	2	11	0	31	2	0	3	2	.600	0	4	2.76
	7 Min. YEARS		185	37	8	74	468	1960	472	209	176	30	19	13	18	93	11	326	14	10	32	26	.552	3	10	3.38

Hector Roa

Bats: Both **Throws:** Right **Pos:** 2B **Ht:** 5'11" **Wt:** 170 **Born:** 06/11/69 **Age:** 26

			BATTING															BASERUNNING				PERCENTAGES		
Year	Team	Lg	G	AB	H	2B	3B	HR	TB	R	RBI	TBB	IBB	SO	HBP	SH	SF	SB	CS	SB%	GDP	Avg	OBP	SLG
1990	Pulaski	R	21	92	32	3	2	3	48	23	14	5	1	17	1	1	0	6	0	1.00	2	.348	.388	.522
	Sumter	A	24	92	20	4	1	0	26	5	7	4	1	12	0	1	0	1	1	.50	3	.217	.250	.283
	Braves	R	13	43	9	1	0	1	13	7	2	5	1	5	1	3	0	4	0	1.00	2	.209	.306	.302
1991	Miami	A	87	280	57	3	5	1	73	32	18	15	1	51	3	3	1	17	9	.65	7	.204	.251	.261
	Macon	A	33	121	37	10	0	2	53	17	16	9	0	22	1	4	2	2	1	.67	1	.306	.353	.438
1992	Durham	A	110	377	105	27	7	8	170	52	46	16	2	55	2	6	2	14	4	.78	4	.279	.310	.451
	Greenville	AA	2	9	3	0	0	0	3	1	2	0	0	3	0	0	0	0	0	.00	0	.333	.333	.333
1993	Greenville	AA	123	447	110	28	4	6	164	50	58	24	0	72	8	2	2	6	7	.46	11	.246	.295	.367
1994	Durham	A	33	125	33	7	0	4	52	15	16	6	0	18	2	0	1	2	3	.40	3	.264	.306	.416
	Greenville	AA	40	146	39	6	1	5	62	17	22	3	0	24	2	1	4	2	4	.33	1	.267	.284	.425
	5 Min. YEARS		486	1732	445	89	20	30	664	219	201	87	6	279	20	21	12	54	29	.65	34	.257	.298	.383

Joe Roa

Pitches: Right **Bats:** Right **Pos:** P **Ht:** 6'2" **Wt:** 180 **Born:** 10/11/71 **Age:** 23

			HOW MUCH HE PITCHED						WHAT HE GAVE UP													THE RESULTS					
Year	Team	Lg	G	GS	CG	GF	IP	BFP	H	R	ER	HR	SH	SF	HB	TBB	IBB	SO	WP	Bk	W	L	Pct.	ShO	Sv	ERA
1989	Braves	R	13	4	0	4	37.1	156	40	18	12	2	0	1	0	10	1	21	3	0	2	2	.500	0	0	2.89
1990	Pulaski	R	14	11	3	1	75.2	313	55	29	25	3	2	1	2	26	0	49	2	2	4	2	.667	1	0	2.97
1991	Macon	A	30	18	4	2	141	556	106	46	33	6	0	3	5	33	4	96	3	0	13	3	.813	2	1	2.11
1992	St. Lucie	A	26	24	2	0	156.1	647	176	80	63	9	6	6	6	15	1	61	0	1	9	7	.563	1	0	3.63
1993	Binghamton	AA	32	23	2	0	167.1	693	190	80	72	9	2	4	10	24	0	73	3	2	12	7	.632	1	0	3.87
1994	Binghamton	AA	3	3	0	0	20	82	16	6	4	0	2	2	1	1	0	11	1	2	2	1	.667	0	0	1.80
	Norfolk	AAA	25	25	5	0	167.2	703	184	82	65	16	3	12	4	34	0	74	4	0	8	5	.500	0	0	3.49
	6 Min. YEARS		143	108	16	7	765.1	3150	769	341	274	45	15	29	28	143	7	385	16	7	50	30	.625	5	1	3.22

Sid Roberson

Pitches: Left **Bats:** Left **Pos:** P **Ht:** 5'9" **Wt:** 170 **Born:** 09/07/71 **Age:** 23

			HOW MUCH HE PITCHED						WHAT HE GAVE UP													THE RESULTS					
Year	Team	Lg	G	GS	CG	GF	IP	BFP	H	R	ER	HR	SH	SF	HB	TBB	IBB	SO	WP	Bk	W	L	Pct.	ShO	Sv	ERA
1992	Helena	R	9	8	1	1	65	276	68	32	25	8	3	1	2	18	0	65	4	1	4	4	.500	0	0	3.46
1993	Stockton	A	24	23	6	0	166	684	157	68	48	8	7	3	12	34	0	87	6	4	12	8	.600	1	0	2.60
1994	El Paso	AA	25	25	8	0	181.1	771	190	70	57	7	5	7	17	48	3	119	4	1	15	8	.652	0	0	2.83
	3 Min. YEARS		58	56	15	1	412.1	1731	415	170	130	23	15	11	31	100	3	271	14	6	31	20	.608	1	0	2.84

Brett Roberts

Pitches: Right **Bats:** Right **Pos:** P **Ht:** 6'7" **Wt:** 225 **Born:** 03/24/70 **Age:** 25

			HOW MUCH HE PITCHED						WHAT HE GAVE UP													THE RESULTS					
Year	Team	Lg	G	GS	CG	GF	IP	BFP	H	R	ER	HR	SH	SF	HB	TBB	IBB	SO	WP	Bk	W	L	Pct.	ShO	Sv	ERA
1991	Elizabethtn	R	6	6	1	0	28	112	21	8	7	0	0	0	0	10	0	27	2	4	3	0	1.000	0	0	2.25

Year	Team	Lg	G	GS	CG	GF	IP	BFP	H	R	ER	HR	SH	SF	HB	TBB	IBB	SO	WP	Bk	W	L	Pct.	ShO	Sv	ERA
1992	Kenosha	A	7	6	0	1	22.2	105	23	18	14	4	1	0	0	15	0	23	1	0	1	1	.500	0	0	5.56
1993	Ft.Myers	A	28	28	3	0	173.2	772	184	93	84	5	5	5	4	86	5	108	10	2	9	16	.360	0	0	4.35
1994	Fort Myers	A	21	21	1	0	116.2	520	123	71	56	5	4	8	3	47	3	75	8	0	6	7	.462	0	0	4.32
	Nashville	AA	5	5	0	0	20	102	30	18	15	1	0	1	1	12	1	11	0	0	2	1	.667	0	0	6.75
	4 Min. YEARS		67	66	5	1	361	1611	381	208	176	15	10	14	8	170	9	244	21	6	21	25	.457	0	0	4.39

Chris Roberts

Pitches: Left Bats: Right Pos: P   **Ht: 6'0" Wt: 180 Born: 06/25/71 Age: 24**

			HOW MUCH HE PITCHED						WHAT HE GAVE UP											THE RESULTS					
Year	Team	Lg	G	GS	CG	GF	IP	BFP	H	R	ER	HR	SH	SF	HB	TBB	IBB	SO	WP	Bk	W	L	Pct.	ShO	Sv	ERA
1993	St.Lucie	A	25	25	3	0	173.1	703	162	64	53	3	2	4	7	36	0	111	2	1	13	5	.722	2	0	2.75
1994	Binghamton	AA	27	27	2	0	175.1	751	164	77	64	11	8	5	6	77	1	128	12	1	13	8	.619	2	0	3.29
	2 Min. YEARS		52	52	5	0	348.2	1454	326	141	117	14	10	9	13	113	1	239	14	2	26	13	.667	4	0	3.02

Jason Robertson

Bats: Left Throws: Left Pos: OF   **Ht: 6'2" Wt: 200 Born: 03/24/71 Age: 24**

			BATTING													BASERUNNING				PERCENTAGES		
Year	Team	Lg	G	AB	H	2B	3B	HR	TB	R	RBI	TBB	IBB	SO	HBP	SH	SF	SB	CS	SB%	GDP	Avg	OBP	SLG
1989	Yankees	R	58	214	61	12	5	0	83	27	31	28	0	28	0	0	4	4	4	.50	2	.285	.362	.388
1990	Greensboro	A	133	496	125	22	5	6	175	71	44	67	2	110	2	4	1	21	13	.62	8	.252	.343	.353
1991	Pr William	A	131	515	136	21	6	3	178	67	54	53	2	138	2	1	4	32	9	.78	9	.264	.333	.346
1992	Pr William	A	68	254	61	6	4	5	90	34	34	31	0	55	1	1	3	14	6	.70	7	.240	.322	.354
	Albany	AA	55	204	44	12	1	3	67	18	33	10	0	44	2	2	2	9	3	.75	5	.216	.257	.328
1993	Albany	AA	130	483	110	29	4	6	165	65	41	43	3	126	4	3	2	35	12	.74	7	.228	.295	.342
1994	Albany-Colo	AA	124	432	94	10	7	11	151	54	53	50	3	120	1	5	4	20	10	.67	6	.218	.301	.350
	6 Min. YEARS		699	2598	631	112	32	34	909	336	290	282	10	621	14	16	20	135	57	.70	43	.243	.318	.350

Mike Robertson

Bats: Left Throws: Left Pos: OF-1B   **Ht: 6'0" Wt: 180 Born: 10/09/70 Age: 24**

			BATTING													BASERUNNING				PERCENTAGES		
Year	Team	Lg	G	AB	H	2B	3B	HR	TB	R	RBI	TBB	IBB	SO	HBP	SH	SF	SB	CS	SB%	GDP	Avg	OBP	SLG
1991	Utica	A	13	54	9	2	1	0	13	6	8	5	0	10	0	0	0	2	1	.67	0	.167	.237	.241
	South Bend	A	54	210	69	16	2	1	92	30	26	18	3	24	3	3	3	7	6	.54	5	.329	.385	.438
1992	Sarasota	A	106	395	99	21	3	10	156	50	59	50	3	55	7	1	3	5	7	.42	8	.251	.343	.395
	Birmingham	AA	27	90	17	8	1	1	30	6	9	10	1	19	0	1	0	0	1	.00	1	.189	.267	.333
1993	Birmingham	AA	138	511	138	31	3	11	208	73	73	59	4	97	3	0	8	10	5	.67	10	.270	.344	.407
1994	Birmingham	AA	53	196	62	20	2	3	95	32	30	31	4	34	2	0	2	6	3	.67	5	.316	.411	.485
	Nashville	AAA	67	213	48	8	1	8	82	21	21	15	4	27	3	0	0	0	3	.00	4	.225	.286	.385
	4 Min. YEARS		458	1669	442	106	13	34	676	218	226	188	19	266	18	5	17	30	26	.54	34	.265	.342	.405

Rod Robertson

Bats: Both Throws: Right Pos: SS-OF   **Ht: 5'9" Wt: 175 Born: 01/16/68 Age: 27**

			BATTING													BASERUNNING				PERCENTAGES		
Year	Team	Lg	G	AB	H	2B	3B	HR	TB	R	RBI	TBB	IBB	SO	HBP	SH	SF	SB	CS	SB%	GDP	Avg	OBP	SLG
1986	Bend	A	65	248	60	5	2	1	72	40	25	28	0	51	4	5	0	18	7	.72	3	.242	.329	.290
1987	Spartanburg	A	92	300	63	10	3	1	82	39	20	12	2	65	6	5	1	14	4	.78	4	.210	.254	.273
1988	Spartanburg	A	124	430	104	12	1	8	142	54	39	13	0	83	9	5	2	29	14	.67	7	.242	.278	.330
1989	Clearwater	A	118	385	102	14	1	4	130	49	32	26	1	51	4	10	5	24	10	.71	8	.265	.314	.338
1990	Reading	AA	51	189	39	3	0	1	45	16	12	6	0	26	3	2	2	7	9	.44	2	.206	.240	.238
	Clearwater	A	58	204	44	7	1	2	59	17	21	18	1	30	2	5	2	8	3	.73	7	.216	.283	.289
1991	Reading	AA	117	416	102	19	0	9	148	52	51	33	0	74	2	6	4	20	6	.77	9	.245	.301	.356
1992	London	AA	64	243	58	12	0	7	91	26	34	15	0	34	3	4	1	13	5	.72	5	.239	.290	.374
	Toledo	AAA	70	222	46	6	1	5	69	23	22	15	2	41	2	3	2	8	5	.62	2	.207	.261	.311
1993	Toledo	AAA	121	409	96	13	2	12	149	54	48	27	1	77	3	5	4	15	7	.68	5	.235	.284	.364
1994	Orlando	AA	25	87	21	4	2	2	35	14	8	6	0	12	1	1	0	5	3	.63	1	.241	.298	.402
	Iowa	AAA	88	263	66	18	2	12	124	36	36	11	0	44	3	5	1	5	8	.38	4	.251	.288	.471
	9 Min. YEARS		993	3396	801	123	15	64	1146	420	348	210	7	588	42	56	24	166	81	.67	57	.236	.287	.337

Don Robinson

Bats: Left Throws: Right Pos: OF   **Ht: 6'0" Wt: 185 Born: 01/16/72 Age: 23**

			BATTING													BASERUNNING				PERCENTAGES		
Year	Team	Lg	G	AB	H	2B	3B	HR	TB	R	RBI	TBB	IBB	SO	HBP	SH	SF	SB	CS	SB%	GDP	Avg	OBP	SLG
1990	Braves	R	41	118	23	3	2	0	30	13	15	13	0	36	1	5	0	5	2	.71	1	.195	.280	.254
1991	Pulaski	R	54	189	54	9	0	3	72	42	23	20	2	44	0	1	0	22	7	.76	1	.286	.354	.381
1992	Macon	A	113	399	98	17	2	1	122	42	41	28	0	118	5	6	3	20	10	.67	9	.246	.301	.306
1993	Durham	A	117	390	89	11	3	10	136	52	47	45	1	112	3	5	3	15	9	.63	10	.228	.311	.349
1994	Greenville	AA	120	358	90	23	2	13	156	49	46	32	5	74	5	2	4	11	10	.52	7	.251	.318	.436
	5 Min. YEARS		445	1454	354	63	9	27	516	198	172	138	8	384	14	19	10	73	38	.66	28	.243	.313	.355

Ken Robinson

Pitches: Right Bats: Right Pos: P Ht: 5'9" Wt: 175 Born: 11/03/69 Age: 25

Year	Team	Lg	G	GS	CG	GF	IP	BFP	H	R	ER	HR	SH	SF	HB	TBB	IBB	SO	WP	Bk	W	L	Pct.	ShO	Sv	ERA
1991	Medcne Hat	R	6	2	0	3	11.2	51	12	8	5	1	1	0	0	5	0	18	2	4	0	1	.000	0	0	3.86
1992	Myrtle Bch	A	20	0	0	9	38.1	162	25	12	12	2	0	1	3	30	0	45	4	0	1	0	1.000	0	1	2.82
1993	Hagerstown	A	40	0	0	24	71.2	314	74	43	37	6	2	4	6	31	1	65	5	1	4	7	.364	0	7	4.65
1994	Hagerstown	A	10	0	0	6	19.2	78	15	8	7	1	1	2	0	4	0	27	2	0	4	1	.800	0	1	3.20
	Dunedin	A	5	0	0	2	10	39	6	2	2	1	0	0	0	4	0	16	0	0	1	1	.500	0	0	1.80
	Syracuse	AAA	30	3	0	5	55.1	235	46	27	23	4	0	3	1	25	1	48	1	0	4	2	.667	0	0	3.74
	4 Min. YEARS		111	5	0	49	206.2	879	178	100	86	15	4	10	10	99	2	219	14	5	14	12	.538	0	9	3.75

Scott Robinson

Pitches: Right Bats: Right Pos: P Ht: 6'2" Wt: 200 Born: 11/15/68 Age: 26

Year	Team	Lg	G	GS	CG	GF	IP	BFP	H	R	ER	HR	SH	SF	HB	TBB	IBB	SO	WP	Bk	W	L	Pct.	ShO	Sv	ERA
1990	Billings	R	12	12	0	0	58.2	278	63	53	35	3	0	3	1	35	1	38	7	0	4	3	.571	0	0	5.37
1991	Cedar Rapds	A	20	19	2	0	126.2	537	122	57	53	5	7	4	2	48	3	75	4	0	8	9	.471	1	0	3.77
1992	Chston-Vw	A	13	13	6	0	99.1	387	73	28	19	3	2	2	0	25	2	80	1	0	8	2	.800	3	0	1.72
	Chattanooga	AA	13	13	1	0	83	340	82	38	35	7	6	4	2	26	0	51	4	0	7	2	.778	1	0	3.80
1993	Indianapols	AAA	9	9	0	0	47.2	219	55	43	34	14	2	2	1	24	2	29	1	3	2	5	.286	0	0	6.42
	Chattanooga	AA	20	18	0	0	112	480	114	60	44	12	6	4	5	40	1	58	5	0	6	5	.545	0	0	3.54
1994	Phoenix	AAA	47	2	0	9	87.1	388	103	57	48	7	3	6	4	34	4	45	8	1	9	5	.643	0	0	4.95
	5 Min. YEARS		134	86	9	9	614.2	2629	612	336	268	51	26	25	15	232	13	376	30	4	44	31	.587	5	0	3.92

Raul Rodarte

Bats: Right Throws: Right Pos: SS Ht: 5'11" Wt: 190 Born: 04/09/70 Age: 25

Year	Team	Lg	G	AB	H	2B	3B	HR	TB	R	RBI	TBB	IBB	SO	HBP	SH	SF	SB	CS	SB%	GDP	Avg	OBP	SLG
1991	Peninsula	A	65	216	48	4	1	0	54	19	14	32	0	56	0	1	2	5	1	.83	5	.222	.320	.250
1992	Peninsula	A	94	290	72	8	6	2	98	37	22	35	2	37	1	3	2	15	10	.60	7	.248	.329	.338
1993	Riverside	A	106	402	116	19	1	5	152	79	48	51	0	66	0	6	2	13	14	.48	7	.289	.367	.378
1994	Jacksonvlle	AA	34	91	22	3	1	3	36	13	13	8	1	15	1	3	0	2	2	.50	2	.242	.310	.396
	Riverside	A	39	156	50	6	4	4	76	29	37	15	1	31	2	1	1	5	2	.71	3	.321	.385	.487
	4 Min. YEARS		338	1155	308	40	13	14	416	177	134	141	4	205	4	14	7	40	29	.58	24	.267	.347	.360

Felix Rodriguez

Pitches: Right Bats: Right Pos: P Ht: 6'1" Wt: 190 Born: 12/05/72 Age: 22

Year	Team	Lg	G	GS	CG	GF	IP	BFP	H	R	ER	HR	SH	SF	HB	TBB	IBB	SO	WP	Bk	W	L	Pct.	ShO	Sv	ERA
1993	Vero Beach	A	32	20	2	7	132	570	109	71	55	15	6	3	6	71	1	80	9	6	8	8	.500	1	0	3.75
1994	San Antonio	AA	26	26	0	0	136.1	588	106	70	61	8	6	7	4	88	3	126	4	5	6	8	.429	0	0	4.03
	2 Min. YEARS		58	46	2	7	268.1	1158	215	141	116	23	12	10	10	159	4	206	13	11	14	16	.467	1	0	3.89

Frankie Rodriguez

Pitches: Right Bats: Right Pos: P Ht: 6'0" Wt: 175 Born: 12/11/72 Age: 22

Year	Team	Lg	G	GS	CG	GF	IP	BFP	H	R	ER	HR	SH	SF	HB	TBB	IBB	SO	WP	Bk	W	L	Pct.	ShO	Sv	ERA
1992	Lynchburg	A	25	25	1	0	148.2	619	125	56	51	11	5	2	6	65	0	129	6	3	12	7	.632	0	0	3.09
1993	New Britain	AA	28	26	4	1	170.2	722	147	79	71	17	2	2	4	78	4	151	7	3	7	11	.389	1	0	3.74
1994	Pawtucket	AAA	28	28	8	0	186	789	182	95	81	18	3	4	8	60	0	160	5	0	8	13	.381	1	0	3.92
	3 Min. YEARS		81	79	13	1	505.1	2130	454	230	203	46	10	8	18	203	4	440	18	6	27	31	.466	2	0	3.62

Luis Rodriguez

Bats: Right Throws: Right Pos: SS Ht: 5'11" Wt: 165 Born: 08/15/70 Age: 24

Year	Team	Lg	G	AB	H	2B	3B	HR	TB	R	RBI	TBB	IBB	SO	HBP	SH	SF	SB	CS	SB%	GDP	Avg	OBP	SLG
1991	Elmira	A	77	272	70	10	2	1	87	48	23	32	0	45	3	2	4	29	4	.88	6	.257	.338	.320
1992	Lynchburg	A	128	516	115	14	4	1	140	59	27	25	0	84	3	7	3	11	6	.65	11	.223	.261	.271
1993	New Britain	AA	99	355	81	16	4	0	105	37	31	16	0	52	4	4	5	7	7	.50	8	.228	.266	.296
1994	Sarasota	A	15	49	11	0	0	0	11	4	5	4	0	9	0	2	0	1	0	1.00	3	.224	.283	.224
	New Britain	AA	6	20	3	0	1	0	5	1	0	0	0	7	0	0	0	0	0	.00	1	.150	.150	.250
	Pawtucket	AAA	64	169	43	4	1	4	61	16	18	5	0	22	0	7	2	3	3	.50	9	.254	.273	.361
	4 Min. YEARS		389	1381	323	44	12	6	409	165	104	82	0	219	10	22	14	51	20	.72	38	.234	.279	.296

Ruben Rodriguez

Bats: Right Throws: Right Pos: C Ht: 6'1" Wt: 180 Born: 08/04/64 Age: 30

Year	Team	Lg	G	AB	H	2B	3B	HR	TB	R	RBI	TBB	IBB	SO	HBP	SH	SF	SB	CS	SB%	GDP	Avg	OBP	SLG
1991	London	AA	14	39	11	4	0	2	21	3	3	5	0	8	0	1	0	0	1	.00	3	.282	.364	.538
	New Britain	AA	23	61	16	1	0	1	20	8	6	3	0	11	1	0	1	1	0	1.00	0	.262	.308	.328
1992	Pawtucket	AAA	17	44	10	3	0	0	13	3	1	2	1	11	0	0	0	0	0	.00	0	.227	.261	.295

Year	Team	Lg	G	AB	H	2B	3B	HR	TB	R	RBI	TBB	IBB	SO	HBP	SH	SF	SB	CS	SB%	GDP	Avg	OBP	SLG
	New Britain	AA	39	119	30	14	0	0	44	10	14	3	0	15	3	4	1	1	0	1.00	3	.252	.286	.370
1993	Pawtucket	AAA	32	97	31	5	0	1	39	12	10	1	0	14	2	0	0	1	1	.50	4	.320	.340	.402
1994	Pawtucket	AAA	18	48	13	4	0	0	17	6	6	1	0	6	0	1	0	0	0	.00	0	.271	.286	.354
	New Britain	AA	3	9	1	0	0	0	1	0	1	0	0	1	0	0	0	0	0	.00	0	.111	.111	.111
	4 Min. YEARS		146	417	112	31	0	4	155	42	41	15	1	66	6	6	1	3	2	.60	13	.269	.303	.372

Steve Rodriguez

Bats: Right   Throws: Right   Pos: 2B   Ht: 5'9"   Wt: 170   Born: 11/29/70   Age: 24

			BATTING															BASERUNNING				PERCENTAGES		
Year	Team	Lg	G	AB	H	2B	3B	HR	TB	R	RBI	TBB	IBB	SO	HBP	SH	SF	SB	CS	SB%	GDP	Avg	OBP	SLG
1992	Winter Havn	A	26	87	15	0	0	1	18	13	5	9	0	17	2	3	0	4	1	.80	3	.172	.265	.207
1993	Lynchburg	A	120	493	135	26	3	3	176	78	42	31	0	69	4	8	3	20	13	.61	15	.274	.320	.357
1994	New Britain	AA	38	159	45	5	2	0	54	25	14	9	0	14	1	3	1	8	4	.67	3	.283	.324	.340
	Pawtucket	AAA	62	233	70	11	0	1	84	28	21	14	0	30	1	3	2	11	3	.79	6	.300	.340	.361
	3 Min. YEARS		246	972	265	42	5	5	332	144	82	63	0	130	8	17	6	43	21	.67	27	.273	.320	.342

Vic Rodriguez

Bats: Right   Throws: Right   Pos: 2B   Ht: 5'11"   Wt: 173   Born: 07/14/61   Age: 33

			BATTING															BASERUNNING				PERCENTAGES		
Year	Team	Lg	G	AB	H	2B	3B	HR	TB	R	RBI	TBB	IBB	SO	HBP	SH	SF	SB	CS	SB%	GDP	Avg	OBP	SLG
1977	Bluefield	R	53	188	55	10	4	3	82	28	23	7	0	30	0	8	1	2	1	.67	7	.293	.316	.436
1978	Bluefield	R	59	209	67	4	2	2	81	26	28	8	0	23	0	1	4	0	0	.00	7	.321	.339	.388
1979	Miami	A	67	228	70	10	2	1	87	23	31	18	2	19	2	3	1	2	0	1.00	6	.307	.361	.382
1980	Alexandria	A	33	130	39	4	2	2	53	20	15	13	0	17	2	0	1	5	0	1.00	3	.300	.370	.408
	Charlotte	AA	19	65	15	0	0	0	15	4	4	3	1	6	0	3	0	1	0	1.00	2	.231	.265	.231
	Miami	A	49	184	60	10	2	2	80	21	21	18	1	16	0	1	3	1	2	.33	8	.326	.380	.435
1981	Charlotte	AA	138	553	169	22	1	9	220	68	65	37	0	51	1	7	3	5	4	.56	13	.306	.348	.398
1982	Charlotte	AA	47	165	48	13	0	3	70	17	18	14	2	14	1	1	2	0	1	.00	6	.291	.346	.424
	Rochester	AAA	87	300	74	10	2	0	88	26	18	11	0	31	0	7	1	3	3	.50	11	.247	.272	.293
1983	Charlotte	AA	140	571	170	26	1	14	240	80	77	26	1	44	0	7	3	2	5	.29	21	.298	.327	.420
1984	Rochester	AAA	132	478	131	22	6	6	183	54	46	32	0	53	3	7	4	0	1	.00	23	.274	.321	.383
1985	Las Vegas	AAA	127	462	144	31	3	11	214	56	58	20	4	41	1	9	4	0	2	.00	10	.312	.339	.463
1986	Louisville	AAA	56	191	52	9	0	1	64	13	18	10	0	22	0	1	0	0	1	.00	5	.272	.308	.335
1987	Louisville	AAA	116	422	124	33	2	3	170	44	54	15	2	42	3	0	8	0	0	.00	18	.294	.317	.403
1988	Portland	AAA	139	562	162	27	8	9	232	67	69	34	1	48	2	6	5	2	2	.50	16	.288	.328	.413
1989	Portland	AAA	120	465	146	34	3	10	216	63	50	35	2	45	4	1	2	2	1	.67	18	.314	.366	.465
1990	Portland	AAA	12	39	11	1	0	1	15	4	2	2	0	5	0	0	0	0	0	.00	3	.282	.317	.385
1991	Portland	AAA	83	270	82	17	0	6	117	36	32	20	0	22	2	4	4	0	0	.00	7	.304	.351	.433
1992	Scranton/wb	AAA	48	155	43	8	2	1	58	14	27	3	0	20	0	1	0	0	0	.00	4	.277	.291	.374
1993	Scranton/wb	AAA	118	442	135	24	3	12	201	59	64	17	0	40	3	6	3	2	4	.33	18	.305	.333	.455
1994	Edmonton	AAA	84	273	76	13	0	6	107	28	46	11	0	23	5	1	5	1	2	.33	13	.278	.313	.392
1984	Baltimore	AL	11	17	7	3	0	0	10	4	2	0	0	2	0	0	0	0	0	.00	0	.412	.412	.588
1989	Minnesota	AL	6	11	5	2	0	0	7	2	0	0	0	1	0	0	0	0	0	.00	0	.455	.455	.636
	18 Min. YEARS		1727	6352	1873	328	43	102	2593	751	766	354	16	612	29	74	54	28	29	.49	219	.295	.332	.408
	2 Maj. YEARS		17	28	12	5	0	0	17	6	2	0	0	3	0	0	0	0	0	.00	0	.429	.429	.607

Bryan Rogers

Pitches: Right   Bats: Right   Pos: P   Ht: 6'1"   Wt: 170   Born: 10/30/67   Age: 27

			HOW MUCH HE PITCHED						WHAT HE GAVE UP										THE RESULTS					
Year	Team	Lg	G	GS	CG	GF	IP	BFP	H	R	ER	HR	SH	SF	HB	TBB	IBB	SO	WP	Bk	W	L	Pct.	ShO	Sv	ERA
1988	Kingsport	R	15	2	0	5	31.1	135	30	23	22	1	0	0	1	14	1	35	1	4	2	3	.400	0	0	6.32
1989	Columbia	A	14	4	0	6	43.1	181	36	16	15	1	5	0	2	14	0	36	0	1	3	2	.600	0	3	3.12
1990	St. Lucie	A	29	19	5	6	148.2	599	127	66	51	3	2	8	4	26	0	96	7	1	9	8	.529	0	4	3.09
1991	Williamsprt	AA	41	0	0	32	61	267	73	33	32	5	5	2	1	18	1	33	1	0	6	8	.429	0	15	4.72
1992	Binghamton	AA	22	0	0	10	35.1	152	37	21	17	4	2	1	1	7	0	20	0	0	3	2	.600	0	1	4.33
	St. Lucie	A	17	0	0	6	30.2	123	24	12	10	1	3	1	2	7	2	17	1	0	2	4	.333	0	2	2.93
1993	Binghamton	AA	62	0	0	40	84.2	347	80	29	22	4	5	4	0	25	2	42	4	0	5	4	.556	0	8	2.34
1994	Norfolk	AAA	20	0	0	4	30	133	35	19	18	4	1	2	1	10	2	8	0	0	2	2	.500	0	1	5.40
	Binghamton	AA	41	0	0	21	60	236	49	17	11	1	3	0	1	14	5	46	2	0	5	1	.833	0	11	1.65
	7 Min. YEARS		261	25	5	130	525	2173	491	236	198	24	26	18	13	135	13	333	16	6	37	34	.521	0	44	3.39

Charlie Rogers

Pitches: Left   Bats: Left   Pos: P   Ht: 6'0"   Wt: 180   Born: 08/21/68   Age: 26

			HOW MUCH HE PITCHED						WHAT HE GAVE UP										THE RESULTS					
Year	Team	Lg	G	GS	CG	GF	IP	BFP	H	R	ER	HR	SH	SF	HB	TBB	IBB	SO	WP	Bk	W	L	Pct.	ShO	Sv	ERA
1990	Miami	A	14	10	2	1	72	312	57	26	21	3	4	1	3	49	1	64	4	14	2	5	.286	0	1	2.63
1991	Miami	A	22	20	0	2	107.1	472	107	54	48	5	7	3	9	50	0	71	3	5	6	7	.462	0	0	4.02
1992	Stockton	A	54	0	0	34	80	313	65	28	25	3	4	2	2	26	3	64	2	4	4	4	.500	0	17	2.81
1993	El Paso	AA	48	2	0	35	72.1	283	50	17	14	2	8	2	2	23	6	55	1	0	4	3	.571	0	23	1.74
1994	New Orleans	AAA	21	0	0	11	22.2	112	34	16	16	7	0	1	0	10	1	11	2	0	1	1	.500	0	1	6.35
	5 Min. YEARS		159	32	2	83	354.1	1492	313	141	124	20	23	9	16	158	11	265	12	23	17	20	.459	0	42	3.15

Jimmy Rogers

Pitches: Right Bats: Right Pos: P　　　　Ht: 6'2" Wt: 190 Born: 01/03/67 Age: 28

			HOW MUCH HE PITCHED						WHAT HE GAVE UP										THE RESULTS					
Year	Team	Lg	G	GS	CG	GF	IP	BFP	H	R	ER	HR	SH	SF	HB	TBB	IBB	SO	WP	Bk	W	L	Pct.	ShO	Sv	ERA
1987	St.Cathmes	A	13	12	0	0	56.1	241	46	33	21	4	2	0	4	24	0	60	5	0	2	4	.333	0	0	3.36
1988	Myrtle Bch	A	33	32	2	0	188.1	803	145	84	70	10	1	6	5	95	1	198	15	6	18	4	.818	0	0	3.35
1989	Knoxville	AA	32	30	1	0	158	718	136	89	80	12	4	3	5	132	1	120	14	3	12	10	.545	0	0	4.56
1990	Knoxville	AA	31	29	2	0	173.1	789	179	98	86	8	6	12	6	104	1	113	12	4	9	12	.429	1	0	4.47
1991	Knoxville	AA	28	27	4	0	168.1	706	139	70	62	7	4	3	6	90	0	122	11	1	7	11	.389	3	0	3.31
1993	Knoxville	AA	19	19	0	0	100.1	431	107	54	45	9	3	2	2	33	1	80	5	0	7	7	.500	0	0	4.04
1994	Syracuse	AAA	31	10	0	5	94	404	82	51	48	7	0	5	0	49	1	69	4	0	5	4	.556	0	0	4.60
	7 Min. YEARS		187	160	9	5	938.2	4092	834	479	412	57	20	31	28	527	5	762	66	14	60	52	.536	4	0	3.95

Lamarr Rogers

Bats: Right Throws: Right Pos: 2B　　　　Ht: 5'8" Wt: 165 Born: 06/24/71 Age: 24

						BATTING											BASERUNNING				PERCENTAGES		
Year	Team	Lg	G	AB	H	2B	3B	HR	TB	R	RBI	TBB	IBB	SO	HBP	SH	SF	SB	CS	SB%	GDP	Avg	OBP	SLG
1992	Bend	A	66	231	67	13	3	2	92	41	21	53	0	31	2	3	2	22	7	.76	1	.290	.424	.398
1993	Central Val	A	112	406	107	14	2	2	131	68	33	68	1	54	4	7	4	29	15	.66	10	.264	.371	.323
1994	New Haven	AA	111	376	100	18	4	2	132	57	35	56	0	51	2	6	2	7	8	.47	8	.266	.362	.351
	3 Min. YEARS		289	1013	274	45	9	6	355	166	89	177	1	136	8	16	8	58	30	.66	19	.270	.381	.350

Dave Rohde

Bats: Both Throws: Right Pos: SS　　　　Ht: 6' 2" Wt: 180 Born: 05/08/64 Age: 31

						BATTING											BASERUNNING				PERCENTAGES		
Year	Team	Lg	G	AB	H	2B	3B	HR	TB	R	RBI	TBB	IBB	SO	HBP	SH	SF	SB	CS	SB%	GDP	Avg	OBP	SLG
1986	Auburn	A	61	207	54	6	4	2	74	41	22	37	1	37	0	1	2	28	9	.76	2	.261	.370	.357
1987	Osceola	A	103	377	108	15	1	5	140	57	42	50	1	58	4	10	0	12	6	.67	4	.286	.376	.371
1988	Columbus	AA	142	486	130	20	2	4	166	76	53	81	1	62	5	4	7	36	4	.90	14	.267	.373	.342
1989	Columbus	AA	67	254	71	5	2	2	86	40	27	41	0	25	1	5	2	15	5	.75	6	.280	.379	.339
	Tucson	AAA	75	234	68	7	3	1	84	35	30	32	1	30	1	7	5	11	5	.69	4	.291	.371	.359
1990	Tucson	AAA	47	170	60	10	2	0	74	42	20	40	0	20	1	1	0	5	2	.71	7	.353	.479	.435
1991	Tucson	AAA	73	253	94	10	4	1	115	36	40	52	3	34	5	2	5	15	6	.71	4	.372	.479	.455
1992	Colo Sprngs	AAA	121	448	132	17	14	4	189	85	55	57	1	60	4	8	2	13	8	.62	7	.295	.378	.422
1993	Buffalo	AAA	131	464	113	22	2	11	172	64	48	50	3	46	3	5	6	4	5	.44	11	.244	.317	.371
1994	Buffalo	AAA	101	273	62	11	1	1	78	24	23	38	4	35	1	4	4	7	4	.64	7	.227	.320	.286
1990	Houston	NL	59	98	18	4	0	0	22	8	5	9	2	20	5	4	1	0	0	.00	3	.184	.283	.224
1991	Houston	NL	29	41	5	0	0	0	5	3	0	5	0	8	0	2	0	0	0	.00	1	.122	.217	.122
1992	Cleveland	AL	5	7	0	0	0	0	0	0	0	2	1	3	0	0	0	0	0	.00	0	.000	.222	.000
	9 Min. YEARS		921	3166	892	123	35	31	1178	500	360	478	15	407	25	47	33	146	54	.73	66	.282	.377	.372
	3 Maj. YEARS		93	146	23	4	0	0	27	11	5	16	3	31	5	6	1	0	0	.00	4	.158	.262	.185

Dan Rohrmeier

Bats: Right Throws: Right Pos: OF　　　　Ht: 6'0" Wt: 185 Born: 09/27/65 Age: 29

						BATTING											BASERUNNING				PERCENTAGES		
Year	Team	Lg	G	AB	H	2B	3B	HR	TB	R	RBI	TBB	IBB	SO	HBP	SH	SF	SB	CS	SB%	GDP	Avg	OBP	SLG
1987	Peninsula	A	68	243	80	13	2	5	112	43	34	29	0	37	2	2	3	2	3	.40	3	.329	.401	.461
1988	Tampa	A	114	421	109	28	8	5	168	53	50	27	2	58	1	1	5	11	7	.61	4	.259	.302	.399
1989	Sarasota	A	25	74	16	2	0	1	21	11	4	12	0	15	0	1	1	1	0	1.00	2	.216	.322	.284
	Charlotte	A	18	65	20	3	1	1	28	9	11	7	0	8	1	0	1	0	1	.00	1	.308	.378	.431
	Tulsa	AA	57	210	67	3	4	5	93	24	27	11	0	20	1	4	0	5	8	.38	5	.319	.356	.443
1990	Tulsa	AA	119	453	138	24	7	10	206	76	62	37	0	51	0	1	4	13	11	.54	14	.305	.354	.455
1991	Tulsa	AA	121	418	122	20	2	5	161	67	62	60	1	57	4	4	7	3	2	.60	14	.292	.380	.385
1992	Memphis	AA	123	433	140	33	2	6	195	54	69	26	2	46	4	0	4	3	7	.30	11	.323	.364	.450
	Omaha	AAA	8	29	7	1	0	1	11	4	5	3	0	4	0	0	0	0	1	.00	0	.241	.313	.379
1993	Omaha	AAA	118	432	107	23	3	17	187	51	70	23	0	59	3	1	7	2	1	.67	10	.248	.286	.433
1994	Memphis	AA	112	436	118	34	4	18	206	64	72	31	3	80	6	0	3	2	2	.50	15	.271	.326	.472
	Chattanooga	AA	17	66	22	7	0	0	29	9	10	5	0	5	0	0	0	1	0	.00	5	.333	.375	.439
	8 Min. YEARS		900	3280	946	191	29	74	1417	465	476	271	8	440	22	14	36	42	44	.49	84	.288	.343	.432

Roberto Rojas

Bats: Left Throws: Left Pos: OF　　　　Ht: 6'0" Wt: 185 Born: 11/23/70 Age: 24

						BATTING											BASERUNNING				PERCENTAGES		
Year	Team	Lg	G	AB	H	2B	3B	HR	TB	R	RBI	TBB	IBB	SO	HBP	SH	SF	SB	CS	SB%	GDP	Avg	OBP	SLG
1991	Niagara Fls	A	7	13	3	1	0	0	4	2	0	1	0	6	0	0	0	1	0	1.00	0	.231	.286	.308
	Bristol	R	38	103	18	3	0	0	21	10	5	14	0	38	0	4	0	6	3	.67	2	.175	.274	.204
1992	Bristol	R	57	214	61	8	3	0	75	38	11	27	2	46	0	1	0	32	11	.74	2	.285	.365	.350
1993	Fayettevlle	A	120	492	125	17	6	1	157	68	29	41	1	118	2	5	1	30	16	.65	2	.254	.313	.319
1994	Lakeland	A	39	121	36	3	3	2	51	17	19	15	1	31	0	1	3	6	7	.46	3	.298	.367	.421
	Trenton	AA	62	167	32	1	2	1	40	20	12	17	0	49	0	6	0	19	8	.70	2	.192	.266	.240
	4 Min. YEARS		323	1110	275	33	14	4	348	155	76	115	4	288	2	17	4	94	45	.68	11	.248	.318	.314

221

David Rolls

Bats: Right Throws: Right Pos: C   Ht: 6'0" Wt: 195 Born: 10/01/66 Age: 28

							BATTING											BASERUNNING				PERCENTAGES		
Year Team	Lg	G	AB	H	2B	3B	HR	TB	R	RBI	TBB	IBB	SO	HBP	SH	SF	SB	CS	SB%	GDP	Avg	OBP	SLG
1988 Eugene	A	35	111	19	5	0	3	33	14	10	19	0	44	3	0	0	2	0	1.00	1	.171	.308	.297
1990 Eugene	A	45	128	36	5	0	5	56	24	13	21	0	27	6	1	2	1	1	.50	2	.281	.401	.438
1991 Salt Lake	R	66	224	73	21	1	4	108	58	47	48	0	37	8	0	6	4	3	.57	4	.326	.451	.512
1992 Charlotte	A	77	211	62	15	2	9	108	31	33	22	0	42	5	0	0	1	5	.17	4	.294	.374	.512
1993 Tulsa	AA	72	221	53	9	0	5	77	23	23	22	0	51	6	2	2	1	2	.33	4	.240	.323	.348
1994 Tulsa	AA	92	293	71	19	0	6	108	40	32	26	0	71	12	4	3	2	0	1.00	11	.242	.326	.369
6 Min. YEARS		387	1188	314	74	3	32	490	190	158	158	0	272	40	7	13	11	11	.50	26	.264	.366	.412

Brian Romero

Pitches: Left Bats: Right Pos: P   Ht: 6'1" Wt: 185 Born: 11/03/68 Age: 26

		HOW MUCH HE PITCHED						WHAT HE GAVE UP											THE RESULTS					
Year Team	Lg	G	GS	CG	GF	IP	BFP	H	R	ER	HR	SH	SF	HB	TBB	IBB	SO	WP	Bk	W	L	Pct.	ShO	Sv	ERA
1989 Butte	R	10	7	0	3	45.1	190	36	11	9	0	0	1	3	23	1	41	4	2	5	0	1.000	0	0	1.79
1990 Gastonia	A	15	15	1	0	91	360	54	17	15	2	1	0	2	35	0	87	3	0	9	2	.818	0	0	1.48
Charlotte	A	12	12	2	0	74.1	283	45	19	14	0	2	1	2	24	0	72	4	4	7	2	.778	0	0	1.70
1991 Tulsa	AA	23	14	2	5	94	422	92	61	52	11	2	1	9	52	1	79	5	3	6	5	.545	0	1	4.98
1992 Tulsa	AA	13	11	0	0	52.1	232	62	31	26	10	3	0	0	20	0	44	2	0	2	5	.286	0	0	4.47
1993 Tulsa	AA	21	18	1	1	94.1	412	98	47	41	4	2	4	4	34	2	72	1	7	5	6	.455	0	0	3.91
1994 Tulsa	AA	7	6	1	0	34.2	136	30	9	8	2	2	1	1	11	0	24	1	0	3	1	.750	0	1	2.08
6 Min. YEARS		101	83	7	9	486	2035	437	195	165	29	12	8	21	199	4	419	20	17	37	21	.638	1	1	3.06

Mandy Romero

Bats: Both Throws: Right Pos: C   Ht: 5'11" Wt: 196 Born: 10/19/67 Age: 27

							BATTING											BASERUNNING				PERCENTAGES		
Year Team	Lg	G	AB	H	2B	3B	HR	TB	R	RBI	TBB	IBB	SO	HBP	SH	SF	SB	CS	SB%	GDP	Avg	OBP	SLG
1988 Princeton	R	30	71	22	6	0	2	34	7	11	13	0	15	1	0	0	1	0	1.00	0	.310	.424	.479
1989 Augusta	A	121	388	87	26	3	4	131	58	55	67	4	74	6	3	6	8	5	.62	10	.224	.343	.338
1990 Salem	A	124	460	134	31	3	17	222	62	90	55	3	68	5	2	4	0	2	.00	10	.291	.370	.483
1991 Carolina	AA	98	323	70	12	0	3	91	28	31	45	4	53	1	2	2	1	2	.33	9	.217	.313	.282
1992 Carolina	AA	80	269	58	16	0	3	83	28	27	29	0	39	1	1	2	0	3	.00	10	.216	.292	.309
1993 Buffalo	AAA	42	136	31	6	1	2	45	11	14	6	1	12	0	1	1	0	1	1.00	5	.228	.259	.331
1994 Buffalo	AAA	7	23	3	0	0	0	3	3	1	2	0	1	0	1	0	0	0	.00	2	.130	.200	.130
7 Min. YEARS		502	1670	405	97	7	31	609	197	229	217	12	262	14	10	15	11	12	.48	46	.243	.332	.365

Marc Ronan

Bats: Left Throws: Right Pos: C   Ht: 6'2" Wt: 190 Born: 09/19/69 Age: 25

							BATTING											BASERUNNING				PERCENTAGES		
Year Team	Lg	G	AB	H	2B	3B	HR	TB	R	RBI	TBB	IBB	SO	HBP	SH	SF	SB	CS	SB%	GDP	Avg	OBP	SLG
1990 Hamilton	A	56	167	38	6	0	1	47	14	15	15	0	37	1	0	3	1	2	.33	3	.228	.290	.281
1991 Savannah	A	108	343	81	10	1	0	93	41	45	37	1	54	4	3	1	11	2	.85	13	.236	.317	.271
1992 Springfield	A	110	376	81	19	2	6	122	45	48	23	2	58	1	0	4	4	5	.44	11	.215	.260	.324
1993 St.Pete	A	25	87	27	5	0	0	32	13	6	6	0	10	0	3	2	0	0	.00	1	.310	.347	.368
Arkansas	AA	96	281	60	16	1	7	99	33	34	26	2	47	2	3	3	1	3	.25	4	.214	.282	.352
1994 Louisville	AAA	84	269	64	11	2	2	85	32	21	12	2	43	2	2	2	3	1	.75	9	.238	.274	.316
1993 St. Louis	NL	6	12	1	0	0	0	1	0	0	0	0	5	0	0	0	0	0	.00	0	.083	.083	.083
5 Min. YEARS		479	1523	351	67	6	16	478	178	169	119	7	249	10	11	15	20	13	.61	41	.230	.288	.314

Gabriel Rosario

Bats: Right Throws: Right Pos: INF   Ht: 6'0" Wt: 150 Born: 10/19/70 Age: 24

							BATTING											BASERUNNING				PERCENTAGES		
Year Team	Lg	G	AB	H	2B	3B	HR	TB	R	RBI	TBB	IBB	SO	HBP	SH	SF	SB	CS	SB%	GDP	Avg	OBP	SLG
1991 Medicne Hat	R	49	164	41	3	1	0	46	23	21	16	0	33	0	2	2	6	4	.60	4	.250	.313	.280
1992 Myrtle Bch	A	23	33	6	2	0	0	8	2	1	1	1	5	0	0	0	2	0	1.00	2	.182	.206	.242
Dunedin	A	54	186	49	7	1	0	58	24	18	14	1	27	5	6	0	2	5	.29	4	.263	.332	.312
1993 Knoxville	AA	1	4	2	0	0	0	2	0	0	0	0	1	0	0	0	0	1	.00	1	.500	.500	.500
Dunedin	A	72	219	49	3	3	0	58	19	18	7	0	24	4	6	0	12	6	.67	9	.224	.261	.265
1994 Knoxville	AA	8	5	0	0	0	0	0	1	0	0	0	2	0	0	0	0	0	.00	0	.000	.000	.000
4 Min. YEARS		207	611	147	15	5	0	172	69	58	38	2	92	9	14	2	22	16	.58	20	.241	.294	.282

Scott Rose

Pitches: Right Bats: Right Pos: P   Ht: 6'3" Wt: 200 Born: 05/12/70 Age: 25

		HOW MUCH HE PITCHED						WHAT HE GAVE UP											THE RESULTS					
Year Team	Lg	G	GS	CG	GF	IP	BFP	H	R	ER	HR	SH	SF	HB	TBB	IBB	SO	WP	Bk	W	L	Pct.	ShO	Sv	ERA
1990 Athletics	R	9	1	0	4	18.1	69	12	5	3	0	0	0	0	3	0	21	1	0	0	0	.000	0	2	1.47
Modesto	A	6	0	0	3	14	61	14	5	2	0	0	0	0	6	1	10	2	0	0	0	.000	0	1	1.29
1991 Modesto	A	13	13	0	0	67.2	306	66	45	33	7	3	3	3	38	0	31	7	1	3	3	.500	0	0	4.39
1992 Madison	A	8	8	1	0	36	154	35	22	17	2	1	2	2	10	0	15	3	1	2	2	.500	0	0	4.25
Reno	A	20	9	0	2	64	314	97	73	60	11	2	2	2	37	3	29	4	0	2	4	.333	0	0	8.44

Year	Team	Lg	G	GS	CG	GF	IP	BFP	H	R	ER	HR	SH	SF	HB	TBB	IBB	SO	WP	Bk	W	L	Pct.	ShO	Sv	ERA
1993	San Berndno	A	28	25	1	0	173.1	765	184	110	82	16	6	8	10	63	6	73	10	0	9	10	.474	1	0	4.26
1994	Huntsville	AA	41	0	0	25	73	328	87	44	38	2	9	4	2	24	8	43	9	0	6	10	.375	0	3	4.68
	5 Min. YEARS		125	56	2	34	446.1	1997	495	304	235	38	21	19	18	181	19	222	36	2	22	29	.431	1	6	4.74

John Rosengren

Pitches: Left Bats: Left Pos: P Ht: 6'4" Wt: 190 Born: 08/10/72 Age: 22

			HOW MUCH HE PITCHED						WHAT HE GAVE UP											THE RESULTS					
Year	Team	Lg	G	GS	CG	GF	IP	BFP	H	R	ER	HR	SH	SF	HB	TBB	IBB	SO	WP	Bk	W	L	Pct.	ShO	Sv	ERA
1992	Bristol	R	14	3	0	3	23	113	16	21	20	2	0	5	0	30	0	28	6	2	0	3	.000	0	0	7.83
1993	Niagara Fls	A	15	15	0	0	82	333	52	32	22	3	1	4	6	38	0	91	6	1	7	3	.700	0	0	2.41
1994	Lakeland	A	22	22	4	0	135.2	569	113	51	38	4	2	4	7	56	0	101	3	2	9	6	.600	3	0	2.52
	Trenton	AA	3	3	0	0	17.1	79	21	15	14	2	1	1	0	11	0	7	0	1	0	2	.000	0	0	7.27
	3 Min. YEARS		54	43	4	3	258	1094	202	119	94	11	4	14	13	135	0	227	15	6	16	14	.533	3	0	3.28

Joe Rosselli

Pitches: Left Bats: Right Pos: P Ht: 6'1" Wt: 170 Born: 05/28/72 Age: 23

			HOW MUCH HE PITCHED						WHAT HE GAVE UP											THE RESULTS					
Year	Team	Lg	G	GS	CG	GF	IP	BFP	H	R	ER	HR	SH	SF	HB	TBB	IBB	SO	WP	Bk	W	L	Pct.	ShO	Sv	ERA
1990	Everett	A	15	15	0	0	78.1	340	87	47	41	10	0	2	0	29	0	90	4	0	4	4	.500	0	0	4.71
1991	Clinton	A	22	22	2	0	153.2	640	144	70	53	5	4	8	1	49	0	127	11	4	8	7	.533	0	0	3.10
1992	San Jose	A	22	22	4	0	149.2	614	145	50	40	7	2	2	2	46	1	111	2	4	11	4	.733	2	0	2.41
1993	Shreveport	AA	4	4	0	0	23	96	22	9	8	1	1	0	0	7	0	19	1	0	0	0	.000	0	0	3.13
1994	Shreveport	AA	14	14	2	0	90.2	350	67	24	19	2	6	2	0	17	0	54	1	0	7	2	.778	2	0	1.89
	Phoenix	AAA	13	13	0	0	74.2	322	96	46	41	10	6	1	1	15	0	35	1	1	1	8	.111	0	0	4.94
	5 Min. YEARS		90	90	8	0	570	2362	561	246	202	35	18	15	4	163	1	436	20	9	31	26	.544	2	0	3.19

Rico Rossy

Bats: Right Throws: Right Pos: 2B Ht: 5'10" Wt: 175 Born: 02/16/64 Age: 31

			BATTING														BASERUNNING				PERCENTAGES		
Year	Team	Lg	G	AB	H	2B	3B	HR	TB	R	RBI	TBB	IBB	SO	HBP	SH	SF	SB	CS	SB%	GDP	Avg	OBP	SLG
1985	Newark	A	73	246	53	14	2	3	80	38	25	32	1	22	1	3	1	17	7	.71	13	.215	.307	.325
1986	Miami	A	38	134	34	7	1	1	46	26	9	24	0	8	1	6	1	10	6	.63	4	.254	.369	.343
	Charlotte	AA	77	232	68	16	2	3	97	40	25	26	0	19	2	8	1	13	5	.72	2	.293	.368	.418
1987	Charlotte	AA	127	471	135	22	3	4	175	69	50	43	0	38	3	3	1	20	9	.69	20	.287	.349	.372
1988	Buffalo	AAA	68	187	46	4	0	1	53	12	20	13	0	17	0	0	1	1	5	.17	4	.246	.294	.283
1989	Harrisburg	AA	78	238	60	16	1	2	84	20	25	27	0	19	3	0	2	2	4	.33	5	.252	.333	.353
	Buffalo	AAA	38	109	21	5	0	0	26	11	10	18	1	11	1	1	2	4	0	1.00	4	.193	.308	.239
1990	Buffalo	AAA	8	17	3	0	1	0	5	3	2	4	0	2	0	1	1	1	0	1.00	4	.176	.318	.294
	Greenville	AA	5	21	4	1	0	0	5	4	0	1	0	2	0	0	0	0	2	.00	1	.190	.227	.238
	Richmond	AAA	107	380	88	13	0	4	113	58	32	69	1	43	3	7	2	11	6	.65	12	.232	.352	.297
1991	Richmond	AAA	139	482	124	25	1	2	157	58	48	67	1	46	5	13	3	4	8	.33	12	.257	.352	.326
1992	Omaha	AAA	48	174	55	10	1	4	79	29	17	34	0	14	0	2	3	3	5	.38	5	.316	.422	.454
1993	Omaha	AAA	37	131	39	10	1	5	66	25	21	20	1	19	3	0	1	3	2	.60	1	.298	.400	.504
1994	Omaha	AAA	120	412	97	23	0	11	153	49	63	61	1	60	5	5	4	9	10	.47	14	.235	.338	.371
1991	Atlanta	NL	5	1	0	0	0	0	0	0	0	0	0	1	0	0	0	0	0	.00	0	.000	.000	.000
1992	Kansas City	AL	59	149	32	8	1	1	45	21	12	20	1	20	1	7	1	0	3	.00	6	.215	.310	.302
1993	Kansas City	AL	46	86	19	4	0	2	29	10	12	9	0	11	1	1	0	0	0	.00	0	.221	.302	.337
	10 Min. YEARS		963	3234	827	166	13	40	1139	442	347	439	6	320	27	49	23	98	69	.59	97	.256	.347	.352
	3 Maj. YEARS		110	236	51	12	1	3	74	31	24	29	1	32	2	8	1	0	3	.00	6	.216	.306	.314

Steve Rowley

Pitches: Right Bats: Right Pos: P Ht: 6'0" Wt: 175 Born: 05/25/68 Age: 27

			HOW MUCH HE PITCHED						WHAT HE GAVE UP											THE RESULTS					
Year	Team	Lg	G	GS	CG	GF	IP	BFP	H	R	ER	HR	SH	SF	HB	TBB	IBB	SO	WP	Bk	W	L	Pct.	ShO	Sv	ERA
1989	Butte	R	11	11	3	0	59	263	52	32	27	5	0	0	8	37	0	62	9	3	4	2	.667	2	0	4.12
1990	Charlotte	A	5	5	0	0	23.2	107	19	16	14	0	1	0	1	21	1	7	3	1	0	4	.000	0	0	5.32
	Gastonia	A	13	13	1	0	81.2	350	66	36	23	2	1	4	4	46	1	79	6	1	6	3	.667	0	0	2.53
1991	Charlotte	A	8	8	1	0	44.2	195	38	15	14	1	0	1	3	32	0	28	0	0	7	1	.875	0	0	2.82
	Tulsa	AA	10	8	0	0	43.1	202	48	32	29	5	1	3	6	27	0	24	6	0	2	4	.333	0	0	6.02
1992	Tulsa	AA	3	1	0	0	7	34	7	6	6	1	1	0	0	7	0	8	1	0	0	0	.000	0	0	7.71
1993	Tulsa	AA	20	19	0	0	92.1	410	103	71	62	13	1	3	5	33	1	63	10	1	8	7	.533	0	0	6.04
1994	Tulsa	AA	29	9	0	11	71.1	328	76	52	49	14	1	5	5	45	2	63	7	1	3	6	.333	0	0	6.18
	6 Min. YEARS		99	74	5	11	423	1889	409	260	224	41	6	16	32	248	5	334	44	7	30	27	.526	2	0	4.77

Matt Ruebel

Pitches: Left Bats: Left Pos: P Ht: 6'2" Wt: 180 Born: 10/16/69 Age: 25

			HOW MUCH HE PITCHED						WHAT HE GAVE UP											THE RESULTS					
Year	Team	Lg	G	GS	CG	GF	IP	BFP	H	R	ER	HR	SH	SF	HB	TBB	IBB	SO	WP	Bk	W	L	Pct.	ShO	Sv	ERA
1991	Welland	A	6	6	0	0	27.2	113	16	9	6	3	0	1	4	11	0	27	0	3	1	1	.500	0	0	1.95
	Augusta	A	8	8	2	0	47	202	43	26	20	2	1	0	2	25	0	35	3	0	3	4	.429	1	0	3.83
1992	Augusta	A	12	10	1	1	64.2	268	53	26	20	1	3	0	5	19	0	65	2	1	5	2	.714	0	0	2.78
	Salem	A	13	13	1	0	78.1	344	77	49	41	13	6	5	3	43	0	46	6	1	1	6	.143	0	0	4.71
1993	Salem	A	19	1	0	4	33.1	168	34	31	22	6	3	0	3	32	3	29	8	2	1	4	.200	0	0	5.94

Year	Team	Lg	G	GS	CG	GF	IP	BFP	H	R	ER	HR	SH	SF	HB	TBB	IBB	SO	WP	Bk	W	L	Pct.	ShO	Sv	ERA
	Augusta	A	23	7	1	6	63.1	276	51	28	17	2	1	3	5	34	4	50	1	0	5	5	.500	1	0	2.42
1994	Carolina	AA	6	3	0	0	16.1	78	28	15	12	3	1	1	3	3	0	14	0	0	1	1	.500	0	0	6.61
	Salem	A	21	13	0	0	86.1	374	87	49	33	9	2	3	7	27	0	72	4	1	6	6	.500	0	0	3.44
	4 Min. YEARS		108	61	5	11	417	1823	389	233	171	39	17	13	30	194	7	338	26	8	23	29	.442	2	0	3.69

Tim Rumer

Pitches: Left   Bats: Left   Pos: P   Ht: 6'3"   Wt: 205   Born: 08/08/69   Age: 25

			HOW MUCH HE PITCHED						WHAT HE GAVE UP											THE RESULTS					
Year	Team	Lg	G	GS	CG	GF	IP	BFP	H	R	ER	HR	SH	SF	HB	TBB	IBB	SO	WP	Bk	W	L	Pct.	ShO	Sv	ERA
1990	Yankees	R	12	12	2	0	74	291	34	23	14	1	1	1	3	20	0	88	4	3	6	3	.667	0	0	1.70
1991	Ft.Laudrdle	A	24	23	3	0	149.1	623	125	59	48	6	9	3	5	49	2	112	7	1	10	7	.588	2	0	2.89
1992	Pr William	A	23	23	1	0	128	538	122	61	51	8	6	5	5	34	2	105	0	1	10	7	.588	0	0	3.59
	Columbus	AAA	1	1	0	0	1	3	0	0	0	0	0	0	0	0	0	1	0	0	0	0	.000	0	0	0.00
1994	Albany-Colo	AA	25	25	2	0	150.2	639	127	61	52	10	2	4	9	75	0	130	7	0	8	10	.444	1	0	3.11
	4 Min. YEARS		85	84	8	0	503	2094	408	204	165	25	18	12	22	178	4	436	18	5	34	27	.557	3	0	2.95

Matt Rundels

Bats: Right   Throws: Right   Pos: 2B   Ht: 5'11"   Wt: 180   Born: 04/26/70   Age: 25

			BATTING															BASERUNNING				PERCENTAGES		
Year	Team	Lg	G	AB	H	2B	3B	HR	TB	R	RBI	TBB	IBB	SO	HBP	SH	SF	SB	CS	SB%	GDP	Avg	OBP	SLG
1992	Jamestown	A	75	277	71	6	2	6	99	43	28	25	0	43	5	2	3	32	11	.74	2	.256	.326	.357
1993	Burlington	A	64	203	55	7	4	4	82	36	17	38	1	36	5	3	1	14	7	.67	5	.271	.397	.404
	Wst Plm Bch	A	8	26	3	0	1	0	5	2	2	3	1	4	0	0	1	3	1	.75	0	.115	.200	.192
	Harrisburg	AA	34	117	40	5	0	6	63	27	17	14	0	31	2	0	0	8	2	.80	1	.342	.421	.538
1994	Harrisburg	AA	112	330	73	9	6	6	112	53	31	51	4	79	2	2	3	19	7	.73	7	.221	.326	.339
	3 Min. YEARS		293	953	242	27	13	22	361	161	95	131	6	193	14	7	8	76	28	.73	15	.254	.350	.379

Troy Rusk

Bats: Left   Throws: Right   Pos: 1B   Ht: 6'3"   Wt: 225   Born: 09/24/67   Age: 27

			BATTING															BASERUNNING				PERCENTAGES		
Year	Team	Lg	G	AB	H	2B	3B	HR	TB	R	RBI	TBB	IBB	SO	HBP	SH	SF	SB	CS	SB%	GDP	Avg	OBP	SLG
1990	Princeton	R	59	194	47	7	2	10	88	31	33	52	2	66	3	0	1	0	1	.00	1	.242	.408	.454
1991	Spartanburg	A	19	67	19	5	0	2	30	9	11	7	0	16	0	0	1	0	1	.00	4	.284	.347	.448
1992	Spartanburg	A	52	182	49	12	0	7	82	25	37	21	0	44	1	0	2	1	1	.50	1	.269	.345	.451
	Clearwater	A	68	240	57	12	1	6	89	23	33	24	0	52	2	1	1	1	0	1.00	4	.238	.311	.371
1993	Clearwater	A	61	199	59	8	1	10	99	30	40	23	0	55	0	1	0	0	3	.00	11	.296	.369	.497
	Reading	AA	41	144	35	6	1	6	61	14	26	11	0	45	0	0	2	0	0	.00	3	.243	.293	.424
1994	Reading	AA	42	113	21	4	0	6	43	14	17	16	2	35	0	1	0	0	0	.00	2	.186	.287	.381
	5 Min. YEARS		342	1139	287	54	5	47	492	146	197	154	4	313	6	3	7	2	6	.25	22	.252	.342	.432

John Russell

Bats: Right   Throws: Right   Pos: OF   Ht: 6'0"   Wt: 195   Born: 01/05/61   Age: 34

			BATTING															BASERUNNING				PERCENTAGES		
Year	Team	Lg	G	AB	H	2B	3B	HR	TB	R	RBI	TBB	IBB	SO	HBP	SH	SF	SB	CS	SB%	GDP	Avg	OBP	SLG
1984	Portland	AAA	93	350	101	22	5	19	190	75	77	44	0	91	6	0	3	1	0	1.00	10	.289	.375	.543
1985	Portland	AAA	16	49	15	2	2	4	33	8	11	13	3	15	1	0	0	0	0	.00	0	.306	.460	.673
1987	Maine	AAA	44	143	29	6	1	7	58	15	24	22	0	37	0	1	1	2	3	.40	7	.203	.307	.406
1988	Maine	AAA	110	394	90	18	0	13	147	50	52	29	2	108	4	0	3	4	2	.67	3	.228	.286	.373
1990	Okla City	AAA	6	22	9	4	0	2	19	7	6	2	0	3	0	0	0	0	0	.00	2	.409	.458	.864
1992	Tulsa	AA	46	163	42	11	0	10	83	26	27	17	1	42	5	0	1	0	4	.00	6	.258	.344	.509
1994	Louisville	AAA	2	4	0	0	0	0	0	0	0	1	0	1	0	0	0	0	0	.00	0	.000	.200	.000
1984	Philadelphia	NL	39	99	28	8	1	2	44	11	11	12	2	33	0	0	3	0	1	.00	3	.283	.351	.444
1985	Philadelphia	NL	81	216	47	12	0	9	86	22	23	18	0	72	0	0	0	2	0	1.00	5	.218	.278	.398
1986	Philadelphia	NL	93	315	76	21	2	13	140	35	60	25	2	103	3	1	4	0	1	.00	6	.241	.300	.444
1987	Philadelphia	NL	24	62	9	1	0	3	19	5	8	3	0	17	0	1	0	0	1	.00	4	.145	.185	.306
1988	Philadelphia	NL	22	49	12	1	0	2	19	5	4	3	0	15	1	0	0	0	0	.00	2	.245	.302	.388
1989	Atlanta	NL	74	159	29	2	0	2	37	14	9	8	1	53	1	0	4	0	0	.00	4	.182	.225	.233
1990	Texas	AL	68	128	35	4	0	2	45	16	8	11	2	41	0	1	0	1	0	1.00	3	.273	.331	.352
1991	Texas	AL	22	27	3	0	0	0	3	3	1	1	0	7	0	0	1	0	0	.00	0	.111	.138	.111
1992	Texas	AL	7	10	1	0	0	0	1	1	2	1	0	4	1	0	1	0	0	.00	0	.100	.231	.100
1993	Texas	AL	18	22	5	1	0	1	9	1	3	2	0	10	0	0	0	0	0	.00	0	.227	.292	.409
	7 Min. YEARS		317	1125	286	63	8	55	530	181	197	128	6	297	16	1	8	7	9	.44	28	.254	.337	.471
	10 Maj. YEARS		448	1087	245	50	3	34	403	113	129	84	7	355	6	2	10	3	3	.50	26	.225	.282	.371

Lee Russell

Pitches: Right   Bats: Right   Pos: P   Ht: 6'2"   Wt: 175   Born: 08/20/70   Age: 24

			HOW MUCH HE PITCHED						WHAT HE GAVE UP											THE RESULTS					
Year	Team	Lg	G	GS	CG	GF	IP	BFP	H	R	ER	HR	SH	SF	HB	TBB	IBB	SO	WP	Bk	W	L	Pct.	ShO	Sv	ERA
1990	Mariners	R	19	5	0	3	55	251	50	33	19	1	0	3	6	27	1	51	1	1	5	1	.833	0	0	3.11
1991	Bellingham	A	15	15	0	0	95.1	414	85	48	31	6	3	1	1	43	1	77	13	0	6	7	.462	0	0	2.93
1992	Peninsula	A	27	26	2	1	157.1	665	132	76	55	4	6	3	8	59	4	130	5	1	7	10	.412	1	0	3.15
1993	Jacksnville	AA	17	17	0	0	89.2	400	115	67	55	14	2	2	2	32	1	52	5	0	4	9	.308	0	0	5.52
1994	Jacksnville	AA	36	3	0	19	71.2	314	82	44	36	8	3	2	0	25	5	39	5	0	1	9	.100	0	3	4.52
	5 Min. YEARS		114	66	2	23	469	2044	464	268	196	33	14	11	17	186	12	349	29	2	23	36	.390	1	3	3.76

Paul Russo

Bats: Right Throws: Right Pos: 3B Ht: 5'11" Wt: 215 Born: 08/26/69 Age: 25

					BATTING												BASERUNNING				PERCENTAGES		
Year	Team	Lg	G	AB	H	2B	3B	HR	TB	R	RBI	TBB	IBB	SO	HBP	SH	SF	SB	CS	SB%	GDP	Avg	OBP	SLG
1990	Elizabethtn	R	62	221	74	9	3	22	155	58	67	38	5	56	1	0	2	4	1	.80	3	.335	.431	.701
1991	Kenosha	A	125	421	114	20	3	20	200	60	100	64	4	105	7	0	10	4	1	.80	5	.271	.369	.475
1992	Orlando	AA	126	420	107	13	2	22	190	63	74	48	0	122	1	2	5	0	0	.00	17	.255	.329	.452
1993	Portland	AAA	83	288	81	24	2	10	139	43	47	29	0	69	0	0	6	0	1	.00	10	.281	.341	.483
1994	Salt Lake	AAA	35	115	34	7	0	3	50	18	17	12	0	28	2	0	3	0	3	.00	4	.296	.364	.435
	Nashville	AA	82	299	68	14	3	10	118	43	40	31	1	77	3	3	0	1	0	1.00	11	.227	.306	.395
	5 Min. YEARS		513	1764	478	87	13	87	852	285	345	222	10	457	14	5	26	9	6	.60	50	.271	.352	.483

Jason Ryan

Pitches: Right Bats: Both Pos: P Ht: 6'2" Wt: 180 Born: 01/23/76 Age: 19

			HOW MUCH HE PITCHED						WHAT HE GAVE UP									THE RESULTS					
Year	Team	Lg	G	GS	CG	GF	IP	BFP	H	R	ER	HR	SH	SF	HB	TBB	IBB	SO	WP	Bk	W	L	Pct.	ShO	Sv	ERA
1994	Cubs	R	7	7	0	0	33	143	32	19	15	2	1	1	2	4	0	30	5	0	1	2	.333	0	0	4.09
	Huntington	R	4	4	1	0	26	93	7	1	1	0	1	0	1	8	0	32	0	0	2	0	1.000	1	0	0.35
	Orlando	AA	2	2	0	0	11	45	6	3	3	1	0	0	1	6	0	12	0	0	2	0	1.000	0	0	2.45
	1 Min. YEARS		13	13	1	0	70	281	45	23	19	3	2	1	4	18	0	74	5	0	5	2	.714	1	0	2.44

Kevin Ryan

Pitches: Right Bats: Right Pos: P Ht: 6'1" Wt: 187 Born: 09/23/70 Age: 24

			HOW MUCH HE PITCHED						WHAT HE GAVE UP									THE RESULTS					
Year	Team	Lg	G	GS	CG	GF	IP	BFP	H	R	ER	HR	SH	SF	HB	TBB	IBB	SO	WP	Bk	W	L	Pct.	ShO	Sv	ERA
1991	Bluefield	R	14	11	0	3	76.1	315	71	26	22	3	0	3	1	24	0	71	6	4	5	4	.556	0	1	2.59
	Kane County	A	1	1	0	0	9.1	35	6	1	1	0	1	0	1	2	0	8	0	0	0	0	.000	0	0	0.96
1992	Frederick	A	27	25	2	1	148.2	666	175	88	78	11	3	4	2	63	1	103	16	3	7	12	.368	0	0	4.72
1993	Bowie	AA	16	15	2	1	88.1	401	106	67	52	8	2	4	1	34	0	40	5	2	3	10	.231	0	0	5.30
	Frederick	A	15	2	0	4	33.1	136	28	11	9	3	1	0	2	9	0	23	3	0	0	3	.000	0	1	2.43
1994	Bowie	AA	41	4	0	14	81	351	86	40	33	8	7	2	2	30	2	37	9	0	8	2	.800	0	1	3.67
	4 Min. YEARS		114	58	4	23	437	1904	472	233	195	33	14	13	9	162	3	282	39	9	23	31	.426	0	3	4.02

Kevin Rychel

Pitches: Right Bats: Right Pos: P Ht: 5'9" Wt: 176 Born: 09/24/71 Age: 23

			HOW MUCH HE PITCHED						WHAT HE GAVE UP									THE RESULTS					
Year	Team	Lg	G	GS	CG	GF	IP	BFP	H	R	ER	HR	SH	SF	HB	TBB	IBB	SO	WP	Bk	W	L	Pct.	ShO	Sv	ERA
1989	Pirates	R	13	13	0	0	67	296	52	40	23	0	3	2	9	31	0	79	6	4	1	6	.143	0	0	3.09
1990	Augusta	A	27	23	0	0	129	615	127	79	59	3	5	4	8	87	0	105	26	6	10	4	.714	0	0	4.12
1991	Salem	A	11	11	0	0	49.1	230	48	44	33	7	1	4	3	27	0	34	10	3	1	7	.125	0	0	6.02
	Augusta	A	8	6	1	1	32.1	151	30	24	20	1	0	2	7	24	0	26	11	0	1	3	.250	1	0	5.57
1992	Augusta	A	13	0	0	8	16	74	12	12	8	0	2	0	0	12	1	16	0	0	1	3	.250	0	2	4.50
	Salem	A	37	0	0	25	39.1	182	37	22	17	4	3	2	4	27	3	35	9	0	2	3	.400	0	7	3.89
1993	Salem	A	53	2	0	11	73	333	68	41	32	3	1	2	10	44	2	86	27	0	5	4	.556	0	0	3.95
1994	Carolina	AA	36	3	0	11	74.2	331	69	45	39	5	2	3	8	42	0	52	12	0	5	3	.625	0	1	4.70
	6 Min. YEARS		198	58	1	56	480.2	2212	443	307	231	23	17	19	49	294	6	433	101	13	26	33	.441	1	10	4.33

Brian Sackinsky

Pitches: Right Bats: Right Pos: P Ht: 6'4" Wt: 220 Born: 06/22/71 Age: 24

			HOW MUCH HE PITCHED						WHAT HE GAVE UP									THE RESULTS					
Year	Team	Lg	G	GS	CG	GF	IP	BFP	H	R	ER	HR	SH	SF	HB	TBB	IBB	SO	WP	Bk	W	L	Pct.	ShO	Sv	ERA
1992	Frederick	A	5	3	0	0	10.1	55	20	15	15	3	0	1	0	6	0	10	4	0	0	3	.000	0	0	13.06
	Bluefield	R	5	5	0	0	27.2	124	30	15	11	0	0	0	2	9	0	33	2	0	2	2	.500	0	0	3.58
1993	Albany	A	9	8	0	0	50.2	217	50	29	18	2	0	4	0	16	0	41	5	0	3	4	.429	0	0	3.20
	Frederick	A	18	18	1	0	121	512	117	55	43	13	3	3	2	37	2	112	17	1	6	8	.429	0	0	3.20
1994	Bowie	AA	28	26	4	0	177	721	165	73	66	24	5	9	0	39	0	145	6	0	11	7	.611	0	0	3.36
	3 Min. YEARS		65	60	5	0	386.2	1629	382	187	153	42	8	17	4	107	2	341	34	1	22	24	.478	0	0	3.56

Steve Sadecki

Pitches: Right Bats: Right Pos: P Ht: 6'1" Wt: 190 Born: 05/14/70 Age: 25

			HOW MUCH HE PITCHED						WHAT HE GAVE UP									THE RESULTS					
Year	Team	Lg	G	GS	CG	GF	IP	BFP	H	R	ER	HR	SH	SF	HB	TBB	IBB	SO	WP	Bk	W	L	Pct.	ShO	Sv	ERA
1991	Gastonia	A	16	16	1	0	78	333	70	34	30	5	4	1	3	43	0	67	3	5	4	4	.500	1	0	3.46
1992	Gastonia	A	21	3	0	4	42.2	190	42	23	21	1	0	1	3	25	4	49	2	2	4	3	.571	0	1	4.43
	Charlotte	A	16	12	1	1	72.2	297	61	24	15	1	6	6	0	20	0	49	0	2	5	7	.417	0	0	1.86
1993	Charlotte	A	24	0	0	5	40.1	165	40	9	9	0	2	0	2	11	0	37	0	0	3	2	.600	0	1	2.01
	Tulsa	AA	9	0	0	7	16	68	16	10	7	2	1	1	0	4	0	12	0	0	0	1	.000	0	1	3.94
	Okla City	AAA	12	2	1	3	20.1	98	22	17	16	4	1	1	3	15	1	13	1	0	0	3	.000	0	0	7.08
1994	Tulsa	AA	34	1	0	16	78.2	321	66	32	25	7	3	3	4	33	2	49	6	2	6	2	.750	0	2	2.86
	Okla. City	AAA	7	0	0	2	12.2	54	14	6	6	1	0	1	1	4	0	5	0	0	3	0	1.000	0	0	4.26
	4 Min. YEARS		139	34	3	38	361.1	1526	331	155	129	21	17	14	16	155	7	281	12	11	25	22	.532	1	5	3.21

Brian Saltzgaber

Bats: Right Throws: Right Pos: C Ht: 5'11" Wt: 175 Born: 03/31/68 Age: 27

Year	Team	Lg	G	AB	H	2B	3B	HR	TB	R	RBI	TBB	IBB	SO	HBP	SH	SF	SB	CS	SB%	GDP	Avg	OBP	SLG
1990	Niagara Fls	A	53	178	40	5	1	2	53	23	20	31	0	24	3	1	1	17	9	.65	6	.225	.347	.298
1991	Fayetteville	A	111	375	98	16	0	2	120	54	30	60	1	61	5	2	6	11	11	.50	5	.261	.365	.320
1992	Lakeland	A	106	334	81	17	2	2	108	42	28	48	1	47	5	10	4	9	10	.47	9	.243	.343	.323
1993	London	AA	87	241	51	9	1	2	68	28	17	41	1	59	5	1	2	13	3	.81	2	.212	.336	.282
1994	Trenton	AA	26	71	12	3	0	1	18	6	4	7	0	18	1	0	1	3	4	.43	1	.169	.250	.254
	5 Min. YEARS		383	1199	282	50	4	9	367	153	99	187	3	209	19	14	14	53	37	.59	23	.235	.344	.306

Todd Samples

Bats: Right Throws: Right Pos: OF Ht: 6'2" Wt: 185 Born: 08/01/69 Age: 25

Year	Team	Lg	G	AB	H	2B	3B	HR	TB	R	RBI	TBB	IBB	SO	HBP	SH	SF	SB	CS	SB%	GDP	Avg	OBP	SLG
1990	Jamestown	A	59	183	45	6	4	1	62	22	13	13	0	48	4	2	1	13	6	.68	3	.246	.308	.339
1991	Sumter	A	130	505	131	29	6	12	208	82	63	47	0	124	8	1	10	25	14	.64	5	.259	.326	.412
1992	Rockford	A	117	410	98	21	6	3	140	52	34	25	2	83	7	2	3	29	10	.74	7	.239	.292	.341
1993	Stockton	A	122	401	106	21	3	6	151	63	48	28	1	63	10	8	4	36	12	.75	7	.264	.325	.377
1994	Stockton	A	26	80	19	4	1	0	25	12	7	12	0	23	3	0	1	2	3	.40	2	.238	.354	.313
	El Paso	AA	80	218	55	16	6	1	86	31	26	20	1	46	4	1	2	7	7	.50	1	.252	.324	.394
	5 Min. YEARS		534	1797	454	97	26	23	672	262	191	145	4	387	36	14	21	112	52	.68	25	.253	.318	.374

Alex Sanchez

Pitches: Right Bats: Right Pos: P Ht: 6'2" Wt: 190 Born: 04/08/66 Age: 29

Year	Team	Lg	G	GS	CG	GF	IP	BFP	H	R	ER	HR	SH	SF	HB	TBB	IBB	SO	WP	Bk	W	L	Pct.	ShO	Sv	ERA
1987	St.Cathmes	A	17	17	0	0	95.1	401	72	33	28	3	0	0	5	38	0	116	6	0	8	3	.727	0	0	2.64
	Myrtle Bch	A	1	0	0	1	3	11	2	1	1	1	0	0	0	0	0	4	0	0	0	0	.000	0	1	3.00
1988	Knoxville	AA	24	24	2	0	149.1	622	100	56	42	8	1	2	3	74	0	166	5	7	12	5	.706	0	0	2.53
	Syracuse	AAA	10	10	1	0	57.2	258	47	26	23	8	3	2	0	43	1	57	4	3	4	3	.571	0	0	3.59
1989	Syracuse	AAA	28	27	1	0	169.2	697	125	68	59	14	1	5	1	74	0	141	11	5	13	7	.650	1	0	3.13
1990	Syracuse	AAA	22	22	1	0	112	521	111	77	71	15	7	8	4	79	1	65	5	0	5	9	.357	0	0	5.71
1991	Syracuse	AAA	14	5	0	8	28	153	33	33	32	2	1	2	1	35	0	12	14	0	1	4	.200	0	1	10.29
	Knoxville	AA	14	11	0	2	58.2	253	43	26	20	3	1	2	2	36	2	38	8	2	4	2	.667	0	0	3.07
1992	Baseball Cy	A	15	13	3	0	78.2	328	61	33	30	2	4	0	4	41	0	42	5	1	6	5	.545	2	0	3.43
	Memphis	AA	1	1	0	0	6	25	4	4	4	0	1	0	1	2	0	6	0	0	0	1	.000	0	0	6.00
1993	Memphis	AA	15	10	0	4	70	299	64	36	34	5	2	0	1	35	0	47	2	1	1	4	.200	0	0	4.37
	Omaha	AAA	16	9	1	3	51	231	62	46	46	7	2	1	0	28	1	31	6	0	2	8	.200	0	0	8.12
1994	Calgary	AAA	20	13	0	2	79	365	89	58	48	8	0	8	2	42	2	48	9	0	3	3	.500	0	0	5.47
	Wichita	AA	4	0	0	2	4	23	4	3	3	0	0	0	0	5	0	4	0	0	0	0	.000	0	0	6.75
1989	Toronto	AL	4	3	0	0	11.2	61	16	13	13	1	0	2	0	14	0	4	1	0	0	1	.000	0	0	10.03
	8 Min. YEARS		201	162	9	22	962.1	4185	817	500	441	76	23	30	24	532	7	777	75	19	59	54	.522	3	2	4.12

Yuri Sanchez

Bats: Left Throws: Right Pos: SS Ht: 6'1" Wt: 165 Born: 11/11/73 Age: 21

Year	Team	Lg	G	AB	H	2B	3B	HR	TB	R	RBI	TBB	IBB	SO	HBP	SH	SF	SB	CS	SB%	GDP	Avg	OBP	SLG
1992	Bristol	R	36	102	18	2	2	0	24	11	5	21	0	41	0	1	0	5	3	.63	1	.176	.317	.235
1993	Fayetteville	A	111	340	69	7	6	0	88	53	30	73	0	125	2	7	3	20	9	.69	3	.203	.344	.259
1994	Lakeland	A	89	254	59	5	5	1	77	41	19	39	0	75	4	5	1	21	8	.72	6	.232	.342	.303
	Trenton	AA	28	78	16	2	2	0	22	7	2	11	0	25	0	2	0	4	1	.80	0	.205	.303	.282
	3 Min. YEARS		264	774	162	16	15	1	211	112	56	144	0	266	6	15	4	50	21	.70	10	.209	.336	.273

Tracy Sanders

Bats: Left Throws: Right Pos: OF Ht: 6'2" Wt: 200 Born: 07/26/69 Age: 25

Year	Team	Lg	G	AB	H	2B	3B	HR	TB	R	RBI	TBB	IBB	SO	HBP	SH	SF	SB	CS	SB%	GDP	Avg	OBP	SLG
1990	Burlington	R	51	178	50	12	1	10	94	38	34	33	0	36	2	0	1	10	3	.77	2	.281	.397	.528
	Kinston	A	10	32	14	3	0	2	23	6	9	7	0	6	0	0	0	1	1	.50	0	.438	.538	.719
1991	Kinston	A	118	421	112	20	8	18	202	80	63	83	4	95	6	2	2	8	5	.62	9	.266	.393	.480
1992	Canton-Akm	AA	114	381	92	11	3	21	172	66	87	77	3	113	3	4	3	3	6	.33	8	.241	.371	.451
1993	Canton-Akm	AA	42	136	29	6	2	5	54	20	20	31	1	30	1	0	1	4	1	.80	1	.213	.361	.397
	Wichita	AA	77	266	86	13	4	13	146	44	47	34	1	67	2	0	1	6	5	.55	2	.323	.403	.549
1994	Binghamton	AA	101	275	66	20	4	8	118	44	37	60	1	88	3	0	5	8	6	.57	1	.240	.376	.429
	5 Min. YEARS		513	1689	449	85	25	75	809	298	297	325	10	435	17	6	13	40	27	.60	23	.266	.387	.479

Mo Sanford

Pitches: Right Bats: Right Pos: P Ht: 6'6" Wt: 220 Born: 12/24/66 Age: 28

Year	Team	Lg	G	GS	CG	GF	IP	BFP	H	R	ER	HR	SH	SF	HB	TBB	IBB	SO	WP	Bk	W	L	Pct.	ShO	Sv	ERA
1988	Reds	R	14	11	0	1	53	217	34	24	19	6	0	1	0	25	1	64	3	4	3	4	.429	0	1	3.23

Year Team	Lg	G	GS	CG	GF	IP	BFP	H	R	ER	HR	SH	SF	HB	TBB	IBB	SO	WP	Bk	W	L	Pct.	ShO	Sv	ERA
1989 Greensboro	A	25	25	3	0	153.2	629	112	52	48	8	4	2	2	64	0	160	6	3	12	6	.667	1	0	2.81
1990 Cedar Rapds	A	25	25	2	0	157.2	628	112	50	48	15	3	2	4	55	1	180	8	1	13	4	.765	1	0	2.74
1991 Chattanooga	AA	16	16	1	0	95.1	395	69	37	29	7	4	3	1	55	2	124	1	0	7	4	.636	1	0	2.74
Nashville	AAA	5	5	2	0	33.2	140	19	7	6	0	0	0	1	22	0	38	3	0	3	0	1.000	2	0	1.60
1992 Chattanooga	AA	4	4	1	0	26.2	101	13	5	4	2	0	0	2	6	0	28	1	0	4	0	1.000	1	0	1.35
Nashville	AAA	25	25	0	0	122	549	128	81	77	22	6	5	3	65	1	129	2	0	8	8	.500	0	0	5.68
1993 Colo Sprngs	AAA	20	17	0	1	105	456	103	64	61	8	3	6	4	57	2	104	7	1	3	6	.333	0	0	5.23
1994 Salt Lake	AAA	37	11	0	9	125.2	553	121	74	68	21	1	9	8	52	0	141	5	1	7	5	.583	0	4	4.87
1991 Cincinnati	NL	5	5	0	0	28	118	19	14	12	3	0	0	1	15	1	31	4	0	1	2	.333	0	0	3.86
1993 Colorado	NL	11	6	0	1	35.2	166	37	25	21	4	4	2	0	27	0	36	2	1	1	2	.333	0	0	5.30
7 Min. YEARS		171	139	9	11	872.2	3668	711	394	360	89	21	28	25	401	7	968	36	10	60	37	.619	6	5	3.71
2 Maj. YEARS		16	11	0	1	63.2	284	56	39	33	7	4	2	1	42	1	67	6	1	2	4	.333	0	0	4.66

Julio Santana

Pitches: Right Bats: Right Pos: P   Ht: 6'0" Wt: 175 Born: 01/20/73 Age: 22

		HOW MUCH HE PITCHED						WHAT HE GAVE UP												THE RESULTS				
Year Team	Lg	G	GS	CG	GF	IP	BFP	H	R	ER	HR	SH	SF	HB	TBB	IBB	SO	WP	Bk	W	L	Pct.	ShO	Sv	ERA
1993 Rangers	R	26	0	0	12	39	153	31	9	6	0	0	0	1	7	0	50	1	0	4	1	.800	0	7	1.38
1994 Charlstn-Wv	A	16	16	0	0	91.1	383	65	38	25	3	0	4	7	44	0	103	7	1	6	7	.462	0	0	2.46
Tulsa	AA	11	11	2	0	71.1	290	50	26	23	1	1	2	2	41	0	45	2	0	7	2	.778	0	0	2.90
2 Min. YEARS		53	27	2	12	201.2	826	146	73	54	4	1	6	10	92	0	198	10	1	17	10	.630	0	7	2.41

Ruben Santana

Bats: Right Throws: Right Pos: 2B   Ht: 6'2" Wt: 175 Born: 03/07/70 Age: 25

		BATTING												BASERUNNING				PERCENTAGES		
Year Team	Lg	G	AB	H	2B	3B	HR	TB	R	RBI	TBB	IBB	SO	HBP	SH	SF	SB	CS	SB%	GDP	Avg	OBP	SLG
1990 Peninsula	A	26	80	17	1	0	0	18	3	5	1	0	22	1	0	0	6	1	.86	1	.213	.232	.225
Bellingham	A	47	155	39	3	2	4	58	22	13	18	2	39	6	0	1	10	9	.53	1	.252	.350	.374
1991 San Berndno	A	108	394	119	16	4	3	152	55	43	26	4	74	6	9	5	34	12	.74	4	.302	.350	.386
Jacksnville	AA	5	15	3	1	0	1	6	2	3	1	0	3	0	0	0	0	0	.00	0	.200	.250	.400
1992 Peninsula	A	113	401	118	19	4	8	169	54	61	21	0	54	9	6	1	17	16	.52	8	.294	.343	.421
1993 Jacksnville	AA	128	499	150	21	2	21	238	79	84	38	7	101	9	3	5	13	8	.62	2	.301	.358	.477
1994 Jacksonvlle	AA	131	501	148	25	4	7	202	62	68	28	1	62	11	3	4	10	7	.59	9	.295	.344	.403
5 Min. YEARS		558	2045	594	85	16	44	843	277	277	133	14	355	42	21	16	90	53	.63	25	.290	.344	.412

Frank Santangelo

Bats: Both Throws: Right Pos: 2B   Ht: 5'10" Wt: 165 Born: 10/24/67 Age: 27

		BATTING												BASERUNNING				PERCENTAGES		
Year Team	Lg	G	AB	H	2B	3B	HR	TB	R	RBI	TBB	IBB	SO	HBP	SH	SF	SB	CS	SB%	GDP	Avg	OBP	SLG
1989 Jamestown	A	2	6	3	1	0	0	4	0	0	1	0	0	0	0	0	1	0	1.00	0	.500	.571	.667
Wst Plm Bch	A	57	173	37	4	0	0	41	18	14	23	1	12	4	6	0	3	3	.50	5	.214	.320	.237
1990 Wst Plm Bch	A	116	394	109	19	2	0	132	63	38	51	2	49	5	8	2	22	7	.76	5	.277	.365	.335
1991 Harrisburg	AA	132	462	113	12	7	5	154	78	42	74	0	45	7	13	4	21	7	.75	6	.245	.355	.333
1992 Indianapols	AAA	137	462	123	25	0	5	163	83	34	62	4	58	7	13	2	12	11	.52	9	.266	.360	.353
1993 Ottawa	AAA	131	453	124	21	2	4	161	86	45	59	4	52	14	8	4	18	8	.69	10	.274	.372	.355
1994 Ottawa	AAA	119	413	104	28	1	5	149	62	41	59	0	64	9	10	3	7	9	.44	11	.252	.355	.361
6 Min. YEARS		694	2363	613	110	12	19	804	390	214	329	11	280	46	68	15	84	45	.65	46	.259	.359	.340

Gerald Santos

Pitches: Right Bats: Right Pos: P   Ht: 5'10" Wt: 175 Born: 07/09/69 Age: 25

		HOW MUCH HE PITCHED						WHAT HE GAVE UP												THE RESULTS				
Year Team	Lg	G	GS	CG	GF	IP	BFP	H	R	ER	HR	SH	SF	HB	TBB	IBB	SO	WP	Bk	W	L	Pct.	ShO	Sv	ERA
1991 Johnson Cty	R	24	0	0	24	32.1	127	25	8	8	1	1	1	2	5	0	55	4	1	2	0	1.000	0	13	2.23
1992 Springfield	A	63	1	0	58	69.1	279	40	20	16	1	5	2	5	26	1	107	7	2	4	4	.500	0	35	2.08
1993 Arkansas	AA	57	0	0	19	82	364	80	36	24	8	7	2	3	41	11	65	12	2	3	6	.333	0	3	2.63
1994 Arkansas	AA	43	0	0	10	63.2	282	62	33	22	1	5	3	3	32	2	33	5	2	3	3	.500	0	0	3.11
4 Min. YEARS		187	1	0	111	247.1	1052	207	97	70	11	18	8	13	104	14	260	28	7	12	13	.480	0	51	2.55

Nelson Santovenia

Bats: Right Throws: Right Pos: C   Ht: 6'3" Wt: 210 Born: 07/27/61 Age: 33

		BATTING												BASERUNNING				PERCENTAGES		
Year Team	Lg	G	AB	H	2B	3B	HR	TB	R	RBI	TBB	IBB	SO	HBP	SH	SF	SB	CS	SB%	GDP	Avg	OBP	SLG
1984 Jacksnville	AA	90	255	55	9	0	5	79	27	29	44	2	30	0	4	2	0	3	.00	12	.216	.329	.310
1985 Indianapols	AAA	28	75	16	2	0	0	18	5	4	7	0	11	0	0	1	1	1	.50	0	.213	.277	.240
Jacksnville	AA	57	184	40	6	0	2	52	15	15	14	1	18	1	4	3	2	0	1.00	10	.217	.272	.283
1986 Jacksnville	AA	31	72	22	7	0	4	41	15	11	19	0	7	1	2	0	0	1	.00	0	.306	.457	.569
Indianapols	AAA	18	57	12	1	0	1	16	6	2	5	0	13	0	1	0	0	0	.00	1	.211	.274	.281
1987 Jacksnville	AA	117	394	110	17	0	19	184	56	63	36	1	58	5	1	3	3	4	.43	13	.279	.345	.467
1988 Indianapols	AAA	27	91	28	5	0	2	39	9	13	4	0	16	1	1	1	0	0	.00	2	.308	.340	.429
1990 Indianapols	AAA	11	44	14	2	0	1	19	3	10	1	0	7	1	0	0	0	0	.00	1	.318	.340	.432
1991 Indianapols	AAA	61	194	51	7	1	6	78	23	26	21	1	24	0	0	2	0	2	.00	10	.263	.332	.402

Year	Team	Lg	G	AB	H	2B	3B	HR	TB	R	RBI	TBB	IBB	SO	HBP	SH	SF	SB	CS	SB%	GDP	Avg	OBP	SLG
1992	Vancouver	AAA	91	281	74	16	0	6	108	24	42	37	2	49	0	3	3	0	0	.00	6	.263	.346	.384
1993	Omaha	AAA	81	274	65	13	0	11	111	33	42	12	1	50	3	0	7	0	1	.00	4	.237	.270	.405
1994	Omaha	AAA	45	145	24	5	0	3	38	12	18	14	1	28	0	1	4	0	0	.00	4	.166	.233	.262
1987	Montreal	NL	2	1	0	0	0	0	0	0	0	0	0	0	0	0	0	0	0	.00	0	.000	.000	.000
1988	Montreal	NL	92	309	73	20	2	8	121	26	41	24	3	77	3	4	4	2	3	.40	4	.236	.294	.392
1989	Montreal	NL	97	304	76	14	1	5	107	30	31	24	2	37	3	2	4	2	1	.67	12	.250	.307	.352
1990	Montreal	NL	59	163	31	3	1	6	54	13	28	8	0	31	0	0	5	0	3	.00	5	.190	.222	.331
1991	Montreal	NL	41	96	24	5	0	2	35	7	14	2	2	18	0	0	4	0	0	.00	4	.250	.255	.365
1992	Chicago	AL	2	3	1	0	0	1	4	1	2	0	0	0	0	0	0	0	0	.00	0	.333	.333	1.333
1993	Kansas City	AL	4	8	1	0	0	0	1	0	0	0	0	2	0	0	0	0	0	.00	0	.125	.222	.125
	10 Min. YEARS		657	2066	511	90	1	60	783	228	275	214	9	311	12	17	27	6	12	.33	67	.247	.318	.379
	7 Maj. YEARS		297	884	206	42	4	22	322	77	116	59	7	165	6	6	17	4	7	.36	25	.233	.281	.364

Mike Sarbaugh

Bats: Right Throws: Right Pos: 2B **Ht: 6'0" Wt: 180 Born: 04/25/67 Age: 28**

						BATTING												BASERUNNING				PERCENTAGES		
Year	Team	Lg	G	AB	H	2B	3B	HR	TB	R	RBI	TBB	IBB	SO	HBP	SH	SF	SB	CS	SB%	GDP	Avg	OBP	SLG
1989	Brewers	R	4	14	5	0	0	0	5	3	3	3	0	2	1	0	1	0	0	.00	0	.357	.474	.357
	Helena	R	24	84	28	8	0	2	42	17	9	7	0	16	2	1	1	0	0	.00	0	.333	.394	.500
	Beloit	A	16	48	7	3	0	0	10	4	4	1	0	15	2	0	0	0	0	.00	1	.146	.196	.208
1990	Reno	A	121	454	132	22	7	6	186	78	67	46	1	76	12	1	5	14	12	.54	12	.291	.368	.410
	Kinston	A	2	8	3	0	0	1	6	2	3	2	0	1	1	0	0	0	0	.00	0	.375	.545	.750
1991	Canton-Akrn	AA	5	15	1	0	0	0	1	1	1	1	0	4	0	1	0	1	0	1.00	0	.067	.125	.067
	Kinston	A	76	262	65	13	1	7	101	39	33	33	1	48	2	1	2	3	1	.75	8	.248	.334	.385
1992	Canton-Akrn	AA	38	120	28	5	0	2	39	19	18	8	0	21	2	3	0	1	2	.33	2	.233	.292	.325
1993	Canton-Akrn	AA	85	277	69	13	5	6	110	29	31	20	1	44	0	0	4	3	2	.60	7	.249	.296	.397
1994	Charlotte	AAA	4	5	1	0	0	0	1	0	0	0	0	0	0	0	0	0	0	.00	0	.200	.200	.200
	Canton-Akrn	AA	80	265	72	9	2	7	106	35	38	24	0	45	3	4	2	0	0	.00	9	.272	.337	.400
	6 Min. YEARS		455	1552	411	73	15	31	607	227	207	145	3	272	25	11	15	22	17	.56	39	.265	.334	.391

Jason Satre

Pitches: Right Bats: Right Pos: P **Ht: 6'1" Wt: 180 Born: 08/24/70 Age: 24**

					HOW MUCH HE PITCHED					WHAT HE GAVE UP										THE RESULTS				
Year	Team	Lg	G	GS	CG	GF	IP	BFP	H	R	ER	HR	SH	SF	HB	TBB	IBB	SO	WP	Bk	W	L	Pct.	ShO	Sv	ERA
1988	Reds	R	11	10	0	0	47	201	31	16	13	0	1	5	2	29	0	44	6	3	0	3	.000	0	0	2.49
1989	Greensboro	A	27	27	2	0	133.2	603	128	95	85	7	4	4	5	87	0	106	14	4	7	13	.350	0	0	5.72
1990	Chston-Wv	A	24	22	3	0	116	504	99	70	61	8	3	5	3	75	1	105	16	3	6	12	.333	1	0	4.73
1991	Cedar Rapds	A	21	20	4	1	132.2	551	101	48	38	5	6	4	2	67	1	130	6	0	8	6	.571	2	1	2.58
	Chattanooga	AA	8	8	0	0	44	195	37	26	25	7	1	0	2	26	0	44	6	1	1	7	.125	0	0	5.11
1992	Chattanooga	AA	14	11	0	2	58	247	56	42	35	7	1	2	1	26	1	36	4	0	3	5	.375	0	0	5.43
1993	Rochester	AAA	15	15	0	0	80	371	87	57	52	12	1	3	6	45	0	42	9	0	4	5	.444	0	0	5.85
	Bowie	AA	13	13	2	0	84	344	68	35	29	7	0	2	4	20	0	65	2	1	7	3	.700	0	0	3.11
1994	Rochester	AAA	37	15	1	5	130.1	578	126	80	72	21	2	6	9	67	5	73	8	1	6	7	.462	0	0	4.97
	7 Min. YEARS		170	141	12	8	825.2	3594	733	469	410	74	19	31	34	442	8	645	71	12	42	61	.408	3	1	4.47

Chris Saunders

Bats: Right Throws: Right Pos: 3B **Ht: 6'2" Wt: 200 Born: 07/19/70 Age: 24**

						BATTING												BASERUNNING				PERCENTAGES		
Year	Team	Lg	G	AB	H	2B	3B	HR	TB	R	RBI	TBB	IBB	SO	HBP	SH	SF	SB	CS	SB%	GDP	Avg	OBP	SLG
1992	Pittsfield	A	72	254	64	11	2	2	85	34	32	34	0	50	1	1	5	5	2	.71	5	.252	.337	.335
1993	St.Lucie	A	123	456	115	14	4	4	149	45	64	40	4	89	1	1	4	6	7	.46	10	.252	.311	.327
1994	Binghamton	AA	132	499	134	29	0	10	193	68	70	43	0	96	4	2	7	6	6	.50	12	.269	.327	.387
	3 Min. YEARS		327	1209	313	54	6	16	427	147	166	117	4	235	6	4	16	17	15	.53	27	.259	.323	.353

Doug Saunders

Bats: Right Throws: Right Pos: 2B **Ht: 6' 0" Wt: 172 Born: 12/13/69 Age: 25**

						BATTING												BASERUNNING				PERCENTAGES		
Year	Team	Lg	G	AB	H	2B	3B	HR	TB	R	RBI	TBB	IBB	SO	HBP	SH	SF	SB	CS	SB%	GDP	Avg	OBP	SLG
1988	Mets	R	16	64	16	4	1	0	22	8	10	9	0	14	0	2	0	2	3	.40	4	.250	.342	.344
	Little Fls	A	29	100	30	6	1	0	38	10	11	6	0	15	0	1	0	1	4	.20	2	.300	.340	.380
1989	Columbia	A	115	377	99	18	4	4	137	53	38	35	2	78	3	4	3	5	5	.50	5	.263	.328	.363
1990	St. Lucie	A	115	408	92	8	4	1	111	52	43	43	0	96	2	7	2	24	10	.71	7	.225	.301	.272
1991	St. Lucie	A	70	230	54	9	2	2	73	19	18	25	0	43	4	5	0	5	6	.45	6	.235	.320	.317
1992	Binghamton	AA	130	435	108	16	2	5	143	45	38	52	0	68	1	5	4	8	12	.40	9	.248	.327	.329
1993	Norfolk	AAA	105	356	88	12	6	2	118	37	24	44	1	63	3	7	1	6	5	.55	13	.247	.334	.331
1994	Binghamton	AA	96	338	96	19	4	8	147	48	45	43	2	63	0	6	4	3	4	.43	6	.284	.361	.435
1993	New York	NL	28	67	14	2	0	0	16	8	0	3	0	4	0	3	0	0	0	.00	2	.209	.243	.239
	7 Min. YEARS		676	2308	583	92	24	22	789	272	227	257	5	440	13	37	14	54	49	.52	48	.253	.329	.342

Rich Sauveur

Pitches: Left **Bats:** Left **Pos:** P   **Ht:** 6' 4" **Wt:** 185 **Born:** 11/23/63 **Age:** 31

					HOW MUCH HE PITCHED				WHAT HE GAVE UP									THE RESULTS					
Year	Team	Lg	G	GS	CG	GF	IP	BFP	H	R	ER	HR	SH	SF	HB	TBB	IBB	SO	WP	Bk	W	L	Pct.	ShO	Sv	ERA
1984	Pr William	A	10	10	0	0	54.2	240	43	22	19	5	2	1	1	31	0	54	3	0	3	3	.500	0	0	3.13
	Nashua	AA	10	10	2	0	70.2	291	54	27	23	4	4	1	3	34	1	48	2	4	5	3	.625	2	0	2.93
1985	Nashua	AA	25	25	4	0	157.1	666	146	73	62	7	9	6	3	78	2	85	7	4	9	10	.474	2	0	3.55
1986	Nashua	AA	5	5	2	0	38	141	21	5	5	1	1	0	1	11	0	28	1	1	3	1	.750	1	0	1.18
	Hawaii	AAA	14	14	6	0	92	391	73	40	31	3	2	0	6	45	1	68	4	8	7	6	.538	1	0	3.03
1987	Harrisburg	AA	30	27	7	0	195	825	174	71	62	9	7	9	9	96	3	160	9	7	13	6	.684	1	0	2.86
1988	Jacksnville	AA	8	0	0	4	6.2	32	7	5	3	0	0	0	0	5	0	8	0	0	0	2	.000	0	1	4.05
	Indianapols	AAA	43	3	0	18	81.1	318	60	26	22	8	5	1	1	28	5	58	3	3	7	4	.636	0	10	2.43
1989	Indianapols	AAA	8	0	0	4	9.2	44	10	8	8	1	0	1	0	6	0	8	0	0	0	1	.000	0	1	7.45
1990	Miami	A	11	6	1	2	40.2	178	41	16	15	2	2	0	4	17	0	34	0	3	0	4	.000	0	0	3.32
	Indianapols	AAA	14	7	0	0	56	232	45	14	12	1	2	2	3	25	0	24	1	3	2	2	.500	0	0	1.93
1991	Tidewater	AAA	42	0	0	21	45.1	188	31	14	12	0	4	0	0	23	5	49	3	3	2	2	.500	0	6	2.38
1992	Omaha	AAA	34	13	1	7	117.1	467	93	54	42	8	3	5	2	39	1	88	4	4	7	6	.538	0	0	3.22
1993	Indianapols	AAA	5	5	0	0	34.2	146	41	10	7	2	2	0	2	7	2	21	0	0	2	0	1.000	0	0	1.82
1994	Indianapols	AAA	53	1	0	30	67	268	47	25	21	7	4	0	1	23	4	65	1	0	3	3	.500	0	12	2.82
1986	Pittsburgh	NL	3	0	0	0	12	57	17	8	8	3	1	0	2	6	0	6	0	2	0	0	.000	0	0	6.00
1988	Montreal	NL	4	0	0	0	3	14	3	2	2	1	0	0	0	2	0	3	0	0	0	0	.000	0	0	6.00
1991	New York	NL	6	0	0	0	3.1	19	7	4	4	1	2	0	2	2	0	4	0	0	0	0	.000	0	0	10.80
1992	Kansas City	AL	8	0	0	2	14.1	65	15	7	7	1	0	0	2	8	1	7	0	1	0	1	.000	0	0	4.40
	11 Min. YEARS		312	126	23	86	1066.1	4427	886	410	344	58	47	26	36	468	24	798	38	40	63	53	.543	7	30	2.90
	4 Maj. YEARS		21	3	0	2	32.2	155	42	21	21	6	3	0	4	18	1	20	0	3	0	1	.000	0	0	5.79

Will Scalzitti

Bats: Right **Throws:** Right **Pos:** C   **Ht:** 6'0" **Wt:** 190 **Born:** 08/29/72 **Age:** 22

						BATTING												BASERUNNING				PERCENTAGES		
Year	Team	Lg	G	AB	H	2B	3B	HR	TB	R	RBI	TBB	IBB	SO	HBP	SH	SF	SB	CS	SB%	GDP	Avg	OBP	SLG	
1992	Bend	A	62	230	66	16	0	7	103	35	40	20	0	40	1	2	1	0	2	.00	9	.287	.345	.448	
1993	Central Val	A	75	248	60	10	0	2	76	25	17	17	1	40	1	3	1	0	1	.00	6	.242	.292	.306	
1994	Colo. Sprng	AAA	1	1	0	0	0	0	0	0	0	0	0	1	0	0	0	0	0	.00	0	.000	.000	.000	
	Central Val	A	81	297	75	13	0	9	115	27	37	16	0	56	4	2	1	0	3	.00	8	.253	.299	.387	
	New Haven	AA	10	30	7	0	0	1	10	2	6	0	0	4	0	0	0	0	0	.00	0	.233	.233	.333	
	3 Min. YEARS		229	806	208	39	0	19	304	89	100	53	1	141	6	7	3	0	6	.00	23	.258	.308	.377	

Gene Schall

Bats: Right **Throws:** Right **Pos:** OF   **Ht:** 6'3" **Wt:** 190 **Born:** 06/05/70 **Age:** 25

						BATTING												BASERUNNING				PERCENTAGES		
Year	Team	Lg	G	AB	H	2B	3B	HR	TB	R	RBI	TBB	IBB	SO	HBP	SH	SF	SB	CS	SB%	GDP	Avg	OBP	SLG	
1991	Batavia	A	13	44	15	1	0	2	22	5	8	3	2	16	0	0	0	0	1	.00	1	.341	.383	.500	
1992	Spartanburg	A	77	276	74	13	1	8	113	44	41	29	0	52	3	2	2	3	2	.60	8	.268	.342	.409	
	Clearwater	A	40	133	33	4	2	4	53	16	19	14	0	29	4	1	3	1	2	.33	2	.248	.331	.398	
1993	Reading	AA	82	285	93	12	4	15	158	51	60	24	0	56	10	0	3	2	1	.67	15	.326	.394	.554	
	Scranton/wb	AAA	40	139	33	6	1	4	53	16	16	19	1	38	7	1	1	4	2	.67	2	.237	.355	.381	
1994	Scranton-Wb	AAA	127	463	132	35	4	16	223	54	89	50	5	86	6	0	6	9	1	.90	11	.285	.358	.482	
	4 Min. YEARS		379	1340	380	71	12	49	622	186	233	139	8	277	30	4	15	19	9	.68	39	.284	.360	.464	

Scott Schanz

Pitches: Right **Bats:** Right **Pos:** P   **Ht:** 6'2" **Wt:** 190 **Born:** 04/02/69 **Age:** 26

					HOW MUCH HE PITCHED				WHAT HE GAVE UP									THE RESULTS					
Year	Team	Lg	G	GS	CG	GF	IP	BFP	H	R	ER	HR	SH	SF	HB	TBB	IBB	SO	WP	Bk	W	L	Pct.	ShO	Sv	ERA
1990	Bellingham	A	7	1	0	3	8	33	7	4	4	0	0	0	0	3	0	3	0	0	1	0	1.000	0	0	4.50
1991	Peninsula	A	27	20	2	4	122.1	558	136	85	70	11	5	6	7	78	1	59	2	3	2	17	.105	0	0	5.15
1992	San Berndno	A	38	5	0	16	77.2	368	84	53	46	8	2	2	4	51	1	68	8	0	1	5	.167	0	2	5.33
1993	Jacksnvlle	AA	49	3	0	21	102	424	77	38	29	11	8	6	2	51	5	81	5	0	7	4	.636	0	1	2.56
1994	Jacksnvlle	AA	19	2	0	9	34.2	150	34	21	16	4	3	3	0	17	4	24	7	0	1	1	.500	0	1	4.15
	5 Min. YEARS		140	31	2	53	344.2	1533	338	201	165	34	18	17	13	200	11	235	22	3	12	27	.308	0	4	4.31

Curt Schmidt

Pitches: Right **Bats:** Right **Pos:** P   **Ht:** 6'6" **Wt:** 223 **Born:** 03/16/70 **Age:** 25

					HOW MUCH HE PITCHED				WHAT HE GAVE UP									THE RESULTS					
Year	Team	Lg	G	GS	CG	GF	IP	BFP	H	R	ER	HR	SH	SF	HB	TBB	IBB	SO	WP	Bk	W	L	Pct.	ShO	Sv	ERA
1992	Jamestown	A	29	1	1	19	63.1	261	42	21	19	1	3	0	5	29	2	61	6	1	3	4	.429	1	2	2.70
	Wst Plm Bch	A	3	0	0	2	5	18	3	0	0	0	0	0	0	1	0	3	0	0	0	0	.000	0	0	0.00
1993	Expos	R	1	1	0	0	5	16	1	0	0	0	0	0	0	0	0	7	0	0	1	0	1.000	0	0	0.00
	Wst Plm Bch	A	44	2	0	22	65.1	285	63	32	23	3	5	1	0	25	3	51	1	1	4	6	.400	0	5	3.17
1994	Harrisburg	AA	53	0	0	26	71.2	291	51	19	15	4	6	4	0	29	1	75	4	0	6	2	.750	0	5	1.88
	3 Min. YEARS		130	4	1	69	210.1	871	160	72	57	8	14	5	5	84	6	197	11	2	14	12	.538	1	12	2.44

Jason Schmidt

Pitches: Right Bats: Right Pos: P Ht: 6'5" Wt: 185 Born: 01/29/73 Age: 22

Year	Team	Lg	G	GS	CG	GF	IP	BFP	H	R	ER	HR	SH	SF	HB	TBB	IBB	SO	WP	Bk	W	L	Pct.	ShO	Sv	ERA
1991	Braves	R	11	11	0	0	45.1	193	32	21	12	0	0	1	0	23	0	44	8	0	3	4	.429	0	0	2.38
1992	Macon	A	7	7	0	0	24.2	119	31	18	11	2	0	1	1	19	0	33	2	2	0	3	.000	0	0	4.01
	Pulaski	R	11	11	0	0	58.1	258	55	38	26	4	0	1	3	31	0	56	3	0	3	4	.429	0	0	4.01
1993	Durham	A	22	22	0	0	116.2	508	128	69	64	12	4	2	8	47	3	110	4	1	7	11	.389	0	0	4.94
1994	Greenville	AA	24	24	1	0	140.2	599	135	64	57	9	6	2	6	54	1	131	9	0	8	7	.533	0	0	3.65
	4 Min. YEARS		75	75	1	0	385.2	1677	381	210	170	27	10	7	20	174	4	374	26	3	21	29	.420	0	0	3.97

Philip Schneider

Pitches: Left Bats: Left Pos: P Ht: 6'1" Wt: 215 Born: 04/26/71 Age: 24

Year	Team	Lg	G	GS	CG	GF	IP	BFP	H	R	ER	HR	SH	SF	HB	TBB	IBB	SO	WP	Bk	W	L	Pct.	ShO	Sv	ERA
1993	Bend	A	4	0	0	4	7	23	1	1	0	0	0	0	0	0	0	9	0	0	1	0	1.000	0	0	0.00
	Central Val	A	19	0	0	4	37.2	165	30	16	13	3	6	0	1	25	0	42	1	0	8	1	.889	0	0	3.11
1994	New Haven	AA	31	21	2	1	135.2	561	117	54	47	8	9	3	2	47	0	94	1	2	10	8	.556	1	0	3.12
	2 Min. YEARS		54	21	2	9	180.1	749	148	71	60	11	15	3	3	72	0	145	2	2	19	9	.679	1	0	2.99

Mike Schooler

Pitches: Right Bats: Right Pos: P Ht: 6'3" Wt: 220 Born: 08/10/62 Age: 32

Year	Team	Lg	G	GS	CG	GF	IP	BFP	H	R	ER	HR	SH	SF	HB	TBB	IBB	SO	WP	Bk	W	L	Pct.	ShO	Sv	ERA
1985	Bellingham	A	10	10	0	0	55.1	0	42	24	18	5	0	0	2	15	0	48	1	1	4	3	.571	0	0	2.93
1986	Wausau	A	26	26	6	0	166.1	700	166	83	62	20	3	3	4	44	0	171	10	2	12	10	.545	1	0	3.35
1987	Chattanooga	AA	28	28	3	0	175	748	183	87	77	14	2	5	6	48	1	144	4	7	13	8	.619	2	0	3.96
1988	Calgary	AAA	26	0	0	21	33.2	139	33	19	12	2	5	1	0	6	1	47	3	1	4	4	.500	0	8	3.21
1991	Jacksnville	AA	11	2	0	3	11.1	50	13	9	7	2	0	1	0	3	0	12	0	0	1	1	.500	0	0	5.56
1992	Calgary	AAA	1	1	0	0	2	8	2	0	0	0	0	0	0	0	0	0	0	0	0	0	.000	0	0	0.00
	Bellingham	A	2	1	0	0	3	12	1	2	0	0	0	0	0	0	0	3	0	0	0	0	.000	0	0	0.00
1993	Okla City	AAA	28	0	0	20	45.2	205	59	33	30	3	1	1	0	11	3	31	5	2	1	3	.250	0	5	5.91
1994	Wichita	AA	22	9	0	7	57.2	261	82	37	30	1	6	3	0	12	3	37	2	0	0	8	.000	0	0	4.68
1988	Seattle	AL	40	0	0	33	48.1	214	45	21	19	4	2	3	1	24	4	54	4	1	5	8	.385	0	15	3.54
1989	Seattle	AL	67	0	0	60	77	329	81	27	24	2	3	1	2	19	3	69	6	1	1	7	.125	0	33	2.81
1990	Seattle	AL	49	0	0	45	56	229	47	18	14	5	3	2	1	16	5	45	1	0	1	4	.200	0	30	2.25
1991	Seattle	AL	34	0	0	23	34.1	138	25	14	14	2	1	1	0	10	0	31	2	1	3	3	.500	0	7	3.67
1992	Seattle	AL	53	0	0	36	51.2	232	55	29	27	7	4	3	1	24	6	33	0	0	2	7	.222	0	13	4.70
1993	Texas	AL	17	0	0	0	24.1	111	30	17	15	3	2	0	0	10	1	16	1	0	3	0	1.000	0	0	5.55
	8 Min. YEARS		154	77	9	51	550	2123	581	294	236	47	17	14	12	139	8	493	25	13	35	37	.486	3	13	3.86
	6 Maj. YEARS		260	0	0	197	291.2	1253	283	126	113	23	15	10	5	103	19	248	14	3	15	29	.341	0	98	3.49

Brad Schorr

Pitches: Right Bats: Right Pos: P Ht: 6'3" Wt: 189 Born: 01/21/72 Age: 23

Year	Team	Lg	G	GS	CG	GF	IP	BFP	H	R	ER	HR	SH	SF	HB	TBB	IBB	SO	WP	Bk	W	L	Pct.	ShO	Sv	ERA
1990	Mets	R	12	8	0	4	57.2	221	44	23	19	0	1	1	2	7	0	47	2	2	2	3	.400	0	3	2.97
1991	Kingsport	R	11	11	3	0	71.2	293	53	40	25	6	0	2	9	16	1	69	5	0	5	6	.455	0	0	3.14
	Pittsfield	A	2	2	0	0	13.2	54	13	4	3	0	0	1	1	5	0	3	0	0	2	0	1.000	0	0	1.98
1992	Columbia	A	27	27	2	0	160	696	169	96	85	13	3	3	10	48	0	106	16	2	12	6	.667	1	0	4.78
1993	St.Lucie	A	27	26	4	1	181.2	770	192	87	75	8	9	8	10	52	1	75	7	4	11	10	.524	0	0	3.72
1994	St. Lucie	A	17	17	4	0	110.1	455	100	45	40	6	6	3	4	34	3	47	4	2	10	4	.714	3	0	3.26
	Binghamton	AA	10	9	0	0	51.1	229	59	36	32	6	1	1	2	19	0	22	2	0	4	4	.500	0	0	5.61
	5 Min. YEARS		106	100	13	5	646.1	2718	630	331	279	39	20	19	38	181	5	369	36	10	46	33	.582	4	3	3.88

Bruce Schreiber

Bats: Right Throws: Right Pos: 2B Ht: 6'0" Wt: 185 Born: 05/04/67 Age: 28

Year	Team	Lg	G	AB	H	2B	3B	HR	TB	R	RBI	TBB	IBB	SO	HBP	SH	SF	SB	CS	SB%	GDP	Avg	OBP	SLG
1989	Princeton	R	64	224	78	15	8	2	115	31	38	20	2	31	0	0	2	7	4	.64	3	.348	.398	.513
1990	Salem	A	134	552	160	24	5	4	206	71	48	33	2	109	9	5	7	6	4	.60	11	.290	.336	.373
1991	Carolina	AA	108	325	79	11	1	1	95	25	22	21	0	64	1	3	2	4	4	.50	7	.243	.289	.292
1992	Salem	A	33	107	20	3	4	2	37	9	8	10	1	21	1	1	0	1	1	.50	0	.187	.263	.346
	Carolina	AA	81	256	68	5	4	0	81	14	15	10	0	39	0	4	2	5	7	.42	5	.266	.291	.316
	Buffalo	AAA	9	18	2	1	0	0	3	3	1	3	0	9	0	0	0	0	0	.00	1	.111	.238	.167
1993	Buffalo	AAA	15	40	8	1	0	0	9	0	2	2	0	11	0	1	0	0	0	.00	1	.200	.238	.225
	Carolina	AA	94	296	77	11	3	2	100	42	28	20	1	50	2	9	3	1	2	.33	10	.260	.308	.338
1994	Carolina	AA	14	45	16	7	0	0	23	7	6	5	2	5	0	0	2	1	0	.00	2	.356	.420	.511
	6 Min. YEARS		552	1863	508	78	25	11	669	202	168	124	8	339	13	23	16	24	23	.51	39	.273	.320	.359

Steve Schrenk

Pitches: Right Bats: Right Pos: P Ht: 6'3" Wt: 185 Born: 11/20/68 Age: 26

Year	Team	Lg	G	GS	CG	GF	IP	BFP	H	R	ER	HR	SH	SF	HB	TBB	IBB	SO	WP	Bk	W	L	Pct.	ShO	Sv	ERA
1987	White Sox	R	8	6	1	0	28.1	115	23	10	3	0	3	0	2	12	0	19	2	1	1	2	.333	1	0	0.95
1988	South Bend	A	21	18	1	1	90	417	95	63	50	4	0	3	13	37	0	58	7	2	3	7	.300	0	0	5.00
1989	South Bend	A	16	16	1	0	79	353	71	44	38	6	2	0	8	44	1	49	9	0	5	2	.714	1	0	4.33
1990	South Bend	A	20	14	2	2	103.2	419	79	44	34	7	3	3	11	25	0	92	7	1	7	6	.538	1	0	2.95
1991	White Sox	R	11	7	0	2	37	144	30	20	12	0	1	0	5	6	0	39	1	0	1	3	.250	0	0	2.92
1992	Sarasota	A	25	22	4	2	154	621	130	48	35	1	4	6	7	40	2	113	7	6	15	2	.882	2	1	2.05
	Birmingham	AA	2	2	0	0	12.1	59	13	5	5	0	0	1	1	11	0	9	1	0	1	1	.500	0	0	3.65
1993	Birmingham	AA	8	8	2	0	61.2	224	31	11	8	2	1	1	1	7	0	51	3	0	5	1	.833	1	0	1.17
	Nashville	AAA	21	20	0	0	122.1	526	117	61	53	11	5	2	3	47	3	78	6	3	6	8	.429	0	0	3.90
1994	Nashville	AAA	29	28	2	0	178.2	769	175	82	69	15	10	4	6	69	3	134	14	1	14	6	.700	1	0	3.48
	8 Min. YEARS		161	141	13	7	867	3647	764	388	307	46	29	20	57	298	9	642	57	14	58	38	.604	7	1	3.19

Lance Schuermann

Pitches: Left Bats: Left Pos: P Ht: 6'2" Wt: 200 Born: 02/07/70 Age: 25

Year	Team	Lg	G	GS	CG	GF	IP	BFP	H	R	ER	HR	SH	SF	HB	TBB	IBB	SO	WP	Bk	W	L	Pct.	ShO	Sv	ERA
1991	Butte	R	30	0	0	16	43.2	203	45	29	22	0	2	2	1	34	2	46	6	7	4	4	.500	0	4	4.53
1992	Miracle	A	51	5	0	17	86.1	390	87	51	45	1	5	9	2	56	1	68	7	2	4	7	.364	0	2	4.69
1993	Charlotte	A	46	0	0	24	65.1	256	40	20	15	1	3	5	1	28	2	59	2	0	1	4	.200	0	16	2.07
1994	Tulsa	AA	27	27	3	0	175.2	743	182	87	80	21	9	7	7	49	2	124	3	2	10	11	.476	0	0	4.10
	4 Min. YEARS		154	32	3	57	371	1592	354	187	162	23	19	23	11	167	7	297	18	11	19	26	.422	0	22	3.93

Jerry Schunk

Bats: Right Throws: Right Pos: SS Ht: 5'11" Wt: 186 Born: 10/05/65 Age: 29

Year	Team	Lg	G	AB	H	2B	3B	HR	TB	R	RBI	TBB	IBB	SO	HBP	SH	SF	SB	CS	SB%	GDP	Avg	OBP	SLG
1986	St.Cathmes	A	71	272	75	12	0	7	108	39	33	21	2	25	2	6	3	18	6	.75	8	.276	.329	.397
1987	Dunedin	A	98	358	88	15	2	4	119	40	39	17	0	38	2	4	0	11	4	.73	9	.246	.282	.332
1988	Dunedin	A	87	343	88	17	2	5	124	36	28	19	0	30	2	8	1	11	7	.61	10	.257	.299	.362
1989	Knoxville	AA	95	270	65	13	4	4	98	32	31	17	0	19	3	8	5	6	3	.67	4	.241	.288	.363
1990	Knoxville	AA	85	274	79	13	1	3	103	32	31	9	0	25	3	14	3	8	7	.53	9	.288	.315	.376
	Syracuse	AAA	26	100	24	4	0	0	28	8	7	3	0	10	0	1	0	1	2	.33	3	.240	.262	.280
1991	Syracuse	AAA	92	327	81	9	0	5	105	34	29	8	0	26	4	10	0	0	3	.00	8	.248	.274	.321
1992	Syracuse	AAA	122	417	109	16	1	2	133	40	26	20	1	21	0	12	6	2	3	.40	13	.261	.291	.319
1993	Portland	AAA	118	397	107	28	1	2	143	53	47	18	1	23	5	13	4	5	3	.63	15	.270	.307	.360
1994	Portland	AA	92	327	90	17	0	7	128	34	35	25	2	20	3	4	1	1	7	.13	8	.275	.331	.391
	9 Min. YEARS		886	3085	806	144	11	39	1089	348	306	157	6	237	24	76	25	63	45	.58	87	.261	.300	.353

Gary Scott

Bats: Right Throws: Right Pos: 3B Ht: 6'0" Wt: 175 Born: 08/22/68 Age: 26

Year	Team	Lg	G	AB	H	2B	3B	HR	TB	R	RBI	TBB	IBB	SO	HBP	SH	SF	SB	CS	SB%	GDP	Avg	OBP	SLG
1989	Geneva	A	48	175	49	10	1	10	91	33	42	22	2	23	9	0	2	4	1	.80	2	.280	.385	.520
1990	Winston-Sal	A	102	380	112	22	0	12	170	63	70	29	4	66	14	5	6	17	3	.85	7	.295	.361	.447
	Charlotte	AA	35	143	44	9	0	4	65	21	17	7	1	17	0	0	3	3	4	.43	3	.308	.333	.455
1991	Iowa	AAA	63	231	48	10	2	3	71	21	34	20	2	45	6	3	2	0	6	.00	11	.208	.286	.307
1992	Iowa	AAA	95	354	93	26	0	10	149	48	48	37	1	48	6	4	5	3	1	.75	8	.263	.338	.421
1993	Indianapols	AAA	77	284	60	12	1	3	83	39	18	21	0	33	4	2	2	2	1	.67	7	.211	.273	.292
	Portland	AAA	54	189	55	8	4	1	74	26	28	27	0	33	7	1	6	3	1	.75	8	.291	.389	.392
1994	Phoenix	AAA	121	426	122	24	3	9	179	55	58	35	3	61	10	1	4	4	7	.36	14	.286	.352	.420
1991	Chicago	NL	31	79	13	3	0	1	19	8	5	13	4	14	3	1	0	0	1	.00	2	.165	.305	.241
1992	Chicago	NL	36	96	15	2	0	2	23	8	11	5	1	14	0	1	0	0	1	.00	3	.156	.198	.240
	6 Min. YEARS		595	2182	583	121	11	52	882	306	315	198	13	326	56	16	30	36	24	.60	60	.267	.339	.404
	2 Maj. YEARS		67	175	28	5	0	3	42	16	16	18	5	28	3	2	0	0	2	.00	5	.160	.250	.240

Scott Scudder

Pitches: Right Bats: Right Pos: P Ht: 6'2" Wt: 190 Born: 02/14/68 Age: 27

Year	Team	Lg	G	GS	CG	GF	IP	BFP	H	R	ER	HR	SH	SF	HB	TBB	IBB	SO	WP	Bk	W	L	Pct.	ShO	Sv	ERA
1986	Billings	R	12	8	0	1	52.2	0	42	34	28	1	0	0	3	36	0	38	8	0	1	3	.250	0	0	4.78
1987	Cedar Rapds	A	26	26	0	0	153.2	660	129	86	70	16	8	2	7	76	0	128	15	3	7	12	.368	0	0	4.10
1988	Cedar Rapds	A	16	15	1	0	102.1	405	61	30	23	3	2	1	2	41	0	126	5	0	7	3	.700	1	0	2.02
	Chattanooga	AA	11	11	0	0	70	290	53	24	23	7	1	3	1	30	0	52	5	0	7	0	1.000	0	0	2.96
1989	Nashville	AAA	12	12	3	0	80.2	339	54	27	24	6	2	3	3	48	0	64	1	1	6	2	.750	3	0	2.68
1990	Nashville	AAA	11	11	1	0	80.2	315	53	27	21	1	0	1	0	32	0	60	0	3	7	1	.875	0	0	2.34
1992	Colo Spmgs	AAA	1	1	0	0	3	14	4	3	2	0	0	0	0	2	0	1	1	0	0	1	.000	0	0	6.00
1993	Charlotte	AAA	23	22	2	0	136	597	148	92	76	21	0	7	7	52	1	64	5	0	7	7	.500	0	0	5.03

231

Year Team		G	GS	CG	GF	IP	BFP	H	R	ER	HR	SH	SF	HB	TBB	IBB	SO	WP	Bk	W	L	Pct.	ShO	Sv	ERA
1994 Buffalo	AAA	35	20	2	3	147.1	646	178	100	92	20	5	7	4	39	0	77	13	1	5	10	.333	0	1	5.62
1989 Cincinnati	NL	23	17	0	3	100.1	451	91	54	50	14	7	2	1	61	11	66	0	1	4	9	.308	0	0	4.49
1990 Cincinnati	NL	21	10	0	3	71.2	316	74	41	39	12	3	1	3	30	4	42	2	2	5	5	.500	0	0	4.90
1991 Cincinnati	NL	27	14	0	4	101.1	443	91	52	49	6	8	3	6	56	4	51	7	0	6	9	.400	0	1	4.35
1992 Cleveland	AL	23	22	0	0	109	509	134	80	64	10	6	4	2	55	0	66	7	0	6	10	.375	0	0	5.28
1993 Cleveland	AL	2	1	0	1	4	20	5	4	4	0	0	0	1	4	0	1	0	0	0	1	.000	0	0	9.00
8 Min. YEARS		147	126	9	4	826.1	3266	722	423	359	75	18	24	27	356	1	610	53	8	47	39	.547	4	1	3.91
5 Maj. YEARS		96	64	0	11	386.1	1739	395	231	206	42	24	10	13	206	19	226	16	3	21	34	.382	0	1	4.80

Kyle Sebach

Pitches: Right Bats: Right Pos: P Ht: 6'4" Wt: 195 Born: 09/06/71 Age: 23

		HOW MUCH HE PITCHED						WHAT HE GAVE UP												THE RESULTS					
Year Team	Lg	G	GS	CG	GF	IP	BFP	H	R	ER	HR	SH	SF	HB	TBB	IBB	SO	WP	Bk	W	L	Pct.	ShO	Sv	ERA
1991 Angels	R	13	11	1	1	64.2	296	62	49	45	4	2	3	7	39	1	58	7	2	3	5	.375	0	0	6.26
1992 Quad City	A	13	13	0	0	61.1	274	52	31	27	5	0	0	8	40	0	50	8	1	3	4	.429	0	0	3.96
Boise	A	13	8	0	3	40.2	215	50	42	34	0	0	6	8	34	0	41	9	1	1	5	.167	0	1	7.52
1993 Cedar Rapds	A	26	26	4	0	154	678	138	73	52	7	4	7	14	70	1	138	10	2	6	9	.400	0	0	3.04
1994 Lake Elsino	A	10	10	3	0	73	306	67	35	28	5	2	2	4	24	1	39	5	0	3	4	.429	0	0	3.45
Midland	AA	16	16	4	0	112.2	494	129	69	58	11	2	4	9	40	0	85	3	0	5	5	.500	2	0	4.63
4 Min. YEARS		91	84	12	4	506.1	2263	498	299	244	32	10	22	50	247	3	411	42	6	21	32	.396	2	1	4.34

Tate Seefried

Bats: Left Throws: Right Pos: 1B Ht: 6'4" Wt: 180 Born: 04/22/72 Age: 23

		BATTING												BASERUNNING				PERCENTAGES		
Year Team	Lg	G	AB	H	2B	3B	HR	TB	R	RBI	TBB	IBB	SO	HBP	SH	SF	SB	CS	SB%	GDP	Avg	OBP	SLG
1990 Yankees	R	52	178	28	3	0	0	31	15	20	22	0	53	2	0	1	2	1	.67	6	.157	.256	.174
1991 Oneonta	A	73	264	65	19	0	7	105	40	51	32	0	66	2	0	7	12	3	.80	6	.246	.325	.398
1992 Greensboro	A	141	532	129	23	5	20	222	73	90	51	0	166	2	1	3	8	8	.50	12	.242	.310	.417
1993 Pr William	A	125	464	123	25	4	21	219	63	89	50	4	150	2	3	6	8	8	.50	8	.265	.335	.472
1994 Albany-Colo	AA	118	444	100	14	2	27	199	63	83	48	4	149	5	1	2	1	5	.17	12	.225	.307	.448
5 Min. YEARS		509	1882	445	84	11	75	776	254	333	203	8	584	13	5	19	31	25	.55	44	.236	.312	.412

Chris Seelbach

Pitches: Right Bats: Right Pos: P Ht: 6'4" Wt: 180 Born: 12/18/72 Age: 22

		HOW MUCH HE PITCHED						WHAT HE GAVE UP												THE RESULTS					
Year Team	Lg	G	GS	CG	GF	IP	BFP	H	R	ER	HR	SH	SF	HB	TBB	IBB	SO	WP	Bk	W	L	Pct.	ShO	Sv	ERA
1991 Braves	R	4	4	0	0	15	65	13	7	7	3	1	0	0	6	0	19	3	1	0	1	.000	0	0	4.20
1992 Macon	A	27	27	1	0	157.1	662	134	65	58	11	3	5	9	68	0	144	5	1	9	11	.450	0	0	3.32
1993 Durham	A	25	25	0	0	131.1	590	133	85	72	15	4	4	7	74	1	112	10	0	9	9	.500	0	0	4.93
1994 Greenville	AA	15	15	2	0	92.2	363	64	26	24	3	5	3	4	38	2	79	5	0	4	6	.400	0	0	2.33
Richmond	AAA	12	11	0	0	61.1	273	68	37	33	6	2	3	0	36	2	35	3	0	3	5	.375	0	0	4.84
4 Min. YEARS		83	82	3	0	457.2	1953	412	220	194	38	15	15	20	222	5	389	26	2	25	32	.439	0	0	3.82

Jose Segura

Pitches: Right Bats: Right Pos: P Ht: 5'11" Wt: 180 Born: 01/26/63 Age: 32

		HOW MUCH HE PITCHED						WHAT HE GAVE UP												THE RESULTS					
Year Team	Lg	G	GS	CG	GF	IP	BFP	H	R	ER	HR	SH	SF	HB	TBB	IBB	SO	WP	Bk	W	L	Pct.	ShO	Sv	ERA
1984 Kinston	A	16	14	2	1	97.1	402	88	48	43	7	2	3	1	35	1	55	7	0	7	4	.636	1	0	3.98
Knoxville	AA	12	12	1	0	69	322	75	47	34	4	2	1	0	47	1	26	8	1	4	6	.400	0	0	4.43
1985 Kinston	A	34	15	1	10	110.1	499	109	62	51	9	1	3	7	69	4	73	7	1	4	13	.235	1	1	4.16
1986 Knoxville	AA	24	17	1	3	106.2	491	101	72	50	7	0	7	6	72	1	55	11	1	4	7	.364	0	2	4.22
1987 Syracuse	AAA	43	12	0	12	107	499	136	90	78	13	2	10	1	59	2	54	14	1	5	8	.385	0	4	6.56
1988 Vancouver	AAA	20	19	0	0	111	507	127	69	56	4	5	7	0	60	0	39	3	6	6	6	.500	0	0	4.54
1989 Vancouver	AAA	44	0	0	32	66.2	263	50	21	17	0	1	3	0	19	2	52	1	3	1	2	.333	0	17	2.30
1990 Vancouver	AAA	40	0	0	27	54.2	246	49	34	31	0	2	5	1	35	1	47	6	0	1	3	.250	0	8	5.10
1991 Phoenix	AAA	32	0	0	27	39.1	177	46	15	15	4	3	3	1	17	2	21	3	0	5	5	.500	0	4	3.43
1992 Nashville	AAA	22	0	0	11	31.2	140	33	16	14	0	1	1	1	18	1	16	3	0	1	1	.500	0	1	3.98
1994 Columbus	AAA	5	0	0	3	4.2	22	5	5	1	0	0	0	0	3	0	3	0	0	0	0	.000	0	0	1.93
1988 Chicago	AL	4	0	0	1	8.2	52	19	17	13	1	0	0	0	8	0	2	2	3	0	0	.000	0	0	13.50
1989 Chicago	AL	7	0	0	2	6	34	13	11	10	2	2	1	0	3	1	4	0	0	0	1	.000	0	0	15.00
1991 San Francisco	NL	11	0	0	2	16.1	72	20	11	8	1	1	0	0	5	0	10	2	0	0	1	.000	0	0	4.41
10 Min. YEARS		292	89	5	126	798.1	3568	819	479	390	48	19	43	18	434	15	441	63	13	38	56	.404	2	37	4.40
3 Maj. YEARS		22	0	0	5	31	158	52	39	31	4	3	1	0	16	1	16	4	3	0	2	.000	0	0	9.00

Keith Seiler

Pitches: Left Bats: Left Pos: P Ht: 6'1" Wt: 180 Born: 11/17/67 Age: 27

		HOW MUCH HE PITCHED						WHAT HE GAVE UP												THE RESULTS					
Year Team	Lg	G	GS	CG	GF	IP	BFP	H	R	ER	HR	SH	SF	HB	TBB	IBB	SO	WP	Bk	W	L	Pct.	ShO	Sv	ERA
1990 Yankees	R	16	0	0	12	20.2	80	18	5	5	1	2	0	0	3	2	23	1	2	2	1	.667	0	4	2.18
Ft.Lauderdle	A	8	0	0	4	16	66	13	1	1	0	2	0	0	6	3	15	2	1	0	0	.000	0	0	0.56
1991 Greensboro	A	52	0	0	18	68	293	61	36	21	2	5	2	3	27	5	64	1	0	7	5	.583	0	3	2.78
Columbus	AAA	2	0	0	1	2.1	10	3	1	1	0	0	0	0	1	0	1	0	0	0	0	.000	0	0	3.86
1992 Pr William	A	16	0	0	13	17	79	21	13	12	1	0	1	0	11	0	11	2	0	0	2	.000	0	5	6.35
Ft. Laud	A	9	0	0	6	15	68	19	7	3	1	1	1	0	6	0	1	1	0	0	0	.000	0	0	1.80

232

	Lg	G	GS	CG	GF	IP	BFP	H	R	ER	HR	SH	SF	HB	TBB	IBB	SO	WP	Bk	W	L	Pct.	ShO	Sv	ERA
Columbus	AAA	3	0	0	2	4.1	19	5	2	2	0	0	0	0	2	0	2	0	0	0	0	.000	0	0	4.15
1993 Pr William	A	31	0	0	16	43.2	192	47	26	19	2	4	1	1	9	0	21	2	0	3	3	.500	0	1	3.92
Columbus	AAA	1	0	0	0	2	11	2	3	3	1	0	1	0	2	1	1	0	0	0	0	.000	0	1	13.50
1994 Albany-Colo	AA	48	0	0	21	62	284	82	36	29	5	4	3	0	22	4	47	8	0	3	5	.375	0	2	4.21
5 Min. YEARS		186	0	0	93	251	1102	271	130	96	13	18	9	4	89	15	189	16	3	15	16	.484	0	15	3.44

Bill Selby

Bats: Left Throws: Right Pos: SS   **Ht: 5'9" Wt: 190 Born: 06/11/70 Age: 25**

						BATTING										BASERUNNING				PERCENTAGES		
Year Team	Lg	G	AB	H	2B	3B	HR	TB	R	RBI	TBB	IBB	SO	HBP	SH	SF	SB	CS	SB%	GDP	Avg	OBP	SLG
1992 Elmira	A	73	275	72	16	1	10	120	38	41	31	6	53	2	2	2	4	4	.50	3	.262	.339	.436
1993 Lynchburg	A	113	394	99	22	1	7	144	57	38	24	2	66	3	2	7	1	2	.33	6	.251	.294	.365
1994 Lynchburg	A	97	352	109	20	2	19	190	58	69	28	0	62	5	2	2	3	1	.75	7	.310	.367	.540
New Britain	AA	35	107	28	5	0	1	36	15	18	15	0	16	0	0	6	0	1	.00	2	.262	.336	.336
3 Min. YEARS		318	1128	308	63	4	37	490	168	166	98	8	197	10	6	17	8	8	.50	18	.273	.332	.434

Rick Sellers

Bats: Right Throws: Right Pos: C   **Ht: 6'0" Wt: 210 Born: 02/22/67 Age: 28**

						BATTING										BASERUNNING				PERCENTAGES		
Year Team	Lg	G	AB	H	2B	3B	HR	TB	R	RBI	TBB	IBB	SO	HBP	SH	SF	SB	CS	SB%	GDP	Avg	OBP	SLG
1989 Niagara Fls	A	29	71	18	3	1	2	29	17	6	17	0	22	0	2	0	3	0	1.00	0	.254	.398	.408
1990 Fayetteville	A	130	430	100	13	4	7	142	48	57	61	2	102	2	1	8	5	3	.63	9	.233	.325	.330
1991 Lakeland	A	71	244	67	8	2	8	103	33	32	26	0	63	3	0	2	3	3	.50	3	.275	.349	.422
1992 London	AA	103	329	88	17	1	9	134	38	51	36	0	67	2	2	4	2	0	1.00	7	.267	.340	.407
1993 London	AA	72	239	63	11	0	6	92	31	31	45	2	55	0	0	0	5	3	.63	11	.264	.380	.385
Toledo	AAA	18	46	13	4	1	2	25	6	7	3	0	8	1	0	0	0	1	.00	1	.283	.340	.543
1994 Indianapols	AAA	58	180	47	13	0	1	63	23	18	25	1	41	0	1	2	0	1	.00	4	.261	.348	.350
6 Min. YEARS		481	1539	396	69	9	35	588	196	202	213	5	358	8	6	16	18	11	.62	35	.257	.347	.382

Jamie Sepeda

Pitches: Right Bats: Right Pos: P   **Ht: 6'2" Wt: 200 Born: 12/08/70 Age: 24**

		HOW MUCH HE PITCHED						WHAT HE GAVE UP										THE RESULTS					
Year Team	Lg	G	GS	CG	GF	IP	BFP	H	R	ER	HR	SH	SF	HB	TBB	IBB	SO	WP	Bk	W	L	Pct.	ShO	Sv	ERA
1992 Batavia	A	5	5	0	0	32.1	126	22	7	4	0	1	0	1	9	0	31	0	4	0	0	.000	0	0	1.11
Clearwater	A	6	6	0	0	35	145	33	14	14	0	3	0	1	12	0	27	1	0	2	3	.400	0	0	3.60
1993 Clearwater	A	26	26	2	0	160	694	165	81	64	8	5	7	5	63	3	97	7	5	9	9	.500	2	0	3.60
1994 Clearwater	A	5	5	1	0	32.1	133	32	13	11	2	0	0	0	6	0	20	1	0	2	1	.667	1	0	3.06
Reading	AA	29	11	0	3	97.1	448	108	67	54	10	9	3	1	55	3	61	6	2	4	7	.364	0	0	4.99
3 Min. YEARS		71	53	3	3	357	1546	360	182	147	20	18	10	8	145	6	236	15	11	17	20	.459	3	0	3.71

Basil Shabazz

Bats: Right Throws: Right Pos: OF   **Ht: 6'0" Wt: 190 Born: 01/31/72 Age: 23**

						BATTING										BASERUNNING				PERCENTAGES		
Year Team	Lg	G	AB	H	2B	3B	HR	TB	R	RBI	TBB	IBB	SO	HBP	SH	SF	SB	CS	SB%	GDP	Avg	OBP	SLG
1991 Johnson Cty	R	40	117	24	3	0	0	27	18	11	16	0	38	2	2	1	4	7	.36	2	.205	.309	.231
1992 Johnson Cty	R	56	223	51	7	2	3	71	33	20	28	1	75	0	1	2	43	11	.80	1	.229	.312	.318
1993 Springfield	A	64	239	71	12	2	4	99	44	18	29	2	66	2	2	0	29	16	.64	1	.297	.378	.414
1994 St. Pete	A	80	308	72	8	2	0	84	50	27	50	1	99	3	4	3	44	18	.71	3	.234	.346	.273
Arkansas	AA	45	171	30	5	1	3	46	18	10	15	1	60	0	0	0	13	6	.68	8	.175	.242	.269
4 Min. YEARS		285	1058	248	35	7	10	327	163	86	138	5	338	7	9	3	133	58	.70	15	.234	.326	.309

Mike Sharperson

Bats: Right Throws: Right Pos: 3B-2B   **Ht: 6'3" Wt: 205 Born: 10/04/61 Age: 33**

						BATTING										BASERUNNING				PERCENTAGES		
Year Team	Lg	G	AB	H	2B	3B	HR	TB	R	RBI	TBB	IBB	SO	HBP	SH	SF	SB	CS	SB%	GDP	Avg	OBP	SLG
1984 Knoxville	AA	140	542	165	25	7	4	216	86	48	48	2	66	1	4	1	20	13	.61	10	.304	.361	.399
1985 Syracuse	AAA	134	536	155	19	7	1	191	86	59	71	2	75	2	3	4	14	15	.48	5	.289	.372	.356
1986 Syracuse	AAA	133	519	150	18	9	4	198	86	45	69	1	67	7	4	1	17	13	.57	15	.289	.379	.382
1987 Syracuse	AAA	88	338	101	21	5	5	147	67	29	40	0	41	1	2	1	14	10	.58	5	.299	.374	.435
1988 Albuquerque	AAA	56	210	67	10	2	0	81	55	30	31	0	25	1	1	1	19	6	.76	7	.319	.407	.386
1989 Albuquerque	AAA	98	359	111	15	7	3	149	81	48	66	2	46	2	4	3	17	12	.59	9	.309	.416	.415
1994 Pawtucket	AAA	37	131	39	10	0	0	49	16	13	21	1	17	0	0	2	5	3	.63	3	.298	.390	.374
Iowa	AAA	31	90	25	3	2	5	47	16	16	9	0	14	2	0	3	3	2	.60	1	.278	.346	.522
1987 Toronto	AL	32	96	20	4	1	0	26	4	9	7	0	15	1	1	0	2	1	.67	2	.208	.269	.271
Los Angeles	NL	10	33	9	2	0	0	11	7	1	4	1	5	0	0	0	0	0	.00	1	.273	.351	.333
1988 Los Angeles	NL	46	59	16	1	0	0	17	8	4	1	0	12	1	2	1	0	1	.00	1	.271	.290	.288
1989 Los Angeles	NL	27	28	7	3	0	0	10	2	5	4	1	7	0	1	1	0	1	.00	1	.250	.333	.357
1990 Los Angeles	NL	129	357	106	14	2	3	133	42	36	46	6	39	1	8	3	15	6	.71	5	.297	.376	.373
1991 Los Angeles	NL	105	216	60	11	2	2	81	24	20	25	0	24	1	10	0	1	3	.25	2	.278	.355	.375
1992 Los Angeles	NL	128	317	95	21	0	3	125	48	36	47	1	33	0	5	3	2	2	.50	9	.300	.387	.394
1993 Los Angeles	NL	73	90	23	4	0	2	33	13	10	5	0	17	1	1	0	2	0	1.00	3	.256	.299	.367
7 Min. YEARS		717	2725	813	121	39	22	1078	493	285	355	7	351	16	18	16	109	74	.60	55	.298	.380	.396
7 Maj. YEARS		550	1196	336	60	5	10	436	148	121	139	9	152	5	27	9	22	14	.61	23	.281	.356	.365

Jon Shave

Bats: Right Throws: Right Pos: SS Ht: 6' 0" Wt: 180 Born: 11/04/67 Age: 27

							BATTING										BASERUNNING				PERCENTAGES		
Year	Team	Lg	G	AB	H	2B	3B	HR	TB	R	RBI	TBB	IBB	SO	HBP	SH	SF	SB	CS	SB%	GDP	Avg	OBP	SLG
1990	Butte	R	64	250	88	9	3	2	109	41	42	25	0	27	3	2	4	21	7	.75	8	.352	.411	.436
1991	Gastonia	A	55	213	62	11	0	2	79	29	24	20	0	26	1	3	0	11	9	.55	3	.291	.355	.371
	Charlotte	A	56	189	43	4	1	1	52	17	20	18	1	30	5	2	4	7	7	.50	3	.228	.306	.275
1992	Tulsa	AA	118	453	130	23	5	2	169	57	36	37	1	59	4	7	5	6	7	.46	10	.287	.343	.373
1993	Okla City	AAA	100	399	105	17	3	4	140	58	41	20	0	60	2	9	1	4	3	.57	12	.263	.301	.351
1994	Okla. City	AAA	95	332	73	15	2	1	95	29	31	14	1	61	5	12	5	6	2	.75	6	.220	.258	.286
1993	Texas	AL	17	47	15	2	0	0	17	3	7	0	0	8	0	0	3	1	3	.25	0	.319	.306	.362
	5 Min. YEARS		488	1836	501	79	14	12	644	231	194	134	3	263	20	35	19	55	35	.61	42	.273	.326	.351

Curtis Shaw

Pitches: Left Bats: Left Pos: P Ht: 6'2" Wt: 190 Born: 08/16/69 Age: 25

			HOW MUCH HE PITCHED						WHAT HE GAVE UP									THE RESULTS					
Year	Team	Lg	G	GS	CG	GF	IP	BFP	H	R	ER	HR	SH	SF	HB	TBB	IBB	SO	WP	Bk	W	L	Pct.	ShO	Sv	ERA
1990	Sou Oregon	A	17	9	0	3	66.1	274	54	28	26	4	1	0	3	30	0	74	5	1	4	6	.400	0	0	3.53
1991	Madison	A	20	20	1	0	100.1	457	82	45	29	1	1	1	6	79	1	87	11	0	7	5	.583	0	0	2.60
1992	Modesto	A	27	27	2	0	177.1	749	146	71	60	5	7	7	6	98	0	154	12	1	13	4	.765	0	0	3.05
1993	Huntsville	AA	28	28	2	0	151.2	676	141	98	83	8	2	3	14	89	2	132	19	4	6	16	.273	1	0	4.93
1994	Huntsville	AA	7	7	0	0	42	181	39	22	21	1	4	1	1	20	0	33	3	0	2	1	.667	0	0	4.50
	Tacoma	AAA	32	8	0	7	82	396	98	69	63	10	5	6	7	61	0	46	11	2	2	6	.250	0	0	6.91
	5 Min. YEARS		131	99	5	10	619.2	2733	560	333	282	29	20	18	37	377	3	526	61	8	34	38	.472	1	0	4.10

John Shea

Pitches: Left Bats: Right Pos: P Ht: 6'6" Wt: 210 Born: 06/23/66 Age: 29

			HOW MUCH HE PITCHED						WHAT HE GAVE UP									THE RESULTS					
Year	Team	Lg	G	GS	CG	GF	IP	BFP	H	R	ER	HR	SH	SF	HB	TBB	IBB	SO	WP	Bk	W	L	Pct.	ShO	Sv	ERA
1986	St.Cathmes	A	14	2	0	5	49	218	44	24	20	2	1	0	0	29	0	59	3	0	3	1	.750	0	0	3.67
1987	Myrtle Bch	A	26	23	1	1	140	604	147	67	54	13	3	3	5	42	1	92	2	3	11	5	.688	1	0	3.47
1988	Knoxville	AA	13	0	0	5	18.1	92	23	14	11	1	2	2	1	12	0	14	3	2	1	3	.250	0	1	5.40
	Dunedin	A	24	18	1	2	122.2	498	115	43	30	4	8	1	1	25	0	83	5	15	4	6	.400	1	2	2.20
1989	Knoxville	AA	31	29	3	1	190.1	803	183	79	57	14	6	2	6	57	1	96	4	6	9	12	.429	1	0	2.70
1990	Syracuse	AAA	40	0	0	26	81.2	363	83	45	33	9	3	1	4	40	4	58	5	2	8	5	.615	0	3	3.64
1991	Syracuse	AAA	35	24	3	5	172	767	198	104	87	15	4	11	8	78	2	76	4	3	12	10	.545	0	2	4.55
1992	Syracuse	AAA	25	21	1	2	118	546	151	92	81	8	3	6	5	49	1	50	8	1	8	8	.500	1	0	6.18
1993	New Britain	AA	48	0	0	12	56.2	241	48	27	23	2	3	1	2	22	3	62	5	1	4	2	.667	0	1	3.65
	Pawtucket	AAA	12	3	0	1	36	170	51	31	28	6	1	2	0	19	0	20	1	0	2	2	.500	0	0	7.00
1994	El Paso	AA	40	0	0	9	53.1	233	52	17	14	0	0	2	1	25	4	50	5	0	5	2	.714	0	3	2.36
	9 Min. YEARS		308	120	9	69	1038	4535	1095	543	438	74	34	31	33	398	16	660	45	33	67	56	.545	3	11	3.80

Andy Sheets

Bats: Right Throws: Right Pos: SS Ht: 6'2" Wt: 180 Born: 11/19/71 Age: 23

							BATTING										BASERUNNING				PERCENTAGES		
Year	Team	Lg	G	AB	H	2B	3B	HR	TB	R	RBI	TBB	IBB	SO	HBP	SH	SF	SB	CS	SB%	GDP	Avg	OBP	SLG
1993	Riverside	A	52	176	34	9	1	1	48	23	12	17	1	51	0	6	4	2	2	.50	4	.193	.259	.273
	Appleton	A	69	259	68	10	4	1	89	32	25	20	1	59	3	4	2	7	7	.50	3	.263	.320	.344
1994	Riverside	A	31	100	27	5	1	2	40	17	10	16	0	22	0	1	0	6	1	.86	1	.270	.371	.400
	Calgary	AAA	26	93	32	8	1	2	48	22	16	11	0	20	1	0	1	1	1	.50	7	.344	.415	.516
	Jacksonville	AA	70	232	51	12	0	0	63	26	17	20	0	54	2	6	1	3	5	.38	4	.220	.286	.272
	2 Min. YEARS		248	860	212	44	7	6	288	120	80	84	2	206	6	17	8	19	16	.54	19	.247	.315	.335

Chris Sheff

Bats: Right Throws: Right Pos: OF Ht: 6'3" Wt: 210 Born: 02/04/71 Age: 24

							BATTING										BASERUNNING				PERCENTAGES		
Year	Team	Lg	G	AB	H	2B	3B	HR	TB	R	RBI	TBB	IBB	SO	HBP	SH	SF	SB	CS	SB%	GDP	Avg	OBP	SLG
1992	Erie	A	57	193	46	8	2	3	67	29	16	32	1	47	1	1	1	15	2	.88	5	.238	.348	.347
1993	Kane County	A	129	456	124	22	5	5	171	79	50	58	2	100	2	3	5	33	10	.77	11	.272	.353	.375
1994	Brevard Cty	A	32	118	44	8	3	1	61	21	19	17	0	23	0	0	1	7	2	.78	2	.373	.449	.517
	Portland	AA	106	395	101	19	4	3	137	50	30	31	0	76	0	3	2	18	4	.82	13	.256	.308	.347
	3 Min. YEARS		324	1162	315	57	11	14	436	179	115	138	3	246	3	7	9	73	18	.80	34	.271	.348	.375

Scott Sheldon

Bats: Right Throws: Right Pos: SS Ht: 6'3" Wt: 185 Born: 11/28/68 Age: 26

							BATTING										BASERUNNING				PERCENTAGES		
Year	Team	Lg	G	AB	H	2B	3B	HR	TB	R	RBI	TBB	IBB	SO	HBP	SH	SF	SB	CS	SB%	GDP	Avg	OBP	SLG
1991	Sou Oregon	A	65	229	58	10	3	0	74	34	24	23	0	44	2	3	1	9	5	.64	5	.253	.325	.323
1992	Madison	A	74	279	76	16	0	6	110	41	24	32	1	78	1	3	4	5	4	.56	2	.272	.345	.394
1993	Madison	A	131	428	91	22	1	8	139	67	67	49	3	121	8	3	8	8	7	.53	8	.213	.300	.325
1994	Huntsville	AA	91	268	62	10	1	0	74	31	28	28	1	69	7	7	3	7	1	.88	4	.231	.317	.276
	4 Min. YEARS		361	1204	287	58	5	14	397	173	143	132	5	312	18	16	16	29	17	.63	19	.238	.319	.330

Keith Shepherd

Pitches: Right Bats: Right Pos: P Ht: 6' 2" Wt: 197 Born: 01/21/68 Age: 27

Year	Team	Lg	HOW MUCH HE PITCHED						WHAT HE GAVE UP										THE RESULTS				
			G	GS	CG	GF	IP	BFP	H	R	ER	HR	SH	SF	HB	TBB	IBB	SO	WP	Bk	W	L	Pct.	ShO	Sv	ERA
1990	Reno	A	5	5	0	0	25	120	22	25	15	1	3	1	2	18	0	16	6	1	1	4	.200	0	0	5.40
	Watertown	A	24	0	0	19	54.1	235	41	22	15	1	4	0	4	29	1	55	9	1	3	3	.500	0	3	2.48
1991	South Bend	A	31	0	0	21	35.1	140	17	4	2	0	3	0	1	19	2	38	5	1	1	2	.333	0	10	0.51
	Sarasota	A	18	0	0	8	39.2	166	33	16	12	0	3	1	2	20	0	24	1	0	1	1	.500	0	2	2.72
1992	Birmingham	AA	40	0	0	30	71.1	282	50	19	17	1	4	1	1	20	2	64	7	1	3	3	.500	0	7	2.14
	Reading	AA	4	3	0	1	22.2	87	17	7	7	1	2	0	1	4	1	9	0	0	0	1	.000	0	0	2.78
1993	Colo Sprngs	AAA	37	1	0	20	67.2	339	90	61	51	2	2	4	4	44	2	57	15	0	3	6	.333	0	8	6.78
1994	Colo. Sprng	AAA	18	0	0	6	29.2	148	40	33	30	4	0	0	3	22	0	21	8	0	0	1	.000	0	1	9.10
	Pawtucket	AAA	6	4	0	2	20.2	101	37	22	21	3	0	0	0	9	0	8	5	0	0	3	.000	0	0	9.15
	Sarasota	A	20	0	0	16	21	87	12	7	7	1	2	1	1	12	0	21	0	1	0	0	.000	0	7	3.00
1992	Philadelphia	NL	12	0	0	6	22	91	19	10	8	0	4	3	0	6	1	10	1	0	1	1	.500	0	2	3.27
1993	Colorado	NL	14	1	0	3	19.1	85	26	16	15	4	1	1	1	4	0	7	1	0	1	3	.250	0	1	6.98
	5 Min. YEARS		203	13	0	123	387.1	1705	359	216	177	14	23	8	19	197	8	313	56	5	12	24	.333	0	38	4.11
	2 Maj. YEARS		26	1	0	9	41.1	176	45	26	23	4	5	4	1	10	1	17	2	0	2	4	.333	0	3	5.01

Don Sheppard

Bats: Right Throws: Right Pos: OF Ht: 6'2" Wt: 180 Born: 05/02/71 Age: 24

Year	Team	Lg	BATTING													BASERUNNING				PERCENTAGES		
			G	AB	H	2B	3B	HR	TB	R	RBI	TBB	IBB	SO	HBP	SH	SF	SB	CS	SB%	GDP	Avg	OBP	SLG
1989	White Sox	R	26	82	15	4	0	0	19	11	4	7	0	28	0	1	0	4	4	.50	1	.183	.247	.232
1990	White Sox	R	46	151	27	6	1	0	35	15	6	12	0	39	0	1	0	12	5	.71	2	.179	.239	.232
1991	South Bend	A	83	178	37	5	2	1	49	24	11	21	0	57	1	1	1	7	2	.78	2	.208	.294	.275
1992	Salinas	A	114	377	96	17	4	2	127	50	43	40	0	101	0	1	7	3	27	14	.66	10	.255	.324	.337
1993	Dunedin	A	39	116	36	4	2	0	44	12	10	17	1	26	0	2	0	6	4	.60	2	.310	.398	.379
	Knoxville	AA	72	249	70	11	1	2	89	32	27	14	0	70	1	2	2	5	5	.50	3	.281	.320	.357
1994	Syracuse	AAA	26	57	7	0	0	0	7	5	2	12	0	28	0	1	2	4	2	.67	0	.123	.268	.123
	Knoxville	AA	39	82	14	3	1	0	19	7	3	12	0	29	0	3	0	2	3	.40	0	.171	.277	.232
	6 Min. YEARS		445	1292	302	50	11	5	389	156	106	135	1	378	2	18	8	67	39	.63	20	.234	.305	.301

Darrell Sherman

Bats: Left Throws: Left Pos: OF Ht: 5' 9" Wt: 160 Born: 12/04/67 Age: 27

Year	Team	Lg	BATTING													BASERUNNING				PERCENTAGES		
			G	AB	H	2B	3B	HR	TB	R	RBI	TBB	IBB	SO	HBP	SH	SF	SB	CS	SB%	GDP	Avg	OBP	SLG
1989	Spokane	A	70	258	82	13	1	0	97	70	29	58	2	29	1	3	2	58	7	.89	1	.318	.459	.376
1990	Riverside	A	131	483	140	10	4	0	158	99	35	89	2	51	12	6	2	74	26	.74	7	.290	.411	.327
	Las Vegas	AAA	4	12	0	0	0	0	0	1	1	1	0	2	0	0	0	1	0	1.00	0	.000	.077	.000
1991	Wichita	AA	131	502	148	17	3	3	180	93	48	74	1	28	9	2	6	43	21	.67	7	.295	.391	.359
1992	Wichita	AA	64	220	73	11	2	6	106	60	25	40	2	25	9	2	2	26	7	.79	6	.332	.450	.482
	Las Vegas	AAA	71	269	77	8	1	3	96	48	22	42	0	41	3	1	1	26	5	.84	3	.286	.387	.357
1993	Las Vegas	AAA	82	272	72	8	2	0	84	52	11	38	0	27	2	7	1	20	10	.67	1	.265	.358	.309
1994	Colo. Sprng	AAA	28	49	11	0	0	0	11	5	5	8	2	8	2	0	0	1	3	.25	3	.224	.356	.224
1993	San Diego	NL	37	63	14	1	0	0	15	8	2	6	0	8	3	1	1	2	1	.67	0	.222	.315	.238
	6 Min. YEARS		581	2065	603	67	13	12	732	426	176	350	9	211	50	20	16	249	79	.76	28	.292	.404	.354

Tommy Shields

Bats: Right Throws: Right Pos: SS Ht: 6' 0" Wt: 185 Born: 08/14/64 Age: 30

Year	Team	Lg	BATTING													BASERUNNING				PERCENTAGES		
			G	AB	H	2B	3B	HR	TB	R	RBI	TBB	IBB	SO	HBP	SH	SF	SB	CS	SB%	GDP	Avg	OBP	SLG
1986	Watertown	A	43	153	44	6	1	4	64	25	25	17	0	36	7	1	3	15	6	.71	3	.288	.378	.418
	Pr William	A	30	112	31	7	1	1	43	17	12	9	0	16	5	1	1	4	1	.80	5	.277	.354	.384
1988	Salem	A	45	156	49	5	0	3	63	20	25	16	0	24	6	1	2	10	3	.77	5	.314	.394	.404
	Harrisburg	AA	57	198	61	4	2	2	75	30	21	14	1	25	3	2	1	7	3	.70	5	.308	.361	.379
1989	Harrisburg	AA	123	417	120	13	4	5	156	66	47	25	3	62	9	2	3	17	5	.77	11	.288	.339	.374
1990	Buffalo	AAA	123	380	94	20	3	2	126	42	30	21	1	72	2	6	3	12	6	.67	11	.247	.288	.332
1991	Rochester	AAA	116	412	119	18	3	6	161	69	52	32	1	73	11	5	3	16	8	.67	11	.289	.354	.391
1992	Rochester	AAA	121	431	130	23	3	10	189	58	59	30	1	71	6	4	4	13	7	.65	5	.302	.352	.439
1993	Iowa	AAA	84	314	90	16	1	9	135	48	48	26	1	46	6	2	2	10	6	.63	9	.287	.351	.430
1994	Iowa	AAA	111	327	86	16	5	5	127	47	33	43	0	60	18	4	4	9	11	.45	9	.263	.375	.388
1992	Baltimore	AL	2	0	0	0	0	0	0	0	0	0	0	0	0	0	0	0	0	.00	0	.000	.000	.000
1993	Chicago	NL	20	34	6	1	0	0	7	4	1	2	0	10	0	0	1	0	0	.00	1	.176	.222	.206
	8 Min. YEARS		853	2900	824	128	23	47	1139	422	352	233	8	486	73	28	26	113	56	.67	74	.284	.350	.393
	2 Maj. YEARS		22	34	6	1	0	0	7	4	1	2	0	10	0	0	1	0	0	.00	1	.176	.222	.206

Steve Shifflett

Pitches: Right Bats: Right Pos: P Ht: 6' 1" Wt: 210 Born: 01/05/66 Age: 29

Year	Team	Lg	HOW MUCH HE PITCHED						WHAT HE GAVE UP										THE RESULTS				
			G	GS	CG	GF	IP	BFP	H	R	ER	HR	SH	SF	HB	TBB	IBB	SO	WP	Bk	W	L	Pct.	ShO	Sv	ERA
1989	Appleton	A	18	2	0	5	39	171	34	25	18	1	1	1	2	19	2	13	8	3	3	3	.500	0	0	4.15

235

Year	Team	Lg	G	GS	CG	GF	IP	BFP	H	R	ER	HR	SH	SF	HB	TBB	IBB	SO	WP	Bk	W	L	Pct.	ShO	Sv	ERA
1990	Appleton	A	57	0	0	34	82.2	330	67	35	27	3	6	2	3	28	4	40	1	1	6	5	.545	0	10	2.94
1991	Memphis	AA	59	1	0	35	113	460	105	34	27	4	8	3	5	22	6	78	1	3	11	5	.688	0	9	2.15
1992	Omaha	AAA	32	0	0	29	43.2	165	30	8	8	0	4	3	0	15	1	19	0	2	3	2	.600	0	14	1.65
1993	Omaha	AAA	43	0	0	27	56	257	78	34	31	7	4	5	0	15	3	31	2	0	3	3	.500	0	5	4.98
1994	Omaha	AAA	45	1	0	16	92.1	401	99	42	38	7	5	2	6	24	3	39	1	0	3	5	.375	0	2	3.70
1992	Kansas City	AL	34	0	0	15	52	221	55	15	15	6	4	1	2	17	6	25	2	1	1	4	.200	0	2	2.60
	6 Min. YEARS		254	4	0	146	426.2	1784	413	178	149	22	28	16	16	123	19	220	13	9	29	23	.558	0	40	3.14

Jeff Shireman

Bats: Both Throws: Right Pos: SS Ht: 5'8" Wt: 165 Born: 03/20/66 Age: 29

						BATTING											BASERUNNING				PERCENTAGES		
Year	Team	Lg	G	AB	H	2B	3B	HR	TB	R	RBI	TBB	IBB	SO	HBP	SH	SF	SB	CS	SB%	GDP	Avg	OBP	SLG
1988	Johnson Cty	R	52	189	64	8	1	2	80	41	19	23	1	15	0	1	1	4	2	.67	1	.339	.408	.423
1989	Springfield	A	121	379	94	7	0	1	104	39	37	55	1	31	1	6	8	8	4	.67	10	.248	.339	.274
1990	St. Pete	A	123	416	106	10	1	0	118	61	37	87	0	34	1	0	4	11	13	.46	12	.255	.382	.284
1991	Arkansas	AA	117	368	89	12	1	1	106	49	28	45	0	32	0	4	3	2	4	.33	20	.242	.322	.288
1992	Louisville	AAA	66	186	37	6	0	0	43	24	11	20	0	18	0	3	1	0	0	.00	6	.199	.275	.231
1993	Arkansas	AA	107	333	95	20	1	2	121	32	32	25	3	43	1	5	4	3	7	.30	7	.285	.333	.363
1994	Arkansas	AA	69	150	27	7	0	0	34	12	13	14	0	15	0	3	0	0	2	.00	4	.180	.250	.227
	7 Min. YEARS		655	2021	512	70	3	6	606	252	177	269	5	188	3	22	21	28	32	.47	60	.253	.339	.300

Scott Shockey

Bats: Left Throws: Left Pos: 1B Ht: 6'2" Wt: 230 Born: 07/04/67 Age: 27

						BATTING											BASERUNNING				PERCENTAGES		
Year	Team	Lg	G	AB	H	2B	3B	HR	TB	R	RBI	TBB	IBB	SO	HBP	SH	SF	SB	CS	SB%	GDP	Avg	OBP	SLG
1989	Sou Oregon	A	32	112	38	5	0	3	52	21	26	18	0	19	2	1	2	2	4	.33	1	.339	.433	.464
1990	Madison	A	71	253	66	16	2	10	116	45	43	26	3	60	5	2	4	2	5	.29	1	.261	.337	.458
	Modesto	A	51	200	65	13	0	9	105	32	50	13	2	48	2	0	6	1	0	1.00	6	.325	.362	.525
	Tacoma	AAA	13	43	12	4	1	0	18	1	7	0	0	7	0	1	0	0	0	.00	3	.279	.279	.419
1991	Huntsville	AA	70	229	55	9	1	4	78	26	31	40	2	54	4	2	2	1	1	.50	6	.240	.360	.341
1993	Tacoma	AAA	21	71	18	5	0	1	26	2	12	8	0	17	1	0	0	1	0	1.00	11	.254	.338	.366
	Modesto	A	97	350	106	20	1	20	188	62	87	64	3	70	6	2	3	1	1	.50	11	.303	.416	.537
1994	Huntsville	AA	28	100	21	6	0	1	30	10	12	12	1	19	1	1	0	2	0	1.00	3	.210	.298	.300
	5 Min. YEARS		383	1358	381	78	5	48	613	199	268	181	11	294	21	8	18	10	11	.48	28	.281	.369	.451

Steve Shoemaker

Pitches: Right Bats: Right Pos: P Ht: 6'3" Wt: 195 Born: 02/24/70 Age: 25

			HOW MUCH HE PITCHED						WHAT HE GAVE UP										THE RESULTS					
Year	Team	Lg	G	GS	CG	GF	IP	BFP	H	R	ER	HR	SH	SF	HB	TBB	IBB	SO	WP	Bk	W	L	Pct.	ShO	Sv	ERA
1991	Athletics	R	8	5	0	2	29.2	127	31	16	13	1	0	0	0	15	0	26	2	4	2	1	.667	0	0	3.94
1992	Madison	A	22	11	2	3	83.1	356	98	56	47	5	4	3	2	18	0	56	5	2	2	5	.286	0	1	5.08
	Modesto	A	10	9	1	0	61.1	256	59	25	21	6	3	2	1	15	0	50	0	0	4	2	.667	0	0	3.08
1993	San Berndno	A	24	23	1	0	126.2	574	146	92	76	16	1	7	3	56	1	116	3	0	9	6	.600	1	0	5.40
1994	Huntsville	AA	36	2	0	11	62.2	273	65	30	23	2	4	1	2	21	3	47	3	0	2	2	.500	0	2	3.30
	4 Min. YEARS		100	50	4	16	363.2	1586	399	219	180	30	11	13	8	125	4	295	13	6	19	16	.543	1	3	4.45

Brian Shouse

Pitches: Left Bats: Left Pos: P Ht: 5'11" Wt: 175 Born: 09/26/68 Age: 26

			HOW MUCH HE PITCHED						WHAT HE GAVE UP										THE RESULTS					
Year	Team	Lg	G	GS	CG	GF	IP	BFP	H	R	ER	HR	SH	SF	HB	TBB	IBB	SO	WP	Bk	W	L	Pct.	ShO	Sv	ERA
1990	Welland	A	17	1	0	7	39.2	177	50	27	23	2	3	2	3	7	0	39	1	2	4	3	.571	0	2	5.22
1991	Augusta	A	26	0	0	25	31	124	22	13	11	1	1	1	3	9	1	32	5	0	2	3	.400	0	8	3.19
	Salem	A	17	0	0	9	33.2	147	35	12	11	2	2	0	0	15	2	25	1	0	2	1	.667	0	3	2.94
1992	Carolina	AA	59	0	0	33	77.1	323	71	31	21	3	8	2	2	28	4	79	4	1	5	6	.455	0	4	2.44
1993	Buffalo	AAA	48	0	0	14	51.2	218	54	24	22	7	0	3	2	17	2	25	1	0	1	0	1.000	0	0	3.83
1994	Buffalo	AAA	43	0	0	20	52	212	44	22	21	6	4	2	1	15	4	31	0	0	3	4	.429	0	0	3.63
1993	Pittsburgh	NL	6	0	0	1	4	22	7	4	4	1	0	1	0	2	0	3	1	0	0	0	.000	0	0	9.00
	5 Min. YEARS		210	1	0	108	285.1	1201	276	129	109	21	18	10	11	91	13	231	12	3	17	17	.500	0	19	3.44

Joe Siddall

Bats: Left Throws: Right Pos: C Ht: 6'1" Wt: 197 Born: 10/25/67 Age: 27

						BATTING											BASERUNNING				PERCENTAGES		
Year	Team	Lg	G	AB	H	2B	3B	HR	TB	R	RBI	TBB	IBB	SO	HBP	SH	SF	SB	CS	SB%	GDP	Avg	OBP	SLG
1988	Jamestown	A	53	178	38	5	3	1	52	18	16	14	1	29	1	4	2	5	4	.56	5	.213	.272	.292
1989	Rockford	A	98	313	74	15	2	4	105	36	38	26	2	56	6	5	4	8	5	.62	3	.236	.304	.335
1990	Wst Plm Bch	A	106	348	78	12	1	0	92	29	32	20	0	55	1	10	2	6	7	.46	7	.224	.267	.264
1991	Harrisburg	AA	76	235	54	6	1	1	65	28	23	23	2	53	1	2	3	8	3	.73	7	.230	.298	.277
1992	Harrisburg	AA	95	288	68	12	0	2	86	26	27	29	1	55	3	1	3	4	4	.50	7	.236	.310	.299
1993	Ottawa	AAA	48	136	29	6	0	1	38	14	16	19	5	33	0	3	2	2	2	.50	6	.213	.306	.279
1994	Ottawa	AAA	38	110	19	2	1	3	32	9	13	10	2	21	2	7	2	1	1	.50	3	.173	.250	.291
1993	Montreal	NL	19	20	2	1	0	0	3	0	1	1	1	5	0	0	0	0	0	.00	1	.100	.143	.150
	7 Min. YEARS		514	1608	360	58	8	12	470	160	165	141	13	302	14	32	18	34	26	.57	36	.224	.289	.292

236

Joe Silva

Ht: 6'6" Wt: 180 Born: 12/19/73 Age: 21

Year Team	Lg	G	GS	CG	GF	IP	BFP	H	R	ER	HR	SH	SF	HB	TBB	IBB	SO	WP	Bk	W	L	Pct.	ShO	Sv	ERA
1992 Blue Jays	R	12	12	0	0	59.1	231	42	23	15	1	0	1	2	18	0	78	1	2	6	4	.600	0	0	2.28
1993 Hagerstown	A	24	24	0	0	142.2	581	103	50	40	6	0	4	4	62	0	161	9	1	12	5	.706	0	0	2.52
1994 Dunedin	A	8	7	0	0	43	188	41	32	18	4	2	6	0	24	0	41	5	0	0	2	.000	0	0	3.77
Knoxville	AA	16	16	1	0	91.1	381	89	47	42	9	2	2	3	31	0	71	4	0	4	8	.333	1	0	4.14
3 Min. YEARS		60	59	1	0	336.1	1381	275	152	115	20	4	13	9	135	0	351	19	3	22	19	.537	1	0	3.08

Bill Simas

Ht: 6'3" Wt: 200 Born: 11/28/71 Age: 23

Year Team	Lg	G	GS	CG	GF	IP	BFP	H	R	ER	HR	SH	SF	HB	TBB	IBB	SO	WP	Bk	W	L	Pct.	ShO	Sv	ERA
1992 Boise	A	14	12	0	1	70.2	320	82	44	31	0	2	4	3	29	2	39	4	1	6	5	.545	0	1	3.95
1993 Cedar Rapds	A	35	6	0	19	80	376	93	60	44	8	5	4	3	36	1	62	4	1	5	8	.385	0	6	4.95
1994 Midland	AA	13	0	0	11	15.1	52	5	1	1	0	0	0	0	2	0	12	0	0	2	0	1.000	0	0	0.59
Lake Elsino	A	37	0	0	27	47	194	44	17	11	2	3	2	3	10	1	34	3	2	5	2	.714	0	13	2.11
3 Min. YEARS		99	18	0	58	213	942	224	122	87	10	10	10	9	77	4	147	11	4	18	15	.545	0	26	3.68

Enoch Simmons

Ht: 6'4" Wt: 215 Born: 09/28/67 Age: 27

Year Team	Lg	G	AB	H	2B	3B	HR	TB	R	RBI	TBB	IBB	SO	HBP	SH	SF	SB	CS	SB%	GDP	Avg	OBP	SLG
1988 Athletics	R	45	150	46	9	3	1	64	42	23	40	0	26	3	2	3	18	2	.90	3	.307	.454	.427
1989 Modesto	A	2	5	0	0	0	0	0	0	0	0	0	2	0	0	0	0	0	.00	0	.000	.000	.000
Sou Oregon	A	69	257	57	9	1	1	71	31	23	32	0	69	6	2	2	10	7	.59	4	.222	.320	.276
1990 Madison	A	117	359	66	10	1	3	87	47	29	47	0	98	4	5	2	17	6	.74	10	.184	.284	.242
1991 Modesto	A	130	443	107	13	3	2	132	81	38	92	2	97	4	2	2	28	15	.65	9	.242	.375	.298
1992 Reno	A	74	246	64	10	2	1	81	46	45	43	1	37	4	1	2	7	7	.50	4	.260	.376	.329
1993 Huntsville	AA	43	140	32	7	0	3	48	24	20	17	0	39	1	0	4	5	2	.71	3	.229	.309	.343
Athletics	R	4	13	7	1	0	1	11	4	3	3	0	2	0	0	0	1	0	1.00	0	.538	.625	.846
Modesto	A	26	86	18	2	0	2	26	12	14	17	0	16	1	0	1	2	2	.50	3	.209	.343	.302
1994 Tacoma	AAA	29	74	16	3	0	2	25	12	6	10	1	22	0	3	0	0	0	.00	1	.216	.310	.338
Huntsville	AA	46	164	41	13	1	0	56	19	14	21	2	30	2	1	0	3	2	.60	6	.250	.342	.341
7 Min. YEARS		585	1937	454	77	11	16	601	318	215	322	6	438	25	16	16	91	43	.68	43	.234	.348	.310

Scott Simmons

Ht: 6'2" Wt: 200 Born: 08/15/69 Age: 25

Year Team	Lg	G	GS	CG	GF	IP	BFP	H	R	ER	HR	SH	SF	HB	TBB	IBB	SO	WP	Bk	W	L	Pct.	ShO	Sv	ERA
1991 Hamilton	A	15	14	0	0	90.1	376	82	34	26	4	0	2	1	25	0	78	1	2	6	4	.600	0	0	2.59
1992 Springfield	A	27	27	2	0	170.1	699	160	63	53	10	9	3	2	39	0	116	10	2	15	7	.682	1	0	2.80
1993 St.Pete	A	13	12	1	1	78.2	326	70	38	30	1	4	4	0	31	0	54	6	1	4	5	.444	0	0	3.43
Arkansas	AA	13	10	0	0	76.2	306	68	26	23	1	2	2	0	18	3	35	4	0	6	3	.667	0	0	2.70
1994 Arkansas	AA	26	26	2	0	162.1	663	148	63	49	4	10	4	3	39	1	115	4	1	7	11	.389	1	0	2.72
4 Min. YEARS		94	89	5	1	578.1	2370	528	224	181	20	25	15	6	152	4	398	25	6	38	30	.559	2	0	2.82

Richie Simon

Ht: 6'2" Wt: 200 Born: 11/29/65 Age: 29

Year Team	Lg	G	GS	CG	GF	IP	BFP	H	R	ER	HR	SH	SF	HB	TBB	IBB	SO	WP	Bk	W	L	Pct.	ShO	Sv	ERA
1986 Auburn	A	15	15	1	0	89.1	374	76	35	29	9	1	2	3	34	0	54	6	0	4	6	.400	0	0	2.92
1987 Osceola	A	5	5	0	0	22.2	99	26	14	12	2	1	0	0	12	0	9	0	1	1	3	.250	0	0	4.76
Auburn	A	16	16	1	0	107.2	461	104	41	31	4	1	0	1	43	1	80	5	0	8	2	.800	1	0	2.59
1988 Asheville	A	23	23	6	0	149	644	144	71	55	11	4	2	5	53	1	100	6	3	9	9	.500	1	0	3.32
Osceola	A	6	6	3	0	41.2	172	38	18	13	3	1	2	0	16	2	19	1	1	2	2	.500	1	0	2.81
1989 Osceola	A	19	19	1	0	121	511	126	60	51	5	3	4	5	33	0	66	5	5	6	8	.429	0	0	3.79
1990 Columbus	AA	49	1	0	12	86.2	379	88	41	32	8	3	3	3	34	2	59	5	2	5	2	.714	0	2	3.32
1991 Jackson	AA	56	0	0	43	70.1	289	55	23	17	3	5	2	3	30	4	54	3	0	4	2	.667	0	20	2.18
1992 Tucson	AAA	9	0	0	6	19.2	94	26	13	11	2	1	1	0	11	2	12	1	0	0	1	.000	0	1	5.03
Jackson	AA	34	1	0	12	48.2	210	40	27	21	8	1	4	6	25	1	30	2	1	3	4	.429	0	4	3.88
1993 Shreveport	AA	52	0	0	50	54	242	56	32	26	2	4	4	4	24	4	38	5	0	2	7	.222	0	26	4.33
1994 Shreveport	AA	26	0	0	10	42	186	45	28	20	3	0	5	0	17	0	33	5	0	2	4	.333	0	1	4.29
9 Min. YEARS		310	86	12	133	852.2	3661	824	403	318	60	25	29	30	332	17	554	44	13	46	50	.479	3	54	3.36

Doug Simons

Ht: 6'0" Wt: 170 Born: 09/15/66 Age: 28

Year Team	Lg	G	GS	CG	GF	IP	BFP	H	R	ER	HR	SH	SF	HB	TBB	IBB	SO	WP	Bk	W	L	Pct.	ShO	Sv	ERA
1988 Visalia	A	17	16	5	1	107.1	467	100	59	47	10	4	3	5	46	0	123	6	1	6	5	.545	2	0	3.94
1989 Visalia	A	14	14	1	0	90.2	372	77	33	15	4	1	4	5	33	1	79	4	1	6	2	.750	0	0	1.49

	Lg	G	GS	CG	GF	IP	BFP	H	R	ER	HR	SH	SF	HB	TBB	IBB	SO	WP	Bk	W	L	Pct.	ShO	Sv	ERA
Orlando	AA	14	14	3	0	87.1	374	83	39	37	7	2	2	2	37	0	58	1	2	7	3	.700	0	0	3.81
1990 Orlando	AA	29	28	5	0	188	765	160	76	53	13	9	4	6	43	2	109	7	1	15	12	.556	0	0	2.54
1992 Indianapols	AAA	32	14	2	6	120	481	114	45	41	7	2	6	2	25	1	66	3	0	11	4	.733	1	0	3.08
1993 Ottawa	AAA	34	13	1	6	115.2	487	134	67	61	13	2	1	2	16	2	75	3	0	7	7	.500	0	0	4.75
1994 Omaha	AAA	17	17	0	0	96.1	405	97	56	49	20	3	0	5	26	0	43	3	1	5	8	.385	0	0	4.58
1991 New York	NL	42	1	0	11	60.2	258	55	40	35	5	9	4	2	19	5	38	3	0	2	3	.400	0	1	5.19
1992 Montreal	NL	7	0	0	2	5.1	35	15	14	14	3	1	1	2	0	6	1	0	0	0		.000	0	1	23.63
6 Min. YEARS		157	116	17	13	805.1	3351	765	375	303	74	23	20	27	226	6	553	27	6	57	41	.582	3	0	3.39
2 Maj. YEARS		49	1	0	13	66	293	70	54	49	8	10	5	3	21	5	44	4	0	2	3	.400	0	1	6.68

Mitch Simons

Bats: Right Throws: Right Pos: 2B **Ht: 5'9" Wt: 170 Born: 12/13/68 Age: 26**

						BATTING									BASERUNNING				PERCENTAGES		
Year Team	Lg	G	AB	H	2B	3B	HR	TB	R	RBI	TBB	IBB	SO	HBP	SH	SF	SB	CS	SB%	GDP	Avg	OBP	SLG
1991 Jamestown	A	41	153	47	12	0	1	62	38	16	39	1	20	0	2	2	23	5	.82	1	.307	.443	.405
Wst Plm Bch	A	15	50	9	2	1	0	13	3	4	5	0	8	0	0	0	1	0	1.00	0	.180	.255	.260
1992 Albany	A	130	481	136	26	5	1	175	57	61	60	0	47	7	2	10	34	12	.74	6	.283	.364	.364
1993 Wst Plm Bch	A	45	156	40	4	1	1	49	24	13	19	0	9	3	1	2	14	8	.64	3	.256	.344	.314
Harrisburg	AA	29	77	18	1	1	0	21	5	5	7	0	14	0	2	1	2	0	1.00	1	.234	.294	.273
1994 Nashville	AA	102	391	124	26	0	3	159	46	48	39	0	38	6	3	5	30	9	.77	6	.317	.383	.407
4 Min. YEARS		362	1308	374	71	8	6	479	173	147	169	1	136	16	10	20	104	34	.75	17	.286	.369	.366

Joel Skinner

Bats: Right Throws: Right Pos: C **Ht: 6'4" Wt: 204 Born: 02/21/61 Age: 34**

						BATTING									BASERUNNING				PERCENTAGES		
Year Team	Lg	G	AB	H	2B	3B	HR	TB	R	RBI	TBB	IBB	SO	HBP	SH	SF	SB	CS	SB%	GDP	Avg	OBP	SLG
1984 Denver	AAA	42	141	40	6	0	10	76	27	27	13	1	31	1	1	4	1	0	1.00	1	.284	.340	.539
1985 Buffalo	AAA	115	390	94	13	0	12	143	47	59	41	0	115	4	0	1	0	0	.00	16	.241	.319	.367
1987 Columbus	AAA	49	178	43	10	2	6	75	19	27	10	0	44	1	1	2	0	1	.00	1	.242	.283	.421
1992 Canton-Akrn	AA	8	20	6	0	0	1	9	2	5	0	0	3	0	0	0	0	0	.00	0	.300	.300	.450
1993 Canton-Akrn	AA	15	46	11	3	0	2	20	6	5	6	0	16	0	1	0	0	0	.00	1	.239	.327	.435
1994 Charlotte	AAA	6	15	4	1	0	0	5	1	2	2	0	4	1	0	0	0	0	.00	1	.267	.389	.333
1983 Chicago	AL	6	11	3	0	0	0	3	2	1	0	0	1	0	0	0	0	0	.00	2	.273	.273	.273
1984 Chicago	AL	43	80	17	2	0	0	19	4	3	7	0	19	0	0	1	1	0	1.00	2	.213	.273	.238
1985 Chicago	AL	22	44	15	4	1	1	24	9	5	5	0	13	0	1	0	0	0	.00	2	.341	.408	.545
1986 Chicago	AL	60	149	30	5	1	4	49	17	20	9	0	43	1	2	1	1	0	1.00	2	.201	.250	.329
New York	AL	54	166	43	4	0	1	50	6	17	7	0	40	0	0	1	0	4	.00	4	.259	.287	.301
1987 New York	AL	64	139	19	4	0	3	32	9	14	8	0	46	1	4	2	0	0	.00	9	.137	.187	.230
1988 New York	AL	88	251	57	15	0	4	84	23	23	14	0	72	0	6	1	0	0	.00	3	.227	.267	.335
1989 Cleveland	AL	79	178	41	10	0	1	54	10	13	9	0	42	1	1	0	1	1	.50	3	.230	.271	.303
1990 Cleveland	AL	49	139	35	4	1	2	47	16	16	7	0	44	0	0	0	0	0	.00	2	.252	.288	.338
1991 Cleveland	AL	99	284	69	14	0	1	86	23	24	14	1	67	1	4	2	0	2	.00	4	.243	.279	.303
6 Min. YEARS		235	790	198	33	2	31	328	102	125	72	1	213	7	3	7	1	1	.50	22	.251	.316	.415
9 Maj. YEARS		564	1441	329	62	3	17	448	119	136	80	1	387	4	18	8	3	7	.30	40	.228	.269	.311

Joe Slusarski

Pitches: Right Bats: Right Pos: P **Ht: 6'4" Wt: 195 Born: 12/19/66 Age: 28**

		HOW MUCH HE PITCHED						WHAT HE GAVE UP										THE RESULTS					
Year Team	Lg	G	GS	CG	GF	IP	BFP	H	R	ER	HR	SH	SF	HB	TBB	IBB	SO	WP	Bk	W	L	Pct.	ShO	Sv	ERA
1989 Modesto	A	27	27	4	0	184	753	155	78	65	15	5	3	8	50	0	160	13	1	13	10	.565	1	0	3.18
1990 Huntsville	AA	17	17	2	0	108.2	471	114	65	54	9	2	9	3	35	0	75	5	0	6	8	.429	0	0	4.47
Tacoma	AAA	9	9	0	0	55.2	241	54	24	21	3	1	3	2	22	0	37	1	1	4	2	.667	0	0	3.40
1991 Tacoma	AAA	7	7	0	0	46.1	182	42	20	14	4	0	0	0	10	0	25	0	2	4	2	.667	0	0	2.72
1992 Tacoma	AAA	11	10	0	0	57.1	249	67	30	24	6	0	5	1	18	1	26	1	0	2	4	.333	0	0	3.77
1993 Tacoma	AAA	24	21	1	0	113.1	501	133	67	60	6	3	7	1	40	1	61	2	0	7	5	.583	1	0	4.76
1994 Tacoma	AAA	7	7	0	0	37.1	167	45	28	25	6	0	3	3	11	0	24	1	0	2	3	.400	0	0	6.03
Reading	AA	5	4	0	0	23.1	97	26	15	12	2	2	0	0	5	0	17	0	1	1	2	.333	0	0	4.63
Scranton-Wb	AAA	10	4	0	3	38	172	50	36	33	8	1	2	3	10	0	29	2	0	2	3	.400	0	0	7.82
1991 Oakland	AL	20	19	1	0	109.1	486	121	69	64	14	0	3	4	52	1	60	4	0	5	7	.417	0	0	5.27
1992 Oakland	AL	15	14	0	1	76	338	85	52	46	15	1	5	6	27	0	38	0	1	5	5	.500	0	0	5.45
1993 Oakland	AL	2	1	0	0	8.2	43	9	5	5	1	2	0	0	11	3	1	0	0	0	0	.000	0	0	5.19
6 Min. YEARS		117	106	7	3	664	2833	685	363	308	59	14	32	21	201	2	454	25	5	41	39	.513	2	0	4.17
3 Maj. YEARS		37	34	1	1	194	867	215	126	115	30	3	8	10	90	4	99	4	1	10	12	.455	0	0	5.34

Mark Small

Pitches: Right Bats: Right Pos: P **Ht: 6'3" Wt: 205 Born: 11/12/67 Age: 27**

		HOW MUCH HE PITCHED						WHAT HE GAVE UP										THE RESULTS					
Year Team	Lg	G	GS	CG	GF	IP	BFP	H	R	ER	HR	SH	SF	HB	TBB	IBB	SO	WP	Bk	W	L	Pct.	ShO	Sv	ERA
1989 Auburn	A	10	3	0	4	19.2	87	17	13	11	3	0	1	1	11	0	23	3	0	0	1	.000	0	2	5.03
1990 Asheville	A	34	0	0	16	52	252	54	36	24	2	4	3	4	37	1	34	9	0	3	4	.429	0	6	4.15
1991 Osceola	A	26	0	0	10	44.2	172	30	10	8	2	1	4	3	19	1	44	2	0	3	0	1.000	0	2	1.61
1992 Osceola	A	22	20	1	2	105	435	97	56	45	8	3	3	0	38	0	69	5	1	5	9	.357	0	0	3.86
1993 Jackson	AA	51	0	0	18	84.2	361	71	34	30	8	3	3	3	41	6	64	8	2	7	2	.778	0	5	3.19

Year Team	Lg	G	GS	CG	GF	IP	BFP	H	R	ER	HR	SH	SF	HB	TBB	IBB	SO	WP	Bk	W	L	Pct.	ShO	Sv	ERA
1994 Jackson	AA	16	0	0	9	21	97	22	16	9	1	1	2	1	10	2	14	4	0	3	1	.750	0	3	3.86
Tucson	AAA	41	0	0	12	70	321	88	48	41	9	3	3	2	34	2	30	13	0	8	5	.615	0	4	5.27
6 Min. YEARS		200	23	1	71	397	1725	379	213	168	33	20	15	12	190	16	278	44	3	29	22	.569	0	17	3.81

Rueben Smiley

Bats: Left Throws: Left Pos: OF **Ht: 6'4" Wt: 195 Born: 08/27/68 Age: 26**

					BATTING												BASERUNNING				PERCENTAGES		
Year Team	Lg	G	AB	H	2B	3B	HR	TB	R	RBI	TBB	IBB	SO	HBP	SH	SF	SB	CS	SB%	GDP	Avg	OBP	SLG
1988 Pocatello	R	50	185	53	3	3	1	65	40	16	31	3	33	0	0	1	7	6	.54	2	.286	.387	.351
1989 Clinton	A	125	451	94	13	3	0	113	53	26	30	0	72	5	7	2	22	9	.71	10	.208	.264	.251
1990 San Jose	A	135	455	121	9	5	3	149	78	48	40	0	105	10	7	4	25	7	.78	9	.266	.336	.327
1991 Shreveport	AA	104	318	73	8	4	5	104	57	31	55	9	58	2	5	0	37	7	.84	3	.230	.347	.327
1992 Shreveport	AA	93	316	81	12	5	6	121	38	35	21	8	71	4	1	1	19	6	.76	4	.256	.310	.383
Phoenix	AAA	17	37	8	3	0	0	11	5	2	3	0	9	1	1	0	0	2	.00	0	.216	.293	.297
1993 Phoenix	AAA	99	313	94	16	7	7	145	58	37	15	3	67	0	0	1	24	3	.89	6	.300	.331	.463
1994 Phoenix	AAA	69	227	68	8	4	2	90	36	20	14	3	35	1	0	0	10	6	.63	3	.300	.343	.396
7 Min. YEARS		692	2302	592	72	31	24	798	365	215	209	26	450	23	21	9	144	46	.76	37	.257	.324	.347

Brandon Smith

Bats: Right Throws: Right Pos: C **Ht: 6'2" Wt: 200 Born: 03/09/73 Age: 22**

					BATTING												BASERUNNING				PERCENTAGES		
Year Team	Lg	G	AB	H	2B	3B	HR	TB	R	RBI	TBB	IBB	SO	HBP	SH	SF	SB	CS	SB%	GDP	Avg	OBP	SLG
1991 Athletics	R	36	111	21	3	0	1	27	16	10	16	0	24	3	1	2	1	3	.25	0	.189	.303	.243
1992 Athletics	R	11	19	5	1	0	0	6	1	4	1	0	1	0	1	0	0	0	.00	0	.263	.300	.316
1994 Norfolk	AAA	2	4	1	0	0	0	1	1	1	0	0	1	0	0	0	1	0	1.00	0	.250	.250	.250
Pittsfield	A	18	54	8	2	0	1	13	2	3	0	0	18	1	0	2	0	0	.00	0	.148	.158	.241
3 Min. YEARS		67	188	35	6	0	2	47	20	18	17	0	44	4	2	4	2	3	.40	2	.186	.263	.250

Bubba Smith

Bats: Right Throws: Right Pos: 1B **Ht: 6' 2" Wt: 225 Born: 12/18/69 Age: 25**

					BATTING												BASERUNNING				PERCENTAGES		
Year Team	Lg	G	AB	H	2B	3B	HR	TB	R	RBI	TBB	IBB	SO	HBP	SH	SF	SB	CS	SB%	GDP	Avg	OBP	SLG
1991 Bellingham	A	66	253	66	14	2	10	114	28	43	13	1	47	2	0	2	0	2	.00	9	.261	.300	.451
1992 Peninsula	A	137	482	126	22	1	32	246	70	93	65	7	138	5	0	5	4	10	.29	13	.261	.352	.510
1993 Jacksnville	AA	37	137	30	8	0	6	56	12	21	7	0	52	2	0	1	0	3	.00	1	.219	.265	.409
Riverside	A	5	19	8	3	0	0	11	5	3	7	0	3	0	0	0	0	0	.00	1	.421	.577	.579
Winston-Sal	A	92	342	103	16	0	27	200	55	81	35	1	109	7	0	4	2	0	1.00	3	.301	.374	.585
1994 Chattanooga	AA	4	9	0	0	0	0	0	0	0	0	0	7	0	0	0	0	0	.00	0	.000	.000	.000
Charlstn-Sc	A	100	354	83	26	1	15	156	38	59	20	1	113	5	0	2	1	2	.33	9	.234	.283	.441
4 Min. YEARS		441	1596	416	89	4	90	783	208	300	147	10	469	21	1	14	7	17	.29	41	.261	.328	.491

Chris Smith

Bats: Right Throws: Right Pos: SS **Ht: 5'11" Wt: 180 Born: 01/14/74 Age: 21**

					BATTING												BASERUNNING				PERCENTAGES		
Year Team	Lg	G	AB	H	2B	3B	HR	TB	R	RBI	TBB	IBB	SO	HBP	SH	SF	SB	CS	SB%	GDP	Avg	OBP	SLG
1992 Boise	A	53	189	41	12	3	1	62	20	27	16	0	25	2	0	4	2	1	.67	4	.217	.280	.328
1993 Cedar Rapds	A	70	246	64	11	2	5	94	29	39	28	2	35	3	1	1	1	2	.33	5	.260	.342	.382
Palm Sprngs	A	40	154	43	7	2	2	60	27	21	16	0	20	1	0	0	3	4	.43	3	.279	.351	.390
1994 Midland	AA	110	421	110	17	4	3	144	61	56	34	0	72	5	1	3	2	7	.22	8	.261	.322	.342
3 Min. YEARS		273	1010	258	47	11	11	360	137	143	94	2	152	11	2	8	8	14	.36	20	.255	.323	.356

Chuck Smith

Pitches: Right Bats: Right Pos: P **Ht: 6'1" Wt: 175 Born: 10/21/69 Age: 25**

		HOW MUCH HE PITCHED					WHAT HE GAVE UP										THE RESULTS					
Year Team	Lg	G	GS	CG	GF	IP	BFP	H	R	ER	HR	SH	SF	HB	TBB	IBB	SO	WP	Bk	W	L	Pct.	ShO	Sv	ERA
1991 Astros	R	15	7	1	2	59.1	272	56	36	23	2	3	0	7	37	0	64	7	5	4	3	.571	0	0	3.49
1992 Asheville	A	28	20	1	3	132	596	128	93	76	14	5	4	4	78	1	117	4	7	9	9	.500	0	1	5.18
1993 Quad City	A	22	17	2	3	110.2	488	109	73	57	16	3	2	6	52	0	103	7	4	7	5	.583	0	0	4.64
1994 Jackson	AA	2	0	0	0	6	30	6	6	3	0	2	0	0	5	0	7	0	0	0	0	.000	0	0	4.50
Osceola	A	35	2	0	11	84.2	376	73	41	35	2	2	2	2	49	3	60	7	3	4	4	.500	0	1	3.72
4 Min. YEARS		102	46	4	19	392.2	1762	372	249	194	34	15	8	19	221	4	351	25	20	24	21	.533	0	1	4.45

Ed Smith

Bats: Right Throws: Right Pos: 1B-OF **Ht: 6'4" Wt: 220 Born: 06/05/69 Age: 26**

					BATTING												BASERUNNING				PERCENTAGES		
Year Team	Lg	G	AB	H	2B	3B	HR	TB	R	RBI	TBB	IBB	SO	HBP	SH	SF	SB	CS	SB%	GDP	Avg	OBP	SLG
1987 White Sox	R	32	114	27	3	0	2	36	10	18	6	0	28	2	0	0	3	3	.50	1	.237	.287	.316
1988 South Bend	A	130	462	107	14	1	3	132	51	46	51	3	87	5	2	2	5	5	.50	9	.232	.313	.286
1989 South Bend	A	115	382	94	20	2	8	142	52	49	43	4	84	7	0	4	7	9	.44	10	.246	.330	.372
1990 Sarasota	A	63	239	46	10	3	4	74	22	23	11	0	61	7	1	3	0	3	.00	6	.192	.246	.310
Birmingham	AA	72	247	61	14	3	1	84	22	23	22	0	49	0	3	4	2	1	.67	10	.247	.304	.340
1991 Sarasota	A	54	198	43	7	0	3	59	27	27	15	1	52	3	2	1	4	3	.57	2	.217	.280	.298

Year Team	Lg	G	AB	H	2B	3B	HR	TB	R	RBI	TBB	IBB	SO	HBP	SH	SF	SB	CS	SB%	GDP	Avg	OBP	SLG
Beloit	A	61	218	57	13	2	4	86	31	37	21	2	41	1	1	3	5	2	.71	5	.261	.325	.394
1992 Stockton	A	99	355	93	21	4	11	155	57	57	49	0	72	1	0	1	6	6	.50	8	.262	.357	.437
El Paso	AA	22	86	25	5	0	2	36	11	15	8	0	20	1	0	1	0	1	.00	2	.291	.354	.419
1993 El Paso	AA	118	419	123	23	6	8	182	64	69	38	4	97	3	0	2	13	5	.72	13	.294	.355	.434
1994 Orlando	AA	115	401	104	17	5	16	179	51	60	37	1	75	4	0	3	4	11	.27	14	.259	.326	.446
8 Min. YEARS		881	3121	780	147	26	62	1165	398	424	301	16	666	37	9	25	49	49	.50	80	.250	.321	.373

Frank Smith

Bats: Right **Throws:** Right **Pos:** OF **Ht:** 6'2" **Wt:** 185 **Born:** 08/11/72 **Age:** 22

					BATTING												BASERUNNING				PERCENTAGES		
Year Team	Lg	G	AB	H	2B	3B	HR	TB	R	RBI	TBB	IBB	SO	HBP	SH	SF	SB	CS	SB%	GDP	Avg	OBP	SLG
1990 Dodgers	R	50	162	36	3	0	1	42	18	17	24	2	46	1	0	1	6	1	.86	3	.222	.324	.259
1991 Great Falls	R	50	179	47	7	3	6	78	40	37	26	0	57	2	1	0	1	1	.50	5	.263	.362	.436
1992 Great Falls	R	22	69	15	0	2	1	22	9	7	7	0	16	1	1	0	1	1	.50	2	.217	.299	.319
Yakima	A	15	49	11	2	0	3	22	7	6	3	0	15	2	0	0	1	0	1.00	5	.224	.296	.449
1993 Bakersfield	A	102	299	77	11	3	5	109	36	30	32	0	91	2	0	3	1	7	.13	4	.258	.330	.365
1994 San Antonio	AA	27	59	16	1	2	1	24	11	4	3	0	14	0	0	1	0	1	.00	3	.271	.302	.407
Vero Beach	A	52	170	49	9	1	1	63	22	24	25	0	35	0	0	3	6	0	1.00	0	.288	.374	.371
5 Min. YEARS		318	987	251	33	11	18	360	143	125	120	2	274	8	2	8	16	11	.59	22	.254	.337	.365

Greg Smith

Bats: Both **Throws:** Right **Pos:** 2B **Ht:** 5'11" **Wt:** 170 **Born:** 04/05/67 **Age:** 28

					BATTING												BASERUNNING				PERCENTAGES		
Year Team	Lg	G	AB	H	2B	3B	HR	TB	R	RBI	TBB	IBB	SO	HBP	SH	SF	SB	CS	SB%	GDP	Avg	OBP	SLG
1985 Wytheville	R	51	179	42	6	2	0	52	28	15	20	1	27	2	3	1	8	1	.89	1	.235	.317	.291
1986 Peoria	A	53	170	43	6	3	2	61	24	26	19	1	45	1	2	0	9	2	.82	2	.253	.332	.359
1987 Peoria	A	124	444	120	23	5	6	171	69	56	62	5	96	4	7	5	26	9	.74	11	.270	.361	.385
1988 Winston-Sal	A	95	361	101	12	2	4	129	62	29	46	2	50	2	6	3	52	12	.81	5	.280	.362	.357
1989 Charlotte	AA	126	467	138	23	6	5	188	59	64	42	1	52	6	9	4	38	13	.75	8	.296	.358	.403
1990 Iowa	AAA	105	398	116	19	1	5	152	54	44	37	1	57	2	4	1	26	14	.65	8	.291	.354	.382
1991 Albuquerque	AAA	48	161	35	3	2	0	42	25	17	10	1	30	0	1	1	11	0	1.00	1	.217	.262	.261
1992 Toledo	AAA	128	445	104	15	3	7	146	56	46	46	0	72	3	4	2	24	3	.89	11	.234	.308	.328
1993 Iowa	AAA	131	500	141	27	1	9	197	82	54	53	1	61	3	9	8	25	11	.69	11	.282	.349	.394
1994 New Orleans	AAA	115	411	95	21	4	1	127	57	38	45	1	57	6	9	3	34	10	.77	8	.231	.314	.309
1989 Chicago	NL	4	5	2	0	0	0	2	1	2	0	0	1	0	0	0	0	0	.00	0	.400	.500	.400
1990 Chicago	NL	18	44	9	2	1	0	13	4	5	2	0	5	0	1	1	1	0	1.00	1	.205	.234	.295
1991 Los Angeles	NL	5	3	0	0	0	0	0	1	0	0	0	2	0	1	0	0	0	.00	0	.000	.000	.000
10 Min. YEARS		976	3536	935	155	29	39	1265	516	389	380	14	547	29	54	28	253	75	.77	72	.264	.338	.358
3 Maj. YEARS		27	52	11	2	1	0	15	6	7	2	0	7	1	2	1	1	0	1.00	1	.212	.250	.288

Ira Smith

Bats: Right **Throws:** Right **Pos:** OF **Ht:** 5'11" **Wt:** 185 **Born:** 08/04/67 **Age:** 27

					BATTING												BASERUNNING				PERCENTAGES		
Year Team	Lg	G	AB	H	2B	3B	HR	TB	R	RBI	TBB	IBB	SO	HBP	SH	SF	SB	CS	SB%	GDP	Avg	OBP	SLG
1990 Great Falls	R	50	142	37	7	3	1	53	31	28	25	0	32	3	2	3	8	6	.57	3	.261	.376	.373
1991 Vero Beach	A	52	176	57	5	3	1	71	27	24	18	0	30	2	0	0	15	3	.83	7	.324	.393	.403
1992 Bakersfield	A	118	413	119	17	4	7	165	79	45	48	3	56	6	8	6	26	14	.65	12	.288	.366	.400
San Antonio	AA	6	11	4	0	1	0	6	3	1	1	0	2	0	0	0	0	0	.00	0	.364	.417	.545
1993 Rancho Cuca	A	92	347	120	30	6	7	183	71	47	55	1	41	5	2	3	32	16	.67	7	.346	.439	.527
Wichita	AA	13	39	9	0	1	0	11	7	4	4	0	9	0	1	0	0	2	.00	2	.231	.302	.282
1994 Wichita	AA	107	358	115	17	6	7	165	58	41	53	2	59	3	3	6	6	12	.33	5	.321	.407	.461
5 Min. YEARS		438	1486	461	76	24	23	654	276	190	204	6	229	19	16	18	87	53	.62	36	.310	.396	.440

Jason Smith

Bats: Right **Throws:** Right **Pos:** 1B **Ht:** 6'4" **Wt:** 225 **Born:** 09/12/70 **Age:** 24

					BATTING												BASERUNNING				PERCENTAGES		
Year Team	Lg	G	AB	H	2B	3B	HR	TB	R	RBI	TBB	IBB	SO	HBP	SH	SF	SB	CS	SB%	GDP	Avg	OBP	SLG
1993 Bend	A	46	152	32	5	0	9	64	22	36	24	1	59	4	0	0	1	2	.33	1	.211	.333	.421
1994 New Haven	AA	7	14	4	0	1	0	6	2	0	2	0	2	2	0	0	0	0	.00	0	.286	.444	.429
Asheville	A	108	356	92	22	0	17	165	48	57	50	1	117	10	0	4	2	0	1.00	8	.258	.362	.463
2 Min. YEARS		161	522	128	27	1	26	235	72	93	76	2	178	16	0	4	3	2	.60	9	.245	.356	.450

Jeff Smith

Pitches: Right **Bats:** Right **Pos:** P **Ht:** 6'0" **Wt:** 195 **Born:** 05/30/70 **Age:** 25

		HOW MUCH HE PITCHED					WHAT HE GAVE UP										THE RESULTS					
Year Team	Lg	G	GS	CG	GF	IP	BFP	H	R	ER	HR	SH	SF	HB	TBB	IBB	SO	WP	Bk	W	L	Pct.	ShO	Sv	ERA
1991 Eugene	A	15	15	0	0	77.2	347	89	46	34	6	5	3	3	21	0	74	5	5	3	8	.273	0	0	3.94
1992 Appleton	A	24	10	0	4	82.2	340	79	38	35	8	2	4	1	27	0	58	3	3	6	3	.667	0	0	3.81
Baseball Cy	A	2	2	0	0	7	33	10	6	5	0	1	0	0	1	0	6	0	0	0	1	.000	0	0	6.43
1993 Wilmington	A	51	0	0	39	64	275	66	33	28	4	3	1	4	25	2	60	6	1	2	7	.222	0	24	3.94
1994 Wilmington	A	41	0	0	36	50	203	49	23	21	10	0	0	0	5	1	48	0	0	2	1	.667	0	13	3.78
Memphis	AA	1	0	0	1	1	4	0	0	0	0	0	0	0	1	0	0	0	0	0	0	.000	0	1	0.00
4 Min. YEARS		134	27	0	80	282.1	1202	293	146	123	27	9	8	8	80	3	246	14	9	13	20	.394	0	38	3.92

Ottis Smith

Pitches: Left **Bats:** Right **Pos:** P **Ht:** 6'1" **Wt:** 160 **Born:** 01/28/71 **Age:** 24

			HOW MUCH HE PITCHED					WHAT HE GAVE UP										THE RESULTS					
Year	Team	Lg	G	GS	CG	GF	IP	BFP	H	R	ER	HR	SH	SF	HB	TBB	IBB	SO	WP	Bk	W	L	Pct.	ShO	Sv	ERA
1990	Mets	R	13	13	3	0	79.1	318	53	21	13	1	1	0	4	28	0	89	6	5	6	5	.545	1	0	1.47
1991	Pittsfield	A	15	15	2	0	103.1	437	89	49	30	5	0	3	5	42	0	79	4	1	7	2	.778	2	0	2.61
1992	Columbia	A	18	12	1	4	95.1	390	75	39	32	5	2	1	3	38	0	94	6	4	6	6	.500	0	2	3.02
	St. Lucie	A	11	11	2	0	65.1	282	63	33	23	6	1	3	3	20	0	39	3	4	4	5	.444	1	0	3.17
1993	Norfolk	AAA	5	3	0	1	18.1	82	22	14	13	3	0	1	0	10	0	11	1	0	0	2	.000	0	0	6.38
	St.Lucie	A	22	21	0	1	133.2	581	140	65	53	6	3	5	8	48	2	83	8	3	10	7	.588	0	0	3.57
1994	Orlando	AA	26	18	2	2	123	516	138	51	42	4	4	5	4	22	1	63	6	0	8	4	.667	2	0	3.07
	5 Min. YEARS		110	93	10	8	618.1	2606	580	272	206	30	11	18	27	208	3	458	34	17	41	31	.569	6	2	3.00

Shad Smith

Pitches: Right **Bats:** Right **Pos:** P **Ht:** 6'4" **Wt:** 220 **Born:** 05/21/67 **Age:** 28

			HOW MUCH HE PITCHED					WHAT HE GAVE UP										THE RESULTS					
Year	Team	Lg	G	GS	CG	GF	IP	BFP	H	R	ER	HR	SH	SF	HB	TBB	IBB	SO	WP	Bk	W	L	Pct.	ShO	Sv	ERA
1990	Ft.Laudrdle	A	1	0	0	1	2.2	12	2	0	0	0	0	0	0	2	0	1	0	0	0	0	.000	0	0	0.00
	Greensboro	A	16	13	0	1	85	357	69	41	34	5	2	2	6	32	3	54	8	0	4	7	.364	0	0	3.60
1991	Greensboro	A	38	17	1	9	121	532	130	67	54	4	4	3	5	43	1	69	6	0	4	8	.333	0	1	4.02
1992	Pr William	A	36	2	0	12	81	373	89	46	32	4	4	5	3	38	1	54	1	3	1	3	.250	0	0	3.56
1993	Shreveport	AA	24	13	0	5	95.2	409	95	43	40	6	3	2	4	37	1	65	3	0	6	3	.667	0	0	3.76
1994	Phoenix	AAA	5	5	0	0	26.1	132	40	31	27	6	1	0	2	10	1	9	0	0	1	2	.333	0	0	9.23
	Shreveport	AA	21	21	2	0	136.2	543	125	61	52	12	5	3	4	25	0	68	4	0	6	9	.400	1	0	3.42
	5 Min. YEARS		141	71	3	28	548.1	2358	550	289	239	37	20	15	24	187	7	320	22	3	22	32	.407	1	1	3.92

Sloan Smith

Bats: Both **Throws:** Right **Pos:** OF **Ht:** 6'4" **Wt:** 215 **Born:** 11/29/72 **Age:** 22

			BATTING													BASERUNNING				PERCENTAGES		
Year	Team	Lg	G	AB	H	2B	3B	HR	TB	R	RBI	TBB	IBB	SO	HBP	SH	SF	SB	CS	SB%	GDP	Avg	OBP	SLG
1993	Oneonta	A	34	116	23	5	1	1	33	14	10	15	0	33	6	3	1	3	2	.60	1	.198	.319	.284
1994	Oneonta	A	38	138	34	5	5	0	49	24	16	25	0	41	2	1	0	2	1	.67	1	.246	.370	.355
	Greensboro	A	79	269	51	4	3	5	76	35	26	42	2	98	2	3	3	13	5	.72	4	.190	.301	.283
	Albany-Colo	AA	7	23	4	2	1	0	8	4	5	3	0	6	0	0	0	0	0	.00	1	.174	.269	.348
	2 Min. YEARS		158	546	112	16	10	6	166	77	57	85	2	178	10	7	4	18	8	.69	7	.205	.321	.304

Tim Smith

Pitches: Right **Bats:** Right **Pos:** P **Ht:** 6'4" **Wt:** 190 **Born:** 08/09/68 **Age:** 26

			HOW MUCH HE PITCHED					WHAT HE GAVE UP										THE RESULTS					
Year	Team	Lg	G	GS	CG	GF	IP	BFP	H	R	ER	HR	SH	SF	HB	TBB	IBB	SO	WP	Bk	W	L	Pct.	ShO	Sv	ERA
1990	Elmira	A	23	2	2	16	66	282	62	33	27	0	6	5	2	25	1	52	5	2	4	6	.400	0	5	3.68
1991	Lynchburg	A	25	25	8	0	174.2	706	149	60	42	6	3	8	9	34	2	103	9	0	12	9	.571	2	0	2.16
1992	New Britain	AA	27	25	2	1	154	690	186	104	91	5	2	6	8	53	3	71	7	5	3	20	.130	1	0	5.32
1993	New Britain	AA	28	28	3	0	180.1	766	192	91	76	9	6	6	11	44	5	81	5	4	7	13	.350	1	0	3.79
1994	New Britain	AA	28	26	1	1	154.2	687	186	113	99	16	6	9	11	38	1	104	11	0	6	14	.300	1	0	5.76
	5 Min. YEARS		131	106	16	18	729.2	3131	775	401	335	36	23	34	41	194	12	411	37	11	32	62	.340	5	5	4.13

Tim Smith

Pitches: Right **Bats:** Right **Pos:** P **Ht:** 6'2" **Wt:** 185 **Born:** 10/24/69 **Age:** 25

			HOW MUCH HE PITCHED					WHAT HE GAVE UP										THE RESULTS					
Year	Team	Lg	G	GS	CG	GF	IP	BFP	H	R	ER	HR	SH	SF	HB	TBB	IBB	SO	WP	Bk	W	L	Pct.	ShO	Sv	ERA
1991	Sou Oregon	A	14	13	1	0	75.1	330	78	52	27	5	1	4	2	17	1	79	7	2	5	2	.714	1	0	3.23
	Madison	A	1	1	0	0	3.2	20	7	4	4	2	1	0	0	2	0	4	0	0	0	1	.000	0	0	9.82
1992	Reno	A	28	26	1	1	158	708	192	107	88	14	4	5	3	62	5	131	9	0	11	10	.524	0	0	5.01
	Tacoma	AAA	2	2	1	0	11.1	47	10	9	9	1	0	0	0	4	0	7	0	0	1	1	.500	0	0	7.15
1993	San Berndno	A	16	15	2	0	88.1	371	84	47	43	13	3	2	2	45	3	72	2	1	6	4	.600	1	0	4.38
	Tacoma	AAA	6	4	0	0	22.2	107	31	18	18	2	0	0	0	11	1	16	2	0	3	0	1.000	0	0	7.15
	Huntsville	AA	9	6	1	1	43	184	46	22	16	5	1	1	1	18	0	31	4	0	1	3	.250	1	0	3.35
1994	Huntsville	AA	2	0	0	2	4.1	14	1	1	1	0	1	0	0	1	0	3	1	0	0	1	.000	0	1	2.08
	Tacoma	AAA	24	5	0	9	51	233	54	37	33	11	2	2	1	25	0	36	4	1	4	4	.500	0	1	5.82
	4 Min. YEARS		102	72	6	13	457.2	2014	503	297	239	53	13	14	9	185	10	379	29	4	31	26	.544	3	2	4.70

Chris Snopek

Bats: Right **Throws:** Right **Pos:** 1B **Ht:** 6'1" **Wt:** 185 **Born:** 09/20/70 **Age:** 24

			BATTING													BASERUNNING				PERCENTAGES		
Year	Team	Lg	G	AB	H	2B	3B	HR	TB	R	RBI	TBB	IBB	SO	HBP	SH	SF	SB	CS	SB%	GDP	Avg	OBP	SLG
1992	Utica	A	73	245	69	15	1	2	92	49	29	52	4	44	2	1	4	14	4	.78	4	.282	.406	.376
1993	South Bend	A	22	72	28	8	1	5	53	20	18	15	0	13	3	0	2	1	1	.50	1	.389	.500	.736
	Sarasota	A	107	371	91	21	4	10	150	61	50	65	2	67	1	3	6	3	2	.60	2	.245	.354	.404
1994	Birmingham	AA	106	365	96	25	3	6	145	58	54	58	3	49	5	3	5	9	4	.69	7	.263	.367	.397
	3 Min. YEARS		308	1053	284	69	9	23	440	188	151	190	9	173	11	7	17	27	11	.71	14	.270	.382	.418

Mark Sobolewski

Bats: Right Throws: Right Pos: 3B   Ht: 5'11" Wt: 185 Born: 02/10/70 Age: 25

										BATTING										BASERUNNING				PERCENTAGES		
Year	Team	Lg	G	AB	H	2B	3B	HR	TB	R	RBI	TBB	IBB	SO	HBP	SH	SF	SB	CS	SB%	GDP	Avg	OBP	SLG
1992	Sou Oregon	A	68	262	76	18	0	7	115	44	38	33	0	52	3	1	3	2	4	.33	8	.290	.372	.439
1993	Modesto	A	130	507	116	23	3	8	160	66	60	42	0	100	8	9	9	0	4	.00	12	.229	.293	.316
1994	Huntsville	AA	133	503	127	37	5	8	198	83	58	49	1	98	13	6	5	2	6	.25	11	.252	.332	.394
	3 Min. YEARS		331	1272	319	78	8	20	473	193	156	124	1	250	24	16	17	4	14	.22	31	.251	.325	.372

Steven Soliz

Bats: Right Throws: Right Pos: C   Ht: 5'10" Wt: 180 Born: 01/27/71 Age: 24

										BATTING										BASERUNNING				PERCENTAGES		
Year	Team	Lg	G	AB	H	2B	3B	HR	TB	R	RBI	TBB	IBB	SO	HBP	SH	SF	SB	CS	SB%	GDP	Avg	OBP	SLG
1993	Watertown	A	56	209	62	12	0	0	74	30	35	15	0	41	1	2	3	2	1	1.00	3	.297	.342	.354
1994	Kinston	A	51	163	43	7	1	3	61	26	19	16	0	32	1	2	1	3	1	1.00	1	.264	.331	.374
	Canton-Akm	AA	18	54	10	1	0	0	11	4	0	2	0	9	1	1	0	0	0	.00	4	.185	.228	.204
	2 Min. YEARS		125	426	115	20	1	3	146	60	54	33	0	82	3	5	4	5	1	1.00	7	.270	.324	.343

Don Sparks

Bats: Right Throws: Right Pos: 1B   Ht: 6'2" Wt: 185 Born: 06/19/66 Age: 29

										BATTING										BASERUNNING				PERCENTAGES		
Year	Team	Lg	G	AB	H	2B	3B	HR	TB	R	RBI	TBB	IBB	SO	HBP	SH	SF	SB	CS	SB%	GDP	Avg	OBP	SLG
1988	Pr William	A	70	267	66	14	0	3	89	22	28	8	0	51	4	1	1	1	0	1.00	8	.247	.279	.333
1989	Pr William	A	115	449	126	32	1	6	178	52	65	24	2	85	2	0	4	1	2	.33	20	.281	.317	.396
1990	Columbus	AAA	16	51	6	3	0	0	9	3	2	2	0	10	1	0	0	0	0	.00	3	.118	.167	.176
	Albany	AA	112	418	110	20	5	4	152	48	52	33	2	70	4	0	5	3	4	.43	14	.263	.320	.364
1991	Columbus	AAA	52	152	39	6	2	0	49	11	25	12	0	27	4	3	2	0	0	.00	7	.257	.324	.322
1992	Albany	AA	134	505	158	31	2	14	235	64	72	30	2	71	2	0	6	2	2	.50	14	.313	.349	.465
1993	Columbus	AAA	128	475	135	33	7	11	215	63	72	29	0	83	4	1	6	2	3	.00	14	.284	.327	.453
1994	Columbus	AAA	139	515	140	21	6	7	194	60	63	42	3	76	4	2	8	2	7	.22	17	.272	.327	.377
	7 Min. YEARS		766	2832	780	160	23	45	1121	323	379	180	9	473	25	7	34	9	18	.33	97	.275	.321	.396

Greg Sparks

Bats: Left Throws: Left Pos: 1B   Ht: 6'0" Wt: 185 Born: 03/31/64 Age: 31

										BATTING										BASERUNNING				PERCENTAGES		
Year	Team	Lg	G	AB	H	2B	3B	HR	TB	R	RBI	TBB	IBB	SO	HBP	SH	SF	SB	CS	SB%	GDP	Avg	OBP	SLG
1984	Spokane	A	67	269	68	13	4	4	101	34	37	17	1	65	0	1	6	1	2	.33	2	.252	.290	.374
1985	Reno	A	123	436	123	23	1	7	169	57	73	36	0	89	1	2	3	4	4	.50	10	.282	.336	.388
1986	Charleston	A	105	344	81	18	1	10	131	40	59	35	1	61	1	1	2	4	3	.57	7	.235	.306	.381
1987	Madison	A	58	222	66	15	1	3	92	25	41	26	3	38	0	1	4	3	1	.75	6	.297	.365	.414
	Huntsville	AA	57	172	48	9	1	4	71	18	28	14	0	35	1	0	2	1	0	1.00	2	.279	.333	.413
1988	Huntsville	AA	124	421	98	21	0	8	143	47	50	48	6	117	3	3	4	5	5	.50	6	.233	.313	.340
1989	Salinas	A	108	356	92	24	1	9	145	38	54	44	4	92	1	0	5	1	5	.17	4	.258	.337	.407
1990	Albany	AA	129	455	112	24	1	19	195	66	77	42	1	118	5	1	3	0	2	.00	6	.246	.315	.429
1991	Carolina	AA	69	220	60	11	0	5	86	19	35	39	5	55	1	0	4	0	2	.00	3	.273	.379	.391
	Buffalo	AAA	55	128	23	7	0	3	39	13	16	12	0	31	0	2	2	1	0	1.00	4	.180	.246	.305
1992	London	AA	106	384	89	19	1	25	185	57	73	57	2	114	2	0	3	1	0	1.00	6	.232	.332	.482
	Toledo	AAA	23	72	13	1	0	2	20	6	4	4	0	26	0	1	1	0	1	.00	0	.181	.221	.278
1993	Pawtucket	AAA	58	198	34	6	0	4	52	7	21	14	0	54	2	1	2	0	3	.00	4	.172	.231	.263
	Canton-Akm	AA	35	117	27	9	0	4	48	11	23	18	2	33	0	1	3	0	1	.00	4	.231	.326	.410
1994	New Haven	AA	88	243	45	8	0	8	77	27	28	33	4	80	1	0	3	1	0	1.00	3	.185	.282	.317
	11 Min. YEARS		1205	4038	979	208	11	115	1554	465	619	439	29	1008	18	14	47	22	29	.43	63	.242	.316	.385

Steve Sparks

Pitches: Right Bats: Right Pos: P   Ht: 6'0" Wt: 180 Born: 07/02/65 Age: 29

			HOW MUCH HE PITCHED						WHAT HE GAVE UP												THE RESULTS					
Year	Team	Lg	G	GS	CG	GF	IP	BFP	H	R	ER	HR	SH	SF	HB	TBB	IBB	SO	WP	Bk	W	L	Pct.	ShO	Sv	ERA
1987	Helena	R	10	9	2	0	57.2	256	68	44	30	8	3	1	4	20	1	47	5	0	6	3	.667	0	0	4.68
1988	Beloit	A	25	24	5	0	164	688	162	80	69	8	4	2	7	51	2	96	5	5	9	13	.409	1	0	3.79
1989	Stockton	A	23	22	3	0	164	660	125	55	44	6	0	1	10	53	0	126	6	0	13	5	.722	2	0	2.41
1990	El Paso	AA	7	6	0	1	30.1	143	43	24	22	4	0	1	1	15	0	17	2	0	1	2	.333	0	0	6.53
	Stockton	A	19	19	5	0	129.1	549	136	63	53	4	4	3	8	31	0	77	7	1	10	7	.588	1	0	3.69
1991	El Paso	AA	4	4	0	0	17	90	30	22	18	1	0	0	0	9	0	10	2	1	1	2	.333	0	0	9.53
	Stockton	A	24	24	8	0	179.2	762	160	70	61	4	3	4	7	98	2	139	13	0	9	10	.474	2	0	3.06
1992	El Paso	AA	28	22	3	3	140.2	613	159	99	84	11	6	10	8	50	1	79	6	3	9	8	.529	0	1	5.37
1993	New Orleans	AAA	29	28	7	0	180.1	767	174	89	77	17	4	9	5	80	1	104	7	2	9	13	.409	1	0	3.84
1994	New Orleans	AAA	28	27	5	0	183.2	787	183	101	91	23	2	4	11	68	0	105	14	3	10	12	.455	1	0	4.46
	8 Min. YEARS		197	185	38	4	1246.2	5315	1240	647	549	86	26	35	61	475	7	800	67	15	77	75	.507	8	1	3.96

Vernon Spearman

Bats: Left **Throws:** Left **Pos:** OF   **Ht:** 5'10" **Wt:** 160 **Born:** 12/17/69 **Age:** 25

						BATTING										BASERUNNING				PERCENTAGES		
Year	Team	Lg	G	AB	H	2B	3B	HR	TB	R	RBI	TBB	IBB	SO	HBP	SH	SF	SB	CS	SB%	GDP	Avg	OBP	SLG
1991	Yakima	A	71	248	72	8	0	0	80	63	17	50	0	37	4	7	1	56	9	.86	1	.290	.416	.323
1992	Vero Beach	A	73	276	84	13	1	0	99	50	16	26	1	25	1	3	1	33	14	.70	5	.304	.365	.359
	San Antonio	AA	48	185	52	3	3	0	61	24	11	15	0	16	1	6	1	18	9	.67	2	.281	.337	.330
1993	San Antonio	AA	56	162	42	4	2	0	50	22	13	11	0	21	1	5	0	13	4	.76	3	.259	.310	.309
	Albuquerque	AAA	62	185	47	6	5	0	63	31	15	17	0	28	0	4	0	11	4	.73	4	.254	.317	.341
1994	San Antonio	AA	105	331	88	14	3	0	108	43	24	39	0	39	2	15	0	21	15	.58	2	.266	.347	.326
	4 Min. YEARS		415	1387	385	48	14	0	461	233	96	158	1	166	9	40	3	152	55	.73	17	.278	.355	.332

Stan Spencer

Pitches: Right **Bats:** Right **Pos:** P   **Ht:** 6'3" **Wt:** 195 **Born:** 08/02/68 **Age:** 26

			HOW MUCH HE PITCHED					WHAT HE GAVE UP									THE RESULTS					
Year	Team	Lg	G	GS	CG	GF	IP	BFP	H	R	ER	HR	SH	SF	HB	TBB	IBB	SO	WP	Bk	W	L	Pct.	ShO	Sv	ERA
1991	Harrisburg	AA	17	17	1	0	92	389	90	63	45	4	6	2	4	30	0	66	2	3	6	1	.857	0	0	4.40
1993	High Desert	A	13	13	0	0	61.2	265	67	33	28	4	0	2	3	18	0	38	1	0	4	4	.500	0	0	4.09
1994	Brevard Cty	A	6	5	0	1	20	84	20	9	7	0	0	1	1	6	0	22	1	0	1	0	1.000	0	0	3.15
	Portland	AA	20	20	1	0	124	505	113	50	48	12	4	6	2	30	2	96	3	1	9	4	.692	0	0	3.48
	3 Min. YEARS		56	55	2	1	297.2	1243	290	146	128	22	8	11	10	84	2	222	7	4	20	9	.690	0	0	3.87

Dennis Springer

Pitches: Right **Bats:** Right **Pos:** P   **Ht:** 5'10" **Wt:** 185 **Born:** 02/12/65 **Age:** 30

			HOW MUCH HE PITCHED					WHAT HE GAVE UP									THE RESULTS					
Year	Team	Lg	G	GS	CG	GF	IP	BFP	H	R	ER	HR	SH	SF	HB	TBB	IBB	SO	WP	Bk	W	L	Pct.	ShO	Sv	ERA
1987	Great Falls	R	23	5	1	13	65.2	290	70	38	21	3	4	2	2	16	2	54	4	0	4	3	.571	0	6	2.88
1988	Bakersfield	A	32	20	6	7	154	657	135	75	56	13	8	7	5	62	4	108	12	1	13	7	.650	4	2	3.27
	Vero Beach	A	1	1	0	0	5.2	25	6	3	3	0	0	0	0	2	0	4	0	0	0	0	.000	0	0	4.76
1989	San Antonio	AA	19	19	4	0	140	583	128	58	49	13	10	2	4	46	2	89	3	0	6	8	.429	1	0	3.15
	Albuquerque	AAA	8	7	0	0	41	193	58	28	22	5	1	0	0	14	0	18	1	0	4	1	.800	0	0	4.83
1990	Albuquerque	AAA	2	2	0	0	6.1	37	10	4	4	1	0	0	2	7	0	2	0	0	0	0	.000	0	0	5.68
	San Antonio	AA	24	24	3	0	163.1	691	147	76	60	8	5	6	1	73	0	77	7	1	8	6	.571	0	0	3.31
1991	San Antonio	AA	30	24	2	0	164.2	725	153	96	81	18	6	11	5	91	2	138	7	0	10	10	.500	0	0	4.43
1992	San Antonio	AA	18	18	4	0	122	525	114	61	59	6	3	2	4	49	3	73	4	0	6	7	.462	0	0	4.35
	Albuquerque	AAA	11	11	1	0	62	269	70	45	39	7	4	1	4	22	0	36	3	0	2	7	.222	0	0	5.66
1993	Albuquerque	AAA	35	18	0	5	130.2	591	173	104	87	18	5	6	2	39	1	69	7	1	3	8	.273	0	0	5.99
1994	Reading	AA	24	19	2	3	135	567	125	74	51	11	8	5	1	44	1	118	14	0	5	8	.385	0	2	3.40
	8 Min. YEARS		227	168	23	28	1190.1	5153	1189	662	532	103	54	42	30	465	15	786	62	3	61	65	.484	5	10	4.02

Steve Springer

Bats: Right **Throws:** Right **Pos:** 2B   **Ht:** 6' 0" **Wt:** 190 **Born:** 02/11/61 **Age:** 34

						BATTING										BASERUNNING				PERCENTAGES		
Year	Team	Lg	G	AB	H	2B	3B	HR	TB	R	RBI	TBB	IBB	SO	HBP	SH	SF	SB	CS	SB%	GDP	Avg	OBP	SLG
1984	Jackson	AA	103	362	99	21	3	5	141	41	40	24	3	50	2	0	6	6	4	.60	16	.273	.322	.390
1985	Tidewater	AAA	126	479	125	20	4	7	174	59	56	34	2	72	1	6	5	9	5	.64	16	.261	.308	.363
1986	Tidewater	AAA	117	440	120	19	6	4	163	52	46	30	0	74	1	5	0	10	5	.67	16	.273	.321	.370
1987	Tidewater	AAA	132	467	131	23	4	7	183	65	54	41	6	78	3	4	5	6	3	.67	10	.281	.339	.392
1988	Tidewater	AAA	97	337	88	15	0	2	109	42	25	29	0	66	0	2	1	4	0	1.00	7	.261	.319	.323
	Vancouver	AAA	27	105	28	4	1	2	40	15	9	4	1	17	0	2	0	1	2	.33	4	.267	.294	.381
1989	Vancouver	AAA	137	520	144	21	3	8	195	61	56	26	1	83	3	7	5	8	8	.50	11	.277	.312	.375
1990	Colo Sprngs	AAA	73	252	70	21	5	6	119	39	42	17	1	48	0	0	8	6	3	.67	6	.278	.314	.472
	Las Vegas	AAA	22	72	18	5	0	2	29	7	10	7	0	19	0	1	2	0	1	.00	2	.250	.309	.403
1991	Calgary	AAA	109	412	106	25	2	17	186	62	70	28	5	76	0	3	2	8	2	.80	14	.257	.303	.451
1992	Tidewater	AAA	117	427	124	16	0	16	188	57	70	22	1	85	0	0	3	9	4	.69	12	.290	.323	.440
1993	Norfolk	AAA	131	484	129	22	4	13	198	52	69	31	8	85	3	2	3	5	6	.45	13	.267	.313	.409
1994	Toledo	AAA	135	511	134	23	4	13	204	73	77	35	2	79	0	1	3	19	15	.56	9	.262	.308	.399
1990	Cleveland	AL	4	12	2	0	0	0	2	1	1	0	0	6	0	0	1	0	0	.00	0	.167	.154	.167
1992	New York	NL	4	5	2	1	0	0	3	0	0	0	0	1	0	0	0	0	0	.00	0	.400	.400	.600
	11 Min. YEARS		1326	4868	1316	235	36	102	1929	625	624	328	30	832	13	33	37	91	58	.61	136	.270	.316	.396
	2 Maj. YEARS		8	17	4	1	0	0	5	1	1	0	0	7	0	0	1	0	0	.00	0	.235	.222	.294

Scott Stahoviak

Bats: Left **Throws:** Right **Pos:** 3B   **Ht:** 6' 5" **Wt:** 208 **Born:** 03/06/70 **Age:** 25

						BATTING										BASERUNNING				PERCENTAGES		
Year	Team	Lg	G	AB	H	2B	3B	HR	TB	R	RBI	TBB	IBB	SO	HBP	SH	SF	SB	CS	SB%	GDP	Avg	OBP	SLG
1991	Visalia	A	43	158	44	9	1	1	58	29	25	22	2	28	3	2	0	9	3	.75	3	.278	.377	.367
1992	Visalia	A	110	409	126	26	3	5	173	62	68	82	2	66	3	0	2	17	6	.74	6	.308	.425	.423
1993	Nashville	AA	93	331	90	25	1	12	153	40	56	56	2	95	1	1	4	10	2	.83	5	.272	.375	.462
1994	Salt Lake	AAA	123	437	139	41	6	13	231	96	94	70	5	90	5	0	6	6	8	.43	12	.318	.413	.529
1993	Minnesota	AL	20	57	11	4	0	0	15	1	1	3	0	22	0	0	0	0	2	.00	2	.193	.233	.263
	4 Min. YEARS		369	1335	399	101	11	31	615	227	243	230	11	279	12	3	12	42	19	.69	26	.299	.403	.461

Matt Stairs

Bats: Left   Throws: Right   Pos: 3B   Ht: 5' 9"   Wt: 180   Born: 02/27/69   Age: 26

					BATTING											BASERUNNING				PERCENTAGES		
Year	Team	Lg	G	AB	H	2B	3B	HR	TB	R	RBI	TBB	IBB	SO	HBP	SH	SF	SB	CS	SB%	GDP	Avg	OBP	SLG
1989	Jamestown	A	14	43	11	1	0	1	15	8	5	3	0	5	0	0	0	1	2	.33	0	.256	.304	.349
	Wst Plm Bch	A	36	111	21	3	1	1	29	12	9	9	0	18	0	1	1	0	0	.00	3	.189	.248	.261
	Rockford	A	44	141	40	9	2	2	59	20	14	15	3	29	2	2	1	5	4	.56	4	.284	.358	.418
1990	Wst Plm Bch	A	55	184	62	9	3	3	86	30	30	40	4	19	5	0	2	15	2	.88	5	.337	.463	.467
	Jacksnville	AA	79	280	71	17	0	3	97	26	34	22	1	42	3	0	5	5	3	.63	6	.254	.310	.346
1991	Harrisburg	AA	129	505	168	30	10	13	257	87	78	66	8	47	3	2	3	23	11	.68	14	.333	.411	.509
1992	Indianapls	AAA	110	401	107	23	4	11	171	57	56	49	3	61	4	4	2	11	11	.50	10	.267	.351	.426
1993	Ottawa	AAA	34	125	35	4	2	3	52	18	20	11	1	15	2	1	0	4	1	.80	3	.280	.348	.416
1994	New Britain	AA	93	280	98	25	2	9	154	44	61	53	7	38	3	0	5	10	7	.59	10	.309	.407	.486
1992	Montreal	NL	13	30	5	2	0	0	7	2	5	7	0	7	0	0	1	0	0	.00	0	.167	.316	.233
1993	Montreal	NL	6	8	3	1	0	0	4	1	2	0	0	1	0	0	0	0	0	.00	1	.375	.375	.500
	6 Min. YEARS		594	2107	613	121	24	46	920	302	307	268	27	274	22	10	19	74	41	.64	55	.291	.374	.437
	2 Maj. YEARS		19	38	8	3	0	0	11	3	7	7	0	8	0	0	1	0	0	.00	1	.211	.326	.289

Larry Stanford

Pitches: Right   Bats: Right   Pos: P   Ht: 6'3"   Wt: 205   Born: 09/24/67   Age: 27

			HOW MUCH HE PITCHED					WHAT HE GAVE UP										THE RESULTS					
Year	Team	Lg	G	GS	CG	GF	IP	BFP	H	R	ER	HR	SH	SF	HB	TBB	IBB	SO	WP	Bk	W	L	Pct.	ShO	Sv	ERA
1989	Oneonta	A	15	15	1	0	80	335	75	41	34	5	3	5	4	30	0	60	6	1	4	3	.571	1	0	3.83
1990	Ft.Laudrdle	A	57	0	0	53	61.2	244	41	15	9	1	7	2	0	18	2	59	7	5	3	1	.750	0	29	1.31
1991	Albany	AA	52	0	0	41	62	262	41	18	13	2	5	6	0	36	3	61	12	0	2	3	.400	0	24	1.89
1992	Columbus	AAA	2	0	0	2	2	10	2	3	1	0	1	0	0	1	0	5	2	0	0	1	.000	0	1	4.50
1994	New Haven	AA	6	0	0	1	8	41	12	8	8	0	2	0	0	7	1	6	0	0	0	1	.000	0	0	9.00
	5 Min. YEARS		132	15	1	97	213.2	892	171	85	65	8	18	13	4	92	6	191	27	6	9	9	.500	1	54	2.74

Kennie Steenstra

Pitches: Right   Bats: Right   Pos: P   Ht: 6'5"   Wt: 220   Born: 10/13/70   Age: 24

			HOW MUCH HE PITCHED					WHAT HE GAVE UP										THE RESULTS					
Year	Team	Lg	G	GS	CG	GF	IP	BFP	H	R	ER	HR	SH	SF	HB	TBB	IBB	SO	WP	Bk	W	L	Pct.	ShO	Sv	ERA
1992	Geneva	A	3	3	1	0	20	76	11	4	2	0	0	0	0	3	0	12	0	1	3	0	1.000	0	0	0.90
	Peoria	A	12	12	4	0	89.2	364	79	29	21	5	2	1	3	21	1	68	4	3	6	3	.667	2	0	2.11
1993	Daytona	A	13	13	1	0	81.1	317	64	26	23	2	3	2	8	12	1	57	2	1	5	3	.625	1	0	2.55
	Iowa	AAA	1	1	0	0	6.2	32	9	5	5	2	0	0	0	4	0	6	0	0	1	0	1.000	0	0	6.75
	Orlando	AA	14	14	2	0	100.1	427	103	47	40	4	4	2	9	25	0	60	5	2	8	3	.727	2	0	3.59
1994	Iowa	AAA	3	3	0	0	13	68	24	21	19	2	0	2	2	4	0	10	0	0	1	2	.333	0	0	13.15
	Orlando	AA	23	23	2	0	158.1	654	146	55	46	12	9	3	9	39	4	83	4	1	9	7	.563	1	0	2.61
	3 Min. YEARS		69	69	10	0	469.1	1938	436	187	156	27	18	10	31	108	6	296	15	8	33	18	.647	6	0	2.99

Mike Stefanski

Bats: Right   Throws: Right   Pos: C   Ht: 6'2"   Wt: 190   Born: 09/12/69   Age: 25

					BATTING											BASERUNNING				PERCENTAGES		
Year	Team	Lg	G	AB	H	2B	3B	HR	TB	R	RBI	TBB	IBB	SO	HBP	SH	SF	SB	CS	SB%	GDP	Avg	OBP	SLG
1991	Brewers	R	56	206	76	5	5	0	91	43	43	22	0	22	5	0	6	3	2	.60	4	.369	.431	.442
1992	Beloit	A	116	385	105	12	0	4	129	66	45	55	1	81	4	3	3	9	4	.69	11	.273	.367	.335
1993	Stockton	A	97	345	111	22	2	10	167	58	57	49	2	45	5	1	2	6	1	.86	15	.322	.411	.484
1994	El Paso	AA	95	312	82	7	6	8	125	59	56	32	0	80	0	2	5	4	3	.57	5	.263	.327	.401
	4 Min. YEARS		364	1248	374	46	13	22	512	226	201	158	3	228	14	6	16	22	10	.69	35	.300	.380	.410

Rod Steph

Pitches: Right   Bats: Right   Pos: P   Ht: 5'11"   Wt: 185   Born: 08/27/69   Age: 25

			HOW MUCH HE PITCHED					WHAT HE GAVE UP										THE RESULTS					
Year	Team	Lg	G	GS	CG	GF	IP	BFP	H	R	ER	HR	SH	SF	HB	TBB	IBB	SO	WP	Bk	W	L	Pct.	ShO	Sv	ERA
1991	Princeton	R	7	7	1	0	46.1	186	37	19	16	1	0	1	4	11	0	52	4	3	2	3	.400	1	0	3.11
	Cedar Rapds	A	8	7	3	0	56.2	229	46	19	16	5	2	0	4	15	1	46	3	4	4	3	.571	2	0	2.54
1992	Cedar Rapds	A	27	27	1	0	154.1	668	157	86	74	18	3	4	6	54	0	136	11	2	12	9	.571	1	0	4.32
1993	Winston-Sal	A	28	28	4	0	167.2	717	166	101	73	21	6	3	8	57	0	130	14	0	7	11	.389	2	0	3.92
1994	Thunder Bay	IND	13	13	3	0	88.1	354	68	30	24	5	3	1	4	17	0	76	5	0	8	1	.889	2	0	2.45
	Canton-Akrn	AA	3	3	1	0	20	89	27	13	12	2	1	0	0	4	0	6	1	0	1	2	.333	0	0	5.40
	4 Min. YEARS		86	85	13	0	533.1	2243	501	268	215	52	15	9	26	158	1	446	38	9	34	29	.540	8	0	3.63

Garrett Stephenson

Pitches: Right   Bats: Right   Pos: P   Ht: 6'4"   Wt: 185   Born: 01/02/72   Age: 23

			HOW MUCH HE PITCHED					WHAT HE GAVE UP										THE RESULTS					
Year	Team	Lg	G	GS	CG	GF	IP	BFP	H	R	ER	HR	SH	SF	HB	TBB	IBB	SO	WP	Bk	W	L	Pct.	ShO	Sv	ERA
1992	Bluefield	R	12	3	0	0	32.1	141	35	22	17	4	0	1	1	7	0	30	4	1	3	1	.750	0	0	4.73
1993	Albany	A	30	24	3	3	171.1	697	142	65	54	6	1	4	5	44	0	147	3	5	16	7	.696	2	1	2.84
1994	Frederick	A	18	17	1	0	107.1	450	91	62	48	13	2	5	5	36	2	133	2	4	7	5	.583	0	0	4.02
	Bowie	AA	7	7	1	0	36.2	161	47	22	21	2	0	1	0	11	1	32	3	2	3	2	.600	1	0	5.15
	3 Min. YEARS		67	51	5	3	347.2	1449	315	171	140	25	3	11	11	98	3	342	12	12	29	15	.659	3	1	3.62

244

Phil Stephenson

Bats: Left Throws: Left Pos: 1B Ht: 6' 1" Wt: 200 Born: 09/19/60 Age: 34

Year	Team	Lg	G	AB	H	2B	3B	HR	TB	R	RBI	TBB	IBB	SO	HBP	SH	SF	SB	CS	SB%	GDP	Avg	OBP	SLG
1984	Tacoma	AAA	124	398	120	25	1	10	177	70	69	85	9	54	0	6	3	15	4	.79	14	.302	.422	.445
1985	Tacoma	AAA	56	171	36	11	0	5	62	30	24	46	1	32	0	1	2	5	1	.83	1	.211	.374	.363
	Midland	AA	50	176	52	14	0	7	87	39	41	35	3	27	1	0	0	5	2	.71	4	.295	.415	.494
1986	Pittsfield	AA	140	423	115	29	2	12	184	72	68	129	8	67	2	3	8	30	18	.63	9	.272	.438	.435
1987	Iowa	AAA	105	298	91	24	2	10	149	53	56	62	2	56	1	2	7	4	6	.40	9	.305	.418	.500
1988	Iowa	AAA	118	426	125	28	11	22	241	69	81	50	9	76	1	2	5	9	5	.64	9	.293	.365	.566
1989	Iowa	AAA	84	290	87	17	3	13	149	52	62	58	9	41	1	0	4	28	3	.90	4	.300	.414	.514
1991	Las Vegas	AAA	7	18	4	0	1	0	6	1	5	1	0	1	0	0	1	0	0	.00	1	.222	.250	.333
	Wichita	AA	12	34	16	5	0	0	21	4	8	6	1	2	0	0	2	0	0	.00	2	.471	.524	.618
1992	Las Vegas	AAA	63	205	68	10	2	8	106	51	43	34	3	28	0	2	5	1	1	.50	7	.332	.418	.517
1993	Omaha	AAA	20	72	22	7	1	4	43	12	8	5	0	12	0	0	0	0	0	.00	3	.306	.351	.597
1994	Louisville	AAA	118	391	105	30	2	8	163	51	55	69	2	67	0	0	3	4	3	.57	4	.269	.376	.417
1989	Chicago	NL	17	21	3	0	0	0	3	0	0	2	0	3	0	0	0	1	0	1.00	0	.143	.217	.143
	San Diego	NL	10	17	6	0	0	2	12	4	2	3	0	2	0	0	0	0	0	.00	0	.353	.450	.706
1990	San Diego	NL	103	182	38	9	1	4	61	26	19	30	1	43	0	0	1	2	1	.67	3	.209	.319	.335
1991	San Diego	NL	11	7	2	0	0	0	2	0	0	2	0	3	0	0	0	0	0	.00	0	.286	.444	.286
1992	San Diego	NL	53	71	11	2	1	0	15	5	8	10	0	11	0	0	0	0	0	.00	0	.155	.259	.211
	10 Min. YEARS		897	2902	841	200	25	99	1388	504	520	580	47	463	6	16	40	101	43	.70	67	.290	.404	.478
	4 Maj. YEARS		194	298	60	11	2	6	93	35	29	47	1	62	0	0	1	3	1	.75	3	.201	.309	.312

Matt Stevens

Pitches: Right Bats: Right Pos: P Ht: 6'1" Wt: 200 Born: 01/20/67 Age: 28

| | | | HOW MUCH HE PITCHED | | | | | | WHAT HE GAVE UP | | | | | | | | | THE RESULTS | | | | | |
Year	Team	Lg	G	GS	CG	GF	IP	BFP	H	R	ER	HR	SH	SF	HB	TBB	IBB	SO	WP	Bk	W	L	Pct.	ShO	Sv	ERA
1989	Batavia	A	16	4	0	6	45.2	185	35	11	10	2	2	0	2	13	2	48	2	0	5	1	.833	0	0	1.97
1990	Spartanburg	A	14	0	0	8	29	118	24	12	7	1	1	0	0	10	0	31	2	1	0	2	.000	0	2	2.17
	Clearwater	A	10	0	0	8	12	43	4	1	1	1	0	0	0	4	1	9	0	0	1	1	.500	0	1	0.75
	Reading	AA	25	0	0	12	44.1	196	43	23	14	5	4	2	0	20	6	34	4	0	3	3	.500	0	4	2.84
1991	Clearwater	A	38	0	0	32	39.2	154	16	7	4	0	3	0	0	18	1	49	1	0	0	3	.000	0	17	0.91
	Reading	AA	25	0	0	11	40.1	162	35	16	16	5	1	1	0	11	1	31	2	0	5	1	.833	0	2	3.57
1992	Scranton/wb	AAA	9	0	0	3	13	61	19	11	9	1	0	0	0	4	0	11	1	0	1	0	1.000	0	0	6.23
	Reading	AA	46	0	0	37	58.2	250	65	31	26	3	3	3	0	16	4	43	3	0	4	4	.500	0	12	3.99
1993	Portland	AAA	53	0	0	16	81.2	352	75	27	18	2	2	3	1	35	3	60	6	1	5	3	.625	0	2	1.98
1994	Salt Lake	AAA	42	0	0	13	60.1	271	77	43	39	9	1	0	1	25	3	41	7	0	4	1	.800	0	2	5.82
	6 Min. YEARS		278	4	0	146	424.2	1792	393	182	144	29	17	9	4	156	21	357	28	2	28	19	.596	0	42	3.05

Todd Steverson

Bats: Right Throws: Right Pos: OF Ht: 6'2" Wt: 185 Born: 11/15/71 Age: 23

Year	Team	Lg	G	AB	H	2B	3B	HR	TB	R	RBI	TBB	IBB	SO	HBP	SH	SF	SB	CS	SB%	GDP	Avg	OBP	SLG
1992	St.Cathrnes	A	65	225	47	9	0	6	74	26	24	26	0	83	1	0	3	23	7	.77	2	.209	.290	.329
1993	Dunedin	A	106	413	112	32	4	11	185	68	54	44	2	118	1	3	1	15	12	.56	3	.271	.342	.448
1994	Knoxville	AA	124	415	109	24	5	9	170	59	38	71	2	112	1	1	1	20	11	.65	3	.263	.371	.410
	3 Min. YEARS		295	1053	268	65	9	26	429	153	116	141	4	313	3	4	5	58	30	.66	8	.255	.343	.407

Andy Stewart

Bats: Right Throws: Right Pos: C Ht: 5'11" Wt: 205 Born: 12/05/70 Age: 24

Year	Team	Lg	G	AB	H	2B	3B	HR	TB	R	RBI	TBB	IBB	SO	HBP	SH	SF	SB	CS	SB%	GDP	Avg	OBP	SLG
1990	Royals	R	21	52	10	4	0	0	14	5	1	9	1	13	3	3	0	3	0	1.00	0	.192	.344	.269
1991	Baseball Cy	A	78	276	64	16	1	3	91	30	36	7	1	59	4	4	2	6	4	.60	6	.232	.260	.330
1992	Baseball Cy	A	94	283	73	13	1	4	100	31	38	21	1	45	2	4	1	3	8	.27	4	.258	.313	.353
1993	Wilmington	A	110	361	100	20	3	8	150	54	42	26	0	88	8	0	1	7	1	.88	6	.277	.338	.416
1994	Wilmington	A	94	360	114	24	3	17	195	53	66	30	4	56	13	2	4	0	2	.00	11	.317	.386	.542
	Memphis	AA	20	72	17	1	0	0	18	10	5	3	1	5	4	1	1	0	0	.00	3	.236	.300	.250
	5 Min. YEARS		417	1404	378	78	8	32	568	183	188	96	8	266	34	14	9	19	15	.56	30	.269	.329	.405

Brady Stewart

Bats: Right Throws: Right Pos: SS Ht: 5'11" Wt: 180 Born: 05/04/69 Age: 26

Year	Team	Lg	G	AB	H	2B	3B	HR	TB	R	RBI	TBB	IBB	SO	HBP	SH	SF	SB	CS	SB%	GDP	Avg	OBP	SLG
1990	Eugene	A	34	85	14	2	0	0	16	15	2	10	0	16	0	2	0	6	0	1.00	3	.165	.253	.188
1991	Appleton	A	51	158	40	9	0	0	49	14	9	17	0	32	0	2	2	1	2	.33	3	.253	.322	.310
	Baseball Cy	A	40	123	29	6	0	1	38	13	8	11	0	38	2	3	0	2	1	.67	5	.236	.309	.309
1992	Baseball Cy	A	62	204	37	4	1	0	43	26	5	19	0	57	0	5	0	7	2	.78	5	.181	.251	.211
	Appleton	A	14	45	13	1	0	0	14	4	2	6	0	8	0	1	0	1	2	.33	2	.289	.373	.311
1993	Wilmington	A	87	258	56	6	0	0	62	22	21	14	0	61	3	5	1	7	8	.47	4	.217	.264	.240
1994	Memphis	AA	56	161	28	2	1	0	32	14	3	17	0	41	0	3	1	5	0	1.00	2	.174	.251	.199
	5 Min. YEARS		344	1034	217	30	2	1	254	108	50	94	0	253	5	21	4	29	15	.66	24	.210	.278	.246

Carl Stewart

Pitches: Right Bats: Right Pos: P Ht: 6'3" Wt: 190 Born: 12/08/70 Age: 24

Year	Team	Lg	G	GS	CG	GF	IP	BFP	H	R	ER	HR	SH	SF	HB	TBB	IBB	SO	WP	Bk	W	L	Pct.	ShO	Sv	ERA
1988	Billings	R	1	0	0	1	1	6	2	1	0	0	0	0	0	1	0	1	2	0	0	0	.000	0	0	0.00
	Reds	R	2	0	0	1	2	10	2	3	3	0	0	1	0	2	0	2	2	0	0	0	.000	0	0	13.50
1990	Billings	R	14	14	0	0	73.2	315	51	41	34	4	1	5	5	47	0	64	15	0	3	4	.429	0	0	4.15
1991	Chston-Wv	A	24	24	2	0	136.1	607	117	73	69	6	2	5	4	88	0	135	18	1	8	12	.400	0	0	4.56
1992	Chston-Vw	A	27	26	1	1	164.2	713	147	76	65	6	3	5	3	84	1	167	25	0	6	10	.375	0	0	3.55
1993	Chston-Wv	A	2	2	0	0	10.2	42	4	2	1	0	0	0	3	4	0	9	2	0	0	0	.000	0	0	0.84
	Chattanooga	AA	10	10	1	0	53.2	242	57	35	30	6	1	2	4	24	0	47	4	0	3	4	.429	0	0	5.03
	Winston-Sal	A	14	14	1	0	80.2	340	65	38	29	9	1	2	5	35	0	69	5	0	5	2	.714	0	0	3.24
1994	Chattanooga	AA	9	6	0	2	41.2	197	44	28	25	2	4	3	3	30	3	33	6	0	1	6	.143	0	0	5.40
	6 Min. YEARS		103	96	5	5	564.1	2472	489	297	256	33	12	21	30	315	4	527	79		26	38	.406	0	0	4.08

Kurt Stillwell

Bats: Both Throws: Right Pos: SS Ht: 5'11" Wt: 180 Born: 06/04/65 Age: 30

Year	Team	Lg	G	AB	H	2B	3B	HR	TB	R	RBI	TBB	IBB	SO	HBP	SH	SF	SB	CS	SB%	GDP	Avg	OBP	SLG
1984	Cedar Rapds	A	112	382	96	15	1	4	125	63	33	70	1	53	1	3	5	24	9	.73	3	.251	.365	.327
1985	Denver	AAA	59	182	48	7	4	1	66	28	22	21	2	23	0	3	0	5	3	.63	3	.264	.340	.363
1986	Denver	AAA	10	30	7	0	0	0	7	2	2	2	0	4	0	0	0	2	0	1.00	2	.233	.281	.233
1994	Indianapols	AAA	93	337	91	22	5	8	147	46	49	30	2	55	3	1	7	1	1	.50	5	.270	.329	.436
1986	Cincinnati	NL	104	279	64	6	1	0	72	31	26	30	1	47	2	4	0	6	2	.75	5	.229	.309	.258
1987	Cincinnati	NL	131	395	102	20	7	4	148	54	33	32	2	50	2	2	2	4	6	.40	5	.258	.316	.375
1988	Kansas City	AL	128	459	115	28	5	10	183	63	53	47	0	76	3	6	3	6	5	.55	7	.251	.322	.399
1989	Kansas City	AL	130	463	121	20	7	7	176	52	54	42	2	64	3	5	3	9	6	.60	3	.261	.325	.380
1990	Kansas City	AL	144	506	126	35	4	3	178	60	51	39	1	60	4	4	7	0	2	.00	11	.249	.304	.352
1991	Kansas City	AL	122	385	102	17	1	6	139	44	51	33	5	56	1	5	4	3	4	.43	8	.265	.322	.361
1992	San Diego	NL	114	379	86	15	3	2	113	35	24	26	9	58	1	4	6	4	1	.80	6	.227	.274	.298
1993	San Diego	NL	57	121	26	4	0	1	33	9	11	11	2	22	1	2	0	4	3	.57	2	.215	.286	.273
	California	AL	22	61	16	2	2	0	22	2	3	4	0	11	0	1	2	2	0	1.00	1	.262	.299	.361
	4 Min. YEARS		274	931	242	44	10	13	345	139	106	123	5	135	4	7	12	32	13	.71	13	.260	.345	.371
	8 Maj. YEARS		952	3048	758	147	30	33	1064	350	306	264	22	444	17	33	27	38	29	.57	49	.249	.310	.349

Don Strange

Pitches: Right Bats: Right Pos: P Ht: 6'0" Wt: 195 Born: 05/26/67 Age: 28

Year	Team	Lg	G	GS	CG	GF	IP	BFP	H	R	ER	HR	SH	SF	HB	TBB	IBB	SO	WP	Bk	W	L	Pct.	ShO	Sv	ERA
1989	Pulaski	R	27	0	0	20	33	136	27	9	9	1	0	1	0	6	2	39	4	1	3	0	1.000	0	5	2.45
1990	Sumter	A	46	0	0	41	54.1	208	34	6	4	0	1	3	3	12	3	53	2	0	4	1	.800	0	24	0.66
1991	Durham	A	38	0	0	32	40.1	172	39	13	8	1	2	2	1	8	1	51	7	0	0	0	.000	0	19	1.79
	Greenville	AA	4	0	0	1	4.2	23	9	7	7	1	0	0	0	2	0	8	1	0	1	0	1.000	0	1	13.50
1992	Greenville	AA	48	0	0	41	60	234	43	19	16	3	0	1	1	19	3	58	3	0	5	3	.625	0	18	2.40
1993	Greenville	AA	27	0	0	24	24.2	109	27	11	10	3	0	2	0	9	1	27	2	0	1	1	.500	0	18	3.65
	Richmond	AAA	34	0	0	19	46.1	200	45	24	20	1	2	1	0	19	6	34	4	0	1	2	.333	0	4	3.88
1994	Richmond	AAA	12	1	0	8	20.1	100	31	15	15	2	1	4	1	7	4	18	2	0	2	1	.667	0	0	6.64
	Memphis	AA	14	0	0	11	21	80	11	4	4	3	1	0	1	6	1	18	0	0	0	0	.000	0	6	1.71
	6 Min. YEARS		250	1	0	197	304.2	1262	266	108	93	15	7	14	7	88	21	306	25	1	17	8	.680	0	92	2.75

Chad Strickland

Bats: Right Throws: Right Pos: C Ht: 6'1" Wt: 185 Born: 03/16/72 Age: 23

Year	Team	Lg	G	AB	H	2B	3B	HR	TB	R	RBI	TBB	IBB	SO	HBP	SH	SF	SB	CS	SB%	GDP	Avg	OBP	SLG
1990	Royals	R	50	163	36	7	0	0	43	14	12	11	0	24	0	2	4	6	2	.75	5	.221	.264	.264
1991	Appleton	A	28	81	14	4	0	1	21	5	5	2	0	12	0	1	1	2	1	.67	0	.173	.190	.259
	Eugene	A	34	118	19	7	0	1	29	13	11	13	0	16	2	2	2	1	1	.50	1	.161	.252	.246
1992	Appleton	A	112	396	101	16	1	2	125	29	49	12	0	37	1	0	5	2	5	.29	6	.255	.275	.316
1993	Wilmington	A	122	409	102	16	6	2	136	51	46	23	0	46	3	7	9	4	3	.57	7	.249	.288	.333
1994	Memphis	AA	114	379	82	14	2	6	118	37	47	17	1	40	3	5	3	1	3	.25	8	.216	.254	.311
	5 Min. YEARS		460	1546	354	64	9	12	472	149	170	78	1	175	9	17	24	16	15	.52	27	.229	.266	.305

Scott Stricklin

Bats: Left Throws: Right Pos: C Ht: 5'11" Wt: 180 Born: 02/17/72 Age: 23

Year	Team	Lg	G	AB	H	2B	3B	HR	TB	R	RBI	TBB	IBB	SO	HBP	SH	SF	SB	CS	SB%	GDP	Avg	OBP	SLG
1993	Elizabethtn	R	38	125	28	2	0	1	33	18	15	16	0	17	0	4	1	1	0	1.00	3	.224	.310	.264
	FtWayne	A	9	31	2	0	0	0	2	1	0	4	0	7	0	0	0	0	0	.00	0	.065	.171	.065
1994	Salt Lake	AAA	2	2	0	0	0	0	0	0	0	0	0	0	0	0	0	0	0	.00	0	.000	.000	.000
	Fort Wayne	A	65	182	55	12	0	2	73	18	19	30	3	38	0	2	1	1	3	.25	2	.302	.399	.401
	Nashville	AA	16	38	9	4	0	0	13	4	1	7	0	11	0	0	0	0	1	.00	0	.237	.356	.342
	2 Min. YEARS		130	378	94	18	0	3	121	41	35	57	3	73	0	6	2	2	4	.33	5	.249	.346	.320

Mark Strittmatter

Bats: Right Throws: Right Pos: C Ht: 6'1" Wt: 200 Born: 04/04/69 Age: 26

Year	Team	Lg	G	AB	H	2B	3B	HR	TB	R	RBI	TBB	IBB	SO	HBP	SH	SF	SB	CS	SB%	GDP	Avg	OBP	SLG
1992	Bend	A	35	101	26	6	0	2	38	17	13	12	0	28	3	0	0	0	4	.00	2	.257	.353	.376
1993	Central Val	A	59	179	47	8	0	2	61	21	15	31	0	29	2	2	3	3	0	1.00	8	.263	.372	.341
	Colo Spngs	AAA	5	10	2	1	0	0	3	1	2	0	0	2	1	0	0	0	0	.00	2	.200	.273	.300
1994	New Haven	AA	73	215	49	8	0	2	63	20	26	33	1	39	9	3	4	1	2	.33	7	.228	.349	.293
	3 Min. YEARS		172	505	124	23	0	6	165	59	56	76	1	98	15	5	7	4	6	.40	19	.246	.357	.327

Tanyon Sturtze

Pitches: Right Bats: Right Pos: P Ht: 6'5" Wt: 190 Born: 10/12/70 Age: 24

Year	Team	Lg	G	GS	CG	GF	IP	BFP	H	R	ER	HR	SH	SF	HB	TBB	IBB	SO	WP	Bk	W	L	Pct.	ShO	Sv	ERA
1990	Athletics	R	12	10	0	1	48	232	55	41	29	3	0	2	5	26	0	30	5	2	2	5	.286	0	0	5.44
1991	Madison	A	27	27	0	0	163	685	136	77	56	5	6	6	5	58	5	88	10	5	10	5	.667	0	0	3.09
1992	Modesto	A	25	25	1	0	151	656	143	72	63	6	5	5	4	78	1	126	5	0	7	11	.389	0	0	3.75
1993	Huntsville	AA	28	28	1	0	165.2	734	169	102	88	16	3	11	6	85	2	112	11	1	5	12	.294	1	0	4.78
1994	Huntsville	AA	17	17	1	0	103.1	435	100	40	37	5	3	4	3	39	1	63	1	0	6	3	.667	0	0	3.22
	Tacoma	AAA	11	9	0	2	64.2	294	73	36	29	5	0	1	2	34	2	28	6	0	4	5	.444	0	0	4.04
	5 Min. YEARS		120	116	3	3	695.2	3036	676	368	302	40	17	29	25	320	11	447	38	8	34	41	.453	1	0	3.91

Chris Stynes

Bats: Right Throws: Right Pos: SS Ht: 5'9" Wt: 170 Born: 01/19/73 Age: 22

Year	Team	Lg	G	AB	H	2B	3B	HR	TB	R	RBI	TBB	IBB	SO	HBP	SH	SF	SB	CS	SB%	GDP	Avg	OBP	SLG
1991	Blue Jays	R	57	219	67	15	1	4	96	29	39	9	0	38	1	1	0	10	3	.77	1	.306	.336	.438
1992	Myrtle Bch	A	127	489	139	36	0	7	196	67	46	16	1	43	8	14	4	28	14	.67	8	.284	.315	.401
1993	Dunedin	A	123	496	151	28	5	7	210	72	48	25	2	40	3	4	4	19	9	.68	12	.304	.339	.423
1994	Knoxville	AA	136	545	173	32	4	8	237	79	79	23	4	36	7	5	4	28	12	.70	12	.317	.351	.435
	4 Min. YEARS		443	1749	530	111	10	26	739	247	212	73	7	157	19	24	12	85	38	.69	33	.303	.336	.423

William Suero

Bats: Right Throws: Right Pos: 2B Ht: 5'9" Wt: 175 Born: 11/07/66 Age: 28

Year	Team	Lg	G	AB	H	2B	3B	HR	TB	R	RBI	TBB	IBB	SO	HBP	SH	SF	SB	CS	SB%	GDP	Avg	OBP	SLG
1986	Medicne Hat	R	64	273	76	7	5	2	99	39	28	15	0	36	3	4	2	13	4	.76	7	.278	.321	.363
1987	St.Cathrnes	A	77	297	94	12	4	4	126	43	24	35	1	35	1	2	1	23	11	.68	3	.316	.389	.424
1988	Myrtle Bch	A	125	493	140	21	6	6	191	88	52	49	2	72	4	3	6	21	7	.75	4	.284	.350	.387
1989	Dunedin	A	51	206	60	10	5	2	86	35	17	16	0	32	3	1	0	9	3	.75	3	.291	.351	.417
	Knoxville	AA	87	324	84	17	5	4	123	42	29	34	0	50	3	2	0	7	4	.64	2	.259	.335	.380
1990	Knoxville	AA	133	483	127	29	7	16	218	80	60	78	3	78	7	6	2	40	21	.66	5	.263	.372	.451
1991	Syracuse	AAA	98	393	78	18	1	1	101	49	28	38	0	51	7	4	3	17	13	.57	9	.198	.279	.257
	Denver	AAA	20	70	27	3	2	0	34	20	15	10	0	8	0	2	1	3	0	1.00	3	.386	.457	.486
1992	Denver	AAA	75	276	71	10	9	1	102	42	25	31	1	33	1	3	2	16	9	.64	5	.257	.332	.370
1993	New Orleans	AAA	46	124	28	4	1	1	37	14	13	21	0	17	1	2	3	8	7	.53	3	.226	.336	.298
1994	Carolina	AA	18	77	25	4	0	1	32	15	7	6	0	14	3	0	0	3	3	.50	1	.325	.395	.416
	Buffalo	AAA	85	268	63	15	4	3	95	27	23	15	2	35	3	4	0	5	5	.50	10	.235	.283	.354
1992	Milwaukee	AL	18	16	3	1	0	0	4	4	0	2	0	1	1	0	0	1	1	.50	2	.188	.316	.250
1993	Milwaukee	AL	15	14	4	0	0	0	4	0	0	1	0	3	0	0	0	0	1	.00	1	.286	.333	.286
	9 Min. YEARS		879	3284	873	150	49	41	1244	494	321	348	9	461	36	33	20	165	87	.65	55	.266	.341	.379
	2 Maj. YEARS		33	30	7	1	0	0	8	4	0	3	0	4	1	0	0	1	2	.33	3	.233	.324	.267

Grant Sullivan

Pitches: Left Bats: Left Pos: P Ht: 6'5" Wt: 210 Born: 03/19/70 Age: 25

Year	Team	Lg	G	GS	CG	GF	IP	BFP	H	R	ER	HR	SH	SF	HB	TBB	IBB	SO	WP	Bk	W	L	Pct.	ShO	Sv	ERA
1991	Oneonta	A	15	15	2	0	94.1	414	92	56	45	2	3	3	5	38	2	45	5	5	6	6	.500	0	0	4.29
1992	Greensboro	A	13	13	0	0	82.1	351	87	35	20	3	3	6	3	21	0	53	7	1	4	6	.400	0	0	2.19
	Ft. Laud	A	12	11	0	0	69.1	310	83	37	31	1	3	4	5	27	0	27	5	0	3	7	.300	0	0	4.02
1993	Pr William	A	34	15	0	4	96.1	447	122	74	63	8	1	3	3	44	0	35	9	0	3	8	.273	0	1	5.89
1994	Tampa	A	22	0	0	6	38.2	183	43	28	22	2	2	3	2	27	1	27	1	1	1	0	1.000	0	0	5.12
	Albany-Colo	AA	3	0	0	1	6.1	32	8	5	5	2	0	0	0	7	0	2	1	0	1	0	1.000	0	0	7.11
	4 Min. YEARS		99	54	5	11	387.1	1737	435	235	186	18	12	19	18	164	3	189	28	7	18	27	.400	0	1	4.32

Mike Sullivan

Pitches: Right Bats: Right Pos: P Ht: 6'3" Wt: 195 Born: 01/27/68 Age: 27

Year	Team	Lg	G	GS	CG	GF	IP	BFP	H	R	ER	HR	SH	SF	HB	TBB	IBB	SO	WP	Bk	W	L	Pct.	ShO	Sv	ERA
1989	Batavia	A	24	0	0	18	45.2	195	41	22	15	6	2	1	1	13	1	42	5	0	4	1	.800	0	5	2.96
1990	Spartanburg	A	22	0	0	18	36	164	39	19	18	1	4	2	0	17	0	28	5	2	4	3	.571	0	4	4.50
	Clearwater	A	13	0	0	11	14.2	57	8	2	2	0	0	1	1	4	0	16	1	0	2	1	.667	0	3	1.23
1991	Clearwater	A	36	7	0	20	76	320	58	29	22	3	1	6	2	36	2	64	4	0	6	3	.667	0	11	2.61

Year	Team	Lg	G	GS	CG	GF	IP	BFP	H	R	ER	HR	SH	SF	HB	TBB	IBB	SO	WP	Bk	W	L	Pct.	ShO	Sv	ERA
1992	Reading	AA	34	0	0	13	44.2	204	56	34	24	5	2	1	1	18	2	27	3	2	2	1	.667	0	0	4.84
	Clearwater	A	24	0	0	21	25.2	96	16	3	3	0	0	1	1	2	1	24	0	0	2	0	1.000	0	10	1.05
1993	Reading	AA	31	0	0	12	45.1	191	42	20	17	2	1	2	2	13	3	29	5	1	0	3	.000	0	4	3.38
1994	Reading	AA	11	0	0	3	14	65	12	10	8	2	2	1	2	13	2	11	1	1	0	1	.000	0	0	5.14
	New Britain	AA	38	0	0	18	51.2	232	55	32	24	1	2	1	3	20	1	34	1	0	2	6	.250	0	3	4.18
	6 Min. YEARS		233	7	0	134	353.2	1524	327	171	133	20	14	16	13	136	12	275	25	6	22	19	.537	0	44	3.38

William Sullivan

Pitches: Right Bats: Right Pos: P Ht: 6'3" Wt: 210 Born: 03/13/71 Age: 24

			HOW MUCH HE PITCHED						WHAT HE GAVE UP										THE RESULTS						
Year	Team	Lg	G	GS	CG	GF	IP	BFP	H	R	ER	HR	SH	SF	HB	TBB	IBB	SO	WP	Bk	W	L	Pct.	ShO	Sv	ERA
1993	Billings	R	18	7	2	9	54	224	33	13	10	1	3	0	6	25	0	79	2	5	5	0	1.000	2	3	1.67
1994	Chattanooga	AA	34	13	2	16	121.1	508	101	60	46	8	2	1	6	40	1	111	5	4	11	7	.611	0	7	3.41
	2 Min. YEARS		52	20	4	25	175.1	732	134	73	56	9	5	1	12	65	1	190	7	9	16	7	.696	2	10	2.87

John Sutherland

Pitches: Right Bats: Right Pos: P Ht: 6'2" Wt: 185 Born: 10/11/68 Age: 26

			HOW MUCH HE PITCHED						WHAT HE GAVE UP										THE RESULTS						
Year	Team	Lg	G	GS	CG	GF	IP	BFP	H	R	ER	HR	SH	SF	HB	TBB	IBB	SO	WP	Bk	W	L	Pct.	ShO	Sv	ERA
1991	Yankees	R	4	1	0	0	7.2	31	5	6	5	0	0	1	0	3	0	5	0	1	0	2	.000	0	0	5.87
1992	Oneonta	A	4	1	0	1	15.2	61	10	2	2	1	1	0	0	2	0	16	0	0	3	0	1.000	0	0	1.15
	Greensboro	A	14	3	0	1	34	144	29	17	15	2	2	0	1	12	0	27	3	0	3	2	.600	0	0	3.97
1993	San Berndno	A	43	1	0	24	70.1	314	73	46	39	7	2	0	0	37	2	59	1	0	3	7	.300	0	4	4.99
1994	Albany-Colo	AA	31	4	0	11	63.2	276	62	35	27	6	1	1	2	25	2	49	1	0	6	4	.600	0	1	3.82
	4 Min. YEARS		96	10	0	37	191.1	826	179	106	88	16	6	2	3	79	4	156	9	1	15	15	.500	0	5	4.14

Glenn Sutko

Bats: Right Throws: Right Pos: C Ht: 6'3" Wt: 225 Born: 05/09/68 Age: 27

			BATTING														BASERUNNING				PERCENTAGES		
Year	Team	Lg	G	AB	H	2B	3B	HR	TB	R	RBI	TBB	IBB	SO	HBP	SH	SF	SB	CS	SB%	GDP	Avg	OBP	SLG
1988	Billings	R	30	84	13	2	1	1	20	3	8	14	0	38	1	3	2	3	1	.75	2	.155	.277	.238
1989	Greensboro	A	109	333	78	21	0	7	120	44	41	47	1	105	4	0	3	1	3	.25	5	.234	.333	.360
1990	Cedar Rapds	A	4	10	3	0	0	0	3	0	0	0	0	2	1	0	0	0	0	.00	1	.300	.364	.300
	Chattanooga	AA	53	174	29	7	1	2	44	12	11	8	1	66	1	0	0	1	1	.50	2	.167	.208	.253
1991	Chattanooga	AA	23	63	18	3	0	3	30	12	11	9	2	20	0	2	0	0	0	.00	1	.286	.375	.476
	Nashville	AAA	45	134	28	2	1	3	41	9	15	22	3	67	0	0	0	1	0	1.00	3	.209	.321	.306
1992	Chattanooga	AA	64	198	37	4	0	10	71	24	27	17	1	90	1	1	2	3	2	.60	1	.187	.252	.359
1993	Winston-Sal	A	31	1	0	0	0	0	0	1	0	0	0	0	0	0	0	0	0	.00	0	.000	.000	.000
1994	New Orleans	AAA	27	77	17	2	0	2	25	10	10	8	1	22	0	0	0	0	1	.00	1	.221	.294	.325
	Beloit	A	59	186	41	9	2	4	66	28	21	35	2	80	1	1	2	3	1	.75	4	.220	.344	.355
1990	Cincinnati	NL	1	1	0	0	0	0	0	0	0	0	0	1	0	0	0	0	0	.00	0	.000	.000	.000
1991	Cincinnati	NL	10	10	1	0	0	0	1	0	1	2	0	6	0	0	0	0	0	.00	0	.100	.250	.100
	7 Min. YEARS		445	1260	264	50	5	32	420	143	144	160	11	490	9	7	9	12	9	.57	20	.210	.301	.333
	2 Maj. YEARS		11	11	1	0	0	0	1	0	1	2	0	7	0	0	0	0	0	.00	0	.091	.231	.091

Makato Suzuki

Pitches: Right Bats: Right Pos: P Ht: 6'4" Wt: 195 Born: 05/31/75 Age: 20

			HOW MUCH HE PITCHED						WHAT HE GAVE UP										THE RESULTS						
Year	Team	Lg	G	GS	CG	GF	IP	BFP	H	R	ER	HR	SH	SF	HB	TBB	IBB	SO	WP	Bk	W	L	Pct.	ShO	Sv	ERA
1992	Salinas	A	1	0	0	0	1	3	0	0	0	0	0	0	0	0	0	1	0	0	0	0	.000	0	0	0.00
1993	San Berndno	A	48	1	0	35	80.2	351	59	37	33	5	3	2	2	56	4	87	12	2	4	4	.500	0	12	3.68
1994	Jacksonvlle	AA	8	0	0	1	12.2	58	15	4	4	1	0	1	0	6	0	10	0	0	1	0	1.000	0	1	2.84
	3 Min. YEARS		57	1	0	36	94.1	412	74	41	37	6	3	3	2	62	4	98	12	2	5	4	.556	0	13	3.53

Steve Swail

Bats: Right Throws: Right Pos: C Ht: 6'3" Wt: 200 Born: 04/28/67 Age: 28

			BATTING														BASERUNNING				PERCENTAGES		
Year	Team	Lg	G	AB	H	2B	3B	HR	TB	R	RBI	TBB	IBB	SO	HBP	SH	SF	SB	CS	SB%	GDP	Avg	OBP	SLG
1989	Pulaski	R	31	78	17	4	0	0	21	12	6	8	0	16	0	1	0	2	0	1.00	1	.218	.291	.269
1990	Burlington	A	33	75	11	2	0	0	13	9	3	10	0	24	1	2	0	0	0	.00	0	.147	.256	.173
1991	Durham	A	32	50	5	0	0	0	5	2	1	1	0	15	0	0	0	0	1	.00	0	.100	.118	.100
1992	Durham	A	9	7	2	0	0	0	2	2	0	1	0	2	0	1	0	0	0	.00	0	.286	.375	.286
	Macon	A	5	5	2	0	0	0	2	2	2	1	0	0	0	0	0	0	0	.00	0	.400	.500	.400
	Greenville	AA	5	14	3	0	0	0	3	0	0	1	0	5	0	0	0	0	0	.00	0	.214	.267	.214
1993	Durham	A	48	133	35	6	0	1	44	16	12	12	0	39	1	2	0	1	3	.25	6	.263	.329	.331
1994	Greenville	AA	38	105	14	1	0	0	15	7	7	12	0	39	0	1	1	0	1	.00	3	.133	.220	.143
	6 Min. YEARS		201	467	89	13	0	1	105	50	31	46	0	141	2	7	1	3	5	.38	11	.191	.266	.225

Pedro Swann

Bats: Left Throws: Right Pos: OF Ht: 6'0" Wt: 195 Born: 10/27/70 Age: 24

			BATTING														BASERUNNING				PERCENTAGES		
Year	Team	Lg	G	AB	H	2B	3B	HR	TB	R	RBI	TBB	IBB	SO	HBP	SH	SF	SB	CS	SB%	GDP	Avg	OBP	SLG
1991	Idaho Falls	R	55	174	48	6	1	3	65	35	28	33	0	45	2	1	2	8	5	.62	4	.276	.393	.374

Year Team	Lg	G	AB	H	2B	3B	HR	TB	R	RBI	TBB	IBB	SO	HBP	SH	SF	SB	CS	SB%	GDP	Avg	OBP	SLG
1992 Pulaski	R	59	203	61	18	1	5	96	36	34	32	3	33	7	0	1	13	6	.68	6	.300	.412	.473
1993 Durham	A	61	182	63	8	2	6	93	27	27	19	0	38	1	0	0	6	12	.33	2	.346	.411	.511
Greenville	AA	44	157	48	9	2	3	70	19	21	21	0	23	1	1	0	2	2	.50	5	.306	.347	.446
1994 Greenville	AA	126	428	121	25	2	10	180	55	49	46	2	85	4	0	2	16	9	.64	14	.283	.356	.421
4 Min. YEARS		345	1144	341	66	8	27	504	172	159	139	5	224	15	2	5	45	34	.57	31	.298	.380	.441

Dave Swartzbaugh

Pitches: Right Bats: Right Pos: P   Ht: 6'2" Wt: 195 Born: 02/11/68 Age: 27

| | | HOW MUCH HE PITCHED | | | | | | WHAT HE GAVE UP | | | | | | | | | | | THE RESULTS | | | | | |
Year Team	Lg	G	GS	CG	GF	IP	BFP	H	R	ER	HR	SH	SF	HB	TBB	IBB	SO	WP	Bk	W	L	Pct.	ShO	Sv	ERA
1989 Geneva	A	18	10	0	1	75	338	81	59	41	5	0	3	1	35	1	77	8	1	2	3	.400	0	0	4.92
1990 Peoria	A	29	29	5	0	169.2	736	147	88	72	11	1	3	7	89	1	129	10	4	8	11	.421	2	0	3.82
1991 Peoria	A	5	5	1	0	34.1	145	21	16	7	0	2	1	2	15	1	31	2	2	0	5	.000	0	0	1.83
Winston-Sal	A	15	15	2	0	93.2	379	71	22	19	3	5	1	1	42	1	73	4	0	10	4	.714	1	0	1.83
Charlotte	AA	1	1	0	0	5.1	25	6	7	6	1	0	0	0	3	1	5	1	0	0	1	.000	0	0	10.13
1992 Charlotte	AA	27	27	5	0	165	689	134	78	67	13	5	10	9	62	2	111	5	1	7	10	.412	2	0	3.65
1993 Iowa	AAA	26	9	0	5	86.2	385	90	57	51	16	6	4	5	44	1	69	6	0	4	6	.400	0	1	5.30
Orlando	AA	10	9	1	0	66	268	52	33	31	5	2	1	3	18	0	59	2	0	1	3	.250	0	0	4.23
1994 Iowa	AAA	10	0	0	1	19.1	94	24	18	18	8	1	2	1	15	1	14	2	0	1	0	1.000	0	0	8.38
Orlando	AA	42	1	0	11	79	327	70	36	29	7	5	3	4	19	2	70	0	0	2	4	.333	0	2	3.30
6 Min. YEARS		183	106	14	18	794	3386	696	414	341	69	27	28	33	342	11	638	40	8	35	47	.427	5	3	3.87

Denny Sweeney

Pitches: Left Bats: Left Pos: P   Ht: 6'0" Wt: 187 Born: 08/06/69 Age: 25

| | | HOW MUCH HE PITCHED | | | | | | WHAT HE GAVE UP | | | | | | | | | | | THE RESULTS | | | | | |
Year Team	Lg	G	GS	CG	GF	IP	BFP	H	R	ER	HR	SH	SF	HB	TBB	IBB	SO	WP	Bk	W	L	Pct.	ShO	Sv	ERA
1991 Elizabethtn	R	16	2	0	6	57.2	262	52	39	19	4	2	0	4	25	2	64	5	3	2	3	.400	0	2	2.97
1992 Kenosha	A	31	0	0	16	50.1	215	50	23	19	2	3	0	5	9	0	49	2	1	1	2	.333	0	2	3.40
1993 Ft.Myers	A	39	13	1	7	114.2	503	110	56	50	5	8	1	5	55	1	77	6	2	8	7	.533	0	0	3.92
1994 Nashville	AA	27	0	0	8	33	168	51	28	26	3	1	2	2	18	1	25	4	1	1	2	.333	0	0	7.09
4 Min. YEARS		113	15	1	37	255.2	1148	263	146	114	14	14	3	16	107	4	215	17	7	12	14	.462	0	4	4.01

Mark Sweeney

Bats: Left Throws: Left Pos: OF   Ht: 6'1" Wt: 195 Born: 10/26/69 Age: 25

| | | BATTING | | | | | | | | | | | | | | | BASERUNNING | | | | PERCENTAGES | | |
Year Team	Lg	G	AB	H	2B	3B	HR	TB	R	RBI	TBB	IBB	SO	HBP	SH	SF	SB	CS	SB%	GDP	Avg	OBP	SLG
1991 Boise	A	70	234	66	10	3	4	94	45	34	51	2	42	5	1	3	9	5	.64	7	.282	.416	.402
1992 Quad City	A	120	424	115	20	5	14	187	65	76	47	3	85	4	6	5	15	11	.58	6	.271	.346	.441
1993 Palm Sprngs	A	66	245	87	18	3	3	120	41	47	42	6	29	2	0	3	9	6	.60	4	.355	.449	.490
Midland	AA	51	188	67	13	2	9	111	41	32	27	3	22	6	0	4	1	1	.50	5	.356	.444	.590
1994 Midland	AA	14	50	15	3	0	3	27	13	18	10	2	10	0	1	2	1	1	.50	3	.300	.403	.540
Vancouver	AAA	103	344	98	12	3	8	140	59	49	59	3	50	1	1	3	3	3	.50	5	.285	.394	.407
4 Min. YEARS		424	1485	448	76	16	41	679	264	256	236	19	238	22	9	20	38	27	.58	30	.302	.400	.457

Scott Talanoa

Bats: Right Throws: Right Pos: 1B   Ht: 6'5" Wt: 240 Born: 11/12/69 Age: 25

| | | BATTING | | | | | | | | | | | | | | | BASERUNNING | | | | PERCENTAGES | | |
Year Team	Lg	G	AB	H	2B	3B	HR	TB	R	RBI	TBB	IBB	SO	HBP	SH	SF	SB	CS	SB%	GDP	Avg	OBP	SLG
1991 Helena	R	37	127	37	10	0	6	65	24	29	29	2	32	3	0	2	1	2	.33	4	.291	.429	.512
1992 Beloit	A	106	357	82	18	0	13	139	57	56	49	1	109	2	3	2	7	4	.64	3	.230	.324	.389
1993 Beloit	A	87	258	74	12	0	25	161	55	66	71	6	86	8	0	4	5	3	.63	3	.287	.449	.624
1994 El Paso	AA	127	429	111	20	1	28	217	89	88	77	6	138	9	0	4	1	2	.33	11	.259	.380	.506
4 Min. YEARS		357	1171	304	60	1	72	582	225	239	226	15	365	22	3	12	14	11	.56	21	.260	.386	.497

Amaury Talemaco

Pitches: Right Bats: Right Pos: P   Ht: 6'3" Wt: 180 Born: 01/19/74 Age: 21

| | | HOW MUCH HE PITCHED | | | | | | WHAT HE GAVE UP | | | | | | | | | | | THE RESULTS | | | | | |
Year Team	Lg	G	GS	CG	GF	IP	BFP	H	R	ER	HR	SH	SF	HB	TBB	IBB	SO	WP	Bk	W	L	Pct.	ShO	Sv	ERA
1992 Huntington	R	12	12	2	0	76.1	318	71	45	34	6	2	1	2	17	0	93	7	0	3	5	.375	0	0	4.01
Peoria	A	2	1	0	0	5.2	31	9	5	5	0	0	0	1	5	0	5	0	0	0	1	.000	0	0	7.94
1993 Peoria	A	23	23	3	0	143.2	602	129	69	55	9	2	6	5	54	0	133	8	0	8	11	.421	0	0	3.45
1994 Daytona	A	11	11	2	0	76.2	313	62	35	29	4	4	2	4	23	0	59	3	3	7	3	.700	0	0	3.40
Orlando	AA	12	12	2	0	62.2	264	56	29	24	6	4	2	4	20	0	49	3	0	3	5	.375	0	0	3.45
3 Min. YEARS		60	59	9	0	365	1528	327	183	147	25	12	11	16	119	0	339	21	3	21	25	.457	0	0	3.62

Jeffrey Tam

Pitches: Right Bats: Right Pos: P   Ht: 6'1" Wt: 185 Born: 08/19/70 Age: 24

| | | HOW MUCH HE PITCHED | | | | | | WHAT HE GAVE UP | | | | | | | | | | | THE RESULTS | | | | | |
Year Team	Lg	G	GS	CG	GF	IP	BFP	H	R	ER	HR	SH	SF	HB	TBB	IBB	SO	WP	Bk	W	L	Pct.	ShO	Sv	ERA
1993 Pittsfield	A	21	1	0	13	40.1	180	50	21	15	0	0	1	1	7	0	31	1	3	3	3	.500	0	0	3.35
1994 Columbia	A	26	0	0	26	28	115	23	14	4	0	1	0	2	6	0	22	0	2	1	1	.500	0	18	1.29
St. Lucie	A	24	0	0	22	26.2	99	13	0	0	0	0	0	3	6	1	15	1	2	0	0	.000	0	16	0.00
Binghamton	AA	4	0	0	4	6.2	35	9	6	6	0	2	1	0	5	0	7	0	0	0	0	.000	0	0	8.10
2 Min. YEARS		75	1	0	62	101.2	429	95	41	25	0	2	1	7	24	1	75	2	7	4	4	.500	0	34	2.21

Jimmy Tatum

Bats: Right   Throws: Right   Pos: C   Ht: 6'2"   Wt: 200   Born: 10/09/67   Age: 27

Year	Team	Lg	G	AB	H	2B	3B	HR	TB	R	RBI	TBB	IBB	SO	HBP	SH	SF	SB	CS	SB%	GDP	Avg	OBP	SLG
1985	Spokane	A	74	281	64	9	1	1	78	21	32	20	0	60	5	4	1	0	1	.00	7	.228	.290	.278
1986	Charleston	A	120	431	112	19	2	10	165	55	62	41	2	83	2	4	5	2	4	.33	11	.260	.324	.383
1987	Chston-Sc	A	128	468	131	22	2	9	184	52	72	46	2	65	8	4	9	8	5	.62	16	.280	.348	.393
1988	Wichita	AA	118	402	105	26	1	8	157	38	54	30	2	73	5	6	3	2	3	.40	5	.261	.318	.391
1990	Canton-Akm	AA	30	106	19	6	0	2	31	6	11	6	1	19	1	0	2	1	0	1.00	2	.179	.226	.292
	Stockton	A	70	260	68	16	0	12	120	41	59	13	0	49	8	0	4	4	5	.44	7	.262	.312	.462
1991	El Paso	AA	130	493	158	27	8	18	255	99	128	63	5	79	15	2	20	5	7	.42	21	.320	.399	.517
1992	Denver	AAA	130	492	162	36	3	19	261	74	101	40	3	87	9	4	11	8	9	.47	11	.329	.382	.530
1993	Colo Sprngs	AAA	13	45	10	2	0	2	18	5	7	2	0	9	1	0	0	0	1	.00	3	.222	.271	.400
1994	Colo. Sprng	AAA	121	439	154	43	1	21	262	76	97	44	4	84	5	1	10	2	2	.50	6	.351	.408	.597
1992	Milwaukee	AL	5	8	1	0	0	0	1	0	0	1	0	2	0	0	0	0	0	.00	0	.125	.222	.125
1993	Colorado	NL	92	98	20	5	0	1	28	7	12	5	0	27	1	0	2	0	0	.00	0	.204	.245	.286
	9 Min. YEARS		934	3417	983	206	18	102	1531	467	623	305	19	608	59	25	65	32	37	.46	89	.288	.350	.448
	2 Maj. YEARS		97	106	21	5	0	1	29	7	12	6	0	29	1	0	2	0	0	.00	0	.198	.243	.274

Bob Taylor

Pitches: Right   Bats: Right   Pos: P   Ht: 6'3"   Wt: 225   Born: 03/25/66   Age: 29

Year	Team	Lg	G	GS	CG	GF	IP	BFP	H	R	ER	HR	SH	SF	HB	TBB	IBB	SO	WP	Bk	W	L	Pct.	ShO	Sv	ERA
1984	Paintsville	R	16	4	0	7	47.1	220	59	31	23	5	1	1	0	21	2	42	5	0	2	1	.667	0	0	4.37
1985	Helena	R	8	0	0	2	14	0	12	12	10	1	0	0	1	10	0	12	4	0	0	0	.000	0	0	6.43
1989	Pocatello	R	29	1	0	20	57.2	229	46	12	8	0	3	2	2	11	2	74	2	0	3	2	.600	0	10	1.25
1990	Clinton	A	31	0	0	30	35.1	156	29	13	6	2	1	2	4	16	0	42	2	0	5	2	.714	0	17	1.53
	San Jose	A	13	0	0	9	20.1	100	24	19	16	1	2	2	1	15	2	18	1	0	3	2	.600	0	2	7.08
1991	San Jose	A	9	0	0	8	10.2	49	14	6	6	0	0	0	0	4	0	13	2	0	0	1	.000	0	4	5.06
	Shreveport	AA	39	2	0	14	67.1	291	62	33	31	5	6	2	2	30	6	68	3	2	3	3	.500	0	2	4.14
1992	Shreveport	AA	34	1	1	10	60.1	253	60	22	17	1	3	3	0	17	4	56	3	1	4	2	.667	0	1	2.54
	Phoenix	AAA	20	0	0	7	30	133	33	14	8	2	0	0	2	10	2	28	2	0	4	1	.800	0	0	2.40
1993	Phoenix	AAA	49	12	0	11	144.1	636	166	85	68	15	6	3	4	49	4	110	7	2	10	8	.556	0	2	4.24
1994	Phoenix	AAA	61	1	0	30	97.1	415	98	57	50	16	5	2	4	32	6	86	4	0	7	5	.583	0	10	4.62
	8 Min. YEARS		309	21	1	148	584.2	2482	603	304	243	48	27	17	20	215	28	549	35	5	41	27	.603	0	48	3.74

Scott Taylor

Pitches: Right   Bats: Right   Pos: P   Ht: 6'3"   Wt: 200   Born: 10/03/66   Age: 28

Year	Team	Lg	G	GS	CG	GF	IP	BFP	H	R	ER	HR	SH	SF	HB	TBB	IBB	SO	WP	Bk	W	L	Pct.	ShO	Sv	ERA
1989	Wausau	A	16	16	6	0	106.1	445	92	49	38	5	3	2	6	37	1	65	8	3	9	7	.563	2	0	3.22
	Williamsprt	AA	10	7	1	1	40.2	185	49	26	26	6	1	5	1	20	1	22	2	0	1	4	.200	0	0	5.75
1990	San Berndno	A	34	21	1	3	126.1	596	148	100	76	17	0	3	7	69	0	86	10	1	8	8	.500	0	1	5.41
1991	Durham	A	24	16	2	5	111.1	452	94	32	27	3	6	2	2	33	3	78	10	0	10	3	.769	0	3	2.18
	Greenville	AA	8	7	1	0	43	191	49	25	20	4	1	1	2	16	2	26	6	0	3	4	.429	1	0	4.19
1992	Greenville	AA	22	4	0	6	39	172	44	31	29	6	0	3	3	18	0	20	3	0	1	1	.500	0	1	6.69
	El Paso	AA	11	9	0	0	54.1	224	45	21	21	5	3	1	0	19	1	37	2	1	4	2	.667	0	0	3.48
1993	El Paso	AA	17	16	1	1	104.1	434	105	53	44	4	2	2	11	31	2	76	0	0	6	6	.500	0	0	3.80
	New Orleans	AAA	12	8	1	3	62.1	244	48	17	16	3	5	1	2	21	1	47	1	1	5	1	.833	0	0	2.31
1994	New Orleans	AAA	28	27	4	0	165.2	720	177	88	79	12	4	5	12	59	2	106	3	0	14	9	.609	1	0	4.29
	6 Min. YEARS		182	131	17	19	853.1	3663	851	442	376	65	25	25	46	323	13	563	45	6	61	45	.575	4	5	3.97

Scott Tedder

Bats: Left   Throws: Left   Pos: OF   Ht: 6'4"   Wt: 195   Born: 06/01/66   Age: 29

Year	Team	Lg	G	AB	H	2B	3B	HR	TB	R	RBI	TBB	IBB	SO	HBP	SH	SF	SB	CS	SB%	GDP	Avg	OBP	SLG
1988	White Sox	R	58	214	73	13	0	0	86	30	25	28	1	16	1	2	2	8	1	.53	5	.341	.416	.402
1989	Sarasota	A	121	386	105	18	0	0	123	56	38	73	1	65	2	9	4	14	9	.61	11	.272	.387	.319
1990	Sarasota	A	121	381	108	6	2	0	118	65	47	90	6	46	0	2	3	13	9	.59	15	.283	.418	.310
	Birmingham	AA	2	3	1	0	0	0	1	1	0	2	0	1	0	0	0	0	0	.00	0	.333	.600	.333
1991	Sarasota	A	42	149	50	5	1	0	57	25	17	29	2	19	0	4	3	6	4	.60	5	.336	.436	.383
	Birmingham	AA	95	337	99	14	3	0	119	34	32	51	0	38	0	3	0	5	4	.56	7	.294	.387	.353
1992	Birmingham	AA	126	429	101	15	3	1	125	54	47	65	2	34	2	4	7	2	6	.25	7	.235	.334	.291
1993	Birmingham	AA	39	118	30	5	0	1	38	20	12	19	0	15	0	2	1	1	4	.20	2	.254	.355	.322
	Nashville	AAA	47	111	32	5	0	3	46	24	15	14	0	15	0	1	0	2	2	.50	0	.288	.368	.414
1994	Birmingham	AA	86	257	68	14	4	2	96	35	27	58	1	32	0	2	1	8	3	.73	2	.265	.399	.374
	Orlando	AA	34	99	32	6	0	0	38	16	12	30	1	13	0	1	2		4	.20	3	.323	.473	.384
	7 Min. YEARS		771	2484	699	101	13	7	847	360	272	459	17	294	5	30	23	60	52	.54	57	.281	.391	.341

250

John Tejcek

Bats: Right Throws: Right Pos: OF Ht: 5'10" Wt: 185 Born: 07/16/71 Age: 23

Year	Team	Lg	G	AB	H	2B	3B	HR	TB	R	RBI	TBB	IBB	SO	HBP	SH	SF	SB	CS	SB%	GDP	Avg	OBP	SLG
1993	Riverside	A	64	241	69	12	2	4	97	42	36	28	0	46	4	4	2	4	4	.50	8	.286	.367	.402
1994	Calgary	AAA	17	62	17	4	0	1	24	5	5	5	0	18	1	0	0	4	0	1.00	0	.274	.338	.387
	Riverside	A	49	178	55	9	0	5	79	33	31	12	1	47	2	1	4	5	1	.83	3	.309	.352	.444
	Jacksonville	AA	38	123	33	5	0	2	44	18	9	8	0	31	0	1	1	7	1	.88	1	.268	.311	.358
	2 Min. YEARS		168	604	174	30	2	12	244	98	84	53	1	142	7	6	7	20	6	.77	12	.288	.349	.404

Fausto Tejero

Bats: Right Throws: Right Pos: C Ht: 6'2" Wt: 205 Born: 10/26/68 Age: 26

Year	Team	Lg	G	AB	H	2B	3B	HR	TB	R	RBI	TBB	IBB	SO	HBP	SH	SF	SB	CS	SB%	GDP	Avg	OBP	SLG
1990	Boise	A	39	74	16	2	0	0	18	14	7	23	2	23	2	3	3	1	0	1.00	0	.216	.402	.243
1991	Quad City	A	83	244	42	7	0	1	52	16	18	14	0	52	4	3	1	0	1	.00	5	.172	.228	.213
1992	Edmonton	AAA	8	17	4	1	0	0	5	0	0	4	0	2	1	2	0	0	2	.00	0	.235	.409	.294
	Midland	AA	84	266	50	11	0	2	67	21	30	11	0	63	4	5	3	1	2	.33	6	.188	.229	.252
1993	Palm Sprngs	A	7	20	6	2	0	0	8	2	1	2	0	1	0	1	0	0	1	.00	0	.300	.364	.400
	Vancouver	AAA	20	59	9	0	0	0	9	2	2	4	1	12	1	2	1	1	1	.50	0	.153	.215	.153
	Midland	AA	26	69	9	1	1	1	15	3	7	8	0	17	2	1	1	0	0	.00	3	.130	.238	.217
1994	Midland	AA	50	150	32	3	0	5	50	17	24	15	0	31	1	1	2	2	2	.50	6	.213	.286	.333
	Vancouver	AAA	16	45	9	2	0	0	11	6	6	4	0	9	0	2	1	1	1	.50	1	.200	.260	.244
	5 Min. YEARS		333	944	177	29	1	9	235	81	95	85	2	210	15	20	12	6	10	.38	21	.188	.262	.249

Anthony Telford

Pitches: Right Bats: Right Pos: P Ht: 6'0" Wt: 184 Born: 03/06/66 Age: 29

Year	Team	Lg	G	GS	CG	GF	IP	BFP	H	R	ER	HR	SH	SF	HB	TBB	IBB	SO	WP	Bk	W	L	Pct.	ShO	Sv	ERA
1987	Newark	A	6	2	0	3	17.2	72	16	2	2	0	0	0	0	3	0	27	0	0	1	0	1.000	0	0	1.02
	Hagerstown	A	2	2	0	0	11.1	46	9	2	2	0	0	0	1	5	0	10	0	0	1	0	1.000	0	0	1.59
	Rochester	AAA	1	0	0	0	2	9	0	0	0	0	0	0	0	3	0	3	1	0	0	0	.000	0	0	0.00
1988	Hagerstown	A	1	1	0	0	7	24	3	0	0	0	0	0	0	0	0	10	0	0	1	0	1.000	0	0	0.00
1989	Frederick	A	9	5	0	2	25.2	116	25	15	12	1	1	2	2	12	0	19	2	0	2	1	.667	0	1	4.21
1990	Frederick	A	8	8	1	0	53.2	207	35	15	10	1	0	0	4	11	1	49	4	0	4	2	.667	0	0	1.68
	Hagerstown	AA	14	13	3	1	96	384	80	26	21	3	5	3	3	25	1	73	4	0	10	2	.833	1	0	1.97
1991	Rochester	AAA	27	25	3	0	157.1	666	166	82	69	18	5	3	4	48	2	115	7	1	12	9	.571	0	0	3.95
1992	Rochester	AAA	27	26	3	1	181	766	183	89	84	15	4	4	6	64	0	129	9	2	12	7	.632	0	0	4.18
1993	Rochester	AAA	38	6	0	12	90.2	397	98	51	43	10	2	4	3	33	3	66	6	0	7	7	.500	0	2	4.27
1994	Richmond	AAA	38	20	3	0	142.2	607	183	82	67	17	4	4	4	41	2	111	1	0	10	6	.625	1	0	4.23
1990	Baltimore	AL	8	8	0	0	36.1	168	43	22	20	4	0	2	1	19	0	20	1	0	3	3	.500	0	0	4.95
1991	Baltimore	AL	9	1	0	4	26.2	109	27	12	12	3	0	1	0	6	1	24	1	0	0	0	.000	0	0	4.05
1993	Baltimore	AL	3	0	0	2	7.1	34	11	8	8	3	0	0	1	3	0	6	1	0	0	0	.000	0	0	9.82
	8 Min. YEARS		171	108	13	19	785	3294	763	364	310	65	21	20	27	245	9	612	34	3	60	34	.638	2	3	3.55
	3 Maj. YEARS		20	9	0	6	70.1	311	81	42	40	10	0	3	2	26	1	50	3	0	3	3	.500	0	0	5.12

David Tellers

Pitches: Right Bats: Right Pos: P Ht: 5'10" Wt: 175 Born: 03/13/68 Age: 27

Year	Team	Lg	G	GS	CG	GF	IP	BFP	H	R	ER	HR	SH	SF	HB	TBB	IBB	SO	WP	Bk	W	L	Pct.	ShO	Sv	ERA
1990	Welland	A	20	0	0	16	39.2	148	23	9	6	2	1	1	0	7	0	53	1	2	4	2	.667	0	5	1.36
1991	Carolina	AA	11	0	0	9	13.1	64	18	8	7	1	1	0	0	6	4	9	1	0	0	2	.000	0	1	4.72
	Salem	A	40	0	0	28	71	279	54	16	11	1	4	4	2	20	4	61	0	3	6	4	.600	0	10	1.39
1992	Carolina	AA	16	0	0	6	25.1	103	23	11	10	2	1	1	2	9	2	23	1	0	2	1	.667	0	2	3.55
	Salem	A	32	5	0	24	74	302	72	32	30	9	3	0	2	14	4	63	0	0	3	7	.300	0	10	3.65
1993	Duluth-Supr	IND	38	0	0	20	51.1	225	57	17	14	2	2	0	3	19	6	40	1	1	7	3	.700	0	9	2.45
1994	New Haven	AA	41	1	0	22	71.2	285	57	31	27	8	2	0	3	12	2	56	2	2	1	6	.143	0	9	3.39
	5 Min. YEARS		198	6	0	125	346.1	1406	304	124	105	25	14	6	12	87	22	305	6	8	23	25	.479	0	46	2.73

J.J. Thobe

Pitches: Right Bats: Right Pos: P Ht: 6'6" Wt: 200 Born: 11/19/70 Age: 24

Year	Team	Lg	G	GS	CG	GF	IP	BFP	H	R	ER	HR	SH	SF	HB	TBB	IBB	SO	WP	Bk	W	L	Pct.	ShO	Sv	ERA
1993	Columbus	A	19	19	2	0	132	523	105	36	28	6	2	4	1	25	0	106	3	1	11	2	.846	0	0	1.91
	Kinston	A	4	4	0	0	23	102	26	11	8	1	0	4	1	9	0	11	1	0	1	2	.333	0	0	3.13
1994	W. Palm Bch	A	2	2	0	0	12	50	14	5	5	0	1	1	1	2	0	4	0	0	1	1	.500	0	0	3.75
	Harrisburg	AA	21	21	1	0	120.2	513	129	73	58	12	6	5	2	24	0	57	7	0	7	8	.467	0	0	4.33
	2 Min. YEARS		46	46	3	0	287.2	1188	274	125	99	19	9	14	5	60	0	178	11	1	20	13	.606	0	0	3.10

Tom Thobe

Pitches: Left Bats: Left Pos: P Ht: 6'5" Wt: 195 Born: 09/03/69 Age: 25

			HOW MUCH HE PITCHED						WHAT HE GAVE UP										THE RESULTS					
Year Team	Lg	G	GS	CG	GF	IP	BFP	H	R	ER	HR	SH	SF	HB	TBB	IBB	SO	WP	Bk	W	L	Pct.	ShO	Sv	ERA
1993 Macon	A	43	0	0	22	70.1	299	70	25	21	0	6	1	2	16	1	55	8	0	7	5	.583	0	5	2.69
1994 Greenville	AA	51	0	0	27	63.2	263	56	21	18	3	5	2	0	26	2	52	6	2	7	6	.538	0	9	2.54
2 Min. YEARS		94	0	0	49	134	562	126	46	39	3	11	3	2	42	3	107	14	2	14	11	.560	0	14	2.62

Carlos Thomas

Pitches: Right Bats: Right Pos: P Ht: 6'4" Wt: 215 Born: 08/06/68 Age: 26

			HOW MUCH HE PITCHED						WHAT HE GAVE UP										THE RESULTS					
Year Team	Lg	G	GS	CG	GF	IP	BFP	H	R	ER	HR	SH	SF	HB	TBB	IBB	SO	WP	Bk	W	L	Pct.	ShO	Sv	ERA
1991 Yakima	A	16	2	0	5	34.1	158	26	18	15	0	0	1	0	33	0	42	4	2	2	0	1.000	0	0	3.93
1992 Yakima	A	15	15	0	0	83	378	72	64	47	8	0	2	13	50	0	59	5	5	3	8	.273	0	0	5.10
1993 Bakersfield	A	38	8	0	7	97.2	444	89	51	47	8	2	5	4	75	0	82	12	0	5	9	.357	0	1	4.33
1994 San Antonio	AA	26	0	0	12	42	188	37	20	16	2	3	3	0	29	5	32	3	0	2	5	.286	0	3	3.43
Bakersfield	A	15	1	0	8	28.2	129	27	21	17	1	4	1	1	22	0	17	6	0	2	2	.500	0	1	5.34
4 Min. YEARS		110	26	0	32	285.2	1297	251	174	142	19	9	12	18	209	5	232	30	7	14	24	.368	0	5	4.47

John Thomas

Bats: Left Throws: Right Pos: OF Ht: 5'11" Wt: 195 Born: 09/09/68 Age: 26

			BATTING														BASERUNNING				PERCENTAGES		
Year Team	Lg	G	AB	H	2B	3B	HR	TB	R	RBI	TBB	IBB	SO	HBP	SH	SF	SB	CS	SB%	GDP	Avg	OBP	SLG
1990 Hamilton	A	33	118	32	8	0	3	49	20	14	15	0	30	1	0	2	9	3	.75	1	.271	.353	.415
Springfield	A	39	152	38	11	0	1	52	19	12	10	0	36	0	0	0	3	3	.50	4	.250	.296	.342
1991 St. Pete	A	115	429	128	13	10	3	170	51	46	35	0	71	5	0	3	8	8	.50	17	.298	.356	.396
1992 Arkansas	AA	115	408	111	18	5	10	169	49	49	21	0	91	1	0	3	3	6	.33	16	.272	.307	.414
1993 Louisville	AAA	108	377	104	15	1	9	148	30	40	15	4	75	3	0	1	1	1	1.00	9	.276	.308	.393
1994 Louisville	AAA	102	321	77	18	2	17	150	34	54	23	2	80	2	0	1	3	3	.43	12	.240	.293	.467
5 Min. YEARS		512	1805	490	83	18	43	738	203	215	119	6	383	12	0	11	27	24	.53	59	.271	.319	.409

Keith Thomas

Bats: Right Throws: Right Pos: OF Ht: 6'1" Wt: 180 Born: 09/12/68 Age: 26

			BATTING														BASERUNNING				PERCENTAGES		
Year Team	Lg	G	AB	H	2B	3B	HR	TB	R	RBI	TBB	IBB	SO	HBP	SH	SF	SB	CS	SB%	GDP	Avg	OBP	SLG
1986 Reds	R	42	145	31	1	2	2	42	24	13	23	0	57	3	2	1	18	6	.75	1	.214	.331	.290
1987 Billings	R	45	142	36	6	2	4	58	22	24	7	1	45	0	1	0	11	4	.73	1	.254	.289	.408
1988 Greensboro	A	108	438	105	12	4	4	137	63	26	17	0	122	2	4	0	30	6	.83	2	.240	.271	.313
1989 Modesto	A	93	330	70	5	2	6	97	36	29	24	1	102	2	3	0	19	10	.66	5	.212	.270	.294
1990 Modesto	A	62	215	48	7	0	4	67	24	14	14	0	65	1	0	2	16	10	.62	4	.223	.272	.312
Madison	A	44	142	30	3	1	3	44	21	20	10	0	43	0	1	2	12	1	.92	3	.211	.260	.310
1991 Madison	A	13	44	9	1	0	0	10	4	4	3	0	11	0	1	0	3	1	.75	1	.205	.255	.227
Appleton	A	74	232	62	10	4	7	101	32	28	12	0	60	2	3	2	21	5	.81	1	.267	.306	.435
1992 Salem	A	104	372	103	24	4	16	191	54	51	18	2	90	5	1	6	30	7	.81	12	.277	.314	.513
Carolina	AA	22	78	23	2	4	4	45	13	15	7	0	23	0	0	0	9	1	.90	2	.295	.353	.577
1993 Salem	A	25	94	25	8	0	4	45	17	11	7	0	30	2	1	1	8	1	.89	1	.266	.330	.479
Carolina	AA	94	336	80	9	2	15	138	40	52	22	0	110	2	1	4	12	8	.60	2	.238	.286	.411
1994 Wichita	AA	109	307	73	13	4	7	115	38	33	32	1	82	5	1	1	46	10	.82	7	.238	.319	.375
9 Min. YEARS		835	2875	695	101	33	76	1090	388	327	196	5	840	24	20	18	235	70	.77	42	.242	.294	.379

Larry Thomas

Pitches: Left Bats: Right Pos: P Ht: 6'1" Wt: 190 Born: 10/25/69 Age: 25

			HOW MUCH HE PITCHED						WHAT HE GAVE UP										THE RESULTS					
Year Team	Lg	G	GS	CG	GF	IP	BFP	H	R	ER	HR	SH	SF	HB	TBB	IBB	SO	WP	Bk	W	L	Pct.	ShO	Sv	ERA
1991 Utica	A	11	10	0	0	73.1	288	55	22	12	2	3	2	0	25	0	61	3	0	1	3	.250	0	0	1.47
Birmingham	AA	2	2	0	0	6	28	6	3	2	0	0	0	0	4	1	2	0	0	0	0	.000	0	0	3.00
1992 Sarasota	A	8	8	0	0	55.2	220	44	14	10	1	1	0	0	7	1	50	2	0	5	0	1.000	0	0	1.62
Birmingham	AA	17	17	3	0	120.2	474	102	32	26	4	4	2	1	30	2	72	5	0	8	6	.571	0	0	1.94
1993 Nashville	AAA	18	18	1	0	100.2	441	114	73	67	15	3	6	1	32	4	67	4	1	4	6	.400	0	0	5.99
Sarasota	A	8	8	3	0	61.2	247	52	19	17	3	2	0	0	15	1	27	1	1	4	2	.667	2	0	2.48
Birmingham	AA	1	1	0	0	7	33	9	5	4	1	0	0	1	1	1	5	0	0	0	1	.000	0	0	5.14
1994 Birmingham	AA	24	24	1	0	144	642	159	96	74	17	4	6	5	53	0	77	11	2	5	10	.333	0	0	4.63
4 Min. YEARS		89	86	8	2	569	2373	541	264	212	43	17	16	8	167	9	361	26	4	27	28	.491	2	0	3.35

Mike Thomas

Pitches: Left Bats: Left Pos: P Ht: 6'1" Wt: 175 Born: 09/02/69 Age: 25

			HOW MUCH HE PITCHED						WHAT HE GAVE UP										THE RESULTS					
Year Team	Lg	G	GS	CG	GF	IP	BFP	H	R	ER	HR	SH	SF	HB	TBB	IBB	SO	WP	Bk	W	L	Pct.	ShO	Sv	ERA
1989 Mets	R	8	8	0	5	31.1	127	23	5	5	0	0	1	2	14	0	34	2	0	2	0	1.000	0	0	1.44
Kingsport	R	6	3	0	3	19.1	90	13	16	14	1	2	0	1	17	0	17	1	0	1	2	.333	0	0	6.52
1990 Pittsfield	A	28	3	0	13	64	270	51	23	19	3	2	3	3	29	3	80	6	0	3	3	.500	0	3	2.67

Year Team	Lg	G	GS	CG	GF	IP	BFP	H	R	ER	HR	SH	SF	HB	TBB	IBB	SO	WP	Bk	W	L	Pct.	ShO	Sv	ERA
1991 Columbia	A	30	0	0	27	41	179	28	15	11	1	3	1	2	30	2	59	3	2	4	2	.667	0	15	2.41
Sumter	A	19	0	0	15	27.1	125	25	13	12	0	1	1	1	18	0	30	5	2	4	1	.800	0	5	3.95
1992 Rockford	A	28	17	1	8	113	473	98	52	45	8	3	7	6	51	0	108	5	4	5	9	.357	0	2	3.58
1993 Wst Plm Bch	A	25	0	0	19	27.1	123	19	13	10	0	3	0	2	23	2	28	1	0	1	3	.250	0	9	3.29
Harrisburg	AA	25	0	0	14	32.1	150	34	18	17	3	2	1	1	19	2	40	1	2	2	2	.500	0	6	4.73
1994 El Paso	AA	50	0	0	32	66.1	296	57	36	25	6	7	3	4	42	3	59	6	2	3	3	.400	0	20	3.39
6 Min. YEARS		219	26	1	136	422	1833	348	191	158	22	23	17	22	243	12	455	30	12	24	25	.490	0	60	3.37

Royal Thomas

Pitches: Right Bats: Right Pos: P Ht: 6'2" Wt: 187 Born: 09/03/69 Age: 25

		HOW MUCH HE PITCHED						WHAT HE GAVE UP													THE RESULTS				
Year Team	Lg	G	GS	CG	GF	IP	BFP	H	R	ER	HR	SH	SF	HB	TBB	IBB	SO	WP	Bk	W	L	Pct.	ShO	Sv	ERA
1987 Utica	A	19	6	0	7	76	308	67	23	16	1	2	2	0	18	3	62	3	1	6	0	1.000	0	2	1.89
1988 Clearwater	A	9	2	0	4	19	95	24	21	19	0	3	2	3	14	2	6	3	2	0	4	.000	0	2	9.00
Spartanburg	A	22	22	7	0	145.2	611	134	74	49	7	6	3	7	47	0	67	7	1	6	13	.316	2	0	3.03
1989 Clearwater	A	27	21	11	0	154	630	141	70	57	7	6	6	1	39	1	49	1	0	11	9	.550	3	0	3.33
1990 Riverside	A	27	27	1	0	166	740	209	103	87	11	4	6	4	49	3	93	10	0	9	13	.409	0	0	4.72
1991 High Desert	A	27	27	4	0	155	699	178	108	91	15	4	6	5	61	2	99	9	1	8	13	.381	0	0	4.70
1992 Wichita	AA	41	14	0	6	125.1	573	151	104	88	12	5	5	6	51	3	91	8	1	7	7	.500	0	2	6.32
1993 San Antonio	AA	47	6	0	16	109.2	475	116	58	48	11	6	6	3	44	5	52	4	0	4	6	.400	0	2	3.94
1994 Greenville	AA	46	0	0	18	85.1	367	90	38	30	4	5	2	1	28	3	48	2	1	6	4	.600	0	2	3.16
8 Min. YEARS		265	125	23	51	1036	4498	1110	599	475	68	41	38	30	351	22	567	47	7	57	69	.452	5	10	4.13

Fletcher Thompson

Bats: Left Throws: Right Pos: 2B Ht: 5'11" Wt: 180 Born: 09/14/68 Age: 26

		BATTING												BASERUNNING				PERCENTAGES		
Year Team	Lg	G	AB	H	2B	3B	HR	TB	R	RBI	TBB	IBB	SO	HBP	SH	SF	SB	CS	SB%	GDP	Avg	OBP	SLG
1990 Auburn	A	59	199	56	8	3	0	70	35	21	37	3	45	6	5	2	19	9	.68	2	.281	.406	.352
1991 Burlington	A	116	428	116	15	3	5	152	85	33	104	0	116	5	5	2	34	16	.68	2	.271	.417	.355
1993 Jackson	AA	98	316	93	15	2	4	124	64	29	55	2	83	1	7	1	23	12	.66	6	.294	.399	.392
1994 Jackson	AA	121	388	102	14	2	4	132	69	31	58	2	106	10	4	0	28	13	.68	5	.263	.373	.340
4 Min. YEARS		394	1331	367	52	10	13	478	253	114	254	7	350	22	21	5	104	50	.68	15	.276	.399	.359

Jason Thompson

Bats: Left Throws: Left Pos: 1B Ht: 6'4" Wt: 200 Born: 06/13/71 Age: 24

		BATTING												BASERUNNING				PERCENTAGES		
Year Team	Lg	G	AB	H	2B	3B	HR	TB	R	RBI	TBB	IBB	SO	HBP	SH	SF	SB	CS	SB%	GDP	Avg	OBP	SLG
1993 Spokane	A	66	240	72	25	1	7	120	36	38	37	6	47	1	0	5	3	2	.60	3	.300	.389	.500
1994 Rancho Cuca	A	68	253	91	19	2	13	153	57	63	37	4	58	3	0	3	1	1	.50	5	.360	.443	.605
Wichita	AA	63	215	56	17	2	8	101	35	46	28	2	77	3	1	1	0	1	.00	5	.260	.352	.470
2 Min. YEARS		197	708	219	61	5	28	374	128	147	102	12	182	7	1	9	4	4	.50	13	.309	.397	.528

Paul Thoutsis

Bats: Left Throws: Right Pos: OF Ht: 6'1" Wt: 185 Born: 10/23/65 Age: 29

		BATTING												BASERUNNING				PERCENTAGES		
Year Team	Lg	G	AB	H	2B	3B	HR	TB	R	RBI	TBB	IBB	SO	HBP	SH	SF	SB	CS	SB%	GDP	Avg	OBP	SLG
1984 Winston-Sal	A	90	299	67	9	2	2	86	32	26	32	3	55	4	2	1	1	1	.50	6	.224	.306	.288
1985 Winter Havn	A	75	209	48	6	0	1	57	18	18	18	1	44	3	1	0	0	3	.00	2	.230	.300	.273
1986 Greensboro	A	106	364	105	16	3	15	172	83	77	77	3	57	6	1	11	0	0	.00	4	.288	.410	.473
1987 Winter Havn	A	105	336	83	14	2	7	122	47	41	35	3	50	7	2	2	2	1	.67	6	.247	.329	.363
New Britain	AA	1	4	0	0	0	0	0	0	0	0	0	0	0	0	0	0	0	.00	0	.000	.000	.000
1988 Springfield	A	28	92	25	3	0	0	28	5	12	8	2	10	0	0	2	0	0	.00	4	.272	.324	.304
Arkansas	AA	7	9	3	0	0	0	3	0	2	0	0	0	0	0	1	0	0	.00	0	.333	.300	.333
St. Pete	A	30	91	25	4	0	0	29	14	8	14	3	7	0	0	1	0	1	.00	1	.275	.368	.319
1989 St.Pete	A	74	243	70	10	3	2	92	21	21	22	2	17	5	0	3	0	1	.00	6	.288	.355	.379
1990 Arkansas	AA	101	266	75	14	5	5	114	25	37	12	2	37	1	0	3	0	2	.00	3	.282	.312	.429
1992 New Britain	AA	108	327	79	21	3	4	118	31	47	24	2	46	4	1	4	0	5	.00	6	.242	.298	.361
1993 New Britain	AA	64	213	62	12	2	0	78	17	21	27	1	24	0	1	2	0	2	.00	4	.291	.368	.366
Pawtucket	AAA	60	216	69	10	1	4	93	30	27	24	1	28	2	1	0	1	1	.50	9	.319	.393	.431
1994 Pawtucket	AAA	94	304	68	10	1	10	110	28	40	37	4	56	1	2	6	3	0	1.00	9	.224	.305	.362
10 Min. YEARS		943	2973	779	129	22	50	1102	351	377	330	27	431	33	11	37	7	17	.29	59	.262	.339	.371

Gary Thurman

Bats: Right Throws: Right Pos: OF Ht: 5'10" Wt: 175 Born: 11/12/64 Age: 30

		BATTING												BASERUNNING				PERCENTAGES		
Year Team	Lg	G	AB	H	2B	3B	HR	TB	R	RBI	TBB	IBB	SO	HBP	SH	SF	SB	CS	SB%	GDP	Avg	OBP	SLG
1984 Charleston	A	129	478	109	6	8	6	149	71	51	81	1	127	8	1	3	44	17	.72	6	.228	.347	.312
1985 Ft. Myers	A	134	453	137	9	9	0	164	68	45	68	1	93	4	3	4	70	18	.80	7	.302	.395	.362
1986 Memphis	AA	131	525	164	24	12	7	233	88	62	57	0	81	0	4	3	53	18	.75	4	.312	.378	.444
Omaha	AAA	3	2	1	0	0	0	1	1	0	2	0	0	0	0	0	2	0	1.00	0	.500	.750	.500
1987 Omaha	AAA	115	450	132	14	9	8	188	88	39	48	0	84	3	5	3	58	7	.89	4	.293	.363	.418
1988 Omaha	AAA	106	422	106	12	6	3	139	77	40	38	2	80	4	8	3	35	12	.74	6	.251	.317	.329
1989 Omaha	AAA	17	64	14	3	2	0	21	5	3	7	0	18	0	0	0	5	4	.56	0	.219	.296	.328

Year	Team	Lg	G	AB	H	2B	3B	HR	TB	R	RBI	TBB	IBB	SO	HBP	SH	SF	SB	CS	SB%	GDP	Avg	OBP	SLG
1990	Omaha	AAA	98	381	126	14	8	0	156	65	26	31	1	68	4	6	2	39	15	.72	6	.331	.385	.409
1994	Nashville	AAA	130	470	124	17	12	5	180	76	60	35	1	85	10	4	3	20	7	.74	6	.264	.326	.383
1987	Kansas City	AL	27	81	24	2	0	0	26	12	5	8	0	20	0	1	0	7	2	.78	1	.296	.360	.321
1988	Kansas City	AL	35	66	11	1	0	0	12	6	2	4	0	20	0	0	0	5	1	.83	0	.167	.214	.182
1989	Kansas City	AL	72	87	17	2	1	0	21	24	5	15	0	26	0	2	1	16	0	1.00	0	.195	.311	.241
1990	Kansas City	AL	23	60	14	3	0	0	17	5	3	2	0	12	0	1	0	1	1	.50	2	.233	.258	.283
1991	Kansas City	AL	80	184	51	9	0	2	66	24	13	11	0	42	1	3	1	15	5	.75	4	.277	.320	.359
1992	Kansas City	AL	88	200	49	6	3	0	61	25	20	9	0	34	1	6	0	9	6	.60	3	.245	.281	.305
1993	Detroit	AL	75	89	19	2	2	0	25	22	13	11	0	30	0	1	1	7	0	1.00	2	.213	.297	.281
	8 Min. YEARS		863	3245	913	99	66	29	1231	539	326	367	6	636	33	31	21	326	98	.77	42	.281	.358	.379
	7 Maj. YEARS		400	767	185	25	6	2	228	118	61	60	0	184	2	14	3	60	15	.80	12	.241	.297	.297

Jerrey Thurston

Bats: Right Throws: Right Pos: C Ht: 6'4" Wt: 200 Born: 04/17/72 Age: 23

			BATTING															BASERUNNING				PERCENTAGES		
Year	Team	Lg	G	AB	H	2B	3B	HR	TB	R	RBI	TBB	IBB	SO	HBP	SH	SF	SB	CS	SB%	GDP	Avg	OBP	SLG
1990	Padres	R	42	144	33	6	1	0	41	22	16	14	0	37	0	2	0	4	1	.80	1	.229	.297	.285
1991	Chston-Sc	A	42	137	14	2	0	0	16	5	4	9	0	50	0	1	1	1	1	.50	3	.102	.156	.117
	Spokane	A	60	201	43	9	0	1	55	26	20	20	1	61	2	2	2	2	2	.50	2	.214	.289	.274
1992	Waterloo	A	96	263	37	7	0	0	44	20	14	12	0	73	2	6	2	1	0	1.00	4	.141	.183	.167
1993	Wichita	AA	78	197	48	10	0	2	64	22	22	14	0	62	6	3	0	2	0	1.00	5	.244	.313	.325
1994	Wichita	AA	77	238	51	10	2	4	77	30	28	19	1	73	8	2	1	1	4	.20	8	.214	.293	.324
	5 Min. YEARS		395	1180	226	44	3	7	297	125	104	88	2	356	18	16	6	11	8	.58	21	.192	.257	.252

Tony Tijerina

Bats: Both Throws: Right Pos: C Ht: 6'0" Wt: 185 Born: 12/19/69 Age: 25

			BATTING															BASERUNNING				PERCENTAGES		
Year	Team	Lg	G	AB	H	2B	3B	HR	TB	R	RBI	TBB	IBB	SO	HBP	SH	SF	SB	CS	SB%	GDP	Avg	OBP	SLG
1991	Pittsfield	A	44	144	35	5	1	0	42	16	17	15	0	13	4	1	2	1	1	.50	3	.243	.327	.292
1992	St. Lucie	A	32	81	18	2	0	0	20	7	6	5	0	14	2	0	0	0	0	.00	1	.222	.284	.247
1993	Capital City	A	53	175	54	9	3	0	69	15	21	14	0	25	0	2	3	3	5	.38	3	.309	.354	.394
1994	Binghamton	AA	27	88	23	5	1	1	33	10	12	2	0	23	0	1	0	0	0	.00	3	.261	.278	.375
	4 Min. YEARS		156	488	130	21	5	1	164	48	56	36	0	75	6	4	5	4	6	.40	10	.266	.321	.336

Ozzie Timmons

Bats: Right Throws: Right Pos: OF Ht: 6'2" Wt: 205 Born: 09/18/70 Age: 24

			BATTING															BASERUNNING				PERCENTAGES		
Year	Team	Lg	G	AB	H	2B	3B	HR	TB	R	RBI	TBB	IBB	SO	HBP	SH	SF	SB	CS	SB%	GDP	Avg	OBP	SLG
1991	Geneva	A	73	294	65	10	1	12	113	35	47	18	0	39	2	0	4	4	3	.57	1	.221	.267	.384
1992	Charlotte	AA	36	122	26	7	0	3	42	13	13	12	0	26	1	1	0	2	2	.50	2	.213	.289	.344
	Winston-Sal	A	86	305	86	18	0	18	158	64	56	58	3	46	2	4	4	11	0	1.00	5	.282	.396	.518
1993	Orlando	AA	107	359	102	22	2	18	182	65	58	62	3	80	2	2	1	5	11	.31	6	.284	.392	.507
1994	Iowa	AAA	126	440	116	30	2	22	216	63	66	36	0	93	1	3	2	0	3	.00	12	.264	.319	.491
	4 Min. YEARS		428	1520	395	87	5	73	711	240	240	186	6	284	8	10	11	22	19	.54	26	.260	.341	.468

Ken Tirpack

Bats: Left Throws: Right Pos: 1B Ht: 6'0" Wt: 186 Born: 10/03/69 Age: 25

			BATTING															BASERUNNING				PERCENTAGES		
Year	Team	Lg	G	AB	H	2B	3B	HR	TB	R	RBI	TBB	IBB	SO	HBP	SH	SF	SB	CS	SB%	GDP	Avg	OBP	SLG
1992	Elizabethtn	R	61	228	76	13	2	9	120	42	42	31	2	36	5	0	5	1	2	.33	3	.333	.416	.526
1993	Ft.Wayne	A	127	473	139	34	3	9	206	71	70	68	4	103	6	1	4	1	4	.20	10	.294	.385	.436
1994	Nashville	AA	37	127	28	7	0	1	38	14	13	11	1	19	2	0	0	0	1	.00	4	.220	.293	.299
	Fort Myers	A	68	234	63	15	1	4	92	24	29	23	0	43	0	0	6	3	1	.75	7	.269	.327	.393
	3 Min. YEARS		293	1062	306	69	6	23	456	151	154	133	7	201	13	0	17	5	8	.38	24	.288	.369	.429

Dave Tokheim

Bats: Left Throws: Left Pos: OF Ht: 6'1" Wt: 185 Born: 05/25/69 Age: 26

			BATTING															BASERUNNING				PERCENTAGES		
Year	Team	Lg	G	AB	H	2B	3B	HR	TB	R	RBI	TBB	IBB	SO	HBP	SH	SF	SB	CS	SB%	GDP	Avg	OBP	SLG
1991	Batavia	A	40	158	51	12	3	2	75	28	21	9	0	20	1	2	1	6	2	.75	1	.323	.361	.475
1992	Clearwater	A	106	396	93	12	6	4	129	40	41	30	4	40	5	2	2	10	12	.45	4	.235	.296	.326
1993	Clearwater	A	41	155	51	8	2	0	63	27	11	14	4	17	2	1	1	7	5	.58	1	.329	.390	.406
	Reading	AA	65	257	75	11	6	2	104	30	25	12	0	36	0	3	0	6	6	.57	3	.292	.323	.405
1994	Reading	AA	126	438	132	17	6	13	200	56	47	27	2	70	4	1	3	12	10	.55	10	.301	.345	.457
	4 Min. YEARS		378	1404	402	60	23	21	571	181	145	92	10	183	12	9	7	43	35	.55	21	.286	.334	.407

Dilson Torres

Pitches: Right Bats: Right Pos: P Ht: 6'1" Wt: 215 Born: 05/31/70 Age: 25

			HOW MUCH HE PITCHED					WHAT HE GAVE UP										THE RESULTS					
Year	Team	Lg	G	GS	CG	GF	IP	BFP	H	R	ER	HR	SH	SF	HB	TBB	IBB	SO	WP	Bk	W	L	Pct.	ShO	Sv	ERA
1993	St.Cathmes	A	17	0	0	12	23	98	21	13	8	3	1	0	6	6	0	23	2	0	1	4	.200	0	3	3.13
1994	Wilmington	A	15	9	0	5	59.1	239	47	15	9	5	3	2	0	15	0	49	2	2	7	2	.778	0	2	1.37
	Memphis	AA	10	9	0	0	59	229	47	15	12	3	2	1	5	10	0	47	1	0	6	0	1.000	0	0	1.83
	2 Min. YEARS		42	18	0	17	141.1	566	115	43	29	11	6	3	5	31	0	119	5	2	14	6	.700	0	5	1.85

254

Paul Torres

Bats: Right Throws: Right Pos: 1B-OF Ht: 6'3" Wt: 210 Born: 10/19/70 Age: 24

Year	Team	Lg	G	AB	H	2B	3B	HR	TB	R	RBI	TBB	IBB	SO	HBP	SH	SF	SB	CS	SB%	GDP	Avg	OBP	SLG
1989	Wytheville	R	54	191	45	9	1	7	77	34	38	32	0	55	6	0	2	2	4	.33	3	.236	.359	.403
1990	Peoria	A	36	123	30	4	1	5	51	18	18	13	0	33	2	1	0	1	1	.50	2	.244	.326	.415
	Geneva	A	77	271	72	23	1	10	127	46	45	39	1	72	10	2	5	9	3	.75	2	.266	.372	.469
1991	Winston-Sal	A	27	87	10	1	0	2	17	9	7	11	0	30	2	0	1	4	0	1.00	3	.115	.228	.195
	Peoria	A	99	352	75	24	2	13	142	60	50	48	2	91	9	3	0	6	2	.75	7	.213	.323	.403
1992	Winston-Sal	A	134	458	109	15	6	14	178	55	78	60	2	114	5	2	7	4	4	.50	10	.238	.328	.389
1993	Daytona	A	100	353	98	17	5	13	164	63	43	52	0	94	8	1	3	5	4	.56	5	.278	.380	.465
	Orlando	AA	19	55	14	4	0	3	27	10	10	7	0	18	0	0	0	3	0	1.00	1	.255	.339	.491
1994	Orlando	AA	61	160	38	2	1	10	72	21	26	31	1	41	2	1	2	2	6	.25	5	.238	.364	.450
	Daytona	A	26	90	28	6	3	4	52	12	20	11	2	26	0	0	1	4	1	.80	1	.311	.382	.578
6 Min. YEARS			633	2140	519	105	20	81	907	328	335	304	8	574	44	10	21	40	25	.62	40	.243	.346	.424

Robert Toth

Pitches: Right Bats: Right Pos: P Ht: 6'2" Wt: 180 Born: 07/30/72 Age: 22

Year	Team	Lg	G	GS	CG	GF	IP	BFP	H	R	ER	HR	SH	SF	HB	TBB	IBB	SO	WP	Bk	W	L	Pct.	ShO	Sv	ERA
1990	Royals	R	7	7	0	0	38	148	34	8	7	1	0	0	2	4	0	22	3	0	2	2	.500	0	0	1.66
1991	Baseball Cy	A	13	10	0	0	63.2	263	53	24	20	1	5	1	2	23	2	42	0	0	2	3	.400	0	0	2.83
1992	Appleton	A	23	22	2	1	127.1	515	111	58	48	9	6	5	5	34	0	100	3	0	7	6	.538	0	0	3.39
1993	Wilmington	A	25	24	0	1	151.2	609	129	57	49	13	5	2	3	40	1	129	7	1	8	7	.533	0	0	2.91
1994	Wilmington	A	11	7	3	1	59.1	234	52	14	12	3	2	0	2	9	0	36	0	0	6	1	.857	2	0	1.82
	Memphis	AA	20	12	0	4	88.2	372	89	46	41	13	3	1	7	24	0	61	14	0	5	8	.385	0	1	4.16
5 Min. YEARS			99	82	5	7	528.2	2141	468	207	177	40	21	9	21	134	3	390	27	1	30	27	.526	2	1	3.01

Jason Townley

Bats: Right Throws: Right Pos: C Ht: 6'2" Wt: 220 Born: 06/18/69 Age: 26

Year	Team	Lg	G	AB	H	2B	3B	HR	TB	R	RBI	TBB	IBB	SO	HBP	SH	SF	SB	CS	SB%	GDP	Avg	OBP	SLG
1987	St.Cathrnes	A	60	177	31	4	1	6	55	21	17	27	0	47	2	0	3	1	1	.50	2	.175	.287	.311
1988	Dunedin	A	2	7	2	0	0	0	2	0	1	0	0	1	0	0	0	0	0	.00	0	.286	.286	.286
	Myrtle Bch	A	5	15	6	2	0	1	11	4	3	1	0	4	0	0	0	0	0	.00	0	.400	.438	.733
	St.Cathrnes	A	64	225	49	4	0	5	68	19	18	30	1	65	1	1	1	2	4	.33	0	.218	.311	.302
1989	Dunedin	A	51	155	33	8	0	1	44	16	12	20	0	42	1	2	0	0	0	.00	5	.213	.307	.284
1990	Dunedin	A	119	397	116	22	1	11	173	58	63	41	0	82	3	5	3	1	2	.33	10	.292	.360	.436
1991	Knoxville	AA	81	213	42	8	0	0	50	12	13	31	0	56	1	10	1	0	4	.00	2	.197	.301	.235
1992	Knoxville	AA	56	185	43	11	0	2	60	7	20	14	0	48	1	4	0	1	1	.50	1	.232	.290	.324
1993	Dunedin	A	2	4	2	0	0	0	2	1	1	1	0	0	0	0	0	0	0	.00	1	.500	.600	.500
1994	Syracuse	AAA	78	187	51	6	0	3	66	25	27	24	3	54	0	2	1	2	0	1.00	8	.273	.354	.353
8 Min. YEARS			518	1565	375	65	2	29	531	163	175	189	4	399	9	24	9	7	12	.37	37	.240	.323	.339

Mark Tranbarger

Pitches: Left Bats: Left Pos: P Ht: 6'2" Wt: 205 Born: 09/17/69 Age: 25

Year	Team	Lg	G	GS	CG	GF	IP	BFP	H	R	ER	HR	SH	SF	HB	TBB	IBB	SO	WP	Bk	W	L	Pct.	ShO	Sv	ERA
1991	Johnson Cty	R	4	0	0	0	8	37	11	7	2	0	0	0	2	0	0	6	1	1	1	0	1.000	0	0	2.25
	Cardinals	R	23	0	0	4	29.1	115	22	5	4	0	1	2	0	4	0	37	3	1	3	0	1.000	0	0	1.23
1992	Springfield	A	42	0	0	17	49.2	220	47	27	20	4	1	3	3	24	0	38	2	1	1	0	1.000	0	2	3.62
1993	Savannah	A	56	1	0	11	66	276	56	25	23	3	3	2	3	29	0	50	2	0	5	2	.714	0	1	3.14
1994	Chattanooga	AA	12	0	0	6	10	46	12	6	6	0	0	1	1	4	0	9	1	0	0	1	.000	0	0	5.40
	Winston-Sal	A	37	1	0	24	39.2	174	36	18	15	3	1	0	3	19	3	31	3	0	4	3	.571	0	12	3.40
4 Min. YEARS			174	2	0	62	202.2	868	184	88	70	10	6	8	12	80	3	171	12	3	14	6	.700	0	16	3.11

Mark Tranberg

Pitches: Right Bats: Right Pos: P Ht: 6'4" Wt: 210 Born: 02/28/69 Age: 26

Year	Team	Lg	G	GS	CG	GF	IP	BFP	H	R	ER	HR	SH	SF	HB	TBB	IBB	SO	WP	Bk	W	L	Pct.	ShO	Sv	ERA
1992	Batavia	A	11	0	0	4	20	103	23	20	18	5	0	0	2	15	1	25	4	1	0	2	.000	0	0	8.10
1993	Spartanburg	A	11	11	4	0	81.2	318	54	24	18	5	0	2	1	21	0	83	3	0	8	1	.889	1	0	1.98
	Clearwater	A	14	13	2	0	75.2	316	78	26	21	1	2	1	3	18	0	59	2	0	7	3	.700	0	0	2.50
1994	Clearwater	A	9	8	4	0	63.1	221	33	6	1	0	3	1	1	11	1	41	3	0	7	1	.875	3	0	0.14
	Reading	AA	24	15	0	3	94	441	122	76	63	15	3	4	5	37	1	60	1	3	3	12	.200	0	0	6.03
3 Min. YEARS			69	47	10	7	334.2	1399	310	152	121	26	8	8	12	102	3	268	16	3	25	19	.568	4	0	3.25

Jody Treadwell

Pitches: Right Bats: Right Pos: P Ht: 6'0" Wt: 190 Born: 12/14/68 Age: 26

Year	Team	Lg	G	GS	CG	GF	IP	BFP	H	R	ER	HR	SH	SF	HB	TBB	IBB	SO	WP	Bk	W	L	Pct.	ShO	Sv	ERA
1990	Vero Beach	A	16	8	2	5	80.1	316	59	17	16	2	3	1	1	22	6	80	2	3	9	1	.900	1	1	1.79

Year	Team	Lg	G	GS	CG	GF	IP	BFP	H	R	ER	HR	SH	SF	HB	TBB	IBB	SO	WP	Bk	W	L	Pct.	ShO	Sv	ERA
1991	San Antonio	AA	10	10	1	0	61	271	73	41	32	7	2	1	4	22	1	43	0	2	3	3	.500	0	0	4.72
	Bakersfield	A	17	14	0	0	91.1	392	92	46	38	8	2	0	4	34	2	84	7	1	5	4	.556	0	0	3.74
1992	San Antonio	AA	29	4	2	4	76	331	74	40	35	3	2	3	4	40	4	68	6	2	3	5	.375	1	1	4.14
1993	Albuquerque	AAA	39	10	0	6	105.1	481	119	58	55	7	3	2	7	52	7	102	11	2	5	4	.556	0	0	4.70
1994	Albuquerque	AAA	33	24	0	4	158.2	676	151	78	75	11	5	5	2	10	59	3	114	7	1	10	6	.625	0	2	4.25
	5 Min. YEARS		144	70	5	19	572.2	2467	568	280	251	38	17	9	30	229	23	491	33	11	35	23	.603	2	4	3.94

Chad Tredaway

Bats: Both   Throws: Right   Pos: 2B-3B   **Ht: 6'0"   Wt: 180   Born: 06/18/72   Age: 23**

							BATTING										BASERUNNING				PERCENTAGES		
Year	Team	Lg	G	AB	H	2B	3B	HR	TB	R	RBI	TBB	IBB	SO	HBP	SH	SF	SB	CS	SB%	GDP	Avg	OBP	SLG
1992	Geneva	A	73	270	81	19	2	5	119	39	31	24	1	24	3	3	5	6	4	.60	3	.300	.358	.441
1993	Daytona	A	66	242	62	12	0	0	74	32	21	27	2	25	0	3	4	4	3	.57	1	.256	.326	.306
1994	Orlando	AA	45	146	38	3	0	1	34	13	15	10	0	20	1	1	3	2	0	1.00	3	.192	.244	.233
	Daytona	A	77	284	69	14	3	5	104	26	28	23	0	39	1	4	1	1	5	.17	6	.243	.301	.366
	3 Min. YEARS		261	942	240	48	5	11	331	110	95	84	3	108	5	11	13	13	12	.52	13	.255	.315	.351

Chris Tremie

Bats: Right   Throws: Right   Pos: C   **Ht: 6'0"   Wt: 200   Born: 10/17/69   Age: 25**

							BATTING										BASERUNNING				PERCENTAGES		
Year	Team	Lg	G	AB	H	2B	3B	HR	TB	R	RBI	TBB	IBB	SO	HBP	SH	SF	SB	CS	SB%	GDP	Avg	OBP	SLG
1992	Utica	A	6	16	1	0	0	0	1	1	0	0	0	5	0	0	0	0	0	.00	0	.063	.063	.063
1993	White Sox	R	2	4	0	0	0	0	0	0	0	0	0	0	0	0	0	0	0	.00	0	.000	.000	.000
	Sarasota	A	14	37	6	1	0	0	7	2	5	2	0	4	3	0	0	0	0	.00	1	.162	.262	.189
	Hickory	A	49	155	29	6	1	1	40	7	17	9	0	26	4	1	0	0	0	.00	5	.187	.250	.258
1994	Birmingham	AA	92	302	68	13	0	2	87	32	29	17	0	44	6	3	2	4	1	.80	3	.225	.278	.288
	3 Min. YEARS		163	514	104	20	1	3	135	42	51	28	0	79	13	4	2	4	1	.80	9	.202	.260	.263

Mike Triessl

Bats: Right   Throws: Right   Pos: C   **Ht: 6'1"   Wt: 215   Born: 02/27/71   Age: 24**

							BATTING										BASERUNNING				PERCENTAGES		
Year	Team	Lg	G	AB	H	2B	3B	HR	TB	R	RBI	TBB	IBB	SO	HBP	SH	SF	SB	CS	SB%	GDP	Avg	OBP	SLG
1993	Riverside	A	3	3	1	0	0	0	1	1	0	0	0	0	0	0	0	0	0	.00	0	.333	.333	.333
	Appleton	A	34	81	15	5	0	1	23	9	8	14	0	32	2	3	1	0	0	.00	0	.185	.316	.284
1994	Calgary	AAA	5	11	3	1	0	0	4	1	0	0	0	3	0	1	0	0	0	.00	0	.273	.273	.364
	Riverside	A	54	129	30	4	2	4	50	20	19	12	0	38	1	0	0	1	0	1.00	6	.233	.303	.388
	2 Min. YEARS		96	224	49	10	2	5	78	31	27	26	0	73	3	4	1	1	0	1.00	6	.219	.307	.348

George Tsamis

Pitches: Left   Bats: Right   Pos: P   **Ht: 6' 2"   Wt: 190   Born: 06/14/67   Age: 28**

			HOW MUCH HE PITCHED						WHAT HE GAVE UP											THE RESULTS					
Year	Team	Lg	G	GS	CG	GF	IP	BFP	H	R	ER	HR	SH	SF	HB	TBB	IBB	SO	WP	Bk	W	L	Pct.	ShO	Sv	ERA
1989	Visalia	A	15	13	3	1	94.1	387	85	36	32	10	3	0	2	34	0	87	9	3	6	3	.667	0	0	3.05
1990	Visalia	A	26	26	4	0	183.2	731	168	62	45	4	3	2	4	61	0	145	7	1	17	4	.810	3	0	2.21
1991	Orlando	AA	1	1	0	0	7	28	3	2	0	0	0	0	0	4	0	5	0	0	0	0	.000	0	0	0.00
	Portland	AAA	29	27	2	0	167.2	716	183	75	61	11	8	6	5	66	0	75	7	1	10	8	.556	1	0	3.27
1992	Portland	AAA	39	22	4	6	163.2	700	195	78	71	12	4	5	5	51	1	71	2	0	13	4	.765	1	1	3.90
1993	Portland	AAA	3	3	0	0	14	74	27	15	13	2	0	1	0	5	0	10	0	0	1	2	.333	0	0	8.36
1994	Jacksonville	AA	13	5	0	3	43.1	181	41	24	20	5	2	1	2	14	1	18	1	0	3	3	.500	0	0	4.15
	Calgary	AAA	2	0	0	0	2	13	7	5	4	1	0	0	0	0	0	0	0	0	0	0	.000	0	0	18.00
1993	Minnesota	AL	41	0	0	18	68.1	309	86	51	47	9	2	6	3	27	5	30	1	1	1	2	.333	0	1	6.19
	6 Min. YEARS		128	97	13	10	675.2	2830	709	297	246	45	20	15	18	235	2	411	26	5	50	24	.676	5	1	3.28

Greg Tubbs

Bats: Right   Throws: Right   Pos: OF   **Ht: 5' 9"   Wt: 178   Born: 08/31/62   Age: 32**

							BATTING										BASERUNNING				PERCENTAGES		
Year	Team	Lg	G	AB	H	2B	3B	HR	TB	R	RBI	TBB	IBB	SO	HBP	SH	SF	SB	CS	SB%	GDP	Avg	OBP	SLG
1984	Braves	R	18	58	21	4	3	0	31	13	3	15	0	5	0	0	1	5	2	.71	0	.362	.486	.534
	Anderson	A	50	174	53	5	2	2	68	25	11	27	0	29	1	3	0	19	6	.76	0	.305	.401	.391
1985	Sumter	A	61	239	85	11	7	6	128	53	36	33	0	36	2	1	3	30	18	.63	2	.356	.433	.536
	Durham	A	70	266	75	15	6	8	126	44	32	36	0	52	3	2	1	29	12	.71	6	.282	.373	.474
1986	Greenville	AA	144	536	144	21	7	5	194	95	56	107	2	74	3	10	3	31	22	.58	14	.269	.391	.362
1987	Greenville	AA	141	540	145	19	7	3	187	97	40	86	2	86	2	7	1	24	19	.56	9	.269	.370	.346
1988	Greenville	AA	29	101	24	1	1	0	27	13	12	13	0	20	1	0	1	4	0	1.00	1	.238	.330	.267
	Richmond	AAA	78	228	56	14	2	2	80	43	11	28	0	38	1	3	1	8	8	.50	5	.246	.329	.351
1989	Greenville	AA	11	27	5	0	0	0	5	4	1	8	0	4	0	0	0	3	0	1.00	0	.185	.371	.185
	Richmond	AAA	115	405	122	10	11	4	166	64	35	47	0	49	1	5	0	19	15	.56	10	.301	.375	.410
1990	Richmond	AAA	11	23	5	0	0	0	5	3	1	11	0	6	0	1	0	0	2	.00	0	.217	.471	.217
	Harrisburg	AA	54	213	60	6	5	3	85	35	21	23	0	35	0	1	1	8	1	.89	7	.282	.350	.399
1991	Buffalo	AAA	121	373	102	18	11	3	151	71	34	48	1	62	5	5	2	34	11	.76	11	.273	.362	.405
1992	Buffalo	AAA	110	430	126	20	5	7	177	69	42	57	2	64	3	3	2	20	19	.51	6	.293	.378	.412
1993	Indianapolis	AAA	97	334	102	21	4	10	161	59	45	42	3	65	2	1	3	15	11	.58	4	.305	.383	.482

Year Team	Lg	G	AB	H	2B	3B	HR	TB	R	RBI	TBB	IBB	SO	HBP	SH	SF	SB	CS	SB%	GDP	Avg	OBP	SLG
1994 Buffalo	AAA	133	504	142	22	3	2	176	58	45	44	1	71	1	3	4	13	9	.59	8	.282	.338	.349
1993 Cincinnati	NL	35	59	11	0	0	1	14	10	2	14	0	10	1	0	0	3	1	.75	0	.186	.351	.237
11 Min. YEARS		1243	4451	1267	187	74	55	1767	746	425	625	11	696	25	45	22	262	155	.63	83	.285	.374	.397

Mike Tucker

Bats: Left Throws: Right Pos: SS   Ht: 6'2" Wt: 185 Born: 06/25/71 Age: 24

					BATTING												BASERUNNING				PERCENTAGES		
Year Team	Lg	G	AB	H	2B	3B	HR	TB	R	RBI	TBB	IBB	SO	HBP	SH	SF	SB	CS	SB%	GDP	Avg	OBP	SLG
1993 Wilmington	A	61	239	73	14	2	6	109	42	44	34	4	49	2	0	4	12	2	.86	0	.305	.391	.456
Memphis	AA	72	244	68	7	4	9	110	38	35	42	0	51	6	3	4	12	5	.71	1	.279	.392	.451
1994 Omaha	AAA	132	485	134	16	7	21	227	75	77	69	2	111	3	2	6	11	3	.79	6	.276	.366	.468
2 Min. YEARS		265	968	275	37	13	36	446	155	156	145	6	211	11	5	14	35	10	.78	7	.284	.379	.461

Scooter Tucker

Bats: Right Throws: Right Pos: C   Ht: 6'2" Wt: 205 Born: 11/18/66 Age: 28

					BATTING												BASERUNNING				PERCENTAGES		
Year Team	Lg	G	AB	H	2B	3B	HR	TB	R	RBI	TBB	IBB	SO	HBP	SH	SF	SB	CS	SB%	GDP	Avg	OBP	SLG
1988 Everett	A	45	153	40	5	0	3	54	24	23	30	0	34	3	0	3	0	0	.00	0	.261	.386	.353
1989 Clinton	A	126	426	105	20	2	3	138	44	43	58	2	80	9	3	4	6	5	.55	11	.246	.346	.324
1990 San Jose	A	123	439	123	28	2	5	170	59	71	71	4	69	13	2	6	9	3	.75	14	.280	.391	.387
1991 Shreveport	AA	110	352	100	29	1	4	143	49	49	48	1	58	5	6	2	3	4	.43	8	.284	.376	.406
1992 Tucson	AAA	83	288	87	15	1	1	107	36	29	28	1	35	3	1	2	5	1	.83	12	.302	.368	.372
1993 Tucson	AAA	98	318	87	20	2	1	114	54	37	47	8	37	2	2	2	1	5	.17	7	.274	.369	.358
1994 Tucson	AAA	113	408	131	38	1	14	213	64	80	48	2	56	6	2	5	3	2	.60	9	.321	.396	.522
1992 Houston	NL	20	50	6	1	0	0	7	5	3	3	0	13	2	1	0	1	1	.50	2	.120	.200	.140
1993 Houston	NL	9	26	5	1	0	0	6	1	3	2	0	3	0	0	0	0	0	.00	0	.192	.250	.231
7 Min. YEARS		698	2384	673	155	9	31	939	330	332	330	18	369	41	16	24	27	20	.57	69	.282	.376	.394
2 Maj. YEARS		29	76	11	2	0	0	13	6	6	5	0	16	2	1	0	1	1	.50	2	.145	.217	.171

Lee Tunnell

Pitches: Right Bats: Right Pos: P   Ht: 6'0" Wt: 180 Born: 10/30/60 Age: 34

		HOW MUCH HE PITCHED						WHAT HE GAVE UP									THE RESULTS					
Year Team	Lg	G	GS	CG	GF	IP	BFP	H	R	ER	HR	SH	SF	HB	TBB	IBB	SO	WP	Bk	W	L	Pct.	ShO	Sv	ERA
1985 Hawaii	AAA	7	7	2	0	46.2	0	32	12	12	2	0	0	1	24	0	29	3	0	4	1	.800	2	0	2.31
1986 Hawaii	AAA	27	26	2	0	142.1	667	180	106	95	9	5	3	5	81	1	95	14	0	4	11	.267	0	0	6.01
1987 Louisville	AAA	6	6	1	0	37	156	33	16	14	3	0	0	0	19	0	32	2	0	4	1	.800	1	0	3.41
Springfield	A	1	1	0	0	2.2	11	4	1	1	0	0	0	0	0	0	3	0	0	1	0	1.000	0	0	3.38
1988 Louisville	AAA	24	20	0	0	135.1	581	136	69	58	7	6	7	3	55	1	60	8	11	6	8	.429	0	0	3.86
1989 Portland	AAA	25	5	0	10	66.1	273	56	24	20	2	2	6	1	23	2	58	2	2	2	4	.333	0	4	2.71
1990 Tucson	AAA	33	20	2	6	124.1	556	144	76	66	5	8	1	0	48	4	59	4	0	6	7	.462	0	2	4.78
1994 New Haven	AA	17	0	0	5	29	116	23	7	6	0	1	0	1	7	1	25	3	1	3	1	.750	0	1	1.86
Colo. Spmg	AAA	11	0	0	2	10.1	53	15	14	13	2	0	1	0	7	1	10	0	0	0	2	.000	0	0	11.32
1982 Pittsburgh	NL	5	3	0	2	18.1	75	17	8	8	1	1	0	2	5	0	4	0	0	1	1	.500	0	0	3.93
1983 Pittsburgh	NL	35	25	5	4	177.2	731	167	81	72	15	2	6	2	58	3	95	11	5	11	6	.647	3	0	3.65
1984 Pittsburgh	NL	26	6	0	5	68.1	317	81	44	40	6	4	1	0	40	6	51	6	2	1	7	.125	0	1	5.27
1985 Pittsburgh	NL	24	23	0	1	132.1	565	126	70	59	11	3	2	1	57	4	74	3	0	4	10	.286	0	0	4.01
1987 St. Louis	NL	32	9	0	3	74.1	335	90	45	40	5	3	4	1	34	7	49	2	5	4	4	.500	0	0	4.84
1989 Minnesota	AL	10	0	0	4	12	59	18	8	8	1	0	0	0	6	1	7	0	0	1	0	1.000	0	0	6.00
7 Min. YEARS		151	85	7	23	594	2413	623	325	285	30	22	18	11	264	10	371	36	16	29	36	.446	3	7	4.32
6 Maj. YEARS		132	66	5	19	483	2082	499	256	227	39	13	13	6	200	21	280	22	12	22	28	.440	3	1	4.23

Frank Turco

Bats: Right Throws: Right Pos: 2B   Ht: 5'11" Wt: 165 Born: 07/03/68 Age: 26

					BATTING												BASERUNNING				PERCENTAGES		
Year Team	Lg	G	AB	H	2B	3B	HR	TB	R	RBI	TBB	IBB	SO	HBP	SH	SF	SB	CS	SB%	GDP	Avg	OBP	SLG
1990 Rangers	R	5	10	3	1	0	0	4	1	1	1	0	2	0	0	0	0	1	.00	0	.300	.364	.400
Gastonia	A	5	8	1	0	0	0	1	2	0	1	0	1	0	0	0	0	0	.00	0	.125	.222	.125
Erie	A	29	83	18	5	0	3	32	12	9	8	0	16	1	2	1	1	0	1.00	1	.217	.290	.386
1991 Reno	A	38	104	18	3	1	0	23	7	4	7	0	28	2	3	1	3	0	1.00	3	.173	.237	.221
Bend	A	60	215	51	14	3	1	74	33	26	27	0	36	2	0	0	9	8	.53	3	.237	.328	.344
1992 Charlotte	A	93	264	60	12	5	3	91	29	23	18	0	68	1	3	3	14	2	.88	2	.227	.276	.345
1993 Tulsa	AA	118	423	113	13	2	8	154	45	39	27	0	86	1	5	2	13	8	.62	8	.267	.311	.364
1994 Tulsa	AA	95	302	79	15	3	7	121	43	33	25	1	82	1	7	2	18	7	.72	4	.262	.318	.401
5 Min. YEARS		443	1409	343	63	14	22	500	172	135	114	1	319	8	20	9	58	26	.69	21	.243	.302	.355

Brian Turner

Bats: Left Throws: Left Pos: 1B   Ht: 6'2" Wt: 210 Born: 06/09/71 Age: 24

					BATTING												BASERUNNING				PERCENTAGES		
Year Team	Lg	G	AB	H	2B	3B	HR	TB	R	RBI	TBB	IBB	SO	HBP	SH	SF	SB	CS	SB%	GDP	Avg	OBP	SLG
1989 Yankees	R	50	188	39	7	3	1	55	29	28	20	0	30	2	2	3	5	2	.71	4	.207	.286	.293
1990 Greensboro	A	37	118	24	5	1	0	31	14	5	16	0	29	0	1	0	3	2	.60	1	.203	.299	.263
Oneonta	A	69	227	56	13	1	0	71	28	24	36	1	49	2	1	1	7	4	.64	1	.247	.353	.313

257

Year	Team	Lg	G	AB	H	2B	3B	HR	TB	R	RBI	TBB	IBB	SO	HBP	SH	SF	SB	CS	SB%	GDP	Avg	OBP	SLG
1991	Greensboro	A	123	424	113	17	2	8	158	58	63	59	1	93	2	2	4	10	11	.48	4	.267	.356	.373
1992	Ft. Laud	A	127	454	107	16	1	7	146	39	54	46	2	103	0	5	5	3	8	.27	13	.236	.303	.322
1993	San Berndno	A	109	406	132	23	3	21	224	69	68	49	4	75	2	2	3	4	2	.67	3	.325	.398	.552
1994	Albany-Colo	AA	2	4	2	0	0	0	2	1	1	1	1	0	0	0	0	1	0	1.00	0	.500	.600	.500
	Tampa	A	118	420	101	24	3	10	161	63	64	63	3	84	4	1	4	2	1	.67	7	.240	.342	.383
	6 Min. YEARS		635	2241	574	105	14	47	848	301	307	290	12	463	12	14	20	35	30	.54	33	.256	.342	.378

Ryan Turner

Bats: Right Throws: Right Pos: OF Ht: 6'4" Wt: 200 Born: 04/24/69 Age: 26

			BATTING															BASERUNNING				PERCENTAGES		
Year	Team	Lg	G	AB	H	2B	3B	HR	TB	R	RBI	TBB	IBB	SO	HBP	SH	SF	SB	CS	SB%	GDP	Avg	OBP	SLG
1991	Bend	A	65	241	76	16	1	3	103	37	43	32	0	48	9	1	1	2	3	.40	7	.315	.413	.427
1992	Visalia	A	118	413	110	22	6	7	165	70	62	49	2	71	4	0	9	14	8	.64	13	.266	.343	.400
1993	Central Val	A	112	422	124	23	1	13	188	64	67	62	2	88	5	2	3	11	5	.69	16	.294	.388	.445
1994	New Haven	AA	38	123	24	5	0	2	35	13	10	11	0	33	1	0	3	1	1	.50	2	.195	.261	.285
	4 Min. YEARS		333	1199	334	66	8	25	491	184	182	154	4	240	19	3	16	28	17	.62	38	.279	.365	.410

Shane Turner

Bats: Left Throws: Right Pos: 2B Ht: 5'10" Wt: 190 Born: 01/08/63 Age: 32

			BATTING															BASERUNNING				PERCENTAGES		
Year	Team	Lg	G	AB	H	2B	3B	HR	TB	R	RBI	TBB	IBB	SO	HBP	SH	SF	SB	CS	SB%	GDP	Avg	OBP	SLG
1985	Oneonta	A	64	228	56	7	3	0	69	35	26	35	2	44	3	1	2	12	0	1.00	2	.246	.351	.303
1986	Ft.Laudrdle	A	66	222	71	12	2	2	93	48	36	51	1	35	3	4	3	12	8	.60	6	.320	.448	.419
1987	Columbus	AAA	25	76	17	0	2	0	21	10	7	5	0	16	0	1	0	2	1	.67	2	.224	.272	.276
	Albany	AA	20	73	23	3	1	1	31	19	8	12	0	3	1	1	1	2	1	.67	3	.315	.414	.425
	Reading	AA	74	283	96	16	6	3	133	50	47	21	1	35	3	1	1	3	6	.33	5	.339	.390	.470
1988	Maine	AAA	38	117	21	3	1	0	26	10	9	7	0	21	1	3	2	2	2	.50	1	.179	.228	.222
	Reading	AA	78	295	88	11	6	3	120	52	21	26	3	53	7	6	2	14	2	.88	3	.298	.367	.407
1989	Reading	AA	46	141	28	5	1	1	38	18	11	27	1	27	2	0	0	13	3	.81	2	.199	.335	.270
	Rochester	AAA	59	194	43	6	1	2	57	31	19	19	1	33	1	4	1	6	4	.60	5	.222	.293	.294
1990	Hagerstown	AA	10	38	9	1	0	0	10	5	1	0	0	10	0	0	0	1	0	1.00	1	.237	.237	.263
	Rochester	AAA	86	209	59	7	0	1	69	29	19	25	2	41	0	7	2	3	5	.38	4	.282	.356	.330
1991	Rochester	AAA	110	404	114	13	2	1	134	49	57	47	1	75	3	1	2	6	7	.46	13	.282	.360	.332
1992	Calgary	AAA	76	242	68	17	3	0	91	31	26	35	1	46	3	2	1	10	8	.56	7	.281	.377	.376
1993	Calgary	AAA	86	323	98	22	1	0	122	46	38	32	1	57	7	2	5	6	5	.55	12	.303	.373	.378
1994	Phoenix	AAA	12	27	4	1	1	0	7	3	0	6	0	6	0	0	0	0	2	.00	1	.148	.303	.259
	Rochester	AAA	28	87	17	4	0	0	21	11	9	16	0	22	2	0	2	2	0	1.00	4	.195	.327	.241
	Birmingham	AA	26	97	23	4	0	0	27	8	13	9	0	12	0	0	0	0	0	.00	1	.237	.302	.278
1988	Philadelphia	NL	18	35	6	0	0	0	6	1	1	5	0	9	0	0	0	0	0	.00	1	.171	.275	.171
1991	Baltimore	AL	4	1	0	0	0	0	0	0	0	0	0	0	0	0	0	0	0	.00	0	.000	.000	.000
1992	Seattle	AL	34	74	20	5	0	0	25	8	5	9	0	15	0	2	2	2	1	.67	4	.270	.341	.338
	10 Min. YEARS		904	3056	835	132	30	14	1069	455	347	373	14	536	36	33	24	94	54	.64	71	.273	.357	.350
	3 Maj. YEARS		56	110	26	5	0	0	31	9	6	14	0	24	0	2	2	2	1	.67	5	.236	.317	.282

Dave Tuttle

Pitches: Right Bats: Right Pos: P Ht: 6'3" Wt: 190 Born: 09/29/69 Age: 25

			HOW MUCH HE PITCHED					WHAT HE GAVE UP									THE RESULTS					
Year	Team	Lg	G	GS	CG	GF	IP	BFP	H	R	ER	HR	SH	SF	HB	TBB	IBB	SO	WP	Bk	W	L	Pct.	ShO	Sv	ERA
1992	Chston-Vw	A	17	16	0	0	97.1	416	87	46	42	5	0	6	1	53	1	93	4	0	3	5	.375	0	0	3.88
1993	Chston-Wv	A	13	13	0	0	81.1	343	66	37	32	3	1	1	3	36	1	74	6	1	8	3	.727	0	0	3.54
	Winston-Sal	A	15	15	2	0	86.1	388	98	61	53	8	3	2	1	39	0	58	6	0	7	7	.500	1	0	5.53
1994	Chattanooga	AA	14	14	0	0	84	377	82	60	42	8	4	2	7	48	5	54	10	0	2	9	.182	0	0	4.50
	Winston-Sal	A	13	13	2	0	76.2	315	58	26	18	8	0	0	3	27	0	64	2	0	5	2	.714	0	0	2.11
	3 Min. YEARS		72	71	4	0	425.2	1839	391	230	187	32	8	11	15	203	7	343	28	1	25	26	.490	1	0	3.95

Mike Twardoski

Bats: Left Throws: Left Pos: 1B Ht: 5'11" Wt: 185 Born: 07/13/64 Age: 30

			BATTING															BASERUNNING				PERCENTAGES		
Year	Team	Lg	G	AB	H	2B	3B	HR	TB	R	RBI	TBB	IBB	SO	HBP	SH	SF	SB	CS	SB%	GDP	Avg	OBP	SLG
1986	Batavia	A	63	202	62	12	0	6	92	33	17	43	2	25	0	2	1	11	3	.79	4	.307	.427	.455
1987	Kinston	A	85	267	77	16	2	3	106	45	38	73	0	50	2	0	5	3	3	.50	9	.288	.438	.397
1988	Kinston	A	132	450	145	26	3	6	195	80	87	117	6	59	0	0	10	21	8	.72	17	.322	.454	.433
1989	Canton-Akm	AA	113	380	104	19	2	0	127	56	36	77	2	47	0	4	4	7	7	.50	12	.274	.393	.334
1990	New Britain	AA	127	413	121	34	3	1	164	72	45	95	4	46	0	7	2	4	3	.57	11	.293	.424	.397
1991	Winter Havn	A	4	14	2	1	0	0	3	2	2	0	0	1	0	0	1	0	0	.00	0	.143	.133	.214
	Pawtucket	AAA	110	367	93	20	2	4	129	52	26	62	4	65	3	14	1	0	1	.00	7	.253	.365	.351
1992	Pawtucket	AAA	121	389	113	23	4	13	183	55	49	92	4	56	1	9	6	1	5	.17	10	.290	.422	.470
1993	Norfolk	AAA	131	427	120	15	2	9	166	66	38	69	6	65	1	2	4	9	11	.45	10	.281	.379	.389
1994	Pawtucket	AAA	111	382	108	15	1	13	164	61	49	56	5	38	1	4	1	8	2	.80	11	.283	.375	.429
	9 Min. YEARS		997	3291	945	181	19	55	1329	522	387	684	33	452	8	42	35	64	43	.60	91	.287	.407	.404

258

Brad Tyler

Bats: Left Throws: Right Pos: 3B Ht: 6'2" Wt: 175 Born: 03/03/69 Age: 26

Year	Team	Lg	G	AB	H	2B	3B	HR	TB	R	RBI	TBB	IBB	SO	HBP	SH	SF	SB	CS	SB%	GDP	Avg	OBP	SLG
1990	Wausau	A	56	187	44	4	3	2	60	31	24	44	2	45	2	1	2	11	4	.73	2	.235	.383	.321
1991	Kane County	A	60	199	54	10	3	3	79	35	29	44	1	25	1	1	2	5	3	.63	0	.271	.402	.397
	Frederick	A	56	187	48	6	0	4	66	26	26	33	3	33	2	1	1	3	2	.60	0	.257	.372	.353
1992	Frederick	A	54	185	47	11	2	3	71	34	22	43	2	34	2	1	4	9	3	.75	2	.254	.393	.384
	Hagerstown	AA	83	256	57	9	1	2	74	41	21	34	2	45	2	1	0	23	5	.82	5	.223	.318	.289
1993	Bowie	AA	129	437	103	23	17	10	190	85	44	84	2	89	1	1	3	24	11	.69	2	.236	.358	.435
1994	Rochester	AAA	101	314	82	15	8	7	134	38	43	38	2	69	2	1	0	7	4	.64	4	.261	.345	.427
	5 Min. YEARS		539	1765	435	78	34	31	674	290	209	320	14	340	12	7	12	82	32	.72	15	.246	.364	.382

Tim Unroe

Bats: Right Throws: Right Pos: SS Ht: 6'3" Wt: 200 Born: 10/07/70 Age: 24

Year	Team	Lg	G	AB	H	2B	3B	HR	TB	R	RBI	TBB	IBB	SO	HBP	SH	SF	SB	CS	SB%	GDP	Avg	OBP	SLG
1992	Helena	R	74	266	74	13	2	16	139	61	58	47	1	91	4	1	1	3	4	.43	2	.278	.393	.523
1993	Stockton	A	108	382	96	21	6	12	165	57	63	36	0	96	7	3	4	9	10	.47	8	.251	.324	.432
1994	El Paso	AA	126	474	147	36	7	15	242	97	103	42	2	107	5	0	9	14	6	.70	6	.310	.366	.511
	3 Min. YEARS		308	1122	317	70	15	43	546	215	224	125	3	294	16	4	14	26	20	.57	16	.283	.359	.487

Ugueth Urbina

Pitches: Right Bats: Right Pos: P Ht: 6'2" Wt: 170 Born: 02/15/74 Age: 21

Year	Team	Lg	G	GS	CG	GF	IP	BFP	H	R	ER	HR	SH	SF	HB	TBB	IBB	SO	WP	Bk	W	L	Pct.	ShO	Sv	ERA
1991	Expos	R	10	10	3	0	63	252	58	34	16	2	0	0	4	10	0	51	2	3	3	3	.500	1	0	2.29
1992	Albany	A	24	24	5	0	142.1	582	111	68	51	14	2	5	4	54	0	100	4	4	7	13	.350	2	0	3.22
1993	Burlington	A	16	16	4	0	108.1	436	78	30	24	7	2	1	7	36	1	107	6	5	10	1	.909	1	0	1.99
	Harrisburg	AA	11	11	3	0	70	298	66	32	31	5	4	2	5	32	1	45	1	1	4	5	.444	1	0	3.99
1994	Harrisburg	AA	21	21	0	0	120.2	497	96	49	44	11	4	7	3	43	0	86	6	1	9	3	.750	0	0	3.28
	4 Min. YEARS		82	82	15	0	504.1	2065	409	203	166	39	12	15	23	175	2	389	19	14	33	25	.569	5	0	2.96

Marc Valdes

Pitches: Right Bats: Right Pos: P Ht: 6'0" Wt: 170 Born: 12/20/71 Age: 23

Year	Team	Lg	G	GS	CG	GF	IP	BFP	H	R	ER	HR	SH	SF	HB	TBB	IBB	SO	WP	Bk	W	L	Pct.	ShO	Sv	ERA
1993	Elmira	A	3	3	0	0	9.2	46	8	9	6	0	0	0	3	7	0	15	0	0	0	2	.000	0	0	5.59
1994	Kane County	A	11	11	2	0	76.1	315	62	30	25	3	4	1	8	21	0	68	3	0	7	4	.636	0	0	2.95
	Portland	AA	15	15	0	0	99	411	77	31	28	5	3	1	8	39	1	70	4	3	8	4	.667	0	0	2.55
	2 Min. YEARS		29	29	2	0	185	772	147	70	59	8	7	2	19	67	1	153	7	3	15	10	.600	0	0	2.87

Pedro Valdez

Bats: Left Throws: Left Pos: OF Ht: 6'1" Wt: 160 Born: 06/29/73 Age: 22

Year	Team	Lg	G	AB	H	2B	3B	HR	TB	R	RBI	TBB	IBB	SO	HBP	SH	SF	SB	CS	SB%	GDP	Avg	OBP	SLG
1991	Huntington	R	50	157	45	11	1	0	58	18	16	17	3	31	2	1	5	5	1	.83	7	.287	.354	.369
1992	Peoria	A	33	112	26	7	0	0	33	8	20	7	3	32	0	0	4	0	0	.00	1	.232	.268	.295
	Geneva	A	66	254	69	10	0	5	94	27	24	3	1	33	3	2	2	4	5	.44	2	.272	.286	.370
1993	Peoria	A	65	234	74	11	1	7	108	33	36	10	4	40	0	5	4	2	2	.50	3	.316	.339	.462
	Daytona	A	60	230	66	16	1	8	108	27	49	9	1	30	2	0	5	3	4	.43	8	.287	.313	.470
1994	Orlando	AA	116	365	103	14	4	1	128	39	37	20	3	45	2	2	1	2	6	.25	10	.282	.322	.351
	4 Min. YEARS		390	1352	383	69	7	21	529	152	182	66	15	211	9	10	21	16	18	.47	31	.283	.316	.391

Julio Valera

Pitches: Right Bats: Right Pos: P Ht: 6'2" Wt: 215 Born: 10/13/68 Age: 26

Year	Team	Lg	G	GS	CG	GF	IP	BFP	H	R	ER	HR	SH	SF	HB	TBB	IBB	SO	WP	Bk	W	L	Pct.	ShO	Sv	ERA
1986	Kingsport	R	13	13	2	0	76.1	356	91	58	44	5	4	0	0	29	2	64	4	1	3	10	.231	1	0	5.19
1987	Columbia	A	22	22	2	0	125.1	522	114	53	39	7	2	1	4	31	0	97	6	0	8	7	.533	2	0	2.80
1988	Columbia	A	30	27	8	3	191	775	171	77	68	8	5	7	4	51	3	144	9	6	15	11	.577	0	1	3.20
1989	St.Lucie	A	6	6	3	0	45	173	34	5	5	1	2	0	0	6	1	45	0	0	4	2	.667	2	0	1.00
	Jackson	AA	19	19	6	0	137.1	566	123	47	38	4	7	3	8	36	2	107	10	0	10	6	.625	2	0	2.49
	Tidewater	AAA	2	2	0	0	13	52	8	3	3	1	0	0	1	5	0	10	1	0	1	1	.500	0	0	2.08
1990	Tidewater	AAA	24	24	9	0	158	648	146	58	53	12	6	5	5	39	3	133	7	5	10	10	.500	2	0	3.02
1991	Tidewater	AAA	26	26	3	0	176.1	739	152	79	75	12	8	6	6	70	4	117	8	3	10	10	.500	1	0	3.83
1992	Tidewater	AAA	1	1	0	0	6	25	5	0	0	0	0	0	0	2	0	7	2	0	1	0	1.000	0	0	0.00
1994	Lake Elsino	A	2	2	0	0	9.2	45	14	10	10	0	0	0	1	3	0	11	1	0	1	1	.500	0	0	9.31
	Midland	AA	3	3	0	0	19	79	17	8	8	2	0	1	0	9	0	15	0	0	1	0	1.000	0	0	3.79
	Vancouver	AAA	11	11	0	0	59.2	269	70	40	35	9	2	3	3	20	1	43	4	1	1	3	.250	0	0	5.28
1990	New York	NL	3	3	0	0	13	64	20	11	10	1	0	0	0	7	0	4	0	0	1	1	.500	0	0	6.92
1991	New York	NL	2	0	0	1	2	11	1	0	0	0	0	0	0	4	1	3	0	0	0	0	.000	0	0	0.00
1992	California	AL	30	28	4	0	188	792	188	82	78	15	6	2	2	64	5	113	5	0	8	11	.421	2	0	3.73

1993 California	AL	19	5	0	8	53	246	77	44	39	8	4	1	2	15	2	28	2	0	3	6	.333	0	4	6.62
8 Min. YEARS		159	156	33	3	1016.2	4249	945	446	378	61	36	26	32	301	16	793	52	16	65	61	.516	10	1	3.35
4 Maj. YEARS		54	36	4	9	256	1113	286	137	127	24	10	3	4	90	8	148	7	0	12	18	.400	2	4	4.46

Kerry Valrie

Bats: Right Throws: Right Pos: OF   Ht: 5'10" Wt: 195 Born: 10/31/68 Age: 26

								BATTING										BASERUNNING				PERCENTAGES		
Year	Team	Lg	G	AB	H	2B	3B	HR	TB	R	RBI	TBB	IBB	SO	HBP	SH	SF	SB	CS	SB%	GDP	Avg	OBP	SLG
1990	Utica	A	42	149	28	4	1	0	34	14	10	8	1	46	1	1	0	12	6	.67	4	.188	.234	.228
1991	South Bend	A	87	331	71	11	2	6	104	47	29	23	1	78	3	3	0	32	6	.84	3	.215	.272	.314
1992	South Bend	A	79	314	81	12	2	5	112	34	37	16	0	53	1	0	4	22	15	.59	6	.258	.293	.357
	Sarasota	A	51	174	41	9	0	1	53	13	23	14	0	42	1	0	2	13	1	.93	2	.236	.293	.305
1993	Sarasota	A	115	386	82	14	2	12	136	47	52	17	1	81	4	2	7	19	7	.73	6	.212	.249	.352
1994	Birmingham	AA	119	423	121	27	3	3	163	59	58	34	4	75	4	4	4	29	10	.74	3	.286	.342	.385
5 Min. YEARS			493	1777	424	77	10	27	602	214	209	112	7	375	14	8	17	127	45	.74	21	.239	.286	.339

Doug Vanderweele

Pitches: Right Bats: Right Pos: P   Ht: 6'3" Wt: 200 Born: 03/18/70 Age: 25

			HOW MUCH HE PITCHED						WHAT HE GAVE UP												THE RESULTS					
Year	Team	Lg	G	GS	CG	GF	IP	BFP	H	R	ER	HR	SH	SF	HB	TBB	IBB	SO	WP	Bk	W	L	Pct.	ShO	Sv	ERA
1991	Everett	A	15	15	0	0	87	371	73	42	19	1	1	3	8	35	1	65	12	7	6	4	.600	0	0	1.97
1992	Clinton	A	9	9	0	0	51	228	61	33	28	5	2	2	2	24	1	39	7	3	3	3	.500	0	0	4.94
	San Jose	A	16	15	1	0	87.1	387	77	49	36	7	3	2	8	50	1	51	4	2	6	4	.600	0	0	3.71
	Phoenix	AAA	1	0	0	0	1.2	8	3	2	2	0	0	0	0	0	0	1	1	0	0	0	.000	0	0	10.80
1993	Shreveport	AA	1	0	0	0	2	7	0	0	0	0	0	0	0	0	0	3	0	0	0	0	.000	0	0	0.00
	San Jose	A	25	24	3	1	171	728	188	78	74	17	12	5	3	55	3	106	8	2	10	6	.625	0	0	3.89
1994	San Jose	A	8	8	0	0	51.2	215	46	21	16	3	4	1	5	10	0	33	0	0	3	3	.500	0	0	2.79
	Shreveport	AA	21	21	1	0	125.1	533	146	62	53	7	7	3	3	32	2	55	4	0	6	9	.400	0	0	3.81
4 Min. YEARS			96	92	5	1	577	2477	594	287	228	40	29	16	29	206	8	352	36	14	34	29	.540	0	0	3.56

Ben VanRyn

Pitches: Left Bats: Left Pos: P   Ht: 6'5" Wt: 195 Born: 08/09/71 Age: 23

			HOW MUCH HE PITCHED						WHAT HE GAVE UP												THE RESULTS					
Year	Team	Lg	G	GS	CG	GF	IP	BFP	H	R	ER	HR	SH	SF	HB	TBB	IBB	SO	WP	Bk	W	L	Pct.	ShO	Sv	ERA
1990	Expos	R	10	9	0	0	51.2	205	44	13	10	0	0	0	2	15	0	56	0	0	5	3	.625	0	0	1.74
1991	Sumter	A	20	20	0	0	109.1	506	122	96	79	14	3	7	6	61	0	77	10	4	2	13	.133	0	0	6.50
	Jamestown	A	6	6	1	0	32.1	143	37	19	18	1	0	0	2	12	0	23	4	0	3	3	.500	0	0	5.01
1992	Vero Beach	A	26	25	1	0	137.2	583	125	58	49	4	5	8	2	54	1	108	4	5	10	7	.588	1	0	3.20
1993	San Antonio	AA	21	21	1	0	134.1	557	118	43	33	5	4	1	3	38	1	144	2	4	14	4	.778	0	0	2.21
	Albuquerque	AAA	6	6	0	0	24.1	120	35	30	29	1	1	2	0	17	0	9	0	0	1	4	.200	0	0	10.73
1994	Albuquerque	AAA	12	9	0	0	50.2	251	46	42	36	6	3	1	0	24	1	44	0	1	4	1	.800	0	0	6.39
	San Antonio	AA	17	17	0	0	102.1	418	93	42	34	5	3	1	0	35	0	72	2	0	8	3	.727	0	0	2.99
5 Min. YEARS			118	113	3	1	642.2	2783	649	343	288	36	19	20	15	256	3	533	22	14	47	38	.553	1	0	4.03

Hector Vargas

Bats: Right Throws: Right Pos: 3B   Ht: 5'11" Wt: 155 Born: 06/03/66 Age: 29

								BATTING										BASERUNNING				PERCENTAGES		
Year	Team	Lg	G	AB	H	2B	3B	HR	TB	R	RBI	TBB	IBB	SO	HBP	SH	SF	SB	CS	SB%	GDP	Avg	OBP	SLG
1986	Yankees	R	61	212	50	6	0	0	56	27	25	33	0	28	3	3	2	10	11	.48	5	.236	.344	.264
1987	Pr William	A	34	53	12	0	0	0	12	8	2	5	0	5	0	1	0	1	1	.50	3	.226	.293	.226
	Oneonta	A	15	43	12	4	1	0	18	4	7	2	0	6	1	0	2	1	2	.33	0	.279	.313	.419
	Albany	AA	44	130	29	3	0	1	35	18	10	15	0	30	0	5	0	3	2	.60	1	.223	.303	.269
1988	Ft.Lauderdle	A	3	14	2	0	0	0	2	2	3	0	0	4	0	0	0	0	0	.00	0	.143	.143	.143
	Oneonta	A	46	143	37	5	2	0	46	24	16	13	0	23	0	0	2	11	0	1.00	7	.259	.316	.322
1989	Pr William	A	5	11	2	1	0	0	3	2	0	3	0	4	0	1	0	0	0	.00	1	.182	.357	.273
	Peninsula	A	84	288	75	8	3	3	98	44	27	35	2	41	2	0	3	35	13	.73	11	.260	.341	.340
	Ft.Lauderdle	A	19	53	17	2	1	0	21	6	3	3	0	15	0	0	1	2	2	.50	1	.321	.351	.396
1990	Ft.Lauderdle	A	117	429	132	20	9	0	170	48	61	30	1	68	3	4	11	21	11	.66	8	.308	.349	.396
1991	Albany	AA	106	345	96	16	3	1	121	49	39	45	0	65	5	2	10	23	5	.82	10	.278	.368	.351
1992	Albany	AA	116	417	125	26	9	1	172	64	41	48	0	73	2	2	0	25	13	.66	7	.300	.375	.412
1993	Ottawa	AAA	36	93	17	3	1	0	22	10	6	15	1	25	1	2	0	3	3	.50	2	.183	.303	.237
	Canton-Akrn	AA	29	90	20	2	0	1	25	9	8	12	0	22	0	0	2	3	0	1.00	1	.222	.308	.278
1994	Bowie	AA	123	428	134	33	3	3	197	73	58	68	3	66	9	1	6	5	7	.42	9	.313	.413	.460
9 Min. YEARS			838	2749	760	129	32	15	998	388	306	327	7	475	26	21	31	143	70	.67	66	.276	.355	.363

Julio Vargas

Bats: Right Throws: Right Pos: SS   Ht: 5'10" Wt: 150 Born: 09/10/74 Age: 20

								BATTING										BASERUNNING				PERCENTAGES		
Year	Team	Lg	G	AB	H	2B	3B	HR	TB	R	RBI	TBB	IBB	SO	HBP	SH	SF	SB	CS	SB%	GDP	Avg	OBP	SLG
1993	Athletics	R	50	195	56	6	6	0	74	46	25	15	1	37	0	1	2	12	6	.67	3	.287	.335	.379
1994	Tacoma	AAA	1	1	0	0	0	0	0	0	0	0	0	0	0	0	0	0	0	.00	0	.000	.000	.000
	Athletics	R	48	176	38	7	2	0	49	22	16	12	0	40	0	1	2	4	5	.44	3	.216	.263	.278
2 Min. YEARS			99	372	94	13	8	0	123	68	41	27	1	78	0	2	4	16	11	.59	6	.253	.300	.331

Jim Vatcher

Bats: Right **Throws:** Right **Pos:** OF   **Ht:** 5' 9" **Wt:** 165 **Born:** 05/27/66 **Age:** 29

Year	Team	Lg	G	AB	H	2B	3B	HR	TB	R	RBI	TBB	IBB	SO	HBP	SH	SF	SB	CS	SB%	GDP	Avg	OBP	SLG
1987	Utica	A	67	249	67	15	2	3	95	44	21	28	0	31	2	2	1	10	5	.67	5	.269	.346	.382
1988	Spartanburg	A	137	496	150	32	2	12	222	90	72	89	1	73	8	9	3	26	13	.67	10	.302	.414	.448
1989	Clearwater	A	92	349	105	30	5	4	157	51	46	41	0	49	2	0	2	7	3	.70	11	.301	.376	.450
	Reading	AA	48	171	56	11	3	4	85	27	32	26	1	29	1	0	4	2	0	1.00	6	.327	.411	.497
1990	Scr Wil-Bar	AAA	55	181	46	12	4	5	81	30	22	32	1	33	0	1	2	1	4	.20	4	.254	.363	.448
1991	Las Vegas	AAA	117	395	105	28	6	17	196	67	67	53	3	76	3	3	2	4	12	.25	14	.266	.355	.496
1992	Las Vegas	AAA	111	280	77	15	3	8	122	41	35	39	4	60	3	6	2	2	6	.25	1	.275	.367	.436
1993	Las Vegas	AAA	103	293	93	17	2	7	135	36	45	35	0	46	4	5	2	3	4	.43	7	.317	.395	.461
1994	Norfolk	AAA	112	316	74	20	1	10	126	41	48	36	1	56	1	4	2	2	4	.33	4	.234	.313	.399
1990	Philadelphia	NL	36	46	12	1	0	1	16	5	4	4	0	6	0	0	0	0	0	.00	1	.261	.320	.348
	Atlanta	NL	21	27	7	1	1	0	10	2	3	1	0	9	0	0	0	0	0	.00	0	.259	.286	.370
1991	San Diego	NL	17	20	4	0	0	0	4	3	2	4	0	6	0	0	0	1	0	1.00	0	.200	.333	.200
1992	San Diego	NL	13	16	4	1	0	0	5	1	2	3	0	6	0	0	0	0	0	.00	0	.250	.368	.313
	8 Min. YEARS		842	2730	773	180	28	70	1219	427	388	379	11	453	24	30	20	57	51	.53	64	.283	.373	.447
	3 Maj. YEARS		87	109	27	3	1	1	35	11	11	12	0	27	0	1	0	1	0	1.00	1	.248	.322	.321

Marcos Vazquez

Pitches: Right **Bats:** Right **Pos:** P   **Ht:** 5'10" **Wt:** 170 **Born:** 11/05/68 **Age:** 26

Year	Team	Lg	G	GS	CG	GF	IP	BFP	H	R	ER	HR	SH	SF	HB	TBB	IBB	SO	WP	Bk	W	L	Pct	ShO	Sv	ERA
1987	Braves	R	12	12	1	0	70.1	308	68	35	29	1	1	4	4	35	2	46	5	1	3	5	.375	0	0	3.71
1988	Sumter	A	32	18	1	6	133	611	145	93	79	15	6	6	7	76	1	74	8	10	7	11	.389	0	0	5.35
1989	Sumter	A	25	25	4	0	156.2	661	144	78	57	9	2	7	4	56	0	98	4	2	10	10	.500	1	0	3.27
	Burlington	A	2	2	0	0	11	52	13	11	8	1	1	1	0	4	0	10	1	0	0	0	.000	0	0	6.55
1990	Durham	A	12	11	1	0	57	255	60	33	24	6	0	0	5	29	1	28	6	0	4	2	.667	0	0	3.79
	Burlington	A	15	13	5	1	87.2	366	89	50	37	2	2	2	1	20	0	41	8	2	6	5	.545	0	0	3.80
1991	Macon	A	14	14	3	0	92	373	61	35	26	2	2	0	5	40	0	75	10	0	7	4	.636	1	0	2.54
	Durham	A	4	4	0	0	24	109	30	9	7	0	0	0	0	11	0	12	2	0	3	0	1.000	0	0	2.63
1992	Greenville	AA	14	14	1	0	73.1	310	81	38	35	6	2	4	2	30	0	38	7	0	6	4	.600	0	0	4.30
	Durham	A	15	9	0	2	74.2	310	53	24	18	5	0	2	2	32	1	53	4	2	5	0	1.000	0	0	2.17
1993	Greenville	AA	43	4	0	16	82	366	96	47	42	1	9	2	2	37	7	61	3	2	4	5	.444	0	3	4.61
1994	Chattanooga	AA	29	19	1	3	131	558	121	60	51	8	8	4	4	52	2	71	8	2	8	7	.533	1	0	3.50
	8 Min. YEARS		217	145	17	28	992.2	4288	961	513	413	56	33	32	36	422	14	607	66	21	63	53	.543	3	3	3.74

Guillermo Velasquez

Bats: Left **Throws:** Right **Pos:** 1B   **Ht:** 6' 3" **Wt:** 225 **Born:** 04/23/68 **Age:** 27

Year	Team	Lg	G	AB	H	2B	3B	HR	TB	R	RBI	TBB	IBB	SO	HBP	SH	SF	SB	CS	SB%	GDP	Avg	OBP	SLG
1987	Chston-Sc	A	102	295	65	12	0	3	86	32	32	16	0	65	0	1	0	2	0	1.00	13	.220	.260	.292
1988	Chston-Sc	A	135	520	149	28	3	11	216	55	90	34	9	110	1	3	9	1	1	.50	6	.287	.326	.415
1989	Riverside	A	139	544	152	30	2	9	213	73	69	51	4	91	2	0	10	4	3	.57	14	.279	.338	.392
1990	Wichita	AA	105	377	102	21	2	12	163	48	72	35	5	66	1	0	4	1	1	.50	9	.271	.331	.432
1991	Wichita	AA	130	501	148	26	3	21	243	72	100	48	6	75	1	0	7	4	2	.67	6	.295	.354	.485
1992	Las Vegas	AAA	136	512	158	44	4	7	231	68	99	44	8	94	1	0	9	3	1	.75	7	.309	.359	.451
1993	Las Vegas	AAA	30	129	43	6	1	5	66	23	24	10	1	19	1	0	2	0	0	.00	2	.333	.380	.512
1994	Charlotte	AAA	18	52	11	3	0	1	17	7	4	10	1	9	0	0	1	0	0	.00	1	.212	.333	.327
	New Britain	AA	23	70	15	2	0	0	17	6	9	12	1	15	0	0	2	0	0	.00	0	.214	.321	.243
1992	San Diego	NL	15	23	7	0	0	1	10	1	5	1	0	7	0	0	0	0	0	.00	0	.304	.333	.435
1993	San Diego	NL	79	143	30	2	0	3	41	7	20	13	2	35	0	0	1	0	0	.00	3	.210	.274	.287
	8 Min. YEARS		818	3000	843	172	15	69	1252	384	497	260	35	544	7	4	44	15	9	.63	58	.281	.335	.417
	2 Maj. YEARS		94	166	37	2	0	4	51	8	25	14	2	42	0	0	1	0	0	.00	3	.223	.282	.307

Quilvio Veras

Bats: Both **Throws:** Right **Pos:** 2B   **Ht:** 5'9" **Wt:** 165 **Born:** 04/03/71 **Age:** 24

Year	Team	Lg	G	AB	H	2B	3B	HR	TB	R	RBI	TBB	IBB	SO	HBP	SH	SF	SB	CS	SB%	GDP	Avg	OBP	SLG
1990	Mets	R	30	98	29	3	3	1	41	26	5	19	0	16	3	1	1	16	8	.67	1	.296	.421	.418
	Kingsport	R	24	94	36	5	0	1	44	21	14	13	1	14	1	1	0	9	5	.64	1	.383	.463	.468
1991	Kingsport	R	64	226	76	11	4	1	98	54	16	36	0	28	7	5	0	38	11	.78	3	.336	.442	.434
	Pittsfield	A	5	15	4	0	1	0	6	3	2	5	0	1	0	0	0	2	0	1.00	0	.267	.450	.400
1992	Columbia	A	117	414	132	24	10	2	182	97	40	84	3	52	9	5	3	66	35	.65	5	.319	.441	.440
1993	Binghamton	AA	128	444	136	19	7	2	175	87	51	91	0	62	9	4	5	52	23	.69	3	.306	.430	.394
1994	Norfolk	AAA	123	457	114	22	4	0	144	71	43	59	2	56	4	6	4	40	18	.69	8	.249	.338	.315
	5 Min. YEARS		491	1748	527	84	29	7	690	359	171	307	6	229	33	22	13	223	100	.69	21	.301	.413	.395

Jacob Viano

Pitches: Right Bats: Right Pos: P Ht: 5'10" Wt: 170 Born: 09/04/73 Age: 21

Year	Team	Lg	G	GS	CG	GF	IP	BFP	H	R	ER	HR	SH	SF	HB	TBB	IBB	SO	WP	Bk	W	L	Pct.	ShO	Sv	ERA
			HOW MUCH HE PITCHED						WHAT HE GAVE UP												THE RESULTS					
1993	Rockies	R	22	1	0	8	33	136	24	15	12	1	0	1	3	6	0	32	6	0	2	2	.500	0	1	3.27
1994	Asheville	A	41	0	0	35	53.1	219	36	11	8	3	4	0	2	24	4	58	9	0	4	1	.800	0	23	1.35
	New Haven	AA	8	0	0	5	11.1	51	7	7	3	0	0	1	0	8	0	14	1	0	0	3	.000	0	0	2.38
	2 Min. YEARS		71	1	0	48	97.2	406	67	33	23	4	4	2	5	38	4	104	16	0	6	6	.500	0	24	2.12

Joey Vierra

Pitches: Left Bats: Left Pos: P Ht: 5'7" Wt: 170 Born: 01/31/66 Age: 29

Year	Team	Lg	G	GS	CG	GF	IP	BFP	H	R	ER	HR	SH	SF	HB	TBB	IBB	SO	WP	Bk	W	L	Pct.	ShO	Sv	ERA
			HOW MUCH HE PITCHED						WHAT HE GAVE UP												THE RESULTS					
1987	Reds	R	14	0	0	0	21	78	11	4	2	0	1	1	0	5	0	29	0	0	1	2	.333	0	8	0.86
	Tampa	A	9	0	0	6	8	40	14	11	9	3	1	0	1	3	0	7	0	0	1	1	.500	0	1	10.13
1988	Greensboro	A	34	0	0	24	41.1	162	30	13	11	0	3	0	1	8	2	42	6	3	2	1	.667	0	7	2.40
1989	Cedar Rapds	A	47	0	0	28	74.1	293	43	22	14	4	1	1	4	20	3	81	3	1	5	3	.625	0	7	1.70
1990	Nashville	AAA	49	0	0	17	57.2	246	55	25	21	6	7	4	0	25	2	37	1	0	3	3	.500	0	1	3.28
1991	Nashville	AAA	62	2	0	15	95.2	412	81	60	46	8	4	1	6	43	2	84	5	2	5	4	.556	0	2	4.33
1992	Chattanooga	AA	1	1	0	0	6	23	5	0	0	0	1	0	0	0	0	3	0	0	1	0	1.000	0	0	0.00
	Nashville	AAA	52	3	0	19	81.2	336	65	29	27	6	2	2	2	28	2	62	6	1	4	1	.800	0	0	2.98
1993	San Antonio	AA	9	0	0	4	11.2	53	14	7	7	1	3	0	1	4	1	6	1	0	1	0	1.000	0	1	5.40
	Albuquerque	AAA	29	0	0	15	33	155	38	22	18	3	4	0	2	18	6	24	4	1	0	4	.000	0	1	4.91
1994	Birmingham	AA	27	6	1	7	66.2	271	60	23	22	1	5	2	3	19	1	63	4	2	4	2	.667	1	1	2.97
	Nashville	AAA	19	0	0	10	21.1	96	25	11	9	2	0	2	1	11	1	18	2	0	0	0	.000	0	3	3.80
	8 Min. YEARS		352	12	1	156	518.1	2165	441	227	186	34	32	13	21	184	20	456	32	10	27	21	.563	1	32	3.23

Hector Villanueva

Bats: Right Throws: Right Pos: C Ht: 6'1" Wt: 220 Born: 10/02/64 Age: 30

Year	Team	Lg	G	AB	H	2B	3B	HR	TB	R	RBI	TBB	IBB	SO	HBP	SH	SF	SB	CS	SB%	GDP	Avg	OBP	SLG
			BATTING															BASERUNNING				PERCENTAGES		
1985	Peoria	A	65	193	45	7	0	1	55	22	19	27	0	36	3	2	1	0	2	.00	7	.233	.335	.285
1986	Winston-Sal	A	125	412	131	20	2	13	194	58	100	81	3	42	2	2	12	6	4	.60	12	.318	.422	.471
1987	Pittsfield	AA	109	391	107	31	0	14	180	59	70	43	1	38	1	2	3	3	4	.43	8	.274	.345	.460
1988	Pittsfield	AA	127	436	137	24	3	10	197	50	75	71	6	58	4	2	8	5	4	.56	9	.314	.408	.452
1989	Iowa	AAA	120	444	112	25	1	12	175	46	57	32	2	95	1	1	2	1	1	.50	6	.252	.303	.394
1990	Iowa	AAA	52	177	47	7	1	8	80	20	34	19	2	36	1	1	0	0	1	.00	4	.266	.340	.452
1991	Iowa	AAA	6	25	9	3	0	2	18	2	9	1	1	6	0	0	1	0	0	.00	0	.360	.370	.720
1992	Iowa	AAA	49	159	38	8	0	9	73	21	35	20	0	36	0	1	2	0	1	.00	4	.239	.320	.459
1993	Louisville	AAA	40	124	30	9	0	5	54	13	20	16	1	18	1	0	0	0	0	.00	5	.242	.331	.435
1994	Ottawa	AAA	26	93	20	5	0	4	37	12	11	12	0	18	1	0	0	0	0	.00	2	.215	.308	.398
1990	Chicago	NL	52	114	31	4	1	7	58	14	18	4	2	27	2	0	0	1	0	1.00	3	.272	.308	.509
1991	Chicago	NL	71	192	53	10	1	13	104	23	32	21	1	30	0	0	1	0	0	.00	3	.276	.346	.542
1992	Chicago	NL	51	112	17	6	0	2	29	9	13	11	2	24	0	0	0	0	0	.00	3	.152	.228	.259
1993	St. Louis	NL	17	55	8	1	0	3	18	7	9	4	1	17	0	0	0	0	0	.00	3	.145	.203	.327
	10 Min. YEARS		719	2454	676	139	7	78	1063	303	430	322	16	383	14	11	31	15	17	.47	59	.275	.359	.433
	4 Maj. YEARS		191	473	109	21	2	25	209	53	72	40	6	98	2	0	1	1	0	1.00	14	.230	.293	.442

Ron Villone

Pitches: Left Bats: Left Pos: P Ht: 6'3" Wt: 230 Born: 01/16/70 Age: 25

Year	Team	Lg	G	GS	CG	GF	IP	BFP	H	R	ER	HR	SH	SF	HB	TBB	IBB	SO	WP	Bk	W	L	Pct.	ShO	Sv	ERA
			HOW MUCH HE PITCHED						WHAT HE GAVE UP												THE RESULTS					
1993	Riverside	A	16	16	0	0	83.1	375	74	47	39	5	1	1	4	62	0	82	7	3	7	4	.636	0	0	4.21
	Jacksnville	AA	11	11	0	0	63.2	269	49	34	30	6	1	2	1	41	3	66	9	0	3	4	.429	0	0	4.24
1994	Jacksonville	AA	41	5	0	19	79.1	360	56	37	34	7	1	4	5	68	3	94	9	0	6	7	.462	0	8	3.86
	2 Min. YEARS		68	32	0	19	226.1	1004	179	118	103	18	3	7	10	171	6	242	25	3	16	15	.516	0	8	4.10

George Virgilio

Bats: Both Throws: Right Pos: 2B Ht: 5'9" Wt: 170 Born: 02/15/71 Age: 24

Year	Team	Lg	G	AB	H	2B	3B	HR	TB	R	RBI	TBB	IBB	SO	HBP	SH	SF	SB	CS	SB%	GDP	Avg	OBP	SLG
			BATTING															BASERUNNING				PERCENTAGES		
1990	Pulaski	R	58	220	57	9	2	3	79	35	21	27	2	19	1	3	0	7	4	.64	9	.259	.343	.359
1991	Pulaski	R	15	54	19	5	0	0	24	8	7	3	0	6	2	1	1	3	0	1.00	0	.352	.400	.444
	Macon	A	46	148	28	4	2	1	39	17	17	13	0	19	1	0	1	4	2	.67	2	.189	.258	.264
1992	Macon	A	112	370	84	17	5	1	114	30	34	44	2	59	1	3	2	18	17	.51	12	.227	.309	.308
1994	Harrisburg	AA	89	243	63	16	1	1	96	29	41	26	0	36	2	1	2	1	1	.50	5	.259	.333	.395
	4 Min. YEARS		320	1035	251	51	10	10	352	119	120	113	4	139	7	8	6	33	24	.58	28	.243	.320	.340

262

Joe Vitiello

Bats: Right **Throws:** Right **Pos:** OF **Ht:** 6'2" **Wt:** 215 **Born:** 04/11/70 **Age:** 25

					BATTING												BASERUNNING				PERCENTAGES		
Year	Team	Lg	G	AB	H	2B	3B	HR	TB	R	RBI	TBB	IBB	SO	HBP	SH	SF	SB	CS	SB%	GDP	Avg	OBP	SLG
1991	Eugene	A	19	64	21	2	0	6	41	16	21	11	1	18	1	0	2	1	1	.50	0	.328	.423	.641
	Memphis	AA	36	128	27	4	1	0	33	15	18	23	0	36	1	0	1	0	0	.00	2	.211	.333	.258
1992	Baseball Cy	A	115	400	113	16	1	8	155	52	65	46	1	101	7	0	8	0	5	.00	11	.283	.360	.388
1993	Memphis	AA	117	413	119	25	2	15	193	62	66	57	2	95	5	0	5	2	0	1.00	8	.288	.377	.467
1994	Omaha	AAA	98	352	121	28	3	10	185	46	61	56	1	63	7	1	3	3	2	.60	15	.344	.440	.526
	4 Min. YEARS		385	1357	401	75	7	39	607	191	231	193	5	313	21	1	19	6	8	.43	36	.296	.387	.447

Joe Vitko

Pitches: Right **Bats:** Right **Pos:** P **Ht:** 6'8" **Wt:** 210 **Born:** 02/01/70 **Age:** 25

			HOW MUCH HE PITCHED					WHAT HE GAVE UP									THE RESULTS					
Year	Team	Lg	G	GS	CG	GF	IP	BFP	H	R	ER	HR	SH	SF	HB	TBB	IBB	SO	WP	Bk	W	L	Pct.	ShO	Sv	ERA
1989	Mets	R	8	5	1	2	41	170	28	20	15	0	0	2	1	16	0	33	4	3	4	1	.800	0	0	3.29
	Pittsfield	A	5	5	1	0	29.2	119	24	6	3	1	0	0	2	8	0	29	1	0	2	1	.667	1	0	0.91
1990	Columbia	A	16	12	4	2	90.1	367	70	29	25	3	3	2	1	30	0	72	12	1	8	1	.889	2	1	2.49
1991	St. Lucie	A	22	22	5	0	140.1	549	102	40	35	6	2	1	4	39	1	105	6	1	11	8	.579	2	0	2.24
1992	Binghamton	AA	26	26	4	0	165	696	163	76	64	11	2	1	12	53	0	89	7	0	12	8	.600	3	0	3.49
1993	Mets	R	1	1	0	0	3	11	1	0	0	0	0	0	0	1	0	2	1	0	0	0	.000	0	0	0.00
	St.Lucie	A	2	2	0	0	7	25	4	1	1	0	0	0	0	1	0	5	0	0	0	0	.000	0	0	1.29
1994	Binghamton	AA	11	10	0	1	58	259	65	41	41	8	2	1	4	31	1	36	5	1	2	5	.286	0	0	6.36
1992	New York	NL	3	0	0	1	4.2	29	12	11	7	1	0	1	0	6	1	6	1	0	0	1	.000	0	0	13.50
	6 Min. YEARS		91	83	15	5	534.1	2196	457	213	184	29	9	7	24	179	2	371	36	6	39	24	.619	8	1	3.10

Mark Voisard

Pitches: Right **Bats:** Right **Pos:** P **Ht:** 6'5" **Wt:** 210 **Born:** 11/04/69 **Age:** 25

			HOW MUCH HE PITCHED					WHAT HE GAVE UP									THE RESULTS					
Year	Team	Lg	G	GS	CG	GF	IP	BFP	H	R	ER	HR	SH	SF	HB	TBB	IBB	SO	WP	Bk	W	L	Pct.	ShO	Sv	ERA
1992	Bend	A	26	1	0	5	53	233	51	28	26	5	2	2	3	29	2	65	4	0	5	2	.714	0	2	4.42
1993	Central Val	A	21	14	0	1	82.1	365	72	58	56	6	0	2	1	53	0	61	6	0	3	6	.333	0	0	6.12
1994	Central Val	A	18	4	0	4	46.2	197	29	18	9	2	3	0	3	22	2	38	3	2	3	2	.600	0	2	1.74
	New Haven	AA	30	1	0	27	43.1	174	34	9	8	1	2	2	0	17	5	36	3	1	3	2	.600	0	15	1.66
	3 Min. YEARS		95	20	0	37	225.1	969	186	113	99	14	7	6	7	121	9	200	16	3	14	12	.538	0	19	3.95

Derek Wachter

Bats: Right **Throws:** Right **Pos:** OF **Ht:** 6'2" **Wt:** 195 **Born:** 08/28/70 **Age:** 24

					BATTING												BASERUNNING				PERCENTAGES		
Year	Team	Lg	G	AB	H	2B	3B	HR	TB	R	RBI	TBB	IBB	SO	HBP	SH	SF	SB	CS	SB%	GDP	Avg	OBP	SLG
1991	Brewers	R	51	186	59	16	5	6	103	52	42	40	1	59	1	0	4	3	0	1.00	1	.317	.433	.554
1992	Beloit	A	111	363	98	17	9	10	163	53	61	43	1	113	1	5	3	6	5	.55	9	.270	.346	.449
1993	Stockton	A	115	420	123	20	4	22	217	75	108	64	2	93	6	3	11	3	3	.50	7	.293	.385	.517
1994	El Paso	AA	30	117	45	9	5	0	64	14	24	13	0	24	2	0	3	3	0	1.00	2	.385	.444	.547
	New Orleans	AAA	65	221	63	15	1	5	95	33	39	24	1	57	3	4	3	3	0	1.00	6	.285	.359	.430
	4 Min. YEARS		372	1307	388	77	24	43	642	227	274	184	5	346	13	12	24	18	8	.69	25	.297	.383	.491

Scott Wade

Bats: Right **Throws:** Right **Pos:** OF **Ht:** 6'2" **Wt:** 200 **Born:** 04/26/63 **Age:** 32

					BATTING												BASERUNNING				PERCENTAGES		
Year	Team	Lg	G	AB	H	2B	3B	HR	TB	R	RBI	TBB	IBB	SO	HBP	SH	SF	SB	CS	SB%	GDP	Avg	OBP	SLG
1984	Winter Havn	A	48	157	38	10	0	2	54	24	15	26	0	36	1	0	1	3	2	.60	3	.242	.351	.344
1985	Winter Havn	A	104	320	67	13	3	7	107	42	37	49	5	80	4	1	3	12	8	.60	3	.209	.319	.334
1986	New Britain	AA	123	414	110	23	1	9	162	54	51	54	0	102	8	0	7	31	12	.72	4	.266	.356	.391
1987	Pawtucket	AAA	108	355	90	12	4	16	158	51	60	32	1	123	3	0	6	11	9	.55	3	.254	.316	.445
1988	Pawtucket	AAA	114	396	94	17	2	10	145	42	37	24	2	118	4	3	1	7	2	.78	8	.237	.287	.366
1989	Pawtucket	AAA	104	345	82	20	2	12	142	39	35	34	1	81	0	2	1	6	3	.67	8	.238	.305	.412
1990	Pawtucket	AAA	105	303	70	12	4	11	123	34	41	27	0	97	5	4	1	9	8	.53	6	.231	.304	.406
1991	Scranton-Wb	AAA	112	309	81	14	1	9	136	48	43	33	0	70	3	1	2	4	5	.44	8	.262	.337	.440
1992	Syracuse	AAA	18	45	7	2	0	0	9	3	3	5	0	12	2	0	1	0	0	.00	2	.156	.264	.200
	Iowa	AAA	72	227	54	14	0	14	110	38	38	28	2	57	4	3	7	5	3	.63	4	.238	.323	.485
1993	Iowa	AAA	47	147	25	8	0	3	42	14	15	12	0	42	2	1	2	9	3	.75	2	.170	.239	.286
	Portland	AAA	11	37	12	3	1	0	17	6	4	2	0	10	2	0	0	0	1	.00	2	.324	.390	.459
	Norfolk	AAA	23	79	15	3	1	6	38	10	13	5	0	32	0	0	0	0	0	.00	1	.190	.238	.481
1994	Scranton-Wb	AAA	31	75	14	5	0	3	28	6	9	7	0	29	1	0	0	1	0	1.00	3	.187	.265	.373
	11 Min. YEARS		1020	3209	759	156	25	102	1271	411	401	338	11	889	39	15	32	98	56	.64	57	.237	.314	.396

Terrell Wade

Pitches: Left **Bats:** Left **Pos:** P **Ht:** 6'3" **Wt:** 204 **Born:** 01/25/73 **Age:** 22

			HOW MUCH HE PITCHED					WHAT HE GAVE UP									THE RESULTS					
Year	Team	Lg	G	GS	CG	GF	IP	BFP	H	R	ER	HR	SH	SF	HB	TBB	IBB	SO	WP	Bk	W	L	Pct.	ShO	Sv	ERA
1991	Braves	R	10	2	0	0	23	112	29	17	16	0	0	1	0	15	0	22	3	2	2	0	1.000	0	0	6.26

Year	Team	Lg	G	GS	CG	GF	IP	BFP	H	R	ER	HR	SH	SF	HB	TBB	IBB	SO	WP	Bk	W	L	Pct.	ShO	Sv	ERA
1992	Idaho Falls	R	13	11	0	0	50.1	257	59	46	36	5	4	5	2	42	0	54	5	0	1	4	.200	0	0	6.44
1993	Macon	A	14	14	0	0	83.1	336	57	16	16	1	0	1	1	36	0	121	11	0	8	2	.800	0	0	1.73
	Durham	A	5	5	0	0	33	137	26	13	12	3	0	0	1	18	0	47	0	1	2	1	.667	0	0	3.27
	Greenville	AA	8	8	1	0	42	179	32	16	15	6	1	0	1	29	0	40	2	0	2	1	.667	1	0	3.21
1994	Greenville	AA	21	21	0	0	105.2	444	87	49	45	7	3	2	0	58	0	105	8	0	9	3	.750	0	0	3.83
	Richmond	AAA	4	4	0	0	24	103	23	9	7	1	0	1	0	15	0	26	0	0	2	2	.500	0	0	2.63
	4 Min. YEARS		75	65	1	0	361.1	1568	313	166	147	23	9	11	5	213	0	415	30	3	26	13	.667	1	0	3.66

Aubrey Waggoner

Bats: Left   Throws: Right   Pos: OF   Ht: 5'11"   Wt: 185   Born: 12/06/66   Age: 28

			BATTING															BASERUNNING				PERCENTAGES		
Year	Team	Lg	G	AB	H	2B	3B	HR	TB	R	RBI	TBB	IBB	SO	HBP	SH	SF	SB	CS	SB%	GDP	Avg	OBP	SLG
1985	White Sox	R	49	142	27	6	2	1	40	33	10	49	3	40	1	3	2	12	7	.63	2	.190	.397	.282
1986	Appleton	A	60	188	34	2	0	3	45	25	7	23	1	46	3	3	0	29	4	.88	2	.181	.280	.239
	White Sox	R	34	81	23	3	3	1	35	22	12	27	0	13	2	0	2	18	1	.95	0	.284	.464	.432
	Peninsula	A	20	72	14	0	3	0	20	7	9	14	0	24	1	1	0	4	3	.57	2	.194	.333	.278
1987	Peninsula	A	115	426	113	15	4	12	172	82	51	87	2	88	5	4	2	52	23	.69	8	.265	.394	.404
1988	Birmingham	AA	13	40	8	2	2	0	14	6	1	11	0	11	1	0	1	4	5	.44	1	.200	.377	.350
	Tampa	A	43	126	28	3	6	3	52	19	15	21	0	34	1	0	2	11	2	.85	2	.222	.333	.413
1989	Birmingham	AA	114	302	69	23	6	4	116	66	35	76	1	74	9	2	1	25	12	.68	1	.228	.397	.384
1990	Birmingham	AA	81	276	71	17	4	5	111	57	32	56	1	60	2	2	1	11	9	.55	1	.257	.385	.402
1991	Vancouver	AAA	50	156	32	4	4	1	47	23	10	19	0	39	2	1	1	5	3	.63	0	.205	.298	.301
	Birmingham	AA	69	248	57	11	4	3	85	39	21	54	2	56	1	2	0	20	6	.77	1	.230	.370	.343
1992	Greenville	AA	90	237	64	14	3	14	126	51	45	70	1	81	1	0	3	21	12	.64	0	.270	.434	.532
	Richmond	AAA	7	22	5	1	0	1	9	2	6	3	0	6	0	0	0	1	0	1.00	0	.227	.320	.409
1993	Calgary	AAA	13	38	10	2	1	2	20	9	4	15	0	17	0	0	0	3	0	1.00	0	.263	.472	.526
	Jacksnville	AA	34	102	25	8	2	3	46	29	7	40	0	34	0	0	1	7	3	.70	0	.245	.455	.451
1994	Ottawa	AAA	11	17	4	0	0	1	7	4	5	5	0	5	0	0	0	1	1	.50	0	.235	.409	.412
	Greenville	AA	53	158	44	5	3	4	67	28	14	33	1	57	0	1	3	10	6	.63	3	.278	.397	.424
	10 Min. YEARS		856	2631	628	116	47	58	1012	502	284	603	12	685	29	19	19	234	97	.71	21	.239	.384	.385

Jimmy Waggoner

Bats: Left   Throws: Right   Pos: SS   Ht: 5'11"   Wt: 185   Born: 04/17/67   Age: 28

			BATTING															BASERUNNING				PERCENTAGES		
Year	Team	Lg	G	AB	H	2B	3B	HR	TB	R	RBI	TBB	IBB	SO	HBP	SH	SF	SB	CS	SB%	GDP	Avg	OBP	SLG
1989	Sou Oregon	A	54	200	54	7	0	1	64	35	18	35	0	40	0	1	1	5	6	.45	0	.270	.377	.320
1990	Modesto	A	35	86	14	3	0	0	17	13	5	21	1	25	2	2	0	1	1	.50	1	.163	.339	.198
	Madison	A	39	114	28	3	0	1	34	16	8	26	0	18	0	1	1	4	3	.57	3	.246	.383	.298
1991	Modesto	A	86	241	54	4	2	2	68	34	19	70	0	67	2	4	1	3	1	.75	7	.224	.401	.282
1992	Reno	A	93	317	98	18	0	11	149	75	57	87	2	50	4	1	3	2	5	.29	4	.309	.460	.470
	Huntsville	AA	6	16	1	0	0	0	1	0	0	0	0	2	0	0	0	0	0	.00	1	.063	.063	.063
1993	Huntsville	AA	57	129	18	3	0	1	24	12	8	29	0	38	0	0	1	2	2	.50	5	.140	.296	.186
1994	Huntsville	AA	70	173	36	1	1	1	42	19	9	37	1	44	1	4	1	0	3	.00	4	.208	.349	.243
	6 Min. YEARS		440	1276	303	39	3	17	399	204	124	305	4	284	9	13	8	17	21	.45	24	.237	.386	.313

Don Wakamatsu

Bats: Right   Throws: Right   Pos: C   Ht: 6' 2"   Wt: 210   Born: 02/22/63   Age: 32

			BATTING															BASERUNNING				PERCENTAGES		
Year	Team	Lg	G	AB	H	2B	3B	HR	TB	R	RBI	TBB	IBB	SO	HBP	SH	SF	SB	CS	SB%	GDP	Avg	OBP	SLG
1985	Billings	R	58	196	49	7	0	0	56	20	24	25	2	36	0	5	2	1	0	1.00	7	.250	.332	.286
1986	Tampa	A	112	361	100	18	2	1	125	41	66	53	2	66	5	0	8	6	1	.86	11	.277	.370	.346
1987	Cedar Rapds	A	103	365	79	13	1	7	115	33	41	30	1	71	3	2	3	3	3	.50	9	.216	.279	.315
1988	Chattanooga	AA	79	235	56	9	1	1	70	22	26	37	0	41	0	1	2	0	1	.00	5	.238	.339	.298
1989	Birmingham	AA	92	287	73	15	0	2	94	45	45	32	0	54	7	5	5	7	6	.54	4	.254	.338	.328
1990	Vancouver	AAA	62	187	49	10	0	0	59	20	13	13	1	35	7	1	1	2	2	.50	2	.262	.332	.316
1991	Vancouver	AAA	55	172	34	8	0	4	54	20	19	12	0	39	1	4	2	0	0	.00	3	.198	.251	.314
1992	Albuquerque	AAA	60	167	54	10	0	2	70	22	15	15	0	23	4	1	0	0	1	.00	5	.323	.392	.419
1993	Albuquerque	AAA	54	181	61	11	1	7	95	30	31	15	2	31	4	0	4	0	1	.00	3	.337	.392	.525
1994	Okla. City	AAA	1	2	0	0	0	0	0	0	0	0	0	1	0	0	0	0	0	.00	0	.000	.000	.000
1991	Chicago	AL	18	31	7	0	0	0	7	2	0	1	0	6	0	0	0	0	0	.00	0	.226	.250	.226
	10 Min. YEARS		676	2153	555	101	5	24	738	253	280	232	8	397	31	19	27	19	15	.56	49	.258	.335	.343

Tim Wakefield

Pitches: Right   Bats: Right   Pos: P   Ht: 6' 2"   Wt: 195   Born: 08/02/66   Age: 28

			HOW MUCH HE PITCHED						WHAT HE GAVE UP												THE RESULTS				
Year	Team	Lg	G	GS	CG	GF	IP	BFP	H	R	ER	HR	SH	SF	HB	TBB	IBB	SO	WP	Bk	W	L	Pct.	ShO	Sv	ERA
1989	Welland	A	18	1	0	11	39.2	168	30	17	15	1	2	1	2	21	0	42	9	0	1	1	.500	0	2	3.40
1990	Salem	A	28	28	2	0	190.1	824	187	109	100	24	7	6	10	85	2	127	11	0	10	14	.417	0	0	4.73
1991	Buffalo	AAA	1	1	0	0	4.2	23	8	6	6	3	0	0	0	1	0	4	0	0	0	1	.000	0	0	11.57
	Carolina	AA	26	25	8	1	183	741	155	68	59	13	6	3	9	51	6	120	2	1	15	8	.652	1	0	2.90
1992	Buffalo	AAA	20	20	6	0	135.1	559	122	52	46	10	3	7	3	51	1	71	9	0	10	3	.769	1	0	3.06

Year	Team	Lg	G	GS	CG	GF	IP	BFP	H	R	ER	HR	SH	SF	HB	TBB	IBB	SO	WP	Bk	W	L	Pct.	ShO	Sv	ERA
1993	Carolina	AA	9	9	1	0	56.2	265	68	48	44	5	2	4	5	22	0	36	3	0	3	5	.375	0	0	6.99
1994	Buffalo	AAA	30	29	4	0	175.2	824	197	127	114	27	13	11	23	98	0	83	16	0	5	15	.250	1	0	5.84
1992	Pittsburgh	NL	13	13	4	0	92	373	76	26	22	3	6	4	1	35	1	51	3	1	8	1	.889	1	0	2.15
1993	Pittsburgh	NL	24	20	3	1	128.1	595	145	83	80	14	7	5	9	75	2	59	6	0	6	11	.353	2	0	5.61
	6 Min. YEARS		132	113	21	12	785.1	3404	767	427	384	83	33	32	52	329	9	483	50	1	44	47	.484	3	2	4.40
	2 Maj. YEARS		37	33	7	1	220.1	968	221	109	102	17	13	9	10	110	3	110	9	1	14	12	.538	3	0	4.17

Joe Waldron

Pitches: Left   Bats: Left   Pos: P   **Ht: 6'0"   Wt: 180   Born: 07/04/69   Age: 25**

			HOW MUCH HE PITCHED						WHAT HE GAVE UP											THE RESULTS					
Year	Team	Lg	G	GS	CG	GF	IP	BFP	H	R	ER	HR	SH	SF	HB	TBB	IBB	SO	WP	Bk	W	L	Pct.	ShO	Sv	ERA
1990	Spokane	A	21	1	0	4	46.2	244	61	45	32	2	3	1	3	40	0	42	5	2	1	4	.200	0	0	6.17
1991	Chston-Sc	A	38	16	0	13	147.1	628	135	72	61	9	5	7	2	59	4	141	4	9	10	6	.625	0	5	3.73
1992	Waterloo	A	49	2	0	15	94.2	416	113	63	52	9	3	2	2	32	3	73	7	2	7	3	.700	0	1	4.94
1993	Waterloo	A	16	1	1	5	32	132	19	11	9	1	2	2	1	19	2	30	3	0	3	3	.500	0	1	2.53
	Rancho Cuca	A	30	0	0	8	35	155	43	28	23	6	0	0	1	11	0	31	0	2	1	2	.333	0	0	5.91
1994	Harrisburg	AA	2	0	0	0	2.1	8	1	0	0	0	0	0	0	0	0	0	0	1	0	0	.000	0	0	0.00
	W. Palm Bch	A	34	0	0	13	51	202	42	10	9	2	2	1	3	15	0	56	2	2	4	3	.571	0	3	1.59
	5 Min. YEARS		190	20	1	58	409	1785	414	229	186	29	15	13	12	176	9	373	21	18	26	21	.553	0	10	4.09

Jim Walewander

Bats: Both   Throws: Right   Pos: 3B   **Ht: 5'10"   Wt: 155   Born: 05/02/61   Age: 34**

			BATTING														BASERUNNING				PERCENTAGES		
Year	Team	Lg	G	AB	H	2B	3B	HR	TB	R	RBI	TBB	IBB	SO	HBP	SH	SF	SB	CS	SB%	GDP	Avg	OBP	SLG
1984	Lakeland	A	137	502	136	16	2	0	156	70	36	64	2	40	6	8	3	47	18	.72	15	.271	.358	.311
1985	Lakeland	A	129	499	141	13	7	0	168	80	36	48	4	28	2	1	6	30	10	.75	7	.283	.344	.337
	Birmingham	AA	14	45	13	0	1	0	15	3	2	2	0	3	0	1	0	0	1	.00	0	.289	.319	.333
1986	Glens Falls	AA	124	440	107	10	6	1	132	59	31	43	4	54	2	4	2	25	11	.69	11	.243	.312	.300
1987	Toledo	AAA	59	210	57	9	1	0	68	27	12	28	1	31	1	1	0	18	11	.62	3	.271	.360	.324
1988	Toledo	AAA	4	11	5	2	0	0	7	4	2	3	0	3	0	1	0	2	1	.67	0	.455	.571	.636
1989	Toledo	AAA	133	484	109	15	3	7	151	53	38	60	3	72	6	6	4	32	10	.76	9	.225	.316	.312
1990	Columbus	AAA	131	368	92	14	5	1	119	80	31	90	1	67	11	6	4	49	13	.79	4	.250	.408	.323
1991	Columbus	AAA	126	408	92	11	3	3	118	81	38	69	1	68	5	7	3	54	19	.74	5	.225	.342	.289
1992	Okla City	AAA	44	124	26	7	0	0	33	20	10	17	0	18	2	3	2	5	2	.71	1	.210	.310	.266
1993	Vancouver	AAA	102	351	107	12	1	1	124	77	43	60	1	57	9	5	3	36	6	.86	8	.305	.416	.353
1994	Edmonton	AAA	52	168	32	5	0	0	37	19	12	16	0	22	1	2	2	10	2	.83	1	.190	.262	.220
	Midland	AA	25	86	27	4	0	0	31	13	9	15	0	15	0	1	2	10	1	.91	0	.314	.408	.360
1987	Detroit	AL	53	54	13	3	1	1	21	24	4	7	0	6	0	2	0	2	1	.67	2	.241	.328	.389
1988	Detroit	AL	88	175	37	5	0	0	42	23	6	12	0	26	0	10	1	11	4	.73	1	.211	.261	.240
1990	New York	AL	9	5	1	1	0	0	2	1	1	0	0	0	0	0	0	1	1	.50	0	.200	.200	.400
1993	California	AL	12	8	1	0	0	0	1	2	3	5	0	1	0	0	0	1	1	.50	0	.125	.429	.125
	11 Min. YEARS		1080	3696	944	118	29	13	1159	586	300	515	17	478	45	46	31	318	105	.75	64	.255	.351	.314
	4 Maj. YEARS		162	242	52	9	1	1	66	50	14	24	0	33	0	12	2	15	7	.68	3	.215	.284	.273

Dane Walker

Bats: Left   Throws: Right   Pos: OF   **Ht: 5'10"   Wt: 180   Born: 11/16/69   Age: 25**

			BATTING														BASERUNNING				PERCENTAGES		
Year	Team	Lg	G	AB	H	2B	3B	HR	TB	R	RBI	TBB	IBB	SO	HBP	SH	SF	SB	CS	SB%	GDP	Avg	OBP	SLG
1991	Athletics	R	29	118	43	3	0	2	52	37	22	24	1	11	2	1	0	12	1	.92	5	.364	.479	.441
	Modesto	A	22	66	18	2	1	0	22	11	5	14	0	9	0	1	1	2	3	.40	2	.273	.395	.333
1992	Madison	A	82	287	85	13	2	3	111	56	23	42	0	57	1	4	2	23	10	.70	6	.296	.386	.387
	Reno	A	31	122	34	6	0	0	40	24	3	23	1	23	1	0	0	8	7	.53	4	.279	.397	.328
1993	Modesto	A	122	443	131	22	1	9	182	94	67	94	0	55	0	7	1	16	16	.50	6	.296	.418	.411
1994	Modesto	A	9	27	11	4	0	1	18	6	16	10	0	5	0	1	1	0	0	.00	2	.407	.553	.667
	Huntsville	AA	47	153	42	10	0	0	52	21	10	24	0	29	1	6	1	6	7	.46	3	.275	.374	.340
	4 Min. YEARS		342	1216	364	60	4	15	477	249	146	231	2	189	5	20	6	67	44	.60	28	.299	.412	.392

Hugh Walker

Bats: Left   Throws: Right   Pos: OF   **Ht: 5'11"   Wt: 210   Born: 02/09/70   Age: 25**

			BATTING														BASERUNNING				PERCENTAGES		
Year	Team	Lg	G	AB	H	2B	3B	HR	TB	R	RBI	TBB	IBB	SO	HBP	SH	SF	SB	CS	SB%	GDP	Avg	OBP	SLG
1988	Royals	R	63	242	58	9	6	0	79	41	24	34	5	50	11	0	1	27	4	.87	0	.240	.358	.326
1989	Appleton	A	103	344	88	13	3	6	125	38	40	35	1	74	11	0	0	13	17	.43	5	.256	.344	.363
1990	Baseball Cy	A	128	463	113	15	6	4	152	51	54	32	5	107	5	0	4	28	17	.62	4	.244	.298	.328
1991	Memphis	AA	117	407	94	16	6	4	134	40	43	29	3	107	12	1	2	11	9	.55	5	.231	.300	.329
1992	Memphis	AA	23	74	15	4	1	1	24	9	5	9	0	31	4	0	0	0	5	.00	1	.203	.322	.324
	Baseball Cy	A	78	278	72	15	7	5	116	38	31	22	0	71	7	0	2	11	8	.58	2	.259	.327	.417
1993	Wilmington	A	126	450	116	20	3	21	205	66	71	34	4	106	11	1	7	14	14	.50	10	.258	.321	.456
1994	Memphis	AA	91	277	72	11	4	7	112	42	38	22	1	58	8	0	1	12	8	.60	6	.260	.331	.404
	7 Min. YEARS		729	2535	628	103	36	48	947	325	306	217	19	604	69	2	17	116	82	.59	33	.248	.322	.374

Mike Walker

Pitches: Right Bats: Right Pos: P Ht: 6' 1" Wt: 195 Born: 10/04/66 Age: 28

			HOW MUCH HE PITCHED						WHAT HE GAVE UP													THE RESULTS					
Year	Team	Lg	G	GS	CG	GF	IP	BFP	H	R	ER	HR	SH	SF	HB	TBB	IBB	SO	WP	Bk	W	L	Pct.	ShO	Sv	ERA
1986	Burlington	R	14	13	1	0	70.1	339	75	65	46	9	2	5	4	45	0	42	1	0	4	6	.400	0	0	5.89
1987	Waterloo	A	23	23	8	0	145.1	637	133	74	58	11	4	3	13	68	1	144	14	0	11	7	.611	1	0	3.59
	Kinston	A	3	3	0	0	20.2	91	17	7	6	0	0	2	0	14	0	19	2	0	3	0	1.000	0	0	2.61
1988	Williamsprt	AA	28	27	3	1	164.1	717	162	82	68	11	5	3	9	74	1	144	17	2	15	7	.682	0	0	3.72
1989	Colo Sprngs	AAA	28	28	4	0	168	772	179	124	108	21	8	7	14	93	0	97	12	0	6	15	.286	0	0	5.79
1990	Colo Sprngs	AAA	18	12	0	2	79	374	96	62	49	6	3	9	7	36	5	50	6	0	2	7	.222	0	0	5.58
	Canton-Akrn	AA	1	1	0	0	7	29	4	0	0	0	0	0	0	4	0	3	0	0	1	0	1.000	0	0	0.00
1991	Canton-Akrn	AA	45	1	0	34	77.1	347	68	36	24	2	5	1	7	45	6	42	13	0	9	4	.692	0	11	2.79
1992	Toledo	AAA	42	1	0	16	78.2	384	102	62	51	5	3	2	8	44	6	44	7	1	2	8	.200	0	4	5.83
1993	Orlando	AA	16	2	0	6	28.1	138	42	26	23	4	3	0	6	9	4	21	5	1	2	3	.400	0	1	7.31
	Iowa	AAA	12	0	0	3	23.1	97	22	8	7	1	0	2	2	9	0	11	3	0	1	1	.500	0	0	2.70
1994	Iowa	AAA	56	0	0	37	87.1	367	80	33	29	2	4	3	4	34	8	56	8	1	6	2	.750	0	8	2.99
1988	Cleveland	AL	3	1	0	0	8.2	42	8	7	7	0	1	0	0	10	0	7	0	0	0	1	.000	0	0	7.27
1990	Cleveland	AL	18	11	0	2	75.2	350	82	49	41	6	4	2	6	42	4	34	3	1	2	6	.250	0	0	4.88
1991	Cleveland	AL	5	0	0	3	4.1	22	6	1	1	0	0	0	1	2	1	2	0	0	0	1	.000	0	0	2.08
	9 Min. YEARS		286	111	16	99	949.2	4292	994	579	469	72	37	37	74	475	31	673	88	5	62	60	.508	1	25	4.44
	3 Maj. YEARS		26	12	0	5	88.2	414	96	57	49	6	5	2	7	54	5	43	3	1	2	8	.200	0	0	4.97

Mike Walker

Pitches: Right Bats: Right Pos: P Ht: 6' 3" Wt: 205 Born: 06/23/65 Age: 30

			HOW MUCH HE PITCHED						WHAT HE GAVE UP													THE RESULTS					
Year	Team	Lg	G	GS	CG	GF	IP	BFP	H	R	ER	HR	SH	SF	HB	TBB	IBB	SO	WP	Bk	W	L	Pct.	ShO	Sv	ERA
1986	Watertown	A	16	16	2	0	103.1	477	116	71	52	8	4	5	7	46	1	81	8	1	4	10	.286	0	0	4.53
1987	Harrisburg	AA	4	4	0	0	15	74	20	17	15	2	0	0	0	9	0	9	4	1	0	2	.000	0	0	9.00
	Salem	A	21	21	4	0	135.2	581	140	67	56	14	6	2	0	57	1	91	8	0	12	5	.706	1	0	3.71
1988	Harrisburg	AA	13	13	2	0	74.1	308	76	40	29	8	3	2	2	15	0	47	4	4	2	7	.222	2	0	3.51
	Salem	A	5	5	1	0	37	160	42	17	13	3	1	0	1	9	0	29	3	0	2	2	.500	0	0	3.16
	Buffalo	AAA	8	8	2	0	55	217	52	18	17	3	3	3	1	8	1	26	1	0	2	3	.400	0	0	2.78
1989	Buffalo	AAA	3	3	0	0	17	74	12	13	10	2	2	0	0	13	0	5	2	0	0	1	.000	0	0	5.29
	Calgary	AAA	18	17	2	0	88	412	119	74	63	15	4	4	2	37	3	46	7	2	6	7	.462	1	0	6.44
1990	Calgary	AAA	25	24	3	0	144.2	637	176	92	86	16	4	6	3	45	0	64	7	0	5	11	.313	0	0	5.35
1992	Jacksonville	AA	11	11	0	0	62	261	63	38	33	6	2	1	3	18	0	40	3	1	3	3	.500	0	0	4.79
	Calgary	AAA	12	6	1	1	41	189	50	26	24	5	3	0	1	19	1	24	2	0	5	1	.833	0	0	5.27
1993	Calgary	AAA	28	27	3	0	169.2	741	197	91	76	11	4	7	5	47	2	131	10	0	13	8	.619	1	0	4.03
1994	Phoenix	AAA	7	7	0	0	36	172	57	32	28	6	1	0	2	14	0	22	2	0	0	4	.000	0	0	7.00
	Okla. City	AAA	13	9	0	1	53	259	70	55	43	9	2	2	1	29	1	33	5	0	5	4	.556	0	0	7.30
1992	Seattle	AL	5	3	0	1	14.2	74	21	14	12	4	1	1	0	9	3	5	1	0	0	3	.000	0	0	7.36
	8 Min. YEARS		184	171	20	2	1031.2	4562	1190	651	545	108	39	32	28	366	10	648	66	9	59	68	.465	5	0	4.75

Peter Walker

Pitches: Right Bats: Right Pos: P Ht: 6'2" Wt: 195 Born: 04/08/69 Age: 26

			HOW MUCH HE PITCHED						WHAT HE GAVE UP													THE RESULTS					
Year	Team	Lg	G	GS	CG	GF	IP	BFP	H	R	ER	HR	SH	SF	HB	TBB	IBB	SO	WP	Bk	W	L	Pct.	ShO	Sv	ERA
1990	Pittsfield	A	16	13	1	1	80	346	74	43	37	2	0	4	3	46	0	73	1	0	5	7	.417	0	0	4.16
1991	St. Lucie	A	26	25	1	0	151.1	641	145	77	54	9	9	5	4	52	2	95	7	3	10	12	.455	0	0	3.21
1992	Binghamton	AA	24	23	4	1	139.2	605	159	77	64	9	3	2	3	46	0	72	5	2	7	12	.368	0	0	4.12
1993	Binghamton	AA	45	10	0	33	99.1	423	89	45	38	6	6	1	5	46	1	89	5	0	4	9	.308	0	19	3.44
1994	St. Lucie	A	3	0	0	2	4	16	3	2	1	1	0	0	0	1	0	5	0	0	0	0	.000	0	0	2.25
	Norfolk	AAA	37	0	0	19	47.2	207	48	22	21	3	3	2	0	24	2	42	3	0	2	4	.333	0	3	3.97
	5 Min. YEARS		151	71	6	56	522	2238	518	266	215	30	21	14	15	215	5	376	21	5	28	44	.389	0	22	3.71

Donnie Wall

Pitches: Right Bats: Right Pos: P Ht: 6'1" Wt: 180 Born: 07/11/67 Age: 27

			HOW MUCH HE PITCHED						WHAT HE GAVE UP													THE RESULTS					
Year	Team	Lg	G	GS	CG	GF	IP	BFP	H	R	ER	HR	SH	SF	HB	TBB	IBB	SO	WP	Bk	W	L	Pct.	ShO	Sv	ERA
1989	Auburn	A	12	8	3	2	65.1	250	45	17	13	2	0	1	3	12	0	69	2	3	7	0	1.000	1	1	1.79
1990	Asheville	A	28	22	1	3	132	586	149	87	76	18	5	6	9	47	1	111	10	0	6	8	.429	0	1	5.18
1991	Burlington	A	16	16	3	0	106.2	421	73	30	24	4	4	2	4	21	1	102	5	0	7	5	.583	1	0	2.03
	Osceola	A	12	12	4	0	77.1	295	55	22	18	3	3	2	2	11	1	62	1	0	6	3	.667	2	0	2.09
1992	Osceola	A	7	7	0	0	41	166	37	13	12	1	1	1	2	8	0	30	2	0	3	1	.750	0	0	2.63
	Jackson	AA	18	18	2	0	114.1	479	114	51	45	6	2	4	2	26	2	99	4	1	9	6	.600	0	0	3.54
	Tucson	AAA	2	2	0	0	8	35	11	1	1	0	0	0	0	1	0	2	0	0	0	0	.000	0	0	1.13
1993	Tucson	AAA	25	22	0	2	131.2	567	147	73	56	11	7	4	2	35	3	89	4	3	6	4	.600	0	0	3.83
1994	Tucson	AAA	26	24	2	0	148.1	634	171	80	73	9	4	9	3	35	2	84	4	0	11	8	.579	2	0	4.43
	6 Min. YEARS		146	131	15	7	824.2	3433	802	381	318	54	26	29	27	196	10	648	32	7	55	35	.611	6	2	3.47

B.J. Wallace

Pitches: Left Bats: Right Pos: P   Ht: 6'4" Wt: 195 Born: 05/18/71 Age: 24

Year Team	Lg	G	GS	CG	GF	IP	BFP	H	R	ER	HR	SH	SF	HB	TBB	IBB	SO	WP	Bk	W	L	Pct.	ShO	Sv	ERA
1993 Wst Plm Bch	A	25	24	0	0	137.1	579	112	61	50	2	7	5	11	65	0	126	5	6	11	8	.579	0	0	3.28
1994 Harrisburg	AA	8	8	1	0	43	190	34	27	23	5	3	0	1	27	0	30	3	0	1	3	.250	1	0	4.81
2 Min. YEARS		33	32	1	0	180.1	769	146	88	73	7	10	5	12	92	0	156	8	6	12	11	.522	1	0	3.64

Derek Wallace

Pitches: Right Bats: Right Pos: P   Ht: 6'3" Wt: 200 Born: 09/01/71 Age: 23

Year Team	Lg	G	GS	CG	GF	IP	BFP	H	R	ER	HR	SH	SF	HB	TBB	IBB	SO	WP	Bk	W	L	Pct.	ShO	Sv	ERA
1992 Peoria	A	2	0	0	1	3.2	13	3	2	2	0	1	0	0	1	0	2	0	2	0	1	.000	0	0	4.91
1993 Daytona	A	14	12	0	1	79.1	342	85	50	37	6	6	2	2	23	2	34	5	11	5	6	.455	0	1	4.20
Iowa	AAA	1	1	0	0	4	20	8	5	5	0	0	1	0	1	0	2	0	0	0	0	.000	0	0	11.25
Orlando	AA	15	15	2	0	96.2	418	105	59	54	12	5	0	10	28	3	69	9	4	5	7	.417	0	0	5.03
1994 Orlando	AA	33	12	1	19	89.1	391	95	61	57	11	3	4	10	31	3	49	6	4	2	9	.182	0	8	5.74
Iowa	AAA	5	0	0	2	4.1	21	4	4	2	0	0	0	0	4	0	3	1	0	0	1	.000	0	0	4.15
3 Min. YEARS		70	40	3	23	277.1	1205	300	181	157	29	15	7	22	88	8	159	21	21	12	24	.333	0	10	5.09

Anthony Ward

Pitches: Left Bats: Left Pos: P   Ht: 6'1" Wt: 190 Born: 06/09/67 Age: 28

Year Team	Lg	G	GS	CG	GF	IP	BFP	H	R	ER	HR	SH	SF	HB	TBB	IBB	SO	WP	Bk	W	L	Pct.	ShO	Sv	ERA
1988 St.Cathrnes	A	18	12	0	4	72.1	331	75	50	36	6	5	3	5	41	1	64	7	9	2	8	.200	0	0	4.48
1989 Myrtle Bch	A	16	13	1	1	69	310	73	49	40	6	1	3	2	36	0	46	3	2	5	5	.286	0	1	5.22
1990 Dunedin	A	27	26	1	0	181.1	718	150	63	57	8	8	0	8	39	0	137	8	3	14	6	.700	0	0	2.83
1991 Knoxville	AA	31	18	1	2	128	549	122	64	53	7	4	4	10	53	2	110	7	3	6	10	.375	0	0	3.73
1992 Knoxville	AA	6	2	0	0	19.2	82	18	7	6	0	1	1	2	6	0	21	1	0	1	0	1.000	0	0	2.75
Syracuse	AAA	20	11	1	3	73.1	353	100	69	56	14	3	5	5	34	0	46	2	1	2	9	.182	0	0	6.87
1993 Knoxville	AA	11	0	0	6	21	89	17	5	4	1	2	0	0	10	0	23	0	1	1	1	.500	0	3	1.71
Syracuse	AAA	35	1	0	12	41.1	190	37	22	17	7	5	3	4	25	3	45	1	0	1	2	.333	0	1	3.70
1994 Syracuse	AAA	64	3	0	14	57	264	63	37	35	3	1	3	3	35	1	41	7	0	1	3	.250	0	1	5.53
7 Min. YEARS		228	86	4	42	663	2886	655	366	304	52	30	22	39	279	7	533	36	19	30	44	.405	0	6	4.13

Ricky Ward

Bats: Right Throws: Right Pos: 3B   Ht: 5'11" Wt: 170 Born: 08/30/70 Age: 24

Year Team	Lg	G	AB	H	2B	3B	HR	TB	R	RBI	TBB	IBB	SO	HBP	SH	SF	SB	CS	SB%	GDP	Avg	OBP	SLG
1990 Everett	A	39	149	39	11	1	1	55	22	22	17	0	28	3	1	1	7	6	.54	4	.262	.347	.369
1991 Clinton	A	126	442	123	22	1	11	180	64	64	58	3	68	7	2	7	13	13	.50	9	.278	.366	.407
1992 San Jose	A	88	335	100	28	1	3	139	49	53	21	2	34	3	4	9	6	8	.43	7	.299	.337	.415
Shreveport	AA	1	3	0	0	0	0	0	0	0	0	0	1	0	0	0	0	0	.00	0	.000	.000	.000
1993 San Jose	A	41	143	26	4	0	0	30	17	12	13	0	14	2	3	3	2	2	.50	6	.182	.255	.210
Shreveport	AA	33	90	23	8	0	0	31	8	5	7	0	8	1	1	0	0	1	.00	3	.256	.316	.344
1994 Nashville	AA	49	150	28	7	0	6	53	23	20	14	0	24	1	2	1	0	1	.00	7	.187	.259	.353
5 Min. YEARS		377	1312	339	80	3	21	488	186	176	130	5	177	17	13	21	28	31	.47	36	.258	.328	.372

Jeff Ware

Pitches: Right Bats: Right Pos: P   Ht: 6'3" Wt: 190 Born: 11/11/70 Age: 24

Year Team	Lg	G	GS	CG	GF	IP	BFP	H	R	ER	HR	SH	SF	HB	TBB	IBB	SO	WP	Bk	W	L	Pct.	ShO	Sv	ERA
1992 Dunedin	A	12	12	1	0	75.1	319	64	26	22	1	3	0	3	30	0	49	7	3	5	3	.625	1	0	2.63
1994 Knoxville	AA	10	10	0	0	38	175	50	32	29	5	0	2	2	16	0	31	1	0	0	7	.000	0	0	6.87
2 Min. YEARS		22	22	1	0	113.1	494	114	58	51	6	3	2	5	46	0	80	8	3	5	10	.333	1	0	4.05

Jim Waring

Pitches: Right Bats: Left Pos: P   Ht: 6'2" Wt: 180 Born: 09/19/69 Age: 25

Year Team	Lg	G	GS	CG	GF	IP	BFP	H	R	ER	HR	SH	SF	HB	TBB	IBB	SO	WP	Bk	W	L	Pct.	ShO	Sv	ERA
1991 Auburn	A	21	7	0	12	61	265	70	39	26	5	4	2	2	10	1	56	2	0	0	4	.000	0	3	3.84
1992 Burlington	A	20	20	2	0	122	476	100	42	30	9	2	0	4	19	0	104	5	3	11	7	.611	0	0	2.21
Asheville	A	3	3	1	0	20	74	11	2	1	0	0	0	1	4	0	20	1	0	1	1	.500	0	0	0.45
1993 Osceola	A	4	0	0	0	17.1	72	16	5	5	0	0	0	0	6	0	16	1	0	1	1	.500	0	0	2.60
1994 Osceola	A	11	10	1	0	76.2	318	77	31	18	5	5	3	1	12	1	36	1	0	4	2	.667	1	0	2.11
Jackson	AA	17	17	1	0	102.1	426	101	46	40	12	3	1	4	19	0	60	2	0	7	8	.467	1	0	3.52
4 Min. YEARS		76	57	5	12	399.1	1631	375	165	120	31	14	6	12	70	2	292	12	3	24	23	.511	2	3	2.70

Mike Warner

Bats: Left Throws: Left Pos: OF   Ht: 5'10" Wt: 170 Born: 05/09/71 Age: 24

Year Team	Lg	G	AB	H	2B	3B	HR	TB	R	RBI	TBB	IBB	SO	HBP	SH	SF	SB	CS	SB%	GDP	Avg	OBP	SLG
1992 Idaho Falls	R	10	33	9	3	0	1	15	4	6	3	0	5	0	0	0	1	0	1.00	0	.273	.333	.455

Year	Team	Lg	G	AB	H	2B	3B	HR	TB	R	RBI	TBB	IBB	SO	HBP	SH	SF	SB	CS	SB%	GDP	Avg	OBP	SLG
	Macon	A	50	180	50	7	2	1	64	40	8	34	0	28	0	3	0	21	4	.84	2	.278	.393	.356
1993	Durham	A	77	263	84	18	4	5	125	55	32	50	3	45	2	3	3	29	12	.71	4	.319	.428	.475
	Greenville	AA	5	20	7	0	2	0	11	4	3	2	0	4	0	0	0	2	1	.67	0	.350	.409	.550
1994	Durham	A	88	321	103	23	8	13	181	80	44	51	1	50	2	1	1	24	10	.71	3	.321	.416	.564
	Greenville	AA	16	55	18	5	0	1	26	13	3	9	0	5	1	0	0	3	0	1.00	0	.327	.431	.473
	3 Min. YEARS		246	872	271	56	16	21	422	196	96	149	4	137	5	7	4	80	27	.75	9	.311	.413	.484

Ron Warner

Bats: Right Throws: Right Pos: SS　　　**Ht: 6'3" Wt: 185 Born: 12/02/68 Age: 26**

Year	Team	Lg	G	AB	H	2B	3B	HR	TB	R	RBI	TBB	IBB	SO	HBP	SH	SF	SB	CS	SB%	GDP	Avg	OBP	SLG
1991	Hamilton	A	71	219	66	11	3	1	86	31	20	28	0	43	3	4	1	9	2	.82	4	.301	.386	.393
1992	Savannah	A	85	242	53	8	1	0	63	30	12	29	2	63	1	5	2	2	3	.40	5	.219	.303	.260
1993	St.Pete	A	103	311	90	8	3	4	116	42	37	31	2	39	5	7	4	5	1	.83	9	.289	.359	.373
1994	Arkansas	AA	95	233	56	14	1	4	84	28	25	39	5	57	1	2	0	1	1	.50	4	.240	.352	.361
	4 Min. YEARS		354	1005	265	41	8	9	349	131	94	127	9	202	10	18	7	17	7	.71	22	.264	.350	.347

Brian Warren

Pitches: Right Bats: Right Pos: P　　　**Ht: 6'1" Wt: 165 Born: 04/26/67 Age: 28**

Year	Team	Lg	G	GS	CG	GF	IP	BFP	H	R	ER	HR	SH	SF	HB	TBB	IBB	SO	WP	Bk	W	L	Pct.	ShO	Sv	ERA
1990	Bristol	R	1	1	0	0	4	17	4	1	1	0	0	0	0	2	0	0	0	1	0	0	.000	0	0	2.25
	Niagara Fls	A	12	10	1	2	62.1	258	53	26	15	3	0	2	4	15	0	62	2	0	2	6	.250	0	0	2.17
1991	Fayetteville	A	10	1	0	0	25.2	99	18	6	6	0	0	0	2	5	0	28	3	2	3	1	.750	0	0	2.10
	Lakeland	A	17	16	4	0	103.1	406	86	34	29	3	6	1	1	15	1	75	6	3	8	2	.800	2	0	2.53
1992	London	AA	25	25	3	0	147.1	606	146	66	54	10	1	0	5	32	1	83	7	0	7	9	.438	2	0	3.30
1993	London	AA	22	1	0	13	29.1	125	36	19	19	6	0	1	0	9	0	21	1	0	3	3	.500	0	5	5.83
	Toledo	AAA	24	1	0	11	36.2	160	40	17	14	3	0	1	2	11	2	26	3	0	2	2	.500	0	0	3.44
1994	Indianapols	AAA	55	0	0	14	80.1	329	82	33	28	4	4	4	3	16	4	56	3	0	5	2	.714	0	1	3.14
	5 Min. YEARS		166	55	8	40	489	2000	465	202	166	29	11	9	17	105	8	351	25	6	30	25	.545	4	6	3.06

John Wasdin

Pitches: Right Bats: Right Pos: P　　　**Ht: 6'2" Wt: 195 Born: 08/05/72 Age: 22**

Year	Team	Lg	G	GS	CG	GF	IP	BFP	H	R	ER	HR	SH	SF	HB	TBB	IBB	SO	WP	Bk	W	L	Pct.	ShO	Sv	ERA
1993	Athletics	R	1	1	0	0	3	13	3	1	1	0	0	0	1	0	0	1	0	0	0	0	.000	0	0	3.00
	Madison	A	9	9	0	0	48.1	185	32	11	10	1	3	0	1	9	1	40	2	3	2	3	.400	0	0	1.86
	Modesto	A	3	3	0	0	16.1	68	17	9	7	0	0	0	0	4	0	11	0	0	0	3	.000	0	0	3.86
1994	Modesto	A	6	4	0	2	26.2	102	17	6	5	2	0	0	2	5	0	30	0	0	3	1	.750	0	0	1.69
	Huntsville	AA	21	21	0	0	141.2	571	126	61	54	13	3	4	2	29	2	108	7	0	12	3	.800	0	0	3.43
	2 Min. YEARS		40	38	0	2	236	939	195	88	77	16	6	4	6	47	3	190	9	3	17	10	.630	0	0	2.94

Scott Watkins

Pitches: Left Bats: Left Pos: P　　　**Ht: 6'3" Wt: 180 Born: 05/15/70 Age: 25**

Year	Team	Lg	G	GS	CG	GF	IP	BFP	H	R	ER	HR	SH	SF	HB	TBB	IBB	SO	WP	Bk	W	L	Pct.	ShO	Sv	ERA
1992	Kenosha	A	27	0	0	11	46.1	196	43	21	19	4	2	1	3	14	0	58	1	0	2	5	.286	0	1	3.69
1993	Ft.Wayne	A	15	0	0	8	30.1	124	26	13	11	0	1	2	1	9	0	31	0	1	2	0	1.000	0	1	3.26
	Ft.Myers	A	20	0	0	10	27.2	125	27	14	9	0	2	0	0	12	0	41	2	1	2	2	.500	0	3	2.93
	Nashville	AA	13	0	0	3	16.2	75	19	15	11	2	0	1	1	7	0	17	2	1	0	1	.000	0	0	5.94
1994	Nashville	AA	11	0	0	8	13.2	60	13	9	7	1	1	2	0	4	0	11	1	0	1	0	1.000	0	3	4.61
	Salt Lake	AAA	46	0	0	26	57.1	269	73	46	43	10	4	5	1	28	5	47	1	1	2	6	.250	0	3	6.75
	3 Min. YEARS		132	0	0	66	192	849	201	118	100	17	10	11	6	74	5	205	7	4	9	14	.391	0	11	4.69

Ron Watson

Pitches: Right Bats: Left Pos: P　　　**Ht: 6'5" Wt: 240 Born: 09/12/68 Age: 26**

Year	Team	Lg	G	GS	CG	GF	IP	BFP	H	R	ER	HR	SH	SF	HB	TBB	IBB	SO	WP	Bk	W	L	Pct.	ShO	Sv	ERA
1990	Angels	R	20	0	0	8	33	141	26	14	12	0	0	0	1	14	0	21	2	2	2	3	.400	0	0	3.27
1991	Boise	A	18	3	0	7	26	131	35	28	18	1	0	0	3	15	0	27	3	0	0	1	.000	0	0	6.23
1992	Quad City	A	40	0	0	25	70	298	43	20	10	2	6	4	4	42	3	69	11	1	8	5	.615	0	10	1.29
1993	Midland	AA	36	0	0	18	46.1	217	39	22	20	2	3	0	6	43	2	41	8	0	2	1	.667	0	3	3.88
1994	Midland	AA	52	0	0	44	57.1	259	54	29	24	2	3	1	3	37	1	53	6	0	0	6	.000	0	17	3.77
	5 Min. YEARS		166	3	0	102	232.2	1046	197	113	84	7	12	5	17	151	6	211	30	3	12	16	.429	0	30	3.25

Jim Wawruck

Bats: Left Throws: Left Pos: OF　　　**Ht: 5'11" Wt: 185 Born: 04/23/70 Age: 25**

Year	Team	Lg	G	AB	H	2B	3B	HR	TB	R	RBI	TBB	IBB	SO	HBP	SH	SF	SB	CS	SB%	GDP	Avg	OBP	SLG
1991	Orioles	R	14	45	17	1	1	0	20	6	6	6	0	4	0	0	0	2	2	.50	0	.378	.451	.444
	Frederick	A	22	83	23	3	0	0	26	15	7	7	0	14	1	1	0	10	0	1.00	2	.277	.341	.313
1992	Frederick	A	102	350	108	18	4	8	158	61	46	47	2	69	2	1	5	11	8	.58	9	.309	.389	.451
1993	Bowie	AA	128	475	141	21	5	4	184	59	44	43	3	66	1	5	2	28	11	.72	7	.297	.355	.387

268

Year	Team	Lg	G	AB	H	2B	3B	HR	TB	R	RBI	TBB	IBB	SO	HBP	SH	SF	SB	CS	SB%	GDP	Avg	OBP	SLG
1994	Rochester	AAA	114	440	132	20	7	9	193	63	53	32	1	77	4	1	2	17	2	.89	6	.300	.351	.439
	4 Min. YEARS		380	1393	421	63	17	21	581	204	156	135	6	230	8	8	9	68	23	.75	24	.302	.365	.417

Melvin Wearing

Bats: Right **Throws:** Right **Pos:** 1B   **Ht:** 6'3" **Wt:** 230 **Born:** 04/19/67 **Age:** 28

						BATTING												BASERUNNING				PERCENTAGES		
Year	Team	Lg	G	AB	H	2B	3B	HR	TB	R	RBI	TBB	IBB	SO	HBP	SH	SF	SB	CS	SB%	GDP	Avg	OBP	SLG
1989	Erie	A	60	171	43	6	1	10	81	26	22	45	3	51	1	1	2	0	1	.00	4	.251	.406	.474
1990	Wausau	A	106	339	86	9	2	18	149	45	56	72	2	101	4	0	2	0	7	.46	11	.254	.388	.440
	Frederick	A	22	79	26	5	2	2	41	13	14	9	0	19	0	0	2	0	1	.00	2	.329	.389	.519
1991	Frederick	A	94	335	88	14	3	11	141	46	53	54	4	74	7	1	4	1	2	.33	9	.263	.373	.421
	Hagerstown	AA	35	107	32	6	0	3	47	18	24	17	0	28	4	0	0	1	0	1.00	2	.299	.414	.439
1992	Hagerstown	AA	83	275	71	15	2	5	105	27	46	38	2	72	2	0	3	8	2	.80	12	.258	.349	.382
	Rochester	AAA	58	187	61	16	2	4	93	33	45	33	1	45	3	0	5	2	1	.67	9	.326	.425	.497
1993	Rochester	AAA	112	379	89	14	2	14	149	52	61	55	3	109	5	0	6	5	1	.83	11	.235	.335	.393
1994	Rochester	AAA	28	90	21	6	0	6	45	15	11	17	0	35	2	0	2	0	1	.00	1	.233	.360	.500
	Thunder Bay	IND	47	169	47	11	0	5	73	24	21	23	1	43	1	0	3	2	0	1.00	3	.278	.362	.432
	6 Min. YEARS		645	2131	564	102	12	78	924	299	353	363	16	577	29	2	29	25	16	.61	64	.265	.375	.434

Ben Weber

Pitches: Right **Bats:** Right **Pos:** P   **Ht:** 6'4" **Wt:** 180 **Born:** 11/17/69 **Age:** 25

				HOW	MUCH	HE	PITCHED				WHAT	HE	GAVE	UP						THE	RESULTS			
Year	Team	Lg	G	GS	CG	GF	IP	BFP	H	R	ER	HR	SH	SF	HB	TBB	IBB	SO	WP	Bk	W	L	Pct.	ShO	Sv	ERA
1991	St.Cathmes	A	16	14	1	2	97.1	417	105	43	35	3	4	2	4	24	2	60	7	2	6	3	.667	0	0	3.24
1992	Myrtle Bch	A	41	1	0	23	98.2	406	83	27	18	1	2	3	7	29	3	65	7	0	4	7	.364	0	6	1.64
1993	Dunedin	A	55	0	0	36	83.1	355	87	36	27	4	9	0	7	25	5	45	7	1	8	3	.727	0	12	2.92
1994	Dunedin	A	18	0	0	14	26.1	110	25	8	8	1	6	0	1	5	3	19	1	0	3	2	.600	0	3	2.73
	Knoxville	AA	25	10	0	6	95.2	400	103	49	40	8	3	1	2	16	0	55	4	0	4	3	.571	0	0	3.76
	4 Min. YEARS		155	25	1	81	401.1	1688	403	163	128	17	24	6	21	99	13	244	26	3	25	18	.581	0	21	2.87

Weston Weber

Pitches: Right **Bats:** Right **Pos:** P   **Ht:** 6'0" **Wt:** 175 **Born:** 01/05/64 **Age:** 31

				HOW	MUCH	HE	PITCHED				WHAT	HE	GAVE	UP						THE	RESULTS			
Year	Team	Lg	G	GS	CG	GF	IP	BFP	H	R	ER	HR	SH	SF	HB	TBB	IBB	SO	WP	Bk	W	L	Pct.	ShO	Sv	ERA
1986	Medford	A	13	13	0	0	68	0	64	42	26	4	0	0	4	28	0	69	5	1	5	5	.500	0	0	3.44
1987	Madison	A	9	8	0	0	46.2	203	44	21	18	4	0	2	1	27	0	38	2	1	4	1	.800	0	0	3.47
1988	Modesto	A	17	17	1	0	98	440	91	59	44	7	4	5	2	54	0	81	14	1	6	7	.462	0	0	4.04
1989	Huntsville	AA	15	2	0	4	34	161	34	25	20	2	1	3	1	29	0	17	0	3	3	2	.600	0	0	5.29
	Modesto	A	11	11	1	0	69	293	60	32	25	1	3	2	3	34	1	49	4	1	3	6	.333	0	0	3.26
	Tacoma	AAA	6	0	0	2	11	48	8	9	9	1	0	0	0	7	0	6	0	1	0	0	.000	0	0	7.36
1990	Tacoma	AAA	35	2	0	9	63	291	64	44	35	4	2	4	4	43	2	35	3	0	5	2	.714	0	1	5.00
	Portland	AAA	4	1	0	1	10	52	15	10	9	0	0	1	1	5	0	7	0	0	0	0	.000	0	0	8.10
1991	Huntsville	AA	34	0	0	17	54	240	57	23	13	1	1	2	4	18	1	26	4	1	2	3	.400	0	3	2.17
	Tacoma	AAA	15	0	0	11	31.2	129	28	14	7	0	1	1	2	7	0	15	1	1	2	0	1.000	0	1	1.99
1992	Tacoma	AAA	52	0	0	23	94	421	95	45	43	6	9	3	8	53	9	51	10	0	4	5	.444	0	2	4.12
1993	Jacksnville	AA	17	0	0	8	26.2	109	25	6	5	1	0	1	1	7	1	12	2	0	2	1	.667	0	1	1.69
1994	Calgary	AAA	32	24	2	1	158.2	734	216	118	105	24	0	5	4	53	4	108	3	2	12	8	.600	0	0	5.96
	9 Min. YEARS		260	78	4	76	764.2	3121	801	448	359	55	21	29	36	365	18	514	48	12	48	40	.545	0	8	4.23

Tom Wegmann

Pitches: Right **Bats:** Right **Pos:** P   **Ht:** 6'0" **Wt:** 190 **Born:** 08/29/68 **Age:** 26

				HOW	MUCH	HE	PITCHED				WHAT	HE	GAVE	UP						THE	RESULTS			
Year	Team	Lg	G	GS	CG	GF	IP	BFP	H	R	ER	HR	SH	SF	HB	TBB	IBB	SO	WP	Bk	W	L	Pct.	ShO	Sv	ERA
1990	Mets	R	1	0	0	1	3		0	0	0	0	0	0	0	0	0	3	0	1	0	0	.000	0	0	0.00
	Kingsport	R	14	12	4	1	84.1	342	53	34	24	8	1	2	1	30	0	103	10	7	5	4	.556	2	0	2.56
1991	Columbia	A	7	6	1	0	48	172	21	7	3	1	0	0	1	9	0	69	0	1	5	0	1.000	1	0	0.56
	St. Lucie	A	13	11	0	1	61	239	46	19	17	0	3	0	1	14	0	69	1	6	4	3	.571	0	1	2.51
1992	Tidewater	AAA	7	6	0	0	36.2	165	38	19	18	3	0	1	3	17	0	38	5	1	2	3	.400	0	0	4.42
	Binghamton	AA	27	11	2	4	97.2	384	73	29	28	5	2	1	4	27	1	93	3	2	9	2	.818	0	1	2.58
1993	Norfolk	AAA	44	2	0	14	86.1	356	68	33	31	8	7	1	1	34	8	99	4	1	5	3	.625	0	2	3.23
1994	Rochester	AAA	54	0	0	32	83	374	86	37	34	6	1	4	0	46	10	68	11	0	5	1	.833	0	10	3.69
	5 Min. YEARS		167	48	7	53	498	2035	385	178	155	31	14	9	11	177	19	542	34	19	35	16	.686	3	14	2.80

Chris Weinke

Bats: Left **Throws:** Left **Pos:** 1B   **Ht:** 6'3" **Wt:** 205 **Born:** 07/31/72 **Age:** 22

						BATTING												BASERUNNING				PERCENTAGES		
Year	Team	Lg	G	AB	H	2B	3B	HR	TB	R	RBI	TBB	IBB	SO	HBP	SH	SF	SB	CS	SB%	GDP	Avg	OBP	SLG
1991	St.Cathmes	A	75	271	65	9	1	3	85	31	41	41	1	61	0	3	4	12	9	.57	1	.240	.335	.314
1992	Myrtle Bch	A	135	458	110	16	2	13	169	61	63	70	7	89	6	4	5	4	9	.31	6	.240	.345	.369
1993	Dunedin	A	128	476	135	16	2	17	206	68	98	66	8	78	2	1	4	8	6	.57	7	.284	.370	.433
1994	Knoxville	AA	139	526	133	23	2	8	184	61	87	45	6	121	0	4	5	12	4	.75	10	.253	.309	.350
	4 Min. YEARS		477	1731	443	64	7	41	644	221	289	222	22	349	8	12	18	36	28	.56	24	.256	.340	.372

269

Bill Wengert

Pitches: Right Bats: Right Pos: P   Ht: 6'5" Wt: 210 Born: 01/04/67 Age: 28

		HOW MUCH HE PITCHED						WHAT HE GAVE UP												THE RESULTS					
Year Team	Lg	G	GS	CG	GF	IP	BFP	H	R	ER	HR	SH	SF	HB	TBB	IBB	SO	WP	Bk	W	L	Pct.	ShO	Sv	ERA
1988 Great Falls	R	14	6	0	1	45	202	44	28	18	4	2	1	0	23	0	42	2	1	3	3	.500	0	0	3.60
1989 Bakersfield	A	21	15	0	0	91.1	408	104	59	48	7	2	6	4	44	0	66	7	1	2	7	.222	0	0	4.73
1990 Vero Beach	A	22	7	0	6	74.2	320	66	40	32	5	0	4	4	36	1	47	4	0	5	1	.833	0	0	3.86
1991 Vero Beach	A	30	13	2	8	127	511	100	36	29	3	2	4	6	42	2	114	8	4	7	6	.538	2	3	2.06
1992 Vero Beach	A	5	5	0	0	22.2	104	31	14	13	5	1	2	1	6	0	15	2	0	1	0	1.000	0	0	5.16
San Antonio	AA	10	7	0	0	50.1	212	48	20	18	3	2	0	0	13	0	43	2	0	2	3	.400	0	0	3.22
1993 Wichita	AA	28	25	3	1	162.1	693	167	86	74	16	8	8	8	43	3	106	15	2	7	7	.500	1	0	4.10
1994 Wichita	AA	35	16	0	10	112.2	516	145	81	68	10	6	4	5	35	2	85	9	0	6	7	.462	0	2	5.43
7 Min. YEARS		165	94	5	26	686	2966	705	364	300	53	23	29	28	242	8	518	49	8	33	34	.493	3	5	3.94

Don Wengert

Pitches: Right Bats: Right Pos: P   Ht: 6'3" Wt: 205 Born: 11/06/69 Age: 25

		HOW MUCH HE PITCHED						WHAT HE GAVE UP												THE RESULTS					
Year Team	Lg	G	GS	CG	GF	IP	BFP	H	R	ER	HR	SH	SF	HB	TBB	IBB	SO	WP	Bk	W	L	Pct.	ShO	Sv	ERA
1992 Sou Oregon	A	6	5	1	0	37	144	32	6	6	1	1	0	1	7	0	29	1	1	2	0	1.000	0	0	1.46
Madison	A	7	7	0	0	40	176	42	20	15	2	2	0	2	17	0	29	1	0	3	4	.429	0	0	3.38
1993 Madison	A	13	13	2	0	78.2	322	79	30	29	5	4	4	1	18	0	46	6	0	6	5	.545	0	0	3.32
Modesto	A	12	12	0	0	70.1	299	75	42	37	8	1	1	3	29	0	43	4	1	3	6	.333	0	0	4.73
1994 Modesto	A	10	7	0	3	42.2	174	40	15	14	1	2	1	1	11	0	52	1	0	4	1	.800	0	2	2.95
Huntsville	AA	17	17	1	0	99.1	411	86	43	36	14	0	0	4	33	1	92	3	1	6	4	.600	0	0	3.26
3 Min. YEARS		65	61	4	3	368	1526	354	156	137	31	10	6	12	115	1	291	16	3	24	20	.545	0	2	3.35

Mickey Weston

Pitches: Right Bats: Right Pos: P   Ht: 6'1" Wt: 180 Born: 03/26/61 Age: 34

		HOW MUCH HE PITCHED						WHAT HE GAVE UP												THE RESULTS					
Year Team	Lg	G	GS	CG	GF	IP	BFP	H	R	ER	HR	SH	SF	HB	TBB	IBB	SO	WP	Bk	W	L	Pct.	ShO	Sv	ERA
1984 Columbia	A	32	2	0	20	63.2	272	58	27	13	2	6	1	2	27	6	40	5	0	6	5	.545	0	2	1.84
1985 Lynchburg	A	49	3	1	24	100.1	407	81	29	24	4	3	2	0	22	2	62	4	1	6	5	.545	1	10	2.15
1986 Jackson	AA	34	4	0	7	70.2	308	73	40	34	9	3	2	4	27	3	36	3	0	4	4	.500	0	2	4.33
1987 Jackson	AA	58	1	0	21	82	346	96	39	31	4	0	1	1	18	5	50	6	1	8	4	.667	0	3	3.40
1988 Jackson	AA	30	14	4	4	125.1	507	127	50	31	3	8	5	0	20	4	61	4	0	8	5	.615	0	2	2.23
Tidewater	AAA	4	4	2	0	29.2	115	21	6	5	0	3	0	1	5	1	16	1	0	2	1	.667	1	0	1.52
1989 Rochester	AAA	23	14	2	7	112	445	103	30	26	6	2	2	1	19	0	51	1	0	8	3	.727	1	4	2.09
1990 Rochester	AAA	29	12	2	13	109.1	432	93	36	24	3	1	2	0	22	0	58	3	0	11	1	.917	0	6	1.98
1991 Syracuse	AAA	27	25	3	1	166	710	193	85	69	7	4	5	3	36	1	60	10	0	12	6	.667	0	0	3.74
1992 Scranton/wb	AAA	26	24	2	1	170.2	683	165	65	59	12	5	5	3	29	2	79	4	1	10	6	.625	1	1	3.11
1993 Norfolk	AAA	21	20	3	1	127.1	542	149	77	60	10	3	2	2	18	2	41	4	0	10	9	.526	0	0	4.24
1994 New Haven	AA	9	0	0	9	12	48	10	2	1	1	0	0	0	2	1	11	2	0	2	1	.667	0	2	0.75
Colo. Sprng	AAA	37	0	0	14	53.1	252	80	40	37	7	2	2	0	17	0	30	2	0	5	5	.500	0	1	6.24
1989 Baltimore	AL	7	0	0	2	13	55	18	8	8	1	0	0	1	2	0	7	0	0	1	0	1.000	0	1	5.54
1990 Baltimore	AL	9	2	0	4	21	94	28	20	18	6	1	0	0	6	1	9	1	0	0	1	.000	0	0	7.71
1991 Toronto	AL	2	0	0	2	2	8	1	0	0	0	0	0	0	1	1	1	0	0	0	0	.000	0	0	0.00
1992 Philadelphia	NL	1	1	0	0	3.2	19	7	5	5	1	0	0	1	1	0	0	0	0	0	1	.000	0	0	12.27
1993 New York	NL	4	0	0	0	5.2	30	11	5	5	0	0	0	1	1	0	2	0	0	0	0	.000	0	0	7.94
11 Min. YEARS		379	123	16	122	1222.1	5067	1249	526	414	68	40	29	17	262	27	595	49	3	92	55	.626	4	31	3.05
5 Maj. YEARS		23	3	0	8	45.1	206	65	38	36	8	1	0	3	11	2	19	1	0	1	2	.333	0	1	7.15

Steve Whitaker

Pitches: Left Bats: Left Pos: P   Ht: 6'6" Wt: 225 Born: 04/15/70 Age: 25

		HOW MUCH HE PITCHED						WHAT HE GAVE UP												THE RESULTS					
Year Team	Lg	G	GS	CG	GF	IP	BFP	H	R	ER	HR	SH	SF	HB	TBB	IBB	SO	WP	Bk	W	L	Pct.	ShO	Sv	ERA
1991 San Jose	A	6	6	0	0	29.1	129	25	15	11	2	0	3	1	25	0	21	3	1	2	1	.667	0	0	3.38
1992 San Jose	A	26	26	3	0	148.1	648	157	80	69	7	6	5	6	86	2	83	10	0	8	9	.471	0	0	4.19
1993 San Jose	A	22	21	1	1	127.1	582	106	70	54	9	2	6	5	114	0	94	7	0	8	10	.444	0	0	3.82
Shreveport	AA	4	1	0	2	8.1	38	5	1	1	0	1	0	0	7	0	12	0	0	1	0	1.000	0	0	1.08
1994 Shreveport	AA	27	26	1	0	154.2	648	140	69	58	13	7	6	5	68	0	108	3	0	11	8	.579	1	0	3.38
4 Min. YEARS		85	80	5	3	468	2045	433	235	193	31	16	20	17	300	2	318	23	1	30	28	.517	1	0	3.71

Billy White

Bats: Right Throws: Right Pos: 2B   Ht: 6'0" Wt: 185 Born: 07/03/68 Age: 26

		BATTING															BASERUNNING				PERCENTAGES		
Year Team	Lg	G	AB	H	2B	3B	HR	TB	R	RBI	TBB	IBB	SO	HBP	SH	SF	SB	CS	SB%	GDP	Avg	OBP	SLG
1989 Geneva	A	68	254	82	19	1	3	112	44	29	43	0	36	3	2	1	16	5	.76	9	.323	.425	.441
1990 Winston-Sal	A	134	505	136	15	2	5	170	85	54	70	3	108	9	9	3	25	8	.76	13	.269	.366	.337
1991 Charlotte	AA	123	396	106	16	3	3	137	52	50	66	2	72	4	4	5	13	9	.59	9	.268	.374	.346
1992 Charlotte	AA	121	403	102	12	0	4	126	57	33	46	0	90	3	6	4	10	8	.56	9	.253	.331	.313
1993 Daytona	A	38	125	42	9	2	3	64	19	22	16	0	23	5	4	1	2	0	1.00	2	.336	.429	.512
Orlando	AA	40	120	29	11	1	2	48	14	14	15	1	28	0	2	2	1	2	.33	2	.242	.321	.400
1994 New Haven	AA	82	236	58	13	0	1	74	31	22	37	0	48	2	4	1	0	3	.00	11	.246	.351	.314
6 Min. YEARS		606	2039	555	95	9	21	731	302	224	293	6	405	26	31	17	67	35	.66	54	.272	.368	.359

Chris White

Pitches: Right Bats: Right Pos: P Ht: 6'0" Wt: 180 Born: 09/15/69 Age: 25

		HOW MUCH HE PITCHED						WHAT HE GAVE UP											THE RESULTS					
Year Team	Lg	G	GS	CG	GF	IP	BFP	H	R	ER	HR	SH	SF	HB	TBB	IBB	SO	WP	Bk	W	L	Pct.	ShO	Sv	ERA
1991 Auburn	A	26	0	0	17	46.2	205	46	25	19	3	1	1	3	18	2	38	3	5	2	3	.400	0	9	3.66
1992 Asheville	A	41	13	0	22	117.1	496	122	51	44	4	0	3	3	29	3	103	7	5	13	4	.765	0	8	3.38
1993 Osceola	A	13	12	1	0	88.1	364	88	37	33	8	0	3	2	19	1	51	1	2	6	3	.667	0	0	3.36
Jackson	AA	16	11	0	1	60	283	80	54	49	3	3	3	3	25	2	44	5	2	3	5	.375	0	1	7.35
1994 Jackson	AA	52	0	0	11	66.2	282	60	32	26	4	2	2	2	23	6	61	2	1	4	5	.444	0	2	3.51
4 Min. YEARS		148	36	1	51	379	1630	396	199	171	22	6	12	13	114	14	297	18	15	28	20	.583	0	20	4.06

Derrick White

Bats: Right Throws: Right Pos: 1B Ht: 6' 1" Wt: 220 Born: 10/12/69 Age: 25

		BATTING														BASERUNNING				PERCENTAGES		
Year Team	Lg	G	AB	H	2B	3B	HR	TB	R	RBI	TBB	IBB	SO	HBP	SH	SF	SB	CS	SB%	GDP	Avg	OBP	SLG
1991 Jamestown	A	72	271	89	10	4	6	125	46	49	40	0	46	7	0	2	8	3	.73	8	.328	.425	.461
1992 Harrisburg	AA	134	495	137	19	2	13	199	63	81	40	3	73	7	0	2	17	3	.85	16	.277	.338	.402
1993 Wst Plm Bch	A	6	25	5	0	0	0	5	1	1	2	0	2	0	0	0	2	0	1.00	0	.200	.231	.200
Ottawa	AAA	67	249	70	15	1	4	99	32	29	20	2	52	3	0	1	10	7	.59	10	.281	.341	.398
Harrisburg	AA	21	79	18	1	0	2	25	14	12	5	0	17	2	0	1	2	0	1.00	2	.228	.287	.316
1994 Ottawa	AAA	47	99	21	4	0	0	25	13	9	8	1	25	1	1	1	4	1	.80	3	.212	.275	.253
Portland	AA	74	264	71	13	2	4	100	39	34	28	1	52	3	0	2	14	7	.67	5	.269	.343	.379
1993 Montreal	NL	17	49	11	3	0	2	20	6	4	2	1	12	1	0	0	2	0	1.00	1	.224	.269	.408
4 Min. YEARS		421	1482	411	62	9	29	578	208	215	142	7	267	23	1	9	57	21	.73	44	.277	.348	.390

Jimmy White

Bats: Left Throws: Right Pos: OF Ht: 6'1" Wt: 170 Born: 12/01/72 Age: 22

		BATTING														BASERUNNING				PERCENTAGES		
Year Team	Lg	G	AB	H	2B	3B	HR	TB	R	RBI	TBB	IBB	SO	HBP	SH	SF	SB	CS	SB%	GDP	Avg	OBP	SLG
1990 Astros	R	52	180	44	6	4	0	58	32	18	29	1	51	1	0	2	11	8	.58	2	.244	.349	.322
1991 Asheville	A	128	437	112	22	2	8	162	66	43	43	2	133	5	0	2	12	15	.44	8	.256	.329	.371
1992 Burlington	A	102	370	106	20	7	1	143	39	47	38	0	84	2	1	6	17	13	.57	7	.286	.351	.386
Asheville	A	24	83	28	6	1	2	42	12	14	7	1	15	0	0	0	5	0	1.00	0	.337	.389	.506
1993 Osceola	A	125	447	123	9	12	7	177	80	37	54	1	120	5	0	3	24	17	.59	1	.275	.358	.396
1994 Osceola	A	48	174	55	14	6	5	96	37	21	21	1	43	3	0	0	9	3	.75	2	.316	.399	.552
Jackson	AA	64	211	62	7	7	8	107	30	26	12	0	68	0	1	3	1	5	.17	7	.294	.327	.507
5 Min. YEARS		543	1902	530	84	39	31	785	296	206	204	6	514	16	2	16	79	61	.56	27	.279	.351	.413

Sean Whiteside

Pitches: Left Bats: Left Pos: P Ht: 6'4" Wt: 190 Born: 04/19/71 Age: 24

		HOW MUCH HE PITCHED						WHAT HE GAVE UP											THE RESULTS					
Year Team	Lg	G	GS	CG	GF	IP	BFP	H	R	ER	HR	SH	SF	HB	TBB	IBB	SO	WP	Bk	W	L	Pct.	ShO	Sv	ERA
1992 Niagara Fls	A	15	11	0	0	69.2	289	54	26	19	2	1	2	0	24	0	72	7	5	8	4	.667	0	0	2.45
1993 Fayetteville	A	24	16	0	4	100.2	443	113	68	52	8	0	5	3	41	0	85	18	0	3	5	.375	0	0	4.65
1994 Lakeland	A	13	0	0	6	31.1	126	21	6	4	1	0	0	0	12	0	39	4	0	0	2	.000	0	2	1.15
Trenton	AA	25	0	0	16	36.2	155	26	13	10	2	2	2	1	15	2	31	4	1	2	2	.500	0	5	2.45
3 Min. YEARS		77	27	0	26	238.1	1013	214	113	85	12	4	9	4	92	2	227	33	6	13	13	.500	0	7	3.21

Ryan Whitman

Pitches: Right Bats: Right Pos: P Ht: 6'2" Wt: 180 Born: 01/04/72 Age: 23

		HOW MUCH HE PITCHED						WHAT HE GAVE UP											THE RESULTS					
Year Team	Lg	G	GS	CG	GF	IP	BFP	H	R	ER	HR	SH	SF	HB	TBB	IBB	SO	WP	Bk	W	L	Pct.	ShO	Sv	ERA
1990 Expos	R	14	0	0	13	23	83	14	3	3	0	0	0	1	0	0	23	0	0	1	0	1.000	0	3	1.17
1992 Erie	A	20	0	0	4	44.2	176	33	13	9	3	0	1	2	20	0	41	3	0	6	2	.750	0	0	1.81
1993 High Desert	A	12	5	0	2	50.2	220	49	26	21	3	1	2	0	21	0	31	2	0	8	2	.800	0	0	3.73
1994 Wichita	AA	13	4	0	1	36.1	175	56	39	35	3	1	1	0	17	1	16	3	2	1	3	.250	0	0	8.67
Rancho Cuca	A	10	0	0	4	16	79	25	16	14	1	0	3	1	5	0	11	0	0	0	0	.000	0	0	7.88
4 Min. YEARS		69	9	0	24	170.2	733	177	97	82	10	2	7	4	63	1	122	8	2	16	7	.696	0	3	4.32

Mike Whitten

Pitches: Left Bats: Left Pos: P Ht: 6'4" Wt: 200 Born: 12/27/68 Age: 26

		HOW MUCH HE PITCHED						WHAT HE GAVE UP											THE RESULTS					
Year Team	Lg	G	GS	CG	GF	IP	BFP	H	R	ER	HR	SH	SF	HB	TBB	IBB	SO	WP	Bk	W	L	Pct.	ShO	Sv	ERA
1992 Erie	A	11	0	0	3	16	76	17	13	11	2	0	0	1	15	0	13	5	0	1	0	1.000	0	0	6.19
1993 High Desert	A	43	0	0	33	52.2	223	44	20	13	0	4	1	0	30	3	26	3	1	5	2	.714	0	13	2.22
1994 Portland	AA	27	0	0	4	37	181	44	24	20	3	1	3	2	23	5	27	6	0	1	3	.250	0	4	4.86
Brevard Cty	A	23	0	0	13	36	149	30	15	9	0	4	2	0	13	1	21	1	0	0	3	.000	0	4	2.25
3 Min. YEARS		104	0	0	53	141.2	629	135	72	53	5	9	6	3	81	9	87	15	1	7	8	.467	0	17	3.37

Chris Widger

Bats: Right **Throws:** Right **Pos:** C **Ht:** 6'3" **Wt:** 195 **Born:** 05/21/71 **Age:** 24

Year	Team	Lg	G	AB	H	2B	3B	HR	TB	R	RBI	TBB	IBB	SO	HBP	SH	SF	SB	CS	SB%	GDP	Avg	OBP	SLG
1992	Bellingham	A	51	166	43	7	2	5	69	28	30	22	0	36	1	0	5	8	1	.89	4	.259	.340	.416
1993	Riverside	A	97	360	95	28	2	9	154	43	58	19	0	64	3	3	4	5	4	.56	8	.264	.303	.428
1994	Jacksonville	AA	116	388	101	15	3	16	170	58	59	39	4	69	5	0	2	8	7	.53	7	.260	.334	.438
	3 Min. YEARS		264	914	239	50	7	30	393	129	147	80	4	169	9	3	11	21	12	.64	19	.261	.323	.430

Pat Wiegandt

Pitches: Left **Bats:** Left **Pos:** P **Ht:** 5'11" **Wt:** 180 **Born:** 12/09/67 **Age:** 27

Year	Team	Lg	G	GS	CG	GF	IP	BFP	H	R	ER	HR	SH	SF	HB	TBB	IBB	SO	WP	Bk	W	L	Pct.	ShO	Sv	ERA
1989	Martinsville	R	9	9	0	0	45.2	187	44	22	13	4	2	0	1	15	0	47	0	0	2	5	.286	0	0	2.56
1990	Spartanburg	A	10	0	0	8	18.1	66	12	2	2	0	0	0	0	2	0	17	0	0	2	0	1.000	0	2	0.98
	Clearwater	A	33	4	0	16	75.2	316	70	33	22	4	4	3	3	37	2	52	6	3	4	8	.333	0	4	2.62
1991	Clearwater	A	11	0	0	5	10.1	47	14	7	4	0	0	0	0	3	0	11	2	0	0	1	.000	0	1	3.48
	Reading	AA	48	0	0	5	81	341	66	26	24	4	3	2	1	40	2	50	5	1	2	3	.400	0	1	2.67
1992	Scranton/wb	AAA	1	0	0	1	1	4	0	0	0	0	0	0	0	1	0	2	0	0	0	0	.000	0	0	0.00
	Reading	AA	56	0	0	12	81.2	354	66	31	27	3	5	1	1	48	5	65	8	1	6	3	.667	0	2	2.98
1993	Reading	AA	56	0	0	16	73.1	326	75	41	29	3	7	2	0	44	7	60	5	1	6	2	.750	0	0	3.56
1994	Scranton-Wb	AAA	6	0	0	1	4.2	30	11	8	7	0	1	1	1	3	0	3	0	0	0	0	.000	0	0	13.50
	Reading	AA	52	0	0	16	52.1	219	49	23	18	4	2	3	2	19	1	35	1	1	2	4	.333	0	1	3.10
	6 Min. YEARS		282	13	0	80	444	1890	407	193	146	22	24	12	9	212	17	342	27	7	24	26	.480	0	10	2.96

Jim Wiley

Pitches: Right **Bats:** Left **Pos:** P **Ht:** 6'3" **Wt:** 195 **Born:** 12/25/68 **Age:** 26

Year	Team	Lg	G	GS	CG	GF	IP	BFP	H	R	ER	HR	SH	SF	HB	TBB	IBB	SO	WP	Bk	W	L	Pct.	ShO	Sv	ERA
1989	Yankees	R	11	10	0	0	56.1	231	50	21	18	1	0	0	4	12	0	53	5	2	3	4	.429	0	0	2.88
1990	Pr William	A	22	22	0	0	114	510	121	67	55	5	1	2	4	51	1	76	5	3	5	9	.357	0	0	4.34
1991	Ft.Laudrdle	A	4	4	0	0	22.1	100	27	15	15	2	0	0	0	8	0	15	1	1	0	0	.000	0	0	6.04
	Yankees	R	3	3	0	0	7.2	35	11	7	3	0	0	0	0	0	0	9	2	0	0	2	.000	0	0	3.52
1992	Yankees	R	4	3	0	1	22.1	89	15	5	4	0	0	0	2	4	0	21	0	0	2	1	.667	0	0	1.61
	Ft. Laud	A	11	10	2	0	62.1	270	74	39	29	4	2	1	3	18	0	23	2	0	4	4	.500	0	0	4.19
1993	Pr William	A	36	12	0	7	91.1	424	114	69	48	9	2	6	2	39	0	54	5	1	2	8	.200	0	1	4.73
1994	Albany-Colo	AA	7	0	0	2	13	60	19	11	10	0	0	1	0	4	1	5	3	1	1	0	1.000	0	0	6.92
	6 Min. YEARS		98	64	2	10	389.1	1719	431	234	182	21	5	10	15	136	2	256	23	8	17	28	.378	0	1	4.21

Curt Wilkerson

Bats: Both **Throws:** Right **Pos:** 2B **Ht:** 5'9" **Wt:** 175 **Born:** 04/26/61 **Age:** 34

Year	Team	Lg	G	AB	H	2B	3B	HR	TB	R	RBI	TBB	IBB	SO	HBP	SH	SF	SB	CS	SB%	GDP	Avg	OBP	SLG
1994	Omaha	AAA	27	91	23	5	0	0	28	8	7	7	0	17	0	0	0	0	1	.00	3	.253	.306	.308
	Ottawa	AAA	13	43	9	3	0	0	12	3	5	2	0	7	0	0	1	0	0	.00	0	.209	.239	.279
1983	Texas	AL	16	35	6	0	1	0	8	7	1	2	0	5	0	0	0	3	0	1.00	0	.171	.216	.229
1984	Texas	AL	153	484	120	12	0	1	135	47	26	22	0	72	2	12	2	12	10	.55	7	.248	.282	.279
1985	Texas	AL	129	360	88	11	6	0	111	35	22	22	0	63	4	6	3	14	7	.67	7	.244	.293	.308
1986	Texas	AL	110	236	56	10	3	0	72	27	15	11	0	42	1	0	1	9	7	.56	2	.237	.273	.305
1987	Texas	AL	85	138	37	5	3	2	54	28	14	6	0	16	2	0	0	6	3	.67	2	.268	.308	.391
1988	Texas	AL	117	338	99	12	5	0	121	41	28	26	3	43	2	3	2	9	4	.69	7	.293	.345	.358
1989	Chicago	NL	77	160	39	4	2	1	50	18	10	8	0	33	0	1	1	4	2	.67	3	.244	.278	.313
1990	Chicago	NL	77	186	41	5	1	0	48	21	16	7	2	36	0	3	0	2	2	.50	4	.220	.249	.258
1991	Pittsburgh	NL	85	191	36	9	1	2	53	20	18	15	0	40	0	0	4	2	1	.67	2	.188	.243	.277
1992	Kansas City	AL	111	296	74	10	1	2	92	27	29	18	3	47	1	7	4	18	7	.72	4	.250	.292	.311
1993	Kansas City	AL	12	28	4	0	0	0	4	1	0	1	0	6	0	0	0	2	0	1.00	1	.143	.172	.143
	1 Min. YEARS		40	134	32	8	0	0	40	11	12	9	0	24	0	0	1	0	1	.00	4	.239	.285	.299
	11 Maj. YEARS		972	2452	600	78	23	8	748	272	179	138	8	403	12	32	17	81	43	.65	39	.245	.286	.305

Cary Williams

Bats: Right **Throws:** Right **Pos:** OF **Ht:** 6'3" **Wt:** 175 **Born:** 06/14/67 **Age:** 28

Year	Team	Lg	G	AB	H	2B	3B	HR	TB	R	RBI	TBB	IBB	SO	HBP	SH	SF	SB	CS	SB%	GDP	Avg	OBP	SLG
1989	Clearwater	A	52	187	50	14	0	2	70	35	14	16	0	31	9	1	2	9	4	.69	2	.267	.350	.374
1990	Clearwater	A	63	245	64	12	3	1	85	20	21	7	0	33	2	2	1	2	2	.50	7	.261	.286	.347
	Reading	AA	49	179	43	10	0	2	59	16	18	7	0	32	3	2	0	0	3	.00	4	.240	.280	.330
1991	Reading	AA	116	421	117	21	3	6	162	55	62	27	3	69	6	3	5	12	1	.92	6	.278	.327	.385
1992	Scranton/wb	AAA	112	373	83	18	3	7	128	38	40	15	0	66	7	3	4	7	4	.64	5	.223	.263	.343
1993	Scranton/wb	AAA	78	232	50	15	2	0	69	27	14	23	0	27	3	3	2	3	4	.43	8	.216	.292	.297
1994	Scranton-Wb	AAA	4	12	2	1	0	0	3	1	1	0	0	2	1	0	0	0	0	.00	0	.167	.231	.250
	Reading	AA	48	120	23	6	1	3	40	8	17	6	0	22	1	1	1	1	1	.50	5	.192	.234	.333
	6 Min. YEARS		522	1769	432	97	12	21	616	200	187	101	3	282	32	15	15	34	19	.64	37	.244	.295	.348

Jeff Williams

Pitches: Right **Bats:** Right **Pos:** P **Ht:** 6'4" **Wt:** 230 **Born:** 04/16/69 **Age:** 26

		HOW MUCH HE PITCHED						WHAT HE GAVE UP									THE RESULTS					
Year Team	Lg	G	GS	CG	GF	IP	BFP	H	R	ER	HR	SH	SF	HB	TBB	IBB	SO	WP	Bk	W	L	Pct.	ShO	Sv	ERA
1990 Bluefield	R	9	0	0	9	11.1	48	7	3	2	0	0	0	1	5	0	14	1	0	2	0	1.000	0	0	1.59
Frederick	A	16	0	0	13	25	115	23	17	13	2	0	2	2	17	0	31	1	0	2	1	.667	0	1	4.68
1991 Frederick	A	12	0	0	11	16.2	68	17	6	5	1	1	1	0	6	0	20	0	0	1	2	.333	0	6	2.70
Hagerstown	AA	39	0	0	29	55.1	247	52	23	16	1	2	3	0	32	1	42	6	0	3	5	.375	0	17	2.60
1992 Hagerstown	AA	36	15	3	16	123	579	148	91	66	9	5	6	6	70	0	82	15	1	8	10	.444	0	6	4.83
1993 Rochester	AAA	33	5	0	11	86	389	95	59	55	10	2	7	4	47	3	59	8	1	2	5	.286	0	1	5.76
1994 Albuquerque	AAA	3	0	0	0	4.1	21	7	4	4	0	0	0	0	3	0	3	0	0	0	1	.000	0	0	8.31
Calgary	AAA	40	1	0	16	69.2	328	88	53	43	4	1	4	2	43	3	30	11	0	3	3	.500	0	0	5.56
5 Min. YEARS		188	21	3	105	391.1	1795	437	256	204	27	11	23	15	223	7	282	42	2	21	27	.438	0	31	4.69

Matt Williams

Pitches: Left **Bats:** Both **Pos:** P **Ht:** 6'0" **Wt:** 175 **Born:** 04/12/71 **Age:** 24

		HOW MUCH HE PITCHED						WHAT HE GAVE UP									THE RESULTS					
Year Team	Lg	G	GS	CG	GF	IP	BFP	H	R	ER	HR	SH	SF	HB	TBB	IBB	SO	WP	Bk	W	L	Pct.	ShO	Sv	ERA
1993 Kinston	A	27	27	2	0	153.1	672	125	65	54	6	7	5	8	100	0	134	12	6	12	12	.500	1	0	3.17
1994 Canton-Akrn	AA	5	4	0	1	23.2	112	30	22	20	3	1	3	1	14	0	9	1	0	0	3	.000	0	0	7.61
High Desert	A	5	5	0	0	18	101	33	29	26	7	2	3	1	13	1	10	2	0	1	4	.200	0	0	13.00
Kinston	A	15	15	1	0	81.1	358	86	63	55	17	0	2	2	33	0	67	4	2	4	6	.400	0	1	6.09
2 Min. YEARS		52	51	3	1	276.1	1243	274	179	155	33	10	13	12	160	1	220	19	8	17	25	.405	1	1	5.05

Reggie Williams

Bats: Both **Throws:** Right **Pos:** OF **Ht:** 6'1" **Wt:** 185 **Born:** 05/05/66 **Age:** 29

		BATTING															BASERUNNING				PERCENTAGES		
Year Team	Lg	G	AB	H	2B	3B	HR	TB	R	RBI	TBB	IBB	SO	HBP	SH	SF	SB	CS	SB%	GDP	Avg	OBP	SLG
1988 Everett	A	60	223	56	8	1	3	75	52	29	47	0	43	3	0	2	36	10	.78	5	.251	.385	.336
1989 Clinton	A	68	236	46	9	2	3	68	38	18	29	0	66	3	5	1	14	9	.61	1	.195	.290	.288
Boise	A	42	153	41	5	1	3	57	33	14	24	0	29	2	0	1	18	5	.78	2	.268	.372	.373
1990 Quad City	A	58	189	46	11	2	3	70	50	12	39	0	60	4	2	1	24	6	.80	2	.243	.382	.370
1991 Palm Sprngs	A	14	44	13	1	0	1	17	10	2	21	0	15	1	1	0	6	5	.55	0	.295	.530	.386
Midland	AA	83	319	99	12	3	1	120	77	30	62	2	67	0	5	3	21	9	.70	3	.310	.419	.376
1992 Edmonton	AAA	139	519	141	26	9	3	194	96	64	88	1	110	3	7	8	44	14	.76	9	.272	.375	.374
1993 Vancouver	AAA	130	481	132	17	6	2	167	92	53	88	2	99	5	9	6	50	17	.75	7	.274	.388	.347
1994 Albuquerque	AAA	104	288	90	15	8	4	133	55	42	33	1	62	0	1	2	21	10	.68	6	.313	.381	.462
1992 California	AL	14	26	6	1	1	0	9	5	2	1	0	10	0	0	0	2	0	.00	0	.231	.259	.346
7 Min. YEARS		698	2452	664	104	32	23	901	503	264	431	6	551	21	30	24	234	85	.73	35	.271	.381	.367

Shad Williams

Pitches: Right **Bats:** Right **Pos:** P **Ht:** 6'0" **Wt:** 185 **Born:** 03/10/71 **Age:** 24

		HOW MUCH HE PITCHED						WHAT HE GAVE UP									THE RESULTS					
Year Team	Lg	G	GS	CG	GF	IP	BFP	H	R	ER	HR	SH	SF	HB	TBB	IBB	SO	WP	Bk	W	L	Pct.	ShO	Sv	ERA
1992 Quad City	A	27	26	7	0	179.1	748	161	81	65	14	6	6	7	55	0	152	9	1	13	11	.542	0	0	3.26
1993 Midland	AA	27	27	2	0	175.2	758	192	100	92	16	6	6	3	65	1	91	9	1	7	10	.412	0	0	4.71
1994 Midland	AA	5	5	1	0	32.1	112	13	4	4	1	0	0	1	4	0	29	2	0	3	0	1.000	1	0	1.11
Vancouver	AAA	16	16	1	0	86	386	100	61	44	14	3	2	3	30	0	42	6	0	4	6	.400	1	0	4.60
3 Min. YEARS		75	74	11	0	473.1	2004	466	246	205	45	15	14	14	154	1	314	26	2	27	27	.500	2	0	3.90

Slim Williams

Pitches: Left **Bats:** Left **Pos:** P **Ht:** 6'7" **Wt:** 232 **Born:** 05/18/65 **Age:** 30

		HOW MUCH HE PITCHED						WHAT HE GAVE UP									THE RESULTS					
Year Team	Lg	G	GS	CG	GF	IP	BFP	H	R	ER	HR	SH	SF	HB	TBB	IBB	SO	WP	Bk	W	L	Pct.	ShO	Sv	ERA
1984 Great Falls	R	8	0	0	3	11	0	10	14	11	0	0	0	0	16	0	9	1	0	0	1	.000	0	0	9.00
Dodgers	R	2	0	0	0	3	20	4	4	0	0	0	0	0	4	0	1	0	0	0	0	.000	0	0	0.00
1985 Dodgers	R	13	13	1	0	66.2	306	54	35	28	1	3	2	2	55	0	58	5	4	4	4	.500	1	0	3.78
1986 Vero Beach	A	30	6	0	16	60	285	47	35	29	1	6	3	1	66	2	40	8	4	1	1	.500	0	0	4.35
1987 Visalia	A	13	13	2	0	85	373	66	38	21	5	6	1	5	62	2	81	10	0	7	4	.636	0	0	2.22
1988 Visalia	A	37	0	0	28	51	221	41	23	21	2	4	2	2	33	0	55	5	3	3	4	.429	0	12	3.71
1989 Orlando	AA	43	0	0	39	53.1	240	50	23	18	3	1	1	0	35	1	62	1	2	6	4	.600	0	14	3.04
Portland	AAA	16	0	0	8	23.2	112	24	15	11	0	0	1	0	18	0	22	2	1	3	2	.600	0	3	4.18
1990 Portland	AAA	51	3	0	27	84	388	73	64	47	4	3	6	3	74	2	62	7	1	4	6	.400	0	3	5.04
1991 Phoenix	AAA	30	28	3	1	160	748	192	120	106	17	3	5	1	93	0	69	12	5	7	9	.438	0	0	5.96
1993 Orlando	AA	15	14	0	0	90.2	377	84	29	25	4	5	0	2	38	1	65	2	2	5	5	.500	0	0	2.48
Iowa	AAA	17	13	0	1	78	329	74	32	30	5	5	2	1	37	0	49	3	2	5	3	.625	0	0	3.46
1994 Harrisburg	AA	1	1	0	0	4	18	3	1	0	0	0	0	0	2	0	5	0	0	0	0	.000	0	0	0.00
Ottawa	AAA	27	11	1	3	99.1	448	105	60	50	5	2	3	1	53	1	57	7	0	9	2	.818	1	1	4.53
10 Min. YEARS		303	102	7	126	869.2	3865	827	493	397	47	38	26	18	586	9	636	63	24	54	45	.545	2	33	4.11

Todd Williams

Pitches: Right Bats: Right Pos: P   Ht: 6'3" Wt: 185 Born: 02/13/71 Age: 24

Year	Team	Lg	G	GS	CG	GF	IP	BFP	H	R	ER	HR	SH	SF	HB	TBB	IBB	SO	WP	Bk	W	L	Pct.	ShO	Sv	ERA
1991	Great Falls	R	28	0	0	14	53	232	50	26	16	1	0	0	1	24	1	59	4	1	5	2	.714	0	8	2.72
1992	Bakersfield	A	13	0	0	13	15.2	64	11	4	4	1	1	0	0	7	1	11	0	0	0	0	.000	0	9	2.30
	San Antonio	AA	39	0	0	34	44	196	47	17	16	0	4	1	1	23	6	35	3	0	7	4	.636	0	13	3.27
1993	Albuquerque	AAA	65	0	0	50	70.1	321	87	44	39	2	0	1	1	31	6	56	6	0	5	5	.500	0	21	4.99
1994	Albuquerque	AAA	59	0	0	36	72.1	299	78	29	25	5	1	3	6	17	3	30	6	1	4	2	.667	0	13	3.11
	4 Min. YEARS		204	0	0	147	255.1	1112	273	120	100	9	6	5	9	102	17	191	19	2	21	13	.618	0	64	3.52

Antone Williamson

Bats: Left Throws: Right Pos: 3B   Ht: 6'1" Wt: 185 Born: 07/18/73 Age: 21

Year	Team	Lg	G	AB	H	2B	3B	HR	TB	R	RBI	TBB	IBB	SO	HBP	SH	SF	SB	CS	SB%	GDP	Avg	OBP	SLG
1994	Helena	R	6	26	11	2	1	0	15	5	4	2	0	4	0	0	0	0	0	.00	1	.423	.464	.577
	Stockton	A	23	85	19	4	0	3	32	6	13	7	0	19	0	1	3	0	1	.00	1	.224	.274	.376
	El Paso	AA	14	48	12	3	0	1	18	8	9	7	0	8	0	0	1	0	0	.00	1	.250	.339	.375
	1 Min. YEARS		43	159	42	9	1	4	65	19	26	16	0	31	0	1	4	0	1	.00	3	.264	.324	.409

Travis Willis

Pitches: Right Bats: Right Pos: P   Ht: 6'2" Wt: 185 Born: 11/28/68 Age: 26

Year	Team	Lg	G	GS	CG	GF	IP	BFP	H	R	ER	HR	SH	SF	HB	TBB	IBB	SO	WP	Bk	W	L	Pct.	ShO	Sv	ERA
1989	Geneva	A	16	15	5	1	100.1	415	92	55	38	7	2	1	8	21	3	93	5	3	4	7	.364	0	0	3.41
1990	Peoria	A	31	22	6	4	163	682	152	78	59	6	8	7	14	41	1	93	9	6	10	11	.476	3	0	3.26
	Winston-Sal	A	2	2	0	0	4.1	30	13	12	10	2	0	0	2	3	0	2	0	2	0	1	.000	0	0	20.77
1991	Winston-Sal	A	53	0	0	48	73.1	315	74	36	33	2	2	2	3	25	1	60	7	0	6	4	.600	0	4	4.05
1992	Iowa	AAA	3	0	0	2	7	32	9	6	6	4	1	0	0	3	0	1	1	0	1	1	.500	0	0	7.71
	Charlotte	AA	46	0	0	22	61.2	252	55	23	20	2	2	2	1	16	3	34	5	0	5	3	.625	0	4	2.92
1993	Orlando	AA	61	1	0	57	82.1	357	91	37	26	2	10	3	2	22	6	56	8	0	8	6	.571	0	24	2.84
1994	Buffalo	AAA	56	0	0	10	76.1	329	89	42	36	7	1	3	0	26	3	42	3	0	6	3	.667	0	1	4.24
	6 Min. YEARS		268	40	11	144	568.1	2412	575	289	228	32	26	18	30	157	17	381	38	11	40	36	.526	3	55	3.61

Brandon Wilson

Bats: Right Throws: Right Pos: SS   Ht: 6'1" Wt: 175 Born: 02/26/69 Age: 26

Year	Team	Lg	G	AB	H	2B	3B	HR	TB	R	RBI	TBB	IBB	SO	HBP	SH	SF	SB	CS	SB%	GDP	Avg	OBP	SLG
1990	White Sox	R	11	41	11	1	0	0	12	4	5	4	0	5	0	1	1	3	1	.75	1	.268	.326	.293
	Utica	A	53	165	41	2	0	0	43	31	14	28	0	45	0	3	2	14	5	.74	1	.248	.354	.261
1991	South Bend	A	125	463	145	18	6	2	181	75	49	61	2	70	2	7	4	41	11	.79	3	.313	.392	.391
	Birmingham	AA	2	10	4	1	0	0	5	3	2	0	0	2	0	0	0	0	0	.00	0	.400	.400	.500
1992	Sarasota	A	103	399	118	22	6	4	164	68	54	45	2	64	4	5	2	30	16	.65	4	.296	.371	.411
	Birmingham	AA	27	107	29	4	0	0	33	10	4	4	0	16	0	0	0	5	0	1.00	1	.271	.297	.308
1993	Birmingham	AA	137	500	135	19	5	2	170	76	48	52	0	77	3	4	3	43	10	.81	7	.270	.341	.340
1994	Nashville	AAA	114	370	83	16	3	0	120	42	26	30	0	67	3	10	2	13	5	.72	4	.224	.286	.324
	5 Min. YEARS		572	2055	566	83	20	13	728	309	202	224	4	346	12	30	14	149	48	.76	21	.275	.348	.354

Craig Wilson

Bats: Right Throws: Right Pos: 2B   Ht: 5'11" Wt: 210 Born: 11/28/64 Age: 30

Year	Team	Lg	G	AB	H	2B	3B	HR	TB	R	RBI	TBB	IBB	SO	HBP	SH	SF	SB	CS	SB%	GDP	Avg	OBP	SLG
1984	Erie	A	72	282	83	18	4	7	130	53	46	29	0	27	4	1	2	10	4	.71	8	.294	.366	.461
1985	Springfield	A	133	504	132	16	4	8	180	64	52	47	0	67	1	4	6	33	14	.70	12	.262	.323	.357
1986	Springfield	A	127	496	136	17	6	1	168	106	49	65	0	49	1	9	4	44	12	.79	11	.274	.357	.339
1987	St. Pete	A	38	162	58	6	4	0	72	35	28	14	0	5	0	0	0	12	8	.60	3	.358	.409	.444
	Louisville	AAA	21	70	15	2	0	1	20	10	8	3	0	5	0	2	1	0	2	.00	1	.214	.243	.286
	Arkansas	AA	66	238	69	13	1	1	87	37	26	30	1	19	1	3	2	9	6	.60	5	.290	.369	.366
1988	Louisville	AAA	133	497	127	27	2	1	161	59	46	54	1	46	0	6	4	6	4	.60	13	.256	.326	.324
1989	Arkansas	AA	55	224	71	12	1	1	88	41	40	21	1	14	1	3	1	8	5	.62	4	.317	.377	.393
	Louisville	AAA	75	278	81	18	3	1	108	37	30	14	0	25	2	3	1	1	3	.25	5	.291	.329	.388
1990	Louisville	AAA	57	204	57	9	2	2	76	30	28	28	0	15	1	5	6	5	3	.63	3	.279	.360	.373
1992	Louisville	AAA	20	81	24	5	1	0	31	13	5	5	0	8	0	1	0	3	2	.60	2	.296	.337	.383
1993	Omaha	AAA	65	234	65	13	1	3	89	26	28	20	0	24	1	1	1	7	4	.64	6	.278	.336	.380
1994	Okla. City	AAA	65	227	59	6	0	4	77	23	27	23	4	24	1	6	2	1	2	.33	14	.260	.328	.339
1989	St. Louis	NL	6	4	1	0	0	0	1	1	1	1	0	2	0	0	0	0	0	.00	0	.250	.400	.250
1990	St. Louis	NL	55	121	30	2	0	0	32	13	7	8	0	14	0	0	2	0	0	.00	2	.248	.290	.264
1991	St. Louis	NL	60	82	14	2	0	0	16	5	13	6	2	10	0	0	2	1	0	.33	2	.171	.222	.195
1992	St. Louis	NL	61	106	33	6	0	0	39	6	13	10	2	18	0	2	1	1	2	.33	4	.311	.368	.368
1993	Kansas City	AL	21	49	13	1	0	1	17	6	3	6	0	6	0	1	0	1	1	.50	1	.265	.357	.347
	10 Min. YEARS		927	3497	977	162	29	30	1287	534	408	353	7	328	13	44	30	139	69	.67	87	.279	.345	.368
	5 Maj. YEARS		203	362	91	11	0	1	105	31	37	32	4	50	0	3	5	2	5	.29	13	.251	.308	.290

Desi Wilson

Bats: Left   Throws: Left   Pos: OF   Ht: 6'7"   Wt: 230   Born: 05/09/68   Age: 27

Year	Team	Lg	G	AB	H	2B	3B	HR	TB	R	RBI	TBB	IBB	SO	HBP	SH	SF	SB	CS	SB%	GDP	Avg	OBP	SLG
1991	Rangers	R	8	25	4	2	0	0	6	1	7	3	0	2	0	0	1	0	0	.00	0	.160	.241	.240
1992	Butte	R	72	253	81	9	4	5	113	45	42	31	1	45	1	0	0	13	11	.54	1	.320	.396	.447
1993	Charlotte	A	131	511	156	21	7	3	200	83	70	50	4	90	7	0	2	29	11	.73	18	.305	.374	.391
1994	Tulsa	AA	129	493	142	27	0	6	187	69	55	40	5	115	2	0	1	16	14	.53	14	.288	.343	.379
	4 Min. YEARS		340	1282	383	59	11	14	506	198	174	124	10	252	10	0	4	58	36	.62	33	.299	.364	.395

Gary Wilson

Pitches: Right   Bats: Right   Pos: P   Ht: 6'3"   Wt: 180   Born: 01/01/70   Age: 25

Year	Team	Lg	G	GS	CG	GF	IP	BFP	H	R	ER	HR	SH	SF	HB	TBB	IBB	SO	WP	Bk	W	L	Pct.	ShO	Sv	ERA
1992	Welland	A	13	4	0	5	42.1	170	27	9	5	0	1	0	1	13	1	40	1	0	3	2	.600	0	0	1.06
	Augusta	A	7	7	0	0	41.2	177	43	22	17	2	3	3	3	7	0	27	1	1	2	3	.400	0	0	3.67
1993	Salem	A	15	15	0	0	78.1	356	102	58	50	15	1	1	2	25	0	54	3	0	5	5	.500	0	0	5.74
	Augusta	A	20	6	0	4	51	229	66	35	31	4	1	1	3	11	0	42	3	0	3	7	.300	0	0	5.47
1994	Salem	A	6	6	1	0	35	147	41	12	9	2	0	0	0	4	0	26	3	0	3	1	.750	1	0	2.31
	Carolina	AA	22	22	7	0	161.2	654	144	55	46	11	8	5	10	37	0	97	2	0	8	5	.615	2	0	2.56
	3 Min. YEARS		83	60	8	9	410	1733	423	191	158	34	14	10	19	97	1	286	13	2	24	23	.511	3	0	3.47

Nigel Wilson

Bats: Left   Throws: Left   Pos: OF   Ht: 6'1"   Wt: 185   Born: 01/12/70   Age: 25

Year	Team	Lg	G	AB	H	2B	3B	HR	TB	R	RBI	TBB	IBB	SO	HBP	SH	SF	SB	CS	SB%	GDP	Avg	OBP	SLG
1988	St.Cathrnes	A	40	103	21	1	2	2	32	12	11	12	0	32	4	1	1	8	4	.67	0	.204	.308	.311
1989	St.Cathrnes	A	42	161	35	5	2	4	56	17	18	11	0	50	4	1	0	8	2	.80	1	.217	.284	.348
1990	Myrtle Bch	A	110	440	120	23	9	16	209	77	62	30	3	71	6	2	2	22	12	.65	4	.273	.326	.475
1991	Dunedin	A	119	455	137	18	13	12	217	64	55	29	4	99	9	4	7	26	11	.70	4	.301	.350	.477
1992	Knoxville	AA	137	521	143	34	7	26	269	85	69	33	5	137	7	2	2	13	8	.62	2	.274	.325	.516
1993	Edmonton	AAA	96	370	108	26	7	17	199	66	68	25	7	108	10	1	2	8	3	.73	6	.292	.351	.538
1994	Edmonton	AAA	87	314	97	24	1	12	159	50	62	22	3	79	10	0	4	2	3	.40	3	.309	.369	.506
1993	Florida	NL	7	16	0	0	0	0	0	0	0	0	0	11	0	0	0	0	0	.00	0	.000	.000	.000
	7 Min. YEARS		631	2364	661	131	41	89	1141	371	345	162	22	576	50	11	18	87	43	.67	19	.280	.337	.483

Steve Wilson

Pitches: Left   Bats: Left   Pos: P   Ht: 6'4"   Wt: 224   Born: 12/13/64   Age: 30

Year	Team	Lg	G	GS	CG	GF	IP	BFP	H	R	ER	HR	SH	SF	HB	TBB	IBB	SO	WP	Bk	W	L	Pct.	ShO	Sv	ERA
1985	Burlington	A	21	10	0	4	72.2	317	71	44	37	11	1	4	2	27	1	76	1	3	3	5	.375	0	0	4.58
1986	Tulsa	AA	24	24	2	0	136.2	617	117	83	74	10	5	8	7	103	0	95	12	6	7	13	.350	0	0	4.87
1987	Charlotte	A	20	17	1	1	107	442	81	41	29	5	0	2	3	44	0	80	5	2	9	5	.643	1	0	2.44
1988	Tulsa	AA	25	25	5	0	165.1	698	147	72	58	14	6	4	8	53	1	132	3	1	15	7	.682	3	0	3.16
1991	Iowa	AAA	25	16	1	4	114	482	102	55	49	11	0	1	7	45	2	83	7	0	3	8	.273	0	0	3.87
1993	Albuquerque	AAA	13	12	0	0	51.1	220	57	29	25	5	4	1	2	14	0	44	4	2	0	3	.000	0	0	4.38
1994	New Orleans	AAA	51	3	0	15	76.2	332	78	39	37	5	1	2	4	33	1	67	5	1	8	6	.571	0	1	4.34
1988	Texas	AL	3	0	0	1	7.2	31	7	5	5	1	0	0	0	4	1	1	0	0	0	0	.000	0	0	5.87
1989	Chicago	NL	53	8	0	9	85.2	364	83	43	40	6	5	4	1	31	5	65	0	1	6	4	.600	0	2	4.20
1990	Chicago	NL	45	15	1	5	139	597	140	77	74	17	9	3	2	43	4	95	2	1	4	9	.308	0	1	4.79
1991	Chicago	NL	8	0	0	2	12.1	53	13	7	6	1	0	1	0	5	1	9	0	0	0	0	.000	0	0	4.38
	Los Angeles	NL	11	0	0	3	8.1	28	1	0	0	0	0	0	0	4	0	5	0	0	0	0	.000	0	2	0.00
1992	Los Angeles	NL	60	0	0	18	66.2	301	74	37	31	6	5	4	1	29	7	54	7	0	2	5	.286	0	0	4.18
1993	Los Angeles	NL	25	0	0	4	25.2	120	30	13	13	2	1	0	1	14	4	23	3	0	1	0	1.000	0	1	4.56
	7 Min. YEARS		179	107	9	24	723.2	3108	653	363	309	61	17	22	33	319	9	577	37	15	45	47	.489	4	1	3.84
	6 Maj. YEARS		205	23	1	42	345.1	1494	348	182	169	33	20	12	5	130	24	252	12	2	13	18	.419	0	6	4.40

Thomas Wilson

Bats: Right   Throws: Right   Pos: OF   Ht: 6'3"   Wt: 185   Born: 12/19/70   Age: 24

Year	Team	Lg	G	AB	H	2B	3B	HR	TB	R	RBI	TBB	IBB	SO	HBP	SH	SF	SB	CS	SB%	GDP	Avg	OBP	SLG
1991	Oneonta	A	70	243	59	12	2	4	87	38	42	34	2	71	3	0	5	4	4	.50	6	.243	.337	.358
1992	Greensboro	A	117	395	83	22	0	6	123	50	48	68	0	128	3	1	8	2	1	.67	8	.210	.325	.311
1993	Greensboro	A	120	394	98	20	1	10	150	55	63	91	0	112	4	3	8	5	5	.29	5	.249	.388	.381
1994	Albany-Colo	AA	123	408	100	20	1	7	143	54	42	58	2	100	6	4	4	4	6	.40	6	.245	.345	.350
	4 Min. YEARS		430	1440	340	74	4	27	503	197	195	251	4	411	16	8	25	12	16	.43	25	.236	.350	.349

Randy Wilstead

Bats: Left   Throws: Left   Pos: 1B   Ht: 6'4"   Wt: 200   Born: 04/05/68   Age: 27

Year	Team	Lg	G	AB	H	2B	3B	HR	TB	R	RBI	TBB	IBB	SO	HBP	SH	SF	SB	CS	SB%	GDP	Avg	OBP	SLG
1990	Jamestown	A	56	180	48	11	1	4	73	24	21	25	3	43	2	0	0	1	1	.50	0	.267	.362	.406
1991	Rockford	A	121	421	107	26	4	6	159	59	57	58	11	72	1	1	5	2	2	.50	7	.254	.342	.378
	Wst Plm Bch	A	1	1	0	0	0	0	0	0	0	0	0	0	0	0	0	0	0	.00	0	.000	.000	.000

Year	Team	Lg	G	AB	H	2B	3B	HR	TB	R	RBI	TBB	IBB	SO	HBP	SH	SF	SB	CS	SB%	GDP	Avg	OBP	SLG
1992	Wst Plm Bch	A	129	449	128	27	3	8	185	56	71	47	8	68	3	0	4	7	7	.50	12	.285	.354	.412
1993	Wst Plm Bch	A	60	201	67	19	3	3	101	33	35	39	6	39	1	0	2	3	1	.75	3	.333	.440	.502
	Harrisburg	AA	45	108	28	7	0	4	47	10	15	12	2	21	0	0	1	1	1	.50	2	.259	.331	.435
1994	Harrisburg	AA	122	374	110	27	3	13	182	71	64	72	4	83	7	0	3	3	6	.33	7	.294	.414	.487
	5 Min. YEARS		534	1734	488	117	14	38	747	253	263	253	34	326	14	1	15	17	18	.49	31	.281	.375	.431

Chris Wimmer

Bats: Right **Throws:** Right **Pos:** SS   **Ht:** 5'11" **Wt:** 170 **Born:** 09/25/70 **Age:** 24

Year	Team	Lg	G	AB	H	2B	3B	HR	TB	R	RBI	TBB	IBB	SO	HBP	SH	SF	SB	CS	SB%	GDP	Avg	OBP	SLG
1993	San Jose	A	123	493	130	21	4	3	168	76	53	42	1	72	8	7	6	49	12	.80	6	.264	.328	.341
1994	Shreveport	AA	126	462	131	21	3	4	170	63	49	25	2	56	8	5	4	21	13	.62	7	.284	.329	.368
	2 Min. YEARS		249	955	261	42	7	7	338	139	102	67	3	128	16	12	10	70	25	.74	13	.273	.328	.354

Darrin Winston

Pitches: Left **Bats:** Right **Pos:** P   **Ht:** 6'0" **Wt:** 195 **Born:** 07/06/66 **Age:** 28

Year	Team	Lg	G	GS	CG	GF	IP	BFP	H	R	ER	HR	SH	SF	HB	TBB	IBB	SO	WP	Bk	W	L	Pct.	ShO	Sv	ERA
1988	Jamestown	A	14	7	0	5	44	194	47	28	24	3	3	2	0	19	0	29	2	4	2	4	.333	0	2	4.91
1989	Rockford	A	47	0	0	30	65	256	52	16	11	0	3	3	0	11	0	70	7	1	7	1	.875	0	16	1.52
1990	Jacksnville	AA	47	0	0	20	63	246	38	16	15	3	5	2	0	28	2	45	4	0	6	2	.750	0	7	2.14
1991	Indianapols	AAA	27	0	0	4	31	143	26	10	5	3	6	2	1	21	5	23	2	0	1	0	1.000	0	0	1.45
1993	Harrisburg	AA	24	0	0	9	44.2	206	53	30	23	4	4	4	2	19	2	36	3	0	1	0	1.000	0	1	4.63
	Wst Plm Bch	A	8	2	1	3	24.2	88	18	6	4	0	0	0	0	3	0	21	0	0	2	0	1.000	0	0	1.46
1994	Harrisburg	AA	25	0	0	11	35.1	144	32	12	6	3	3	0	2	9	3	27	0	0	4	2	.667	0	0	1.53
	Ottawa	AAA	23	0	0	9	28.1	116	27	15	12	6	1	0	0	10	1	17	0	0	2	0	1.000	0	0	3.81
	6 Min. YEARS		215	9	1	91	336	1393	293	133	100	22	25	13	5	120	13	268	18	5	25	9	.735	0	26	2.68

Rob Wishnevski

Pitches: Right **Bats:** Right **Pos:** P   **Ht:** 6'1" **Wt:** 215 **Born:** 01/02/67 **Age:** 28

Year	Team	Lg	G	GS	CG	GF	IP	BFP	H	R	ER	HR	SH	SF	HB	TBB	IBB	SO	WP	Bk	W	L	Pct.	ShO	Sv	ERA
1987	St.Cathmes	A	16	15	1	0	88	359	58	18	15	2	3	2	6	39	1	71	6	0	7	2	.778	0	0	1.53
1988	Dunedin	A	34	29	0	1	171.1	738	159	92	74	10	5	1	14	61	2	107	19	6	11	11	.500	0	1	3.89
1989	Knoxville	AA	14	11	0	2	66.1	278	50	23	17	4	2	3	4	26	0	36	4	0	6	1	.857	0	0	2.31
	Syracuse	AAA	16	12	2	2	89.1	372	83	44	39	6	2	3	9	25	0	32	8	1	5	5	.500	1	0	3.93
1990	Syracuse	AAA	9	8	0	0	48.2	229	65	40	36	6	0	1	0	23	1	28	2	0	2	5	.286	0	0	6.66
	Knoxville	AA	20	17	1	3	105.2	439	84	54	45	7	6	2	4	39	0	74	10	3	6	3	.667	1	1	3.83
1991	Knoxville	AA	31	10	0	11	101	439	78	46	33	2	3	3	9	53	5	58	11	1	6	8	.429	0	3	2.94
	El Paso	AA	7	0	0	3	16	71	17	8	7	1	2	1	1	6	3	9	1	0	4	0	1.000	0	1	3.94
1992	El Paso	AA	13	0	0	13	17.1	62	7	2	2	0	0	0	1	4	0	16	2	0	1	0	1.000	0	9	1.04
	Denver	AAA	44	1	0	27	77	357	87	49	43	4	6	3	3	39	7	64	7	0	9	6	.600	0	3	5.03
1993	New Orleans	AAA	52	0	0	33	70.1	296	68	34	32	9	3	2	9	17	2	72	3	1	5	3	.625	0	10	4.09
1994	Louisville	AAA	41	20	2	10	146.1	633	131	69	64	12	9	3	16	59	2	105	13	0	9	8	.529	1	1	3.94
	8 Min. YEARS		297	123	6	105	997.1	4273	887	479	407	63	41	24	76	391	23	672	86	12	71	52	.577	3	28	3.67

Bill Wissler

Pitches: Right **Bats:** Right **Pos:** P   **Ht:** 6'3" **Wt:** 205 **Born:** 08/27/70 **Age:** 24

Year	Team	Lg	G	GS	CG	GF	IP	BFP	H	R	ER	HR	SH	SF	HB	TBB	IBB	SO	WP	Bk	W	L	Pct.	ShO	Sv	ERA
1992	Kenosha	A	21	7	1	3	74	294	52	22	11	0	2	1	3	16	0	59	5	6	4	3	.571	1	0	1.34
	Orlando	AA	13	13	5	0	82.1	333	74	36	34	9	3	3	2	18	0	56	2	5	3	8	.273	1	0	3.72
1993	Nashville	AA	29	25	2	1	175.1	731	169	88	77	23	5	6	6	48	2	115	7	0	10	10	.500	0	0	3.95
1994	Salt Lake	AAA	53	3	0	24	92.1	434	125	68	65	14	5	3	4	37	7	64	2	1	5	6	.455	0	5	6.34
	3 Min. YEARS		116	48	8	28	424	1792	420	214	187	46	15	13	15	119	9	294	16	12	22	27	.449	2	5	3.97

Shannon Withem

Pitches: Right **Bats:** Right **Pos:** P   **Ht:** 6'3" **Wt:** 185 **Born:** 09/21/72 **Age:** 22

Year	Team	Lg	G	GS	CG	GF	IP	BFP	H	R	ER	HR	SH	SF	HB	TBB	IBB	SO	WP	Bk	W	L	Pct.	ShO	Sv	ERA
1990	Bristol	R	14	13	0	0	62	288	70	43	37	4	0	0	5	35	1	48	12	2	3	9	.250	0	0	5.37
1991	Fayettevlle	A	11	11	0	0	47.2	241	71	53	45	2	2	0	0	30	0	19	8	0	2	6	.250	0	0	8.50
	Niagara Fls	A	8	3	0	2	27	115	26	12	10	0	0	2	2	11	0	17	2	0	1	2	.333	0	0	3.33
1992	Fayettevlle	A	22	2	0	8	38	173	40	23	20	3	2	2	4	20	0	34	9	2	1	3	.250	0	2	4.74
1993	Lakeland	A	16	16	2	0	113	462	108	47	43	5	1	5	5	24	0	62	3	0	10	2	.833	1	0	3.42
1994	Trenton	AA	25	25	5	0	178	735	190	80	68	10	4	4	4	37	0	135	5	2	7	12	.368	1	0	3.44
	5 Min. YEARS		96	70	7	11	465.2	2014	505	258	223	24	9	13	20	157	1	315	39	6	24	34	.414	2	2	4.31

Mat Witkowski

Bats: Right **Throws:** Right **Pos:** 2B   **Ht:** 6'0" **Wt:** 175 **Born:** 02/05/70 **Age:** 25

Year	Team	Lg	G	AB	H	2B	3B	HR	TB	R	RBI	TBB	IBB	SO	HBP	SH	SF	SB	CS	SB%	GDP	Avg	OBP	SLG
1988	Padres	R	51	201	65	5	3	0	76	37	25	16	1	32	3	2	1	17	6	.74	1	.323	.380	.378

Year	Team	Lg	G	AB	H	2B	3B	HR	TB	R	RBI	TBB	IBB	SO	HBP	SH	SF	SB	CS	SB%	GDP	Avg	OBP	SLG
	Spokane	A	1	1	0	0	0	0	0	1	0	0	0	1	0	0	0	0	0	.00	0	.000	.000	.000
1989	Chston-Sc	A	119	448	127	18	5	0	155	67	44	65	4	81	4	8	1	26	15	.63	4	.283	.378	.346
1990	Waterloo	A	128	470	119	24	2	1	150	75	55	59	3	104	6	5	7	19	14	.58	13	.253	.339	.319
1991	High Desert	A	129	485	129	17	8	6	180	80	56	60	2	81	6	6	3	24	11	.69	13	.266	.352	.371
1992	Wichita	AA	125	431	117	13	4	6	156	61	48	33	2	80	4	2	4	11	11	.50	8	.271	.326	.362
	Las Vegas	AAA	5	16	3	0	1	0	5	1	0	3	0	2	0	0	0	0	0	.00	1	.188	.316	.313
1993	Las Vegas	AAA	91	286	81	6	3	1	96	49	35	33	1	42	0	4	0	10	2	.83	8	.283	.357	.336
1994	Las Vegas	AAA	7	12	2	0	0	0	2	1	1	0	0	3	0	1	0	1	0	1.00	0	.167	.167	.167
	Wichita	AA	88	284	73	9	1	3	93	31	27	23	1	49	1	4	3	10	8	.56	8	.257	.312	.327
	7 Min. YEARS		744	2634	716	92	27	17	913	403	291	292	14	475	24	32	19	118	67	.64	56	.272	.348	.347

Steve Wojciechowski

Pitches: Left   Bats: Left   Pos: P Ht: 6'2" Wt: 185 Born: 07/29/70 Age: 24

			HOW MUCH HE PITCHED						WHAT HE GAVE UP												THE RESULTS					
Year	Team	Lg	G	GS	CG	GF	IP	BFP	H	R	ER	HR	SH	SF	HB	TBB	IBB	SO	WP	Bk	W	L	Pct.	ShO	Sv	ERA
1991	Sou Oregon	A	16	11	0	1	67	311	74	45	28	4	4	2	1	29	2	50	6	1	2	5	.286	0	0	3.76
1992	Modesto	A	14	14	0	0	66.1	282	60	32	26	2	2	3	1	27	0	53	5	2	6	3	.667	0	0	3.53
1993	Modesto	A	14	14	1	0	84.2	341	64	29	24	3	3	2	0	36	0	52	1	1	8	2	.800	1	0	2.55
	Huntsville	AA	13	13	1	0	67.2	310	91	50	40	6	1	5	2	30	1	52	5	1	4	6	.400	1	0	5.32
1994	Huntsville	AA	27	26	1	1	177	716	148	72	61	7	7	3	0	62	1	114	10	2	10	5	.667	0	0	3.10
	4 Min. YEARS		84	78	3	2	462.2	1960	437	228	179	22	17	15	4	184	4	321	27	7	30	21	.588	2	0	3.48

Jerry Wolak

Bats: Right   Throws: Right   Pos: OF Ht: 5'10" Wt: 170 Born: 07/27/70 Age: 24

			BATTING															BASERUNNING				PERCENTAGES		
Year	Team	Lg	G	AB	H	2B	3B	HR	TB	R	RBI	TBB	IBB	SO	HBP	SH	SF	SB	CS	SB%	GDP	Avg	OBP	SLG
1988	White Sox	R	41	144	46	6	0	0	52	18	10	7	0	17	0	1	1	10	6	.63	2	.319	.349	.361
1989	Utica	A	57	223	61	13	5	0	84	28	24	12	0	35	4	1	0	12	4	.75	3	.274	.322	.377
1990	South Bend	A	121	352	98	17	0	1	118	48	28	37	1	68	6	4	2	11	15	.42	8	.278	.355	.335
1991	Sarasota	A	110	326	95	17	1	3	123	36	22	14	0	62	3	13	0	22	8	.73	3	.291	.327	.377
1992	Sarasota	A	90	332	96	23	5	5	144	47	39	14	4	54	5	9	2	17	14	.55	3	.289	.326	.434
	Birmingham	AA	46	169	50	13	1	0	65	18	13	8	0	25	2	1	0	5	2	.71	4	.296	.335	.385
1993	Birmingham	AA	137	525	160	35	4	9	230	78	64	26	2	95	8	2	4	16	12	.57	11	.305	.345	.438
1994	Nashville	AAA	111	394	101	21	2	8	150	42	35	15	0	75	4	7	2	6	4	.60	7	.256	.289	.381
	7 Min. YEARS		713	2465	707	145	18	26	966	315	235	133	7	431	32	38	11	99	65	.60	41	.287	.330	.392

Bob Wolcott

Pitches: Right   Bats: Right   Pos: P Ht: 6'0" Wt: 190 Born: 09/08/73 Age: 21

			HOW MUCH HE PITCHED						WHAT HE GAVE UP												THE RESULTS					
Year	Team	Lg	G	GS	CG	GF	IP	BFP	H	R	ER	HR	SH	SF	HB	TBB	IBB	SO	WP	Bk	W	L	Pct.	ShO	Sv	ERA
1992	Bellingham	A	9	7	0	2	22.1	105	25	18	17	4	0	0	2	19	0	17	3	2	0	1	.000	0	0	6.85
1993	Bellingham	A	15	15	1	0	95.1	386	70	31	28	7	1	2	6	26	1	79	6	1	8	4	.667	0	0	2.64
1994	Calgary	AAA	1	1	0	0	6	25	6	2	2	1	0	0	0	3	0	5	0	0	0	1	.000	0	0	3.00
	Riverside	A	26	26	5	0	180.2	761	173	75	57	11	4	4	5	50	4	142	5	0	14	8	.636	1	0	2.84
	3 Min. YEARS		51	49	6	2	304.1	1277	274	126	104	23	5	6	13	98	5	243	14	3	22	14	.611	1	0	3.08

Joel Wolfe

Bats: Right   Throws: Right   Pos: OF Ht: 6'3" Wt: 205 Born: 06/18/70 Age: 25

			BATTING															BASERUNNING				PERCENTAGES		
Year	Team	Lg	G	AB	H	2B	3B	HR	TB	R	RBI	TBB	IBB	SO	HBP	SH	SF	SB	CS	SB%	GDP	Avg	OBP	SLG
1991	Sou Oregon	A	59	251	76	17	3	2	105	49	34	25	0	28	3	0	0	19	5	.79	8	.303	.373	.418
1992	Reno	A	122	463	118	18	5	1	149	80	44	59	1	72	0	4	2	19	13	.59	15	.255	.338	.322
1993	Modesto	A	87	300	105	29	1	6	154	54	56	51	0	42	6	0	6	18	14	.56	5	.350	.446	.513
	Huntsville	AA	36	134	40	6	0	3	55	20	18	13	1	24	0	1	0	6	3	.67	5	.299	.361	.410
1994	Huntsville	AA	121	436	120	26	3	5	167	65	57	61	2	79	4	6	7	26	10	.72	13	.275	.364	.383
	4 Min. YEARS		425	1584	459	96	12	17	630	268	209	209	4	245	13	11	15	88	45	.66	46	.290	.374	.398

Mike Wolff

Bats: Right   Throws: Right   Pos: OF Ht: 6'1" Wt: 195 Born: 12/19/70 Age: 24

			BATTING															BASERUNNING				PERCENTAGES		
Year	Team	Lg	G	AB	H	2B	3B	HR	TB	R	RBI	TBB	IBB	SO	HBP	SH	SF	SB	CS	SB%	GDP	Avg	OBP	SLG
1992	Boise	A	68	244	66	12	1	11	113	49	39	32	1	60	6	1	2	5	5	.50	0	.270	.366	.463
1993	Cedar Rapds	A	120	407	100	18	5	17	179	63	72	74	1	104	2	5	5	8	8	.50	4	.246	.361	.440
1994	Midland	AA	113	397	115	30	1	13	186	64	58	54	3	91	6	5	6	10	9	.53	4	.290	.378	.469
	3 Min. YEARS		301	1048	281	60	7	41	478	176	169	160	5	255	14	11	13	23	22	.51	8	.268	.368	.456

Doug Wollenburg

Bats: Right   Throws: Right   Pos: SS Ht: 6'2" Wt: 185 Born: 10/11/70 Age: 24

			BATTING															BASERUNNING				PERCENTAGES		
Year	Team	Lg	G	AB	H	2B	3B	HR	TB	R	RBI	TBB	IBB	SO	HBP	SH	SF	SB	CS	SB%	GDP	Avg	OBP	SLG
1992	Idaho Falls	R	69	257	78	10	1	4	102	43	43	24	1	29	4	1	2	11	5	.69	5	.304	.369	.397
1993	Durham	A	113	361	108	21	4	5	152	49	42	27	2	61	6	13	3	6	7	.46	4	.299	.355	.421
1994	Greenville	AA	91	246	57	15	2	2	82	31	19	20	0	44	7	7	4	3	4	.43	9	.232	.303	.333
	3 Min. YEARS		273	864	243	46	7	11	336	123	104	71	3	134	17	21	9	20	16	.56	18	.281	.344	.389

Jason Wood

Bats: Right Throws: Right Pos: SS   Ht: 6'1" Wt: 170 Born: 12/16/69 Age: 25

Year	Team	Lg	G	AB	H	2B	3B	HR	TB	R	RBI	TBB	IBB	SO	HBP	SH	SF	SB	CS	SB%	GDP	Avg	OBP	SLG
1991	Sou Oregon	A	44	142	44	3	4	3	64	30	23	28	0	30	2	2	3	5	2	.71	0	.310	.423	.451
1992	Modesto	A	128	454	105	28	3	6	157	66	49	40	1	106	4	3	5	5	4	.56	15	.231	.296	.346
1993	Huntsville	AA	103	370	85	21	2	3	119	44	36	33	0	97	2	9	3	2	4	.33	7	.230	.294	.322
1994	Huntsville	AA	134	468	128	29	2	6	179	54	84	46	1	83	6	5	15	3	6	.33	9	.274	.336	.382
	4 Min. YEARS		409	1434	362	81	11	18	519	194	192	147	2	316	14	19	26	15	16	.48	31	.252	.323	.362

Ted Wood

Bats: Left Throws: Left Pos: OF   Ht: 6'2" Wt: 178 Born: 01/04/67 Age: 28

Year	Team	Lg	G	AB	H	2B	3B	HR	TB	R	RBI	TBB	IBB	SO	HBP	SH	SF	SB	CS	SB%	GDP	Avg	OBP	SLG
1989	Shreveport	AA	114	349	90	13	1	0	105	44	43	51	2	72	6	10	3	9	7	.56	8	.258	.359	.301
1990	Shreveport	AA	131	456	121	22	11	17	216	81	72	74	5	76	7	4	2	17	8	.68	8	.265	.375	.474
1991	Phoenix	AAA	137	512	159	38	6	11	242	90	109	86	4	96	4	0	10	12	7	.63	13	.311	.407	.473
1992	Phoenix	AAA	110	418	127	24	7	7	186	70	63	48	4	74	4	2	5	9	9	.50	5	.304	.377	.445
1993	Ottawa	AAA	83	231	59	11	4	1	81	39	21	38	3	54	2	2	1	12	2	.86	4	.255	.364	.351
1994	Ottawa	AAA	125	412	115	25	8	13	195	63	59	48	7	79	2	2	5	4	5	.44	13	.279	.353	.473
1991	San Francisco	NL	10	25	3	0	0	0	3	0	1	2	0	11	0	1	0	0	0	.00	0	.120	.185	.120
1992	San Francisco	NL	24	58	12	2	0	1	17	5	3	6	0	15	1	2	0	0	0	.00	4	.207	.292	.293
1993	Montreal	NL	13	26	5	1	0	0	6	4	3	3	1	3	0	3	0	0	0	.00	0	.192	.276	.231
	6 Min. YEARS		700	2378	671	133	37	49	1025	387	367	345	25	451	25	20	26	63	38	.62	51	.282	.375	.431
	3 Maj. YEARS		47	109	20	3	0	1	26	9	7	11	1	29	1	6	0	0	0	.00	4	.183	.264	.239

Chris Woodfin

Pitches: Right Bats: Right Pos: P   Ht: 6'1" Wt: 190 Born: 02/23/68 Age: 27

| | | | HOW MUCH HE PITCHED | | | | | WHAT HE GAVE UP | | | | | | | | | | THE RESULTS | | | | | |
Year	Team	Lg	G	GS	CG	GF	IP	BFP	H	R	ER	HR	SH	SF	HB	TBB	IBB	SO	WP	Bk	W	L	Pct.	ShO	Sv	ERA
1991	White Sox	R	13	1	0	10	26.1	104	19	7	7	0	1	0	0	7	0	24	0	0	1	0	1.000	0	4	2.39
	South Bend	A	3	0	0	2	4.2	24	5	4	3	0	1	1	0	5	3	5	3	0	0	2	.000	0	1	5.79
1992	South Bend	A	36	0	0	19	59.1	258	53	27	18	1	6	0	4	27	1	82	6	0	3	6	.333	0	5	2.73
1993	White Sox	R	4	0	0	2	5	17	1	1	0	0	0	0	0	0	0	7	0	0	1	0	1.000	0	0	0.00
	South Bend	A	11	0	0	7	16.2	63	10	3	3	1	0	0	1	3	0	34	0	0	0	0	.000	0	4	1.62
1994	Pr. William	A	29	0	0	26	28.2	130	21	16	6	1	1	2	1	18	1	43	4	0	2	4	.333	0	12	1.88
	Birmingham	AA	13	0	0	13	15	63	9	5	5	0	0	0	0	9	1	19	1	0	1	1	.500	0	8	3.00
	4 Min. YEARS		109	1	0	79	155.2	659	118	63	42	3	9	3	6	69	6	214	14	0	8	13	.381	0	34	2.43

Tyrone Woods

Bats: Right Throws: Right Pos: OF   Ht: 6'1" Wt: 190 Born: 08/19/69 Age: 25

Year	Team	Lg	G	AB	H	2B	3B	HR	TB	R	RBI	TBB	IBB	SO	HBP	SH	SF	SB	CS	SB%	GDP	Avg	OBP	SLG
1988	Expos	R	43	149	18	2	0	2	26	12	12	7	0	47	0	0	2	2	4	.33	3	.121	.158	.174
1989	Jamestown	A	63	209	55	6	4	9	96	23	29	20	1	59	2	0	3	8	9	.47	5	.263	.329	.459
1990	Rockford	A	123	455	110	27	5	8	171	50	46	45	1	121	1	0	3	5	7	.42	13	.242	.310	.376
1991	Wst Plm Bch	A	96	295	65	15	3	5	101	34	31	28	0	85	3	0	3	4	4	.50	5	.220	.292	.342
1992	Rockford	A	101	374	109	22	3	12	173	54	47	34	4	83	1	0	6	15	6	.71	6	.291	.347	.463
	Wst Plm Bch	A	15	56	16	1	2	1	24	7	7	6	0	15	1	0	1	2	1	.67	1	.286	.359	.429
	Harrisburg	AA	4	4	0	0	0	0	0	0	0	0	0	3	0	0	0	0	0	.00	0	.000	.000	.000
1993	Harrisburg	AA	106	318	80	15	1	16	145	51	59	35	0	77	2	2	1	4	1	.80	8	.252	.329	.456
1994	Ottawa	AAA	88	294	66	12	0	6	96	34	30	26	4	76	2	0	3	2	1	.67	8	.224	.289	.327
	Harrisburg	AA	38	133	42	16	2	5	77	23	28	13	2	29	1	0	2	2	1	.67	3	.316	.376	.579
	7 Min. YEARS		677	2287	561	116	20	64	909	288	289	214	12	595	13	2	24	44	34	.56	52	.245	.310	.397

Tracy Woodson

Bats: Right Throws: Right Pos: 3B   Ht: 6'3" Wt: 216 Born: 10/05/62 Age: 32

Year	Team	Lg	G	AB	H	2B	3B	HR	TB	R	RBI	TBB	IBB	SO	HBP	SH	SF	SB	CS	SB%	GDP	Avg	OBP	SLG
1984	Vero Beach	A	76	256	56	9	0	4	77	29	36	27	2	41	6	0	4	7	4	.64	5	.219	.304	.301
1985	Vero Beach	A	138	504	126	30	4	9	191	55	62	50	6	78	9	5	8	10	5	.67	12	.250	.324	.379
1986	San Antonio	AA	131	495	133	27	3	18	220	65	90	33	7	59	5	1	1	4	1	.80	11	.269	.320	.444
1987	Albuquerque	AAA	67	259	75	13	2	5	107	37	44	17	0	22	2	0	4	1	1	.50	12	.290	.333	.413
1988	Albuquerque	AAA	85	313	100	21	1	17	174	46	73	39	4	48	2	1	4	1	3	.25	8	.319	.394	.556
1989	Albuquerque	AAA	89	325	95	21	0	14	158	49	59	32	2	40	4	0	3	2	1	.67	7	.292	.360	.486
1990	Vancouver	AAA	131	480	128	22	5	17	211	70	81	50	2	70	6	0	5	6	4	.60	18	.267	.340	.440
1991	Richmond	AAA	120	441	122	20	3	6	166	43	56	28	0	43	2	3	8	1	4	.20	18	.277	.317	.376
1992	Louisville	AAA	109	412	122	23	2	12	185	62	59	24	2	46	2	5	4	4	5	.44	7	.296	.335	.449
1994	Rochester	AAA	75	279	66	15	1	5	98	26	36	16	0	32	0	0	1	2	0	1.00	11	.237	.277	.351
	Louisville	AAA	43	158	55	16	1	7	94	29	26	11	2	12	0	0	0	0	1	.00	6	.348	.391	.595
1987	Los Angeles	NL	53	136	31	8	1	1	44	14	11	9	2	21	2	0	1	1	1	.50	2	.228	.284	.324
1988	Los Angeles	NL	65	173	43	4	1	3	58	15	15	7	1	32	1	0	2	1	2	.33	4	.249	.279	.335

	Lg	G	AB	H	2B	3B	HR	TB	R	RBI	TBB	IBB	SO	HBP	SH	SF	SB	CS	SB%	GDP	Avg	OBP	SLG
1989 Los Angeles	NL	4	6	0	0	0	0	0	0	0	0	0	1	0	0	0	0	0	.00	2	.000	.000	.000
1992 St. Louis	NL	31	114	35	8	0	1	46	9	22	3	0	10	1	1	0	0	0	.00	1	.307	.331	.404
1993 St. Louis	NL	62	77	16	2	0	0	18	4	2	1	0	14	0	0	1	0	0	.00	1	.208	.215	.234
10 Min. YEARS		1064	3922	1078	217	22	114	1681	511	622	327	27	491	38	15	42	38	27	.58	118	.275	.333	.429
5 Maj. YEARS		215	506	125	22	2	5	166	42	50	20	3	78	4	1	4	2	3	.40	10	.247	.279	.328

Steve Worrell

Pitches: Left Bats: Left Pos: P Ht: 6'2" Wt: 190 Born: 11/25/69 Age: 25

		HOW MUCH HE PITCHED						WHAT HE GAVE UP							THE RESULTS									
Year Team	Lg	G	GS	CG	GF	IP	BFP	H	R	ER	HR	SH	SF	HB	TBB	IBB	SO	WP	Bk	W	L	Pct.	ShO	Sv	ERA
1992 White Sox	R	2	0	0	2	3	10	1	0	0	0	0	0	0	0	0	5	0	0	0	0	.000	0	2	0.00
Utica	A	4	0	0	2	10	45	11	5	4	0	0	1	1	2	0	10	3	0	1	0	1.000	0	1	3.60
South Bend	A	14	0	0	5	22.1	91	17	2	0	0	1	0	0	7	0	21	0	0	1	1	.500	0	2	0.00
1993 South Bend	A	36	0	0	24	59	231	37	12	11	0	7	0	2	23	3	57	2	0	4	2	.667	0	10	1.68
1994 Pr. William	A	26	0	0	20	48	199	37	23	19	6	1	1	3	19	1	47	2	1	4	2	.667	0	3	3.56
Birmingham	AA	7	0	0	1	10.1	35	2	0	0	0	0	0	0	5	0	6	0	0	1	0	1.000	0	0	0.00
3 Min. YEARS		89	0	0	54	152.2	611	105	42	34	6	9	2	6	56	4	146	7	1	11	5	.688	0	18	2.00

Craig Worthington

Bats: Right Throws: Right Pos: 3B Ht: 6' 0" Wt: 200 Born: 04/17/65 Age: 30

		BATTING															BASERUNNING				PERCENTAGES		
Year Team	Lg	G	AB	H	2B	3B	HR	TB	R	RBI	TBB	IBB	SO	HBP	SH	SF	SB	CS	SB%	GDP	Avg	OBP	SLG
1985 Bluefield	R	39	129	44	9	1	7	76	33	20	10	1	19	2	3	1	3	2	.60	3	.341	.394	.589
1986 Hagerstown	A	132	480	144	35	1	15	226	85	105	82	7	58	2	0	8	7	12	.37	12	.300	.399	.471
1987 Rochester	AAA	109	383	99	14	1	7	136	46	50	32	3	62	2	3	2	0	2	.00	10	.258	.317	.355
1988 Rochester	AAA	121	430	105	25	1	16	180	53	73	39	2	93	0	0	6	3	1	.75	13	.244	.303	.419
1991 Rochester	AAA	19	57	17	4	0	2	27	10	9	6	0	8	1	0	0	0	0	.00	3	.298	.375	.474
1992 Colo Sprngs	AAA	90	319	94	25	0	6	137	47	57	33	1	67	4	1	3	0	1	.00	11	.295	.365	.429
1993 Iowa	AAA	132	469	128	23	0	13	190	63	66	59	3	91	1	1	2	1	1	.50	15	.273	.354	.405
1994 Iowa	AAA	122	365	105	18	0	17	174	58	69	55	4	74	6	3	2	4	4	.50	15	.288	.388	.477
1988 Baltimore	AL	26	81	15	2	0	2	23	5	4	9	0	24	0	0	0	1	0	1.00	2	.185	.267	.284
1989 Baltimore	AL	145	497	123	23	0	15	191	57	70	61	2	114	4	3	1	1	2	.33	10	.247	.334	.384
1990 Baltimore	AL	133	425	96	17	0	8	137	46	44	63	2	96	3	7	3	1	2	.33	13	.226	.328	.322
1991 Baltimore	AL	31	102	23	3	0	4	38	11	12	12	0	14	1	1	0	0	1	.00	3	.225	.313	.373
1992 Cleveland	AL	9	24	4	0	0	0	4	0	2	2	0	4	0	0	0	0	0	.00	0	.167	.231	.167
8 Min. YEARS		764	2632	736	153	4	83	1146	395	449	316	21	472	18	11	24	18	23	.44	82	.280	.358	.435
5 Maj. YEARS		344	1129	261	45	0	29	393	119	132	147	4	252	8	11	4	3	6	.33	28	.231	.323	.348

Julian Yan

Bats: Right Throws: Right Pos: 1B Ht: 6'4" Wt: 190 Born: 07/24/65 Age: 29

		BATTING															BASERUNNING				PERCENTAGES		
Year Team	Lg	G	AB	H	2B	3B	HR	TB	R	RBI	TBB	IBB	SO	HBP	SH	SF	SB	CS	SB%	GDP	Avg	OBP	SLG
1986 St.Cathrnes	A	73	282	77	7	2	15	133	40	49	25	1	72	2	0	1	2	1	.67	5	.273	.335	.472
1987 Myrtle Bch	A	132	481	111	21	2	17	187	67	71	41	1	129	8	0	5	3	3	.50	7	.231	.299	.389
1988 Dunedin	A	136	498	124	21	5	16	203	55	75	37	3	115	14	0	5	0	1	.00	12	.249	.316	.408
1989 Dunedin	A	133	460	115	21	5	24	218	68	72	47	5	130	10	1	4	2	4	.33	7	.250	.330	.474
1990 Knoxville	AA	113	389	95	18	3	15	164	55	48	25	1	108	6	0	4	2	1	.67	7	.244	.297	.422
1991 Knoxville	AA	103	351	98	16	3	16	168	45	61	22	0	108	5	3	2	4	4	.33	9	.279	.329	.479
1992 Knoxville	AA	111	392	106	23	4	16	185	51	49	28	6	93	6	0	5	1	5	.17	12	.270	.325	.472
1993 Syracuse	AAA	91	278	74	9	5	7	114	30	36	14	0	91	1	1	3	3	2	.60	6	.266	.301	.410
1994 Syracuse	AAA	34	81	21	4	2	2	35	13	11	9	0	17	0	0	0	2	1	.67	4	.259	.333	.432
9 Min. YEARS		926	3212	821	140	31	128	1407	424	472	248	17	863	52	5	29	17	22	.44	69	.256	.317	.438

Kip Yaughn

Pitches: Right Bats: Right Pos: P Ht: 6'1" Wt: 180 Born: 07/20/69 Age: 25

		HOW MUCH HE PITCHED						WHAT HE GAVE UP							THE RESULTS									
Year Team	Lg	G	GS	CG	GF	IP	BFP	H	R	ER	HR	SH	SF	HB	TBB	IBB	SO	WP	Bk	W	L	Pct.	ShO	Sv	ERA
1990 Wausau	A	10	10	0	0	51	226	46	32	30	5	1	3	3	29	0	47	7	2	2	4	.333	0	0	5.29
1991 Frederick	A	27	27	1	0	162	721	168	84	71	15	1	4	7	76	0	155	11	3	11	8	.579	0	0	3.94
1992 Hagerstown	AA	18	18	5	0	116.1	465	88	52	45	6	0	2	6	33	0	106	4	3	7	8	.467	0	0	3.48
1993 High Desert	A	6	6	0	0	21	101	25	17	16	3	0	4	3	13	0	13	3	0	0	0	.000	0	0	6.86
Edmonton	AAA	1	1	0	0	5	19	6	0	0	0	0	0	0	1	0	2	0	0	1	0	1.000	0	0	0.00
1994 Portland	AA	36	14	0	7	108.1	480	112	70	57	14	6	8	9	51	2	83	1	3	7	7	.500	0	3	4.74
5 Min. YEARS		98	76	6	7	463.2	2012	445	259	219	43	8	21	28	203	2	406	26	11	28	27	.509	0	3	4.25

Eric Yelding

Bats: Right Throws: Right Pos: SS-OF Ht: 5'11" Wt: 165 Born: 02/22/65 Age: 30

		BATTING															BASERUNNING				PERCENTAGES		
Year Team	Lg	G	AB	H	2B	3B	HR	TB	R	RBI	TBB	IBB	SO	HBP	SH	SF	SB	CS	SB%	GDP	Avg	OBP	SLG
1984 Medicne Hat	R	67	304	94	14	6	4	132	61	29	26	0	46	0	0	3	31	11	.74	3	.309	.361	.434
1985 Kinston	A	135	526	137	14	4	2	165	59	31	33	0	70	4	5	3	62	26	.70	4	.260	.307	.314
1986 Ventura	A	131	560	157	14	4	4	197	83	40	33	0	84	0	6	2	41	18	.69	6	.280	.319	.352
1987 Knoxville	AA	39	150	30	6	1	0	38	23	7	12	0	25	1	1	1	10	5	.67	4	.200	.262	.253
Myrtle Bch	A	88	357	109	12	2	1	128	53	31	18	0	30	4	1	4	73	13	.85	5	.305	.342	.359

Year Team	Lg	G	AB	H	2B	3B	HR	TB	R	RBI	TBB	IBB	SO	HBP	SH	SF	SB	CS	SB%	GDP	Avg	OBP	SLG
1988 Syracuse	AAA	138	556	139	15	2	1	161	69	38	36	3	102	0	2	0	59	23	.72	4	.250	.296	.290
1991 Tucson	AAA	11	43	17	3	0	0	20	6	3	4	0	4	2	0	0	4	2	.67	0	.395	.469	.465
1992 Tucson	AAA	57	218	63	8	5	0	81	30	23	13	0	50	0	2	1	17	9	.65	6	.289	.328	.372
Vancouver	AAA	36	120	26	3	0	0	29	17	6	13	0	17	0	4	2	15	2	.88	2	.217	.289	.242
1994 Iowa	AAA	29	73	18	2	0	0	20	10	6	3	0	17	0	0	0	4	2	.67	2	.247	.276	.274
1989 Houston	NL	70	90	21	2	0	0	23	19	9	7	0	19	1	2	2	11	5	.69	2	.233	.290	.256
1990 Houston	NL	142	511	130	9	5	1	152	69	28	39	1	87	0	4	5	64	25	.72	11	.254	.305	.297
1991 Houston	NL	78	276	67	11	1	1	83	19	20	13	3	46	0	3	1	11	9	.55	4	.243	.276	.301
1992 Houston	NL	9	8	2	0	0	0	2	1	0	0	0	3	0	0	0	0	0	.00	0	.250	.250	.250
1993 Chicago	NL	69	108	22	5	1	1	32	14	10	11	2	22	0	4	0	3	2	.60	3	.204	.277	.296
8 Min. YEARS		731	2907	790	91	27	12	971	411	214	191	6	445	11	21	15	316	111	.74	36	.272	.318	.334
5 Maj. YEARS		368	993	242	27	7	3	292	122	67	70	6	177	1	13	8	89	41	.68	20	.244	.292	.294

Mark Yockey

Pitches: Left   Bats: Left   Pos: P   Ht: 6'3"   Wt: 200   Born: 05/25/68   Age: 27

		HOW MUCH HE PITCHED						WHAT HE GAVE UP												THE RESULTS					
Year Team	Lg	G	GS	CG	GF	IP	BFP	H	R	ER	HR	SH	SF	HB	TBB	IBB	SO	WP	Bk	W	L	Pct.	ShO	Sv	ERA
1990 Everett	A	23	1	0	14	46.2	197	45	22	20	2	2	1	3	15	0	53	0	5	5	2	.714	0	3	3.86
1991 Clinton	A	36	2	0	7	65	283	60	29	21	0	2	3	1	27	0	72	2	1	3	2	.600	0	1	2.91
1992 Shreveport	AA	42	1	0	13	50	224	53	23	23	2	3	6	2	28	4	35	1	0	4	2	.667	0	0	4.14
1993 Shreveport	AA	48	0	0	19	71.2	286	60	23	17	2	5	0	3	20	0	60	2	1	3	6	.333	0	4	2.13
1994 Portland	AA	18	0	0	8	28	140	39	26	24	8	0	1	3	18	1	24	0	0	1	1	.000	0	0	7.71
5 Min. YEARS		167	4	0	61	261.1	1130	257	123	105	14	12	11	12	108	5	244	5	7	15	13	.536	0	8	3.62

Dmitri Young

Bats: Both   Throws: Right   Pos: SS   Ht: 6'2"   Wt: 215   Born: 10/11/73   Age: 21

		BATTING															BASERUNNING				PERCENTAGES		
Year Team	Lg	G	AB	H	2B	3B	HR	TB	R	RBI	TBB	IBB	SO	HBP	SH	SF	SB	CS	SB%	GDP	Avg	OBP	SLG
1991 Johnson Cty	R	37	129	33	10	0	2	49	22	22	21	1	28	2	0	2	2	1	.67	1	.256	.364	.380
1992 Springfield	A	135	493	153	36	6	14	243	74	72	51	3	94	5	0	4	14	13	.52	9	.310	.378	.493
1993 St.Pete	A	69	270	85	13	3	5	119	31	43	24	3	28	2	0	5	3	4	.43	7	.315	.369	.441
Arkansas	AA	45	166	41	11	2	3	65	13	21	9	1	29	2	0	0	4	4	.50	5	.247	.294	.392
1994 Arkansas	AA	125	453	123	33	2	8	184	53	54	36	14	60	5	1	3	0	3	.00	6	.272	.330	.406
4 Min. YEARS		411	1511	435	103	13	32	660	193	212	141	22	239	16	1	14	23	25	.48	28	.288	.352	.437

Pete Young

Pitches: Right   Bats: Right   Pos: P   Ht: 6'0"   Wt: 225   Born: 03/19/68   Age: 27

		HOW MUCH HE PITCHED						WHAT HE GAVE UP												THE RESULTS					
Year Team	Lg	G	GS	CG	GF	IP	BFP	H	R	ER	HR	SH	SF	HB	TBB	IBB	SO	WP	Bk	W	L	Pct.	ShO	Sv	ERA
1989 Jamestown	A	18	10	0	8	65	269	63	18	14	2	0	1	5	14	0	62	6	0	5	2	.714	0	4	1.94
1990 Wst Plm Bch	A	39	12	0	25	109.1	453	106	36	30	4	3	3	2	27	1	62	6	0	8	3	.727	0	19	2.47
1991 Sumter	A	1	0	0	0	1	5	1	1	1	0	0	0	0	1	0	2	0	0	0	0	.000	0	0	9.00
Harrisburg	AA	54	0	0	29	90	368	82	28	26	9	4	1	2	24	4	74	1	0	7	5	.583	0	13	2.60
1992 Indianapolis	AAA	36	0	0	20	48.2	216	53	19	19	5	4	3	1	21	3	34	0	0	6	2	.750	0	7	3.51
1993 Ottawa	AAA	48	0	0	16	72.1	311	63	32	30	5	5	4	6	33	10	46	2	0	4	5	.444	0	1	3.73
1994 Pawtucket	AAA	2	0	0	1	6.1	26	7	3	2	1	0	0	0	0	0	4	0	0	0	0	.000	0	0	2.84
New Britain	AA	51	7	0	14	100.1	435	98	57	48	10	4	4	6	38	1	62	6	1	2	3	.400	0	3	4.31
1992 Montreal	NL	13	0	0	6	20.1	85	18	9	9	0	0	2	1	9	2	11	0	0	0	0	.000	0	0	3.98
1993 Montreal	NL	4	0	0	2	5.1	20	4	2	2	1	1	0	0	2	0	3	0	0	1	0	1.000	0	0	3.38
6 Min. YEARS		249	29	0	113	493	2083	473	194	170	35	20	15	22	158	19	346	21	1	32	20	.615	0	47	3.10
2 Maj. YEARS		17	0	0	8	25.2	105	22	11	11	1	1	2	1	9	2	14	1	0	1	0	1.000	0	0	3.86

Ray Young

Pitches: Right   Bats: Right   Pos: P   Ht: 6'3"   Wt: 180   Born: 05/27/64   Age: 31

		HOW MUCH HE PITCHED						WHAT HE GAVE UP												THE RESULTS					
Year Team	Lg	G	GS	CG	GF	IP	BFP	H	R	ER	HR	SH	SF	HB	TBB	IBB	SO	WP	Bk	W	L	Pct.	ShO	Sv	ERA
1984 Great Falls	R	13	8	0	0	47.1	0	53	46	38	4	0	0	2	46	0	47	3	3	3	2	.600	0	0	7.23
1985 Bakersfield	A	19	17	0	1	85.1	0	61	73	54	7	0	0	8	111	0	81	12	1	1	9	.100	0	0	5.70
1986 Bakersfield	A	12	8	0	3	38	205	47	43	39	3	0	2	2	47	0	27	7	2	1	5	.167	0	0	9.24
1987 Dunedin	A	34	5	0	15	95.1	411	62	34	28	3	6	3	2	72	1	69	10	3	3	2	.600	0	0	2.64
1988 Modesto	A	25	19	0	1	98.2	493	70	78	61	3	0	8	4	142	0	78	28	11	8	7	.533	0	0	5.56
1989 Huntsville	AA	29	27	2	0	146.2	653	112	78	64	2	6	4	3	109	0	163	12	12	13	6	.684	2	0	3.93
1990 Tacoma	AAA	28	27	1	0	165	736	155	87	77	8	5	7	4	105	1	137	9	16	14	7	.667	1	0	4.20
1993 Las Vegas	AAA	14	0	0	8	20.2	100	29	15	13	1	4	0	0	8	0	20	3	0	1	2	.333	0	2	5.66
1994 Edmonton	AAA	2	2	0	0	10	45	13	6	6	1	1	0	0	2	0	8	2	0	0	0	.000	0	0	5.40
Tacoma	AAA	8	4	0	2	23.2	120	33	21	19	4	1	1	1	17	2	16	2	2	1	3	.250	0	0	7.23
9 Min. YEARS		184	117	3	30	730.2	2763	635	481	399	36	23	25	26	659	4	646	88	50	45	43	.511	3	2	4.91

Ramon Zapata

Bats: Right   Throws: Right   Pos: INF   Ht: 5'8"   Wt: 155   Born: 01/14/71   Age: 24

		BATTING															BASERUNNING				PERCENTAGES		
Year Team	Lg	G	AB	H	2B	3B	HR	TB	R	RBI	TBB	IBB	SO	HBP	SH	SF	SB	CS	SB%	GDP	Avg	OBP	SLG
1991 Pirates	R	23	78	24	4	1	0	30	23	7	18	0	5	0	1	2	11	1	.92	1	.308	.429	.385

Year Team	Lg	G	AB	H	2B	3B	HR	TB	R	RBI	TBB	IBB	SO	HBP	SH	SF	SB	CS	SB%	GDP	Avg	OBP	SLG
1992 Augusta	A	99	302	55	11	2	0	70	41	22	54	0	75	1	5	2	10	13	.43	3	.182	.306	.232
Welland	A	8	24	5	1	0	0	6	1	0	2	0	9	1	0	0	0	1	.00	1	.208	.296	.250
1993 Augusta	A	81	235	58	10	3	2	80	31	32	37	0	47	3	3	3	6	7	.46	4	.247	.353	.340
1994 Carolina	AA	21	61	16	2	2	1	25	5	7	2	0	13	0	1	0	0	1	.00	2	.262	.286	.410
Salem	A	74	230	66	11	0	4	89	41	25	31	0	36	1	6	1	3	4	.43	6	.287	.373	.387
4 Min. YEARS		306	930	224	39	8	7	300	142	93	144	0	185	6	16	8	30	27	.53	17	.241	.344	.323

Gregg Zaun

Bats: Both   Throws: Right   Pos: C   Ht: 5'10"   Wt: 170   Born: 04/14/71   Age: 24

		BATTING															BASERUNNING				PERCENTAGES		
Year Team	Lg	G	AB	H	2B	3B	HR	TB	R	RBI	TBB	IBB	SO	HBP	SH	SF	SB	CS	SB%	GDP	Avg	OBP	SLG
1990 Wausau	A	37	100	13	0	1	1	18	3	7	7	0	17	1	2	0	0	0	.00	2	.130	.194	.180
Bluefield	R	61	184	57	5	2	2	72	29	21	23	1	15	1	0	1	5	5	.50	2	.310	.388	.391
1991 Kane County	A	113	409	112	17	5	4	151	67	51	50	1	41	2	3	4	4	4	.50	10	.274	.353	.369
1992 Frederick	A	108	383	96	18	6	6	144	54	52	42	0	45	3	1	7	3	5	.38	10	.251	.324	.376
1993 Bowie	AA	79	258	79	10	0	3	98	25	38	27	4	26	1	0	1	4	7	.36	7	.306	.373	.380
Rochester	AAA	21	78	20	4	2	1	31	10	11	6	0	11	0	0	2	0	0	.00	1	.256	.302	.397
1994 Rochester	AAA	123	388	92	16	4	7	137	61	43	56	2	72	4	3	3	4	2	.67	5	.237	.337	.353
5 Min. YEARS		542	1800	469	70	20	24	651	249	223	211	8	227	12	9	18	20	23	.47	37	.261	.339	.362

Clint Zavaras

Pitches: Right   Bats: Right   Pos: P   Ht: 6'1"   Wt: 175   Born: 01/04/67   Age: 28

		HOW MUCH HE PITCHED						WHAT HE GAVE UP												THE RESULTS					
Year Team	Lg	G	GS	CG	GF	IP	BFP	H	R	ER	HR	SH	SF	HB	TBB	IBB	SO	WP	Bk	W	L	Pct.	ShO	Sv	ERA
1985 Bellingham	A	12	11	0	0	56.1	0	49	37	35	2	0	0	1	47	1	62	11	0	4	7	.364	0	0	5.59
1986 Wausau	A	17	17	0	0	91.1	404	68	45	34	5	0	2	8	67	0	98	11	2	6	6	.500	0	0	3.35
1987 Salinas	A	26	26	2	0	139.2	612	102	87	69	6	2	8	8	101	0	180	22	0	7	12	.368	2	0	4.45
1988 Vermont	AA	24	24	2	0	128.2	544	115	67	56	10	1	3	10	54	3	120	6	0	10	7	.588	1	0	3.92
1989 Calgary	AAA	21	19	1	1	110.1	488	105	77	74	10	3	6	8	56	1	89	3	3	6	9	.400	0	0	6.04
1991 San Berndno	A	11	11	0	0	40.1	192	35	25	17	2	1	3	3	37	0	38	7	0	1	3	.250	0	0	3.79
Jacksnville	AA	6	6	0	0	31.1	140	36	18	16	2	1	0	2	10	0	21	2	0	2	2	.500	0	0	4.60
1992 Calgary	AAA	4	4	0	0	13.2	76	24	22	20	1	0	1	0	12	0	5	2	0	1	2	.333	0	0	13.17
Jacksnville	AA	20	20	0	0	109	504	109	68	64	12	6	2	9	67	3	88	7	1	3	11	.214	0	0	5.28
1993 Colo Spmgs	AAA	6	0	0	1	8	40	5	3	2	0	1	1	0	11	0	9	0	0	0	0	.000	0	0	2.25
1994 Calgary	AAA	9	9	0	0	36.1	188	58	40	37	7	0	2	4	22	1	19	0	0	1	3	.250	0	0	9.17
Jacksonvlle	AA	6	6	0	0	34.2	152	44	20	19	4	0	1	2	10	2	20	2	0	1	1	.500	0	0	4.93
1989 Seattle	AL	10	10	0	0	52	231	49	33	30	4	4	1	2	30	1	31	1	0	1	6	.143	0	0	5.19
9 Min. YEARS		162	153	5	2	799.2	3340	750	509	443	61	15	29	55	494	11	749	73	6	42	63	.400	3	0	4.99

Mike Zimmerman

Pitches: Right   Bats: Right   Pos: P   Ht: 6'0"   Wt: 180   Born: 02/06/69   Age: 26

		HOW MUCH HE PITCHED						WHAT HE GAVE UP												THE RESULTS					
Year Team	Lg	G	GS	CG	GF	IP	BFP	H	R	ER	HR	SH	SF	HB	TBB	IBB	SO	WP	Bk	W	L	Pct.	ShO	Sv	ERA
1990 Welland	A	9	0	0	7	13.1	58	8	4	1	0	1	0	1	9	0	22	1	1	2	0	1.000	0	2	0.68
Salem	A	19	0	0	13	25.2	122	28	19	17	1	1	1	5	16	3	24	3	2	1	1	.500	0	5	5.96
1991 Salem	A	49	1	0	44	70	344	51	47	34	1	2	1	14	72	2	63	20	0	4	2	.667	0	9	4.37
1992 Carolina	AA	27	27	1	0	153	673	141	82	65	10	8	7	7	75	2	107	13	4	4	15	.211	0	0	3.82
1993 Carolina	AA	33	0	0	23	45	198	40	26	18	2	1	1	4	21	2	30	2	1	2	3	.400	0	9	3.60
Buffalo	AAA	33	0	0	8	46.1	199	45	23	21	5	4	2	0	28	3	32	2	0	3	1	.750	0	1	4.08
1994 Carolina	AA	16	0	0	15	16.1	72	13	6	5	1	1	0	1	8	0	9	2	0	2	2	.500	0	9	2.76
Buffalo	AAA	19	0	0	4	23.1	99	25	10	9	0	2	0	2	13	1	14	3	0	0	1	.000	0	0	3.47
Edmonton	AAA	9	7	0	1	38.2	179	33	19	15	0	1	3	5	29	0	23	7	1	5	1	.833	0	1	3.49
5 Min. YEARS		214	35	1	115	431.2	1944	384	236	185	20	21	15	39	271	13	324	53	9	23	26	.469	0	39	3.86

Alan Zinter

Bats: Both   Throws: Right   Pos: C   Ht: 6'2"   Wt: 190   Born: 05/19/68   Age: 27

		BATTING															BASERUNNING				PERCENTAGES		
Year Team	Lg	G	AB	H	2B	3B	HR	TB	R	RBI	TBB	IBB	SO	HBP	SH	SF	SB	CS	SB%	GDP	Avg	OBP	SLG
1989 Pittsfield	A	12	41	15	2	1	2	25	11	12	12	0	4	0	0	1	0	0	.00	0	.366	.500	.610
St.Lucie	A	48	159	38	10	0	3	57	17	32	18	2	31	1	1	5	0	1	.00	5	.239	.311	.358
1990 St. Lucie	A	98	333	97	19	6	7	149	63	63	54	1	70	1	0	1	8	1	.89	10	.291	.386	.447
Jackson	AA	6	20	4	1	0	0	5	2	1	3	0	11	0	0	0	1	0	1.00	1	.200	.304	.250
1991 Williamsprt	AA	124	422	93	13	6	9	145	44	54	59	1	106	3	2	2	3	3	.50	10	.220	.319	.344
1992 Binghamton	AA	128	431	96	13	4	16	167	63	50	70	5	117	4	0	7	0	0	.00	7	.223	.337	.387
1993 Binghamton	AA	134	432	113	24	4	24	217	68	87	90	7	105	1	0	5	1	0	1.00	4	.262	.386	.502
1994 Toledo	AAA	134	471	112	29	5	21	214	66	58	69	4	185	7	0	0	13	5	.72	9	.238	.344	.454
6 Min. YEARS		684	2309	568	111	27	82	979	334	357	375	20	629	17	3	19	26	11	.70	40	.246	.353	.424

Eddie Zosky

Bats: Right **Throws:** Right **Pos:** SS **Ht:** 6' 0" **Wt:** 180 **Born:** 02/10/68 **Age:** 27

Year	Team	Lg	G	AB	H	2B	3B	HR	TB	R	RBI	TBB	IBB	SO	HBP	SH	SF	SB	CS	SB%	GDP	Avg	OBP	SLG
1989	Knoxville	AA	56	208	46	5	3	2	63	21	14	10	0	32	0	2	1	1	1	.50	4	.221	.256	.303
1990	Knoxville	AA	115	450	122	20	7	3	165	53	45	26	1	73	5	6	3	3	13	.19	7	.271	.316	.367
1991	Syracuse	AAA	119	511	135	18	4	6	179	69	39	35	1	82	5	7	5	9	4	.69	11	.264	.315	.350
1992	Syracuse	AAA	96	342	79	11	6	4	114	31	38	19	0	53	1	7	4	3	4	.43	10	.231	.270	.333
1993	Hagerstown	A	5	20	2	0	0	0	2	2	1	2	0	1	0	0	1	0	0	.00	1	.100	.174	.100
	Syracuse	AAA	28	93	20	5	0	0	25	9	8	1	0	20	4	2	3	0	1	.00	1	.215	.248	.269
1994	Syracuse	AAA	85	284	75	15	3	7	117	41	37	9	0	46	2	6	5	3	1	.75	8	.264	.287	.412
1991	Toronto	AL	18	27	4	1	1	0	7	2	2	0	0	8	0	1	0	0	0	.00	1	.148	.148	.259
1992	Toronto	AL	8	7	2	0	1	0	4	1	1	0	0	2	0	0	1	0	0	.00	0	.286	.250	.571
6 Min. YEARS			504	1908	479	74	23	22	665	226	182	102	2	307	17	30	22	19	24	.44	42	.251	.292	.349
2 Maj. YEARS			26	34	6	1	2	0	11	3	3	0	0	10	0	1	1	0	0	.00	1	.176	.171	.324

Jon Zuber

Bats: Left **Throws:** Left **Pos:** 1B **Ht:** 6'1" **Wt:** 175 **Born:** 12/10/69 **Age:** 25

Year	Team	Lg	G	AB	H	2B	3B	HR	TB	R	RBI	TBB	IBB	SO	HBP	SH	SF	SB	CS	SB%	GDP	Avg	OBP	SLG
1992	Batavia	A	22	88	30	6	3	1	45	14	21	9	1	11	1	0	1	1	1	.50	1	.341	.404	.511
	Spartanburg	A	54	206	59	13	1	3	83	24	36	33	1	31	1	0	1	3	1	.75	6	.286	.386	.403
1993	Clearwater	A	129	494	152	37	5	5	214	70	69	49	5	47	0	3	4	6	6	.50	15	.308	.367	.433
1994	Reading	AA	138	498	146	29	5	9	212	81	70	71	4	71	1	1	5	2	4	.33	11	.293	.379	.426
3 Min. YEARS			343	1286	387	85	14	18	554	189	196	162	11	160	3	4	11	12	12	.50	33	.301	.378	.431

Single-A & Rookie Stats

This section is one of our favorite parts of the book, and full of hidden gems. Take, for instance, that fellow Mark Littell who pitched in one game for Stockton in 1994. Hmm, name sounds familiar. And 42 years old! Can it be—yes, it's the same Mark Littell who pitched for the Royals back in the 1970s, and who gave up that big home run to Chris Chambliss. It seems that Littell is now a pitching coach in the Brewer system, and there was one day when the Stockton club ran out of pitchers, so all of a sudden it was, "You're in there, Mark." He showed those kids a thing or two, also, pitching a hitless inning and picking up the win. He did give up a balk, but heck, Mark was pitching back in the days when Luis Tiant was allowed to do his mumbo-jumbo on the mound (at least by most American League umpires). Nice work, old-timer.

As always, we still have a few guys with NA for age. This is because Howe didn't have the age in their database when we needed the stats in early October. The abbreviations are the same as in the Career section. Note: Players from the independent leagues (Northern, North Central and Frontier) are not included in this book.

1994 Batting -- Single-A and Rookie Leagues

Player	Lg	A	G	AB	H	2B	3B	HR	TB	R	RBI	TBB	IBB	SO	HBP	SH	SF	SB	CS	SB%	GDP	Avg	OBP	SLG
Abad,Fausto,Sarasota	A	22	111	354	102	20	0	2	128	39	35	42	4	58	5	5	5	2	12	.14	9	.288	.367	.362
Abad,Irvin,Blue Jays	R	22	51	180	39	4	11	0	65	26	17	17	0	40	0	3	1	13	3	.81	3	.217	.283	.361
Abbott,Jeffrey,White Sox	R	22	4	15	7	1	0	1	11	4	3	4	0	0	0	0	0	2	1	.67	1	.467	.579	.733
Hickory			63	224	88	16	6	6	134	47	48	38	1	33	1	1	1	2	1	.67	4	.393	.481	.598
Abbs,Steven,Johnson Cty	R	23	47	153	41	15	1	5	73	31	27	13	0	35	10	0	2	2	0	1.00	0	.268	.360	.477
Abell,Antonio,Cardinals	R	20	30	77	8	0	0	0	8	8	3	8	0	35	1	1	0	2	3	.40	0	.104	.198	.104
Abreu,Guillermo,Elizabethtn	R	19	22	69	13	1	2	0	18	9	8	6	0	10	1	0	0	0	0	.00	1	.188	.263	.261
Abreu,Nelson,Cubs	R	18	44	135	27	4	4	0	39	12	9	11	0	30	1	0	0	3	3	.50	2	.200	.265	.289
Huntington	R	18	7	24	5	0	0	0	5	2	1	0	0	7	0	1	0	0	1	.00	1	.208	.208	.208
Acevedo,Juan,Rockies	R	18	21	54	9	0	1	0	11	2	2	1	0	21				3	1	.75	0	.167	.211	.204
Adams,Jason,Pittsfield	A	23	33	78	12	1	0	0	13	7	6	11	0	32	3	2	0	2	2	.50	1	.154	.283	.167
Adams,Bill,Vero Beach	A	26	63	129	26	2	1	0	30	19	7	17	0	47	1	4	1	6	6	.50	2	.202	.297	.233
Adolfo,Carlos,Vermont	A	19	67	252	67	10	3	6	101	41	33	28	0	60	0	0	0	11	7	.61	5	.266	.335	.401
Agbayani,Benny,St. Lucie	A	23	119	411	115	13	5	5	153	72	63	58	2	67	10	1	5	8	6	.57	9	.280	.378	.372
Akers,Chad,Charlstn-Sc	A	23	133	490	135	23	1	4	172	65	35	52	1	49	2	2	3	41	16	.72	14	.276	.346	.351
Albaladejo,Randy,Quad City	A	22	26	65	9	2	0	0	11	9	8	6	0	20	1	2	1	1	1	.50	0	.138	.219	.169
Auburn	A	22	35	112	25	3	0	1	31	12	15	6	0	12	1	0	0	1	0	1.00	4	.223	.273	.277
Albarado,Marc,Utica	A	23	47	129	29	6	1	3	46	18	22	13	1	40	1	0	2	2	0	1.00	5	.225	.297	.357
Albert,Chernan,White Sox	R	19	54	161	35	4	2	2	49	22	9	29	0	48	2	0	0	8	6	.57	2	.217	.344	.304
Alcantara,Isreal,W. Palm Bch	A	22	125	471	134	26	4	15	213	65	69	26	0	130	3	1	3	9	3	.75	6	.285	.324	.452
Alderman,Kurt,Vermont	A	24	44	141	43	8	2	1	58	26	24	11	0	30	6	0	2	1	1	.50	2	.305	.375	.411
Aldridge,Steve,Greensboro	A	23	50	147	35	3	0	2	44	22	18	29	0	31	3	3	0	2	2	.50	4	.238	.374	.299
Alfonzo,Robert,St. Lucie	A	22	2	1	0	0	0	0	0	0	0	0	0	0	0	0	0	0	0	.00	0	.000	.000	.000
Kingsport	R	22	28	83	20	0	0	0	20	6	7	9	0	12	1	0	0	1	0	1.00	0	.241	.323	.241
Alguacil,Jose,Clinton	A	22	74	245	51	13	0	1	87	40	25	13	0	42	5	11	1	6	6	.50	2	.290	.337	.355
Everett	A	22	45	169	36	7	0	0	43	24	7	10	1	41	8	3	0	18	4	.82	4	.213	.289	.254
Alimena,Charles,Clinton	A	23	78	261	70	18	1	2	96	41	40	34	2	64	3	4	0	2	1	.67	4	.268	.359	.368
San Jose	A	23	25	60	18	3	0	0	21	7	5	6	2	14	2	3	0	0	0	.00	3	.300	.382	.350
Aljian,Reed,Lake Elsino	A	23	8	14	2	0	0	0	2	1	0	1	0	6	0	0	0	0	0	.00	2	.143	.200	.143
Boise			7	8	0	0	0	0	0	1	0	0	0	5	2	0	0	0	0	.00	0	.000	.200	.000
Allamo,Efrain,Rockies	R	18	23	54	9	1	0	0	10	3	1	1	0	16	0	0	0	1	2	.33	2	.167	.182	.185
Allen,Marlon,Princeton	R	22	20	64	16	2	0	6	36	15	17	9	0	21	2	0	1	0	0	.00	0	.250	.355	.563
Allen,Matt,W. Palm Bch	A	25	44	110	24	1	0	1	28	14	17	21	0	31	2	0	3	3	3	.50	1	.218	.346	.255
Allison,Christopher,Utica	A	23	39	144	48	4	3	0	58	19	16	10	0	16	1	4	2	11	3	.79	3	.333	.376	.403
Allison,Fritz,Elmira	A	23	37	116	26	3	1	2	37	18	13	9	0	33	6	0	0	0	0	.00	4	.224	.313	.319
Almond,Greg,Madison	A	24	97	303	71	15	4	4	100	37	30	29	1	76	2	1	3	1	3	.25	5	.234	.303	.330
Almonte,Wady,Orioles	R	20	42	120	24	2	0	2	32	11	9	8	0	22	1	2	0	2	0	1.00	2	.200	.256	.267
Alongi,Douglas,Peoria	A	24	21	60	11	3	0	0	14	16	1	10	0	17	0	2	0	1	1	.50	5	.183	.300	.233
Alvarado,Basilio,Expos	R	23	30	100	25	4	0	0	29	5	4	2	0	19	0	0	1	1	0	1.00	2	.250	.262	.290
Alvarez,Rafael,Twins	R	18	32	101	32	5	0	2	43	15	10	18	0	14	1	2	0	4	2	.67	4	.317	.425	.426
Alzuelde,Daniel,Angels	R	23	44	138	33	7	3	0	46	16	18	16	0	23	2	6	2	0	1	.00	6	.239	.323	.333
Amador,Manuel,Spartanburg	A	19	91	341	85	14	3	6	123	54	42	30	2	65	8	3	2	5	3	.63	4	.249	.323	.361
Amaya,Edilberto,White Sox	R	19	14	25	4	1	0	0	5	4	2	1	0	7	1	0	0	0	0	.00	1	.160	.222	.200
Ambrosina,Pete,Johnson Cty	R	21	29	94	17	0	0	1	20	14	9	7	0	24	5	2	3	4	5	.44	0	.181	.266	.213
Amerson,Gordon,Padres	R	18	44	164	46	5	2	0	55	27	22	29	0	51	0	0	0	9	2	.82	2	.280	.389	.335
Abezcua,Adan,Auburn	A	21	32	99	26	9	0	0	35	12	9	4	0	21	4	1	1	0	1	.00	2	.263	.315	.354
Amman,Matthew,Welland	A	21	67	200	47	3	1	2	58	23	15	27	1	64	2	3	2	20	11	.65	9	.235	.329	.290
Amos,Chris,Ogden	A	23	25	95	21	8	0	0	29	15	6	10	2	19	1	2	0	0	1	.00	6	.221	.302	.305
Anderson,Charlie,Madison	A	25	127	437	113	26	5	10	179	61	45	31	4	119	5	3	2	9	8	.53	9	.259	.314	.410
Andino,Luis,Martinsvlle	R	20	25	45	6	1	0	0	7	2	5	4	0	22	1	2	0	0	0	1.00	0	.133	.220	.156
Andrews,Jeffery,Billings	R	22	30	88	17	3	0	0	20	7	9	2	0	30	0	1	0	0	1	.00	2	.193	.209	.227
Angeli,Douglas,Spartanburg	A	24	43	165	40	8	0	0	48	16	14	15	0	29	0	0	1	5	3	.63	4	.242	.304	.291
Clearwater	A	24	77	265	69	14	2	1	90	25	26	23	0	39	0	5	0	2	2	.50	6	.260	.319	.340
Anson,Fred,Mariners	R	20	16	35	3	0	0	0	3	2	3	2	0	10	0	0	0	0	1	.00	1	.086	.135	.086
Apicella,James,Everett	A	22	53	202	54	8	4	1	73	32	21	15	1	54	5	2	1	1	0	1.00	5	.267	.332	.361
Arambula,Chris,Cardinals	R	23	44	171	52	8	1	0	62	17	13	11	1	31	1	0	3	0	2	.00	5	.304	.344	.363
Arano,Eloy,Bristol	R	21	52	164	43	4	0	0	47	14	15	14	2	30	1	2	1	8	1	.89	2	.262	.322	.287
Aranzamendi,Alex,Kane County	A	21	25	75	19	3	0	3	31	11	16	3	0	20	1	0	1	1	0	1.00	1	.253	.280	.413
Arias,Amador,Winston-Sal	A	23	75	193	46	7	0	2	59	25	15	11	0	33	1	3	1	7	6	.54	2	.238	.282	.306
Arias,David,Mariners	R	19	53	167	41	10	1	2	59	14	20	14	2	46	2	1	4	1	4	.20	2	.246	.305	.353
Arias,Georgie,Lake Elsino	A	22	134	514	144	28	3	23	247	89	80	58	1	111	5	3	4	6	3	.67	9	.280	.356	.481
Arias,Ramon,Red Sox	R	21	4	9	1	0	0	0	1	0	0	2	0	1	0	0	0	0	0	.00	1	.111	.273	.111
Arias,Rogelio,Rockies	R	19	45	158	37	3	1	0	42	13	15	6	0	12	1	0	2	3	3	.50	0	.234	.263	.266
Arrollado,Courtney,Red Sox	R	20	37	140	27	6	1	0	35	18	8	4	0	17	1	2	2	2	2	.50	3	.193	.215	.250
Arvelo,Thomas,Kingsport	R	19	38	132	24	5	1	0	33	22	17	23	0	29	3	4	2	1	0	1.00	2	.182	.313	.250
Pittsfield	A	21	13	43	11	1	0	0	12	4	2	3	0	15	1	0	0	1	2	.33	1	.256	.319	.279
Asche,Michael,Welland	A	23	55	204	49	5	1	4	68	22	25	13	0	30	1	3	0	6	3	.67	2	.240	.289	.333
Asencio,Fernando,Great Falls	R	21	67	277	91	19	4	4	130	41	53	26	3	32	2	0	3	14	15	.48	4	.329	.386	.469
Ashby,Chris,Yankees	R	20	45	163	55	8	1	5	80	28	38	21	0	20	1	1	3	2	0	1.00	6	.337	.410	.491
Greensboro	A	20	6	16	2	0	0	0	2	0	2	2	0	6	0	0	0	0	0	.00	0	.125	.222	.188
Astacio,Onofre,Twins	R	19	17	45	11	1	2	0	16	10	4	4	0	11	2	0	0	7	1	.88	1	.244	.333	.356
Augustine,Andy,Bellingham	A	22	49	138	31	3	0	0	34	18	10	21	0	34	4	2	0	2	2	.50	4	.225	.339	.246
Austin,Jacob,Salem	A	25	117	437	131	14	2	21	212	60	77	42	0	76	11	3	5	11	6	.65	11	.300	.372	.485
Avalos,Gilbert,Peoria	A	22	85	275	74	16	2	1	97	54	30	33	0	56	7	7	1	11	11	.50	4	.269	.361	.407
Aven,Bruce,Watertown	A	22	61	220	73	14	5	5	112	49	33	20	0	45	12	2	5	12	3	.80	0	.332	.409	.509
Avila,Rolando,Bluefield	R	21	56	200	55	14	1	1	74	41	17	28	0	30	8	3	3	28	7	.80	2	.275	.381	.370
Azuaje,Jesus,Columbus	A	22	118	450	127	20	1	7	170	77	57	69	0	72	5	6	0	21	7	.75	6	.282	.384	.378

1994 Batting -- Single-A and Rookie Leagues

Player	Lg	A	G	AB	H	2B	3B	HR	TB	R	RBI	TBB	IBB	SO	HBP	SH	SF	SB	CS	SB%	GDP	Avg	OBP	SLG
Baber,Larue,Springfield	A	23	24	64	13	1	0	0	14	2	6	4	0	21	1	1	2	3	2	.60	3	.203	.254	.219
Rancho Cuca	A	23	74	233	55	12	2	1	74	30	25	27	0	71	1	4	3	14	9	.61	4	.236	.314	.318
Babin,Brady,Marlins	R	19	15	62	12	3	0	1	18	7	10	3	0	7	1	0	1	1	0	1.00	1	.194	.239	.290
Kane County	A	19	12	38	8	2	1	0	12	4	5	1	0	10	0	1	1	0	0	.00	1	.211	.225	.316
Bady,Edward,Vermont	A	23	44	141	35	5	5	2	56	19	21	12	0	51	2	5	0	11	6	.65	3	.248	.316	.397
Baez,Raul,Utica	A	24	30	77	9	2	0	0	11	6	5	9	0	12	0	1	0	4	1	.80	1	.117	.207	.143
Bagley,Sean,White Sox	R	19	16	25	4	0	0	0	4	1	1	1	0	6	1	1	0	1	0	1.00	1	.160	.222	.160
Baker,Jason,Fort Wayne	A	22	114	377	92	17	2	3	122	46	26	36	2	53	3	1	1	9	7	.56	6	.244	.314	.324
Bakner,Brett,Lethbridge	R	23	39	124	21	4	0	2	31	14	10	10	1	25	2	1	0	1	5	.17	3	.169	.243	.250
Bako,Paul,Winston-Sal	A	23	90	289	59	9	1	3	79	29	26	30	0	81	4	8	0	2	2	.50	6	.204	.299	.273
Balfe,Ryan,Bristol	R	19	43	121	26	3	0	1	32	12	11	23	0	38	1	1	1	2	4	.33	1	.215	.342	.264
Balint,Robert,Bristol	R	21	22	44	6	3	0	0	9	6	3	2	0	17	2	0	0	1	0	1.00	2	.136	.208	.205
Ballara,Juan,St. Pete	A	23	71	226	46	12	5	5	83	33	15	18	1	60	2	1	0	1	0	1.00	7	.204	.266	.367
Bamberger,Kris,Brewers	R	21	31	68	8	0	0	0	8	5	1	13	0	27	2	1	1	0	2	.00	0	.118	.274	.118
Bando,Sal,New Jersey	A	24	23	66	12	4	0	1	19	6	7	9	0	21	1	0	1	0	0	.00	1	.182	.286	.288
Madison	A	24	3	7	0	0	0	0	0	0	0	1	0	3	1	0	0	0	0	.00	0	.000	.222	.000
Banks,Brian,Stockton	A	24	67	246	58	9	1	4	81	29	28	38	2	46	2	3	2	3	8	.27	8	.236	.340	.329
Beloit	A	24	65	237	71	13	1	9	113	41	47	29	5	40	2	1	2	11	1	.92	3	.300	.375	.477
Banks,Ronald,W. Michigan	A	23	73	245	52	15	1	6	87	31	27	30	0	52	4	2	3	8	4	.67	3	.212	.305	.355
Barbary,Travis,Great Falls	R	23	17	45	8	3	0	0	11	6	5	14	0	18	0	1	0	1	0	1.00	0	.178	.373	.244
Barger,Michael,Appleton	A	24	136	541	160	22	6	0	194	90	34	42	1	48	8	6	23	40	18	.69	9	.296	.354	.359
Barker,Glen,Fayettevlle	A	24	74	267	61	13	5	1	87	38	30	33	0	79	9	2	1	41	13	.76	5	.228	.332	.326
Lakeland	A	24	28	104	19	5	1	2	32	10	6	4	0	34	2	0	0	5	3	.63	2	.183	.227	.308
Barnden,Myles,Albany	A	23	52	176	45	8	0	0	53	27	26	34	0	40	5	0	0	5	4	.56	2	.256	.387	.301
Frederick	A	23	16	35	3	0	0	0	3	0	3	4	0	11	2	0	0	0	0	.00	0	.086	.220	.086
Barnes,Kelvin,Cubs	R	20	54	162	35	9	1	0	46	18	25	16	0	53	1	3	0	10	8	.56	0	.216	.291	.284
Barnhardt,Steven,Red Sox	R	19	17	47	13	3	1	0	18	5	8	4	1	7	2	0	0	0	0	.00	0	.277	.358	.383
Bartee,Kimera,Frederick	A	22	130	514	150	22	4	10	210	97	57	56	1	117	7	14	4	44	9	.83	7	.292	.367	.409
Barton,Byron,Cubs	R	21	11	26	7	1	1	1	13	3	5	4	0	4	1	0	0	1	0	1.00	0	.269	.387	.500
Huntington	R	21	7	26	10	2	0	0	12	2	1	0	0	5	0	0	0	1	1	.50	0	.385	.385	.462
Barwick,Lyall,Cedar Rapds	A	24	51	142	35	8	2	2	53	17	13	15	0	25	0	5	0	2	1	.67	5	.246	.318	.373
Bass,Jason,Jamestown	A	21	48	162	44	9	4	5	76	23	18	22	1	52	2	0	0	4	3	.57	2	.272	.366	.469
Bass,Jason,Braves	R	19	49	173	25	8	0	0	33	14	4	15	0	33	2	0	1	5	8	.38	2	.145	.220	.191
Basso,Mike,Rancho Cuca	A	30	14	33	10	1	0	4	23	10	9	7	0	3	0	0	0	1	0	1.00	2	.303	.425	.697
Bates,Fletcher,Mets	R	NA	52	183	39	5	3	5	65	23	29	33	0	49	0	0	1	4	3	.57	1	.213	.327	.355
St. Lucie	A	NA	7	24	6	1	1	1	12	2	4	1	0	5	0	0	0	0	0	.00	0	.250	.280	.500
Batista,Dario,Bellingham	A	22	47	144	30	5	0	0	35	19	16	16	2	20	1	3	0	8	5	.62	3	.208	.292	.243
Batista,Juan,Burlington	A	22	33	121	24	3	1	4	41	13	16	12	0	41	1	0	0	0	0	.00	0	.198	.276	.339
Batista,Tony,Modesto	A	21	119	466	131	26	3	17	214	91	68	54	1	108	4	5	2	7	7	.50	10	.281	.359	.459
Batiste,Darnell,Burlington	R	19	19	47	7	2	0	0	9	4	1	3	0	16	0	0	0	3	1	.75	2	.149	.273	.191
Baugh,Gavin,Kane County	A	21	65	219	50	9	1	3	70	32	21	10	0	69	1	3	2	3	0	1.00	3	.228	.263	.320
Bautista,Juan,Orioles	R	23	21	65	10	2	2	0	16	4	3	2	0	19	1	1	0	1		.75	3	.154	.191	.246
Bautista,Juan,Johnson Cty	R	22	61	208	52	16	1	4	82	28	31	16	1	55	3	0	3	9	5	.64	3	.250	.309	.394
Bazzani,Matthew,Mets	R	21	30	83	16	3	3	1	28	7	9	4	0	19	3	0	2	1	1	.50	1	.193	.250	.337
Bearden,Douglas,White Sox	R	19	46	165	36	4	1	1	45	15	12	4	0	30	1	1	2	1	1	.50	4	.218	.238	.273
Beaumont,Hamil,Yankees	R	20	33	108	20	5	1	3	36	15	11	14	0	48	1	1	0	0	1	.00	1	.185	.285	.333
Becker,David,Medicne Hat	A	20	33	92	20	1	0	0	21	10	7	18	0	37	4	5	0	6	3	.67	2	.217	.368	.228
Beeney,Ryan,Oneonta	A	22	30	103	31	5	1	1	41	17	7	12	0	19	2	0	1	3	2	.60	0	.301	.381	.398
Bell,Michael,Charlstn-Wv	A	20	120	475	125	22	6	6	177	58	58	47	1	76	3	1	6	16	12	.57	14	.263	.330	.373
Belliard,Ronald,Brewers	R	19	39	143	42	7	3	0	55	32	27	14	1	25	3	2	1	7	0	1.00	1	.294	.366	.385
Bellum,Donnie,Madison	A	NA	89	264	61	10	3	2	83	29	27	25	1	45	3	0	5	14	8	.64	6	.231	.300	.314
Beltre,Eddy,Hickory	A	22	28	75	16	3	0	0	19	4	8	6	1	12	1	4	0	2	2	.50	3	.213	.280	.253
Benbow,Lou,Dunedin	A	24	28	69	8	3	0	0	11	7	5	6	0	17	2	1	0	1	2	.33	4	.116	.208	.159
St. Lucie	A	24	15	34	9	1	0	0	10	2	3	10	0	10	1	2	0	1	2	.33	0	.265	.444	.294
Berblinger,Jeffrey,Savannah	A	24	132	479	142	27	7	8	207	86	67	52	0	85	25	6	5	24	5	.83	8	.296	.390	.432
Berg,David,Kane County	A	24	121	437	117	27	8	9	187	80	53	54	0	80	8	15	6	8	6	.57	10	.268	.354	.428
Bergeron,Greg,Lethbridge	R	22	51	166	44	4	1	0	50	29	21	29	1	31	9	5	3	9	9	.50	7	.265	.396	.301
Bernhardt,Steven,Central Val	A	24	68	204	52	9	0	0	61	23	14	23	0	21	0	3	1	3	3	.25	3	.255	.329	.299
Berry,Jeff,Sarasota	A	24	17	44	7	0	0	0	7	2	1	1	0	6	2	0	0	0	0	.00	1	.159	.213	.159
Berry,Michael,Burlington	A	24	94	334	105	18	1	10	155	67	45	53	0	59	1	1	1	7	3	.70	3	.314	.409	.464
Berteotti,Jerry,Yakima	A	24	19	26	3	1	0	0	4	3	2	2	0	4	2	0	1	0	0	.00	2	.115	.226	.154
Betances,Junior,Helena	R	22	66	212	56	8	3	2	76	37	21	34	1	38	1	6	0	12	6	.67	1	.264	.365	.358
Betancourt,Rafael,Red Sox	R	20	24	63	7	0	0	0	7	7	3	6	0	19	0	0	2	1	0	1.00	1	.111	.183	.111
Bethea,Scott,High Desert	A	26	107	373	111	21	3	2	144	65	47	44	3	51	4	4	6	13	10	.57	9	.298	.372	.386
Bethke,Jamie,High Desert	A	22	22	70	18	5	0	0	23	10	4	6	0	9	0	0	0	0	0	.00	2	.257	.333	.329
Betts,Todd,Watertown	A	22	65	227	74	18	2	10	126	49	53	54	2	29	4	1	2	3	2	.60	1	.326	.460	.555
Betzsold,Jim,Watertown	A	22	66	212	61	18	0	12	115	48	46	53	1	68	15	1	4	3	3	.50	2	.288	.457	.542
Beyna,Terry,Auburn	A	22	27	75	23	4	0	1	30	12	12	10	0	10	2	1	0	0	0	.00	0	.307	.402	.400
Bierek,Kurt,Greensboro	A	22	133	467	118	24	6	14	196	78	73	69	2	101	8	2	3	8	1	.89	10	.253	.356	.420
Biermann,Steve,Savannah	A	23	51	96	22	0	0	0	22	9	7	23	0	24	3	1	0	5	1	.67	2	.229	.393	.229
Biernat,Joeseph,Peoria	A	24	111	390	96	16	6	7	145	56	36	27	3	77	5	4	2	8	9	.47	4	.246	.302	.372
Bifone,Peter,Spokane	A	23	68	268	70	12	0	4	94	32	25	20	3	36	3	1		5	2	.71	4	.261	.318	.351
Bigler,Jeff,Clearwater	A	25	104	366	103	21	1	5	141	41	49	54	3	47	1	0	4	1	1	.50	10	.281	.372	.385
Biltimier,Michael,Bakersfield	A	24	92	306	84	18	1	14	146	46	42	33	3	84	4	1	3	5	3	.63	9	.275	.350	.477
Bingham,David,Hickory	A	24	45	163	42	7	3	2	61	25	24	15	0	44	10	0	2	1	3	.25	2	.258	.353	.374
Ogden	R	24	51	183	60	5	2	4	81	47	34	28	0	41	12	0	3	20	4	.83	4	.328	.442	.443
Bishop,Timothy,Mets	R	21	10	32	6	1	0	1	9	2	2	2	0	6	0	0	0	1		.00	2	.188	.235	.281

1994 Batting -- Single-A and Rookie Leagues

			BATTING															BASERUNNING				PERCENTAGES		
Player	Lg	A	G	AB	H	2B	3B	HR	TB	R	RBI	TBB	IBB	SO	HBP	SH	SF	SB	CS	SB%	GDP	Avg	OBP	SLG
Bishop,Teddy,Bellingham	A	22	34	85	21	4	1	3	36	13	11	14	0	38	2	0	0	2	2	.50	2	.247	.366	.424
Black,Keith,St. Pete	A	25	84	203	44	6	0	1	53	29	11	29	0	38	2	7	0	7	4	.64	1	.217	.321	.261
Blair,Brian,Charlstn-Wv	A	23	121	411	102	21	0	7	144	65	38	53	1	90	3	2	4	30	8	.79	7	.248	.335	.350
Blasingame,Kent,Clearwater	A	26	106	395	100	12	7	6	144	61	37	29	2	90	9	6	3	18	16	.53	8	.253	.317	.365
Blum,Geoffrey,Vermont	A	22	63	241	83	15	1	3	109	48	38	33	0	21	3	1	1	5	5	.50	4	.344	.428	.452
Bocachica,Hiram,Expos	R	19	43	168	47	9	0	5	71	31	16	15	0	42	2	2	0	11	4	.73	1	.280	.346	.423
Bogle,Brian,Huntington	R	22	46	140	39	7	1	5	63	17	20	8	1	41	3	0	2	8	2	.80	2	.279	.327	.450
Boka,Ben,Pittsfield	A	22	38	133	26	7	1	0	35	10	13	5	0	44	1	2	0	0	1	.00	2	.195	.230	.263
Bokemeier,Mathew,Hudson Vall	A	22	72	262	54	12	0	1	69	24	24	11	0	50	2	0	2	4	5	.44	5	.206	.242	.263
Bolognese,Keith,Danville	R	23	47	154	43	9	0	2	58	18	23	15	2	34	0	1	1	2	3	.40	1	.279	.341	.377
Bonilla,Ramon,Athletics	R	20	37	122	25	3	0	0	28	13	12	3	0	31	2	1	2	1	0	1.00	4	.205	.233	.230
Bonnici,James,Riverside	A	23	113	397	111	23	3	10	170	71	71	58	0	81	18	0	3	1	2	.33	14	.280	.393	.428
Booker,Kevin,Hickory	A	23	85	296	67	15	4	1	93	32	28	20	2	74	6	1	2	11	7	.61	5	.226	.287	.314
Boone,Aaron,Billings	R	22	67	256	70	15	5	7	116	48	55	36	3	35	3	0	6	6	3	.67	7	.273	.362	.453
Booty,Joshua,Marlins	R	20	10	36	8	1	0	0	11	5	2	5	0	8	0	1	0	1	0	1.00	2	.222	.317	.306
Elmira	A	20	4	16	4	1	0	0	5	1	1	0	0	4	0	0	0	0	1	.00	0	.250	.250	.313
Borel,James,Bristol	R	23	50	168	48	10	2	1	65	44	18	35	0	26	0	2	0	18	6	.75	0	.286	.409	.387
Borges,Mariano,Pirates	R	22	6	23	8	3	0	0	11	5	3	2	0	2	0	0	0	0	1	.00	3	.348	.400	.478
Welland	A	22	51	136	31	3	2	0	38	10	12	4	0	34	4	4	0	7	6	.54	3	.228	.271	.279
Borges,Victor,Cubs	R	18	40	136	19	2	0	0	21	20	5	10	0	19	0	5	0	2	2	.50	2	.179	.250	.198
Borrero,Richie,Sarasota	A	22	44	145	28	8	0	3	45	15	14	9	0	50	4	1	0	0	1	.00	0	.193	.259	.310
Boryczewski,Marty,Lethbridge	R	22	38	116	24	3	1	0	29	10	11	5	0	25	1	0	0	5	1	.83	2	.207	.246	.250
Borzello,Mike,Savannah	A	24	1	4	0	0	0	0	0	0	0	0	0	1	0	0	0	0	0	.00	0	.000	.000	.000
Madison	A	24	3	9	3	0	0	0	3	0	1	1	0	2	0	1	0	0	0	.00	0	.333	.400	.333
Bostic,Dwain,Cardinals	R	20	16	39	9	0	0	0	9	2	5	6	1	11	2	0	0	0	0	.00	0	.231	.354	.231
Boston,D.J.,Dunedin	A	23	119	433	125	20	1	7	168	59	52	55	2	65	0	2	5	19	9	.68	8	.289	.365	.388
Boulware,Benjamin,White Sox	R	23	4	12	2	0	0	0	2	2	0	1	0	1	2	0	0	1	0	1.00	0	.167	.333	.167
Hickory	A	23	100	337	112	19	2	4	147	56	36	28	0	45	9	4	4	8	6	.57	3	.332	.394	.436
Bourne,Charles,Blue Jays	R	20	52	191	44	8	1	2	60	35	19	25	0	45	1	2	0	35	9	.80	0	.230	.323	.314
Bowen,Jae,Johnson City	R	24	58	8	4	0	2	0	10	7	5	10	0	22	1	0	1	0	0	.00	0	.138	.282	.207
Bowers,Ray,Quad City	A	21	127	467	120	21	3	15	192	60	63	39	2	143	12	1	5	14	8	.64	7	.257	.327	.411
Bowles,John,Utica	A	20	38	135	33	10	0	0	43	19	10	22	2	24	1	0	1	1	2	.33	0	.244	.352	.319
Bowman,Delshon,Orioles	R	19	36	57	6	1	1	0	9	7	1	10	0	19	3	0	1	2	4	.33	1	.105	.271	.158
Boyette,Tony,Princeton	R	19	61	223	52	14	0	5	81	27	35	27	0	56	3	0	2	3	2	.60	10	.233	.322	.363
Braddy,Junior,Red Sox	R	23	51	198	70	11	1	2	89	30	43	19	2	20	0	0	3	12	4	.75	5	.354	.405	.449
Sarasota	A	23	8	26	9	1	0	0	10	2	2	3	0	5	0	0	0	1	0	1.00	0	.346	.414	.385
Bradish,Michael,Pr. William	A	27	20	56	12	5	0	0	17	8	4	6	0	17	0	0	0	2	2	.50	3	.214	.290	.304
Bradley,London,Daytona	A	24	5	7	0	0	0	0	0	3	0	4	0	2	0	1	0	0	0	.00	1	.000	.364	.000
Bragga,Matt,Butte	R	22	63	243	82	10	1	5	109	47	48	25	2	32	3	0	1	4	0	1.00	4	.337	.404	.449
Brainard,Matthew,Spartanburg	A	24	51	180	41	3	2	6	66	23	20	22	1	60	2	0	1	4	1	.80	2	.228	.317	.367
Brandon,Jelani,Eugene	A	21	76	292	80	12	3	5	113	37	38	43	3	86	2	0	2	7	4	.64	4	.274	.369	.387
Brannon,Tony,Red Sox	R	20	44	160	35	3	0	0	38	17	11	13	1	21	1	3	0	2	4	.33	2	.219	.282	.238
Branyan,Russell,Burlington	R	19	55	171	36	10	0	5	61	21	13	25	2	64	4	0	1	4	2	.67	3	.211	.323	.357
Bray,Notorris,Giants	R	21	53	198	48	4	6	0	64	33	12	16	0	44	6	2	1	16	10	.62	3	.242	.317	.323
Brede,Brent,Fort Myers	A	22	116	419	110	21	4	2	145	49	45	63	3	60	0	1	3	18	4	.82	7	.263	.358	.346
Breuer,Jim,Yakima	A	21	41	135	31	8	0	2	45	14	14	7	0	55	4	0	0	2	2	.50	3	.230	.288	.333
Brewer,Buford,Bend	A	23	33	122	32	2	0	2	40	12	21	13	1	18	4	0	3	2	4	.33	2	.262	.345	.328
Brewer,Brett,Danville	R	20	54	182	47	7	0	4	66	26	17	5	1	51	5	2	1	14	3	.82	9	.258	.295	.363
Bridgers,Brandon,Albany	A	22	119	446	116	25	4	3	158	64	44	46	0	77	5	6	6	39	27	.59	3	.260	.332	.354
Bridges,William,Quad City	A	23	117	447	135	20	4	1	166	66	53	38	3	29	3	8	4	14	11	.56	9	.302	.358	.371
Briggs,Stoney,Rancho Cuca	A	23	121	417	112	22	2	17	189	63	76	54	1	124	9	2	7	14	13	.52	7	.269	.359	.453
Bright,Brian,Sarasota	A	25	4	11	2	0	0	0	2	0	0	1	0	3	0	0	0	0	0	.00	1	.182	.250	.182
Lynchburg	A	25	21	75	9	1	0	1	13	4	5	6	0	11	0	0	1	0	1	.00	0	.120	.185	.173
Brinkley,Josh,W. Palm Bch	A	21	2	5	0	0	0	0	0	0	0	0	0	1	0	0	0	0	0	.00	0	.000	.000	.000
Expos	R	21	8	27	3	0	0	0	3	3	1	1	0	5	0	0	0	0	0	.00	0	.111	.200	.111
Vermont	A	21	7	19	5	1	0	0	6	5	1	1	0	5	0	0	0	0	0	.00	0	.263	.300	.316
Burlington	A	21	11	30	7	0	0	0	7	2	2	3	0	7	4	1	1	0	0	.00	0	.233	.368	.233
Brissey,Jason,Peoria	A	22	54	152	28	6	2	0	38	21	14	19	0	47	2	1	2	1	2	.33	0	.184	.282	.250
Brito,Diolis,Cubs	R	21	28	81	27	2	0	0	29	14	10	9	0	11	3	1	0	5	5	.50	1	.333	.419	.358
Brito,Domingo,Martinsville	R	19	32	73	9	2	0	0	11	5	3	7	0	31	1	1	0	1	2	.33	1	.123	.200	.151
Broach,Donald,Billings	R	23	63	270	84	11	1	3	106	55	38	24	0	40	7	3	1	17	12	.59	7	.311	.381	.393
Brooks,Eddie,Salem	A	22	30	98	22	5	0	4	39	14	15	11	0	38	1	2	0	0	1	.00	4	.224	.309	.398
Augusta	A	22	40	126	20	3	0	2	29	14	9	17	0	35	2	3	1	3	1	.75	0	.159	.267	.230
Brooks,Rayme,High Desert	A	22	95	326	89	20	3	20	175	55	76	45	0	102	7	0	4	2	3	.40	3	.273	.369	.537
Broome,Corey,Fayetteville	A	23	18	62	9	0	2	0	13	5	11	8	0	19	0	0	0	0	0	.00	2	.145	.243	.210
Brophy,E.J.,Clearwater	A	25	49	126	23	3	0	3	35	17	17	20	0	24	2	3	1	0	0	.00	3	.183	.302	.278
Brown,Adrian,Augusta	A	21	79	308	80	17	1	1	102	41	18	14	0	38	0	6	0	19	12	.61	2	.260	.292	.331
Brown,Armann,Fort Wayne	A	22	10	38	10	2	0	0	12	8	4	2	0	12	2	2	1	3	1	.75	0	.263	.326	.316
Twins	R	22	5	16	2	1	0	0	3	1	0	1	0	4	1	0	0	0	0	.00	0	.125	.222	.188
Brown,Derek,Orioles	R	18	32	73	12	3	0	0	15	8	3	11	0	23	1	0	0	2	1	.67	0	.164	.279	.205
Brown,Drew,Lethbridge	R	23	7	26	3	0	0	0	3	4	2	2	0	5	0	0	0	0	1	.00	0	.115	.179	.115
Brown,Emil,Athletics	R	20	32	86	19	1	1	3	31	13	12	13	0	12	4	0	0	5	1	.83	2	.221	.350	.360
Brown,Jerome,Twins	R	19	36	129	30	7	1	3	48	19	17	9	1	30	3	1	1	3	4	.43	3	.233	.296	.372
Brown,Kevin,Hudson Vall	A	22	68	232	57	19	1	6	96	33	32	23	0	86	4	0	0	1	0	1.00	4	.246	.317	.414
Brown,Ray,Billings	R	22	60	218	80	19	3	9	132	50	49	27	0	32	10	0	5	1	5	.38	5	.367	.450	.606
Brown,Ronald,Kane County	A	25	109	411	109	22	3	9	164	51	75	26	1	75	4	0	5	4	2	.67	14	.265	.312	.399
Brown,Roosevelt,Idaho Falls	R	19	48	160	53	8	1	3	72	28	22	17	0	15	1	0	2	8	6	.57	2	.331	.397	.450

286

1994 Batting -- Single-A and Rookie Leagues

						BATTING												BASERUNNING				PERCENTAGES		
Player	Lg	A	G	AB	H	2B	3B	HR	TB	R	RBI	TBB	IBB	SO	HBP	SH	SF	SB	CS	SB%	GDP	Avg	OBP	SLG
Brown,Shawn,Lakeland	A	24	101	342	76	10	0	4	98	36	30	21	2	53	7	2	2	10	3	.77	13	.222	.280	.287
Brown,Todd,Bluefield	R	23	4	8	2	0	0	0	2	2	0	0	0	1	2	0	0	1	0	1.00	0	.250	.400	.250
Albany	A	23	38	111	26	3	1	0	31	10	7	6	0	32	2	2	0	13	6	.68	1	.234	.286	.279
Brown,Vick,Greensboro	A	22	117	382	88	8	1	0	98	69	20	73	0	79	4	4	1	27	10	.73	6	.230	.359	.257
Brown,Willie,Kane County	A	24	112	364	84	20	2	11	141	61	47	47	4	131	4	1	4	15	4	.79	7	.231	.322	.387
Brunner,Mike,Blue Jays	R	23	21	60	12	2	0	1	17	5	4	5	0	12	0	1	0	1	0	1.00	3	.200	.262	.283
Brunson,Larry,Fayetteville	A	20	103	348	75	9	1	0	86	75	28	78	0	76	6	7	1	50	16	.76	4	.216	.367	.247
Lakeland	A	20	11	39	7	0	0	1	10	4	3	5	0	11	0	0	0	3	2	.60	0	.179	.273	.256
Bryan,Leonardo,Angels	R	22	38	101	26	4	2	1	37	10	17	6	0	26	1	1	2	2	4	.33	2	.257	.300	.366
Buchanan,Carlos,Oneonta	A	21	50	177	40	9	2	4	65	28	26	24	2	53	6	0	2	5	3	.63	2	.226	.335	.367
Buchanan,Shawn,South Bend	A	26	39	130	23	4	1	0	29	18	12	24	0	36	1	1	3	8	3	.73	0	.177	.304	.223
Pr. William	A	26	34	90	24	2	0	3	35	18	13	16	0	24	1	1	2	2	1	.67	2	.267	.380	.389
Buckley,Mathew,Boise	A	22	19	38	3	1	0	0	4	1	2	3	0	5	0	0	0	0	0	.00	2	.079	.146	.105
Lake Elsino	A	22	2	2	0	0	0	0	0	0	0	0	0	0	0	0	0	0	0	.00	0	.000	.000	.000
Bugg,Jason,High Desert	A	24	103	332	86	26	2	7	137	56	38	49	2	72	4	2	5	6	4	.60	7	.259	.356	.413
Buhner,Shawn,Bellingham	A	22	53	153	44	12	0	4	68	19	19	16	1	39	0	0	4	4	2	.67	0	.288	.347	.444
Bunkley,Antuan,Twins	R	19	41	136	31	5	1	1	41	12	20	8	0	24	3	0	3	0	2	.00	5	.228	.280	.301
Burchel,Brad,Helena	R	23	32	94	33	10	0	2	49	17	22	13	0	29	2	1	2	3	2	.60	1	.351	.432	.521
Burgos,Carlos,Eugene	A	23	53	160	43	7	0	1	53	18	19	18	3	31	3	0	1	0	1	.00	4	.269	.352	.331
Burguillos,Carlos,Lakeland	A	23	80	227	50	7	1	1	62	20	19	20	0	32	0	4	1	5	6	.45	6	.220	.282	.273
Burke,Alan,Clearwater	A	24	107	374	80	24	1	6	124	44	49	27	0	84	4	8	3	3	1	.75	7	.214	.272	.332
Burke,James,Cedar Rapds	A	23	127	469	124	24	1	1	153	57	47	40	3	64	12	4	8	6	8	.43	15	.264	.333	.326
Burke,Stoney,Beloit	A	24	9	12	1	0	0	0	1	1	2	1	0	7	0	1	0	0	0	.00	0	.083	.154	.083
Burrough,Butch,Albany	A	24	56	194	50	13	4	7	92	25	31	29	0	54	2	0	1	1	3	.25	5	.258	.358	.474
Burrows,Mike,Mariners	R	19	52	186	54	8	6	3	83	21	25	10	2	44	2	1	2	4	2	.67	4	.290	.330	.446
Burton,Essex,Pr. William	A	26	131	503	143	22	10	3	194	94	50	67	1	88	5	6	6	66	19	.78	5	.284	.370	.386
Bustos,Saul,Williamsprt	A	22	72	221	41	12	3	3	68	29	27	29	0	50	1	8	3	4	2	.67	4	.186	.280	.308
Butler,Garrett,Yankees	R	19	52	152	32	3	1	0	37	22	12	22	0	55	4	4	1	9	6	.60	7	.211	.324	.243
Byington,Jimmie,Rockford	A	21	105	328	82	14	3	1	105	44	48	26	0	64	5	0	5	14	7	.67	5	.250	.310	.320
Caballero,Javier,Orioles	R	19	23	56	7	4	0	0	11	4	7	1	0	15	1	0	2	0	1	.00	2	.125	.150	.196
Cabrera,Alex,Peoria	A	23	121	432	120	25	1	24	219	57	73	19	4	92	16	0	4	2	8	.20	4	.278	.329	.507
Cabrera,Carlos,Hagerstown	A	21	35	112	24	3	2	0	31	15	3	11	0	23	1	2	1	0	2	.00	0	.214	.288	.277
St. Cathrns	A	21	56	190	39	6	0	0	45	15	15	6	0	24	2	0	1	8	3	.73	2	.205	.236	.237
Cabrera,Jairo,Bluefield	R	23	34	107	29	4	1	0	35	15	12	10	1	21	0	2	1	1	2	.33	4	.271	.331	.327
Cabrera,Orlando,Expos	R	21	22	73	23	4	1	0	29	13	11	5	0	8	0	1	0	5	0	1.00	1	.315	.359	.397
Cady,Todd,Elmira	A	22	44	162	31	10	0	3	50	12	19	10	1	47	2	0	1	0	1	.00	4	.191	.246	.309
Cairo,Miguel,Bakersfield	A	21	133	533	155	23	4	2	192	76	48	34	3	37	6	15	4	44	23	.66	9	.291	.338	.360
Calderon,Ricardo,Giants	R	19	49	189	30	8	1	0	40	15	14	8	0	64	0	0	1	1	4	.20	0	.159	.192	.212
Callan,Brett,Osceola	A	23	47	109	15	3	0	1	21	17	4	24	0	34	3	2	0	0	1	.00	6	.138	.309	.193
Cameron,Mike,Pr. William	A	22	131	468	116	15	17	6	183	86	48	60	2	101	8	2	0	22	10	.69	6	.248	.343	.391
Camilli,Jason,Expos	R	19	53	212	54	4	3	0	64	33	13	31	1	44	0	0	1	5	6	.45	4	.255	.348	.302
Camilo,Jose,Marlins	R	18	54	188	52	7	0	0	59	34	27	19	0	33	1	0	4	4	2	.67	2	.277	.340	.314
Campanis,Jim,Lake Elsino	A	27	53	179	48	7	0	8	79	21	21	18	0	35	2	0	1	1	0	1.00	2	.268	.340	.441
Campos,Jesus,Burlington	A	21	12	44	6	0	0	0	6	1	1	1	0	7	0	0	0	0	1	.00	0	.136	.156	.136
Expos	R	21	3	11	4	0	0	0	4	0	3	1	0	0	0	0	0	0	0	.00	1	.364	.385	.364
W. Palm Bch	A	21	62	240	66	11	2	0	81	37	16	17	1	23	0	1	1	13	2	.87	5	.275	.322	.338
Cancel,David,White Sox	R	21	45	131	26	5	3	3	46	12	14	11	0	28	0	0	1	9	1	.90	2	.198	.259	.351
Cancel,Robinson,Brewers	R	19	29	70	12	0	0	0	12	6	8	9	1	19	2	0	2	0	2	.00	2	.171	.277	.171
Candelaria,Ben,Hagerstown	A	20	3	13	3	0	0	1	6	2	3	0	0	4	0	0	0	0	0	.00	0	.231	.231	.462
St. Cathrns	A	20	71	250	66	15	1	2	89	36	37	35	1	55	1	3	1	8	4	.67	6	.264	.355	.356
Canizaro,Jason,San Jose	A	21	126	464	117	16	2	15	182	77	69	46	1	98	5	0	3	12	6	.67	7	.252	.324	.392
Cannaday,Aaron,Augusta	A	23	86	261	54	10	1	6	84	27	32	27	0	104	4	0	5	8	3	.73	2	.207	.286	.322
Canot,Andres,Rangers	R	19	8	20	4	2	0	0	6	0	3	1	0	6	0	0	0	0	0	.00	0	.200	.238	.300
Cantrell,Derrick,Brewers	R	22	55	191	48	7	2	1	62	35	26	16	0	33	12	1	5	23	5	.82	3	.251	.339	.325
Cantu,Mike,St. Pete	A	26	60	232	48	10	0	4	70	15	26	15	0	45	3	0	2	1	0	1.00	7	.207	.262	.302
Clearwater	A	26	46	176	43	13	0	9	83	23	36	13	0	54	3	3	3	0	0	.00	5	.244	.303	.472
Cappuccio,Carmine,Pr. William	A	25	101	401	117	30	1	12	185	71	60	25	1	53	9	2	4	8	4	.67	7	.292	.344	.461
Cardenas,Epifanio,Kinston	A	23	95	325	77	13	2	4	106	38	33	26	0	44	2	1	5	6	3	.67	7	.237	.293	.326
Cardenas,Johnny,Riverside	A	24	58	178	37	3	0	1	43	16	13	14	1	36	3	3	1	0	1	.00	6	.208	.276	.242
Cardona,Alex,Cardinals	R	20	18	46	10	2	0	0	12	5	5	2	0	5	1	0	0	1	0	1.00	0	.217	.265	.261
Cardona,Richard,Jamestown	A	19	19	46	12	2	0	0	14	6	5	7	0	9	0	0	0	0	0	.00	2	.261	.358	.304
Carey,Todd,Lynchburg	A	23	105	363	85	14	2	13	142	42	42	49	0	77	3	1	2	1	4	.20	2	.234	.329	.391
Carmona,Cesarin,Rancho Cuca	A	18	3	2	0	0	0	0	0	0	0	0	0	1	0	0	0	0	0	.00	0	.000	.000	.000
Padres	R	18	35	130	26	3	4	0	37	19	8	18	0	57	4	0	2	17	2	.89	0	.200	.312	.285
Carone,Richard,Hickory	A	24	67	209	50	10	1	7	83	37	37	33	1	54	3	1	1	1	1	.50	6	.239	.350	.397
Carpenter,Jerry,Boise	A	23	24	55	14	2	0	1	19	5	9	3	0	16	0	2	0	1	0	1.00	2	.255	.293	.345
Carpenter,Matthew,Bend	A	22	35	95	18	3	0	3	30	8	10	7	0	26	2	2	0	0	0	.00	5	.189	.260	.316
Carr,Jeffrey,Athletics	R	21	25	55	9	1	0	0	10	7	3	10	0	13	4	0	1	0	1	.00	0	.164	.329	.182
Carr,Jeremy,Rockford	A	24	121	437	112	19	5	1	134	85	32	60	1	59	16	2	4	52	22	.70	8	.256	.364	.307
Carranza,Pete,Asheville	A	23	117	411	116	34	0	9	177	70	52	38	3	58	4	1	2	3	1	.75	7	.282	.347	.431
Carrasquel,Domingo,Stockton	A	23	3	6	0	0	0	0	0	0	0	0	0	0	0	0	0	0	0	.00	0	.000	.000	.000
Helena	R	23	41	135	38	2	0	0	40	33	16	22	1	17	3	3	1	6	2	.75	1	.281	.391	.296
Carrigg,Mike,Ogden	R	22	55	219	72	14	1	0	88	44	30	21	1	33	1	2	1	14	2	.88	2	.329	.388	.402
Carroll,Douglas,Bellingham	R	22	28	79	19	1	0	0	20	6	10	7	0	10	2	0	1	0	1	.00	2	.241	.315	.253
Carvajal,Jhonny,Charlstn-Sc	A	20	67	198	45	6	0	0	51	27	13	19	0	25	2	2	3	12	3	.80	3	.227	.297	.258
Princeton	R	20	53	218	59	10	4	2	83	35	29	14	2	38	5	5	3	31	11	.74	0	.271	.325	.381
Carvajal,Jovino,Cedar Rapds	A	26	121	503	147	23	8	6	204	82	54	40	3	76	1	3	1	68	25	.73	5	.292	.345	.406

1994 Batting -- Single-A and Rookie Leagues

Player	Lg	A	G	AB	H	2B	3B	HR	TB	R	RBI	TBB	IBB	SO	HBP	SH	SF	SB	CS	SB%	GDP	Avg	OBP	SLG
Casanova,Papo,Rancho Cuca	A	22	123	471	160	27	2	23	260	83	120	43	2	97	9	0	3	1	4	.20	16	.340	.403	.552
Castaldo,Gregg,Frederick	A	24	83	232	61	5	6	8	102	39	32	27	0	51	7	6	3	2	0	1.00	8	.263	.353	.440
Castaneda,Hector,Albany	A	23	54	150	50	6	0	2	62	22	17	24	1	20	0	4	0	5	0	1.00	6	.333	.425	.413
Castillo,Alberto,Everett	A	19	53	160	36	5	0	3	50	16	21	21	0	56	0	0	0	0	0	.00	1	.225	.313	.313
Castillo,Braulio,Osceola	A	27	17	60	11	5	0	0	16	5	6	5	1	19	1	0	0	0	0	.00	3	.183	.254	.267
Castillo,Luis,Marlins	R	NA	57	216	57	8	0	0	65	49	16	37	0	36	1	2	2	31	12	.72	1	.264	.371	.301
Castle,Ryan,Williamsprt	A	23	8	7	2	1	0	0	3	1	0	2	0	2	1	0	0	2	1	.67	0	.286	.500	.429
Castro,Dennis,Elmira	A	22	9	20	6	1	0	1	10	5	4	5	0	5	1	0	0	0	0	.00	1	.300	.462	.500
Castro,Francisco,Great Falls	R	20	47	150	45	3	2	0	52	38	18	35	0	27	3	3	2	14	9	.61	1	.300	.437	.347
Castro,Jose,Athletics	R	20	42	150	42	5	3	1	56	27	11	22	0	34	0	1	0	17	7	.71	0	.280	.386	.373
Castro,Luis,Rockies	R	19	21	52	8	2	0	0	10	5	7	6	0	18	4	3	0	5	1	.83	2	.154	.290	.192
Castro,Ramon,Astros	R	19	37	123	34	7	0	3	50	17	14	17	1	14	2	0	0	5	5	.50	4	.276	.373	.407
Castro,Ruben,Elizabethtn	R	19	29	96	28	1	0	0	29	13	8	11	0	9	0	1	0	1	1	.50	1	.292	.364	.302
Catalanotto,Frank,Fayetteville	A	21	119	458	149	24	8	3	198	72	56	37	1	54	3	5	1	4	5	.44	4	.325	.379	.432
Catlett,David,Macon	A	21	8	20	1	0	0	0	1	1	0	2	0	6	0	0	1	1	1	.50	0	.050	.136	.050
Idaho Falls	A	21	60	231	62	11	5	2	89	38	42	21	2	49	11	0	1	18	6	.75	5	.268	.355	.385
Cavanagh,Mike,Clinton	A	25	88	267	63	21	0	5	99	37	33	21	1	85	3	9	4	4	0	1.00	5	.236	.299	.371
Cawhorn,Gerad,Columbus	A	22	90	287	67	11	1	11	113	38	47	31	0	73	10	8	2	4	2	.67	6	.233	.327	.394
Cedeno,Edguardo,Rockford	A	22	40	140	36	9	1	4	59	27	20	10	0	38	2	2	0	4	0	1.00	4	.257	.316	.421
Eugene	A	22	43	124	24	7	2	2	41	17	15	9	0	48	1	5	0	4	4	.50	1	.194	.254	.331
Cedeno,Jose,Central Val	A	20	8	23	4	0	0	0	4	1	1	2	0	7	0	0	0	0	0	.00	1	.174	.240	.174
Bend	A	20	27	66	15	2	1	4	31	9	15	6	0	32	2	1	1	1	0	1.00	1	.227	.307	.470
Cepeda,Malcom,Eugene	A	22	41	107	27	8	0	2	41	12	17	18	1	35	4	0	1	3	2	.60	2	.252	.377	.383
Cephas,Ben,Beloit	A	22	19	35	7	1	0	1	11	7	6	3	1	9	1	0	0	1	3	.25	1	.200	.282	.314
Helena	R	22	54	206	63	8	4	0	79	35	16	12	0	30	3	2	0	29	9	.76	1	.306	.353	.383
Cerio,Steve,St. Pete	A	25	78	234	60	15	1	5	92	18	27	17	0	44	3	0	2	0	0	.00	6	.256	.313	.393
Cervantes,Ray,San Bernrdo	A	24	91	264	54	6	1	2	68	26	12	26	0	73	1	1	1	5	5	.50	5	.205	.277	.258
Chaddrick,Thad,Vermont	A	24	4	12	2	0	0	0	2	2	1	4	0	4	0	0	0	0	0	.00	0	.167	.375	.167
Chambers,Bradley,Cubs	R	21	41	108	20	5	0	0	25	12	6	11	0	21	1	1	0	0	2	.00	1	.185	.267	.231
Chambers,Mack,Burlington	R	22	64	222	52	14	0	0	66	34	14	31	1	56	6	4	2	20	10	.67	4	.234	.341	.297
Columbus	A	22	1	1	1	0	0	0	1	0	0	0	0	0	0	0	0	0	0	.00	0	1.000	1.000	1.000
Champion,James,Fort Wayne	A	21	60	189	46	8	0	4	66	16	20	19	3	44	1	0	2	4	1	.80	5	.243	.313	.349
Chapman,Eric,Columbus	A	23	57	163	38	9	5	1	60	27	8	15	1	37	1	1	0	11	2	.85	5	.233	.302	.368
Charbonnet,Mark,W. Palm Bch	A	24	103	323	86	18	6	1	119	44	32	25	2	69	3	3	2	7	7	.50	2	.266	.323	.368
Charles,Frank,Charlotte	A	26	79	254	67	17	1	2	92	23	33	16	1	52	3	5	2	2	3	.40	2	.264	.313	.362
Charles,Justin,Elmira	A	24	44	134	28	8	0	3	45	20	16	9	1	33	1	0	1	1	2	.33	7	.209	.282	.336
Charles,Steve,Blue Jays	R	20	21	55	8	2	0	0	10	7	5	14	0	23	3	1	0	1	0	1.00	1	.145	.347	.182
Chavez,Eric,Frederick	A	24	124	388	103	26	3	23	204	75	82	65	0	100	3	2	8	3	2	.60	5	.265	.369	.526
Cheff,Tyler,Burlington	R	24	20	58	14	2	1	0	18	4	6	5	1	11	2	0	2	1	1	.67	1	.241	.313	.310
Watertown	A	24	3	12	2	1	0	0	3	1	0	0	0	4	0	0	0	0	0	.00	0	.167	.167	.250
Choate,Jon,Watertown	A	21	37	121	28	4	1	0	34	15	11	14	0	30	1	1	0	0	1	.00	3	.231	.314	.281
Christmon,Andrew,Fayettevlle	A	23	88	283	64	11	4	8	107	35	29	33	2	103	3	1	1	7	3	.70	2	.226	.313	.378
Christopher,Claude,Savannah	A	23	119	433	115	16	3	3	146	55	41	52	2	65	9	1	3	20	5	.80	11	.266	.354	.337
Clapinski,Chris,Brevard Cty	A	23	65	157	45	12	3	1	66	33	13	23	2	28	3	7	1	3	2	.60	2	.287	.386	.420
Clark,Howie,Frederick	A	21	2	7	1	1	0	0	2	1	0	0	0	2	0	0	0	0	0	.00	0	.143	.143	.286
Albany	A	21	108	353	95	22	7	2	137	56	47	51	3	58	7	4	1	5	4	.56	7	.269	.371	.388
Clark,Kevin,Utica	A	22	57	185	47	10	2	2	65	31	12	19	1	50	6	0	1	2	3	.40	2	.254	.341	.351
Claudio,Patricio,Kinston	A	23	121	454	111	16	2	1	134	56	24	42	1	117	6	4	2	34	20	.63	6	.244	.315	.295
Claus,Marc,Fort Myers	A	24	24	56	12	1	0	0	13	5	8	4	0	14	1	0	0	1	0	1.00	3	.214	.279	.232
Clifford,Jim,Appleton	A	25	92	262	63	15	2	10	112	37	40	31	0	92	14	1	1	8	6	.57	4	.240	.351	.427
Cline,Pat,Cubs	R	20	3	0	0	0	0	0	0	0	0	0	0	0	0	0	0	0	0	.00	0	.000	.000	.000
Clyburn,Danny,Salem	A	21	118	461	126	19	0	22	211	57	90	20	2	96	0	0	5	4	5	.44	7	.273	.300	.458
Coach,Calvin,Johnson Cty	R	22	48	123	24	1	1	0	27	23	14	16	0	20	2	2	0	18	7	.72	1	.195	.298	.220
Coe,Kevin,Cubs	R	19	37	125	35	4	2	1	46	17	13	9	0	33	4	1	1	3	6	.33	2	.280	.345	.368
Coffee,Gary,Royals	R	20	44	114	28	4	2	1	39	14	17	18	0	32	4	0	0	0	0	.00	4	.246	.365	.342
Colburn,Brian,Twins	R	19	33	125	40	4	1	0	46	23	10	15	1	19	1	0	0	9	4	.69	2	.320	.394	.368
Cole,Abdul,Marlins	R	19	37	124	26	9	0	1	38	27	12	16	0	33	4	1	3	6	3	.67	3	.210	.313	.306
Coleman,Michael,Red Sox	R	19	25	95	26	6	1	3	43	15	15	10	0	20	3	0	1	5	3	.63	4	.274	.358	.453
Utica	A	19	23	65	11	2	0	1	16	16	3	14	0	21	0	3	0	11	1	.92	0	.169	.316	.246
Collier,Dan,Lynchburg	A	24	84	299	67	16	0	11	116	39	40	16	1	134	8	1	1	5	2	.71	6	.224	.281	.388
Collier,Lou,Augusta	A	21	85	318	89	17	4	7	135	48	40	25	0	53	8	0	3	32	10	.76	4	.280	.345	.425
Salem	A	21	43	158	42	4	1	6	66	25	16	15	0	29	6	2	2	5	8	.38	4	.266	.348	.418
Collins,Mike,Butte	R	22	43	145	33	4	1	0	39	18	14	12	0	42	2	3	1	10	3	.77	2	.228	.294	.269
Collum,Gary,Columbia	A	23	97	383	97	12	4	2	123	48	31	26	0	74	5	2	2	29	10	.74	3	.253	.308	.321
Colon,Hector,Madison	A	23	65	171	45	4	0	1	52	28	28	27	0	26	1	6	0	18	4	.82	4	.263	.367	.304
Columna,Jose,Macon	A	20	19	50	10	0	0	0	10	5	0	3	0	14	0	0	0	1	0	1.00	4	.200	.245	.200
Durham	A	20	6	3	0	0	0	0	0	1	0	1	0	2	0	0	0	0	0	.00	0	.000	.000	.000
Braves	R	20	12	34	10	0	0	1	13	1	1	4	0	9	0	0	0	0	1	.00	1	.294	.368	.382
Comeaux,Edward,Hudson Vall	A	22	69	223	50	7	4	0	65	29	26	29	0	46	5	4	2	26	10	.72	6	.224	.324	.291
Conger,Jeff,Salem	A	23	111	362	83	8	3	9	124	65	37	53	0	105	9	6	4	13	8	.62	5	.229	.339	.343
Conner,Decomba,Princeton	R	21	46	158	53	7	5	7	91	45	19	24	3	39	0	1	2	30	4	.88	0	.335	.418	.576
Contreras,Efrain,New Jersey	A	22	52	169	31	3	0	2	40	26	20	25	1	25	2	0	1	2	0	1.00	4	.183	.291	.237
Conway,Jeff,Spokane	A	22	44	121	27	5	0	1	35	13	11	14	0	31	1	2	2	1	1	.56	1	.223	.304	.289
Cook,David,Mets	R	19	31	113	32	8	1	1	45	10	13	8	0	20	1	0	0	1	2	.33	3	.283	.336	.398
Cook,Hayward,Elmira	A	23	63	227	62	10	8	5	103	36	29	20	0	45	2	1	1	6	5	.54	1	.273	.336	.454
Cook,Jason,Appleton	A	23	51	172	43	5	4	3	65	23	18	23	0	34	0	1	0	3	3	.50	7	.250	.338	.378
Cook,Steve,Cedar Rapds	A	23	87	277	71	16	1	5	104	43	40	41	0	66	4	5	2	5	3	.63	5	.256	.358	.375

									BATTING										BASERUNNING				PERCENTAGES		
Player	Lg	A	G	AB	H	2B	3B	HR	TB	R	RBI	TBB	IBB	SO	HBP	SH	SF		SB	CS	SB%	GDP	Avg	OBP	SLG
Coolbaugh,Mike,Dunedin	A	23	122	456	120	33	3	16	207	53	66	28	3	94	7	3	4		3	4	.43	14	.263	.313	.454
Cooney,Kyle,Great Falls	R	22	44	163	49	10	2	2	69	28	15	5	1	22	6	0	2		1	3	.25	0	.301	.341	.423
Cooper,Tim,Tampa	A	24	92	283	73	13	7	8	124	44	41	47	1	68	3	2	3		2	2	.50	5	.258	.366	.438
Coquillette,Trace,Burlington	A	21	5	17	3	1	0	0	4	2	0	1	0	4	0	0	0		1	0	1.00	0	.176	.222	.235
Vermont	A	21	70	252	77	11	5	9	125	54	52	23	0	40	8	1	6		7	2	.78	5	.306	.374	.496
Cora,Manuel,Riverside	A	23	115	411	124	13	9	0	155	50	46	17	0	49	1	11	2		7	5	.58	4	.302	.329	.377
Cordero,Pablo,Giants	R	22	22	77	23	3	0	1	29	18	11	7	2	13	2	0	0		7	2	.78	0	.299	.372	.377
Clinton	A	22	17	53	7	0	0	0	7	3	2	1	0	17	0	1	0		1	0	1.00	1	.132	.148	.132
Cordova,Luis,Brevard Cty	A	24	23	80	18	2	0	2	26	9	7	5	1	13	0	1	0		1	1	.50	0	.225	.271	.325
Corey,Bryan,Jamestown	A	21	41	85	13	1	1	0	16	14	3	13	0	27	2	1	0		2	3	.40	0	.153	.280	.188
Corso,Christopher,Kane County	A	24	3	8	3	0	0	0	3	0	2	1	0	3	0	0	0		0	0	.00	0	.375	.444	.375
Cossins,Timothy,Hudson Vall	A	25	6	17	2	1	0	1	6	1	2	0	0	4	0	0	0		0	0	.00	1	.118	.118	.353
Charlotte	A	25	10	28	3	0	0	0	3	2	2	4	0	6	0	1	0		1	0	1.00	1	.107	.219	.107
Costello,Brian,Spartanburg	A	20	126	456	107	17	2	6	146	58	65	40	2	122	5	2	4		13	10	.57	8	.235	.301	.320
Costic,Tim,Fort Wayne	A	24	68	235	56	13	1	4	83	28	29	11	0	60	3	0	3		4	3	.57	8	.238	.278	.353
Coulter,Shannon,Eugene	A	22	30	116	25	4	0	1	32	22	14	19	0	16	2	2	1		5	4	.56	0	.216	.333	.276
Cowsill,Brendon,Angels	R	20	19	55	9	3	2	0	16	6	6	4	0	21	0	0	0		1	0	1.00	4	.164	.220	.291
Cox,Steven,W. Michigan	A	20	99	311	75	19	2	6	116	37	32	41	3	95	4	1	3		2	6	.25	5	.241	.334	.373
Cox,Robert,Mets	R	19	27	97	21	4	0	0	25	14	11	10	0	24	0	0	1		0	1	.00	1	.216	.290	.258
Cradle,Cobi,Charlstn-Sc	A	23	112	412	114	19	5	1	146	80	28	60	3	59	6	6	4		43	12	.78	7	.277	.373	.354
Princeton	R	23	17	61	19	3	2	1	29	17	6	16	1	12	3	1	0		14	4	.78	0	.311	.475	.475
Cradle,Rickey,Dunedin	A	22	114	344	88	14	3	10	138	65	39	59	0	87	9	0	1		20	10	.67	5	.256	.378	.401
Craigue,Nathan,Twins	R	19	32	104	32	4	0	0	36	21	10	12	1	14	2	0	0		2	0	1.00	0	.308	.390	.346
Crawford,Rich,Brevard Cty	A	25	17	25	5	0	1	0	7	3	3	6	0	8	2	0	0		0	0	.00	0	.200	.394	.280
Creelman,Mark,Marlins	R	20	24	69	9	1	0	0	10	8	6	9	0	24	0	0	2		1	0	1.00	1	.130	.225	.145
Cromer,Brandon,Hagerstown	A	21	80	259	35	8	5	6	71	25	26	25	0	98	0	2	3		0	2	.00	4	.135	.209	.274
Cromer,David,W. Michigan	A	24	102	349	89	20	5	10	149	50	58	33	1	76	4	3	2		11	10	.52	5	.255	.325	.427
Cropper,Roger,Mariners	R	22	32	105	22	0	1	0	24	13	6	10	0	38	3	2	0		9	1	.90	0	.210	.297	.229
Crutchfield,David,Cubs	R	20	29	88	20	3	2	0	27	10	9	6	0	22	0	2	1		3	2	.60	0	.227	.274	.307
Cruz,Brian,Macon	A	24	60	128	25	6	0	1	34	14	14	29	0	34	3	6	2		1	2	.33	3	.195	.356	.266
Danville	R	24	11	23	3	1	0	0	4	3	2	1	0	6	3	0	0		0	0	.00	0	.130	.259	.174
Cruz,Devei,Giants	R	20	18	53	16	8	0	0	24	10	5	5	0	3	1	1	1		0	1	.00	1	.302	.367	.453
Cruz,Francis,Padres	R	20	41	136	31	2	3	1	42	15	13	10	0	60	3	0	1		5	2	.71	1	.228	.293	.309
Cruz,Jacob,San Jose	A	21	31	118	29	7	0	0	36	14	12	9	0	22	2	2	0		0	2	.00	6	.246	.305	.305
Cuellar,Jose,Appleton	A	25	54	154	33	5	1	1	43	17	17	19	0	32	0	0	1		0	0	.00	5	.214	.295	.279
Cuevas,Eduardo,Springfield	A	21	106	350	104	14	4	2	132	45	40	12	0	52	2	7	6		11	10	.52	5	.297	.319	.377
Culp,Matt,Watertown	A	22	8	27	7	5	0	0	12	4	4	2	0	3	1	0	1		0	1	.00	1	.259	.333	.444
Burlington	R	22	26	76	19	4	0	5	38	10	11	12	0	21	4	1	0		2	0	1.00	0	.250	.380	.500
Culp,Randy,Expos	R	20	23	88	11	2	0	1	16	2	3	3	0	25	0	0	0		4	0	.00	4	.125	.154	.182
Cumberbatch,Abdiel,San Berndo	A	23	21	80	15	1	1	0	18	12	8	9	0	23	0	1	1		4	2	.67	0	.188	.267	.225
Cunnigan,Donn,Pirates	R	22	16	52	12	3	0	0	15	7	3	10	0	14	0	0	0		1	2	.33	0	.231	.355	.288
Cunningham,Earl,Lake Elsino	A	25	36	108	23	4	0	5	42	14	15	6	0	50	0	1	1		1	1	.50	1	.213	.252	.389
Cedar Rapds	A	25	40	136	30	5	0	8	59	21	21	6	0	43	5	0	0		1	2	.33	0	.221	.279	.434
Curtis,Kevin,Orioles	R	19	12	38	15	5	0	1	23	3	4	6	0	4	0	0	0		1	0	1.00	1	.395	.477	.605
Albany	A	19	20	67	15	3	0	1	21	5	7	8	0	14	1	0	0		0	0	.00	1	.224	.325	.313
D'Ambrosia,Mark,Huntington	R	21	30	71	14	4	1	0	20	7	10	13	1	28	3	0	0		0	2	.00	3	.197	.345	.282
D'Amico,Jeff,W. Michigan	A	20	9	36	10	3	0	0	13	5	3	4	0	7	1	0	1		2	2	.50	0	.278	.357	.361
D'Aquila,Thomas,Bluefield	R	22	59	190	42	10	1	12	90	37	38	32	1	59	1	1	1		8	3	.73	3	.221	.335	.474
Daedelow,Craig,Orioles	R	19	46	116	26	2	0	0	28	19	8	19	0	20	2	1	0		6	1	.86	0	.224	.343	.241
Dailey,Jason,Idaho Falls	R	22	3	12	3	0	0	0	3	0	1	1	0	3	1	0	0		0	1	.00	1	.250	.308	.250
Dalton,Carl,Madison	A	23	129	466	112	33	5	12	191	69	77	53	2	104	4	2	6		11	6	.65	11	.240	.319	.410
Damon,Johnny,Wilmington	A	21	119	472	149	25	13	6	218	96	75	62	6	55	8	5	7		44	9	.83	4	.316	.399	.462
Danapilis,Eric,Fayettevlle	A	24	115	381	96	19	1	23	186	71	83	54	0	114	14	0	0		5	2	.71	12	.252	.360	.488
Daniels,Moe,Lake Elsino	A	24	79	237	62	6	3	7	95	55	36	49	0	85	1	5	0		18	6	.75	7	.262	.390	.401
Dantzler,Eric,Giants	R	22	49	173	40	6	2	0	50	23	27	33	2	46	1	0	3		13	2	.87	1	.231	.352	.289
Darden,Antonio,Elmira	A	21	50	175	46	8	5	1	67	34	20	18	0	30	6	1	0		6	3	.67	5	.263	.352	.383
Darr,Michael,Bristol	R	19	44	149	41	6	0	1	50	23	18	23	1	22	1	0	0		4	4	.50	3	.275	.376	.336
Darwin,Brian,Sou. Oregon	A	21	26	59	11	1	0	0	12	3	6	6	0	17	2	1	1		3	0	1.00	1	.186	.279	.203
Dasilva,Manny,Sou. Oregon	A	22	63	216	69	20	2	3	102	30	39	17	0	42	6	3	4		2	4	.33	7	.319	.379	.472
Daubach,Brian,St. Lucie	A	23	129	450	123	30	2	6	175	52	74	58	5	120	5	3	4		14	9	.61	3	.273	.360	.389
Daunic,Willie,St. Cathrns	A	24	66	232	50	5	0	0	55	22	20	27	0	34	1	5	1		2	1	.67	4	.216	.299	.237
Davalillo,David,Angels	R	20	54	231	58	8	3	3	81	28	31	12	0	39	0	4	1		1	1	.50	4	.251	.287	.351
Davenport,Jeff,Sarasota	A	24	10	16	3	1	0	0	4	2	1	0	0	4	0	0	0		1	0	1.00	1	.188	.188	.250
Lynchburg	A	24	14	45	8	2	0	1	13	1	4	1	0	13	0	0	0		2	0	.00	2	.178	.196	.222
Davidson,Cleatus,Twins	R	18	24	85	15	1	0	0	16	8	5	9	0	19	0	1	1		3	1	.75	0	.176	.253	.188
Davila,Victor,Hagerstown	A	22	77	266	65	10	2	8	103	35	31	18	2	59	3	0	2		2	1	.67	3	.244	.298	.387
Davis,Albert,Pirates	R	18	38	128	36	5	3	1	50	23	15	20	0	28	1	0	2		7	2	.78	2	.281	.377	.391
Davis,Edward,Bakersfield	A	24	56	198	51	7	1	7	81	25	22	18	0	67	4	2	0		8	10	.44	3	.258	.332	.409
Vero Beach	A	24	61	192	33	5	0	3	47	20	16	10	0	65	2	2	1		5	4	.56	4	.172	.220	.245
Davis,Josh,Padres	R	19	33	121	35	3	0	0	38	19	6	7	0	24	2	0	1		2	2	.50	1	.289	.336	.314
Davis,Melvin,Clinton	A	23	98	318	87	19	5	1	119	44	25	20	1	60	5	5	3		9	10	.47	6	.274	.324	.374
Davis,Thomas,Albany	A	22	61	216	59	10	1	5	86	35	35	18	0	52	2	4	4		4	4	.50	3	.273	.331	.398
Dawson,Charles,Idaho Falls	R	23	36	133	40	7	2	5	66	31	28	17	0	14	1	0	3		4	3	.57	3	.301	.377	.496
Dean,Chris,Bellingham	A	22	72	270	79	16	0	9	122	50	30	26	1	65	8	3	2		15	7	.68	6	.290	.367	.449
Dean,Mark,New Jersey	A	24	60	186	38	7	0	0	45	24	17	14	0	34	2	0	1		6	6	.50	5	.204	.262	.242
Deares,Gregory,Madison	A	24	65	227	63	17	4	4	100	32	29	26	1	40	1	0	1		2	3	.40	7	.278	.353	.441
Deboer,Robert,Sou. Oregon	A	24	45	129	33	4	0	4	49	23	21	18	0	43	2	0	1		7	0	1.00	4	.256	.353	.380

1994 Batting -- Single-A and Rookie Leagues

													BATTING						BASERUNNING				PERCENTAGES		
Player	Lg	A	G	AB	H	2B	3B	HR	TB	R	RBI	TBB	IBB	SO	HBP	SH	SF	SB	CS	SB%	GDP	Avg	OBP	SLG
DeBruhl,Randy,Charlstn-Sc	A	25	59	140	25	4	0	6	47	14	16	13	0	66	3	2	0	0	0	.00	4	.179	.263	.336
DeJesus,Jose,Cubs	R	20	50	172	35	8	2	2	53	27	22	9	0	57	2	2	3	1	1	.50	1	.203	.247	.308
DeJesus,Malvin,Fayetteville	A	23	66	189	39	7	1	1	51	21	14	32	0	34	1	3	1	19	6	.76	3	.206	.323	.270
Dekneef,Mike,Appleton	A	25	32	101	20	3	0	0	23	7	7	7	0	15	2	2	1	2	2	.50	2	.198	.261	.228
de la Cruz,Lorenzo,Hagerstown	A	23	125	457	111	20	4	19	196	72	62	30	1	152	6	1	0	12	8	.60	13	.243	.298	.429
Delafield,Glenn,Greensboro	A	23	88	305	70	5	2	4	91	41	23	40	0	90	4	2	0	11	12	.48	11	.230	.327	.298
Delaney,Donovan,Eugene	A	21	63	234	63	16	1	6	99	35	33	13	3	50	7	2	4	7	0	1.00	4	.269	.322	.423
De La Rosa,Elvis,Bristol	R	20	31	91	15	3	1	2	26	10	7	11	0	23	0	0	0	1	1	.50	1	.165	.255	.286
Lakeland	A	20	2	3	0	0	0	0	0	0	0	0	0	2	0	0	0	0	0	.00	0	.000	.000	.000
Deleon,Jose,Bellingham	A	21	50	152	33	7	0	0	40	13	17	1	1	26	1	1	1	2	2	.50	2	.217	.226	.263
DeLeon,Robert,Rancho Cuca	A	24	123	435	110	21	3	7	158	53	74	22	1	64	6	1	11	3	3	.50	8	.253	.291	.363
DeLeon,Santos,Bellingham	A	21	56	167	37	8	0	0	45	24	10	13	1	50	2	4	0	18	1	.95	2	.222	.286	.269
Delgado,Ariel,Angels	R	18	38	105	15	1	1	0	18	14	3	6	0	19	3	1	0	5	2	.71	8	.143	.211	.171
Delgado,Jose,Danville	R	20	27	94	22	4	0	0	26	13	7	10	1	11	1	1	2	4	3	.57	1	.234	.308	.277
Braves	R	20	23	79	14	1	0	0	15	11	3	12	0	10	0	0	0	5	2	.71	0	.177	.286	.190
Duran,Wilson,Mariners	R	20	39	149	56	5	4	0	69	30	10	15	0	24	1	0	0	13	5	.72	2	.376	.436	.463
Appleton	A	20	9	31	6	0	0	0	6	2	0	0	0	8	0	0	0	0	0	.00	2	.194	.194	.194
Delossantos,Juan,Mariners	R	19	11	37	9	0	0	0	9	3	2	1	0	13	1	1	0	0	0	.00	1	.243	.282	.243
Delvecchio,Nick,Yankees	R	25	4	13	5	0	0	0	5	1	0	2	0	3	0	0	0	0	0	.00	0	.385	.467	.385
Tampa	A	25	27	95	27	3	0	7	51	17	18	11	0	20	1	0	0	0	0	.00	0	.284	.361	.537
DeMark,Dominic,Rockies	R	21	39	123	31	7	0	2	44	17	20	7	0	36	6	0	1	0	0	.00	3	.252	.321	.358
Denbow,Don,Everett	A	22	63	227	56	5	2	12	101	44	41	39	0	92	2	0	1	3	1	.75	1	.247	.361	.445
Denman,Ralph,Danville	R	22	24	81	18	5	0	0	23	12	7	6	0	17	0	0	0	3	3	.50	0	.222	.276	.284
Dennis,Brian,Williamsprt	A	23	50	141	35	6	0	4	53	20	17	11	3	30	15	2	2	2	5	.29	5	.248	.361	.376
Depastino,Joe,Utica	A	21	51	172	46	11	1	5	74	23	31	22	1	41	3	1	1	5	2	.71	4	.267	.357	.430
Dermendziev,Tony,Asheville	A	22	72	187	35	6	0	7	62	22	22	12	1	49	1	1	0	6	4	.60	0	.187	.239	.332
Derosso,Anthony,Red Sox	R	19	46	168	42	6	0	4	60	23	22	12	0	33	5	0	3	1	0	1.00	1	.250	.314	.357
Derotal,Francisco,Spokane	A	21	20	54	8	3	0	0	11	5	5	4	0	21	1	1	1	2	1	.33	2	.148	.213	.204
Padres	R	21	4	12	0	0	0	0	0	0	1	0	0	4	0	0	1	0	0	.00	1	.000	.000	.000
De Simone,Ray,Charlstn-Wv	A	22	72	216	43	6	0	0	49	25	16	25	0	38	2	2	3	8	7	.53	4	.199	.285	.227
Diaz,Freddie,Lake Elsino	A	22	110	350	100	29	1	5	146	48	64	35	0	71	4	7	6	4	4	.50	5	.286	.352	.417
Diaz,Cesar,Columbia	A	20	66	225	55	13	1	7	91	26	27	21	0	46	5	0	2	3	2	.60	3	.244	.320	.404
Diaz,Edwin,Charlstn-Wv	A	20	122	413	109	22	7	11	178	52	60	22	0	107	8	8	9	11	14	.44	7	.264	.308	.431
Diaz,Einar,Columbus	A	22	120	491	137	23	2	16	212	67	71	17	0	34	21	1	1	4	4	.50	18	.279	.330	.432
Diaz,Javier,Asheville	A	20	36	88	23	4	0	1	30	9	9	8	1	23	0	2	0	2	1	.67	6	.261	.323	.341
Diaz,Ivan,Cardinals	R	20	21	62	17	0	0	0	17	8	4	4	0	13	1	1	0	1	0	1.00	4	.274	.328	.274
Diaz,Linardo,Martinsvlle	R	20	56	200	47	5	2	2	62	33	22	20	0	44	2	1	0	13	6	.68	4	.235	.311	.310
Diaz,Lino,Rockford	A	24	127	414	131	23	1	4	168	57	44	32	4	33	14	2	5	11	6	.65	14	.316	.381	.406
Dickerson,Bobby,Fayetteville	A	23	83	255	51	9	2	2	70	36	22	32	0	91	2	0	0	6	5	.55	2	.200	.294	.275
Dieguez,Mike,Huntington	R	22	61	192	51	21	1	0	74	14	17	32	1	28	2	1	1	3	4	.43	6	.266	.365	.385
Dietz,Steve,Fayetteville	A	24	56	165	33	4	1	0	39	27	21	35	1	37	1	3	1	11	4	.73	1	.200	.342	.236
Difilippo,John,Princeton	R	21	24	22	5	1	0	0	6	10	2	6	0	5	1	0	0	5	3	.63	1	.227	.414	.273
Dijol,Julio,Cubs	R	NA	21	42	4	1	0	0	5	6	4	10	0	19	3	1	0	1	0	1.00	0	.095	.309	.119
Dillingham,Daniel,Eugene	A	21	37	134	29	4	0	3	42	16	17	12	2	33	3	1	0	4	3	.57	1	.216	.295	.313
Dilone,Juan W.,Michigan	A	22	106	352	81	15	5	12	142	66	48	46	3	110	4	5	3	29	12	.71	3	.230	.323	.403
Disalle,Javier,Orioles	R	19	11	29	8	2	0	0	10	4	5	1	0	7	0	0	0	0	1	.00	3	.276	.300	.345
Dishington,Nate,Cardinals	R	20	51	179	51	15	3	4	84	36	36	22	2	58	5	0	2	1	1	.50	2	.285	.375	.469
Dixon,Colin,San Bernrdo	A	26	126	477	134	31	1	19	224	79	79	39	0	92	16	7	4	4	2	.67	14	.281	.353	.470
Dobrolsky,Bill,Beloit	A	25	72	197	52	12	0	3	73	29	25	35	0	55	3	5	0	1	1	.50	4	.264	.383	.371
Doezie,Troy,Ogden	R	21	28	74	13	3	0	2	22	11	13	8	0	27	2	2	3	0	1	.00	0	.176	.264	.297
Dolney,Daniel,Osceola	A	19	4	9	1	0	0	0	1	0	0	1	0	1	0	0	0	0	0	.00	0	.111	.200	.111
Astros	R	19	32	73	18	2	2	0	24	8	9	9	1	11	3	3	1	2	0	1.00	0	.247	.349	.329
Domino,Rob,Billings	R	24	58	192	63	9	0	3	81	37	32	24	1	32	1	1	4	3	4	.57	6	.328	.398	.422
Donati,John,Boise	A	22	70	233	74	19	1	11	128	62	57	53	3	61	5	0	5	4	0	1.00	5	.318	.446	.549
Dorencz,Mark,Quad City	A	23	45	122	23	3	2	1	33	21	11	14	0	24	0	4	1	2	1	.67	4	.189	.272	.270
Dorsey,Jim,Pittsfield	A	22	21	82	26	9	0	0	35	16	18	5	0	11	0	1	1	3	1	.75	1	.317	.352	.427
Doster,David,Clearwater	A	24	131	480	135	42	4	13	224	76	74	54	3	71	11	3	8	12	7	.63	12	.281	.362	.467
Doty,Derrin,Cedar Rapds	A	25	60	229	74	12	0	5	101	43	34	25	1	52	4	0	0	20	4	.83	5	.323	.398	.441
Lake Elsino	A	25	64	238	65	12	0	7	98	41	24	21	1	46	5	5	1	12	5	.71	7	.273	.345	.412
Doucette,Darren,Madison	A	24	69	157	33	6	1	4	53	17	17	31	1	45	3	1	2	0	0	.00	1	.210	.347	.338
Dowler,Demetrius,Daytona	A	23	126	481	136	17	3	9	186	80	62	36	2	83	6	10	3	15	7	.68	6	.283	.338	.387
Drent,Brian,White Sox	R	21	31	70	13	2	1	1	20	6	4	11	0	25	0	1	0	2	5	.29	1	.186	.296	.286
Driskell,Jeff,Jamestown	A	23	48	163	48	9	3	5	78	18	29	9	0	37	1	2	3	0	2	.00	4	.294	.330	.479
Dukart,Derek,Oneonta	A	23	83	234	69	8	0	0	77	25	33	19	0	36	2	1	1	2	0	1.00	8	.295	.350	.329
Duke,Darrick,Springfield	A	24	114	392	92	11	3	5	124	60	51	54	1	85	8	2	2	27	14	.66	1	.235	.336	.316
Duke,Mitch,Charlstn-Sc	A	25	82	225	48	5	2	2	63	19	17	36	0	35	2	2	1	0	0	.00	8	.213	.326	.280
Dumas,Christopher,Mariners	R	20	37	112	22	5	0	2	33	16	8	11	0	34	3	1	0	5	1	.83	2	.196	.286	.295
Dumas,Mike,Beloit	A	24	100	331	102	7	0	0	109	66	36	62	0	59	3	10	1	41	16	.72	4	.308	.421	.329
Dunavan,Chad,Appleton	A	22	37	118	25	4	2	5	48	14	20	3	0	49	2	1	1	2	0	1.00	6	.212	.244	.407
Duncan,Mark,Lethbridge	R	23	70	270	89	11	5	1	113	61	37	17	1	45	17	1	2	16	11	.59	3	.330	.402	.419
Duncan,Robert,Braves	R	19	21	54	8	2	0	0	10	2	1	8	0	21	4	0	0	2	0	1.00	1	.148	.303	.185
Dunn,Todd,Beloit	A	24	129	429	94	13	2	23	180	72	63	50	3	131	6	4	4	18	8	.69	6	.219	.307	.420
Dunwoody,Todd,Kane County	A	20	15	45	5	0	0	1	8	7	1	5	0	17	0	1	0	2	0	1.00	1	.111	.200	.178
Marlins	R	20	46	169	44	6	6	1	65	32	25	21	1	28	4	1	1	11	3	.79	1	.260	.354	.385
Duplessis,Dave.W. Palm Bch	A	25	115	389	101	24	2	8	153	49	58	48	5	108	10	0	4	4	4	.50	6	.260	.351	.393
Durkin,Chris,Osceola	A	24	103	329	77	21	1	4	112	46	31	53	3	86	3	0	5	20	9	.69	5	.234	.341	.340
Duross,Gabe,Peoria	A	23	119	465	136	27	2	6	185	48	95	13	4	26	5	1	4	3	4	.43	16	.292	.316	.398

1994 Batting -- Single-A and Rookie Leagues

			BATTING															BASERUNNING				PERCENTAGES		
Player	Lg	A	G	AB	H	2B	3B	HR	TB	R	RBI	TBB	IBB	SO	HBP	SH	SF	SB	CS	SB%	GDP	Avg	OBP	SLG
Durrington,Trent,Angels	R	19	16	52	14	3	0	1	20	13	2	11	0	16	1	0	0	5	1	.83	1	.269	.406	.385
Durrwachter,Douglas,Billings	R	23	65	236	67	11	3	1	87	48	25	28	0	43	5	2	3	13	6	.68	5	.284	.368	.369
Durso,Joe,Hagerstown	A	24	104	382	116	25	3	11	180	77	67	61	2	66	2	1	2	6	2	.75	5	.304	.400	.471
Duva,Brian,Watertown	A	22	48	170	45	4	2	3	62	28	27	13	1	26	2	1	3	11	1	.92	3	.265	.319	.365
Eaddy,Keith,Albany	A	24	28	86	25	7	0	2	38	14	8	7	0	24	1	0	0	2	2	.50	0	.291	.358	.442
Frederick	A	24	43	106	16	3	0	2	25	13	12	19	0	47	1	1	1	1	0	1.00	2	.151	.283	.236
Eaglin,Mike,Macon	A	22	26	77	18	0	0	0	18	8	5	9	0	18	2	2	0	7	2	.78	1	.234	.330	.234
Ealy,Tracey,San Jose	A	23	46	162	37	6	2	3	56	22	22	22	0	38	1	3	1	3	5	.38	2	.228	.323	.346
San Bernrdo	A	23	41	149	45	5	0	3	59	20	9	20	0	37	3	2	0	10	2	.83	2	.302	.395	.396
Ebbert,Chad,Padres	R	21	17	54	9	4	0	0	13	4	5	7	1	11	0	0	0	0	1	.00	0	.167	.262	.241
Ebel,Dino,Bakersfield	A	29	2	3	1	0	0	0	1	0	0	0	0	0	0	0	0	0	0	.00	0	.333	.333	.333
Eddie,Steven,Charlstn-Sc	A	24	132	470	116	28	1	1	149	40	57	24	0	82	4	4	6	1	5	.17	11	.247	.286	.317
Edens,Larry,Williamsprt	A	24	23	74	19	1	3	1	29	10	10	12	0	21	0	0	0	6	3	.67	0	.257	.360	.392
Edwards,Aaron,Welland	A	21	69	274	66	8	3	1	83	32	19	14	0	53	5	1	4	18	6	.75	6	.241	.286	.303
Edwards,Randy,Asheville	A	21	23	61	12	4	0	1	19	4	5	9	0	18	0	1	0	0	1	.00	1	.197	.292	.311
Eierman,John,Lynchburg	A	25	38	123	24	2	0	5	41	14	17	10	0	31	1	1	0	1	0	1.00	3	.195	.261	.333
High Desert	A	25	74	291	94	19	1	6	133	35	46	14	0	61	1	0	2	2	2	.50	4	.323	.354	.457
Eldridge,Brian,Modesto	A	25	39	102	23	0	3	2	35	12	12	17	1	22	1	1	3	0	1	.00	2	.225	.333	.343
W. Michigan	A	25	49	184	48	11	1	1	64	28	15	17	3	29	3	2	1	3	0	1.00	3	.261	.332	.348
Elliott,Greg,Osceola	A	25	100	339	92	21	4	1	124	38	36	43	0	49	2	2		4	3	.57	9	.271	.355	.366
Ellis,Kevin,Peoria	A	23	105	386	109	18	4	14	177	65	67	42	3	93	7	0	2	3	1	.75	8	.282	.362	.459
Ellsworth,Ben,Savannah	A	24	54	73	13	2	0	0	15	15	3	6	0	22	0	2	0	0	4	.00	2	.178	.241	.205
Encarnacion,Juan,Fayettevlle	A	19	24	83	16	1	1	1	22	6	4	8	1	36	1	0	0	1	1	.50	2	.193	.272	.265
Bristol	R	19	54	197	49	7	1	4	70	16	31	13	1	54	1	1	1	9	2	.82	2	.249	.310	.355
Lakeland	A	19	3	6	2	0	0	0	2	1	0	0	0	3	1	0	0	0	0	.00	0	.333	.429	.333
Engle,Daniel,Mets	R	20	20	53	11	0	1	1	16	6	3	9	0	13	1	2	0	0	0	.00	3	.208	.333	.302
Ennis,Wayne,Princeton	R	18	29	71	10	3	0	0	13	10	8	6	0	27	1	2	1	6	1	.86	1	.141	.215	.183
Ephan,Larry,Charlstn-Wv	A	24	101	314	78	18	1	5	113	42	41	71	0	62	5	0	2	5	5	.00	3	.248	.393	.360
Epperson,Chad,St. Lucie	A	23	50	148	32	7	0	2	45	15	10	16	2	42	0	1	2	1	2	.33	2	.216	.289	.304
Escalet,Ruberto,Helena	R	23	15	33	4	0	0	0	4	3	5	3	2	0	0	0	1	0	1	1.00	0	.121	.189	.121
Brewers	R	23	31	106	33	2	0	1	38	20	19	16	1	19	0	1	0	4	3	.57	0	.311	.426	.358
Espada,Angel,Braves	R	20	26	73	16	2	0	0	18	11	1	8	0	11	0	1	0	7	5	.58	0	.219	.296	.247
Espinal,Juan,Springfield	A	20	118	386	95	27	3	14	170	66	50	36	1	102	3	4	5	0	2	.00	2	.246	.312	.440
Espy,Cecil,San Bernrdo	A	32	43	171	32	10	0	1	45	12	12	17	0	55	0	0	0	4	2	.67	2	.187	.261	.263
Estalella,Bobby,Spartanburg	A	20	86	299	65	19	1	9	113	34	41	31	0	85	1	1	4	0	1	.00	5	.217	.290	.378
Clearwater	A	20	13	46	12	1	0	2	19	3	9	3	0	17	0	2	1	0	0	.00	0	.261	.300	.413
Estrada,Josue,Burlington	A	20	119	416	93	12	3	5	126	52	39	36	0	140	3	7	3	8	3	.73	6	.224	.288	.303
Estrada,Osmani,Charlotte	A	26	131	501	128	29	4	4	177	64	30	57	0	60	11	7	5	8	10	.44	10	.255	.341	.353
Eusebio,Ralph,Huntington	R	22	4	11	0	0	0	0	0	2	1	2	0	2	1	0	0	1	0	1.00	0	.000	.214	.000
Evans,Jason,South Bend	A	24	97	355	94	15	3	6	133	53	48	47	3	70	2	8	5	8	8	.50	3	.265	.350	.375
Evans,Matthew,Lakeland	A	23	124	436	106	20	1	6	146	38	53	65	4	82	2	1	0	3	2	.60	11	.243	.344	.335
Evans,Michael,Rockford	A	22	72	219	42	13	0	9	82	26	31	28	1	53	4	0	0	2	1	.67	6	.192	.295	.374
Evans,Pat,Watertown	A	22	27	82	21	1	2	0	26	6	12	12	1	17	1	0	0	1	0	1.00	0	.256	.358	.317
Evans,Stan,Clearwater	A	24	73	205	45	10	0	1	58	27	23	25	1	40	3	3	4	3	4	.43	1	.220	.308	.283
Evans,Tom,Hagerstown	A	20	95	322	88	16	2	13	147	52	51	51	1	80	1	1	1	2	1	.67	3	.273	.373	.457
Everson,Darin,Burlington	A	24	39	117	31	10	1	7	64	23	32	12	1	30	2	1	1	0	0	.00	2	.265	.341	.547
Faccione,Christopher,Fayettevlle	A	24	120	448	113	23	9	14	196	66	60	41	3	84	4	3	3	30	13	.70	12	.252	.319	.438
Faggett,Ethan,Red Sox	A	24	41	117	34	2	2	1	43	14	17	12	0	33	2	0	0	10	7	.59	2	.291	.366	.368
Fagley,Dan,Marlins	R	20	14	41	6	1	0	0	7	4	2	7	0	15	1	0	0	0	1	.00	1	.146	.286	.171
Failla,Paul,Boise	A	22	62	208	46	7	1	0	55	37	30	46	0	41	0	4	4	7	2	.78	4	.221	.357	.264
Faircloth,Wayne,South Bend	A	24	4	9	2	0	0	0	2	0	0	2	0	5	1	0	0	0	0	.00	0	.222	.417	.222
Faircloth,Kevin,Yakima	A	25	51	169	34	1	1	0	37	33	14	24	0	46	4	4	2	11	1	.92	0	.201	.312	.219
Fairman,Andy,Stockton	A	25	50	185	44	13	0	5	72	29	24	18	1	27	2	2	3	4	0	1.00	4	.238	.308	.389
Fana,Chico,Martinsvle	R	21	2	5	1	1	0	0	2	0	1	0	0	3	0	0	0	0	0	.00	0	.200	.200	.400
Fantauzzi,John,Rancho Cuca	A	23	32	108	25	2	0	4	39	15	12	13	0	30	0	1	1	1	1	.50	0	.231	.311	.361
Springfield	A	23	68	231	70	12	0	5	97	32	40	26	1	54	6	1	5	0	3	.00	5	.303	.381	.420
Farlow,Kevin,Lake Elsino	A	26	8	23	3	0	0	0	3	1	1	1	0	7	0	0	0	0	0	.00	0	.130	.167	.130
Farner,Matt,Blue Jays	R	20	10	35	9	0	0	0	9	4	1	3	0	10	0	0	0	3	2	.60	0	.257	.316	.257
Farrell,Jon,Salem	A	23	123	445	120	21	4	11	182	67	42	41	1	91	4	0	1	11	2	.85	8	.270	.336	.409
Farris,Mark,Welland	A	20	45	164	47	7	1	1	59	16	17	20	0	35	2	0	2	2	5	.00	2	.287	.371	.360
Augusta	A	20	14	49	6	0	0	1	9	2	2	1	0	15	2	0	0	0	0	.00	1	.122	.173	.184
Fasano,Salvatore,Rockford	A	23	97	345	97	16	1	25	190	61	81	33	4	66	16	0	5	8	3	.73	10	.281	.366	.551
Wilmington	A	23	23	90	29	7	0	7	57	15	32	13	0	24	0	0	3	0	0	.00	3	.322	.408	.633
Feauto,Brett,Batavia	A	24	6	19	4	0	0	0	4	2	3	1	0	8	1	0	1	0	1	1.00	0	.211	.273	.211
Felch,Jim,Danville	R	24	16	36	7	3	0	0	10	4	5	9	1	15	0	0	0	0	0	.00	1	.194	.356	.278
Idaho Falls	R	24	13	45	12	1	0	0	13	3	4	1	0	6	0	1	0	1	0	1.00	0	.267	.283	.289
Felder,Ken,Stockton	A	24	121	435	119	21	2	10	174	56	60	32	1	112	11	5	4	4	4	.50	6	.274	.336	.400
Feliz,Pedro,Giants	R	18	38	119	23	0	0	0	23	7	3	2	0	20	2	3	4	2	3	.40	3	.193	.220	.193
Fenton,Cary,Vermont	A	22	47	156	37	5	0	0	42	20	12	20	1	30	7	5	0	13	5	.72	1	.237	.350	.269
Ferguson,Jeffrey,Fort Wayne	A	22	22	89	23	7	1	1	35	15	6	11	0	18	1	0	0	4	1	.80	1	.258	.347	.393
Fermin,Carlos,Lakeland	A	21	39	114	19	0	0	0	19	8	8	5	0	16	0	1	0	1	2	.33	5	.167	.202	.167
Fernandez,Antonio,Spokane	A	22	68	265	62	11	1	1	78	23	37	23	2	56	3	0	5	5	5	.17	8	.234	.297	.294
Fernandez,Jose,Expos	R	20	44	168	39	8	0	5	62	27	23	13	0	33	2	1	1	11	1	.92	2	.232	.293	.369
Fernandez,Randy,Cardinals	R	21	15	42	11	1	0	0	12	4	5	8	0	14	0	0	0	3	3	.50	0	.262	.380	.286
Ferrier,Ross,Pittsfield	A	23	54	192	56	9	8	1	84	22	35	23	2	41	3	0	0	5	5	.50	0	.292	.376	.438
Fick,Chris,San Bernrdo	A	25	44	144	32	10	1	7	65	20	28	15	0	47	3	1	0	2	3	.40	2	.222	.309	.451
Figueroa,Danny,Asheville	A	21	28	74	16	4	0	1	23	7	5	3	0	26	1	0	0	2	1	.67	0	.216	.326	.311

1994 Batting -- Single-A and Rookie Leagues

| | | | BATTING | | | | | | | | | | | | | | | | BASERUNNING | | | | PERCENTAGES | | |
Player	Lg	A	G	AB	H	2B	3B	HR	TB	R	RBI	TBB	IBB	SO	HBP	SH	SF	SB	CS	SB%	GDP	Avg	OBP	SLG
Bend	A	21	48	122	29	10	0	2	45	15	11	20	0	47	5	1	1	7	6	.54	2	.238	.365	.369
Fink,Marc,Brewers	R	18	11	35	7	0	0	1	10	1	4	2	0	13	1	0	0	0	0	.00	0	.200	.263	.286
Fithian,Grant,Tampa	A	23	5	11	2	1	0	0	3	1	0	1	0	3	0	0	0	0	0	.00	1	.182	.250	.273
Fitzpatrick,Will,Beloit	A	24	119	390	95	24	0	12	155	39	52	60	6	98	2	0	5	2	1	.67	4	.244	.344	.397
Flannelly,Tim,Tampa	A	24	1	3	3	1	0	0	4	0	1	1	0	0	0	0	0	0	0	.00	0	1.000	1.000	1.333
Flores,Jose,Batavia	A	22	68	229	58	7	3	0	71	41	16	41	0	31	6	2	2	23	8	.74	3	.253	.378	.310
Fonville,Chad,San Jose	A	24	68	283	87	9	6	0	108	58	26	34	0	34	4	5	0	22	8	.73	5	.307	.389	.382
Foote,Derek,Danville	R	20	19	54	9	3	0	1	15	4	5	4	0	25	1	1	0	0	0	.00	1	.167	.237	.278
Ford,Eric,Utica	A	23	49	148	30	8	0	1	41	13	25	6	0	29	3	0	3	2	2	.50	0	.203	.244	.277
Forkner,Timothy,Quad City	A	22	124	429	128	23	4	6	177	57	57	57	3	72	7	10	8	6	8	.43	10	.298	.383	.413
Fortin,Troy,Fort Wayne	A	20	1	4	0	0	0	0	0	0	0	0	0	0	0	0	0	0	0	.00	0	.000	.200	.000
Elizabethtn	R	20	63	221	68	17	1	8	111	48	40	41	3	28	7	0	0	1	2	.33	8	.308	.431	.502
Foster,James,Albany	A	23	121	421	112	29	3	8	171	61	56	54	0	59	11	0	6	5	3	.63	13	.266	.360	.406
Foster,Jason,Angels	R	22	9	31	5	1	0	0	6	5	3	3	0	10	2	1	0	0	0	.00	0	.161	.278	.194
Foster,Jeffrey,Burlington	A	23	85	313	67	11	0	9	105	43	35	29	0	84	1	2	2	6	2	.75	8	.214	.284	.335
Francisco,David,Modesto	A	22	130	499	138	18	5	9	193	86	48	61	0	110	9	11	2	29	18	.62	1	.277	.364	.387
Francisco,Vicente,W.Michigan	A	22	131	452	112	19	0	0	131	43	41	40	0	69	0	14	6	16	16	.50	4	.248	.305	.290
Franklin,James,Yankees	A	24	38	127	34	0	0	0	34	16	11	19	0	26	1	1	0	1	6	.14	3	.268	.367	.268
Franklin,James,Braves	R	20	6	19	3	0	0	0	3	0	0	0	0	4	1	0	0	0	0	.00	0	.158	.200	.158
Idaho Falls	R	20	40	132	24	4	2	0	32	16	18	16	0	31	1	1	0	6	2	.75	1	.182	.273	.242
Fraraccio,Dan,Pr.William	A	24	26	80	19	1	1	1	25	10	7	3	0	19	0	1	1	0	1	1.00	1	.238	.262	.313
White Sox	R	24	3	2	1	0	0	0	1	0	0	1	0	1	0	0	0	0	0	.00	0	.500	.667	.500
Frazier,Ronald,Royals	R	20	41	124	26	4	1	2	38	17	14	9	0	30	3	3	1	11	2	.85	3	.210	.277	.306
Frazier,Terance,Modesto	A	26	64	179	41	10	1	1	56	25	10	15	0	33	1	2	1	2	4	.33	3	.229	.291	.313
Freeburg,Ryan,Central Val	A	24	94	300	72	20	1	10	124	32	40	33	1	121	9	4	1	3	4	.43	7	.240	.332	.413
Freeman,Richard,Huntington	R	23	64	218	49	10	3	0	65	23	30	35	0	22	3	0	7	12	6	.67	6	.225	.331	.298
Freeman,Sean,Jamestown	A	23	67	222	65	14	1	2	87	22	31	19	3	46	4	0	4	2	2	.50	0	.293	.353	.392
Freire,Alejandro,Astros	R	20	29	83	25	4	0	1	32	8	13	5	0	17	3	2	2	5	1	.83	0	.301	.355	.386
French,Anton,Cardinals	R	19	52	204	45	8	8	2	75	30	29	16	1	53	0	0	2	11	3	.79	0	.221	.275	.368
Frias,Hanley,High Desert	A	21	124	452	115	17	6	3	153	70	59	41	1	74	2	5	3	37	12	.76	9	.254	.317	.338
Frias,Reddy,St.Cathrns	A	NA	73	270	67	6	4	0	81	40	19	41	0	61	4	8	0	23	11	.68	1	.248	.356	.300
Fric,Sean,Peoria	A	22	19	56	15	4	0	0	19	8	4	7	0	16	0	1	0	1	2	.33	1	.268	.349	.339
Williamsprt	A	22	66	230	61	18	4	5	102	39	25	30	1	43	2	0	4	9	5	.64	6	.265	.350	.443
Friedman,Jason,Sarasota	A	25	124	469	154	35	11	7	232	60	87	22	9	74	1	1	12	2	3	.40	3	.328	.351	.495
Friedrich,Steven,Hickory	A	22	29	87	14	5	0	1	22	8	10	8	0	35	1	3	2	0	1	.00	1	.161	.235	.253
Butte	R	22	51	203	55	9	5	3	83	27	31	12	0	60	1	1	3	6	1	.86	5	.271	.311	.409
Froschauer,Trevor,Osceola	A	22	4	10	3	0	0	0	3	2	0	1	0	5	0	0	0	0	0	.00	0	.300	.364	.300
Quad City	A	22	48	144	30	8	0	6	56	14	22	19	0	61	6	0	2	0	0	.00	0	.208	.322	.389
Frye,Danny,Winston-Sal	A	25	86	287	54	15	1	10	101	38	28	38	0	89	2	1	0	2	7	.22	7	.188	.287	.352
Fuller,Aaron,Sarasota	A	23	118	414	108	17	2	2	135	89	28	82	1	90	5	14	2	45	13	.78	7	.261	.388	.326
Fussell,Denny,Billings	R	24	49	153	50	8	2	1	65	27	20	19	1	32	1	0	1	4	1	.80	4	.327	.402	.425
Gabriel,Denio,Orioles	R	19	7	28	8	2	0	0	10	2	2	0	0	7	1	0	0	1	1	.50	0	.286	.310	.357
Bluefield	R	19	52	168	33	6	4	0	47	22	10	7	0	36	0	2	2	13	6	.68	3	.196	.226	.280
Gagliano,Emanuel,San Bernrdo	A	24	62	213	43	11	1	2	62	15	14	20	0	62	1	3	0	1	0	1.00	6	.202	.274	.291
Gainey,Bryon,Mets	R	19	47	179	41	8	1	5	66	26	28	17	0	54	3	1	5	0	1	.00	5	.229	.299	.369
Kingsport	R	19	10	32	5	0	0	3	14	4	7	4	1	16	0	0	0	0	2	.00	0	.156	.250	.438
Galan,Manolo,Orioles	R	20	24	40	5	0	0	0	5	0	2	6	0	7	0	2	0	0	0	.00	1	.125	.239	.125
Galarza,Joel,Giants	R	21	29	87	17	2	2	1	26	9	9	9	1	20	2	1	2	3	3	.50	1	.195	.280	.299
Clinton	A	21	19	61	15	1	0	1	19	8	7	8	0	14	1	0	0	2	2	.50	2	.246	.343	.311
Galligani,Marcel,W.Michigan	A	24	43	116	24	5	0	3	38	12	15	15	0	44	2	1	0	3	3	.50	1	.207	.308	.328
Gallone,Santy,Spartanburg	A	23	103	341	96	27	0	6	141	52	37	36	0	47	10	3	0	6	2	.75	9	.282	.367	.413
Gambill,Chad,Bend	A	19	58	194	42	11	1	4	67	16	27	15	0	61	0	2	2	4	2	.67	5	.216	.268	.345
Gann,Stephen,Charlstn-Sc	A	25	129	475	130	30	2	10	194	60	72	20	3	90	9	1	3	6	4	.60	6	.274	.314	.408
Garcia,Adrian,Durham	A	22	72	169	40	6	0	5	61	19	21	24	1	65	1	0	0	2	0	1.00	0	.237	.335	.361
Garcia,Amaury,Marlins	R	NA	58	208	65	9	3	0	80	46	25	33	0	49	2	1	2	10	3	.77	4	.313	.408	.385
Garcia,Apostol,Bristol	R	18	47	130	20	3	0	0	23	20	8	18	0	35	5	5	0	18	9	.67	0	.154	.281	.177
Lakeland	A	18	6	15	4	0	0	0	4	0	0	3	0	3	0	0	0	1	1	.50	0	.267	.267	.267
Garcia,Carlos,Twins	R	19	35	127	33	6	2	1	46	16	12	6	0	25	1	2	1	10	0	1.00	1	.260	.296	.362
Garcia,Eduard,Huntington	R	20	20	46	5	1	0	2	12	6	3	6	0	17	1	1	0	2	0	1.00	0	.109	.226	.261
Cubs	R	20	11	22	5	1	0	0	6	1	1	1	0	6	0	0	0	0	0	.00	0	.227	.261	.273
Garcia,Eric,Angels	R	20	3	6	0	0	0	0	0	0	0	0	0	1	0	0	0	0	0	.00	1	.000	.000	.000
Garcia,Freddy,St.Cathrns	A	22	73	260	74	10	2	13	127	46	40	33	1	57	2	1	3	1	3	.25	6	.285	.366	.488
Garcia,Guillermo,St.Lucie	A	23	55	203	48	9	1	1	62	22	23	13	1	24	3	2	0	0	2	.00	6	.236	.292	.305
Garcia,Karin,Vero Beach	A	19	121	452	120	28	10	21	231	72	84	37	8	112	1	0	6	8	3	.73	7	.265	.319	.511
Garcia,Jason,Danville	R	23	57	198	41	8	2	0	53	22	17	25	0	72	1	4	1	9	4	.69	6	.207	.298	.268
Garcia,Julio,Oneonta	A	22	11	22	3	0	0	0	3	3	1	8	0	7	1	1	0	2	0	.00	2	.136	.387	.136
Garcia,Luis,Jamestown	A	20	67	239	47	8	2	1	62	21	19	8	0	48	1	6	3	6	9	.40	4	.197	.223	.259
Garcia,Miguel,Watertown	A	21	23	55	10	1	0	1	14	12	7	11	0	15	1	0	0	1	0	1.00	1	.182	.328	.255
Burlington	R	21	10	34	7	1	0	0	8	4	0	7	0	1	0	1	0	5	2	.71	1	.206	.289	.235
Garcia,Osmel,New Jersey	A	21	71	264	71	8	2	1	86	54	29	26	0	35	8	1	1	24	7	.77	4	.269	.349	.326
Garcia,Vincente,Asheville	A	20	123	397	87	22	1	4	123	41	44	35	0	56	5	6	3	5	10	.33	9	.219	.289	.310
Garciaparra,Anthony,Sarasota	A	21	28	105	31	8	1	1	44	20	16	10	0	8	1	3	2	5	2	.71	2	.295	.356	.419
Gargiulo,Michael,Bluefield	R	20	41	129	26	5	0	2	37	16	17	14	0	30	0	1	1	2	0	1.00	4	.202	.274	.287
Garman,Sean,New Jersey	A	21	39	109	27	3	0	0	30	11	11	16	0	28	1	0	1	1	2	.67	3	.248	.346	.275
Garrett,Bryan,Columbus	A	23	16	34	6	0	0	0	6	6	1	4	0	8	0	2	0	9	1	1.00	0	.176	.263	.176
Garrow,Dave,Fort Myers	A	24	58	156	35	4	0	0	39	18	10	25	0	29	6	5	0	7	7	.50	1	.224	.349	.250
Gatti,Dominic,Hudson Vall	A	23	47	136	40	2	2	0	46	28	11	26	0	12	5	0	0	14	10	.58	2	.294	.425	.338

1994 Batting -- Single-A and Rookie Leagues

			BATTING															BASERUNNING				PERCENTAGES		
Player	Lg	A	G	AB	H	2B	3B	HR	TB	R	RBI	TBB	IBB	SO	HBP	SH	SF	SB	CS	SB%	GDP	Avg	OBP	SLG
Gavello,Tim,Ogden	R	23	69	266	86	20	1	7	129	68	54	49	3	31	10	3	4	12	8	.60	3	.323	.441	.485
Gay,Brad,Stockton	A	22	59	168	26	1	0	0	27	7	9	12	0	53	1	5	1	0	1	.00	1	.155	.214	.161
Gazarek,Marty,Williamsprt	A	22	45	181	68	13	0	2	87	22	18	6	0	17	2	3	0	14	7	.67	2	.376	.402	.481
Peoria	A	22	23	89	29	6	0	1	38	18	12	2	0	14	3	0	2	2	3	.40	4	.326	.354	.427
Genden,Eric,Marlins	R	20	58	194	56	12	0	4	82	35	34	38	2	45	10	0	2	0	0	.00	4	.289	.426	.423
German,Juan,Athletics	R	20	51	164	41	3	2	2	54	27	29	23	0	57	6	3	1	1	2	.33	1	.250	.361	.329
Gerteisen,Aaron,Madison	A	22	33	89	19	2	1	1	26	14	14	14	0	24	0	2	0	6	3	.67	1	.213	.320	.292
New Jersey	A	22	69	249	63	7	2	0	74	38	21	32	0	28	3	3	3	17	9	.65	7	.253	.343	.297
Giardi,Mike,Everett	A	22	26	54	13	5	0	0	18	12	7	12	0	12	0	1	0	1	1	.50	3	.241	.379	.333
Gibralter,David,Sarasota	A	20	51	184	35	5	1	4	54	20	18	6	1	41	1	0	0	1	2	.33	2	.190	.220	.293
Utica	A	20	62	222	57	11	0	5	83	31	32	14	2	40	5	1	2	3	1	.75	5	.257	.313	.374
Gibson,Derrick,Bend	A	20	73	284	75	19	5	12	140	47	57	29	5	102	9	0	1	14	4	.78	4	.264	.350	.493
Gil,Daniel,Peoria	A	20	20	60	13	1	0	0	14	4	2	3	0	12	0	0	0	3	1	.75	2	.217	.254	.233
Williamsprt	A	20	9	25	4	1	0	0	5	2	2	2	0	2	0	1	0	0	0	.00	1	.160	.207	.200
Huntington	R	20	50	158	35	5	0	3	49	28	19	16	0	29	7	1	2	5	1	.83	3	.222	.317	.310
Gill,Steven,W. Palm Bch	A	26	80	264	66	15	4	2	95	31	28	27	3	42	6	4	2	14	4	.78	2	.250	.331	.360
Gilmore,Kale,Butte	R	22	65	247	76	17	4	10	131	43	46	36	1	68	4	0	3	7	3	.70	2	.308	.400	.530
Gipner,Mark,Greensboro	A	21	4	11	1	0	0	0	1	1	1	5	0	4	0	0	0	0	0	.00	1	.091	.375	.091
Oneonta	A	21	46	136	29	4	1	0	35	10	11	22	0	32	1	2	0	3	1	.75	3	.213	.327	.257
Gipson,Charles,Riverside	A	22	128	481	141	12	3	1	162	102	41	76	4	67	12	7	2	34	15	.69	8	.293	.401	.337
Giudice,John,Asheville	A	24	66	252	73	12	1	9	114	36	22	17	1	56	5	0	0	6	5	.55	2	.290	.347	.452
Central Val	A	24	53	195	55	13	2	4	84	30	33	18	1	55	6	2	2	6	2	.75	3	.282	.357	.431
Glass,Chip,Watertown	A	24	60	237	73	8	6	2	99	51	22	26	1	34	0	1	1	12	10	.55	1	.308	.375	.418
Goldberg,Lonnie,Charlstn-Wv	A	24	67	198	46	10	1	0	58	24	10	15	0	55	0	5	0	6	1	.86	2	.232	.286	.293
Goligoski,Jason,Hickory	A	23	135	499	135	18	7	1	170	98	67	99	0	82	9	5	9	17	5	.77	7	.271	.394	.341
Golston,Toraino,Butte	R	22	30	93	26	3	0	1	32	13	15	20	0	18	0	0	0	0	4	.00	0	.280	.400	.344
Gomez,Paul,Mets	R	22	4	16	3	1	0	1	7	3	2	1	0	2	0	0	0	1	1	.50	0	.188	.235	.438
Columbia	A	22	12	32	9	2	0	0	11	3	3	4	0	8	0	2	0	2	0	1.00	0	.281	.361	.344
Kingsport	R	22	15	44	9	1	0	2	16	4	5	5	0	10	1	0	0	2	0	1.00	1	.205	.300	.364
Gonzalez,Mario,Charlstn-Wv	A	24	71	23		2	0	0	25	19	4	13	0	10	2	1	1	6	3	.67	1	.324	.437	.352
Gonzalez,Mauricio,Central Val	A	23	104	358	92	14	2	4	122	42	41	18	1	58	0	9	5	5	0	1.00	13	.257	.289	.341
Gonzalez,Ricardo,Charlstn-Sc	A	25	3	6	2	0	0	0	2	1	0	0	0	0	0	0	0	0	0	.00	1	.333	.333	.333
Gonzalez,Raul,Wilmington	A	21	115	414	108	19	8	9	170	60	51	45	2	50	2	2	4	0	4	.00	8	.261	.333	.411
Gonzalez,Wikleman,Pirates	R	21	41	143	48	8	2	4	72	25	26	13	1	13	3	1	1	2	4	.33	3	.336	.400	.503
Goodwin,Rawlin,Red Sox	R	25	89	30	3	1	1	0	38	9	9	4	0	7	1	1	0	2	2	.33	2	.337	.372	.427
Gordon,Adrian,Elizabethtn	R	21	55	188	61	7	0	12	104	38	46	28	0	45	6	1	1	14	2	.88	1	.324	.426	.553
Gordan,Herman,Blue Jays	R	20	33	102	20	2	0	0	22	16	5	13	0	25	0	1	0	11	2	.85	1	.196	.287	.216
Graham,John,Lynchburg	A	24	78	254	70	11	1	4	95	34	30	22	2	59	3	1	2	4	2	.67	3	.276	.338	.374
Graham,Tim,High Desert	A	23	117	417	127	23	7	18	218	77	65	61	1	114	1	4	1	13	10	.57	5	.305	.394	.523
Grass,Darren,Spokane	A	23	48	166	43	6	0	6	67	20	24	12	0	36	5	1	2	0	1	.00	4	.259	.324	.404
Greeley,Jim,Boise	A	20	60	177	47	9	1	4	70	22	32	19	0	32	4	2	4	0	3	.00	7	.266	.343	.395
Green,Bert,Johnson Cty	R	21	54	199	48	5	0	0	53	32	11	25	1	61	0	4	2	22	7	.76	0	.241	.323	.266
Greene,Todd,Lake Elsino	A	21	133	524	158	39	4	35	306	98	124	64	12	96	4	0	3	10	3	.77	12	.302	.378	.584
Grieve,Benjamin,Sou. Oregon	A	19	72	252	83	13	0	7	117	44	50	51	7	48	10	0	3	2	2	.50	6	.329	.456	.464
Griffin,Chad,Athletics	R	19	40	118	30	2	3	3	47	15	15	11	1	41	0	1	1	3	2	.60	2	.254	.315	.398
Griffin,Juan,Astros	R	19	35	80	18	5	1	0	25	14	4	5	0	24	3	6	0	6	3	.67	1	.225	.295	.313
Grinstead,Carl,Butte	R	22	3	10	0	0	0	0	0	0	0	0	0	6	0	0	0	0	0	.00	0	.000	.000	.000
Grissom,Antonio,W. Palm Bch	A	25	101	309	69	9	4	6	98	39	27	36	1	53	1	0	3	17	12	.59	6	.223	.304	.317
Gross,Rafael,Great Falls	R	20	65	258	60	11	9	4	101	39	35	26	1	48	9	3	3	9	4	.69	6	.233	.321	.391
Grotewold,Jeff,San Bernrdo	A	29	32	117	36	10	0	6	64	19	25	15	0	29	2	0	0	0	3	.00	4	.308	.390	.547
Grubb,Dennis,Greensboro	A	24	39	103	19	1	0	0	20	9	8	13	1	25	2	0	0	7	2	.78	2	.184	.288	.194
Gubanich,Creighton,Modesto	A	23	108	375	88	20	3	15	159	53	55	54	0	102	7	5	2	5	4	.56	9	.235	.340	.424
Guerrero,Rafael,Columbia	A	20	105	371	92	11	2	4	119	43	28	20	1	64	4	3	3	13	3	.81	6	.248	.291	.321
Guerrero,Vladimir,Expos	R	19	37	137	43	13	3	5	77	24	25	11	0	18	2	0	3	0	7	.00	0	.314	.362	.562
Guerrero,Wilton,Vero Beach	A	20	110	402	118	11	4	1	140	55	32	29	0	71	1	10	2	23	20	.53	2	.294	.341	.348
Gugino,Mark,Elmira	A	22	50	178	55	10	3	0	71	26	20	29	0	30	2	1	0	6	4	.60	4	.309	.410	.399
Guiel,Aaron,Cedar Rapds	A	22	127	454	122	30	1	18	208	84	82	64	2	93	6	5	7	21	7	.75	7	.269	.364	.458
Guiliano,Matthew,Martinsvlle	R	23	58	190	42	5	0	5	62	33	16	24	0	57	7	3	2	16	3	.84	4	.221	.327	.326
Guillen,Jose,Pirates	R	19	30	110	29	4	1	4	47	17	11	7	0	15	6	0	0	2	1	.67	0	.264	.341	.427
Guillen,Jose,W. Michigan	A	22	34	102	23	4	1	0	29	18	10	20	0	24	0	4	1	9	4	.69	1	.225	.350	.284
Modesto	A	22	87	267	70	11	5	0	91	37	29	40	0	58	1	11	2	11	3	.79	7	.262	.358	.341
Gulan,Mike,St. Pete	A	24	120	466	113	30	2	8	171	39	56	26	2	108	2	0	6	2	8	.20	8	.242	.282	.367
Gulseth,Mark,Giants	R	23	7	20	5	2	0	0	7	7	2	8	0	3	0	0	0	0	1	.00	0	.250	.464	.350
Clinton	A	23	35	102	24	2	1	1	31	6	9	12	0	23	0	0	1	2	0	1.00	1	.235	.313	.304
Gump,Christopher,Clinton	A	24	31	92	26	5	1	1	36	16	13	23	0	20	4	4	0	4	0	1.00	1	.283	.438	.391
Gutierrez,Rick,Watertown	A	25	65	249	65	7	1	2	80	48	21	39	1	40	0	3	1	25	5	.83	4	.261	.360	.321
Guzman,Ismael,Jamestown	A	24	16	46	9	4	0	0	13	1	5	0	0	11	0	1	0	0	0	.00	0	.196	.196	.283
Gyselman,Jeffrey,Batavia	A	24	2	7	2	0	0	0	2	2	1	0	0	2	0	0	0	0	0	.00	0	.286	.286	.714
Spartanburg	A	24	12	28	2	0	0	0	2	4	2	3	0	8	0	0	0	0	0	.00	1	.071	.161	.071
Haag,Jeffrey,Watertown	A	24	4	11	0	0	0	0	0	1	1	0	0	5	0	0	0	0	0	.00	0	.000	.000	.000
Haar,Richard,W. Palm Bch	A	24	4	7	2	1	0	0	3	3	1	4	0	0	0	0	0	0	0	.00	0	.286	.500	.429
Haas,Matthew,Vermont	A	23	49	173	47	5	0	1	55	27	20	18	0	27	3	1	3	3	1	.75	2	.272	.345	.318
Hacopian,Derek,Kinston	A	25	21	70	21	9	0	0	30	9	4	7	1	8	2	0	1	0	0	.00	2	.300	.380	.429
Hagen,Sean,Pirates	R	20	39	142	32	8	1	1	45	21	12	16	0	34	3	0	2	5	1	.83	2	.225	.313	.317
Hagge,Kirk,Bristol	R	19	25	57	9	0	0	0	9	7	5	11	0	25	1	0	0	0	3	.00	1	.158	.304	.158
Halbruner,Rick,Blue Jays	R	21	60	219	40	12	1	6	72	17	36	12	2	63	4	1	4	2	0	1.00	4	.183	.234	.329
Halemanu,Joshua,Auburn	A	21	56	197	40	13	1	6	73	17	25	16	0	67	1	0	1	1	2	.33	3	.203	.265	.371

1994 Batting -- Single-A and Rookie Leagues

Player	Lg	A	G	AB	H	2B	3B	HR	TB	R	RBI	TBB	IBB	SO	HBP	SH	SF	SB	CS	SB%	GDP	Avg	OBP	SLG
Haley,Bradley,Pittsfield	A	23	28	93	21	2	0	1	26	8	14	11	1	21	3	1	0	1	2	.33	3	.226	.327	.280
Hall,Carl,Vermont	A	24	53	194	40	4	4	2	58	32	20	21	0	38	3	3	2	4	1	.80	2	.206	.291	.299
Hall,Darran,Princeton	R	19	48	90	17	1	1	0	20	22	5	33	0	29	2	2	1	19	6	.76	2	.189	.413	.222
Hall,Ronnie,Bend	A	19	67	233	63	9	4	7	101	43	34	28	2	62	10	1	1	24	11	.69	3	.270	.371	.433
Hall,Ryan,Johnson Cty	R	23	57	178	43	8	0	6	69	32	33	35	2	28	2	1	2	1	1	.50	2	.242	.369	.388
Hall,Todd,Hickory	A	23	7	14	1	0	0	0	1	0	0	1	0	1	0	0	0	0	1	.00	1	.071	.133	.071
South Bend	A	23	16	54	13	4	0	1	20	7	9	7	0	11	2	0	1	0	1	.00	1	.241	.344	.370
Pr. William	A	23	21	52	11	1	1	0	14	3	6	7	0	12	0	0	1	0	0	.00	3	.212	.300	.269
Hallead,John,Rockies	R	19	28	80	15	1	0	0	16	8	2	4	0	34	2	1	1	6	0	1.00	1	.188	.241	.200
Ham,Kevin,Boise	A	20	66	193	44	10	0	2	60	24	20	21	0	76	4	5	2	6	3	.67	2	.228	.314	.311
Hamburg,Leon,Sou. Oregon	A	20	60	185	44	8	1	5	69	31	24	29	1	52	5	3	5	0	0	.00	4	.238	.348	.373
Hamilton,Joe,Utica	A	20	52	166	43	7	2	3	63	23	21	32	2	41	2	1	4	3	2	.60	2	.259	.377	.380
Hamlin,Jonas,Beloit	A	25	133	495	124	29	1	14	197	63	88	39	2	124	6	1	9	14	9	.61	10	.251	.308	.398
Hammer,Ben,Astros	A	21	48	133	40	4	0	0	44	24	17	9	0	21	4	4	2	7	5	.58	2	.301	.358	.331
Hampton,Michael,Billings	R	23	65	228	59	9	1	4	82	34	40	33	0	51	1	1	7	11	5	.69	1	.259	.346	.360
Hampton,Robert,Medicne Hat	R	19	29	101	18	4	0	1	25	12	7	6	0	33	0	0	0	1	0	1.00	1	.178	.224	.248
Hanel,Marcus,Salem	A	23	87	286	70	9	1	5	96	36	27	14	0	54	6	5	3	3	2	.60	5	.245	.291	.336
Hanlon,Larry,Charlstn-Wv	A	23	59	181	43	11	0	2	60	24	15	23	0	30	5	1	2	5	4	.56	4	.238	.336	.331
Hansen,Elston,San Bernrdo	A	23	64	218	64	14	4	10	116	30	34	28	0	52	6	1	3	7	4	.64	7	.294	.389	.532
Greensboro	A	23	20	75	19	3	0	7	43	12	14	7	0	26	1	1	0	1	1	.50	1	.253	.325	.573
Hansen,Jed,Eugene	A	22	66	235	57	8	2	3	78	26	17	24	2	56	8	2	1	6	4	.60	1	.243	.332	.332
Harley,Alquentin,Rancho Cuca	A	23	96	333	105	17	5	8	156	74	35	55	0	45	5	4	2	19	6	.76	6	.315	.418	.468
Harmer,Francis,Orioles	R	20	35	108	28	5	2	0	37	11	4	13	0	21	0	0	0	0	0	.00	0	.259	.339	.343
Harmes,Kris,Dunedin	A	24	105	403	116	34	4	11	191	56	71	36	7	59	5	1	5	2	6	.25	4	.288	.350	.474
Harmon,Brian,Great Falls	R	19	60	223	55	10	4	5	88	37	48	30	0	56	1	1	3	2	0	1.00	3	.247	.335	.395
Harper,Otis,Cardinals	R	20	31	90	17	1	1	0	20	8	9	4	0	25	1	0	0	3	2	.60	1	.189	.232	.222
Harris,Eric,Sou. Oregon	A	22	50	121	36	11	0	7	68	24	28	12	0	44	3	2	2	2	2	.50	2	.298	.370	.562
Harris,Ghainbria,Augusta	A	22	89	305	66	20	2	4	102	30	40	17	0	56	3	0	5	3	6	.33	2	.216	.261	.334
Harriss,Robin,Watertown	A	23	49	168	41	5	0	4	58	19	25	16	0	16	1	3	4	1	0	1.00	5	.244	.307	.345
Hartung,Andy,Daytona	A	26	32	110	21	5	0	3	35	14	15	18	0	19	0	1	1	3	0	1.00	4	.191	.302	.318
Hartwell,Eddie,Clinton	A	23	51	145	39	6	0	0	45	17	21	22	2	28	4	4	1	3	2	.60	4	.269	.378	.310
Hastings,Lionel,Elmira	A	22	73	282	77	17	0	5	109	39	43	28	0	48	4	3	4	4	5	.44	3	.273	.343	.387
Hatfield,Rick,Asheville	A	20	93	281	50	5	0	2	61	20	23	16	2	55	2	4	0	1	2	.33	10	.178	.227	.217
Hattig,Keith,Boise	A	21	9	29	6	0	0	0	6	4	1	6	0	6	0	3	0	2	1	.67	0	.207	.343	.207
Angels	R	21	41	137	33	3	1	2	44	19	18	19	1	25	1	4	1	3	1	.75	2	.241	.335	.321
Hawkins,Kraig,Tampa	A	23	108	437	104	7	1	0	113	72	29	61	1	105	2	3	0	37	19	.66	6	.238	.334	.259
Hawkins,Wesley,Albany	A	23	93	303	71	18	2	4	105	32	39	30	0	74	8	2	5	10	8	.56	11	.234	.315	.347
Hayes,Heath,Watertown	A	23	46	147	38	5	1	4	57	31	27	22	0	31	1	0	3	3	1	.75	4	.259	.353	.388
Hayward,Joseph,High Desert	A	24	78	206	36	7	2	1	50	33	20	35	0	44	3	0	1	2	1	.67	7	.175	.302	.243
Hearn,Sean,Dunedin	A	24	40	149	46	14	1	5	77	15	26	7	2	35	0	0	1	4	4	.50	4	.309	.338	.517
Heath,Jason,Bellingham	A	24	49	129	35	10	1	2	53	16	22	5	0	28	2	0	3	4	1	.80	2	.271	.302	.411
Hecker,Doug,Sarasota	A	24	115	431	119	28	1	13	188	53	70	29	4	95	8	0	4	2	2	.50	8	.276	.331	.436
Hedpeth,Dennis,Great Falls	R	22	23	78	14	1	0	1	18	14	6	6	0	10	2	3	1	2	0	1.00	1	.179	.253	.231
Held,Daniel,Spartanburg	A	24	130	484	123	32	1	18	211	69	69	52	2	119	9	1	11	2	0	1.00	11	.254	.331	.436
Helms,Ryan,White Sox	R	19	25	59	10	2	0	0	12	5	3	14	0	11	0	0	0	1	0	1.00	0	.169	.329	.203
Helms,Wesley,Braves	R	19	56	184	49	15	1	4	78	22	29	22	0	36	4	0	1	6	1	.86	3	.266	.355	.424
Hemphill,Bret,Boise	A	23	71	252	74	16	1	3	101	44	36	40	2	53	1	1	6	1	1	.50	6	.294	.385	.401
Hence,Sam,Kinston	A	24	88	290	65	11	2	5	95	33	37	6	0	60	7	1	3	6	3	.67	6	.224	.255	.328
Henderson,Juan,Cedar Rapds	A	21	94	318	74	14	1	2	96	41	31	26	0	64	7	11	1	13	9	.59	4	.233	.304	.302
Henderson,Lee,Springfield	A	24	43	133	30	10	0	0	40	15	14	13	0	40	2	3	1	0	1	.00	4	.226	.302	.301
Rancho Cuca	A	24	25	55	14	2	0	3	25	9	7	5	0	18	0	0	0	0	0	.00	1	.255	.317	.455
Hendricks,Ryan,Bluefield	R	22	59	187	42	6	1	4	62	24	26	37	1	65	5	0	4	3	2	.60	3	.225	.361	.332
Henley,Robert,Burlington	A	22	98	346	104	20	1	20	186	72	67	49	1	91	10	1	3	1	2	.33	8	.301	.400	.538
Henry,Antoine,Savannah	A	22	120	436	107	19	4	8	158	64	46	67	0	91	18	6	3	19	17	.53	6	.245	.366	.362
Henry,Santiago,Dunedin	A	22	109	408	103	22	6	6	155	56	46	19	2	99	7	2	4	9	4	.69	7	.252	.295	.380
Herdman,Eli,Twins	R	19	33	109	17	4	0	0	21	7	4	13	0	22	0	0	1	0	1	.00	2	.156	.244	.193
Hernaiz,Juan,Vero Beach	A	20	2	1	0	0	0	0	0	0	0	0	0	1	0	0	0	0	0	.00	0	.000	.500	.000
Hernandez,Carlos,Astros	R	19	51	192	62	10	1	0	74	45	23	19	0	22	4	2	1	25	7	.78	1	.323	.394	.385
Hernandez,Luis,Pittsfield	A	23	65	233	62	5	1	0	69	44	18	32	0	36	3	3	2	12	4	.75	4	.266	.359	.296
Hernandez,Mike,Yakima	A	23	26	42	6	1	0	0	9	4	4	12	0	14	1	0	2	0	0	.00	0	.143	.345	.214
Herrera,Jose,Modesto	A	22	103	370	106	20	3	11	165	59	56	38	3	76	10	5	6	21	12	.64	5	.286	.363	.446
Herrick,Jason,Cedar Rapds	A	21	109	339	85	18	5	7	134	62	51	42	2	92	3	2	6	10	3	.77	8	.251	.333	.395
Hickey,Mike,Riverside	A	25	130	487	137	23	7	10	204	75	90	68	5	94	6	5	5	15	8	.65	12	.281	.373	.419
Hickman,Charles,Rockford	A	24	122	408	94	17	3	8	141	51	53	30	2	84	6	0	4	2	2	.50	6	.230	.290	.346
Hicks,Jamie,Idaho Falls	R	23	5	21	8	1	0	0	9	4	0	0	0	4	0	0	1	1	0	1.00	0	.381	.381	.429
Macon	A	23	31	95	23	4	1	0	29	8	7	3	0	15	2	1	0	0	0	.00	2	.242	.277	.305
Hidalgo,Jose,Orioles	R	20	44	104	30	5	1	1	40	12	9	5	1	13	3	0	1	0	0	.00	3	.288	.336	.385
Hidalgo,Richard,Quad City	A	19	124	476	139	47	6	12	234	68	76	23	1	80	7	1	4	12	12	.50	9	.292	.331	.492
Hightower,Vee,Peoria	A	23	46	147	35	6	4	1	52	28	10	28	1	30	2	1	1	6	3	.67	3	.238	.365	.354
Hill,Michael,Hudson Vall	A	24	30	70	10	2	0	1	15	9	5	3	0	19	5	0	1	3	0	1.00	0	.143	.228	.214
Hilo,Johnny,Great Falls	R	21	58	204	53	11	0	1	67	27	34	40	1	31	0	0	0	6	6	.50	1	.260	.375	.328
Hilt,Scott,Fort Wayne	A	22	43	125	35	6	0	2	47	13	11	16	1	40	3	0	1	0	1	.00	2	.280	.372	.376
Hinds,Collin,Mariners	R	21	39	100	13	3	1	1	21	4	10	8	1	42	8	1	1	3	2	.60	1	.130	.248	.210
Hinds,Rob,Tampa	A	24	110	405	118	10	3	1	137	63	32	31	0	76	4	7	3	24	11	.69	8	.291	.345	.338
Hinton,Steve,Burlington	A	25	41	147	42	9	1	10	83	28	26	18	2	22	2	0	0	1	1	.50	4	.286	.363	.565
W. Palm Bch	A	25	22	72	11	2	1	0	15	4	6	9	1	17	0	2	1	1	0	1.00	1	.153	.244	.208
Hiraldo,Jerry,Kingsport	R	20	36	115	22	2	0	1	27	14	11	15	0	21	0	1	1	1	1	.50	2	.191	.285	.235

294

1994 Batting -- Single-A and Rookie Leagues

Player	Lg	A	G	AB	H	2B	3B	HR	TB	R	RBI	TBB	IBB	SO	HBP	SH	SF	SB	CS	SB%	GDP	Avg	OBP	SLG
Hobbie,Matthew,Burlington	R	20	33	111	19	0	1	3	30	13	10	19	0	24	1	0	1	7	4	.64	0	.171	.295	.270
Hodge,James,Beloit	A	22	24	48	5	1	0	1	9	4	3	14	0	25	0	0	0	0	0	.00	1	.104	.306	.188
Helena	R	22	14	33	4	0	0	0	4	3	1	2	0	15	0	0	0	0	0	.00	0	.121	.171	.121
Hodge,Roy,Frederick	A	24	127	450	130	27	4	9	192	70	64	57	0	73	3	3	4	8	6	.57	12	.289	.370	.427
Hodson,Blair,Columbus	A	23	77	233	54	8	1	1	67	27	23	18	1	48	1	1	1	4	2	.67	7	.232	.289	.288
Hofer,Raymond,Idaho Falls	R	20	41	161	45	7	0	2	58	16	20	6	0	28	1	0	2	4	1	.80	1	.280	.306	.360
Holdren,Nathan,Asheville	A	23	111	377	89	19	0	28	192	56	74	28	1	129	10	0	0	3	4	.43	5	.236	.306	.509
Holin,Andrew,Huntington	R	23	38	124	29	3	1	4	46	10	16	7	0	40	2	0	2	0	0	.00	2	.234	.281	.371
Holland,Rodney,Williamsprt	A	24	32	106	27	3	2	2	40	15	13	20	0	25	2	1	1	6	3	.67	1	.255	.380	.377
Holley,Jack,St.Cathrns	A	18	19	46	8	0	0	0	8	6	3	7	1	9	0	2	0	1	1	.50	2	.174	.283	.174
Hollins,Damon,Durham	A	21	131	485	131	28	0	23	228	76	88	45	0	115	4	2	3	12	7	.63	9	.270	.335	.470
Holt,Kevin,Lethbridge	R	23	68	250	76	17	2	2	103	36	43	33	2	36	2	0	3	10	3	.77	4	.304	.385	.412
Hoover,Raymond,Rockies	R	20	25	59	7	0	0	1	10	2	2	5	0	25	0	0	0	0	0	.00	2	.119	.188	.169
Horn,Jeff,Fort Myers	A	24	34	100	28	3	0	0	31	10	9	8	1	11	3	0	1	0	2	.00	6	.280	.348	.310
Hostetler,Brian,Stockton	A	25	98	309	84	17	0	5	116	45	47	45	2	45	4	4	3	3	1	.75	3	.272	.369	.375
House,Mitch,Augusta	A	23	76	253	74	14	3	6	112	46	37	46	0	68	8	0	1	8	3	.73	2	.292	.416	.443
Salem	A	23	45	152	43	2	1	7	68	19	24	13	0	38	5	0	1	2	5	.29	2	.283	.357	.447
Houser,Jeremy,Bend	A	20	60	203	39	6	2	0	49	21	12	14	0	30	2	0	1	4	4	.50	3	.192	.250	.241
Howard,Rich,Butte	R	22	62	237	70	9	1	0	81	50	23	42	0	14	3	2	1	7	8	.47	15	.295	.406	.342
Huff,Lawrence,Martinsvlle	R	23	39	143	36	2	1	1	43	24	7	29	0	20	6	1	0	17	4	.81	3	.252	.399	.301
Batavia	A	23	20	67	15	1	0	0	16	13	2	12	1	10	0	2	0	5	0	1.00	1	.224	.342	.239
Hughes,Robert,Vermont	A	23	37	108	25	1	1	1	31	16	11	11	0	24	1	2	1	2	0	1.00	4	.231	.306	.287
Hugo,Sean,Albany	A	22	59	183	55	17	4	4	92	34	33	37	2	33	3	2	2	4	4	.50	3	.301	.422	.503
Hunt,Kenya,Spokane	A	22	46	151	34	6	1	1	45	21	11	11	0	54	1	0	0	7	2	.78	5	.225	.289	.298
Hunter,Scott,Great Falls	R	19	64	237	75	12	4	2	101	45	28	25	1	40	5	4	3	17	5	.77	1	.316	.389	.426
Hunter,Torii,Fort Wayne	A	19	91	335	98	17	1	10	147	57	50	25	1	80	10	0	2	8	10	.44	5	.293	.358	.439
Huntley,Brian,Huntington	R	21	16	41	7	1	0	0	8	8	3	7	0	13	1	1	1	3	1	.75	0	.171	.300	.195
Williamsprt	A	21	23	62	17	1	0	0	18	13	2	11	0	10	2	4	0	2	4	.33	2	.274	.400	.290
Hurst,Jimmy,Pr. William	A	23	127	455	126	31	6	25	244	90	91	72	4	128	4	0	5	15	8	.65	9	.277	.377	.536
Hurst,Roy,Williamsprt	A	22	47	135	33	7	3	0	46	15	19	6	0	20	3	3	0	1	0	1.00	3	.244	.292	.341
Hust,Gary,Modesto	A	23	72	236	50	10	2	8	88	36	44	29	1	99	6	0	5	4	5	.44	4	.212	.308	.373
Hutchins,Norman,Angels	R	19	43	136	26	4	1	0	32	8	7	3	0	44	1	1	1	5	2	.71	0	.191	.213	.235
Hutchison,Tom,Butte	R	21	53	160	46	3	1	0	51	42	23	42	1	18	7	10	1	22	11	.67	3	.288	.452	.319
Iapoce,Anthony,Brewers	R	21	55	222	55	7	2	0	66	37	25	15	0	43	5	3	1	16	3	.84	1	.248	.309	.297
Iatarola,Aaron,Cedar Rapds	A	23	102	313	71	19	2	12	130	41	45	30	1	88	5	2	2	6	3	.67	3	.227	.303	.415
Ibanez,Raul,Appleton	A	22	91	327	102	30	3	7	159	55	59	32	3	37	2	0	2	10	5	.67	3	.312	.375	.486
Ibarra,Jesus,Everett	A	22	67	252	57	15	1	10	104	32	37	34	0	82	1	0	0	0	5	.00	5	.226	.321	.413
Ignash,Reggie,Burlington	R	19	36	106	19	1	0	1	23	7	11	7	0	40	2	0	1	4	3	.57	2	.179	.241	.217
Ingram,Darron,Princeton	R	19	46	131	26	5	1	2	39	13	11	19	0	50	1	1	1	4	1	.20	2	.198	.303	.298
Irvis,Damon,Twins	R	19	31	85	18	0	0	0	18	8	8	14	0	13	0	1	0	4	4	.50	2	.212	.323	.212
Isom,Daleon,Mariners	R	19	21	47	5	1	0	0	6	3	2	3	0	17	0	0	1	3	5	.38	1	.106	.157	.128
Izquierdo,Sergio,White Sox	R	22	18	52	15	2	0	0	17	4	16	4	0	2	0	1	1	1	1	.50	3	.288	.333	.327
Hickory	A	22	5	15	0	0	0	0	0	2	0	3	0	1	1	0	0	0	0	.00	0	.000	.211	.000
Jackson,Gavin,Sarasota	A	21	108	321	77	6	1	0	85	46	27	33	0	40	7	12	0	9	10	.47	1	.240	.324	.265
Jackson,Joseph,Boise	A	23	45	136	34	5	1	0	41	24	9	7	0	24	1	8	0	1	1	.50	1	.250	.292	.301
Jackson,Karun,Peoria	A	24	12	36	12	2	1	1	19	6	3	1	0	6	1	2	0	2	2	.50	0	.333	.368	.528
Jackson,Rodney,Padres	R	20	30	98	21	2	2	0	27	19	5	4	0	32	5	0	0	7	1	.88	3	.214	.280	.276
Jackson,Ryan,Elmira	A	22	72	276	80	18	1	6	118	46	41	22	1	40	1	0	6	4	3	.57	2	.290	.338	.428
Jaime,Angel,Vero Beach	A	22	127	482	136	15	9	6	187	85	38	38	1	64	4	10	6	16	10	.62	8	.282	.336	.388
Jarrett,Lincoln,Bend	A	23	74	279	67	13	0	0	80	31	15	24	0	45	2	4	2	4	4	.50	6	.240	.303	.287
Jasco,Elinton,Huntington	R	20	66	241	61	9	2	1	77	39	10	29	0	60	2	7	2	36	20	.64	0	.253	.336	.320
Jefferson,Dave,Marlins	R	20	27	98	22	1	1	1	28	11	15	4	0	16	0	1	1	0	0	.00	3	.224	.255	.286
Jelsovsky,Craig,Mets	R	19	37	118	30	3	0	0	33	20	8	12	0	19	4	2	0	4	3	.57	2	.254	.343	.280
Jenkins,Brett,Clinton	A	25	12	42	8	1	0	1	12	5	10	10	0	13	1	0	0	2	0	1.00	1	.190	.346	.286
San Jose	A	25	48	175	47	10	1	5	74	21	23	15	1	41	3	2	3	2	1	1.00	4	.269	.332	.423
San Bernrdo	A	25	4	16	4	2	0	1	9	3	2	1	0	2	0	0	0	0	0	.00	1	.250	.294	.563
Jenkins,Demetrish,Winston-Sal	A	22	106	379	92	16	0	7	129	57	33	55	1	81	6	1	3	19	7	.73	9	.243	.345	.340
Jennings,Lance,Wilmington	A	23	92	316	78	14	0	7	113	46	39	25	1	62	5	10	3	1	0	1.00	8	.247	.309	.358
Jennings,Robin,Daytona	A	23	128	476	133	24	5	8	191	54	60	45	5	54	4	4	4	2	10	.17	13	.279	.344	.401
Jensen,Blair,Burlington	R	19	31	73	10	1	0	0	11	5	2	12	0	24	2	1	1	3	1	.75	4	.137	.273	.151
Jensen,Jeffrey,Batavia	A	22	72	270	70	6	3	1	85	24	27	13	0	41	4	3	1	4	1	.80	7	.259	.302	.315
Jensen,Marcus,San Jose	A	22	118	418	101	18	0	7	140	56	47	61	5	100	8	2	6	1	1	.50	9	.242	.345	.335
Jimenez,Elvis,Rockies	R	19	42	151	43	10	5	1	66	21	15	6	0	36	3	0	0	5	3	.63	4	.267	.306	.410
Jimenez,Oscar,Rockford	A	20	113	349	85	15	2	6	122	62	27	44	1	93	20	1	1	9	7	.56	2	.244	.360	.350
Jimenez,Ruben,Johnson Cty	R	19	38	125	25	1	0	0	26	24	10	31	0	42	2	4	0	11	4	.73	1	.200	.367	.208
Johns,Keith,St. Pete	A	23	122	464	106	20	0	3	135	52	47	37	1	49	2	12	4	18	9	.67	7	.228	.286	.291
Johnson,Artis,Huntington	R	22	60	206	56	13	1	1	74	21	20	12	0	22	2	1	1	7	6	.46	2	.272	.317	.359
Johnson,Todd,Kinston	A	24	36	96	20	1	1	0	23	8	7	6	0	20	1	1	2	1	0	1.00	2	.208	.257	.240
Johnson,Damon,Medicne Hat	R	19	38	121	29	7	0	3	45	11	18	5	0	49	0	1	1	2	1	.33	0	.240	.268	.372
Johnson,Earl,Springfield	A	23	136	533	149	11	3	1	169	80	43	37	0	94	3	13	4	80	25	.76	2	.280	.328	.317
Johnson,Heath,Twins	R	18	22	60	12	3	0	0	15	4	6	11	0	23	1	0	0	2	0	1.00	0	.200	.333	.250
Johnson,Jack,Pr. William	A	25	22	57	9	2	0	1	14	6	5	1	0	17	0	1	1	0	0	.00	0	.158	.169	.246
Johnson,James,Spokane	A	22	66	252	53	9	1	3	73	42	21	30	0	67	1	0	2	39	5	.89	1	.210	.296	.290
Johnson,Jason,Rangers	R	19	57	188	39	8	3	0	53	20	10	30	0	60	2	0	0	11	8	.58	2	.207	.320	.282
Johnson,J.J.,Lynchburg	A	21	131	515	120	28	4	14	198	66	51	36	3	132	1	1	4	4	7	.36	9	.233	.288	.384
Johnson,Joaquin,Braves	R	18	29	69	5	0	0	0	5	1	1	11	0	39	2	0	0	0	2	.00	2	.072	.220	.072
Johnson,Keith,Bakersfield	A	24	64	210	42	12	1	2	62	19	19	16	0	49	5	3	2	13	7	.65	3	.200	.270	.295

295

1994 Batting -- Single-A and Rookie Leagues

				BATTING															BASERUNNING				PERCENTAGES		
Player	Lg	A	G	AB	H	2B	3B	HR	TB	R	RBI	TBB	IBB	SO	HBP	SH	SF	SB	CS	SB%	GDP	Avg	OBP	SLG
Johnson,Mark,White Sox	R	19	32	87	21	5	0	0	26	10	14	14	0	15	3	0	0	1	1	.50	0	.241	.365	.299
Johnson,Michael,Columbia	A	24	9	15	3	1	0	0	4	1	0	2	0	6	0	1	0	0	0	.00	0	.200	.294	.267
Pittsfield	A	24	16	56	11	2	0	0	13	5	3	1	0	9	0	0	0	0	0	.00	1	.196	.211	.232
Johnson,Shelby,Mariners	R	21	12	21	7	0	0	0	7	2	4	1	0	8	0	0	0	0	0	.00	0	.333	.364	.333
Johnston,Tom,Ogden	R	22	37	94	14	2	0	0	16	14	7	22	0	40	2	1	0	1	2	.33	0	.149	.322	.170
Jones,Andy,Braves	R	18	27	95	21	5	1	2	34	22	10	16	2	19	2	0	0	5	2	.71	3	.221	.345	.358
Danville	R	18	36	143	48	9	2	1	64	20	16	9	0	25	3	0	1	16	9	.64	0	.336	.385	.448
Jones,Ben,Fort Wayne	A	21	100	335	91	15	0	1	109	43	24	29	1	49	4	0	0	19	9	.68	4	.272	.337	.325
Jones,Donny,High Desert	A	22	23	61	12	3	0	0	15	7	2	3	1	19	2	1	0	0	0	.00	2	.197	.258	.246
Jones,Gary,Bend	A	23	47	156	41	3	1	1	49	26	12	25	0	15	1	0	0	10	2	.83	3	.263	.369	.314
Jones,Keith,Madison	A	24	113	383	104	23	2	2	137	66	25	38	1	52	7	7	1	24	17	.59	4	.272	.347	.358
Jones,Grier,Fort Wayne	A	24	81	259	64	16	0	6	98	38	52	34	0	54	6	3	5	2	0	1.00	6	.247	.342	.378
Jones,John,Sou. Oregon	A	22	48	94	18	2	1	2	28	11	11	12	0	28	2	0	0	0	0	.00	1	.191	.296	.298
Jones,Pookie,Bend	A	23	52	193	62	10	0	10	102	30	24	19	2	40	7	0	1	4	2	.67	1	.321	.400	.528
Central Val	A	23	13	50	15	3	0	0	18	8	3	3	0	14	2	0	0	1	1	.50	0	.300	.357	.360
Jones,Robert,Bristol	R	22	34	101	21	4	3	1	34	13	11	11	1	26	0	0	2	6	0	1.00	7	.208	.281	.337
Jones,Ryan,Hagerstown	A	20	115	402	96	29	1	18	179	60	72	45	0	124	6	0	5	1	0	1.00	6	.239	.321	.445
Jones,Shane,Ogden	R	23	71	287	73	17	3	10	126	54	52	18	0	68	6	1	6	4	0	.00	3	.254	.306	.439
Jones,Terry,Central Val	A	24	129	536	157	20	1	2	185	94	34	42	1	85	1	10	4	44	12	.79	12	.293	.345	.345
Jorgensen,Randall,Riverside	A	23	110	368	97	13	1	3	121	45	42	39	2	63	5	5	2	2	3	.33	19	.264	.341	.329
Juarez,Raul,Twins	R	19	26	84	9	2	1	1	16	9	4	9	0	27	2	0	0	1	1	.50	0	.107	.211	.190
Judge,Mike,Helena	R	23	51	149	49	15	2	5	83	34	41	25	1	20	4	2	4	5	3	.63	2	.329	.429	.557
Jumonville,Joseph,Savannah	A	24	127	480	125	26	2	7	176	53	57	13	1	58	3	2	7	2	7	.22	10	.260	.280	.367
Kail,Joseph,Hudson Vall	A	22	21	55	16	0	0	1	19	8	3	5	0	14	2	0	0	1	1	.50	0	.291	.371	.345
Charlstn-Wv	A	22	15	55	6	2	0	0	8	6	4	3	0	11	0	1	0	2	0	1.00	1	.109	.155	.145
Kapano,Corey,Lake Elsino	A	25	81	299	87	17	4	9	139	35	53	31	1	62	3	0	4	1	5	.17	7	.291	.359	.465
Kearney,Chad,Martinsville	R	19	19	35	3	0	0	0	3	4	0	3	0	23	1	0	0	1	0	1.00	0	.086	.179	.086
Keefe,Jim,Augusta	A	21	50	124	33	3	0	0	36	16	7	13	1	27	3	5	0	11	7	.61	5	.266	.350	.290
Welland	A	21	27	87	20	4	0	0	24	6	9	4	0	17	0	3	0	2	5	.29	0	.230	.264	.276
Keel,David W.Michigan	A	22	90	224	48	12	4	3	77	32	30	50	1	46	1	1	1	7	1	.61	9	.214	.359	.344
Keene,Andre,San Jose	A	24	68	220	53	6	2	3	72	43	40	44	1	51	4	2	2	9	1	.90	3	.241	.374	.327
Clinton	A	24	41	143	43	7	0	9	77	27	37	28	0	30	2	0	1	12	8	.60	7	.301	.420	.538
Keifer,Gregory,Everett	A	22	27	53	12	3	1	1	20	7	5	5	0	20	0	1	0	1	0	1.00	1	.226	.293	.377
Keister,Don,St. Lucie	A	24	75	237	69	8	0	0	77	36	22	46	4	21	1	2	1	14	14	.50	4	.291	.407	.325
Kelley,Erskine,Augusta	A	24	100	368	92	16	5	9	145	43	42	30	1	95	4	0	1	17	8	.68	7	.250	.313	.394
Kelley,Rodd,Boise	A	22	51	129	32	5	0	0	37	23	6	26	0	20	2	1	1	5	5	.50	0	.248	.380	.287
Kendall,Jeremey,Spartanburg	A	23	133	515	148	32	7	8	218	98	60	57	1	128	23	4	6	62	27	.70	3	.287	.379	.423
Kennedy,Jesse,Danville	R	21	54	162	44	12	1	3	67	30	16	30	0	48	1	0	1	15	7	.68	0	.272	.387	.414
Kerr,Brian,Bluefield	R	19	3	9	0	0	0	0	0	0	0	0	0	6	0	0	0	0	0	.00	0	.000	.000	.000
Orioles	R	19	35	121	30	4	1	0	36	13	9	10	0	29	1	0	0	4	1	.80	2	.248	.311	.298
Kerr,James,Yankees	R	20	38	142	29	1	1	1	35	13	16	11	0	35	1	3	0	2	2	.50	3	.204	.266	.246
Greensboro	A	20	9	28	4	1	0	0	5	3	0	2	0	8	1	0	0	1	0	1.00	0	.143	.226	.179
Kessler,Dave,Cedar Rapids	A	25	11	29	5	1	1	0	8	3	3	3	0	7	0	2	0	0	0	.00	0	.172	.250	.276
Key,Jeffrey,Spartanburg	A	20	25	87	19	2	1	1	26	7	14	7	1	39	1	0	1	0	0	.00	0	.218	.281	.299
Batavia	A	20	49	185	50	6	7	3	79	25	32	14	2	41	1	1	2	11	1	.92	5	.270	.322	.427
Killeen,Tim,Modesto	A	24	101	365	87	18	3	16	159	53	75	49	2	107	2	2	5	5	2	.71	3	.238	.328	.436
Killen,Brent,Lakeland	A	25	83	272	73	21	2	0	98	29	37	54	6	43	0	0	6	1	2	.33	7	.268	.383	.360
Kimsey,Keith,Lakeland	A	22	121	448	100	19	3	12	161	47	58	29	0	136	3	0	3	4	3	.57	17	.223	.273	.359
King,Andre,Macon	A	21	129	496	122	22	6	4	168	80	38	34	1	139	15	12	2	31	10	.76	3	.246	.313	.339
King,Anthony,Huntington	R	24	2	6	2	1	0	0	3	0	0	0	0	2	0	0	0	0	0	.00	0	.333	.333	.500
King,Brett,San Jose	A	22	48	188	47	8	2	1	62	24	11	19	1	62	4	1	0	6	8	.43	0	.250	.332	.330
Clinton	A	22	68	261	57	13	2	5	89	45	30	23	1	86	2	3	2	12	3	.80	2	.218	.285	.341
King,Clay,San Jose	A	25	94	259	64	13	0	8	101	39	43	23	1	52	0	3	3	1	0	.00	8	.247	.303	.390
King,Hank,Lake Elsino	A	24	7	12	0	0	0	0	0	0	0	1	0	4	0	0	0	0	0	.00	1	.000	.077	.000
Cedar Rapids	A	24	23	60	13	3	0	0	16	9	3	4	0	12	1	1	0	0	0	.00	1	.217	.277	.267
King,Kevin,Blue Jays	R	21	26	88	20	3	1	1	28	5	10	7	0	27	1	0	1	6	0	1.00	2	.227	.289	.318
King,Thomas,Williamsprt	A	24	11	30	9	1	0	1	13	3	6	7	0	8	1	1	0	2	0	.00	0	.300	.447	.433
Kingman,Brendan,Kane County	A	22	93	334	81	15	3	3	111	41	38	24	0	67	4	4	0	2	3	.40	4	.243	.301	.332
Kingsale,Gene,Orioles	R	18	50	168	52	2	3	0	60	26	9	18	0	24	2	1	1	15	8	.65	1	.310	.381	.357
Kingston,Mark,Daytona	A	25	109	370	83	14	1	4	111	42	35	34	1	79	6	1	4	2	1	.33	12	.224	.297	.300
Kinney,Michael,Bakersfield	A	23	41	109	22	1	1	1	28	10	18	17	1	44	5	0	0	8	5	.62	0	.202	.336	.257
Kiraly,John,Columbia	A	22	116	397	96	21	2	4	133	47	34	47	6	105	4	1	3	1	4	.20	8	.242	.326	.335
Kirgan,Christopher,Bluefield	R	22	58	209	58	8	3	7	93	34	29	27	1	53	0	0	4	1	0	1.00	4	.278	.354	.445
Kirtlan,Josh,Ogden	R	22	64	194	51	11	3	5	83	38	35	18	2	60	7	1	3	6	2	.75	1	.263	.342	.428
Klassen,Danny,Beloit	A	19	133	458	119	20	3	6	163	61	54	58	0	123	12	17	3	28	14	.67	3	.260	.356	.356
Knauss,Tom,Fort Wayne	A	21	120	404	76	15	3	12	133	43	45	26	2	110	4	2	5	1	4	.20	3	.188	.241	.329
Knight,Shawn,Spokane	A	23	16	50	14	3	0	0	17	10	7	11	0	11	1	0	0	4	2	.67	0	.280	.419	.340
Knott,John,Macon	A	24	135	474	136	33	3	17	226	91	74	66	0	118	18	7	6	38	9	.81	9	.287	.390	.477
Knowles,Brian,High Desert	A	23	98	346	101	16	3	3	132	58	44	35	0	89	5	3	3	10	7	.59	11	.292	.362	.382
Knowles,Eric,Greensboro	A	21	125	439	114	31	3	2	157	68	42	62	1	104	3	4	7	11	5	.69	10	.260	.350	.358
Koehler,Jim,Riverside	A	24	108	371	91	18	1	15	156	53	67	32	2	103	9	0	6	4	1	.80	2	.245	.316	.420
Koerick,Thomas,White Sox	R	22	41	129	29	5	0	0	42	15	16	11	0	43	8	0	2	4	0	1.00	3	.225	.320	.326
Koeyers,Ramsey,W. Palm Bch	A	20	79	241	62	11	1	3	84	27	31	21	0	61	1	3	0	3	3	.50	0	.257	.319	.349
Kofler,Eric,Yankees	R	19	48	161	39	4	3	0	49	16	18	22	0	32	1	1	0	1	2	.33	0	.242	.337	.304
Konerko,Paul,Yakima	A	19	67	257	74	15	2	6	111	25	58	36	4	52	6	0	0	1	0	1.00	7	.288	.379	.432
Koonce,Graham,Bristol	R	20	44	120	25	4	0	0	29	15	15	28	1	25	3	0	0	4	0	1.00	6	.208	.364	.242
Kopriva,Dan,Winston-Sal	A	25	90	290	90	15	1	11	140	57	36	49	0	39	9	3	2	7	5	.58	7	.310	.423	.483

1994 Batting -- Single-A and Rookie Leagues

Player	Lg	A	G	AB	H	2B	3B	HR	TB	R	RBI	TBB	IBB	SO	HBP	SH	SF	SB	CS	SB%	GDP	Avg	OBP	SLG
Koscielniak,Dwain,Spokane	A	22	2	5	1	0	0	0	1	0	1	4	0	1	0	0	0	0	1	.00	0	.200	.556	.200
Padres	R	22	55	201	53	3	2	3	69	33	29	21	1	39	2	0	5	8	2	.80	3	.264	.341	.343
Koskie,Cordel,Elizabethtn	R	22	34	107	25	2	1	3	38	13	10	18	0	27	2	0	0	0	0	.00	3	.234	.354	.355
Krause,Scott,Helena	R	21	63	252	90	18	3	4	126	51	52	18	2	49	9	1	2	13	6	.68	2	.357	.416	.500
Kruger,Andrew,Bristol	R	22	29	96	28	4	2	0	36	17	10	7	0	14	3	1	0	10	4	.71	1	.292	.358	.375
Fayetteville	A	22	24	78	19	2	0	0	21	6	4	8	1	6	1	1	0	3	3	.50	1	.244	.322	.269
Kuilan,Hector,Marlins	R	19	40	141	22	7	0	0	29	11	17	6	0	15	0	2	0	0	1	.00	4	.156	.188	.206
Kurek,Christopher,Red Sox	R	23	2	4	2	0	0	0	2	0	1	0	0	0	0	0	0	0	0	.00	0	.500	.500	.500
Utica	A	23	31	93	19	1	1	1	25	11	10	1	0	30	3	2	0	0	0	.00	3	.204	.237	.269
Labarca,Argenis,Princeton	R	20	13	40	7	1	0	1	11	1	3	3	0	4	0	2	0	0	1	.00	1	.175	.233	.275
Charlstn-Sc	A	20	25	70	14	3	0	0	17	3	5	5	0	9	0	0	0	0	0	.00	3	.200	.253	.243
Lachance,Vince,Burlington	A	23	85	289	73	17	1	3	101	34	32	35	0	73	7	3	4	5	6	.45	3	.253	.343	.349
Lackey,Steve,Pittsfield	A	20	3	4	1	0	0	0	1	1	0	2	0	0	0	2	0	0	0	.00	0	.250	.500	.250
Kingsport	R	20	56	187	37	6	1	0	45	22	7	24	1	31	3	3	0	2	2	.50	2	.198	.299	.241
Ladd,Jeff,St. Cathrns	A	24	59	203	66	13	0	12	115	43	44	44	2	60	3	0	1	2	1	.67	2	.325	.450	.567
Hagerstown	A	24	41	140	37	4	0	8	65	20	25	21	0	48	5	1	0	4	1	.80	6	.264	.380	.464
Ladjevich,Richard,Bellingham	A	23	68	235	73	12	0	1	88	36	31	22	1	39	22	1	1	3	4	.43	5	.311	.418	.374
Lakovic,Greg,Twins	R	20	11	32	5	0	1	0	7	2	4	7	0	10	0	0	1	0	0	.00	0	.156	.300	.219
Elizabethtn	R	20	6	12	0	0	0	0	0	1	0	3	0	7	0	0	0	0	0	.00	1	.000	.200	.000
Lamar,Johnny,Charlstn-Sc	A	25	58	193	44	12	0	2	62	17	23	10	0	30	0	0	3	2	1	.67	9	.228	.262	.321
Lamb,David,Albany	A	22	92	308	74	9	2	0	87	37	29	32	0	40	2	6	0	4	1	.80	4	.240	.316	.282
Landaker,David,Astros	R	21	37	128	39	9	3	0	54	16	16	14	1	22	3	0	2	9	1	.90	0	.305	.381	.422
Landers,Mark,Medicne Hat	R	23	60	210	60	12	0	5	87	23	42	29	2	49	2	0	5	1	1	.50	3	.286	.370	.414
Landrum,Tito,Bakersfield	A	24	87	327	80	13	1	16	143	49	50	20	1	83	7	0	2	11	8	.58	3	.245	.301	.437
Landry,Lonny,Jamestown	A	20	30	108	30	8	0	2	44	24	9	20	1	28	2	2	0	13	3	.81	1	.278	.400	.407
Landry,Todd,Stockton	A	22	105	356	95	12	6	8	143	55	49	28	0	53	5	4	4	4	1	.80	10	.267	.326	.402
Lane,Ryan,Elizabethtn	R	20	59	202	48	13	0	3	70	32	18	26	0	47	2	3	2	4	3	.57	4	.238	.328	.347
Langdon,Trajan,Spokane	A	19	17	52	8	2	0	0	10	4	2	2	0	21	0	1	0	0	0	.00	1	.154	.185	.192
Lantigua,Eduardo,Bakersfield	A	21	53	208	48	7	3	5	76	25	23	7	1	46	2	0	3	3	4	.43	3	.231	.259	.365
Kinston	A	21	68	236	60	9	3	11	108	33	35	23	1	50	5	1	0	8	7	.53	6	.254	.333	.458
Lantigua,Miguel,Mets	R	21	35	117	18	2	0	0	20	9	7	11	0	45	0	0	0	5	0	.00	0	.154	.227	.171
Lanza,Michael,Bellingham	A	21	61	186	51	7	0	1	61	26	18	19	1	35	2	4	2	7	5	.58	3	.274	.344	.328
Larkin,James,Utica	A	24	3	7	3	0	0	0	3	0	0	2	0	2	0	0	0	0	0	.00	0	.429	.556	.429
Larkin,Stephen,Hudson Vall	A	21	66	237	47	10	1	2	65	26	22	30	1	47	1	0	3	10	5	.67	3	.198	.288	.274
Larocca,Gregory,Spokane	A	21	42	158	46	9	2	0	59	20	14	14	0	18	2	2	0	7	2	.78	4	.291	.356	.373
Rancho Cuca	A	22	28	85	14	5	1	1	24	7	8	7	0	11	2	1	1	3	1	.75	2	.165	.242	.282
Latham,Chris,Bakersfield	A	22	52	191	41	5	2	2	56	29	15	28	1	49	2	4	0	28	7	.80	2	.215	.321	.293
Yakima	A	22	71	288	98	19	8	5	148	69	32	55	7	66	2	3	0	33	20	.62	1	.340	.449	.514
Lauterhahn,Michael,Huntington	R	22	60	189	42	8	2	0	54	32	14	51	1	56	1	4	1	19	13	.59	5	.222	.388	.286
Law,Khris,Athletics	R	20	43	128	32	7	2	1	46	17	13	9	0	29	2	1	0	6	3	.67	3	.250	.309	.359
Lawson,David,Appleton	A	22	27	84	13	0	0	1	16	12	2	13	1	29	0	1	0	0	2	.00	0	.155	.268	.190
Lawton,Matthew,Fort Myers	A	23	122	446	134	30	1	7	187	79	51	80	3	64	2	2	3	42	19	.69	7	.300	.407	.419
Lea,Corey,Augusta	A	22	6	13	2	0	0	0	2	1	0	1	0	4	1	0	0	1	0	1.00	0	.154	.267	.154
LeBron,Ruben,Red Sox	R	19	42	144	39	8	0	0	47	27	14	10	0	18	0	3	4	15	4	.79	0	.271	.310	.326
Leclair,Paul,Kingsport	R	22	27	93	20	4	0	4	36	13	12	5	0	25	0	1	0	2	2	.50	0	.215	.255	.387
Columbia	A	22	8	13	1	0	0	0	1	1	0	1	0	7	0	2	0	1	0	1.00	0	.077	.143	.077
Ledee,Ricky,Greensboro	A	20	134	484	121	23	9	22	228	87	71	91	4	126	4	3	6	10	11	.48	7	.250	.369	.471
Lee,Carlos,White Sox	R	19	29	56	7	1	0	0	8	6	1	4	0	8	0	0	0	0	1	.00	0	.125	.183	.143
Lee,Charles,W. Palm Bch	A	23	10	28	4	0	0	0	4	2	1	2	0	6	0	0	0	1	0	1.00	0	.143	.200	.143
Burlington	A	23	80	275	65	16	0	8	105	36	38	17	0	75	2	3	2	11	6	.65	6	.236	.284	.382
Lee,Derrek,Rancho Cuca	A	19	126	442	118	19	2	8	165	66	53	42	2	95	7	0	6	18	14	.56	11	.267	.336	.373
Leger,Gus,Angels	R	20	20	53	11	1	0	0	12	5	5	0	0	22	1	0	1	0	1	.00	0	.208	.218	.226
Leger,Tim,Welland	A	21	10	36	7	1	0	0	8	6	1	3	0	7	2	0	0	3	0	1.00	0	.194	.293	.222
Legree,Keith,Fort Myers	A	23	55	186	45	8	1	4	67	16	15	23	1	52	1	0	2	8	3	.73	6	.242	.325	.360
Lemons,Richard,Columbus	A	23	88	272	73	13	5	9	123	47	46	35	0	92	2	0	0	12	4	.75	2	.268	.356	.452
Leon,Geraldo,Cardinals	R	18	46	161	37	3	2	0	44	16	17	11	0	51	3	1	4	1	4	.20	4	.230	.285	.273
Lesher,Brian,Modesto	A	24	117	393	114	21	0	14	177	76	68	81	5	84	8	0	8	11	11	.50	8	.290	.414	.450
Levias,Andres,Hickory	A	21	64	203	49	3	2	0	56	31	16	18	0	36	3	3	2	9	6	.60	4	.241	.310	.276
Lewis,Tyrone,Vero Beach	A	21	26	83	15	2	1	0	19	3	8	3	0	17	1	2	2	0	0	.00	3	.181	.213	.229
Lewis,Andreaus,Charlstn-Wv	A	21	16	39	8	1	0	1	12	7	1	9	0	13	4	0	0	3	2	.60	0	.205	.404	.308
Burlington	R	21	36	99	27	5	2	1	39	12	12	14	0	38	5	0	0	7	3	.70	0	.273	.390	.394
Lewis,Dwight,Idaho Falls	R	21	46	157	48	6	1	5	71	25	24	14	0	43	2	0	1	4	2	.67	3	.306	.368	.452
Lewis,Kevin,Columbia	A	23	52	142	28	5	0	2	39	13	17	10	0	45	1	2	1	1	1	.50	2	.197	.267	.275
Lewis,Marc,Red Sox	R	20	97	188	61	13	2	3	90	32	32	10	0	19	1	2	4	16	3	.84	4	.325	.363	.457
Lynchburg	A	20	8	32	6	1	0	1	10	3	5	3	0	4	0	0	0	2	0	1.00	0	.188	.257	.313
Lewis,Mark,Vermont	A	23	59	173	38	2	0	0	40	23	13	24	0	27	6	5	4	4	2	.67	4	.220	.329	.231
Lewis,Robert,Columbus	A	24	51	132	24	8	0	3	41	20	21	26	0	32	5	1	1	2	2	.50	3	.182	.335	.311
Lezeau,James,Bend	A	22	44	110	23	4	0	2	33	17	9	13	0	51	0	0	0	2	0	1.00	0	.209	.286	.300
Lidle,Kevin,Lakeland	A	23	56	187	49	13	2	6	84	26	30	19	0	46	4	1	1	1	1	.50	2	.262	.341	.449
Liepa,John,Lethbridge	R	23	31	81	18	0	2	0	22	17	5	12	0	13	2	1	0	2	0	1.00	1	.222	.333	.272
Linares,Ruben,Orioles	R	20	39	95	21	2	1	0	25	3	6	6	0	19	0	1	1	2	0	1.00	3	.221	.265	.263
Lindsey,Rodney,Padres	R	19	48	172	46	3	0	0	49	29	19	11	0	59	9	0	0	15	8	.65	2	.267	.344	.285
Link,Charles,Frederick	A	24	120	429	104	19	3	7	150	67	51	44	2	66	3	5	6	10	6	.63	5	.242	.313	.350
Little,Mark,Hudson Vall	A	22	54	208	61	15	5	3	95	33	27	22	1	38	1	0	4	14	5	.74	4	.293	.357	.457
Livesey,Steve,San Bernrdo	A	26	4	8	1	0	0	0	1	1	0	1	0	1	0	0	0	0	0	.00	1	.125	.222	.125
Livesey,Shanetone,Osceola	A	21	108	373	84	15	3	1	108	36	43	34	2	46	2	0	4	10	5	.67	7	.225	.291	.290
Llanos,Victor,Savannah	A	22	87	284	62	14	1	3	87	23	37	16	1	62	2	1	1	4	1	.80	6	.218	.263	.306

297

1994 Batting -- Single-A and Rookie Leagues

Player	Lg	A	G	AB	H	2B	3B	HR	TB	R	RBI	TBB	IBB	SO	HBP	SH	SF	SB	CS	SB%	GDP	Avg	OBP	SLG
Lobaton,Jose,Oneonta	A	21	66	239	54	9	2	0	67	34	15	22	0	55	3	3	2	14	7	.67	7	.226	.297	.280
Loduca,Paul,Bakersfield	A	23	123	455	141	32	1	6	193	65	68	52	2	49	3	0	4	16	9	.64	5	.310	.381	.424
Loeb,Marc,Dunedin	A	25	39	108	25	7	1	0	34	7	7	15	0	23	1	0	1	2	2	.50	3	.231	.328	.315
Lofton,James,Billings	R	21	66	282	91	11	10	4	134	64	47	26	0	46	1	4	3	18	5	.78	2	.323	.378	.475
Lombard,George,Braves	R	19	40	129	18	2	0	0	20	10	5	18	0	47	3	0	0	10	4	.71	1	.140	.260	.155
Long,Justin,Elmira	A	23	14	32	4	1	0	0	5	3	0	2	0	9	0	0	0	0	1	.00	1	.125	.176	.156
Marlins	R	23	40	143	39	5	2	5	63	21	27	11	0	34	2	1	1	2	1	.67	1	.273	.329	.441
Long,R.D.,Tampa	A	24	94	257	61	9	2	6	92	44	33	43	1	66	2	0	2	37	9	.80	3	.237	.349	.358
Long,Ryan,Wilmington	A	22	123	494	130	25	5	11	198	69	68	16	0	72	8	3	3	7	3	.70	4	.263	.296	.401
Long,Terrence,Kingsport	R	19	60	215	50	9	2	12	99	39	39	32	0	52	4	0	1	9	3	.75	2	.233	.340	.460
Lopez,Carlos,Mariners	R	20	42	136	29	2	0	0	31	12	12	9	1	22	0	1	1	1	0	1.00	3	.213	.260	.228
Lopez,Jose,Mets	R	19	45	164	53	10	1	2	71	34	31	13	0	30	2	1	1	2	1	.67	1	.323	.364	.433
Kingsport	R	19	4	15	4	3	0	1	10	1	1	0	0	0	0	0	0	0	0	.00	1	.267	.267	.667
Lopez,Mendy,Royals	R	20	59	235	85	19	3	5	125	56	50	22	0	27	3	2	5	19	2	.90	5	.362	.415	.532
Lopez,Rene,Fort Myers	A	23	109	383	101	12	1	7	136	48	48	46	1	66	2	0	7	3	3	.50	12	.264	.340	.355
Lopez,Richard,Johnson Cty	R	21	55	192	39	15	0	2	50	29	14	24	0	31	0	3	1	8	4	.67	6	.203	.290	.260
Lopez,Roberto,Stockton	A	23	5	16	2	1	0	0	3	2	1	3	0	1	0	0	0	1	1	.50	0	.125	.263	.188
Lorenzo,Wilson,Red Sox	R	23	9	18	3	0	0	0	3	1	2	2	0	4	0	0	0	0	0	.00	1	.167	.250	.167
Lucca,Lou,Brevard Cty	A	24	130	441	125	29	1	8	180	62	76	72	2	73	4	0	6	3	7	.30	18	.283	.384	.408
Luciano,Virgilio,Rangers	R	19	45	152	31	8	3	1	48	17	13	8	0	39	1	1	1	6	2	.75	1	.204	.247	.316
Lugo,Jesus,Cardinals	R	20	49	200	70	7	2	3	90	28	30	8	0	18	0	2	1	2	0	1.00	6	.350	.373	.450
Luna,Brian,Brewers	R	20	43	151	42	9	5	3	70	27	24	25	2	32	4	0	2	2	0	1.00	1	.278	.390	.464
Luna,Richard,Salem	A	21	14	31	5	0	0	0	5	6	0	5	0	9	0	0	0	1	0	.00	0	.161	.278	.161
Augusta	A	21	41	105	21	1	0	0	22	14	6	15	0	21	5	3	1	11	5	.69	2	.200	.320	.210
Lunar,Fernando,Braves	R	18	33	100	24	0	2	3	35	9	12	1	0	13	3	1	0	0	0	.00	1	.240	.267	.350
Luuloa,Keith,Angels	R	20	28	97	29	4	1	1	38	14	10	8	0	14	4	1	3	3	4	.43	0	.299	.366	.392
Luzinski,Ryan,Vero Beach	A	21	112	379	99	18	3	11	156	48	61	33	1	91	5	1	5	2	1	.67	11	.261	.325	.412
Lyde,Alfredo,Pirates	R	20	36	122	24	3	1	2	35	13	12	10	0	45	2	0	0	3	2	.60	3	.197	.269	.287
Lyman,Jason,Columbus	A	25	30	69	15	4	1	0	21	10	3	9	0	22	2	0	1	3	0	1.00	1	.217	.321	.304
Lynch,Mike,Lethbridge	R	23	52	124	24	2	1	3	37	16	14	31	0	48	1	0	0	11	4	.73	3	.194	.359	.298
Macero,Victor,Cubs	R	18	37	94	14	1	0	0	15	5	10	3	0	28	1	0	0	2	2	.50	1	.149	.184	.160
Machado,Robert,Pr. William	A	22	93	312	81	17	1	11	133	45	47	27	0	68	4	2	1	1	0	1.00	10	.260	.326	.426
Macias,Jose,Expos	R	21	31	104	28	8	2	1	43	23	6	14	0	15	0	0	0	4	1	.80	2	.269	.356	.413
Macon,Leland,Charlstn-Wv	A	22	126	438	105	14	1	5	136	43	42	40	1	94	14	3	2	17	18	.49	10	.240	.322	.311
Madden,Joseph,Batavia	A	24	6	17	2	1	0	0	3	2	3	5	0	5	0	0	0	2	0	1.00	1	.118	.318	.176
Spartanburg	A	24	36	116	30	5	1	0	37	11	9	11	0	24	2	0	0	4	2	.67	1	.259	.333	.319
Mader,Chris,Hickory	A	24	74	268	69	11	2	9	111	38	41	27	1	48	6	1	5	0	2	.00	9	.257	.333	.414
Madsen,Dan,Peoria	A	24	33	116	36	6	2	3	55	22	14	15	1	17	2	3	2	11	3	.79	3	.310	.393	.474
Daytona	A	24	92	294	59	7	4	9	96	42	39	47	0	74	6	3	5	11	10	.52	10	.201	.318	.327
Madsen,David,Madison	A	23	121	416	122	26	0	9	175	62	81	63	1	72	7	1	8	3	6	.33	7	.293	.389	.421
Magdaleno,Ricky,Winston-Sal	A	20	127	437	114	22	2	13	179	52	49	49	1	80	0	2	4	7	9	.44	9	.261	.333	.410
Magee,James,Macon	A	20	111	357	97	17	2	1	121	29	34	18	0	71	8	1	4	12	8	.60	5	.272	.318	.339
Magee,Wendell,Batavia	A	22	63	229	64	12	4	2	90	42	35	16	1	24	4	1	2	10	2	.83	5	.279	.335	.393
Mahalik,John,Burlington	A	23	9	30	5	0	0	0	5	1	3	1	0	5	0	1	0	0	1	.00	0	.167	.194	.167
W. Palm Bch	A	23	63	161	43	9	2	0	56	30	12	29	0	20	4	4	2	4	4	.50	4	.267	.388	.348
Mahay,Ron,Sarasota	A	24	105	367	102	18	0	4	132	43	46	39	3	67	2	7	4	3	5	.38	9	.278	.347	.360
Majeski,Brian,Great Falls	R	23	27	112	37	7	2	0	48	24	19	4	0	21	2	4	0	6	0	1.00	3	.330	.364	.429
Malin,Edgar,White Sox	R	20	8	13	1	0	1	0	3	2	1	1	0	7	0	0	0	0	0	.00	0	.077	.143	.231
Malloy,Marty,Durham	A	22	118	428	113	22	1	6	155	53	35	52	2	69	2	2	3	18	12	.60	9	.264	.344	.362
Malone,Scott,Charlotte	A	24	100	325	81	16	2	1	104	43	36	49	2	43	2	5	3	7	7	.50	4	.249	.348	.320
Mandel,Brett,Ogden	R	26	4	5	0	0	0	0	0	0	1	0	0	4	0	0	0	0	0	.00	0	.000	.000	.000
Mangham,Rodney,Astros	R	23	55	174	62	11	4	0	81	38	29	16	1	22	5	4	5	14	4	.78	3	.356	.415	.466
Manrique,Marco,Frederick	A	23	64	206	50	10	1	4	74	22	28	10	0	26	1	1	5	2	0	1.00	5	.243	.279	.359
Marabella,Tony,Expos	R	22	7	24	10	4	0	0	14	2	3	6	0	1	0	0	0	0	0	.00	0	.417	.533	.583
Burlington	A	22	38	137	35	6	0	4	53	22	18	16	0	16	0	1	1	0	2	.00	4	.255	.331	.387
Marine,Del,Fayetteville	A	23	85	284	73	18	0	7	112	32	33	30	1	55	6	1	2	4	6	.40	7	.257	.339	.394
Markiewicz,Brandon,Lake Elsino	A	23	18	65	14	1	1	0	17	3	3	1	0	11	1	2	0	1	0	1.00	3	.215	.239	.262
Boise	A	23	21	88	29	3	3	0	38	15	9	3	0	12	1	0	1	0	1	.00	0	.330	.355	.432
Cedar Rapds	A	23	5	15	3	0	0	0	3	2	1	1	1	4	0	0	1	0	1	.00	2	.200	.235	.200
Marks,Lance,Macon	A	23	55	164	37	12	1	5	66	20	32	12	0	43	0	2	3	5	2	.71	1	.226	.274	.402
Marquez,Jesus,Appleton	A	22	76	276	80	9	3	3	104	37	34	22	1	44	1	1	4	9	9	.50	2	.290	.340	.377
Marrero,Elieser,Savannah	A	21	116	421	110	16	3	21	195	71	79	39	3	92	5	2	5	4	5	.56	6	.261	.328	.463
Marsh,Roy,Auburn	A	21	55	187	48	7	0	2	61	52	13	49	0	39	4	1	0	15	5	.75	2	.257	.419	.326
Marshall,Jason,Wilmington	A	25	48	149	44	9	1	0	55	17	12	12	0	24	1	3	2	0	0	.00	5	.295	.348	.369
Marte,Pedro,Columbus	A	23	21	40	7	0	0	0	7	4	3	3	0	10	0	1	0	2	3	.40	1	.175	.233	.175
Martin,Andy,Madison	A	24	26	97	25	5	0	5	45	14	24	14	0	22	0	0	0	0	1	.00	1	.258	.348	.464
Martin,Ariel,Huntington	R	23	8	23	6	2	0	3	17	5	6	1	0	7	0	0	1	0	0	.00	0	.261	.280	.739
Martin,Eric,Everett	A	23	12	35	5	2	0	0	7	4	1	6	0	10	0	0	0	0	0	.00	0	.143	.268	.200
Martin,Jeff,Lynchburg	A	24	34	99	24	4	0	3	37	14	12	8	0	37	2	0	1	1	0	1.00	2	.242	.309	.374
Sarasota	A	24	51	164	40	9	1	6	69	24	21	16	1	54	2	1	1	0	3	.00	1	.244	.315	.421
Martin,Lincoln,Frederick	A	23	102	341	83	15	6	2	116	64	37	52	1	62	6	12	1	15	5	.75	8	.243	.352	.340
Martin,Matt,Winston-Sal	A	25	6	7	1	0	0	0	1	1	1	1	0	2	0	0	0	0	0	.00	0	.143	.250	.143
Martin,Michael,Jamestown	A	23	60	187	47	5	1	0	54	27	21	15	0	17	3	5	2	8	4	.67	4	.251	.314	.289
Martin,Ryan,Danville	R	19	33	79	18	3	0	1	24	8	8	9	0	28	3	3	2	0	1	.00	1	.228	.323	.304
Martinez,Angel,Dunedin	A	22	122	450	117	14	6	7	164	50	52	22	1	79	11	3	1	1	3	.25	15	.260	.310	.364
Martinez,Dalvis,Jamestown	A	21	61	201	51	16	6	2	85	38	16	26	0	59	3	2	1	3	4	.43	3	.254	.345	.423
Martinez,Erik,Spokane	A	23	50	174	36	7	1	1	48	20	13	11	0	36	3	2	1	15	2	.88	3	.207	.284	.276

298

1994 Batting -- Single-A and Rookie Leagues

Player	Lg	A	G	AB	H	2B	3B	HR	TB	R	RBI	TBB	IBB	SO	HBP	SH	SF	SB	CS	SB%	GDP	Avg	OBP	SLG
Martinez,Felix,Wilmington	A	21	117	400	107	16	4	2	137	65	43	30	0	91	3	12	2	19	8	.70	10	.268	.322	.343
Martinez,Gabriel,Stockton	A	21	112	364	90	18	3	0	114	37	32	17	1	66	4	4	4	19	11	.63	8	.247	.285	.313
Martinez,Gregory,Beloit	A	23	81	224	62	8	1	0	72	39	20	25	1	32	3	6	1	27	11	.71	4	.277	.356	.321
Martinez,Humberto,Red Sox	R	20	31	74	14	2	0	0	16	6	4	2	0	23	1	2	1	1	1	.50	2	.189	.218	.216
Martinez,Luis,Expos	R	20	30	97	16	4	0	0	20	11	6	11	0	29	2	1	0	1	1	.50	2	.165	.259	.206
Martinez,Obed,Padres	R	19	26	95	26	1	2	0	31	11	10	2	0	19	1	2	0	3	2	.60	2	.274	.296	.326
Martinez,Pablo,Giants	R	19	31	65	12	2	0	0	14	1	5	3	0	20	0	0	0	3	2	.60	1	.185	.221	.215
Martinez,Ramon,Rockford	A	22	6	18	5	0	0	0	5	3	3	4	0	2	0	1	0	1	0	1.00	1	.278	.409	.278
Wilmington	A	22	90	325	87	13	2	2	110	40	35	35	0	25	4	20	5	6	3	.67	14	.268	.341	.338
Martins,Eric,Sou. Oregon	A	22	56	236	78	16	3	4	112	47	34	23	1	36	5	2	0	17	10	.63	4	.331	.402	.475
W. Michigan	A	22	18	71	22	4	1	0	28	11	7	5	0	12	0	1	2	1	2	.33	2	.310	.346	.394
Marval,Raul,Everett	A	19	29	99	21	5	0	1	29	9	12	4	0	22	1	1	3	4	4	.50	3	.212	.243	.293
Clinton	A	19	81	273	60	9	3	0	75	27	28	16	0	75	2	4	6	4	5	.44	5	.220	.263	.275
Mastrullo,Michael,Burlington	R	20	35	84	22	2	1	0	26	11	6	20	0	37	1	3	1	4	3	.57	1	.262	.406	.310
Mateo,Franklin,Brewers	R	NA	16	70	26	6	1	0	34	13	3	7	0	8	0	0	0	6	3	.67	1	.371	.429	.486
Helena	R	NA	45	128	41	3	1	0	46	29	14	22	0	17	1	1	1	13	7	.65	2	.320	.421	.359
Mathews,Byron,South Bend	A	24	84	305	69	10	4	1	90	41	29	27	0	73	4	3	4	16	11	.59	4	.226	.294	.295
Pr. William	A	24	24	96	27	6	1	2	41	17	13	6	0	18	1	0	0	6	2	.75	0	.281	.330	.427
Mathews,Jon,Rockies	R	22	4	15	5	0	0	0	5	0	2	0	0	0	0	0	0	1	0	1.00	0	.333	.333	.333
Bend	A	22	15	39	36	3	0	0	39	12	13	25	1	25	1	0	0	3	1	.75	2	.259	.356	.281
Mathis,Joe,Bellingham	A	20	53	158	39	4	3	2	55	21	17	16	0	45	2	3	0	13	5	.72	0	.247	.324	.348
Matos,Domingo,W. Palm Bch	A	23	75	277	57	10	1	6	87	24	34	12	1	70	1	2	2	2	2	.50	6	.206	.240	.314
Matos,Julius,Watertown	A	20	43	138	34	2	2	0	40	13	18	13	0	33	0	0	3	2	2	.60	6	.246	.307	.290
Matos,Malvin,Charlotte	A	23	69	242	57	13	2	5	89	22	33	14	0	59	1	1	4	3	9	.25	2	.236	.276	.368
Matos,Pasqual,Macon	A	20	11	29	5	2	0	0	7	1	2	0	0	10	1	0	0	1	0	1.00	0	.172	.200	.241
Idaho Falls	R	20	43	157	40	7	1	7	70	22	29	2	0	39	0	1	2	7	2	.78	7	.255	.261	.446
Matthews,Gary,Spokane	A	20	52	191	40	6	1	0	48	23	18	19	1	58	2	0	1	3	5	.38	4	.209	.286	.251
Matvey,Michael,Savannah	A	23	122	444	112	26	3	3	153	61	65	44	1	99	9	9	3	4	9	.31	16	.252	.330	.345
Maxwell,Jason,Daytona	A	23	116	368	85	18	2	10	137	71	32	55	0	96	8	6	2	7	7	.50	6	.231	.342	.372
Mayber,Chan,Rockies	R	22	45	170	39	5	1	0	46	21	8	12	0	33	2	4	1	4	3	.57	2	.229	.286	.271
Mayes,Craig,Clinton	A	25	49	155	32	5	1	1	42	13	14	11	1	33	0	2	1	0	2	.00	4	.206	.257	.271
San Berndro	A	25	50	191	48	5	0	2	59	20	21	17	1	35	1	0	0	2	2	.50	3	.251	.316	.309
Maynor,Tonka,Welland	A	23	59	197	51	9	2	0	64	21	21	17	1	40	9	1	2	2	0	1.00	1	.259	.342	.325
Maysonet,Jose,Blue Jays	R	19	53	181	44	10	3	0	60	27	15	25	0	51	1	2	1	18	6	.75	3	.243	.337	.331
Dunedin	A	19	2	1	0	0	0	0	0	0	0	0	0	1	0	0	0	0	0	.00	0	.000	.000	.000
McAfee,Leland,Pirates	R	22	34	131	25	5	2	0	34	10	17	3	0	19	3	0	2	8	2	.80	2	.191	.223	.260
McAllister,Troy,Oneonta	A	24	2	5	0	0	0	0	0	0	0	2	0	3	1	0	0	0	0	.00	0	.000	.375	.000
Greensboro	A	24	1	0	0	0	0	0	0	1	0	0	0	0	0	0	0	0	0	.00	0	.000	.000	.000
Tampa	A	24	1	2	0	0	0	0	0	1	0	1	0	0	0	0	0	0	0	.00	0	.000	.333	.000
McBride,Charles,Macon	A	21	81	296	100	21	6	13	172	60	54	29	0	80	0	4	3	17	4	.81	5	.338	.393	.581
McCalmont,James,Elizabethtn	R	23	62	242	60	9	1	7	92	46	31	27	0	30	8	1	2	2	1	.67	5	.248	.341	.380
McCarthy,Kevin,Mets	R	18	14	51	10	0	1	0	12	6	5	4	0	9	0	0	1	2	1	.33	2	.196	.255	.235
McCartney,Sommer,Elmira	A	22	37	80	14	4	0	0	18	3	5	3	1	16	1	1	0	0	1	.00	1	.175	.214	.225
McCloughan,Scot,Dunedin	A	24	6	20	6	3	0	0	9	4	3	1	0	1	0	0	0	1	0	.00	1	.300	.333	.450
Hagerstown	A	24	57	223	66	12	4	3	95	32	32	16	2	38	3	3	1	8	4	.67	4	.296	.350	.426
McClure,Craig,White Sox	R	19	49	135	32	9	2	1	48	27	16	17	0	44	2	0	0	10	2	.83	1	.237	.331	.356
McCroskey,Jackie,Princeton	R	21	57	189	43	9	4	3	69	27	25	18	0	49	2	0	2	7	6	.54	2	.228	.299	.365
McCubbin,Shane,Burlington	A	22	22	66	16	4	1	0	22	7	4	6	0	27	3	0	0	0	0	.00	2	.242	.333	.333
Vermont	A	22	57	202	49	12	1	5	78	29	23	13	0	45	6	0	2	2	1	.67	4	.243	.305	.386
McDonald,Immanuel,Athletics	R	21	51	154	37	4	4	2	55	29	10	15	0	42	5	1	0	7	6	.54	4	.240	.328	.357
McDonald,Jason,W. Michigan	A	23	116	404	96	11	9	2	131	67	31	81	1	87	4	9	4	52	23	.69	5	.238	.369	.324
McDonald,William,Johnson Cty	R	22	59	199	49	12	0	6	79	32	31	27	3	36	5	2	2	3	1	.75	9	.246	.346	.397
McDougal,Mike,Cardinals	R	20	21	74	20	6	0	0	26	13	6	8	0	16	1	0	0	2	1	.67	0	.270	.349	.351
McEwing,Joe,Madison	A	22	90	346	102	24	2	4	152	58	47	32	4	53	1	5	3	18	15	.55	5	.324	.380	.439
St. Pete	A	22	50	197	49	7	0	1	59	22	20	19	0	32	1	4	0	8	4	.67	4	.249	.314	.299
McGehee,Michael,Cubs	R	19	23	61	12	1	0	0	13	7	5	8	0	15	0	0	1	0	1	.00	1	.197	.286	.213
Peoria	A	19	3	5	1	0	0	0	1	0	1	1	0	1	0	0	0	0	0	.00	0	.200	.333	.200
McGinn,Shaun,Batavia	A	23	21	71	11	3	0	0	14	2	5	3	0	16	0	0	0	0	2	.00	1	.155	.189	.197
McGonigle,Bill,Helena	R	23	4	8	2	0	0	0	2	1	1	1	0	2	0	0	0	0	0	.00	0	.250	.333	.250
Beloit	A	23	14	36	9	3	0	0	12	5	1	2	0	4	1	0	0	0	1	.00	1	.250	.308	.333
McGuire,Ryan,Lynchburg	A	23	137	489	133	29	0	10	192	70	73	79	2	77	2	4	7	10	9	.53	19	.272	.371	.393
McInnes,Christopher,Beloit	A	24	121	381	84	5	5	1	102	73	30	55	0	79	4	20	2	45	4	.92	6	.220	.324	.268
McKinnis,Leroy,Springfield	A	23	121	421	117	30	3	9	180	70	67	44	1	84	12	0	5	3	2	.60	8	.278	.359	.428
McKinnon,Sandy,South Bend	A	21	117	462	111	9	4	3	137	64	28	32	0	83	4	7	3	36	14	.72	7	.240	.293	.297
McKinnon,Tom,Madison	A	22	45	161	45	7	3	5	73	18	32	3	2	43	3	0	5	4	3	.57	4	.280	.297	.453
McLamb,Brian,Greensboro	A	22	32	110	30	7	0	0	37	13	14	6	0	31	3	1	2	3	3	.50	2	.273	.322	.336
Oneonta	A	22	71	262	48	10	2	1	65	31	20	12	0	59	5	2	5	8	3	.73	4	.183	.229	.248
McLendon,Craig,Rangers	R	19	32	92	14	0	0	0	14	9	5	9	0	18	1	1	0	1	1	.50	4	.152	.233	.152
McMillan,Thomas,Cardinals	R	19	34	101	22	7	0	1	32	13	6	12	0	36	1	0	1	5	3	.63	2	.218	.304	.317
McMillon,William,Kane County	A	23	137	496	125	25	3	17	207	88	101	84	2	99	10	1	9	7	3	.70	13	.252	.366	.417
McMullen,Jon,Spartanburg	A	21	65	256	76	14	2	12	130	42	53	15	0	56	4	0	3	1	2	.33	4	.297	.342	.508
McNally,Sean,Eugene	A	22	74	278	69	16	2	3	98	44	30	24	1	66	4	2	2	4	7	.36	5	.248	.315	.353
McNeal,Pepe,Burlington	R	19	31	99	13	0	0	0	13	8	3	8	0	30	2	3	0	2	1	.67	3	.131	.211	.131
McQueen,Conrad,Mets	R	20	7	25	6	1	0	0	7	0	4	1	0	7	0	0	0	0	0	.00	0	.240	.269	.280
McSparin,Paul,Pirates	R	21	22	59	4	0	0	1	7	5	2	8	0	17	4	1	1	1	1	.50	0	.068	.222	.119
McWhite,Raymond,Danville	R	21	61	213	35	17	0	1	55	26	20	26	1	75	3	1	2	13	5	.72	7	.164	.262	.258
Mealing,Allen,Helena	R	21	61	168	46	6	4	2	66	29	18	21	1	53	1	3	1	8	6	.57	7	.274	.356	.393

1994 Batting -- Single-A and Rookie Leagues

Player	Lg	A	G	AB	H	2B	3B	HR	TB	R	RBI	TBB	IBB	SO	HBP	SH	SF	SB	CS	SB%	GDP	Avg	OBP	SLG
Mediavilla,Ricky,Savannah	A	25	79	231	45	6	3	1	60	28	13	12	0	24	16	2	1	7	6	.54	5	.195	.281	.260
Medina,Alger,Brewers	R	21	12	24	6	0	0	1	9	2	4	4	0	8	0	1	0	1	0	1.00	0	.250	.345	.375
Medina,Ricardo,Daytona	A	23	54	137	31	5	1	3	47	10	20	10	0	16	1	1	3	1	0	1.00	4	.226	.278	.343
Medrano,Anthony,Blue Jays	R	20	6	22	8	4	0	1	15	2	5	1	0	0	0	0	0	0	0	.00	0	.364	.391	.682
Dunedin	A	20	60	199	47	6	4	4	73	20	21	12	0	26	3	3	1	3	3	.50	4	.236	.288	.367
Meggers,Mike,Winston-Sal	A	24	114	418	95	25	2	25	199	62	80	31	0	139	1	0	7	6	2	.75	8	.227	.278	.476
Meilan,Tony,Great Falls	R	23	27	59	22	3	0	1	28	10	10	9	0	6	2	2	2	1	1	.50	2	.373	.458	.475
Mejia,Miguel,Albany	A	20	22	58	10	1	1	0	13	6	3	5	0	20	1	1	1	5	5	.50	0	.172	.246	.224
Bluefield	R	20	50	191	51	5	5	2	72	34	24	17	0	39	1	5	1	32	9	.78	2	.267	.329	.377
Melendez,Enrique,Rockies	R	19	37	130	27	5	1	1	37	16	5	7	0	43	2	1	2	0	1	.00	1	.208	.255	.285
Melendez,Osmin,Orioles	R	20	48	151	36	5	2	0	45	21	18	22	1	11	1	0	2	7	3	.70	1	.238	.335	.298
Melhuse,Adam,Hagerstown	A	23	118	422	109	16	3	11	164	61	58	53	3	77	1	1	6	6	8	.43	13	.258	.338	.389
Meluskey,Mitch,Kinston	A	21	100	319	77	16	1	3	104	36	41	49	0	62	2	2	4	3	4	.43	4	.241	.342	.326
Mendez,Carlos,Rockford	A	21	104	363	129	26	2	5	174	45	51	13	2	50	5	4	2	0	0	.00	11	.355	.382	.479
Mendez,Emilio,Peoria	A	22	42	89	18	2	1	0	22	5	4	7	0	22	4	6	1	0	0	.00	1	.202	.287	.247
Williamsprt	A	22	32	90	15	1	0	0	16	4	7	3	0	19	0	2	1	1	2	.33	3	.167	.191	.178
Mendez,Rodolfo,Royals	R	20	59	222	68	12	6	2	98	52	34	32	0	33	3	2	3	22	6	.79	3	.306	.396	.441
Mendez,Sergio,Augusta	A	21	88	331	91	15	2	7	131	36	38	10	1	70	4	0	1	7	4	.64	4	.275	.303	.396
Mendoza,Jesus,White Sox	R	20	13	43	11	2	0	0	13	2	3	2	0	4	0	0	1	3	2	.60	2	.256	.283	.302
Menechino,Frank,South Bend	A	24	106	379	113	21	5	5	159	77	48	78	1	70	9	3	2	15	8	.65	8	.298	.427	.420
Mepri,Sal,Princeton	R	18	14	21	2	0	0	0	2	0	0	2	0	8	0	0	0	0	1	.00	0	.095	.174	.095
Meran,Jorge,Vermont	A	20	8	22	4	2	0	0	6	1	3	0	0	5	0	0	0	0	0	.00	1	.182	.182	.273
Expos	R	20	33	119	26	4	5	0	40	7	17	5	0	16	0	1	2	2	2	.50	3	.218	.246	.336
Mercedes,Feliciano,Frederick	A	21	43	139	33	3	2	0	40	17	19	10	0	34	0	4	3	4	4	.50	2	.237	.283	.288
Orioles	R	21	3	10	3	1	0	0	4	1	2	0	0	0	0	0	0	0	0	.00	0	.300	.273	.400
Mercedes,Guillermo,Charlotte	A	21	132	443	98	7	1	0	107	44	37	47	0	67	5	11	4	14	13	.52	9	.221	.301	.242
Mercedes,Juan,Williamsprt	A	21	7	26	4	0	0	0	4	3	0	1	0	10	0	0	0	0	1	.00	1	.154	.185	.154
Merila,Mark,Spokane	A	23	58	198	50	11	2	1	68	36	14	49	0	30	0	2	2	8	4	.67	3	.253	.398	.343
Merloni,Louis,Sarasota	A	24	113	419	120	16	2	1	143	59	63	36	4	57	7	7	10	5	2	.71	11	.286	.345	.341
Meskauskas,John,Rockies	R	22	1	3	1	0	0	0	1	0	0	1	0	1	0	0	0	0	0	.00	0	.333	.500	.333
Bend	A	22	22	51	7	1	0	1	11	8	2	4	0	19	1	0	0	1	0	1.00	2	.137	.214	.216
Metcalfe,Michael,Bakersfield	A	22	69	275	78	10	0	0	88	44	18	28	0	34	1	4	2	41	13	.76	6	.284	.350	.320
Meza,Larry,St. Pete	A	22	89	257	61	6	3	3	82	33	17	23	3	31	1	3	3	7	2	.78	5	.237	.299	.319
Michael,Jeffry,Frederick	A	23	80	258	73	12	1	1	90	28	24	12	1	33	1	0	0	7	7	.50	2	.283	.317	.349
Micucci,Michael,Williamsprt	A	22	43	105	20	2	0	0	22	16	8	8	0	16	4	5	3	3	2	.60	1	.190	.267	.210
Mifflin,Brian,Mets	R	21	35	129	26	3	3	3	44	12	14	4	0	42	1	0	0	2	0	1.00	2	.202	.231	.341
Millan,Adan,Batavia	A	23	17	53	17	4	0	0	21	10	11	10	0	6	1	0	1	0	1	.00	1	.321	.431	.396
Spartanburg	A	23	48	153	41	12	0	4	65	20	29	33	1	21	1	0	1	1	1	.50	6	.268	.399	.425
Millan,Bernie,Stockton	A	24	126	489	147	21	3	1	177	56	51	22	1	39	0	13	3	8	6	.57	13	.301	.329	.362
Millan,Jorge,Johnson City	R	21	24	57	12	1	0	0	13	6	8	6	0	9	0	3	1	0	1	.00	1	.211	.303	.228
Millar,Kevin,Kane County	A	23	135	477	144	35	2	19	240	75	93	74	2	88	13	0	4	3	3	.50	12	.302	.405	.503
Milledge,Tony,Cardinals	R	19	22	71	18	3	0	0	21	4	3	1	0	13	1	0	0	2	1	.67	1	.254	.274	.296
Miller,Jason,Rangers	R	17	38	121	23	5	1	0	30	11	11	23	1	14	0	0	0	2	2	.50	2	.190	.319	.248
Miller,Roger,San Jose	A	28	48	165	33	8	0	2	47	19	15	19	0	20	4	1	2	0	0	.00	4	.200	.295	.285
Miller,Roy,Riverside	A	23	42	99	20	4	1	1	29	17	12	12	0	23	7	0	0	3	1	.75	2	.202	.325	.293
Miller,Ryan,Pittsfield	A	22	68	277	71	11	1	1	87	37	23	16	1	37	4	3	2	3	3	.50	0	.256	.304	.314
Milliard,Ralph,Kane County	A	21	133	515	153	34	2	8	215	97	67	68	2	63	9	4	7	10	10	.50	6	.297	.384	.417
Millican,Kevin,Hudson Vall	A	21	71	255	62	16	1	8	104	33	44	35	2	74	2	2	2	6	2	.75	7	.243	.338	.408
Millwood,Terry,Twins	R	19	5	15	2	0	0	0	2	1	2	3	0	4	0	0	0	0	0	.00	0	.133	.263	.133
Miralth,Charles,Idaho Falls	R	23	44	163	45	3	2	1	55	26	19	8	0	24	0	1	2	1	2	.33	5	.276	.306	.337
Miranda,Alejandro,Sou. Oregon	A	23	73	222	67	11	4	1	89	41	23	22	3	54	8	1	1	1	2	.33	6	.302	.383	.401
Mitchell,Don,Osceola	A	25	119	455	109	14	4	0	131	47	36	34	1	56	2	5	3	20	13	.61	7	.240	.294	.288
Mitchell,Rivers,Bristol	R	23	43	147	38	2	1	0	42	22	18	21	0	35	3	1	1	12	4	.75	2	.259	.360	.286
Mobilia,William,Batavia	A	24	35	112	29	8	2	1	44	17	10	15	0	29	3	1	1	1	2	.33	2	.259	.359	.393
Moeder,Tony,Cedar Rapds	A	23	117	410	110	20	0	18	184	64	64	45	1	89	8	2	2	7	4	.64	10	.268	.351	.449
Moen,Rob,Kane County	A	24	4	10	0	0	0	0	0	1	1	1	0	3	0	1	0	0	0	.00	2	.000	.083	.000
Molina,Ben,Cedar Rapds	A	20	48	171	48	8	0	3	65	14	16	8	0	12	3	1	0	1	2	.33	3	.281	.324	.380
Molina,Jose,Peoria	A	20	78	253	58	13	1	0	76	31	33	24	1	61	4	5	4	4	3	.57	5	.229	.302	.300
Molina,Luis,Appleton	A	21	7	21	3	1	0	0	4	2	1	3	0	3	1	0	0	1	0	1.00	0	.143	.280	.190
Bellingham	A	21	47	100	21	3	0	0	24	13	10	17	0	25	8	3	1	4	2	.67	0	.210	.365	.240
Monds,Wonderful,Durham	A	22	18	53	11	2	0	2	19	7	10	2	1	11	0	0	0	5	0	1.00	3	.208	.232	.358
Macon	A	22	104	365	106	23	12	10	183	70	41	22	0	82	9	8	2	42	9	.82	6	.290	.344	.501
Monroe,Darryl,Jamestown	A	23	52	170	33	8	0	1	44	16	17	14	1	29	6	3	2	8	5	.62	5	.194	.276	.259
Montero,Danny,Daytona	A	21	19	44	8	1	0	0	9	4	6	5	0	11	0	0	0	0	0	.00	2	.182	.265	.205
Huntington	R	21	42	107	20	7	0	0	25	20	12	8	0	29	2	0	0	3	3	.50	1	.187	.256	.234
Montero,Joselin,Marlins	R	19	17	49	8	0	1	0	10	2	3	4	0	17	1	0	0	0	0	.00	2	.163	.241	.204
Montilla,Miguel,Cubs	R	21	22	62	12	1	0	0	13	13	2	10	0	19	1	2	0	9	1	.90	3	.194	.315	.210
Moody,Mario,Cubs	R	21	22	56	12	1	1	0	15	11	3	5	0	9	3	4	0	10	0	1.00	0	.214	.313	.268
Moore,David,White Sox	R	20	17	40	5	1	0	1	9	5	7	7	0	15	1	0	0	2	2	.50	0	.125	.271	.225
Moore,Mark,W. Michigan	A	24	106	340	93	27	2	9	151	49	53	42	2	79	10	1	3	4	6	.40	10	.274	.360	.444
Moore,Boo,Lynchburg	A	25	17	56	12	3	0	1	18	7	5	5	0	14	3	0	2	0	0	.00	1	.214	.303	.321
Moore,William,White Sox	R	22	4	10	1	0	0	0	1	1	1	0	0	6	0	0	0	0	0	.00	0	.100	.182	.100
Hickory	A	22	60	230	57	5	2	1	69	43	26	33	1	28	1	7	3	10	6	.63	7	.248	.341	.300
Mora,Melvin,Osceola	A	23	118	435	120	29	4	8	181	57	46	37	1	60	10	3	3	24	16	.60	8	.282	.352	.426
Morales,Hery,Kingsport	R	22	40	135	27	5	1	1	37	17	11	15	0	24	2	1	0	2	0	1.00	3	.200	.289	.274
Morales,Jesus,Mets	R	22	15	53	12	1	0	0	13	8	3	5	0	18	0	1	1	0	0	.00	3	.226	.288	.245
Kingsport	R	22	21	59	14	1	0	0	15	5	2	4	0	15	0	2	0	1	1	.50	1	.237	.286	.254

300

1994 Batting -- Single-A and Rookie Leagues

						BATTING												BASERUNNING				PERCENTAGES		
Player	Lg	A	G	AB	H	2B	3B	HR	TB	R	RBI	TBB	IBB	SO	HBP	SH	SF	SB	CS	SB%	GDP	Avg	OBP	SLG
Morales,William,W. Michigan	A	22	111	380	101	26	0	13	166	47	51	36	4	64	3	3	2	3	5	.38	12	.266	.333	.437
Morel,Plinio,Savannah	A	24	7	17	2	0	0	0	2	1	0	0	0	3	2	1	0	0	0	.00	1	.118	.211	.118
Madison	A	24	39	110	23	5	0	0	28	12	9	9	0	17	0	0	0	1	0	1.00	1	.209	.269	.255
Moreno,Erik,Macon	A	25	23	54	7	1	0	0	8	4	3	9	0	8	0	2	0	1	2	.33	2	.130	.254	.148
Moreno,Jorge,Fayetteville	A	22	74	230	49	12	2	4	77	29	24	17	0	73	1	5	2	4	2	.67	4	.213	.268	.335
Moreno,Victor,Royals	R	19	9	18	2	0	0	0	2	3	0	3	0	6	0	0	0	0	0	.00	0	.111	.238	.111
Morgan,David,Medicne Hat	A	23	16	50	14	1	0	1	18	4	5	2	0	12	2	0	0	0	1	.00	1	.280	.333	.360
Morgan,Kevin,St. Lucie	A	24	132	448	122	8	3	1	139	63	47	37	0	62	7	9	3	7	7	.50	5	.272	.335	.310
Morillo,Cesar,Wilmington	A	23	16	55	9	1	0	0	10	3	4	5	1	17	1	0	1	1	0	1.00	1	.164	.242	.182
Rockford	A	21	70	242	68	11	2	2	89	23	25	15	2	35	2	1	2	4	3	.57	6	.281	.326	.368
Morreale,John,Beloit	A	23	70	144	39	3	2	0	46	27	12	21	0	40	1	6	0	5	5	.50	3	.271	.367	.319
Morris,Donald,Blue Jays	R	19	11	34	6	1	0	0	7	3	2	2	0	9	0	0	0	1	2	.33	0	.176	.222	.206
Morris,Gregory,Boise	A	23	74	260	74	18	1	0	94	45	38	50	1	54	3	0	4	12	3	.80	6	.285	.401	.362
Morris,Jon,Spokane	A	23	2	9	2	0	0	0	2	2	1	1	0	2	0	0	0	0	0	.00	0	.222	.300	.222
Springfield	A	23	41	99	20	3	0	0	23	8	8	13	0	34	2	3	1	0	1	.00	0	.202	.304	.232
Morris,Robert,Peoria	A	22	101	362	128	33	1	7	184	61	64	53	4	63	7	10	2	7	7	.50	10	.354	.443	.508
Morrow,Nick,Billings	R	23	66	246	82	16	4	14	148	60	56	33	1	46	2	0	1	6	2	.75	1	.333	.415	.602
Moschetti,Michael,Sou. Oregon	A	20	59	201	45	7	2	2	62	33	21	20	0	66	11	1	2	8	7	.53	3	.224	.325	.308
Mosquera,Julio,Medicne Hat	R	20	59	229	78	17	1	2	103	33	44	18	3	35	3	0	0	3	3	.50	4	.341	.393	.450
Mota,Alfonso,Angels	R	21	45	154	53	8	7	1	78	37	19	26	0	34	4	2	0	5	1	.83	1	.344	.451	.506
Mota,Guillermo,St. Lucie	A	21	1	4	0	0	0	0	0	1	0	0	0	0	0	0	0	0	0	.00	0	.000	.000	.000
Kingsport	R	21	65	245	60	10	2	9	101	40	37	20	0	78	4	4	0	5	4	.56	5	.245	.312	.412
Mota,Santo,Madison	A	23	137	474	131	19	3	4	168	77	46	56	0	84	2	13	3	28	29	.49	4	.276	.353	.354
Motte,James,Fort Wayne	A	23	129	480	116	22	3	8	168	66	47	36	1	109	1	4	4	12	9	.57	9	.242	.294	.350
Moultrie,Pat,Hagerstown	A	22	79	303	67	9	4	4	96	43	37	13	0	50	1	5	1	20	7	.74	2	.221	.255	.317
Mowry,David,Springfield	A	23	61	215	51	10	0	13	100	27	47	18	2	52	3	0	5	0	1	.00	4	.237	.299	.465
Rancho Cuca	A	23	56	202	47	9	1	7	79	26	38	14	2	55	2	0	2	1	0	1.00	1	.233	.286	.391
Moyle,Mike,Butte	R	23	49	189	68	18	3	5	107	43	52	27	0	36	2	0	2	4	1	.80	8	.360	.441	.566
Mucker,Kelcey,Elizabethtn	R	20	64	240	57	10	0	6	85	23	31	22	1	65	2	0	1	2	2	.50	0	.238	.303	.354
Mueller,William,San Jose	A	24	120	431	130	20	9	5	183	79	72	103	11	47	3	1	6	4	8	.33	15	.302	.435	.425
Mullen,Adam,Braves	R	19	20	56	9	1	0	0	10	5	3	2	0	22	3	1	0	1	0	1.00	2	.161	.230	.179
Mumma,Robert,South Bend	A	24	25	73	14	1	0	2	21	9	11	15	1	13	0	0	0	0	0	.00	0	.192	.330	.288
Hickory	A	24	23	76	21	3	0	1	27	10	6	7	0	19	1	1	0	0	0	.00	0	.276	.341	.355
Mummau,Robert,Dunedin	A	23	21	50	11	1	0	0	12	5	6	4	0	15	0	1	0	0	2	.00	0	.220	.278	.240
Hagerstown	A	23	46	169	50	10	2	1	67	20	24	10	0	32	2	0	3	2	2	.50	4	.296	.337	.396
Muro,Peter,Ogden	R	23	23	83	20	1	1	0	23	12	7	3	0	15	5	2	0	2	1	.67	1	.241	.308	.277
Murphy,James,Lynchburg	A	23	117	456	113	19	4	0	140	64	26	45	1	72	3	2	2	27	19	.59	13	.248	.318	.307
Sarasota	A	23	2	7	1	0	0	0	1	0	0	0	0	2	0	0	0	1	0	1.00	0	.143	.143	.143
Murphy,Jeff,St. Pete	A	24	49	139	27	5	0	0	32	11	8	22	1	37	3	1	2	2	0	1.00	4	.194	.313	.230
Murphy,Mike,Dunedin	A	23	125	469	129	11	4	1	151	57	34	55	3	106	9	4	3	31	10	.76	9	.275	.360	.322
Murphy,Quinn,Burlington	R	19	26	69	16	3	0	0	19	10	9	12	0	33	0	0	0	3	3	.50	1	.232	.346	.275
Murphy,Sean,Watertown	A	23	1	2	0	0	0	0	0	0	0	0	0	1	0	0	0	0	0	.00	0	.000	.000	.000
Columbus	A	23	8	7	0	0	0	0	0	1	1	4	0	3	0	0	1	1	0	1.00	0	.000	.333	.000
Murphy,Steve,Wilmington	A	24	102	353	87	15	7	1	119	57	37	45	0	63	4	9	4	23	4	.85	3	.246	.335	.337
Myers,Aaron,Rockies	R	19	43	150	32	5	1	4	51	11	20	10	0	46	1	0	1	0	1	.00	1	.213	.265	.340
Myers,Rod,Wilmington	A	22	126	457	120	20	4	12	184	76	65	67	3	93	6	12	1	31	11	.74	7	.263	.363	.403
Myrow,John,Central Val	A	23	128	521	143	26	2	8	197	81	73	27	1	85	7	3	3	26	5	.84	16	.274	.314	.378
Nadeau,Michael,Bluefield	R	21	56	188	40	8	2	0	52	18	18	10	0	31	8	3	4	7	1	.88	3	.213	.276	.277
Nava,Marlo,Fort Wayne	A	22	86	324	88	11	1	1	104	43	23	15	0	52	3	6	2	1	1	.50	10	.272	.308	.321
Navarro,Cesar,Giants	R	19	21	79	17	1	1	0	20	8	5	3	0	18	1	0	1	3	2	.60	0	.243	.280	.286
Navas,Jesus,White Sox	R	20	25	59	10	0	0	0	10	4	6	6	0	11	0	1	2	1	2	.33	4	.169	.239	.169
South Bend	A	20	12	43	6	0	0	0	6	2	0	0	0	9	0	0	1	1	2	.33	1	.140	.140	.140
Neal,Michael,Kinston	A	23	101	378	99	21	1	5	137	51	38	40	1	94	3	3	1	8	12	.40	6	.262	.336	.362
Nelson,Bryant,Quad City	A	21	45	156	38	6	0	1	47	20	6	11	0	15	0	0	0	3	5	.38	3	.244	.293	.301
Auburn	A	21	65	261	84	16	7	6	132	53	35	11	0	13	1	3	1	2	1	.67	9	.322	.350	.506
Nelson,Charles,Yakima	A	23	63	212	68	8	5	0	86	53	25	57	3	49	0	4	2	30	5	.86	3	.321	.461	.406
Nelson,Tray,Oneonta	A	22	21	40	5	1	0	0	6	8	2	7	0	17	1	1	1	3	1	.75	2	.125	.265	.150
Newell,Brett,Danville	R	22	66	228	60	9	0	0	69	35	20	39	0	53	13	3	1	5	5	.50	7	.263	.399	.303
Newhouse,Andre,South Bend	A	22	104	350	100	13	2	2	123	67	46	40	1	72	7	2	4	26	4	.87	5	.284	.365	.349
Newman,Wayne,Danville	R	22	48	129	28	4	1	4	46	20	12	13	0	31	2	3	0	9	7	.56	3	.217	.299	.357
Newstrom,Douglas,Vero Beach	A	23	119	405	117	22	5	2	155	47	46	59	3	51	2	0	5	4	5	.44	5	.289	.378	.383
Nicholas,Darrell,Helena	R	23	15	61	23	3	2	0	30	18	13	10	0	10	1	0	0	11	3	.79	0	.377	.472	.492
Beloit	A	23	59	221	63	8	3	1	80	33	35	22	0	54	1	1	2	17	4	.81	4	.285	.347	.362
Niethammer,Marc,Burlington	A	23	92	301	50	10	1	12	98	31	30	30	2	124	4	2	1	0	0	.00	5	.166	.250	.326
Nihart,Tim,Elizabethtn	R	22	2	7	2	0	0	0	2	1	3	0	0	1	0	0	0	0	0	.00	0	.286	.286	.429
Fort Wayne	A	22	14	38	9	1	0	0	10	3	7	2	0	7	0	0	0	0	2	.00	1	.237	.262	.263
Niles,David,Rockies	R	18	35	98	24	2	0	0	26	8	4	24	1	35	0	0	1	3	2	.60	1	.245	.390	.265
Nitschke,Bear,Martinsvlle	R	24	14	49	9	1	0	0	10	6	6	9	1	9	0	1	0	1	0	1.00	0	.184	.305	.204
Batavia	A	24	19	61	9	0	0	0	9	5	6	4	1	15	1	1	0	1	0	1.00	2	.148	.212	.148
Nixon,Trot,Lynchburg	A	21	71	264	65	12	0	12	113	33	43	44	1	53	3	1	3	10	3	.77	5	.246	.357	.428
Nobles,Ivan,Blue Jays	R	20	33	115	27	4	2	0	35	18	12	15	0	33	2	1	0	12	0	1.00	0	.235	.333	.304
Noriega,Kevin,Yankees	R	21	20	60	15	5	0	0	20	8	5	13	1	10	1	0	1	2	0	1.00	1	.250	.387	.333
Greensboro	A	21	9	28	7	1	0	0	8	3	3	2	0	9	0	0	0	0	0	.00	0	.250	.300	.286
Norman,Eric,Red Sox	R	21	7	25	8	2	1	0	12	7	4	3	0	0	2	1	0	1	1	.50	0	.320	.433	.480
Norman,Ken,Fort Myers	A	23	106	368	86	12	3	2	110	49	30	34	1	83	6	1	2	32	6	.84	7	.234	.307	.299
Northeimer,James,Batavia	A	22	45	144	38	9	2	2	57	16	20	14	2	22	4	1	3	0	5	.00	3	.264	.339	.396
Norton,Chris,Savannah	A	24	126	439	116	11	2	26	209	75	82	73	4	144	4	3	2	6	4	.60	11	.264	.373	.476

1994 Batting -- Single-A and Rookie Leagues

Player	Lg	A	G	AB	H	2B	3B	HR	TB	R	RBI	TBB	IBB	SO	HBP	SH	SF	SB	CS	SB%	GDP	Avg	OBP	SLG
Norton,Gregory,South Bend	A	22	127	477	137	22	2	6	181	73	64	62	4	71	2	2	3	5	3	.63	7	.287	.369	.379
Nova,Pasqual,Padres	R	20	48	164	25	9	2	3	47	17	19	10	0	87	8	0	1	8	2	.80	1	.152	.235	.287
Nunez,Isaias,Johnson Cty	R	21	67	225	53	13	6	5	93	31	32	36	1	40	0	2	2	4	7	.36	6	.236	.338	.413
Nunez,Primitivo,Augusta	A	18	8	12	2	0	0	0	2	2	0	2	0	7	0	0	0	0	0	.00	0	.167	.286	.167
Nunez,Primitivo,Pirates	R	18	34	112	25	1	1	0	28	12	7	7	0	28	1	1	0	4	1	.80	0	.223	.275	.250
Nunez,Ramon,Durham	A	22	124	453	125	23	0	17	199	59	62	38	1	98	2	0	4	4	9	.31	9	.276	.332	.439
Nunez,Sergio,Royals	R	20	59	232	92	9	7	5	130	64	24	32	0	17	6	0	4	37	12	.76	2	.397	.474	.560
Nunnally,Jon,Kinston	A	23	132	483	129	29	2	22	228	70	74	64	3	125	3	1	3	23	11	.68	5	.267	.354	.472
O'Brien,John,Batavia	A	22	71	263	63	17	3	3	95	34	33	18	2	45	7	2	2	6	4	.60	4	.240	.303	.361
O'Donnell,T.J.,Sarasota	A	24	8	23	4	0	0	0	4	1	2	0	0	1	0	0	0	1	0	1.00	2	.174	.174	.174
O'Neill,Doug,Ogden	R	25	70	259	72	21	4	10	131	55	53	45	0	101	0	3	2	10	6	.63	2	.278	.382	.506
Oakland,John,Central Val	A	24	89	315	81	18	0	4	111	24	40	25	3	39	4	0	4	0	0	.00	12	.257	.316	.352
Ocasio,Freddy,Asheville	A	24	41	100	32	6	0	1	41	13	12	10	0	9	1	4	3	0	0	.00	2	.320	.377	.410
Ogden,Jamie,Fort Myers	A	23	69	251	66	12	0	7	99	32	22	16	0	52	2	1	1	12	8	.60	1	.263	.311	.394
Oglesby,Luke,Rockford	A	24	79	188	47	6	1	0	55	30	22	12	1	44	3	10	1	29	8	.78	1	.250	.304	.293
Ojeda,Miguel,Welland	A	20	48	142	27	6	0	2	39	11	8	5	0	30	2	2	0	1	0	1.00	0	.190	.228	.275
Olinde,Chad,Williamsprt	A	23	56	202	51	7	0	1	61	20	15	15	0	31	2	3	2	5	3	.63	5	.252	.308	.302
Oliveros,Leonardo,Martinsvle	R	19	18	50	13	0	0	0	13	1	6	0	0	11	1	0	3	0	0	.00	2	.260	.259	.260
Ollison,Scott,Clearwater	A	23	64	149	33	4	1	0	39	15	9	18	0	27	1	4	1	6	5	.55	4	.221	.308	.262
Olstead,Nate,Butte	R	23	63	225	81	10	4	2	105	40	50	40	6	40	5	0	1	6	2	.75	8	.360	.465	.467
Opatkiewicz,Ryan,Huntington	R	20	53	157	35	5	1	0	42	18	10	16	0	18	3	3	1	6	3	.67	1	.223	.305	.268
Oram,Jonathan,Watertown	A	21	48	149	41	6	2	3	60	23	26	11	0	26	3	4	1	2	2	.50	3	.275	.337	.403
Ordaz,Luis,Charlstn-Sc	A	19	9	31	7	0	0	0	7	3	0	1	0	4	1	1	0	1	0	1.00	1	.226	.273	.226
Princeton	R	19	60	211	52	12	3	0	70	33	12	10	1	27	2	5	1	7	5	.58	2	.246	.286	.332
Ordonez,Magglio,Hickory	A	21	132	490	144	24	5	11	211	86	69	45	1	57	1	2	3	16	7	.70	11	.294	.353	.431
Orie,Kevin,Daytona	A	22	6	17	7	3	1	1	15	4	5	8	1	4	1	0	0	0	1	.00	0	.412	.615	.882
Ortega,Randy,W. Michigan	A	22	74	222	53	11	0	2	70	26	30	29	1	42	6	1	2	3	0	1.00	3	.239	.340	.315
Ortiz,Asbel,Rangers	R	19	47	116	15	7	1	0	24	12	12	15	0	35	2	0	2	1	3	.25	3	.129	.237	.207
Ortiz,Nicky,Sarasota	A	21	81	283	76	18	3	2	106	34	40	21	1	57	3	6	3	7	2	.78	11	.269	.323	.375
Ortiz,Pedro,Orioles	R	18	34	94	13	1	0	0	14	6	4	4	0	18	1	0	2	1	0	1.00	3	.138	.178	.149
Ortman,Benjamin,Central Val	A	24	57	183	39	14	2	2	63	33	15	30	0	49	1	1	1	6	2	.75	4	.213	.326	.344
Asheville	A	24	60	233	63	13	1	3	87	29	18	23	1	48	0	2	3	20	8	.71	4	.270	.332	.373
Osentowski,Jared,Columbia	A	22	16	38	4	2	0	0	6	2	4	8	0	8	1	1	1	1	0	.00	1	.105	.271	.158
Pittsfield	A	22	30	101	18	3	0	0	21	5	7	7	0	16	2	0	0	3	1	.75	1	.178	.245	.208
Otanez,Willis,Vero Beach	A	22	131	476	132	27	1	19	218	77	72	53	2	98	4	0	7	4	2	.67	10	.277	.350	.458
Ottavinia,Paul,Burlington	A	22	49	187	38	8	0	2	52	17	21	7	0	28	0	0	2	5	1	.83	2	.203	.230	.278
Owens,Walter,Burlington	R	22	25	87	18	2	3	0	26	16	4	7	0	23	1	3	2	8	3	.73	2	.207	.268	.299
Butte	R	22	18	48	9	1	0	0	10	3	3	4	0	8	1	2	2	3	3	.50	0	.188	.264	.208
Oyas,Danny,Charlstn-Sc	A	22	45	165	46	10	0	5	71	19	24	10	0	29	1	2	2	5	5	.50	5	.279	.320	.430
Ozario,Yudith,Pittsfield	A	20	66	246	70	3	2	0	77	41	17	15	0	54	1	1	2	24	7	.77	1	.285	.326	.313
Ozoria,Claudio,W. Palm Bch	A	23	36	116	26	5	3	1	40	15	9	3	0	19	4	3	0	3	2	.60	1	.224	.268	.345
Pachot,John,Burlington	A	20	100	351	89	17	0	1	109	37	26	13	1	46	3	5	4	1	2	.33	12	.254	.283	.311
Paez,Isreal,Twins	R	18	35	129	37	3	0	1	43	15	20	6	0	17	2	0	1	4	4	.50	5	.287	.326	.333
Paez,Raul,Salem	A	21	17	50	11	5	0	0	16	8	8	5	0	9	0	0	0	0	0	.00	1	.220	.291	.320
Welland	A	21	45	155	39	5	0	1	47	17	12	11	0	20	2	1	1	3	1	.75	4	.252	.308	.303
Pagan,Angel,Albany	A	21	34	95	20	4	0	0	24	15	9	14	0	24	3	1	2	10	3	.77	0	.211	.325	.253
Bluefield	R	21	46	133	33	6	0	0	39	18	13	23	0	19	1	4	3	12	4	.75	3	.248	.356	.293
Pagee,Shawn,Jamestown	A	24	21	51	8	3	0	0	11	5	3	7	0	12	2	0	0	0	0	.00	0	.157	.283	.216
Pages,Javier,W. Palm Bch	A	23	19	57	17	5	0	2	28	10	9	11	0	18	1	0	1	0	0	.00	0	.298	.414	.491
High Desert	A	23	34	101	19	0	0	3	28	8	14	11	1	32	2	0	0	0	0	.00	0	.188	.278	.277
Pallino,John,Lethbridge	R	23	57	182	41	9	0	1	53	20	24	30	0	30	0	1	0	5	5	.50	7	.225	.335	.291
Palmer,James,Yankees	R	20	50	164	35	8	1	1	48	21	23	26	0	41	7	1	0	1	1	.50	1	.213	.345	.293
Parker,Corey,Fayettevlle	A	24	83	240	51	10	1	4	75	26	36	42	2	59	5	0	3	2	3	.40	3	.213	.338	.313
Parra,Franklin,Charlotte	A	23	106	431	115	19	8	6	168	61	35	16	1	68	2	3	3	10	7	.59	5	.267	.294	.390
Patel,Manish,Appleton	A	23	95	315	79	9	4	1	99	48	28	27	1	42	9	5	1	5	9	.36	6	.251	.327	.314
Patterson,Jacob,Elizabethtn	R	21	63	231	62	11	0	18	127	37	53	37	3	69	2	0	2	1	0	1.00	3	.268	.371	.550
Patterson,Jarrod,Kingsport	R	21	36	112	29	5	2	5	53	12	18	12	2	39	1	0	0	2	0	1.00	1	.259	.336	.473
Pittsfield	A	21	29	106	19	6	1	1	30	8	15	10	0	34	0	0	2	1	0	1.00	1	.179	.246	.283
Patton,Gregory,Lynchburg	A	23	63	216	48	8	3	6	80	30	21	27	0	49	1	1	1	0	1	.00	5	.222	.310	.370
Patton,Scott,White Sox	R	21	1	4	2	0	0	0	2	2	3	1	0	0	0	0	0	1	0	1.00	0	.500	.600	.500
Hickory	A	21	11	40	12	1	0	1	16	4	6	2	0	14	1	0	0	1	1	.50	2	.300	.349	.400
Patzke,Jeff,Hagerstown	A	21	80	271	55	10	1	4	79	43	22	36	1	57	3	2	3	7	3	.70	4	.203	.300	.292
Paul,Kortney,Eugene	A	23	49	155	33	9	1	0	44	18	9	13	1	43	2	0	0	3	7	.30	3	.213	.282	.284
Paulino,Arturo,Athletics	R	20	44	141	39	8	3	1	56	13	22	11	0	40	1	2	3	11	4	.73	1	.277	.327	.397
Paulino,Nelson,Durham	A	22	82	204	39	9	0	1	51	17	9	18	0	28	1	4	2	11	9	.55	1	.191	.258	.250
Payano,Gustavo,Royals	R	22	21	60	17	2	0	0	19	16	7	13	0	7	3	1	1	6	2	.75	0	.283	.429	.317
Rockford	A	22	8	24	5	1	0	0	6	1	3	0	0	8	0	0	1	0	0	.00	0	.208	.200	.250
Payne,Kenneth,Rangers	R	21	55	179	35	12	0	6	65	21	24	14	1	59	8	0	1	0	1	.00	2	.196	.282	.363
Pearson,Cory,Charlstn-Wv	A	20	105	366	84	16	3	4	118	57	27	43	0	89	24	1	1	36	19	.65	3	.230	.348	.322
Pearson,Eddie,Pr. William	A	21	130	502	139	28	3	12	209	58	80	45	1	80	3	0	3	0	0	.00	11	.277	.338	.416
Pearson,Kevin,Elizabethtn	R	22	37	125	27	3	1	3	41	25	13	18	0	22	7	0	1	2	0	1.00	4	.216	.344	.328
Pecorilli,Aldo,St. Pete	A	24	135	508	141	26	3	18	227	76	78	56	4	69	4	1	3	13	9	.59	7	.278	.352	.447
Peeples,Michael,Blue Jays	R	18	47	172	40	5	3	0	51	22	11	13	1	25	4	3	2	17	5	.77	0	.233	.298	.297
Peer,Jeff,Vermont	A	23	17	69	19	3	2	1	29	8	12	1	0	15	2	1	0	1	0	1.00	1	.275	.306	.420
Peguero,J.,San Bernrdo	A	30	129	533	154	18	0	25	247	91	76	21	1	104	8	1	4	11	5	.69	13	.289	.324	.463
Peguero,Julio,Riverside	A	26	28	99	38	2	1	2	48	16	23	11	0	17	1	4	1	3	4	.43	2	.384	.446	.485
Pena,Elvis,Rockies	R	18	49	171	39	5	2	0	48	31	9	35	0	47	6	1	0	20	12	.63	1	.228	.377	.281

1994 Batting -- Single-A and Rookie Leagues

Player	Lg	A	G	AB	H	2B	3B	HR	TB	R	RBI	TBB	IBB	SO	HBP	SH	SF	SB	CS	SB%	GDP	Avg	OBP	SLG
Pena,Francisco,Twins	R	18	23	76	17	3	0	0	20	6	4	6	0	14	1	1	0	0	0	.00	1	.224	.289	.263
Perez,Jhonny,Astros	R	18	36	144	46	12	2	1	65	37	27	15	1	16	1	1	1	18	3	.86	4	.319	.385	.451
Perez,Neifi,Central Val	A	20	134	506	121	16	7	1	154	64	35	32	1	79	2	19	5	9	7	.56	6	.239	.284	.304
Perez,Nelson,Giants	R	19	46	130	33	6	1	0	41	15	9	2	0	35	1	0	0	2	5	.29	1	.254	.271	.315
Perez,Richard,Daytona	A	22	99	325	77	9	1	0	88	45	21	22	0	54	1	10	0	8	5	.62	14	.237	.295	.271
Perez,Tomas,Burlington	A	21	119	465	122	22	1	8	170	76	47	48	3	78	1	4	5	8	10	.44	2	.262	.329	.366
Perez,Wilman,Marlins	R	20	29	75	16	5	0	0	21	17	11	17	0	37	2	0	0	3	3	.50	1	.213	.372	.280
Perry,Chan,Burlington	R	22	52	185	58	16	1	5	91	28	32	18	0	28	1	0	4	6	0	1.00	9	.314	.370	.492
Person,Wilton,Idaho Falls	R	21	39	135	47	9	0	1	59	27	15	11	2	8	0	1	4	5	0	1.00	1	.348	.387	.437
Peterson,Charles,Augusta	A	21	108	415	106	14	6	4	144	55	40	35	2	78	3	0	2	27	18	.60	7	.255	.316	.347
Petersen,Nate,Quad City	A	23	68	215	59	11	2	4	86	27	21	14	3	29	2	0	1	1	3	.25	7	.274	.323	.400
Petite,Brett,Daytona	A	24	23	51	13	1	1	0	16	3	6	2	0	11	1	2	0	0	1	.00	0	.255	.296	.314
Petrulis,Paul,Columbia	A	23	105	347	83	15	0	1	101	44	20	45	0	63	1	9	0	8	4	.67	11	.239	.328	.291
Pettiford,Torrey,Batavia	A	22	8	22	2	1	0	0	3	5	0	3	0	0	0	0	0	1	0	1.00	1	.091	.200	.136
Martinsvlle	R	22	39	144	33	6	1	1	44	24	10	11	0	35	0	0	2	8	3	.73	2	.229	.284	.306
Phillips,Christopher,Fort Myers	A	23	89	270	60	9	0	2	75	37	18	35	0	58	1	4	4	15	3	.83	6	.222	.310	.278
Phillips,Darren,Blue Jays	R	19	21	52	10	3	0	0	13	6	5	5	0	19	0	3	0	0	1	.00	0	.192	.263	.250
Phillips,Gary,Clinton	A	23	124	438	109	23	4	9	167	62	50	40	3	98	6	5	4	4	7	.36	6	.249	.318	.381
Phillips,Steve,San Berndo	A	27	66	233	69	15	1	8	110	44	42	46	2	79	2	0	2	1	4	.20	4	.296	.413	.472
Pichardo,Sandy,Columbia	A	20	118	420	108	6	7	2	134	48	30	36	0	99	6	9	2	34	28	.55	3	.257	.323	.319
Pickett,Eric,Braves	R	19	43	144	28	4	2	4	48	13	15	20	1	42	2	1	0	1	2	.33	1	.194	.301	.333
Pico,Brandon,Peoria	A	21	112	400	107	21	5	10	168	70	61	39	0	74	4	10	3	11	8	.58	9	.268	.336	.420
Picollo,John,Oneonta	A	21	5	13	1	0	0	0	1	0	0	1	0	6	0	0	0	0	0	.00	0	.077	.143	.077
Pierre-Louis,Danton,Martinsvlle	R	20	53	161	34	5	0	2	45	20	14	24	3	36	2	1	1	4	1	.80	2	.211	.319	.280
Pierzynski,Anthony,Twins	R	18	43	152	44	8	1	1	57	21	19	12	0	19	0	0	2	0	3	.00	3	.289	.337	.375
Pimentel,Wander,St. Pete	A	22	25	38	7	3	0	1	13	4	8	5	0	13	0	3	0	1	0	1.00	0	.184	.279	.342
Pineiro,Michael,Central Val	A	23	39	127	22	5	0	0	27	9	6	8	0	24	1	1	1	1	1	.50	4	.173	.226	.213
San Berndo	A	23	18	69	19	5	1	2	32	9	14	8	1	15	1	0	0	1	0	1.00	4	.275	.359	.464
Pinoni,Scott,Eugene	A	22	52	190	49	12	1	6	81	15	37	14	2	57	4	0	4	2	0	1.00	1	.258	.316	.426
Pinto,Rene,Yankees	R	17	40	134	38	8	3	1	55	15	18	10	0	26	3	0	3	0	1	.00	3	.284	.340	.410
Pitts,Jon,Charlotte	A	23	15	43	7	1	1	0	10	2	3	1	0	8	0	1	0	0	0	.00	4	.163	.182	.233
Pitts,Kevin,Vero Beach	A	22	64	197	41	6	4	1	58	19	15	5	0	55	5	1	1	1	0	1.00	8	.208	.245	.294
Pitts,Shedrick,Royals	R	19	43	76	13	1	1	0	16	13	9	9	0	29	1	1	2	2	2	.50	0	.171	.261	.211
Podsednik,Scott,Rangers	R	19	60	211	48	7	1	1	60	34	17	41	0	34	3	2	3	18	5	.78	1	.227	.357	.284
Poe,Charles,Pr.William	A	23	130	469	126	21	3	14	195	72	83	51	2	103	5	2	7	14	2	.88	9	.269	.345	.416
Pointer,Corey,Braves	R	19	27	77	11	4	0	1	8	8	4	8	0	31	2	0	0	2	1	.67	2	.143	.241	.234
Polanco,Felipe,Augusta	A	19	17	58	12	1	1	0	15	9	8	6	0	13	1	0	0	7	3	.70	1	.207	.292	.259
Welland	A	19	48	159	32	4	0	1	39	19	9	6	0	36	3	0	0	16	6	.73	4	.201	.244	.245
Polanco,Placido,Cardinals	A	19	32	127	27	4	0	1	34	17	10	7	0	15	1	0	0	4	2	.67	2	.213	.259	.268
Polanco,Raul,Cubs	R	18	41	90	15	5	1	0	22	9	3	10	0	34	3	1	0	5	2	.71	1	.167	.272	.244
Polidor,Wilfredo,South Bend	A	21	97	355	101	14	2	3	128	43	36	10	0	40	3	4	2	1	2	.33	9	.285	.308	.361
Pollock,Jason,Ogden	R	24	10	21	6	2	0	0	8	5	3	2	0	10	2	0	0	0	1	.00	0	.286	.400	.381
Polo,Jim,Williamsprt	A	22	39	113	17	4	0	0	21	14	16	28	0	22	1	3	0	8	3	.73	2	.150	.324	.186
Pomierski,Joe,Bellingham	A	21	55	152	27	4	0	4	43	20	25	16	2	46	1	1	3	2	3	.40	2	.178	.256	.283
Pond,Simon,Expos	R	18	40	147	38	7	0	0	45	18	15	16	1	25	1	1	0	3	1	.50	4	.259	.329	.306
Poor,Jeffrey,Giants	R	21	6	11	5	1	0	0	6	2	5	2	0	0	0	0	1	0	0	.00	1	.455	.500	.545
Everett	A	21	32	98	27	5	0	1	35	7	14	13	1	24	3	1	0	0	0	.00	8	.276	.377	.357
Porter,Kedric,Orioles	R	20	43	103	23	3	0	0	26	15	8	11	0	10	3	1	0	8	0	1.00	3	.223	.316	.252
Porter,Marquis,Peoria	A	22	66	221	60	11	2	6	93	40	29	27	0	59	2	6	4	6	5	.55	5	.271	.350	.421
Post,Dave,Bakersfield	A	21	31	106	25	5	1	0	32	16	9	13	0	9	3	0	0	6	4	.60	2	.236	.326	.302
Yakima	A	21	70	263	77	14	1	1	96	46	27	56	3	42	5	1	5	18	5	.78	3	.293	.419	.365
Powell,Corey,Osceola	A	24	132	480	116	22	2	5	157	46	60	28	1	88	7	0	6	4	4	.50	25	.242	.290	.327
Powell,Gordon,Stockton	A	23	63	212	53	10	3	3	78	27	23	7	0	54	3	2	1	3	1	.75	2	.250	.283	.368
Powell,Lejon,Everett	A	21	41	165	51	15	1	5	83	31	25	19	1	47	4	0	2	27	1	.96	1	.309	.389	.503
San Jose	A	21	4	4	2	0	1	0	4	0	0	0	0	0	0	0	0	0	0	.00	0	.500	.500	1.000
Pozo,Yohel,Bend	A	21	45	137	26	9	0	0	35	13	13	6	0	20	1	4	1	0	0	.00	7	.190	.228	.255
Prater,Steve,Kane County	A	22	50	160	35	9	1	1	49	20	12	11	0	43	3	2	2	1	1	.50	3	.219	.278	.306
Pratt,Wesley,Auburn	A	22	60	227	73	9	4	2	96	30	40	16	0	34	2	1	1	6	1	.86	12	.322	.370	.423
Prensi,Dagoberto,Medicne Hat	R	22	66	265	72	8	5	3	99	41	32	15	3	71	3	1	0	12	2	.86	5	.272	.318	.374
Preston,Doyle,Princeton	R	22	62	227	53	10	4	5	86	38	36	36	1	67	2	0	1	9	4	.69	2	.233	.342	.379
Pridy,Todd,Brevard Cty	A	24	132	482	121	36	5	13	206	64	89	56	5	116	4	0	6	6	1	.86	16	.251	.330	.427
Priest,Chris,Lethbridge	R	23	72	280	86	15	5	14	153	55	55	26	2	62	10	0	2	19	6	.76	1	.307	.384	.546
Prieto,Alejandro,Royals	R	19	18	60	18	5	0	2	29	15	17	2	1	5	4	0	1	1	0	1.00	0	.300	.358	.483
Prieto,Christian,Rancho Cuca	A	22	102	353	87	10	3	1	106	64	29	52	1	49	5	6	4	29	11	.73	3	.246	.348	.300
Prieto,Columbus	A	22	124	378	81	14	8	8	135	67	39	65	3	87	15	4	0	21	10	.68	6	.214	.352	.357
Pritchard,Stephen,Helena	R	22	65	195	45	12	0	1	60	37	28	27	1	38	4	1	2	3	4	.43	2	.231	.333	.308
Probst,Alan,Quad City	A	24	113	375	87	14	1	9	130	50	41	37	3	98	2	3	2	5	2	.29	8	.232	.302	.347
Prybylinski,Don,St. Pete	A	27	32	83	21	2	0	0	23	5	2	8	0	19	3	2	0	0	0	.00	5	.253	.340	.277
Pullen,Shane,Martinsvle	R	22	64	221	75	16	0	3	100	33	39	32	2	39	4	1	3	13	10	.57	5	.339	.427	.452
Purdy,Alan,Salem	A	24	32	82	18	1	0	1	22	10	7	8	0	15	1	3	0	2	1	.67	2	.220	.304	.268
Pyle,John,Rangers	R	23	5	18	3	2	0	0	5	1	1	1	0	2	1	0	0	0	0	.00	0	.167	.286	.278
Querecuto,Juan,Dunedin	A	25	170	42	7	0	3	58	9	20	7	0	28	1	2	2	0	1	.00	6	.247	.278	.341
Raasch,Glen,Cubs	R	26	2	5	2	1	0	0	3	3	3	1	0	0	0	0	0	0	0	.00	0	.400	.500	.600
Peoria	A	26	25	72	16	2	0	2	24	9	12	9	0	22	2	0	0	1	0	1.00	1	.222	.305	.333
Rackley,Keifer,Riverside	A	24	64	236	71	14	1	10	117	43	43	25	1	46	5	1	1	6	1	.86	6	.301	.375	.496
Radmanovich,Ryan,Fort Myers	A	23	26	85	16	4	0	2	26	11	9	7	0	19	2	0	0	3	1	.75	0	.188	.266	.306
Fort Wayne	A	23	101	383	105	20	6	19	194	64	69	45	3	98	3	1	1	19	14	.58	7	.274	.354	.507

303

1994 Batting -- Single-A and Rookie Leagues

				BATTING															BASERUNNING				PERCENTAGES		
Player	Lg	A	G	AB	H	2B	3B	HR	TB	R	RBI	TBB	IBB	SO	HBP	SH	SF	SB	CS	SB%	GDP	Avg	OBP	SLG
Raifstanger,John,Sarasota	A	22	8	18	0	0	0	0	0	2	0	0	0	8	0	0	0	0	0	.00	0	.000	.000	.000
Utica	A	22	40	130	31	5	0	1	39	20	10	16	1	20	2	3	0	1	6	.14	2	.238	.331	.300
Raleigh,Matt,Burlington	A	24	114	398	109	18	2	34	233	78	83	75	3	138	5	0	3	6	2	.75	8	.274	.393	.585
Ramirez,Alex,Columbus	A	20	125	458	115	23	3	18	198	64	57	26	0	100	4	0	4	7	5	.58	11	.251	.295	.432
Ramirez,Angel,Hagerstown	A	22	117	454	127	17	14	9	199	71	51	21	2	103	7	4	3	21	14	.60	3	.280	.320	.438
Ramirez,Anibal,Bellingham	A	21	7	18	3	0	0	0	3	0	2	3	0	3	0	1	0	0	1	.00	0	.167	.286	.167
Mariners	R	21	41	143	33	4	0	0	37	13	9	8	0	17	1	1	2	4	2	.67	5	.231	.273	.259
Ramirez,Daniel,Mets	R	21	44	176	50	10	2	0	64	26	29	11	0	23	3	0	0	7	5	.58	4	.284	.337	.364
Ramirez,Hiram,Clinton	A	22	55	180	58	12	0	7	91	30	23	18	1	47	2	1	0	0	1	.00	4	.322	.390	.506
Ramirez,Juan,Kingsport	R	22	47	163	32	2	0	3	43	29	14	18	0	45	2	0	0	2	0	1.00	5	.196	.284	.264
Ramirez,Richard,Watertown	A	19	6	21	1	0	0	0	1	1	1	2	0	4	0	0	0	0	0	.00	1	.048	.130	.048
Burlington	R	19	22	60	11	2	0	1	16	5	3	4	0	12	2	1	0	2	2	.50	0	.183	.258	.267
Ramirez,Roberto,Riverside	A	25	117	430	129	28	7	14	213	70	79	25	0	88	4	1	4	8	4	.67	9	.300	.341	.495
Ramos,Eddy,Quad City	A	22	126	460	117	24	4	12	185	54	56	19	1	95	1	4	2	17	5	.77	11	.254	.284	.402
Ramos,Noel,Orioles	R	18	47	156	33	7	0	5	55	22	22	17	0	54	2	0	0	1	0	1.00	8	.212	.297	.353
Rash,Joshua,Yakima	A	21	51	153	35	10	1	1	50	21	21	19	2	48	2	3	2	4	2	.67	7	.229	.318	.327
Rasmussen,Nathan,Great Falls	R	20	33	92	20	5	1	1	30	21	5	12	0	23	3	1	1	0	2	.00	1	.217	.324	.326
Raymondi,Michael,Twins	R	19	21	56	15	2	1	0	19	6	12	11	0	17	2	0	3	1	0	1.00	1	.268	.389	.339
Redington,Tom,Lake Elsino	A	26	129	469	139	31	1	13	211	72	66	71	1	85	5	1	4	6	4	.60	14	.296	.392	.450
Redmond,Mike,Kane County	A	24	92	306	83	10	0	1	96	39	24	26	0	31	9	6	2	3	4	.43	10	.271	.344	.314
Brevard Cty	A	24	12	42	11	4	0	0	15	4	2	3	0	4	1	0	0	0	0	.00	1	.262	.326	.357
Reed,Kenneth,Albany	A	23	18	52	9	2	0	2	17	6	6	4	0	16	1	0	0	0	2	.00	3	.173	.246	.327
Reese,Matthew,W. Michigan	A	24	101	298	77	21	2	2	108	45	43	42	3	70	3	3	4	7	5	.58	6	.258	.352	.362
Reeves,Glenn,Kane County	A	21	102	370	95	15	3	3	125	65	34	66	0	76	2	5	0	5	4	.56	15	.257	.372	.338
Reilly,John,St. Cathrns	A	22	20	53	13	1	1	0	16	5	4	8	0	11	0	0	0	3	0	1.00	0	.245	.344	.302
Rengifo,Daliene,White Sox	R	18	18	14	2	0	0	0	2	3	0	2	0	3	0	0	0	1	1	.50	0	.143	.250	.143
Rennhack,Mike,Quad City	A	20	127	449	102	14	1	10	148	54	48	50	2	83	2	8	5	12	5	.71	14	.227	.304	.330
Renteria,Edgar,Brevard Cty	A	19	128	439	111	15	1	0	128	46	36	35	2	56	0	2	2	6	11	.35	14	.253	.307	.292
Reyes,Jimmy,South Bend	A	23	69	238	67	8	2	1	82	28	36	23	0	48	2	2	3	6	5	.55	0	.282	.346	.345
Reyes,Jose,Augusta	A	22	5	14	4	2	0	0	6	4	3	0	0	4	1	0	0	0	0	.00	0	.286	.444	.429
Pirates	R	22	16	30	8	1	1	0	11	5	6	10	0	5	0	0	0	0	1	.00	0	.267	.450	.367
Reyes,Michael,Elmira	A	23	55	145	28	5	1	1	38	21	7	17	0	51	3	0	0	2	2	.50	3	.193	.291	.262
Reyes,Winston,Martinsvlle	R	21	54	173	45	12	0	5	72	29	21	16	0	60	1	2	1	5	5	.50	1	.260	.325	.416
Reynolds,Paul,Cubs	R	21	2	3	1	0	0	0	1	0	0	0	0	0	0	0	0	0	0	.00	0	.333	.333	.333
Reynolds,Paul,Rockies	R	22	35	114	22	4	1	0	28	8	11	8	0	40	4	1	2	2	2	.50	2	.193	.270	.246
Rhone,Oscar,Rockford	A	23	81	242	52	7	2	1	66	23	23	15	0	59	2	5	2	4	5	.44	3	.215	.264	.273
Rice,Charles,Pirates	R	19	56	204	60	16	2	6	98	34	43	29	1	43	7	0	1	6	5	.55	0	.294	.398	.480
Rich,Anthony,Quad City	A	22	48	131	30	2	0	0	32	12	5	5	0	24	1	6	0	2	0	1.00	1	.229	.263	.244
Richardson,Brian,Vero Beach	A	19	19	52	12	0	1	0	14	3	3	4	0	15	0	0	0	3	1	1.00	2	.231	.276	.269
Yakima	A	19	70	266	62	15	0	5	92	35	44	35	1	82	1	0	0	12	4	.75	3	.233	.325	.346
Richardson,Eric,Hickory	A	22	54	177	44	0	2	2	54	32	11	26	0	47	1	1	1	18	6	.75	0	.249	.345	.305
South Bend	A	22	29	100	23	3	0	0	26	7	8	9	0	24	0	0	0	2	3	.40	2	.230	.294	.260
Richardson,Jeff,Sou. Oregon	A	22	58	151	34	5	2	1	46	26	20	23	0	53	1	7	2	14	1	.93	4	.225	.328	.305
Richardson,Scott,Stockton	A	24	131	495	131	25	3	2	168	76	33	73	0	64	1	9	0	49	12	.80	10	.265	.360	.339
Ridenour,James,White Sox	R	24	1	2	0	0	0	0	0	0	0	0	0	0	0	0	0	0	0	.00	0	.000	.000	.000
Ridner,Dusty,Williamsprt	A	23	3	4	0	0	0	0	0	1	0	1	0	3	0	0	0	1	0	1.00	0	.000	.200	.000
Riemer,Matthew,Albany	A	22	36	99	24	8	0	1	35	9	9	9	0	20	2	3	0	3	1	.75	3	.242	.318	.354
Frederick	A	22	43	11	3	0	0	0	14	5	8	1	0	15	5	1	0	2	1	.67	1	.256	.347	.326
Riggs,Adam,Great Falls	R	22	62	234	73	20	3	5	114	55	44	31	1	38	4	2	2	19	8	.70	2	.312	.399	.487
Yakima	A	22	4	7	2	1	0	0	3	1	0	0	0	1	0	0	0	0	0	.00	0	.286	.286	.429
Rincones,Wuamner,White Sox	R	21	23	66	19	5	0	0	24	10	3	8	0	7	0	0	1	2	2	.50	1	.288	.360	.364
Hickory	A	21	25	78	17	3	0	1	23	12	13	11	0	20	0	0	1	2	0	.00	2	.218	.311	.295
Rios,Armando,Clinton	A	23	119	407	120	23	4	8	175	67	60	59	2	69	4	1	7	16	12	.57	7	.295	.384	.430
Rios,Eduardo,Vero Beach	A	22	133	529	139	28	8	13	222	70	79	24	1	85	8	2	6	2	5	.29	15	.263	.302	.420
Ripplemeyer,Brad,Durham	A	25	62	200	44	10	1	3	65	23	14	28	0	59	3	1	1	2	4	.33	6	.220	.325	.325
Rivera,Miguel,Johnson Cty	R	21	64	232	55	10	5	4	87	43	33	30	0	41	5	5	3	8	4	.67	3	.237	.333	.375
Rivera,Ruben,Greensboro	A	21	105	400	115	24	3	28	229	83	81	47	1	125	8	0	2	36	5	.88	6	.288	.372	.573
Tampa	A	21	34	134	35	4	3	5	60	18	20	8	0	38	1	0	0	12	5	.71	7	.261	.308	.448
Rivera,Santiago,Springfield	A	22	61	135	29	7	1	0	38	16	13	22	0	46	0	5	2	3	1	.75	7	.215	.321	.281
Spokane	A	22	20	70	21	4	0	0	25	10	8	11	0	21	2	0	0	1	2	.33	0	.300	.410	.357
Rivera,Wilfredo,Utica	A	21	56	186	48	11	2	0	63	25	20	9	0	33	2	2	7	1	1	.50	3	.258	.289	.339
Rivers,Jonathan,Medicne Hat	R	22	55	190	46	3	1	3	60	26	23	24	0	42	4	1	0	7	5	.58	0	.242	.339	.316
Roberge,John,Great Falls	R	22	63	256	82	17	1	1	104	55	42	20	0	22	5	2	5	24	4	.86	7	.320	.374	.406
Yakima	A	22	4	8	3	1	0	0	4	1	0	0	0	3	1	0	0	1	0	1.00	0	.375	.444	.500
Roberson,Gerald,Idaho Falls	R	20	53	208	60	10	2	0	74	40	24	19	0	39	6	0	2	19	10	.66	2	.288	.362	.356
Roberts,David,Jamestown	A	23	54	178	52	7	2	0	63	33	12	29	4	27	1	3	1	12	8	.60	0	.292	.392	.354
Roberts,John,Springfield	A	21	81	269	76	11	2	9	118	62	44	44	2	79	20	1	4	30	10	.75	4	.283	.415	.439
Rancho Cuca	A	21	50	167	42	3	1	6	65	26	30	23	1	47	7	0	1	13	6	.68	2	.251	.364	.389
Roberts,Lonell,Dunedin	A	24	118	490	132	18	3	3	165	74	31	32	3	104	3	2	4	61	12	.84	4	.269	.316	.339
Robertson,Dean,Orioles	R	19	38	57	14	4	0	0	18	12	8	5	0	12	0	0	0	2	0	1.00	0	.246	.306	.316
Robinson,Anthony,Pirates	R	19	43	145	29	6	1	0	37	30	10	19	0	22	4	0	0	6	5	.55	4	.200	.304	.255
Robinson,Daniel,Brevard Cty	A	24	123	432	111	20	4	4	151	50	53	41	3	99	5	2	6	1	2	.33	10	.257	.324	.350
Robinson,Darek,New Jersey	A	22	74	286	76	8	2	0	88	35	39	28	1	40	1	3	4	2	3	.40	9	.266	.329	.308
Robinson,Hassan,Auburn	A	23	43	149	36	3	0	0	39	13	12	2	0	12	3	2	1	4	1	.80	5	.242	.261	.262
Robinson,Dwight,St. Lucie	A	25	129	388	88	11	1	5	116	39	31	63	5	92	3	8	3	6	3	.67	6	.227	.338	.299
Robledo,Nilson,South Bend	A	26	103	373	106	25	4	9	166	63	69	39	0	97	3	2	1	0	1	.00	8	.284	.352	.445
Robles,Juan,Royals	R	23	5	7	2	0	0	0	2	0	0	1	0	0	0	0	0	0	0	.00	0	.286	.375	.286

304

1994 Batting -- Single-A and Rookie Leagues

Player	Lg	A	G	AB	H	2B	3B	HR	TB	R	RBI	TBB	IBB	SO	HBP	SH	SF	SB	CS	SB%	GDP	Avg	OBP	SLG
Wilmington	A	23	12	15	0	0	0	0	0	0	0	1	0	3	0	0	0	0	0	.00	1	.000	.063	.000
Robles,Oscar,Astros	R	19	55	165	54	5	1	0	61	40	19	32	0	17	2	10	0	14	9	.61	5	.327	.442	.370
Robles,Rafael,New Jersey	A	22	57	174	37	6	1	0	45	27	24	29	0	44	0	0	1	4	3	.57	6	.213	.324	.259
Robson,Adam,Padres	R	22	18	62	18	3	1	2	29	8	11	15	0	18	1	0	0	0	0	.00	2	.290	.416	.468
Spokane	A	22	17	54	9	1	0	0	10	3	3	10	1	23	2	0	0	1	2	.33	1	.167	.318	.185
Rocha,Juan,Royals	R	21	44	131	35	11	0	3	55	26	27	18	0	27	1	1	2	12	4	.75	2	.267	.355	.420
Roche,Marlon,Astros	R	20	41	146	46	7	3	0	59	27	22	20	0	26	1	1	0	10	5	.67	3	.315	.401	.404
Rockmore,Thurston,Lethbridge	R	24	70	278	85	14	0	3	108	56	30	37	0	34	3	0	1	31	15	.67	5	.306	.392	.388
Rodriguez,Adam,Fayetteville	A	24	46	164	42	14	1	5	73	25	23	15	2	28	1	0	0	2	2	.50	2	.256	.322	.445
Rodriguez,Hector,New Jersey	A	23	36	105	26	5	0	0	31	16	14	20	0	24	1	0	2	0	0	.00	3	.248	.367	.295
Rodriguez,Javier,Mariners	R	21	34	98	25	2	1	2	35	10	8	7	0	17	1	0	0	0	0	.00	3	.255	.311	.357
Rodriguez,Jose,Rockies	R	18	1	4	0	0	0	0	0	0	0	0	0	0	0	0	0	0	0	.00	0	.000	.000	.000
Rodriguez,Maximo,Brevard Cty	A	21	12	40	5	1	0	2	12	4	12	1	0	16	1	0	0	0	0	.00	1	.125	.167	.300
Marlins	A	21	5	21	4	1	0	0	5	3	2	1	0	4	1	0	0	0	0	.00	1	.190	.261	.238
Elmira	A	21	51	170	40	9	1	2	57	20	19	8	0	42	1	0	0	3	1	.75	4	.235	.274	.335
Rodriguez,Miguel,Helena	R	20	10	16	6	0	0	1	9	3	3	3	1	2	0	0	0	0	0	.00	0	.375	.474	.563
Brewers	R	20	28	85	18	6	2	0	28	10	13	7	1	18	1	0	3	0	1	.00	2	.212	.271	.329
Rodriguez,Miguel,Athletics	R	20	48	162	39	5	3	1	53	23	18	31	0	37	0	3	2	7	3	.70	2	.241	.359	.327
Rodriguez,Nerio,South Bend	A	22	18	59	13	4	0	0	17	4	8	2	0	14	2	0	3	0	2	.00	1	.220	.258	.288
Pr. William	A	22	6	19	4	1	1	0	7	2	1	1	0	9	0	1	0	0	0	.00	0	.211	.250	.368
Rodriguez,Noel,Quad City	A	21	64	242	68	11	1	4	93	28	29	11	1	56	1	0	2	0	3	.00	4	.281	.315	.384
Rodriguez,Roman,Stockton	A	26	6	9	2	0	0	0	2	3	0	2	0	1	0	0	1	0	0	1.00	0	.222	.417	.222
Lake Elsino	A	26	25	84	26	1	1	1	32	10	5	6	0	16	1	3	0	1	1	.50	0	.310	.363	.381
San Bernrdo	A	26	25	79	16	1	1	1	22	11	7	15	0	15	1	0	0	2	1	.67	2	.203	.337	.278
Rodriguez,Saul,Angels	R	21	35	111	29	4	2	1	40	16	18	27	0	21	2	0	0	3	2	.60	1	.261	.414	.360
Rodriguez,Victor,Marlins	R	18	24	96	31	0	0	0	33	13	17	7	0	7	0	0	3	2	0	1.00	3	.323	.358	.344
Rodrigues,Cecil,Beloit	A	23	38	116	33	5	0	3	47	16	24	13	1	29	0	3	2	10	3	.77	3	.284	.351	.405
Stockton	A	23	56	205	54	12	3	3	81	29	19	25	1	48	2	6	0	14	3	.82	1	.263	.349	.395
Roggendorf,Christian,St. Cathns	A	23	60	189	33	8	0	0	41	13	18	19	0	40	3	0	2	1	1	.50	1	.175	.258	.217
Rogue,Francisco,Brewers	R	19	38	112	23	3	3	0	32	11	15	4	1	21	0	0	3	2	0	.33	0	.205	.227	.286
Rojas,Christian,Princeton	R	20	59	184	42	5	0	5	62	28	18	11	0	47	2	3	0	1	4	.20	0	.228	.279	.337
Roland,William,Royals	R	21	57	208	57	8	5	3	84	33	35	29	0	36	2	1	1	7	1	.88	0	.274	.367	.404
Rolen,Scott,Spartanburg	A	20	138	513	151	34	5	14	237	83	72	55	4	90	4	1	7	6	8	.43	8	.294	.363	.462
Roman,Melvin,Everett	A	20	71	245	59	8	1	1	72	43	14	44	1	65	4	1	1	21	10	.68	4	.241	.364	.294
Romano,Scott,Tampa	A	23	120	419	127	35	3	20	228	88	87	59	2	55	15	1	6	5	3	.63	3	.303	.403	.544
Romay,Willie,Brevard Cty	A	24	43	122	28	5	3	2	45	22	17	20	1	36	0	0	4	5	4	.56	5	.230	.329	.369
Romero,Marty,Yankees	R	18	7	13	3	0	0	0	3	1	1	0	0	3	0	0	0	0	0	.00	0	.231	.231	.231
Reyes,Jose,Vero Beach	A	20	38	126	29	6	0	2	41	15	13	9	0	19	1	2	0	0	2	.00	2	.230	.287	.325
Bakersfield	A	20	70	260	71	19	1	7	113	36	36	19	0	53	3	1	0	15	5	.75	3	.273	.330	.435
Rondon,Alexander,Athletics	R	20	39	136	33	4	2	4	53	26	24	13	0	32	2	0	3	2	0	1.00	3	.243	.312	.390
Root,Derek,Astros	R	20	47	169	46	8	1	0	56	21	35	8	2	18	1	0	3	2	1	.67	5	.272	.304	.331
Root,Mitch,Jamestown	A	21	38	106	37	7	0	1	47	14	21	12	0	21	1	0	2	1	2	.33	4	.349	.413	.443
Roper,Chad,Fort Myers	A	22	92	337	81	17	0	4	110	32	44	32	3	76	4	0	7	7	8	.47	8	.240	.308	.326
Rosado,Juan,Expos	R	20	50	181	44	13	2	2	67	29	14	17	0	27	2	1	2	5	0	1.00	4	.243	.312	.370
Rosado,Luis,Yankees	R	19	27	82	17	2	1	0	21	9	6	5	0	30	1	0	0	2	0	1.00	0	.207	.261	.256
Rosar,Greg,Butte	R	23	43	167	52	6	1	3	69	26	28	9	0	35	1	0	2	1	0	1.00	2	.311	.346	.413
Rosario,Eliezer,Padres	R	19	26	96	23	4	2	0	31	7	7	6	0	21	0	0	3	6	6	.50	0	.240	.276	.323
Rosario,Felix,Medicne Hat	R	23	61	222	64	13	2	6	99	49	26	40	0	56	1	2	1	17	6	.74	0	.288	.398	.446
Rosario,Victor,Stockton	A	28	22	70	16	2	0	2	24	8	11	2	0	15	2	1	0	1	2	.33	0	.229	.270	.343
Rose,Pete,Hickory	A	25	32	114	25	4	1	0	31	14	12	13	2	18	2	3	2	0	0	.00	3	.219	.305	.272
White Sox	R	25	2	4	2	0	0	0	2	1	1	0	0	0	0	0	0	0	0	.00	0	.500	.500	.500
Pr. William	A	25	45	146	41	3	1	4	58	18	22	18	0	15	0	2	3	0	1	.00	2	.281	.353	.397
Roskos,John,Elmira	A	20	39	136	38	7	0	4	57	11	23	27	0	37	0	0	2	0	1	.00	0	.279	.394	.419
Ross,Tony,Auburn	A	20	45	135	39	3	5	0	52	24	14	23	0	21	0	2	0	14	6	.70	1	.289	.392	.385
Rounsifer,Aaron,Red Sox	A	21	16	56	18	5	0	1	26	8	1	8	1	9	0	0	0	2	0	.00	0	.321	.333	.464
Royster,Aaron,Martinsvlle	R	22	54	168	46	11	2	7	82	31	39	28	1	47	2	0	1	7	4	.64	2	.274	.382	.488
Ruby,Jeremy,Angels	R	19	1	1	0	0	0	0	0	0	0	2	0	1	0	0	0	0	0	.00	0	.000	.667	.000
Ruff,Tony,Danville	R	22	15	49	9	0	1	1	13	7	5	5	0	15	1	0	0	2	0	1.00	1	.184	.273	.265
Padres	R	22	11	44	15	1	3	1	25	10	3	3	0	6	0	1	0	1	2	.33	0	.341	.383	.568
Ruiz,Cesar,Bristol	R	22	14	41	5	0	1	1	10	7	3	7	1	18	1	1	1	0	0	.00	0	.122	.260	.244
Rumfield,Toby,Winston-Sal	A	22	123	462	115	11	4	29	221	79	88	48	1	107	0	0	7	2	3	.40	9	.249	.318	.478
Rupp,Brian,St. Pete	A	23	129	438	115	19	4	2	148	40	34	61	1	77	0	5	0	9	3	.75	20	.263	.353	.338
Rupp,Chad,Fort Wayne	A	23	85	257	63	20	0	15	128	46	50	50	0	79	6	0	3	2	0	1.00	0	.245	.368	.498
Rushdan,Rasheed,Rockies	R	19	44	142	21	0	0	0	25	7	9	9	0	43	5	0	3	4	4	.50	4	.148	.220	.176
Russell,Jason,Martinsvlle	R	21	37	101	28	4	1	1	37	24	10	31	1	23	7	2	0	3	2	.40	1	.277	.475	.366
Rutz,Ryan,Hudson Vall	A	22	65	235	58	2	0	1	63	26	19	21	1	31	3	3	0	15	7	.68	2	.247	.317	.268
Ryan,Robbie,Lethbridge	R	24	66	228	58	10	2	5	87	35	35	26	0	48	5	3	4	12	5	.71	8	.254	.338	.382
Ryder,Steve,Huntington	R	22	41	98	17	1	0	0	18	6	8	10	0	29	7	2	0	7	2	.78	1	.173	.296	.184
Sadler,Donnie,Red Sox	R	20	53	206	56	8	6	1	79	52	16	23	0	27	3	1	3	32	8	.80	1	.272	.349	.383
Saffer,Jon,Vermont	A	21	70	263	83	18	5	3	120	44	43	33	1	47	1	1	1	14	3	.82	1	.316	.393	.456
Sagmoen,Marc,Charlotte	A	24	122	475	139	25	10	3	193	74	47	37	2	56	3	1	3	15	10	.60	15	.293	.346	.406
Salazar,Marlon,Giants	R	19	22	66	10	1	0	0	11	3	5	4	0	25	1	0	1	0	0	.00	0	.152	.208	.167
Salcedo,Edwin,Tampa	A	24	20	69	17	1	1	3	29	14	9	7	0	23	4	0	0	1	0	1.00	0	.246	.350	.420
San Bernrdo	A	24	41	141	30	2	1	14	76	20	33	7	0	76	3	0	1	3	3	.25	1	.213	.265	.539
Salzano,Jerry,Beloit	A	24	19	57	10	2	0	0	12	10	1	7	0	12	4	0	0	3	1	.25	2	.175	.309	.211
Williamsprt	A	20	75	283	80	15	3	2	107	33	37	15	0	44	8	1	2	5	5	.50	4	.283	.334	.378
Samuel,Quvia,Oneonta	A	21	50	165	38	6	1	4	58	19	16	15	1	53	2	0	0	3	0	1.00	7	.230	.302	.352

1994 Batting -- Single-A and Rookie Leagues

Player	Lg	A	G	AB	H	2B	3B	HR	TB	R	RBI	TBB	IBB	SO	HBP	SH	SF	SB	CS	SB%	GDP	Avg	OBP	SLG
Samuels,Scott,Brevard Cty	A	24	89	281	65	11	0	3	85	35	25	46	1	70	4	1	1	11	5	.69	7	.231	.346	.302
Sanchez,Gordon,Tampa	A	24	7	22	1	0	0	0	1	0	2	3	1	4	0	1	0	0	0	.00	0	.045	.160	.045
Sanchez,Marcos,Padres	R	20	42	148	37	10	2	1	54	26	17	12	0	44	2	0	0	6	2	.75	2	.250	.315	.365
Sanchez,Santiago,Mets	R	20	28	88	28	2	2	0	34	14	9	12	0	17	2	0	0	0	1	.00	1	.318	.412	.386
Sanchez,Victor,Auburn	A	23	58	219	63	15	0	3	87	33	35	13	1	40	4	0	1	0	0	.00	7	.288	.338	.397
Sanders,Tony,St. Cathrns	A	21	74	258	66	17	3	6	107	36	45	27	0	53	1	4	2	8	7	.53	2	.256	.326	.415
Sanders,Rod,Princeton	R	21	13	11	2	1	0	0	3	2	0	2	0	2	0	0	0	1	0	1.00	1	.182	.308	.273
Charlstn-Sc	A	21	46	106	19	3	0	1	25	7	12	3	0	36	2	0	1	1	2	.33	1	.179	.214	.236
Sanders,William,Sou. Oregon	A	23	39	100	26	7	1	1	38	12	13	5	1	37	0	1	1	1	0	1.00	1	.260	.292	.380
Sanderson,David,Kingsport	R	22	41	167	46	7	0	4	65	29	26	11	0	34	1	3	0	7	1	.88	2	.275	.324	.389
Pittsfield	A	22	7	27	6	0	0	0	6	1	2	1	0	7	0	0	0	1	0	1.00	0	.222	.250	.222
Sanford,Chance,Salem	A	23	127	474	130	32	6	19	231	81	78	56	0	95	2	1	4	12	6	.67	7	.274	.351	.487
Santa,Roberto,Hudson Vall	A	23	57	170	43	7	0	0	50	14	14	17	0	19	5	1	5	0	0	.00	5	.253	.330	.294
Santa,Sergio,Cardinals	R	19	43	138	33	6	4	0	47	17	9	13	0	41	0	1	1	1	2	.33	4	.239	.303	.341
Santana,Francis,Giants	R	19	14	35	3	0	0	0	3	2	0	1	0	14	0	0	0	0	0	.00	0	.086	.111	.086
Santana,Jose,Osceola	A	23	92	301	67	8	1	4	89	32	25	17	2	42	4	3	3	2	4	.33	4	.223	.271	.296
Santana,Ramon,Astros	R	21	25	67	12	2	0	1	17	6	4	4	0	20	0	0	1	1	1	.50	1	.179	.222	.254
Santana,Raul,High Desert	A	23	36	126	27	8	0	1	38	18	12	11	0	27	0	2	1	1	2	.33	2	.214	.275	.302
W. Palm Bch	A	23	40	124	30	8	1	1	43	19	18	14	0	23	1	0	1	2	1	.67	4	.242	.321	.347
Santiago,Arnold,Burlington	R	20	39	105	28	6	0	0	34	10	16	7	1	20	1	0	1	2	3	.40	3	.267	.316	.324
Santini,Aaron,Fort Wayne	A	23	33	79	8	1	2	0	13	10	4	7	0	24	2	2	1	0	1	.00	1	.101	.191	.165
Santos,Edgardo,Expos	R	21	44	153	39	8	0	0	47	16	19	19	1	7	0	0	1	1	0	.00	4	.255	.335	.307
Santos,Leigh,Butte	R	23	24	52	10	3	0	1	16	6	5	11	0	20	1	0	1	2	0	1.00	0	.192	.338	.308
Santucci,Steven,Madison	A	23	37	95	16	2	0	0	18	12	7	9	0	26	0	3	1	2	1	.67	2	.168	.238	.189
New Jersey	A	23	70	261	75	9	5	1	97	31	37	33	0	39	2	3	2	13	5	.72	9	.287	.369	.372
Sapp,Shon,Red Sox	R	19	19	50	9	2	0	1	14	3	3	9	0	16	3	0	0	1	0	1.00	1	.180	.339	.280
Sasser,Robert,Idaho Falls	R	20	58	219	50	9	6	2	77	32	26	19	3	58	1	0	1	13	1	.93	3	.228	.292	.352
Saturnino,Sherton,Macon	A	23	76	239	65	15	2	6	102	27	34	5	0	73	4	2	1	14	6	.70	2	.272	.297	.427
Sauer,John,Cubs	R	20	23	51	11	1	0	0	12	7	8	7	0	19	0	2	0	0	0	.00	1	.216	.310	.235
Sauritch,Christopher,Bluefield	R	23	4	16	4	1	0	0	5	1	1	0	0	3	0	0	0	0	0	.00	0	.250	.333	.313
Albany	A	23	28	70	11	2	0	0	13	9	4	8	0	20	5	3	0	5	0	1.00	1	.157	.289	.186
Sauve,Erik,Hudson Vall	A	23	60	181	43	7	1	0	52	24	14	28	0	16	7	0	0	4	4	.50	6	.238	.361	.287
Savary,Scott,Billings	R	22	31	91	22	6	0	0	28	20	13	11	0	22	2	0	2	3	0	1.00	3	.242	.330	.308
Charlstn-Sc	A	22	14	46	11	1	1	0	14	6	0	2	0	11	1	0	0	2	0	1.00	1	.239	.286	.304
Saylor,Jamie,Quad City	A	20	92	321	84	16	2	2	110	57	22	28	2	65	7	1	1	14	5	.74	4	.262	.333	.343
Sbrocco,Jon,Clinton	A	24	64	214	53	8	0	0	61	48	22	42	1	27	6	7	1	6	3	.67	3	.248	.384	.285
Schaaf,Bob,Yakima	A	22	31	82	26	2	1	0	30	11	9	14	0	16	1	0	2	4	1	.80	2	.317	.423	.366
Schmidt,Keith,Macon	A	24	9	16	0	0	0	0	0	0	0	2	0	7	0	0	0	0	0	.00	0	.000	.111	.000
Schmidt,Tom,Central Val	A	22	99	334	81	8	1	9	118	36	50	52	2	100	8	2	2	3	4	.43	3	.243	.356	.353
Schmitz,Michael,Tampa	A	24	3	8	1	0	0	0	1	0	1	0	0	2	0	0	0	0	0	.00	0	.125	.222	.125
Greensboro	A	24	117	432	97	18	1	5	139	42	60	30	0	97	5	1	6	2	2	.50	11	.225	.279	.322
Schneider,Daniel,Everett	A	23	40	136	32	6	2	1	45	17	18	9	0	34	1	0	1	2	0	1.00	6	.235	.286	.331
Schreiber,Stanley,Pirates	R	19	35	103	28	1	1	0	31	13	11	10	0	27	3	1	0	1	2	.33	1	.272	.353	.301
Schreimann,Eric,Martinsville	R	20	51	165	28	11	0	1	42	17	19	11	0	27	2	1	2	4	2	.67	1	.170	.228	.255
Schroeder,John,Twins	R	19	40	144	39	9	1	3	59	15	23	11	0	40	2	0	0	1	0	1.00	1	.271	.331	.410
Schwab,Christopher,Burlington	A	20	45	163	22	0	0	3	31	6	10	14	0	74	0	0	0	2	0	1.00	6	.135	.202	.190
Expos	R	20	38	144	29	8	1	3	48	19	22	21	2	44	0	0	1	0	0	.00	0	.201	.301	.333
Vermont	A	20	28	103	22	3	0	1	28	14	12	12	0	32	0	1	2	2	1	.67	1	.214	.291	.272
Schwenke,Matthew,Bakersfield	A	22	42	131	22	3	0	1	28	7	14	6	0	41	3	0	0	0	0	.00	3	.168	.221	.214
Scioscia,Mike,Charlotte	A	36	1	2	1	0	0	0	1	0	0	0	0	0	0	0	0	0	0	.00	0	.500	.500	.500
Scolaro,Donald,Auburn	A	23	42	132	33	3	2	1	43	21	10	4	0	32	5	5	0	3	0	1.00	0	.250	.298	.326
Scopio,Joseph,Cubs	R	22	8	28	10	3	0	0	13	6	4	8	0	3	0	0	0	2	1	.67	0	.357	.500	.464
Williamsprt	A	22	22	59	11	0	0	0	11	6	3	7	0	14	0	1	0	1	2	.29	0	.186	.273	.186
Sears,Jayson,Angels	R	19	2	3	0	0	0	0	0	0	0	4	0	3	0	0	0	0	0	.00	0	.000	.571	.000
Secrist,Reed,Salem	A	25	80	221	54	12	0	10	96	29	35	22	0	58	1	2	2	2	2	.50	4	.244	.314	.434
Sefcik,Kevin,Clearwater	A	24	130	516	147	29	8	2	198	83	46	49	2	43	7	4	5	30	13	.70	7	.285	.351	.384
Seguignol,Fernando,Oneonta	A	20	73	266	77	14	9	2	115	36	32	16	1	61	2	0	0	4	6	.40	4	.289	.335	.432
Segura,Juan,Salem	A	21	13	35	6	2	1	0	10	3	0	4	0	6	1	0	1	1	0	1.00	1	.171	.256	.286
Augusta	A	21	97	324	71	11	0	0	82	29	28	12	0	81	1	4	1	4	5	.44	4	.219	.249	.253
Seitzer,Brad,Beloit	A	25	102	343	86	13	0	11	132	45	53	58	1	78	3	6	4	2	2	.50	7	.251	.360	.385
Sell,Donald,Yakima	A	24	54	172	52	12	3	3	79	29	21	16	1	37	0	1	0	12	3	.80	6	.302	.362	.459
Selmo,Feliberto,Macon	A	21	71	179	37	4	1	1	46	17	12	11	0	55	1	5	3	5	3	.63	3	.207	.255	.257
Senkowitz,Mark,Lynchburg	A	24	31	102	24	4	0	2	34	12	11	2	0	19	4	2	0	1	0	1.00	3	.235	.278	.333
Serra,Jose,Albany	A	22	106	357	87	13	0	1	103	35	26	30	0	64	7	7	2	33	8	.80	4	.244	.313	.289
Sierra,Nestor,Bellingham	A	23	67	245	68	9	0	4	89	30	32	22	2	45	1	2	3	3	2	.40	5	.278	.336	.363
Sexson,Rich,Columbus	A	20	130	488	133	25	2	14	204	88	77	37	2	89	14	0	5	7	3	.70	5	.273	.338	.418
Sexton,Christopher,Charlstn-Sc	A	23	133	467	140	21	4	5	184	82	59	91	3	67	2	6	6	18	11	.62	9	.300	.412	.394
Shankle,Ronald,Lethbridge	R	21	43	139	26	7	0	3	42	20	14	13	0	46	2	5	1	2	1	.67	4	.187	.265	.302
Sharp,Scott,Princeton	R	22	46	159	42	9	2	4	67	22	21	16	0	53	0	1	1	4	2	.67	1	.264	.330	.421
Shatley,Andrew,Blue Jays	R	23	51	166	36	5	0	2	47	20	15	19	0	49	6	0	1	3	2	.60	1	.217	.314	.283
Sheffield,Tony,Utica	A	21	62	213	56	11	5	0	77	29	14	25	0	71	1	2	0	6	4	.60	2	.263	.343	.362
Shelley,Jason,Braves	R	20	8	25	4	0	0	0	4	0	1	0	0	11	0	0	0	0	0	.00	0	.160	.160	.160
Shepherd,Brian,Everett	A	22	11	29	7	0	1	0	9	7	3	7	0	5	1	0	0	1	0	1.00	3	.241	.395	.310
Clinton	A	22	8	11	0	0	0	0	0	0	0	1	0	7	0	0	0	0	0	.00	0	.000	.083	.000
Giants	R	22	15	46	8	3	0	0	11	4	5	8	0	13	1	0	0	0	2	.00	0	.174	.309	.239
Shiotani,Kazuhiko,Bristol	R	21	10	14	0	0	0	0	0	0	0	0	0	6	0	0	0	0	0	.00	0	.000	.000	.000
Shipman,Mike,Batavia	A	21	13	40	11	5	0	0	16	2	3	1	0	8	1	0	0	0	1	.00	0	.275	.310	.400

306

1994 Batting -- Single-A and Rookie Leagues

Player	Lg	A	G	AB	H	2B	3B	HR	TB	R	RBI	TBB	IBB	SO	HBP	SH	SF	SB	CS	SB%	GDP	Avg	OBP	SLG
Shirley,Al,Columbia	A	21	127	437	93	14	5	23	186	67	56	50	2	208	6	2	3	23	6	.79	2	.213	.300	.426
Shores,Scott,Batavia	A	23	72	264	66	10	5	6	104	46	32	27	0	54	4	3	2	19	7	.73	3	.250	.327	.394
Short,Richard,Bluefield	R	22	64	229	69	8	0	4	89	39	35	22	1	23	2	0	2	4	6	.40	3	.301	.365	.389
Shugars,Shawn,Hudson Vall	A	23	18	45	12	3	0	0	15	6	8	9	0	7	1	0	0	0	0	.00	0	.267	.400	.333
Shumpert,Derek,Oneonta	A	19	75	239	54	7	1	0	63	21	22	26	0	86	1	4	1	10	11	.48	5	.226	.303	.264
Sievers,Jason,Clinton	A	23	12	21	5	0	0	0	5	3	2	3	0	7	0	2	0	0	0	.00	0	.238	.333	.238
High Desert	A	23	42	128	16	2	0	0	18	7	7	12	0	27	1	5	2	0	0	.00	4	.125	.203	.141
Silvia,Brian,New Jersey	A	23	67	218	66	18	4	6	110	35	42	34	3	44	13	0	3	4	2	.67	4	.303	.422	.505
Simmons,Chris,Ogden	R	23	40	106	31	2	2	1	40	20	11	14	0	22	1	2	1	2	5	.29	2	.292	.377	.377
Simmons,Edwon,Orioles	R	19	47	106	23	3	1	0	28	16	16	16	0	17	5	1	0	7	2	.78	1	.217	.344	.264
Simmons,Mark,Cedar Rapds	A	22	84	272	69	6	0	2	81	35	30	36	1	76	0	4	2	13	7	.65	6	.254	.339	.298
Simon,Randall,Macon	A	20	106	358	105	23	1	10	160	45	54	6	2	56	1	1	2	7	6	.54	7	.293	.305	.447
Simonton,Benji,Clinton	A	23	67	237	64	16	4	14	130	47	57	52	3	73	5	1	0	10	3	.77	1	.270	.412	.549
San Jose	A	23	68	259	77	20	0	14	139	41	51	32	0	86	5	1	1	0	2	.00	5	.297	.384	.537
Simonton,Cy,Mariners	R	18	20	62	15	0	1	0	17	10	4	6	1	13	1	0	0	2	3	.40	0	.242	.319	.274
Simpson,Jeramie,Mets	R	20	31	101	24	3	4	0	35	20	12	12	0	15	2	2	2	4	1	.80	2	.238	.325	.347
Simpson,Jay,Lake Elsino	A	25	89	262	60	16	3	2	88	41	18	16	1	67	3	3	0	17	3	.85	4	.229	.281	.336
Sims,Michael,Brevard Cty	A	24	74	230	57	9	0	0	66	22	29	22	0	32	2	3	2	3	2	.60	13	.248	.316	.287
Sims,Wesley,Charlotte	A	23	92	312	68	8	3	3	91	26	32	36	4	51	2	5	2	9	3	.75	5	.218	.301	.292
Singleton,Christopher,San Jose	A	22	113	425	106	17	5	2	139	51	49	27	0	62	3	5	3	19	6	.76	9	.249	.297	.327
Sisco,Steve,Wilmington	A	25	76	270	74	11	4	3	102	41	32	37	0	39	2	6	4	5	6	.45	2	.274	.361	.378
Skeels,Mark,Brevard Cty	A	25	29	85	13	2	0	0	15	8	10	24	0	24	0	0	1	0	1	.00	3	.153	.333	.176
Smith,Brett,Ogden	R	23	33	114	38	10	2	1	55	21	19	4	0	20	2	1	0	2	0	1.00	1	.333	.367	.482
Smith,Craig,Stockton	A	23	68	228	59	11	1	0	72	17	27	11	0	40	4	2	1	5	2	.71	1	.259	.303	.316
Smith,Dan,Daytona	A	25	38	116	19	6	0	0	25	8	4	12	0	21	0	1	0	2	1	.67	4	.164	.242	.216
Stockton	A	23	5	17	1	0	0	0	1	2	0	1	0	6	0	2	0	0	0	.00	0	.059	.111	.059
Smith,David,Sarasota	A	23	1	2	1	0	0	0	1	0	0	0	0	1	0	0	0	0	0	.00	0	.500	.500	.500
Smith,Demond,Lake Elsino	A	22	12	26	3	0	1	0	5	1	1	4	0	8	0	1	0	4	4	.00	1	.115	.233	.192
Boise	A	22	71	279	78	9	7	5	116	60	45	43	2	57	2	7	4	26	9	.74	0	.280	.375	.416
Smith,John,St. Lucie	A	25	111	390	97	17	2	18	172	59	70	45	3	113	6	3	2	13	9	.59	4	.249	.334	.441
Smith,John,Astros	R	18	38	112	22	4	1	0	28	11	8	4	0	25	0	1	2	6	4	.60	2	.196	.220	.250
Smith,John,Kabisa,Pirates	R	19	19	69	12	3	0	2	21	10	10	2	0	18	0	0	2	0	2	.00	2	.174	.192	.304
Smith,Keith,Bristol	R	19	42	143	36	3	0	0	39	25	16	17	0	31	1	7	2	15	7	.68	1	.252	.331	.273
Fayetteville	A	19	13	55	11	3	0	0	14	0	0	1	0	12	0	2	0	1	1	.00	1	.200	.200	.255
Smith,Larry,Royals	R	20	44	98	19	2	1	2	29	17	10	16	0	28	1	2	0	1	0	1.00	1	.194	.313	.296
Smith,Matthew,Royals	R	19	32	101	24	5	3	1	38	13	12	12	2	26	1	0	0	1	0	1.00	1	.238	.325	.376
Smith,Mike,High Desert	A	21	132	512	149	23	6	21	247	96	94	73	2	89	5	4	5	28	15	.65	13	.291	.382	.482
Smith,Bobby,Durham	A	21	127	478	127	27	2	12	194	49	71	41	1	112	4	1	0	18	7	.72	19	.266	.329	.406
Smith,Rodiquez,Yankees	R	19	56	196	56	7	4	1	74	41	18	41	1	51	1	2	0	20	4	.83	2	.286	.412	.378
Greensboro	A	19	7	20	1	0	0	0	1	2	0	3	0	7	0	0	0	0	0	1.00	1	.050	.174	.050
Smith,Ronald,Williamsprt	A	23	4	9	0	0	0	0	0	0	1	1	0	2	0	0	0	0	0	.00	0	.000	.100	.000
Smith,Coleman,Peoria	A	25	31	48	10	2	0	0	12	13	6	12	0	15	3	1	1	2	0	1.00	1	.208	.391	.250
Smith,Scott,Appleton	A	23	60	178	38	5	0	2	51	26	13	23	0	46	4	1	1	3	4	.43	2	.213	.316	.287
Smith,Sean,Macon	A	21	81	242	56	7	2	1	70	23	26	19	2	47	3	6	0	3	2	.60	5	.231	.295	.289
Snook,Robert,Helena	R	21	26	31	2	0	0	0	2	1	0	5	0	16	0	3	0	1	0	.00	0	.065	.194	.065
Snyder,Jared,Cubs	R	25	10	29	5	2	0	0	7	3	4	1	0	5	1	1	1	0	0	.00	1	.172	.219	.241
Solano,Fausto,St. Cathrns	A	21	73	288	77	11	3	2	100	49	19	32	0	47	1	6	1	19	10	.66	4	.267	.342	.347
Solomon,Steve,Clearwater	A	23	131	497	150	29	5	9	216	88	62	51	7	71	10	5	5	21	11	.66	12	.302	.375	.435
Soper,Steven,Medicne Hat	R	23	59	219	52	7	2	1	66	40	21	11	1	53	8	3	4	10	3	.77	4	.237	.293	.301
Sorg,Jay,Princeton	R	22	58	164	34	3	1	4	51	14	23	15	1	44	0	0	1	5	6	.45	1	.207	.272	.311
Soriano,Fred,Modesto	A	20	22	53	3	0	0	0	3	8	1	7	0	21	3	1	0	2	1	.67	2	.057	.206	.057
W. Michigan	A	20	78	201	45	2	1	1	52	30	16	21	0	70	12	12	0	23	7	.77	3	.224	.333	.259
Soriano,Jose,Sou. Oregon	A	21	60	176	38	8	2	3	59	34	23	11	0	48	3	4	4	12	5	.71	3	.216	.268	.335
Sosa,Gamalier,Angels	R	21	40	136	33	3	0	0	36	18	14	21	1	31	0	1	1	3	1	.75	4	.243	.340	.265
Soto,Manuel,White Sox	R	22	19	48	9	0	0	0	9	8	4	5	0	13	0	2	0	8	4	.67	0	.188	.264	.188
South Bend	A	22	11	38	7	2	0	0	9	3	2	2	0	12	0	1	0	0	0	.00	0	.184	.225	.237
Soto,Wilson,Brewers	R	20	56	196	42	6	0	4	60	37	22	21	1	46	3	2	1	27	2	.93	1	.214	.299	.306
Southard,Scott,Kane County	A	23	95	310	71	12	0	0	83	33	36	40	0	34	1	6	4	3	2	.60	11	.229	.315	.268
Sowards,Ryan,Great Falls	R	21	45	149	40	10	3	1	59	29	27	20	0	24	1	1	2	2	2	.50	3	.268	.357	.396
Sparks,Rodney,Eugene	A	23	42	137	35	3	0	0	38	11	10	21	0	39	1	0	0	3	2	.60	3	.255	.372	.277
Spencer,Shane,Tampa	A	23	90	334	97	22	3	8	149	44	53	30	0	53	1	1	1	5	3	.63	8	.290	.350	.446
Spiegel,Richard,Danville	R	21	46	152	42	9	0	9	78	26	26	15	1	33	0	1	1	2	2	.50	3	.276	.339	.513
Spiezio,Scott,Modesto	A	22	127	453	127	32	4	14	211	84	68	88	4	72	7	3	9	5	0	1.00	15	.280	.399	.466
Spoyd,Richard,Helena	R	21	1	0	0	0	0	0	0	0	0	0	0	0	0	0	0	0	0	.00	0	.000	.000	.000
Springfield,Brent,Pirates	R	19	45	164	45	3	6	1	63	33	29	21	1	34	4	1	1	12	2	.86	0	.274	.368	.384
Spry,Shane,Hickory	A	19	3	3	0	0	0	0	0	0	3	0	0	2	0	0	0	0	0	.00	1	.000	.500	.000
White Sox	R	19	46	138	36	8	2	1	51	25	7	17	0	23	1	1	0	4	1	.80	3	.261	.346	.370
Stadler,Mike,Burlington	R	20	22	70	12	3	0	3	24	7	8	7	0	26	1	0	0	0	2	.00	0	.171	.256	.343
Stamison,Michael,Sou. Oregon	A	23	59	194	47	14	0	4	73	29	33	23	1	66	2	2	3	3	1	.75	5	.242	.324	.376
Stanczak,John,Charlotte	A	24	93	320	74	18	2	4	108	32	41	31	1	75	3	4	5	2	6	.25	5	.231	.303	.338
Stanley,B.J.,Johnson Cty	R	21	22	46	4	1	0	0	5	6	3	8	0	8	0	1	0	1	0	1.00	0	.087	.222	.109
Stare,Lonny,Clinton	A	24	38	76	22	3	2	0	29	12	5	4	0	14	1	1	0	2	3	.40	0	.289	.333	.382
Stasio,Chris,Everett	A	24	20	39	10	3	0	0	13	6	1	3	0	14	0	0	1	0	0	.00	0	.256	.302	.333
Staton,Tarrence,Welland	A	20	12	45	8	3	0	0	11	4	4	0	0	7	0	0	0	5	0	1.00	1	.178	.178	.244
Pirates	R	20	11	39	10	3	0	0	16	3	5	1	0	8	1	0	0	2	0	1.00	0	.256	.293	.410
Augusta	A	20	37	125	27	6	1	0	35	9	5	10	0	38	0	1	1	6	1	.86	5	.216	.272	.280
Steed,David,Yakima	A	NA	48	147	37	5	2	5	61	24	24	28	0	43	5	1	0	1	2	.33	4	.252	.389	.415

307

1994 Batting -- Single-A and Rookie Leagues

																			BATTING				BASERUNNING				PERCENTAGES		
Player	Lg	A	G	AB	H	2B	3B	HR	TB	R	RBI	TBB	IBB	SO	HBP	SH	SF	SB	CS	SB%	GDP	Avg	OBP	SLG
Stevens,Ted,Vermont	A	22	6	8	2	0	0	0	2	3	1	2	0	2	0	0	0	0	0	.00	0	.250	.400	.250
San Bernrdo	A	22	9	31	5	2	0	1	10	5	2	2	0	9	1	0	0	0	0	.00	1	.161	.235	.323
Stevenson,Chad,Bristol	R	19	34	83	13	2	0	1	18	11	7	18	0	17	1	1	0	0	1	.00	5	.157	.314	.217
Stewart,Shannon,Hagerstown	A	21	56	225	73	10	5	4	105	39	25	23	1	39	1	2	2	15	11	.58	3	.324	.386	.467
Stingley,Derek,Spartanburg	A	24	96	270	58	4	6	1	77	40	22	15	0	86	7	2	1	24	9	.73	3	.215	.273	.285
Stone,Craig,Medicne Hat	R	19	57	213	57	10	0	4	79	31	27	13	0	56	7	1	2	3	2	.60	4	.268	.328	.371
Stovall,Darond,St. Pete	A	22	134	507	113	20	6	15	190	68	69	62	3	154	0	2	5	24	8	.75	10	.223	.305	.375
Strange,Michael,Medicne Hat	R	21	55	177	44	7	3	1	60	30	20	22	0	50	6	2	2	4	2	.67	3	.249	.348	.339
Stratton,John,Lynchburg	A	24	22	57	17	2	1	0	21	6	2	7	0	13	1	0	0	1	0	1.00	0	.298	.385	.368
Strauss,Jon,Oneonta	A	22	2	2	0	0	0	0	0	0	1	0	0	1	1	0	0	0	0	.00	0	.000	.333	.000
Yankees	R	1	1	0	0	0	0	0	0	0	0	1	0	0	1	0	0	0	0	.00	0	.000	.000	.000
Stuart,Rich,Angels	R	18	38	109	30	2	2	2	42	12	13	14	0	31	0	4	1	1	0	1.00	1	.275	.355	.385
Stuckenschneide,Eric,Yakima	A	23	58	190	57	13	4	3	87	40	39	45	3	43	5	3	0	22	4	.85	2	.300	.446	.458
Stumberger,Darren,Watertown	A	22	69	256	66	13	1	10	111	47	52	35	0	56	3	1	7	0	0	.00	3	.258	.346	.434
Sturdivant,Marcus,Appleton	A	21	113	413	104	12	7	2	136	50	36	33	1	43	4	4	0	20	17	.54	7	.252	.313	.329
Suarez,Sadiel,Braves	R	19	21	62	7	2	0	0	9	7	1	8	0	21	0	0	0	2	1	.67	4	.113	.214	.145
Subero,Carlos,Rockford	A	23	63	208	46	10	1	1	61	20	16	7	0	35	1	5	1	1	1	.50	2	.221	.249	.293
Suplee,Ray,Tampa	A	24	101	338	87	15	3	6	126	42	54	42	0	84	12	1	5	0	3	.00	4	.257	.355	.373
Sutherland,Alex,Appleton	A	23	94	330	84	17	2	3	114	24	40	19	0	70	3	2	2	2	6	.25	4	.255	.299	.345
Sutton,Larry,Wilmington	A	25	129	480	147	33	1	26	260	91	94	81	10	71	6	1	9	2	1	.67	7	.306	.406	.542
Swafford,Derek,Welland	A	20	16	64	24	4	3	0	34	8	11	6	1	13	0	1	0	8	3	.73	2	.375	.429	.531
Augusta	A	20	51	189	36	9	4	1	56	16	16	11	0	71	5	0	1	12	5	.71	2	.190	.252	.296
Sweeney,Mike,Rockford	A	21	86	276	83	20	3	10	139	47	52	55	4	43	9	0	4	0	1	.00	8	.301	.427	.504
Sweet,Jon,Welland	A	23	51	154	39	8	0	0	47	17	17	17	1	20	5	1	1	0	3	.00	1	.253	.345	.305
Swift,Scott,Giants	R	24	52	188	56	8	2	0	68	23	18	33	3	23	1	1	2	19	4	.83	2	.298	.402	.362
Silvestri,Tony,Brevard Cty	A	24	82	267	56	4	1	0	62	24	12	20	1	25	6	6	1	5	3	.63	4	.210	.279	.232
Takayoshi,Todd,Lake Elsino	A	24	7	18	3	0	0	0	3	2	1	3	1	1	0	0	0	1	1	.50	1	.167	.286	.167
Cedar Rapds	A	24	95	302	93	16	1	8	135	42	46	44	7	43	2	1	2	2	2	.50	8	.308	.397	.447
Tatis,Fernando,Rangers	R	20	60	212	70	10	2	6	102	34	32	25	4	33	3	0	2	20	4	.83	4	.330	.405	.481
Tawwater,Darren,Cardinals	R	22	34	106	27	8	0	5	50	18	13	13	0	37	6	0	0	0	0	.00	3	.255	.368	.472
Taylor,Byron,New Jersey	A	22	15	13	0	0	0	0	0	2	0	4	0	8	0	0	0	0	2	.00	1	.000	.235	.000
Taylor,Jim,Kinston	A	24	76	217	51	14	0	5	80	30	19	29	0	63	2	2	1	3	4	.43	2	.235	.329	.369
Taylor,Mike,New Jersey	A	24	70	258	76	8	3	0	90	43	23	41	2	38	0	1	5	6	2	.75	5	.295	.385	.349
Taylor,Sam,Boise	A	23	10	16	1	0	0	0	1	4	1	4	0	6	0	0	0	2	0	1.00	0	.063	.250	.063
Charlstn-Sc	A	23	21	68	16	3	0	1	22	11	7	5	0	9	0	2	0	3	0	.00	0	.235	.288	.324
Tebbs,Nathan,Utica	A	22	70	219	44	5	0	0	49	18	23	11	0	34	1	4	1	9	4	.69	1	.201	.241	.224
Teel,Garett,Bakersfield	A	27	1	3	0	0	0	0	0	0	0	0	0	0	0	0	0	0	0	.00	0	.000	.000	.000
Teeters,Brian,Eugene	A	22	52	209	56	8	4	4	84	38	17	20	2	60	2	1	2	20	6	.77	1	.268	.335	.402
Tena,Dario,Augusta	A	22	27	106	26	1	0	0	27	16	3	5	0	16	0	4	0	13	8	.62	2	.245	.279	.255
Salem	A	22	67	173	43	4	0	0	47	26	8	9	0	27	0	2	1	11	8	.58	3	.249	.284	.272
Terilli,Joe,Daytona	A	26	78	202	46	10	0	0	56	18	11	37	1	33	3	6	3	6	1	.86	7	.228	.351	.277
Terrell,Matthew,St. Lucie	A	23	103	336	84	8	4	1	103	30	31	28	2	113	5	8	2	20	10	.67	5	.250	.315	.307
Terry,Antonio,Billings	R	19	43	136	33	1	0	1	37	20	10	11	0	43	0	0	0	5	3	.63	1	.243	.299	.272
Tessicini,David,Clinton	A	22	23	64	18	0	0	1	21	13	11	9	0	19	0	1	1	1	2	.33	0	.281	.365	.328
Everett	A	22	51	170	43	5	1	3	59	22	22	26	2	31	6	3	1	3	0	1.00	3	.253	.369	.347
Texidor,Jose,Charlotte	A	23	131	501	129	24	5	5	178	69	68	48	0	80	3	1	4	3	11	.21	6	.257	.324	.355
Therrien,Dominic,High Desert	A	23	3	11	3	2	0	0	5	3	2	0	0	2	0	0	0	0	0	.00	0	.273	.273	.455
Thielen,Duane,San Jose	A	23	9	33	2	0	0	0	2	4	1	1	0	15	1	0	0	1	0	1.00	0	.061	.114	.061
Clinton	A	23	69	247	60	9	5	12	115	39	29	15	0	94	3	2	0	8	4	.67	3	.243	.294	.466
Thobe,Steven,Welland	A	23	46	151	29	11	0	1	43	14	10	12	0	33	2	0	0	1	0	1.00	3	.192	.261	.285
Thomas,Brian,Charlotte	A	24	124	450	127	26	9	5	186	60	61	55	4	122	5	5	8	23	9	.72	6	.282	.361	.413
Thomas,Byron,Kingsport	R	22	42	155	37	3	3	0	46	20	11	12	0	27	0	1	1	8	3	.73	1	.239	.292	.297
Thomas,Gregory,Kinston	A	22	103	351	67	14	2	15	130	46	42	26	0	97	5	2	2	5	2	.71	4	.191	.255	.370
Thomas,Juan,South Bend	A	23	119	446	112	20	6	18	198	57	79	27	2	143	9	0	5	3	4	.43	13	.251	.304	.444
Thomas,Mike,Rancho Cuca	A	23	9	20	4	1	0	0	5	3	2	0	0	4	0	0	0	0	0	.00	1	.200	.200	.250
Springfield	A	23	35	98	17	3	0	1	23	11	9	2	0	29	3	0	0	1	1	.50	2	.173	.214	.235
Thomas,Rod,Charlstn-Sc	A	21	110	343	72	20	4	10	130	35	47	24	0	115	3	1	1	12	5	.71	2	.210	.265	.379
Thomas,Tim,Lakeland	A	25	100	328	78	15	1	2	101	40	34	66	4	95	7	1	4	3	2	.60	6	.238	.373	.308
Thomason,Shane,Mariners	R	22	25	83	18	2	0	0	20	6	1	0	0	28	1	0	0	0	4	.00	1	.217	.226	.241
Thompson,Leroy,Columbus	A	20	106	345	87	12	8	8	139	54	51	42	2	100	3	1	2	1	5	.17	3	.252	.337	.403
Thompson,William,Lakeland	A	24	82	274	58	17	0	7	96	28	28	24	0	61	4	1	2	4	3	.57	8	.212	.283	.350
Tidick,Michael,White Sox	R	24	18	42	8	2	0	0	10	4	0	4	0	9	1	0	0	0	1	.00	2	.190	.277	.238
Tiffany,Ted,Angels	R	21	42	99	25	4	0	0	29	19	5	19	0	28	0	3	0	7	0	1.00	1	.253	.373	.293
Tiller,Bradley,Burlington	R	19	45	123	19	0	2	1	26	9	5	7	0	43	4	2	0	3	3	.50	1	.154	.224	.211
Tillman,Bennie,Idaho Falls	R	22	39	130	38	5	2	0	47	21	20	16	1	33	0	1	1	6	2	.75	0	.292	.370	.362
Timmons,Shayne,St. Cathms	A	23	19	54	10	2	0	0	12	0	5	2	0	15	0	1	0	1	1	.50	1	.185	.214	.222
Tinoco,Luis,Mariners	R	20	14	41	8	0	0	0	8	4	2	9	0	11	2	0	1	0	0	.00	2	.195	.358	.195
Tinsley,Charles,Martinsvlle	R	20	39	103	10	1	1	1	16	8	4	10	1	62	1	1	0	3	2	.60	0	.097	.184	.155
Tolbert,Andrew,Idaho Falls	R	19	36	118	31	5	4	0	44	14	11	13	0	18	5	0	0	8	1	.89	3	.263	.360	.373
Topping,Daniel,Giants	R	19	36	129	34	7	2	1	48	9	17	6	1	29	3	1	1	0	3	.00	5	.264	.305	.372
Torborg,Dale,Kingsport	R	23	19	45	13	2	0	1	18	4	7	1	0	11	1	2	0	0	0	.00	0	.289	.319	.400
Torok,John,Batavia	A	22	18	49	15	0	1	0	17	13	5	10	0	7	0	0	0	7	1	.88	1	.306	.424	.347
Spartanburg	A	22	42	127	25	1	2	1	33	13	15	17	1	16	1	1	0	0	0	.00	0	.197	.297	.260
Torres,Tony,Brevard Cty	A	25	98	368	93	14	7	4	133	58	39	39	1	67	2	3	3	17	6	.74	6	.253	.325	.361
Torres,Jaime,Greensboro	A	22	89	322	87	22	1	6	129	27	63	13	0	39	8	0	3	4	4	.50	17	.270	.308	.401
Toth,Dave,Durham	A	25	72	165	40	11	0	2	57	23	20	19	0	28	1	1	1	1	0	1.00	4	.242	.323	.345
Tovar,Edgar,San Bernrdo	A	21	82	340	108	16	1	10	156	58	40	24	0	29	6	4	0	13	6	.68	3	.318	.373	.459

308

1994 Batting -- Single-A and Rookie Leagues

Player	Lg	A	G	AB	H	2B	3B	HR	TB	R	RBI	TBB	IBB	SO	HBP	SH	SF	SB	CS	SB%	GDP	Avg	OBP	SLG
W. Palm Bch	A	21	30	123	40	9	1	3	60	15	23	5	1	13	1	1	0	4	0	1.00	2	.325	.357	.488
Towle,Justin,Charlstn-Sc	A	21	83	221	49	9	0	2	64	27	19	26	1	59	2	1	0	2	6	.25	8	.222	.309	.290
Winston-Sal	A	21	2	7	1	0	0	0	1	1	0	0	0	2	0	0	0	0	0	.00	1	.143	.143	.143
Towner,Kyle,Bellingham	A	22	56	138	22	1	0	0	23	17	9	22	0	30	4	2	2	19	6	.76	0	.159	.289	.167
Townsend,Chad,High Desert	A	23	64	247	73	12	3	9	118	39	46	19	1	43	3	0	2	1	2	.33	6	.296	.351	.478
Kinston	A	23	64	229	52	6	0	10	88	29	43	27	3	49	5	0	1	2	1	.67	1	.227	.321	.384
Trammell,Gary,Auburn	A	23	70	272	82	10	4	3	109	44	47	22	0	23	0	2	6	15	7	.68	3	.301	.347	.401
Trammell,Thomas,Jamestown	A	23	65	235	70	18	6	5	115	37	41	23	0	32	4	0	4	9	7	.56	1	.298	.365	.489
Trapaga,Julio,Durham	A	20	74	217	44	10	0	2	60	28	17	19	0	69	1	3	4	1	2	.33	3	.203	.266	.276
Treanor,Matthew,Royals	R	19	46	99	18	5	0	1	26	17	12	14	1	23	3	1	1	1	1	.50	2	.182	.299	.263
Trimble,Robin,Greensboro	A	23	60	195	38	2	1	1	45	10	9	19	1	52	0	0	2	2	1	.67	3	.195	.264	.231
Oneonta	A	23	32	101	23	4	0	1	30	7	17	7	0	20	3	1	0	0	0	.00	1	.228	.292	.297
Troilo,Jason,Oneonta	A	22	7	15	2	1	0	0	3	0	1	4	0	3	0	1	0	0	0	.00	0	.133	.316	.200
Greensboro	A	22	22	58	11	3	0	0	14	5	6	5	0	16	1	0	0	0	0	.00	0	.190	.266	.241
Truby,Chris,Quad City	A	21	36	111	24	4	1	2	36	12	19	3	0	29	2	0	2	1	1	.50	3	.216	.246	.324
Auburn	A	21	73	282	91	17	6	7	141	56	61	23	0	48	3	1	8	20	4	.83	8	.323	.370	.500
Tucker,Robert,Lake Elsino	A	24	12	34	3	0	0	0	3	2	2	3	0	11	1	1	0	0	0	.00	1	.088	.184	.088
Tunison,Rich,Fort Myers	A	26	60	146	25	0	1	1	30	12	9	6	0	36	1	3	0	4	2	.67	2	.171	.209	.205
Turlais,John,Kingsport	R	23	30	101	18	2	0	1	23	11	11	9	0	19	0	1	1	2	1	.67	4	.178	.243	.228
Turner,Rocky,Pittsfield	A	23	53	177	35	2	2	0	41	20	9	12	0	49	3	6	2	11	6	.65	1	.198	.258	.232
Twist,Jeffrey,Bend	A	22	7	19	5	1	0	1	9	1	3	0	0	6	1	0	0	1	0	1.00	0	.263	.300	.474
Asheville	A	22	15	36	6	0	0	0	6	4	0	4	0	13	0	0	0	0	0	.00	1	.167	.250	.167
Twitty,Sean,Tampa	A	24	11	28	8	3	0	1	14	4	3	6	0	6	2	0	1	0	0	.00	0	.286	.432	.500
Tyler,Joshua,Brewers	R	21	54	193	52	4	3	0	62	35	24	30	0	34	6	4	1	8	4	.67	6	.269	.378	.321
Tyrus,Jason,Spokane	A	23	49	147	34	2	1	1	41	14	17	15	0	47	0	7	1	11	4	.73	3	.231	.301	.279
Ugueto,Hector,Savannah	A	21	48	118	21	2	0	0	23	13	5	11	0	35	3	1	0	0	3	.00	2	.178	.261	.195
Ugueto,Jesus,Madison	A	22	66	215	54	10	2	1	71	18	20	12	0	32	0	3	4	6	8	.43	4	.251	.286	.330
Ullian,David,Spokane	A	22	45	161	35	4	1	1	44	13	19	16	2	31	3	1	1	2	1	.67	6	.217	.298	.273
Underwood,Devin,Red Sox	R	21	24	67	20	1	0	1	24	8	6	3	0	12	3	1	0	0	0	.00	2	.299	.356	.358
Unrat,Christopher,Charlstn-Wv	A	24	64	192	41	10	0	7	72	28	24	29	1	73	3	0	1	1	3	.25	3	.214	.324	.375
Urso,Joe,Lake Elsino	A	24	134	494	138	30	4	2	182	67	46	78	4	66	14	4	4	10	6	.63	8	.279	.379	.368
Utting,Benjamin,Idaho Falls	R	19	59	227	54	2	2	0	60	43	22	30	0	37	0	5	0	13	3	.81	6	.238	.327	.264
Valdes,David,Yakima	A	24	27	54	13	1	0	0	14	10	5	10	0	5	0	1	0	3	0	1.00	6	.241	.359	.259
Valdez,Mario,White Sox	R	20	53	157	37	11	2	2	58	20	25	30	0	28	2	0	1	0	6	.00	3	.236	.363	.369
Valdez,Miguel,Macon	A	15	49	11	3	0	1	0	17	3	4	1	0	17	0	0	1	0	1	.00	1	.224	.240	.347
Danville	R	20	52	164	41	8	1	1	54	19	16	24	2	35	0	1	1	11	8	.58	3	.250	.344	.329
Valdez,Trovin,Albany	A	21	20	65	17	0	2	0	21	10	4	1	0	17	2	0	1	9	1	.90	1	.262	.290	.323
Bluefield	R	21	55	184	53	7	3	3	75	43	18	11	1	26	5	5	5	20	6	.77	1	.288	.337	.408
Valenti,Jon,Athletics	R	21	53	195	56	9	5	2	81	27	27	19	1	34	3	0	2	4	4	.50	6	.287	.356	.415
Valentin,Jose,Elizabthtn	R	19	54	210	44	5	0	9	76	23	27	15	0	44	2	0	0	1	2	.33	9	.210	.263	.362
Valenzuela,Derek,Charlstn-Sc	A	22	1	0	0	0	0	0	0	0	0	0	0	0	1	0	0	0	0	.00	0	.000	1.000	.000
Valette,Ramon,Fort Myers	A	23	122	404	97	21	1	4	132	50	49	22	0	80	5	3	1	19	7	.73	9	.240	.287	.327
Vallarelli,Mike,Boise	A	23	5	5	1	0	0	0	1	0	1	0	0	1	0	0	0	0	0	.00	0	.200	.167	.200
Vanpelt,Dennis,Boise	A	23	56	165	47	13	0	2	66	32	38	30	5	36	0	1	5	1	1	.50	6	.285	.385	.400
Vaninetti,Geno,Hagerstown	A	20	27	90	14	2	0	1	19	8	10	6	0	30	0	0	1	1	2	.33	1	.156	.208	.211
Medicne Hat	R	20	47	145	24	8	0	5	47	18	22	7	0	63	5	2	2	0	0	.00	8	.166	.226	.324
Vaske,Terry,Williamsprt	A	24	19	62	10	2	0	2	18	7	7	8	0	21	0	0	0	1	0	1.00	0	.161	.257	.290
Vasquez,Chris,Charlstn-Sc	A	23	28	98	20	2	1	1	27	9	7	2	0	11	0	0	1	1	1	.50	2	.204	.218	.276
Winston-Sal	A	23	69	217	60	11	1	5	88	31	29	13	0	43	0	0	1	3	2	.60	4	.276	.316	.406
Vasquez,Daniel,Rangers	R	21	56	204	61	8	4	9	104	29	39	13	0	54	2	0	3	12	7	.63	4	.299	.342	.510
Hudson Vall	A	21	4	17	2	1	0	0	3	1	1	0	0	5	0	0	1	1	1	.50	0	.118	.118	.176
Vasquez,Diomedes,Blue Jays	R	22	14	53	10	1	0	0	11	6	4	1	0	12	0	0	0	2	3	.40	2	.189	.204	.208
St. Cathrns	A	22	32	93	19	4	1	1	28	10	5	4	0	23	2	1	2	1	2	.33	0	.204	.253	.301
Vasut,Tony,Peoria	A	22	29	85	23	4	2	1	34	7	6	13	0	28	0	1	1	2	1	.67	1	.271	.364	.400
Vatter,Scott,Butte	R	23	12	28	7	1	0	0	8	11	6	9	0	11	1	0	0	5	0	1.00	0	.250	.447	.286
Vaughn,Derek,Lake Elsino	A	25	13	36	6	2	0	0	8	5	1	2	0	9	0	1	0	2	0	1.00	0	.167	.211	.222
Cedar Rapds	A	25	70	170	46	6	0	5	67	26	18	22	1	32	3	4	1	14	7	.67	5	.271	.362	.394
Vega,Ramon,Giants	R	21	48	155	40	9	4	3	66	21	13	20	0	43	7	1	2	2	3	.40	3	.258	.364	.426
Velandia,George,Lakeland	A	20	22	60	14	4	0	0	18	8	3	6	0	14	0	3	1	0	2	.00	0	.233	.299	.300
Springfield	A	20	98	290	71	14	0	4	97	42	36	21	0	46	4	6	3	5	6	.45	8	.245	.302	.334
Velazquez,Edgard,Asheville	A	19	119	447	106	22	3	11	167	50	39	23	0	120	3	3	2	9	9	.50	14	.237	.278	.374
Velazquez,Jose,Yankees	R	19	54	197	46	9	1	1	60	26	27	28	1	30	2	0	2	1	2	.33	4	.234	.332	.305
Velez,Jose,St. Pete	A	22	100	279	73	8	0	2	87	30	22	15	2	18	3	4	3	6	3	.67	9	.262	.303	.312
Venezia,Daniel,Fort Wayne	A	23	103	342	69	10	4	1	90	31	22	20	0	48	1	2	1	16	6	.73	7	.202	.247	.263
Venezia,Richard,Welland	A	21	49	124	24	0	1	0	26	7	12	19	0	34	0	1	0	6	6	.50	4	.194	.299	.210
Ventura,Leonardo,Sou. Oregon	A	21	29	76	14	4	0	1	21	7	9	6	0	32	2	0	1	0	1	.00	2	.184	.247	.276
Veras,Iluminado,Angels	R	20	17	48	10	4	0	0	14	4	5	3	0	9	0	1	0	1	0	1.00	1	.208	.255	.292
Veras,Juan,Rangers	R	20	56	193	38	5	1	0	45	27	8	19	0	39	1	1	1	19	5	.79	1	.197	.272	.233
Verduzco,Steven,Osceola	A	20	102	322	80	20	0	1	103	50	34	37	0	58	3	9	4	20	5	.80	8	.248	.328	.320
Vessel,Andrew,Charlstn-Wv	A	20	114	411	99	23	2	8	150	40	55	29	0	102	10	1	4	7	10	.41	3	.241	.304	.365
Vickers,Randal,Mariners	R	19	20	55	8	2	1	1	15	5	6	2	0	28	1	0	0	3	0	1.00	1	.145	.186	.273
Vidro,Jose,W. Palm Bch	A	20	125	465	124	30	2	4	170	57	49	51	4	56	5	3	3	8	2	.80	5	.267	.344	.366
Vielleux,William,Cubs	R	21	47	111	28	8	0	1	43	22	19	20	0	38	3	1	0	3	1	.67	1	.252	.381	.387
Vilchez,Jose,Twins	R	19	33	113	25	5	1	1	35	11	6	3	0	28	0	0	0	1	0	1.00	0	.221	.241	.310
Villa,William,Blue Jays	R	19	20	65	16	1	0	1	20	8	6	2	0	10	0	1	0	3	0	1.00	0	.246	.265	.308
Villalobos,Carlos,Mariners	R	20	51	175	51	6	2	4	73	17	29	11	1	34	2	2	2	6	0	1.00	8	.291	.337	.417
Villano,Michael,Everett	A	23	23	57	16	4	0	1	23	8	8	8	0	14	0	0	2	1	1	.50	1	.281	.364	.404

1994 Batting -- Single-A and Rookie Leagues

			BATTING																BASERUNNING				PERCENTAGES		
Player	Lg	A	G	AB	H	2B	3B	HR	TB	R	RBI	TBB	IBB	SO	HBP	SH	SF	SB	CS	SB%	GDP	Avg	OBP	SLG
Villaran,Miguel,Brewers	R	19	19	27	6	1	0	0	7	1	3	0	0	13	2	0	0	0	1	.00	0	.222	.276	.259
Vinas,Julio,South Bend	A	22	121	466	118	31	1	9	178	68	75	43	4	75	4	6	6	0	2	.00	9	.253	.318	.382
Vindivich,John,Auburn	A	23	59	203	61	12	6	1	88	32	22	20	2	50	0	2	3	11	3	.79	3	.300	.358	.433
Vindivich,Paul,Rockford	A	21	35	107	27	8	0	0	35	7	13	8	0	28	2	1	2	1	4	.20	0	.252	.311	.327
Eugene	A	21	45	143	27	1	1	2	36	12	10	7	0	51	2	2	1	1	3	.25	2	.189	.235	.252
Vinyard,Derek,Sarasota	A	24	80	262	69	4	1	0	75	37	16	24	1	50	2	10	4	12	3	.80	1	.263	.325	.286
Vizcaino,Julian,Cedar Rapds	A	21	10	21	1	0	0	1	4	3	1	4	0	9	0	1	0	0	0	.00	1	.048	.200	.190
Vizcaino,Romulo,Fort Wayne	A	21	45	168	40	2	0	0	42	14	19	13	0	27	2	0	1	1	4	.20	1	.238	.299	.250
Elizabethtn	R	21	57	226	62	12	1	5	91	51	31	33	1	33	2	0	3	9	2	.82	10	.274	.367	.403
Vlasis,Chris,Savannah	A	25	94	260	57	6	2	2	73	46	30	30	1	57	1	2	6	20	7	.74	2	.219	.304	.281
Vollmer,Scott,Hickory	A	24	110	420	115	24	4	7	168	52	81	39	2	63	4	4	6	0	1	.00	17	.274	.337	.400
Waco,David,Spartanburg	A	25	31	90	22	4	0	2	32	13	10	15	0	20	3	3	1	0	3	.00	4	.244	.367	.356
Clearwater	A	25	40	115	39	12	2	3	64	20	31	17	0	14	1	3	2	0	0	.00	1	.339	.422	.557
Waldrop,Tom,Durham	A	25	97	289	62	13	1	12	113	41	54	29	2	89	5	2	2	2	5	.29	4	.215	.295	.391
Walker,John,Utica	A	23	16	48	13	1	0	0	14	9	2	10	0	10	0	2	0	5	0	1.00	0	.271	.397	.292
Sarasota	A	23	11	36	9	1	0	0	10	1	7	2	0	5	1	2	1	1	1	.50	2	.250	.300	.278
Lynchburg	A	23	19	61	9	2	0	0	11	7	1	9	0	10	1	0	0	1	1	.50	0	.148	.268	.180
Walker,Roderic,Rangers	R	19	50	160	35	3	3	1	47	28	16	15	0	40	1	0	3	16	8	.67	0	.219	.285	.294
Walker,Steve,Daytona	A	23	20	61	12	3	0	1	18	5	9	3	0	25	1	0	0	4	1	.80	1	.197	.246	.295
Peoria	A	23	90	266	57	13	5	2	86	38	22	20	3	83	3	6	0	15	5	.75	5	.214	.277	.323
Walker,Todd,Fort Myers	A	22	46	171	52	5	2	10	91	29	34	32	0	15	0	0	4	6	3	.67	4	.304	.406	.532
Walker,Shon,Augusta	A	21	78	242	55	6	1	4	75	38	26	62	3	84	1	0	1	29	6	.83	1	.227	.382	.310
Wallace,Brian,Appleton	A	23	110	385	91	15	3	4	124	44	45	19	2	91	5	0	8	11	11	.50	3	.236	.276	.322
Wallace,Joe,Madison	A	23	36	84	23	5	0	2	34	15	11	19	0	23	3	0	1	1	1	.50	1	.274	.421	.405
Walls,Eric,Rockford	A	22	85	255	81	13	4	1	105	56	32	31	1	43	2	3	1	24	16	.60	6	.318	.394	.412
Wampler,Samuel,Martinsvlle	R	20	18	52	6	2	0	0	8	5	5	7	0	17	0	0	0	0	0	.00	2	.115	.220	.154
Ward,Daryle,Bristol	R	20	48	161	43	6	0	5	64	17	30	19	4	33	0	1	1	5	1	.83	3	.267	.343	.398
Warner,Bryan,Burlington	R	20	63	224	64	11	2	8	103	29	35	10	1	35	5	0	1	11	6	.65	2	.286	.329	.460
Warner,Ken,Macon	A	20	82	241	54	9	0	1	66	28	12	27	0	55	1	6	0	3	7	.30	4	.224	.305	.274
Warner,Randy,Columbia	A	21	125	457	124	26	5	11	193	52	73	45	2	123	6	1	5	5	7	.42	4	.271	.341	.422
Warren,Leotis,Pirates	R	20	54	202	62	14	5	0	86	32	24	9	1	61	6	0	2	6	2	.75	4	.307	.352	.426
Waszgis,B.J.,Frederick	A	24	122	426	120	16	3	21	205	76	100	65	2	94	5	3	4	1	1	.86	3	.282	.380	.481
Wathan,Dusty,Mariners	R	21	35	86	18	2	0	1	23	14	7	11	0	13	3	0	0	0	0	.00	0	.209	.320	.267
Watkins,William,Winston-Sal	A	22	132	524	152	24	5	27	267	107	83	62	3	84	7	1	6	31	13	.70	8	.290	.369	.510
Watson,Kevin,Everett	A	22	49	197	52	11	6	3	84	20	34	21	2	55	1	0	4	5	4	.56	6	.264	.332	.426
Watson,Marty,Charlstn-Wv	A	20	120	433	102	24	6	16	186	53	67	33	0	149	2	3	1	10	5	.67	1	.236	.292	.430
Watts,Josh,Batavia	A	20	14	50	15	2	0	0	17	5	10	4	0	13	1	0	0	1	1	.67	1	.300	.357	.340
Watts,Richard,Welland	A	22	45	135	28	8	1	1	41	21	13	19	0	45	4	1	2	1	1	.50	3	.207	.319	.304
Weathersby,Leonard,Royals	R	20	26	60	14	3	1	0	19	5	8	7	0	15	1	0	1	2	2	.50	1	.233	.319	.317
Weaver,Colby,Idaho Falls	R	22	26	75	17	2	2	0	23	9	7	15	0	15	6	1	0	2	4	.33	2	.227	.396	.307
Welch,James,Royals	R	21	32	63	17	3	0	1	23	8	14	7	0	10	1	0	2	0	0	.00	0	.270	.342	.365
Welles,Robert,Jamestown	A	22	24	57	12	2	0	1	17	7	5	0	0	18	2	1	0	0	0	.00	1	.211	.237	.298
Wells,Forry,Bend	A	24	37	117	30	8	0	1	41	19	13	23	2	29	4	0	0	9	1	.90	2	.256	.396	.350
Wells,Mark,Bend	A	23	11	42	12	4	0	3	25	7	9	7	1	14	1	0	0	2	0	1.00	1	.286	.400	.595
Asheville	A	23	59	216	57	9	0	11	99	28	37	20	1	72	3	2	2	4	3	.57	2	.264	.332	.458
Wells,Beck,Charlstn-Wv	A	24	82	244	59	12	1	4	85	23	23	25	0	45	4	1	2	3	3	.50	4	.242	.320	.348
West,Thomas,Spokane	A	23	6	22	2	0	0	1	5	3	3	1	0	5	1	0	0	0	0	.00	0	.091	.167	.227
Springfield	A	23	61	189	42	8	0	4	62	20	30	30	2	51	4	0	0	1	1	.50	0	.222	.338	.328
Whatley,Edwin,Williamsprt	A	23	71	230	56	9	3	2	77	35	25	36	3	32	4	1	1	10	4	.71	6	.243	.354	.335
Wheeler,Ryan,Boise	A	31	63	11	0	0	0	11	5	7	16	0	15	3	5	1	3	1	.75	0	.175	.361	.175
White,Andre,Kinston	A	24	84	245	60	5	1	3	76	31	27	17	1	42	2	6	0	6	6	.50	5	.245	.299	.310
White,Chad,Osceola	A	24	94	286	66	8	1	1	79	29	29	25	2	43	6	7	2	8	9	.47	5	.231	.304	.276
White,Donnie,St. Lucie	A	23	118	463	132	17	9	5	182	73	44	38	2	97	5	9	4	31	9	.78	7	.285	.343	.393
White,Eric,Columbus	A	22	84	276	70	15	2	5	104	39	38	31	0	42	1	1	4	6	2	.75	4	.254	.327	.377
White,James,Batavia	A	22	57	10	0	0	0	10	7	2	5	0	15	3	2	0	1	2	.33	0	.175	.277	.175
White,Jason,Modesto	A	25	113	379	78	14	2	22	162	53	62	47	4	138	3	5	0	1	1	.50	5	.206	.298	.427
White,Kelly,Jamestown	A	23	54	188	43	9	4	2	66	28	28	19	1	36	0	1	1	3	2	.60	4	.229	.298	.351
White,Clay,Giants	R	22	10	24	6	1	0	0	7	2	3	1	0	5	0	0	0	0	1	.00	2	.250	.280	.292
White,Walt,Elmira	A	23	70	215	57	7	0	0	64	41	19	27	0	45	4	2	1	0	2	.00	4	.265	.356	.298
Whitehurst,Todd,Pittsfield	A	23	75	288	79	10	8	5	120	49	54	29	4	58	3	1	5	12	4	.75	5	.274	.342	.417
Whittaker,Jerry,White Sox	R	21	13	36	15	4	2	0	23	6	4	3	0	5	1	0	0	1	0	1.00	0	.417	.475	.639
Hickory	A	21	41	152	38	8	0	3	55	17	23	9	0	37	2	0	1	2	2	.50	4	.250	.299	.362
Wiegandt,Bryan,Spartanburg	A	22	45	141	29	9	0	1	41	16	8	9	0	30	5	3	0	1	0	1.00	5	.206	.277	.291
Weiser,Mike,Idaho Falls	R	22	6	22	9	0	0	0	9	3	4	3	0	3	1	0	0	0	0	1.00	1	.409	.480	.409
Macon	A	22	41	76	14	2	0	0	16	9	4	3	0	18	3	1	1	0	0	.00	1	.184	.241	.211
Wilkerson,Adrian,Brewers	R	20	50	199	58	4	1	0	64	32	19	14	0	41	1	0	1	13	8	.62	4	.291	.340	.322
Williams,Antonio,Braves	R	19	24	80	7	0	0	0	7	1	2	1	0	31	0	0	1	2	1	.67	1	.088	.098	.088
Williams,Curtis,Johnson Cty	R	22	32	79	15	2	0	0	17	11	3	14	0	25	1	1	0	5	5	.50	0	.190	.319	.215
Williams,Keith,San Jose	A	23	128	504	151	30	8	21	260	91	97	60	2	102	4	0	8	4	3	.57	8	.300	.373	.516
Williams,Ed,Savannah	A	23	92	305	69	10	1	1	84	30	20	32	0	74	1	1	4	2	7	.22	7	.226	.301	.275
Williams,George,W. Michigan	A	26	63	221	67	20	1	8	113	40	48	44	3	47	8	1	0	6	3	.67	3	.303	.436	.511
Williams,Glenn,Braves	R	17	24	89	18	2	0	2	26	8	7	9	0	32	0	0	1	4	1	.80	0	.202	.273	.292
Danville	R	17	24	79	20	2	0	1	25	11	9	8	0	20	3	4	0	2	4	.33	4	.253	.344	.316
Williams,Harold,Hickory	A	24	137	535	162	27	3	24	267	99	104	53	6	103	11	1	3	1	1	.50	12	.303	.375	.499
Williams,Drew,Helena	R	23	67	227	55	9	1	12	102	44	53	41	4	55	3	2	1	6	3	.67	3	.242	.364	.449
Williams,Juan,Durham	A	22	122	394	86	14	0	19	157	55	57	54	1	131	1	0	4	7	10	.41	2	.218	.311	.398
Williams,Mark,New Jersey	A	24	33	89	13	4	0	0	17	5	8	18	0	31	0	2	1	0	0	.00	2	.146	.287	.191

1994 Batting -- Single-A and Rookie Leagues

Player	Lg	A	G	AB	H	2B	3B	HR	TB	R	RBI	TBB	IBB	SO	HBP	SH	SF	SB	CS	SB%	GDP	Avg	OBP	SLG
Williams,Norman,Butte	R	21	62	248	68	8	3	0	82	49	27	12	1	33	4	3	2	16	8	.67	1	.274	.316	.331
Williams,Ray,Hudson Vall	A	21	34	87	13	2	1	0	17	15	6	4	0	24	0	2	0	8	2	.80	3	.149	.187	.195
Williamson,Joel,Augusta	A	25	35	76	19	3	0	1	25	9	8	9	0	20	2	2	0	1	1	.50	2	.250	.345	.329
Williamson,Matthew,Martinsvlle	R	22	8	34	12	0	0	1	15	7	5	4	0	9	1	0	0	8	0	1.00	2	.353	.436	.441
Batavia	A	22	46	170	45	8	0	0	53	26	16	13	1	43	4	3	1	5	3	.63		.265	.330	.312
Williamson,Tyler,Eugene	A	22	35	113	19	1	0	1	23	8	6	6	0	28	0	0	0	1	0	1.00	4	.168	.210	.204
Wills,Shawn,Spartanburg	A	25	20	67	11	1	1	1	17	6	4	3	0	18	0	1	0	3	0	1.00	1	.164	.200	.254
Wilson,Chris,Helena	R	24	55	129	31	2	0	1	36	25	14	15	0	27	5	4	0	14	5	.74	2	.240	.342	.279
Wilson,Craig,Pr. William	A	24	131	496	131	36	4	4	187	70	66	58	2	44	6	5	6	1	2	.33	16	.264	.345	.377
Wilson,Enrique,Columbus	A	19	133	512	143	28	12	10	225	82	72	44	5	34	6	0	4	21	13	.62	7	.279	.341	.439
Wilson,Leslie,Billings	R	24	49	124	36	2	1	3	49	22	19	19	0	22	5	0	0	5	1	.83	3	.290	.405	.395
Wilson,Preston,Columbia	A	20	131	474	108	17	4	14	175	55	58	20	0	135	3	0	3	13	10	.57	4	.228	.262	.369
Wilson,Todd,Everett	A	23	55	213	66	14	0	4	92	29	32	10	2	41	2	0	1	3	1	.75	4	.310	.345	.432
Wilson,Vance,Pittsfield	A	22	44	166	51	12	0	2	69	22	20	5	2	27	5	0	1	4	1	.80	1	.307	.343	.416
Wilson,Pookie,Brevard Cty	A	24	125	483	129	12	4	1	152	81	29	50	1	49	3	8	3	26	14	.65	4	.267	.338	.315
Wingate,Ervan,Bakersfield	A	21	63	176	44	8	2	3	65	31	15	23	0	39	2	4	3	1	4	.20	5	.250	.338	.369
Winget,Jeremy,Ogden	R	22	71	277	103	22	4	6	151	66	74	41	2	48	2	0	6	16	14	.53	1	.372	.448	.545
Winston,Todd,Osceola	A	25	50	84	16	2	0	1	21	10	6	15	1	19	1	3	0	2	5	.29	1	.190	.320	.250
Winterlee,Scott,Kingsport	R	24	3	11	6	1	1	0	9	4	2	0	0	1	0	0	0	0	0	.00	1	.545	.545	.818
Mets	R	24	7	21	7	1	0	1	11	2	5	2	0	2	0	0	0	1	0	1.00	0	.333	.391	.524
Wipf,Mark,Columbia	A	22	99	358	91	25	8	9	159	38	49	23	5	92	3	1	1	14	10	.58	6	.254	.304	.444
Wiseley,Michael,Lakeland	A	24	126	467	130	20	5	0	160	69	36	49	1	60	7	1	4	14	11	.56	10	.278	.353	.343
Witt,Kevin,Medicne Hat	R	19	60	243	62	10	4	7	101	37	36	15	0	52	1	1	1	4	1	.80	3	.255	.300	.416
Wittig,Paul,Vero Beach	A	21	40	100	25	3	1	1	33	8	16	7	0	22	2	2	0	0	0	.00	2	.250	.312	.330
Wojnarowicz,Corey,Lethbridge	R	24	43	124	31	4	3	1	44	19	11	24	0	25	0	0	0	3	3	.50	3	.250	.372	.355
Wolff,Michael,Albany	A	22	55	185	54	11	0	1	68	26	19	12	0	23	9	1	2	5	1	.83	5	.292	.361	.368
Wood,Tony,Braves	R	22	37	120	24	1	0	0	25	8	8	11	0	17	2	1	0	6	1	.86	5	.200	.278	.208
Woodridge,Richard,Springfield	A	24	96	261	65	9	0	2	80	33	33	34	0	30	2	6	3	14	9	.61	3	.249	.337	.307
Woods,Ken,San Jose	A	24	90	336	100	18	3	6	142	58	49	45	0	43	4	3	3	15	7	.68	3	.298	.384	.423
Wooten,William,Fayetteville	A	22	121	439	118	25	1	3	154	45	61	27	0	84	11	3	4	1	3	.25	11	.269	.324	.351
Wright,Ronald,Braves	R	19	45	169	29	9	0	1	41	10	16	10	0	21	0	0	0	1	0	1.00	3	.172	.218	.243
Wright,Terry,Butte	R	24	57	226	76	8	2	0	88	46	21	27	1	16	1	3	1	15	8	.65	1	.336	.408	.389
Wuerch,Jason,San Bernrdo	A	23	100	325	75	10	1	1	90	38	25	40	1	71	3	2	1	7	6	.54	7	.231	.320	.277
Wyngarden,Brett,Lakeland	A	24	11	23	7	0	0	1	10	4	4	3	0	7	1	0	0	1	0	1.00	0	.304	.407	.435
Fayetteville	A	24	22	62	14	2	0	1	19	10	3	3	1	12	3	1	0	1	0	1.00	1	.226	.294	.306
Yard,Bruce,Bakersfield	A	23	27	81	18	2	0	1	23	7	7	10	1	8	0	2	0	2	1	.67	3	.222	.308	.284
Vero Beach	A	23	43	135	35	7	0	1	45	13	10	14	0	12	1	2	2	0	0	.00	2	.259	.329	.333
Yedo,Carlos,Oneonta	A	21	38	122	41	11	2	4	68	18	22	17	2	34	2	0	0	0	0	.00	2	.336	.426	.557
Yeske,Kyle,Albany	A	25	79	254	63	12	2	1	82	30	21	28	0	74	5	0	3	5	1	.83	3	.248	.332	.323
Young,Delwyn,Appleton	A	31	14	36	11	2	1	1	18	7	5	5	0	4	1	0	0	1	0	1.00	1	.306	.405	.500
Young,Kevin,Boise	A	23	63	240	56	7	2	2	73	29	30	15	0	35	7	1	3	8	4	.67	5	.233	.294	.304
Yselonia,John,Augusta	A	23	101	358	88	20	2	5	127	30	41	28	2	66	2	1	0	11	2	.85	3	.246	.304	.355
Zahner,Kevin,Vero Beach	A	22	46	123	32	4	0	0	36	11	9	5	1	13	0	2	2	0	0	.00	2	.260	.285	.293
Zaletel,Brian,Clinton	A	24	87	330	81	17	2	12	138	39	57	18	1	85	3	1	1	2	2	.50	2	.245	.290	.418
Zambrano,Jose,Lynchburg	A	24	70	247	69	12	1	7	104	36	31	29	0	61	3	3	2	1	1	.50	4	.279	.359	.421
Zambrano,Victor,Yankees	R	20	50	175	36	5	1	0	43	23	16	13	0	43	1	2	1	6	2	.75	3	.206	.263	.246
Zanolla,Daniel,Ogden	R	24	27	76	27	7	2	1	41	17	14	6	0	10	1	2	2	2	2	.50	0	.355	.400	.539
Zellers,Kevin,Yakima	A	24	51	183	37	7	2	3	57	25	27	22	0	48	2	2	2	9	0	1.00	5	.202	.292	.311
Zerpa,Mauro,White Sox	R	20	30	87	22	2	0	0	28	6	7	6	0	12	2	2	0	3	0	1.00	1	.253	.316	.322
Zonca,Chris,Martinsvlle	R	23	23	67	14	3	0	1	20	5	8	11	1	16	2	0	0	0	0	.00	3	.209	.338	.299
Zorrilla,Julio,Mets	R	NA	43	162	46	5	1	0	53	37	10	22	0	19	3	4	1	5	4	.56	3	.284	.378	.327
Zorrilla,Miguel,Twins	R	20	23	69	10	3	0	0	13	8	4	4	0	25	2	0	0	2	0	1.00	1	.145	.213	.188
Zuleta,Julio,Huntington	R	20	6	15	1	0	0	0	1	0	2	4	0	4	0	0	0	0	0	.00	1	.067	.263	.067
Cubs	R	20	30	100	31	0	0	0	32	11	8	8	0	18	2	0	0	5	1	.83	0	.310	.373	.320
Zuniga,David,Columbia	A	24	77	182	44	1	3	0	51	35	17	37	0	40	2	8	0	7	9	.44	2	.242	.376	.280
Zwisler,Joshua,Beloit	A	20	18	57	12	3	0	0	15	3	4	7	0	8	0	0	0	2	1	.67	0	.211	.297	.263
Helena	R	20	63	228	73	15	0	6	106	47	43	21	3	23	0	1	2	7	4	.64	4	.320	.375	.465

1994 Pitching -- Single-A and Rookie Leagues

Player	Lg	A	G	GS	CG	GF	IP	BFP	H	R	ER	HR	SH	SF	HB	TBB	IBB	SO	WP	Bk	W	L	Pct.	ShO	Sv	ERA
Abramavicius,Jason,Augusta	A	25	4	0	0	0	8	34	6	4	0	0	1	0	0	4	1	9	0	0	1	0	1.000	0	0	0.00
Salem	A	25	33	13	0	4	109.1	462	103	51	39	9	6	4	5	32	1	60	7	0	5	8	.385	0	0	3.21
Abreu,Jose,Giants	R	20	20	0	0	19	28	117	22	4	4	0	2	0	1	11	1	36	2	0	6	0	1.000	0	7	1.29
Abreu,Winston,Braves	R	18	13	11	0	1	57.1	257	57	35	26	2	0	5	4	24	0	53	3	4	0	8	.000	0	0	4.08
Adachi,Tomojiro,Bristol	R	20	19	0	0	7	36	157	37	20	18	7	2	2	1	15	0	24	4	1	2	3	.400	0	0	4.50
Adair,Scott,Mets	R	19	12	12	2	0	70	297	68	32	17	0	2	0	4	21	0	36	2	2	6	3	.667	1	0	2.19
Adam,Justin,Royals	R	20	4	0	0	0	5.1	29	6	8	8	1	0	0	1	5	0	4	1	0	0	1	.000	0	0	13.50
Adams,Terry,Daytona	A	22	39	7	0	21	84.1	383	87	47	41	5	4	2	4	46	3	64	8	1	9	10	.474	0	7	4.38
Adkins,Rob,St. Cathrns	A	23	4	0	0	0	5.1	30	4	8	7	0	1	0	0	12	0	2	1	0	0	0	.000	0	0	11.81
Adkins,Tim,Hagerstown	A	21	35	0	0	7	70.2	299	64	37	29	2	6	4	2	33	1	75	4	0	3	3	.500	0	2	3.69
Agostinelli,Peter,Clearwater	A	26	64	0	0	23	70.1	301	79	38	35	3	8	2	1	14	6	34	1	0	2	3	.400	0	5	4.48
Agosto,Stevenson,Angels	R	19	13	1	0	7	26.1	125	27	18	13	1	3	1	3	14	0	26	6	1	2	0	.000	0	0	4.44
Agramonte,Freddy,Great Falls	R	21	15	8	0	2	52	259	60	49	38	4	2	6	8	38	0	48	7	2	2	6	.250	0	1	6.58
Aguirre,Jose,Lake Elsino	A	21	3	0	0	1	2.2	13	3	1	1	0	1	0	0	2	0	1	0	1	0	0	.000	0	0	3.38
Cedar Rapds	A	21	38	0	0	12	73	310	54	25	22	2	3	1	3	40	4	82	11	0	4	2	.667	0	5	2.71
Alexander,Eric,Savannah	A	24	25	18	0	0	104.2	453	124	62	53	18	5	2	6	27	0	73	3	0	3	10	.231	0	0	4.56
Alexis,Julio,Cardinals	R	21	13	5	0	1	46	205	62	26	19	0	0	1	1	7	0	34	1	1	4	4	.500	0	0	3.72
Alfonseca,Antonio,Kane County	A	22	32	9	0	7	86.1	361	78	41	39	5	2	3	2	21	1	74	14	0	6	5	.545	0	0	4.07
Alger,Kevin,Spartanburg	A	25	1	0	0	0	2	8	1	1	1	0	0	0	0	0	0	0	0	0	0	0	.000	0	0	4.50
Clearwater	A	25	23	1	0	5	53	233	46	25	21	5	1	1	3	30	3	38	0	1	3	2	.600	0	0	3.57
Allen,Cedric,Princeton	R	23	13	10	1	2	73	284	48	18	11	2	3	2	4	17	0	62	1	2	6	1	.857	1	1	1.36
Allen,Damon,Salem	A	31	4	0	0	2	3.2	29	9	10	8	2	0	0	2	5	0	3	0	0	0	0	.000	0	0	19.64
Allen,Ron,Lynchburg	A	22	9	0	0	6	8	43	13	11	9	3	0	1	0	4	0	4	2	0	1	0	1.000	0	0	10.13
Almanzar,Carlos,Medicne Hat	R	21	14	14	0	0	84.2	351	82	38	27	2	7	1	1	19	0	77	3	2	7	4	.636	0	0	2.87
Altman,Christopher,Clinton	A	24	9	4	0	1	30.1	150	21	24	22	1	1	2	3	38	0	30	19	0	1	3	.250	0	0	6.53
Giants	R	24	10	0	0	2	8.2	52	9	11	8	0	0		4	13	0	9	3	0	2	2	.500	0	0	8.31
Alvarado,Luis,Elizabethtn	R	20	20	0	0	8	31.1	143	40	20	16	5	3	2	0	10	1	26	2	0	1	2	.333	0	0	4.60
Alvarez,Ivan,San Jose	A	25	21	1	0	5	57	254	67	42	40	7	1	2	4	27	0	46	5	0	4	1	.800	0	0	6.32
Ambrose,John,White Sox	R	20	11	10	1	0	46.2	195	34	21	19	4	1	2	6	24	0	43	4	3	1	2	.333	0	0	3.66
Hickory	A	20	3	1	0	1	12.2	58	16	11	10	1	0	0	0	6	0	7	0	0	1	1	.500	0	0	7.11
Aminoff,Matthew,Bellingham	A	23	9	0	0	2	13.2	65	14	11	10	3	1	1	0	10	2	12	3	0	0	1	.000	0	0	6.59
Appleton	A	23	10	1	0	3	27	123	25	15	13	2	3	0	4	17	0	18	0	1	1	0	1.000	0	0	4.33
Amos,Chad,Sarasota	A	23	6	0	0	3	8	33	9	2	2	1	2	0	0	2	0	3	0	0	1	1	.500	0	0	2.25
Lynchburg	A	23	37	0	0	22	55.2	229	44	18	15	7	2	0	3	17	0	60	2	1	5	3	.625	0	6	2.43
Andersen,Mark,Marlins	R	23	3	0	0	2	5.1	24	2	0	0	0	0	0	1	2	0	5	1	0	0	0	.000	0	0	0.00
Kane County	A	23	15	0	0	5	19	90	17	13	7	1	1	1	1	12	1	13	6	0	1	1	.500	0	0	3.32
Anderson,Eric,Royals	R	20	7	2	0	1	24	85	12	0	0	0	0	1	0	5	0	21	3	1	3	0	1.000	0	0	0.00
Anderson,Eric,Elizabethtn	R	22	17	3	0	7	28	135	36	20	14	1	1	0	2	20	0	25	6	0	3	3	.500	0	0	4.50
Anderson,James,Pirates	R	19	10	10	0	0	56.1	230	35	21	10	1	2	1	2	27	0	66	5	1	5	1	.833	0	0	1.60
Anderson,John,Auburn	A	21	25	1	0	8	55.2	256	60	37	24	4	4	2	4	20	2	46	5	0	4	2	.667	0	3	3.88
Anderson,Matt,Albany	A	24	13	10	0	0	64.1	255	45	19	17	1	1	0	2	23	0	60	3	1	7	2	.778	0	0	2.38
Frederick	A	24	9	9	0	0	44.1	212	47	38	30	4	0	5	5	27	1	41	3	0	3	4	.429	0	0	6.09
Anderson,Mike,Charlotte	A	23	32	0	0	8	57.2	261	63	34	31	4	3	2	3	32	0	31	5	0	1	3	.250	0	0	4.84
Anderson,Tom,Osceola	A	25	20	0	0	12	20.1	110	24	23	20	1	3	0	3	22	2	25	5	1	1	1	.500	0	0	8.85
Anderson,Bill,Rancho Cuca	A	23	22	2	0	5	62.1	265	64	36	31	2	2	0	3	24	0	70	2	4	7	0	1.000	0	0	4.48
Anez,Maycoll,White Sox	R	18	2	0	0	2	2	16	7	7	7	0	0	0	0	3	0	1	0	0	0	0	.000	0	0	31.50
Angel,Jason,Winston-Sal	A	23	16	1	1	3	40.2	182	42	27	24	2	1	3	1	24	1	19	4	0	0	3	.000	0	0	5.31
Antolick,Jeff,Tampa	A	24	28	14	2	1	103.1	436	93	51	42	2	5	1	1	43	3	83	11	0	9	6	.600	0	0	3.66
Antonini,Adrian,Batavia	A	22	20	0	0	5	30.1	140	38	19	16	1	0	0	1	12	0	24	5	0	3	0	1.000	0	0	4.75
Apana,Matthew,Riverside	A	24	26	26	3	0	165.1	694	142	63	52	8	5	3	4	70	0	137	5	0	14	4	.778	3	0	2.83
Aquino,Julio,Great Falls	R	22	16	12	0	2	81.1	346	105	46	41	3	0	1	2	9	0	55	6	1	3	4	.429	0	0	4.54
Arellano,Carlos,Burlington	R	20	16	5	2	1	55.1	236	39	18	16	0	2	0	1	30	0	29	7	1	5	1	.833	1	0	2.60
Arffa,Steven,Pittsfield	A	22	14	14	1	0	88.1	372	91	46	35	5	1	5	4	13	1	56	4	1	6	5	.545	0	0	3.57
Arguto,Samuel,Fayettevlle	A	24	47	0	0	24	66.1	315	72	54	45	13	4	8	1	44	5	45	7	2	1	7	.125	0	2	6.11
Arias,Alfredo,St. Cathrns	A	22	17	1	0	10	50.2	212	41	24	21	3	0	3	3	15	0	39	12	4	1	2	.333	0	0	3.73
Arias,Wagner,Beloit	A	20	26	25	4	0	166.1	702	135	76	66	20	1	5	6	66	2	135	15	4	11	8	.579	1	0	3.57
Armendariz,Jesse,Williamsprt	A	23	15	2	0	6	24.1	118	32	24	19	2	0	0	3	13	0	15	4	0	1	1	.500	0	0	7.03
Arnold,Jim,Durham	A	21	25	25	0	0	145	656	144	96	75	26	3	1	14	79	4	91	8	4	7	7	.500	0	0	4.66
Arrandale,Matthew,Savannah	A	24	19	19	5	0	133.1	559	112	36	26	2	1	2	4	21	1	121	3	0	15	3	.833	1	0	1.76
St. Pete	A	24	9	9	0	0	59	244	65	26	22	0	4	2	1	11	0	29	2	1	3	4	.429	0	0	3.36
Arroyo,Luis,Springfield	A	21	16	16	1	0	99.2	434	86	50	38	8	5	2	1	47	4	76	4	4	8	2	.800	0	0	3.43
Rancho Cuca	A	21	10	10	0	0	54.1	243	62	33	29	6	1	1	3	30	0	34	2	0	3	4	.429	0	0	4.80
Asher,Ray,Red Sox	R	20	7	0	0	2	8.2	34	5	2	0	0	1	1	1	1	0	7	0	0	0	0	.000	0	0	0.00
Aswegan,Cecil,Butte	R	22	26	1	0	15	35.1	191	55	56	52	4	3	5	3	35	2	38	5	2	1	6	.143	0	0	13.25
Atkinson,Neil,Rockford	A	24	51	0	0	19	74.1	295	64	21	21	1	3	4	1	16	2	82	6	1	7	1	.875	0	5	2.54
Atwater,Joseph,Pittsfield	A	20	15	15	3	0	99	437	113	60	47	4	1	2	4	27	2	58	10	1	4	9	.308	0	0	4.27
Augustine,Rob,High Desert	A	24	28	8	1	10	75	359	80	65	53	5	3	2	4	61	2	60	12	2	5	4	.556	0	0	6.36
Kinston	A	24	6	0	0	3	5	31	5	4	3	0	0	0	2	8	0	8	2	0	0	0	.000	0	0	5.40
Ayala,Fernando,Great Falls	R	23	20	1	0	13	30.2	145	39	23	18	4	1	2	4	14	0	25	1	3	0	2	.000	0	0	5.28
Aybar,Manuel,Cardinals	R	20	13	13	1	0	72.1	295	69	25	17	0	2	4	4	9	0	79	4	3	6	1	.857	0	0	2.12
Bailey,Mike,South Bend	A	24	29	0	0	21	54.2	225	49	26	21	5	2	1	1	18	1	46	3	1	4	5	.444	0	7	3.46
Bajda,Michael,Jamestown	A	21	21	0	0	8	40	198	43	32	24	4	0	3	6	32	0	28	3	4	1	3	.250	0	0	5.40
Baker,Derek,Pittsfield	A	22	26	0	0	20	39.2	167	28	7	7	0	2	1	0	28	1	34	3	0	1	0	1.000	0	11	1.59
Baker,Donald,Ogden	R	NA	4	0	0	0	7.2	39	15	10	10	1	1	1	2	9	0	5	1	0	0	0	.000	0	0	11.74
Baker,Jared,Rancho Cuca	A	24	27	27	1	0	141.2	650	134	86	60	11	2	4	20	75	3	129	8	1	9	10	.474	0	0	3.81
Baker,Jason,Vermont	A	20	13	13	0	0	61.2	279	55	44	33	4	0	2	5	40	0	21	20	0	6	5	.545	0	0	4.82
Balbuena,Roberto,Cubs	R	22	14	6	0	5	38.2	177	39	18	16	0	1	3	4	17	2	31	0	1	3	5	.375	0	2	3.72

1994 Pitching -- Single-A and Rookie Leagues

Player	Lg	A	G	GS	CG	GF	IP	BFP	H	R	ER	HR	SH	SF	HB	TBB	IBB	SO	WP	Bk	W	L	Pct.	ShO	Sv	ERA
Baldwin,Scott,W. Michigan	A	25	25	20	0	2	112.1	491	90	55	43	3	6	6	3	62	0	112	13	6	7	8	.467	0	1	3.45
Baldwin,William,White Sox	R	24	1	0	0	1	1	5	1	1	1	0	0	0	1	0	0	1	0	0	0	0	.000	0	0	9.00
Ballance,Dale,Lethbridge	R	22	15	14	0	0	93.1	412	100	70	48	7	2	4	4	34	0	57	10	1	5	6	.455	0	0	4.63
Banks,Jim,Modesto	A	25	42	0	0	27	57	237	38	17	15	1	2	3	0	29	2	76	4	3	3	1	.750	0	15	2.37
Barbao,Joe,Batavia	A	23	22	0	0	18	31.1	131	35	12	9	0	3	0	0	4	2	26	0	0	2	2	.500	0	6	2.59
Barker,Jeffrey,Jamestown	A	21	13	13	0	0	63.2	275	65	33	28	1	3	4	5	14	0	62	2	2	3	3	.500	0	0	3.96
Barker,Richard,Huntington	R	22	17	0	0	6	39.1	187	36	35	26	3	2	2	7	25	0	22	2	3	2	4	.333	0	0	5.95
Barkley,Brian,Red Sox	R	19	4	3	0	0	18.2	71	11	7	2	1	1	0	0	4	0	14	2	1	0	0	.000	0	0	0.96
Barksdale,Joe,Red Sox	R	21	15	1	0	5	27.1	144	34	32	22	0	2	1	6	16	0	14	5	1	0	1	.000	0	0	7.24
Barnes,Keith,Asheville	A	20	27	24	0	1	146.1	660	168	95	87	10	7	7	10	61	1	96	15	1	8	9	.471	0	2	5.35
Barnes,John,Rancho Cuca	A	22	2	2	0	0	5.1	28	10	7	6	0	1	0	0	2	0	5	1	0	0	0	.000	0	0	10.13
Barnes,Larry,Brewers	R	18	9	8	0	0	22.2	122	29	32	23	3	0	1	1	19	0	35	14	0	0	5	.000	0	0	9.13
Barnes,Monte,Yankees	R	21	11	0	0	7	19	90	25	16	8	1	2	1	1	3	0	7	0	2	0	1	.000	0	0	3.79
Baron,Jim,Springfield	A	21	25	23	0	0	105.2	515	121	83	75	14	2	3	7	76	2	73	14	3	6	6	.500	0	0	6.39
Barrett,Mark,Spokane	A	23	19	1	0	10	26.2	118	17	13	10	1	0	0	1	20	0	31	2	0	0	1	.000	0	0	3.38
Barrick,Troy,Savannah	A	23	4	0	0	4	5	21	2	1	1	0	1	0	1	4	0	4	0	0	0	1	.000	0	2	1.80
New Jersey	A	22	26	1	0	20	29	148	35	19	16	0	5	0	3	22	0	25	3	0	2	3	.400	0	13	4.97
Barrios,Manuel,Quad City	A	20	43	0	0	11	65	295	73	44	43	4	5	2	7	23	4	63	8	2	0	6	.000	0	4	5.95
Barylak,Alex,Williamsprt	A	22	25	0	0	18	30	140	39	26	23	3	0	0	3	13	0	22	1	0	0	1	.000	0	5	6.90
Bates,Shawn,Orioles	R	20	15	0	0	11	31.2	136	23	15	11	1	1	1	2	16	0	31	4	1	2	1	.667	0	3	3.13
Bluefield	R	20	4	0	0	2	6	32	12	7	6	1	0	1	0	4	1	6	1	1	0	0	.000	0	0	9.00
Batista,Mario,Pirates	R	20	4	3	0	0	20.2	83	14	6	5	0	0	0	1	8	0	17	1	1	1	0	1.000	0	0	2.18
Battaglia,Charles,Rangers	R	20	10	6	0	2	31	136	30	14	10	3	2	1	1	7	0	17	3	3	2	2	.500	0	0	2.90
Battles,Robert,Savannah	A	23	26	22	0	2	124.1	523	120	71	58	11	7	3	3	25	2	78	0	3	5	8	.385	0	0	4.20
Bawlson,Jeffrey,Angels	R	21	3	1	0	1	7.1	39	14	10	8	0	0	0	0	5	0	5	0	0	0	1	.000	0	0	9.82
Baxter,Herb,Vero Beach	A	23	45	0	0	20	56.1	242	45	26	24	2	0	2	3	35	1	48	4	4	1	2	.333	0	0	3.83
Bearden,Brent,St. Cathrns	A	23	18	0	0	11	36.2	147	29	20	15	3	2	2	2	7	0	42	4	0	3	1	.750	0	2	3.68
Beashore,Gary,Peoria	A	24	9	0	0	1	21.2	97	21	10	10	1	3	2	2	11	0	10	5	0	1	0	1.000	0	0	4.15
Beaumont,Matthew,Boise	A	22	12	10	0	0	64	268	52	27	25	2	4	2	7	22	1	77	3	0	3	3	.500	0	0	3.52
Becerra,Juan,Rangers	R	19	18	0	0	9	25.2	112	20	15	9	1	4	0	2	13	1	15	1	0	3	1	.750	0	2	3.16
Beck,Christopher,Bellingham	A	23	15	11	0	1	59.1	268	66	46	36	3	3	2	2	26	1	57	10	2	2	4	.333	0	0	5.46
Beck,Greg,Helena	R	22	18	2	0	11	43.2	191	42	26	21	4	3	2	2	20	1	41	3	0	4	3	.571	0	4	4.33
Beck,Johnny,Martinsvlle	R	22	22	0	0	10	33.1	145	38	17	15	4	1	0	0	14	1	23	4	0	3	1	.750	0	2	4.05
Becker,Kevin,Lynchburg	A	22	6	0	0	2	9.1	52	17	13	8	1	1	0	2	4	0	11	2	1	0	0	.000	0	0	7.71
Utica	A	22	5	1	0	0	7.2	38	9	4	4	0	1	0	0	4	0	6	1	0	0	1	.000	0	0	4.70
Becker,Tom,Yankees	R	20	7	7	0	0	31.2	147	26	24	10	0	1	0	0	23	0	29	5	0	1	3	.250	0	0	2.84
Beddinger,Douglas,Twins	R	20	14	10	1	2	60.1	262	60	27	21	1	0	1	3	21	0	45	13	4	0	6	.000	0	0	3.13
Beebe,Hans,Mets	R	20	13	0	0	11	27.2	113	26	11	9	2	0	1	0	7	0	22	0	0	1	0	1.000	0	4	2.93
Beech,Lucas,Batavia	A	23	4	3	0	1	18.2	80	9	4	4	0	1	0	4	12	0	27	0	0	2	1	.667	0	0	1.93
Spartanburg	A	23	10	10	4	0	69.2	274	51	23	20	7	0	1	4	23	0	83	5	3	4	4	.500	1	0	2.58
Beltran,Alonso,Dunedin	A	23	7	5	0	0	25.1	109	22	13	13	4	0	2	1	10	0	10	1	0	2	1	.667	0	0	4.62
Bennett,Bob,W. Michigan	A	24	6	4	0	1	24.2	103	23	8	6	1	2	0	2	6	0	23	0	0	2	0	.000	0	1	2.19
Modesto	A	24	20	10	0	4	80.2	332	75	31	27	2	1	0	1	25	0	71	5	1	8	2	.800	0	0	3.01
Bennett,Shayne,Sarasota	A	23	15	8	0	4	48.1	216	46	31	24	1	2	1	3	27	0	28	1	1	1	6	.143	0	3	4.47
Bennett,Ricky,South Bend	A	25	4	0	0	2	8	38	14	4	4	0	0	0	0	2	0	2	0	0	0	0	.000	0	1	4.50
Benny,Peter,Brewers	R	19	16	2	0	4	58	263	59	35	22	3	2	1	4	30	1	65	9	0	5	3	.625	0	3	3.41
Benson,Jeremy,Oneonta	A	22	18	1	0	7	32	135	23	13	7	0	3	1	1	12	1	36	2	0	0	1	.000	0	3	1.97
Benz,Jacob,Vermont	A	23	28	0	0	12	46	188	24	11	8	1	1	2	4	19	3	36	1	0	4	1	.800	0	3	1.57
Berlin,Mike,Fayettevlle	A	24	6	1	0	1	13.1	47	8	1	0	0	0	0	2	2	0	9	2	0	2	0	1.000	0	1	0.00
Lakeland	A	24	27	5	0	8	81.2	350	80	35	29	4	6	0	5	34	2	55	8	0	6	5	.545	0	1	3.20
Bernal,Manuel,Royals	R	21	19	0	0	13	28.1	125	25	13	4	0	1	1	1	11	2	14	2	0	4	3	.571	0	3	1.27
Berry,Jason,Yankees	R	21	2	0	0	1	4	14	3	1	1	0	0	0	0	0	0	5	0	0	1	0	1.000	0	0	2.25
Oneonta	A	21	13	0	0	3	23.1	104	21	16	12	1	0	1	1	9	0	27	1	1	2	1	.333	0	1	4.63
Greensboro	A	21	4	0	0	3	5.1	24	5	0	0	0	0	0	0	2	1	2	0	0	0	0	.000	0	2	0.00
Bettencourt,Justin,Bristol	R	21	11	9	0	0	44	190	39	28	20	3	3	1	1	25	0	39	5	1	2	4	.333	0	0	4.09
Beverlin,Jason,W. Michigan	A	21	17	1	0	5	41	168	32	12	8	0	1	0	2	14	0	48	3	4	3	2	.600	0	1	1.76
Bieniasz,Derek,Mariners	R	21	11	11	0	0	51.2	201	42	15	8	0	2	2	4	9	0	55	2	3	3	3	.500	0	0	1.39
Bigham,Dave,Fort Myers	A	24	53	1	0	26	67.1	306	62	30	26	5	5	2	3	39	3	53	4	0	6	2	.750	0	6	3.48
Billingsley,Marvin,Osceola	A	22	36	1	0	11	45.1	254	52	53	43	1	0	3	11	55	2	28	12	2	0	3	.000	0	0	8.54
Binversie,Brian,Oneonta	A	22	3	0	0	1	3	13	2	0	0	0	0	0	0	0	0	2	1	0	0	0	.000	0	0	0.00
Birsner,Roark,Cubs	R	19	9	6	1	2	39	165	30	14	10	1	1	1	3	16	1	40	2	0	3	2	.600	0	0	2.31
Daytona	A	19	2	2	0	0	6.2	36	10	9	9	0	1	0	2	7	0	4	2	0	0	2	.000	0	0	12.15
Black,David,San Bernrdo	A	26	14	0	0	6	25.2	110	27	20	18	1	1	1	0	9	0	9	1	2	0	0	.000	0	0	6.31
Black,Jayson,Red Sox	R	19	16	0	0	5	32.2	145	37	18	15	0	1	3	0	13	0	15	2	1	3	1	.750	0	0	4.13
Blackwell,Richard,Welland	A	22	6	0	0	1	12.1	55	14	8	4	1	0	0	0	1	0	13	0	0	1	1	.500	0	0	2.92
Blair,Donnie,Stockton	A	23	14	14	0	0	81.2	330	85	36	31	8	4	2	1	9	2	47	0	1	5	4	.556	0	0	3.42
Blais,Mike,Lynchburg	A	25	10	0	6	77.1	354	99	66	57	12	2	2	1	18	0	46	3	1	1	6	.143	0	1	6.63
Blake,Todd,Savannah	A	24	62	0	0	19	69.2	302	67	34	29	5	3	4	2	27	4	61	6	0	3	5	.375	0	2	3.75
Blanco,Alberto,Quad City	A	19	27	19	0	3	117	520	118	70	61	13	4	4	5	66	0	101	11	3	7	9	.438	0	0	4.69
Blanco,Rosmel,Cubs	R	21	8	7	0	0	28	146	38	27	19	0	1	0	3	21	0	21	3	1	0	0	.000	0	0	6.11
Bland,Nathan,Great Falls	R	20	2	1	0	1	9.1	37	6	2	1	0	1	0	1	3	0	12	1	0	0	0	.000	0	0	0.96
Bakersfield	A	20	12	9	0	0	50.1	228	58	31	30	10	3	0	1	27	0	19	2	1	2	6	.250	0	0	5.36
Blazier,Ronald,Clearwater	A	23	29	29	0	0	173.1	715	177	73	65	15	4	6	9	36	1	120	2	1	13	5	.722	0	0	3.38
Bledsoe,Randy,New Jersey	A	23	9	2	0	3	20.2	94	24	19	17	1	2	0	1	11	0	15	4	0	0	2	.000	0	0	7.40
Bluma,James,Eugene	A	23	26	0	0	23	36.1	133	19	5	4	0	1	1	0	6	0	35	0	0	2	1	.667	0	12	0.99
Wilmington	A	23	7	0	0	7	9.2	34	7	2	1	0	0	0	0	0	0	5	0	0	4	0	1.000	0	2	0.93
Blyleven,Todd,Boise	A	22	12	5	0	3	45.2	197	43	14	11	2	2	1	4	14	0	53	5	0	4	2	.667	0	0	2.17

313

1994 Pitching -- Single-A and Rookie Leagues

Player	Lg	A	G	GS	CG	GF	IP	BFP	H	R	ER	HR	SH	SF	HB	TBB	IBB	SO	WP	Bk	W	L	Pct.	ShO	Sv	ERA
Lake Elsino	A	22	8	6	0	0	42.1	182	38	20	14	4	0	4	2	17	0	33	2	0	1	2	.333	0	0	2.98
Bobbitt,Greg,Peoria	A	24	19	19	2	0	114.1	503	126	63	53	6	3	5	10	34	0	82	5	3	8	7	.533	1	0	4.17
Daytona	A	24	9	4	0	3	26.1	111	27	14	13	2	0	0	1	7	0	22	1	0	1	2	.333	0	0	4.44
Bock,Jeffrey,Durham	A	24	39	11	1	7	101.2	461	123	83	66	21	3	4	5	34	4	68	7	1	4	8	.333	1	1	5.84
Bogle,Sean,Williamsprt	A	21	15	6	0	1	33.2	165	34	31	28	1	0	1	3	33	0	23	4	2	1	1	.500	0	0	7.49
Bogott,Kurtiss,Red Sox	R	22	3	2	0	0	13.2	49	7	1	1	0	0	0	1	3	0	12	2	0	1	0	1.000	0	0	0.66
Lynchburg	A	22	6	6	0	0	26.1	127	32	23	18	1	1	1	1	14	0	14	2	0	2	3	.400	0	0	6.15
Bojan,Tim,W. Michigan	A	25	38	5	0	13	82.1	361	56	44	30	4	4	2	6	60	0	80	2	2	7	3	.700	0	3	3.28
Bonanno,Robert,Boise	A	24	6	6	0	0	39.2	155	23	11	6	1	0	0	2	10	0	41	2	0	5	0	1.000	0	0	1.36
Cedar Rapids	A	24	9	9	0	0	51	219	56	25	25	4	1	2	4	16	1	40	6	1	3	2	.600	0	0	4.41
Bonilla,Welnis,Red Sox	R	19	25	0	0	24	39.2	159	32	6	5	0	0	1	0	11	0	24	3	1	5	0	1.000	0	14	1.13
Bourgeois,Steven,Clinton	A	22	20	20	0	0	106.1	464	97	57	43	16	4	2	7	54	0	88	11	0	8	5	.615	0	3	3.64
San Jose	A	22	7	7	0	0	36.2	167	40	22	22	4	1	1	1	22	0	27	5	0	4	0	1.000	0	0	5.40
Bovee,Mike,Wilmington	A	21	28	26	0	0	169.2	675	149	58	50	10	4	3	4	32	0	154	8	1	13	4	.765	0	0	2.65
Bowen,Mitchel,Brevard Cty	A	22	35	1	0	13	72	305	61	31	24	5	5	2	0	31	2	52	4	0	7	3	.700	0	0	3.00
Bowers,Shane,Fort Wayne	A	23	27	11	1	9	81.2	333	76	32	30	3	5	1	6	18	1	72	8	0	6	4	.600	0	3	3.31
Fort Myers	A	23	13	0	0	5	17.2	85	28	7	7	1	0	0	0	4	0	19	2	0	0	0	.000	0	0	3.57
Bowie,Micah,Braves	R	20	6	5	0	1	29.2	124	27	14	10	1	0	2	1	5	0	35	1	0	3	0	.000	0	0	3.03
Danville	R	20	7	5	0	0	32.2	141	28	16	13	4	2	3	3	13	1	38	2	0	3	1	.750	0	0	3.58
Bowman,Paul,Kingsport	R	22	10	3	0	3	16.2	85	24	23	18	2	0	0	4	6	0	14	2	0	0	2	.000	0	0	9.72
Box,Shawn,Peoria	A	22	12	11	3	0	73.2	304	66	33	29	3	2	4	3	20	0	61	5	0	3	2	.600	0	0	3.54
Boyd,Jason,Martinsville	R	22	14	13	1	0	69	306	65	46	32	6	0	1	4	32	0	45	7	6	3	7	.300	0	0	4.17
Boynewicz,Jim,Burlington	A	25	46	0	0	26	80	341	80	48	39	6	2	6	3	18	1	44	6	0	4	3	.571	0	9	4.39
Brabant,Daniel,Columbus	A	22	36	7	0	10	99.1	419	86	41	37	9	5	4	3	40	1	120	5	0	8	5	.615	0	1	3.35
Brandow,Derek,Dunedin	A	25	29	21	0	3	140.1	593	122	59	50	6	4	5	2	58	0	123	11	1	7	6	.538	0	1	3.21
Brandt,Dale,Yankees	R	21	13	0	0	8	22	93	13	7	5	0	0	0	3	5	0	26	2	1	0	2	.000	0	1	2.05
Oneonta	A	21	7	0	0	6	9	49	17	10	9	0	2	0	1	4	0	8	0	0	0	2	.000	0	0	9.00
Breitenstein,Kevin,Welland	A	23	2	0	0	0	4	20	3	4	3	1	0	0	2	1	0	2	0	0	0	0	.000	0	0	6.75
Brennan,Shawn,Idaho Falls	R	21	1	0	0	0	0	1	0	1	0	0	0	0	0	1	0	0	0	0	0	0	.000	0	0	0.00
Brewer,Brian,Albany	A	23	26	16	2	6	123.1	529	127	65	54	5	3	4	2	42	0	92	9	2	6	8	.429	0	1	3.94
Brewer,Nevin,Rockford	A	23	44	0	0	40	64.1	250	43	9	7	2	2	1	3	19	0	69	3	0	7	1	.875	0	20	0.98
Brewington,Jamie,Clinton	A	23	10	10	0	0	53	226	46	29	29	5	1	3	2	24	0	62	7	1	2	4	.333	0	0	4.92
San Jose	A	23	13	13	0	0	76	310	61	38	27	3	2	2	2	25	0	65	7	1	7	3	.700	0	0	3.20
Briggs,Anthony,Braves	R	21	1	0	0	0	4	14	1	0	0	0	0	0	0	1	0	1	0	0	0	0	.000	0	0	0.00
Idaho Falls	R	21	20	0	0	5	49.2	227	58	30	22	1	2	2	2	21	2	45	6	0	2	3	.400	0	1	3.99
Brincks,Mark,South Bend	A	25	10	1	0	3	25	114	29	14	12	2	2	2	1	10	0	17	2	3	1	1	.500	0	0	4.32
Pr. William	A	25	1	0	0	0	4	18	6	3	2	0	0	1	0	1	0	1	0	0	0	0	.000	0	0	4.15
Briscoe,Janos,Rangers	R	22	13	0	0	4	25.1	111	20	15	9	1	0	0	0	12	0	17	2	3	2	0	1.000	0	0	3.20
Brixey,Dustin,Royals	R	21	18	1	0	6	31	130	26	12	8	0	1	0	1	13	0	18	4	1	3	0	1.000	0	0	2.32
Brohawn,Michael,San Jose	A	22	4	4	0	0	16.2	80	27	15	13	2	1	0	2	5	0	13	1	0	0	2	.000	0	0	7.02
Brooks,Wesley,Lynchburg	A	23	28	28	4	0	172.2	751	176	104	92	19	2	8	6	64	3	117	5	4	12	12	.500	1	0	4.80
Broome,Curtis,Hickory	A	23	32	15	0	10	120.2	534	144	77	62	13	4	4	4	31	2	74	4	2	5	5	.500	0	3	4.62
Broome,John,Williamsprt	A	22	21	4	0	6	55	250	58	34	23	6	1	4	4	22	1	55	5	0	1	5	.167	0	0	3.76
Brothers,John,Winston-Sal	A	25	37	3	0	8	74.2	383	82	70	59	10	4	5	7	74	1	45	7	0	5	4	.556	0	0	7.11
Brower,James,Hudson Vall	A	22	4	4	1	0	19.2	83	14	10	7	0	0	2	1	6	0	15	0	1	2	1	.667	0	0	3.20
Charlstn-Wv	A	22	12	12	3	0	78.2	312	52	18	15	2	1	1	5	26	1	84	6	0	7	3	.700	2	0	1.72
Brown,Alvin,Lakeland	A	24	4	0	0	3	7	49	11	8	7	0	0	0	0	7	0	9	1	0	0	0	.000	0	0	9.00
Fayettevlle	A	24	33	12	1	11	97.2	441	61	60	47	3	4	0	7	83	0	109	27	2	6	7	.462	1	0	4.33
Brown,Chad,Dunedin	A	23	52	0	0	20	78	326	59	29	28	1	4	3	0	41	1	56	3	2	6	7	.462	0	4	3.23
Brown,Charlie,Tampa	A	21	1	0	0	0	2.1	13	5	3	3	0	0	0	0	2	0	2	0	0	0	0	.000	0	0	11.57
Oneonta	A	21	17	0	0	11	21	95	20	14	12	0	1	0	0	12	1	22	3	0	2	1	.667	0	0	5.14
Brown,Dickie,High Desert	A	24	18	18	4	0	114.2	487	114	57	49	10	3	4	8	37	1	100	5	0	4	4	.500	1	0	3.85
Kinston	A	24	7	7	1	0	41	171	33	21	18	5	1	0	2	14	0	40	0	0	4	2	.667	0	0	3.95
Brown,Cory,Albany	A	22	28	15	2	9	121	527	116	61	51	6	1	4	7	52	1	106	3	1	6	10	.375	0	3	3.79
Brown,Dan,Clearwater	A	26	50	0	0	19	52	211	43	13	9	1	3	1	0	22	4	37	1	2	2	0	1.000	0	0	1.56
Brown,Darold,Idaho Falls	R	21	14	14	0	0	71	307	70	35	29	4	0	1	5	34	2	58	5	0	4	7	.364	0	0	3.68
Brown,Willard,Cedar Rapids	A	23	27	27	5	0	176	728	158	89	74	6	6	4	12	45	2	129	4	6	6	9	.400	2	0	3.78
Brownson,Mark,Rockies	R	20	19	4	0	6	54.1	224	48	18	10	2	2	2	3	6	0	72	2	2	4	1	.800	0	3	1.66
Bruce,Tim,Appleton	A	22	9	0	0	4	9	45	8	7	7	2	1	1	0	10	1	10	1	0	1	0	1.000	0	0	7.00
Brunson,William,Winston-Sal	A	25	30	23	3	3	165	711	161	83	73	22	5	7	12	58	2	109	6	4	12	7	.632	0	0	3.98
Bryant,Adam,Billings	R	23	23	0	0	16	41.1	164	32	15	13	0	2	1	3	11	0	49	4	2	3	1	.750	0	4	2.83
Bryant,Christopher,Cubs	R	19	7	2	0	4	24	102	18	7	5	0	0	1	1	9	1	24	3	1	1	0	1.000	0	0	1.88
Huntington	R	19	7	3	0	1	21.1	96	17	10	7	1	3	0	1	12	0	19	9	0	2	2	.500	0	0	2.95
Buckles,Brandall,Hudson Vall	A	24	27	0	0	24	45.2	173	31	10	7	0	0	2	2	8	0	51	1	0	3	1	.750	0	18	1.38
Buddie,Mike,Tampa	A	24	25	24	0	0	150.1	643	143	75	67	7	5	8	5	66	2	113	4	1	12	5	.706	0	0	4.01
Budz,Edward,St. Cathrns	A	23	19	0	0	18	18.2	82	20	8	8	0	1	2	3	11	2	11	2	1	2	1	.667	0	6	3.86
Buhs,Matthew,Rangers	R	21	18	2	0	4	36	170	41	28	24	0	5	2	4	24	0	23	1	0	0	3	.000	0	0	6.00
Bullinger,Kirk,St. Pete	A	25	39	0	0	18	53.2	220	37	16	7	0	4	0	1	20	5	50	4	0	2	0	1.000	0	6	1.17
Bullock,Craig,St. Lucie	A	23	41	0	0	22	51	211	52	18	14	1	3	2	1	11	4	18	0	1	3	3	.500	0	2	2.47
Bullock,Joshua,Burlington	A	24	19	1	0	10	25	116	34	22	17	3	0	2	2	12	1	19	0	2	2	3	.400	0	0	6.12
Bunch,Melvin,Wilmington	A	23	15	12	0	0	61	252	52	30	23	8	1	1	0	15	0	62	2	0	5	3	.625	0	0	3.39
Burciaga,Manuel,Royals	R	21	19	0	0	4	30.2	145	23	22	17	2	1	1	2	31	1	19	3	0	5	1	.833	0	0	4.99
Burdick,Morgan,Bend	A	20	4	4	0	0	14.2	77	20	18	12	1	0	0	1	13	0	8	3	1	0	1	.000	0	0	7.36
Rockies	R	20	10	9	0	0	50	224	48	29	24	1	0	1	5	18	0	30	4	1	3	6	.333	0	0	4.32
Burger,Robert,Martinsville	R	19	7	5	0	0	19	83	20	13	12	3	0	0	1	8	0	13	4	1	2	1	.500	0	0	5.68
Burke,Ethan,Mets	R	19	9	0	0	6	17.2	75	16	7	5	1	0	2	0	9	1	9	1	0	3	3	.500	0	0	2.55
Burley,Rick,Rockford	A	22	29	15	0	9	118.2	491	101	49	44	4	7	7	7	40	5	81	8	4	5	3	.625	0	3	3.34

1994 Pitching -- Single-A and Rookie Leagues

Player	Lg	A	G	GS	CG	GF	IP	BFP	H	R	ER	HR	SH	SF	HB	TBB	IBB	SO	WP	Bk	W	L	Pct.	ShO	Sv	ERA
Burlingame,Dennis,High Desert	A	25	31	26	2	1	143.2	688	179	130	110	15	6	9	7	104	2	96	19	2	5	11	.313	0	0	6.89
Burt,Christopher,Helena	R	22	18	5	0	9	44	191	43	30	24	3	4	2	6	13	0	42	4	4	2	4	.333	0	3	4.91
Busby,Mike,St. Pete	A	22	26	26	1	0	151.2	663	166	82	75	11	8	5	14	49	1	89	5	2	6	13	.316	0	0	4.45
Bush,Craig,Utica	A	21	16	10	1	2	65.2	295	77	37	24	0	3	4	5	22	1	43	4	2	1	6	.143	0	0	3.29
Bussa,Todd,Fayetteville	A	22	5	0	0	2	15	62	10	1	0	0	1	0	2	4	0	13	2	0	2	0	1.000	0	1	0.00
Lakeland	A	22	28	1	0	13	53	244	67	30	28	4	3	3	2	25	2	27	5	1	3	5	.375	0	1	4.75
Butcher,Jason,Bakersfield	A	25	2	0	0	1	1.2	14	3	5	4	1	0	0	0	6	0	3	0	0	0	0	.000	0	0	21.60
Yakima	A	25	12	3	0	3	29	134	32	19	13	2	2	1	5	10	1	30	5	3	2	1	.667	0	0	4.03
Buteaux,Shane,White Sox	R	23	12	10	0	0	55	236	60	33	26	0	2	4	5	15	0	28	4	5	1	5	.167	0	0	4.25
Butler,Jason,Durham	A	24	13	3	0	2	27.1	132	28	21	18	6	2	1	0	18	2	12	6	2	2	2	.500	0	0	5.93
Butler,Mike,Lake Elsino	A	24	43	4	0	7	87.1	387	97	56	45	8	7	2	7	35	3	75	3	1	6	5	.545	0	2	4.64
Butler,Shane,Williamsprt	A	24	2	0	0	2	2	8	2	0	0	0	0	0	0	1	0	2	0	0	0	0	.000	0	0	0.00
Peoria	A	24	4	0	0	1	5.2	29	7	6	5	1	1	0	1	6	1	4	1	0	0	1	.000	0	0	7.94
Byrd,Matthew,Durham	A	24	29	0	0	20	37.1	156	22	20	19	7	0	0	2	19	2	39	5	0	2	4	.333	0	3	4.58
Byrdak,Timothy,Eugene	A	21	15	15	0	0	73.1	302	60	33	25	6	2	2	4	20	0	77	1	1	4	5	.444	0	0	3.07
Byrne,Earl,Cubs	R	23	4	1	0	1	11	41	5	3	2	0	1	1	0	6	0	11	0	1	1	1	.500	0	0	1.64
Cabrera,Jose,Kinston	A	23	24	24	0	0	133.2	575	134	84	66	15	6	3	5	43	0	110	5	5	4	13	.235	0	0	4.44
Cafaro,John,Albany	A	22	30	1	0	15	68.1	304	73	41	37	3	3	4	8	27	4	53	7	4	3	5	.375	0	3	4.87
Cain,Travis,Danville	R	19	13	10	0	1	49	239	38	42	27	4	1	2	4	52	0	61	6	1	2	6	.250	0	0	4.96
Cain,Sheldon,Madison	A	24	54	5	0	26	85	364	85	48	37	8	2	2	3	23	3	76	4	3	2	5	.286	0	2	3.92
Calderon,Jose,Brewers	R	19	12	0	0	4	14.2	76	19	15	11	0	2	0	0	12	0	17	3	2	1	0	1.000	0	0	6.75
Caldwell,David,Burlington	R	20	10	10	0	0	42	206	38	40	34	1	0	1	3	46	0	44	7	2	2	5	.286	0	0	7.29
Call,Mike,Pr. William	A	26	27	26	8	0	170.1	720	181	89	76	17	9	5	5	38	1	87	10	0	10	12	.455	2	0	4.02
Callahan,Damon,Princeton	R	19	8	7	0	0	50	209	38	16	9	1	1	2	3	13	0	41	3	0	7	0	1.000	0	0	1.62
Camacho,Daniel,Bakersfield	A	21	10	0	0	4	22.1	86	9	3	3	0	0	1	0	15	1	25	5	0	0	0	.000	0	0	1.21
Campbell,Camp,Columbus	A	24	3	0	0	0	7	34	8	8	7	0	1	1	3	2	0	4	1	0	0	0	.000	0	0	9.00
Campbell,Richard,Eugene	A	23	13	0	0	4	15.1	72	12	9	8	1	0	1	0	15	0	20	2	1	1	0	1.000	0	0	4.70
Campbell,Ryan,Astros	R	20	18	0	0	6	34.2	150	41	17	12	1	0	2	0	8	0	32	0	0	4	0	1.000	0	1	3.12
Cardona,Isbel,Clinton	A	23	8	0	0	4	10	69	15	24	15	1	0	0	1	24	0	9	0	0	0	0	.000	0	0	13.50
Everett	A	23	18	5	0	6	48.1	229	51	33	21	2	0	1	5	30	2	46	5	0	3	1	.750	0	0	3.91
Carl,Todd,Brevard Cty	A	22	3	0	0	0	4.2	24	6	4	4	0	0	0	0	5	0	2	1	0	0	0	.000	0	0	7.71
Elmira	A	22	21	0	0	11	21.2	103	25	12	10	0	0	4	1	12	0	18	5	0	0	1	.000	0	2	4.15
Carmona,Rafael,Riverside	A	22	50	0	0	48	67.1	264	48	22	21	3	1	0	4	19	0	63	3	0	8	2	.800	0	21	2.81
Carmona,William,Winston-Sal	A	23	8	0	0	6	8.1	34	6	2	2	0	0	0	0	4	0	5	0	0	0	0	.000	0	0	2.16
Princeton	R	23	7	7	0	0	35	158	34	22	17	1	1	1	4	21	0	32	9	2	2	2	.500	0	0	4.37
Charlstn-Sc	A	23	14	2	0	7	33	144	26	19	19	0	0	2	2	19	2	24	8	1	3	2	.600	0	1	5.18
Carpenter,Brian,Bakersfield	A	22	22	0	0	14	36	162	39	23	18	0	0	1	2	16	0	33	0	1	0	1	.000	0	1	4.50
Carpenter,Brian,St. Pete	A	24	26	20	0	3	131.2	572	152	76	70	16	2	5	7	38	1	76	2	1	12	7	.632	0	0	4.78
Carpenter,Chris,Medicne Hat	R	20	15	15	0	0	84.2	366	76	40	26	3	2	3	8	39	0	80	9	2	6	3	.667	0	0	2.76
Carrasco,Jose,Boise	A	21	3	2	0	0	10.1	45	11	8	8	2	0	0	0	3	0	9	2	0	0	0	.000	0	0	6.97
Cedar Rapds	A	21	2	0	0	0	4	21	7	5	5	3	0	0	0	2	0	4	0	0	0	0	.000	0	0	11.25
Carrasco,Troy,Fort Wayne	A	20	28	28	2	0	160.2	683	159	88	73	14	5	1	4	60	0	146	9	0	10	10	.500	1	0	4.09
Carroll,Dave,Madison	A	22	27	26	0	0	137	626	170	101	79	13	11	4	3	62	1	85	6	2	6	11	.353	0	0	5.19
Carruth,Jason,Lethbridge	R	23	13	13	0	0	75.1	342	85	53	39	3	3	1	8	27	1	55	5	1	5	6	.455	0	0	4.66
Cartaya,Anibal,Orioles	R	19	10	0	0	6	22	105	22	11	9	1	1	0	2	13	0	18	3	2	0	1	.000	0	1	3.68
Carter,Lance,Eugene	A	20	8	7	0	1	26.1	118	28	17	16	2	1	3	1	15	0	23	4	3	1	0	1.000	0	0	5.47
Royals	R	20	5	5	0	0	31	110	19	1	1	1	1	0	0	3	0	36	1	0	3	0	1.000	0	0	0.29
Caruso,Gino,Stockton	A	25	43	9	0	14	105.2	465	97	56	42	6	6	6	9	49	3	89	7	1	8	2	.800	0	0	3.58
Caruthers,Clayton,Billings	R	22	14	14	1	0	81	357	85	47	35	2	1	3	3	36	1	63	7	0	5	3	.625	0	0	3.89
Casey,Ryan,Huntington	R	22	19	0	0	5	46.1	191	37	18	15	2	3	1	2	19	0	43	12	3	3	1	.750	0	3	2.91
Castillo,Carlos,White Sox	R	20	12	12	0	0	59	239	53	20	17	4	2	2	2	10	0	57	3	4	4	3	.571	0	0	2.59
Hickory	A	20	3	1	0	2	12	42	3	0	0	0	0	0	1	2	0	17	0	0	2	0	1.000	0	0	0.00
Castillo,Mariano,San Jose	A	24	45	0	0	15	106.2	448	106	49	41	10	9	2	2	27	2	81	5	0	10	7	.588	0	0	3.46
Castro,Antonio,Angels	R	23	11	1	0	9	18.2	81	22	6	6	0	0	0	0	6	0	16	2	0	1	0	1.000	0	4	2.89
Boise	A	23	2	0	0	2	2	9	2	1	1	0	0	0	0	1	0	4	0	0	0	0	.000	0	0	4.50
Cedar Rapds	A	23	10	0	0	6	17	74	15	12	10	1	2	1	0	7	0	8	2	1	1	1	.500	0	1	5.29
Castro,Gamalier,Cubs	R	19	13	0	0	7	25	107	21	10	4	0	0	2	3	12	0	18	6	1	2	0	1.000	0	2	1.44
Cather,Michael,Charlotte	A	24	44	0	0	37	60.1	270	56	33	26	2	3	3	2	40	3	53	1	0	8	6	.571	0	0	3.88
Centrano,Jose,Vermont	A	21	21	0	0	14	32.2	139	29	11	8	2	1	0	1	8	0	33	1	0	2	0	1.000	0	5	2.20
Challinor,John,Bakersfield	A	20	23	2	0	6	50	211	46	27	25	6	3	1	1	24	0	36	15	0	4	3	.571	0	0	4.50
Yakima	A	20	16	6	0	3	54.2	227	46	34	23	5	1	1	3	17	2	45	0	1	4	2	.667	0	0	3.79
Chamberlain,Matthew,Salem	A	23	22	22	2	0	125	521	137	90	74	14	6	3	5	38	1	73	8	1	5	11	.313	0	0	5.79
Chantres,Carlos,White Sox	R	19	16	2	0	3	35	150	28	21	14	2	1	0	3	13	0	29	6	1	1	0	1.000	0	0	3.60
Chapman,Jeffry,Twins	R	19	13	13	0	0	70.1	292	64	34	20	1	0	4	6	17	0	42	11	3	5	6	.455	0	0	2.56
Charles,Israel,Royals	R	22	11	8	0	3	40.2	184	42	26	16	0	0	2	2	17	0	33	3	2	3	2	.600	0	0	3.54
Charlton,Aaron,Clinton	A	22	19	7	0	4	57.1	244	64	42	35	4	4	0	3	17	0	43	14	1	1	5	.167	0	0	5.49
Chavarria,David,Hudson Vall	A	22	14	0	0	6	17.1	82	17	11	5	0	0	0	2	17	0	14	3	1	0	2	.000	0	1	2.60
Chavez,Tony,Lake Elsino	A	24	12	0	0	7	13.1	75	21	19	15	0	2	1	2	11	2	12	2	0	0	5	.000	0	1	10.13
Cedar Rapds	A	24	39	1	0	34	50	222	48	33	24	0	3	2	2	28	4	52	7	0	4	3	.571	0	16	4.32
Chavez,Carlos,Albany	A	22	5	0	0	3	9.1	41	9	3	3	0	0	0	0	7	0	4	0	0	1	0	1.000	0	0	2.89
Bluefield	R	22	13	13	2	0	85.2	346	58	38	28	11	2	5	6	32	0	92	12	1	7	5	.583	1	0	2.94
Cheek,Jeff,St. Cathms	A	25	5	0	0	0	10.1	53	13	11	8	0	0	2	0	5	0	8	0	1	1	1	.500	0	0	6.97
Chen,Bruce,Braves	R	18	9	7	0	2	42.2	180	42	21	18	2	0	2	2	3	0	26	3	0	1	4	.200	0	1	3.80
Chew,Greg,Welland	A	21	17	0	0	6	22	104	22	14	12	2	0	1	2	13	0	20	2	0	1	1	.500	0	0	4.84
Chouinard,Bobby,Modesto	A	23	29	20	0	5	145.2	599	147	53	42	9	5	8	2	32	1	74	5	1	12	5	.706	0	0	2.59
Chrisman,Jim,Wilmington	A	24	26	0	0	24	33	133	21	13	7	5	1	1	1	6	1	31	1	0	1	6	.143	0	8	1.91
Christman,Scott,Pr. William	A	23	20	20	2	0	116	497	116	64	49	7	3	2	4	44	0	94	5	4	6	11	.353	0	0	3.80

1994 Pitching -- Single-A and Rookie Leagues

			HOW MUCH HE PITCHED						WHAT HE GAVE UP												THE RESULTS					
Player	Lg	A	G	GS	CG	GF	IP	BFP	H	R	ER	HR	SH	SF	HB	TBB	IBB	SO	WP	Bk	W	L	Pct.	ShO	Sv	ERA
Christmas,Mo,Macon	A	21	31	16	5	6	138	558	123	55	43	8	1	7	5	22	0	101	5	0	9	4	.692	3	0	2.80
Cindrich,Jeff,Tampa	A	24	42	0	0	19	53.2	246	57	26	23	3	4	3	2	30	4	59	4	0	5	3	.625	0	1	3.86
Cintron,Jose,Boise	A	19	13	13	0	0	75.2	314	67	37	32	5	3	4	2	21	1	53	1	0	5	3	.625	0	0	3.81
Civit,Xavier,Vermont	A	22	14	10	0	3	59.2	274	52	38	27	3	1	2	4	40	0	38	4	0	5	2	.714	0	0	4.07
Clark,Chris,Padres	R	20	17	1	0	6	33.2	153	35	17	12	2	1	0	2	18	0	25	5	0	0	0	.000	0	1	3.21
Clelland,Rick,Burlington	A	23	39	0	0	8	59.1	282	64	51	43	10	3	1	4	47	1	47	12	0	2	0	1.000	0	0	6.52
Clement,Matthew,Spokane	A	20	2	2	0	0	7.1	39	8	7	5	0	0	0	1	11	0	4	1	1	1	1	.500	0	0	6.14
Padres	R	20	13	13	0	0	67	286	65	38	33	0	1	0	6	17	0	76	10	0	8	5	.615	0	0	4.43
Clemons,Christopher,White Sox	R	22	3	2	0	0	7	27	5	3	3	0	0	1	0	1	0	5	0	0	0	0	.000	0	0	3.86
Hickory	A	22	12	12	0	0	69.1	290	74	37	34	5	4	2	5	18	0	42	6	0	4	2	.667	0	0	4.41
Clinkscales,Sherar,Royals	R	25	11	0	0	2	13.1	67	10	7	6	0	0	0	3	18	0	18	4	0	0	0	.000	0	0	4.05
Rockford	A	25	14	0	0	3	12.2	60	8	12	11	1	0	1	1	15	0	9	3	0	2	0	1.000	0	1	7.82
Cloude,Kenneth,Mariners	R	20	12	7	0	2	52.1	209	36	22	12	1	2	2	6	19	0	61	9	0	3	4	.429	0	0	2.06
Cobb,Trevor,Elizabethtn	R	21	12	12	1	0	78.2	318	61	33	25	2	4	0	5	19	0	68	8	1	9	1	.900	1	0	2.86
Cochran,Jim,Savannah	A	26	2	0	0	0	1	10	5	6	6	1	0	0	2	0	0	0	0	0	0	1	.000	0	0	54.00
Cochrane,Christopher,Sou Oreg	A	22	28	0	0	26	33.1	141	26	16	14	0	2	3	4	14	2	33	2	0	2	5	.286	0	14	3.78
Coe,Brent,Blue Jays	R	20	17	0	0	3	21.2	98	24	13	7	0	1	2	0	15	0	13	6	0	1	1	.500	0	1	2.91
Coe,Keith,Boise	A	21	3	0	0	0	4	33	9	13	13	1	0	2	1	9	0	1	2	0	0	0	.000	0	0	29.25
Angels	R	21	6	0	0	2	8.1	42	11	6	6	0	1	0	1	4	0	10	4	0	0	1	.000	0	0	6.48
Cole,James,Beloit	A	24	27	27	3	0	173.1	742	177	76	64	14	7	5	8	53	0	150	14	4	18	5	.783	1	0	3.32
Cole,Jason,Vermont	A	22	14	0	0	8	13	61	11	4	2	0	2	2	3	5	0	7	2	1	1	0	1.000	0	3	1.38
Collett,John,Bellingham	A	23	2	0	0	0	3.1	16	1	5	1	0	0	0	1	2	0	2	0	0	0	0	.000	0	0	2.70
Collins,Edward,Brewers	R	18	10	6	0	3	38.2	174	33	18	7	0	1	0	5	14	0	33	7	0	3	3	.500	0	2	1.63
Collins,Zachary,Idaho Falls	R	22	10	5	0	1	30.1	142	30	21	12	3	0	0	0	22	0	17	2	1	1	2	.333	0	1	3.56
Colmenares,Luis,Rockies	R	20	4	0	0	11	14.1	70	16	7	4	1	0	0	3	4	1	20	3	0	1	0	1.000	0	5	2.51
Colomez,Jesus,Cubs	R	20	9	0	0	1	17.2	100	33	27	17	1	1	0	0	8	1	11	0	1	1	1	.500	0	0	8.66
Colon,Bartolo,Burlington	R	20	12	12	0	0	66	291	46	32	23	3	2	1	4	44	0	84	6	2	7	4	.636	0	0	3.14
Colon,Julio,Bakersfield	A	22	8	8	0	0	44.2	196	47	30	28	8	0	0	3	23	0	36	4	1	1	5	.167	0	0	5.64
Great Falls	R	22	9	6	0	0	41.2	170	29	17	10	1	0	0	0	18	0	45	7	0	6	2	.750	0	0	2.16
Vero Beach	A	22	4	3	0	0	16.2	67	14	7	7	1	0	0	0	7	0	11	1	0	1	1	.500	0	0	3.78
Conley,Curt,Central Val	A	24	57	0	0	17	71.2	337	78	44	42	5	3	0	2	48	6	59	10	3	4	7	.364	0	3	5.27
Conner,Scott,Frederick	A	23	53	0	0	22	73.1	325	65	34	29	5	4	1	5	49	2	61	8	0	2	1	.667	0	8	3.56
Connolly,Chris,Wilmington	A	24	37	0	0	12	63	258	40	18	12	1	2	4	2	33	1	30	4	1	8	3	.727	0	0	1.71
Connors,Chad,Charlstn-Sc	A	23	19	0	0	5	40	159	26	14	12	3	1	3	4	12	1	34	2	0	1	1	.500	0	0	2.70
Winston-Sal	A	23	28	0	0	18	45.2	169	20	7	6	2	0	0	1	17	0	32	0	0	2	2	.500	0	11	1.18
Constantinides,Nick,Bristol	R	23	9	1	0	1	14.2	81	25	20	16	2	0	0	2	11	1	11	2	1	0	2	.000	0	0	9.82
Contreras,Marco,Ogden	R	23	16	4	0	5	37.2	183	64	31	27	4	3	1	0	15	3	27	3	2	3	2	.600	0	0	6.45
Conway,Keith,Madison	A	22	55	0	0	21	58	252	49	21	18	2	1	4	0	37	3	71	3	3	1	2	.333	0	3	2.79
Cook,Jacob,Red Sox	R	20	11	11	0	0	58.2	257	55	24	22	2	1	1	3	31	0	54	4	1	6	3	.667	0	0	3.38
Cook,Kenny,Bakersfield	A	22	23	0	0	8	38.2	174	40	26	19	3	2	0	4	17	0	28	5	1	0	0	.000	0	0	4.42
Cook,Rodney,Rangers	R	24	22	0	0	20	31	128	23	7	4	0	1	0	6	7	0	39	0	0	1	1	.500	0	12	1.16
Cook,Scott,Everett	A	24	27	0	0	9	41.2	199	42	32	30	3	0	2	3	28	1	47	3	1	2	1	.667	0	1	6.48
Cooper,David,Mariners	R	20	11	8	0	0	42	199	45	35	28	1	1	7	5	31	0	28	15	0	0	8	.000	0	0	6.00
Cope,Craig,Mets	R	19	9	2	0	3	19.1	91	16	16	4	1	1	0	0	14	0	21	5	0	0	2	.000	0	1	1.86
Cope,Robin,Appleton	A	22	25	3	0	12	48.1	262	68	58	45	4	1	1	8	40	1	29	8	1	0	4	.000	0	0	8.38
Coppinger,John,Bluefield	R	21	14	13	0	1	73.1	302	51	24	20	5	0	3	2	40	0	88	5	0	4	3	.571	0	0	2.45
Corn,Chris,Oneonta	A	23	21	2	0	7	50.2	222	49	22	21	4	2	1	3	19	2	51	3	1	1	1	.500	0	1	3.73
Coronado,Osvaldo,Mets	R	21	3	1	0	1	16.1	67	15	8	7	0	0	1	0	1	0	15	2	0	1	1	.500	0	0	3.86
Corps,Edwin,San Jose	A	22	29	29	0	0	168.1	731	180	95	74	6	5	6	20	43	1	91	4	1	10	6	.625	0	0	3.96
Corral,Ruben,Blue Jays	R	19	3	0	0	4	19	84	20	12	12	1	1	0	2	6	0	21	3	0	3	0	1.000	0	0	5.68
Correa,Jose,Twins	R	23	3	0	0	0	4	17	4	1	1	0	0	0	0	6	0	0	0	0	0	0	.000	0	0	2.25
Fort Myers	A	23	8	4	0	3	24.2	118	34	22	18	4	0	1	2	9	0	18	1	0	0	4	.000	0	0	6.57
Correia,Joseph,Twins	R	18	1	1	0	0	3	16	7	4	4	0	0	0	0	1	0	1	0	0	0	1	.000	0	0	12.00
Corrigan,Cory,Savannah	A	23	29	9	1	7	80	329	84	37	25	6	2	1	4	13	0	64	3	2	3	4	.429	0	0	2.81
Cosman,Jeffrey,Columbia	A	24	20	20	3	0	136.1	557	125	52	42	4	4	0	10	34	0	120	16	1	9	7	.563	0	0	2.77
St. Lucie	A	24	7	7	2	0	48.1	203	42	14	11	1	4	0	3	20	2	31	0	0	3	2	.600	1	0	2.05
Costa,Tim,Spartanburg	A	24	17	17	2	0	116.1	487	109	60	46	11	5	0	13	31	0	106	4	2	6	9	.400	0	0	3.56
Clearwater	A	24	8	8	1	0	47	204	44	25	22	3	0	1	0	31	0	27	1	0	3	5	.375	0	0	4.21
Coyle,Bryan,Great Falls	R	19	12	4	0	4	31	135	33	18	16	1	0	1	3	16	0	24	3	1	1	2	.333	0	1	4.65
Craig,Casey,Mariners	R	19	12	0	0	4	21	106	28	21	12	0	0	1	3	9	1	12	0	1	0	3	.000	0	0	5.14
Creamer,Gerry,Sarasota	A	25	28	1	0	6	42	187	43	25	23	3	1	3	2	20	1	23	7	0	0	4	.000	0	1	4.93
Creek,Ryan,Quad City	A	22	21	15	0	3	74	356	86	62	41	6	5	3	14	41	2	66	9	3	3	5	.375	0	0	4.99
Crills,Bradley,Bluefield	R	21	13	9	1	0	63	248	48	28	18	7	4	2	5	12	1	36	5	0	3	3	.500	1	0	2.57
Crine,Dennis,White Sox	R	20	10	7	0	3	41	172	41	25	12	1	0	2	1	9	0	25	2	0	4	1	.200	0	0	2.63
South Bend	A	20	6	1	0	0	19	82	19	5	5	1	1	1	2	5	0	8	1	0	1	1	.500	0	0	2.37
Crossley,Chad,Astros	R	23	8	0	0	3	18.2	74	11	6	0	0	1	0	3	5	0	19	0	0	2	0	1.000	0	0	0.00
Auburn	A	23	14	1	0	8	31.1	136	26	10	7	0	0	2	4	14	0	37	0	0	1	0	1.000	0	0	2.01
Croushore,Rich,Madison	A	24	62	0	0	14	94.1	410	90	49	43	5	4	2	5	46	2	103	10	4	6	6	.500	0	4	4.10
Crow,Paul,Appleton	A	22	16	0	0	8	15.1	80	25	15	12	4	2	3	1	7	4	11	1	0	2	0	1.000	0	2	7.04
Crowther,Brent,Bend	A	23	13	9	0	1	56	271	68	41	29	2	0	4	9	24	0	44	8	3	3	5	.375	0	0	4.66
Crowther,John,Blue Jays	R	21	5	0	0	1	6.2	38	9	10	5	0	0	0	2	5	0	8	1	0	0	1	.000	0	0	6.75
St. Cathrns	R	21	12	0	0	6	13	79	23	18	17	2	1	1	2	10	0	10	4	1	0	2	.000	0	0	11.77
Cruise,Mark,Johnson Cty	R	22	26	0	0	9	32.2	133	27	11	7	0	3	1	2	10	5	27	1	0	3	2	.600	0	2	1.93
Crump,Jody,Johnson Cty	R	22	15	3	0	3	35.2	152	39	17	12	3	1	1	1	10	0	28	4	0	1	1	.500	0	3	3.03
Cubillan,Darwin,Yankees	R	20	13	8	1	0	57.1	222	45	16	15	1	4	1	0	16	0	48	2	1	4	2	.667	1	0	2.35
Greensboro	A	20	1	0	0	0	2	15	6	5	4	0	0	0	0	2	0	1	0	0	0	0	.000	0	0	18.00
Culberson,Don,Daytona	A	24	18	6	0	6	47.1	241	49	46	35	1	4	1	8	49	1	47	9	1	0	4	.000	0	0	6.65

1994 Pitching -- Single-A and Rookie Leagues

Player	Lg	A	G	GS	CG	GF	IP	BFP	H	R	ER	HR	SH	SF	HB	TBB	IBB	SO	WP	Bk	W	L	Pct.	ShO	Sv	ERA
Peoria	A	24	7	7	0	0	39.2	174	33	22	18	2	2	3	2	25	0	28	4	0	1	6	.143	0	0	4.08
Culp,Wesley,Danville	R	20	18	5	0	5	58.1	280	67	51	30	3	4	3	8	28	3	38	5	0	0	6	.000	0	0	4.63
Cumberland,Chris,Greensboro	A	22	22	22	1	0	137.2	559	123	55	45	9	4	2	4	41	0	95	11	2	14	5	.737	1	0	2.94
Cunnane,Will,Kane County	A	21	32	16	5	6	138.2	540	110	27	22	2	4	1	6	23	4	106	5	1	11	3	.786	4	1	1.43
Cunningham,Scott,New Jersey	A	23	29	0	0	6	48.1	216	55	27	25	1	0	2	4	24	0	36	3	1	9	0	1.000	0	0	4.66
Curren,Tighe,Johnson Cty	R	21	22	0	0	5	31.2	130	26	13	10	4	1	0	2	7	0	30	6	0	1	1	.500	0	1	2.84
Czanstkowski,Thomas,Quad Cty	A	22	39	3	0	18	63.1	309	92	58	48	6	1	1	2	36	0	41	11	1	1	4	.200	0	1	6.82
D'Allessandro,Marc,Rockies	R	19	14	14	1	0	66.2	294	71	39	28	0	2	2	4	27	1	72	4	4	2	6	.250	0	0	3.78
D'amato,Brian,High Desert	A	23	16	0	0	10	26.2	128	39	26	22	4	2	1	1	11	0	15	3	0	2	3	.400	0	1	7.43
Lynchburg	A	23	12	0	0	2	21	91	19	16	12	1	1	1	1	13	0	13	1	0	0	1	.000	0	1	5.14
D'andrea,Mike,Durham	A	25	27	26	1	0	158	674	167	85	74	19	3	4	6	49	1	133	7	3	9	10	.474	0	0	4.22
Dabalak,Darin,Spartanburg	A	22	23	0	0	12	35.1	145	26	12	12	1	1	1	1	16	1	23	4	0	2	3	.400	0	5	3.06
Dace,Derek,Astros	R	20	11	11	1	0	59	245	55	26	22	2	5	2	1	21	0	52	2	3	2	3	.400	0	0	3.36
Dafun,Kekoa,Angels	R	20	8	8	4	0	61.2	252	54	23	22	2	0	1	3	18	0	67	1	1	5	2	.714	1	0	3.21
Cedar Rapids	A	20	3	3	0	0	17	78	18	12	7	1	0	1	1	6	0	14	2	0	1	0	1.000	0	0	3.71
Lake Elsino	A	20	2	2	0	0	13	54	11	4	2	0	0	0	1	7	0	11	1	1	1	1	.500	0	0	1.38
Daigle,Timothy,Bluefield	R	23	20	0	0	13	30.1	125	23	9	5	2	1	2	0	7	0	28	4	0	0	1	.000	0	4	1.48
Dale,James,New Jersey	A	22	15	15	0	0	73	333	79	44	37	2	3	2	3	38	0	75	10	0	2	7	.222	0	0	4.56
Dalton,Brian,Helena	R	23	19	1	0	10	43	174	33	16	10	2	4	0	1	20	3	35	6	0	4	3	.571	0	0	2.09
Daniels,John,Bellingham	A	21	20	2	0	3	41.1	196	49	22	17	4	2	2	4	21	0	42	3	2	2	2	.500	0	1	3.70
Daniels,Lee,Dunedin	A	24	49	0	0	41	60	258	55	30	25	3	3	1	3	26	0	48	5	2	3	6	.333	0	15	3.75
Dark,David,Cubs	R	24	1	0	0	0	1	6	2	1	1	0	0	0	0	1	0	0	0	0	0	0	.000	0	0	9.00
Darley,Ned,Winston-Sal	A	24	10	10	0	0	40	195	54	36	33	2	0	1	1	24	0	25	3	0	2	3	.400	0	0	7.43
DaSilva,Fernando,Burlington	A	23	28	25	4	0	162.1	702	179	96	79	20	2	8	6	51	2	126	9	0	9	8	.529	2	0	4.38
Davenport,Joseph,Blue Jays	R	19	7	1	0	2	11	48	12	5	4	0	0	1	1	7	0	2	1	1	0	0	.000	0	0	3.27
Davey,Thomas,Medicne Hat	R	21	14	14	0	0	65	318	76	59	37	3	2	2	3	59	0	35	11	0	2	8	.200	0	0	5.12
Davidson,Rod,Pirates	R	21	8	0	0	1	17.1	76	14	9	5	1	0	1	0	11	0	18	4	0	1	0	1.000	0	0	2.60
Davis,Arthur,Angels	R	20	13	13	2	0	96.1	402	91	41	27	5	1	3	1	32	0	70	5	1	7	6	.538	1	0	2.52
Boise	A	20	1	1	0	0	5	27	10	9	8	1	1	0	0	4	0	1	1	0	0	1	.000	0	0	14.40
Davis,Jeffrey,Charlstn-Wv	A	22	45	0	0	43	49.2	214	53	25	22	3	0	1	2	11	0	72	2	1	2	3	.400	0	19	3.99
Davis,Kane,Welland	A	20	15	15	2	0	98.1	400	90	36	29	4	2	3	2	32	1	74	7	1	5	5	.500	0	0	2.65
Davis,Keith,Spokane	A	22	16	11	0	0	64.1	304	76	51	40	6	1	3	9	34	0	48	6	2	2	7	.222	0	0	5.60
Davis,Ray,Madison	A	22	27	27	1	0	167	691	149	68	55	9	5	5	7	58	2	127	2	3	12	10	.545	1	0	2.96
Dawley,Joey,Bluefield	R	23	11	2	0	5	23.2	110	20	18	15	2	0	1	1	18	0	18	4	0	1	2	.333	0	2	5.70
Albany	A	23	5	0	0	4	7.1	37	7	6	5	0	0	1	1	7	1	4	1	0	0	0	.000	0	0	6.14
Day,Steven,Clinton	A	24	52	0	0	28	91.2	407	85	54	45	3	6	3	2	57	2	64	11	0	2	3	.400	0	1	4.42
Debrino,Rob,Fort Wayne	A	21	50	0	0	34	72.1	312	77	44	35	5	1	2	3	28	2	58	5	0	5	3	.625	0	11	4.35
Declue,Brian,Cedar Rapds	A	24	22	3	0	9	62.1	271	67	28	26	4	1	1	4	13	2	56	6	2	6	1	.857	0	0	3.75
DeHart,Rick,W. Palm Bch	A	25	30	20	3	5	136.1	566	132	61	51	12	7	2	3	34	0	88	7	1	9	7	.563	2	0	3.37
Dejesus,Cesar,Pirates	R	19	7	0	0	5	14.2	82	21	22	15	0	0	1	3	11	0	6	3	1	1	0	1.000	0	0	9.20
Delacruz,Feleles,Medicne Hat	R	21	13	0	0	3	17.2	87	15	13	10	1	0	0	2	17	1	9	7	1	0	0	.000	0	0	5.09
De La Maza,Roland,Columbus	A	23	21	21	1	0	112.2	473	102	59	37	13	5	4	6	38	0	97	3	2	13	2	.867	0	0	2.96
de la Rosa,Maximo,Columbus	A	23	14	14	0	0	75.1	310	49	33	28	2	1	1	10	38	0	71	5	2	4	2	.667	0	0	3.35
Kinston	A	23	13	13	0	0	69.2	324	82	56	39	7	2	4	4	38	0	53	3	2	0	11	.000	0	0	5.04
DeLeon,Elcidio,Welland	A	23	3	0	0	1	5.1	21	3	3	3	0	0	0	0	4	0	4	2	0	1	0	1.000	0	0	5.06
Augusta	A	23	19	1	0	2	37.1	171	35	25	20	1	1	1	4	20	1	48	4	0	0	3	.000	0	0	4.82
Delgado,Ernesto,Brevard Cty	A	19	1	1	0	0	6	25	3	3	2	0	1	2	0	4	0	1	1	0	0	0	.000	0	0	3.00
Marlins	R	19	4	2	0	2	16	71	15	10	6	0	0	0	0	5	0	18	1	0	1	1	.500	0	1	3.38
Delzine,Domingo,Charlstn-Wv	A	22	38	0	0	16	69.1	292	66	37	33	7	2	1	5	13	1	59	5	1	1	4	.200	0	0	4.28
Dempsey,John,Wilmington	A	23	6	0	0	1	9.1	50	13	8	4	1	0	2	1	7	0	3	2	1	1	0	1.000	0	0	3.86
Royals	R	23	2	0	0	0	5	22	7	2	2	0	0	0	0	1	0	4	0	0	0	0	.000	0	0	3.60
Demyan,Kirk,Columbia	A	23	9	0	0	4	16.2	89	31	25	24	4	0	0	2	9	0	10	3	0	0	0	.000	0	0	12.96
Dennis,Shane,Spokane	A	23	12	12	1	0	77.1	322	70	38	35	5	4	3	3	25	0	80	2	2	1	7	.125	1	0	4.07
Springfield	A	23	3	3	0	0	17	61	5	2	2	1	0	0	0	8	0	10	0	0	1	0	1.000	0	0	1.06
Desabrias,Mark,Padres	R	19	5	0	0	1	7.1	34	8	7	3	0	0	0	2	3	0	4	3	0	1	0	1.000	0	0	3.68
Desantis,Dominic,Clearwater	A	26	23	1	0	5	45.1	200	51	29	23	3	4	0	5	14	2	35	4	0	5	3	.625	0	0	4.57
Dessellier,Christopher,Mariners	R	21	16	0	0	1	26.1	112	15	7	5	0	0	0	4	18	0	38	5	0	1	0	1.000	0	0	1.71
Detmers,Kristren,Madison	A	21	16	16	0	0	90.1	380	88	45	34	4	1	1	4	31	0	74	0	1	5	7	.417	0	0	3.39
Deutsch,Curry,Welland	A	22	15	0	0	3	26.1	128	33	26	19	0	1	1	1	18	0	14	3	0	0	2	.000	0	0	6.49
Devereaux,Chad,Frederick	A	22	41	0	0	11	69	274	55	26	26	12	4	2	0	20	3	77	4	0	3	5	.375	0	2	3.39
Devries,Andrew,Huntington	R	22	7	1	0	3	12.1	73	26	18	12	2	1	0	3	5	0	12	0	1	0	1	.000	0	0	8.76
Cubs	R	22	6	0	0	4	12.1	52	9	2	1	0	1	0	1	4	0	9	0	0	1	0	1.000	0	3	0.73
DeWalt,Mark,Red Sox	R	20	14	0	0	5	14.2	94	20	26	21	1	0	2	7	23	0	8	15	0	0	1	.000	0	0	12.89
DeWitt,Martin,Asheville	A	22	37	0	0	21	53.1	254	52	40	33	2	3	0	4	43	2	42	6	0	2	3	.400	0	0	5.57
Diaz,Jairo,Cubs	R	19	9	8	0	1	41.2	178	33	21	17	1	2	0	0	14	0	44	1	1	2	2	.500	0	0	3.67
Williamsprt	A	19	3	1	0	1	5.1	27	8	1	0	0	0	0	0	4	0	6	1	0	0	0	.000	0	0	13.50
Dickens,John,Wilmington	A	24	38	3	1	7	77.2	321	69	40	37	7	5	3	4	21	1	56	3	1	4	2	.667	1	4	4.29
Dickson,Jason,Boise	A	22	9	7	0	1	44.1	190	40	22	19	3	1	0	2	18	1	37	3	2	3	1	.750	0	1	3.86
Dillinger,John,Augusta	A	21	23	22	1	1	119.2	524	107	77	57	5	6	2	3	54	1	118	8	5	5	9	.357	0	0	4.29
Dillon,Chad,Giants	R	19	13	13	0	0	52	222	36	26	21	0	1	1	5	32	0	54	6	2	4	5	.444	0	0	3.63
Dingman,Craig,Yankees	R	21	17	1	0	11	32	135	27	17	12	0	7	2	1	9	0	51	4	0	0	5	.000	0	0	3.38
Dinnen,Kevin,Columbus	A	23	26	0	0	13	47.2	202	44	14	11	1	1	1	4	21	1	42	0	0	3	1	.750	0	2	2.08
Dinyar,Eric,Jamestown	A	21	28	0	0	19	45.1	191	38	20	17	1	0	3	4	11	1	30	6	1	5	1	.833	0	5	3.38
Diorio,Michael,Astros	R	22	2	0	0	0	2.1	19	5	6	6	1	0	0	0	3	0	2	0	1	0	0	.000	0	0	23.14
Osceola	A	23	13	7	0	0	44	191	48	24	14	4	1	2	0	11	0	27	2	0	3	2	.600	0	0	2.86
Dixon,Gary,Spokane	A	23	32	0	0	26	45.1	189	31	8	6	0	1	3	1	24	5	81	2	0	2	1	.667	0	11	1.19
Dixon,James,Hickory	A	22	24	10	0	7	99	449	114	58	40	12	3	5	9	28	0	73	6	1	5	4	.556	0	1	3.64

1994 Pitching -- Single-A and Rookie Leagues

Player	Lg	A	G	GS	CG	GF	IP	BFP	H	R	ER	HR	SH	SF	HB	TBB	IBB	SO	WP	Bk	W	L	Pct.	ShO	Sv	ERA
Pr.,William	A	22	6	1	1	1	19	84	21	14	14	2	0	1	0	10	1	13	1	2	1	1	.500	0	0	6.63
Dodd,Robert,Batavia	A	22	14	7	0	2	52	209	42	16	13	0	2	1	2	14	1	44	4	0	2	4	.333	0	1	2.25
Dolejsi,Dale,Bristol	R	22	24	0	0	11	36.2	161	33	20	16	2	2	1	2	18	1	17	4	2	3	1	.750	0	1	3.93
Dolson,Andy,Dunedin	A	25	2	0	0	0	4	15	4	1	1	0	0	0	0	0	0	3	0	0	0	0	.000	0	0	2.25
Doman,Roger,Dunedin	A	22	32	12	0	11	103.1	460	119	72	60	10	2	7	3	40	0	64	12	0	3	9	.250	0	2	5.23
Domenico,Brian,Sou. Oregon	A	22	17	8	0	0	57.1	284	65	49	37	2	3	4	2	42	0	39	18	0	1	2	.333	0	0	5.81
Done,Jose,Watertown	A	19	14	14	1	0	76.1	330	76	46	37	9	1	2	5	35	0	44	5	0	6	4	.600	0	0	4.36
Donovan,Scot,Watertown	A	22	23	0	0	20	24.1	111	24	12	9	1	0	0	0	13	1	19	3	0	2	2	.500	0	10	3.33
Doorneweerd,Dave,Salem	A	22	25	15	2	3	103.2	444	95	53	42	13	1	2	7	36	2	91	0	0	6	9	.400	0	0	3.65
Dougherty,Anthony,Watertown	A	22	26	0	0	13	40.2	178	33	20	13	0	3	0	4	19	2	37	3	2	6	1	.857	0	2	2.88
Doughty,Brian,Appleton	A	20	12	7	1	2	38.2	173	44	32	25	8	1	0	1	19	0	14	6	1	1	5	.167	0	0	5.82
Mariners	R	20	7	6	0	0	37	154	36	15	11	0	0	1	4	4	0	27	1	0	1	3	.250	0	0	2.68
Dowhower,Deron,Elizabethtn	R	23	12	12	0	0	62.1	278	45	37	22	3	3	3	1	38	0	73	29	1	5	4	.556	0	0	3.18
Downs,John,Wilmington	A	24	16	1	0	8	28.2	121	24	12	12	4	0	0	1	12	0	35	1	0	2	1	.667	0	1	3.77
Doyle,Tom,Riverside	A	25	9	0	0	5	14	68	21	20	19	0	0	0	3	11	0	12	1	2	0	0	.000	0	0	15.55
Dressendorfer,Kirk,Athletics	R	26	6	6	0	0	12.1	45	3	1	0	0	0	0	1	4	0	17	0	0	1	0	.000	0	0	0.00
Drewien,Daniel,Springfield	A	22	45	0	0	15	62.1	268	44	26	25	6	4	3	4	36	5	63	6	2	3	4	.429	0	9	3.61
Drews,Matthew,Oneonta	A	20	14	14	1	0	90	369	76	31	21	1	1	2	8	19	0	69	3	0	7	6	.538	1	0	2.10
Driskill,Daniel,Jamestown	A	24	3	0	0	1	6.2	31	8	8	4	0	0	0	0	1	0	2	0	1	0	0	.000	0	0	5.40
Driskill,Travis,Columbus	A	23	62	0	0	59	64.1	267	51	25	18	2	5	2	1	30	4	88	6	0	5	5	.500	0	35	2.52
Droll,Jeff,Hickory	A	24	12	0	0	6	21	101	24	11	9	1	2	0	2	12	0	22	2	0	1	1	.500	0	0	3.86
South Bend	A	24	20	0	0	13	27	120	22	13	12	1	1	1	0	20	0	15	4	0	0	0	.000	0	4	4.00
Drumheller,Al,Greensboro	A	23	30	0	0	18	58	253	50	27	19	3	2	1	2	32	1	73	5	2	2	2	.333	0	2	2.95
Drysdale,Brooks,Cedar Rapds	A	24	16	0	0	15	19.2	72	9	1	1	0	0	1	0	3	1	27	1	0	1	1	.500	0	7	0.46
Duda,Steven,Stockton	A	24	13	9	2	1	57	251	71	34	32	4	5	1	3	17	0	32	2	2	2	6	.250	0	0	5.05
Beloit	A	24	27	0	0	18	41.2	176	42	17	15	1	5	0	2	13	5	42	4	1	3	3	.500	0	10	3.24
Dudeck,Dave,Lethbridge	R	22	24	0	0	11	30.1	149	32	22	14	1	0	5	4	16	4	28	10	0	3	2	.600	0	4	4.15
Duffy,Ryan,Welland	A	22	8	0	0	6	10.2	49	12	7	6	1	3	0	1	3	0	6	1	0	1	1	.500	0	1	5.06
Duncan,Devohn,Spokane	A	20	11	11	0	0	61	250	43	16	10	1	1	2	5	36	0	69	7	2	4	2	.667	0	0	1.48
Duncan,Sean,White Sox	R	22	16	0	0	10	24	94	18	5	4	1	1	0	0	6	1	21	3	0	0	1	.000	0	2	1.50
Hickory	A	22	7	0	0	4	13	54	9	7	6	1	1	1	0	7	0	14	0	0	0	0	.000	0	0	4.15
Dunlap,Travis,Wilmington	A	23	16	0	0	3	23.1	106	26	15	9	4	0	1	0	13	1	12	2	0	1	1	.500	0	0	3.47
Dunn,Cordell,Pirates	R	19	11	1	0	3	22.2	112	22	20	15	0	3	1	2	19	0	4	4	0	1	3	.250	0	0	5.96
Duran,Ignacio,Springfield	A	24	26	13	0	3	86.2	390	87	69	45	9	8	0	4	37	3	81	3	2	7	7	.500	0	0	4.67
Duran,Roberto,Bakersfield	A	22	42	4	0	29	65.1	300	61	43	35	5	3	4	5	48	0	86	6	0	6	5	.545	0	10	4.82
Durocher,Jayson,Vermont	A	20	15	15	3	0	99	422	92	40	34	0	0	3	2	44	1	74	11	1	9	2	.818	1	0	3.09
Dutch,John,Sarasota	A	22	12	2	0	3	23	100	22	10	9	1	0	3	9	9	0	11	1	2	1	0	1.000	0	0	3.52
Dyess,David,Orioles	R	22	10	0	0	6	20	77	14	3	2	0	0	0	1	4	0	25	1	5	1	0	1.000	0	2	0.90
Dijkhoff,Radhomes,Orioles	R	20	12	12	1	0	73	307	69	34	27	2	0	5	0	17	0	67	4	1	3	6	.333	0	0	3.33
Dzafic,Zack,Lynchburg	A	27	10	0	0	7	10.1	52	14	4	4	0	2	0	1	7	0	5	2	0	0	1	.000	0	0	3.48
Eaddy,Brad,Bakersfield	A	25	6	0	0	4	7.1	31	5	3	3	0	0	0	1	5	0	8	1	0	0	2	.000	0	0	3.68
Great Falls	R	25	18	2	0	8	40.2	195	55	37	32	5	1	2	2	18	3	40	4	1	3	2	.600	0	0	7.08
Ebert,Derrin,Braves	R	18	10	7	1	2	43	176	40	18	14	4	0	0	1	8	0	25	1	3	1	3	.250	1	0	2.93
Eddings,Jeff,Great Falls	R	24	21	1	0	16	30.1	128	22	7	3	0	1	1	2	7	0	30	0	1	1	1	.500	0	7	0.89
Yakima	A	24	2	0	0	0	3	15	3	2	1	0	1	0	0	1	0	3	0	0	0	1	.000	0	0	3.00
Eden,William,Rockies	R	22	1	0	0	0	2	6	0	0	0	0	0	0	0	0	0	2	0	0	1	0	1.000	0	0	0.00
Bend	A	22	16	0	0	5	30.1	140	39	26	23	1	2	1	0	14	0	31	6	1	2	3	.400	0	2	6.82
Edgar,Dwaine,Oneonta	A	22	14	0	0	4	13.2	84	22	22	16	0	3	0	2	20	0	12	3	4	0	2	.000	0	1	10.54
Edsell,Geoff,Cedar Rapds	A	23	17	17	4	0	125.1	538	109	54	42	10	5	0	6	65	1	84	10	4	11	5	.688	1	0	3.02
Lake Elsino	A	23	9	7	0	1	40	174	38	21	18	3	0	0	0	24	1	26	3	2	2	2	.500	0	0	4.05
Eggert,Dave,W. Palm Bch	A	25	40	0	0	18	37.2	156	40	19	16	2	2	3	0	15	0	32	1	1	3	1	.750	0	3	3.82
Eggleston,Scott,Spartanburg	A	20	13	9	0	2	53	240	61	42	28	7	1	3	4	23	0	36	6	3	3	2	.600	0	0	4.75
Ehler,Daniel,Kane County	A	20	27	27	0	0	162.1	689	170	75	66	13	5	4	14	36	0	101	7	3	10	6	.625	0	0	3.66
Elarton,Vincent,Astros	R	19	5	5	0	0	28	92	9	0	0	0	0	0	0	5	0	28	1	0	4	0	1.000	0	0	0.00
Quad City	A	19	9	9	0	0	54.2	220	42	23	20	4	2	2	1	18	0	42	3	1	4	1	.800	0	0	3.29
Elsbernd,David,Hickory	A	24	6	6	0	0	36.2	160	37	22	14	4	0	2	6	4	0	23	0	2	3	2	.600	0	0	3.44
Emerson,Scott,Frederick	A	23	28	22	2	0	129.2	573	141	78	61	6	5	5	4	62	1	87	4	1	8	8	.500	0	0	4.23
Engle,Tom,Mets	R	24	2	1	0	0	5.2	33	10	10	9	0	0	0	0	5	0	8	2	0	0	1	.000	0	0	14.29
Columbia	A	24	17	1	0	0	94	397	92	50	44	10	3	5	7	30	1	65	9	1	5	6	.455	0	0	4.21
Epstein,Ian,Athletics	R	24	13	5	0	3	55.2	223	39	15	9	1	3	1	0	36	0	55	2	1	5	1	.833	0	1	1.46
Erwin,Scott,Athletics	R	27	7	5	0	0	14	59	13	9	8	1	1	0	0	4	0	21	2	0	1	1	.500	0	0	5.14
Escalante,Simon,Cardinals	R	18	19	1	0	2	32.2	136	29	15	8	0	1	1	2	10	0	19	2	0	3	1	.750	0	0	2.20
Escamilla,Jaime,Hudson Vall	A	23	24	3	0	11	57.2	238	35	27	16	2	4	2	4	25	1	72	6	3	5	5	.500	0	3	2.50
Escobar,Jose,Blue Jays	R	19	11	10	1	0	57	251	56	23	17	0	0	1	0	18	0	64	5	3	4	2	.667	0	0	2.35
Estavil,Mauricio,Batavia	A	23	11	0	0	5	39.1	184	43	23	17	1	1	4	5	17	0	31	7	2	3	2	.600	0	1	3.89
Estes,Buck,Mariners	R	22	5	5	0	0	20	86	19	7	7	0	1	0	1	6	0	31	7	0	0	3	.000	0	0	3.15
Appleton	A	22	5	4	0	1	19.2	92	19	13	10	1	2	1	2	17	0	28	4	0	0	2	.000	0	0	4.58
Etheridge,Roger,Charlstn-Sc	A	23	10	10	0	0	58.1	258	64	35	29	6	4	1	4	27	0	42	2	0	2	2	.500	0	0	4.47
Macon	A	23	7	4	0	1	33	150	39	17	13	3	0	1	2	8	0	19	1	0	3	1	.750	1	0	3.55
Durham	A	23	9	9	1	0	64.1	245	41	12	10	2	2	1	0	16	0	36	3	0	6	2	.750	1	0	1.40
Etler,Todd,Charlstn-Sc	A	21	7	7	1	0	47.2	190	48	17	14	4	1	0	2	3	1	31	0	0	4	2	.667	1	0	2.64
Winston-Sal	A	21	19	19	1	0	106	479	141	84	76	25	1	5	3	31	0	61	5	1	5	11	.313	0	0	6.45
Evangelista,Alberto,Danville	R	21	13	0	0	2	17.1	67	8	6	4	2	1	1	0	7	1	24	0	1	0	0	.000	0	0	2.08
Macon	A	21	10	0	0	1	16.2	76	14	9	8	2	2	0	1	11	0	17	1	0	1	0	1.000	0	0	4.32
Evans,Bart,Wilmington	A	24	26	26	0	0	145	587	107	53	48	7	4	4	8	61	0	145	10	0	10	3	.769	0	0	2.98
Evans,Jim,Osceola	A	24	34	1	0	21	51.2	237	59	44	39	2	4	3	3	30	3	30	5	3	1	7	.125	0	9	6.79
Evans,Sean,Salem	A	24	51	0	0	34	55.2	273	55	40	24	1	4	2	7	34	3	49	7	0	3	7	.300	0	9	3.88

1994 Pitching -- Single-A and Rookie Leagues

Player	Lg	A	G	GS	CG	GF	IP	BFP	H	R	ER	HR	SH	SF	HB	TBB	IBB	SO	WP	Bk	W	L	Pct.	ShO	Sv	ERA
Evenhus,Jason,Ogden	R	24	14	7	1	4	54.1	253	75	45	37	4	3	4	6	5	0	37	2	1	3	4	.429	0	1	6.13
Eyre,Scott,South Bend	A	23	19	18	2	1	111.2	481	108	56	43	7	2	4	3	37	0	111	8	3	8	4	.667	0	0	3.47
Faile,William,Braves	R	20	15	1	0	7	31.2	160	45	38	29	0	0	2	2	21	0	18	9	0	0	2	.000	0	1	8.24
Idaho Falls	R	20	3	0	0	1	5.1	32	5	9	7	1	0	2	2	7	0	2	1	0	1	0	1.000	0	0	11.81
Faino,Jeff,Lynchburg	A	22	40	8	0	9	97.1	441	107	66	59	16	4	4	1	41	1	93	3	1	1	9	.100	0	3	5.46
Falls,Curt,Lethbridge	R	21	19	1	0	5	35.1	162	31	21	14	0	3	2	2	26	0	32	7	0	0	2	.000	0	0	3.57
Falmier,Ryan,Rangers	R	20	5	4	0	1	22.1	110	37	27	24	2	1	1	2	8	0	11	3	0	1	4	.200	0	0	9.67
Falteisek,Steve,W. Palm Bch	A	23	27	24	1	0	159.2	658	144	72	45	3	0	6	3	49	0	91	11	4	9	4	.692	0	0	2.54
Fansler,Stan,Rangers	R	30	4	0	0	2	6	23	5	3	2	1	0	0	0	3	0	7	0	0	0	0	.000	0	0	3.00
Fargas,Hector,Rancho Cuca	A	21	3	0	0	0	6.1	35	12	5	5	0	0	1	0	3	0	4	0	0	0	0	.000	0	0	7.11
Springfield	A	21	36	0	0	8	64.2	282	58	45	38	7	1	4	5	32	1	50	5	1	3	2	.600	0	0	5.29
Farmer,Craig,Lethbridge	R	23	28	0	0	26	34.1	150	27	20	14	0	0	3	1	14	0	45	14	1	2	2	.500	0	13	3.67
Farmer,Jon,Marlins	R	21	4	1	0	2	16	60	9	5	3	1	0	0	0	2	0	15	2	0	2	0	1.000	0	1	1.69
Kane County	A	21	9	7	0	1	43.2	177	41	21	21	2	1	2	1	4	0	22	2	0	3	3	.500	0	1	4.33
Farnsworth,Shane,Ogden	R	22	8	7	0	0	30.2	149	39	24	17	0	0	1	3	16	1	18	2	1	3	1	.750	0	0	4.99
Farr,Mark,Marlins	R	21	12	2	0	7	37.2	151	25	9	8	2	1	0	1	14	1	43	4	2	4	0	1.000	0	2	1.91
Farson,Brian,Augusta	A	22	30	0	0	9	38.2	166	35	19	15	1	4	2	1	11	1	49	5	0	2	5	.286	0	0	3.49
Faulkner,Edward,Huntington	R	20	14	0	0	5	21.2	93	18	15	7	2	1	1	0	10	0	15	2	1	1	3	.250	0	0	2.91
Feingold,Leon,Butte	A	22	13	1	0	5	20.2	115	20	31	22	1	1	3	3	24	1	19	5	2	1	1	.500	0	0	9.58
Felix,Antonio,White Sox	R	18	5	0	0	2	5	30	9	8	5	1	0	1	1	5	0	3	0	2	0	1	.000	0	0	9.00
Fennell,Barry,Cubs	R	18	11	11	0	0	47.2	224	59	39	33	2	5	3	0	21	0	39	5	1	0	6	.000	0	0	6.23
Fereira,Marcos,White Sox	R	20	11	1	0	6	18.1	80	20	13	13	2	2	0	1	10	0	6	0	0	1	3	.250	0	1	6.38
Fermin,Ramon,Modesto	A	22	29	18	0	8	133	565	129	71	53	12	3	3	9	42	1	120	16	1	9	6	.600	0	5	3.59
Fernandes,James,Sarasota	A	23	9	5	0	3	24.1	128	43	35	33	6	1	0	1	18	1	11	2	3	1	4	.200	0	0	12.21
Fernandez,Fernando,Bend	A	20	21	0	0	8	32.1	171	51	35	26	8	0	3	0	21	0	30	4	2	1	1	.500	0	0	7.24
Fernandez,Jared,Utica	A	23	21	1	0	15	30	144	43	18	12	4	0	0	2	8	2	24	0	1	1	1	.500	0	4	3.60
Fernandez,Osvaldo,Riverside	A	25	14	13	1	0	84.2	353	67	33	27	8	1	2	3	37	0	80	3	4	8	2	.800	1	0	2.87
Fidge,Darren,Elizabethtn	R	20	29	0	0	28	39	146	19	5	3	1	1	0	3	10	0	43	0	0	2	2	.500	0	16	0.69
Filbeck,Ryan,Kane County	A	22	44	0	0	13	53.1	229	57	34	31	3	6	2	4	16	1	39	6	0	3	2	.600	0	1	5.23
Fiore,Tony,Spartanburg	A	23	28	28	9	0	166.2	719	162	94	76	10	2	5	4	77	1	113	19	1	12	13	.480	1	0	4.10
Fitzer,Doug,Riverside	A	25	20	0	0	7	37	150	30	12	9	1	0	0	0	13	0	19	3	0	2	0	1.000	0	0	2.19
Fitzpatrick,Dave,South Bend	A	22	10	0	0	6	15.1	65	16	9	6	0	3	1	0	6	0	9	0	0	1	1	.500	0	1	3.52
Fitzpatrick,Ken,Rockford	A	20	26	13	0	6	106.2	475	115	64	47	5	5	1	6	43	2	52	10	0	4	7	.364	0	1	3.97
Flury,Patrick,Rockford	A	22	34	0	0	18	55	254	61	27	24	3	2	2	5	33	2	41	3	2	1	3	.250	0	2	3.93
Foderaro,Kevin,Johnson Cty	R	22	10	10	0	0	54.2	231	57	23	14	4	0	2	2	10	0	46	2	2	2	2	.500	0	0	2.30
Fontana,Michael,Cedar Rapds	A	25	5	1	0	2	15.1	76	24	21	17	5	0	0	2	11	0	13	2	0	0	2	.000	0	0	9.98
Forbes,Adam,White Sox	R	20	12	2	0	1	33.2	153	35	14	11	1	0	0	1	21	0	29	2	1	2	3	.400	0	0	2.94
Ford,Benjamin,Yankees	R	19	18	0	0	11	34	143	27	13	9	0	0	0	6	8	0	31	3	0	2	0	.500	0	3	2.38
Fordham,Thomas,Hickory	A	21	17	17	1	0	109	452	101	47	38	10	1	1	3	30	1	121	5	4	10	5	.667	1	0	3.14
South Bend	A	21	11	11	1	0	74.2	315	82	46	36	4	4	3	0	14	0	48	4	0	4	4	.500	1	0	4.34
Forster,Pete,Twins	R	20	12	11	0	0	62.2	256	40	27	17	3	2	1	6	37	0	44	6	0	2	5	.286	0	0	2.44
Forster,Scott,Vermont	A	23	12	9	0	0	52.2	236	38	32	19	0	0	1	4	34	0	39	6	2	1	6	.143	0	0	3.25
Fortune,Gresham,Butte	R	22	17	2	0	8	23.1	132	36	39	30	3	0	2	5	19	1	8	5	0	0	3	.000	0	0	11.57
Foshie,Joshua,Marlins	R	22	3	0	0	0	8	32	5	3	3	1	0	0	2	1	0	8	1	0	2	1	.667	0	0	3.38
Foster,Kris,Expos	R	20	18	5	0	5	52.1	229	34	21	9	3	0	1	5	32	0	65	3	2	4	2	.667	0	0	1.55
Foster,Mark,Spartanburg	A	23	32	0	0	25	42.1	192	41	23	21	0	5	1	4	24	0	40	10	3	4	2	.667	0	11	4.46
Clearwater	A	23	16	1	0	5	26.2	118	28	13	10	0	0	0	0	14	0	22	0	1	2	0	.500	0	1	3.38
Foulke,Keith,Everett	A	22	4	4	0	0	19.1	79	17	4	2	0	1	0	2	3	0	22	0	0	2	0	1.000	0	0	0.93
Fox,Chad,Winston-Sal	A	24	25	25	1	0	156.1	674	121	77	67	18	5	5	9	94	0	137	20	1	12	5	.706	0	0	3.86
France,Aaron,Welland	A	21	7	5	0	1	24	98	22	12	6	1	0	1	3	6	0	16	1	1	2	0	.000	0	0	2.25
Franek,Thomas,Spartanburg	A	24	28	7	0	15	71.2	306	79	36	28	5	3	2	3	11	2	54	4	1	3	4	.429	0	6	3.52
Franklin,James,Charlstn-Wv	A	23	18	0	0	5	24.1	106	24	12	8	1	0	0	1	12	0	30	1	0	2	1	.667	0	0	2.96
Franklin,Jay,Daytona	A	26	5	0	0	2	10	49	14	8	7	1	1	0	1	4	1	9	2	0	0	0	.000	0	0	6.30
Franklin,Joel,Billings	R	22	9	9	0	0	45.1	199	41	25	20	3	2	1	4	25	1	26	3	2	3	3	.500	0	0	3.97
Franko,Kristin,San Jose	A	24	21	21	0	0	100.1	466	126	84	68	15	4	4	7	41	0	66	5	1	7	9	.438	0	0	6.10
Clinton	A	24	7	6	0	0	35.1	174	52	34	28	5	1	5	0	20	0	19	6	1	1	3	.250	0	0	7.13
Frascatore,Steven,New Jersey	A	23	12	0	0	0	21.1	100	26	16	15	1	2	0	0	8	0	13	4	0	1	1	.500	0	0	6.33
Freehill,Michael,Boise	A	24	28	0	0	19	45	179	37	20	16	2	4	0	1	10	5	38	2	1	3	6	.333	0	8	3.20
Freeman,Christopher,Dunedin	A	22	17	3	0	5	50.2	205	44	16	14	1	2	2	0	21	1	45	5	2	3	2	.600	0	1	2.49
Fregosi,Danny,Orioles	R	21	8	2	0	4	18.2	78	16	12	11	0	0	1	0	7	0	27	5	0	2	1	.667	0	0	5.30
Freitas,Mike,Padres	R	25	4	0	0	2	6	23	2	1	1	0	0	0	0	3	0	7	1	0	1	0	1.000	0	0	1.50
Fritz,Charles,Idaho Falls	R	23	6	0	0	2	14.2	70	21	11	9	1	2	0	0	5	0	14	0	0	2	0	1.000	0	0	5.52
Frontera,Chad,Everett	A	22	13	12	0	0	59.2	273	60	35	23	3	1	2	7	27	2	50	6	0	4	4	.500	0	0	3.47
Frost,Brady,Vermont	A	23	16	0	0	11	28.1	130	34	19	13	3	0	1	0	7	0	13	3	0	0	4	.000	0	4	4.13
Fuduric,Anton,Bristol	R	20	11	9	0	0	39.1	198	44	38	29	7	1	3	5	30	0	17	7	0	0	2	.000	0	0	6.64
Fuller,Stephen,Astros	R	20	8	1	0	3	14.1	71	17	13	11	1	1	1	0	12	0	13	2	0	1	1	.500	0	0	6.91
Fultz,Aaron,Fort Myers	A	21	28	28	3	0	168.1	745	193	95	81	9	6	4	7	60	5	132	9	2	9	10	.474	0	0	4.33
Fussell,Christopher,Orioles	R	19	14	8	0	2	56.1	245	53	30	26	2	1	4	4	24	0	65	6	1	2	3	.400	0	0	4.15
Gaillard,Julian,Lakeland	A	24	30	9	0	8	92	389	82	37	29	3	1	2	10	29	0	51	3	1	6	1	.857	0	2	2.84
Galindez,Luis,Padres	R	24	1	0	0	0	1	3	0	0	0	0	0	0	0	1	0	1	0	0	0	0	.000	0	0	0.00
Gamboa,Javier,Eugene	A	21	16	14	0	1	62	277	58	45	40	8	1	2	7	29	0	62	6	2	0	5	.000	0	0	5.81
Gambs,Chris,Clinton	A	21	13	4	0	1	33.1	157	37	27	22	3	1	3	0	29	1	21	3	0	0	0	.000	0	0	5.94
San Jose	A	21	4	0	0	2	5	26	6	9	8	1	1	0	0	6	0	4	0	0	0	0	.000	0	0	14.40
Gann,Charlie,Idaho Falls	R	19	25	1	0	11	54	260	76	50	39	8	6	3	8	14	0	24	8	0	1	3	.250	0	0	6.50
Gapski,Mark,Watertown	A	24	14	11	0	2	76.1	339	83	41	37	2	1	2	8	30	0	47	4	2	6	3	.667	0	0	4.36
Garcia,Alfredo,Huntington	R	21	8	4	0	3	30	129	35	23	15	3	0	0	1	6	0	28	0	0	1	4	.200	0	1	4.50
Williamsport	A	21	8	7	3	1	45.1	190	41	16	15	1	1	3	1	17	1	39	4	1	3	3	.500	1	1	2.98

1994 Pitching -- Single-A and Rookie Leagues

Player	Lg	A			HOW MUCH HE PITCHED									WHAT HE GAVE UP									THE RESULTS					
			G	GS	CG	GF	IP	BFP	H	R	ER	HR	SH	SF	HB	TBB	IBB	SO	WP	Bk	W	L	Pct.	ShO	Sv	ERA
Garcia,Ariel,White Sox	R	19	10	8	1	1	50	200	52	20	19	1	1	1	1	4	0	34	3	1	4	3	.571	0	0	3.42
Garcia,Eddy,Princeton	R	19	12	10	0	1	57	254	61	37	30	4	2	4	4	24	0	36	5	4	5	1	.833	0	0	4.74
Garcia,Frank,Cardinals	R	21	27	0	0	25	29.2	116	16	7	4	0	1	0	3	7	0	39	0	0	1	1	.500	0	18	1.21
Garcia,Jose,Braves	R	20	17	8	1	9	52	229	55	37	34	4	1	3	1	21	2	37	3	1	3	7	.300	0	0	5.88
Garcia,Luis,Charlotte	A	25	36	0	0	25	51.2	197	38	15	14	6	1	0	0	9	3	46	2	0	2	3	.400	0	7	2.44
Garcia,Ramon,Welland	A	21	2	0	0	1	1.2	10	2	3	2	0	0	0	1	2	0	1	1	0	0	0	.000	0	0	10.80
Garcia-luna,Francisco,Augusta	A	22	11	11	1	0	58	253	62	31	22	2	2	2	2	16	0	44	6	0	1	5	.167	0	0	3.41
Garrelts,Jason,Marlins	A	22	11	9	2	0	51.1	208	38	24	15	3	1	1	2	17	0	58	2	0	4	1	.800	0	0	2.63
Garrett,Harold,Springfield	A	20	21	20	0	0	102.1	454	93	67	54	8	2	5	6	54	2	79	9	2	7	4	.636	0	0	4.75
Garrett,Jeff,Ogden	R	23	24	0	0	10	59.2	267	69	45	32	5	1	4	4	16	1	48	6	5	2	3	.400	0	4	4.83
Garrett,Neil,Asheville	A	20	29	23	1	0	132	605	158	101	88	23	2	6	8	76	1	100	2	5	7	11	.389	0	0	6.00
Gaskill,Derek,Helena	R	21	2	0	0	1	2.2	16	8	4	4	1	0	0	0	1	0	3	0	0	0	0	.000	0	0	13.50
Brewers	R	21	19	0	0	0	28	129	29	18	11	0	1	2	4	16	0	19	6	0	2	1	.667	0	0	3.54
Gaspar,Cade,Lakeland	A	21	8	8	0	0	30.2	128	28	25	19	6	2	2	3	8	0	25	0	1	1	3	.250	0	0	5.58
Gates,Sean,Padres	R	23	9	0	0	6	12.2	52	7	5	2	0	0	0	1	9	0	7	2	0	0	0	.000	0	1	1.42
Gautreau,Mike,New Jersey	A	23	11	0	0	5	11.2	57	12	11	6	1	1	2	1	5	0	9	2	0	0	1	.000	0	3	4.63
Savannah	A	23	2	0	0	0	5	23	6	3	2	0	0	1	0	1	0	2	0	0	1	0	1.000	0	0	3.60
Gay,Steven,Ogden	R	23	18	1	0	11	24.2	114	27	18	14	2	0	1	2	11	0	21	2	1	2	3	.400	0	4	5.11
Gendron,Jonnie,Welland	A	21	15	11	0	0	71	311	76	50	40	6	2	3	7	30	0	42	7	0	2	8	.200	0	0	5.07
Genke,Mike,Spartanburg	A	24	36	0	0	13	64	259	53	42	17	4	3	2	2	15	0	49	5	0	2	2	.500	0	2	2.39
Geraldo,Antonio,Blue Jays	R	20	15	6	0	5	45.2	192	41	28	22	2	1	2	5	17	0	49	8	2	3	2	.600	0	4	4.34
Gerhart,Bert,Charlstn-Wv	A	22	28	25	6	0	163.2	679	151	81	63	16	2	2	15	39	1	118	5	5	11	12	.478	0	0	3.46
Giard,Ken,Durham	A	22	20	0	0	4	30.1	146	31	23	23	4	1	1	0	27	1	39	3	0	2	4	.333	0	0	6.82
Giles,Thomas,Elmira	A	20	8	0	0	3	12.1	55	14	8	6	0	3	0	0	6	2	10	2	0	0	1	.000	0	0	4.38
Marlins	R	20	12	0	0	8	19.2	83	16	7	6	1	0	1	0	9	0	15	0	0	1	2	.333	0	3	2.75
Gilmore,Joel,Clearwater	A	25	20	19	1	1	119.1	495	121	57	43	11	0	4	4	20	3	72	4	1	9	6	.600	0	1	3.24
Giron,Emiliano,Princeton	R	23	21	0	0	14	56.2	235	31	20	14	4	6	4	5	26	2	77	7	1	4	3	.571	0	5	2.22
Giuliano,Joseph,Braves	R	19	14	12	0	0	66.1	299	85	51	39	4	1	3	2	14	0	48	6	2	3	6	.333	0	0	5.29
Glasscock,Jon,San Bernrdo	A	28	11	8	0	0	30.2	154	47	37	33	7	2	0	4	13	0	17	1	0	1	5	.167	0	0	9.68
Glauber,Keith,New Jersey	A	23	17	10	0	3	68.2	289	67	36	32	3	4	2	2	26	1	51	8	0	4	6	.400	0	0	4.19
Glover,John,Blue Jays	R	18	2	0	0	0	1.1	13	4	8	7	1	0	0	1	4	0	2	1	1	0	0	.000	0	0	47.25
Gobert,Christopher,Danville	R	19	12	0	0	2	19.1	89	20	13	12	2	0	0	2	13	0	22	4	0	0	0	.000	0	0	5.59
Goedde,Roger,Pirates	R	19	9	9	1	0	47.1	199	41	26	11	0	0	0	1	19	0	35	5	4	2	3	.400	0	0	2.09
Goedhart,Darrell,Clearwater	A	24	21	1	0	4	38	161	34	23	15	1	2	0	1	17	4	33	6	0	2	3	.400	0	0	3.55
Goergen,Todd,Clearwater	A	27	8	0	0	2	11	48	10	3	3	0	0	0	0	5	1	4	0	0	0	0	.000	0	0	2.45
Gogolewski,Christopher,Rangers	R	21	6	6	1	0	30.2	119	26	8	4	1	0	0	0	5	0	22	0	5	3	2	.600	1	0	1.17
Hudson Vail	A	21	7	7	1	0	40.1	164	34	22	18	1	2	1	3	12	0	31	2	3	3	3	.500	0	0	4.02
Gogolin,Elton,W. Michigan	A	23	11	0	0	3	18.1	83	13	6	3	0	1	1	0	14	0	23	0	2	0	0	.000	0	1	1.47
Gold,Steve,Helena	R	21	15	3	0	5	36.2	163	37	23	23	5	1	4	2	16	0	22	4	3	2	1	.667	0	2	5.65
Golden,Matthew,New Jersey	A	23	13	11	0	2	60	263	70	34	33	4	3	2	4	12	0	45	6	0	5	3	.625	0	0	4.95
Gomes,Wayne,Clearwater	A	22	23	21	1	0	104.1	474	85	63	55	5	2	4	3	82	2	102	27	4	6	8	.429	1	0	4.74
Gomez,Alexander,Angels	R	20	15	0	0	5	29	117	20	8	8	0	1	1	3	13	1	24	4	1	0	0	.000	0	1	2.48
Gomez,Augustine,Hickory	A	21	32	0	0	19	59.1	233	41	20	20	3	2	1	2	30	0	53	2	0	5	1	.833	0	3	3.03
Gomez,Dennys,Clinton	A	24	6	0	0	2	11	49	11	8	6	1	1	1	0	5	1	3	1	0	0	2	.000	0	0	4.91
Everett	A	24	21	0	0	13	35.1	159	34	14	10	2	4	2	3	17	4	37	4	1	4	1	.800	0	2	2.55
Gongora,Gordy,Danville	R	20	21	0	0	8	31	138	32	16	12	1	3	1	0	9	0	17	0	1	1	2	.333	0	2	3.48
Gontkosky,Robert,Columbia	A	22	36	4	0	14	70.2	327	75	38	28	6	2	3	8	37	1	67	3	1	2	7	.222	0	5	3.57
Gonzalez,Generoso,Bristol	R	19	17	3	0	4	36	165	30	22	17	3	0	1	5	23	0	23	7	2	1	1	.500	0	0	4.25
Gonzalez,Geremis,Peoria	A	20	13	13	1	0	71.1	325	86	53	44	4	2	3	7	32	0	39	5	2	1	6	.125	0	0	5.55
Williamsprt	A	20	16	12	1	2	80.2	357	83	46	38	6	3	3	10	23	0	64	4	1	4	6	.400	1	1	4.24
Gonzalez,Jess,Lethbridge	R	23	12	2	0	6	28	126	31	23	21	2	1	3	1	12	1	26	0	0	1	1	.500	0	1	6.75
High Desert	A	23	3	0	0	1	12.2	47	9	2	2	1	0	0	0	1	0	10	0	0	0	0	.000	0	0	1.42
Gonzalez,Jhonny,Rockies	R	18	20	0	0	13	28.1	122	25	14	8	0	1	1	2	12	1	31	1	1	1	4	.200	0	3	2.54
Gonzalez,Juan,Helena	R	20	2	0	0	1	5.1	26	9	1	1	0	0	1	0	1	0	3	1	0	1	0	1.000	0	0	1.69
Brewers	R	20	14	14	0	0	86.2	370	96	47	32	1	0	5	6	23	0	68	16	1	5	3	.625	0	0	3.32
Gonzalez,Laril,Rockies	R	19	16	1	0	7	28.2	135	28	24	15	1	1	2	2	21	2	23	9	0	3	2	.600	0	0	4.71
Gonzalez,Santo,Rockies	R	18	18	0	0	4	25.2	116	16	17	16	1	1	0	6	23	1	26	8	0	1	3	.250	0	0	5.61
Gooch,Amie,Rockies	R	18	15	9	0	1	58	238	45	28	17	0	2	2	0	16	0	66	12	1	2	4	.333	0	0	2.64
Goodrich,Jon,Bend	A	22	3	1	0	0	11.2	49	11	4	3	0	1	0	0	4	0	9	0	0	0	0	.000	0	0	2.31
Asheville	A	22	21	0	0	9	49	217	50	32	24	7	3	1	2	24	2	41	5	1	0	3	.000	0	2	4.41
Gordon,Mike,Greensboro	A	23	23	22	0	0	107.1	501	128	88	77	15	1	3	8	54	0	116	11	1	2	10	.167	0	0	6.46
Gosch,Grant,Astros	R	20	1	0	0	0	0	3	0	3	3	0	0	0	0	4	0	0	2	1	0	0	.000	0	0	0.00
Gottsch,Jerry,Butte	R	23	20	1	0	4	44.1	207	51	33	30	3	1	4	1	31	2	35	8	1	1	2	.333	0	0	6.09
Gourdin,Tom,Fort Wayne	A	21	29	1	0	11	52.2	251	75	50	42	2	2	0	5	24	0	32	11	2	2	3	.400	0	1	7.18
Grace,Mike,Spartanburg	A	25	15	15	0	0	80.1	345	84	50	43	6	4	1	8	20	1	45	0	2	5	5	.500	0	0	4.82
Graham,Steven,Danville	R	23	18	0	0	8	36	151	26	18	13	0	3	2	2	14	2	37	6	1	3	1	.750	0	3	3.25
Granata,Chris,Watertown	A	23	22	1	0	7	49.2	203	44	23	19	3	2	0	1	11	1	39	1	0	1	2	.333	0	2	3.44
Granger,Gregory,Fayetteville	A	22	26	24	1	0	160.1	666	138	72	59	12	5	2	12	47	0	118	15	4	9	7	.563	0	0	3.31
Grant,Brian,St. Cathrns	A	22	15	15	0	0	84.1	360	75	41	34	2	1	2	2	35	0	90	7	2	5	3	.625	0	0	3.63
Grasser,Craig,Savannah	A	25	56	0	0	49	58.2	244	45	20	12	3	2	0	6	20	1	87	3	1	2	2	.500	0	37	1.84
Green,Christopher,Bellingham	A	20	28	0	0	15	34	156	33	23	16	1	6	1	3	17	4	25	5	0	2	3	.400	0	3	4.24
Green,David,Astros	R	20	18	0	0	7	23	96	16	11	7	0	1	1	1	16	0	12	6	4	2	1	.667	0	0	2.74
Green,Jason,Macon	A	21	10	8	0	1	29	150	36	32	29	4	0	1	0	40	0	40	9	0	0	3	.000	0	0	9.00
Danville	R	21	11	11	0	0	56	254	26	29	18	2	1	2	2	60	1	83	8	2	5	4	.556	0	0	2.89
Greene,Jake,Kane County	A	23	15	0	0	2	20.2	103	22	25	14	2	1	2	1	12	0	12	3	1	0	2	.000	0	0	6.10
Elmira	A	23	5	0	0	1	8	32	3	1	0	0	0	0	0	6	0	10	1	0	0	0	.000	0	1	0.00
Grenert,Geoff,Cedar Rapds	A	24	45	2	0	15	93	404	81	46	36	9	3	4	5	38	7	74	7	2	6	6	.500	0	3	3.48

1994 Pitching -- Single-A and Rookie Leagues

Player	Lg	A	G	GS	CG	GF	IP	BFP	H	R	ER	HR	SH	SF	HB	TBB	IBB	SO	WP	Bk	W	L	Pct.	ShO	Sv	ERA
Grennan,Steven,Columbia	A	24	47	0	0	22	69.1	299	40	22	18	4	3	0	14	41	3	100	9	1	4	4	.500	0	1	2.34
Grieve,Timothy,Eugene	A	23	25	0	0	6	58	227	28	12	10	1	3	1	3	26	0	84	1	1	7	1	.875	0	1	1.55
Griffin,Ryan,Albany	A	21	17	0	0	15	26.1	119	23	12	11	1	1	1	2	18	1	20	2	0	0	2	.000	0	8	3.76
Bluefield	R	21	16	9	2	4	65.2	276	58	32	27	3	1	3	2	19	0	43	6	0	6	4	.600	0	0	3.70
Griffith,Jeremy,White Sox	R	19	4	0	0	1	7.2	33	7	2	2	0	0	0	2	4	0	2	2	2	0	0	.000	0	0	2.35
Grimm,John,Lakeland	A	24	44	0	0	37	53.2	222	37	19	15	3	2	0	1	31	2	65	2	1	4	3	.571	0	19	2.52
Grote,Jason,Giants	R	20	18	0	0	5	28.2	132	26	15	11	2	4	2	0	16	2	35	1	0	2	2	.500	0	2	3.45
Grundy,Phillip,Rockford	A	22	27	26	0	0	151.1	622	135	65	54	6	1	4	1	51	3	116	14	0	15	8	.652	0	0	3.21
Grzanich,Mike,Quad City	A	22	23	22	3	1	142.2	598	145	55	49	5	2	1	11	43	2	101	5	0	11	7	.611	0	0	3.09
Grzelaczyk,Kenny,Rancho Cuca	A	24	23	8	0	4	69	311	76	51	42	6	0	3	1	34	1	51	4	2	0	5	.000	0	1	5.48
Guerra,Esmili,Peoria	A	23	11	0	0	5	18.2	78	11	6	2	0	1	1	0	6	0	8	0	1	1	0	1.000	0	1	0.96
Guerra,Mark,Pittsfield	A	23	14	14	2	0	94	392	105	47	36	4	4	5	4	21	1	62	2	2	7	6	.538	0	0	3.45
Gulledge,Derek,Bluefield	R	22	3	0	0	2	7	30	7	5	5	1	0	1	0	4	0	10	3	0	1	0	1.000	0	0	6.43
Gunderson,Michael,Auburn	A	22	2	2	0	0	5.2	31	8	6	6	0	0	1	0	9	0	4	0	0	0	1	.000	0	0	9.53
Gunnett,Chris,Lethbridge	R	24	19	2	0	6	39.1	185	49	28	24	3	1	4	3	21	1	25	2	3	1	2	.333	0	1	5.49
High Desert	A	24	6	0	0	6	7.1	31	6	1	0	0	0	0	0	4	1	2	0	0	1	0	1.000	0	1	0.00
Gutierrez,Alfredo,Brewers	R	19	18	0	0	6	23.1	102	23	10	8	1	1	1	3	11	0	15	2	0	0	2	.000	0	2	3.09
Guzik,Robbie,St. Lucie	A	25	9	0	0	7	8	37	9	5	3	1	0	0	0	4	0	8	1	0	0	0	.000	0	7	3.38
German,Domingo,Padres	R	20	13	13	0	0	70	309	65	39	32	1	1	2	11	25	0	55	5	2	8	4	.667	0	0	4.11
Haas,Dave,Lakeland	A	29	5	3	0	0	20	90	23	9	8	0	2	3	3	8	0	4	0	0	1	0	1.000	0	0	3.60
Hacen,Abraham,Orioles	R	24	7	0	0	3	15.2	73	21	13	11	0	1	1	0	8	0	13	1	0	0	1	.000	0	0	6.32
Hackett,Jason,Orioles	R	20	14	10	0	2	50.2	266	81	66	48	3	1	1	3	28	0	34	16	1	0	8	.000	0	0	8.53
Hackman,Luther,Rockies	R	20	12	12	0	0	55.2	234	50	21	13	1	0	0	1	16	0	63	1	1	1	3	.250	0	1	2.10
Hagan,Danny,Charlstn-Sc	A	23	27	22	1	2	128.2	571	137	68	54	9	4	6	9	59	0	96	17	2	8	10	.444	1	1	3.78
Halama,John,Auburn	A	23	6	3	0	3	28	107	18	5	4	1	2	0	0	5	0	21	1	1	4	1	.800	0	1	1.29
Quad City	A	23	9	9	1	0	51.1	222	63	31	26	2	3	0	2	18	1	37	3	0	3	4	.429	1	0	4.56
Hale,Chad,Lynchburg	A	23	20	0	0	13	24.1	102	28	12	10	2	2	0	0	9	1	15	2	1	0	3	.000	0	1	3.70
Hale,Shane,Albany	A	21	11	10	0	0	55.1	239	54	31	25	3	2	2	5	22	0	52	2	5	2	3	.400	0	0	4.07
Frederick	A	26	11	11	0	0	62	277	68	38	34	10	4	3	3	30	0	49	5	3	4	1	.571	0	0	4.94
Hall,Billy,Astros	R	21	12	0	0	8	19.1	74	7	7	4	0	2	0	0	5	0	24	0	0	5	1	.833	0	0	1.86
Quad City	A	21	9	0	0	4	13.2	63	11	8	5	1	4	1	0	7	1	20	5	1	1	2	.333	0	0	3.29
Hall,Yates,New Jersey	A	22	10	8	0	0	48.1	192	32	13	10	1	4	0	0	21	0	50	5	1	3	2	.600	0	0	1.86
Halperin,Michael,St. Cathrns	A	21	9	1	0	5	24	86	11	5	3	0	0	1	0	5	0	19	2	0	2	1	.667	0	1	1.13
Hagerstown	A	21	6	6	0	0	30	116	25	4	4	1	1	0	0	7	0	27	3	1	2	1	.667	0	1	1.20
Hamilton,Paul,Martinsvlle	A	23	19	2	0	3	34.2	161	49	28	23	7	2	0	0	8	0	25	1	3	3	4	.429	0	0	5.97
Hamm,Eric,Cubs	R	22	4	0	0	3	10.1	47	10	5	4	0	0	0	3	4	0	4	0	0	2	1	.667	0	0	3.48
Hancock,Brian,Stockton	A	24	1	0	0	0	1.1	8	4	4	4	0	0	0	0	1	0	0	0	0	0	0	.000	0	0	27.00
Handy,Russell,Burlington	A	20	4	4	0	0	17	85	25	22	19	2	0	0	3	9	0	12	0	1	1	3	.250	0	0	10.06
Vermont	A	20	14	14	1	0	67.1	315	73	53	34	3	2	7	6	33	0	51	4	0	4	5	.444	1	0	4.54
Hansen,Brent,Sarasota	A	23	8	7	0	1	40.1	167	37	15	13	0	0	1	0	15	0	27	3	0	2	2	.500	0	0	2.90
Hanson,Craig,Rancho Cuca	A	24	49	2	0	13	83	374	78	37	29	9	2	2	1	47	4	83	9	0	7	5	.583	0	3	3.14
Hanson,Kristofor,Columbus	A	23	18	18	1	0	101.2	417	93	50	42	10	2	2	6	22	0	75	3	1	6	7	.462	0	0	3.72
Harpe,Daniel,Spokane	A	20	1	0	0	0	2	10	3	2	2	0	0	0	0	0	0	3	1	0	0	0	.000	0	0	9.00
Padres	R	20	14	1	0	6	23	114	23	18	14	0	1	0	2	11	0	33	13	0	1	1	.500	0	1	5.48
Harris,James,Lake Elsino	A	23	26	26	5	0	168.1	719	157	94	71	12	5	6	8	62	1	149	14	2	10	10	.500	1	0	3.80
Harrison,Brian,San Bernrdo	A	28	23	1	0	8	58.1	258	61	28	25	5	5	2	2	29	1	65	4	0	5	1	.833	0	3	3.86
Hart,Jason,Peoria	A	23	20	0	0	10	37.1	149	29	17	15	4	1	1	0	7	0	33	3	0	4	2	.667	0	3	3.62
Daytona	A	23	26	0	0	23	37.1	150	26	11	7	1	0	2	2	6	0	39	3	0	3	3	.500	0	12	1.69
Hartgrove,Lyle,Utica	A	23	6	0	0	5	13.1	56	11	3	3	0	1	0	0	5	0	11	0	3	1	1	.500	0	1	2.03
Sarasota	A	23	18	0	0	8	30	128	34	12	11	2	1	0	1	3	0	18	0	1	1	2	.000	0	0	3.30
Hartman,Peter,Charlotte	A	24	26	24	0	1	128.1	575	132	70	65	8	4	5	4	77	0	107	15	6	5	11	.313	0	0	4.56
Hartmann,Richard,New Jersey	A	21	11	0	0	5	17.1	73	17	9	8	1	0	0	0	7	0	18	2	0	2	0	1.000	0	0	4.15
Hartnett,William,Osceola	A	24	35	17	1	9	129.1	542	112	66	56	10	4	8	6	47	3	85	3	4	4	13	.235	0	4	3.90
Hartshorn,Tyson,Blue Jays	R	20	10	10	0	0	54.1	209	38	15	11	0	0	1	1	17	1	52	2	0	2	3	.400	0	0	1.82
Hartung,Michael,Williamsprt	A	22	4	0	0	2	5	30	9	7	4	0	0	0	1	5	0	2	0	0	0	0	.000	0	0	7.20
Huntington	R	22	16	0	0	12	22.2	89	14	8	6	2	1	0	0	5	0	23	0	0	0	2	.000	0	0	2.38
Hartvigson,Chad,Everett	A	22	12	1	0	1	40.2	168	34	16	15	5	1	0	0	14	3	51	4	2	2	2	.500	0	0	3.32
Harvell,Albert,Charlstn-Sc	A	23	41	8	0	11	92	423	104	55	40	6	3	3	5	48	4	67	7	0	3	7	.300	0	0	3.91
Haught,Gary,Modesto	A	24	39	1	0	13	70.2	292	66	35	34	8	6	1	2	26	0	52	2	0	4	3	.571	0	2	4.33
Hause,Brendan,Sou. Oregon	A	20	13	6	0	3	58	239	46	18	13	0	1	2	3	23	1	55	3	4	4	1	.800	0	2	2.02
W. Michigan	A	20	4	2	0	0	13.1	59	16	9	8	1	3	1	0	6	0	5	0	0	0	1	.000	0	0	5.40
Hausmann,Isaac,Rangers	R	19	9	0	0	3	16.1	72	16	9	4	1	0	0	3	4	1	13	0	0	1	1	.500	0	0	2.20
Havens,Jeff,Williamsprt	A	22	4	0	0	0	6.1	32	12	8	8	0	1	0	0	2	0	2	0	0	0	0	.000	0	0	11.37
Hayward,Steve,Lynchburg	A	24	27	21	0	3	133.2	612	160	95	67	10	4	13	8	54	2	87	19	2	4	14	.222	0	1	4.51
Hebbert,Allan,Elmira	A	22	8	7	0	0	29.1	149	37	27	26	4	0	0	2	16	0	16	4	0	3	3	.500	0	0	7.98
Hebel,Jon,Charlstn-Sc	A	24	7	1	0	1	13	64	11	15	13	1	0	0	0	14	0	9	1	0	0	0	.000	0	0	9.00
Heflin,Bronson,Batavia	A	23	14	13	1	0	83	353	85	38	33	5	5	0	6	20	0	71	11	2	6	5	.545	0	0	3.58
Heiserman,Rick,Watertown	A	22	7	0	0	2	11.2	48	6	3	3	0	0	1	0	5	0	6	2	2	1	0	1.000	0	0	2.31
Heisler,Laurence,Spartanburg	A	26	21	0	0	7	41.1	185	46	23	20	3	1	2	3	16	1	36	5	1	2	0	1.000	0	1	4.35
Helfrich,Christopher,Sou Oregon	A	23	23	3	0	8	42.2	208	49	38	33	4	2	4	4	28	1	33	3	0	2	1	.667	0	0	6.96
Helvey,Robert,Johnson Cty	R	23	25	0	0	14	27	129	25	20	18	3	0	0	2	18	2	36	5	0	5	3	.625	0	3	6.00
Henderson,Chris,Central Val	A	23	51	4	0	26	73	340	72	47	44	6	2	4	0	50	3	72	15	0	5	3	.625	0	7	5.42
Henderson,Lester,Medicne Hat	R	23	19	0	0	5	31	155	41	27	20	1	1	3	3	19	0	27	2	0	1	2	.333	0	1	5.81
Hennis,Randy,Brevard Cty	A	29	6	4	0	0	22.2	101	27	15	14	2	0	0	0	6	0	12	0	1	3	1	.750	0	0	5.56
Henrickson,John,Lethbridge	R	22	13	10	1	1	59	285	71	46	40	1	2	3	6	24	0	55	8	5	4	4	.444	1	0	6.10
Henrikson,Dan,Clinton	A	26	16	1	0	4	36.2	167	44	26	21	2	3	2	2	15	0	25	3	0	2	0	1.000	0	1	5.15
San Jose	A	26	31	1	0	14	67.2	291	67	32	28	8	3	1	2	24	2	60	3	0	2	5	.286	0	3	3.72

1994 Pitching -- Single-A and Rookie Leagues

Player	Lg	A	G	GS	CG	GF	IP	BFP	H	R	ER	HR	SH	SF	HB	TBB	IBB	SO	WP	Bk	W	L	Pct.	ShO	Sv	ERA
Herbert,Russell,White Sox	R	23	4	2	0	1	13	46	6	3	3	0	0	0	0	3	0	19	0	0	0	1	.000	0	1	2.08
Hickory	A	23	8	7	0	1	36.2	154	33	14	14	3	1	0	2	15	0	34	1	2	2	1	.667	0	0	3.44
Heredia,Felix,Kane County	A	19	24	8	1	11	68	306	86	55	43	7	3	4	3	14	0	65	6	0	4	5	.444	0	3	5.69
Herges,Matt,Vero Beach	A	25	48	3	1	12	111	476	115	45	41	8	8	2	4	33	3	61	3	3	8	9	.471	0	3	3.32
Hermanson,Mike,Rancho Cuca	A	23	25	18	0	2	94.2	444	100	68	65	11	5	2	11	54	2	78	12	1	2	6	.250	0	0	6.18
Hernandez,Rudy,White Sox	R	18	4	0	0	2	4	18	4	3	2	0	0	0	0	3	0	1	0	0	0	1	.000	0	0	4.50
Hernandez,Santos,Clinton	A	22	32	0	0	11	48	201	47	23	20	5	6	2	4	10	1	48	4	4	5	7	.417	0	4	3.75
Hermann,Gary,Clearwater	A	25	1	1	0	0	1.2	6	1	0	0	0	0	0	0	0	0	1	0	0	0	0	.000	0	0	0.00
Hibbard,William,Blue Jays	R	19	19	0	0	12	32.1	137	32	14	8	1	2	0	0	8	1	23	1	1	3	5	.375	0	3	2.23
Hijus,Erik,St. Lucie	A	22	26	26	3	0	160.2	709	159	85	71	8	6	10	5	90	3	140	10	8	11	10	.524	1	0	3.98
Hill,Shane,Butte	R	23	21	8	4	10	79	360	110	61	49	10	0	1	8	9	3	46	8	0	4	6	.400	0	1	5.58
Hill,Jason,Boise	A	23	23	0	0	8	29.2	135	31	14	10	2	0	1	1	16	3	37	2	2	4	3	.571	0	2	3.03
Hill,Kendall,Braves	R	20	15	1	0	3	37	175	43	29	25	0	3	4	0	20	0	23	2	1	0	2	.000	0	0	6.08
Hill,Shawn,Peoria	A	25	51	0	0	49	50	203	30	20	17	2	2	1	2	19	3	65	1	1	3	3	.500	0	25	3.06
Hiller,Joseph,Beloit	A	23	14	0	0	5	17.1	82	18	12	11	1	1	2	0	13	2	14	1	1	2	2	.500	0	0	5.71
Hillis,Jon,Helena	R	23	14	0	0	4	21.1	116	29	26	22	1	1	2	2	21	0	16	13	0	1	3	.250	0	0	9.28
Hillman,Gregory,Peoria	A	25	26	26	4	0	157	688	182	107	86	17	8	7	2	52	0	142	6	6	8	11	.421	0	0	4.93
Hinchliffe,Brett,Appleton	A	20	27	27	3	0	173.2	721	140	79	62	16	7	4	10	50	4	160	5	2	11	7	.611	1	0	3.21
Hingle,Larry,Lake Elsino	A	24	15	0	0	9	26.1	121	28	15	11	2	0	3	0	15	0	13	3	0	0	0	.000	0	1	3.76
Osceola	A	24	17	0	0	8	22	95	17	5	2	1	3	1	0	11	3	10	0	0	2	1	.667	0	0	0.82
Hinson,Dean,High Desert	A	23	32	0	0	22	45	224	52	41	32	4	0	3	7	30	0	37	4	0	3	3	.500	0	7	6.40
Lake Elsino	A	23	3	0	0	1	4	19	6	3	3	1	0	0	1	0	0	3	0	0	0	0	.000	0	0	6.75
Hmielewski,Chris,W. Palm Bch	A	24	41	1	0	10	78.2	327	75	41	37	7	0	6	0	32	0	54	9	1	3	2	.600	0	3	4.23
Hoalton,Brandon,Idaho Falls	R	21	13	11	0	2	54	239	62	35	28	3	2	3	4	22	0	35	7	4	2	2	.500	0	1	4.67
Hobson,Daren,Sarasota	A	23	7	0	0	5	5.1	25	4	3	3	0	0	0	0	6	0	4	0	0	0	0	.000	0	0	5.06
Red Sox	R	23	3	0	0	2	2.1	13	4	4	4	0	0	0	0	2	0	2	0	0	0	1	.000	0	1	15.43
Hodges,Kevin,Rockford	A	22	24	17	2	6	114.1	466	96	53	43	5	3	0	9	35	1	83	7	3	9	6	.600	1	3	3.38
Hoffman,Edson,Ogden	R	24	20	2	0	8	34.1	155	44	22	15	2	0	0	0	10	0	27	3	0	2	2	.500	0	0	3.93
Hogan,Sean,Williamsprt	A	23	2	0	0	0	5.1	23	2	1	1	0	0	0	0	6	0	7	0	0	1	0	1.000	0	0	1.69
Hogue,Jay,Ogden	R	22	5	5	0	0	23	103	29	18	14	1	1	2	0	14	0	15	0	0	2	2	.500	0	0	5.48
Holcomb,Shawn,Angels	R	21	1	0	0	1	1	5	1	1	1	0	0	0	0	1	0	1	0	0	0	1	.000	0	0	9.00
Holden,Stephen,Athletics	R	21	16	0	0	5	28.1	150	40	26	24	0	0	1	6	24	1	20	10	0	1	1	1.000	0	0	7.62
Holland,Joel,Marlins	R	23	12	0	0	5	20.2	102	24	22	13	1	2	2	0	15	1	16	14	0	1	1	.500	0	0	5.66
Hollins,Jessie,Daytona	A	25	4	0	0	2	5	26	7	4	4	0	0	0	1	3	0	2	0	0	0	0	.000	0	0	7.20
Hollins,Stacy,Modesto	A	22	29	22	0	3	143.1	610	133	57	54	10	4	2	8	55	1	131	7	1	13	6	.684	0	0	3.39
Hollis,Ronald,Yakima	A	21	15	9	0	3	61.1	275	63	34	27	5	2	0	4	23	2	52	5	1	4	2	.667	0	1	3.96
Holtz,Michael,Boise	A	22	22	0	0	16	35	143	22	4	2	0	2	0	1	11	2	59	3	1	0	0	.000	0	11	0.51
Homan,John,Ogden	R	22	4	3	0	0	11	62	27	17	14	2	0	1	2	5	0	6	1	0	0	0	.000	0	0	11.45
Hook,Jeffrey,Astros	R	20	11	11	0	0	46	209	40	32	26	2	2	1	5	26	0	46	5	4	0	4	.000	0	0	5.09
Hornbeck,Ryan,Everett	A	22	6	2	0	0	11.1	58	10	12	7	2	0	1	6	8	0	11	0	1	1	1	.500	0	0	5.56
Horton,Eric,Medicne Hat	R	24	19	0	0	1	37.1	176	38	26	20	1	1	0	4	26	1	34	6	2	4	2	.667	0	1	4.82
Hostetler,Jeff,High Desert	A	24	10	0	0	3	17.1	98	24	24	17	3	1	0	1	16	0	14	1	0	0	0	.000	0	0	8.83
Hostetler,Marcus,Macon	A	25	46	0	0	34	73.1	311	57	19	13	2	3	0	5	30	6	84	5	0	5	4	.556	0	9	1.60
Howard,Christopher,Bend	A	23	24	0	0	8	32.1	159	42	25	17	6	3	1	2	17	1	28	3	0	2	3	.400	0	0	4.73
Howard,Jim,Macon	A	21	7	7	0	0	24.1	113	27	13	11	0	1	4	0	10	0	17	3	0	2	3	.400	0	0	4.07
Howard,Tom,Marlins	R	19	11	4	0	2	32	157	28	22	21	0	1	0	2	34	0	37	8	0	1	2	.333	0	1	5.91
Howell,Ken,San Bernrdo	A	34	11	8	0	0	47	214	55	35	29	7	2	2	4	20	0	43	4	1	1	4	.200	0	0	5.55
Hower,Daniel,Hudson Vall	A	22	14	7	0	6	26.2	135	26	21	17	1	1	1	1	27	0	23	4	0	1	2	.333	0	0	5.74
Howry,Bobby,Everett	A	21	5	5	0	0	19	97	29	19	15	3	0	1	1	10	2	16	5	0	0	4	.000	0	0	7.11
Clinton	A	21	9	8	0	0	49.1	219	61	29	23	1	3	4	3	16	0	22	4	2	2	3	.250	0	0	4.20
Howze,Ben,Daytona	A	25	8	1	0	2	20.1	92	28	11	11	1	1	0	1	8	1	6	4	0	0	1	.000	0	0	4.87
Hoy,Wayne,St. Cathrns	A	24	3	0	0	1	4	19	7	1	0	0	0	0	0	1	0	1	0	1	0	0	.000	0	0	0.00
Hubbard,Mark,Greensboro	A	25	26	26	2	0	149.1	642	162	69	59	11	1	5	7	46	0	139	4	3	13	7	.650	1	0	3.56
Tampa	A	25	2	1	0	1	6.2	33	9	6	3	2	0	1	0	2	0	5	0	0	0	1	.000	0	0	4.05
Huber,Aaron,Sou. Oregon	A	22	17	7	0	3	55.2	265	72	49	36	6	2	4	5	23	0	35	6	3	2	2	.400	0	1	5.82
Huffman,Jason,Eugene	A	22	2	0	0	1	2.1	13	5	3	1	0	1	0	0	1	0	2	0	0	0	0	.000	0	0	3.86
Huffman,Jeffrey,Utica	A	23	16	6	0	0	53.1	234	58	33	28	1	1	0	2	21	1	50	5	0	1	3	.250	0	0	4.72
Humphrey,Richard,Astros	R	24	4	0	0	0	7	30	7	3	1	0	1	0	1	3	0	8	0	0	1	0	1.000	0	0	1.29
Osceola	A	24	3	0	0	0	6	32	8	8	7	0	0	4	0	3	0	5	0	0	0	0	.000	0	0	10.50
Humphry,Trevor,Spartanburg	A	23	12	0	0	5	16.1	76	20	14	12	1	2	0	0	6	0	15	0	0	1	1	.500	0	0	6.61
Hunt,William,Fayetteville	A	24	41	2	0	16	93	394	76	34	27	3	10	1	5	51	3	84	5	2	4	5	.444	0	2	2.61
Hunter,Richard,Martinsvlle	R	20	18	0	0	8	38	153	31	19	19	3	1	2	0	9	1	39	1	0	3	2	.600	0	2	4.50
Huntsman,Brandon,Orioles	R	19	12	10	0	1	40	189	29	21	20	2	1	1	7	36	0	36	6	0	2	4	.333	0	0	4.50
Huntsman,Scott,Brewers	R	22	4	0	0	4	3.2	12	1	0	0	0	0	0	0	0	0	3	0	0	0	0	.000	0	0	0.00
Helena	R	22	17	0	0	10	20	99	28	19	15	2	3	1	1	11	1	22	1	0	0	1	.000	0	5	6.75
Hurtado,Edwin,Hagerstown	A	25	33	16	1	9	134.1	553	118	53	44	8	0	4	1	46	0	121	6	2	11	2	.846	0	2	2.95
Iddon,Brant,Mariners	R	19	11	8	0	2	36.1	155	32	18	14	1	1	1	3	10	1	34	3	1	2	2	.500	0	0	3.47
Iglesias,Mike,Vero Beach	A	22	19	14	1	3	89.2	376	87	46	42	9	2	4	1	29	2	50	4	1	3	6	.333	0	0	4.22
Inman,Bert,San Bernrdo	A	24	16	16	0	0	74	340	78	57	53	8	3	5	5	58	0	62	11	0	2	9	.182	0	0	6.45
Ippolito,Robert,Bellingham	R	22	25	0	0	11	40	170	29	14	12	2	2	0	6	19	0	47	1	0	3	3	.500	0	6	2.70
Isom,Jeffrey,Augusta	A	22	13	0	0	3	15	70	17	8	4	1	0	1	0	5	0	13	5	0	0	0	.000	0	0	2.40
Springfield	A	22	24	0	0	14	34	134	29	8	5	1	1	1	0	6	2	29	4	0	0	3	.000	0	3	1.32
Jacobs,Dwayne,Braves	R	18	12	1	0	6	28.2	135	35	29	26	0	1	3	3	19	0	14	8	0	1	2	.333	0	0	8.16
Jacobs,Michael,Red Sox	R	22	13	4	0	1	30.1	142	38	26	25	1	1	2	0	19	0	20	6	0	1	3	.400	0	0	7.42
Jacobs,Russell,Mariners	R	20	8	1	0	2	13.1	52	9	4	4	0	0	1	0	5	0	12	1	0	0	0	.000	0	0	2.70
Jacobs,Ryan,Macon	A	21	27	18	1	2	121.2	532	105	54	39	9	4	2	3	62	2	81	6	1	8	7	.533	1	1	2.88
Jacobson,Kelton,Jamestown	A	24	10	5	0	2	27.2	121	29	15	9	2	0	1	0	9	1	18	1	2	2	1	.667	0	0	2.93

1994 Pitching -- Single-A and Rookie Leagues

Player	Lg	A	G	GS	CG	GF	IP	BFP	H	R	ER	HR	SH	SF	HB	TBB	IBB	SO	WP	Bk	W	L	Pct.	ShO	Sv	ERA
Janzen,Marty,Greensboro	A	22	17	17	0	0	104	431	98	57	45	8	0	0	2	25	1	92	2	1	3	7	.300	0	0	3.89
Jarvis,Jason,Oneonta	A	21	19	7	0	6	65.1	259	40	20	17	0	1	1	3	18	1	78	2	2	4	2	.667	0	2	2.34
Greensboro	A	21	2	0	0	2	6.2	32	8	3	3	0	0	0	0	5	0	7	0	0	1	0	1.000	0	0	4.05
Jarvis,Matt,Frederick	A	23	31	14	0	3	103.2	459	92	58	48	7	5	2	9	48	0	67	3	0	10	4	.714	0	1	4.17
Jaye,Robert,Great Falls	R	22	2	0	0	0	4.1	21	6	4	1	0	0	0	0	0	0	3	0	0	0	0	.000	0	0	2.08
Jenkins,Arthur,Spokane	A	23	18	11	0	0	69	323	81	51	41	2	2	1	3	38	1	71	6	0	3	6	.333	0	0	5.35
Jenkins,Jonathan,Frederick	A	27	3	0	0	0	5	24	4	3	3	0	0	0	1	5	1	5	0	1	0	0	.000	0	0	5.40
Jersild,Aaron,Dunedin	A	26	34	14	3	3	142	586	130	58	50	10	6	5	2	41	0	112	6	6	11	6	.647	1	0	3.17
Jerzembeck,Michael,Tampa	A	23	16	16	0	0	68.2	274	59	27	24	6	1	2	2	22	0	45	2	1	4	3	.571	0	0	3.15
Jesperson,Bob,Charlstn-Sc	A	26	4	0	0	1	10	43	10	3	2	0	0	1	0	2	0	14	2	0	0	0	.000	0	0	1.80
Winston-Sal	A	26	41	0	0	26	52.2	231	48	28	25	5	3	1	3	22	1	46	11	0	2	5	.286	0	7	4.27
Johns,Clarence,Johnson Cty	R	22	15	0	0	6	32	150	28	26	17	3	2	1	3	18	1	33	0	0	5	2	.714	0	1	4.78
Johnson,Carl,Kinston	A	24	19	0	0	8	24	135	38	32	26	3	3	2	5	18	0	23	7	0	0	2	.000	0	1	9.75
Johnson,Jason,Augusta	A	21	20	19	1	0	102.2	465	119	67	46	5	4	4	7	32	0	69	12	2	2	12	.143	0	0	4.03
Johnson,Jason,Central Val	A	24	21	20	2	0	103.2	435	98	57	41	7	5	4	5	37	3	70	8	4	5	11	.313	2	0	3.56
Johnson,Michael,Medicne Hat	R	19	9	9	0	0	36.1	170	48	31	18	2	2	0	1	22	0	8	8	1	1	3	.250	0	0	4.46
Johnson,Phil,Cubs	R	20	8	0	0	4	11.1	56	12	10	10	0	1	0	0	10	1	9	6	0	2	0	1.000	0	1	7.94
Johnson,Ronald,Johnson Cty	R	23	12	12	0	0	67	286	66	30	20	6	2	0	2	16	0	60	1	2	5	3	.625	0	0	2.69
Johnson,Scott,Elmira	A	20	16	4	0	4	40.1	179	46	29	20	0	3	3	4	8	1	26	4	0	2	2	.500	0	0	4.46
Johnson,Steve,St. Pete	A	25	34	3	0	7	81	353	93	46	38	5	1	5	5	20	1	41	2	1	4	5	.444	0	1	4.22
Johnston,Sean,Mets	R	19	2	1	0	1	10	33	0	0	0	0	0	0	0	4	0	13	0	0	1	0	1.000	0	1	0.00
Kingsport	R	19	6	6	0	0	29	123	22	14	10	1	0	1	1	15	0	27	3	1	2	3	.400	0	0	3.10
Johnston,Sean,Pr. William	A	24	27	27	3	0	165	717	185	89	83	9	7	5	4	61	1	81	6	0	15	6	.714	1	0	4.53
Jones,Dan,Pirates	R	25	4	0	0	1	6.2	34	7	7	3	0	1	0	2	4	0	6	0	0	0	1	.000	0	0	4.05
Jones,Jeff,Spokane	A	21	13	4	0	3	32	153	41	27	18	2	0	1	5	10	0	21	2	2	1	3	.250	0	0	5.06
Jones,Bobby,Stockton	A	23	26	26	2	0	147.2	638	131	90	69	12	4	4	4	64	0	147	5	2	6	12	.333	0	0	4.21
Jordan,Jason,Jamestown	A	22	7	7	1	0	37.1	160	34	18	7	0	2	0	1	11	0	20	3	1	2	3	.400	1	0	1.69
Fayetteville	A	22	7	7	0	0	42	160	31	12	10	2	0	0	0	10	0	29	3	0	4	0	1.000	0	0	2.14
Juhl,Mike,Clearwater	A	25	18	0	0	11	22.2	110	30	18	14	0	2	4	0	13	4	14	1	1	0	4	.000	0	0	5.56
Karns,Timothy,Orioles	R	23	20	0	0	13	53.1	226	44	25	21	2	2	1	5	22	0	33	5	0	3	1	.750	0	3	3.54
Karvala,Kyle,Martinsvlle	R	24	21	0	0	8	40.2	167	29	17	12	1	2	2	1	16	0	48	3	0	5	1	.833	0	2	2.66
Kauflin,David,Bristol	R	19	12	12	0	0	64.2	268	60	33	25	4	5	2	6	14	1	31	4	0	1	3	.250	0	0	3.48
Kaufman,Bradley,Springfield	A	23	31	20	3	4	145.1	602	124	62	54	9	5	3	4	63	6	122	14	1	10	9	.526	0	0	3.34
Kaysner,Brent,Royals	R	21	3	0	0	0	1.1	15	6	7	7	0	0	1	1	4	0	1	0	0	0	0	.000	0	0	47.25
Keehn,Andrew,Rockies	R	20	19	0	0	9	30.1	147	35	17	14	1	0	3	4	20	1	30	5	0	2	0	1.000	0	0	4.15
Keenan,Brad,Charlstn-Sc	A	24	17	0	0	9	20.1	104	25	19	15	1	3	0	1	22	2	13	8	0	1	1	.500	0	1	6.64
Keith,Jeff,Everett	A	23	28	0	0	14	54.2	220	30	21	17	0	1	3	3	29	1	63	6	0	4	1	.800	0	2	2.80
Kell,Robert,Charlstn-Wv	A	24	38	0	0	17	54.2	228	43	27	24	6	4	2	3	21	0	57	7	0	4	2	.667	0	2	3.95
Kelley,Jason,Huntington	R	19	8	8	0	0	33	142	19	17	13	0	0	1	3	20	1	21	6	5	2	2	.500	0	0	3.55
Kelly,Jeffrey,Pirates	R	20	11	7	0	1	46.1	207	54	26	21	4	0	2	1	12	0	24	0	3	0	5	.000	0	0	4.08
Kelly,John,Pittsfield	A	22	8	7	0	0	35	160	38	14	13	0	0	2	2	21	0	25	2	0	4	2	.667	0	0	3.34
Kenady,Jason,Bakersfield	A	21	5	0	0	1	7.2	42	12	11	11	2	0	2	0	6	0	5	1	0	0	1	.000	0	0	12.91
Yakima	A	21	15	7	0	5	62.2	265	54	22	20	1	3	2	4	28	1	60	2	3	3	2	.600	0	1	2.87
Kendrick,Scott,Williamsprt	A	19	3	3	0	0	11	53	15	13	8	1	0	0	0	6	0	7	8	0	0	3	.000	0	0	6.55
Huntington	R	19	10	7	0	0	47	205	47	29	21	4	2	0	0	18	1	33	4	3	2	2	.500	0	0	4.02
Kennedy,Gregory,Lynchburg	A	23	24	11	1	5	76	352	100	51	42	6	2	2	1	30	0	43	10	0	4	6	.400	0	0	4.97
High Desert	A	23	9	2	0	3	20.1	104	32	26	25	4	1	1	1	19	1	7	4	0	0	0	.000	0	0	11.07
Kennedy,Scott,Blue Jays	R	22	4	0	0	3	5	23	4	5	4	0	1	0	0	3	0	1	1	0	0	0	.000	0	0	7.20
Bristol	R	22	6	0	0	3	11.1	50	12	4	2	0	0	0	0	7	0	8	2	0	1	0	1.000	0	0	1.59
Kenny,Sean,Columbia	A	22	45	0	0	22	70.2	307	74	36	27	6	2	1	6	20	2	57	2	5	4	3	.571	0	6	3.44
Kerley,Collin,Daytona	A	25	40	1	0	21	68.1	297	68	37	35	1	1	4	2	24	4	63	11	0	1	4	.200	0	2	4.61
Kermode,Alfred,Burlington	A	24	39	17	1	19	128.2	553	123	72	59	10	4	9	4	47	3	88	8	1	6	7	.462	1	6	4.13
Kester,Timothy,Osceola	A	23	24	22	2	0	134	580	159	85	73	7	8	5	8	30	5	71	3	0	5	12	.294	0	0	4.90
Keusch,Joseph,Hudson Vall	A	24	14	0	0	6	24	104	28	20	18	0	1	4	3	3	0	25	2	0	0	1	.000	0	0	6.75
Khoury,Tony,Peoria	A	24	15	0	0	5	29	122	22	16	14	2	1	2	2	16	0	26	0	1	0	1	.000	0	0	4.34
Kindall,Scott,Kingsport	R	22	15	0	0	7	29.1	125	20	9	6	3	0	1	2	14	0	29	3	0	0	1	.000	0	2	1.84
St. Lucie	A	22	7	0	0	5	7.1	25	5	2	2	1	0	0	1	2	0	3	0	0	0	0	.000	0	0	2.45
Kindler,Tom,Springfield	A	24	30	19	1	0	130	566	112	75	56	11	3	4	11	58	2	121	17	3	7	9	.438	1	0	3.88
King,Curtis,New Jersey	A	24	5	4	0	0	20.2	92	19	7	6	0	0	1	0	11	0	14	2	1	1	0	1.000	0	0	2.61
Savannah	A	24	8	8	2	0	53	202	37	14	11	4	2	1	4	9	0	40	1	0	4	1	.800	2	0	1.87
King,William,Sou. Oregon	A	22	1	1	0	0	3	10	1	0	0	0	0	0	0	1	0	2	0	0	0	0	.000	0	0	0.00
W. Michigan	A	22	17	1	0	8	44.2	183	35	11	9	2	2	0	1	19	1	25	0	1	2	1	.667	0	4	1.81
Kirkland,Kris,Batavia	A	25	13	0	0	10	14.1	64	15	7	5	0	0	0	0	6	0	8	0	0	2	3	.400	0	3	3.14
Spartanburg	A	25	2	0	0	2	2	7	1	0	0	0	0	0	0	0	0	0	0	0	0	0	.000	0	0	0.00
Kitchen,Ronald,Albany	A	23	18	0	0	17	38.2	151	29	7	1	0	2	1	1	6	0	27	0	0	5	0	.500	0	5	0.23
Klamm,Ted,Salem	A	25	16	15	0	0	67	316	90	62	59	17	1	1	6	23	0	50	8	2	2	7	.222	0	0	7.93
Charlstn-Sc	A	25	10	0	0	5	13	68	19	10	8	1	0	1	1	9	0	15	0	1	1	0	1.000	0	0	5.54
Kline,Steven,Columbus	A	22	28	28	2	0	185.2	744	153	67	62	14	1	2	7	36	0	174	6	2	18	5	.783	1	0	3.01
Knieper,Aaron,Burlington	A	23	35	19	1	2	127.1	590	154	90	70	11	2	8	12	60	0	67	17	6	4	8	.333	0	0	4.95
Knighton,Toure,Charlstn-Wv	A	19	25	25	1	0	117	544	130	97	82	13	1	11	10	67	1	83	10	1	3	12	.200	1	0	6.31
Knowles,Greg,St. Pete	A	26	37	0	0	14	51.2	230	61	31	25	5	3	2	1	14	2	29	4	0	3	5	.375	0	14	4.35
Knox,Jeff,Cedar Rapds	A	22	14	4	1	0	41.2	203	61	45	30	9	3	3	3	16	3	31	5	0	1	3	.250	0	0	6.48
Boise	A	22	16	16	0	0	87.1	396	110	62	48	4	4	3	8	29	3	52	1	2	6	5	.545	0	0	4.95
Koehler,P.K.,Braves	R	21	12	0	0	10	20	98	23	17	8	0	1	1	1	12	0	12	4	1	3	2	.400	0	1	3.60
Idaho Falls	R	21	3	2	0	0	15	66	17	10	9	3	0	0	1	4	0	5	2	0	1	0	1.000	0	0	5.40
Koenig,Matthew,Kingsport	R	22	15	1	1	5	34.1	161	36	23	19	1	0	0	4	16	0	31	1	0	3	1	.750	0	0	4.98
Konieczki,Dominic,Fort Myers	A	26	47	0	0	15	74	336	74	44	29	1	3	2	3	36	5	74	10	1	3	5	.375	0	4	3.53

1994 Pitching -- Single-A and Rookie Leagues

Player	Lg	A	G	GS	CG	GF	IP	BFP	H	R	ER	HR	SH	SF	HB	TBB	IBB	SO	WP	Bk	W	L	Pct.	ShO	Sv	ERA
Kopitzke,Chad,Beloit	A	23	20	0	0	9	37	145	25	16	11	4	0	0	3	7	0	24	1	0	2	1	.667	0	1	2.68
Stockton	A	23	21	0	0	9	32.2	143	37	15	14	2	3	1	1	12	1	17	0	1	1	3	.250	0	0	3.86
Koppe,Clinton,Billings	R	21	14	14	1	0	89.1	360	85	48	42	4	3	3	2	23	3	61	4	2	9	2	.818	0	0	4.23
Kotes,Chris,Dunedin	A	26	26	24	2	0	148.2	616	134	54	50	7	5	4	5	55	0	91	5	1	10	6	.625	1	0	3.03
Krablin,Justin,Kingsport	R	21	13	0	0	7	27.2	118	33	20	15	3	2	1	0	4	0	21	4	0	2	2	.500	0	1	4.88
Kramer,Dan,Red Sox	R	24	3	0	0	0	2.1	9	2	0	0	0	0	0	0	0	0	2	0	0	0	0	.000	0	0	0.00
Sarasota	A	24	16	0	0	5	14.1	60	8	5	2	1	0	0	0	9	0	12	2	1	2	0	1.000	0	3	1.26
Kramer*,Jeffrey,Helena	R	21	16	10	0	6	70.1	309	62	23	16	0	4	1	6	28	2	82	11	4	5	2	.714	0	2	2.05
Kramer,Scott,Watertown	A	21	14	4	0	3	37.1	171	36	23	18	1	0	0	5	19	0	38	3	1	2	2	.500	0	0	4.34
Krause,Kevin,Daytona	A	21	1	1	0	0	5.1	22	5	3	3	1	0	0	0	0	0	1	0	0	0	1	.000	0	0	5.06
Williamsprt	A	21	10	0	0	4	19.1	92	27	14	9	0	1	0	0	7	0	18	2	0	1	1	.500	0	0	4.19
Cubs	R	21	5	0	0	3	7.1	32	6	4	3	0	0	0	1	4	1	9	0	0	0	1	.000	0	0	3.68
Kroon,Marc,Rancho Cuca	A	22	26	26	0	0	143.1	655	143	86	77	14	4	9	11	81	1	153	9	3	11	6	.647	0	0	4.83
Krueger,Robert,Appleton	A	23	44	0	0	14	51.2	216	43	26	21	6	4	1	2	19	1	54	2	0	2	1	.667	0	0	3.66
Kubinski,Timothy,W. Michigan	A	23	30	23	1	4	158.2	677	168	82	64	8	13	4	7	36	0	126	8	10	14	6	.700	0	0	3.63
Kummerfeldt,Jason,Winston-Sal	A	25	8	6	0	0	34	156	44	24	22	3	1	3	5	8	0	29	0	1	2	2	.500	0	0	5.82
Kurnik,Michael,Eugene	A	24	17	0	0	5	31	139	21	15	9	2	3	1	5	20	0	32	1	0	1	2	.333	0	0	2.61
Kurtz,Rodd,Peoria	A	22	31	21	2	5	142.1	634	184	89	69	8	6	7	5	25	2	84	4	8	7	10	.412	0	1	4.36
Kyslinger,Dan,Stockton	A	23	30	21	0	4	115	512	125	73	63	9	2	8	5	47	3	92	7	1	7	5	.583	0	2	4.93
Lachappa,Matt,Springfield	A	20	20	20	1	0	116.2	504	107	61	53	15	8	3	12	44	3	98	9	0	6	8	.385	0	0	4.09
LaGarde,Joseph,Vero Beach	A	20	25	15	0	3	105.2	446	101	57	49	5	2	3	7	41	0	66	8	1	6	8	.429	0	0	4.17
Lair,Scott,Johnson Cty	R	21	15	4	0	0	40	169	35	26	17	4	1	2	2	15	0	34	1	1	2	0	1.000	0	0	3.83
Lake,Kevin,Everett	A	22	10	7	0	1	46	196	46	21	18	2	2	1	0	18	0	44	2	0	4	4	.500	0	0	3.52
Lane,Aaron,Albany	A	24	35	0	0	30	54.2	232	42	20	14	0	1	3	2	24	0	56	4	3	3	2	.600	0	11	2.30
Frederick	A	24	5	0	0	5	7.1	32	10	3	3	1	0	0	0	3	0	6	1	0	1	1	.500	0	2	3.68
Lane,Michael,Bluefield	R	24	2	0	0	0	5	23	6	5	4	2	0	0	1	2	0	3	0	0	0	0	.000	0	0	7.20
Lankford,Frank,Greensboro	A	24	54	0	0	27	82.1	352	79	37	27	3	6	1	1	18	3	74	7	1	7	6	.538	0	2	2.95
Lapka,Rick,Princeton	R	23	19	0	0	6	43	191	44	28	22	0	1	3	6	17	1	46	5	3	3	2	.600	0	2	4.60
Lapoint,Jason,Expos	R	24	3	0	0	3	5	22	7	2	2	1	0	0	1	1	0	4	1	0	0	0	.000	0	1	3.60
Burlington	A	24	23	0	0	9	30.2	126	33	13	13	1	3	1	1	7	0	16	0	0	1	0	1.000	0	0	3.82
Largussa,Levon,Dunedin	A	24	6	5	0	0	16.1	76	14	12	8	1	0	1	1	16	0	10	3	0	0	2	.000	0	0	4.41
Larkin,Andy,Kane County	A	21	21	21	3	0	140	577	125	53	44	6	3	3	19	27	0	125	4	0	9	7	.563	1	0	2.83
Larocca,Todd,Orioles	R	22	1	0	0	0	3.1	10	0	0	0	0	0	0	0	0	0	3	0	0	0	0	.000	0	0	0.00
Bluefield	R	22	9	0	0	5	13.1	64	20	11	10	0	2	0	2	4	1	13	3	0	1	2	.333	0	1	6.75
Larock,Scott,Bend	A	22	16	7	0	0	63.2	267	71	30	27	5	2	1	3	11	0	45	1	4	3	5	.375	0	0	3.82
Central Val	A	22	4	3	0	0	21	87	23	7	5	1	0	0	0	2	0	17	0	0	2	1	.667	0	0	2.14
Larosa,Mark,W. Palm Bch	A	26	2	0	0	0	2	9	3	0	0	0	0	0	0	0	0	1	0	0	1	0	1.000	0	0	0.00
Expos	R	26	10	0	0	2	12	49	9	3	2	0	0	0	1	3	0	12	1	0	1	0	1.000	0	0	1.50
Larson,Toby,Pittsfield	A	22	21	1	0	9	46.1	187	34	18	15	1	1	2	1	13	0	40	2	1	2	4	.667	0	4	2.91
Lasbury,Robert,Asheville	A	22	25	3	0	0	52.1	261	74	48	39	3	3	1	3	29	1	32	10	1	5	0	1.000	0	0	6.71
Lavenia,Mark,Huntington	R	22	25	0	0	23	31.1	139	22	14	9	1	1	1	1	17	0	32	4	2	3	5	.375	0	2	2.59
Lawrence,Matt,Cubs	R	23	2	0	0	2	5	34	10	12	4	0	0	1	1	4	0	3	1	1	1	0	1.000	0	0	7.20
Lawrence,Sean,Salem	A	24	12	12	0	0	72	312	76	38	21	8	1	2	3	18	0	66	2	0	4	2	.667	0	0	2.63
Leach,Jarman,Spokane	A	22	23	3	0	4	54.2	256	66	28	26	3	1	1	2	30	0	36	3	0	2	3	.400	0	0	4.28
Leach,Matthew,Elizabethtn	R	22	15	0	0	6	24	125	24	26	19	3	1	0	2	27	0	23	5	0	0	2	.000	0	0	7.13
LeBron,Jose,Padres	R	24	5	0	0	1	5.2	20	1	1	0	0	1	1	0	1	0	7	0	0	1	0	1.000	0	0	0.00
Lee,Anthony,Daytona	A	24	3	1	0	1	7.2	40	7	8	7	1	0	2	1	8	0	11	2	2	0	0	.000	0	0	8.22
Lee,Bradley,Rangers	R	20	4	1	0	0	7	26	3	0	0	0	0	0	1	1	0	3	0	0	0	0	.000	0	0	0.00
Lee,Jeremy,Blue Jays	R	20	4	1	0	0	17.1	67	12	3	3	0	0	0	1	3	0	9	1	0	0	0	.000	0	1	1.56
St. Cathms	A	20	12	4	0	0	38.2	164	31	19	16	2	3	1	4	14	0	27	3	0	2	3	.400	0	0	3.72
Legault,Kevin,Fort Myers	A	24	26	26	1	0	154.2	693	196	87	73	8	6	4	5	52	5	68	9	0	7	11	.389	0	0	4.25
Legrow,Robert,Batavia	A	24	5	5	0	0	30	126	33	11	9	1	1	0	1	4	0	14	2	0	2	1	.667	0	0	2.70
Spartanburg	A	24	12	1	0	6	30.2	133	30	11	11	1	1	1	0	17	1	16	1	0	1	0	1.000	0	0	3.23
Lehman,Toby,South Bend	A	23	34	16	0	7	120.2	533	113	70	56	7	4	6	8	65	0	78	8	2	9	5	.643	0	4	4.18
Lehoisky,Russel,Fort Wayne	A	24	36	14	0	11	117	547	121	83	60	10	6	5	5	88	1	67	22	2	5	7	.417	0	0	4.62
Leibee,Skye,Sou. Oregon	A	21	18	8	0	3	60.2	287	64	40	33	2	2	4	4	38	1	65	11	2	3	2	.600	0	0	4.90
Leiber,Zane,White Sox	R	21	3	0	0	1	3.1	14	2	1	1	0	0	1	0	1	0	3	0	0	0	1	.000	0	0	2.70
Lemp,Chris,Frederick	A	23	52	0	0	47	66.1	284	53	28	20	6	6	2	4	29	1	60	6	0	5	5	.500	0	21	2.71
Leon,Michael,Vermont	A	23	7	0	0	3	12	65	20	17	10	2	0	0	2	5	0	10	1	1	0	2	.000	0	0	7.50
Leonhart,David,Pittsfield	A	24	22	0	0	11	30.2	145	32	35	26	0	2	1	4	21	0	27	7	0	0	3	.000	0	0	7.63
Leroy,John,Macon	A	20	10	9	0	0	47.1	173	36	21	20	2	0	1	0	20	0	44	1	5	3	3	.500	0	0	4.46
Leshnock,Donnie,Greensboro	A	24	44	3	0	16	80.2	361	81	40	31	2	4	4	5	42	3	62	9	0	4	4	.500	0	0	3.46
Lesperance,Frank,Butte	R	23	13	8	0	0	46	219	61	45	37	6	0	2	0	24	1	24	6	0	2	1	.667	0	0	7.24
Lewis,Edward,Quad City	A	23	35	0	0	14	56.2	272	78	50	44	9	1	3	6	25	0	44	9	4	3	4	.429	0	0	6.99
Leystra,Jeff,St. Cathms	A	22	16	0	0	13	28.2	123	31	18	13	2	0	1	0	7	0	26	2	1	1	4	.200	0	4	4.08
Licursi,Richard,High Desert	A	24	14	14	1	0	77.1	359	91	56	48	12	5	2	6	45	1	61	6	7	3	8	.273	0	0	5.59
Lynchburg	A	24	17	11	0	0	61	281	72	45	35	11	2	2	2	31	0	53	1	2	1	8	.111	0	0	5.16
Lidle,Cory,Stockton	A	22	25	1	0	12	42.2	200	60	32	21	2	0	0	1	13	1	38	1	0	1	2	.333	0	4	4.43
Beloit	A	23	13	9	1	0	69	279	65	24	20	4	4	2	1	11	0	62	6	0	3	4	.429	1	0	2.61
Lindemann,Wayne,South Bend	A	25	16	16	3	0	111.1	466	108	52	35	5	4	6	1	21	1	69	0	0	8	3	.727	0	0	2.83
Pr. William	A	25	10	9	0	0	47.1	234	65	55	49	10	2	4	3	32	0	23	1	0	1	0	1.000	0	0	9.32
Linebarger,Keith,Fort Wayne	A	24	23	0	0	10	45.1	177	24	11	10	1	2	4	3	21	0	41	4	0	3	0	1.000	0	4	1.99
Fort Myers	A	24	16	0	0	10	27	138	39	22	18	0	1	2	1	14	0	21	2	0	2	2	.500	0	1	6.00
Linehan,Andy,Elmira	A	19	5	0	0	3	9.1	34	4	2	2	0	0	0	1	3	0	3	0	0	1	0	1.000	0	0	1.93
Linfante,Rob,Butte	R	23	18	2	0	6	39	189	57	44	40	5	0	1	8	20	0	38	4	0	0	0	.000	0	0	9.23
Lintern,John,Everett	A	23	20	7	0	4	64	290	64	37	27	11	1	3	8	31	5	58	5	2	2	4	.333	0	0	3.80
Liriano,Orlando,Cubs	R	19	1	0	0	1	2	8	2	0	0	0	0	0	0	1	0	1	0	0	1	0	1.000	0	0	0.00

1994 Pitching -- Single-A and Rookie Leagues

			HOW MUCH HE PITCHED						WHAT HE GAVE UP												THE RESULTS					
Player	Lg	A	G	GS	CG	GF	IP	BFP	H	R	ER	HR	SH	SF	HB	TBB	IBB	SO	WP	Bk	W	L	Pct.	ShO	Sv	ERA
Lisio,Joseph,Kingsport	R	21	21	0	0	19	23.1	100	22	9	7	3	1	0	2	7	0	22	1	0	2	3	.400	0	9	2.70
Lister,Marty,Winston-Sal	A	23	6	0	0	4	5	33	7	7	3	0	1	1	0	11	1	4	1	0	0	2	.000	0	2	5.40
Quad City	A	23	46	0	0	32	47	207	31	18	15	0	1	1	0	37	1	54	2	1	2	4	.333	0	13	2.87
Littell,Mark,Stockton	A	42	1	0	0	1	1	4	0	0	0	0	0	0	0	1	0	0	0	0	1	0	1.000	0	0	0.00
Lloyd,John,Cedar Rapds	A	21	20	12	3	1	93	401	98	52	48	9	4	3	3	28	1	59	10	3	5	5	.500	1	1	4.65
Locey,Anthony,Peoria	A	24	26	0	0	10	35	153	38	20	16	1	3	1	0	14	1	42	4	0	1	2	.333	0	1	4.11
Lock,Daniel,Auburn	A	22	11	11	0	0	59	246	46	21	15	3	2	2	4	20	0	47	3	0	3	1	.750	0	0	2.29
Locklear,Jeff,San Jose	A	25	12	8	0	3	42.1	190	52	35	24	7	2	1	2	11	0	16	1	0	2	2	.500	0	0	5.10
Clinton	A	25	7	7	0	0	38.2	166	38	19	14	5	5	3	0	13	0	23	0	4	5	2	.714	0	0	3.26
Loetzsch,Tyson,Angels	R	19	15	12	1	1	73	313	83	45	28	2	2	3	6	16	0	45	3	0	4	7	.364	0	0	3.45
Logan,Christopher,Spokane	A	24	25	0	0	9	35.2	176	43	28	26	2	1	2	7	22	1	40	4	1	2	1	.667	0	0	6.56
Logan,Marcus,New Jersey	A	23	13	13	2	0	64	274	53	32	28	3	2	2	4	27	0	53	10	1	5	4	.556	1	0	3.94
Loiselle,Richard,Rancho Cuca	A	23	27	27	0	0	156.2	704	160	83	69	12	7	6	11	76	2	120	12	0	9	10	.474	0	0	3.96
Loiz,Niuman,Astros	R	21	13	13	1	0	67.2	266	43	21	14	0	3	1	4	17	0	57	2	1	6	1	.857	1	0	1.86
Lombardi,John,Albany	A	22	24	23	0	0	126.1	569	144	86	56	14	2	6	0	53	0	88	5	2	8	9	.471	0	0	3.99
Long,Joey,Rancho Cuca	A	24	46	0	0	17	52	248	69	36	27	3	6	2	1	22	1	52	8	0	2	4	.333	0	3	4.67
Long,Joe,Tampa	A	24	32	1	0	7	49	221	61	27	19	2	1	3	3	20	2	21	4	1	1	3	.250	0	0	3.49
Lopez,Andres,Eugene	A	22	17	12	0	0	78.2	346	85	39	24	1	2	3	4	21	0	74	4	0	4	6	.400	0	0	2.75
Lopez,Johan,Auburn	A	20	14	14	2	0	76.2	339	86	49	41	4	2	4	4	24	0	74	7	3	7	5	.583	1	0	4.81
Lopez,Orlando,Peoria	A	22	42	5	0	9	93.1	406	87	48	41	5	4	3	7	35	2	106	6	5	7	2	.778	0	1	3.95
Lott,Brian,Princeton	R	23	14	14	2	0	94	391	97	39	33	5	4	1	4	20	0	61	9	3	6	4	.600	2	0	3.16
Love,Farley,Cubs	R	22	3	0	0	0	3.2	22	1	6	5	0	0	1	0	8	0	4	0	0	0	0	.000	0	0	12.27
Lovinger,Kevin,New Jersey	A	23	35	0	0	5	52.1	211	36	13	9	3	3	0	2	19	1	71	3	0	1	0	1.000	0	1	1.55
Lowe,Benjamin,Blue Jays	R	21	22	1	0	5	22.1	104	20	16	11	0	4	0	2	14	1	27	1	1	2	1	.667	0	1	4.43
Lowe,Jason,Sou.Oregon	A	22	18	9	0	3	69.2	304	56	38	29	5	1	3	7	45	2	62	10	1	5	3	.625	0	2	3.75
Lowry,James,Burlington	R	20	17	0	0	3	26.1	118	17	15	10	0	1	1	2	22	0	32	4	0	1	3	.250	0	0	3.42
Loynd,Mike,W. Palm Bch	A	31	24	0	0	3	31.1	130	22	12	11	1	3	1	1	17	1	37	2	0	5	2	.714	0	0	3.16
Lucchetti,Larry,St.Pete	A	26	23	14	0	1	98.2	416	102	49	36	5	1	1	2	40	1	39	4	2	4	4	.500	0	0	3.28
Luckert,Gabriel,Giants	R	19	15	0	0	5	34	142	26	12	9	0	1	3	3	9	3	31	6	0	1	2	.333	0	0	2.38
Ludwick,Eric,St.Lucie	A	23	27	27	3	0	150.1	671	162	102	76	6	1	12	6	77	1	77	3	5	7	13	.350	0	0	4.55
Luft,Tommy,Athletics	R	24	2	2	0	0	6	33	8	6	4	0	0	0	0	3	0	3	1	0	0	1	.000	0	0	6.00
Lukasiewicz,Mark,Hagerstown	A	22	29	17	0	5	98	449	108	70	52	8	6	4	7	51	0	84	8	0	3	6	.333	0	0	4.78
Lundberg,Bryan,Batavia	A	23	5	0	0	1	8	38	10	8	7	0	1	0	2	2	0	5	1	0	0	1	.000	0	0	7.88
Lundquist,David,Hickory	A	22	27	27	3	0	178.2	759	170	88	69	15	4	3	12	43	0	133	8	2	13	10	.565	2	0	3.48
Lutt,Jeff,Augusta	A	23	22	0	0	3	36	166	37	23	18	3	2	1	2	15	0	35	3	0	2	2	.500	0	0	4.50
Lynch,James,Astros	R	19	20	2	0	11	42.1	177	29	20	10	0	1	1	6	20	1	35	3	1	5	2	.714	0	5	2.13
Lyons,Curt,Charlstn-Sc	A	20	12	11	0	0	65.1	276	64	30	28	2	1	1	8	22	0	55	12	0	3	6	.333	0	0	3.86
Princeton	R	20	4	4	0	0	27.1	104	16	9	6	0	1	0	2	2	0	28	2	0	1	1	.500	0	0	1.98
Lyons,Steve,St.Lucie	A	24	31	6	1	5	83	369	84	55	50	2	2	1	9	41	5	30	7	0	7	2	.778	0	0	5.42
Columbia	A	24	3	3	1	0	22.1	94	21	15	9	1	1	0	1	7	0	15	3	0	0	2	.000	0	0	3.63
Maberry,Louis,Winston-Sal	A	24	14	0	0	7	25.1	109	25	19	19	5	0	2	1	14	1	23	1	0	0	0	.000	0	0	6.75
Macey,Fausto,Giants	R	19	9	9	0	0	50	194	37	14	12	0	2	2	0	8	0	26	1	0	2	2	.500	0	0	2.16
Everett	A	19	5	5	0	0	27.2	120	30	12	11	1	1	0	0	8	0	22	1	2	1	2	.667	0	0	3.58
Machmer,Matt,Cubs	R	20	6	0	0	3	8.1	37	9	4	4	0	1	0	0	4	0	10	0	0	0	1	.000	0	1	4.32
Maduro,Calvin,Frederick	A	20	27	26	0	1	152.1	636	132	86	72	18	3	3	4	59	0	137	10	4	9	8	.529	0	0	4.25
Magee,Jamie,Braves	R	20	7	0	0	0	11.1	65	9	15	14	0	0	0	0	22	0	7	8	0	0	0	.000	0	0	11.12
Magnelli,Anthony,Madison	A	24	15	1	0	7	31	141	38	18	15	5	1	1	2	7	0	23	2	0	1	3	.250	0	0	4.35
Magre,Peter,Charlstn-Sc	A	23	47	1	0	20	67.1	292	57	35	32	7	1	5	2	38	6	53	4	3	4	3	.571	0	6	4.28
Mainville,Martin,Expos	R	29	7	7	0	0	46	175	30	5	5	0	1	1	2	8	0	48	3	0	4	0	1.000	0	0	0.98
W. Palm Bch	A	29	1	1	0	0	5	21	5	1	1	0	0	0	0	1	0	4	0	0	1	0	1.000	0	0	1.80
Majors,Shane,Princeton	R	19	10	5	0	3	34.1	159	34	22	11	2	0	1	3	23	3	24	5	2	3	1	.750	0	0	2.88
Maldonado,Jay,Hagerstown	A	22	40	0	0	16	75.1	323	69	44	33	6	6	4	4	24	1	65	8	1	6	5	.545	0	7	3.94
Mallicoat,Rob,Rancho Cuca	A	30	2	0	0	0	2.2	10	3	1	1	0	0	0	0	1	0	3	0	1	1	0	1.000	0	0	3.38
Mallory,Trevor,Hagerstown	A	23	27	26	0	0	150.2	669	162	97	79	16	4	9	6	64	0	95	7	1	9	11	.450	0	0	4.72
Malloy,Charles,Utica	A	23	13	9	1	0	54.2	229	44	25	20	0	2	3	2	30	0	46	4	3	6	2	.750	1	0	3.29
Maloney,Sean,Beloit	A	24	51	0	0	41	59	272	73	42	36	3	2	5	4	10	5	53	6	1	2	6	.250	0	22	5.49
Mamott,Joseph,Utica	A	21	16	12	0	0	67	306	61	43	33	1	7	3	9	45	0	46	9	0	3	7	.300	0	0	4.43
Manley,Kevin,Mets	R	19	11	1	0	3	15.2	92	23	22	13	0	0	0	0	23	0	14	6	0	0	1	.000	0	0	7.47
Mann,James,Blue Jays	R	20	11	9	0	0	53	236	54	28	22	1	3	1	3	26	1	41	0	1	3	2	.600	0	0	3.74
Manning,David,Charlotte	A	23	20	20	0	0	97	438	119	69	60	5	4	3	6	39	0	46	8	3	4	11	.267	0	0	5.57
Manning,Derek,W. Michigan	A	24	29	23	2	4	154	617	120	52	39	4	7	1	3	42	0	118	3	3	11	7	.611	1	2	2.28
Manning,Leonard,Martinsvle	R	23	15	4	1	1	45	208	40	26	18	3	0	4	3	32	2	57	10	2	2	4	.333	0	0	3.60
Manning,Michael,Hudson Vall	A	23	8	0	0	2	9.1	57	22	21	15	1	0	3	3	9	0	11	1	0	0	0	.000	0	0	14.46
Manon,Julio,Johnson Cty	R	21	5	0	0	0	8.2	43	11	8	8	2	0	0	0	5	0	7	1	0	0	0	.333	0	0	8.31
Cardinals	R	21	14	0	0	4	16	69	20	9	9	0	0	0	0	9	0	18	1	2	0	1	.000	0	1	5.06
Mantei,Matt,Appleton	A	21	48	0	0	43	48	201	42	14	11	2	2	2	1	21	3	70	6	0	5	3	.833	0	26	2.06
Marenghi,Matthew,Bluefield	R	22	15	11	0	0	65.2	274	68	21	19	3	2	0	3	15	1	50	7	2	6	3	.667	0	0	2.60
Markham,Andy,Burlington	A	22	25	25	3	0	117	528	142	101	89	14	0	4	8	48	1	69	5	4	5	15	.250	0	0	6.85
Marquardt,Scott,Savannah	A	22	23	23	2	0	142.2	581	106	66	57	16	3	4	10	49	0	118	11	1	13	5	.722	2	0	3.60
Marrero,Kenny,Jamestown	A	25	27	0	0	15	55.1	222	43	14	13	3	5	1	2	18	2	54	4	1	4	1	.800	0	8	2.11
Marte,Beneris,Giants	R	19	14	0	0	6	21.2	89	25	9	6	2	1	1	0	10	6	12	0	0	0	0	.000	0	2	2.49
Martin,Jeff,Clinton	A	22	55	0	0	50	89	372	81	34	28	3	5	4	6	24	6	104	7	2	5	5	.500	0	20	2.83
San Jose	A	22	1	0	0	1	2	7	1	0	0	0	0	0	0	0	2	0	0	0	0	0	.000	0	0	0.00
Martin,Jerry,Charlotte	A	23	28	27	1	0	164.2	665	133	52	38	6	2	4	4	68	0	80	8	7	13	6	.684	5	0	2.08
Martin,Michael,Johnson Cty	R	21	12	12	0	0	77.2	326	73	29	16	6	1	3	3	15	1	57	0	1	7	2	.778	0	0	1.85
Martinez,Cesar,Sarasota	A	22	6	1	0	1	14.1	69	20	11	10	1	0	1	0	7	0	10	1	0	1	0	1.000	0	0	6.28

325

1994 Pitching -- Single-A and Rookie Leagues

Player	Lg	A	G	GS	CG	GF	IP	BFP	H	R	ER	HR	SH	SF	HB	TBB	IBB	SO	WP	Bk	W	L	Pct.	ShO	Sv	ERA
High Desert	A	22	15	15	1	0	85	391	103	63	50	14	1	3	5	30	0	52	5	0	3	8	.273	0	0	5.29
Martinez,Fausto,Mariners	R	20	17	0	0	4	29.2	127	31	16	13	0	2	1	4	8	0	18	0	0	2	0	1.000	0	0	3.94
Martinez,Javier,Huntington	R	18	9	8	0	1	35	147	24	20	15	1	1	2	3	21	0	31	9	2	2	1	.667	0	0	3.86
Martinez,Johnny,Burlington	R	22	11	11	1	0	70	305	73	45	31	4	2	1	3	16	1	72	8	3	2	6	.250	0	0	3.99
Kinston	A	22	2	2	0	0	8	34	10	7	7	1	0	1	0	4	0	3	0	0	0	0	.000	0	0	7.88
Martinez,Ozzie,Bristol	R	20	16	5	0	2	49	203	36	23	20	6	0	3	0	25	0	41	2	3	2	4	.333	0	1	3.67
Martinez,Sean,San Bernrdo	A	24	4	0	0	2	7	32	10	7	6	0	0	0	0	2	0	3	1	1	0	0	.000	0	0	7.71
Mascia,Dan,Rangers	R	24	10	0	0	0	12	56	12	8	6	0	0	0	0	11	0	6	1	1	1	0	1.000	0	0	4.50
Maskivish,Joseph,Welland	A	23	28	0	0	21	28	115	19	8	6	0	1	1	2	10	0	27	2	0	2	0	1.000	0	14	1.93
Masse,Daniel,Billings	R	21	13	0	0	3	24.1	130	35	19	15	1	0	5	1	18	0	18	3	0	0	0	.000	0	0	5.55
Mathews,Delmer,Macon	A	20	26	18	0	2	117.2	540	133	73	59	9	2	7	8	50	2	92	6	0	10	7	.588	0	0	4.51
Matos,Jose,Asheville	A	20	3	3	0	0	8.1	46	15	12	9	3	0	0	0	8	0	5	1	0	0	2	.000	0	0	9.72
Bend	A	20	21	0	0	12	26.1	139	38	33	28	5	0	4	3	19	0	14	2	1	0	3	.000	0	1	9.57
Matranga,Jeff,St. Pete	A	24	63	0	0	26	87.1	367	76	30	23	4	5	2	3	30	7	76	1	1	8	5	.615	0	3	2.37
Mattes,Troy,Expos	R	19	12	11	0	0	55.2	221	35	25	21	2	0	0	3	21	0	51	7	0	3	2	.600	0	0	3.40
Matthews,Mike,Columbus	A	21	23	23	0	0	119.2	502	120	53	41	8	3	3	7	44	1	99	7	3	6	8	.429	0	0	3.08
Mattos,Anthony,Everett	A	23	26	0	0	19	48	204	40	21	20	4	0	1	0	22	5	66	3	0	2	3	.400	0	3	3.75
Mattson,Craig,Augusta	A	21	54	0	0	36	70	309	65	38	28	3	0	2	4	30	1	78	16	1	6	5	.545	0	2	3.60
Matulevich,Jeff,Madison	A	25	47	0	0	46	50.2	217	40	24	16	2	3	1	5	21	1	40	6	0	3	4	.429	0	30	2.84
Matznick,Dan,White Sox	R	23	2	2	0	0	7	28	3	1	1	0	0	0	0	2	0	11	0	0	0	0	.000	0	0	1.29
South Bend	A	23	5	5	0	0	21	97	20	16	15	1	0	2	3	11	0	16	3	0	0	3	.000	0	0	6.43
Maurer,Michael,Sou. Oregon	A	22	17	8	0	5	63.1	285	68	42	25	2	4	4	5	20	1	67	7	3	2	6	.250	0	3	3.55
Maye,Steve,San Bernrdo	A	30	43	9	0	13	132	565	123	62	50	12	3	7	11	44	0	108	6	0	4	5	.444	0	4	3.41
Mayer,Aaron,Angels	R	20	15	14	1	0	84.1	383	84	56	41	3	1	4	13	41	0	77	9	3	4	8	.333	0	0	4.38
Mays,Marcus,Kane County	A	21	27	13	1	4	94.2	396	89	51	46	11	2	3	3	30	3	51	5	1	4	6	.400	0	1	4.37
Mayse,Robbie,Orioles	R	21	9	0	0	4	14	76	23	19	17	0	1	3	1	11	0	6	3	0	0	2	.000	0	1	10.93
Mazzone,Tony,Idaho Falls	R	22	15	12	0	1	61.1	310	100	76	52	10	0	1	5	18	2	49	2	0	1	6	.143	0	0	7.63
McAdams,Dennis,Asheville	A	21	22	1	0	11	30	141	37	24	21	1	2	2	5	16	1	23	6	0	3	1	.750	0	2	6.30
Bend	A	21	23	5	0	9	52	233	50	34	24	5	6	2	6	26	0	41	2	0	2	2	.500	0	3	4.15
McBride,Jonathan,St. Cathrns	A	21	13	13	1	0	69.2	302	81	39	33	4	1	1	4	12	0	30	5	0	4	4	.500	0	0	4.26
McBride,Rodney,Twins	R	20	8	1	0	3	21.2	85	18	5	4	0	0	0	0	1	0	12	1	0	1	1	.500	0	3	1.66
McCaffrey,Dennis,Cardinals	R	19	12	0	0	4	14.2	66	12	10	5	1	1	1	2	8	0	15	5	0	0	1	.000	0	0	3.07
McClinton,Patrick,Asheville	A	23	23	0	0	9	32.2	141	26	8	5	1	1	2	1	17	0	28	0	1	1	1	.500	0	1	1.38
McClurg,Clint,Martinsvle	R	21	14	10	0	1	53	237	43	34	27	5	1	2	5	33	0	48	12	0	6	2	.750	0	0	4.58
McCommon,Jason,Vermont	A	23	24	3	0	13	48	196	47	20	19	1	0	3	0	15	2	47	7	1	3	4	.429	0	4	3.56
McCormack,Andrew,South Bend	A	21	27	26	4	1	188	797	209	86	74	15	8	5	6	51	1	115	6	3	9	11	.450	1	0	3.54
McDill,Allen,Columbia	A	23	19	19	1	0	111.2	461	101	52	44	11	5	2	4	38	2	102	9	1	9	6	.600	0	0	3.55
McDonald,Matthew,Athletics	R	21	14	7	0	1	55.2	240	44	24	21	1	0	2	3	31	1	78	8	2	4	4	.500	0	0	3.40
McEntire,Ethan,Kingsport	R	19	13	13	0	0	87.1	352	62	38	25	4	5	2	6	29	0	69	7	4	4	4	.500	0	0	2.58
McFarlane,Toby,Fayetteville	A	23	44	0	0	13	77.1	342	70	45	43	11	4	1	10	41	0	66	14	0	2	2	.500	0	5	5.00
McGarity,Jeremy,Madison	A	24	62	0	0	15	90.2	394	91	51	40	3	8	4	8	36	5	53	9	1	3	3	.500	0	0	3.97
McGinn,Mark,Lethbridge	R	21	12	1	0	5	13	86	13	21	18	0	1	1	5	27	0	10	13	0	0	2	.000	0	0	12.46
McGraw,Doug,Osceola	A	23	19	2	0	3	44.1	208	57	30	30	8	2	1	2	25	0	31	7	0	1	3	.250	0	0	6.09
McKenzie,David,Charlstn-Sc	A	24	17	17	5	0	105.2	434	105	50	43	6	3	4	2	20	0	65	2	0	8	5	.615	1	0	3.66
McKinion,Mickey,Hickory	A	21	28	0	0	12	40	193	48	35	23	7	3	0	5	16	0	54	4	1	3	5	.375	0	1	5.18
McKinley,Leif,Lynchburg	A	23	13	0	0	6	27.1	124	37	19	17	2	0	0	1	7	1	15	3	0	0	1	.000	0	0	5.60
High Desert	A	23	24	0	0	15	37	166	55	31	29	4	2	3	0	6	0	28	6	0	4	3	.571	0	2	7.05
McLain,Mike,San Jose	A	25	47	0	0	38	88	369	80	34	27	3	3	4	9	24	2	81	9	0	3	4	.429	0	13	2.76
McLaughlin,Dennis,Utica	A	22	25	0	0	12	34.1	152	37	9	9	1	2	0	3	14	1	37	0	0	3	1	.750	0	3	2.36
McMillan,Leonard,Giants	R	21	13	9	0	2	50.1	203	37	18	15	2	2	3	0	19	0	35	5	2	2	1	.667	0	0	2.68
McMullen,Michael,Clinton	A	21	14	1	0	5	24.1	122	34	25	17	5	1	1	1	14	0	22	4	2	1	3	.250	0	0	6.29
Giants	R	21	10	9	0	0	49	205	47	21	18	2	2	3	3	15	1	40	3	0	3	3	.500	0	0	3.31
McNeill,Kevin,Johnson Cty	R	24	13	13	0	0	72.2	310	75	37	32	9	5	1	1	26	1	53	6	0	3	4	.429	0	0	3.96
Meadows,Matthew,Marlins	R	19	8	7	0	0	37	151	34	9	8	1	0	0	1	6	0	33	0	0	3	0	1.000	0	0	1.95
Mear,Richard,Cardinals	R	19	6	6	0	0	24.1	102	16	8	7	0	0	1	1	16	0	30	4	1	1	0	1.000	0	0	2.59
Medina,Rafael,Oneonta	A	20	14	14	1	0	73.1	319	67	54	38	7	2	5	1	35	0	59	7	3	3	7	.300	0	0	4.66
Meier,Pat,Princeton	R	22	3	3	0	0	13.2	68	19	11	10	0	0	2	1	9	2	13	1	1	0	2	.000	0	0	6.59
Charlstn-Sc	A	22	15	3	0	2	30	128	30	26	24	0	0	1	1	14	1	22	5	0	1	5	.167	0	0	7.20
Meiners,Doug,Hagerstown	A	21	26	26	4	0	153	655	170	82	57	7	1	5	5	40	0	104	8	0	8	10	.444	2	0	3.35
Meinershagen,Adam,Dunedin	A	19	16	1	0	0	101.2	453	115	62	54	10	3	5	5	42	0	52	8	1	6	6	.500	0	0	4.78
Mejia,Carlos,Lynchburg	A	21	6	0	0	2	8.2	47	13	11	10	4	1	0	0	6	0	5	1	0	0	0	.000	0	1	10.38
Utica	A	21	18	3	0	5	49.2	210	41	20	11	1	1	1	2	19	1	47	2	0	4	2	.667	0	0	1.99
Mejia,Felix,Yankees	R	19	4	0	0	0	5.2	29	1	4	3	0	1	0	2	10	0	4	1	1	0	1	.000	0	0	4.76
Mejia,Jorge,Red Sox	R	22	7	0	0	3	13.1	56	12	6	5	0	0	2	0	6	0	9	1	0	1	0	1.000	0	1	3.38
Lynchburg	A	22	10	0	0	2	21.1	85	20	9	8	1	0	0	0	6	0	5	0	0	0	0	.000	0	0	3.38
Mendez,Manuel,Cardinals	R	21	24	0	0	9	22.1	95	20	11	11	0	1	0	1	7	0	32	1	0	1	0	1.000	0	0	4.43
Mendoza,David,Blue Jays	R	19	9	8	0	0	43.2	183	38	20	17	1	2	1	5	14	0	46	3	1	2	2	.500	0	0	3.50
Mendoza,Ramiro,Tampa	A	23	22	21	1	1	134.1	560	133	54	45	7	5	3	2	35	1	110	2	3	12	6	.667	0	0	3.01
Mendoza,Rey,Marlins	R	24	2	0	0	0	4.1	16	1	0	0	0	0	0	0	2	0	6	0	0	0	0	.000	0	0	0.00
Brevard City	A	24	10	9	1	0	37	183	47	33	26	2	3	1	2	26	0	26	4	2	1	3	.250	0	0	6.32
Mercado,Gabriel,Brewers	R	22	1	1	0	0	3	14	3	2	2	0	0	0	0	3	0	2	0	0	0	0	.000	0	0	6.00
Helena	R	22	14	12	1	0	75.1	323	71	48	39	5	2	2	3	31	3	45	5	2	7	2	.778	0	0	4.66
Mercado,Hector,Osceola	A	21	25	25	1	0	136.2	601	123	75	60	5	11	4	1	79	4	88	9	3	6	13	.316	1	0	3.95
Merrill,Ethan,Utica	A	23	13	4	0	2	44.2	176	36	16	7	0	0	1	0	11	0	35	2	0	2	3	.400	0	1	1.41
Merritt,James,Marlins	R	20	3	1	0	0	3	20	6	5	5	0	0	0	0	5	0	2	0	0	0	0	.000	0	0	15.00
Mesa,Rafael,Burlington	R	21	29	0	0	27	30	126	19	15	11	1	1	1	4	14	2	33	4	0	1	0	1.000	0	13	3.30
Kinston	A	21	3	0	0	2	2.1	9	0	0	0	0	0	0	0	2	0	6	0	0	0	0	.000	0	0	0.00

1994 Pitching -- Single-A and Rookie Leagues

Player	Lg	A	G	GS	CG	GF	IP	BFP	H	R	ER	HR	SH	SF	HB	TBB	IBB	SO	WP	Bk	W	L	Pct.	ShO	Sv	ERA
Metheney,Michael,Clearwater	A	24	12	11	0	0	63.1	275	77	42	35	6	2	0	1	18	1	28	1	2	3	5	.375	0	0	4.97
Spartanburg	A	24	8	8	2	0	50.1	202	43	17	14	2	2	1	0	12	0	30	3	0	3	4	.429	0	0	2.50
Meyer,Alan,Padres	R	20	1	0	0	0	1	6	1	1	1	0	0	0	0	3	0	1	0	0	0	0	.000	0	0	9.00
Meyer,David,Oneonta	A	23	9	9	2	0	49.2	206	45	30	16	1	3	0	0	17	0	30	7	0	3	4	.429	0	0	2.90
Greensboro	A	23	5	5	0	0	32.2	127	25	9	7	0	1	1	3	14	0	25	0	0	4	1	.800	0	0	1.93
Tampa	A	23	1	1	0	0	3	17	7	5	5	2	0	0	0	2	0	4	1	0	0	1	.000	0	0	15.00
Meyer,Jay,Pr.William	A	24	3	0	0	1	5.1	27	8	6	5	1	0	0	0	5	0	1	0	0	1	0	1.000	0	0	8.44
Hickory	A	24	23	0	0	10	44.1	188	39	19	13	6	3	1	0	16	0	32	2	0	2	1	.667	0	2	2.64
Meyhoff,Jason,Elizabethtn	R	22	20	1	0	7	33.1	142	24	16	12	1	1	0	1	13	1	35	8	4	3	2	.600	0	0	3.24
Michalak,Christian,W. Michigan	A	24	15	10	0	2	67	291	66	32	29	3	4	2	8	28	0	38	2	3	5	3	.625	0	0	3.90
Modesto	A	24	17	10	1	3	77.1	310	67	28	25	13	2	3	3	20	1	46	4	3	5	3	.625	0	2	2.91
Micknich,Steve,Elmira	A	23	7	0	0	6	7.1	28	3	1	0	0	0	0	0	4	0	8	0	0	0	0	.000	0	0	0.00
Miles,Chad,Elmira	A	22	11	9	0	1	42	207	46	32	23	1	1	4	4	33	0	14	10	1	0	6	.000	0	0	4.93
Miller,Dan,Ogden	R	23	18	17	2	0	112	481	139	64	59	7	3	1	3	23	0	94	5	0	10	2	.833	0	0	4.74
Miller,Eric,St. Pete	A	24	57	0	0	51	58.1	238	40	15	13	2	2	0	4	24	0	66	7	0	1	2	.333	0	37	2.01
Miller,Jerrod,Idaho Falls	R	19	3	3	0	0	11.2	58	14	15	15	2	0	0	1	11	0	11	5	0	0	1	.000	0	0	11.57
Miller,Shawn,Fort Wayne	A	22	22	5	0	6	61	270	72	36	24	4	3	1	3	14	0	39	3	0	0	4	.000	0	0	3.54
Million,Doug,Rockies	R	19	3	3	0	0	12	46	8	3	2	0	0	0	0	3	0	19	2	0	1	0	1.000	0	0	1.50
Bend	A	19	10	10	0	0	57.2	246	50	23	15	4	1	0	4	21	0	75	4	0	5	3	.625	0	0	2.34
Millwood,Kevin,Macon	A	20	12	4	0	4	32.2	165	31	31	21	4	2	1	2	32	1	24	4	0	0	5	.000	0	1	5.79
Danville	R	20	13	5	0	2	46	211	42	25	19	4	4	1	2	34	2	56	1	0	3	3	.500	0	1	3.72
Mimnaugh,Scott,Sou. Oregon	A	24	6	0	0	1	6.2	36	9	13	11	1	0	0	0	8	2	5	0	0	0	1	.000	0	0	14.85
Minor,Thomas,New Jersey	A	23	35	0	0	16	48.1	202	41	14	9	1	3	1	4	13	1	48	0	2	4	1	.800	0	6	1.68
Mirando,Walter,Marlins	R	NA	11	9	0	1	58.1	227	44	14	11	1	1	3	2	18	0	53	6	1	6	2	.750	0	0	1.70
Mitchell,Alvin,Utica	A	23	14	12	2	1	70.1	299	74	41	35	5	0	2	7	25	0	41	3	0	4	4	.500	1	0	4.48
Mitchell,Courtney,Martinsvlle	R	22	17	0	0	5	27.1	135	31	28	20	3	1	3	2	22	0	27	11	1	0	1	.000	0	0	6.59
Mitchell,Jeffrey,Expos	R	23	19	0	0	5	26.2	127	33	23	21	1	2	1	3	12	0	18	3	1	1	0	1.000	0	2	7.09
Mitchell,Kelvin,Mariners	R	20	16	0	0	4	32.2	135	20	14	7	1	0	1	3	9	0	48	2	1	3	1	.750	0	2	1.93
Mitchell,Steve,San Bernrdo	A	22	9	2	0	0	10	66	15	18	15	2	0	0	1	20	0	8	4	0	0	1	.000	0	0	13.50
Mittauer,Casey,Oneonta	A	22	26	0	0	20	38.2	165	32	10	7	0	1	0	1	13	2	31	2	0	3	3	.500	0	4	1.63
Mix,Derek,Spokane	A	21	22	6	0	12	52	264	56	42	36	5	0	4	11	49	2	56	17	1	4	5	.444	0	0	6.23
Mix,Gregory,Brevard Cty	A	23	44	0	0	22	78	314	65	29	27	2	4	4	2	20	2	51	1	0	6	2	.750	0	4	3.12
Moehler,Brian,Lakeland	A	23	26	25	5	0	164.2	687	153	66	55	3	7	7	6	65	0	92	8	3	12	12	.500	2	0	3.01
Mojica,Gonzalo,Burlington	R	18	10	10	1	0	42.2	215	50	53	30	4	4	2	5	30	0	42	11	5	0	8	.000	0	0	6.33
Montane,Ivan,Appleton	A	22	29	26	1	0	159	680	132	79	68	13	4	6	12	82	0	155	19	2	8	9	.471	1	0	3.85
Montelongo,Joseph,Williamsprt	A	21	12	9	2	1	70.1	295	54	29	20	2	2	2	5	33	1	57	5	6	3	5	.375	1	0	2.56
Peoria	A	21	2	2	1	0	17	64	15	4	4	0	0	0	0	1	0	11	1	2	1	1	.500	0	0	2.12
Montgomery,Josh,Butte	R	24	14	8	0	2	40.2	200	58	47	38	5	2	1	1	20	0	30	12	4	0	7	.000	0	0	8.41
Montgomery,Steve,Royals	R	21	12	0	0	6	17.1	68	12	6	3	0	0	0	0	5	0	12	1	0	1	1	.500	0	3	1.56
Montoya,Wilmer,Watertown	A	21	11	11	1	0	49	199	39	18	14	2	2	2	4	23	0	50	3	1	3	2	.600	0	0	2.57
Moody,Eric,Hudson Vall	A	24	15	12	1	1	89	355	82	32	28	2	2	3	2	18	1	68	3	4	7	3	.700	0	0	2.83
Mooney,Eric,Eugene	A	23	9	3	0	2	22	98	25	16	10	0	4	2	1	10	1	10	2	1	0	1	.000	0	0	4.09
Moore,Joel,Central Val	A	22	25	24	0	0	133	607	149	78	67	8	6	1	8	64	1	89	12	1	11	8	.579	0	0	4.53
Moore,Warren,Bellingham	A	22	11	10	1	0	61.2	247	48	18	18	4	0	2	2	24	0	73	4	0	5	2	.714	0	0	2.63
Moores,Jon,Elmira	A	22	20	1	0	6	31.2	141	31	21	20	1	5	2	2	18	1	24	3	0	1	3	.250	0	0	5.68
Moraga,David,Expos	R	19	14	0	0	7	23.2	100	23	11	4	0	3	1	0	8	1	13	4	2	3	5	.375	0	2	1.52
Morales,Armando,Charlstn-Sc	A	24	15	11	0	2	62.2	264	52	29	27	8	0	3	2	26	0	55	7	0	4	3	.571	0	0	3.88
Morel,Ramon,Augusta	A	20	28	27	2	0	168.2	689	157	69	53	8	2	4	12	24	0	152	20	0	10	7	.588	1	0	2.83
Moreno,Julio,Orioles	R	19	4	2	0	0	8.1	41	14	14	11	2	0	2	0	1	0	6	0	0	0	2	.000	0	0	11.88
Morgan,Eric,Bellingham	A	22	12	0	0	3	22.2	99	19	10	10	2	0	0	3	9	0	25	3	1	4	2	.667	0	1	3.97
Morones,Geno,Daytona	A	24	16	16	2	0	99.2	399	87	37	30	3	1	1	2	28	0	69	3	0	5	3	.625	2	0	2.71
Morse,Paul,Elizabethtn	R	22	7	0	0	5	7.1	35	8	7	6	2	0	1	2	3	0	8	0	0	0	0	.000	0	0	7.36
Fort Wayne	A	22	16	0	0	11	20.1	97	27	15	13	2	1	0	2	10	0	17	0	0	0	3	.000	0	3	5.75
Mortimer,Michael,Hudson Vall	A	24	14	10	0	1	61	276	64	32	26	5	2	1	7	27	0	51	8	2	3	4	.429	0	0	3.84
Morvay,Joseph,Charlstn-Wv	A	24	37	1	0	11	71	303	50	27	22	4	4	1	4	30	1	85	4	0	2	4	.333	0	2	2.79
Moses,Michael,Charlstn-Sc	A	24	25	8	0	5	82.1	370	83	50	43	8	3	3	9	42	3	73	8	0	4	9	.308	0	0	4.70
Moses,Shane,Helena	R	22	2	2	0	0	9	38	10	4	3	0	0	0	0	3	0	2	1	0	1	0	1.000	0	0	3.00
Brewers	R	22	9	0	0	4	38.1	167	49	24	21	2	2	2	0	7	0	42	5	0	3	2	.600	0	0	4.93
Moss,Damian,Danville	R	18	12	12	1	0	60.1	265	30	28	24	1	1	0	14	55	0	77	12	3	2	5	.286	1	0	3.58
Mott,Thomas,Elizabethtn	R	21	8	6	1	1	37.2	161	31	17	12	2	2	1	4	15	0	15	1	1	4	3	.571	0	0	2.87
Mounce,Anthony,Astros	R	20	11	11	0	0	59.2	246	56	24	18	1	2	1	1	18	0	72	2	2	4	2	.667	0	0	2.72
Muir,Harry,Hagerstown	A	22	33	1	0	17	64	300	74	50	48	8	6	1	5	33	1	41	3	2	5	6	.455	0	1	6.75
Mull,Blaine,Royals	R	18	3	3	0	0	15	56	8	1	0	0	0	0	0	2	0	8	0	0	2	0	1.000	0	0	0.00
Munda,Steve,San Bernrdo	A	25	24	22	0	0	100	517	155	118	108	21	4	3	4	68	0	80	12	4	5	13	.278	0	0	9.72
Murphy,Matthew,Brewers	R	24	4	0	0	0	19.1	77	18	6	4	0	0	0	0	7	0	16	0	0	1	2	.000	0	0	1.86
Stockton	A	24	9	9	0	0	48.1	218	59	32	29	3	5	3	3	16	0	25	0	0	1	3	.250	0	0	5.40
Murray,Heath,Spokane	A	22	15	15	2	0	99.1	408	101	46	32	6	6	2	5	18	0	78	4	3	5	6	.455	1	0	2.90
Murray,James,Giants	A	20	10	0	0	2	15	60	12	8	7	0	0	0	0	3	0	19	0	0	0	0	.000	0	0	4.20
Everett	A	20	6	1	0	1	12.1	56	15	10	10	3	0	0	0	5	0	14	2	0	0	1	.000	0	1	7.30
Myers,Jason,Clinton	A	21	26	26	2	0	146.2	616	150	77	69	14	8	5	4	36	0	100	8	0	10	6	.625	0	0	4.23
Myers,Tom,Frederick	A	25	12	0	0	2	13.2	68	11	10	10	0	0	0	2	17	1	13	3	0	0	0	.000	0	0	6.59
Najera,Noe,Watertown	A	24	21	1	0	6	34	161	36	20	17	1	2	1	3	22	4	37	4	0	2	1	.667	0	2	4.50
Nape,John,Lethbridge	R	22	14	14	0	0	80.2	377	102	66	58	5	5	1	3	42	0	46	8	1	2	6	.250	0	0	6.47
Narcisse,Tyrone,Osceola	A	23	26	26	0	0	146	633	153	91	79	7	5	5	11	57	2	86	9	4	7	11	.389	1	0	4.87
Nate,Scott,Brewers	R	21	16	0	0	0	20.2	92	19	11	6	0	2	2	0	10	0	24	5	1	1	1	.500	0	2	2.61
Navarro,Richard,Lakeland	A	25	30	2	0	12	44.1	197	42	27	25	2	2	2	2	20	0	47	2	0	1	4	.200	0	0	5.08
Neese,Joshua,Lakeland	A	23	1	1	0	0	3.1	16	3	3	2	0	0	0	0	3	0	2	0	0	0	0	.000	0	0	5.40

1994 Pitching -- Single-A and Rookie Leagues

Player	Lg	A	G	GS	CG	GF	IP	BFP	H	R	ER	HR	SH	SF	HB	TBB	IBB	SO	WP	Bk	W	L	Pct.	ShO	Sv	ERA
Neier,Chris,Asheville	A	23	31	0	0	9	56.1	247	61	28	23	4	5	5	3	19	1	49	1	0	2	2	.500	0	1	3.67
Central Val	A	23	19	0	0	10	27.2	113	28	10	9	1	0	1	0	4	1	23	4	0	1	0	1.000	0	4	2.93
Neilson,Mike,Watertown	A	24	3	0	0	1	3.1	16	3	2	2	0	0	0	1	2	0	3	0	0	0	0	.000	0	1	5.40
Neiman,Josh,Padres	R	20	14	6	0	2	52.1	222	52	27	20	2	2	1	5	7	0	45	4	2	2	3	.400	0	2	3.44
Nelson,Earl,Macon	A	23	26	2	0	14	61	244	44	12	5	2	3	0	3	20	1	55	7	0	3	3	.500	0	0	0.74
Nelson,Rodney,Royals	R	20	12	12	1	0	70.2	281	50	18	14	1	0	2	3	21	0	51	5	0	9	0	1.000	1	0	1.78
Nestor,Donald,Boise	A	23	22	0	0	12	36	158	40	18	13	0	2	1	4	9	1	29	5	0	1	1	.500	0	2	3.25
Newell,Brandon,Columbia	A	23	45	0	0	20	64.2	262	50	25	17	3	3	3	6	17	1	59	5	1	5	1	.833	0	6	2.37
Newman,Damon,Sou. Oregon	A	21	11	6	0	2	37.2	169	30	17	16	2	1	1	4	28	0	32	6	1	3	3	.500	0	0	3.82
Newton,Christopher,Jamestown	A	22	29	0	0	10	42.2	181	33	17	8	0	5	0	2	17	1	33	3	0	4	3	.571	0	0	1.69
Newton,Geronimo,Riverside	A	21	2	1	0	0	8	32	5	4	4	2	0	0	0	3	0	4	0	1	0	0	.000	0	0	4.50
Bellingham	A	21	21	8	0	4	60	255	43	19	14	1	2	2	2	36	3	43	8	3	3	4	.429	0	0	2.10
Nieto,Antonio,Billings	R	22	21	2	0	11	44.1	175	33	21	11	1	1	0	4	10	0	31	2	2	1	1	.500	0	3	2.23
Nieves,Ernie,Lake Elsino	A	24	27	0	0	17	39.2	181	42	25	19	3	2	2	2	24	2	33	3	1	1	3	.250	0	1	4.31
Nix,Jim,Winston-Sal	A	24	29	28	1	1	169	753	168	103	86	23	6	9	9	87	1	139	10	2	11	10	.524	0	0	4.58
Noguchi,Shigeki,Central Val	A	21	26	21	2	1	137.2	571	112	50	39	7	3	3	2	56	1	161	13	2	8	3	.727	1	0	2.55
Nolte,Eric,San Bernrdo	A	31	54	0	0	38	89.2	425	105	62	53	14	4	2	5	43	0	110	5	0	3	2	.600	0	7	5.32
Norman,Scott,Fayettevlle	A	22	25	25	4	0	165	672	148	63	51	9	3	4	4	41	0	95	12	0	14	7	.667	2	0	2.78
Lakeland	A	22	3	3	1	0	18.1	77	19	7	6	2	1	1	5	9	0	9	2	0	2	0	1.000	1	0	2.95
Nowak,Steve,Jamestown	A	24	26	0	0	13	57.1	258	53	29	23	3	4	1	6	27	0	33	13	0	2	4	.333	0	2	3.61
Nunez,Clemente,Brevard Cty	A	20	19	16	2	1	98.2	407	86	45	34	8	5	2	1	24	0	66	3	1	6	5	.545	1	0	3.10
Nunez,Maximo,Blue Jays	R	22	20	0	0	15	24.2	119	32	23	11	0	1	1	1	10	0	17	2	2	1	5	.167	0	2	4.01
Nutt,Steve,Spartanburg	A	23	21	0	0	7	30.1	145	32	20	17	3	1	3	3	23	0	24	2	1	1	2	.333	0	1	5.04
Nuttle,Jamison,Pirates	R	23	7	0	0	2	12	53	9	6	2	0	0	0	0	6	0	9	2	0	0	1	.000	0	0	1.50
Augusta	A	23	2	0	0	0	3.1	14	3	2	2	1	0	0	1	1	0	1	0	0	0	0	.000	0	0	5.40
Nyari,Peter,Batavia	A	23	14	10	0	2	52	216	33	22	16	2	1	1	1	35	0	59	2	1	5	1	.833	2	0	2.77
Nye,Ryan,Batavia	A	22	13	12	1	0	71.2	301	64	27	21	3	1	0	6	15	0	71	2	1	7	2	.778	0	0	2.64
Nygaard,Chris,Expos	R	23	21	0	0	13	34	136	22	11	9	1	0	0	2	10	1	31	2	1	1	3	.250	0	7	2.38
O'Brien,Brian,Fort Wayne	A	23	45	0	0	20	89.2	374	81	38	32	7	5	4	3	29	1	72	7	2	11	2	.846	0	3	3.21
O'Brien,Mark,Charlotte	A	22	4	2	0	0	6	37	13	13	12	2	1	0	0	6	0	4	2	1	0	2	.000	0	0	18.00
Hudson Vall	A	22	14	14	3	0	89.1	379	88	42	33	1	3	2	2	29	2	60	8	7	5	6	.455	1	0	3.32
O'Donnell,Erik,Central Val	A	25	23	0	0	5	51.2	239	70	36	27	7	3	2	2	15	2	23	5	0	4	4	.500	0	0	4.70
O'Flynn,Gardner,Hudson Vall	A	23	20	0	0	6	30.2	140	34	12	10	0	3	1	2	12	0	25	0	0	2	2	.500	0	0	2.93
O'Hearn,Paul,Ogden	R	24	17	16	6	1	123.2	526	118	49	42	1	1	4	14	38	1	99	6	1	8	5	.615	1	1	3.06
O'Laughlin,Chad,San Bernrdo	A	23	5	4	0	1	16.1	98	39	34	27	4	1	4	1	7	0	8	1	0	0	3	.000	0	0	14.88
O'Malley,Paul,Auburn	A	22	9	9	1	0	44.2	205	51	30	27	3	1	1	5	18	0	38	7	2	3	4	.429	0	0	5.44
Ocasio,Mark,Rangers	R	20	12	10	1	0	51.2	241	65	41	24	5	0	4	5	19	1	26	4	0	4	4	.500	0	0	4.18
Ochsenfeld,Chris,Great Falls	R	18	8	3	0	1	25.1	118	23	18	10	1	1	3	1	15	0	22	3	2	1	0	1.000	0	0	3.55
Oehrlein,David,Savannah	A	25	12	12	0	0	76.1	298	52	22	18	2	1	4	4	22	0	62	3	0	8	1	.889	0	0	2.12
St. Pete	A	25	12	12	0	0	76	308	67	27	25	6	3	2	2	23	0	64	2	0	6	2	.750	0	0	2.96
Ogden,Jason,South Bend	A	25	17	0	0	8	30.2	132	27	15	14	3	1	1	3	16	0	24	4	0	3	1	.750	0	4	4.11
Pr. William	A	25	11	0	0	7	18.2	92	25	18	14	3	2	3	0	12	0	9	7	0	0	3	.000	0	0	6.75
Ohme,Kevin,Fort Wayne	A	24	2	2	0	0	7	29	7	2	2	0	0	0	1	0	0	8	0	0	1	0	1.000	0	0	2.57
Oiler,David,Twins	R	24	4	0	0	1	4.1	24	7	5	5	0	0	0	0	3	0	8	2	0	1	0	1.000	0	0	10.38
Fort Myers	A	24	6	0	0	3	10	47	15	5	4	0	0	1	0	2	0	9	0	0	0	0	.000	0	0	3.60
Ojeda,Erick,Mets	R	19	13	13	2	0	65.1	283	66	36	26	5	0	2	1	21	0	59	5	2	3	4	.429	0	0	3.58
Oldham,Robert,Burlington	R	21	15	4	0	6	34	167	32	30	23	2	2	1	4	31	0	39	5	1	1	6	.143	0	0	6.09
Olivier,Richard,Yankees	R	20	4	0	0	2	9.1	34	5	5	2	1	1	1	0	0	0	10	0	0	0	1	.000	0	1	1.93
Olivo,Gary,Giants	R	21	11	0	0	5	13	70	11	14	13	0	0	1	1	18	0	14	5	1	1	1	.500	0	0	9.00
Olson,Chris,Spartanburg	A	23	9	6	0	1	35.2	174	41	31	23	5	2	1	2	26	0	29	4	1	3	2	.250	0	0	5.80
Olszewski,Eirc,Idaho Falls	R	20	15	13	0	0	67.1	345	91	67	55	8	2	3	3	57	1	51	13	0	3	7	.300	0	0	7.35
Ontiveros,Art,Lethbridge	R	23	15	15	0	0	77.2	364	102	66	49	5	0	2	8	24	3	48	9	8	3	7	.300	0	0	5.68
Orellano,Rafael,Red Sox	R	22	4	3	0	0	13.1	50	6	3	3	0	0	0	0	4	0	10	1	2	1	0	1.000	0	0	2.03
Sarasota	A	22	16	16	2	0	97.1	375	68	28	26	5	1	0	4	25	0	103	2	3	11	3	.786	1	0	2.40
Ormonde,Troy,Huntington	R	20	11	7	0	1	44.2	199	39	24	14	0	2	1	4	29	0	51	7	8	0	2	.000	0	0	2.82
Oropesa,Eddie,Vero Beach	A	23	19	10	1	3	72	285	54	24	17	2	3	2	4	25	2	67	2	0	4	3	.571	0	0	2.13
Oropeza,Igor,Watertown	A	22	13	13	0	0	76.1	327	69	32	18	1	1	1	6	21	0	76	4	2	8	2	.800	0	0	2.12
Ortiz,Steven,Burlington	R	22	14	0	0	6	26.1	135	34	26	21	4	2	4	1	23	0	20	6	0	0	1	.000	0	0	7.18
Ottmers,Marc,Madison	A	23	10	10	0	0	48	221	46	29	24	6	2	4	1	34	0	59	2	4	2	4	.333	0	0	4.50
Paasch,Stephan,Batavia	A	22	18	6	0	3	57.2	244	50	28	19	2	3	3	1	24	0	49	10	0	3	3	.500	0	0	2.97
Pace,Scotty,Elmira	A	23	13	12	2	0	70.2	307	73	35	32	3	3	0	3	27	2	50	7	0	3	7	.300	0	0	4.08
Pacheco,Alexander,Burlington	A	21	37	4	0	19	68.1	302	79	51	39	6	7	2	6	22	1	69	5	0	3	8	.273	0	5	5.14
W. Palm Bch	A	21	9	0	0	0	12	47	9	3	3	1	0	0	4	0	0	12	2	0	1	0	1.000	0	0	2.25
Pack,Steve,Kingsport	R	21	12	11	3	0	74	293	61	20	14	3	2	2	2	15	0	57	7	1	6	3	.667	0	0	1.70
Columbia	A	21	1	1	0	0	3.2	13	9	7	7	1	1	1	0	1	0	0	0	0	0	0	.000	0	0	17.18
Padilla,Roy,Red Sox	R	19	15	12	0	0	72.1	325	68	39	24	0	0	2	6	34	0	52	9	0	6	1	.857	0	0	2.99
Padron,Oscar,Astros	R	21	8	2	0	2	21.2	88	19	6	5	0	0	1	3	9	0	15	0	1	1	0	1.000	0	1	2.08
Auburn	A	21	6	6	0	0	31.1	154	36	25	20	6	1	2	5	20	1	29	4	0	1	3	.250	0	0	5.74
Paige,Carey,Macon	A	21	19	19	1	0	105.2	440	87	32	20	3	2	2	5	33	2	119	3	2	8	6	.571	0	0	1.70
Durham	A	21	6	6	0	0	28.2	130	31	19	15	2	0	2	0	13	0	25	0	0	2	2	.500	0	0	4.71
Palmer,Brett,Burlington	R	20	13	1	0	4	35.2	169	34	24	18	2	1	3	0	25	0	27	2	0	1	0	1.000	0	0	4.54
Paluk,Jeffrey,Yakima	A	22	16	7	0	4	55	237	47	29	22	2	1	3	8	20	1	52	6	2	1	4	.200	0	2	3.60
Paniagua,Jose,W. Palm Bch	A	21	26	26	1	0	141	606	131	82	57	6	5	4	8	54	2	110	13	2	9	9	.500	0	0	3.64
Parisi,Mike,Elmira	A	22	13	13	3	0	78.1	328	64	32	26	3	3	1	9	26	0	56	5	1	5	5	.500	1	0	2.99
Parker,Freddie,Cardinals	R	21	5	0	0	0	6.2	33	8	8	8	0	0	1	1	6	0	4	3	0	0	0	.000	0	0	10.80
Parkins,Rob,San Bernrdo	A	31	44	6	1	15	122	530	137	62	52	5	4	1	0	43	2	103	11	1	7	4	.636	1	3	3.84
Parotte,Frisco,Yankees	R	19	13	0	0	8	25.2	99	17	10	7	0	2	1	1	3	0	31	1	2	5	1	.833	0	1	2.45

328

1994 Pitching -- Single-A and Rookie Leagues

Player	Lg	A	G	GS	CG	GF	IP	BFP	H	R	ER	HR	SH	SF	HB	TBB	IBB	SO	WP	Bk	W	L	Pct.	ShO	Sv	ERA
Oneonta	A	19	6	0	0	2	10.2	56	13	11	7	1	0	2	0	1	8	2	9	1	0	0	2	.000	0	0	5.91
Parris,Steve,Salem	A	27	17	7	0	1	57	247	58	24	23	7	0	2	6	21	1	48	1	0	3	3	.500	0	0	3.63
Patterson,Jim,San Bernrdo	A	24	42	17	1	9	133.1	606	170	103	89	13	3	5	10	40	4	96	12	1	7	14	.333	0	0	6.01
Paugh,Richard,Welland	A	23	26	1	0	9	35.1	144	24	5	5	0	5	0	1	12	0	34	2	2	1	3	.250	0	3	1.27
Paul,Andy,Stockton	A	23	16	7	0	4	49	223	56	30	21	4	2	4	1	19	1	38	7	2	3	4	.429	0	1	3.86
Pauls,Matthew,Rangers	R	20	19	0	0	8	35.2	142	28	10	6	1	1	0	0	4	0	19	0	1	2	2	.500	0	2	1.51
Pavano,Carl,Red Sox	R	19	9	7	0	0	44	176	31	14	9	1	0	1	1	7	0	47	4	1	4	3	.571	0	0	1.84
Pavicich,Paul,Elizabethtn	R	22	12	2	1	2	35.1	145	24	16	16	4	3	2	1	20	1	35	0	0	3	1	.750	0	1	4.08
Pavlovich,Anthony,Brewers	R	20	19	0	0	15	27.1	109	24	7	5	1	1	2	1	8	0	29	3	0	2	1	.667	0	8	1.65
Paz,Ivan,Rockies	R	21	17	0	0	3	24.2	126	32	31	27	1	0	1	1	20	1	22	4	3	0	1	.000	0	1	9.85
Peery,Noah,Columbia	A	23	20	0	0	13	33	150	27	20	17	2	1	1	5	20	0	24	6	1	2	3	.400	0	0	4.64
Pelatowski,Keith,Williamsprt	A	23	24	6	0	11	44.2	207	59	42	28	3	2	3	0	13	0	25	2	3	4	5	.444	0	0	5.64
Pelka,Brian,Welland	A	23	3	3	0	0	18	68	12	4	4	0	0	0	1	2	0	10	1	2	1	0	1.000	0	0	2.00
Pena,Alex,Bluefield	R	22	18	0	0	14	41.2	149	16	6	3	1	0	0	1	6	1	35	3	0	5	2	.714	0	3	0.65
Pena,Jim,San Bernrdo	A	30	16	3	0	10	39	167	37	17	17	4	1	1	1	11	0	29	2	0	3	4	.429	0	0	3.92
Percibal,William,Albany	A	21	28	28	3	0	169.1	744	160	80	67	9	1	3	1	90	0	132	13	4	13	9	.591	2	0	3.56
Perez,Edward,Royals	A	18	0	0	0	10	27.2	123	31	19	16	2	1	1	2	12	0	27	0	0	1	1	.500	0	2	5.20
Perez,Gil,Welland	A	22	5	0	0	2	9.1	34	5	1	1	0	1	0	0	1	0	9	0	0	0	1	.000	0	0	0.96
Augusta	A	22	20	0	0	3	38.2	185	44	37	35	5	4	1	2	19	3	26	7	1	1	3	.250	0	0	8.15
Perez,Hilario,Sarasota	A	22	7	6	0	0	32.2	144	42	26	25	2	0	1	0	9	0	11	0	0	1	2	.333	0	0	6.89
Utica	A	22	14	14	1	0	77.2	332	75	35	28	1	3	2	3	23	0	31	8	0	6	5	.545	1	0	3.24
Perez,Juan,Athletics	R	22	14	4	0	7	47.1	216	66	30	23	1	0	3	0	14	0	41	3	0	3	2	.600	0	1	4.37
Perez,Julio,Burlington	A	21	8	8	0	0	46.1	193	38	11	7	0	0	0	3	19	2	47	1	6	3	3	.500	0	1	1.36
Watertown	A	21	6	6	1	0	35	153	37	17	14	2	2	1	1	13	0	24	1	0	1	2	.333	0	0	3.60
Perez,Luis,Twins	R	22	18	0	0	9	24.1	162	48	58	39	3	2	1	4	33	0	20	11	0	0	3	.000	0	0	14.42
Perez,Luis,Hudson Vall	A	21	20	3	0	5	52.1	239	54	38	26	1	2	4	3	21	1	28	4	0	1	3	.250	0	0	4.47
Perez,Dario,Wilmington	A	25	31	4	0	12	61	259	63	38	36	9	0	2	2	15	2	56	3	0	3	3	.500	0	2	5.31
Perisho,Matt,Cedar Rapds	A	20	27	27	0	0	147.2	689	165	90	71	11	7	7	4	88	0	107	8	3	12	9	.571	0	0	4.33
Perkins,Daniel,Fort Wayne	A	20	12	12	0	0	50.2	229	61	38	35	3	3	1	4	22	1	34	4	1	1	8	.111	0	0	6.22
Elizabethtn	R	20	10	9	1	0	54	223	51	31	22	2	2	1	7	14	0	34	9	1	0	2	.000	0	0	3.67
Perkins,Scott,Helena	R	23	15	11	0	1	76.1	332	56	34	26	5	3	1	9	52	0	76	12	1	5	1	.833	0	0	3.07
Petcka,Joe,St. Lucie	A	24	12	1	0	5	25.2	120	22	17	12	1	0	0	0	27	1	16	5	1	0	2	.000	0	2	4.21
Columbia	A	23	11	10	1	0	52.1	264	61	55	44	10	5	1	5	38	0	42	10	0	0	9	.000	0	0	7.57
Peters,Christopher,Salem	A	23	3	0	0	1	3.1	16	5	5	5	2	0	0	1	1	0	2	1	0	1	0	1.000	0	0	13.50
Augusta	A	23	54	0	0	29	60.2	268	51	34	29	1	5	2	2	33	2	83	7	0	4	5	.444	0	4	4.30
Peters,John,Elizabethtn	A	23	3	0	0	2	5.2	21	3	0	0	0	0	1	0	1	0	8	0	0	0	0	.000	0	0	0.00
Fort Wayne	A	23	16	0	0	5	25.1	110	21	12	7	2	0	2	0	11	1	32	4	1	1	2	.333	0	1	2.49
Peterson,Dean,Sarasota	A	22	21	20	6	0	141	572	141	65	57	9	7	8	2	26	0	94	4	0	9	7	.563	3	0	3.64
Peterson,Jayson,Huntington	R	19	9	8	0	0	39.1	192	45	27	22	2	2	2	3	32	0	32	9	1	1	5	.167	0	0	5.03
Petroff,Daniel,Boise	A	21	8	8	0	0	44.1	183	35	18	14	1	3	0	3	19	2	41	0	2	3	2	.600	0	0	2.84
Pett,Jose,Dunedin	A	19	15	15	1	0	90.2	389	103	47	38	1	5	5	3	20	0	49	3	4	4	8	.333	0	0	3.77
Pettiet,Chris,Blue Jays	R	19	7	2	0	3	8	52	16	20	14	1	0	3	0	13	0	4	5	0	0	1	.000	0	0	15.75
Pettit,Doug,Brevard Cty	A	25	40	0	0	31	46.2	194	37	13	13	4	4	1	2	13	1	38	1	1	3	3	.500	0	14	2.51
Phelps,Tom,Burlington	A	21	23	23	1	0	118.1	534	143	91	73	9	7	7	5	48	1	82	7	0	8	8	.500	1	0	5.55
Phillip,Craig,Red Sox	R	23	3	0	0	3	2.2	11	1	2	1	1	0	1	0	1	0	0	0	0	0	1	.000	0	1	3.38
Phillips,Jason,Augusta	A	21	23	23	1	0	108.1	531	118	97	81	4	3	4	12	88	1	108	21	3	6	12	.333	0	0	6.73
Phillips,Jonny,Auburn	A	23	20	1	0	6	35	185	49	36	35	9	3	2	6	29	0	35	4	0	1	1	.500	0	0	9.00
Phillips,Marc,Eugene	A	23	16	5	0	5	35	180	42	36	20	2	3	4	3	26	0	28	2	0	1	4	.200	0	0	5.14
Phipps,Chris,Martinsvile	R	21	13	13	1	0	76	325	70	45	31	8	3	1	1	30	0	42	5	0	3	5	.375	0	0	3.67
Pickett,Ricky,Charlstn-Sc	A	25	28	0	0	19	27.1	121	14	8	6	1	0	4	2	20	0	48	4	0	1	1	.500	0	13	1.98
Winston-Sal	A	25	21	0	0	17	24	112	16	11	10	0	1	1	2	23	1	33	2	0	2	1	.667	0	0	3.75
Pickford,Kevin,Augusta	A	20	2	2	0	0	8.2	37	9	6	4	1	0	0	0	5	0	7	1	0	0	1	.000	0	0	4.15
Welland	A	22	15	15	1	0	84.2	377	86	52	46	7	1	6	5	36	0	52	2	2	5	8	.385	1	0	4.89
Pickich,Jeffrey,Augusta	A	23	13	0	0	5	17.2	75	17	7	6	0	0	0	0	5	0	25	4	0	1	0	1.000	0	2	3.06
Pierce,Marvin,Burlington	R	20	19	0	0	3	30	153	36	23	23	2	0	0	5	20	2	30	12	1	1	0	1.000	0	0	6.90
Pierson,Jay,Pr. William	A	24	28	28	3	0	189.1	785	183	85	70	22	10	3	6	48	0	117	11	2	14	8	.636	1	0	3.33
Pike,Dave,Charlotte	A	24	22	8	0	5	54.2	266	57	41	38	4	3	2	7	44	0	28	12	1	2	5	.286	0	0	6.26
Pinango,Simon,Red Sox	R	21	12	12	0	0	68.1	279	62	29	25	1	2	3	3	16	0	53	3	0	4	3	.571	0	0	3.29
Pineda,Leonel,Marlins	R	18	12	11	1	1	66.1	282	66	30	22	2	1	1	3	15	0	49	3	1	2	2	.500	0	0	2.98
Pisciotta,Scott,W. Palm Bch	A	22	4	4	0	0	21	93	20	12	11	1	0	2	2	14	1	11	8	0	0	3	.000	0	0	4.71
Burlington	A	22	40	4	0	15	73.2	325	69	46	36	6	1	1	5	39	2	64	10	0	2	4	.333	0	0	4.40
Pitcher,Scott,W. Palm Bch	A	27	18	1	0	7	24.2	118	33	21	20	2	0	1	0	12	1	23	5	0	0	3	.000	0	0	7.30
Pittsley,Jim,Wilmington	A	21	27	27	1	0	161.2	673	154	73	57	15	3	9	4	42	0	171	2	1	11	5	.688	1	0	3.17
Pivaral,Hugo,Vero Beach	A	18	22	20	1	0	97.1	423	102	55	39	6	5	2	6	29	0	90	6	5	6	5	.545	0	0	3.61
Great Falls	R	18	3	2	0	0	10	42	8	4	3	0	0	1	3	3	0	12	1	0	1	0	1.000	0	0	2.70
Place,Mike,Durham	A	24	10	3	0	2	22.2	109	39	21	18	6	1	1	0	4	1	12	0	1	0	3	.000	0	0	7.15
Macon	A	24	4	4	0	0	23.2	93	15	5	5	2	1	0	1	7	0	19	1	0	3	0	1.000	0	0	1.90
Plaster,Allen,Modesto	A	24	45	0	0	30	51.1	214	27	21	11	3	2	1	1	31	2	71	5	0	6	2	.750	0	13	1.93
Ploeger,Tim,High Desert	A	23	43	2	0	10	102	509	145	101	90	17	1	6	7	54	1	92	9	2	1	6	.143	0	1	7.94
Plumlee,Christopher,Butte	R	23	4	0	0	0	3	31	7	16	16	0	0	2	1	13	0	4	7	0	0	0	.000	0	0	48.00
Polak,Richard,Yankees	R	28	3	0	0	1	4	14	3	0	0	0	0	0	0	0	0	5	0	0	0	0	.000	0	0	0.00
Tampa	A	28	1	0	0	0	1.2	7	3	1	1	0	0	0	0	1	0	0	0	0	0	0	.000	0	0	5.40
Ponson,Sidney,Orioles	R	18	12	10	1	0	73	300	68	30	24	5	1	3	2	17	0	53	2	4	4	3	.571	0	0	2.96
Pontbriant,Matt,Augusta	A	23	21	21	2	0	126.1	551	134	65	43	7	3	4	5	41	0	76	8	0	3	8	.273	0	0	3.06
Pontes,Daniel,Savannah	A	24	17	14	0	0	91.2	369	80	43	30	4	3	0	5	17	0	81	9	1	6	5	.500	0	0	2.95
Pool,Bruce,Yankees	R	24	3	0	0	2	4	24	10	7	4	0	0	0	0	0	0	4	0	0	0	0	.000	0	0	9.00
Tampa	A	24	3	0	0	0	5	19	3	1	0	0	0	0	0	0	0	4	0	0	0	0	.000	0	0	0.00

1994 Pitching -- Single-A and Rookie Leagues

Player	Lg	A	G	GS	CG	GF	IP	BFP	H	R	ER	HR	SH	SF	HB	TBB	IBB	SO	WP	Bk	W	L	Pct.	ShO	Sv	ERA
Pool,Matthew,Bend	A	21	6	6	0	0	30.2	132	28	13	11	1	1	0	2	14	0	28	0	1	1	1	.500	0	0	3.23
Asheville	A	21	9	8	0	1	58	236	51	21	18	4	0	1	1	18	0	40	4	1	4	3	.571	0	1	2.79
Pooschke,Mark,Giants	R	20	15	0	0	3	21.2	101	22	13	8	0	0	1	1	15	0	15	6	0	0	3	.000	0	1	3.32
Porzio,Mike,Cubs	R	22	7	0	0	6	13.2	64	19	10	9	0	0	0	1	6	0	5	0	0	0	3	.000	0	1	5.93
Poupart,Melvin,Mets	R	20	15	1	0	14	33	135	26	12	9	0	1	1	2	18	0	28	3	1	2	3	.400	0	5	2.45
Powell,Jay,Frederick	A	23	26	20	0	2	123.1	552	132	79	68	13	4	3	1	54	0	87	12	2	7	7	.500	0	1	4.96
Powell,Jeremy,Expos	R	19	9	9	1	0	43	171	37	16	14	1	0	1	2	14	0	36	2	2	2	2	.500	0	0	2.93
Powell,John,Charlotte	A	24	17	12	2	0	81.1	327	61	38	32	4	6	0	4	28	1	85	2	4	2	8	.200	0	0	3.54
Prado,Jose,Bakersfield	A	23	28	28	0	0	163.1	684	159	75	64	8	3	3	5	56	0	143	11	5	15	9	.625	0	0	3.53
Prater,Christopher,Everett	A	22	14	14	0	0	67.1	303	94	47	39	4	4	1	3	16	1	53	2	1	3	7	.300	0	0	5.21
Pratt,Richard,Hickory	A	24	29	23	3	3	165	661	138	51	37	9	5	4	3	29	0	153	1	1	11	6	.647	1	0	2.02
Prejean,Alex,White Sox	R	20	15	0	0	2	30.2	141	25	13	10	2	1	0	2	25	2	28	2	1	4	1	.800	0	1	2.93
Premack,Clayton,Lethbridge	R	22	17	0	0	6	25.2	132	30	28	23	0	2	4	2	25	1	24	7	0	1	0	1.000	0	1	8.06
Presley,Kirk,St. Lucie	A	NA	2	2	0	0	8.2	45	12	7	4	0	2	0	2	6	1	3	0	0	1	1	.500	0	0	4.15
Pittsfield	A	NA	14	14	0	0	90	402	86	46	38	3	1	2	5	41	2	51	7	0	5	6	.455	1	0	3.80
Press,Gregg,Elmira	A	23	14	12	0	0	64.2	293	77	30	26	3	4	4	2	17	1	56	7	2	3	4	.429	0	0	3.62
Preston,George,Beloit	A	21	9	3	0	3	19.1	103	25	18	16	0	1	1	3	20	0	20	4	1	0	0	.000	0	0	7.45
Helena	R	21	13	13	0	0	64.1	317	66	60	48	4	2	1	3	57	0	54	10	3	2	4	.333	0	0	6.72
Price,Tom,Great Falls	R	23	19	0	0	10	38	164	40	20	13	3	2	5	2	9	2	22	5	0	3	4	.429	0	0	3.08
Priest,Eddie,Billings	R	21	13	13	2	0	85	333	74	31	24	3	1	0	1	14	0	82	2	1	7	4	.636	0	0	2.54
Proctor,William,South Bend	A	24	34	0	0	25	57.1	252	53	33	20	0	5	3	1	25	1	51	5	1	4	4	.500	0	3	3.14
Puffer,Brandon,Twins	R	19	18	0	0	16	35.1	157	33	18	12	1	0	1	4	19	0	40	6	1	2	2	.500	0	2	3.06
Pumphrey,Kenneth,Mets	R	18	10	8	0	0	57.1	244	51	27	23	6	1	4	3	16	0	42	6	3	1	3	.250	0	0	3.61
Putrich,Josh,Huntington	R	21	7	6	0	0	37.2	161	32	18	15	1	2	1	2	16	0	30	3	1	3	1	.750	0	0	3.58
Williamsprt	A	21	5	4	0	0	24.1	105	28	17	14	3	0	2	2	8	0	16	3	0	2	2	.500	0	0	5.18
Puttmann,Shannon,Welland	A	23	13	1	0	7	19.1	112	21	27	16	1	4	0	6	20	2	10	8	0	0	1	.000	0	0	7.45
Quillin,Ty,Pittsfield	A	23	20	0	0	11	24.2	135	24	29	20	0	4	4	7	26	0	27	5	0	0	1	.000	0	0	7.30
Quinones,Rene,Winston-Sal	A	25	44	0	0	9	70.2	331	84	48	41	6	1	2	5	40	2	31	9	1	2	3	.400	0	1	5.22
Quirk,John,Hickory	A	24	22	5	0	7	58	261	54	41	37	8	3	4	1	39	0	27	3	0	5	3	.625	0	0	5.74
Pr. William	A	24	3	0	0	1	4.1	20	2	5	5	1	2	0	0	5	0	2	0	0	0	0	.000	0	0	10.38
Radlosky,Robert,Twins	R	21	11	11	0	0	56.1	234	54	28	21	1	0	3	3	19	0	52	4	7	3	4	.429	0	0	3.36
Raggio,Brady,New Jersey	A	22	4	4	0	0	27	115	28	7	5	0	2	0	0	4	0	20	1	0	3	0	1.000	0	0	1.67
Madison	A	22	11	11	1	0	67.1	277	63	31	24	8	3	2	3	14	1	66	3	0	4	3	.571	0	0	3.21
Rain,Steven,Huntington	R	20	14	10	1	1	68	272	55	26	20	2	2	2	2	19	0	55	4	4	3	3	.500	1	0	2.65
Raines,Kenneth,Idaho Falls	R	22	25	0	0	19	50.1	207	44	25	17	1	3	2	2	13	0	49	3	0	4	2	.667	0	7	3.04
Rajotte,Jason,W. Michigan	A	22	36	0	0	23	47.2	208	47	28	22	0	2	1	1	20	6	31	2	1	0	0	.000	0	7	4.15
Ralston,Kristopher,Wilmington	A	23	20	18	2	0	109.1	448	84	36	29	11	2	2	5	38	0	102	4	2	10	4	.714	0	0	2.39
Rama,Shelby,Spartanburg	A	23	30	10	1	12	97.1	437	110	58	47	7	3	2	5	43	1	66	7	2	5	7	.417	1	1	4.35
Ramirez,Hector,St. Lucie	A	22	27	27	6	0	194	802	202	86	74	10	10	6	5	50	2	110	6	8	11	12	.478	1	0	3.43
Ramirez,Rafael,Cardinals	R	20	12	11	0	1	71.1	292	66	38	25	1	0	1	4	8	0	51	13	0	5	3	.625	0	0	3.15
Ramos,Cesar,Columbus	A	21	17	0	0	9	30.2	142	30	20	16	1	4	2	3	12	2	24	3	3	1	3	.250	0	0	4.70
Kinston	A	21	21	0	0	4	36	176	45	27	21	1	0	3	6	20	0	14	2	2	3	4	.429	0	1	5.25
Ramos,Edgar,Quad City	A	20	22	16	1	4	98.2	429	110	59	49	3	2	1	3	30	1	92	6	0	2	8	.200	0	1	4.47
Rangel,Julio,Yankees	R	19	5	0	0	2	7.1	34	7	6	2	0	0	0	1	1	0	9	1	0	0	0	.000	0	0	2.45
Rapozo,Brett,Padres	R	23	4	0	0	2	6	34	11	10	8	0	0	0	2	4	0	3	4	1	0	0	.000	0	0	12.00
Rath,Alfred,Vero Beach	A	22	13	11	0	0	62.2	261	55	26	19	3	3	3	2	23	0	50	4	0	5	6	.455	0	0	2.73
Rathbun,Jason,Greensboro	A	22	14	5	0	2	43	187	36	22	19	3	3	1	2	22	0	35	4	3	2	3	.400	0	0	3.98
Tampa	A	22	4	2	1	1	17.2	67	10	3	3	0	0	0	0	7	0	10	0	0	1	0	1.000	1	0	1.53
Ratliff,Christopher,Giants	R	22	5	5	0	0	24.2	103	18	6	5	1	1	0	2	11	0	17	7	0	2	0	1.000	0	0	1.82
Clinton	A	22	12	4	0	5	31.1	152	38	30	24	5	1	3	3	18	0	17	5	1	0	4	.000	0	0	6.89
Rawitzer,Kevin,Rockford	A	24	15	15	0	0	76.1	329	80	27	21	5	0	4	3	27	1	75	6	1	5	2	.714	0	0	2.48
Wilmington	A	24	7	1	0	2	17.2	79	18	10	9	0	1	0	0	11	0	13	1	0	0	1	.000	0	0	4.58
Ray,Kenneth,Rockford	A	20	27	18	0	6	128.2	516	94	34	26	5	4	1	0	56	2	128	18	2	10	4	.714	0	3	1.82
Rayer,Anthony,Expos	R	21	17	3	0	6	40.2	174	31	21	16	3	0	0	1	27	0	36	9	4	2	2	.500	0	1	3.54
Rector,Robert,Giants	R	20	9	5	0	0	30.1	117	19	8	4	0	1	1	0	8	0	37	2	2	2	1	.333	0	0	1.19
Reed,Brandon,Bristol	R	20	13	13	0	0	78	337	82	41	31	3	1	3	9	10	0	68	4	0	3	5	.375	0	0	3.58
Reed,Brian,Butte	R	23	16	16	6	0	114.1	484	124	63	53	9	4	6	11	19	0	108	1	6	9	6	.600	0	0	4.17
Reed,Chris,Charlstn-Sc	A	21	26	25	1	1	145.2	650	156	90	78	12	3	3	11	72	2	99	9	1	11	7	.611	0	0	4.82
Reed,Jason,Yakima	A	22	16	7	0	3	63	258	50	24	20	2	2	2	1	22	0	52	2	0	4	0	1.000	0	0	2.86
Reed,Kenneth,Martinsville	R	20	14	0	0	9	17	93	24	28	24	3	0	1	1	16	1	14	12	0	0	0	.000	0	1	12.46
Reed,Steven,Cardinals	R	19	12	0	0	2	13	59	16	8	8	2	2	4	1	4	0	10	1	1	0	0	.000	0	0	5.54
Rehkopf,Rob,Williamsprt	A	23	13	0	0	5	31.1	150	40	26	22	1	1	1	4	18	0	16	1	2	2	2	.500	0	0	6.32
Reichenbach,Eric,St. Lucie	A	24	3	0	0	0	4.2	24	7	6	3	0	0	0	1	4	0	2	0	0	0	0	.000	0	0	5.79
Reichstein,Derek,Elmira	A	22	6	5	0	0	27	129	29	18	14	3	0	2	1	15	2	12	2	1	1	2	.333	0	0	4.67
Reid,Rayon,Pirates	R	21	3	3	0	0	16	66	18	6	4	0	0	0	2	1	0	10	3	0	1	0	1.000	0	0	2.25
Welland	A	21	11	11	1	0	70	294	69	40	34	4	3	2	5	19	0	42	3	2	3	8	.273	0	0	4.37
Reinheimer,Christian,Johnsn Cty	R	24	13	0	0	1	16.1	79	17	10	8	1	0	0	0	19	0	11	4	1	0	1	.000	0	0	4.41
Rekar,Bryan,Central Val	A	23	22	19	0	2	111.1	465	120	52	43	3	4	5	2	31	2	91	12	3	6	6	.500	0	0	3.48
Remington,Jake,Padres	R	19	18	6	1	4	46.1	185	36	16	12	0	2	1	1	11	0	45	4	0	3	3	.500	0	0	2.33
Renfroe,Chad,Lynchburg	A	21	19	16	0	1	90.2	404	97	51	45	7	1	4	5	35	1	67	2	2	7	4	.636	0	0	4.47
Resendez,Oscar,High Desert	A	23	33	14	2	10	120.2	564	112	86	76	12	2	3	4	88	0	91	9	1	2	11	.154	1	2	5.67
Resz,Gregory,Greensboro	A	23	7	0	0	7	7.2	32	6	3	3	0	0	0	0	2	0	14	1	0	0	0	.000	0	2	3.52
Tampa	A	23	18	0	0	18	18.2	79	21	8	3	0	0	1	1	4	0	20	0	0	0	2	.000	0	6	1.45
Revenig,Todd,Athletics	R	26	4	4	0	0	7.2	33	7	4	3	1	1	0	0	2	0	6	0	0	0	0	.000	0	0	3.52
Reyes,Dennis,Vero Beach	A	18	9	9	0	0	41.2	199	58	37	31	6	1	1	0	18	0	25	1	1	4	4	.333	0	0	6.70
Great Falls	R	18	14	9	0	2	66.2	294	71	37	28	0	0	0	6	25	0	70	10	1	7	1	.875	0	0	3.78
Reyes,Pedro,Pirates	R	18	1	0	0	1	0	5	2	0	0	0	0	0	0	1	0	1	0	0	0	0	.000	0	0	0.00

1994 Pitching -- Single-A and Rookie Leagues

Player	Lg	A	G	GS	CG	GF	IP	BFP	H	R	ER	HR	SH	SF	HB	TBB	IBB	SO	WP	Bk	W	L	Pct.	ShO	Sv	ERA
Reinozo,Querbin,Charlstn-Wv	A	21	22	2	0	6	44.2	218	68	41	35	10	0	4	5	9	0	36	3	0	2	2	.500	0	0	7.05
Rhine,Kendall,Auburn	A	24	8	0	0	2	19.2	92	18	14	11	1	0	0	3	11	0	15	6	1	0	1	.000	0	0	5.03
Rhodes,Joe,Orioles	R	20	8	1	0	5	14.2	69	19	14	13	1	0	3	0	9	0	10	4	0	2	1	.667	0	0	7.98
Ricabal,Daniel,Yakima	A	22	27	0	0	27	29	111	17	4	1	0	1	1	1	10	2	32	1	2	5	1	.833	0	12	0.31
Rich,Bart,Kane County	A	24	38	0	0	23	40.1	180	33	21	18	1	0	1	1	25	3	53	10	0	2	3	.400	0	5	4.02
Richardson,David,Marlins	R	21	10	0	0	7	15.2	70	16	6	3	0	0	0	0	7	0	7	4	0	1	1	.500	0	1	1.72
Richardson,Kasey,Twins	R	18	12	11	1	0	58.1	227	42	25	20	2	1	0	3	18	0	59	5	0	2	4	.333	1	0	3.09
Richey,Jeff,San Jose	A	25	49	0	0	40	84.1	350	70	30	20	4	7	6	6	32	2	87	1	2	3	4	.429	0	19	2.13
Ricken,Raymond,Oneonta	A	21	10	10	0	0	50.1	206	45	25	20	1	1	1	2	17	1	55	6	3	2	3	.400	0	0	3.58
Greensboro	A	21	5	5	0	0	25	109	27	13	13	1	0	1	0	12	0	19	3	0	1	2	.333	0	0	4.68
Riedling,John,Billings	R	19	15	5	0	2	44.1	221	62	36	27	0	2	2	3	28	0	27	7	0	4	1	.800	0	0	5.48
Rife,Jackie,Martinsvlle	R	20	6	5	0	1	22	114	33	30	23	4	0	0	2	19	1	22	1	0	0	3	.000	0	0	9.41
Rigby,Bradley,Modesto	A	22	11	1	0	3	23.2	101	20	10	10	0	1	1	2	10	1	28	1	0	2	1	.667	0	0	3.80
Riley,Darren,Butte	R	25	8	7	0	0	36.1	182	53	37	30	1	3	2	7	17	2	24	2	0	0	4	.000	0	0	7.43
Rinaldi,Gregg,Pirates	R	22	2	0	0	1	3	15	3	3	1	0	0	0	0	2	0	0	0	0	1	0	1.000	0	0	3.00
Rios,Dan,Greensboro	A	22	37	0	0	34	41.1	164	32	4	4	1	2	0	3	13	1	36	3	0	3	2	.600	0	17	0.87
Tampa	A	22	9	0	0	8	10.1	41	6	2	0	0	0	1	1	4	0	11	0	0	0	0	.000	0	2	0.00
Rios,Michael,Sou. Oregon	A	23	8	1	0	2	11	50	12	9	3	1	0	0	0	6	0	14	2	0	0	1	.000	0	1	2.45
Ritter,Jason,Eugene	A	20	25	0	0	3	54.2	255	51	37	29	5	3	4	4	41	1	43	7	3	2	4	.333	0	0	4.77
Rivera,Oscar,Appleton	A	23	7	0	0	4	13	69	18	12	8	1	2	1	1	6	1	10	0	0	1	3	.250	0	0	5.54
Roach,Pete,Yakima	A	24	8	4	0	2	40	147	24	5	3	0	0	0	1	6	0	32	0	1	3	1	.750	0	0	0.68
Vero Beach	A	24	7	6	0	0	36.2	157	41	20	18	0	0	1	1	12	0	19	1	1	2	3	.400	0	0	4.42
Robbins,Bennie,Braves	R	18	6	0	0	0	15	66	15	5	4	0	0	0	2	3	0	12	0	2	0	1	.000	0	0	2.40
Robbins,Jason,Billings	R	22	14	14	4	0	85.2	364	63	39	30	2	2	0	9	35	2	76	4	0	11	1	.917	1	0	3.15
Robbins,Phillip,Yankees	R	19	8	3	0	0	23	102	21	16	13	2	1	3	1	15	0	14	1	0	0	2	.000	0	0	5.09
Roberts,Franklin,Marlins	R	20	9	0	0	4	12	63	13	11	4	1	2	0	2	13	1	7	1	0	2	2	.500	0	0	3.00
Roberts,Raymond,Eugene	A	22	29	0	0	13	48.2	203	43	18	10	4	1	2	3	14	0	58	3	0	4	2	.667	0	5	1.85
Rodriguez,Dave,Bristol	A	20	4	4	0	0	20.2	81	9	9	9	1	0	1	2	8	0	17	2	0	1	2	.333	0	0	3.92
Robinson,Martin,Yankees	R	18	10	10	0	0	46	212	58	32	20	1	6	2	2	16	0	27	7	4	2	3	.400	0	0	3.91
Rocker,John,Danville	R	NA	12	12	1	0	63.2	285	50	36	25	4	3	4	6	38	1	72	13	4	1	5	.167	0	0	3.53
Rodriguez,Chris,Daytona	A	23	15	0	0	13	17.2	85	27	10	10	1	1	1	1	9	2	10	3	0	0	1	.000	0	2	5.09
Peoria	A	23	10	0	0	3	15	74	23	13	10	3	1	1	1	5	0	11	1	0	1	1	.500	0	0	6.00
Rodriguez,Frankie,Stockton	A	22	26	24	3	0	151	627	139	67	57	6	6	9	13	52	1	124	6	0	10	9	.526	1	0	3.40
Rodriguez,Luis,Giants	R	19	14	1	0	2	18	98	22	21	11	0	0	2	4	14	1	16	4	1	3	3	.250	0	0	5.50
Rodriguez,Salvador,Yankees	R	20	1	1	0	0	3	11	2	0	0	0	0	0	0	2	0	4	0	0	0	0	.000	0	0	0.00
Tampa	A	20	2	2	0	0	9	38	12	7	7	3	1	0	1	3	0	2	0	0	1	0	1.000	0	0	7.00
Rodriguez,Victor,Blue Jays	R	21	11	11	0	0	49	222	48	35	31	0	4	1	4	34	0	40	5	1	1	6	.143	0	0	5.69
Roettgen,Mark,Cardinals	R	18	11	8	0	1	42	186	39	26	23	3	0	3	2	22	0	43	10	1	3	2	.600	0	0	4.93
Rogers,Jason,Bluefield	R	22	9	8	0	1	39	158	39	14	10	0	1	0	0	10	0	30	7	1	1	2	.333	0	0	2.31
Rolish,Chad,Modesto	A	22	7	0	0	2	8	49	17	16	14	3	1	0	0	9	2	2	1	0	0	0	.000	0	0	15.75
Sou. Oregon	A	22	11	1	0	6	23.2	105	21	12	5	0	2	0	3	10	1	23	2	0	2	1	.667	0	0	1.90
Rolocut,Brian,Yakima	A	21	15	6	0	1	58.1	256	52	33	25	5	1	2	3	35	0	54	13	2	4	1	.800	0	0	3.86
Roman,Juan,Expos	R	19	23	1	0	11	39.2	182	36	30	20	1	4	3	3	19	0	28	13	7	3	3	.500	0	1	4.54
Romano,Mike,Hagerstown	A	23	18	18	2	0	108.1	453	91	47	37	10	2	3	9	40	0	90	5	2	10	2	.833	0	0	3.07
Roque,Tony,St. Lucie	A	23	2	0	0	0	3	15	2	1	0	0	1	0	0	3	1	2	0	0	0	0	.000	0	0	0.00
Columbia	A	23	15	15	1	0	86.1	353	73	26	23	6	1	3	4	30	1	74	7	1	6	3	.667	0	0	2.40
Rosado Hornedo,Jose,Royals	R	20	14	12	0	2	64.2	246	45	14	9	0	3	2	2	7	0	56	0	0	6	2	.750	0	0	1.25
Rose,Brian,Bend	A	22	24	4	0	8	60	263	49	28	24	1	1	2	9	26	1	75	4	1	3	4	.400	0	0	3.60
Rose,Tim,Cubs	R	20	13	1	0	0	31.1	137	27	20	15	0	0	0	5	14	1	14	0	4	3	1	.750	0	0	4.31
Rosenbohm,Jim,Clinton	A	21	24	22	0	0	114.1	517	129	74	65	10	5	1	12	48	1	77	5	2	3	10	.231	0	0	5.12
Ross,Jeremy,Marlins	R	21	14	1	0	6	33.1	132	23	11	9	1	0	1	1	11	0	32	8	1	2	2	.500	0	0	2.43
Rossiter,Mike,Athletics	R	22	2	0	0	1	3.2	20	8	6	2	0	1	0	0	0	0	3	1	0	0	1	.000	0	0	4.91
Rowland,Thad,Lynchburg	A	24	18	7	1	5	56.2	241	59	18	18	4	0	2	1	16	0	46	3	1	4	1	.800	1	1	2.86
Ruch,Robert,Elizabethtn	R	22	4	4	0	0	20.2	84	19	7	5	2	0	1	0	8	0	19	2	0	2	1	.667	0	0	2.18
Fort Wayne	A	22	10	5	0	3	29.2	141	39	26	22	3	4	4	0	15	1	19	2	0	2	4	.400	0	0	6.67
Ruess,Matthew,Jamestown	A	22	15	15	0	0	84.2	361	81	42	32	5	1	1	1	39	0	64	3	1	5	5	.500	0	0	3.40
Ruiz,Rafael,White Sox	R	20	13	0	0	7	15	62	11	4	3	1	2	0	0	6	1	13	0	0	1	1	.500	0	2	1.80
Runion,Tony,Columbus	A	23	35	8	1	7	119	486	89	40	33	5	4	0	11	39	3	140	10	0	8	6	.571	0	2	2.50
Runion,Jeff,Charlstn-Wv	A	20	9	9	0	0	41.1	180	34	24	23	6	0	1	4	19	0	36	4	3	2	3	.400	0	0	5.01
Runyan,Paul,Princeton	R	23	16	6	0	7	54.1	239	59	36	25	2	2	1	3	16	2	38	5	2	2	5	.286	0	0	4.14
Runyan,Sean,Auburn	A	21	14	14	2	0	95.1	396	90	49	37	5	1	1	2	19	0	66	12	1	7	5	.583	1	0	3.49
Rusch,Glendon,Rockford	A	20	28	17	1	5	114	485	111	61	59	5	6	5	6	34	2	122	7	1	8	5	.615	1	1	4.66
Rusciano,Chris,Macon	A	23	2	0	0	0	3.1	14	6	6	6	0	0	0	0	2	0	0	0	0	0	1	.000	0	0	16.20
Idaho Falls	R	23	24	0	0	19	39	178	47	30	23	2	1	3	2	17	2	31	4	0	1	4	.200	0	0	5.31
Rush,Tony,Oneonta	A	22	4	0	0	3	4	25	6	9	7	0	0	0	1	5	0	5	1	0	0	0	.000	0	0	15.75
Rushworth,Jim,W. Palm Bch	A	23	23	0	0	13	23.2	120	34	17	13	2	2	0	0	16	2	16	4	0	0	4	.000	0	4	4.94
Ruskey,Jason,Bellingham	A	22	23	0	0	9	27.2	133	33	10	8	1	0	5	2	5	2	24	3	0	2	1	.667	0	1	2.60
Russell,Michael,Braves	R	18	12	6	0	0	29.2	157	30	29	24	1	0	5	5	36	0	21	11	1	1	3	.250	0	0	7.28
Rutledge,Murry,Charlstn-Sc	A	23	5	2	0	1	10.2	55	12	11	11	0	0	2	1	11	0	7	2	0	0	2	.000	0	0	9.28
Ruyak,Todd,Kinston	A	24	13	0	0	3	24	107	22	15	13	3	0	1	1	12	0	17	4	1	0	0	.000	0	0	4.88
High Desert	A	24	27	4	0	10	64	304	91	55	46	10	4	6	1	28	1	50	3	0	0	4	.000	0	1	6.47
Ryan,Michael-sean,Rangers	R	19	11	5	0	1	30	143	37	26	19	2	0	2	3	15	0	14	3	0	0	3	.000	0	0	5.70
Ryan,Robert,Hudson Vall	A	24	14	14	0	0	83.2	352	73	40	27	2	3	5	6	36	1	63	5	6	5	5	.500	0	0	2.90
Ryan,Matt,Augusta	A	23	34	0	0	31	41	174	33	14	6	0	1	0	4	7	1	49	0	0	2	1	.667	0	13	1.32
Salem	A	23	10	0	0	16	28.1	120	27	12	6	0	0	0	2	8	1	13	2	0	2	1	.500	0	7	1.91
Saccavino,Paul,Fort Myers	A	25	36	9	1	6	103.1	457	104	54	43	4	3	5	6	49	4	85	10	0	5	4	.556	0	1	3.75
Sacharko,Mark,Astros	R	19	19	0	0	10	32	125	18	12	11	1	1	0	1	13	0	28	1	1	1	1	.500	0	2	3.09

1994 Pitching -- Single-A and Rookie Leagues

Player	Lg	A	G	GS	CG	GF	IP	BFP	H	R	ER	HR	SH	SF	HB	TBB	IBB	SO	WP	Bk	W	L	Pct.	ShO	Sv	ERA
Sadler,Aldren,Beloit	A	23	16	16	5	0	99	428	96	48	39	9	3	3	3	51	1	79	13	0	7	4	.636	1	0	3.55
Sailors,Jim,Madison	A	22	13	4	0	4	24.2	164	39	41	33	3	2	1	5	48	1	27	11	1	1	4	.200	0	0	12.04
New Jersey	A	22	13	4	0	2	28.2	134	26	23	11	1	1	0	1	21	0	25	5	2	1	1	.500	0	0	3.45
Saipe,Michael,Bend	A	21	16	16	0	0	84.1	363	73	52	39	7	3	4	7	34	0	74	6	2	3	7	.300	0	0	4.16
Salado,Tim,Ogden	R	23	21	1	0	7	43.1	196	52	31	22	3	2	2	2	12	0	43	2	1	3	1	.750	0	0	4.57
Salamon,John,Beloit	A	23	33	0	0	17	48	219	27	17	14	2	2	3	4	52	0	54	5	1	3	1	.750	0	6	2.63
Salazar,Michael,Fayettevlle	A	24	35	11	0	9	105.2	441	97	47	36	6	1	3	4	36	1	103	4	2	3	5	.375	0	1	3.07
Salcedo,Jose,Stockton	A	22	41	4	0	15	88	410	101	67	53	17	4	3	12	32	2	49	6	0	2	5	.286	0	5	5.42
Salcedo,Mateo,Pirates	R	21	20	0	0	18	28.2	121	31	9	8	1	2	3	0	7	2	15	2	0	1	2	.333	0	2	2.51
Salmon,Fabian,Beloit	A	23	36	3	0	9	80.2	367	87	62	60	12	6	1	10	36	3	56	6	1	3	3	.500	0	0	6.69
Sampson,Benjamin,Fort Wayne	A	20	25	25	0	0	139.2	617	149	72	59	10	7	5	5	60	0	111	5	4	6	9	.400	0	0	3.80
Sanchez,Jesus,Kingsport	R	20	13	12	3	0	87.1	346	61	27	19	2	1	1	4	24	0	71	7	1	7	4	.636	0	0	1.96
Sanchez,Jose,Riverside	A	22	10	10	0	0	45.1	212	54	44	38	6	0	3	1	25	0	48	3	1	1	7	.125	0	0	7.54
Appleton	A	22	11	10	0	0	56.1	263	63	40	37	1	6	3	4	27	0	54	5	4	4	4	.500	0	0	5.91
Sanders,Lance,Spartanburg	A	24	9	0	0	6	10.2	49	14	9	8	2	0	1	0	3	0	14	0	0	0	0	.000	0	0	6.75
Batavia	A	24	4	0	0	1	6.2	31	9	4	4	1	0	0	1	2	0	6	0	0	0	0	.000	0	0	5.40
Saneaux,Francisco,Albany	A	21	26	21	1	4	106	501	97	93	77	8	2	5	12	91	0	100	15	3	4	12	.250	0	0	6.54
Santaella,Alexis,Greensboro	A	23	24	15	0	2	103	456	118	57	48	6	2	4	5	42	0	74	17	1	7	7	.500	0	0	4.19
Santamaria,Silverio,Sarasota	A	25	27	0	0	13	41.2	192	36	28	22	2	2	2	3	28	0	39	10	1	4	3	.571	0	1	4.75
Santamaria,William,Mets	R	19	9	5	2	0	42	157	21	10	8	1	0	1	1	13	0	46	1	0	4	1	.800	2	0	1.71
Kingsport	R	19	1	1	0	0	6	22	4	2	2	0	1	1	0	1	0	2	0	0	0	0	.000	0	0	3.00
Santana,Manuel,Salem	A	22	42	0	0	15	64.1	308	85	51	40	9	0	2	2	29	2	45	4	1	2	1	.667	0	0	5.60
Santana,Marino,Bellingham	A	23	15	15	1	0	80	331	68	35	28	3	1	1	3	26	0	88	10	3	6	3	.667	0	0	3.15
Santiago,Antonio,Red Sox	R	18	14	3	0	6	40	169	39	18	14	2	0	1	2	8	0	23	4	7	3	0	1.000	0	0	3.15
Santiago,Jose,Royals	R	20	10	1	0	7	19	84	17	7	5	1	0	0	1	7	0	10	2	1	1	0	1.000	0	2	2.37
Santiago,Sandi,San Bernrdo	A	25	12	12	0	0	58	256	58	42	38	8	4	2	1	28	0	45	2	1	2	3	.400	0	0	5.90
Santos,Henry,Fayetteville	A	22	15	15	0	0	82.2	356	76	44	36	11	1	1	3	42	0	57	3	0	4	8	.333	0	0	3.92
Lakeland	A	22	11	11	0	0	52.2	276	88	52	45	11	6	1	4	34	0	35	5	2	1	6	.143	0	0	7.69
Santos,Rafael,Pirates	R	19	17	0	0	17	20	84	12	5	1	0	1	1	3	11	1	11	0	0	2	2	.500	0	5	0.45
Sartain,David,High Desert	A	25	14	6	0	4	34.1	166	38	28	26	4	0	0	6	28	0	32	1	0	2	2	.500	0	0	6.82
Sasaki,Kenny,Central Val	A	NA	27	4	0	8	52	244	40	36	27	1	2	3	6	51	4	55	19	2	2	4	.333	0	1	4.67
Sauerbeck,Scott,Pittsfield	A	23	21	0	0	9	48.1	200	39	16	11	0	3	1	1	19	2	39	4	0	3	1	.750	0	1	2.05
Saugstad,Mark,High Desert	A	24	5	0	0	2	7.1	38	10	10	10	1	2	1	1	6	0	3	1	0	0	0	.000	0	0	12.27
Saunders,Tony,Brevard Cty	A	21	10	10	1	0	60	237	54	24	21	4	2	1	2	9	0	46	2	0	5	5	.500	0	0	3.15
Sawyer,Zack,W. Michigan	A	22	40	6	0	23	86.1	377	66	41	33	6	5	2	3	49	1	79	8	3	4	5	.444	0	3	3.44
Scafa,Bob,Yakima	A	22	22	0	0	6	36.2	142	24	7	7	0	2	1	3	12	5	32	3	1	3	2	.600	0	1	1.72
Scarpitti,Jeff,Eugene	A	24	14	0	0	7	15.2	80	21	16	14	3	1	2	1	11	1	15	2	0	2	3	.400	0	0	8.04
Schaffner,Eric,Yankees	R	20	11	11	0	0	59.1	248	63	30	25	3	2	0	1	17	0	49	5	0	2	5	.286	0	0	3.79
Scheffer,Aaron,Bellingham	A	19	2	0	0	0	3	16	4	4	2	0	0	1	0	3	0	5	0	0	0	0	.000	0	0	6.00
Mariners	R	19	24	0	0	20	32.1	127	18	11	7	1	1	1	2	10	0	26	4	1	2	2	.500	0	6	1.95
Scheffler,Craig,Vero Beach	A	23	24	1	0	4	41.1	183	33	23	17	3	3	1	3	30	2	28	4	1	0	0	.000	0	0	3.70
Yakima	A	23	21	0	0	5	40.1	164	30	13	9	2	2	0	1	15	0	43	2	0	8	2	.800	0	1	2.01
Schenbeck,Tommy,Stockton	A	23	56	0	0	24	91.2	400	84	45	32	4	5	3	2	38	3	82	9	1	4	10	.286	0	6	3.14
Schiefelbein,Michael,Everett	A	23	13	13	0	0	61.1	285	58	38	30	4	2	3	4	48	0	50	7	0	2	4	.333	0	0	4.40
Schlomann,Brett,Yankees	R	20	10	10	1	0	54	230	56	22	18	1	4	1	0	16	0	51	2	0	6	3	.667	0	0	3.00
Oneonta	A	20	1	1	0	0	5	24	4	3	1	1	0	1	0	4	0	6	0	0	0	0	.000	0	0	5.40
Schlutt,Jason,Springfield	A	23	27	0	0	17	35	164	41	26	23	3	4	3	0	19	6	27	4	1	3	0	1.000	0	2	5.91
Rancho Cuca	A	23	16	0	0	7	25	116	30	21	21	6	1	0	1	11	1	21	3	2	1	0	1.000	0	0	7.56
Schmidt,Jeff,Lake Elsino	A	24	39	11	0	14	92	395	94	54	42	8	7	0	4	28	2	70	4	6	1	5	.167	0	12	4.11
Schmitt,Christopher,Beloit	A	24	14	0	0	3	22.2	125	29	27	12	1	1	1	2	25	0	24	5	0	1	1	.500	0	0	4.76
Schmitt,Todd,Rancho Cuca	A	25	53	0	0	50	50.2	215	43	15	11	2	5	1	2	24	1	45	2	1	2	4	.333	0	29	1.95
Schneider,Jeff,St. Cathrns	A	22	8	0	0	3	8	47	16	13	13	2	0	1	2	5	0	6	3	1	0	1	.000	0	1	14.63
Schneider,Thomas,Vermont	A	22	2	1	0	0	6	28	6	4	4	0	0	1	2	1	0	3	0	0	0	1	.000	0	0	6.00
Burlington	A	22	30	15	0	7	107.1	495	137	92	70	9	6	4	4	40	0	83	17	1	6	10	.375	0	0	5.87
Schooler,Aaron,Elizabethtn	R	22	5	3	0	0	9	40	9	9	8	1	1	1	1	3	0	2	2	0	0	1	.000	0	0	8.00
Schroeder,Rodney,Padres	R	20	15	7	0	3	53	236	51	32	20	1	0	3	7	19	0	46	4	1	3	5	.375	0	0	3.40
Schulte,Troy,Auburn	A	23	24	0	0	19	36	153	39	9	8	1	1	2	1	6	1	32	5	0	2	2	.500	0	7	2.00
Schutz,Carl,Durham	A	23	53	0	0	47	53.1	240	35	30	29	6	4	1	4	46	1	81	10	0	3	3	.500	0	20	4.89
Scott,Ronald,Savannah	A	23	43	0	0	19	56.2	274	52	50	38	4	2	2	4	54	4	39	10	5	3	3	.500	0	1	6.04
Seip,Rod,Charlstn-Wv	A	21	31	18	1	4	133.1	588	140	82	68	13	5	5	7	43	2	133	2	0	3	14	.176	0	1	4.59
Sellers,Jeff,Central Val	A	31	4	0	1	0	5	17	1	0	0	0	0	0	0	1	0	7	0	0	0	0	.000	0	0	0.00
Sellner,Aaron,Twins	R	21	19	1	0	8	43	188	37	19	11	0	0	1	3	25	0	41	5	6	3	2	.600	0	1	2.30
Senior,Shawn,Lynchburg	A	23	13	13	0	0	76.1	338	73	45	30	6	3	2	2	34	1	62	5	1	4	4	.500	0	0	3.54
Sarasota	A	23	14	13	0	0	83.1	360	82	33	28	6	2	0	2	47	0	58	8	2	8	3	.727	0	0	3.02
Serafini,Dan,Fort Myers	A	21	23	23	2	0	136.2	600	149	84	70	11	7	5	6	57	1	130	7	1	9	9	.500	1	0	4.61
Severino,Jose,Cardinals	R	21	24	0	0	6	33	137	22	12	9	1	0	1	6	11	0	46	8	0	5	1	.833	0	2	2.45
Sexton,Jeff,Watertown	A	21	10	0	0	5	23	95	19	3	1	0	1	0	0	7	2	16	3	1	1	0	1.000	0	3	0.39
Columbus	A	23	14	2	0	6	30	121	17	13	12	2	1	0	3	9	2	35	1	0	1	0	1.000	0	0	3.60
Shafer,Bill,Macon	A	22	27	0	0	15	51.2	205	40	12	8	0	2	3	4	4	0	47	1	0	0	0	.000	0	8	1.39
Durham	A	22	23	0	0	12	25.2	107	21	11	9	2	2	0	0	9	0	21	2	1	2	1	.667	0	2	3.16
Shaffer,Travis,St. Lucie	A	26	32	2	0	9	69.2	299	72	28	26	5	1	5	6	27	6	37	2	0	4	2	.667	0	1	3.36
Shagena,Randy,Elmira	A	23	21	1	0	7	46.1	206	52	30	22	3	2	3	1	18	0	32	6	0	3	2	.600	0	1	4.27
Sharer,Anthony,Pirates	R	19	13	3	0	4	40.1	188	60	36	33	6	1	5	3	6	0	12	4	1	2	4	.333	0	1	7.36
Shaver,Anthony,Astros	R	23	4	0	0	1	7	29	5	0	0	0	0	0	0	4	0	8	0	1	0	0	.000	0	0	0.00
Osceola	A	23	23	0	0	15	35.1	142	33	13	9	0	1	1	4	18	1	14	2	0	2	2	.500	0	2	2.29
Sheehan,Chris,Wilmington	A	26	28	0	0	10	59.1	237	49	22	16	4	4	0	1	17	2	55	5	0	6	1	.857	0	4	2.43
Shelby,Anthony,Yankees	R	21	8	8	0	0	42.1	177	33	19	5	1	2	0	0	16	0	51	1	1	3	1	.750	0	0	1.06

1994 Pitching -- Single-A and Rookie Leagues

Player	Lg	A	G	GS	CG	GF	IP	BFP	H	R	ER	HR	SH	SF	HB	TBB	IBB	SO	WP	Bk	W	L	Pct	ShO	Sv	ERA
Oneonta	A	21	5	5	1	0	25.1	115	33	16	13	0	0	2	1	7	0	13	2	0	1	3	.250	0	0	4.62
Sheldon,Shane,Brewers	R	22	10	0	0	7	10	47	6	7	6	1	0	0	2	7	0	15	1	0	0	0	.000	0	0	5.40
Shenk,Larry,Frederick	A	26	49	0	0	22	66.1	292	62	42	35	9	5	1	1	32	0	76	4	0	8	3	.727	0	2	4.75
Shoemaker,Stephen,Oneonta	A	22	12	12	0	0	58.2	262	62	32	28	2	1	1	3	28	0	46	5	1	3	5	.375	0	0	4.30
Short,Barry,Mets	R	21	10	7	0	1	62.1	252	49	21	17	3	1	0	1	19	0	49	9	0	5	2	.714	0	0	2.45
Kingsport	R	21	1	1	0	0	5.1	22	5	0	0	0	0	0	0	3	0	3	0	0	1	0	1.000	0	0	0.00
Shrum,Dennis,Auburn	A	23	23	0	0	21	37	153	28	17	10	1	2	4	3	11	3	25	2	0	5	2	.714	0	7	2.43
Shumate,Jacob,Danville	R	19	12	7	0	1	31.2	175	30	34	29	0	1	5	8	52	0	29	15	0	0	4	.000	0	0	8.24
Sick,David,Boise	A	23	26	0	0	7	42.2	207	46	26	17	3	0	2	7	29	0	45	3	1	2	2	.500	0	0	3.59
Sides,Craig,Kinston	A	22	13	4	0	2	25	118	38	23	21	2	1	1	1	8	0	18	2	0	1	1	.500	0	0	7.56
Sievert,Mark,St. Cathrns	A	22	14	14	1	0	81.2	319	59	30	28	4	1	3	1	28	0	82	4	0	7	4	.636	1	0	3.09
Sikes,Jason,Martinsvle	R	19	3	3	0	0	11	49	12	6	3	0	0	1	0	7	0	4	4	0	0	2	.000	0	0	2.45
Sikes,Ken,Yakima	A	22	16	10	0	3	68.1	286	41	22	20	4	1	3	4	40	0	86	5	0	3	3	.500	0	3	2.63
Siler,Jeff,Lakeland	A	24	3	0	0	2	3.2	14	3	1	1	1	0	0	0	1	0	4	0	0	1	0	1.000	0	0	2.45
Bristol	R	24	13	0	0	11	22.1	75	10	3	2	1	1	1	1	6	2	26	1	1	2	2	.500	0	5	0.81
Jamestown	A	24	3	0	0	1	5	22	4	4	4	0	0	0	0	4	0	5	0	0	0	0	.000	0	1	7.20
Silva,Luis,Athletics	R	20	14	8	1	3	72.2	299	61	26	23	5	0	0	2	16	1	88	5	1	5	3	.625	0	0	2.85
Simmons,Carlos,Rangers	R	21	15	10	0	0	50.2	206	40	16	14	2	2	0	0	13	0	39	2	0	4	2	.667	0	0	2.49
Simmons,John,Durham	A	24	40	0	0	11	67.2	295	67	35	33	8	2	3	2	31	2	47	5	1	3	2	.600	0	2	4.39
Sinacori,Chris,Vero Beach	A	24	47	0	0	26	71	335	69	47	43	8	0	7	11	51	1	39	11	0	2	3	.400	0	3	5.45
Sinclair,Steve,Hagerstown	A	23	38	1	0	16	105	458	127	53	44	9	4	5	2	25	0	75	3	0	9	2	.818	0	3	3.77
Singer,Thomas,Dunedin	A	26	33	6	1	0	74.1	361	79	59	53	5	4	2	5	61	1	48	12	1	2	3	.400	0	0	6.42
Singleton,Kendrick,Expos	R	19	4	0	0	1	3.1	18	0	4	3	0	1	0	0	6	0	5	0	0	0	0	.000	0	1	8.10
Singleton,Scott,Spokane	A	20	31	0	0	6	44.1	194	41	24	19	4	6	1	4	20	0	39	3	0	2	3	.400	0	0	3.86
Sinnes,David,Hagerstown	A	24	55	0	0	53	61	249	50	20	13	1	2	3	2	16	0	52	6	0	2	3	.400	0	37	1.92
Sirotka,Mike,South Bend	A	24	27	27	8	0	196.2	824	183	99	67	11	9	6	3	58	1	173	7	2	12	9	.571	2	0	3.07
Skinner,John,Princeton	R	20	8	0	0	1	10.2	66	18	17	10	0	3	0	2	9	4	4	3	1	0	1	.000	0	0	8.44
Charlstn-Sc	A	20	7	0	0	4	11.1	53	14	5	4	0	1	0	2	5	0	2	1	0	0	0	.000	0	0	3.18
Skjerpen,Trevor,Welland	A	22	17	0	0	10	22.1	92	19	9	8	3	0	0	3	9	0	11	2	1	2	1	.667	0	3	3.22
Augusta	A	22	8	0	0	2	7.1	41	8	4	4	0	0	0	0	9	0	3	1	0	0	0	.000	0	0	4.91
Skrmetta,Matthew,Jamestown	A	22	17	15	1	1	93.2	389	74	42	33	4	2	3	7	37	0	56	2	3	5	3	.625	0	0	3.17
Skuse,Nicholas,Boise	A	23	18	8	0	3	54.1	241	67	35	31	5	1	2	4	17	0	53	6	2	4	2	.667	0	0	5.13
Slade,Shawn,Cedar Rapds	A	24	42	0	0	25	58.2	249	50	21	18	3	6	2	1	25	4	56	2	3	5	4	.556	0	3	2.76
Slamka,John,Rockies	R	21	4	3	0	0	17.1	68	12	5	4	0	1	0	0	5	0	11	3	0	1	2	.333	0	0	2.08
Bend	A	21	9	9	0	0	50.2	229	61	40	23	2	4	1	0	12	0	34	3	0	1	6	.143	0	0	4.09
Smith,Andrew,Modesto	A	20	2	0	0	1	7	27	6	5	5	1	0	0	0	2	0	3	0	0	0	0	.000	0	0	6.43
Sou. Oregon	A	20	16	7	0	2	52.2	246	56	46	29	1	4	2	2	27	2	32	9	2	4	4	.500	0	1	4.96
Smith,Brook,Clinton	A	23	17	9	0	2	54.1	277	74	63	61	5	3	3	3	45	1	38	8	3	1	7	.125	0	0	10.10
Giants	R	23	2	0	0	0	4.2	18	5	1	1	0	0	0	0	4	0	4	0	0	0	0	.000	0	0	1.93
Everett	A	23	6	0	0	4	8.2	39	3	1	1	0	0	0	1	10	0	9	2	0	0	0	.000	0	0	1.04
Smith,Byrond,Albany	A	22	29	12	2	10	121	516	127	67	51	13	2	1	11	32	0	96	7	1	8	9	.471	0	1	3.79
Smith,Cameron,Fayetteville	A	21	26	26	1	0	133.2	619	133	100	90	10	6	5	18	86	0	128	17	1	5	13	.278	0	0	6.06
Smith,Scotty,Charlotte	A	24	31	21	2	0	139.2	576	132	62	55	9	3	5	3	34	2	88	1	2	7	4	.636	0	0	3.54
Smith,Daniel,Charlstn-Wv	A	19	27	27	4	0	157.1	715	171	111	86	12	5	2	19	55	0	86	5	2	7	10	.412	0	0	4.92
Smith,Eric,Clearwater	A	25	54	0	0	37	59	257	50	22	19	2	1	0	0	34	3	32	6	0	2	2	.500	0	15	2.90
Smith,John,Sou. Oregon	A	23	19	2	0	1	26	122	26	18	12	2	1	2	2	17	4	25	3	1	1	2	.333	0	1	4.15
Smith,Justin,Batavia	A	23	5	0	0	1	5.2	29	10	5	3	0	1	0	1	2	0	2	0	0	0	0	.000	0	0	4.76
Smith,Jake,Princeton	R	23	23	0	0	21	29.1	128	20	16	4	0	1	0	0	17	2	23	3	0	0	1	.000	0	8	1.23
Smith,Keilan,St. Cathrns	A	23	15	15	2	0	94	396	81	43	33	5	3	8	5	38	0	56	8	0	3	4	.429	2	0	3.16
Smith,Mason,Medicne Hat	R	22	13	0	0	3	24.1	109	30	18	18	1	1	0	1	8	1	21	2	2	1	1	.500	0	2	6.66
Smith,Sean,Yankees	A	23	5	0	0	2	7.2	38	8	12	7	1	0	0	0	7	0	5	0	0	0	0	.000	0	0	8.22
Smith,Ramon,Medicne Hat	R	21	14	0	0	9	16	83	20	14	13	0	0	0	1	16	0	25	7	0	0	1	.000	0	0	7.31
Smith,Randall,Medicne Hat	R	22	20	5	0	11	64	268	58	36	24	3	2	4	5	20	0	53	6	3	5	4	.556	0	4	3.38
Smith,Randy,St. Cathrns	A	22	13	11	0	0	59.1	256	59	35	34	6	1	0	5	23	0	39	2	1	3	4	.429	0	0	5.16
Smith,Ryan,Appleton	A	21	21	21	5	0	144.1	589	129	54	45	10	4	5	12	28	0	82	7	0	10	6	.625	1	0	2.81
Smith,Toby,Rockford	A	23	29	16	0	12	121	489	104	50	44	8	3	3	4	31	1	91	14	2	11	9	.550	0	4	3.27
Smith,Roy,Mariners	R	19	11	5	0	1	45	164	30	9	8	2	1	1	1	4	0	35	2	0	3	1	.750	0	0	1.60
Smock,Greg,Modesto	A	24	3	0	0	2	3.2	18	2	3	3	1	0	0	1	5	0	0	2	0	0	0	.000	0	0	7.36
Fayettevlle	A	24	11	0	0	6	13.1	75	8	16	15	3	0	2	2	26	0	9	4	0	0	0	.000	0	0	10.13
Smyley,Doug,Ogden	R	22	21	1	0	9	35.2	155	39	21	9	2	1	2	1	9	0	27	4	0	1	1	.500	0	2	2.27
Snyder,John,Lake Elsino	A	20	26	26	2	0	159	698	181	101	79	16	5	5	6	56	0	108	11	2	10	11	.476	0	0	4.47
Sobik,Trad,Bristol	R	19	4	4	0	0	15.2	59	7	2	0	0	0	1	0	5	0	16	1	0	1	1	.500	0	0	0.00
Lakeland	A	19	1	1	0	0	3	16	5	5	5	1	1	0	1	2	0	2	0	0	0	0	.000	0	0	15.00
Sobkoviak,Jeff,Asheville	A	23	17	0	0	9	32.1	149	31	14	10	5	3	0	4	16	3	24	2	0	2	2	.500	0	3	2.78
Central Val	A	23	34	0	0	5	59.1	268	66	36	30	7	3	2	2	22	1	51	2	0	4	0	1.000	0	0	4.55
Soderstrom,Stephen,San Jose	A	23	8	8	0	0	40.2	179	34	20	19	2	2	1	4	26	0	40	4	1	2	3	.400	0	0	4.20
Sodowsky,Clint,Lakeland	A	22	19	18	1	1	110.1	466	111	58	47	5	2	2	6	34	0	73	12	0	6	3	.667	1	0	3.83
Sollecito,Gabriel,Fayetteville	A	22	46	0	0	45	57	238	47	21	18	1	2	2	10	15	2	52	1	0	4	3	.571	0	18	2.84
Solomon,Dave,Billings	R	23	23	0	0	16	42.2	179	34	19	16	2	4	0	1	26	4	37	4	0	3	4	.429	0	8	3.38
Sosa,Helpis,Athletics	R	22	15	11	0	3	79.1	346	100	46	38	7	0	3	4	11	2	76	10	0	6	3	.667	0	1	4.31
Sosa,Jose,Augusta	A	22	24	2	0	11	48.2	207	49	29	21	2	0	0	6	15	0	44	5	1	2	3	.400	0	0	3.88
Salem	A	22	17	0	0	5	24.1	107	24	12	10	1	0	1	1	10	1	16	3	0	1	0	1.000	0	0	3.70
Soto,Daniel,Burlington	A	21	19	0	0	9	31.2	143	33	19	15	6	0	0	0	9	0	15	0	2	1	2	.333	0	3	4.26
Expos	R	21	3	0	0	2	3	15	5	2	0	0	1	0	0	1	0	3	0	0	1	0	1.000	0	0	0.00
Soult,Dave,Clinton	A	24	5	0	0	2	12.2	59	12	5	5	2	1	0	1	6	1	10	3	0	2	0	1.000	0	1	3.55
South,Carl,Great Falls	R	20	15	6	0	3	42	219	53	46	38	3	0	1	5	35	1	32	17	1	1	4	.200	0	1	8.14
Spade,Matthew,Welland	A	22	15	11	0	1	81.1	322	65	29	22	3	3	2	5	17	0	52	3	3	5	2	.714	0	0	2.43

1994 Pitching -- Single-A and Rookie Leagues

Player	Lg	A	G	GS	CG	GF	IP	BFP	H	R	ER	HR	SH	SF	HB	TBB	IBB	SO	WP	Bk	W	L	Pct.	ShO	Sv	ERA
Spang,R.J.,Mets	R	20	9	0	0	8	18.2	69	10	6	5	1	0	0	1	5	1	14	2	0	2	1	.667	0	2	2.41
Sparma,Blase,Durham	A	24	30	17	0	4	109	491	131	89	69	16	3	6	10	43	1	49	13	0	4	9	.308	0	0	5.70
Spenrath,Chris,Butte	R	23	17	12	1	4	85.2	403	111	78	55	11	0	4	9	33	1	50	9	0	4	8	.333	0	0	5.78
Spiller,Derron,St. Pete	A	25	50	0	0	15	68.1	308	70	33	25	1	4	2	4	34	2	49	4	0	4	1	.800	0	0	3.29
Spingola,Donald,Kingsport	R	22	7	0	0	3	11.2	60	12	12	9	0	0	1	1	9	0	10	3	1	0	0	.000	0	0	6.94
Spykstra,Dave,Yakima	A	21	30	7	0	2	41.2	193	43	22	17	1	1	2	1	33	0	32	7	0	3	1	.750	0	2	3.67
Stadelhofer,Michael,Twins	R	21	18	1	0	8	44	204	42	34	19	0	1	3	1	29	1	29	8	2	2	3	.400	0	1	3.89
Stafford,Jerry,Brevard Cty	A	25	28	3	0	13	62	269	72	29	23	0	3	1	3	22	0	52	2	1	1	1	.500	0	1	3.34
Standish,Scott,Greensboro	A	22	26	9	2	2	99	392	74	31	22	5	0	1	4	22	0	92	2	1	5	4	.556	0	0	2.00
Tampa	A	22	5	4	0	0	29	113	18	7	7	4	1	2	2	5	0	36	2	0	2	1	.667	0	0	2.17
Stanifer,Robby,Elmira	A	23	9	8	1	0	49	211	54	17	14	2	0	1	2	12	1	38	2	3	2	1	.667	0	0	2.57
Brevard Cty	A	23	5	5	0	0	24.1	115	32	20	17	2	1	1	3	10	0	12	2	1	1	2	.333	0	0	6.29
Stanton,Ed,Madison	A	23	5	0	0	1	6.2	32	6	6	2	2	0	0	0	8	0	4	0	0	0	0	.000	0	0	2.70
Stark,Zachary,Marlins	R	20	12	3	0	6	32.1	132	28	14	11	1	0	0	2	10	2	27	1	0	4	3	.571	0	0	3.06
Starling,Marcus,Elizabethtn	R	22	10	8	0	0	41.1	191	39	29	18	2	3	3	4	25	0	34	3	2	2	4	.333	0	0	3.92
Steed,Rick,Dunedin	A	24	30	0	0	17	44	195	33	14	13	1	2	1	1	30	1	55	10	1	3	1	.750	0	4	2.66
Stein,William,Johnson Cty	R	21	13	13	1	0	59.2	242	44	21	19	4	4	2	1	24	0	69	3	0	4	1	.800	0	0	2.87
Steinert,Robert,Hagerstown	A	23	25	25	0	0	120.2	522	108	59	48	12	2	3	8	50	0	141	6	0	8	4	.667	0	0	3.58
Steinke,Brock,Osceola	A	20	9	6	0	1	31	148	40	31	24	5	1	2	1	11	0	26	0	3	3	3	.500	0	0	6.97
Astros	R	20	4	3	0	0	17	69	15	4	2	1	2	0	1	6	0	9	2	0	1	0	1.000	0	0	1.06
Stephenson,Brian,Williamsprt	A	21	5	5	0	0	19	80	17	9	9	2	0	2	4	4	0	13	1	1	0	2	.000	0	0	4.26
Peoria	A	21	6	6	2	0	42.1	180	41	18	15	3	3	0	6	6	1	29	1	0	3	1	.750	0	0	3.19
Stepner,Josh,Athletics	R	23	14	0	0	12	34.1	150	30	17	10	2	4	1	1	14	4	29	1	1	3	3	.500	0	2	2.62
Stevenson,Jason,Huntington	R	20	5	1	0	1	10.2	47	12	5	5	2	3	1	0	6	0	5	1	0	1	1	.500	0	1	4.22
Cubs	R	20	5	5	0	0	25	112	31	12	7	1	3	1	0	4	0	19	3	0	1	1	.500	0	0	2.52
Stewart,Christopher,Savannah	A	23	55	0	0	21	60.1	244	32	15	11	1	4	4	2	29	7	70	8	0	4	4	.500	0	3	1.64
Stewart,David,Batavia	A	23	12	0	0	9	16.1	66	10	4	3	0	1	0	0	6	0	15	2	1	1	1	.500	0	2	1.65
Stewart,Rachaad,Orioles	R	20	1	1	0	0	3	15	6	5	5	0	0	1	0	0	0	3	0	2	0	0	.000	0	0	15.00
Bluefield	R	20	14	3	0	7	43.1	171	34	11	8	0	2	1	2	10	0	43	4	3	3	1	.750	0	0	1.66
Stewart,Scott,Rangers	R	19	14	8	0	3	54.1	221	47	22	17	1	1	0	2	12	0	62	7	9	4	1	.800	0	1	2.82
Stoecklin,Tony,Durham	A	24	40	9	0	10	88.2	400	82	50	43	8	6	1	8	46	3	55	5	7	4	4	.500	0	0	4.36
Stone,Matthew,Blue Jays	R	20	10	1	0	4	14.2	70	17	10	7	1	2	2	1	11	0	13	1	0	1	1	.500	0	0	4.30
Stone,Ricky,Great Falls	R	20	13	7	0	4	50.2	232	55	40	25	5	0	1	2	24	0	48	9	2	2	2	.500	0	0	4.44
Strade,Sean,Medicne Hat	R	22	20	0	0	6	30	145	35	23	17	4	1	3	0	15	1	30	2	0	2	0	1.000	0	0	5.10
Strong,Joe,San Bernrdo	A	32	12	11	0	0	53.2	246	60	46	40	11	0	4	3	27	0	43	6	2	2	4	.400	0	0	6.71
Stubbs,Jerald,Vermont	A	23	22	3	1	3	60.1	262	59	23	16	2	3	0	8	16	0	45	1	2	4	2	.667	0	0	2.39
Stull,Everett,W. Palm Bch	A	23	27	26	3	0	147	627	116	60	54	3	7	3	12	78	0	165	15	6	10	10	.500	1	0	3.31
Stumpf,Brian,Martinsvlle	R	23	20	0	0	17	24	103	21	3	3	1	1	0	0	9	1	25	4	0	0	1	.000	0	12	1.13
Batavia	A	23	6	0	0	4	6	30	8	5	4	0	3	0	0	3	1	5	0	0	1	1	.500	0	1	6.00
Sullivan,Dan,Riverside	A	25	34	2	0	8	69.2	316	86	43	33	6	2	2	0	23	3	36	6	0	2	3	.400	0	0	4.26
Suppan,Jeffrey,Sarasota	A	20	27	27	4	0	174	712	153	74	63	10	6	2	6	50	0	173	9	1	13	7	.650	2	0	3.26
Surratt,Jamie,Savannah	A	24	45	1	0	6	70.2	280	50	16	15	5	5	3	1	25	0	75	1	1	5	1	.833	0	1	1.91
Sutton,Derek,Pittsfield	A	22	15	8	2	5	64	284	72	31	25	5	3	1	1	30	0	22	8	4	3	3	.500	2	0	3.52
Swan,Tyrone,Spartanburg	A	26	28	28	1	0	171.1	750	175	107	85	19	3	1	8	80	1	167	17	1	12	10	.545	1	0	4.46
Swanson,Skeeter,Columbia	A	22	25	22	1	0	133.1	576	128	83	63	13	4	5	7	52	0	114	14	1	5	12	.294	0	0	4.25
Szimanski,Thomas,Bellingham	A	22	17	0	0	9	23	97	17	9	6	0	1	2	2	16	2	20	4	3	2	0	1.000	0	1	2.35
Tagle,Hank,South Bend	A	27	37	0	0	29	46.1	197	41	25	21	7	4	2	4	14	1	49	4	1	4	3	.571	0	4	4.08
Tajima,Toshio,San Bernrdo	A	27	34	1	0	15	74	351	102	66	61	16	3	4	9	23	0	53	3	6	2	2	.500	0	0	7.42
Tapia,Benito,White Sox	R	21	16	2	0	10	31	141	36	15	8	0	1	1	2	11	0	21	0	0	2	0	1.000	0	3	2.32
Tapia,Elias,Great Falls	R	19	14	4	0	3	35.2	174	39	32	26	1	1	3	4	28	0	21	10	2	1	4	.200	0	0	6.56
Tatar,Jason,Fort Wayne	A	20	27	27	2	0	150.1	662	147	72	62	10	10	6	5	67	1	163	9	2	5	11	.313	0	0	3.71
Tatis,Ramon,Kingsport	R	22	13	4	0	8	40.2	187	35	25	15	2	2	1	2	31	0	36	5	2	1	3	.250	0	0	3.32
Tatrow,Danny,Johnson Cty	R	22	2	0	0	0	1.2	10	3	2	2	0	0	0	0	3	0	0	0	0	0	0	.000	0	0	10.80
Taulbee,Andrew,San Jose	A	22	13	13	0	0	71	300	66	28	21	5	5	1	6	20	0	51	4	0	4	3	.571	0	0	2.66
Taylor,Tommy,Frederick	A	24	32	0	0	16	43.1	207	54	29	21	5	2	2	2	18	1	48	3	0	4	1	.800	0	2	4.36
Kinston	A	24	3	3	0	0	14.1	61	9	5	5	1	1	0	0	8	0	13	3	0	0	0	.000	0	0	3.14
Telgheder,Jim,Sarasota	A	24	33	10	0	9	84	345	85	52	49	7	7	3	2	17	1	43	1	2	5	5	.500	0	4	4.93
Temple,Jason,Pirates	R	20	12	11	0	0	58	260	54	42	29	6	2	3	2	35	0	44	5	0	2	5	.286	0	0	4.50
Tenaglia,Steve,Royals	R	21	6	0	0	1	10.1	42	11	2	2	0	0	1	0	2	0	11	1	0	1	0	1.000	0	0	1.74
Theodile,Jason,Hickory	A	22	19	16	2	1	86.1	383	81	53	46	7	1	2	2	47	0	68	11	1	7	4	.636	0	0	4.80
Theron,Greg,Appleton	A	21	33	0	0	15	69.2	303	62	37	32	7	2	6	7	27	1	57	3	1	5	1	.833	0	0	4.13
Thibert,John,Lake Elsino	A	25	45	0	0	23	60	245	50	31	24	4	3	0	4	27	3	47	10	1	3	3	.500	0	2	3.60
Thomas,Jason,Danville	R	23	7	0	0	7	8.1	39	9	2	1	0	4	0	0	4	0	11	0	0	0	0	.000	0	1	1.08
Macon	A	23	19	0	0	10	25.2	115	18	13	7	0	2	1	0	18	0	19	2	0	1	0	1.000	0	3	2.45
Thomas,Nate,Cubs	R	21	15	5	0	3	18.1	69	13	5	5	1	0	0	2	6	0	15	0	0	0	0	.000	0	0	2.45
Thomas,Robert,Great Falls	R	23	13	6	0	3	50	239	52	38	32	3	1	0	7	31	0	48	4	3	2	4	.333	0	1	5.76
Thornforde,Jim,Greensboro	A	24	12	11	0	0	49	242	58	48	45	5	3	3	3	43	0	32	5	1	2	5	.286	0	0	8.27
San Bernrdo	A	24	17	6	0	0	30.1	192	59	66	57	6	2	5	3	36	0	29	6	0	0	5	.000	0	0	16.91
Thompson,David,Fort Wayne	A	23	6	0	0	0	9.2	46	14	7	7	1	1	0	1	2	0	8	2	1	0	0	.000	0	0	6.52
Thompson,Gregory,Yakima	A	19	14	7	0	0	37.1	195	49	34	28	1	2	3	3	32	1	21	5	4	1	4	.200	0	0	6.75
Thompson,John,Bellingham	A	22	15	15	1	0	82	354	63	40	33	6	0	4	3	44	0	78	19	3	4	5	.444	0	0	3.62
Thompson,Mark,Danville	R	24	28	0	0	22	40	160	30	8	3	1	1	0	1	10	3	42	2	0	4	1	.800	0	5	0.68
Thomson,John,Asheville	A	21	19	15	1	0	88.1	361	70	34	28	3	2	1	0	33	1	79	1	0	6	6	.500	1	0	2.85
Central Val	A	21	9	8	0	0	49.1	201	43	20	18	0	0	2	1	18	1	41	3	1	3	1	.750	0	0	3.28
Thornton,Arthur,Kane County	A	25	27	27	2	0	164.2	696	150	81	65	12	2	5	15	51	2	118	9	1	7	14	.333	2	0	3.55
Thurman,Michael,Vermont	A	21	2	2	0	0	6.2	28	6	4	4	0	0	0	0	2	0	3	0	0	0	1	.000	0	0	5.40
Thurmond,Travis,Boise	A	21	8	0	0	3	13	50	8	3	3	1	0	2	0	6	0	17	1	0	1	0	1.000	0	0	2.08

334

1994 Pitching -- Single-A and Rookie Leagues

Player	Lg	A	HOW MUCH HE PITCHED G	GS	CG	GF	IP	BFP	WHAT HE GAVE UP H	R	ER	HR	SH	SF	HB	TBB	IBB	SO	WP	Bk	THE RESULTS W	L	Pct.	ShO	Sv	ERA
Angels	R	21	6	5	0	1	31	132	25	15	9	1	1	1	2	11	0	39	8	0	1	3	.250	0	0	2.61
Cedar Rapids	A	21	2	0	0	0	4.2	19	3	1	1	1	0	0	0	3	0	2	0	0	1	0	1.000	0	0	1.93
Tidwell,Jason,Brevard Cty	A	23	24	21	1	0	137.2	583	133	70	60	5	4	6	6	43	0	96	3	2	11	8	.579	0	0	3.92
Tijerina,Tano,Beloit	A	21	3	1	0	2	6.1	37	13	13	11	1	0	0	0	5	0	3	2	1	0	1	.000	0	0	15.63
Helena	R	21	17	4	0	4	42.2	204	56	37	23	3	0	1	5	17	0	34	6	1	3	2	.600	0	0	4.85
Tipton,Kenneth,Royals	R	23	8	3	0	1	23.1	92	23	13	10	1	0	1	1	2	0	10	3	0	2	1	.667	0	0	3.86
Eugene	A	23	7	2	0	1	15	77	19	16	16	2	1	1	0	12	0	4	4	0	0	2	.000	0	0	9.60
Titus,Brian,Helena	R	22	19	0	0	7	24.2	113	21	15	12	2	1	1	2	17	2	15	7	2	2	1	.667	0	1	4.38
Tomberlin,Lance,Huntington	R	21	2	0	0	2	3	18	6	4	0	0	0	0	1	2	0	2	0	0	0	0	.000	0	0	0.00
Toney,Michael,Medicne Hat	R	21	28	0	0	27	34.1	144	20	8	4	1	0	1	3	18	1	36	2	1	1	1	.500	0	18	1.05
Torres,Luis,Padres	R	19	15	2	0	5	34	146	31	15	9	0	0	2	2	12	0	24	3	1	2	3	.400	0	1	2.38
Touchett,Sean,Elmira	A	22	22	0	0	20	34.2	165	30	21	18	2	3	3	1	29	2	55	6	0	1	4	.200	0	6	4.67
Towns,Ryan,Rockford	A	23	34	2	0	10	64.1	271	55	22	21	5	3	3	3	31	1	54	1	0	5	1	.833	0	1	2.94
Townsend,Richard,Salem	A	24	50	0	0	11	63.2	278	66	41	38	8	3	2	2	29	2	52	8	1	6	5	.545	0	1	5.37
Trevino,Ricardo,Lethbridge	R	24	21	0	0	5	30.1	150	32	35	29	0	0	3	1	27	0	20	7	3	2	2	.500	0	1	8.60
Trimarco,Michael,Albany	A	23	26	0	0	14	63	259	53	30	22	2	0	1	0	24	0	41	4	1	1	2	.333	0	2	3.14
Trinidad,Hector,Daytona	A	21	28	27	0	0	175.2	726	171	72	63	8	7	3	7	40	0	142	3	1	11	9	.550	1	0	3.23
Trisler,John,Clearwater	A	25	27	22	4	1	156.2	641	148	68	57	12	7	8	8	36	0	72	4	2	8	10	.444	0	0	3.27
Troutman,Mike,Vero Beach	A	22	43	0	0	10	78.1	328	69	39	34	6	3	2	1	35	5	66	5	1	3	2	.600	0	0	3.91
Trumpour,Andy,Kingsport	R	21	11	11	0	0	59.2	249	54	26	18	5	0	0	2	20	0	46	7	1	4	4	.500	0	0	2.72
Tucker,Brett,Clinton	A	23	29	0	0	11	63.2	287	72	37	29	10	5	3	3	24	0	47	6	1	3	3	.500	0	2	4.10
Tucker,Julien,Auburn	A	22	14	14	3	0	84.1	355	72	30	21	4	1	3	5	30	0	63	13	0	8	3	.727	0	0	2.24
Turnier,Aaron,Macon	A	24	16	0	0	9	25.1	107	23	10	8	0	0	1	2	10	0	24	7	0	0	1	.000	0	0	2.84
Durham	A	24	26	0	0	11	43	197	31	16	13	2	3	1	1	36	3	39	7	0	3	2	.600	0	3	2.72
Turrentine,Richard,Yankees	R	24	6	0	0	1	8.2	40	10	8	7	1	1	0	1	4	0	11	2	0	0	0	.000	0	0	7.27
Tampa	A	24	10	0	0	2	14.2	70	14	10	10	0	1	0	2	13	0	10	3	0	1	0	1.000	0	0	6.14
Tweedlie,Brad,Winston-Sal	A	23	10	5	0	1	29.1	161	48	47	40	7	1	3	3	19	0	18	4	0	1	4	.200	0	0	12.27
Charlstn-Sc	A	23	8	8	0	0	38	173	42	27	24	4	2	0	2	20	0	30	9	2	3	4	.429	0	0	5.68
Twiggs,Greg,Daytona	A	23	45	0	0	14	70.1	316	70	44	34	4	4	3	3	33	2	45	3	1	3	4	.429	0	0	4.35
Tyner,Marcus,Idaho Falls	R	23	11	11	2	0	65	288	78	35	28	1	1	3	7	17	0	50	6	0	4	4	.500	1	0	3.88
Tynon,Don,Elmira	A	24	24	1	0	5	41	194	48	33	25	5	4	1	3	18	1	29	5	0	5	2	.714	0	0	5.49
Tyrrell,Jim,Sarasota	A	22	7	0	0	3	6	45	16	15	10	0	1	0	2	6	0	4	0	0	0	1	.000	0	0	15.00
Utica	A	22	27	0	0	20	39.1	160	25	14	8	0	1	2	2	18	0	37	5	0	3	1	.750	0	7	1.83
Upchurch,David,Eugene	A	23	18	8	0	0	62.2	275	66	29	17	4	2	1	5	17	0	52	2	1	2	1	.667	0	0	2.44
Updike,Jon,Mariners	R	22	19	0	0	15	24.2	106	18	9	6	2	2	1	3	15	1	21	3	0	0	0	.000	0	2	2.19
Urbina,Red,W. Michigan	A	21	6	0	0	1	6.2	46	18	16	14	1	0	2	0	9	1	3	0	0	0	2	.000	0	0	18.90
Athletics	R	21	5	4	0	1	21	89	25	9	9	2	2	2	1	4	0	11	0	0	1	1	.500	0	1	3.86
Urso,Sal,Riverside	A	23	30	1	0	12	34.2	156	44	27	23	4	1	2	3	14	0	26	3	0	1	2	.333	0	0	5.97
Valdez,Carlos,San Jose	A	23	36	17	0	10	123.2	536	109	70	62	7	3	6	12	61	0	116	6	0	8	6	.571	0	0	4.51
Valdez,Eugenio,Athletics	R	18	19	0	0	8	43.1	181	44	16	11	2	3	2	1	11	5	24	4	0	2	3	.400	0	5	2.28
Valdez,Ken,Angels	R	20	14	0	0	11	19.1	80	11	10	4	0	0	0	0	10	0	19	5	0	1	0	1.000	0	1	1.86
Valdez,Orlando,Giants	R	20	16	0	0	4	21.2	98	22	18	7	1	1	3	1	6	0	17	2	1	1	0	1.000	0	1	2.91
Valdez,Doug,Butte	R	23	17	6	1	6	50.1	230	78	42	40	5	0	0	3	12	1	20	1	1	2	2	.500	0	0	7.15
Valdez,Victor,Quad City	A	22	32	1	0	15	58.1	242	51	30	27	6	2	2	6	17	0	41	6	2	2	4	.333	0	1	4.17
Valley,Jason,Batavia	A	22	14	12	1	1	65.1	291	77	48	34	2	2	2	3	26	0	28	2	2	3	5	.375	0	0	4.68
Vandermark,John,Batavia	A	23	16	0	0	7	21.1	92	11	12	8	2	1	0	2	16	0	25	3	2	1	1	.500	0	1	3.38
Vanhof,John,Bellingham	A	21	15	15	2	0	90	376	72	28	23	2	1	0	3	38	0	97	11	1	7	3	.700	1	0	2.30
Vanlanduyt,Jules,Huntington	R	23	3	0	0	1	5	30	9	8	6	1	0	0	0	5	0	4	1	1	0	0	.000	0	0	10.80
Vaught,Jay,Watertown	A	23	14	13	2	0	82.1	340	73	38	30	5	3	5	3	16	1	50	3	6	7	4	.636	0	0	3.28
Vazquez,Archie,Hickory	A	23	50	0	0	48	67	264	37	14	9	5	3	1	1	22	0	78	6	0	7	3	.700	0	28	1.21
Vazquez,Javier,Expos	R	19	15	11	1	0	67.2	260	37	25	19	0	1	3	15	0	56	9	2	5	2	.714	1	0	2.53	
Vegil,Aaron,Princeton	R	20	9	0	0	2	11.2	55	13	10	5	2	1	0	0	7	0	8	2	3	2	1	.667	0	0	3.86
Charlstn-Sc	A	20	7	0	0	1	9	43	12	4	4	0	1	0	0	3	0	7	1	1	0	0	.000	0	0	4.00
Veras,Dario,Rancho Cuca	A	22	59	0	0	13	79	332	66	28	18	7	7	0	6	25	9	56	2	0	9	2	.818	0	3	2.05
Viegas,Randy,Pirates	R	19	12	11	1	0	67.2	286	55	33	31	6	0	1	7	31	0	44	2	2	2	3	.400	0	0	4.12
Villarreal,Modesto,Royals	R	19	17	8	0	2	50.2	212	49	18	11	2	1	1	3	9	0	40	3	0	4	0	1.000	0	0	1.95
Viner,Brandon,Red Sox	R	22	5	0	0	1	5	28	12	6	6	1	0	0	0	6	0	4	0	0	0	0	.000	0	0	10.80
Vogelgesang,Joe,St. Cathrns	A	24	3	0	0	0	6	31	9	8	8	0	0	0	4	0	0	4	0	0	0	2	.000	0	0	12.00
Volkert,Oreste,Medicne Hat	R	20	18	0	0	6	42.1	192	60	32	25	1	4	1	1	11	1	29	5	1	3	2	.600	0	2	5.31
Volkman,Keith,Angels	R	18	15	0	0	8	24	113	20	11	9	1	0	1	3	18	0	24	4	2	0	0	.000	0	0	3.38
Vukson,John,Yakima	A	19	14	1	0	0	16	82	11	17	13	0	0	0	4	23	0	15	8	0	1	0	1.000	0	0	7.31
Wagner,Bret,New Jersey	A	22	3	3	0	0	12.1	53	10	9	7	0	0	0	0	4	0	13	0	0	1	0	1.000	0	0	5.11
Savannah	A	22	7	7	0	0	44	161	27	8	6	2	0	1	0	6	0	43	3	1	4	1	.800	0	0	1.23
Wagner,Joe,Beloit	A	23	28	28	0	0	185.1	793	178	99	81	10	8	3	6	62	3	137	20	1	13	9	.591	1	0	3.93
Wagner,Matthew,Appleton	A	23	15	1	0	7	32.2	129	23	8	3	2	2	0	1	8	1	48	4	2	4	2	.667	0	0	0.83
Wagner,Billy,Quad City	A	23	26	26	2	0	153	640	99	71	56	9	7	6	8	91	0	204	12	9	8	9	.471	0	0	3.29
Walania,Alan,Kane County	A	24	23	0	0	6	33.1	161	38	34	26	7	1	2	8	9	0	33	6	1	1	3	.250	0	0	7.02
Waldrep,Arthur,Bend	A	23	5	5	0	0	28.2	122	34	14	13	1	0	0	4	3	0	14	0	2	1	2	.333	0	0	4.08
Asheville	A	23	12	4	0	5	35.2	160	43	25	17	4	0	1	6	18	0	21	2	1	1	2	.333	0	0	4.29
Walkden,Mike,Bakersfield	A	22	3	0	0	1	4	17	5	3	3	1	0	0	0	3	0	0	0	0	0	0	.000	0	0	6.75
Walker,James,Frederick	A	24	26	17	0	1	113.2	492	121	60	55	19	5	4	5	40	0	81	4	5	5	5	.500	0	0	4.35
Walker,Jim,Quad City	A	24	32	18	0	4	125	569	133	80	58	10	14	3	16	42	2	104	5	1	8	10	.444	0	1	4.18
Walker,Jason,Watertown	A	23	18	0	0	10	23	96	21	12	6	1	4	1	1	9	2	12	1	0	2	1	.667	0	2	2.35
Walker,Wade,Peoria	A	23	28	28	4	0	178.1	789	192	108	79	11	6	9	8	72	0	117	17	4	14	12	.538	1	0	3.99
Wallace,Kent,Tampa	A	23	39	0	0	17	77.2	310	60	23	18	2	2	3	3	22	4	61	2	0	6	3	.667	0	7	2.09
Walls,Douglas,Asheville	A	21	21	21	1	0	106.1	470	81	68	59	6	3	7	8	71	1	111	16	5	6	10	.375	0	0	4.99
Walsh,Matthew,W.Michigan	A	22	30	22	0	2	133.2	547	118	62	51	9	3	3	4	38	0	98	4	5	10	5	.667	0	1	3.43

1994 Pitching -- Single-A and Rookie Leagues

			HOW MUCH HE PITCHED						WHAT HE GAVE UP												THE RESULTS					
Player	Lg	A	G	GS	CG	GF	IP	BFP	H	R	ER	HR	SH	SF	HB	TBB	IBB	SO	WP	Bk	W	L	Pct.	ShO	Sv	ERA
Walter,Michael,Quad City	A	20	23	0	0	10	28.1	134	27	18	13	0	2	2	1	20	1	28	4	1	2	2	.500	0	3	4.13
Walters,Brett,Spokane	A	20	2	0	0	1	1.2	9	4	1	1	0	1	0	0	0	0	2	1	0	0	0	.000	0	0	5.40
Padres	R	20	14	6	0	8	45.1	175	28	15	11	1	2	0	0	8	0	45	3	0	2	2	.500	0	6	2.18
Ward,Bryan,Kane County	A	23	47	0	0	40	55.2	235	46	27	21	4	3	4	2	21	2	62	2	0	3	4	.429	0	11	3.40
Ward,Kerry,Pirates	R	20	9	2	0	3	25.1	124	37	27	22	0	1	0	3	7	0	22	5	0	1	4	.200	0	0	7.82
Ward,Duane,Dunedin	A	31	3	1	0	0	4	16	4	2	2	0	0	0	0	0	0	4	0	0	1	0	1.000	0	0	4.50
Warembourg,Larry,Bend	A	23	28	0	0	23	38.2	177	47	21	16	1	5	1	1	15	4	31	1	2	2	2	.500	0	3	3.72
Warrecker,Theodore,Burlington	R	22	12	0	0	5	19.2	99	12	16	12	0	2	2	6	21	2	26	10	1	0	2	.000	0	0	5.49
Warren,Deshawn,Cedar Rapids	A	21	22	21	0	1	98	432	76	43	37	3	3	3	2	76	2	88	13	2	7	4	.636	0	0	3.40
Watkins,Jason,Pr. William	A	25	42	0	0	25	76.2	326	59	31	23	5	9	0	2	35	5	76	4	1	5	3	.625	0	2	2.70
Weaver,Eric,Vero Beach	A	21	7	7	0	0	24	109	28	20	18	3	0	0	1	9	1	22	1	0	1	3	.250	0	0	6.75
Webb,Douglas,Brewers	R	21	1	0	0	1	1	3	1	0	0	0	0	0	0	0	0	1	0	0	0	0	.000	0	0	0.00
Stockton	A	21	29	0	0	12	35	179	38	33	21	2	1	4	2	27	0	34	5	4	0	2	.000	0	0	5.40
Weber,David,Williamsprt	A	20	15	14	0	0	70.2	336	92	65	60	3	2	6	6	33	2	44	8	7	1	9	.100	0	0	7.64
Weber,Eric,Bristol	R	20	14	3	0	7	32.1	140	28	18	10	1	3	1	3	11	0	21	3	0	3	3	.500	0	0	2.78
Weber,Lenny,Burlington	R	22	19	0	0	5	27.2	130	29	16	14	2	2	1	1	15	0	35	7	1	0	0	.000	0	1	4.55
Weber,Neal,W. Palm Bch	A	22	25	24	1	0	135	566	113	58	48	8	4	4	4	62	0	134	7	5	9	7	.563	0	0	3.20
Wehn,Kevin,Bend	A	22	3	0	0	2	6	22	4	1	1	0	0	0	0	0	0	3	0	0	1	0	1.000	0	0	1.50
Asheville	A	22	20	0	0	9	39.2	197	49	36	27	4	0	3	3	22	0	29	3	0	2	2	.500	0	3	6.13
Weidert,Christopher,Expos	R	21	12	12	0	0	63.2	259	43	25	20	3	0	3	3	24	0	53	3	1	5	3	.625	0	0	2.83
Weinberg,Todd,Sou. Oregon	A	23	17	9	0	3	68	306	65	36	27	2	7	3	4	31	3	73	4	0	7	3	.700	0	1	3.57
Weiss,Marc,Billings	R	21	25	0	0	15	43.1	195	41	19	14	2	4	0	4	22	2	30	5	3	4	1	.800	0	3	2.91
Welch,David,Kinston	A	25	60	1	0	18	94	419	109	50	42	11	3	2	3	31	1	73	0	3	5	2	.714	0	2	4.02
Welch,Michael,Columbia	A	22	24	24	5	0	159.2	667	151	81	64	14	7	5	11	33	0	127	5	0	7	11	.389	2	0	3.61
Welch,Robert,Red Sox	R	19	6	2	0	1	14.2	63	10	5	4	0	1	0	2	7	0	20	1	0	2	1	.667	0	0	2.45
Welch,Travis,Johnson Cty	R	21	30	1	0	27	35.2	143	24	12	10	2	0	0	1	17	2	39	2	0	3	2	.600	0	17	2.52
Wells,David,Macon	A	23	42	0	0	18	78.2	333	71	40	28	6	3	3	6	20	1	71	9	1	6	2	.750	0	3	3.20
West,Adam,Cardinals	R	21	12	12	0	0	66	267	53	26	22	3	2	1	7	24	0	54	8	1	5	5	.500	0	0	3.00
West,Kenyon,Marlins	R	19	11	5	0	3	36.2	143	27	10	8	1	0	2	0	14	0	16	6	0	4	1	.800	0	0	1.96
Westbrook,Destry,Quad City	A	24	27	0	0	12	46.1	205	48	25	23	3	2	2	2	23	1	50	3	0	0	2	.000	0	1	4.47
Westcott,Christian,Utica	A	22	1	0	0	0	1	6	3	2	1	0	0	0	0	0	0	1	0	0	0	0	.000	0	0	9.00
Wharton,Joseph,Greensboro	A	24	13	0	0	7	15.1	61	8	5	5	1	0	0	1	9	0	20	3	2	0	0	.000	0	0	2.93
Wheeler,Earl,Charlotte	A	25	36	11	0	7	104	449	118	60	51	5	2	8	2	28	1	45	4	0	2	4	.333	0	0	4.41
Whisenant,Matt,Brevard Cty	A	24	28	26	0	0	160	679	125	71	60	7	6	7	9	82	2	103	18	1	6	9	.400	1	0	3.38
Whitaker,Anthony,W. Michigan	A	23	37	5	0	12	79	345	83	41	36	7	1	1	6	25	2	56	5	1	3	4	.429	0	2	4.10
White,Darell,Springfield	A	23	46	0	0	15	75.1	344	74	47	40	6	1	3	2	46	2	74	7	0	4	1	.800	0	1	4.78
White,Kyle,Springfield	A	25	25	6	0	7	55.2	283	80	57	45	9	3	3	2	31	0	48	3	0	2	8	.200	0	0	7.28
Whiteman,Greg,Jamestown	A	22	15	15	1	0	75.2	328	72	39	34	2	2	0	0	35	0	67	7	2	6	5	.545	1	0	4.04
Whiteman,Tony,Bristol	R	24	23	0	0	17	34.1	159	44	27	22	2	2	1	2	11	0	29	0	2	4	1	.800	0	2	5.77
Fayettevlle	A	24	1	0	0	1	4	23	8	3	3	0	1	0	0	3	1	1	0	0	0	0	.000	0	0	6.75
Witfill,Mike,Daytona	A	20	1	1	0	0	5.1	30	9	8	8	1	1	0	0	4	0	4	0	0	0	1	.000	0	0	13.50
Cubs	R	20	13	6	0	4	36.1	173	38	34	26	2	2	4	1	18	0	16	2	0	0	4	.000	0	0	6.44
Whitten,Charles,Kinston	A	23	27	27	0	0	153.1	634	127	78	73	21	4	5	4	64	0	148	9	0	9	10	.474	0	0	4.28
Wicks,Rosloe,Mets	R	18	12	1	0	5	25	107	18	9	3	0	1	0	2	10	0	16	3	0	3	0	1.000	0	0	1.08
Wiley,Chad,Charlotte	A	23	42	0	0	9	72	321	71	29	25	3	3	2	4	37	0	63	6	1	4	6	.400	0	1	3.13
Wilkerson,Steve,Charlstn-Sc	A	22	46	0	0	32	55.2	251	42	33	26	4	2	4	7	38	2	39	7	0	0	4	.000	0	15	4.20
Princeton	R	22	9	0	0	5	10.2	51	8	6	6	1	1	0	3	8	1	13	4	0	1	0	1.000	0	1	5.06
Wilkins,Marc,Salem	A	24	28	28	0	0	151	657	155	84	62	15	6	3	22	45	0	90	14	1	8	5	.615	0	0	3.70
Williams,Brian,Bellingham	A	23	10	0	0	3	16.2	88	23	19	14	0	1	1	0	18	2	14	9	0	0	0	.000	0	0	7.56
Williams,Greg,Columbus	A	23	37	0	0	12	73.1	312	49	32	28	2	1	4	5	52	0	84	8	1	6	1	.857	0	1	3.44
Williams,Jeff,Columbus	A	25	42	1	0	15	42	203	58	34	25	6	0	0	5	16	0	41	3	2	2	0	1.000	0	5	5.36
Williams,Juan,Elizabethtn	R	21	9	9	0	0	50	212	50	29	25	5	2	1	0	22	0	43	4	0	2	2	.500	0	0	4.50
Williard,Brian,Cedar Rapids	A	22	12	12	3	0	74.2	326	90	44	39	5	5	5	3	15	0	54	5	0	3	5	.375	2	0	4.70
Lake Elsino	A	22	5	5	0	0	23.1	108	42	17	17	3	0	1	0	4	0	12	1	0	2	1	.667	0	0	6.56
Willming,Gregory,Charlstn-Wv	A	24	34	2	0	18	81.2	381	109	56	42	12	3	2	8	21	2	61	4	2	4	8	.667	0	1	4.63
Wilson,Michael,Fayettevlle	A	22	14	14	0	0	57.1	271	74	49	35	3	0	2	12	23	0	28	14	3	2	10	.167	0	0	5.49
Jamestown	A	22	5	4	0	0	15	65	16	9	8	1	0	0	1	8	0	4	2	0	1	2	.333	0	0	4.80
Wilson,Paul,Mets	R	22	3	3	0	0	12	47	8	4	4	0	0	1	0	4	0	13	0	2	0	0	.000	0	0	3.00
St. Lucie	A	22	8	8	0	0	37.1	160	32	23	21	3	0	1	3	17	1	37	0	5	0	5	.000	0	0	5.06
Wilson,Ricardo,Twins	R	18	15	0	0	11	25.1	113	25	17	15	2	0	1	0	14	0	17	5	1	0	1	.000	0	0	5.33
Wilson,Stewart,Cubs	R	21	4	0	0	0	6.1	25	3	1	0	0	0	0	1	4	0	5	0	1	0	0	.000	0	0	0.00
Wilstead,Judd,Beloit	A	22	26	9	0	10	75	344	82	48	38	5	6	1	7	36	2	46	2	1	5	6	.455	0	0	4.56
Wimberly,Larry,Martinsvlle	R	19	13	13	0	0	69.2	281	55	24	20	6	2	2	3	25	0	67	5	1	3	2	.600	0	0	2.58
Winchester,Martin,Appleton	A	22	29	7	0	4	63.1	303	68	49	38	6	4	6	5	43	1	45	4	0	2	5	.286	0	1	5.40
Windham,Michael,Madison	A	23	21	21	1	0	121.2	526	119	67	58	12	1	3	9	49	0	88	10	3	10	7	.588	0	0	4.29
Winkle,Kenneth,Eugene	A	23	14	10	0	0	45.2	208	37	32	16	2	2	0	3	23	0	61	6	0	4	4	.500	0	0	3.15
Winslett,Dax,Bakersfield	A	23	27	27	0	0	159.1	686	163	89	79	13	10	4	6	57	0	111	12	1	10	11	.476	0	0	4.46
Wise,William,Braves	R	19	15	0	0	7	29.1	153	28	30	21	1	1	3	4	34	0	17	8	1	1	2	.333	0	0	6.44
Witasick,Gerald,Madison	A	22	18	18	2	0	112.1	443	74	36	29	5	5	3	2	42	0	141	5	0	10	4	.714	0	0	2.32
Witte,Trey,Riverside	A	25	25	0	0	4	54.1	235	57	29	26	2	1	2	5	15	2	45	3	0	4	3	.571	0	0	4.31
Wolff,Bryan,Springfield	A	23	60	0	0	47	63.2	298	46	43	38	3	7	1	0	58	4	99	11	4	3	8	.273	0	24	5.37
Wolff,Thomas,Kingsport	R	21	11	3	1	2	37.2	157	28	19	13	2	1	2	4	14	0	38	5	2	4	0	1.000	1	0	3.11
Wollins,Paul,Idaho Falls	R	23	13	0	0	7	32.2	145	31	21	17	0	0	0	4	22	0	15	11	0	1	0	1.000	0	1	4.68
Wood,Mike,Spartanburg	A	24	10	0	0	7	15	64	13	6	4	1	1	2	0	6	0	9	2	0	0	1	.000	0	0	2.40
Batavia	A	24	2	0	0	1	3.1	13	4	1	1	0	0	0	0	1	0	4	0	0	0	0	.000	0	0	2.70
Woodall,Brent,Peoria	A	24	24	0	0	14	37	179	53	39	32	4	1	4	2	16	1	30	2	0	0	1	.000	0	0	7.78
Woodall,Kevin,Rangers	R	23	9	8	1	0	45.1	182	33	18	15	1	0	1	6	19	0	24	1	0	4	2	.667	0	0	2.98

1994 Pitching -- Single-A and Rookie Leagues

Player	Lg	A	G	GS	CG	GF	IP	BFP	H	R	ER	HR	SH	SF	HB	TBB	IBB	SO	WP	Bk	W	L	Pct.	ShO	Sv	ERA
Charlotte	A	23	6	6	0	0	35.1	160	31	17	15	3	1	4	4	27	0	19	4	1	3	2	.600	0	0	3.82
Woodard,Steven,Brewers	R	20	15	12	2	1	82.2	336	68	29	22	3	2	3	4	13	1	85	8	1	8	0	1.000	0	0	2.40
Woodring,Jason,Burlington	A	21	12	0	0	1	19.2	96	27	15	10	2	1	2	1	12	1	13	1	2	0	2	.000	0	0	4.58
Expos	R	21	2	0	0	0	1.1	10	3	3	2	1	0	0	0	2	0	2	0	1	0	0	.000	0	0	13.50
Woods,Brian,South Bend	A	24	20	18	2	2	115.1	499	108	65	50	9	5	3	5	49	0	107	10	4	4	12	.250	0	0	3.90
Woodson,Kerry,Mariners	R	26	4	4	0	0	18.2	82	18	13	13	0	1	1	5	5	0	14	2	0	1	1	.500	0	0	6.27
Riverside	A	26	9	9	0	0	45.2	191	41	24	22	4	3	1	6	14	0	19	1	0	2	4	.333	0	0	4.34
Worley,Robert,Riverside	A	24	40	0	0	35	48.1	218	47	29	23	3	3	0	1	32	2	37	3	1	2	2	.500	0	8	4.28
Worley,Roger,Orioles	R	19	3	3	0	0	6.2	36	9	11	8	2	0	0	2	3	0	4	2	1	0	2	.000	0	0	10.80
Wright,Howard,Astros	R	24	8	0	0	5	11	47	3	5	1	0	0	0	0	8	0	4	1	1	2	0	1.000	0	1	0.82
Wright,Jamey,Asheville	A	20	28	27	2	0	143.1	655	188	107	95	6	5	4	16	59	1	103	9	5	7	14	.333	0	0	5.97
Wright,Jaret,Burlington	R	19	4	4	0	0	13.1	62	13	10	8	1	0	1	2	9	0	16	0	0	0	1	.000	0	0	5.40
Wright,Scott,Batavia	A	25	4	0	0	2	8.2	45	9	8	6	0	0	1	0	10	0	6	3	0	0	0	.000	0	0	6.23
Wunsch,Kelly,Beloit	A	22	17	17	0	0	83.1	400	88	69	57	11	4	3	13	47	1	77	6	0	3	10	.231	0	0	6.16
Helena	R	22	9	9	1	0	51	238	52	39	29	7	1	2	10	30	0	37	6	1	4	2	.667	0	0	5.12
Wyatt,Cortez,Williamsprt	A	22	22	2	0	5	46.1	220	58	47	38	2	3	2	6	19	0	23	7	2	2	3	.400	0	1	7.38
Yan,Esteban,Macon	A	21	28	28	4	0	170.2	696	155	85	62	15	4	3	13	34	1	121	4	6	11	12	.478	3	0	3.27
Yarbough,Jason,Martinsvlle	R	21	4	0	0	2	3.1	31	13	15	8	1	1	0	3	3	0	2	0	1	0	0	.000	0	0	21.60
York,Charles,Kinston	A	24	41	12	0	12	106	491	120	74	63	14	0	2	8	52	0	87	9	1	6	6	.500	0	0	5.35
Young,Brian,Lynchburg	A	26	4	0	0	0	6.1	30	8	5	5	1	1	0	0	3	0	6	0	0	0	0	.000	0	0	7.11
Young,Danny,Salem	A	23	10	0	0	2	18.2	94	32	17	16	2	0	1	0	9	0	12	3	0	2	0	1.000	0	0	7.71
Augusta	A	23	21	9	0	3	66.2	290	58	32	25	2	2	3	2	33	0	73	6	1	2	5	.286	0	0	3.38
Young,Reginald,Medicne Hat	R	20	15	15	0	0	70.2	331	86	55	42	8	3	1	6	46	0	59	6	1	3	5	.375	0	0	5.35
Zavershnik,Michael,Blue Jays	R	19	4	0	0	1	6.1	27	10	6	6	1	1	0	0	2	0	4	1	0	0	0	.000	0	0	8.53
Zedalis,Craig,Danville	R	22	18	0	0	7	32.1	123	22	6	6	0	1	1	2	5	1	25	2	0	4	0	1.000	0	1	1.67
Macon	A	22	9	0	0	9	9.1	40	11	7	6	1	3	0	0	4	1	5	2	0	1	1	.500	0	0	5.79
Zerbe,Chad,Vero Beach	A	23	18	18	1	0	98.1	412	88	50	37	6	0	4	2	32	0	68	6	0	5	5	.500	0	0	3.39
Ziegler,Shane,Bluefield	R	23	7	0	0	4	11	44	11	6	6	2	0	0	1	1	0	8	0	2	1	1	.500	0	1	4.91
Zolecki,Michael,Central Val	A	23	10	8	0	0	35.2	150	27	14	11	0	1	1	1	23	1	30	1	0	0	1	.000	0	0	2.78
Zonger,Steve,W. Michigan	A	25	22	0	0	19	22.2	93	11	6	6	1	0	0	3	13	1	26	3	0	2	1	.667	0	9	2.38
Modesto	A	25	23	0	0	9	35.2	151	34	10	9	1	1	1	0	17	1	41	2	0	2	1	.667	0	0	2.27
Zubiri,Jon,Columbus	A	20	17	16	1	1	91.2	398	83	54	50	10	2	2	10	31	0	64	6	0	6	6	.500	1	0	4.91

Team Stats

American Association Batting - AAA

Team	G	AB	H	2B	3B	HR	TB	R	RBI	TBB	IBB	SO	HBP	SH	SF	SB	CS	SB%	GDP	Avg	OBP	SLG
Omaha	144	4809	1312	238	42	150	2084	747	685	574	23	836	71	39	53	156	78	.67	101	.273	.355	.433
New Orleans	144	4736	1273	259	51	79	1871	714	647	579	28	875	56	68	47	187	73	.72	116	.269	.352	.395
Indianapolis	143	4891	1331	300	43	136	2125	705	657	461	27	928	45	37	48	70	39	.64	107	.272	.337	.434
Louisville	142	4744	1273	294	41	131	2042	697	641	491	31	872	40	43	33	67	54	.55	127	.268	.340	.430
Iowa	143	4722	1313	292	32	134	2071	683	631	386	29	836	68	72	44	91	81	.53	99	.278	.339	.439
Nashville	144	4868	1260	256	41	149	2045	677	639	397	27	831	95	53	45	98	48	.67	96	.259	.324	.420
Oklahoma City	144	4822	1278	252	48	107	1947	646	608	482	25	971	55	49	44	95	52	.65	117	.265	.336	.404
Buffalo	144	4782	1230	250	34	65	1743	536	499	402	40	765	37	61	30	121	57	.68	117	.257	.318	.364
Total	574	38374	10270	2141	332	951	15928	5405	5007	3772	230	6914	467	422	344	885	482	.65	880	.268	.338	.415

American Association Pitching - AAA

Team	G	GS	CG	GF	IP	BFP	H	R	ER	HR	SH	SF	HB	TBB	IBB	SO	WP	Bk	W	L	Pct.	ShO	Sv	ERA
Nashville	144	144	13	131	1281	5484	1224	587	502	94	63	35	38	515	46	1041	62	11	83	61	.576	12	46	3.53
Indianapolis	143	143	11	132	1282	5388	1267	595	516	114	58	25	32	391	34	849	53	7	86	57	.601	13	50	3.62
New Orleans	144	144	13	131	1250.2	5371	1271	658	593	128	38	34	77	473	18	857	85	10	78	66	.542	9	33	4.27
Buffalo	144	144	7	137	1252.1	5404	1311	673	599	117	59	57	60	439	16	761	52	3	55	89	.382	5	31	4.30
Louisville	142	142	8	134	1236.2	5435	1266	694	628	110	61	50	76	494	33	934	99	12	74	68	.521	7	48	4.57
Omaha	144	144	14	130	1243.2	5429	1320	713	615	144	48	37	63	473	13	794	60	7	68	76	.472	6	34	4.45
Iowa	143	143	11	132	1229.2	5341	1258	720	632	125	48	49	65	464	41	823	75	11	69	74	.483	7	32	4.63
Oklahoma City	144	144	13	131	1252	5532	1353	765	670	119	47	57	56	523	29	855	79	23	61	83	.424	11	27	4.82
Total	574	574	90	484	10028	43384	10270	5405	4755	951	422	344	467	3772	230	6914	565	84	574	574	.500	70	301	4.27

International League Batting - AAA

Team	G	AB	H	2B	3B	HR	TB	R	RBI	TBB	IBB	SO	HBP	SH	SF	SB	CS	SB%	GDP	Avg	OBP	SLG
Rochester	141	4752	1263	258	44	141	2032	731	666	470	17	850	57	23	46	118	40	.75	102	.266	.336	.428
Charlotte	142	4766	1305	221	32	132	1986	721	670	532	44	710	50	29	46	80	40	.67	124	.274	.350	.417
Syracuse	142	4741	1330	238	30	116	1976	673	621	441	36	870	23	43	44	108	45	.71	113	.281	.342	.417
Columbus	142	4615	1194	228	42	137	1917	671	620	526	22	993	30	30	46	104	78	.57	97	.259	.335	.415
Pawtucket	142	4864	1285	219	20	147	1985	668	618	530	36	853	31	41	36	95	60	.61	133	.264	.338	.408
Ottawa	142	4692	1199	265	39	106	1860	664	604	565	35	920	37	38	44	97	51	.66	119	.256	.337	.396
Toledo	142	4743	1256	222	35	138	1962	634	592	418	19	1056	40	22	32	205	98	.68	85	.265	.328	.414
Richmond	141	4845	1275	238	38	120	1949	633	573	406	32	765	36	33	51	118	59	.67	105	.263	.322	.402
Norfolk	142	4756	1177	226	34	80	1711	617	544	488	27	864	37	64	44	146	85	.63	90	.247	.320	.360
Scranton-wb	142	4758	1184	280	25	95	1799	586	544	449	30	854	52	37	43	71	51	.58	102	.249	.318	.378
Total	709	47532	12468	2395	339	1212	19177	6598	6052	4825	298	8735	393	360	432	1142	607	.65	1070	.262	.333	.403

International League Pitching - AAA

Team	G	GS	CG	GF	IP	BFP	H	R	ER	HR	SH	SF	HB	TBB	IBB	SO	WP	Bk	W	L	Pct.	ShO	Sv	ERA
Richmond	141	141	8	133	1273.2	5354	1222	583	503	97	48	39	21	466	42	981	46	6	80	61	.567	12	46	3.55
Norfolk	142	142	23	119	1261.1	5310	1252	590	499	106	41	50	51	405	26	730	49	6	67	75	.472	10	29	3.56
Pawtucket	142	142	18	124	1272.2	5421	1219	644	553	141	26	32	36	466	16	927	58	5	78	64	.549	8	38	3.91
Charlotte	142	142	14	128	1233.2	5252	1187	647	562	142	44	48	47	425	20	914	78	2	77	65	.542	6	41	4.10
Columbus	142	142	9	133	1216.2	5291	1252	658	555	100	35	37	40	466	16	803	72	8	74	68	.521	6	36	4.11
Toledo	142	142	6	136	1232.2	5356	1241	665	557	123	38	50	38	474	33	962	53	5	63	79	.444	9	26	4.07
Ottawa	142	142	6	136	1238.2	5460	1294	691	581	126	39	44	36	544	42	822	64	4	70	72	.493	5	40	4.22
Syracuse	142	142	5	137	1206.2	5302	1241	697	599	122	27	44	32	504	24	803	52	5	71	71	.500	3	43	4.47
Rochester	141	141	10	131	1218.1	5376	1277	701	609	136	23	46	40	541	45	912	77	8	67	74	.475	7	33	4.50
Scranton-wb	142	142	17	125	1237	5431	1283	722	643	119	39	42	52	534	34	881	77	4	62	80	.437	9	26	4.68
Total	709	709	116	593	12391.1	53553	12468	6598	5661	1212	360	432	393	4825	298	8735	626	53	709	709	.500	75	358	4.11

Pacific Coast League Batting - AAA

Team	G	AB	H	2B	3B	HR	TB	R	RBI	TBB	IBB	SO	HBP	SH	SF	SB	CS	SB%	GDP	Avg	OBP	SLG
Calgary	143	5107	1567	357	33	198	2584	961	900	552	23	826	41	20	52	78	42	.65	151	.307	.376	.506
Salt Lake	144	5095	1577	313	45	134	2382	941	885	545	22	802	58	20	58	103	59	.64	135	.310	.379	.468
Albuquerque	139	4911	1517	269	55	168	2400	892	828	498	28	808	46	39	46	124	67	.65	126	.309	.375	.489
Colorado Springs	139	4815	1435	307	45	156	2300	846	791	504	27	879	45	29	43	104	56	.65	119	.298	.367	.478
Tucson	144	4992	1474	305	58	115	2240	822	766	524	36	825	45	47	56	123	60	.67	127	.295	.364	.449
Las Vegas	144	4905	1378	244	42	153	2165	759	702	545	25	986	51	59	45	90	50	.64	126	.281	.356	.441
Vancouver	142	4778	1399	263	45	96	2040	757	710	489	17	803	42	42	63	97	68	.59	110	.293	.359	.427
Edmonton	142	4886	1404	298	38	147	2219	743	690	411	17	855	57	35	46	131	55	.70	121	.287	.347	.454
Phoenix	143	4902	1413	257	62	102	2100	737	679	399	22	826	62	32	40	121	71	.63	128	.288	.347	.428
Tacoma	142	4878	1363	261	27	96	1966	666	603	415	24	850	47	53	49	111	68	.62	132	.279	.339	.403
Total	711	49269	14527	2874	450	1365	22396	8124	7554	4882	241	8460	494	376	498	1082	596	.64	1275	.295	.361	.455

Pacific Coast League Pitching - AAA

Team	G	GS	CG	GF	IP	BFP	H	R	ER	HR	SH	SF	HB	TBB	IBB	SO	WP	Bk	W	L	Pct.	ShO	Sv	ERA
Vancouver	142	142	17	125	1217.1	5331	1327	704	613	146	36	50	68	433	19	843	77	7	77	65	.542	7	36	4.53
Phoenix	143	143	2	141	1239.2	5477	1441	749	650	139	48	52	41	457	30	805	66	6	70	72	.493	10	38	4.72
Tacoma	142	142	7	135	1245.1	5510	1350	761	659	132	33	49	44	541	16	771	64	15	61	81	.430	8	33	4.76
Albuquerque	139	139	1	138	1230.2	5475	1432	778	670	112	32	29	57	481	28	887	84	8	83	56	.597	4	44	4.90
Tucson	144	144	5	139	1267.2	5619	1478	791	675	118	44	55	35	442	30	814	66	2	81	63	.563	5	39	4.79
Edmonton	142	142	9	133	1222.1	5476	1459	811	716	130	37	50	47	462	7	844	78	8	67	75	.472	7	28	5.27
Salt Lake	144	144	6	138	1249.2	5643	1476	834	736	157	38	54	52	495	23	862	71	8	74	70	.514	0	30	5.30
Colorado Springs	139	139	13	126	1199	5492	1492	862	764	141	41	40	55	489	25	814	66	9	70	69	.504	7	29	5.73
Las Vegas	144	144	9	135	1245.2	5737	1511	888	751	127	43	54	48	561	30	960	81	6	56	87	.392	7	25	5.43
Calgary	143	143	5	138	1251.1	5765	1561	946	818	163	26	63	47	521	33	860	91	10	71	72	.497	4	36	5.88
Total	711	711	74	637	12368.2	55525	14527	8124	7052	1365	378	496	494	4882	241	8460	744	79	710	710	.500	59	338	5.13

Eastern League Batting - AA

Team	G	AB	H	2B	3B	HR	TB	R	RBI	TBB	IBB	SO	HBP	SH	SF	SB	CS	SB%	GDP	Avg	OBP	SLG
Bowie	142	4732	1335	264	35	101	1972	750	658	465	24	775	40	42	60	192	71	.73	113	.282	.347	.417
Binghamton	141	4856	1344	274	37	95	1977	695	640	471	23	805	25	54	55	103	77	.57	94	.277	.340	.407
Harrisburg	139	4629	1236	240	30	128	1920	692	636	528	23	995	43	50	38	140	91	.61	103	.267	.345	.415
Canton-akron	142	4663	1241	233	32	114	1880	660	613	465	19	948	46	48	40	99	64	.61	99	.266	.336	.403
New Haven	140	4589	1160	219	22	105	1738	638	584	519	35	965	49	49	40	99	59	.63	119	.253	.332	.379
Albany	141	4562	1144	200	37	116	1766	609	560	529	26	1024	47	52	39	119	79	.60	91	.251	.332	.387
New Britain	140	4554	1123	219	35	93	1691	602	546	526	19	886	46	35	47	76	74	.51	100	.247	.328	.371
Portland	141	4729	1194	232	24	93	1753	600	542	455	13	923	35	54	28	100	72	.58	110	.252	.321	.371
Reading	140	4668	1180	196	40	97	1747	587	537	410	18	849	44	42	38	96	68	.59	111	.253	.317	.374
Trenton	140	4437	1015	191	31	84	1520	527	473	412	15	981	46	40	23	128	68	.65	90	.229	.300	.343
Total	703	46419	11972	2268	323	1026	17964	6360	5789	4780	215	9151	421	466	408	1152	723	.61	1030	.258	.330	.387

Eastern League Pitching - AA

Team	G	GS	CG	GF	IP	BFP	H	R	ER	HR	SH	SF	HB	TBB	IBB	SO	WP	Bk	W	L	Pct.	ShO	Sv	ERA
Bowie	142	142	19	123	1220	5140	1175	569	481	114	41	37	24	395	14	1043	68	12	84	58	.592	8	34	3.55
New Haven	140	140	17	123	1218.2	5143	1110	577	466	87	50	37	30	421	18	927	39	20	77	63	.550	16	36	3.44
Binghamton	141	141	16	125	1261.1	5372	1188	593	502	97	54	37	60	497	28	943	62	14	82	59	.582	9	40	3.58
Albany	141	141	10	131	1218.2	5228	1201	597	492	86	42	42	44	442	21	931	86	16	71	70	.504	5	30	3.63
Harrisburg	139	139	7	132	1222	5183	1095	603	506	108	50	35	28	496	6	963	66	6	88	51	.633	12	45	3.73
Trenton	140	140	24	116	1174.1	5091	1241	624	536	85	41	40	31	450	14	737	56	16	55	85	.393	6	23	4.11
Canton-akron	142	142	14	128	1216.2	5284	1189	660	560	107	41	39	41	533	28	820	69	10	69	73	.486	9	33	4.14
New Britain	140	140	5	135	1202	5281	1277	690	577	91	40	41	53	471	15	931	65	7	59	81	.421	8	18	4.32
Portland	141	141	5	136	1235.2	5417	1246	718	619	130	49	49	71	523	44	928	56	15	60	81	.426	8	35	4.51
Reading	140	140	5	135	1220.2	5368	1250	729	613	121	58	51	39	532	27	928	82	13	58	82	.414	4	36	4.52
Total	703	703	122	581	12190	52507	11972	6360	5352	1026	466	408	421	4780	215	9151	649	129	703	703	.500	85	330	3.95

Southern League Batting - AA

Team	G	AB	H	2B	3B	HR	TB	R	RBI	TBB	IBB	SO	HBP	SH	SF	SB	CS	SB%	GDP	Avg	OBP	SLG
Carolina	140	4734	1263	255	39	78	1830	642	585	408	41	808	57	51	53	104	68	.60	87	.267	.329	.387
Huntsville	138	4451	1116	232	31	73	1629	613	548	528	15	871	62	64	62	129	74	.64	103	.251	.334	.366
Knoxville	140	4614	1221	210	55	63	1730	612	545	427	26	890	54	45	33	203	96	.68	80	.265	.332	.375
Chattanooga	140	4611	1210	233	27	83	1746	608	544	446	20	877	49	49	41	146	85	.63	92	.262	.331	.379
Jacksonville	137	4524	1181	231	20	131	1845	602	558	359	12	784	57	49	34	124	72	.63	91	.261	.321	.408
Memphis	137	4547	1136	218	27	109	1735	595	550	407	30	821	57	45	36	96	65	.60	93	.250	.317	.382
Nashville	140	4644	1163	218	19	125	1794	594	552	418	20	1006	51	39	34	124	61	.67	85	.250	.317	.386
Birmingham	139	4572	1132	228	32	40	1544	584	508	483	22	754	52	39	36	155	79	.66	82	.248	.324	.338
Greenville	136	4435	1124	224	25	90	1668	539	483	375	26	828	51	55	43	121	81	.60	92	.253	.316	.376
Orlando	137	4421	1146	187	33	76	1627	489	442	370	21	774	43	64	28	84	107	.44	97	.259	.321	.368
Total	692	45553	11692	2236	308	868	17148	5878	5315	4221	233	8413	533	500	400	1286	788	.62	902	.257	.324	.376

Southern League Pitching - AA

Team	G	GS	CG	GF	IP	BFP	H	R	ER	HR	SH	SF	HB	TBB	IBB	SO	WP	Bk	W	L	Pct.	ShO	Sv	ERA
Greenville	136	136	6	130	1181.2	4982	1124	528	460	77	53	33	34	423	23	878	67	11	73	63	.537	12	44	3.50
Huntsville	138	138	7	131	1208.2	5106	1133	536	461	71	57	31	30	455	37	847	60	11	81	57	.587	9	46	3.43
Orlando	137	137	11	126	1172.1	4926	1128	561	478	90	68	36	65	342	27	715	50	8	59	78	.431	11	28	3.67
Nashville	140	140	12	128	1221	5170	1169	564	461	74	38	39	52	398	7	917	69	8	74	66	.529	9	37	3.42
Chattanooga	140	140	14	126	1214.1	5139	1091	575	462	86	55	33	51	455	31	904	72	14	67	73	.479	8	33	3.42
Memphis	137	137	2	135	1203	5098	1178	581	481	81	44	52	50	396	21	822	78	4	75	62	.547	9	37	3.60
Birmingham	139	139	6	133	1208.2	5220	1193	615	498	86	39	38	66	458	25	843	86	10	65	74	.468	9	27	3.71
Carolina	140	140	19	121	1230.1	5264	1230	619	511	101	55	40	72	384	13	888	62	4	74	66	.529	8	33	3.74
Knoxville	140	140	8	132	1194.1	5200	1201	646	518	99	50	55	61	462	12	851	76	6	64	76	.457	10	29	3.90
Jacksonville	137	137	15	122	1168	5107	1245	653	563	103	41	43	52	448	37	748	80	12	60	77	.438	5	34	4.34
Total	692	692	100	592	12002.1	51212	11692	5878	4893	868	500	400	533	4221	233	8413	700	90	692	692	.500	90	348	3.67

Texas League Batting - AA

Team	G	AB	H	2B	3B	HR	TB	R	RBI	TBB	IBB	SO	HBP	SH	SF	SB	CS	SB%	GDP	Avg	OBP	SLG
El Paso	136	4654	1316	238	87	80	1968	833	734	551	21	1019	50	31	46	131	83	.61	90	.283	.362	.423
Midland	136	4583	1247	246	37	84	1819	739	669	573	25	873	51	56	51	110	67	.62	100	.272	.356	.397
Tulsa	136	4446	1144	236	30	90	1710	581	521	433	16	955	46	53	32	106	81	.57	94	.257	.327	.385
Wichita	136	4541	1183	206	41	90	1741	572	512	441	33	975	52	34	44	153	87	.64	108	.261	.330	.383
Shreveport	136	4427	1160	249	22	68	1657	569	504	411	39	788	52	78	43	141	67	.68	89	.262	.329	.374
Jackson	135	4332	1135	207	47	80	1676	561	517	372	28	916	40	44	41	107	83	.56	89	.262	.323	.387
San Antonio	136	4474	1139	248	32	84	1703	550	490	411	28	866	45	71	30	113	80	.59	85	.255	.322	.381
Arkansas	135	4325	1015	210	34	92	1569	511	451	444	42	898	33	44	24	67	54	.55	96	.235	.309	.363
Total	543	35782	9339	1840	330	668	13843	4916	4398	3636	232	7290	369	411	311	928	602	.61	751	.261	.333	.387

Texas League Pitching - AA

Team	G	GS	CG	GF	IP	BFP	H	R	ER	HR	SH	SF	HB	TBB	IBB	SO	WP	Bk	W	L	Pct.	ShO	Sv	ERA
Shreveport	136	136	9	127	1181.1	4884	1112	515	427	77	49	37	34	343	11	781	56	6	73	63	.537	9	40	3.25
Jackson	135	135	8	127	1148.2	4880	1032	536	424	82	50	30	54	439	38	941	81	7	74	61	.548	13	48	3.32
Arkansas	135	135	12	123	1170	4911	1100	546	437	78	62	30	35	360	20	940	52	8	68	67	.504	11	35	3.36
San Antonio	136	136	0	136	1191.2	5101	1109	569	471	53	59	37	36	543	44	999	62	21	62	74	.456	6	35	3.56
Tulsa	136	136	15	121	1169.1	4934	1117	594	516	120	39	39	42	452	25	870	57	20	63	73	.463	6	37	3.97
El Paso	136	136	14	122	1204.1	5263	1281	655	564	83	45	47	61	509	33	817	68	12	88	48	.647	8	52	4.21
Wichita	136	136	3	133	1186.2	5303	1284	739	604	84	71	47	37	522	43	966	87	8	54	82	.397	7	32	4.58
Midland	136	136	13	123	1182.1	5241	1306	761	641	91	36	44	70	468	18	976	91	15	61	75	.449	5	28	4.88
Total	543	543	74	469	9434.1	40517	9341	4915	4084	668	411	311	369	3636	232	7290	554	97	543	543	.500	65	298	3.90

California League Batting - A

Team	G	AB	H	2B	3B	HR	TB	R	RBI	TBB	IBB	SO	HBP	SH	SF	SB	CS	SB%	GDP	Avg	OBP	SLG
Rancho Cucamonga	136	4606	1253	221	34	123	1911	775	709	501	15	1023	70	28	55	153	76	.67	85	.272	.349	.415
Riverside	136	4626	1307	213	47	87	1875	772	699	528	24	905	83	43	44	128	56	.70	117	.283	.363	.405
High Desert	136	4686	1263	236	42	134	1985	764	709	525	12	1033	50	33	39	139	79	.64	103	.270	.347	.424
Lake Elsinore	136	4662	1249	251	33	120	1926	719	641	556	20	948	50	51	38	140	65	.68	95	.268	.350	.413
San Jose	136	4636	1231	217	42	92	1808	719	644	580	25	912	59	35	46	100	58	.63	100	.266	.351	.390
Modesto	136	4474	1150	220	37	135	1849	718	646	631	22	1127	66	57	47	108	71	.60	82	.257	.354	.413
San Bernardino	136	4616	1177	211	19	131	1819	648	584	473	9	1139	67	37	21	101	59	.63	105	.255	.332	.394
Bakersfield	136	4557	1193	218	29	86	1727	623	529	415	20	913	70	44	31	263	133	.66	75	.262	.331	.379
Stockton	136	4554	1180	214	29	63	1641	601	519	419	9	836	55	64	33	141	69	.67	90	.259	.327	.360
Central Valley	136	4583	1203	213	22	62	1646	595	520	380	12	893	55	59	42	114	57	.67	113	.262	.324	.359
Total	680	46000	12206	2214	334	1033	18187	6934	6200	5008	168	9729	625	451	396	1387	723	.66	965	.265	.343	.395

California League Pitching - A

Team	G	GS	CG	GF	IP	BFP	H	R	ER	HR	SH	SF	HB	TBB	IBB	SO	WP	Bk	W	L	Pct.	ShO	Sv	ERA
Modesto	136	136	1	135	1199.2	4964	1058	482	414	84	39	26	45	390	14	1016	70	17	96	40	.706	16	55	3.11
Riverside	136	136	12	124	1198.1	5096	1126	574	482	87	30	29	46	423	11	944	50	18	87	49	.640	16	31	3.62
Central Valley	136	136	4	132	1196.1	5238	1182	634	504	81	43	33	47	551	33	1033	130	26	65	71	.478	10	39	3.79
Bakersfield	136	136	3	133	1198	5150	1136	641	542	103	47	33	48	542	4	1012	124	14	69	67	.507	4	37	4.07
San Jose	136	136	0	136	1206.1	5193	1200	656	535	92	55	41	85	426	10	928	61	11	74	62	.544	4	40	3.99
Rancho Cucamonga	136	136	2	134	1199.1	5362	1187	671	560	100	45	38	83	588	26	1079	79	19	77	59	.566	6	44	4.20
Lake Elsinore	136	136	14	122	1194.1	5165	1218	680	533	92	50	38	67	440	21	898	75	26	65	71	.478	5	32	4.02
Stockton	136	136	2	138	1186.2	5220	1229	697	549	86	59	51	67	457	22	938	64	16	54	82	.397	6	29	4.16
San Bernardino	136	136	2	134	1186.1	5522	1435	940	819	146	45	51	70	563	9	984	98	19	48	88	.353	1	22	6.21
High Desert	136	136	13	123	1191.1	5581	1435	959	828	162	39	55	67	628	18	897	97	16	45	91	.331	4	18	6.25
Total	680	680	59	621	11957	52491	12206	6934	5766	1033	452	395	625	5008	168	9729	848	182	680	680	.500	72	347	4.34

341

Carolina League Batting - A

Team	G	AB	H	2B	3B	HR	TB	R	RBI	TBB	IBB	SO	HBP	SH	SF	SB	CS	SB%	GDP	Avg	OBP	SLG
						BATTING										BASERUNNING				PERCENTAGES		
Frederick	137	4567	1228	212	36	127	1893	758	691	528	14	903	68	60	43	159	65	.71	77	.269	.350	.414
Wilmington	138	4683	1290	233	52	103	1936	735	654	507	27	755	64	85	49	139	51	.73	85	.275	.351	.413
Winston-salem	137	4549	1154	202	22	202	2006	726	664	516	12	1047	47	25	43	121	74	.62	84	.254	.333	.441
Prince William	136	4590	1229	234	52	102	1873	723	642	480	13	867	50	29	35	147	53	.74	89	.268	.341	.408
Salem	139	4623	1242	204	27	140	1920	706	637	431	4	919	67	33	38	104	74	.58	94	.269	.337	.415
Durham	136	4485	1113	227	17	140	1794	617	569	460	14	1029	37	19	27	122	86	.59	88	.248	.321	.400
Lynchburg	139	4633	1150	214	22	117	1759	600	542	498	13	1014	54	29	28	72	58	.55	98	.248	.326	.380
Kinston	138	4515	1094	212	19	106	1662	584	516	438	15	1036	56	28	29	123	86	.59	63	.242	.315	.368
Total	550	36645	9500	1738	247	1037	14843	5449	4915	3858	112	7570	443	308	292	987	547	.64	678	.259	.335	.405

Carolina League Pitching - A

Team	G	GS	CG	GF	IP	BFP	H	R	ER	HR	SH	SF	HB	TBB	IBB	SO	WP	Bk	W	L	Pct.	ShO	Sv	ERA
		HOW MUCH THEY PITCHED					WHAT THEY GAVE UP												THE RESULTS					
Wilmington	138	138	7	131	1221.1	5003	1045	491	402	105	30	26	32	359	9	1089	52	9	94	44	.681	15	40	2.96
Prince William	136	136	6	131	1177.1	5076	1178	640	523	110	60	31	41	459	12	861	77	14	71	65	.522	9	32	4.00
Frederick	137	137	3	134	1187.2	5183	1143	676	562	128	49	37	50	531	13	1036	72	20	75	61	.551	6	39	4.26
Durham	136	136	5	131	1180.2	5169	1164	688	583	161	34	31	63	510	30	903	90	20	66	70	.485	6	32	4.44
Kinston	138	138	6	132	1176.1	5175	1157	716	583	128	30	36	59	508	1	1008	87	19	60	78	.435	5	33	4.46
Salem	139	139	5	134	1191.2	5302	1281	727	569	134	38	33	88	424	18	904	88	7	64	75	.460	4	37	4.30
Winston-salem	137	137	9	128	1184.2	5314	1196	743	642	146	30	49	71	607	15	887	91	10	67	70	.489	6	37	4.88
Lynchburg	139	139	6	133	1194	5344	1336	768	636	125	37	49	39	460	14	882	79	17	52	87	.374	4	30	4.79
Total	550	550	61	489	9513.2	41566	9500	5449	4500	1037	308	292	443	3858	112	7570	636	116	549	550	.500	55	280	4.26

Florida State League Batting - A

Team	G	AB	H	2B	3B	HR	TB	R	RBI	TBB	IBB	SO	HBP	SH	SF	SB	CS	SB%	GDP	Avg	OBP	SLG
						BATTING										BASERUNNING				PERCENTAGES		
Tampa	132	4364	1171	192	46	108	1779	698	623	504	13	877	57	22	36	160	61	.72	83	.268	.349	.408
Clearwater	135	4504	1198	251	39	70	1737	632	562	462	23	725	53	54	46	114	67	.63	95	.266	.338	.386
Brevard County	139	4513	1148	205	34	48	1565	596	515	520	21	820	44	37	43	102	66	.61	119	.254	.334	.347
Vero Beach	135	4505	1182	197	49	82	1723	594	542	375	17	885	40	41	52	80	59	.58	89	.262	.321	.382
Sarasota	133	4371	1174	210	26	48	1580	582	527	395	30	820	54	73	49	99	64	.61	82	.269	.333	.361
St. Lucie	137	4453	1165	168	30	49	1540	578	505	473	26	892	53	64	29	135	94	.59	72	.262	.338	.346
Dunedin	133	4480	1184	223	36	77	1710	575	515	389	23	889	63	27	33	160	74	.68	97	.264	.330	.382
Ft. Myers	134	4376	1113	193	21	62	1534	551	483	516	17	802	37	23	45	186	82	.69	101	.254	.335	.351
West Palm Beach	132	4302	1090	213	32	60	1547	549	482	401	19	853	51	34	32	106	64	.62	70	.253	.322	.360
Charlotte	136	4504	1141	208	50	39	1566	546	480	437	16	767	41	52	43	98	90	.52	81	.253	.322	.348
Daytona	134	4357	1069	182	35	64	1513	543	482	459	13	826	55	53	32	77	67	.53	115	.245	.323	.347
St. Petersburg	139	4610	1101	199	26	68	1556	531	470	471	20	895	32	49	35	142	69	.67	105	.239	.312	.338
Osceola	135	4252	1035	208	27	37	1408	506	444	415	15	753	52	38	36	136	78	.64	103	.243	.316	.331
Lakeland	132	4190	994	183	39	48	1399	487	433	474	21	921	45	26	30	99	66	.60	104	.237	.319	.334
Total	943	61781	15765	2832	490	860	22157	7968	7063	6291	274	11725	677	593	541	1694	1001	.63	1316	.255	.328	.359

Florida State League Pitching - A

Team	G	GS	CG	GF	IP	BFP	H	R	ER	HR	SH	SF	HB	TBB	IBB	SO	WP	Bk	W	L	Pct.	ShO	Sv	ERA
		HOW MUCH THEY PITCHED					WHAT THEY GAVE UP												THE RESULTS					
Tampa	132	132	12	122	1128.2	4778	1080	511	409	61	30	42	40	401	18	922	51	11	80	52	.606	15	34	3.26
West Palm Beach	132	132	9	123	1132.1	4767	1023	514	417	50	39	35	41	451	8	965	99	25	71	60	.542	12	39	3.31
Brevard County	139	139	11	128	1205	5004	1040	516	429	52	50	44	48	406	10	883	55	14	78	61	.561	15	32	3.20
Lakeland	132	132	12	121	1121.1	4809	1087	531	433	56	45	38	58	456	10	794	70	13	63	68	.481	14	29	3.48
Clearwater	135	135	12	123	1185.1	4970	1115	537	443	71	39	32	38	414	35	767	63	18	72	62	.537	12	28	3.36
St. Lucie	137	137	25	112	1186.2	5003	1112	544	447	51	37	45	56	469	38	714	45	33	71	65	.522	13	40	3.39
St. Petersburg	139	139	4	135	1248	5272	1216	554	457	64	45	32	57	401	20	891	49	14	74	65	.532	10	48	3.30
Charlotte	136	136	5	131	1187.2	5076	1122	566	490	67	41	40	45	513	17	810	74	26	60	76	.441	5	28	3.71
Dunedin	133	133	8	125	1172.2	5030	1111	570	485	66	48	49	30	499	7	854	90	21	65	68	.489	7	32	3.72
Sarasota	133	133	13	120	1153	4935	1150	606	510	67	43	28	44	424	4	851	68	22	69	64	.519	11	37	3.98
Ft. Myers	134	134	10	124	1176	5201	1255	609	495	57	45	41	46	464	35	913	75	4	71	63	.530	6	40	3.79
Daytona	134	134	16	118	1166.1	5034	1172	609	519	58	38	36	57	406	18	822	79	13	61	73	.455	13	30	4.00
Vero Beach	135	135	6	129	1167.2	5017	1124	610	516	76	36	37	54	480	19	849	70	10	60	75	.444	10	25	3.98
Osceola	135	135	7	128	1130.2	5011	1158	691	551	64	57	42	63	507	35	690	73	23	46	89	.341	6	24	4.39
Total	943	943	148	795	16361.1	69907	15765	7968	6601	860	593	541	677	6291	274	11725	961	256	941	941	.500	149	466	3.63

Midwest League Batting - A

Team	G	AB	H	2B	3B	HR	TB	R	RBI	TBB	IBB	SO	HBP	SH	SF	SB	CS	SB%	GDP	Avg	OBP	SLG
Kane County	139	4575	1182	238	29	88	1742	705	626	541	11	909	69	50	52	66	42	.61	113	.258	.342	.381
Peoria	138	4605	1232	241	41	94	1837	697	619	468	25	968	83	74	36	105	87	.55	97	.268	.343	.399
Cedar Rapids	139	4630	1221	229	23	103	1805	689	600	496	23	947	64	53	32	189	88	.68	88	.264	.341	.390
Clinton	139	4643	1192	231	35	91	1766	689	610	503	19	1130	62	69	32	104	80	.57	81	.257	.335	.380
South Bend	139	4725	1234	207	36	66	1711	687	609	491	16	967	55	41	49	128	74	.63	77	.261	.335	.362
Springfield	140	4555	1167	201	27	73	1641	674	594	485	10	1015	82	53	55	196	99	.66	69	.256	.335	.360
Rockford	139	4563	1222	218	31	78	1736	669	576	423	23	837	9	37	42	173	87	.67	93	.268	.328	.380
Beloit	140	4440	1117	182	20	89	1606	669	582	603	23	1095	53	84	41	230	89	.72	70	.252	.345	.362
Burlington	137	4547	1106	202	14	140	1756	648	575	476	13	1169	49	32	38	62	41	.60	82	.243	.319	.386
Madison	139	4511	1175	239	32	70	1688	639	570	493	18	908	43	48	46	148	117	.56	79	.260	.336	.374
West Michigan	139	4508	1116	245	35	78	1665	637	558	596	26	1023	69	64	34	191	112	.63	77	.248	.342	.369
Appleton	139	4600	1217	211	50	74	1750	635	549	398	15	857	62	31	32	147	114	.56	75	.265	.329	.380
Quad City	138	4612	1193	226	31	85	1736	612	537	374	21	924	55	55	40	103	74	.58	91	.259	.319	.376
Ft. Wayne	139	4643	1144	215	24	89	1674	602	528	427	17	1002	54	25	40	106	75	.59	78	.246	.315	.361
Total	972	64157	16518	3085	428	1218	24113	9252	8133	6774	260	13751	809	716	569	1948	1179	.62	1170	.257	.333	.376

Midwest League Pitching - A

Team	G	GS	CG	GF	IP	BFP	H	R	ER	HR	SH	SF	HB	TBB	IBB	SO	WP	Bk	W	L	Pct.	ShO	Sv	ERA
Rockford	139	139	5	134	1201.2	5003	1067	494	421	55	39	33	52	431	22	1003	100	16	89	50	.640	17	44	3.15
West Michigan	139	139	3	136	1220	5214	1103	577	464	61	63	28	57	483	14	971	61	42	74	65	.532	8	36	3.42
Kane County	139	139	14	125	1203.1	5085	1138	591	491	78	39	36	94	324	17	955	91	8	71	68	.511	14	26	3.67
South Bend	139	139	20	119	1222.2	5237	1201	634	491	78	55	47	41	422	7	938	71	20	72	67	.518	8	30	3.61
Madison	139	139	5	134	1184.2	5138	1147	635	506	87	49	34	57	516	19	1037	75	25	66	73	.475	9	32	3.84
Appleton	139	139	18	121	1193.2	5169	1096	636	503	97	52	46	92	473	18	1025	86	24	75	64	.540	9	35	3.79
Cedar Rapids	139	139	16	123	1222	5337	1189	647	533	86	52	40	55	525	32	980	101	29	77	62	.554	11	35	3.93
Ft. Wayne	139	139	6	133	1207	5246	1223	647	531	82	56	35	51	494	10	1024	107	18	66	73	.475	10	31	3.96
Beloit	140	140	20	120	1196.1	5270	1176	669	556	98	50	34	76	518	24	991	111	18	76	64	.543	8	39	4.18
Peoria	138	138	19	119	1198.2	5244	1273	698	564	78	51	54	64	406	12	946	76	31	68	70	.493	5	32	4.23
Quad City	138	138	7	131	1195	5281	1207	702	577	81	55	36	82	537	16	1088	102	31	57	81	.413	5	25	4.35
Springfield	140	140	6	134	1197.1	5315	1111	723	588	111	54	38	59	616	42	1050	111	25	69	71	.493	9	40	4.42
Clinton	139	139	2	137	1195.1	5335	1260	766	635	108	65	53	62	556	13	902	134	26	57	82	.410	4	29	4.78
Burlington	137	137	10	127	1179.2	5269	1327	833	666	118	36	55	67	473	14	841	102	21	55	82	.401	5	25	5.08
Total	972	972	151	821	16817.1	73143	16518	9252	7526	1218	716	569	909	6774	260	13751	1328	334	972	972	.500	122	459	4.03

South Atlantic League Batting - A

Team	G	AB	H	2B	3B	HR	TB	R	RBI	TBB	IBB	SO	HBP	SH	SF	SB	CS	SB%	GDP	Avg	OBP	SLG
Hickory	140	4705	1278	206	44	82	1818	747	671	537	18	873	74	47	50	99	59	.63	107	.272	.352	.386
Columbus	138	4636	1178	213	51	111	1826	718	615	476	14	881	90	27	26	136	64	.68	85	.254	.334	.394
Hagerstown	136	4510	1136	201	51	121	1802	675	596	440	15	1080	42	25	33	107	68	.61	74	.252	.322	.400
Spartanburg	139	4629	1169	238	34	96	1763	659	586	466	15	1063	86	25	43	137	74	.65	80	.253	.329	.381
Greensboro	140	4525	1086	196	31	100	1644	638	564	586	13	1109	58	25	42	140	67	.68	108	.240	.332	.363
Savannah	137	4520	1118	181	31	83	1610	630	552	470	13	936	2	44	35	114	77	.60	94	.247	.316	.356
Fayetteville	137	4491	1083	206	40	77	1600	625	542	533	15	1056	72	37	26	191	89	.68	76	.241	.330	.356
Macon	137	4511	1180	245	38	86	1759	616	548	343	6	1048	79	67	36	210	83	.72	67	.262	.322	.390
Albany	137	4411	1142	235	35	50	1597	610	515	505	7	878	95	42	37	184	90	.67	83	.259	.345	.362
Charleston-sc	137	4457	1073	215	29	75	1571	567	485	480	4	1044	89	30	38	161	114	.59	69	.241	.324	.352
Charleston-wv	140	4578	1136	225	22	66	1603	565	500	423	12	899	46	33	38	148	76	.66	104	.248	.316	.350
Asheville	134	4350	1088	226	8	122	1696	546	496	373	14	1029	59	29	26	77	59	.57	88	.250	.316	.390
Augusta	137	4509	1083	192	33	58	1515	537	452	402	10	1069	60	29	29	230	104	.69	68	.240	.309	.336
Columbia	135	4358	1055	176	41	80	1553	534	454	405	16	1138	47	45	29	152	96	.61	53	.242	.311	.356
Total	962	63190	15805	2955	488	1207	23357	8667	7576	6439	172	14103	899	505	488	2086	1120	.65	1156	.250	.326	.370

South Atlantic League Pitching - A

Team	G	GS	CG	GF	IP	BFP	H	R	ER	HR	SH	SF	HB	TBB	IBB	SO	WP	Bk	W	L	Pct.	ShO	Sv	ERA
Savannah	137	137	10	127	1201.1	4928	1022	504	402	89	34	34	58	356	19	1044	65	12	82	55	.599	11	45	3.01
Columbus	138	138	6	132	1200	5030	1054	543	447	85	36	28	84	417	14	1158	67	16	87	51	.630	11	43	3.35
Macon	137	137	11	126	1181.2	5059	1061	546	410	75	36	34	64	437	17	1003	77	15	73	64	.533	16	28	3.12
Columbia	135	135	14	121	1152.2	4941	1081	603	471	95	42	30	93	413	11	998	102	16	59	76	.437	9	31	3.68
Greensboro	140	140	5	135	1211.1	5204	1179	604	494	77	32	30	53	468	10	1053	91	19	71	69	.507	10	34	3.67
Hickory	140	140	9	131	1228.2	5236	1163	605	481	110	40	31	58	385	3	1025	61	16	86	54	.614	12	39	3.52
Albany	137	137	10	127	1157.1	5034	1106	621	491	65	21	36	54	520	10	935	75	27	63	74	.460	10	35	3.82
Fayetteville	137	137	7	130	1185.2	5132	1058	623	516	87	43	32	92	556	12	947	130	16	62	75	.453	7	23	3.92
Hagerstown	136	136	7	129	1190.2	5124	1181	624	495	89	41	47	51	433	3	997	68	9	80	56	.588	4	53	3.74
Charleston-wv	140	140	8	132	1202.1	5269	1184	658	561	89	34	44	83	548	24	926	119	11	65	75	.464	9	38	4.20
Spartanburg	139	139	19	120	1202.1	5197	1192	659	532	95	40	31	63	472	9	957	99	19	67	72	.482	6	25	3.98
Charleston-sc	137	137	15	122	1180	5151	1157	676	548	108	27	37	99	411	9	1046	65	16	56	81	.409	6	23	4.18
Augusta	137	137	8	129	1183.1	5233	1169	694	523	53	40	33	71	468	12	1110	139	14	50	86	.368	7	21	3.98
Asheville	134	134	5	129	1139.1	5100	1198	707	591	90	39	41	76	555	19	904	93	21	60	73	.451	9	39	4.67
Total	962	962	134	828	16616.2	71638	15805	8667	6962	1207	505	488	999	6439	172	14103	1251	227	961	961	.500	127	477	3.77

Appalachian League Batting - R

Team	G	AB	H	2B	3B	HR	TB	R	RBI	TBB	IBB	SO	HBP	SH	SF	SB	CS	SB%	GDP	Avg	OBP	SLG
Princeton	66	2244	534	96	27	45	819	360	270	267	9	578	26	25	17	143	64	.69	26	.238	.324	.365
Elizabethton	66	2176	557	92	7	74	885	356	316	285	8	437	41	6	19	36	14	.72	60	.256	.350	.407
Johnson City	68	2168	485	94	14	33	706	349	262	301	8	477	36	30	23	96	51	.65	32	.224	.325	.326
Bluefield	68	2148	537	88	21	35	772	344	258	238	6	442	35	26	33	135	46	.75	33	.250	.330	.359
Martinsville	68	2179	497	88	8	31	694	311	240	281	10	591	40	18	14	104	45	.70	35	.228	.325	.318
Kingsport	66	2187	498	71	15	48	743	309	253	225	4	507	24	25	6	60	23	.72	33	.228	.306	.340
Danville	67	2220	535	114	7	29	750	304	231	253	9	549	40	21	14	107	65	.62	43	.241	.328	.338
Bristol	63	2027	466	64	11	17	603	279	226	278	11	475	28	26	13	113	47	.71	35	.230	.329	.297
Huntington	67	2093	484	95	13	20	665	260	203	257	4	459	40	23	27	112	67	.63	42	.231	.323	.318
Burlington	65	2103	471	85	13	33	681	243	202	237	6	588	44	18	17	98	54	.64	41	.224	.313	.324
Total	332	21545	5064	887	136	365	7318	3115	2461	2622	75	5103	354	218	183	1004	476	.68	380	.235	.325	.340

Appalachian League Pitching - R

Team	G	GS	CG	GF	IP	BFP	H	R	ER	HR	SH	SF	HB	TBB	IBB	SO	WP	Bk	W	L	Pct.	ShO	Sv	ERA
Bluefield	68	68	6	62	573.2	2352	471	235	184	40	15	19	25	184	5	503	64	10	39	29	.574	7	15	2.89
Kingsport	66	66	11	55	571	2404	479	235	190	31	15	13	34	209	0	467	55	13	36	30	.545	8	13	2.99
Johnson City	68	68	1	67	593	2533	550	285	210	51	23	13	21	213	12	530	37	7	42	26	.618	6	24	3.19
Elizabethton	66	66	4	62	557.2	2399	483	302	222	35	27	16	33	248	3	491	79	10	36	30	.545	5	17	3.58
Princeton	66	66	3	63	601.2	2597	540	307	212	24	30	21	45	229	17	506	64	22	41	25	.621	5	20	3.17
Bristol	63	63	0	63	535	2324	496	308	237	41	20	21	39	219	5	388	48	13	27	36	.429	5	11	3.99
Huntington	67	67	2	65	574.1	2503	500	320	229	29	27	15	34	275	2	490	73	34	28	39	.418	7	8	3.59
Danville	67	67	2	65	583	2623	461	333	239	30	25	27	54	394	15	634	76	13	28	39	.418	4	9	3.69
Martinsville	68	68	3	65	583.1	2591	574	385	290	58	15	19	24	283	7	518	85	13	32	36	.471	1	22	4.47
Burlington	65	65	4	61	566.1	2611	510	379	282	26	21	19	44	368	9	576	91	24	23	42	.354	3	15	4.48
Total	332	332	36	296	5739	24937	5064	3115	2295	365	218	183	354	2622	75	5103	672	159	332	332	.500	51	154	3.60

Arizona League Batting - R

Team	G	AB	H	2B	3B	HR	TB	R	RBI	TBB	IBB	SO	HBP	SH	SF	SB	CS	SB%	GDP	Avg	OBP	SLG
Brewers	56	1894	479	62	22	11	618	304	237	197	8	402	48	9	26	108	36	.75	26	.253	.334	.326
Athletics	56	1821	454	61	30	20	635	265	218	196	2	445	34	13	18	69	39	.64	34	.249	.331	.349
Padres	55	1842	452	56	28	11	597	264	190	165	2	568	46	3	15	90	36	.71	28	.245	.321	.324
Angels	55	1836	444	66	25	12	596	249	198	210	2	426	22	29	15	44	22	.67	39	.242	.325	.325
Cardinals	56	1900	476	79	21	16	645	247	203	156	5	474	25	6	15	41	27	.60	31	.251	.313	.339
Giants	55	1835	426	72	21	6	558	212	168	171	9	438	29	15	19	71	44	.62	35	.232	.305	.304
Mariners	56	1853	443	53	18	16	580	200	169	138	8	462	34	13	15	54	28	.66	33	.239	.301	.313
Rockies	55	1738	369	50	15	9	560	173	132	142	1	486	38	11	12	57	35	.62	35	.212	.284	.274
Total	222	14719	3543	499	180	101	4705	1914	1515	1375	37	3701	276	99	135	534	267	.67	261	.241	.315	.320

Arizona League Pitching - R

Team	G	GS	CG	GF	IP	BFP	H	R	ER	HR	SH	SF	HB	TBB	IBB	SO	WP	Bk	W	L	Pct.	ShO	Sv	ERA
Mariners	56	56	0	56	486	2029	396	219	156	7	14	21	48	165	3	464	58	7	21	35	.375	6	10	2.89
Giants	55	55	0	55	491	2099	405	219	160	10	17	22	30	205	8	451	55	7	29	26	.527	7	11	2.93
Cardinals	56	56	1	55	490	2058	448	229	175	11	10	17	34	141	0	478	59	10	34	22	.607	3	21	3.21
Athletics	56	56	1	55	483.1	2091	489	235	185	25	14	15	19	146	14	473	47	5	32	24	.571	8	10	3.44
Padres	55	55	1	54	471	2027	423	245	180	7	12	12	41	153	1	432	63	7	28	27	.509	3	18	3.44
Angels	55	55	8	47	481.1	2089	463	250	182	15	10	17	41	191	1	423	52	9	23	32	.418	3	11	3.40
Rockies	55	55	1	54	468	2050	434	253	182	11	8	14	33	191	8	492	62	13	23	32	.418	7	13	3.50
Brewers	56	56	2	54	497	2164	485	264	183	15	14	17	30	183	2	488	80	7	32	24	.571	2	15	3.31
Total	222	222	14	208	3867.2	16607	3543	1914	1403	101	99	135	276	1375	37	3701	476	65	222	222	.500	39	109	3.26

Gulf Coast League Batting - R

Team	G	AB	H	2B	3B	HR	TB	R	RBI	TBB	IBB	SO	HBP	SH	SF	SB	CS	SB%	GDP	Avg	OBP	SLG
Royals	59	2012	567	98	30	29	812	377	306	253	4	367	38	15	25	123	34	.78	25	.282	.369	.404
Astros	59	1961	563	101	23	9	737	341	270	196	8	347	33	36	22	129	53	.71	32	.287	.358	.376
Marlins	59	1937	477	77	14	14	624	325	251	240	3	408	30	10	24	72	29	.71	36	.246	.335	.322
Pirates	60	1978	497	87	27	23	707	298	246	197	4	433	48	5	17	64	36	.64	23	.251	.331	.357
Red Sox	60	2034	538	85	19	19	718	292	242	155	5	326	32	15	24	101	40	.72	36	.265	.323	.353
Mets	59	1946	481	71	23	20	658	287	235	201	0	430	22	14	22	33	29	.53	28	.247	.321	.338
Expos	59	1986	487	101	17	23	691	266	208	196	5	375	13	5	18	46	25	.65	36	.245	.315	.348
Yankees	59	1888	460	65	18	13	600	255	220	247	3	454	25	16	11	47	29	.62	40	.244	.337	.318
Cubs	60	1867	409	69	17	6	530	247	190	184	0	494	31	29	8	64	38	.63	25	.219	.299	.284
Rangers	60	1866	416	77	19	24	603	243	189	214	6	433	26	5	18	106	46	.70	24	.223	.309	.323
Blue Jays	60	1874	411	69	24	16	576	243	187	192	3	475	23	20	15	132	38	.78	23	.219	.298	.307
Twins	60	1992	476	76	13	14	620	238	204	192	3	419	26	8	16	54	27	.67	36	.239	.312	.311
White Sox	60	1887	422	76	22	13	581	232	182	220	0	408	28	10	11	70	41	.63	35	.224	.312	.308
Orioles	59	1915	433	66	14	10	557	222	164	193	2	377	28	8	12	61	28	.69	39	.226	.304	.291
Braves	59	1831	330	66	4	16	452	163	124	184	3	470	30	5	5	59	31	.66	32	.180	.265	.247
Total	446	28974	6967	1184	284	249	9466	4029	3218	3064	49	6216	433	201	248	1161	524	.69	470	.240	.320	.327

Gulf Coast League Pitching - R

Team	G	GS	CG	GF	IP	BFP	H	R	ER	HR	SH	SF	HB	TBB	IBB	SO	WP	Bk	W	L	Pct.	ShO	Sv	ERA
Royals	59	59	1	58	521.1	2157	427	197	140	12	8	12	27	175	3	413	36	6	47	12	.797	11	14	2.42
Marlins	59	59	3	56	512	2145	423	213	157	19	9	11	19	201	6	456	64	5	38	21	.644	3	10	2.76
Astros	59	59	2	57	510.2	2107	396	216	153	10	23	11	25	201	1	464	29	21	41	18	.695	7	11	2.70
Expos	59	59	3	56	518.2	2151	385	227	167	15	13	13	29	203	2	467	60	24	35	24	.593	7	20	2.90
Mets	59	59	6	53	508	2133	432	233	161	20	7	12	16	174	1	411	48	11	32	27	.542	8	13	2.85
White Sox	60	60	2	58	508.1	2161	465	240	182	20	14	13	36	182	14	399	37	21	20	40	.333	1	12	3.22
Rangers	60	60	3	57	510.2	2198	483	263	191	22	8	15	37	173	3	357	28	23	32	28	.533	7	18	3.37
Yankees	59	59	2	57	500	2136	460	265	173	13	34	12	22	172	0	473	40	13	26	32	.448	7	8	3.11
Red Sox	60	60	0	60	526	2287	489	269	209	12	8	19	35	209	0	396	62	19	40	20	.667	4	18	3.58
Blue Jays	60	60	1	59	501	2179	487	294	219	10	23	16	31	227	4	436	48	14	26	34	.433	2	11	3.93
Twins	60	60	2	58	513	2237	481	302	208	14	6	16	36	248	1	416	77	25	22	38	.367	3	7	3.65
Pirates	60	60	2	58	509	2246	493	308	220	29	12	20	27	221	3	348	45	12	25	35	.417	2	8	3.89
Cubs	60	60	1	59	498	2257	500	311	232	11	21	17	34	219	9	397	37	16	25	34	.424	5	14	4.19
Orioles	59	59	2	57	504.1	2245	511	323	263	23	10	28	28	216	0	434	62	18	23	36	.390	3	10	4.69
Braves	59	59	2	57	498.1	2290	535	368	292	19	5	33	31	243	2	349	67	16	13	46	.220	3	5	5.27
Total	446	446	32	414	7639.1	32929	6967	4029	2967	249	201	248	433	3064	49	6216	740	244	445	445	.500	73	179	3.50

Northwest League Batting - R

Team	G	AB	H	2B	3B	HR	TB	R	RBI	TBB	IBB	SO	HBP	SH	SF	SB	CS	SB%	GDP	Avg	OBP	SLG
Yakima	76	2654	715	134	31	34	1013	446	366	438	24	654	41	25	21	162	52	.76	49	.269	.379	.382
Boise	76	2574	671	124	18	30	921	437	371	385	13	555	35	40	41	82	34	.71	50	.261	.359	.358
Southern Oregon	76	2574	686	136	16	50	1004	425	376	301	14	695	69	32	31	79	40	.66	56	.267	.355	.390
Everett	76	2600	653	126	20	47	960	370	323	306	11	719	39	13	19	91	29	.76	63	.251	.337	.369
Bellingham	76	2551	633	106	5	30	839	341	289	256	12	578	62	30	25	105	52	.67	44	.248	.329	.329
Bend	76	2562	622	118	14	53	927	335	300	278	14	642	53	16	19	95	40	.70	52	.243	.327	.362
Eugene	76	2627	636	116	17	39	903	329	289	261	20	699	49	17	20	67	42	.61	36	.242	.320	.344
Spokane	76	2579	599	102	11	22	789	318	256	279	9	607	38	22	20	110	46	.71	52	.232	.314	.306
Total	304	20721	5215	962	132	305	7356	3001	2570	2504	117	5149	386	195	196	791	335	.70	402	.252	.340	.355

Northwest League Pitching - R

Team	G	GS	CG	GF	IP	BFP	H	R	ER	HR	SH	SF	HB	TBB	IBB	SO	WP	Bk	W	L	Pct.	ShO	Sv	ERA
Bellingham	76	76	5	71	673.1	2921	593	318	251	32	21	21	37	320	17	673	96	20	42	34	.553	4	20	3.35
Yakima	76	76	0	76	696.1	2987	586	321	249	30	22	21	48	328	16	641	64	20	49	27	.645	7	25	3.22
Boise	76	76	0	76	679.1	2936	655	343	275	36	25	19	50	248	19	647	41	13	44	32	.579	7	24	3.64
Everett	76	76	0	76	670.2	2999	664	377	300	50	18	21	46	325	27	667	57	10	37	39	.487	5	15	4.03
Eugene	76	76	0	76	682.2	3003	620	378	269	43	27	31	46	307	3	680	47	13	35	41	.461	3	20	3.55
Spokane	76	76	3	73	676.2	3035	691	385	309	37	24	24	59	340	9	662	64	14	30	46	.395	6	12	4.11
Bend	76	76	0	76	676	3060	736	438	331	50	26	23	51	274	6	584	47	20	29	47	.382	2	14	4.41
Southern Oregon	76	76	0	76	673	3074	670	441	323	27	32	36	49	362	20	595	86	13	38	38	.500	3	25	4.32
Total	304	304	8	296	5428	24015	5215	3001	2307	305	195	196	386	2504	117	5149	502	123	304	304	.500	37	155	3.83

New York-Penn League Batting - R

Team	G	AB	H	2B	3B	HR	TB	R	RBI	TBB	IBB	SO	HBP	SH	SF	SB	CS	SB%	GDP	Avg	OBP	SLG
Watertown	74	2504	680	112	25	56	1010	446	386	343	7	483	45	17	31	77	31	.71	44	.272	.365	.403
Vermont	75	2564	686	106	29	35	955	416	348	275	2	508	48	26	28	83	36	.70	49	.268	.346	.372
Auburn	76	2550	724	124	35	33	1017	411	350	219	3	422	31	25	27	92	32	.74	60	.284	.345	.399
New Jersey	75	2447	611	90	19	11	772	353	292	329	7	439	34	21	32	80	40	.67	62	.250	.343	.315
Pittsfield	75	2578	663	101	26	15	861	349	286	211	12	529	42	23	24	92	42	.69	27	.257	.321	.334
Batavia	74	2394	599	100	30	19	816	340	276	229	10	439	45	24	19	99	40	.71	42	.250	.325	.341
Elmira	73	2388	600	120	20	33	859	337	280	236	4	525	38	9	17	33	32	.51	44	.251	.326	.360
Jamestown	74	2444	621	130	30	27	892	334	283	243	11	509	34	27	24	71	54	.57	41	.254	.327	.365
St. Catharines	74	2386	588	98	15	36	824	321	284	285	5	487	20	30	12	78	45	.63	30	.246	.330	.345
Utica	72	2339	567	107	15	22	770	311	257	235	10	514	32	25	26	66	32	.67	36	.242	.317	.329
Hudson Valley	74	2430	570	106	16	24	780	311	258	263	6	492	43	10	24	106	53	.67	47	.235	.317	.321
Williamsport	75	2395	580	102	22	25	801	308	258	259	7	442	48	38	21	81	58	.58	45	.242	.326	.334
Oneonta	75	2383	580	100	26	19	789	294	254	249	6	594	36	16	17	55	39	.59	53	.243	.322	.331
Welland	74	2427	568	89	15	14	729	254	215	197	4	518	43	26	13	101	53	.66	43	.234	.301	.300
Total	520	34229	8637	1485	323	369	11875	4785	4027	3573	94	6901	539	317	315	1114	587	.65	623	.252	.330	.347

New York-Penn League Pitching - R

Team	G	GS	CG	GF	IP	BFP	H	R	ER	HR	SH	SF	HB	TBB	IBB	SO	WP	Bk	W	L	Pct.	ShO	Sv	ERA
Utica	72	72	5	67	612	2651	595	223	192	14	21	19	39	249	6	455	44	14	35	37	.486	9	17	3.28
Batavia	74	74	3	71	621.2	2683	595	302	229	20	27	12	36	230	6	518	54	11	40	34	.541	3	18	3.32
Watertown	74	74	5	69	642.1	2767	599	310	238	28	19	13	39	251	13	498	40	17	48	26	.649	5	21	3.33
Jamestown	74	74	3	71	650	2802	593	322	244	26	24	17	35	263	5	476	49	18	42	32	.568	7	16	3.38
New Jersey	75	75	2	73	652.2	2851	631	333	274	23	33	15	32	273	3	579	71	8	43	32	.573	5	24	3.78
Hudson Valley	74	74	6	68	646.2	2777	602	338	253	16	23	33	41	243	6	527	47	27	37	37	.500	3	21	3.52
Welland	74	74	4	70	648	2769	600	338	266	34	26	20	49	233	3	442	47	14	30	44	.405	3	21	3.69
Auburn	76	76	8	68	641.2	2820	629	339	266	42	21	26	45	238	7	528	70	8	45	31	.592	4	19	3.73
Oneonta	75	75	5	70	623.2	2708	577	340	254	23	24	17	28	247	10	555	50	16	30	45	.400	4	14	3.67
St. Catharines	74	74	4	70	633	2706	590	341	291	35	15	25	35	229	1	492	59	12	35	39	.473	10	17	4.14
Pittsfield	75	75	10	65	660	2881	662	349	273	22	19	26	32	260	9	437	54	5	37	38	.493	3	18	3.72
Elmira	73	73	6	67	613.2	2761	636	349	284	28	32	32	35	274	13	457	69	8	30	43	.411	3	11	4.17
Vermont	75	75	6	67	656.1	2901	651	369	256	21	17	29	44	293	7	476	64	12	42	33	.560	3	19	3.51
Williamsport	75	75	6	69	635.2	2912	718	469	376	37	16	31	49	290	5	461	62	26	26	49	.347	5	12	5.32
Total	520	520	73	447	8937.1	38989	8637	4785	3727	369	317	315	539	3573	94	6901	780	196	520	520	.500	67	248	3.75

Pioneer League Batting - R

Team	G	AB	H	2B	3B	HR	TB	R	RBI	TBB	IBB	SO	HBP	SH	SF	SB	CS	SB%	GDP	Avg	OBP	SLG
Ogden	72	2524	750	156	26	49	1105	528	458	306	12	564	57	21	36	97	55	.64	31	.297	.381	.438
Billings	72	2521	754	121	30	50	1085	492	413	293	7	474	38	12	34	95	47	.67	47	.299	.376	.430
Helena	72	2476	711	119	21	42	998	477	392	308	15	472	40	31	21	138	64	.68	31	.287	.372	.403
Great Falls	72	2537	724	142	35	28	1020	469	389	303	8	418	45	28	32	118	59	.67	39	.285	.368	.402
Butte	72	2522	759	110	26	30	1011	464	392	328	12	458	36	24	21	108	52	.68	52	.301	.386	.401
Idaho Falls	72	2506	686	97	32	28	931	394	340	229	8	464	35	10	21	120	46	.72	45	.274	.340	.372
Lethbridge	72	2388	626	100	22	35	875	392	312	295	7	473	54	17	17	126	69	.65	51	.262	.354	.366
Medicine Hat	72	2478	640	108	18	42	910	365	330	225	9	658	46	19	20	69	31	.69	42	.258	.329	.367
Total	288	19952	5650	953	210	304	7935	3581	3026	2287	78	3981	351	162	202	871	423	.67	338	.283	.364	.398

Pioneer League Pitching - R

Team	G	GS	CG	GF	IP	BFP	H	R	ER	HR	SH	SF	HB	TBB	IBB	SO	WP	Bk	W	L	Pct.	ShO	Sv	ERA
Billings	72	72	8	64	631.2	2706	596	328	253	21	22	15	35	251	13	503	46	12	50	22	.694	4	20	3.60
Helena	72	72	2	70	630.1	2850	623	405	316	44	29	21	53	338	12	526	89	22	44	28	.611	3	18	4.51
Ogden	72	72	9	63	631.1	2833	772	421	329	35	17	26	40	187	7	494	46	18	41	31	.569	3	13	4.69
Medicine Hat	72	72	0	72	639.1	2902	687	423	302	31	26	19	39	337	6	525	76	18	36	36	.500	2	27	4.25
Great Falls	72	72	0	72	639.2	2918	695	438	335	34	13	29	48	293	6	557	88	17	34	38	.472	2	15	4.71
Idaho Falls	72	72	2	70	625.1	2895	751	475	366	48	22	22	42	286	9	461	81	5	30	42	.417	2	16	5.27
Lethbridge	72	72	1	71	622.1	2920	705	499	391	28	19	36	48	319	11	471	100	23	29	43	.403	2	19	5.65
Butte	72	72	12	60	618	2943	821	592	492	63	14	34	46	276	14	444	73	18	24	48	.333	1	1	7.17
Total	288	288	34	254	5038	22967	5650	3581	2784	304	162	202	351	2287	78	3981	599	133	288	288	.500	19	129	4.97

Leader Boards

Brian Hunter. Billy Ashley. Joe Vitiello. Marc Newfield. Bill Pulsipher. If you're interested in minor league prospects, you've probably heard these names by now. All five players were ranked among the top prospects in baseball in 1994, and all of them appear at the top of at least one leader board on the pages that follow. Of, course, you'll also see names like Russ Morman and Mike Simms—veteran minor leaguers whose days as top prospects have long since passed. But even those fellows shouldn't be completely dismissed. Remember what a "veteran minor leaguer" named Geronimo Berroa did when given a chance in in 1994?

Players who split time between AAA and AA have combined numbers. The Batting Boards are for players with a minimum of 365 total plate appearances. The Pitching Boards are for pitchers who threw at least 109 innings.

Team Abbreviations

ABQ - Albuquerque	IND - Indianapolis	PAW - Pawtucket
ALB - Albany	IWA - Iowa	PHX - Phoenix
ARK - Arkansas	JCK - Jackson	POR - Portland (PCL)
BIR - Birmingham	JAX - Jacksonville	PRT - Portland (EAST)
BNG - Binghamton	KNX - Knoxville	REA - Reading
BOW - Bowie	LON - London	RMD - Richmond
BUF - Buffalo	LOU - Louisville	ROC - Rochester
CAN - Canton-Akron	LVG - Las Vegas	SAN - San Antonio
CAR - Carolina	MDL - Midland	SHR - Shreveport
CGY - Calgary	MEM - Memphis	SLK - Salt Lake
CHR - Charlotte	NBR - New Britain	SWB - Scranton-WB
CNG - Chattanooga	NHV - New Haven	SYR - Syracuse
COL - Columbus	NO - New Orleans	TAC - Tacoma
CSP - Colorado Springs	NOR - Norfolk	TCN - Tucson
EDM - Edmonton	NSH - Nashville (SOU)	TOL - Toledo
ELP - El Paso	NVL - Nashville (AMAS)	TRE - Trenton
GRV - Greenville	OKC - Oklahoma City	TUL - Tulsa
HRB - Harrisburg	OMA - Omaha	VAN - Vancouver
HVL - Huntsville	ORL - Orlando	WCH - Wichita
	OTT - Ottawa	

League Abbreviations

AMAS - American Association	PCL - Pacific Coast League
EAST - Eastern League	SOU - Southern League
INT - International League	TEX - Texas League

Triple-A/Double-A Batting Leaders

Batting Average

Player	Team	League	
Hunter, Brian	TCN	PCL	.372
Cordova, Martin	SLK	PCL	.358
Tatum, Jimmy	CSP	PCL	.351
Bragg, Darren	CGY	PCL	.350
Morman, Russ	EDM	PCL	.350
Newfield, Marc	CGY	PCL	.349
Ashley, Billy	ABQ	PCL	.345
Vitiello, Joe	OMA	AMAS	.344
Green, Shawn	SYR	INT	.344
McIntosh, Tim	SLK	PCL	.338
Coomer, Ron	ABQ	PCL	.338
Pye, Eddie	ABQ	PCL	.335
Faneyte, Rikkert	PHX	PCL	.334
Hosey, Dwayne	OMA	AMAS	.333
Obando, Sherman	ROC	INT	.330

On-Base Percentage

Player	Team	League	
Vitiello, Joe	OMA	AMAS	.440
Carter, Jeff	SLK	PCL	.438
Hunter, Brian	TCN	PCL	.432
Bragg, Darren	CGY	PCL	.430
Ashley, Billy	ABQ	PCL	.428
Cordova, Martin	SLK	PCL	.426
Hosey, Dwayne	OMA	AMAS	.424
Willard, Jerry	CGY	PCL	.423
Pritchett, Chris	MDL	TEX	.421
Tedder, Scott	ORL	SOU	.421
Basse, Mike	ELP	TEX	.421
Pye, Eddie	ABQ	PCL	.419
Wilstead, Randy	HRB	EAST	.414
Several tied at			.413

Slugging Percentage

Player	Team	League	
Ashley, Billy	ABQ	PCL	.701
Phillips, J.R.	PHX	PCL	.631
Hosey, Dwayne	OMA	AMAS	.628
Obando, Sherman	ROC	INT	.603
Tatum, Jimmy	CSP	PCL	.597
Newfield, Marc	CGY	PCL	.593
Cordova, Martin	SLK	PCL	.592
Manto, Jeff	ROC	INT	.586
Young, Ernie	HVL	SOU	.582
Maas, Kevin	IND	AMAS	.580
Morman, Russ	EDM	PCL	.574
Prince, Tom	ABQ	PCL	.573
Brito, Bernardo	SLK	PCL	.572
Simms, Mike	TCN	PCL	.568
Nieves, Melvin	LVG	PCL	.564

Home Runs

Player	Team	League	
Ashley, Billy	ABQ	PCL	37
Raven, Luis	VAN	PCL	31
Manto, Jeff	ROC	INT	31
Denson, Drew	NVL	AMAS	30
Brito, Bernardo	SLK	PCL	29
Talanoa, Scott	ELP	TEX	28
Johnson, Charles	PRT	EAST	28
Phillips, J.R.	PHX	PCL	27
Davis, Glenn	OMA	AMAS	27
Hosey, Dwayne	OMA	AMAS	27
Seefried, Tate	ALB	EAST	27
Busch, Mike	ABQ	PCL	27
Maas, Kevin	IND	AMAS	26
Several tied at			25

Runs Batted In

Player	Team	League	
Coomer, Ron	ABQ	PCL	123
Brito, Bernardo	SLK	PCL	122
Raven, Luis	VAN	PCL	116
Ashley, Billy	ABQ	PCL	105
Denson, Drew	NVL	AMAS	103
Unroe, Tim	ELP	TEX	103
Anderson, Garret	VAN	PCL	102
Manto, Jeff	ROC	INT	100
Clark, Tony	TOL	INT	99
Davis, Glenn	OMA	AMAS	97
Tatum, Jimmy	CSP	PCL	97
McIntosh, Tim	SLK	PCL	96
Stahoviak, Scott	SLK	PCL	94
Simms, Mike	TCN	PCL	93
Several tied at			92

Stolen Bases

Player	Team	League	
Goodwin, Curtis	BOW	EAST	59
Moore, Kerwin	HVL	SOU	54
Goodwin, Tom	OMA	AMAS	50
Hunter, Brian	TCN	PCL	49
Penn, Shannon	TOL	INT	45
Holifield, Rick	REA	EAST	44
Barker, Tim	NO	AMAS	41
Womack, Tony	BUF	AMAS	41
Veras, Quilvio	NOR	INT	40
Massarelli, John	EDM	PCL	39
Owens, Eric	CNG	SOU	38
Jackson, Damian	CAN	EAST	37
McCracken, Quinton	NHV	EAST	36
Noland, J.D.	CSP	PCL	35
Several tied at			34

Triple-A/Double-A Batting Leaders

Catchers Batting Average

Player	Team	League	
Tatum, Jimmy	**CSP**	**PCL**	.351
McIntosh, Tim	SLK	PCL	.338
Tucker, Eddie	TCN	PCL	.321
Lyons, Barry	IND	AMAS	.309
Laker, Tim	OTT	INT	.309
Merullo, Matt	CHR	INT	.300
Lampkin, Tom	PHX	PCL	.300
Willard, Jerry	CGY	PCL	.288
Hubbard, Mike	ORL	SOU	.286
Levis, Jesse	CHR	INT	.285
Prince, Tom	ABQ	PCL	.285
McGinnis, Russ	OMA	AMAS	.282
Borrelli, Dean	TAC	PCL	.279
Lutz, Brent	KNX	SOU	.272
Johnson, Charles	PRT	EAST	.264

First Basemen Batting Average

Player	Team	League	
Morman, Russ	**EDM**	**PCL**	.350
Vitiello, Joe	OMA	AMAS	.344
Perry, Herb	CHR	INT	.327
Hansen, Terrel	CGY	PCL	.320
Ball, Jeff	JCK	TEX	.316
Bowie, Jim	TAC	PCL	.314
Pritchett, Chris	MDL	TEX	.309
Lopez, Luis	RMD	INT	.305
Raven, Luis	VAN	PCL	.304
Garcia, Omar	NOR	INT	.302
Belk, Tim	CNG	SOU	.301
Phillips, J.R.	PHX	PCL	.300
Santana, Ruben	JAX	SOU	.295
Kirkpatrick, Jay	ABQ	PCL	.295
Wilstead, Randy	HRB	EAST	.294

Second Basemen Batting Average

Player	Team	League	
Pye, Eddie	**ABQ**	**PCL**	.335
Hajek, Dave	TCN	PCL	.324
Carter, Jeff	SLK	PCL	.324
Raabe, Brian	SLK	PCL	.321
Stynes, Chris	KNX	SOU	.317
Simons, Mitch	NSH	SOU	.317
Vargas, Hector	BOW	EAST	.313
Hecht, Steve	PHX	PCL	.311
Higgins, Kevin	LVG	PCL	.309
Garrison, Webster	CSP	PCL	.302
Graffanino, Anthony	GRV	SOU	.300
Durham, Ray	NVL	AMAS	.296
Rodriguez, Steve	PAW	INT	.293
Hall, Billy	LVG	PCL	.292
Johnson, Erik	PHX	PCL	.292

Third Basemen Batting Average

Player	Team	League	
Coomer, Ron	**ABQ**	**PCL**	.338
Stahoviak, Scott	SLK	PCL	.318
Byington, John	NO	AMAS	.310
Unroe, Tim	ELP	TEX	.310
Capra, Nick	EDM	PCL	.304
Manto, Jeff	ROC	INT	.297
Chimelis, Joel	SHR	TEX	.295
Bell, David	CHR	INT	.293
Jorgensen, Terry	PRT	EAST	.289
Worthington, Craig	IWA	AMAS	.288
Quinones, Luis	JAX	SOU	.287
Scott, Gary	PHX	PCL	.286
Greene, Willie	IND	AMAS	.285
Sveum, Dale	CGY	PCL	.282
Jackson, Chuck	OKC	AMAS	.278

Shortstops Batting Average

Player	Team	League	
Grudzielane, Mark	**HRB**	**EAST**	.322
Alfonzo, Edgar	BOW	EAST	.309
Holbert, Ray	LVG	PCL	.300
Alfonzo, Edgar	BNG	EAST	.293
Castro, Juan	SAN	TEX	.288
Bates, Jason	CSP	PCL	.286
Gonzalez, Alex	SYR	INT	.284
Montoyo, Charlie	SWB	INT	.282
Loretta, Mark	NO	AMAS	.282
Mordecai, Mike	RMD	INT	.280
Faries, Paul	PHX	PCL	.280
Hocking, Dennis	SLK	PCL	.279
Several tied at			.274

Outfielders Batting Average

Player	Team	League	
Hunter, Brian	**TCN**	**PCL**	.372
Cordova, Martin	SLK	PCL	.358
Bragg, Darren	CGY	PCL	.350
Newfield, Marc	CGY	PCL	.349
Ashley, Billy	ABQ	PCL	.345
Green, Shawn	SYR	INT	.344
Faneyte, Rikkert	PHX	PCL	.334
Hosey, Dwayne	OMA	AMAS	.333
Obando, Sherman	ROC	INT	.330
Young, Ernie	HVL	SOU	.329
Palmeiro, Orlando	VAN	PCL	.328
Lennon, Patrick	NBR	EAST	.326
Perez, Danny	ELP	TEX	.325
Beamon, Cliff	CAR	SOU	.323
Several tied at			.321

Triple-A/Double-A Batting Leaders

Hits

Player	Team	League	
Hunter, Brian	TCN	**PCL**	191
Coomer, Ron	ABQ	PCL	181
Bragg, Darren	CGY	PCL	175
Stynes, Chris	KNX	SOU	173
Goodwin, Curtis	BOW	EAST	171
Bullett, Scott	IWA	AMAS	163
Battle, Allen	LOU	AMAS	163
Anderson, Garret	VAN	PCL	162
Lydy, Scott	TAC	PCL	160
Lopez, Luis	RMD	INT	159
Raven, Luis	VAN	PCL	158
McIntosh, Timothy	SLK	PCL	157
Byington, John	NO	AMAS	157
Hajek, David	TCN	PCL	157
Grudzielane, Mark	HRB	EAST	157

Doubles

Player	Team	League	
Newfield, Marc	CGY	**PCL**	44
Battle, Allen	LOU	**AMAS**	44
Chimelis, Joel	SHR	TEX	43
Tatum, Jimmy	CSP	PCL	43
Anderson, Garret	VAN	PCL	42
Rohrmeier, Dan	CNG	SOU	41
Stahoviak, Scott	SLK	PCL	41
Kirkpatrick, Jay	ABQ	PCL	41
Simms, Mike	TCN	PCL	39
Aude, Rich	BUF	AMAS	38
Tucker, Eddie	TCN	PCL	38
Several tied at			37

Triples

Player	Team	League	
Perez, Danny	ELP	**TEX**	17
Durham, Ray	NVL	AMAS	12
Harris, Mike	ELP	TEX	12
Holifield, Rick	REA	EAST	12
Thurman, Gary	NVL	AMAS	12
Bowers, Brent	KNX	SOU	11
Massarelli, John	EDM	PCL	10
Hecht, Steve	PHX	PCL	10
Several tied at			9

Extra Base Hits

Player	Team	League	
Simms, Mike	TCN	**PCL**	69
Malave, Jose	NBR	EAST	68
Newfield, Marc	CGY	PCL	65
Tatum, Jimmy	CSP	PCL	65
Manto, Jeff	ROC	INT	64
Denson, Drew	NVL	AMAS	63
Obando, Sherman	ROC	INT	63
Coomer, Ron	ABQ	PCL	62
Raven, Luis	VAN	PCL	61
Durham, Ray	NVL	AMAS	61
Jennings, Doug	IND	AMAS	61
Several tied at			60

Plate Appearances per Strikeout

Player	Team	League	
Raabe, Brian	SLK	**PCL**	48.45
Hajek, Dave	TCN	PCL	22.83
Higgins, Kevin	LVG	PCL	22.55
Byington, John	NO	AMAS	19.17
Ramos, Ken	TCN	PCL	17.59
Capra, Nick	EDM	PCL	17.36
Stynes, Chris	KNX	SOU	16.22
Lopez, Luis	RMD	INT	13.12
Brooks, Jerry	ABQ	PCL	12.62
Bowie, Jim	TAC	PCL	12.37
Fleming, Carlton	ALB	EAST	12.08
Otero, Ricky	BNG	EAST	12.08
Ledesma, Aaron	NOR	INT	11.71
Twardoski, Mike	PAW	INT	11.68
Simons, Mitch	NSH	SOU	11.68

Switch-Hitters Batting Average

Player	Team	League	
Hosey, Dwayne	OMA	**AMAS**	**.333**
Carter, Jeff	SLK	PCL	.324
Cedeno, Roger	ABQ	PCL	.321
Nieves, Mel	LVG	PCL	.308
Barry, Jeff	BNG	EAST	.304
Durham, Ray	NVL	AMAS	.296
Otero, Ricky	BNG	EAST	.294
Hall, Billy	LVG	PCL	.292
Quinones, Luis	JAX	SOU	.287
Tavarez, Jesus	PRT	EAST	.286
Bates, Jason	CSP	PCL	.286
Penn, Shannon	TOL	INT	.284
Candaele, Casey	IND	AMAS	.282
Sveum, Dale	CGY	PCL	.282
Hocking, Dennis	SLK	PCL	.279

Triple-A/Double-A Pitching Leaders

Earned Run Average

Player	Team	League	
Acevedo, Juan	**NHV**	**EAST**	2.37
Beatty, Blaine	CNG	SOU	2.38
Woodall, Brad	RMD	INT	2.42
Grott, Matt	IND	AMAS	2.55
Bolton, Rodney	NVL	AMAS	2.56
Wilson, Gary	CAR	SOU	2.56
Barcelo, Marc	NSH	SOU	2.65
Radke, Brad	NSH	SOU	2.66
Ruffcorn, Scott	NVL	AMAS	2.72
Johns, Doug	TAC	PCL	2.72
Simmons, Scott	ARK	TEX	2.72
Birkbeck, Mike	RMD	INT	2.73
Keyser, Brian	NVL	AMAS	2.73
Perez, Carlos	OTT	INT	2.77
Several tied at			2.83

Wins

Player	Team	League	
Acevedo, Juan	**NHV**	**EAST**	17
Ratekin, Mark	VAN	PCL	15
Ruffcorn, Scott	NVL	AMAS	15
Tavarez, Julian	CHR	INT	15
Roberson, Sid	ELP	TEX	15
Woodall, Brad	RMD	INT	15
Beltran, Rigoberto	LOU	AMAS	15
Frascatore, John	LOU	AMAS	15
Several tied at			14

Saves

Player	Team	League	
Clontz, Brad	**RMD**	**INT**	38
Reyes, Alberto	HRB	EAST	35
Jones, Stacy	SHR	TEX	34
St.Claire, Randy	SYR	INT	33
Holman, Shawn	OTT	INT	31
Huisman, Rick	JCK	TEX	31
Phoenix, Steve	HVL	SOU	29
Smith, Willie	LOU	AMAS	29
Clark, Terry	RMD	INT	26
Bottalico, Ricky	REA	EAST	25
Johnson, Dane	NVL	AMAS	24
Croghan, Andy	COL	INT	24
Osuna, Al	ABQ	PCL	23
Dougherty, Jim	TCN	PCL	21
Thomas, Mike	ELP	TEX	20

Games Pitched

Player	Team	League	
St.Claire, Randy	**SYR**	**INT**	65
Ward, Anthony	SYR	INT	64
Lancaster, Les	SYR	INT	64
Christopher, Mike	TOL	INT	63
Clontz, Brad	RMD	INT	63
McFarlin, Terric	LVG	PCL	63
McCready, James	BNG	EAST	63
Florence, Don	PAW	INT	61
Clark, Terry	RMD	INT	61
Pierce, Jeff	PAW	INT	61
Taylor, Bob	PHX	PCL	61
Rogers, Bryan	BNG	EAST	61
Christianse, Jason	BUF	AMAS	61
Phillips, Tony	CGY	PCL	60
Reyes, Alberto	HRB	EAST	60

Complete Games

Player	Team	League	
Rasmussen, Dennis	**OMA**	**AMAS**	10
Rodriguez, Frank	PAW	INT	8
Roberson, Sid	ELP	TEX	8
Wilson, Gary	CAR	SOU	7
Beatty, Blaine	CNG	SOU	6
Ogea, Chad	CHR	INT	6
Miller, Trever	TRE	EAST	6
Gutierrez, Jim	JAX	SOU	6
Wendell, Turk	IWA	AMAS	6
Minchey, Nate	PAW	INT	6
Hillman, Eric	NOR	INT	6
Frascatore, John	LOU	AMAS	6
Several tied at			5

Shutouts

Player	Team	League	
Beatty, Blaine	**CNG**	**SOU**	4
Ruffcorn, Scott	NVL	AMAS	3
Wendell, Turk	IWA	AMAS	3
Woodall, Brad	RMD	INT	3
Several tied at			2

Triple-A/Double-A Pitching Leaders

Strikeouts

Player	Team	League	
Haynes, Jimmy	**BOW**	**EAST**	**191**
Dishman, Glenn	LVG	PCL	177
Pulsipher, Bill	BNG	EAST	171
Gallaher, Kevin	TCN	PCL	170
Beatty, Blaine	CNG	SOU	162
Acevedo, Juan	NHV	EAST	161
Rodriguez, Frank	PAW	INT	160
Baldwin, James	NVL	AMAS	156
Bennett, Joel	PAW	INT	154
Barcelo, Marc	NSH	SOU	153
Mlicki, Dave	CHR	INT	152
Perez, Carlos	OTT	INT	151
Barber, Brian	LOU	AMAS	149
Several tied at			145

Strikeouts per 9 IP — Starters

Player	Team	League	
Barber, Brian	**LOU**	**AMAS**	**11.05**
Gallaher, Kevin	TCN	PCL	9.58
Haynes, Jimmy	BOW	EAST	9.19
Bennett, Joel	PAW	INT	9.14
Wade, Terrell	RMD	INT	9.09
Dishman, Glenn	LVG	PCL	8.74
Baldwin, James	NVL	AMAS	8.67
Cromwell, Nate	LVG	PCL	8.67
Bergman, Sean	TOL	INT	8.44
Mlicki, Doug	JCK	TEX	8.44
Schmidt, Jason	GRV	SOU	8.38
Rodriguez, Felix	SAN	TEX	8.32
Acevedo, Juan	NHV	EAST	8.30
Mlicki, Dave	CHR	INT	8.27
Taylor, Kerry	LVG	PCL	8.19

Strikeouts per 9 IP — Relievers

Player	Team	League	
Benitez, Armando	**BOW**	**EAST**	**13.31**
Beckett, Robert	LVG	PCL	12.58
Huisman, Rick	JCK	TEX	11.26
Burgos, Enrique	OMA	AMAS	10.86
Percival, Troy	VAN	PCL	10.77
Ricci, Chuck	SWB	INT	10.22
Christianse, Jason	BUF	AMAS	10.20
Bottalico, Richard	REA	EAST	10.11
Pierce, Jeff	PAW	INT	10.02
Borowski, Joseph	BOW	EAST	9.95
Croghan, Andy	COL	INT	9.79
Jordan, Rick	KNX	SOU	9.79
Hall, Drew	TOL	INT	9.53
Schmidt, Curt	HRB	EAST	9.42
Drahman, Brian	EDM	PCL	9.25

Innings Pitched

Player	Team	League	
Pulsipher, Bill	**BNG**	**EAST**	**201.0**
Perez, Carlos	OTT	INT	198.0
Beatty, Blaine	CNG	SOU	196.1
Roa, Joe	NOR	INT	187.2
Haynes, Jimmy	BOW	EAST	187.0
Radke, Brad	NSH	SOU	186.1
Rodriguez, Frank	PAW	INT	186.0
Woodall, Brad	RMD	INT	185.2
Brock, Russell	TAC	PCL	184.1
Sparks, Steve	NO	AMAS	183.2
Barcelo, Marc	NSH	SOU	183.1
Dishman, Glenn	LVG	PCL	182.1
Roberson, Sid	ELP	TEX	181.1
Ratekin, Mark	VAN	PCL	180.1
Schrenk, Steve	NVL	AMAS	178.2

Opponent Batting Average — Starters

Player	Team	League	
Beatty, Blaine	**CNG**	**SOU**	**.206**
Mlicki, Doug	JCK	TEX	.211
Person, Robert	BNG	EAST	.219
Rodriguez, Felix	SAN	TEX	.219
Acevedo, Juan	NHV	EAST	.219
Arteaga, Ivan	SAN	EAST	.223
Ruffcorn, Scott	NVL	AMAS	.225
Minchey, Nate	SAN	INT	.229
Wojciechows, Steve	HVL	SOU	.230
Wendell, Turk	KNX	AMAS	.230
Woodall, Brad	GRV	INT	.230
Rumer, Tim	ALB	EAST	.231
Spoljaric, Paul	LVG	SOU	.234
Mitchell, Larry	REA	EAST	.234
Several tied at			.235

Opponent Batting Average — Relievers

Player	Team	League	
Benitez, Armando	**BOW**	**EAST**	**.160**
Huisman, Rick	JCK	TEX	.181
Christianse, Jason	BUF	AMAS	.194
Sauveur, Rich	IND	AMAS	.195
Rightnowar, Ron	NO	AMAS	.197
Gavaghan, Sean	LVG	SOU	.197
Stidham, Phil	TOL	INT	.198
Bailey, Cory	PAW	INT	.199
Clontz, Brad	RMD	INT	.200
Schmidt, Curt	HRB	EAST	.202
Burgos, Enrique	OMA	AMAS	.208
Bauer, Matt	TOL	INT	.211
Borowski, Joe	BOW	EAST	.213
Dunbar, Matt	COL	INT	.214
Edenfield, Ken	VAN	PCL	.218

1994 Park Data

Yet another STATS/Howe exclusive! A year ago, for the first time ever, we presented conclusive evidence that many minor league parks affect hitters to an even greater degree than do most parks in the majors. That's vital information for someone assessing the major league chances of say, minor league vet Jeff Manto, who had a big year for Rochester in 1994. We're not saying that Manto's numbers (31 HR, 27 of them in 329 AB at Rochester) should be discounted. But the big numbers he put up were compiled under extremely hitter-friendly conditions: Rochester's park produced 32 percent more homers than the average International League park.

The Index is a way a measuring each park's effects on hitters and pitchers by comparing home and road performance, with an index of 100 indicating a neutral park. A home run index of 105 and a doubles index of 93 indicates that the team's home ballpark increases homers by 5% while decreasing doubles by 7%.

The numbers in this section are for 1994 only.

American Association — AAA

Buffalo
	G	Avg	AB	R	H	2B	3B	HR	SO
Home	72	.266	4804	563	1277	269	29	65	747
Road	72	.265	4766	646	1264	257	43	117	779
Index	—	100	101	87	101	104	67	55	95

Indianapolis
	G	Avg	AB	R	H	2B	3B	HR	SO
Home	72	.266	4943	653	1317	283	46	131	876
Road	71	.265	4829	647	1281	296	40	119	901
Index	—	100	101	100	101	93	112	108	95

Iowa
	G	Avg	AB	R	H	2B	3B	HR	SO
Home	72	.271	4767	717	1290	308	38	149	836
Road	71	.274	4670	686	1281	269	37	110	823
Index	—	99	101	103	99	112	101	133	100

Louisville
	G	Avg	AB	R	H	2B	3B	HR	SO
Home	71	.274	4820	755	1319	278	44	134	959
Road	71	.261	4678	636	1220	300	35	107	847
Index	—	105	103	119	108	90	122	122	110

Nashville
	G	Avg	AB	R	H	2B	3B	HR	SO
Home	70	.260	4710	659	1226	231	42	126	946
Road	74	.252	4991	605	1258	264	36	117	926
Index	—	103	100	115	103	93	124	114	108

New Orleans
	G	Avg	AB	R	H	2B	3B	HR	SO
Home	72	.267	4624	657	1236	275	48	96	855
Road	72	.269	4860	715	1308	259	48	111	877
Index	—	99	95	92	94	112	105	91	102

Oklahoma City
	G	Avg	AB	R	H	2B	3B	HR	SO
Home	72	.267	4835	656	1291	256	50	83	932
Road	72	.277	4835	755	1340	267	47	143	894
Index	—	96	100	87	96	96	106	58	104

Omaha
	G	Avg	AB	R	H	2B	3B	HR	SO
Home	73	.270	4871	745	1314	241	35	167	763
Road	71	.278	4745	715	1318	229	46	127	867
Index	—	97	100	101	97	103	74	128	86

International League — AAA

Charlotte
	G	Avg	AB	R	H	2B	3B	HR	SO
Home	71	.261	4754	697	1239	208	23	159	798
Road	71	.267	4698	671	1253	236	43	115	826
Index	—	98	101	104	99	87	53	137	95

Columbus
	G	Avg	AB	R	H	2B	3B	HR	SO
Home	73	.257	4746	672	1219	259	54	117	921
Road	69	.268	4579	657	1227	216	27	120	875
Index	—	96	98	97	94	116	193	94	102

Norfolk
	G	Avg	AB	R	H	2B	3B	HR	SO
Home	70	.242	4640	513	1121	210	35	63	821
Road	72	.268	4879	694	1308	236	36	123	773
Index	—	90	98	76	86	94	102	54	112

Ottawa
	G	Avg	AB	R	H	2B	3B	HR	SO
Home	71	.251	4699	604	1179	248	30	86	852
Road	71	.274	4790	751	1314	270	28	146	890
Index	—	91	98	80	90	94	109	60	96

Pawtucket
	G	Avg	AB	R	H	2B	3B	HR	SO
Home	71	.268	4900	713	1312	244	12	182	924
Road	71	.247	4823	599	1192	221	37	106	856
Index	—	108	102	119	110	109	32	169	108

Richmond
	G	Avg	AB	R	H	2B	3B	HR	SO
Home	71	.267	4842	598	1293	207	31	88	845
Road	70	.252	4783	618	1204	229	37	129	901
Index	—	106	100	95	106	89	83	67	93

Rochester
	G	Avg	AB	R	H	2B	3B	HR	SO
Home	70	.278	4748	748	1321	259	45	158	923
Road	71	.258	4730	684	1219	253	29	119	839
Index	—	108	102	111	110	102	155	132	110

Scranton-wb
	G	Avg	AB	R	H	2B	3B	HR	SO
Home	71	.260	4731	674	1230	290	38	87	822
Road	71	.258	4789	634	1237	244	29	127	913
Index	—	101	99	106	99	120	133	69	91

Syracuse
	G	Avg	AB	R	H	2B	3B	HR	SO
Home	70	.274	4710	706	1289	247	40	115	823
Road	72	.271	4726	664	1282	234	28	123	850
Index	—	101	103	109	103	106	143	94	97

Toledo
	G	Avg	AB	R	H	2B	3B	HR	SO
Home	71	.266	4762	673	1265	223	31	157	1006
Road	71	.260	4735	626	1232	256	45	104	1012
Index	—	102	101	108	103	87	68	150	99

Pacific Coast League — AAA

Albuquerque
	G	Avg	AB	R	H	2B	3B	HR	SO
Home	71	.307	5025	872	1543	273	49	125	867
Road	68	.295	4762	798	1406	264	53	155	828
Index	—	104	101	105	105	96	88	76	99

Calgary
	G	Avg	AB	R	H	2B	3B	HR	SO
Home	71	.311	5073	992	1580	351	31	197	768
Road	72	.301	5142	915	1548	308	47	164	918
Index	—	103	100	110	104	116	67	122	85

Colorado Springs
	G	Avg	AB	R	H	2B	3B	HR	SO
Home	68	.322	4766	930	1536	312	50	169	781
Road	71	.283	4912	778	1391	296	42	128	912
Index	—	114	101	125	115	109	123	136	88

Edmonton
	G	Avg	AB	R	H	2B	3B	HR	SO
Home	71	.295	4785	789	1411	349	49	151	832
Road	71	.292	4981	765	1452	263	47	126	867
Index	—	101	96	103	97	138	109	125	100

Las Vegas
	G	Avg	AB	R	H	2B	3B	HR	SO
Home	72	.294	5086	874	1494	282	51	161	1035
Road	72	.288	4850	773	1395	263	49	119	911
Index	—	102	105	113	107	102	99	129	108

Phoenix
	G	Avg	AB	R	H	2B	3B	HR	SO
Home	72	.290	4977	705	1442	261	70	118	869
Road	71	.294	4803	781	1412	295	43	123	762
Index	—	99	102	89	101	85	157	93	110

Salt Lake
	G	Avg	AB	R	H	2B	3B	HR	SO
Home	72	.300	5099	913	1532	286	36	166	822
Road	72	.304	5000	862	1521	307	52	125	842
Index	—	99	102	106	101	91	68	130	96

Tacoma
	G	Avg	AB	R	H	2B	3B	HR	SO
Home	71	.260	4836	634	1257	254	20	96	859
Road	71	.298	4885	793	1456	264	33	132	762
Index	—	87	99	80	86	97	61	73	114

Tucson
	G	Avg	AB	R	H	2B	3B	HR	SO
Home	72	.297	5001	771	1487	284	65	96	790
Road	72	.291	5033	842	1465	313	40	137	849
Index	—	102	99	92	102	91	164	71	94

Vancouver
	G	Avg	AB	R	H	2B	3B	HR	SO
Home	71	.269	4621	644	1245	222	29	86	837
Road	71	.302	4901	817	1481	301	44	156	809
Index	—	89	94	79	84	78	70	58	110

Southern League — AA

Birmingham

	G	Avg	AB	R	H	2B	3B	HR	SO
Home	69	.251	4611	602	1156	219	28	45	778
Road	70	.255	4580	597	1169	230	31	81	819
Index	—	98	102	102	100	95	90	55	94

Carolina

	G	Avg	AB	R	H	2B	3B	HR	SO
Home	69	.264	4592	613	1212	251	32	72	881
Road	71	.264	4853	648	1281	227	38	107	815
Index	—	100	97	97	97	117	89	71	114

Chattanooga

	G	Avg	AB	R	H	2B	3B	HR	SO
Home	70	.252	4527	583	1141	226	29	69	896
Road	70	.251	4629	600	1160	225	22	100	885
Index	—	101	98	97	98	103	135	71	104

Greenville

	G	Avg	AB	R	H	2B	3B	HR	SO
Home	70	.256	4510	548	1156	225	32	90	895
Road	66	.250	4364	519	1092	207	26	77	811
Index	—	102	97	100	100	105	119	113	107

Huntsville

	G	Avg	AB	R	H	2B	3B	HR	SO
Home	71	.250	4614	580	1152	221	23	75	894
Road	67	.251	4369	569	1097	224	23	69	824
Index	—	99	100	96	99	93	95	103	103

Jacksonville

	G	Avg	AB	R	H	2B	3B	HR	SO
Home	66	.266	4527	636	1202	241	10	137	747
Road	71	.271	4519	619	1224	242	35	97	785
Index	—	98	106	111	106	99	29	141	95

Knoxville

	G	Avg	AB	R	H	2B	3B	HR	SO
Home	71	.267	4803	641	1281	233	53	84	891
Road	69	.260	4383	617	1141	191	41	78	850
Index	—	102	106	101	109	111	118	98	96

Memphis

	G	Avg	AB	R	H	2B	3B	HR	SO
Home	68	.249	4395	564	1096	212	23	119	799
Road	69	.259	4708	612	1218	260	35	71	844
Index	—	96	95	94	91	87	70	180	101

Nashville

	G	Avg	AB	R	H	2B	3B	HR	SO
Home	70	.245	4571	564	1119	217	32	93	976
Road	70	.257	4716	594	1213	219	29	106	947
Index	—	95	97	95	92	102	114	91	106

Orlando

	G	Avg	AB	R	H	2B	3B	HR	SO
Home	68	.267	4403	547	1177	191	46	84	656
Road	69	.248	4432	503	1097	211	28	82	833
Index	—	106	101	110	109	91	165	103	79

Eastern League — AA

Albany

	G	Avg	AB	R	H	2B	3B	HR	SO
Home	73	.253	4677	590	1181	224	23	102	1017
Road	68	.257	4523	616	1164	218	36	100	938
Index	—	98	96	89	95	99	62	99	105

Binghamton

	G	Avg	AB	R	H	2B	3B	HR	SO
Home	71	.270	4774	654	1287	235	32	98	848
Road	70	.259	4803	634	1245	252	33	94	900
Index	—	104	98	102	102	94	96	105	95

Bowie

	G	Avg	AB	R	H	2B	3B	HR	SO
Home	70	.272	4578	678	1245	235	16	133	860
Road	72	.264	4797	641	1265	257	40	82	958
Index	—	103	98	109	101	96	42	170	94

Canton-akron

	G	Avg	AB	R	H	2B	3B	HR	SO
Home	72	.258	4660	614	1202	204	30	87	823
Road	70	.265	4632	706	1228	233	38	134	945
Index	—	97	98	85	95	87	78	65	87

Harrisburg

	G	Avg	AB	R	H	2B	3B	HR	SO
Home	67	.256	4538	650	1162	212	35	137	965
Road	72	.251	4665	645	1169	242	32	99	993
Index	—	102	105	106	107	90	112	142	100

New Britain

	G	Avg	AB	R	H	2B	3B	HR	SO
Home	70	.249	4510	575	1122	230	37	65	918
Road	70	.271	4717	717	1278	234	34	119	899
Index	—	92	96	80	88	103	114	57	107

New Haven

	G	Avg	AB	R	H	2B	3B	HR	SO
Home	71	.242	4730	620	1144	233	31	75	1046
Road	69	.252	4464	595	1126	202	29	117	846
Index	—	96	103	101	99	109	101	80	117

Portland

	G	Avg	AB	R	H	2B	3B	HR	SO
Home	72	.264	4884	705	1289	265	46	132	942
Road	69	.252	4568	613	1151	204	29	91	909
Index	—	105	102	110	107	121	215	136	97

Reading

	G	Avg	AB	R	H	2B	3B	HR	SO
Home	71	.264	4829	730	1273	221	35	137	932
Road	69	.256	4524	586	1157	197	31	81	845
Index	—	103	104	121	107	105	106	158	103

Trenton

	G	Avg	AB	R	H	2B	3B	HR	SO
Home	66	.252	4239	544	1067	209	38	60	800
Road	74	.252	4726	607	1189	229	30	109	918
Index	—	100	101	100	101	102	141	61	97

Texas League — AA

Arkansas

	G	Avg	AB	R	H	2B	3B	HR	SO
Home	68	.241	4249	528	1025	215	26	84	862
Road	67	.242	4498	530	1090	227	44	86	976
Index	—	100	93	96	93	100	63	103	93

El Paso

	G	Avg	AB	R	H	2B	3B	HR	SO
Home	68	.289	4598	806	1327	284	90	63	907
Road	68	.273	4657	682	1270	232	47	100	929
Index	—	106	99	118	104	124	194	64	99

Jackson

	G	Avg	AB	R	H	2B	3B	HR	SO
Home	67	.248	4306	527	1069	188	34	77	979
Road	68	.253	4332	570	1098	227	35	85	878
Index	—	98	101	94	99	83	98	91	112

Midland

	G	Avg	AB	R	H	2B	3B	HR	SO
Home	66	.289	4516	811	1304	295	46	95	913
Road	70	.266	4689	689	1247	210	48	80	936
Index	—	109	102	125	111	146	100	123	101

San Antonio

	G	Avg	AB	R	H	2B	3B	HR	SO
Home	70	.246	4566	487	1121	209	46	45	956
Road	66	.260	4333	632	1127	248	30	92	909
Index	—	94	99	73	94	80	146	46	100

Shreveport

	G	Avg	AB	R	H	2B	3B	HR	SO
Home	67	.248	4414	506	1093	215	33	61	783
Road	69	.266	4434	578	1179	228	23	84	786
Index	—	93	103	90	95	95	144	73	100

Tulsa

	G	Avg	AB	R	H	2B	3B	HR	SO
Home	69	.255	4491	601	1146	216	27	135	974
Road	67	.258	4314	574	1115	229	38	75	851
Index	—	99	101	102	100	91	68	173	110

Wichita

	G	Avg	AB	R	H	2B	3B	HR	SO
Home	68	.270	4642	650	1254	218	28	108	916
Road	68	.268	4525	661	1213	239	65	66	1025
Index	—	101	103	96	103	89	42	160	87

California League — A

Bakersfield

	G	Avg	AB	R	H	2B	3B	HR	SO
Home	68	.259	4483	643	1161	214	9	105	924
Road	68	.256	4554	621	1168	199	39	84	1001
Index	—	101	98	104	99	109	23	127	94

Central Valley

	G	Avg	AB	R	H	2B	3B	HR	SO
Home	68	.271	4616	628	1253	199	20	70	947
Road	68	.250	4529	601	1132	194	31	73	979
Index	—	109	102	104	111	101	63	94	95

High Desert

	G	Avg	AB	R	H	2B	3B	HR	SO
Home	68	.288	4880	968	1406	278	58	186	954
Road	68	.281	4597	755	1292	251	43	110	976
Index	—	103	106	128	109	104	127	159	92

Lake Elsinore

	G	Avg	AB	R	H	2B	3B	HR	SO
Home	68	.264	4656	719	1229	269	39	86	884
Road	68	.271	4576	680	1238	224	24	126	962
Index	—	96	102	106	99	118	160	67	90

Modesto

	G	Avg	AB	R	H	2B	3B	HR	SO
Home	68	.243	4365	604	1059	187	22	133	1091
Road	68	.251	4573	596	1149	207	33	86	1052
Index	—	97	95	101	92	95	70	162	109

Rancho Cucamonga

	G	Avg	AB	R	H	2B	3B	HR	SO
Home	68	.274	4621	759	1266	236	37	116	1022
Road	68	.256	4592	687	1174	203	26	107	1080
Index	—	107	101	110	108	116	141	108	94

Riverside

	G	Avg	AB	R	H	2B	3B	HR	SO
Home	68	.263	4507	617	1186	203	47	58	889
Road	68	.266	4684	729	1247	233	35	116	960
Index	—	99	96	85	95	91	140	52	96

San Bernardino

	G	Avg	AB	R	H	2B	3B	HR	SO
Home	68	.280	4749	799	1330	224	23	167	1116
Road	68	.275	4660	789	1282	243	41	110	1007
Index	—	102	102	101	104	90	55	149	109

San Jose

	G	Avg	AB	R	H	2B	3B	HR	SO
Home	68	.250	4502	608	1126	202	44	54	988
Road	68	.277	4716	767	1305	231	30	130	852
Index	—	90	95	79	86	92	154	44	121

Stockton

	G	Avg	AB	R	H	2B	3B	HR	SO
Home	68	.258	4621	589	1190	202	35	58	914
Road	68	.270	4519	709	1219	229	32	91	860
Index	—	95	102	83	96	86	107	62	104

Carolina League — A

Durham

	G	Avg	AB	R	H	2B	3B	HR	SO
Home	69	.270	4543	678	1176	209	21	171	973
Road	67	.246	4473	627	1101	203	22	130	959
Index	—	105	99	105	104	101	94	130	100

Frederick

	G	Avg	AB	R	H	2B	3B	HR	SO
Home	67	.250	4416	653	1103	190	20	115	960
Road	70	.272	4667	781	1268	227	33	140	979
Index	—	92	99	87	91	88	64	87	104

Kinston

	G	Avg	AB	R	H	2B	3B	HR	SO
Home	69	.235	4528	614	1063	184	25	112	1060
Road	69	.263	4525	686	1188	222	24	122	984
Index	—	89	100	90	89	83	104	92	108

Lynchburg

	G	Avg	AB	R	H	2B	3B	HR	SO
Home	70	.270	4814	741	1302	259	36	121	999
Road	69	.259	4573	627	1184	236	34	121	897
Index	—	104	104	116	106	104	101	95	106

Prince William

	G	Avg	AB	R	H	2B	3B	HR	SO
Home	69	.260	4492	617	1166	246	47	84	840
Road	67	.271	4579	746	1241	224	36	128	888
Index	—	96	95	80	91	112	133	67	96

Salem

	G	Avg	AB	R	H	2B	3B	HR	SO
Home	70	.292	4921	871	1436	274	38	170	922
Road	69	.246	4416	562	1087	178	32	104	901
Index	—	119	110	153	130	138	107	147	92

Wilmington

	G	Avg	AB	R	H	2B	3B	HR	SO
Home	70	.244	4522	537	1103	192	38	62	885
Road	68	.261	4717	689	1232	218	31	146	959
Index	—	93	93	76	87	92	128	44	96

Winston-salem

	G	Avg	AB	R	H	2B	3B	HR	SO
Home	66	.261	4409	738	1151	184	22	202	931
Road	71	.255	4695	731	1199	230	35	146	1003
Index	—	102	101	109	103	85	57	147	99

Florida State League — A

Brevard County

	G	Avg	AB	R	H	2B	3B	HR	SO
Home	70	.237	4514	505	1069	192	28	47	869
Road	69	.251	4454	607	1119	201	34	53	834
Index	—	94	100	82	94	94	81	88	103

Charlotte

	G	Avg	AB	R	H	2B	3B	HR	SO
Home	69	.242	4589	506	1112	224	41	53	856
Road	67	.265	4351	606	1151	203	54	53	721
Index	—	92	102	81	94	105	72	95	113

Clearwater

	G	Avg	AB	R	H	2B	3B	HR	SO
Home	69	.258	4675	597	1208	229	40	73	762
Road	66	.259	4274	572	1105	208	28	68	730
Index	—	100	105	100	105	101	131	98	95

Daytona

	G	Avg	AB	R	H	2B	3B	HR	SO
Home	69	.244	4579	582	1119	207	39	61	886
Road	65	.262	4275	570	1122	195	36	61	762
Index	—	93	101	96	94	99	101	93	109

Dunedin

	G	Avg	AB	R	H	2B	3B	HR	SO
Home	68	.265	4648	638	1230	223	34	87	922
Road	65	.252	4232	507	1065	192	26	56	821
Index	—	105	105	120	110	106	119	141	102

Ft. Myers

	G	Avg	AB	R	H	2B	3B	HR	SO
Home	68	.256	4515	548	1158	186	30	54	882
Road	66	.271	4465	612	1210	218	40	65	833
Index	—	95	98	87	93	84	74	82	105

Lakeland

	G	Avg	AB	R	H	2B	3B	HR	SO
Home	62	.259	3899	511	1011	178	37	61	744
Road	70	.238	4503	507	1070	197	29	43	971
Index	—	109	98	114	107	104	147	164	88

Osceola

	G	Avg	AB	R	H	2B	3B	HR	SO
Home	68	.239	4241	532	1015	188	36	34	732
Road	67	.271	4352	665	1178	224	33	67	711
Index	—	88	96	79	85	86	112	52	106

St. Lucie

	G	Avg	AB	R	H	2B	3B	HR	SO
Home	68	.264	4318	573	1141	183	32	48	753
Road	69	.251	4528	549	1136	206	33	52	853
Index	—	105	97	106	102	93	102	97	93

St. Petersburg

	G	Avg	AB	R	H	2B	3B	HR	SO
Home	70	.247	4659	542	1150	205	43	56	848
Road	69	.249	4685	543	1167	213	31	76	938
Index	—	99	98	98	97	97	139	74	91

Sarasota

	G	Avg	AB	R	H	2B	3B	HR	SO
Home	66	.276	4296	659	1187	210	31	57	817
Road	67	.254	4470	529	1137	188	35	58	854
Index	—	109	96	126	106	116	92	102	100

Tampa

	G	Avg	AB	R	H	2B	3B	HR	SO
Home	65	.264	4181	590	1105	204	40	84	860
Road	67	.258	4445	619	1146	203	38	85	939
Index	—	103	97	96	99	107	112	105	97

Vero Beach

	G	Avg	AB	R	H	2B	3B	HR	SO
Home	67	.272	4520	668	1229	212	29	111	890
Road	68	.245	4394	536	1077	196	46	47	844
Index	—	111	104	126	116	105	61	230	103

West Palm Beach

	G	Avg	AB	R	H	2B	3B	HR	SO
Home	64	.249	4147	517	1031	191	30	34	904
Road	68	.249	4353	546	1082	188	27	76	914
Index	—	100	101	101	101	107	117	47	104

Midwest League — A

Appleton

	G	Avg	AB	R	H	2B	3B	HR	SO
Home	66	.262	4441	650	1162	221	38	88	945
Road	73	.247	4660	621	1151	220	40	83	937
Index	—	106	105	116	112	105	100	111	106

Beloit

	G	Avg	AB	R	H	2B	3B	HR	SO
Home	73	.257	4668	761	1199	206	21	109	1089
Road	67	.251	4364	577	1094	183	17	78	997
Index	—	102	96	121	101	105	115	131	102

Burlington

	G	Avg	AB	R	H	2B	3B	HR	SO
Home	67	.268	4517	762	1212	219	12	155	988
Road	70	.262	4665	719	1221	263	38	103	1022
Index	—	103	101	111	104	86	33	155	100

Cedar Rapids

	G	Avg	AB	R	H	2B	3B	HR	SO
Home	71	.250	4643	639	1159	210	26	100	966
Road	68	.269	4650	697	1251	230	27	89	961
Index	—	93	96	88	89	91	96	113	101

Clinton

	G	Avg	AB	R	H	2B	3B	HR	SO
Home	71	.263	4770	728	1253	226	29	90	1091
Road	68	.268	4470	727	1199	223	40	109	941
Index	—	96	102	96	100	95	68	77	109

Ft. Wayne

	G	Avg	AB	R	H	2B	3B	HR	SO
Home	69	.259	4674	606	1209	225	26	81	1005
Road	70	.253	4579	643	1158	207	30	90	1021
Index	—	102	104	96	106	106	85	88	96

Kane County

	G	Avg	AB	R	H	2B	3B	HR	SO
Home	70	.256	4605	637	1177	220	31	77	885
Road	69	.251	4562	659	1143	229	25	89	979
Index	—	102	100	95	102	95	123	86	90

Madison

	G	Avg	AB	R	H	2B	3B	HR	SO
Home	68	.249	4297	565	1068	219	32	77	976
Road	71	.267	4695	709	1254	239	33	80	969
Index	—	93	96	83	89	100	106	105	110

Peoria

	G	Avg	AB	R	H	2B	3B	HR	SO
Home	70	.275	4782	740	1317	274	42	85	976
Road	68	.265	4491	655	1188	237	18	87	938
Index	—	104	103	110	106	109	219	92	96

Quad City

	G	Avg	AB	R	H	2B	3B	HR	SO
Home	70	.260	4678	678	1218	223	35	92	1026
Road	68	.262	4505	636	1182	219	34	74	986
Index	—	99	101	104	100	98	99	120	100

Rockford

	G	Avg	AB	R	H	2B	3B	HR	SO
Home	70	.254	4474	568	1135	215	27	44	897
Road	69	.254	4536	595	1154	201	22	89	943
Index	—	100	97	94	97	106	124	50	96

South Bend

	G	Avg	AB	R	H	2B	3B	HR	SO
Home	69	.266	4670	661	1244	220	44	71	901
Road	70	.252	4726	660	1191	212	32	73	1004
Index	—	106	100	102	106	105	139	96	91

Springfield

	G	Avg	AB	R	H	2B	3B	HR	SO
Home	68	.257	4430	721	1140	198	37	100	1025
Road	72	.244	4672	676	1138	194	28	84	1040
Index	—	106	100	113	106	106	139	126	104

West Michigan

	G	Avg	AB	R	H	2B	3B	HR	SO
Home	70	.227	4508	536	1025	209	28	49	981
Road	69	.261	4582	678	1194	228	44	90	1013
Index	—	87	97	78	85	93	65	55	98

South Atlantic League — A

Albany

	G	Avg	AB	R	H	2B	3B	HR	SO
Home	70	.253	4513	606	1141	227	39	34	892
Road	67	.257	4301	625	1107	217	42	81	921
Index	—	98	100	93	99	100	88	40	92

Asheville

	G	Avg	AB	R	H	2B	3B	HR	SO
Home	68	.269	4461	669	1200	237	7	123	950
Road	66	.254	4277	584	1086	199	22	89	983
Index	—	106	101	111	107	114	31	133	93

Augusta

	G	Avg	AB	R	H	2B	3B	HR	SO
Home	67	.239	4476	568	1072	199	45	39	1084
Road	70	.254	4654	663	1180	222	44	72	1095
Index	—	94	100	90	95	93	106	56	103

Columbia

	G	Avg	AB	R	H	2B	3B	HR	SO
Home	66	.251	4291	574	1075	203	32	99	1078
Road	69	.240	4430	563	1061	203	52	76	1058
Index	—	105	101	107	106	103	64	134	105

Charleston-sc

	G	Avg	AB	R	H	2B	3B	HR	SO
Home	67	.249	4506	631	1122	217	37	88	1075
Road	70	.245	4528	612	1108	209	27	95	1015
Index	—	102	104	106	106	104	138	93	106

Charleston-wv

	G	Avg	AB	R	H	2B	3B	HR	SO
Home	71	.261	4612	630	1204	234	33	60	852
Road	69	.247	4526	593	1116	223	32	95	973
Index	—	106	99	103	105	103	101	62	86

Columbus

	G	Avg	AB	R	H	2B	3B	HR	SO
Home	69	.252	4641	698	1169	215	55	113	1022
Road	69	.238	4459	563	1063	172	32	83	1017
Index	—	106	104	124	110	120	165	131	97

Fayetteville

	G	Avg	AB	R	H	2B	3B	HR	SO
Home	70	.232	4468	604	1038	189	36	66	1017
Road	67	.249	4426	644	1103	211	33	98	986
Index	—	93	97	90	90	89	106	67	102

Greensboro

	G	Avg	AB	R	H	2B	3B	HR	SO
Home	71	.243	4656	612	1131	214	24	90	1101
Road	69	.253	4488	630	1134	189	34	87	1061
Index	—	96	101	94	97	109	68	100	100

Hagerstown

	G	Avg	AB	R	H	2B	3B	HR	SO
Home	69	.265	4667	697	1236	226	47	119	1081
Road	67	.246	4393	602	1081	207	35	91	996
Index	—	106	103	112	111	103	126	123	102

Hickory

	G	Avg	AB	R	H	2B	3B	HR	SO
Home	71	.262	4794	705	1257	203	50	110	982
Road	69	.256	4632	647	1184	232	23	82	916
Index	—	103	101	106	103	85	210	130	104

Macon

	G	Avg	AB	R	H	2B	3B	HR	SO
Home	68	.243	4403	519	1069	197	35	74	1042
Road	69	.255	4594	643	1172	252	36	87	1009
Index	—	95	97	82	93	82	101	89	108

Savannah

	G	Avg	AB	R	H	2B	3B	HR	SO
Home	67	.226	4238	515	956	157	22	98	942
Road	70	.250	4727	619	1184	205	41	74	1038
Index	—	90	94	87	84	85	90	148	101

Spartanburg

	G	Avg	AB	R	H	2B	3B	HR	SO
Home	68	.254	4464	639	1135	237	26	94	985
Road	71	.258	4755	679	1226	214	35	97	1035
Index	—	99	96	98	97	118	79	103	101

New York-Penn League — A

Auburn

	G	Avg	AB	R	H	2B	3B	HR	SO
Home	38	.280	2497	401	698	121	40	47	446
Road	38	.258	2543	349	655	118	20	28	504
Index	—	109	98	115	107	104	204	171	90

Batavia

	G	Avg	AB	R	H	2B	3B	HR	SO
Home	37	.245	2393	319	586	92	24	11	453
Road	37	.256	2379	323	608	100	25	28	504
Index	—	96	101	99	96	91	95	39	89

Elmira

	G	Avg	AB	R	H	2B	3B	HR	SO
Home	36	.247	2349	305	581	113	13	30	493
Road	37	.270	2425	381	655	112	30	31	489
Index	—	92	100	82	91	104	45	100	104

Hudson Valley

	G	Avg	AB	R	H	2B	3B	HR	SO
Home	37	.232	2469	303	574	112	23	21	517
Road	37	.249	2397	346	598	100	20	19	502
Index	—	93	103	88	96	109	112	107	109

Jamestown

	G	Avg	AB	R	H	2B	3B	HR	SO
Home	36	.249	2429	336	605	123	29	31	491
Road	38	.246	2477	320	609	109	15	22	494
Index	—	101	104	111	105	115	197	144	101

Oneonta

	G	Avg	AB	R	H	2B	3B	HR	SO
Home	37	.241	2261	296	545	78	31	11	561
Road	38	.244	2510	338	612	108	17	31	588
Index	—	99	93	90	91	80	202	39	106

Pittsfield

	G	Avg	AB	R	H	2B	3B	HR	SO
Home	38	.261	2563	354	670	121	20	12	485
Road	37	.256	2559	344	655	115	31	25	481
Index	—	102	98	100	100	105	64	48	101

St. Catharines

	G	Avg	AB	R	H	2B	3B	HR	SO
Home	37	.240	2399	311	576	100	4	42	506
Road	37	.252	2387	351	602	94	33	29	473
Index	—	95	101	89	96	106	12	144	106

Utica

	G	Avg	AB	R	H	2B	3B	HR	SO
Home	37	.239	2382	306	569	98	19	22	491
Road	35	.260	2280	306	593	110	23	14	478
Index	—	92	99	95	91	85	79	150	98

Watertown

	G	Avg	AB	R	H	2B	3B	HR	SO
Home	38	.271	2553	406	692	107	17	50	550
Road	36	.245	2395	350	587	102	19	34	431
Index	—	111	101	110	112	98	84	138	120

Welland

	G	Avg	AB	R	H	2B	3B	HR	SO
Home	37	.242	2412	262	583	95	15	23	481
Road	37	.238	2455	310	585	108	22	25	479
Index	—	101	98	91	100	90	69	94	102

Northwest League — A

Bellingham

	G	Avg	AB	R	H	2B	3B	HR	SO
Home	38	.224	2480	281	555	86	6	34	613
Road	38	.259	2591	378	671	128	21	28	639
Index	—	86	96	74	83	70	30	127	100

Bend

	G	Avg	AB	R	H	2B	3B	HR	SO
Home	38	.269	2661	442	715	131	15	61	557
Road	38	.249	2587	331	643	120	13	42	669
Index	—	108	103	134	111	108	112	141	81

Boise

	G	Avg	AB	R	H	2B	3B	HR	SO
Home	38	.257	2602	382	670	113	20	33	628
Road	38	.256	2565	398	656	122	20	33	574
Index	—	101	101	96	102	91	99	99	108

Eugene

	G	Avg	AB	R	H	2B	3B	HR	SO
Home	38	.234	2608	325	611	117	17	32	724
Road	38	.248	2605	382	645	121	17	50	655
Index	—	95	100	85	95	97	100	64	110

Everett

	G	Avg	AB	R	H	2B	3B	HR	SO
Home	38	.258	2620	379	676	127	17	60	734
Road	38	.250	2569	368	641	121	16	37	652
Index	—	103	102	103	105	103	104	159	110

Southern Oregon

	G	Avg	AB	R	H	2B	3B	HR	SO
Home	38	.267	2569	447	687	130	19	35	618
Road	38	.258	2597	419	669	132	9	42	673
Index	—	104	99	107	103	100	213	84	93

Spokane

	G	Avg	AB	R	H	2B	3B	HR	SO
Home	38	.252	2575	363	648	126	12	27	631
Road	38	.248	2592	340	642	93	15	32	638
Index	—	102	99	107	101	136	81	85	100

Yakima

	G	Avg	AB	R	H	2B	3B	HR	SO
Home	38	.251	2606	382	653	132	26	23	645
Road	38	.248	2615	385	648	125	21	41	650
Index	—	101	100	99	101	106	124	56	100

1994 AAA Lefty-Righty Stats

As was the case with our park data, last year's *Minor League Handbook* included platoon breakdowns for Class AAA hitters and pitchers for the first time ever. It was full of fascinating information. For instance, Chicago Cub pitching prospect Steve Trachsel, a right-handed pitcher, actually performed much better against left-handed hitters (.215 opponents average) at the AAA level in 1993 than he did against righties (.297). A fluke? The Cubs, and the National League, found out that it wasn't. As was the case in AAA, Trachsel dominated lefty hitters at the major league level (.212 opponents average), but had some problems with righties (.268).

Howe Sportsdata, which provides this information, will be adding more detail in future years. But these numbers, by themselves, can help you identify the prospects from the suspects. Ever wonder why some well-hyped lefty swinger hasn't gotten the major league call? His splits may tell you the answer.

The section includes batting splits for all hitters with 100 or more AAA at-bats last season and pitching splits for all hurlers with 100 or more AAA opponent at-bats in 1994.

AAA Batting vs. Left-Handed and Right-Handed Pitchers

	vs Left			vs Right		
Player - Team	H	AB	Avg	H	AB	Avg
Alexander - Rochester	26	115	.226	79	306	.258
Allanson - Vancouver	7	35	.200	29	103	.282
Allred - Richmond	5	37	.135	33	132	.250
Alvarez - Nashville	14	58	.241	34	165	.206
Amaro - Charlotte	21	50	.420	37	131	.282
Anderson - Vancouver	44	153	.288	120	355	.338
Andrews - Ottawa	41	140	.293	72	313	.230
Armas - Tacoma	26	90	.289	101	353	.286
Ashley - Albuquerque	24	82	.293	110	306	.359
Aude - Buffalo	35	123	.285	108	390	.277
Baez - Rochester	33	127	.260	50	228	.219
Barbara - Albuquerque	1	7	.143	58	161	.360
Barker - New Orleans	38	142	.268	78	292	.267
Barnes - Toledo	13	51	.255	20	77	.260
Barnwell - Columbus	11	68	.162	11	44	.250
Basse - New Orleans	15	62	.242	52	175	.297
Bates - Colo. Sprng	28	110	.255	100	337	.297
Battle - Louisville	33	111	.297	129	405	.319
Battle - Syracuse	52	154	.338	91	363	.251
Becker - Salt Lake	17	64	.266	72	218	.330
Bell - Charlotte	49	168	.292	90	310	.290
Bellinger - Phoenix	40	111	.360	49	224	.219
Bieser - Scranton-WB	11	54	.204	49	168	.292
Blosser - Pawtucket	27	111	.243	64	239	.268
Borrelli - Tacoma	22	76	.289	81	293	.276
Bournigal - Albuquerque	20	48	.417	49	160	.306
Bowie - Tacoma	20	84	.238	109	327	.333
Bragg - Calgary	41	140	.293	134	360	.372
Brito - Salt Lake	36	101	.356	99	336	.295
Brogna - Norfolk	10	65	.154	53	193	.275
Brooks - Albuquerque	33	99	.333	92	291	.316
Brown - Iowa	1	8	.125	30	119	.252
Brown - Richmond	22	84	.262	50	186	.269
Bruno - Las Vegas	34	120	.283	83	331	.251
Bryant - Calgary	44	147	.299	89	269	.331
Buccheri - Tacoma	34	100	.340	102	348	.293
Buford - Rochester	33	125	.264	89	326	.273
Bullett - Iowa	27	125	.216	132	396	.333
Burnitz - Norfolk	23	106	.217	52	208	.250
Busch - Albuquerque	30	122	.246	91	338	.269
Byington - New Orleans	55	153	.359	100	347	.288
Caceres - Omaha	23	62	.371	41	174	.236
Cameron - Buffalo	8	46	.174	16	90	.178
Canate - Syracuse	9	38	.237	19	115	.165
Candaele - Indianapols	45	152	.296	99	359	.276
Canseco - New Orleans	31	131	.237	62	269	.230
Capra - Edmonton	32	87	.368	84	295	.285
Carey - Rochester	6	44	.136	35	124	.282
Carter - Salt Lake	42	141	.298	107	319	.335
Carter - Iowa	36	118	.305	86	302	.285
Castellano - Colo. Sprng	11	33	.333	31	87	.356
Cedeno - Albuquerque	29	93	.312	94	290	.324
Cianfrocco - Las Vegas	10	28	.357	24	84	.286
Cirillo - New Orleans	22	71	.310	50	165	.303
Cockrell - Colo. Sprng	31	84	.369	54	187	.289
Colbert - Charlotte	27	101	.267	19	79	.241
Cole - Colo. Sprng	29	104	.279	56	180	.311
Colon - Iowa	36	117	.308	83	318	.261
Coolbaugh - Louisville	29	82	.354	68	251	.271
Coomer - Albuquerque	53	132	.402	128	403	.318
Cooper - Indianapols	24	74	.324	49	152	.322
Cordova - Salt Lake	40	110	.364	98	275	.356
Correia - Vancouver	33	111	.297	70	263	.266
Cox - Iowa	25	81	.309	55	221	.249
Cromer - Louisville	30	94	.319	83	322	.258
Cron - Charlotte	36	130	.277	45	220	.205
Cruz - Tacoma	8	36	.222	62	182	.341
Cruz - Toledo	11	71	.155	64	232	.276
Cummings - Buffalo	16	54	.296	39	125	.312
Dalesandro - Vancouver	14	47	.298	49	152	.322
Dascenzo - Norfolk	18	60	.300	50	186	.269
Daugherty - Syracuse	15	41	.366	35	108	.324
Davis - Okla. City	35	114	.307	83	276	.301
Davis - Okla. City	15	66	.227	34	151	.225
Davis - Omaha	38	123	.309	94	339	.277
Davis - Columbus	44	137	.321	71	279	.254
Deak - Las Vegas	29	111	.261	57	187	.305
Deak - Louisville	35	120	.292	96	363	.264
Decker - Edmonton	19	52	.365	82	207	.396
Dejardin - Columbus	10	49	.204	11	70	.157
Delarosa - Salt Lake	28	105	.267	50	181	.276
Delgado - Syracuse	32	116	.276	66	191	.346
Denson - Nashville	39	145	.269	94	360	.261
Diaz - Pawtucket	11	35	.314	28	81	.346
Dismuke - Indianapols	17	66	.258	87	325	.268
Dodson - New Orleans	13	52	.250	53	196	.270
Dostal - Rochester	13	54	.241	52	172	.302
Ducey - Okla. City	24	104	.231	86	307	.280
Dunn - Salt Lake	22	75	.293	80	255	.314
Durant - Salt Lake	27	103	.262	75	240	.313
Durham - Nashville	47	157	.299	109	370	.295
Eenhoorn - Columbus	28	120	.233	54	223	.242
Everett - Edmonton	25	78	.321	83	243	.342
Fabregas - Vancouver	8	46	.174	37	161	.230
Faneyte - Phoenix	30	84	.357	92	281	.327
Faries - Phoenix	44	144	.306	97	359	.270
Fariss - Edmonton	32	105	.305	86	309	.278
Faulkner - Rochester	8	23	.348	15	82	.183
Felix - Tacoma	5	26	.192	18	105	.171
Fernandez - Phoenix	16	57	.281	23	86	.267
Figueroa - Ottawa	22	81	.272	31	138	.225
Finn - New Orleans	18	81	.222	49	150	.327
Flaherty - Toledo	16	55	.291	23	96	.240
Flores - Charlotte	38	123	.309	30	125	.240
Forbes - Vancouver	24	85	.282	66	230	.287
Fordyce - Norfolk	15	50	.300	45	179	.251
Fox - Tacoma	13	30	.433	47	161	.292
Franco - Iowa	19	92	.207	102	345	.296
Fulton - Toledo	6	24	.250	30	135	.222
Gainer - Colo. Sprng	8	43	.186	61	233	.262
Garcia - Norfolk	20	75	.267	35	152	.230
Gardner - Ottawa	10	40	.250	38	146	.260
Garner - Scranton-WB	10	39	.256	40	148	.270
Garrison - Colo. Sprng	45	141	.319	110	364	.302
Geisler - Scranton-WB	10	63	.159	26	116	.224
Giambi - Tacoma	5	29	.172	51	147	.347
Giannelli - Syracuse	18	60	.300	76	267	.285
Gil - Okla. City	33	122	.270	88	368	.239
Gilbert - Scranton-WB	37	169	.219	101	369	.274
Giles - Charlotte	32	108	.296	104	324	.321
Giovanola - Richmond	16	65	.246	81	279	.290
Givens - Toledo	19	91	.209	47	192	.245
Glenn - New Orleans	4	33	.121	33	122	.270
Goff - Buffalo	9	42	.214	61	235	.260
Gonzales - Charlotte	2	28	.071	28	105	.267
Gonzalez - Syracuse	39	127	.307	85	310	.274
Goodwin - Omaha	33	121	.273	97	302	.321
Grebeck - Vancouver	15	48	.313	23	80	.288
Green - Syracuse	45	136	.331	104	297	.350
Greene - Indianapols	37	125	.296	87	310	.281
Greer - Okla. City	7	22	.318	28	90	.311
Guerrero - Tucson	20	76	.263	64	214	.299
Hajek - Tucson	43	139	.309	110	338	.325
Hall - Las Vegas	23	81	.284	52	200	.260
Haney - Iowa	19	71	.268	69	232	.297
Harris - Okla. City	41	139	.295	75	341	.220
Haselman - Calgary	19	51	.373	35	112	.313
Hatcher - Tucson	27	106	.255	75	239	.314
Hatteberg - Pawtucket	16	61	.262	40	177	.226
Hecht - Phoenix	16	77	.208	90	256	.352
Helfand - Tacoma	3	21	.143	33	157	.210
Hernandez - Columbus	14	54	.259	22	80	.275
Higgins - Las Vegas	21	70	.300	113	364	.310
Higginson - Toledo	32	143	.224	99	333	.297
Hinzo - Calgary	10	35	.286	25	107	.234
Hocking - Salt Lake	44	115	.383	66	279	.237
Holbert - Las Vegas	33	116	.284	95	309	.307
Hollandsworth - Albuq.	25	106	.236	118	397	.297
Horn - Columbus	9	51	.176	39	146	.267
Hosey - Omaha	41	106	.387	93	293	.317
Hosey - Vancouver	25	114	.219	72	260	.277
Houston - Richmond	14	59	.237	62	253	.245
Howard - Calgary	26	86	.302	41	180	.228
Howard - Albuquerque	16	62	.258	63	205	.307
Howell - Norfolk	10	47	.213	32	136	.235
Howitt - Nashville	17	52	.327	42	179	.235
Hubbard - Colo. Sprng	27	82	.329	89	238	.374
Hughes - Richmond	22	77	.286	27	151	.179
Humphreys - Columbus	45	174	.259	76	313	.243
Hunter - Tucson	58	140	.414	132	370	.357
Huskey - Norfolk	33	136	.243	75	338	.222
Huson - Okla. City	11	53	.208	80	249	.321
Ingram - Toledo	34	119	.286	56	195	.287
Jackson - Okla. City	25	88	.284	74	265	.279
Jackson - Vancouver	26	76	.342	79	282	.280
Jennings - Indianapols	30	119	.252	99	317	.312
Jeter - Columbus	8	31	.258	36	95	.379
Johnson - Phoenix	36	112	.321	79	279	.283
Jones - Colo. Sprng	32	116	.276	86	263	.327
Jones - Phoenix	36	110	.327	75	289	.260
Jones - Charlotte	16	70	.229	85	313	.272
Jordan - Scranton-WB	27	86	.314	64	228	.281
Kellner - Tucson	18	58	.310	69	236	.292
Kelly - Richmond	18	79	.228	64	234	.274
Kelly - Richmond	20	76	.263	31	113	.274
Kessinger - Indianapols	34	120	.283	66	277	.238
Kmak - Norfolk	28	84	.333	38	180	.211
Knabenshue - Buffalo	5	17	.294	33	114	.289
Knapp - Omaha	8	27	.296	26	124	.210
Koslofski - Omaha	18	78	.231	48	226	.212
Kowitz - Richmond	26	100	.260	114	366	.311
Kremblas - Indianapols	17	71	.239	19	79	.241
Kremers - New Orleans	5	32	.156	30	128	.234
Kunkel - Toledo	28	119	.235	58	227	.256
Laker - Ottawa	50	150	.333	78	266	.293
Lampkin - Phoenix	28	115	.243	108	338	.320
Leach - Columbus	34	148	.230	82	296	.277
Ledesma - Norfolk	30	108	.278	88	323	.272
Lee - Ottawa	43	145	.297	94	313	.300
Leiper - Buffalo	22	63	.349	67	281	.238
Leonard - Phoenix	25	82	.305	68	232	.293
Levasseur - Calgary	17	58	.293	11	56	.196
Levis - Charlotte	31	112	.277	75	260	.288
Lewis - Charlotte	28	113	.248	56	212	.264
Lewis - Rochester	18	68	.265	35	105	.333
Lieberthal - Scranton-WB	24	91	.264	44	198	.222
Lindeman - Norfolk	14	37	.378	31	86	.360
Lindsey - Nashville	7	43	.163	27	121	.223
Lis - Syracuse	36	99	.364	57	220	.259
Litton - Pawtucket	32	106	.302	38	147	.259
Lockett - Scranton-WB	15	66	.227	45	197	.228
Lockhart - Las Vegas	11	56	.196	95	275	.345
Loretta - New Orleans	10	63	.159	19	75	.253
Lovullo - Calgary	15	60	.250	47	151	.311
Luce - Okla. City	11	53	.208	29	116	.250
Lyden - Edmonton	16	70	.229	69	219	.315
Lydy - Tacoma	36	90	.400	124	417	.297
Lyons - Indianapols	43	131	.328	90	300	.300
Mabry - Louisville	27	116	.233	96	358	.268
Mack - Calgary	23	86	.267	94	318	.296
Makarewicz - Tucson	14	43	.326	34	125	.272
Maksudian - Iowa	25	58	.431	39	137	.285
Manahan - Calgary	25	91	.275	59	204	.289
Marrero - Ottawa	3	47	.064	59	207	.285
Marsh - Scranton-WB	40	116	.345	78	323	.241
Martin - Ottawa	31	129	.240	57	237	.241
Martin - Nashville	16	55	.291	28	117	.239
Martinez - Columbus	10	56	.179	73	244	.299
Martinez - Nashville	41	139	.295	86	332	.259
Martinez - Tacoma	29	111	.261	108	425	.254
Marzano - Scranton-WB	21	103	.204	38	173	.220
Massarelli - Edmonton	25	89	.281	84	328	.256
Masse - Columbus	27	83	.325	30	138	.217
Masteller - Salt Lake	9	37	.243	93	302	.308
Matheny - New Orleans	12	52	.231	27	129	.209

AAA Batting vs. Left-Handed and Right-Handed Pitchers

Player - Team	vs Left			vs Right		
	H	AB	Avg	H	AB	Avg
Matos - Tacoma	27	73	.370	76	263	.289
McCarty - Salt Lake	12	58	.207	35	128	.273
McCoy - Okla. City	33	96	.344	75	255	.294
McDavid - Las Vegas	31	135	.230	99	342	.289
McGinnis - Omaha	34	90	.378	62	249	.249
McIntosh - Salt Lake	45	128	.352	112	336	.333
McNeely - Pawtucket	51	195	.262	54	258	.209
Mejia - Colo. Sprng	22	82	.268	56	192	.292
Mercedes - Tacoma	11	55	.200	28	150	.187
Merullo - Charlotte	32	120	.267	92	295	.312
Miller - Tucson	15	70	.214	72	264	.273
Millette - Edmonton	33	98	.337	74	308	.240
Milstien - Nashville	7	47	.149	34	127	.268
Moler - Scranton-WB	12	47	.255	23	94	.245
Montalvo - Syracuse	21	76	.276	20	103	.194
Montgomery - Tucson	30	97	.309	55	234	.235
Montoyo - Scranton-WB	32	128	.250	75	252	.298
Moore - Richmond	32	78	.410	48	140	.500
Mordecai - Richmond	38	110	.345	69	272	.254
Morman - Edmonton	31	95	.326	111	311	.357
Mota - Colo. Sprng	7	35	.200	23	89	.258
Mota - Omaha	26	89	.292	65	265	.245
Mouton - Columbus	16	50	.320	48	154	.312
Munoz - Pawtucket	48	173	.277	87	342	.254
Munoz - Vancouver	10	34	.294	52	153	.340
Murray - Pawtucket	36	174	.207	68	287	.237
Natal - Edmonton	9	28	.321	23	87	.264
Navarro - Norfolk	11	35	.314	35	132	.265
Nevin - Tucson	35	109	.321	80	328	.244
Newfield - Calgary	52	124	.419	98	306	.320
Nieves - Las Vegas	36	113	.319	89	293	.304
Noboa - Buffalo	24	80	.300	42	153	.275
Noland - Colo. Sprng	6	37	.162	67	164	.409
Nuneviller - Scranton-WB	30	91	.330	39	172	.227
O'Leary - New Orleans	8	45	.178	65	176	.369
Obando - Rochester	42	135	.311	91	265	.343
Offerman - Albuquerque	16	52	.308	58	172	.337
Oliva - Richmond	28	88	.318	66	283	.233
Olmedo - Richmond	35	136	.257	54	251	.215
Ortiz - Nashville	40	114	.351	55	232	.237
Ortiz - Pawtucket	37	100	.370	62	214	.290
Ortiz - Phoenix	15	77	.195	85	287	.296
Osik - Buffalo	20	95	.211	33	159	.208
Owens - Colo. Sprng	21	68	.309	48	189	.254
Palmeiro - Vancouver	36	125	.288	113	331	.341
Pappas - Louisville	5	48	.104	36	157	.229
Paquette - Tacoma	12	39	.308	58	206	.282
Parker - Norfolk	22	77	.286	39	151	.258
Pedre - Pawtucket	22	109	.202	21	88	.239
Pedrique - Edmonton	13	54	.241	42	177	.237
Pegues - Indianapolis	33	80	.413	38	165	.230
Peltier - Okla. City	20	82	.244	92	336	.274
Pemberton - Toledo	35	127	.276	74	233	.318
Penn - Toledo	52	165	.315	74	279	.265
Perez - Syracuse	45	142	.317	110	368	.299
Perezchica - Columbus	15	44	.341	15	58	.259
Perry - Charlotte	36	112	.321	85	261	.326
Petagine - Tucson	7	53	.132	69	187	.369
Pevey - Syracuse	13	40	.325	57	219	.260
Phillips - Phoenix	25	98	.255	83	262	.317
Pirkl - Calgary	31	104	.298	81	249	.325
Pledger - Iowa	8	26	.308	57	204	.279
Posada - Columbus	24	128	.188	51	185	.276
Pose - New Orleans	28	111	.252	89	311	.286
Prager - Louisville	5	23	.217	36	152	.237
Pride - Ottawa	11	58	.190	66	242	.273
Prince - Albuquerque	19	70	.271	75	260	.288
Pulliam - Las Vegas	31	108	.287	40	206	.194
Pye - Albuquerque	29	84	.345	92	277	.332
Quinlan - Scranton-WB	22	69	.319	41	193	.212
Quinones - Calgary	29	79	.367	43	157	.274
Quintana - Buffalo	13	49	.265	12	57	.211
Raabe - Salt Lake	48	136	.353	104	338	.308
Ramirez - Charlotte	32	142	.225	65	275	.236
Ramos - Las Vegas	35	93	.376	67	217	.309
Ramos - Tucson	13	59	.220	105	332	.316
Randa - Omaha	31	110	.282	92	336	.274
Raven - Vancouver	22	97	.227	78	231	.338
Ready - Ottawa	13	50	.260	13	77	.169
Richardson - Louisville	17	72	.236	45	167	.269
Riles - Vancouver	23	72	.319	75	248	.302
Robertson - Nashville	4	21	.190	44	192	.229
Rodriguez - Calgary	15	33	.455	21	82	.256
Rodriguez - Pawtucket	17	68	.250	29	97	.299
Rodriguez - Pawtucket	26	91	.286	44	142	.310
Rodriguez - Pawtucket	26	91	.286	16	76	.211
Rodriguez - Edmonton	18	67	.269	59	209	.282
Rohde - Buffalo	19	80	.238	43	191	.225
Ronan - Louisville	10	44	.227	53	221	.240
Rossy - Omaha	32	105	.305	62	299	.207
Russo - Salt Lake	10	30	.333	24	85	.282
Saenz - Nashville	32	102	.314	68	281	.242
Santangelo - Ottawa	30	135	.222	73	270	.270
Santovenia - Omaha	4	39	.103	20	103	.194
Schall - Scranton-WB	37	121	.306	93	334	.278
Scott - Phoenix	37	116	.319	85	310	.274
Sellers - Indianapolis	19	55	.345	28	125	.224
Shave - Okla. City	29	103	.282	44	232	.190
Shields - Iowa	26	80	.325	60	244	.246
Siddall - Ottawa	1	21	.048	18	89	.202
Silvestri - Columbus	28	114	.246	71	280	.254
Singleton - New Orleans	4	33	.121	33	100	.330
Smiley - Phoenix	11	48	.229	57	179	.318
Smith - New Orleans	30	127	.236	64	281	.228
Smith - Rochester	32	131	.244	76	303	.251
Snow - Vancouver	17	47	.362	39	142	.275
Sojo - Calgary	2	14	.143	31	88	.352
Sparks - Columbus	47	170	.276	93	345	.270
Springer - Toledo	44	169	.260	90	342	.263
Stahoviak - Salt Lake	29	94	.309	110	343	.321
Staton - Las Vegas	20	69	.290	55	202	.272
Stephenson - Louisville	20	80	.250	85	310	.274
Stillwell - Indianapols	28	97	.289	63	240	.263
Suero - Buffalo	18	78	.231	43	187	.230
Sveum - Calgary	30	112	.268	81	281	.288
Sweeney - Vancouver	22	80	.275	75	264	.284
Tatum - Colo. Sprng	48	125	.384	104	309	.337
Thomas - Louisville	27	103	.262	51	219	.233
Thoutsis - Pawtucket	10	78	.128	57	222	.257
Thurman - Nashville	34	144	.236	90	326	.276
Timmons - Iowa	32	109	.294	84	330	.255
Tomberlin - Pawtucket	16	49	.327	47	140	.336
Townley - Syracuse	25	84	.298	26	103	.252
Tubbs - Buffalo	38	137	.277	102	359	.284
Tucker - Omaha	35	152	.230	98	325	.302
Tucker - Tucson	39	98	.398	90	306	.294
Turang - Calgary	34	95	.358	61	182	.335
Twardoski - Pawtucket	31	116	.267	77	266	.289
Tyler - Rochester	14	57	.246	68	257	.265
VanBurkleo - Colo. Sprng	24	100	.240	89	317	.281
Vatcher - Norfolk	31	107	.290	43	209	.206
Veras - Norfolk	35	128	.273	79	329	.240
Vitiello - Omaha	34	95	.358	82	249	.329
Wachter - New Orleans	18	79	.228	45	142	.317
Walewander - Edmonton	9	37	.243	23	131	.176
Wawruck - Rochester	33	117	.282	98	318	.308
Wedge - Pawtucket	31	100	.310	41	150	.273
Wehner - Buffalo	19	84	.226	81	242	.335
White - Ottawa	22	65	.338	21	99	.212
Whitmore - Edmonton	21	99	.212	98	322	.304
Willard - Calgary	26	82	.317	81	289	.280
Williams - Las Vegas	15	60	.250	62	159	.390
Williams - Albuquerque	26	70	.371	64	218	.294
Wilson - Nashville	27	114	.237	56	256	.219
Wilson - Okla. City	20	73	.274	39	154	.253
Wilson - Edmonton	17	66	.258	80	248	.323
Wolak - Nashville	35	126	.278	66	268	.246
Womack - Buffalo	19	105	.181	74	306	.242
Wood - Ottawa	35	117	.299	80	291	.275
Woods - Ottawa	18	97	.186	47	193	.244
Worthington - Iowa	28	80	.350	76	284	.268
Young - Tacoma	5	19	.263	24	83	.289
Young - Louisville	24	73	.329	76	249	.305
Young - Buffalo	11	40	.275	51	184	.277
Zaun - Rochester	26	124	.210	64	261	.245
Zinter - Toledo	45	171	.263	67	300	.223
Zosky - Syracuse	29	90	.322	46	194	.237

AAA Pitching vs. Left-Handed and Right-Handed Batters

	vs Left			vs Right		
Player - Team	H	AB	Avg	H	AB	Avg
Abbott - Omaha	32	89	.360	23	110	.209
Acre - Tacoma	11	40	.275	13	66	.197
Adkins - Rochester	30	70	.429	33	129	.256
Alberro - Okla. City	31	103	.301	48	160	.300
Allen - Colo. Sprng	42	120	.350	66	197	.335
Allison - Tacoma	38	140	.271	166	490	.339
Anderson - Iowa	52	180	.289	82	257	.319
Anderson - Louisville	6	37	.162	25	82	.305
Anderson - New Orleans	17	58	.293	23	62	.371
Ausanio - Columbus	18	85	.212	27	133	.203
Bailey - Pawtucket	17	90	.189	27	131	.206
Baldwin - Nashville	70	294	.238	74	314	.236
Ballard - Buffalo	12	39	.308	58	184	.315
Baptist - Syracuse	21	100	.210	124	399	.311
Barber - Louisville	26	134	.194	53	184	.288
Bark - Richmond	16	103	.155	112	374	.299
Barton - Phoenix	10	42	.238	41	156	.263
Batchelor - Louisville	31	96	.323	54	208	.260
Bauer - Toledo	8	56	.143	21	76	.276
Bell - Tucson	35	114	.307	174	571	.305
Beltran - Louisville	19	80	.238	128	457	.280
Bennett - Vancouver	29	126	.230	42	208	.202
Bergman - Toledo	62	271	.229	85	322	.264
Berumen - Las Vegas	34	123	.276	66	204	.324
Birkbeck - Richmond	66	269	.245	79	333	.237
Blomdahl - Toledo	91	290	.314	101	369	.274
Bochtler - Las Vegas	42	157	.268	74	242	.306
Bohanon - Okla. City	17	71	.239	89	316	.282
Bolton - Nashville	59	218	.271	49	216	.227
Borbon - Richmond	13	67	.194	53	223	.238
Borland - Scranton-WB	22	86	.256	13	92	.141
Boucher - Ottawa	19	85	.224	91	350	.260
Boze - New Orleans	93	311	.299	89	338	.263
Brennan - Iowa	37	133	.278	62	200	.310
Brink - Phoenix	47	163	.288	93	323	.288
Brito - New Orleans	20	91	.220	14	96	.146
Brock - Tacoma	55	203	.271	60	251	.239
Brosnan - Albuquerque	17	47	.362	58	195	.297
Bross - Indianapolis	38	172	.221	48	227	.211
Brow - Syracuse	33	127	.260	44	175	.251
Brumley - Okla. City	46	159	.289	63	238	.265
Bruske - Tucson	17	61	.279	30	99	.303
Bryant - Salt Lake	30	124	.242	138	441	.313
Buckels - Louisville	29	106	.274	43	184	.234
Burgos - Omaha	11	51	.216	33	157	.210
Burns - Calgary	46	135	.341	87	297	.293
Burrows - Okla. City	33	97	.340	42	208	.202
Bustillos - Albuquerque	23	74	.311	34	104	.327
Butcher - Vancouver	11	40	.275	20	78	.256
Byrd - Charlotte	16	51	.314	17	81	.210
Campbell - Salt Lake	15	58	.259	24	95	.253
Campbell - Las Vegas	62	196	.316	108	360	.300
Carlson - Phoenix	70	217	.323	112	394	.284
Carper - Columbus	67	214	.313	61	242	.252
Carter - Scranton-WB	6	41	.146	16	68	.235
Carter - Pawtucket	70	215	.326	64	245	.261
Castillo - Iowa	22	92	.239	35	158	.222
Castillo - Norfolk	12	46	.261	23	64	.359
Chapin - Edmonton	39	148	.264	71	226	.314
Chiamparino - Las Vegas	18	58	.310	27	92	.293
Christiansen - Buffalo	4	44	.091	15	69	.217
Christopher - Toledo	32	99	.323	44	185	.238
Cimorelli - Louisville	21	70	.300	43	165	.261
Clark - Richmond	31	117	.265	41	188	.218
Clayton - Columbus	40	136	.294	63	223	.283
Combs - Scranton-WB	34	113	.301	133	431	.309
Converse - Calgary	54	145	.372	51	160	.319
Cornelius - Ottawa	70	270	.259	79	303	.261
Costello - Phoenix	57	167	.341	85	299	.284
Courtright - Indianapols	33	127	.260	106	391	.271
Crabtree - Syracuse	48	165	.291	77	252	.306
Creek - Louisville	5	21	.238	32	85	.376
Cross - Syracuse	85	318	.267	88	359	.245
Curry - Okla. City	29	101	.287	47	146	.322
Czaikowski - Colo. Sprng	18	67	.269	36	163	.221

	vs Left			vs Right		
Player - Team	H	AB	Avg	H	AB	Avg
Daal - Albuquerque	4	21	.190	34	107	.318
Darwin - Calgary	20	95	.211	41	173	.237
Davis - Calgary	7	30	.233	28	121	.231
Dedrick - Rochester	43	141	.305	55	238	.231
DeJesus - Omaha	25	78	.321	26	130	.200
Delossantos - Buffalo	25	88	.284	21	95	.221
Delucia - Indianapols	13	55	.236	9	89	.101
DeSilva - Albuquerque	32	105	.305	58	177	.328
Dettmer - Okla. City	23	78	.295	36	113	.319
Diaz - Ottawa	13	36	.361	28	83	.337
DiPoto - Charlotte	14	52	.269	23	82	.280
Dixon - Louisville	11	67	.164	37	154	.240
Dougherty - Tucson	26	83	.313	44	159	.277
Drahman - Edmonton	29	95	.305	31	140	.221
Draper - Las Vegas	39	122	.320	53	171	.310
Dunne - Scranton-WB	18	62	.290	18	59	.305
Dyer - Buffalo	14	58	.241	19	71	.268
Edenfield - Vancouver	27	112	.241	42	204	.206
Eiland - Columbus	55	248	.222	86	301	.286
Fischen - Ottawa	13	65	.200	40	159	.252
Ellis - Nashville	69	211	.327	57	204	.279
Fajardo - Okla. City	16	76	.211	28	115	.243
Farrell - New Orleans	30	81	.370	80	276	.290
Ferry - Indianapols	22	60	.367	25	75	.333
Finnvold - Pawtucket	16	55	.291	16	100	.160
Flener - Syracuse	5	22	.227	33	122	.270
Fletcher - Scranton-WB	69	241	.286	75	298	.252
Florence - Pawtucket	20	84	.238	46	146	.315
Florie - Las Vegas	30	104	.288	46	171	.269
Foster - Iowa	11	54	.204	10	54	.185
Frascatore - Louisville	35	129	.271	39	163	.239
Fraser - Edmonton	23	81	.284	43	149	.289
Frazier - Columbus	45	172	.262	63	227	.278
Fritz - Vancouver	20	83	.241	41	128	.320
Frohwirth - Pawtucket	21	71	.296	28	134	.209
Fyhrie - Omaha	48	135	.356	51	194	.263
Gaddy - Scranton-WB	34	144	.236	127	488	.260
Gallaher - Tucson	26	85	.306	29	122	.238
Gamez - Phoenix	19	78	.244	102	308	.331
Ganote - Syracuse	43	140	.307	36	165	.218
Garagozzo - Columbus	7	35	.200	37	135	.274
Garcia - Albuquerque	22	72	.306	47	162	.290
Gardner - Tucson	40	140	.286	55	158	.348
George - New Orleans	23	71	.324	34	108	.315
Goetz - Okla. City	41	153	.268	61	221	.276
Gohr - Toledo	23	105	.219	52	181	.287
Gonzales - Toledo	27	100	.270	115	365	.315
Gorecki - Albuquerque	55	159	.346	70	260	.269
Gozzo - Norfolk	12	46	.261	10	59	.169
Green - Scranton-WB	93	323	.288	86	305	.282
Greer - Norfolk	11	41	.268	24	82	.293
Grimsley - Charlotte	26	125	.208	32	141	.227
Grott - Indianapols	18	116	.155	88	314	.280
Guardado - Salt Lake	29	98	.296	142	491	.289
Gunderson - Norfolk	7	34	.206	18	98	.184
Hamilton - Las Vegas	26	94	.277	43	138	.312
Hammaker - Nashville	9	41	.220	15	69	.217
Hancock - Buffalo	24	101	.238	78	237	.329
Haney - Omaha	27	96	.281	98	341	.287
Hansell - Albuquerque	38	161	.236	71	293	.242
Harriger - Las Vegas	82	254	.323	134	407	.329
Harris - Calgary	50	150	.333	87	269	.323
Hartgraves - Tucson	30	96	.313	76	290	.262
Hartsock - Louisville	18	58	.310	23	74	.311
Hathaway - Las Vegas	21	88	.239	100	305	.328
Hawblitzel - Colo. Sprng	68	233	.292	132	427	.309
Hawkins - Salt Lake	40	116	.345	52	195	.267
Haynes - Ottawa	28	120	.233	43	198	.217
Helling - Okla. City	71	239	.297	82	281	.292
Henderson - Ottawa	62	232	.267	61	237	.257
Henry - Salt Lake	32	87	.368	40	143	.280
Hillman - Norfolk	11	58	.190	92	336	.274
Hines - Columbus	21	95	.221	66	228	.289
Hitchcock - Columbus	8	26	.308	45	174	.259
Holman - Calgary	25	63	.397	44	116	.379

	vs Left			vs Right		
Player - Team	H	AB	Avg	H	AB	Avg
Holman - Ottawa	24	110	.218	41	148	.277
Holzemer - Vancouver	20	84	.238	130	403	.323
Hook - Phoenix	41	118	.347	68	242	.281
Hope - Buffalo	47	181	.260	51	207	.246
Hutton - Columbus	12	57	.211	19	72	.264
Ilsley - Iowa	24	99	.242	105	383	.274
Jacome - Norfolk	23	88	.261	115	399	.288
James - Vancouver	28	137	.204	73	226	.323
Jarvis - Indianapols	58	204	.284	78	318	.245
Jimenez - Tacoma	39	117	.333	43	167	.257
Johns - Tacoma	27	125	.216	87	362	.240
Johnson - Nashville	15	55	.273	25	110	.227
Johnstone - Edmonton	14	58	.241	32	107	.299
Jones - Charlotte	25	89	.281	37	147	.252
Karl - New Orleans	9	58	.155	83	275	.302
Keyser - Nashville	63	249	.253	60	256	.234
Kiefer - New Orleans	48	224	.214	58	220	.264
Kilgo - Indianapols	27	82	.329	52	174	.299
King - Calgary	12	55	.218	34	97	.351
Knox - Louisville	24	92	.261	156	496	.315
Knudsen - Toledo	25	94	.266	31	155	.200
Krivda - Rochester	24	120	.200	125	484	.258
Kutzler - Omaha	54	160	.338	57	222	.257
Lancaster - Syracuse	40	128	.313	55	224	.246
Layana - Ottawa	25	93	.269	44	142	.310
Leary - Ottawa	25	98	.255	47	122	.385
Lee - Iowa	22	80	.275	44	157	.280
Lemon - Edmonton	48	132	.364	72	219	.329
Leskanic - Colo. Sprng	51	197	.259	78	294	.265
Lima - Toledo	60	232	.259	64	295	.217
Lira - Toledo	78	262	.298	93	343	.271
Lomon - Richmond	63	274	.230	96	295	.325
Long - Edmonton	105	290	.362	119	403	.295
Looney - Ottawa	34	103	.330	100	383	.261
Lopez - Charlotte	53	219	.242	83	324	.256
Lorraine - Vancouver	17	75	.227	145	495	.293
Luebbers - Iowa	67	248	.270	82	279	.294
Lynch - Charlotte	19	73	.260	43	147	.293
Maldonado - Tacoma	18	60	.300	39	108	.361
Manuel - Rochester	83	263	.316	78	296	.264
Marquez - Nashville	25	104	.240	23	130	.177
Marshall - Colo. Sprng	16	60	.267	33	102	.324
Mathews - Edmonton	40	123	.325	48	205	.234
Maxcy - Toledo	15	68	.221	16	91	.176
McFarlin - Las Vegas	31	99	.313	45	166	.271
McGehee - Rochester	75	271	.277	90	314	.287
McMurtry - Tucson	51	201	.254	68	283	.240
Meier - Colo. Sprng	62	175	.354	83	251	.331
Melendez - Pawtucket	34	118	.288	40	164	.244
Menendez - Phoenix	4	30	.133	20	72	.278
Milacki - Omaha	35	136	.257	56	192	.292
Miller - Edmonton	76	227	.335	88	289	.304
Miller - Buffalo	33	107	.308	32	95	.337
Minchey - Pawtucket	44	224	.196	84	336	.250
Minor - Buffalo	14	70	.200	33	127	.260
Mintz - Phoenix	12	48	.250	28	95	.295
Minutelli - Tucson	20	66	.303	67	189	.354
Misuraca - Salt Lake	29	95	.305	59	179	.330
Mitchell - Okla. City	33	132	.250	47	173	.272
Mlicki - Charlotte	76	262	.290	103	385	.268
Moeller - Omaha	23	90	.256	57	168	.339
Mohler - Tacoma	12	59	.203	57	206	.277
Mongiello - Nashville	54	157	.344	40	173	.231
Moody - Okla. City	8	29	.276	32	124	.258
Moore - Colo. Sprng	29	87	.333	38	132	.288
Morman - Tucson	19	77	.247	66	215	.307
Morrison - Vancouver	54	142	.380	59	226	.261
Morton - Norfolk	14	88	.159	110	415	.265
Munoz - Scranton-WB	12	60	.200	15	62	.242
Munoz - Salt Lake	74	258	.287	106	322	.329
Mutis - Edmonton	10	26	.385	31	97	.320
Myers - Edmonton	8	44	.182	70	210	.333
Neidlinger - Louisville	28	74	.378	23	83	.277
Newlin - Edmonton	27	67	.403	35	99	.354
Nichols - Omaha	78	255	.306	85	305	.279

AAA Pitching vs. Left-Handed and Right-Handed Batters

Player - Team	vs Left H	AB	Avg	vs Right H	AB	Avg	Player - Team	vs Left H	AB	Avg	vs Right H	AB	Avg
Nichting - Albuquerque	20	54	.370	41	124	.331	St Claire - Syracuse	18	113	.159	39	134	.291
Novoa - Iowa	19	96	.198	132	439	.301	Stevens - Salt Lake	16	57	.281	25	105	.238
O'Donoghue - Rochester	38	111	.342	104	327	.318	Stevens - Salt Lake	23	88	.261	54	156	.346
Ogea - Charlotte	73	259	.282	73	349	.209	Stidham - Toledo	14	80	.175	34	160	.213
Ojala - Columbus	22	111	.198	135	473	.285	Sturtze - Tacoma	29	90	.322	44	167	.263
Olivares - Louisville	19	92	.207	28	97	.289	Swan - Charlotte	11	44	.250	42	118	.356
Olsen - Nashville	35	132	.265	34	136	.250	Tavarez - Charlotte	75	272	.276	92	404	.228
Oquist - Rochester	21	72	.292	33	124	.266	Taylor - Las Vegas	68	244	.279	107	375	.285
Osteen - Tacoma	23	100	.230	146	460	.317	Taylor - Phoenix	33	122	.270	67	256	.262
Painter - Colo. Sprng	12	59	.203	78	258	.302	Taylor - New Orleans	66	258	.256	113	394	.287
Parra - Albuquerque	79	237	.333	111	348	.319	Telford - Richmond	81	248	.327	67	306	.219
Parrett - Omaha	18	76	.237	16	69	.232	Telgheder - Norfolk	75	297	.253	81	311	.260
Patrick - Tacoma	18	59	.305	32	125	.256	Thompson - Colo. Sprng	64	196	.327	105	361	.291
Patterson - Scranton-WB	41	154	.266	61	209	.292	Tomlin - Buffalo	17	53	.321	53	157	.338
Pavlik - Okla. City	14	55	.255	12	55	.218	Torres - Phoenix	43	136	.316	42	170	.247
Pedraza - Colo. Sprng	18	52	.346	42	104	.404	Treadwell - Albuquerque	49	212	.231	102	388	.263
Pennington - Rochester	20	81	.247	48	230	.209	Trombley - Salt Lake	36	107	.336	39	141	.277
Percival - Vancouver	32	95	.337	31	129	.240	Urbani - Louisville	7	22	.318	44	154	.286
Perez - Ottawa	18	82	.220	112	377	.297	Valdes - Albuquerque	18	61	.295	26	111	.234
Perez - Okla. City	88	313	.281	105	373	.282	Valdez - Pawtucket	32	143	.224	58	226	.257
Perschke - Iowa	27	96	.281	24	105	.229	Valera - Vancouver	31	118	.263	49	145	.338
Petkovsek - Tucson	74	237	.312	102	333	.306	Vanegmond - Pawtucket	39	172	.227	71	285	.249
Pettitte - Columbus	15	55	.273	86	316	.272	VanLandingham - Phnix	7	39	.179	14	70	.200
Phillips - Syracuse	53	199	.266	73	237	.308	VanRyn - Albuquerque	12	37	.324	63	186	.339
Phillips - Calgary	57	146	.390	76	263	.289	Veres - Iowa	20	77	.260	23	126	.183
Pierce - Omaha	12	50	.240	67	226	.296	Vosberg - Tacoma	5	43	.116	34	139	.245
Pierce - Pawtucket	19	92	.207	34	135	.252	Wakefield - Buffalo	85	338	.251	112	341	.328
Plantenberg - Calgary	21	69	.304	106	351	.302	Walker - Norfolk	16	62	.258	32	116	.276
Potts - Richmond	15	84	.179	60	230	.261	Wall - Tucson	74	244	.303	97	339	.286
Pugh - Indianapolis	34	103	.330	25	104	.240	Walton - Colo. Sprng	21	90	.233	58	161	.360
Quantrill - Scranton-WB	26	113	.230	29	104	.279	Ward - Syracuse	16	74	.216	47	148	.318
Quirico - Columbus	14	73	.192	49	174	.282	Warren - Indianapols	30	102	.294	52	200	.260
Ratekin - Vancouver	70	208	.337	89	292	.305	Watkins - Salt Lake	21	71	.296	52	160	.325
Ratliff - Iowa	17	52	.327	22	68	.324	Wayne - Albuquerque	23	59	.390	58	170	.341
Remlinger - Norfolk	13	45	.289	44	191	.230	Weber - Calgary	102	268	.381	114	404	.282
Rhodes - Rochester	11	60	.183	59	276	.214	Wegmann - Rochester	28	105	.267	58	218	.266
Ricci - Scranton-WB	31	91	.341	29	150	.193	Wendell - Iowa	63	237	.266	71	344	.206
Ridenour - Edmonton	49	161	.304	62	237	.262	Wertz - Charlotte	20	91	.220	33	142	.232
Rightnowar - New Orlns.	28	130	.215	34	184	.185	Weston - Colo. Sprng	32	85	.376	50	151	.331
Ritz - Colo. Sprng	6	48	.125	24	94	.255	White - Ottawa	12	41	.293	64	229	.279
Rivera - Columbus	16	58	.276	18	69	.261	Williams - Scranton-WB	44	160	.275	43	145	.297
Roa - Norfolk	83	281	.295	101	369	.274	Williams - Vancouver	41	147	.279	66	222	.297
Robinson - Syracuse	18	90	.200	28	116	.241	Williams - Albuquerque	29	99	.293	49	173	.283
Robinson - Phoenix	34	112	.304	69	229	.301	Willis - Buffalo	29	102	.284	60	197	.305
Rodriguez - Pawtucket	69	288	.240	107	404	.265	Wilson - New Orleans	24	92	.261	52	195	.267
Rogers - Norfolk	9	36	.250	26	83	.313	Winston - Ottawa	12	40	.300	15	65	.231
Rogers - New Orleans	11	36	.306	23	65	.354	Wishnevski - Louisville	59	209	.282	72	337	.214
Rogers - Syracuse	41	153	.268	41	197	.208	Wissler - Salt Lake	43	128	.336	82	257	.319
Roper - Indianapolis	20	100	.200	28	114	.246	Woodall - Richmond	24	107	.224	135	585	.231
Rosselli - Phoenix	17	45	.378	79	253	.312	Zavaras - Calgary	25	57	.439	33	103	.320
Ruffcorn - Nashville	62	305	.203	77	312	.247							
Sager - Las Vegas	25	67	.373	32	103	.311							
Salkeld - Calgary	37	122	.303	41	155	.265							
Sanchez - Calgary	29	112	.259	60	201	.299							
Sanford - Salt Lake	46	178	.258	75	305	.246							
Satre - Rochester	55	197	.279	71	297	.239							
Sauveur - Indianapols	17	85	.200	30	155	.194							
Scheid - Edmonton	17	81	.210	93	312	.298							
Schrenk - Nashville	83	309	.269	92	371	.248							
Scudder - Buffalo	80	264	.303	91	307	.296							
Seelbach - Richmond	34	103	.330	34	129	.264							
Seminara - Norfolk	49	167	.293	59	217	.272							
Service - Indianapols	14	56	.250	21	147	.143							
Shaw - Tacoma	24	71	.338	74	246	.301							
Shifflett - Omaha	43	131	.328	56	232	.241							
Shouse - Buffalo	18	76	.237	26	114	.228							
Simons - Omaha	18	72	.250	79	299	.264							
Small - Tucson	28	103	.272	63	196	.321							
Smith - Phoenix	16	44	.364	24	75	.320							
Smith - Tacoma	21	86	.244	33	117	.282							
Smith - Louisville	8	58	.138	17	103	.165							
Smithberg - Tacoma	24	91	.264	51	192	.266							
Sparks - New Orleans	80	324	.247	103	378	.272							
Spoljaric - Syracuse	11	28	.393	36	164	.220							
Springer - Vancouver	32	109	.294	45	209	.215							

Major League Equivalencies

Before I came to work for STATS, I spent four years working with Bill James. One of my chores each fall, when the final minor league stats came out in *Baseball America*, was to input the stat lines for every player who saw significant time at the Double- or Triple-A level. Took me about a week, but it was a welcome break from actually having to think.

Anyway, after some twists and turns in a BASIC program that Bill wrote about a decade ago, those minor-league statistics were transformed into Major League Equivalencies (MLEs). As Bill described them in last year's *Minor League Handbook*:

> These numbers are not intended to be projections or predictions of who will do what in the major leagues next season, or in any other season. They are, however, just one step away from that: they represent the major league equivalent of what the player has done in the minor leagues.

A few years ago, STATS took over the actual running of the MLE programs, but they're basically the same as they have always been. The basic principle is this: take the minor league stats, and adjust them for the context—the league and the ballparks, both minor and major—to come up with a close approximation of what the player would have done last season, *had he been in the major leagues with his parent club*. And given a chance to play in the majors, most players approximate their MLEs. Obviously, players have fluke years in the minors, just as they do in the majors—Tuffy Rhodes' 1993 MLEs showed him slugging .482, far better than anything he'd done before, and in 1994 he slugged just .387. But we also showed Manny Ramirez with a .538 slugging percentage, and Rafael Bournigal with a .277 SLG. Given a chance in the majors last season, they finished at .521 and .267, respectively.

Numerous "baseball men" have long maintained that minor league hitting stats don't really mean anything, but over the last 10 years Bill and STATS have proved that they *do* mean something, quite a lot actually, if you know how to look at them. So take a few minutes and look at Bob Abreu (Astros), Darren Bragg (Mariners) and Marty Cordova (Twins), just three of the relatively-unknown prospects whose MLEs suggest a quality major league future.

— *Rob Neyer*

Major League Equivalencies for 1994 AAA/AA Batters

Batter	Age	Avg	G	AB	R	H	2B	3B	HR	RBI	BB	SO	SB	CS	OBP	SLG
ANGELS																
Anderson,Garret	23	.281	123	477	56	134	33	3	9	77	20	97	2	3	.310	.419
Boykin,Tyrone	27	.199	119	407	47	81	16	1	3	45	43	83	5	11	.276	.265
Cohick,Emmitt	26	.220	96	313	29	69	19	2	6	44	19	106	1	4	.265	.351
Correia,Rod	27	.240	106	359	40	86	9	1	4	36	18	56	5	7	.276	.304
Fabregas,Jorge	25	.192	66	203	12	39	4	0	0	18	8	26	0	1	.223	.212
Forbes,P.J.	27	.248	90	302	29	75	16	1	0	30	16	44	2	2	.286	.308
Grebeck,Brian	27	.264	93	292	36	77	18	0	1	25	27	49	0	3	.326	.336
Harkrider,Timothy	23	.232	112	388	49	90	14	0	0	35	37	54	7	14	.299	.268
Hosey,Steve	26	.226	112	358	50	81	17	1	13	45	34	118	5	7	.293	.388
Jackson,John	28	.256	102	340	46	87	12	2	1	28	34	38	11	12	.324	.312
Monzon,Jose	26	.212	83	269	29	57	13	1	3	25	14	55	0	1	.251	.301
Ortiz,Bo	25	.258	107	387	56	100	21	1	9	51	23	61	10	5	.300	.388
Palmeiro,Orlando	26	.287	117	432	59	124	22	2	0	35	42	48	13	6	.350	.347
Perez,Eddie	25	.260	61	208	27	54	11	1	5	28	25	55	5	4	.339	.394
Pritchett,Chris	25	.264	127	432	61	114	19	1	4	65	54	93	2	3	.346	.340
Ramirez,J.D.	28	.247	123	425	57	105	20	1	10	41	30	102	1	4	.297	.369
Raven,Luis	26	.266	132	492	78	131	16	4	23	84	18	146	6	1	.292	.455
Riles,Ernest	34	.269	99	308	40	83	15	4	11	43	34	71	1	3	.342	.451
Riley,Marquis	24	.243	97	367	50	89	9	1	0	20	22	64	19	9	.285	.272
Smith,Chris	21	.223	110	400	43	89	13	1	2	40	20	77	1	7	.260	.275
Sweeney,Mark	25	.251	117	375	53	94	11	1	8	48	48	62	1	4	.336	.349
Wolff,Mike	24	.248	113	375	45	93	23	0	10	41	32	97	6	9	.307	.389
ASTROS																
Abreu,Bob	21	.277	118	386	51	107	23	6	12	61	30	91	8	9	.329	.461
Ball,Jeff	26	.290	111	345	55	100	27	2	9	48	24	83	6	7	.336	.458
Chavez,Raul	22	.200	89	245	14	49	6	0	0	18	12	46	0	0	.237	.224
Colon,Dennis	21	.253	118	368	31	93	15	4	3	44	12	48	6	4	.276	.340
Evans,Tim	26	.239	98	238	19	57	7	2	0	20	10	50	0	2	.270	.286
Groppuso,Mike	25	.240	118	341	41	82	14	1	9	39	25	109	4	6	.292	.367
Guerrero,Juan	28	.240	89	271	28	65	13	3	4	31	16	49	0	1	.282	.354
Hajek,Dave	27	.272	129	449	45	122	23	2	4	45	18	25	8	6	.300	.359
Hatcher,Chris	26	.246	108	325	35	80	22	2	6	47	12	99	3	0	.273	.382
Hunter,Brian	24	.315	128	470	72	148	22	4	5	32	33	57	32	12	.360	.411
Kellner,Frank	28	.246	106	276	20	68	10	2	0	22	29	45	3	3	.318	.297
McNabb,Buck	22	.252	125	441	56	111	23	4	0	22	18	70	11	16	.281	.322
Miller,Orlando	26	.211	93	318	34	67	12	3	5	35	10	84	2	2	.235	.314
Montgomery,Ray	25	.211	103	313	32	66	15	3	4	32	22	59	3	2	.263	.316
Mota,Gary	24	.216	108	305	39	66	11	2	7	45	41	89	8	6	.309	.334
Nevers,Tom	23	.244	125	435	45	106	23	1	6	52	22	113	7	4	.280	.343
Nevin,Phil	24	.215	118	418	43	90	16	0	6	50	35	111	1	1	.276	.297
Petagine,Roberto	24	.262	65	229	34	60	15	0	5	28	22	59	1	0	.327	.393
Ramos,Ken	28	.251	121	367	52	92	15	3	0	20	47	29	14	5	.336	.308
Simms,Mike	28	.232	118	401	57	93	31	3	13	60	35	101	5	4	.294	.421
Thompson,Fletcher	26	.239	121	376	58	90	12	1	3	26	41	119	20	7	.314	.301
Tucker,Scooter	28	.267	113	378	41	101	30	0	8	51	30	61	1	1	.321	.410
White,Jimmy	22	.266	64	203	25	54	6	4	6	22	8	76	0	4	.294	.424
ATHLETICS																
Armas,Marcos	25	.246	113	419	44	103	20	2	13	56	14	126	0	2	.270	.396
Beard,Garrett	26	.230	88	270	33	62	12	0	5	30	28	48	2	5	.302	.330

Major League Equivalencies for 1994 AAA/AA Batters

Batter	Age	Avg	G	AB	R	H	2B	3B	HR	RBI	BB	SO	SB	CS	OBP	SLG
Borrelli,Dean	28	.240	101	350	24	84	16	0	2	32	24	69	0	1	.289	.303
Bowie,Jim	30	.273	109	388	51	106	19	1	5	51	39	41	1	2	.340	.366
Buccheri,James	26	.266	121	425	45	113	6	1	2	30	32	48	24	9	.317	.299
Cruz,Fausto	23	.278	65	205	20	57	15	0	0	13	13	34	1	2	.321	.351
Giambi,Jason	24	.233	108	352	48	82	22	0	6	55	39	68	0	0	.309	.347
Hart,Chris	26	.209	117	354	39	74	10	3	7	45	17	111	5	7	.245	.314
Lydy,Scott	26	.273	135	479	76	131	29	1	12	56	45	116	16	6	.336	.413
Martinez,Manuel	24	.219	137	511	59	112	19	2	6	46	21	77	13	10	.250	.299
Mashore,Damon	25	.201	59	204	21	41	8	1	2	18	9	59	4	1	.235	.279
Matos,Francisco	25	.267	86	318	31	85	7	0	0	23	10	34	12	9	.290	.289
Molina,Izzy	24	.194	116	377	27	73	14	1	6	44	12	51	4	1	.219	.284
Moore,Kerwin	24	.219	132	479	85	105	12	2	3	29	72	111	42	16	.321	.271
Paquette,Craig	26	.246	65	232	30	57	9	1	12	37	10	51	2	3	.277	.448
Sheldon,Scott	26	.208	91	260	27	54	8	0	0	24	21	76	5	1	.267	.238
Simmons,Enoch	27	.210	75	229	25	48	12	0	1	16	22	56	2	2	.279	.275
Sobolewski,Mark	25	.226	133	486	73	110	31	3	6	51	36	108	1	6	.280	.340
Wolfe,Joel	25	.249	121	421	57	105	21	1	4	50	45	87	20	7	.322	.333
Wood,Jason	25	.248	134	452	47	112	24	1	4	74	34	91	2	6	.300	.332
Young,Ernie	25	.293	101	341	53	100	19	2	15	60	37	78	3	11	.362	.493
BLUE JAYS																
Adriana,Sharnol	24	.215	86	214	25	46	7	0	2	18	28	50	5	6	.306	.276
Battle,Howard	23	.262	139	507	63	133	25	6	13	65	35	86	20	7	.310	.412
Bowers,Brent	24	.261	127	464	46	121	17	9	3	43	15	81	11	7	.284	.356
Brito,Tilson	23	.253	139	467	54	118	16	6	4	50	26	73	25	9	.292	.338
Butler,Rich	22	.246	147	484	54	119	11	4	4	42	33	102	11	10	.294	.310
Canate,William	23	.209	130	469	46	98	16	0	0	32	22	84	12	6	.244	.243
Crespo,Felipe	22	.256	129	493	65	126	29	3	8	43	42	103	15	5	.314	.375
Delgado,Carlos	23	.303	85	300	45	91	10	0	18	50	36	61	0	0	.378	.517
Giannelli,Ray	29	.272	114	320	37	87	18	0	9	44	42	81	0	0	.356	.413
Gonzalez,Alex	22	.269	110	428	60	115	21	3	11	50	46	97	18	6	.340	.409
Green,Shawn	22	.329	109	423	71	139	26	2	12	53	35	57	14	6	.380	.485
Lis,Joe	26	.276	89	312	46	86	19	0	10	43	21	41	2	0	.321	.433
Lutz,Brent	25	.258	111	365	49	94	15	4	7	36	25	108	14	9	.305	.378
Perez,Robert	26	.287	128	498	55	143	27	2	9	57	23	80	3	6	.319	.404
Pevey,Marty	33	.256	96	254	25	65	12	1	5	27	17	58	1	2	.303	.370
Steverson,Todd	23	.248	124	407	52	101	23	4	8	33	53	121	14	5	.335	.383
Stynes,Chris	22	.301	136	532	70	160	31	3	7	70	17	38	21	8	.322	.410
Weinke,Chris	22	.240	139	517	54	124	22	1	7	77	33	130	9	3	.285	.327
Zosky,Eddie	27	.248	85	278	35	69	14	2	6	32	7	48	2	0	.267	.378
BRAVES																
Ayrault,Joe	23	.211	107	342	31	72	21	0	5	32	13	76	1	1	.239	.316
Brown,Jarvis	28	.238	71	260	31	62	9	2	3	22	26	35	5	2	.308	.323
Caraballo,Ramon	26	.194	94	310	29	60	3	3	8	24	13	57	4	9	.226	.300
Gillis,Tim	27	.224	128	434	41	97	19	1	7	39	32	93	1	5	.277	.320
Giovanola,Ed	26	.247	123	413	46	102	18	1	7	35	29	61	5	3	.296	.346
Graffagnino,Anthony	23	.279	124	427	54	119	25	1	6	42	34	55	19	7	.332	.384
Grijak,Kevin	24	.251	100	339	32	85	17	0	9	47	13	41	1	2	.278	.381
Houston,Tyler	24	.219	97	302	25	66	13	1	3	25	11	44	2	2	.246	.298
Hughes,Troy	24	.215	108	307	29	66	13	0	2	22	28	59	5	1	.281	.277
Kelly,Mike	25	.235	82	302	34	71	12	2	11	34	23	97	5	5	.289	.397

Major League Equivalencies for 1994 AAA/AA Batters

Batter	Age	Avg	G	AB	R	H	2B	3B	HR	RBI	BB	SO	SB	CS	OBP	SLG
Kowitz,Brian	25	.271	124	447	51	121	25	3	6	43	31	53	14	5	.318	.380
Lopez,Luis	30	.276	133	500	50	138	28	1	14	59	25	43	2	1	.310	.420
Moore,Bobby	29	.297	87	300	35	89	6	1	4	18	18	31	6	6	.336	.363
Mordecai,Mike	27	.253	99	368	50	93	21	0	11	43	26	50	9	6	.302	.399
O'Connor,Kevin	26	.253	126	459	40	116	17	0	2	27	22	71	16	6	.287	.303
Oliva,Jose	24	.228	99	359	39	82	14	0	19	48	18	93	1	1	.265	.426
Olmeda,Jose	27	.205	109	375	37	77	16	3	3	29	21	73	10	3	.247	.288
Perez,Eddie	27	.235	113	375	28	88	13	1	7	37	13	47	0	0	.260	.331
Robinson,Don	23	.232	120	349	40	81	20	1	11	37	21	76	7	9	.276	.390
Swann,Pedro	24	.262	126	416	45	109	22	1	8	40	31	88	10	8	.313	.377
Wollenburg,Doug	24	.213	91	240	25	51	13	1	1	15	13	45	2	3	.253	.288
BREWERS																
Barker,Timothy	27	.239	128	422	59	101	22	4	4	36	64	101	32	11	.340	.339
Basse,Michael	25	.271	117	358	62	97	10	5	1	37	58	87	25	9	.373	.335
Byington,John	27	.283	134	487	59	138	29	2	7	72	30	30	6	1	.325	.394
Byrd,Jim	26	.179	83	235	20	42	6	0	1	17	11	62	2	6	.215	.217
Canseco,Ozzie	30	.212	117	391	45	83	26	0	11	56	46	145	2	4	.295	.363
Castleberry,Kevin	27	.238	74	239	32	57	5	4	0	26	16	53	8	6	.286	.293
Cirillo,Jeff	25	.282	61	227	37	64	16	1	8	38	23	40	3	0	.348	.467
Dodson,Bo	24	.213	105	315	38	67	13	0	1	29	42	65	1	2	.305	.263
Finn,John	27	.262	76	221	30	58	10	0	1	20	29	22	11	9	.348	.321
Glenn,Leon	25	.217	115	359	47	78	18	2	8	41	24	129	10	6	.266	.345
Harris,Mike	25	.237	105	354	56	84	18	7	3	45	35	72	8	5	.306	.353
Lofton,Rod	27	.290	92	334	52	97	21	2	1	40	16	72	15	5	.323	.374
Loretta,Mark	23	.246	120	419	50	103	17	3	0	39	27	48	6	4	.291	.301
O'Leary,Troy	25	.301	63	216	36	65	16	3	6	36	27	38	8	1	.379	.486
Perez,Danny	24	.284	115	415	65	118	16	10	4	54	28	84	6	4	.330	.400
Pose,Scott	28	.256	124	414	50	106	11	4	0	43	39	54	16	5	.320	.302
Riggs,Kevin	26	.257	66	218	28	56	8	1	0	16	29	41	2	6	.344	.303
Samples,Todd	25	.216	80	208	23	45	13	3	0	19	12	49	5	6	.259	.308
Singleton,Duane	22	.250	80	260	39	65	12	4	1	28	27	62	11	7	.321	.338
Smith,Greg	28	.208	115	399	47	83	18	2	0	31	38	59	28	9	.277	.263
Stefanski,Mike	25	.226	95	297	43	67	5	3	5	41	20	85	2	2	.274	.313
Talanoa,Scott	25	.222	127	409	66	91	17	0	20	65	49	147	0	1	.306	.411
Unroe,Tim	24	.270	126	448	72	121	30	4	10	76	26	114	10	5	.310	.422
Wachter,Derek	24	.286	95	322	37	92	20	2	4	49	28	84	4	0	.343	.398
CARDINALS																
Battle,Allen	26	.290	132	503	86	146	40	5	4	57	49	83	17	6	.353	.414
Biasucci,Joe	25	.247	112	352	44	87	17	0	14	47	42	101	0	6	.327	.415
Bradshaw,Terry	26	.265	136	498	77	132	27	6	12	57	47	81	13	9	.328	.416
Cholowsky,Dan	24	.217	131	451	56	98	17	3	13	50	54	118	16	5	.301	.355
Coolbaugh,Scott	29	.280	94	322	50	90	22	4	15	62	32	70	2	4	.345	.512
Cromer,Tripp	27	.251	124	406	44	102	21	6	7	41	27	86	3	5	.298	.384
Deak,Darrel	25	.250	133	472	54	118	21	1	14	61	41	106	0	1	.310	.388
Diggs,Tony	28	.210	105	286	32	60	12	3	0	12	16	36	5	5	.252	.273
Ellis,Paul	26	.226	102	279	27	63	8	0	5	38	29	35	0	0	.299	.308
Holbert,Aaron	22	.290	59	231	40	67	9	5	1	18	11	25	7	6	.322	.385
Lewis,Anthony	24	.222	109	405	59	90	17	0	16	54	22	98	1	0	.262	.383
Mabry,John	24	.240	122	463	63	111	27	0	12	56	26	68	1	5	.280	.376
Pappas,Erik	29	.179	64	201	27	36	6	1	5	25	24	44	1	2	.267	.294

Major League Equivalencies for 1994 AAA/AA Batters

Batter	Age	Avg	G	AB	R	H	2B	3B	HR	RBI	BB	SO	SB	CS	OBP	SLG
Radziewicz,Doug	26	.215	121	339	32	73	15	1	7	39	36	67	0	0	.291	.327
Richardson,Jeff	29	.238	89	240	24	57	11	0	3	17	13	38	0	0	.277	.321
Ronan,Marc	25	.218	84	262	26	57	10	1	1	17	10	43	2	0	.246	.275
Stephenson,Phil	34	.245	118	379	42	93	27	1	6	45	57	68	3	2	.344	.369
Thomas,John	26	.218	102	312	28	68	16	1	13	45	19	81	2	3	.263	.401
Warner,Ron	26	.234	95	231	27	54	13	0	3	24	32	59	0	0	.327	.329
Woodson,Tracy	32	.251	118	422	44	106	27	0	8	49	21	44	1	0	.287	.372
Young,Dmitri	21	.265	125	449	52	119	32	1	7	53	30	61	0	2	.311	.388
Young,Gerald	30	.284	83	310	47	88	26	2	4	29	40	27	9	9	.366	.419
CUBS																
Brown,Brant	24	.256	127	461	46	118	27	4	4	31	27	92	7	14	.297	.358
Bullett,Scott	26	.282	135	511	58	144	24	2	10	53	14	115	18	7	.301	.395
Carter,Mike	26	.262	122	405	43	106	21	1	5	23	10	45	11	13	.280	.356
Colon,Cris	26	.248	123	420	41	104	27	1	10	42	10	71	1	1	.265	.388
Cox,Darron	27	.238	99	290	27	69	13	0	2	20	21	49	3	1	.289	.303
Franco,Matt	25	.253	128	423	49	107	28	2	9	55	40	69	2	2	.317	.392
Glanville,Doug	24	.246	130	472	45	116	20	1	5	44	17	52	18	7	.272	.324
Gomez,Rudy	26	.237	91	224	22	53	9	0	2	13	13	48	2	6	.278	.304
Haney,Todd	29	.263	83	293	37	77	19	0	2	27	21	30	6	5	.312	.348
Hubbard,Mike	24	.269	104	349	44	94	12	2	11	33	21	62	4	6	.311	.410
Kieschnick,Brooks	23	.268	126	459	49	123	23	2	12	47	24	83	2	4	.304	.405
Peterson,Chris	24	.209	117	368	29	77	11	2	1	22	27	95	5	10	.263	.258
Pledger,Kinnis	26	.255	92	290	39	74	17	1	7	32	23	74	3	4	.310	.393
Robertson,Rod	27	.226	113	340	40	77	18	2	12	34	12	58	6	9	.253	.397
Sharperson,Mike	33	.263	68	213	25	56	11	1	4	22	24	31	5	3	.338	.380
Shields,Tommy	30	.237	111	316	36	75	14	3	4	25	33	62	6	10	.309	.339
Smith,Ed	26	.244	115	393	43	96	15	3	16	51	27	80	2	10	.293	.420
Tedder,Scott	29	.264	120	348	43	92	18	2	1	33	64	47	5	5	.379	.336
Timmons,Ozzie	24	.241	126	427	49	103	26	1	20	51	28	97	0	2	.288	.447
Valdez,Pedro	22	.268	116	358	33	96	12	2	0	31	14	48	1	5	.296	.313
Worthington,Craig	30	.263	122	353	45	93	15	0	15	53	42	77	2	3	.342	.433
DODGERS																
Abbe,Chris	24	.237	73	228	20	54	11	0	5	21	17	58	0	1	.290	.351
Ashley,Billy	24	.282	107	354	55	100	13	1	21	63	31	121	3	4	.340	.503
Beauchamp,Kash	32	.223	88	233	26	52	11	0	4	23	18	52	1	3	.279	.322
Blanco,Henry	23	.208	132	394	30	82	19	1	4	32	37	71	4	6	.276	.292
Brooks,Jerry	28	.260	115	358	45	93	16	0	9	47	18	35	2	1	.295	.380
Busch,Mike	26	.210	126	429	43	90	16	1	15	49	29	106	1	3	.260	.357
Castro,Juan	23	.263	123	430	46	113	20	2	3	37	22	70	3	7	.299	.340
Cedeno,Roger	20	.261	104	352	50	92	11	1	2	29	30	59	18	8	.319	.315
Coomer,Ron	28	.276	127	489	53	135	23	2	12	73	15	65	2	3	.298	.405
Demetral,Chris	25	.236	108	356	37	84	21	1	4	33	24	47	3	2	.284	.334
Hollandsworth,Todd	22	.229	132	468	48	107	21	2	11	54	27	100	9	9	.271	.353
Howard,Matt	27	.239	88	247	26	59	8	2	0	19	8	13	9	8	.263	.287
Ingram,Garey	24	.232	101	341	58	79	20	1	6	23	30	66	13	5	.294	.349
Kirkpatrick,Jay	25	.266	126	436	51	116	33	0	14	63	32	98	1	2	.316	.438
Lott,Billy	24	.268	122	433	51	116	20	2	9	52	22	107	15	6	.303	.386
Maness,Dwight	21	.196	57	209	27	41	4	2	4	17	17	57	10	17	.257	.292
Moore,Mike	24	.202	72	247	27	50	10	0	4	27	15	80	8	7	.248	.291
Offerman,Jose	26	.268	56	205	25	55	4	1	0	18	21	50	5	4	.336	.298

Major League Equivalencies for 1994 AAA/AA Batters

Batter	Age	Avg	G	AB	R	H	2B	3B	HR	RBI	BB	SO	SB	CS	OBP	SLG
Prince,Tom	30	.226	103	305	36	69	21	0	11	32	30	70	1	2	.296	.403
Pye,Eddie	28	.273	100	330	47	90	13	2	1	25	28	45	6	6	.330	.333
Spearman,Vernon	25	.243	105	321	36	78	11	1	0	20	27	41	15	6	.302	.283
Williams,Reggie	29	.253	104	265	33	67	9	2	2	25	19	65	13	5	.303	.325
EXPOS																
Andrews,Shane	23	.229	137	445	63	102	23	1	11	67	63	132	4	4	.325	.360
Benitez,Yamil	22	.226	126	455	43	103	16	2	11	68	22	143	12	14	.262	.343
Dauphin,Phil	26	.234	114	320	29	75	14	3	6	29	26	60	6	8	.292	.353
Figueroa,Bien	31	.217	85	254	21	55	12	0	0	22	14	32	1	0	.257	.264
Fitzpatrick,Robert	26	.219	95	302	29	66	11	0	6	25	18	83	2	3	.263	.315
Grudzielanek,Mark	25	.287	122	464	68	133	34	1	7	49	27	70	22	8	.326	.409
Hardge,Mike	23	.195	121	437	44	85	9	1	4	31	35	116	19	7	.254	.247
Horne,Tyrone	24	.253	90	297	41	75	13	0	6	35	31	98	7	12	.323	.357
Hymel,Gary	27	.219	77	224	26	49	14	0	8	26	5	71	0	0	.236	.388
Kipila,Jeff	29	.226	95	261	31	59	16	0	7	24	24	52	0	0	.291	.368
Laker,Tim	25	.282	118	408	54	115	30	1	8	56	37	100	8	5	.342	.419
Lee,Derek	28	.274	131	446	49	122	33	6	9	59	52	85	8	5	.349	.435
Marrero,Oreste	25	.220	88	246	32	54	13	4	5	24	23	58	0	0	.286	.366
Martin,Chris	27	.215	113	363	35	78	22	0	2	31	27	48	3	3	.269	.292
Northrup,Kevin	25	.285	125	421	54	120	25	0	9	53	33	56	5	2	.337	.409
Pride,Curtis	26	.231	82	290	44	67	15	2	6	25	31	85	16	6	.305	.359
Rundels,Matt	25	.192	112	318	39	61	8	3	4	23	32	84	12	6	.266	.274
Santangelo,Frank	27	.229	119	401	49	92	28	0	3	32	47	67	5	8	.310	.322
Virgilio,George	24	.227	89	233	21	53	15	0	3	30	16	38	0	0	.277	.330
Wilstead,Randy	27	.261	122	357	53	93	24	1	9	47	45	88	1	5	.343	.409
Wood,Ted	28	.252	125	397	50	100	23	5	9	47	38	82	2	4	.317	.403
Woods,Tyrone	25	.226	126	412	44	93	25	1	7	43	28	110	2	0	.275	.342
GIANTS																
Bellinger,Clay	26	.223	106	318	33	71	12	0	4	34	12	58	4	0	.252	.299
Benard,Marvin	24	.296	125	442	60	131	30	2	3	44	24	62	18	7	.333	.394
Chimelis,Joel	27	.277	127	466	68	129	40	0	9	66	31	62	6	5	.322	.421
Christopherson,Eric	26	.234	88	261	27	61	20	0	5	36	32	58	3	0	.317	.368
Cookson,Brent	25	.290	76	241	33	70	19	2	10	41	16	75	3	0	.335	.510
Ehmann,Kurt	24	.228	124	417	42	95	19	0	0	36	20	91	6	2	.263	.273
Faneyte,Rikkert	26	.283	94	339	42	96	13	3	4	39	20	66	9	5	.323	.375
Faries,Paul	30	.235	124	473	53	111	17	2	1	34	19	55	20	7	.264	.285
Hecht,Steve	29	.263	112	339	53	89	13	4	6	32	21	56	13	4	.306	.378
Johnson,Erik	29	.244	106	360	29	88	15	1	0	31	23	59	1	5	.290	.292
Jones,Dax	24	.234	111	376	37	88	20	2	2	35	14	44	10	7	.262	.314
Lampkin,Tom	31	.252	118	424	52	107	26	4	5	48	28	51	5	6	.299	.368
Leonard,Mark	30	.248	89	294	35	73	15	1	7	33	34	55	1	1	.326	.378
McFarlin,Jason	25	.265	106	298	34	79	10	2	4	26	13	33	16	6	.296	.352
Miller,Barry	26	.259	124	405	50	105	25	1	11	67	51	89	1	1	.342	.407
Mirabelli,Doug	24	.204	85	250	21	51	7	0	3	22	27	51	2	0	.282	.268
Murray,Calvin	23	.215	129	470	61	101	18	3	1	32	36	86	24	9	.271	.272
Ortiz,Ray	27	.230	122	343	35	79	15	4	6	38	12	81	0	4	.256	.350
Phillips,J.R.	25	.254	95	338	47	86	23	2	18	54	30	100	2	4	.315	.494
Scott,Gary	26	.240	121	400	37	96	19	1	6	40	23	64	2	6	.281	.338
Smiley,Rueben	26	.250	69	212	24	53	6	2	1	13	9	36	6	5	.281	.311
Wimmer,Chris	24	.266	126	451	58	120	19	2	3	45	19	59	16	6	.296	.337

Major League Equivalencies for 1994 AAA/AA Batters

Batter	Age	Avg	G	AB	R	H	2B	3B	HR	RBI	BB	SO	SB	CS	OBP	SLG
INDIANS																
Bell,David	22	.275	134	469	57	129	16	2	16	76	35	55	1	5	.325	.420
Bruett,J.T.	27	.235	110	302	36	71	12	1	2	25	31	38	5	5	.306	.301
Bryant,Pat	22	.222	124	370	53	82	13	1	10	46	35	91	16	6	.289	.343
Cron,Chris	31	.216	103	343	43	74	18	0	20	62	28	108	0	1	.275	.443
Flores,Miguel	24	.256	87	242	30	62	9	0	1	26	19	30	6	6	.310	.306
Giles,Brian	24	.296	128	423	64	125	17	2	14	50	47	62	6	5	.366	.444
Harvey,Raymond	26	.276	137	496	57	137	23	3	5	63	45	92	0	5	.336	.365
Jackson,Damian	21	.254	138	520	74	132	27	3	4	40	44	126	27	10	.312	.340
Jones,Tim	32	.246	115	382	51	94	16	1	6	36	37	66	7	2	.313	.340
Levis,Jesse	27	.268	111	366	47	98	19	0	9	51	47	40	1	0	.351	.393
Lewis,Mark	25	.243	86	321	48	78	15	0	7	29	30	49	1	4	.308	.355
Marini,Marc	25	.259	91	324	50	84	20	1	15	57	37	65	1	4	.335	.466
Martindale,Ryan	26	.275	86	269	35	74	13	2	5	35	19	56	2	2	.323	.394
Maxwell,Pat	25	.244	75	250	26	61	7	0	0	16	11	33	6	4	.276	.272
Meade,Paul	26	.234	107	389	43	91	20	3	2	36	17	81	3	6	.266	.316
Merullo,Matt	29	.281	112	406	45	114	19	4	10	64	21	48	1	0	.316	.421
Mitchell,Tony	24	.248	130	484	61	120	23	0	23	78	30	118	4	1	.292	.438
Perry,Herb	25	.307	102	365	58	112	19	2	11	60	35	56	6	4	.368	.460
Pough,Clyde	25	.273	121	411	60	112	26	2	18	60	37	103	2	2	.333	.477
Proctor,Brian	26	.272	104	309	35	84	23	0	5	31	35	55	0	5	.346	.395
Ramirez,Omar	24	.217	134	411	57	89	19	1	7	38	46	44	11	7	.295	.319
Sarbaugh,Mike	28	.251	84	263	30	66	8	1	6	33	17	47	0	0	.296	.357
MARINERS																
Adams,Tommy	25	.212	71	245	26	52	12	0	6	16	17	61	5	7	.263	.335
Barron,Tony	28	.272	110	397	52	108	19	2	16	48	19	94	13	4	.305	.451
Bragg,Darren	25	.297	126	462	71	137	29	3	11	54	44	78	18	6	.358	.444
Bryant,Scott	27	.269	105	387	44	104	28	1	12	55	25	72	0	1	.313	.439
Diaz,Eddy	23	.229	104	332	36	76	20	0	6	35	15	25	9	4	.262	.343
Griffey,Craig	24	.201	106	319	31	64	13	0	2	24	24	75	14	5	.257	.260
Hansen,Terrel	28	.296	112	398	48	118	21	0	18	67	13	98	1	3	.319	.485
Howard,Chris	29	.207	75	251	26	52	8	0	6	28	17	72	0	0	.257	.311
Kounas,Tony	27	.237	68	207	22	49	14	0	5	19	11	35	0	0	.275	.377
Mack,Quinn	29	.243	114	379	40	92	26	0	3	32	20	54	6	6	.281	.335
Manahan,Tony	26	.238	78	277	30	66	18	0	2	23	15	24	4	1	.277	.325
Newfield,Marc	22	.296	107	398	56	118	38	1	11	53	27	63	0	2	.341	.480
Pirkl,Greg	24	.265	87	328	44	87	18	0	13	46	15	63	0	0	.297	.439
Pozo,Arquimedez	21	.269	119	435	59	117	31	0	11	46	23	47	8	7	.306	.416
Quinones,Luis	33	.248	117	383	50	95	24	0	9	42	31	75	2	2	.304	.381
Santana,Ruben	25	.274	131	486	53	133	25	2	5	58	20	69	7	6	.302	.364
Sheets,Andy	23	.227	96	313	36	71	19	0	1	24	21	81	2	4	.275	.297
Sveum,Dale	31	.236	102	369	45	87	19	1	14	49	32	109	0	0	.297	.407
Turang,Brian	28	.287	68	268	32	77	15	2	3	25	11	43	3	3	.315	.392
Widger,Chris	24	.239	116	377	49	90	15	2	13	50	29	76	5	6	.293	.393
Willard,Jerry	35	.244	110	349	55	85	24	0	15	51	58	76	0	0	.351	.441
MARLINS																
Brumley,Mike	32	.239	85	293	35	70	19	1	7	26	23	70	4	3	.294	.382
Capra,Nick	37	.257	109	358	46	92	21	3	4	26	28	26	16	6	.311	.366
Christian,Eddie	23	.201	65	219	19	44	9	0	0	15	12	56	0	4	.242	.242
Clark,Tim	26	.234	135	466	46	109	25	0	10	47	32	121	2	7	.283	.352

Major League Equivalencies for 1994 AAA/AA Batters

Batter	Age	Avg	G	AB	R	H	2B	3B	HR	RBI	BB	SO	SB	CS	OBP	SLG
Decker,Steve	29	.336	73	238	24	80	18	0	7	31	18	25	0	1	.383	.500
Everett,Carl	25	.288	78	299	41	86	13	1	7	30	13	69	10	13	.317	.408
Fariss,Monty	27	.241	129	390	54	94	26	2	13	39	37	104	1	4	.307	.418
Johnson,Charles	23	.233	132	425	47	99	25	0	20	58	47	104	2	5	.309	.433
Jorgensen,Terry	28	.256	124	450	47	115	19	0	10	52	25	54	0	4	.295	.364
Lyden,Mitch	30	.250	84	272	33	68	17	0	11	42	7	78	1	0	.269	.434
Malinoski,Chris	27	.203	87	217	16	44	6	0	2	11	19	40	0	3	.267	.258
Martinez,Ramon	25	.211	132	483	43	102	14	1	0	32	18	113	21	8	.240	.244
Massarelli,John	29	.219	120	392	43	86	14	5	2	23	22	76	25	10	.261	.296
Millette,Joe	28	.221	118	384	26	85	17	1	2	24	8	77	3	5	.237	.286
Morman,Russ	33	.300	114	377	45	113	24	1	12	53	24	65	5	0	.342	.464
O'Halloran,Greg	27	.231	104	372	38	86	19	3	5	38	23	76	1	3	.276	.339
Pedrique,Al	34	.194	74	217	13	42	7	0	0	11	22	33	0	2	.268	.226
Rodriguez,Vic	33	.233	84	257	18	60	10	0	3	30	7	24	0	2	.254	.307
Schunk,Jerry	29	.243	92	313	24	76	14	0	5	25	16	21	0	7	.280	.335
Sheff,Chris	24	.224	106	379	36	85	16	0	3	22	19	82	12	4	.261	.290
Tavarez,Jesus	24	.252	89	337	44	85	9	5	1	23	22	68	13	5	.298	.318
White,Derrick	25	.223	121	349	37	78	14	1	2	30	24	82	11	8	.273	.287
Whitmore,Darrell	26	.239	115	397	47	95	19	2	13	39	27	80	9	3	.288	.395
Wilson,Nigel	25	.262	87	294	32	77	19	0	7	40	14	83	1	3	.295	.398

METS

Batter	Age	Avg	G	AB	R	H	2B	3B	HR	RBI	BB	SO	SB	CS	OBP	SLG
Alfonzo,Edgardo	21	.262	127	477	70	125	29	1	11	59	43	58	9	11	.323	.396
Barry,Jeffrey	26	.274	110	372	38	102	19	2	6	54	23	66	7	12	.316	.384
Brogna,Rico	25	.226	67	252	28	57	12	3	10	32	13	65	0	3	.264	.417
Burnitz,Jeromy	26	.221	85	307	50	68	13	3	12	43	43	86	14	6	.317	.401
Castillo,Berto	25	.220	90	304	26	67	11	0	5	33	27	49	0	3	.284	.306
Dascenzo,Doug	31	.255	68	239	26	61	11	0	3	23	19	24	4	8	.310	.339
Davis,Jay	24	.291	111	323	42	94	12	2	3	33	9	42	6	3	.310	.368
Fordyce,Brook	25	.242	66	223	22	54	11	2	2	28	16	27	0	0	.293	.336
Fully,Edwards	23	.220	83	209	21	46	8	1	3	17	5	37	2	5	.238	.311
Garcia,Omar	23	.276	131	456	54	126	19	3	3	57	30	69	7	9	.321	.351
Graham,Greg	26	.195	83	220	21	43	7	0	0	21	21	51	1	1	.266	.227
Hare,Shawn	28	.259	93	297	37	77	18	0	8	31	41	73	6	6	.349	.401
Howell,Pat	26	.212	97	212	29	45	11	1	0	5	16	55	9	6	.268	.274
Huskey,Butch	23	.211	127	464	51	98	20	2	8	50	32	92	12	7	.262	.315
Jacobs,Frank	27	.256	121	414	50	106	22	0	10	53	34	69	1	1	.313	.382
Kmak,Joe	32	.233	86	258	24	60	4	0	4	27	27	53	1	3	.305	.295
Ledesma,Aaron	24	.255	119	420	43	107	17	0	2	49	24	43	14	8	.295	.310
Otero,Ricky	23	.265	128	510	76	135	25	6	5	45	33	52	24	10	.309	.367
Parker,Rick	32	.248	73	222	25	55	8	0	1	14	25	40	7	5	.324	.297
Sanders,Tracy	25	.211	101	265	34	56	17	2	6	29	40	94	5	6	.315	.358
Saunders,Chris	24	.240	132	480	53	115	24	0	7	55	29	102	4	6	.283	.333
Saunders,Doug	25	.255	96	325	38	83	16	2	6	35	29	67	2	4	.316	.372
Vatcher,Jim	30	.214	112	308	35	66	17	0	8	42	31	58	1	4	.286	.347
Veras,Quilvio	24	.231	123	446	62	103	19	3	0	37	51	58	32	13	.310	.287

ORIOLES

Batter	Age	Avg	G	AB	R	H	2B	3B	HR	RBI	BB	SO	SB	CS	OBP	SLG
Alexander,Manny	24	.220	111	410	49	90	19	3	4	30	12	68	21	8	.242	.310
Alfonzo,Edgar	28	.286	124	448	65	128	30	0	10	63	29	66	9	8	.329	.420
Arnold,Ken	26	.244	86	221	25	54	7	0	4	23	16	50	2	5	.295	.330
Baez,Kevin	28	.208	110	346	39	72	14	0	1	33	31	53	1	7	.273	.257

Major League Equivalencies for 1994 AAA/AA Batters

Batter	Age	Avg	G	AB	R	H	2B	3B	HR	RBI	BB	SO	SB	CS	OBP	SLG
Buford,Damon	25	.241	111	435	70	105	17	2	13	52	27	83	21	9	.286	.379
Devarez,Cesar	25	.290	73	241	37	70	11	2	5	41	5	26	5	2	.305	.415
Dostal,Bruce	30	.258	87	221	37	57	8	1	0	28	36	49	5	3	.362	.303
Goodwin,Curt	22	.268	142	582	91	156	15	5	1	32	29	81	42	17	.303	.316
Lewis,T.R.	24	.258	72	236	30	61	12	0	6	30	16	48	4	1	.306	.386
Lindsey,Doug	27	.219	73	210	21	46	9	0	4	18	10	45	0	0	.255	.319
Lukachyk,Rob	26	.271	108	362	59	98	16	4	9	46	34	62	23	9	.333	.412
Manto,Jeff	30	.271	131	428	66	116	25	1	25	81	59	76	1	2	.359	.509
McClain,Scott	23	.221	133	416	61	92	25	0	10	50	53	93	4	3	.309	.353
Millares,Jose	27	.204	89	225	20	46	11	0	2	33	9	40	2	2	.235	.280
Obando,Sherman	25	.297	109	384	53	114	30	4	16	54	23	54	0	1	.337	.521
Ochoa,Alex	23	.278	134	503	66	140	21	1	12	71	36	70	20	8	.327	.396
Smith,Mark	25	.220	114	422	54	93	22	0	15	52	27	90	2	3	.267	.379
Tyler,Brad	26	.234	101	303	30	71	12	5	6	34	30	71	4	4	.303	.366
Vargas,Hector	29	.288	123	413	63	119	28	2	7	50	50	69	3	7	.365	.416
Wawruck,Jim	25	.272	114	423	49	115	16	4	7	42	25	79	12	2	.313	.378
Zaun,Gregg	24	.211	123	375	48	79	12	2	6	34	44	73	2	2	.294	.301
PADRES																
Bream,Scott	24	.267	109	318	30	85	6	1	4	26	26	86	12	8	.323	.330
Bruno,Julio	22	.215	123	424	30	91	19	1	4	33	15	87	2	5	.241	.292
Bush,Homer	22	.262	59	233	26	61	9	2	2	10	6	41	14	5	.280	.343
Curtis,Randy	24	.216	89	264	27	57	7	1	4	18	22	87	9	10	.276	.295
Deak,Brian	27	.243	99	280	26	68	14	0	9	32	37	76	0	1	.331	.389
Drinkwater,Sean	24	.208	91	288	25	60	14	1	4	29	13	42	2	0	.243	.306
Gennero,Brad	23	.246	128	479	53	118	15	4	13	45	24	94	5	4	.282	.376
Hall,Billy	26	.245	99	367	37	90	11	1	2	22	27	84	21	10	.297	.297
Hardtke,Jason	23	.204	75	245	19	50	11	0	4	21	13	47	0	2	.244	.298
Higgins,Kevin	28	.258	119	403	46	104	19	0	1	28	29	23	0	2	.308	.313
Holbert,Ray	24	.251	118	398	43	100	15	2	6	33	32	103	17	6	.307	.344
Lockhart,Keith	30	.267	89	307	39	82	11	2	4	27	16	38	1	4	.303	.355
McDavid,Ray	23	.224	128	447	54	100	18	2	9	39	42	115	14	5	.290	.333
Nieves,Melvin	23	.261	111	380	51	99	12	2	19	58	37	144	0	2	.326	.453
Pulliam,Harvey	27	.193	95	300	30	58	7	0	15	33	13	68	0	1	.227	.367
Ramos,John	29	.276	114	290	32	80	19	0	7	29	25	43	0	0	.333	.414
Smith,Ira	27	.285	107	340	43	97	14	3	6	30	33	63	3	12	.349	.397
Staton,David	27	.231	79	255	24	59	7	0	9	30	28	65	0	0	.307	.365
Thomas,Keith	26	.209	109	296	28	62	10	2	6	24	20	87	30	11	.259	.318
Thompson,Jason	24	.228	63	206	26	47	14	1	6	34	17	82	0	1	.287	.393
Thurston,Jerry	23	.187	77	230	22	43	8	1	3	21	12	78	0	4	.227	.270
Williams,Eddie	30	.304	59	204	30	62	9	0	15	34	15	35	0	0	.352	.569
Witkowski,Mat	25	.222	95	284	23	63	7	0	2	20	14	55	6	8	.258	.268
PHILLIES																
Bennett,Gary	23	.212	63	203	11	43	8	0	2	18	10	28	0	0	.249	.281
Bieser,Steve	27	.248	93	222	35	55	12	0	0	12	14	44	8	6	.292	.302
Brito,Luis	24	.202	86	277	28	56	6	1	2	17	9	42	2	3	.227	.253
Edwards,Jay	26	.212	75	241	27	51	2	2	2	24	9	54	7	2	.240	.261
Fisher,David	25	.231	118	402	48	93	23	2	5	35	41	71	3	5	.302	.336
Geisler,Phil	25	.223	128	426	38	95	15	0	5	43	32	111	3	7	.277	.293
Gilbert,Shawn	30	.235	141	533	68	125	31	2	5	44	55	93	14	5	.306	.328
Gomez,Mike	24	.228	82	246	25	56	10	1	0	13	3	18	3	0	.237	.276

Major League Equivalencies for 1994 AAA/AA Batters

Batter	Age	Avg	G	AB	R	H	2B	3B	HR	RBI	BB	SO	SB	CS	OBP	SLG
Hayden,Dave	25	.232	87	228	23	53	8	0	3	20	19	61	2	0	.291	.307
Holifield,Rick	25	.225	131	436	54	98	16	8	8	42	32	127	30	10	.278	.353
Jordan,Kevin	25	.269	81	305	37	82	21	0	10	48	24	30	0	1	.322	.436
Lieberthal,Mike	23	.215	84	289	19	62	15	0	0	27	17	31	0	0	.258	.266
Lockett,Ron	25	.211	90	261	28	55	9	0	4	15	9	60	4	3	.237	.291
Marsh,Tom	29	.248	114	436	44	108	29	3	7	49	11	62	3	5	.266	.376
Marzano,John	32	.193	88	274	21	53	18	1	0	16	20	34	1	2	.248	.266
McConnell,Chad	24	.215	88	261	25	56	8	2	5	35	17	94	4	4	.263	.318
Moler,Jason	25	.249	122	417	44	104	20	2	4	44	36	51	6	6	.309	.336
Montoyo,Charlie	29	.261	114	376	54	98	27	0	7	39	62	65	2	2	.365	.388
Nuneviller,Thomas	26	.243	129	445	46	108	24	1	5	47	24	60	4	1	.281	.335
Quinlan,Tom	27	.220	76	255	32	56	11	1	7	19	23	98	2	1	.284	.353
Schall,Gene	25	.264	127	450	45	119	33	2	13	75	42	93	6	0	.327	.433
Tokheim,Dave	26	.280	126	425	47	119	16	4	11	40	19	77	8	9	.311	.414
Zuber,Jon	25	.273	138	484	69	132	28	3	7	59	51	78	1	3	.342	.386
PIRATES																
Allensworth,Jermaine	23	.220	118	440	53	97	24	5	0	28	27	84	11	14	.266	.298
Aude,Rich	23	.258	138	504	56	130	35	2	12	67	35	87	6	5	.306	.407
Beamon,Trey	21	.297	112	418	58	124	16	6	4	39	23	56	18	7	.333	.392
Bonifay,Ken	24	.199	95	282	30	56	19	1	4	23	22	62	2	1	.257	.316
Brown,Mike	23	.227	117	366	41	83	22	1	5	37	31	100	2	1	.287	.333
Cameron,Stanton	25	.246	126	451	56	111	28	2	11	58	30	109	9	2	.293	.390
Encarnacion,Angelo	22	.265	67	219	21	58	15	0	2	26	7	29	1	2	.288	.361
Espinosa,Ramon	23	.245	82	282	37	69	14	2	1	33	7	40	9	10	.263	.319
Goff,Jerry	31	.230	79	269	23	62	17	0	3	27	27	67	0	0	.301	.327
Johnson,Mark	27	.251	111	375	58	94	18	1	18	71	48	95	4	6	.336	.448
Krevokuch,Jim	26	.215	107	325	29	70	15	0	3	34	15	44	1	3	.250	.289
Leiper,Tim	28	.242	114	339	30	82	18	1	3	33	17	40	2	3	.278	.327
Marx,Tim	26	.270	77	230	26	62	10	1	5	35	14	31	0	3	.311	.387
Munoz,Omer	29	.286	79	276	25	79	13	0	4	32	8	31	1	4	.306	.377
Noboa,Junior	30	.263	67	232	22	61	8	0	0	15	11	11	3	6	.296	.297
Osik,Keith	26	.193	83	254	23	49	14	0	4	28	23	43	0	1	.260	.295
Polcovich,Kevin	25	.213	125	395	38	84	12	1	1	27	27	74	6	4	.263	.256
Ratliff,Daryl	25	.253	78	245	32	62	6	1	0	24	16	36	8	4	.299	.286
Rohde,Dave	31	.207	101	266	20	55	10	0	0	19	32	36	5	4	.292	.244
Suero,William	28	.233	103	335	35	78	17	2	2	24	16	50	5	8	.268	.313
Tubbs,Greg	32	.258	133	488	49	126	20	2	1	38	37	74	10	9	.310	.314
Wehner,John	28	.279	88	319	44	89	17	2	5	37	27	37	16	6	.335	.392
Womack,Tony	25	.200	106	410	34	82	8	1	0	15	16	79	31	12	.230	.224
Young,Kevin	26	.253	60	221	22	56	13	3	4	23	12	47	4	2	.292	.394
RANGERS																
Aurilia,Rich	23	.225	129	453	66	102	17	5	10	56	44	80	7	12	.294	.351
Cairo,Sergio	24	.263	123	448	47	118	23	0	11	75	33	95	0	2	.314	.388
Clinton,Jim	28	.221	75	222	20	49	3	0	0	14	5	62	8	3	.238	.234
Davis,Doug	32	.209	75	211	21	44	9	0	2	23	29	61	1	1	.304	.280
Davis,Butch	37	.284	106	370	52	105	21	7	4	48	17	46	14	4	.315	.411
Ducey,Rob	30	.249	115	393	60	98	25	7	14	57	65	95	6	4	.356	.455
Edwards,Mike	25	.251	104	338	38	85	15	4	5	36	36	60	1	4	.324	.364
Gil,Benji	22	.229	139	475	54	109	18	4	7	48	28	127	10	7	.272	.328
Harris,Donald	27	.223	127	466	51	104	12	3	11	51	22	113	4	11	.258	.333

Major League Equivalencies for 1994 AAA/AA Batters

Batter	Age	Avg	G	AB	R	H	2B	3B	HR	RBI	BB	SO	SB	CS	OBP	SLG
Huson,Jeff	30	.282	83	294	41	83	18	1	0	23	26	33	13	4	.341	.350
Jackson,Chuck	32	.257	97	342	39	88	20	0	5	42	35	55	1	2	.326	.360
Lowery,Terrell	24	.279	129	491	88	137	33	7	6	53	49	122	26	9	.344	.411
Luce,Roger	26	.246	108	353	43	87	18	1	5	33	16	102	1	1	.279	.346
Magallanes,Ever	29	.243	118	400	48	97	23	0	3	41	32	50	3	7	.299	.323
McCoy,Trey	28	.282	101	341	47	96	26	0	11	58	36	68	0	0	.350	.455
Morrow,Timmie	25	.188	86	292	34	55	13	2	5	30	15	68	4	5	.228	.298
Nelson,Rob	31	.254	79	272	25	69	13	0	10	48	35	92	0	0	.339	.412
Peltier,Dan	27	.250	125	408	54	102	19	3	7	52	44	90	3	2	.323	.363
Rolls,David	28	.234	92	290	39	68	18	0	5	31	21	76	1	0	.286	.348
Shave,Jon	27	.203	95	325	25	66	13	1	0	27	12	64	4	1	.231	.249
Turco,Frank	26	.254	95	299	42	76	14	2	5	32	21	88	14	6	.303	.365
Wilson,Craig	30	.240	65	221	20	53	5	0	2	23	20	25	0	1	.303	.290
Wilson,Desi	27	.282	129	489	68	138	26	0	5	54	33	123	12	13	.328	.366
RED SOX																
Blosser,Greg	24	.251	97	346	43	87	22	0	13	45	37	102	7	2	.324	.428
Brown,Randy	25	.214	114	384	44	82	14	1	6	25	22	110	6	4	.256	.302
Colon,Felix	24	.218	129	435	44	95	25	1	6	45	51	111	2	2	.300	.322
Crowley,Jim	25	.180	76	217	21	39	2	0	6	20	20	61	1	2	.249	.272
Hatteberg,Scott	25	.234	98	303	26	71	18	0	5	22	31	60	1	1	.305	.343
Housie,Wayne	30	.218	112	344	32	75	17	0	4	34	27	67	1	7	.275	.302
Juday,Robert	24	.188	93	313	36	59	18	0	0	14	41	68	1	6	.282	.246
Lennon,Patrick	27	.315	114	422	69	133	32	3	14	57	35	103	8	8	.368	.505
Litton,Greg	30	.261	74	253	35	66	19	1	7	40	21	44	1	0	.318	.427
Malave,Jose	24	.290	122	459	75	133	39	4	20	79	38	87	2	6	.344	.523
McNeely,Jeff	25	.218	117	450	50	98	15	3	3	28	41	106	9	15	.283	.284
Munoz,Jose	27	.250	129	511	49	128	18	0	5	34	44	62	8	11	.310	.315
Murray,Glenn	24	.212	130	458	61	97	17	0	20	53	46	142	6	2	.284	.380
Ortiz,Luis	25	.297	81	310	39	92	15	1	5	30	24	30	0	3	.347	.400
Pedre,Jorge	28	.199	75	231	19	46	9	0	4	22	7	38	0	2	.223	.290
Rappoli,Paul	23	.273	109	352	44	96	14	3	3	34	37	60	12	9	.342	.355
Rodriguez,Steve	24	.279	100	384	44	107	16	1	0	29	17	46	12	5	.309	.326
Stairs,Matt	26	.305	93	315	38	96	26	1	7	52	39	41	6	6	.381	.460
Thoutsis,Paul	29	.213	94	300	23	64	10	0	8	33	31	59	2	0	.287	.327
Twardoski,Mike	30	.273	111	377	50	103	15	0	10	40	47	40	5	1	.354	.393
Wedge,Eric	27	.272	77	250	36	68	14	0	15	49	42	50	0	0	.377	.508
REDS																
Belk,Tim	25	.282	124	418	57	118	33	2	9	77	48	47	9	7	.356	.435
Buckley,Troy	27	.219	75	215	13	47	10	0	2	17	6	33	0	0	.240	.293
Candaele,Casey	34	.259	131	495	55	128	29	4	3	43	29	64	6	5	.300	.352
Cooper,Gary	30	.298	76	218	36	65	17	1	9	30	33	58	5	2	.390	.509
Dismuke,Jamie	25	.245	121	380	42	93	20	0	12	41	41	52	0	0	.318	.392
Franklin,Micah	23	.260	79	273	41	71	16	0	10	35	27	80	1	1	.327	.429
Gibralter,Steve	22	.255	133	451	63	115	27	2	13	56	38	118	7	7	.313	.410
Gordon,Keith	26	.247	100	304	43	75	15	1	7	37	19	101	8	6	.291	.372
Greene,Willie	23	.265	114	423	64	112	22	0	21	67	49	89	6	3	.341	.466
Jennings,Doug	30	.276	130	424	64	117	31	2	21	77	64	106	4	3	.371	.507
Kessinger,Keith	28	.228	115	382	31	87	18	1	2	40	33	59	2	0	.289	.296
Koelling,Brian	26	.244	111	386	53	94	10	3	2	27	20	80	23	8	.281	.301
Kremblas,Frank	28	.227	90	286	26	65	10	2	0	21	14	74	7	5	.263	.276

Major League Equivalencies for 1994 AAA/AA Batters

Batter	Age	Avg	G	AB	R	H	2B	3B	HR	RBI	BB	SO	SB	CS	OBP	SLG
Lyons,Barry	35	.285	114	417	53	119	23	0	12	55	24	60	0	1	.324	.427
Maas,Kevin	30	.262	111	374	59	98	23	2	22	51	33	74	1	2	.322	.511
Merchant,Mark	26	.291	106	320	27	93	13	1	5	50	32	46	0	1	.355	.384
Mottola,Chad	23	.226	118	394	39	89	18	0	6	36	24	70	6	11	.270	.317
Owens,Eric	24	.237	134	511	65	121	16	2	2	32	43	89	29	10	.296	.288
Pegues,Steve	27	.266	63	237	30	63	14	7	5	24	5	44	7	2	.281	.447
Pennyfeather,William	27	.247	103	385	44	95	24	1	6	39	22	68	10	3	.287	.361
Reese,Calvin	22	.253	134	474	69	120	22	2	11	43	34	77	16	6	.303	.378
Rohrmeier,Dan	29	.261	129	490	63	128	38	0	17	70	28	88	1	1	.301	.443
Stillwell,Kurt	30	.248	93	327	38	81	20	3	7	41	27	54	0	0	.305	.391
ROCKIES																
Bates,Jason	24	.259	125	441	47	114	17	4	7	53	44	57	2	6	.326	.363
Bolick,Frank	29	.259	120	398	69	103	19	0	23	68	63	88	1	3	.360	.480
Brito,Jorge	29	.262	84	263	26	69	15	1	7	37	20	75	1	0	.314	.407
Case,Mike	26	.268	118	373	46	100	20	2	7	38	33	104	7	4	.328	.389
Cockrell,Alan	32	.285	96	305	40	87	17	1	11	49	23	65	1	1	.335	.456
Cole,Stu	29	.276	97	275	27	76	19	1	4	26	16	46	4	3	.316	.396
Counsell,Craig	24	.280	83	300	46	84	20	1	4	36	32	33	3	1	.349	.393
Echevarria,Angel	24	.261	58	207	24	54	6	0	9	31	13	48	1	4	.305	.420
Gainer,Jay	28	.217	94	272	26	59	11	1	6	23	18	63	1	3	.266	.331
Garrison,Webster	29	.276	128	496	66	137	28	3	10	47	33	66	12	5	.321	.405
Gomez,Fabio	27	.279	90	251	41	70	19	0	3	31	24	67	2	3	.342	.390
Hubbard,Trent	29	.336	79	307	54	103	19	3	6	26	32	41	18	7	.398	.476
Jones,Chris	29	.296	98	372	54	110	19	2	16	52	25	74	8	2	.340	.487
Kosco,Bryn	28	.241	132	478	62	115	24	3	20	88	51	130	1	2	.314	.429
List,Paul	29	.259	81	274	44	71	13	1	9	39	27	72	0	2	.326	.412
McCracken,Quinton	25	.284	136	549	92	156	29	5	5	38	42	74	28	11	.335	.383
Mejia,Roberto	23	.256	73	273	37	70	21	1	4	25	15	50	4	4	.295	.385
Noland,J.D.	26	.301	108	415	52	125	17	4	4	66	21	60	25	15	.335	.390
Owens,Jay	26	.245	77	249	30	61	9	5	4	30	23	67	1	3	.309	.369
Rogers,Lamarr	24	.274	111	380	55	104	18	4	2	34	48	53	5	8	.355	.358
Sparks,Greg	31	.182	88	242	26	44	8	0	7	27	28	83	0	0	.267	.302
Strittmatter,Mark	26	.235	73	217	19	51	8	0	2	25	28	40	0	2	.322	.300
Tatum,Jimmy	27	.323	121	421	53	136	37	0	16	68	32	86	1	2	.371	.525
Van Burkleo,Ty	31	.239	128	410	63	98	24	2	14	60	59	114	2	4	.335	.410
White,Billy	26	.252	82	238	30	60	13	0	1	21	32	50	0	3	.341	.319
ROYALS																
Burton,Darren	22	.238	97	365	44	87	12	3	1	30	23	52	7	6	.284	.296
Caceres,Edgar	31	.246	67	228	28	56	6	3	1	13	11	22	3	3	.280	.311
Canale,George	29	.212	114	416	44	88	24	1	8	41	34	80	4	1	.271	.332
Caraballo,Gary	23	.227	127	418	36	95	20	0	6	48	21	70	4	3	.264	.318
Davis,Glenn	34	.249	129	450	56	112	28	0	16	71	41	74	2	3	.312	.418
Garber,Jeff	28	.268	77	231	28	62	12	1	4	30	25	54	4	5	.340	.381
Goodwin,Tom	26	.279	113	412	49	115	15	6	1	25	16	59	35	13	.306	.352
Halter,Shane	25	.207	129	483	49	100	22	0	4	28	26	103	7	14	.248	.277
Hiatt,Phil	26	.271	114	409	47	111	25	3	11	54	27	121	8	8	.317	.428
Hosey,Dwayne	28	.300	112	387	70	116	22	8	14	59	44	81	18	7	.371	.506
Koslofski,Kevin	28	.191	93	298	31	57	7	2	3	28	27	89	6	4	.258	.258
McGinnis,Russ	32	.247	98	328	54	81	19	0	14	51	46	63	0	3	.340	.433
Mota,Jose	30	.233	100	347	44	81	12	6	0	23	34	39	17	6	.302	.303

Major League Equivalencies for 1994 AAA/AA Batters

Batter	Age	Avg	G	AB	R	H	2B	3B	HR	RBI	BB	SO	SB	CS	OBP	SLG
Norman,Les	26	.237	119	410	45	97	20	3	8	46	28	54	4	8	.285	.359
Randa,Joe	25	.247	127	438	48	108	25	1	6	37	21	48	3	2	.281	.349
Rossy,Rico	31	.209	120	398	36	83	21	0	6	46	44	59	6	10	.287	.307
Strickland,Chad	23	.199	114	371	30	74	13	1	4	38	11	40	0	3	.223	.272
Tucker,Mike	24	.245	132	465	55	114	15	6	12	57	50	110	7	3	.318	.381
Vitiello,Joe	25	.313	98	336	34	105	26	2	6	45	41	62	2	2	.387	.455
Walker,Hugh	25	.241	91	270	34	65	10	3	4	30	15	59	8	8	.281	.344
TIGERS																
Brady,Pat	29	.208	93	269	20	56	4	0	4	29	32	71	4	5	.292	.268
Clark,Tony	23	.274	132	485	63	133	24	0	29	105	49	149	1	4	.341	.503
Cruz,Ivan	27	.243	97	301	35	73	9	1	16	42	28	88	0	0	.307	.439
Decillis,Dean	27	.255	88	294	35	75	16	1	7	34	25	43	1	2	.313	.388
Dellicarri,Joe	28	.220	116	314	39	69	15	2	1	28	31	65	6	5	.290	.290
DuBose,Brian	24	.225	108	378	52	85	9	2	11	44	29	103	10	10	.280	.347
Givens,Jim	27	.222	105	279	24	62	5	3	0	10	30	68	13	10	.298	.262
Gonzalez,Pete	25	.257	76	202	26	52	10	0	3	25	29	44	2	7	.351	.351
Higginson,Bob	24	.268	137	471	80	126	25	2	25	66	46	104	13	8	.333	.488
Ingram,Riccardo	28	.275	90	309	38	85	14	3	9	55	24	47	9	6	.327	.427
Kunkel,Jeff	33	.238	103	341	45	81	15	0	11	44	7	86	17	6	.253	.378
Mashore,Justin	23	.220	131	449	68	99	12	4	8	48	33	129	25	10	.274	.318
Mendenhall,Kirk	27	.218	125	417	64	91	15	2	9	40	45	104	22	8	.294	.329
Milne,Darren	24	.242	113	363	41	88	10	1	7	39	25	76	9	5	.291	.333
Pemberton,Rudy	25	.293	99	355	48	104	11	2	12	57	18	65	24	9	.327	.437
Penn,Shannon	25	.272	114	437	62	119	11	4	2	32	30	102	36	14	.319	.330
Perona,Joe	25	.216	107	357	42	77	22	2	5	28	28	54	0	5	.273	.331
Pratte,Evan	26	.258	87	318	41	82	16	0	5	36	25	59	1	3	.312	.355
Rendina,Mike	24	.227	116	387	50	88	14	0	13	50	27	83	1	1	.278	.364
Springer,Steve	34	.252	135	504	72	127	20	3	13	76	35	83	15	15	.301	.381
Zinter,Alan	27	.230	134	466	65	107	24	3	24	57	69	197	10	5	.329	.448
TWINS																
Becker,Rich	23	.280	71	268	43	75	19	2	1	25	28	59	4	1	.348	.377
Brito,Bernardo	31	.269	108	413	57	111	21	1	19	82	20	127	2	0	.303	.462
Byrd,Tony	24	.235	132	511	58	120	26	6	6	35	30	123	22	8	.277	.344
Carter,Jeff	31	.285	122	435	71	124	16	5	3	47	62	83	17	6	.374	.366
Cepicky,Scott	28	.220	96	305	41	67	10	2	7	30	31	71	6	4	.292	.334
Cordova,Martin	25	.318	103	362	46	115	22	3	12	44	26	66	11	6	.363	.494
Davenport,Adell	27	.230	123	453	51	104	20	0	18	66	21	120	0	1	.264	.393
de la Rosa,Juan	26	.237	89	274	27	65	13	2	2	31	11	51	0	2	.267	.321
Duncan,Andres	23	.249	122	394	46	98	16	0	8	43	23	106	16	6	.290	.350
Dunn,Steve	25	.272	90	313	41	85	18	1	10	49	16	79	0	0	.307	.431
Durant,Mike	25	.261	103	326	45	85	21	3	2	34	24	49	6	3	.311	.362
Gerald,Ed	24	.269	112	391	60	105	16	7	12	48	34	116	11	5	.327	.437
Hazlett,Steve	25	.289	123	454	59	131	32	1	12	50	30	107	7	3	.333	.443
Hocking,Denny	25	.245	112	376	41	92	13	5	3	38	19	60	9	7	.281	.330
Masteller,Dan	27	.265	98	321	35	85	23	2	5	39	14	28	2	1	.296	.396
McIntosh,Tim	30	.297	118	437	59	130	30	0	11	65	17	50	0	0	.324	.442
Miller,Damian	25	.262	103	325	33	85	10	0	7	32	28	55	3	6	.320	.357
Moore,Tim	23	.242	123	433	46	105	27	0	16	62	31	141	7	10	.293	.416
Raabe,Brian	27	.281	123	448	52	126	23	2	1	33	34	11	6	8	.332	.348
Russo,Paul	25	.233	117	407	52	95	20	3	10	48	33	112	0	3	.291	.371

Major League Equivalencies for 1994 AAA/AA Batters

Batter	Age	Avg	G	AB	R	H	2B	3B	HR	RBI	BB	SO	SB	CS	OBP	SLG
Simons,Mitch	26	.312	102	388	43	121	27	0	2	45	31	41	23	9	.363	.397
Stahoviak,Scott	25	.282	123	415	65	117	36	4	8	63	48	95	4	8	.356	.446
WHITE SOX																
Alvarez,Clemente	27	.197	87	218	15	43	7	0	2	11	14	49	0	2	.246	.257
Brady,Doug	25	.232	127	505	52	117	15	5	3	41	28	61	24	9	.272	.299
Coleman,Kenneth	28	.185	80	200	30	37	6	1	2	24	29	40	2	4	.288	.255
Coughlin,Kevin	24	.239	112	360	45	86	9	0	0	23	29	44	3	8	.296	.264
Denson,Drew	29	.242	138	491	78	119	27	1	25	86	46	76	2	2	.307	.454
Disarcina,Glenn	25	.238	118	441	44	105	23	1	6	50	18	77	7	5	.268	.336
Durham,Ray	23	.271	133	509	74	138	28	7	13	55	37	92	24	9	.321	.430
Fryman,Troy	23	.207	123	435	48	90	19	2	5	38	23	92	1	5	.247	.294
Gonzalez,Paul	26	.205	77	219	18	45	7	2	4	20	19	68	2	2	.269	.311
Hood,Randy	26	.208	90	212	26	44	9	0	0	17	16	38	5	3	.263	.250
Howitt,Dann	31	.232	66	224	25	52	13	0	6	30	15	49	2	0	.280	.371
Jordan,Michael	32	.189	127	429	40	81	15	0	2	45	38	119	21	8	.255	.238
Martinez,Domingo	27	.249	131	458	47	114	19	1	18	67	31	104	1	1	.297	.413
Nunez,Rogelio	25	.278	66	205	20	57	6	1	0	18	5	39	5	3	.295	.317
Ortiz,Javier	32	.253	111	336	41	85	17	1	13	46	29	57	5	1	.312	.426
Robertson,Mike	24	.247	120	397	45	98	25	1	8	43	35	62	4	6	.308	.375
Saenz,Olmedo	24	.239	107	372	40	89	23	1	10	49	24	58	2	2	.285	.387
Snopek,Chris	24	.246	106	357	51	88	22	2	5	48	43	51	6	4	.328	.361
Thurman,Gary	30	.241	130	456	63	110	14	7	4	50	29	87	14	5	.287	.329
Tremie,Chris	25	.209	92	296	28	62	11	0	1	25	12	46	2	1	.240	.257
Turner,Shane	32	.181	66	204	17	37	6	0	0	17	22	40	1	2	.261	.211
Valrie,Kerry	26	.269	119	413	52	111	24	2	2	51	25	78	21	8	.311	.351
Wilson,Brandon	26	.205	114	361	35	74	14	1	4	21	24	68	9	5	.255	.283
Wolak,Jerry	24	.235	111	383	35	90	18	1	6	29	12	77	4	4	.258	.334
YANKEES																
Barnwell,Richard	27	.214	105	323	42	69	11	2	3	21	23	88	12	6	.266	.288
Carpenter,Bubba	26	.276	123	387	45	107	13	0	13	49	46	75	6	5	.353	.411
Davis,Russ	25	.255	117	404	66	103	27	1	21	60	53	96	2	7	.341	.483
Eenhoorn,Robert	27	.219	99	334	33	73	9	1	4	34	12	44	1	2	.246	.287
Fleming,Carlton	23	.231	117	372	37	86	11	0	0	35	41	38	15	6	.308	.261
Fox,Andy	24	.214	121	467	71	100	19	2	11	41	50	108	16	6	.290	.334
Hill,Lew	26	.217	82	253	34	55	12	1	9	31	19	78	2	5	.272	.379
Humphreys,Mike	28	.228	135	474	72	108	22	0	6	44	55	95	21	8	.308	.312
Jeter,Derek	21	.342	69	240	37	82	12	1	3	25	29	31	16	6	.413	.438
Leach,Jalal	26	.241	132	432	48	104	16	5	5	48	33	110	10	12	.295	.336
Luke,Matt	24	.275	63	233	32	64	10	1	8	38	22	53	4	4	.337	.429
Martinez,Chito	29	.257	94	292	41	75	14	3	15	41	41	83	0	1	.348	.479
Masse,Billy	28	.237	71	215	32	51	15	0	4	12	26	44	0	6	.320	.363
McNamara,Jim	30	.183	69	202	8	37	3	0	0	12	5	43	0	1	.203	.198
Mouton,Lyle	26	.289	133	464	62	134	34	3	14	67	33	111	8	7	.336	.466
Perezchica,Tony	29	.300	72	260	46	78	15	4	9	38	17	56	1	3	.343	.492
Posada,Jorge	23	.220	92	305	40	67	11	1	10	41	27	83	3	5	.283	.361
Robertson,Jason	24	.208	124	427	51	89	9	4	11	50	40	127	15	6	.276	.326
Seefried,Tate	23	.218	118	440	60	96	13	1	27	79	38	157	0	5	.280	.436
Silvestri,Dave	27	.230	114	383	62	88	17	1	21	72	71	134	13	11	.350	.444
Sparks,Don	29	.250	139	500	52	125	19	3	5	55	36	79	1	7	.300	.330
Wilson,Thomas	24	.232	123	401	51	93	19	0	6	40	46	106	3	6	.311	.324

About the Companies Who Produced This Book

About STATS Inc.

My name is Rob Neyer, and I envy Steve Moyer. Steve, our longtime Director of Operations, used to have the assignment of writing the annual "About STATS, Inc." I use the word "writing" loosely, because with the change of a few commas here and there, the same "About STATS, Inc." seemed to appear year after year. It wasn't Steve's fault; it's just that there wasn't much new to report, because STATS' growth was almost entirely related to one sport—baseball.

Now it's my job to write about STATS. Regrettably for me but happily for you, I've got a tougher time than Steve ever did. Why? Well, we're still growing—a year ago, we were ranked 144th on the "Inc. 500" list of fastest-growing privately-held companies—and it's far more than just baseball now. In 1992, we inaugurated our in-dpeth coverage of football, and you can see the results all over the place, from TNT's and ESPN's NFL coverage to *Pro Football Revealed*, our first football book.

But it goes beyond baseball and football. Starting this fall, STATS has reporter networks covering both the NHL *and* the NBA, so you can imagine the kinds of products we'll soon have ready. Immediately available is our real-time coverage, via STATS On-Line. Given a computer, a modem, and a reasonable fee, you can follow literally *any* game in any of the four major professional leagues, *as it happens*.

Of course, STATS is the leader in innovative fantasy games, from *Bill James Fantasy Baseball* to *BJFB: The Winter Game* to *STATS Fantasy Football* to *STATS Fantasy Hoops*. Can *STATS Fantasy Pucks* be far behind?

That's just the start. All the big players are looking to build on-ramps to the info superhighway, and STATS will be both building our own and providing construction materials for the others. How will we do it? Aside from our brilliant staff, everything depends on two things: our customers, and our network of diligent and dedicated reporters. If you'd like to be a customer (again), a reporter, or both, write us at:

STATS, Inc.
8131 Monticello Ave.
Skokie, IL 60076-3300

. . . or call us at 1-800-63-STATS (outside the U.S., make that 708-676-3322). We're looking forward to having you along for the ride.

About Howe Sportsdata

Howe Sportsdata International has been keeping statistics on professional baseball since 1910. Currently, Howe is the official statistician of all 17 U.S.-based National Association Professional Baseball Leagues and three independent leagues: the Northern, Frontier and North Central (although those stats are not contained in this book). They also compile statistics for the Arizona Fall League, the Hawaiian Winter League and winter baseball leagues located in Mexico, Puerto Rico, the Dominican Republic, Venezuela and Australia. In addition, Howe keeps the official statistics of the Continental Basketball Association, all professional minor hockey leagues and the National Professional Soccer League.

Originally based in Chicago, Illinois, Howe Sportsdata International is now located in Boston, Massachusetts on the historic Fish Pier, maintaining 24-hour/seven-days-per-week operation during the baseball season. Howe also maintains a satellite office in San Mateo, California. Howe is responsible for maintaining statistics for more than 250 teams who collectively play nearly 13,000 games a year.

Howe also provides statistical information to all 28 major league teams and to major media outlets such as *USA Today*, *The Sporting News*, *Baseball America*, the Associated Press and *Sports Illustrated*. Howe also counts as its customers many leading newspapers, of which the following are but a small representative sample: *The Los Angeles Times*, *The Detroit Free Press*, *The Miami Herald* and both the *Chicago Sun-Times* and the *Chicago Tribune*. For more information about Howe, write to:

Howe Sportsdata International
Boston Fish Pier, West Building #2, Suite 306
Boston, Massachusetts 02110

Appendix

Minor League Team	Organization	League	Level
Albany	Yankees	Eastern League	AA
Albany	Orioles	South Atlantic League	A
Albuquerque	Dodgers	Pacific Coast League	AAA
Angels (Mesa)	Angels	Arizona League	R
Appleton	Mariners	Midwest League	A
Arkansas	Cardinals	Texas League	AA
Asheville	Rockies	South Atlantic League	A
Astros (Kissimmee)	Astros	Gulf Coast League	R
Athletics (Scottsdale)	Athletics	Arizona League	R
Auburn	Astros	New York-Penn League	A
Augusta	Pirates	South Atlantic League	A
Bakersfield	Dodgers	California League	A
Batavia	Phillies	New York-Penn League	A
Bellingham	Mariners	Northwest League	A
Beloit	Brewers	Midwest League	A
Bend	Rockies	Northwest League	A
Billings	Reds	Pioneer League	R
Binghamton	Mets	Eastern League	AA
Birmingham	White Sox	Southern League	AA
Blue Jays (Dunedin)	Blue Jays	Gulf Coast League	R
Bluefield	Orioles	Appalachian League	R
Boise	Angels	Northwest League	A
Bowie	Orioles	Eastern League	AA
Braves (W.Palm Beach)	Braves	Gulf Coast League	R
Brevard County	Marlins	Florida State League	A
Brewers (Chandler)	Brewers	Arizona League	R
Bristol	Tigers	Appalachian League	R
Buffalo	Pirates	American Association	AAA
Burlington	Expos	Midwest League	A
Burlington	Indians	Appalachian League	R
Butte	Independent	Pioneer League	R
Calgary	Mariners	Pacific Coast League	AAA
Canton-Akron	Indians	Eastern League	AA
Cardinals (Chandler)	Cardinals	Arizona League	R
Carolina	Pirates	Southern League	AA
Cedar Rapids	Angels	Midwest League	A
Central Valley	Rockies	California League	A
Charleston-SC	Rangers	South Atlantic League	A
Charleston-WV	Reds	South Atlantic League	A
Charlotte	Indians	International League	AAA
Charlotte	Rangers	Florida State League	A
Chattanooga	Reds	Southern League	AA
Clearwater	Phillies	Florida State League	A
Clinton	Giants	Midwest League	A
Colorado Springs	Rockies	Pacific Coast League	AAA
Columbia	Mets	South Atlantic League	A
Columbus	Yankees	International League	AAA
Columbus	Indians	South Atlantic League	A
Cubs (Kissimmee)	Cubs	Gulf Coast League	R
Danville	Braves	Appalachian League	R
Daytona	Cubs	Florida State League	A
Dunedin	Blue Jays	Florida State League	A
Durham	Braves	Carolina League	A
Edmonton	Marlins	Pacific Coast League	AAA
El Paso	Brewers	Texas League	AA
Elizabethton	Twins	Appalachian League	R
Elmira	Marlins	New York-Penn League	A
Eugene	Royals	Northwest League	A
Everett	Giants	Northwest League	A
Expos (St. Lucie)	Expos	Gulf Coast League	R
Fayetteville	Tigers	South Atlantic League	A
Frederick	Orioles	Carolina League	A
Fort Myers	Twins	Florida State League	A
Fort Wayne	Twins	Midwest League	A
Giants (Scottsdale)	Giants	Arizona League	R
Great Falls	Dodgers	Pioneer League	R
Greensboro	Yankees	South Atlantic League	A
Greenville	Braves	Southern League	AA
Hagerstown	Blue Jays	South Atlantic League	A
Harrisburg	Expos	Eastern League	AA
Helena	Brewers	Pioneer League	R
Hickory	White Sox	South Atlantic League	A
High Desert	Independent	California League	A
Hudson Valley	Rangers	New York-Penn League	A
Huntington	Cubs	Appalachian League	R
Huntsville	Athletics	Southern League	AA
Idaho Falls	Braves	Pioneer League	R
Indianapolis	Reds	American Association	AAA
Iowa	Cubs	American Association	AAA
Jackson	Astros	Texas League	AA
Jacksonville	Mariners	Southern League	AA
Jamestown	Tigers	New York-Penn League	A
Johnson City	Cardinals	Appalachian League	R
Kane County	Marlins	Midwest League	A
Kingsport	Mets	Appalachian League	R
Kinston	Indians	Carolina League	A

Minor League Team	Organization	League	Level
Knoxville	Blue Jays	Southern League	AA
Lake Elsinore	Angels	California	A
Lakeland	Tigers	Florida State League	A
Las Vegas	Padres	Pacific Coast League	AAA
Lethbridge	Independent	Pioneer League	R
Louisville	Cardinals	American Association	AAA
Lynchburg	Red Sox	Carolina League	A
Macon	Braves	South Atlantic League	A
Madison	Cardinals	Midwest League	A
Mariners (Peoria)	Mariners	Arizona League	R
Marlins (Melbourne)	Marlins	Gulf Coast League	R
Martinsville	Phillies	Appalachian League	R
Medicine Hat	Blue Jays	Pioneer League	R
Memphis	Royals	Southern League	AA
Mets (St. Lucie)	Mets	Gulf Coast League	R
Midland	Angels	Texas League	AA
Modesto	Athletics	California League	A
Nashville	Twins	Southern League	AA
Nashville	White Sox	American Association	AAA
New Britain	Red Sox	Eastern League	AA
New Haven	Rockies	Eastern League	AA
New Jersey	Cardinals	New York-Penn League	A
New Orleans	Brewers	American Association	AAA
Norfolk	Mets	International League	AAA
Ogden	Independent	Pioneer League	R
Oklahoma City	Rangers	American Association	AAA
Omaha	Royals	American Association	AAA
Oneonta	Yankees	New York-Penn League	A
Orioles (Sarasota)	Orioles	Gulf Coast League	R
Orlando	Cubs	Southern League	AA
Osceola	Astros	Florida State League	A
Ottawa	Expos	International League	AAA
Padres (Peoria)	Padres	Arizona League	R
Pawtucket	Red Sox	International League	AAA
Peoria	Cubs	Midwest League	A
Phoenix	Giants	Pacific Coast League	AAA
Pirates (Bradenton)	Pirates	Gulf Coast League	R
Pittsfield	Mets	New York-Penn League	A
Portland	Marlins	Eastern League	AA
Prince William	White Sox	Carolina League	A
Princeton	Reds	Appalachian League	R
Quad City	Astros	Midwest League	A
Rancho Cucamonga	Padres	California League	A
Rangers (Pt. Charlotte)	Rangers	Gulf Coast League	R
Reading	Phillies	Eastern League	AA
Red Sox (Fort Myers)	Red Sox	Gulf Coast League	R
Richmond	Braves	International League	AAA

Minor League Team	Organization	League	Level
Riverside	Mariners	California League	A
Rochester	Orioles	International League	AAA
Rockford	Royals	Midwest League	A
Rockies (Chandler)	Rockies	Arizona League	R
Royals (Fort Myers)	Royals	Gulf Coast League	R
Salem	Pirates	Carolina League	A
Salt Lake	Twins	Pacific Coast League	AAA
San Antonio	Dodgers	Texas League	AA
San Bernardino	Independent	California League	A
San Jose	Giants	California League	A
Sarasota	Red Sox	Florida State League	A
Savannah	Cardinals	South Atlantic League	A
Scranton-WB	Phillies	International League	AAA
Shreveport	Giants	Texas League	AA
South Bend	White Sox	Midwest League	A
Southern Oregon	Athletics	Northwest League	A
Spartanburg	Phillies	South Atlantic League	A
Spokane	Padres	Northwest League	A
Springfield	Padres	Midwest League	A
St. Catharines	Blue Jays	New York-Penn League	A
St. Lucie	Mets	Florida State League	A
St. Petersburg	Cardinals	Florida State League	A
Stockton	Brewers	California League	A
Syracuse	Blue Jays	International League	AAA
Tacoma	Athletics	Pacific Coast League	AAA
Tampa	Yankees	Florida State League	A
Toledo	Tigers	International League	AAA
Tucson	Astros	Pacific Coast League	AAA
Trenton	Tigers	Eastern League	AA
Tulsa	Rangers	Texas League	AA
Twins (Fort Myers)	Twins	Gulf Coast League	R
Utica	Red Sox	New York-Penn League	A
Vancouver	Angels	Pacific Coast League	AAA
Vermont	Expos	New York-Penn League	A
Vero Beach	Dodgers	Florida State League	A
Watertown	Indians	New York-Penn League	A
Welland	Pirates	New York-Penn League	A
West Michigan	Athletics	Midwest League	A
West Palm Beach	Expos	Florida State League	A
White Sox (Sarasota)	White Sox	Gulf Coast League	R
Wichita	Padres	Texas League	AA
Williamsport	Cubs	New York-Penn League	A
Wilmington	Royals	Carolina League	A
Winston-Salem	Reds	Carolina League	A
Yakima	Dodgers	Northwest League	A
Yankees (Tampa)	Yankees	Gulf Coast League	R

383

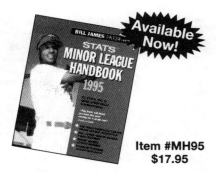

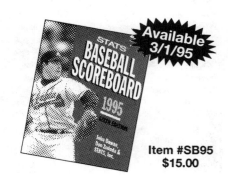

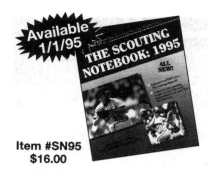
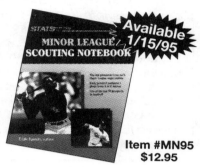

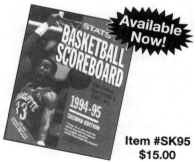
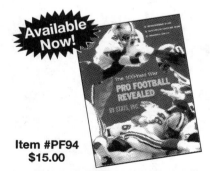

STATS INC Order Form

Name_____ Phone_____
Address_____ Fax_____
City_____ State_____ Zip_____

Method of Payment (U.S. Funds Only):

❏ Check/Money Order   ❏ Visa   ❏ MasterCard

Cardholder Name_____

Credit Card Number_____ Exp. _____

Signature_____

BOOKS

Qty	Product Name	Item #	Price	Total
	STATS 1995 Major League Handbook	HB95	$17.95	
	1995 Major League Hndbk. (Comb-bnd)	HC95	$19.95	
	STATS 1995 Projections Update	PJUP	$9.95	
	The Scouting Notebook: 1995	SN95	$16.00	
	STATS 1995 Player Profiles	PP95	$17.95	
	1995 Player Profiles (Comb-bound)	PC95	$19.95	
	STATS 1995 Minor Lg. Scouting Ntbk.	MN95	$12.95	
	STATS 1995 Minor League Handbook	MH95	$17.95	
	1995 Minor League Hndbk. (Comb-bnd)	MC95	$19.95	
	STATS 1995 BVSP Match-Ups!	BP95	$6.99	
	STATS 1995 Baseball Scoreboard	SB95	$15.00	
	STATS 1994-95 Basketball Scoreboard	SK95	$15.00	
	Pro Football Revealed-The 100 Yd. War	PF94	$15.00	
	For previous editions, circle appropriate years:			
	Major League Handbook 91 92 93 94		$9.95	
	The Scouting Report 92 94		$16.00	
	Player Profiles 93 94		$9.95	
	Minor League Handbook 92 93 94		$9.95	
	BVSP Match-Ups! 94		$3.99	
	Baseball Scoreboard 91 92 93 94		$9.95	
	Basketball Scoreboard 94		$9.95	

FANTASY GAMES & STATSfax

Qty	Product Name	Item #	Price	Total
	BJFB: The Winter Game	WG	$129.00	
	How to Win The Winter Game (book)	WGBK	$16.95	
	Winter Game STATSfax	WFX5	$20.00	
	STATS Fantasy Hoops	SFH	$85.00	
	SFH STATSfax/5-day	SFH5	$20.00	
	SFH STATSfax/7-day	SFH7	$25.00	
	STATS Fantasy Football	SFF	$59.00	
	SFF STATSfax/3-day	SFF3	$15.00	
	Bill James Fantasy Baseball	BJFB	$89.00	
	BJFB STATSfax/5-day	SFX5	$20.00	
	BJFB STATSfax/7-day	SFX7	$25.00	

STATS ON-LINE

Qty	Product Name	Item #	Price	Total
	STATS On-Line/Basic Plan	ONLE	$30.00	
	STATS On-Line/Full Access Plan	ONLP	$90.00	

**For faster service, call
1-800-63-STATS or 708-676-3322, or fax
this form to STATS at
708-676-0821**

1st Fantasy Team Name (ex. Colt 45's):_____ _____
   What Fantasy Game is this team for?_____
2nd Fantasy Team Name (ex. Colt 45's):_____ _____
   What Fantasy Game is this team for?_____

NOTE: $1.00/player is charged for all roster moves and transactions.

For Bill James Fantasy Baseball & BJFB: The Winter Game:
Would you like to play in a league drafted by Bill James?   ❏ Yes   ❏ No

TOTALS

	Price	Total
Product Total (excl. Fantasy Games and On-Line)		
For first class mailing in U.S. add:	+$2.50/book	
Canada—all orders—add:	+$3.50/book	
Order 2 or more books—subtract:	-$1.00/book	
IL residents add 8.5% sales tax		
Subtotal		
Fantasy Games & On-Line Total		
GRAND TOTAL		

FREE Information Kits:

❏ STATS Reporter Networks
❏ BJFB: The Winter Game
❏ Bill James Fantasy Baseball
❏ STATS On-Line
❏ STATS Fantasy Hoops
❏ STATS Fantasy Football
❏ STATS Year-end Reports
❏ STATSfax

MH95

Mail to: STATS, Inc., 8131 Monticello Ave., Skokie, IL 60076-3300